ALTERNATIVE ROCK

Dave Thompson

MILLER FREEMAN BOOKS
San Francisco

Published by Miller Freeman Books
600 Harrison Street, San Francisco, CA 94107
An imprint of Music Player Network, www.MusicPlayer.com
Publishers of Guitar Player, Bass Player, Keyboard, Gig, MC2,
and EQ Magazines

Distributed to the book trade in the U.S and Canada
by Publisher's Group West
1700 Fourth Street, Berkeley, CA 94710

Distributed to the music trade in the U.S. and Canada
by Hal Leonard Publishing
P.O. Box 13819, Milwaukee, WI 53213

Design by Wilsted & Taylor Publishing Services
Cover design by Richard Leeds
Front cover photo of Henry Rollins: Jay Blakesberg
Back cover photo of Billie Joe Armstrong of Green Day:
© Jim Steinfeldt/Chansley Entertainment Archives

Library of Congress Cataloging-in-Publication Data

Thompson, Dave.
      Alternative rock / by Dave Thompson.
       p. cm. — (Third ear)
      Includes bibliographical references, discographies, and
      index.
      ISBN 0-87930-607-6 (alk. paper)
       1. Alternative rock music—History and criticism.
      2. Alternative rock music—Discography. I. Title.
      II. Series.

      ML3534.T543 2000
      781.66—dc21   00-058249

Printed in the United States of America
00 01 02 03 04 05   5 4 3 2 1

CONTENTS

PERFORMERS

A

B

C

Acknowledgments

Any book this size necessarily demands the help and dedication of an army of people. I'd like to thank everybody who threw something into the pot, but most especially Jo-Ann Greene and Amy Hanson, co-writers of many of the reviews included within.

For other material contributions, thanks to Gaye Black, Boz Boorer, Mark Brennan, Leslie Carter, Rob Cherry, Kevin Coral, Veronique Cordier, John Donovan, Mick Farren, Klaus Fleischer, Rick Gershon, Bill Glahn, Eric Goulden, Matt Green, Dave Hawes, Johnny Indovina, Brian James, Christian Koeppel, Ivan and Lynette Kral, Laurie, Jackie Leven, Greg Loescher, Athan Maroulis, Betsy Martin, Tyson Meade, Barb Mitchell, Andrew Oldham, Brian Perera, Jason Pettigrew, Bill Rieflin, Roderick Romero, Yvonne Ruskin, Mark St. John, Julian St. Paul, Mike Scharman, Alan Lee Shaw, TV Smith, James Stevenson Nils Stevenson, Ken Stringfellow, Thomas Thorn and Wendy Weissberg.

Finally, to everybody else who helped bring the beast to life — my agent, Sherrill Chidiac; Dorothy Cox, Michelle Dowdy, Nancy Tabor, and all at Miller Freeman Books; Anchorite Man, Back Ears (whose ears are on backwards), Bateerz and family (not forgetting the Crab), Blind Pew, Barb East, Ella, the Gremlins who live in the furnace, K-Mart (not the store), Geoff Monmouth, Nutkin, Rita & Eric, Snarleyyow, Sprocket, and Neville Viking.

Introduction

Alternative Rock, as it is understood today, was born in the mid-1970s, at a point when "Rock Around the Clock" was closer in time than "Anarchy in the UK" is today; when the demise of the Beatles was as fresh in that generation's minds as the death of Kurt Cobain is in ours (fresher, in fact; five years, compared to just over six); and when bands like Emerson, Lake, and Palmer, 10cc, and the Electric Light Orchestra were still looked towards as heralds of rock'n'roll's next objective — *not* because they were actually capable of delivering it, but because nobody knew where else to look.

Then, in 1975, three things occurred to change all that, forever.

First, although nobody even dreamed of it having any significance whatsoever, was the release of former Velvet Underground frontman Lou Reed's latest album, 64 minutes of tuneless sonic distortion titled *Metal Machine Music*.

Second was the arrival of *Horses*, the debut album by New York street poetess Patti Smith, produced by Reed's old Velvets' bandmate John Cale.

And the third, across the ocean in London, was the emergence of the Sex Pistols — whose manager, Malcolm McLaren, had just returned from a few months in New York, checking out the underground talent.

Even regarded collectively, the linkage was little more than cosmetic and certainly nothing more than coincidental. None had any precedent (although earnest rock historians raced to find some anyway); none had any past beyond the individual performers' own. What they did have, and what they were willing to share with anyone who listened, was an electrifyingly prophetic vision of the future.

Within little more than a year, Reed's buzzing, cacophonous slab of noise was informing the first tentative steps of a world of would-be electronic pioneers; Smith's scream of consciousness babelogue was opening the floodgates through which the entire New York underbelly would pour into the limelight; and the Sex Pistols were unleashing a horde of like-minded musical hooligans to forge a music, a fashion, and most of all, an attitude which — with Reed and Smith holding tight to their hand — rewrote the rule book in hateful crayon strokes, eight miles high.

And rule one was — there were no more rules.

The first time *Rolling Stone* magazine caught punk auteurs the Slits in concert in 1977, writer Charles Young was astonished to hear, mid-set and in full view of a clubful of music fans, the guitarist strike a discordant chord, celebrate "fucking hell, listen to this!", and then do it again, deliberately.

To ears schooled in the venerable academy that was rock in the mid-1970s, her response, and that of her bandmates and audience, was incomprehensible. To those already tutored by the cataclysms of Reed, Smith, and Rotten, however, that discordance meant something — liberation from the morals and mores of an earlier musical age, freedom to experiment far beyond the established boundaries of rock, and a direct link to countless possible musical futures.

The fall-out was apparent immediately — the mutation of punk into American hardcore and European Oi!; fusion with reggae, ska, and early Motown; the birth of the gothic and industrial scenes; and the contrary juxtapositions of electronic pop and tribal rhythm. Prior to 1975, rock'n'roll was a catch-all term big enough to embrace any number of fleeting sub-genres. Thereafter, it barely covered half of what was going on. The rest was left to fend for itself.

For a time, the new music was called just that, "New Musik" — the misspelling intended to imply its futuristic tendencies. "New Wave" was popular for a time, before the media leaped upon it as a definable style in its own right; and "Indie" (short for independent record companies) remained current even after the major labels began signing the same bands. "Post punk" served well in the early 1980s; "post-modern" was adopted towards the end of that decade; "college rock" had its day in the sun. But somewhere around the mid-1980s, the word "alternative" began creeping into the vocabulary and, by the dawn of the 1990s, it had all but taken over.

It was never the most appropriate term for the music it described, and became increasingly less so as the music itself began crossing into the mainstream. What, one could not help but ask, was alternative about a band — U2, REM, or Nirvana for example — whose records sold in the millions, whose tours could sell out sports fields? Or, equally pervasively, why were a band like Motorhead considered a heavy metal act when their rudiments were clearly rooted in a raw punk ethic, while Pearl Jam were called alternative, when the opposite was true?

This book does not intend to answer those questions, simply because they are unanswerable. The likes of REM, U2, Duran Duran, and Nine Inch Nails — regular chart-toppers one and all — each have their own place in the story of alternative music, just as the Cows, the Raunchettes, Punk Lurex OK, and Thee Headcoatees have theirs.

The goal, then, was not to chronicle every performer ever to be categorized an "alternative rock" act, but to isolate a sampling of those who have made the greatest contributions to what we now call by that name.

From the outset, chronological parameters needed to be established. Even a cursory glance at the multitude of other reference works which document the subject will reveal some startling (and sometimes, disagreeable) inclusions — from Abba and David Bowie to Neil Young and Frank Zappa. Both the historical and cultural boundaries of alternative have been pushed back so far that they almost pre-date rock'n'roll itself. (Sun Ra is not featured in this book.)

Most of the above artists (and many more besides) are discussed here. Strictly speaking, however, inclusions have been limited exclusively to those performers who have emerged since 1975 — the only exceptions will be found in the work of certain producers, profiled for their involvement in the seminal records of the past quarter century, regardless of whether they were working beforehand.

Of the 400+ performers, producers, and record labels profiled here, perhaps a quarter were the proverbial no-brainers, the cornerstones upon which all modern understanding of alternative music is built — Steve Albini, the Sex Pistols, Sonic Youth, Wire, Nirvana, and so forth are simply too well known to have been ignored.

Just as many, however, have been included because they *were* ignored, though they should have become well known. Others still have been selected as representatives of musical styles which have yet to throw up any true front-runners; yet others because somewhere in their catalog, there lurks that one gem, that one shining moment of unimpeachable style and substance, that to overlook them would be unforgivable.

Each individual entry follows the same format, opening with the original (or earliest-documented line-up) of the band profiled, birthdates/places (when known), and instruments played. Thereafter, full career synopses include subsequent line-up changes and major career events.

Included wherever possible are chart positions for both albums and singles, for the US (positions taken from Joel Whitburn's *Top Pop Albums* and *Top Pop Singles/Billboard*) and UK (positions taken from *The Guinness Book of...Hit Albums* and *...Hit Singles/Music Week*). UK-independent chart positions are also provided for the years 1980–89, the cut-off date following chart compiler Barry Lazell's own logic that by the early 1990s, the chart was on its way to becoming "a farce... as the major record companies decided that having an indie hit was a good way of breaking a new act. So they began forming their own... labels which went through independent distribution." (*Indie Hits 1980–89*; Cherry Red Books, UK)

DISCOGRAPHIES

LP/CD listings are as complete as possible. All are US releases except where noted — UK, Germany, Australia, Japan, etc. In those instances where an album appeared internationally in a prior year to the US release, this original release is given, with the domestic issue listed only where the title and/or contents differ.

The availability of releases is not addressed. As labels dig deeper into the vault in search of fresh material for reissue, even long-deleted albums which were once considered unsalable are now returning to the racks (and often disappearing again soon after).

Neither are different formats (vinyl, tape, CD, etc.) considered. In general, pre-1986 releases were originally available on vinyl and cassette only; post 1986, CDs came to dominate, although many releases continued to appear on vinyl (some exclusively).

The discographies strive to differentiate between albums intended to showcase fresh material — a group's "new album" — and those (*Selected Compilations and Archive Releases*) which collect previously unreleased material from early in a band's career, rare and unavailable cuts, or greatest hits/"best of" selections. These listings are generally complete, but do omit titles which either duplicate or are superceded other collections.

Where relevant, solo, side project, and other related releases follow the main band discography; the growing trend for name remixes is also addressed by the inclusion of remix discographies for many of today's most active practitioners.

Producer discographies are, for the most part, selective — few producers have confined their activities to one style of music, no matter how broad that style might be, and in the interests of both space and relevance, it was necessary to remove many albums and artists which clearly fall beyond the scope of this book. In certain cases, however, earlier (pre-1975) releases have been allowed to stand where it is likely that the records themselves influenced at least part of that producer's future work. Generally, solo albums by individual producers are not listed.

Label listings are similarly selective, generally concentrating upon the company's first 50–100 releases, as it is during this span that a label most frequently resolves its own future character. Other cut-off points include the absorption of an indie into a major; a change in ownership or control; or a major change in direction. All label discographies, however, are as complete as possible for the period under discussion.

REVIEWS AND RATINGS

Reviews of selected albums are included as a general guide to the band's music and impact. Albums are rated on a scale of **1**–**9**, with **1** representing a very poor release, and **9** the best in the band's catalog. It should be noted that these ratings apply only within an individual band's discography — a rating of **7** in one band's catalog does not necessarily imply it is superior to a **5** in another's band.

Similarly, a rating of **1** is not intended to suggest that an album is one of the worst ever made (although it probably is), simply that it is the worst the band in question has ever made. The majority of releases are rated between **5**–**7**, indicating that while the band may not have attained its (potential) peak, the album is definitely worthy.

In addition, a rating of **10** has been awarded to those albums which can be considered essential listening, not only for their content, but also for their historical and/or cultural impact. [For the full listing, see the "10 Star Album List" on page 817.]

Where a band is profiled, all relevant reviews are included within the discographies that follow. A number of other acts, otherwise absent from the book, are discussed within individual producer or label listings. Because singles and EPs are included for reference and completeness only, they are not rated.

Sources

Much of the groundwork for this book was laid over two decades of writing about and listening to the bands included in this book — I have on occasion "sampled" my own past work, including reviews and interviews published in the following: *Alternative Press, Bikini, CD Now, City Heat, Goldmine, huH, Live! Music Review, Melody Maker, Mojo, Pandemonium, Record Collector, The Rocket*, and *Rolling Stone*. Other interview material was supplied by Jo-Ann Greene and Amy Hanson.

Among the reference books most frequently consulted, the following were constant companions: *VH-1 Rock Stars Encyclopedia* by Dafydd Rees and Luke Crampton (DK Publishing), *The Great Rock Discography* by Martin Strong (Canongate Publishing), *Rock Family Trees* by Pete Frame (Omnibus Press), *Top Pop Albums* and *Top Pop Singles* by Joel Whitburn (Record Research), *Guinness Book of Hit Albums* and *Guinness Book of Hit Singles* by Rice/Gambaccini/Rice (Guinness Publishing), the *Trouser Press Record Guide* ed. Ira Levin (Collier), *Good Vibrations: A History of Record Production* by Mark Cunningham (Sanctuary), and

the *International Discography of the New Wave* by B George and Martha Defoe.

For the background and development of individual genres and scenes, *Black Leather Jacket* by Mick Farren (Abbeville), *Vacant* by Nils and Ray Stevenson (Thames & Hudson), *High on Rebellion* by Yvonne Sewall-Ruskin (Thunder's Mouth), *Straight Outa Bristol* by Phil Johnson (Sceptre), *Destroy* by Alvin Gibbs (Britannia), *Unknown Legends of Rock'n'Roll* by Richie Unterberger (Miller Freeman), *Techno Rebels* by Dan Sicko (Billboard Books), *This Ain't No Disco: The Story of CBGB* by Roman Kozak (Faber & Faber), *All Ages: Reflections on Straight Edge* by Beth Lahickey (Revelation), *Make The Music Go Bang: The Early LA Punk Scene*, ed. Don Snowden (Griffin), and *Encyclopedia of North West Music* by James Bush (Sasquatch).

For specific band histories and details, those biographies noted at the end of individual entries are generally recommended.

ESSAYS
An Older Alternative

ROTTEN RADIO

On July 16, 1977, London's Capital Radio invited the Antichrist to come into the studio and play a few records. And across the city, the napalm blast of Johnny Rotten's breath could be felt before needle even touched vinyl.

Punk had come to destroy, to purge, to sweep the musical landscape clean of the excesses of the past, and Rotten was the High Priest of all that the new breed held holy. The first time his eventual bandmates met him, he was wearing a Pink Floyd T-shirt, with the words "I hate" crudely scrawled across it, and when he spoke of rock's past, it was with a shrug, a sneer, and a rolling of the eyes. "Boring old farts."

On the radio that night, though, the iconoclasm failed to materialize, and in doing so, hit home even harder than it ever could have if Rotten had read the script. For there were Boring Old Farts... and there were farting old bores. And there really was a difference.

Cuts by David Bowie and Gary Glitter catered to Rotten's own youth as a pop consumer; Aswad, the Gladiators, and Dr. Alimantado summed up his love of reggae. The Chieftains reflected upon his London Irish upbringing, with the kind of music which would have ricochetted round the Lydon living room every time there was a family get-together.

1960s Freak Beat champions, the Creation, captured the fuzz and buzz of garage rock, fed through the same tinny amplifiers which punk rock distorted its own thuggish riffery through. And Neil Young's "Revolution Blues" at least adhered to some form of harsh apocalyptic imagery, a slice of Manson-abilia so misanthropic that when Young toured with Crosby, Stills, and Nash, they allegedly begged him not to perform it. A little over a decade later, Young would be adopted again by a new generation, rising up this time in the soul of Grunge, and seeing in Young a kindred spirit (musically and, apparently, sartorially) despite ten years in the commercial dumper. Rotten doubtless admired very different qualities to those which set Eddie Vedder's heart racing. But he would have taken the same journey through the darkness to arrive at his conclusions.

Rotten's other inclusions, too, have been validated by time. The late Tim Buckley would enjoy one resurrection in 1984, after This Mortal Coil covered his "Song to the Siren,"

and another ten years later, even as his son, Jeff, was establishing his own career.

Kevin Coyne, a former mental hospital orderly, whose entire solo career had been cripplingly idiosyncratically informed by the experience; Peter Hammill, resolutely introspective, deliriously obscure, purveyor of aural self-flagellation since the dogdays of the hippy era; both found longevity and appreciation long after their original '70s stamping grounds were levelled.

German avant-gardists Can have hovered over the experimental fringes of punk, electro, and industrial for so long that it's easy to believe that their first Anglo acolytes are now approaching pensionable age.

And Captain Beefheart has continued to defy both commercial fame and critical acclaim by refusing to even make new records. His last "new" release of the 20th century was a five-disc box set devoted in the main to the out-takes from his fourth album, 1969's *Trout Mask Replica*. Three decades on from its original release, at a time when every last one of the 1960s' other sonic excesses has been embraced and absorbed by mainstream pop politics, *Trout Mask Replica* remained as uncompromisingly "out there" as its name insisted it should be.

Rotten knew precisely what effect his choices would have on an audience gagging for noise and nihilism. But he was also unrepentant. Heading off peer pressure at the pass, he launched an offensive immediately. "A lot of [Punk] is real rubbish. I mean, real rubbish, and just giving it a terrible name"; then he told co-host Tommy Vance to "just play the records... they speak for themselves."

Ninety minutes later, and almost 25 years on, Rotten's choices still resonate with the passion which he insisted informed his own music — and which, possibly coincidentally, but certainly not accidentally — informed the story of punk, new wave... the alternative scene itself.

It is a relatively simple story, confused only by the modern era's obsession with thinking up new labels for its children, and its childrens' children too: ska-punk, grunge-funk, gothic-industrial, metal hip hop... then creating magazines, radio shows, and industry awards for each of them.

It is straightforward, too, in its ability to accommodate such offspring, and in doing so, to push its own historical parameters ever further back, through the early 1970s, into the late 1960s, back to the garage band heartland of mid-decade America or the beat boom snarling of post-Beatles Britain. What is surprising, perhaps, is just how willingly history embraces those discoveries.

When '60s wildmen the Pretty Things came back to life in 1998, almost 20 years after their last new album, a lot of younger critics called them a barbaric precursor of punk. But the relationship was much more personal than that — guitarist Dick Taylor remembered how "John Lydon used to come and see us with his mom at the 100 Club"; fellow ex-Pistol Glen Matlock recorded a single with the band; and Taylor concluded, "If you think about our very early stuff, there's certainly a very strong resemblance. The garage bands certainly nodded in our direction, and out of garage comes punk. Captain Sensible said we were one of his favorite bands."

The Pretty Things, the Gladiators, Neil Young, Kevin Coyne, Can, Aswad, the Chieftains, Gary Glitter, Captain Beefheart, the Creation, David Bowie, Dr. Alimantado, Tim Buckley... if Rotten had been granted another 90 minutes, he could have added Jacques Brel, the Deviants, T.Rex, Dillinger, the Fugs, Stockhausen, Syd Barrett, the Mothers Of Invention, Roxy Music, Alex Chilton, Alex Harvey, Prince Buster, Gram Parsons, Skip Spence, the Modern Lovers, Joe Meek, Scott Walker, Cockney Rebel, Hawkwind, Red Crayola, Amon Duul II, Tapper Zukie, the New York Dolls, Iggy Pop, Roky Erickson, the Pink Fairies, the MC5.

All played their part, all made their mark, and most of them have reappeared — in spirit or in song, if not in living person — in the annals of rock in the last 25 years.

Of all the bands to be reborn, revitalized, or revisited in that period, however, one stands head and shoulders above them all — Year Zero in terms of all that would come to pass. That band was the Velvet Underground, a group whose members not only foresaw and foreshadowed the future during the band's own lifetime, they then stuck around long to ensure that the seeds they sowed came to life.

VELVET GOLDMINE — MORE THAN JUST A MOVIE

Put in the starkest terms, the Velvet Underground were the most influential band to come out of white rocking America — ever. Elvis Presley may have set the ball rolling in the first place, but it was his hips and that sneer which did it really, and by the time he truly understood what was going on, he was already on his way to Colonel Tom's reprocessing plant.

Bob Dylan had a suck on the cigar as well, but four great albums in a quarter of a century, and a handful of folkie classics doesn't cut any ice in this neck of the woods... does it, Mr. Jones?

So who's left? The Grateful Dead? Boring. Bruce Springsteen? Double boring. The Byrds? Do they even count as rock'n'roll? Probably not, but neither did the Velvets, and that's what was so important about them. Take a snap poll of every band who's meant anything to anyone with half a brain cell between them, and you can bet your life they cut their teeth on "Sweet Jane," progressed on to "Heroin," and still go to bed at night with a picture of "Sister Ray" by the nightlight.

Bowie wrote a song, which was openly inspired by the Velvets ("Queen Bitch"); Bryan Ferry recorded one by them ("What Goes On"). Jane's Addiction covered "Rock and Roll," the Sisters of Mercy used to encore with "Sister Ray," there's a bootleg of Patti Smith crooning "Pale Blue Eyes," and both Tracy Thorn and REM have had stabs at "Femme Fatale." But the Velvet Underground were more than a pop group, more than a lifestyle, they were life in itself. The names changed, the music changed, but for four years, four albums, a few hundred gigs, and a never-ending conveyor belt's worth of sleazoid debauchery stories, the Velvets picked up everything anyone could ever want to know about rock'n'roll and shoved it in their faces. With feeling.

The Velvet Underground were born of Lou Reed and John Cale's fascination with experimental music, but they were bred amid the claustrophobic paranoia of Andy Warhol's New York Factory, and like that star-crossed parent, emerged a band of a million moods.

One moment sweet and tender, when Nico sang "I'll Be Your Mirror," or Lou intoned "New Age"; suddenly bright and poppy, through the first album's "Sunday Morning," or the last one's "Who Loves the Sun?"; then bleak — "Waiting for the Man," macabre — "Lady Godiva's Operation," nihilistic — "Heroin," or just plain cataclysmic. Seventeen minutes of "Sister Ray," eight more of "European Son to Delmore Schwarz," and about two minutes into "I Heard Her Call My Name," right after Reed realized (for the second time) that his mind has just split open, a screech of guitar noise runs the heart attack drums to the end of the song, and ensures the listener's mind, too, will split before they get there.

Brian Eno, rising through 1972 as the other-worldly electro-whiz in Roxy Music, once estimated that no more than 100 people ever heard the Velvet Underground — "but they all went out and formed bands." And their second album, 1968's *White Light White Heat*, was the template which most of them gravitated towards.

It boasted just six tracks, but almost all the ingredients of the next three decades are there, in the discordant guitars and exploding inevitability; in a sleeve as black as the blackout it was met with; and in the imagery the band wore like a worn suit of clothes.

There was Reed, five foot something of state-sponsored zombie gone wrong — "I had 24 shock treatments when I was 17," he once remarked. "I suppose it made me write things like 'Lady Godiva's Operation'." There was Cale the mad scientist — when the blade comes down through Waldo's head at the end of "The Gift," you can hear the Welshman grin-kerthunk. There was Tucker — elfin, smirking, the tightest timekeeper in the business, tomboy grown into tomcat. And there was guitarist Sterling Morrison, never speaking, seldom moving, the most sinister one of them all.

"The Velvets do have a certain sordid image," Tucker — by the early 1990s, Born Again in the Lord and raising a family in the south — admitted. "But it's a media misrepresentation. We weren't like that at all." Only "Sister Ray," the litany of death, drugs, and depravity which closed *White Light White Heat* bothered her, and only one lyric at that. "She's still sucking on my ding-dong," sang Reed. "Lou should have thought of a different word," responded Tucker.

America, on the other hand, wished he'd thought of a different job. Three of the band's albums flopped so hard, they'd have broken a weaker act's back (chart placings of #177 and #199, respectively, for their first two albums were earned almost exclusively from north-east coast sales). Their fourth album was so heavily remixed by their manager that Reed himself could stand it no more. He walked, the album bombed, and nobody gave either of them a second thought.

Nobody, that is, aside from a young David Bowie, a struggling singer-songwriter of no fixed musical abode, who emerged as the single most powerful, and in many ways, most influential icon of the entire 1970s.

In and of himself, Bowie did nothing more than amplify whispers that were already touching ears in small doses, elevating fringe interests to the edge of mainstream acceptance. But the very act of amplification was a revolution, and the only trick was knowing precisely when to unleash it.

Bowie had been following Lou Reed's progress since his own ex-manager came back from New York with a tape of the Velvets' first album in 1966. By 1968, little magpie David had written "Little Toy Soldier" and copped half of the Velvets' "Venus In Furs" for the chorus. In 1971, he came up with "Hang onto Yourself," and was accused by the *New Musical Express* of rewriting "Sweet Jane." Then he dedicated his next album's "Queen Bitch" to "Velvet Lou — some white heat returned"; Bowie knew precisely what he'd borrowed from the Velvets and when he burst into the pop consciousness in 1972, he made that debt plain as day.

That year, Bowie and guitarist Mick Ronson co-produced Reed's second solo album, 1972's *Transformer*, introducing a whole new generation of innocents to the twilight shenanigans of Max's Kansas City. Then, with one legend rehabilitated — *Transformer* went Top 30 in America, a single,

"Walk on the Wild Side," hit #16 — Bowie got to work on another, Iggy Pop and the Stooges.

Four years had elapsed since the Stooges howled out of Ann Arbor, MI; four years, two albums, and a death-defying litany of depravity, degradation, and semi-self immolation. The Stooges didn't play gigs, it was said, they simply made a lot of noise while their singer rolled in broken glass. They didn't perform songs, they committed out aural sabotage while Iggy slashed his chest. And Pop himself wasn't a rock'n'roll singer, he was a human ashtray, stubbing out cigarettes on his own flesh.

Bowie pulled the Stooges out of obscurity, took them to London, got them a record deal, then sent them into the studio to set the legend to music. They emerged with a statement of molten rock defiance called *Raw Power*; he remixed it to such impenetrable density, that 20 years on, Iggy himself redid the job and missed the point entirely. *Raw Power* was an important album *because* it sounded so bad and because, in 1973, people simply didn't make records that sounded like that. Anybody that did, then, was either demented — or a pioneer. Or both, which is why, though neither *Raw Power* nor *Transformer* really fit the glam rock bag into which rock history subsequently forced them, both were as much at home in there as they would be anywhere else.

So much of rock music is about projecting an image. Glam rock simply amplified the requirement a thousand-fold. Bowie knew that when he created Ziggy ("Z" — the last, "Iggy" — the Stooge) Stardust, the plastic monster rock star with which he first rose to superstardom; Bryan Ferry knew it too, when he designed Roxy Music as space-age mutants at a '50s hop prog nightclub; and Pop and Reed were certainly aware of it, having already spent their careers building a lifetime's worth of free lunch-worthy legends.

Musically, their latest offerings were simply extensions of their last — sordid city ruminations from Reed, nihilistic hard rock bellowing from Pop. But those album sleeves! Lou in kohl and pancake, dicing with Bowie's own professed bisexuality by stuffing a banana down his road-manager's trousers and sticking his picture on the LP's back cover; Iggy in topless, lean animal splendor, and a pair of gold lame trousers so tight that you couldn't remove them with paint stripper. Kids, buying those albums because of Bowie's involvement, may well have hated both of them. But the sleeves would be pinned to their walls for years after.

Glam rock, as a genuine musical force, was a purely British phenomenon, one which never translated into American streets, primarily because America wasn't set up to handle it. It took its musical impetus from wherever it could — most of T.Rex's best records sounded like revved up Chuck Berry, the best of Bowie's were indeed rewritten from the Velvet Underground. But culturally, it emerged from an event which would not truly be parallelled in the US for years to come — Britain's legalization of adult homosexuality in 1969; an event promptly celebrated in song by the Kinks' vivacious "Lola" (whose composer Ray Davies, incidentally, was allegedly the title character in the Velvets' "Sister Ray"), and teasingly acknowledged through 1971 by the coyly flamboyant Marc Bolan.

Indeed, it was no coincidence whatsoever that each of the movement's major acts were either fronted, or highlighted, by a certain sexual ambiguity: Bowie and Bolan led the pack, but Mud had Rob Davies, all perm and pout and dangling ear-rings; Sweet had Steve Priest, camp chorus lines, and an eye for flirtatious vivacity; Roxy Music had Eno, leonine androgyny in feathers, frills, and ladies' shoes; and Gary Glitter seemed utterly indiscriminating when he asked, in song, if you wanted to touch him *"there."*

For a little under two years, from the spring of '72 to the winter of '73, an entire generation of British teens grew up for whom Gary Glitter's "Rock'n'Roll," Mott the Hoople's "All the Young Dudes," and Roxy's "Virginia Plain" were the cornerstones of a revolution every bit as potent as Elvis' hips, the Beatles' wigs, and the Haight-Asbury trips which had transfixed their forebears. But those things had merely challenged society one level at a time. Glam confronted it on every stage possible.

Not for the first time in rock history was the music a poor second to the packaging, but in the past, only a privileged few could have got away with it. Glam, however, liberated the halt, the lame, the ugly, and the hopeless, until glitter and a pair of platform boots really were all one needed to bring a sprinkling of fairydust to the most disparate of careers.

Bluesy Rod Stewart, owlish Elton John, sensitive Leo Sayer — they all flirted with glam rock, and glam just flirted right on back. Years later, all three would date their own megastardom to the days when getting dressed really meant dressing up, and heading down to a market which functioned on a level so transparent that you could indulge it to whatever level you liked — lifestyle, image, or simply a couple of neat promo tricks with which to flesh out an otherwise skeletal corpse.

Precisely the same equation, of course, would fire punk rock half a decade on. But whereas punk couched its rebellion in rags and tatters, glam glittered in all the finery it could muster — outrageous platform boots, star spangled jackets, crazy color, and rhinestone raunch. Then, when that was accomplished and the last fleck of silver was strategically arranged on immaculate cheekbone, people could get down to the serious stuff.

It was glam's fascination with, and validation of, the gay lifestyle which cracked the doors through which punk's first openly homosexual artists would emerge in the late 1970s — the Tom Robinson Band's "Glad To Be Gay" opus became an utterly unexpected, but almost predictable, Top 20 hit in 1978.

But the shattering of sartorial stereotyping also laid the foundations for the chrysalis of creativity from which punk's most outlandish icons would emerge — as the triumph of style over substance, art over ability, magic over musicianship, gave hope to auteur instrumentalists everywhere. And that was where the New York Dolls sashayed into the picture.

RECOMMENDED LISTENING

Glam Rock Exploding 10 key tributes

MARC ALMOND The Idol (LP *Fantastic Star*)

CARTER USM Glam Rock Cops (45)

FABULON In the Mood (LP *All Girls Are Pretty*)

LONDON SUEDE Trash (LP *Coming Down*)

MARILYN MANSON Dope Show (LP *Mechanical Animals*)

MORRISSEY Glamorous Glue (LP *Your Arsenal*)

NANCY BOY Are Friends Electric? (EP)

PLACEBO Nancy Boy (LP *Placebo*)

ANDI SEX GANG Heaven Shines for You (EP)

THRILL KILL KULT Sex on Wheels (LP *Sexplosion*) .

VELVET UNDERGROUND

LPs

1967 THE VELVET UNDERGROUND AND NICO (Verve)

1968 WHITE LIGHT WHITE HEAT (Verve)

1969 THE VELVET UNDERGROUND (Verve)

1970 LOADED (Atlantic)

1973 SQUEEZE (Polydor)

1993 LIVE MCMXCII (Sire)

Selected Compilations and Archive Releases

1972 LIVE AT MAX'S KANSAS CITY (22 AUGUST 1970) (Atlantic)

1979 1969 – THE VELVET UNDERGROUND LIVE (Mercury)

1985 VU – RARE 1968-69 (Polydor)

1986 ANOTHER VIEW (Polydor)

1995 PEEL SLOWLY AND SEE (Polydor)

RECOMMENDED LISTENING

Covering the Velvets 10 crucial covers of the Velvets; individually and collectively

BAUHAUS Rosegarden Funeral of Sores (B-side)

NICK CAVE All Tomorrow's Parties (LP *Kicking Against the Pricks*)

CLOCK DVA "Black Angel's Death Song" (B-side)

HUMAN DRAMA Caroline Says II (LP *Pin Ups*)

MARC AND THE MAMBAS Caroline Says (LP *Untitled*)

TOM ROBINSON BAND Waiting for the Man (LP *Castaway Club vol 3*)

RUNAWAYS Rock'n'Roll (LP *The Runaways*)

SIOUXSIE AND THE BANSHEES Gun (LP *Through the Looking Glass*)

SLITS Sister Ray (LP *The Official Bootleg*)

TUBEWAY ARMY White Light White Heat (LP *Tubeway Army*)

THE STOOGES

The Stooges represent one of the great treasures of American rock'n'roll. From the primal scream of their early (late '60s) battering, when their *Stooges* debut and *Funhouse* follow-up sent audiences either running for cover or (less likely), staring in rapt admiration, through to the last dance of the fast disintegrating *Raw Power* line-up, Iggy and the Stooges took music to extremes which the human ear could never contemplate and which the human mind could barely understand.

A fiery exorcism of all that the pre-punk era had become, and all that the post-punk years would aspire to, the Stooges were originally discovered when Elektra Records head Jac Holzmann traveled to Detroit to sign the MC5 and was induced to catch the Stooges as well. He wound up signing both bands, but while MC5 have since ascended into the halls of legend on the strength of their rhetoric and a single, thunderous, debut album (followed by two subsequent discs of almost overwhelmingly rockist mediocrity), it was the Stooges who pinpointed the future.

Their debut, produced by former Velvet Underground bassist John Cale, was released in September, 1969, and promptly ushered in two songs which remained touchstones of three chord slobbering banality (as England's *New Musical Express* later put it) a full decade later — "No Fun" and "I Wanna Be Your Dog." A year later, *Funhouse* added "TV Eye," "Dirt," and "1970" to the litany of legends, and if the Stooges hadn't broken up shortly after its release, swamped by drug and personal problems, their next album would have been even greater.

The Stooges were never made for the long haul though. "Our first big gig was at the Grande Ballroom [in Detroit], supporting Blood, Sweat, and Tears," Iggy reminisced. "We played two songs, 'Goodbye Bozos' which later became 'Little Doll,' and 'Asthma Attack.' I used to get really fuelled up on two grams of bikers' speed, five trips of acid and as much grass as could be inhaled before the gig. I found this concoc-

tion was effective enough to completely lose my senses, then we'd gather like a football team and hype ourselves up to a point where we'd scream 'okay guys, whadda we gonna do? KILL KILL KILL.' Then we'd hit the stage."

That was in 1968. By 1970, the Stooges' reputation was complete. "Half the audience walked out after five minutes," sniffed the *Omaha Sentinel*'s live reviewer. "Two hundred years ago, people would have been locked up for acting like that. Now he's a star," growled *Record World*. And *Entertainment World* got down and dirty with the cause for all the distaste. "[Iggy] tosses himself off on stage, runs into the middle of the audience, leaps onto a table, grabs a burning candle vase and lifts it high above his head. For a moment, it looks as if he'll put it back down — dear God, make him put it back down. But no, instead he lowers it over his chest and very slowly spills all its melted wax over his naked chest."

Neither was the nightmare confined to US journalists. "Iggy Pop sells sickness, rampant paranoia and mindless drivel," snarled the *NME*'s Linda Solomon, "the worst kind of psycho drama, as graceful as a maimed octopus, a lean and slimy caveman who had fallen into a bottle of peroxide."

The Stooges split shortly after guitarist James Williamson was lured into their orbit. When the band reunited two years later, encouraged by the patronage of the then-rising David Bowie, it was to Williamson that the surviving original band members (Pop, and the rhythm section of Ron and Scott Asheton) returned.

Flown first to London, then back to L.A., the Stooges would spend much of the next year in the studio, trying with increasing despair and desperation to hone their own vision into something which Bowie's manager, Tony DeFries, would deem acceptable. "We recorded things like 'Fresh Rag,' 'Gimme Some Skin,' 'Sick of You,' 'Scene of the Crime,' 'Tight Pants' and 'Search and Destroy,'" Iggy remembered. "And DeFries freaked. It was far too violent to be associated with David. He let us keep 'Search and Destroy' and the riff to 'Tight Pants' (which became 'Shake Appeal'), then sent us back into the studio."

Released in summer 1973, *Raw Power*'s impact on all which would follow remains indelible. Listened to today, it still boasts a primal immediacy which was seriously lacking, if not absolutely unique, in the annals of the glam-sodden early '70s. For most people, after all, it was David Bowie's patronage which alerted them to the Stooges; he "mixed" *Raw Power* for its ultimate consumption, and the band's dissatisfaction with his efforts went onto become as legendary as the album itself — particularly when it became evident that it didn't matter what the Stooges sounded like. They still wouldn't get played on the radio, and despite the support of both Bowie and his management, they were never going to knock James Taylor off the chart.

The group whiled away their time lazing by the massive heart shaped swimming pool installed by the house's previous owner, Carole Lombard, with just Lee Childers, his secretary Suzi HaHa and a wall caked in fans' graffiti for company. Childers' primary responsibility was to keep the band away from drugs, a monumental task as he recalls it, and one which Iggy and the Stooges were not going to assist him with. Indeed, Childers soon realized that the best he could hope for was to regulate their intake and pray that when he packed them off every morning to the workshop where they rehearsed, they would return in the evening. Otherwise, he would be forced to tour L.A., hunting through the bars and alleyways to locate whichever hole it was that the band had chosen to collapse into that night.

Yet he sympathized with their dilemma. Iggy was a performer, but for months he couldn't perform. Nobody knew what the group were rehearsing for, they simply rehearsed. When Childers asked DeFries why they weren't working, the reply was that the band wasn't ready for it; in almost eighteen months on the Mainman payroll, the band played just two gigs, one in London in July, 1972, and one in Detroit which came close to not even taking place. The night before the show, at the Ford Auditorium, Iggy and guitarist James Williamson disappeared. DeFries later found them crashed out in an alleyway, having pawned all their equipment, including the three-quarter size guitar Iggy had custom built, to buy methadone.

Says Childers, "Iggy was totally crazy by now. He did a local radio interview, he took all his clothes off in the studio and started waving his naked body out of the window, telling passers-by that he was the greatest dancer in the world. He was weird, he was abusive...and the show was a great success. Then he was sent back to L.A. to sit again." Finally, DeFries heard that Jerry Wald, Helen Reddy's manager, had expressed an interest in taking the band off his hands. DeFries leaped on his offer like the Godsend it was. He told Childers to sack the band immediately. Unfortunately, as Childers succinctly puts it, "Jerry Wald thought Helen Reddy was weird. He hadn't seen anything yet!" Wald remained on the scene for little more than a week; the Stooges lived on the street for the rest of the year.

But they also toured America, and continued rehearsing that projected next album, taping every sound which they dreamed of making, and building up a barrage of material which remains the bedrock of the group's reputation. There was talk, briefly, of Todd Rundgren coming in to produce them, but like so much else in the Stooges' universe, talk is cheap. They would do the job themselves — guitarist James Williamson, the Ron and Scott Asheton rhythm section, keyboard player Scott Thurston and Iggy himself scheming the

screaming which would become the unwritten rule of the band's immediate future.

There was no shortage of material, albeit material which exists in a twilight zone which is uniquely its own; a land of desperate nihilism shot through with a rage so tangible that you can still touch it, 25 years on. One by one, the band's lifelines had vanished... Bowie, their friend; Mainman, their management; CBS, their label. On the road, shows booked in the first flush of optimism were degenerating into weird, wired violence. The Stooges had a reputation for drama, danger, and destruction, and audiences wanted nothing less. What could the band do but oblige?

In Los Angeles in late 1973, the Stooges played ten shows in five nights at the Whiskey, and Iggy almost died from physical exhaustion. At Max's Kansas City, he threw a glass on the stage, then rolled in the shards. "My heart is broken," he told the crowd, then he picked up more glass and tried to show it to them.

Beaten, battered, and bruised, the Stooges were sinking, and they not only knew it, they almost welcomed their fate. Songs like "Rubber Legs," "Till the End of the Night," and "She Creature of the Hollywood Hills" captured the band at its most drug-crazed and disillusioned, recording a giant Fuck You to the world, songs which would — with the live "Metallic KO" album standing as their last will and testament — establish the Stooges' worst reputation.

But a studio take of that album's "Cock In My Pocket" proved that the deathwish which allegedly developed over the band's final months, was already firmly in place long before that. "It's like an Eddie Cochran thing," Iggy mused. "Nobody sits down and writes a song called 'I Got My Cock In My Pocket,' but that was basically what I carried around to keep myself alive, so I just stood up at the mike and there it was."

The desultory autobiography of "Open Up and Bleed" oozed the same disillusion and despair. The Stooges regularly ended their live set with this song, drifting from harmonica-fuelled slow blues into a cacophony of protesting feedback, as the band left the stage but didn't tell their instruments. In the studio, armageddon crept in far more quietly. But it was there all the same. And then there was Bo Diddley's "I'm a Man," rewriting the riff which created the Stooges' own "Sick of You," but drawing, too, on energies and emotions which were already old when the world itself was still young.

The nature of the Stooges' last rehearsals and recordings screamed out of the tapes. Reissued on countless occasions over the past 15 years, the sound is sometimes variable, the quality occasionally low-fi. But there's a slovenly majesty to the proceedings all the same, a sense that the world might have trampled across the Stooges' hopes, but at least they could still dream if they wanted.

Quite what they were dreaming of, however, was to be left unsaid. Early in 1974, the Stooges fell apart for the last time, unnoticed, unmourned, unloved, and Iggy himself vanished underground, crawling and vomiting his way down the last corridor of rock'n'roll mythology.

"The name Iggy Pop was synonymous with shit. The guy who'd be tied up in a bag and thrown out of a window two floors up at a Deep Purple gig. The guy whose girlfriend ran off with Robert Plant. The guy who Ian Hunter said would never make it because he had no talent." It would be another four years before Iggy could relay all that to an English journalist, then smile the smile of the truly triumphant. "But I'm still here. Where's Ian Hunter today?"

LPs

1969 THE STOOGES (Elektra)
1970 FUNHOUSE (Elektra)
1973 RAW POWER (Columbia)

Selected Compilations and Archive Releases

1975 METALLIC KO (Skydog — France)
1978 KILL CITY (Bomp)
1995 ROUGH POWER (Bomp)
1996 YOUR PRETTY FACE IS GOING TO HELL (Trident UK)
1997 CALIFORNIA BLEEDING (Bomp)
1999 THE COMPLETE FUN HOUSE SESSIONS (Rhino)
2000 DOUBLE DANGER (Bomp)

RECOMMENDED LISTENING

Stooged Again 10 essential Iggy/Stooges covers
THE CHURCH Endless Sea (LP *Box of Birds*)
DAMNED I Feel Alright (1970) (LP *Damned Damned Damned*)
EMF Search and Destroy (EP)
JOAN JETT I Wanna Be Your Dog (LP *Up Your Alley*)
MISSION 1969 (LP *Resurrection*)
PETER MURPHY Fun Time (LP *Love Hysteria*)
SEX PISTOLS No Fun (45)
SIOUXSIE & THE BANSHEES Passenger (LP *Through the Looking Glass*)
SKY CRIES MARY We Will Fall (LP *Enter at the Axis*)
WYLDE RATTZ (Mark Arm, Ron Asheton, Steve Shelley, Mike Watt) TV Eye (original soundtrack *Velvet Goldmine*)
We Will Fall: A Tribute To Iggy Pop (Royalty, 1997) Features the Misfits, Joey Ramone, 7 Year Bitch, Joan Jett, Lenny Kaye, Jayne County, Sugar Ray, etc.

THE DEVIANTS

The Social Deviants were the archetypal rebels, icons in search of an iconoclast. Their leader, the corkscrew-haired Mick Farren, started life in greasy anti-social groups with names like the Mafia, playing hard-drinking R&B a few circuits down from the nascent Rolling Stones and Pretty Things. But while those early bands aspired to rise above their station, the Deviants seemed determined to sink below it.

Punk before anyone figured out how to spell it, heavy before anyone applied the term to metal, the Deviants (they dropped the Social before their first album) closed the 1960s ranked among rock's most timeless, unsung heroes — with three albums which remain the acid test for anyone who associates that decade with love and peace.

Despite their obvious ambition ("most bands wanted to get fucked up most nights. We wanted to get fucked up every night!"), the Deviants spent most of 1966 hurtling between ill (or non-) paying gigs, and Farren admitted that they might have run hopelessly aground had he and drummer Russell Hunter not stumbled across the ever-enterprising owner of *IT* magazine, Nigel Samuel.

Maybe it was the Deviants' flair which appealed; they were, after all, the only band around who boasted two bassists ("because we already had one, then another one wanted to join and because we liked him, we said yes"). Maybe it was their company. Or maybe it was their drugs.

Samuel handed over seven hundred pounds, and when the Deviants recorded their debut album *Ptoof!* (mutant R&B heavily influenced by everything from the Mothers of Invention to the Fugs, and two years ahead of the Stooges and the MC5 — the two bands most commonly likened to the Deviants), he set up a label to release it on, Underground Impresarios.

There was no major label distribution deal waiting in the wings; instead, the album was distributed through the underground press, it was sold at gigs, and when Farren got a job at the legendary nightclub UFO, he sold it there as well. In the end, some 8,000 copies were passed into circulation, more than enough for Decca, the home of the Stones, to pick it up for a major release. The Deviants had arrived.

Bassist Cord Rees quit in May 1967; Farren, Hunter, and guitarist Sid Bishop were joined by Farren's flatmate Duncan Sanderson, and keyboard player Dennis Hughes, and in this form, the Deviants summoned up the energy to make a second album, *Disposable*.

Farren once described the result as "a methedrine monster," a series of freak-form jams which did or didn't resolve themselves into riffs seemingly at random. The sound of the

Deviants had always hinted at violence, but *Disposable* went beyond simple contemplation. Indeed, if ever a record should have been charged with assault....

Certainly it took just one listen for Decca to determine that once was more than enough. The band was summarily dropped and *Disposable* turned up on another self-made indy, Stable; Sid Bishop was replaced by Canadian guitarist Paul Rudolph, and the Deviants soldiered on.

In short order, they headlined a show on the steps of St. Paul's Cathedral, doing their bit for Christian Aid Week; hit every festival they could crash their way into; and grabbed a proper record deal, with the newly-launched Transatlantic. It didn't dawn on them that a label whose specialty was English folk would not really have much idea what to do with a still-stoned, daily-drunken gang of hippies, whose third (self-titled) album was wrapped inside a picture of a heavily made-up nun suggestively tonguing a vaguely phallic icepop.

The Deviants was recorded during July 1969, to stand as the Deviants' statement of intent... and that of the entire counter-culture. "For the past 13 years," wrote Farren in the album's liner notes, "Rock & Roll has been the secret language of a generation, despite lapses into gibberish and sidetracks into academic obscurity. Rock & Roll is a secret language that the rulers cannot understand." The generation gap, the clichéd division of young from old which was once blamed for every breakdown in societal communication, was suddenly no longer a simple gap; now it was a yawning void.

But it was not a chronological battle any more. It was ideological. You could be 18, and gung-ho in 'Nam; you could be 50, and out of your tree on acid. Age was no longer at issue. It was vision which mattered, and the Deviants had it in abundance.

"We are the people who pervert your children," confessed Farren in "The People Suite" (a two minute suite! Brilliant!), as Rudolph's guitar leaped from speaker to speaker, but worldwide parenthood didn't have much time left to worry.

When the group's manager suggested that Paul Rudolph be given a homecoming concert in Vancouver, Canada, the Deviants gladly agreed. Money was tight, and the band could only afford one-way air tickets. But they were playing three nights at the Colonial Ballroom, and that sounded impressive. Sure they'd make enough for their return trip... wouldn't they?

No. The shows were a disaster, and suddenly, Rudolph, Sanderson, and Hunter found themselves stranded in North America, living off whatever local largess they could find, and instead of saving their money, using it to finance a journey south... to the Promised Land: San Francisco. They later told writer Pete Frame that they'd been "looking for the pot of gold." Instead, they simply found the pot, and spent most of their time getting high, while Farren returned to Britain for a highly successful career in writing, as a music journalist, a sci-fi novelist and, in 1974, the only genuinely readable rock'n'roll novel ever published, the barely varnished truth of *The Tale of Willy's Rats*.

He still recorded occasionally, as well; an EP for Stiff in 1978 (as punk finally embraced his past reputation) was followed by *Vampires Stole My Lunch Money*, a deliciously abandoned solo album which featured contributions from Chrissie Hynde, Wilko Johnson (Dr. Feelgood) and the Pink Fairies' Larry Wallis.

By the mid-1980s, Farren had reformed the Deviants, originally for chaotic annual gatherings in London, but increasingly through the 1990s, as a regular musical outlet. Still anarchic, still attacking, still astonishing, the Deviants' gigs are still like minor apocalypses and their albums still come out on local independents — Bomp in the US, Captain Trip in Japan. In fact, Farren himself has admitted, the only real difference is, he's a lot older now, and he's just got even crankier.

LPs

1967 PTOOF (Decca UK)
1968 DISPOSABLE (Sable UK)
1969 THE DEVIANTS (Sire)
1996 EATING JELLO WITH A HEATED FORK (Bomp/Alive)
1999 THE DEVIANTS HAVE LEFT THE PLANET (Captain Trip — Japan)
1999 BARBARIAN PRINCES LIVE IN JAPAN 1999 (Captain Trip — Japan)

Selected Compilations and Archive Releases

1996 FRAGMENTS OF BROKEN PROBES (Captain Trip — Japan)
2000 THIS VINYL IS CONDEMNED (Total Energy)

UDO LINDENBERG

When Udo Lindenberg first stepped into a solo career, after two years spent playing drums with the German psychedelic blues band, the New City Preachers, few observers could ever have predicted that 30 years on, he would be entrenched as the single most influential musician in his homeland's rock history. Indeed, at the time, most people simply saw him as an impudent musical mischief-maker, obsessed by history's past mistakes and parallels, but who'd be off as soon as he'd annoyed enough famous people.

Hallmarked as they were by Lindenberg's uniquely querulous musical temperament, his first two solo albums, *Lindenberg* (1971) and *Daumen Im Wind* (1972) did little to disavow them of this impression. His third, however, confirmed that Lindenberg was no ordinary troublemaker. Accompanied by his Panikorchester backing band, the monumental *Alles Klar Auf Der Andreas Doria* revealed a savagely psychotic urban street rocker stepping smartly into the role he has occupied ever since — the arch-provocateur of German rock, a fiercely political, angrily questioning artist whose lyrics constantly targeted and satirized a post-war Germany constructed, as he saw it, from many of the same bricks as its wartime predecessor.

Colliding that imagery with such recurrent themes as the doomed liner *Titanic*; the resurgency of Nazism among both German and foreign youth; the Berlin Wall ("for playing tennis, it's too tall"); and extreme nationalism, Lindenberg swiftly established himself as both a vicious and a wildly popular thorn in the authorities' side.

With two, sometimes three new albums appearing every year, and such singles as "Good Life City," "Reeperbahn," and "Russei" maintaining his presence in the German Top 40, by 1976 Lindenberg was unquestionably the most significant domestic artist on the German scene as it unknowingly prepared to greet the age of punk — an age, of course, for which Lindenberg had spent half a decade laying out the welcome mat. Indeed, although his appeal never translated into English-speaking markets, by 1977, Lindenberg's albums were readily available in the UK. The jacket imagery of that year's *No Panik on the Titanic* alone dovetailed perfectly with the prevalent musical mood — a top-hatted, green-faced madman cackling ferociously as the liner sank beneath a fiery sky.

Five years later, with Lindenberg now signed to Island Records in Britain, the single "Berlin" — an English language distillation of much of Lindenberg's apocalyptic vision — received regular late-night radio airplay. Packaged in a sleeve depicting a collage of National Front/Nazi-related news cuttings, the single slipped effortlessly into the climate of warning being fostered by Rock Against Racism and the Anti-Nazi League.

Lindenberg was not only a force for agitation, however. He did much to encourage at least some dialogue between the East German authorities and the then-Communist country's music-starved youth, visiting the country in 1983 and meeting with Erich Honnecker in 1987. He visited the Soviet Union, and was selected as West Germany's sole contribution to the BBC telecast of Live Aid. In fact, as he moved closer towards middle-age (he turned 50 in 1996), Lindenberg embraced the role of elder statesman as readily as he had once accepted the mantel of young punk, a role in which his influence upon the various skeins of German alternative music remains unparalleled among homegrown performers.

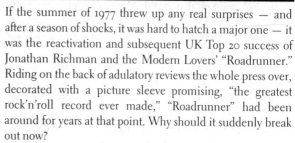

ROCK AND ROLL WITH THE MODERN LOVERS

If the summer of 1977 threw up any real surprises — and after a season of shocks, it was hard to hatch a major one — it was the reactivation and subsequent UK Top 20 success of Jonathan Richman and the Modern Lovers' "Roadrunner." Riding on the back of adulatory reviews the whole press over, decorated with a picture sleeve promising, "the greatest rock'n'roll record ever made," "Roadrunner" had been around for years at that point. Why should it suddenly break out now?

Well, for starters, it was at least one of the greatest rock'n'roll records ever made, but it was also one of the simplest, which is why — from the moment it was released on 1975's *Beserkley Chartbusters* label comp — Richman's musical tour of his hometown, Boston, MA, slipped into the rehearsal room repertoire of every aspiring young band in the UK. By the time the song reappeared, first on a 1975 single, then (a different version) on 1976's oft-delayed release of the band's three-year-old debut album, and finally (both versions) in 1977, "Roadrunner" was already a legend. The hit was simply the sound of a generation grabbing a piece of it.

The Modern Lovers story was short. As a teen, band leader Jonathan Richman had devoted himself to the Velvet Underground, trailing them around the east coast with studious devotion. "I would watch them rehearse," Richman remembered. "I saw them do about 100 live shows, plus rehearsal time. I was a kid hanging out, and an obnoxious one at that." But John Cale was impressed enough that he would later produce Richman's first serious demos, and Tucker loved him so much that she cut a duet with him.

The Velvets broke up in August 1970; the Modern Lovers formed in September. The continuity was that smooth and, as the band developed, it was seamless as well. By the time journalist Lillian Roxon caught up with them in 1972, the Modern Lovers (aka Dance Band of the Highway, aka The Highway Dance Band — it took Richman a while to decide) were at least as intense as their frontman's mentors, and opinions were just as divided over them.

"Jonathan attracted a real diverse bunch of people," original bassist Rolfe Anderson recalled. "When we were on stage at Cambridge YMCA, people were spitting at us out of the balcony, throwing cans at us. It was such a neat dichotomy, 'cos there were other people who really loved us." Anderson himself admitted he very nearly didn't join the band — "when I first heard Jonathan's voice, I said, 'uh-oh! This guy's a singer?'" Roxon, however, loved the band and wasn't afraid to say so.

Rolfe was out of the band by then; in 1972, he was replaced by Ernie Brooks from another Boston group, Albatross. Bandmate Jerry Harrison (keyboards — later of the Talking Heads) followed, and with future Cars founder David Robinson on drums, the Modern Lovers were thrust into the spotlight. Within days of Roxon's review, marveled Harrison, "all these people were coming to see us, all these articles were being written...."

Warner Brothers were the first label to make a serious attempt to catch the band. The Modern Lovers were opening for Aerosmith and the WB executives arrived just in time to see... Aerosmith. Unperturbed, the band arranged a second show in the basement of Harrison's house. Robinson's father, who owned a liquor store, supplied the drinks, and 35 people were invited to attend. Then a 36th arrived, a girl who nobody knew, who spent the entire evening heckling the band.

Still, Warners were impressed and, with the band's newly acquired management, Shifman and Larson (of Loggins & Messina fame), sensing a bidding war, both Warners and A&M were persuaded to fly the band to L.A. for auditions. Alan Mason produced the three-song A&M demo; Velvet John Cale handled the Warners session and the band.

The band returned to the east coast. There they hooked up with entrepreneur Kim Fowley and banged out another album's worth of material before the news that Warners wanted to sign the band pulled them back to Burbank in summer 1973, for a return engagement with Cale. This time, however, it was a disaster. They recorded two songs, they completed neither. Richman's idea of the band's sound was changing and neither producer nor band seemed to like what they heard — skeletal quasi-nursery rhymes about abominable snowmen, bank tellers, and insects.

Cale split to launch a solo career (and record his own version of Richman's "Pablo Picasso") and Fowley flew in to try and salvage something. But the 20 tracks of demos which he squeezed out of the band were scarcely any more successful. By the time the band blew a label showcase, opening for Tower of Power, even their managers had had enough.

Weeks later, Warners informed the band they were letting them go. The official reason was the vinyl shortage caused by the Arab oil embargo — there simply wasn't enough wax around to risk on an untried new band. But just as likely, Warners knew a disintegrating group when they saw one, and by February 1974, the Modern Lovers had indeed collapsed.

Back in Boston, Richman hooked up with former Velvets drummer Mo Tucker and local legend Willie Alexander, to record a new version of a Velvet Underground out-take, "I'm Sticking with You." But it would be spring before another label moved for Richman, the San Francisco-based Beserkley, not only offering a record deal, but also proposing buying the Warners and A&M tapes, and compiling another album from them. Richman agreed, and returned to California, to record the four tracks which would emerge on *Beserkley Chartbusters*: "It Will Stand," "Government Center," "New Teller," and "Roadrunner."

A new Modern Lovers was formed around labelmates the Rubinoos' Curly Keranen; a new sound was forged around the stark simplicity of Richman's new songs. And one posthumous album (plus an ever-lengthening string of quasi-legal live tapes and out-takes) is all that remain of the original band.

Those albums, however, are precious. For at a time when the roots of punk were still not even a glimmer in the eyes of the glam-addled New York Dolls; when the Stooges were locked in their last dark dance with disintegration; and all else was singer-songwriting introspection and gloom, the Modern Lovers were a glass-shattering, peace-destroying, cacophony, granted immortality by just one song, but time and again transcending even that state.

Besides, the spirit, if not the sound, of the Modern Lovers would live on in Richman. Paring down music and lyric but never losing sight of all he originally held dear, even at his most musically obstinate, he remained the same kid who used to follow the Velvets, the same dreamer who wrote "Pablo Picasso," the same genius who came up with "Roadrunner." And he probably still has the radio on.

Punk: New York

To begin with, it wasn't punk rock.

It was art, it was anger, it was boredom ricochetting from arena to club, it was even — as CBGBs club owner Hilly Kristal was want to tag the music oozing from his Bowery bar — street rock. But it wasn't punk rock. That, if you went by the pages of the music press, was still the preserve of the snotty singer-songwriters who'd been emerging elsewhere on the sub-big time mainstream.

Hindsight might be outraged, but there are writers around the U.S. who still remember when Nils Lofgren was "punk," Bruce Springsteen was "punk," Graham Parker was "punk," and the unfathomable racket leeching from the underbelly of New York was just the out-of-tune strummings of so many no-name wanna-bes. And it was only when you dug a little deeper that you realized just how many of them there were.

From the outset, there were two very separate streams of consciousness at work, each with its own set of ethics, each with its own ax to grind. The first came howling out of the Mercer Arts Center, backing onto the old Broadway Central Hotel, where bands with names like Wayne County, Suicide, Teenage Lust, and the New York Dolls strutted their sordid variations on an unsalable theme of glam rock. The second, grimier and gruntier, but a little arty and smarter as well, would make its nest in the Bowery — the Dictators, the Ramones, Patti Smith, Television... dreams and dreamers all.

And the only thing that any of them had in common was: not one of them ever imagined that fate, and sundry seismic reverberations out of England would one day see them conspiring together. Nor that such grim pits could be the catalyst that caused the ensuing explosion — and for a while, they were right, because one day, the Mercer fell in on itself, while Eric Emerson and his Magic Tramps were rehearsing there. But no one was hurt, so they dusted themselves down, and the party moved a few blocks to Max's Kansas City, and the fates continued to conspire from there.

Max's was a legend long before the Velvet Underground recorded their final, live album there, in summer 1970. It opened in December 1965, a restaurant/bar on Park Avenue South, just off Union Square, but few people stopped by to eat and drink alone. The Warhol circus had a sideshow there, the cream of New York arts held court there, and the rest of the planet could only look on in starstruck obeisance. It was, Andy Warhol once said, "the exact spot where pop art and Pop Life came together in the sixties," and over the next decade, Max's ruled that world.

In one corner, David Bowie with his spidery retinue of Martians and mayhem; in the other, the Dolls, all gratuitous sleaze and too many late nights; in another, Alice Cooper... and in the back room, whatever you wanted, whenever you wanted it. It was a sign of how many people took advantage of that offer that, when financial problems threatened to close the club, it was saved by the artists who hung there. Andy Warhol donated a soup can, Michael Steiner, Richard van Buren, David Budd, Roy Lichtenstein, Bridgid Polk — more than 60 of New York's finest — gifted pieces of original art to be auctioned to keep Kansas City in Manhattan.

Owner Mickey Ruskin opened Max's upstairs bar in 1969 to cater wholly to live rock bands, and that became a mecca as well. Bob Marley played his first-ever US shows there, opening for the then equally unknown Springsteen; Aerosmith, Billy Joel, and Garland Jeffreys passed through; Iggy Pop did four nights in knee boots, leather pants, and very little else; Alice Cooper played in a negligee, with paper cones for breasts. And Tim Hardin played there the night a baby elephant urinated on the stage. Hardin finished the song, looked at the elephant, and sighed "everybody's a critic." It's an indication of just how magical Max's was that although everyone remembers Hardin's response, but few even wondered what the elephant was doing there in the first place.

The New York Dolls were the closest thing Max's ever had to a house band, and with good reason. Even if no other city in America would touch them, their city loved them with a flaming passion and the Dolls reciprocated by playing Max's three nights a week, almost every week.

But then Ruskin bowed out in December 1974, and as a light went out on the New York underground, it was strange, Johnny Thunders remarked years later, but a lot of the heart went out of his band at the same time.

It wasn't necessarily an internal dynamic. Ruskin, his widow Yvonne reflected, "really cared about the welfare of other people. He was a true patron of the artists, and was a father figure to LOTS of people. He was the Papa Bear of the counter-culture scene in NYC. He offered lots of encouragement and his generosity provided people a safe sanction from which to flourish. That's why, when Mickey owned Max's, it was definitely a home away from home. You never went without a meal, or even money if you needed it. Mickey was always there to listen and offer a helping hand. He was a hard act to follow."

When Ruskin left, a lot of the Dolls' sense of security went with him, and by the spring of 1974, the band were right back where they started, playing mini-tours of New York City (Club 82, Mothers, back to Club 82...) and saving up songs for their second album, *Too Much, Too Soon.* Indeed.

Max's would reopen for business the following year and reestablish itself as a primo rock venue. But if one believes in Fate, it was no coincidence whatsoever that Ruskin should quit Max's just as Hilly Kristal opened CBGB OMFUG (Country, BlueGrass and Blues and Other Music For Undernourished Gourmandizers). The torch of pioneering patronage which Ruskin had carried so proudly aloft could not have fallen into safer hands.

It lay deep in the heart of the Bowery, fronting the first floor of the biggest flophouse in Manhattan, opened on the site of a club which English journalist Mick Farren remembered having "the worst drag queens on the planet"...in other words, when it came to location, CBGBs had nothing whatsoever going for it. Inside, however, was a revelation.

A long, dark room — essentially an alleyway between the bar on one side and tables on the other — CBGBs boasted some of the cheapest drinks in town, the best burgers in the city, a killer chili (to rival Max's famous chick peas), and owner Hilly Kristal's never-less-than-amazing eye for new bands. It was, said Patti Smith, "basically a hole in the wall," and when Television played there in spring 1974, "there was just a trickling in of people." However, within weeks that trickle became a flood. Of onlookers and participants.

Television told Patti Smith about the place, and she started playing there regularly. The Ramones stumbled across it, playing their first gig opening for the Marbles on New Talent night, and getting invited back almost before they'd finished their set. Blondie emerged and became regulars as well, even as they tried to decide whether the New Musical Express was really being encouraging when it called them "a competent garage band... fronted by a squeaky bath toy."

When Patti Smith Group guitarist Ivan Kral and friend Amos Poe decided to capture New York on film, inevitably they went to CBs to shoo. They emerged with Blank Generation, one of the crucial documents of the age.

The Dictators were the first of the CBGBs regulars to land a "real" record deal — in fact, they'd already signed to Epic before they made their CBGBs debut, establishing themselves firmly as the elder statesmen of a very young scene. Legs McNeil, co-founder of Punk magazine, remembered studying the Dictators' album sleeve while his own dream was still in the pre-publication stage — "it showed them in black leather jackets in front of a White Castle. I think there is also a line in a Dictators' song where someone is called a 'local punk'."

"I can't even remember the number of times the Dictators played at CBGBs," vocalist Handsome Dick Manitoba once admitted. "[But] when I want to feel melancholy and good, I look at the memorabilia of those days. CBGBs was like a home place. No class, on the Bowery, but the same

people who worked there were the same people who came there. It was a rock'n'roll club" — and its denizens would fight to the death for its glory, especially in the face of the reopened Max's. Indeed, heckling Wayne County from the side of the stage one night, Manitoba touched so many nerves that he wound up in hospital with a broken collarbone — and County was slapped with an assault charge, after walloping him with a microphone stand.

Yet the Dictators were considered outsiders as well, as though their very existence a nanosecond or two before the rest of the scene solidified somehow excluded them from full membership of the CBGBs society. For, while the Dictators were celebrating the release of their Go Girl Crazy debut, the rest of CBGBs was playing the Festival of Unsigned Bands.

In late June 1975, ads appeared in the New York locals Village Voice and Soho News announcing auditions. CBGBs had been open little more than 18 months at that point, but already it had established itself as the focal point of the city's convolutions. The Ramones, Television, Talking Heads, Blondie, and Mink DeVille were more than merely up-and-running by now. Patti Smith was so hot that to many local critics, she was CBGBs — and that was the impetus behind the Festival: Hilly Kristal's belief that Smith was just one of so many deserving bands playing the club on a regular basis. "The [critics] were not paying attention to the other bands. They acted like there was nothing here."

Scheduling the festival for what was traditionally a quiet period on the New York scene (the summer dogdays immediately following the Newport Jazz festival), Kristal wasn't expecting too much of a response — the ad for the auditions also carried a splash for an upcoming Ramones/Talking Heads show, and the total attendance was no more than 100.

But the auditions were the cue for every aspiring musician in metropolitan New York to swiftly lash something down on tape and mail it in, a barrage which Kristal painstakingly played through, trying to pick "what I thought were the most interesting bands, the bands that were playing pretty well at this point, and had a little bit of direction that was their own."

By early July, a provisional running order for the event — now officially titled the CBGBs Festival of Unsigned Bands — saw 30 bands onstage between 11:30 and 5 AM every night for twelve nights. By the time the whole thing was over, Kristal had added three further shows, simply to meet the demand for repeat performances. And while not one of the acts would land a record deal as a direct consequence of the Festival, most at least knew they'd made their mark. "The papers wrote about it," Kristal recalled. "It was a really big lift... [not] just to CBGBs, but to this whole new scene in music, which you could call punk or new wave. We called it street rock."

The Festival was a massive success; so massive that when it came time to follow through for the next generation of unsigned, fresh talent, Kristal knew the only way was up — a *Live at CBGBs* album.

Max's Kansas City had already made a move in the same direction, recording a string of representative evenings for release as *Max's Kansas City 76*. It was a strong line-up as well — opening with Wayne County, performing the club anthem "Max's Kansas City," Pere Ubu, Suicide, the Fast, Harry Toledo, the John Collins Band, and Cherry Vanilla all filed through — and in terms of imminent break-out bands, Max's not only had a full hand, they also had enough reserve talent to fill a second volume the following year.

CBGBs, on the other hand, was the victim of its own success. "The Ramones were signed and Television were about to be," Kristal mourned. "I didn't have any choice." He tried recording Blondie "but it came out badly. We went over it, and we wanted it to happen. It just didn't work. We did Talking Heads too, but my agreement was that they could bow out if they didn't want to do it later." They didn't.

Of the club regulars, that left *Hair* actress Annie Golden's Shirts, Tuff Darts, and Mink DeVille, bands which had already been round the record companies once with no takers (all these would be snapped up in the new year), and the Miamis. Echoing the recipe for the previous year's Festival of Unknown Bands, Kristal ran another ad announcing auditions, then culled the cream to complete the album. He was rewarded with the Laughing Dogs, Sun, Stuart's Hammer, and Manster — names which left even CBGBs regulars scratching their heads and asking "who?"

Elsewhere, however, the club's cachet was strong enough that the album sold on the CBGBs brandname alone. With Kristal distributing the album himself, the first pressing of *Live at CBGBs* had already sold a few thousand copies to a European importer and a few thousand more out of the club itself, when Atlantic Records, left behind in the dash for the CBs bands, came in and purchased the rights to the album itself. It wound up selling around 40,000 copies — "not bad for a double album," enthused Kristal; and not at all bad for one stuffed with unknowns.

It was the bands who weren't on the album, however, who would take CBGBs' name the furthest. Patti Smith's *Horses* was released in the fall of 1975, and scored across the US and overseas, too. Richard Hell's "Blank Generation" was licensed for Europe by Stiff Records; and in spring 1976, the Ramones unleashed their debut album, a blaze of supersonic riffery, street-smart badinage, and punctuating every burst of adrenalined fuzz with the inimitable count-in one-two-three-four. Even before the band hit Britain for their first

shows in July 1976, their reputation alone boded more than a simple gig. By the time they left, the Ramones had remade the future in their own ragged image.

Subsequent histories crediting "da Bruddahs" with kick-starting British punk are disproved by chronology alone. The Sex Pistols, the Jam, the Stranglers, and the Damned were already up and running. The Clash were rehearsing, and the Adverts were advertising.

"Nobody had heard a Ramones record at that point in England," Damned drummer Rat Scabies explained. "It was barely out, and hadn't been imported. But we'd seen the photographs of the Heartbreakers, Television, and people. You get the look, and interpret it in your own way, and I think the difference was the whole New York scene was based much more around art and poetry, Allen Ginsberg. Whereas in England, we really didn't have any money, we were all [unemployed], life was in the literal sense, not the romantic one."

But the Ramones' presence, their very existence, undoubtedly helped. A cross-section of the audience at the Ramones' July 4, 1976 show at the London Roundhouse reveals any number of future punk musicians and icons, drawn by the UK media's championing of the band as a counterpart to the scene exploding on the London underground. The Ramones did not create that scene. But they did confirm it.

STRANDED IN THE CONCRETE JUNGLE

America had never seen anything like the New York Dolls. Neither had it ever wanted to. Extolling a hybrid howl which stretched from the Stones to the Stooges, from Berry to Bolan, from Alice to Abba, they then wrapped it up in an attitude which was part trash, part princess, and utterly degenerate. Boston rocker Willie Alexander once gave his pre-pubescent nephew a Dolls record for Christmas, then sat back smiling while the other adults in the room stared in horror. Men in lipstick? What was he trying to do to the child?

Educate him. Musically, the Dolls were a revelation, but visually, they were a revolution and those were the shots which people heard loudest. The best legend was how they came to look like they did — desperate to land a regular gig, it is said, the infant band applied to the transvestite 84 Club in Manhattan, dressing up for the first time simply to add power to their argument.

In fact, they'd been planning the outrage from the start, after one Johnny Volume joined a Manhattan bar band called Actress. He changed his name to Johnny Thunders, the band became the New York Dolls, and having added vocalist David Johansen, the Dolls' great unveiling came in March 1972, at the Diplomat Hotel in Times Square. They'd even invited a few media types down, Danny Fields included, and when he raved about their outfits — "Have You Seen Your Mother"-era Stones colliding with a drunken housewives' convention — the band was set on course.

Fields and '60s entrepreneur turned '70s visionary Marty Thau notwithstanding, few people in the music industry liked the Dolls. Even among the Dolls' own friends; for everyone who saw them as the future of rock, there was another who thought they were the worst thing on ten legs. The Rolling Stones came close to signing them to their own label, until Jagger decided they were "'orrible." But Rod Stewart was so infatuated that he arranged for the Dolls to fly to England to support him before they even had a record contract, and the four New Yorkers who would soon become KISS were equally impressed. Ace Frehley once admitted, "the Dolls were the hottest thing around and we always wished we could be the Dolls because we were nobody at the time. But we weren't physically like the Dolls, who were small, skinny guys, so we decided to come on in black and silver instead."

The Dolls landed in London in 1972 and for a time, it looked as though they might actually stay. But the death of drummer Billy Murcia from a heroin overdose sent them back to New York to draft in drummer Jerry Nolan — whose vivid pink kit Murcia had been borrowing. It was the notoriety which followed Murcia's death which finally prompted Mercury to step in with an offer for the band. The Dolls signed, and after "auditioning" twenty different producers, they settled for Todd Rundgren.

At this point, the band's set consisted largely of covers: Eddie Cochran's "Something Else," Bo Diddley's "Pills," Archie Bell's "Showdown," Sonny Boy Williamson's "Don't Start Me Talking," and the Kinks' "All Day and All of the Night." With Rundgren at the helm, however, the group swiftly settled down to developing their own self-composed repertoire — and sessions taped at Planet Studios in 1973 testify to the ease with which the Dolls took to the songwriting process. By the time their eponymous debut album finally appeared in August 1973, it was already the yardstick by which all future glitter-trash merchants would be measured.

Not that there were too many contenders for the Dolls' throne. While the album reached #116, and an opening spot on the latest Mott The Hoople tour certainly exposed the Dolls to a massive audience, America was proving stubbornly resilient to their charms.

Europe was no better. Just as so many other American hopefuls have discovered to their own cost, British audiences preferred to measure the Dolls up against local talent, then write them off as lacking. The French liked them, but in a land where Jerry Lewis was still spoken of in God-like tones, even the Dolls themselves weren't overly impressed. "Five minutes off the plane in Paris," British journalist Nick Kent reported, "walking towards the airport entrance, Johnny Thunders throws up. Bl-a-a-a-a-a-g-g-h-h!"

But they had an impact regardless. British singer-songwriter Graham Parker recalled, "I remember watching [BBC television's] Old Grey Whistle Test when the New York Dolls were on, in 1973 or whenever, and [host] Bob Harris saying 'I'm sorry, but I really don't like that.' He said it on the air after they played, and I think that must have inspired a lot of kids into saying 'well, we fucking do, this is what we want to see, not bloody Osibisa'; I can imagine a lot of kids... whatever became the Sex Pistols, I think they saw that performance and realized there was something beyond Progressive Music."

To those kids, the Dolls epitomized the cult of the outsider — even at the height of their posthumous punk-era fame; after all, the Dolls were rarely feted for their music or dress sense. It was for applying that music (and dress sense) to an American scene which patently had no time for them. Like the Stooges and the Velvets before them, the Dolls conjured an imagery which could not help but hit home, a sense of society *in extremis*.

Future Sex Pistols manager and trendy Chelsea haberdasher Malcolm McLaren understood that when he joined the Dolls in the US in fall 1974 to pick up the strands of a relationship launched the previous summer, when he and partner Vivienne Westwood were in New York, trying to shop Westwood's latest clothes designs — retro '50s chic meets *A Clockwork Orange*. They never took a single order, but the Dolls were impressed, and they all kept in touch. A year later, they asked him to become their manager.

McLaren redesigned the Dolls, dressed them as Communists and was kind of surprised that nobody outside Manhattan really took to the new look. Indeed, while such slogans as "better Red than dead" and a stage draped in Communist paraphernalia might have been a great joke among the New York art set, in the great American heartland, nobody even thought of laughing. How different, McLaren pondered, it would be if he could apply that same sense of outrage to Britain, with its centralized media and fad-hungry press, and a public who knew what to follow, without being sheep. How different, and how eminently saleable.

He flew home in summer 1975, and six months later, he launched the Sex Pistols. The Dolls' dream had been of subverting the system from without, but the system was too strong. McLaren learned from his own mistakes. You had to kick the door down from the inside.

RECOMMENDED LISTENING

WAYNE COUNTY Paranoia Paradise (EP)
DICTATORS California Sun (LP *Go Girl Crazy*)
HEARTBREAKERS Chinese Rocks (LP *LAMF*)

RICHARD HELL Blank Generation (45)
THE RAMONES Beat on the Brat (LP *Ramones*)
PATTI SMITH GROUP Hey Joe (45)
SUICIDE Cheree (LP *Suicide*)
TALKING HEADS Psycho Killer (LP *Talking Heads* 77)
TELEVISION Little Johnny Jewel (45)
CHERRY VANILLA I Know How to Hook (LP *Bad Girl*)

NEW YORK DOLLS

LPs

1973 NEW YORK DOLLS (Mercury)
1974 TOO MUCH TOO SOON (Mercury)

Selected Compilations and Archive Releases
1981 LIPSTICK KILLERS — MERCER ST SESSIONS
1984 RED PATENT LEATHER

IGGY IN EXILE

"You may not recognize me, but my name's Iggy Pop. I've just been worked over for a week by a Transylvanian masseuse in San Francisco…" and so Iggy Pop broke a silence which stretched back more than two years, turning up unannounced at a Patti Smith gig at the L.A. Roxy in January 1976, and then vanishing back into legend again.

What a legend it was becoming though. More active in obscurity than he'd ever been when he had a record deal, Iggy's name had been attached to more abortive possibilities than probably even he was aware of: a UK tour in May 1974; an album for Elton John's Rocket label; and a new band with the Doors' Ray Manzarek.

He guested at the 1974 Jim Morrison commemoration gig at the Whiskey in Hollywood, and the New York Dolls' Death of Glitter festival; he was trussed up in a bag and thrown out of a window at a Deep Purple aprés show party; he gouged a hole in his own chest at the opening night of his play *Murder of the Virgin*, while his ex-guitarist whipped him with electrical flex; and he started a new album with Stooges guitarist James Williamson. They never finished it, though, and when Iggy shambled out of the studio leaving nine tracks unfinished, he probably thought they never would.

Unfinished music was the order of the day. In May 1975, David Bowie and his backing singer, Geoffrey MaCormack (aka Warren Peace) had dragged Iggy into an L.A. studio to record an archetype for what would one day become the gratuitously autobiographical "Turn Blue." But he walked out of that as well and, though he promised to return to the stu-

dio later, he never did. Afterwards, he phoned his mentor to apologize. Bowie told him to piss off. "I hope he's not dead," Bowie mused later on. "He's got a good act."

He wasn't dead, but he was close. Thrown out of James Williamson's apartment after one transgression too many, Iggy got a fistful of downers from an obliging L.A. doctor, dropped by a local diner — and dropped into somebody's dinner.

The cops gave him a choice — jail or hospital; he chose the hospital, then discharged himself and hitched a ride out of town. The next thing he knew, he was puking vivid green bile on a sidewalk somewhere. That's when even he knew he'd had enough. He checked himself into a psychiatric institute, which is where Bowie picked him up again in spring 1976, hauling him away from the Transylvanian masseuse, to join his latest tour entourage.

Bowie's initial idea was to record a one-off single with Iggy. Based around a lurching riff his guitarist had concocted, Bowie had written just one verse of "Sister Midnight" when he showed the song to Pop. The speed with which Iggy completed that lyric, then reeled off enough material for half a dozen more, convinced Bowie that they should set their sights on an album.

"Bowie gave me a chance to apply myself, because he thinks I have some talent," Iggy mused. "I think he respected me for putting myself in a loony bin. He was the only guy who came to visit me, nobody else came. Not even my so-called friends in L.A. But David came."

The monolith which became *The Idiot* started life at the Chateau D'Heurouville, outside Paris, where Bowie was recording his own *Low* album. From there, the party moved to Munich, and finally Berlin, by the Wall, where they completed a record which the watching Eno would promptly describe as "an experience akin to being encased in a block of concrete"… but which so thoroughly reinvented the Pop legend that when he toured the UK and US in spring '77, he didn't even need to roll in broken glass anymore. The music was immolating enough.

The Idiot was released in March 1977, but any fears his label, RCA, might have entertained about the album's reception had long since been quashed by circumstances elsewhere.

Iggy hung over the nascent British Punk scene like a predatory bat. Indeed, he'd been a part of the British pop psyche for so long that even without the Bowie connection, his past self-destruction had become part of the language. His refusal to indulge in similar terror tactics now only embedded them even deeper. Before *The Idiot* was even released, The Damned had recorded the Stooges' "I Feel Alright," the Pistols had covered "No Fun," and The Adverts' Gaye Advert had glued his photo to her bass.

French imports of the first two Stooges albums, the only available pressings for six years or more, were selling out everywhere, finally prompting domestic reissues that spring. *Metallic KO*, a quasi-bootleg document of the final Stooges concert, all breaking glass and rampant Hell's Angels, was omnipresent. Even a hastily repackaged budget reissue of *Raw Power* made the UK Top 50, and everybody marveled at just how densely packed the monster sounded. Presumably, David Bowie had remixed the Stooges' tapes to make them sound like the noises in his head. Apparently, he'd had a migraine that day.

The Idiot climbed to #30 in the UK; its successor, *Lust For Life*, #28 six months later, statistics which indicated just how thoroughly punk had changed the face of British music. Nine months earlier, Iggy Pop seemed as likely to have a hit record as he was to walk on the moon. Maybe even less. Now he'd had three in one year. But when the national press, ever-hungry for a handle for the reborn Pop, rechristened him the Godfather of Punk, his retort was one of exquisite disdain. "I'm not a Punk anymore. I'm a damned man."

Undeterred, the audience for Iggy's two London shows in March 1977 represented a virtual punk pilgrimage. No less than the Ramones' first visit eight months previous, there was nowhere else you'd dream of being.

Ex-Pistol Glen Matlock and the Damned's Brian James were there, opening the friendship which would see them join Iggy's 1978 *New Values* and 1979 *Soldier* bands respectively. Howard Devoto, ex-Buzzcock was there, handing Iggy a copy of that band's *Spiral Scratch* EP and telling him, "I've got all your records. Now you've got all mine."

The Adverts, who would open Iggy's next UK tour; The Vibrators, who supported on this one; Siouxsie and the Banshees, Johnny Rotten — the whole gang was there. And David Bowie, ivory-tinkler throughout the tour, was completely ignored as a new generation filed in to pay homage to their hero. It was probably then that one realized just how great a debt punk owed the Pop. And how little he wanted in return. "The present generation don't owe me anything. I did it all for myself."

Anarchy in the UK

The Ramones inherited England, but was England actually worth inheriting?

A social study of the UK as the 1970s rolled towards their cleavage makes depressing reading, a litany of labor disputes and soaring unemployment, rampant inflation and racial unrest.

The Irish Republican Army was at its violent peak, actively and accurately targeting soft British cities. A dying socialist government was grinding to a halt, the far Right was raising its inner city profile. As the 30th anniversary of the end of World War II rolled around, Britain looked more like the loser than ever, an apocalyptic battlefield waiting to happen. And the sun just kept on shining.

The summer of 1975 was one of the hottest on record; a garden-killing, drought-inducing scorcher which left the cities baking in their own thick smog. The following year,1976, it would be even worse. Once, kids hung out on street corners because it was something to do. Now they did it because there was nothing else to do. It was too bloody hot.

The hit records of the age sum up its redundancy — fat Greek balladeers, aging Country & Westerners, singing prime-time comedians, the interminable bloat of "Bohemian Rhapsody." "In 1974–75, there weren't a lot of lulls in the tedium," Banshee Siouxsie reflected. "There was Roxy Music, but Bowie was past it, Lou Reed was... losing it. There was Sparks, thank goodness for them, and it was really important to see them on television, they were one of the few bands you'd see and say 'thank God there's something good on,' in amongst all this idiocy. But that was it."

The Damned's Brian James felt the same way about the Heavy Metal Kids, a knowing wink of rock and raucousness wrapped up in space age Dickensian rags and tatters. "They kinda filled a little bit of a gap among all that pomp of the early 1970s. You had the hippie side, you had the Glam thing that was taking itself so very seriously, and then there was Gary Holton and his boys, just being silly."

But even at their peak — three albums by Sparks, a dynamic debut by the Kids — both bands were out on an increasingly precarious limb. It was the time of slick production and production-line disco, faceless heavy metal and introspective singer-songwriters; nothing you could sing to and even less you'd want to dance to. Great Pop is the voice of the people set to music, but when it's too hot to sing, and you're too tired to play.... If it wasn't for Thin Lizzy's, "The Boys Are Back in Town," that entire summer of 1976 would have been a stinking, sweltering, wasteland. But even Lizzy didn't really know who the boys would turn out to be — nor

where the final part of the ultimate equation would be drawn from.

Unseen for several years, but finally latched onto by the press around the end of 1974, a whole new generation of bands had grown up around (or more precisely, within) the British pub circuit, creating ripples at least as powerful as those radiating out of the New York City bar equivalent. It was, of course, called *pub rock*, and it was a revelation.

Throughout the early-mid 1970s, the rock concert circuit in Britain was firmly in the thrall of a handful of organizations, each one jealously guarding its stable of name bands by allowing management and record companies to continue filtering in a steady trickle of "up and coming" acts. If a band didn't have those initial contacts, though, the chances of them breaking into even the lower echelons of the conventional touring circus declined accordingly. So they went for the unconventional one instead — to the network of pubs which pocked British cities, and which always wanted someone to entertain the punters. In the past, they'd relied on informal weekend talent shows. Now they booked bands. And so long as the drinkers kept on buying drinks....

By the time the music press figured out what was really going on, the scene was already strong enough to have warranted a few major label signings — Ace went to Anchor, and scored a hit with "How Long," the Hammersmith Gorillas signed with Page One, Ducks Deluxe joined RCA, Brinsley Schwarz joined UA, Kilburn and the High Roads signed with Warners.

They'd broken through to the theaters as well — through January/February 1975, Dr. Feelgood, Kokomo, and Chili Willi and the Red Hot Peppers launched a full scale invasion of the UK with the Naughty Rhythms Tour. It was one of the biggest hits of the year, and it turned the hitherto unknown Feelgoods into superstars. And with good reason.

Spiraling out of the oil refining wasteland of Canvey Island, on the edge of east London, the Feelgoods fired a solid battery of short, sharp R&B; primal Rolling Stones if they'd found speed instead of acid. Totally retro in their wedding suits and R&B chops, they were tight, aggressive, and they looked so tough they could beat you up from 15 yards, and they wouldn't even spill their drinks. "Hiroshima in a pint glass" is how the *NME* once described them, but even that was an understatement. The Feelgoods probably didn't even drink from pint glasses, they chewed their beer straight from the hops — and that included guitarist Wilko Johnson, a solid teetotaler. Johnson mimed machine gun attacks while he played; Lee Brilleaux sang with the savagery of some terrible jungle cat growl; and the rhythm section thought it was the San Andreas fault. And at their best (and for two albums/three years, they were always at their best), the Feelgoods unleashed a sonic firestorm which established them among the most popular live bands in the country... without even one hit single to sustain them. Just a couple of years later, punk rock passed by the Feelgoods without a second glance, but the soil would have been a lot rockier if they hadn't tilled it first.

If the Feelgoods had any real competition, it was Eddie and the Hot Rods — a band which did make the transition from R&B to punk (or at least, if we jump ahead a few chords, to new wave), but whose roots, and indeed forte, lay inside those same sweaty pubs and clubs. The difference was, whereas the Feelgoods, irrespective of their real ages, gave the impression of purist maturity, the Rods were very young, very loud and very, very snotty. They even had a song (later the title of their first album) called "Teenage Depression," and early in 1976, it was a potent rallying cry.

The Rods made one mistake, though, and in a lot of ways, it was one too many. On February 12, 1976, the unknown Sex Pistols were booked to support the Rods at the London Marquee — and they stole the show, smashing the headliners' gear in the process, and hurling obscenities at the crowd. Or so Hot Rod Dave Higgs complained afterwards.

"They can't play or nothing, they just insult the audience. They wrecked our PA, we waited for them to apologize, but they had fucked off." It would be another few months before anyone realized that that was precisely the point of these punk rockers: the fact that they couldn't "play or nothing," and they wouldn't have admitted it if they could. But the world wasn't ready for that revelation, and so the pub rock explosion continued. Again, it was only later that anyone realized that, though the generation of musicians who were bloodied by punk was not entirely blooded in the pubs, enough of them certainly were. Ducks Deluxe, whose Sean Tyla would go on to write one of the seminal proto-punk classics, "Styrofoam," fathered new wave maestros the Motors; Brinsley Schwarz featured future Damned/Wreckless Eric producer Nick Lowe; Chili Willi and the Red Hot Peppers boasted Elvis Costello sideman Pete Thomas on drums; Costello himself came out of Flip City; Ace's keyboard player, Paul Carrack, joined Squeeze; the 101ers' guitarist, Joe Mellor, formed the Clash. And then there was Roogalator, who blueprinted so much of the new wave's early focal points that even they never knew for certain what had happened.

Of all the acts signed to the soon-to-be-seminal Stiff Records in 1976, during the six months between its pub rock birth and the first, Damned-led stirring of its punk rock heyday, few had the critical punch of Roogalator. The *New Musical Express* spread the band over its center pages in December 1975, and asked "is this the future of rock'n'roll?". Record companies prostrated themselves at the band's feet and everywhere the band turned, there was an endless procession of would-be managers, agents, and A&R men telling them, "you're the biggest thing since Springsteen, and we'll sell Roogalator pajamas."

They were almost right as well, except Roogalator themselves would never reap the benefits. Within six months of Roogalator's *All Aboard* EP debut, Elvis Costello had borrowed Cincinnati-born vocalist Danny Adler's glasses and haircut, and launched himself as an even Angrier Young Man. Within a year, keyboard player Nick Plytas was working with the Tom Robinson Band and Lene Lovich (and eventually wound up in the house band on the *Jonathan Ross Show*). And within two, Roogalator had shattered, with just that early EP and a latter-day album to show for three years of non-stop touring.

Adler's forte, at least through Roogalator's early peak, was conjuring a very English sounding music from some distinctly American-sounding imagery — his songs echoed with references to Amtrak and the mid-west, while the band's best known number (courtesy of that Stiff EP) was the unequivocally titled "Cincinnati Fatback."

It was pure synchronicity, then, that rising at almost exactly the same time was an artist whose approach was the precise reversal of Roogalator's, a writer who took his suburban English sensibilities, and welded them to a solidly American sound: Graham Parker. And the press adored him as well. Parker himself fought grimly against the pub rock tag. Emerging in mid-1975 with his band, the Rumour (themselves made up from sundry Brinsley Schwarz, Bontemps Roulez, and Ducks Deluxe alumni), Parker joined Adler in absolutely predicting the direction in which great swathes of the forthcoming punk storm would move, translating onto his vinyl the emotions which had hitherto been confined to other people's rhetoric. "I was angry at the way pop music was," Parker reflected, "I was angry with the flatulence of it all and I thought what I was doing should be the kind of music people were into, instead of still lying down in the dark listening to *Dark Side of the Moon*, and they all jump when the alarm bell goes off and they all roll a joint."

Across two albums in a year, *Howling Wind* and *Heat Treatment*, Parker's ferocious soul rock hybrid ("angry Motown" he called it) left British critics agape, and traditional rockers aghast. Maybe Bob Dylan did describe Parker's "(Hey Lord) Don't Ask Me Questions" as one of the greatest songs he'd ever heard, but Parker's take-no-prisoners assault upon all that had once been deemed holy wasn't simply sacrilegious, it was positively iconoclastic.

Up there again with Lofgren, Adler, Patti Smith, Bob Seger (championed, oddly but convincingly by the Hot

Rods), and Springsteen, then just breaking through in Britain with his white tee and leathers, Parker represented a new breed of rocker — "punks" in the sense that Hollywood's Dead End Kids were punks, city-smart street urchins with guitars instead of switchblades, lyrics instead of graffiti. For a few months through the spring of 1976, the word "punk" turned up a lot in the UK music press, and it had nothing to do with the Pistols or safety pins. Then the real thing happened and the Rumour just groaned. "Our attitude to Punk was, we were kind of jolted. We were in a field of one, we were the happening kids, we were outrageous doing things like 'Can't Hurry Love' really aggressively; doing reggae with this angry attitude; we had it all together, and suddenly we were not the only ballgame, there was this thing called the Sex Pistols, and it was — 'oh my God, what's going on?'"

For a few months, Parker and punk marched hand in hand. "Until punk, we were not reaching a mass audience; we weren't really solidifying what we had, we were still a press act in a way. But when punk happened, we increased our audience. We'd play some gigs where the whole front rows were swarming with kids spitting at us because they had read somewhere that I was the godfather of punk or the grandfather of punk, and so we did start to attract a wider audience."

The group scored their first hits, and toured with Thin Lizzy, a gruelling blitzkrieg across the UK which saw that band, too, earn even more grudging punk respect, simply through their choice of support. Like the Dictators in New York, however, the Rumour could also be considered a throwback to an earlier age. No matter that the likes of Nick Lowe, Elvis Costello, and Kilburn and the High Roads' Ian

Graham Parker

© Jim Steinfeldt/Chansley Entertainment Archives

Dury were now riding punk's coattails to glory, the fact is, they also emerged with its birth pangs, part and parcel of an exciting new movement. Graham Parker and the Rumour, on the other hand, were already onto their third album. "At the time," Parker continued, "I thought it was good I was before everyone else, because I thought everyone would remember that. The attitude of the music I was doing would be reflected in what was going on. I thought because I was first, that was great, I started it."

But of course it didn't work like that, and Parker himself still remembers the moment when underground acceptance finally passed him over. It wasn't when the Rumour opened for Bob Dylan at Blackbushe Aerodrome, it wasn't their highly publicized signing to Arista Records, and the ensuing *Squeezing Out Sparks* smash hit. It was just another night in London, when the Rumour played the Roundhouse.

"That's when I knew the wind was finally changing. Pere Ubu and Devo opened for us and after the gig, all the press ran backstage. And I remember standing at my dressing door, and they all ran past me, straight into Devo and Pere Ubu's dressing room. It was like a cartoon, and I thought 'uh-huh, something's changed here.'"

What had changed was the perception of what pub rock itself had changed into two years earlier. Pub rock's importance is not as much for who it produced, but for what it allowed to be produced. Even remembering Graham Parker's hatred of *Dark Side of the Moon*, few of this new generation of bands were reacting solely against the increasingly horsefaced convolutions of the rock'n'roll elite — the ELPs, ELOs, and REO Speedwagons of that poor benighted world.

True, there was no room for any of those bands' nonsense in the pubs, no time for three-hour synth epics or interminable drum solos, just a non-stop diet of driving rock'n'roll, a savage beat and scything guitars and musicians who dressed like the boy next door. But pub rockers were still proud of their instrumental prowess, still thought that complicated chord changes were something to write home about, and when the Hot Rods condemned the Sex Pistols' lack of musicianship, that's precisely what they were talking about. The Flamin' Groovies, poster children of the early *Sniffin' Glue* fanzine, would bite the same dust six months later, when they attacked the Damned's lack of musical virtuosity. And when the Sex Pistols signed with A&M in 1977, and the label's roster turned out to complain, it wasn't the singer-songwriters who roared the loudest, it was the left-over '70s prog rockers whose own peregrinations were suddenly under threat. After all, if musical virtuosity didn't sell any more — what was the point of that classical education?

The Sex Pistols were incompetent, even manager Malcolm McLaren knew that. They could barely play, Johnny

Rotten could not sing, and right at the start, their songs were simply a succession of atrociously rendered covers, held together by Rotten's genuinely caustic personality. But their incompetence was also a virtue, their ugliness a beauty. It was an age, after all, when the Tate Gallery's decision to exhibit a pile of bricks as a work of "modern art" was still capable of inspiring fiery controversy. To the people who could see the point of those bricks, the Pistols were not that great a departure.

"The scene already kind of existed," Damned drummer Rat Scabies recollected. "It wasn't like 'oh wow here's the Sex Pistols, I'm going to and be a punk.' It was, 'oh, here's one of the other groups that are kind of on the edge of what we're doing'." And what they were doing was provoking a reaction among people who thought that music was made by musicians. The first press coverage which the Pistols received dwelled more on the fights which they started with their audience, than with anything so mundane as the music; the first time punk rock itself made the headlines was when a girl lost an eye at the 100 Club Festival. Rock'n'roll had become a steady job, staffed, even at grassroots level, by wide-eyed careerists for whom plugging in an instrument wasn't much more of an emotional trip than plugging in a typewriter. And at the start, the kids with whom McLaren and his assistant, Bernie Rhodes surrounded themselves were no different. Within the ranks of both the Pistols and Rhodes' London SS, only Rotten could realistically claim never to have entertained daydreams of incipient pop stardom. Of the others — the Pistols' Cook, Jones, and Matlock, and the SS's Brian James, Tony James and Mick Jones — all started out worshipping the pop icons of their recent past.

Once they had been deconditioned, however; once the allure of "making it" had been replaced by the notion of smashing "it" first, then things started to change. And they started that night at the Marquee, when the Sex Pistols incurred the Hot Rods' wounded wrath.

For the first time in its history, rock'n'roll was experiencing a generation gap within itself. For the first time, its elders were looking down on their uncultured offspring and chiding, "kids today." And for the first time, those kids just looked right back at them and laughed.

THE STRANGLERS

The Stranglers weren't punk, but they sure made the right noises. Born in 1974 as The Guildford Stranglers, operating out of a tiny Surrey village called Chiddington and not really looking capable of progressing out of it, the band might have spent its entire career in the shadows of the pub and club scene if events elsewhere had not conspired to inflate them.

Neither did the band members themselves — Hugh Cornwell (vocals, guitar), Jean Jacques Burnel (bass), aged drummer Jet Black and keyboard player Dave Greenfield — have particularly high hopes. By their own admission, they were a terrible band. "We still had good songs... but we were terrible" — and audiences appeared to agree. The handful of venues which booked the Stranglers once, would seldom book them again and, while late 1975 saw them having graduated to the lower London circuit, supporting the likes of comedy troupers Albertos Y Los Trios Paranoias at the pubs and dives, it took the first stirrings of punk to give the Stranglers an audience they could... not identify with, but at least play to.

Indeed, by the summer of 1976, the Stranglers were opening for the Flamin' Groovies and the Ramones at the Roundhouse and Dingwalls, while their press debut came in the first ever issue of *Sniffin' Glue*, an enthusiastic Mark P opining, "their sound is 1976. The Stranglers are a pleasure to boogie to — sometimes they sound like the Doors, other times like Television, but they've got an ID of their own."

DJ John Peel was not so convinced, although he did admit that behind the quartet's piss-poor musicianship, there was "a compelling seediness." And audiences awaiting Patti Smith at Hammersmith Odeon in the fall weren't impressed either, walking out almost *en masse* before the band had even started to "boogie." Unperturbed and certainly unrepentant, the Stranglers landed their own headlining UK tour through November 1976, and finally things began to click, even for folk unimpressed in the past. Maybe it was the extra gigging; maybe they'd simply decided to rehearse. But though the songs were the same, and the sound and the noise, somehow it now seemed listenable. Even enjoyable.

They courted and won the punk crowd (including the notorious Finchley Boys gang), at the same time as United Artists swooped where no other label cared to tread, and signed the band. And in December 1976, work commenced on the Stranglers' first album — a wild set intended to echo their now compulsive live performance, with extra effects thrown in for atmosphere.

The group seemed hellbent on causing controversy. Aware of the public disquiet over this new punk music, and anxious to do something about it, the Greater London Council decided to start keeping a close eye on the antics of these little snotnoses. So, when they heard that Hugh Cornwell had recently been sighted wearing a T-shirt which, parodying the famed Ford logo, featured the word "Fuck," the Council immediately demanded the band guarantee that their next London gig (at the Roundhouse, supporting the Climax Blues Band) be conducted without any further lewdness.

The show's promoter agreed, but Cornwell didn't. As the band's set approached its climax, Cornwell revealed the T-shirt and told the audience what had been said. He took the shirt off and the band played on. Then, as they kicked into their next song, he put it on again. The management cut the power and the band was finished for the night.

The Stranglers' first single, "Grip," was released in February 1977, selling over 2,000 copies in its first week and eventually peaking at #44 in the chart... a good start. A John Peel session followed and in March, the album arrived, abandoning its original title of "Dead on Arrival" in favor of the more atmospheric IV Rattus Norvegicus.

The record rocketed to #4, an astonishing achievement until one realized that it was also an astonishing album. The Stranglers had arrived, and it seemed they could do no wrong. "Peaches," a deliriously sexist account of a day at the seaside, gave the Stranglers a major hit (and 20+ years later, would be co-opted as the theme tune to a BBC cookery program!), simultaneously becoming the first British chart smash ever to include the word "clitoris" in its lyric.

It was ironic, then, that the next Stranglers controversy revolved not around their choice of words, but the manner in which they presented them. The picture sleeve for the "Peaches" single, its credits written in blackmail-note-style cut-out lettering, had to be withdrawn after some folk complained that it was an incitement to crime!

So were the Stranglers as disgusting as they were painted? Probably. They were certainly old enough to know how offensive their macho ramblings were; but they were also cynical enough to know that offensiveness often helped sell records. And while nobody would say their audience only bought the records so they could hear women being abused, when one's prime audience is teenaged (and male), a bit of titillation couldn't hurt. "Making love to the Mersey Tunnel with a sausage," after all, was only one of their finer lyrical moments.

The band's problems continued. A dose of flu saw the Stranglers' first post-"Peaches" UK tour get off to a very shaky start as Cornwell was forced to postpone the first show, then collapsed following the second. Two shows more were cancelled in the wake of the riots when the Clash played the London Rainbow and every other club owner got paranoid that the punks might do the same to him. And when shows went ahead, they didn't go according to plan. In Cleethorpes, Burnel demanded the audience stop fighting one another, and suggested they fight him instead. Of course they did. At another gig, he was bitten on the leg — hard; and at the band's hotel one night, a clash with local police left the bassist with a battered hand and a few more canceled gigs to contend with.

More trouble. The French army, noting that Burnel's parents were also French, decided JJ was ripe for a spot of military service. For a few days there, the hard man of punk looked like he might never squirm out of that one... but he did, and the band celebrated with their third hit single, "Something Better Change." (They also proved that they could behave themselves around the fairer sex when they backed singer Celia Gollin on her debut single, a terrific version of "Mony Mony" credited to Celia and the Mutations.)

No More Heroes, the band's second album (and fourth single) followed, a hurried disappointment highlighted by "I Feel Like a Wog", "Bring on the Nubiles," and an abysmal studio rehash of "Peasant in the Big Shitty" — pre-deal favorites one and all. But, of course, the headlines weren't far away, after it was revealed that one song, "Dagenham Dave," was the Stranglers' ode to an old-time fan who, distraught at been ousted in the band's affections by the Finchley mob, took the only way out and killed himself.

On the road, too, trouble followed the band like a well-oiled magnet. In Sweden, they clashed with the local Teddy Boys, the Raggere. In England, they tangled with the police. But the music kept coming. Radio One taped one of the band's Roundhouse gigs for broadcast and later, for the live LP, X Cert — a fairly accurate portrayal of the band as they prepared to close the book on the first stage of their development; Warner Brothers taped their Hope & Anchor Festival appearance for a two-album live set, Front Row Festival.

A secret tour of small venues took the band through the winter of 1977; away from the big stage, they were at last able to start introducing new material into the set, including "5 Minutes" — released as a single in January 1978, and "Nice'n'Sleazy," its follow-up. Then came a tour of North America and, in April, the third Stranglers' album.

Black and White, released — of course — in both black and limited edition white vinyl, was a marked improvement on its predecessor. "5 Minutes" was absent, which confused a few pop-spotters, but "Nice'n'Sleazy" and a churning assassination of Dionne Warwick's "Walk on By" both made it on, together with "Sweden (All Quiet on the Eastern Front)", an account of the band's ongoing relationship with the Raggere. The live album followed, prefacing the release of Burnel's first (and somewhat overdone) solo album *Euroman Cometh*; a handful of summer festival shows, however, proved that neither ideas nor unity were lacking in the Stranglers' camp and, when the band opened for the Who at Wembley, all but two tracks from the first two albums had disappeared from view.

Now it was *Black and White* and the forthcoming *The Raven* which dominated the band's set; a new, less dense and distinctly more pop-oriented sound which paved the way for the astonishing commercial (if not critical) renaissance the Stranglers were to experience during the early 1980s. Like so many other bands of the era, they had finally turned their backs on punk. Unlike so many others, they replaced it with something just as valuable.

SNIFFIN' GLUE/ATV

It was the old, old story. Bored bank clerk falls in love with punk rock, types and handscrawls a few pages about it, xeroxes a fanzine, sells it at gigs, creates a monster, starts a new fashion. The first issue of Mark Perry's *Sniffin' Glue* appeared in July 1976 and, as much as the music it aimed to document, it fired a new fashion.

That first issue's cover flagged the Ramones and the Blue Oyster Cult; the Punk Reviews page visited the Flamin' Groovies and the Stranglers; and the intro warned of the treats to follow — the Nazz and Todd Rundgren, Roogalator, the Raspberries, the Mothers of Invention, and the Count Bishops. There really wasn't much punk around in those days. By Christmas 1976, however, there was barely a mention of any band more than six months old, and not a hint of Perry's early interests.

Other 'zines followed, most in the spirit of *Sniffin' Glue's* own violent intimacy; others stepping even further out of the realms of either musical or literary conformity. Most, however, followed the one tried and trusted dictate of 'zinedom — as the *NME* put it, "a fanzine must be passionate, hectic, glorious, and inconsequential." Most were. But none repeated the impact of *Sniffin' Glue*.

Perry's baby grew with the scene it championed, and for a year, *Sniffin' Glue* ruled the British fanzine roost. When Perry slammed the Jam, his words were so sainted that Paul Weller retaliated by burning the offending issue on stage. And when he recommended that readers go to the news agent and spit inside a copy of *ZigZag* to disgust that magazine's traditional hippy readership... readers did.

But Perry was growing tired of simply writing about bands — he wanted to step out and be written about himself. His last group, the hopefully-named New Beatles, had done

nothing whatsoever; his next, Alternative TV, could scarcely do any worse.

Harry Murlowski, *Sniffin' Glue's* assistant editor, came up with the band name, said Perry; "[we] were walking past a theater and Harry said, 'it's like alternative TV.' It was such a sharp and weird thing to say."

Featuring Perry on vocals, ex-Generation X drummer John Towe, Mickey Smith (bass), and former Nobodies' guitarist Alex Fergusson, ATV formed in March 1977, rehearsing at Throbbing Gristle's studios in Hackney, where they recorded their first single, a flexidisc of "Love Lies Limp" to be given away with the final issue of *Sniffin' Glue*, in August 1977. Two months later, on May 6, 1977, ATV made their live debut in Nottingham.

The first lineup splintered almost immediately, Smith quitting to be replaced by one of Perry's New Beatles' chums, Tyrone Thomas, and on June 5, ATV opened for Wayne County's Electric Chairs, in Brighton. Six gigs later, Towe quit (he went on to join Rage (with future White Cat Eddie Cox, and Killing Joke's Martin Glover); but not before *Sounds* described the band as "the Velvet Underground on Social Security." Towe was replaced by Chris Bennett and the band carried on gigging, at the same time as preparing their debut album.

They were caught rehearsing in *The Punk Rock Movie*, the cinema verite documentary of punk's first savage summer; more exposure came in December, when the "How Much Longer" single appeared on Perry's own Deptford Fun City wing of Miles Copeland's Illegal Records set up. *The Image Has Cracked* the group's live and studio debut album, appeared the following spring, and proved to be very aptly named.

Thanks to all that *Sniffin' Glue* stood for, listeners expected Perry to uphold the same tenets of punk purity as he'd demanded from others; *Image*, however, was vigorously divisive, an album which *ZigZag* magazine promptly (but so accurately) condemned as "an LP of easy exits and extended bluffs."

ATV, however, were not to be distracted. With a break only for a May 1978 reissue of "Love Lies Limp," Perry rocketed on towards the Throbbing Gristle sound which by now captivated him — and seemingly, him alone. By the time of *Vibing Up the Senile Man (Part One)*, the second ATV album, and its accompanying single, "The Force Is Blind," only Perry remained from the original band; only bassist Dennis Burns remained from any of those which had followed. And of ATV's original, punk-era press disciples, even *Sounds* found the album unlistenable.

Unperturbed, Perry, Burns, and Dave George took the new album out on the road, but an end of sorts was already in sight. Snarled Perry, "there's too many bands already playing their greatest hits on stage without ATV doing it as well. I mean, it would be taking advantage if we went on playing 'Action' and getting away with it. We thought audiences would appreciate the fact that ATV were trying to progress, and we're trying to write new music on stage."

For the most part, they thought wrong, and in March 1979, on stage at Chelmsford, ATV called it a day. Side one of the *Scars on Sunday* album preserved highlights from this final show; side two introduced the Good Missionaries, the band which would pick up exactly where ATV left off, only without the incumbrance of such an historically resonant name.

But, of course, it wasn't the end really. The first ATV reunion, with Fergusson back on board, occurred as early as 1981; another kept Perry amused through the second half of the decade; and in 1999, Perry celebrated the release of his 20th album, under the born-yet-again name of Alternative TV.

MOTORHEAD

This is your brain. This is your brain on Motorhead. And if you couldn't tell the difference, then congratulations. It's already too late.

Mot-or-head. Have any three syllables ever possessed more power... to shock, to horrify, to outrage... than they? Born in 1975 from the wreckage of Lemmy Kilminster's dismissal from Hawkwind, Motorhead was the bassist's revenge, not only on the band which sacked him and the label which let them, but also on anyone and everyone who thought that good taste and decency were what rock was all about.

They didn't play gigs, they ripped the top of your head off and stirred the contents with drumsticks. They didn't give interviews, they ripped the top of the journalist's head off and stirred that up as well. And they didn't make records because their label of the time, UA, put one ear to the tape box containing their masters, and buried it in a lead lined vault. If punk hadn't come snarling round the corner, Motorhead would probably have broken up on the spot, unloved, unheard, unmourned. Instead, their white light was reprieved to roam the outer fringes of the punk rock consciousness, while the rest of the world wondered how they could be stopped. Early singles appeared through Stiff (UK) and Skydog (France), and nobody paid them much heed-least of all Stiff, who deleted "White Line Fever" before it was even released. But then they signed to Chiswick and never had to look back. Their first single, "Motorhead," was big, their first album was bigger, and by the new year, Motorhead had been picked up by the Bronze mini major, and were selling out shows wherever they went.

Their albums charted, they scored hit singles, from pariahs to princes in under twelve months, Motorhead had

pulled off the impossible. Today, the entire face of modern metal, from the spangled eyesores of '80s America through the ghetto rabble rousers of the post-Nirvana '90s, owes its everything to Motorhead. The difference is, compared to Motorhead, they all sound like the Carpenters. Forget the Sex Pistols, the Beatles, and Presley. If you really want to look on the true face of rock, clock Lemmy. Even his warts kick ass.

The original Motorhead menage — Lemmy, Lucas Fox and Larry Wallis, moonlighting from the recently revitalized Pink Fairies — remains the ultimate realization of all that rock'n'roll should portend. A bare-fanged threat to the order of things; a slobbering, slavering, three-headed monster, Motorhead were to the British rock scene what the Blue Oyster Cult were to America — a similar grasp on the importance of imagery, a similar disregard for the niceties of society. The difference was, Motorhead meant it — their first ever gig saw them opening for the BOC in London. They blew the headliners home.

Produced by Dave Edmunds, Motorhead's first 1975 recordings were electrifying; Lemmy's raw throat sucking the last link with life from his own past with Hawkwind, even as he fed it to the yowling fledgling of his future. It was an unearthly combination. Motorhead pulled in one direction, Edmunds pulled in another, then they both let go at the same time, and the result flew out of the middle someplace. Edmunds' characteristic widescreen wall of sound leavening vast empty spaces within the Motorhead roar; Motorhead's aural approximation of a methadone comedown hanging out with Phil Spector to shoot some holes in the breeze.

They cut four songs: "Leaving Here," the Motown R&B stomper which Lemmy would have remembered from his days in the British beat boom, the self-fulfilling "Motorhead" (which Lemmy had already recorded before, with Hawkwind), the Fairies anthem "City Kids," and Wallis' savage "On Parole." The band's label, UA, hated them all.

Edmunds quit the sessions, and Motorhead moved on. Working now with former Four Pennies Merseybeater Fritz Fryer, nine songs were completed, including another brace of Lemmy-led Hawkwind classics, the eerie "The Watcher" and "Lost Johnny," the pharmaceutical nightmare he wrote with ex-Deviant Mick Farren. Unfortunately, UA loathed the new tapes almost as much as they loathed the first ones; Motorhead were dropped, and we would never hear their like again — at least until they reemerged. But Motorhead rarely recaptured those glories again. They got louder, of course, and faster and harder, and maybe that made them a little more dangerous. But they had an audience now, and they knew what it wanted. It was when they didn't know that they were at their best, because they didn't seem to care, either. Those early tapes have since been released under the title *On Parole*. Somehow, that only seems appropriate.

Stiff Records

In early spring 1976, in the "records for sale" section of the music press classifieds, a new record company announced its birth. It demanded no fanfare, and made no extravagant promises, but anybody who had followed pub rockers Brinsley Schwarz through their seven year career would have paid attention regardless. "So It Goes" was the debut single by Schwarz songwriter Nick Lowe; it was also — although nobody could have known this at the time — the maiden release for what would become the most exciting record label of the late 1970s.

Never before had a label garnered its supporters not only through its artists, but also through its own identity. Stiff collectors bought Stiff records regardless of their musical merit and, most later agreed, it would be 3 years and 50+ new releases before the label let them down. Which wasn't at all bad for a company only intended to be a showcase for a few passing pub rockers, launched by Brinsley's manager Dave Robinson and Dr. Feelgood road manager Jake Riviera, with a £400 loan from his employers.

From the start, however, Stiff set about doing things differently. "Mono, enhanced stereo," insisted the credits to Lowe's debut. "The world's most flexible record label," pledged the company's logo. "Artistic breakthrough: double b-side!" bellowed the first release by the Tyla Gang; and further witticisms quickly followed. When David Bowie released a new album called *Low*, Lowe responded with an EP called *Bowi*. Fleetwood Mac released *Rumours*, and the Rumour released *Max*. And then there was the promotional button which insisted, "if it ain't Stiff, it ain't worth a fuck" — a legend which proved so instantly popular that bootleg versions were appearing on the streets within weeks, and Stiff's reputation was guaranteed. Bootleg buttons, indeed.

"So It Goes" arrived with what remains the most sensible catalog number in recorded history: a plaintive, pleading BUY ONE. It only followed, therefore, that subsequent releases would exhort even more grandiose purchases: the Pink Fairies — BUY TWO, Roogalator — BUY THREE... by the time the label finally closed, in 1987, they were up to BUY 259.

Things moved quickly. In October 1976, Stiff signed the Damned and unleashed "New Rose" (BUY SIX — and a lot of people did); the first record by any British punk band, beating the Sex Pistols' "Anarchy In The U.K." by three full weeks and precipitating some of the most perplexed reviews in the history of the written word.

Few journalists knew what to make of the Damned's one minute and 99 seconds (well, that's what the label said) of adrenalined noise; fewer still comprehended the blistered blitzkrieg cover of the Beatles' "Help" which turned up on the b-side. But within weeks, Stiff had landed major label distribution; within months, the label was opening its own retail outlet. By summer 1977, Elvis Costello was threatening to score his first chart hit; by fall, the Live Stiffs tour was the hottest ticket on the concert circuit, and names like the Damned, the Adverts, Ian Dury, and Wreckless Eric were by-words for the wider pastures roamed by the new wave cognoscenti.

Indeed, it took Stiff no time at all to transform itself from a pub rock nursing home to a punk rock institution, and that without changing the company's outlook one iota. Stiff still released records by other company's artists — the *A Bunch of Stiff Records* sampler included contributions from Graham Parker (Mercury) and Dave Edmunds (Swansong). Stiff still trawled the halls of musical eccentricity in search of the next Max Wall (a vaudevillian comedian), Humphrey Ocean (an established and respected artist), or Jona Lewie (a wacky keyboard player with an outstanding haircut). And Stiff still made "mistakes" which an amateur might have avoided.

The most famous involved the Damned's debut album, *Damned Damned Damned*, which shipped with a photograph of Eddie and the Hot Rods on the back cover instead of the intended Damned portrait. But even before that, Stiff's art department was coyly disaster prone, as they proved when Roogalator's "Cincinnati Fatback" appeared packaged within a pastiche of the Beatles' *With the Beatles* album, accurate down to the trademarked logo on the back.

Its owners, EMI, promptly threatened legal action unless the pirated image was removed; Stiff responded by deleting the single and suddenly, the company had a brand new maxim. "We're a record company, not a museum," Riviera announced and no Stiff release could ever be considered safe again — including ones which hadn't even been released yet. Motorhead's "Leaving Here" single was deleted from the Stiff catalog immediately before it reached the stores; Ian Dury's summer 1977 "Sex and Drugs and Rock and Roll," was withdrawn just as it seemed poised to enter the chart.

Stiff finally hit the Top 40 with Elvis Costello three months later. Indeed, it was obvious from the outset that Costello, whose "Less than Zero" debut arrived in March 1977, was a cut above the rest of the pack — even after one of the national tabloids picked up on the references to "Mr. Oswald with his swastika tattoo" and asked whether Elvis was a Nazi sympathizer. It was obvious, too, that with the best will in the world, Stiff would not be able to keep him forever.

He left Stiff in early 1978 — not, however, for the brighter vistas of a major label, but for Jake Riviera's next venture, the Radar label. Nick Lowe and Liverpudlian powerpoppers the Yachts followed, but with Dave Robinson remaining in charge at Stiff, there really was no cause for concern.

Through the fall of 1978, Mickey Jupp, Lene Lovich, Jona Lewie, Wreckless Eric, and schoolgirl country singer Rachel Sweet were put aboard a railroad train and despatched around Britain on the latest Live Stiffs package tour. It was never going to be as successful as its predecessor (it actually lost £10,000), despite making it to the US (which the first tour never did), but it did heighten awareness of the label in an enterprising fashion, and precipitated Lovich and Lewie, at least, into the public eye.

Her "Lucky Number" made #3 in February 1979; Lewie's "Stop the Cavalry" topped the chart in 1980; even Wreckless Eric Goulden, for so long the label's Artist Most Likely To, was threatening to fulfill his potential at last, first with a fabulous pop song called — plaintively — "Pop Song"; then when Cliff Richard covered his yearning "Broken Doll."

The label's A&R department was on top of the world as well. The Adverts had moved onto Anchor and begun running up a string of hit singles. Jane Aire and the Belvederes, signed amid the same wave of Akron-mania that recruited Rachel Sweet and Devo (and prompted the *Akron Compilation* sampler), moved to Virgin. The Members, a band signed to Stiff's One Off subsidiary under the banner of "we'll sign 'em, and if they're no good, dump 'em back in the gutter," joined them there. With Kirsty MacColl emerging as one of the songwriting greats of new decade (her "They Don't Know" became comedienne Tracy Ullman's first hit), it was hard to detect a single black cloud in the firmament.

But there were some, and once they appeared, they stayed ominously overhead. Even as Madness, Dave Stewart & Barbara Gaskin, Tenpole Tudor, the Belle-Stars, the Pogues, and indeed, Tracy Ullman, launched the company into its most fevered period of hitmaking ever, the third and final Stiff label package tour, *Son of Stiff*, sank like a stone — its failure all the more noticeable for the amount of effort which went into marketing it. There was even a movie made of the affair, preserving Joe "King" Carrusco, Dirty Looks, Any Trouble, the Equators, and Tenpole Tudor for future posterity. Unfortunately, future posterity didn't care.

Something had changed. No longer a wired delinquent selling silliness to the masses, Stiff suddenly seemed to have become a business, in the business of doing business. It had become a "real" record company. And though the label would live on for another six years and continue releasing new records for a little longer than that, few of its original cachets would stay the course — and even fewer of its original motives. Once indeed, it was true that if it wasn't Stiff, it wasn't worth a fuck. Now, even if it was Stiff, there was no guarantee that it would be worth anything any more.

The label's decline could be charted across any sampling of its post-1980 releases, but still there were moments of sheer, shining glory — isolated moments of musical majesty from John Otway (a demented retelling of "The Green Green Grass of Home"); a brace of classics by Department S; unlikely efforts from the Untouchables and the immortally-named Pookiesnackenburger. And when it did all wrap up, it was with breathtakingly circular purity, as the label's first ever friend became its last ever signing, and Dr. Feelgood came back to reclaim their £400.

Since then, of course, Stiff has remained on the release sheets, across a string of compilations, and reissues spread between a dozen different labels worldwide, and each one harking back to the original days of grind and glory... the Damned's "New Rose" and the Adverts' "One Chord Wonders," primal Costello and early Wreckless Eric, Dury bemoaning "What a Waste" and Lovich demanding "Say When," Max Wall's "England's Glory" and Larry Wallis' "Police Car"... and the days when Dave Robinson's explanation for Stiff's existence genuinely did ring true.

"If major record companies were really good," he cheerfully admitted, "then we wouldn't be here."

STIFF RECORDS LABEL DISCOGRAPHY 1976-78 SINGLES

BUY *prefix*

1. NICK LOWE — So It Goes
2. PINK FAIRIES — Between the Lines
3. ROOGALATOR — Cincinnati Fatback
4. TYLA GANG — Styrofoam
5. LEW LEWIS — Caravan Man
6. THE DAMNED — New Rose
7. RICHARD HELL — Blank Generation
8. PLUMMET AIRLINES — Silver Shirt
9. MOTORHEAD — Leaving Here
10. THE DAMNED — Neat Neat Neat
11. ELVIS COSTELLO — Less than Zero
12. MAX WALL — England's Glory
13. THE ADVERTS — One Chord Wonders
14. ELVIS COSTELLO — Alison
15. ELVIS COSTELLO — Red Shoes
16. WRECKLESS ERIC — Whole Wide World
17. IAN DURY — Sex and Drugs and Rock and Roll

18. THE DAMNED — Problem Child
19. THE YACHTS — Suffice to Say
20. ELVIS COSTELLO — Watching the Detectives
21. NICK LOWE — Halfway to Paradise
22. LARRY WALLIS — Police Car
23. IAN DURY — Sweet Gene Vincent
24. THE DAMNED — Don't Cry Wolf
25. WRECKLESS ERIC — Reconnez Cherie
26. JANE AIRE AND THE BELVEDERES — Yankee Wheels
27. IAN DURY — What a Waste
28. THE BOX TOPS — The Letter
29. HUMPHREY OCEAN — Whoops A Daisy
30. JONA LEWIE — The Baby, She's on the Street
31. JUST WATER — Singing in the Rain
32. LENE LOVICH — I Think We're Alone Now
33. WAZMO NARIZ — Tele Tele Telephone
34. WRECKLESS ERIC — Take the KASH
35. LENE LOVICH — Home
36. MICKY JUPP — Old Rock'n'Roller
37. JONA LEWIE — Hallelujah Europa
38. IAN DURY — Hit Me With Your Rhythm Stick
39. RACHEL SWEET — BABY
40. WRECKLESS ERIC — Crying Waiting Hoping
41. BINKY BAKER AND THE PIT ORCHESTRA — Toe Knee Black Burn
42. LENE LOVICH — Lucky Number
43. THE RUMOUR — Frozen Years
44. RACHEL SWEET — I Go to Pieces
45. THE RUMOUR — Emotional Traffic
46. LENE LOVICH — Say When
47. KIRSTY MACCOLL — They Don't Know
48. LEW LEWIS — Lucky Seven
49. WRECKLESS ERIC — Hit'n'Miss Judy
50. IAN DURY — Reasons to be Cheerful (part 3)

Other Prefixes

BOY 1 DEVO — Satisfaction
BOY 2 DEVO — Be Stiff
DAMNED 1 THE DAMNED — Stretcher Case Baby
DEA/SUK 1 WAYNE KRAMER — Rambling Rose
DEV 1 DEVO — Mongoloid

FREEB 2 various artists — Excerpts from Stiff's Greatest Hits
FREEB 1 IAN DURY — Sex and Drugs and Rock and Roll
NAZZ 1 WAZMO NARIZ — Who Eez Wazmo Nariz?
OFF 2 ERNIE GRAHAM — Romeo and the Lonely Girl
OFF 1 THE SUBS — Gimme Your Heart
OFF 4 THE REALISTS — I've Got a Heart
OFF 3 THE MEMBERS — Solitary Confinement
UPP 1 MICKY JUPP — Nature's Radio

EPs

DEAL

LAST 1 NICK LOWE — Bowi
LAST 2 ALBERTO Y LOS TRIOS PARANOIAS — Snuff Rock
LAST 3 unreleased (WRECKLESS ERIC — Picadilly Menial)
LAST 4 MICK FARREN — Screwed Up
LAST 5 THE SPORTS — Who Listens to the Radio?
ODD 2 various artists — Be Stiff
ODD 1 DEVO — Be Stiff
TRAIN 1 various artists — You're Either On the Train or Off It

ALBUMS

SEEZ prefix

0. various artists — Heroes and Cowards
1. The DAMNED — Damned Damned Damned
2. various artists — A Bunch of Stiffs
3. ELVIS COSTELLO — My Aim Is True
4. IAN DURY — New Boots and Panties
5. THE DAMNED — Music for Pleasure
6. WRECKLESS ERIC — Wreckless Eric
7. LENE LOVICH — Stateless
8. JONA LEWIE — On the Other Hand There's a Fist
9. WRECKLESS ERIC — Wonderful World Of
10. MICKY JUPP — Juppanese
11. unreleased (JANE AIRE AND THE BELVEDERES)
12. RACHEL SWEET — Fool Around
13. THE RUMOUR — Frogs, Sprouts, Clogs and Krauts
14. IAN DURY AND THE BLOCKHEADS — Do It Yourself
15. THE SPORTS — Don't Throw Stones

Live at the BBC — The John Peel Sessions

The BBC archives have been described as the last great untapped resource in rock'n'roll history. No matter that the last 15 years have seen vast swathes of previously unreleased music exhumed from the vault, still the two hundred-plus "At the Beeb," "Radio One in Concert," and "Peel Sessions" collections released to date represent only the tip of the iceberg.

In 1993, it was estimated that since the inception of BBC Radio One in September 1967, some 1,500 different bands had recorded around 8,000 largely unreleased performances. Since that time, of course, the figure has only increased — despite the reasons behind the actual concept of sessions having been forgotten more than a decade ago.

The use of exclusive radio sessions is a relic of British radio's earliest years, and the Musicians' Union's fears that the invention posed a serious threat to its membership. Most musicians in the 1920s and 1930s looked to concert work for their livelihood, with recording a bonus which few could rely upon. It only followed, therefore, that if the public wanted to hear music being played, they would go out to dances and nightclubs. The idea that suddenly, they could stay at home and have all the top hits piped directly through to them was terrifying. If people could listen to music on the radio, after all, why would they bother going out to shows?

The answer to that question was supplied by "needletime," a piece of legislation enforced by the Musicians' Union to regulate the amount of time which could be devoted to broadcasting gramophone records. The BBC, a state-sponsored organization which held the monopoly on British broadcasting until the early 1970s, had no alternative but to comply.

Even as its most lenient, needletime was harsh. Little more than twelve hours of pre-recorded music was allowed per week throughout the BBC's entire operation (domestic and abroad), with even top music shows restricted to just half an hour of disc spinning per three or four hour broadcast. The rest of the program would thus be devoted to live performances.

By the early 1960s and the dawn of Britain's rock'n'roll era, the Union had relaxed its regulations a little, but still, the demands remained stern. The legendary *Saturday Club*, the source for many of the now famous (and oft-bootlegged) early Beatles, Rolling Stones, and Yardbirds performances, was allocated just 45 minutes of needletime per two hours of airtime.

Things weren't much better when the BBC launched its pop music station, Radio One, in 1967. DJ John Peel's name today is synonymous with BBC radio sessions, but that is because he, too, had three hours of show to fill, and barely half of that could be plugged with records. New sessions would be taped, old ones would be repeated, anything to comply with the regulations. But by the time needletime was finally abolished in 1988, the session had become so entrenched within the Peel Show's make-up that nobody even dreamed of abandoning it.

Peel himself was born in Liverpool, England, although his radio career began in Dallas, TX in 1962, and took off when his audience realized his geographical connections to the home of the Beatles. He relocated to the west coast in 1965, where he "discovered" one of the finest American psychedelic bands of all, the Misunderstood, then returned to England to launch his *Perfumed Garden* show on the pirate Radio London.

When the authorities moved against the illegal broadcasters in summer 1967, Peel was one of several DJs offered a post in the new regime and that fall, he became one of the first hosts of *Top Gear*, "the program which looks beyond the horizons of pop." The first of the live sessions which would become the show's most lasting legacy was broadcast on October 1, 1967.

Today, new bands still mail their demos in to Peel, hoping that he will call them in and set them on the road to fame; better established bands still consider a BBC session the ideal showcase for a new album's worth of songs.

Most BBC sessions are recorded in one day and from the modern listener's point of view, that in itself is fascinating. The Cure's Robert Smith spoke of recording the group's *Wild Mood Swings* album, "and taking three weeks to get the snare sound right." At the BBC in December 1978, for the Cure's first ever Peel session, he had three minutes. Then, and now, it was a fast-paced, furious atmosphere and the results (generally broadcast within a week of the recording) can be fascinating — performances caught almost midway between the live environment and the studio. Working with tough, no-nonsense BBC producers who know exactly what needs to be done, and how long it takes, even the greatest perfectionist musician has to simply buckle down and get the job done.

Still, many artists believe they reached a peak of sorts under the BBC gun. Robyn Hitchcock described the

Egyptians' final BBC session as "the best stuff we ever did. It was live, it was mixed by our soundman who's Finnish, and there were about 20 people in the other room drinking wine and coffee and they'd just hold their glasses still for three minutes while we did a take, then we'd do another one. That last session, I think, is the real heart of the Egyptians."

The Only Ones' John Perry concurred. "When somebody who'd never heard the [band] wanted to know what we sounded like, I'd always play them the Peel sessions in preference to the studio albums. They're rougher, but there's more feel. You could do more or less whatever you wanted —nobody was at all put out when I wanted to record the sound of my Strat being thrown around the room for the end of 'Oh No,' they just went out and set up the appropriate mikes."

Through the early-mid 1970s, Peel was one of the few BBC DJs who were not afraid to go out on a limb. He broadcast late, 10:00 pm on weekday evenings, and thought nothing of devoting great swathes of his show to a new album by one of the bands he held holy, or a session by someone that his listeners had probably never heard of. When the first stirrings of punk rock began making themselves felt, it was inevitable that Peel would investigate. Indeed, the first "punk" record aired on the John Peel Show was the Ramones' debut album in May 1976. Peel himself had only just got hold of the record, "and [that night], I put in five or six tracks from it. I immediately got a lot of letters from people saying 'you must never do that again,' and of course, that always excites me."

By late August, Peel was playing Nick Lowe's Stiff Records debut "Sound of the City" on a nightly basis; on September 29, he opened the show with the Saints' "I'm Stranded" (and then played Stevie Wonder's new album in its entirety). On October 12, the Vibrators became the first of the new wave bands to record a session; the Doctors of Madness followed; and on November 30, the Damned brought pure punk rock screaming into studios which just weeks, even days before, such doughty warriors as folkie Alan Hull, the Climax Chicago Blues Band, and Stackridge had made their own.

"John Peel was underground radio," Damned drummer Rat Scabies recalled. "It was the only show, on two hours a night, that would play anything that wasn't mainstream chart, commercial success. That was why it was the hippest show, because it was the only one that would play anything. He was the first one that played 'New Rose' on the radio, it was alright. He was championing the cause, it wasn't like it was a commercial set-up."

Even with Peel's patronage, however, the Damned were not in for an easy ride. "The very first session that we did, because it was 'punk rock outrage,' the first engineer walked off the session on the grounds that we had amplifiers six feet tall. The whole day, we had this constant parade of people walking into the control room and staring at us... and then walking out again. You have to understand, it was a bit spooky, because it was very hip for the conservative public to refuse to have anything to do with punk rock. The smart thing to do was to deliver the goods and fucking let them know it was something valid and here to stay."

The band cut five tracks, "New Rose," "Neat Neat Neat," "Stab Yor Back," "So Messed Up," and "I Fall" and, over the next nine years, the Damned would make six more appearances on the Peel show, including some of their most inspired performances.

"You'd get the gear in there at 11 or something, then fuck about getting sound together for an hour or so, and then they'd always stop for lunch. That was one of the big appeals about the Peel sessions, you could always eat cheap in the canteen. That's important when you're on 30 quid a week. After that you'd lay down the tracks, then you'd mix.

We always had a thing, because the engineers always liked to be finished by 7 or 8, we found out... I think it was Terry Riley, was the only person who'd ever kept the engineers there past midnight. When we did the 'Curtain Call' session (recorded 10/6/80), we made a point of staying there til past midnight so we could be the other people that had done it. And that session was the one I enjoyed most, that I thought sounded best."

Through 1977, even as punk made greater and greater inroads into the UK chart consciousness, Peel remained its greatest champion, forever one step ahead of even the hippest of his fellow DJs. The Adverts and the Jam both cut four sessions in little more than two years; Siouxsie and the Banshees recorded two before they even had a record deal; and the Clash recorded one, although it would never be broadcast. According to Peel, "[they] did the backing tracks, but couldn't do the vocals — they said the equipment wasn't up to the expected standards, which I thought wasn't a terribly revolutionary gesture."

On another occasion, it was the band who weren't up to the "expected standard," as engineer Nick Gomm discovered when the Slits recorded their first Peel session (9/19/77). "It was everyone hitting anything as loudly as possible; vaguely in time, there was a sort of rhythm there, and then this maniac shrieking on top. Onstage at that time it probably sounded quite good, but when it came out over little speakers, fairly quietly, it was just painful. The tuning of the guitars was all over the place. We couldn't stand listening to these guitars, they were so badly out of tune. So myself and the other engineer [Bill Aitken], both guitarists to a certain degree, had to go out and retune them ourselves."

The onus of selecting bands for the sessions fell squarely on Peel and producer John Walters. Both were regular gig-goers, with Walters taking his brief so seriously that he referred to punk shows as "lack-of-talent-spotting" — the "lack of (conventional, serious musicianly) talent," of course, being what he and Peel found so delightful about punk.

Both, too, possessed a definite sense of what "belonged" on their show. Discussing his reluctance to air a session by the Police in 1978 (he was eventually overruled by Peel), Walters explained, "if you follow the philosophy of the program, they shouldn't have been on. They summed up conformity, whereas punk was all about non-conformity." The April 1979 appearance on the show of Crass, simultaneously making their first (and last!) appearance on Radio One, confirmed Walters' stance. Few bands were less conformist than Crass.

The oddest things could grab the pair's attention. Peel was intrigued by the Slits because any band that could rile the tabloid press with their name alone had to have something going for them; John Walters went to see Adam and the Ants, and ended up booking their manager, Jordan, for the show. "[She] came on stage for one number, painted face, hair standing up about a foot in the air, and began to shriek. I thought 'get that girl into the studio and let her shriek to the nation'."

Gang of Four, the Raincoats, Bauhaus, and the Birthday Party all recorded Peel sessions long before the vast majority of listeners had even heard of them, while May 1978 saw Peel broadcast the first ever session by the Fall — a band which remains one of the best-kept secrets of the modern era, despite having now recorded more Peel sessions than any other band in history. In 1998, the band recorded their 20th, and Peel himself has acknowledged, "they're the great miracle of my musical life. I just adore them — if they made a bad record, I wouldn't know. All they have to do is turn up and that's enough."

Through the 1980s, Peel's position as king of the BBC sessions remained secure, but it was no longer unchallenged. Other DJs, too, were regularly airing new bands — Tommy Vance, who wrapped up what was then called the New Wave of British Heavy Metal; Richard Skinner, who brought in Depeche Mode and TV Smith's Explorers; Janice Long, with Fine Young Cannibals, Gaye Bikers on Acid, and the Mission; and Simon Mayo, who introduced the Pixies to the listening public.

But still Peel remained out in front, his crystalline vision of what truly mattered to the underground landscape confirmed by his response to a controversy which erupted, ironically enough, around one of the BBC's safer broadcasters, David Jensen, and a band (and song) which Peel himself had first broadcast three months earlier.

In August 1983, the Smiths recorded a session for Jensen's show, turning in performances of "Accept Yourself," "I Don't Owe You Anything," and "Pretty Girls Make Graves," plus a reprise of "Reel Around the Fountain," from that earlier Peel session. The recording took place on August 12. Thirteen days later, *The Sun* tabloid newspaper reported that the BBC was in "uproar" following the realization that one of the songs, as reporter Nick Ferrari put it, "contains clear references to picking up kids for sexual kicks."

Of course it didn't, and it is unlikely whether anybody at the BBC even thought it did. But such exposure in the biggest selling newspaper in the country could not help but force a reaction. Jensen's producer, Mike Hawkes, withdrew the song from the session broadcast; the band's label, Rough Trade, cancelled its release as the next Smiths single; and John Walters was so outraged by the entire debacle that he promptly invited the band back into the studio to record another session the following month. He also ensured that a Smiths session would either be recorded or repeated every two or three weeks for the next seven months, a policy which would be rewarded when the Smiths established themselves, as Peel himself has since remarked, as one of the most crucial bands of the entire 1980s.

"The most interesting bands for me are the ones in which you can detect no echo of the past, which is why the Smiths are so significant, because when you first heard them you couldn't say, 'they've been listening to so and so'."

Increasingly, as the 1980s progressed, however, Peel found it harder and harder to make that same claim for other groups. "There were the sons of Joy Division, then the sons of the Cure and the sons of Killing Joke, and you get to the point where you think, 'actually I've heard enough of that particular noise.' It's always a relief when you move on, rather like snakes shedding their skin."

Through the late 1980s, Peel loudly championed the new generation of British and American hardcore bands —with the British Extreme Noise Terror and Napalm Death, and the American Doctor and the Crippens becoming regular studio guests. Indeed, when Peel's managers, Clive and Shirley Selwood, announced plans to launch a new label, Strange Fruit, dedicated solely to exhuming relics from what was then (1987) 20 years worth of Peel Sessions, two volumes of *Hardcore Holocaust* were numbered among their flagship releases.

Not every session by every band has been available for release. To begin with, every musician involved in the session has to give their approval beforehand; a process which can be, and has been, snarled by an artist's internal politics (attempts to chronicle David Bowie's BBC sessions have constantly foundered on this rock), record company attitudes, and the players' own memories of the sessions. Brett

Anderson, vocalist with London Suede, acknowledged that when his band is approached on the subject, "it's very much a case by case basis. Some performances were better than others."

Other bands, however, approved the release of old sessions because they highlighted a side to the group which might otherwise have been lost forever, as they experimented with their own songs, or tried out other people's. Billy Bragg fans still rave about the near-impromptu rendition of "Route 66" which he performed for Peel in August 1983, replacing the song's traditional lyric with a guide to the route between two eastern English towns.

The Damned performed a riotous Gary Numan parody in 1979; and during 1982, Peel himself prevailed upon every band who passed through to record a version of Rodgers and Hammerstein's "You'll Never Walk Alone" for a compilation album he was hoping to release. The album never materialized, but the recordings, by Vice Squad, Pete Wylie's Wah!, the Three Johns, the Gymslips, the Diagram Brothers, and more are archived, awaiting their day in the sun. (Vice Squad's alone has seen release, on their *Punk Rock Panties* collection.)

Those groups who have given carte blanche to release entire blocks of sessions, then, are indeed a minority, albeit an increasingly impressive one. The Only Ones, the Ruts, the Adverts, New Order, Stiff Little Fingers, and Joy Division were numbered among the earliest acts to acknowledge the historical value of the full canon. The success of the initial *Peel Sessions* releases was such that conventional record labels, too, soon acknowledged the worth of the BBC archives, and began contracting directly with the BBC for releases.

TVT released a four-CD collection of XTC recordings; 4AD compiled one disc of the Pixies; while Strange Fruit itself span off a host of similarly themed labels, catering for live recordings from other BBC music shows, the *In Concert* and *Old Grey Whistle Test* series, or dedicated to specific genres — world music, heavy metal, and so on.

Yet the major appeal of the BBC sessions, and the Peel Sessions in particular, remains their exclusivity. More than anything else, a session preserves a moment in time in a band's history with a quality and a veracity which nothing else, neither live recordings nor studio out-takes, can emulate. They show a band simultaneously on its best behavior and at its most crazily vulnerable, working simply for that moment, with nothing else on its mind. And that honesty remains the sessions' greatest asset... that, and the almost illicit thrill of knowing that the music you are listening to was never recorded with posterity in mind. So far as the BBC was concerned, needletime was an irritant. It created an institution in spite of itself.

JOHN PEEL SESSIONS INDEX 1977-79

1/4/77: CHRIS SPEDDING
1/12/77: PIRATES (1)
1/14/77: BOWLES BROTHERS
1/17/77: BOYS OF THE LOUGH (1)
1/21/77: LITTLE BOB STORY (1)
1/25/77: BE BOP DELUXE (1)

2/4/77: JOHN MARTYN (1)
2/7/77: ANDY FAIRWEATHER LOWE
2/10/77: LEO KOTTKE
2/14/77: ROCKPILE
2/18/77: ROY HARPER (1)
2/21/77: EDDIE AND THE HOT RODS (1)
2/22/77: JUNE TABOR (1)
2/28/77: PLUMMET AIRLINES

3/3/77: STEVE GIBBONS BAND (1)
3/7/77: STRANGLERS (1)
3/17/77: SUPERCHARGE
3/18/77: A BAND CALLED O
3/18/77: KEVIN COYNE (1)

4/6/77: VIV STANSHALL (1)
4/11/77: CHAPMAN WHITNEY STREETWALKERS
4/12/77: MICHAEL CHAPMAN (1)
4/12/77: RACING CARS (1)
4/19/77: MIKE HERON'S REPUTATION
4/20/77: GENERATION X (1)
4/21/77: PETER HAMMILL (1)
4/22/77: MOTORS (1)
4/22/77: THIS HEAT (1)
4/26/77: NIC JONES
4/27/77: FABULOUS POODLES (1)
4/29/77: THE ADVERTS (1)

5/2/77: THE JAM (1)
5/3/77: MEDICINE HEAD
5/10/77: CARAVAN
5/13/77: JOHN MCLAUGHLIN AND SHAKTI
5/14/77: CRUELLA DE VILLE
5/16/77: THE DAMNED (2)
5/20/77: RADIO STARS (1)
5/23/77: FRANKIE MILLER (1)
5/23/77: VIV STANSHALL (2)
5/24/77: NEIL INNES

6/3/77: FIVE HAND REEL (1)
6/3/77: THE RUMOUR
6/6/77: TYLA GANG (1)
6/17/77: UFO
6/20/77: MOON
6/21/77: BOB SARGEANT
6/22/77: THE VIBRATORS (1)
6/24/77: XTC (1)
6/27/77: CHELSEA 91)

7/1/77: CHARLIE FEATHERS
7/4/77: STEVE GIBBONS BAND (2)
7/7/77: MOVIES
7/11/77: COUNTRY JOE MCDONALD
7/13/77: MODELS
7/15/77: MARTIN SIMPSON
7/21/77: GENERATION X (2)
7/22/77: LITTLE BOB STORY (2)
7/25/77: THE JAM (2)
7/26/77: CORTINAS
7/27/77: COUNT BISHOPS

8/1/77: ELVIS COSTELLO AND THE ATTRACTIONS (1)
8/2/77: DICK GAUGHAN
8/3/77: BOOMTOWN RATS (1)
8/8/77: THE BOYS (1)
8/15/77: BLUE
8/17/77: IVOR CUTLER (1)
8/22/77: THIN LIZZY
8/23/77: COLOSSEUM II
8/29/77: SQUEEZE (1)
8/30/77: THE ADVERTS (2)
8/31/77: GARY BOYLE

9/1/77: ROOGALATOR
9/13/77: STRANGLERS (2)
9/16/77: ALBERTOS Y LOS TRIOS PARANOIAS
9/19/77: THE BUZZCOCKS (1)
9/20/77: ONLY ONES (1)
9/21/77: MOTORS (2)
9/26/77: XTC (2)
9/27/77: THE SLITS (1)
9/29/77: STEEL PULSE (1)

10/10/77: DR. FEELGOOD (1)
10/10/77: PIANO RED
10/11/77: WRECKLESS ERIC (1)
10/13/77: DOWNLINERS SECT
10/14/77: NEW HEARTS
10/14/77: BILLY BOY ARNOLD
10/17/77: EDDIE AND THE HOT RODS (2)

10/18/77: KILLJOYS (1)
10/20/77: TYLA GANG (2)
10/24/77: SUBWAY SECT (1)
10/27/77: THE LURKERS (1)
10/28/77: SKREWDRIVER

11/2/77: VAN DER GRAAF GENERATOR
11/7/77: RICH KIDS (1)
11/7/77: TOM ROBINSON BAND (1)
11/8/77 LOUISIANA RED
11/14/77: QUEEN
11/14/77: PIRATES (2)
11/16/77: NATIONAL HEALTH
11/18/77: RADIO STARS (2)
11/22/77: PHIL MANZANERA & 801
11/24/77: THIS HEAT 2)
11/28/77: ULTRAVOX
11/30/77: THE ZEROS

12/2/77: SUBURBAN STUDS
12/5/77: SIOUXSIE AND THE BANSHEES (1)
12/6/77: SHAM 69
12/12/77: ATV (1)
12/13/77: DRONES
12/16/77: MARTIN CARTHY
12/19/77: VIV STANSHALL (3)
12/30/77: REZILLOS (1)

1/5/78: HIDING PLACE
1/13/78: BANDOGGS
1/16/78: JOHN MARTYN (2)
1/17/78: MICHAEL CHAPMAN (2)
1/19/78: METAL URBAIN (1)
1/24/78: THE STUKAS
1/30/78: ADAM AND THE ANTS
1/31/78: WIRE (1)

2/1/78: JUNE TABOR (2)
2/3/78: DE DANNANN
2/6/78: BE BOP DELUXE (2)
2/10/78: ROBIN AND BARRY DRANSFIELD
2/13/78: KILLJOYS (2)
2/14/78: ROCKS
2/15/78: PATRICK FITZGERALD (1)
2/20/78: MAGAZINE (1)
2/22/78: THE WASPS (1)
2/23/78: SIOUXSIE AND THE BANSHEES (2)
2/27/78: DEKE LEONARD AND ICEBERG

3/1/78: KEVIN COYNE (2)
3/6/78: THE VIBRATORS (2)

3/6/78: X-RAY SPEX (1)

3/8/78: WRECKLESS ERIC (2)

3/14/78: MEKONS (1)

3/20/78: ELVIS COSTELLO AND THE ATTRACTIONS (2)

3/21/78: BOTHY BAND

3/23/78: THE FLYS (1)

3/31/78: FIVE HAND REEL (2)

4/3/78: THE WHITE CATS (1)

4/3/78: RICH KIDS (2)

4/4/78: GAY AND TERRY WOODS

4/5/78: VIV STANSHALL (4)

4/12/78: IVOR CUTLER (2)

4/13/78: STIFF LITTLE FINGERS (1)

4/14/78: ONLY ONES (2)

4/17/78: BUZZCOCKS (2)

4/19/78: LANDSCAPE

4/24/78: THE LURKERS (2)

4/26/78: THE SMIRKS

4/27/78: STEEL PULSE (2)

5/3/78: CRABS

5/3/78: MATUMBI (1)

5/3/78: THE ZONES (1)

5/15/78: THE BOYS (2)

5/15/78: SQUEEZE (2)

5/17/78: DIRE STRAITS

5/19/78: THE SKIDS (1)

5/22/78: THE SLITS (2)

5/22/78: BRITISH LIONS

5/26/78: BOOMTOWN RATS (2)

5/31/78: UK SUBS (1)

6/1/78: BOYS OF THE LOUGH (2)

6/5/78: FRANKIE MILLER (2)

6/8/78: REZILLOS (2)

6/15/78: THE FALL (1)

6/19/78: PIRANHAS (3)

6/23/78: HITS

6/26/78: OTWAY-BARRETT

6/28/78: MICKEY JUPP

7/3/78: REGGAE REGULAR (1)

7/3/78: CHELSEA (2)

7/4/78: PRICE FAR I & CREATION REBEL

7/5/78: RAB NOAKES

7/10/78: DESPERATE BICYCLES

7/10/78: PENETRATION (1)

7/13/78: PATRICK FITZGERALD (2)

7/17/78: ADAM AND THE ANTS (2)

7/20/78: KING

7/24/78: CARPETTES (1)

7/25/78: VIV STANSHALL (5)

7/27/78: ATV (2)

7/31/78: MAGAZINE (2)

8/1/78: LEYTON BUZZARDS (1)

8/7/78: THE LURKERS (3)

8/7/78: SPIZZ OIL

8/9/78: TANZ DER YOUTH

8/10/78: POP GROUP

8/15/78: TYLA GANG (3)

8/16/78: HUMAN LEAGUE

8/21/78: ROY HARPER (2)

8/21/78: PREFECTS (1)

8/25/78: THE WHITE CATS (2)

8/29/78: PRAG VEC (1)

8/30/78: PUNISHMENT OF LUXURY (1)

9/1/78: THE SKIDS (2)

9/11/78: RACING CARS (2)

9/11/78: THE ADVERTS (3)

9/13/78: HOT WATER

9/15/78: UK SUBS (2)

9/18/78: DR. FEELGOOD (2)

9/18/78: STIFF LITTLE FINGERS (2)

9/22/78: THE ZONES (2)

9/25/78: MOTORHEAD

10/2/78: MEKONS (2)

10/3/78: WIRE (2)

10/4/78: RADIO STARS (3)

10/10/78: REGGAE REGULAR 2)

10/16/78: THE UNDERTONES (1)

10/18/78: SPLIT ENZ

10/19/78: MOLESTERS (1)

10/23/78: BUZZCOCKS (3)

10/24/78: THE YACHTS (1)

10/25/78: METAL URBAIN (2)

10/25/78: FABULOUS POODLES (2)

10/27/78: SWELL MAPS (1)

10/30/78: ANGELIC UPSTARTS

10/30/78: ELVIS COSTELLO AND THE ATTRACTIONS (3)

11/1/78: 999

11/6/78: JOHN COOPER CLARKE

11/8/78: CRISIS

11/13/78: X-RAY SPEX (2)

11/13/78: MATUMBI (2)

11/16/78: HERE AND NOW

11/19/78: MEKONS (3)

11/21/78: THE FLYS (2)

11/23/78: XTC (3)
11/27/78: LENE LOVICH (1)
11/28/78: PAUL BRADY
11/29/78: THE WAILING COCKS

12/4/78: SUBWAY SECT (2)
12/5/78: FINGERPRINTZ
12/6/78: THE FALL (2)
12/11/78: THE CURE (1)
12/12/78: IAN DURY & THE BLOCKHEADS
12/13/78: SCRITTI POLITTI (1)
12/13/78: CIMARRONS
12/21/78: CARPETTES (2)

1/3/79: ONLY ONES (3)
1/8/79: THE DAMNED (3)
1/15/79: PREFECTS (2)
1/16/79: TUBEWAY ARMY
1/18/79: GANG OF FOUR (1)
1/22/79: LEYTON BUZZARDS (2)
1/23/79: MEMBERS (1)
1/29/79: THE RUTS (1)
1/30/79: THE LURKERS (4)

2/5/79: THE UNDERTONES (2)
2/6/79: MOLESTERS (2)
2/7/79: PRAG VEC (2)
2/14/79: GENERATION X (3)
2/14/79: JOY DIVISION (1)
2/20/79: THE WASPS (2)
2/21/79: PIRANHAS (1)
2/21/79: LAURA LOGIC
2/22/79: MONOCHROME SET (1)
2/26/79: THE SKIDS (3)
2/26/79: JOE JACKSON
2/27/79: IVOR CUTLER (3)

3/5/79: EDDIE AND THE HOT RODS (3)
3/6/79: BIG IN JAPAN
3/7/79: PENETRATION (2)
3/12/79: TOM ROBINSON BAND 2)
3/21/79: SPIZZ ENERGI (1)
3/22/79: NEON

4/2/79: ADAM AND THE ANTS (3)
4/2/79: FRANKIE MILLER (3)
4/4/79: GAFFA
4/5/79: NEON HEARTS
4/9/79: ROY HILL BAND (2)
4/10/79: THE SHAPES
4/10/79: CRASS

4/16/79: SIOUXSIE AND THE BANSHEES (3)
4/17/79: PATRICK FITZGERALD (3)
4/26/79: GLAXO BABIES
4/30/79: SHAKE

5/1/79: RAINCOATS
5/7/79: THE SKIDS (4)
5/8/79: LINTON KWESI JOHNSON
5/9/79: RESISTANCE
5/14/79: MAGAZINE (3)
5/16/79: THE CURE (2)
5/21/79: THE RUTS (2)
5/22/79: SWELL MAPS (2)
5/23/79: STEVE ELGIN & THE FLATBACKERS
5/28/79: BUZZCOCKS (4)
5/29/79: SPECIALS (1)
5/30/79: PUNISHMENT OF LUXURY (2)

6/3/79: EXPELAIRES
6/7/79: THE NEWS
6/18/79: WAYNE COUNTY & THE ELECTRIC CHAIRS
6/20/79: AGONY COLUMN
6/21/79: DISTRIBUTORS
6/25/79: GARY NUMAN
6/27/79: LEYTON BUZZARDS (3)
6/27/79: ROY HILL BAND (1)
6/28/79: UK SUBS (3)

7/2/79: THE YACHTS (2)
7/4/79: SCRITTI POLITTI (2)
7/5/79: MONITORS
7/7/79: GANG OF FOUR (2)
7/9/79: CHORDS
7/11/79: THE VAPORS
7/16/79: PURPLE HEARTS
7/18/79: NIKKI AND THE DOTS
7/19/79: THE RUSSIANS
7/25/79: SECRET AFFAIR (1)
7/26/79: PIRANHAS (2)
7/30/79: POLICE
7/30/79: PSYCHEDELIC FURS

8/6/79: JIMMY NORTON'S EXPLOSION
8/9/79: CRAVATS
8/13/79: LOUDON WAINWRIGHT III
8/13/79: STEEL PULSE (3)
8/14/79: DOLLY MIXTURE
8/15/79: COCKNEY REJECTS
8/20/79: MERTON PARKAS
8/22/79: ECHO AND THE BUNNYMEN
8/27/79: MADNESS

9/3/79: ORCHESTRAL MANOEUVRES IN THE DARK
9/6/79: MONOCHROME SET (2)
9/7/79: CHELSEA (3)
9/10/79: QUADS
9/12/79: FLOWERS
9/13/79: THE PRATS
9/17/79: STIFF LITTLE FINGERS (3)
9/18/79: WIRE (3)
9/19/79: KEVIN COYNE (3)
9/24/79: PETER HAMMILL (2)
9/24/79: THE DODGEMS
9/25/79: SHOES FOR INDUSTRY
9/26/79: ELTI FITS
9/28/79: WILKO JOHNSON

10/1/79: MEMBERS (2)
10/1/79: FUN BOY THREE
10/4/79: VITUS DANCE
10/8/79: THE FLYS (3)
10/9/79: AU PAIRS
10/15/79: XTC (4)
10/15/79: THE TEARDROP EXPLODES
10/17/79: A CERTAIN RATIO
10/22/79: THE SELECTER
10/22/79: SPECIALS (2)
10/25/79: COMSAT ANGELS
10/29/79: THE DAMNED (4)
10/29/79: KILLING JOKE

11/5/79: THE BEAT
11/5/79: THE JAM (3)
11/12/79: THE ADVERTS (4)
11/21/79: THE TRANSMITTERS
11/26/79: PINK MILITARY
11/26/79: SECRET AFFAIR (2)
11/27/79: SPIZZ ENERGI (2)
11/29/79: THE PASSIONS

12/5/79: THE ADICTS
12/10/79: JOY DIVISION (2)
12/10/79: LENE LOVICH (2)
12/17/79: PIL
12/17/79: NOTSENSIBLES
12/24/79: VIV STANSHALL (6)

STRANGE FRUIT LABEL LISTING 1975-99 SESSION RELEASES

001 NEW ORDER 6/1/82
002 THE DAMNED 5/10/77
003 SCREAMING BLUE MESSIAHS 7/27/84
004 STIFF LITTLE FINGERS 9/12/78
005 SUDDEN SWAY 11/16/83
006 WILD SWANS 5/1/82
007 MADNESS 8/14/79
008 GANG OF FOUR 1/9/79
009 WEDDING PRESENT 2/11/86
010 TWA TOOTS 10/22/83
011 THE RUTS 5/14/79
012 SIOUXSIE AND THE BANSHEES 11/29/79
013 JOY DIVISION 1/31/79
014 THE PRIMEVALS 9/8/85
016 THE UNDERTONES 1/21/79
017 X-MAL DEUTSCHLAND 4/30/85
018 THE SPECIALS 5/23/79
019 STUMP 1/26/86
020 BIRTHDAY PARTY 4/21/81
021 THE SLITS 9/19/77
022 SPIZZ OIL 8/1/78
023 JUNE BRIDES 10/22/85
025 THE PREFECTS 1/8/79
026 YEAH YEAH NOH 1/19/86
027 BILLY BRAGG 7/27/83
028 THE FALL 11/27/78
029 GIRLS AT OUR BEST 2/17/81
030 REDSKINS 10/9/82
032 TUBEWAY ARMY 1/10/79
033 JOY DIVISION 11/26/79
034 THE ADVERTS 4/25/77
035 MIGHTY WAH 8/22/84
036 THE TRIFFIDS 5/5/85
038 THAT PETROL EMOTION 6/11/85
039 NEW ORDER 1/26/81
040 THE DAMNED 11/30/76
041 WIRE 1/18/78
042 ELECTRO HIPPIES 7/12/87
044 THE BUZZCOCKS 9/7/77
045 CUD 6/16/87
046 THE VERY THINGS 12/17/83
047 ULTRAVOX 11/21/77
048 EXTREME NOISE TERROR 11/10/87
049 NAPALM DEATH 9/13/87
050 THE CURE 12/4/78
052 THE NIGHTINGALES 10/1/80

053 INTENSE DEGREE 2/28/88
054 THE STUPIDS 5/12/78
055 THE SMITHS 5/18/83
056 BOLT THROWER 1/3/88
057 HALF MAN HALF BISCUIT 11/10/85
058 BIRTHDAY PARTY 12/2/81
060 ECHO AND THE BUNNYMEN 8/15/79
062 THE ROOM 4/14/85
063 ETON CROP 10/1/85
066 SIOUXSIE AND THE BANSHEES 2/6/78
067 AMAYENGE 7/5/88
069 UNSEEN TERROR 3/22/88
070 FOUR BROTHERS 9/11/88
071 A GUY CALLED GERALD 10/30/88
072 INSPIRAL CARPETS 3/26/89
073 CARCASS 12/13/88
074 GO BETWEENS 10/21/84
075 THE ASSOCIATES 8/24/81
076 COLOURBLIND JAMES EXPERIENCE 10/18/88
077 HAPPY MONDAYS 2/31/89
078 PRONG 1/22/89
079 PROPHECY OF DOOM 1/28/90
080 THE JAM 4/25/77

PEEL SESSIONS ALBUMS (MULTIPLE SESSIONS)

SFRLP 100 various artists — The Sampler
SFPSD 049 NAPALM DEATH
SFPMA 202 GARY NUMAN/TUBEWAY ARMY
SFPMA 203 DOOM
SFPMA 204 FSK
SFPMA 205 THAT PETROL EMOTION
SFPMA 206 A WITNESS
SFPMA 207 THE SLITS
SFPMA 208 EXTREME NOISE TERROR
SFPMA 209 NEW FAST AUTOMATIC DAFFODILS
SFPMA 210 JESUS AND MARY CHAIN
SFM 211 BABES IN TOYLAND
SFM 212 various artists — Amphetamine Reptile Collection
SFM 213 various artists — Clawfist Collection
SFM 214 various artists — Hut Collection
SFM 215 FLUKE
SFR 101 various artists — Hardcore Holocaust vol I
SFR 102 THE ONLY ONES
SFR 103 THE UNDERTONES
SFR 104 THE BUZZCOCKS
SFR 105 MICRODISNEY
SFR 106 STIFF LITTLE FINGERS

SFR 107 GANG OF FOUR
SFR 108 WIRE
SFR 109 THE RUTS
SFR 110 NEW ORDER
SFR 111 JOY DIVISION
SFR 113 various artists — Hardcore Holocaust vol II
SFR 114 THE CHAMELEONS
SFR 115 ADAM AND THE ANTS
SFR 116 BOLT THROWER
SFR 117 BILLY BRAGG
SFR 118 THE ORB
SFR 119 various artists — Too Pure
SFR 120 NAPALM DEATH
SFR 121 THE DAMNED
SFR 122 WEDDING PRESENT
SFR 123 UNSANE
SFR 124 MEGA CITY FOUR
SFR 125 VOODOO QUEENS
SFR 126 various artists — Sub Pop Collection
SFR 127 SENSELESS THINGS
SFR 128 BAND OF SUSANS
SFR 129 various artists — Planet Dog Collection
SFR 131 various artists — Nation Compilation
SFR 132 MISTY IN ROOTS
SFR 133 TRUMAN'S WATER
SFR 200 various artists — 21 Years Of Alternative Radio
SFR 202 various artists — Manchester: So Much To Answer For
SFR 204 various artists — Winters Of Discontent
SFR 205 various artists — New Season

NIRVANA AT THE BBC

NOVEMBER 22, 1989: JOHN PEEL (RECORDED) LOVE BUZZ/ABOUT A GIRL/POLLY/SPANK THRU

Nirvana's first European tour, with Seattle's Tad, comprised a gruelling 36 shows in just 42 days through October–December 1989, with the band trooping into the BBC's Maida Vale Studio 4 on October 26, less than a week after touchdown, to record a session for the John Peel show.

With ex-Mott The Hoople drummer Dale Griffin in the producer's chair and Kurt Cobain in particularly fine form, the trio hammered down a blistering four track session, comprising versions of their debut single "Love Buzz," "Spank Thru" from the *Sub Pop* 200 compilation, "Polly," a new song they had recently attempted recording for the *Blew* EP, and "About a Girl" from the band's recently released debut album, *Bleach.*

The session went unaired for close to a month, finally going out on November 22, a fortnight before the band went home. The tour itself was not a particularly happy outing, with the final show, at the Charing Cross Astoria's Lame Fest on December 3, ranking amongst the worst and the best gigs Nirvana ever played, depending upon who you believe. A review in the following week's *Melody Maker* even predicted the line-up changes which would shortly be rocking the band, although it was drummer Chad Channing who departed, not "the lanky, rubberlegged, frog like bassist."

NOVEMBER 3, 1990: JOHN PEEL (RECORDED) SON OF A GUN/MOLLY'S LIPS/D7/ TURNAROUND

Drummer Dave Grohl had been with Nirvana for mere weeks before he was scooped up and taken to Europe for the band's second continental tour, this time opening for L7. A new single, coupling "Sliver" and "Dive," was imminent, but the tour was also timed to keep the band occupied while their own future fell into place. The management company Gold Mountain, and a clutch of major record labels were all in hot pursuit of the group, with Geffen and Charisma rapidly emerging as the favorites.

All that, of course, was a long way away as the band settled into the European tour with a return visit to Studio 3 at the BBC's Maida Vale complex on October 21, 1990, a surprisingly welcome highlight. Once again, Dale Griffin was in the producer's chair.

Three of the four songs which Nirvana recorded that afternoon have since been given an official release. "Son of a Gun," "Molly's Lips," and a thunderously crooked version of Devo's "Turnaround" all featured on the *Incesticide* rarities compilation, leaving only the cover of the Wipers' "D7" out in the cold —it would, however, be featured on the Australian *Hormoanin'* compilation, before resurfacing on the b-side of the "Lithium" CD single.

NOVEMBER 3, 1991: JOHN PEEL (RECORDED) DUMB/DRAIN/ENDLESS NAMELESS

Nirvana's third BBC session was recorded a full two months before broadcast, on September 3, 1991, at the tail end of the last minute rush of advance publicity and festival shows before *Nevermind* blew the band's lives out of the water.

Utilizing Maida Vale Studio 5, and the now familiar embrace of Dale Griffin, Nirvana previewed the forthcoming album with versions of "Drain You" and "Endless Nameless," the latter a freeform jam which wasn't even credited on the record and appears on the BBC's own records under the name "No Title as Yet." The other cut, the older "Dumb," was more conventional.

NOVEMBER 18, 1991: MARK GOODIER (RECORDED) POLLY/BEEN A SON/ SOMETHING IN THE WAY/ ANEURYSM

Returning from their European dates, Nirvana were back in the UK on November 3, the same day as the John Peel session was finally broadcast. Aside from a string of long, sold-out shows, the band was also booked for a wealth of television appearances which included, amongst others, an anarchic rendering of "Smells Like Teen Spirit" on *Top of the Pops*, and a deliriously raw performance on the *Jonathan Ross Show*. Both are featured on Nirvana's official live video, *Live! Tonight! Sold Out!*.

The band returned to the BBC's Maida Vale Studios on November 9, to record their first session for the Mark Goodier Show. Working with producers Miti Adhikari and John Taylor in Studio 4, they turned in the very accomplished, but slightly tour-fatigued versions of "Been a Son" and "Aneurysm" which would subsequently appear on *Incesticide*, and a punked-up rendering of "Polly" which that same collection would subtitle "[New Wave]." It's ironic, then, that the best of the batch should be the unreleased fourth performance: a moody, atmospheric take on "Something in the Way."

Following Cobain's death in April 1994, the BBC broadcast a full tribute to the singer, airing all four Peel and Goodier sessions in their entirety plus excerpts from Nirvana's Halloween 1991 Seattle show. Although this was not a BBC recording (and was in any case largely superceded by *From the Muddy Banks of the Wishkah*), British fans, at least, implicitly associate the show with the band's Peel and Goodier legacy, while the BBC broadcast was itself the source for bootlegged versions of an early live version of "Oh, The Guilt" (from Nirvana's split single with Jesus Lizard) and the unreleased "Talk to Me."

Rock Against Racism

"Do we have any foreigners in the audience tonight?" Eric Clapton took the stage drunk, and seemed progressively worse for wear as the show went on. "If so, please put up your hands. I think we should vote for Enoch Powell." Onstage at the Birmingham Odeon, in the immigrant heart of Britain's midlands, the guitarist formerly known as God openly pledged his support to a right wing politician best known for advocating the forced repatriation of Britain's black population.

It was August 5, 1976, and Clapton had inadvertently thrown another log onto the fires of the incipient punk explosion. The very next week, all three British music papers (*Sounds*, *Melody Maker*, and the *New Musical Express*) carried a letter signed by Red Saunders, David Widgery, and Syd Shelton, announcing the organization of "a rank and file movement against the racist poison in music. We urge support for Rock Against Racism." In the next seven days, the letter drew 140 responses from the public. Over the next seven years, it changed the face of Britain.

Rock Against Racism remains the most single-minded and, in that singlemindedness, successful force for political change in the history of music. In allying itself so early and so potently, with the forces of punk rock, it became all but inseparable from that movement — a rallying point so powerful that even when all the other punk tenets had come crumbling down and it was apparent that unemployment, poverty, and hunger were not about to be swept away with guitars, there was still one fight which could be won. And though racism itself might not have been destroyed, the culture of ignorance which is its most fertile breeding ground was certainly given less raw materials to work with.

Clapton himself swiftly recanted — he was drunk, he said, he claimed he was joking, and eventually, even his fiercest detractors conceded that sometimes, one can say things which fall completely out of context, usually because one has not actually put them into context in the first place. Clapton was publicly reacting to a private incident (an Arab pinching his wife's bottom in public), but when he admitted he was wrong, he never asked for forgiveness. For in so brutally focusing attention upon an issue which had been smoldering beneath the surface of British society for 20 years, he helped society itself take a step which as many years worth of "concerned citizenry" had never been able to put into action.

Rock Against Racism (RAR) hosted its first concert at a London pub in November 1976 — a couple of unknown bands; a wall stacked with literature, leaflets, and buttons; and an audience shuffling around not quite certain how they ought to behave. Would there be speeches? Would there be hand-holding and massed choruses of "We Shall Overcome"? Or would there simply be a lot of music, a little private discussion, and — for the first time in radical politics — an organization which was content to let the people take action, while their leaders benignly looked on? Most people guessed the first two, a few held out hope for the third. The few were proven correct.

Initially by word of mouth, but later through its own *Temporary Hoarding* magazine, RAR cried out for political activism. But it did not preach, it did not bully, and it did not argue. Like the Trotsky-ist Socialist Workers Party (SWP) upon which it was most obviously modeled, RAR's tactics were simple — focusing attention upon struggles and issues, then using those struggles to build support for itself. Either you were for its cause, or against it. What you did next was your own concern.

Of course, not everybody was supportive of such methods, particularly when it became apparent that the new operation had borrowed more than its mannerisms from the SWP. RAR actually operated out of SWP-owned premises and was frequently featured in the pages of the party's *Socialist Worker* newspaper. Inevitably, the right wing drew its own conclusions, and condemned the whole thing as a leftist plot, a full-scale Communist take-over of the nation's confused youth.

In fact, RAR had little patience for party politics, seeing in the machinations of even liberal government policies further barriers against the progress of its own issues. "Other battles are fought with ballots and bullets," the audience at one RAR pub gig was told. "Ours is fought with Belts And Braces" — and out came the band of the same name, fervent supporters of the RAR cause. As RAR co-founder Widgery explained, "the music came first and was more exciting. It provided the creative energy and the focus in what became a battle for the soul of young working class England."

The almost wholly ideological agenda set out at RAR's founding conference in January 1977 was to change little over the next five years. Across the country, but most prominently in the areas which past waves of immigration had designated racial melting pots, the far right wing National Front was conducting a campaign which did indeed seek to indoctrinate great swathes of British youth, its tactics wavering between simple intimidation, and outright physical damage.

Asian and black households were being targeted constantly, with graffiti and stones, with punches and bottles, sometimes even with firebombs. But not, of course, by the Front's members themselves, for they were far too smart for such criminal activities. It was the people their message spread out to — the teenage workers canned from their jobs "because a black would do it for half the wage"; the blue collar home-owners whose property values had plummeted "because a Pakistani family had moved in down the block"; the skinhead kid whose sister had been knocked up by a Rasta. They were the ones who heard the Front's rhetoric, and translated it into action with knuckleheaded ease.

Such attacks were rarely reported in the media or, if it could be helped, to the police. If you can't trust your own neighbors, after all, how could you trust your neighbors' police force? Better to try and sort it yourself. So fear bred ferocity, beatings bred belligerence.

In August 1976, the Clash's Joe Strummer, together with bandmate Paul Simenon and manager Bernie Rhodes, attended the Notting Hill Carnival in west London. It was just three weeks since Eric Clapton's outburst, and with 60 arrests and some 450 reported injuries, the carnival's annual celebration of West Indian immigrant life swiftly degenerated into the largest UK riot since 1958.

Fired by Rhodes' revolutionary vision, and Strummer's love of reggae, the Clash contingent believed themselves at one with the Rastas, their personal outlaw fantasies receiving a major boost when the trio were stopped by the law. "We got searched by policemen looking for bricks," Strummer recalled. But their dreams came crashing back to earth a little later, when they were cornered in an alley, "and we got searched by Rastas looking for pound notes."

The situation changed rapidly, however. "Before the Rock Against Racism thing really got going," Chelsea vocalist Gene October recalled, "if you were white, there were parts of town you simply didn't go into, because the blacks would kick the shit out of you — not because they were racist, but because you might be. The black kids wanted to mix and later, after punk happened and Rock Against Racism got going, they could — you'd walk past a bunch of Rastas and they'd be fine, 'how you going, mate?' You'd get black kids at punk shows, punk kids at reggae shows — that simply couldn't have happened a year earlier. That's how much Rock Against Racism changed things."

In August 1977, just a year after that first RAR missive appeared in the press, the movement was vast enough to mobilize a massive army to block and harass a National Front march through predominantly black Lewisham, in south London. Inevitably, the event ended in vast numbers of arrests and injuries; inevitably, too, RAR were portrayed in the press as the troublemakers, storming an hitherto peaceful, legal, and democratic exercise. But it was the marchers who went home bloodied and beaten, and the protestors who celebrated into the night.

Through 1977–78, RAR was everywhere. Its most important displays were the vast Anti-Nazi League rallies which saw entire city blocks transformed into semi-carnivals, thousands of marchers moving through some of London's most racially sensitive areas, en route to free concerts featuring the cream of the punk and reggae community — the April 1978 march which ended with a Clash concert in Victoria Park and the Alexandra Palace festival a year later, were simply the largest of these.

Smaller scale benefits and events were being staged on a weekly basis, some featuring genuinely exciting headline material — Aswad, Matumbi, the Tom Robinson Band, Elvis Costello, Stiff Little Fingers; others offering little more than what was, at the time, considered standard pub and club fare — the Enchanters, the Carol Grimes Band, Milk, the still emergent Ruts. Some raised money, some raised hackles — the National Front regularly picketed such concerts. But all raised awareness.

The Front tried to fight back, using fire against fire. But few bands would openly align themselves with the movement, and those that did — Skrewdriver were one of the first — frequently found themselves unwelcome anywhere else. Attempts by the Front to claim the Sex Pistols for their own were fiercely denounced by Johnny Rotten; a more logical claim on Sham 69, whose partisan skinhead following really did seem the Front's natural constituency, was likewise exploded when vocalist Jimmy Pursey became one of RAR's most vociferous supporters.

Neither was London alone the focal point of activity. In Coventry, the nascent Specials were early adherents to the RAR banner; in Birmingham, so were UB40 and it was this wellspring of regional activity which allowed RAR, through the summer of 1978, to stage what amounted to a touring festival, traveling the country with a revolving door full of participating bands.

By 1978, too, *Temporary Hoarding* was selling over 12,000 issues a month, and RAR was operating its own record label out of an address in Artesley, in rural Bedfordshire. But the organization was not resting back on its laurels. Indeed, with a General Election just around the corner in May 1979, RAR was girding itself for the biggest fight of its short life.

The battle was fought in every available forum. The *New Musical Express* interviewed Red Saunders, and barely interrupted him once; while *Sounds* ran a memorable feature reminding its readers that it wouldn't only be black entertainers who would suffer if the National Front ever got into power. Musicians as far from the racial stereotype as Joe Strummer (born in Ankara, Turkey), the Police's Stewart Copeland (Alexandria, Egypt), the Electric Chairs' Henry Padovani (Corsica), Japan's Mick Karn (Greek descent), even that perennial parental favorite, Cliff Richard (Lucknow, India), would come under fire as well.

Such tactics were heavy-handed, but they needed to be. At the 1974 election, the Front ran 54 candidates, and though none were elected, still the party came away with 3.3 percent of the vote. In 1979, they were fielding 303 potential Members of Parliament. Mathematically, the implications were terrifying.

In March 1979, RAR and the Anti-Nazi League combined to launch the Militant Entertainment tour, climaxing with an all-day festival at the Alexandra Palace. Other, smaller events were planned for elsewhere around the country in the lead-up to the election.

The following month, a Front march through the predominantly Asian suburb of Southall was broken up by demonstrators, and suddenly even the mainstream press seemed to realize precisely what was at stake, when a schoolteacher, Blair Peach, was killed by a blow to the head from a Special Patrol Group officer. The irony of a pacifist being killed by a policeman protecting fascists was inescapable. Ten days later, when the country turned out to vote, the Front was utterly annihilated. Within a year, the party had all but crumbled.

RAR's greatest accomplishment was not the death of racism, because of course, racism did not die with the end of the National Front, any more than RAR would perish now that the Front had been destroyed.

What it did do was ensure that an entire generation of youth, beset though it was by mass unemployment and seemingly endemic hopelessness, did not succumb to the blandishments of the far right — blandishments which have led to the scapegoating of religious and ethnic minorities since the dawn of civilization.

Thus, even as racism as a political creed slipped back beneath the covers of British political life — where 1979's electoral victor, Margaret Thatcher's Conservative Party, would certainly keep it warm — so RAR only strengthened, as an organization, but more importantly, as the institutionalized ideology it had always set out to become.

The rise of the 2-Tone label in Britain in 1979 only increased the organization's hold on British youth, while the launch of RAR-USA by *Trouser Press* journalist Kathy Frank and Michael Masucci saw the birth of a grassroots movement whose principles still flourish today, in the form of the broadly-targeted Canadian Artists Against Racism, and the more specialized Spirit of Unity (reggae), Ska Against Racism, and Rappers Against Racism.

These are the victories which RAR sought when it was launched; these are the ones which remain its immortal legacy. Racism, as Red Saunders once remarked, will probably never be destroyed. "But if it can be defeated often enough, that could be good enough."

Punky Reggae Party

The sound systems were pumping the whole summer long, and into the winter as well. All down London's Portobello Road, the ribbon of market traders and antique stores which links seedy Ladbroke Grove to chintzy Notting Hill, their insistent offbeat hung heavy in the air, rising above the babel of Jamaican patois and west London slang, blending with the traffic on the Westway overpass.

1976 had been a long, hot summer. Drought and water shortages frayed moods already savaged by the unrelenting heat. Old people were dying in their homes from sunstroke and thirst, young people were fighting in the streets from boredom and bad temper. At the end of August, the annual Notting Hill carnival (a weekend-long celebration of Jamaican immigrant society) exploded into the worst rioting seen in London in two decades, since the same area went up in flames in the late 1950s, and triggered author Colin MacInnes to write the *Absolute Beginners* Mod bible.

Once again, the cultural melting pot was approaching the boiling point, and if you listened closely, the word was that next year would be even harder. For next year, 1977, the two sevens would clash, and in Rastafarian iconography that meant just one thing — armageddon.

Joseph Hill and Culture's *Two Sevens Clash* remains one of the crucial reggae long players of the mid-1970s; a prophecy of merciless destruction which gripped Britain's West Indian population as fervently and fearfully as it did Jamaica's. Inevitably, that same sensation of foreboding and fear — but also of anticipation and excitement — would communicate itself further afield.

In the annals of musical history, 1977 would become the year of punk, the explosion of musical nihilism which irrevocably changed the shape of a nation. Its ingredients were manifold, drawn from across the rock'n'roll spectrum of course, but also from the cultural microcosms which comprised contemporary British society. The Jamaican community, with its focal points in the underprivileged underbellies of the country's biggest cities, and its long-established principles of righteous rebellion, would inevitably become drawn into the stew.

Joe Strummer and Mick Jones, middle class white boys slumming it in the shadow of the Westway as they pieced together their new band, the Clash, were a common sight on Portobello Road, thumbing through the racks of Jamaican imports. Johnny Rotten, the iconoclastic frontman of the Sex Pistols, was a known dub freak — when the Pistols signed to Virgin Records in the spring of 1977, the label's support of reggae was a key element in the decision.

Gene October of Chelsea, Tony James of Generation X, T.V. Smith of the Adverts, a whole generation of white musicians brought up on the imported sounds of Keith Hudson, Rupie Edwards, King Tubby, and Augustus Pablo — most of them shopping from the little reggae store beneath the arch of Ladbroke Grove subway station — was preparing to fuse the roar of punk with the rhythms of reggae. For them, *Two Sevens Clash* was not a warning. It was a manifesto, and one which DJ Don Letts, spinning discs at the punk mecca Roxy club, was destined to consummate.

"When the Roxy started," Letts reflected, "there were literally no punk records to play... so I had to play something I liked, which was reggae. I guess I did turn a few people onto it. The crowd wanted to hear more reggae. We turned each other on through our different cultures. They liked me because I gave them access to Jamaican culture, and they turned me on to a white culture that didn't fucking exist before they came along."

All that was needed now was for somebody to bring the two together. Which is when the Clash decided to record Junior Murvin's "Police and Thieves"; the white punk's answer to the Jamaicans' hope.

"Now I think what a bold brass neck we had to cover it," vocalist Joe Strummer marvelled years later. "But I'm glad we did, because... it led onto great things in the future with Lee Perry and Bob Marley hearing it, and being hip enough to know we'd brought our own music to the party."

Built around a dramatic Mick Jones rearrangement, with two guitars playing the on and off-beats ("any other group," explained Strummer, "would've played on the offbeat [alone], trying to assimilate reggae"), "Police and Thieves" almost never made it onto the Clash's self-titled debut album. In the event, it *made* the album, and before the end of the year, Perry himself would be producing the Clash's next single, "Complete Control."

Bob Marley greeted the Year of Judgement with what was simultaneously his most commercial, and his most apocalyptic vision yet, "Exodus." One week after the Sex Pistols topped the British chart with "God Save the Queen," "Exodus" became Marley's fourth hit in under two years and, in the prevalent mood of the time, his most important.

The neo-Nazi National Front party was flexing its muscles that year and, when the Birmingham suburb of Handsworth went up in smoke in the aftermath of a NF rally, it was *Exodus* which provided the soundtrack to the resistance, the imploring of "Natural Mystic," the optimism of "Three Little Birds," the embattled defiance of "Exodus" itself.

The movement of Jah people began. Over the next two years, as Britain's hastily born Anti-Nazi League battled the fascists in the country's city centers, Marley's music would rise above the sounds of destruction — a beacon of hope, the clarion call of resistance.

Of course, *Exodus* was no less symbolic to Marley himself. Much of it was recorded in Miami, Florida, where Marley and his family fled following an attempt on his life in December 1976. His belief that the would-be assassins were politically motivated gave *Exodus* an irrevocable flavoring, his private despair and desperation shot through with the stubborn resistance of the unwilling exile.

Unwittingly and initially unknowingly, however, Marley also delivered the rallying cry which would feed the flames of freedom which burned an entire ocean away. But he was not slow in comprehending the ramifications of the rebellion.

No sooner had Lee Perry recorded with the Clash, then he was excitedly telling Bob Marley all about it. The pair promptly recorded "Punky Reggae Party," a celebration uniting black and white, punk and Rasta, with an inseparability which remained as powerful two decades later, in the hybrid sounds of Rancid, Sublime, and NOFX, as it was back then, through the dub-heavy thrashing of the Slits and the Clash. More than that, however, it was the sound of Marley showering approval upon his latest crop of acolytes, and they, of course, responded in kind.

The Slits' version of John Holt's paranoid classic "Man Next Door"; Stiff Little Fingers' faithful take on Marley's own "Johnny Was"; the Members' softly skanking "Off Shore Banking Business"; all and more were as much a statement of Roots solidarity as they were a show of punk intent.

Before the end of 1977, Matumbi, Steel Pulse (whose "Handsworth Rebellion" developed fully formed from the transplanted Babylon of that year's Birmingham riots), and Aswad had all evolved onto the punk scene. From Jamaica via New York City, Tapper Zukie erupted through the patronage of Patti Smith, and in the clubs and pubs, Dillinger's "Cocaine on my Brain" was positively endemic.

Poet Linton Kwesi Johnson burst through with a commentary on police persecution of Britain's West Indian youth which led first, to wideranging outrage, then to at least some minor revisions in the law.

Producer Adrian Sherwood took the first tentative steps on the journey which would establish his On-U dub sound among the primal forces of the next decade. Rolling Stone Keith Richards demonstrated that even Boring Old Farts understood part of the equation, with a magnificent solo rendition of Jimmy Cliff's "The Harder They Come." And Misty In Roots proved the traffic was not all one way by using their own label, People Unite, to launch the Ruts, the most accomplished punk/reggae crossover of them all.

The importance of this cross-fertilization, as Marley and Perry were amongst the first to appreciate, lay in the fact that punk in Britain was not simply a musical phenomenon. Indeed, at its purest heart, music was simply the vehicle by which more pressing social and political concerns were being brought into the open.

It was that which led the British authorities to strive so ferociously to suppress punk's first stirrings — banning the bands, closing their clubs, arresting its icons. Punk was, first and foremost, the sound of the rebellious streets and, if its blood ties with reggae were forged through a mutual distrust of the establishment, they were cemented by the establishment's heavy-handed attempts at repression. Young Rastas always were an easy target for opportunistic police harassment. Now young punks joined them on the wanted list.

The disparate forces at work through this tumultuous year finally crested in October 1977, when Bob Marley arrived in the UK to play a weeklong season at London's Rainbow Theatre. Punks and Rastas led the rush for tickets, maintaining an uneasy preparedness as uglier factions crossed over from Skinhead culture — rightly or wrongly synonymous with the racist political right. In the meantime, the media, previewing the shows, and the cops, policing them, prepared for a bloodbath.

The simple positioning of police vans and the flying phalanx of lawmen which would dive into the crowd at preordained intervals, to emerge with another struggling innocent in bondage, suggested something beyond simply crowd control. It was more like divide and conquer, setting brother against brother, skin against Skin, protecting society by crushing its roots. "Kill it before it grows," a line from Marley's "I Shot the Sheriff," rang with special resonance at the Rainbow.

The venue's own security, too, was edgily aggressive, sending a fresh wave of tangible emotion out across the crowd. By the time Marley and the Wailers themselves appeared onstage, an audience gathered in that state of peaceful union which Bob Marley fought so hard for had long since fractured into glowering factions, through which the police passed like an avenging angel. That most of the arrests that night were for minor (marijuana) drug offenses only exacerbated the law's total lack of understanding of the situation.

From the stage, Marley took in that same situation with a glance. Talking to the British press later, he condemned the police, condemned the bouncers, condemned the handful of kids who attended the shows looking for trouble or worse. But he praised the audience which ensured that by and large, they didn't find it. Through a set dominated by *Exodus* the album, and crowned by "Exodus" the song, Marley first steadied, then utterly salved the troubled waters lapping to the lip of the stage. And by the time "Punky Reggae Party" came around, that's exactly what it was — a seething partyl-ike celebration of release, relief, and joy, which drew and then threw the anger aside. Even the cops were dancing. Well, some of them were.

The warring tribes would never again come together with such pronounced unity as they did at the Rainbow; but neither would they sunder with such potentially violent intensity either. The Clash's Joe Strummer still sensed the divide inside Hammersmith Palais for a Prince Far I show a short while later (he wrote a song about the experience too), but he knew he was safe there all the same; that nothing would happen if he didn't let it.

Homegrown reggae artists found vast, wide acceptance on stages normally walked by punks; when Rock Against Racism staged their biggest rally yet, at Alexandra Palace in the spring of 1979, it could have choked the bill with reggae and no one would have complained. As it was, the biggest cheer of the evening was reserved for Scottish rocker Alex Harvey, who eschewed his own catalog of hard hits and favorites to lead the crowd through an impassioned rendition of Marley's "Big Tree, Small Axe."

In February 1978, meanwhile, Althea (Forest) and Donna (Reid)'s "Uptown Top Ranking" became the first Jamaican record to make #1 in Britain since Dave and Ansell Collins, seven years before. A shrill cry of female emancipation catapulting out of the male dominated culture of the Rasta mainstream, "Uptown Top Ranking" was the first blow in the next round of cultural conflicts which would unite black and white, Jamaican and Englishman, against the traumas of tradition; another step in the evolution to a higher state of being and another story entirely.

The two sevens had already clashed by then, and armageddon had been averted, fought with fire and the sheer strength of togetherness. The future could — and would — fight its own wars.

RECOMMENDED LISTENING

THE CLASH Armagiddon Time (LP *London Calling*)

CULTURE Two Sevens Clash (LP *Two Sevens Clash*)

BOB MARLEY Exodus (LP *Exodus*)

NEW AGE STEPPERS Fade Away (45)

MAX ROMEO War in a Babylon (LP *War in a Babylon*)

THE RUTS Jah Wars (LP *The Crack*)

THE SLITS Man Next Door (45)

STEEL PULSE Ku Klux Klan (LP *Handsworth Revolution*)

PETER TOSH Legalize It (LP *Legalize It*)

TAPPA ZUKIE MPLA (LP *MPLA*)

Don't Call Me Ska-Face

The reemergence of Britain's skinhead culture after half a decade in the shadows was, in retrospect, inevitable. Punk, after all, was already tamed, and just as society always needs a scapegoat, anti-society always needs a focus. Nevertheless, only the most bigoted opponent could draw anything but coincidental conclusions from the simultaneous rise of the National Front, the public face of the '70s Nazi revival and, for a short time, a potential Great Power in British political circles.

As many skinhead outfits, after all, allied themselves with the socialist Anti-Nazi League, as they did the Front, and from that allegiance came new direction, politically, culturally, and musically. For by actively encouraging the already formative mutation of punk and reggae, an entire new union was forged from two new musical forces. Oi! was one, 2-Tone was the other, and if they sometimes seemed mutually incompatible, they were also irrevocably symbiotic.

Without 2-Tone, and the rest of the punk-ska half-breed which history now lumps under that one, convenient, corporate banner, Oi! — the most familiar term under which the mutant meeting of Third Generation punks and Blank Generation skinheads would take place — could never have flourished as it did.

Both came from the streets, both spoke to "the kids," both offered an escape from the disenfranchisement which was the everyday life of the young working class. And if the conflicting ideologies which powered them served primarily to reinforce the historical stereotypes of the time, they also harkened back to an earlier age.

The headlines, of course, concentrated on the trouble which did attend certain skinhead gatherings, focused on the bad apples who openly sided with the Front, delighted in recounting tales of unquestionable racist violence. But they missed the countless corollaries, and that was where 2-Tone came in, redressing the balance, then upsetting it entirely.

2-Tone exerted a peculiar influence over its audience. Outside shows Nazi-daubed skins would harass the "n-word loving" passers-by with NF leaflets, wit, and weapons. Inside, however, it was the skins who gave the performers the most encouragement, transforming entire theaters into vast, swirling skank machines, reliving the days 15 years before, when the Mods — in terms of demeanor, if not exactly dress, the Skins' closest antecedent — were the standard bearers of ska and rocksteady, as those musics swept the UK from their homeland, Jamaica. Then, as now, color became irrelevant; then as now, the audience was, indeed, truly two-toned.

In the inferno of outrage which greeted the emergence of genuinely hard-core racist Skin bands, the existence of this other breed was overlooked entirely. And though one cannot rightfully say which was the minority faction, it's impossible to determine which was the majority either. Because, whatever the conclusion, a Specials' gig really was just an excuse for everyone to get down together, regardless of color or cult, and when the "Skinhead Moonstomp" went on sale, it danced straight up the UK chart.

2-Tone was the name which was given to the music, but 2-Tone was also a record label and together, they became a way of life. Founded by Specials vocalist Jerry Dammers as an outlet for his own assemblage's then-unique brand of ska-punk, 2-Tone tapped so swiftly into a national mood that by the time the label released its first single, the Specials' Prince Buster tribute "Gangsters," 2-Tone was already a definable brand name.

The climate into which 2-Tone so stylishly skanked was a weird one. Oi! was indeed rising from the ashes of first wave punk, but 1979 was also the summer of Mod, a ghost laid to rest in the mid-1960s but reborn first by Paul Weller's obsession with his old Who and Small Faces records, then by the Who's own revitalization around the movie version of their 1973 Mod concept album, "Quadrophenia."

2-Tone, too, traced its antecedents back to that same era of original Mod, but with a socio-political edge which not only screamed out of the band's own records, but was also apparent in the countless cover versions which they peppered their repertoire with. When the Specials revived Dandy Livingstone's laconic "A Message to You, Rudy," they also revived the emotions which made the song so important when it was first released, appealing to a new generation whose own social prospects were as appalling as the original Jamaican Rude Boys'.

Unemployment was soaring, inflation was rising, living standards had bottomed out. Caught between the existing menace of an incumbent socialist government which lost its direction years before, and the imminent peril of Margaret Thatcher's fundamentalist conservatism, British youth stared into a bleak no-future which even the Sex Pistols could not have envisaged. The only real dilemma was, what they were going to do about it — embrace the essentially negative (and oft-times nihilistic) weariness of Oi! or wrap their troubles in dreams?

"The establishment like these divisions," Sham's Jimmy Pursey mused. "That there's Teds [Teddy Boys] fighting the Hell's Angels fighting the skinheads fighting so and so. If they ever thought the kids didn't care what they wore or thought, but were just one against one thing — them — they'd be really scared. This way, with 27 identities, they know they've got us beat." 2-Tone, blending those identities into one amorphous mass, was not to be so easily tamed.

The label itself reflected Dammers' ambitions for the music the Specials were making. Learning the importance of presentation from a short-lived alliance with Clash manager Bernie Rhodes, he and bandmates Neville Staples and Lynval Golding began piecing together the kind of image which they thought a ska band should have: half Jamaican Rude Boy, half London Skinhead, part Mod, part punk, black and white pop art, cubes and arrows, pork-pie hats, two-tone tonics and mohair jackets, crombies, Harringtons, Ben Shermans, Doc Martens...and, presiding over the entire montage, Walt Jabsco, the distinctive black and white rude boy image which Jerry lifted from an old photo of Peter Tosh, and who would come to symbolize 2-Tone in every area it touched.

By the end of May 1979, the first pressing of "Gangsters"/"The Selecter" was sold out, and distributors Rough Trade were furiously trying to keep up with the demand for more. The Specials themselves were inescapable — BBC radio DJ John Peel adored them, and played "Gangsters" every chance he got. The music press was lionizing them, describing the Specials as the most exciting thing to hit music since the Sex Pistols, and though that was hardly a unique compliment (was there a band in the land who hadn't received it?), this time they seemed to mean it.

The most important advance, though, was the rapidity with which the Specials began to acquire their own crowd; that, after all, was what the cohesion of their own image was intended to do; that was what sorted the men from the boys.

On April 8, 1979, the Specials opened for the UK Subs and the Damned at the London Lyceum. Fiery street punks, the Subs had long since cultivated a skinhead/Oi! cult following, but their own brand of adrenalined terrace chanting only appealed on the most basic level — it was great to sing along with, and great for pogoing, too. But like their decade-old forebears, the new breed of skins wanted to dance as well. They flirted with reggae, and bought "Uptown Top Ranking" by the binful. Then the Specials stormed out with an entire setful of the stuff; new songs, old songs, and songs like "Gangsters" and "Too Much Too Young" which sat in the middle. How could they fail?

The Specials' singles hit the mainstream too, and a slew of other bands emerged in their wake — Selecter, Madness, UB40, the [English] Beat, led by the twin figureheads of Dave Wakeling and Rankin' Roger. Everywhere, ska became a national obsession, and while 2-Tone led the field, it was by no means the only game in town. The creation of Secret Affair's I-Spy label in stark imitation of 2-Tone, and its immediate recruitment of the newly reemerged ska lagend Laurel Aitken, exacerbated the mania even further.

Vince Seggs of punk-reggae masters the Ruts, recalled how vocalist Malcolm Owen, "really got into the ska look, the hats, and clothes. It was a real cross-over point — Malcolm, in his inimitable way, started to wear a pork-pie hat and a mauve two-tone suit. It was a bit of a fashion thing, but it was kinda normal really, because I came out of ska and Motown, that's what I listened to as a kid, and with cross-fertilization and all that, blah blah, gigs with Misty In Roots, all the reggae bands in London, it was kind of normal that 2-Tone would come out of that. And as the 2-Tone thing picked up, we were getting some of that crowd come along to see us."

Aitken himself felt nothing but admiration for the new generation of rudies. "Lots of people said that the [Specials] were ripping off the original sound of ska, but I wouldn't say that because lots of black people don't want to play ska. So it was great for me to see Jerry Dammers and his posse doing what they were doing, because a lot of black people weren't interested in it. I don't know why."

Former Planets trombonist Rico Rodriguez, drawn into the new wave by the Specials themselves, agreed with Aitken. "Some writers... they say that the Specials is stealing reggae and ska from the black man. But this is just pure foolishness, just pure fuckery, the things they say. For when I lived in Jamaica... I was playing this music and was a most loved and respected musician in Jamaica. So would I be playing with the Specials if the things these people say are true?"

Like Aitken, Rico's reemergence did much to earn the so-called ska revival a respect which its Mod counterpart could never gain, and as 2-Tone's own commercial stock continued to soar, so even fresher talents began to stir.

The Walkie Talkies, formed by Liverpool guitarist (and future Mission frontman) Wayne Hussey, were one of the first non-2-Tone bands to get off the blocks, releasing their "Rich and Nasty" single shortly before Christmas 1979. They were quickly followed by Diversion, with a cracking take on Prince Buster's "Rough Rider," the all-instrumental Ska-Dows, and the utterly demented Bad Manners. There were the Akrylykz, featuring future Fine Young Cannibal Roland Gift; Graduate, the West Country aggregation which would one day metamorphose into Tears For Fears; Paul "King" Sampson's Reluctant Stereotypes; Vaughn Toulouse's Guns For Hire.

Things were moving quickly; too quickly, according to some observers. The Bodysnatchers were signed to 2-Tone in 1980; signed, too, to appear in the *Dance Craze* ska movie which Jerry Dammers was currently making, but Dave Wakeling, already a weary veteran of the whole shebang, complained "every record company's going fucking mad over this 2-Tone thing. Look what's happening to the Bodysnatchers. They're going to get killed because they're not ready for it.

People are waiting for the 2-Tone mistake, and it won't be long."

The "2-Tone mistake," of course, did not necessarily mean a mistake made by 2-Tone. So rapidly had ska taken off, so vast was its infant catalog, that any miscalculation within its ranks could not help but reflect badly on the entire genre. When a string of dates on the Specials/Madness tour the previous fall was disrupted by warring skinheads, the mainstream news crews were quick to castigate this latest youth cult. Now, as once enthusiastic media ears began to discern (or maybe just imagine) a noticeable slackening off in the frenetic pace of the 2-Tone sound, the music press, too, commenced its backlash.

Last in, first out. The Bodysnatchers were still climbing the chart when the first salvo hit — when "Do the Rock Steady" peaked at #22, it was lowest chart position yet attained by a 2-Tone release. Then the guns turned on the rank and file, harmless innocents like the Army, the Charlie Parkas, the MPs, the Skavengers, the Tigers, and the Viewers.

Regardless of quality (and some of these outsiders were very good indeed), the signal lack of success which awaited them fired further sordid cynicism towards the ska movement as a whole, as though the 2-Tone tag and the imagery alone were what sold the label's records, with the actual music a wearisome by-product. And sadly, there was some truth to such accusations.

Having departed 2-Tone after one single apiece, only Madness and the English Beat had gone on to hit the rock and pop mainstream. The Selecter quit 2-Tone in the summer of 1981, complaining about the over-commercialization of the company, and all but vanished from view for a decade. There were no commercial rewards, either, for Cairo, the Rent Boys, Mix Blood, the Gangsters, Mobster, the Ska City Rockers (another Roland Gift outfit), T and the Unknown, or for Boff, signed to R.A.K. and then changing their name (to Boss) when it was pointed out that their original choice was a not-so-obscure colloquialism for "fuck." Everywhere, the dream was collapsing, and it was doing so under its own weight. Shortly before her group walked away, Selecter's Pauline Black complained that the majority of tapes sent into 2-Tone were simply clones, "that a lot of bands feel that to get a deal on 2-Tone, they have to make only a certain type of music." Yet, as Jerry Dammers never tired of pointing out, commercial success was simply an occasional by-product of musical success — and not necessarily a pleasant one, either. Remembering the Oklahoma morning when he was awakened from a sound sleep with the news that "Too Much Too Young" was #1, he reflected, "I just went back to sleep. I could not face it." He had created the monster he always

dreamed of. What he wasn't expecting was the burden of responsibility with which that monster, would present him.

The Specials' audience was rowdy and getting rowdier. Suddenly, Jerry Dammers was the media-appointed spokesman for every incident of youth violence and from there, it was such a swift promotion to media-appointed scapegoat that when genuine accidents did occur, he found himself being called upon to defend them too.

In Skegness, two nights into the Specials' spring 1980 UK tour, the stage collapsed beneath the weight of so many celebrating fans. "Mindless hooligans!" screamed the press. "Skinhead riot!" "Really good kids [who] just want to be part of it," responded Jerry, and he was right. But sometimes, being right isn't enough. You need to be listened to as well.

In July 1980, a proposed 2-Tone festival in London was cancelled in the face of "local opposition." When the Specials toured Japan, the show's promoter and the band's own publicist were thrown into jail, accused of inciting a stage invasion. Disastrous events on the band's fall 1980 UK tour, hammered further nails into the 2-Tone coffin, as rival gangs descended upon the gigs to air whatever grievances they could come up with.

Desperate to break its own mold, 2-Tone signed the Swinging Cats, an almost comically unstable dance act, then sent them out on that same ill-tempered tour with the Specials. And as the New Musical Express wondered, "is the 2-Tone quality control on holiday or what?," the Specials themselves announced they were going to take the next six months off, to consider what they wanted to do next.

Surveying the wreckage which lay all around, it was hard to argue with them. The Swinging Cats broke up before the tour was even over; the Bodysnatchers watched their second single scrape to a lowly #50, then followed suit (minus vocalist Rhoda Dakar and bassist Nicky Summers, they resurfaced as the Belle Stars); and the Specials' own "farewell — for now" show at a massive CND rally in Trafalgar Square, was scrapped when the Department of the Environment refused them permission to use their live P.A.

Instead, the group prepared for hibernation with a record which simultaneously summed up the quagmire into which they were sinking — and that which was slowly sucking the life out of Britain as a whole, Bob Dylan's "Maggie's Farm" savagely reworked and targeted roundly at Margaret Thatcher. It reached #4, but all it really proved, arriving as it did just months after the English Beat implored the same woman to "Stand Down Margaret," was that even the British Prime Minister was now a greater force in contemporary music than 2-Tone.

Despite their announcement, the Specials continued gigging throughout the spring of 1981, regularly convening to support sundry non-aligned anti-nuclear organizations;

Anti-Racist and Anti-Fascist benefits; an unemployment march which wound up in London on May Day, having set out from Liverpool a week earlier; and in late June, a massive benefit in Coventry, aimed at raising money for an Asian student murdered earlier in the year in an apparently racist attack.

The following week, the group played a free festival in the Yorkshire town of Rotherham, and seven days after that, on the first weekend of July 1981, they headed into Leeds to headline the Northern Carnival Against Racism, the biggest event staged by RAR since 1979. It was a capricious fate indeed which ordained that as the performers relaxed in their hotel on the evening before the show, events in London were proving that even a concert of this magnitude might not be enough to stamp out the cancer of racism.

On July 3, 1981, Oi! finally erupted out of the secret fears of Britain's immigrant community and into the headlines. That evening, the Business, Last Resort, and the 4 Skins arrived at a scheduled show in the predominantly Asian suburb of Southall, to find a gang of 300 Asian youths had taken control of the entire neighborhood, to protect it against the expected insurgence of skinheads. Street skirmishes had already brought the police into the area, but rather than risk igniting an already volatile situation, the law decided to await developments — and watched while a crowd of 2,000 Asians gathered around the evening's venue, a pub called the Hambrough Tavern.

Not until the bricks started flying through the pub windows did the police move in and, by then, it was already too late. A police van was commandeered and set alight, then driven, medieval fireship style, through the doors of the pub. It remains a miracle that nobody was killed in the ensuing conflagration, but the charred memory of the Hambrough Tavern remains a potent image in the annals of post-punk Britain, a symbol of the moment when the posturing of pop finally tore the fabric of reality.

Neither did it matter who was at fault. Though the Asian kids engineered this particular confrontation, so-called skinheads had started more than enough of their own in the past. So, for that matter, had the police — three months earlier, the south London neighborhood of Brixton exploded in far more widespread rioting than this. The Southall riot was different, though; nobody "started" it, no one pushed the button. It was, simply, the culmination of years of antagonism, years of fear, and, within the Asian community, years of allowing the pressure to build and build and build. That night, it finally exploded.

"The next day," the Business' Mickey Fitz recalled, "we were recording and the police came in to interview us. They went, 'look boys, you're getting the blame regardless. No matter what comes out, you guys are getting the blame and

we do feel sorry for you, but because you were playing in what they cast as an Asian area, you're the scapegoats."

Up in Leeds, of course, the Carnival Against Racism went ahead, more impassioned than it might ordinarily have been, but with a depressing air of futility as well. Southall was not an isolated incident, even if its consequences were unique. But was race even the issue any longer? Or was the problem deeper than skin color; deeper, even, than creed and culture?

Prime Minister Thatcher's social and economic practices had bitten deep into the British way of life. Unemployment continued spiralling from one record high to another; social security benefits were being slashed across the board. It was hopelessness, not hatred, which was burning up Britain, and what was the establishment doing to make things better? It was staging a Royal Wedding, the marriage of Prince Charles and Lady Diana Spencer, and how nice that the country could afford to spend a million pounds on pomp and circumstance, when half the people who'd be watching the event on TV couldn't afford to toast the happy couple. And the other half couldn't afford a TV. For weeks, disaffected commentators were saying that something had to give. Now, suddenly, it had.

That same night, just as the Specials took the stage in Leeds, rioting broke out in Toxteth, a black neighborhood in Liverpool. It would take the authorities 48 hours to quell the battle. Three nights later, Toxteth's tinderbox twin in Manchester's Moss Side exploded. Bristol's St. Pauls followed; Wood Green in London; Nottingham, Coventry, Birmingham, Northampton.... Daily, the sun arose on the blackened carnage of another outbreak of rioting, the shattered glass of broken store windows, the buckled plastic of firebombed riot shields, the crippled steel of burned out cars; nightly, another neighborhood went up in the roar of flames, the shattering of glass, the distressed howl of the emergency sirens.

Rudie ran riot. Blacks with whites with Asians with everyone. An entire generation united by frustration and rage and anger and most of all, impotence, and it was as though the whole country had taken to the streets, to take back the streets, rising up against the Charles and Dianas and the Thatchers and her lackeys; against the faceless bureaucrats who talked of economy then spent millions on Concorde; who talked of tightening belts while they let out their trousers.

And while Nero fiddled and Rome burned, the rude boys scored their greatest hit yet, the spectral lament of the Specials' "Ghost Town."

No record has ever nailed a moment so accurately, no zeitgeist was ever so thoroughly zapped. With a symmetry which would have been utterly chilling if it wasn't so breathtakingly perfect, the Specials' lament for a club, a town, an entire country which had been closed and left to ruin and rats, topped the British chart for four long, fiery weeks. And really, the Specials had to break up almost immediately afterwards, because they could never, ever, have followed it up.

No one could. Nothing could.

RECOMMENDED LISTENING — THE SKA REVIVAL

BOOMTOWN RATS House on Fire (LP *V Deep*)

THE ENGLISH BEAT Stand Down Margaret (45)

FINE YOUNG CANNIBALS Good Thing (LP *Fine Young Cannibals*)

FUN BOY THREE The Lunatics Have Taken Over the Asylum (LP *Fun Boy 3*)

THE JAM Absolute Beginners (45)

ARTHUR KAY AND THE ORIGINALS Ska Wars (45)

MADNESS One Step Beyond (LP *One Step Beyond*)

SELECTER Missing Words (LP *Too Much Pressure*)

SPECIALS Gangsters (LP *The Specials*)

UB40 One in Ten (LP *Present Arms*)

CHORDS Maybe Tomorrow (45)

JOLT Watcha Gonna Do About It (45)

LAMBRETTAS Poison Ivy (45)

LONG TALL SHORTY 70's Boy (B-side)

LOW NUMBERS Keep in Touch (45)

MERTON PARKAS You Need Wheels (45)

NEW HEARTS Just Another Teenage Anthem (45)

PURPLE HEARTS Millions Like Us (45)

SECRET AFFAIR Time for Action (45)

SQUIRE Walking Down the Kings Road (45)

THE YOUNG MOD'S FORGOTTEN GLORY — LONDON, 1979

The music press had been gearing up for something to happen, long before it ever did. The divergent streams of punk rock on the one hand, and 2-Tone on the other, had been threatening to clash since they first shared a stage. One had the look, in the porkpie hats and tightly-tailored suits of the Specials, Madness and co.; the other had the sound, in the Pop Art rock of the Jam, the Small Faces-esque roar of the Pistols. Mod, the fashion leaders were determined, was a revival just waiting to happen.

The heyday of the original Mods was back in the early-mid 1960s. It was a time of turmoil, British youth discovering its own voice for the very first time, and letting it out in a blur of amphetamined nights and street-fighting days. A lifestyle where fashion was king, and — as journalist Nik Cohn so deftly remarked — "if you were caught in last night's sweater, you were dead."

Mod rose, and enjoyed its day in the media sun. Pitched battles with rival rockers disturbed the sleepy calm of British public holidays; bands like the Who, the Small Faces, and the Birds blared out of radio and TVs alike. When they moved on, so did fashion, but the undercurrents remained, swirling behind the scenes, and waiting... just waiting.

Ska, punk, and the Who — in 1979, Pete Townshend announced that the group's 1973 album, *Quadrophenia*, was to be the subject of a major movie, a recounting of his own youth and that of an entire generation. Scooters, Parkas, Union Jacks... the uniform of a bygone age was faithfully recreated on film, and from there, it was but a small step out onto the streets. Mod exploded back onto the British rock scene with a fury could have predicted, and as it exploded, the bands poured out like a lucky Vegas jackpot.

There was a touching innocence to most of them, although of course, a few people were out to make a quick buck of the fashion. The Nips' "Happy Song" claimed to be produced by one P. Weller, although it wasn't the Jam's Paul, and it probably wasn't Shane MacGowan's Nips either. But it was still a great record, and that's what bound the Mod crowd together.

Even among their wildest supporters, few people claimed that the sound of most of the Mod bands was anything stunningly original. But it was exciting as hell. Taking their cue from the sounds of the 1960s, only vaguely revved up with a dash of modern technology, authenticity was the key word — an authentic look, an authentic logo (arrows and roundels, the symbols of the original movement, were everywhere), and most of all, authentic sounds. Most of the records could have been conceived in the white heat of Mod's original explosion, a process which burgeoned until what once seemed retro was actually well-crafted timelessness.

Windmilling guitar chords, danceable rhythms, a sense — if not a taste — of a heartful of speed pumping through an endless nightclub, even the bandnames belonged to an earlier era: Dexy's Midnight Runners and the Purple Hearts were both named for Mod drugs of choice; Long Tall Shorty for the song which every band played; the Untouchables for the TV show everybody watched. The Killermeters' vocalist, Vic Vespa, was named for a scooter.

But if the past was being pillaged, it got something in return; a new sense of its own identity, a rebirth which restored some great classic oldies to the hearts and minds of the modern age. When the Bridgehouse pub in east London's canning town held its first Mod Mayday on May 1, 1979, half the bands were still playing cover versions. When they returned the following year, most of them had record deals, and burned up the chart like Lambrettas with legs. It was, in the words of the Secret Affair, a time for action, and no matter how fleetingly, their call to arms was obeyed.

Mod didn't last; how could it? So ephemeral, so delicate, and so bound up in the business of fashion that the fashion itself was simply a passing fancy, by 1982, half the best bands had already split, and the rest were getting their kicks elsewhere. Tracing rock history through its own chronological order, a minor psychedelic revival came around next, and the next time anyone caught sight of Vic Vespa, he'd already changed his name.

But Mod's spirit prevailed. How could it do anything else? And today, when the original Mods are well into middle-age, it remains a vibrant memory, and a fiery inspiration. Ready! Steady! Go!

COMPLETE 2-TONE LABEL LISTING

7" Singles

1/2 SPECIALS/Selecter split single

3 MADNESS — The Prince

4 SELECTER — On My Radio

5 SPECIALS — A Message to You Rudy

6 THE BEAT — Tears of a Clown

7 ELVIS COSTELLO — I Can't Stand Up for Falling Down (withdrawn)

7 THE SPECIAL AKA — live EP

8 SELECTER — 3 Minute Hero

9 BODYSNATCHERS — Let's Do Rock Steady

10 SELECTER — Missing Words

11 SPECIALS — Rat Race

12 BODYSNATCHERS — Easy Life

13 SPECIALS — Stereotype

14 SWINGING CATS — Easy

15 RICO — Sea Cruise

16 SPECIALS — Do Nothing

17 SPECIALS — Ghost Town

18 RHODA W/THE SPECIAL AKA — The Boiler

19 RICO W/THE SPECIAL AKA — Jungle Music

20 APOLLINAIRES — The Feeling's Gone

21 HIGSONS — Tear the Whole Thing Down

22 APOLLINAIRES — Envy the Love

23 SPECIAL AKA — War Crimes

24 HIGSONS — Run Me Down

25 SPECIAL AKA — Racist Friend

26 SPECIAL AKA — Nelson Mandela

27 SPECIAL AKA — What I Like Most About You Is Your Girlfriend

28 FRIDAY CLUB — Window Shopping

29 JB'S ALL STARS — The Alphabet Army

Albums

5001 SPECIALS — Specials

5002 SELECTER — Too Much Pressure

5003 SPECIALS — More Specials

5004 various artists — Dance Craze

5005 RICO — That Man is Forward

5006 RICO — Jama

5007 various artists — This Are Two Tone

5008 SPECIAL AKA — In the Studio

5009 various artists — The Two Tone Story

Hardcore

Hardcore started as a genre and turned into a lifestyle. It started as punk rock and ended up an art form. And to its critics, it started as a joke, and never got funny. But it wound up the single most important development in American rock since the 1960s, with an impact which is as real today as it ever was in the past.

"Hardcore," said Barry Hensler, frontman of Michigan punks Big Chief, "came to scrape off the Styxes and the Speedwagons and the remnant punk bullshit. Only when that was done could people get on with something different." A role call of the bands, performers, and establishments to have emerged, or escaped, from the hailstorm agrees with him — cult icons Fugazi, fronted by Minor Threat's Ian MacKaye; Bob Mould and Grant Hart of Hüsker Dü; the Beastie Boys and the Red Hot Chili Peppers; performer, poet, and publisher Henry Rollins; record labels Alternative Tentacles, Slash, and SST. They all exploded from the furious quickfire of the hardcore movement and, almost without exception, all retain the values which made it a part of their lives to begin with.

"Hardcore had such an emotionally potent impact on the connection between the heart and soul and gut" revealed the Peppers' Anthony Kiedis. "I remember thinking, if music can make me this sexually excited, this emotionally excited, this physically compelled to thrust my body back and forth across the floor, wouldn't that be a wonderful thing to make other people feel with your own music?" Within weeks of that revelation, Kiedis was onstage.

Two bands lay at the heart of hardcore — on the east coast, Bad Brains, a jazz-funk fusion band operating out of Washington DC as the first wave of imported punk rock swept over the ocean from Britain; on the west coast, turned on their head by the possibilities the music was screaming out at them, Black Flag, converted to speed by the primal Ramones and then pushing the pedal down through the metal. Both groups built fiercesome local reputations, neither ever made friends with the critics.

In some ways, the scene did have parallels elsewhere. In Britain, where the Oi! movement was first gathering momentum around bands like Cockney Rejects, the Business, the Anti Nowhere League, and Discharge, the same emotions were united in their rejection of the first wave of punk bands' lemming-leap into the safety net of the establishment. "Betrayed?" asked the Rejects' Micky Geggus in 1979, "yeah, course I feel betrayed. It's like everything's gone back to what it was like in '74 and '75. But I honestly think it's started again. The feeling's come back again."

In America, the feeling had never left. The difference was, the punk movement in Britain was always rooted in disaffection first, ability much later. In the US, the speed with which a band could play was a point of living honor, because you had to be able to stop playing that quickly as well, to turn on a dime in mid riff and change tempo, graceful assault and balletic battery. And the more out of control it sounded, the more control a band needed to take.

The absence of grace, of course, was matched by the lack of grandiosity. The first single by Bad Brains, "Pay to Cum," lasted just one minute and 24 seconds. Even the Dickies weren't that precipitous. Five of the 15 tracks on Black Flag's debut album clocked in at under two minutes as well — one, "Spray Paint the Walls," lasted just 32 seconds, which meant it took longer to read the 16 lines of lyrics than it did to play the song. So why bother reading?

Punk hit Los Angeles with all the force of a tsunami, like "the big one" the city had been living in fear of ever since someone realized they'd built the place on one of the country's most unstable fault lines, in one of its most notorious fire zones, across one of its most active tornado belts (not many people know that). One minute everything was all Linda Ronstadt and Stevie Nicks and welcome to the Hotel California, the next — all the kids had green hair, and they spat instead of rolling another joint.

None of that was new to the Damned's Brian James, but when his band became the first British punk group to play L.A., in the spring of '77, it amazed him all the same. "We were expecting to scare a bunch of Dead-heads. In the end, I think they were just as scary as we were."

From the outset, punk was different from other Californian crazes. For a start, it took an entire generation whose laidback indifference was the result of years of careful breeding and, for the first time, gave them something worth fighting for.

Contemporary analysts were always baffled that punk gained such a firm foothold in the Promised Land — who wants anarchy when you've got palm trees and swimming pools? To the punks themselves, though, the flags had been going up for years.

"I thought punk had something to offer me because it was other people that felt as I did," Bad Religion's Greg Graffin recalled. "I just didn't fit into the [California] lifestyle. If you could see the photos from that era... the people were not trying to look like they fit in, they were weird, but authentic people. I remember feeling like, who cares, I don't have enough money to buy Levis, I'm just going to wear my truskins. And I had a couple of t-shirts that I tried to make punk by writing FUCK on them. They were white t-shirts that I tried to dye black, but I didn't know what I was doing, but I wore them to death."

One day his grandmother, a deeply religious, very conservative mid-westerner, bought him a leather jacket because she knew he wanted one, and knew it would last for a very long time. "What she didn't know was, I was going to mutilate the thing, put spikes in it, and paint a skull on the back, which I did the first week I had it."

In July 1977, the Starwood banned punk after the Weirdoes staged a July 4 party and torched the American flag. The Troubadour followed suit after a Bags show ended with every table being upturned. And no sooner had the Starwood revoked its own injunction than a bouncer got stabbed at a Fear gig, and the posters all came down again. By the end of 1977, remembered Tony Secunda, English manager of Latino punks The Plugz, the last place left open was the Masque, and that was only because the law hadn't figured out what it was yet. "It was a vacant basement underneath the Hollywood Center, which was run by this crazed half-Scot, half-Irishman named Brendan Mullen. He was walking home one night, and he literally tripped over it, fell down the stairs and thought it would make a good rehearsal space."

It was never an "official" club, and that's what lent the Masque its mystique and its freedom. Bands would book in to rehearse, invite their friends down to watch them, and Mullen would sit at the door charging a couple of bucks admission.

A Black Flag gig rung down the curtain on the Masque — the LAPD finally padlocked the basement's paint-tattooed doors during summer 1978, the latest blow in what had already become a running battle between culture and cop. Mullen himself didn't mind too much, though; he just went round the corner to West Sunset, and opened Club Lingerie. And the slam dancers took it from there.

According to a now infamous story in the *LA Times*, slam dancing — that peculiar and peculiarly violent form of dancing which picked up where the London pogo left off — was birthed at the Fleetwood, a club on Huntington Beach. It quickly swept outward from there though, to consume the whole city and bring fresh life and bitter outrage to every middle-aged, middle-class neurosis which punk had ever bred. Less responsible media followed gratuitously in the *Times*' shock-horror wake, and with good reason. Why, after all, should a society look to itself in its search for solutions to its problems, when there was an entire culture beyond it, which literally begged to be scapegoated?

When Black Flag played a free concert in Polliwog Park, they caused a riot with their very appearance. In Huntington Beach, the police department habitually referred to punk bands as gangs, and their fans, therefore, as gang members.

Black Flag responded by tagging every available surface with their distinctive flying banner logo. The law hit back by placing the band under virtual 24-hour surveillance.

Unsolved murders were lain at punk's door and in the pages of an increasingly hysterical tabloid press, Nazi Surf Punk Psychos became the biggest bogeyman since Charles Manson's creepy-crawly nightstalkers. A generation before, society had been divided over the length of the Beatles' hair. Now it was divided over the color, and it was against this backdrop of unreasoning, unrelenting hatred that hardcore made its final, shuddering, transformation, out of the shadows and into... isolation.

The conflicts which forced Bad Brains to flee their hometown with just the bitterly self-explanatory "Banned in DC" to show for their pains, were the same as constricted other bands, in other cities, into equally tiny boxes — their own clubs, their own labels, their own dances, even their own sports. Inevitably, they would form their own network as well.

When Bad Religion's Greg Graffin handed a tape of his band's first demos to Circle Jerks drummer Lucky Lehrer, his first stop was the K-ROQ studios, to guest on the Rodney Bingenheimer show. Lehrer played the tape over the air, warts and all, then told the listening world Bad Religion were his friends. Graffin and co. took it from there.

In 1978, Black Flag frontman Greg Ginn launched the SST label because no other record company in town would even let him in the door. His own band's "Nervous Breakdown" was the first release; San Pedro natives Mike Watt and D. Boon's Minutemen had the second; Saccharine Trust's "Paganicons" became the third band to release music on SST. By the time Black Flag finally gave up on trying to get gigs around their hometown, and set out on a nationwide tour instead, SST was already an established player on the hardcore scene, and had just been joined by the Dischord label, formed by Minor Threat's Ian MacKaye.

Like Bad Brains, and like Black Flag's new vocalist, Henry Rollins, MacKaye was from DC. But there the comparisons ended. In L.A., hardcore was a gratuitous noise — "we were going to make as large a racket, piss as many people off, go apeshit as we could," as Black Flag/Circle Jerks founder Keith Morris succinctly put it. In DC, however, there was a definite agenda, and MacKaye was the person who set it.

His latest band, Minor Threat, had released just one EP, but "Straight-Edge" not only summarized MacKaye's own rage and bitterness — "at the way [his last band] Teen Idles were ridiculed [locally], my friends, this family of punk rockers that I belonged to, the way we were treated" — it encapsulated the mood of almost everyone who heard it, establishing that for all the negative connotations of appearances, hardcore was desperately affirmative.

"We use the negatives for a positive outcome," Greg Graffin confirmed. "That is to provoke people to think about something themselves, which ultimately makes them feel better about themselves. When you can figure something out on your own, it empowers you."

"Straight-Edge," however, went beyond simple empowering. The song became a lifestyle, the lifestyle became the law. Fiercely puritanical, "Straight-Edge" embraced a creed of almost zero tolerance towards drugs, alcohol, even towards meat eating (Ian MacKaye became a vegetarian in 1984), and smoking. It was the ultimate in teen rebellion, the rejection of symbols which had lain at the core of "mainstream" youth disobedience since the dawn of time, in favor of an attitude which the most straight-laced adult could never have a problem with — which, of course, guaranteed that they would.

It wasn't a wholly unprecedented stance. A decade and a half before, Britain's Mod scene had taken a similar stand against the truisms of youth delinquency — the Who's Pete Townshend reflected, "we made the establishment uptight, we made our parents uptight, and our employers uptight, because although they didn't like the way we dressed, they couldn't accuse us of not being smart. We had short hair and were clean and tidy."

Unwitting and unrelated though the comparison may have been, straight-edge took that same subversion and twisted it even further. For such prohibitions were not wholly altruistic — they also addressed a problem which had been escalating on the US music scene since the mid-1970s: the draconian liquor licensing laws which forbade access to music, simply because one wasn't old enough to drink. In Europe, anybody was permitted onto licensed premises, anybody could go see a band, and so long as they didn't drink, no one minded. Straight-edge demanded the same right be granted to American youth

The creed rapidly took on broader ramifications, regardless. From Boston, SS Decontrol (SSD), black-clad behemoths in headbands, emerged with a militancy which even took their peers aback. In concert, the band even encouraged fans to knock drinks and cigarettes out of other onlookers' hands, and Ian MacKaye marveled, "we were bad kids, we got into fights and stuff, but we were nice and sort of goofy. SSD were pretty grim. They were really hard."

Few other pioneers took things to such extremes, but still it was with the release of "Straight Edge" that both MacKaye and his label discovered their audience. Soon, MacKaye was trading tapes and letters with fans as far afield as Nevada, Massachusetts, New York, California — and in every one, there was a hardcore scene.

Each one developed in its own universe. It might have been a chance encounter with English punk vinyl; it might have been the Ramones; it might have been exposure to the Plasmatics — speed punk New Yorkers fronted by the outrageous Wendy O'Williams, whose nihilistic sense of theater made KISS look like a Nativity play. But almost without exception, the bands erupting across the country were convinced they were alone in their strivings. Only as Dischord and SST gained wider distribution, and bands emerged from their own hometown environs to take their message elsewhere, could hardcore even begin to coalesce — and then, only after the individual bands had gotten over the shock of finding others like them.

Out of Reno, NV, came 7 Seconds — whose own label, Positive Force, would eventually become a major player on the independent scene. From San Francisco, Flipper followed the Dead Kennedys into the realms of utter dislocation, by playing the fastest music on earth at the slowest speed they could. From Missoula, MT, Deranged Diction (featuring a very pre-Pearl Jam Jeff Ament) slid into Seattle with similar intent — "one of the fastest bands around," recalled Mudhoney's Mark Arm, "who then became the slowest band on earth... and the weirdest."

From Detroit, Negative Approach; from Minneapolis, Dogbreath, the mach 10 classic metal band which accelerated into the Replacements; from the twin city of St. Paul, Hüsker Dü. The Meat Puppets moseyed out of Phoenix; from Austin, Millions of Dead Cops — later tastefully abbreviated to MDC, but never losing the abrasive idealism of their original name.

Only in the cities that could arguably claim to have started the ball rolling was there any semblance of coherence, a sense of a "scene" expanding with its audience, bands begetting bands. In L.A., Social Distortion, the Mau Maus, 45 Grave, Suicidal Tendencies, Legal Weapon, Bad Religion, Leaving Trains, and TSOL (True Sounds Of Liberty) burst through so quickly that shortly, even the tiniest club was hosting what amounted to a hardcore festival at every show, cramming six or seven bands a night on the stage — and all the while, SST maintained a running commentary on their development.

It was the same story in DC. Ian MacKaye's younger brother Alex formed Faith in 1981, while Dischord ensured even greater continuity with a succession of — if not inspired, at least encouraging — signings, local and otherwise. Government Issue, the Necros, Youth Brigade, Iron Cross, and Void all had records out by 1983, while the Stahl brothers' Scream (immortalized almost a decade later when latter-day drummer Dave Grohl was recruited to Nirvana) were responsible for one of 1982's most dynamic albums, the still-frenzied *Still Screaming*.

Boston was one of the first cities to develop a scene to rival the established epicenters, an entire universe erupting out of SSD's debut *The Kids Will Have Their Say* EP, and confirming itself with the release of 1982's *This is Boston, Not L.A.* compilation.

Featuring dynamic, and extraordinarily individualistic contributions from Gang Green — the kingpins of the rapidly emerging skate-punk scene; Jerry's Kids' six songs in seven minutes; and DYS (featuring Dag Nasty's Dave Smalley), *This Is Boston* may not have been the first regional hardcore compilation released, but like the same city's *Mashing Up the Nation* ska collection four years later (and the *Live At The Rat* punk showcase five years before), it proved that Boston certainly knew a pulse when it felt one.

One factor continued to link the swirl of new bands — the problem of finding places to play. "Banned in DC" was neither a hollow boast nor an isolated complaint. Commercial pariahs, social outcasts, hardcore bands developed in isolation, and remained there. A handful of established venues ventured into the waters, but swiftly backed out again when they realized precisely what they were letting themselves in for — an unrestrained orgy of under-age moshers, with no sense of propriety, let alone property.

Vandalism ran hand in hand with violence — in New York, CBGBs began demanding $150 deposit from every band that played, simply to cover the inevitable damage to the bathrooms. Simultaneously, bar profits plummeted even as door takings soared — disastrous for a business whose survival (and staff wages) depended far more on the former than the latter. Add on the need for extra security and, even before the local neighborhood watch roused itself into action, hardcore shows were frequently far more trouble than they were worth, to the clubs at any rate. To the audiences, however, hardcore was a way of life which they would follow to the death — or at least, disfigurement. Not every stage diver would be caught by the crowd.

Other venues backed out as much because of the bands as their audiences, as their rivalry, too, took on wider connotations. By the late 1980s, the hatred between Boston's Slapdash and New York's Waste of Youth was even reflected in the band's lyrics; a few years earlier, fans — and members — of SSD and DYS would paint Xs on their foreheads when they played in New York, so they'd know not to punch one another when the pit finally exploded.

Of course, the outsiders' obsession with the violence inherent in hardcore completely overlooked the good that came out of it: the sense of community which bound its followers, which congregated around the skateparks of inner city America. But there was some accuracy, too, in the doomsayers' predictions that hardcore, at least in its earliest flowering, was destined to burn out sooner rather than later.

Bad Religion were the first big name to slip. According to Greg Graffin, "we were getting disillusioned. When we started in 1980, the scene... was so much more accepting, so much more open, so much more liberal. People didn't care what you looked like, there was no affiliation, no factions. Then, for some reason, around late '82, it started to get this gang mentality which sadly is still with us today, where people started affiliating with different punk scenes in southern California. You had the Huntington Beach people, the Hollywood people, and they all thought they should band together and fight each other. Whereas I just wanted to play the music and be a part of something I thought was very liberal and rewarding.

"So, since the scene kind of let us down, we in turn — not knowingly, [but certainly] in retrospect — we let the scene down too, by going into the studio and doing a record we just wanted to do without worrying about the constraints of our styles, not worrying about the marketing." The result was *Into the Unknown*, a keyboard-heavy prog rock jamboree — not that dissimilar to TSOL's *Beneath the Shadows* in its own way, but somehow construed as much more of a departure.

The band themselves were so shocked by their creation that they broke up shortly after and there, too, they found themselves in surprising company. Bad Brains also shattered in 1982, Minor Threat in 1983, SSD and DYS in 1985. The Minutemen fell apart after D.Boon died in an Arizona car crash in December the same year. The Replacements redirected themselves towards Big Star, other bands towards big labels.

Black Flag shattered, said Greg Ginn, when suddenly "people started seeing money in indy rock and... we couldn't go out on a limb anymore." Hüsker Dü shattered after venturing onto one limb too many. Even relatively minor players like New York's Beastie Boys were bound elsewhere, experimenting with rap and hip hop, or simply growing up and growing out.

But the streets were still starving, and by the summer of 1985, New York-based skinhead bands like the Cro-Mags, Agnostic Front, and Murphy's Law had already set the stage for the next generation of hardcore acts. By 1987, Letch Patrol, Crackdown, and Youth of Today were making even SSD's old straight-edge philosophies seem liberal.

Some of the old guard tried to rebel against this new line of thinking — Ian MacKaye even tried to organize a full-fledged backlash: the so-called Revolution Summer, which would wrestle back control of the genre through a veritable conspiracy of new bands — Fire Party, Rites of Spring, Mission Impossible, his own Embrace. "Skinheads hated Embrace," he mused proudly, "because they wanted Minor Threat."

But by March 1986, Embrace had collapsed, crushed by its own irrelevance to what the hardcore audience wanted. Rites of Spring followed a year later, when vocalist Guy Piccioto joined MacKaye in a new band, Fugazi. Lunch Meat metamorphosed into Soulside; for the valiant souls who manned the last barricades, the summer of revolution sank into a winter of discontent; and hardcore thrashed on, harder than ever.

THEY CALLED IT OI!

Jimmy Pursey was never the subtlest lyricist, as anyone who ever sat through Sham 69's *That's Life* concept album will know. But from the moment they appeared, crop-topped bootboys with the rabble-riling songs which sprayed like spit and graffiti, Sham 69 spread their message like plague was out of fashion. Playing street-smart punk with a foot-stomping rhythm, Sham was the sound of inner-city boredom, burned through with guitars like oxy-acetylene and vocals barked like the riot act.

"If the kids (stomp stomp) are united (stomp stomp) they will never (stomp stomp) be divided," and though Sham themselves never intended to nurture a supporting army of neo-Nazi skinheads, if ever a counter-culture found a voice to be vile with, this was it. Everything which has ever been written about Oi! (the most familiar term under which the mutant meeting of third generation punk and blank generation skins would take place) sprang from Sham — including, in a roundabout fashion, its name.

Sham's core audience drew heavily from the amorphous anti-culture of British soccer supporters, among whose repertoire of chants Sham songs swiftly rooted. There they flourished alongside other such evergreens as "You'll Never Walk Alone," a revised "Land of Hope & Glory," and the Bohemian Rhapsody of them all, "Oggie Oggie Oggie — Oi! Oi! Oi!"

It was brutal; it was simplistic; it was deafening. In America, a similar brew picked up speed and became hardcore. In Britain, it simply got louder — in terms of both volume and volubility.

Musically, the stage was already set for something this shattering to emerge. By early 1978, punk in the spirit it was originally spat was a source of intense disillusion for anybody still captivated by those founding ideals. Under those terms, the refuge offered by the burgeoning street punk/Oi! movement was undeniably attractive and, when Sham continued vocal in their rejection of the crasser elements of the so-called Sham Army, the Army revolted.

"Hersham Boys, Hersham Boys, lace-up boots and corduroys," sang Pursey of the suburban kids with whom he'd grown up. "Hersham Boys, Hersham Boys, ribbons and bows and cuddly toys," responded the new breed of city kids and, as Sham slipped into last year's headlines, a new breed rose to fill their Doc Martens.

The Angelic Upstarts, Cock Sparrer, Infa-Riot, the 4-Skins... overnight they emerged, as Oi! didn't simply identify its own self, it isolated it too; a confrontational roar which challenged complacency, defied convention, and seemed at its most potent in the same working class neighborhoods which the National Front targeted for political disruption — black and Asian communities on the fringe of inner cities.

It was not a deliberate policy. "Think about it," cautioned Business vocalist Micky Fitz. "Those were the areas which the bands came from as well and it's very difficult to say to Sparrer or the Foreskins, why are you playing there? 'Because I bloody live there, that's why.'"

But still Oi! shows were characterized by busloads of Skins descending from all over the country in vehicles daubed in Nazi/NF graffiti; violence still almost habitually disrupted the bands' shows. Despite the members' own protestations of innocence, two-thirds of Skrewdriver's summer

'78 tour was cancelled after venues were unable to get insurance against the expected damage and destruction. And where they did play, entire local communities went on petrified stand-by as their neighborhoods filled with marauding youths whose tattoos and t-shirts alone indicated their political persuasion.

Fitz continues "what eventually brought Oi! down was the split in the skinhead scene, where you had plain normal skins that just wanted to listen to the music, wear the clothes and have a really good time, and then the right wing hijacked the imagery, and when there was trouble at one of those shows and the media showed pictures of skinheads, everybody got the blame."

How ironic, then, that most of the bands swept up under the Oi! banner were harmless. The Toy Dolls had a major hit with the nursery favorite "Nellie the Elephant" and no one ever saw that as a threat. Max Splodge and his Splodgenessabounds would have made an unconvincing menace to society, even without the silly name. And nobody was ever intimidated by Peter and the Test Tube Babies. Indeed, there was only ever a handful of bands who even thought of espousing any rhetoric harsher than the standard tear-down-the-government line which was as old as the hills to begin with.

To an inflamed media, however, the litany of beatings, burnings, and all-round bashings which marred the Skinhead community's best-publicized contacts with civilization told a different story. Record labels suffered inexplicable equipment failures when an Oi! band's demo tape landed on the desk. Promoters would suddenly remember a pressing prior engagement when bands came looking for gigs. Journalists would lose their notebooks when it was time to write reviews. By the end of the 1980s, Oi! was dead, killed by a very well-orchestrated conspiracy of silence.

"The Business did the odd tour in the 1980s," Micky Fitz continued, "and made a few more records, the *Welcome to the Real World* album in 1988, but we did our last show in '89, then split because there really was nothing happening. Then suddenly, I got a call from this guy in Germany, 'do you want to tour?' Yeah, we'd never toured there before, but we arrive and all they're doing is talking about hardcore, and we're going 'hardcore? What's this hardcore?' They say you must know Sick of it All, Slapshot, Mad Ball... er no, they haven't been to England. And suddenly we realized how far we were behind things, that the English are so far behind America and Germany that it's unbelievable. Now we've toured with all those bands, and the whole scene's come back to life."

The Futurists: England 1980-82

They've been called everything from emotionless mannequins plying dark, electronic isolation; to the most important noise in rock since Chuck Berry first let rip on a guitar. Their music has been described as the last frontier of recorded sound, and man's first step towards his technological destiny. They are the robots on the autobahn, the showroom dummies on the space lab, the voice of energy, endless, endless.... They are Kraftwerk, and they redefined rock'n'roll.

Other names may have made a greater splash in both musical and commercial terms, others might have kicked youth, society, and culture into an entirely different gear. But when debating the single most influential band of the late 1970s, Kraftwerk win hands down.

History has not recorded whose idea it was to edit down the original 22-minute title track to the fourth Kraftwerk album to a snappy three minute single; nor does it recall the look on the faces of the sales reps who were handed advance copies of it and told to do their job. But few records have ever seemed so unlikely, so unsuited, so *unsingle-like* as "Autobahn." And few have turned all those presumptions so thoroughly on their heads. Top 30 in America, Top 20 in the UK, "Autobahn" became the surprise hit of the year, of the decade. Even the popular misinterpretation of the record's lyric (it really did sound as though Ralf Hutter and Florian Schneider were singing "fun fun fun on the autobahn," conjuring up visions of grinning Teutonic Beach Boys) could not camouflage its alien nature.

Kraftwerk toured in the wake of their "Autobahn" success; played shows across Europe and the US, even appeared on *Midnight Special*, and then vanished from view. They spent a year establishing their own Kling Klang label, and adding the finishing touches to an arsenal of electronic instruments which would ultimately replace even the unweildy synthesizers they were carrying around. *Radioactivity*, their next album, was very much a testing ground for this impressive array of tricks, and though the album in no way lived up to the enormity of its predecessor, it showed that success had in no way gone to Kraftwerk's head.

Although the US and Britain in general now regarded Kraftwerk as archetypal European one-hit wonders, the group's own following was surprisingly vocal. In Britain, the incipient punk movement was drawing at least some of its energy from Kraftwerk's own peculiar rejection of traditional rock'n'roll values, and making its preferences known both in interviews and on club dancefloors.

Even more prominently, David Bowie was loudly singing the group's praises. His 1976 *Station to Station* tour featured a lengthy pre-show tape of Kraftwerk's music — Bowie had,

in fact, asked the group to open the shows, but they turned him down. Instead, Bowie himself relocated to Germany and, over the next 12 months, worked with Brian Eno and Iggy Pop on three albums which would themselves pave the way for Kraftwerk's own subsequent breakthrough, simply by echoing musical and notional ideas which Kraftwerk themselves had already used.

Across the course of Bowie's *Low* and *"Heroes"* albums, and Pop's *"The Idiot,"* Kraftwerk's influence rings even louder than Bowie's own voice — a debt which Bowie himself acknowledged when he titled one track (from *"Heroes"*) after Florian — "V2 Schneider." Bowie also recorded the album's title track in the same three languages as Kraftwerk would render their "Showroom Dummies" single: German, French, and English. Kraftwerk, for their part, mentioned their meeting in the title track of their next album. They appeared strangely unimpressed.

Kraftwerk were far from idle during this bout of superstar cheerleading. Throughout late 1976, even as Bowie worked on *Low*, they were at Kling Klang, putting the finishing touches to that next album, *Trans-Europe Express*.

As much as the Sex Pistols and their fellow punk conspirators, no less than the deaths of Elvis Presley and Marc Bolan, *Trans-Europe Express* remains locked inside the curious cultural melting pot which was 1977; is, in turn, symptomatic of all that was to be wrought during that tumultuous year. Not since the peak of psychedelia precisely ten years before had musical tastes seemed so ripe for experimentation, and with that experimentation, change and transformation.

Without exception, the seeds of the musical preoccupations of the next decade, electronic and industrial, grunge and rave, were sewn during 1977 and, though history records it as the Year of Punk alone, there really was so much more going on.

The first of Bowie's Berlin albums, *Low*, appeared in January 1977, followed in March by Pop's *The Idiot*. Three months after that, Donna Summer and producer Giorgio Moroder topped worldwide charts with "I Feel Love," a sonic pulse which finally consummated the same marriage of electronics and disco which Kraftwerk ("Tanzmuzik," from their third album, *Ralf and Florian*) and Can ("I Want More," an insistently sibillant summer 1976 UK hit) had already proposed. And in between times, its influence and impact already pre-determined, Kraftwerk released *Trans-Europe Express*.

The album was greeted, initially, with disbelief. To many people, Kraftwerk were still the Teutonic Beach Boys of old, and first impressions were of that earlier hit having simply been rerouted down a railroad track, with clattering metal replacing hissing rubber, and the travelogue dictated not by the freedom of the road, but the iron discipline of the tracks.

Pairing rhythm and melody to their lowest common denominator, an icy delivery against which Hutter and Schneider's vocals sounded almost tuneful, *Trans-Europe Express* was bright, brutal, brittle; a robotic denunciation not only of humanity, but of humankind itself.

But Kraftwerk were by no means finished. *The Man Machine*, the following year, made even *Trans-Europe Express* seem somehow old-fashioned. Rooted in an exploration of man's relationship with machinery, and the possibilities that a blending of the two might imbibe, Kraftwerk's seventh album leaped into the UK Top 10. The band announced they would not be touring, but despatched ambassadors out regardless — a pair of essential singles, "The Robots" and "Neon Lights," which made infinitely more sense on the dancefloor than Kraftwerk themselves would in the clubs. And if the dances those records evoked were jerky, spasmodic, robotic, then that, too, was preordained.

Staging a pair of press conferences in Paris and New York, Kraftwerk themselves took a back seat to the entire proceedings. Their places were taken by robots, automatic doppelgangers, the final demonstration of the machine's precedence over man. And while the critics went into overdrive, slamming Kraftwerk's distant coldness, the fringes of the punk scene knew precisely what they were talking of.

New Yorkers Suicide reduced even Kraftwerk's symphonies to minimalist poetry, a duet for disassociated voice and cold waves of sound. Ultravox! traveled to Cologne to record their next album — their first, the Eno-produced *Ultravox*, had already proclaimed "I Want to be a Machine"; now Kraftwerk's own early producer Connie Plank was going to show them how to accomplish that ambition. Months later Japan headed for Munich to record with Giorgio Moroder. Both bands already had synthesizers. Now they wanted the Germans to show them what to do with them.

Londoners Rikki Sylvan and his Last Days of Earth hissed menacing slabs of electronics into songs about the apocalypse and alienation. Fledgling producer Daniel Miller returned from a DJ-ing stint in Switzerland to reinvent himself as the Normal and cut "TVOD," a physical love affair between man and television set. Even punk noisemakers Tubeway Army weren't immune, as they proved when frontman Gary Numan walked into his record company offices with a clutch of new demos, recreating himself as an automated icicle who prayed to the aliens.

Everywhere, musicians were dropping the guitars they'd picked up two years earlier and picked up synthesizers instead. Prices dropped as interest soared — soon, even the most impecunious new band seemed to be sporting their own brand new synth, and the mysterious noise maker of just a few years before was now beeping and burping everywhere one turned. And then Gary Numan soared to #1 with "Are Friends Electric," and even the instrument's novelty status became redundant. Numan was a star and the Nu-men were taking over.

The scene which Numan opened up for public inspection had, like the music itself, been quietly percolating in the London clubs for close to a year, centered around Billy's, a Friday night "Club for Heroes" discotheque based out of Gossips nightclub. Hosted since June 1978, by DJs Dave Claridge and Rusty Egan (the latter ex-Glen Matlock's Rich Kids), Billy's revolved around a diet of non-stop Bowie, Kraftwerk, Roxy Music, *The Idiot*, and film scores; that, and doorman Steve Strange's increasingly unpredictable notions of what somebody should look like before he'd let them enter.

Punk dress codes, once so liberal, had constricted to the point of cliche. Leather jacket, bondage trousers, ripped T-shirt, the obligatory safety pins — it was all so formal, a uniform of numbing predictability. Billy's was different; Billy's wouldn't let anyone in unless they'd made an effort to look a little different — and the greater the effort, the greater the rewards.

For once inside, the building's dingy exterior opened up into a sea of posing, preening, prancing, beautiful people in beautiful... clothes was the wrong word, for some turned up near naked, others extemporized from whatever they found in the linen closet. But the studs'n'spikes crowd who'd turned punk into a parade ground never got in, and Strange was big and intimidating enough to make sure they couldn't simply gatecrash either.

The movement was exclusive — it didn't even have a title. *The Face*, the magazine which did most to keep tabs on the Billy's scene, opted for the Cult With No Name. The traditional music press toyed with the New Romantics and the Now Crowd; someone else came up with Futurists, and once Billy's expanded to take over Tuesday nights as well and changed its name to Blitz, the Blitz Kids summed things up for a while as well. But only for a while.

An even more exclusive niterie, an even brighter butterfly, Blitz was a screaming day-glo beacon in the dark of post-punk London. David Bowie dropped by there, first to record his impressions in the hit "Boys Keep Swinging," then later, looking for extras for his "Ashes to Ashes" video. Suddenly, Steve Strange was on *Top of the Pops*.

So was Gary Numan, as he followed "Are Friends Electric?" with "Cars" and "Complex"; and so were a band who supported him on his fall 1979 tour then exploded to prominence in the aftermath: Orchestral Manoeuvres in the Dark. The queue outside Blitz grew longer, and was about to get longer still.

In fall 1979, Strange, Egan, and fellow Rich Kids refugee Midge Ure began working together as Visage. Ultravox's Billy Currie came in on keyboards (weeks later, Ure would become that band's newest member); Magazine's John McGeogh, Barry Adamson, and Dave Formula rounded out the rest of the band, and over the next year — around Magazine and Ultravox's own mounting activities — the team pieced together their first album.

They needed to move quickly. At the same time as Blitz's owners were putting together their band, a bunch of the club's clients were doing the same. The eternally flamboyant Boy George O'Dowd, fresh from a shortlived dalliance with the infant Bow Wow Wow, was rehearsing with former Damned drummer Jon Moss in a new band tentatively named Sex Gang Children.

Adam Ant, who'd been playing dress-up since the days when even the punk mecca Roxy was still a gay club called Chaguarama's, was experimenting with pirate jackets and Cherokee warpaint. Kate Garner and Jeremy Healy had already started calling themselves Haysi Fantayzee, and preparing an image long before they'd written any songs. And five self-styled "flash geezers who liked having their picture taken and wearing clothes to be looked at," were themselves gazing wistfully towards the drum riser and thinking that would be the ultimate thrill, "to get up on a stage and have everyone in the club looking at you." From Gary Kemp's longing, Spandau Ballet were born.

Spandau Ballet played their first live show at Billy's; accompanied the club to Blitz; then pulled off a string of shows deliberately staged in the most attention-grabbing venues they could find — aboard the floating HMS Belfast naval museum; at another "exclusive" night club, Le Beat Route; at singer Toyah Wilcox's Mayhem Studio in Battersea. "The alternative," guitarist Gary Kemp explained, "would have been to go down to the Marquee and say, 'here's a cassette, can we have a gig?' But how could we expect the people that like us to come down and see us support Saxon?"

Like the Sex Gang Children (who changed their name to Culture Club before they'd even played a gig) and Adam and his Ants, Spandau Ballet came out of Blitz, but they were not the sound of Blitz. There, the DJ soundtrack remained much the same as it had always been; hefty slices of classic electro-rooted rock, whose pallete only expanded as fast as bands like the Human League, Orchestral Manoeuvres in the Dark, Ultravox, Japan, and Simple Minds issued new albums.

What these new bands did was take the sounds, but ally them to their own ideas. Boy George talked of Culture Club as a dub-powered excursion into the realms of white reggae; Adam took Burundi drum rhythms and applied them to positive pop; and Spandau delved into a heavy funk groove which the New Musical Express, in March 1980 — still safe amid those days before the phrase had any other meaning — unhesitatingly described as "soaring Gothic dance that conjures up everything except rock'n'roll."

Through summer 1980, Spandau took their show across southern and central England — not touring in the traditional manner, but renting coaches and buses and piling in with their fans, the Spandarlings, as the press was already calling them, for more "special" concerts in the places least likely. By the time the roadshow hit the midlands city of Birmingham in October, for an afternoon show at the local Botanical Gardens, there couldn't have been a fashion-conscious kid in the country unaware of them.

Birmingham was a smart target for the band's early aspirations. Not only did a thriving urban scene rival London for flamboyance — Martin Degville, later frontman with Sigue Sigue Sputnik, was already a colorful figurehead — but there was also a burgeoning underground of bands, constantly gigging and forever looking for a route out of town. Reggae-ska crossovers UB40 found one, by hitching their star to the 2-Tone bandwagon; now Fashion and Duran Duran were waiting for theirs.

They found it courtesy of Spandau Ballet. Duran bassist John Taylor recalled, "there was an article in Sounds about [them]. The [band are] describing the music that they're making, and they're referred to as part of a 'New Romantic' movement. And I say to the guys, 'Hey look, check this out, it sounds like these guys are doing the same kind of thing that we are.' Just in terms of them taking these Euro beats, it was just about this kind of white European dance style with guitars.

"Actually, we were nothing like that music, but when you looked at it on paper, it seemed that way. It was just pure opportunism really, to take the [New Romantic] label and stick it into the song "Planet Earth," but we called up the girl who wrote the piece, Betty Page, and said, 'Hey, we're part of this New Romantic movement you're talking about, but we're in Birmingham, why don't you come up and see us?' So, she did, and that was the first article that got written about the band."

Spandau Ballet signed with Chrysalis two days after the Birmingham show; Duran Duran joined EMI days before their Sounds feature was published; and the Londoners kept their noses in front. While Spandau's first single, the pounding "To Cut a Long Story Short," climbed to #5 in January 1981, selling 23,000 copies a day, Duran's "Planet Earth" braked at #12. Elsewhere, Visage's "Fade to Grey" made #8, Ultravox's "Vienna" was #2. Even the bands who refused to acknowledge this New Romantic movement had to admit that there was something going on.

It kept going, too. Clubs on the very fringes of London — Croc's in Rayleigh, Scamps in Southend — staged regular Futurist nights, under the aegis of another of the original Blitz kids, Stevo. But whereas other DJs were content simply spinning the discs, Stevo wanted to make them as well. For a few months now, he'd been compiling a weekly Futurist chart for *Sounds*, based on requests at the clubs and his own immaculate tastes, and as he packed up his gear at the end of a night, another pile of home demos would cascade onto his turntables from bands who'd heard the music Stevo played and hoped he'd find the same qualities in theirs.

A lot of what he was given was rubbish, but some showed genuine promise — not enough, maybe, to interest a real record label, but certainly enough to demand a wider hearing. Through the fall of 1980, Stevo rounded up tapes from every band he could, scouring the grapevine for word of anyone he'd missed, and by the end of January 1981, he was ready for action.

The Some Bizzare Album, its title deliberately retaining Stevo's own original spelling mistake (which, in turn, was retained for the name of his record label), was released on January 31, 1981; the definitive anthology of the Futurist scene. Not one of the twelve bands had a deal at the time — within a couple of years, however, four would have scored major hits: Depeche Mode, The The, Blancmange, and Soft Cell, while four more: Naked Lunch, B-Movie, the Fast Set, and Blah Blah Blah — at least had their own records out.

Neither had Stevo even scratched the top of the iceberg. The same day as his album was released, Sheffield's Thompson Twins were self-releasing their first single, "Perfect Game"; within a month, keyboard player Thomas Dolby had issued his "Urges." And just down the road from Billy's, a new club was unearthing talents from even further left of center.

Former frontman with the Doctors of Madness, Richard Strange originally opened the Cabaret Futura as a venue for performances of his own mixed media *Phenomenal Rise* stageshow. Other acts — handpicked by Strange from those he deemed most relevant to the Cabaret's own ambience — followed, and Strange himself made no secret of the fact that through these fringes of the Futurist movement, he detected the imprimateur of his own former band.

"While I would never be so presumptuous as to say we were responsible totally for the direction [music] did take in the late 1970s, I think we were very influential, and that influence is becoming more apparent in the bands that have emerged in the past few years, people like Joy Division, the Skids, and Simple Minds." The latter indeed acknowledged their particular debt when they introduced a live cover of the Velvet Underground's "Waiting for the Man" as a song written by Richard Strange; the Skids' Richard Jobson became a Cabaret regular, performing spoken word demolitions of everyone from Sylvia Plath to Ultravox ("India," he'd imperiously announce midway through "India Song," "it means nothing to me, either").

Positive Noise, Kissing the Pink, and Everest the Hard Way all played appreciative sets to art-ridden audiences, and when Strange finally closed the Cabaret in 1982, it was in the knowledge that he had already passed the baton on. Founded by a handful of the Cabaret Futura's own most colorful denizens, the Batcave opened just a few weeks after the Cabaret closed, a focal point for Futurism's own most unexpected convolution, into the Dali-esque darkness of Goth.

Through the first half of 1981, while Stevo's first discoveries scored their breakthrough hits (Depeche Mode made #57 with "Dreaming of Me" in the spring, Soft Cell marched to #1 with "Tainted Love" that summer), Duran Duran and Spandau continued setting the pace — not for the New Romantics and Futurists now, though, for but for a whole new era of teenybop fervor, unseen since the heyday of the Bay City Rollers.

It took them both by surprise. Spandau, in particular, doggedly maintained their hybrid-funk dance rock well into the year, peaking with "Musclebound" and "Chant Number One" before finally caving in to market pressures in early 1982. But Duran, too, found the new attention shocking, all the more so since Nick Rhodes insisted "it was the last thing we ever thought would happen, because the content of our songs was hardly something that was going to appeal to a teen audience."

"Brighton was the first date of the UK tour that we did with the release of the first album," continued John Taylor. "The curtains opened, and there was this sea of screaming girls, it completely threw me off my balance. I had no idea. It was like somebody pulling the rug out from under you, because one was used to putting all the energy out, and suddenly having this huge surge or energy coming at you, it was extraordinary. And that set the base for the next three years."

Suddenly crowned the princes of a new rock aristocracy, the "wild nobility" which Adam Ant's "Ant Music" had predicted just six short months before, Duran Duran exited the Futurist scene almost before they'd had a chance to put anything back into it — but precisely at the same moment that Kraftwerk returned to take it back for themselves.

Three years had elapsed since their last album, *Man Machine*, years during which Kraftwerk completely re-equipped their Kling Klang studios with computers, and barely paid any attention to what was happening in the outside world. They just got on with their music — a new album titled *Computer World* — and when they did reemerge, it was to discover that their detractors had been trampled to death.

Britain was in the grip of synthesizer mania, guitars and drums had been wiped from the planet, and even as *Computer World* moved up the chart, so the band's UK record company began reactivating Kraftwerk's back catalog.

Trans-Europe Express reappeared in the album chart, and emboldened, EMI decided to release a couple of singles. "Pocket Calculator" first, and then "Computer Love." Both did moderately well, grazing the Top 40, then slipping out of view again. But DJs kept on playing "Computer Love," and when they got bored, they just flipped it over, and played its b-side, the three year old "The Model" instead. And suddenly sales started flickering again. By early winter 1981, EMI had officially reissued the single with "The Model" as the a-side, and it started to climb.

On January 9, 1982, "The Model" entered the UK chart at #21. The following week, it breached the Top 10; on January 23, it hit #2. It slipped one place the week after that, but it was only a hiccup. On February 6, "The Model" hit #1, and suddenly Kraftwerk weren't simply the first German band ever to top the British chart, they were the biggest thing in sight. Had they only followed it up, they might have remained so.

"I think it was EMI's idea to release 'The Model' again," Kraftwerk's Wolfgang Flur recalled. "We'd already had some success with it, but sometimes a song has to go together with the times, with influences and fashion, before it can be recognized, whereas three years before, it was maybe too far ahead of its time. Somebody in EMI had the idea and he was absolutely right.

"We'd just had *Computer World* out, and it was strange, seeing such an old song doing well, when the new one wasn't doing so well" — so strange, in fact, that Flur quit the band shortly after, admitting, "the success of 'The Model' gave me the answer to the question I had in my heart, that it was the older [Kraftwerk] things which had more romanticism, more melody, warmer sounds, more humor, which functioned better. I felt that, and it gave me the insight I needed."

His bandmates retreated, away from the garish glare of the limelight, away from the record company pressures and the media's demands, away from these strange quirks of timing which could push them to the peak, then kick them all the way down again. The future was left, once again, to the Futurists, and of course, they kept on coming.

The Human League, sundered by a down the middle break-up in early 1981, regrouped and reemerged stronger than ever with the chart-topping "Don't You Want Me." Vince Clarke's Yaz/Yazoo, formed from a similarly cataclysmic split within the ranks of Depeche Mode, scored with "Only You." American aspirants Ministry emerged with a debut album, *No Sympathy*, which highlights some of Al

Jourgensen's most humanely listenable confections. A Flock of Seagulls conquered America, and Boy George's Culture Club took on the world.

"Looking back at that period now," Duran Duran's Nick Rhodes reflected, "I think really what it was about was, a style movement that came out of punk and glam rock. What we did took the original punk ethic, and bind it up with the electronic music of Kraftwerk and Giorgo Moroder and all that disco stuff as well, which we sort of liked some of, mixed in with glam rock. All of that together resulted in the New Romantic ethos."

And as for what came out of it... "the new music," John Taylor announced in 1981, "is music played by young people with a positive and fresh approach, who are giving value for money, and aren't flying plastic pigs above Bingley Hall. But if people don't buy our records because we haven't got frilly shirts on, I'm not interested."

RECOMMENDED LISTENING

A FLOCK OF SEAGULLS Wishing (LP *Listen*)

ABC Poison Arrow (LP *Lexicon of Love*)

DEPECHE MODE See You (LP *A Broken Frame*)

DURAN DURAN Save A Prayer (LP *Rio*)

HAYSI FANTAYZEE John Wayne is Big Leggy (45)

HUMAN LEAGUE Empire State Human (LP *Reproduction*)

M Pop Musik (LP *Official Secrets*)

OMD Enola Gay (LP *Organisation*)

SPANDAU BALLET Musclebound (LP *Diamond*)

TUBEWAY ARMY Are "Friends" Electric? (LP *Replicas*)

THE KRAUTROCK CONNECTION

Krautrock. It's a faintly disreputable sounding term, redolent of the attitudes of an age gone by, when rock'n'roll's Anglo-American hegemony was utterly unimpeded and the notions of even a vaguely viable musical (rock musical) form emerging from elsewhere was so risible as to be unintelligible.

Yet it is also a strangely evocative term, one which conjures, as Julian Cope once mused, "a powerful pre-punk attitude achieved by the pioneering few — the Ur-punk, those at the very beginning. Krautrock is what punk would have been if Johnny Rotten alone had been in charge."

Rotten does not disagree. His favorite album was Can's *Tago Mago*, and "in the beginning, I hated the music the Sex Pistols were playing." He came around because, in tiny ways, he was able to introduce the disciplines of one into the chaos of the other, even as Krautrock itself, in the shape of Kraftwerk, Can, and Neu, eased itself into the same space.

In late 1977, the UK music paper *Sounds* ran a piece heralding "New Musick" — the dub of King Tubby, the "postpunk" of Siouxsie and the Banshees, and the electronics which merged from west (Pere Ubu and Throbbing Gristle) to east (Kraftwerk again) and pointed to a future which wasn't a million miles from what Rotten would then go onto create with Public Image Ltd.

Can's Holger Czukay would be courted by such English musicians as Brian Eno, Jon Hassell, David Sylvian, and PIL's own Jah Wobble, while 1997 brought *Sacrilege*, a Can remix project which brought in tributes from as far afield as Sonic Youth, UNKLE, Daniel Miller, and System 7 alongside the expected Eno and Wobble. The result, though not guaranteed to appeal to Can purists, nevertheless indicated just how broadly influential the group had been — and no doubt will remain.

What made Krautrock so important, however, was not the vistas to which it might lead, but those which it had left behind. At the end of World War II, afterall, it wasn't simply Germany's cities which had been laid waste by the victorious allies. Much of the country's very culture had been destroyed as well, and though Germany rebuilt, that one essential building block remained unobtainable. By the mid-1960s, the sound of young Germany was the same as young everywhere else: imported British beat bands, borrowed American protest songs, and a few rising local songwriters (Udo Lindenberg paramount among them) who were able to rhyme in English.

Things started to change around 1967, when the possibilities inherent in improvised rock music first began to impact on the scene. Things began to change consciously a little after that, on the wings of a new wave of young German artists, born too late to have experienced the horrors of the war, but not so late that they were willing to accept life in the shadow of their country's conquerors.

Deconstructing the principles of western rock, subverting first, the necessity of lyrics, then the dominance of conventional instrumentation, and finally the need for traditional structure, bands like Tangerine Dream, Amon Duul, Ash Ra Tempel, Cluster, Faust, and Guru Guru may (as western rock historians insist) have taken their lead from Pink Floyd, the Soft Machine, and sundry other psychedelic soundweavers. But it was where they took that lead which really mattered, into a cosmic meltdown which may not have fit anybody's idea of a truly indigenous German musical form, but would become one anyway.

The catalyst around which Germany's musical renaissance would be built was a young man who had spent much of his early adulthood outside of Germany, in Austria with the Vienna Symphony Orchestra, and in New York with avant-garde composer LaMonte Young. These were the experiences, far removed from any notions of pop or even rock, which prompted Irmin Schmidt to form Can when he returned to his native Cologne in 1968, and linked up with another occasional exile, Holger Czukay.

Czukay spent 1966 teaching in Switzerland. He, too, had a firm grounding in the avant-garde, having studied and worked with Karlheinz Stockhausen, only to collide with his students' love of the early Pink Floyd and Velvet Underground and have his very understanding of music torn out from under his feet. "Something like 'Sister Ray'," he mused, "seemed very wild and spontaneous."

Originally christened Inner Space, the band started life using precisely the same musical instruments as their former western idols. But then they started to mess with them — removing the guitar and leaving the feedback; stripping the melody, but layering the drums; removing the vocals, but adding a flute.

Their early recordings were rough, their early line-up unstable. Inner Space's first single, "Kama Sutra," was credited only to Schmidt; an album, *Canaxis 5*, was Czukay and a friend, Rolf Dammers, feeding assorted ethnic disciplines through a box of bleeping, hissing tricks. But still they were moving forward, so that by the time the newly christened Can released their own debut album, *Monster Movie* in August 1969, they had already crossed a rubicon which their Anglo-American counterparts would not bridge for several months more. "Yoo Doo Right" (covered, many years later, by Thin White Rope) was not simply a twenty minute excursion which occupied one entire side of the album, although that in itself was a feat. It was merely an excerpt of a solid twelve hour improvisation!

Neither was it a fluke. Can's next release, *Soundtracks* (their first for UK major label Liberty), comprised a series of largely disconnected pieces originally intended as a stop-gap before the band's official second album was released, but which pulled even further away from the band's beginnings. *Monster Movie*, Julian Cope deadpanned (in his masterful history, *Krautrocksampler*), was the sound of Can "desperately trying not to play the Velvets' 'European Son'"; *Soundtracks* was them wondering whether they'd ever be able to play it again.

Almost two years elapsed before Can released their next album — 1971's *Tago Mago* combined one disc of relatively conventional song structures (the Jesus and Mary Chain later covered "Mushroom Head"), with another of free form improvisation, canting, chanting, churning; then they followed up with *Ege Bamyasi Okraschoten*, a single disc distillation of all its predecessor's high points, and spawning a #1 single as well, as "Spoon" devoured the German chart.

It would be four years more before Can — in a very different incarnation — had a British hit under their belt, with the insistent sibilance of "I Want More." But as *Ego Bamyasi* made the rounds of encouraging ears, even this distant success seemed somehow closer to hand. Richard Williams, the *Melody Maker* journalist who already had the discovery of Roxy Music to his credit, now began championing Can. The difference was: whereas his love of Roxy had been a voice in the wilderness, Can seemed to appeal to everyone.

It was unfortunate, then, that at this precise moment, guitarist Michael Karoli was stricken with a perforated ulcer, forcing Can off the road (and, as it transpired, out of the studio) for several months. They returned in early 1973 with a well-received UK tour, but another six months were to elapse before their next album, *Future Days*, by which time the momentum which had propelled the band so far was on the point of exhaustion.

For while they were away, another power had swept out of Germany and it, too, was soon poised on the brink of a breakthrough. The difference was, whereas Can made music for the heart and soul (Japanese-born vocalist Damo Suzuki was even regarded as a sex symbol in some quarters), Dusseldorf-based Kraftwerk didn't even have hearts and souls. Just machines.

Having first united in the shortlived Organisation, Ralf Hutter and Florian Schneider, the group's organist and flautist, formed Kraftwerk in 1970 as a trio — the third member of which was their own recording studio. Like Can, who were already operating out of their own private environment, the duo realized that the only way to approach the music they wanted to make was to do so in their own time, on their own territory. The remaining members of the band followed later.

The name which Hutter and Schneider chose for the band, too, was somehow ominous. Dusseldorf lies within Germany's industrial heartland, in the shadow of a myriad power plants. Power plant in German is Kraftwerk.

From the outset, then, Kraftwerk knew what they wanted to do — and their first album, *Kraftwerk*, spelled it out, ruthlessly signposting the immense influence they were to have, not solely on electronic music, but on rock'n'roll in general. Put simply, Kraftwerk would be to the 1980s and 1990s all that Chuck Berry was to the decades before. And if *Trans-Europe Express* was their "Johnny B Goode," and *Autobahn* their "Rock and Roll Music," the least that can be said for *Kraftwerk* is that it was their "Maybelline."

Over the next two years, Kraftwerk continued refining that original visison. For their second self-titled album, recorded after a split which saw bandmates Klaus Dinger and Michael Rother quit to form their own band, Neu!, Hutter and Schneider replaced guitars with a drum machine. For their third, *Ralf and Florian*, they brought further electronics to the fore.

Synthesizers, Hutter and Schneider were sure, had infinitely more potential than had been demonstrated so far; the freaky whooshes of Hawkwind, the morose contemplations of Tangerine Dream, the pompous pounding of Keith Emerson. These elements were all old hat, even before they'd been worn. Kraftwerk were looking for new applications, new purposes, new pop. They lay all three bare with their fourth album, 1975's Anglo-American monster hit *Autobahn*, and ushered in a future which the band members themselves could barely have envisaged.

The Birth of Goth

In the beginning, there was darkness. The light of punk was flickering, the fires of fury were dying. Where once there was hope, there now lurked despair; where once there was promise, there now lay shattered dreams. In 1977, rock'n'roll awaited renewal. By 1979, it had the Pop Group and a clutch of similarly drab, dour introverts, all utterly preoccupied with what better-bred critics called the blackest side of the human psyche.

The Cure were publicly moving towards the sickened ultimatum of *Pornography*; the Psychedelic Furs were transfixing the underground with a freak-form frenzy which even their greatest albums would never recapture; Siouxsie and the Banshees were writing metal postcards from the edge of their own nervous breakdowns.

Nowhere was safe from the creeping miasma. Once hotbeds of jangling, chiming pop, the northern English cities of Liverpool and Manchester had both grafted their distinct native sensibilities (the Beatles versus the Hollies, Oasis versus Stone Roses) onto an awakened fascination with moping minorchords. While dark raincoat sales went through the roof, Liverpool's Echo and the Bunnymen, Big in Japan and Teardrop Explodes, and Manchester's The Fall, A Certain Ratio, and Magazine all took their first tentative steps into daylight, with Joy Division — named for the enforced brothels established in the holocaust concentration camps — swiftly establishing themselves as the pack's undisputable leaders.

From the outset, there was something darkly compulsive about the Joy Division — the suspicion that the psychic traumas which comprised vocalist Ian Curtis' best lyrics were written from something more than simple imagination; the suspicion, too, that the epileptic dance he indulged in on stage might not be entirely an act. The singer would be dead, hanged by his own hand, before the world learned the true extent of Curtis' private hell, severe epilepsy included, but even before then, Joy Division appealed because they confronted issues which nobody else did. And because their music sounded so miserable.

The defining moment in Joy Division's development (although they were swift to distance themselves from it once it became apparent where it was leading) came when the band's manager, television presenter Tony Wilson, publicly described their music as "gothic rock."

The term itself was not his own invention; indeed, it had been swirling around the edges of rock consciousness for close to a decade at that point, waiting for a movement it could stick to. Nico, the icicle-voiced valkyrie with the original Velvet Underground, had rejoiced beneath the same tag back in 1971, when poor sales of her *Marble Index* solo album prompted producer John Cale to muse, "you can't sell suicide." Since then, "gothic" had raised its head on more than one occasion, but to anybody who was really paying attention, the Nico connection remained the best.

Joy Division shared many of the same values as hallmarked *Marble Index* — a droning density which dominated both the performance and the production, and a sense that the very sound conveyed secrets which could utterly liberate the listener... or utterly destroy him. Where Joy Division departed from Nico's archetype was in the nature of their own personal reference points. Born in Cologne, Germany in 1938, and thus living through both the best and worst days of World War II, Nico's world view was irrevocably rooted in the contradictions of her native culture: the psychic strength of imagery and image; and its corollary, the brute force bombing with which the Allies smashed it. Joy Division, as their name implies, shared her fascination with the symbolism of the Third Reich. But they grew up in the peace and prosperity of 1960s Britain — a world in which total war was an abstract concept, to be studied alongside the films of Werner Herzog or the philosophies of Friedrich Nietzsche. Yet the war, described for them by their grandparents and schoolbooks, impacted Joy Division just as strongly. "I was brought up by my grandparents," guitarist Bernard Sumner recalled, "and they told me about the war, about all the sacrifices people had made so that we could be free. We had a room upstairs with gasmasks and sandbags and English flags, tin helmets. The war left a big impression on me." And that impression, whether consciously or not, bled through the band's music and into their audience, to become a cornerstone of what Tony Wilson called gothic rock.

For Joy Division were not alone in their exploitation of Nazi symbolism. At her first ever concert, at the 100 Club Punk Festival in September 1976, Siouxsie (of the Banshees fame) danced almost topless in a swastika armband, while reciting the Lord's Prayer — religion colliding with religious intensity to create a new breed of blasphemy. Church groups condemned the group for their music, libertarian idealists condemned their imagery.

Siouxsie responded with a disinterested shrug and the Banshees followed up with a version of the Beatles' "Helter Skelter" — shameless in its invocation of all that Charles Manson had perceived in the song. But the group toned down its look and lyrics regardless, and concentrated — like Joy Division, equally fearful of being tarred with the Fascist brush — on making the same points with sound.

"A lot of [what we were doing] was just sort of accident," Banshees bassist Steve Severin revealed, "us attempting to find something of our own. Our influences were the Roxy Musics, David Bowies, T. Rexs, a twisted sexuality, a black humor which was different." Beyond a general delight in denting industry preconceptions, neither was there any sense of actually forging a fresh musical direction, much less fathering a whole new genre. Like Joy Division, like the Slits and the Pop Group, Siouxsie and the Banshees were shooting in the dark.

Severin continued, "we weren't being calculated about it. When we were making *The Scream* [the Banshees' epochal debut album], we didn't tell the guitarist, 'oh, you have to play an A sharp minor there, and it'll be really spooky.' We'd say 'make it a cross between the Velvet Underground and the shower scene from *Psycho*.'"

But again like Joy Division, the Banshees made no attempt to disguise their own influences. *The Scream* was titled for an Edward Munch painting; their first German hit, "Mittageisen (Metal Postcard)" lifted its key lyrics from a speech by wartime Luftwaffe chief Hermann Goering, and was dedicated to anti-Nazi artist John Heartfield. "Playground Twist" was pure Alfred Hitchcock; and "Voices" and "The Staircase (Mystery)" were deliberate nods in the direction of 18th century romance novelist Ann Radcliffe — all mysterious tapping and creaking doors, and a fear not of darkness, but of what that darkness disguised.

All were startlingly different songs, but each was bound by a common claustrophobia; a nagging sense that there was something more than simple open spaces between Siouxsie's ice queen vocals and the echo-swamped guitars. "A lot of what we were doing, if you have to put a name to it, was intended to be resonant, rather than innovate," Severin continued. "We read a lot, we watched a lot of movies, and we tried to interest people in the same kind of things."

What those "same kind of things" boiled down to, of course, was a fascination with darkness — physical, psychic, and emotional. *Psycho* meets the Velvet Underground to start with, but a lot of other, personal, elements as well. *New Musical Express* journalist Paul Morley once said of Joy Division (and it was equally true of the Banshees), "their music could worm through the words of Sterling and Gibson... could buzz around the up-sense and down-data of Ballard or Burroughs... could form a soundtrack for Godard or Bergman... but NOT Tarantino." In order for such bands' success — their existence, even — to become something more than an isolated phenomenon, however, they needed a market to tap into; an audience which wanted theater with its thoughtfulness. They achieved it — or rather, had it achieved *for* them — with the arrival into the post-punk con-

sciousness of author Anne Rice's book, *Interview With The Vampire*.

A shockingly modernistic reclamation of the reality and the sexually-pregnant romance that earlier European vampire traditions took for granted, the novel was published in 1976 — musically the dawn of the punk era, but culturally, early into a burgeoning fascination with the occult launched three years previous by the success of *The Exorcist*. *Interview With The Vampire*, however, shared little common ground with such a gory archetype.

No sinister cartoon bloodsucker, Rice's vampire unquestionably adhered to many of the basic tenets of modern literary vampirism. But his very inhumanity was flavored with humanity, a need for acceptance, a hunger for love, and an unfulfillable desire for companionship — why else would he have even agreed to be interviewed?

It was an audacious combination, but it worked brilliantly — *Interview With The Vampire* was scarcely on the streets before its hero, Louie, was recruiting a whole new generation of the figuratively Undead. And while its absorption into the musical bloodstream was slow, moving by word of mouth rather than deed and example, by 1979, its influence was unquestionably making itself felt.

Richard Jackson, a punk fan growing up in the northern English town of Hull, extolled his love of the book as almost evangelical, particularly after he discovered that the Damned's vocalist (the vespertine Dave Vanian) was also an acolyte. And as Jackson began looking around "for music which made me feel the same way the book did," it swiftly transpired that he wasn't alone in his quest.

A former gravedigger with his own long-standing penchant for dressing as a vampire, Dave Vanian contributed little of his image to his band's actual sound — through the late 1970s at least, the Damned remained the same buzzsaw blur of three chord invective they were when they first set foot on a stage. But the Vanian persona was pervasive regardless, all the more so once audiences began emulating his dress sense.

"Long before there was a recognized gothic look," Damned guitarist Brian James recalled, "there were fans turning up at shows dressed like Dave — which was brilliant at the time, because it lifted us right out of the typical punk rock band thing. Other groups had the safety pins and the spitting and the bondage trousers, but you went to a Damned show, and half the local cemetery would be propped up against the stage."

Drummer Rat Scabies agreed. "The Vanian dollies, that's what we used to call them. Dave's whole thing, right from day one, had been that he was kind of a vampire bloke. The thing about that was he was always like that, it wasn't something he put on just before he went onstage, it was the way he was when he got up in the morning, went to bed, working on the car. He was fairly committed to that look, that was why he was the cool guy to pick up on, and that's why we stuck with him, because everyone would say, 'ah, look at him, he's funny,' but he really wasn't, he was probably the most genuine person, he really is a fucking fruitcake. Plus he was a pretty good looking guy, he was pretty hot property.

"When [the goth] thing started coming out, it seemed to me, yeah his time has come round, and the shockwaves had gone far enough now that the average girlie pop fan is relating to an image and a singer in a band. It was definitely due, and that was the time for it to happen."

The Damned themselves would be wholeheartedly embracing this audience soon enough, with such early 1980s hits as "Grimly Fiendish" and "Thanks for the Night" amply repaying the Undead for their devotion. In 1977/78, however, the band defiantly remained the jokers in what would eventually be termed the proto-goth pack, providing the visuals which a fast swelling audience was looking for, but leaving the task of breaking fresh musical ground to a handful of other, more eclectic concerns — the Banshees and Joy Division at the fore. Everywhere one looked, it seemed, somebody was striking another minor chord, and moping about in the dark, and fans like Richard Jackson had indeed found their ideal.

It would be foolish, of course, to even attempt to credit *Interview With The Vampire* with responsibility for what was now coalescing, any more than Marion Bradley's Arthurian bestseller *The Mists Of Avalon* kickstarted the upsurge of interest in New Age/Celtic mythology of the 1980s. But it did supply a focal point for people of a certain mindset, and *Interview With The Vampire* fulfilled the same function — not so much seeking out new travelers, as offering a firm direction to existing ones. It would be inaccurate, too, to paint the incipient scene as possessing anything even remotely resembling a deliberate ethos. Several journalists have suggested that goth, or at least the post-punk floundering which preceded goth, was in part caused by the angst that followed the collapse of punk; a sense of futility because punk hadn't changed the world after all, and if it couldn't do it, nothing could. While the older kids were angry, their younger brothers and sisters were just depressed.

To depict goth as some kind of musical Hemlock Society, however, is to miss the point of the movement altogether, even in its earliest flowering. Punk, by its very nature, had appealed to society's extroverts; even within its self-proclaimed parish of pariahs, and its championing of the individual and the misfit, the gaudy hair colors and exhibitionist costumes which were the punk "uniform" offered no ready role for the kid who wanted to simply sit at the back, dressed in black, lighting candles, and contemplating Thanatos in all His awesome guises. Once the media came into the pic-

ture, and punk itself was subverted by its own subversive imagery, then the chances of pondering loftier concepts than the injustice of unemployment were even scarcer. "It's not that goths enjoy being depressed," journalist Julian Saint-Paul wrote in 1980. "They just don't like seeming happy."

But no less than the medieval legends which form so much of the modern goth iconography, the musical moods and elements required by the experience were already being set in stone from the start. All they needed now was to be refined, which was where Bauhaus — memorably described in *Melody Maker* as a mass of "reheated Banshees leftovers with just a hint of not-unappetizing Joy Division" — would enter the picture.

Bauhaus' first single, "Bela Lugosi's Dead," was released in mid-1979, or close to a year before anybody bar the Banshees and Joy Division had even hinted at consigning such a sound to vinyl — ten, palpably intense minutes of sinister scratching and scraping, guitars like fingernails, vocals like an open artery. Quite simply, "Bela Lugosi's Dead" was utterly unlike anything anyone had ever heard before, anything anyone had ever done before.

It was also, singer Peter Murphy insisted, "a very tongue-in-cheek song; the essence of the song, if you peel back the first layer, is very tongue-in-cheek-'Bela Lugosi's dead, undead,' it's hilarious. But [it] sounds extremely serious, very heavyweight and quite dark, and the mistake we made is that we also performed it with such naive seriousness. That's what pushed the audience into seeing it as a much more serious thing. The intention going into the performance actually overshadowed the humor of it."

Having taken that first step, however, there was no going back. At first, the movement which sprang from this burgeoning bucket of archetypes was nameless. "It took about a year and a half [for the media to catch on]" Murphy continued. "And about a year for us to realize that we were actually drawing quite a large audience, post-punks who were gelling into something which we called the wildebeests. We played a festival, Futurama in Leeds, and we toddled on to do our little bit, make way for the headliners, and suddenly there was this noise like a distant stampede coming towards us, and there they all were, these wildebeests flooding in. And we just thought 'My God! What have we done?'"

What they had done was complete the equation which would cause a million adolescent manias to suddenly, and irrevocably, coalesce. Dave Vanian had provided the look, the Banshees supplied the menace, and Joy Division the angst. Now Bauhaus instilled the intellectual discipline, and the spore from which a new culture could be spawned. They name-dropped Sartori and St. Vitus' dance; they sang of stigmata martyrs and lilies and remains; and the passion of lovers, they knew, was for death. Their very name was taken from a Weimar-era German school of architecture — albeit one whose modernist tendency ran totally counter to the spirit of what would become termed as the gothic movement. "Bauhaus probably had more to do with starting goth," Scabies reflected. "I don't know if they were though. Murphy did look a little bit like Dave Vanian. But I don't give a fuck, I like a good horror movie, I enjoy being frightened, and like old castles the same as anything else. It was kind of irrelevant, and fashion's a disposable item."

But Bauhaus' stance also raised critical hackles. Reviewing the group's second single, January 1980's "Dark Entries," and having first filed Bauhaus alongside a host of other groups who used Joy Division as the stencil for their strivings, a *Sounds* reviewer mused, "I like it, but something tells me I should be worried. Do these 'new Joy Division Bands' have a social conscience? Where does the pose end, and the real, aware art begin?" He was not to know (could not have known, in those politically charged years immediately after punk) that for the moment, the pose was the art. Social consciences were out of fashion already.

For Rocco, guitarist with the deliciously vampiric-sounding Flesh for Lulu, "the gothic thing started with bands like Bauhaus, the Banshees, a general tribe of people walking around in black clothes and black spiky hair. For me, it was like listening to a Nico record, that atmosphere... and also the drug thing, of course. Getting heavily into the wrong ones, it was all part of that."

It was astonishing how quickly the musical mood turned, from the chaos of punk to the contemplation of the inner self; from mach ten mayhem to mackintoshes. Many of the early bands being swept into the gothic pigeonhole affected a raincoat-clad look of studied dreariness, and made music, they deadpanned, and matched the English climate.

Twenty years later, following the Littleton, Colorado school shooting which briefly catapulted gothic culture into a very unwelcome spotlight, the "Trench Coat Mafia" would become the epitome of a nation's fear. In London, Liverpool, and Manchester, in 1979, however, the swiftly-dubbed Raincoat Brigade was simply a byword for young men who took themselves just a little bit too seriously, made music to match, and chose their heroes and heroines very carefully indeed. Especially their heroines.

In 1978, Nico abandoned her latest comeback attempt after she was jeered and bombarded offstage by audiences which simply couldn't understand what a wheezing harmonium and a voice marinaded in the dust of crumbling shadows could possibly have had in common with Lou Reed and the group which recorded "Sister Ray." But "two years later," Nico boasted, "new English bands were begging me to join them onstage. They would say things like 'we are goths, but you are gothic,' and if I liked them, I would do it." One of the

bands she liked was Bauhaus, joining them onstage in her recently-adopted hometown of Manchester for a ragged version of the Velvets' own "Waiting for the Man." Nico would die in 1987, after a fall from her bicycle, but seven years later, Peter Murphy still agreed with what his teenaged self had told her. "Nico was gothic. But she was Mary Shelley gothic to everyone else's Hammer Horror film gothic. They all did Frankenstein, but Nico's was real."

Through the winter of 1979/80, new groups were forming daily it seemed, each arriving early enough that by the time the media finally got wind of what was happening, any one of them could pontificate from a position of apparent authority; each introducing a new piece to the jigsaw. Often, it was a band's name alone which would alert an audience to its musical potential — Theatre of Hate, with its implications of surrealist suffering; Gene Loves Jezebel, conjuring images of Biblical harlotry; and the self explanatory Southern Death Cult, whose vocalist, Ian Astbury, readily acknowledges that it was the emergence of Bauhaus which prompted his own band's first efforts. But even he was unaware of just how quickly the jaws of fashion would snap closed — so quickly that within two years, he had been forced to abbreviate the band's name twice, first to Death Cult and finally to the Cult, simply to shake free of the associated baggage.

"The goth tag started as a bit of a joke. One of the groups coming up at the same time as Southern Death Cult was Sex Gang Children with Andi Sex Gang — who I used to call the Gothic Goblin, because he was a little guy, and he's dark, he used to like Edith Piaf and this macabre music, and he lived in a building in Brixton called Visigoth Towers. So he was the little Gothic Goblin, and his followers were goths. That's where goth came from." And by late 1980, in the pages of the British music press, it had stuck, surfacing first in reviews of Bauhaus' *In the Flat Field* debut album ("Gothick-Romantick pseudo-decadence" — the *NME*), and then adhering to any flat black surface one could name.

Gene Loves Jezebel co-founder Michael Aston was more understanding. "We absolutely didn't start as a goth band. But there's a very powerful history behind us being from southern Wales — the whole of Camelot, the singing, the mining. The people look to the past, its legends, its poetry, all that had an impact on us, and I think that put us into the gothic context. Plus our music was very, very moody, dark, and very lyrical." Again, the stereotypes slip into place. Happy people don't dress all in black, happy people don't listen to Edith Piaf, happy people don't read poetry, happy people don't base their musical statements around Benedictine chants and Indian mantras. Discussing *Faith*, the Cure's megalithic third album and one which he himself would later describe as the aural equivalent to wearing sackcloth and ashes, Robert Smith admitted, "I like a lot of music which is built around repetition, musics built around slow changes [that] allow you to draw things out." Meditative, melancholy, mesmeric chants and mantras, he continued, fit that bill.

Where the stereotype led, the archetypes followed. Soon, no well-dressed follower of this new wave of bands would even dream of leaving the house in color, by daylight, in anything less than full make-up and undertaker drag. Add the hint of transvestitism which has never lost the power to shock in terms of teenaged fashion, and of course, that well-thumbed copy of Ann Rice to read on the train; throw in a pack of clove cigarettes, to imbue the proceedings with a touch of European glamor, and by early 1980, the gothic "look" was as obsessive as the music.

"It was paradoxical," Murphy continues, "because on the one hand, it was an audience which we had created through our own efforts, which is every band's dream. But on the other, we were a little perturbed, curious, and confused — why does our audience look like this?" One evening before a show, Murphy was walking through London's Camden Town with Bauhaus' lighting technician, watching the audience as it flitted to the venue. "I turned round and said 'God, people really do look strange these days,' and he just laughed — 'how can you say... YOU'RE saying OTHER people look strange?'"

Yet though there was a uniform, and a uniform system of beliefs setting in, still there was an individuality to goth which cut, and continues to cut, through the accusations of cliche. Clothing was trademark black, but stylistically it ran the gamut of fashions, from Regency-era frills and lace to pre-millennial fetish and leather; from fishnet sluttishness to winding cloth zombie chic, with room on the fringe for rib-cage necklaces and glow-in-the-dark skull and crossbone T-shirts. For some it was vaudeville, to others, vestment, but it was also, Andi Sex Gang enthused, "the epitome of human spirit" — even when that spirit simply donned the darkness for weekends and days off, then spent a few hours sitting round local graveyards, waiting for the next fashion bandwagon to rumble through. "It's become a way of life for so many people," Christian Death's Rozz Williams mused. "It's kind of baffling. How do these people maintain it? Wake up, 'have to put in my fangs, do my hair.... Got to make it down to the graveyard before it's closed.' It really gets bad when people get stuck just in that, where they can't go outside of that. Sometimes I'll be trying out new material, and people will be screaming out for 'Romeo Distress,' and I think, 'go home, play the record, and don't come back, please.' God forbid I end up going on a *Sound and Vision* tour like David Bowie, except instead of singing the old songs, I'll have to sacrifice virgins and summon up demons every night."

Williams committed suicide (on April 1, 1998), before that particular nightmare could come true. Nevertheless, in the 17 years before that, since Christian Death first broke out of Los Angeles, every aspect of the band's being, from Williams' desperately ambiguous sexuality, to the project's very name, melded into the gothic image — even though Williams himself never imagined such a thing. "I thought if we were lucky, people would think we were like the Cramps or Alice Cooper. That's what I was into."

Indeed, the Cramps had been popularizing B-movie rock imagery for some four years at that point, essentially working around the same sense of campy kitsch as Dave Vanian in England, only substituting Roger Corman for Hammer Horror. And they were huge in L.A., where Christian Death, 45 Grave, and the Superheroines were the kingpins on what the local media called the "death rock scene." It was a name which the musicians themselves approved of. Williams admitted, "The Cramps were a major influence, only we didn't like rockabilly. We liked Alice Cooper, David Bowie, and the Sex Pistols. So death rock, as we saw it, was taking the visual and lyrical aspect of the Cramps, and attaching it to rock'n'roll. Only people started calling it gothic rock instead, and it ended up going to a very different place than we had intended."

Ferociously theatrical and utilizing stage sets and costumes to a level unseen on an American stage since the heyday of KISS, Christian Death's taste for the macabre was echoed in everything they did, from the songs they wrote to the philosophies they expounded in interviews. Williams spoke openly of a crushingly religious upbringing and his disdain, now, for organized religion. He described life as a Bacchanalian quest to experience everything that was available spiritually, sexually, and chemically.

"America's always been ruled by extremes," Williams reasoned. "Look at the Punks, look at the bikers, look at the Hippies. Altamont couldn't have happened anywhere else. Manson couldn't have been Belgian. We just came along at a time when everything else of value had already been ripped to shreds. Religion was the only thing left to destroy."

He might also have pointed out that through the 1980s, much of American political life was dominated by the raised voices of the religious right, with rock'n'roll a favorite, and apparently easy, target. It was one of the proudest days of Williams' life, he said, when Christian Death's first album, *Only Theatre of Pain*, was featured on a religious television program which his own parents used to watch. "They did a special on Satanic influences in rock. They had our record on, and they broke it." It only followed, therefore, that although he always insisted that the band's name was far more of a joke than a statement of intent, Christian Death came to epitomize that impious stream of gothic thought which remains most people's first (and only) impression of the scene. And in so doing, the group's blasphemy became as integral to the American gothic scene as "Be Bop A Lula" was to '50s rock'n'roll.

By 1981–82, goth — or at least, a black-clad profundity which the trans-Atlantic music press insisted labeling as such — was breaking out everywhere and in every guise: Australia's Birthday Party, allying the young Nick Cave's horror vocals to some of the gothiest song titles ever ("Release the Bats" — how could anyone resist?); Scotland's Cocteau Twins hurtling through ethereal cobwebs of drone and soundscape; Dead Can Dance and the Dancing Did... so many bands, so many nuances.

Edgar Allen Poe and Bram Stoker, never completely overlooked by changing tastes, but nevertheless tarred with the brush of old-fashioned stuffiness, were utterly rehabilitated: the Banshees devoted a song to Poe, the Stranglers gifted him with an entire album, *The Raven*.

The ailing midnight theater circuit found new life through the resuscitation of poorly preserved and barely watchable prints of vintage horror classics, Lugosi's *Dracula* of course, *The Cabinet of Dr. Caligari*, *Nosferatu the Vampire*... anything to which the cachet of gothic glamor could reasonably be attached. The bloodsoaked kitsch of Vincent Price, Christopher Lee and Peter Cushing's '60s-era Hammer Horror movies was revived as an entire generation set aside the received wisdom of past critics and complainants, and decided to discover for itself the nature of past beasts.

Siouxsie encouraged such voyages. "When I was young, the only books I used to read were those cheap horror paperbacks, the ones by Herbert van Thal. My favorite movies are Hammer films, especially the ones with Vincent Price. The way he acts is so corny and obvious, but still he's amazingly effective. You should never be afraid to be corny."

And while there was undoubtedly a great deal of simple one-up-man-ship going on — the timeless race to prove "I was a goth before you were a goth" — there was a great deal of sincere interest and appreciation born as well, a sincerity which found its voice within the frantic blur of activity and expression that was the Batcave.

The Batcave (the new movement's first purpose-built spiritual home/nightclub) was located in Dean Street, in the heart of London's Soho district, at the convergence of multiple tourist routes. The famed Marquee Club was just round one corner; the St. Moritz afterhours bar round another. Some of London's best known pubs and niteries were numbered amongst the Batcave's neighbors, yet even the new venue's founders, the band Specimen, were surprised (and delighted) by the black-slicked audience which formed a silent, shuffling procession through the winding streets of Soho .

Nik Fiend, later to form his own band, Alien Sex Fiend, but at this time, simply an employee at the club, recalled, "the Batcave was intended to be an alternative to whatever else was happening at the time, an alternative independent. It was the perfect outlet for doing something that made no sense. I was always into Alice Cooper, but I was also into Salvador Dali, so for me it was an opportunity to do something that was visually exciting, to an audience which was equally visually exciting.

"It was this mental idea of loads of people, photographers, clothes designers, musicians, artists, people from all different walks of life all thrown in together, everybody helps everybody through. The people that we knew at the inception of The Batcave really were a diverse group, which is something Mrs. Fiend (Nik's somewhat abruptly named wife) and I often commented upon. But other people, the media, just shut that out because they didn't want to hear it. They wanted goth to be goth. But really, the Batcave was the meeting place for a thousand, million, fragments."

Some of those fragments would be apparent on the first Batcave compilation album, released two years later and featuring contributions from as far afield as Killing Joke bassist Youth's new band Brilliant and industrialists Test Department, alongside the inevitable (but themselves ferociously disparate) Specimen and Alien Sex Fiend.

Other bands, however, were desperately trying to distance themselves from the whole movement. Steve Severin was adamant, "all the time the goth thing was growing up alongside us, we were doing something completely different to what the audience imagined we were doing." But the Banshees were lucky; they were able to keep moving, diversifying, and changing. Bauhaus, however, split, shattered — Peter Murphy mourned, "because the gothic tag was always there, and of course, we eventually found ourselves playing to our reputation. We were just clicking with energy, but when it came down to thinking about what we were doing, we realized that we were pandering to the audience, to what we thought the audience would like." Other groups, too, either sundered or spun away. Joy Division broke up following Ian Curtis' suicide in May 1980, to be reborn as dancefloor terrorists New Order. The Cure chose to deliberately self-destruct (then reform as introspective eccentrics), rather than attempt to follow the consumptive despair of their last album, 1982's *Pornography*. The Cult and Gene Loves Jezebel made fresh starts in America, where both would enjoy decidedly non-gothy hits through the mid-late 1980s. Almost without exception, the bands which epitomized goth by their very disparity, abandoned it once the walls began closing in. But there was still a demand for the music, and in 1983, the Sisters of Mercy stepped into the breach to fill it.

Wayne Hussey — who, with vocalist Andrew Eldritch, was responsible for writing many of the Sisters' most immediately identifiable early anthems before breaking away to form his own band, the Mission — agreed. "The Sisters probably were goth, and The Mission as well. If you looked at us... visually, we weren't a goth band. People took one element of the way I dressed, the way Andrew dressed, or maybe they saw we had an armful of bangles, whatever. And they mixed it all up. But songs like 'Sacrilege' and 'Serpent's Kiss' were pretty incriminating, weren't they?" On a stage choked with dry ice, their music regimented by the relentless heartbeat of a drum machine, and the black and hat-clad Andrew Eldritch's sepulchral intonations rising above the dizzying swirl of the guitars, the Sisters were the final consummation of the gothic musical ethos. "The Sisters represent goth," Cleopatra Records chief Brian Perera marveled, "in the same way as the Rolling Stones represent rock." Peter Murphy agreed. "The Sisters probably were the consummate goth band. The Sisters were formed for goths by goths, and by God, they were goth." But it was Steve Severin who put it best, wrapping up precisely how far the music had traveled from its experimentally artful origins. "There were no bands left doing it, so the kids started doing it themselves. With the Sisters of Mercy, suddenly the audience was onstage itself."

RECOMMENDED LISTENING

SIOUXSIE AND THE BANSHEES Voices (B-side)

BAUHAUS Bela Lugosi's Dead

JOY DIVISION She's Lost Control (LP *Unknown Pleasures*)

THE CURE Faith (LP *Faith*)

ALIEN SEX FIEND Ignore the Machine (45)

SOUTHERN DEATH CULT Moya (B-side)

THE MISSION Wake (RSV) (B-side)

GENE LOVES JEZEBEL Shaving My Neck (EP)

BIRTHDAY PARTY Jennifer's Veil (EP)

SISTERS OF MERCY Colours (LP *Floodland*)

The Industrial Gothic Complex

Few musical terms have ever been so open to interpretation as "industrial music," as Genesis P-Orridge, one of the movement's own progenitors, once explained. "There's an irony in the word 'industrial' because there's the music industry. And then there's the joke [Throbbing Gristle] often used to make in interviews about churning out records like motorcars — that sense of industrial. Up until then, the music had been...based on the blues and slavery, and we thought it was time to update it to at least Victorian times — the Industrial Revolution."

Whatever it meant, however, "industrial music" would become one of the most readily identified, and most misunderstood forms in modern rock history — a sound which could range from the clattering pop of Depeche Mode's "People Are People," to the impenetrable buzz of Premature Ejaculation; from the harsh "aggro" of Ministry, to the dense swamps of Current 93, and on through a sprawling army of electronic and percussive auteurs and mavericks who worked so far left of musical center that even their melodies rejected conventional mores.

It was San Francisco artist Monte Cazazza who coined the phrase, "Industrial music for industrial people," in conversation with Throbbing Gristle, and they who put a sound to his ideas. "When we finished [our] first record," P-Orridge said, "we went outside and we suddenly heard trains going past and little workshops under the railway arches and the lathes going and electric saws and we suddenly thought, 'we haven't actually created anything at all, we've just taken it in subconsciously and re-created it."

The theory behind the music was based around taking risks. "Sometimes," P-Orridge mused, "I think we've given birth to a monster, uncontrollable, thrashing, spewing forth mentions of Auschwitz for no reason. It's funny because when I really think about it, the original half-dozen who started it all off are still the best ones, like [Cabaret Voltaire], Boyd Rice... the first wave. But I suppose that's inevitable, it's the old story, like in the '60s — Zappa was completely different to Beefheart who was completely different to the Doors who were completely different to the Velvet Underground. And we were completely different to the Cabs, and Boyd was totally different and Z'ev is different.

"We've all got a quite clear individual style linked to our individual lives, whereas now [industrial performers] all sound like each other, and more than each other, they sound like weedy fragments that they've honed in on, of one of the other people. The staggering thing [in September 1982], is that 'industrial' has become a word that is used worldwide — there are record sections in shops in Japan that say 'Industrial Music'. Journalists now use 'industrial' as a term like they would 'blues'. It's become part of the vocabulary. And I'm sure most of them have totally forgotten where it came from!"

It was the emergence (and subsequent arrival on British shores) of the German groups DAF, and Einsturzende Neubauten; Australia's S.P.K.; the arrival, too, of Jim Thirlwell's manifold Foetus variations; and Boyd Rice's nihilistic Non persona, which gave an hitherto mutually-exclusive scene its first genuinely fresh impetus, and empowered others to maintain the momentum. All took their impetus not from chords and choruses but from pure sound, with the German contingent adopting the pure sonics of the hammering of the metal worker, the pounding of the construction site, the roaring of engines. The ensuing soundscapes frequently defied even the most liberal interpretation of "music," but would become an integral part of it regardless.

As early as 1982, Germany's Die Krupps took the first steps toward hybridization. Their first single, "Stahlwerksymphony" juxtaposed factory sounds with experimental keyboard melodies, and while the group retained their metal-on-metal percussive edge, still the marriage with synthi-pop melodies was astounding. But it was Depeche Mode who truly grasped the bull by the horns, rewiring a studio Synclavier to regurgitate not the instrument's own pre-programmed sounds and effects, but a string of soundtracks far removed from anything hitherto applied to a "simple" pop record.

Depeche Mode's Martin Gore was one of the witnesses to Einsturzende Neubauten's first ever UK show, a self-explanatory Metal Concerto, staged at London's ICA in early 1983. "The power and excitement of it was brilliant," he enthused afterwards, and already he was contemplating how to use "the ideas in a different context, in the context of pop."

"Every band has to start taking risks to progress, [although] it's pretty much in the lap of the gods whether [anyone] will understand the changes," mused Nitzer Ebb's Bon Harris in 1990. Seven years earlier, Depeche Mode had taken that same belief further than any band in their position had ever journeyed before.

Recording in Berlin, Depeche Mode hauled in sounds from across the spectrum of everyday life — an airline hostess running through the pre-take-off safety drill, a bass drum hit with a piece of metal, an acoustic guitar plucked with a German coin. "We made a conscious decision to become harder musically," Alan Wilder explained. "So we thought, what sounds really hard and nasty? And of course we decided on metal."

The record which introduced this melange to Depeche Mode's public, 1984's "People Are People," would become their first ever US Top 40 hit, made the UK Top 5, and topped the chart in Germany — an irony which was not lost on either the band, or their detractors. *NME* journalist Don Watson called Depeche Mode "a smoothed out SPK," but could not help but admire the "search for diversity" which characterized their *Some Great Reward* album; *Sounds'* Johnny Waller christened them Britain's "most subversive pop group"; and a host of younger musicians received their first lesson in the principles of Industrial from the clanging, clattering cacophony of Depeche Mode's latest single. The band remains the catalyst around which many of the groups from the mid-1980s and beyond were created.

With the spotlight, of course, there came diversification. Industrial's own natural boundaries became increasingly blurred as the 1980s progressed, until even pure ambient, spontaneous, and improvisational music forms were considered as valid a point of reference as any. Both the modern dance and decades-old progressive rock scenes were hijacked as influences, while heavy metal became an inalienable element in the industrial brew as guitars made a loud and shatteringly distorted comeback. The search, after all, was not for "fashionable" music, but for loud and outspoken noise.

"People take the label to describe music," said Throbbing Gristle's Cosey Fanni Tutti. "Industrial for [us] embraced everything we did, every activity. It wasn't just the music, it was a philosophy. It was a seriousness of what life is about. That has nothing to do with what is called industrial now. It was so anti-music to call something industrial." Bandmate Chris Carter was equally disparaging. "Industrial music stopped when Throbbing Gristle and Industrial Records packed up. And there's been nothing truly Industrial since then. There aren't any true Industrial bands."

He was correct, too, at least in the context of industrial as he understood and pioneered it — even those bands which grew out of Throbbing Gristle's primal assault, Carter and Fan Tutti's Chris & Cosey, P-Orridge's Psychic TV and Peter Christopherson's Coil, stretched the boundaries considerably further than their own project would ever have permitted. The early '90s' commercial breakthroughs, in swift succession (Ministry, Nine Inch Nails, Skinny Puppy, and KMFDM) however, told a different story.

Like Depeche Mode, Ministry, Puppy, and NIN all developed out of an earlier fascination with electronic pop. Trent Reznor started his musical life in the early 1980s with the Exotic Birds — Cleveland's biggest techno-dance act. Al Jourgensen's Ministry devised their first dance hits from a musical homebase unabashedly modeled upon Depeche Mode and A Flock of Seagulls. And both Skinny Puppy's

cEVIN Key and Numb's Don Gordon emerged from Vancouver synthipoppers Images in Vogue.

Germany's KMFDM, on the other hand, moved into the frame from the opposite direction, beginning life as another unrepentant cacophony of percussion and drilling (their first ever live show co-starred a battalion of construction workers), but swiftly tangling those roots amid a smorgasbord of similarly noisy, but often quite disparate musical themes — heavy metal, thrash, and sundry dance routines.

Vocalist Sasha Konietzko recalled, "we had used shitloads of guitars since we started in 1984. We did a show with Missing Foundation in Hamburg, where we had five guitars and half the crowd walked out because they couldn't bear them. [But] distorted guitars and layers of guitars are one of the subliminal sounds that really goes straight through the brain to the emotions of people, and I don't exclude myself. If you hear the sound of four guitars just chugging along, it does something. It has an ultra-brutal violence that is a very good basis to start a mixture. And then you add some drums, add some bass stuff...."

Signing to Chicago's Wax Trax label, KMFDM linked with producer Adrian Sherwood in 1988 to cut *Don't Blow Your Top*, a spartan album which, like most of Sherwood's work, highlighted the producer as much as the band. The following year's *UAIOE*, however, was considerably more representative of KMFDM's true motives, all the more so when they followed up with the defining "Virus" and "God-like" singles.

The group were introduced to America by Ministry when the two bands toured together in 1989. Konietzko continued, "Al Jourgensen was doing a lot of promotion before that infamous tour in '89–90, the KMFDM/Ministry tour. People were asking him, 'what is KMFDM, what do we have to expect here?' And he said, 'KMFDM are like a battalion of guitars marching through Europe'." Ministry's own embrace of guitars, the sound of their then fermenting *Psalm 69* album, followed that experience.

"I use more guitars and more guitars because I like guitars," Konietzko explained. "It's actually a nice challenge to have a lot of guitars and really embed them in the music. Just really have them back there driving it without being too prominent." And as for the complaint that sometimes, there were too many guitars, Konietzko was unrepentant. "Kids write us and say, 'take the guitars out, we want pure synth music.' Hey, then go buy Depeche Mode."

KMFDM's revision of what industrial music meant was not necessarily a welcome one. Die Krupps' Jurgen Engler explained, "if you were to ask me five years ago if KMFDM, NIN, or Ministry were industrial, I would have told you no. You know why? Because they don't have any connection with what industrial was about in the early days. It's an

American form of industrial. Here in Europe, it was always experimental music, it wasn't rock music, which is all that is, and even we are now."

"Industrial is evolving," Konietzko countered. "But I don't consider myself industrial. If I was to give myself a label it would be industrial-alternative-electronic-crossover-rock and danceabilly. All the music is coming somewhere, it's not really going anywhere, it doesn't matter where it goes or where it comes from. The only thing is, we should have fun while doing it. And we did. I couldn't give a damn if 10,000 people liked it or 40,000 or one million."

By the early-mid 1990s, such defiance, both musical and verbal, had become the public face of industrial music. Yet, while purists — Metal Men's Eric Muhs among them — continued to believe, "instruments are a crutch for people who can't make noise"; and bands like Sister Machine Gun, Gravity Kills, Stabbing Westward, and Die Warzau brought a melodicism to industrial which lay at ever starker odds to the music's own roots; there lay a middle ground which simply defied categorization, even as the media itself flocked to tuck everything into a single tidy box. The Electric Hellfire Club epitomized that defiance.

Named for the libertine gentleman's club whose rumored degeneracy alternately outraged and titillated 18th century England, the Electric Hellfire Club were formed by former Thrill Kill Kult mainstay Thomas Thorn (aka Buck Ryder) and keyboard player Shane Lassen in early 1991 — against a television backdrop of the first bombing raid of the Gulf War. It was a suitably apocalyptic dawn for a band who would soon bring a whole new definition to such an over-used expression.

Vocalist Thorn explained, "Electric Hellfire Club was part of the 'second generation' of 'industrial bands'... that is to say, we grew up with (or in my case, in) groups like Ministry, Front 242, Thrill Kill Kult, etc. who pioneered the genre. I worked retail promo at the Wax Trax label during 1989–90 when it was all starting to peak, but I got very sick of eating, drinking and sleeping industrial. At the end of the day I was going home and dragging out AC/DC or Judas Priest records. Then, when I grew weary of TKK's disco obsession and decided to go out on my own, the original concept for Hellfire was to combine that sort of heavy metal sensibility with electro-dance elements. I am not sure how successful we were...but whatever we ended up creating was at very least, unique."

Hellfire were unapologetically Satanic. Their live set included everything from Lassen's Halloween horns to Thorn's ritual shredding of a Bible; a philosophy which would place them firmly on the furthest fringes of even rock's self-acclaimed outsiders — as Thorn discovered (to his undying amusement) when Hellfire toured with Danzig.

"That tour was just crazy, because a lot of those places in the Carolinas, people would be going 'yeah, y'all rock, this is real good.' And then at the very end of the set, we'd do the song 'Age of Fire,' which has the 'God is Dead, Satan Lives' thing, and I'd come out in this black pope's outfit and tear up a Bible. Now, these people went insane, throwing beer bottles, spitting, threatening to kill us. Then after the show, some of them would come up and say 'that's not right, you can't tear the Bible up,' and I'd be — 'what are you doing at a Danzig show then?' And these people would go 'Glenn Danzig's not into that devil shit'... so why's he's got all these inverted crosses everywhere? 'Well, he's singing like that to warn people'."

Signing to Cleopatra, Hellfire's first album *Burn Baby Burn*, emerged in 1993, an industrial complex of traumatized techno, bad trip psychedelia, and blistered heavy metal, wrapped up with lyrics which questioned orthodoxy — musical, religious, and cultural — in every guise the band could find it.

"I owe a lot of Hellfire's success to the lessons I learned in TKK," Thorn continued. "Primarily that there are NO rules. Mixing styles and genres was one of the keys to Thrill Kill's success, and that was a consideration in the format of the Hellfire sound. Dance tunes, metal anthems, pop songs...and various combinations thereof. Different elements of our sound appealed to different people.

"You've got to remember that [when we started], there was no Marilyn Manson, so it wasn't like we were going 'oh well....' There was a void, for the people who were into the philosophy from the standpoint of the Black Metal people but who didn't want to listen to music that sounded like a jet engine."

A fascination with at least the mechanics of Satanic ritual was nothing new in rock'n'roll, but even compared to the metal acts which preceded them, Hellfire were different. They really did mean it, even when caricaturing the imagery across a sequence of wryly chosen cover versions. But their takes on Pink Floyd's "Lucifer Sam," the Rolling Stones' "Sympathy for the Devil," AC/DC's "Highway to Hell," Motley Crue's "Shout at the Devil," Bauhaus' "Bela Lugosi's Dead," and the Cure's "Killing An Arab" suggested more than simply the ritualistic appeasement of their audience's demands for more songs about dying and the devil.

It also indicated a healthy understanding of the true visceral appeal of rock'n'roll *regardless* of how the media tries to categorize it. After almost a decade in the Club, Thorn admitted he was "still complimented when someone calls us 'a poor excuse for an industrial band' (usually someone born after 1978), and laugh when we are called a 'goth band.' I smile when the MUSE computer at record chains categorizes us as HARDCORE/PUNK. A local paper recently referred to us as Black Metal. In my opinion, the industry's inability to pigeon-hole us has been part of what has kept us alive and constantly changing."

That inability, of course, was never restricted to Hellfire's observers alone, nor to the relatively tight confines of a putatively industrial audience. Through the mid 1990s, Hellfire did epitomize a breed of band who had taken the public perception of industrial to an entirely new plateau, but by the end of their decade, even their fusion had been superceded (commercially, if not musically) by such trans-genre heavyweights as Type O Negative, Coal Chamber, and, of course, Marilyn Manson.

The marriage of goth and industrial, initiated by Reznor but swiftly consummated by those others, initially had little to do with musical styles — again, it was a philosophical conjoining, embellished by the existence of both musical forms on the edge of convention. Yet it became so deeply rooted that, by the mid-1990s, the general public was no more able to distinguish between gothic and industrial species than between different genus of kangaroo.

For some bands, the cross-fertilization of imagery (if not always purity) offered a welcome adjunct to already flourishing reference points — "there's also a lot to be said," acknowledged Thorn, "for a rock group all dandied-up in psycho-goth-adelia, who are bigger and meaner than any of the shaved-head, stompy-boot aggro industrial boys around."

From their peaks of already lofty ambivalence, self-confessedly serious goths treated such extremes with absolute disdain, regarding Nine Inch Nails' Trent Reznor as little more than a pretentious modernist who wallowed in ugliness, the living corollary to Goth's own (albeit equally stereotyped) ideal of 19th-century Romanticism and beauty.

At the same time, however, a great many people who might never have dreamed of investigating the goth lifestyle were drawn at least into its periphery by Reznor, and in his footsteps, self-styled Antichrist Superstar showman Marilyn Manson. Still, it was inconceivable to even the most morbidly pessimistic observer that it would be this same apparently superficial coterie who would, with the internet a willing partner in their own fantasies, present the gothic-industrial complex with its first taste of widespread media condemnation.

"The beauty of the internet," Christian Death's Rozz Williams mused, "is that it gives everybody a voice. You don't have to shout to be heard. The problem is that it tends only to be the extreme cases who want to be heard in the first place, so you log onto what looks like a gothic site, and you're as likely going to read about mutilation, fetishism, mass murder and Hitler, as you are about vampire novels and the best place to buy little gargoyles. I can imagine a lot of people getting some very strange ideas about it all."

These "strange ideas" were already making their presence felt. In Washington DC in December 1996, a 26-year-old self-styled vampire, Jon C. Bush, was charged with raping and sexually molesting 13 girls, all aged between 13 and 16, under the guise of initiating them into his own "vampire club." In January 1997, 17-year-old Alex Barayni was a member of a gothic role-playing club, the Dark Ballad Gaming Society, when he and a friend butchered a family of four in Bellevue, WA. In March 1998, four so-called teenage vampires in Dallas were charged with desecrating, and then burning a church.

By the time two disaffected teens walked into the cafeteria of their Littleton high school the following April and fired the first shots of a massacre which would leave 12 students, one teacher, and both gunmen dead, the internet contained enough digital DNA to damn an entire generation — one which was as ill-prepared for the beckoning firestorm as the small Colorado town itself.

In the media, on television, and in the newspapers, the public was treated to hastily compiled and generally poorly researched "investigations" into the savage "new" industrial/gothic cult which was poisoning America's children — a confused litany of armageddon prophecy, Race War ritual, and vampiric bloodletting, set to the beat of this ferocious industrial metal holocaust.

KMFDM, whose song lyrics were found all over the gunmen's apocalyptic website, found themselves issuing a public apology for events which they never dreamed were possible. Marilyn Manson, whose scheduled concert in nearby Denver the following week was cancelled within hours of the massacre, then postponed his entire tour rather than face a grieving America with a message which was now so maligned. Stores and record labels devoted to both the music and the culture hurried to distance themselves from the witch hunt, and the handful of courageous voices which were raised in dissent were swiftly drowned beneath the hysterical baying.

Across America, where rapprochement should have followed the grieving, ignorance, prejudice, and hypocrisy flourished instead. Gothic clothing was banned from school campuses across the country, and there were reports of gothic kids and clubs alike being targeted by "concerned" citizens — themselves as full of hate, it seemed, as the boys whose actions they so deplored.

Of course the fuss would die down; if there is one positive thing to be said for tabloid journalism, it is that instant hysteria demands instant gratification, and once that's achieved, the spotlight moves on. But still the scars of those few crazy weeks would linger on, in the distinctly poor performances of new albums by Ministry and Nine Inch Nails later in the year, in the authorities' increased watchfulness for anything resembling "deviant" behavior, and in Marilyn Manson's personal pledge for his own activities in the era to come.

His next album, he swore, would be "the most dark and violent music we've ever done, probably because of the abuse in the media. I thought if I was going to get blamed for something, I'd give them a real reason. This album will make them wish that I was never born."

RECOMMENDED LISTENING

EINSTURZENDE NEUBAUTEN Yu-Gung (LP *Halber Mensch*)

ELECTRIC HELLFIRE CLUB Book of Lies (LP *Calling Dr Luv*)

KMFDM Godlike (LP *Naive*)

MINISTRY New World Order (LP *Psalm 69*)

NINE INCH NAILS March of the Pigs (LP *Downward Spiral*)

NON Medici Mass (LP *Receive the Flame*)

NUMB Cash (LP *Christmeister*)

SKINNY PUPPY Testure (LP *Vivisect VI*)

THROBBING GRISTLE We Hate You (LP *The Best Of... Vol 2*)

YOU'VE GOT FOETUS ON YOUR BREATH Wash It Off (LP *Deaf*)

Sampling

When it first appeared in the early 1980s, many people saw the sampler as just another fancy toy, something which could lift pre-recorded sounds from one source, then transplant them some place else. Of course, it had other applications; transforming sounds, not aping them, or even creating whole new ones. But how such possibilities could be translated into the physical composition of music was another matter entirely.

In the early 1960s, English producer Joe Meek would spend hours isolating individual sounds: the fizzing of a shorted-out electrical cable, the clatter of a fork on a table, the flushing of a lavatory, and then manipulating them electronically to create a new texture. He reveled in the idea of people hearing his latest recordings, and never knowing what they were listening to.

A decade later, following up their multi-million selling *Dark Side of the Moon* album, Pink Floyd attempted recording an entire album without using a single conventional instrument, relying instead on household objects. Again, the idea was to manipulate familiar objects into an unfamiliar context. And a decade after that, Boyd Rice and Frank Tovey did indeed record an entire LP, *Easy Listening for the Hard of Hearing*, through exploring the tonal possibilities of everyday pieces of furniture. (In other words, they banged them a lot.)

Neither they, nor Floyd, nor Meek, however, could ever have envisioned a day when such pioneering was to become common practice; nor one in which the physical task of compiling the sounds into something approaching music could be done at the push of a button. But then, they never had a sampler at their side. "The first polyphonic samplers completely changed pop music," recalled Don Gordon of Canadian industrialists Numb. "For the first time, whole textures, whole things, could exist that never could before. That was the beginning of sampling technology."

The grandfather of samplers was the Fairlight, a device which first came into being in the mid-1970s through the efforts of electronic music enthusiasts and designers Peter Vogel, Tony Furse, and Kim Ryrie, founder of *Electronics Today International* magazine. "We [originally] set out to develop real time pure syntheses technology that allowed us to control every parameter of the sound," Ryrie reflected. "We wanted to digitally create sounds that were very similar to acoustic musical instruments, and that had the same amount of control as a player of an acoustic instrument has over his or her instrument."

That project failed and, at first, the notion of utilizing real life sounds struck the team as somehow cheating. Though it gave them "the complexity of sound that we had failed to create digitally," it did not allow the amount of control which they sought. "We could only control things like attack, sustain, vibrato and decay of a sample and this was a very, very severe limitation of the original goal that we had set ourselves."

Still, they continued to develop the system, wearily acknowledging that it was better than nothing and, by 1979, they were ready to begin marketing it — uncertain whether anybody would even want the thing. The sound quality was poor, the equipment was barely portable and even the lowest frequency samples lasted no more than a couple of seconds. But having packaged it up with a collection of eight-inch 500Kb floppy discs, each one containing 22 stored sounds, the team found widespread excitement for their "orchestra in a box," and widespread condemnation too.

Professional musicians' organizations around the world swiftly realized the precise threat which it implied. An orchestra in a box, indeed — with all the instruments already on disc, who would ever require another "live" musician? Entire bands could be digitally canned and, long before many musicians had even heard of the Fairlight, Britain's Musicians Union were already predicting a day when synthesizers and their ilk would take over from the musician completely. Taking steps to avert it, they distributed free "Keep Music Live" buttons and stickers in a desperate attempt to preserve rock's latest endangered species — the musician who actually knew how to make music.

The first "name" rock performer to investigate the Fairlight's potential was Peter Gabriel — then in the midst of recording his third solo album. Vogel organized a demonstration at the studio where Gabriel and producer Steve Lillywhite were working; Gabriel promptly employed Vogel himself to operate what the ensuing album's liner notes call a "Computer Musical Instrument" (CMI). The Fairlight's future was assured.

With Gabriel himself overseeing the UK importation and distribution of the Fairlight, the instrument exploded into prominence. Former Led Zeppelin bassist John Paul Jones purchased the first one; Kate Bush, the Buggles duo of Trevor Horn and Geoff Downes, Thomas Dolby, Stevie Wonder, Todd Rundgren and Pink Floyd's Rick Wright followed. The Fairlight's designers, however, remained alert to their creation's flaws, even as the world of rock'n'roll flocked to sing its praises, namely that while the machine could make sounds (and store up to 50,000 notes), it could not convey expression.

Some musicians promptly turned that fallibility to their own advantage, just as they always had when faced with an apparent impossibility. Even to practiced users, electronic instruments in general operated with a certain degree of trial and error. Don Gordon continued, "the first samplers... were pretty primitive, it didn't [always] sound like what you programmed. It might have been a piano you were sampling, but when it came back at you it didn't sound like one anymore. So instead of pretending it was going to be a piano, fuck it, make it more of what it isn't."

For some musicians, such distortions often had as much appeal as the original sounds they'd been pursuing — early experimental bands like Portion Control and Nocturnal Emissions filled their recordings with these weird electronic "mistakes," and were to be very influential not only in the budding industrial scene, but across the electronic spectrum. Most musicians, however, still required accuracy in their art and so, in 1982, Fairlight unveiled the CMI Series II, together with a whole new software application, Page R.

The program laid out musical notes as an on-screen graphic, so easily manipulated by the operator that, once an initial sequence of sounds was stored, entire musical sequences could be pieced together with a mere handful of keystrokes. It was a development which so completely changed the face of music-making that even Fairlight's own official history acknowledged, "in an echo of the punk era, Page R... hailed the impending democratization of music creation. [No longer] the exclusive domain of accomplished keyboard players and 'serious' musicians, the Fairlight could now be used by anyone who wanted to make music."

Unfortunately, although it was unquestionably an aid to producing music, the Fairlight also made it very easy to overproduce. Discussing his 1989 album, *Enchanted*, Marc Almond reflected, "recording it was a very cold experience, it was very much a studio album, working with two producers who were into computers and technology. It was very much the way of doing things at that time, it was the way of making a 'modern record.' I wanted to use an Egyptian orchestra, I'm very much into the organic side of things, playing real things and have some kind of adventure. So we did that, then they'd chop it all up and put it in a Fairlight and use a little sample of it. The producers were very much into making a coldly produced record, and it was a very boring experience."

"Computers focus you in on all the wrong things," agreed Siouxsie and the Banshees' Budgie. "You start to worry about minute pitching differences. When the band first started, they never knew about concert pitch... or tuning. No one had a tuner, it was 'okay, that's an E because it's the bottom string.' We recorded *Superstition* with Stephen Hague because it was a perverse idea, he'd worked with New Order, the Pet Shop Boys... we should have been warned. Stephen's

a computer fiend, and when you're working with computers, there's no need to stop. You can constantly readjust, rejig, you can move notes left and right.

"But somehow, computers don't seem to belong in the recording studio and, if they are there, they should be in the back somewhere. They should help you tap your creative energy, not *be* the creative energy. It certainly didn't work with us."

Even the computer's own advocates were aware of the procedure's failings. Speaking for the wealth of more experimentally-minded musicians who valued the bleeps and squawks of the earlier instruments, Depeche Mode vocalist Dave Gahan complained, "I look at a lot of other people that use sampled sounds in disappointment nowadays. They just seem to hire a Fairlight, sample a few orchestral sounds, and that's it. It all seems rather boring."

His own band championed the Synclavier, an instrument which also allowed the manipulation of samples, but took a lot of the ice-cold precision out of their use. Like the Fairlight, the Synclavier was a child of the mid-1970s. It was developed in 1975 at Dartmouth College, New Hampshire, by Sydney Alonso, Cameron Jones, and Jon Appleton, and marketed the following year by the specially-formed New England Digital Corporation.

Since that time, it had become increasingly common in both rock and electronic music, so when Depeche Mode ordered their first one in 1982, recalled producer Daniel Miller "we already knew all about it, and had loads of ideas as to what we could do with it."

One of these ideas involved what Miller described as "the psychological effect of recording sounds in their own acoustical space, and using them" — the clatter of pipes being banged against a fence by the band members, while an irate night watchman yelled for them to stop, for example, created what Alan Wilder described as a very usable "CREESH-OY!". Another very workable tactic, Miller recalled, involved heading down to a disused railroad station and making as much noise as they could. "One day we grabbed a stereo tape recorder and sampled a bunch of things — old metal, bottles breaking, things running into walls — then brought them back to the studio and put them into the Synclavier."

Conventional instruments were used, but they were often hideously distorted. Had Depeche songwriter Martin Gore not appeared on German television with a guitar slung around his neck, few viewers would ever have guessed that the band's latest single, "Love, In Itself," featured samples of that same instrument. Yet it is also indicative of the hostility which sampling was engendering among "traditional" musicians that, when Depeche Mode sampled a shawm (a Chinese oboe) for "Everything Counts," Gore revealed, "people wrote to us to say they felt cheated that we hadn't spent three months learning how to play [it]."

As the 1980s progressed, of course, sampling became such an integral part of modern music that few people even give its use, or implications, a second thought. The dance music scene of the early 1990s was especially heavily influenced by the procedure; indeed, according to Cop International label head Christian Koeppel, "the introduction of the sampler as an instrument, and not just a reproduction tool, was the biggest step of musical evolution of the 90s.

"It spawned a whole new generation of sounds and especially beats — suddenly, people were able to put together very strong rhythmical patterns that would have required shitloads of musicians if you wanted to recreate them acoustically; plus, through sampling, you have the ability to grab whatever sound pleases you, and transform it into your own instrument. That definitely expanded the horizons, and it enabled people to work cross-genre, blending styles in ways that have been unimaginable."

Prodigy dancer Maxim continued, "[by] 1992, in the dance scene, everybody was sampling from everything, going through every record collection they could think of." In England, especially, "the country is so small and contains so many cultures, an individual will take in so many experiences in music, they'll just sample so much in their lifetime."

Neither would increased legislation surrounding the use of samples dampen enthusiasm for the process. Through the late 1980s, an increasing number of new releases lifted ever larger — or at least, more integral — portions of other peoples' recordings for their own, and with that growth came increasing unease regarding both the legal and ethical status of the procedure.

As early as 1986, Sigue Sigue Sputnik were forced to rerecord elements of their debut album for American release, after it was pointed out that nobody had yet cleared any of the samples included — many of the celebrity voices heard on the finished disc were ultimately supplied by mimics.

The following year, Abba were able to suppress the Justified Ancients of Mu's 1987 (What the Fuck's Going On) album, over the unlicensed presence of elements of their "Dancing Queen" hit; and in 1991, Irish singer-songwriter Gilbert O'Sullivan set a landmark precedent when a judge ruled that rapper Biz Markie's unauthorized sampling of the veteran's "Alone Again (Naturally)" constituted nothing short of theft.

Padraic Ogl of gothic kingpins Thanatos, too, was foiled by the need to clear musical samples. Working on the band's *Blisters* album, Ogl and collaborator William Tucker concocted one track "that was all samples from [David Bowie's] *Low*... one of the ambient tracks rearranged via sampling, with vocals and some other sampled stuff." The track was eventually left off the album "because we didn't have time to clear the samples."

The issue of copyright reached its apex, however, in 1997, with the release of the Verve's "Bitter Sweet Symphony." The use of a sample from the Andrew Loog Oldham Orchestra's baroque interpretation of the Rolling Stones' "The Last Time" saw compositional, production, and performance credits taken away from the Verve, and handed to the original recording's creators and publishers. Historically, the Verve will be remembered for releasing one of the late 1990s' most powerful singles. The moment in time which "Bitter Sweet Symphony" defined, however, was not simply an artistic one. It was a legal one too, and one whose true ramifications will unquestionably shape the first years of the 21st century.

"I truly believe that sampling is totally cool as long as you don't 'borrow' whole phrases or hooks," Christian Koeppel continued. "If the most integral part of your music is something you lifted from somebody else, then you need to rethink what you're doing. Either that, or join a covers band." The plethora of tribute groups which emerged through the mid-late 1990s proved he wasn't alone in his thinking either.

But he also cautions, "there is a major difference between sampling other people's music, meaning to isolate an existing sequence and somehow employ it elsewhere, and simply sampling, which means taking individual sounds which might have nothing whatsoever to do with music in the first place, like the sound of raindrops or a car passing by, and turning them into music. And it is important, when people talk about whether sampling has been good or bad for music, that they know which one they mean."

Video: An Eighties Revolution

It was one of the greatest miscasts in the history of rock: a song mourning the murder of one golden age being hijacked to welcome the assassin of another.

Buggles' "Video Killed the Radio Star" (dir. Russell Mulcahy) was never anything but a quirky, sad lament for the death of pop's years of innocence, the years before television swept all before it. On August 1, 1981, however, it was the first video ever screened on the newborn MTV and, if the cable channel's instigators even stopped to contemplate the irony they were party to, they never let it show. Buggles passed into history as co-instigators of a new age in music and television; Music Television simply passed into a new age.

Launched at the now-bargain price of $20 million, the fledgling network's first steps were uncertain. Originally the dream of ex-Monkee Mike Nesmith, but now the brainchild of Robert Pitman, Executive Vice President of the Warner Amex Satellite Entertainment Company (WASEC), MTV took months, sometimes years, to finally break into all of America's key markets, culturally, and commercially. In the station's first 18 months of operation, total advertising revenue was just $7 million.

Neither did the music industry immediately embrace what seemed to many to be a distinctly ill-considered venture. Few bands actively made videos in the very early 1980s, meaning MTV's programming would at best consist of a few dozen oldies, a handful of show reels, and a bunch of nostalgic TV clips if it was lucky.

Yet within three years, *Rolling Stone* was warning its readers that, "video is taking over popular culture," and in August 1984, MTV became a public corporation, boasting ad revenues of $1 million a week and contracts with four record companies for exclusive rights to all their new music videos. In addition, a second MTV channel, VH-1, had been launched in response to rival broadcaster Ted Turner's pledge to inaugurate his own competing 24 hour music channel. Not quite overnight, but certainly faster than anyone expected, MTV completely redefined the concept of music marketing in the US, to the point where to eschew rock's latest medium would be to abandon the fastest and largest promotional tool in the country.

For bands and record companies alike, the changes were brutal. Suddenly, choosing a director was as vital as choosing a producer; selecting a location was on a par with selecting a studio; and the importance of a storyboard, of course, outweighed even the lyrics of the song. In short, the music was no longer the medium, nor even the message. Indeed, in those instances where a band simply acted along with their director's instructions, the music was barely even necessary,

just a pleasant little soundtrack to someone else's whim. A great video could sell a dreadful record. A bad one couldn't have shifted the greatest song on earth. And the handful of entrepreneurs who did foresee that would soon be buried beneath the hundreds who claimed they did.

The first band ever to seriously harness the music video, or film short as it was originally termed, were the Beatles, following their decision to quit touring in 1966. The Rolling Stones and the Kinks had both experimented with the medium prior to that, but with little commercial success — the Stones' "Have You Seen Your Mother, Baby," featured the band in matronly drag and was banned from television at home and abroad; the Kinks' "Dead End Street" starred the band as undertakers and was buried on the grounds of bad taste.

The Beatles, on the other hand, made their films specifically for broadcast, to plug the void their concerts and regular TV appearances once filled, and in summer 1973, preparing for *his* retirement from live performance, David Bowie followed suit, shooting the most notable of his early videos, for the "Life on Mars?" single.

Video remained a substitute for "the real thing" two years later, when Queen unveiled "Bohemian Rhapsody," a six minute mini-epic wrapped around their latest single and shot, the band bashfully confessed, because the song was too complicated to try and perform on television.

In later years, it would become fashionable to describe the admittedly complex and effects-laden "Bohemian Rhapsody" as the founding father of rock video as a serious media — thus ignoring such equally pioneering, but less seen earlier works as Bowie's "John I'm Only Dancing" (1972) and the Rolling Stones' "We Love You" (from 1967, the first genuinely storyboarded promo film). And it is true that for the remainder of the decade, few of the bands that did venture into video territory did so with anything other than a staged performance. Director Julien Temple's clip of the Sex Pistols' "Pretty Vacant" (1977) earned notoriety simply because it marked the band's first appearance on *Top of the Pops*; while both Siouxsie and the Banshees and the Jam, both of whom made regular videos through the late 1970s, confined their theatrical urges to some neat lighting effects.

In 1979, Blondie and director David Mallett shot videos for all twelve tracks on the band's latest album, *Eat to the Beat*, an astonishingly extravagant gesture. But it was David Bowie, with the videos excerpted from his *Lodger* and *Scary Monsters* albums in 1979/80, who restored video as a genuinely creative movement; the Boomtown Rats who consolidated its re-emergence, and Adam and the Ants who truly brought it back to prominence.

Bowie, after all, worked with as much regard for his own artistic mindset as his audience's needs, draping his videos either with heavy symbolism — or at least, something which passed for heavy symbolism. The significance of the bizarrely-costumed Bowie, New Romantic figurehead Steve Strange, and sundry others being pursued down the beach by a bulldozer has never been satisfactorily explained, by either artist or his myriad observers ("Ashes to Ashes," 1980).

The Rats, too, required the viewer to be "in on the joke." Breathtaking though it was, the video for "Someone's Looking at You" played on vocalist Bob Geldof's passing resemblance to the young Mick Jagger by paying tribute to the Stone's first movie role, *Performance*. Coupled with the air of unbridled paranoia permeating the song, it was a stunningly effective piece of work, but a stiflingly elitist one as well.

It was left to Adam Ant, then, to spell out video's true potential, and he did so with a passion. The three singles which most clearly delineate his period of greatest impact were "Stand and Deliver," "Prince Charming," and "Ant Rap." Ant's reference points were distinctly British, purposefully insular (singer Lulu and actress Diana Dors were wholly homebased icons), and unashamedly nostalgic — the dandy highwayman, the handsome prince, and the knight in shining armor were staples of UK pantomime, even if they did translate into other cultures as well.

The end results were so eyecatching, however, that such observations were absolutely worthless. A blur of color, action, and extravagance, Ant's videos were designed to entertain, but they were also designed to sell — not just a single song, but a complete package; of Adam, his Ants, and an entire Insect Nation. Antmusic was a way of life and the videos were the point of entry.

Which was the principle behind MTV.

MTV was, first and foremost, a pure marketing phenomenon. Its founders and the labels who most actively encouraged them (primarily, but not exclusively, those with vested interests in those UK acts), were painfully aware of the shortcomings of American radio at that time — the ever-decreasing volume of new acts being broken countrywide (as opposed to those who simply squeaked through with a single hit); aware, too, of the pitifully tiny number of available television outlets for "new" acts.

Such dedicated outlets as *Midnight Special* (which was, in any case, retiring as of May 1, 1981) and *Solid Gold* notwithstanding, the primary national outlet for anything more challenging than the mainstream was NBC's *Saturday Night Live*, then a precocious five-year-old still on the cusp of cutting edge comedy, and renowned for having music acts to match.

Appearances, however, were deceptive. The *SNL* season which immediately preceded the launch of MTV unveiled just three acts who could even politely be called "new": Prince, whose third album was slowly climbing the chart; Cheap Trick, whose sixth was about to be released; and Joe "King" Carrasco, an Austin Tex-Mex garage act who never got beyond the "promising" status. Punk rock and its polite American cousin new wave had already given rock itself a much needed nudge; now the marketing departments needed a similar one.

According to Duran Duran's John Taylor, "our manager was... certainly the only Englishman that had a dialogue with WASEC before MTV hit the airwaves. I think that the conversations he had, and the kind of videos we delivered, for example 'Save a Prayer' and 'Hungry Like the Wolf' [both dir. Russell Mulcahy] were a direct result of those conversations, the WASEC directors saying, 'Yeah, we're going to do this thing, but quite frankly, all the historical stuff we have is kind of tame, and we don't have anything that's exciting, new.'

"MTV had to be progressive, because nobody wanted to watch Black Sabbath videos all night and there was no video for 'Stairway to Heaven.' If MTV had had its way, they would have simply reflected the most popular radio format, which was rock radio at that time. But they couldn't do that because the videos didn't exist. So they had to take what was offered to them and I think we were the first band to really give them something that was a turn-on for the viewers, because it was colorful, real and fun. Those videos evoked the kind of mood that Pepsi tries to evoke with every commercial they make — youth, vibrancy, energy."

The band were touring the US with Blondie when the musicians themselves encountered MTV for the first time. Nick Rhodes recalled, "we went to the offices in New York, which I remember was just a few rooms — I knew all the members of staff, the people that owned it, everything else, almost on first name terms, there was only like 16 of them. At the time MTV was available in three states, it wasn't even available in Manhattan. It was in New Jersey, Texas somewhere, and some place in Florida and that was it.

"It was a very new idea, but we had our videos, and we thought this was great, because in England you could only get your video played once if you were lucky, that was it. There was no place for them to play. So we started building this relationship with MTV, and obviously it worked... they liked the 'Hungry Like the Wolf' video, and the 'Save a Prayer' video that we shot in Sri Lanka on a shoe string budget — it cost I think 35,000 pounds for three videos. We had these things, and we were very proud of them, and MTV was playing them and getting great reaction in those markets."

One of the first records which MTV could claim to have broken — albeit only within its early, limited catchment areas — was performance artist Laurie Anderson's spectral "O Superman" (dir. Josh White), borne on a video which *Time* magazine, no less, praised as "a satellite transmission from a forbidden planet." Although America would remain one of the few western nations where "O Superman" was not a major commercial hit, still its hypnosis remains one of the early 1980s' most vivid audio-visual memories.

Duran Duran's own video career began slowly. Even the most notorious (and accordingly, seldom seen) of their early singles, summer 1981's "Girls on Film" (dir. Kevin Godley and Lol Creme) offered little more than a passing commentary upon the band, particularly after the musicians themselves were despatched to the sidelines of a screen full of mud-wrestling *Penthouse* pets.

Indeed, through early 1982, A Flock of Seagulls and Haircut 100 both had a more powerful video presence than Duran Duran. From the moment "Hungry Like the Wolf" hit the screens in May 1982, however, Duran Duran became the living embodiment of MTV, the band who, more than any of the myriad others who followed them, epitomized all that MTV represented — an escape from the scripted scriptures of traditional music television; an escape from mundanity and madness; an oasis of calm culture in a string of increasingly exotic locations.

But such accolades do not come free of charge. "I hated doing videos," Andy Taylor revealed later. "John and I used to get drunk and go and hide. Then get sick and get diarrhea. It was like jungle to jungle, I'm riding on elephants and swimming in the water they pissed in, and I got really sick, I got a virus, and had to go to hospital for 4 days once we got back to the UK, that's my memory of making the videos."

John Taylor continued, "the videos were equal parts fun and absolute nightmare. I don't think you ever really know when you're doing something and we never had time to sit back and say, 'hey didn't we do a great job there?' Because we were always onto the next thing. I think we always had a bit of a dismissive attitude towards the videos anyway.

"I got two Grammys for videos [for Best Video Shortform and Best Video Album, 1983], but I don't really count them as Grammys. So when people ask if I've had any Grammys, I'll say, 'yes, but they're for videos.' Not really appreciating what the videos were doing for us, giving us an audience basically, we were like, 'I don't want to talk about fucking videos all time, what about the music, man?'."

The 1983 Grammys were the first to reflect MTV's impact, not only in the videos categories — where fellow British invaders A Flock of Seagulls were among the losing nominees — but also elsewhere across the rock spectrum. Culture Club, Eurythmics, and Men Without Hats, all

MTV-friendly artists, battled it out for Best New Artist; Culture Club again were nominated for Best Pop Performance; and Pat Benatar, one of the first American rockers to appreciate the burgeoning power of video, won Best Female Rock Vocal.

The first acts to follow Duran Duran's lead into truly extravagant videos were, of course, Michael Jackson and David Bowie, both of whom took the medium to new heights with their long-form epics *Thriller* and *Jazzing for Blue Jean*. Close behind them, however, in terms of both extravagance and subsequent impact were Frankie Goes to Hollywood, whose "Relax" video would become one of the most talked about releases of 1984 — and that was without many people actually even seeing the thing.

Passing a storyline dreamed up by band members Holly Johnson and Paul Rutherford onto director Bernard Rose, and then toning down *his* ideas for mass consumption, Frankie set to work on a four minute extravaganza which they intended would represent everything they dreamed that Frankie could be. Everything.

"We wanted it to be really lavish," Rutherford enthused, "a spectacle in itself and not just an advert for the single," Johnson outlined the plot. "The idea is that there's this virginal character, Frankie, and his girlfriend's just left him. He's never had sex and he's walking down the street and gets lured into an orgy scene by this character in black. It's going to be a club scene, the sort of clubs we like going to. It's going to be Emperor Nero in this club, a huge man who gets his whole body shaved for sexual kicks and feeds people to tigers and lions."

The video opened, in fact, with Johnson being drawn through the streets of East London on a rickshaw pulled by ZTT record label head Paul Morley, wearing Mickey Mouse ears. "Frankie has apparently asked to be taken to a nightclub," explained *The Face* magazine. "Anyone daft enough to ask Paul Morley in Mickey Mouse ears to take them to a club of his choosing probably deserves what follows."

What followed, however, would remain a well-guarded secret. Like the infamous "Sex Dwarf" video shot by Soft Cell and director Tim Pope three years earlier (a gore-spattered epic in which singer Marc Almond took a chainsaw to the contents of a slaughterhouse while an array of scantily-clad dancers reveled in the detritus), "Relax" was banned even before it premiered, with ZTT distributors Island Records insisting yet another promo be shot, this time a conventional "in concert" effort.

But like the record it accompanied, the video would become a legend regardless, all the more so when Frankie bounced back with "Two Tribes" (dir. Godley/Creme), an equally depraved fantasy sequence — only this time the protagonists were really at loggerheads. At the height of US

President Reagan's cold war jitters, Frankie pitched a presidential lookalike into a no-holds-barred wrestling bout with his opposite number in the Soviet Union, President Chernenhko.

Ineffectually refereeing the bout from between the colliding bodies, Johnson maintained a running commentary on the battle through the words of the song, adding extracts from the British Government's nuclear precaution guide, the "Protect & Survive" leaflet, to the chaos. Of course, it was greeted with another ban, with only Britain's Channel Four ever screening the full video during the song's own lifetime, tucked away at midnight with a studio discussion of the song's message to demonstrate responsible broadcasting.

The fact these videos could not be seen, in rotation on MTV or simply popping up on network television, of course was self-defeating in some ways — and immensely profitable in others. Home video releases, restricted by considerably less squeamish guidelines than broadcasters, would always provide one lifeline (although "Sex Dwarf" failed to turn up even on Soft Cell's own hits collection). More importantly than that, however, the publicity resulting from a well-documented ban was often equal to the exposure obtained when a video went into full rotation; it, too, created a cachet around the artist and a reputation for subversion which might pack even greater power.

London Suede vocalist Brett Anderson recalled the video shot to accompany his band's 1994 single, "We Are the Pigs" — a *Clockwork Orange*-esque landscape of shadowy arsonists and masked urban warriors. "That video, it's not MTV friendly, it's not anything friendly, it's not *Hammer House of Horror* friendly. I was totally, totally dead set that 'We Are the Pigs' should be the single. All the record company were coming down and saying, 'Please, let's have 'New Generation.' I was saying 'No, this has got to be the single,' and I just went off on this stupid fucking thing. But it's one of the few videos that I actually love, I'd say out of all the videos we'd made to that point, I liked three of them; 'Animal Nitrate,' I like that one, I like 'So Young'. The rest of them veered from embarrassing to barely acceptable."

Anderson was not alone in the condemnation of (much of) what the public is encouraged to see as an extension of his own art — for the simple reason that often, it isn't that at all.

Some artists do hold out for full control of their videos — Björk, for example, is adamant, "maybe it's that very female thing, 'I will kill for my kids, do what the fuck you want with me, but if you touch my kids you're dead.' But that's how I feel about my songs. When I take a song to a video director and tell him, 'okay, the song is about this,' it's like taking your son to the doctor. He takes him away from you and looks after him, and does things to him... what I try

to do with all the people I work with is, make sure they're people who are in tune with what you want. That's the reason I want to work with them in the first place, because they're special."

For many other artists, however, video is something buried away in the fine print of a contract, and it's only when they first come to make one that they discover precisely what all the gobbledegook actually means. "You're given a budget, you're given a director, and you're given the position you've got to stand in." Following a string of well-received indy videos, shot on a shoestring with a hand-held Super 8 camera, Robyn Hitchcock signed with major label A&M in 1988, and suddenly found things were going to be very different indeed from then on. "A&M said 'we'd like you to make videos on 16mm and sync your voice up, and mime to this. But I'd never mimed to anything in my life, mainly because we couldn't afford it. So I turned round and said, 'I don't see why I should' and we had this great long legal wrangle about how many things I had to mime to.

"We made three or four videos for A&M, and it was a bit depressing because they weren't nearly as good as the home-made ones which we made with bits of string ['Raymond Chandler Evening' dir. Tony Moon] and out-of-sync vocals. Basically I felt the more money that went into the video, the less it showed what we were about. I think we got very good stuff on 8mm — it wasn't expensive, but it didn't make us look cheap. I think we looked and sounded cheaper the more money that was spent on us."

Mighty Mighty Bosstones vocalist Dicky Barrett shared his disillusion. "We're at the point now where we make the videos in a day. We don't care about them, we keep our eyes focused on the song. We spent so much time writing songs, we spent so much time getting our live performance the way we like it, and we spend a day making these videos, one day and it's fun. Then you give it to somebody and they put it in a box and they send it over to MTV, and they don't play it."

Again as early as 1984, there were a lot of bands uttering a similar complaint. Urban/black music was absolutely underrepresented on MTV until a posse of artists led by David Bowie coerced the station into revising its original rock-only formula by threatening to withhold their own new releases. (Michael Jackson was the first major beneficiary of the policy change.)

"New" music, too, was becoming increasingly squeezed out as the decade progressed and the rock and metal mainstream embraced the concept of marketing through video. By 1987, the very genre which launched MTV as the upstart in a sea of musical mediocrity was confined to a single one hour slot, anodynely dubbed *The New Video Hour*. There, and only there, the likes of Art of Noise, David Byrne, and Laurie Anderson — acts already marginalized in the American mainstream consciousness — were further ghettoized, despite (or cynically, maybe because) their work frequently validating the very use of video as an adjunct to the music in the first place.

There, too, one might catch a glimpse of the handful of directors whose own innovations would ultimately earn that greatest of video compliments, and be reduced to an overused cliche. Polish director Zbigniew Rybczynski (Art of Noise's "Close to the Edit," Grandmaster Flash's "Sign of the Times," Simple Minds' "All the Things She Said"), Rudi Dolezal and Hannes Rossacher (Falco's "Rock Me Amadeus") and Stephen R. Johnson (Talking Heads' "Road to Nowhere," Peter Gabriel's "Sledgehammer") all spent the mid-1980s working within the precepts of *The New Video Hour*.

The void laid bare by the mainstream's co-opting of "popular" video, and the continued ghettoization of MTV's own programming schedules, was best illustrated by British director Tim Pope. Pope himself was no stranger to MTV audiences — his eye for color and movement was one of the key elements in the success of both Men Without Hats' 1983 #3 "The Safety Dance" and, deeper into the decade, Talk Talk's "It's My Life."

It was his videos with the Cure, however, which set the highest standards, not only for their own individual quality, nor because — like those early Adam Ant creations — they first created, then sustained, an instantly identifiable image around the band. Rather, it was because within that attendant image, there was infinitesimal room for maneuver. Once one had seen ZZ Top's sunglasses, beards, and custom car a few times, there was little else to add to them. Similarly, Billy Idol's pouting leather Boy Elvis; Cyndi Lauper's teenaged tantrum; and David Lee Roth's lovable arch buffoon were readily identifiable, but restrictively one dimensional.

The Cure, however, shifted with the wind; clowning with love cats at one shoot, crawling with caterpillars in another, and locked in a wardrobe as it fell over a cliff in a third. By the time of the band's MTV breakthrough in 1987, the station's programmers had five full years of increasingly bizarre antics to air to a now breathless audience.

Duran Duran's Nick Rhodes once remarked, "when we came out, videos were new, it was a blank canvas, and we could paint whatever we wanted on it." Cure vocalist Robert Smith agreed with him. "Our early videos are very much what people expected the Cure to be like, 'A Forest' [dir. Dave Hillier] and all that. The advantage we had when we first started doing things with Tim Pope was that no one had really done that much, and in the world of video, anything you thought of was new." By 1994, when the partnership was finally sundered, that was no longer true, but in the meantime, the two parties were responsible for some genuinely innovative work — even if, occasionally, things did not go exactly as planned.

In 1985, "In Between Days" was announced with a video depicting the band being assailed by an array of grotesquely colored socks. Smith explained, "I [told] Tim that we'd like flashes of color going when I was singing, and he said, 'what, color like my socks? And I said 'yeah.' And that obviously stuck in his mind because socks are cheap and easy to come by. He tells us that he told the animators to use fluorescent socks in the color scheme and they took him at this word. And they spent thousands of pounds drawing all those socks, frame by frame. Bloody mental! 8,000 pounds — it's outrageous."

Two years later, for "Why Can't I Be You," Pope himself was celebrating an unearthly coup — "this is it! The video I've always wanted to make! The Cure DANCING! I can't believe I'm seeing this! They're FINISHED!". In fact, they were just beginning; with *The New Video Hour* behind it, "In Between Days" had debuted the Cure into the *Billboard* Top 100 (at #99); now, "Why Can't I Be You" spun to #54.

Months later, "Just Like Heaven" would break the band in the Top 40, and when 1989 brought "Love Song" — it didn't matter (though bassist Simon Gallup liked to mutter otherwise) that Pope spent two days making the stalactites which surround the seated, singing Smith. "It was #2 in America," said Smith, "and the video made me look glamorous, and it's the only one ever to do that. And it made the song."

Such triumphs of the video-maker's art were never, however, a goal which MTV or any other tele-video medium (NBC's *Friday Night Videos*, ABC's *Hot Tracks*, HBO's *Video Jukebox*, Britain's *The Chart Show* and *Max Headroom*) ever felt obliged to pursue. Indeed, they were the exception, and would remain so for as long as mediocrity (or at least, a suitably low common denominator) continued to pull in the advertising revenue.

When an artist the caliber of Kate Bush, for example, could not be guaranteed regular airtime for her work (thus condemning her masterful "Cloudbursting" epic to the retail and rental domains alone, and making an absolute mockery of the "Greatest Ever..." countdowns which periodically occupy program makers), what hope did anyone have whose dreams encompassed challenging tastes as well as technique?

"I'm pushing for MTV to get off their ass," Perry Farrell announced as he and partner Casey Niccoli prepared to shoot Jane's Addiction's first video in 1988. "Videos have become formulated, and I'm not one to conform because I really don't see that as an end, I see that as a beginning, because there's just so much more you can do." Excerpted from a 24 minute mini-movie, *Soul Kiss*, "Mountain Song" debuted the band in the MTV viewing room — and was promptly declined, the moment the first exposed female nipple hove into view.

Farrell was unrepentant. The nudity was included "because [it is] part of the expression. You might not like it and it might not be worth a shit, but that's what I foresaw for the video." MTV could screen it "with all the bits," he said, or they could "get out of my face... and it'll be seen in the clubs where the kids go." MTV got out of his face.

That there was an alternative venue for videos — one which "the kids" took more seriously than the moving wallpaper of television — was a heresy which few industry mavens took an enlightened view of. Surprisingly, then, MTV had already predicted, if not quite pre-empted, such a development with the creation of the wholly genre-specific programming which would dominate the station's output through the late 1980s and into the 1990s — *Yo! MTV Raps* for the rap fans, *Headbangers Ball* for the metal crowd, and succeeding the new video hour, *120 Minutes* for the alternative crew.

All had their audiences, all — in many parts of the country — were the best those audiences could hope for. But attempts to broaden those programs' bases even further were invariably doomed to failure.

Englishman Dave Kendall first presented *120 Minutes* during summer 1989, while regular host Kevin Seale was away on assignment. By 1993, through the mainstream mushrooming of alternative rock, however, Kendall was so firmly entrenched in the show's hotseat that for many people, he *was* alternative rock... or at least, its media face. Even more unusually, he was also one of the best people for such a job — although few people realized that until he was peremptorily replaced during a 1993 shuffle of staff and VJs.

"I parted company with MTV partly because I was just haranguing them more than they liked about making the show musically stronger. I went out of my way to get videos like the Justified Ancients of Mu and Alien Sex Fiend on and they were refused. Sometimes I was successful — Sister Machine Gun and Murder Inc would never have got on if I hadn't pushed. But in the end... I wasn't prepared to see [the concept] diluted, watered down and frittered away."

In the early days of the show, he continued, "a lot of the videos were shot with grainy images, because bands had no money to do otherwise" — a style pioneered, ironically, by Queen/Mellencamp director Bruce Gowers. "Suddenly that became really hip, [and] you got $100,000 [videos] looking like they cost $5,000" — which of course squeezed out the ones that genuinely were shot on a shoestring.

The snow/skateboarding fraternity understood this when product and exhibition videos began applying punk and ska soundtracks to their action-packed footage. Though they were frequently done without any input from the bands themselves, unquestionably such offerings helped raise the bands' own profile among a seriously committed, and well-targeted audience. In 1989, a full five years before their *Smash* album rendered them post-modern superstars, the inclusion of the Offspring's "A Thousand Days" in one such film was responsible for a massive upswing in that band's fortunes, and journalist Jo-Ann Greene explained, "I think all the '90s punk bands give some credit to the board videos for their breakthroughs, because even if you never got to actually see the band in the film, you still heard their music — and on MTV you got neither. Those videos were a major introduction into the mass market at a time when neither TV nor radio would give punk and ska the time of day."

Beyond the punk circuit, video and computer games became another key arena, particularly for techno and electronic acts. It was no coincidence whatsoever that many of the videos featured on MTV's late night *Amp*, dedicated to the electro boom, utilized imagery and graphic techniques pioneered within and familiar from another discipline entirely. Indeed, as marketing has grown increasingly sophisticated, the humble rock video is even beginning to get left behind as bands and record companies discover ever more inventive ways of getting a song across to the public, without going to the expense of making a video which may or may not even make it into rotation.

Movie soundtrack tie-ins, sports and wrestling, and the internet have all made inroads into what had hitherto been the exclusive preserve of the rock video, not only offering invaluable exposure to an audience measured in millions, but often allowing specific demographics to be targeted with military precision. Not only that, but such avenues often also operate with far fewer moral strictures than a conventional broadcaster, granting both visual and lyrical freedom to artists.

Such practices have dribbled into mainstream videomaking. Like Perry Farrell and "Mountain Song," London Suede's "We Are the Pigs" remains an extreme example of an accepted act purposefully making an unacceptable video.

Other acts, however, have exercised the same notions, not for the sake of outrage alone, but also to prove artistic points of their own. Radiohead's 1995 video for "High and Dry," for instance, was shot by the then, completely untried Brock Cunningham, and guitarist Jonny Greenwood admitted that the band were going out on a limb when they commissioned it.

"We got all these scripts and ideas from these newer directors and took them to the record company and said, 'wanna do this?, wanna do that?' and they said, 'No, no you can't do that.' So in the end, we just did it. We kind of kept sticking our neck out and we were lucky. It worked. All bands were complaining about doing videos and consequently everyone was doing really bad videos. We decided to start enjoying them instead and trying to do them well."

REM, too, took to video-making with dramatic zeal, and this despite spending much of the 1980s positively rebelling against the genre. Vocalist Michael Stipe reflected, "we were making these videos, paying a lot of money to have them made, and they were not being played anywhere. It was dumb. The 'anti' attitude was not flying." By the end of the decade, he was the only one in the band who could even tolerate videos, a position which was validated when he realized, around the same time, that "videos are, I think, a great way to get my ideas across."

Stipe was rewarded, as it were, with three entries in *Rolling Stone*'s "100 Best Rock Videos of All Time" (#3: "Losing My Religion" [dir. Tarsem], #41: "Man on the Moon" [dir. Peter Care], #93 "Orange Crush" [dir. Matt Mahurin]); and if plaudits such as these remain the final criteria of a video's worth and impact, then it is the success of bands like REM, the Cure, Radiohead, and U2 — so perfectly captured by directors of the caliber of Wim Wenders, Kevin Godley and Anton Corbijn — who justify the less profiled efforts of the myriad artists who never find themselves on MTV and VH-1. Yet who, in turn, nevertheless validate the very existence of such channels as anything beyond a simple marketing tool.

And that validation dates back to the modern medium's own earliest days, when rock video was young, MTV was younger, and Duran Duran ruled the airwaves.

"Without MTV," mused Nick Rhodes, "it possibly would have taken us a little longer at radio. Where would MTV be without us? Somebody else would've been there, is the simple answer, but I think we did make the channel much more interesting, and I think that helped make other videos more interesting. Before us, all the other videos were just people playing in front of a video camera."

RECOMMENDED VIEWING

BJÖRK Human Behavior (dir. Michel Gondry)

BOOMTOWN RATS Someone's Looking at You (dir. David Mallet)

KATE BUSH "Cloudbursting" (dir. KB/David Garfath/Julian Doyle)

DAFT PUNK "Da Funk" (dir. Spike Jonze)

DURAN DURAN "Wild Boys" (dir. Russell Mulcahy)

LONDON SUEDE "We Are the Pigs" (dir. Howard Greenhalgh)

PULP This is Hardcore (dir. Doug Nichol)

REM "Losing My Religion" (dir. Tarsem)

TIM POPE "I Want to Be a Tree" (dir. Tim Pope)

WHITE TOWN "Your Woman" (dir. Mark Adcock)

KEY ALTERNATIVE VIDEO DIRECTORS 1977–99

[Videographies are generally complete within the scope of this book.]

MATTHEW AMOS

1990	Right Here, Right Now — JESUS JONES
1991	There's No Other Way (version 2) — BLUR
1992	Connected — STEREO MC's
1993	Step It Up — STEREO MC'S
1993	The Drowners — SUEDE
1994	Hypocrite — LUSH
1994	Jailbird — PRIMAL SCREAM

PAUL ANDRESEN

1992	Insane Clown Posse — INSANE CLOWN POSSE
1993	Savory — JAWBOX
1993	Carwash Hair (co-dir. George Dougherty) — MERCURY REV
1994	Something for Joey — MERCURY REV
1994	Cooling Card — JAWBOX
1994	Destroy Before Reading (co-dir. David Landis) — JESUS LIZARD
1994	Pop Heiress Dies — CHAINSAW KITTENS
1996	Super-fire (co-dir. Nancy Bardawil) — GIRLS AGAINST BOYS
1997	Volcano Girls (co-dir. Nancy Bardawil) — VERUCA SALT
1997	S.O.S. — THE SUICIDE MACHINES
1997	Long Long Time — LOVE SPIT LOVE
1999	Denial — SEVENDUST

CHRIS APPLEBAUM

1994	Songs About Girls — CATHERINE
1994	Can't Put My Finger on It — WEEN
1995	Now They'll Sleep — BELLY
1995	Good — BETTER THAN EZRA
1995	Hell of a Hat — THE MIGHTY MIGHTY BOSSTONES
1996	A Common Disaster — COWBOY JUNKIES
1996	Counting Blue Cars — DISHWALLA
1996	Destination Ursa Major — SUPERDRAG
1997	The Impression That I Get — THE MIGHTY MIGHTY BOSS-TONES
1997	Sink to the Bottom — FOUNTAINS OF WAYNE
1997	Under Your Skin — LUSCIOUS JACKSON
1997	Royal Oil — THE MIGHTY MIGHTY BOSSTONES
1998	Closing Time — SEMISONIC
1998	Singing in My Sleep — SEMISONIC
1998	Hooch (v2: Bank Robbery) — EVERYTHING
1999	Circles — SOUL COUGHING

TIM ARMSTRONG

1994 Nihilism — RANCID

1994 Salvation (co-dir. Mark Kohr) — RANCID

1995 Ruby Soho (co-dir. Jim Guerinot) — RANCID

VAUGHAN (ARNELL) & ANTHEA (BENTON)

1986 Brand New Lover — DEAD OR ALIVE

1988 Wishing Well (v2) — TERENCE TRENT D'ARBY

1993 Blow Your Mind — JAMIROQUAI

1995 Space Cowboys — JAMIROQUAI

VAUGHAN ARNELL

1997 Alright — JAMIROQUAI

1997 Angels (v1) — ROBBIE WILLIAMS

1998 Let Me Entertain You — ROBBIE WILLIAMS

1998 Millennium (v1) — ROBBIE WILLIAMS

MARTIN ATKINS

1987 Strangelove (v2)— DEPECHE MODE

1987 Little Fifteen — DEPECHE MODE

1989 Nightmares — VIOLENT FEMMES

1989 You Happy Puppet — 10,000 MANIACS

1990 Groovy Train — THE FARM

1991 Get the Message — ELECTRONIC

1992 The Rising Sun — THE FARM

1992 Heavy Liquid — THEE HYPNOTICS

1994 Messiah — THE FARM

1995 The Only One — GOO GOO DOLLS

MEIERT AVIS

1980 I Will Follow (v1) — U2

1981 Gloria — U2

1982 A Celebration — U2

1982 New Year's Day — U2

1983 Two Hearts Beat As One — U2

1985 The Unforgettable Fire — U2

1985 King for a Day — THOMPSON TWINS

1985 Revolution — THOMPSON TWINS

1985 In a Lifetime (co-dir. Bono/Edge) — BONO & CLANNAD

1987 With or Without You (v1) — U2

1987 Where the Streets Have No Name — U2

1989 All I Want Is You — U2

1989 This Side of Love — TERENCE TRENT D'ARBY

1990 To Know Someone Deeply Is to Know — TERENCE TRENT D'ARBY

1990 Billy, Don't Fall in Love with Me — TERENCE TRENT D'ARBY

1991 Til She Comes — PSYCHEDELIC FURS

1993 Without a Trace — SOUL ASYLUM

1994 Touch Me Fall — INDIGO GIRLS

LANCE BANGS

1995 The Diamond Sea (co-dir. Spike Jonze/Dave Markey/Steve Paine/Angus Wall) — SONIC YOUTH

1996 How the West Was Won — REM

1997 Busy Child (v1) — THE CRYSTAL METHOD

1999 Dirty Dream Number Two — BELLE & SEBASTIAN

1999 Spit on a Stranger — PAVEMENT

1999 Last Ride In — GREEN DAY

NANCY BARDAWIL

1996 Super-fire (co-dir. Paul Andresen) — GIRLS AGAINST BOYS

1997 Volcano Girls (co-dir. Paul Andresen) — VERUCA SALT

1997 Shutterbug — VERUCA SALT

1997 More Than This — 10,000 MANIACS

1998 Iris — GOO GOO DOLLS

1998 Celebrity Skin — HOLE

1998 Slide — GOO GOO DOLLS

1999 Dizzy — GOO GOO DOLLS

1999 Black Balloon — GOO GOO DOLLS

STEVE BARRON

1980 Dog Eat Dog (live) — ADAM AND THE ANTS

1981 Love Action (I Believe in Love) — HUMAN LEAGUE

1981 Penthouse and Pavement — HEAVEN 17

1981 Don't You Want Me? — THE HUMAN LEAGUE

1982 Antmusic (co-dir. Daniel Kleinman) — ADAM AND THE ANTS

1982 It Ain't What You Do... (it's the Way That You Do It) — FUN BOY THREE

1982 Real Men — JOE JACKSON

1982 Let Me Go — HEAVEN 17

1982 Steppin' Out — JOE JACKSON

1983 Mad World — TEARS FOR FEARS

1983 Breaking Us in Two — JOE JACKSON

1983 (Keep Feeling) Fascination — THE HUMAN LEAGUE

1983 Pale Shelter — TEARS FOR FEARS

1984 It's a Miracle — CULTURE CLUB

1984 Louise — THE HUMAN LEAGUE

1984 Electric Dreams — PHIL OAKEY/GIORGIO MORODER

1985 Take on Me (v2) — A-HA

1985 The Sun Always Shines on TV — A-HA

1986 Train of Thought — A-HA

1986 Hunting High and Low — A-HA

1986 Cry Wolf — A-HA

1987 Manhattan Skyline — A-HA

1991 Crying in the Rain — A-HA

SAMUEL BAYER

1991 Smells Like Teen Spirit — NIRVANA

1992 Tones of Home (v1) — BLIND MELON

1993 No Rain — BLIND MELON

1994 Elemental — TEARS FOR FEARS

1994 Change (v1) — BLIND MELON

1994 Albatross — CORROSION OF CONFORMITY (COC)

1994 Unyielding Conviction — FISHBONE

1994 Zombie — THE CRANBERRIES

1994 Doll Parts — HOLE

1995 Ode to My Family — THE CRANBERRIES

1995 Star — THE CULT

1995 I Saw the Light — THE THE

1995 I Can't Be with You — THE CRANBERRIES

1995 Ridiculous Thoughts [as Freckles Flynn] — THE CRANBERRIES

1995 Vow — GARBAGE

1995 The Break — URGE OVERKILL

1995 Bullet with Butterfly Wings — THE SMASHING PUMPKINS

1995 Gotta Get Away — THE OFFSPRING

1996 Honky's Ladder — AFGHAN WHIGS

1996 Only Happy When It Rains — GARBAGE

1996 Stupid Girl — GARBAGE

1999 Ends — EVERLAST

1999 Coma White — MARILYN MANSON

1999 Angels (v3) — ROBBIE WILLIAMS

EVAN BERNARD

1995 Root Down (v1) — THE BEASTIE BOYS

1995 Flavor — THE JON SPENCER BLUES EXPLOSION & BECK

1995 Uninvited — RUTH RUTH

1996 Kinda Love — THE JON SPENCER BLUES EXPLOSION

1997 The Outdoor Type — THE LEMONHEADS

1997 Blister in the Sun — VIOLENT FEMMES

1997 The Harder They Come — RANCID

1997 Tell It to the Kids — BIS

1998 You Get What You Give — NEW RADICALS

1999 Nice Guys Finish Last — GREEN DAY

1999 Army — BEN FOLDS FIVE

1999 Rendez-vu — BASEMENT JAXX

ADAM BERNSTEIN

1986 Put Your Hand Inside the Puppet Head — THEY MIGHT BE GIANTS

1986 Don't Let's Start — THEY MIGHT BE GIANTS

1986 (She Was A) Hotel Detective — THEY MIGHT BE GIANTS

1988 Punk Rock Girl — THE DEAD MILKMEN

1989 Hey Ladies — THE BEASTIE BOYS

1989 Ana — THEY MIGHT BE GIANTS

1989 They'll Need a Crane — THEY MIGHT BE GIANTS

1989 Love Shack — THE B-52'S

1989 Roam — THE B-52'S

1990 Birdhouse in Your Soul — THEY MIGHT BE GIANTS

1991 American Music — VIOLENT FEMMES

1992 The Statue Got Me High — THEY MIGHT BE GIANTS

1993 Push the Little Daisies — WEEN

1993 Hang on to Your Ego — FRANK BLACK

1993 Saturday Night — NED'S ATOMIC DUSTBIN

1994 Headache — FRANK BLACK

1994 Peter Bazooka — THE DEAD MILKMEN

NICO BEYER

1993 Evangeline — COCTEAU TWINS

1994 Snail Shell — THEY MIGHT BE GIANTS

1995 This Is Music — THE VERVE

1995 Destination Eschaton — THE SHAMEN

BIG TV (AKA ANDY DELANEY & MONTY WHITEBLOOM)

1988 Love Truth & Honesty — BANANARAMA

1990 We Love You — RYUICHI SAKAMOTO

1990 Violence of Summer — DURAN DURAN

1990 Serious — DURAN DURAN

1991 Crazy — SEAL

1992 These Are the Days — 10,000 MANIACS

1993 Sweet Harmony — THE BELOVED

1993 Do You Love Me Like You Say ? — TERENCE TRENT D'ARBY

1994 Famine — SINEAD O'CONNOR

1994 Speed — BILLY IDOL

1996 Wrong — EVERYTHING BUT THE GIRL

GAVIN BOWDEN

1995 Warped — RED HOT CHILI PEPPERS

1995 Piranha — TRIPPING DAISY

1996 Aeroplane — RED HOT CHILI PEPPERS

1996 Pepper — THE BUTTHOLE SURFERS

1996 Coffee Shop — RED HOT CHILI PEPPERS

1996 On a Rope — ROCKET FROM THE CRYPT

1996 Charlie Brown's Parents — DISHWALLA

1996 Failure — ORANGE 9MM

1996 Scooby Snacks (v2) — FUN LOVIN' CRIMINALS

1997 Medicine — ORBIT

1997 The End of Something — ROLLINS BAND

1998 No Shelter — RAGE AGAINST THE MACHINE

1999 Leech — EVE 6

1999 Anthem for the Year 2000 — SILVERCHAIR

JAMES BROWN

1997 Ain't Talkin' 'bout Dub — APOLLO FOUR FORTY

1997 Raw Power — APOLLO FOUR FORTY

1998 Not Alone — BERNARD BUTLER

DEREK BURBIDGE

1978 Roxanne (v1) — THE POLICE

1978 So Lonely — THE POLICE

1979 Can't Stand Losing You (v2) — THE POLICE

1979 Message in a Bottle — THE POLICE

1979 Walking on the Moon — THE POLICE

1980 Cars — GARY NUMAN

1980 Don't Stand So Close to Me (v1) — THE POLICE
1980 De Do Do Do, De Da Da Da — THE POLICE
1981 Our Lips Are Sealed — THE GO-GO'S
1981 Invisible Sun — THE POLICE
1981 Every Little Thing She Does Is Magic — THE POLICE
1981 Spirits in the Material World — THE POLICE

BILL BUTT
1991 Only Love Can Break Your Heart — ST. ETIENNE

CARINA CAMAMILE
1984 I Want to Be a Cowboy — BOYS DON'T CRY

DONALD CAMMELL
1984 Pride (first Version) — U2

PETER CARE
1983 Resistance (co-dir. Peter Anderson) — CLOCK DVA
1984 Hypnotize — SCRITTI POLITTI
1985 Shake the Disease — DEPECHE MODE
1985 Vanity Kills (v2) — ABC
1985 It's Called a Heart — DEPECHE MODE
1986 Stripped — DEPECHE MODE
1986 Venus — BANANARAMA
1986 Final Solution — PETER MURPHY
1986 More Than Physical — BANANARAMA
1991 Radio Song — REM
1992 Drive — REM
1992 Man on the Moon — REM
1993 The Sidewinder Sleeps Tonite — REM
1993 Regret — NEW ORDER
1994 Say Something (v2) — JAMES
1994 What's the Frequency, Kenneth? — REM
1997 Electrolite (co-dir. Spike Jonze) — REM

GERALD V. CASALE
1980 Whip It — DEVO
1980 Touch and Go — THE CARS
1980 Panorama — THE CARS
1981 Beautiful World — DEVO
1995 I'll Stick Around — FOO FIGHTERS

PETER CHRISTOPHERSON
1986 Heartland — THE THE
1986 Infected — THE THE
1987 The Mercy Beat — THE THE
1988 Chains of Love — ERASURE
1988 A Little Respect — ERASURE
1989 Stop! — ERASURE
1990 Waifs and Strays — MARC ALMOND
1991 Say Hello, Wave Goodbye '91 — MARC ALMOND

1991 Tainted Love '91 — MARC ALMOND
1992 Pinion (v1) — NINE INCH NAILS
1992 Wish (v1) — NINE INCH NAILS
1992 Help Me I Am in Hell (v1) — NINE INCH NAILS
1992 King of Trash — GAVIN FRIDAY
1992 Gave Up (v1) — NINE INCH NAILS
1992 Rhythm of Time — FRONT 242
1992 New World Order (N. W. O.) — MINISTRY
1992 Falling Off the Edge of the World — GAVIN FRIDAY
1993 Just One Fix — MINISTRY
1993 Freedom — RAGE AGAINST THE MACHINE
1993 Bombtrack — RAGE AGAINST THE MACHINE
1994 March of the Pigs (v1) — NINE INCH NAILS
1994 March of the Pigs [live] — NINE INCH NAILS
1994 The Sun Does Rise — JAH WOBBLE'S INVADERS OF THE HEART FEATURING DOLORES O'RIORDAN
1994 Lies — STABBING WESTWARD
1994 Becoming More Like God — JAH WOBBLE
1995 Stories (v1) — THERAPY?
1995 Age of Panic — SENSER
1996 Bulls on Parade — RAGE AGAINST THE MACHINE
1996 People of the Sun — RAGE AGAINST THE MACHINE
1997 One Angry Dwarf and 200 Solemn Faces — BEN FOLDS FIVE
1998 Comin' Back — THE CRYSTAL METHOD
1999 Keep Away — GODSMACK
1999 Welcome to the Fold — FILTER
1999 It's Saturday — MARCY PLAYGROUND

JEM COHEN
Talk About the Passion — REM

ROMAN COPPOLA
1994 Deep Sleep Motel — NANCY BOY
1994 Voodoo Lady — WEEN
1995 Walking Contradiction — GREEN DAY
1995 Lump (v1/2) — THE PRESIDENTS OF THE UNITED STATES OF AMERICA
1995 Sick of Myself — MATTHEW SWEET
1995 Piss Bottle Man — MIKE WATT & EVAN DANDO
1995 We're the Same — MATTHEW SWEET
1996 Peaches — THE PRESIDENTS OF THE UNITED STATES OF AMERICA
1996 Waiting (v1/2) — THE RENTALS
1996 Mach 5 — THE PRESIDENTS OF THE UNITED STATES OF AMERICA
1998 Revolution 909 — DAFT PUNK
1998 Honey — MOBY
1998 Gangster Tripping — FATBOY SLIM
1999 Praise You (co-dir. Spike Jonze) — FATBOY SLIM

ANTON CORBIJN
1983 Hockey — PALAIS SCHAUMBURG

1984 Beat Box — THE ART OF NOISE
1984 Dr. Mabuse — PROPAGANDA
1984 Seven Seas — ECHO AND THE BUNNYMEN
1984 Red Guitar — DAVID SYLVIAN
1984 Pride (v3) — U2
1984 The Ink in the Well — DAVID SYLVIAN
1985 Bring on the Dancing Horses — ECHO AND THE BUNNYMEN
1986 A Question of Time — DEPECHE MODE
1987 The Game — ECHO AND THE BUNNYMEN
1987 Strangelove (v1) — DEPECHE MODE
1987 Lips Like Sugar — ECHO AND THE BUNNYMEN
1987 Never Let Me Down Again — DEPECHE MODE
1987 Bedbugs and Ballyhoo — ECHO AND THE BUNNYMEN
1988 Behind the Wheel — DEPECHE MODE
1988 Atmosphere — JOY DIVISION
1988 Headhunter — FRONT 242
1989 Faith and Healing — IAN MCCULLOCH
1989 Personal Jesus — DEPECHE MODE
1990 Enjoy the Silence — DEPECHE MODE
1990 Killer Wolf — DANZIG
1990 Policy of Truth — DEPECHE MODE
1990 World in My Eyes — DEPECHE MODE
1991 Tragedy (for You) — FRONT 242
1991 Halo — DEPECHE MODE
1991 Lover Lover Lover — IAN MCCULLOCH
1992 One (v1) — U2
1992 Straight to You — NICK CAVE AND THE BAD SEEDS
1992 Dirty Black Summer — DANZIG
1993 I Feel You — DEPECHE MODE
1993 Heart Shaped Box — NIRVANA
1993 Walking in My Shoes — DEPECHE MODE
1993 Condemnation — DEPECHE MODE
1994 In Your Room — DEPECHE MODE
1994 Liar — ROLLINS BAND
1994 Mockingbirds — GRANT LEE BUFFALO
1994 One Caress — DEPECHE MODE
1995 My Friends — RED HOT CHILI PEPPERS
1997 Barrel of a Gun — DEPECHE MODE
1997 It's No Good — DEPECHE MODE
1997 Useless — DEPECHE MODE
1997 Please (v1) — U2
1999 Goddess on a Hiway — MERCURY REV
1999 Opus 40 (v1) — MERCURY REV

CHRIS CUNNINGHAM
1995 Light Aircraft on Fire — THE AUTEURS
1995 Second Bad Vilbel — AUTECHRE
1996 Back with the Killer Again — THE AUTEURS
1996 36 Degrees — PLACEBO
1997 The Next Big Thing — JESUS JONES
1997 Fighting Fit — GENE

1997 No More Talk — DUBSTAR
1997 Come to Daddy — APHEX TWIN
1998 Only You — PORTISHEAD
1999 All Is Full of Love — BJÖRK
1999 Window Licker — APHEX TWIN
1999 Afrika Shox — LEFTFIELD AND AFRIKA BOMBAATAA

GREGORY DARK
1997 Wrong Way (co-dir. Josh Fischel) — SUBLIME
1997 Doin' Time (co-dir. Josh Fischel) — SUBLIME
1999 Blue Monday — ORGY
1999 Hero — The Verve Pipe

TAMRA DAVIS
1989 Netty's Girl — THE BEASTIE BOYS
1990 Kool Thing — SONIC YOUTH
1991 Dirty Boots — SONIC YOUTH
1992 100% (co-dir. Spike Jonze) — SONIC YOUTH
1993 No Alternative Girls — HOLE & LUSCIOUS JACKSON & FREE KITTEN & HUGGY BEAR & BIKINI KILL
1993 Daughters of the Kaos — LUSCIOUS JACKSON
1994 Big Gay Heart — THE LEMONHEADS
1994 Bull in the Heater (co-dir. Kim Gordon) — SONIC YOUTH
1994 City Song — LUSCIOUS JACKSON
1994 It's About Time — THE LEMONHEADS
1995 All Hail Me — VERUCA SALT
1999 Ladyfingers — LUSCIOUS JACKSON

JONATHAN DAYTON & VALERIE FARIS
1992 Pets — PORNO FOR PYROS
1994 Gun (Jim Rose Sideshow Version) — SOUNDGARDEN
1994 Rocket — THE SMASHING PUMPKINS
1995 Star 69 — REM
1995 I Don't Want to Grow Up — THE RAMONES
1995 Tongue — REM
1996 1979 — THE SMASHING PUMPKINS
1996 Spider-Man — THE RAMONES
1996 Tonight, Tonight — THE SMASHING PUMPKINS
1997 The End Is the Beginning Is the End (co-dir. Joel Schumacher) — THE SMASHING PUMPKINS
1997 All Around the World — OASIS
1998 Perfect — THE SMASHING PUMPKINS
1999 She's Got Issues — THE OFFSPRING

JONATHAN DEMME
1984 Once in a Lifetime (v2) — TALKING HEADS
1984 Genius of Love (v2) — TOM TOM CLUB
1985 Perfect Kiss — NEW ORDER
1985 Sun City (co-dir. Hart Perry/Godley & Creme) — ARTISTS UNITED AGAINST APARTHEID

BARRY DEVLIN

1984 Pride (v2) — U2

1985 A Sort of Homecoming — U2

1985 Bad — U2

1987 In God's Country — U2

1987 I Still Haven't Found What I'm Looking For — U2

NIGEL DICK

1983 I Think I'll Get My Haircut — JONA LEWIE

1984 Baby Now That I've Found You — ANY TROUBLE

1984 Greatness and Perfection of Love — JULIAN COPE

1984 You Don't Love Me — MARILYN

1984 Drag Me Down — BOOMTOWN RATS

1984 Illuminations — SWANSWAY

1984 One Better Day — MADNESS

1984 Mother's Talk (v1) — TEARS FOR FEARS

1984 Shout — TEARS FOR FEARS

1984 Dave — BOOMTOWN RATS

1984 Do They Know It's Christmas? — BAND AID

1984 Xmas '84 — STIFF ALL STARS

1985 Things Can Only Get Better — HOWARD JONES

1985 Everybody Wants to Rule the World — TEARS FOR FEARS

1985 Head Over Heels — TEARS FOR FEARS

1985 Norwich — STIFF ALL STARS

1985 Life in One Day — HOWARD JONES

1985 One Year On — BAND AID

1985 I Believe — TEARS FOR FEARS

1986 Mother's Talk (v2) — TEARS FOR FEARS

1986 This Is the World Calling — BOB GELDOF

1987 Twilight World — SWING OUT SISTER

1987 Fooled by a Smile — SWING OUT SISTER

1989 Sweet Soul Sister — THE CULT

1990 Beatles and Stones — HOUSE OF LOVE

1990 Famous Last Words — TEARS FOR FEARS

1991 Diane — MATERIAL ISSUE

1991 Stand by Love — SIMPLE MINDS

1994 Time Won't Let Me — THE SMITHEREENS

1995 Rewrite — EVERLASTING

1995 Rock'n'roll Star — OASIS

1995 Wonderwall — OASIS

1995 Bury My Heart at Wounded Knee — INDIGO GIRLS

1996 Israel's Son (v1/v2) — SILVERCHAIR

1996 Don't Look Back in Anger — OASIS

1996 Champagne Supernova — OASIS

1996 Angel Mine — COWBOY JUNKIES

1996 Cup of Tea — VERVE PIPE

1996 The Beautiful Struggle — THE BORROWERS

1996 Tattva — KULA SHAKER

1996 When the Angels Sing — SOCIAL DISTORTION

1997 Gone Away — THE OFFSPRING

1997 Bottle Rockets — THE CUNNINGHAMS

1997 Wide Open Space — MANSUN

1997 Don't Go Away — OASIS

1999 At My Most Beautiful — REM

DARREN DOANE

1994 Homesick (co-dir. Pennywise) — PENNYWISE

1995 Go — DANCE HALL CRASHERS

1995 Same Old Story — PENNYWISE

1997 Chick Magnet — MXPX

1997 Cashed In — PULLEY

1997 Little Man — SUPERTONES

1997 Dammit (co-dir. Ken Daurio) — BLINK 182

1997 Supertones Strike Back — SUPERTONES

1997 Doin' Time — MXPX

1998 Josie (v2) (co-dir. Ken Daurio) — BLINK 182

1998 Jolene — SPRING HEELED JACK USA

1999 Lovely Denver Mint — JIMMY EAT WORLD

1999 Potential for a Fall — SICK OF IT ALL

RUDI DOLEZAL & HANNES ROSSACHER

1986 Rock Me Amadeus — FALCO

1986 Vienna Calling — FALCO

DOM & NIC

1994 Caught by the Fuzz — SUPERGRASS

1994 Mansize Rooster — SUPERGRASS

1995 Lenny — SUPERGRASS

1995 Alright — SUPERGRASS

1995 Time — SUPERGRASS

1995 Bluetonic — THE BLUETONES

1996 Going Out — SUPERGRASS

1996 Marblehead Johnson — THE BLUETONES

1996 Setting Sun — THE CHEMICAL BROTHERS

1996 The Box — ORBITAL

1997 Richard III — SUPERGRASS

1997 Sun Hits the Sky — SUPERGRASS

1997 Block Rockin' Beats — THE CHEMICAL BROTHERS

1997 Cheapskate — SUPERGRASS

1997 D'you Know What I Mean? — OASIS

1997 Come Back Brighter — REEF

1997 I'm Afraid of Americans (remix) — DAVID BOWIE & TRENT REZNOR

1998 Late in the Day — SUPERGRASS

1998 Heroes — THE WALLFLOWERS

1998 Ava Adore — THE SMASHING PUMPKINS

1999 Hey Boy, Hey Girl — THE CHEMICAL BROTHERS

CLARK EDDY

1994 If You Don't Love Me (I'll Kill Myself) — PETE DROGE

1995 All Wrong — GOD LIVES UNDERWATER

1996 What I Got (v1/2) — SUBLIME

1997 All I Wanted Was a Skateboard — SUPER DELUXE

1998 Busy Child (v2) — THE CRYSTAL METHOD

NICK EGAN

1993 Ordinary World — DURAN DURAN

1993 Sugar Kane — SONIC YOUTH

1994 Supersonic (v2) — OASIS

1995 Live Forever (v2) — OASIS

1995 Perfect Day — DURAN DURAN

1995 Vibrator — TERENCE TRENT D'ARBY

1995 Inbetweener — SLEEPER

1995 Sleep Well Tonight — GENE

1995 White Lines (Don't Do It) — DURAN DURAN

1995 Judy Staring at the Sun — CATHERINE WHEEL

1996 Bored — DEFTONES

1996 Desperately Wanting — BETTER THAN EZRA

1997 Love Is the Law — THE SEAHORSES

1997 Ready or Not — MANBREAK

1998 Bloodclot (co-dir. Rancid) — RANCID

JOHN FLANSBURGH

1992 The Guitar (The Lion Sleeps Tonight) — THEY MIGHT BE GIANTS

1993 Los Angeles — Frank Black

1993 Hang on to Your Ego (co-dir. Adam Bernstein) — FRANK BLACK

1995 A Girl Like You — EDWYN COLLINS

1996 Soundtrack to Mary (co-dir. Norwood Cheek) — SOUL COUGHING

1999 Doctor Worm — THEY MIGHT BE GIANTS

JAMES FRY

1993 I Was Born on Xmas day — ST. ETIENNE

1994 Pale Movie — ST. ETIENNE

CHRIS GABRIN

1982 The Hanging Garden — THE CURE

1982 Don't Go — YAZ

1983 Temptation — HEAVEN 17

1983 Time (Clock of the Heart) — CULTURE CLUB

1983 Watching — THOMPSON TWINS

1983 Church of the Poison Mind — CULTURE CLUB

1984 Turn to You (co-dir. Mary Lambert) — THE GO-GO'S

GRANT GEE

1997 Six — MANSUN

1997 No Surprises — RADIOHEAD

1999 Toilet Trouble — RADIOHEAD

1999 Tender — BLUR

1999 Palo Alto — RADIOHEAD

ANDREA GIACOBBE

1997 Dirt — DEATH IN VEGAS

1998 Push It — GARBAGE

1999 Revolution Action (v2) — ATARI TEENAGE RIOT

DUNCAN GIBBINS

1983 Who's That Girl? — EURYTHMICS

JONATHAN GLAZER

1995 Karmacoma — MASSIVE ATTACK

1995 The Universal (v1) — BLUR

1996 Street Spirit — RADIOHEAD

1996 Virtual Insanity — JAMIROQUAI

1997 Into My Arms (co.dir. Nick Cave) — NICK CAVE AND THE BAD SEEDS

1997 Cosmic Girl (v2) — JAMIROQUAI

1997 Karma Police — RADIOHEAD

1998 Rabbit in Your Headlights — UNKLE FEATURING THOM YORKE

KEVIN GODLEY & LOL CREME

1981 Girls on Film — DURAN DURAN

1981 Fade to Grey (v1) — VISAGE

1981 Mind of a Toy — VISAGE

1982 Temporary Beauty — GRAHAM PARKER

1982 Synchronicity II (short) — THE POLICE

1982 I Want to Be Free — TOYAH

1982 Thunder in the Mountains — TOYAH

1983 Victims — CULTURE CLUB

1983 Synchronicity (live) — THE POLICE

1983 Every Breath You Take — THE POLICE

1983 Wrapped Around Your Finger — THE POLICE

1983 Forbidden Colours — DAVID SYLVIAN

1984 Relax (v3) — FRANKIE GOES TO HOLLYWOOD

1984 Two Tribes (v1/2) — FRANKIE GOES TO HOLLYWOOD

1984 Everything Must Change — PAUL YOUNG

1984 The Power of Love (v1/2) — FRANKIE GOES TO HOLLY-WOOD

1985 A View to a Kill — DURAN DURAN

1985 Don't Mess with Doctor Dream — THOMPSON TWINS

1986 Sun City (co-dir. Jonathan Demme/Hart Perry) — ARTISTS UNITED AGAINST APARTHEID

1986 Everybody Have Fun Tonight — WANG CHUNG

1986 Don't Stand So Close to Me '86 — THE POLICE

1986 All Fall Down — ULTRAVOX

1987 I Want to Hear It From You — GO WEST

KEVIN GODLEY

1992 Even Better Than the Real Thing (v1) — U2

1993 Numb (v1) — U2

1993 Lemon (v3) — U2

1994 Girls and Boys — BLUR

1994 In the Name of the Father — GAVIN FRIDAY & BONO

1995 Hold Me, Thrill Me, Kiss Me, Kill Me (co.dir. Maurice Linnane) — U2

1995 I'll Do Ya — WHALE

1996 Mission: Impossible — ADAM CLAYTON & LARRY MULLEN

1996 You, Me & World War III — GAVIN FRIDAY

1997 Dream — FOREST FOR THE TREES

1997 Soldier's Daughter — TONIC

1998 The Sweetest Thing — U2

1999 Forever — THE CHARLATANS

1999 New Day (v2) — WYCLEF JEAN, FEATURING BONO

MICHEL GONDRY

1992 Two Worlds Collide — INSPIRAL CARPETS

1992 Les Voyages Immobiles — ETIENNE DAHO

1993 She Kissed Me — TERENCE TRENT D'ARBY

1993 Human Behaviour — BJÖRK

1994 Fire on Babylon — SINEAD O'CONNOR

1995 Protection — MASSIVE ATTACK, FEATURING TRACY THORN

1995 Army of Me — BJÖRK

1995 Isobel — BJÖRK

1996 Hyperballad — BJÖRK

1997 Feel It — NENEH CHERRY

1997 Around the World — DAFT PUNK

1997 Everlong — FOO FIGHTERS

1997 Joga — BJÖRK

1997 Deadweight — BECK

1997 Bachelorette — BJÖRK

1999 Let Forever Be — The Chemical Brothers

STUART A. GOSLING

1997 Chemical #1 — JESUS JONES

1997 High (v1) — FEEDER

1997 You're Gorgeous — BABYBIRD

1998 Breakbeat Era — RONI SIZE

1999 Insomnia — FEEDER

BRIAN GRANT

1979 Pop Muzik — M

1979 Blind Among the Flowers — THE TOURISTS

1979 Laugh and Walk Away — THE SHIRTS

1979 I Only Wanna Be with You — THE TOURISTS

1979 Christmas Day — SQUEEZE

1980 Kool in the Kaftan — B.A. ROBERTSON

1980 That's the Way the Money Goes — M

1980 Quiet Life — JAPAN

1980 Geno — DEXY'S MIDNIGHT RUNNERS

1980 To Be or Not to Be — B.A. ROBERTSON

1980 To Cut a Long Story Short — Spandau Ballet

1980 Towers of London — XTC

1980 Flight 19 — B.A. ROBERTSON

1981 The Freeze — SPANDAU BALLET

1981 Uninvited Guests — KIT HAIN

1981 Kids in America (v1) — KIM WILDE

1981 Saint Saens on the Radio — B.A. ROBERTSON

1981 The Race Is On — DAVE EDMUNDS & STRAY CATS

1981 Chequered Love — KIM WILDE

1981 Doors of My Heart — THE BEAT

1981 Jimmy Jones — THE VAPORS

1981 She's Got Claws — GARY NUMAN

1981 Little Miss Prissy — STRAY CATS

1981 Open Your Heart — HUMAN LEAGUE

1981 Hold Me — B.A. ROBERTSON

1981 Cambodia — KIM WILDE

1982 Ball and Chain — XTC

1982 Senses Working Overtime — XTC

1982 Rhythm of the Jungle — THE QUICK

1982 Black Coffee in Bed — SQUEEZE

1982 Talk Talk (v2) — TALK TALK

1982 View From a Bridge — KIM WILDE

1982 You Little Fool — ELVIS COSTELLO AND THE ATTRACTIONS

1982 The Look of Love (part One) (v1) — ABC

1982 Nobody's Fool — HAIRCUT 100

1982 For What It's Worth — HOLLY BETH VINCENT

1982 European Female — THE STRANGLERS

1983 Love on Your Side — THOMPSON TWINS

1983 Midnight Summer Dream — THE STRANGLERS

1983 My Foolish Friend — TALK TALK

1983 Vienna (live) — ULTRAVOX

1983 Saved by Zero — THE FIXX

1984 New Moon on Monday — DURAN DURAN

1986 Sinful — PETE WYLIE

1986 Secret Separation — THE FIXX

1989 A Girl Like You — THE SMITHEREENS

CARLOS GRASSO

1993 Low — CRACKER

1994 Eurotrash Girl — CRACKER

1994 Get Off This — CRACKER

1994 El Dorado Motorhome — GRANT LEE BUFFALO

1994 Fuzzy — GRANT LEE BUFFALO

1994 Lone Star — GRANT LEE BUFFALO

1994 Stuck Here Again — L7

1994 Live Forever (v1) — OASIS

1995 Infected — BAD RELIGION

1995 Honey Don't Think — GRANT LEE BUFFALO

1995 Summer — BUFFALO TOM

1995 Demagogue — URBAN DANCE SQUAD

1995 Promises Broken — SOUL ASYLUM

HOWARD GREENHALGH

1989 So Alive — LOVE & ROCKETS

1989 Head On — THE JESUS AND MARY CHAIN

1990 Heaven or Las Vegas — COCTEAU TWINS

1990 Iceblink Luck — COCTEAU TWINS

1990 Deluxe — LUSH

1991 Rush — BIG AUDIO DYNAMITE II

1993 Can You Forgive Her? — PET SHOP BOYS

1993 Jean the Birdman — DAVID SYLVIAN & ROBERT FRIPP

1993 Go West — PET SHOP BOYS

1993 Go West (part 2) — PET SHOP BOYS

1993 I Wouldn't Normally Do This Kind of Thing — PET SHOP BOYS

1994 Liberation — PET SHOP BOYS

1994 Absolutely Fabulous (co-dir. Bob Spiers) — PET SHOP BOYS

1994 Yesterday, When I Was Mad — PET SHOP BOYS

1994 The Wild Ones — LONDON SUEDE

1995 Paninaro '95 — PET SHOP BOYS

1996 Before — PET SHOP BOYS

1996 Walking on the Milky Way — ORCHESTRAL MANOEUVRES IN THE DARK

1996 Single Bilingual — PET SHOP BOYS

1996 Nancy Boy — PLACEBO

1997 A Red Letter Day — PET SHOP BOYS

1997 Chase (v1/2) — TRANCE ATLANTIC AIR WAVES

1998 Post-modern Sleaze — SNEAKER PIMPS

1999 Beat Mama — CAST

1999 Lately — SKUNK ANANSIE

1999 Everything Will Flow — LONDON SUEDE

1999 New York City Boy — PET SHOP BOYS

BRIAN GRIFFIN

1994 Sulky Girl — ELVIS COSTELLO AND THE ATTRACTIONS

1998 Only When I Lose Myself — DEPECHE MODE

MICK HAGGERT Y

1981 We Got the Beat (live) (co-dir. C D Taylor) — THE GO-GO'S

1982 Vacation (co-dir. C D Taylor) — THE GO-GO'S

1983 Legal Tender (co-dir. C D Taylor) — B-52'S

1983 Song for Future Generations (co-dir. C D Taylor) — B-52'S

1985 Children of the Revolution — VIOLENT FEMMES

1993 I Held Her in My Arms — VIOLENT FEMMES

1994 Harness Up (Soul's on Fire) — DIED PRETTY

HAMMER & TONGS (GARTH JENNINGS/NICK GOLDSMITH/ DOMINIC LEUNG)

1996 Weak — SKUNK ANANSIE

1996 Nice Guy Eddie — SLEEPER

1997 Help the Aged — PULP

1998 A Little Soul — PULP

1999 'B' Line — LAMB

1999 Right Here, Right Now — FATBOY SLIM

1999 Pumping on Your Stereo — SUPERGRASS

1999 Coffee & TV — BLUR

PHILIP HARDER

1993 Come See About Me — AFGHAN WHIGS

1993 Miles Iz Ded — AFGHAN WHIGS

1994 X — BAILTERSPACE

1995 Sweet 69 — BABES IN TOYLAND

1995 Shame — LOW

1996 Over the Ocean — LOW

1997 Red House — SHUDDER TO THINK

1997 Brimful of Asha — CORNERSHOP

1997 Sleep on the Left Side — CORNERSHOP

1999 Just My Imagination — THE CRANBERRIES

JOHN HILLCOAT

1981 Nick the Stripper (co-dir. Paul Goldman) — BIRTHDAY PARTY

1988 Veronica (co-dir. Evan English) — ELVIS COSTELLO

1990 The Ship Song — NICK CAVE AND THE BAD SEEDS

1992 Jack the Ripper — NICK CAVE AND THE BAD SEEDS

1992 I Had a Dream Joe — NICK CAVE AND THE BAD SEEDS

1994 Do You Love Me? — NICK CAVE AND THE BAD SEEDS

1994 Loverman — NICK CAVE AND THE BAD SEEDS

1994 Bizarre Love Triangle (co-dir. Polly Borland) — FRENTE!

1994 Saturn V — INSPIRAL CARPETS

1995 O Baby — SIOUXSIE AND THE BANSHEES

1995 Stargazer — SIOUXSIE AND THE BANSHEES

1995 Going South — THE WOLFGANG PRESS

1996 Kevin Carter — MANIC STREET PREACHERS

1996 Alisha Rules the World — ALISHA'S ATTIC

1996 Australia — MANIC STREET PREACHERS

1996 She Makes My Nose Bleed — MANSUN

1998 Church of Noise — THERAPY?

1998 Lonely Crying Only — THERAPY?

1998 All You Good Good People — EMBRACE

1998 You Don't Care About Us — PLACEBO

DAVE HILLIER

1981 Play for Today — THE CURE

1981 A Forest — THE CURE

SIMON HILTON

1991 A Touch of the Night — WILLIAM ORBIT

1995 I'm a Believer — EMF & VIC & BOB

1998 Let Down [unreleased] — RADIOHEAD

WAYNE ISHAM

1981 Pretty in Pink — PSYCHEDELIC FURS

1995 Don't Cry — SEAL

PHIL JOANOU

1989 When Love Comes to Town — U2

1992 One (v1) — U2

1992 Wild Horses — U2

SPIKE JONZE

1992 100% (co-dir. Tamra Davis) — SONIC YOUTH

1993 Cannonball (co-dir. Kim Gordon) — THE BREEDERS

1993 High in Highschool — CHAINSAW KITTENS

1993 Country at War — X

1994 Ditch Digger — ROCKET FROM THE CRYPT

1994 Old Timer — THAT DOG

1994 Divine Hammer (co-dir. Kim Gordon/Kim Deal) — THE BREEDERS

1994 Sabotage — THE BEASTIE BOYS

1994 I Can't Stop Smiling — VELOCITY GIRL

1994 Big Train — MIKE WATT

1994 If I Only Had a Brain — MC 900 FT. JESUS

1994 Feel the Pain — DINOSAUR, JR.

1994 Sure Shot (co-dir. Nathanial Hornblower) — THE BEASTIE BOYS

1995 Freedom of '76 — WEEN

1995 Car Song — ELASTICA

1995 Crush with Eyeliner — REM

1995 It's Oh So Quiet — BJÖRK

1995 The Diamond Sea (co-dir. Lance Bangs/ Dave Markey/Steve Paine/Angus Wall) — SONIC YOUTH

1996 Drop — THE PHARCYDE

1997 Electrolite (co-dir. Peter Care) — REM

1997 Da Funk — DAFT PUNK

1997 Shady Lane — PAVEMENT

1997 Elektrobank — THE CHEMICAL BROTHERS

1997 Liberty Calls — MIKE WATT

1998 Root Down (v2) — THE BEASTIE BOYS

1998 Home — SEAN LENNON

1998 Praise You (co-dir. Roman Coppola) — FATBOY SLIM

NEIL JORDAN

1987 Red Hill Mining Town — U2

JOSEPH KAHN

1993 Crossfire — DIE KRUPPS

1993 Fatherland — DIE KRUPPS

1995 Bloodsuckers — DIE KRUPPS & BIOHAZARD

1995 Locusts — SPAHN RANCH

1995 To the Hilt — DIE KRUPPS

1997 Last Cup of Sorrow — FAITH NO MORE

1998 Space Lord — MONSTER MAGNET

1998 Powertrip — MONSTER MAGNET

1998 Living Dead Girl — (co-dir. Rob Zombie) ROB ZOMBIE

DEAN KARR

1994 Clean My Wounds — CORROSION OF CONFORMITY (COC)

1996 Sweet Dreams (Are Made of This) — MARILYN MANSON

1996 Jurassitol — FILTER

1996 Sworn and Broken — THE SCREAMING TREES

1997 Out of My Mind — DURAN DURAN

1997 Villains — THE VERVE PIPE

1997 My Own Summer (shove It) — THE DEFTONES

1999 Shock the Monkey — COAL CHAMBER

1999 Voodoo — GODSMACK

KEEF (AKA KEITH MACMILLAN & JOHN WEAVER)

1978 Wuthering Heights — KATE BUSH

1978 Denis — BLONDIE

1978 Them Heavy People — KATE BUSH

1978 (I'm Always Touched by Your) Presence Dear — BLONDIE

1978 Detroit 442 — BLONDIE

1978 The Man with the Child in His Eyes — KATE BUSH

1978 Picture This — BLONDIE

1978 Hammer Horror — KATE BUSH

1979 Wow — KATE BUSH

1980 Breathing — KATE BUSH

1980 Babooshka — KATE BUSH

1980 Army Dreamers — KATE BUSH

1981 Rapture — BLONDIE

1982 Cheers Then — BANANARAMA

1983 Na Na Hey Kiss Him Goodbye — BANANARAMA

1986 Sanctify Yourself — SIMPLE MINDS

PAUL KELLY

1992 Avenue — ST. ETIENNE

1993 Hobart Paving — ST. ETIENNE

1993 You're in a Bad Way — ST. ETIENNE

1994 Like a Motorway — ST. ETIENNE

1995 He's on the Phone — ST. ETIENNE

KEVIN KERSLAKE

1986 Shadow of a Doubt — SONIC YOUTH

1987 Beauty Lies in the Eyes — SONIC YOUTH

1989 Candle — SONIC YOUTH

1990 In Bloom (v1/2) — NIRVANA

1990 Halah — MAZZY STAR

1992 Come As You Are — NIRVANA

1992 Lithium (co-dir. Mark Racco) — NIRVANA

1993 Otha Fish — THE PHARCYDE

1993 Superdeformed — MATTHEW SWEET

1993 The Ghost at Number One — JELLYFISH

1993 Sliver — NIRVANA

1993 Soul to Squeeze — RED HOT CHILI PEPPERS

1993 Cherub Rock — THE SMASHING PUMPKINS

1994 Fade Into You (v2) — MAZZY STAR

1995 She's a River — SIMPLE MINDS

1995 Hey Man, Nice Shot — FILTER

1995 Bright Yello Gun — THROWING MUSES

1995 Dose — FILTER

1995 She's Lost Control — GIRLS AGAINST BOYS

1996 Brain Stew/Jaded — GREEN DAY

1996 Flowers in December — MAZZY STAR

1997 Halls of Illusion — INSANE CLOWN POSSE

1997 The Meaning of Life — THE OFFSPRING

1998 Sometimes It Hurts — STABBING WESTWARD

1998 Sherry Fraser — MARCY PLAYGROUND

JON KLEIN

1991 The Fly (co-dir. Richie Smyth) — U2

1992 Teethgrinder — THERAPY?

1992 Your Town — DEACON BLUE

1993 Will We Be Lovers? — DEACON BLUE

1993 Nausea — THERAPY?

1993 Screamager — THERAPY?

1993 Religion — FRONT 242

1994 Stay Together — LONDON SUEDE

1994 Here She Comes — DANIEL ASH

1994 Millenium — KILLING JOKE

1995 Roll with It — OASIS

1996 Twinkle — WHIPPING BOY

MARK KOHR

1993 DMV — PRIMUS

1993 Mr. Krinkle — PRIMUS

1993 Longview — GREEN DAY

1993 My Name Is Mud — PRIMUS

1994 Basket Case — GREEN DAY

1994 When I Come Around — GREEN DAY

1994 Here and Now — LETTERS TO CLEO

1994 Salvation (co-dir. Tim Armstrong) — RANCID

1994 Kinder Words — THE MIGHTY MIGHTY BOSSTONES

1995 Down to This — SOUL COUGHING

1995 Stuck with Me — GREEN DAY

1995 Enough — DANCE HALL CRASHERS

1995 Geek Stink Breath — GREEN DAY

1995 Fireman — JAWBREAKER

1996 Just a Girl — NO DOUBT

1996 You Make Me Feel Like a Whore — EVERCLEAR

1996 The Distance — CAKE

1997 Volcano — THE PRESIDENTS OF THE UNITED STATES OF AMERICA

1997 I Will Survive — CAKE

1997 Tape Loop — MORCHEEBA

1997 Sell Out — REEL BIG FISH

1997 The Rascal King — THE MIGHTY MIGHTY BOSSTONES

1997 Hitchin' a Ride — GREEN DAY

1997 Everything to Everyone (co-dir. Art Alexis) — EVERCLEAR

1997 Time of Your Life (Good Riddance) — GREEN DAY

1998 Wrong Thing, Right Then — THE MIGHTY MIGHTY BOSS-TONES

1998 Redundant — GREEN DAY

1999 One Man Army — OUR LADY PEACE

KAREN LAMOND

1996 No One Speaks — GENEVA

1997 God Bless — LAMB

1997 Gorecki — LAMB

1998 The Incidentals — ALISHA'S ATTIC

1998 I Wish I Were Here — ALISHA'S ATTIC

1998 Ma Solituda — CATHERINE WHEEL

MATT MAHURIN

1987 With or Without You (v2) — U2

1988 Sweet Jane (v1) — COWBOY JUNKIES

1988 All Night Long — PETER MURPHY

1988 Orange Crush — REM

1992 Hit Song — PETER MURPHY

1993 Love Is Blindness — U2

1993 Take a Walk — URGE OVERKILL

1993 Dear Ol' Dad — BLIND MELON

1993 Runaway Wind — PAUL WESTERBURG

1994 Die Laughing — THERAPY?

1995 The Scarlet Thing in You — PETER MURPHY

1995 Rosealia (v2) — BETTER THAN EXRA

1996 Gold Dust Woman — HOLE

DAVID MALLET

1978 Hanging on the Telephone — BLONDIE

1979 I Don't Like Mondays — BOOMTOWN RATS

1979 Dreaming — BLONDIE

1979 The Hardest Part — BLONDIE

1979 Union City Blue — BLONDIE

1979 Shayla — BLONDIE

1979 Eat to the Beat — BLONDIE

1979 Accidents Never Happen — BLONDIE

1979 Die Young Stay Pretty — BLONDIE

1979 Slow Motion — BLONDIE

1979 Atomic (v1) — BLONDIE

1979 Sound-a-sleep — BLONDIE

1979 Victor — BLONDIE

1979 Living in the Real World — BLONDIE

1980 Call Me (v1) — BLONDIE

1982 White Wedding — BILLY IDOL

1984 Eyes Without a Face — BILLY IDOL

1984 Catch My Fall — BILLY IDOL

1985 Relax (v5) — FRANKIE GOES TO HOLLYWOOD

1986 To Be a Lover — BILLY IDOL

MIKE MANSFIELD

1982 Goody Two Shoes — ADAM ANT

1982 Charlotte Sometimes — CURE

McG

1996 Santeria — SUBLIME
1997 Walkin' on the Sun — SMASH MOUTH
1997 Why Can't We Be Friends? — SMASH MOUTH
1998 Mungo City — SPACEHOG
1998 The Way — FASTBALL
1998 Can't Get Enough of You — SMASH MOUTH
1998 Pretty Fly (for a White Guy) — THE OFFSPRING
1998 One-Hit Wonder — EVERCLEAR
1999 Why Don't You Get a Job? — THE OFFSPRING
1999 All Star — SMASH MOUTH

MIKE MILLS

1996 Men in Black — FRANK BLACK
1998 Sexy Boy — AIR
1998 Legacy — MANSUN
1998 Kelly, Watch the Stars — AIR
1998 Party Hard — PULP
1998 All I Need — AIR
1999 Run On — MOBY

SIMON MILNE

1982 Destination Unknown — MISSING PERSONS
1982 Today — TALK TALK
1983 Too Shy — KAJAGOOGOO
1983 Union of the Snake — DURAN DURAN
1984 The Lebanon — THE HUMAN LEAGUE
1984 Life on Your Own — THE HUMAN LEAGUE
1985 Do Not Disturb — BANANARAMA

MICHAEL MINER

1984 Wake Me Up Before You Go Go — WHAM!
1985 West End Girls — PET SHOP BOYS
1986 Wicked Ways — BLOW MONKEYS

MARIA MOCHNACZ

1992 Dress — PJ HARVEY
1992 Sheela-Na-Gig — PJ HARVEY
1993 50 Ft. Queenie — PJ HARVEY
1993 Man Size — PJ HARVEY
1994 Down by the Water — PJ HARVEY
1995 C'mon Billy — PJ HARVEY
1995 Send His Love to Me — PJ HARVEY
1996 Is That All There Is? — PJ HARVEY
1996 That Was My Veil — PJ HARVEY & JOHN PARRISH
1998 A Perfect Day Elise — PJ HARVEY
1998 The Wind — PJ HARVEY

ROCKY MORTON

1981 Genius of Love (v1) (co-dir. Annabel Jankel) — TOM TOM CLUB

1982 The Pleasure of Love (co-dir. Annabel Jankel) — TOM TOM CLUB
1988 Blind (co-dir. Annabel Jankel) — TALKING HEADS
1996 Guilty — GRAVITY KILLS
1996 Pretty Vacant — SEX PISTOLS
1996 Enough — GRAVITY KILLS
1999 Stitches — ORGY

DAVID MOULD

1992 Pop Scene — BLUR
1992 Hey Jealousy — GIN BLOSSOMS
1994 To the End (v1) — BLUR
1995 Connection — ELASTICA
1995 Charity — SKUNK ANANSIE
1995 Stutter (v2) — ELASTICA
1995 Sandcastles — BOMB THE BASS
1995 High and Dry (v1) — RADIOHEAD
1996 Kelly's Heroes — BLACK GRAPE
1996 Trash (v1) — LONDON SUEDE
1997 Say What You Want (v1) — TEXAS
1997 She's a Star — JAMES
1997 Place Your Hands — REEF
1997 Dominoid — MOLOKO
1997 Stand by Me — OASIS
1998 Stay — BERNARD BUTLER
1998 Change of Heart — BERNARD BUTLER
1999 I Know What I'm Here For — JAMES
1999 Burning Down the House — TOM JONES AND THE CARDIGANS
1999 Rhythm & Blues Alibi — GOMEZ

RUSSELL MULCAHY

1979 Video Killed the Radio Star — THE BUGGLES
1979 Circus of Death — THE HUMAN LEAGUE
1979 Empire State Human — THE HUMAN LEAGUE
1980 Turning Japanese — VAPORS
1981 Vienna (v1) — ULTRAVOX
1981 Planet Earth (co-dir. Perry Haines) — DURAN DURAN
1981 Musclebound — SPANDAU BALLET
1981 Nightboat — DURAN DURAN
1981 Chant No. 1 (live) — SPANDAU BALLET
1981 The Thin Wall — ULTRAVOX
1981 Paint Me Down — SPANDAU BALLET
1981 The Voice (v1) — ULTRAVOX
1981 My Own Way — DURAN DURAN
1982 Instinction — SPANDAU BALLET
1982 Hungry Like the Wolf — DURAN DURAN
1982 Lonely in Your Nightmare — DURAN DURAN
1982 Talk Talk (v1) — TALK TALK
1982 Only the Lonely — THE MOTELS
1982 Take the L Out of Lover — THE MOTELS
1982 Save a Prayer (v1) — DURAN DURAN

1982 Rio — DURAN DURAN

1983 Is There Something I Should Know? — DURAN DURAN

1983 True — SPANDAU BALLET

1983 Total Eclipse of the Heart — BONNIE TYLER

1984 The Reflex (v1) — DURAN DURAN

1984 The War Song — CULTURE CLUB

1984 The Wild Boys — DURAN DURAN

1985 Save a Prayer (live) — DURAN DURAN

1985 Shame — THE MOTELS

1985 Call Me — GO WEST

SOPHIE MULLER

1987 You Have Placed a Chill in My Heart — EURYTHMICS

1987 I Need a Man — EURYTHMICS

1987 Beethoven (I Love to Listen To) — EURYTHMICS

1988 Wide Eyed Girl — EURYTHMICS

1988 Break My Heart — SHAKESPEAR'S SISTER

1989 You're History — SHAKESPEAR'S SISTER

1989 Don't Ask Me Why — EURYTHMICS

1989 Run Silent — SHAKESPEAR'S SISTER

1989 Angel — EURYTHMICS

1990 King & Queen of America (v2) — EURYTHMICS

1990 Emperor's New Clothes (v2) — SINEAD O'CONNOR

1991 Thank You World (co-dir. Karl Wallinger & Jake Tilson) — WORLD PARTY

1991 Coast Is Clear — CURVE

1991 Goodbye Cruel World — SHAKESPEAR'S SISTER

1992 Stay — SHAKESPEAR'S SISTER

1992 Fait Accompli — CURVE

1992 I Don't Care — SHAKESPEAR'S SISTER

1992 Hello (Turn Your Radio On) — SHAKESPEAR'S SISTER

1993 Venus As a Boy — BJÖRK

1994 Miss World — HOLE

1994 Sometimes Always — JESUS AND MARY CHAIN, FEATURING HOPE SANDOVAL

1994 Come On — JESUS AND MARY CHAIN

1995 Ten Storey Love Song — STONE ROSES

1996 13th — THE CURE

1996 I Can Drive — SHAKESPEAR'S SISTER

1996 Don't Speak — NO DOUBT

1997 Beetlebum — BLUR

1997 Excuse Me, Mr — NO DOUBT

1997 Song 2 — BLUR

1997 Sunday Morning — NO DOUBT

1997 On Your Own — BLUR

1997 Chinese Burn — CURVE

1997 Oi to the World — NO DOUBT

1998 Be Strong Now — JAMES IHA

1998 What If — LIGHTNING SEEDS

1999 When I Grow Up (v1/v2) — GARBAGE

1999 Secret Smile — SEMISONIC

1999 You Stole the Sun From My Heart — MANIC STREET PREACHERS

1999 Chiquitita — SINEAD O'CONNOR

1999 Hanging Around — THE CARDIGANS

MARK NEALE

1993 Lemon (v1/2) — U2

1994 Sunflower (v2) — PAUL WELLER

1995 Never — ELECTRAFIXION

1995 Christianity — THE WOLFGANG PRESS

1996 Spaceman — BABYLON ZOO

1997 The Freshmen — THE VERVE PIPE

1998 I Will Still Be Laughing — SOUL ASYLUM

DOUG NICHOL

1991 Des Attractions Desirade — ETIENNE DAHO

1993 Un Homme Mer — ETIENNE DAHO

1993 Rue Des Petits — ETIENNE DAHO

1996 Touts Les Gouts Sont Dans Ma Nature — ETIENNE DAHO/JACQUES DUTRONC

1998 This is Hardcore — PULP

1998 Le Premeir Jour — ETIENNE DAHO

1998 I Deal — ETIENNE DAHO

1999 Mystical Machine Gun — KULA SHAKER

ARTHUR PIERSON

1981 Radio Free Europe — REM

MARK PELLINGTON

1992 One (v2) — U2

1992 Television: The Drug of a Nation — DISPOSABLE HEROES OF HYPOCRISY

1995 Waydown — CATHERINE WHEEL

1995 Kickin' — WHALE

1996 Ladykillers — LUSH

1999 We're in This Together — NINE INCH NAILS

JESSE PERETZ

1992 It's a Shame About Ray — THE LEMONHEADS

1993 Tom Boy — BETTIE SERVEERT

1994 Shocker in Gloomtown — THE BREEDERS

1994 Flashlight — FUZZY

1994 Hit Liquor — SHUDDER TO THINK

1996 Big Me — FOO FIGHTERS

1996 Popular — NADA SURF

1999 Learn to Fly — FOO FIGHTERS

TIM POPE

1982 Let's Go to Bed — THE CURE

1983 The Safety Dance — MEN WITHOUT HATS

1983 The Walk — THE CURE

1983 The Lovecats — THE CURE

1984 It's My Life — TALK TALK
1984 The Caterpillar — THE CURE
1984 Such a Shame — TALK TALK
1984 Magic — THE CARS
1984 I Want to Be a Tree — TIM POPE
1984 Dum Dum Girl (v1/2) — TALK TALK
1985 When All's Well — EVERYTHING BUT THE GIRL
1985 In Between Days — THE CURE
1985 Close to Me — THE CURE
1985 Life's What You Make It — TALK TALK
1986 Killing an Arab — THE CURE
1986 Living in Another World — TALK TALK
1986 Jumping Someone Else's Train — THE CURE
1986 Boys Don't Cry (v1) — THE CURE
1986 A Night Like This — THE CURE
1987 Slow Train to Dawn — THE THE
1987 Why Can't I Be You? — THE CURE
1987 Catch — THE CURE
1987 Just Like Heaven — THE CURE
1988 Hot, Hot, Hot — THE CURE
1988 I Believe in You — TALK TALK
1989 Lullaby (v1) — THE CURE
1989 Fascination Street (v1) — THE CURE
1989 Proud to Fall — IAN MCCULLOCH
1989 Lovesong — THE CURE
1990 Jealous of Youth (live) — THE THE
1990 Pictures of You — THE CURE
1990 Never Enough — THE CURE
1990 Close to Me (closet Remix) — THE CURE
1992 The Sweetest Drop — PETER MURPHY
1992 Friday I'm in Love (v1) — THE CURE
1992 Not Sleeping Around — NED'S ATOMIC DUSTBIN
1997 Wrong Number — THE CURE

BOB RICKER D
1982 Other Voices — THE CURE
1982 Primary — THE CURE

DAVE ROBINSON
1979 One Step Beyond — MADNESS
1982 House of Fun — MADNESS
1982 Our House — MADNESS
1984 They Don't Know — TRACY ULLMAN

MARK ROBINSON
1979 Brass in Pocket — PRETENDERS

MAFK ROMANEK
1986 Sweet Bird of Truth — THE THE
1994 Closer — NINE INCH NAILS
1995 Strange Currencies — REM

1996 Little Trouble Girl — SONIC YOUTH
1996 Novocaine for the Soul — EELS
1996 Devil's Haircut — BECK
1997 The Perfect Drug — NINE INCH NAILS

PEDRO ROMHANYI
1988 She Drives Me Crazy (v2) — FINE YOUNG CANNIBALS
1989 In the Ghetto — BEATS INTERNATIONAL
1990 Real, Real, Real — JESUS JONES
1990 My Book — THE BEAUTIFUL SOUTH
1991 Let Love Speak Up Itself — THE BEAUTIFUL SOUTH
1992 Hit — THE SUGARCUBES
1992 Old Red Eyes Is Back — THE BEAUTIFUL SOUTH
1992 Always the Last to Know — DEL AMITRI
1992 Uh Huh, Oh Yeah — PAUL WELLER
1992 Walkabout — THE SUGARCUBES
1992 Babies — PULP
1993 Animal Nitrate — LONDON SUEDE
1993 Into Tomorrow — PAUL WELLER
1993 Give It All Away — WORLD PARTY
1993 Sunflower (v1) — PAUL WELLER
1994 Do You Remember the First Time? — PULP
1994 Wild Wood — PAUL WELLER
1994 Change — THE LIGHTNING SEEDS
1994 Parklife — BLUR
1994 Lucky You — THE LIGHTNING SEEDS
1994 Hung Up — PAUL WELLER
1995 X-French Tee Shirt— SHUDDER TO THINK
1995 Driving with the Brakes On — DEL AMITRI
1995 Common People — PULP
1995 Changing Man — PAUL WELLER
1995 Dream a Little Dream — THE BEAUTIFUL SOUTH
1995 Mis-shapes — PULP
1995 I'm Only Sleeping — SUGGS
1996 Three Lions — THE LIGHTNING SEEDS
1996 A Design for Life — MANIC STREET PREACHERS
1996 The Beautiful Ones — LONDON SUEDE
1996 Disco 2000 — PULP
1997 Saturday Night — LONDON SUEDE
1997 Blackbird on a Wire — THE BEAUTIFUL SOUTH
1997 Lazy — LONDON SUEDE
1997 You Showed Me — THE LIGHTNING SEEDS
1997 Summertime — THE SUNDAYS
1997 Did It Again — KYLIE MINOGUE
1997 History Repeating — PROPELLERHEADS & SHIRLEY BASSEY
1999 I Don't Know What You Want — PET SHOP BOYS

ZBIGNIEW RYBCZYNSKI
1984 All I Wanted — BELFEGORE
1984 Close (to the Edit) (v1) — THE ART OF NOISE
1985 Hell in Paradise — YOKO ONO

1985 P. Machinery — PROPAGANDA

1985 Alive and Kicking — SIMPLE MINDS

1986 All the Things She Said — SIMPLE MINDS

1986 Opportunities (v2) — PET SHOP BOYS

1987 Dragnet — ART OF NOISE

1988 Bleu Comme Toi — ETIENNE DAHO

ROCKY SCHENCK

1982 Fish Heads (co-dir. Bill Paxton/Joan Farber/Paul Kaufman) — BARNES AND BARNES

1990 Alice Everyday — BOOK OF LOVE

1991 That Is Why — JELLYFISH

1994 Gentlemen — AFGHAN WHIGS

1994 Backwater — MEAT PUPPETS

1994 Lady in the Front Row — RED KROSS

1995 Vertigogo — COMBUSTIBLE EDISON

1995 Born with a Tail — SUPERSUCKERS

1995 Where the Wild Roses Grow — NICK CAVE AND THE BAD SEEDS & KYLIE MINOGUE

1996 Love Untold — PAUL WESTERBERG

1996 Henry Lee — NICK CAVE AND THE BAD SEEDS & PJ HARVEY

1999 Yoo Hoo — IMPERIAL TEEN

JAKE SCOTT

1993 Everybody Hurts — REM

1994 Disarm — THE SMASHING PUMPKINS

1994 Am I Wrong? — LOVE SPIT LOVE

1995 All I Ask of Myself Is That I Hold Together — NED'S ATOMIC DUSTBIN

1995 Fake Plastic Trees — RADIOHEAD

1995 On Your Own — THE VERVE

1995 Morning Glory — OASIS

1996 In the Meantime — SPACEHOG

1996 When You're Gone — THE CRANBERRIES

1997 Staring at the Sun (v1) — U2

1999 Be There — UNKLE, FEATURING IAN BROWN

1999 New — NO DOUBT

STEPHANE SEDNAOUI

1991 Mysterious Ways — U2

1992 Give It Away — RED HOT CHILI PEPPERS

1992 Breaking the Girl — RED HOT CHILI PEPPERS

1993 Today — SMASHING PUMPKINS

1993 Big Time Sensuality — BJÖRK

1994 Sly — MASSIVE ATTACK

1995 Pumpkin — TRICKY

1995 Garbage — QUEER

1996 Milk — GARBAGE

1996 Possibly Maybe — BJÖRK

1996 Hey Dude — KULA SHAKER

1996 Gangster Moderne — MC SOLAAR

1996 Le Nouveau Western — MC SOLAAR

1997 Discoteque — U2

DREW SENTIVAN

1997 Nude Beach (live) — THE SCOFFLAWS

1997 I Wasn't Going to Call You Anyway — THE TOASTERS

1997 Pay Some Dues — SPRING HEELED JACK USA

1997 High School — ISAAC GREEN & THE SKOLARS

1997 Don't Let the Bastards Grind You Down — THE TOASTERS

1998 Running Right Through the World — THE TOASTERS

FLORIA SIGISMONDI

1994 The Birdman — OUR LADY PEACE

1996 The Beautiful People — MARILYN MANSON

1996 Anna — PURE

1996 Tourniquet — MARILYN MANSON

1997 Black Eye — FLUFFY

1997 Makes Me Wanna Die — TRICKY

1997 (Can't You) Trip Like I Do — FILTER, FEATURING THE CRYSTAL METHOD

1998 Can't Get Loose — BARRY ADAMSON

TOM STERN

1990 Taste the Pain (co-dir. Alex Winter) — RED HOT CHILI PEPPERS

1995 Dopehat — MARILYN MANSON

WALTER STERN

1994 No Good (Start the Dance) — THE PRODIGY

1995 Poison — THE PRODIGY

1995 Hymn — MOBY

1995 Life Is Sweet — THE CHEMICAL BROTHERS & TIM BURGESS

1995 Voodoo People (v1) — THE PRODIGY

1995 Evidence — FAITH NO MORE

1996 Firestarter — THE PRODIGY

1997 Breathe — THE PRODIGY

1997 Bittersweet Symphony (v1) — THE VERVE

1997 Risingson — MASSIVE ATTACK

1998 Teardrop — MASSIVE ATTACK

1998 Angel — MASSIVE ATTACK

BENJAMIN STOKES

1988 Stigmata (co-dir. Al Jorgensen) — MINISTRY

1988 Flashback — MINISTRY

1989 Down in It (co-dir. Eric Zimmerman) — NINE INCH NAILS

1992 Edge of No Control — MEAT BEAT MANIFESTO

1993 Opal Mantra — THERAPY?

1996 Asbestos Lead Asbestos — MEAT BEAT MANIFESTO

1997 Toxygene — THE ORB

1997 Welcome to My Mind — PSYKOSONIK

1997 Helter Skelter '97 — MEAT BEAT MANIFESTO

1999 Bad Blood — MINISTRY

MARK SZASZY

1994 Supersonic (v1) — OASIS

1994 Shakermaker — OASIS

1994 Missing You — EVERYTHING BUT THE GIRL

1994 Cigarettes & Alcohol — OASIS

1994 Whatever — OASIS

1999 Five Fathoms — EVERYTHING BUT THE GIRL

TARSEM

1991 Losing My Religion — REM

GAVIN TAYLOR

1983 Sunday Bloody Sunday — U2

JULIEN TEMPLE

1981 Tears Are Not Enough (v1) — ABC

1982 See You — DEPECHE MODE

1982 Do You Really Want to Hurt Me? — CULTURE CLUB

1982 Leave in Silence — DEPECHE MODE

1983 Rock This Town — STRAY CATS

1983 Come on Eileen — DEXY'S MIDNIGHT RUNNERS

1983 Stray Cat Strut — STRAY CATS

1983 Mantrap (opening Theme) — ABC

1983 Show Me — ABC

1983 Many Happy Returns — ABC

1983 The Look of Love (part One) (v2) — ABC

1983 4ever 2gether — ABC

1983 All of My Heart (v2) — ABC

1983 Mantrap Theme — ABC

1983 Poison Arrow (v2) — ABC

1983 Tears Are Not Enough (v2) — ABC

1983 Mantrap (closing Theme) — ABC

1986 Don't Need a Gun — BILLY IDOL

1993 For Tomorrow — BLUR

1993 Come Undone — DURAN DURAN

1993 Adam in Chains — BILLY IDOL

1993 Too Much Information — DURAN DURAN

TONY VAN DEN ENDE

1982 Child Come Away — KIM WILDE

1985 Moments in Love — ART OF NOISE

1985 Money's Too Tight (to Mention) — SIMPLY RED

1985 Rain — THE CULT

1985 Revolution — THE CULT

1985 Holding Back the Years — SIMPLY RED

1998 El President — DRUGSTORE, FEATURING THOM YORKE

MARTIN WALLACE

1994 On (co-dir. Jarvis Cocker) — APHEX TWIN

1997 Rented Rooms — TINDERSTICKS

1999 Can We Start Again? — TINDERSTICKS

WIM WENDERS

1990 Night and Day — U2

1993 Stay (Faraway So Close) — U2

JOSH WHITE

1981 O! Superman — LAURIE ANDERSON

HYPE WILLIAMS

1996 Home — DEPECHE MODE

ALEX WINTER

1990 Taste the Pain (co-dir. Tom Stern) — RED HOT CHILI PEPPERS

1994 Milktoast — HELMET

1995 Verklemmt — FOETUS

1997 Exactly What You Wanted — HELMET

1997 Bug Powder Dust — BOMB THE BASS & JUSTIN WARFIELD

1997 One to One Religion — BOMB THE BASS

WIZ

1991 You Love Us — MANIC STREET PREACHERS

1992 Stinkin' Thinkin' — THE HAPPY MONDAYS

1992 Love's Sweet Exile — MANIC STREET PREACHERS

1993 Metal Mikey (v2) — LONDON SUEDE

1993 Too Young to Die — JAMIROQUAI

1993 Moving — LONDON SUEDE

1993 She's Not Dead — LONDON SUEDE

1994 Emergency on Planet Earth — JAMIROQUAI

1994 Jesus Hairdo — THE CHARLATANS

1995 Hypnotised — SIMPLE MINDS

1995 Loose (v1/2) — THERAPY?

1995 Diane — THERAPY?

1997 Man That You Fear — MARILYN MANSON

1997 He's Dead — LONDON SUEDE

1998 My Star — IAN BROWN

1998 If You Tolerate This, Then Your Children Will Be Next — MANIC STREET PREACHERS

1998 Inertia Creeps — MASSIVE ATTACK

1999 Out of Control — THE CHEMICAL BROTHERS

ROB ZOMBIE

1995 Electric Head, Part 2 (The Ecstasy) — WHITE ZOMBIE

1995 Super Charger Heaven — WHITE ZOMBIE

1996 I'm Your Boogieman — WHITE ZOMBIE

1997 Toyko Vigilante #1 — POWERMAN 5000

1998 Dragula — ROB ZOMBIE

1998 Living Dead Girl (v1/2) (co-dir. Joseph Kahn) — ROB ZOMBIE

1999 Superbeast (Girl Riding on a Motorcycle Mix) — ROB ZOMBIE

Millionaires Against Hunger

The first news reports out of Ethiopia were sickening in their brutality, damning in their simplicity. While the rest of the world was looking elsewhere, watching the Russians watching the Americans watching the Chinese watching the Russians; while President Reagan launched troops into Grenada, and the IRA sent its bombers after Thatcher, an entire African nation was literally starving to death.

A handful of European aid workers were doing their best, but that was never going to be good enough. The BBC film crew which entered the first refugee camp had expected to see suffering; what they discovered was absolute carnage, and when people switched on the news that night in November 1984, that was what they were presented with. Absolute carnage.

Few of the people watching the report would forget it that evening, or even the next day. Charities around the UK reported that donations rose substantially in the days immediately following the broadcast. But they also knew that another few weeks would bring another few disasters — lesser ones, to be sure, but heartrending all the same, and Ethiopia would be forgotten again, just another African dustbowl.

It is a matter of historical record today how Boomtown Rats vocalist Bob Geldof watched that report and was almost instantly inspired to launch first Band Aid, then Live Aid — individually and collectively, the largest, most successful, and still the best known music-driven charity efforts the world has ever seen. "Do They Know It's Christmas," written by Geldof and Ultravox vocalist Midge Ure, would become the highest selling single in British chart history; "We Are The World," its American doppelganger, would grasp a similar accolade in the US (it was eventually outsold by Elton John's "Candle In the Wind 97").

But whereas USA for Africa relied on the hoariest American mainstream acts for its vocal and musical punch — Dylan, Springsteen, Tina Turner, Stevie Wonder, the Jackson Family, Harry Belafonte, and Waylon Jennings, Band Aid concentrated on the young stars of the day, Spandau Ballet, Duran Duran, Bananarama, U2, Culture Club, Frankie Goes to Hollywood, Wham!, Style Council, Heaven 17 — the MTV generation in American TV talk. And whereas USA for Africa took six weeks to be released, Band Aid was out in six days. One event was pure Hollywood. The other was pure punk.

Even Geldof, pleased beyond words that his dream had come so far, could not help but acknowledge the difference. "The contrast between the British and American recordings could not have been more dramatic," he reflected. "Where in London, everybody rolled up looking pretty much as they would look on most Sundays at home, in L.A. the whole affair was 'showbiz'."

That same demographic demon would haunt the ensuing Live Aid festival as well. In London, the bulk of the talent on display had emerged within the past five years, an entire new generation of musicians stepping forward to relight the flames of idealism which had burned so brightly through the '60s, then been rekindled so dramatically by punk. In Philadelphia, it was the '60s revisited, or at least the early-mid 1970s, with the only even halfway "new" acts on stage being those Britons whose private schedules had simply placed them in the US at the time. Geldof had said beforehand that he didn't care who played so long as they were capable of making the money pour in. But it was a savage indictment of the state of American music in the mid-1980s all the same; and a glowing testament to the vitality of Britain's.

Band Aid was even born on the set of Britain's hippest TV show — Geldof's wife, Paula Yates, presented *The Tube*, a weekly rock magazine show notorious for venturing closer to the edge than any other. Frankie Goes to Hollywood and Sigue Sigue Sputnik were both debuted on *The Tube*; Foetus made his first UK TV appearance there; and Ultravox were headlining the night that Geldof concocted Band Aid — Midge Ure was actually on set the first time Geldof called him.

Geldof already had the ghost of the song, a projected Boomtown Rats ballad called "It's My World." The Rats, however, were in the commercial doldrums; their latest album, *In the Long Grass*, had already been preceded by three absolute flop singles, and nobody held out hope for the LP. He had a name for the new project as well, the Bloody Do-Gooders, although that would probably have to be changed, along with the words to the song.

Spending the next three days on the phone, Geldof had completed the cast of participants before "Do They Know It's Christmas" was finally written and had finalized most of the industry machinations which needed to be smoothed — production, art, distribution, the Musicians Union, the media, the routing of royalties towards the right destinations. The single was recorded on November 25; director Nigel Dick completed the video on November 27; it was on *Top of the Pops* on November 29. Two weeks later, "Do They Know It's Christmas" entered the UK chart at #1, and remained at the top for five weeks.

In the new year, Geldof and Ure paid their first visit to Ethiopia, accompanying the first shipment of relief; they returned home and Geldof immediately launched a new

Boomtown Rats tour, encoring every night with "Do They Know It's Christmas" and raising a further 50,000 pounds — the tour's entire profit — for Band Aid. Now it was time to put his next plan into action, staging the whole thing again as a festival.

Other nations had already followed Band Aid's lead — Austria Fur Afrika, USA for Africa, Chanteurs Sans Frontieres (France), Bryan Adams' Northern Lights (Canada), Germany, Japan, Australia. Geldof later estimated 25 Band Aid-type projects appeared around the world, topping their national charts and raising more money for the fund. "Do They Know It's Christmas" itself had raised 8 million pounds by mid-March; "We Are the World" $6.5 million by mid-May. Unfortunately, as Geldof pointed out, there were 22 million people starving. After reckoning in transportation, distribution, and administrative costs, $18 million would keep them alive for about three weeks.

Organizing Live Aid was much like organizing Band Aid — only on a far grander scale. It was not the first such operation; in 1971 George Harrison took over Madison Square Garden for the Concerts for Bangla-Desh benefit; eight years later, UNICEF organized four nights of Concerts for the People of Kampuchea at London's Hammersmith Odeon, drawing in appearances from the Pretenders, the Clash, Ian Dury, the Specials, and Elvis Costello, alongside such older acts as the Who, Robert Plant, Rockpile, and Paul McCartney.

That was the kind of line-up which Geldof envisioned, although his dream far surpassed either of those earlier ventures. Nothing less than a full global telethon was required, the action switching back and forth between stages around the world while telephone hotlines collected pledges and donations. He wanted television to broadcast the event, sponsors to underwrite it, advertisers to further boost the profits.

Transportation had to be sorted out for the artists. Promoters Bill Graham and Harvey Goldsmith were recruited to handle such mechanics as selecting the optimum venues. Geldof himself began contacting artists, everyone who appeared on the Band Aid and USA for Africa recordings; everyone who'd wanted to, but been unavailable at the time; and everyone who'd come along afterwards to ask why they'd not been invited in the first place. The first time Geldof told Harvey Goldsmith he wanted 50 bands, the promotor joked, "there aren't 50 bands on the whole planet." In fact, they ended up with close to 100.

Broadcast in its near entirety by the BBC in Britain, and MTV in the US, Live Aid took place on July 13, 1985, live from London's Wembley Stadium and Philadelphia's JFK. Similar events occurred simultaneously in Sydney, Vienna, Moscow, Cologne and the Hague. Appropriately, the first song played was "Rocking All Over the World," by veteran British boogie band Status Quo.

In terms of TV coverage, then, the UK event would run uninterrupted through the English afternoon, the US and US stages would then alternate through the evening, before the broadcast closed with the Americans alone. And as with any event of such magnitude, there were problems, judgmental as well as technical. Adam Ant had time to perform just one song, and the world was waiting for one of the monster hits of a few years before. Instead, he announced his latest single, "Vive le Rock," and the following week, while virtually every other act who performed that day saw their records climb the UK chart, Ant alone watched his go down.

Bob Dylan, equally ill-advisedly, concluded an already disastrously ramshackle acoustic set with the admonition, "it would be nice if some of this money went to the American farmers." As Geldof angrily retorted, "Something so simplistic and crowd pleasing... crass, stupid and nationalistic... was beyond belief. There is a difference between losing your livelihood and losing your life."

Geldof's Rats lost their vocal mikes during "Rat Trap"; Paul McCartney during 'Let It Be." Elvis Costello intended performing the Beatles' "All You Need Is Love" but didn't know the words, so he wrote them on his hand. And Bono forgot there were other bands besides U2 on the bill, and turned in one of the most memorable performances of the day.

"I remember getting carried away with myself on stage," Bono reflected. "I forgot it was a tight 15 minute thing on TV and I thought it was just U2 playing. As a result we didn't get to do 'Pride (In the Name of Love),' and ['Bad'] went on for seven minutes because I saw someone getting squashed down front and I was wanting to go down there. I wanted some sort of gesture that included the crowd because they seemed as important to me as the people behind the stage.

"The next few days were the blackest depression! I saw the TV film back and I thought I'd made a big mistake and misjudged the situation. I went out and drove for days. I couldn't really speak to anyone. And when I got back, I found people were saying the bit they remembered was U2."

U2's performance was indeed impressive — only Bryan Ferry of the "older" acts came close to touching their spontaneity; only Duran Duran, Style Council, and Paul Young approached their set with the same sense of adventure. And when Joan Baez took the JFK stage and greeted "you children of the eighties" with the promise, "this is your Woodstock and it's long overdue," her sentiments were as misplaced as Dylan's. Beyond bringing together a vast number of people for a festival of music, the two events had nothing whatsoever in common. Woodstock was the intended signal for a countercultural revolution; Live Aid was a technological money machine — "Millionaires Against Hunger," as the then unknown Red Hot Chili Peppers remarked in a second album out-take. Woodstock was designed to free peoples' consciousness; Live Aid was intended to jar their conscience.

And while Woodstock would ultimately prove the last of its breed, Live Aid was only the beginning, proof that rock'n'roll wasn't a mean ol' monster after all, and that it cared for the whole world. Barely two months after Live Aid, the first Farm Aid benefit sprang out of Dylan's closing remarks. Less than a year later, Amnesty International's Conspiracy of Hope concert tour traveled the world in aid of human rights, and was followed in 1988 by the similarly far-reaching Human Rights Now! outing.

Artists United Against Apartheid resurrected many of the ideals of Rock Against Racism earlier in the decade, but targeted their energies exclusively at the then-incumbent South African government (a point also taken by the Free Nelson Mandela campaign). The Beastie Boys' Free Tibet concerts in the mid-late 1990s focused attention upon China's occupation of that country; the Concert for Peace 2000 networked 2,000 concerts worldwide into one massive benefit for the reconstruction of Kosovo.

In humanitarian terms alone, Band Aid began a revolution; in musical terms... cynics say it started a bandwagon, but so long as that bandwagon continued distributing largesse to the needy, did it matter how altruistic its founding motives were? Or how musically valid it might actually prove? "Do They Know It's Christmas" really wasn't that bad a record — and certainly it was more palatable than the superstar bleating of its American counterpart.

But when producers Stock, Aitken, and Waterman took it upon themselves to reconvene Band Aid in 1989, rerecording the original hit with that year's crop of rising young stars, the ensuing reprise was pitiful. The string of other x-Aid records which followed in the original's wake, raising funds for everything from the victims of a North Sea ferry disaster (Ferry Aid) to those killed in the Bradford soccer stadium fire, did not raise the quality any higher.

All, however, made a difference to their intended beneficiaries, and in an age when many traditional charities are themselves in need of charitable aid, such gestures were an invaluable fillup to people attempting to rebuild shattered lives.

The Band Aid Trust finally closed down in January 1992, having raised a total $144,124,694. It had survived for seven years — "it was only meant to last seven weeks" said Geldof, "but I hadn't counted on the fact that hundreds of millions of people would respond, and I hadn't reckoned on over $100 million." Back in 1986, he said he didn't want Band Aid to become an institution. It didn't. It became an inspiration.

THE LIVE AID PROGRAM

(times in GMT)

12.02 STATUS QUO
12.19 STYLE COUNCIL
12.44 BOOMTOWN RATS
13.00 ADAM ANT
13.06 INXS (video from Melbourne)
13.16 ULTRAVOX
13.34 LOUDNESS (video from Japan)
13.47 SPANDAU BALLET
13.51 BERNIE WATSON (US)
14.02 JOAN BAEZ (US)
14.07 ELVIS COSTELLO
14.10 THE HOOTERS (US)
14.11 OPUS (video from Austria)
14.22 NIK KERSHAW
14.32 FOUR TOPS (US)
14.38 BB KING (video from the Hague)
14.45 BILLY OCEAN (US)
14.52 OZZY OSBOURNE & BLACK SABBATH (US)
14.55 SADE
15.12 RUN DMC (US)
15.12 YU ROCK MISSION (video from Belgrade)
15.18 STING
15.27 RICK SPRINGFIELD (US)
15.27 PHIL COLLINS
15.47 REO SPEEDWAGON (US)
15.50 HOWARD JONES
15.55 AUTOGRAPH (VIDEO FROM MOSCOW)
16.07 BRYAN FERRY
16.07 CROSBY STILLS NASH & YOUNG (US)
16.24 UDO LINDENBERG (video from Cologne)
16.26 JUDAS PRIEST (US)
16.38 PAUL YOUNG
16.48 PAUL YOUNG & ALISON MOYET
17.00 UK/US LINK-UP
17.02 BRYAN ADAMS (US)
17.20 U2 (UK)
17.40 BEACH BOYS (US)
18.00 DIRE STRAITS/STING (UK)
18.26 GEORGE THOROGOOD W/BO DIDDLEY/ALBERT COLLINS (US)
18.44 QUEEN (UK)
19.03 DAVID BOWIE & MICK JAGGER (pre-recorded video)
19.07 SIMPLE MINDS (US)
19.22 DAVID BOWIE (UK)
19.41 PRETENDERS (US)
20.00 THE WHO (UK)
20.20 SANTANA/PAT METHENY (US)

20.50 ELTON JOHN (UK)

20.57 ASFORD SIMPSON/TEDDY PRENDERGRASS (US)

21.05 ELTON JOHN/KIKI DEE (UK)

21.09 ELTON JOHN/KIKI DEE/WHAM (UK)

21.30 MADONNA (US)

21.48 FREDDY MERCURY & BRIAN MAY (UK)

21.51 PAUL MCCARTNEY (UK)

21.56 UK Finale

22.14 TOM PETTY (US)

22.30 KENNY LOGGINS (US)

22.49 THE CARS (US)

23.07 NEIL YOUNG (US)

23.43 POWER STATION (US)

00.21 THOMPSON TWINS (US)

00.39 ERIC CLAPTON (US)

01.04 PHIL COLLINS (US)

01.13 PAGE/PLANT/JONES (US)

01.47 DURAN DURAN (US)

02.15 PATTI LABELLE (US)

02.50 HALL & OATES, KENDRICKS, RUFFIN

03.15 MICK JAGGER

03.28 MICK JAGGER & TINA TURNER

03.39 BOB DYLAN, KEITH RICHARD, RON WOOD

03.55 US Finale

Art or Obscenity — Punk Rock Meets the PMRC

The Dead Kennedys had been testing America's morality for years — their very name was an affront to certain segments of the population, while the string of lethal singles which spun out of the band's San Francisco hometown offered blast after blast of confrontational outrage, each one guaranteed to send someone else's blood pressure soaring. When the band decided to package their latest album, 1985's *Frankenchrist*, with a free poster, reproducing Swiss-born artist H.R. Giger's *Penis Landscape #20*, the ten sets of copulating genitalia it depicted seemed mild compared to some of the band's calculations.

In Los Angeles, however, the mother of one teenaged purchaser thought otherwise. Enough that her own flesh and blood (her 14-year-old daughter bought the record for her 11-year-old brother) would be listening to such seditious rants as "MTV Get Off the Air," "Soup is Good Food," and "Goons of Hazard"; why should they have to look at a bunch of disembodied penises and vaginas while they were doing so?

Her initial complaint to the attorney general of California was taken up by the L.A. city attorney's office — a sequence of events which would plunge the Dead Kennedys, and their label Alternative Tentacles, into a landmark First Amendment (free speech) conflict which destroyed the band and came close to destroying the label. But it also tested the true strength of the first genuinely powerful regulatory body in the history of rock music, the Parental Music Resource Center (PMRC). Tested, and found sorely wanting.

Like *Frankenchrist*, the PMRC sprang into life in 1985 after three Washington DC housewives, Susan Baker, Pam Howar, and Tipper Gore, quite independently caught themselves actually paying attention to the lyrics of songs which their children, their friends and, in Howar's case, their aerobics instructors were blissfully, unconcernedly, listening to.

They were shocked. There was Sheena Easton, the Scottish songbird recently taken under Prince's wing, merrily discussing the virtues of her sugar walls. There was Prince himself, extolling the virtues of his "Darling Nikki," masturbating with a magazine in a hotel lobby. There was Judas Priest suggesting they be eaten alive and, of course, there was Frankie Goes to Hollywood, prolonging their erections by relaxing. "Anything goes," Howar said of current musical lyricism. "It's no holds barred." The women drew up a shortlist of music's favorite vices — promiscuity, sado-masochism, rebellion, drugs, and the occult — and on May 13, they organized a meeting in a local church, to discuss the menace of "Porn Rock."

Of course, the trio were not the first body to organize against what many people perceived as rock'n'roll's penchant for depraved imagery. Precisely ten years earlier, in 1975, *Time* magazine ran an exposé of "sex rock" highlighted by the 22 consecutive orgasms Donna Summer appeared to enjoy during her disco hit "Love to Love You, Baby." The following year, Rod Stewart's "Tonight's the Night" was censored for radio after sensitive ears objected to his request "spread your wings and let me come inside."

The Reverend Jesse Jackson, national president of the civil rights group People United to Save Humanity (PUSH), waded into the controversy, suggesting that his own group would be willing to organize boycotts against record companies who weren't able to clean up their act themselves. There was, he insisted, a "definite correlation" between the increasing number of unwanted teen pregnancies and "songs advocating sex without responsibility."

In 1977, *Variety* opened a second front when it imported the British establishment's loathing of "the new pop menace" punk rock with a seething condemnation of the music's "mindless violence, gutter language and crass excesses." Later that same year, the US press at large watched with interest as the Sex Pistols went on both media and judicial trial for the use of the word "bollocks" in their debut album title.

By the time the Washington wives had mobilized themselves, however, such controversies appeared mild by comparison with what was currently going on. The innuendo of early rock rebels had become overt, the off-color banter had become explicit pornography. The Beatles wanted to hold your hand, WASP (like Nine Inch Nails years later) wanted to fuck you like an animal. "Some rock groups advocate Satanic rituals," hissed the invitation to their first meeting. "Others sing of killing babies..." and others, still, recommended "open rebellion against parental... authority."

All of which was shocking enough, but worse was to come — for the music industry, at least. After all, people complained about the contents of song lyrics all the time. But this time, the complainants were somewhat better connected than the average "Outraged of Oshkosh" — Mrs. Gore was married to Tennessee Senator Al Gore; Mrs. Howar was the wife of a major DC construction company owner; and Mrs. Baker's husband was President Reagan's treasury secretary, James Baker.

Christening themselves the Parental Music Resource Center, the wives' message swiftly found fertile ground. *Newsweek* pondered "the tasteless, graphic and gratuitous sexuality saturating the airwaves and filtering into our homes." *US News & World Report* wondered "why we allow this filth?". The *Washington Post* praised the women for taking a stand against 'filth, violence, sado-masochism and explicit sex."

There were even some musicians willing to come out in support of the campaign. "I am fully in favor of censorship in music," admitted former Velvet Underground drummer Maureen Tucker. "As a parent, my feeling is that every record in a store should be required to have a lyric sheet that a parent can read before their kids buy the record. I think that's a parent's right when their kid is 13, 14, especially when records and CDs are so expensive. I've thrown out tapes that my kids have bought — 'no, you can't listen to that,' and they've just spent $10 on it, which is a lot of money in this household. That's how strongly I feel about it."

More direct action followed. In late May, the National Association of Broadcasters circulated over 800 radio station group owners, informing them of the PMRC's intention to lobby Congress for controls on the content of new music. They then contacted 41 record labels, asking them to include a lyric sheet with all new releases so station programmers "could clearly understand what words are being sung." MCA promptly pulled the latest single by One Way, the ironically titled "Let's Talk," on the grounds that it was indeed too suggestive for airplay.

By late summer, radio across the country was reviewing its airplay policies. MTV met with the PMRC, if only to emphasize that its own standards were already higher than "many other music video outlets" — the station's banning of the Rolling Stones' "She Was Hot," in which the fly buttons popped off a bulging male crotch, was doubtless a case in point. And on August 6, one day after the Recording Industry Association of America (RIAA) announced that its members would be willing to consider placing stickers warning of explicit lyrics on certain record sleeves, the Senate Commerce Committee announced they would be holding a hearing on "Porn Rock" in September. Mrs. Gore's husband, Senator Al, would be one of the members of the impartial panel.

The PMRC promptly rejected the RIAA's proposal as too arbitrary, and issued its own set of suggested guidelines. A uniform rating system was demanded, comparable to that employed by Hollywood — except instead of 300 or so movies a year, the music industry would be forced to individually grade around 30,000 songs. Artists should be assessed not only by the content of their records, but also by the standards they set in concerts that minors might attend.

Explicit or otherwise controversial record sleeves should be placed out of sight, in the manner of X-Rated movies or pornographic magazines; and albums should be loudly emblazoned with a single sticker warning of the record's overall content — "O" for occult, "V" for violence, "D/A" for drugs and alcohol, "X" for sex and bad language. Frank Zappa, one of the group's most vociferous opponents, suggested that they might also want to consider "a large yellow 'J' on material written or performed by Jews."

September finally brought the publication of the PMRC's list of rock's greatest offenders — Motley Crue, Black Sabbath, AC/DC, Venom, Van Halen, Twisted Sister, Cyndi Lauper, Prince, Madonna... music, Mrs. Gore would tell the Senate Committee, which "is curling my hair." And she, Mrs. Gore said, was "a fairly with-it person." One could only imagine what it was doing to sour old squares.

The PMRC continued attracting influential support, but so did the opposition. Danny Goldberg, owner of the management company Gold Mountain, announced the formation of the Musical Majority under the auspices of the ACLU, to resist the PMRC, with Los Angeles Mayor Tom Bradley becoming the first elected official to join his campaign. Four record company heads were asked to attend the Senate hearings — none showed, and only one even bothered responding to the invitation. The RIAA continued to be adamant that stickers remained the only viable option, and on November 1, a joint press conference announced that agreement had been reached.

Of the RIAA's 44 member companies, 22 (between them accounting for around 80% of all US record sales) would highlight "explicit" albums either with a parental advisory label, or by publishing unexpurgated lyrics on the back of the LP sleeve, to allow concerned citizens to make their own decision. Other issues were left undecided — including whether an album jacket emblazoned with this particular solution's expected expletives was at all appropriate viewing for anybody else who might chance upon it.

Nevertheless, both the PMRC and their allies at the Parent Teachers Association (PTA) proclaimed themselves delighted with the agreement — as was French singer Serge Gainsbourg, who became the first artist ever to be stickered in the US when his *Love on the Beat* album arrived with the warning, "Parental Advisory — Explicit French Lyrics."

The Dead Kennedys were not among the bands immediately targeted by the PMRC, neither was Alternative Tentacles among the labels to agree that they would follow the stickering guidelines. Indeed, as the organization's published list of targets made apparent, the most disturbing music of all — that being made on the fringes of even the alternative world's furthest reaches — had escaped the PMRC's attention altogether. Tipper? Meet Genesis P. Nevertheless, when *Frankenchrist* appeared in December 1985, it bore the appropriate sticker, and by the standards recently set in Washington, that should have been enough.

The law and the PMRC, however, felt different. Following the initial complaint, and at the PMRC's express bequest, Biafra's home was raided at 6 AM on April 15, 1986, by nine members of both the Los Angeles and San Francisco police departments, representing Biafra and the original complainant's home forces. The dawn visitors went away empty-handed, but still Biafra and Alternative Tentacles label manager Michael Bonanno were charged with distributing harmful matter to minors, an offense which carried a maximum penalty of a year in prison, or a $2,000 fine.

Only twice before, back in 1966, had the music industry been successfully prosecuted for obscenity, when the US Supreme Court upheld obscenity convictions leveled against the mail order distributors of an instrumental percussion album titled *Erotica*, and a spoken word collection of poems by the Frenchman Pierre Louys.

However, deputy city attorney Michael Guarino was confident that the tide had turned. Talking to the *L.A. Times*, he claimed that his office had an entire file full of dossiers on musicians that they were intending to prosecute once the Alternative Tentacles case had been won.

It would take more than nine months for the case to come to trial, a period during which both the group and label were pushed to the brink of extinction. Legal fees were hardship enough, but American retail appeared to have already found the band guilty. Stores which had hitherto carried Dead Kennedys records without a murmur were now backing away; Alternative Tentacles itself appeared to have been blacklisted.

A full schedule of 1986 releases was eventually cut back to just nine: seven albums, one EP, and a bitter commentary on events from The Dead Kennedys themselves, *Bedtime for Democracy*. Released in December, it would be the band's final recording.

The following year was even slower as Biafra awaited trial. Yet when the court date finally arrived, in mid-August, 1987, it was all but an anti-climax. The singer's defense included the claim that the poster was intended to illustrate, both literally and figuratively, the album's own concept of "people screwing each other over." Prosecuting the case, Guarino countered by describing the inclusion of the poster "absolutely irresponsible," adding to the jury's own discomfort (and evermore outraged sense of proportion) by comparing artist Giger to Richard Ramirez, the suspected "night stalker" serial killer.

An increasingly surreal debate was only exacerbated by events in a neighboring court room where a bitter child custody battle was very audibly underway, while the public gallery in Biafra's trial was crammed with his own fans, turning out in full punk regalia. Even the lawyers found themselves inexorably drawn into the comedy. On the final day in court, one of the defense team took Guarino's photograph with a joke camera — he pressed the shutter, and a penis popped out of the lens.

Talking a decade later, Guarino explained, "obscenity laws dictate that you can't distribute material that meets the established definition of prurient, and that you can't distribute hard-core material to children. I agreed that the Giger insert was inappropriate for distribution to kids, and I assumed the jury would be asked to decide that question." What he didn't foresee was that the judge would allow the poster's context, in terms of the album's lyrics, to figure in the debate. When he did, Guarino confessed, "I knew the case wasn't worth following."

After two and a half weeks of trial, the jurors broke to consider their verdict. Little more than a day later they returned to declare themselves stalemated. The judge promptly declared a mistrial and threw out the case. The whole affair ended with an ecstatic Biafra surrounded by jurors, all requesting autographed copies of the offending poster.

Victory, however, didn't come cheaply — as he told reporters later, "I've been wearing Lenny Bruce's shoes for over a year, and I don't think they fit very well." Not only had he lost his band, his marriage, too, had crumbled. Alternative Tentacles' legal fees topped $80,000; Biafra's own amounted to more than $55,000.

The British-based No More Censorship Defence Fund pitched in; so, through a battery of benefit concerts and exhibitions, did the worlds of hardcore punk and art. But unlike so many other rockers who found themselves in dire financial straits, Biafra had not been able to rely on the goodwill of his peers for support. According to *Rolling Stone*, Frank Zappa, Steve Van Zandt, and Jefferson Starship's Paul Kantner were the only high-profile rock artists to contribute to his defense fund, — all three acknowledging that despite the battle's public depiction as a First Amendment issue, there were political points at stake as well.

Not for the first time, afterall, was a notorious thorn in the authoritarian side being assailed through utterly unrelated means — Biafra's own example of Lenny Bruce, an anti-establishment comedian hounded for drug offenses, was equally applicable to a host of others, from Beatle John Lennon to MC5 manager John Sinclair.

"Make enough trouble on one side of the law," as Lords of the New Church vocalist Stiv Bators put it, "and they'll find a way of placing you on the other." Van Zandt (the former E

Street Band guitarist who coordinated 1985's "Sun City" anti-apartheid movement) condemned the entire music industry for simply sitting by and watching as society itself pressed artists "not to be so controversial. The controversy supposedly has to do with sex or drugs or Satanism, [but] it also extends to political issues. The Jim Morrisons or the Jimi Hendrixes of the world, maybe they wouldn't be signed now."

"I think they assumed I was some Sid Vicious idiot who would plead guilty and pay a $50 fine and then they could use that precedent against major-label artists," mused Biafra. "[Guarino himself] called [the trial] a 'cost-effective way of sending a message' on TV at the time — in other words, let's bash a small independent in hopes of getting rid of Ozzy, Judas Priest, and Prince." Instead, the trial set a valuable precedent for a plethora of future controversies, including the rash of rap acts which sundry local authorities deemed should follow Biafra up the courthouse path. In the words of 2 Live Crew's own rigorously persecuted (and unanimously acquitted) contribution to the art vs. obscenity debate, however, freedom of speech really did allow performers to be *as nasty as they wanna be.*

Michael Guarino, too, later acknowledged that the whole business was a gross error of judgement. Now the Director of Clinical Programs at JFK University in Orinda, CA, he told *Addicted to Noise* in 1997, "in retrospect, I think it's more important for [District Attorneys] offices and US Attorneys offices to focus on the tremendous amount of conflict of interest at the top, the accountants, the lawyers, the politicians, and get out of the area of freedom of expression."

Or, as Jello Biafra put it, "history is never on the side of the censor. Just ask Allen Ginsberg or Socrates."

[FOOTNOTE: Seven years later, a federal judge dismissed another artwork charge involving Alternative Tentacles, after the Philadelphia Fraternal Order of Police (FOP) and police sergeant John Whalen filed a $2.2 million defamation suit revolving around the Crucifucks' 1992 album *Our Will Be Done*. The sleeve depicted Whalen posing as an officer gunned down in the line of duty — a commentary, explained Biafra, "about the widespread problem of police brutality in America." The Judge agreed that the image was not, and could never be construed as, a personal assault upon Whalen himself.]

Also see the entry for "ALTERNATIVE TENTACLES," in "PRODUCERS & LABELS" on page 741.

Gilman Street

Since 1987, Berkeley's 924 Gilman Street Project has lit a beacon for alternative culture across San Francisco and the Bay Area. Non-profit, volunteer-run, all-ages, drug and alcohol free, the venue-come-community center has devoted itself exclusively to promoting up-and-coming (and frequently unsigned) bands from across the musical spectrum, often under the umbrella of a variety of benefits, from Rock Against Racism and Food Not Bombs, to battered womens' shelters and gay rights.

It also established itself as the hub of the new wave of punk bands to emerge out of California through the early-mid 1990s — Green Day, NOFX, Offspring, and Rancid were all nurtured by Gilman Street. So were Jon Ginoli's pioneering San Francisco queercore band Pansy Division and, through the last weeks of the decade, there was no indication that the class of '99 — the Gods Hate Kansas, the Plus Ones, Severed Head of State, Scratchabit, and the Capitalist Casualties — was going to prove any less dynamic than that of '89.

The Gilman Street phenomenon was only possible because of the nascent scene that had already formed in Bayside. Like London in 1976, there was a sudden flowering of bands, a surge of energy that was literally uncontainable — although Larry Livermore, ex-guitarist with late '80s Bay Area heroes The Lookouts and one of the original organizers of Gilman Street would cringe at the comparison.

Some 20 years older than the teenaged musicians he associated with, Livermore explains, "Because of my age [39 at the time], I had a much larger historical perspective on the whole scene. The Gilman Street scene had more in common with the early hippies than it did with the early punks. They were essentially very negative and reactionary, 'we hate everything, we want to destroy everything.' The Gilman Street punks were really about building something, they made their own club out of nothing, they ran it on volunteer labor, and it's still going. It's like a miracle, nobody's ever made any money out of it, and very few institutions of that size survive without a profit motive. But it has, and it's changed the face of pop music."

The moment there was a place to play, the bands came out of the woodwork. Many were still in high school (the Lookouts' own drummer, Tre Cool, was just 13); others just seemed to wander in off the street. The Offspring played one of their first shows under that name (they were previously known as Manic Subsidal) at Gilman Street, traveling up from their Orange County homebase for the occasion, and soon became a semi-regular attraction, opening for the likes of L7 and Fugazi.

El Sobrante natives Isocracy, on the other hand, debuted after frontman (and high school senior) John Kiffmeyer called Livermore, to ask how the Lookouts got so many shows. Livermore told him to bring his newly-formed band down to the next Lookouts' show, and they could play a few songs as opener. "Isocracy was as much a performance art show as music," Livermore reflected. "They'd bring all these props and garbage they found out in the suburbs and throw it at the audience, who'd throw it back." The band eventually broke up over creative differences — half the members wanted to become serious musicians. The others just wanted to continue having fun.

Another early recruit was the Mr. T Experience, the Berkeley band formed by UC Berkeley graduate Dr. Frank in the mid-1980s around a tight hybrid of Ramones, Descendants, and Buzzcocks-shaped pop punk. According to Livermore, "they were the first of the new punk bands that didn't just want to be tough and fight and nasty. Basically punk had strangled itself by this time with all this hostile, macho energy, and we were the new kind of guy that was nice and we liked people, and we thought it was fun to play and go to shows. We weren't violent at all, we were just the opposite, people put us down for being wimpy and sissies."

Gilman Street didn't care. So far as the organizers were concerned, "we had our own little universe with the best music in the world, even though nobody, even across the bay in San Francisco, took us seriously. We were just a bunch of goofy kids... not all of us were young, but it was the attitude. The old time punks in the city were very hardcore and mean, and they thought it was all kid's stuff, a joke."

Livermore, of course, disagreed with such pronouncements. "I started saying this back in '87, but it was a lot like what happened in the '60s. I came into San Francisco at the tail end of the hippie thing, but there was enough left for me to see that spirit, and that was what was going on at Gilman.

"There were all these kids that never had any outlet for their creativity, and had never been taken seriously because the East Bay (they used to call it East Berlin), it was the unwanted step-sister of the glamorous San Francisco/Bay area. It's basically working class, it's never been thought of as any sort of cultural area except for the university, and yet there sprung up this whole new kind of music, and a real rivalry as the kids would get a great kick of making fun of the old farts in San Francisco who hadn't done anything since the late '70s or early '80s. It was a positive kind of rebellion." And it was that which was reflected in sound of the bands that created the original Gilman Street scene.

"I've never understood music without a melody," Mr. T frontman Dr. Frank explained. "There are a lot of people that think rock music should be tough and mean and evil... [who] want the music they're listening to, to sound as ugly as they want people to think their lives are. But I think without a melody, it's not really music, so then it's just all attitude."

It was to preserve this policy of "music first" that Livermore launched the Lookout label. The imprint originally surfaced in spring 1987, with the release of his own band's first album, *One Planet One People*; it lay moribund for the remainder of the year, but by early 1988, he was already reconsidering Lookout Records' future.

The *Maximum Rock'n'Roll* fanzine set the ball rolling with the *Turn It Around* collection, the seminal document of Gilman Street's early days: Corrupted Morals, Sweet Baby Jesus, Isocracy, Crimpshrine, Operation Ivy, Stikky, Bugger All, and Sewer Trout all made it on, alongside future punk legends No Use For a Name. Now Livermore was looking to take things even further.

"In the fall a friend, David Hayes (later head of Very Small Records and Too Many Records) and I started talking about putting out more records because of all the new bands that had come up in Berkeley at that time." The pair went into partnership, and in January 1988, Lookout was relaunched with four 7" EPs, including Isocracy's *Bedtime for Isocracy*, Crimpshrine's *Sleep, What's That?*, and Operation Ivy's *Hectic*.

Formed by guitarist Tim Armstrong and bassist Matt Freeman, Operation Ivy debuted at Gilman Street in spring 1987, opening for MDC. A tight ska-punk band at a time when the west coast's only other active practitioners, Fishbone and the Untouchables, were seeking other directions entirely, Operation Ivy became firm Gilman Street favorites — were, in fact, all but synonymous with the venue for much of their career. Livermore himself personally became convinced that Operation Ivy would be the next band to break out — and remained so even when it became clear that the band would rather break up.

Freeman recalled, "I remember quite specifically [Larry] telling me that Operation Ivy was going to be one of those bands like the Dead Kennedys that keep selling more records after we break up. I said, 'Whatever, Larry, I think you did too much acid in the hippy days dude.' He's since proved me wrong. I've actually talked to him since and said, 'You were totally right'."

Few early Lookout signings packed the same punch as Operation Ivy, but by the end of 1988, Gilman Street was nevertheless well enough established to sustain a full length Lookout compilation: the double LP *The Thing That Ate Floydd*.

Thirty-four bands contributed, ranging from such Lookout faithfuls as Op Ivy, Isocracy, Sweet Baby Jesus, the Mr. T Experience and, of course, the Lookouts; through future headliners No Use For a Name, Steelpole Bathtub, and the Vagrants; and onto those bands whom even local history only dimly recalls — the immortally named Boo! Hiss! PFFTLB, and Eyeball and Kamala and the Karnivores (formed by Berkeley scenestress and promotor Kamala Parks). Other releases, too, flourished. The Yeastie Girlz — Jane, Cammie, and Kate — landed a record deal after serenading passers-by on Gilman Street itself with the à cappella rap "You Suck." Neurosis, the Surrogate Brains, Cringer, and Fuel followed.

Operation Ivy broke up in May 1989; two years later, Freeman and Armstrong later linked with another Gilman Street regular, drummer Brett Reed, as Rancid and therein hangs a true Gilman Street legend.

One night in 1991, an unknown new band appeared onstage at the venue. Nobody knew their names, nobody knew their repertoire. But they were called Smog, and they were destined to become one of the longest lasting legends of America's '90s punk scene, particularly after Rancid's success ensured that Reed would become the only member of the band not to embrace a future of obscurity.

Rather, he would fight to perpetuate Smog's almighty legacy, as a press release for Rancid's second album made clear. "Through hard work, persistence and an explosive debut LP on Epitaph, Rancid has managed to do the impossible; they were able to shake the legendary image and sound of Smog. This record is a testament to that victory."

Immediately, the music industry leaped aboard this tantalizing detail. "Suddenly we started seeing all these ads for gigs, 'ex-Smog'," marveled Matt Freeman. Music encyclopedias would repeat Smog's fame, carefully differentiating them from Bill Callahan's long-running Drag City label act (who did, coincidentally, share a Kill Rock Stars label compilation with the early Rancid), isolating instead Smog's indisputable punk rock heritage. The first time MTV aired a Rancid video, the VJ proudly and solemnly informed the world that Reed was once in Smog, one of *the* primal California punk acts.

Unfortunately, Smog were never that. Indeed, their sole legacy was a tape of one rehearsal; their sole claim to fame, as even Reed admitted, was his own future role in Rancid. The only reason for bringing up Smog in the first place was to fill in between mentions of his bandmates' pedigree — Operation Ivy and the spin-off Dance Hall Crashers (Armstrong and Freeman), and the UK Subs (Lars Frederikson). Irony, however, does not always translate well.

The first Gilman Street band to gravitate to a major label was Sweet Baby Jesus, who joined with Slash/Warner just weeks after Operation Ivy folded. They went little further, but still their elevation would have far-reaching consequences, particularly once they shortened their name to the less controversial Sweet Baby and prompted one of the bands they'd left behind, ex-Isocracy bassist John Kiffmeyer's Sweet Children, to change theirs', on the very eve of the release of their Lookout debut EP. *1000 Hours* was ultimately released under the name Green Day.

By mid-1990, new Lookout releases were appearing with delirious regularity — one month alone brought debuts from Crimpshrine frontman Jeff Ott's new band, Fifteen; the Mr. T Experience; Green Day's *Slappy*; and the first vinyl manifestation of Brent's TV, a '50s' styled rock'n'roll outfit whose guerilla assaults on laundromats the length and breadth of the west coast were already becoming legendary. Descending upon unsuspecting towns, the band would first call all the local venues in search of a show; then, if they couldn't get one, they'd simply set up beside the nearest washing machine.

Despite the success of both the club and Lookout, however, Gilman Street remained a fraught enterprise. The local authorities in particular seemed adamant to have the club closed — a campaign which only really lost steam in 1999, at the conclusion of a massive letter-writing campaign organized through the club's website.

Stubbornly undeterred, however, Gilman Street continued plying Berkeley youth with punk. 1991 brought the first Lookout release from Screeching Weasel, *Maximum Rock'n'Roll* columnist Ben Weasel's Chicago-based punk band, who themselves had been making regular pilgrimages to Gilman Street since 1988 — and once caused considerable consternation when Weasel stripped naked while supporting Op Ivy. The band broke up on a regular basis, but a split EP with Born Against was followed by the band's third album, *My Brain Hurts* (plus a reissue of their second, *Boogada Boogada Boogada*) — and despite their volatility, Screeching Weasel would become one of Lookout's own longest serving acts.

The following year, 1992, brought the club's first supergroup, Pinhead Gunpowder. The brain child of Crimpshrine's Aaron Cometbus and featuring members of Fuel and Monsula, plus Green Day's Billie Joe Armstrong, Pinhead Gunpowder debuted on the Lookout compilation, *Can of Pork* in 1992 and followed the next year with their own *Fahizah* EP on Lookout.

Pansy Division, too, were taking off — one of the few self-confessedly all-gay bands in America (and certainly on the American punk scene), their combination of tight pop-punk and fierce lyrics were all encased in a blistering sense of humor — as they proved with the EP *Nine Inch Males*, and a cover of Hüsker Dü's "The Biggest Lie." (Similarly topical was *Touch My Joe Camel*, a commentary on the prevalent belief that the beloved tobacco icon was, in fact, a thinly disguised phallus. With humps.)

It would be Green Day, however, who finally put Gilman Street firmly on the US punk map; two Lookout albums had sold over 50,000 copies apiece (only Operation Ivy's *Energy* outperformed them), and in 1994, the band moved to Reprise.

The band tried their hardest to keep Gilman Street out of their early press, even as Lookout's Wat Tyler celebrated Armstrong's burgeoning celebrity with the *I Wanna Be Billie Joe* EP, and Pansy Division prepared for their first national tour, opening for Green Day. "Majors want to monopolize on every underground that's happening, and I don't want our town to get exploited," Armstrong said. "I'm taking myself down, and I'm not taking anyone else with me!" Media feeding frenzies, after all, had destroyed enough indigenous scenes as it was, wiping out entire city's musical scenes. What chance did a single club stand?

But really there was no way around at least a degree of mainstream attention, as Livermore noted. "I understood [Green Day's] intention, I think that they meant extremely well. Their ideals and intentions were noble, but their understanding of it was a bit naive. In a sense, even by refusing to talk about it, they drew attention to it.

"I think they realized that if they were going to have success, they were going to have a big impact on the scene. They were trying to minimize it, because that scene meant everything to them; it's what saved them from the drudgery of a really alienated and useless youth. Really, except for music, those guys weren't going much of any place, and they'll be the first to tell you that. So they loved the scene. However, there's no way their success could fail to impact on it."

And maybe it did. Less than six months after Green Day's *Dookie* hit the Top 200, Offspring's *Smash* had joined it there. Six months on from that, Rancid, too, were chartbound. But success seems only to have bound the scene even tighter, to have deepened the devotion which kept Gilman Street alive in the first place. And five years after it became a household name, Gilman Street remains as pure as it was at the start.

The Moon-Ska Stomp

"You have to keep generating to a new audience," Moon Ska label chief Rob "Bucket" Hingley declared, "and ska music has that ability. Every so often, it brings up a whole new core audience. That has a lot to do with the fact that the music itself is so vital."

Back in 1983, of course, few people would have agreed with him. The 2-Tone movement which thrust ska back into the media spotlight was dead. The Specials and the Selecter had crashed and burned; Madness were off doing music halls someplace, and Bad Manners were still struggling unknowns. But Bucket wasn't going to let a little thing like the wholesale death of a dream put him off. His first band, Not Bob Marley, debuted his first record label, Ice Bear Records. When the band became the Toasters, the label became Moon and, in 1985, America's first ever dedicated ska label made its debut with a single by German ska legend Dieter Osten, and the Toasters' own *Recriminations* E.P.

Originally cut as a demo (with producer Stanley Turpentine — aka singer Joe Jackson), it was a primitive recording, but it was to become a prominent landmark regardless. Local sales earned the Toasters a residency at CBGB's; that, in turn, opened stages elsewhere across the city and, by 1986, there were enough bands dancing to a similar beat that Moon could scoop up the best of them for a showcase compilation, the aptly titled *New York Beat* .

It wasn't exclusively a ska collection — even the best-intentioned movement needs time to gather steam. Neither was it necessarily ska as any past practitioner might have recognized it. Hardcore and punk both filtered through the participants' influences; a brittle, battle-scarred edge which defied simple categorization, while the presence of a couple of straightforward mod groups, who didn't even nod in the direction of ska, only confused the brew even further. But still *New York Beat* would become the touchstone of the future, not only offering inspiration and support to other nascent ska communities across the US, but also proving that there really was life still left in the old warrior.

A few of the bands on the collection wouldn't last the pace — tight, aggressive units like City Beat, Beat Brigade, Too True, and the Boilers would all hustle off to ska heaven before the end of the decade. But a couple were built to last — the Toasters, of course, and King Django, the ska-crazed alias of one Jeff Baker, publisher of the metropolis' first ever ska 'zine, *Rude Awakening*. And with the success of *New York Beat* adding to the swirling live excitement, it quickly became clear that Moon had the potential to be something far more than a mere vanity label for Toasters' releases. The following year, then, Moon conceived a series of split 7" sin-gles, highlighting some of the best acts on the label's doorstep. The Toasters and Beat Brigade kicked off what was initially intended to be a six record set, followed by Legal Gender (who promptly changed their name to the N.Y. Citizens), and the Scene.

Financing problems ultimately halted the remainder of the series; Moon was still finding its feet in terms of economics as much as enterprise, and the Toasters' first two albums, *Ska-boom* and *Thrill Me Up*, would both be licensed to the Celluloid independent, simply because Moon couldn't afford to release them itself. Yet even that was not a safe haven. A chain reaction of closures and bankruptcies through 1987 saw Moon lose most of its key distributors, followed by Celluloid itself. With the band's finances wrecked, and plans in ruin, only the possibility of a German tour kept the Toasters alive and only a deal with that country's Pork-Pie label gave them the money to carry on.

Returning home, Bucket arranged a low-key domestic cassette release for *Thrill Me Up*, for the band to sell at gigs, and as group and label pulled themselves back up, he resolved that neither the Toasters, nor any of the other bands he still intended attracting to Moon would ever come so close to disaster again. If Moon was to survive, it would do so with a self-sufficiency which has remained the label's creed ever since — that no artist involved with Moon would ever suffer the financial and emotional hardships incurred by labels and distributors collapsing.

The New York Citizens were the first to benefit from Bucket's new found resolve, with the 1988 release of their first album, *On the Move*. An aggressive mix of melodic 2-Tone, funk, and chantalong hardcore, *On the Move* was a precursor indeed of both the skacore and skafunk of the future and a total contrast to what was initially planned to be Moon's next release, the *Rockin' Steady* debut album by the Boilers. Unlike the New York Citizens — or just about any other act in town at the time — the Boilers preferred to keep their 2-Tone pure.

Sadly, a string of mishaps ensured that *Rockin' Steady* would only ever appear in Britain, and there only briefly. Its Moon release never happened, and the Boilers folded with only their contribution to *New York Beat* to their domestic credit, a pitiful legacy for such great promise. But the New York Citizens lived on and, in late 1989, they released their second record, the *Stranger Things Have Happened* EP — a title which could just as readily been applied to Moon's next release.

New York might have been the hub of American ska during this period, but it was by no means the be all and end all.

Isolated though it remained, the syncopated beat was pulsing across the country — as the Toasters discovered when their touring began taking them further afield.

A burgeoning Boston scene was already known — less than a year after *New York Beat*, the first wave of Boston ska bands highlighted the *Mash It Up* compilation. Other bands, however, hailed from considerably further afield, and in 1988, Moon released *Skaface*, a compilation which reached across to the west coast in search of fresh ska talent.

Let's Go Bowling, Skankhead, and Donkey Show all made notable showings, while the album also debuted future superstars No Doubt, then boasting two female vocalists and a live set comprised almost exclusively of Specials and Selecter covers (their one original song was the self-explanatory "No Doubt"). *Skaface* was a revelatory collection, stunning everyone who still believed the ska movement was a distinctly east coast regional thing (it hadn't seemed large enough to be called a phenomenon); stunning, too, the doomsayers who believed that Moon still lived on borrowed time. The label had survived, and was growing stronger all the time. And so was the music it promulgated.

From New Jersey, Bigger Thomas and the Steadys would prove unquestioned highlights of the *New York City Ska Live* compilation, an historic Cat Club collection which showcased just how vibrant East Coast ska had become and how disparate its practitioners were. But Moon no longer wanted, nor even needed, to simply trawl through local waters. Suddenly, every city in the country seemed to have its own burgeoning ska scene, and Moon was the first port of call for almost every one.

All around the country, promoters were anxiously searching for local talent to match with the visiting New Yorkers. When the Toasters hit Philadelphia, Public Service immediately handed over their debut, *Somebody Scream*; Moon released it on cassette in 1990. When they arrived in DC in 1992, they encountered the Skunks. Back in California, enough bands had now broken through to fill an entire album with west coast ska: 1992's *California Ska-Quake* — a set which not only introduced a host of bands destined to become key players on the 1990s American ska scene, but also highlighted the dichotomous relationship which exists between the east and west coasts.

While the east, or at least Moon's share of it, continued to lean towards the old supercharged 2-Tone sound and its own immediate offshoots, the west was never bound by so readily definable a tradition. Rather, it evolved from a variety of sources, not least of all jazz-based swing, early Jamaican ska, mento, and punk as well.

The jazz-inflected Jump with Joey made one of their rare American appearances on the album; Hepcat turned in a typically high-quality Heptones-esque smoothie; the long

moribund Dance Hall Crashers announced their much-anticipated relaunch; and Skankin' Pickle dropped by to show what had happened to *Skaface* heroes, Skankhead. They'd changed their name in 1989, and self-released a debut album, *Skafunkrastapunk* in 1991, debuting their own Dill Records label with a set whose title pretty much summed up their sound... or at least part of it. They forgot to squeeze in the metal.

The now entrenched Moon notwithstanding, Dill would rapidly become one of the premier US ska labels, not only through Skankin' Pickles' own releases, but also via a chain of inspired outside signings. Hawaii's Tantra Monsters, the Rabies, the Rudiments, and the now legendary San Francisco-based Janitors Against Apartheid would all confirm the basic tenets of Dill's *modus operandi* — there's ska, there's punk, and there's a world in between of esotericism and weirdness. Skankin' Pickle's own final releases were an EP, followed by an album's worth of quite unexpected covers, ranging from Bad Brains and Bad Manners, to Oingo Boingo and Devo.

Elsewhere, too, California ska was thriving, even as *California Ska-Quake* arrived to acquaint the rest of the country with the western state of affairs. Tazy Phyllipz and Albino Brown, the DJ masterminds behind K-UCI's *The Ska Parade*, were already a landmark in Orange County, with an impressive roster of stars and wannabes regularly playing live on their show (and then being creamed off for 1994's 28-track *Step On It: The Best of the Ska Parade Radio Show* compilation). From punks playing ska like the Voodoo Glow Skulls, to ska in its original form, courtesy of the legendary Roland Alphonso; from traditionalists like Jump with Joey to unrepentant third wavers like the Skeletones; the sampler (and accompanying video) captured the Californian explosion in all its glorious diversity. And now, it seemed, the rest of the American music scene was finally catching up.

By 1993, Moon (or Moon Ska, as the label was rechristened, following the objections of a rival, older Moon label in Tennessee) was diversifying furiously, its appetite for ska fed by a massive grassroots movement which flourished across the nation, and further nourished by college radio, fanzines, even a hint of mainstream interest. It was time to put the whole thing on the road.

Through fall 1993, the Skavoovie package tour scoured the US and Canada. Headlined by the reformed delights of the '60s pioneers the Skatalites, and 2-Tone veterans Selecter, alongside Special Beat and the Toasters, together with an ever-changing roster of regional talent, in every city the scene was the same, an auditorium crammed with fans and a backstage stuffed with bands — some preparing to perform, some simply hoping to. Moon and Bucket remained a magnet for every demo tape in town.

Out of Connecticut bounded Spring-Heeled Jack. From Philadelphia, Ruder Than You; from Grand Rapids, Michigan, Mustard Plug — suddenly, there was a thriving midwestern ska scene thrusting into the spotlight, spilling off the Jump Up! label's invaluable *American Skathic* showcase, and inspiring Moon Ska to release *Skarmageddon*, the first in a series of compilations showcasing ska acts from all across America — MU330, Mustard Plug, Skapone, the Invaders, Weaker Youth Ensemble, the Pacers....

Spawn of Skarmageddon followed and again it shone the spotlight on the midwest — Michigan's Superdot, Illinois' Slaphappy, and St. Louis trad/jazz fusionists Isaac Green and the Skalars — who would swiftly become one of Moon Ska's mightiest new signings, alongside the inimitable Pietasters.

Formed in DC in 1990, the Pietasters had already self-released their eponymous debut, and through 1994–95, the group toured incessantly. Indeed, if some acts are patently not made for the long haul out of obscurity, there are others for whom the attendant trials and tribulations are very much the stuff of life... bands like the Pietasters, who can look back on their career-so-far and shudder, "there was six years of drinking and driving around the country to get us where we are now." Vocalist Steve Jackson grimaced in 1997, "we're road hardened veterans of the seedy underbelly of club entertainment."

By the time the Pietasters released their second album, *Oohlooloo*, even the national music media was sniffing around their dessert tray. But though both press reaction and sales were good, that wasn't enough for some of the octet's members. Suddenly, the only thing that "the band most likely to" through 1994–95 were likely to do was splinter. "We were in a transition," Jackson reflected, "because people wanted to do different things with their lives. They thought it was a dumb idea to be in a band that didn't make any money. Those of us with poor judgement carried on" — and promptly landed a tour with the Mighty Mighty Bosstones. A deal with Rancid frontman Tim Armstrong's Hellcat label followed, and the Pietasters haven't looked back since.

Ska broke in America in 1996. MTV and the media had already been paying ever closer attention for a couple of years; inevitably the major labels would follow. The Mighty Mighty Bosstones came through first, but others quickly followed, so fast and furious that within a year, most ska purists were mourning the day the world ever heard of their music.

Bosstones' frontman Dicky Barrett shared the dismay, all the more so since his band were frequently singled out as the act which made ska "fashionable" again. Oozing with irony, he told *Billboard*, "I am the fucking puppeteer. I am the great fucking Jim Henson. All of the ska musicians you hear are merely my Muppets." Talking to *Alternative Press* in early 1997, however, he was considerably more resigned. "[Record companies] put together bands all the time; there's ska bands being constructed right now by some marketing genius and record-label weasels who are gonna try and cash in on what's going on. Some may even exist right now, although I don't want to point any fingers."

The Bosstones weren't, of course, the only beneficiaries of ska's mainstream emergence. No Doubt slammed home with 1996's US chart-topping *Tragic Kingdom*; Goldfinger hit with "Here in Your Bedroom"; Reel Big Fish scored with "Sell Out"; Less Than Jake with *Losing Streak*; Save Ferris with a wholesomely radio-friendly cover of Dexy's "Come On, Eileen." Suddenly Moon Ska was no longer the only game in town. Capitol, Warners, BMG, and Sony all had their ska bins too.

In fact, ska broke both because of and despite the Mighty Mighty Bosstones' own accelerating rise. On the one hand, they unquestionably introduced great swathes of the American public to the new wave of "ska," even if a lot of what hit was in actuality a desperately watered-down approximation of what had been building in the underground. On the other hand, it was a need to tell the world what the music really sounded like which inspired other bands to try and make as big an impression as the Mighty Mighty Bosstones had. If the public wouldn't listen to *Don't Know How to Party*, maybe they'd listen to something else.

Over at Moon Ska, the mood was seriously defiant. Angrily hitting out at what "true" ska aficionados justifiably saw as the corporate take-over of their music, the label all but doubled its output and raised the stakes even further with some genuinely uncompromising releases — including some which the label itself wasn't always aware of.

Rocksteady aficionado Chris Murray formed King Apparatus in his native Toronto in the late 1980s. 2-Tone based, but with elements of rock and punk floating freely throughout, the group debuted with the *Loud Party* cassette, then scored a local hit with their single "Made for TV." Their follow-up LP, *King Apparatus* and constant touring brought them Canadian acclaim, while distribution through Moon Ska introduced them to America. Indeed, King Apparatus would become the first foreign concern ever to be signed by the label, although that wasn't honor enough. Murray wanted to take ska to the limit, and when King Apparatus broke up, he did.

Moving to California, and rechristening himself Venice Shoreline Chris, the singer recorded an LP in his own four-track studio, utilizing nothing more than an old Hammond organ and an acoustic guitar, which doubled as percussion. The result, *The Four Track Adventures of Venice Shoreline Chris*, was so far removed from the typical Moon Ska record that even Bucket was taken aback.

The songs themselves were superb, with a truly traditional sound. But was the outside world ready for lo-fi? Probably not. Bucket asked Murray to rerecord the album in a more conventional manner, but though the singer complied, he still made his point. Somewhere in the manufacturing process, between the tapes being delivered to the pressing plant and Moon receiving finished copies of the album, an extra track crept onto the album, a plaintive (and defiantly poorly-recorded) plea that the album be released as it was originally conceived.

Moon Ska's catalog continued to grow. The Busters (from Germany), Spitfire (Russia), Skaferlatine (France), Mr. Review (the Netherlands), and the Porkers (Australia) joined the roster; and when a Toasters tour of South America introduced Bucket to the vivacious world of Latino ska, of course he wanted to share it with Stateside ska fans as well, via the *100% Latin Ska Compilation*.

He picked up the debut (and sadly, posthumous) album by Agent 99, one of the hits of the May 1994 Oi! Ska festival in New York, and possibly the only ska band ever to employ a very prominent flute; then followed that with the first ruminations of the New York Ska-Jazz Ensemble supergroup. The brainchild of Toasters Rick Faulkner and Fred Reiter, the Ensemble featured fellow Toaster John McCain, ex-Scofflaw Victor Rice, Skatalite Devon James, and ska sessionman extraordinaire Cary Brown, plus such stellar guests as the Skatalites' Tommy McCook and Hepcats Greg Lee and Alex Desert. The result was a Big Apple ska album cut through with authentic jazz passages.

Surely the most bizarre addition of all, however, was Mephiskapheles, the world's only known skanking Satanists. Moon Ska's Noah Wildman recalled, "The sound of Mephiskapheles was pretty unprecedented for the NYC ska scene — even today, they stick out like a sore thumb. Basically bouncing trad ska off of punk, jazz, oi!, alternarock and a hefty dose of '80s cheese-metal, and a singer whose vocal style is somewhere between Dicky Barrett and a Death Metal croaker, makes for some captivating listening."

Produced by Bill Laswell, Mephiskapheles' *God Bless Satan* album initially appeared on the band's own Pass the Virgin label; licensed to Moon Ska (where it was granted the catalog number 666) the LP garnered a rash of rave reviews, and more besides. Mephiskaphales' cover of "The Bumble Bee Tuna Song" was elected one of the Top Ten Worst Ska Songs of All Time when the readers of *Skatastrophy* fanzine were asked to vote upon such a heady issue, and the group promptly agreed. As trombonist Greg Robinson declared, "it's a really annoying tune, but we've got to play it."

And play it they did, first in front of fervid hometown crowds, then around the US as Mephiskapheles toured with punk veterans The Buzzcocks. By 1996, Europe, too, had fallen beneath the band's spell and, before the year was out, Mephiskapheles found themselves with three hit singles in Hawaii... including, inevitably, the "Bumble Bee Tuna Song."

Mephiskapheles also rounded up a couple of firsts for Moon Ska. Their arrival marked the first time the label received complaints from the religiously outraged, while they also became first Moon Ska project to be aired on MTV when Rancid hosted *120 Minutes*. After a decade plus spent shouting the odds from the most remote sidelines of the US music industry, Moon Ska had finally tasted "the big time." And all the credit was promptly deflected onto anybody else they could think of.

"I give credit to everybody that believes in it basically," Bucket explained. "There's been a lot of people over the years that have had their shoulder to the wheel to see that ska music got promoted, and people didn't forget about it. And mainly to the bands that have been for a long time playing — I don't just mean the Toasters, but bands like Bim Skala Bim and others who were out there in the cold. But mostly, the music itself, because it's irrepressible.

"The new kids that come in, no matter what the point of entry is, through 2-Tone, punk, or skacore, all of a sudden they're exposed to the fact that there's more to it than just this one band, there's a whole subculture of this stuff. They get interested and start tracing it back and maybe rediscover the Skatalites, rediscover Laurel Aitken, and that's really refreshing for me because that's what it's really all about.

"The roots of the music is with these guys, so it's fitting that kids can get into it through ska-core, and graduate from that through the 2-Tone bands or whatever, to get to the roots of the music. I think that's what's really rewarding. It's nice to see that happening."

ISAAC GREEN & THE SKALARS Don't Count
HEPCAT Open Season Is Closed

ICE BEAR/MOON SKA LABEL DISCOGRAPHY — THE FIRST CENTURY

TOAST 1/2 THE TOASTERS — Beat Up 7"
TOAST 3/4 EAST OF EDEN — Sea of Happiness 7"
TOAST 5/6 THE TOASTERS — Recriminations EP
TOAST 7/8 KILL ME — Kill Me LP
TOAST 9/10 various artists — New York Beat — Hit and Run LP
TOAST 11/12 EAST OF EDEN — Dieter Osten LP
TOAST 13/14 THE TOASTERS/BEAT BRIGADE split 7"
TOAST 15/16 LEGAL GENDER/THE SCENE split 7"
013 THE TOASTERS — Skaboom LP
017 NEW YORK CITIZENS — On the Move LP
018 THE BOILERS — Rockin' Steady LP
019 various artists — Skaface LP
020 NEW YORK CITIZENS — Stranger Things Have Happened
021 THE TOASTERS — Thrill Me Up LP
022 various artists — NY Ska Live
023 THE TOASTERS — This Gun For Hire LP
024 DANCE HALL CRASHERS — 1989–92 LP
025 BIGGER THOMAS — Mboy Yknow LP
026 PUBLIC SERVICE — Somebody Scream LP
027 LET'S GO BOWLING — Music to Bowl By LP
028 THE SCOFFLAWS — The Scofflaws LP
029 KING APPARATUS — King Apparatus LP
030 THE BUSTERS — Couch Potato LP
031 various artists — California Ska-quake LP
032 HEPCAT — Out of Nowhere LP
033 THE TOASTERS — New York Fever LP
034 THE SKUNKS — Chaos in Skunkville LP
035 URBAN BLIGHT — Urban Blight LP
036 THE BUSTERS — Dead or Alive
037 REGATTA 69 — Regatta 69 LP
038 RUDER THAN YOU — Big Step LP
039 PIETASTERS — Pietasters LP
040 THE SKUNKS — Mixed Nuts LP
041 various artists — Skarmageddon LP
042 MUSTARD PLUG — Big Daddy Multitude LP
043 THE TOASTERS — Dub 56 LP
044 THE ARSENALS — Stomp LP
045 THE TOASTERS — Live in LA EP
046 MU330 — Press LP
047 MUDSHARKS — Crackin' Porcelain LP
048 THE ALLSTONIANS — Go You! LP
049 THE FIASCOS/OTIS REEM split 7"
050 NEVILLE STAPLES — Skanktastic LP

051 THE SCOFFLAWS — Spider in My Bed 7"
052 THE SCOFFLAWS — In Hi Fi LP
053 THE PORKERS — Grunt LP
054 various artists — 100% Latin Ska LP
055 MAGADOG — Magadog LP
056 New York Citizens — The Truth About LP
057 NEW YORK SKA-JAZZ ENSEMBLE — New York Ska Jazz Ensemble LP
058 various artists — Spawn of Skarmageddon LP
059 PIETASTERS — Oolooloo LP
060 NEW YORK SKA JAZZ ENSEMBLE — Blow Wind Blow 7"
061 LAUREL AITKEN — The Bluebeat Years LP
062 SKAVOOVIE AND THE EPITONES — Fat Footin' LP
063 THE TOASTERS — Chuck Berry 7"
064 BLUEBEATS — Hardest Working Man 7"
065 LET'S GO BOWLING — Mr Twist LP
666 MEPHISKAPHELES — God Bless Satan LP
067 THE SLACKERS — Better Late Than Never LP
068 SPRING-HEELED JACK — Static World View LP
069 AGENT 99 — Agent 99 LP
070 LOS PIES NEGROS — Moviendo Los Pies LP
071 VENICE SHORELINE CHRIS — The Four Track Adventures Of LP
072 various artists — Closer Than You LP
073 THE SLACKERS — Tonight 7"
074 LET'S GO BOWLING — You Take Me 7"
075 THE PIETASTERS — Ocean 7"
076 RUDER THAN YOU — Horny for Ska LP
077 various artists — Skank Down Under LP
078 various artists — California Skaquake 2 LP
079 THE SKUNKS — No Apologies LP
080 LOS HOOLIGANS — Traditions LP
081 THE PIETASTERS — The Pietasters Are Strapped Live LP
082 unissued
083 THE TOASTERS — Hard Band Fe Dead LP
084 unissued
085 unissued
086 ISAAC GREEN & THE SKALARS — Skoolin' with the Skalars LP
087 HOUSE OF RHYTHYM — In a Different Style LP
088 THE TROJANS — Trojan Warriors for Your Protection LP
089 INSPECTER 7 — Agent 86 7"
090 various artists — Latin Ska vol 2 LP
091 THE BLUEBEATS — Dance with Me LP
092 NEW YORK SKA-JAZZ ENSEMBLE — Low Blow
093 THE ALLSTONIANS — The Allston Beat LP
094 MAGADOG — DUI-N-I LP
095 BUFORD O'SULLIVAN — I Can't Decide EP
096 MU330 — Jason 7"
097 THE SCOFFLAWS — Live vol 1 LP
098 SKAVOOVIE & THE EPITONES — Riverboat 7"
099 various artists — New York Beat vol 2 LP
100 unreleased

JUMP UP LABEL DISCOGRAPHY

01 various artists — American Skathic vol 1 LP
02 various artists — American Skathic vol 2 LP
03 various artists — Death of American Skathic LP
04 PARKA KINGS — 23 Skidoo LP
05 SUSPECT BILL — Bill Me later LP
06 various artists — Return of American Skathic LP
07 TELEGRAPH — 10 Songs & Then Some LP
08 EXCEPTIONS — Five Finger Discount LP
09 HOT STOVE JIMMY — Salute LP
10 ECLECTICS — Idle Worship LP
11 GREENHOUSE — Tomorrow the World LP
12 PARKA KINGS — Bienvenidos LP
13 GANGSTER FUN — Pure Fun LP
14 ADJUSTERS — Politics of Style LP
15 DEALS GONE BAD — Large & In Charge LP
16 TELEGRAPH — Quit Your Band LP
17 SKAPONE — Brand New Flavor LP
18 various artists — Smash Your Radio LP
19 RUNFORYERLIFE — Runforyerlife LP
20 FIRST GRADE CRUSH — It's Not You LP
21 unreleased
22 PEACOCKS — In Without Knocking LP
23 THUMPER — Songs from the Grave LP
24 PARKA KINGS — Where's the Afterparty? LP
25 ORANGETREE — Fixing Stupid LP
26 DR MANETTE — The Same Thing LP
27 HOT STOVE JIMMY — Theme LP
28 TEENAGE FRAMES — 1% Faster LP
29 MEGASUPERULTRA — Power Pop Art LP
30 DEALS GONE BAD — Overboard LP

ASIAN MAN LABEL DISCOGRAPHY

01 LESS THAN JAKE — Pezcore LP
02 various artists — Misfits of Ska LP
03 unreleased
04 B LEE BAND — B Lee Band LP
05 LINK 80 — 17 Reasons LP
06 various artists — Misfits of Ska 2 LP
07 MU330 — Press LP
08 MU330 — Chimps on Parade LP
09 SLAPSTICK — 25 Songs LP
10 MEALTICKET — Lisa Marie LP
11 THE BROADWAYS — Big City LP
12 SLOW GHERKIN — Double Happiness LP
13 TUESDAY — Early Summer LP
14 LINK 80 — Killing Katie LP
15 BLUE MEANIES/MU330 — split 7"
16 MU330 — Crab Rangoon LP
17 UNSTEADY — Double or Nothing LP
18 POTSHOT — Pots'n'Shots LP
19 TUESDAY — Freewheelin' LP
20 THE CHINKEES — Karaoke with the Chinkees EP
21 THE BROADWAYS — Broken Star LP
22 THE CHINKEES — Are Coming LP
23 FIVE IRON FRENZY — Miniature Golf Course EP
24 LET'S GO BOWLING — Freeway Lanes LP
25 JOHNNY SOCKO — Full Trucker Effect LP

The Bristol Sound — From Pop Group to Pop Stars

Few bands were so universally despised as the Pop Group. Apparently motiveless, seemingly humorless, and certainly tuneless, the gray-garbed guerrillas were theoretically flawless in the newsprint plaudits of sundry UK music critics.

But anybody venturing down to find out what they actually sounded like was seldom in for anything less than an evening of shuffling discomfort, in the company of four self-confessed musical incompetents for whom the hint of a rhythm was sufficient to sustain another five minutes of bad-mannered bashing; whose lyrics gashed slogans across the cacophony; whose very existence — as musical entertainment, at least — was an affront to anyone born with ears.

Even as they progressed and improved, even once they began releasing records, still the Pop Group sat on the furthest extremes of even the bleak slabs of concrete which passed as punk experimentalism. They fell out of the sky like a two-headed cow and, when their debut single swore, "western values mean nothing to her," much the same sentiment could be applied to the Pop Group. Musical values meant nothing to them.

Alongside fellow dub into dirge pioneers the Slits, however, the Pop Group created a hydra-headed legacy which would haunt the dislocation dance for the next ten years. "People like Steve Albini keep going on about the Pop Group," vocalist Mark Stewart reflected years later, "Al [Jourgensen] from Ministry.... But a lot of people refer back to the Pop Group stuff, not because they were fans, but because it opened up a lot of directions for people, and gave them the possibility of experimenting a lot. Maybe it paved the way for a lot of things."

The Pop Group imploded in 1981, but they never really died. Stewart alone ensured that, linking with producer Adrian Sherwood and, as he admitted, basically carrying on as before. "It wasn't as if I left the band behind, because you can hear it continuing. If you were a psychiatrist, you could study the lyrics and attitudes and stuff, and you'd see I haven't really changed, I've still got the same Bolshi, arrogant attitude I had when I was 14. I don't feel any different than I did in the Pop Group, I'm still ranting and raving about stuff."

Indeed, his first move as a solo artist was to form the dub reggae band which, if one rolls back the roughness which was the Pop Group's best disguise, was one of the things which they'd been trying to become, around the time of their second album. Except what this new group created wasn't reggae either. Stewart continued, "when I was 14, 15, we were buying New York Dolls albums, but I was also buying really heavy dub, and I was going to black clubs in Bristol from the age of 12. With the Pop Group, from the word go, I wanted a funk sound, but specifically I wanted a reggae producer, so we got in the best English reggae producer, Dennis Bovell. There's lots of dub techniques on the Pop Group's stuff."

The Pop Group's home town of Bristol already had a flourishing reggae scene. As one of the principle ports for both 18th century slavery and 20th century immigration, Bristol embraced racial integration earlier than almost any other city in Britain — and it showed in the music.

Bands like Black Roots, Talisman, and Restriction were local superstars; neighborhoods like St. Pauls and Clifton hosted the hottest sound system shows; and record stores like Revolver dispensed the newest reggae and dub titles. And then there was the Dug Out, the catalyzing Clifton club where the city's musical mavericks learned to mix and match their influences to the tapestry of local preoccupations. Revolver Records' own Grant Marshall was the DJ, mixing reggae and dub with punk, funk, and electro; adding hip hop to the brew once those records began percolating into the country, jazz as that started seeping back into cool.

It was at the Dug Out where Nellee Hooper, Miles Johnson, Rob Chant and Rob Smith (later to unite as Smith and Mighty) first started congregating regularly, joining Marshall behind the turntable in the first loose incarnations of what would become the Wild Bunch — swiftly joined by Robert el Naja and Andrew Vowles, the posse eventually morphed into Massive Attack.

The shattered remains of the Pop Group were there, too — Gareth Sager and Bruce Smith, wondering what would happen if they mixed James Brown with Fela Kuti and called it Rip Rig & Panic; Dan Katsis, on the verge of birthing the Glaxo Babies; and Stewart, on the cusp of releasing the dark dub *Learning to Cope with Cowardice* album and already pondering plots even further afield.

In 1982, Stewart contacted Keith LeBlanc and Doug Wimbish, the rhythm section which powered the early Sugarhill rap scene. They were playing with Grandmaster Flash at the time, "cutting all the early rap stuff that we were trying to copy with the Pop Group. Fantastic! And they were open enough to meet this crazy kid from Bristol and start making these weird kind of disjointed records."

Cementing themselves into place as the latest incarnation of Stewart's Mafia backing band (then reinventing themselves as the Tackhead Sound System, with one of Stewart's closest friends, Gary Clail), Wimbish and LeBlanc became a pervading local influence by their very presence. Their links with Stewart, himself already assuming a father figure role on the whole Dug Out scene, only flung the door open wider.

"Although hip hop was American, and we were British, there was never that sense of not understanding it," the Wild Bunch's Miles Johnson reflected. "We were West Indians dealing with reggae and they were dealing with soul, everybody had the same struggles, the same search for enjoyment. What I liked about punk, although it sounded a bit fake, was the same as I liked about hip hop. You didn't have a regular rhythm, and you could be creative with it."

Grant Marshall continued, "punk and reggae never sounded similar but they shared a way of thinking. There was an anarchistic feeling about both. Jamaican culture has always been rebellious; it's always been about taking risks."

That creativity, and those risks, were to be expressed as powerfully within the audience as they were up in the DJ booth; and among the musicians who forged the bond between the two, its impact was even more pronounced.

Neneh Cherry was the Stockholm-born daughter of West African percussionist Amadu Jah, dividing her childhood between Sweden and New York with her artist mother Moki, and step-father Don Cherry. She arrived in London in 1980 to find Don adopted by both the Slits and the Pop Group, and an entire scene bubbling around her very pedigree. "She was like this Scandinavian punk," Mark Stewart recalled, "chilling out in Bristol...." Almost immediately upon hitting town, Cherry was performing with a ska band, the Nails; soon she was guesting (alongside her father) with the Slits, and when her boyfriend Bruce Smith finally formed Rip Rig & Panic in 1981, Cherry was first choice vocalist.

As the decade rolled on, so did the action — indefatigable, intense, and utterly incestuous. Mark Stewart's brother, Charles, led Reborn to an ironically still-born career with Island Records — one single and a complete-but-cancelled album was the sum of their output. Smith & Mighty co-produced Massive Attack's "Any Love" first single, then produced a full, flop album by its exquisite guest vocalist, Carlton. Massive Attack themselves received an inestimable boost when Del Naja and Vowles were recruited to work with Cherry and her new partner, Cameron McVey, on her *Raw Like Sushi* debut album.

With worldwide sales in excess of two million, and the hits "Buffalo Stance" and "Manchild," *Raw Like Sushi* introduced at least a theoretical Bristol scene to the world at large;

musically, it had still to prove itself, but behind the scenes, clearly the city was hopping.

Mark Stewart cut what is generally regarded as the first manifestation of what would become "the Bristol sound" when he gave Smith and Mighty 500 pounds for their recent reinvention of Satie's "Gymnopedies #1," grafted *West Side Story*'s "Somewhere" over the basic theme, and then concocted a new lyric, "Stranger Than Love."

Dampening down Stewart's customary musical assault to a muted mutant dub daze, drifting on beats and dreamy samples, slow enough to be laid back, dark enough to sound disturbingly sinister — all that could subsequently be called "trip-hop" was present. But "Stranger Than Love" (from 1987's *Mark Stewart* album) would stand utterly alone until the Dust Brothers employed similar tricks on the Beastie Boys' *Paul's Boutique* in 1989 — possibly coincidence, but just as easily absolute symbiosis. This decade's end closure of the links between hip-hop and its Bristolian heritage would in turn pave the way for the first local strivings of the 1990s. And it was Stewart again who grasped the golden ring in 1992. He just neglected to let anybody hear it.

"I was in Bristol, and I started to record another album. [And] if it had come out, it would have been the first of what they call the Bristol Beat. It was a year or two ahead, and a lot of the musicians on it later became Portishead, Tricky and masses of stuff, that sound continued through those people. But I immediately got bored with it." He scrapped the record and moved into what he perceived to be the more immediately exciting acid-techno scene, "but out of those sessions Tricky was born. I helped him do his first single, made the music, and put him up on his little ladder."

Stewart had known the erstwhile Adrian Thaws since the boy was at high school, and had been pushing him to do something for almost as long. Indeed, the first time Stewart ever heard Smith & Mighty's "Gymnopedies #1," when the duo made their debut live at the Apres-Ski Party behind the Bristol Hippodrome, "I pushed Tricky on stage, which was the first time anybody got him to rap publicly."

Having made his debut, the self-styled Tricky Kid alternated a life of juvenile delinquency with regular gigs with Shockwave, a local sound system, and an early incarnation of hip-hop heroes the Fresh Four, before resurfacing on Massive Attack's *Blue Lines* album. In 1991, he linked with producer Geoff Barrow to cut "Nothing's Clear," rapping over a sampled piano line from the *Betty Blue* soundtrack, for the Bristol charity album, *The Hard Sell*. It would be 1993, however, before his solo career got underway, when he reunited with Stewart and, with 15-year-old singer Martina, cut "Aftermath."

Released on Tricky's own Naive label, the single brought him to the attention of Island Records. The following year, he unveiled *Maxinquaye*, one of the three strands of the beast which the media — already inspired by Massive Attack and Geoff Barrow's similarly insurgent Portishead — would now dub trip-hop.

While Portishead (or Porter's Head, as a 1992 *Billboard* review of Neneh Cherry's *Homebrew* dubbed her occasional collaborators) grew out of the studios which had already spawned early efforts by Massive Attack and the Tricky Kid, history's temptation was always to credit producer Barrow, session arranger Adrian Utley, and pub band vocalist Beth Gibbons as the catalyst which melded the entire Bristol scene.

There is truth to that portrait — like Massive's Del Naja, Barrow had been an integral part of the Neneh Cherry/Cameron McVey team, while his seemingly perpetual presence at the Coach House studios ensured that any musician who passed through those doors would find themselves side-by-side with him at some point. At the same time, however, the simple manipulation of beats and samples into what would become the instantly identifiable (and immediately much-imitated) world of trip-hop was never the work of one person, or even one group of people. Rather, it was distillation of so many past points of input that the opened ear could indeed track back to the Pop Group and discern the first stirrings; trace them through Adrian Sherwood and Mark Stewart's New Age Steppers cooperative; stab a pin into any point on the city's early-mid 80s musical map, and unravel another skein of sound and ambition. And besides, even as the rest of the world was greeting this new music, all three of the scene's appointed pioneers were furiously struggling against the pigeonhole.

But it was already too late. A music industry which prides itself on keeping pace with its creations, of course, was swift to leap aboard the trip-hop bandwagon. Morcheeba emerged with a sultry strand of the dislocated beat; New York indy scamps Spacehog dipped into the waters with the loping "One of These Days." trip-hop, journalist Phil Johnson discovered, was everywhere, "in the post-rave aesthetic of blunted beats put out by bedroom mixers like those on James Lavelle's Mo-Wax label, or in the work of Leftfield, the Chemical Brothers, and too many white dub warriors to mention."

Still, the progenitors of the Bristol sound battled against its very existence. No less than his mentor, Mark Stewart, drawing back from the brink before most people knew it was even there, Tricky pushed the furthest out, following *Maxinquaye* with the loopy demo-esque *Nearly God*, before embarking upon a string of convolutions which have elevated his appetite for activity to Prince-like proportions.

Portishead, on the other hand, struggled hardest, before themselves admitting that their sophomore album was little more than a dry repeat of their first, and not truly finding a fresh voice until 1999, when they collaborated with Tom Jones for one cut on his Reload album — the big band soul of "Motherless Child."

And Massive Attack shrugged the whole hype aside and denounced the entire musical field as a media-made fabrication, which of course it was in a way — the term "trip-hop" was itself conjured by *Mix Mag*. They began the evacuation almost immediately, passing their mastertapes onto Ariwa Studios dub demon Mad Professor (aka Neil Fraser) to remix as he saw fit.

Under his nimble fingers and sizzling brain, the hitherto genre-defining *Protection* album was reinvented with dozy dub grooves augmented by smashing loops and big beats — a monstrous, magical looking glass as if Alice Cooper had gone to Wonderland instead of Lewis Carroll's little friend. By the time Massive Attack released their third album, 1998's seething *Mezzanine*, trip-hop was the last thing on their minds. And by the time people heard it, they had no alternative but to agree.

RECOMMENDED LISTENING

AUDIOWEB Into My World (LP *Audioweb*)

BABY FOX Ladybird (LP *A Normal Family*)

DJ KRUSH Skin Against Skin (LP *Milight*)

HOOVERPHONIC Inhaler (LP *A New Stereophonic Sound Spectacular*)

MC SOLAAR Nouveau Western (LP *Prose Combat*)

MASSIVE ATTACK Heat Miser (LP *Protection*)

MORCHEEBA Trigger Hippy (LP *Who Can You Trust*)

PORTISHEAD Glory Box (LP *Dummy*)

MARK STEWART Stranger Than Love (LP *Mark Stewart*)

TRICKY Hell Is Around the Corner (LP *Maxinquaye*)

Agit-Punk in Britain — The Eighties and Beyond

The 1980s dawned damp and drab, but mostly disappointing. People fall for it every time, go to bed thinking things will be different, that the zeitgeist would be zapping from the first day of the decade, but they wake up and Pink Floyd are still number one. Can I have an alarm call for when something good happens?

Punk came to destroy. What nobody expected was that it would hang around so long after. The Clash, the Jam, Buzzcocks, Generation X, the Stranglers — they were all still out there kicking and hitting, especially hitting, as the Jam took up residence at the top of the UK charts, and the hordes of Mod bowed down at their feet. The only healthy movement in sight was the unhealthy moping which drained down from the north, the Liverpudlian wearers of raincoats and ashes.

Polar in outlook, polarizing in appeal, bands like The Teardrop Explodes, Echo and the Bunnymen, and (from 35 miles down the road in Manchester), Joy Division, and the Fall, were never going to be challenging the Jam, but that wasn't really their point. It was enough that they were out there, challenging the things that the Jam now stood for, and it was crushingly ironic that, at a time when the British music press spoke of Positive Punk, the upstart genre's most pressing talents tended to stress negative strengths.

Beyond the confines of British rock's own politics, however, the real world just rumbled on. 1981 brought riots, 1982 brought war. That spring, outraged by Argentina's latest assault on the peaceful sovereignty of a penguin colony in the South Atlantic, Prime Minister Thatcher embroiled the UK within the last colonial war of the century, simultaneously drumming the nation up to such a state of patriotic fervor that when Crass came out to loudly protest the conflict, with an anti-war flexi disc, even the music papers condemned their treachery. By the time the band got round to asking Thatcher, "How Does It Feel (To Be the Mother of a Thousand Dead)," the government itself was planning legal action against the band.

The non-specific railings of U2 and the nascent Alarm aside, the first "conventional" act to openly attack the conflict was New Model Army — rent-a-row agit-proppers whose unspoken motto of "if it rhymes, we'll complain about it" had already established them as the logical heirs of a Protest Punk crown which reached back to Bob Dylan, and was last seen hanging out with Paul Weller. Their "Spirit of the Falklands," swiftly followed as it was by Billy Bragg's

"Between the Wars," voiced the growing public unease at the knowledge that not only may the war have been avoidable, it might even have been unnecessary.

Kirk Brandon's Spear of Destiny weighed in with "Mickey," the sad tale of a vet who came home in slightly more pieces than he left in, while ex-Advert TV Smith launched his now thriving (but then distinctly underexposed) solo career with "War Fever," a snarling jab at the ease with which the population was riled to begin with. "Your little flag is stuck in the ground, you take sides...."

It is one of recent history's greatest ironies that punk's greatest foes, Britain's eternally incumbent Conservative Government, was to remain its most potent lifeline through the remainder of the decade. The Falklands War notwithstanding, the Thatcher/Major regime's progressive annihilation of Britain's welfare, health care, and social security systems, and the attendant miseries of joblessness, homelessness and, if you were old enough and sick enough, ultimately lifelessness, found their most vociferous opposition in the spirit of punk.

Clause 28, a piece of legislation aimed at curbing homosexuality in the community, drew embittered responses from across the musical spectrum, straight and gay. A new "Poll Tax" system designed to replace property taxes brought an equally voluble reaction, all the more so after its enacting was accompanied by the country's worst public riots since 1981. And a law aimed at shooting down unlicensed raves succeeded in uniting even the traditionally cut-throat electro-dance scene against a common enemy.

Several of TV Smith's most powerful latter-day songs drew their ammunition directly from government pronouncements, while Tom Robinson's Living in a Boom Time album emerged an equally effective manifesto of disaffection. Similarly, New Model Army maintained a constant barrage of critical observation throughout the decade (and into the next one), one which, at its height, also formed the missing link between punk — the music — and its philosophically more developed cousin, the unaccompanied poets of the early 80s' "ranting" movement.

Indeed, though there was no denying the sheer instrumental pizzazz at New Model Army's disposal, it was the likes of Attila the Stockbroker, John Cooper Clarke, Seething Wells and Army frontman Slade the Leveller's ladyfriend Joolz, whose verbal broadsides found the fondest echo in their vitriol. In fact, Joolz and New Model Army frequently shared live billing, and though her own rent-a-rollicking approach to societal wrongs was not always guaranteed a fair hearing by the prepared-to-pogo masses, it was at least bottled off in context.

Attila, on the other hand, seldom got bottled off, primarily because he looked like he'd enjoy it. Visually resembling the kind of kid who used to bully Henry Rollins in weight-lifting class, Attila was never less than an esoteric lunatic, verging on sheer comic genius even when his subject matter was serious.

His first album, *Ranting at the Nation*, remains alternately horribly dated (the triple threat of Communism, Margaret Thatcher, and Depeche Mode fans named Nigel) and uproariously funny (ditto) — it is also, however, a veritable time capsule of British life and lies in the very early 1980s. Subsequently arming himself with a wealth of eastern European medieval instruments, time and subsequent recordings saw him lose none of that original edge or bite, while his later move onto the folk circuit lost him none of his topical power either.

The very purpose of folk music, after all, is to relate, and relate to, the beliefs and dreams of the common people. If its traditional roots have grown increasingly fossilized since the advent of recording technology and the attendant scholarly need to pinpoint and preserve the "definitive" version of every song, it remains a thriving, if oft-overlooked, adjunct to contemporary music. The fact that this adjunct is better known today as punk rock is a matter for the musicologists of the future to sort out.

If Attila headed the humorist's assault on Thatcher's increasingly unappetizing vision of Britain, Seething Wells (later to become NME journalist Stephen Wells) led the strong-arm division. According to legend, he took to poetry only after discovering there wasn't a band on earth who could play as loud as he shouted, and that despite his having emerged from British punk's then thriving oi! offspring. In fact, it was the oi! movement which maintained the strongest focus on the political situation of the age, with Wells' contributions to the 1982 compilation *Jobs Not Yops* (Youth Opportunity Programs, a Thatcherite scheme to send kids out for unpaid work experience, at the same time as knocking them off the unemployment register) swiftly establishing him at the forefront of the movement.

Elsewhere, the Anti-Nowhere League's "Streets of London" so savagely updated the old folkie standard that for many bands (New Model Army excepted), an entirely new avenue of thought was opened and the mid-'80s railings of oi!'s last surviving progenitors today read like a text book of Tory crimes.

Unfortunately, few people read it. Oi! itself was sinking, crushed by the overtones of racist violence which still attended its furthest extremes, and the positivity which attended its finest outpourings died with it, buried beneath so much bad press and misunderstanding. By the mid-1980s, it was lost forever, to be replaced by — nothing. Indeed, at a time when British royalty bestowed its blessing upon pop, and pop royalty threw crumbs to the starving Ethiopians, there simply was no room in the mainstream for anything more profound than the blandest stab at social comment — which is why Paul Hardcastle's "19," mourning a war which Britain never even fought, could remain at #1 for five weeks, while Billy Bragg's "Between the Wars" (discussing those she had) barely spent that long in the Top 75.

Even Sigue Sigue Sputnik, former Generation X-er Tony James' presciently techno-inflected attempt to fight complacency from within, was swiftly unmasked and sent on its way, while Frankie Goes to Hollywood's own attempts at subverting the norm were simply sucked wholesale into the circus they had originally set out to circumvent.

In commercial terms, the decades which have clicked off since punk first breathed the fiery breath of wholesale rejuvenation across a decaying music scene have seen everything change — and nothing change. In 1988 and again in 1998, the biggest hits were still the blandest confections, the biggest bands were still the benighted dinosaurs and the biggest mouths (all of which had grown up with punk, then grown out of it too) were marginal sideshows at best, dancing just on one side of oblivion.

So, when Chumbawamba — whose own career had seen them regularly flirting with precisely that musical arena — scored a massive worldwide hit with "Tubthumping" in 1997, they did more than provide the 1990s with one of its most memorable (and, by the same token, ultimately annoying) hit singles. They also cemented into place one of the most extraordinary ironies of the age: self-confessed anarchists suddenly living the highlife of TV appearances, industry parties, and flash-looking videos.

To old fans who'd been attracted to the band for their politics, "Tubthumping" and its reasonably successful follow-up, "Amnesia," were tantamount to betrayal; to new fans who'd come in with the hits, the politics themselves were little more than a gimmick. To Chumbawamba themselves, their new visibility offered them the opportunity to finally put into practice a belief system which had never been accepted within even the "alternative" corners of the modern music industry — but which had sustained Chumbawamba for 15 years at that point, and would do so even more thereafter.

"In Britain, in particular, the press absolutely hated us," said vocalist Dunstan Bruce. "We're too extreme for a lot of press." But he also mused, "power isn't just about huge record sales and units and markets. It's also about small victories and personal relationships and things in daily life which happen all the time. So our power in the music industry changes year to year, but when someone writes to us from a small town in Italy or Nebraska to say thanks for what we're doing with our music, then that makes it all worthwhile and satisfying." And the fact was, the success of "Tubthumping," and its parent album, *Tubthumper* (Chumbawamba's tenth), ensured that their music would get into small towns in Italy and Nebraska — and with it, their message.

Chumbawamba formed in Paris in 1982, a three-piece busking Clash and Undertones covers with an acoustic guitar and a basic drum kit. Returning to their hometown of Leeds, the trio took over a vacant house with some friends and began plotting a larger scale project; never a band, more a collective; never a career, more a way of life which just happened to have music at its heart.

Their early influences were as obvious as they were uncompromising. Musically, the Slits and the Fall made comfortable bedfellows for the auteur anger of Chumbawamba's music; socially, the anarchist stance of Crass was one with which all (eventually) eight band members could agree with, all the more so after Crass' own absorption into mainstream politics as media-appointed spokesmen for grumbling alternative lifestyle-rs forced that band to break up in 1984.

Having already appeared on the second of Crass' *Bullshit Detector* compilations, Chumbawamba effortlessly joined the handful of other politically-literate commentators who were now slipping into the void bared by Crass' passing; readily, too, they picked up the banner of disaffection and questioning which Crass had once flown so high.

There, however, the comparisons ended. Crass confronted political policy head on and ultimately found themselves influencing those policies to the point where the British government actually circulated a memo warning its members not to rise to Crass' antagonism. Chumbawamba agitated from the sidelines. Crass forced the British government to permit open discussion of its conduct during the Falklands War. Chumbawamba watched as vocalist Danbert Nobacon emptied a bucket of iced water over Deputy Prime Minister John Prescott at the 1998 BRITS awards ceremony, in protest at a supposedly socialist government's mistreatment of 500 striking Liverpool dockers.

Aligning themselves, then, with grassroots rebellion as opposed to open revolution, Chumbawamba became a common sight at the anti-nuclear peace camps which sprang up around southern England during the 1980s; a vital, vocal power in the workers' rights struggle against the tentacles of corporate disenfranchisement and money. And in the circles within which they themselves moved, a veritable powerhouse of ideas and reform.

Those circles, however, were far removed from anything even remotely resembling the music industry. Forming their own label, Agit-Prop, Chumbawamba's first single, "Revolution," was financed by the members' day-jobs. Their first shows were arranged around domestic commitments. But still Chumbawamba's debut album made waves, as *Pictures of Starving Children Sell Records* arrived to puncture the self-satisfied glow of smugness which radiated from the UK industry in the wake of Live Aid while the label's projected final release (before Chumbawamba joined One Little Indian), *Jesus H Christ*, would not even get into the stores, after distributors and stores alike took exception to its subject matter.

Instead the band released *Shhh*, underlining the kneejerk nature of the previous album's fate by featuring many of the same songs, and simply changing the focus of a few key lyrics, away from religion and towards the bigotry which religion encourages. Even these controversies, however, seemed muted when compared with the tempestuous reaction to 2000's "Passenger List for Doomed Flight #1721," the B-side of the band's "She's Got All the Friends That Money Can Buy" 45.

From the band's point of view, the targets of this latest release — political hypocrisy, corporate greed, military bullying, and cultural imperialism — were the same as those which they had always pursued, as the song bid a not-so-fond adieu to what the band described as "a list of the people we'd most like to see disappear from our lives, from all powerful political liars to gruesomely rich businessmen to hideously egotistical pop and TV stars. And there we are at the airport, knowing the aeroplane is doomed, waving a smug bye-bye."

Other things had changed, however — a consequence both of the heightened visibility which "Tubthumping" induced, and of the increasingly narrow bottleneck into which modern society has forced the concept of free speech. Reaction to "Passenger List," was immediate and violent, ranging from hate-mail condemning the band's "tastelessness" through to DJs threatening to drop the band from their playlists "because of our 'hateful stance against Bono'" [one of the song's named targets].

Chumbawamba's own response to such violence continued, "25 years ago... Malcolm McLaren and cohorts preceded the formation of the Sex Pistols by setting out a list of the things they hated. The list they came up with, peppered with politicians, pop stars etc... is a good way of drawing a very definite line. What's the difference between the stale Mick Jagger rock excess tedium of the '70s and the passive compliance of pop in 2000?

"One difference might be that people are less tolerant of radical ideas than they ever were in the '70s, that we've all been stunned into silence by fancy sounding focus groups and their boring, boring lies. 'I did not go to war to divert attention from my relations with that woman.' Remember that one?"

Chumbawamba are unique. Advance interest in their first post-*Tubthumping* album, 2000's *WYSIWYG (What You See Is What You Get)*, was sufficient to push it into the upper echelons of the chart regardless of its ultimate commercial performance. Politically, they remained a voice in the wilderness, but it was at least it was a wilderness which was willing to listen, even if it didn't necessarily pay attention.

Elsewhere, however, the voices which shout the loudest (and TV Smith, New Model Army, Tom Robinson, and Kirk Brandon still number among them) are those which have either dropped off the commercial radar altogether, or never climbed aboard it in the first place, and now exist in a cultural underground which simply cannot — or will not — contend with the Backstreet Boyz and Spice Girls of this world.

It is in their hands, nevertheless, that the links between punk rock past and present remain purest, and there that the folk of the current generation is being created.

The '90s saw (and did not, sadly, recoil from) more Class of '76-type reunions than any mere calendar should ever have to contend with, but their Zimmer-framed recreations of all that once was so holy rarely meant more than a few bucks in the bank and a few more memories mashed in the festival mud. Punk rock, despite what their bank managers might tell them, is not something which can be recreated and revisited. It is the unquenchable spirit of rebellion and rage, an eternal questioning of values and virtue. It is the voice of the people, raised loudly for their benefit. It is the power of the moment, and when that moment has passed, the power passes too.

But like the clichéd old T-shirt insisted, punk will never die.

RECOMMENDED LISTENING

ATTILA THE STOCKBROKER Libyan Students from Hell (LP *Libyan Students from Hell*)

BOY GEORGE No Clause 28 (45)

CHUMBAWAMBA/A STATE OF MIND We Are the World (45)

CRASS Sheep Farming in the Falklands (45)

FRANKIE GOES TO HOLLYWOOD Two Tribes (45)

NEW MODEL ARMY 51st State (LP *The Ghost of Cain*)

POGUE MO CHONE Dark Streets of London (45)

TOM ROBINSON Yuppie Scum (LP Living in a Boom Time)

TV SMITH'S CHEAP Third Term (LP *RIP*)

SPEAR OF DESTINY Mickey (LP *World Service*)

Rock in the Rain — 20 Essential Festivals, 1975–99

CBGBS FESTIVAL OF UNSIGNED BANDS

NEW YORK, NY (1975) The first and most notable of three festivals staged during 1975–76, spotlighting the unsigned talent which called the Bowery club home. Subsequent events were staged over Christmas 1975, and late summer 1976.

7/16-8/3 Ramones, Tuff Darts, Blondie, Talking Heads, White Lightning, Jelly Roll, Pretty Poison, Mink DeVille, Sniper, Antenna, Planets, Day Old Bread, Rainbow Daze, Mantis, Ice, Patrick David Kelly & Toivo, Demons, John Collins, Johnny's Dance Band, Trilogy, Heartbreakers, the Shirts, Stagger Lee, Mad Brook, Seven Wind, Uncle Son, Sting Rays, Johnny's Dance Band, Hambone Sweets, Silent Partners, Punch, Dancer, Television, Marbles, Ruby & the Rednecks, Uneasy Sleeper

COACHELLA VALLEY MUSIC AND ARTS FESTIVAL

EMPIRE POLO FIELD, INDIO, CA (1999) Staged in California's self-styled "city of festivals," Coachella was billed as the largest "European-styled" rock festival ever staged in the US — "European style" apparently meaning that bands appeared on several stages around the vast grounds, rather than the mere two or three already familiar from other events. Organized by the Goldenvoice agency in L.A., the festival presented a powerful cross-section of current alternative talent, although most of the pre-show attention seemed aimed towards Morrissey, and rumors that he and former Smiths guitarist Johnny Marr were planning to reunite at the show — even Indio's own *Desert Sun* newspaper joined in the speculation. In the event, the pair apparently never even saw one another.

10/9-10 Perfect Circle, Bis, Medeski Martin & Wood, Perry Farrell, Morrissey, Chemical Brothers, Beck, At the Drive In, the Bicycle Thief, IQU, Super Furry Animals, Modest Mouse, Art of Noise, Spiritualized, Underworld, Christopher Lawrence, the Wiseguys, Simply Jeff, Cornelius, Breakbeat Era, Jurassic 5, u-Ziq, Money Mark, Cibo Matto, Pavement, Ben Harper, Rage Against the Machine, Tool, Ugly Duckling, Gil Scott Heron, Spearhead, Innerzone Orchestra, Moby, the Angel, BT, Banco De Gaia, Fantastic Plastic Machine, Lamb, Thievery Corporation, Gus Gus, A-Trak, LTJ Bukem, Rob Hall, Autechre

FUTURAMA

LEEDS, ENGLAND (1980–82) Staged by Leeds promotor and F Club owner John Keenan, Futurama was the first national event to acknowledge the growing schism in the punk/new wave scene, as what the press called the "New Musik" consciousness began pushing through.

1980 (Leeds, England) 9/13-14 Siouxsie and the Banshees, Echo and the Bunnymen, U2, Wasted Youth, Clock DVA, Altered Images, Blah Blah Blah, the Mirror Boys, Vena Cava, Acrobats of Desire, Danse Crazy, Music For Pleasure, the Distributors, Soft Cell, Eaten Alive by Insects, Gary Glitter, Athletico Spizz 80, Psychedelic Furs, Hazel O'Connor, 4-be-2s, Young Marble Giants, Soft Boys, Durutti Column, Classix Nouveaux, Notsensibles, Desperate Bicycles, Frantic Elevators, the Flowers, Boots for Dancing, Brian Brain, Vice Versa, Artery, Naked Lunch, Or Was He Pushed, Household Name

1981 (Stafford, England) 9/5-6 Gang of Four, Bauhaus, Human Condition, the Passions, Theatre of Hate, OK Jive, the Sound, 23 Skidoo, the Lines, Felt, Revenna & the Magnetics, A Flock of Seagulls, Ponderosa Glee Boys, Another Colour, Sisters of Mercy, Really, My Silent War, Simple Minds, Bow Wow Wow, Doll by Doll, Richard Strange, Modern Eon, Eyeless in Gaza, Diagram Brothers, Virgin Prunes, Blue Orchids, UK Decay, Havana Let's Go, Section 25, Higsons, Ludus, Martian Dance, B-Movie, Everest the Hard Way, the Teaset, Cry, Vena Cava

1982 (Leeds, England) 9/11-12 the Damned, Dead or Alive, Southern Death Cult, New Order, Durutti Column, China Crisis, Thomas Dolby, Danse Society, March Violets, Gene Loves Jezebel, Three Courgettes, A Flock of Seagulls, Cook Da Books, Dalek I Love You, Blancmange, Blue Poland, the Alarm, Brilliant, Icicle Works, Three D, Fish in Sea, Sleeping Figures, Ideal

FAMILY VALUES

(1998–present) Inspired by their experiences on the final Lollapalooza outing, Korn and manager Jeff Kwantinetz launched the Family Values tour in fall 1998, as a showcase for the new breed of hip hop-infused metal which they, of course, epitomized.

1998 9/29-10/14 Korn, Limp Bizkit, Ice Cube, Orgy, Rammstein

1999 9/21–11/22 Limp Bizkit, Primus, Crystal Method, DMX, System of a Down, Staind, Filter, Method Man, Red Man

GATHERING OF THE TRIBES

MOUNTAIN VIEW, CA and COSTA MESA, CA, 1990 In October 1990, Cult vocalist Ian Astbury staged two days of the Gathering of the Tribes, a watershed event which brought together artists from across the modern musical spectrum, with one sense of purpose and direction.

The Cramps, the Indigo Girls, the Charlatans, Queen Latifah, Steve Jones, the American Indian Dance Theater, Soundgarden, and Michelle Shocked... the names weren't even that important. It was the vision which united them and the success with which they met which mattered; that, and the knowledge that Astbury had accomplished at his first attempt an alchemy which other people, professional agents and bookers and promoters, had been seeking for the past 15 years — a festival of alternative rock, which addressed the needs of an alternative audience.

Astbury explained, "I made the observation that there was a complete lack of harmony between young musicians. The communal spirit that had come through punk rock didn't exist any more. I was really intrigued by NWA when they came out, they reminded me of punk, they were so radical, and I liked Ice T, and Soundgarden, and I thought, there's all these groups around, these counter-culture groups, and no one's hearing them outside of their own camps. They're all in their little boxes, they don't recognize each other's presence, there's no linkage between rap and rock, between rock and alternative, and certainly not folk or traditional.

"Everything was very formatted, nothing was crossing over, and I just thought it would be amazing if we could bring together all these different groups for a concert, to show people as a whole what was going on with our generation, so we wouldn't have to deal with Phil Collins and Bruce Springsteen any longer. It would be a concert showcasing all the different options, showing the linkage."

Over the next nine months, the Gathering of the Tribes fell into place. "I came up with the idea of bringing in socio-environmental groups, because it was the same thing as the bands, 300 organizations all working to save the rainforest, but all hating each other at the same time." The Bill Graham Organization became involved, introducing the then revolutionary concept of adding performance artists, theater groups, and cutting edge technology to the sideshows.

Only when Astbury began working out the finer musical details did the first cracks begin appearing, as the Gathering became snarled in private feuds between the booking agencies he needed to be cooperating with to fulfill his dream. "I talked to Lenny Kravitz, Slash, I spent six hours with Axl Rose, I approached Red Hot Chili Peppers, Jane's Addiction, Soundgarden, Iggy Pop, Happy Mondays... everyone seemed so keen. But what I didn't know was that all their different agencies — they

were the same as the bands and the environmental groups, all at war with one another, and this time, there was no way to make them work together.

"Suddenly all these acts started dropping out, word was going out that they shouldn't do this, it would be bad for their careers, all that bullshit. Happy Mondays aren't interested in doing it, the Red Hot Chili Peppers aren't interested, Jane's Addiction aren't interested and I was left wondering what the fuck is going on? All these people who said they wanted to do it are pulling out. It was really bizarre."

Still, the Gathering did go ahead, over two days (October 6 and 7) at the Shoreline Amphitheater in Mountain View, California, and the Pacific Amphitheater in Costa Mesa, and Astbury reflected, "it was an incredible success. We felt that we'd done something. We were even planning another one. And then Lollapalooza came along, and they all said it was based on the Reading Festival. Well fuck, that's been going on for twenty years, why do it six months after this event, why not do it six months previous? End of argument."

GLASTONBURY FESTIVAL

GLASTONBURY, ENGLAND (1971–present) Staged within one of England's most mystic corners, the legendary birthplace of King Arthur, the first Glastonbury festival, Glastonbury Fayre, was held in September 1970, when Michael Eavis, owner of the Worthy Farm dairy farm, arranged a free concert featuring the cream of the late '60s underground: Tyrannosaurus Rex, Al Stewart, and Quintessence among them.

The Fayre returned the following year, stretching over five days and featuring performances from Melanie, Hawkwind, Fairport Convention, David Bowie, Brinsley Schwarz and more. The event would also be documented on both film and record, but despite its obvious success, there would be no repeat performance for six more years. Then, in 1978, a group of travelers heading for the Stonehenge festival were rerouted to Worthy Farm by rumors that Glastonbury had been revived. It hadn't, but Eavis allowed them to stage a festival on his property regardless, and was rewarded by a magical performance from Nik Turner's Sphinx as they, too, made their way to Stonehenge.

Glastonbury officially returned in 1979, with a show headlined by Peter Gabriel (on a stage donated by Genesis), and again two years later, with New Order and Hawkwind topping the bill. Since that time, it has missed only two years: 1991, after the previous year's show was the scene of a massed confrontation between festival security and so-called New Age Travelers, and in 1996, when the organizer simply felt like taking a break.

In that period, Glastonbury would rise first to rival, then absolutely eclipse Reading (which in any case spent much of the 1980s fighting to stay alive), while never losing sight of its own initial founding principle of fighting the commercialization of the "conventional" festival. The price of admission, rising though it did from 7 pounds in 1979, to 85 pounds twenty years later, included donations to the Campaign for Nuclear Disarmament

(CND), Greenpeace, Oxfam, and WaterAid — organizations which have benefited to the tune of 3 million pounds in that same period.

1993 6/25-27 (including) Velvet Underground, Belly, Teenage Fanclub, London Suede, Dodgy, the Verve, Jamiroquai, Ozric Tentacles, Stereo MCs, the Orb, Back to the Planet, Mega City 4, Lemonheads, Spiritualized

1994 6/24-26 (including) Ride, Rage Against the Machine, St. Etienne, Jah Wobble, Nick Cave, Levellers, Paul Weller, James, World Party, Spin Doctors, Elvis Costello, Galliano, Mary Black, Tindersticks, Peter Gabriel, Beastie Boys, Boo Radleys, Manic Street Preachers, Pretenders, Echobelly, Oasis, Chumbawamba, Pulp, Radiohead, Blur, Spiritualized, African Headcharge, Transglobal Underground, Senser, M People, Björk, Orbital, Trash Can Sinatras, Tom Robinson, Gorky's Zygotic Mynci, Glenn Tilbrook

1995 6/23-25 (including) Simple Minds, PJ Harvey, Oasis, Black Crowes, Page & Plant, Jamiroquai, the Cure, Orbital, Lightning Seeds, Goldie, Dodgy, Elastica, Sleeper, Supergrass, Shed 7, the Verve, Ash, Prodigy, Menswear, Skunk Anansie, Shamen, Eat Static, System 7, Darren Emerson, Plastikman, Fluke, Carl Cox, Massive Attack Sound System, Portishead, Billy Bragg, John Otway, Mike Scott, Nick Lowe

1997 6/27-29 (including) Phish, Echo and the Bunnymen, the Levellers, Beck, Supergrass, the Prodigy, Republica, Nanci Griffith, Ray Davies, Cast, Dodgy, Ocean Colour Scene, Radiohead, Sheryl Crow, Catatonia, Kenickie, Placebo, Ash, Divine Comedy, Reef, Dharmas, Stereolab, Chemical Brothers, Kula Shaker, Super Furry Animals, Mansun, Massive Attack, David Byrne, Finlay Quaye, Lamb, Galliano, Herbaliser, Aphex Twin, the Orb, System 7, DJ Rap, Primal Scream, Reprazent, Daft Punk, Bentley Rhythm Ace, Ninja Tune, Nick Lowe, Billy Bragg, Beth Orton, Bootleg Beatles, Steve Harley, Andy White

1998 6/26-28 (including) Foo Fighters, James, Lightning Seeds, My Life Story, Primal Scream, Catatonia, Embrace, Matchbox 20, Rialto, Rocket from the Crypt, Supernaturals, Warm Jets, Faithless, Cornershop, Portishead, Asian Dub Foundation, Dawn of the Replicants, Ian Brown, Scott 4, Unbelievable Truth, Wireless, Girl Eats Boy, Fluke, Cut La Roc, Monkey Mafia, Darren Emerson, Luke Slater, Billy Nelson, Moby, Chemical Brothers, Blur, Mansun, Robbie Williams, Stereophonics, Tori Amos, Tricky, Catherine Wheel, Deftones, Kenickie, Marion, Monaco, Placebo, St. Etienne, Cornershop, Drug Store, Gomez, Jesus and Mary Chain, the Shack, Finitribe, Autechre, Spring Heel Jack, Fatboy Slim, Lo Fidelity All Stars, Plastikman, Nick Lowe, World Party, Loop Guru, Ozric Tentacles, Attila the Stockbroker, Nick Cave, Pulp, Sonic Youth, Space, Audioweb, Bentley Rhythm Ace, Bernard Butler, Mighty Bosstones, Spiritualized, Divine Comedy, Mad Professor, Baby Bird, Julian Cope, Chip Taylor, Eddi Reader, John Otway

1999 6/25-27 (including) Bjorn Again, Ian Dury, Blondie, Hole, Beautiful South, REM, Queens of the New Stone Age, Gay Dad, dEUS, Wilco, Pavement, Gomez, Kula Shaker, Lamb, Fat Boy Slim, Chemical Brothers, Airbus, Add N To (X), Built to Spill, Tom Robinson, Billy Bragg, Joe Strummer, Ash, Texas, Underworld, Manic Street Preachers, Hurricane #1, Creatures, Travis, the Cardigans, Super Furry Animals, Cast, Freestylers, Orbital, Praga Khan, Dot Allison, Shack, Death in Vegas, Ultrasound, Patti Smith, the Corrs, Skunk Anansie, Tindersticks, Mercury Rev, Mogwai, Jurassic 5, Dodgy, Kitachi, Sneaker Pimps.

HOLIDAYS IN THE SUN

BLACKPOOL, ENGLAND (1996–present) Organized by Darren Russell Concerts, the first Holidays in the Sun festival, in Blackpool in 1996, was staged to mark the 20th anniversary of punk rock itself, priding itself on bringing together as many of the original era's survivors as was possible, with the entire event to be documented on video and disc.

The recently resuscitated Sex Pistols — whose fourth single, of course, titled the event, were conspicuous by their absence, but the response from other bands (and the audience) was such that DRC had no hesitation in making the festival an annual event, albeit with many of the same bands appearing every year. Smaller, similar, events also began taking place in London and abroad.

8/96 (including) Slaughter & the Dogs, Drones, Not-Sensibles, Ex-Ray Spex, Anti-Nowhere League, Chron Gen, the Vibrators, Hank, Eater, Spizz Energi, TV Smith, Erase Today, Special Duties, One way System, Funeral Dress, Major Accident, External menace, Sic Boy Federation, Mere Dead Men, the Blood, V2, B-Bang Cider, the Lurkers, Suburban Studs, USSR, Radio Stars, Zounds, the Crack, 999, Alternative TV, the Carpettes, Buzzcocks, Sham 69, Capo Regime, the Proles, English Dogs, Splodgenessabounds, Krill, the Casualties, Walking Abortions, Do Public Toys, the Stains, Salford Jets, Eddie Mooney, GBH

HORDE

(1992-98) Horizons of Rock Developing Everywhere was founded in 1992 by a committee fronted by Blues Traveler frontman John Popper, Phish, Widespread Panic, and Bruce Hampton of the Aquarium Rescue Unit. "We tried to keep it as idealistic as possible," Hampton recalled. "No management, no booking agency, just the bands. [We] didn't have huge followings at the time, so we said 'let's put them together'."

That idealism was to be HORDE's greatest asset in its infancy; that, and an anonymity which ensured that long after a voracious mainstream had devoured other traveling festivals, HORDE would continue incognito, selling out venues, but never shedding its principles. It would be 1994, after two years of touring, before the organizational muscle of the Bill Graham Presents agency was brought in to handle the day-to-day running of the tour, and Heidi Kelso, part of the original organizing team, later marveled, "the greatest thing about HORDE is that it created its own thing. We didn't have corporate sponsorship, and nobody really directed the course of the way this tour has grown."

But it did grow, from eight shows in 1992, to a record 42 in 1997; from an unrepentant jam band line-up the first time around, to a sprawling cross section headlined by Neil Young, and highlighted by Sky Cries Mary.

1992 7/9-12, 8/6-9; 1993 7/3-8/15; 1994 7/15-9/4; 1995 8/3-9/3 (above including) Big Head Todd, Sean Kelly, Blues Traveler, Jimmy Cliff, Freddie Jones, Sheryl Crow, Warren Haynes, the Mother Hips, Cycomotogoat, the Ugly Americans, the Allman Brothers, Widespread Panic, Aquarium Rescue Unit, Spin Doctors, Bela Fleck, Phish

1996 7/6-9/1 (including) Blues Traveler, Dave Matthews Band, Lennie Kravitz, Natalie Merchant, Rusted Root, Taj Mahal, Neil Young (1 show)

1997 7/11-8/20 (including) Beck, Ben Folds Five, Big Head Todd & the Monsters, Cake Like, Kula Shaker, Leftover Salmon, Medeski Martin & Wood, Morphine, Neil Young & Crazy Horse, Primus, Sky Cries Mary, Soul Coughing, Squirrel Nut Zippers, Toad the Wet Sprocket

1998 7/9-9/5 (including) Blues Traveler, Alana Davis, Barenaked Ladies, Ben Harper, Dead Girls & Other Stories, Smashing Pumpkins, Marcy Playground, Fastball

LILITH FAIR

Lilith fair was conceived by Canadian singer-songwriter Sarah McLachlan, as a multi-artist showcase of female talent — a marginal affair in the eyes of the music press, until the second year out (1998) saw it emerge the most successful multi-artist tour of the year, grossing over $28 million in 52 shows.

Traditionally, few artists appeared throughout the entire tour, the majority simply playing a handful of shows as their schedules allowed — others would guest at single venues. In 1999, Sinead O'Connor, Stevie Nicks, Emmylou Harris, and Winona Judd all made special appearances.

1997 7/5-8/24 (including) Wild Strawberries, Shawn Colvin, Sheryl Crow, Indigo Girls, Lisa Loeb, Sarah McLachlan, Suzanne Vega, Patty Griffin, Emm Gryner, K's Choice, Kelly Willis, Tara MacLean, Beth Orton, Victoria Williams, Emmylou Harris,

1998 6/19-8/31 (including) Sinead Lohan, Shawn Colvin, Sixpence None the Richer, Indigo Girls, Dead Girls & Other Stories, Queen Latifah, Wild Strawberries, Lisa Loeb, Tara MacLean, Victoria Williams, Sarah McLachlan, Me'shell Ndegeocello, Liz Phair, Suzanne Vega, Trish Murphy, Patty Griffin, Emm Gryner, K's Choice, Kendall Payne,

1999 7/8-8/31 (including) Sandra Bernhard, Shawn Colvin, Deborah Cox, Sheryl Crow, Dixie Chicks, Indigo Girls, Queen Latifah, Lisa Loeb, Luscious Jackson, Martina McBride, Sarah McLachlan, Monica, Mya, Me'shell Ndegeocello, Liz Phair, the Pretenders, Suzanne Vega, Battershell, Dance Hall Crashers, Sinead Lohan, Tara MacLean, Aimee Mann, Medieval Baebes, Beth Orton, Kendall Payne, Sixpence None the Richer, Wild Strawberries, Victoria Williams, Kelly Willis

LOLLAPALOOZA

(1991-98) With Perry Farrell's determination to break up Jane's Addiction an open secret, the drive to make their final tour something special became an obsession, not only for Farrell, but also for their agent, Marc Giger and his Triad booking agency. "They told me I could do whatever I wanted," Farrell recalled, so he did — a multi-media event encompassing "music, art and military discoveries as forms of entertainment."

Defiant in the face of Astbury and his supporters, Farrell insisted he got the idea from for Lollapalooza Britain's Reading Festival and the series of festivals staged in the Mojave Desert by Desolation Agency during the early-mid 1980s. There was, however, one major difference. Reading was held in the same field every year. The Mojave shows moved around, but still they remained static. Even the Gathering of the Tribes had played only two venues. Farrell's show would encompass the entire US.

Taking the name Lollapalooza from an old episode of *The Three Stooges*, Farrell involved himself in every aspect of the venture from recruiting the bands to setting up the merchandising and information booths which would pepper the festival grounds. He dreamed of crossing the political spectrum, so Greenpeace and Refuse and Resist were invited, but so were the National Rifle Association and the US Army. There would be carnival stalls, fairground rides, makeshift theaters, and circus acts. And there would be music. Lots of it.

Two of Farrell's original choices for Lollapalooza '91, the Red Hot Chili Peppers and Nick Cave, would turn him down — although significantly, both would play subsequent tours. Other acts, however, were as excited by the venture as Farrell himself. "This is a pioneering tour," rapper Ice-T explained. "To be able to pack arena shows... it's a very educational experience. Everybody's taking a pill they're not used to."

"There was a lot of thought about mixing and matching [the bands into] a multi-faceted bill," Farrell continued. "I wanted to integrate, racially integrate, musically integrate, and I think it's a good start."

Even before the first show, July 18, 1991, he talked of trying to maintain Lollapalooza as an annual event, and fears that his ambition might be thwarted by the recession then cutting into the music industry were assuaged as soon as tickets went on sale. Detroit sold out in minutes, Chicago sold 32,000 tickets; just 8 out of the 18 shows did not sell out, and with a total gross of $8.5 million, Lollapalooza ended 1991 as the 25th most profitable tour of the year.

Singlehandedly, that month of shows completely transformed the summer touring industry, both at home and abroad. It also redefined American youth culture for the next decade at least. Reflecting upon just one of the sideshow acts at Lollapalooza '91, the pierced and branded Body Manipulations team, Living Color's Vernon Reid told *Rolling Stone*, "I truly believe Lollapalooza was the beginning of extreme body art. Piercing started to go mainstream with that tour."

So, the musicians on the bus believed, did alternative rock. "There was always an ongoing debate about what this tour meant for [it]," Reid continued. "Just like Woodstock signalled the end of the hippie era, was this the beginning of the end of 'alternative' as an outside thing?"

Once again a scene had developed, one in which, as Ice-T put it, "groups... have pioneered a certain form of music [but] none... get played on the radio." He was speaking specifically for the seven bands aboard the tour, but he encompassed the entire alternative universe all the same. When Lollapalooza '91 swept the country, Nirvana's *Nevermind* had still to be released; grunge was still an inexplicable term flapping around the pages of *Melody Maker*; Pearl Jam was still a reference to the peyote preserves made by an unknown Seattle vocalist's Native American grandmother.

Planning for the second tour began almost as soon as the first one ended, in October 1991, whittling an initial shortlist of 70 bands down to seven, but this time not only scheming a musical and cultural extravaganza of unearthly ramifications. He also needed to out — Lollapalooza Lollapalooza itself.

It was this constant need to continually better past performances which would, ultimately, bring the curtain down on Lollapalooza. The critical sniping began almost as soon as the line-up for the second tour was announced, first as the bands on the bill were compared (generally unfavorably) with their "equivalents" on the previous outing, then when disquieting murmurings about Triad's role in the entire affair began to surface.

Although Farrell ostensibly took a free hand in deciding who would be on the bill, complaints that Triad's acts dominated the festival first arose in 1991, after Henry Rollins claimed that despite being personally invited aboard by Farrell, his band was not confirmed on the bill until they signed with Triad. Now the Ramones' Joey Ramone was publicly acknowledging that his band had been excluded from the '92 roster because they weren't a Triad act, while fellow outsiders L7, too, were refused entry, despite the vociferous (and public) support of the headlining Red Hot Chili Peppers. "A lot of what Lollapalooza is," Ramone reflected, "is a real political situation."

Farrell himself seemed to distance himself from Lollapalooza '92; even removing his own new band, Porno for Pyros, from the

running (in fact, they would play one show, taking the newly-instituted second stage for a short set on the festival's opening day). The following year, he was even further removed — bowing out after the massive William Morris Agency swallowed Triad, and he suddenly discovered that all his ideas and suggestions for the outing "were kind of brushed aside. I just have to grit my teeth and pray that I don't get embarrassed too many times.

"People just stopped thinking it really was more than just a rock'n'roll concert. To me, [Lollapalooza] is more about youth culture, but they just thought, 'okay, now that we've got it established, let's just fill in the bands'." Attempts to persuade Sting, Neil Young, and the reformed Velvet Underground to join Lollapalooza '93 were doomed to failure, leaving the tour to set off without an established headliner (metal act Alice in Chains would close the show), while Lollapalooza '94 would be even more disastrously stigmatized when the headlining Nirvana's Kurt Cobain killed himself, before the band's participation had even been officially confirmed.

The original organizational team of Geiger, Farrell, and Ted Gardner were back at the center of things for Lollapalooza '94, bent on re-establishing the event, in Geiger's words, as "the beacon for all things alternative."

The loss of Nirvana, however, effectively beheaded the outing, and though the Festival lived on for three more years, it had also outlived its own usefulness. Once, Lollapalooza had been an only child, scampering around America with the biggest bag of toys in the world. Now, there were multi-artist packages emerging from every direction — John Popper's HORDE, Sarah McLachlin's Lilith Fair, Ozzy Osborne's Ozzfest, the punk-packed Warped — all taking another piece of the pie which had once been Lollapalooza's alone.

As late as April 1998, the team were still scrambling for even a halfway attractive headlining act for that year's festival, but with Radiohead, Garbage, Green Day, and Marilyn Manson among those who declined the honor, there was clearly no way they could proceed. And no way they could be faulted for their decision to call it quits, as Gary Bongiovani, editor of the tour monitor *Pollstar* magazine, explained. "The industry is probably better off that [they] decided not to go out with a weak lineup and fail. Obviously they were not comfortable with the talent they had, and rather than fall on their sword, they decided not to do it."

1991 7/18–8/29 Jane's Addiction, Siouxsie and the Banshees, Living Color, Nine Inch Nails, Ice-T, Butthole Surfers, Rollins Band

1992 7/18–9/13 Red Hot Chili Peppers, Pearl Jam, Jesus and Mary Chain, Soundgarden, Ministry, Ice Cube, Lush

1993 Alice in Chains, Arrested Development, Babes in Toyland [replaced by Tool], Front 242, Fishbone, Dinosaur Jr.

1994 Smashing Pumpkins, George Clinton, the Beastie Boys, the Breeders, A Tribe Called Quest, Nick Cave, Green Day [replaced by the Boredoms]

1995 7/4–8/9 Sonic Youth, Hole, Cypress Hill, Sinead O'Connor [replaced by Elastica], Beck, Jesus Lizard, Mighty Mighty Bosstones, Pavement, Moby

1996 6/27–8/3 Psychotica, Screaming Trees, Rancid, Violent Femmes, Ramones, Soundgarden, Metallica

1997 Tool, James, Tricky, Snoop Doggy Dogg, Korn, Prodigy, Orbital

MOJAVE EXODUS

MOJAVE DESERT, CA (1983–85) A series of annual events launched by Stuart Swezey, head of L.A. underground agency Desolation Center, the Mojave Exodus (1983), the Mojave Aus-zug (1984), and the Gila Monster Jamboree (1985) highlighted talent perceived elsewhere as "difficult" — the Minutemen, Ein-sturzende Neubauten, and making their first ever west coast appearance at the third event, Sonic Youth. Perry Farrell's first band Psi Com were on the bill at the latter, and the singer later acknowledged, that was where "the spirit of Lollapalooza came from, that's where I cut my teeth."

MONT DE MARSEN PUNK FESTIVAL

MONT DE MARSEN, FRANCE (1976–77) As head of the French Skydog label, Marc Zermati had been pioneering "street rock" for at least two years. The first quasi-bootleg pressings of Iggy and the Stooges' seminal live *Metallic KO* album were a Skydog release, together with a string of releases by French bands operat-ing within the same frame of pub rock reference as the UK scene.

Lining up some half dozen of the best, then extending invita-tions across the English Channel to the two UK independent labels whose vision seemed most to echo his, Stiff and Chiswick, Zermatti hatched the first punk rock festival — so titled because even the French knew which way the musical wind was blowing.

The result, predictably, was a chaotic meeting of two very sep-arate mindsets: the pub rock ethos of Little Bob Story, Nick Lowe, and the recently revitalized Pink Fairies (heroes, five years and as many line-up changes before, of the British free hippy fes-tival circuit), clashing with the punk energies of the Damned and the Boys. Eddie and the Hot Rods, fresh from badmouthing the Sex Pistols all over the UK media, sat squarely in the middle.

Staged at Mont de Marsen, about an hour's drive south of Bordeaux, the Punk Rock Festival was a disaster from a musical point of view. The musicians fought among themselves, no more than 150 curious locals rattled around a 5,000 capacity bullring, and the only event of any significance to come out of the entire affair was when Damned bassist Ray Burns was renamed "fucking Captain Sensible" while pretending to be an airline pilot on the coach.

An attempt to replay the festival the following year was unsuc-cessful, despite strong performances from two bands who — until the day before the show — had actually been one: ex-Rings gui-tarist and drummer Alan Lee Shaw and Rod Latter appeared as the Maniacs, vocalist Twink under his old band name, the Pink Fairies.

1976 8/21 Nick Lowe, Pink Fairies, Eddie and the Hot Rods, Hammersmith Gorillas, Tyla Gang, Count Bishops, the Boys, the Damned, Shakin' Street, Little Bob Story, Bijou, Il Baritz, Kalfont Rockchaud

100 CLUB FESTIVAL

LONDON, ENGLAND (1976) Little more than one month after the Mont de Marsen punk festival, London's 100 Club staged its own full scale punk rock festival, an event hatched by Sex Pistols manager Malcolm McLaren and 100 Club promotor Ron Watts. Spread across two sold-out nights, headlined by the Pistols, the Clash, and the Damned, and giving first-ever performances to Subway Sect and Siouxsie and the Banshees, the 100 Club Festi-val was the moment when punk finally hit the national media.

A glass thrown towards the stage during the Damned's set shattered on a pillar and took out a girl's eye, a tragic accident but one which confirmed what the press had been pondering all along, that this latest breed of musical rebels were the most bar-baric yet. And that confirmed what McLaren had been hoping for all along, that punk rock, street rock, call-it-what-you-would rock, was more than just a handful of bands. It was a full-fledged movement.

9/20 Sex Pistols, Clash, Subway Sect, Siouxsie and the banshees

9/21 the Damned, Chris Spedding & the Vibrators, Stinky Toys, Buzzcocks

ORGANIC FESTIVAL

BIG BEAR, SAN BERNADINO, CA (1996) An all-night outdoor rave festival, arguably the largest legal event of its kind ever staged.

6/22 (including) Orb, Chemical Brothers, Orbital, Underworld, Meat Beat Manifesto, Loop Guru, DJ Trance

READING FESTIVAL

READING, ENGLAND (1961–present) The oldest, continually-running outdoor rock festival is Britain's Reading, first staged in 1961 at the Richmond Athletic grounds as the National Jazz festi-val, and staged religiously every August since then, with just one two year hiatus (1984/85), when the necessary permits became suddenly unobtainable.

The festival did not actually move to the town with which it is now synonymous until 1971, when organizer Harold Pendle-ton was invited to take part in a local, government-sponsored celebration of Reading itself. According to Pendleton, nobody on the council realized that the original festival's jazz remit had long since faded from view, to be replaced first by R&B, then straightforward rock — the most recent festival, in Plumpton in 1970, saw the likes of Black Sabbath, Deep Purple, and Van Der Graaf Generator on the bill, with only veteran jazzman Chris Barber upholding the festival's founding principles.

Still, a bill highlighted by Genesis, Arthur Brown, Wishbone Ash, and Rory Gallagher passed off without problem, despite one national newspaper warning local residents to beware "the way-out impact of thousands of hippies" descending upon their "picture postcard village," and the following year, Pendleton was invited back to the town to stay.

Through the 1970s, the newly-rechristened National Jazz, Blues, and Rock Festival would come to dominate the UK live circuit, a three-day celebration of almost idealistic quality. Whatever machinations may have gone on behind the scenes, as record companies and promoters battled to have their acts scheduled on the bill, the festival never seemed to bow to the forces of commerce or greed. No mindless pop or manufactured hype; when a label finally did succeed in sponsoring a day at Reading, in 1976, it was Virgin Records, the darlings of the prog rock underground, with a roster which ran from the space rock of Gong to the reggae of U-Roy.

Perhaps cognizant of the fact that it took a certain kind of band to function on all cylinders on a stage in a field, beset by whatever the elements chose to fling at it, Reading paid little heed to the music rising out of the UK pub circuit through the early 1970s. Chilli Willi and the Red Hot Peppers appeared in 1974, Dr. Feelgood in 1975, Eddie and the Hot Rods in 1976, all as low on the bill as their current status demanded and, without exception, failing to impress.

Pub rock, the Reading consensus insisted, should stay in the pubs, and so it was that the Festival, having been present at the birth of every significant development in British rock from the Beat Boom to Psychedelia, from the Blues Revival to Prog Rock, was looking the other way entirely when punk first stepped onto the scene.

Reading, 1977, then, was headlined by Uriah Heep, Thin Lizzy and the Sensational Alex Harvey Band, with Aerosmith, Hawkwind, and the Doobie Brothers following them up. Eddie and the Hot Rods, the Motors (a band formed from the wreckage of Ducks Deluxe and the Snakes), and Graham Parker's Rumour highlighted the Pub Rock quotient.

The only remotely new, or at least new wave, bands in sight were electro cold warriors Ultravox, and Wayne County's Electric Chairs, whose transvestite toilet humor was never going to translate to the bedenimmed hordes of rockers awaiting them. The band was met by a hail of mud, cans, and insults which did not let up until they left the stage.

The following year saw the organizers make a more concerted bid for new wave acceptance. The first night was the crucial one, with Ultravox, Sham 69, Penetration, and Radio Stars all leading up to the headlining Jam. Saturday passed off relatively unpunked, and then Sunday returned to the fray with Chelsea, Squeeze, John Otway, and the Tom Robinson Band, before the Patti Smith Group wound things up. And then the reviews came

in, reminding everybody once again that punk was an indoor pursuit. Indeed, if the Sham fans hadn't spent much of the weekend throwing stuff at anything which moved, the entire weekend would have been completely unmemorable.

For 1979, the Police and the Cure were about as punky as the festival would ever again be; by 1980, the event had been wholly absorbed by the resurgent New Wave of British Heavy Metal; and by the end of the decade, Reading was dying on the vine, gamely plodding forward every year with another mix'n'match blend of hopefuls, has-beens, and never were's. Status Quo and the Stranglers topped the bill in 1987, Starship and Uriah Heep in 1988; but then promotor Pendleton handed the booking over to the upstart Mean Fiddler Organization, already an innovative power on the London club scene, and suddenly Reading was alive again.

Completely overhauling the festival's booking policy, the new promoters not only set out attracting new music, they also persuaded DJ John Peel to compere a festival he'd not even attended in a decade. Within two years, even before the Pendletons left the scene in 1992, Reading was rendered unrecognizable from the hard rocking monster it had so recently become... even the toilet and catering facilities were upgraded.

The most dramatic expansion of all, however, came in 1999, when Mean Fiddler announced a parallel event to be staged in the northern city of Leeds, over the same weekend as Reading, and featuring many of the same bands.

1989 (including) Sugarcubes, the Pogues, the Mission, the Wonder Stuff, My Bloody Valentine, Jesus Jones, Tackhead, the Butthole Surfers

1990 (including) Inspiral Carpets, Nick Cave, the Pixies, Mudhoney, Faith No More, the Cramps

1991 (including) Iggy Pop, James, Sisters of Mercy, Blur, De La Soul, Sonic Youth, Carter USM, Hole, Nirvana, Teenage Fanclub, Flowered Up

1992 (including) Nirvana, the Wonder Stuff, Public Enemy

1993 (including) Porno For Pyros, The The, Siouxsie and the Banshees, New Order, Blur, Big Star, Boo Radleys, the Grid, One Dove

1994 (including) Primal Scream, Red Hot Chili Peppers, Manic Street Preachers, Pulp, Radiohead, Soundgarden, Elastica, Tindersticks, Jeff Buckley

1995 (including) Smashing Pumpkins, Hole, Green Day, Björk, Paul Weller, Beck, Gene, Foo Fighters, Reef, Ash, Cast, Neil Young

1996 (including) Rage Against the Machine, Black Grape, Stone Roses, Prodigy, Garbage, Ash, Offspring, Underworld, Rocket from the Crypt, Sonic Youth, Dubstar, Julian Cope, Space, Babybird, Mansun, Kenickie, Geneva

1997 (including) London Suede, Manic Street Preachers, Metallica, the Orb, Space, Stereolab, Marilyn Manson, the Verve, Audioweb, Boo Radleys, Catatonia, Embrace, Bentley Rhythm Ace, Cornershop

1998 (including) Beastie Boys, Prodigy, Garbage, New Order, Ash, Mansun, Supergrass, Echo and the Bunnymen, Bluetones, Super Furry Animals, Travis, Spiritualized, Gomez, Stereophonics

1999 (including) Charlatans, Blur, Red Hot Chili Peppers, Chemical Brothers, Catatonia, Offspring, Reef, Echo and the Bunnymen, Fun Lovin' Criminals, Divine Comedy, Terrorvision, Space, Pavement, Gene, Dandy Warhols, Sebadoh, Arab Strap, Auteurs, Black Box Recorder, Elastica, Jim's Super Stereo World, My Life Story, Paradise Motel

SOCIAL CHAOS

(1999) "It's the first old school punk tour the States has seen," promotor Randy Wolpin said shortly before Social Chaos got underway. "The bands that invented the sound that made Green Day's Billie Joe Armstrong a millionaire," replied *Alternative Press*. But while several of the bands originally scheduled to appear dropped out (the Exploited and Peter & the Test Tube babies among them); and others fell by the wayside as the tour went on (D.R.I., Gang Green, and the Anti Heroes), still Social Chaos pulled off some remarkable coups, including "classic line-up" reunions for the UK Subs and Chelsea.

7/15-8/8 TSOL, UK Subs, DOA, Chelsea, Business, Vice Squad, Vibrators, LES Stitches, One Way System, Anti-Heroes, Gang Green, Sloppy Seconds, Murphy's Law, DRI.

STONEHENGE

SALISBURY, ENGLAND Free midsummer night festivals had been staged within the archaeological treasure of Stonehenge since the early 1970s; Hawkwind's Nik Turner recalled "chancing upon the first one, which was encouraged and publicized by Radio Caroline, almost by chance. I was passing Stonehenge and there were all these people there, sitting around the stones smoking chillums and getting wrecked."

Music followed the people organically. One person might bring a guitar, another might bring a band — by 1975, people were bringing generators and lighting rigs, while 1978 saw Turner's latest band, Sphinx, set up their full stage extravaganza amid the ancient stones. "We went on at 4 am, and it was must have been fantastic for the people who were there; suddenly this great magic show turned up, with dancers, it was really very competent, really electric!"

Concerns that the midsummer revellers might — and indeed had — damage the stones themselves eventually led to the monument itself being roped off, and the festival outlawed. Still it went on, however, a magnet first for rock, then for punk rock's disenfranchised outsiders. Crass played in 1980, until a gang of bikers

took exception to their hardnosed political rhetoric; sundry members of Hawkwind and associated bands were a permanent fixture, and every year, it seemed, would bring together another band of like-minded souls, simply to make music for the masses gathered to watch the sun break over the ancient stones.

Ozric Tentacles formed there in 1983; Omnia Opera were present two years later, when the authorities' attempts to shut the festival down exploded into open warfare; and attempts to divert the Stonehenge crowd to the better organized (ticketed) festival taking place simultaneously at Glastonbury simply left the highways of southwestern England clogged with bands of wandering minstrels and musicians, spreading the text of free festival even further afield.

TORONTO HEATWAVE

TORONTO, CANADA (1980) Despite being billed as the first-ever North American festival to devote itself to new wave music, the event was plagued by disappointment. The headlining Clash pulled out, the attendance came in at around half the anticipated 100,000. "By the time we got to Punkstock, we were 50,000 wrong," punned the watching *New Musical Express*. While both the Talking Heads, premiering their new, extended ten-strong line-up, and Elvis Costello and the Attractions (who opened their set by announcing, "Hello, we're the Clash") turned in powerful performances, still the over-riding impression was one of drab anti-climax.

8/23 (including) Elvis Costello, Talking Heads, B-52's, the Pretenders, Holly & the Italians, Rockpile, the Rumour, Teenage Head

US FESTIVAL

SAN BERNADINO, CA (1982–83) The Unuson (or Unite Us In A Song) festival was conceived by Apple Computers' Steve Wozniak. Billed as the Woodstock of the West, it attempted to learn from the mistakes of other events by firmly segregating its roster between the veterans, the mainstream, and the new wave.

Reasonably successful in 1982, the policy backfired in 1983, when the amount of money paid to the headlining Clash ($500,000) received considerably more attention than the quality of the music they, or any of the other participants, served up.

Having squabbled with the organizers and other acts all day, the Clash themselves took the stage two hours late to play a bedraggled 80 minute set which did nothing to quell rumors that the band was on the edge of splitting up (it was, in fact, the final gig the band would play before Mick Jones' departure).

Vocalist Joe Strummer himself later pinpointed all that was misguided about the event (and, contrarily, noble about the Clash's involvement) when he complained, "I'm not going to have some millionaire restaging Woodstock for his ego gratification and tax loss in his backyard and get away with it. Don't tell me you can recreate Woodstock in the Me Generation of cocaine California in 1983."

1982 9/3 (including) Police, Talking Heads, B-52's, Ramones, Gang of Four, English Beat

1983 5/28 (including) the Clash, Men at Work, Stray Cats

WOODSTOCK, NY

(1969, 1979, 1989, 1994, 1999) Thirty years on from the original festival, on a farm in upstate New York at the height of the Vietnam War, the spirit of Woodstock remained a palpable presence on the American psyche. It was the peak of the '60s experience — a decade born of trust had been betrayed times out of number, but still youth fought for the dream that had once been there for the taking. Woodstock, half a million people gathered for three days of peace and love and music, was the pinnacle of their achievement, and no matter how many years had passed since then, that achievement surely still meant something.

The first attempt to reprise Woodstock, in 1970, was abandoned, while a Woodstock Reunion on the tenth anniversary of the original festival, was a sparsely attended, poorly promoted wash-out. 1989 brought a more concerted attempt to celebrate the festival, but passed by with little more than MTV screening unseen footage from the original event.

It would be 1994, then, before a truly successful recreation of the event (if not the spirit) of Woodstock was staged. One, on the site of the 1969 show featuring survivors from that first weekend; the other, in nearby Saugerties, uniting 33 bands who might, in another lifetime, have dignified the first (and a handful, Bob Dylan included, who had refused to appear there).

Green Day, triumphant in the mud which piled up against anything or anyone which remained standing still for more than a minute, stole the show; other performers — Blind Melon, the Cranberries, the Rollins Band — confirmed their ascendancy. The inevitability of a 30th anniversary event was apparent even before the clean-up teams had finished mopping up the 25th.

"Woodstock has become the Olympics of live music," announced co-organizer Michael Lang. "Every five years we can step out of ourselves and celebrate diversity, great music and each other." But Woodstock '99 was a long way from Woodstock '69 — both physically (Rome, NY, is nowhere near Woodstock itself) and spiritually; and a long way from Glastonbury, Lollapalooza, HORDE, even Reading at its soul-sapping mid-80s low. Peace and love, the much-bandied watchwords of the Woodstock generation, come at a price of course, but $150 per ticket and $4 for a bottle of water at the height of a scorching August was asking a lot of the most committed pacifist, particularly at the end of a decade which had seen the very concept of a rock festival turned on its head.

No longer content to simply sit in a field (or in this case, a former air force base) and get off on the vibes (man), the Woodstock '99 generation wanted distraction, needed amusement, demanded excitement. And if the festival organizers weren't going to provide those things, the audience was going to find them anyway.

It is true, as Moby told the BBC, that "you don't have a festival based on peace and love, and invite Kid Rock and Insane Clown Posse." Of all the flashpoints during the three day event, the most serious occurred during appearances by bands whose very existence was founded on aggression — rehabilitation counsellor David Schneider later reported witnessing a gang rape while Korn was performing, while another rape was alleged during Limp Bizkit's set.

Later, it was pointed out that Woodstock was not the only legendary festival celebrating its 30th anniversary that year. On December 6, 1969, the Rolling Stones wound up their latest, greatest, tour of North America with a free concert at a disused speedway stadium in Livermore, CA. It was not their first choice of venue — originally scheduled for the better appointed Sears Point Raceway, the organizers discovered just 20 hours before showtime that the site was no longer available. They moved then, and in so doing, they presented the lexicon of rock'n'roll with a new word. That word was Altamont.

Nobody celebrated the 30th anniversary of Altamont, or the one murder, several rapes, and countless beatings which occurred as the Stones' Hell's Angels security team kept the peace with pool cues and meaty fists. No misguided promoter sat up late night on the telephone, inviting the cream of modern rock to come recreate a night which has gone down in history as the darkest in the history of rock'n'roll festivals.

But as the fire tenders arrived to quench the 13 conflagrations blazing across the Woodstock 99 festival grounds; as the police received the first reports of assault from still tearful young women; and the paramedics took away the last of the 120 hospital cases collected over the three day weekend, including one man allegedly crushed beneath a toppled van, it was not too hard to imagine that someone, somewhere, had got their anniversaries muddled up. This was Woodstock, after all. And things like that just didn't happen there.

1994 8/12-14 (including) Del Amitri, Live, James, Sheryl Crow, Blues Traveler, Collective Soul, Violent Femmes, Blind Melon, Cypress Hill, Rollins Band, Primus, Cranberries, Youssou n'Dour, Nine Inch Nails, Metallica, Aerosmith, the WOMAD Performers with Peter Gabriel, Green Day, Neville Brothers, Arrested Development, Porno for Pyros, Red Hot Chili Peppers, the Orb, Orbital

1999 7/23-25 (including) Umbilical Bros, Buck Cherry, Insane Clown Posse, George Clinton, Jamiroquai, Sheryl Crow, DMX, Offspring, Korn, Guster, Ice Cube, Chemical Brothers, Tragically Hip, Kid Rock, Rage Against the Machine, Limp Bizkit, Metallica, Mike Ness, Our Lady Peace, Sevendust, Godsmack, Megadeth, Brian Setzer Orchestra, Elvis Costello, Creed, Red Hot Chili Peppers

Twenty Essential Alternative Rock Movies

1. BLANK GENERATION (1976)

dir. Ivan Kral/Amos Poe

In 1975, something was coalescing within the NYC music scene and Ivan Kral, the newly-recruited guitarist for the Patti Smith Group, decided to film it. "I didn't really have any goal for the movie," he insisted, "except as some kind of a document to look back on. I did it more as a fan than anything else." But still he emerged with the first film ever made about punk rock, *Blank Generation*.

Working over a period of some three months, Kral and partner Amos Poe filmed virtually every band they could find, playing every club they could get their equipment into — then edited the whole thing down in one day.

"I just cut wherever was proper, and didn't think about it," Kral explained. "I didn't have five assistants, it was just myself in this cramped little room, figuring out which bands were important enough. Like we know, the Ramones happened, and so did Blondie, Television, Patti [Smith], Talking Heads; so it was just an obvious choice, the rest of the bands were just kind of a fill in."

The end result was the quintessential document of NYC's early punk scene. Other groups featured include the New York Dolls, the Heartbreakers, Wayne County, the Shirts, Marbles, Tuff Darts, and Harry Toledo. The only thing missing was a soundtrack. A synchronous sound camera was far too expensive, so the film makers dubbed either demos (including the original demo of Richard Hell and Voidoids' "Blank Generation" over the credits) or, in the case of the Ramones, a live tape. Only the Patti Smith Group were granted high quality — they, after all, had an album out.

Blank Generation did play at selected cinemas, but a new problem swiftly arose. "Pretty soon the prints were coming back to the distributor without segments of the Ramones or Blondie." Not surprising as the bands' popularity grew, but that created another problem. "We were afraid they'd all sue us, so we decided to just put it on a shelf and release it as a curiosity once in a while. Just use it as part of the document of that time." Since then, segments have appeared in both foreign and American music TV documentaries, including Time Life's *History of Punk Rock*, while 1977 would bring a 25 minute successor-of-sorts, *Punking Out*, shot exclusively at CBGBs.

2. THE PUNK ROCK MOVIE (1977)

dir. Don Letts

3. PUNK IN LONDON (1977)

dir. Wolfgang Buld

By spring, 1977, London punks couldn't pogo without sending a filmcrew flying. "The media was jumping all over it," Slaughter and the Dogs' Mick Rossi recalled. "It was such a vicious, forceful movement that at gigs, it wouldn't be uncommon to see filmcrews, photographers and people with video cameras."

They came from all over the world — Europe, America, Australia, even Japan, each shoving their way through the crowded clubs to secure footage of punk rock live and in the flesh. Rossi wasn't even aware there was a *Punk Rock Movie* "until I saw a little ad in the *NME* saying it was playing at the Scala, and saw us listed as one of the bands featured! It was very chaotic at the time."

Letts, a staple of the punk scene, and German Buld were shooting shoulder to shoulder much of the time — at least until they finally came to an agreement not to film the same shows and bands. Letts — already a familiar face on the local scene — inevitably came out on top, not only capturing the Sex Pistols at their Screen on the Green show, but also crucial early footage of the Clash, Siouxsie and the Banshees, Generation X, and the Slits, as well as such up and coming acts as X Ray Spex and Eater, and visiting New Yorkers Wayne County and the Heartbreakers.

In contrast, *Punk in London* featured mostly second stringers, although Buld did manage to shoot some live Clash and Adverts footage, alongside X Ray Spex, the Lurkers, the Jam at the 100 Club, the Boomtown Rats at the Marquee, and Kevin Rowland's Killjoys. The live footage was then cut through with interviews with Mark P (Perry), editor of the fanzine *Sniffin' Glue*, and Chelsea leader, Gene October, generally mundane interludes which did much to defuse the power of the rest of the film.

Nevertheless, Buld, too, emerged with a seminal document, one of the principle sources for subsequent punk documentary footage and, double-billed with *The Punk Rock Movie*, the next best thing to being there.

4. JUBILEE (1978)

dir. Derek Jarman

Jubilee was deeply silly and horribly meaningful, sinking under its own symbolism as the likes of Adam Ant, Ants manager and Sex store figurehead Jordan, and a deliciously decadent Wayne County (brutally microphoned to death by Jordan and her *Clockwork Orange*-esque cohorts) wandered around, wondering quite what they'd done to be drawn into such a production.

Ah, but the soundtrack (all of the above, plus Toyah, Suzi Pinns, and Eno) was great, and with Jarman's view of the punk scene emerging every bit as outrageous as any of his future movies, it was all very good fun... provided you didn't think about it too hard.

5. BURNING BOREDOM (1978)

dir. Wolfgang Buld

Keen to maintain his punk career following the success of *Punk In London*, Buld reunited with the Adverts during their fall 1978, German tour, using that as the backdrop for his next movie. "The plot was basically us going to Germany and doing three gigs," bassist Gaye Advert recalled. "We didn't have to learn a script though. It was basically about these two teenagers, Ian and Karen, who were supposed to be fans of ours and the events that then happened — these two kids are supposed to have met us in a restaurant, and they tag along to the gig."

The majority of the movie is in German, except for scenes with the band who didn't speak the language. To complicate matters further, Karen spoke almost no English, leaving Buld to translate back and forth — no easy task when everybody is improvising furiously. No surprise, then, that an already turgid plotline does little to sustain the viewer. The Adverts' live performances, however, are dynamic, and *Burning Boredom* did provide a springboard for Buld's future career. Today he is a respected director, responsible for many of Germany's best music documentaries.

6. QUADROPHENIA (1979)

dir. Franc Roddam

The movie which kickstarted the entire UK Mod revival, and laid the groundwork for the 2-Tone craze as well, this magnificent recreation of the Who's 1973 album of the same name was once rumored to be starring Johnny Rotten, Billy Idol, and Sham 69.

In the end, their roles went to Phil Daniels (later to become both an established actor *and* the voice on Blur's "Park Life"), Sting (previously seen portraying a singing garage mechanic in Christopher Petit's *Radio On*), and the

Cross Section, a proto-Mod combo who went precisely nowhere in the movie's aftermath. But the casting really wasn't that important. *Quadrophenia* perfectly encapsulated the era it was depicting; a time of frustration, disappointment, and old world values still to be consumed by the vision of youth. Up there with Michael Apted's 1974 death of a rock star epic *Stardust*, it remains one of the greatest rock movies ever made.

Roddam, the Who's unanimous choice for director, had never made a feature film before, although his BBC television play, *Dummy* — the story of a deaf teenaged prostitute — had made a major impression on the Who, not least for its mischievous play on the title of their own sensorily-impaired little whore. Still his recruitment was an inspired decision.

Newsweek called *Quadrophenia* "a damn good movie," even as American audiences left the theaters baffled by the fast-paced cockney accents and fast moving portrayal of a lifestyle which had no equivalent in American culture. Who biographer Richard Barnes describes it as "one of the most realistic and entertaining films about adolescence ever to come from the British film industry." Indeed, it would take another 15 years, and the release of *Trainspotting*, before another British movie made such a dramatic and defining impact upon the American movie scene.

The movie version of *Quadrophenia* seldom appears as much more than a footnote in biographies of the Who, an oversight which not only overlooks, but actually negates, the vast impact it was to have on the band's subsequent standing. Since the album's original release, the band had arguably spent close to half a decade in creative and critical freefall. The movie, in so firmly linking past with present, then, was nothing less than the Philosopher's Stone for which Townshend had been searching for over a decade; the event which made sense of his restless search for meaning within his own career.

Understandably uncomfortable with the popular notion that his last record was always better than his next (a common failing in both the public and media's perception of the Who), but equally, painfully, aware that he had spent the mid-late 1960s singlehandedly breeding the flock of pop albatrosses which now hung around his neck, Townshend finally realized, with the movie *Quadrophenia*, that rock history is relative.

If a mood he captured in 1973 could still be current six years later, then it only followed that a record he made 20 years ago would still be brand new to somebody hearing it for the first time today. And with that knowledge, Townshend was finally free, from *Tommy*, from "My Generation," from the Who itself. Though the band would soldier on for another couple of albums and another few misjudged years, still it can be said that the Who themselves ended with

Quadrophenia. They broke up when Jimmy's motorbike hit the water in the final moments of the film.

7. ROCK'N'ROLL HIGH SCHOOL (1979)

dir. Alan Arkush

PJ Soles stars, but it's the Ramones' movie through and through, as Arkush recreates the same high school lives and loves which made *Grease* such a hit for John Travolta, then drops da bruddahs into the thick of it.

Some genuinely inspired moments emerge from producer Roger Corman's backpack of tricks (including a race of scientifically-altered giant white mice), while the soundtrack serves up a potpourri which wanders from Fleetwood Mac to Todd Rundgren, the MC5 to Eno, and then drops Eddie and the Hot Rods, Nick Lowe, and the Velvet Underground into the brew. The Ramones provided the bulk of the fare, however, 14 tracks including the custom-written title theme.

8. DECLINE OF WESTERN CIVILIZATION (1980)

dir. Penelope Spheeris

Spheeris began her UCLA career studying behavioral psychology, switching to film-making following the death of her husband, cameraman Robert Schoeller, and a subsequent meeting with director Albert Brooks. Early work included directing shorts for *Saturday Night Live*, and production on Brooks' *Real Life* in 1979. The following year, she began work on *Decline...*, a cinéma vérité document of the L.A. punk scene.

Completed on a budget of $125,000 (its successor, the metal-based *Part Two*, cost $1 million), *Decline...* captured primal performances by Black Flag, X, Catholic Guilt, and the Circle Jerks, plus the fast disintegrating, but still crucial Germs. Indeed, while *Decline...* was guilty of sacrificing grit and realism for neat angles and lighting, it remedied those faults with some genuinely high-quality footage of bands which, at that point, had scarcely mastered the intricacies of making records.

Two years later, Spheeris returned to the L.A. punk scene for *Suburbia*, a drama following the misadventures of a group of punk outcasts, drawn at least in part from the city's own punk community. The one-legged Andre was a familiar sight at local shows; so was Mike B the Flea, bassist with local punx Fear (but soon to find greater renown as a Red Hot Chili Pepper). However, Spheeris' own daughter, Anna, took another part, while the punks' communal hang-out was "decorated" by professional Hollywood set designers, characters who had patently learned all they knew from tabloid television punk exposés. And *Suburbia* never rose above that level.

Only the live footage (including some fabulous TSOL and Fear performances) captured any of the turmoil and immediacy Spheeris' cameras were pursuing, shot at a disused theater on Sunset, the remainder labored under many of the same symbolic misapprehensions as Jarman's *Jubilee*, only with considerably less subtlety. When Jarman wanted to portray youth on the rampage, he had them lob a molotov cocktail at an innocent homeowner. Spheeris intercut scenes of a pack of wild dogs.

9. RUDE BOY (1980)

dir. Jack Hazan/David Mingay

Although it would be 1980 before it was released, *Rude Boy* was filmed across the summer and fall of 1978. Like Derek Jarman, whose *Jubilee* was released that same year, the Clash didn't want to so much document punk, as analyze Britain's current climate. Unlike Jarman, they wanted people to understand their points as well. So, the rise of the National Front and the subsequent formation of Rock Against Racism were portrayed through footage of riots and marches, and via two separate subplots as well.

The major storyline, meanwhile, followed the fate of Ray Gange, a real-life acquaintance of Strummer's and the living embodiment of "wayward youth," confronted with the chance — through the auspices of the Clash — to escape the hopelessness of his life. And if the movie had gone according to plan, that is what would have happened. The Clash were even planning to call the movie *Rudie Can't Fail* — because, of course, he couldn't.

But he did. Working without scripts, allowing the cameras to keep rolling both backstage and off-duty, Gange simply did not appear to grasp the concept. He argued, he fought, he made some alarming social faux pas and eventually, even the Clash had to concede defeat. By the time the movie itself was released, further squabbles — this time with the movie's backers — had seen the band totally disassociate themselves from the project, and few reviewers could blame them.

For all its problems, however, *Rude Boy* did brutally capture reality. The Clash are followed onstage and off, from rehearsal studio to their court appearances for shooting pigeons, and on into the recording studio. The performance shots in particular were phenomenal, towering above the live footage found in most other movies of the day, and of sufficient quality that much of *Rude Boy*'s soundtrack would appear on the Clash's official live album, a full 20 years later.

Gange himself, meanwhile, was thoroughly unlikable, a user who has nothing to give in return, and by the end of the film, he symbolizes little more than youthful closed-mindedness and ignorance. In that sense, he perfectly epitomized Thatcher's Britain; self-important, self-involved, and totally selfish — which means, in a circuitously bizarre fashion, *Rude Boy* absolutely succeeded in fulfilling its initial brief, capturing in microcosm all the tensions boiling beneath Britain's post-punk surface.

The anti-Nazi marches were real, as were the riots, and though the scene where Gange is hassled by the police was staged, still it was a fact of life for punks and minorities. Elsewhere, incoming Prime Minister Margaret Thatcher's Tory Conference law and order speech was the British equivalent of the Nuremberg Rally, and no less sinister. *Rude Boy* actually ends with her election into office — an image so chilling that it still sends shivers down the spines of those that lived through her regime.

10. GREAT ROCK AND ROLL SWINDLE (1980)

dir. Julien Temple

In January 1978, director Lech Kowalski caught a glimpse of the sheer destructive force of punk when he filmed the Sex Pistols' American tour and ruthlessly captured the band disintegrating before the camera's lens. Horrifying, funny, and heartbreaking, the movie documented the true hell of the tour, and the band's implosion. A year later, Temple and Pistols manager Malcolm McLaren put the finishing touches to their own version of events, *The Great Rock'n'Roll Swindle*. There was no similarity.

Temple was no stranger to the Pistols, although you'd never know it to look at him. London born, Cambridge educated, and a graduate of the National Film School, he had nevertheless worked for Glitterbest, the Sex Pistols' management company, in which capacity he shot reels of live footage at the many Pistols' gigs over the fall of '76, and on the Anarchy Tour in early '77.

At the time, Pistol's manager Malcolm McLaren wasn't even sure what he wanted to do with it all, and the first Pistols movie, the succinctly-titled *Sex Pistols Number 1*, simply comprised a kaleidoscope of the band's TV appearances, including the infamous *Today* show, *So It Goes*, *Young Nation*, the Janet Street-Porter interview and a host of news reports relating to the band. The 30-minute short ended with newsreel footage of Queen Elizabeth II's coronation, with the Pistols' "God Save the Queen" overdubbed. (Much of this material, plus unused footage, was subsequently compiled for 2000's *Filth and the Fury* documentary.)

By late 1977, however, McLaren's vision was more cohesive. According to Temple, "we decided to come up with a framework to use the documentary footage that we had collected. We'd been working on ideas, and came up with this idea of the Swindle: ten lessons that Malcolm would give, because at this stage Malcolm was beginning to get really bad press.

"So the presentation was designed to make him seem very evil; blowing Malcolm up into a much more prescient figure, having pre-thought everything out and planned it all, really masterminded the whole thing. Whereas, it was really a much more spontaneous reaction to a series of crises each time. I mean there was an overall momentum of ideas that hung the thing together, but it certainly wasn't pre-planned."

Temple succeeded far beyond McLaren's dream, and today, *Swindle* is viewed by many as the truth. In reality, the greatest swindle of all was the manager's rewriting of history in his own favor.

11. PUNK CAN TAKE IT (1980)

dir. Julien Temple

As a postscript to that movie, Temple shot the UK Subs' *Punk Can Take It* immediately after the completion of *Swindle* in '79, including cameo appearances by *Swindle* co-stars Eddie "Tenpole" Tudor and Helen of Troy, alongside excellent live footage of the then fast rising UK Subs at the Lyceum and the Cambridge May Ball.

The incidental scenes were tied together by narrator John Snagge, who — not so coincidentally — was the voice of the Pathe newsreels during the Second World War; the gist of the movie, according to Temple's direction, was the parallel between blitz era Britain and the ferocious attacks punk was attempting to withstand.

The media, big business, and sell-out bands were all the enemies that were trying to level the scene. The UK Subs were one of the few resisting the tide of corruption. Former Subber Nicky Garratt admitted, "there was a side of me that thought it was pretty corny, because it was just things that people had said over and over again. But it was a political statement and I think it was good because the World War II theme seemed to make sense."

The movie also ends on an upbeat note, for punks would, to paraphrase Sir Winston Churchill, fight them on the beaches, in the streets, at the label headquarters, and all they needed fear was fear itself. For no matter how heavy the artillery, punk really could take it. Who knew then that for most of the combatants, the battle was already over?

12. DANCE CRAZE (1981)

dir. Joe Massot

Oops! A 2-Tone documentary which utterly failed to match even a modicum of the passion which the music itself had generated — all the more so since it didn't actually appear until the dance craze itself was dead and buried. Bad Manners, the English Beat, and Madness prevent it from being a total 2-Tone label propaganda device; Selecter, the Specials, and the Bodysnatchers wrest the crown back again, while a smattering of '50s- and '60s-era TV and newsreel spots attempt to place the modern rude boys into an historical context.

True to the title, the movie is the view from the dance floor, meaning much of the in-concert action is seen around the heads of by-standers. But a few moments of inspired live material, notably the Specials' "Too Much Too Young" and Madness' "Razor Blade Alley," do show through, and the accompanying soundtrack album was dynamite.

13. URGH! A MUSIC WAR (1981)

dir. Michael White

Essentially a massive in-concert video showcasing the talents employed by Miles Copeland's IRS management company and brother Ian's FBI booking agency, *Urgh* coordinated a five-week series of live shows in L.A., New York, Paris, and London, during August/September 1980, featuring the cream of the new wave, then filmed and recorded all of them.

The resulting album and video were at least as seamless as any past live festival documentary; where they exceeded even the standards of *Woodstock*, *Monterey Pop*, and *Isle of Wight* (the late 1960s/early 1970s benchmarks for such productions) in the sheer consistency, extravagance, and versatility of the acts showcased.

Toyah, OMD, Oingo Boingo, Echo and the Bunnymen, XTC, Klaus Nomi, Gary Numan, the Surf Punks, the Cramps, Pere Ubu, Splodgenessabounds, UB40, the Go-Gos, Spizz 80, the Dead Kennedys, and Magazine were numbered among the 33 bands showcased, all performing one song apiece. (The Police, featuring the third Copeland brother, Stewart, and the singing mechanic from *Radio On*, got two.)

14. WINGS OF DESIRE (1986)

dir. Wim Wenders

German director Wenders has always been a connoisseur of rock and film — indeed of music and film. Unlike many directors of the time, his forte was to assure and acquire a sonic tapestry that would weave itself indelibly into his visual world, until the very act of watching a Wenders film becomes akin to religious epiphany, so perfectly do sound and vision work in tandem.

But Wenders (pre-1999's *Buena Vista Social Club*) as a rock film director? Yes — without a doubt. He has long been known as a rock'n'roll kind of guy and no film performance captures that quality better, albeit briefly, than *Wings of Desire*.

Scored by Jurgen Kneiper with additional contributions from Laurie Anderson and Nick Cave, the film itself revolves around the universal truths of humanity and love, the story of an angel (Bruno Ganz) who desires only to shake the bonds of immortality in order to love a woman (Solvieg Dommartin), finely wrought against the backdrop of a divided Berlin.

The audience becomes voyeur to the drama that plays out on the screen and Wenders wanted to capture that essence, the rush of real time, the anticipation of union. And in its own way, rock'n'roll is the one vehicle which does capture the brutal truth in being human and being in love, the aural compliment to the dark slide into bliss. And, Wenders knew, there were only two bands who could play the part.

Nick Cave and his Bad Seeds joined fellow Australians Crime and the City Solution on a Berlin soundstage to turn in some of the most memorable rock performances ever captured on film. Added as house bands in a cavernous club where angel becomes flesh and blood, Cave and Crime subtly embodied and mirrored the action on screen within the honesty of their own performances.

Across two scenes and over two songs, while humanity is the putative focus, the music steals the scene. Wenders captured the raw honesty of Crime's "Six Bells Chime" and the brutal truths of Cave's "From Here to Eternity" with perfect clarity. And although the musicians were only indeed "playing a part," their very work was enhanced by the actions around them, somehow making them more real and thereby further blurring the lines between musician and actor, between reality and realism. And in accomplishing that magical fission, Wenders captured two great and unequaled sequences in rock film, proof that the genre doesn't have to be a long barrage of sound. It needs only to transcend that mythical fourth wall, even if just for a moment.

15. ABSOLUTE BEGINNERS (1986)

dir. Julien Temple

Quadrophenia said it best, but the maxim bears repeating. Mod was a fashion out of time. Strangely ephemeral, delicate, neat and ferociously well-dressed, it was less a cult than it was a way of life; less a rebellion than a complete reassessment of the meaning of Youth.

If the Teddy Boys of the 1950s represented the glory of Britain's past, with their studied Edwardian wardrobes updated to include the street-fighting accouterments of the atomic age, Mods were the future. They were the first of the Baby Boomers, conceived in the bloodbath of frenzied wartime sex, and coming of age just as the boundless possibilities of youth first started encroaching on the privileges of adulthood.

In 1960, the very concept of "teenagers" was less than twenty years old, creeping from the pages of the popular science magazine which first coined the term in 1941. But Mod revolutionized it overnight.

The Mod bible, if such god-less, feckless cynicism as the Mods embodied could have a bible, was a thin paperback called "Absolute Beginners," written by a 55-year-old novelist named Colin MacInnes. Set against the ferment of London's 1958 Notting Hill race riots, and published at the dawn of the Age of Mods, in 1959, by the mid-1960s there were kids on the street who'd been carrying it around for so long they could recite it from memory.

Mod music was as matchless as their reading matter (and, of course, their wardrobe). No matter that modern pop history insists that the only Mod musicians who mattered were the Who and the Small Faces, according to the true dictates of the movement, the only sounds that really mattered were the ones the Mods found for themselves — American R&B, pre-Motown soul, and blue beat. Especially blue beat. And with the music, of course, came the lifestyle, one which, again, was born when the battlelines were drawn up at Notting Hill.

The western neighborhood of Notting Hill was the center of London's West Indian community, home to almost 7,000 people or close to 60% of the area's entire population. And they made it their own. All night at the Apollo pub on All Saints Road and in the basement of the Bajay coffee house on Talbot Road; all day at the Fortess cafe on Blenheim Crescent, and non-stop at the impromptu "shebeen" parties which every other house seemed to host, Jamaican music blared out, and Jamaican voices blared out even louder.

This was the neighborhood which, for four days at the height of August, was reduced to a no-go area by stone and bomb throwing white youths, knife and axe waving blacks, and a police force which could only stand around paralyzed by the unprecedented vistas of carnage.

MacInnes cataloged that carnage, and for almost 30 years since then, movie directors and musicians alike had been pondering setting the whole thing to celluloid. It took Julien Temple, however, to envisage setting it to music as well, and even with Paul Weller — the book's loudest advocate even before he wrote a song titled after it — having distanced himself from the entire affair, it was Temple's sheer panache and ambition which carried the day.

With David Bowie appearing as a singing, tap dancing advertising executive, and the future Mrs. Liam Gallagher, Patsy Kensit, alongside him, *Absolute Beginners* transplanted MacInnes' England into *West Side Story*'s Hollywood, ending up with a series of loosely linked, but breathtakingly well-designed and choreographed music videos, awash in a bris-

tling lexicon of iconographical cultural references and in-jokes.

Some of it was painful, some of it was awful. But for two hours in a darkened cinema, the sensory overload of *Absolute Beginners* left even the bitterest observer drained. It had little to do with the book, of course, and even less to do with Mod. But across a star-studded firmament, and a soundtrack to match, *Absolute Beginners* dazzled, danced, and dizzied with color, speed, and action.

Yeah, they said it couldn't be done... but only the critics agreed with them.

16. SINGLES (1992)

dir. Cameron Crowe

A Seattle native, Crowe's vision for *Singles* was simple — to capture the honesty, mood, and feel of his hometown music scene, before fame and fortune blew it all away forever. Indeed, it had already started to happen, which is why so much of *Singles* seems to be locked within a state of utter flux, the identity crisis which automatically accompanies a sudden change in status. Genuine documentary? Or simple role-playing parody? At the time, it didn't matter.

Certainly the ensemble cast which Crowe gathered round him made leading man Matt Dillon a little uneasy — he'd graduated from that sort of film years before. "But then I met Pearl Jam, and that sold me. I thought, okay, I know where I'm goin'. These guys are cool."

Dillon was to be the "star" of Citizen Dick, a local grunge band and a tough stretch for the well-groomed actor. His own short hair was covered by a wig in a more natural Seattle do — long, lank, and unkempt. Pearl Jam's Jeff Ament provided his wardrobe in the knowledge that at least one aspect of the movie would grasp some local flavor, but Crowe, too, was aiming for realism, shooting at many of Seattle's clubs and hangouts, and employing local musicians to simply be themselves.

Ament and fellow Pearl Jam members Eddie Vedder and Stone Gossard were recruited to back Dillon in Citizen Dick; Soundgarden, Alice in Chains, and Tad would all appear as themselves. And, of course, further authenticity was assured by one of Dillon's own most memorable lines. "I just don't like to reduce us to the Seattle scene... We're huge in Europe, right now."

They probably could have been, as well.

17. 1991: THE YEAR THAT PUNK BROKE (1992)

dir. Dave Markey

In 1986, Dave Markey was the drummer with Painted Willie, opening act on the final Black Flag tour and perfectly placed, therefore, to follow the proceedings from behind his camera — the result, *Reality 86ed*, has been described as one of the most authentic rock documentaries of the entire era. It's just a shame it's never been released.

Six years later, Markey was still hanging with a bunch of punks, only now the equation had changed somewhat. Nirvana were #1, Sonic Youth were leading the queue of bands who might soon be joining them. The Ramones were back with their best album in years, Dinosaur Jr. had a major label deal, Babes in Toyland were spearheading the Riot Grrl movement... it was, somebody appears to have said, the year that punk broke.

Of course it wasn't; another three years would need to elapse before the unexpectedly fertile San Francisco Bay Area truly restored punk rock to the headlines — and that revolution would not be televised. In the meantime, however, Markey's hour and a half of primarily live and underlit performance footage at least kept tabs on the best of the up and coming batch, interspersed with some typically punk behavior from its stars.

A period piece before it was even released, but a worthy artifact for all that, *1991* remains the one true document of a tumultuous time. Just don't expect a happy ending.

18. REALITY BITES (1994)

dir. Ben Stiller

Reflecting on her decision — scorned by friends and advisors — to take on *Reality Bites*, Winona Ryder explained, "I have a lot of friends in college who I grew up with... who say movies don't show what we're like. These are regular kids who just go to the movies every other weekend." This, she believed, was a movie for them.

Her character, a chain-smoking class valedictorian named Lelaina, was essentially the post-teenaged version of almost any of the characters Ryder had played in her own adolescence, from *Lucas'* Rina through Dinky Bossetti, and with only a slight stretch of the imagination, even Lydia Deetz of *Beetlejuice* fame. They typified "Generation X" before the term was coined. Lelaina personified it thereafter.

Unemployed and unemployable, apparently unable to do anything, in fact, more than smoke and talk to the Psychic Hotline, Lelaina is finally jerked back to reality by a $400 phone bill. Only then can her true ambition return, a long suppressed dream of making a video documentary about her friends — the roommate who works at the Gap, the slacker with a crummy band and a silly tuft of goatee beard... the end result, as one review put it, was a movie which proved just one thing. "That Generation X may be the first group to

know how boring they are and to make movies about it, paid for out of their allowances."

And that might well be so. But it was also the first movie since *Singles* to take modern youth and "show it like it is." Was it the movie's fault that the view wasn't so pleasant?

19. NATURAL BORN KILLERS (1994)

dir. Oliver Stone

History doesn't record which was the first movie *not* to actually feature the songs included on its soundtrack, but by the early 1990s, the practice was endemic. Movies still begat hits; hits occasionally begat movies (John Waters' *Pretty in Pink* was famously based around the Psychedelic Furs song of the same name); but just as frequently, songs and scenes existed in splendid isolation, right up until the marketing men bade them unite on a soundtrack album.

Nine Inch Nails had certainly had their share of movie moments, all the more so once Trent Reznor's record label, TVT, began exercising their control over his *Pretty Hate Machine*-era material. Reznor himself might not even have known that Oliver Stone had requested that album's "Something I Can Never Have," until Stone also requested another track from its successor, *The Downward Spiral*, but when the pair met at a screening of "A Warm Place," something immediately fell into place.

Stone suggested that Reznor's Nothing label might like to put out the entire soundtrack; when Reznor agreed, the director then asked if he would oversee the entire project. The result, a full integration of all the movie's musical and visual elements, would reinvent the entire genre of rock-related soundtracks. A few other film makers even paid attention.

As the songs intended for *Natural Born Killers* were already in place, Reznor was intended simply to oversee their editing, then write one new song, "Burn," for a particular scene. Reznor, however, decided to take his producer title seriously, and create a soundtrack that would truly parallel the on-screen action, Stone agreed, and Reznor was given free rein over the record.

He actually assembled the soundtrack album while touring Europe with Nine Inch Nails, setting up computers in his hotel rooms, then remixing, re-editing, splicing in dialogue, sequencing, the works. In the process, he estimated that he must have watched the movie a good seventy times, and while it might not have been the same as actually writing a soundtrack, it was almost as creative. And the end results were spectacular, just as Reznor always knew they would be.

The movie wasn't bad either.

20. KURT AND COURTNEY (1997)

dir. Nick Broomfield

The official story was simple. On Friday, April 8, 1994, electrician Gary Smith arrived at Kurt Cobain's home in Seattle's wealthy Madrona neighborhood to install a new security system. He could hear a television on inside the house, but there was no answer at the door, so he got on with his job, tracing the wires along the garage to the upstairs room which had once been used by the Cobains' daughter's nanny, Michael De Witt. Glancing in a window he saw what he initially took to be a tailor's mannequin — and then he saw the blood.

Kurt and Courtney is the story of what happened next, a labyrinth of increasingly surreal claims and counter claims, accusations and accidents... in February 1996, Courtney Love's father, Hank Harrison, pointed the finger of suspicion directly at his daughter, then told director Broomfield that "the more attention that gets paid to what I'm talking about here, the funnier it's going to look if I ended up dead somewhere on the railroad tracks." In April 1997, Mentors vocalist, El Duce, made even harsher accusations to Broomfield's

cameras. Eight days later, he fell in front of an on-coming train.

Kurt and Courtney doesn't necessarily convince anybody that Cobain was cold-heartedly murdered; indeed, Broomfield himself admits, sometime before the movie ends, that he's having problems believing what he's hearing. He didn't stop the cameras, though, and that's what gives *Kurt and Courtney* its edge; the fact that even as the camera is insisting we trust it, the director is slapping his forehead in total disbelief.

"What it comes down to," one of Cobain's former associates told *Mojo* magazine, "is this. Courtney has her story about her life with Kurt and what led up to his death, [fellow Nirvana members Kris Novoselic and Dave Grohl] have theirs, and a lot of other people, who weren't even around at the time, have theirs. And unfortunately, those are the stories which everyone hears. They're the only people who would talk to Nick Broomfield."

And though it spoils a damned good conspiracy story, one has to admit, he's right.

PERFORMERS

A

A CERTAIN RATIO

FORMED 1977 (Manchester, England)

ORIGINAL LINE-UP Simon Topping (vocals); Peter Terrell (guitar); Martin Moscrop (guitar); Jeremy Kerr (bass); Donald Johnson (drums)

Originally lining up as a drummerless quartet, and taking their name from the chorus of Brian Eno's "True Wheel" (from his *Taking Tiger Mountain by Strategy* album), ACR formed for fun and to make noise in keeping with the free-spirited ethos of the post-punk era, but without any set musical agenda. Only as their abilities improved to match their ambitions did a less-anarchic form of spontaneity creep into their work. By early 1979, the band members were writing their own material.

Attracting the interest of the local Factory label (they were, in fact, discovered by Joy Division manager Rob Gretton), by April, ACR were in the studio with producer Martin Hannett, recording their debut single, "All Night Party."

With influences that stretched from the Northern soul records they grew up with, to the extremes leaking out elsewhere on the scene, ACR were hard to ignore — all the more so after the icy regimentation of their drum machine-powered line-up was replaced by powerhouse Donald Johnson. Opting to deliver a half live/half studio debut album, work began (with Hannett) on the studio side in September 1979. A month later, side two was recorded live in London, when ACR opened for Talking Heads at the Electric Ballroom. *The Graveyard and the Ballroom* (#29 UK indy) was released in January 1980 as a limited edition cassette, and swiftly sold out.

"Shack Up," ACR's second single, translated Banbarra's mid-1970s funk anthem into a distinctly English-urban landscape with devastating results. Originally released in Europe only — through Factory's newly-formed Factory Benelux subsidiary — import copies flooded the UK and, later in the year, the record even made a showing on the American dance charts, a staggering development which anticipated labelmates New Order's "Blue Monday" breakthrough by a full three years.

"Flight" (#7 UK indy) followed, and in late 1980, the band was paired with Grace Jones for a pair of songs (including a radical restructuring of Talking Heads' "Houses in Motion") which could have completely redefined both acts' careers. Unfortunately, the union was never sanctioned by Jones' label, Island, and the session was scrapped.

ACR paid their first visit to the US in early 1981 to record a full studio album. *To Each* (#1 UK indy) offered a summary of their career to date, revised through a newly-expanded line-up. Former Occult Chemistry/Twilight Zonerz vocalist Martha Tilson met the band in New York and was immediately brought on board to contribute some punishing vocals, set on the jazzy edge of modern dance.

ACR continued to develop this new sound across their next single, "Waterline" (#10 UK indy), but complaints that they had grown willfully obscure were dispatched by their first release of 1982, the unashamed reggae instrumental "Abracadubra," issued under the pseudonym Sir Horatio. Timed to ride, at least in part, the last embers of the 2-Tone/ska boom, "Abracadubra" was not a musical style to which ACR would return. But still the sense of fun which went into the record's creation held over to their next releases, the "Guess Who" (#23 UK indy) and "Knife Slits Water" (#3 UK indy) singles, and *Sextet* (#53 UK, #1 UK indy).

ACR's third album, *I'd Like to See You Again* (#2 UK indy) followed in November 1982, shortly after Tilson's departure. Apparently intended more as an update of the band's line-up and sound than as a document of their current interests, its proximity to what was already being described as ACR's masterpiece also worked against it. Matters worsened when first, Peter Terrell quit to go on pilgrimage to India, then Simon Topping left to study percussion (he later reappeared in the dance band Quango Quango).

The pair were replaced by keyboard player Andy Connell and vocalist Carol Mackenzie, and ACR dropped into musical free-fall, crowning a distinctly uninspired period with a note-perfect rendition of Stevie Wonder's "Don't You Worry 'Bout a Thing," the B-side of a lackluster new single, "I Need Someone Tonight" (#8 UK indy).

Mackenzie's departure in mid-1984 signalled the group's renaissance. Tony Quigley was recruited from the jazz band (and Factory labelmates), Kalima, and with Jeremy Kerr moving up to take over vocals, ACR relaunched themselves at the Hammersmith Palais in August. By December, "Life's a Scream" (#6 UK indy) had restated almost every last one of the original band's ideals, while its successors, the Mardi

Gras-inflected "Brazilia" (#13 UK indy) and the Ornette Coleman-influenced "Wild Party" (#4 UK indy), introduced even fresher elements to the brew.

Reviewing their headlining appearance at the 1985 ICA Rock Festival in London, *Melody Maker* deadpanned. "ACR kicked off with their new B-side, a start-stop-stomp overlain with some incomprehensible tape babble.... [But] for all their clinical precision, ACR play with none of the cold technicality which disfigures certain of their contemporaries."

It was an excited report, made even more vital by the release of a dramatic best of, *The Old and the New* (#3 UK indy), in the new year. By the time of their next album, a return to the cassette-only format for *Made In America*, ACR were flinging themselves headlong into modern jazz — pastures which were explored even further on 1986's full-blooded *Force* (#2 UK indy), and the "Mickey Way" single.

In 1987, ACR quit Factory for major label A&M, hoping that the larger company's promotional budget would extend beyond Factory's promises-and-prayers approach. Connell split to form Swing Out Sister and the remaining quartet of Martin Moscrop, Kerr, Quigley, and Johnson would spend close to two years out of sight, before resurfacing in June 1989, with the single "The Big E." Two further singles, "Backs to the Wall" and "Your Blue Eyes," appeared on either side of the *Good Together* album, while the accompanying tour would be celebrated in July 1990, with the live *MCR* mini-album, and the superlative "Good Together" single.

ACR also scored their first hit, with the recruitment of New Order's Bernard Sumner and future Fatboy Slim mainman Norman Cook, to remix the ballad "Won't Stop Loving You" (#55 UK), but by late 1990, the band's contract had lapsed, leading to the cancellation of another Cook mix — a remake of "Shack Up." By 1991, ACR were back in the Factory orbit, signing to Rob Gretton's Rob's Records label and unveiling what would become their last album for five years, *Up In Downsville*, and the singles "The Planet," "27 Forever," and "Mello."

Officially abbreviating their name to ACR, the band continued to release singles through 1993 and 1994 — remix-heavy EPs which featured "Turn Me On," "Tekno," and "Shack Up." 1994 also saw the re-release of the band's entire Factory catalog, together with a dynamic remix collection, *Looking for a Certain Ratio*. That, in turn, would inform the band's own future plans, and in 1997, ACR returned with *Change the Station*.

Fronted now by vocalists Lrona Bailey and Denise Johnson, a Manchester-scene veteran with vocal credits ranging from Electronic to Primal Scream and the Pet Shop Boys (she also released a couple of indy singles during 1996), ACR had again proved their durability. 1997, of course, marked the band's 20th anniversary, but more importantly, they also demonstrated how their durability worked, by absorbing — just as they had in the beginning — the spirit of the times, and staying just one step ahead of it.

A Certain Ratio LPs

7 The Graveyard and the Ballroom (Factory) 1980 Half-agitated live, half-somber studio, formative thrashing cut through with delinquent, jerky dance rhythms.

5 To Each (Factory) 1981 Disciplined — but largely indulgent — attempt to plug the void left by Joy Division's passing, through the wringer of ACR's increasingly jazz-funk sensibilities.

8 Sextet (Factory) 1982 Tilson's triumph, as ACR merge crashing disco beats with lurching rhythms and emerge with an album of sometimes awesome power.

5 I'd Like to See You Again (Factory) 1982 Quirk for quirk's sake, jazz for jazz's sake, and possibly, purposefully MOR.

6 Made in America (LIVE) (Dojo — UK) 1986

6 Force (Factory) 1986 The modern jazz dance starts here — tentatively in concert (where a string of early classics are smoothly executed), brutally on disc.

7 Good Together (A&M) 1989 Looking towards the dancefloors, predicting what would one day become acid jazz, a tighter — and certainly less "adult" — disc than anything in seven years.

6 Up in Downsville (Rob's Records — UK) 1992 Calming down again — but still targeted towards the dance floors — ACR remind the world that they are from Madchester.

8 Change the Station (Rob's Records — UK) 1997 Dynamic fusion of classic ACR awkwardness and modern (courtesy of Johnson) electro-soulfulness.

Selected Compilations and Archive Releases

6 The Old and the New (Factory) 1986 Less than perfect compilation bidding farewell to the Tilson era.

7 Lookin' for a Certain Ratio [REMIXES] (Creation) 1994 Electronic, 808 State's Graham Massey, The Other Two, and Sub Sub get to sometimes uncomfortable grips with the ACR back catalog.

A FLOCK OF SEAGULLS

FORMED 1979 *(Liverpool, England)*
ORIGINAL LINE-UP *Mike Score (vocals, keyboards); Paul Reynolds (b. 8/4/62 — guitar); Frank Maudsley (b. 11/10/59 — bass); Ali Score (drums)*

1979 was a fertile time in Liverpool, and an odd one as well. Everywhere, new bands were forming, and each one seemed to have a stranger name: Pete Wylie's Wah! convolutions, Echo and the Bunnymen, Dalek I Love You, The Teardrop

Explodes, Orchestral Manoeuvres in the Dark (OMD), etc. A Flock of Seagulls fit that scene like a glove.

Mike Score had just quit another local group, Tontrix, when he began rehearsing this new band with brother Ali and friends Frank Maudsley and Paul Reynolds. They took over a room above Mike's hair salon, and stayed there for more than a year until former Be Bop Deluxe frontman Bill Nelson heard one of their tapes, and offered them a deal with his Cocteau label.

"(It's Not Me) Talking," (#45 UK indy) was released in June 1981, but it was the evergreen "Telecommunication," the title track of the band's debut EP, which became the more memorable New Wave club hit. And by the end of the year, A Flock of Seagulls were signing a major label deal.

"I Ran (So Far Away)" (#9 US, #43 UK) — punningly political at a time when Iran itself was making headlines around the clock — was chosen for their first single. And with the band's image — designed by the members themselves during downtime at the hairdressing salon — making for some magnificent photos, the total picture was irresistible.

While April 1982, brought the band's self-titled debut album (#10 US, #32 UK), MTV flipped for the Seagulls' video. The rest of America followed, and by summer 1982, A Flock of Seagulls had exploded, blazing a Top 10 single and a monster album into places where the rest of the so-called new romantic pack was still desperately trying to strike a spark. Even before the band's homeland had truly caught on to their sparkling stylisms, America was clutching A Flock of Seagulls to its heart.

"Space Age Love Song" (#30 US, #34 UK) kept the band on the chart. By early 1983, "D.N.A.," another track from that much-acclaimed first album, had won the Grammy for Best Rock Instrumental of the year. "Wishing (I Had a Photograph of You)" (#26 US, #10 UK) made it three smashes in a row, and A Flock of Seagulls' second album, Listen (#16 US, #16 UK), was Top 20 bound as well.

"Nightmares" (#53 UK) and "Transfer Affection" (#38 UK) fared poorly, however, and the group's third album, The Story of a Young Heart (#66 US, #30 UK), was a disappointment, even for fans. Two further singles, 1984's "The More You Live, the More You Love" (#56 US, #26 UK) and 1985's "Who's That Girl" (#66 UK) marked the end of the "classic" Seagulls line-up.

Replacing guitarist Reynolds with Gary Steadnin and adding a second keyboard player, Chris Chryssaphis, the group's fourth album, Dream Come True, appeared in 1986, only for the band to break up shortly thereafter. Score launched a second generation of Seagulls in 1989 with a new single, "Magic," and a well-received American tour, but by the end of the year, they too had split.

A third Flock formed in 1995, lining-up as Score, Ed Berner (guitar), Dean Pichette (bass), and AJ Mazzetti (drums). A new album, "The Light at the End of the World" (featuring the six-year-old "Magic" and new single "Burning Up"), was released and the band toured ferociously. A string of personnel changes followed, resolving themselves by early 1998 into a line-up of Score, Joe Rodriguez (guitar), Lucio Rubino (bass), and Darryl Sons (drums).

A Flock of Seagulls LPs

8 A Flock of Seagulls (Jive) 1982 Six of the ten tracks had already appeared on singles, but still a killer debut. Bouncy pop backed by driving, dancey rhythms and fleshed out by warm, lush keyboards. Little artistic ground is broken, but strong melodies and sharp hooks ensure there's no quibbling. (8)

6 Listen (Jive) 1983 The immortal "Wishing" fits into Listen like a walrus wearing a pair of pants, standing so high above its fellows that even the dreamy "Transfer Affection" and the proto-Goth "Nightmares" pale in comparison.

5 The Story of a Young Heart (Jive) 1984 Bill Nelson returned to produce, but the band was out of ideas and the hit machine was out of gas. Nevertheless, Seagulls achieve another timely first — their contemporaries wouldn't be this pointlessly pop-glossed for another year or so.

3 Dream Come True (Jive) 1986 Few songs, fewer melodies, utterly unmemorable.

6 Light at the End of the World (Sava) 1996 Resurrected for the '80s revival and remembering what made the old days so special, Light offers nothing new for long-time fans, but recaptures some of the dizziness which made the Seagulls flock in the first place.

Selected Compilations and Archive Releases

6 The Best Of (Music Club) 1998 The most complete of several straight-forward collections of the hits, marred only by the fact that the band didn't have that many.

7 Greatest Hits Remixed (Cleopatra) 1999 The '90s mash the '80s, with some decidedly bizarre results.

ADAM AND THE ANTS

FORMED 1977 (London, England)
ORIGINAL LINE-UP Adam Ant Goddard (b. Stewart 11/3/54 — vocals, guitar); Lester Square (guitar); Andy Warren (b. 1961 — bass, vocals); Paul Flanagan (drums)

It was an unexpected encounter with the nascent Sex Pistols which transformed Stuart Goddard, art student, into Adam Ant, pop star — that, followed by four years spent slogging around the U.K. club circuit, while hordes of disbelievers hooted at all he held holy.

In November 1975, Goddard was a member of club circuit hopefuls Bazooka Joe and His Rhythm Hot Shots when the Pistols gate-crashed one of their concerts, played until the plug was pulled, then shrank back into the night, leaving everyone scratching their heads... everyone, that is, except Goddard. Within six months of the meeting, Goddard — with the newly recruited Lester Square — was forming a new band, the B-Sides, intent on pursuing his own vision of the vistas revealed by the Sex Pistols.

Lured in by a classified ad inviting young musicians and Ramones fans to "Beat on the Bass with the B-Sides," Andy Warren and the first of several temporary drummers joined in July 1976. With Paul Flanagan also on board, the band did get around to some recording — laying down a version of Nancy Sinatra's "These Boots Are Made for Walking" — but still the B-Sides were rarely stable enough to leave the rehearsal room, and not yet visionary enough to want to.

That changed in April 1977, when the B-Sides were reborn as Adam and the Ants. Goddard became Adam Ant, the remainder simply adopted Ant as their nom-de-punk, and on April 23, the new band debuted at the Roxy, supporting Siouxsie and the Banshees. Square quit two weeks later to form Monochrome Set, and by May, Ant had put together a new group, with Warren, Mark Ryan (aka Mark Gaumont — guitar), and Dave Barbe (aka Dave Barbarossa — drums).

A handful more gigs through May set the flavor for much of the remainder of the Ants' career: a rollercoaster ride between exhilarating lows — they were thrown offstage just one song ("Beat My Guest") into their second ever show, and unimagined highs — two shows opening for X-Ray Spex at the prestigious Man in the Moon pub in Chelsea were sufficient to earn them their own headlining gig, then back to soul destroying lows — two minutes into the show, the only people left in the room were the friends the band had put on the guest list. and not all of them, either.

One of the friends who did stick around was Pamela "Jordan" Rooke, an assistant at Malcolm McLaren's Sex shop, and the closest thing to a human mannequin the proprietors could have dreamed of — dyed, styled hair piled atop deeply stylized make-up, fishnet legs, and rubber torso — Jordan wore what she sold, sold what she wore, and hit the clubs in the same clothes she'd wear while commuting. A living outrage, she was already twice as eye-catching as half the bands she went to see, and probably twice as famous. She would become the Ants' manager that same evening.

The Ants' workload increased. More support gigs were interrupted by a role in Derek Jarman's punk-inspired movie, *Jubilee*, but it took an appearance on John Peel's BBC radio show in the new year to finally alert the industry to the band's still untapped potential. The Ants signed to Decca in the spring of 1978, one day after Jordan resigned as manager

and the band's most recent recruit, guitarist Johnny Bivouac, quit. After one gig with no guitar, Matthew Ashman (b. 1962, London; d. 11/21/95), was recruited in time to play the Debutantes' Party at the Hard Rock Cafe on June 6, 1978.

The Ants recorded an entire album's worth of material for Decca, including the likes of "Red Scab" and "Cleopatra" (both of which would become internationally renowned in later, re-recorded, form), "Boil in the Bag Man," "Song for Ruth Ellis," and a host of other darkly sexual epics, Decca unleashed the utterly unrepresentative "Young Parisians" as the band's first single, then dropped the band in early 1979.

It would be another nine months before the Ants truly recovered from the shock, after they signed with the Do It indy, and released a new collection of songs, the album *Dirk Wears White Sox* (#1 UK indy). Much of the Decca material had been dropped from the set, to be superceded by a new repertoire — leading off with the "Zerox" single (#1 UK indy), and when two major UK tours through the year saw the band's star climb higher, Ant knew that one more push could see them break through.

In September, the Ants sold out two nights at London's Electric Ballroom. Just days later, however, Warren quit to join Lester Square in the Monochrome Set; he would be replaced by Lee Gorman, around the same time as Ant recruited former Sex Pistols manager Malcolm McLaren to help him revamp the band's image. Ant gave McLaren a thousand pounds, McLaren gave him the bullet. Ant was sacked from his own band, to be replaced by two new singers, a 14-year-old Burmese girl McLaren discovered singing in a north London launderette, Annabella Lu Win (b. Myant Myant Aye, 1966, Rangoon, Burma), and London scenester Boy George O'Dowd. George quit after one gig, but renamed Bow Wow Wow, this new line-up would be launched on a wave of revolutionary superlatives in early 1980.

Immediately, Ant set about forming a new band, built around an unprecedented penchant for color and costume and the same concept of two drummers, as had fired his teenage years hero Gary Glitter through his greatest successes. Chris "Merrick" Hughes (b. London, 3/3/54) Terry Lee Miall (b. London, 11/8/58) were joined by bassist Kevin Mooney and ex-Models guitarist Marco Pirroni (b. London, 4/27/59), a founding member of both Chelsea (singer Gene October settled upon the name the week after Pirroni quit), and Siouxsie and the Banshees.

The new-look Ants first completed their obligations to Do It, a re-recording of the album's "Car Trouble" (#1 UK indy), then set about seeking a new manager, a new label, and a new lease on life. Ant was sick of being put on by pirates. Now he was going to be a bigger pirate than all of them, and what was surprising was how quickly — and effectively —

the whole thing happened for him. One moment, Ant was the punk pariah, a standing joke even amongst his fans; the next, he was inciting everyone to unplug the jukebox and join his insect nation. And they were doing it!

Ant's manifesto was simple. "We perform and work for a future age. We are optimists and, being so, we reject the 'blank generation' ideal. We acknowledge the fanzine as the only legitimate form of journalism and consider the established press to be little more than talentless clones, guilty of extreme laziness. We believe that a writer has the right to draw upon any source material, however offensive or distasteful it might seem. We have NO interest in politics; we identify with no movement or sect other than our own. We are interested in sexmusic, entertainment action and excitement, and anything young and new."

Harnessing the capabilities of video before most people were even dimly aware of them, Ant constructed his own stardom with surprising rapidity — and abandoned it equally swiftly. He seemed to erupt out of nowhere, burn briefly, then erupt back into obscurity, and that was what made the whole thing so magical.

In August 1980, the rambunctious "Kings of the Wild Frontier" (#48 UK) marked the Ants' CBS debut; two Top 5 hits "Dog Eat Dog" (#4 UK) in November, and "Ant Music" (#2 UK) in the new year, were followed by the chart-topping "Stand and Deliver" (#1 UK) and "Prince Charming" (#1 UK).

Both their sophomore set, November 1980's *Kings of the Wild Frontier* (#44 US, #1 UK) and the following year's *Prince Charming* (#94 US, #2 UK), ranked among the biggest selling albums of the year, and a string of early Ants singles were reissued to different shades of chart-bound glory: "Young Parisians" (#9 UK), "Car Trouble" (#33 UK), "Zerox" (#45 UK), "Deutscher Girls" (#13 UK), and "Kings of the Wild Frontier" (#2 UK). Meanwhile, *Dirk Wears White Sox*, rose to #16 in January 1981, over a year after it was released.

Then, as suddenly as the dream had come to life, it was over. Ant replaced Mooney with former Vibrators/Roxy Music bassist Gary Tibbs (b. London, 1/25/58), and the lyrics to "Ant Rap" (#3 UK) were both a tribute to the soldier ants, and their farewell. Retaining Pirroni alone as his songwriting partner, Ant scattered the Ants and, though the bubble seemed far from bursting right away, by the time his solo debut, "Goody Two Shoes" (#12 US, #1 UK), gave Adam his American breakthrough, his greatest achievements already seemed far, far behind him.

His videos, once a stampede of excitement and energy, were now muted shadows, under-budgeted and overtaken by the erstwhile New Romantics: Duran Duran, Depeche Mode, the Human League, and Spandau Ballet. Wham!

snatched away Adam's teenybait following; Frankie Goes to Hollywood snatched away the rhythm nation he'd so painstakingly constructed. Ant wasn't even old hat any more — just a tatty ski mask which had seen better days.

A comparatively under-performing new album, *Friend or Foe* (#16 US, #5 UK), was joined by the similarly disappointing singles "Friend or Foe" (#9 UK) and "Desperate but Not Serious" (#66 US). "Puss N' Boots" (#5 UK) rallied, but "Strip" (#42 US, #41 UK) stalled after Ant refused to amend its risque lyrics for UK airplay. "Apollo 9" (#13 UK) proved a poor reminder of the Phil Collins-produced *Strip* album (#65 US, #20 UK), and Ant would never see the business end of the Top 10 again.

Not only that, but his performance at Live Aid in 1985 was so poorly received that, according to the following week's *Melody Maker*, sales of his latest single, "Vive Le Rock" (#50 UK), actually went down in the days after the festival — at a time when recordings by every other performer went through the roof.

Ant and Pirroni made one attempt to stop the rot, recruiting former T. Rex/Bowie producer Tony Visconti to handle their next album, also titled *Vive Le Rock* (#131 US, #42 UK). "They wanted the T.Rex sound, a 1985 version, and I was almost reluctant to do it," Visconti admitted. "But with today's technology it can very easily be updated, so I went ahead and did it, and it was a lot of fun."

But *Vive Le Rock* performed as poorly as its herald and, when CBS dropped him the following year, Ant turned away from music entirely. While Pirroni joined Spear of Destiny and moved heavily into session work, Ant concentrated his energies on acting, landing roles in TV's *The Equalizer*, Kimberley Foster's *Love Bites*, Arnold Schwarzenegger's *Last Action Hero*, and John Frankenheimer's *Tales from the Crypt*.

Interrupting this routine with just one new album, 1990's *Manners and Physique* (#57 US, #19 UK), and singles "Room at the Top" (#17 US, #13 UK) and "Can't Set Rules About Love" (#47 UK), Ant passed close to a decade "quietly appearing with Dennis Hopper, Harry Dean Stanton, Bruce Dern, and Sharon Stone in a dozen or so films, which have been teaching me my craft as an actor." He was also studying with Harry Mastrogeorge.

In 1993, buoyed by a hit placing for the *Antmusic* (#6 UK) retrospective, Ant ventured back onto the road, and recorded a new album, *Persuasion*, with Chic maestro Bernie Edwards. His label, MCA, shelved it. Two more years passed, "then one day in a cafe in Piccadilly, I turned to Marco and said 'fuck this, let's write a new bastard album.'"

Ant re-emerged in 1994, riding the publicly-stated admiration of Trent Reznor (a cover of "Physical (You're So)" appears on Nine Inch Nails' *Broken* mini-album). Towards the end of the year, work began on a new album, with Pirroni, plus ex-Ruts drummer Dave Ruffy (the pair worked together on Sinead O'Connor's debut album), bassist Bruce Witkin and multi-instrumentalist Morrissey mainstay Boz Boorer. Again Ant toured, a three-month jaunt which cloaked the US in resurgent Antmania, then returned to England for two London date — Ant's first UK shows since Live Aid.

He was rewarded with minor chart placings for the album *Wonderful* (#143 US, #24 UK), and two singles, "Wonderful" (#39 US, #32 UK) and "Gotta Be a Sin" (#48 UK), then retreated again.

Adam and the Ants LPs

9 Dirk Wears White Sox (Do It — UK) 1979 Even at the height of Antmania, it was no surprise that this quirk-laden collection of deliberately anti-social pokes at S&M freaks, religious devotees, handicapped zoo-goers, and delinquent motor cars never took the world by storm. No surprise, but an incredible injustice.

9 Kings of the Wild Frontier (Epic) 1980 Not since the days of Gary Glitter had a band had their anthemic shout so resoundingly answered by an entire nation. The percussion led the Ants' invasion, a tribal assault shifting from Burundi trances to war-fevered tattoo, the backdrop to a tapestry of high-energy punk, exhilarating pop, western twang, sea chanties, and artsy Wire-esque judder.

4 Prince Charming (Epic) 1981 Two classic 45s ("Stand and Deliver" and the title track) mask a disappointingly redundant album which reaches its nadir with "Mile High Club," "S.E.X." and — although the intent was pure — "Ant Rap." Great jacket, though.

Adam Ant LPs

3 Friend or Foe (Epic) 1982 Adam's solo debut made more of the latter than former — and that despite going gold on the back of "Goody Two Shoes." The Doors cover ("Hello, I Love You") was a big mistake.

5 Strip (Epic) 1983 When he's camp, he's kingly, when he's coy, he's less convincing. The title track was a masterpiece of innuendo (or not), but Phil Collins' co-production had more gloss than a paint shop, and no amount of stripping could wipe that out.

3 Vive le Rock (Epic) 1985 Bowie/Bolan producer Tony Visconti was on hand to recapture the vintage be-bop boogie bounce, and Ant and Pirroni were in full 50s retro mood. But the rebirth miscarried in the nasty 80s sheen, and there's more cock-up than Cochran about this sad affair.

4 Manners and Physique (MCA) 1990 Prince's pal Andre Cymone tries reinventing the Ant as a sexy dancefloor demagogue. Adam tries to let him, but even "Room at the Top" had too much space to let.

4 Wonderful (Capitol) 1995 If Boy George had made this album, we'd call it a return to late Culture Club standards, with all the dire forebodings which that brings to mind. But because it's Adam, and he once meant so much, we persevere. Sadly.

Selected Compilations and Archive Releases

7 Antics in the Forbidden Zone (Sony) 1991 Career spanning epic with horrifyingly diminishing returns as cruel chronology kicks in.

8 The Peel Sessions (Strange Fruit) 1991 Primal Ants, with invigorating versions of a dozen pre-*Wild Frontier* classics.

6 B-side Babies (Sony) 1995 Early Ant hits were great, with killer cuts on both sides of the single. *Forbidden Zone* wrapped up half the story, *Babies* neatly completes it. Again, however, time passes too quickly.

Bow Wow Wow LPs

7 Your Cassette Pet (EMI — UK) 1980 Eight track mini-album following the "C30 C60 C90 — Go!" formula of breathless Antisms and Annabelle's yelping.

7 See Jungle! See Jungle! Go Join Your Gang Yeah! City All Over, Go Ape Crazy (RCA) 1981 Never has calculation sounded so good. The boys pound out the tribal beats, the girl admits she's a puppet and a bimbo, reverse pop psychology at its cutting edge best. and of course it worked a charm.

5 When the Going Gets Tough (RCA) 1983 Losing manager McLaren and all the attendant baggage, Bow Wow Wow keep the rudiments of their sound, but lose the tsunami of outrage and provocation.

6 Live in Japan [LIVE] (Receiver UK) 1997 15 tracks of frenzied woofery, in front of a suitably garrulous audience.

Selected Compilations and Archive Releases

8 I Want Candy (RCA) 1981 US edition including the crucial *Last of the Mohicans* EP, plus three remixes, one reprise from *See Jungle*, and two new tracks. A fair round up, climaxing with the hauntingly hypnotic "Baby Oh No."

8 I Want Candy (EMI — UK) 1982

7 Twelve Original Recordings (Harvest) 1982 The UK edition of *Candy* reprised *Your Cassette Pet* plus the *Mohicans* EP and a few non-album singles. *12 Original Recordings* hacked off two tracks for the US market.

6 Best Of (RCA) 1996 The hits, the misses, the desperate attempts to claw something back.

7 Wild in America (Cleopatra) 1998 Invigorating modern remix collection, highlighted by a fabulous take on "Technology" — Blondie meets the Mission!

Further Reading

Adam and the Ants by Chris Welch (Star Books, UK, 1991).

ADVERTS

FORMED 1976 (London, England)
ORIGINAL LINE-UP TV Smith (b. Tim Smith North Tawton, England, 4/5/56 — vocals); Gaye Advert (b. Gaye Black Bideford, England, 8/26/56 — bass); Howard Pickup (b. Howard Boak b. 1951, d. 7/96 — guitar); Laurie Driver (b. Laurie Muscat — drums).

With TV Smith and Gaye Advert having moved to London from their native Devon in summer 1976, The Adverts made their live debut at the Roxy Club in January 1977, to immediate impact. The band attracted a manager, publishing magnate Michael Dempsey, immediately following their first show; they were recorded for the forthcoming *Live at the Roxy, London, WC2* punk compilation album at their second; and they landed a record deal at their third, when they were introduced to Stiff Records by Damned guitarist Brian James.

By the time they played their tenth show, the Adverts' debut single, "One Chord Wonders," was Single of the Week in the *New Musical Express*, and the band were preparing for their first nationwide tour — opening for the Damned and starring on what is still one of the greatest concert posters ever made. The Damned, it said, "can play three chords. The Adverts can play one. Hear all four at...." When the Adverts signed to the major label Anchor/Bright in June 1977, they were already regarded as one of the very best things to have hit punk so far, with one of the most captivating bassists.

Gaye Advert's face adorned the first single sleeve, and much of the band's early press. The most photogenic figure on the entire British Punk scene, her panda-eye make-up and omnipresent leather jacket defined the face of female Punkdom until well into the next decade, even as her dogged refusal to play along with her sex-symbol status helped redefine the role of women in rock. No longer just a pretty face, no longer a novelty for the media to drool at, cool to the point of absolute indifference, Advert proved that you could be a woman and still be a vital component of a band.

If she remained the focal point of the band, despite barely moving the whole time she was on stage, Smith was its raging heart, spitting out the fail-safe succession of songs which still delineate punk's hopes, aspirations and, ultimately, regrets. "New Church," "Great British Mistake," and "Bombsite Boy" were flawless anthems of DIY disaffection, nailed down by great crunching choruses and drums like dustbin lids.

Single of the Week across the music press, "Gary Gilmore's Eyes" (#18 UK), was based on the American killer's request that his eyes be donated to medical science following his execution, and won plaudits for everything

from the most memorable chant of a year which already bristled with memorable chants, to accusations of ghoulish sickness. By early August, the record was selling upwards of 3,000 copies a week, crashing into the Top 20 in time for Gaye Advert's 21st birthday.

Inexplicably, neither a British tour with Iggy Pop nor a third successive Single of the Week, could help the follow-up 45, "Safety in Numbers," into the chart, but the new year saw success as "No Time to Be 21" (#34 UK) was followed swiftly by the band's first album, *Crossing the Red Sea with The Adverts* (#38 UK), in February.

A monstrous tour took in practically every available stage in Britain, then zipped overseas for shows in Ireland and Europe. An American tour was on the horizon, and even the departure of Laurie Driver on the eve of the album's release could not dent the Adverts' equilibrium. John Towe, late of Chelsea and Generation X, stepped in for the tour, before the Maniacs' Rod Latter took over in May. The Adverts looked unstoppable.

Of course, they weren't. Jumping labels to RCA after Bright's American parent, ABC, refused to grant *Red Sea* a US release let alone encourage the group to tour, the band was suddenly relegated to a major label backwater. In September 1978, "Television's Over," The Adverts' first single in ten months, slipped past all but unnoticed. In June 1979, the quasi-unplugged "My Place," followed it into oblivion.

Working now with producer Tom Newman (of *Tubular Bells* fame!), the Adverts' second album, *Cast of Thousands*, was completed in late summer, as the band returned to the road. Augmenting the line-up with another Oldfield associate, Tim Cross (keyboards), The Adverts played a handful of shows through the early fall, but things were clearly falling apart.

Latter and Howard Pickup both quit in the weeks leading up to the album's November 1979, release, and after a handful more gigs with the hastily recruited guitarist Paul Martinez and his brother Rick (drums) filling in, Smith and Advert called it quits as well. By the time *Cast of Thousands* finally hit the streets, not only was there no band to promote it, there wasn't even one to explain it.

The band shattered. Advert and Pickup left music altogether; Latter linked with fellow ex-Maniac Alan Lee Shaw and the Damned's Brian James in the Severed Dwarves, before forming the Lone Sharks. Smith and Cross reunited in TV Smith's Explorers.

The Adverts' back catalog, meanwhile, took on a life of its own. Some half a dozen reissues of *Crossing the Red Sea* would pass before Smith finally remastered it to his own satisfaction in 1997; two posthumous live albums would be spread over innumerable compilations, and an alternate take of "Gary Gilmore's Eyes" (#5 UK indy) would hit in 1983. An archive release of the band's first John Peel session, from April 1977, would also prove successful (#19 UK indy).

Also see the entry for "TV SMITH" on page 635.

The Adverts LPs

10 Crossing the Red Sea with The Adverts (Bright — UK) 1978 Recorded at Abbey Road studios with producer John Leckie, *Red Sea* was the first album by one of punk's founding fathers to absorb the lessons of the previous twelve months and acknowledge that simply raising your voice and shouting didn't cut the ice anymore.

Like the Sex Pistols' *Bollocks* before it, *Red Sea* was weighted down with past singles — mostly re-recorded — preserving the band's live set in more or less its entirety. Indeed, though it would remain unreleased until 1997, the album's original concept ran for close to one hour, and did, in fact, include every song The Adverts knew. If content was unsurprising, though, the execution was heart-stopping, a snakepit of jarring staccato rhythm which wasn't always obvious in concert, but underpinned The Adverts' sound regardless. Even at their most rudimentary (the opening crash of "One Chord Wonders" is certainly that) *Red Sea* echoed with a widescreen amplification which utterly defied the conventional tinny-amp claustrophobia of The Adverts' peers — even The Clash used to make out they recorded in a box.

Red Sea, contrarily, was as wide as its title was long, with a mix to match its ambition. Plus, the closing "Great British Mistake" packs a self-destructive boleric finale which continues to expound upon the sordid demise of punk, long after Smith has run out of words.

9 Cast of Thousands (RCA — UK) 1979 Grandiose experiment or ambitious conceit? Bloody-minded self-destruction, or courageous reinvention? Symphonic in an age of minimalism, literate in a time of liturgy, the keys-heavy *Cast of Thousands* remains a startling anomaly amidst the conformity of its era — a punk in the truest meaning of the word.

Selected Compilations and Archive Releases

6 Live and Loud!! (Link — UK) 1989
6 Live at the Roxy 1977 (Receiver — UK) 1990 Great gigs, good sound, and churning buzzsaws from springtime shows in Nottingham and (title notwithstanding) Birmingham respectively.

9 The Wonders Don't Care (New Millennium — UK) 1997 Following from an earlier EP release, excellent BBC session versions of most of the band's classic numbers, from the hit "Gary Gilmore's Eyes" to the storming "Television's Over." But it's the final session, with future Robert Plant sideman Paul Martinez on guitar, and the Mike Oldfield Band's Tim Cross on keyboards, which really proves The Adverts' point. Punk rock was all about adventure, right? That line-up was as adventurous as it gets.

8 Singles Collection (Anagram — UK) 1997 Straightforward document of the band's A- and B-sides.

8 Best Of (Anagram — UK) 1998 Scarily similar to above, with a few choice album cuts to relieve the familiarity.

Further Reading
The Life and Times of TV Smith by Dave Thompson (private 1988).

AFGHAN WHIGS

FORMED 1986 *(Cincinnati, OH)*
ORIGINAL LINE-UP *Greg Dulli (b. 5/11/65, Ohio — vocals, guitar); Rick McCollum (b. 7/14/65, Kentucky — guitar); John Curley (b. 3/15/65, Trenton, NJ — bass); Steve Earle (b. 3/28/66, Cincinnati — drums)*

According to legend, the Afghan Whigs were formed on Halloween 1986, in an Athens, Ohio police cell. Greg Dulli was cooling off after running away with a policeman's hat; Rick McCollum was banged up as well and, having whiled away their captivity playing cards, they stuck together when they got out.

So much for legend. In fact, Dulli, McCollum, and Steve Earle were all students at the University of Cincinnati, while John Curley was a photography intern at the *Cincinnati Enquirer* newspaper. He and Dulli met at a friend's apartment building, and were soon playing together in a punk band, the Black Republicans.

The Afghan Whigs — a name the quartet claimed to have borrowed from a Florida-based white Muslim motorcycle gang — officially formed in 1986. Landing a residency at The Squeeze Inn, a local lesbian bar, the band worked the local circuit, then pooled their resources to record and release their first album, *Big Top Halloween*, on their own Ultrasuede label, in 1988.

A word-of-mouth hit littered with 12 already spellbinding Dulli originals, it was followed up with a cut on the local Man-Cub label's *Where the Hell Are the Good Scissors?* compilation — much of which was recorded at the band's own Ultra Sound Studios. (Dulli, Curley, and McCollum were also involved in the Bucking Straps' "Doin' Lines.")

The album brought the Whigs to the attention of Seattle's Sub Pop label — a cult concern still struggling to impact outside of its own north-western environs at that time. Although the Whigs' return to action would be slowed when Dulli contracted pneumonia, their arrival — initially for a one off contribution to Sub Pop's Singles Club project ("I Am the Sticks") — was seen as one way of broadening the label's horizons. Instead, as Sub Pop itself took off, it narrowed the Whigs', slamming them into a generic Seattle scene-shaped box which could not have been further from the band's musical intentions.

The "Sister Brother" single and *Up in It* album, featuring a cover of Paul K and the Weathermen's "Amphetamines and Coffee," was released in April 1990; a formative effort which clashed classic soul with a rude post-hardcore indy guitar buzz — all far removed from anything remotely resembling grunge, but enough to peg the band there in the critical esteem.

Sub Pop obviously agreed. The Whigs next single, "Retarded," made an appearance on the compilation *The Grunge Years*, alongside contributions from Nirvana, L7, Beat Happening, Babes in Toyland, the Walkabouts, Screaming Trees, Tad, Love Battery, and Dickless, and bowing temporarily to the inevitable, the Whigs unleashed *Congregation* and the "Turn on the Water" single in early 1992.

A new single, the Supremes' "My World Is Empty Without You," preceded the Whigs' first statement of their true concerns — the magical *Uptown Avondale* EP. Covers of Freda Payne's "Band of Gold" and the Supremes' "Come See About Me" were both included. Dulli later reflected of his love for soul, "there is no more emotional music that I've ever heard. Even the restraint in soul music feels like it's ready to burst at the seams, and when it does, you know exactly what that person is feeling."

A split single with fellow Cincinnati band Ass Ponys in late 1992 ended the Whigs' Sub Pop career. The band signed to Elektra in 1993 — the label's enthusiasm for the band encompassing even Dulli's insistence that he be allowed to direct the band's videos and produce their records. The fall release of the MTV hit "Debonair," a well-received national TV debut on *Conan O'Brien*, and in October, the *Gentlemen* (#58 UK) album, proved they had made the right decision. It was Dulli who was uncertain, coming close to scrapping the album for fear that its contents might be too personal. His bandmates dissuaded him, but still the result was an emotional firestorm.

Following the *What Jail Is Like* EP in 1994, in 1996 a new album, *Black Love* (#79 US), continued this exploration. Intending the songs to "unravel cinematically," Dulli explained, "the music is more important than it used to be, the lyrics are less direct, less aggressive."

The album was originally demoed shortly before the band — with new drummer Paul Buchignani replacing Earle — headed out on tour in March 1995. Then, as Dulli put it, "we took seven of the songs along, just to see what would happen to them." The end result, as the band intended, was a fuller, better rounded concept of how the songs could sound — a concept which in turn flavored the remainder of *Black Love*, and even leaked into the latest of the band's covers collection, a Tom Waits-like rendering of "If I Only Had a Heart" (from The Wizard of Oz), and a more faithful take on Barry White's "Can't Get Enough of Your Love" (for the *Beautiful Girls* movie soundtrack).

The singles "Honky's Ladder" and "Going to Town" made a strong stab at giving the band a hit single, but the failure of the album to break them out of the cult niche they had inhabited for so long, was taking its toll. The group completed a tour with Neil Young, and then effectively broke up.

Although it was never intended as a full-time project, Dulli formed a new band, the Twilight Singers, with Harold Chichester (of Howlin' Maggie) and Seattle-ite Shawn Smith (Brad, Satchel), and recorded an album, *Twilight*. Its release was still pending (and thus, promptly cancelled) when the Whigs re-emerged with another new drummer, Michael Horrigan (b. 1965); a new label, Columbia; and a whole new ethic.

Titled for the four members' birth years, *1965* (#176 US), was recorded at Daniel Lanois' studio in New Orleans. The band was determined to create a record as upbeat and lusty as past releases had been acclaimed as down and depressed. The degree to which they succeeded could be measured by the response to the Whigs' April 1999 tour with Aerosmith. "Their fans seemed to like us," was the group's utterly modest response to a five week triumph.

Again, the accompanying singles were well-received — "Somethin' Hot" in November 1998 and "66" in May 1999. However, the tour itself was not without incident. In December, Dulli was injured in an altercation following the band's Austin, TX show; a string of shows were cancelled while he recovered before the band returned to action, live and in the studio (their cover of Al Green's "Beware" was a *Blair Witch Project* soundtrack highlight).

Afghan Whigs LPs

🔳 **Up in It (Sub Pop) 1990** Coming on now like the missing link between third album *Replacements* and mid-period Chameleons UK, Dulli's tortured tales of woe and self-loathing found an immediate echo amid the Gen X crowd.

🔳 **Congregation (Sub Pop) 1991** According to one reviewer, *Congregation* sounded like everyone involved wanting to kill each other. The band didn't disagree. What higher recommendation could there be?

🔳 **Gentlemen (Elektra) 1993** Alternately reflective (Dulli had just broken up with his girlfriend), bleak and raw, *Gentlemen* was then shot through with the same love of R&B which flavored the Whigs' earlier recordings, but imbibed with a new and genuine understanding of what made soul music soulful.

🔳 **Black Love (Elektra) 1996** Widescreen, majestic, and at times symphonic, if *Gentlemen* was (as Dulli claimed) the Whigs' *Astral Weeks*, *Black Love* was their *Sgt. Pepper*, a case of the band taking the studio to its limits, and then pushing on.

7 1965 (Columbia) 1998 A less-than-ideal follow-up to their best album yet, but "66," "Uptown Again," and "The Vampire Lanois" stand proud among the Whigs' finest moments ever.

AIR

FORMED 1995 *(Paris, France)*
ORIGINAL LINE-UP Nicolas Godin (b. Versailles — vocals, electronics); Jean Benoit Dunckel (b. Versailles — vocals, electronics)

Born in Versailles, but introduced in Paris, Nicolas Godin and Jean Benoit Dunckel met when a mutual friend, Alex Gopher, brought Godin into Dunckel's band, Orange. Gopher quit soon after to launch a solo career, and in 1995, Dunckel and Godin changed the band's name to Air. Largely re-equipped with a keyboard-based arsenal, they landed a deal with the Sourcelabs label in France and in Britain with the prestigious Mo'Wax.

Despite frequent comparisons to such seventies' synthesizer mavens as Tomita, Jean-Michel Jarre, and Vangelis, Air made immediate inroads into the European dance scene when their first single, "Modular," landed the duo a memorable UK club hit in November 1995. It also brought them to the attention of Depeche Mode, and Air were one of several outside influences invited to remix the Mode's 1997 single, "Home."

Two further singles, the *Casanova 70* EP in July 1996, and November 1997's "Le Soleil est Pres de Moi" preluded Air's first American release, the self-explanatorily titled *Singles* compilation in July 1997. The October 1999 album, *Premiers Symptones* (#12 UK), also rounded up a number of the band's early club hits. However, it would be 1998 before Air made their US breakthrough, when the single (and ape-laden video) "Sexy Boy" hit the airwaves.

Taken from the group's newly-released *Moon Safari* album (itself a staggering potpourri of Euro-disco rhythms, retro-synth colorings, and good old-fashioned pop), "Sexy Boy" would become one of the crucial dance hits of the late 1990s — its impact heightened by the success of subsequent singles "Kelly Watch the Stars" (#14 UK) and "All I Need" (#29 UK). However two years would elapse before the duo returned in 2000 with the soundtrack to Sophia Coppola's *Virgin Suicides* (#14 UK).

Air LPs

8 Moon Safari (Caroline) 1998 Light electro with a cool space-age theme; ideas and atmospheres collide to wrap up with a hefty dose of pure, pristine pop.

8 Virgin Suicides (Caroline) 2000 Packing no obvious hits, this better-than-average set of dance-flavored movie music at least broke a silence which was getting worrisome.

Selected Compilations and Archive Releases

8 Premiers Symptomes (Astralwerks) 1999 Successor to an earlier five-track *Singles* collection, a seven-track compilation of early singles captures the duo at their most innovative... and their most kitsch. The period film theme air of "Casanova 70" is spot-on.

WILLIE "LOCO" ALEXANDER

BORN 1942 *(Boston, MA)*

The grand old man of East Coast punk, Willie Alexander traced his musical career back to 1964 and the Lost, a Beach Boys-esque garage band who released three singles through Capitol, before breaking up in 1967. Other bands — Grass Menagerie, Bagatelle, and Bluesberry Jam — followed, but, as the Boston *Sweet Potato* fanzine put it, "the trump card in Willie's curriculum vitae is his short stint with the Velvet Underground [in 1972], after the departure of Lou Reed."

Alexander's appearance in their ranks, alongside fellow Grass Menagerie alumni Doug Yule, added little to the band's formidable legend and having recorded one final album, the lackluster *Squeeze*, the Velvets split following a disappointing European tour. Alexander returned to Boston and in March 1974, he joined Jonathan Richman and Velvets drummer Maureen Tucker to record their "I'm Sticking With You" duet. The following year, he was "present in the studio" when Ready Teddy, featuring ex-Lost guitarist Matthew Mackenzie and Bluesberry Jam guitarist Mau Mau, recorded their eponymous debut album. He became a common sight too, sitting in with local bands to play the two songs for which he would later be so justly feted — "Kerouac," an epitaph for the beat writer, and "Mass Ave," his lugubrious ode to "just hanging out."

He started writing the song in 1972, building and revising it, and changing the lyrics almost every time he sang it. "The original first line was 'in your left nostril, how could you be hostile,'" Alexander later explained. "It sounded horrible when I sang it, and things just started changing from that point on."

Working at the time with the Infliktors, Lee Ritter's proto-nihilist punk monster (*Time* selected them as the ultimate representatives of punk in the magazine's summer '77 Youth Crime issue), Alexander knocked the song into recordable shape, then went into the studio with another local outfit — the newly-formed Nervous Eaters — to cut the single.

First released on his own Garage label in January 1977, "Mass Ave" was then reissued nationally through Bomp, by which time the *Live at the Rat* compilation had already served notice that something very intriguing was going on in Boston.

The Real Kids, Third Rail, DMZ, the Boize, Marc Thor, and Sass and Susan joined Alexander on the album and now he had a new group behind him, the Boom Boom Band. Billy Loosigian (guitar), Sev Grossman (bass), and David McLean (drums) accompanied Alexander through three tracks on the album: "Kerouac," "Pup Tune," and the anthemic "At the Rat" ("At the Hop" rewritten for the jumping Beantown punk scene).

Never ceasing to remind people that at age 35, he was already older than most of the Boring Old Farts his acolytes were railing against, Alexander continued gigging through the first half of 1977 and soon found his local fame shifting further afield. A second single, "Hit Her Wid De Axe," followed on Garage; another, "Dirty Eddie," appeared via Somor; and that summer, Alexander signed a production deal with Craig Leon, fresh from producing The Ramones. By fall, the band were sitting on a three-album deal with MCA — and MCA were sitting on the band.

It would be over a year before their first single, "You Beat Me to It," and album, the eponymous set highlighted by another re-recording of "Kerouac" and an oddly wrought cover of "You've Lost That Loving Feeling" (the band's next single), were released. It would be over six months more before *Meanwhile, Back in the States* arrived — its title a reference to the amount of time the band was spending in France, where Alexander's fame had attained legendary proportions.

Sadly, such acclaim was of little use to MCA, who dropped the band in early 1979. The Boom Boom Band broke up soon after and Alexander promptly recorded his first solo single, "Gin," with Lord Manuel (synth), Brad Hallan (bass), and Chuck Myra (drums). He also collaborated with local hero The Count, the Radio Hearts (the 1979 single "BU Baby"), and the Outs (a tremendous version of "Walk Away Renee," included on 1981's *Boston Incest Album* collection).

Gigging regularly, but recording sporadically over the next decade, Alexander turned his attention back to the country which so took him to heart, signing with the French New Rose label and accompanied by Al Lourenzo Drake (drums), releasing the largely-acoustic *Solo Loco*. He then formed a new band, the Confessions, featuring Ready Teddy's Mackenzie, former Lost bassist Walter Powers, and drummer John Dunton-Downer, and toured France through March and April 1982 — an outing captured on the double live *Autre Chose* set. The same line-up, plus another Ready Teddy graduate, Mau Mau, then returned to the US to record *A Girl Like You*.

A reunion with Loosigian brought 1984's *Taxi Stand Diane* EP and Alexander occasionally reformed the Boom Boom Band for benefit shows. His next recordings, though, continued his penchant for working with as many different instrumentalists as possible. The "Burning Candle" single in 1985 featured Mission of Burma's Erik Lindgren (keyboards) alongside Kevin Crudder (cello) and Steve Adams (sax); the 1986 album *Tap Dancing on My Piano* featured harmonica player, Richard Hunter.

In 1988, Alexander returned to conventional band format for *The Dragons Are Still Out*. Accompanied in the studio by Lindgren, plus Boby Bear (drums), Neil Thompson (bass), and Rupert Webster (guitar), he then put together a new live band featuring Bare, Webster, and Scott Baerenwald. Simultaneously, he also began working regularly with Bordeaux band, the Boosters — Gerard Hello (guitar), Christophe Ithurritze (keyboards), Marc Buffau (bass) and Bruno Lechene (drums).

1991 saw Alexander celebrating ten years' worth of increasingly surreal musical accomplishments with the *Willie Loco Boom Boom Ga Ga* collection, a set which also debuted his next project, the Persistence of Memory Orchestra, a two-sax, drum, and piano quartet which draped songs over the most skeletal of frameworks. Featuring Lindgren, Jim Doherty (guitar), Ken Field (sax), and Juan/Danny/Ovel (beatbox), this line-up would also record an eponymous 1994 album.

Willie "Loco" Alexander LPs

7 Solo Loco (New Rose — France) 1981 Primarily acoustic, with the occasional synthesizer burbling into earshot, the cracked voice sounds even more cracked without a rock'n'roll band to roar over.

8 Tap Dancing on My Piano (New Rose — France) 1986 Late night blueswailin', Alexander wanders from self-composed aggrandizement — devoting one ballad to bandmate Boby Bare — to genuinely heart-breaking self-pity, a maudlin "I'm So Lonesome I Could Cry."

7 The Dragons Are Still Out (New Rose — France) 1988 Demonically reckless rock, delightfully mistitled, with a psychedelic title track to leave even acid heads feeling a little displaced. The dragons are back with a vengeance.

9 Persistence of Memory Orchestra (Accurate) 1994 Primal, rootsy fuzz redesigned for minimalist eardrums. "Whatever Happened to Rita Ratt?" is an Alexander classic, the improvised "Fishtown Horrible" rap has a horrible fascination, and "Shopping Cart Louie" is just plain merciless.

Willie Alexander and the Boom Boom Band LPs

8 Willie Alexander and the Boom Boom Band (MCA) 1978 A seminal blend of protopunk and sideways pop-rock, with twists of

R&B, slivers of '60s pop, and a double dose of the Velvets — sonic fuzz and winsomely evocative songs served up with power and flair. The Boom Booms do indeed boom, but it's Alexander's quirkily charming delivery that steals the show.

6 Meanwhile, Back in the States (MCA) 1979 No longer giving a hoot for record company tastes and flavors, the Boom Boom Band unleashed in all their naked joy. Shame they sound so dispirited.

Willie Alexander and the Confessions LPs

8 A Girl Like You (New Rose — France) 1982 From the raunchy sleeve on in, Alexander's blue period sprayed across disheveled rock and disturbed blues. A lot of people rate this Alexander's best album; it isn't, but it tries.

6 Autre Chose [LIVE] (New Rose — France) 1982 An a cappella "Tennessee Waltz" is the weirdest moment; everything else more or less adheres to very loose approximations of the studio counterparts.

Selected Compilations and Archive Releases

7 Greatest Hits (New Rose — UK) 1985

8 Willie Loco Boom Boom Ga Ga (Northeastern) 1991 Respectively, five and 15 years of primal Willie, compiling singles, album tracks, rarities, and the odd unreleased gem for the perfect overview of the Beantown hero's career.

ALIEN SEX FIEND

FORMED 1982 (London, England)
ORIGINAL LINE-UP Nick "Nik Fiend" Wade (vocals); Christine "Mrs. Fiend" Wade (keyboards); Johnny "Ha-Ha" Freshwater (drums); David "Yaxi High-rizer" James (guitar)

Wade's early musical strivings document his love of Alice Cooper. His first band, the Earwigs, were named after one of Cooper's own formative aliases, his second, Mr. and Mrs. Demeanour, for a track on Cooper's *Easy Action* album. Another Wade project, Demon Preacher (later The Demons), got as far as recording a brace of 45s — "Little Miss Perfect" for London's Small Wonder label, and the "Royal Norther" EP for Illegal, and years later landed a third track, "Dead End Kidz," on *Killed by Death* Volume 666.

They went nowhere at the time however, and by early 1982, Wade was working at the newly-opened Batcave, introducing himself to newcomers as Fiend; his wife Christine was promptly rechristened Mrs. Fiend. Linking with Johnny HaHa and Yaxi High-rizer, Nik and Mrs. formed Alien Sex Fiend in late 1982, debuting at the Batcave on December 1, just weeks before they unleashed their first album, the cassette-only *The Lewd, the Mad, the Ugly and Old Nik*.

It was nothing more than a collection of demos and recent live tracks, but still it convinced Cherry Red's Ana-

gram subsidiary to sign the band. 1983 opened with "Ignore the Machine" (#6 UK indy), produced by former Killing Joke bassist Youth, but it was with the release of their first full album, *Who's Been Sleeping in My Brain* (#10 UK indy), that the group came of age, kicking into a solid stream of dementedly high quality psychedelic goth rockers.

Acid Bath (#4 UK indy) followed, while the band also enjoyed a stream of indy chart hits — "Lips Can't Go" (#12 UK indy), "R.I.P." (#4 UK indy), "Dead and Buried" (#4 UK indy), and "E.S.T. (Trip to the Moon)" (#3 UK indy) between mid-1983 and summer 1984.

Recorded following Ha-Ha's departure, the following year's "I'm Doing Time in a Maximum Security Twilight Zone" (#6 UK indy) and the *Maximum Security* album (#100 UK, #5 UK indy) went even further, breaking the band in Japan, where a massively successful tour resulted in the release of a storming live album, *Liquid Head in Tokyo* (#7 UK indy).

As a trio, the band showcased its two predominant moods — psych and fuzz — across the *Impossible Mission* mini album, then completed the darkly monolithic *"It": The Album* (#7 UK indy) and a cover of Johnny Cash's "I Walk the Line" (#12 UK indy) as a trio, before touring the UK as the opening act on Alice Cooper's "Nightmare Returns" tour (replacing the scheduled Zodiac Mindwarp and the Love Reaction).

High-Rizer departed following the *Here Cum Germs* album (#22 UK indy) and Adam Ant-esque title track (#14 UK indy), and an audacious cover of Red Crayola's "Hurricane Fighter Plane"; Fiend and Mrs. celebrated the line-up's ultimate reduction with a raucous anti-Christmas single, "Stuff the Turkey" (#14 UK indy), and opted to continue on as a duo, enabled by electronics and sampling.

Piecing together a new line-up around guitarist Rat Fink Jr. and keyboardist Doc Milton, the band cut a new single, the "Haunted House" medley of past Fiendishness, then took to the road to record the live *Another Planet*. It was followed by *Curse*, featuring *Beavis and Butthead* favorite "Now I'm Feeling Zombified," and emerged sufficiently adventurous to launch Alien Sex Fiend onto the fringes of the slowly-burgeoning early '90s space rock scene — queer bedmates for the likes of Ozric Tentacles and Sky Cries Mary, but appropriate ones as well.

Their version of "Echoes" was a definite high point on the Pink Floyd tribute album *A Saucerful of Pink* (Cleopatra); "Mrs. Fiend Goes to Outer Space" was a milestone amidst the same label's authoritative *Space Daze* anthology; and an in-concert cover of Hawkwind's "Silver Machine" became a near-permanent staple.

Yet still, Alien Sex Fiend could not resist pushing further afield, with the harsh *Open Head Surgery* album, and a wildly successful American tour (itself documented on the *Altered States of America* live album). They then reappeared in 1995 with *Inferno*, the putative soundtrack to a newly released CD-ROM game. The group also launched their own label, 13th Moon, keeping their name alive and alert with the trance-heavy *Evolution* EP and *Nocturnal Emissions* album.

Through the last years of the decade, the Fiends set to work rearranging and revising their now-voluminous back catalog, unveiling a string of compilations and remix collections (in their DJ guise of Fiend at the Controls), which themselves represent some of the most adventurous and dynamic music of the decade — ensuring that even when Alien Sex Fiend aren't moving, they're never standing still.

Alien Sex Fiend LPs

3 Who's Been Sleeping in My Brain (Anagram — UK) 1983 Formative, historic, and almost completely unlistenable melange of crashing, yelling, and sub-punk droning on about comic cut monsters. Pretty horrible, really.

6 Acid Bath (Epitaph — UK) 1984 What a difference a decent studio makes. Adding glam rock and sound effects to the brew, the Fiends' noise takes on some genuinely toe-tapping nuances.

7 Maximum Security (Anagram — UK) 1985 With "Mine's Full of Maggots" serving up mental images which video could never recapture, the Fiends' tightest, toughest album yet is also the most robotically bleak, as a (very '80s) drum machine takes center stage.

7 Liquid Head in Tokyo [LIVE] (Anagram — UK) 1985 Spacey as hell, the Fiends lock into riffs and grooves and then cackle loudly over all of them. A rite of passage for the uninformed, a gorgeous celebration for the convert.

8 "It": The Album (Plague) 1986 Now fully in the thrall of space-adventuring sci-fi electronics, with songs expanding to match the mood, the Fiends begin looking towards mutant dance territory as well.

7 Here Cum Germs (PVC) 1987 "Impossible Mission" is a highlight, the acoustic "Isolation" is a first, and "Boots On" is one of the Fiends' finest. But who can resist a song called "My Brain is in the Cupboard Above the Kitchen Sink"?.

7 Another Planet (Caroline) 1988 The Fiends find a sampler, and the straitened line-up acknowledges that even freaks can have fun. The title track mashes Sputnik riffing with garbled drawl vocals, "Sample My Sausage" should be impossibly rude, and "Wild Green Fiendy Liquid" sounds just like its title says it should.

8 Too Much Acid? [LIVE] (Anagram — UK) 1989 Basically, the singles collection live, and a jolly good time to be had by all.

9 Curse (Sinclair) 1990 "Zombiefied" remains the Fiends' best known, best loved statement of intent, but at least half of *Curse* is just as great, with "Katch 22" approaching manic rock opera pro-

portions and "Ain't Got Time to Bleed" possessing a sinister lope which even the Jesus and Mary Chain guitars can't demystify.

7 Open Head Surgery (Sinclair) 1992 A tougher album than past releases had prepared listeners for, verging on Psychic TV territory in places, but still on the look-out for any braincells missed by previous excursions.

7 The Altered States of America [LIVE] (Futurist) 1993 Eight tracks representing more or less the best of Fiend culminated in a savage "RIP."

6 Inferno (Anagram — UK) 1995 A CD-ROM soundtrack, not necessarily enhanced by the lack of visuals.

5 Nocturnal Emissions (13th Moon — UK) 1998 Something of a mish-mash of ideas and idiosyncracies which would have been better used for remixes and B-sides.

Selected Compilations and Archive Releases

7 All Our Yesterdays (Anagram — UK) 1988

8 Drive My Rocket (Cleopatra) 1994 '80s-era singles collections charting the Fiend's crossover from Goth to club — a little bafflingly as it's not chronological, but Mrs. Fiend supplies helpful liner notes.

7 The Batcave Masters (Cleopatra) 1998 Excellent compilation, drawing from rare singles and album cuts, highlighting the dancier end of the Fiend experience.

9 Fiend at the Controls (Cleopatra) 1999 A genre-spanning 2-CD collection of demos, remixes, and non-CD rarities, notable for dub remixes of 1983's "Under the Thunder" and Red Crayola's legendary "Hurricane Fighter Plane."

DOT ALLISON

BORN *(Edinburgh, Scotland)*

Scottish diva Dot Allison first emerged as the breathless platinum blonde fronting One Dove, heroes of the post-Acid House fall out, in 1991. Formed (as Dove) in Glasgow where Allison was studying Applied Biochemistry at the university, and completed by keyboard players Ian Carmichael and Jim McKinven (ex-Altered Images), One Dove self-released their debut single, "Fallen," in 1991, an instant club hit which was comparable with the best of St. Etienne (if the Happy Mondays had got there first).

A copy made its way to producer and Boys Own label head Andrew Weatherall, who quickly volunteered to produce an entire album — his first outside work since Primal Scream's *Screamadelica*. Preceded by a reissue of "Fallen" and the powerful "Transient Truth," *Morning Dove White* (#30 UK) would appear in summer 1993, only to be lost in the corporate shuffling which scarred the label's dealings with its parent company, London.

As Allison later explained, "they dropped Underworld and the Chemical Brothers, and kept us because they thought we had hit singles." Over the next six months, three 45s — "White Love" (#43 UK), "Breakdown" (#24 UK), and "Why Don't You Take Me" (#30 UK) — proved the short-term wisdom of that decision. But while the band continued gigging, promotion was zero, and after almost three years of inactivity, Allison quit One Dove for a solo career — shortly before a near-fatal car accident left her in a wheelchair for four months.

Back on her feet by mid-1996, Allison moved to London and began recording demos. She signed with Heavenly (Arista in America) in 1997, and worked on what would become her first album which began via a series of fascinating collaborations. Vintage songwriter Hal David (of Burt Bacharach and… fame) was recruited after Allison met the veteran at her publishers' office one day, My Bloody Valentine's Kevin Shields, the Beta Band's Chris Allison, and Primal Scream's Mani would all be drawn in, while boyfriend Richard Fearless, of Death in Vegas, would join Weatherall on production (Allison herself appeared on one track on Death in Vegas' near-simultaneous *Contino Sessions* album.)

January 1999 saw the release of the first single from the sessions, "Tomorrow Never Comes," as a limited edition of 500 copies. "Mo' Pop" followed in March, the album *Afterglow* appeared in October, and earned Allison comparisons which ranged from Nico to Dusty Springfield.

Dot Allison LPs

8 Afterglow (Arista) 1999 Moods swoop from sundry St. Etienne-isms ("Mo' Pop") to the same spectral beauties as haunted the first *This Mortal Coil* album ("Message Persona") — an effective blend which presents Allison in so many different musical lights that *Afterglow*'s greatest achievement might well be its cohesion. Drifting and driving, fading into first gear, swirling and swinging, *Afterglow* is the album which the club scene has been trying to make for a long time.

One Dove LP

7 Morning Dove White (Boys Own) 1993 For the mornings after the rave before, gorgeous dance pop on the edge of dance-pop greatness.

MARC ALMOND

BORN *Peter Marc Almond, 7/9/59 (Southport, England)*

Soft Cell frontman Marc Almond tentatively tested the solo waters in 1981 and 1982 with his Marc and the Mambas project, and two hit albums, *Untitled* (#42 UK) and *Torment and Torreros* (#28 UK). But it took the final demise of Soft Cell, in January 1984, to truly turn Almond's attention towards the future.

His initial response was petulance; the singer announced his retirement in response to the increasingly vitriolic mockery of the music press. However, by May he had reconsidered and re-emerged with the appropriately titled "The Boy Who Came Back" (#52 UK), a taster for his forthcoming solo debut, *Vermin in Ermine* (#36 UK), and the launchpad for what would prove to be a three-year collaboration with producer Mike Hedges. Harnessing the singer's talents as he reined in his musical excesses, Hedges would be responsible for transforming a promising stylist with an eye for sleaze into what Almond himself considers his greatest epithet, "the Judy Garland of the garbage heap."

Buoyed by the well-received album, a second single, "You Have" (#57 UK), and in September, his first solo live performances, Almond swiftly indicated that his immediate career was going to have far more in common with the twilight sleaze of the Mambas project than with the electronic tint of Soft Cell. Indeed, reminded later that he was one half of one of the world's most innovative computer pioneers, Almond simply laughed. "I was lucky I had Dave Ball. I was just the singer"— and that's the role he was to assume solo.

That said, Soft Cell's third and final album, the foreboding *This Last Night in Sodom*, had already hinted at the direction in which Almond's lyric writing was headed. Now with a new band, the Willing Sinners (pianist Annie Hogan, bassist Billy McGee, guitarist Richard Riley, cellist Martin McCarrick, and drummer Stephen Humphries), forming from the ashes of the Mambas, he was free to immerse himself completely in a world of sexual and social decadence.

His cultural touchstones, of course, remained unchanged — Scott Walker (whose "The Plague" was a highlight of Almond's Royal Festival Hall show on September 8), Belgian songwriter Jacques Brel, and the *Berlin*-era Lou Reed remained as powerful in Almond's solo work as they were on the Mambas albums. However, the marked difference was that whereas once Almond had been content to simply cover those artists' songs, now he was making the same point with his own compositions.

The best and earliest indication of this transformation came again in September 1984 when Almond appeared at the *Violent Silence* celebration of the French author Georges Bataille at London's Bloomsbury Theatre. Accompanied by Hogan alone, Almond's performance was as brooding melancholic as Bataille's own prose, and again established a stylistic precedent.

Fears that Almond was taking himself too seriously, however, were allayed in the new year when he announced his intention to stage a week-long cabaret at Raymond's Revue Bar. The most notorious of London's Soho strip clubs, it was a venture which would allow him to revel in the subterranean lifestyles which so informed his songs, at the same time acknowledging the sheer vaudevillian tackiness of it all.

In the event, the shows fell through (an attempt to transfer the performances to the more salubrious Ronnie Scott's Jazz Club also foundered), but Almond maintained a high, light, profile regardless, joining Bronski Beat in April 1985, for a high camp medley of Donna Summer's "I Feel Love" and "Love to Love You Baby," and John Leyton's "Johnny Remember Me" (#3 UK). It became Almond's biggest hit since Soft Cell's "What" three years before.

Almond waited out the summer of 1985 while manager Stevo sought a new distribution deal for his Some Bizzare label — to which Almond was signed directly. The singer punctuated the silence with live work and a second collaboration, "Skin." Credited to the Burmoe Brothers, Almond, and Guy Chambers, it was not a hit, but it did introduce a new element to Almond's vocal arsenal — an empathy with '40s and '50s jazz which would loom ever larger as his career progressed.

Stories of Johnny (#22 UK), his next album, appeared that fall through Virgin, and a single of the title track (#23 UK) was followed by "Love Letters," recorded with the Westminster City School Choir (#68 UK), and "This House Is Haunted" (#55 UK). It was a very pop-oriented set, but Almond would not pursue the soft options which the album appeared to offer. Announcing "my songs stink of back rooms, bar rooms, sweat, semen, saw dust, absinthe from Madrid, mescal, roses, gunpowder and dew drenched oakwood," he claimed his next album would be dedicated to masturbation and his next stage performance would reinvent him as a torch singer.

The aptly titled *Mother Fist and Her Five Daughters* (#41 UK) was highlighted by "St. Judy," dedicated to Judy Garland and further flavored by covers ranging from Juliette Greco's "Undress Me" and Eartha Kitt's "The Heel," to Brecht, Weill, and Brel, while Almond's performances at the Soho Jazz festival and the London Palladium that fall certainly fulfilled his prophecy. But behind the scenes, Virgin were furiously opposed to Almond's new direction, and increasingly alarmed at the sequence of poorly selling singles he was delivering.

Despite a string of stunning videos, "A Woman's Story" (#41 UK), "Ruby Red" (#47), and "Melancholy Rose" (#71 UK) all failed to make a major impression on the chart, and when the parent album finally made its belated appearance in April 1987, it was clear that though Almond was certainly at his creative peak, commercially he had reached the bottom. Virgin's patience was finally exhausted when the singer proposed releasing a double album comprised entirely of covers of French songs, *Baudelaire Meets Brel*. The label

steadfastly refused to entertain the project — that, despite the fact that Almond had already started work on it.

In 1986, Almond commissioned translator Paul Buck to utterly refresh a Brel canon which was in serious danger of collapsing into cliche; two decades had passed since first, Rod McKuen, and later, Mort Shuman, unveiled the first English language versions of the Belgian superstar's work, since then the likes of "If We Only Have Love," "Carousel," and — most pernicious of all — "Seasons in the Sun" had become easy listening standards. Even "If You Go Away," so majestically recounted by Almond on the first Mambas album, had endured assaults from across the AOR spectrum, while those Brel songs which remained firmly within the rock idiom — "Next," "Amsterdam," and "My Death" amongst them — had in turn become so heavily associated with their best known interpreters (the Sensational Alex Harvey Band, Scott Walker, and David Bowie) that nothing short of reinvention could unchain them.

Almond intended providing that reinvention, but while he fought with Virgin, another of Brel's English admirers, Nick Curry, was himself attempting fresh interpretations of the Brel canon, for release under his Momus alias. The critical success of the ensuing *Nicky* EP simply heaped further insult upon Almond's plight, and by fall 1987, Almond and Virgin had parted ways.

Exorcising a few demons via the brutal *Flesh Volcano* collaboration with Foetus, and placing the French album on hold, Almond joined EMI late in the year (again via Some Bizzare) and began work on what would prove to be his commercial renaissance, *The Stars We Are* (#144 US, #41 UK).

Recorded with a new band, La Magia (Hogan, McGee, and Humphries), the album was originally conceived as a collection of duets, and while that scheme eventually faded, still elements of the dream survived — a version of "Kept Boy," recorded with Agnes Brenelle, retained for vinyl pressings of the album; "This House Is a House of Trouble" (#8 UK indy) with Sally Timms and the Drifting Cowgirls, released as a 45 in June 1987; and "Your Kisses Burn," a collaboration with Velvet Underground vocalist Nico, and the last thing she recorded before her death in early 1989.

"Tears Run Rings" (#67 US, #26 UK), "Bitter Sweet" (#40 UK), and "Only the Moment' (#45 UK) provided minor hits, but the most significant cut was a re-creation of Gene Pitney's "Something's Gotten Hold of My Heart" (#1 UK), recorded with Pitney himself, and released as a January 1989 smash hit.

Almond seized the moment to complete work on the French album, modifying the concept now to incorporate two separate discs. The first, *Jacques* (#9 UK indy), was released in December 1989 and Almond promoted it with a string of magical concerts in France, Germany, and the

Netherlands, performing with a solitary pianist, Maurice Horhut. It was an effective gesture, certainly accentuating the personal nature of the performance, but it also helped ensure that this already idiosyncratic project would pass by all but unnoticed.

Almond, however, was unflustered by *Jacques* commercial failure. In fact, he later confessed that he would have been more shocked if it had been a hit. Instead, he reveled in his newfound ability to have, as he put it, "mischievous fun in the mainstream." Abandoning La Magia, Almond returned with *Enchanted* (#52 UK), his most blatantly commercial album since *Stories of Johnny*. However, his observation that "it's actually more demanding than doing the, shall we say, more credible things I've done in the past," was not misplaced. *Enchanted* sold poorly, a fate echoed by two singles, "A Lover Spurned" (#29 UK) and "Desperate Hours" (#45 UK), while a much-ballyhooed reunion with Soft Cell partner Dave Ball on a remix of "Waifs and Strays" missed the chart altogether.

Almond/Some Bizzare changed labels again after this, transferring to Warner Brothers just as the hits- and remixes-packed *Memorabilia* collection (#8 UK) restored Soft Cell to the chart. It was followed by two "new" Soft Cell singles, "Say Hello Wave Goodbye 91" (#38 UK) and a reissued "Tainted Love" (#5 UK). Riding the resultant wave of interest, Almond followed through with a major hit of his own, an electronic version of Brel's "Jacky" (#17 UK).

The track was taken from the Trevor Horn-produced *Tenement Symphony* (#39 UK) album, and while a second reunion with Dave Ball, as co-writer of "My Hand over My Heart" (#33 UK), bottomed out, the third 45 from this latest album, David McWilliams' "Days of Pearly Spencer" (#3 UK), effortlessly restored Almond to chart glory.

He celebrated with his first full concerts in four years — performances in Liverpool in June 1992 and Nottingham in September, which led up to a spectacular Royal Albert Hall performance titled *12 Years of Tears*. Billed as a three-hour retrospective of his entire career, it was the most grandiose performance he had ever given — a riot of costume changes and choreography — captured for both video and CD release.

The live album did not chart, but a single of Charles Aznavour's "What Makes a Man a Man" (#60 UK) garnered considerable airplay, and once again Almond was at a commercial peak. Which meant, of course, that he would follow it with an album of introspective obscurity, resuscitating the second half of the French project and recreating it (with pianist Martin Watkins) as *Absinthe*.

Absinthe was a highwater mark in Almond's development as an artist and interpreter, but it arrived at another low point of his career. After years of tranquilizer use, he was finally coming to terms with something friends had been telling him for some time, "that I had a problem. I can be very much manic depressive at times, and I've gone through periods when I can be very down in my life or very up in my life. I've always felt I've tried to work, even during the black periods in my life I felt I tried to channel that into some creativity. But I became agoraphobic, [which is] why the concerts were so few and far between. Huge chunks of my memory were being wiped out. I'd forget the words to songs. The drugs were affecting my judgement. But I couldn't see it." He was fighting his way out of the haze when he learned that Warners had dropped him from their roster.

Almond had already started work on a new album, first relocating to New York to record with former Soft Cell producer Mike Thorne, then returning to London to reunite with Mike Hedges for the first time since *Mother Fist*. Martin Ware of Heaven 17 and Sigue Sigue Sputnik's Neal X joined the London sessions; John Cale, Chris Spedding, and former New York Doll David Johansen dropped by the New York studio, and with Almond promising a return to the edgier glam punk of Soft Cell's final recordings, successive postponements of *Fantastic Star* were as frustrating for fans as for Almond himself.

With Some Bizzare having re-signed with Mercury, the Almond/Stevo team's first-ever home, the singer watched as the label spent an entire year culling singles from the unreleased album, in the hope of scoring a major hit — "Adored and Explored" (#25 UK), "The Idol" (#44 UK), and "Child Star" (#41 UK). None came close, and finally, abandoning all hope, Mercury released *Fantastic Star* (#54 UK) utterly without fanfare in March 1996, then dropped Almond barely weeks later.

Almond remained out of sight for much of the next two years, although behind the scenes he remained active. He joined '60s veteran PJ Proby for a duet, "Yesterday Has Gone" (#58 UK), but more crucially, he broke with both Some Bizzare and manager Stevo, declaring that he would rather retire than continue with a relationship which had clearly run its course. "I started to grow up and really look at the shit that was happening, and I thought I've got to take the reins back now and get control of it before its' too late."

Despite this new resolution and the ensuing freedom, rumors of new recordings passed as quickly as the tentative release dates which accompanied them, and though Almond signed to the Echo label in early 1998, still it would be well over a year before a new album was released — the acclaimed *Open All Night* — by which time he had left Echo again, and launched his own Bluestar label.

Previewed by the single "Black Kiss," the album appeared in the UK in March 1999 (September in the US), accompanied later in the year by two more singles, "My Love" and

"Tragedy"; a book of Almond's lyrics and poetry, *A Beautiful Twisted Night*; and a shockingly confessional autobiography, *Tainted Life*. That fall, Almond would also play his first US dates in a decade, accompanied by Neal X and bassist Rick May.

Also see the entry for "SOFT CELL" on page 641.

Marc Almond LPs

7 Vermin in Ermine (Some Bizzare/Mercury UK) 1984 Every generation gets the "Hey Jude" it deserves. "Ugly Head" made it for the fashion-conscious '80s.

6 Stories of Johnny (Some Bizzare/Virgin UK) 1985 With a first half much stronger than the second, this set founders in the wake of much of Almond's better stuff, although both "This House Is Haunted" and "Stories of Johnny" rise to star status.

8 Violent Silence (Virgin Europe/Virgin UK) 1986 From a 1984 performance at the Violent Silence festival, Almond turned his vision of Georges Bataille's writing into songs of staggering beauty and stormy rage. Even repeated in the studio, the performance remains one of his most powerful, marked most notably by "Healthy as Hate" and Annie Hogan's "Blood Tide".

9 Mother Fist and Her Five Daughters (Some Bizzare/Virgin UK) 1987 An absolute stunner, *Fist* captures Almond on a defiant upswing, delivering songs with a strength not seen since the Mambas. He spits out "Mother Fist," tempers his rage with the aching "There Is a Bed," while the wicked duo "Melancholy Rose" and "Ruby Red" showcase him at his most melody-whipped lascivious.

6 The Stars We Are (Capitol) 1988 Less a cohesive album than a collection of nifty singles, this disc of harmless pop is held together on the strength of "Tears Run Rings" and "Something's Gotten Hold of My Heart" — which remains one of Almond's best covers ever.

8 Jacques (Some Bizzare UK) 1989 A full disc of Brel interpretations fully capturing Almond's love for his subject. Finely wrought and beautifully rendered, Brel comes alive once more across old favorites, "The Bulls" and "If You Go Away" (from the Mambas era), and through a clutch of new translations showcasing both Brel and Almond's massive vision.

9 Enchanted (Capitol) 1990 Sea shanty cabaret with a flamenco heart, this is Almond's best latter period album; from "Waifs and Strays" through "Toreador in the Rain" and "Orpheus in Red Velvet," *Enchanted* is a twisted sonic landscape through which the songs flow together effortlessly, while remaining strong on their own. A triumph!

5 Tenement Symphony (Reprise) 1991 Best known for "The Days of Pearly Spencer" and "Jacky," *Symphony* encapsulates good ideas, but remains hopelessly scattered in delivery, and horribly dilettante in its address.

8 Twelve Years of Tears [LIVE] (Reprise) 1992 A glorious performance brimful with infectious energy, *12 Years* captures every-

thing that makes Almond special. From his disco-fied "Jacky" to the impassioned rendition of "What Makes a Man," *Tears* showcases Almond not only as a flawless performer, but also, given the devotion of the audience, the master of his domain.

9 Absinthe (Some Bizzare UK) 1993 Recorded as a companion to *Jacques*, this collection of wrenching French-tinged cabaret/torch has the feel of a subversive Gilbert and Sullivan opera; both carnival and carnivore, lush strings and piano convey pained beauty while Almond's voice soars over a world of smoky clubs, of love never experienced, and glass after endless glass of Pernod. Or, indeed, absinthe.

8 Fantastic Star (Mercury UK) 1996 Almond back-to-basics, like he woke up and wondered if he could reform Soft Cell with Dr. and the Medics — the disco glam revival started here and "The Idol" is the most savage denouement of the day, namechecking rock's most sainted corpses with an exaggerated savagery Almond hasn't unleashed since "Uglyhead." But with its guitars and its grinding stomp, it was maybe too near the knuckle to give the pop kids the bone.

8 Open All Night (Instinct) 1999 Beautiful and brutal, the king back in his castle. The mood is delightful, and the cohesively wide scope creates a place where Creatures and Sneeker Pimps percolate through the fixtures. Combining Almond's best stylistic elements and just the right amount of electronic wizardry, the songs are his most personal yet, but they also seem somewhat protected — because it's still too scary to look too deep into his soul.

Selected Compilations and Archive Releases

8 Singles 1984-87 (Virgin) 1987

6 Memorabilia — The Singles (Some Bizzare UK) 1991 A little bit of Soft Cell, a little bit of Almond, this singles compilation features '91 remixes of "Memorabilia" and "Say Hello Wave Goodbye," as well as a Grid (Dave Ball) remix of the fabulous "Waifs and Strays." That's the good news. The bad news is, the remixes sound more dated than the originals.

8 1992 A Virgin's Tale 1 (Virgin)
8 1992 A Virgin's Tale 2 (Virgin)
7 1995 Treasure Box (EMI UK) Three compilations concentrating on non-album singles and B¬sides, plus some demos and rarities on *Treasure Box*; fascinating flotsam with some genuinely powerful cover versions — "The Plague" "Salty Dog" — and remixes.

4 Le [Sic] Magia in Concert (Thirsty Ear) 1999 From the typo in the title to the zero production and horrible sound, a festering sore of a drab disappointment.

Marc and the Mambas LPs

9 Untitled (Some Bizzare) 1981 Bearing the sordid soul which Soft Cell simply wouldn't permit, Almond's own "Untitled" stands effortlessly alongside the masters — Lou Reed, Scott Walker, and Syd Barrett — but it's the blazing torch of Brel's "If

You Go Away" which dominates; a fabulous vocal accompanied only by Hogan's raw piano.

10 Torment and Torreros 1983 "The sound of a nervous breakdown on record," Almond joked years later, and it's difficult not to disagree. Now embracing the seediness which Soft Cell only flirted with, four sides of vinyl alternated between psychic exorcism and physical relief, a shock indeed for the pop kids lured into earshot even by "Numbers" and *The Art of Falling Apart*. There, afterall, the excesses remained on the tight leash of suggestion. From the garage flamenco of the instrumental "Blood Wedding" to the jagged industrialism of "A Million Manias," the Mambas had no such inhibitions.

The inevitable Brel number, "The Bulls," isn't just one of the Belgian's most vividly symbolic songs, it's also one of the hardest to execute accurately, but Almond pulls it off partly because his vocal range is already accustomed to skipping from flippant boredom to impassioned disturbance, but also because those are the very extremes which the Mambas' own nightmare gothic cabaret revolves around.

At times, the mood is tender if tortured — the insistently downbeat "Black Heart" is a spectral "Say Hello"-toned ballad; "In My Room," an old Walker Brothers chestnut, actually takes on fresh pathos in Almond's arms; and the Steve Severin/Robert Smith-composed "Torment" could be a dry run for some later Siouxsie and the Banshees ballad. There's also the dramatically torrid finale, "Beat Out That Rhythm on a Drum," deliciously lackadaisical, light-hearted, and lazy, even with the firelight dancing and the gypsy girls aflame.

But "The Animal with You" is nihilistic nastiness, half sung, half sneered, and powered by the bitter demand, "what have you ever done for me?" And "Lesion" (as in "your love leaves a...") is so wrapped up in its own fury that the very instrumentation sounds like domestic abuse. Then there's "Catch a Falling Star," gratuitously scatological and so sourly autobiographical that a lot of other stars had to turn the other cheek.

Torment is not an easy album to live with, but it must have been even more difficult to create — to go that far out on both a commercial limb and a self-indulgent whim. The album is probably one side too long, the production is certainly less than halfway complete, and even occasional conspirator Foetus sounds a little perplexed by the madness around him. But still Almond manages to pull it off, and he's still around today to prove it.

Further Reading

Tainted Life by Marc Almond (Sidwick & Jackson 1999).

APHEX TWIN

BORN *Richard James, 8/13/71 (Cornwall, England)*

Björk's "King of Creativity" moved to London from his native Cornwall in 1989, a teenaged DJ lured by the then-burgeoning rave scene, and aiming his own musical efforts directly into the heart of the movement.

Quickly establishing himself amongst the most inventive DJs on the circuit, both via performance and his appearance (as Dice Man) on the Warp label's highly influential *Artificial Intelligence* album, Richard James linked with fellow electronics maven Tom Middleton, and issued the *Analogue Bubblebath* EP under the name AFX in September 1991. Early the following year, a second volume was recorded by James alone, garnering airplay on the London pirate radio station, KISS FM, and securing a cult club hit for one cut in particular, the excitable "Didgeridoo" (#55 UK) — a track purposefully designed to drive the audience into the chill-out room.

Signing to the Belgian R&S label, James re-recorded "Didgeridoo" for release under his Aphex Twin alias (debuted the previous year with a self-titled EP of chill house) and was promptly rewarded with a major dancefloor hit. The rush-released *Xylem Tube* EP follow-up was less successful, but forever seeking new outlets for his prolific output, James now formed his own Rephlex label with Grant Wilson-Claridge and began releasing a series of desperately limited edition singles under the Caustic Window alias.

Under the name Polygon Window, he also participated in the Warp label's *Artificial Intelligence* series of albums (alongside fellow ambient-techno pioneers Autechre, B12, Black Dog, and FUSE), contributing the *Surfing on Sine Waves* album. "Quoth" (#49 UK) became Polygon Window's first hit in April 1993.

However, the greatest attention was reserved for Aphex Twin's own long-promised debut album, the putatively retrospective 2-LP *Selected Ambient Works '85–'92*. James once remarked that he was amazed when he first heard techno and acid, because he'd been making the same kind of music himself for years (he bought his first synth at age 12) and had been creating cassettes of it for his friends for almost as long. Whether or not the album really did reach back across seven years of recording and writing was immaterial. Still, it was an astounding snapshot of his development, indicating James' debt to the early ambient work of Brian Eno, at the same time as pioneering a techno root which was without precedent.

James both furthered and parodied, his debut's aims two years later, with the 2-CD/3-LP *Selected Ambient Works Volume 2* (#11 UK). His major label (Sire) debut arrived at a time when the American dance scene, in particular, was awash with minimalist ambient constructions — Aphex Twin was simply more minimalist and ambient than any of them.

The album only narrowly missed the UK Top 10, while James' oft-stated desire to have a major hit single saw him turning out some genuinely dramatic dance music, both under his own collection of names, and also in the guise of remixing other artists. The Cure, Curve, Jesus Jones, Meat

Beat Manifesto, and St. Etienne all enjoyed Aphex Twin/Richard James remixes during this period, several of which bore no apparent resemblance whatsoever to the original piece of music.

In 1993, a third LP-length volume of *Analogue Bubblegum* further muddied James' musical reputation, turning in a hardhitting assemblage of head-banging techno, and it was this theme which dominated James' first American tour (alongside Moby and Orbital) later in the year. In the event, James came off the road deeply rueing the experience — his performances were frequently so violent that he ended up destroying much of his own equipment!

Still seeking that elusive Top 10 hit, Aphex Twin released "On" (#32 UK) in December 1993. The single remains significant in that it reunited James first with Tom Middleton (in his Reload guise), then introduced the public to Michael Paradinas, soon to join the Rephlex stable as u-Ziq.

Other Rephlex signings during 1993–94 included the Kosmik Kommando (aka Mike Dred) and Kinesthesia/Cylob (Chris Jeffs), while 1996 would see James and u-Ziq collaborate on the impressive *Expert Knob Twiddlers* album, playfully credited to Mike and Rich. Other James pseudonyms — their activities confined to singles, EPs, and remixes — include Blue Calx, Gak, Joyrex, Q- Chastik, Power Pill, and Metapharstic.

Following up the success of *Selected Ambient Works 2*, James next released a compilation of his early R&S singles (plus a dynamic remix for Mescalinum United), the aptly named *Classics*, then scored his third British hit with the wheeze-laden "Ventolin" (#49 UK), a tribute to the asthma drug of the same name (James himself had suffered from the condition since childhood).

1995 also saw the release of Aphex Twin's third — and most adventurous — album, the sweeping *I Care Because You Do*. Heavily influenced by such modern composers as Philip Glass, the album did in fact come to Glass' attention, and Aphex Twin's next single, "Donkey Rhubarb," included an orchestral version of the album's "Icct Hedral" arranged by Glass himself.

James was still capable of hitting out with brutal strength, however, as he proved with *Hangable Auto Bulb*, an experimental hybrid of hardcore electronics and pulsing jungle. This particular theme would be continued across Aphex Twin's next EP, *Girl/Boy* (#64 UK), and album, *Richard D. James Album*, an exhausting collection which appeared, ironically, to have left James as drained as his listeners.

Since that time, just two new Aphex Twin releases, both EPs, have materialized — 1997's harsh *Come to Daddy* and 1999's *Windowlicker*. Both transplanted pounding electronic harshness into a remorseless drum'n'bass landscape, creating an oxymoronic hybrid of genuinely anti-social dance music.

Aphex Twin LPs

9 **1993 Selected Ambient Works 85–92 (R&S UK)**

8 **1994 Selected Ambient Works Vol. 2 (Sire)** Mindblowing electronics from James' pre-fame bedroom tapes. Defying labels, *Works'* title only partially describes these tracks, which also zig into spacey noodling before zagging to trance. Volume 2 heads off in a new direction — more reverent, somber, and almost classical in feel.

8 **I Care Because You Do (Sire) 1995** Reinventing himself yet again, *Care* is James at his most eclectic, pulling together calm, serene moments then launching into battering and bruising beat-heavy tracks. The moods run the emotional gamut, the rhythms shifting from trancey to hip-hoppish, while the electronics conjure up sounds barely recognizable to the human ear.

8 **Richard D. James Album (Elektra) 1996** His most accomplished and experimental set to date, exploring disjointed rhythms and more extreme sounds. It makes for disconcerting listening, especially as James incorporates a dizzying array of styles and effects (from toys to power tools) into the tracks, making *James* an excursion back in time even as it launches the artist himself into a brand new musical milieu. Possibly.

Selected Compilations and Archive Releases

7 **Classics (R&S UK) 1995** Early works, including the *Didgeridoo* and *Xylem Tube* EPs.

7 **51/13 Aphex Singles Collection (Wea Australia) 1996** A round-up of later EP tracks, the Philip Glass version of "Icct Hedral" included.

AFX LP

6 **Analogue Bubblebath Vol. 3 (Rephlex) 1992** It does indeed bubble, as well as burble, bleep, pulse, and pound in a mindblowing journey into the underbelly of electronics. Rhythms build, then disappear; atmospheres coalesce, then are ripped apart; tatters of rave take center stage only be ignominiously turfed off. A highly experimental, and at times, almost uncomfortable, listen. But never boring.

Mike and Rich LP

7 **Expert Knob Twiddlers (Rephlex UK) 1996**

Polygon Window LP

8 **Surfing on Sine Waves (Wax Trax) 1993** Sound as perpetual motion, beats, samples, and snippets of melody simply circle around and around, constantly shifting, transforming, fading — a process which gives the music an almost iridescent quality. Most of the tracks travel to trancey ports, but a few do journey into darkly ominous spaces. "Other worldly" doesn't begin to sum this up.

Richard James — Selected Productions/Remixes
1992 MESCALINUM UNITED — We Have Arrived [MULTIPLE MIXES] (R&S)
1992 MEAT BEAT MANIFESTO — Mindstream (Play It Again Sam)
1993 JESUS JONES — Zeroes and Ones (Food)
1993 CURVE — Falling Free (Anxious)
1993 SOFT BALLET — Sand Lowe (Alfa)
1993 ST. ETIENNE — Your Head My Voice (Heavenly)
1993 ST. ETIENNE — Who Do You Think You Are (Heavenly)
1994 SEEFEEL — Time to Find Me [MULTIPLE MIXES] (Too Pure)
1994 NAV KATZE — Ziggy (Victor)
1994 BEATNIKS — Une Femme N'est Pas Un Homme (VAP)
1994 GAK — Gak EP (Warp)
1994 NAV KATZE — Change (Victor)
1995 PHILLIP BOA & THE VOODOO CLUB — Turnips (Motor)
1995 WAGON CHRIST — Spotlight (Rising High)
1995 BUCK TICK — In the Glitter (Invitation)
1995 NINE INCH NAILS — The Beauty of Being Numb (TVT)
1995 GAVIN BRYARS — Raising the Titanic [MULTIPLE MIXES] (Point)
1996 DIE FANTASTISCHEN VIER — Krieger (Sony)
1996 KINESTHESIA — Triachus (Rephlex)
1996 NOBUKAZU TAKEMURA — Let My Fish Loose (99)
1996 MIKE FLOWERS POPS — Debase (LO)
1997 PHILLIP GLASS — Heroes (Point)
1997 GENTLE PEOPLE — Journey (Rephlex)
1997 DMX KREW — You Can't Hide Your Love (Rephlex)
1997 BECK — Richard's Hairpiece (DGC)

AQUA

FORMED [as Joyspeed] 1996 (Copenhagen, Denmark)
ORIGINAL LINE-UP Rene Dif (b. 10/17/67, Denmark — vocals); Lene Grawford Bystrom (b. 10/2/73, Tonsberg, Norway — vocals); Claus Norreen (b. 6/5/70, Copenhagen — keyboards); Soeren Rasted (b. Copenhagen, 6/13/69 — keyboards)

Aqua came together around the keyboards and drum machine-playing duo of Claus Norreen and Soeren Rasted, who themselves met back in 1989 when they were working at a gas station together. Recruited to record the soundtrack for a Danish film, *Fraekke Frida*, they then brought in DJ rapper/vocalist Rene Dif, Norwegian singer and TV host Lene Grawford Bystrom, and once the soundtrack was complete, formed a band together — Joyspeed.

It was not a particularly well-starred outfit. Their one single, "Itzy Bitzy," spent a week on the Swedish charts before disappearing and Joyspeed took the hint. Changing their name and revamping their image, they became Aqua in late 1995, signed to the Danish label Universal Music, and released their first single (a track from their maiden demo), "Roses Are Red" that September.

The name change did the trick. An immediate monstrous smash, "Roses Are Red," dominated the Danish chart for two months, earning a platinum record in the process. The follow-up, "My Oh My" in February 1997 was even more successful, going gold within just six days as it became the fastest-selling Danish single of all time. But it was "Barbie Girl," a biting social comment dressed up as utter sonic nonsense, which brought Aqua the international breakthrough.

A chart-topper around the world, "Barbie Girl" (#1 US, #1 UK) sold over 340,000 copies in its first two days of release in America, and not even a highly publicized bout of legal letter-writing between the band and the manufacturers of the real-life Barbie Doll could dampen its ardor. The band's debut album, *Aquarium* (#1 US, #1 UK), followed, topping the Danish chart for 11 weeks and disgorging three further massive hits, "Dr. Jones" (#1 UK), "Turn Back Time" (#1 UK), and "Lollipop" (#17 US).

The group toured the US and Europe in the wake of the hit, concluding the outing with a short Scandinavian tour through fall 1998 and a headline performance in front of 70,000 people at Copenhagen's Tivoli Gardens. They resumed operations in September 1999, playing a secret show in San Francisco to preview material from the forthcoming *Aquarius* album. A new single, "Cartoon Heroes" (#7 UK), followed in early 2000.

Aqua LPs

7 Aquarium (MCA) 1997 Plastic pop for perfect people. The first listen to Aqua's dance-friendly saccharin is enough to put even a non-diabetic into a sugar coma, but these wily Scandinavians are not the happy, snappy airheads that their music (and some of their lyrics) suggests. Their deconstruction of the not-so-innocent fun to be had with Barbie dolls suggests that there's something more going on here.

8 Aquarium (MCA) 2000 Full of underwater love songs, torrid torch tracks, and a herd of stomping club numbers, *Aquarius* has it all, including unabashed bubblegum and sensual salsa. A little less sticky-sweet than *Aquarium*, and more overt in intention, Aqua carries on spoofing Western culture with "Cartoon Heroes," splatter flicks a la "Halloween," and (most surreal of all) "Freaky Friday," which finds our heroine awaking to discover her life's turned into a country song, all lyrically lampooned to perfection.

Further Reading

The Official Book by Jacqui Smith (Back Stage, 1998).

ART OF NOISE

FORMED 1983 (London, England)

ORIGINAL LINE-UP *Gary Langan* (engineer); *Anne Dudley* (b. London, 5/7/56 — keyboards); *JJ Jeczalik* (b. 5/11/55 — programmer); *Paul Morley* (texts); *Trevor Horn* (producer)

Child prodigy Anne Dudley, an award-winning composer by the age of 12, first met producer Trevor Horn when the pair worked together in a dance band during the 1970s. Later, while he scored a worldwide #1 with Buggles' "Video Killed the Radio Star," and subsequently joined prog giants Yes, Dudley resurfaced as a member of Cindy and the Saffrons (alongside actress Joanne Whalley [Kilmer]), scoring a UK hit with a version of the Shangri-Las' "Past, Present, Future" (#53 UK) in early 1983.

That same year, she reunited with Horn, following the birth of his ZTT label and with Gary Langan and JJ Jeczalik on board, began experimenting with a Fairlight sampler. By late summer, with ZTT Marketing executive and former *New Musical Express* journalist Paul Morley also part of the group, Art of Noise became the first musicians to be signed to ZTT.

Taking their name from Italian Luigi Rossolo's futurist manifesto, *L'Arte Dei Rumori*, AON's initial intention was to simply construct instrumental sound collages utilizing the vast and then untapped resources opened up by sampling. Despite such obscure intentions, however, AON found themselves scoring instant success.

In April 1984, the quintet's *Into Battle with the Art of Noise* EP, leading off with "Beatbox," commenced an astonishingly successful assault on the American R&B Top 10. "Moments in Love" (#51 UK), their next 45, would subsequently achieve worldwide fame when it became part of the playlist for Madonna's marriage to Sean Penn. But it was with "Close (to the Edit)" (#8 UK) in the new year that AON finally arrived. The single won the Best Editing and Most Experimental categories at the second MTV video awards, and in 1996, it returned to the chart when it was sampled for Prodigy's UK chart-topper "Firestarter."

The group's debut album, *(Who's Afraid of) The Art of Noise* (#85 US, #27 UK), was also successful, but AON's relations with ZTT were souring, largely as a consequence of the label's utterly idiosyncratic marketing strategies. With Horn and Morley as bound up in the burgeoning success of Frankie Goes to Hollywood as they were in pursuing AON's own efforts, the group splintered and by late 1984, Dudley, Jeczalik and Langan had quit ZTT and signed AON to Chrysalis' China subsidiary (co-founded by Derek Green, famously the man who sacked the Sex Pistols from A&M Records).

The move paid immediate dividends. "Legs" (#69 UK) was followed by a highly stylized version of Duane Eddy's "Peter Gunn" (#50 US, #8 UK) and featured the veteran guitarist as special guest. It was named Best Rock Instrumental at the following year's Grammy awards.

"Paranoimia" (#34 US, #12 UK), a collaboration with television android Max Headroom, followed. While the release of the group's second album, *In Visible Silence* (#53 US, #18 UK), prompted them to undertake their first-ever tour of Japan and America (plus a single date in Britain), its success also launched AON into a spate of television, movie, and commercial work, itself culminating in their next single, "Dragnet 88" (#60 UK), taken from the soundtrack to the Tom Hanks/Dan Ackroyd movie of the same name.

AON's third album, *In No Sense? Nonsense!* (#124 US, #55 UK), followed in late 1987. A year later, the group scored their biggest hit ever when they teamed with Tom Jones for a cover of Prince's "Kiss" (#5 UK, #31 US). There would be just one more AON single, "Yebo" (#63 UK), featuring Mahlathini and the Mahotella Queens, in August 1989, before the band broke up.

A compilation (their second in under a year), *The Best of the Art of Noise* (#83 US, #55 UK) kept the group's name alive, however, and over the next decade, a string of remixes and collections would be released to some success — the singles "Art of Love" (#67 UK), "Instruments of Darkness" (#45 UK), and "Shades of Paranoimia" (#53 UK) included.

Dudley would remain the most visible member of the group. In March 1990, she conducted the orchestra at Yoko Ono's Lennon tribute concert in Liverpool and by September she was working with Killing Joke frontman Jaz Coleman on the *Songs from the Victorious City* album.

Thereafter, often combining the roles of producer, arranger, composer, and musician, she would work with artists as far afield as the Moody Blues, Boy George, k.d. lang, Five Star, New Edition, and Phil Collins (with whom she collaborated on the *Buster* movie soundtrack). Other movie successes included *The Crying Game*, *The Pope Must Die*, and Academy Award-winning *The Full Monty*.

In 1997, work began on a new AON album around a revised nucleus of Dudley, Horn, Morley, and former 10cc/Godley and Creme mainstay Lol Creme who also directed the album's first video, "Metaphore." Describing the resultant *The Seduction of Claude Debussy* as "the soundtrack to a film that wasn't made about the life of Claude Debussy," AON also claimed, "it's a soundtrack to the apprehension and wonder there is as we slip from one century to another. When we got back together, we noticed that in pop music, rock and dance, everyone plunders the recent past. We wanted to go further in the past than most pop music, in order to go further into the future."

The Art of Noise LPs

7 (Who's Afraid of) The Art of Noise? (ZTT) 1984 Rhythms, soundbytes, and collage rock to create a soundscape that alternately fascinates and irritates. Like one, you'll love it all.

7 In Visible Silence (China) 1986 More of the same, but "Peter Gunn" is a masterful distillation of it all regardless.

4 In No Sense? Nonsense! (China) 1987 Ambitious to a fault, the traditional AON sound is subverted beneath orchestras, choirs, superstar buddies, and samples reaching back through its own past doings. Perplexing and plodding in equal doses.

1 Below the Waste (China) 1989 With esotericism even further to the fore, the AON world music symphony. Background music for when you leave the house.

3 The Seduction of Claude Debussy (ZTT) 1999 AON regroup to create a tribute to composer Debussy, and one wonders, what did he do to deserve this? Game show host narration and overblown orchestration ensure "Seduction" is the worst possible form of self-indulgence... the type that even the self doesn't enjoy.

Selected Compilations and Archive Releases

3 The Ambient Collection (China) 1990 Remixer Youth (Killing Joke) wallpapers AON's China catalog

7 The Fon Mixes (China) 1991 The rave generation struts their stuff across 13 remixes of the electronic masters' music. DJ stars of the day (Carl Cox), rising club heroes (The Prodigy, LFO, Rhythmatic), established names (808 State's Graham Masset, Cabaret Voltaire's Richard H. Kirk's side project Sweet Exorcist), and engineers/producers (Youth, Robert Gordon, Mark Brydon) all work their magic, overseen by Mark Gamble, who offers up three remixes of his own.

7 The Best Of (Offbeat) 1994 This is not a band to rediscover, no matter how many high-profile samples they've inspired.

ASH

FORMED *1994 (Downpatrick, North Ireland)*
ORIGINAL LINE-UP *Mark Hamilton (b. 1977 — bass); Rick "Rock" McMurray (drums); Tim Wheeler (b. 1/4/77 — guitar, vocals)*

One of the brightest bands to break through in the Britpop afterglow of the mid-1990s, the roots of Ash date back to 1989 and a barely-teenaged heavy metal band called Vietnam, comprising of Mark Hamilton, Tim Wheeler, and friends Cookie (vocals) and Andy (drums).

Vietnam folded in 1992, around the same time as Hamilton and Wheeler discovered The Stooges, courtesy of another local band, Laser Gun Nun. Although elements of their past would still be surfacing in the duo's music almost a decade later ("I'd Give You Anything" from Ash's 1977 debut album, heartily plunders Black Sabbath's "NIB"), metal was clearly a dead end compared to Laser Gun Nun's ambitious grunge sound.

"People liked them and didn't like us," Wheeler reflected and by early 1994, the pair had linked with drummer Rick McMurray as Ash, a sprightly punk pop band, ironically claiming influences which were as old as Hamilton and Wheeler themselves were. Born in 1977, they took their lead from the bands of that same era — but the date had another significance, too. It was also the year in which the original *Star Wars* movie was released and staunch sci-fi fans that they were, they were not going to let the coincidence go unremarked.

After a self-produced demo introduced them to veteran radio plugger Steve Tavener in 1993, Ash's debut came with one track, "Season," on a four-track compilation of local bands (*Raptor Presents*) released that October. But it was "Jack Names the Planets," their debut single, which proved the ideal showcase for the group's fast-fermenting identity. Released as a 12" single on the local La La Land label, the 1,000 copies pressed seemed to all find influential ears — DJ Mark Radcliffe, who slammed the single onto the airwaves; the journalists who raved about the band in print; and the major label A&R men who descended upon Ash like locusts.

In May 1994, with a re-pressing of "Jack" now on the streets, Ash signed to Infectious Records and were immediately rewarded with a Top 5 indy chart hit, "Petrol," recorded with Elastica producer Mark Waterman. The group would subsequently tour Britain with Elastica.

"Uncle Pat" followed, together with a mini-album, *Trailer*, by which time Ash's infectious playfulness had attracted US interest too. They eventually joined Reprise, themselves flush from the success of the similarly pop-punk powered Green Day, and 1995 brought a Stateside release for *Trailer*.

The band's next single, "Kung Fu" (#57 UK), hit in March 1995. It was followed by the *Girl from Mars* EP (#11 UK), a Top 20 entry achieved just as Ash launched their first full European tour. That in turn was rounded off with a triumphant performance at the Glastonbury Festival, just two days after Wheeler and Hamilton completed their A-Level school exams. Similarly successful showings at T in the Park, Reading and Roskilde followed while Ash also visited Japan, Australia, and the US, and the year wrapped up with a second Top 20 entry, "Angel Interceptor" (#14 UK).

1977, Ash's debut album followed in the new year, on the back of "Goldfinger" (#5 UK). The album entered the British chart at #1 and the band launched into a season of almost non-stop gigging — captured on 1997's *Live at the Wireless* recounting of an Australian radio broadcast. They also became the first band ever to headline two nights at the

Glastonbury Festival, crowning the triumph with another Top 10 hit, "Oh Yeah" (#6 UK).

Breaks in the schedule allowed them to recruit second guitarist Charlotte Hatherley (ex-Night Nurse) in August 1997 and record the title theme to the movie *A Life Less Ordinary*. Ash would also become heavily involved in the Omagh Fund, a charity established to aid victims of an August 1998, terrorist bombing in the Northern Irish town. "I'm Gonna Fall," a track earmarked for Ash's second album, would appear on the Fund's *Across the Bridge of Hope* benefit album shortly before Christmas.

The much-anticipated second album, *Nu Clear Sounds*, finally materialized in Britain in late 1998 (fall 1999 in America) with both LP and the "Jesus Says" single effortlessly sweeping into the national press' end-of-year Best Ofs. Fears that success might somehow dampen Ash's edge, however, were quelled by the appearance of a new single, "Numbskull," and its accompanying video, a cautionary tale of group sex, drug abuse, and nudity, directed by Damon Tiernan and promptly banned by every video broadcaster in Europe. Incidentally, the single's B-sides further explored the band's musical roots with covers of Nirvana's "Blew" and Mudhoney's "Who You Drivin' Now."

Ash LPs

7 1977 (Reprise) 1996 Refusing to pick a genre and stick with it, Ash pull their disparate styles together by gluing the joins with a coat of indie rock — which amazingly does the trick.

7 Live at the Wireless [LIVE] (Death Star UK) 1997 A blistering recounting of an October 1996 Australian radio concert.

8 Nu Clear Sounds (Reprise) 1999 Further tightening the screws, Ash move towards a more classic British pop-rock sound, interspersed with highly entertaining diversion into punk, dreamy pop and even techno, a new clear sound of explosive power.

Selected Compilations and Archive Releases

6 Trailer (Infectious UK) 1994

6 Trailer (Expanded Version) (Reprise) 1995 A hint of Britpop savvy, a dash of older Indy-American fuzz, beaten and blended into something which cites The Buzzcocks as an influence, but can also sound like Black Sabbath.

AUTEURS

FORMED 1992 *(London, England)*
ORIGINAL LINE-UP *Luke Haines (b. 10/7/67, Walton On Thames — vocals, guitar); Glenn Collins (b. 2/7/68, Cheltenham — drums); Alice Readman (b. 1967, Harrow)*

Thoroughly misunderstood by the British press (who aligned them with a long expected glam revival) and the Americans (who simply compared them to the London Suede) The Auteurs would straddle the 1990s as one of the most subtly idiosyncratic bands around — a combination of irresistible pop hooks and palpable darkness. Interviewed in July 1999, Luke Haines claimed the song which best described him was the Adverts' "One Chord Wonders" and if the song's intent be explored beyond its title, he might well be correct.

The Auteurs formed when Haines and Alice Readman broke up their late-1980s band, the Servants, following one album in 1990. The pair linked with ex-Dog Unit drummer Collins, and the Auteurs debuted at London's Euston Rails Club in April 1992. They signed to Virgin's Hut subsidiary and released their first single, "Showgirl," in December.

New Wave (#35 UK), The Auteurs' debut album, was released in January 1993 with the band sound having been expanded by the arrival of cellist James Banbury. It was a remarkable record, one of the year's most acclaimed albums, the blueprint for much of what would subsequently be termed "Brit-pop," and a well-chosen finalist in that year's Mercury Music Awards (it missed out on the Best Album award by a single vote).

Collins was replaced by Barney Crockford that summer, and in November, The Auteurs' next single, "Lenny Valentino" (#41 UK), gave them their first hit single. "Chinese Bakery" (#42) followed, but *Now I'm a Cowboy* (#27 UK), The Auteurs' second album, would surely have improved on its eventual placing had Haines not broken both his ankles and had been unable to undertake any meaningful promotion.

It would be over a year before The Auteurs returned with the sinister *Back with the Killer* EP (#45 UK) in January 1996 — a silence broken only by *The Auteurs Vs u-Ziq* remixes collection, which paired them with Aphex Twin protege Michael Paradinas. It was an unlikely combination, born from a remix of "Lenny Valentino" and expanded over three other tracks — "Daughter of a Child," "Chinese Bakery," and "Underground Movies." The result would be named Album of the Week in both *Melody Maker* and the *New Musical Express*, earning comparisons with Global Communications' similarly revolutionary reassemblage of Chapterhouse's *Blood Music*.

Predictions that The Auteurs would pursue the electronic direction further with their next album were dashed when Haines' announced their decision to record with producer Steve Albini. "Next week," smirked a cynical *Alternative Press*, "Jellyfish with Billy Childish."

The doubters were proven correct. A single, "Light Aircraft on Fire" (#58 UK) and the 1996 *After Murder Park* album both sold poorly, and following one final single, the *Kid's Issue* EP in May 1996, Haines announced the end of the band.

Haines alone resurfaced as Baader Meinhof, a terrorist pop interface named for the 1970s German revolutionaries who had long been a source of extremist rock fantasy (former Velvet Underground chanteuse Nico regularly dedicated "Deutschland Uber Alles" to Andreas Baader). With the entire project developing from a single track on *After Murder Park*, "Tombstone," Baader Meinhof's eponymous debut album appeared in September 1996; a jarring collection which lived up to both its maker's reputation and its own pretensions.

A second Haines solo project, Black Box Recorder (Haines joined by former Jesus and Mary Chain drummer John Moore, and vocalist Sarah Nixey) appeared in mid-1998 (a year later in America). Accompanied by the "Child Psychology" single and a gripping Clio Barnard video, a string of London club residencies and news of a swiftly recorded second album maintained Black Box Recorder's profile into the new year. Constant comparisons with The Auteurs continued to haunt Haines, however, and 1999 saw the old band name resuscitated, with a single paying tribute to '70s glam band, the Rubettes. A new album, *How I Learned to Love the Bootboys*, followed — a full length exploration, and possibly exorcism, of the ghosts of Haines' Glam-era childhood.

The Auteurs LPs

⑧ **New Wave (Hut) 1993** A university thesis on how to build Brit-pop, shot through with such startlingly intelligent perversity that the end result is more of a template than a tribute. "Junk Shop Clothes" and "Showgirl" stand out loudly.

⑧ **Now I'm a Cowboy (Hut) 1994** "Lenny Valentino" says it all — casual, suave, camp, and knowing — the rest of the album simply follows in its semi-sordid wake and there's a sinister edge coming through which remains deliciously shocking long after the initial fission has faded.

⑥ **After Murder Park (Hut) 1996** Under Steve Albini's roughshod tutelage, The Auteurs emerge all but unrecognizable — aggressive and angular, but with sufficient melodicism to suggest that whatever else they'd been doing since their last album, ignoring the Beatles wasn't part of it. Ignoring everyone else, however, certainly was.

⑨ **How I Learned to Love the Boot Boys (Hut — UK) 1999** The opening "The Rubettes" and the Gary-Glitter-Goes-Punk "Your Gang Our Gang" are almost obsessive; Haines goes back to his childhood with a chilling eye for the little bits which most folk forget, and that includes the music. A very English album, of course, but a universal horror haunts its dusty corners.

⑧ **The Servants Disinterest (Fire) 1990** Bland post-Go-Betweens mopery, with Haines an anonymous guitarist.

Baader Meinhof LP

⑨ **Baader Meinhof (Hut) 1996** Simultaneously miles removed from, and inextricably involved with the parent concern; sensu-

ously sinister and bitterly poppy; terrorist pop of the highest measure.

Black Box Recorder LPs

⑧ **England Made Me (Hut) 1998** Sliding effortlessly in alongside the rest of Haines' murky, maggot-ridden catalog with a heart-breaking "Seasons in the Sun," *England* actually peaks with a slug slowed-down "Uptown Top Ranking" — although quite how (or why) such an hitherto unflappable statement of joyous defiance could be turned into a funeral is another matter entirely.

⑧ **The Facts of Life (Nude — UK) 2000** "The Art of Driving" is the signature hit, but throughout this slinky, sexy, summer-storm collection, art itself becomes art form.

AVENGERS

FORMED 1977 *(San Francisco, CA)*
ORIGINAL LINE-UP *Penelope Houston (vocals); Greg Westermark (guitar); Johnathan Postal (bass); Danny Furious (drums)*

If the Avengers have any regrets, it is that the band was long dead and buried before they received even a modicum of the applause and attention they deserved during their lifetime. A mere two singles comprised the Avengers' recorded legacy, together with a handful of live cuts and studio out-takes — sufficient material for two highly-rated compilation albums — but scarcely the epitaph they deserve.

Formed mere months before the Sex Pistols hit San Francisco and slamming out the *Car Crash* EP just weeks later, the Avengers were so highly rated that they were invited to open the Pistols' Winterland show on January 14, 1978. Pistol Steve Jones was certainly impressed; in 1979, he accompanied The Avengers (now comprising Penelope Houston, Danny Furious, guitarist Greg Ingraham, and bassist Jimmy Wilsey) into the studio to cut a second EP, *The American in Me*. Houston was so unhappy with the results that she re-recorded her vocals after he'd gone.

The group broke up shortly after, but their two EPs rank among the prime building blocks of American hardcore — much of what would transpire on that scene through the 1980s could be lain at least partially at the Avengers' door. However, Houston's performance also contained broad hints of the versatility she would display a few years later, following her re-emergence with a new folk-inflected band, 30, and a similarly themed solo album, *Birdboys*, produced in part by occasional Resident Snakefinger.

Despite a string of remarkable solo albums, highlighted by the Stones-ey, Beggars Banquet-esque *The Whole World* in 1993, and her powerful, occasionally Grace Slick-like vocals, Houston's reinvention would never stand in the way of her original intentions. And in 1999, following the highly acclaimed release of an album's worth of unreleased

Avengers' material, the group reunited for a similarly well-received US tour.

Selected Compilations and Archive Releases

8 Avengers 1977–79 (CD Presents) 1983
9 Died for Your Sins (Lookout) 1999 Compared with everything else coming out of California in the late 1970s, 14 and 21 tracks respectively do the Avengers few favors. The difference is, the Avengers did a lot of it first.

Penelope Houston LPs

6 Birdboys (Subterranean) 1988 Produced by Snakefinger, a strongly folk-flavored, acoustic rocker which doesn't necessarily match Houston's still fiery delivery.

7 500 Lucky Pieces (ID) 1992 Self-released cassette featuring original versions of several songs destined to resurface on *The Whole World* and *Cut You*.

9 The Whole World (Heyday) 1993
8 Karmal Apple (Normal) 1994 Suddenly everything comes good — the material strengthens, Houston's attitude softens — but the ensuing collision is less of a compromise than a collusion. The instrumentation sounds less esoteric than it actually is, which itself proves she knows what she's doing, while the songs provide an effective (and blameless) echo of what would one day be dubbed "alt-folk." Or something equally meaningless.

8 Crazy Baby (Return to Sender — Germany) 1994 Distinctly downbeat collaboration with master of minimalism Pat Johnson.

8 Cut You (Reprise) 1996 In giving a full release to such joys as "Sweetheart" and "Fall Back" from *500 Lucky Pieces*, *Cut You* can't be faulted for rerecording them. Alongside highlights from her other three albums, it can. Few of the revamps are actually better than their forebears, but several are equals and the title track has a dynamic will of its own.

3 Tongue (WB) 1999 Generally disappointing stab at positing a future for The Avengers; hardcore powerpop posturing for no discernable purpose.

Selected Compilations and Archive Releases

8 Silk Purse (From a Sow's Ear) (Return to Sender — Germany) 1994 A limited edition live and out-takes set, crowned by Alex Chilton's never-so-lovely "Take Care."

AZTEC CAMERA

FORMED 1980 *(East Kilbride, Scotland)*
ORIGINAL LINE-UP *Roddy Frame (b. 1/29/64, East Kilbride — vocals, guitar); Alan Welsh (bass); Dave Mulholland (drums)*

Formed from the ashes of schoolboy Roddy Frame's punk band, the Forensics, Aztec Camera emerged in 1981 at the forefront of what looked, briefly but impressively, like the next wave of British pop, headlining the Scotland-based Postcard labels roster of intense, and critically adored, post-punk mopers.

The band's first major line-up change had occurred before anybody south of the border even knew their name, when Campbell Owens replaced Alan Welsh in late 1980. The band contributed a track to a cassette given free with *Urban Development* fanzine, and in December, Postcard head Alan Horne caught Aztec Camera opening for the Revillos at the Bungalow Bar in Paisley. He signed them days later.

With its first issue of the new year, *Sounds* music paper was ready to introduce Aztec Camera to the world, courtesy of a debut single, "Just Like Gold" (#10 UK indy), and journalist Dave McCullough's infectious — and well-placed — enthusiasm.

With guitars which sometimes jangled, and lyrics which hung just on the positive side of lachrymose, a second superlative single, "Mattress of Wire" (#8 UK indy) and the excellent "Hot Club of Christ" (on the *Ghosts of Christmas Past* compilation) left Aztec Camera poised on the edge of the major breakthrough. Growing apart from Postcard, however, Aztec Camera's original intention of "releasing as many records as we can," as Frame put it, was swiftly subsumed beneath a need to take stock of their situation.

A proposed Postcard album, *Green Jacket Grey*, was abandoned — so was drummer Dave Mulholland — and Aztec Camera relocated to London. Blair Cunningham was briefly drafted in from Haircut 100, before Frame recruited former Ruts drummer Dave Ruffy. Then, with keyboardist Bernie Clark augmenting the line-up, Frame, Owens, and Aztec Camera prepared to create a masterpiece, with the band's major label (Rough Trade in the UK; Sire in the US) debut, *High Land Hard Rain* (#129 US, #22 UK, #1 UK indy) and another hit single, "From Pillar to Post" (#4 UK indy).

Patronizing references to Frame's youth, which pepper subsequent analyses of Aztec Camera's first records, are misleading. Just 17 when he cut the *Postcard* singles, 18 when "Oblivious" (#47 UK, #1 UK indy) gave him his first UK hit single in January 1983, Frame's talents were no more prodigious than those of a horde of other young musicians breaking through the UK scene at that particular time.

Where he did rise head and shoulders above most of the prevailing newcomers was in his ability to grasp the musical standards of an earlier, predominantly mid-late '60s, age and ally them to lyrics and cultural values which were pure teen adrenalin, a captivating brew which deserved more than the string of modest hits that marked the band's homeland high spot — "Walk Out to Winter" (#64 UK, #3 UK indy) — and a reissue of "Oblivious" on WEA (#18 UK). Under the guise of the French Impressionists, Aztec Camera also released a

Christmas single that year, covering the Residents' "Santa Dog."

Aztec Camera underwent another line-up change in the new year, with only Ruffy surviving from the last incarnation, to work alongside former Bluebells bassist Craig Gannon, Orange Juice/Josef K guitarist Malcolm Ross, and keyboard player Guy Fletcher. With the revised band came a reshaping of Frame's original fire and vision and, plainly taking much of his lead from Elvis Costello, Frame began constructing the far wordier, if no less obsessively introspective canvas which would materialize on his second album, *Knife* (#175 US, #14 UK).

Heralded by the September 1984 single, "All I Need Is Everything" (#34 UK), and produced by Dire Straits mainman Mark Knopfler (a marriage which guaranteed musical standards to match Frame's lyrical aspirations), *Knife* was simultaneously both Frame's artistic highpoint, and his low. By 1984, Aztec Camera had been almost completely overshadowed by the emergence of The Smiths, a band who took much of Frame's original premise and promise, and translated it into terms no less grandiose but far more accessible than Frame's increasingly complicated projections.

Frame responded with the space-filling *Backwards and Forwards* live EP (#181 US), bringing with it a quite unexpected cover of Van Halen's "Jump" and another series of line-up changes. Again, Ruffy alone survived; the new line-up was completed by bassist Marcus Miller, guitarist Steve Jordan, and former System keyboard player David Frank.

It was an accomplished line-up, but in 1987 *Love* (#193 US, #10 UK) was a backward step into pop cliché, an attempt to make a record which would work on American radio (the studio sessions were built around *Letterman* regular Will Lee and disco king Dan Hartman). Neither was it immediately successful. *Love* (#49 UK) fared very disappointingly, while a single, "Deep Wide and Tall," failed to chart altogether.

However, in March 1988, "How Men Are" (#25 UK), "Somewhere in My Heart" (#3 UK), and "Working in a Goldmine" (#31 UK) saw interest in Aztec Camera soar to new peaks — embracing a reissue of "Deep and Wide and Tall" (#55 UK) and culminating with two sold-out shows at London's Royal Albert Hall.

Aztec Camera returned in 1990, with only latter-day live bassist Paul Powell retained from any previous Aztec Camera line-up. He was joined by Frank Santoh (drums) and Gary Sanctuary (keyboards) for *Stray* (#22 UK) and the "Crying Scene" (#70 UK) single. A star-studded return to form, *Stray* featured guest appearances from Orange Juice frontman Edwyn Collins, Squeeze keyboard player Paul Carrack, and former Clash/Big Audio Dynamite leader Mick Jones (singing lead vocals on the deliciously BAD soundalike "Good Morning Britain," #19 UK).

Aztec Camera played a short US tour that fall, and the following summer took an all-acoustic show on the road in the UK. Frame would also launch a partnership with Edwyn Collins, debuting at the Edinburgh Festival in August 1991, and consummated by the single "Spanish Horses" (#52 UK). He also worked with Welsh veteran Andy Fairweather Low, on a cover of Amen Corner's "If Paradise Is Half as Nice" (released on the *Ruby Trax* benefit album in 1992) before linking with Ryuichi Sakamoto for the next Aztec Camera album, *Dreamland* (#21 UK) and single "Dream Sweet Dreams" (#67 UK). The partnership would be continued over onto Sakamoto's *Sweet Revenge* album in 1994.

In November 1995, *Frestonia*, produced by former Madness producers Clive Langer and Alan Winstanley, proved Frame's worst-performing album yet — it also marked the end of both Aztec Camera and Frame's relationship with Warners.

Opting to continue on as a solo artist, Frame signed with Go! Discs, then took a year off, reveling for the first time in his newfound freedom from the writing/recording/touring routine. By the time he was ready to resume, Go! Discs had been bought out by the Polygram major and label head Andy McDonald was operating his own Independent label. Frame transferred, and in 1998, scored immediate hits with "Reason for Living" (#45 UK) and *The North Star* (#55 UK). He departed Independent soon after.

Aztec Camera LPs

9 High Land, Hard Rain (Sire) 1983 Haunting, hopeful, and howling. Pop this brittle should be treated like fine crystal.

8 Knife (Sire) 1984 The dubious recruitment of producer Mark Knopfler turned out to be a godsend as Frame's earlier fragility starts turning towards darker, earthen energies.

5 Love (Sire) 1987

8 Stray (Sire) 1990 "The Crying Scene" and "Notting Hill Blues" alone repair the damage of *Love*'s big sheen over-production, while the chalk'n'cheese duet with Big Audio Dynamite's Mick Jones ("Good Morning Britain") has a crass charm of its own.

6 Dreamland (Sire) 1993

7 Frestonia (Reprise) 1995 Frame has been bruised, battered, and a bit disillusioned by time, but he's still a hopeless romantic at heart. *Frestonia* perfectly captures that state as the vividly emotional lyrics and delivery take centerstage and the evocative melodies complete the perfect tableaus.

Selected Compilations and Archive Releases

7 New Live and Rare (WEA) 1998

7 Spanish Horses (WEA) 1992

7 Covers and Rare (WEA) 1993 Japanese collections rounding up rare live recordings, remixes, and B-sides.

⑥ **Live on the Test [LIVE] (Windsong — UK) 1995** Sadly, a less-than-inspired reminder that even the best bands have an off day — and sometimes they're recorded.

⑨ **The Best Of (WEA) 1999** Either a predictable package of single hits and misses or a slab of solid genius. Depends what you're looking for.

Roddy Frame LP

⑥ **North Star (Independente) 1998**

B

BAD BRAINS

FORMED 1979 (Washington DC)
ORIGINAL LINE-UP H.R. (b. Paul Hudson, 2/11/56, London,
England — vocals); Dr. Know (b. Gary Miller, 9/15/58, Washington DC — guitar); Darryl Aaron Jenifer (b. 10/22/60, Washington DC — bass); Earl Hudson (b. 12/17/57, Alabama —
drums)

The single most influential hardcore band to emerge from
the late-1970s America, the four members of Bad Brains were
playing together in a jazz fusion band, Mind Power, when
they were introduced to punk rock in 1979. Immediately the
band reinvented themselves, taking their new name from a
Ramones song, while reinventing an attitude partially from
the visceral excitement of this new direction, partly from the
Rastafarianism which all four members espoused.

The ensuing collision alone would have been sufficient
to mark Bad Brains out in an American scene still struggling
to absorb the white reggae lessons of the Clash and the Ruts;
the fact that Bad Brains themselves were black only inverted
the equation. Over the past two years, punk had prided itself
on its distance from society. Bad Brains' emergence, and the
problems they encountered as a black band on a white circuit, served to remind even the movement's most patient
martyrs that prejudice is not only a fashion statement.

Having celebrated the difficulties they encountered in
Washington with "Banned in DC," Bad Brains moved to
New York, and within a matter of months they were invited
to England to tour with the recently reformed Damned. Selling off much of their equipment to pay for their airfare, the
band arrived in Britain only to be sent home again when
their work permits were refused.

January 1980, saw Bad Brains release their first single, the
immediate classic "Pay to Cum," on their own eponymous
label; it would be close to two years before Bad Brains followed it up, with the *Bad Brains* EP, released on the Dead
Kennedy's Alternate Tentacles label. However, the band was
recording constantly, a clutch of demos and studio dates preserved on 1996's *Black Dot* album and 1997's *The Omega Sessions* EP, brutal reminders of the group's original savagery.

December 1982, finally saw Bad Brains release their first
album, an eponymous half-live, half-studio collection
through the cassette-only ROIR label (*Bad Brains* has subsequently been reissued as *Attitude*); and even after its appearance, the group's reputation continued to rest largely upon

their dynamic live shows and the hardcore dub marriage of
which they remained the undisputed masters.

Linking with Cars' mainman Ric Ocasek, undertaking
one of his earliest outside production jobs, Bad Brains began
work on their first full studio album later in 1982. Like their
stage show, both *Rock for Light* and the *I and I Survive* EP
(#48 UK indy) clashed Bad Brains' instinctive hardcore zeal
with powerful, and often overwhelmingly positive Rastafarian reggae. When the group broke up shortly after the
album's release, it was this latter course which HR (now
known as Ras Hailu Gabriel Joseph I) chose to follow.

Best summarized by the *HR Tapes 1984–86* compilation,
HR's solo career was largely forgettable, leading to accusations that his return to Bad Brains in 1986 was motivated by
money. The ensuing album *I Against I*, however, swiftly
demolished that notion as Bad Brains turned in what
remains their masterpiece, an album which finally answered
one of the rock historians' favorite "what if's" — what if Jimi
Hendrix had lived long enough to collaborate with Bob Marley?

The tour which followed, too, was spellbinding, and
would be documented across three separate live albums,
1988's *Live*, 1990's *The Youth Are Getting Restless*, and 1991's
Spirit Electricity. Bad Brains themselves, however, would
sunder the moment the tour was over — HR and brother
Earl returning to the singer's solo career, while Jenifer and
Know soldiered on with former Faith No More vocalist
Chuck Moseley and Cro-Mags drummer Mackie. This line-
up never recorded and by the time Bad Brains returned to
the studio in 1989, the Hudsons were back on board,
although the ensuing *Quickness* album and *Spirit Electricity*
EP did them few favors.

The Hudsons departed again, Mackie returned to the
band, alongside vocalist Israel Joseph-I and in 1993 the new-
look Bad Brains signed to Epic for *Rise*. Within a year, however, the Hudsons had again been encouraged to return, this
time with the offer of a deal with Madonna's Maverick label.
With producer Ocasek also back on board, Bad Brains
recorded *God of Love*, toured, and then split up again. Over
the next three years, HR devoted himself to his Human
Rights project, concentrating on reggae and light punk,
while Jenifer hooked up with Shining Path, a band formed
by former Bad Brains roadies Chip Love and Danny Ilchuck.
In late 1998, however, the original Bad Brains line-up
regrouped yet again. Rechristening themselves Soul Brains
in a bid to escape the negative connotations of their earlier
alias, the band debuted with a southwestern tour in October

and continued gigging through 1999, apparently preparatory to releasing a new album early in 2000.

Bad Brains LPs

6 Bad Brains (Roir) 1982 A re-recorded "Pay to Cum" fronts an aggression-packed mashing of hardcore and roots reggae.

6 Rock for Light (PVC) 1983 More re-recordings; five *Bad Brains* numbers resurface under producer Ric Ocasek's guidance, for a brighter sound... but still a gut-wrenching blur.

9 I Against I (SST) 1986 Taking its title track from one of the group's earliest recordings (a ragged version subsequently surfaced on *The Omega Sessions*), *I* championed all of the band's musical ideas and directions, while an indication of its intensity can be gleaned from "Sacred Love" — HR phoned his vocals into the studio from a DC prison, following a marijuana bust midway through the album sessions.

5 Live (SST) 1988 From 1987, less a document than a confirmation, scarred by a reggae revamp of the Beatles' "Day Tripper."

3 Quickness (Caroline) 1989 Too much adequate rock, not enough superlative reggae. Just one track to remind you this isn't a bad Dead Kennedys.

6 The Youth Are Getting Restless (Caroline) 1990

6 Spirit Electricity (SST) 1991 1987 live revisited, again and oddly, again.

2 Rise (Epic) 1993 Joseph I is no HR and thrash is no substitute for emotion. Get past those stumbling blocks and *Rise* still sinks.

4 God of Love (Maverick) 1995

Selected Compilations and Archive Releases

7 Black Dots (Caroline) 1996 A 1979-era studio recounting of Bad Brains' then-current live set.

8 Omega Tapes (Caroline) 1997 Unreleased 1980 studio recordings.

HR LPs

5 It's About Luv (SST) 1995 Half punk, half reggae, but noticeably less supercharged than the usual Bad Brains amalgam. Appended by the *Keep out of Reach* EP, *Luv* was subsequently reissued as *HR Tapes 84–86*.

6 Human Rights (SST) 1986 The production is the superstar, but at least the songs and performance try to keep up. The first techno-calypso fusion?

5 Singin' in the Heart (SST) 1989

3 Charge (SST) 1990 HR's reggae-retro album, high on Rastafarian evangelism, but contrarily low on sonic sincerity.

Selected Compilations and Archive Releases

8 Anthology (SST) 1998 Even underachievement has its rewards — the best of the bits adding up to a surprisingly cohesive whole.

BAD RELIGION

FORMED 1980 *(San Fernando Valley, CA)*
ORIGINAL LINE-UP *Greg Graffin (vocals); Brett Gurewitz (guitar); Jay Bentley (bass); Jay Ziskrout (drums)*

Formed at high school in 1980 around a nucleus of Greg Graffin, Jay Ziskrout, and former Quarks guitarist Brett Gurewitz, Bad Religion were originally a trio, going so far as to work out three songs — "Sensory Overload," "World War III," and "Politics" — before realizing they needed a bassist.

Their friend Jay Bentley apparently couldn't play bass at the time of his recruitment; he had, however, just mastered a one-string version of "Smoke on the Water" on guitar and his recruitment was enough to encourage the band to cut its first demo. A copy found its way to Circle Jerks drummer Lucky Lehrer, who played it while guesting on KROQ one evening, a full two weeks before Bad Religion were scheduled to make their live debut at Joey's Kills in Burbank.

Sadly, the exposure didn't help. The show was cancelled at the last minute due to a near-total lack of audience and instead, Bad Religion played their first show opening for Social Distortion some weeks later. In late summer 1981, the band recorded their debut EP, *6 Songs*, for release on their own Epitaph label (named for Graffin's favorite King Crimson song).

2,000 copies were pressed and proved successful enough to fund the band's debut album, produced by former Sparks guitarist Jim Mankey. *How Could Hell Be Any Worse* was recorded in under a week, during which time drummer Fiskrout quit to be replaced by Peter Finestone. The album would prove a success and the band continued gigging — registering, as they did so, a general downswing in the mood of the Southern California punk scene. By the time Bad Religion came to record their second album, the members were convinced that punk was dead, and it was time to move on.

The sessions for *Into the Unknown* were fraught at the best of times and positively disastrous at the worst. Horrified at Graffin's indulgent over-use of a Roland Juno 6 keyboard, Bentley quit the band midway through recording the first song (he was replaced by Paul Dedona). Finestone left to attend school in England with another Valley musician, Davey Goldman, filling in. By the time the album was complete, Bad Religion were in shreds. And when the record flopped disastrously, band, and label, both folded.

Bentley alone remained actively playing with Wasted Youth, TSOL, and Cathedral of Tears. In 1985, however, Graffin and Finestone resurfaced as Bad Religion, cutting the *Back to the Unknown* EP with Circle Jerks guitarist Greg Hetson (a guest on *How Could Hell*) and one of Bentley's predecessors in Wasted Youth, bassist Tim Galegos. This line-up toured heavily over the next year before Galegos left and Bentley returned to the ranks.

Months later, Gurewitz, having recovered from the drug problems which had forced him even further out of the picture, agreed to stand in for Hetson at one show and ended up enjoying it so much that he too returned to the line-up.

The reunited Bad Religion debuted with *Suffer*, recording at Gurewitz's own studio, Westbeach Recorders, and released on the revitalized Epitaph — the label's second release following on from the debut album by L7. The following year, 1989, Bad Religion released *No Control* and it was obvious that things were beginning to happen. *Suffer* had sold approximately 4,000 copies, an excellent run for a tiny label. *No Control* shipped 12,000.

Reflecting on the indy punk scene of the time, Bentley explained, "at the time you had two heavies, Alternative Tentacles (run by the Dead Kennedys Jello Biafra) and SST (Black Flag's label). But they'd been around so long that they had a catalogue of like 900 records, so they could pretty much run their thing of being what they were. Then all of a sudden, there was Dischord (Fugazi, Ian MacKay's label) and Epitaph that were out there selling their records. Fugazi would put out a record and sell 50,000 out the door, and we'd be, 'Wow!' Then we put out *No Control* and sold around 60,000. It was funny, because even with no contact, we were playing this game from east and west coast, how big can this get? How many can we really do? How far can we push this before something happens?"

Taking advantage of their newfound popularity, 1990 brought the 80–85 collection, catching up on Bad Religion's earlier material (the title was a misnomer; the band recorded nothing in either 1980 or 1985). It sold over 100,000, a figure which 1991's *Back to the Grain* — alive with the group's now trademark harmonies — was quick to improve upon. Bad Religion were in demand. One especially persistent suitor, Bentley recalled, was the keyboard player from Bruce Springsteen's E Street Band. "He wanted us to rerecord *Against the Grain* with HIM producing it, and HIM rewriting the songs. That was the funniest thing I'd ever seen. He even brought this guy with him that had a bag full of money."

Finestone quit at this point, to concentrate on another band he'd been involved in, the Fishermen. Like Bad Religion, they were hotly tipped; unlike Bad Religion, they had a major label deal. However, the band split before their debut album was released and Finestone later re-appeared with a new punk band, Fifi, on his own label, Low Blow Records.

With long-time fan Bobby Schayer now on drums, Bad Religion's next album, *Generator*, was recorded in January 1991 as the first shots of the Gulf War were fired. Appalled at the spectacle of the ensuing superpower gang rape, the band promptly turned over two of their new songs to an anti-war

EP being prepared by Tim Yohanon of *Maximum Rock'N'Roll*, "Fertile Crescent" and "Heaven Is Falling," tracks which would also appear on *Generator* but in the meantime firmly established the band's political stance in the eyes of a market which was only just beginning to discover their history.

The long-threatened breakthrough finally came with *Recipe for Hate*, the album Schayer succinctly described as Bad Religion's *Sergeant Pepper*. Guest appearances from Johnette Napolitano, Clawhammer's Jon Wahl and Chris Bagarazzi, Greg Leisz from k.d. lang's band, and Pearl Jam's Eddie Vedder sweetened the record's reception even further and as sales soared stratospherically (close to 200,000), Bad Religion took their next step up, departing Epitaph for the major label pastures of Atlantic.

The decision to quit Epitaph wasn't simply motivated by the band's own needs. The label too was becoming swamped beneath the immensity of the Bad Religion experience, to the detriment of a now swiftly growing stable of other artists. And it is no coincidence that no sooner was the label free to deal with acts other than Bad Religion that both the Offspring and Rancid commenced their own dizzying ascents.

Accompanied by the MTV hits "Atomic," "American Jesus," and the title track — Bad Religion's Atlantic debut — 1994's *Stranger than Fiction*, would become their biggest seller yet. But it would also be Gurewitz's last with the group. Citing both personal differences within the band and a need to maintain a presence at Epitaph, he announced his decision following the band's latest tour.

He was replaced by Brian Baker, ex-Minor Threat, and a formative member of Glen Danzig's first post-Misfits group, Samhain. Incidentally, the week he was invited to join Bad Religion, he was also asked to fill in for Peter Holsapple in REM's live band. "That's me in the corner," Baker later punned, "choosing Bad Religion."

The reconfigured group debuted in 1995 with a new album, *The Gray Race*, and a gritty new live set, *Tested*. Their latest UK tour paid dividends when their latest single, "21st Century" (#41 UK), became their first ever hit in that country while the two albums bowled over even older fans, who suddenly noticed they really didn't miss Gurewitz that much.

Bentley agreed, acknowledging that "making [*Tested*] was very much like making *Suffer*, there was no pressure for it to be anything. We were just having fun, it was right back to where we were eight years ago, because we're doing it because we want to, not because we have some contractual obligation."

Another "fun" project caught the band in the studio with Die Toten Hosen vocalist Campino recording the mighty "Raise Your Voice" for a compilation accompanying the German leg of the Warped tour in 1999, and 1998's wryly titled

No Substance (#78 US) confirmed the group's continued commitment. But it was the 2000's union with producer Todd Rundgren which truly indicated their recent growth — an explosion of sound and unrepentant dynamism which established Bad Religion not simply as the godfathers of American punk, but as genuinely powerful pioneers of modern American rock in general.

Bad Religion LPs

6 How Could Hell Be Any Worse (Epitaph) 1982 Slightly more melodic than most of the LA hardcore crew but just as fast and furious; clashing standard punky stop/start songs with a barely disguised debt to '70s hard rock. But listen close, and there's just a hint of things to come.

7 Into the Unknown (Epitaph) 1983 The great, lost Bad Religion album, with Graffin's auteur keyboards colliding punk and proto-synthi-pop, before sailing off into distinctly softer, rockier pastures and prescient soaring harmonies. "I think *Unknown* is like early REM," Graffin mused later. "And if it had come a couple of years later, it probably would have been as popular as them." Unfortunately....

7 Suffer (Epitaph) 1988 Fast, furious, edgy, insightful lyrics about the state of the world... it all started here. A hint of harmonies, a mass of melodies, *Suffer* marks the true dawn of the band's slow rise to stardom.

7 No Control (Epitaph) 1989 Polishing their sound to a fine gleam, *No Control* is even tighter than *Suffer*, with even stronger songs.

8 Agaist the Grain (Epitaph) 1990 This album goes anywhere but. The now-trademarked multi-part harmonies emerge full born, and though the songs remain frenetic,the sound is brighter, bigger, verging on anthemic.

8 Generator (Epitaph) 1992 No longer feeling obligated to break the speed of sound on every track, Bad Religion offer up complexity and experiment while the slower tempos actually let you hear what the band are singing about — a valid consideration for a band with so much to say.

9 Recipe for Hate (Atlantic) 1993 Continuing to intellectually question America's blind view of itself and the rest of the world, Bad Religion wrap themselves in some of their strongest songs ever and bring in some surprising guests as well. An obvious next step on from *Generator*, a little bit cleaner, a tiny taste brighter, and a major league breakthrough which deserved every plaudit.

8 Stranger than Fiction (Atlantic) 1994 While *Recipe* went for poppy, *Fiction* goes for polish, helped by bringing in an outside producer, Andy Wallace, for the first time. Aggression and drama spar at mid-punk pace while the themes remain as acerbic as ever.

9 The Gray Race (Atlantic) 1996 With Gurewitz gone, Bad Religion have a lot to prove. But his replacement, ex-Minor Threat/Dag Nasty Baker, not only brings new blood to the band, but also some superior guitar work. Gritty classics, tougher than recent offerings, dance on an edge not visited since the days of *Generator*.

8 Tested [LIVE] (Atlantic) 1997 From the 1996 US/European tours, *Tested* was recorded directly onto 8-track from the onstage mikes — no overdubs, no high-end mixing consoles, just pure unadulterated music. If you've ever wondered what an onstage band think they themselves sound like, this is it. Disconcerting the first listen, energizing thereafter, few live albums have been this brave.

8 No Substance (Atlantic) 1998 Shared song-writing credits make this Bad Religion's most eclectic album ever, eagerly exploring new sounds and styles... ah, *Into the Unknown* II! Only better.

9 The New America (Atlantic) 2000 Astonishing collaboration with producer Todd Rungren opens the band's already wide-screen sound into a whole new dimension of sonic insanity.

Selected Compilations and Archive Releases

6 80–85 (Epitaph) 1991 Ignore the omission of *Into the Unknown*, and it's a solid round-up of pre-*Suffer* EPs, compilations, and the full debut album.

7 All Ages (Epitaph) 1995 Another compilation album, seeding pre-*Recipe* classics with a bumper crop of previously unreleased live material.

Greg Graffin LP

7 American Lesion (Polypterus) 1998 Graffin departs the angry world of punk for a personal, introspective record filled with acoustic guitars and soft rock songs. Emotional instead of political, but tough going for hidebound headbangers.

CHRIS BAILEY

BORN *(Kenya, Africa)*

The son of a British army officer, Chris Bailey arrived in Brisbane, Australia in the mid-'60s when his parents decided to emigrate from their Belfast, Northern Ireland home. In 1974, Bailey and friend Ed Kuepper formed their first band together, the Saints, and by 1976 the group was legendary throughout the Australian underground, a twisted tsunami of mutated old Rolling Stones riffs and damaged Stooges half-breeds. (A slew of early Saints recordings appeared on the 1995 collection, *The Most Primitive Band in the World*. The title was not an exaggeration.)

Nick Cave, an impressed teenage witness to the ensuing chaos, described the Saints as "so misanthropic, it was unbelievable. They were so loud!" And even though Bailey himself now reckons that "thousands, literally thousands" of musicians have passed through the ranks of the Saints since then, the band remains the same — misanthropic, unbelievable, and loud.

The Saints announced their existence with one of the classic singles of the era, 1976's "Stranded," released on their own Fatal label. The UK-based Power Exchange indy picked it up early in the new year, coupling it on single with Stanley Frank's "S'cool Daze," and encouraged by a slew of salutory reviews, the Saints moved to London.

EMI's Harvest subsidiary promptly snatched them up, and in May 1977, the band's major label debut single, "Erotic Neurotic," and album, *Stranded*, were released. Weeks later, the Saints' first major gig saw them opening for the Ramones and Talking Heads at the Roundhouse in June.

Bailey, however, was never "terribly fond of the punky-rock scene in England. "We took it all very seriously; it was the end of the Vietnam period, the height of that idealistic 'we're not going to sell out, bah humbug' thing, talking revolution and all that kind of thing. And you only had to spend two days on the Kings Road to realize that wasn't true."

October saw the band hit out at current preoccupations with their new single, a version of "River Deep Mountain High," but it was the new year which truly brought the Saints' distaste home. Accompanied by the single "This Perfect Day" (#34 UK), *Eternally Yours*, the Saints' second album, appeared in 1978 and went out of its way to reflect their stance — from the exaggeratedly "fat man with beer gut" cover photo and Bailey's decidedly unpunky long, stringy hair, through to the souped-up R&B in the grooves.

Even though the band were one of the hits of the Hope & Anchor's Front Line festival shows, contributing a biting "Demolition Girl" to the ensuing live album, their record company clearly hated them. Bailey continued, "it was all very corporate and we got into a lot of trouble for not wearing the right clothes, having the right haircuts... if we had come up fifteen years later, we'd maybe have been part of that grunge scene, but timing has never been one of the Saints' big things." Or, as another of the band's 1978 singles warned the label, "Know Your Product."

EMI lost interest, and while a new single, "Security," emerged in November 1978, the Saints' third album, *Prehistoric Sounds*, was left to die, and the band was dropped to roam the wilderness of quasi-legal European cult labels.

Kuepper quit the band, heading out for an idiosyncratic solo career which has included its own nod to the past, in the form of the ironically-named Aints, but Bailey persevered with the Saints, swiftly putting together a new group with Barrington (guitar), Janine Hall (bass), and Mark Birmingham (drums). In April 1980, the EP *Paralytic Tonight, Dublin Tomorrow*, debuted the band through the French label, Lost Records; November 1980, "Always" appeared on Larrikin; and in February 1981, *Monkey Puzzle* emerged on Lost.

With Lords of the New Church guitarist Brian James guesting on guitar, *Out in the Jungle* saw the Saints out on a high note (their final tour in 1984 was subsequently preserved on *Live in a Mud Hut*) and Bailey launched a solo career with the semi-acoustic *Casablanca*. He followed it with the all-covers *What We Did on Our Holidays*, but he reformed the Saints in 1987 and signed with TVT, just as the label began emerging onto the rock scene after beginning life concentrating on television themes only.

Lining up now as Bailey, Iain Sheddin, Arturo LaRizza, Barrington Francis, and Joe Chiofalo, a new album, *All Fools Day*, brought the band its first US tour. But when a mass of legal problems arose, utterly stilting the band's development, Bailey persevered for one more album, 1989's *Prodigal Son*, then abandoned the group for a solo career.

Three Bailey solo albums followed — *Demons, Savage Entertainment*, and *54 Days at Sea* — while he also toured the US with Concrete Blonde in 1994. But he was hankering for volume again. "I've been making fairly acoustic, quite lovely little records, but a few years back I was going through a songwriting session with a friend, and she banned me from bringing in an acoustic guitar. And I kind of had vague plans to do something Saints-wise, so...." So he gathered together the umpteenth line-up of a bona fide rock'n'roll legend, plugged in, and let rip.

Now based in Amsterdam, Holland, Bailey's conspirators were predominantly Dutch — Mons Wieslander (guitar), Ian Walsh (guitar), Joakim Tack (bass), and Andreas Jornvill (drums). Their activities, *The Howling* and *Everybody Knows the Monkey*, remain Bailey's personal vision "of what bands should be, and I think it was a matter of rediscovering how much fun you can have, just plugging in without too many effects. It's very hard for me to be objective about my work as a songwriter, the people you work with tend to cover you. But I wanted to make the kind of records I'd have made if I hadn't made any other records."

Chris Bailey LPs

7 Casablanca (New Rose, France) 1983 Or, backstage at the folk bar, a loose, and sometimes lonely sounding guitar and voice job, with just enough rawness to keep your nerves on edge.

9 What We Did on Our Holidays (New Rose, France) 1984 A dynamic collection of rock/soul/folk flavored covers, with a bonus reprise of *Casablanca*'s stand-out "Wait Till Tomorrow"(retitled "Ghost Ships"). Bailey may not be the only guy whose voice can handle both Marvin Gaye *and* Jacques Brel, but he's one of the precious few who can throw in Wilson Pickett as well.

6 Demons (New Rose, France) 1991 Closer to the recently reformed and re-sundered Saints than the solo glories of old, a pause as opposed to priceless.

10 **Savage Entertainment (New Rose, France) 1992** With another version of "Wait Till Tomorrow"/"Ghost Ships"setting sail, no one can accuse Bailey of not knowing a classic when he writes one. Only now it has a boat-load of company.

Lyrically, *Savage Entertainment* adheres to those proven Bailey bugbears of loneliness and lunacy, themes which resurface even in the drunkenly cavorting "Getting Friendly with the Devil" and the sexually frank title track (a sly revision, incidentally, of Roxy Music's "Dreamhome" trick. Ferry's lover had an air valve; Bailey's has a two pin plug.)

Musically too, *Savage Entertainment* continues down familiar solo roads, although orchestral dramas and lashings of cello now cavort around the wide open spaces — in lesser hands, such excess could be unbearably pompous and occasionally ("Do They Come from You"), he does make even ELO sound humble.

Bailey rarely falls for the obvious ploy though, and the very next cut, the wry "Life's a Comedy," is so painfully sparse that even the lone electric guitar sounds like overkill. Indeed, as strong as the songs are, the arrangements run them close and if Bob Dylan made this record, he'd have called it *Blood on the Tracks*. It really is that special.

9 **54 Days at Sea (New Rose, France) 1994** A traumatic twin to *Savage Entertainment*, apparently constructed in the aftermath of a broken marriage, but typically expanding the palette to absorb a lot of other tragedies too. Bleak even when it tries to be bloated, an emotional whirlpool which never relents.

The Saints LPs

8 **(I'm) Stranded (Sire) 1977** The title track was a punk classic, but the rest of their debut album put the Saints in firm Eddie and the Hot Rods' territory, a frenetic pub band with oodles of attitude. Even across the hottest R&B stompers, Kuepper's leads are too long and dinosaur-screaming, although when he's riffing *a la* hyperspeed Keith Richard, he's as cool and convincing as Bailey's snotty snarl.

8 **Eternally Yours (Sire) 1978** An unabashed R&B love letter, with definite touches of the Dolls and Small Faces, slash'n'trash chaos and some brilliant acoustics.

7 **Prehistoric Sounds (Harvest) 1981** Punishingly direct album, emphasizing not only that the Saints were on their way out, but also why — Kuepper and Bailey's futures had very different paths to trace and from "Everything's Fine" to "The Chameleon," the crossroads are lit with neon.

6 **The Monkey Puzzle (New Rose, France) 1981**

5 **Out in the Jungle... (Flicknife, UK) 1982**

7 **A Little Madness to Be Free (New Rose, France) 1984** Cut more in the mould of Bailey's recent solo albums than one would expect from the Saints, the arrangements nevertheless pale in the face of the brand name's inherent drama.

5 **Live in a Mud Hut (New Rose, France) 1985** Generally muddy recounting of the 1984 comeback tour.

8 **All Fools Day (TVT) 1987** A dark, driving behemoth whose horizons broadened to incorporate some genuinely powerful bluesy-soulful howlers.

7 **Prodigal Son (TVT) 1988** The US edition got yet another version of "Ghost Ships," but a weak one which reflected poorly on the rest of the album. Hunt out the import and "Fire and Brimstone," "Grain of Sand," and"Shipwreck" would dignify any best-of-Bailey.

9 **Howling (Amsterdamned) 1997** The first all-new album in almost a decade saw sole-surviving Saint Bailey fearlessly up-ending the garage-punk-blues cookbook, plugging everything through an amp stack which can't help but smoke. *Howling* does indeed howl. It also growls, screams, and bellows.

8 **Everybody Knows the Monkey (Amsterdamned) 1998** Timeless trash rock sets the scene with "What Do You Want," so if you don't like being slapped round the head by delinquent three-chord slobber, look elsewhere. If you do, there's a beautifully rancorous sheen and Bailey remains the only man who would rhyme "corporate zoo" with "vestibule."

Selected Compilations and Archive Releases

7 **The Best of The Saints (Razor) 1986**

7 **Scarce Saints (Raven, Australia) 1989** 1976–78 compilations highlighted by the non-album singles. *Scarce* drops one side's worth of studio material in favor of unreleased live from 1977 and 1981.

8 **The New Rose Years (Fan Club, France) 1989** Neat companion to the regular albums, with EP, live, and compilation cuts to keep the interest high.

8 **Songs of Salvation 1976–1988 (Raven, Australia) 1991**

9 **The Most Primitive Band in the World (Hot, Australia) 1995** In early 1974, the Ramones were still rehearsing, the Sex Pistols were still led by a guy named Wally, but the Saints were already roaring and recording in Ed Kuepper's folks' garage. The sound is strong, the material is mighty, and "Stranded" sounds like a prototype for the next 25 years of rock'n'roll.

9 **Know Your Product (EMI, UK) 1996** Dramatic 22-track anthology combines great swathes of *Stranded* and *Eternally Yours* (sadly skimps on *Prehistoric Sounds*) with out-takes and single-only cuts.

Ed Kuepper/The Aints LPs

7 **Ascension (Hot, Australia) 1991** Hooliganism, heavy garage punk at its damn-near finest.

6 **Very Live (SLSQ) (Aint, Australia) 1991** The subtitled SLSQ means "slightly limited sound quality." But if you can get past that, you discover what happens when a punk legend decides to take his own legacy out for the night, and realizes it just wasn't punky enough. The Saints' "I'm Stranded" has rarely sounded so despairing, "Erotic Neurotic" is rendered psychotic, and "River Deep Mountain High" becomes a completely level playing field.

despairing, "Erotic Neurotic" is rendered psychotic, and "River Deep Mountain High" becomes a completely level playing field.

6 AutoCannibalism (Hot/Cargo) 1992 Six track mini-album heavily influenced by US grunge

Selected Compilations and Archive Releases

7 Shelf Life Unlimited!! Hotter than Blazing... (Hot, Australia) 1995

Ed Kuepper/The Laughing Clowns LPs

8 Law of Nature (Hot, Australia) 1983 A kaleidoscope of brilliance; all "Red River Rock" honks and stray guitars which bounce off the drums and burrow into your soft bits.

8 Ghosts of an Ideal Wife (Hot, Australia) 1985 Recorded while the studio was being demolished, which fit because the band was collapsing too. Still, country bar-room blues have rarely sounded so desperate.

Ed Kuepper LPs

8 Electrical Storm (Hot, Australia) 1986 Retaining the Laughing Clowns' signature saxes, but a relaxed,almost folk-ridden collection, the archetypal Acquired Taste. Well worth the effort, though.

6 Rooms of the Magnificent (Hot, Australia) 1987 With Paul Smith, Diane Spence, and Glad Reed all aboard, a Laughing Clowns reunion in everything but name, with a (sadly unremarkable) eye on the kind of territory REM borrowed from elsewhere in the '80s.

8 Everybody's Got To (Capitol) 1988 Widescreen guitars punch through ten solid slabs of powerful pop. An almighty triumph; an unfeasible flop.

7 Today Wonder Wonder (Hot, Australia) 1990 Stripped bare and homely, instrumental credits include a cardboard box, of course.

7 Honey's Steel Gold (Hot, Australia) 1991 Shockingly loose, exhilaratingly electric, and the first Australian indy album ever to crack the national Top 30.

9 Black Ticket Day (Hot, Australia) 1992 Recorded with the Elektra String Quartet, Kuepper's most restlessly inquisitive albums slams archetypal songs into utterly disconcerting landscapes.

8 Serene Machine (Hot, Australia) 1993 Charmingly laid-back neo-acoustic set, encapsulated by the closing "Married to My Lazy Life." Except it isn't really that lazy, as the party-pounding "Reasons" has already chased you around the block.

9 Character Assassination (Restless) 1994 Dry, solo recordings, stripped-back production, then a mass of arrangements and instrumentation were dropped into place. The result — studio production with the air of home demos.

7 King in the Kindness Room (Hot, Australia) 1995 Kuepper's own website put it best — "imagine Throbbing Gristle jamming with Leonard Cohen on MTV Unplugged."

8 I Was a Mail Order Bridegroom (Hot, Australia) 1995 Kuepper unplugged, running through past favorites — his own (The Saints' "Messing with the Kid" included) and other peoples'.

6 Exotic Mail Order Moods (Hot, Australia) 1995 A mail order-only companion to *Bridegroom*, but this time mangled with samples, backbeat, and tortured guitar. Fittingly, the deranged cover of Bowie's "Man Who Sold the World" is subtitled in memory of Nirvana's own version, "Poor Kurt — He's Second Fiddle to This."

7 Frontierland (Hot, Australia) 1996 A bizarre marriage between '60s psych and '90s electro, with Dixieland, reggae, and country peeking around the edges.

5 Starstruck (Hot, Australia) 1997 28-track instrumental album, suitably subtitled "music for films and adverts." Cuts range in length from 30 seconds to 9 minutes, but build into a collage crammed with elements of past Kuepper compositions.

8 With a Knapsack on My Back [LIVE] (Hot, Australia) 1997 Dynamic radio recording from Germany.

6 Cloudland (Hot, Australia) 1998 Limited edition all-instrumentals album.

7 Ed Kuepper & His Oxley Creek Playboys Live [LIVE] (Hot —Australia) 1998

6 Bluehouse (Hot, Australia) 1998 Another instrumentals-only collection.

Selected Compilations and Archive Releases

8 Butterfly Net (Hot, Australia) 1994 From *Electrical Storm* to *Black Ticket Day*, a collection apparently aimed at proving why *Melody Maker* just called him a God — because it might be true, of course.

8 Heart of New Wave (Pok, Greece) 1995 Highly regarded overview of Kuepper's entire post-Saints career.

7 The Wheelie Bin Affair (Hot, Australia) 1997 16-track collection of non-album singles, 1992–97.

7 Reflections of Ol' Golden Eye (Hot, Australia) 1998 Collection drawn largely from rarities and limited edition album releases.

BAILTER SPACE

FORMED 1986 *(Christchurch, New Zealand)*
ORIGINAL LINE-UP *Alister Parker (vocals, guitar); John Halvorsen (vocals, bass); Hamish Kilgour (drums)*

The roots of Bailter Space lay within the stream of antipodean bands who emerged at the tail end of the 1970s, operated in near-total isolation, then blew onto the Anglo-American scene during the early-mid 1980s, fully formed and utterly dislocated from any conventional line of musical thought. Their eventual incorporation into these new markets owed more to the malleability of those markets than to any deliberate compromise on the musicians' part — again, an approach epitomized by Bailter Space.

The band grew out of an earlier, Christchurch-based band, The Gordons. Formed by Alister Parker, John Halvorsen, and Brent McLachlan, after the trio met at an art gallery, The Gordons played their first gig just one week later, a tribute to what Parker described as the "sort of telepathic communication" which existed between the musicians. "It was very spontaneous, and like nothing I'd ever heard before. There was a feeling that we could be very illogical with our thinking when we were playing. There was no talking, we just exchanged these quiet stares and played."

The *Future Shock* EP in 1980, and an eponymous album two years later, brought this remarkable band's story to a close; the Gordons split in 1982 and it would be another four years before Parker returned to music, when he reunited with Halvorsen, then linked with Hamish Kilgour (ex-the Clean and the Great Unwashed), to form Nelsh Bailter Space. McLachlan was brought in as producer, and the *Nelsh Bailter Space* EP and "New Man" single appeared on New Zealand's Flying Nun label late in 1987.

Kilgour quit during the band's first visit to New York in 1988, forming a new band, Monsterland. Of course McLachlan replaced him and in this form, Bailter Space (they dropped the Nelsh when Kilgour left) set about recording *Tanker*, their debut album, and the *Grader Spader* EP, later in the year. Both established Bailter Space on the forefront of rock experimentalism.

Thermos followed two years later, and in 1990, Bailter Space signed to the American Matador label. The group relocated to the US soon after, and set about reintroducing themselves with the relentless *The Aim* EP. Released as two separate 45s in Britain, *The Aim* received two Single of the Week awards from *Melody Maker*.

With the change in scenery came a change in direction. Elements of the band's next album, *Robot World*, and the out-takes which partially comprised the *BEIP* EP, echoed an unholy collision between Beatle harmonies and Velvet Underground dissonance — indeed, Parker spoke of getting into "the harmonic value of distortion; we started to be very particular about where we set the instruments up and the angles the sounds were bouncing at. From these harmonic experiments I became more interested in the actual melodic content of the music," a consequence which *Vortura* took to extremes that were as unexpected as they were exhilarating.

Having completed that experiment, however, Bailter Space's next album, *Wammo*, saw the group returning to its most wildly sonic roots — the album was so called because seven of its ten tracks were themselves originally titled "Wammo" (another, the band's latest single, was simply titled "Splat"). This process reached its crescendo with 1997's *Capsule*, and the accompanying *Retro* EP, before Bailter Space launched another abrupt change in direction with the *Photon* EP and a new album, 1999's *Solar 3*.

See also the entry for "CLEAN," on page 273.

Bailter Space LPs

8 Tanker (Flying Nun, NZ) 1988 *Tanker* drew immediate comparisons with Sonic Youth — primarily because Sonic Youth was one of the few bands around making such colossal demands on the listener. Terms like "darkly insistent," "determinedly linear," and "irresistibly propulsive" remain the best ways of describing an utterly indescribable lesson in post-Velvets noisemaking.

5 Thermos (Flying Nun, NZ) 1990

7 Robot World (Matador) 1993 Keep quaffing the Kraftwerk and it'll all make sense in the end.

8 Vortura (Matador) 1994 Blistering blasts of white noise disfigure the icy landscapes of last time out — not the ultimate Bailter Space experience, but certainly the most archetypal.

8 Wammo (Matador) 1995 In space, no one can hear you make a concept album. But in Bailter Space, it doesn't matter and the end result emerges their most conventional hook-laden missive yet.

6 Capsule (Turnbuckle) 1997

7 Solar 3 (Turnbuckle) 1999 An eerie techno/electronic approximation of the band's mid-period stylisms — the fuzz and guitar drones a backdrop for the shimmering, simmering melodies. Almost defiantly, *Solar 3* winds through dark aggression, hypnotic trance, brooding sorrow and on into glimmering pop.

BANANARAMA

FORMED 1980 (London, England)
ORIGINAL LINE-UP *Siobhan Fahey (b. 9/10/57, London, England — vocals); Sarah Dallin (b. 12/17/61, Bristol, England — vocals); Keren Woodward (b. 4/2/61, Bristol, England — vocals)*

Journalism student Sarah Dallin and BBC accountant Keren Woodward met Siobhan Fahey at the London College of Fashion, where Fahey too was studying journalism. The trio began singing together for fun, usually turning up at pubs and clubs, and providing entertainment during intermissions between the scheduled acts. They were also using the rehearsal studio where Sex Pistols Steve Jones and Paul Cook were breaking in their own new band, the Professionals, and Woodward later reflected of those early shows, "[they] made us realize that everybody else was as bored as us." In the age of post-punk seriousness, when every new band seemed set on having even less fun than Joy Division, "everything was dreary, and just the sight of people like us up there enjoying ourselves dancing around was enough."

A handful of guest appearances followed, including a stint playing maracas with the Monochrome Set in November 1980. Department S vocalist Vaughan Toulouse cited the still-unnamed group as his Tip for the Top in a *New Musical Express* feature and by early 1981, the trio made a few club appearances singing and dancing along to a demo tape which Paul Cook produced with them. "Aie a Mwana," a mid-'70s disco stomper originally recorded by Black Blood, took off quickly and when Demon Records boss Clive Banks announced he wanted to release it, the girls (having hastily named themselves Bananarama) agreed.

The single appeared in August 1981, a seductive antidote to a summer which was otherwise exploding with every imaginable tension. It was the year that many British inner-cities erupted in the flames of riot and unrest when the Specials' foreboding "Ghost Town" topped the chart and when the whole country seemed teetering on the edge of oblivion. And then Bananarama burst into view — cheery, cheeky, cute, and irresistible — and attracting attention in the unlikeliest of places.

Both Elvis Costello and Paul Weller were loudly singing their praises (Weller had them open four Christmas shows for The Jam that year, and contributed one song, "Dr Love," to their debut album), while the Fun Boy Three — fresh from the breakup of The Specials — invited Bananarama to sing backup on their forthcoming debut album.

The two groups wound up recording six songs together, beginning with the duet "It Ain't What You Do (It's the Way That You Do It)" (#4 UK), which became the Fun Boys' next single, and "Really Saying Something" (#5 UK), which became Bananarama's. Despite promises to the contrary, however, the two groups would not work together again; instead, Bananarama followed up with "Shy Boy" (#83 UK, #4 US) backed with what became their signature song, "Don't Call Us (Boy Trouble)."

Turning down a sudden spate of modeling offers from Britain's notoriously girl-hungry tabloid press, Bananarama came into their own with their next release — their first self-composed effort, "Cheers Then" (#45 UK). It indicated a musical depth and ability which utterly contradicted the trio's burgeoning public image as fun-loving banana girls; a depth which would be reinforced by their debut album, *Deep Sea Skiving* (#63 US, #7 UK).

Aside from the Weller track, the album featured six band compositions, including "Young at Heart," later a UK #1 for the Bluebelles, while the album's cover of Steam's "Na Na Hey Hey Kiss Him Goodbye" (#5 UK) continued Bananarama's domination of the British chart. "Cruel Summer"

(#9 US, #8 UK — covered in 1998 by Scandinavian superstars Ace of Base — #10 US) followed, but work on their second album kept the group out of the spotlight for much of the next eight months.

The ominous "Robert De Niro's Waiting" (#95 US, #3 UK) relaunched them early in 1984 and clearly introduced a new sensibility. Bananarama themselves seriously resisted releasing "De Niro" as a single, arguing that "the record company wanted it because it's the closest to the breezy pop we're known for." But that was only true if you didn't listen to it.

Bananarama (#30 US, #16 UK) was released that spring 1984 and did indeed mark a radical departure for the group — as performers and as writers. "Rough Justice" (#23 UK) was a hardnosed look at domestic violence. "King of the Jungle," was a lament for a band friend, Thomas Reilly (brother of Stiff Little Fingers drummer Jim), shot and killed by a British soldier in Belfast the previous August.

Unfortunately, the band's sudden serious streak did not translate into record sales. "Hot Line to Heaven" (#58 UK), "The Wild Life" (#70 US), and "Do Not Disturb" (#31 UK) fared poorly and Bananarama retreated for close to a year, working with producers Stock, Aitken, and Waterman on a new sound and a new image. They returned in May 1986, armed with a smash-hit cover of Shocking Blue's "Venus" (#1 US, #8 UK).

Two albums, *True Confessions* (#15 US, #46 UK) and *Wow* (#44 US, #27 UK), were accompanied by a chain of further hit singles — "More than Physical" (#73 US, #41 UK), "Trick of the Light" (#76 US, #32 UK), "I Heard a Rumour" (#4 US, #14 UK), "Love in the First Degree" (#48 US, #3 UK), and "I Can't Help It" (#47 US, #20 UK). The group worked with Daryl Hall on the soundtrack to *The Secret of My Success* and discussed revamping "What's New Pussycat" with the Cure.

It was, of course, all a long way from the street smart social comment which the trio had been espousing a mere twelve months before. And for Fahey, the one band member most likely to question the sacrifices of success, it was just a little too far for comfort. She still wanted to make records, she said, but she was more interested in improving her tennis playing with boyfriend David Stewart (of the Eurythmics). The pair married on August 1, 1987, and months later, Fahey left the group. (She would later surface in Shakespear's Sister with former Eric Clapton Band vocalist Marcella "Detroit" Levy.)

Fahey was replaced by ex-Shillelagh Sisters Jacqui O'Sullivan (b. 8/7/60, London); she debuted on the first of a string of increasingly insubstantial singles released through the remainder of 1988 — "I Want You Back" (#5 UK), "Love Truth and Honesty" (#89 US, #23 UK), and "Nathan Jones"

(#15 UK). *The Greatest Hits Collection* (#151 US, #3 UK) opened 1989 and effectively closed Bananarama's hit-making career. A March 1989 charity remake of the Beatles' "Help" (#3 UK) credited to Bananarama/La Na Nee Nee Noo Noo and co-starring comediennes Dawn French and Jennifer Saunders, would be their final Top 10 hit.

A remix of "Cruel Summer" (#19 UK) was followed by a union with Killing Joke's Youth, for the "Only Your Love" (#27 UK) single in August 1990. It would be six months more before a follow-up materialized, as "Preacher Man" (#20 UK) and a cover of the Doobie Brothers' "Long Train Running" (#30 UK) preceded the band's fifth album, *Pop Life* (#42).

The record was barely on the streets when O'Sullivan quit in September 1991, leaving Dallin and Woodward to continue on as a duo, now reunited with the similarly abridged production team of Stock and Waterman. "Movin' On" (#24 UK), "Last Thing on My Mind" (#71 UK), and a magnificent cover of Andrea True Connection's "More More More" (#24 UK) preceded Bananarama's next album, April 1993's *Please Yourself* (#46 UK).

Suggestions that Bananarama themselves had been forgotten by the public, however, were shot down when "Young at Heart," from their debut album, took the Bluebells to #1 — even as founder member Fahey enjoyed a chart renaissance of her own with Shakespear's Sister. Their "Stay" topped the UK chart for eight weeks in early 1992; the album *Hormonally Yours* (#56 US, #3 UK) won the Outstanding Contemporary Song Collection award at the 1993 Ivor Novellos. Shakespear's Sister's May 1993 split was actually announced from the winner's rostrum at that event.

A barely-noticed 1995 album *Ultra Violet* notwithstanding, it would be 1998 before Bananarama re-emerged when Fahey rejoined her bandmates (and Adam and the Ants guitarist Marco Pirroni) for a deliciously camp, one-off revival of Abba's "Waterloo" for inclusion in Channel 4 television's *A Song for Eurotrash* extravaganza.

For the group which started for nothing more than laughs, the wheel had come full circle. But for the single most important British girl group of the 1980s — forebearers of everything from Kenickie to the Spice Girls, Elastica to Shampoo — one couldn't help but feel cheated. Bananarama were worth so much more than that.

Bananarama LPs

10 **Deep Sea Skiving (London) 1983** They were never the simple pop conveyor belt their critics claimed they were — or rather, they were, but without any of the negative connotations which such a phrase intended. Rather, the string of flawless singles which preceded (and accompanied) the album's release were simply the easiest points of entry.

But even the soaring "Na Na Hey Hey Kiss Him Goodbye" and the kinda-cloying "Shy Boy" were more than 'nana-by-number sing-alongs; while "Really Saying Something" (cut with the post-Specials Fun Boy Three) and the truly tribal "Aie a Mwana"(produced by Sex Pistol Paul Cook) evidenced a dance-floor sensibility drawn directly from Bananarama's own pre-record deal reality.

The heart of *Skiving*, however, lay in the three self-composed numbers which contrarily stood at total odds with the public perception of the band: the resigned "What a Shambles," the bittersweet "Cheers Then," and the yearning "Wish You Were Here." None may have been more than teenage diary entries set to suitably minor key melodies, but what more should they have been?

Disregard Barry Blue's momentarily fashionable '80s disco production and hone in on voices and harmonies alone, and the Brill Building couldn't have put things more directly. Add "Boy Trouble (Don't Call Us)" and the galloping "Young at Heart"(later covered for a UK chart-topper by Scotland's Bluebelles), then imagine if the Shangri-Las could write as well as they pouted. Bananarama really were that good.

9 **Bananarama (London) 1984** Preluded by Bananarama's own admission that they were sick of their image, a collection as hard as their faces on the cover, lightened only by the exquisite harmonies which cut through even the darkest moments — the deeply traumatized "Robert De Niro's Waiting," the abuse-scarred disturbance of "Rough Justice," and the shattered resignation of "Cruel Summer." Again, the pure pop production detracts from the despair — *Bananarama*'s strongest point, then, was that it made its points despite that.

3 **True Confessions (London) 1986**

2 **Wow (London) 1987** The megahit "Venus" reinvented Bananarama completely, and it was downhill all the way. The best of both albums (the latter recorded with Jacqui O'Sullivan a faint shadow of Siobhan's towering magnificence) was condensed on *Greatest Hits* and even that was way too much.

4 **Pop Life (London) 1991**

3 **Please Yourself (London) 1992**

5 **Ultra Violet (Curb) 1995**

Selected Compilations and Archive Releases

7 **Greatest Hits (London) 1988** Commercially flawless but ultimately one-dimensional portrait of the artist as... oh yeah, a simple pop conveyor belt.

Shakespear's Sister LPs

7 **Sacred Heart (London) 1989**

8 **Hormonally Yours (London) 1992**

BAUHAUS

FORMED 1979 *(Northampton, England)*
ORIGINAL LINE-UP *Peter Murphy (b. 7/11/57 , Northampton —*
vocals); Daniel Ash (b. 7/31/57, Northampton — guitar);
David J (b. David Haskins, 4/24/57, Northampton — bass);
Kevin Haskins (b. 7/19/56, Northampton — drums)

Few bands ever exerted such a profound influence as Bauhaus, and the few that have are legends: Velvet Underground, Iggy Pop and the original Stooges, David Bowie (back when he was still Ziggy), and the Sex Pistols. Indeed, Bauhaus' own influences adhered strongly to that same unholy quartet. Daniel Ash still describes the first time he saw David Bowie on TV in 1972 as the single most important moment in his musical life, adding that the main reason he started hanging out with Peter Murphy in the first place was because Murphy looked like Bowie. In a high school playground in the provincial English town of Northampton, such distinctions were important.

Not that Bauhaus ever set out to rewrite musical history, of course. Their earliest gigs were simply chaos — the band gate-crashed other bands' shows, insisting they were friends of the support group, and played until they were thrown out or switched off.

Shamelessly theatrical, Bauhaus emerged in 1979 at the tail-end of the punk explosion, seeing themselves as a simple reaction to the increasingly po-faced seriousness of the groups that were breaking through around them. It was the age of Joy Division, Echo and the Bunnymen, and primal Simple Minds, dour, unsmiling doom-merchants whose only ambition, it seemed, was to dress their entire audience in trenchcoats.

Bauhaus had no such pretensions but they changed the way people dressed regardless, changed the way they thought, and utterly altered the course of British underground music through the early 1980s.

Having recorded the sequence of early demos later released on the *In the Studio* mini-album, Bauhaus' first single, "Bela Lugosi's Dead" (#8 UK indy), was released by the independent Small Wonder label in mid-1979, effectively kick-starting gothic rock a full two years before the media realized what was happening. In January 1980, "Dark Entries" (#17 UK indy) confirmed the ignition.

With "Terror Couple Kill Colonel" (#22 UK indy) and a cover of T. Rex's "Telegram Sam" (#3 UK indy) keeping the band on the singles chart, Bauhaus' first album, *In the Flat Field* (#72 UK, #1 UK indy), followed in October 1980. Dominating the indy listings for 105 weeks, it was more than a simple record, it was a clarion call to the host of bands now emerging around the banner Bauhaus had so inadvertently raised — Southern Death Cult, the Sex Gang Children, and Alien Sex Fiend. Suddenly, Bauhaus found themselves the pied pipers of a whole new movement. They hated the attention, loathed being lumped into a genre — gothic rock — that they had never intended even entering, let alone creating.

Peter Murphy of Bauhaus

© Jim Steinfeldt/Chansley Entertainment Archives

The dilemma didn't show, though. With the release of *Mask* (#30 UK) in 1981, Bauhaus began threatening way beyond the cosy confines of the indy listings. "Kick in the Eye" (#59 UK), an EP of the same title (#45 UK), and "The Passions of Lovers" (#56 UK) all emerged from the band's live repertoire as 45 rpm *pieces de resistance*, while June 1982's "Spirit" (#42) became such a favorite that Bauhaus would re-record it for their forthcoming third album.

Still, when Bauhaus did finally break through to a mass audience, after two years of slowly building their appeal, it was with what Ash described as another joke, first hatched during a John Peel session. "We were so sick of people saying we sounded like David Bowie, that we went out and recorded one of his songs, and made it sound as close to the original as we could." That was "Ziggy Stardust" (#15 UK), which gave Bauhaus their first top 20 hit and ensured that their next two singles, "Lagartija Nick" (#44 UK) and the mystifying "She's in Parties" (#26 UK), would receive similar attention.

Their third album, too, would profit from Bauhaus' humor. *The Sky's Gone Out* (#4 UK) became the band's most successful album yet and their most diverse as well — a well-rounded attempt to lift themselves far beyond the confines of gothic rock, even as their audience strived to pen them in. That those expectations still succeeded in killing the group was the one unresolved issue to haunt the members over the next 15 years.

Bauhaus shattered following one final album — one which was very eclectic, and largely acoustic. The group knew it was dying even as the record was made, and bowed out with a farewell concert (subsequently released as *Rest in Peace*) one week before *Burning from the Inside* (#13 UK) was released.

The band split in two — Murphy as a solo artist, his bandmates as Love and Rockets — and both enjoyed considerable success. The legacy of Bauhaus, however, was never far away, as a string of repetitive, but generally well-received compilations appeared through the 1980s. The group even returned to the chart in 1989 with *Swing the Heartache* (#169 US), a collection of the band's BBC sessions.

Throughout the 1990s, "Bauhaus to Reform" rumors circulated the goth community, particularly in America where neither band nor gothic music itself had ever completely fallen out of fashion. The four band members finally regrouped in 1998 for a four-month US/European tour, releasing the live *Gotham* album the following fall.

Also see the entries for "LOVE AND ROCKETS" on page 468, and "PETER MURPHY" on page 511.

Bauhaus LPs

9 In the Flat Field (4AD) 1980 An edgy epic piled high with some of Bauhaus' best-loved performances — the drily hypnotic "Spy in the Cab," the sonically unparalleled "Dark Entries" — and it's getting increasingly difficult to figure out what the goths saw in it all.

8 Mask (Beggars Banquet) 1981 Bauhaus' second album pushed even further beyond its predecessor's parameters, embracing the kind of artistic destiny which their old idol, David Bowie, would spend the next 15 years searching for; a blend of savage rock and controlled emotion, art as a heart attack.

10 The Sky's Gone Out (Beggars Banquet) 1982 From the droning "Silent Hedges" to the drifting "Exquisite Corpse," and peaking with the three-part paranoid ramblings of "The Three Shadows," Bauhaus' masterpiece owed nothing to anything else happening at the time.

"Spirit," re-recorded from a near hit single, and spot-on covers of Bowie's "Ziggy Stardust" and Eno's pulsating "Third Uncle" were the compass points from which the album set out, but it was the shattered riffola of "In the Night," the rank Sinatra of "All We Ever Wanted," and again, "The Three Shadows," performance art with poisoned paintbrush, which directed the traffic.

Black humor, bloated hubris and utterly preposterous imagery ("I slice off those rosy cheeks indeed") mass on the edge of musical apocalypse, and even the pretentiousness has a prettiness of its own. All they ever wanted was everything — and that's what they delivered.

8 Press the Eject and Give Me the Tape [LIVE] (Beggars Banquet) 1982 Over its original 11 tracks (and six CD bonus cuts) reveals a dimension that the band's studied studio work could never recapture — the sheer driving force of a band which simply couldn't afford to relax.

8 Burning from the Inside (Beggars Banquet) 1983 Bauhaus' final album, and the amputations are audible. Songs like "King Volcano" and "Slice of Life" showed just how far, and how far apart, the band members had grown; they were the sound of a band falling apart and making sure their decay was preserved on tape.

6 Gotham [LIVE] (Metropolis) 1999 Taken from 1998's Resurrection tour, the greatest hits played live like they never had been before — correctly. Live and studio versions of Dead Can Dance's "Severance" offer the only new song in sight. A second appeared on 2000's *Heavy Metal 2* soundtrack.

Selected Compilations and Archive Releases

7 1979–1983 (Beggars Banquet) 1985 Four albums into two; Bauhaus from cradle to grave, but "Bela Lugosi"'s alive, not dead.

8 Swing the Heartache — The BBC Sessions (Beggars Banquet) 1989 A better compilation with a tougher edge — all they did for the BBC.

7 Rest in Peace — The Final Concert (NEMO) 1993 The final concert indeed, in all its dry-iced and damp-eyed splendor. A well-paced set leaves no stone unturned, suffers few departures, and wraps up with a six-song encore which left the venue breathless.

6 Live in the Studio 1979 (Beggars Banquet) 1997 An eight-track, 25-minute rehearsal inadvertently taped by the band and never recorded over. Raw, rough, and blistered by the shattered promise of punk's sordid dream, it captures Bauhaus before anything else got its claws in them. Interestingly,"Honeymoon Croon" sounded like a psychotic "My Sharona."

8 Crackle (Beggars Banquet) 1998 A fairly standard best-of package, except... "Bela" makes its long-playing debut and still sounds as staggering as it did first time out. Elsewhere, 16 tracks only gnaw the surface of the true best-of Bauhaus.

Further Reading

Dark Entries: Bauhaus & Beyond by Ian Shirley (SAF, UK, 1994).

BEASTIE BOYS

FORMED *1982 (New York, NY)*
ORIGINAL LINE-UP *Michael Diamond (b. 11/20/65, New York — vocals); Adam Yauch (b. 8/15/67, Brooklyn — bass); John Berry (guitar); Kate Schellenbach (b. 1/5/66, New York — drums)*

Nobody who caught the Beastie Boys' earliest performances — a beer-soaked barrage of noise and obscenity spewing from the stage at Yauch's 15th birthday party in 1982 — could ever have predicted that within a decade, the band would rank amongst the most influential American acts of the alternative era; that they would be almost singlehandedly responsible for pulling hip-hop culture off the streets and into the strip malls; that, almost two decades after they began, the Beastie Boys would be a phenomenon which transcended cultural boundaries as effortlessly as their music once trashed musical ones. In fact, most people who caught them early on were more concerned that they never catch them again.

The band formed from the ashes of the Young Aborigines, featuring John Berry, Kate Schellenbach (both later to reappear in Luscious Jackson), Jeremy Shatten, and Mike Diamond. Adam Yauch replaced Shatten and, as the Beastie Boys, the band set about establishing themselves on the New York hardcore scene. At a time when hardcore was accelerating far beyond its original roots in punk, to the point where speed and scatology alone appeared to concern the music's progenitors, the Beastie Boys were faster, and ruder, than most; a blur of unfocussed rage and ranting which was preserved, if not truly caged, on their debut release, 1982's *Polly Wog Stew*.

It was with the arrival of former Adam Horovitz, ex-the Young and the Useless, that the Beastie Boys' vision began to shift away from the frenzy of hardcore and into an area roughly defined by rap culture — "Cooky Puss" (#17 UK indy), the 1983 single which unveiled the Beasties' new direction, was widely regarded as simply another white boy parody, but dismiss the juvenilia and the Beasties — now lining up as Mike D (Diamond), MCA (Yauch, who also doubled as Nathaniel Hornblower, the band's video director), and King Ad-Rock (Horovitz) — were suddenly revealed as able, and absolutely unselfconscious, practitioners.

That much was apparent from the band members' willingness to acknowledge — even celebrate — their own white, middle-class roots. Rap was great, but so were punk and metal, and the Beasties' achievement would be to blend all three together in a sound which would slash racial boundaries and stereotypes to shreds. Of course it was the juvenilia which caught the ear first, a relentless wall of raucous obnoxiousness, descending into crude sexuality and mindless teen rebellion.

Signing to Def Jam, a street label founded by fellow NYU alumni Rick "RR" Rubin and rap promoter Russell Simmons, and with turntable DJ Doctor Dre added to the band's arsenal, the *Rock Hard* EP (produced by Rubin) was a celebration of all this. Featuring a wild AC/DC sample, "Rock Hard" would become one of the band's most readily recognizable tracks.

The Beasties' next single, "She's on It," was released just as the band joined Madonna's "Virgin" tour, and immediately ran into trouble. According to Mike D, "it was one of the two songs that we would perform to the boos and shocked expressions of her audience every night." Apparently it was Madonna's intervention alone which prevented the band from being thrown off the tour, but even she could not have realized precisely what the band was on the verge of achieving.

Licensed to Ill (#1 US, #7 UK), the Beastie Boys' debut album, would be popularly acclaimed as the first rap album to ever top the US chart. Leading off with "Fight for Your Right (to Party)" (#7 US, #11 UK), following through with "No Sleep Till Brooklyn" (#14 UK), a reissue of "She's on It" (#10 UK), "Girls" (#34 UK), and "Brass Monkey" (#48 US), a powerhouse album was rendered even more impressive by the ease with which the Beasties themselves slipped into the knuckleheaded, beer-swilling roles which their music seemingly demanded they take.

By the time the Beastie Boys arrived in Switzerland for the 1986 Montreaux Pop Festival, the album was on its way to selling 4 million copies and their Stateside superstardom was already assured. European notoriety could not be far behind — particularly after one of the band's press aides planted a story in the sensation-hungry UK tabloids alleging that the Beasties had been introduced to a group of sick children and laughed at them.

According to London's *Daily Mirror*, "the world's nastiest pop group... taunted leukemia victims, calling them cripples... their sickening jibes at young cancer sufferers have made them outcasts on the eve of their first British tour."

Further increasingly preposterous allegations followed: in Montreaux, they wrecked a hotel bar and threw beer at other guests; in Hamburg, they daubed feces on their hotel room walls; in Paris, they started a riot; and everywhere the band went, Volkswagon owners were left speechless with rage, as rampaging fans tore the VW logos off the hoods of their vehicles in emulation of the clunky pendants their new heroes habitually sported.

British hotels announced that the group was not welcome in their establishments; politician Geoffrey Dickens demanded, "I want these diabolical creatures banned from these shores." But the Beasties were unfazed. "Sure we're nasty," Def Jam's Simmons responded. "We're exactly what American teenagers have been for the past 30 years." Except that wasn't the intention. Yauch reflected, "we actually became what we'd set out to make fun of. By drinking so much beer and acting like sexist macho jerks, we actually became just that."

The band toured America, now headlining the same size venues they'd opened for Madonna in. They were featured in Run DMC's *Tougher than Leather* movie; Horovitz made his appearances in TV's *The Equalizer* and the movies *Lost Angels* and *The Santa Ana Project*; in the UK, a novelty act, Morris and the Minors, charted with a Beasties parody,

"Stutter Rap (No Sleep Till Bedtime)" (#4 UK), and even when it emerged that the entire Montreaux incident had simply been fabricated by an over-zealous PR officer, still the cachet of callous, rebellious youth clung to the Beasties like a well-loved cardigan.

It was still intact three years later when the band finally emerged from a long, bitter estrangement from Rubin and Simmons with a new album, a new label (Capitol), a new sound, and a new attitude. Which is probably why *Paul's Boutique* (#14 US, #44 UK) was such a disappointment when it arrived... and such a delight to rediscover once the shock had worn off.

Despite charting high, sales of *Paul's Boutique* and the attendant single "Hey Ladies" (#36 US) dropped off swiftly. It is only hindsight which has re-evaluated the album, to a point where it is now widely regarded amongst the most crucial releases of the era. Certainly its impact on the hip-hop scene is incalculable — a blending of so many of the movement's own disparate threads and completely unshackled by the barriers by which the scene's own originators still abided. At the time, the Beasties had little alternative but to lurch into another lengthy hiatus.

A three year layoff followed, during which the Beasties established their own studio and Grand Royal label before finally re-emerging with *Check Your Head* (#10 US) in 1992 and the singles "So What'cha Want" (#93 US) and "Pass the Mic" (#47 UK). Guest appearances from Biz Markie and Ted Nugent (together during the aptly titled "The Biz Versus

© Henry Diltz/Chansley Entertainment Archives

the Nuge") and a triumphantly nostalgic assault upon the Boys' own hardcore past, "Time for Livin'," established the opposing poles from which the album would work, although it would soon become apparent that *Check Your Head* was little more than a dry run for the Beasties next move, the genre-busting *Ill Communication* (#1 US, #10 UK).

A blistering album, *Ill Communication* stated for all time that the Beastie Boys had finally transcended every generic pigeonhole there was, simply by sampling pieces of all of them. A British tour climaxed with a phenomenal Glastonbury Festival set in June 1994, just as the band's latest single, "Get It Together" (#19 UK), became their first major hit in seven years (it was followed by "Sure Shot" — #27 UK); and while the Beasties stole the show at 1994's Lollapalooza tour, the world's first acid-funk-jazz-hardcore-rap-techno-lounge album established the Beasties' inalienable right to wander wherever their musical inclination took them.

The band's outside interests, too, were spreading even further afield. Following their creation of the annual Tibetan Freedom Concerts, the mini-albums *Root Down* (#50 US) and *The In Sound from Way Out* (#45 US) were the most overt manifestation of this freedom — the first a raucous live collection and the second an instrumental collection which took the mid-'90s fascination for space-age bachelor pad music, then overlaid it with Afro Funk Lite.

1998's *Hello Nasty* (#1 US, #1 UK) and the singles "Intergalactic" (#28 US, #5 UK) and "Body Movin'" (#15 UK) continued to prove how thoroughly the Beasties had absorbed the lessons and the freedoms now available to them — a conclusion backed up by the revolutionary nature of their final release of the century, the near-career-spanning anthology, *The Sound of Science* (#19 US).

Available in its "official" form through conventional commercial outlets, the album was also obtainable via the internet, with purchasers able to personally select their own 40 strong track listing from the 150 available on the site.

Beastie Boys LPs

9 Licensed to Ill (Def Jam) 1986 An anthemic smorgasbord of adolescence and stupidity, gleefully spray painting goonish graffiti across America's fat-head frat-boy consciousness.

10 Paul's Boutique (Capitol) 1989 Gone were the brainless party chants; gone was the abrasive rock-from-the-city-streets rhythm. Opening (and closing) with a presentiment of everything which would one day be called trip-hop, *Paul's Boutique* linked the Beasties with the Dust Brothers production team of John King and Mike Simpson, themselves hot from their recent collaborations with Tone Loc and Young MC. According to Simpson, the Dust Brothers wrote 95% of the new album's music ("and the Beasties wrote 95% of the lyrics"), a collaboration which utterly reinvented the Beastie Boys on the cutting edge of avant-garde hip-hop and shed the specter of their Def Jam days for good.

7 Check Your Head (Capitol) 1992 More of the same, although in simply repeating, rather than refining, the avant-garde edge of *Boutique*, *Head* paled poor in honest comparison.

9 Ill Communication (Grand Royal) 1994 Stellar throughout, the glorious cheese of a '70s revival hit hard in the head by the Beastie's own rap vision. Where would 1994 have been without "Sure Shot" and "Sabotage"?

8 Hello Nasty (Grand Royal) 1998 A dramatic celebration of the Beasties' old-school past, even as it constructed a newer-than-new school future... then mashed them both together into one invigorating whole.

Selected Compilations and Archive Releases

6 Some Old Bullshit (Grand Royal) 1994 A collection of early, and long out-of-print hardcore releases — most of which weren't particularly good even at the time.

9 The Sound of Science (Grand Royal) 1999 Though all but ignoring life before *Paul's Boutique*, 42 tracks trace the Beasties from "Cookie Puss" on — with a few rarities, oddballs, and slabs of pure idiocy (Elton John's "Bennie and the Jets") to interrupt the innovation.

Further Reading

Rhyming & Stealing: A History of... by Angus Batey (Omnibus,UK, 1998).

BEAT HAPPENING

FORMED 1984 *(Olympia, WA)*
ORIGINAL LINE-UP *Calvin Johnson (vocals, guitar); Heather Lewis (vocals, guitar); Bret Lunsford (vocals, drums)*

Although the group itself had effectively already disbanded by the time Nirvana and co. thrust Seattle into the forefront of American mainstream attention, the pioneering enterprises of Beat Happening nevertheless served as a reminder that not every sound emanating from the Pacific Northwest needed to be ground into the pigeonhole-marked grunge — at the same time as proving that grunge itself had antecedents which utterly defied conventional wisdom.

Formed in Olympia by KAOS radio DJ Calvin Johnson and Heather Lewis in 1982 (Bret Lunsford joined the following year), and debuting with a friend named Heather Laura, as Laura, Heather and Calvin, on the Seattle Sub Pop label's 1983 sampler *Sub Pop 9*, Beat Happening challenged orthodoxy on every level available.

The simple three-piece line-up eschewed bass in a manner which echoed, but never aped, the Cramps' own experiments in that direction. Indeed, the resultant sound was as delicately spectral as the Cramps was forebodingly off-center, and across two five-song cassette releases, the *Beat Happening* and *Three Tea Breakfast* EPs (the latter partially written and recorded while the band members vacationed in Japan), Beat Happening created a virtuous, but purposefully un-virtuostic sound, both divorced from, but desperately dedicated to, capturing a punk ethic which echoed back to the earliest days of PNW garage rock.

Linking, unsurprisingly, with local messiah Greg Sage of the Wipers, work began on Beat Happening's debut album, live and low-fi, in December 1983. The first two cuts recorded became their debut single, "Our Secret"; further sessions the following fall would make it onto the finished album.

That even the band's fans described the 18.23 minute-long result as "amateurishly charming" was an unfortunate by-product of the process; Beat Happening's primary objective was to make records which retained the freshness of the ideas that spawned the songs in the first place. This lack of complication and contrivance would remain Beat Happening's touchstone for the remainder of their career.

Regular gigs at the Tropicana in Olympia saw the band play their hometown at least once a month through 1984. The band were also regulars on new K compilations, of course. New releases, however, remained thin on the ground. It would be 1987 before the second Beat Happening single arrived, "Look Around," followed by "Honey Pot" in the new year.

Capturing the same aura of unamplified amplification as Jonathan Richman's Modern Lovers experimented with on their wryly titled *Rock and Roll With* album, 1988's *Crashing Through* EP and *Jamboree* album were the first Beat Happening records to receive large-scale distribution, thanks to a link-up between Johnson's K label and the rapidly expanding Sub Pop label in Seattle. (Johnson was a contributor to the original Sub Pop fanzine, several years before Beat Happening's first release.)

Further exposure was granted by the involvement of producers Steve Fisk, Mark Lanegan, and Gary Lee Connor, with an EP split between Beat Happening and the latter pair's Screaming Trees, which enjoyed enough sufficient action to guarantee a warm welcome for the band's own next single, the classic "Foggy Eyes," and album.

Unfortunately, 1989's *Black Candy* dropped the ball somewhat, and though tours with Fugazi during 1990 and 1991 were well-received, it would be two years before a new Beat Happening album, *Dreamy* (and the "Red Head Walking" and "Nancy Sin" singles), emerged to paper over the cracks. (In the interim, the 26-track *1983–85* was released to round up the band's pre-Sub Pop catalog while the group maintained their penchant for appearing on compilations.) The higher the group's profile seemed to climb, the less interest the band members — Johnson in particular — seemed to have.

The K label was flourishing, while Johnson was also a prime mover behind the International Pop Underground Festival in Olympia in 1991. Over 50 bands — including the Melvins, L7, Seaweed, Bikini Kill, the Fastbacks, and Billy Childish — appeared. (Highlights of the festival later appeared on a K double album.)

Johnson also moved towards the formation of two new musical projects — the Halo Benders (with Doug Martsch of Built to Spill and producer Fisk) and Dub Narcotic. Following the 1991 "Seahunt" single, there would be just one further Beat Happening album, then, 1992's *You Turn Me On*, and the accompanying single, "Not a Care in the World."

Assurances that Beat Happening have not broken up continue to be issued from K; in the meantime, Johnson has maintained a profile through collaborations with Beck (1994's *One Foot in the Grave* LP), Pansy Division, and more.

Beat Happening LPs

6 Beat Happening (K) 1985

8 Jamboree (Sub Pop/K) 1988 A rougher, more varied set than the defiantly monotone debut, where ghosts of The Cramps and the grunge-to-come collide in deft delirium.

4 Black Candy (Sub Pop/K) 1989 Though the title track kicks critical ass, the rest of the album sounds like BH didn't actually know they were making it. Or that someone was taping the rehearsal.

8 Dreamy (Sub Pop/K) 1991

7 You Turn Me On (Sub Pop/K) 1992 While still determinedly minimalistic, *Turn* is indeed a turning point, as Beat Happening exhibit a maturity and sound quality never dreamt of in the past.

Selected Compilations and Archive Releases

7 1983–85 (K) 1990 26 tracks trace from the first single through EPs to the first album, and on into the world of out-takes and exclusive compilation cuts. Draining, but complete.

BECK

BORN *Beck Campbell, 7/8/70 (Kansas City, KS)*

The son of former Warhol superstar Bibbe Hansen and blue-grass musician David Campbell, Hansen is also the grandson (and grand-nephew) of Al and Channing Hansen, members of the anti-art situationist movement of the late 1960s. He dropped out of high school in the ninth grade, performed with a poetry troupe called Youthless, and in 1989, traveled to New York where he worked the Lower East Side folk circuit.

He returned to L.A. in 1990, playing coffee bars and small clubs, before forming the band Ten Ton Lid with Martha Atwell, concentrating on American folk music. He was again working solo, however, when he was spotted at the Silverlake Coffee House by Bong Load label chief Tom Rothrock.

Hansen's first single, "To See That Woman of Mine," followed in late 1992, backed by the similarly classic "MTV Makes Me Want to Smoke Crack." It was followed in January 1993 by the fruits of a recent session with hip-hop producer Karl Stephenson, "Loser." Originally released as a limited edition (500 copies) 12-inch single, "Loser" initially appeared to pass by unnoticed.

A cassette-only 17-song album, *Golden Feelings*, and the defiantly low-fi EP, *Western Harvest Field by Moonlight* followed, but elsewhere, "Loser" was beginning to pick up steam. It caught the imagination of Seattle alternative radio station KNDD DJ Marco Collins, who slammed it into rotation, KROQ in LA followed, and suddenly radio programmers across America were playing it.

Courted by a slew of record labels, Hansen eventually signed with Geffen, having first ensured that not only would he have complete control over what they released in his name, he also had the right to take material to other, independent, labels. They agreed, and having rewarded them with the most inevitable hit of the year, "Loser" (#10 US, #15 UK), Hansen then delivered a debut album which was recorded for $200 and had already been available as a privately released cassette.

Mellow Gold (#13 US, #41 UK), the flagship album of the underground low-fi movement, followed "Loser" up the charts, riding on the back of a slew of almost slavishly rave reviews. The singles "Beercan" and "Pay No Mind" followed, together with a phenomenally successful tour featuring the Presidents of the United States of America as Hansen's backing band. Of course the novelty aura which surrounded that band did nothing to dampen the feeling that Hansen, too, was a mere passing fad, all the more so after Hansen and Presidents' guitarist Chris Ballew reinvented themselves as Caspar and the Mollusc, and released the "Twig" single. (The pair also guested on the Geraldine Fibbers' "Blue Cross.")

The singer, however, was not playing ball. He started work on his second Geffen album almost immediately. In the meantime, a handful of oddball indy releases were unleashed to keep collectors busy — *Stereopathic Soul Manure*, a compilation of home demos dating back to 1988, and the *One Foot in the Grave* collaboration with Beat Happening's Calvin Johnson. (Hansen also released a single on Johnson's K label, "It's All in Your Mind".)

Hansen's second Geffen album, *O-de-lay* (#16 US, #17 UK) was to prove even bigger than its predecessor. "What Walt Whitman did for riverboat captains," one critic wrote, "Beck does for Karaoke and jeans." Hansen insisted that his studio was right in between two others — one holding Black Sabbath, the other the Muppets. "I was sort of in the middle of the sandwich," he said, adding that he and the Dust Brothers tapped into both studios, then smuggled the results onto the album — "on a subliminal level."

With both Noel Gallagher and Aphex Twin providing remixes, "Devil's Haircut" (#94 US, #22 UK) hit in mid-1996; further singles "Where It's At" (#61 US, #35 UK), "The New Pollution" (#78 US, #14 UK), and "Sissyneck" (#24 UK) were accompanied by a string of high-profile live shows, including the first Tibetan Freedom festival in San Francisco and a series of sold-out European shows in the fall.

"Where It's At" won Best Male Video at the 1996 MTV awards, while "Devil's Haircut" and "New Pollution" would scoop five more in 1997 between them. Then, with the commercial response sewn up, *Odelay* became one of the critics' most-lauded albums of the year. Hansen was nominated for three Grammys, and took two of them: Best Alternative Performance and Best Male Rock Perfomance. He also received "Artist of the Year" awards from *Rolling Stone* and *Spin* in America; *Mojo* and *Q* in the UK.

Although Hansen's commercial profile remained high through 1997/98, with the singles "Jack Ass" (#73 US), "Deadweight" (#23 UK), and "Tropicalia" (#39 UK) contractual wranglings between Hansen and both Geffen and Bongload did much to mar the release of 1998's *Mutations* (#13 US, #24 UK).

Recorded with Radiohead producer Nigel Godrich and featuring string arrangements by his own father, Hansen personally considered the album to be an experimental side project; certainly he insisted Geffen had no right to release it as a full album and while the dispute was eventually settled amicably, future releases were on hold for some months. At one point, Hansen even stopped work in the studio, although he continued touring across the US through late 1997 and on to Australia in January 1998.

He also dropped out of a projected collaboration with rapper Puff Daddy, rather than take part in the intended remake of Elton John's "Bennie and the Jets," and turned down the lead role in John Waters' *Pecker*. He preferred, he said, "to go where the wind blows me."

In May 1998, Hansen premiered *Playing with Matches*, a performance art piece composed with his grandfather, while he spent much of the second half of the year on the road in the US and Australia. He continued working in the studio, however, and in mid-1999, surprised all observers by announcing a new album to be released by Geffen, before Christmas.

Midnite Vultures (#34 US, #19 UK) and the accompanying single "Sexxlaws" were recorded between July 1998 and June 1999 with the Dust Brothers co-producing two tracks ("Debra" and "Hollywood Freaks"). Evidence of just how deeply he had become embedded in the American psyche, however, was provided when he became the sole remotely contemporary artist invited to appear at Radio City Music Hall's centenary celebrations in New York City in January 2000. (He was also asked to entertain the masses in Times Square on New Year's Eve, but turned it down.)

Beck LPs

6 Golden Feelings (Sonic Enemy) 1993 Cassette-only presentation of the low-fi birth of Beck.

5 A Western Harvest Field by Moonlight (Fingerpaint) 1994

7 Mellow Gold (DGC) 1994 If Beck is a spokesman for the postmodern crowd, then this platter presents the patter in the guise of old-time folk, shot through with a hefty dose of idiosyncratic grandeur. Plus, of course, it gave Generation X something else to complain about, as the media hijacked the anthemic "Loser".

6 One Foot in the Grave (K) 1994 All guitar-picking, folk-singing, and string-twanging; an old-time down-home songfest with Beat Happening's Calvin Johnson lending his pipes to the brew.

7 Odelay (DGC) 1996 An action-packed speedway of hip-hop, folk, funk, and blues, *Odelay* was produced by the Dust Brothers, the revered mixmasters who piloted the Beastie Boys through the labyrinthine delights of *Paul's Boutique*. Echoing that album's glorious irreverence, *Odelay* gleefully mines the '70s, '80s, and '90s for their — and its own — best moments.

6 Mutations (Geffen) 1998 Originally intended for independent release, *Mutations* rounds up four years worth of unreleased (and sometimes unformed) songs, recorded live in the studio with Radiohead producer Nigel Godrich.

5 Midnite Vultures (Geffen) 1999 Busily mines the kind of territory Love & Rockets might have pursued if Prince took over their production — then lifts Marilyn Manson for "Get Real Paid" just to keep the retro beast at bay. Sadly, *Vultures'* best ideas are the loops and sound effects.

Selected Compilations and Archive Releases

5 Stereopathic Soul Manure (Flipside) 1994 Patchy collection of material cut between 1988 and 1994.

Further Reading

Lord Only Knows by Steven Hamer (Omnibus, UK, 1998).

BELLE AND SEBASTIAN

FORMED *1996 (Glasgow, Scotland)*

ORIGINAL LINE-UP *Stuart Murdoch (b. 1967 — vocals); Stuart David (bass); Chris Geddes (keyboards); Isobel Campbell (cello); Sarah Martin (violin); Stevie Jackson (guitar, vocals); Richard Colburn (drums)*

Belle (Stuart Murdoch) and Sebastian (Stuart David) met in an all-night cafe in January 1996. According to legend, they recruited the first five musicians they found and started playing shows in the oddest places they could — libraries, church crypts, and house parties — keeping the proceedings alive by rehearsing as little as possible.

Murdoch, at the time, was attending a music business course being run at Glasgow's Stowe College by former Associates frontman Alan Rankine. One of the course's aims was to take two songs by one of the class and follow them through from recording to release as a single on Rankine's own Electric Honey label. When the class elected one of Murdoch's demo tapes for the honor, he gathered up Belle and Sebastian, spent three days in the studio, and emerged with sufficient material for an entire album.

Tigermilk was released by Electric Honey in summer 1996, a limited edition of 1,000 copies which sold out within months (the album would finally be reissued in 1999, by which time copies of the original were selling for upwards of $600 on the collectors market), while BBC radio disc jockeys John Peel and Mark Radcliffe waxed deliriously about the music.

The band was shocked. "We thought it was okay," Colburn admitted. But July brought the band's first BBC radio session, for Radcliffe, "then record companies and fans started calling, and we thought 'My God, what have we done?'" Belle and Sebastian signed with the Jeepster label in August 1996, and in November, rush-released their sophomore album, *If You're Feeling Sinister*.

Blessed with vocals straight out of Donovan's '60s, and a musical echo of vintage Boomtown Rats, topped off by a West Coast vibe tinged with unbridled Scots romanticism, the band's eclectic appeal was exacerbated by a handful of darkly appropriate gigs with Tindersticks. According to *Alternative Press*, "the songs catapult themselves out of the kind of void the Pogues might have filled, if they'd tippled cappucino instead of... name your poison." *Spin* preferred a more pedestrian collision between Beat Happening and Tindersticks.

Plans for an American release of *Sinister* in early 1997 convinced Belle and Sebastian to delay a conventional follow-up album in favor of a triptych of EPs: *Dogs on Wheels* — incredibly, the band's first ever 7-inch (#58 UK), comprising a clutch of early demos; *Lazy Line Painter Jane* (#41 UK); and 3.6.9. *Seconds of Light* (#32 UK). All three would finally receive a US release in 2000.

Each of the EPs dented the UK chart at the same time as *Sinister* was stirring up the US college listings; one San Francisco station would place the album at #5 in its year's end Top 100, the highest placed British band on the listing. Belle and Sebastian made their American debut at the CMJ festival in September 1997.

Accompanied by the single "This Is Just a Modern Rock Song," *The Boy with the Arab Strap* (#12 UK), Belle and Sebastian's intriguingly named third album, followed in 1998, cornering the market in lachrymose post-Nick Drakery, but adding little to either of its predecessors.

A fascinating solo album from Campbell, *The Green Fields of Foreverland*, kept the homefires burning, together with the much anticipated reissue of *Tigermilk* (#12 UK). The band also made their long-awaited British television debut on *Apocalypse Tube*, broadcast on cable on November 20, 1999 and as part of Channel 4's millennial celebrations on January 1, 2000 previewing material set for their fourth album. Meanwhile, Stuart David's first novel, *Nalda Said* (IMP), was published in late 1999.

Belle and Sebastian LPs

[9] Tigermilk (Electric Honey) 1996 Three years of unavailability saw original pressings of this album soar in value on the collectors' market — then it was reissued and its stock rocketed too. A gentle masterpiece, utterly in debt to Nick Drake (and a bit of Donovan too), but also utterly unique, from the wry liner biography to the Yes riff semi-ripped for "You're Just a Baby." The manic spite of the opening "The State I Am In" buoys the occasional sag; that and the slickly loose instrumentation, harmonies which haunt the fringe of fear, and a wealth of emotionally crippled reflection.

[7] If You're Feeling Sinister (Enclave) 1996 Wailing harps and Motown bass defy you to call it easy listening, but still Murdoch's vocals are a distinctly Donovan-esque reminder of a simpler era you never knew existed.

[8] The Boy with the Arab Strap (Matador) 1998 Light as a feather and fragile as glass, in anyone else's hands, *Boy* would be precocious, and bore-dering on fey. B&S, however, transform even those qualities into delicate breezy pop, accented by orchestral strings and then pumped up with hints of rock, a postcard for the '90s.

[7] Fold Your Hands, Child, You Walk Like a Peasant (Matador) 2000 Minor-key comedown as the same sad lovers sing the same sad refrains and "Nice Day For a Sulk" seems aptly voiced indeed.

Isobel Campbell LP

[6] The Green Fields of Foreverland (Jeepster) 1999 Sparse pianos and flutes echo low (and Low) and anyone who thought "Afterhours" was the best thing the Velvets ever did will have a brand new friend indeed.

BELLY

FORMED 1992 *(Providence, RI)*
ORIGINAL LINE-UP *Tanya Donelly (b. 7/14/66 — vocals, guitar); Thomas Gorman (b. 5/20/66 — guitar); Fred Absong (bass); Chris Gorman (b. 7/29/67 — drums)*

Tanya Donelly is for all intents and purposes a one-woman alternative rock cottage industry, and her band, Belly, was the perfect example of the fast-rising and combusting star ethic of the 1990's alternative scene, reflective of the sorry trend of becoming a smash hit just in time to see the kids move on to the next big thing. Given time, the band could have become a mainstay of the mid-decade's better output.

Donelly first came to note as a member of Throwing Muses, a vital part of the burgeoning 1980's East Coast music scene. Formed by Donelly, her half-sister Kristin Hersh (guitar, vocals), Elaine Adamedes (bass), and David Narcizo (drums), the band didn't really get going until 1985 when Leslie Langston (bass) replaced Adamedes as the band geared up for their first full album release. Preceded by the single "Chains Change" (#6 UK indy), September 1986's *Throwing Muses* (#7 UK indy) saw the band readily capturing college radio and the underground vibe, and a fame which quickly spread up and down the coast,

The Fat Skier (#2 UK indy), *House Tornado* (#3 UK indy), and *Hunkpapa* (#59 UK, #2 UK indy) followed, together with a second European hit single, "Dizzy" (#4 UK); Donelly, however, would leave in 1992 following *The Real Ramona* (#26 UK), while Hersh would also depart to carve her own successful, solo career.

She had already tested the extra-curricular waters — albeit briefly — when Donelly and Pixies guitarist/vocalist, Kim Deal, united as the Breeders in Boston in 1990. Initially working with bassist Josephine Woods (ex-Perfect Disaster) and drummer Shannon Doughty (b. Britt Walford, aka Mike Hunt, ex-Slint), the band existed solely as a creative outlet that was very separate from their other projects, and released their first album, *Pod* (#22 UK), in May 1990.

Donelly would stay through the recording of the EP *Safari* before she quit both to form her new band, Belly. (Like the Throwing Muses, the Breeders would continue apace throughout the nineties with Deal's sister Kelly replacing Donelly.) Belly, though, was not just another alt-rock super group — it was the realization of Donelly's vision. After a start in very late 1991, the band released the *Slowdust* EP in June 1992. Produced by Gil Norton (Pixies), the EP masterfully introduced the band's hypnotic, edgy, rock sound to an already expectant crowd — her past alone assured Donelly a strong fanbase.

The band's next release, the *Gepetto* EP, debuted in November. Belly, meanwhile, were busy putting the finishing touches to their first full-length, *Star* (#59 US, #2 UK), for release in January 1993. Written almost exclusively by Donelly, it spawned several singles — the defining "Feed the Tree" (#95 US, #32 UK) was followed by a remixed version of "Gepetto" (#49 UK) and "Low Red Moon".

Crashing the Grammy awards that year, the band were given a critical nod with a nomination for Best New Act. By 1994, *Star* had gone gold, and the band were bowing to accolades from fans and critics alike. They won "Best Modern Rock Act" at the Boston Music Awards while *Star* took "Debut Album of the Year" as Belly became the perfect demonstration of the ease with which good alternative bands could cross over into the mainstream while still retaining their own vision and sound.

Absong left the band in May 1993 and was replaced by bassist Gail Greenwood (b. 3/10/60), as the band headed back to the studio, this time at Island Records' Compass Point hideaway in the Bahamas, to begin work on their follow-up set. *King* (#57 US, #6 UK) hit the streets in February 1995 and what the band hoped would catapult them further into the annals of alternative history, instead backfired when the album was declared both a commercial and critical failure. Two singles were peeled from the set, "Now They'll Sleep" (#28 UK) in January 1995, while the prophetic "Seal My Fate" (#35 UK) followed the album in July.

Belly continued to tour, but never quite rebounded or regained momentum after *King*. A US outing with the fast-rising Catherine Wheel saw the English band steal the show on a nightly basis, despite the close friendship between the two groups. Donelly would even appear as guest vocalist on Catherine Wheel's "Judy Staring at the Sun" single, and perhaps it was indicative of how far her star had fallen, when that became her hosts' first non-charting single since their debut, four years before.

Belly disbanded in the summer of 1996. Greenwood joined L7, while Donelly embarked on a solo career, launched with *Lovesongs for Underdogs* (#36 UK) and the singles "Pretty Deep" (#55 UK) and "The Bright Light" (#64 UK).

Belly LPs

7 Star (Sire) 1993 Eschewing art school politic for pure pop hooks and catchy beats, Belly forge fresh ground by reprising three tracks from the *Slow Dust* EP ("Dusted," "Slow Dog," and "Low Red Moon") then filling the gaps with friends and relatives of the inescapable "Feed the Tree".

8 King (Sire) 1995 With former Who producer Glyn Johns at the helm, powerful, poppy, and Brit-slick as only a Boston band can be.

Tanya Donelly Solo LPs

6 Lovesongs for Underdogs (Sire) 1997

Breeders LPs

4 Pod (4AD) 1990 Steve Albini's production was as much an emotional crutch for Deal as a musical outlet for Donelly — or so it sounds. Rougher than it should have been, the set is dominated by a sense of Pixies castoffs, with barely a thrown-out muse in sight.

8 Last Splash (4AD) 1993 Much better. *Splash* makes waves, a raw punk ethic driven through with pure pop and good old guitar hooks. Add a dose of '70's retro and the massive "Cannonball" smash, and voilà — success.

Throwing Muses LPs

7 Throwing Muses (Sire) 1986

5 House Tornado (Sire) 1988

6 Hunkpapa (Sire) 1989

8 The Real Ramona (Sire) 1991

6 Red Heaven (Sire) 1992

7 The Curse (live) (Sire) 1992

4 University (Sire) 1995

4 Limbo (Rykodisc) 1996

Selected Compilations and Archive Releases

7 In a Doghouse (Rykodisc) 1998

BEVIS FROND

BORN *Nick Saloman, 1953 (London, England)*

As the putative head of a psychedelic revival which the Anglophone press has spent 20 years predicting, but which has still to fully materialize, and as co-publisher of the *Ptolemaic Terrascope* fanzine which itself has done much to whip those predictions into shape, the Bevis Frond remains one of the great unsung, but seldom under-estimated, heroes of the freak-pop underground. Utterly independent, and certainly untouched by even the vaguest commercial reasoning, the one man Frond has devoted his career to an increasingly surreal series of albums and recordings, any one of which can be described as representative, all of which are superlatively individual.

More than three decades have elapsed since the schoolboy Saloman formed the Bevis Frond Museum in 1967, yet band and intentions remain as pure as they ever were in his childlike imagination — a point proven when 1987's *Through the Looking Glass* retrospective unearthed one song from a tape he made twenty years before. According to Saloman, it was better than anything else on the record.

Saloman actually made his vinyl debut supplementing the folk duo Oddsocks on the 1975 album *Men of the Moment* but it would be 1980 before he emerged in his own right, fronting the Von Trap Family across a well-received EP, *Brand New Thrill*, and a few gigs around London and the south. When that band broke up in 1981, Saloman formed Room 13 from the wreckage and was then forced to retrieve his own life from a similar mess, after an accident involving his motorbike and a road-working hole in the road.

Severely injured and forced to wait three years before receiving any compensation, Saloman was thus out of action until 1986 — a period during which he stockpiled the songs which would eventually begin appearing on the first Bevis Frond album in 1987.

Working on a newly purchased portastudio, Saloman reactivated the Woronzow label he formed for the Von Trap Family in 1980, then pressed up 250 copies of the album, *Miasma*. A copy found its way to the psychedelic specialist record store, Funhouse, in Margate who ordered as many copies as Saloman could provide — "so I pressed up another 250 and it just kept selling."

A maddening hotchpotch of Hendrix, Howe, and howling, *Miasma* was recorded for fun. *Inner Marshland*, the second Bevis Frond album, was made in the knowledge that Saloman now had an audience — and a hungry one. Before the end of 1987, Saloman had recorded and released two more albums, *Lord of the Dark Skies*, credited to the Outskirts of Infinity and featuring Saloman, guitarist Barri Watts, and drummer Rick Gunther, and the two-disc retrospective *Bevis Through the Looking Glass*, featuring out-takes from its predecessors, plus glimpses back into Saloman's musical past.

1988 opened with the so aptly named *Acid Jam*, a guitar workout performed by Bevis Frond, Mick Wills, and the Outskirts of Infinity. The album caused considerable discontent among Saloman's followers, none of whom seemed to have been expecting his normally concise whimsy to be so drastically diverted. (Wills' audience, too, was shocked — he was better known for the gentle folk of another Woronzow release, *Fern Hill*.)

Saloman made amends, however, first with a pair of singles, "African Violets" and "High in a Flat," presented free with the magazine *Freakbeat*; then with *Triptych*, a return to songwriting form which perfectly complimented *Miasma* and *Marshland*. As the last of Saloman's portastudio recordings, Bevis Frond's right to the vacant lot perched in the cultural wasteland between Syd Barrett and Lewis Carroll rests exclusively upon the magical might of this record.

Saloman launched *Ptolemaic Terrascope* in 1989 with a free Bevis Frond single, "The 99th Very Last Time." Months later, "Somewhere Else" graced issue three, while a deal with the US-based Reckless label saw the entire Bevis Frond catalog revitalized on CD in 1988–89.

1990's *Any Gas Faster* celebrated the extra exposure with a tight, but noticeable, sonic upgrade, as Saloman moved operations to an outside studio. He also made his live debut, accompanied by Ron Goodway (guitar), Martin Crowley (drums), and former Hawkwind bassist Adrian Shaw for a string of sporadic, but increasingly regular, shows — one, in Copenhagen, Denmark, was excerpted on one side of the US *Earsong* EP.

1990's "Sexorcist" split single (with the Walking Seeds) passed unnoticed by all but devoted collectors. 1991's *New River Head*, however, was a disappointing set following the promise of its predecessor — the appearance of its outtakes on the US *A Gathering of Fronds* compilation, and the *Snow* EP, the second of two successive *Ptolemaic Terrascope* giveaway singles, was scarcely a blessing. However, in concert, Bevis Frond continued to impress.

Having already recorded an album with former Pink Fairies drummer and legend Twink, Saloman's next band was originally intended to feature the veteran, alongside Shaw and Bari Watts (guitar). The drummer departed, however, on the eve of Bevis Frond's 1991 European tour, to be replaced by Rick Gunter of Outskirts of Infinity. (Former Camel drummer Andy Ward would replace him in 1995.) It was a fabulously successful outing, so much so that a second tour of European festivals followed while Saloman's personal star would be so bolstered sufficiently to finance a solo acoustic tour of the continent in early 1994.

A dispute over the US release of 1992's *London Stone* saw Saloman depart Reckless after the label told him it "wasn't up to my usual standard." He returned to the pastures of import-only Woronzow releases and immediately set to work on *Beatroots*, a sixties beat-inflected set intended to prove that even Fronds can have fun — one of the most frequent criticisms of his regular work was that it lacked jokes.

Preluded by the Frond's own *Summer Holiday* EP of Cliff Richard covers (featuring Saloman's daughter, Debbie, on vocals on one cut) and released under the near-anagrammatical pseudonym of Fred Bison, *Beatroots* would become one of Saloman's most instantly enjoyable albums ever. A similarly entertaining version of "Live for Today" (also covered by the Lords of the New Church) appeared as a single in Italy in 1993.

Saloman nevertheless spent the early 1990s in a disorientating musical limbo; his obvious enjoyment of live work seemingly distracting him from the studio. However, 1995's *Superseeder* (and accompanying "Dolly Bug" and "Sociopath" singles) saw his gift for songwriting — as opposed to noise-making — return and with a new US deal linking him to Flydaddy, Saloman rounded out the decade with a trilogy of albums as captivating as any past block of work.

Son of Walter was the first in the sequence in 1996. The following year brought the critically acclaimed *North Circular Road* album, named for the ring road which passes Saloman's Walthamstow home, the "Little Town Pier" 45, and a split single with Sandoz Lime. There was also another single, "Off My Shoes," included with the latest issue of *Ptolemaic Terrascope* and news that the magazine was running into serious financial problems led to an event that indicated just how deeply Saloman's fans cared for him.

An independently arranged benefit for the magazine was staged in Providence, RI, in August 1997, inducing the Bevis Frond's first ever US performance; Terrastock has since become an annual event — with Bevis Frond, of course, annual headliners.

Bevis Frond was back in the US the following year for a string of shows climaxing with the San Francisco gig excerpted on a 1999 live album. Saloman also collaborated with northwest singer-songwriter Mary Lou Lord, contributing six songs to her *Got No Shadow* album, and consummating a relationship born when he and Ward wrote and played Lord's 1996 single, "Martian Saints."

Back in Britain, Bevis Frond toured with the 1960s' protest rock veteran Country Joe McDonald, with a second live album, *Eat Flowers and Kiss Babies*, again following in 1999. For his own part, Saloman continued gigging including — of course — an appearance at 1999's Terrastock, staged in London on the release of the Bevis Frond's third Flydaddy album, *Vavona Burr*. A short US tour followed.

Bevis Frond LPs

8 Miasma (Reckless) 1987 Hinting at all manner of past influences with psych and freakbeat paramount in mind, Bevis Frond emerges onto an unsuspecting scene with what would — though few folk knew it at the time — wind up one of the best underground albums of the 1980s.

8 Inner Marshland (Reckless) 1987 One of the greatest Bevis album sleeves ever and a headlong plunge into the psychedelic swamps he only paddled his paws in last time.

2 Acid Jam (Woronzow UK) 1987 Three over-long and undeniably acidic guitar instrumentals; the eminently disposable sound of musicians with too much time on their hands. Or glue. Surely they could put their instruments down occasionally?

9 Triptych (Reckless) 1988 If any one album can be called the Bevis Frond's masterpiece; if, indeed, psychedelia has any place in the modern home, *Triptych*, with its 19-minute "Tangerine Infringement Beak" and a glorious "Hey Joe" coda, offers both epics and snatches to take first place.

6 Any Gas Faster (Reckless) 1990 The shortest ever Bevis Frond album — 15 songs in 50 minutes. Also the rockiest, as the

constraints of a "real" studio apparently deter him from the expected DIY experimentation.

4 New River Head (Reckless) 1991 Occasionally Saloman takes things too far; an agony of electronic retching — the sort of noise Frank Zappa used to reserve for Vanilla Fudge impersonations.

8 London Stone (Woronzow UK) 1992 Deliriously perverse, Nick Saloman encapsulates virtually the entire history of British music in 12 songs; folk-rock, hard rock, prog-rock, psychedelia, British Beat, garage punk, dark pop, and shoegazing all find a place within, although the moody melodies and insightful lyrics give *Stone* a solid sound all its own.

4 It Just Is (Woronzow UK) 1993 A double CD dedicated to the recently deceased guitar legend Ollie Halsall, but scarcely doing either Bevis Frond or Halsall any favors. It just is... but you'll probably wish it wasn't.

4 Sprawl (Woronzow UK) 1994 Nine tracks on the CD, 15 on vinyl, with "Right On (Hippy Dream)" clocking in at a fiercesome 21 minutes. Unfortunately, the album was very sensibly titled.

7 Superseeder (Woronzow UK) 1995 Recorded with Saloman's live band of Shaw, Ward, and Watts, a disjointed set which meanders from eastern cadence ("Superseeded") to western punkiness (the single, "Dolly Bug") and peaks just past the halfway mark with 17 minutes of guitar-burned "House of Mountains."

6 Acoustic Action (Woronzow) 1996 Folky, faintly hippy, acoustic album recorded with regular Bevis Frond bassist Adrian Shaw.

6 Son of Walter (Flydaddy) 1996 Great songs. Shame he had to record them so appallingly.

7 North Circular (Flydaddy) 1999 Two CDs (three LPs) pack 27 songs of generally high quality rock — and a bizarre lack of psychedelia. An unexpectedly pleasant deviation.

6 Vavona Burr (Flydaddy) 1999 Country Joe McDonald opens the album, parodying his "Fish Cheer" of Woodstock fame with a similar "Frond Cheer." From there on, *Vavona Burr* meanders through several shades of Frond, from crushing metallisms to gentle torch. A mixed, but merry, bag.

7 Live at the Great American Music Hall [LIVE] (Flydaddy) 1999 12 tracks recorded during Bevis Frond's 1998 US outing.

Selected Compilations and Archive Releases

6 Bevis Through the Looking Glass (Reckless)1987 Double album rampage through Saloman's unused stockpile of songs, fragments, and freak-outs. Includes the youthful Frond's 1967 opus "Alister Jones."

5 Auntie Winnie Album (Reckless) 1989 A somewhat disjointed collection of non-specific archive oddities.

6 A Gathering of Fronds (Reckless) 1992 Collection marred by the inclusion of 30 extra, hitherto vinyl-only minutes of the superfluous *New River Head*. Otherwise, a glorious succession of out-of-print singles, flexis, and compilation cuts.

⑧ Vaultscan Vols. 1/2 (Woronzow) 1997
⑧ Livewired Vols. 1/2 (Woronzow) 1997
⑧ Radioactivity (Woronzow) 1997 Cassette only collections of unreleased studio, live and radiomaterial recorded between 1986–95. For completists only.

Nick and Nick and the Psychotic Drivers LP

⑤ Nick and Nick and the Psychotic Drivers (Contempo) 1988 Deliciously deranged blast through such nuggets as "Dick, I've Lost My Sun" and "Amedeo Tortella's Bathroom." Not for the faint of heart.

Bevis and Twink LP

② Magic Ear (Woronzow UK) 1990 Acid noise. Both parties have done a lot better.

Magic Muscle LP

⑥ Gulp (Woronzow UK) 1991 Bassist Shaw brings fellow Hawkwind graduate Simon House and Edgar Broughton Band drummer Steve Broughton along to recreate the hazy days of early 1970s hippy-space-jam bands. Very successfully as well.

The Fred Bison Five LP

⑧ Beatroots (Woronzow UK) 1992 Garage rock at its greasy-grimiest. No freak-outs, just lots of freakbeat.

Doctor Frond LP

⑤ Doctor Frond (Magic Gnome) 1998 Jams recorded while Saloman was guesting on the latest album by blues-rockers band Dr Brown.

Bevis Frond/Country Joe MacDonald LP

⑥ Eat Flowers and Kiss Babies (Woronzow) 1999 Recorded live in London and Aberdeen during 1998. Great version of "Fixin' to Die."

B-52's

FORMED 1976, *(Athens, GA)*
ORIGINAL LINE-UP *Fred Schneider (b. 7/1/1956, Newark, NJ — vocals, keyboards); Kate Pierson (b. 4/27/1948, Weehawken, NJ — vocals, organ, bass); Cindy Wilson (b. 2/28/57, Athens — vocals, percussion, guitar); Ricky Wilson (b. 3/19/53, Athens — guitar); Keith Strickland (b. 10/26/53, Athens — drums)*

The B-52's are the only band to capture a transient moment, make it wholly their own, and make it last forever. Initially, the band were just a bunch of friends — people all doing their own thing. Schneider had played in local bands Night Soil and Bridge Mix, while Pierson was a folkie in the Sun

Donuts, and the others were working stiffs. By the very end of 1976, however, the quintet had gelled as a band — with minimal musical experience.

Taking the band's name from the glorious Southern slang for the good old bouffant hair-do, the B-52's' Pierson and Wilson adopted the style as well, wigged their hair higher than high and in the process defined an instant visual image for the band. It was one that would endure, making them as recognizable in 1999 as it did back then.

Regularly gigging, the band's wacky sixties beach blanket ethic wrapped itself around the new wave of the late seventies and was an instant Athens area smash. Playing first over backing tapes, the band quickly nailed a set and headed up to New York with a demo tape and a one-off gig at Max's Kansas City. Although the show was fair at best, the band were asked back and in the summer of 1978, they returned to begin a residency at the club.

With funds from a friend, Danny Beard, the band formed their own Boo-Fant imprint through the Athens DB label and recorded the anthemic "Rock Lobster," released in the fall of 1978. The song was an instant hit and would become a sonic catch phrase for an entire generation of revellers. Utterly unique, it snagged attention across the UK (where DJ John Peel was an early champion of the band) and the US, before catching the ear of Island president Chris Blackwell, who promptly offered the band a deal. The band signed with Island for Europe, Warners in the US, and in April 1979, the band flew to Island's Compass Point Studios in the Bahamas to commence recording.

It was a whirlwind session. Their eponymous album (#56 US, #22 UK) was out by July and charted worldwide. A re-recorded "Rock Lobster' (#56 US, #37 UK) became a hit while that same month heralded the band's official UK debut, with a show on July 8 at the Lyceum Ballroom in London, sharing the bill with the Tourists, featuring future Eurythmics Annie Lennox and Dave Stewart.

With the album out and a runaway success, the band opened 1980 with an adventurous tour. The B-52's first scoured the United States, spurred on by the success of the single. This was duly followed by stints in Japan and Australia. In August, they appeared at the Heatwave Festival in Toronto, Canada, before they wrapped up the year with another UK tour, highlighted by three dates at London's Hammersmith Odeon in December.

In the midst of so much jet-setting, the band returned to Compass Point to begin their follow-up with producer Rhett Davies (Roxy Music, Brian Eno). Fans had a taste with the July single "Give Me Back My Man" (#61 UK) before the album, *Wild Planet* (#18 US, #18 UK), emerged in September following roughly the same format as before. By the following April, it had been certified gold.

Singles were duly dispatched, with "Private Idaho" (#74 US) the first to appear in October — the song had been a live performance staple as far back as the Max's Kansas City days. "Dirty Back Road" followed in November while the wacky "Quiche Lorraine" rung in the new year. And although the band wouldn't have a new project unveiled until 1982, a superlative mini-album, *The Party Mix* (#55 US, #36 UK), was released in July. It featured remixes of classics from the first two albums and spawned one single, the party-mixed "Give Me Back My Man".

Now solidly locked into the retro sci-fi sound of their first two albums, the B-52's themselves were desperately trying to determine their next step — one in which, they hoped, would allow them to grow up without growing away from their fame. With this in mind, they linked with Talking Heads frontman David Byrne, certain that at worst, they would decipher a new direction. Recording at Skyline Studios, trying to capture a more "sophisticated" sound, the resulting mini-LP, *Mesopotamia* (#35 US, #18 UK), was released in February 1982 — and was solidly panned by critics and fans, who, it seemed, wanted the B-52's to remain what they had been.

The album's two singles, "Deep Sleep" and "Mesopotamia," failed to chart, and although *Mesopotamia* became the band's highest charting record yet, it was also their poorest selling.

Taking a brief break to refresh themselves, Pierson, Cindy Wilson, and Strickland recorded several tracks with Melon, a conglomeration consisting of Adrian Belew and members of the Japanese band the Plastics. The two songs, "Honeydew" and "I Will Call You (And Other Famous Last Words)," would eventually turn up on the EP *Snakeman Show* "*Senso Hantai*" in Japan only.

The band determined to rebound in 1983 with the release of their third full-length, *Whammy!* (#29 US, #33 UK), supported by the memorable "Song for a Future Generation" (#63 UK) and "Legal Tender" (#81 US) singles. The band were quiet during the year, however, and in 1984, without any explanation, dropped from sight to take a long sabbatical.

In fact, Ricky Wilson was seriously ill — he had been diagnosed with AIDS and by 1984 his health was beginning to fail badly. Prevailing attitudes in the US at that time, however, ensured that the band would keep his illness secret for as long as possible.

Through the band's enforced absence, Schneider took the year to record an album under his one-off alter ego, Shake Society. In January 1985, however, the entire band reconvened to perform at the Rock in Rio festival in Rio De Janeiro, Brazil, and six months later, the B-52's were back in the studio. But Wilson's health was again deteriorating at an alarming rate. He finally lost his battle with the disease on October 12, 1985.

The band would largely remain out of sight for the next year. But their debut *B-52's* was reissued in 1986 and hit platinum, with a reissue of "Rock Lobster" (#12 UK) reacquainting audiences with the band's signature sound, just as they prepared to re-emerge in their own right.

Dedicated to Ricky, *Bouncing off the Satellites* (#85 US, #74 UK) was released in the fall of 1986 in the US; a year later in Britain. Poorly promoted, it would spawn two singles, "Wig" in June 1987 and "Summer of Love" in September but both remained as low profile as the band itself. Still recovering from Wilson's loss, the remaining members of the B-52's weren't even certain that they wanted to continue on as a band.

Finally, after much contemplation and soul searching, they did decide to carry on, as a quartet with Strickland taking over on guitar, and adding various musicians to round out the sound in session and on tour. The band reconvened, this time working with producers Don Was and Nile Rodgers, former Gang of Four bassist Sara Lee, keyboard player Pat Irwin, and future David Bowie drummer Zach Alford.

The result, 1989's stunning *Cosmic Thing* (#4 US, #8 UK), came in the middle of a dance revival, a genre to which the B-52's felt thoroughly connected. Thus emboldened, the album tore through the charts as single after single was peeled off through 1989 and 1990. The B-52's were back on their game, as inspired, many said, as they were back in 1979. The album would go double platinum in March 1990.

"Love Shack" (#3 US, #2 UK) was rushed into heavy rotation on MTV and eventually won "Best Group Video" and "Best Art Direction" at the MTV Video Awards in September 1990. Accompanied by an equally deserving video, "Channel Z" (#61 UK) and "Roam" (#3 US, #17 UK) capped the year on record; the B-52's themselves wrapped it up by headlining MTV's New Year's Eve party.

With "Deadbeat Club" (#30 US) becoming the fourth single from the album and Pierson guesting on Iggy Pop's first ever US hit, "Candy" (#28 UK), the band was seldom out of sight through 1990. They kicked the year off with three huge sell-out performances at Radio City Music Hall in New York in February; in April, they took part in the annual Earth Day celebration in New York; and in June, they launched a massive US tour, under the banner *Summer of 1990*.

Mesopotamia was remixed during the summer for a reissue in the new year (#184 US), but the year was highlighted by a special performance on August 13, 1990, in Inglewood, CA, playing a sold out AIDS awareness show. They raised $345,000 for various AIDS groups. The band — primarily through Schneider — would continue to support AIDS awareness. Schneider co-hosted The Haoui Party: Music

People United for AIDS Relief benefit with Ice-T at 1992's New Music Seminar and 1993 he participated in a benefit sponsored by LIFEbeat to raise funds for people who have been diagnosed with HIV.

Aside from a remixed version of Schneider's six-year-old *Monster* (#85 US), 1991 was another quiet year. The band made known their support of the anti-fur movement, contributing a song to *Tame Yourself*, a PETA-sponsored benefit album (two years earlier, the B-52's participated in the Rock Against Fur benefit at the Palladium in New York in March 1989; two years later in 1993, Pierson would be charged for taking part in an anti-fur demonstration at the offices of Vogue in New York).

But the band was shaking itself out. In March 1992, the B-52's played a New York fundraiser for Democrat Jerry Brown — without Cindy Wilson. Now essentially a trio, the remaining B-52's retired to the studio, again with Don Was, to record another album, *Good Stuff* (#16 US, #8 UK), released in the spring of 1992.

Augmented by the returning Irwin, Julee Cruise (vocals), Tracy Wormworth (bass), and Sue Hadjopoulos (drums), the band again launched extensive tours of the US and Europe, shot through with single releases: "Good Stuff" (#28 US, #21 UK), "Tell It Like It T-I-IS" (#61 UK), a Moby remix of "Is That You Mo-Dean?", and "Hot Pants Explosion."

They again disappeared following the tour but surfaced anew in 1994, reinvented as the BC-52's for an appearance in the movie remake of *The Flinstones* and recording the film's title track "(Meet) The Flinstones" (#33 US, #3 UK). If the band were generally inactive, however, Schneider was not, continuing his solo venture with another album in 1997, *Just Fred*. He also appeared at the 1997 Grammy Awards, dispelling growing rumors that the band had split up.

In fact, they had just gotten back together again and in October 1997, Wilson rejoined the band for a show in their hometown, Athens. The following June, Warners released the first B-52's retrospective, *Time Capsule — Songs for a Future Generation* (#93 US) in June. It featured two new tracks and was followed by a full US tour with the Pretenders.

B-52's LPs

9 **The B-52's (WB) 1979** Alien part-animals from a galaxy far, far away, the B-52's materialize ready for a good time and dressed to kill (beehives can be lethal) in the latest fashion — from 1962. The music was equally out of time, from the Peter Gunnish "Planet Claire," the psychobilly psychedelic "Rock Lobster," and into the '60s via the frantic "Dance This Mess Around," and a touching cover of "Down Town." But in the best Beach Blanket Babes Meet the Monsters from Mars tradition, the final scene still sees the bonfire lit, the radio on, and the whole world realizes

these weirdos are kinda goofy — but fun. And so the invasion began.

7 **Wild Planet (WB) 1980** While never quite reaching the dizzying heights of their debut, the B-52's party on, and the opening track even provides instruction, or at least cliff notes, to help you follow their lead. The lyrical themes continue down the same surreal path (best of the batch — the ode to errant poodle "Quiche Lorraine"), even as the music now treads a more tried and true path. "Strobe light" and "Give Me Back My Man" (mildly rude chorus, by the way) best recapture the extremes of the past.

5 **Whammy! (WB) 1983** After the moody diversion of the *Mesopotamia* mini-album, all downbeat drifting and sultry assault, it's back to Planet Boisterous, and two more gems for the greatest hits machine, "Legal Tender" and "Song for a Future Generation." Unfortunately, that's pretty much all there is.

5 **Bouncing off the Satellites (WB) 1986** Poignantly dedicated to the late Ricky Wilson, *Satellites* moves with the last few years' ups and downs. Fabulous for "Wig," but elsewhere the smile is clearly slipping somewhat.

8 **Cosmic Thing (Reprise) 1989** A scintillating renewal, the B-52's tapped into the late 1980's dance sensibility with a squawking, squealing vengeance. Repetition dulled the greatest joys, but still "Love Shack" and "Channel Z" are capable of unexpectedly creeping up and making you grin. And even "Roam" is not as bad as its video made out. Smart fun throughout.

3 **Good Stuff (Reprise) 1992** Never trust albums which tell you how great they're going to be. They never are.

Selected Compilations and Archive Releases

8 **Party Mix/Mesopotamia (Reprise) 1991** Two post-*Wild Planet* mini-albums; awkward bedfellows but oddly appealing anyway — *Party Mix* with its boisterous reprises of the first two album's greatest bits, *Mesopotamia* with producer David Byrne glowering disapprovingly at any inclination to have fun.

8 **Time Capsule — Songs for a Future Generation (Reprise) 1998**

Fred Schneider LPs

1 **Fred Schneider (Reprise) 1991** Recorded in the mid-1980s, but canned until "Love Shack" demanded more product. Unreleased albums are like a cancer — they itch and ache and burn holes in the pocket, and the fans want to hear them, and one day, some day, at the time of most opportune commercial visibility... *they appear*. Which is when we remember that sometimes there's a good reason for leaving something on the shelf. It gives the dust bunnies something to laugh at.

3 **Just Fred (Reprise) 1996** It had to be an improvement on its predecessor and with a backing band drawn from a who's who of indy cults, it was. Punkier than expected, rawer than imagined; but still Fred cries out for something more — a foil, a straight man, a buffer... some songs?

Further Reading

The B-52's by Della Martini (Music Sales, 1990).

BIG AUDIO DYNAMITE

FORMED 1984, (London, England)

ORIGINAL LINE-UP Mick Jones (b. 6/26/53, London — guitar, vocals); Don Letts (keyboards); Dan Donovan (keyboards); Leo Williams (bass); Greg Roberts (drums)

Mick Jones' departure from The Clash was never as surprising, nor as catastrophic as the media liked to paint it — not for Jones, anyway. Always the most active extra-curricular Clashman, it was during one of his outside production jobs, working with Theatre of Hate on their "Westworld" project, that Jones first glimpsed the possibilities which life beyond The Clash could unleash, and across his last albums with the band, 1980's *Sandanista* (most notably "The Magnificent Seven") and 1982's *Combat Rock*, Jones' electro-hip-hop ambition screamed louder than words.

Still it took Jones some two and a half years to piece together his first post-Clash project, working most closely with Roxy Club DJ and film maker Don Letts on a project which Joe Strummer, the first time he heard the rough mixes, described as "the worst load of shit I've ever heard in my life." Talking with the *New Musical Express*, Strummer recalled telling Jones, "do yourself a favor. Don't put it out."

Early names for the new band included Real Westway and the Top Risk Action Company before Jones finally settled on Big Audio Dynamite. The line-up, too, seemed to be in a constant state of confusion. Letts was joined by another Roxy Club alumni, barman (and ex-Basement Five bassist) Leo Williams, but an attempt to bring former Clash drummer Topper Headon into the frame around Christmas 1983, foundered when Headon, hopelessly lost within the drug habit which forced him from The Clash, refused to clean up for the occasion.

Eventually drummer Greg Roberts was acquired through a newspaper ad while photographer Dan Donovan came in after he let slip that he played keyboards — the son of '60s snapper Terence Donovan, he was actually shooting the band's first album cover at the time he made the admission.

By October 1984, Big Audio Dynamite were playing their first live shows around London, and the following spring they toured Europe with U2 and with ex-Generation X bassist Tony James engineering the band's sound. It was his job, Jones said, "to take the group, rip it apart and make it something different every night." James quit soon after the event to concentrate on his own new band, Sigue Sigue Sputnik, but the seeds of his sonic rebelliousness remained. When Big Audio Dynamite entered the studio to begin work on what would become *This Is Big Audio Dynamite* (#103 US, #27 UK), dub remix producer Paul Smyrkle was brought in to continue the good work.

Both live and on vinyl, Big Audio Dynamite was a departure, not only from the rock which Jones had so effortlessly dashed off with The Clash, but from most white musical avenues altogether. A wildchild collision of hip-hop, punk, and rock, into which BAD inserted movie themes and dialogue, spoken word soundbytes and beats and rhythms, the album either enthralled or repelled, and the first single, "The Bottom Line," passed by completely unnoticed. With the release of "E=MC2" (#11 UK) in April 1986, however, all criticism was stilled.

A dynamic collage based upon, and sampling, the career of director Nic Roeg, "E=MC2" was packed with both aural (and, on the accompanying video, visual) reminders of such movie classics as *Walkabout, Performance, Don't Look Now*, and *The Man Who Fell to Earth*. The first UK rock hit to feature sampling, the single's performance equalled The Clash's best ever performance to date. "Medicine Show" (#29 UK) and "C'mon Every Beatbox" (#51 UK) followed it chartwards, and the band's reinvigorated debut album remained on the chart for almost seven months.

Throughout 1986, rumors of a Clash reunion seemed to be everywhere, all the more so after Strummer joined Jones on the video for "Medicine Show." Jones reciprocated by playing guitar and producing Strummer's "Love Kills" solo single and by August, the pair were busily writing songs which would appear on the second BAD album, *No 10 Upping Street* (#119 US, #11 UK).

Ultimately, Strummer would take co-writing credits on five of the album's nine tracks, including the minor hit "V Thirteen" (#49 UK) and shared the production credits as well. But hopes that the partnership might flourish further fell by the wayside as a second single, "Sightsee MCI," failed to chart, and BAD returned to the studio to begin work on their third album. (A Clash connection did live on, however, in the use of a Paul Simenon painting for the cover.)

Fully conscious of all the electronic gimmickry he had unleashed, Jones previewed the album with the anti-sampling single "Just Play Music" (#51 UK). Indeed, *Tighten Up Vol 88* (#102 US, #33 UK), titled after a series of ska compilations released in the UK in the early 1970s, represented a considerable departure for the band. Largely abandoning electronics, Jones instead drew upon more traditional rock and soul-based roots, flavored with some of his best guitar playing in years. But with the band having established itself by virtue of its eclecticism, such a return found little favor in the marketplace and crashed out of the chart after just three weeks. A second single, "Other 99," bombed.

BAD toured the UK through the summer but further plans were placed on hold when Jones contracted a virulent bout of chicken pox from his four-year-old daughter Lauren, one which affected his throat and lungs, and left him in a coma for 15 days. He also suffered nerve damage and for some months there was doubt whether he would ever play guitar or sing again. Not until the following summer was he able to return to work and in September 1989, Big Audio Dynamite released their fourth album, *Megatop Phoenix* (#87 US, #26 UK), and accompanying single, "Contact."

Drawing heavily from the acid house culture percolating beneath the surface of the UK underground, *Megatop Phoenix* was, in its way, as revolutionary as *This Is Big Audio Dynamite* had been four years earlier. But whereas the fruits of that album were immediately apparent, in the rise (on both sides of the Atlantic) of an army of followers and acolytes which ranged from the Beastie Boys to Sigue Sigue Sputnik, *Megatop Phoenix* offered commentary on a scene which was already flourishing, drew its immediate focus from an already existing musical form (De La Soul's *Three Feet High and Rising* was Jones' constant companion), and ultimately failed to add anything new to what the scene's denizens already knew was out there.

Again the album could muster nothing more than a brief three weeks in the chart and while the group did undertake successful tours of Britain and the US, by early 1990, BAD had fallen apart.

Letts, Williams, and Roberts quit to form their own band, Screaming Target (Roberts and Williams later reconvened as Dreadzone); Jones began piecing together a new incarnation of BAD called, with self-explanatory simplicity, BAD II.

Bassist Gary Stonadge, guitarist Nick Hawkins, DJ Zonka, and former Sigue Sigue Sputnik drummer Chris Kavanagh came in, the latter joining just weeks before Dan Donovan quit to join the reformed Sputnik (he too subsequently appeared in Dreadzone). Then, with Jones enjoying a surprise hit as guest vocalist on the new Aztec Camera single, "Good Morning Britain" (#19 UK), BAD II debuted in London on August 10, 1990.

Two months later, an album of what initially appeared to be quickly recorded demos, *Kool Aid* (#55 UK), hit the streets, continuing Jones' fascination with acid house but adding a new, fresh dimension to matters by aurally equating the new movement with the punk scene of 15 years before.

Neither was it any coincidence that Jones should release such a streetwise reaffirmation of his own punk credentials at a time when the former members of The Clash were in negotiation with Levis over the use of Jones' "Should I Stay or Should I Go" in a new advertising campaign. The ensuing single made #1 in Britain (a track on the *Screaming Target* album, sung by Pretenders' vocalist Chrissie Hynde,

comments on this with the line "the wild one's selling jeans") and the white riot seemed an awfully long time ago.

From the outset, BAD II claimed *Kool Aid* was intended as nothing more than a stopgap gesture to the fans and that a proper full album would be forthcoming in the new year. That was *The Globe* (#76 US, #63 UK), essentially a dramatically remixed and revised version of *Kool Aid* released in July and packing a bonus in the shape of "Rush" (#32 US), a rearranged version of *Kool Aid*'s "Change of Atmosphere."

"Rush" would make #1 in Australia, "The Globe" (#72 US, #63 UK) was a club hit worldwide while *The Globe* itself topped the American college radio charts, selling over a quarter of a million copies in the process. Its failure in Britain appeared utterly irrelevant.

BAD II should have followed up immediately. Instead, following a slot on MTV's controversial *120 Minutes* tour, appearing alongside Public Image Ltd, and new hopes Blind Melon and Live, the band took much of the next year off. A video compilation in 1992 and a few gigs with U2 (including the Australian leg of the Zooropa tour) the following year marked the sum of BAD II's activity, while hopes of a new album in early 1994 receded with every passing month.

But the group did perform at the Mick Ronson memorial concert in London in May, and a Mick Jones solo single, "Repetitive Beats," was released under the name of Retribution as part of a unified underground protest against the British government's incoming Criminal Justice Bill.

Finally, in November 1994, "Looking for a Song" (#68 UK) and *Higher Power* were released, debuting the new, abridged band name Big Audio but offering little of lasting merit, and nothing even vaguely possessing the revolutionary zeal for which Jones was still, even as he approached middle age, revered by confused youth. Jones, too, sensed the album's irrelevance, and returned to the studio almost immediately to create *F-Punk*.

Marking a return to the old Big Audio Dynamite name — marking, too, a return to the high energy, low boredom threshold of early BAD — *F-Punk* (its title a pun on George Clinton's P-Funk) was a no frills techno-punk album; an acknowledgement of the immutability of his past and the possibilities of the future. The addition of keyboard player Andrew Shapps, DJ and former Beat vocalist Rankin' Roger, Joe Attard, Bob Wond, and Darryl Fulstow to the line-up brought further abandon to the live show and as the Big Audio Dynamite Soundsystem, the group moved almost entirely away from the notion of conventional gigs, staging massive celebrations of dance and rhythm instead.

A new album, *Entering the Ride*, was recorded but left unreleased until 1999 saw it appear via the band's newly inaugurated website. Instead, BAD began showcasing at their own Club Maximum in London, finally bringing to fruition the dream of an all-encompassing, all-powerful, electronic dance machine which Jones himself had envisioned at the start of the BAD adventure.

Also see the entries for the "CLASH" on page 270 and "JOE STRUMMER" on page 661.

Big Audio Dynamite LPs

9 This Is Big Audio Dynamite (Columbia) 1985 A shattering (at the time) blend of soundscapes shot through with snatches of speech, movie dialogue, and stray Hollywood themes, together with the immortal "E=MC2" and "Medicine Show."

7 Number 10 Upping Street (Columbia) 1986 "Come On Every Beatbox" starts things off in thunderous fashion, but the much-anticipated reunion with co-writer Joe Strummer leaves a sense of disappointment which time cannot erase.

7 Tighten Up Volume 88 (Columbia) 1988 Stripping back the electro, a fairly basic soul rock album, powerful in its own way but a little too generic for a band which once pushed the boundaries so far.

6 Megatop Phoenix (Columbia) 1989 Dance-crazed, acid-drenched return to the first album form, marred only by the fact that a lot of other people had already done the same things last week.

7 Kool Aid (CBS UK) 1990

5 The Globe (Columbia) 1991 With the band revamped as BAD II, hit singles "Rush" and "The Globe" presents a distorting memory of how good the album should have been; *Kool Aid*, while basically little more than its demos, ultimately deserves far more credit than it received.

5 Higher Power (Columbia) 1994 Sporting yet another truncation, Big Audio (no dynamite, so you can't say they never warned you) remain artful, cultural scavengers. The closer you get to the ensuing junkyard sculptures, the more clever they appear. But step back and it's a tottering pile of detritus in search of something to do. Good title track though.

6 F-Punk (Radioactive) 1995 Sporting a new rhyming dictionary, Jones' lyrics (utilitarian at best) plummet to Dr. Seuss juvenility without the wit or charm. Still, *F-Punk* is much more coherent than its overly clever predecessor, even as it presents a similar montage of musical and vocal fragments and styles. At least this time, BAD pulled them into songs which are worth a second play.

8 Entering the Ride (Internet Release) 1999 Surprisingly vital, electrifying electro roots rock slammed through with a total disregard for contemporary fashion — and sounding all the fresher because of it.

Selected Compilations and Archive Releases

7 Lost Treasures of Big Audio Dynamite I and II (Sony, Japan) 1993 Priceless rarities collection, slightly hamstringed by the amount of filler which creeps in among the remixes and extensions.

5 Super Bad (Columbia) 1995 Buy the first album, download the last, grab a few 12-inch singles from the rest of the career, and *Super Bad* becomes super redundant.

Screaming Target LP

7 Hometown Hi-Fi (Island) 1991

Dreadzone LPs

8 360 Degrees (Creation) 1993

6 Second Light (Virgin) 1995

7 Biological Radio (Virgin) 1997

BIG BLACK

FORMED 1982 *(Evanston, IL)*
ORIGINAL LINE-UP *Steve Albini*

An experiment into sound that made hardcore punk seem melodic, Big Black's music was alternately hailed as pure, inspired genius — or utterly nihilistic self-indulgence. Either way, it fulfilled Steve Albini's intention of creating an environment so full of noise that sonic collapse was the inevitable result. He succeeded, using a drum machine, his own wiles, and little else, on Big Black's first release, the *Lungs* EP in fall 1982.

Adding ex-Naked Raygunners members Santiago Durango (guitars) and Jeff Pezzati (bass) to the mix, Albini completed the band's line-up by replacing the drum machine with Pat Byrne. Big Black then recorded two more EP's, *Bulldozer* in 1983, and in April 1985, *Racer-X* on the Homestead label. Never known for their prolific output, the band followed the EP over a year later with two singles, "Il Duce" and "Heartbeat".

Pezzati was replaced by Dave Riley (ex-Savage Beliefs) and Byrne was usurped by a new drum machine in 1986 when Big Black recorded their first full-length, *Atomizer* (#16 UK indy). Collectors demand for early Big Black, meanwhile, was assuaged when Homestead coupled "Lungs" and "Bulldozer" into one package, *Hammer Party* (#11 UK indy), shortly before the band shifted to Touch and Go, the label with which Albini — already establishing himself on the other side of the production booth — remains indelibly associated today.

Big Black released the "Headache" EP (#3 UK indy) in June 1987. Weak musically, it stirred controversy and generated news nonetheless. The original issue boasted a cover so offensive (a full color shot of an accident victim's head) that the album was initially released shrouded in a black sleeve. Albini, too, kept Big Black's buzz afloat issuing the quasi-bootleg EP "Sound of Impact" (#7 UK indy). A limited edition recounting of a typically brutal live performance, the album was released without any mention of Big Black at all. One listen, however, and it was immediately obvious who the culprits were.

Durango left the band to begin a study of law (he would later record under the moniker Arsenal, releasing two EPs, "Manipulator" and "Factory Smog"). He was replaced by Melvyn Belli as Big Black prepared to record what would become their final album. *Songs About Fucking* (#1 UK indy), released in July 1987, was followed the next month by an odd single as the band coupled a version of Albini's childhood heroes, Cheap Trick's "He's a Whore," with a mystifying Big Black-ified rendition of Kraftwerk's classic, "The Model" (#2 UK indy).

Albini disbanded Big Black shortly after, ostensibly to concentrate further on outside production. He wasn't through with making music though. "My profession is as a recording engineer," he explained. "But my passion is as a performing rock musician." He formed a new band with Scratch Acid rhythm section Dave William Sims (bass) and Rey Washam (drums), and deliberately set out to unsettle and enrage the general public, by dubbing the project Rapeman. A decade had elapsed since an English band, the Raped, had been universally castigated for their apparent insensitivity — Rapeman would discover that if anything, the climate had become even frostier for such provocative gestures.

Though the trio recorded three singles, "Hated Chinee," "Budd" (#2 UK indy), and "Inki's Butt Crack," and an album, *Two Nuns and a Black Mule* (#4 UK indy), they would never overcome the hostility which their name aroused, and finally broke up in 1989. Again Albini retreated behind the scenes, grafting his purposefully ugly aural sculptures onto the steady stream of bands who visited his Illinois studios, but by 1993, the urge returned, and he re-emerged with a new project, Shellac. Accompanied by Bob Weston (bass, ex-Volcano Suns) and Todd Trainer (drums, ex-Rifle Sport), the band debuted with 1993's "The Rude Gesture" single, swiftly following through with "Uranus" and "The Bird is the Most Popular Finger."

An album, *At Action Park*, was followed by a European tour highlighted by a new 45, "Billiardspielerlied," given away at the band's show in Bremen, Germany on August 24, 1995 and a *Melody Maker* review which noted of their riotous London show, "Shellac appear to be a magnet for assholes."

Back home, a version of the metal classic "Jailbreak" was contributed to an AC/DC tribute album; a split single with Mule followed in 1997, but purposefully under-achieving, another year would elapse before the band's second album, *Terraform*.

Also see the entry for "STEVE ALBINI" in "PRODUCERS & LABELS," on page 739.

Big Black LPs

8 Atomizer (Homestead) 1986 Themes of small-town wasteland reflect an utter hopelessness which in turn is certainly reflected in the music. An acquired, but rewarding, taste of what life would be like if your ears were full of blood.

6 Songs About Fucking (Touch and Go) 1987 A posthumous album with more of the same, Big Black's wall of sound never fails to bludgeon.

Selected Compilations and Archive Releases

8 The Hammer Party (Homestead) 1986 Fantastic compilation of the first two EPs, when Big Black were louder, angrier, and even rawer than ever, introducing the pure genius of "Dead Billy" and "Steelworker" to an open-mouthed audience.

7 The Rich Man's Eight-Track Tape (Homestead) 1987 A compilation of the first LP plus the *Headache* EP and the "Heartbeat" single.

6 Pig Pile [LIVE] (Touch and Go) 1992

Rapeman LP

7 Two Nuns and a Pack Mule (Blast First) 1988 Confrontational follow-up to BB, this album is the next logical progression for the sound as Albini grows up.

Shellac LPs

5 Shellac at Action Park (Touch and Go) 1994 Definitely an album made by engineers and producers; what *Park* lacks in musical prime it more than makes up for in sonic perfection — albeit inhumanely loudly.

6 Terraform (Touch and GO) 1998

BIKINI KILL

FORMED 1992 (Olympia, WA)

ORIGINAL LINE-UP *Kathleen Hanna (b. 6/9/69 — vocals); Billy Boredom (b. William Karren, 3/10/65 — guitar); Kathi Wilcox (b. 11/19/69 — bass); Tobi Vail (b. 7/20/69 — drums)*

Dismissing indy rock as sexist and the Riot Grrl movement as meaningless in the face of their own espoused "Revolution Girl Style Now" rhetoric, Bikini Kill grew out of the editorial team behind the feminist fanzine *Bikini Kills*. Evergreen College students Kathleen Hanna, Tobi Vail, and Kathi Wilcox began publishing in the late 1980s, and initially saw the band as a vehicle for the 'zine's own radical views on the masculine hegemony of alternative rock — and as a forum for other women to speak out.

One feature of early shows was an open mike forum; another, itself purposefully divisive, was to confine the (primarily male) slam dancers to the sides of the stage to allow would-be participants to remain at the front.

Allying themselves with the similarly intentioned Bratmobile and Heavens to Betsy, Bikini Kill added guitarist Billy Boredom and debuted with a self-released cassette of their first album, titled after their already stated agenda, in 1991. Later in the year, they signed with local iconoclasts Kill Rock Stars and over the next year, isolated tracks leaked out on various compilations — the caustically ironic "Suck My Left One" on *There's a Dyke in the Pit* and "Feels Blind" on *Kill Rock Stars* — while the group also went into the studio with Fugazi frontman Ian MacKaye to re-record elements of their debut album for a self-titled EP.

The spirited "Boy"/"Girl" split single with Slim Moon was succeeded in 1992 by another collaboration, the *Yeah Yeah Yeah/Our Troubled Youth* album, split with the like-minded British band, Huggy Bear. The two bands toured Britain together the following year, introducing an entire new audience to what the UK press, nevertheless, insisted on dubbing Riot Grrl — a phrase which blossomed to incorporate almost any other punk-inflected band with female membership (Babes in Toyland, L7, Hole) and ultimately became so meaningless that when the Spice Girls emerged three years later, the media lost no time in dubbing them, too, Riot Grrl.

Returning to the US, Bikini Kill hooked up with producer Joan Jett to record the classic "Rebel Girl" 45 (Hanna would co-write one song, "Spinster," for Jett's *Pure and Simple* album), and the following year *Pussy Whipped* became the band's first full album. A re-recording of "Rebel Girl" highlighted a dramatic manifesto, but it was ironic that having spearheaded the feminist movement in the first place, Bikini Kill were now rapidly being left behind.

Although the members continued active elsewhere (Hanna appeared on Mike Watt's latest album; Wilcox, Boredom, and Vail worked as the Frumpies), Bikini Kill themselves did not record for almost two years after *Pussy Whipped*. They re-emerged in 1995 with two new singles, the "Anti Pleasure Dissertation" EP in May and "I Like Fucking"/"I Hate Danger" in September, both preludes to a new album, 1996's *Reject All Americans*.

Having been instrumental in organizing a virtual press black-out to prevent any further dilution of their ethic, however, Bikini Kill returned to a considerably straitened audience. The group finally disbanded in 1998, just as a compilation of their singles celebrated their existence.

Bikini Kill LPs

9 Revolution Girl Style Now (Bikini Kill) 1991 Rough recording quality doesn't change the fact that the only truly essential BK album is the one they created while building their own crowd themselves — not having one thrust upon them by everyone else.

4 Yeah Yeah Yeah/Our Troubled Youth (w/Huggy Bear) (Kill Rock Stars) 1992 One side apiece, with BK's efforts again scarred by anapparent inability to turn the volume down.

7 Pussy Whipped (Kill Rock Stars) 1994 With "Rebel Girl" having already turned up on single and EP, it leaps onto album for the first time and wipes the floor with its colleagues. Still, with just 24 minutes of playing time, *Pussy Whipped* makes up in energy what it lacks in quality.

5 Reject All American (Kill Rock Stars) 1996 Unfocussed after the first few minutes; uninteresting a few minutes after that, although "RIP" touches a few new nerves.

Selected Compilations and Archive Releases

9 The CD Version of the First Two Albums (Kill Rock Stars) 1994

7 Singles (Kill Rock Stars) 1998 Starts hot, winds up cool, but a solid document nonetheless.

BIM SKALA BIM

FORMED 1983 *(Boston, MA)*
ORIGINAL LINE-UP *Dan Vitale (vocals); Ephraim LaSalle (guitar); Mark Ferranti (bass); John Ferry (trombone), Robin DuCot (keyboards); Chris Kramtch (drums)*

Bim Skala Bim share with The Toasters the honor of being America's longest running ska act, with hometown Boston coming in just behind New York in documenting its infant ska scene with a compilation album; *Mash It Up Volume One* appeared in 1986, less than a year after The Toasters-led *New York Beat*.

Playing their first gig just two weeks after they formed, Bim Skala Bim's first months together were characterized by regular line-up changes — Chris Kramtsch was replaced by John Sullivan, Ephraim LaSalle by Will Cluster — and a lot of local gigging. The group broke up in October 1984, but reformed ten months later with drummer Jay Potts, guitarist Jim Jones, keyboard player John Cameron, and second vocalist Lauren Fleischer joining original members Dan Vitale, Mark Ferranti, and John Ferry. Potts quit after a month (he later resurfaced with Catholic Guilt) to be replaced by Jim Arhleger, and in this form, the band recorded their first, self-titled album in October 1985.

By the time of its April 1986, release, however, further line-up changes had altered the group's disposition — Jackie Starr replaced Fleischer, Vince Nobile (trombone) replaced Ferry (he later joined Detroit ska sensations Gangster Fun, but returned to Bim in 1999) — and the band recruited percussionist Rick Barry. Powered now by the twin vocals of Vitale and Jackie Starr, Bim returned to the studio with legendary producer Jimmy Miller, emerging with a new single,

"Edge of a Knife." The band also appeared on the seminal *Mash It Up* compilation of Boston bands.

Another honor came when Bim became the first Boston ska act to break into the New York circuit when they landed a track on Moon's 1988 *Skaface* compilation. Indeed, with constant touring only honing their edge even further, Bim Skala Bim were now powerful enough to give any other US ska combo a run for its money, as they proved by finishing second at that year's WBCN's Rock'n'Roll Rumble.

But Bim's greatest success was coming in Europe. *NME* called them the best ska band in America and *Boston Bluebeat* (as their debut was retitled) was selling strongly across the continent. The band also headlined London's International Ska Festival. Such success brought Bim Skala Bim a US deal with Celluloid, who released the sophomore *Tuba City* in 1988, but the departure of Starr (for southern California band Donkey Show) and the demise of Celluloid saw a straitened Bim follow through with the low-key archival collection *How's It Goin'*, the first release on their own wryly tuitled uNsiGnEd ReCoRDs, soon to be renamed Big Indie Beat, or BIB.

The band gigged through 1991, returning to the studio in early 1992 to begin work on their next full album, *Bones* and what would become Bim's finest moment — when 1991 brought the band a surprise success with a cover of Pink Floyd's "Brain Damage." A major hit on the college radio circuit, this unrepresentative, unexpected, and ultimately unwanted, victory took some time to live down.

It did, however, earn BIB a distribution deal through Relativity, and over the next two years, Bim would reissue much of their back catalog, together with the genre-defining *The Shack* compilation album, alongside the consolidatory *Live At The Paradise*, recorded at a hometown show with new keyboard player John Cameron, and preserving Bim's high energy, crowd-rousing performance for all time.

While the group continued gigging, a number of side projects — Vitale's Steady Earnest, Elevator (later the Joint Chiefs), and the short-lived Santa among them — also took to the road and the studio; Bim themselves would release their own next albums, *Eyes and Ears* and *Universal* (with trombonist Mark Paquin), at two-year intervals to better accomodate their unrelenting live schedule. 1999 saw them slightly break step, recording (but not releasing) a new album titled for its cover of the ska classic, "Easy Skanking," and also working on a Bim Skala Bim CD-ROM.

Bim Skala Bim LPs

6 Bim Skala Bim (Fonograff) 1985 A considerably more reggae than ska- driven collection, but still setting Bim up among the prime practitioners on the infant US scene.

8 Tuba City (Celluloid) 1989 Closer to modern expectations, a frequently stunning collection made even greater by a guest appearance from Skatalite Rol and Alphonso.

7 Bones (BIB) 1991 Pink Floyd's "Brain Damage" gets the big Bim treatment, but "Wandering Soul" and "In Our Midst" are the real stars of the show.

8 Live at the Paradise (BIB) 1993 Perfectly recapturing the party feeling of Bim live, and with a hometown Boston crowd in full cry, the band pull out the stops with a powerhouse set, spanning all four past albums plus a couple that never made it onto disc.

7 Eyes and Ears (BIB) 1995 Embracing reggae, calypso, and the sweet pop sounds of the '60s, plus a solid stab at rock with the harmony washed "Set Me Up," *Eyes* is Bim at their multi-faceted best.

7 Universal (BIB) 1997

Selected Compilations and Archive Releases

7 How's It Going (BIB) 1990

7 American Playhouse (BIB) 1997 Comprises cuts from *Tuba*, *Bones*, and *Eyes*

6 The One that Got Away 1999 Ten years of outtakes and B-sides

Steady Earnest LPs

7 Out of Line (BIB) 1994 A heady mix of rootsy ska and rocksteady; twinned with punk, pop, and soul, Steady Earnest's melody-driven, dance-inspiring sound stayed traditional amid the most modern trappings.

6 Take It Take It Take It [LIVE] (BIB) 1994

BIOSPHERE

BORN *Geir Jenssen (Tromso, Norway)*

Jenssen discovered electronic music through the music of New Order, Depeche Mode, Wire, and Brian Eno. "Hearing [it]," he recalled, "was like discovering a new universe. A universe which I wanted to be a part of." By 1983, he had invested in his first synthesizer and began experimenting with music that reflected his academic interests. "I get a lot of inspiration from what I learned from my archeology studies. Studying the Ice Age and Stone Age has definitely influenced my music."

In 1984, Jenssen released his first album, the cassette-only, limited edition *Likvider*, credited to E-Man and two years later he formed his first band, Bel Canto, with Nils Johansen, intending to create their own "Arctic" sound. Joined by vocalist Anneli Drecker, the group's first demo tape earned considerable local applause, and the following year Bel Canto bought an inter-rail ticket each and set off to meet their favorite record companies. They eventually signed with Belgium's Crammed Discs (Nettwerk in the US) and that fall, the band relocated to Brussels.

Jenssen did not remain in the city for long, returning to Tromso and maintaining his band work via the mails. 1987 brought the album *White-Out Conditions* and three singles, the *Blank Sheets* EP, "Dreaming Girl," and the title track. However, by the time of Bel Canto's second album, *Birds of Passage*, Jenssen was also working on his own solo project using a sampler for the first time.

Under the name of Bleep, this material was subsequently released by Crammed's SSR subsidiary as *The North Pole by Submarine*, accompanied by the singles "Sure Be Glad When You're Dead" (under the name I Said Bleep) and "In Your System." Subsequent Bleep singles included "A Byte of AMC" (1990) and "The Launchpad" (1991); another Bleep track, "Lukenia" (from the *Norsk Epleslang* compilation), would be reworked as "Cygnus A" for Jenssen's next project, Biosphere.

Although Johansen and Drecker returned to Norway in the summer of 1990, Jenssen quit Bel Canto soon after and set about recording the first Biosphere releases, a 12" single titled "The Fairy Tale" and the album, *Microgravity*. SSR rejected both as unmarketable, only for the tiny Norwegian Origo Sound label to pick them up and score sizeable European club hits in 1991. Biosphere's music slipped right into the chill-out rooms, and with Jenssen's own homebase lying 500 miles inside the Arctic Circle, there was a pun there which few DJs could resist.

In 1992, Jenssen was one of several European artists invited to participate in Hector Zazou's *Sahara Blue* project — "I'll Strangle You," Jenssen's contribution to the set, would also be released as a single in Belgium.

In 1993, the *Baby Satellite* EP brought together three remixes of the album's "Baby Interphase," a stopgap release, while Jenssen prepared the next Biosphere album, 1994's *Patashnik* (Russian for "the traveller"). He also recorded as Cosmic Explorer, hitting in Belgium with the EP *The Hubble*. His homeland renown, meanwhile, saw him score the Norwegian movies *Eternal Stars* (1993) and *Insomnia* (1997). A collaboration with German ambient composer Peter Narnlook resulted in the well-received *Fires of Ork* (and a single of the title track) and Jenssen would also work with Jah Wobble's Invaders of the Heart and Bobby Bird of Higher Intelligence Agency.

Biosphere, however, remained Jenssen's best-known alias. An EP drawn from *Patashnak*, *The SETI Project* proved

a club hit in late 1994 while he scored a bona fide UK chart hit with "Novelty Waves" (#51 UK) following its appearance in a Levi commercial. The following year, he signed with Eno's All Saints label and released *Substrata*, a cycle inspired partly by a climbing expedition to Nepal he undertook in May 1994 and partly by the birth of his daughter, Andrea, midway through the sessions.

Bel Canto LPs

⑥ **White Out Conditions (Nettwerk) 1987** Bleak, but not glacial; hard but not unyielding; but maybe too purely atmospheric for comfort.

⑥ **Birds of Paradise (Nettwerk) 1989**

⑥ **Shimmering Warm and Bright (Crammed) 1991** Their first without Jenssen, but more of the sounds are so well described by the title.

Bleep LP

⑧ **The North Pole by Submarine (SSR) 1990** Deep dance textures, but touched with sufficient sensitivity to make just as much sense from the armchair.

Biosphere LPs

⑦ **Microgravity (Apollo) 1992**

⑧ **Patashnik (Apollo) 1994** The one with the Levi's hit on it! Captivating post-ambient whispers resolving themselves into lovely, strange sounds.

⑨ **Substrata (All Saints) 1997** Glacial images grind through the wind, frostbitten beards and ice-caked footsteps — sparse tunes play beneath seemingly solid melodies, but the ground is never as safe as it looks and one false footfall... and you're finished. Grimly beautiful, chilling, chaotic; passages heat your feet by the fire but the Yeti are still howling outside the door, and you wonder if you'll ever feel truly warm again. A magnificent album but if you're going to play it when you're on your own... take a packed lunch.

Geir Jenssen LP

⑥ **Soundtrack — Insomnia (Origo) 1997**

Geir Jenssen/Pete Namlook LP

⑦ **The Fires of Ork (Apollo) 1994** More dramatic than past Jenssen projects, and certainly more unsettling, but no other dramatic surprises.

Geir Jenssen/Bobby Bird LP

⑥ **Polar Frequencies (Apollo) 1996**

BIRTHDAY PARTY

FORMED *(as Boys Next Door)* 1975 *(Melbourne, Australia)*
ORIGINAL LINE-UP *Nick Cave (b. 9/22/57, Warraknabeal, Australia — vocals); Mick Harvey (b. 9/29/58, Rochester, Australia — guitar); Tracy Pew (bass); Phill Calvert (drums)*

Having made his recorded debut at age 13 when his local church choir cut a Christmas single of "Silent Night" and "Oh, Little Town of Bethlehem," Nick Cave was attending Caulfield Grammar School in Wangaratta, near Melbourne, when he met Tracy Pew, Phill Calvert, and Mick Harvey.

Under the name Boys Next Door, the quartet began jamming together, subsisting on what Cave remembered as "a couple of our own songs, but basically it was just Alex Harvey's stuff, and a bit of Alice Cooper..." a diet which served them in good stead as the first flames of punk licked the Australian music scene. "We'd played concerts before the punk thing happened and we could play reasonably well, and we were playing kind of raucous noisy gigs anyway. It didn't take that much to change our sound in order that we were a punk rock group."

With the band now based in Melbourne, by late 1977, Boys Next Door's local fame had reached the ear of Suicide, an Australian indie label, who included three of their early songs ("Masturbation Generation," "Boy Hero," and "These Boots Are Made for Walking") on a March 1978 compilation, *Lethal Weapons*. A single of "These Boots" was also released and shortly after, the Mushroom label offered Boys Next Door the chance to record an album.

Unfortunately, Cave mourned, "we were given a producer who didn't have a clue. We had a manager who took us into the office one day and said 'Listen, boys, I've been on to the phone to London, punk's out, power pop's in,' and he had these diagrams of clothes he wanted us to wear. [And we had] a record company, who had absolutely no idea about anything." Still unreleased in its original form, *Brave Exhibitions* was scarcely representative of the band from the outset. By the time the sessions ended, it could have been by a different band entirely.

Taking out their frustrations on the stage, Boys Next Door developed into one of the most violent acts Australia had ever seen — so out of control that there was barely a venue in the region that would book them. Still they persevered, and having been joined by guitarist Rowland Howard, the group returned to the studio to try and salvage *Brave Exhibitions*.

They failed, but an album was drawn from the sessions anyway. *Door Door* appeared, much to the group's chagrin, in May 1979. Far more to their tastes was a split single cut with fellow Melbourne band, the Models, and released on a tiny local label, but credited to the almost anagrammatical

Torn Ox Bodies, to avoid problems with their label, Mushroom.

Not until year's end were Boys Next Door able to extricate themselves from the Mushroom deal, and in December, Missing Link released the *Hee Haw* EP. Unfortunately, once again the band found label politics overwhelming their own sense of self and figuring that one Australian label was probably very much like another, there was only one thing left to do — they would leave Australia.

Boys Next Door played their final Australian show on February 16, 1980 at the Crystal Ballroom in Melbourne, marking the occasion with two new singles — "Happy Birthday," credited to the familiar band name, and "Mr Clarinet" (#43 UK indy) by The Birthday Party. Less than six months later, the group was in London with the local music press falling over itself to praise them.

Signing a single to 4AD, "The Fiend Catcher" (#21 UK indy) was released in October followed in April by the *Prayers on Fire* album (#4 UK indy), both accompanied by intensive (and intense) gigging. Never less than an uncompromising ball of yowling sound and frantic energy, "angry young men spewing forth their bile" as Harvey later put it, the Birthday Party's violence and vision were utterly without peer — groundbreaking and ballbreaking in equal quantities, but backbreaking as well, as gigs in Europe and a brief American tour were bookended by a seemingly endless slog around Britain. Outwardly outrageous, appearing to thrive on such a workload, internally the band was cracking loudly.

The "Release the Bats" single (#3 UK indy) and a union with Lydia Lunch (captured on the *Drunk on the Pope's Blood* live EP, #2 UK indy) preceded the band's return to Australia in early 1982 to record their next album. The very fabric of the band was beginning to unravel and a change in locale, they hoped, might hold the fraying ends together. It couldn't. Despite completing both their own album and a single, "After the Fireworks," with the Go-Betweens (themselves still planning their own move to London), the Birthday Party continued collapsing.

First, Pew was jailed on a drunk driving charge and missed the group's return to Britain. Then, Calvert quit (he reappeared in the Psychedelic Furs) just weeks after the release of *Junkyard* (#73 UK, #1 UK indy) *and* on the eve of the band's next tour. With Harvey filling in on drums and both Magazine bassist Barry Adamson and Rowland Howard's brother Harry replacing Pew, the Birthday Party hit the road, only to discover that their goth-trimmed audience, too, was moving on.

It was time for the band to move on as well. "We abhorred everything about London," Cave later recalled. "We found it to be one of the greatest disappointments of our lives. After living in Australia and reading constantly about London, what an amazingly exciting place it was, we finally got there and found this horrible, very constipated society."

Emboldened by a meeting with the German industrial band Einsturzende Neubauten and encouraged by the friendship of that band's guitarist, Blixa Bargeld, the Birthday Party (with Pew back on board) abandoned London and moved to Berlin. One last EP, the presciently titled *Bad Seed* EP (#3 UK indy), ended their relationship with 4AD in June 1983, and that fall, the Birthday Party signed to Mute.

Ensconced in Hansa studios, however, even the optimism engendered by these changes could not paper over the cracks. Internal relationships continued deteriorating, personal ambitions were broadening — Pew was talking about leaving music behind and returning to Australia to study, Cave was contemplating taking his now fast-maturing vision into new, solo pastures at the same time as nursing a heroin habit which only made communication even harder. Even the addition of Bargeld as a party guest could not disguise the fact that *Mutiny* (#3 UK indy) was the end of the group.

An Australian tour was booked, then thrown into disarray when Harvey announced he was quitting the band. Hastily recruiting Marching Girls drummer Des Hefner, the Birthday Party completed the tour, only for Howard to announce his own departure, to form Crime and the City Solution. Too crippled to continue, the Birthday Party officially disbanded in July 1983.

Although the band members would all troupe in and out of Cave's solo career, the Birthday Party themselves have never reunited, although two volumes of John Peel Sessions (#7, #11 UK indy) and the *It's Still Living* live album (#19 UK), preluded a reformation of sorts in September 1992, when Cave reconvened the majority of the band for three songs during a London solo gig. The death of Pew, from a powerful epileptic seizure on November 7, 1986, however, precluded anything more than tentative reunions; a second would take place in the studio in 1999, after the band regained control of their back catalog and mixed the *Live 1981–82* anthology for fall release.

Also see the entries for "NICK CAVE" on page 245 and "CRIME AND THE CITY SOLUTION" on page 298.

Birthday Party/Boys Next Door LPs

5 Door Door (Mushroom — Australia) 1979 Six tracks from the Karsky sessions, four more with Rowland Howard, and one track, "After a Fashion," which is so closely modelled on Television's "Marquee Moon" that it seems churlish even to mention it.

7 The Boys Next Door/The Birthday Party (Mushroom — Australia) 1980 "Mr Clarinet" and "The Friend Catcher" prove that even the notion of a strangely split disc was taking advantage of the band's own indecision; with feedback and fury now fully to the fore, the conflagration was already underway.

The Birthday Party LPs

8 Prayers on Fire (4AD UK) 1981 So much of the Brit-goth '80s rested on Birthday Party's initial formula that a lot of the intensity has been burned away now — to leave an unexpected melodicism, tangible emotions and readily discernable lyrics. At the time, though... well, you can still see why it made such a difference.

9 Junkyard (4AD UK) 1982 With the definitive rampage through "Big Jesus Trash Can" still echoing from a demonic John Peel session, *Junkyard* initially seemed less frenzied than its predecessor. But the understatement pays off as *Junkyard* peels away the mythology which was already alive around the band, and replaces it with a psychoses that was wholly their own, and infinitely more terrifying.

Selected Compilations and Archive Releases

8 The Mutiny/The Bad Seed (4AD — UK) 1989 "Deep in the Wood," "Sonny's Burning" and the awe-inspiring "Jennifer's Veil" highlight this pairing of two post-*Junkyard* EPs.

9 Hits (4AD — UK) 1992 That's "hits" as in physical violence, as opposed to those things you get when you sell lots of records, although in terms of posthumous impact and importance, there's barely a soul who would pick this disc up without some idea of what they'll find..."Release the Bats," "Zoo Music Girl," "Swampland"... the ultimate introduction.

8 It's Still Living — Live (Missing Link — Australia) 1985
7 Live 1981-82 (4AD UK) 1999 *Living* catches the cataclysm first hand; the band approved, remixed and modeled *Live* has better sound, stronger performances, but seems ever-so-slightly out to impress.

Further Reading

The Birthday Party & Other Adventures by Robert Brokenmouth (Omnibus, UK, 1996).

BJÖRK

BORN *Björk Gudmundsdottir, 11/21/65 (Reykjavik, Iceland)*

Although Björk's first "solo" international hit came when she linked with 808 State on April 1991's "Ooops" (#42 UK) and had already become established in her native Iceland through the previous year's *Gling-Glo* set, it took the demise of her band, the Sugarcubes, to acclimatize the public to the concept of her solo career — that, and a phenomenally successful new album, *Debut* (#61 US, #3 UK).

Released within nine months of the demise of the Sugarcubes, the album itself sold over two and a half million copies worldwide, simultaneously spawning four successive hit singles: "Human Behaviour" (#36 UK, the subject of an astonishing dance mix by Underworld), "Venus as a Boy"

(#29 UK), "Big Time Sensuality" (#88 US, #17 UK), and "Violently Happy" (#13 UK).

She would co-write the title track to Madonna's 1994 *Bedtime Stories* album (Björk's own version was released as "Sweetest Dream"), she combined with David Arnold for "Play Dead" (#12 UK) from the *Young Americans* movie soundtrack, and she wrapped up a frenetic year by scooping the Best Solo Artist and Object of Desire categories in the annual *NME BRAT* awards and International Newcomer and International Female Solo Artist at the BRITS. It was a very hectic beginning for what has proven one of the most individualistic careers of the 1990s.

In the aftermath of such successes, Björk moved to London's Belsize Park, to be closer to the musicians and scene which was now so important to her, and to work on a series of collaborations for a follow-up album, the three million-selling *Post* (#32 US, #2 UK). Nellee Hooper, Graham Massey, Tricky, and Howie B all played their part in this remarkable record; further talents lent their names to the remix collection *Telegram* (#66 US, #59 UK).

While Björk began the *Post* tour with a headlining appearance at the Reading Festival, a slew of accompanying hit singles descended — "Army of Me" (#10 UK), from the

© Jim Steinfeldt/Chansley Entertainment Archives

Tank Girl soundtrack, "Isobel" (#23 UK), the Christmas novelty "It's Oh So Quiet" (#4 UK), "Hyperballad" (#8 UK), and "Possibly Maybe" (#13 UK) all kept Björk in the chart through 1995–96; while Spike Jonze's video for "It's Oh So Quiet" won Best Choreography at the MTV Video Awards.

But success would not come without a price. With her superstardom ensuring she was fair game for the notoriously voracious British tabloid press, Björk's private life became an open book to readers of the less scrupulous papers, while her public behavior fell beneath an equally bright spotlight.

On tour in the US, she lost her voice, and was forced to cancel four shows through nervous exhaustion. In Thailand, passing paparazzi snapped her beating on one of their numbers, reporter Julie Kaufman, after repeated requests to be left in peace were ignored. In Israel, another tabloid photographer returned home with what were apparently photos of a topless Björk sunbathing on the beach. And back in England, only the vigilance of a post office worker caught the package addressed to her, mailed by an Hispanic-American "fan," and designed to spray acid over whoever opened the package. Claiming that he sent the package in protest at Björk's then on-going relationship with the Jamaican-Scot performer Goldie, the sender committed suicide immediately after mailing the bomb. Björk's own latest single, "I Miss You" (#36 UK), was playing in the background while he did it.

While a pair of limited edition 12" singles remixing *Post* cuts "Possibly Maybe" and "Enjoy" led up to the Christmas 1996 release of *Telegram*, Björk began work on what would become *Homogenic*. She previewed four of the new songs at the 1996 Tibetan Freedom concert: "All Neon Like," "Joga" (a song co-authored with Tricky which had already appeared on his *Nearly God* album), "Hunter," and "Pluto."

The original plan was to record with RZA of the Wu Tang Clan, creating an album which Björk insisted would comprise "strings and fat beats, and nothing else. So I did the string arrangements, and then I wanted fat beats. But he was just so busy that we couldn't hook up. He was finishing the Wu Tang album and that was taking ages, and when we did finally meet up in New York, I'd already done the album."

Described by Björk as "truly Icelandic, filthy Troll techno," *Homogenic* (#28 US, #4 UK) emerged as her most well-rounded album yet, proof positive of a remark she made earlier in the year, before the album's completion. "From far far away, I look like a kooky chick who sings along with fax machines. I don't think of me that way, no way, but at the same time, I do want to take noises from the modern day, which some people think are ugly, and make pop tunes out of them." In other words, "I want everybody to sing along with fax machines."

A European tour scheduled for fall 1997, was cancelled after Björk succumbed to a kidney infection. In her absence, "Joga" and "Bachelorette" (#21 UK) were released as singles, while she recovered in time for the Grammys, where she was nominated for Best Alternative Music Performance, and the BRITS, where she took Best International Female Artist for the second time. "Bachelorette" would also win the Best Art Direction gong at the MTV awards.

Björk spent spring 1998 touring the US — in April, she joined Joni Mitchell at the Walden Woods benefit in LA to duet on "What Is This Thing Called Love?"; in May, she sold out two nights at New York's Hammerstein Ballroom; and year's end brought two more singles, "Hunter" and a Beck remix of "Alarm Call" (#33 UK). However, another incident involving a fan — this time a Spaniard who broke into her mother's home — left Björk seriously contemplating retirement. "This is worse than the mail bomb. Maybe I have to stop releasing my music." She told the Swedish newspaper *Expressen*, "before I was 26, my motto was never to let anyone hear my music."

Björk would spend much of the next year recording the soundtrack to Lars Von Trier's *Dancer in the Dark*; Björk also made her acting debut in the film, opposite Catherine Deneuve. Another movie collaboration for the soundtrack to Spike Jonze's *Being John Malkovich*, paired her with LFO's Marc Bell and appeared as an MP3 internet download on her own website in November 1999, shortly before Björk played her first live shows of the year with the Brodsky Quartet in London on December 9 and 11. She wrapped up the year by appearing at the Voices of Europe 2000 concert in Reykjavik, Iceland.

Also see the entry for "SUGARCUBES" on page 665.

Björk LPs

7 Debut (Elektra) 1993 Very much a disc of two parts, the undisguised epics ("Venus as a Boy," "Violently Happy," and "Human Behaviour") which would stand alone whatever the company, and a crop of lesser efforts ("Come to Me," "One Day") which need all the nurturing producer Nellee Hooper can muster. All's well that ends well, though, and *Debut* emerges with unparalleled strength.

8 Post (Elektra) 1995 Spreading the workload among various producers, *Post* has a more scattershot feel, but a broadened appeal, as detailed across "Hyper Ballad," "Army of Me," and the deranged big-band anarchy of "It's Oh So Quiet."

7 Celebrating Wood and Metal (One Little Indian — UK) 1996 Fan club only release culling tracks from Björk's oddly sparse *MTV Unplugged* performance.

9 Homogenic (Elektra) 1997 Aiming for a flavor of "filthy troll techno" and an album which reflects the land where she grew up, Björk contrarily turns in a collection of internationalist mag-

nificence — in many ways the summary of all she'd strived for before.

Selected Compilations and Archive Releases

6 Best Mixes from Debut (One Little Indian — UK) 1994

6 Telegram (Elektra) 1996 The originals were perfect enough. Underworld's marathon remake of "Human Behaviour" notwithstanding, little here adds to any of them.

Further Reading

Björkography by Martin Aston (Simon & Schuster 1999).

FRANK BLACK

BORN 1/1/65 *(Long Beach, CA)*

The artist formerly known as Black Francis had already started work on his first solo album when he told his fellow Pixies that the fairytale was over. Linking with keyboard player Eric Drew Feldman (ex-Captain Beefheart, Pere Ubu), who himself sessioned on the Pixies' *Trompe le Monde* album, Black created an eponymous set (#117 US, #9 UK), which at its finest, preserved all the Pixies' own best points, then layered them with a melodic sense which that band only occasionally aimed for. Could the Pixies have made this record, he was asked shortly after its release. "No," he replied. "Eric and I wouldn't have let them."

This same dogged determination to do things his way pursued Black through 1994's *Teenager of the Year* (#131 US), a generally superior album which performed absolutely appallingly. After just two weeks on the chart, and despite spawning the hit "Headache" (#53 UK), it fell away, and Black quit Elektra (4AD in the UK) soon after.

Signing with American, his third solo album, *The Cult of Ray* (#127 US), was a hard-rocking set which suggested a whole new direction for Black, but clearly a popular one. "Men in Black" (#37 UK) and "I Don't Want to Hurt You" (#63 UK) both gained significant airplay, but Black's similarly intentioned next album was barely complete when his US label, American, ceased operations in early 1997.

Recorded live to two tracks in just four days, and intended to introduce his new backing band to the world — bassist Dave McCaffrey, guitarist Lyle Workman, and drummer Scott Boutier — the *Frank Black and the Catholics* album eventually found a European release early in 1998.

It would be close to a year more before he found a US outlet, via SpinArt. The wait was worthwhile, however. Released at a time when Pixies nostalgia was at a peak, thanks to recently released retrospectives of both their official and radio work, *Frank Black & the Catholics* dismissed all such notions with two of Black's finest ever songs, "All My

Ghosts" (also released as a single) and "The Man Who Was Too Loud."

Two further singles, "I Gotta Move" and "Dog Gone," were released from the album while the band toured the US, then returned to the studio to record their second album. Now lining up with McCaffrey, Boutier, and new guitarist Rich Gilbert (ex-Boston legends Human Sexual Response), *Pistolero* took a little longer to record than its predecessor (ten days), but packed a similar sense of personal exorcism and spiritual rejuvenation. Again he toured heavily, although UK fans were disappointed when his European itinerary included only one British show in London.

Also see the entry for the "PIXIES" on page 547.

Frank Black LPs

8 Frank Black (4AD) 1993 A sharper eye for pop notwithstanding, a not-quite-there invention. Although the Beach Boys' "Hang onto Your Ego" proves he knew what people were saying about him.

8 Teenager of the Year (4AD) 1994 More experimental, with some critics detecting a definite streak of Beefheart in the weirder moments. But it's just as likely the rest of the exorcism, with "(I Want to Live on an) Abstract Plain" and "Space Is Gonna Do Me Good" both packing hidden subtexts for those who doubted the rebirth.

4 The Cult of Ray (WB) 1996 New band, new sound, new absolute dearth of inspiration. Oh, dear. Well that scuppers that theory, doesn't it?

9 Frank Black & The Catholics (Play It Again) 1998 Or maybe it just cleared the air for it. "Do You Feel Bad About It" has a deceptive bounce to it, while the semi-surreal "King and Queen of Siam" would make a great Samuel Beckett story, if the despair was played for giggles. And then there's "The Man Who Was Too Loud," the story of a guy who used to indulge in high-octane indy cult heroics, then... but you can probably guess the rest.

9 Pistolero (Spinart) 1999 Black is the kind of curmudgeon you wish you could have for an uncle. Musically, he's as bad-tempered as a bear, stamping through a landscape of songs whose overall message appears to be, shit or get off the pot. And with a folkier, but at the same time rockier vibe than one might have expected from past Black albums, his apparent impatience with anything that stands in his way does conjure up images of pickup trucks, six packs of beer, and a gun rack with a big dog tied to it. Good job he's currently making the best albums of his career-so-far then.

BLACK FLAG

FORMED *1977 (Los Angeles, CA)*
ORIGINAL LINE-UP *Greg Ginn (b. Greg Pettibone, 6/8/54 — guitar); Keith Morris (vocals); Chuck Dukowski (bass); Robo (drums)*

Black Flag emerged from the punk-whipped streets of Los Angeles in 1977, the most prominent and committed of the wave of groups whose stated purpose was to relieve local youth from the traditional sounds of California rock. Mixing the simplicity of The Ramones with the passion of the Sex Pistols was the easy part; far more challenging was snapping the conditioning of their audience to encourage people to listen to the new band as well as mosh to it, a pre-requisite which was never easy to enforce even amongst founder Ginn's own bandmates.

Greg Ginn's first recruit was drummer Keith Morris, who switched to vocals when he couldn't afford a drum kit. Robo joined the following year, together with bassist Chuck Dukowsky, hijacked from a band who shared rehearsal space with Black Flag, but gigs were harder to find. Armed with a 15-song repertoire, the band played anywhere they could, from parties and garages to the Standard Oil refinery in El Segundo to the Sunday afternoon Lunch on the Grass in Manhattan Park. Black Flag were booked on the understanding that they were a Fleetwood Mac cover band.

Although there was a flourishing local punk scene, dominated by the Dangerhouse and Slash labels, and a handful of venues willing to adopt the bands, still it would be 1978 before Ginn decided Black Flag could make their first record — and another year before they could afford to release it. With Ginn's brother Raymond Pettibone on board as resident artist, designing the band's posters and record sleeve, "Nervous Breakdown" was finally released on Ginn's own SST label, shortly before Morris quit to form the Circle Jerks.

His replacement, Ron Reyes (b. Chavo Pederast) would stay around long enough to record the five-track *Jealous Again* EP in August 1980, before he was replaced by former Redd Kross guitarist Dez Cadena.

That fall, Black Flag were filmed for Penelope Spheeris' *Decline of Western Civilization* movie and in December 1980, Black Flag undertook their first US tour. It was in Washington DC on that first outing that the band met the young Ian MacKaye, just launching his new band, Minor Threat, and one of his former roadies, State of Alert vocalist Henry Rollins (b. Henry Garfield, 2/13/61, Washington DC). They kept in touch, and when Black Flag returned to the East Coast the following summer, Rollins joined them onstage for one song.

The band were impressed, all the more so since Cadena had been talking about giving up vocals for rhythm guitar, and soon after, Rollins was Black Flag's new vocalist. He quit his job, sublet his apartment, sold almost everything he owned, and joined the band mid-tour.

Two new Black Flag singles, the three-track *Six Pack* EP (#16 UK indy) and a raw version of "Louie Louie," had already been recorded before he joined (so had the band's contribution to the *Chunks* compilation). Rollins' vinyl debut would come when the band recorded their first album, *Damaged*, on the eve of their first British tour in late 1981 — itself a traumatic affair which saw the band roundly heckled everywhere they played. The UK punk scene, after all, had never been tolerant of its American counterpart, and Black Flag's appearance at London's Lyceum, sandwiched between the Oi! pontifications of the Anti Nowhere League and the cartoon punch of the Damned, was a masterpiece of mismatching.

Further shows with Chelsea and back in London with the Exploited and Honey Bane were no better, but it was in Leeds, halfway up the bill at a pre-Christmas punk festival, that Black Flag truly encountered the xenophobic disdain of their hosts. The only Americans on a bill comprising of many of the country's most potent punk acts — the UK Subs, Vice Squad, and Chron Gen among them — Black Flag's performance was met with a violent silence.

Originally scheduled for release on the Unicorn label, *Damaged* was issued in January 1982 through SST, after Unicorn's parent label, MCA, deemed it unacceptable for release — a quote from the company chairman, "as a parent... I found it an anti- parent record," was stickered over MCA's logo on 25,000 record sleeves, but MCA were not finished with the band yet.

Citing breach of contract, SST and Black Flag were to be bound up in legal affairs for the next two years, with the band unable to record until the dispute was solved. An attempt to circumvent the injunction with the *TV Party* EP (#30 UK indy) and *Everything Went Black* collection of unreleased material, issued through SST without any reference to the band themselves, only aggravated the situation further.

Throughout this period, the band kept going. Robo quit and while Bill Stevenson of the Descendents filled in for a show or two, a long succession of replacement drummers would also play with the band before future Danzig drummer Chuck Biscuits made the final commitment. Dukowski then quit shortly before work began on Black Flag's second album, *My War* (#5 UK indy), in early 1983; Ginn would handle bass on the album, under the alias Dale Nixon, before Kira Roessler joined at the end of the year.

With so much lost time to make up, Black Flag gigged heavily throughout 1984, setting a record of sorts when in one 24-hour period, they played three shows in three separate states. They also released two albums, *Slip It In* (#8 UK indy) and *Family Man* (#14 UK indy), a disc split between instrumentals, and Rollins' spoken word material. 1985 was even more hectic, with an EP of further instrumentals, *The Process of Weeding*, sandwiched by two conventional collections, *Loose Nut* and *in My Head*.

Much of the group's early momentum, however, had been irrevocably drained by their legal difficulties and the financial problems which followed, while the departures of Stevenson and Roessler (to be replaced by Anthony Martinez and C'el) further disrupted the group's equilibrium. Certainly Black Flag's next American tour — a mammoth undertaking split into three legs as it sought to cover every last inch of the country — found the group in increasing disarray.

Ginn, in particular, was feeling the pressure; also on the bill was Gone, a three-piece instrumental band that he formed with Simeon Cain and Andrew Weiss, and the strain of two high energy performances a night, plus the everyday administration of the SST label was taking its toll. Once the tour was over, Ginn announced he was quitting both Black Flag and Gone, to concentrate on SST. Less than a year later, the Rollins Band — featuring Cain and Weiss — was on the road.

Since that time, rumors of a Black Flag reunion have circulated, but the closest they came to fruition was a 1999 show erroneously billed as Black Flag, but in fact featuring Morris' latest Circle Jerks incarnation. The show's promoter defended the misbilling by insisting that Morris embodied the spirit of Black Flag to him. Ginn responded by labelling the event a "Punk Rock Karaoke Fraud," and in the event, Morris wasn't present either — he fell ill on the eve of the show.

Rollins' own recollections of his Black Flag days, the *Get in the Van* book and audio cassette, appeared in 1994, and earned the performer a Grammy for Best Audio Book.

Also see the entry for "HENRY ROLLINS" on page 706.

Black Flag LPs

9 Damaged (SST) 1991 At the time, Black Flag sounded like a Sham 69 rehearsal, with a madman on guitar. They still do, but *Damaged* remains perhaps the greatest US punk album of them all. High humor wracks the lyrics, though, and the whole thing blisters with a joyous conviction which is almost nostalgic in its sincerity.

6 My War (SST) 1983 Hardcore offered the freedom to start rock'n'roll afresh. Or alternatively, to disappear into a quagmire of tuneless bellowing. You choose.

7 Family Man (SST) 1984 One half instrumental, the other spoken word. Buy two copies, then play one over the other. It rocks.

4 Slip It In (SST) 1984 With a title surely borrowed from Whitesnake or some such, and riffs that look in that direction too, Black Flag teeter on the edge of parody. Or "Paranoid" — and that would be the one by Grand Funk, not Sabbath.

8 Live 84 [LIVE] (SST) 1984 A sudden return to form, as the live arena kicks all the attempted finesse and progression out of the room and concentrates on what Black Flag do best — playing very loudly and very fast.

6 Loose Nut (SST) 1985

5 In My Head (SST) 1985 "This Is Good" stands as a latter-day Black Flag classic, and the rest of *Loose Nut* at least tries to keep up. *In My Head* pales by comparison, and with the band's other interests still making themselves heard (the same year's *Weeding Out* EP served up a slab more proggy instrumentals), the loud stuff began to seem like more of an obligation than an actual calling....

4 Who's Got the 10 1/2 [LIVE] (SST) 1986 With new drummer Martinez on board, Black Flag touch down inPortland, OR for a night of primarily recent music. Occasional high points are effortlessly subdued by a growing penchant for sludge. The split looms closer.

Selected Compilations and Archive Releases

6 Everything Went Black (SST) 1982 Embargo-beating out-takes collection — which, of course, only landed the band in deeper trouble. In terms of the actual music involved, it probably wasn't worth the pain.

9 The First Four Years (SST) 1983 Masterful recounting of the early singles, EPs, compilation tracks, with the *Six Pack* EP sounding more vital than ever.

7 Wasted... Again (SST) 1988 A 12-track mini anthology; adequate but it needed to have been at least three times the length.

Circle Jerks LPs

6 Group Sex (Epitaph) 1981

5 Wild in the Streets (Epitaph) 1982 Still more of a live concern than a studio machine, but the Jerks retain their taste under pressure, turning in the world's first hardcore restructuring of a song by Jackie de Shannon ("Put a Little Love in Your Heart"). But make it quick because there's another song along in 45 seconds.

6 Golden Shower of Hits (Rhino) 1983 "Jerks on 45," of course, remains the favorite, a joyously idiotic, hardcore medley of the songs we love to hate — "AfternoonDelight," "You're Having My Baby," Captain & Tennille. Unfortunately, having mastered the novelty song so well, it's difficult for the band to take the rest of the album as seriously as it deserves.

4 Wonderful (Combat) 1985 A cacophonic blitzkrieg, of course, with subject matter ranging from helping old ladies across the street to the Springsteenesque declaration of patriotism — "American Heavy Metal Weekend." The hardcore band in *Repo Man* have themselves been repossessed.

4 VI (Combat) 1987

Selected Compilations and Archive Releases

8 Gig [LIVE] (Combat) 1992

Further Reading

Get in the Van: On the Road with Black Flag by Henry Rollins (2.13.61, 1994).

BLACK 47

FORMED 1989 *(New York, NY)*

ORIGINAL LINE-UP *Larry Kirwan (vocals, guitar); Chris Byrne (pipes); Fred Parcells (trombone); Geoffrey Blythe (b. Birmingham, England — sax); David Conrad (bass); Thomas Hamlin (drums)*

In 1989, Larry Kirwan was a disillusioned musician (ex-Major Thinkers), enjoying considerable success as a playwright when he became involved in an unauthorized benefit concert staged in Prague, Czechoslovakia for Vaclav Havel's dissidents. Some months before the revolution which liberated that country from Communism, some 12,000 attended the show and Kirwan began looking at rock'n'roll as a vehicle for social change.

Returning to New York, he fell into conversation with New York cop and part-time uilleann piper Chris Byrne, then working with the Irish-American folk band Beyond the Pale. By the end of the evening, the pair had formed Black 47, named for the darkest days of the Irish potato famine which had driven both musicians' forefathers to America.

As a two-piece backed with tapes and a drum machine, the pair devised a set built around a clutch of Kirwan originals, jigs, reels, reggae, and '60s rockers and played their first show in late 1989 at a fund-raising rally in the Bronx, staged for visiting Northern Ireland activist Bernadette Devlin-McAliskey. Their performance was disastrous and the pair were promptly fired from all their subsequent engagements — a predicament which actually worked in their favor, as word got round about an Irish band so unlike any other that even the Irish didn't like them.

By early 1990, Black 47 had a full-time residency at Paddy Reilly's bar and the band line-up began to expand with their following. Thomas Hamlin had played with Kirwan in Major Thinkers, Geoffrey Blythe was a founding member of Kevin Rowland's Dexy's Midnight Runners, and of course, not a show went by without someone stumbling drunkenly up to the statge, demanding they play "Come on Eileen."

They never obliged, but still the result was an intoxicating blend of Afro-Celtic reggae rock which packed the bar whenever the band played. Soon, the band's New York fame alone was sufficient to keep them gigging 200 nights a year, and in 1992, Black 47 self-released their eponymous first album, a fiery encapsulation of all they had achieved in the past year; a three-page write-up in *Newsday* encouraged a deal with EMI's SBK subsidiary, and the following year brought the Ric Ocasek produced *Fire of Freedom* (#176 US).

Fronted by the single "Funky Ceili," an MTV video hit, the album slammed Black 47 into the mainstream, despatching them on their first major US tour and unleashing a second hit, "Maria's Wedding."

It would have been easy and Kirwan admitted, "a lot safer" to simply deliver a Fires of Freedom II as their follow-up album, but instead, Black 47 released *Home of the Brave* — a dark, and considerably more urban selection of songs — and overnight, it seemed, the band's national momentum ceased. The collapse of SBK exacerbated the album's difficulties, while the group also lost two bassists in short succession — David Conrad was replaced by Kevin Jenkins shortly after *Home of the Brave*; Jenkins quit following a highway accident on the way home from a gig in Rhode Island, to be replaced by Andrew Goodsight.

Green Suede Shoes, the band's fourth album, rang down the curtain on their major label career. By decade's end, Black 47 were back confined to New York's Irish circuit, albeit with an amazing story behind them, and a new generation ahead of them. Kirwan's solo album, *Keltic Kids*, was recorded for his own two children, and featured contributions from Roseanne Cash and GE Smith, alongside the members of Black 47.

A live album, bookending a career's worth of Kirwan classics with suitably rearranged versions of Bob Marley's "Three Little Birds" and Bob Dylan's "Like a Rolling Stone," appeared on the Vermont- based Gadfly label in mid-1999; the following year, newly signed to Shanachie, the group released *Trouble in the Land*.

Black 47 LPs

7 Black 47 (Black 47) 1992

8 Fire of Freedom (SBK) 1993 A non-stop crop of rabble-rousing songs embraces reggae, hip-hop, rock, and jazz, entwined with skirling Gaelic melodies and a couple of tracks, "Funky Ceili" and "Maria's Wedding," which have literally written themselves into the Irish-American roots rock experience.

5 Home of the Brave (SBK) 1994 Oh dear. Black 47 didn't want to make the same noises again, so they made some radically different ones. Unfortunately, the old noises were what they did best.

7 Green Suede Shoes (Polygram) 1996 A return to form but nobody was watching. A neglected classic, The Pogues go posh.

8 Live in NYC [LIVE] (Gadfly) 1999 Crank it up loud enough, soak the house with beer and cigarette smoke, and you could almost be there — Wetlands on St. Patrick's Day, 1998, while America's greatest Irish reggae band blast through a hit-packed set. "Funky Ceili" is a bit Bruce Springsteen stadium rock-shaped, but everything else is just as it should be.

8 Trouble in the Land (Shanachie) 2000

Larry Kirwan LP

7 Keltic Kids (self-released) 1997 Too young for Dylan and Marley, too innocent for politics, and too small to reach the volume control? Juvenile jiggery-reelery, alive with magicians, leprechauns, fairy horses, and more.

BLONDIE

FORMED 1974 *(New York, NY)*
ORIGINAL LINE-UP *Debbie Harry (b. 7/1/45, Miami, FL — vocals); Chris Stein (b. 1/5/50, Brooklyn, NY — guitar); Fred Smith (bass); Bill O'Connor (drums)*

Originally (if briefly) named Angel and the Snake, then renamed to capitalize on former Max's waitress Debbie Harry's distinctive platinum coloring, Blondie were formed by Harry following ill-fated stints with Wind in the Willows and the Stilettos, where she first encountered Chris Stein, Fred Smith, and Bill O'Connor.

Taking their cue from the early '60s girl groups who were Harry's own musical motivation, shot through with the trash rock aesthetic of fellow New Yorkers, Wayne County and the New York Dolls, Blondie's earliest recordings (produced by author Alan Betrock and revealed on the 1993 *Blonde and Beyond* compilation) would serve as the mirror for much of what the band was destined to accomplish, ranging from a cover of the Shangri-Las' "Out in the Streets" to the mysterious "Disco Song," a piece of high camp irony which would one day emerge as "Heart of Glass."

Despite the band falling into a regular slot at CBGBs, the line-up remained unstable. Former Luger guitarist Ivan Kral was on board for a time, before he quit to join the better-heeled Patti Smith Group, while the departures of O'Conner and Smith (the latter for fellow Bowery dwellers Television) were overcome by the recruitment of Gary Valentine (bass), Clement Burke (b. 11/24/55, New York — drums), and James Destri (b. 4/13/54 — keyboards).

Blondie were one of the highlights of the 1975 CBGBs festival; twelve months later, club owner Hilly Kristal earmarked them to appear on a proposed document of the CBGBs scene, a double-live album titled *Live at CBGBs*. Session after session ended in disarray and disappointment, however, and Blondie were eventually omitted from the set. Still, their appeal was growing, and that summer, the band linked with producer and ex-Strangelove Richard Gottehrer to record their debut album *Blondie* (and single "X Offender"), released through Private Stock that fall.

The album was not a success, but with Blondie falling into the same liberal New York punk camp as The Ramones, Television, Patti Smith, and Richard Hell, and Harry in particular striking a chord with adolescent watchers, interest in the band was nevertheless significant enough to draw Chrysalis into the hunt for their signature. Buying out the band's Private Stock contract, the label reissued *Blondie* in early 1977 (it finally made the UK chart in March 1979, #75 UK), just as Blondie set out on their first national tour across the US with Iggy Pop, and then Britain, opening for Television.

That latter was an odd, but strangely effective coupling, made all the more alluring by the racey ad campaign unveiled to promote Blondie's latest single. A picture of a distinctly dishevelled looking Harry was accompanied by the slogan "wouldn't YOU like to 'Rip Her to Shreds'?" provoking a hail of outrage from feminists, and distaste from within Blondie's own camp too. In as much as it raised the temperature of the band's UK following, however, the campaign itself was a success.

Valentine was sacked from the band shortly before work began on their second album; he went on to launch a short-lived solo career, while his erstwhile bandmates recruited Frank Infante and former Silverhead bassist Nigel Harrison (b. Princes Risborough, England) and got to work on *Plastic Letters* (#72 US, #10 UK).

A distinctly transitional album, *Plastic Letters* nevertheless spawned Blondie's first two British hits, a cover of Randy and the Rainbows' '60s hit "Denise," resexed "Denis" (#2 UK) in February 1978, and the delicious "(I'm Always Touched by Your) Presence, Dear" (#10 UK) in April. A second tour, headlining this time, upped the band's profile even further, but the United States remained stubbornly oblivious to the group's charms, even after "Picture This" (#12 UK) in August 1978 introduced producer Mike Chapman to an increasingly intoxicating brew.

Parallel Lines (#6 US, #1 UK), Blondie's third album, topped the UK charts some six months before it finally broke through in America, by which time both "Hanging on the Telephone" (#5 UK) and January 1979's "Heart of Glass" (#1 US, #1 UK) had confirmed Blondie's European superstardom. Number one for a month in Britain, "Heart of Glass" would finally top the American chart in April and while it would be another two years before the group returned to such heady heights, still the erstwhile "Disco Song" had finally come good.

"Sunday Girl" (#1 UK), another cut from *Parallel Lines*, kept Blondie at the top in Britain, while a French language version did just as well across the English Channel. "One Way or Another" (#24 US) followed while Blondie's triumphant London Hammersmith Odeon show that fall climaxed with a guest appearance from Robert Fripp, adding twisted guitar through an encore version of David Bowie's "'Heroes'."

Pausing only to headline the 1979/1980 season premiere of *Saturday Night Live* on October 13, Blondie returned to the studio immediately to prepare *Eat to the Beat* (#17 US, #1 UK). Although flawed and rushed, it marked the peak of their commercial achievement regardless. "Dreaming" (#27 US, #2 UK), "The Hardest Part" (#84 US), and the irresistably seductive "Atomic" (#39 US, #1 UK) all emerged among the band's most enduring releases, while Harry and Stein's personal versatility was proven when she starred in, and he scored, Mark Reichart's *Union City Blue* movie (the title theme, included on *Eat to the Beat*, reached #13 UK).

Further evidence of the band's inventiveness arrived in a video companion to *Eat to the Beat*, 11 separate videos shot with director David Mallet, at a time when the video medium was still very much in its commercial infancy. MTV would not debut for close to another two years, British television barely had an hour's worth of dedicated music programming a week, and few houses even possessed video players on either side of the Atlantic. Still the set was a success, commercially and artistically, and in years to come, while other bands struggled to put together their first video resume, Blondie already had close to an hour's worth of first-rate material to fall back on.

In April 1980, another soundtrack collaboration linked Blondie with German disco producer Giorgio Moroder and resulted in their biggest hit since "Heart of Glass" — the pulsing "Call Me" (#1 US, #1 UK). Confident, now, with both their commercial and creative powers, Blondie's next album, *Auto-American* (#7 US, #3 UK), was to prove their most ambitious yet. Since "Heart of Glass," Harry and Stein in particular had embedded themselves in America's modern dance culture, emerging with an album which was both brilliantly realized and strangely patchy.

A cover of the reggae classic "The Tide Is High" (#1 US, #1 UK) brought chart-topping success around the world, but in June 1981, "Rapture" (#1 US, #5 UK) proved strangely divisive, appealing to the group's US audience, but disappointing British fans for whom Harry's performance smacked of patronizing dilettantism. "Rapture" earned the band's lowest chart placing ("Union City Blue" notwithstanding) since "Picture This," and with *Auto-American* also faltering below the band's accustomed peak at the top of the chart, it was clear that the love affair was reaching an end.

While a hits collection (#30 US, #4 UK) did its best to repair the damage, Harry's solo album *Koo Koo* (#25 US, #6 UK) hammered fresh nails into the coffin. Uniting her with Chic masterminds Nile Rodgers and Bernie Edwards, and boasting an HR Giger sleeve which predated the social acceptance of body piercing by a good decade, *Koo Koo*'s primary goal appeared to be to establish Harry's credentials as a "serious" artist within the generally fallow field of urban dance, and to distance her even further from the "classic" Blondie sound. Which meant, of course, that when she returned to it in 1982 with the band's next album, *The Hunter* (#33 US, #9 UK), even diehards had trouble taking it seriously.

Neither of the accompanying singles — "Island of Lost Souls" (#37 US, #11 UK) and "War Child" (#39 UK) touched the Top 10, while the band's latest British tour was cancelled because of poor ticket sales. Even worse, the group was visibly falling apart. In January 1982, even as Blondie's last album was being prepared, Infante threatened legal action after being excluded from the group's latest activities.

Now the members scattered, primarily to session work. Stein launched his own Animal Records label and promptly signed Iggy Pop, while Harry announced an acting career which would be broken only occasionally by new solo records — and which itself was shattered when Stein fell ill with the debilitating blood disease pemphigus. He would remain out of action for the next four years, by which time a new Harry single, "Rush Rush," had already passed by unpromoted and unnoticed.

In 1986, *Rockbird* (#97 US, #31 UK) and "French Kissing in the USA" (#57 US, #8 UK) announced something of a comeback, but two subsequent Harry sets did little — *Def Dumb and Blonde* (#123 US, #12 UK), produced jointly by *Parallel Lines* maestro Chapman and Thompson Twins frontman Tom Bailey, and *Debravation* (#24 UK), produced by Stein, Arthur Baker, and Art of Noise pianist Anne Dudley. Later, Harry worked with the highly acclaimed Jazz Passengers alongside Boy Nathanson, Chris Fowlkes, Brad Jones, BJ Rodriguez, Rob Thomas, and Bill Ware, and guested with the David Byrne less-Talking Heads, the sensibly renamed Heads, on 1996's *No Talking, Just Head* album.

In the meantime, a steady stream of Blondie-related archive and remix projects kept the band's name alive and in 1997, the first reports of a reunion leaked out. Initial rumors that Blondie would appear at Lilith Fair proved false, however, the group did return to the studio in summer 1997, recording two songs with Duran Duran members Nick Rhodes and Warren Cucurullo. Burke and Destri were both invited back into the Harry/Stein axis but hopes of an early release for the new material were dashed by the objections of excluded members Infante and Harrison.

It would be mid-1998 before the matter was resolved and while the band's former label, EMI, readied a new vintage live album and the *Atomic/Atomix* (#13 UK) compilation, the Blondie machine moved into overdrive. A European tour opened in Stockholm on October 26, 1998, and in the new year, the band appeared at the American Music Awards performing "No Exit" with Coolio and members of Wu Tang Clan.

The new album, *No Exit* (#18 US, #5 UK), followed, minus the Duran tracks, but previewed by an instant smash hit single, "Maria" (#82 US, #1 UK). "Nothing is Real but the Girl" followed, before the band's 1999 comeback tour was highlighted on the career-spanning *LIVID*, featuring tracks recorded in the US and UK.

Blondie LPs

8 Blondie (Private Stock) 1976 Sparkling melodies, bouncy beats, clap-along choruses, and enough hooks to wipe out all marine life on the Eastern seaboard, Blondie were cut firmly in the grand tradition of '60s girl groups — even if only one of them was female. But Debbie Harry still ripped all comers to shreds, with a cat fight sexuality and a posse which oozed from the wrong side of the tracks. The world's first pop/punk crossover was indeed a shark in jets' clothing.

8 Plastic Letters (Chrysalis) 1977 "Denis" and "Presence, Dear" were the hits but the whole album rippled with the pop priestess glamor which its debut was just too naive to assimilate. Less exuberant, but just as daring, with a brooding ebullience which couldn't be beat.

9 Parallel Lines (Chrysalis) 1978 A pair of Nerves' covers gave *Parallel Lines* the street credos this time, but even as Blondie continued playing to the punks, the album was aptly titled. For paralleling the punk lite pop tracks ("One Way or Another," "I Know But I Don't Know," and "Hanging on the Telephone"), and veering away from the electro experiment ("Fade Away and Radiate"), Blondie target their soul directly at the mainstream chart with the sweet "Sunday Girl" and the saucy "Heart of Glass." And with everything drenched in you- just-gotta-grin '60s pop class, who was surprised when it blew up so big?

8 Eat to the Beat (Chrysalis) 1979 As an album, it was disappointing. But as a stream of singles which peaked with the heavenly "Atomic," *Eat to the Beat* could hold its head up with the best of the band's past output — primarily because most of it was their best. No longer arch sexpots, no longer coy popsters, Blondie now was the sound of a million cash registers clattering in deliberate harmony, and "Dreaming" and "Shayla" had a sheen which made even Abba sound abrasive.

8 Auto American (Chrysalis) 1980 A desperate lurch out of what was perceived as "the formula," washing up somewhere between the twin embarrassments of "Rapture" and "The Tide is High."

2 The Hunter (Chrysalis) 1982 They should have broken up. Instead, they said goodbye. Unfortunately, no one was listening and "Island of Lost Souls" was less a tired single and more a guided tour of Blondie's fallen empire.

7 No Exit (Beyond) 1999 Imagine an entire album that sounds as great as "Atomic" did, but without the knowing pin-up cuteseiness. Imagine a record that respects all that Blondie represented in the past, but isn't interested in rewriting it. And imagine 14 tracks that eye the future with such honesty and optimism that even the token oldie (the Shangri-Las' "Out in the Street," re-recorded from Blondie's earliest demo tape) looks to Nick Cave for its arrangement, and coolly acknowledges the oxymoron that is a 50-something woman singing a high school sophomore's lyric. Of course "he don't hang around with the gang no more" — he's too busy doing the gardening and listening to the weary, dreamy, and strangely country-ish "The Dream's Lost on Me."

7 Livid (Beyond) 1999 Old hits and new marvels rub shoulders in a hastily packaged souvenir of the recent sold out tours.

Selected Compilations and Archive Releases

4 Once More into the Bleach (Chrysalis) 1988 Generously mixing Blondie's best with the solo Harry's hits, then spoiling the show with some pointless, joyless remixes. And not for the last time, either.

9 The Platinum Collection (Chrysalis) 1993
8 Blonde and Beyond (Chrysalis) 1994 Rock-solid hits and rarities collections featuring primal demos, B-sides, 12-inch mixes, even the original (1976) prototype for what would become "Heart of Glass." The foreign language "Sunday Girl" (the most worthwhile track on *Bleach*) makes a happy reappearance, while a smattering of live covers prove the band's breathless sense of adventure. (9,8)

2 The Remix Project (Chrysalis) 1995 Utah Saints, Black Dog, and Armand Van Helden are among the guilty men; "Heart of Glass," "Dreaming," and "Atomic" are among the victims. Dreadful.

8 Philadelphia 1978/Dallas 1980 [LIVE] (Capitol) 1999 Originally released as the limited edition *Picture This*, stunning sound, a respectful audience, and a contagious joie de vivre drape this non-stop revision of the band's greatest hits plus. Arguably, Blondie never made a bad record until 1981, and they never played that many bad gigs either.

Debbie/Deborah Harry LPs

3 Koo Koo (Chrysalis) 1981
5 Rockbird (Geffen) 1986
4 Def, Dumb and Blonde (Sire) 1989

Jazz Passengers LPs

5 In Love (Highstreet) 1994

6 Individually Twisted (32 Records) 1996 After a brief appearance on *In Love*, Harry moves to the fore of this quasi-ad hoc aggregation to duet with Elvis Costello, and generally sounds more relaxed than at any time since "Call Me."

Further Reading

Making Tracks: The Rise of Blondie by Debbie Harry/Chris Stein/Victor Bockris (Da Capo 1998).

BLUR

FORMED *(as Seymour)* 1988 (Colchester, England)
ORIGINAL LINE-UP *Damon Albarn (b. 3/23/68, Whitechapel, London — vocals); Graham Coxon (b. 3/12/69, Rintein, Germany — guitar); Dave Rowntree (b. 5/8/64, Colchester — drums); Alex James (b. 11/21/68, Boscombe — bass)*

Damon Albarn and Graham Coxon met in Colchester's Stanway Comprehensive choir. Albarn was the son of Soft Machine's stage designer; Coxon was an army brat whose father played in a military band and it was he who wanted to pursue a musical career, playing with a string of local, Colchester area bands. Albarn was more interested in theater and moved to London to study drama. There he did succumb to one musical temptation, forming a synthi-soul duo with Sam Vamplew called Two's a Crowd. Linking with London's Beat Factory studio team Graeme Holdaway and Marijke Bergkamp, the duo recorded some 15 demos before Vamplew departed and Albarn continued working solo.

Joined now by Coxon, playing saxophone, Albarn recorded another set of demos under his own name, before adding fellow Goldsmiths College student Dave Rowntree, guitarist Eddie Deedigan, and a bassist also named Dave. Naming themselves Circus, the band recorded further demos but played just one gig before Deedigan and Dave the bassist quit.

Alex James, another Goldsmith's student, replaced them and in December 1988, Circus were renamed Seymour, in honor of a character Albarn invented during his acting days. Still utilizing the Beat Factory team, Seymour's first demo comprised six tracks, all subsequently released as B-sides to Blur's 1993 "Sunday Sunday" single.

By the summer of 1989, Seymour were playing very occasional shows around London. They also recorded another demo which included "She's So High," the first song the band ever wrote together. One of the tapes made its way to Andy Ross and former Teardrop Explodes member David Balfe, head of Food Records. Intrigued, Balfe caught the band in November at London's Powerhaus, and in March 1990, Seymour signed to the label as Blur. A name change had been one of Food's first demands.

A UK tour opening for The Cramps was followed by a trip to Battery Studio with former Julian Cope producer Steve Lovell and his partner Steve Power. Heavily influenced by Stone Roses (who also used that studio), the swirling psychedelia of "She's So High" (#48 UK) placed Blur firmly into the then-prevalent Baggy genre in October 1990. "There's No Other Way" (#82 US, #8 UK) followed in March 1991, this time produced by Stephen Street (best known then for his work with The Smiths), who was to become a stalwart within the Blur camp. Blur promptly set out on another tour, supported by the newly emerging Catherine Wheel.

"Bang" (#24 UK) in August 1991 was followed by *Leisure* (#7 UK), well received despite Coxon subsequently describing it as "our indie detox album. We got all that Dinosaur [Jr], [My Bloody] Valentine, and C86 bile out of our system." Further tours of Britain and France followed before Blur headed for America for a month long tour in November 1991. Which is where things started going wrong for them.

Blur arrived at almost the same precise moment that the entire American indy scene began its love affair with Nirvana and *Nevermind*, and Albarn recalled, "it went from there being a vague interest in things British, to no interest at all. Having nothing to say as a nihilistic post-modern statement works in Britain, but it did not translate in Texas. It was painfully obvious that things were going wrong."

Even worse awaited upon their return home to discover that their pole position in British pop had been thoroughly usurped by the emergent London Suede. "Pop Scene" (#32 UK), Blur's first single of the new year, sold poorly; its intended follow-up, "Never Clever," was shelved and just to compound their misery, the band's finances were in utter disarray. It was time to go back to the drawing board.

Albarn reflected, "we were forced to become sort of isolated, the only thing we could really relate to were the British bands who'd never done well in America, because they'd had a similar experience to us. I think we strongly identified with people like Julian Cope, Ray Davies, [XTC's] Andy Partridge, Paul Weller, etc, etc." Indeed, Partridge came very close to producing the next Blur album, but three songs into the sessions, the project was shelved. Archetypal Englishman though he was, Partridge was just a little too archetypal for Blur.

Still, Albarn did buy a used tape recorder from the man, and as he took possession of a machine which had played such a great part in XTC's own recorded idiosyncrasies, he said later, he felt as though a "tradition was being handed on to me in a bizarre way. For the first time, I could focus all my disparate influences from theater and '60s pop, because I had enough tracks to put them all together. That fired my musical imagination and I started writing about all these English characters, and then musically I could color them appropriately."

Even after Food suggested they try working with Nirvana producer Butch Vig, Blur did not lose sight of their vision; instead, they returned to Stephen Street and began anew, this time with a provisional title of *British Image 1*. The album eventually emerged as *Modern Life Is Rubbish* (#15 UK).

The title was borrowed from a piece of street grafitti; the album was described by Coxon as "a psychotic view of what our roots were when we were away, a kind of homesickness vision of England. It wasn't really a celebration of England, it was a critique. It wasn't even an accurate vision of England, it was a fantasy England we had in our heads. We were pretty out of it as people, this whole idea of a really perverse kind of Kinks' view of things came around because of that, really."

Nods to the Kinks, Julian Cope, Madness, The Who, The Smiths, the newly-emerged Auteurs, and The Jam's Paul Weller littered the album with almost conceptual glee, a patchwork history of British pop which was greeted with total mystification in the US — just as the band planned. But three successive singles, "For Tomorrow" (#28 UK), "Chemical World" (#28 UK), and "Sunday Sunday" (#26 UK) saw the band at least maintain their equilibrium at home, and by the end of the year, Albarn recalled, "we'd really got something happening in Britain. The record started appearing in end of year polls, not high, but it was there, we sort of regained our integrity for ourselves."

In March 1993, emerging from sessions with producer Stephen Hague, Blur released a taster for their next album, the maddeningly infectious "Girls and Boys" (#5 UK, #59 US). One month later, the group's third album, *Parklife* (#1 UK), arrived to define Brit-pop as the commercial power of the post-grunge 1990s; indeed Albarn was not being immodest when he mused of that album, "it had as much effect on British culture as *Nevermind* did on America."

Three further singles from *Parklife* — "To the End" (#16 UK), "Parklife" (#10 UK), and "End of a Century" (#19 UK) — hit and the only cloud on the horizon was the rapid rise behind them of Oasis, a band which seemingly sprang fully formed from the more streetwise elements of *Parklife*. Indeed, within a year of that album, the two bands were neck and neck in the Brit-pop stakes, a cut-throat, and frequently ill-tempered, competition which the media's sudden obsession with "who's biggest, who's best" only exacerbated.

When Albarn won the patronage of Kink Ray Davies, Oasis picked up with Paul Weller, and both performed with their respected patrons on the BBC's *White Room* show. Albarn co-wrote a song with trip-hop maven Tricky in 1995; Noel Gallagher collaborated with the Chemical Brothers. Now the two bands would release new singles simultaneously on August 26, 1995, and the public could decide which they preferred.

"The tabloids went just completely bananas," recalled Albarn, "and the whole scene went from being a big alternative thing to completely mainstream and getting on the News At 10, and blah, blah, blah. They found my first girlfriend from when I was 15 [she sold them his old love letters], and I'd been hounded by this bitchy little schoolteacher from some village in Leicestershire, I hadn't seen her for 10 years, but she had the lowdown... that absolute crap that only the British seem able to do."

The great day dawned, and history will record Blur as the victor. "Country House" entered the chart at #1, selling 274,000 copies; Oasis' "Roll with It" made #2 (216,000 copies). But with both bands' new albums entering the charts at #1 one month apart, honors remained even until Noel Gallagher let slip a comment which still haunts his public image, wishing AIDS and death upon Albarn and James, "because I fucking hate them." He offered a public apology shortly after, but the damage was done. Oasis might eventually have emerged as the biggest band (they conquered America, after all). But Blur were by far the better one.

The Great Escape (#150 US, #1 UK), the new Blur album, was little more than a consolidation of *Parklife* — an enjoyable, but ultimately disappointing exercise in treading water, whose success did not disguise the fact that Blur themselves were tiring of the whole Brit-pop extravaganza. Albarn later admitted that "the only thing I would have changed in hindsight is that I would have held back *The Great Escape* and put it on [as a play]... a musical about the fall of Olde England."

In a deliberate attempt to escape from pop stardom, Blur withdrew from Britain and spent the next eight months on a world tour; by the time they returned, three further singles from the album — "The Universal" (#5 UK), "Stereotypes" (#7 UK), and "Charmless Man" (#5 UK) — had kept them in the Top 10, but their own horizons had broadened immeasurably.

They talked enthusiastically about the music they encountered during a US tour the previous year, an indy scene which critics pointed out was the antithesis of all the band represented, but which Blur themselves now embraced unflinchingly. "Beetlebum" (#1 UK), the first single from their fifth album, *Blur* (#61 US, #1 UK), was minimalist rock par excellence; while "Song 2" (#2 UK), released while the UK was still reeling from the raucousness of it all, defied all predictions when it exploded out of late-night MTV to become *the* spring break anthem of the year. Two further singles, "On Your Own" (#5 UK) and "MOR" (#15 UK), only took the band even further from their Brit-pop heartland.

Blur, however, had by no means completed their metamorphosis. Coxon, widely regarded as the architect of the band's shift, released an understated solo album, *The Sky is High* (#31 UK), which only muddied the waters even further, while Albarn went on record insisting that *Blur* was banged down with barely a hint of studio finesse, an exorcism which he confessed could only be done once. As far as their musical future went, Blur were still at square one — which meant the only escape was another total shift.

The recruitment of producer William Orbit, fresh from the latest Madonna album, was the first clue towards the record's ultimate destination. So was the news that much of the album was written following Albarn's split with long-term girlfriend Justine Frischmann (of Elastica).

According to Albarn, the band spent the first two weeks in the studio jamming, while Orbit took "every single thing we did, eight hours a day for three weeks, putting it onto Pro Tools — we basically played everything live, but then it's all been mutated, which I found a very, very exciting experience."

13 (#80 US, #1 UK), he said, "was the antithesis of everything we've done in the past. And I know I say this every time, but it's a very different record from anything we've ever done; it's more influenced by people like Otis Redding than Ray Davies, and there's a lot of — not 'yeah yeah baby,' but alluding to that sort of sentiment. It's a totally first person record."

Such ambition did not spike its acceptance. "Tender" (#2 UK) was succeeded by "Coffee and TV" (#11 UK) and "No Distance Left to Run" (#14 UK), while the band ended the year with a Christmas stocking-stuffer box set containing all their UK singles to date. A simultaneous British Tour was similarly devoted to A-sides alone.

Blur LPs

7 Leisure (SBK) 1991 They had all the baggy accessories (Keith Richard's riffs, Beatles' harmonies, lashings of psychedelia) and wore them like a straitjacket but the songs themselves were classic pop gems, waiting to be freed from genre constraints.

8 Modern Life Is Rubbish (SBK) 1993 Blur show off their cleverness on this irony-heavy romp through a fading Britain and all its trappings. The musical echoes of pop icons past (freakbeat, glam, and punk included) drive home the point while simultaneously turning it on its head — art not only imitating life, but becoming it as well.

10 Parklife (SBK) 1994 The first thing to remember is that no one expected Blur to make an album like this. The second is that no one thought Blur were even capable of making an album like this. *Modern Life* hinted at a retro-pop sensibility of some description, but short of selling souls to Satan, there's no way anybody should be able to leap from "Colin Zeal" to "Tracy Jacks" and still have the breath to finish the job. "Girls and

Boys," the psycho-sexual Euro trashery which kicks things off, is part of the language now — a relentless dance floorstomper which epitomizes everything that's great about English pop and everything that's bad about England. It's not exactly a secret, but that's the trick — wry observation tied to wiry composition and Blur's links to the hallowed canons of '60s quintessentia simply cannot be overstated, or under-rated.

From the Mockney pop Cockney exhortations of "Parklife" to the gorgeous "To the End," the best song Paul McCartney never wrote, Blur sharpened their vision of Britain's musical past at the same time as advancing their blueprint for its future. And if *Modern Life* really was the sound of Blur skimming through pop history, *Parklife* was them settling down for some serious revision.

Of course, life was never like this, really, any more than the putatively prototypical Kinks' "Village Green" accurately reflected an earlier era still. But even if the nostalgia's an illusion, Blur's impressions of England and of their youth and dreams is a masterpiece of music, mood, and lyric. And most of all, timing.

8 The Great Escape (Virgin) 1995 While *Parklife* dwelled on the pointless mundanities which comprise modern life (got up, washed the car, fed the cat, bought a new drill attachment), *The Great Escape* spotlighted the end result of the dreams which got left behind — angst, disconnection, depression, and pretension. Occasionally hackneyed ("Stereotypes"), sometimes too obvious ("Ernold Same"), and all too often too clever for its own good, still a soaring and dizzying combination of pounding anthems and heartbreaking ballads offered an easy escape from the portentous themes.

6 Blur (Virgin) 1997 Having dissected Britain culturally and musically, past and present, Blur turn their attention to the US in this lo-fi, allegedly Pavement-inspired indy effort. Notions of C&W, hip-hop, punk rock, and cacophony had all turned up on B-sides before; now they collided with the band's previous penchant for ballads, Bowie, bizarre electronics, lush instrumentation, and the Kinks. The success of "Song 2" suggests this was a good move. The music, however, says otherwise.

7 13 (Virgin) 1999 Off on another tangent, having admitted the last one didn't lead very far, Blur fly off on a musical free-for-all of experiment, excess, and soulful eccentricities. Fueled by a newfound reliance on hardcore electronics, much of *13* is intriguingly stimulating, but only the soaring "Tender" seems truly memorable.

Selected Compilations and Archive Releases

6 The Special Collectors Edition (Food — Japan) 1995 Handy wrap-up of B-sides and oddities. Early purchasers had the opportunity of procuring a Blur dinner plate.

4 Live at the Budokan (Food — Japan) 1996

5 Bustin' and Dronin' — Rarities and Live (Food — Australia) 1999 They got better through the *Blur/13* era, but "classic" period Blur were never much more than an irrelevance live. The *Budokan* set, then, is instantly disposable; *Bustin'* is saved by the B-side reprises.

9 Anniversary Box Set (EMI — UK) 1999 A monstrous, but strangely compelling, 125-song/17-disc wrap-up of all Blur's singles to date, with B-sides, remixes all present and correct, and the inevitable UK multiple format releases sensibly slimmed down to one disc apiece. The repetition gets heavy towards the end; a lot of the remixes don't require more than one listen, and a single disc of A-sides alone would probably suffice for most passing punters. But the artifact value is incredible, and there were some gems buried away on thebacksides — "Rednecks," "Maggie May," " and a chilling French language version of "To the End," plus a handful of innocent Seymour demos.

Graham Coxon LPs

7 The Sky Is Too High (Caroline) 1999 Far removed from the lush sonic pastures of the mothership, *Sky* is a mismash of loud noises and low-fi acoustics, with Coxon's slightly off-kilter vocals and utterly out-of-key lyrics drawling, drooping, and dripping over 11 hapless semi-singsongs. The key is the epic "I Wish," sort of a Buzzcocks sentiment meet Sonic Youth feedback, and Venice Shoreline Chris-alike strumming. An acquired taste, maybe, but a remarkably unpretentious one.

7 The Golden D (Transcopic) 2000

Damon Albarn/Michael Nyman LP

6 Ravenous (Original Soundtrack) (Virgin) 1999 Still aligned with William Orbit, but completely out of sorts with his Blur persona, Albarn gets down and serious on an offbeat, and often eclectic, selection of movie themed instrumentals.

BOMB THE BASS

FORMED 1988 (London, England)
ORIGINAL LINE-UP Tim Simenon (b. 1968, London)

Bomb the Bass emerged in Britain in 1988 amidst the wave of DJ-fired singles then sweeping the club scene (M/A/R/R/S' "Pump Up the Volume" paramount among them). A debut single, "Beat Dis," was released but from the start, Wag Club DJ Tim Simenon knew he was faced with an intensely elitist audience, one which was convinced that the only worthwhile music was coming out of the New York clubs. Simenon accordingly arranged for his releases to ape American imports in every way, including adopting the "white label" approach of not crediting either the artist or the song in the hope of foiling rival DJs. (This subtle subterfuge was only marginally belied by the appearance of the countdown from British television's *Thunderbirds* among the samples.)

Snapped up by Rhythm King, "Beat Dis" (#2 UK, #1 UK indy) was a massive hit in February 1988, and despite the swift unmasking of its maker as a 20-year-old Londoner, its success readily prompted the "Don't Make Me Wait"/"Megablast" (#6 UK, #2 UK indy) follow-up in August, featuring labelmate Merlin, vocalist Lorraine Macintosh, and Massive Attack/Soul II Soul producer Nellee Hooper.

In November, a dense remake of Aretha Franklin's "Say a Little Prayer" (#10 UK, #1 UK indy), with guest vocalist Maureen Walsh, made it three Top 10 smashes in a row, while a Bomb the Bass album, *Into the Dragon* (#18 UK, #3 UK indy), indicated the true strengths of the team of Simenon and co-producer Pascal Gabrel. The release of Neneh Cherry's sassy "Buffalo Stance," produced by Simenon, shortly before Christmas, simply confirmed what a lot of people already knew.

Following a year of such intense activity, Bomb the Bass would go on hiatus, although Simenon himself would remain very active. In the new year, his next Cherry project, "Manchild" (co-written with Massive Attack founder 3D) was a British Top 5 hit, while he also co-produced Adamski's "Killer" chart-topper and Seal's #2 "Crazy." Jonathan Saul Kane, one of Simenon's prime conspirators on *Into the Dragon*, too, resurfaced in 1990 as Depth Charge, a hip-hop instrumentalist whose readily recognizable trademark was the use of sampled soundbytes from his beloved kung fu movies (Kane also records as Octagon Man).

Simenon resumed work as Bomb the Bass in early 1991, scheduling the "Love So True" single before becoming embroiled in a media controversy over the suitability of the projects's name at the height of the Gulf War. The single was hastily recredited to Simenon himself, and Bomb the Bass resufaced instead with the seasonal "Winter in July" (#7 UK).

Neither "The Air You Breathe" (#52 UK) nor "Keep Giving Me Love" (#62 UK) proved convincing follow-up hits, although the *Unknown Territory* (#19 UK) album, effortlessly furthering both Massive Attack and Depth Charge's advances into proto trip-hop territory, eventually crested only one place below its predecessor's peak. Still, Bomb the Bass vanished again, while Simenon returned to production, this time with performers ranging from Björk and Gavin Friday to model Naomi Campbell and INXS vocalist Michael Hutchence (whose posthumously released, self-titled, solo set would feature Simenon, alongside Gang of Four's Andy Gill, and Black Grape mainstay Danny Saber).

1994 brought Bomb the Bass' third album, released on Simenon's own Stoned Heights label. *Clear* was very much an all-star production, featuring contributions from as far afield as Jah Wobble, Justin Warfield, and Sinead O'Connor, whose vocal on the album's "Vampire" would stand among her own finest ever performances. Warfield's "Bug Powder Dust" (#24 UK) rap, Spikey Tee's "Darkheart" (#35 UK), Carlton's "1 to 1 Religion" (#53 UK), and Bernard Fowler's "Sandcastles" (#54 UK), meanwhile, all became minor hits.

Bomb the Bass LPs

7 Into the Dragon (Rhythm King) 1988 Took the DJ out of the clubs and into the studio, where Tim Simenon essentially committed a dance set to vinyl, a show which ranges from fast break beats to hip-hop to acid house, but is best remembered for the hit "Beat Dis."

6 Unknown Territory (Rhythm King) 1991 Despite the presence of "The Air You Breathe," this should be renamed the Unknown Album. Simenon updated his sound and in so doing, cracked the golden egg that would eventually flourish as trip-hop.

9 Clear (4th & Broadway) 1995 Sporting two different mixes for the US and UK, *Clear* was a triumph with Simenon at his best and utilizing all the tricks picked up over his years as producer. Dub-fused-with-trip-hop-fused-with-hip-hop-fused-with-soul. Standout tracks include "Empire" with Sinead O'Connor guesting and "Bug Powder Dust" which introduced the remix team of Kruder & Dorfmeister.

Tim Simenon — Selected Productions

1987 JAMIE MORGAN — Shotgun (Tabu) **6**

1989 MATERIAL — Seven Souls (Virgin) **5**

1989 NENEH CHERRY — Raw Like Sushi (Virgin) **6** She's at her best on "Buffalo Stance" which opens and drives the album; the rest of the tracks never really match that enthusiasm. However, it's an interesting romp as Cherry takes a stab at a myriad of styles.

1991 SEAL — Seal (Sire) **8** With Simenon just one of several producers involved (Trevor Horn and William Orbit also conspired), a potpourri of shifting visions; that, and the presence of "Crazy" and "Killer" ensure any album would struggle to match its potential. But Seal, his voice equally adept at ballad and dance, nevertheless turned in a stunning debut.

1992 25TH OF MAY — Lenin & Mccarty (Arista) **9** These "agitpop" hybridists take out their frustration with the world through their music and their cleverly titled debut is amilitant's dream come true. Transferring anger into savage assaults on politics, society, and lack of justice, Lenin's lyrics sting with barbs sharpened by wit, sardonic irony, and justified outrage. The album may be powered by the hip-hop beats, but the music is an anarcho-riot of classic rock riffs, pop melodies, and enough hooks to hang the government from. An electrifying debut — radio friendly, yet politically threatening.

1996 TIM BOOTH & ANGELO BADALAMENTI — Booth & The Bad Angel (Polygram) **4** Featuring James frontman Booth, the multi-faceted Badalamenti, Brian Eno, Bernard Butler — sadly the parts were worth considerably more than the preposterously over-ambitious whole.

1997 DEPECHE MODE — Ultra (Mute) **7**

BONGWATER

FORMED 1987 *(New York, NY)*

ORIGINAL LINE-UP *Mark Kramer (b. 1958 — guitar, instrumentation); Ann Magnuson (vocals, spoken word)*

The union between Shimmy Disc label founder/producer Mark Kramer (ex-Shockabilly, Butthole Surfers) and performance artist/actress Ann Magnuson was backed by a rotating roster of musicians including Dave Rick (guitar, Phantom

Tollbooth), David Licht (drums, ex-Shockabilly), and Fred Frith (guitar, Henry Cow).

Echoing many of the techniques Kramer first introduced with Shockabilly, including the effective use of politically themed samples and soundbites, over some surprisingly gentle musical themes, Bongwater set about quietly reinventing and deconstructing rock, utilizing Magnuson's wild interpretations of her own vivid dreams.

While Bongwater didn't tour per se, they did shake the rooftops at selected gigs, including an early performance art/beat/happening extravaganza for the Low Culture-High Art opening at the Museum of Modern Art. There, and with their first EP, *Breaking No New Ground!* in 1987, they continued setting things sideways, covering — and simultaneously utterly disassembling — the Moody Blues "Ride My See-Saw."

Double Bummer, the duo's first full-length, was released that same year, its intelligent humor quickly emerging via their cover of glam icon Gary Glitter's "Rock & Roll Pt. 2", to the adroitly titled, "David Bowie Wants Ideas" (the two segue together via an idealistic groupie fantasy sequence). The Led Zeppelin standard "Dazed and Confused," meanwhile, became "Dazed and Chinese," sung, of course, in Mandarin. Its similarity to some of Yoko Ono's stabs at rock reiteration was, of course, as deliberate as the duo's frequent resemblance to *Double White*-era Beatles artiness.

Too Much Sleep debuted in 1990, an opus to dreamtime which followed Bongwater's set path into the annals of psychedelic obscurity. *The Power of Pussy* (1991), on the other hand, brought everything back to earth, from the title track (which featured a duet with B-52's vocalist Fred Schneider) to a take on the Weavers' sing-along standard, "Kisses Sweeter than Wine." Backed by a European tour, the duo accompanied by Shimmy Disc artist Dogbowl (ex-King Missile), *Pussy* would become Bongwater's "best seller", although whether that was due to the content or the cover may long be disputed.

As 1991 continued, the relationship between Kramer and Magnuson splintered, shattered and irreconcilably fell to pieces. The band would end their rollercoaster ride with the post-breakup release of *The Big Sell Out* later that year and a legal battle which saw Shimmy Disc pushed into bankruptcy before it was resolved.

Kramer's workaholic musical career has continued with recordings as, and with, the likes of BALL (later Gumball), Jad Fair, King Missile, and Half Japanese, as well as maintaining Shimmy Disc among the most prolific indy labels in the US.

Bongwater LPs

9 Double Bummer (Shimmy Disc) 1988 Magnificent, if sprawling, trawl through the wasteland of '70s and '80s pop culture, punctuated by some astonishing covers and lifts — Soft Machine's "We Did It Again," the Monkees' "You JustMay Be the One," and "Porpoise Song," and some sampled Yoko Ono rub against the wry "David Bowie Wants Ideas," an ironically disturbed take on Gary Glitter's "Rock'n'Roll" and a few odd deconstructions of the Beatles. "Dazed and Chinese" and "Four Sticks" both highlight a sideways-on Led Zeppelin influence, and the whole thing is a lot more accessible than its makers' reputations might suggest.

8 Too Much Sleep (Shimmy Disc) 1990

8 The Power of Pussy (Shimmy Disc) 1991 Bongwater look to the sex trade with predictable results — although for every "What Kind of Man Reads *Playboy*?" and "Obscene and Pornographic Art" (neither of which, of course, are as weighty as their titles), there's "Nick Cave Dolls" and a fabulous cover of Dudley Moore's "Bedazzled," plus nine minutes of "Folk Song" proving anything but.

7 The Big Sell Out (Shimmy Disc) 1992

Selected Compilations and Archive Releases

8 Box of Bongwater (Shimmy Disc) 1988 Brain-charring wrap-up of the band's entire oeuvre. Not to be consumed in one sitting.

BOO RADLEYS

FORMED 1988 (Liverpool, England)
ORIGINAL LINE-UP *Martin Carr (b. 11/29/68, Thurso, Scotland — vocals, guitar); Sice (b. Simon Rowbottom, 6/18/69, Wallasey, England — vocals, guitar); Tim Brown (b. 2/26/69, Wallasey, England — bass); Steve Hewitt (drums)*

Childhood friends growing up together in the Liverpool suburb of Wallasey, Martin Carr and Sice named the Boo Radleys from a character in *To Kill a Mockingbird* — one of the syllabus books in their English class in high school. With school friend Tim Brown and, following a number of stand-ins, Steve Hewitt in tow, the band debuted at the Victoria bar in New Brighton and recorded their first five-track demo in 1989.

It was a friend of the band, Mark Waring of Dandelion Adventure, who handed the tape to Action Records (his own band recorded for the Preston-based label) and in 1990, the Boos cut *Ichabod and I*, another title steeped in American literary lore, but otherwise echoing the distinctly English sounds of My Bloody Valentine and Ride, undisputed kings of the Shoegazing trance-psychedelic movement.

Rob Cieka (b. 8/4/68, Wolverhampton, England) replaced Hewitt shortly after the band recorded its first BBC radio session in July 1990, and in November the Boos signed to Rough Trade and released the EP *Kaleidoscope*.

With the group still firmly locked into the swirling guitar sound, the Boos' next two releases, the *Every Heaven* and *Boo Up!* EPs were minor indy hits, but it took their switch to Creation (following the collapse of Rough Trade in 1991) to break the pattern of under-achievement. A third EP, *Adrenalin*, accompanied the move before Creation cleared the decks by giving a belated release to *Everything's Alright Forever* (#55 UK), the sophomore album recorded for Rough Trade the previous fall.

Their first UK hit, "Does This Hurt" (backed by the anthemic "Boo! Forever," #67 UK) in June 1992, offered the band further encouragement and over the next two years, regular live work and a burgeoning media profile both conspired to raise the Boos' stock. Then, home from an American tour with Sugar, they returned to the studio to work on the aptly titled *Giant Step* (#17 UK).

The first of the albums to raise the Boos' profile as a fiercely independent and creative force, as opposed to mere court followers, *Giant Step* spawned a string of hits — "I Wish I Was Skinny" (#75 UK), "Barney and Me" (#48 UK), and "Lazarus" (#50 UK). The latter also picked up considerable acclaim in the US, and building upon that success, the Boos became one of the star turns on the second stage at Lollapalooza 94.

Combining an ear for Brit-pop with a taste for Phil Spector-style soul, "Wake Up Boo!" (#9 UK) in early 1995 gave the group their biggest hit yet; the following month, the parent album, *Wake Up!* (#1 UK), proved it was no fluke, launching a summer of solid gigging and unlikely triumphs — opening for Blur at the Mile End Stadium in June, many observers claimed the Boos stole the show, while gigs at the Glastonbury and Reading festivals were equally successful.

"Find the Answer Within" (#37 UK), "It's Lulu" (#25 UK), and "From the Bench at Belvidere" (#24 UK) maintained the album's high European profile, but an American release for the album fell flat. Columbia, Creation's regular US distributor, dropped the band shortly after, and 1996's *C'mon Kids* would not even see a US date for another year — by which time it had already served its stated purpose. Deliberately loud and overly clever, Carr insisted the album was designed solely to rid the Boos of their more recent converts — a statement (as the *Murder Ballads*-era Nick Cave could testify) which is normally guaranteed to increase a band's following.

In the Boos' case, however, the public took Carr at his word. *C'mon Kids* entered the charts high, then fell fast; two singles, "What's in the Box" (#25 UK) and the title track (#18 UK) followed suit. By the time *C'mon Kids* finally reached in America, in March 1998, even the Boos seemed to have forgotten about it. The final Boos album, *Kingsize*, was released in Britain in late 1998 but did not reach the US until spring 1999, by which time the band had already broken up, in February 1999. Carr would re-emerge with a new band, Brave Captain, in August, debuting with the song "The Monk Jumps over the Wall," on the XFM radio station compilation *The Carve-Up*.

Boo Radleys LPs

6 Ichabod and I (Action — UK) 1990

6 Everything's Alright Forever (Creation/Columbia) 1992 The Boos swirl, twirl, and at times outright buzz; it's all a bit of a Blur-y Ride, but the pure pop-to-be still shines through.

7 Giant Step (Creation/Columbia) 1993 Exploding in a dozen different directions, the Boos careen through indy riffs, reggae hooks, raucous rock, and into cacophony, but those perfect pop harmonies keep somersaulting overhead.

8 Wake Up (Creation/Columbia) 1995 Dreaming of the past, the Boos add a plethora of '60s influences to their repertoire — Motown, Beach Boys, and British Beat amongst them — and the world wakes up to the wonders of Boo.

6 C'mon Kids (Mercury) 1997 Transitionally awkward, the Boos' new direction turns out to be less a cul-de-sac than a suicide note.

8 Kingsize (Mercury) 1999 Back to *Wake Up* basics, the dream comes of age. Pulling together their past explorations, then pulling out all the stops, plush production, superb arrangements, and orchestration, exquisite songwriting, mature and insightful lyrics combine into a regal album and a worthy epitaph for this monumental band.

Selected Compilations and Archive Releases

8 Learning to Walk (Rough Trade — UK) 1992 The 1990–91 EPs *Kaleidoscope*, *Every Heaven* and *Boo Up* trace the transition between first and second albums, plus Peel session covers of Love's "Alone Again Or" and New Order's "True Faith."

BOOMTOWN RATS

FORMED 1975 *(Dun Laoghaire, Ireland)*
ORIGINAL LINE-UP *Bob Geldof (b. 10/5/54, Dublin — vocals); Johnny Fingers (b. John Moylett 9/10/56 — keyboards); Pete Briquette (b. Patrick Cusack, 7/2/54 — bass); Gerry Cott (guitar); Gerry Roberts (b. 6/16/54 — guitar); Simon Crowe (drums)*

Formed by freelance music journalist Bob Geldof, first as the Nightlife Thugs, but later in honor of one of the gangs featured in the Woody Guthrie biopic *Bound for Glory*, the Boomtown Rats were originally fronted by guitarist Gerry Roberts with Geldof intending to maintain a machiavellian presence as manager only. By the time news of the London punk scene started filtering across the Irish Sea, however, Geldof had moved to the microphone and in 1976, he led the band to England, settling in the London suburb of Chessington.

A deal with Ensign and a string of low-profile shows around London paved the way for the Rats' late summer 1977 emergence, by which time Geldof had already earned a slice of street credibility when his name was added to the growing litany of punk musicians physically assaulted by outraged members of the public in the aftermath of the Sex Pistols' "God Save the Queen."

Still the Rats intended keeping their fashionable options open, allying themselves with the punk scene only when it suited them, and broadening their horizons the rest of the time. So they gratefully accepted the opening slot at Tom Petty's first London headline shows, then grafitti'd London with the warning "Rats Eat Heartbreakers."

They came close to doing so, as well. Petty, after all, was simply the latest in a long line of old-style American punks, with a bloodline which stretched from James Dean to Springsteen, and nothing more on their minds than cars, girls, and street corner conventions. So, as it transpired, were the Rats, but in transplanting those same concerns to the streets of Dublin, it wasn't only the 24 hour coke machines which went out of the window. Glamor, style, and romance, too, were dispensed with, replaced with adrenalined disillusionment and aimless, angry energy.

The pure punk punch and sentiment of the Rats' debut single, "Looking After Number One" (#11 UK), gave them their chart debut that fall, with "Mary of the 4th Form" (#15 UK) and "She's So Modern" (#12 UK) following in a similarly frenzied fashion. Released in September, their eponymous debut album (#18 UK) revealed a driving rock band directly descended from classic Stones and Thin Lizzy; the brilliantly quirk-laden *Tonic for the Troops* (#112 US, #8 UK) sophomore album, on the other hand, clasped the band's ambition so tightly to its soul that the band's fourth single, the insistently ticking "Like Clockwork" (#6 UK), was almost shocking in its audacity — smarter than your average punk song, new wave in a way which the new wavers themselves were still a few months from discovering.

Punning off both the song's motorik rhythm and its chorus, a *New Musical Express* feature that same year proclaimed, "my mind beats time like Kraftwerk," but Geldof was unrepentant. Both "Like Clockwork" and *Tonic for the Troops* made the Top 10, yet if anyone was surprised about how far and fast the band had advanced, the Rats hadn't even begun to march.

"Rat Trap" (#1 UK) at the end of 1978, remains one of the crucial singles of the era. Over five minutes long at a time when the likes of The Buzzcocks were still winning plaudits for releasing the shortest single ever; divided, almost into suites, or at least movements, "Rat Trap" tumbled straight back into the mid-'70s definition of "punk," Born to Run Revisited, at the same time as paving the way for a slew of similarly visionary efforts from The Jam, Sham 69, *et al.*

There was one crucial difference. "Rat Trap"'s protagonists were real, its scenario was real — this was no sun-blistered New Jersey streetscape, or Mink De Ville-ian Hispanic ghetto. "Rat Trap" was homebase UK, having to turn up "Top of the Pops" to drown out the sound of mum and dad fighting, kebab houses with cheap formica tabletops; mindless, directionless boredom every night. Thin Lizzy touched the same nerve with "The Boys Are Back in Town" two years earlier. But Lizzy's boys still had hope. Geldof's had nothing.

In May 1979, returning from a three-month US tour, the Rats headlined the Loch Lomond festival, the largest outdoor event ever staged in Scotland and in July, the band released Geldof's piece de resistance — "I Don't Like Mondays" (#73 US, #1 UK). The true-life tale of American schoolgirl Brenda Spencer, who took a gun to school "because..." ensured the Rats' superstardom. Adjudged Best Pop Song and Outstanding British Lyric at the Ivor Novello Awards, it became one of the biggest selling 45s in British chart history and when Paul McCartney congratulated Geldof on the honor, the King Rat's response was delicious. Referring to McCartney's own recent chart-topper, "Mull of Kintyre," Geldof shot back "yeah, and I didn't need fucking bagpipes to do it."

With the band's grasp on the emergent video medium as solid and (though history forgets) influential as any better-publicized pioneers, *The Fine Art of Surfacing* (#103 US, #7 UK), the band's third album, arrived bristling with self confidence and loaded with hits. The paranoid anthem "Someone's Looking at You" (#4 UK), its video a Geldof-as-Jagger performance straight out of the Stone's *Performance* movie, and the suicide blonde of the oddly prescient "Diamond Smiles" (#13 UK) kept the band in the chart while the Rats' 1980 world tour would become one of the year's most successful by any act.

Yet time was running out. Although the band's next album, the Tony Visconti produced *Mondo Bongo* (#116 US, #6 UK) spawned its own monster hits in "Banana Republic" (#3 UK) and "Elephant's Graveyard" (#26), it was a messy, inconsistent set — crimes which the Rats had never previously been guilty of, and for which they could never be forgiven. The departure of Gerry Cott only amplified the band's sudden weakness and when their next all-new single, the Phil Spector-esque "Never in a Million Years" (#62 UK) became their first single not to make the Top 30 (and "Charmed Lives," their first not to chart at all), the end was clearly in sight.

1982's *V Deep* (#64 UK) — a dense but lushly produced excursion into no wave dance — crashed, and even the post-ska iconoclasm of "House on Fire" (#24 UK) could do nothing right. By early 1984, the Boomtown Rats were all but finished as a chart act — their final hits, "Tonight" (#73 UK) and "Drag Me Down" (#50 UK), were excerpted from a new album, *In the Long Grass* (#188 US), which even Geldof admitted was dead before it was released.

Although Geldof himself never showed much interest in the trade, predictions that he would turn his hand to acting had been rife even before he took the starring role in the movie version of Pink Floyd's *The Wall* in 1982. The Rats' uncontrolled commercial nosedive only upped the ante. In November 1984, however, all bets were sidelined after the singer caught a BBC TV report on the famine in Ethiopia.

Overnight, he and Ultravox vocalist Midge Ure wrote a benefit song; within days, the pair had gathered 36 of the era's most successful performers into one studio, to record "Do They Know It's Christmas" under the name of Band Aid. The following month, Geldof joined a similar effort in America, USA for Africa and in July 1985, his exhortations were responsible for one of the most successful musical charity events ever staged, Live Aid. The Boomtown Rats, of course, performed during the London segment of the show, the last live appearance of their career, on what Geldof, as he left the stage, described as the greatest day of his life.

Awarded an honorary Knighthood by HM the Queen the following June (and marrying longtime girlfriend Paula Yates two months later), Geldof attempted to pick up the reins of his musical career in November with the *Deep in the Heart of Nowhere* (#130 US, #79 UK) album and "This Is the World Calling" (#82 US, #25 UK) single. Their lowly chart positions belied the fact that Geldof himself continued among the most visible, and highly regarded, entertainers in the world.

A second single, "Love Like a Rocket" (#61 UK), performed no better and it would be four more years before Geldof released another record, the Rupert Hine produced *Vegetarians of Love* (#21 UK) album, and a superb — and wryly autobiographical — single, "The Great Song of Indifference" (#15 UK). Geldof, however, seemed in no apparent hurry to follow up either success, even waiting 18 months before playing his first conventional solo live shows — a string of festivals during the summer of 1992.

A third album, *The Happy Club*, appeared in 1993, but again Geldof's celebrity status could not help it. The album flopped; a single, "Crazy" (#65), barely did any better and while the Rats/Geldof compilation, *Loudmouth* (#10 UK), proved that the music did still matter to some people, Geldof's personal life was now consuming many more column inches than his career.

Wife Yates was publicly dating INXS vocalist Michael Hutchence and the acrimonious divorce and custody battles which followed (the couple had two children) would captivate tabloid readers throughout Britain and Australia. Hutchence's death, an apparent suicide on November 22, 1997, of course, would enter modern folklore as a by-product of the bitter wrangling between the couple although Geldof's reputation, at least, emerged intact from the tragedy.

Boomtown Rats LPs

7 Boomtown Rats (Mercury UK) 1977 "Looking After #1" set the Rats up for punk, but across this slab of vital, driving, pub-rock blues, the naked ambition of "Neon Heart," "Close as You'll Ever Be, " and "Kicks" suggest that Geldof is more than a simple Mick Jagger *look*-alike.

8 Tonic for the Troops (Columbia) 1978 Quirk-ridden dive into the heart of the new wave, the Rats' natural rock basics shifting into clipped riffing and iced delivery: the still crucial "Like Clockwork," the suicide dream of "Living on an Island," and the vicious "She's So Modern" sound oh-so-'78, but it's "Rat Trap" — ironically a hang-over from the first album's stylings — which seals the album's status.

9 The Fine Art of Surfacing (Columbia) 1979 Following "Rat Trap" into the realm of the succinct epic, "Someone's Looking at You," "Diamond Smiles," and of course, "I Don't Like Mondays" are simply the jewels which lead you into the Rats' most fulfilled album yet. "Sleep (Fingers' Lullaby)" is a forgotten classic.

6 Mondo Bongo (Columbia) 1981 A distinctly backward step, although the dark dub stylings of "Elephant's Graveyard" and the home thoughts from abroad lament of "Another Piece of Red" rate highly.

8 V Deep (Columbia) 1982 Back to their best with Spector stylings enveloping "Never in a Million Years," and "House on Fire," a ska-hearted romp which epitomizes this ambitious album's intentions.

6 In the Long Grass (Columbia) 1985 Eminently listenable, but three years past its sell-by date.

Bob Geldof LPs

7 Deep in the Heart of Nowhere (Atlantic) 1986

7 Vegetarians of Love (Atlantic) 1990

6 The Happy Club (Polygram) 1993

Selected Compilations and Archive Releases

7 Greatest Hits (Columbia) 1987 Utilitarian singles collection which never recovers from the brilliance of its best bits, and overlooks a lot of album-track classics.

7 Loudmouth (Mercury Uk) 1994

7 Great Songs of Indifference (Sony) 1997 Two sets essentially echoing *Greatest Hits* mistake, but adding some solo Geldof goodies to bring the tale up-to-date.(7,7)

Further Reading

Is That It? by Bob Geldof/Paul Vallely (Weidenfeld & Nicolson, 1986).

BOY GEORGE

BORN *George O'Dowd, 6/14/61 (Eltham, Kent, England)*

Although the band had yet to formally announce their demise, by mid-1986 Culture Club was widely regarded as a dead issue, with Boy George apparently hell-bent on joining it in the grave. In early July, the singer's brother acknowledged that George was a heroin addict; the following week, George and his clubbing companion Marilyn were arrested and charged with cannabis possession; days later, one of the sidemen employed on the last Culture Club album, keyboard player Michael Rudetski, died of a drug overdose at George's house.

George visited rehab specialist Dr. Meg Patterson for treatment and the following February was able to report his successful recovery on British television's *Wogan* chat show. An immediate hit with the lightly reggaefied "Everything I Own" (#1 UK) in March 1987, however, was a deceptive start to his reborn career. The parent album, *Sold* (#145 US, #29 UK), was followed by three similarly under-performing singles, "Keep Me in Mind" (#29 UK), "Sold" (#24 UK), and "To Be Reborn" (#13 UK), and though George remained a popular media figure, his musical career would never get off the ground in commercial terms.

Creatively, however, he was writing and performing some of the best records of his life. The misguided politicizing of Culture Club's "War Song" was erased by 1988's "No Clause 28" (#57 UK), a caustic attack on recent anti-gay legislation, and though George's conversion to the Hari Krishna sect that same year was widely regarded with cynicism, that too, brought a new depth to his music.

Two further singles that year, "Live My Life" (#40 US, #62 UK), from the *Hiding Out* movie soundtrack, and "Don't Cry" (#60 UK), evidenced that, despite their lowly chart placings. But, George's next two albums, *Tense Nervous Headache* and *Boyfriend*, went unreleased in America, despite the latter spawning another minor hit, "Don't Take My Mind On a Trip" (#68 UK).

Abandoning an attempt to reconvene Culture Club and backed instead by a new band, Jesus Loves You, George rounded out 1989 by forming his own label, More Protein,

and scored a minor hit with the self-released "After the Love" (#68 UK). "Bow Down Mister" (#27 UK) and "Generations of Love" (#35 UK) followed in the new year accompanied by *The Martyr Mantras* (#60 UK). The album was released in the US as a Boy George solo set.

However, the album was badly promoted and sold poorly — a consequence, George reasoned, of his own public image. "I'd given the junk up, now I was into Hari Krishna and vegetarian food. People thought I was insane. In fact, I was ahead of my time, just a few years too early for the whole Krishna thing. I was pipped to the post by Kula Shaker and Madonna."

1992 brought a return to grace when George performed the title theme to the hit movie *The Crying Game* (#15 US, #22 UK), but a new Jesus Loves You single, "Sweet Toxic Love" (#65 UK), flopped in December and by the end of the year both band and the More Protein label had folded.

George spent much of 1993 working on his autobiography, *Take It Like a Man* (co-written with journalist Spencer Bright); he did return to the chart as guest vocalist on PM Dawn's "More than Likely" (#40 UK), however, while a new compilation album, 1994's *At Worst... The Best Of* (#169 US, #24 UK) and *The Devil in Sister George* remixes EP (#26 UK) went some way to assuring another massive flurry of interest when *Take It Like a Man* finally appeared in 1995. But a simultaneous new album, *Cheapness and Beauty* (#44 UK), was unable to ride the momentum, despite featuring a magnificent cover of Iggy Pop's "Funtime" (#45 UK) and subsequent minor hits "Il Adore" (#50 UK) and "Same Thing in Reverse" (#56 UK).

A projected follow-up album was abandoned when George quit Virgin Records in late 1995 (many of the tracks later surfaced on 1999's *Unrecoupable One Armed Bandit* collection). Instead, George linked with the Ministry of Sound label as a remixer. His first collection, 1995's *The Annual*, was a two-CD set split with Pete Tong and included George's own "Same Thing in Reverse" among its 13 Boy-mixed cuts.

Now working as a columnist for the *Daily Express* newspaper and a DJ for the Galaxy Radio Network as well as leading a new live band, Sister Queen, the singer was next sighted fronting the reggae project Dubversive and enjoying a Jamaican hit with a version of Junior Murvin's "Police and Thieves." George also received a Grammy Best Dance Recording nomination for "When Will You Learn," a one-off 12-inch released in late 1997. However, such activity came to a halt in late 1998 when George announced the reformation of Culture Club.

Also see the entry for "CULTURE CLUB" on page 303.

Boy George LPs

4 Sold (Virgin) 1987 Desperate to find life outside Culture Club, George isolates the club, but forgets the culture completely. The soft reggae hit "Everything I Own" is as good as it gets, while the production proves that even new technology can get quickly dated.

6 Tense Nervous Headache (Virgin — UK) 1988 Gorgeous version of "What Becomes of the Broken Hearted," butthe playful "American Boys" notwithstanding, little else matches George's still viable potential.

7 Boyfriend (Virgin — Germany) 1989 Finally catching up with his own abilities, as opposed to those he thought he needed to show, the first "proper" George solo album with "No Clause 28," "Don't Take My Mind on a Trip,"and "I'm Not Sleeping Anymore" dramatically grasping the club sensibility.

7 The Martyr Mantras (Virgin) 1991 George's Jesus Loves You project had its own share of gems, "Generations of Love" and "Love Hurts" among them, plus a Pascal Gabriel remix of "No Clause 28."

9 Cheapness and Beauty (Virgin) 1995 From the opening electro-stomp through Iggy's "Funtime" and on through the heavy punch of "Satan's Butterfly Ball," "Sad," and more, George delivers his most powerful, and certainly best produced album ever — thunderous instrumentation merging with genuinely confident songwriting and vocals. An astonishing rebirth.

Selected Compilations and Archive Releases

3 High Hat (Virgin) 1989 Oddly cobbled collection drawn from *Tense Nervous Headache* and *Boyfriend*, giving an utterly unnecessary reprise to the self-consciously gauche "You Are My Heroin" and dropping "No Clause 28."

8 Spin Dazzle (Virgin — UK) 1992

7 At Worst... The Best Of (Virgin) 1993 Roughly similar collections of both solo and Culture Club hits, with *Spin Dazzle* edging ahead through the inclusion of some excellent remixes (Massive Attack's "One on One" among them).(8,7)

5 The Devil in Sister George (Virgin) 1994 Mini-album highlighting further recent remixes, but an irrelevant sideshow nonetheless.

8 The Unrecoupable One Man Bandit (Back Door) 1999 Largely salvaging the demos from the aborted follow-up to *Cheapness & Beauty*, "GI Josephine" and "Spooky Truth" prove that the masterpiece wasn't a fluke. There's also a stunning version of Bowie's "Suffragette City" to erase the horrors of Culture Club's "Starman."

Further Reading

Take It Like a Man by Boy George/Spencer Bright (Harper Collins, 1995).

BOYS

FORMED 1976 *(London, England)*
ORIGINAL LINE-UP *Matt Dangerfield (guitar, vocals); Casino Steel (keyboards); Duncan "Kid" Reid (bass, vocals); "Honest" John Plain (guitar); Jack Black (drums)*

Matt Dangerfield and Casino Steel emerged from the floating aggregation of auditions and rehearsals which comprised the legendary London SS. Steel was also ex-Hollywood Brats, whose 1975 album *Grown Up Wrong* was widely praised among proto-punk archaeologists.

Tentative gigging throughout 1976 and 1977 landed the band a deal with NEMS and in April 1977, their first single appeared, a carefree anthem of nihilistic cliche called "I Don't Care." "First Time" followed in July and in November, the Boys' debut album, *The Boys* (#50 UK) (recorded in just two days), proved the loyalty of the band's small, but vociferous, live support.

Christmas 1977 brought the first release by what would become the band's annual alter-ego, the Yobs, the seasonal "Run Rudolph Run" 45. Then it was back to the clubs and, in the spring, the studio. *Alternative Chartbusters*, their second album, would be previewed by "Brickfield Nights," the first new Boys single in six months and immediately it was apparent that things had changed appreciably while the band had been away. Abandoning the roughshod adrenaline of their early punk, the Boys now stood on the threshold of power-pop mastery, effortlessly reeling off hook-laden, guitar-driven nuggets; garage rock for the new wave, and as close to perfection in their own direction as the Ramones (with whom the Boys were most frequently compared) were in theirs'.

The band's European profile, building upon both the Hollywood Brats' reputation and the Boys' own persistent work, had exploded. Boysmania swept Holland; graffiti peppered walls in Norway. Still largely overlooked in their homeland, the Boys went into 1979 on the verge of continental superstardom, only for their plans to make a major blow when they parted company with NEMS early into the recording of their third album.

The band signed with Safari and scrapping the original sessions, they traveled to Trondheim, Norway to begin again with producer Bjorn Nesside. After toying with such titles as *Skidmarks*, *Driving Through Cabbages*, and *The Boys' Greatest Tits*, they visited the Norwegian town of Hell and immortalized that instead — *To Hell with the Boys* (#4 UK indy) appeared in October 1979, just as the Boys launched a British tour opening for The Ramones.

Unfortunately, the band's European profile still wasn't translating at home, as two new singles, "Kamikaze" (#9 UK indy) and "Terminal Love" (#32 UK indy), together with a riotously rude Yobs Christmas album flopped and as 1980 dragged on, it became clear that the Boys were losing hope. Lurkers guitarist John Plain joined briefly, but finally, he and Casino Steel took the advice of the band's most recent single, "You Better Move On," (#30 UK indy) and quit.

They were replaced by former X-Ray Spex saxophonist, Rudi, but *Boys Only*, the group's fourth album, offered little evidence that he had done more than replaced Steel's physical presence. Neither the album nor the "Weekend" and "Let It Rain" singles performed well and by March 1981, Reid too had quit. He was replaced by Lurkers vocalist Howard Wall and former Chelsea drummer Chris Bashford for the band's next (sold out) Italian tour, and the band scratched out one final single, "Woch Woch Woch," before folding.

Dangerfield moved into production, working with Toyah (Nick Tauber, producer of the Boys' final album would succeed him) before forming a new band, the Mirrors. Steel returned to Norway, working with a succession of bands before reuniting with Plain in Ian Hunter's Dirty Laundry in 1996 (Plain and Black were also members of the New Guitars, with ex-Lurker Pete Stride).

In 1997, following a partial reunion on Die Toten Hosen's *Learning English* punk tribute, Steel, Plain, Reid, and Dangerfield linked with the German band's vocalist, Campino, for an unplugged best of the Boys collection, *Power Cut*. Japanese punks Michelle Gun Elephant, meanwhile, would score several homeland hits with covers of the Boys' "Soda Pressing" and "Sick on You." MCG were also among the contributors to *Satisfaction Guaranteed*, a Boys tribute released in 1999, which featured the debut by Plain's new band, Honest.

The Boys LPs

6 The Boys (NEMS) 1977

7 Alternative Chartbusters (NEMS) 1978 Pushing past the rent-a-punk barriers of their debut (although "The First Time" was a gem), *Alternative Chartbusters* peaks with "Brickfield Nights," rewriting the rules for solid punk pop-rock.

9 To Hell with the Boys (Safari) 1979 A guitar-frenzied romp through "Saber Dance;" schoolboy French of puerile potency ("Rue Morgue"); an inexplicable flop with"Terminal Love" — *To Hell with the Boys* had it all.

8 Boys Only (Safari) 1980 Power popping with undiminished passion, *Boys Only* peaks not only with the band's own "Weekend" 45, but also a surprising cover of Sam Cooke's "Wonderful World."

Selected Compilations and Archive Releases

5 Live at the Roxy (Link) 1991

6 BBC Radio One in Concert [SPLIT W/VIBRATORS] (Windsong) 1993

8 Complete Punk Singles Collection (Anagram) 1997

7 Punk Rock Rarities (Captain OI!) 1999 Fascinating trawl through the archives, including original single mixes, demos, and the abandoned pre-*Hell* third album in its entirety.

7 Radio One Sessions (Vinyl Japan) 1999 Two Peel sessions and a breathless live performance from 1980.

BILLY BRAGG

BORN *Steven William Bragg, 12/20/57 (Barking, Essex, England)*

As a member of the pub punk band Riff Raff, Bragg had four singles under his belt (including the indy mini-hit "I Wanna Be a Cosmonaut") before he joined the British Army in 1981 — and left again within 90 days.

He returned to music, touring the UK by public transport and honing a folk-punk repertoire of self-composed social commentary — the Paul-Weller-meets-Paul-Simon vibe of "The Busy Girls Buys Beauty" — and wickedly rearranged classics. His version of Bobby Troup's "Route 66," revised for the considerably less magical A13 (trunk road to the sea), was a perpetual live favorite and would also distinguish Bragg's radio debut on the John Peel show in July 1983.

That same month, Bragg's debut album, *Life's a Riot with Spy Vs Spy* was released through his own Utility label, collecting together three afternoons worth of demos recorded for his music publishers. Both session and album were well received and in October, Bragg signed with Go! Discs, who promptly reissued his album (#30 UK, #1 UK indy). The Peel session would appear four years later (#4 UK indy).

Dominating the indy charts until April 1984 when Go! Discs landed major label distribution, the album would sell over 150,000 copies while Bragg himself toured exhaustively. He made his US debut with a short tour in August, following up in 1985 with a string of dates opening for The Smiths, but it was his alignment with the political left in Britain which cemented his reputation as a performer and songwriter.

Throughout the bitter coal miners' strike which tore the UK apart in 1984–85, Bragg was a regular guest at benefit shows, and in October, he was arrested during an anti-apartheid demonstration outside the South African embassy in London. Two years later, he would be charged with criminal damage for cutting a fence during an anti-nuclear demo at a US air force base. Most significantly, however, he was one of the guiding forces behind Red Wedge, a union with the Redskins, Style Council, the Communards, and others, aimed at raising funds for the socialist Labour party's election campaign during 1986–87. Later, he would become a regular at the Earth Day festival.

Such activities inevitably flavored Bragg's music — yet the rhetoric reputation of his *Brewing Up with Billy Bragg* (#16 UK) sophomore album in 1984 and the *Between the Wars EP* (#15 UK) in March 1985 was readily belied when Kirsty MacColl scored with a cover of Bragg's tender "New England" (#7 UK), again in March. "Days Like This" (#43 UK), in early 1986, previewed the *Talking Poetry with the Taxman* (#8 UK) album, both making a lyrical virtue of Britain's mid-'80s slide into Thatcherite disarray. At the same time, however, the import *St Swithins Day EP* (#2 UK indy), singles like "Levi Stubbs' Tears" (#29 UK), and "Greetings to the New Brunette" (#58 UK), featuring Smiths guitarist Johnny Marr and vocalist MacColl, continued to portray him as a songwriter of remarkable sensitivity.

Elsewhere, a charity cover of the Beatles' "She's Leaving Home" (#1 UK) emphasized interpretative powers which Bragg had hitherto buried away on B-sides and live shows (his occasional assaults on Linda Ronstadt's mid-'70s repertoire was an especially well guarded secret, until 1999's *Reaching to the Converted* compilation unearthed versions of both "Heart Like a Wheel" and "The Tatler").

"Waiting for the Great Leap Forward" (#52 UK) followed in September 1988, two months before *Workers Playtime* (#198 US, #17 UK) became Bragg's first US chart entry. The following February, Bragg made his American TV debut on the David Letterman show. He scored another Top 30 hit as guest on pre-Fatboy Slim mastermind Norman Cook's first solo single, "Won't Talk About It" (#29 UK).

Bragg's next album, *The Internationale* (#34 UK), appeared a year later, and he would spend much of 1990 touring, including an eastern European outing with Natalie Merchant and Michael Stipe. He joined REM on a version of Suzanne Vega's "Tom's Diner" for the *Tom's Album* collection and relaunched his own, long-moribund Utility label, signing New Zealand band Dead Famous People and Dolly Mixtures, among others. Such activity paid off when his next album, *Don't Try This at Home* (#8 UK) became his biggest hit since 1986, aided by the singles "Sexuality" (#27 UK) and "You Woke Up My Neighbourhood" (#54 UK), as well as contributions from Stipe and Merchant.

Although he continued gigging, playing both conventional shows and benefits, Bragg would not release another new album for five years. 1992's *Accident Waiting to Happen EP* (#33 UK) alone broke the silence before he finally re-emerged (on a new label, Cooking Vinyl) with 1996/1997's *William Bloke* (#16 UK) and *Bloke on Bloke* (#72 UK) pairing and the singles "Upfield" (#46 UK) and "The Boy Done Good" (#55 UK).

He confirmed his return in 1998 when he teamed with Uncle Tupelo pin-off Wilco to record *Mermaid Avenue* (#90 US, #34 UK), the first of two volumes of previously unreleased Woody Guthrie songs which Bragg was invited to complete following his appearance at the Guthrie tribute concert in New York in 1992. He also played the Rock and Roll Hall of Fame's Woody Guthrie tribute in September 1996, and following the album's release, played Guthrie's 86th birthday celebrations in Okemah, OK. But the widely praised ease with which he moved into territory which hitherto, Bob Dylan alone had been able to call his own, should not have surprised anybody.

Bragg's reinvention of the dustbowl cowboy, after all, was not that far removed from his own beginnings — riding the bus instead of a boxcar, writing his songs as the miles flashed by, then taking them to the people before the ink was even dry. The A13 had stretched to the promised land after all.

Billy Bragg LPs

8 Life's a Riot with Spy Vs Spy (Go! Discs) 1983 Seven-song introduction to the basic Bragg — one man, his guitar, and a tinny little amp — all piling up behind the naked, naïve passion which was his early calling card. "New England" and "Milkman of Human Kindness" grab the plaudits, but there's little to choose between any of them.

9 Brewing Up (Go! Discs) 1984 Slowly adding deftness to both performance and instrumentation (trumpet and organ!), with "St Swithins Day" to lure in the star-crossed lovers.

8 Talking with the Taxman About Poetry (Elektra) 1986 Close enough to masterful to justify the critical consensus that it is Bragg's best album, although only "Greetings to the New Brunette" truly matches the best of its predecessors.

7 Workers Playtime (Elektra) 1988 Oddly subdued, despite the presence of a full band.

8 The Internationale (Elektra) 1990 Disconcerting mini-album, less a full release than a public trial for sundry sonic experiments — the a cappella "Nicaragua Nicaragua" and "I Dreamed I Saw Phil Ochs Last Night"; theBeefheartian Salvation Army which pursues "Marching Song of the Covert Battalions." Thankfully, most work well.

6 Don't Try This at Home (Elektra) 1991

7 William Bloke (Elektra) 1996

6 Bloke on Bloke (Cooking Vinyl — UK) 1997 Return to the acoustic essentials of his best early work, combined with the experiences of fatherhood and aging, a warm and mature album which doesn't even seem to miss the old fire. *Bloke on Bloke* is a mini-album complement which includes a scratchy cover of The Smiths' "Never Had No-One Ever."

9 Mermaid Avenue (Elektra) 1998 Fifteen hitherto unheard Guthrie songs make up this album, but Bragg's own acknowledgement that Guthrie's recording career "was more or less over" by the time he wrote them should not be taken as a warning. A vivacious collaboration with Wilco is musically reminiscent of Dylan *circa* 1970–71, but lyrically as redolent of the songs' own era as anything else Guthrie wrote — and that's as true of the unabashed childrens' songs ("Hoodoo Voodoo") as it is for the epics of a dustbowl Okie childhood ("Way Over Yonder"), and onto the period politics ("Christ for President").

9 Mermaid Avenue Vol 2 (working title) (Elektra) 2000 Further explorations of the unheard Guthrie canon, featuring several songs previewed in a BBC documentary on the making of the first volume. "Airline to Heaven" and "My Flying Saucer" offer highlights, while Natalie Merchant's "I Was Born" is a career highlight.

Selected Compilations and Archive Releases

8 Back to Basics (Elektra) 1987 Compilation featuring the first two albums, plus the *Between the Wars EP*.

8 Reaching to the Converted (Rhino) 1999 B-sides and rarities collections which rises above such an unpromising description to prove one of the best intros to Bragg's ouvre imaginable.

Further Reading

Still Suitable for Miners: The Official Biography by Andrew Collins (Virgin, UK, 1998).

BRIAN JONESTOWN MASSACRE

FORMED *1990 (San Francisco, CA)*
ORIGINAL LINE-UP *Anton Newcombe (vocals, guitar)*

Playing guerilla gigs in attics and parties, Anton Newcombe formed the Brian Jonestown Massacre "in response to a lack of the kind of music I wanted to listen to out there." The first years of the band's existence were spent experimenting with both music and musicians, and unleashing a string of increasingly ambitious singles, 1992's "She Made Me" and 1993's "Convertible" and "Candyfloss" among them. Newcombe also spent this time compiling what became the Brian Jonestown Massacre's first two albums, *Space Girl and Other Favorites*, a compilation of the band's earliest 45s, and *Methadrone*, with guitarist Jeffrey Davies, bassists Rick Maymi and Matt Hollywood, and drummers Brian Glaze and Graham Bonnar.

Claiming inspiration (naturally) from the ghost of Rolling Stone Brian Jones, Newcombe simultaneously threw himself into the creation of two further albums, *Their Satanic Majesties' Second Request* and *Take It from the Man*, recording one by night and one by day. All four albums would see the light of day within little more than a year of one other, during 1995–96, spread between Bomp and Newcombe's own Tangible label.

It was with these latter sessions that the Brian Jonestown Massacre finally arrived at a reasonably steady line-up of Hollywood, Davies, Glaze and Dean Taylor (guitar), Mara Kegal (keyboards), Dawn Thomas (accordion), and Joel Gion (Spokesman for the Revolution). The stability was initially short-lived, however, as the band shattered on stage in Austin, Texas in 1996. Gion and Newcombe alone fulfilled the band's outstanding schedule with an unplugged set, paving the way for the *Thank God for Mental Illness* album, recorded in one day in July for an alleged total cost of $17.36.

Taylor and Hollywood drifted back into the frame and the Massacre would establish themselves as an in-demand opening act, gigging with Mercury Rev, Love and Rockets, Sonic Boom/Spectrum, as well as with Oasis on their first US tour.

A new line-up coalesced around Newcombe, Hollywood, and Gion, featuring Peter Hayes (guitar) and Miranda Richards (guitar, vocals), and the Massacre's sixth album, *Give It Back* was released in early 1997, the prelude to the band's long-awaited switch to a major label later in the year. Returning to the more-or-less classic line-up of Newcombe, Hollywood, Gion, Taylor, and Davies, 1998's *Strung Out in Heaven* appeared on TVT although the group retained its independence sufficiently to unveil a swift follow-up through the tiny Which label, *Bringing It All Back Home Again*.

Brian Jonestown Massacre LPs

7 Methodrone (Bomp) 1995

8 Take It from the Man (Bomp) 1996 Recorded live between November 1996 and February 1996, there are spacey songs, acid-drenched numbers, straight-on proto-rockers, and best of all, an 11-minute "Straight Up and Down" which sums everything up in one monstrous swoop.

7 Their Satanic Majesties' Second Request (Tangible) 1996 BJM come to terms with not just the Stones' psychedelic strivings, but with the entire acid era — and all its attendant casualties. Then they lovingly recreate the whole shebang with appropriate Haight-date instruments and dreamy melodies.

6 Thank God for Mental Illness (Bomp) 1996

8 Give It Back (Bomp) 1997 Never sitting still, veering from loping rock ("Satellite"), to droning folk ("Malela" — Simon & Garfunkel's first album played through the Incredible String Band's most incredible strings), and on to unabashed psilocybic obtuseness, *Give It Back* both follows up the loose ends left by past albums and opens the door to some future thoughts as well.

7 Strung Out in Heaven (TVT) 1998 Best approximating all the joys that the Jesus and Mary Chain once threatened to deliver, time has stood still for the last 30 years and the Massacre range freely across it all. A smorgasbord of alternative realities, suggested solutions, and desperately whacked pop notions.

7 Bringing It All Back Home Again (Which) 1999 Lovelier six-song ghost of the country/acoustic *Mental Illness*.

6 Spacegirl and Other Favorites (Tangible) 1996 Formative noise and proto-psych space monsters unleashed.

BROKEN BONES

FORMED 1983 (Stoke on Trent, England)
ORIGINAL LINE-UP Tony "Bones" Roberts (guitar); Nobby (vocals); Terry "Tezz" Roberts (bass); Cliff (drums)

Broken Bones was formed by Tony Roberts shortly after he quit Discharge, one of the most successful bands to emerge from the Oi! movement that swamped Britain during the early 1980s. "Never Again" gave that band a UK hit single in 1981, while their debut album, *Hear Nothing*, stayed on the chart for five weeks. Clearly destined to follow in those mighty footsteps, Bones unveiled his latest juggernaut in late 1982, setting out on a solid year of gigging leading up to the release, in January 1984, of the *Decapitated* EP (#10 UK indy).

May brought "Crucifix" (#12 UK indy), another three-track monster which, when allied with *Dem Bones* (#5 UK indy), suggested Broken Bones might break out of the punk ghetto all together, and have a serious impact on the mainstream. Live shows became increasingly riotous celebrations; the established music press was paying attention. Not since Punk's heyday in the late 1970s had a band seemed poised for so many great things.

That chance was lost when over a year elapsed before Broken Bones' third single — a year, nevertheless, which saw the band consolidate its vinyl reputation with a never-ending tour. Broken Bones' 1985 live album, *Live at the 100 Club*, remains the acid test for anyone who claims to be a punk today — a record which forges an unimagined middle ground between hardcore, metal, and the apocalypse.

The band's much-anticipated third single, *Seeing Through My Eyes* (#6 UK indy), led off a mini-album which immortalized some of Broken Bones' best-loved songs — "It's Like," "The Point of Agony," the foreboding "Death Is Imminent," and "Decapitated Part 2". But *Seeing Through My Eyes* was to prove Broken Bones' finest moment. Cliff quit, to be replaced by the singularly named Bazz, in time for the defiant "Never Say Die" (#23 UK indy) and the patchy half studio/half live album *F.O.A.D.* ("Fuck Off and Die"). Neither it nor the *Bone Crusher* mini-album, however, even hinted at a return to old glories, and by the time of mid-1987's "Trader in Death" single, Roberts was the only surviving original member of Broken Bones as both brother Terry and Nobby departed.

He recruited Quiv (vocals) and DL Harris (bass) and with the band newly signed to the metal specialist label Music for Nations, Broken Bones embraced a whole new direction, harbingers of the mayhem which passes for metal today, and boasting a defiance which was as much desperate as it was dangerous. By the early 1990s, Broken Bones were essentially no more. Tezz went on to play briefly with Ministry, appearing on their *In Case You Didn't Feel Like Showing Up* live album; he then formed Battalion of Saints. Bones fronts a new generation of Discharge.

Broken Bones LPs
7 Dem Bones (Fall Out) 1984
8 Live 100 Club [LIVE] (Fall Out) 1985 The death-defying roar of the post-Oi! fallout in its native, naked environment.
6 F.O.A.D. (Fall Out) 1987 A two-part recapitulation of "Decapitated" and "Seeing Through My Eyes" highlight an over-long first flirtation with the powers of meaty metal.
5 Losing Control (Heavy Metal Records) 1989
5 Trader in Death (Heavy Metal Records) 1990
3 Stitched Up (Rough Justice) 1991

Selected Compilations and Archive Releases
6 Brain Dead (Rough Justice) 1992 Sensibly sorted "best of" the last three studio albums.
7 Death Is Imminent (Cleopatra) 1993
8 The Complete Singles (Cleopatra) 1997

BUFFALO TOM

FORMED 1986 (Amherst, MA)
ORIGINAL LINE-UP Bill Janovitz (vocals, guitar); Chris Colbourn (bass); Tom Maginnis (drums)

Named in part for drummer Tom Maginnis, Buffalo Tom emerged from Amherst, MA in 1987, around three University of Massachussetts students. Early shows caught them performing as the Buffalo Tom Trio at the Iron Horse folk club in nearby Northampton, and much of the group's debut album would be derived from this primal repertoire.

Close to two years of local gigging elapsed before Buffalo Tom signed with the Megadisc label (who have subsequently licensed their output to both SST and Beggars Banquet), during which period they developed a close relationship with fellow Northampton-ite J Mascis of Dinosaur [Jr]. Employing him as both mentor and producer, and generally echoing the better known cult across their swiftly rearranged debut album material, Buffalo Tom spent the next year waiting while scheduling delays postponed the record's release again and again. They spent the delay in the studio, again with Mascis at the helm, and completed *Birdbrain* shortly after *Buffalo Tom* was finally released.

A sign of the band's already shifting priorities came with a cover of the Psychedelic Furs' "Heaven," one of two predominantly acoustic cuts on the album (the other was a reprise of their debut's "Reason Why"). Their first concentrated blast of touring, too, shaped the band's immediate future, but another year was spent waiting for *Birdbrain* to come out, by which time Buffalo Tom had shifted dramatically away from their recorded sound.

While the entire American music scene, it seemed, finally embraced the cacophonous mud of grunge which Buffalo Tom had certainly helped refine across their first two albums, the group now unearthed a folk-rock sound which would inform both 1992's semi-breakthrough *Let Me Come Over* (#49 UK) and 1993's *Big Red Letter Day* (#185 US, #17 UK). Buffalo Tom ended 1993 as many critics' pick for an imminent breakthrough. But while "Taillights Fade" (from *Come Over*) and "Soda Jerk" (from *Red Letter*) both enjoyed a moment of media attention, neither took off and Buffalo Tom's greatest success would come in the UK, where both albums made the Top 50 and *Red Letter* scraped the Top 20.

The group spent the next year on tour, reaffirming their earlier roots with the hard-hitting, self-co-produced *Sleepy Eyed* (#160 US) — a generally successful attempt to meld their live sound with the studio environment. 1998's *Smitten*, recorded in Woodstock, NY in the depth of winter, pursued this same objective; Bill Janowitz's *Lonesome Billy* solo album, quietly released the previous year, gave continued vent to the folky elements extracted from the band sound. A remarkable consolidation of both streams of thought came about when Buffalo Tom recorded a version of Paul Weller's "Going Underground" for the 1999 Jam tribute album, *Fire and Skill*.

Buffalo Tom LPs

4 Buffalo Tom (SST) 1989

3 Birdbrain (Beggars Banquet) 1990 If it's true that The Pixies really are the new Boxtops, then REM have to be Poco. Which means that anyone who sounds like REM are automatically the Nitty Gritty Dirt Band.

6 Let Me Come Over (Beggars Banquet) 1992 Basic rock'n'whimper — songs start as one, fall into the other, but with only the occasional genuine let-down. The loud bits outweigh the wet ones, and the trademark harmonies are finally beginning to gel.

8 Big Red Letter Day (Beggars Banquet) 1993 Completing the shift into Big Star country, Buffalo Tom jangle and twang with the best of them, filling *Red Letter* with moody melodies lightened by harmonies and the exquisite guitars. College rock rarely sounded this good.

6 Sleepy Eyed (East West) 1995

6 Smitten (Polydor) 1998

Bill Janovitz LP
5 Lonesome Billy (Beggars Banquet) 1997

BULLSHIT DETECTOR
compilation

UK PUNK COMPILATIONS; 1980–83

"Don't expect music when melody is anger, when the message is defiance, three chords are frustration when the words are from the heart." With that promise, Crass launched their own survey of the best of young, unsigned British bands in the immediate aftermath of punk and emerged with one of the most uncompromising documents of the entire era.

Familiar names abound, Chumbawamba, Napalm Death, and Anthrax all contributed to the series during their infancy. Similarly, at least two future superstar drummers — London Suede's Simon Gilbert and Catherine Wheel's Neil Sims — made their recorded debuts within the three-volume *Bullshit Detector* series, with Dead to the World and 1984 respectively.

But the albums' true worth was in registering the sheer depth and weight of anger still percolating beneath the increasingly bland UK street scene, all the more so since few of the bands plunged into the Oi!/hardcore waters which were the traditional preserve of the socially disaffected.

Also see the entry for "CRASS" on page 294.

Bullshit Detector — Directory of Bands
(volume numbers follow in parentheses)
1984 — Break-Up (vol. 2)
A NUL NOISE — Hibashuka (vol. 3)
A GARDENER — A Gardener's Song (vol. 2)
ACTION FROGS — Drumming Up Hope (vol. 1)
ALIENATED — Living in Fear (vol. 3)
ALTERNATIVE — Change It (vol. 1)
AMEBIX — University Challenged (vol. 1)
AMERIKAN ARSENAL — Get Off Your Ass (vol. 2)
ANEEB — Berlin Wall (vol. 3)
ANIMUS — Nuclear Piss (vol. 3)
ANTHRAX — All the Wars (vol. 2)
APF BRIGADE — Anarchist Attack (vol. 1)
ARMCHAIR POWER — Power (vol. 1)
ATTRITION — In Your Mind (vol. 3)
AVERT AVERSION — Oh What a Nice Day (vol. 3)
AWAKE MANKIND — Once upon a Time (vol. 3)
BARBED WIRE — Weapons of War (vol. 3)

BOFFO — Garageland (vol. 2)

BORED — Riot Style (vol. 2)

BRAINWASHED PUPILS — The Demonstration (vol. 3)

CAINE MUTINY — Morning Star (vol. 1)

CAPITAL PUNISHMENT — We've Realized the Truth Now (vol. 2)

CARNAGE — Carnage (vol. 3)

CHUMBAWAMBA — Three Years Later (vol. 2)

CLOCKWORK CRIMINALS — We Are You (vol. 1)

COUNTER ATTACK — Don't Wanna Fight for You (vol. 1)

CRAG — Voice Your Protest (vol. 3)

CRASS — Do They Owe Us a Living (vol. 1)

DANDRUFF — Life in a Whiskey Bottle (vol. 3)

DEAD TO THE WORLD — Action Man (vol. 3)

DEFORMED — Freedom (vol. 2)

DIRECT ACTION — Death Without a Thought (vol. 3)

DISRUPTORS — Napalm (vol. 1)

DISTRUCTORS — Agent Orange (vol. 2)

DOUGIE — War Without Victory (vol. 2)

ERATICS — National Service (vol. 1)

FIFTH COLUMN — Counterfeit Culture (vol. 3)

FRENZY BATTALION — Thalidomide (vol. 1)

FUCK THE CIA — Right Or Wrong (vol. 1)

FUNKY RAYGUNS — The Hare and a Tortoise (vol. 3)

NEALE HARMER — Hard Nut (vol. 3)

HEALTH HAZARD — Picture (vol. 3)

PHIL HEDGEHOG — Radio Times (vol. 3)

ICON — Cancer (vol. 1)

IMPALERS — Sun Sun Sun (vol. 3)

KRONDSTADT UPRISING — Receiver Deceiver (vol. 2)

MALICE — Faceless (vol. 3)

MARKUS ABUSED — The Killing Machine (vol. 3)

METRO YOUTH — Brutalized (vol. 2)

MICHAEL KINGZETT TAYLOR — Paranoia (vol. 3)

MOLOTOV COCKTAIL — Ain't Got a Clue (vol. 2)

NAKED — Mid 1930s (vol. 2)

NAPALM DEATH — The Crucifixion of Possessions (vol. 3)

NO DEFENSES — Work to Consume (vol. 3)

NO LABEL — Let's Get It Right (vol. 2)

NORMALITY COMPLEX — Black Market Shadow (vol. 2)

OMEGA TRIBE — Nature Wonder (vol. 2)

ONE MAN'S MEAT — Your Country Misleads You (vol. 3)

PASSION KILLERS — Start Again (vol. 2)

PEROXIDE — Ministry of Death (vol. 3)

PITS — UK in Dreamland (vol. 2)

POLEMIC SYSTEM — Manipulated Youth (vol. 2)

POLITICIDE — 51st State (vol. 3)

PORNO SQUAD — Khaki Doesn't Go with My Eyes (vol. 1)

POTENTIAL VICTIM — People (vol. 3)

PSEUDO SADISTS — Slaughter of the Innocent (vol. 2)

REALITY CONTROL — The War Is Over (vol. 3)

REBEL A — Genesis Genocide (vol. 3)

RED ALERT — Who Needs Society (vol. 1)

REJECTED — Same Old Songs (vol. 2)

REPUTATIONS IN JEOPARDY — Girls Love Popstars (vol. 1)

RICHARD III — Will You Care? (vol. 3)

RIOT SQUAD — Security System (vol. 2)

SAMMY RUBETTE & SAFETY MARCH — Ballot of Maggie the Maggot (vol. 3)

SCEPTICS — Local Chaos (vol. 1)

SEVENTH PLAGUE — Rubber Bullets (vol. 3)

SIC — Low (vol. 2)

SINYX — Mark of the Beast (vol. 1)

SNIPERS — War Song (vol. 1)

SPEAKERS — Why (vol. 1)

PG MURDERS — Soldiers (vol. 1)

ST. VITUS DANCERS — The Survivor (vol. 2)

STATE OF SHOCK — Excess Youth (vol. 3)

STEGZ — Christus Erectus (vol. 2)

SUCKS — 3 (vol. 1)

SUSPECTS — Random Relations (vol. 2)

ANDY T — Jazz on a Summer's Day/Nagasaki Mon Amour (vol. 1)

TOBY KETTLE — Theatre Comment (vol. 2)

TOTAL CHAOS — Psycho Analysis (vol. 2)

TOXIC EPHEX — Police Brutality (vol. 2)

TOXIC — Tradition of Slaughter (vol. 2)

UNTITLED — We Are Taught to Kill (vol. 3)

VERBAL ASSAULT — Not Yet Ron (vol. 3)

WAITING FOR BARDOT — Voice of UK (vol. 2)

WARNING — Beasts of Friction/Tin Drum (vol. 3)

ROB WILLIAMS — Lies (vol. 3)

XS — Fuck the System (vol. 2)

XTRACT — Fight for Peace (vol. 3)

YOUR FUNERAL — Think About It (vol. 2)

YOUTH IN ASIA — Power and the Glory (vol. 2)

YOUTHANASIA — Power (vol. 3)

KATE BUSH

BORN *Catherine Bush, 7/30/58 (Bexley Heath, England)*

Bush was 14 when she recorded her first demos, financed by a friend of her physician father, Ricky Hooper, who in turn passed them onto an old University friend, Pink Floyd guitarist Dave Gilmour. He recorded further tracks with her, and finally interested EMI in the prodigious schoolgirl.

Keen to nurture the talent rather than package it up for teeny-style gratification, EMI arranged for Bush to take voice, mime, and dance classes while refining her songwriting at home, and on stage — the K.T. Bush Band, featuring brother Paddy, Brian Bath, Del Palmer, and drummer Charlie Morgan — began playing shows around south London in April 1977, debuting at the Rose of Lee pub in Lewisham.

The band continued gigging through the spring, then broke up in June when Bush began work on her debut album. Early plans for a single of "James and the Cold Gun, " a track which had worked well live, were cancelled when Bush unveiled "Wuthering Heights" for release in the new year. An insistently haunting song performed at an utterly disconcerting pitch, "Wuthering Heights" (#1 UK) was a massive hit, despite the general press consensus that its greatest virtue was its novelty value — a condemnation which struck at both song and singer. Despite EMI's own insistence that Bush be marketed with a long-term career in mind, still early promotional pictures emphasized her youth and femininity, with one particularly benippled photograph, already vetoed by Bush as an album sleeve, instead employed for posters and press ads.

The Kick Inside (#3 UK), Bush's first album, and the accompanying "The Man with the Child in His Eyes" (#85 US, #6 UK) did much to repair the damage — the one an astoundingly versatile collection of songs, moods, and impressions; the other, an achingly tender ballad which, had it been at all representative of the rest of Bush's muse, would have tipped her irrevocably into interminable pop adulthood.

Bush, however, was not to be pinned down. All but assuming her production duties herself, she began work on her second album while *Kick Inside* was still in the Top 20, adamant that whatever her first album said about her talents, the new one would say something else entirely — a deliberate policy which would continue to inform her career over the next decade. Furthering the dislocation through her videos, idiosyncratic modern dance and mime extravaganzas only loosely rooted in the song's subject matter, Bush would confirm her creative independence in the public mind long before her actual records began consistently justifying her reputation.

Still, the bizarre "Hammer Horror" (#44 UK) and "Wow" (#14 UK) — an immature, but nevertheless heartfelt assault on her own experiences in the media — proved thoughtful trailers for the sophomore *Lionheart* (#6 UK), and in early 1979, Bush announced her first UK and European tours.

Extravagantly choreographed and rehearsed, with the London show recorded for both video and a possible live album, the March/April 1979, outing ultimately proved so unsatisfying that Bush promptly retired from live work. An EP, *On Stage* (#10 UK), would be the only immediate souvenir of the outing and Bush returned to the studio to concentrate on her third album, *Never Forever* (#1 UK).

A guest appearance on Peter Gabriel's 1980 hit "Games Without Frontiers" (#48 US, #4 UK) increased Bush's credibility at a time when Gabriel himself was still considered a maverick on the margins of the rock avant-garde, while her own anti-nuclear "Breathing" 45 introduced an apocalyptic edginess which likewise fed directly into recent developments on the post-punk scene. At the same time, however, Bush retained the fantastical element which had always been her most entrancing quality, letting it loose across both "Babooshka" (#5 UK) and the festive "December Will Be Magic Again" (#29 UK).

She jerked back to reality with "Army Dreamers" (#16), a song whose topicality was only enhanced by Britain's newly incumbent Conservative government's muttered contemplation of reintroducing the draft. At a time when only the likes of Crass and the bands lining up on the first volume of *Bullshit Detector* were openly commenting upon that particular piece of would-be legislation, Bush's subversion was all the more notable for its unexpectedness.

Bush spent much of 1981 working on new material, unveiling the first fruits in June with the furiously percussive "Sat in Your Lap" (#11 UK). The self-produced *The Dreaming* (#157 US, #3 UK) followed late the following year, her most developed album yet — a dense exploration of both musical and lyrical styles far removed from even the extremes of its predecessors.

The title track, a haunted journey through the Australian bush (#48 UK), the Celtic air of "Night of the Swallow," and the violently cinematic "Get Out of My House" all predicted attitudes which would not percolate into the rock mainstream for some time yet, while the album was highlighted by what became, in turn, the most inexplicable flop single of the year, "There Goes a Tenner." *Smash Hits* journalist Neil Tennant, still a couple of years away from pop fame with the Pet Shop Boys, acknowledged Bush's accomplishments with a review which condemned the album as "very weird," at the same time as complimenting Bush's attempt to "become less accessible."

Bush herself seemed immune to either criticism or praise, performing minimal promotion, then retreating back to her constantly growing home studio. Her baffled US label followed *The Dreaming*'s marginal success with an introductory hits EP, *Kate Bush* (#148 US); the rest of the world just sat back and awaited *Hounds of Love* (#30 US, #1 UK). It was a long wait. Two years in the making, and again previewed by a powerful scene-setting single, "Running Up That Hill" (#30 US, #3 UK), *Hounds of Love* would be granted further strength by the 12-inch remixes Bush prepared for "Hill" and its immediate follow-up, "Cloudbursting" (#20 UK). Extending the mantric mood of both, without any of the space-filling which normally scarred "rock" remixes, both performances were shop windows for Bush's now unimpeachable production talents as much as the songs — with "Cloudbursting" being further dignified by a breathtaking video (co-starring Donald Sutherland) whose omission from sundry year/decade/century's end Best Of charts continues to make a mockery of MTV's claim to even begin to represent the genre fairly.

"Running Up That Hill" brought Bush her US breakthrough in November 1985 with two further singles, "The Hounds of Love" (#18 UK) and "Big Sky" (#37 UK) at least attracting attention on the strengths of their own videos. More importantly, however, Bush's stylistic influence was also making itself felt on the US scene, as a new wave of increasingly self-assertive female musicians began emerging from the college communities which had hitherto been Bush's strongest Stateside foothold.

It would be another two years before the first of these (North Carolina-born Tori Amos) emerged to compete with Bush in the mainstream. In the meantime, Bush celebrated her first hits collection, *The Whole Story* (#76 US, #1 UK), with the bizarre "Experiment IV" (#23 UK) single and self-directed video and scored a simultaneous hit with another collaboration with Gabriel, the winsome "Don't Give Up" (#72 US, #9 UK).

After so much achievement, Bush ended the decade with her first genuinely disappointing record, the folk-inflected *This Sensual World* (#43 US, #2 UK) (subsequently honored by *Q* magazine amongst "50 albums that sound like sex"), and singles of the title track (#12 UK), "Love and Anger" (#38 UK) and "This Woman's Work" (#25 UK). A pointless cover of Elton John's "Rocket Man" (#12 UK), recorded for a Bernie Taupin/Elton John tribute album, broke another silence in 1991; the following year, a sample of "Cloudbursting" dignified British techno ravers Utah Saints' "Something Good" (#98 US, #4 UK). Bush herself returned in 1993 with *The Red Shoes* (#28 US, #2 UK), a star-spangled continuation of *World*'s less excitable maturity — Jeff Beck, Eric Clapton, Prince, and Dave Gilmour were numbered among the guests.

Again, a clutch of less-than-massive singles followed: the title track (#21 UK), the twanging "Rubberband Girl" (#88 US, #12 UK), "Moments of Pleasure" (#26 UK), and "And So Is Love" (#26 UK). Bush also collaborated with harmonica veteran Larry Adler on "The Man I Love" (#27 UK), while 1994 saw her deliver the 50-minute home video *The Lion, the Cross and the Curve* — a reinstatement of her vision, if not accessibility.

Two years later, Bush recorded the Gaelic language "Mna na Heireann" for the Common Ground project but it would be spring 1999 before fresh reports that she was working on a new album arrived, while she would also be contributing soundtrack material to the forthcoming Disney movie *Dinosaur*. Such a lengthy silence, however, did not prevent her from registering in a crop of millennial polls, as the 33rd

"Greatest Star of the 20th century" (*Q* magazine) and the 46th Most Influential Woman in Rock (VH-1).

Kate Bush LPs

9 The Kick Inside (EMI America) 1978 Sexy, sensual, and surprisingly edgy, the songs swing from tough-talkers to exquisite vulnerability without missing a beat; this finely wrought set reintroduced Cathy and Heathcliff via "Wuthering Heights" while Bush's sonic scales astonished fans and dolphins alike.

7 Lionheart (EMI America) 1978 The album set the pace for what would become an unfortunate standard — half an album of stunners and a flip side's worth of filler. Although what's good is unbelievable — especially "Hammer Horror" and "Oh England My Lionheart" — and perhaps that makes the rest pale in comparison.

7 Never Forever (EMI America) 1980 More of a follow-up to the first album, this set finds Bush refining and settling into her sound. The mysterious "Babooshka" and the blatant "Breathing," meanwhile pinpoint the next decade's worth of concerns.

10 The Dreaming (EMI America) 1982 Completely departing Bush's previous formulae, less a collection of songs than a dreamily twisted landscape of beauty and ugliness, melded into one sleepy vision. Half nightmare, half erotic missive, the songs exist exquisitely both alone and (better) within the context of the whole, with the hyper-visual title track itself expanding the canvas beyond anything previously pushed into the world of simple "rock."

"Pull Out the Pin" and the Stephen King-inspired "Get Out of MyHouse" are the ravers, balanced by the utterly surreal balladry of "Houdini" and "Night of the Swallow". And lest the mood become too extreme, she puts it all in perspective with the teasing tones of "There Goes a Tenner," its coda host to one of the loveliest melodic snatches in Bush's entire repertoire.

The Dreaming defined Bush for the future at the same time as redefining her past — there were hints and suggestions if you knew where to look, but the first shock of the percussive "Sat in Your Lap" still resonates, two decades on.

7 The Hounds of Love (EMI America) 1985 Although this album delivered two of Bush's best singles, "Running Up That Hill" and "Cloudbursting," the rest of the set falls short of expectation, albeit with a pleasant shift to subverted Irish traditional jigs. The context seems plain, though, and the subject matter spartan — maybe she was just trying too hard.

5 The Sensual World (Columbia) 1989 All grown up and knowing it. Kudos to Bush for producing such a seductive record; Brownie points, too, for then wrapping that frankness in guarded suggestion. But one does yearn for the days when she'd just let it all fly.

2 The Red Shoes (Columbia) 1993 Bush backtracks far from even where she started, with a clutch of wasted wastrel songs which really should have been left in the vault.

Further Reading

A Visual Documentary by Kevin Cann/Sean Mayes (Omnibus, UK, 1988).

BUTTHOLE SURFERS

FORMED 1979 *(San Antonio, TX)*
ORIGINAL LINE-UP *Gibby Haynes (b. Gibson Haynes, 1957 — vocals); Paul Leary (b. 1958 — guitar)*

The son of TV presenter Mr. Peppermint, Gibby Haynes was an accounting and economics student at Trinity University, San Antonio, TX when he met financing Masters student Paul Leary in 1977. Forming a partnership, the pair's early activities included manufacturing Lee Harvey Oswald bedding for sale to tourists, before the Butthole Surfers formed from the ashes of such Haynes-Leary-led musical projects as the Ashtray Baby Heads and Nine Foot Worm Makes Home Food. The new name itself came from one of the latter band's songs ; a local radio DJ is credited as the first person to (inadvertently) refer to the group by that name.

Moving to California, the band was picked up by Alternative Tentacles in 1981, but it would be two years more before their debut album appeared. Recorded back in San Antonio, *Brown Reason to Live* featured the group's first vaguely stable line-up, with former Hugh Beaumont Experience drummer King Coffey in place for the group's first UK tour, in early 1984. The frantic *Live PCPPEP* live album followed — a dramatic recording, which nevertheless offered a mere fraction of the group's true potency; Haynes' natural showmanship quickly leading them towards a freak show circus-like performance whose influence would soon be apparent as far afield as Ministry, the Red Hot Chili Peppers, and ultimately, the Jim Rose Circus Sideshow.

In May 1984, *Brown Reason* (retitled *Butthole Surfers*) climbed to #21 on the UK indy charts, establishing that country as the band's most profitable market. However, the line-up was still seeking the stability required. to make a prolonged push. A succession of bassists known only by their christian names — Alan, Trevor, Terence — was ended with the recruitment of one-time Shockabilly member Mark Kramer, soon after *Psychic... Powerless... Another Man's Sac* (#12 UK indy) became the Butthole's first release on their new label, Touch and Go.

Reveling in their ability to combine scatological tastelessness with marked chart success, then deface some of rock's

© Jim Steinfeldt/Chansley Entertainment Archives

most sacred icons ("American Woman" was a particularly welcome target), the Buttholes unleashed the *Creamed Corn from the Socket of David* EP (#9 UK indy) and *Rembrandt Pussyhorse* (#9 UK indy) before Kramer quit to form Bongwater.

Bassist Jeff Pinkus and a second drummer, Theresa Nervosa (b. Theresa Naylor), were added to the band as the *Locust Abortion Technician* (#3 UK indy) album and tour came together (the group would also add a full-time naked dancer, Kathleen, rather than hope that the audience would produce one as had been the case in the past). It was this line-up which created the band's most notorious album, 1988's *Hairway to Steven* (#6 UK), with its nine tracks furthering the Led Zeppelin puns by bearing a rude symbol instead of a title.

Topping the UK indy chart for two weeks, the *Widowermaker* EP (#1 UK indy), in November 1989, marked Nervosa's swansong as a Surfer (*Double Live*, #4 UK indy, on the band's own Latino Bugger label also captures this most crazed line-up in action). The following year, having signed to Rough Trade, a new EP, *The Hurdy Gurdy Man*, and album, *Pioughed* (a phonetic acronym for P-Oed or pissed off) (#68 UK), brought the group its biggest success to date.

A well-received showing on the first Lollapalooza through the summer of 1990 followed, while Haynes' Jack Officers side project provoked some underground comment when Kramer's Shimmy Disc released the quaintly titled *Digital Dump* album. But if any one event can be said to have raised the Surfers' profile beyond their traditional cult outrage stakes, it was Haynes' starring role on Ministry's "Jesus Built My Hot Rod" genre-defining single in early 1992. A monster hit, it catapulted Ministry to superstardom and offered similar possibilities to almost anyone associated with them — and that included a bunch of foul-mouthed Texans with an "R"-rated name.

The Surfers were snapped up by Capitol, and in early 1993 released *Independent Worm Saloon* (#154 US, #73 UK), produced by Led Zeppelin veteran John Paul Jones (in 1999, Leary returned a favor and guested on John Paul Jones' *Zooma* solo album).

"Who Was in My Room Last Night," a single (and MTV hit video, featuring Red Hot Chili Pepper Flea), came close to a US chart breakthrough, and while middle American media outlets debated the ethics of the band's name (eventually rechristening them the BH Surfers for in-store displays), the group combined a relentless touring regimen with the latest in a long line of sporadic side projects.

Leary moved into production, handling the Meat Puppets and the Supersuckers among others, while Haynes divided his time between an outrageous stint as DJ with Austin's alternative radio station 101X, and P, a band formed with actor Johnny Depp, recording Abba's "Dancing Queen" as part of their self-titled debut album. Coffey, too, worked on both sides of the board, as head of his own Trance Syndicate label and in partnership with Squid man David McCreeth as Drain.

The Surfers themselves reconvened for *Electric Larryland* (#31 US), their most conventional album ever, and their first major US chart hit, even as the band's traditional following howled its disappointment at the Surfers' apparent abandonment of past tasteless abuse. "Pepper," a UK Top 60 hit that fall, actually echoed the elsewhere-fashionable trip-hop stylings.

With sales of 600,000 behind them, the Butthole Surfers immediately returned to the studio to record a new album, *After the Astronaut*. They emerged with what Leary called their "grand masterpiece... our most pride-worthy effort and our most cohesive album to date." Capitol apparently agreed, but just weeks before the album's April 1998 release, a major disagreement between the band's then-manager and label saw the album — and indeed, the band — placed on indefinite hold.

Label and band finally parted company that summer. Allowing nothing else to go to waste, Capitol promptly gifted *After the Astronaut*'s intended artwork by artist Mark Ryden (but based on a sketch by Leary), to Marcy Playground's *Shapeshifter*.

The Surfers, meanwhile, spent the unexpected downtime negotiating for the return of their back catalog to the band members themselves and planning the launch of their own label.

Butthole Surfers LPs

6 A Brown Reason to Live (Alternative Tentacles) 1983 Mini album makes its point immediately, with the savage yowl of "The Shah Sleeps in Lee Harvey's Grave," and the genre splitting "Hey" — sole lyric an ad nauseam recitation of the title. The Gary Glitter revival starts here?

6 Live Pcppep (Alternative Tentacles) 1984 Dense live recounting of much of *Brown Reason*

7 Psychic... Powerless... Another Man's Sac (Touch and Go) 1985

7 Rembrandt Pussyhorse (Touch and Go) 1986 Originally canned by Alternative Tentacles, a skewed look at the rock of the '70s which, however distortedly, made the Surfers the buttholes they became. Neil Young's "Heart of Gold" provides the opening piano chords, but it's Guess Who's "American Woman" which blazes the trail.

8 Locust Abortion Technician (Touch and Go) 1987 Still teasing the memory banks, "Sweet Loaf" starts out from roughly the same point as Black Sabbath's "Sweet Leaf," but then things go awry — and not only in the delivery. Purposefully recorded in what sounds like a wet swamp, and avoiding even the hint of good taste with the blatant "Kuntz," *Locust* reaches its heart-attack peak with "22 Going On 23," delivered at a tempo completely of the Surfers' own making.

7 Hairway to Seven (Touch and Go) 1988 "I Saw an X Ray of a Girl Passing Gas" and other tales of delinquent delight.

7 Double Live [LIVE] (Touch and Go) 1989

8 Pioughd (Capitol) 1991 With a chorus of "Gary Shandling" (during "Revolution"), the only clear sound in sight, *Pioughd* stands defiantly as theButthole's revenge on any major label which thought it could make pop stars out of them.

6 Independent Worm Saloon (Capitol) 1993 Suddenly, songs to sing and dance to. John Paul Jones' production might have had something to do with clearing the fog, but maybe not. That's the Surfers' charm after all — taking a '60s pop melody, stretching it mercilessly into discordance, then foisting it into a shotgun marriage with funk. Among other things, of course.

9 Electric Larryland (Capitol) 1996 The masters of punk/hard rock weirdness return with this menagerie of kick-ass rockers, moody pop ballads, C&W, speed metal, and in the hit "Pepper," an Eastern-tinged, sardonic pop homage to Jim Carroll. There again, nothing's quite that straightforward,as their clash and crash cross-over coax defenseless little styles out from under the couch, and then bash them over the head. Chock-a-block with twisted makeovers!

Selected Compilations and Archive Releases

6 The Hole Truth... And Nothing Butt (Trance Syndicate) 1995 Rough live and rougher demos, while Gibby's hitherto unknown love for Gordon Lightfoot gets an airing in a vintage radio interview.

Jack Officers LP

6 Digital Dump (Shimmy Disc) 1990 Taking its lead from Daniel Miller's Silicon Teens (or not), a synth and sample heavy collection of daft dance and plastic pop.

Paul Leary LP

3 The History of Dogs (Capitol) 1991 High-principled, but chronologically-challenged political agit-prog.

Drain LPs

5 Pick Up Heaven (Trance Syndicate) 1992

6 Offspeed and in There (Trance Syndicate) 1996

P LP

7 P (Capitol) 1996 Gibby and Depp in total Texas roots rock mode — assuming Texas was redesigned by an Abba-loving Roger Corman. The Swedes' "Dancing Queen" is so perfectly rendered it might not even be funny.

BUZZCOCKS

FORMED 1976 *(Manchester, England)*
ORIGINAL LINE-UP *Pete Shelley (b. Peter McNeish, 4/17/55, Manchester — guitar); Howard Devoto (b. Howard Trafford — vocals); Steve Diggle (bass); John Maher (drums)*

Between late 1977 and their dissolution two years later, The Buzzcocks were the most consistent singles band in Britain, certainly among the groups thrown up by punk. From the early thrash of "Boredom" through the sophistication of "What Do You Know?," the 14 45s produced by the Manchester quartet represented English pop at its most precise; an effortless stream of jukebox classics unheard since the heyday of Marc Bolan's T.Rex, five years previous, and unrepeated until the heyday of Blur 15 years hence.

Howard Devoto and Pete Shelley met at the Bolton Institute of Technology in 1975, where Devoto was advertising for would-be musicians to join him in "working out a version of 'Sister Ray'." Shelley — whose interest in experimental music had already seen him record an album, the subsequently issued *Sky Yen* — and bassist Garth Smith answered his call and with "some guy who played drums," the embryonic Buzzcocks played their first ever gig on April 1, 1976. Unfortunately, while Shelley and Devoto had worked out a set, they hadn't got around to teaching it to their bandmates. The plug was pulled on the band after just three numbers.

Having read about punk rock and the Sex Pistols in the London press, the pair set about bringing this new sensation to Manchester, booking the band for shows in June 1976, then pulling Steve Diggle and John Maher out of the audience that first night to join their own band. When the Pistols returned to Manchester in July, the new-look Buzzcocks opened the show.

The Buzzcocks made their London debut in August, at the bottom of a bill which included both the Pistols and The Clash, at the Islington Screen on the Green. The following month, they played the punk festival at the 100 Club and in October, The Buzzcocks recorded their first demos, sessions which would be split between the band's self-released debut single, the "Spiral Scratch" EP and later, the famous "Time's Up" bootleg (subsequently given an authorized release in the early 1990s). "Spiral Scratch" appeared in January 1977 to rave reviews and a berth in the alternative charts which ended only when the band ran out of records to sell. Days later, Devoto quit The Buzzcocks.

With Shelley moving to vocals (and rhythm guitar), Diggle took over the lead guitar and Garth Smith was recalled as bassist. In this form, The Buzzcocks opened for The Clash on their February 1977 White Riot tour and became regulars at the Roxy Club, contributing two tracks to the *Live at the Roxy* album that spring. They signed to United Artists in

August and in November, "Orgasm Addict" became The Buzzcocks' debut single.

It ran into problems immediately — not the least being a radio ban and a threatened walk-out from record packers at the pressing plant. Undeterred, The Buzzcocks, now featuring Steve Garvey on bass (Smith left on the eve of the band's first major UK tour), followed up with "Oh Shit," although at least they had the sense to relegate the song to the B-side, of "What Do I Get" (#37 UK). The guardians of morality were not deterred, however, and again a pressing plant strike loomed. It was averted when The Buzzcocks made it onto *Top of the Pops* and "What Do I Get" began moving chartwards.

"I Don't Mind" (#55 UK) followed, paving the way for The Buzzcocks' debut album, *Another Music in a Different Kitchen* (#15 UK). Comprised totally of Buzzcocks' originals, many co-penned by Devoto (whose own band, Magazine, was now up and running), the album was promptly acclaimed an instant classic, and over the next twelve months, The Buzzcocks were seldom out of the UK chart.

"Love You More" (#34 UK) in June 1978 was oddly publicized as the shortest single ever made (at one minute and 45 seconds, it wasn't, but it came close), while September brought "Ever Fallen in Love" (#12 UK), the band's biggest hit, and the herald for their bestselling album, *Love Bites* (#13 UK). And finally, the band's past and present collided when Shelley resurrected the same co-written melody for The Buzzcocks' new single, "Promises" (#20), as Devoto had employed for Magazine's debut "Shot by Both Sides."

In March 1979, "Everybody's Happy Nowadays" (#29 UK) coincided with a short UK tour captured for the *Entertaining Friends* home video release; it would be five more months, however, before The Buzzcocks were again sighted, with their album, *A Different Kind of Tension* (#163 US, #26 UK) following up a disappointing new single, Diggle's "Harmony in My Head" (#32 UK) and a reissue of *Spiral Scratch* (#31 UK), aimed at calming a now frenzied collectors market.

The band made its first trip to America, an event celebrated by the release of the now legendary *Singles Going Steady* collection of A- and B-sides, quite possibly the sharpest album to come out of the entire punk era. Then, in November 1979, The Buzzcocks played their last major UK tour, supported by Joy Division. The outing was generally well-received, although The Buzzcocks themselves seemed to be playing with uncharacteristic sloppiness. Never the tightest of live bands, many of the shows appeared so under-rehearsed and careless that it was no surprise when The Buzzcocks announced a year long hiatus at the end of the outing.

The group returned with what they called an installment plan tour — a short string of gigs designed to promote the first of three new singles: "Are Everything" (#61 UK), "Strange Thing," and "Running Free." Neither concerts nor records recaptured the buzz of the earlier band, however, and in the spring of 1981, Pete Shelley went into the studio with producer Martin Rushent to demo songs for the next Buzzcocks' album. He came out with the rudiments of his solo debut. The Buzzcocks were shattered on the spot.

Shelly's interest in electronics was not new. A self-confessed Can fanatic (he penned the sleeve notes to a 1981 compilation), in 1979 he linked with two friends, Francis Cookson and Eric Random, to recreate Robert Fripp/Brian Eno's *No Pussyfooting*, both in concert and on a three-track EP, *Big Noise from the Jungle*. Generally scorned for its improvisational esotericism, the project utilized pre-recorded tapes, drum machines, and random electronics to create a collage of directed noise, much of which could be generated with no human participation whatsoever. In fact, elements of the work dated back to 1974 and *Sky Yen* — as was shown when that set was finally released.

Firmly embraced by more accessible electronics, Shelley's first true solo album, *Homosapien* (#121 US), spawned the majestic club hit single of the same name (later covered by Bay Area queercore champions, Pansy Division) and the minor hit "Telephone Operator" (#66 UK). Unfortunately, neither this album nor its follow-ups, *XL1* (#151 US) and *Heaven and the Sea*, ever lived up to that one song's promise. Shelley's last significant success came with the November 1984 single "Never Again" (#13 UK indy).

Nor did Diggle ever escape the shadow of the band — a point driven home in Europe where promoters insisted on billing his status as an ex-Buzzcock even higher than the name of his current band, Flag of Convenience. Finally bowing to a certain inevitability, he started touring as Buzzcocks FOC, even as The Buzzcocks' own stock burgeoned through Fine Young Cannibals' hit cover of "Ever Fallen in Love," and a well received retrospective boxed set, *Product*.

Late in 1989, Shelley, Diggle, and Garvey, plus former Smiths drummer Mike Joyce reformed The Buzzcocks, initially as a live act, but inevitably gravitating to the studio as well. Joyce quit for Public Image Ltd. and Maher returned briefly, but by the time of the band's first full album, 1993's *Trade Test Transmission*, Shelley and Diggle were joined by Tony Barber (bass) and Phil Barker (drums).

Seldom recapturing the sheer effervescence of the original line-up (*Alternative Press* accused Diggle's contributions to the repertoire as sounding "even more like Bad Company than they used to"), The Buzzcocks nevertheless persevered, releasing an electrifying live album, *French*, in 1995 and a new studio disc, *All Set*, a year later.

The true scale of their achievement was made clear in 1999, however, on the tenth anniversary of the reunion. Not only had The Buzzcocks outlived their original incarnation, they had also been back together longer than they were apart, celebrating the fact with a new album, *Modern*, issued (in Britain) with a bonus disc of their older material "because," said Shelley, "so many of our younger fans have never heard that stuff." Many of them hadn't even been born.

Buzzcocks LPS

10 Another Music in a Different Kitchen (UA UK) 1978 Between the brittle epics of love left in the lurch and the ragged jam duets between drums and fractured guitar, an album which so effortlessly captured The Buzzcocks' stark appeal, that it's almost a shame they ever made another — and difficult to believe that grumpy old Howard Devoto ever played a part in their birth.

Both sides follow the same perfect pattern, opening with the power punch (the insurgent "Fast Cars" and the indolent "I Don't Mind"), building up speed through the razor-sharp mayhem of Shelley's short, sharp shocks, and then peaking with les pieces de resistance, the glorious age-ist *Sixteen*, and the utterly meaningless (and simultaneously, absolutely indispensable) "Moving Away from the Pulsebeat," an excuse for everyone to show what they can do; chaos on the edge of a cliff.

The fact that nobody topples is amazing; the fact that almost six minutes fly past and the whole thing still counts as punk is miraculous. Then you wait through a moment of silence and the whole thing threatens to begin again.

7 Love Bites (UA UK) 1978 It had to be disappointing after the debut, and of course the band didn't let us down. Yet many of the songs are actually sharper — "Ever Fallen in Love," "Just Lust," "ESP" and the immortal "Nostalgia"; while "Late for the Train" at least reiterates most of "Pulsebeat"'s death-defying daring.

8 A Different Kind of Tension (IRS) 1980 Oddly deflated, awkwardly growing, *Tension* veers between shattering brilliance ("I Don't Know What to Do with My Life," "You Say You Don't Love Me") and grinding mediocrity ("Mad Mad Judy," "Sitting Round at Home"), and then explodes through the "Pulsebeat" barrier with a closing salvo — "Money," "Hollow Inside," and "Tension" — which itself is simply the curtain raiser to the epic "I Believe," a devastating statement of vulnerable intent, and the most honest moment yet in a life built on truths.

6 Trade Test Transmissions (Caroline) 1993 A little uncertain as to how to proceed with this reunion business, they crank up the guitars, tone down the uncertainty, and then sling in a song about masturbation for all the orgasm addicts still out there.

7 French [LIVE] (IRS) 1996 Live in France, fast and furious, and searing through their old hits and newer numbers with precision, clarity, and care. Some things have improved with age, then.

7 All Set (IRS) 1996 Returning to what they do best (writing short, sharp, perfect pop songs), *All Set* is a brilliant album — if

totally derivative — but only of themselves, so that's all right then. Rewriting the greatest bits from their first two albums (and nicking one from the Style Council), the tracks jingle along like the sugarland express, and the only pratfalls occur when they try something new. Which just goes to show — stick with what you know.

7 Modern (Go Kart) 1999 Ironically, this is the least modern sounding of all The Buzzcock albums — slower paced and heavily dusted with glitter (think T. Rex, Ziggy, and a hint of old Hoople). When not reworking old riffs in glam style, the group dive into post-punk and new wave before finally coming a cropper when they tackle jungle and splashes of electro.

Selected Compilations and Archive Releases

9 Singles Going Steady (IRS) 1979 So close to perfection, it's painful. With only the eternally irritating "Everybody's Happy Nowadays" to spoil the show, the hits fill one half, the B-sides on the other, and if the likes of "Something's Gone Wrong Again" and "Why Can't I Touch It" had replaced the filler on the same-period *Tension* album, the end result would have been unbeatable.

6 Parts One – Three (IRS) 1984 They went away, then came back six months later with the half-baked notion of an album in installments. Halfway through it, they went away again. It isn't hard to see why.

4 Lest We Forget [LIVE] (Roir) 1988 Recorded live during the band's 1979–80 American tour (apparently on a Walkman by the bar).

4 Live at the Roxy 1977 (Receiver) 1989 Highlighting the entire early 1977 show excerpted for the original *Live at the Roxy, London WC2* sampler — highlighting, too, the sheer tragic travesty of a Buzzcocks gig.

9 Product (Restless) 1989 Catalog-stuffed box set — everything you need, and then some.

6 Time's Up (Document) 1991 Official release for oft-bootlegged formative Devoto-era demos. Guaranteed not to thrill fans of either TheBuzzcock's or Magazine.

8 Operators Manual (IRS) 1991 Eight of the band's nine UK hits are included, plus 17 album tracks proving nothing more than The Buzzcocks' unrelenting brilliance. Unfortunately, that's not enough — the best of the band was dishevelled and dangerous, poised on the sense that it could all fall apart at any moment. *Operators Manual* is too perfect to truly document the ensuing delight.

4 Entertaining Friends [LIVE] (IRS) 1992 1979 live set highlighting the awful dichotomy of a band who made great records, but could never recapture them live.

8 Chronology (EMI — UK) 1997 Utterly bizarre vault scraping exercise which makes no attempt to hide its origins... indeed, it makes a virtue of them — as well it should. While seldom a patch on the album versions, eight sets of demos trace The Buzzcocks' development from cradle to (original) grave, with half a dozen unreleased songs to pinpoint some fascinating might-have-beens.

⑥ **BBC Sessions (EMI UK) 1998** Full career-spanning selections from an archive that actually holds a lot of better material.

Pete Shelley LPs

③ **Sky Yen (Groovy UK) 1979** Recorded in 1974, rough Krautrock stylings that have absolutely *nothing* to do with the rest of his career.

⑥ **Homosapien (Genetic UK) 1981** The title track dwarfs the album in the popular memory, but a lot of the other songs run it close.

⑤ **XL1 (Genetic UK) 1983**

⑤ **Heaven and the Sea (Mercury) 1986**

Flag of Convenience LP

③ **Here's One I Made Earlier (AX-S — UK) 1995**

C

CABARET VOLTAIRE

FORMED 1973 (Sheffield, England)
ORIGINAL LINE-UP Stephen Mallinder (vocals, bass); Chris Watson (electronics); Richard Kirk (guitar, keyboards, wind)

Named for a Dadaist club established in Zurich in 1917, Cabaret Voltaire first began playing together in the early 1970s, working with an oscillator and tape recorders. (Their first ever recording, "Baader Meinhof," subsequently appeared on the compilation *A Factory Sampler*.)

Later, through the music department of Sheffield University, the trio were able to expand their arsenal, and early (1974) Cabaret Voltaire performances included one show at Sheffield University and another at the Edinburgh Arts Festival, where the band itself stayed at home and sent a cassette and a film along instead. "Is That Me," the B-side of 1979's "Nag Nag Nag" (Rough Trade) single, was recorded at one of the band's 1975 shows. Other early work appeared on 1981's *Cabaret Voltaire 1974–76* collection, but the band's first official release was *Limited Edition*, a cassette which was indeed limited — just 25 copies were made.

In June 1977, the trio linked with a loose collective of other Sheffield/Manchester area musicians as the Studs—Martyn Ware, Adi Newton, and Ian Craig Marsh (Future/Human League), Glen Gregory (later Heaven 17), and Haydn Boyes were also involved in a band whose solitary show, opening for Manchester punks The Drones, featured versions of "Louie Louie," Lou Reed's "Vicious," Iggy Pop's "Cock in My Pocket," and one original, "The Drones Want to Come On Now."

The Studs broke up immediately after, but still caught up in the flurry of punk-era excitement, Cabaret Voltaire signed to Rough Trade after the label saw them opening for the Buzzcocks, and in 1978, the group's *Extended Play* EP introduced their vision to the world at large. Though the most important cut was undoubtedly the vicious "Mussolini Head Kick," a cover of Lou Reed's "Here She Comes Now" would stand as perhaps the most accessible track from this entire period.

Indeed, the Velvet Underground remained a constant touchstone for the early Cabaret Voltaire, alongside Can, Stockhausen, Roxy Music and — though one was hard-pressed to detect the influence — James Brown. Furthermore, journalist Biba Kopf would later insist, "the scratch and break elements of hip-hop and rap are partly rooted in the noise terrorism of Cabaret Voltaire..." — an intriguing claim for a band whose most persistent manifesto was, "we do not allow any dancing."

In April 1979, Cabaret Voltaire played a week long residence at the Gibus Club in Paris, while other shows placed them alongside Joy Division. But the opportunity to push even deeper into the punk consciousness, touring alongside the Raincoats and Kleenex, was turned down. They did, however, open for avant garde author William S. Burroughs at an open arts festival, with Richard Kirk explaining, "[we felt] as if we were carrying on the legacy of what [he] did with literature. We were sort of applying it to music in some ways."

Cabaret Voltaire's first full album, *Mix Up* (#12 UK indy) appeared in fall 1979, a deeply experimental piece far removed from the ferocity of the recently-released "Nag Nag Nag" single, and a harbinger of the similarly seemingly haphazard sounds which would characterize the "Silent Command" (#10 UK indy) and "Three Mantras" (#10 UK indy) singles.

The Voice of America (#3 UK indy) and the in-concert *Live at the YMCA 10/27/79* (#2 UK indy) albums continued moving away from the punk arena at the speed of light, and in 1981, Cabaret Voltaire finally hit their peak, in terms of both quality and quantity. The 3 *Crepuscule Tracks* EP (#8 UK indy), a *Live at the Lyceum* cassette (#14 UK indy), and *Red Mecca* (#1 UK indy) testified to the uncompromising creativity which marked Cabaret Voltaire, with "Eddie's Out" (#6 UK indy) emerging as perhaps the highlight of their entire Rough Trade period.

The band next undertook some soundtrack work for the BBC, (released as *Johnny Yesno* — #8 UK indy — in 1983), plus production for Manchester artniks 23 Skidoo, and Tiller Boys conspirator Eric Random. Despite the group's growing acclaim, however, Chris Watson quit in October 1981 to take up a technical post in television (he later resurfaced in the Hafler Trio before abandoning music in the early 1990s).

Kirk and Stephen Mallinder opted not to replace him, instead pulling in a succession of outside musicians to fill the breach — Eric Random played guitar and percussion on 1982's live *Benefit for Solidarity* album (released under the Pressure Company pseudonym). He was also in evidence on *2x45* (#98 UK, #1 UK indy), a double 12" package released in June 1982. (*Hai!*, #5 UK indy, was another live album, recorded in Japan.)

Mallinder and Kirk both launched solo careers, largely pursuing visions even less penetrable than the band's work. Cabaret Voltaire, meanwhile, parted company with Rough

Trade in late 1982, and after a brace of independent singles — "Fool's Game" and a remix of the *Johnny Yesno* cut "Yashar" (#6 UK indy) – the duo signed to Some Bizarre/Virgin (Caroline in the US) in December 1982.

They debuted with the "Just Fascination" 12", perhaps the tightest Cabaret Voltaire release yet. It found the band moving into the same mutant disco-oriented territory which Some Bizzare labelmates Soft Cell (whose Dave Ball produced the record) were mapping out, a feeling which was enlarged by *The Crackdown* (#31 UK) in August 1983, and older fans felt some relief when the group's next few projects — the retrospective *TV Wipeout* video, and solo albums by both members — brought a return to earlier values. However, it was only a matter of time before the Cabs blended their new found interest in dance music with their original sensibilities, and the September 1984 12" single "Sensoria" was certainly a step in that direction. An album, *Micro-phonies* (#69 UK) arrived in October, to be followed by the single which, presumably, proved the band knew what they were talking about a decade earlier, when they first started discussing their influences. It was called "James Brown."

A fascinating collaboration with former Josef K frontman Paul Haig followed, under the banner, The Executioner. The team cut one track, "The Executioner's Theme," for release through Factory Benelux; it never appeared, but remixes of the cut would appear on Haig's *European Sun* collection, and the Crepuscule label compilation *The Quick Neat Job*. Another union paired Cabaret Voltaire with Ministry's Al Jourgensen and Bill Rieflin, plus vocalist Chris Connolly, as Acid Horse, for the deliciously psychotic "No Name No Slogan" 12".

The pattern of video-single-album followed again in 1985, with the *Gasoline in Your Eye* film project (and accompanying double 12" soundtrack single "Drinking Gasoline" — #71 UK), followed by the critically acclaimed "I Want You" 45, and the band's eleventh album, *The Covenant, the Sword, and the Arm of the Lord* (#57 UK).

Harking back more to their first few albums than the neo-mainstream material the band had lately been involved in, *The Covenant* was described by Mallinder as an attempt to regain the duo's "identity. We had to get this out because we didn't want to just slip into duplicating or sophisticating what we had done [before]." However, the more commercial sounds with which the band had dallied were to remain in play, on the "Drain Train" (#5 UK indy) single in 1986 and, cementing Cabaret Voltaire's recently-inked pact with EMI's Parlophone subsidiary, the gentle "Don't Argue" (#69 UK), which became the first of four minor UK hits around the end of the decade.

"Here to Go," produced by Adrian Sherwood, and *The Code* followed, their dramatic reinvention only exaggerated by Rough Trade's release of the *Golden Moments* CD compilation. Yet Cabaret Voltaire were only just beginning their excursions.

Late in 1989, Kirk alone began working in the field of so-called bleep music, teaming up with Sheffield DJ Parrot under the name Sweet Exorcist. "Test One" was a single dance track released in six different mixes over the course of two 12" EPs (Warp). A second Sweet Exorcist project produced the *Clonk* Remix EP at the end of the year, and in January 1991, the album *Clonk's Coming* — both on Warp. (Clonk, incidentally, is a character from the 2000 AD comic book.)

While Kirk remained based in Sheffield, Mallinder moved to London, and he, too, began flirting with the electro-dance scene. In 1988, he launched a new band, Love Street, with Soft Cell's Dave Ball and Mark Brydon, releasing one single, "Galaxy," before dovetailing neatly back into Cabaret Voltaire. By late 1989, the duo were working with house music producer Marshall Jefferson to create the "Hypnotized" (#66 UK) single — available in a staggering eleven different mixes in October 1989. In the new year, at least seven mixes of "Keep On" (#55 UK) followed, while the album *Groovy, Laid Back and Nasty*, and the "Easy Life" single (#61 UK), maintained the barrage, while Cabaret Voltaire toured the house circuit.

With Daniel Miller and A Guy Called Gerald to hand as remixers, Cabaret Voltaire's flirtation with electro-house saw them radically reinvent their reputation, one again. However, the moment was brief — when Cabaret Voltaire left EMI, the desire to make commercial house records left them.

Defecting to Les Disques du Crepescule, *Body and Soul* (and the *What Is Real* EP) in 1991 were recorded in a week, and with their attention to unconventional detail, both found the band moving back into the sort of territory they had traveled at their experimental peak. "It was back to basics," Mallinder said. "We weren't consciously saying 'Oh, we'd better write a few tracks on here that are really catchy,' which you... felt you had to do with the last LP at EMI. We went in with a very different attitude."

Further remix collections, *Percussion Force* and the dynamic *Western Reworks* (plus a single of *Covenant*'s rearranged "I Want You") highlighted more of the band's current eccentricity; the 44-minute *Colours* EP followed suit. Two subsequent albums, *Plasticity* and *International Language*, were even more conscious attempts to return Cabaret Voltaire to their roots — just in time for the band's demise. Recorded in November 1993, Cabaret Voltaire's final release was *The Conversation*, two discs of none too coherent ideas recorded even as the band members were plotting their future paths.

Mallinder moved to Australia in 1995, where he works as Sassi and Loco; Kirk resumed his solo career, and also recorded as Xon, Sandoz, and Electronic Eye. Cabaret Voltaire never formally split, however, and while hopes that Mute would entertain a new album at decade's end were eventually dashed, Kirk was adamant that "there will be a new piece of music. It's amazing how many people want it to happen."

Cabaret Voltaire LPs

5 Limited Edition (Private Cassette) 1976 Think of a can with a few angry insects inside. Shake it to make them even angrier. Place your ear right up close.

6 Mix Up (Rough Trade) 1979 The wide open use of tape loops and "found" noises echoes the early experimental albums recorded by Robert Fripp and Brian Eno. The live "Eyeless Sight" is a surprise highlight.

6 The Voice of America (Rough Trade) 1980

7 Live at the YMCA 10/27/79 [LIVE] (Rough Trade) 1980 8 Live at the Lyceum [LIVE] (Rough Trade) 1981 Away from their still stripped back studio incarnation, the band explode with dance-conscious energy on the nervous edge of industrial funk. The sound quality shakes (*Lyceum* was taped on a Walkman), but the power is undeniable.

8 Red Mecca (Rough Trade) 1981 Tighter and increasingly rhythmic, oddly peaking with Henry Mancini's "Touch of Evil."

6 Benefit for Solidarity [LIVE] (Pressure Co Paradox) 1982

7 Hai! [LIVE] (Rough Trade) 1982

7 Johnny Yesno (Doublevision) 1983 Oddly dissimilar to the accompanying video's soundtrack, although the key "Hallucination Sequence" is intact.

8 The Crackdown (Some Bizaare) 1983 The most accessible of the indy releases ("Crackdown," "Moscow," "Just Fascination"), the CD appends the original vinyl's bonus 12-inch EP.

6 Micro-Phonies (Some Bizaare) 1984

7 The Covenant, the Sword and the Arm of the Lord (Caroline) 1985 Closely following cut-up patterns already explored by The Art of Noise; at times purposefully disruptive dance music powered by a singularly dated sounding synth. The multi-tracked vocals add a touch of sinister ambience to the proceedings, though, and the most successful numbers ("I Want You," the Depeche-like "Warm") are not coincidentally the most settled.

7 The Code (EMI Manhattan) 1987

8 Groovy, Laid Back and Nasty (Parlophone) 1990 Sensibly-titled house explorations, shot through with a genuine warmth.

7 Body and Soul 1991

7 Plasticity (Crepescule) 1992

9 International Language (CV/Plastex) 1993 A festival of pulsing, beats, and bleats, Cabaret Voltaire at their latter day peak.

6 Conversation (Instinct) 1994 Two CDs of generally gentle electro-trance grooves, shot through with inaudible whispers and muttering, but usually with something nasty (and painful sounding) going on just behind the beats.

Selected Compilations and Archive Releases

6 Cabaret Voltaire 1974–76 (Industrial) 1981 Uneasy listening from an attic, includes elements of what later became *Limited Edition*, but demands a lot of patience.

7 Western Works Records (Western Works — Belgium) 1987 Generally awkward but certainly formative demos recorded 1977–79.

6 Golden Moments (Rough Trade) 1987 Heavily weighted towards album tracks, disconcertingly pulled out of context.

7 8 Crepescule Tracks (Crepescule — Belg) 1989 The 3 *Crepescule Tracks* EP, padded with singles and a brilliant, unreleased take on "The Theme from Shaft."

8 Listen Up with the Cabaret Voltaire (Mute) 1990 Sensible compilation of all the band's Rough Trade singles.

6 The Living Legends (Mute) 1990 Compilation of rarities drawn from *NME* cassettes, Factory samplers, etc, plus seven unreleased cuts.

5 Percussion Force (Crepescule) 1991 10-track collection of "Body and Soul" remixes.

8 Western Reworks 1992 (Virgin) 1992 Fabulous remix collection hitting "Ghost Talk," "I Want You," "24–24," "Crackdown" and more.

8 BBC Recordings 1984–86 (New Millenium — UK) 1999 At their peak in the studio and breathtaking live, the band mix the best of both worlds across three shattering sessions, plus live and out-take material.

Stephen Mallinder LP

6 Pow Wow (Fetish) 1982 Strangely futuristic explorations through drum, bass, and gravelly voice.

Chris Watson LPs

6 Stepping into the Dark (Touch) 1996

5 Outside the Circle of Fire (Touch) 1998

5 Bang! An Open Letter (Double Vision) 1994

Hafler Trio LPs

5 Alternation, Perception and Resistance (Layla) 1985 Reissued as *Walk Gently Through the Gates of Joy* (Soleilmoon)

6 A Thirsty Fish (Soleilmoon) 1987

6 Kill the King (Silent) 1991

5 Mastery of Money (Touch) 1992

8 How to Reform Mankind (Touch) 1993

7 One Dozen Economical Stories (Sub Rosa) 1994

4 **Negentropy (Ash International) 1994** Bizarre collection of deconstructed piano samples, recorded by Clock DVA mainstay Adi Newton in Stockholm. Why Stockholm?

3 **Masturbatorium (Touch Tone) 1995** Annie Sprinkle joins the gang.

5 **All That Rises Must Converge (Soleilmoon) 1995**

5 **Four Ways of Saying Five (Soleilmoon) 1995**

7 **Seven Hours Sleep (Soleilmoon) 1995**

7 **Inoutof (Soleilmoon) 1995**

6 **Utterances of Supreme Ventriloquist (Soleilmoon) 1996**

7 **Fuck (Touch) 1997**

4 **Resurrection (Touch) 1997** Awkward live in Sweden set.

Richard Kirk LPs

7 **Disposable Half-Truths (Mute) 1980**

6 **Time High Fiction (Double Vision) 1983** A compilation of past, unreleased, material, awkward to sit through, but as powerful as anything Cabaret Voltaire were currently attempting.

6 **Black Jesus Voice (Rough Trade) 1986**

7 **Ugly Spirit (Rough Trade) 1986**

6 **Hoodoo Talk [W/PETER HOPE] (Native) 1987**

6 **Virtual State (Wax Trax!) 1993**

6 **The Number of Magic (Wax Trax!) 1995**

5 **Knowledge Through Science (Mute) 1998**

5 **Darkness at Noon (Touch) 1999** Noise-based reflection of the then on-going allied assault on Kosovo.

Richard Kirk/Sweet Exorcist LP

7 **Spirit Guide to Low Tech (Touch) 1994**

Richard Kirk/Guy Van Stratten LP

6 **Agents With False Memories (Ash) 1996**

Richard Kirk/Sandoz LPs

8 **Digital Lifeforms (Touch) 1993**

7 **Intensely Radioactive (Touch) 1994**

7 **Every Man Got Dreaming (Touch) 1995**

8 **Dark Continent (Touch) 1996**

7 **God Bless the Conspiracy (Alpha) 1997**

8 **Sandoz in Dub (Touch) 1998**

Richard Kirk/Electronic Eye LPs

6 **Closed Circuit (Beyond) 1994**

6 **The Idea of Justice (Beyond) 1995**

Richard Kirk/Cold Warrior LP

7 **Alphaphone Vol. 1: Step, Write, Run (Touch) 1996**

Alphaphone Label Listing 1997–99
(all Richard Kirk pseudonyms)

Singles

001 PAPADOCTRINE — Flesh Hunter
002 MULTIPLE TRANSMISSION — Earthloop
003 CHEMICAL AGENT — Waterfall
004 ROBOTS+HUMANOIDS — Indigo Octagon
005 INTERNATIONAL ORGANISATION — Shooting Stars
006 COLD WARRIOR — Yellow Square 12-inch albums

1 **6** **NITROGEN — Intoxica**

2 **unreleased**

3 **7** **DARK MAGUS — Night Watchmen**

4 **6** **TRAFFICANTE — Is This Now?**

5 **6** **AL JABR — One Million and Three**

CAMPER VAN BEETHOVEN

FORMED 1983 *(Redlands, CA)*
ORIGINAL LINE-UP *David Lowery (b. 10/10/60, San Antonio — vocals, guitar); Greg Lisher (guitar); Chris Molla (pedal steel); Jonathan Segel (violin); Victor Krummenacher (bass); Chris Pedersen (drums)*

Named by soon-to-depart founder member David McDaniels, and comprising three former members of California club band Box of Laffs (David Lowery, Chris Pedersen, Chris Molla), Camper Van Beethoven are renowned as the first band ever to be described as "alternative" — at a time when most critics were still mulling over such terms as new wave, post punk and post modern. In a statement beloved by subsequent rock historians and iconographers, Lowery reflected, "I remember first seeing that word applied to us. The nearest I could figure is that we seemed like a punk band, but we were playing pop music, so they made up the word 'alternative' for those of us who do that."

In fact, there was little punk — or pop — about the early Camper. With Jonathan Segel's violin and Molla's pedal steel the dominant instruments, and Lowery's lilting half-English vocal stylings sarcastically floating above it all, Camper embraced Americana roots music with a passion which owed as much to the members' esoteric record collections as anything else.

Released on Lowery's own Pitch-A-Tent label, and recorded in two weekends in fall 1984, *Telephone Free Landslide Victory* (#30 UK indy), the group's debut, merged an ethnic approximation of ska, "Border Ska," with a folky cover of Black Flag's "Wasted." Victor Krummenacher's past with jazz pretenders Wrestling Worms also flavored the group's sound. They were indeed alternative, but an alternative to what, no one could say.

"Take the Skinheads Bowling" (#8 UK indy) was a surprise radio hit born of the band's constant touring — introducing the band to European markets via a deal with Rough Trade. Six months later, Camper made their UK debut, while summer 1986's *II/III* album(#8 UK indy) — highlighted by a country-fied cover of Sonic Youth's "I Love Her All the Time" — continued to expand their musical horizons. The album's title, incidentally, referred to the fact that it was originally intended to be two separate records, the band's second and third albums respectively.

With former Shockabilly frontman Eugene Chadbourne temporarily added to supply psychedelic guitar solos, *Camper Van Beethoven* (aka *The Third Album* — #7 UK indy) took their vision to its extremes, with the eclecticism to the fore. "Peace and Love" was shamelessly based upon the Velvet Underground's "The Gift," while a cover of Pink Floyd's "Interstellar Overdrive" finally erupted out of three years of rehearsals and surprise live appearances to defy any further attempts to categorize the group — particularly after "Good Guys and Bad Guys" became the first Camper video to air on MTV.

The union with Chadbourne would subsequently be distinguished by *Camper Van Chadbourne*, an all-covers album issued in 1987; that set, however, preluded a period of comparative silence from the band — the *Vampire Can Mating Oven* EP, wrapping up a few odds and ends, and *Great Big Hits* compilation closed Camper's indy days.

However, their re-emergence on Virgin Records in 1988, with *Our Beloved Revolutionary Sweetheart* (#124 US) and the "Life Is Grand" single, suggested that there was a lot more than a big budget affecting the band. With the *Eye of Fatima* and *Turquoise Jewelry* EPs leading the assault on the radiowaves, and a well-received single, "(I Was Born in a) Laundromat," *Sweetheart* marked Camper's first appearance on the US chart, but disappointed many fans nonetheless.

The departure of Segel in 1989 marked the beginning of the end. He was replaced by Morgan Fichter, whose ethereal fiddle underpinned the band's final album, *Key Lime Pie* (#141 US) and dominated the cult hit cover of Status Quo's "Pictures of Matchstick Men, " but by the end of the year, the group had splintered.

Krummenacher, Pedersen, and Greg Lisher reunited with Segel as the Monks of Doom, a splinter group they originally initiated in 1986. Constantly reiterating many of Camper's key elements, their 1992 *Insect God* EP marked a peak of sorts, by blending the band's own weirdness with covers of Syd Barrett, the Mothers of Invention, and a musical adaptation of author Edward Gorey's title piece. Segal also recorded as Hieronymous Firebrain (with drummer Russ Blackmar) and Jack and Jill (Blackmar and bassist Jane

Thompson). Lowery, the instigator of the none-too-peaceable split, formed Cracker in 1992.

Also see the entry for "CRACKER" on page 290.

Camper Van Beethoven LPs

7 **Telephone Free Landslide Victory (Pitch-A-Tent) 1982**

6 **II/III (IRS) 1986**

9 **Camper Van Beethoven (Pitch-A-Tent) 1986** Cracked grins, jollity, and the best fun you could have in mid-80s America, CVB bounces all over the place, quizzically ruminating on "Joe Stalin's Cadillac" and "Jerry's Daughter," punning on Led Zeppelin ("Five Sticks," "Stairway to Heaven[sic]," and stray references to a bridge), and leaping from cajun to folk to metal to psych... oh, you name it, it's probably here.

5 **Camper Van Chadbourne (Fundamental) 1988** Collaboration with Eugene Chadbourne, with both parties giving too much ground.

6 **Our Beloved Revolutionary Sweetheart (Virgin) 1988** Calmer than their older self, less unself-consciously bizarre, and certainly less prone to go racing off on odd musical tangents. A little disappointing.

8 **Key Lime Pie (Virgin) 1989** Paving the way for some of Cracker's subsequent melancholy, a Camper album almost completely devoid of belly laughs. Dark, then, but never dull, their best selling record is also one of their best.

Selected Compilations and Archive Releases

7 **Camper Vantiquities (IRS) 1993** Camper's finest old bones scraped clean through a succession of occasionally crucial outtakes and oddities. 1987's out-of-print and similarly themed *Vampire Can Mating Oven* is a welcome bonus, for covers of Box O'Laffs' "Ice Cream Every Day" and Ringo Starr's "Photograph."

Monks of Doom LPs

5 **Soundtrack to Film Breakfast On the Beach of Deception (Pitch-A-Tent/IRS) 1987**

4 **The Cosmodemonic Telegraph Company (Pitch-A-Tent) 1989**

5 **Meridian (Baited Breath) 1991**

4 **Forgery (IRS) 1992** Mostly instrument mood music, with a few songs thrown in to spice up the pot. Musically, the group meddled in a variety of other styles, a bit of C&W, a stab at jazz-fusion, a toss of folk, and so on. Even so, *Forgery* lacks the imagination that made Camper special, and will appeal only to the band's hardcore fans.

Jonathan Segel/Hieronymous Firebrain LPs

4 **Storytelling (Pitch-A-Tent) 1989**

4 **Hieronymous Firebrain (Delta) 1991**

3 Here (Magnetic) 1994
4 There (Magnetic) 1994

Jack and Jill LPs
5 Chill and Shrill (Magnetic) 1995
5 Fancy Birdhouse (Magnetic) 1997

Victor Krummenacher/A Great Laugh LP
4 A Great Laugh (Magnetic) 1995

CANDYSKINS

FORMED 1989 *(Oxford, England)*
ORIGINAL LINE-UP *Nick Cope (vocals); Mark Cope (guitar); Nobby Burton (b. Nick Burton, guitar); Karl Shale (bass); John Halliday (drums)*

Founders of the Oxford beat scene which subsequently spawned Radiohead, Supergrass, and Unbelievable Truth, Candyskins emerged in 1989 with the indy favorite "Submarine Song," on the local Long Beach label. "She Blew Me Away" followed in 1990 and the *You Are Here* EP in 1991, before the band signed with Geffen. A reissue of "Submarine Song" became a radio hit that summer. However, it was the wildly triumphant "The Space I'm In" which established the band's power-pop-flavored guitar roar as a staunch MTV favorite during 1991, the title track to the band's debut album.

Widely tipped for a major breakthrough, 1993's *Fun?* spawned a second air play hit, "Wembley," with "Land of Love" following up in style. But two silent years later, the Candyskins were dropped, with legal problems keeping the group out of sight for another year. Finally, in late 1995, new manager Richard Cotton landed a one-off single deal with UK independent Rotator, and was rewarded with the near-hit "Mrs. Hoover" (#65 UK). The inclusion of the ripping "24 Hours" on the *OXCD* collection of Oxford area bands followed, and in June, "Get On" gave the band another indy hit, and led to a tour with Space.

Further minor hits for "Circles" and the reissued "Mrs. Hoover" during 1996 prompted Geffen to reissue *Fun?* that same year, much to the band's chagrin: the Cope brothers were subsequently arrested for spray painting "No Fun" across the label's London offices.

1997's debut Top 40 British hit, "Monday Morning," was accompanied by the UK and Japan-only release of *Sunday Morning Fever*, the band's third album. "Hang Myself on You" followed in April, while October 1997's "Feed It" drew massive radio interest after it was revealed that the song's inspiration was the recent Heavens Gate cult suicide. Gigs with Dodgy, My Life Story, and Del Amitri kept the group's

profile high, while Nick Cope reasoned, "our old management thought we should concentrate on America, which means we neglected Britain. So we had to go back and do all the things a band does to build an audience there."

With bassist Brett Gordon replacing Karl Shale, March 1998, saw Ultimate release "You Better Stop," a non-album prelude to what would indeed become Candyskins' return to the US, as they signed with Velvel for the acclaimed album *Death of a Minor TV Celebrity*, and single "Somewhere Under London." An instant critical success, the album's ultimate fate, sadly, was decided by their label's collapse soon after release.

Candyskins LPs
8 Space I'm In (Geffen) 1991 Starting with the same influences as the rest of Britain's pop bands at the beginning of the '90s (recycled Stones riffs and '60s pop melodies), the Candyskins actually come up with something new; sparkling pop rock tinged with psychedelia round the edges, and accompanied by unusually thoughtful lyrics.

7 Fun? (Geffen) 1993 Still sporting their influences on their sleeves, but no less fun for that, the Candyskins emphasize the rock'n'pop with a bigger sound, riddled with soaring leads, rougher riffs, some genuinely meaty power chords and, of course, "Wembley."

8 Sunday Morning Fever (Ultimate UK) 1997 14 tracks (17 in Japan), and weighed down with a carnival of hits — "Monday Morning," "Car Crash," "24 Hours" and the ubiquitous "Mrs. Hoover," sweeping away the most stubborn cob webs.

8 Death of a Minor TV Celebrity (Velvel) 1998 *Death* heralds the birth of the Candyskins' new sound — a fabulous mix of Brit pop and post-indy punch. The melodies remain strong even if they no longer jangle, and the group's more textured style, wider musical canvas, and moodier lyrics are stunningly sublime.

CARDIGANS

FORMED 1992 *(Jonkopping, Sweden)*
ORIGINAL LINE-UP *Nina Persson (b. Karlskoga, Sweden — vocals); Peter Svensson (guitar); Magnus Sveningsson (bass), Lasse Johansson (keyboards); Bengt Lagerberg (drums)*

Formed by songwriters Peter Svensson and Magnus Sveningsson, heavy metal musicians with a new-found taste for indy pop (House of Love and Charlatans UK in particular), the Cardigans' most immediate selling point was Nina Persson, an art school student who had never sung professionally before joining the band.

Sharing an apartment where they worked ceaselessly on their first demos, the band were picked up by Swedish producer Tore Johansson in 1993, and the following May, signed with the Stockholm label, a dance pop company modeled on Britain's Heavenly set-up.

Despite complaints that it was too dark and serious, their ambitiously scored debut album *Emmerdale*, in February 1994, was subsequently voted Best Swedish album of the year, while the singles "Rise and Shine," in May 1994, and "Black Letter Day," in August, were immediate hits.

Two further Sweden-only singles followed: "Rise and Shine" in September, and "Hey! Get Out of My Way" (backed by a cover of Thin Lizzy's "The Boys Are Back in Town") in May 1995. That same month also saw a UK release for "Carnival" (#72 UK), along with a string of live shows across Europe, paving the way for the Cardigans' international breakthrough — "Carnival," backed by a ferociously rearranged cover of Ozzy Osbourne's "Mr. Crowley," became a summer radio hit in Britain, with the buoyant *Life* (#58 UK) album arriving in October.

Singles flew thick and fast. "Hey, Get Out of My Way" was a massive hit in Japan; a reissue of "Sick and Tired" (#34 UK) was followed by a rerecording of "Rise and Shine" (#29 UK). Persson alone scored a Japanese hit with "Desafinado," and with the small Minty Fresh label having given *Life* a US release, the band made its first Stateside trip that summer of 1996.

In September 1996, *First Band on the Moon* (#18 UK) became the Cardigans' major label debut on both sides of the Atlantic, eventually going gold in the US, and — following the group's first Far Eastern visit — platinum in Japan. "Lovefool" (#2 UK) emerged as America's fourth most played radio hit of 1997, its success establishing the Cardigans as Sweden's most successful musical export since Abba, two decades previous. "Been It" (#56 UK) and "Your New Cuckoo" (#35 UK) wrapped up a tremendous year, and 18 solid months of gigging.

The band took a six month break following the *Moon* world tour, during which the members all took time out to guest with other artists. Sveningsson took over running the band's web site; Persson guested on Shudder to Think's "First Love, Last Rites," and formed a country band called Akamp; Lagerberg and Svensson recorded with Swedish supergroup Paus, featuring Joakim Berg of Kent; Svensson alone joined another local band, the Confusions, and wrote an entry for the Swedish heats of the Eurovision Song Contest.

Returning to Johansson's Country Hell studio in Skurup, the Cardigans then reconvened around their favorite video game, *Gran Turismo* — which eventually gave its name to their fourth album (#151 US, #8 UK) in October 1998, and its theme to their next single, "My Favourite Game" (#14 UK). Conceived as a return to the dark side to the band's original (debut era) intentions, this latest album also brought Persson

into focus as the band's lyricist. The band launched another world tour to coincide, although Sveningsson was absent from the proceedings; pleading road-weariness, he was replaced for the duration by Larry Ljungberg.

Further singles "Erase/Rewind" (#7 UK) "Hanging Round" (#17 UK) saw the band through the first half of 1999, but even with this latest clutch of worldwide hits under their belts, the Cardigans nevertheless maintained their capacity to surprise, joining Welsh veteran Tom Jones for a year's end version of the Talking Heads' "Burning Down the House" (#7 UK).

Cardigans LPs

7 Emmerdale (Trampolene) 1994 The languid account of Black Sabbath's "Sabbath Bloody Sabbath" is a spot of bright humor in a dreamily downbeat concoction.

7 Life (Minty Fresh) 1995 Brighter, sunnier, more like the quirky Cardigans who would soon be conquering the universe.

8 First Band On the Moon (Mercury) 1996 *Not* a masterpiece, although any album which can contain "Lovefool," "Been It," and a rinky-dink return to the Sabbath songbook ("Iron Man") doesn't fall too far short.

8 Gran Turismo (Mercury) 1998 And with that diversion over with, a return to the textures of *Emmerdale*. Colorful claustrophobia.

Selected Compilations and Archive Releases

7 Other Side of the Moon (Polygram — Japan) 1998 Useful remix/B-sides collection.

CARTER THE UNSTOPPABLE SEX MACHINE

FORMED 1987 *(London, England)*
ORIGINAL LINE-UP *Jim Bob (b. Jim Morrison, 11/22/60 — vocals, guitar); Fruitbat (b. Leslie Carter, 2/12/58 — vocals, guitar)*

Jim Bob and Fruitbat met in 1980, when Morrison (ex-Dead Clergy) joined Carter's Ballpoints shortly before they metamorphosed from a punk band into a new romantic combo. The pair then became members of Peter Pan's Playground, and when that band broke up, worked as children entertainers under the name Jamie and Leslie.

In 1984, the pair formed Jamie Wednesday, lining up with Dean Leggitt (drums), Simon Henry (saxophone), and Lyndsey (trumpet). An unapologetically twee quintet, the band's finest moment came with a cover of the 60s' TV theme "White Horses" (#46 UK indy), included on their debut 12", *Vote for Love*, for the Pink label; they followed up with tracks on the *Beast* and *It Sells or It Smells* compilations.

An *NME* feature on the band, in 1986, would later gift its headline to the band Pop Will Eat Itself, but proved of little use to Jamie Wednesday themselves — gigs with The Men They Couldn't Hang, and a second single, "We Three Kings of Orient Aren't," followed through 1986, but by the end of the year the band had splintered.

Still, Jim Bob and Fruitbat persevered, fulfilling the last of Jamie Wednesday's scheduled shows (opening for The Men They Couldn't Hang at the London Astoria) as a drum-machine powered duo, in laughingly unrehearsed emulation of the Beastie Boys. Joined by manic MC Jon Beast, Carter the Unstoppable Sex Machine (their name taken from a local newspaper headline concerning a senior citizen killed by his uncontrollable sex drive) gigged around London — and one show in Manchester — through early 1988, and in August released their debut single, "A Sheltered Life," on the Big Cat indy.

It did nothing, and the pair concentrated on live work for the next year, usually around London, but with the occasional trip further afield, before unleashing "Sheriff Fatman" in November 1989. A word-play heavy attack on slum landlords, the single struck a chord with Britain's reborn agit-prop movement, and in the new year, Carter's debut album, *101 Damnations* confirmed their political potency — at the same time as ensuring their reputation for humor, bad puns, and frenetic punk-inflected electronic dance music.

That spring, Carter became the first western rock band to tour the newly-independent Czechoslovakia, and in June 1990, the success of their new single, "Rubbish," saw the duo sign with Rough Trade. The *Handbuilt for Perverts* EP followed, rounding up the A- and B-sides of the band's last few singles, while a new 45, "Anytime Anyplace Anywhere" came close to topping the UK indychart.

Carter's much-anticipated mainstream breakthrough was postponed, however, when the outbreak of the Gulf War saw their next single, the anti-racist, anti-military "Bloodsports for All" (#48 UK) banned. However, 30 *Something* (#8 UK) hit, hauled its predecessor in its wake (#29 UK), and when Carter played the University of London in March, onlookers were stunned when EMF — riding high at the time with their "Unbelievable" hit — appeared as support band.

Carter signed with Chrysalis following the demise of Rough Trade, prompting hit reissues of "Sheriff Fatman" (#23 UK) and "Rubbish" (#14 UK), and the group's US debut, opening for EMF at the 1991 New Music Seminar, was well received despite the obvious colloquial gulf dividing Carter's lyrics from American understanding.

Back home, Carter's profile continued soaring following a well publicized, live television tussle with TV presenter

Philip Schofield at the 1991 *Smash Hits* awards. More publicity, and a mass outpouring of public sympathy, attended the band after they were sued for paraphrasing a line from the Rolling Stones' "Ruby Tuesday" for the hit "After the Watershed" (#11 UK).

April 1992's "The Only Living Boy in New Cross" (#7 UK), an utterly triumphant commentary on the spread of AIDS, became an MTV favorite in America; and in May 1992, Carter reached their peak with *1992: The Love Album* (#1 UK). "Do Re Mi So Far So Good" (#22 UK) followed, and the duo wrapped up a triumphant twelve months with one of the year's most memorable Christmas singles, a desperately emotional take on "The Impossible Dream"(#21 UK).

The group's live success, too, continued to build — they conquered the Reading Festival that year; but there was also a disquieting element creeping into their following, as Carter shows became better associated with the raucous party atmosphere and attendant madness, than the music, and the often serious messages built into the lyrics. "A certain amount of people latched onto Jon Beast, cycling hats, that side of things," Fruitbat reflected. "When we decided to go a bit strange, they didn't get it."

"A bit strange" was also the band's own summation of *Post Historic Monsters* (#5 UK), 1993's dark and uncompromising album which spawned two hit singles, "Lean on Me I Won't Fall Over" (#16 UK)and "Lenny and Terence" (#40 UK), but never threatened to duplicate the success of its predecessor (the album was released in the US through IRS the following year, following the dismantling of Chrysalis' American office). It was, hindsight would later muse, the beginning of the end.

Attempting to broaden their sound, the duo added a live drummer, Wez (ex-Resque) in February 1994, but a new single, the nightmarishly brilliant semi-autobiographical "Glam Rock Cops" (#24 UK) faltered at home, and was not even issued in America. "Let's Get Tattoos" (#30 UK) and "The Young Offender's Mum" (#34 UK), trailers for the *Worry Bomb* album, fared poorly, while the album itself only just made the UK Top 10, and that despite boasting a bonus live album, recorded during Carter's precedent-setting tour of Croatia earlier in the year. (They were the first major band to perform there following the outbreak of civil war.)

"Born on the 5th of November" (#35 UK), celebrating Britain's traditional Firework Night festival, fell far short of its deserved mark. But the true mark of Carter's decline was drawn from the pathetic performance of *Straw Donkey*, a Greatest Hits reminder that, in terms of classic singles, Carter had now spent eight years streaking ahead of the rest of the pack.

Chrysalis dropped the group, and with Fruitbat incapacitated with a back injury sustained while cleaning the bathtub, Carter spent much of the next year out of sight. They re-emerged with 1997's *A World Without Dave* mini-album, and a new-look six-piece line-up comprising ex-Smash bassist Salv, Wez's brother Steve (guitar) and first, Simon Painter, then Ben Lambert (keyboards). A full UK tour was followed by the wryly-titled and well attended Carter Break America US tour, but Jim Bob and Fruitbat had had enough. Years before, they had agreed that if the group ever stopped being fun, they'd end it. They had now reached that point.

Carter USM played their final show at the Guildford Festival on August 2, 1997, followed it with the low-key release of the band's final recordings, *I Blame the Government*, then went their separate ways.

Jim Bob subsequently formed Jim's Super Stereoworld, whose debut single, the charming "Bonkers in the Nut" and "Could UB the 1 I Waited 4" both made the indy Top 10. Fruitbat's new band, Abdoujaparov, followed with "Baby Food" and "Maria's Umbrella."

Carter the Unstoppable Sex Machine LPs

8 101 Damnations (Big Cat — UK) 1990 Like a Dickensian novel, Carter's debut is the champion of the hopeless and homeless ("Midnight on the Murder Mile"), parasites and prey ("Sheriff Fatman"), their weaknesses and wounds exposed to the cold, harsh light of manic, pun-drenched lyrics and a baggy-blast-goes-vaudeville sound.

9 30 Something (Chrysalis) 1991 A lethal peppering of hilariously twisted cultural references and clichés, draped within a soundtrack scavenged from musical graveyards of virtually every persuasion. "Bloodsport for All," "Shopper's Paradise," and the magnificently maudlin "The Final Comedown" offer something for everyone.

10 1992: The Love Album (Chrysalis) 1992 Nobody can turn a phrase like Carter, but *1992* is magnificent even by their standards, turning words inside out before flipping them firmly onto their heads, all to reinforce the emotional impact of the excruciating scenarios the duo create.

The AIDS farewell "The Only Living Boy in New Cross" and a truly emotional "The Impossible Dream" — one which actually acknowledges its impossibility — pack a contemplative punch unparalleled in pop, while even the so-called gags (the contrarily depressed "Is Wrestling Fixed?"; the political photo-op "Suppose You Gave a Funeral and Nobody Came") raise points that at least demand reflection later.

To dwell on the lyrics alone, though, is to miss the other half of the equation — the blaring symphonic emotion of the music, orchestrated through guitars, voice, and keyboards and then pumped with sampled testosterone. It's a heady brew, an anthemic circus and a monster that wants your heart, soul, and funny bone.

8 Post Historic Monsters (IRS) 1993 Bizarrely dropping the subtlety, but not the witty word play, Carter launch a frontal assault on the things that really bother them — Lenny Kravitz, the theme from *MASH*, Bono, the usual suspects — with their punkiest buzzsaw backing yet. Oddly, the US version adds "Commercial Fucking Suicide" to the running order. Was someone trying to tell them something?

8 Worry Bomb (Chrysalis — UK) 1995 Temporarily label-less in America, Carter bounced back with a song, "The Last Loony Left in Town", which fulfilled all the promise of "Sheriff Fatman" and the sick kid from New Cross. Still tirelessly chronicling the British vaudeville villainy which had now confirmed their US downfall, Carter remain fast'n'funny, pun-crunching, stunning, and the *Worry Bomb* explodes in all directions at once, a breathless bonanza of true punk so pure that it was a black day indeed when the gods passed them over. Or was it a green one? Sometimes, it's so hard to figure out what the kids will want.

8 Doma Sportova — Live at Zagreb (Chrysalis — UK) 1995

7 A World Without Dave (Cooking Vinyl) 1997 The symphonic pulse of "Broken Down in Broken Town," the loping "Johnny Cash," a reprise of "Road Rage"; and "And God Created Brixton" (odds on for a major dance hit) — these songs brag the best hallmarks of vintage USM, but the zing seems to have gone AWOL someplace, and the previously gleeful smash-and-grab montage only occasionally sparkles through the paranoia.

7 I Blame the Government (Cooking Vinyl) 1998 After the desolation that was *Dave*, Carter return with the much more chirpy and cheerful *Government*. With the US edition almost doubling the size of the UK set through the judicious inclusion of recent singles and out-takes, the lyrics once again shine with punchy wit and the frantically guitar-driven music recaptures their old madcap pop flair. They'd already decided to break up, though, so maybe it was just for old time's sake.

Selected Compilations and Archive Releases

7 This Is the Sound of Electric Guitars (Chrysalis — Japan) 1993 Rousing mini-album immortalizing Carter's occasional assaults on other peoples' repertoires — and the Buzzcocks, Generation X, the Jam, and the Smiths never sounded so wired in their lives.

9 Starry Eyed and Bollock Naked (IRS) 1994

9 Straw Donkey (Chrysalis — UK) 1995 Respectively anthologizing Carter's non-album B-sides and ever sparkling singles, from the ferocious "Sheriff Fatman," through the heartbreaking "Only Living Boy in New Cross," on to the stamping "Glam Rock Cops," wrapping up with the tender "Born On the 5th of November"... Were the '90s ever really this inflammatory?

7 Sessions 1991–1997 (Cooking Vinyl — UK) 1999 Studio and live BBC recordings.

CATATONIA

FORMED 1992 (Cardiff, Wales)

ORIGINAL LINE-UP Cerys Matthews (b. 4/10/69, Cardiff — vocals); Mark Roberts (guitar); Paul Jones (bass); Clancy Pegg (keyboards); Dafydd Ieuan (drums)

Barmaid Cerys Matthews was busking around Cardiff when she met Mark Roberts and Paul Jones, ex-local pub band Y Criff (the Body); the name Catatonia was lifted from Aldous Huxley's *The Doors of Perception*, and by the end of 1992, the band were gigging around Cardiff, and preparing to make their recorded debut, on the Ankst label's *Mae Ddoe Yn Ddoe* compilation album.

They had a strained relationship with the label; Ankst was fervently pro-Welsh language, not-quite-insisting that acts performed in their native language alone. Catatonia, however, were equally at home singing in English, and though they would eventually record several more tracks for label comps (including *Ap Elvis, Triskedekaphilia*, and the Beck-inspired *SC4 Makes Me Want to Smoke Crack*), by mid-1993, a performance on Welsh TV had brought Catatonia to the attention of another, less doctrinaire Welsh label, Crai.

Catatonia signed, and in September 1993, released the *For Tinkerbell* EP, an instant *NME* single of the week. It was followed in May by *Hooked*, a similar success, and the cue for the London music industry to begin paying attention. (Both EPs have since been compiled on the 1993/1994 mini-album.) By summer, Rough Trade had invited Catatonia to contribute to the label's on-going Singles Club — "Whale" was released in August, followed in February 1995, by the band's first indy chart smash, "Bleed," on the Nursery indy.

Although several major labels were now keeping tabs on Catatonia, the band themselves were already in negotiation with Blanco Y Negro — Rough Trade head Geoff Travis was that label's A&R man, and his faith in the band overcame any other blandishments thrown Catatonia's way. They finally signed in late 1995, shortly after Clancy Pegg quit to join Crac, and Dafydd Ieuan joined the Super Furry Animals. The pair were replaced by Owen Powell (ex-Crumb Blowers — guitar) and Aled Richards (drums), old friends of Roberts, who arrived just as Catatonia cut their major label debut, the limited edition Christmas 1995 EP.

The new year brought a rerecording of the first EP's "Sweet Catatonia" (#61 UK), and the first signs that Catatonia were destined — or perhaps, doomed — to take their place within the sudden explosion of Welsh bands suddenly cluttering up the UK music press under the dubious soubriquet of taff rock. The Manic Street Preachers, the Super Furry Animals, the Stereophonics and Gorky's Zygotic Mynci also hailed from the principality, and were all enjoying some level of chart success.

With Matthews now habitually sporting a T-shirt emblazoned, "fastrisinglagersoakedriproaringpoptart," for the most part, Catatonia refused to be drawn in — like so many UK media inventions, taff rock was unlikely to stick around for long. However, the exposure, matched with increasingly high profile live shows and radio performances did send "Lost Cat" (#41 UK) soaring in April 1996, and in August, "You've Got a Lot to Answer For" (#35 UK) debuted the band in the Top 40.

Produced by Morrissey/Blur mastermind Stephen Street, and backed by performances at Reading and the Phoenix festival, the single was a trailer for Catatonia's *Way Beyond Blue* debut album (#40 UK), a set whose strong reception was further assured by a reissue of "Bleed" (#46 UK).

Catatonia toured through much of 1997, before returning to the studio with Sugarcubes producer Tommy D, to cut a new track, "Mulder and Scully" — titled, of course, for the *X Files* television characters. The band suggested the track as a single to Blanco Y Negro, only to be told at the time that it wasn't suitable; now, the label returned to them and admitted it was wrong, requesting Catatonia rerecord it for their next album. They came close to refusing — they had far stronger material up their sleeve. But the label prevailed, and after October's "I Am the Mob" (#40 UK) had announced the band's return, "Mulder and Scully" (#3 UK) began its ascent.

Matthews alone also linked with Space to record the immortal duet "The Ballad of Tom Jones" (#4 UK) for inclusion on the Liverpool band's next album. Released as a single in February 1998, the single would further enhance both bands' careers, all the more so after Matthews took to guesting at occasional Space shows, to perform the song — one version, recorded in Wolverhampton, would appear on the B-side of Space's "Begin Again" single (#21 UK), later in the year.

Catatonia themselves played a short, low-key UK tour in February, to coincide with the release of *International Velvet* (#1 UK) — as low-key, that is, as it's possible to be when your latest album is top of the chart. It closed in March, with a live radio broadcast from Newport, and in April 1998, Catatonia made their first trip to the US, on the eve of their next single, the future BRITS Best Single Award winning "Road Rage" (#5 UK).

They returned home for a summer spent playing festivals at home and abroad, most notably Glastonbury in England, and a Versace fashion show in Milan, Italy, while two further singles, "Strange Glue" (#11 UK) and "Game On" (#33 UK) were culled from the album. Then it was back on the road opening for the Manic Street Preachers, before wrapping up the year with an appearance on BBC TV's New Year's Eve show, hosted by former Squeeze pianist Jools Holland.

Among the other guests was Tom Jones, the veteran '60s star contemplating a fresh comeback, with an album's worth of duets. Matthews (and Space) were both invited to participate in the sessions, with Jones and Matthews giving the notion a live rehearsal on the show that night. The ensuing single, "Baby It's Cold Outside" (#17 UK) would appear the following December.

In the meantime, Catatonia's third album was awaiting a title. For a time, the band was very keen on calling it *Catatonia Are Shit*; they eventually settled for *Equally Cursed and Blessed* (#1 UK), trailed by the singles "Dead From the Waist Down" (#7 UK), "Londinium" (#20 UK), and "Karaoke Queen" (#36 UK). The rest of the year, of course, would be spent touring, including their first ever Australian dates, with the band returning to the US in January 2000, to coincide with the Stateside release of the album.

Catatonia LPs

8 Way Beyond Blue (Blanco Y Negro — UK) 1996

9 International Velvet (Blanco Y Negro — UK) 1998 Cerys first: imagine Björk with laryngitis and a lisp, but not sounding like either — "Scully" (as in the murderously catchy "Mulder and...") comes out "Skelly," "grace" comes out "grease," and aside from its breathtaking depth and shape, that's all you need to know about her singing style. And though Catatonia itself sounds like it should be the name of some god-awful mid-western hardcore band, in reality it's the melodic whoop of Sleeper; the comic swagger of Supergrass; the sonic glare of Space; and a stunning album which insists, "embroidery makes me blind."

9 Equally Cursed and Blessed (Atlantic) 2000 Reprising its predecessor's "Mulder and Scully" and "Road Rage" for a US audience that slept through the last one, *Equally Cursed* opens with the unforgettable "Dead From the Waist Down," shoots through "Storm the Palace" and "Bulimic Beats," and matches *Velvet* note for note. Another soaring triumph.

Selected Compilations and Archive Releases

7 The Sublime Magic of Catatonia (Nursery) 1995 European compilation of the *Hooked* EP, plus Nursery and Rough Trade 45s, and a cut from the *Volume* series.

7 1993/1994 (MLL) 1999 Straightforward coupling of the first two EPs.

CATHERINE WHEEL

FORMED 1990 (*Great Yarmouth, England*)
ORIGINAL LINE-UP *Rob Dickinson (b. 7/23/65 — vocals, guitar); Brian Futter (b. 12/7/65 — guitar); David Hawes (bass); Neil Sims (b. 10/4/65 — drums)*

The godfathers of the dense swirl which would emerge from Britain's post-baggy scene formed in 1990 around local garage band graduates Rob Dickinson and Brian Futter, the nucleus of the earlier Ten Angry Men. That band's classic rock repertoire — Black Sabbath's "War Pigs" and "Iron Man," and Rush's "2112" — belied their own ambition, although revelations that Dickinson's cousin and the new band's staunchest supporter was Iron Maiden vocalist Bruce Dickinson went some way towards explaining it.

A year spent rehearsing and demoing introduced Neil Sims, a graduate of *Bullshit Detector* stars 1984; David Hawes followed, the only respondent to an advert placed in a local record store, calling for a bassist "into My Bloody Valentine, Stone Roses."

A seven track demo landed the band their debut gig, at the Norwich Art Centre, on September 24, 1990; the venue's promotor also owned the Wilde Club label, which released the group's first EP, *She's My Friend*. A London showcase followed, bringing with it a rave *NME* review, and by April, Catherine Wheel were touring the country with Blur, promoting their *Painful Thing* EP. Two months later, the group signed with Mercury.

"Black Metallic" (#68 UK), a track previewed on a BBC radio session earlier in the year, became Catherine Wheel's major label debut in November — a revelatory drone which showcased the band's determination to lead the next generation of British shoegazers out of the movement's current miasma. Its success paved the way for the follow-up, "Balloon" (#59 UK) and, as Catherine Wheel completed their first European tour (opening for Smashing Pumpkins), a ready market for their first album, *Ferment* (#36UK), produced by Talk Talk keyboard player Tim Friese Green.

A rerecording of "I Want to Touch You" (#35 UK), from the band's second EP, maintained the momentum, and Catherine Wheel made their US debut that spring. A review in *Alternative Press* had already prepped their audience, insisting, "imagine if Ian Curtis hadn't sunk to despair. Catherine Wheel is what Joy Division could have been, and should have been." Now, as they undertook close to a year of solid Stateside gigging, broken only by lightning trips back to Europe for festival dates, Catherine Wheel were enjoying a MTV hit with "Black Metallic," and growing anticipation for their sophomore album.

1992 closed with 30 *Century Man* (#47 UK), an oddball EP covering three of the band's favored influences, Scott Walker, Hüsker Dü, and Mission of Burma, each one a sonic taster for *Chrome* (#58 UK) — a Gil Norton produced album which began where "Black Metallic" left off, with the dense "Crank" (#66 UK) and "Show Me Mary" (#62 UK), and ended with the Wheel back on the road, relentlessly criss-crossing Europe and America.

After such a relentless schedule, the news that they intended taking 1994 off was no surprise. They returned stronger than before, with a set originally titled *Evolve or Die*, which itself evolved into *Happy Days*, home to another smash video, "Way Down" (#67 UK), and a duet with Belly's Tanya Donelly, "Judy Staring at the Sun." It was an intense record — so much so, Dickinson later confessed, that "we still meet people who aren't very familiar with the last quarter of *Happy Days* because they couldn't manage to wade through that far. The opening kind of wore people down a bit, because it was an abrasive, churning beginning, and I think it led people to get exhausted reasonably quickly."

In November 1995, Catherine Wheel's latest tour (with Belly) was pulled up short after a family emergency sent the band home early. A handful of Canadian shows in January 1996, notwithstanding, the band would effectively disappear following *Happy Days*, a silence punctuated only by the B-sides and out-takes collection *Like Cats and Dogs*.

It would be another year before Catherine Wheel re-emerged with *Adam and Eve*, a considerably shorter, and easier album than its predecessor, recorded over the course of a year with four different producers — Tim Friese-Greene, Garth Richardson, Bob Ezrin, and Dickinson himself.

Staggered US/UK release dates saw *Adam and Eve* released in the US close to a year before it appeared in Britain — by which time, Mercury's failure to promote the album in America had resulted in Catherine Wheel quitting the label following an exhaustive US tour. Beginning December 1997, the band did score three minor hits in their homeland, "Delicious" (#53 UK), "Ma Solituda" (#53 UK), and "Broken Nose" (#48 UK). Hawes departed shortly before they signed with Columbia soon after, and in September 1999, Catherine Wheel began work on the fifth album *Anybody Hurt* at Elvis Costello's studio in Rye, England.

Catherine Wheel LPs

8 Ferment (Mercury) 1992 The lyrics are enigmatic, the atmosphere's a swirl, but the guitars are a righteous roar of rock and a mighty strange brew all round — super sound sculptures in magnificent black metallic.

8 Chrome (Mercury) 1993 Emerging from the sonic shadows of *Ferment*, Dickinson's vocals come to the fore, while the band has a cleaner, brighter sound, even as ribbons of swirling atmospheres continue to stream through.

7 Happy Days (Mercury) 1995 An overly dense opening crushes any hope of playing the album through from start to finish. But if you excise a daft duet with Tanya Donelly (play the merciless "Way Down" twice instead), haunting ballads creep out from beneath the epic monsters, and a whirling battery will indeed emerge.

7 Adam and Eve (Mercury) 1997

8 Anybody Hurt (Columbia) 2000 The departure of bassist Hawes cut much of the tension from the Wheel's sound; so did the decision to bring every song in at under 5 minutes. Such a succinct approach, however, brought a new dimension and direction to the proceedings as the band turned in their most consistent set since *Chrome*.

Selected Compilations and Archive Releases

7 Like Cats and Dogs (Mercury) 1996 The guitars shimmer, shutter, and soar across this collection of the band's UK B-sides, moody and introspective, generally experiments for directions yet to come. Oh, and a Pink Floyd cover which had the lighters flaring every time they played it live in America.

NICK CAVE

BORN 9/22/57 (*Warraknabeal, Australia*)

Following the break-up of the Birthday Party, Nick Cave was sighted only once, when he joined Marc Almond, Lydia Lunch, and Foetus in the Immaculate Consumptives; a Halloween 1983 gathering which played just four shows, in New York and Washington DC, before stepping purposefully into the annals of rock myth and legend.

Cave seemed intent on joining them there. Still based in Berlin, the city where the Birthday Party ended, his next move was to arrange a short Australian tour under the billing, Nick Cave — Man or Myth? Joined by Party colleagues Mick Harvey and Tracy Pew, plus Magazine's Barry Adamson, and Australian guitarist Hugo Race, and premiering new material alongside the expected Birthday Party oldies, the tour received good local notices, but little attention elsewhere. Cave, however, was content, renaming the band The Cavemen (and later, the Bad Seeds), and with Blixa Bargeld replacing Pew, he played a handful of low-key shows around the UK and western Europe through early 1984.

In April 1984, the Bad Seeds made their recorded debut with a session for BBC radio DJ John Peel, while the following month brought the band's first single, Elvis Presley's "In the Ghetto" (#1 UK indy), and the album *From Her to Eternity* (#40 UK, #1 UK indy) — the clearest indications imaginable of why the Birthday Party had to end. Gone were the days of complete cacophony. The disjointed jangle which Cave maintained was now seen to be balanced with a firm blues style and Cave's seedily haunting poetic lyrics.

In November 1984, Cave and the Bad Seeds returned to the studio to record *The Firstborn Is Dead* (#53 UK, #2 UK indy), another installment in the singer's continued fascination with Elvis Presley (the title, of course, referred to Presley's stillborn twin brother Jesse). The first single from the album, the brooding "Tupelo" (#1 UK indy) further illustrated that obsession, while another key to Cave's musical heritage was provided by the cover of Bob Dylan's "Wanted Man," an unreleased track from Dylan's generally despised *Nashville Skyline* sessions. "I love Bob Dylan," Cave admitted years later. "You can forgive and forgive and forgive."

Dylan's hold over Cave and the rest of the band was strong, and apparently reciprocal. Cave actually reworked the lyrics to "Wanted Man" for the album, but in order to be able to include it, had to contact Dylan for approval to release it. With a generosity which would not be repeated until 1996, and The Dunblane charity revision of "Knocking on Heaven's Door," this permission was ultimately forthcoming — although the wait did delay the release of the album.

Still it seemed the band was on a roll, and in August 1986, Cave and the Bad Seeds released what remains their most decisive album, the all-covers *Kicking Against the Pricks* (#89 UK, #1 UK indy). Originally planned as a double album, 23 songs were recorded, of which close to half remain unissued. Still *Kicking Against the Pricks* overflowed with very personalized renditions of songs as disparate as the Seekers' "The Carnival Is Over," Lou Reed's "All Tomorrow's Parties," and Glen Campbell's "By the Time I Get to Phoenix," and demonstrated just how powerful an interpreter Cave had become.

© Jim Steinfeldt/Chansley Entertainment Archives

"The Singer" gave Cave his third successive UK indy chart topper, and 1986 also saw Cave, Harvey, and Bargeld record a soundtrack to John Hillcoat and Evan English's Ghosts... of the Civil Dead movie. Unreleased until 1989, the ensuing piece nevertheless deserves its place amidst Cave's most frighteningly intense recordings, a rank it shares with the album-length double EP set *Your Funeral... My Trial* (#1 UK indy) — which itself would impact upon Cave's cinematic career. Berlin director Wim Wenders was so impressed by one cut, "The Carny," that he invited Cave to contribute a cameo role and two songs for his newest film, *Wings of Desire*.

1987 continued as 1986 left off, with the ever restless Cave continuing to fill his time with any project he could — writing his first novel, *And the Ass Saw the Angel*, recording both his own next album, 1988's *Tender Prey* (#67 UK, #2 UK indy), and an EP with Anita Lane, *Dirty Sings*, and turning in some remarkable one-off live shows around Europe. Almost all, however, were seriously hindered by Cave's drug use, a habit which Cave had never tried to disguise, but which had finally run out of control. Finally, with the threat of possible imprisonment looming, Cave agreed to check into rehab in August 1988.

Following two further singles, "The Mercy Seat" (#3 UK indy) and "Deanna" (#4 UK indy), touring for *Tender Prey* (with the Bad Seeds augmented by Gun Club alumni Kid Congo Powers) was scheduled to start a mere four days after Cave reemerged into the world, newly clean and somewhat unsure of what his life would be like without the comfort of drugs. To his surprise, it would prove to be yet another pivotal point in his career. *Tender Prey* was well-received by the media, while the ensuing tour would produce one of the all-time great road documentaries, *The Road to God Knows Where*, shot during the month-long American leg.

Cave relocated to Sao Paulo, Brazil, following the tour, to settle down with girlfriend Viviane Carniero (the mother of Cave's son, Luke). It was there that he would record his next album, *The Good Son* (#47 UK), and though he worried about how the final record would sound, Cave knew he had taken his music to the next level.

While Britain enjoyed the singles "The Ship Song" and "The Weeping Song," Cave retreated back to Sao Paulo, and his world of reading and writing. Music was on hold for the time being as Cave settled into the role of family man, breaking only to tape a seriously idiosyncratic 80-minute version of "Tower of Song" for a forthcoming Leonard Cohen tribute album. (The released version left some 75 minutes of music on the cutting room floor.)

In October 1991, Cave, Viviane, and Luke traveled to New York, where Cave was constructing the songs that would become his next album, *Henry's Dream* (#29 UK).

Once again, in a departure from the Cave recording norm, a producer (Neil Young's David Briggs) was recruited for the album, at the insistence of his record company. "I spent an evening going through my record collection, looking for the least producer-like producer I could find. I came up with David Briggs. You listen to the Young albums, and they sound like there is no producer. They're extremely raw, and they are what they are — great songs performed in great ways."

Unfortunately, it didn't work that way for Cave; indeed, the band were so displeased with Briggs' handiwork that the album release was delayed so they could go back into the studio and rework the album to their satisfaction. "Our records are far more complex [than Briggs' vision], there's a lot of overdubbing going on, a lot of riding the phasers and pulling out sounds, a lot of orchestration that we do in the mixing stage, which David was not at all interested in. So in the end, we took what we considered to be a quite undynamic sounding record, and remixed it in our own way."

Henry's Dream was finally released in April 1992, attended by "I Had a Dream, Joe" and — incredibly — his first ever UK hit single, "Straight to You" (#68 UK). Cave also recorded a single with Pogue Shane MacGowan, a duet on "What a Wonderful World" (#72 UK) and contributed two more songs to the soundtrack of Wim Wenders' next movie, *Until the End of the World*. Meanwhile, the *Henry's Dream* tour was the most extensive Cave had yet undertaken, and included several appearances at Australia's answer to Lollapalooza, the Big Day Out festival. A live album and video, *Live Seeds* (#67 UK), would subsequently document the outing.

Cave's most resonant collaboration, however, was the virtual Birthday Party reunion which took place at the London Town and Country Club on September 1, 1992. A full-scale Bad Seeds show was interrupted first by a guest appearance from MacGowan, then by Cave announcing "I'd like to give you a history lesson." With Rowland Howard and Mick Harvey representing the Birthday Party, and former Triffids bassist Martin Casey standing in for the recently-deceased Tracy Pew, the audience was regaled with versions of "Wild World," "Dead Joe," and "Nick the Stripper."

Cave and his family relocated to London in 1993, and work began on his next album, *Let Love In* (#12 UK) almost immediately after the tour ended. Alongside the singles "Do You Love Me" (#68 UK), "Loverman," and "Red Right Hand," the album would also receive high praise in America, finally catapulting Cave and the Bad Seeds out of the cult ghetto in which they had previously languished, and elevating them to a level of success they had neither dreamed of, nor actually wanted. Suddenly it was "cool" to like Nick Cave.

Under heavy record company pressure to support the album, the band launched into another extensive tour, of Europe and the US, highlighted — from his US label's point of view, anyway — by a place on the Lollapalooza festival bill. Cave, however, was disgusted. "Lollapalooza was really the most destructive thing I've done in my career. This, in a way, really damaged our band. I never wanted to do it. The pressure was so great that we relented in the end. But it destroyed some of our love for own music." He retaliated with what he claimed he perceived to be the least commercial thing he could ever do, a collection of murder songs which had been kicking around in his head for years.

Decrying his reputation as an alternative Leonard Cohen, Cave explained, "I really didn't want anything more to do with my problems. The idea was really to make a record where I could stand outside of it... and just write a lot of stories. The idea that it would be a record of murder ballads has been around for years with us. It's been around since the beginning of the Bad Seeds." He was adamant, though, that the album was for his fans alone. People who flocked to his banner at Lollapalooza, he was sure, would fall dead away at the first sniff of this new collection. That assumption would prove to be very wrong.

The first single from the album, "Where the Wild Roses Grow" (#11 UK), was aided by a guest appearance from Australian superstar Kylie Minogue. *Murder Ballads* (#8 UK) itself went to #1 in Australia, sold impressively in Britain and Europe, even did well in the US. His bizarre decision to contribute songs to the *X-Files* and *Batman Forever* movie soundtracks only heightened his profile even further, so it was with some relief that Cave plunged himself back into obscurity, contributing to new albums by Current 93 and Barry Adamson, and penning the score to another John Hillcoat movie, *To Have and To Hold*.

Throughout the recording of *Murder Ballads*, Cave was also working on what he saw as the corollary to that set, a collection of piano ballads documenting the birth of a new love — he and Viviane had broken up, and he was now moving into a relationship with PJ Harvey, his co-star on *Murder Ballads'* second hit single, "Henry Lee" (#36 UK).

Whether or not the new songs related directly to Harvey herself, the album was clearly pertinent to the relationship, and though the affair would not outlive the sessions, still the resultant album, *The Boatman's Call* (#155 US, #22 UK), was released in early 1997, to widespread speculation and gossip, both met with a stony silence from Cave.

Two singles, "Into My Arms" (#53 UK) and "(Are You) The One That I've Been Waiting For?" (#67 UK) followed, but 1998's *Best of* (#11 UK) compilation notwithstanding, Cave closed the 20th century with nothing more than a handful of sporadic live shows and benefits, including a La

Monte Young tribute in London in October 1997 and The Glastonbury Festival in 1998. A European tour took the band as far afield as St. Petersburg; while a low-key US tour did much to erase devotees' disappointment with *The Boatman's Call*. Cave also organized 1999's Meltdown Festival at London's Royal Festival Hall.

Also see the entry for "BIRTHDAY PARTY" on page 199.

Nick Cave LPs

8 From Her to Eternity (Mute) Bridging the gap between the Birthday Party and the future, cacophonous, but credibly melodic as well and stunning across "Avalanche," "Saint Huck," and "The Moon Is in the Gutter." The title track dwells among the most sensually disturbing masterpieces ever written and "In the Ghetto" is a stunning taste of Cave's dexterity with covers.

9 The Firstborn Is Dead (Mute) 1985 A dramatic collection delving into a lost world of extrapolated blues. Vibrant and dark, "Tupelo" screams crossroads, dead twins, and bloody rain, while "Blind Lemon Jefferson" and "The Six Strings That Drew Blood" have a panic all of their own.

8 Kicking Against the Pricks (Mute) 1986 The full-on covers collection he'd been threatening for years, full of twisted blues riffs and growling vocals, and private tributes to Leadbelly, Roy Orbison, John Lee Hooker and Alex Harvey. Often spare and stripped to the skeleton, yet full of brutal rough and tumble, Cave not only records some of his favorite songs, but re-invents them as well.

9 Your Funeral... My Trial (Mute) 1986 Part Party, part Cave, and part armageddon, *Trial* blasts through whatever trappings of pretension his growing fame was attaching to him, to revel in the beauty of a title track which is truly chilling. Elsewhere, "Stranger than Kindness" verges on tender, but everything pales in the face of "The Carny," where rot and refuse permeate all. (9)

6 Tender Prey (Mute) 1988 Cave's first post-drug album, *Tender Prey* simply doesn't have the strength of his previous work, as he seemingly searches for a matching new direction. But "The Mercy Seat" crackles with a touch of classic fire and "Deanna" has a sense of dark purpose, so it's not completely a lost cause.

6 Ghosts... of the Civil Dead (Mute) 1989 Largely instrumental soundtrack, cut with Bargeld and Harvey.

7 The Good Son (Mute) 1990 Reprising Alex Harvey's "Hammer Song" (from *Pricks*) and maybe getting a little predictable with "Weeping Song," still the dynamics strip back and the band keeps it simple — the beginning of a new age.

8 Henry's Dream (Mute) 1992 This set roared into existence like an avalanche. Biting, brutal commentary on a pathetic existence, whipped with desert heat and dry bones, the songs hit hard, cut deep and scar permanently. From the opening lullaby "Papa Won't Leave You, Henry" to the delirious "Christina the Astonishing," it's obvious Cave has regained mastery over his voice and vision.

6 Live Seeds [LIVE] (Mute) 1993

9 Let Love In (Mute) 1994 A massive cycle opened and closed by the phenomenal two part "Do You Love Me?", the album is a culmination of a long, fraught process, revolving around any number of key peaks — "Red Right Hand," "Loverman," "Ain't Gonna Rain Anymore" — a triumph which is arguably his best ever.

9 Murder Ballads (Mute) 1996 Hurrah for death! The antithesis of its predecessor, a not-too-serious rumination on historical interpretations of traditional murder balladry, updated for a modern age but locked inside that mythical depression-era mid-west which lies at the heart of Cave's songwriting brain. The brutally graphic "Stagger Lee" and the contrarily lovely "Henry Lee" (featuring PJ Harvey) are closest to their older prototypes; "Lovely Creature" and "The Curse of Millhaven" could be swept back in time to join them. But in case we take it all too seriously, Dylan's "Death Is Not the End" closes the album on a positive note. Probably.

4 The Boatman's Call (Mute) 1997 Religious imagery, devastated love, and the last will and testament of the unrepentant romantic, a nobly-conceived collection of piano ballads hamstrung by impenetrable sluggishness masquerading as emotion. Dry, dull and dilettante.

6 And the Ass Saw the Angel (Mute) 2000 Spoken word selection from Cave's first (and ten years later, only) novel.

6 The Secret Life of the Love Song (King Mob — UK) 2000 Six songs illustrate two spoken word lectures — heaving going at times, but the (new) music is tasteful.

Selected Compilations and Archive Releases

7 The Best of (Mute) 1998 Fairly predictable (if unimpeachable) rendering everything you'd expect, best dignified by the UK-only bonus of a *Boatman's Call*-era live album.

Further Reading

Bad Seed by Ian Johnston (Little Brown & Co, 1997).

CHAINSAW KITTENS

FORMED 1989 *(Norman, OK)*
ORIGINAL LINE-UP *Tyson Meade (b .Todd Meade — vocals); Mark Metzger (guitar); Aaron Preston (bass); Clint Bay (drums)*

Tyson Meade, a glam-rocking sore thumb in mid-70s Bartlesville, OK, was a founding member of Defenestration — the first band out of neighboring Norman before the Flaming Lips, and the first one back again after the *Slow Iguana* EP and the delightfully titled *Dali Does Windows* album went nowhere. Returning to Bartlesville, Meade hooked up with guitarist Mark Metzger, and by 1990, the Chainsaw Kittens were readying their debut album, *Violent Religion*.

Trent Bell followed him into the band for a tour with Smashing Pumpkins, and 1992's Butch Vig produced *Flipped Out in Singapore*, and the *High in High School* EP. Unfortunately, the Kittens began falling apart soon after. Metzger quit; so did Aaron Preston and Clint Bay, who went on to form For Love Not Lisa, leaving Meade and Bell alone to rebuild the momentum the Kittens had lost.

Long time fan Matt Johnson, new to Oklahoma from Wisconsin, heard the band were looking for a bassist and called offering to try out. He also knew all the band's songs, "which impressed us," said Meade, "because we didn't!"

Johnson arrived with his fan's fervor intact. Where the Kittens used to rehearse once a month for an hour, he had them at it for five hours a week. Where Meade and Bell once wrote a new song every-so-often, "now we just couldn't stop!," Meade enthused. "In the end, we wrote so many that we had to go to the record company and tell them we really needed to do something more than a single, but only slightly less than an album."

With drummer Eric Harmon also debuting, 1993's *Angel on the Range* EP introduced a new, flamboyant Kittens, steeped in Meade's glam roots, but with a vibrant slice of modern pop too. It was followed by the album *Pop Heiress Dies* (and accompanying title track single), and the band gigged on, their energy and extravagance increasing with every show. It was indeed a stark contrast to the stripped down feel of the next Kittens-related project, Meade's low-key *Motorcycle Childhood* solo set.

Following the release of the *Candy for You* EP in 1995, the Chainsaw Kittens were amongst the first recruits to Smashing Pumpkins' James Iha and D'arcy Wretzky's Scratchie label. The band released an eponymous album in 1996 and the "Heart Catch Thump" single, but departed the label shortly after. Still gigging and recording, the band nevertheless maintained a low profile until bursting back in 1999 with a cover of "We Got the Beat," for the Go-Gos tribute album, *Unsealed*, and a projected new album, *God Bless the Chainsaw Kittens*.

Chainsaw Kittens LPs

5 Violent Religion (Mammoth) 1990 From acoustic ballads and Byrd-sy pop to raucous, pounding punk, the only central sound is an at-odds glitter glam edge, and a clutch of songs where the Stooges and a hardcore NY Dolls slam smack dab into the Spiders from Mars.

6 Flipped Out in Singapore (Mammoth) 1992 A new rhythm section and the entrance of guitarist Trent Bell herald the arrival of a new big rock sound, although this time the increasingly crucial insidious glam stylings are lost inside the sonics, while the more delicate pop songs collapse under the roar.

8 Pop Heiress (Mammoth) 1994 Third time's a charm (third album, third producer, third rhythm section) and it finally all comes together. Punk pogos on glitter, '60s guitar jangles over pounding rhythms and pop-rockers surf the new wave through a soaring windstorm of fragile melodies and skittering ballads.

6 Chainsaw Kittens (Scratchie) 1996 Strangely muted, with strings and extra keyboards dulling the edge a little. The glitter roots still shine through boldly, but the punk intensity has disappeared, along with most of their jangly pop melodies.

8 The All American (4 Alarm) 2000

Tyson Meade/Defenestration LP

7 Dali Does Windows 1987 The pre-Kitten Meade holds sway through a hectic ragbag of styles and splashes, with his skewered, emotive lyrics hitting hard throughout.

Tyson Meade LP

8 Motorcycle Childhood 1995 Handling most of the instrumentation himself, sparse lo-fi dynamics capture a sitting-on-the-porch-on-a-Sunday-afternoon kind a feel, as Tyson relives loves, lives, and events from his Oklahoma childhood.

CHAMELEONS UK

FORMED 1981 *(Middleton, Manchester)*
ORIGINAL LINE-UP *Mark Burgess (vocals, bass); Dave Fielding (guitar); Reg Smithies (guitar); Brian Schofield (drums)*

With 1982's seminal "In Shreds," the Chameleons — formed the previous year from the wreckage of Mark Burgess' Cliches and Reg Smithie and Dave Fielding's The Years — appeared set to dominate the new decade like no other band of the age.

According to Burgess, the band was born out of a desire to record a session for John Peel; "it wasn't that we saw this as a stepping stone to success or anything, [just that] all the bands we had grown up admiring had all recorded sessions for John Peel, and that was our main incentive."

Peel instinctively sensed their purity. The first tape they sent him, recorded on a boom box without a drummer, elicited a personal request for a studio recording; the band sold everything they owned to finance it, recruited drummer Brian Schofield for the occasion, and hand-delivered the tape to Peel. Three days later, the group were in London, recording at the BBC. Weeks after that, with John Lever replacing Brian Schofield, the Chameleons were signed by Epic, and dispatched to the studio with producer Steve Lillywhite, himself hot off his first successes with U2.

The result, of course, had nothing in common with Ireland's finest. "In Shreds" was a thunderous percussion-driven slab of echo-laden doom pop which left the label utterly perplexed. So they put it out, and forgot all about it.

Close to a year of inactivity followed, during which time, ex-Magazine drummer Martin Jackson temporarily replaced Lever, and the Chameleons escaped Epic and joined Virgin's Statik subsidiary. Any fears that they might have lost their momentum were quashed, however, first by the February 1983, release of a new single, "As High As You Can Go" (#7 UK indy); then by *Script of the Bridge* (#11 UK indy), their debut album.

Faltering only when it came to rerecording "In Shreds" (#11 UK indy), the Chameleons turned in what would swiftly be regarded as one of the early 80s' crucial debut albums — with "Second Skin" in particular placing the band somewhere between the undisputed giants of recent northern memory, Joy Division and Teardrop Explodes. The fact that both had now disbanded only added emphasis to the Chameleons' potential.

Again, the band lapsed into recorded silence — close to two years elapsed before the band followed up, with *What Does Anything Mean, Basically?* (#60 UK, #2 UK indy) and the single "Singing Rule Britannia (While the Walls Close In)" (#2 UK indy); they spent the interim gigging heavily (a live EP reprising "In Shreds" broke the hush), and towards the end of 1985, the band signed with Geffen.

Released in late 1986, *Strange Times* (#44 UK) was the Chameleons' breakthrough album, while encouraging noises from the US (where the band was renamed Chameleons UK to avoid confusion with a similarly-named American group) saw them tour the college circuit acclaim later in the year. The death of manager Tony Fletcher, from a heart attack, however, dealt the Chameleons a blow from which they would not recover. The band shattered — the title of the 1990 EP, *Tony Fletcher Walked on Water*, indicates the depth of their feelings towards a mentor who was all but the fifth member of the group.

While the first in an often confusing string of compilations and live recordings ensured the Chameleons' name would never die, Burgess and Lever regrouped as Sun and the Moon, joined by and Andy Whittaker and The Chameleons' live keyboard player and Andy Clegg (both ex-Music for Aborigines). They recorded a self-titled album for Geffen, but were dropped soon after its release and broke up following the *Alive; Not Dead* EP later in the year.

Fielding and Smithies, too, remained together, issuing a handful of indy singles before their *Rock the Magic Rock* album in 1993. However, it was Burgess whose post-Chameleons work came closest to recapturing the magic of the original band; even threatened to eclipse it. *Zima Junction*, his 1993 solo album, comprised "demos for an album that never was," yet emerged as consistent as the most painstakingly constructed album.

The Chameleons reconvened for live work in early 2000.

Chameleons UK LPs

4 Script of the Bridge (Statik) 1983 Still haunted by the lost brilliance of the original (Steve Lillywhite produced) "In Shreds," *Script* spends too long trying to recapture it, and not enough recounting what else the band can do. Dry and all-too-often depressingly flat, especially when compared to period BBC sessions.

8 What Does Anything Mean Basically? (Statik) 1985 A triumphant rediscovery of all its predecessor lost, with "On the Beach" borrowing more than its title from Neil Young and "One Flesh" heading the team which works cathedral keyboards and echo-swamped guitars to their limit.

8 Strange Times (Geffen) 1986 An enjoyably turgid album which rooted the band firmly within shoe gazer territory — about five years before anyone else found the way in. The overall feel is of deliberate stagnation — none of the songs ever really goes anyplace, although "Swamp Thing" titillated the sensibility of many a youngster at the time. This album should have become a post-punk bible, but instead floundered in its own miasma. Which, given the era, is actually a very positive thing.

Selected Compilations and Archive Releases

7 The Fans and the Bellows (Hybrid) 1986 Near-essential but painfully raw collection of 1981 demos.

9 Peel Sessions (Dutch East Indies Co) 1990 So superior to the regular studio cuts that it's almost the only Chameleons UK anyone needs — a startling reminder indeed of just how many future blueprints the band kept in their carelessly unlocked briefcase.

7 Here Today, Gone Tomorrow (Imaginary — UK) 1992

8 Radio One Evening Show (Dutch East Indies Co) 1993 More key radio sessions from 1982 through 1985. *Here Today* adds a bonus latter-day live disc.

Mark Burgess and John Lever/The Sun and the Moon LP

7 The Sun and the Moon (Geffen) 1988

Mark Burgess and the Sons of God LP

9 Zima Junction (Pivot) 1994 Burgess himself claimed *Zima Junction* merely compiled demos "for an album that was never to be," yet in a strange way, the stripped, cello-led demo feel suits the music better than a band ever could have. While the beautiful "Facades by Glass in E-Minor" applies Philip Glass' theme to a hauntingly realized Shetland burr, then slides into a Bond theme ("You Only Live Twice"), elsewhere Burgess' own songwriting both echoes ("Happy New Life") and refines ("Refugees," "The Great Adventure") the very best of the Chameleons UK.

CHARLATANS UK

FORMED 1989 (Northwich, England)
ORIGINAL LINE-UP Baz Kettley (vocals); Martin Blunt (b. 1965
— bass); Rob Collins (b. 2/23/63, d. 7/23/96 — keyboards); Jon
Brookes (b. 1969 — drums)

Adopting the same loose, organ-led sound as Mancunian
contemporaries Stone Roses, Inspiral Carpets, and Happy
Mondays, but infusing it with an even breezier feel, the
Charlatans were the instantly accessible face of Madchester,
all the more so after they recruited California-born lighting
specialist Captain Whizzo to their ranks. At a time when
other bands in their orbit were still playing at psychedelia,
the Charlatans were bringing it home.

Martin Blunt was the motivating force behind the band.
He began his recording career with Makin' Time, a Wolver-
hampton-based Mod combo whose solitary released album,
Rhythm N' Soul, kept that scene alive in Britain through the
mid-1980s. When Makin' Time split up (shortly after turning
down a tour with Simply Red, in favor of an outing with the
Untouchables), he linked with Jon Brookes, vocalist Fay Hal-
lam, and vocalist Graham Day (ex-Prisoners), to form the
Gift Horses. They broke up in mid-1988, and Blunt and
Brookes moved onto another Wolverhampton band, the
Prime Movers.

There they encountered Baz Kettley, and over the next
six months, the fluctuating line-up was joined by a keyboard
player who died from an OD after just a handful of rehearsals, around the same time as the Prime Movers changed
their name to the Charlatans.

With Rob Collins now moving in on keyboards, the
band's first gig, in Northwich, near Manchester, brought
them to the attention of Omega Records head Steve Harrison; he was also able to get the Charlatans onto bills with the
Stone Roses — unknown then on a national level, but
already the hottest thing in Manchester.

Kettley quit in April 1989, and was replaced immediately
by Tim Burgess (b. 5/30/68, Northwich), vocalist with one of
the Charlatans' own recent support bands, the Electric Crayons (he joined the Charlatans the very same day the Crayons' first single, "Hip Shake Junkie," was released). A second
guitarist, John Baker, joined soon after, and in October, the
band recorded a three-song demo for sale at gigs, led off by
"Indian Rope"; that track would be re-recorded in January,
for release as the band's debut single (#89 UK, #1 UK indy),
on their own Dead Dead Good label.

Prompted, of course, by the UK media's sudden, and all-
pervading, infatuation with what was now being termed the
Madchester scene, Beggars Banquet's Situation 2 subsidiary
stepped in, and in May, "The Only One I Know" (#9 UK)
sold over 100,000 copies — out-performing new releases by

both the Stone Roses and The Inspiral Carpets. It was followed by "Then" (#12 UK), before October saw the release of
the Charlatans' debut album, *Some Friendly* (#73 US, #1
UK), while the band themselves were in the US, playing Ian
Astbury's Gathering of the Tribes festival. (An edited version
of the album's epic "Sproston Green" would become their
first American 45.)

The group's projected next single, "Happen to Die," was
cancelled when the outbreak of the Gulf War made it apparent that the record would never get played by a sensitive UK
media; it was replaced by "Over Rising" (#15 UK), before guitarist Baker quit that spring 1991, to be replaced by Mark Collins, the Inspiral Carpets' former van driver.

Though "Indian Rope" (#57 UK) kept the band's profile
buoyant, a difficult period was exacerbated when Blunt was
diagnosed with severe depression — hitherto, Burgess later
revealed, the group simply thought he hated "Me. In Time"
(#28 UK), the song selected for the group's next single. His
illness caused the band to lie low for much of the year, and
Between 10th and 11th (#173 US, #21 UK) was not released
until March 1992, by which time the Madchester pendulum
had swung the opposite way entirely, and a press backlash
was now in full force.

"Weirdo" (#19 UK) followed, but with the *Tremolo Song*
EP (#44) similarly faltering in July, the Charlatans spent
much of 1992 out of the country, touring the US and the Far
East; when they returned, it was into the arms of the law, as
Collins was arrested as an (albeit unwitting) accomplice in
an armed robbery. In April 1993, he was sentenced to eight
months in prison, to begin in September.

All through the summer, the band worked to complete
their next album, in the studio with producer Steve Hillage;
Burgess alone recorded singles with St. Etienne ("I Was
Born on Christmas Day") and the Chemical Brothers ("Life
Is Sweet" — two years later a *Charlatans vs the Chemical
Brothers* EP would be released, featuring four Chemical
remixes of material from the Charlatans' eponymous fourth
album).

Collins served four months of his sentence before being
released, and plunged straight back into the band, as *Up to
Our Hips* (#8 UK) restored the band's chart fortunes in
March 1994 — adequate consolation for the continued
under-performance of the band's latest singles, "Can't Get
Out of Bed" (#24 UK), "I Never Want an Easy Life" (#38
UK), and "Jesus Hairdo" (#48 UK).

An American tour that spring, too, was a success, and in
December, the Charlatans unveiled a new single, "Crashin'
In" (#31 UK), composed immediately after the band's return
home. It offered a foretaste of their next album, scheduled
for a fall 1995, release, and over the next nine months, "Just

Lookin'" (#32 UK) and "Just When You're Thinkin' Things Over" (#12 UK) maintained the barrage of new material.

Attempts to continue their relationship with producer Hillage broke down during the sessions; the band completed their eponymous fourth album (#1 UK) alone — the set dispatching them on another world tour, lasting through the remainder of 1995. They returned, and went straight back into the studio, Rockfield in South Wales. It was in the midst of these sessions, on July 23, 1996, that Collins was killed in a car accident, returning to the studio from a local pub. According to the coroner's report, his blood alcohol level was twice the legal limit when he died.

Primal Scream's Martin Duffy was brought in to replace him for two festival shows, at Chelmsford and opening for Oasis at Knebworth. Previewing the *Tellin' Stones* album, a single, "One to Another" (#3) followed in September 1996, and in March 1997, Tony Rogers was recruited on a permanent basis, just as "North Country Boy" (#4 UK) and Tellin' Stories (#1 UK) confirmed the band's rebirth. They were followed in June by "How High" (#6 UK), and through the summer, the Charlatans played well-received sets at T in the Park and Phoenix 97, before embarking on their next US tour.

Another hit single, "Tellin' Stories" (#16 UK), preluded the release of the *Melting Pot* compilation (#4); the band then returned to the studio to begin work on a follow-up album they had once doubted would ever be made — Blunt later admitted it was Rogers who kept the band together, fitting in so well at a time when the Charlatans didn't think they could ever "replace" Collins.

Recorded at their own Big Mushroom studios, and previewed by the single "Forever" (#12 UK), *Us and Us Only* (#2 UK) was released in October 1999, following a summer of festival activity, and focused upon the Charlatans' own discovery that "people move on in life." One song, "Senses (Angel on My Shoulder)" dealt specifically with the loss of Collins.

Charlatans UK LPs

⑧ Some Friendly (Beggars Banquet) 1990 Groovy, trippy, dreamy, psychedelic... any '60s adjective will suffice, but what really makes Charlatans UK stand out from the rest of the baggy pack is their occasional nod to Mod (especially the Who); that and Tim Burgess' wistful, delicate vocals. The persistent, pounding rhythms provide the dance appeal even as the organ defines the sound, constantly shifting and transfiguring, bubbling, burbling, funking out or falling into a deep trance.

⑦ Somewhere Between 10th and 11th (Beggars Banquet) 1992 Kings of nuance, Charlatans UK spin this album out of the subtlest of melodies, hanging on to the slightest of hooks, but weaving all together through the incendiary keyboards and guitar interplay.

⑦ Up to Our Hips (Beggars Banquet) 1994 Realized amid the band's internal chaos, *Hips* diversifies the band's trademark sound via R&B riffs and bright, spangling choruses. Producer Steve Hillage does lose some mystery with the cobwebs, but the songs stand up regardless.

⑧ The Charlatans UK (Beggars Banquet) 1995 Having discovered the magical musical elixir, *Charlatans UK* continues precisely where *Hips* left off, only now the group's self-confidence comes into play as well.

⑧ Tellin' Stories (Beggars Banquet) 1997 The band come full circle, but complete half the journey on just the one album, a return to their Madchester roots seasoned with an adept grip of acoustic balladry made all the more poignant by Rob Collins' tragic death.

⑨ Us and Us Only (MCA) 1999 Blunt called it "Dylan and the Band on Ecstasy playing the last night of the Heavenly Social" — in fact, it sounded more like a late '60s Stones album. Still, with Tim's new strident vocals indeed taking on a definite Dylan-esque quality (abetted by the bluesy harmonica), Charlatans UK stitch their influences seamlessly together, and if the songs occasionally yearn for the old psychedelic organ, new member Tony Rogers' strengths are his subtle atmospheres, permeating every pore of the album.

Selected Compilations and Archive Releases

⑧ Melting Pot (Beggars Banquet) 1998 A singles' collection comprising all their British A-sides, with the crucial addition of four B-sides including the Chemical Brothers remix of "Patrol," previously available only on 12-inch.

Further Reading

The Authorized History by Dominic Wills/Tom Sheehan (Virgin, UK, 1999).

CHELSEA

FORMED 1976 (London, England)
ORIGINAL LINE-UP *Gene October (vocals); Billy Idol (b. William Broad, 11/30/55, Stanmore — guitar); Tony James (bass); John Towe (drums)*

Although Gene October had already been rehearsing with a guitarist, Marco Pirroni (later to join Adam and the Ants), it took an advertisement in *Melody Maker* during summer 1976 to recruit what would become the original line-up of Chelsea. Tony James was a founder member of the legendary London SS, John Towe a youthful veteran of sundry local bands, and Billy Idol was already well known on the London scene as a member of the so-called Bromley Contingent, following the Sex Pistols around. He was also a promising philosophy student, and October had to visit the boy's college to meet with the headmaster, before Idol was permitted to drop out to pursue his dream.

Chelsea made their live debut at the London ICA on October 13, 1976, supporting Throbbing Gristle's *Prostitute* exhibit under the name LSD. Playing behind a stripper named Shelley, they played an eleven-song set comprising versions of "Gloria," "For Your Love," "Rebel Rebel," and eight tracks from early Rolling Stones albums.

Within two months, however, this line-up of Chelsea — the first of many, as it transpired — was no more. Coveting October's role as vocalist, Idol led a backstage revolt which culminated with October's own departure in December. The trio formed their own band, Generation X; October pieced together a new Chelsea, with Bob Jessie (bass), Marti Stacey (guitar), and Carey Fortune (drums).

This line-up debuted at the Roxy as support to The Clash in January 1977. Two nights later, they played the Hope and Anchor, and a couple of hours after that, they were back at the Roxy, but though the line-up had energy, it didn't possess stamina. By March, an entirely new line-up had stabilized out of a series of changes, with Fortune now joined by James Stevenson (guitar) and Henry Badowski (bass).

It was this line-up which cut Chelsea's first, and perhaps most potent single, "Right to Work," and while it assaulted the indy chart, Chelsea played every club that would take them, even as the line-up continued to evolve. Shortly before the release of their second single, "High Rise Living," Badowski quit to play sax for Wreckless Eric; Simon Vitesse replaced him, but in September, with only one more recording behind them ("Urban Kids" was included in the *Jubilee* movie soundtrack), Chelsea split — then reformed in January 1978, around the now solid nucleus of October and Stevenson.

With Dave Martin (guitar), Geoff Myles (bass), and Steve J Jones (drums), a new version of "Urban Kids" was recorded for the band's next single in August 1978, although Chelsea's first album, threatened throughout 1977 and 1978, did not appear until the summer of 1979. With Chris Bashford replacing Jones from the "Urban Kids" line-up, the band thrashed through ten of their best, albeit omitting all past singles. In America, IRS pulled "I'm on Fire" for a single, a fitting introduction to the band on the eve of their first American tour.

Chelsea continued gigging into 1980, issuing a new single, "No One's Coming Outside" (#27 UK indy) in February. Two months later, "Look at the Outside" (#37 UK indy) was accompanied by a triumphant show at the Notre Dame Hall in London, with Police bassist Sting a guest performer.

By summer, however, the band was at an end again. Stevenson guested on the first solo single by UK Subs vocalist Charlie Harper, then joined Generation X for their last hurrah (he eventually wound up in Gene Loves Jezebel), while Martin and Myles formed a new band, the Smart. A final Chelsea single, "No Escape" (#39 UK indy) bade farewell, accompanied by the *Alternative Hits* collection (#7 UK indy).

October and Bashford hastily pieced together a temporary line-up to fulfill the band's last few outstanding shows, at the Lyceum with Infra Riot, and a short US tour. By December 1980, however, Chelsea again disbanded, with Bashford quitting the music industry to pursue a career in art and sign writing.

October immediately began planning a new band, built around Nic Austin (guitar), Stephen Corfield (guitar), Tim Griffin (bass), and Sol Mintz (drums), debuting at Gossip's in London on January 7, 1981. A brace of new singles, "Rocking Horse" (#30 UK indy) and "Freemans" (#27 UK indy), followed, together with a UK tour with Chron Gen. Griffin quit in September, the day before a scheduled show at the Fulham Greyhound; he was replaced for the evening by Sting, before Paul "Linc" Lincoln came in for the band's next single, "Evacuate" (#23 UK indy).

Corfield and Mintz were the next to leave — Mintz was replaced by Malcolm Asling, and Chelsea remained a quartet for gigs with visiting Americans Black Flag, and an appearance at the Leeds punk festival in December. Another new single, "War Across the Nation" (#10 UK indy) preceded the *Evacuate* album (#3 UK indy), but even as the band toured on, reaching out to the new Oi! generation via gigs with the Anti-Nowhere League, the Defects, and Chron Gen, Asling quit to join the UK Subs. Geoff Sewell came in for another US tour, and the "Stand Out" single (#20 UK indy), but finally, October announced the band was finished. They played two farewell shows at the London Marquee in December 1982.

Austin formed Bandits at 4 o'Clock; Lincoln joined former Vice Squad vocalist Beki Bondage's newly formed Ligotage; October launched a solo career with a pair of singles, reggae classics "Suffering in the Land" and "Don't Quit." He then reformed Chelsea in 1985, essentially as himself plus a revolving door of musicians. Three albums through the 1980s, *Original Sinners*, *Rocks Off*, and *Underwraps* (featuring former Menace guitarist Steve Tannett), passed by more or less unnoticed; so did a reunion with Austen, for 1993's *The Alternative* and *Traitor's Gate* albums — both recorded with Matt Sargent (bass), and Stuart Soulsby (drums).

Finally, the "classic" line-up of October, Stevenson (now the only full-time musician in the band), Bashford, and Myles convened to join the Social Chaos US tour through summer 1999. A documentary, highlighted by the effervescent October's bottomless supply of anecdotes, was shot while the tour was in progress.

Chelsea LPs

8 Chelsea (Step Forward) 1979 With the ravishing "I'm on Fire" and an utterly unexpected cover of "Many Rivers to Cross" at either extreme, one of *the* key (albeit delayed) debuts of the first wave UK punk scene.

7 Evacuate (Step Forward) 1982

4 Live at the Marquee (Chaos) 1982

5 Original Sinners (Communique) 1985

5 Rocks Off (Jungle) 1987

7 Underwraps (IRS) 1989 While other old punks threw their all into hardcore, metal or worse, Chelsea remained Chelsea. Still classy and clumsy in equal doses, still happiest when the songs are sing-alongs, but aware now of their comparative maturity, the band sounds better than any since the early 1980s, October spits reinvigorated fire, and The Clash's "Somebody Got Murdered" has rarely sounded better.

8 The Alternative (Alter Ego) 1993 The alternative to what? In Chelsea's case, it's an alternative to the techno scene which was engulfing the UK, closing live venues in its wake. For frontman and vocalist Gene October, this is an opportunity to remind the world just what punk was all about — and precisely what the movement was fighting for.

6 Traitors Gate (Weser) 1994

Selected Compilations and Archive Releases

8 No Escape (IRS — US)/Alternative Hits (Step Forward — UK) 1981

7 Just for the Record (Step Forward — UK) 1985 Two "best of's," the first loaded down with the band's best known numbers, the latter sensibly omitting them.

7 Live at the Music Machine 1978 (Released Emotions — UK) 1991 Rough and ready recording of the classic line-up at its peak.

8 Punk Singles Collection 1977–82 (Captain Oi! — UK) 1999
8 Punk Rock Rarities (Captain Oi! — UK) 1999 A straightforward A- and B-sides collection and its mirror image of out-takes, demos, and what sounds suspiciously like the band's best John Peel session. A cover of the Sex Pistols '"Pretty Vacant" packs at least as much power as most of the Pistols' own attempts at the song.

Gene October LP

9 Life and Struggle (Receiver — UK) 1994 Joined by such luminaries as former Chelsea axe man James Stevenson (playing and producing) and ex-Pistol Glen Matlock, October abandons the old punk parties and embarks on a pub crawl instead. It's a wise move, the singer's gruff vocals are ideal for rivvum'n'booze,

and Stevenson's guitar makes a perfect foil. Smoky, rocking good time music, October may have found his perfect niche.

CHEMICAL BROTHERS

FORMED 1992 (Manchester, England)
ORIGINAL LINE-UP Tom Rowlands (b. 1970, Oxford); Ed Simons (b. 1970, London)

Friends already for two years, Tom Rowlands and Ed Simons first worked together while studying history at Manchester University in 1992, taking over the turntable at a friend's wedding while the scheduled DJ took a break. Renaming themselves the Dust Brothers (unaware that an American production team had already taken the same name), the pair landed a regular gig at the Manchester nightclub Naked Under Leather, working regularly through the aftermath of the Madchester explosion.

Rowlands was a member of Ariel at the time, alongside two friends, Matt and Brendan, releasing singles on a label run by a third, Phil Brown. Fiercely independent, the band sold their singles from the back of Brown's car — "Sea of Beats" was followed by "Mustn't Grumble" and "Roller coaster, " and in early 1992, the band signed to DeConstruction. At the same time, however, Rowlands and Simons alone were looking for fresh music for their DJ act and, coming up blank, decided to create their own.

Based around Renegade Soundwave's "In Dub," "Song to the Siren" was recorded on a home hi-fi, with one sampler, one keyboard, and an Atari computer, yet the result would revolutionize the UK dance scene. Simons had 500 copies pressed up, before a meeting with producer/remixer Andrew Weatherall saw the single licensed to Weatherall's own Junior Boy's Own label, and given a monstrous Sabres of Paradise remix. By the end of 1992, Rowlands had quit Ariel, and with remixes for Leftfield and Lionrock under their belt, the Dust Brothers were preparing their next release, the *14th Century Sky* EP, opening with what would become the duo's signature theme, "Chemical Beats."

The *My Mercury Mouth* EP followed, together with a slew of remix work — St. Etienne's "Like a Motorway," the Charlatans' "Patrol," Primal Scream's "Jailbird," and more. The pair made their live debut at Weatherall's Sabresonic Club, then went on the road to DJ Primal Scream's 1994 British tour.

The duo's fame was traveling fast — so fast, in fact, that it reached the ears of the American Dust Brothers, who contacted them, requesting the Englishmen change their name. The pair became the Chemical Brothers later that year, and in early 1995, began a residency at the legendary Heavenly Sunday Social in London. A mix album, *Live at the Heavenly Social*, would appear early the following year.

Signed now to Virgin, the Chemical Brothers released their next single, "Leave Home" (UK #17) in June 1995. Featuring remixes by Weatherall and Underworld, it was quickly followed by *ExitPlanet Dust* — a set which Virgin came close to scrapping after hearing the duo's recent remixes for labelmates the Manic Street Preachers' "La Tristessa Durera." Their techniques were advancing so quickly that *Exit Planet Dust* already sounded dated.

That same month, the Chemicals DJ-ed the dance tent at the Glastonbury Festival; there they encountered Oasis' Noel Gallagher, already a confirmed fan, and now a willing collaborator. Over the next three months, he contributed vocals to a new Chemicals track, "Setting Sun"; scheduled for a fall release, it was ultimately postponed for another year, while Virgin and Oasis' label, EPic, argued over who would release it.(It finally went to Virgin.)

In the meantime, the band undertook a collaboration with Charlatan Tim Burgess, "Life Is Sweet" (#25 UK) — there would also be a *Charlatans vs the Chemical Brothers* EP released, featuring four Chemical remixes of material from the Charlatans' eponymous fourth album. Early 1996 saw the *Loops of Fury* EP (#13 UK), but it was "Setting Sun" (#80 US, #1 UK) which set the pace, with the Chemicals touring almost non-stop through the year, appearing alongside Oasis and The Charlatans at Knebworth, and headlining the Brixton Academy.

A new single, "Block Rockin' Beats" (#1 UK) was released in early 1997, and proved immediately that "Setting Sun" was no Oasis-driven freak. An instant smash, it paved the way for the Chemicals' second album, *Dig Your Own Hole* (#14 US, #1 UK), to repeat the same feat in April. Even more amazingly, the record climbed the charts in America, an achievement which would, of course, open the door for the Prodigy's equally spectacular annexation of US dance floors later in the year.

Singles "Elektrobank" and the limited edition "Private Psychedelic Reel" (featuring Mercury Rev's Jonathan Donahue) followed, while 1998 saw the Chemicals' current DJ-ing set preserved with the release of *Brothers Gonna Work It Out*, a dynamic mix album which blended remixes of their own material ("Not Another Drugstore," "Block Rockin' Beats," "Morning Lemon") with cuts drawn from across the musical spectrum, from Meat Beat Manifesto and The Manics, to the Love Corporation and The Jimmy Castor Bunch.

With the band already on the road, the Chemicals' own next album, *Surrender* (#32 US, #1 UK), arrived in June 1999, bearing collaborations with New Order's Bernard Sumner, Mazzy Star's Hope Sandoval, and Primal Scream's Bobby Gillespie. It was followed by the moody, remix-stacked "Hey Boy, Hey Girl" (#3 UK) and a second collaboration with Oasis' Noel Gallagher, "Let Forever Be" (#9 UK).

Chemical Brothers LPs

8 Exit Planet Dust (Astralwerks) 1995 Rooted firmly to the club culture where they served their phat beat apprenticeship, *Dust* soars through the livid "In Dust We Trust" and "Song to the Siren," then self-defines the future with the astonishing "Chemical Beats."

9 Dig Your Own Hole (Astralwerks) 1997 Darker and richer than its predecessor, *Dig* is a bass-driven monster devouring all in its path, flowing like a tidal wave, the perfect club in a little plastic jewel case. "Block Rocking Beats" and the Oasis-fuelled "Setting Sun" set difficult precedents, but elsewhere, too, the Brothers continue to find intriguing sounds and samples, while toying with a diversity of styles that they easily transform into their own.

7 Surrender (Virgin) 1999

Selected Compilations and Archive Releases

8 Live at the Social Volume One (Heavenly) 1996
7 Brothers Gonna Work It Out (Astralwerks) 1998 The changing face of the Chemical Brothers, one live set from 1996, one mix tape from 1998, both full-speed excitement and energy, both oozing the ideas which would flavor the future.

Chemical Brothers — Remixes 1993–99
1993 LEFTFIELD/LYDON — Open Up (Hard Hands)
1993 ARIEL — T Baby (Deconstruction)
1993 LIONROCK — Packet of Peace (Deconstruction)
1993 SWORDFISH — The Get On (Pandephonium)
1994 CHARLATANS UK — Patrol (Beggars Banquet)
1994 MANIC STREET PREACHERS — Faster [THREE MIXES] (Sony)
1994 MANIC STREET PREACHERS — La Tristesse Durera [TWO MIXES] (Sony)
1994 JUSTIN WARFIELD — Pick Y'All Up [TWO MIXES] (Qwest)
1994 MANIC STREET PREACHERS — Everything Must Go (Sony)
1994 ST. ETIENNE — Like a Motorway [TWO MIXES] (Heavenly)
1994 PRIMAL SCREAM — Jailbird (Creation)
1994 PRODIGY — Voodoo People [TWO MIXES] (Mute)
1995 CHARLATANS UK — Nine Acre Dust (Beggars Banquet)
1995 SANDALS — Feet [TWO MIXES] (FFRR/Opentoe)
1995 SABRES OF PARADISE — Versus Towtruck (Warp)
1995 BOMB THE BASS — Bug Powder Dust (4th & Broadway)
1995 CHARLATANS UK — Chemical Risk Dub (Beggars Banquet)
1996 METHOD MAN — Bring the Pain (Def Jam)
1996 DEEPER THROAT — Mouth Organ featuring Michael Holden (Stumble)
1996 DAVE CLARKE — No-one's Driving (Deconstruction)
1997 REPUBLICA — Out of this World (Deconstruction)
1998 SPIRITUALIZED — I Think I'm in Love [TWO MIXES] (Dedicated)
1998 DUST BROTHERS — Realize (Dreamworks)
1999 MERCURY REV — Delta Sun Bottleneck Stomp (V2)

BILLY CHILDISH

BORN *William Hamper, 1959 (Chatham, Kent, England)*

When Billy Childish made his first venture into the world of recorded sound, in 1979 at the helm of the Pop Rivits, nobody — not even Childish himself — could have prophesied what the next two decades would bring: namely, one of the greatest, and certainly one of the largest, artist catalogs in rock history, a tally which had already reached 50 full-length albums by 1990, and was pushing the century just in time for the millennium.

In that time, the self-confessed dyslexic has also published a small library full of poetry, short stories, and chapbooks, exhibited his artwork around the world, and birthed the Stuckism school of painting, dedicated to overthrowing the shock value "art" of dead cows and piles of excrement.

He also masterminded one of the most courageous independent record labels around, the similarly prolific Hangman; and almost incidentally, sired at least three very separate, and musically disparate musical genres — the Medway Beat boom which brought both his own bands, and the likes of the Prisoners and the Len Bright Combo to prominence; a garage revival which in turn tagged onto the rockabilly boom of the mid-1980s; and grunge, the peculiarly Pacific Northwest-flavored return to guitar rock which, members of Mudhoney were adamant, could never have happened without Childish's own manic input. For that alone, Childish's recruitment to Seattle's Sub Pop label was the least he deserved.

It took Sub Pop's patronage to persuade Childish's homeland media to pay any attention to him. As frontman, successively and often simultaneously, of the Pop Rivits, the Milkshakes, Thee Mighty Caesars, and Thee Headcoats, Childish had been haunting the fringes of the UK music press consciousness for over a decade. But his refusal to map out a career, as opposed to zig-zagging around one, ensured that most magazines didn't even bother to review his latest album, because by the time it appeared in print, Childish would already have another one out.

The very separate characteristics of his sundry identities, however, ensured that there would be very little repetition across those discs — again, a phenomenal achievement given his prolificity. The Pop Rivits' raucous pop was succeeded, in 1981, by the Milkshakes' R&B basement growl; the Blackhands' menacing country-blues by Childish's solo excursions into folk and spoken word; and underpinning everything, a willingness to expose every last aspect of the creative process, via releases for demos, live shows, and anything else which takes his fancy.

Childish formed the Pop Rivits in 1977, after quitting his first (and only) job at the local Chatham dockyard, and getting into St. Martin's College of Art in London, on the strength of 600 or so drawings he'd completed at the docks. He remained there for half a semester, then returned home to begin a fanzine, *Chatham's Burning*. Childish's own metamorphosis from punk auteur to one-man music industry was gradual, best pinpointed by the Pop Rivits' 1981 decision to rename themselves Mickey and the Milkshakes, after Childish linked with Pop Rivits roadie Mickey Hampshire (guitar) and Banana Bertie (drums), themselves already leading a band called the Milkshakes, who occasionally opened for the Pop Rivits.

Unbound by any constraints beyond those they chose to adopt themselves, the Milkshakes would score three minor hits during 1983–84, "Soldiers of Love" (#35 UK indy), a cover of Vince Taylor's "Brand New Cadillac" (#37 UK indy) and "Ambassadors of Love" (#16 UK indy). However, they attracted the most attention in 1984, when they released four albums on the same day — simply because they could. Surprisingly, then, the band's demise the following year was not caused by exhaustion; rather, Childish, Hampshire, and the rhythm section of Bruce Brand, and Russ Wilkins (replaced for a time by John Agnew) had a new band in mind, the not entirely dissimilar Thee Mighty Caesars.

Brand and Wilkins left soon after, to join Eric Goulden's Captains of Industry/Len Bright Combo project. Thee Mighty Caesars, however, continued on, buoyed by Childish's own insistence that "this is Punk Rock/Rhythm and Beat as it should be, three chords, cheap gear and a healthy dose of hatred and contempt for the outside world."

In 1989, Childish launched Thee Headcoats, just as the Sub Pop connection took off. Inspired, equally, by Sherlock Holmes and '60s cult rockers the Downliners Sect, Thee Headcoats originally featured the returning Brand and bassist Ollie Dolat (replaced by Johnny "Tubs" Johnson), and would emerge Childish's most consistent project yet.

Whilst maintaining his tradition of recording everything in his own home studio, the group's actual repertoire maintained a creative edge not always apparent in their R&B rehashes — an adventurousness kept alive, too, by the existence of Thee Headcoatees, an all-girl parallel featuring Childish's girlfriend, Kyra DeConinck. (A similar project, the all-girl Del Monas, shadowed Thee Milkshakes for much of their life.)

Unlike so many other advocates of "lo-fi" recording, however, Childish was less interested in recording bad songs badly, than in utilizing natural spaces and echoes within his work — techniques largely extinguished by modern technology. Although he later upgraded to a spare bedroom at his mother's house, for many years an empty back room in his own home was his favored studio for rock recordings; "the bathroom's best for the blues stuff," he recommended. "The mike goes in the bath."

Despite such ingenuity, coupled with the undeniably restless creativity which is both Childish's greatest asset and his personal curse, he remains all but unknown in the UK — and prefers it that way. "I never speak to the British press, " he admitted in 1990. "They never print what I say, so why bother?' A decade later, he had relented somewhat, and a profile in the *Guardian* newspaper in September 1999, did point out that already that year, he had released ten albums. All the journalist really cared about, though, was an affair Childish had enjoyed 17 years earlier, with controversial conceptual artist Tracey Emin — herself one of the prime targets of Stuckism. The irony of the situation was not lost on Childish.

Also see the entry for "HANGMAN RECORDS" on page 774 in "PRODUCERS & LABELS."

Billy Childish LPs

8 **I've Got Everything Indeed (Hangman — UK) 1987**

7 **I Remember... (Hangman — UK) 1987** Shockingly authentic solo rhythm'n'blues.

8 **Poems of Laughter and Violence (Hangman — UK) 1988** Largely spoken word poetry and prose recitations. Harrowingly intimate.

Selected Compilations and Archive Releases

8 **The 1982 Cassettes (Hangman — UK) 1987** Poor recording quality doesn't disguise the passion, although it's still a shock to realize this apparent vintage field recording of blues from the Medway Delta was made in 1982 in Childish's bathroom.

6 **Fifty Albums Great (Hangman) 1990** Unplugged renditions of the catalog's greatest bits. Oddly lacking a certain passionate fury.

9 **I Am the Billy Childish (Sub Pop) 1991** Two discs, two hours, condensing too many albums to buy in one sitting, into a manageable menage of one cut per platter. That's 50 songs down, just 500 more to go....

7 **The Sudden Fart of Laughter (Dog Meat) 1992**

4 **Der Henkerman — Kitchen Recordings (Tom Produkt) 1992**

5 **Torments Nest (Ay Carrambra) 1993**

8 **Native American Sampler (Sub Pop) 1993** Benefit album drawing from a decade's worth of native American themed songs and spoken word.

8 **Hunger at the Moon (Sympathy for the Record Industry) 1993**

2 **Made with a Passion (Sympathy for the Record Industry) 1996** Very rough demos, buyer beware. Or very forgiving.

8 **Crimes of the Future (Sympathy for the Record Industry) 1999** Seven tracks apiece from *I've Got Everything* and *I Remember*, and tastes from sundry other albums, singles, and compilations (plus three new recordings), 29-track sampler of Childish's very best blues recordings. The rougher recordings are weeded out, although with a voice and guitar sound like this, it's never going to get too slick.

Billy Childish and Dan Melchior LP

7 **Devil in the Flesh (Sympathy for the Record Industry) 1998** More Dan than Billy, but a surging blues package regardless.

Wild Billy Childish and Big Russ Wilkins LP

6 **Laughing Gravy (Empire — UK) 1987**

Billy Childish and Sexton Ming LP

5 **Which Dead Donkey Daddy? (Hangman — UK) 1987**

6 **Plump Prizes and Little Gems (Hangman — UK) 1987**

6 **Ypres 1917 Overture (Hangman — UK) 1987**

5 **The Cheeky Cheese (Damaged Goods — UK) 1999**

Billy Childish and the Black Hands LPs

8 **Play: Capt'n Calypso's Hoodoo Party (Hangman — UK) 1988** Everyone knows how Robert Johnson sold his soul to the devil. Imagine if the devil sold his soul to Robert Johnson?

7 **The Original Chatham Jack (Sub Pop) 1992** Home-made instruments, homemade blues, recorded with a solitary mike on the far side of the bayou. A tight whining hiss that sits and howls majestically.

6 **Live in the Netherlands (Hangman — UK) 1993**

Pop Rivits LPs

6 **Empty Sounds From Anarchy Ranch (Hypocrite — UK) 1979**

7 **Greatest Hits (Hypocrite — UK) 1980** Sloppy, noisy home recordings, the definitive Pop Rivits sound.

Selected Compilations and Archive Releases

7 **Fun in the UK (Jims — UK) 1987** Well chosen compilation from the two original albums.

5 **Live in Germany 1979 (Hangman — UK) 1990**
6 **Chatham's Burning (Damaged Goods — UK) 1997** Mono crashing, bashing, and thundering — there's a band playing somewhere as well.

Thee Milkshakes LPs

5 **Talking 'Bout (Milkshakes — UK) 1981** Actually credited to Mickey (Hampshire) and the Milkshakes, a flaccid garage stomper compared to the marvels to come.

8 **14 Rhythm & Beat Greats (Milkshakes — UK) 1983**

7 After School Session (Upright — UK) 1983 Covers (or they ought to be) heavy, the 'shakes simply hammering through their repertoire with little finesse but a lot of attitude.

8 IV: The Men With the Golden Greats (Milkshakes — UK) 1983 Brooding beat instrumental collection, aggressive, and masterful in equal doses.

7 20 Rock & Roll Hits of the 50s and 60s (Big Beat — UK) 1984

8 In Germany (All City — UK) 1984

7 Nothing Can Stop These Men (Milkshakes — UK) 1984 Two similarly-rooted collections of all-original rockers.

6 They Came They Saw They Conquered (Pink Dust) 1984

8 Thee Knights of Trashe (Milkshakes — UK) 1984

7 The Last Night at the Mic (Empire) 1985

8 Thee Milkshakes vs The Prisoners (Media Burn) 1985 Both twin the 'shakes with the similarly-themed Prisoners for better beer or worse.

7 Live From Chatham [LIVE] (Hangman — UK) 1987

Selected Compilations and Archive Releases

7 Showcase (Brain Eater) 1983

7 The Milkshakes Revenge (Hangman — UK) 1987 Recorded 1984, the "missing" ninth album.

6 The 107 Tapes (Media Burn) 1986 Early (1981) demos and live from a German show in 1983.

8 19th Nervous Shakedown (Big Beat — UK) 1990 The first Milkshakes CD, and a valuable career-long retrospective.

Thee Mighty Caesars LPs

6 Thee Mighty Caesars (Milkshakes — UK) 1985 Oddly transitional set, from the garage trash of Thee Milkshakes to the trashy punk of the new identity.

8 Beware the Ides of March (Big Beat — UK) 1985

7 The Caesars of Trash (Milkshakes — UK) 1986

8 Acropolis Now (Milkshakes — UK) 1986 With organ added to the brew, think Question Mark and some very brutal Mysterions — "you're gonna cry 96 tears or we're gonna find out why."

5 Live in Rome [LIVE] (Big Beat — UK) 1986

6 Wiseblood (Ambassador — UK) 1987

7 John Lennon's Corpse Revisited (Crypt) 1989 The *Sgt Pepper* type cover suggests a new psychedelic direction. It would be wrong.

Selected Compilations and Archive Releases

5 Don't Give Any Dinner to Henry Chinaski (Hangman — UK) 1987 Early demos... you have been warned.

7 Punk Rock Showcase (Hangman — UK) 1987

8 Thusly, Thee Mighty Caesar's Punk Rock Showcase (Crypt) 1988

8 Surely They Were the Sons of God (Crypt) 1989

6 Caesar's Pleasure (Big Beat — UK) 1994

7 Caesar's Remains (Hangman — UK) 1996

Thee Headcoats LPs

6 Headcoats Down (Hangman — UK) 1989

5 Earls of Suavedom (Crypt) 1990

8 The Kids Are All Square — This Is Hip! (Hangman — UK) 1990 Zeroing in on what would become Thee Headcoats' forte, itself an amalgam of Thee Milkshakes, Thee Mighty Caesars, and an obsession with (in no particular order) Sherlock Holmes' hat and The Downliners Sect, possibly Childish's most "conventional" release yet.

7 Heavens to Murgatroyd, It's Thee Headcoats Already (Sub Pop) 1990 Very much intended for the novice (and with the Sub Pop crowd singing his praises, there were many), new material rubs shoulders with re-recorded oldies.

7 Headcoatitude (Shaking Street — UK) 1991

6 Bo in Thee Garage (Hangman — UK) 1991

5 Cavern by the Sea (K) 1991

6 The Wurst Is Yet to Come [LIVE] (Tom Product) 1992

7 Good Times Are Killing Me (Vinyl Japan) 1993

4 Live at the Wild Western Room (Damaged Goods — UK) 1994

9 Conundrum (Super Electro) 1994 The sub-title says it all, "ripping off the non-entities of yesterday, influencing the stars of tomorrow." Opening with the child-molestation of "Every Bit of Me," the Headcoats' blackest album haunts the extremes of emotion, while the garage door slams and the exhaust fumes build in the corner.

6 In Tweed We Trust (Damaged Goods) 1996 After increasing their punk quotient to almost parodic levels, a sharp turn back to the early sound.

8 The Sounds of the Baskerville (Overground) 1996

8 Knights of the Baskervilles (Birdman) 1996 The instrumental credits range from mandolin to onion twine, a harmonica and a rattle, but it's what they do with them that counts, battered urban blues and the amazing "By the Hairs of My Chinny Chin Chin."

7 Jimmy Reed Experience (Get Hip) 1997 (7) Driving tribute to Jimmy Reed, the solo Childish's most potent influence, and it shows.

8 The Messerschmitt Pilot's Severed Hand (Damaged Goods) 1998

8 Brother Is Dead but Fly Is Gone (Vinyl Japan) 1998 Deranged punk tribute collection, which sees Johnny Moped ("Darling, Let's Have Another Baby"), the Buzzcocks, The Clash, and Richard Hell embracing the nuggets from that earlier firestorm, "Louie Louie," "Diddy Wah Diddy," and a couple of oldies once favored by the Sex Pistols, "Don't Give Me No Lip" and "Whatcha Gonna Do About It?"

7 17 Percent — Hendrix Was Not the Only Musician (Sympathy for the Record Industry) 1999 Packaged with a book and a reproduction of Childish's 1972 school report (source of the title), *Hendrix* kicks off with the mildly self-analytical "Art Or Arse," then bad-temperedly bristles on for 13 more songs worth of tried and trusted mettle.

Selected Compilations and Archive Releases

7 Beach Bums Must Die (Crypt) 1990

8 Best. Sherlock Holmes Meets the Punkenstein Monster (Nippon Columbia — JAPAN) 1998

Headcoat Sect LPs

6 Deerstalking Men (Hangman's Daughter — UK) 1996 Garage classics and Childish originals, with Downliner Don Crane growling the vocals.

7 Ready Sect Go (Vinyl Japan) 2000 More of the same, in a killer period jacket.

Thee Headcoatees LPs

7 Girlsville (Hangman — UK) 1991 The female Headcoats (of course), with the boy band backing their post Shangri-La/Shaggs vocals. And no more or less essential than it should be.

7 Have Love Will Travel (Vinyl Japan) 1992

8 Ballad of an Insolent Pup (Vinyl Japan) 1994

7 Bozstik Haze (Vinyl Japan) 1997 Look no further for *the* definitive version of "I Want Candy"... and more besides, of course.

8 Punk Girls (Sympathy for the Record Industry) 1997 Originals clash with classic punk originals, "Ca Plane Pour Moi" and "Teenage Kicks" included.

5 Taylor Meets Thee Headcoatees (Lissy's — UK) 1998 That's Woodie Taylor, star of Headcoatee Holly GoLightly's solo albums, remixing six past classics to uncompromising degrees of weirdness.

8 Here Comes Cessation (Vinyl Japan) 1999

Selected Compilations and Archive Releases

9 The Sisters of Suave (Damaged Goods — UK) 1999 The endearingly saucy "Come Into My Mouth" became a legend even among people who never heard the original single; "My Boyfriend's Learning Karate," on the other hand, is the song Shampoo should have covered if they wanted to get past one half-decent album. Thee Headcoatees' singles collection, 16 tracks strong and the first time on CD for most of them.

Billy Childish and the Singing Loins LP

4 At the Bridge (Damaged Goods — UK) 1993

CHILLS

FORMED 1980 *(Dunedin, New Zealand)*
ORIGINAL LINE-UP *Martin Phillipps (b. 7/2/63, Dunedin, NZ — vocals, guitar); Rachel Phillipps (guitar); Jane Todd (bass); Alan Haig (b. 8/5/61 — drums)*

Martin Phillipps was the 15-year-old guitarist with the Same, one of New Zealand's first ever punk bands, contemporaries of the Enemy and the early Clean, but doomed to shatter without ever recording. From the band's final line-up, however, Phillipps recruited his sister Rachel and future Verlaines mainstay Jane Todd to a new band he was forming with former Clean vocalist Peter Gutteridge, the Chills.

With a firm grasp on Gutteridge's own love for psychedelia, the Chills made their live debut at Dunedin's Coronation Hall, opening for Bored Games and The Clean on November 15, 1980. Gutteridge left soon after; by June 1981, Dodd and Rachel Phillipps, too, had quit, and with the Chills apparently moribund, Martin Phillipps was an ad hoc member of the Clean, playing keyboards on their first single, "Tally Ho!," and on the road.

In July 1981, Phillipps reconvened the Chills with Alan Haig, and two former members of the Bored Games, Fraser Batts (keyboards/guitar) and Terry Moore (b. 10/27/61 — bass). It was this line-up which would record the Chills' vinyl debut, contributing two tracks to April 1982's *Dunedin Double* various artists EP, released by Flying Nun shortly after Haig quit to join the Verlaines. He was replaced by Martyn Bull (b. 6/17/61), while Rachel Phillipps would return to the Chills to replace Battson the eve of a north island tour with the Clean.

She did not remain on board for the full outing; the last dates of the tour saw the Chills appear as a trio, a formation which would record a pair of singles with Chris Knox of the Tall Dwarfs, November 1982's "Rolling Moon" and 1984's "Pink Frost." Future plans, however, were placed on indefinite hold after Bull was diagnosed with leukemia, and over the next six months, the Chills would emerge only when Bull's health permitted.

With Peter Allison on keyboards, the band played a handful of gigs, while Phillipps would also jam with the Clean's David Kilgour, in a new band, Time Flies — the group never played in public however. In June 1983, the Chills finally acknowledged that Bull was unlikely to return to action, and with his blessing, invited Haig to rejoin. The reconstituted band had barely played a handful of shows when the 22-year-old Bull died, on July 18, 1983.

Devastated, the Chills immediately withdrew again, and while Phillipps would play a handful of solo shows through late 1983, it would be December before the band reappeared, with a new lineup of Phillipps, Haig, Allison and Martin Kean (bass), and a new name, A Wrinkle In Time.

That change was short lived; by the time the band joined Flying Nun's Looney tour in early 1984, alongside Children's Hour, The Expendables, and Doublehappys, the group was again the Chills. However, personality problems were gnawing away at the line-up. In the public eye, the Chills were seen as little more than Phillipps' backing band — an understandable mistake given the number of personnel changes which he alone had survived, but a grievous one all the same.

This impression was only increased after "Pink Frost," recorded two years earlier with Martyn Bull, and dedicated to the drummer's memory, became the Chills' first New Zealand hit single. They followed up with "Doledrums," and The Lost EP (#31 UK indy), a collection of recordings from the past year or so, which had never been completed.

The band held together for a handful of London dates in late 1985, and in March 1986, Flying Nun released the Kaleidoscope World (#3 UK indy) compilation in the UK and US, wrapping up many of the band's early recordings, plus a new New Zealand hit single, "I'll Only See You Alone Again." By October, however, Phillipps had pieced together a new Chills line-up, featuring the classically trained ex-Smart Russians keyboard player Andrew Todd (b. 12/15/58), Coconut Rough's Justin Harwood (b. 7/6/65 — bass) and former Verlaine Caroline Easther (b. 11/30/58 — drums).

This line-up would record one of the Chills' best known numbers, "I Love My Leather Jacket" (#25 UK indy), written by Phillipps about the last gift Martyn Bull ever gave him. A #4 in New Zealand, the single's success prompted the Chills to relocate to London in February 1987, and begin a five-week tour of Europe. Then, back in London, they linked with producer Mayo Thompson of Red Crayola, to record their long-awaited debut album, Brave Words (#7 UK indy).

June 1987 saw the Chills play the Glastonbury Festival with a 60,000+ audience — the largest they had ever appeared before. Two months later, they flew to New York to appear at the New Music Seminar. They returned to London for further European and UK tours (they became only the third western band ever to play in East Germany), appeared on the John Peel show, and scored another hit with "House with a Hundred Rooms" (#21 UK indy). They then returned to New Zealand in November, for sell-out tours of that country and Australia.

Easther quit in the new year, suffering ear problems, and was replaced by 17-year-old former Bygone Era drummer James Stephenson; he arrived just as the band set out for another US visit, one which culminated in the Chills becoming the first Flying Nun act ever to join a major overseas label, when they were signed by Slash/Warner Brothers.

Back in London in early 1989, the Chills linked with Pixies producer Gary Smith, to record their sophomore album, Submarine Bells. Very well-received across Europe, and a college chart topper in the US, the album's release launched the band into an intensive spell of gigging, running up another underground smash with "Heavenly Pop Hit," and again, their return to New Zealand was triumphant. In Dunedin, the band were treated to an official mayoral reception, while every show on the tour was a sell-out. Submarine Bells was the country's number one album, and the world appeared to be at the Chills' fingertips. Instead they broke up.

Todd quit first, followed by Harwood (he later resurfaced in Luna); swiftly, Phillipps and Stephenson recruited Terry Moore from the 1981–82 band line-up, and in July 1991, the trio began demoing for their next album. From there, they traveled to Burbank to record with Church/Shriekback producer Gavin MacKillop, also recruiting dB's frontman Peter Holsapple as keyboard player.

Unfortunately, before work began, Stephenson quit, citing homesickness and, apparently, personality clashes with the newcomer; Phillipps and Moore replaced him with Mauro Ruby, adding Lisa Mednick (b. 6/27/57 — keyboards) and ex-Clay Idols Steven Schayer (b. 2/12/65 — backing vocals) to the brew, before beginning work on what would become Soft Bomb. Renowned arranger Van Dyke Parks would also enter the picture, scoring the magical "Water Wolves."

With the first single from the album, "Male Monster from the Id," establishing itself as the most added track on US college radio, the Chills hit the road in July 1992, now lining up as Phillipps, Moore, Mednick, Schayer, and Earl Robertson (b. 4/15/62 — drums). A full 100 shows were on the itinerary, but early into the outing, following shows in New Zealand and Australia, it became apparent that Robertson was not fitting into the band. He was promptly sent home, and replaced by the Abel Tasmans' Craig Mason (b. 7/28/61) — already aboard the entourage as lighting man.

"Double Summer," a new single, arrived as the tour reached the US; unfortunately, line-up problems were still creating waves in the band, while ticket sales were also lower than expected. Still the group might have survived had their record labels not suddenly panicked. Slash announced they would no longer be promoting the album in either the US or the UK, at which point the company's UK distributor, London, withdrew its support for the still upcoming tour. Phillipps responded by breaking up the band following their final US date, and making no secret of the reasons why.

He returned to Dunedin to try and resolve the snake pit of legal, financial, and contractual problems with which he had suddenly been left; somehow he avoided bankruptcy, but musically, his efforts were restricted to occasional solo performances around Dunedin, and a berth in David Kilgour's '60's covers band, the Pop Art Toasters.

While the Chills were remembered with the *Heavenly Pop Hits* compilation, Phillipps worked on a collection of his solo demos and works in progress, *Sketch Book*. When the Clean reformed in early 1995, Phillipps joined as second guitarist; he also compiled a Chills rarities album, and began work on a biography of the band. That April, too, he, Kilgour and Haig played a few shows as the April Fools, and recorded a new song, "Under Your Face," for a benefit album.

In mid-1995, Phillipps moved to Auckland and began putting together a fresh band, with Dominic Blazer (keyboards), Steven Shaw (bass), and ex-Book of Martyrs Jonathan Armstrong (drums). Dubbed Martin Phillipps and The Chills, the group was scheduled to fly to London in July, to begin work on a new album. Phillipps flew in first; when the band attempted to follow him, however, problems with their visas saw Immigration send them straight back home again. Phillipps stayed on, cutting *Sunburnt* with session men Dave Mattacks (ex-Fairport Convention — drums) and Dave Gregory (ex-XTC — bass), and New York producer Craig Leon.

The album did little, and Phillipps returned to New Zealand, and linked again with the band. Blazer quit, to be replaced by Andrew Taylor; by August 1996, the new recruit, too, had departed, alongside Shaw, and a new line-up, featuring Armstrong, Phil Kusabs (bass) and Tom Miskin (drums), played several shows.

October 1999, saw another new line-up of Martin Phillipps and The Chills, featuring Rodney Haworth, Todd Knudson, and James Dickson. A December tour of New Zealand concluded in Auckland on New Year's Eve, opening Split Enz's millennium concert.

Also see the entry for the "CLEAN" on page 273.

The Chills LPs

6 Brave Words (Flying Nun — NZ) 1987 After so many killer singles and EPs (collected on *Kaleidoscope World*), the first full blast of the Chills was disappointing — although "Wet Blanket" and "16 Heart Throbs" would dignify any best-of the band.

8 Submarine Bells (Slash) 1990 Mischievously well-paced set, hard-nosed rockers ("Familiarity Breeds Contempt") and reflective post goth ("Part Past Part Fiction") side-by-side with the most perfectly named song of the year, "Heavenly Pop Hit." (Of course it wasn't.)

8 Softbomb (Slash) 1992 In other hands, "Song for Randy Newman Etc" could have descended into sour grapes territory; for Phillipps, its acknowledgement of so many kindred spirits is both moving and honest. The magnificent "Water Wolves" and the insubstantial but stunning "Double Summer" rate highly, too.

Martin Phillipps and the Chills LPs

5 Sunburnt (Flying Nun — NZ) 1996 Solid, but not too memorable collection scarred by the inadvertent loss of his entire band.

Selected Compilations and Archive Releases

8 Kaleidoscope World (Flying Nun — NZ) 1985 Devastating round-up of early singles and oddities, including the legendary "Pink Frost" and (US editions only) the *Lost* EP.

8 Heavenly Pop Hits (Flying Nun — NZ) 1994

7 Sketch Book Volume One (Flying Nun — NZ) 1999 Rough demos and oddities, but the rudiments for three or four great lost albums.

CHINA CRISIS

FORMED 1979 *(Liverpool, England)*
ORIGINAL LINE-UP *Gary Daly (b. 5/10/62 — vocals, keyboards); Eddie Lundon (b. 6/9/62 — guitar, keyboards)*

Despite forming amid the wave of new bands washing out of Liverpool in the late 1970s, it took China Crisis close to three years of constant local gigging to make a small mark on even the Liverpool scene when they signed to Inevitable (former home of Pete Wylie and Dead or Alive) and released their debut single, "African and White."

An immediate radio hit that summer of 1981, the single attracted Virgin records, who released the band's second single, "Scream Down at Me," in early 1982; that release flopped, but a reissue of "African and White" (#45 UK) in August 1981, set the stage for China Crisis' debut album, *Difficult Shapes and Passive Rhythms* (#21 UK), and a tour with the then-rising, but still savage Simple Minds.

Both placed China Crisis close to the heart of the postpunk dance scene — even the album sleeve designer, Peter Saville, was best known for his work with Joy Division and New Order, while the band's music unquestionably possessed that bleak quirk which hallmarked the mood of the British rock underground. "No More Blue Horizons" mysteriously missed the chart, but two further hits in 1982, "Christian" (#12 UK) and "Tragedy and Mystery" (#46 UK), swiftly consolidated China Crisis' breakthrough,

Previewed by a single of its title track (#48 UK) in October 1983, China Crisis' second album, *Working With Fire and Steel: Possible Pop Songs Volume Two* (#20 UK) contrarily presented a group which was not afraid to mess with the mainstream. Now augmented by Gazza Johnson (bass) and Kevin Wilkinson (drums), the band's sound was broadening immeasurably, away from the dislocating shuffle of their debut. Daly and Lundon's fascination with '70s studio mavens Steely Dan was no secret, but nobody ever expected that interest to be reciprocated. When Dan mainman Walter

Becker agreed to produce their next record, China Crisis' future seemed pre-ordained.

While the singles "Wishful Thinking" (#9 UK) and "Hanna Hanna" (#44 UK) covered their absence, the band spent most of the next year, 1984, recording with Becker, and with both parties painstakingly pursuing perfection, the ensuing (and so wryly titled) *Flaunt The Imperfection* (#9 UK) could not help but emerge among the most anticipated albums of the age — all the more so after its original release in early 1985 was cancelled after the band was involved in an auto accident, while returning from a studio session. Although the worst injury was the broken jaw sustained by Johnson, the group's plans for the next months were pushed back, and it was May before the album finally emerged.

Flaunt the Imperfection marked the peak of China Crisis' studio ambition. The hits "Black Man Ray" (#14 UK), "King in a Catholic Style (Wake Up)" (#19 UK), and "You Did Cut Me" (#54 UK) introduced a whole new sound to the chart (and the nation: China Crisis impersonators would be coming out of the woodwork over the next couple of years). But it was also possible to have too much of such a good-sounding thing. "Highest High," the band's next single, sank without trace, and when China Crisis re-emerged the following year, they, too, had drawn back from the brink of flawless sonics.

What Price Paradise? (#63 UK) was recorded with Clive Langer and Alan Winstanley (Madness, etc); it could not help but strip back from the lush, layered acreage of its predecessor. Yet two singles — "Arizona Sky" (#47 UK) and "Best Kept Secret" (#36 UK) — fared as poorly as the album (a third, "June Bride," flopped), and when it came time to record their next album, China Crisis again opted for a prolonged period of recording. Much of 1987 was spent in Hawaii, recording at George Benson's island set-up, but the ensuing *Diary of a Hollow Horse* (#58 UK) proved the group's least successful (and most expensive) album yet.

Two final singles, "St. Saviour Square" and "Red Letter Day" failed to chart, and in 1990, Virgin bade farewell to China Crisis with a hits collection (#32 UK), and a Steve Procter remix of "African and White." The band itself shattered (Wilkinson later joined Howard Jones' band), but Daly and Lundon elected to continue on together, retaining the China Crisis identity.

They returned in 1994 with the single "Every Day the Same," and a brace of albums which looked back over the last decade even as they looked ahead to the next, the amusingly titled *Warped By Success*, and the live unplugged set *Acoustically Yours* — accompanied by a single of "Black Man Ray." The group also remained active through the remainder of the decade, albeit on a much smaller scale than they once had known. Regular gigs through 1997/98 climaxed with a headline appearance at the Knowsley Summer Arts festival.

China Crisis LPs

8 Difficult Shapes and Passive Rhythms, Some People Think It's Fun to Entertain (Virgin) 1982 Bleak and claustrophobic, the sons of the Bunnymen and kin of Joy Division, taking tentative strides outside their shell with the difficult funk of a rerecorded "African and White," and more in an endearingly similar vein.

7 Working With Fire and Steel: Possible Pop Songs Volume 2 (Virgin) 1983 Angular melancholy heightened by some genuinely perceptive oboe and strings, a producer (Mike Howlett)'s album as much as the band's, but packed with Crisis class.

3 Flaunt the Imperfection (Virgin) 1985 "The World Spins I Am Part of It" is a dead ringer for a contemporary Simple Minds out-take, but whereas Minds were boring and knew it, China Crisis were suddenly laboring under the impression that their newfound pomposity and borrowed belligerence still meant something.

4 What Price Paradise? (Virgin) 1986 Langer-Winstanley turn in a typically bright production, but the band's self-consciousness simply doesn't let up. What price a decent album?

7 Diary of a Hollow Horse (Virgin) 1989 With Becker returning as producer, odds were high that recent failings would be amplified further. Instead, the dying band actually decided to live a little, turning in the dramatic "All My Prayers" and the lovely "St. Saviour's Square."

8 Warped By Success (Stardumb — UK) 1994

5 Acoustically Yours (Telegraph — UK) 1995 After the crushingly lounge-like facelessness of *Warped...*, a return to at least a degree of intemperance — "African and White" is reassuringly funky, "Wishful Thinking" touchingly whimsical, and "Black Man Ray" has a soulful edge marred only by some terrible vocals.

Selected Compilations and Archive Releases

6 China Crisis Collection (Virgin) 1990

6 Diary: A Collection (Virgin) 1992 Remarkably similar best of's, highlighting the original hits, and the band's slow descent.

3 The Best Of (Purple Pyramid) 1998 Drawn from the band's dog days, despite a promising hit-laden track listing, *The Best of* captures a once-great band auditioning for the late night shift at the wine and cheese bar — only to find Style Council got there first.

CHROME

FORMED 1977 (San Francisco, CA)
ORIGINAL LINE-UP Damon Edge (vocals, guitar, synth); John L. Cyborg (b. John Lambdin — vocals, guitar, bass); Gary Spain (vocals, guitar, bass); Mike Low (guitar, synthesizer, bass)

One of the most powerful partnerships in the entire history of the American underground, Helios Creed and Damon Edge first came together as Chrome in 1977, melding acid guitar to corrosive keyboard, and hatching an incendiary roar which ripped apart the San Francisco underground. And though they split in 1983, both Creed and (until his death in 1996) Edge continued draping themselves over the turntables of the world, filling the hardest, darkest punk heart with a sound that was even harder, even darker.

With an original line-up comprising John Cyborg, Gary Spain and Mike Low, Edge had already cut one album as Chrome, the sci-fi folk-inflected *The Visitation*. With Creed replacing Low soon after, however, and with all four musicians wearing their influences — Can, Jimi Hendrix, Captain Beefheart and the Residents — loudly on their sleeves, Chrome's second album, *Alien Soundscapes*, emerged a wild and totally abandoned sequence of frantic noise.

Required listening for anybody trying to understand the relevance of psychedelia to modern society, and an essential grounding in the rudiments of synthesized industrial music through the next generation of rock experimentalism, *Alien Soundscapes* and its immediate successor, *Half Machine Lip Moves* (1979) would pre-empt practically every experimental musical revolution of the next decade.

However, *Half Machine* found the original line-up falling apart — Cyborg would be credited only with "data memory"; Spain's bass appeared on just two tracks. In their stead, Creed and Edge's grating electronics and harsh tapes dominated both the album, and an EP, *Read Only Memory* (#48 UK indy), excerpted from the soundtrack to an obscure French movie, and a surprise British hit in May 1980. Immediately, Chrome found themselves being offered a major label deal, through Britain's Beggars Banquet (themselves then riding high on Gary Numan's recent robotoid success), and Edge and Creed began rebuilding their vision around the brothers John and Hilary Stench, both formerly of Pearl Harbor and the Explosions. (John Stench had previously worked with an early version of Romeo Void, Hilary with the Vitals).

The "New Age" single and *Red Exposure* album in 1980, were followed by a Beggars reissue of *Half Machine Lip Moves*, while the band were also given the financing to shoot their first video, a *Clockwork Orange*-in-San Francisco epic spread across both "New Age" and "Meet You in the Subway."

Neither video would receive any exposure, neither record charted; and by late 1981, Chrome were back in indy territory, releasing the "Inworlds" 12", as a prelude to the *Blood on the Moon* album. Almost immediately after that project was complete, the band then returned to the studio to cut another single, "Firebomb," and album, *Third from the Sun*.

However, the pressures which divided Chrome three years earlier were still impacting upon the band, only now it was Creed and Edge who were at creative and personal loggerheads. By the end of 1982, Chrome were no more, splintering in the aftermath of one final single, "Anorexic Sacrifice."

Edge and Creed both went solo, albeit with less than consistent results. Edge's attempt to reform Chrome (without Creed) was uniformly disappointing, although *Into the Eyes of the Zombie King*, credited to Damon Edge and Chrome, had a few moments of inspired madness. Creed, contrarily, remained constantly fluid, churning out a string of adventurous albums, and indulging in some peculiar partnerships as well. 1989's *The Last Laugh* paired him to excellent effect with Skin Yard's Daniel House — an indication of just how dense the set was.

It was Creed's alliance with former Hawkwind mainstay Nik Turner, however, which truly catapulted the cult into daylight. Midway through 1993, the LA-based Cleopatra label approached Turner about reissuing his 1978 album, *Sphinx Xitintoday*. As it transpired, the decision was not his, but Virgin Records, who weren't interested, so Turner hatched the idea of rerecording the entire set.

Turner did not meet his fellow musicians — Creed, and members of US space rockers Pressurehed — until the album was complete; it was pieced together by mailing tapes back and forth between his base in Wales, Creed's home in Hawaii, and Pressurehed's L.A. headquarters, but Turner enthused, "it worked out so well that we got another record together immediately."

Prophets of Time would become Turner's first full American solo release, his chance to break out of the import cult confines into which his past output had always been consigned. Fresh recordings of the bleak "Children of the Sun," the Radio Actors' "Strontium 90," and a couple of ICU fail safes were included, alongside contributions from Barney Bubbles, Genesis P-Orridge, and Michael Moorcock. But still it was the tour which lifted the most eyebrows. Space Ritual '94 was a recreation of the original Hawkwind's most legendary tour, back in 1972, and one of the most successful revivals of the entire decade — as a live album, *Space Ritual '94* subsequently testified.

Creed remained with Turner through the mid-1990s, supplementing the band's studio and live output with further solo albums of his own. In 1997, however, with a three disc Chrome boxed set on the shelves, and much of the remainder of the band's catalog back on the shelves, Creed reunited with the Stench brothers and Tommy Grenas of Pressurehed (and the Nik Turner band) in a revitalized Chrome. Two new albums were followed by a month-long American tour in spring 1998, itself recounted on one disc within the *Chrome Flashback/Best Of... Live* package.

Chrome LPs

6 The Visitation (Siren) 1977 The sci-fi themes notwithstanding, a relatively laid back beginning, hints of Bay Area folk rock galloping across a proto-punk landscape, promising but scarcely relevant.

7 Alien Soundtracks (Touch & Go) 1978 With Creed now on board, the guitars lift off and take the imagination with them. From hereon in, the chaos will only increase.

8 Half Machine Lip Moves (Siren) 1979 It was the presence of electronics here which won Chrome the attention of UK label Beggars Banquet, then just peaking with Gary Numan. The presence, *not* their deployment. Frantic excursions to the fringe of white noise, a wild blast of disturbance and decay. Stunning.

7 Red Exposure (Siren) 1980

8 Blood on the Moon (Siren) 1981

6 3rd from the Sun (Siren) 1982

Selected Compilations and Archive Releases

6 No Humans Allowed 1982 The Creed/Edge pairing's final recordings, released as the band finally split.

8 Chrome Box (Subterranean) 1982 Six LP box including *Alien Soundtracks, Half Machine, Blood on the Sun, No Humans Allowed* and two discs of unreleased material.

6 Chronicles I&II (Dossier) 1982

5 Raining Milk (Mosquito) 1983 *Chronicles* served up a two LP distillation of the box set material; *Milk* abridged matters even further.

8 Chrome CD Box (Cleopatra) 1996 Essentially a CD version of *The Chrome Box*, but occasionally using *Raining Milk* abridgements, or outright omissions, to make room for rare live and compilation material.

Damon Edge/Chrome LPs

4 Into the Eyes of Zombie Kings (Dossier) 1984

5 The Lyon Concert [LIVE] (Dossier) 1985

3 Another World (Dossier) 1986

4 Dreaming in Sequence (Dossier) 1987

3 Alien Soundtracks 2 (Dossier) 1989

3 Live in Germany (Dossier) 1989

4 Clairaudient Syndro (Dossier) 1994

4 Having a Wonderful Time With the Tripods (Dossier) 1995

Helios Creed/Chrome LPs

7 Retro Transmission (Cleopatra) 1997 Unlike Edge's dangerously flat contributions to the Chrome canon, Creed unhesitat-

ingly returns to basics, unleashing all the madness which was the original band's hallmark.

6 Tidal Forces 1998

7 Chrome Flashback: Best of Chrome Live (Cleopatra) 1999 2-CD set featuring further excerpts from the *CD Box* collection, paired with a vital 1998 live recording.

Damon Edge LPs

3 Alliance (New Rose) 1985

4 The Wind Is Talking (New Rose) 1985

4 Grand Visions (New Rose) 1986

3 Eternity (Dossier) 1986

3 The Surreal Rock (Dossier) 1987

Helios Creed LPs

6 X Rated Fairy Tales (Fundamental) 1985

6 Superior Catholic Finger (Subterranean) 1989

5 The Last Laugh (Amphetamine Reptile) 1989

6 Boxing the Clown (Amphetamine Reptile) 1990

5 Kiss to the Brain (Amphetamine Reptile) 1993

5 Your Choice Live (Your Choice) 1994

8 Busting Through the Van Allan Belt (Cleopatra) 1994 Apparently invigorated and inspired by experiences on the Nik Turner/Hawkwind tour, Creed indeed busts through with his most electrifying solo disc yet, brain-churning space rock fed through some solid song (well, riff) writing.

7 Helios Creed (Cleopatra) 1994

7 Nugg the Transport (Efa) 1997

6 Dark Matter 2 (Efa) 1998

6 Activated Condition (Man's Ruin) 1998

7 Cromagnum Man (Efa) 1998

Selected Compilations and Archive Releases

8 Cosmic Assault (Cleopatra) 1995

Helios Creed/Nik Turner LPs

7 Sphynx (Cleopatra) 1993 Intended to remake a 1978 classic, but furiously updating it too, a duet between flute, pyramid, and space rock freak-show.

8 Prophets of Time (Cleopatra) 1994 More remakes, but ranging this time through Turner's entire catalog (obscurities our specialty) and engineering a cohesion which a simple "best of" collection could never have mustered.

8 Space Ritual 1994 [LIVE] (Cleopatra) 1995 Arguably, the album Hawkwind were threatening to make before Turner's departure sent the band ricochetting off down sundry retro-metal diversions, a statement not of commercial viability or songwriting acumen, but a swirling, howling, roaring mantra which again spiraled through both old and new material.

7 Travellers of Space (Cleopatra) 1995 Label sampler featuring individual and collaborative tracks by Creed, Chrome, Pressurehed, and others associated with Turner's Hawkwind rebirth, issued to coincide with the team's 1995 US tour.

CHUMBAWAMBA

FORMED 1982 *(Leeds, England)*
ORIGINAL LINE-UP *Lou Watts (b. Louise Mary Watts — vocals); Dunstan Bruce (vocals); Boff (b. Billy McCoid — guitar, vocals, clarinet); Midge Hartley (drums)*

Although the band's roots date back to a group of English buskers working the streets of Paris in the late 1970s, performing a bizarre melange of Clash, Undertones, and Beatles songs, the sprawling commune which is Chumbawamba got underway following the musicians' return to England. Taking over a large, derelict house in Leeds, close by Armley jail, the sextet never regarded themselves as a band. Rather, they were a self-contained commune fired by the same anarchist principles as motivated Crass, but considerably less po-faced about it. For them, the point was to have fun, with music and theatrics simply something they did while not tending the vegetable garden (all six members were vegan), sharing the household chores and adding weight of numbers to sundry political causes. Hartley left; she was replaced by 15-year-old Harry Hamer around the same time as other members of the commune drifted into the musical framework. Resident poet Alice Nutter started taking some of the vocals, Mavis Dillon picked up bass guitar, and Danbert Nobacon (b. Alan Whaley) joined as an all-purpose shouter. In this form, Chumbawamba self-released three cassettes for sale at gigs and other gatherings.

In 1982, reacting to the music press' increased coverage of the Oi! movement, Chumbawamba reinvented themselves as Skin Disease, and volunteered a contribution to the forthcoming *Back on the Streets* Oi! compilation EP. "I'm Thick" comprised its title being shouted out 64 times and so accurately encapsulated Oi!'s brutal immediacy that it was promptly accepted for inclusion. The EP's creators' response, once they discovered the truth behind Skin Disease, has not been recorded.

That same year Chumbawamba also contributed a caustic commentary on the incumbent Conservative Government, "Three Years Later," to Crass' *Bullshit Detector Volume Two* compilation, opening an uneasy alliance with the masters, which included a number of gigs together, but ended after Chumbawamba announced they were publishing a fanzine titled after the lack of Crass interviews within — at a time when every 'zine seemed to have some mention of Crass. Crass, apparently, were not amused.

Although the Chumbawamba's stageshow was becoming increasingly more theatrical, involving props and costume changes, dayjobs meant that they could only play at weekends — an imposition which contrarily added much to their appeal, as even the humblest gig became an event of sorts. Nutter was working as a journalist at the time, Bruce at a removals company, Watts was a car mechanic, Hamer a janitor at an old folks home. Pooling their resources, however, Chumbawamba booked a few hours at a local studio and, in September 1985, self-released (on the Agit-Prop label) their debut single, "Revolution" (#4 UK indie). A remarkable effort, which opened with the sound of John Lennon's "Imagine" being torn off the turntable and unceremoniously broken, a copy found its way to DJ John Peel whose enthusiasm proved contagious. Soaring up the indie chart, "Revolution"'s sales were sufficient to enable the members to quit their jobs and devote themselves full-time to Chumbawamba. Increasingly long tours, however, soon forced Dillon to quit — with two small children, the band's constant road trips were too much. He was replaced by Paul Greco.

A couple of tracks gifted to the *Dig This* compilation, including the irony-laced "The Police Have Been Wonderful," opened 1985; Chumbawamba also commented loudly on former heroes the Clash's recent revival by ambushing them when they played Leeds and pouring red paint over them. Elsewhere, the year of Live Aid could not go unremarked upon and Chumbawamba's debut album, the following fall's *Pictures of Starving Children Sell Records* (#2 UK indie), caused an immediate stir among Britain's still self-satisfied media.

A split single with San Francisco band A State of Mind, "We Are the World" (#4 UK indie), and drummer Hamer's vocal debut, "Rich Pop Stars Make Good Socialists" (offered free with *The Catalogue* magazine) added to the controversy, leaving the band universally reviled for their stance. Indeed, with Crass having split two years earlier, Chumbawamba were now perfectly poised to slip into the void which their departure left, that of chief agitators and conscience-prickers in the constantly collaborative world of British Youth Politics.

It was a role which Chumbawamba only partially took to, although a hostile media paid little attention to such subtleties — even when Chumbawamba's own policies dovetailed with their own. 1987's *Never Mind The Ballots: Here's the Rest of Your Life* album (#2 UK indie), targeted at the recent General Election, and the following year's "Smash Clause 28" single (#5 UK indie), aimed at proposed government legislation banning references to homosexuality from the British schools curriculum, both addressed issues which struck at the core of the freedoms which the music press was constantly braying about, but could not salvage Chumbawamba's own media image.

Neither could a disfigured version of the Beatles' "Let It Be," released under the Scab Aid alias just days after *The Sun* tabloid rallied sundry pop stars (as Ferry Aid) to record their own version of the song to benefit victims of a recent ferry disaster. *The Sun* itself had been the subject of a long-running and intensely ugly industrial dispute, the outcome of which would come close to destroying organized labor unions in Britain — Scab Aid, of course, was named after the popular term for the strikebreakers who facilitated that defeat. As the 1980s ended, Chumbawamba remained totally marginalized, a freakish anarchist sideshow whose pronouncements were to be either ignored, or utterly condemned.

In October 1988, Chumbawamba released their first masterpiece, *English Rebel Songs 1381–1914* (#13 UK indie). The band had never balked at cross-referencing musical styles, dipping into punk, reggae, polka, dance, blues, and the avant garde with gay abandon. *Rebel Songs* zeroed in on the folk influences, unearthing — as its title suggested — six hundred years of anti-establishment ballads and laments. While not realigning the band's press, this unfashionably, but curiously effective à cappella album did serve as a cultural reinvention of sorts and Chumbawamba's general profile increased accordingly.

Contributions to the Agit Prop compilations *101 Songs about Sport* and *This Sporting Life* took well-aimed potshots at the wave of patriotism which inflicted England during the run up to the 1990 soccer World Cup. However, the collapse of the label's distributors saw Chumbawamba embroiled in sundry legal hassles for much of 1989 and early 1990 — a period which they devoted to perfecting their latest musical shift, into the heart of dance music. *Slap*, in July 1990, was the first manifestation of this new interest and was considered so drastic a change that *Maximum Rock'n'Roll* magazine, hitherto one of Chumbawamba's most vociferous American supporters, refused to even review it, claiming that "Chumbawamba weren't punk any more."

Undeterred, Chumbawamba began work on another dance album almost immediately, the now-legendary *Jesus H Christ*. Largely based around samples — uncleared, of course — the album was ready for release when the legal letters began arriving. Mindful of an increasing number of past precedents, including the fate suffered by KLF's first album, *Jesus H Christ* was ultimately shelved and another looming lay-off was broken only when Nutter and Watts (as the Passion Killers) joined the anti-Gulf war lobby with the EP, *Four War is Shit Songs*. Chumbawamba themselves would also mastermind *Peasant Revolt*, a various artists EP celebrating the recent anti-government Poll Tax riots. (They also con-

tributed the remarkably Brechtian "Song of the Mother in Debt" to the *Pox Upon the Poll Tax* compilation.)

The band's own next release appeared in January 1992, when "I Never Gave Up" (from the *Slap* LP) was rerecorded as a merciless Pet Shop Boys parody. It was followed in June by *Shhh*, a new album which essentially reprised the abandoned *Jesus H Christ* without the offending samples, and with the lyrics reworked to reflect the band's recent experiences at the hands of creativity's censors.

Two further singles during 1992, "Never Say Di!," dedicated to the then embattled Princess Of Wales and "Behave," rang down the curtain on the Agit Prop label. Increasing problems with distributors Southern peaked when "Behave" was released in Britain while the band were touring the US. They returned home to find it had sunk without trace and decided finally to seek a more stable new home.

The band signed with One Little Indian in early 1993, debuting in September with a joint single with Credit To The Nation (the two bands had toured together in the past). "Enough is Enough" (#56 UK) commented upon the recent election to council office of a member of the avowedly fascist British Nationalist Party and, in becoming Chumbawamba's first ever mainstream hit single, ushered in an entire new era in the band's existence — one which would, of course, peak with the international success of "Tubthumping" four years later.

With the band's line-up now expanding to include guitarist and producer Neil Ferguson (replacing Greco), trumpeter Jude Abbot, and guest vocalist Howard Storey, and fiddle player Geoff Slaphead, Chumbawamba followed through with "Timebomb" (#59 UK) and the *Anarchy* album (#29 UK), a set whose arrival was infinitely amplified when the tabloid press learned of its cover art, a photograph of a baby being born. Incredibly, the record was banned in some stores, repackaged in a plain sleeve by others.

A new single, a rerecording of the album's "Homophobia," featuring the Sisters of Perpetual Indulgence, an order of gay nuns, accompanied the album's release, while the next year was to see the band almost permanently on the road. Pausing only to link with DIY to cut a single protesting the incoming Criminal Justice Act, "Criminal Injustice," Chumbawamba's next album was, sensibly, a live set — *Showbusiness* was recorded in front of a packed hometown audience in 1994 and offered new listeners an action-packed summary of the band's career so far. (*Showbusiness* would be released in the US in 1997, packaged with Noam Chomsky's *Capital Rules* spoken word album, as *For a Free Humanity: For Anarchy*).

A new single, a response to sundry British magazine's newly developed fascination with the homes of the rich and famous, "Ugh! Your Ugly Houses," surprisingly passed by unnoticed in October 1995; the *Swingin' with Raymond* album (#70 UK), too, under-performed. However, their continuing momentum was drawing ever greater attention and, in early 1996, Chumbawamba achieved what had hitherto seemed the impossible — they signed a major label deal.

Back in 1990, Chumbawamba contributed a version of Elvis Presley's "Heartbreak Hotel" to an anti-major label compilation, *Fuck EMI*; six years later, they signed to that same label (Republic/Universal in the US) and, the following year, "Tubthumping" (#6 US, #2 UK) became the most unexpected hit of the year.

Updating the *Rebel Songs* concept with a series of compositions reflecting life in their home county of Yorkshire ("the Third World," as Monty Python so memorably labelled it), the album *Tubthumper* (#3 US, #19 UK) was similarly massive, while two follow-up singles, "Amnesia" (#10 UK) and the soccer-themed "Top of the World (Ole Ole Ole)" (#21 UK) ensured that the specter of one-hit-wonderdom, widely predicted by a shocked UK media, was thoroughly banished.

While their recent back catalog was reactivated in the UK and released for the first time in America, Chumbawamba again toured ceaselessly, breaking the attendant recorded silence with the *Uneasy Listening* compilation and Nobacon's *The Unfairytale* solo album. Of course they also attracted further flak after Nutter was interviewed on national television and appeared to condone fans shoplifting the band's records from the Virgin Megastore. In fact, it was the show's fellow guests who named Virgin, but the store itself was not impressed, promptly pulling *Tubthumper* off the display racks and selling it only from behind the counter.

1999 saw a fan club single dedicated to the electioneering hypocrisy of British Prime Minister Tony Blair (the '60's girl group parody "Tony Blair"), and the following March, the band swung back into action with a new album, *WYSIWYG* (what you see is what you get) and, of course, a controversial new single — or, at least, B-side. Buried away behind "She's Got All the Friends That Money Can Buy," "Passenger List for Doomed Flight #1721" offered a lengthy list of the public figures Chumbawamba most disliked, a litany of politicians, pop stars, and media personalities which ignited a storm of protest in both the UK and US.

March 2000 saw the band return to the stage; increasing the line-up to eleven with the addition of a horn section and playing shows in Leeds (at the last night of the Duchess of York) and London, before embarking upon a summer of European festival shows. A new single, rerecording the earlier "Enough Is Enough," appeared during summer 2000.

Chumbawamba LPs

7 Pictures of Starving Children Sell Records (Agit Prop — UK) 1986 A bitter punk-fuelled rant which needed to be ranted. It all sounds a little dated today, but as another third world disaster flickers onto our screens (and another third rate pop star demands we do something about it), the sentiments spit back with remarkable venom.

7 Never Mind the Ballots... (Agit Prop — UK) 1987 Lyrically and thematically dominated by the British elections, a raw album but one which nevertheless has some contagious moments. The side-long song/suite, however, can get a little wearing.

9 English Rebel Songs (Agit Prop — UK) 1988 At a time when English folk music had been utterly hijacked by earnest beardies in Arran sweaters and a pot of real ale, Chumbawamba retraced the music's footsteps to a time when the songs really did mean something. Spine-chillingly à cappella (a trick which they wouldn't pull off so successfully until 2000's *WYSIWYG* brought a version of the Bee Gees' "NY Mining Disaster 1941"), the band are also to be congratulated for avoiding the staples of the scene — although "The Triumph of General Ludd" (condemning technology) and the WWI-era "Hanging on the Old Barbed Wire" sound as potent in the late 1980s as they ever did in their prime.

7 Slap! (Agit Prop — UK) 1990 Easy to condemn, but easier just to swallow and smile, *Slap!* is the dancefloor reinvention which captured the sheer mania of a great Chumbawamba gig, without the musical polemic or howling crowds.

9 Shhh (Agit Prop — UK) 1992 The Smiths' "Big Mouth Strikes Again" is the most obvious survivor of the *Jesus H Christ* debacle — "Pop Star Kidnap" and "You Can't Trust Anyone Nowadays" the most bitter reminders. No less enjoyable than its doomed all-kinda-covers predecessor threatened to be, *Shhh* is akin to spending an hour in the company of the greatest jukebox in the world, without quite being able to recall what the records are that you're dancing to.

8 Anarchy (One Little Indian — UK) 1994 Anthem follows anthem as "Timebomb" and "Enough is Enough" alone justify purchase and the rousing "Give the Anarchist a Cigarette" lurks within to surprise anyone who thought the singles were as good as it gets.

8 Showbusiness (One Little Indian — UK) 1995 An astonishing live set, capturing the sheer mayhem of a great Chumbawamba show, and the sound of a hometown audience in paroxysms of delight.

6 Swingin' with Raymond (One Little Indian — UK) 1995 Neatly divided between one side of love songs, one side of hate, *Raymond* is the transitional album Chumbawamba should maybe have made five years before. Overlooked, and not altogether mystifyingly.

8 Tubthumper (Republic) 1997 He drinks a whiskey drink, he drinks a lager drink... "Tubthumping"'s paean to the glories of alcohol would become one of the anthems of the late 1990s, but its fullsome melodies and super-slick sound could not disguise the fangs which were bared beneath the surface.

⑨ WYSIWYG (Republic) 2000 No more the offspring of their last LP than Lennie Kravitz is the son of Jimi Hendrix, WYSI-WYG is the sound either of the octet taking deliberate aim at their own 16 feet, or proof that the long-honored Chumba tradition of never making the same album twice remains of more importance than another surprise hit. The opening "Guess What, I'm With Stupid" takes a well-aimed potshot at all the beastly boy bands who have replaced the Chumbas themselves at the topper-most of the poppermost; elsewhere, the band's traditional social/cultural bugbears are slammed through the wringer of a rougher sound than last time, but still an effortlessly pleasing one.

Selected Compilations and Archive Releases

⑦ First Two (Agit Prop — UK) 1992 Much needed reissue of, indeed, the first two albums.

⑦ Portraits of Anarchists (One Little Indian — UK) 1996 Six new songs appear on a CD given away with copies of this photo-book.

⑧ For a Free Humanity — For Anarchy (Mutual Aid) 1997 US release of Showbusiness, with a second disc comprising Noam Chomsky's spoken word Capital Rules.

⑨ Uneasy Listening (EMI — UK) 1999 23-track compilation, the beginners' guide to Chumbawamba.

CHURCH

FORMED 1979 (Canberra, Australia)
ORIGINAL LINE-UP Peter Koppes (b. 1959 — vocals); Steve Kilbey (bass); Nick Ward (drums)

English emigree Steve Kilbey formed the original three piece Church as a vehicle for his own songwriting, relocating the band from hometown Canberra to Sydney in search of a deal. It was there, while working the club circuit to small reward, that the band encountered another Englishman, Marty Wilson-Piper, and soon after, a demo recorded by the quartet landed them a publishing deal with ATV/Northern Songs. That led to a deal with EMI Australia in 1980, and The Church's first single, "She Never Said," appeared late that year.

The band's Byrds-influenced '60s revival sound was spread throughout their debut album, Of Skins and Heart (and the "Two Fast for You" single), a delicate brew which was nevertheless given a far broader impact by American rock specialist Bob Clearmountain, called in to mix the tapes. The union paid off, as the Church's next single, March 1981's "The Unguarded Moment," made the Australian Top 20, swiftly followed by the parent album.

Nick Ward quit shortly before the album's release — his replacement, Richard Ploog, arrived just as the band embarked upon a year of intensive touring and recording, and in March 1982, the Clearmountain-produced Blurred Crusade album arrived to slam the Church towards Australian super stardom, and open European doors to them as well.

The Church made their first fact-finding journey to Britain and Europe in 1982, returning home to watch the five song EP The Church Sing Songs score another hit. Released on the Carrere indy, the dark, neo-Gothic Seance (#18 UK indy) in March 1983, increased the band's international standing even further (the accompanying single, "It's No Reason," proved a minor radio hit the following summer). Ironically, however, Australian audiences were not so taken with the band's new sound and direction, and from here on in, the bulk of the Church's efforts would be directed towards foreign markets.

A return to the Byrds-like groove in breezy pop, two Australian mini-albums, Remote Luxury and Persia, were compiled together as Remote Luxury for Britain and America (where the band signed to WB); there, after all, the strength of the band's potential was readily recognized — "a refreshing antidote to the increasingly frustrating excesses of their nearest contemporary equivalents, REM," enthused Melody Maker, while a short American tour in 1985 drew similar plaudits.

Returning to Australia, the group spent the remainder of 1985 preparing their next album, their first as a collaborative songwriting team, as opposed to a mouthpiece for Kilbey alone. Previewed with the singles "Columbus," "Tantalized," and "Disenchanted," the difference was astounding, unveiled in the much praised Heyday (#146 US), produced by Peter Walsh (of Gene Loves Jezebel fame), and breaching the US chart in June. Home sales, however, were again poor, and following the release of 1987's Hindsight compilation, EMI Australia dropped the band. Bizarrely, Warners and Carrere followed suit, and the Church suddenly found themselves without a deal anywhere in the world.

They finally signed with Mushroom (for Australia) and Arista (worldwide), and close to two years after completing Heyday, the Church began work on its successor, Starfish (#41 US), recorded over a three month period in Los Angeles, with Waddy Wachtel and Greg Ladanyi producing. It was a blatant, if brilliant, attempt to court US radio approval, and it worked — Starfish went gold in the US, spawning the hit "Under the MilkyWay" (#24 US), and setting the band up for a full year of worldwide touring.

Hopes to recruit former Led Zeppelin producer John Paul Jones to handle their next album fell through. Instead, the Church returned to Los Angeles and Wachtel, to record Good Afternoon Fix (#66 US) in 1989. The partnership, however, had run dry, and the departure of Ploog midway through the sessions, to be replaced by a drum machine, only exacerbated an already tense situation.

Two singles, "Metropolis" and "Russian Autumn Heart," flopped and, with The Church themselves unhappy with an album which in no way matched its predecessor, the band brought in former Patti Smith Group drummer Jay Dee Daugherty to replace Ploog, and embarked upon another lengthy world tour. They then returned to Sydney, the American experiment over, to create an album somewhat closer to their hearts.

The result, 1992's *Priest-Aura* (#176 US), would not even begin to recapture the heady days of *Starfish* in commercial terms. It completely bombed in America, evidence enough of the music's retreat back into familiar Church territory, and while the band's long-time fans were delighted, vocalist Peter Koppes' departure following the band's 1992 Australian tour seemed to leave the Church's entire future hanging in the balance — just as it had got back on track.

Two years of silence followed before Kilbey and Wilson Piper, with drummer Tim Powles, emerged from the studio with *Sometime Anywhere*, a darkly experimental album recorded in Kilbey's own Karmic Hit studio in Sydney. It was, as one UK critic put it, "a great big Persian rug of an album" which threw all the band's influences and ideas into the air, then simply followed where it would.

A low-key acoustic American tour (which saw them play at least one show, in Seattle, in a launderette) that summer was followed by the news that Arista had dropped the band. Undeterred, the Church returned to Karmic Hit in late 1995, with vocalist Koppes back on board as a special guest, and prepared for sessions utterly unfettered by commercial demands and expectations.

Already intending to self-release the ensuing album on their own Deep Karma label, the Church created *Magician Among the Spirits*, a darkly humorous and deeply ambitious record whose initial reception utterly belied its long-term strength. Condemned for its pretension, feyness, and gutless prog rockery, *Magician* would require a few more years, and one more album (1998's *Hologram of Baal*) before it fell into place within the Church's repertoire, as subsequent developments on the tribal-ambient scene elsewhere finally alleviated the sheer dislocation that the album's 14-minute title track originally unleashed.

Such developments, of course, were far off in the future when *Magician* first emerged; and were pushed even further out of reach when Deep Karma's US distributor went under, shortly after the album's 1996 release.

With Koppes now back on board full time, the Church toured Australia in 1997, preparing what would become *Hologram of Baal* via sound check jams and rehearsals. Accompanied by the "Lousiana" 45, the Church's first single

in six years, the ensuing album, their first for new US label Thirsty Ear, would emerge an infinitely looser, and far more open soundscape than either of its predecessors, and an instant critical hit.

A swift follow-up brought the band's most audacious, yet simultaneously characteristic album yet, the *Box of Birds* covers collection. Born from an impromptu live encore of Hawkwind's "Silver Machine," and originally scheduled simply as a single (the B-side would be Mott the Hoople's "All the Young Dudes"), the postponement of a planned Church live album, recorded in Sydney in 1997, sent the band tracing instead through 30 years of their own favorite songs in search of those which had most impacted upon what the Church would become.

A *Box of Birds* was completed with nods towards David Bowie, Kevin Ayers, the Sensational Alex Harvey Band, Iggy Pop... the ensuing role call was, perhaps, predictable, but it was also fitting. Looking back over that same era, while the Church's own albums play in the background, who else could they have been listening to?

The Church LPs

7 Of Skins and Heart (Parlophone Australia) 1981 Decidedly Byrds/Beatles-esque enchantment, cut through with just a hint of fashionable darkness.

7 The Blurred Crusade (Parlophone, Australia) 1982 The Church may still have been paying homage to the '60s, but now they swear allegiance to the new wave too. "When You Were Mine" brilliantly blends INXS energy, a bit of Edge-esque guitar, and Ultravox-y synth grandeur with the expected a touch of the Byrds, while elsewhere, that same jangle slips around everything from ethereal ballads to dreamy jams.

7 Seance (Parlophone, Australia) 1983

8 Remote Luxury (WB) 1984 Compiled from two Australian EPs, deliciously out of time collection which asks, where else could you hear the Flying Burrito Brothers rewriting post-Syd Pink Floyd, and still sound like they're making a contemporary statement?

7 Heyday (WB) 1985 Returning to the pop-rock stylings of *Blurred Crusade* and *Seance*, *Heyday* slots comfortably into the halls of goth — which, at that time, required only a touch of introspection, a hint of melancholy or the odd minor chord. Rousing dark rockers, pretty pop (with the inevitable Byrds' references), and enough lyrical mentions of Goddesses, royalty, biblical places, and soul searching to fill Wayne Hussey's songbook.

6 Starfish (Arista) 1988 Slick (and fashionably thin) mid-80s LA production mars what should have been the Church's triumph — great songs, great lyrics, dark heart. But you have to remove a lot of sugar to reach them.

8 Gold Afternoon Fix (Arista) 1990 The culmination of all that had gone before. The guitar work is superb, Kilbey's bass throbs with emotion and Wilson-Piper and Koppes shower fragile melodies, roaring leads, and melancholy acoustics. Awash in moods-soothing lullaby, haunting Spanish melody, epic drama, driving rock, and pop in all its many mutations.

7 Priest Aura (Arista) 1992

8 Sometime Anywhere (Arista) 1994 Bright-eyed exploration of more styles and emotions, the first half pulsing with a hypnosis which reaches almost tribal proportions. The songs glitter across a disc where dream-pop meets hip-hop and country crosses to the Far East, as driving aggression rub shoulders with anthemic spacey instrumentals. A limited edition of the record contained a bonus disc containing 7 further atmospheric tracks.

8 Magician Among the Spirits (Deep Karma — Australia) 1996 Darkly humorous, deeply ambiguous, the self-consciously bizarre conclusion of *Sometime*'s weirder excursions, topped by a peculiar cover of Steve Harley's "Ritz" and defined by "Welcome," name checking all the duo's heroes. You have to love anyone who can rhyme Roger Moore with Joan Crawford.

7 Hologram of Baal (Thirsty Ear) 1998 Sporting a new big sound and renewed energy, *Hologram* is the punchiest album the band have ever recorded. Even as the songs shimmer into extended and expansive dreamscapes, the guitars are poised to pounce and the rhythm section pulses and quivers with life.

7 A Box of Birds (Thirsty Ear) 1999 Reverential (and self-referential) tribute to the band's childhood record collections, from Alex Harvey and Mott to Hawkwind and Iggy.

Selected Compilations and Archive Releases

8 Hindsight (EMI Australia) 1987

7 Conception (Carrere — UK) 1988 Pre-*Heyday* best of's; the 2-LP *Hindsight* is well-planned and executed, the 10-track *Conception* is at least a snappy introduction.

6 A Quick Smoke at Spots (Archives 1986–90) (Arista) 1991

8 Almost Yesterday 1981–1990 (Raven, Australia) 1994

8 Magician Among the Spirits Plus Some (Thirsty Ear) 1999 Long-delayed US release for *Magician* drops "Ritz," adds the 4-track *Comedown* EP.

Steve Kilbey/Donette Thayer-Hex LPs

6 Hex (Rykodisc) 1989

6 Vast Halos (Rykodisc) 1990

Steve Kilbey/Jack Frost LPs

5 Jack Frost (Arista — UK) 1991

6 Snow Job (Beggas Banquet) 1996

Steve Kilbey LPs

6 Unearthed (Enigma) 1986

6 Earthed (Rykodisc) 1987

7 The Slow Crack (Rough Trade) 1987

5 Remindless (Red Eye — Australia) 1990

6 Narcosis (Vicious Sloth — Australia) 1997

Peter Koppes LPs

5 Manchild and Myth (Rykodisc) 1988

6 From the Well (TVT) 1989

6 Snow Job (Beggars Banquet) 1996

6 Love Era/Irony (Immersion — Australia) 1997

Peter Koppes/The Well LPs

5 Water Rites (Worldwater — Australia) 1995

Marty Willson-Piper LPs

6 In Reflection (Chase — Australia) 1987

7 Art Attack (Rykodisc) 1988

7 Rhyme (Rykodisc) 1989

6 Spirit Level (Rykodisc) 1992

CLASH

FORMED 1976 *(London, England)*
ORIGINAL LINE-UP *Joe Strummer (b. John Graham Mellor, 8/21/52, Ankara, Turkey — vocals, guitar); Mick Jones (b. 6/26/55, London — guitar, vocals); Paul Simonon (b. 12/15/56, London — bass); Keith Levene (guitar); Terry Chimes (b. 1/25/55 — drums)*

The Clash came together in spring 1976 after Mick Jones and Paul Simonon (both ex-London SS) recognized Joe Strummer — then vocalist with pub rockers, the 101ers — on the street. Strummer himself was well-aware of his band's limitations; had been ever since he caught the Sex Pistols live earlier in the year, so when Jones and Simonon asked him to throw it in and join them in a new band, he agreed.

Guitarist Keith Levene departed early, and drummer Terry Chimes was eventually replaced by Topper Headon (b. Nick Headon, 5/30/55, Bromley). But with Strummer, Jones, and Simenon at its heart, the Clash were astonishing. Harder and harsher than they ever appeared on vinyl, stronger than they sounded in subsequent live shows, on a good night they could match the Pistols in almost every department.

Early in the new year, Polydor offered the band unlimited studio time in which to record demos; days before contracts were due to be signed, Clash manager Bernie Rhodes defected the band to CBS. The Clash debuted with "White Riot" (#38), one of *the* crucial chants of early 1977, and one which would be joined on the group's eponymous debut album (#12 UK) by even more. "Career Opportunities," "London's Burning," and "1977" encapsulated the mood of the moment with unerring accuracy, and while the media continued to debate the band's sincerity (Strummer was the middleclass son of a diplomat, after all), the Clash tore into action.

"White Riot" was followed by a second album cut, "Remote Control," and in one of the greatest public relations coups of the era, the Clash announced they were livid. They had not been consulted about this second single, neither would they have approved it if they had been. They returned to the studio and cut a new song about the whole situation, with famed Jamaican producer Lee Perry at the controls, then watched as the ironic "Complete Control" (#28) pushed chartwards.

"Clash City Rockers" (#35 UK), the first of several earnest attempts at self-mythology (Jones' idols, Mott the Hoople, were the role model here), was the Clash's first new release of 1978. It was succeeded by the reggae-toned "White Man in Hammersmith Palais" (#32 UK).

Both singles evinced a considerable enlargement on the Clash's original punk thrash. Unfortunately, attempts to broaden out even further, by recruiting Blue Oyster Cult/Dictators producer Sandy Pearlman to handle the band's sophomore album, failed. *Give 'Em Enough Rope* (#128 US, #2 UK) struggled to recapture the passion of its predecessor, but there was no arguing with its success. It also

Joe Strummer of the Clash

© Jim Steinfeldt/Chansley Entertainment Archives

became the first Clash album to find an American release following on from the quite phenomenal import sales of their debut. (A belated release of *The Clash*, with several additional tracks and a free single, followed — #126 US.)

Two singles culled from the album, "Tommy Gun" (#19 UK) and "English Civil War" (#25 UK), kept the band in the English Top 30, even as their own schedule saw them spending ever more time touring the US; *The Cost of Living* EP, fronted by a cover of the Bobby Fuller Four's "I Fought the Law" (#22 UK), followed suit, while the band's *Rude Boy* movie became one of the cult celluloid hits of the age despite the band themselves disowning it.

London Calling (#27 US, #9 UK), the band's third album, was the set which finally established the Clash as something more than a simple punk band. Produced by maverick genius Guy Stevens (who also handled some of the band's early demos, but was recruited primarily because he used to produce Mott), and spread over four sides of vinyl, *London Calling* was a patchwork of personal influences, disparate and, in places, disjointed. But still it emerged a potent directory of post-punk nerve and neuroses, with two singles, "Train in Vain" (#23 US) and "London Calling" (#11 UK), landing the band their first American, and their biggest British hits, respectively.

Hastily following through, EPic prepared a 10" compilation of the band's most recent dance and reggae excursions, *Black Market Clash* (#74 US), but behind the scenes, the Clash appeared in turmoil. Since original manager Bernie Rhodes was fired in late 1978, the band had worked with journalist Caroline Coon and Pink Floyd management company Blackhill Enterprises, only to now be considering a return to Rhodes. Any thoughts that such disruptions might affect their music, however, were firmly quashed when they followed *London Calling*, in December 1980, with a further six sides of vinyl, the epic *Sandanista* (#24 US, #19 UK).

Intended as a snapshot of three solid weeks spent in the studio, and preceded by two hit singles, "Bankrobber" (#12 UK) and the anti-draft "The Call Up" (#40 UK), *Sandanista* — of course — was critically lambasted as over-indulgent. Nevertheless, it would endure as a monument to the sheer creativity of the band, with two singles — "Hitsville UK" (#56 UK), a Motown duet spoof featuring Jones and girlfriend Ellen Foley, and the dance-oriented "Magnificent Seven" (#34 UK) — pinpointing even wider versatility.

And still the Clash weren't exhausted. Despite growing rumors of mounting personal problems (cresting when the increasingly drug-dependent Headon quit, to be replaced by the returning Terry Chimes), the band nevertheless managed two new singles over the next year, "This is Radio Clash" (#47 UK) and "Know Your Rights" (#43 UK), while the album which followed, 1982's *Combat Rock* (#7 US, #2 UK) saw the Clash finally grasp the golden ring.

Regular US tours had already seen the band teetering on the brink of a major breakthrough — now it would happen. *Combat Rock* was aimed unequivocally at the soft, white underbelly of American FM radio, bristling with potential hit singles ("Rock the Casbah" (#8 US, #30 UK,) and "Should I Stay Or Should I Go" (#45 US, #17 UK), firmly rooted in a solid pop base which was anathema to anyone who bought "White Riot."

On October 9, 1982, the Clash played *Saturday Night Live*, idealistically the most "punk" show on American television. But as a well-read Joe Strummer pointed out later, "all that meant was that Elvis [Costello] and Devo were on a few years before us. We'd have been better off playing Johnny Carson." He seemed, too, to intuitively understand that the Clash's moment of triumph would also be the moment of death.

In November 1982, Chimes departed, to be replaced by former Cold Fish drummer Pete Howard; on May 28, 1983, the band played their final show in their "classic" form, at the massive US Festival in San Bernadino, CA. Four months later, in September 1983, Jones departed in a blaze of acrimony.

Stunned by the collapse of the dream, Strummer himself disappeared briefly, before returning to announce that the Clash would continue. Recruiting guitarists Vince White and Nick Sheppard (ex-Cortinas), within four months of Jones' departure, in January 1984, the new look Clash were out on a short British tour. It would be 18 months, however, before they returned to the studio, releasing a single, "This Is England" (#24 UK) and *Cut the Crap* (#88 US, #16 UK) — the final Clash album and, even its makers subsequently acknowledged, a disastrous coda to the band's career. In November 1985, the Clash called it quits.

Jones and Strummer would reunite occasionally, across a 1986 Strummer solo single, and as co-writers of Jones' second Big Audio Dynamite album. Attempts to bring the pair back beneath the Clash banner, however, would constantly fail, despite some monstrous endorsements. Several compilations charted in the UK, together with a steady stream of reissued singles, including a reissued "Should I Stay" (#1 UK), after the song was revived for a Levi commercial in early 1991. Similarly, wild applause greeted the *On Broadway* boxed set, and in 1995, the band were offered up to $7 million to reform for Lollapalooza.

They refused, finally reconvening only to compile 1999's career-spanning *From Here to Eternity* live album (#193 US, #13 UK); thus preserving the knowledge that barring the Adverts, the Slits, and the Jam, the Clash were the only first

generation punk essential not to have been lured back into action in the mid-late 1990s.

Also see the entries for "BIG AUDIO DYNAMITE" on page 192 and "JOE STRUMMER" on page 661.

The Clash LPs

9 The Clash (Epic — UK) 1997 The template for so many future punks, the Clash's eponymous debut epitomized perfect punk, stark simplicity, basic chords and guitar leads which were practically idiot proof. Hard-hitting lyrically, the Clash were instant tinder to the flames of disaffected youth. And though their cover of Junior Murvin's "Police and Thieves" took them far beyond a mere white riot, still the song remained the same.

7 Give 'Em Enough Rope (Epic) 1978 And they'll hang themselves, quipped detractors, although hindsight treats their union with producer Sandy Pearlman more kindly. Longer, comparatively complex songs, and with their initial fury reduced to white hot embers, even the war cries are more personal and situational. Like most transitional albums, *Rope* remains deeply flawed, but it is still powerful.

10 London Calling (Epic) 1979 Meet the new boss, same as the old boss, and here's a double album to prove it. But truly, the Clash needed two discs, because not a groove goes to waste as they chase their own unrelenting ambition across the musical spectrum.

As always, the strongest songs contain the most radical messages — the triumphant call to arms of the title track, the Big Brotherly "Working for the Clampdown," the ominous warning of "Guns of Brixton," the melancholy reminder of revolution lost of "Spanish Bombs." But even the seemingly insignificant filler — "Koka Kola," the recycled ska of "Rudie Can't Fail," Jones' plaintive "Lost in the Supermarket" — had a place in the overall scheme, taking their place alongside the endless cast of characters streaming through the streets, the famous and the forgotten, pushers and losers, the disillusioned and the lost, rastas and admen, heroes and cheats.

Relentless, then, and relentlessly brilliant, the sound of past and present slammed together, and the last great album of the '70s became the first classic record of the '80s.

8 Sandinista! (Epic) 1980 Three LPs this time, and one disc too far. But Strummer still insists that the point wasn't to make an album so much as present a snapshot in time, and the scale of accomplishment is staggering. Creative use of rap, funk, calypso, and '60s pop opens up whole new vistas of possibility, while the multitude of reggae-fied and dubby tracks and covers throb with life and energy. The haunting "The Call Up" is a masterpiece of revolution, and "Hitsville UK" utterly recaptures the mood of classic Motown. The project maybe failed, but the concept remains unimpeachable.

4 Combat Rock (Epic) 1982 And then they went and sold their souls to America, reducing their revolutionary message to the goofiness of "Rock the Casbah" and the limp sarcasm of "Know

Your Rights," ersatz reggae and self-conscious rap, and all wrapped within a sleek production which even daytime radio couldn't resist. One truly great song, the shattered "Straight to Hell," tried hard to salvage the rest, but "Should I Stay Or Should I Go?" asked a question which didn't need answering.

2 Cut the Crap (Epic) 1985 Beneath the spikey-dyed coif of inflamed punk ethics, co-writing songs with his manager, Strummer poked, croaked, and ultimately choked on such lyrical humdingers as "We Are The Clash" ("no you're not," said Little Nicola), "This Is England," and a parade of pointless pickleheads which would have sounded out-of-sorts on a Foreskins B-side. Appended to the once royal name of the Clash, they were positively treasonable.

Selected Compilations and Archive Releases

8 The Clash (Epic) 1979 The so-called "American" version, actually released *after* their second album and doubtless sewing much confusion among the Great American Public. Four key breaths of paint stripper are culled from the UK pressing, to be replaced with the sound of '78/79, key singles which kept the stakes up high, but lost the plot around "I Fought the Law."

8 Black Market Clash (Epic) 1980

7 Story of The Clash Vol 1 (Epic) 1988

9 On Broadway (Epic) 1991 3-CD box culling 63 tracks from albums, singles, and out-takes, and deceptively coherent because of its brevity. The truncated *Sandanista* benefits immeasurably; but *Combat Rock* still gets too much space.

9 Super Black Market Clash (Epic) 1994 Seismic upgrade of the earlier *Black Market Clash*, a welcome airing for the dub experiments, B-sides, and dance tracks which always elevated the Clash so high. The epic "Armagideon Time," the sassy "Capital Radio," and a magnificently dishevelled "Pressure Drop" rank up there with the best of the band.

8 The Singles (Epic) 1996

9 Live: From Here to Eternity (Epic) 1999 Twenty years in the gestation, culling material from the 1978-era *Rude Boy* soundtrack through to the band's last US tours, but retaining such cohesion that it really could be all one show... and one of the greatest shows you ever could have seen. Twenty years, and they still can't be beat.

Further Reading

Last Gang in Town by Marcus Gray (Owl, 1995).

CLEAN

FORMED 1978 *(Dunedin, New Zealand)*
ORIGINAL LINE-UP *Peter Gutteridge (vocals, bass); David Kilgour (b. 9/6/61 — guitar); Hamish Kilgour (drums)*

If the New Zealand punk scene can be said to possess a definable dynasty, it was started by the Clean. In life, the band all-but debuted the seminal Flying Nun label, so beloved of low-fi completists the world over, and worked with Tall Dwarfs founder Chris Knox. In death, they spawned the Chills, the Great Unwashed, the Bats, and Bailter Space. On top of that, their dense sense of what might have happened had the Velvet Underground lived in a garage would turn the heads of musicians as far away as New York (the young Sonic Youth) and the UK (the Jesus and Mary Chain) — countries not normally renowned for the attention paid to minor league antipodean concerns.

The Clean made their live debut in 1978, as support for New Zealand punk godfathers the Enemy; within a year, however, Peter Gutteridge had quit to form a new band, the Chills, to be replaced by Robert Scott. The Chills broke up (temporarily) in June 1981, and the Clean promptly recruited their guitarist, Martin Phillipps (b. 7/2/63), to guest on keyboards. In this form, the Clean cut their debut single, "Tally Ho!," for $60 NZ — the second ever release on Flying Nun (the first, just days earlier, was the Pin Group's "Columbia").

Like the musicians he would be signing over the next two or three years, Flying Nun founder Roger Shepherd was a devoted fan of '60s psych — and the more whacked the better. The Kilgour brothers were heavily into Skip Spence's *Oar* album, two decades before rock lore and CD reissues brought that particular nugget screaming into mass circulation. Such sounds and notions, filtered through the cultural isolation which was part and parcel of New Zealand life in the late 1970s, would become integral to the Clean, and would be rubbing off elsewhere as well.

Flying Nun intended existing hand to mouth, but sales of "Tally Ho!" swiftly disavowed the label of any notions of enduring struggle. The single made New Zealand's national Top 20, more than sufficient to fund the Clean's next release, 1982's *Boodle Boodle Boodle* EP, "produced" by Knox, who owned the 4-track tape recorder they set up in a rented hall, to make the record.

Boodle hit the Top 5 and eventually went gold, and was promptly followed by another EP, the seven song, and amazingly-titled *Great Sounds Great, Good Sounds Good, So-so Sounds So-so, Bad Sounds Bad, Rotten Sounds Rotten*. Yet by the time the Clean's fourth record was released, the EP *Getting Older*, the band had broken up, shattered by the sheer enormity of their fame.

The Kilgours promptly reunited with original vocalist Gutteridge in the Great Unwashed, before Hamish became a founder member of Bailter Space; Scott formed both Electric Blood and the Bats, leading both bands simultaneously until 1988 (when the Bats alone flew on); and Flying Nun released two collections of unissued Clean odds and ends, appropriately-titled *Oddity* and *Oddity 2* — the latter featuring tracks recorded at the very first Clean gig. Further live material emerged on 1986's *Live Dead Clean*, a stunning EP recorded at three shows during 1981–82.

Demand for more, however, could not go unanswered, and on July 13, 1988, The Scott and The Kilgours reunited for a one-off show at London's Fulham Greyhound pub. The show was recorded for posterity, of course; the following year, Flying Nun released the *In a Live* EP, together with the announcement that the band would be remaining together, to tour and then cut what would become, amazingly, their first ever album. *Vehicle* followed, before the band members went their separate ways — Scott returning to the Bats, and forming a new side project with Electric Blood drummer Jimmy Strang, the Magick Heads.

Hamish Kilgour reunited briefly with Bailter Space, before jumping ship during their first US tour, to set up home with his new wife and form Monsterland, with Lisa Siegel and Danny Manetto (the band later became Mad Scene, and Top Cat). His brother formed Stephen, gigged alongside the Chills' Martin Phillipps in the Pop Art Toasters, and cut a solo album, *Here Come the Cars*.

In March 1994, however, the trio were back together again, a pair of loose rehearsals proving sufficient time in which to write half an album's worth of new songs, recorded in two weeks and released later that same year. The band toured New Zealand (with Hamish's Monsterland supporting), but *Modern Rock* was never intended as anything more than another one-off. The tour over, the band disappeared again.

But they could never be said to have broken up. They toured in 1995 with Martin Phillipps on guitar; and in March 1996, with Hamish back in New Zealand, two studio sessions saw the band kick out a full 18 tracks of new material. *Unknown Country* duly followed towards the end of the year.

Also see the entries for "BAILTER SPACE" on page 173 and "CHILLS" on page 259.

The Clean LPs

5 Vehicle (Flying Nun — NZ) 1990 Nine years and a breakup in the making, the Clean's debut album has little in the way of songs (13 in 30 minutes), but a lot of texture and attitude. Not worth waiting for, but it sure feels nice.

4 Modern Rock (Flying Nun — NZ) 1994 Quick before you miss them, a lightning reunion, a few lightning sessions, and an album which races past almost unnoticed.

6 Unknown Country (Flying Nun — NZ) 1996 Another flying visit, but this time something clicked. Still not a patch on what the Clean once were (back before they started making LPs), but a substantial, if esoterically armed, reminder of the early magnificence.

Selected Compilations and Archive Releases

7 Oddities (Flying Nun — NZ) 1983

6 Oddities 2 (Flying Nun — NZ) 1984

9 Compilation (Homestead) 1986 Truly stunning round-up of early EPs and singles, the justification for every great word ever affixed to the Clean's name.

The Great Unwashed LP

8 Clean Out of Our Minds (Flying Nun — NZ) 1983 Lackadaisically loose and loveable collection of barely written folky songs, strummed, banged, and coaxed out of thin air.

Selected Compilations and Archive Releases

7 Singles (Flying Nun — NZ) 1984

David Kilgour LPs

6 Here Come the Cars (NZ) 1991

8 Sugarmouth (Flying Nun — NZ) 1994

7 David Kilgour and the Heavy Eights (Flying Nun — NZ) 1996

Electric Blood LP

6 Electric Easter (Beehive Rebellion — Australia) 1984

Magick Heads LP

6 Before We Go Under (Flying Nun — NZ) 1995

7 Woody (Flying Nun — NZ) 1997

Bats LPs

5 And Here Is "Music for the Fireside' (Flying Nun — NZ) 1985

5 Daddy's Highway (Communion) 1988

6 The Law of Things (Communion) 1990

5 Feat of God (Mammoth) 1991

6 Silverbeet (Mammoth) 1993 Firmly in the tradition of Kitchens of Distinction, Adorable, and sundry other alternative-lite bands, perfect little pop songs for the early '90s. *Silverbeet* just washes along, taking repeated listenings to distinguish the songs, before "Courage" finally leaps out as their most memorable cut.

6 Couchmaster (Mammoth) 1995

CLOCK DVA

FORMED 1979 *(Sheffield, England)*
ORIGINAL LINE-UP Adi Newton *(vocals)*; Steven Taylor *(bass)*; David James Hammond *(guitar)*; Simon Kemp *(keyboards)*

Formed after Adi Newton quit the embryonic Human League, future Clock DVA took their name from the Nadsat language glossary published in Anthony Burgess' A

Clockwork Orange novel ("dva" also means "two" in Russian) and made their earliest recordings of six therapeutic tape loops, as an experiment in ambient audio therapy, in early 1978. Privately released as the *Lomticks of Time* cassette, and followed by the similarly limited *2nd*, Clock DVA nevertheless swiftly gained a reputation for effortlessly straddling the quite disparate musical fences erected on the one hand by Throbbing Gristle, and on the other by Britain's flirtatious early-1980s rediscovery of sixties soul music.

The Small Wonder label came close to releasing their next effort, a five-track EP titled *Sex Works Beyond Entanglement*, in 1979; when the deal fell through, Clock DVA returned to their own devices, and by year's end had completed two further tapes, *Deep Floor* and *Fragment*.

Kemp had quit by now, to be replaced by Roger Quail; with saxophonist Charlie Collins also aboard, the band's earliest conventional releases were raw contributions to the 1980 compilations *Hicks from the Sticks* ("You're Without Sound") and *First 15 Minutes* ("I'm So Hollow"/"Brigade"), before January 1981 brought an utterly uncompromising, utterly improvised debut album, *White Souls in Black Suits*. Released through Throbbing Gristle's Industrial label, within the IRC cassette series, the album was edited down from 15 hours of tape, and also featured a tape montage created with the members of Cabaret Voltaire (whose Western World studio hosted the album's recording).

In February, with Clock DVA newly signed to the Fetish label, a raw London Lyceum show was recorded for future release, two tracks appearing on the label's *Last Testament* sampler. Then, having replaced Hammond with former Young Marble Giants guitarist Paul Widger, June 1981, brought their debut single, "Four Hours" (#32 UK indy), and the less dance-oriented album *Thirst* (#7 UK indy) — greeted by journalist (and future ZTT conspirator) Paul Morley as "the first brilliant album of 1981, and one of the great records of the '80s."

The group immediately began work on a new album, developing themes hinted at across *Thirst*, but with just a handful of tracks completed, Newton and Turner decided to rebuild the band completely. All three fellow members were dismissed (they later reappeared in the disco-fied Box), and Clock DVA was reinvented as the logical successor to Public Image Ltd's epochal *MetalBox* album. A new line-up of John Carruthers (guitar) and Paul Browse (sax) was pieced together, and the band signed to Polydor, but before any serious work could be completed, Turner died tragically (the 1982 B-side "The Voice That Speaks from Within" discusses the circumstances of his death).

Shaken, Newton recruited Mick Ward (bass), Michael Ward (sax), and Nick Sanderson (drums) to the surviving line-up, and the band set to work on the EP *Passions Still*

Aflame, dedicated to Turner's memory, and largely informed by his passing. A second single, "High Holy Disco Mass" (backed by "The Voice...") followed, and in early 1983, Newton, Browse, Carruthers, Sanderson, and bassist Dean Dennis began work on *Advantage*, the band's next album. Working with producer Hugh Jones, and employing a number of different studios (including Ultravox founder John Foxx's The Garden), *Advantage* spawned the "Resistance" and "Breakdown" singles, and prefaced Clock DVA's first major European tour. ("Breakdown" also featured a stupendous cover of the Velvet Underground's "Black Angel's Death Song.")

Joined by backing vocalist Katie Kissoon, Clock DVA were at their dark dance peak, playing sold-out shows across the continent, and Winding up at the Bains Douche in Paris, for the last night. There, director Julien Temple — shooting the Rolling Stones' "Undercover" video at the same venue — caught them in action, and incorporated a glimpse of their performance in the ensuing video. Immediately following the show, however, Newton traveled to Amsterdam, where he was planning to collaborate with an American psychiatrist — he disbanded Clock DVA, and instead formed the Anti Group Communications Project, an industrial jazz project. Carruthers subsequently joined Siouxsie and the Banshees.

Despite pledging to maintain Clock DVA, Newton would not return to the band name until 1988, when he hooked up with Browse and Dennis alone. Signing with Wax Trax (Interfisch in Germany — the band had no UK deal), Clock DVA released a pair of EPs, *The Hacker* and *The Act*, both melding early elements of the original band with the more contemporary innovation of sampling, and emerged with a very Kraftwerk-ian man machine sound and image.

It was not an altogether satisfying mix, but undeterred, Newton continued on this line for 1990's "Sound Mirror" single and *Buried Dreams* album; a conceptual piece which reprised the EPs' title cuts on a record otherwise heavily indebted to Suicide — both the group and the concept.

The live *Traditional Voices*, according to Newton, boasted a little more "soul"; it was recorded with Anti Group engineer Robert Baker replacing Browse.

The group was now signed to only one label worldwide, the Italian Contempo, but the band remained very active over the next two years. The *Man Amplified* and the "Final Programme" single were followed by another full European tour in 1992; the following year saw the release of two further singles, "H. I. T." and their mix-packed *Bitstream* EP, before the icy *Digital Soundtracks* album appeared in 1992. However, *Sign* and the singles "Voice Recognition Test" and "Eternity" in 1993 would mark the end of another era, as Dennis quit following another European tour.

Newton and Baker alone recorded a cut, "Virtual Flesh," for an Italian project titled *The Virtual Reality Handbook*; then, joined by Newton's brother Ari, plus and Rew Mackenzie and Maurizio Fasolo, they toured and released the live *Kinetic Engineering* album. Silent since that time, Newton has concentrated on issuing and restoring the band's archive.

Clock DVA LPs

6 **White Souls in Black Suits (Industrial) 1980** Cassette-only improvisation blurred the group's own intuitive grasp of soul music with the near-constant roar of white noise.

6 **Thirst (Fetish) 1981** The white noise takes over, although the rhythms remain addictive.

8 **Advantage (Polydor) 1983** Finding a solid medium between the extremes of its predecessors, best experienced via the excellent "Breakdown," disintegration and dance collide in an ecstasy of sound.

7 **Buried Dreams (Wax Trax!) 1990** Dark, cacophonous soundtracks mesh with vocal effects and some genuinely disturbing semi-spoken material.

6 **Transitional Voices [LIVE] (Amphetamine Reptile) 1991**

6 **Man Amplified (Contempo — Italy) 1992**

7 **Digital Soundtrack (Contempo — Italy) 1993** Another sharp shift in direction and outlook, critically abandoning density in favor of almost glacial textures.

7 **Sign (Contempo — Italy) 1993** Still locked into their cyber-state existence, infused with shadings of techno and ambience, although still occasionally recapturing the mechanoid sounds of their past.

5 **Kinetic Engineering [LIVE] (K!7 — Germany) 1994**

Selected Compilations and Archive Releases

7 **Collective; The Best of (Cleopatra) 1994** Although the track titles suggest this is a singles collection, it's virtually all unreleased remixes or rare versions of the originals. Arranged chronologically, they chart the band's progress from techno-soul to their early 1990s ice warriorhood.

Adi Newton/Lustmord LP

6 **The Monstrous Soul (Side Effects) 1992** Collaboration with Brian Williams.

Adi Newton/Hafler Trio LPs

4 **Negentropy (Ash International) 1994**

3 **Masturbatorium 1995**

Adi Newton/Psychophysicist LP

3 **Psychophysicist (Side Effects) 1996** Collaboration with Hafler Trio mainstay and Rew Mackenzie.

COAL CHAMBER

FORMED *1994 (Los Angeles, CA)*
ORIGINAL LINE-UP *Dez Fafara (b. Bradley James Fafara — vocals), Meegs (b. Miguel Rascon — guitar); Rayna Foss (bass); Bug (b. Michael Cox — drums)*

Formed by Dez Fafara and Meegs from the wreckage of an earlier band, She's In Pain, Coal Chamber grew out of the same L.A. metal/hip-hop scene as Korn and The Deftones, arriving a little later than their contemporaries, but bearing a vision which swiftly raised them above such company.

Adding Cox and Foss (then roommates with Fafara's future wife), increasingly regular gigs around L.A. soon began attracting attention — Coal Chamber's down-tuned riffing, after all, was simply the most prominent feature in a potpourri of musical activity which reached from punk and goth, to hardcore and hip-hop, while the group's natural theatricality brought together an exhibitionist audience far removed from those other bands' dour followers.

With Fear Factory's Dino Cazares and rising producer Ross Robinson championing their cause, by fall 1994, Coal Chamber were on the verge of signing to Roadrunner. It was, however, a shortlived romance. Weeks later, Farfara quit the band to appease his wife, while his bandmates struggled to find a replacement. After six months, both acknowledged that things weren't working out — Farfara missed playing, Coal Chamber missed playing with him, and the reunited band returned to live work in spring 1995.

The Roadrunner deal was reignited (it was finally signed at Christmas), and early in the new year, 1996, Coal Chamber entered NRG Recording studios with first time producers Jay Gordon and Jay Baumgardner.

Leading off with the instant classic "Loco" (a song about trying to get signed in L.A.), *Coal Chamber* would be released in February 1997, on the heels of the band's triumphant OzzFest outing. There they came to the attention of Sharon Osbourne, managerial wife of Black Sabbath star Ozzy — she took over the band's management soon after, the first new act she had taken on in a decade.

18 months of solid live work included tours with Pantera (at their request of the headliners' drummer, Vinnie Paul) and Type O Negative, pushing album sales towards the half-million mark, and encouraging *Alternative Press*, the following year, to describe the band's projected second set amongst 1999's most eagerly-anticipated releases.

A tour with Insane Clown Posse through the summer of 1999 ended at the headliners' investigation after just two shows; September then brought the Josh Abraham produced *Chamber Music* (#22 US), itself heralded by a heavily-publicized version of Peter Gabriel's "Shock the Monkey," featuring additional vocals from Ozzy Osbourne, and a gripping

Dean Karr video. Other guests on the album included ex-Human Waste Project vocalist Aimee Echo, and Deadsy's Elijah Blue Allman. The band's first full headline tour followed through fall, with bassist Nadja Puelen standing in for Rayna Foss, absent following the birth of her daughter Kayla (Foss is married to Sevendust drummer Morgan Rose).

Coal Chamber LPs

6 Coal Chamber (Roadrunner) 1997 A formative furnace blast at best, although the mini-hit "Loco" suggests more ideas coming quickly down the turnpike.

8 Chamber Music (Roadrunner) 1999 At its best — the deceptively unyielding "Untrue," the Iggy-moodish "Burgundy," and the string-drenched descent of "My Mercy" — *Chamber Music* batters your brain with an intense brutality. But it's bartering for your heart as well, because sensitivity can scream as much as sickness, and *Chamber Music* is loud. Psycho-symphonics for the sad of soul. Oh, and don't forget "Shock the Monkey."

COCTEAU TWINS

FORMED 1982 (Grangemouth, Scotland)
ORIGINAL LINE-UP *Robin Guthrie (b. 1/4/62 — guitar); Elizabeth Fraser (b. 8/29/63 — vocals); Will Heggie (bass)*

Robin Guthrie and Will Heggie formed the original Cocteau Twins in 1981, taking the name from an early (unrecorded) Simple Minds song. Meeting Elizabeth Fraser at the Grangemouth club which all three frequented (Guthrie was DJ on punk nights), the group's early days were tempestuous — Fraser quit very early on, returning after six months when she began dating Guthrie; and they were still "moseying along aimlessly," as Fraser put it, when the trio attended a Birthday Party gig in early 1982. Guthrie got backstage and introduced himself to Phil Calvert; told him about the band, and came away with an address for the 4AD label.

A demo tape received an inviting response, and in the spring of 1982, the Cocteau Twins signed with the label. Work began on their debut album, *Garlands* (#4 UK indy) in June. Dominated by Guthrie's effects-heavy guitar and Fraser's already ethereal voice, a Siouxsie and the Banshees-esque drone which either captivated the listener or bored him senseless, *Garlands* launched a love affair with BBC radio's DJ John Peel which culminated with the 1999 release of *BBC Sessions*, a two CD collection of recordings which ranks amongst the Cocteaus' finest.

Tours with 4AD labelmates Modern English and The Birthday Party raised the Cocteaus' profile higher, but that fall, the first in a long, lush series of Cocteaus EPs, *Lullabies* (#11 UK indy), evinced the first indication of change within the group's sound. With Guthrie complaining that already, *Garlands* "is like a big stone hanging around our necks,"

Lullabies and its successor, *Peppermint Pig* (#2 UK indy) — produced by Alan Rankin of the Associates, the Cocteaus' first and only attempt to work with an outside producer — refined the Cocteaus' sound towards a more individual sound.

Heggie departed following another extensive UK tour (he later resurfaced in Lowlife); Guthrie and Fraser responded on two fronts, with their contributions to 4AD's *This Mortal Coil: It'll End in Tears* (#1 UK indy) artists collective project, and their own *Head Over Heels* (#51 UK, #1 UK indy) album and *Sunburst and Snowblind* EP (#2 UK indy). These releases crystallized the "trademark" Cocteau sound, all the more so after the Fraser-led This Mortal Coil's version of Tim Buckley's "Song to the Siren" was released as a single (#66 UK, #3 UK indy).

Head Over Heels offered an entrancing brew, but was difficult to reproduce live, as the Cocteaus discovered on a European tour with Orchestral Manouvres in the Dark. Accompanied by backing tapes, the pair cut the tour short 8 dates into the 15-show outing, utterly overwhelmed by technical problems. They resolved many of the difficulties in time for a handful of US gigs later in 1983, but by the new year, they were working with former Drowning Craze bassist Simon Reynolds (b. 4/3/62).

He debuted on *The Spangle Maker* EP, led off by "Pearly Dew Drops Drop" (#29 UK, #1 UK indy) in April 1984 — the Cocteaus' biggest success yet, despite the band's refusal to appear on television's *Top of the Pops* ("everyone was cacking themselves at the thought of success," Fraser later explained).

Treasure (#29 UK, #2 UK indy), their third album followed, a bad-tempered record which reflected Guthrie's own dissatisfaction with the way in which the band's image was going. "We were [being] pushed into all that kind of arty-farty-pre-Raphaelite bullshit," he complained, the situation worsened by their own inability to resist. For five years, the Cocteau Twins had pioneered the ethereal minimalist approach which would come to epitomize much of the mid-'80s indy scene. That this would ultimately develop into cliché was inevitable; so was the band's ultimate inability to develop out of the strictures which bound them.

Still, the band's international fame had now developed to the extent that a world tour was called for, taking them to the US and Japan — where Fraser discovered an entire nation convinced that she was already singing in Japanese! "They were brilliant," she continued, "but a bit confused." In fact, on the rare occasions Fraser did discuss her lyrics, she acknowledged nothing more than distorted English, interspersed with old Scots and occasional nonsensical words.

A new EP, *Akei Guinea* (#41 UK, #1 UK indy) launched 1985, as the band attempted to step back from the *Treasure* formula; *Tiny Dynamite* (#52 UK, #1 UK indy) and *Echoes in a Shallow Bay* (#65 UK, #1 UK indy) followed, companion pieces which pulled the band even further afield. Against that backdrop, the release of *The Pink Opaque* compilation in late 1985 seemed somehow self-defeating, particularly as it contained no material recorded after *Treasure*.

However, it also served as an excellent introduction to the Cocteaus' past, and acted as a healthy stopgap while the trio embarked upon a number of extra-curricular activities — a movie soundtrack with Harold Budd, *The Moon and the Melodies* (the team reunited in 1988 for tracks on Budd's *White Arcades* album); sessions with Dif Juz and Felt; and for Reynolds, a weighty appearance on the second *This Mortal Coil* album.

While he labored on that project, Fraser and Guthrie also began work on the fractured and inconsistent *Victorialand* (#10 UK, #1 UK indy); Reynolds returned in time to complete the EP *Love's Easy Tears* (#53 UK, #1 UK indy), then join the duo on their next European tour. An appearance on another 4AD collective project, 1987's *Lonely Is an Eyesore* notwithstanding, it would prove their last indy chart topper. When the group returned from an 18-month hiatus, spent refitting their own studio, they had signed a major label deal with Capitol, and emerged with *Blue Bell Knoll* (#109 US, #15 UK, #1 UK indy), a sophisticated album which, uniquely, the band simply "weren't in the mood" to promote with live work.

Instead they took another break, while Fraser and Guthrie had their first child, daughter Lucy Belle (their September Sound studios would be named after her birth month); Guthrie would also produce early EPs by recent 4AD signing Lush. The break, unfortunately, evidently did not do the Cocteaus any favors, as the following year's "Iceblink Love" (#53 UK) and *Heaven or Las Vegas* (US #99, UK #7) saw the cracks opened by *Victorialand* tear open. Acknowledging that the band had to change, but not yet sure in what way, Fraser even began writing "conventional" lyrics again, admitting all the while, "I was still trying to get out of writing them."

That indecision, coupled with Guthrie's attempts to break a drug habit and what he called "a complete lack of enthusiasm at 4AD"(with whom they remained signed in Britain), resulted in what both members described as the band's weakest album. Within a year, the Cocteaus had quit 4AD (for Fontana), and after another year in the studio, released "Evangeline" (#34 UK) and *Four Calendar Cafe* (#78 US, #13 UK), very much a back to basics collection — albeit one which was marred by the group's continued irritability.

A Christmas single, "Winter Wonderland" (#58), originally recorded for Lucy Belle alone, rounded out 1993; how-ever, Fraser and Guthrie's marriage broke down just as *Four Calendar Cafe* was released, and a lengthy tour through 1994 did little to ease the tensions between them. A single, "Bluebeard" (#33 UK) was released in early 1995 while the band toured the US, but clearly, the Cocteau Twins were reaching an impasse of sorts.

Two EPs, *Twinlights* (#59 UK) and *Otherness* (#59 UK), appeared during 1995, the latter pairing two new tracks with two Mark Clifford remixes, and in March 1996, "Tishbite" (#34 UK) previewed the Cocteaus' new album, *Milk and Kisses* (#99 US, #17UK). Another single, "Violaine" (#56 UK), followed, but the Cocteaus' spring/summer tours of Europe and the US marked the end of their working relationship. Attempts to record one more album ended with Fraser finally announcing she would not be completing her vocals (with 9 of 16 tracks remaining), and the band folded.

Guthrie launched his own record label, Bella Union in 1997; the first release was Simon Raymonde's solo single, "In My Place," in August. Fraser would begin work on a solo album, and contribute vocals to Massive Attack's *Mezzanine* album.

Cocteau Twins LPs

9 Garlands (4AD) 1982 The Cocteaus at their indecipherable best, Fraser's trademark etherealism combining with Guthrie's ferocious energy for a hauntingly raw dreamscape which finds an alternately delightful and edgy medium between the two extremes. The Siouxsie and the Banshees descriptions flew at the time, but really, there's no comparison.

7 Head Over Heels (4AD) 1983 More melody, less buzzing urgency, and less tense density as well. "Musette and Drums" is an admirable stab in the direction of the Cocteaus' future; "In Our Angelhood," contrarily, really does sound like the Banshees.

9 Treasure (4AD) 1984 "Ivo," an apparent ode to label head Watts-Russell, became a de facto hit, "Persephone" a touchstone for even unwilling Cocteaus imitators. Despite their own reservations, and a certain cynical disrespect towards the Cocteaus' supposed "trademark" sound, their second masterpiece.

6 Victorialand (4AD) 1986

7 Blue Bell Knoll (Capitol/4AD) 1988 Too many moments they'd already done before ("Carolyn's Fingers" equals "Akei Guinea"), but it hangs together well despite that. Fraser is in especially fine voice and a handful of songs still readily conjure the images their nonsense title simply.

4 Heaven Or Las Vegas (Capitol/4AD) 1990

6 Four Calendar Cafe (Capitol) 1993 With the opening "Know Who You Are" recycling every trick in the Cocteaus' book, very much a return to basics — even if they are still re-learning what those basics were.

7 Milk and Kisses (Capitol) 1996

Harold Budd, Elizabeth Fraser, Robin Guthrie, and Simon Fraser LP

5 The Moon and the Melodies (4AD) 1986 If you want Budd, there's too much Cocteaus, if you want the Cocteaus, there's too much Budd. Ultimately, a very pleasant irrelevance.

Selected Compilations and Archive Releases

9 The Pink Opaque (4AD) 1986 The be-all and end-all of Cocteaus collections, peaking when they did and wrapping up a lot of essential loose EPs.

8 The Singles Collection (Capitol) 1990 Literally. A CD box set comprising each of the band's EP releases to date with reproduced artwork.

9 BBC Sessions (Rykodisc) 1999 After years of half-life on the underground circuit, the classic Cocteaus Peel sessions combine with a few latter-day shots for the one Twins album which never once goes off the rails. Plus, it's the closest we're likely to get to a live album.

COIL

FORMED *1982 (London, England)*
ORIGINAL LINE-UP *John (aka Jhon) Balance (b. Geoff Rushton); Peter Christopherson; Stephen Thrower*

John Balance was still a member of Psychic TV when he began recording sporadic private cassettes under the names of Zos Kia and Coil; he also released one Zos Kia single, "Rape" (an early version of Coil's "Here to Here".) He was joined by bandmate Peter Christopherson in 1982, and two years later — following their departure from PTV — Balance and Christopherson released the *How to Destroy Angels* EP in Belgium, a one-sided effort comprising 17 minutes of gonging dedicated to the god Mars, and described in the liner notes as "ritual music for the accumulation of male sexual energy."

Signing to Some Bizzare, a label whose flirtations with the pop mainstream (via Soft Cell and The The) belied the strength of experimentation going on elsewhere in its catalog, the duo enlisted Foetus overlord Jim Thirlwell, Virgin Prune Gavin Friday, and Possession's Stephen Thrower, for their debut album, *Scatology* (#7 UK indy).

In 1984, Coil played a now-legendary show with Soft Cell's Marc Almond. "It was great," Christopherson recalled. "Marc was reading poetry while John gave himself enemas of blood onstage. Nick Cave walked out on us saying we were too gay." Coil celebrated the accomplishment with a cover of Soft Cell's "Tainted Love" (#5 UK indy). An accompanying video — with Almond guest starring as the Angel of Death — was banned, although New York's Museum of Modern Art purchased a copy.

Coil spent much of the next year working with director Derek Jarman on the movie and soundtrack *The Angelic Conversation*; 1985 also saw Coil link with Boyd Rice under the name Sickness of Snakes, to record three tracks for *Nightmare Culture*, an album split between themselves and Current 93.

With Christopherson now establishing himself as one of Britain's most creative video directors, working initially within the Some Bizzare stable, but swiftly branching out, another year-plus preceded Coil's next brace of releases, the three-track *Anal Staircase* EP (#6 UK indy) which lent two of its tracks to *Horse Rotorvator* (#3 UK indy), an album which dispensed almost wholly with the danceable percussives of *Scatology*, and moved instead into an exploration of African and Middle Eastern motifs, shot through with chilling morbidity. "When we were recording [it]," Christopherson later admitted, "it was the beginning of the AIDS epidemic and our friends were beginning to die." That situation heavily influenced the record.

In 1987, Coil were contracted to supply a soundtrack to Clive Barker's *Hellraiser* movie; their submission was not used, but *Unreleased Themes from Hellraiser* nevertheless appeared in 1988, and achieved better reviews than either the movie or its eventual soundtrack could ever have dreamed of. Surplus material from this project, together with out-takes from its two predecessors, appeared on 1988's 18-track *Gold Is the Metal With the Broadest Shoulders* collection — remixes and remasters which also debuted Otto Avery in the band's line-up. Also included were several non-album cuts, lifted from past compilations and one-offs, plus a new single, "Animal in Palace." *Unnatural History* continued this archaeological exercise.

Regrouping in 1990, Coil released the singles "Windowpane" and "Wrong Eye," ushering in the musical mood which culminated on *Love's Secret Domain*, a psychotic menage of dance, industrial, and experimental moods which numbered Marc Almond and Annie Anxiety among a galaxy of featured stars. Elsewhere, Coil's long, lonely life on the fringe of experimental music finally came to an end, as the band found themselves being feted by a host of up-and-coming industrial musicians. Trent Reznor signed the band to his Nothing label, while Christopherson was hired to direct new (hit) videos for Nine Inch Nails, Ministry (the controversial "New World Order" and "Just One Fix"), Front 242, and Rage Against the Machine.

Thrower departed Coil in 1991, to be replaced by Dean McCowall, who debuted on the remix EP *The Snow* that same year; it was followed by "Airborne Bells" in 1993, with further singles "Protection" and (as Eskaton) "NASA Arab" during 1994, along with the long awaited (but substantially remixed) soundtrack to *The Angelic Conversation*. A single of the album's "Blue Theme" also appeared, to mark director Jarman's recent death.

Although the band continued to record under the pseudonyms ELPH and Black Light District, it would be 1998 before Coil released new material — a 72-minute sequence of ambient electronic tones, intended, claimed Balance and Christopherson, "to facilitate time travel."

More new material appeared on the *Foxtrots* compilation, alongside contributions from Nurse With Wound and Current 93, with proceeds from the album aiding Balance's on-going alcohol and drug rehabilitation programs. Further one-off releases included a series of limited edition singles released and deleted on successive equinoxes during 1998: *Moon's Milk...* (spring), "Bee Stings" (summer), *Amethyst Deceivers* (fall) and *North* (winter), featuring guests William Breeze, Boyd Rice collaborator Rose McDowall and Robert Lee.

Another EP, *Astral Disaster*, emerged as a very limited edition (99 copies) in 1999; that same year brought *Musick to Play in the Dark Volume One*, with one track, "Red Birds" (recorded with Julian Cope collaborator Thighpaulsandra) based around Nostradamus' prophecy for July 1999. A second volume appeared in January 2000.

Coil LPs

6 Scatology (Some Bizarre) 1984 A lengthy and often despairing percussive symphony, over which layered synthesizers, guitar feedback, and assorted samples emerge with disconcerting regularity.

7 Horse Rotorvator (Some Bizarre) 1986 A very real and personal awareness of mortality haunts Coil's most divisive album — scarred by the AIDS deaths of several band friends and acquaintances, and marred by the overuse of Fairlightbrass, it also features some genuinely innovative sampling and, despite its subject matter, a seductive Mid-Eastern flavor.

7 Unreleased Themes From Hellraiser (Solar Lodge) 1987 Gothic atmospheres, gothic instruments, dark moody instrumentals which are suddenly shattered by the inclusion of a few themes written for commercials. Program the CD for random play, and rediscover madness.

7 Love's Secret Domain (Wax Trax!) 1991 It's the Coil party album, ambient airs colliding with a piece-meal study of modern trends — acid house, hip hop and so on.

7 Time Machines (Eskaton) 1998

8 Musick to Play in the Dark Volume One (Chalice) 1999 Few albums have been so well-titled. But is it a suggestion? Or a warning?

CONSOLIDATED

FORMED 1988 *(San Francisco, CA)*
ORIGINAL LINE-UP *Adam Sherburne (vocals, guitar); Mark Pistel (keyboards); Philip Steir (drums)*

Consolidated formed from the wreckage of Until December, a Bay Area dance band who toured with Gene Loves Jezebel, released a long forgotten album on Columbia (and turned up on the Hi-NRG Dance Classics compilations a full decade later), but were best remembered locally for their in concert cover of Bauhaus' "Bela Lugosi's Dead." They broke up, and with Sherburne realigning his music around a new social conscience (after "crack ethic careerism and total gang-rape ethics took over"), Consolidated spent four years building a ferocious live reputation.

Signing with Nettwerk, they debuted on vinyl with a self-titled EP in October 1989, prompting Britain's *Spiral Scratch* magazine to describe them as a "white Marxist Public Enemy... the unrelenting voice of an enraged generation."

Encouraging their own live performances to become open debates with the audience, Consolidated were as much a political movement as a musical entity, a status they confirmed (albeit less convincingly) when they dedicated April 1990's debut album, *The Myth of Rock*, to Yussef Hawkins. The EP *Dysfunctional Relationship* followed, as the band set out on another major tour, before beginning work on their sophomore set.

While they certainly retained their unremitting pro-rights stance on issues as disparate as women's rights, ethnic minorities, homosexuality, and animals, still Consolidated were a far friendlier concern than in the past — as Sherburne reflected, "we weeded out some of the nihilistic aggression in the music. We don't think people should have to go out and get assaulted just as a matter of attending a cultural function."

Previewed with March 1991's *This Is a Collective* EP, *Friendly Fascism* arrived in April, an immediate *CMJ* Top 10 hit. The singles "Brutal Equation" in June 1991, and "Unity of Oppression" in October were both substantial alternative chart hits — "Unity" even finished #4 on MTV's *120 Minutes'* year's end best of chart, while December 1991, brought the classic "This is Fa$cism," (#25 on *Billboard*'s dance chart; #1 on Rockpool).

September 1992's *Play More Music* album, and the *Tool & Die* and *Warning: Explicit Lyrics* EPs in 1992/93 maintained the band's success, and the band signed to London for 1994's *Business of Punishment* and the "Butyric Acid" single. Neither performed well, however, and the band was dropped.

During the four year lay-off which followed, Steir and Pistel both quit (although the latter would remain a behind-the-scenes collaborator). Sherburne pieced together a new Consolidated in 1996 with bassist Michael Dunne and drummer Todd Bryerton, and realigning the sound towards a considerably less aggressive approach, returned in 1998 with *Dropped*, the first of a two part soundtrack to the John Stoltenberg screenplay, *Cocklash* — and not, as was daftly speculated elsewhere, a belated reaction to their departure from London. Part two, *Tikkun*, followed in October 1999, as Consolidated launched a major European tour.

Consolidated LPs

6 The Myth of Rock (Nettwerk 1990) 1990 Unlike most radicalized bands, Consolidated never shy from offering solutions to problems loudly.

7 Friendly Fascism (Nettwerk 1991) 1991 Again, a hard hitting soundtrack of hip-hop, funk, soul, and hard rock.

7 Play More Music (Nettwerk 1992) 1992

8 Business of Punishment (London) 1994 No punches pulled (as usual), a litany of political, social, and cultural targets readied for lyrical destruction, with irony and sarcasm far to the fore. The music remains marvelously edgy, but the band are now exhibiting a subtle maturity, making this their best album to date.

7 Dropped (Sol 3) 1998 Great myths of modern rock. In a striking change of direction, Consolidated aim their bombs directly at the mainstream, hypnotizing the listener with an assault of radio-friendly tracks across a spread of formats — soul, dub, industrial, blues, funk, electro-pop, and hip-hop — with the music providing a perfect sugar-coating for the hard message in the center. Poignant vignettes, often ironically told from the oppressor's angle, make *Dropped* as big a political bombshell as its predecessors, just a tad more subtle; so the band haven't changed their political spots at all, just camouflaged them.

6 Tikkun 1999

JULIAN COPE

BORN 10/21/57 (Deri, Wales)

Having pulled away from the wreckage of the Teardrop Explodes, Cope accepted Mercury's offer of a solo deal and issued his first single, "Sunshine Playroom" (#64 UK) on the first anniversary of the band's demise (and fifth anniversary of their birth), in November 1983.

Recorded with Steve Lovell, an old friend most recently working as a busker, and Gary Dwyer, from Teardrop

© Jim Steinfeldt/Chansley Entertainment Archives

Explodes, both the single and its parent *World Shut Your Mouth* (#40 UK) album proved minor UK hits, as did a second single, "The Greatness and Perfection of Love" (#52 UK). Cope's time with Mercury was to be limited, however, both by a continued failure to break out of the eccentric cult bag into which he had fallen during Teardrop Explodes' most overtly psychedelic phase, and by persistent rumors of an out-of-control drug problem.

A disastrous show at Hammersmith Palais, which ended with Cope breaking his mike stand and cutting his stomach while quoting English comedy actor Kenneth Williams, exacerbated this reputation. Released the same month that Cope married his American girlfriend Dorian, his second solo album, *Fried* (#87UK) would be his last for Mercury. In mid-1985, his third album, *Skellington* (recorded with brother Joss and friend Donald Ross Skinner), was rejected out of hand by the label. Cope quit soon after.

He resurfaced over a year later, newly signed to Island and sporting a rerecorded version of "World Shut Your Mouth" (#87 US,#19 UK) — "a loser's anthem," as Cope put it, and for Mercury, a dramatic reminder of what they had lost. (An American EP, *Julian Cope*, repeated all the tracks from the UK 7-inch and 12-inch singles — (#109 US.)

With another hit single behind him, February 1987's "Trampolene" (#31 UK), Cope unveiled the masterful *Saint Julian* (US #105, UK#11) in March. It was another Donald Ross Skinner collaboration, with Double DeHarrison (keyboards), Chris Witton (drums), and James Eller (guitar) completing the studio line-up. Immediately upon its release, this same band (with Richard Frost replacing DeHarrison) kicked off a UK tour highlighted by a televised concert at the Westminster Central Halls in London, and a very successful showing at the 1987 Glastonbury Festival.

Cope then began preparing his follow-up, having first persuaded his record company A&R man, Ron Fair, to produce it. Skinner and another friend, Rooster Cosby — hitherto employed for percussion and "strange vibes" — were upgraded to the rhythm section, and all concerned disappeared into the studio for close to a year of mysterious silence.

The hiatus was broken only once, by the "Eve's Volcano" single (#41 UK); however, former Teardrop manager Bill Drummond did score a cult hit with the salutory "Julian Cope Is Dead" single, and perhaps it was that which spurred Cope to prove that he wasn't. In October 1988, he finally re-emerged with the modern funk masterpiece *My Nation Underground* (#155 US, #42 UK). Another minor hit single, "Charlotte Anne" (#35 UK) was followed with a fabulous cover of the Vogues' "5 o'clock World" (#42 UK) and his own "China Doll" (#53 UK), but once again, Cope seemed content to allow another year to drift by in apparent inactivity.

In fact, he was trying to convince Island to release *Skellington*, the long-since rejected third solo album. When they, too, turned it down, he established his own label, and released the set himself. Press reviews — perhaps predictably, given the album's rough treatment at the hands of record companies — were unanimously in praise of the set, and the following month, April 1990, Cope played his first live show in two years in Brixton.

He was joined onstage by Sqwubbsy, his seven-foot-tall alter-ego — a media celebrity since his starring role at the recent Anti Poll Tax march in London. But no matter how bizarre Cope appeared to be, real life always managed to seem even stranger. April also saw the release of another long-since rejected album, the aborted third Teardrop Explodes album, and when this, too, received unstinting critical praise, Cope resolved that henceforth, all his albums would gestate five years before being released.

Of course the plan never came to fruition, although oddball releases would continue, beginning in May 1990, with *Droolian* a limited edition album which Cope intended to be sold only in Austin, TX, as part of a campaign to free the jailed Roky Erickson.

March 1991, brought Cope's first "conventional" album in three years, as the singer launched a projected trilogy of ecologically minded albums with the sprawling *Peggy Suicide* (#23 UK). It was released on the back of the hits "Beautiful Love" (#32 UK), "East Easy Rider," (#51 UK) and "Head" (#57 UK), and supported by Cope's most UK successful tour yet — a triumphant scenario which continued deep into the new year, with yet another reissue for "World Shut Your Mouth" (#44 UK) and a career-spanning compilation, *Floored Genius* (#22 UK).

Cope's next tour, *Head On*, too, drew upon his entire back catalog, spread across three one-hour long sets a night, and culminating with selections from the second part of the trilogy, *Jehovahkill* (#20 UK).

Unfortunately, just five shows into the tour, Cope fell prey to a throat and chest infection. The dates were rescheduled for the following month — just as Island announced that Cope was being released from his contract. An unprecedented wave of scorn washed over the label — Cope was at a creative and critical peak, his profile had never been higher, he was topping end of year readers polls, he had just scored another hit single, "Fear Loves This Place" (#42 UK)... and he was being dropped.

Forming his own Ma-Gog label, Cope and Donald Ross Skinner released their own *Rite* album in the new year, a meditative piece firmly rooted in the Krautrock Cope had enjoyed as a teen (further explorations would emerge on 1994's *Queen Elizabeth*, recorded with sometime Coil collaborator Thighpaulsandra, and later still, on *Rite 2*). Ma-Gog would also release *Skellington Chronicles*, comprising a repackaged *Skellington*, and a second volume of more of the delightful same.

The first volume of Cope's autobiography, *Head On*, was published in 1994, while live work was confined to venues within reach of the prehistoric monuments Cope was researching for a projected new book. Dates in Ireland and the Scottish highlands (with associated appearances at the Edinburgh festival) occupied him through summer 1993; and while work began on a new album, the final part of the trilogy launched by *Peggy Suicide* and *Jehovakill*, a second volume of *Floored Genius*, anthologizing Cope's solo BBC session recordings, maintained his profile.

Autogeddon (#16 UK), the new album, appeared on Echo (American in the US) in mid-1994, and the following year "Try Try Try" (#24 UK) became Cope's first Top 30 single in five years, previewing the astonishing *20 Mothers* (#20 UK) album. Another set of three hour concerts peaked in September 1995, while Cope's latest literary endeavor, the superb *Krautrock Sampler* guide to German rock of the early 1970s, was published that same month. He paid further tribute to the era with a solo show opening for modern space rock pioneers Ozric Tentacles in London in February 1996.

Cope's final releases during this tempestuous period were 1996's singles "I Come from Another Planet Baby" (#34 UK) and "Planetary Sit In" (#34 UK), and the album *Interpreter* (#39 UK), an exhausting disc which, of course, was not without its attendant controversy — Cope had become involved in several ecological protests, and carried one, opposing the Newbury by-pass highway project, onto *Top of the Pops* with him.

However, much of the next three years would be spent away from music, completing a second volume of autobiography, *Repossessed*, and that long-promised guide to megalithic Britain, *The Modern Antiquarian*. A lavishly packaged guide to every prehistoric stone site in Britain, the book was well-received even within the halls of academic research, while Fortean students, too, acknowledged Cope's accomplishment, as he rounded up both historical and mythological lore.

Cope toured the UK through the spring of 1999, reading from *The Modern Antiquarian*; the pre-recorded music which accompanied those performances would emerge at year's end on his latest album, the near-ambient *Odin*.

Julian Cope LPs

9 World Shut Your Mouth (Mercury) 1984 Even without the legendary title track, and with Cope himself still seemingly uncertain just what he ought to be doing, a raggedly confident debut made magical by "The Greatness and Perfection of Love" and the self-defining "An Elegant Chaos."

7 Fried (Mercury) 1984 The delicate "Reynard the Fox" and "Sunspots" emerge as moments of comparative lucidity in an album which really seems to believe its maker's press — addled, confused, damaged... fried? Cope as casualty, and he does it incredibly well.

9 Saint Julian (Island) 1987 "Eve's Volcano," "Saint Julian," and finally, "World Shut Your Mouth." He's done it again.

9 My Nation Underground (Island) 1988 A lot of people might try to medley Petula Clark and the Vogues, but Cope is one of the few who would release it. Not so much an idiosyncratic curtain raiser, however, as precisely the kind of thing most people would expect — so the rest of the album swerves sharply away, most notably towards Cope's latest bout of suspicion about the meaning of his return to pop stardom but also into a head-on collision with a might slab of funk.

8 Skellington (Copeco) 1989 A dozen ditties recorded for younger folk and older souls, but avoiding the pitfalls of whimsey and twee-dom.

7 Droolian (Mofoco) 1990

7 Peggy Suicide (Island) 1991 A return to whatever Cope calls basics, as ecology and madness clash across two LPs worth of increasingly fractured, but neverless than captivating song forms.

7 Jehovakill (Island) 1992

6 Rite (Echo) 1994 Though it does go on way too long, eight instrumentals rank alongside any of the best bands in Cope's then-germinating *Krautrock Sampler* book. They didn't know when to stop either.

6 Queen Elizabeth (Echo) 1994 Collaboration with Current 93 collaborator Thighpaulsandra.

7 Autogeddon (American) 1994 With "I Gotta Walk" offering up a bass-blurged Johnny Cash being molested by old-time synthesizers, the sing along "Ain't No Getting Round..." and the "Freebird 93"-esque "S. T. A. R. C. A. R." posing the disparate points from which *Autogeddon* converges, Cope institutionalized his oddity just as America was coming to terms with his strangeness. Contrary bugger.

8 20 Mothers (Echo) 1995 Sparse, haphazard, and banal with a vengeance, 20 songs written for Cope's young son range from raking techno pop to hardnosed prog. If Jonathan Richman wrote a song called "Crying Babies, Sleepless Nights," you'd know what to expect. When Cope does it, you're left wondering what vegetation and archaeologists have to do with anything?

9 Interpreter (Cooking Vinyl) 1996 "An all purpose mind map to the Marlborough Downs," insists Cope, but psychic geography is only the tip of this joyously shuffling mix of master strokes as Cope reminds us that he's the only songsmith of the past two decades who actively deserves the tag "Beatlesque" — because he's the only one who doesn't spend his time trying to sound like them, which is what made them so important in the first place.

7 Rite 2 (Head Heritage) 1997

Selected Compilations and Archive Releases

🎵 **Floored Genius (Island) 1992** The ultimate primer, from the Teardrop Explodes to *Peggy Suicide*. Until the Cope box set arrives, it'll do nicely.

🎵 **Floored Genius 2 — BBC Sessions (Dutch East Ini) 1994** Solo career-spanning collection of unreleased BBC recordings.

🎵 **Leper Skin (Polygram) 1999** A greatest hits and rarities collection covering Cope's '80s/early '90s years.

Further Reading

Head On/Repossessed by Julian Cope (Temple 2000).

ELVIS COSTELLO

BORN *Declan MacManus, 8/25/54 (London, England)*

Originally a member of pub rock hopefuls Flip City — whose demos landed him a solo deal with Stiff Records in late 1976 — Elvis Costello (his mother's maiden name) recorded his debut album, *My Aim Is True* (#32 US, #14 UK) in 24 hours in early 1977, produced by Nick Lowe and accompanied by Huey Lewis' country rock band Clover.

Two singles, "Less than Zero" and "Alison," were released before Costello even played his first live show (at the London Nashville on April 27), but on vinyl as much as stage, Costello caused an immediate stir — stark and angular, even in those first days of punk his uncompromising anger and literacy combined to create as lethal a musical brew as any, an assault which only gained in potency after Costello pieced together a backing band, the Attractions: Pete Thomas (b. 8/9/54, Sheffield — drums), Steve Nieve (b. Steve Nason — keyboards), and Bruce Thomas (bass). Both Thomases had pre-punk pedigrees, Bruce with the Sutherland Brothers and Quiver, Pete with Chili Willi and The Red Hot Peppers, but still it was a dramatic combination.

"Red Shoes" gave Costello his *Top of the Pops* debut in August 1977, and in November the brooding "Watching the Detectives"(#15 UK), the Attractions' first single together, became a major hit.

That same month, the band embarked upon the now-legendary Live Stiffs tour, a traveling package which also featured labelmates Lowe, Ian Dury, Wreckless Eric, and Larry Wallis, and would be recorded for one of the crucial live albums of the age, Stiff's *Live Stiffs* (#28 UK). The following month, meanwhile, brought a US release for the *My Aim Is True* album, and the whole process began again.

On December 17, 1977, Costello and the Attractions were the last minute replacement for the Sex Pistols on *Saturday Night Live*, turning in a dramatic performance which saw his scheduled opener, the album's "Less than Zero," suddenly cut short as Costello decided to launch the then unrecorded

"Radio Radio" instead. Rebroadcast during *SNL's* 25th birthday celebrations in 1999, the performance seemed tame, but at the time, Costello's apparent anger and disdain for the system was palpable. He was warned he would never work in American TV again, and an awestricken audience adopted him as the embodiment of all this "punk rock" business they'd been reading about.

The ensuing publicity, coupled with the Attractions' apparently voracious appetite for live work, swiftly paid off. A promo album from their first Canadian tour, *Live at El Mocambo*, became one of the hot properties of the age (it would subsequently be granted a full release within the 2 1/2 *Years* boxed set), and in March, 1978, *My Aim is True* charted in America, where it would be certified platinum in 1991.

Two months later, *This Year's Model* (#30 US, #4 UK), Costello's first for the newly-founded Radar label, appeared, trailing the string of quality 45s which ensured the band were seldom far from the UK Top 30. "(I Don't Want to Go to) Chelsea" (#16 UK), "Pump It Up" (#24 UK) and "Radio Radio" (#29 UK) all hit, the latter cresting just as the band prepared to release their third album, *Armed Forces* (#10 US, #2 UK), in January 1979.

Costello's original title for the album was *Emotional Fascism*, a theme which continued to run through the record even after the title was changed. Certainly it made a queer companion to America's other favorite albums that spring, but still *Armed Forces* broke into the US Top 10, the most successful album yet to come out of Britain's new wave. The accompanying Armed Funk tour, too, saw the Attractions set a record of sorts, as they played three sets at three New York clubs in the same evening.

Returning home, where "Oliver's Army" (#2 UK) and "Accidents Will Happen" (#28 UK) had kept his chart profile high, Costello found himself drawn to the burgeoning 2-Tone movement, producing the first album by the Specials and even briefly releasing his own next single on that label, following Radar's collapse at the end of 1979. He subsequently formed his own label, F-Beat, promptly reissuing "I Can't Stand Up for Falling Down" (#4 UK), alongside a new album, the Lowe-produced *Get Happy!* (#11 US, #2 UK) album. Further hit singles "High Fidelity" (#30 UK) and "New Amsterdam" (#36 UK) followed.

Get Happy! would mark the end of Costello's "angry young man" period, the point at which he began developing away from the "new Bob Dylan" tag which had attended him for three years, and more towards "new Van Morrison" territory — a distressing move for die-hard fans, but a necessary one regardless. This maturity first bloomed on 1981's "Clubland" single (#60 UK) and *Trust* album (#28 US, #9 UK), co-produced by Lowe and Squeeze's Glenn Tilbrook.

(Squeeze would support Costello on his next US tour; Costello would then produce their next album, *East Side Story*.)

It was with *Almost Blue* (#50 US, #7 UK), later that same year, that Costello's now legendary love of American country music burst forth. Previewed by a cover of George Jones' "A Good Year for the Roses" (#50 US, #6 UK), the album also included Patsy Cline's "Sweet Dreams" (#42 UK). Recorded in Nashville with Billy Sherrill, *Almost Blue* was a full-on C&W album; one which was accepted in Nashville itself, when Costello played the Grand Ol'Opry during his December tour.

Of course the album heralded yet another abrupt body-swerve, first when Costello performed with the Royal Philharmonic Orchestra in London in January 1982 — spawning a new single, "I'm Your Toy" (#51 UK); then when he and the Attractions returned to the studio, and went right back to basics.

"You Little Fool" (#52 UK) in June 1982 was swiftly followed by the snarling *Imperial Bedroom* album (#30 US, #6 UK), and further hits "From Head to Toe" (#43 UK) and "Man Out of Time"(#58 UK). Costello also supplied the hit title track to the movie "Party Party" (#48 UK), and retained the mood of those releases with 1983's "Everyday I Write the Book" (#36 US, #28 UK), "Let Them All Talk" (#59 UK), and *Punch the Clock* (#24 US,#3 UK). Despite this apparent return to form, however, Costello and The Attractions were clearly moving apart.

Two singles credited to the Imposter, 1983's "Pills and Soap"(#16 UK, #1 UK indy) and 1984's "Peace in Our Time" (#48 UK), were recorded by Costello alone. Though the Attractions were present throughout Costello's next album, 1984's *Goodbye Cruel World* (#35 US, #10 UK) and single, "I Wanna Be Loved" (#25 UK), when it came time to tour America again, Costello left the band at home, hitting the road instead with T-Bone Burnette. The pair would also record together, as the Coward Brothers, while Costello's own next single, "The Only Flame in Town" (#56 US, #71UK), paired him with co-vocalist Daryl Hall.

A solo Costello was one of the surprise stars of 1985's *Live Aid* festival, performing a raw, unplugged version of the Beatles' "All You Need is Love" (introduced as "an old northern English folk song"); the Attractions would also be absent from all but one track on 1986's *The King of America* album (#39 US,#11 UK) — credited to the Costello Show, and featuring contributions from Tom Waits, Hall and Oates, and members of Los Lobos. The album also spawned the singles "Don't Let Me Be Misunderstood" (#33 UK) and "Blue Chair" (#8 UK indy).

Elsewhere in the album's musician credits, Costello himself was hidden beneath his pre-fame identity of Declan MacManus, and "MacManus" would take center stage again

that year, when he married Pogues bassist Caitlin O'Riordan (Costello's first marriage, by which he'd already had a son before he even recorded his first album, ended in the early 1980s).

Old ties were renewed in August 1986, when Costello reunited with both the Attractions and Nick Lowe for a new single, "Tokyo Storm Warning" (#73 UK). (That same month, he made his acting debut in the movie *No Surrender*.) *Blood and Chocolate* (#84 US, #16 UK, #1 UK indy), followed in October. The publication in 1987 of Bruce Thomas' *Big Wheel* autobiography, however, drove a wedge between vocalist and bassist which would linger for the next seven years, and even prompted Costello to respond to Thomas' complaints with the song "How to Be Dumb," from the *Mighty Like a Rose* album.

Signing to Warner Brothers in late 1988, Costello's next album, *Spike* (#32 US, #5 UK), was primarily designed to showcase Costello's newly-acquired writing partner, Paul McCartney. The collaboration actually dated back to 1987, when the pair co-wrote the McCartney B-side "Back On My Feet." Since that time, Costello and McCartney had co-written and performed both *Spike* and McCartney's *Flowers in the Dirt* (#1 UK) albums, with one of their efforts, Costello's "Veronica" (#19 US, #31 UK), winning Best Male Video at the MTV awards that fall. Costello would also be adjudged Best Male Songwriter in *Rolling Stone*'s year end awards, and even returned to *Saturday Night Live*, on March 25, 1989, for a very different performance to the one that got him "banned" twelve years before.

In May 1989, Costello opened his Month of Sundays residency at the London Palladium, to coincide with a new EP, *Baby Plays Around* (#65 UK); he then launched a US tour through the summer, with a band comprising Attraction Pete Thomas, and session stars Marc Ribot, Larry Knechtel, Michael Blair, Jerry Scheff, and Stephen Soles. Knechtel also joined Costello in the studio to begin work on his next album, 1991's *Mighty Like a Rose* (#55 US, #5 UK), alongside former Elvis Presley sideman James Taylor, bassist Rob Wasserman, and *Spike* drummer Jim Keltner.

Two more McCartney/Costello compositions made it onto this latest album, together with the hit "The Other Side of Summer" (#43 UK), while the accompanying US tour opened at the Santa Barbara County Bowl, closed at Madison Square Garden, and incorporated another *Saturday Night Live* performance (5/18/91).

Through 1991–92, Costello contributed to a number of left-field projects — new albums by Sam Phillips and The Chieftains, a Grateful Dead tribute album, the soundtrack to the ten-hour UK TV drama *GBH*, and a version of the Kinks' "Days" for the soundtrack to Wim Wenders' *Until the End of the World* movie. Most bizarre of all, however, was his late

1992 union with the Brodsky Quartet, to record the neo-classical concept set *The Juliet Letters* (#125 US, #18 UK), based upon the true story of a Verona professor who answered letters addressed to one Juliet Capulet.

With wife O'Riordan, Costello would also compose (in one weekend) an entire album for former Transvision Vamp vocalist Wendy James, the startling *Now Ain't the Time for Tears* (#43 UK) — much of that album's belligerence would reappear on his own next album, *Brutal Youth* (#34 US, #2 UK) and, with it, a full reunion with the Attractions (renamed the Distractions for the occasion), in all their original, garage punk clattering glory.

Four vital singles — "Sulky Girl" (#22 UK), "13 Steps Lead Down"(#59 UK) "You Tripped at Every Step," and "London's Brilliant Parade" (#48 UK) — backed up Costello's harshest collection in years; an album, enthused *Alternative Press*, "[which] reminds us why we loved him in the first place, and why he still hates us in return."

That love/hate dynamic remained in place when the same team convened for 1996's *All This Useless Beauty* (#53 US, #28 UK) and accompanying "It's Time" (#28 UK) single. The intervening two years, meanwhile, were consumed by the Costello-supervised reissue of his back catalog, and the long delayed/oft-deferred appearance of *Kojak Variety* (#102 US), a collection of covers recorded in 1991, which had assumed almost mythic proportions in the intervening four years.

All This Useless Beauty was followed by a pair of singles (the title track and "Distorted Angel") highlighting two of the new British bands with whom Costello was currently enamored, Lush and Sleeper — the latter would accompany him on his 1996 American tour, and Costello's patronage was certainly instrumental in the mid-decade rise of songwriter Louise Wener.

Costello himself, however, was equally interested in pursuing classic songsmiths. In 1996, he played live with Bill Frisell; in 1997, he reunited with the Brodsky Quartet for a contribution to the Kurt Weill tribute *September Songs*, and that same year, appeared on David Letterman's show, performing with veteran Burt Bacharach.

The pair would work together again on the soundtrack to *Grace of My Heart*, and subsequently, across a full album, 1998's *Painted from Memory* (#78 US, #32 UK). One track, "I Still Have That Other Girl, " would earn the pair a Grammy for Best Pop Collaboration with Vocals. Costello's continued taste for the unexpected was similarly confirmed by the release of a five EP box set, *Costello and Nieve*, highlighting a string of low key gigs the pair performed in May 1996, drawing from the full range of Costello's career. A quiet 1999, however, brought only a new compilation, *The Very Best of* (#4 UK) and attendant single, "She" (#19 UK).

Elvis Costello LPs

⑨ My Aim Is True (Stiff) 1977 A bilious collection in substance, if not style, slipping so effortlessly into the punk milieu that even the buzz saws were silenced. "Less than Zero" remains a pivotal moment in rock history, the split second when anger, rage, and understated calm became truly comfortable bedfellows, but the lyrical ambiguities still hang like a well-fed bat. Which Oswald was Elvis really on about: pre-war Brit Fascist Moseley or Kennedy killer Lee Harvey? Or both? Or neither? Either way, the conundrum lent further dimension to Costello's already burgeoning mystique, and no matter how many strings his US label daubed over "Alison," punk elephants never forgot.

⑧ Live at El Mocambo [LIVE] (Columbia) 1978 A super-scarce promo until it resurfaced in the *Two and a Half Years* box set, and prima facae evidence for the Attractions being the best live band of the year.

⑩ This Year's Model (Columbia) 1978 Costello's most perfectly realized recording, a genuinely savage album which continues to brood long after it was hatched. The somewhat sliced up US version, dropping key tracks in favor of singles, has long since been superceded by a CD reissue which restores everything to order, but still "Pump It Up" and the frantic "Chelsea" confound their familiarity with the subtlety of a telephone stalker.

"Night Rally," a second cousin to "Less than Zero," is a defiantly vicious slice of anti-Nazi rhetoric which made perfect sense in a British context, but meant little elsewhere; still its paranoia crowns the closing salvo (the ironic "Living in Paradise," the brittle "Lipstick Vogue") with the finality of a funeral.

Honed to perfection by a year of gigging, and with Costello clearly taking his role as punk's pissed-off nerd neighbor as seriously as it deserved, the Attractions never sounded so well-rounded; organ lines scythe like the Doors never existed (and The Cure lifted a lot of them to prove they probably didn't), and the guitar's so spare that it should be in the other room, being questioned by the FBI. They'll never make it talk, though — this album knows too much already.

⑧ Armed Forces (Columbia) 1979 Retaining *Model*'s viciousness, but tempering the bile, *Armed Forces* emerges savagely schizo, brilliant in part, merely petulant in others. But if "Moods for Moderns" was nasty-by-numbers, "Goon Squad" and "Oliver's Army" retain their shuffling awkwardness and Costello threw in enough other clues to prove he knew when the flogged horse was dead. It was time to get happy, and time for a change.

⑦ Get Happy! (Columbia) 1980 Without a pause for breath, 20 songs, 40-odd minutes, and inflections based chiefly on the same mod era fuelling concerns elsewhere at the time. A shock for the fury-freaks, but time heals.

⑦ Trust (Columbia) 1981 Excise "Clubland" and "From a Whisper to a Scream" (a quasi-duet with Squeeze's Glenn Tilbrook) and *Trust* drags with dreadful finality. Restore them and it could live forever.

⑧ Almost Blue (Columbia) 1981 Having flirted with country a few times already, it was inevitable Costello would turn back to it eventually; clearly eyeing his old Gram Parsons albums, a collection of standards played so straight that even the knowing wink is silent, and the whole thing comes *this* close to falling flat on its face. That it doesn't is testament to the unexpected suitability of *that* voice to the songs. A very unlikely triumph.

5 Imperial Bedroom (Columbia) 1982 With Costello now more concerned with writing "great" songs than simply making good albums, *Bedroom* is what the critics call a "return to form" — but was so patently constructed to elicit that response that it's more fun hunting down the weak spots. It's not that hard either.

7 Punch the Clock (Columbia) 1983 In a perfect world, "Everyday I Write the Book" would have been consigned to *Imperial Bedroom*, and *Punch the Clock* would have been better off without it. Both emotionally and spiritually, a return to the *Armed Forces* temperament — "Pills and Soap" and the so gorgeously despairing "Shipbuilding" (subsequently covered by both Robert Wyatt and London Suede) are the centerpiece, "Charm School" the snarler lurking under the table.

4 Goodbye Cruel World (Columbia) 1984 Too slick, too clean, too AOR. Even guest Daryl Hall sounds a little perturbed. The downward spiral starts here.

4 Blood and Chocolate (Columbia) 1986 Largely colorless partial reunion with the Attractions.

7 Spike (WB) 1989 More guests, more musical chairs, more envious looks at the Songwriters Hall of Fame. But with Paul McCartney on board as co-writer and "Veronica" finally giving "Alison" someone to gossip with, the self-consciousness fades and ambition becomes reality.

5 Mighty Like a Rose (WB) 1991 Cruise control locked, air conditioning on, and we're off to the "Other Side of Summer," the best song he should have written in time for *Punch the Clock*. Unfortunately, the rest of the album chooses lesser role models to ape.

8 Brutal Youth (WB) 1994 The frazzled guitars on "Kinder Murder" lead Costello through his most brutal (and youthful) album in ages, so much so that by the time it hits "This is Hell," you wonder where the last 15 years went. *Armed Forces II* has arrived.

8 Kojak Variety (WB) 1995 Originally bumped off the schedule by *Juliet Letters*, a distinctly Dylanish wander through Costello-shaped covers — the Kinks' "Days," Screaming Jay's "Spell," Dylan's own "I Threw It All Away" — and at last, an Elvis record you can play harmonica too.

7 All This Useless Beauty (WB) 1996 Still garrulous after all these years, the tightness of the title track, "Poor Fractured Atlas," and "The Other End of the Telescope" ensure the recent revival is still in hand.

6 Painted From Memory (Mercury) 1998 Much lauded, but ultimately dry collaboration with master songsmith Burt Bacharach. Clever, clean, but sadly soulless.

The Costello Show LP

5 King of America (WB) 1986 Over-wrought superstar pajama party.

Elvis Costello and Richard Harvey LP

6 Original Music From Gbh (Demon — UK) 1991 The TV show, starring Robert Lindsay and Michael Palin, went on a little bit too long. So, oddly, does the soundtrack.

Elvis Costello and The Brodsky Quartet LP

7 The Juliet Letters (WB) 1993 Strangely effective mock classical conceit, Costello's voice and writing genuinely blending with his collaborators' own charms.

Elvis Costello and Bill Frisell LP

7 Deep Dead Blue, Live at Meltdown (Nonesuch) 1996 Country-tinged live show, with excellent performances of "Weird Nightmare," "Poor Napoleon," and "Deep Dead Blue."

Selected Compilations and Archive Releases

8 Taking Liberties (Columbia) 1980
9 Ten Bloody Marys and Ten How's Your Fathers (F Beat — UK) 1980 Similarly-themed collections of non-album cuts, rarities and the *My Aim Is True* era off cut, "Hoover Factory."

7 Best of (Telstar — UK) 1985
7 Best of Elvis Costello and the Attractions (Columbia) 1985
8 Girls Girls Girls (Columbia) 1989 Straightforward passage through the back catalog, with *Girls* edging ahead by virtue of bulk (2CDs) and a less obvious track selection.

9 2 1/2 Years (Rykodisc) 1993 The first three albums, the *El Mocambo* live set, and another disc's worth of bonus tracks, wrapping up Costello's '70s. There's a reason this wasn't called *The Best of Elvis*, but if you think about it seriously, it's not a very good one.

8 The Very Best of (WB) 1999 Like the subtitle says, the best of the Warner Brothers years, and from "My Dark Life" to "London's Brilliant," an entire young generation of studious singer-songwriters can be heard wrestling with their personal muses.

Further Reading
A Biography by Tony Clayton-Lea (From Intl, 1999).

WAYNE COUNTY

BORN *Wayne Rogers, 7/11/47 (Dallas, GA)*

Wayne Rogers arrived in New York from the Georgia county which gave him his stage name in the late 1960s, gravitating into the Andy Warhol circus in time to star in Jackie Curtis' *Femme Fatale* (opposite Patti Smith) and *Pork*, the revolutionary stage show which — among other things — helped the young and unknown David Bowie find his own calling in life.

Rising through the New York art underground, author of such off-off-Broadway epics as *World — Birth of a Nation* and *Wank*, County found his true performing feet in 1972 when he launched Queen Elizabeth, positively the last word in American Glam Rock. Outrageous, scatological and hilariously obscene, County was promptly whisked back to London by Bowie, signed to the superstar's Mainman management team — and then kept under wraps for the next two years, before being let go. One freak on the streets was apparently quite enough.

Back in New York, County formed the Backstreet Boys with guitarist Greg Van Cook and became a regular at Max's Kansas City — two live tracks appeared on 1976's semi-seminal *Max's Kansas City* album. But it was County's re-emergence in London in 1977 which remains one of the defining moments in the development of punk rock, a convention-crushing creation which strained even that genre's taste and tolerance.

Signed to Police manager Miles Copeland's Illegal label, County and Van Cook formed a new band, the Electric Chairs, around bassist Val Haller and drummer Chris Dust, and cut the *Electric Chairs* EP. County alone also starred in Derek Jarman's *Jubilee* movie, performing the stage favorite "(I Was) Fucked By the Devil Last Night" (since retitled "Paranoia Paradise").

Regulars at both the Roxy Club and The Vortex, the Electric Chairs were unbelievable. Other US imports, the debauched Johnny Thunders and the delicious Cherry Vanilla, made it in Britain because they at least pretended to play by punk rules. County, shrieking, shaking, shitting on stage (it was actually dog food, but you'd only know that if you sniffed it), behaved like nothing on earth, even after he dropped the overt drag dress, and came out in city-bum formals. His gigs were freakshows, his songs were sick sermons, and there was barely a better night out to be had in the city.

Moving to the newly-formed Safari label, the Electric Chairs released the immortal "(If You Don't Want to Fuck Me) Fuck Off" single, slamming themselves into the headlines a full six months before the Sex Pistols' "Bollocks" scandal. An indy chart hit despite a total broadcast ban, "Fuck Off" landed at least one fan in court, after she was arrested for wearing a button emblazoned with the song title, while Safari themselves pre-empted the Parental Advisory craze of a decade hence by packaging the song within an EP titled *Blatantly Offensive*.

Riding the publicity, the group followed up with "Eddie and Sheena," a love song aimed at quelling the rising street warfare between punks and Teddy Boys; and "Trying to Get

On the Radio," a blatantly commercial song which was the group's stab at doing precisely that.

While undergoing several line-up changes, as Dust was replaced by JJ Johnson, Haller by Henry Padovani, and Van Cook by fellow Backstreet Boys alumni Eliot Michaels, the group also recorded 3 albums of increasingly tense, extraordinarily excitable shock rock'n'roll, peaking with 1979's *Things Your Mother Never Told You*.

Still credited to Wayne County, despite the singer having now undergone sufficient medical procedures to be considered "Jayne," *Things Your Mother Never Told You* was a deeply ambitious album, produced by Flying Lizards mastermind David Cunningham, and highlighted by "Berlin," a song which compared with Bowie at the height of his own fascination in that city. It would, however, be the group's last record together.

County and Michaels returned to New York after the Electric Chairs' final show at the London Lyceum was broken up by bottle-throwing thugs demanding less new material, and more old favorites. The remainder of the band returned to the studio with Cunningham to record an album of their own (eventually released as a mere single).

Forming a new band around Michaels, bassist Peter Jordan and Drummer Sammy Minelli, County recorded the live *Rock'n'Roll Resurrection* (#18 UK indy) in Toronto on the last night of the '70s, for release in the new year. She then moved to Berlin to complete her sex change; it would be 1983 before County resumed regular live work, returning to London armed with the songs which would eventually emerge on the 1986 album *Private Oyster*.

Now regarded, with some validity, as a vaudevillian novelty act, County's career since that time has relied as much upon live albums, repackaged oldies, and remixes of "Fuck Off" (most recently a Millennium mix, "Fuck Off 2000") as new material. 1989's *Betty Grable's Legs* and 1995's *Deviation* albums would emerge isolated jewels within a sea of reissues, while County's 1995 autobiography, *Man Enough to Be a Woman*, proved one of the most entertaining, and honest, rock reads of the decade.

Jayne/Wayne County LPs

7 The Electric Chairs (Safari — UK) 1978 Brusque and brittle, still firmly in the jaws of punk shock horror and still recalling "Max's Kansas City." "Bad in Bed" would become a live favorite, though, and "Eddie & Sheena" was classic through and through.

8 Storm the Gates of Heaven (Safari — UK) 1978 Moving closer towards a truly savage identity, *Storm* boasts a remarkable sleeve photograph and a devastating version of "I Had Too Much to Dream Last Night." The presumably autobiographical "Man Enough to Be a Woman" and (the presumably not) "Mr. Normal" offered other highlights.

10 Things Your Mother Never Told You (Safari — UK) 1979
With everybody from Patrick Swayze to the reborn Boy George
having gotten into post-*Priscilla* desert queenery, it seems hard to
believe there was ever a time when County, the original
rock'n'roll trash-gender behemoth, should be denied a fair hearing for what he did, rather than what she sounded like.

Forget the trash aesthetic crown which County's early vinyls
catalog conferred without question, *Things* was a genuine post-
punk tour de force; its title track a snarling, nasty denouement of
innocence at the wrong end of town, while "The Boy With the
Stolen Face" — featuring NY chanteuse Patti Paladin — posed a
scenario which wouldn't have been out of place on a Richard
Hell album.

The experimental "C3" and "Waiting for the Marines," both
predict the kind of antics which producer David Cunningham
would later undertake with his own Flying Lizards, but the tour
de force is "Berlin" a sleazoid dip into the backstreet alleyways
and bars of a city which everybody knew was Europe's most
degenerate, but no one really knew why. Now they did, but still
Things kept sending its postcards from the sort of edge which conventional rock'n'roll stars rarely visited. In other words, there
really were things your mother never told you. County lets you in
on some of them.

6 Rock and Roll Resurrection [LIVE] (Safari — UK) 1980 A
pick-up band and a new year's party pin down a ferocious, but
sadly under-rehearsed concert set.

7 Private Oyster (Revolver — UK) 1986 "Are You a Boy or Are
You a Girl" may be retreading old ground, but there's no escaping
the eye for detail which underpins "The Lady Dye Twist" and "I
Fell in Love With a Russian Soldier." Completely overlooked at
the time, but a confident return all the same.

6 Betty Grable's Legs (Jungle — UK) 1989
7 Deviation (CSA — UK) 1995 It's still pure Big Apple punk,
and Jayne's still writing about what she knows best — herself —
thus the rollicking "Transgender Rock'n'Roll" and "That's What
the New Breed Say." And then it's down to business with the tale
of a "Nuclear Age Vampire" and the macabre "Texas Chainsaw
Manicurist," while even her covers take on an aura of danger and
perversion never imagined on the originals.

Selected Compilations and Archive Releases
9 Let Your Backbone Slip (RPM — UK) 1995
8 Rock'n'Roll Cleopatra (Royalty) 1995 The complete story,
told through album cuts, radio sessions, rarities, and out-takes.
Highlights include an unassailable revision of "Too Much to
Dream Last Night," a cracking BBC version of "Berlin," and so
much more.

Further Reading
Man Enough to Be a Woman by Jayne County/Rupert Smith
(Serpent's Tail, 1996).

COWS

FORMED 1986 *(Minneapolis, MN)*
ORIGINAL LINE-UP *Shannon Selberg (vocals, bugle); Thor Eisentrager (guitar); Kevin Rutmanis (bass); Norm Rogers (drums)*

The Cows emerged, in simplest terms, out of a desire to do
something "different." Thor Eisentrager explained, "we
wanted to do something pretty unconventional, and we
worked hard on it. We play music that we like" — in a setting
they enjoyed. With Shannon Selberg haunting thrift stores,
gas stations, and sex shops in search of a stage full of increasingly bizarre toys and props, much of the band's early notice
related as much to the visuals as the music.

In a city already desensitized to noise by Hüsker Dü and
the early Replacements, however, the Cows worked hard to
stand aside from the crowd, and having removed anything
even vaguely resembling the conventions of songwriting
from their sound, the band released their first album, then
sat back while the critics insisted it was a talentless joke.

A rerecording of "Chow" was released as a single in 1988,
debuting the band on the Amphetamine Reptile label which
they would soon come to epitomize, and over the next two
years, two new albums — *Daddy Has a Tail* in July 1989, and
March 1990's *Effete and Impudent Snobs* (and the "Slap
Back" single) placed the Cows in firm minor cult status, both
at home and in the UK. With Tony Oliveri on drums, their
March 1990 tour included an appearance on the John Peel
show, later included on a compilation devoted in its entirety
to the program's Amphetamine Reptile guests.

The group's style began to change with March 1991's
Peacetika. Originally intended to feature 15 songs, it was
eventually cut to just eight (two of the absentees later surfaced on an Australian single, "Woman Inside," and "Theme
from Midnight Cowboy") — a relinquishment of much of
the band's initial intensity in favor of what would become a
more lyrically brutal, but musically less unfathomable brew.

1992 brought the single "Plowed," one of the band's strongest releases. It was followed by the twin peaks of *Cunning
Stunts* and *Sexy Pee Story*, collections which saw Selberg's
rage and abuse channeled into almost conceptual terms.

August 1994's *Orphan's Tragedy* saw the band adopt
another change, broadening their sound out of the claustrophobic clatter of old and moving away from the rants as well.
Indeed, much of the album was instrumental, a shock to fans
who'd grown to rely upon Selberg to always have something
new to complain about, and there were further shocks to
come after Rogers quit in 1996. His last recording with the
band was "Four Things," a contribution to Pandemonium's
Erase Your Head II compilation.

Rogers was replaced by Freddy Votel for the *Whorn*
album, a set which found the Cows, peculiarly (and certainly

despite themselves) poised on the brink of a step forward. They accepted a berth on Lollapalooza '96, through the second half of the outing, and followed up by touring with Tool. And while that step forward never actually happened, still the heightened profile would see the Cows' appeal expand beyond the members' own wildest dreams.

What a relief, then, when their next record arrived, and proved to be just as abrasive as their last; fall 1997 brought the picture disc EP *The Missing Letter Is You*, a prelude to the band's most recent offering, March 1998's *Sorry in Pig Minor*.

Cows LPs

7 Taint Pluribus, Taint Unum (Treehouse) 1987 Tragically badly recorded though it is, the screaming, grinding, honking mess which occasionally pulls itself into something like music sounds *great* at 3 in the morning. "Summertime Bone" on the other hand, sounds like next door's kid practicing the horn.

6 Daddy Has a Tail (Amphetamine Reptile) 1989 An unpleasant reworking of "Shaking All Over" points the Cows in the not entirely unexpected direction of foulness and filth for the sake of it. Again, however, they apparently forgot to use a recording studio when they made it, preferring to hand etch the songs into chewed up pieces of oxide. Difficult.

8 Effete and Impudent Snobs (Amphetamine Reptile) 1990 And then it all comes together around a thing called "Nancy Boy Cocaine Whore Blues," with words and structure and all that weird stuff. Are the Cows losing it? Or is it just another horrid trick?

5 Peacetika (Amphetamine Reptile) 1991 They're losing it and it's a trick. Now locked firmly into a quasi-hardcore discipline — that is, playing the way people say hardcore was created, when they really don't have a clue — even the Cows appear to be losing interest. And after the apocalyptic "Hitting the Wall," who can blame them?

3 Cunning Stunts (Amphetamine Reptile) 1992 From the tired old joke of the title to the tired old noises within...

4 Sexy Pee Story (Amphetamine Reptile) 1993

5 Orphan's Tragedy (Amphetamine Reptile) 1994

7 Whorn (Amphetamine Reptile) 1996 Coming back from the brink, with lyrics to match — now they sound like a very bad-tempered Crass. That is a Good Thing.

7 Sorry in Pig Minor (Amphetamine Reptile) 1998 The Melvins' King Buzzo produced, which goes some way to explaining an album as dense as a wet winter landslide; other than that, it's business at its still-improving usual. "No I'm Not Coming Out" would sound great on *MTV's Death Match*, by the way.

Selected Compilations and Archive Releases

7 Old Gold 1989–91 (Amphetamine Reptile) 1996 Straightforward reissue of *Daddy*, *Effete*, and *Peacetika*

CRACKER

FORMED 1992

ORIGINAL LINE-UP *David Lowery (b. 9/10/60, San Antonio, TX — vocals, guitar); Johnny Hickman (guitar); Bob Rupe (b. 9/16/56, Michigan — bass); Dave Lovering (b. 12/6/61, Boston, MA — drums)*

Coming together in 1992, around a nucleus of ex-Camper Van Beethoven frontman Lowery, Hickman, ex-Silos bassist Rupe, and former Pixie Lovering, Cracker was launched with "Teen Angst (What the World Needs Now)," an impassioned saga of ironic sex and disaffection set to a boiling powerpop soundtrack: "what the world needs now is another folk singer, like I need a hole in the head." Lowery explained, "at the time I wrote it, I was really tired of hearing these angry, cynical, self-loathing songs, so I wrote this song that's perceived by some people as an angry, cynical, self-loathing song. It's a really eloquent little tirade."

Followed into heavy rotation by the equally frenetic "Happy Birthday to Me," "Teen Angst" established Cracker and the eponymous debut album from which both cuts were taken, as a solid songwriting machine, and one whose bite was considerably sharper than its bark.

Returning from tour, Cracker intended recording their second album live in the studio; four songs, including the maniacal "I Ride My Bike," and "Bad Vibes Everybody" were completed before the project was abandoned and converted to the *Tucson* EP. Instead, the group got to work on a new record, the masterful *Kerosene Hat* (#59 US).

Recorded with Davey Faragher and Michael Urbano, replacing Rupe and Lovering, Cracker's country album was an hour long celebration of joyously unbridled redneckery crammed with instant classics like "Eurotrash Girl"; buried away among the hidden songs at the end, a sing along classic wherever the band played live (but a surprisingly unsuccessful single). "Movie Star," "Let's Go for a Ride," "Get Off This" (#41 UK), and "Low" (#64 US, #43 UK) — a song Lowery described as "part 'Wizard of Oz,' part 'Flowers of Evil'" — became alternative radio favorites through 1994. The *New Musical Express* even coined a new genre for the latter, the delightful (but sadly unexplored) "grunge noir."

Despite the album's obvious reference points, Lowery was adamant, "we're not trying to do [country] authentically. We take things and get it wrong, then it becomes something new." Cracker took this process to the next stage with their third album, 1996's *The Golden Age* (#63 US).

The record kicked off with the latest in Lowery's litany of sonic shark attacks (and the album's first single) the blistering "I Hate My Generation." "I'm talking about 35-year-olds," said Lowery, who was in his mid-30s at the time of the interview. "I feel like my generation was the last generation that had expectations, and then shit didn't pan out. Everybody is so fucking bitter. When it got hard, they all gave up, and they're just bitter assholes now."

For him, age had simply given him the chance to write about subjects "I had no business writing about before. Suddenly you actually have experiences with people dying, or fucked up things happening." And while "a lot of people say I'm always cynical, there are [only] two songs out of 12 on this record with maybe an element of cynicism in them." Unsurprisingly, a single called "Nothing to Believe In" did not appeal to the masses; neither did the maudlin "Sweet Thistle Pie."

Despite a two-year break while the band's live routine was interrupted by Lowery's burgeoning career as a producer (Sparklehorse, Joan Osborne, Counting Crows), *Gentleman's Blues* (#182 US) and the singles "Good Life" and "The World is Mine" maintained this same tradition of being old before his time. Still unafraid to wander through whichever musical pastures took their fancy, as though the band's whole goal in life was to ramble, both "My Life Is Totally Boring Without You" and "I Want Out of the Circus" captured Cracker's creaking country blues vibe to perfection.

In fact, Lowery said, "the only thing I feel is a little weird this time, is we keep getting comparisons to Camper. I think *The Golden Age* sounds more like them than this one does. It's a little confusing to me, but it's hard for me to totally judge what our records sound like. The only problem now, of course, is that a lot of younger people read that and they go 'what? Camper What?'"

Also see the entry for "CAMPER VAN BEETHOVEN" on page 237.

Cracker LPs

7 Cracker (Virgin) 1992 Twanging guitars, nods to the blues and Southern rock confirm that Cracker are, at least musically, true to their name. Lowery's typically twisted sting-in-the-tail lyricism is the first point of entry, the radio-friendly "Teen Angst" and "Happy Birthday to Me" are both sly examples of the singer's sardonic talents, but it's "Can I Take My Gun to Heaven" that's the real knee slapper.

9 Kerosene Hat (Virgin) 1993 Expanding to a four piece, Cracker plug in their guitars and rock out. Still musically diversified, still bent on the psychotic side of country blues, *Hat* peaks more often than any other album in Lowery's catalog, with "Low" a particular high, a Dead cover a surprising triumph, and the acoustic twang of the deranged teenaged twang of "Eurotrash Girl" buried away in the hidden tracks at the end.

6 The Golden Age (Virgin) 1996 Drily disappointing, not only in the wake of *Kerosene Hat*, but also in terms of its own approach and content.

7 Gentleman's Blues (Virgin) 1998

Selected Compilations and Archive Releases
8 Garage D'Or (Virgin) 2000 Two CD collection of rarities, hits, and out-takes.

CRAMPS

FORMED *1976 (New York, NY)*
ORIGINAL LINE-UP *Lux Interior (b. Erick Lee Purkhiser, 1948 — vocals); Poison Ivy Rorschach (b. Kirsty Malana Wallace, 1954 — guitar); Brian Gregory (b. Detroit — guitar); Pam Balam (b. Pam Gregory, Detroit — drums)*

Lux Interior and Poison Ivy Rorschach met hitching round California in 1972. He was on the run from a childhood in Ohio, she was escaping Sacramento, so they pooled their vintage record collections, sold clothes and made surfboards, and suddenly it was 1975 and they were in New York.

The Cramps came together almost immediately. Guitarist Gregory worked in the same Upper East Side record store as Interior, his sister Pam had a drum kit (Interior and Rorschach were adamant they didn't need a bassist) and, as songs came together, ambition quickly followed. So did a new drummer — like guitarists, the first of many — Canadian-born Miriam Linna, and on November 1, 1976, the Cramps played their first ever show, opening for Suicide at CBGBs. Ivy changed her guitar strings right before the show, but she didn't know how to tune them — so she didn't even try. The Cramps got three encores.

A year later, the band was getting three encores every time they played — and they were playing a lot. Linna was replaced in July 1977, by Nick Knox (b. Nicholas George Stephanoff; Cleveland, OH — ex-Electric Eels) and with Alex Chilton calling them "the best rock'n'roll band in the world," the Cramps were ready to record.

Chilton took them to Memphis to make their first record; they ended up at Ardent Studios, working in a time capsule recreation of rock'n'roll's spiritual home, and if the ghosts the band sensed there weren't already inside them, they piled in with a passion that evening.

Released in April 1978, on Vengeance, "The Way I Walk" was followed in October by "Human Fly," both singles then being compiled together as 1979's *Gravest Hits* EP, after the Cramps signed with Illegal. The Cramps' first album, *Songs the Lord Taught Us* (#1 UK indy) followed in April 1980, immediately staking its claim as one of the key albums of the early 1980s, single-handedly kick-starting the punkabilly revival which would grow up the antithesis of the (simultaneously breaking) Stray Cats' clean cut retro recreations.

The singles "Fever" (#12 UK indy), "Garbageman," and "Drugtrain" (#5 UK indy) added to the fervor, and while the departure of Gregory in mid-1980 caused some alarm, he was readily replaced, first by Julien Bond, then by ex-Gun Club guitarist Kid Congo Powers (b. Brian Tristan) in 1980, shortly before the release of the masterpiece *Psychedelic Jungle*, and attendant singles "Goo Goo Muck" and "The Crusher."

Sadly, this majestic line-up would accomplish little of vinyl note. Disputes with their record label, simmering through the early 1980s, finally exploded in 1983, with legal volleys which kept the Cramps out of the studio for a full year — and when they did return, it was with a one-off deal with Enigma, and the live EP *Smell of Female* (#74 UK, #4 UK indy), capturing a Peppermint Lounge show from February.

Two singles from the album, "Faster Pussycat" (#7 UK indy) and "I Ain't Nuthin' but a Gorehound," were released in France, before Congo returned to Gun Club in fall, 1983, to be replaced by Ike Knox (b. Mike Metoff). The band then returned to the road for much of the next year, starting work on a new single, "Can Your Pussy Do the Dog" (#1 UK indy) in September — shortly after Fur (b. Jennifur Stokes) became the Cramps' first ever fulltime bass player.

Based around another cover, Del Raney Umbrella's "Can Your Hossie Do the Dog?," "Pussy" became the Cramps' best selling single yet, and ended the year — not, perhaps, altogether surprisingly — as *Playboy* magazine's Single of the Year. But that was only the beginning.

Lux Interior of the Cramps

© Jim Steinfeldt/Chansley Entertainment Archives

With ex-Satan's Cheerleaders bassist Candy Del Mar replacing Fur, 1986's *A Date with Elvis* (#34 UK, #1 UK indy) was only the fourth "new" Cramps album in eight years, but its timing was fortuitous. Rock'n'roll had been getting very soft just lately, what with Band Aid and Live Aid, and old metal-heads with hearing aids; "people were talking about how rock'n'roll is 'good' again," Interior complained loudly.

He wanted to remind them that the only good rock'n'roll is bad rock'n'roll; sexy, dirty, rude, and raucous. Songs like "Kizmiaz" (#15 UK indy) and "What's Inside a Girl?" (#2 UK indy) were all that and more, but the only way you'd know that was if you lived in one of the countries which realized such things needed saying. *A Date with Elvis* couldn't even get an American release.

In 1987, Ramones vocalist Joey appeared on an L.A. radio station to announce that Lux Interior had died of a drug overdose. The Cramps' latest album, the live *Rockin'n'reelin'* set (#4 UK indy), was fresh on the shelves, but the signs that something was wrong had been evident for some months now — a three month European tour had left the Cramps drained, physically and mentally. They were still unable to find an American deal. The sad news was halfway round the world before Ramone had even left the studio... which was how Interior himself got to hear about it. He lived with the news of his demise all evening, then called the radio station the next day. He was resuscitated just in time to stop the European music press from running his obit.

Still it was to be another year before the Cramps were ready to work again; close to three before the results of their latest sessions were made public. But *Stay Sick* (#62 UK) was worth the wait, and a string of singles — "Bikini Girls with Machine Guns," "All Women Are Bad," and "Creature from the Black Leather Lagoon" appeared intent on making sure everyone knew that.

The longest surviving Cramps line-up ever finally sundered in 1991, with the departures of both Nick Knox and Candy Del Mar; they were replaced, respectively, by Jim Sclavunos (ex-Lydia Lunch's Teenage Jesus and the Jerks and an early Sonic Youth) and Slim Chance of the Mad Daddys, whose 1985 *Music for Men* album was produced by Ivy and Lux. This line-up completed the brilliantly titled *Look Mom! No Head* (and "Eyeball in My Martini" single) before Sclavunos departed, in 1992, following the "Blues Fix" single. He resurfaced alongside fellow ex-Cramp Kid Congo in a new band, Congo Norvell.

Sclavunos was replaced briefly by ex-Weirdos and LA Guns drummer Nicky Alexander, before Rocket 88's Harry Drumdini moved into the drumseat for the remainder of the decade. This line-up would record 1994's *Flame Job* album and the singles "Ultra Twist," "Let's Get Picked Up," and "Naked Girl Falling Down the Stairs." Three years later, still intact, the group would sign with Epitaph for *Big Beat from Badsville*.

Slim Chance departed shortly before the Cramps' 1998 Halloween shows; Doran Shelley replaced him through the Christmas period, but departed after a disastrous New Year's Eve gig; ex-Celebrity Skin bassist Sugarpie Jones joined in time for the Cramps' fall 1999 US tour.

Cramps LPs

9 Songs the Lord Taught Us (IRS) 1980 Non-stop graveyard ghoulishness, like a lifetime's worth of '50s b-trash movies injected into your brain all at once. "Garbageman," "Sunglasses After Dark," "Zombie Dance," "Fever"... No longer mere songs, they're an entire dialect.

9 Psychedelic Jungle (A&M) 1981 And again? And again. "Goo Goo Muck," "Voodoo Idol," "The Caveman," "Green Door"... the papers called it psychobilly, but even that was too weak and watery for this.

8 Smell of Female [LIVE] (Enigma) 1983 All new material (new to vinyl anyway), with "Psychotic Reaction" spiraling out to drop things in your wig hat.

5 Date With Elvis (Big Beat) 1986 Never afraid of the human condition, the Cramps' growing interest in all things — smut soaked reaches an occasionally tiresome crescendo, in amid too few good bits.

6 Rockin'n' Reelin' in Auckland, New Zealand [LIVE] (Vengeance) 1987

8 Stay Sick! (Enigma) 1990 While "Journey to the Center of a Girl" and "Creature from the Black Leather Lagoon" looked back at the psychedelic surf trash which marked the early albums, "Women Are Bad" peered into the future — the band's and America's — with Interior the maniacal preacher who's so convincing in his zeal. If it wasn't for the backward messages which sputter through "Journey"... no, no-one could make that mistake. "Your sweet Satan, my ass; in France they wear no underpants and you're just a turkey from Albuquerque." Have you been corrupted yet?

7 Look Mom! No Head (Restless) 1991

7 Flamejob (Epitaph) 1994 The usual blend of swampy rockabilly, shot through with punk, glam, and psychedelia. The surprises lay in the proportions of these basic ingredients, in the disinterred ancient nuggets (an oddly effective "Route 66" included), and in the themes and lyrics. There's plenty of sex, love, weirdness, and wonder, of course, but fresher than they've been for a while, and maybe a little bit more wicked.

7 Big Beat From Badsville (Epitaph) 1997 Twenty years on... an Energizer bunny in mascara and 6" heels, a freak force defying the last laws of nature, and so enticing! "Sheena's in a Goth Gang," "Haulass Hyena," "Super Goo," "Wet Nightmare" — even if this album is a bit slower tempo'd than normal, it's sexier and more sinuous, too. But of course, they haven't changed a bit.

Selected Compilations and Archive Releases

9 ... Off the Bone (Illegal) 1983 The evil twin to *Songs the Lord...*, early singles and the *Gravest Hits* EP in all their bone-chattering glory.

CRANBERRIES

FORMED 1990 *(Limerick, Ireland)*
ORIGINAL LINE-UP *Dolores O'Riordan (b. 9/6/71, Ballybricken, Limerick — vocals, keyboards); Noel Hogan (b. 12/25/71, Moycross, Limerick — guitar); Mike Hogan (b. 4/29/73, Moycross, Limerick — bass); Fergal Lawler (b. 3/4/71, Parteen, Limerick — drums)*

The brothers Noel and Mike Hogan and Fergal Lawler formed their first band, The Cranberry Saw Us during the summer of 1989, with a friend named Niall Quinn — he quit in May 1990, and recommended Dolores O'Riordan as his replacement. Abbreviating their name to coincide with her arrival, "Linger" was the first song the new look group completed, and they made their live debut soon after, in front of 60 people in the basement of a Limerick hotel.

Within a month, the Cranberries were recording their first demo, with local producer Pearse Gilmore; their *Nothing Left at All* tape appeared on their own Xerica label that fall, in an edition of 300.

A second demo brought the band to the attention of Island Records, and following a June 1991 tour with Moose, the band returned to the studio to begin work on their debut single. In October, a second Xerica release (distributed by Island) brought the *Uncertain* EP, but by the new year, attempts to continue working with Gilmore — now acting as the band's manager as well as their producer — ended with the band opting to end their relationship, and begin again. Litigation with Gilmore would finally be settled in 1995; in the meantime, Rough Trade founder Geoff Travis, and former Smiths' producer Stephen Street were enlisted, and the album sessions resumed at Windmill Studios in Dublin, in June 1992.

October brought the "Dreams" single, followed by the minor hit "Linger" (#74 UK) and a UK tour with Belly. The group's first album, *Everybody Else Is Doing It, So Why Can't We?* (#18 US, #64 UK) arrived the following May, to little action in the UK, but immediate success in the US. Working with Street paid off, and with O'Riordan's already idiosyncratic and heavily-accented vocals pushed far to the front, the album soared, accompanied by the reactivated "Linger" (#8 US).

A six week tour with The The, followed by a handful of dates with London Suede, kept the Cranberries in the US throughout much of the year, and the band returned to the UK to find Island preparing to repromote their entire catalog, using stateside success as the launching pad. The plan worked. A reissued "Linger" (#14 UK) was followed by "Dreams" (#42 US, #27 UK), and finally the album topped the UK chart in June 1994, a full 16 months after its release, and just weeks before O'Riordan married Cranberries tour manager Don Burton.

In August, the Cranberries appeared at the Woodstock II event, and October brought their second album, the harder tinged *No Need to Argue* (#6 US, #2 UK). At the same time, the band's latest UK single, a commentary on the Irish troubles, "Zombie" (#14 UK) became a firm radio favorite, particularly after the Cranberries' *Saturday Night Live* appearance, in February 1995. There, an impassioned "Zombie" would emerge one of the most powerful performances that show has ever seen, while the band's spring tour of America, too, saw O'Riordan, in particular, staking her claim to rank among the finest vocalists of her generation.

While the band's European fans had to remain content with a summer festival tour and a string of singles — "Ode to My Family" (#26 UK), "I Can't Be With You," (#23 UK) and "Ridiculous Thoughts" (#20 UK) — the Cranberries spent 1995 on the road in Australia and the US, where Berriesmania was sweeping the country. A free concert in the shadow of the Washington Monument in DC was halted by the police after just one song, as some 10,000 fans turned up, and in late July, *No Need to Argue* was certified quadruple platinum. (Their debut would emulate this feat in the new year.)

The group toured relentlessly, breaking only to record or for such extra-curricular ventures as O'Riordan's appearance alongside Luciano Pavarotti at the War Child benefit in Italy in September. The May 1996, release of the group's third album, *To the Faithful Departed* (#4 US, #2 UK), and the single "Salvation" (#13 UK), of course, simply extended this hectic schedule even further.

Yet the Bruce (Aerosmith) Fairbairn produced set was the group's weakest yet. Apparently sincere sentiments ("Bosnia," "I Just Shot John Lennon," and the Kurt Cobain tribute "I'm Still Remembering") emerged callow and mawkish, and the emotion apparent on the first two albums sounded drained. In August, the band launched a world tour titled after their latest single, "Free to Decide" (#22 US, #33 UK), but just weeks into the outing, the reasons for the album's failings became apparent. The group was exhausted, with O'Riordan, in particular, utterly shattered by the events of the past four years.

In October 1996, amidst rumors of a split, the group's latest European and Australian tours were abandoned, and the Cranberries disappeared from view. It would be more than two years, and a lot of rumors later, before they resurfaced, first with a contribution to the Fleetwood Mac tribute *Legacy*; then with an appearance at the Nobel Peace Prize Concert in Oslo, in December 1998, with their first live show, and a new album set for a fall 1999 release.

Previewed by the single "Promises" (#13 UK), *Bury the Hatchet* (#13 US, #7 UK) — titled for the task which faced the band members as they reconvened — was co-produced over a six month period by the band and Benedict Fenner, the most leisurely sessions the band had ever experienced. The result was an album which utterly swept away the disappointment of its predecessor, and returned the Cranberries to what early fans considered their rightful place; powerful, melodic and timelessly provocative.

Cranberries LPs

8 Everybody Else Is Doing It So Why Can't We (Island) 1993 While the band mine the obvious bits of U2 and The Cure (that bass line simply doesn't know when to stop), O'Riordan's complex keening reaches for notes which simply shouldn't fit (but do), and emotions she shouldn't touch (but does). "Linger" lingers longest, while "How" goes all *Nevermind* on an up-and-under Blondie gymnastic, but really, everybody else is doing a lot of things, none of which truly match the Cranberries.

6 No Need to Argue (Island) 1994 Live, "Zombie" is an explosion of pent-up frustration. On record, it blends seamlessly into an album which daren't raise a finger lest it disturbs the band's burgeoning super stardom. Not quite toothless simplicity (they're saving that for next time), but wet wet wet.

2 To the Faithful Departed (Island) 1996 "I Just Shot John Lennon," sings Dolores, apparently mindless of the fact that she's just shot a hole in her foot as well, as the Cranberries take on the weight of the world then try to solve all the problems with a song. But how many times can you stand in a stadium, and tell 10,000 screaming fans, "and here's one we wrote for Kurt Cobain"? Ha — they should have thought of that before they wrote it.

9 Bury the Hatchet (Polygram) 1999 A suddenly discovered sense of humor is not the sole reason for the Cranberries' utter redemption — O'Riordan's reluctance toward the zombie squawking of old is also praiseworthy. But still this album astounds, as the Cranberries' slip effortlessly into the void left by Lush's late departure, all unlikely lyrical asides and absurdly contagious choruses, and one song ("Copycat") which is so screwed up, you'd never believe it was them.

CRASS

FORMED 1977 (London, England)
ORIGINAL LINE-UP *Steve Ignorant (vocals); Eve Libertine (vocals); Phil Free (guitar); Pete Wright (bass); Penny Rimbaud (drums) plus others — Joy De Vivre; Hari Nana; Ge Sus; Mike Duffield; Virginia Creeper, etc.*

Crass formed as they meant to go on, a rowdy accumulation of friends and neighbors who'd turn up at whatever passed for rehearsals, and played along with whatever was going on. Steve /Ignorant and Penny Rimbaud were the most permanent members, others just came and went.

By spring 1977, the band had gathered enough equipment and sufficient songs to play their first live shows, and Crass launched onto a chaotic career which saw them banned or rejected from as many venues as they appeared at. Unrepentantly adhering to the ethics of punk, Crass purposefully positioned themselves at the furthest end of the spectrum, politically, musically and culturally — "the [Sex] Pistols, The Clash, and all the other muso-puppets weren't doing it at all," Rimbaud decreed. "They helped no one but themselves, started another facile fashion, brought a new lease of life to London's trendy King's Road and claimed they'd started a revolution. Same old story."

Through the winter of 1977, Crass landed a virtual residency at the White Lion in Putney, most often twinned with the equally unknown UK Subs and generally powered by a copious quantities of adrenalin and alcohol; Rimbaud admitted "we were still too scared to play without a bellyful of booze, and invariably we were in such a state that we'd realize halfway through a song that each of us was playing a different one." By early 1978, however, the band members had settled down and realized they could achieve far more if they remained sober.

They began experimenting with mixed media, launched a newspaper, *International Anthem*, and vowed to keep their newly-designed Crass banner flying until the end of 1984 — a date redolent in Orwellian foreboding. They also launched a graffiti campaign which saw London peppered with short, but generally thought-provoking slogans, all inherent to Crass' vision — "fight war, not wars"; "stuff your sexist shit," and of course, the circle-A of anarchy, central to the band's logo, and destined to become one of the most potent symbols of the age.

The band's support of the then-moribund Campaign for Nuclear Disarmament (CND), too, found a willing ear among the country's disenfranchised punks; Crass were, in many ways, singlehandedly responsible for the wholesale revival of that organization's fortunes through 1978/79. Anarcho-pacifism, soon to become synonymous with British punk, was born.

In summer 1978, the band recorded their first album, after Small Wonder records asked them for a single then couldn't decide which song they wanted. Titled for the number pressed, *The Feeding of the Five Thousand* (#6 UK indy) appeared in spring 1979, as a multi-tracked 45, capturing the full Crass live set on vinyl, and while the music press loathed it and its makers with a passion which even 20 years of nostalgia has yet to soften, the band suddenly found themselves selling records. Sham 69 frontman Jimmy Pursey offered his management services ("he told us he could 'market revolution' and that we'd never succeed without his help"), but Crass turned him down. Their dream had no room for either marketing or success.

A single, "Reality Asylum" (#9 UK indy), followed on the band's own Crass label — the song had been intended for inclusion on *Feeding*, but Small Wonder was unable to find a pressing plant willing to actually handle the song's apparently virulent blasphemous sentiments. It was omitted then, and once the single was released, the band discovered why. Stores carrying the record were raided by the police; the band themselves spent an afternoon being interviewed by the Vice Squad; and while the ensuing publicity did win the band a session for John Peel, in April 1979, it was the only one they'd ever be offered.

That summer, Crass released their second album, *Stations of the Crass* (#1 UK indy), its ambitious fold-out sleeve depicting some of their graffiti work at a London subway station. Again it was released on their own label — Small Wonder, having now been raided almost as many times as the band, still supported the Crass, but simply couldn't function amid the disruption which attended their every move. The band were rewarded with a hit which spent a record-breaking 106 weeks on the indy chart, a success which they immediately poured back into Crass Records.

By the end of the year, Donna and the Kebabs had joined the roster, to be followed by releases by the Poison Girls, Zounds, Flux of Pink Indians, Annie Anxiety, Captain Sensible, the pre-Sugarcubes Kukl and more. In addition, the *Bullshit Detector* series of compilations brought recorded debuts to musicians as disparate as future London Suede drummer Simon Gilbert (with Dead to the World) and Catherine Wheel's Neil Sims (1984).

In spring 1980, Crass combined with the Poison Girls for the "Bloody Revolutions" (#1 UK indy) single, supporting the creation of an Anarchist center for Persons Unknown organization and setting in motion an uneasy liaison between old school anarchists and Crass-fired anarcho-punks.

Such associations added to the social stigma surrounding the band themselves. The HMV chain of record stores banned Crass product from the stores after taking exception to a free poster included in this latest single. The band's attempt to play the 1980 Stonehenge festival ended when a gang of bikers descended to beat them up; while Crass's own audience was widely disaffected when the band's next album, 1981's *Penis Envy* (#1 UK indy), emerged a collection of generally gentle feminist anthems, instead of the hail of abusive abrasion they'd been expecting.

Crass also succeeded in further enraging the tabloids after they presented the album's final track, "Our Wedding," to *Loving* magazine as a give-away flexi disc. Totally convinced by the song's apparent sentiments (and unaware that the generous Creative Recording and Sound Services disguised a far more sinister acronym), the magazine offered the song to its readers as "a must have for that happy day." By the time the hoax was revealed, any number of happy couples had adopted a song by Crass as their "special tune."

"Nagasaki Nightmare" (#1 UK indy) in February 1981, "Rival Tribal Rebel Revel," and the *Merry Crassmas* EP (#2 UK indy) preluded the summer 1982 release of Crass' third LP, *Christ: The Album* (#26 UK, #1 UK indy); however, the band was now walking a very fine line between speaking their mind, and genuine sedition.

In spring 1982, Britain went to war with Argentina over the Falkland Islands; when Crass promptly rushed out an anti-war flexi disc, the music press equally promptly denounced them as traitors. Unchastened, the band followed up with "How Does It Feel (To Be the Mother of a Thousand Dead)," openly dedicated to British Prime Minister Margaret Thatcher, and the British government announced the band would be prosecuted under the Obscene Publications Act.

MP Tim Eggar described the song as "the most vicious, scurrilous and obscene record ever recorded"; his brother, *Daily Mirror* rock critic Robin, called it "the most revolting and unnecessary record I have ever heard." Yet the case crumbled after Eggar MP confronted the band on live radio and found his arguments utterly crushed. Not only did the government back down, but an internal memo was circulated ordering all conservative party members to ignore any future provocation from Crass.

Yet the band itself was shaken by the controversy. No more the merry pranksters riling some shadowy Powers That Be, those Powers now had faces — some of them, members of the opposition Labour Party, were even writing the band letters of support. Crass returned their attentions to domestic ills such as homelessness (in late 1982, they played a major, illegal show at the recently closed Zig Zag Club, now a prominent squat), and disputing the already inevitable outcome of the forthcoming General Election. Campaigning not on domestic issues, but on the tide of jingo-ism unleashed by victory in the Falklands, Thatcher was guaranteed victory, but Crass' *Yes Sir, I Will* album (#1 UK indy) at least offered a show of resistance. The election itself would be followed by in June by the self-explanatory "Sheep Farming in the Falklands" (#1 UK indy), and in July by "Who Dunnit?" (#2 UK indy).

Crass were also responsible for leaking the infamous *Thatchergate Tapes* to the world press, a heavily-edited "tele-phone conversation" between Thatcher and US President Ronald Reagan, in which the British leader "confessed" to many of the Falkland War's most notorious incidents. The band considered the whole thing a clumsy, if thought-provoking spoof. At government level, however, the tapes came close to creating an international incident, as the State Department and the media in both countries rushed to blame the Kremlin! It was some months more before a UK newspaper journalist finally traced the true culprits, by which time the damage had been done. Questions were now being asked about the war, opening the way for subsequent official revelations to actually bear out many of the tape's accusations.

The incident made media stars of Crass. American, British, even Russian media demanded interviews and TV appearances; and of course, the band's beliefs and principles became as much a part of the circus as their activities. "We had gained a form of political power," reflected Rimbaud, "and were being treated with a slightly awed respect," in other words, "we had become the very thing that we were attacking." Though Crass remained a target for the law — being found guilty on another obscenity charge came close to bankrupting the band — "we had become bitter where once we had been joyful, pessimistic where once optimism had been our cause."

The "You're Already Dead" single and *Best Before 1984* compilation followed, but that summer, Crass played what was to become their final show, a benefit for Britain's striking miners. Hari Nana quit soon after, and the band folded. The sign-off on their final statement encapsulated their disillusion — "what was once CRASS, but now knows better."

Vocalist Ignorant subsequantly surfaced alongside Current 93; he also joined Crass proteges Conflict during the late 1980s before forming a new band, The Stratford Mercenaries, in 1999. Their debut album, *Sense of Solitude* followed in March 2000.

Also see the entries for "CRASS RECORDS" on page 756 in "PRODUCERS & LABELS" and for the "BULLSHIT DETECTOR compilation" on page 224.

Crass LPs

8 Feeding of the 5,000 (Small Wonder) 1978 You don't play Crass records. They play you.

9 Stations of the Cross (Crass) 1979 One mighty skull-charring slab of undisciplined, raucous adrenalin screeched over buzzsaw guitars and gut-blasting percussion some of the most invigorating (not to mention pure) punk rock ever recorded.

9 Penis Envy (Crass) 1981 Crass' most cohesive, musical, and dare it be said, lovely album, music to soothe the savage beast, and even once the story leaked, "Our Wedding" remained the perfect song for that special day.

8 Christ the Album (Crass) 1982 The title was so guaranteed to offend that the music didn't matter. And so it didn't. You can turn it down, but you can't shut it out.

8 Yes Sir I Will (Crass) 1983

Selected Compilations and Archive Releases

8 Best Before 1984 (Crass) 1984 Selecting a best of Crass is a crapshoot at best. Just buy everything.

CREATURES

FORMED 1981 (London, England)

ORIGINAL LINE-UP Siouxsie Sioux (b. Susan Dallion, 5/27/57, London, England — vocals); Budgie (b. Peter Clark, 8/21/57, St. Helens, England — drums)

The Creatures began life as a side project designed to fill time between the members' regular Siouxsie and the Banshees efforts, an outlet for songs and expressions which had no place in the main band's repertoire — and also, Budgie later admitted, as "a way for Sioux and I to get alone, to figure out who we were. You're pretty blind when love kicks in, so we went mad celebrating something we'd never experienced before."

Debuting in October 1981, with the *Wild Things* EP (#24 UK), memorably packaged in a sleeve featuring both members topless in a Holiday Inn shower, the Creatures seemed doomed to remain a one-off project, as over a year passed without any attempt at a follow-up. But they were resurrected in early 1983, during a scheduled break in the Banshees' career (bassist Steve Severin would while away the same period working with part-time Banshee Robert Smith of The Cure, on the Glove project).

With more time at their disposal, the Creatures completed a full album, *Feast* (#17 UK), and enjoyed two more hits, the insistent swing of "Miss the Girl" (#21 UK) and a cover of Mel Torme's "Right Now" (#14 UK). Then it was back into mothballs until March 1990, when a new single, "Standing There" (#53 UK), and album, *Boomerang* (#197 US), emerged.

Like *Feast*, which the duo taped in Hawaii, the album was recorded "somewhere exotic — because we could." They chose Cadiz, Spain, and like its predecessor, the album reflected the surroundings.

Initially there was no intention to tour — logistically, such an undertaking seemed impossible. Demand for a US outing, however, was so great that finally Siouxsie and Budgie agreed, surrounding themselves with a vast array of computers and machinery, and heading out on a very well-received set of dates.

The tour over, the Creatures were again retired, remaining in mothballs until the Banshees' 1995 break-up. That,

said Budgie, was when he and Siouxsie realized that "a project we'd started as a sideline suddenly became our career, and not a very stable one at that." Hopes that the Banshees' US label, Geffen, would keep the duo on board were dashed, while legal difficulties surrounding the Banshees' demise meant it would be 1996 before anybody could even acknowledge what had happened.

Finally giving up hopes of attracting a new label deal (but with a Creatures compilation, *A Bestiary Of...*, on the streets in 1997), the pair formed Sioux Records from their home base in France, and in 1998, they launched a phenomenally successful US tour with John Cale (producer of the Banshees' final album, *Rapture*).

The first in a stream of limited edition singles and EPs appeared soon after: "Sad Cunt" would be followed by "Eraser Cut" and "2nd Floor" (appearing as a phenomenal Lol Hammond/Girl Eats Boy remix), with "Exterminating Angel" arriving shortly before Christmas, 1,000 copies with hand-painted sleeves ("you couldn't do that on a major label!" Budgie enthused).

Licensed to Instinct in the US, the *Anima Animus* album appeared the following spring, while further singles — "Say" and "Prettiest Thing" — arrived packed with remixes and new material, keeping alive the duo's dream, Budgie explained, of "making it fun to follow a band again, collect their records, look out for special releases and hard to find picture sleeves." A limited edition live album, *Zulu*; an accompanying EP *Now Buy Zulu*, and a remix collection, *Hybrids*, would also appear during the year.

Also see the entry for "SIOUXSIE AND THE BANSHEES" on page 617.

Creatures LPs

7 Feast (Wonderland) 1983 Exotic menage of semi-Hawaiian chanting and percussive effects, over which Siouxsie rehearses increasingly eclectic variants on future Banshee refrains.

7 Boomerang (Geffen) 1989

8 Anima Animus (Instinct) 1999 Budgie's throbbing electronics blip beneath Siouxsie's so blatantly trademarked vocals, but there's a real sense of the Eurythmics here — which is weird, because Lennox and Stewart always sounded like they wanted to be the Banshees. An edgy, disconcerting album, further over the edge than anything Siouxsie's put her name to in years... probably since the first Creatures album in fact.

7 Zulu [LIVE] (Sioux — UK) 1999

8 Hybrids [REMIXES] (Instinct) 1999 How odd. A remix collection which doesn't waste your life away with interminable loops, beats, and false starts to songs which never begin. Rather, Howie B, Black Dog, Superchumbo, and The Beloved (among others) ensure songs remain songs, moods retain their roots and, with most becoming purity, deliver an alternative you'll actually want to listen to some more.

Selected Compilations and Archive Releases

7 A Bestiary of Creatures (Polygram) 1998 The *Wild Things* EP and first album in their entirety.

CRIME AND THE CITY SOLUTION

FORMED 1978 (*Sydney, Australia*)

ORIGINAL LINE-UP *Simon Bonney (vocals); Harry Zanteni (guitar);Phil Kitchener (bass); Dave MacKinnon (sax); Don McLennan (drums)*

Although the group had been together since 1978, when vocalist Simon Bonney and drummer Don McLennan formed the original line-up for gigs around their native Sydney, it would be 1985 before Crime and the City Solution stirred on anything approaching an international level.

The pair passed through two incarnations of Crime prior to their break-up in 1979; Bonney alone reformed the group in 1985, after meeting up with old friend Mick Harvey (b. Rochester, Australia) in Melbourne, following the collapse of his band, the Birthday Party. They recorded some demos together before Harvey returned to London, where Bonney would join him in late 1984. With Rowland Howard's bassist brother Harry, and eventually, Rowland Howard himself joining on guitar (Harvey played drums), the band began gigging, recording *The Dangling Man* EP (#17 UK indy), the following year.

The arrival of former Swell Maps drummer Epic Soundtracks (b. 1960, London; d. 11/22/97) allowed Harvey to move to guitar, and with the Australian media describing Crime's music as "tasteful grunge" — three full years before the same term was applied to some very dissimilar sounds emanating from the Pacific Northwest — the group recorded two mini-albums, *Just South of Heaven* (#3 UK indy) and *Room of Lights* (#14 UK indy), and scored another hit, "The Kentucky Click" (#27 UK indy).

Already, however, the band was unraveling. Bonney moved to Berlin in 1986, with Harvey following; the Howards and Maps, meanwhile, remained in London, a geographical dislocation around which creative differences within the band continued to fester. Finally the UK-based trio split to form their own band, These Immortal Souls — a band name Rowland Howard had first contemplated some two years earlier, during rehearsals with the Laughing Clowns' Geoffrey Wagner and The Moodists' Chris Walsh. Demos were

recorded, but the other musicians' commitments elsewhere brought the project to a halt. Now the band could be resumed.

In Berlin, Bonney and Harvey set about piecing together a new Crime line-up in mid-1987, playing a handful of Berlin shows before embarking on a tour of eastern Europe in April 1988. Lining up with Bonney's wife-to-be Bronwyn Adams (violin), Einsturzende Neubauten guitarist Alexander Hacke, keyboard player Chrisio Haas (ex-D.A.F.), and bassist Thomas Stern, the group released the single "On Every Train" (#20 UK indy) in April 1988, following through with *Shine*, that same year. The band also contributed to the soundtrack to Wim Wenders' *Wings of Desire*.

1989 brought the album *The Bride Ship* and EP *The Shadow of No Man*; the following year's *Paradise Discotheque* trailed the singles "I Have The Gun" and "The Dolphins and The Sharks." But the excitement which surrounded their earliest releases dissipated seemingly with the band's own willingness to pursue the moods which had once characterized their efforts. A shadow of their former selves, Crime finally broke up following a pair of gigs at CBGBs in New York, on August 5 and 6, 1991. *The Adversary* live album captured highlights of these shows. Harvey, already a regular member of Nick Cave's Bad Seeds, would launch a solo career; Bonney would follow.

Also see the entry for "BIRTHDAY PARTY" on page 199.

Crime and the City Solution LPs

9 Just South of Heaven/Room of Lights (Mute) 1986 While Nick Cave was busy polishing his sound, Crime were concerning themselves with jagged cacophony, ragged and rough rock under the auspices of dirty goth. This remains their finest hour: "Right Man, Wrong Man" is sublime while the haunting "Six Bells Chime" is still awe inspiring. The CD includes bonus early tracks from *Just South of Heaven* and *The Dangling Man* EPs, and is an important chronicle of a band who still remain vastly underrated.

7 Shine (Mute) 1988 Time has tempered the tide somewhat, as Crime's sophomore set boasts a slicker, more mellowed sound. The album is nearly the antithesis of its predecessor — empty space and sparse arrangements replacing the crashing melody and urgent hooks of *Lights*. The dirgy laments, too, are different, but the end result is fascinating nonetheless.

7 Bride Ship (Mute) 1989 More of the same, but with an edgy energy as Bronwyn Adam's strings find a stronger place.

6 Paradise Discotheque (Mute) 1990 -A very grown up Crime deliver a very grown up album, impeccably produced and slick. It's good, if fairly generic, although "The Dolphins and The Sharks" retains some of their earlier sparkle, while "The Last Dictator" parts 1–4 are a self-indulgent concept gone entertainingly awry.

Selected Compilations and Archive Releases

6 The Adversary — Live (Mute) 1993 Recordings from Paris, 12/19/90 and Crime's final shows, in New York, 8/5–6, 1991.

These Immortal Souls LPs

7 Get Lost (SST) 1987

7 I'm Never Gonna Die Again (Elektra) 1992 A delicious foray into the morose annals of the slow dirge, Howard whining and sneering his way though a swamp, while Soundtrack's drums beat blood-red behind him.

Simon Bonney LPs

8 Forever (Mute/Elektra) 1992 Bonney comes swaggering, grumbling, through a bag of Cohen- and Cave-shaped clichés, wondering "who will kiss your eyes when you sleep?" Dangerously dull.

7 Everyman (Mute/Elektra) 1995 Still largely acoustic and downbeat as hell, a semi-conceptual walk through the trashcans of America, from Greyhound stations to grizzled old loners, peeping through cardboard coated windows and throwing pennies to the homeless. Coming to terms with Bonney's country leanings is only the first challenge it meets; rehabilitating Bonney is its greatest accomplishment.

Mick Harvey LPs

7 Intoxicated Man (Mute) 1995

8 Pink Elephants (Mute) 1997 Offering his own translations of French wild man Serge Gainsbourg's most iconoclastic creations (including a delicious Nick Cave/Anita Lane version of "Je T'Aime"), Harvey's faintly sozzled maudlinity offers insights into its subject that the Frenchman's native tongue would never permit.

Rowland Howard/Lydia Lunch LPs

10 Shotgun Wedding 1991 The mid-1980s "Some Velvet Morning" single served notice that there was a musical chemistry between Lunch and Howard which neither had enjoyed elsewhere; that it took close to six years more for them to bring it to fruition remains testament to their activities elsewhere.

Produced by Foetus with stunning understatement, *Shotgun Wedding* is first and foremost, a strikingly musical album. No experimentation, no shrieking, not even too much damage, the duo let the songs speak through the textures as much as the lyrics, although there is no shortage of suitable subjects on board.

"In My Time of Dying" gets the definitive reading which neither Dylan nor Zeppelin were capable of delivering, Alice Cooper's "Black Ju Ju" restores the Dead Baby boy to his seething punk origins, and "Incubator" sounds almost Top 40. Elsewhere, the semi-rap "Pigeon Town" and the laconic "Cisco Sunset" proves the further versatility of the team's songwriting acumen, and though this is by far Lunch's most accessible album, if it wasn't by Lunch, that wouldn't seem surprising.

Epic Soundtracks LPs

7 Rise Above (Bar None) 1993

6 Sleeping Star (Bar None) 1994

8 Change My Life (Bar None) 1996

Selected Compilations and Archive Releases

8 Everything Is Temporary (Innerstate) 1999

CRYSTAL METHOD

FORMED 1994 *(Los Angeles, CA)*
ORIGINAL LINE-UP *Scott Kirkland (b. Las Vegas, NV — electronics); Ken Jordan (b. Las Vegas, NV — electronics)*

Crystal Method's acid funk beat was premiered in 1994, on the "Now is the Time" single, a logical progression from Scott Kirland and Ken Jordan's DJ-ing activities on the L.A. rave scene, and released through ex-pat Brits Steven Melrose and Justin King's City of Angels label. It was followed in 1995 by the signature "Keep Hope Alive" tribute to the rave community, and over the next year, regular remixes of both singles would maintain a strong presence on American dance floors.

Crystal Method signed to Geffen's Outpost subsidiary in 1996, immediately setting up as a homegrown response to the recent Chemical Brothers/Prodigy-led British invasion. Their debut album, *Vegas*, would indeed live up to that challenge (it would eventually be certified gold), while the duo's dramatically theatrical live performances went some way towards bettering the imports.

A 14-month US tour followed, interspersed with contributions to such soundtracks as *Lost in Space* and *South Park's Chef Aid*, the latter teaming Crystal Method with Ozzy Osbourne and Ol'Dirty Bastard. Hopes for a swift follow-up album recorded with Motley Crue drummer Tommy Lee were dashed, however, when Kirkland admitted, in spring 1999, that "we haven't really found a niche [in the studio] yet."

Instead, Crystal Method joined Orbital, the Lo Fidelity All-Stars, and DJ John Kelley on July 1999's Community Service Tour, to try out ideas "and just get out of the studio." Still experimenting, they followed that with a berth on September's Family Values outing, alongside Limp Bizkit, Primus, Filter, and more.

Crystal Method LP

9 Vegas (Outpost) 1997 One of the most impressive debuts in the history of the club scene, *Vegas* was a stunning amalgamation of driving rhythms, anthemic vocal snippets, and sublime melodies, wrapped in a hint of darkness, but overcome by the uplifting beats.

CULT

FORMED 1987 (Bradford, England)
ORIGINAL LINE-UP Ian Astbury (b. Heswall, Cheshire, 5/14/62);
Billy Duffy (b. William Duffy 5/12/61, Manchester — guitar)

Raised in Canada, Ian Astbury returned to northern England in 1978, lured by the punk rock scene he'd seen on TV. Moving first to Liverpool, he was involved in several bands (including Send No Flowers), none of which ever got off the ground; then to Belfast, Northern Ireland, where he fronted Children of Lust. By late 1981, he was sharing a house with some like-minded punks in Bradford, and from a chaotic aggregation of personalities and musical preferences, Southern Death Cult began to take shape around Astbury, drummer Haq "Aky" Qureshi, guitarist David "Buzz" Burrows, and bassist Barry Jetson.

Adopting the American Indian imagery he'd learned to love in Canada, but running it first through the wringer of English punk as it transmuted towards the New Romantic look on the one hand, and the still nameless scene epitomized by Bauhaus and Siouxsie and the Banshees on the other, Southern Death Cult were a striking vision, aided by some monstrous good fortune. Their first ever gig, in early 1982, was filmed for a TV show called *What a Life*; their first London gig, opening for Chelsea at the Marquee, was reviewed in *Sounds* — and that first review called them "the Second Coming."

The band were immediately invited on tour with Theatre of Hate; swung from there into a similar outing with Bau-haus. By the end of 1982, Southern Death Cult were confidently selling out their own shows, and released their first single, "Fat Man" (#43 UK, #1 UK indy) in December. It topped the indy listings for two weeks and set the stage for a bidding war that could have set the group up for life. Instead, Astbury broke the band up, and began plotting a new outfit, Death Cult, with Theatre of Hate guitarist Billy Duffy.

Agreeing that the new band should at least try to capitalize on Southern Death Cult's high profile, they dubbed the group Death Cult, linked with drummer Ray Taylor Smith and guitarist-turned-bassist Jamie Stewart from low-grade goth rockers Ritual, and walked straight onto the cover of the *NME*.

Beggars Banquet rush-released the band's debut, the four-track *Brothers Grimm* EP (#2 UK indy), and the following week, Death Cult made their live debut, in Oslo, Norway. "God's Zoo" (#4 UK indy) followed; then, with another Theatre of Hate graduate, Nigel Preston, on drums, the name was truncated even further. "The idea was to make it in America," Astbury unabashedly announced. "And we were never going to do that with a name like Death Cult."

The Cult's *Tube* appearance on January 14, 1984, was stunning. Astbury came on stage with half his face painted, the Hard Rock God stepping out of his Goth Theatrics body. It was an effective device, and one whose visual connotations were only emphasized by the band's next two singles, "Spirit-walker" (#1 UK indy) and "Resurrection Joe" (#74 UK).

In August 1984, the Cult departed for their first professional look at their spiritual homeland, America, playing

© Jim Steinfeldt/Chansley Entertainment Archives

shows in New York and Los Angeles before returning home to watch their debut album, *Dreamtime* (#21 UK), cement their metamorphosis in the public mind, and begin work themselves on the next stage of their transformation.

Introducing the wide-screen rock sound which would come to characterize the band's sound, "Sanctuary" (#15 UK) was released in May 1985, and continued selling so strongly that it returned to the chart six months later. "Rain" (#17 UK) followed. Replacing the increasingly drug-dependent Preston with Big Country's Mark Brzezicki (he would subsequently give way to Les Warner, from Julian Lennon's band), the Cult then cut *Love* (#87 US, #4 UK), a savage amalgam of modern rock and '60s psychedelia which sold over 200,000 copies in Britain, but whose American reception was positively overwhelming.

They played the Christmas 1985 *Saturday Night Live*, then launched a tour which saw the Cult treated like chart-topping heroes. The band resolved that from here on in, all their efforts would go towards ensuring that reception became a reality.

According to the Cult's own mythology, the sessions for what became the *Electric* (#38 US, #4 UK) album passed by with Astbury in an almost perpetual stupor; he himself admits that he was drunk every day of the sessions. "That record is like my evil twin, the Mr. Hyde to *Love*'s Dr. Jekyll, a really dark album. I mean, all we did was drink, I was completely fucking wasted all the time, I don't remember being sober during that period at all."

The album was scrapped, and in November 1986, Astbury and Duffy flew to New York, initially to remix the tapes, but ultimately to rerecord them. In February 1987, four months after *Electric* was originally scheduled, the first fruit of the sessions, "Love Removal Machine" (#18 UK) was finally released. (The abandoned sessions were reserved for UK B-sides.)

With Stewart shifting to rhythm guitar and Kid Chaos (ex-Zodiac Mindwarp) in on bass, the Cult's 1987 US tour was an absolute triumph. *Electric* was Top 40 bound, and MTV could not get enough of the group. Even without breaking the Top 100, "Li'l Devil" (#11 UK) and "Wild Flower" (#24 UK) joined a long line of Cult video smashes, and whatever musical turbulence would be shaping the second half of the hitherto stagnant 1980s, the Cult were clearly going to be part of it.

"The whole scene was changing," Astbury reflected. "I think it was inevitable because of the way punk fell into the '80s, and suddenly Phil Collins was omnipresent, Phil Collins was Buddha, Mick and Keith, Bruce Springsteen, Sting, Eric Clapton... the Live Aid crowd just permeated the eighties, and the younger groups couldn't come through because

there was no way through that hierarchy. I mean, how do you get past Phil Collins?

"Then in the late eighties, groups like Metallica burst through, Guns'n'Roses burst through, we burst through, the rap scene burst through. Suddenly there was something happening again, and whatever it turned out to be, it was a changing of the guard. Goodbye Mr. Spandex Seventies Rocker, hello Mr. Big Hair Eighties Rocker."

The Cult continued touring through 1987–88, headlining over an infant Guns'n'Roses on an outing which was swiftly to ascend to the annals of Rock Legend as the drunken episodes mounted up as quickly as the wrecked hotel bills. By the time the band came off the road in March 1988, the Cult was in total disarray. The most immediate casualties were the band's management team, and Kid Chaos and Les Warner, all of whom were let go. (Chaos, or Haggis as he was now calling himself, immediately formed the Four Horsemen.)

Astbury, Duffy, and Stewart relocated to Los Angeles, recruiting new management, a new rhythm section, and a new producer. They eventually settled on Aerosmith engineer Bob Rock, and with Stewart reverting to bass, session drummer Mick Curry was recruited, and the team headed to Canada to begin work on *Sonic Temple* (#10 US, #3 UK), an album which finally embraced the metal genre, even as the metal fans embraced the band.

Attended by the singles "Fire Woman" (#46 US, #15 UK), "Edie"(#93 US, #32 UK), "Sun King," (#39 UK) and "Sweet Soul Sister"(#42 UK), and with Matt Sorum moving into the drum seat, the Cult set out on their latest world tour on April 29, 1989, beginning with a slot opening for Metallica's "Damaged Justice" jaunt across the US.

"It was," Astbury reflected, "madness, the height of Bacchanalian fucking, living off the vine, white line fever, trashing hotel rooms, groupies... you name it, it was going on. I was right in the heart of this thing and it's going on every fucking night. It was like a bordello every night, traveling in a mobile whorehouse. Everywhere we were, it was happening."

It was in the midst of this that Astbury hatched the vision which would, within two years, be reborn as perhaps the single most influential innovation of the entire decade-to-come, the Gathering of the Tribes festival which not only ignited Perry Farrell's near-identical dream of Lollapalooza, but remains the spiritual fore-father of every travelling festival of the 1990s. Staged in October 1989, Gathering of the Tribes was an extravaganza of cross-cultural, counter-cultural music, art, and politics — a resounding triumph ironically at a time when Astbury's own life was at an all time low.

Sorum and Stewart both quit the group, finances were in disarray, lawsuits were flying from every direction. Astbury's father died, and two weeks later, so did his close friend

Andrew Wood, vocalist with the Seattle band Mother Love Bone. A dispirited new album, 1991's *Ceremony* (#25 US, #9 UK), was recorded with bassist Charley Drayton and *Sonic Temple* drummer Mick Curry, but emerged, in Astbury's words, "a fucking shambles"; two singles, "Wild Hearted Son" (#40 UK) and "Heart of Soul" (#51 UK) were barely noticed. Only as Astbury set about putting his life back together, could he rebuild the band as well.

It was a slow process, encompassing the recruitment of yet another rhythm section for yet another world tour (Kinley Wolfe and Michael Lee), balanced by time spent with his future wife, Heather.

The Cult's resurrection was signaled by the release of a dramatic new single, "The Witch," recorded with Rick Rubin in 1992 for the *Cool World* movie soundtrack. Wolfe and Lee were dismissed, to be replaced by bassist Craig Adams, on the run from the Mission, and Dag Nasty drummer Scott Garrett, and after a clutch of summer 1993 dates (with first, Guns'n'Roses, then Metallica), the band headed to Vancouver, Canada, to begin work on a new album — titled, simply *The Cult* (#69 US, #21 UK).

Two singles, "Coming Down" (#50 UK) and "Star" (#65 UK), sandwiched the album and live work which would take the band across the US, Europe, and Australia. Gene Loves Jezebel guitarist James Stevenson came on board for the tour and, for a time, the Cult was back at its best. But onstage in Rio de Janeiro in March 1995, Astbury shattered the band.

"The Cult was breaking up for quite a long time," the singer reflected. "I was always dismayed that we never lived up to our potential and all. There was constantly struggles within the band, certainly creatively. I always wanted to be more progressive and Billy was evolving more into hard rock guitar. He didn't seem to be able to break out of that mold, that was the conflict right there. And also, we were so incompatible as people, we were like chalk and cheese, completely different people, completely different interests."

The members scattered to the winds. Stevenson returned to Gene Loves Jezebel, and also rejoined Craig Adams and Billy Duffy in former Alarm frontman Mike Peters' new band. Astbury, meanwhile, formed the Holy Barbarians with Lucifer Wing guitarist Patrick Sugg, former Cult drummer Scott Garrett, and his brother, bassist Matt. Demoed in L.A. and recorded in Liverpool, the Holy Barbarians' debut album, *Cream* appeared in 1996, but swiftly vanished.

By 1999, Astbury and Duffy were again working together as the Cult, even as Astbury complete work on his own forthcoming solo debut, *Natural Born Guerilla*. Produced by Masters of Reality frontman Chris Goss, and featuring a reworking of The Cult's own "The Witch," the album was far deeper embroiled in electronica than he had ever gone before. "My fascination has been going on since about 1987–

88, [but] it really wasn't something I could do with the Cult. It wasn't really appropriate."

Nevertheless, the revamped Cult — featuring returning drummer Matt Soren and Porno for Pyros' bassist Martin Lenoble — had little difficulty in handling the challenge. A handful of warm-up shows in southern California in June 1999, were followed by the band's great unveiling at the Tibetan Freedom Concert in Chicago on June 13, the prelude to a 24-date summer tour — and to thoughts of a new Cult album as well.

The Cult LPs

8 Dreamtime (Beggars Banquet — UK) 1984
7 Dreamtime Live (Beggars Banquet — UK) 1984 Still cloaked in the final vestiges of Southern Death Cult's slow transition, "Spiritwalker" and "Resurrection Joe" place the band on a cusp so decisive that you can hear the live album weighing its options.

8 Love (Sire) 1985 "She Sells Sanctuary" was a deceptive, if utterly anthemic, introduction. The true sound of *Love* is found in "Revolution" and "The Big Neon Glitter." Big neon guitars, more like.

8 Electric (Sire) 1987 The sonic assault of "Love Removal Machine," and a terrifying rampage through "Born to be Wild" show the band's heads have finally arrived at their goal. The album which made stars of Guns'n'Roses.

6 Sonic Temple (Sire) 1989 "Edie" exuded a beauty and charm tailor-made for the band's sense of self, but utterly at odds with the remainder of this sadly overwrought creation. The crassly manipulative cliché of "Fire Woman," on the other hand, knew precisely what it was meant to be doing.

4 Ceremony (Sire) 1991 Honest attempt at reinvention, scuppered by an absolute division in the old time unity.

7 The Cult (American) 1994 Sudden change in fortunes, renewed eye on the future, "Coming Down" and "Black Sun" would have dignified the best of the Cult's back catalog, while "Star" still stuns if you play it loud enough.

Selected Compilations and Archive Releases

8 Pure Cult (Beggars Banquet — UK) 1993
7 High Octane Cult (WB) 1996 Vinyl pressings of *Pure Cult* feature a bonus, but a sadly late-in-the-day live set; *High Octane* and *The Singles* just bang out the singles in heart-stopping succession.

7 The Singles (Beggars Banquet) 2000

Southern Death Cult

Selected Compilations and Archive Releases

9 Southern Death Cult (Beggars Banquet) 1984 The singles, the B-sides, the radio sessions, the live cuts, the demos, the kitchen sink, anything to stuff an album full of souvenirs of a band who outlived their usefulness before anyone realized how useful they were.

Holy Barbarians LP
7 Cream (Sire) 1996

Ian Astbury LP
8 Natural Born Guerilla (Beggars Banquet) 1999

CULTURE CLUB

FORMED 1980 (London, England)
ORIGINAL LINE-UP *Boy George (b. George O'Dowd, 6/14/61, Eltham, Kent — vocals); Mikey Craig (b. 2/15/60, Hammersmith, London — bass); Jon Moss (b. 9/11/57, Wandsworth, London — drums); Roy Hay (b. 8/12/61, Southend — guitar)*

Boy George was already a familiar figure around the London clubs when former Sex Pistols manager Malcolm McLaren recruited him to front the early Bow Wow Wow. It was a short lived affair, highlighted by one show at the London Rainbow before George quit, to link with disc jockey Mikey Craig and guitarist John Suede in a new band, In Praise of Lemmings. Name changes saw the band spend some months as Sex Gang Children (a name George subsequently gave to goth figurehead Andi Sex Gang), before settling on Culture Club, following the arrival of Roy Hay and former London/Damned drummer Jon Moss.

George's initial vision was a "tripped out reggae band," roots and technology slamming together into one glorious whole, but when future Pet Shop Boy Neil Tennant, then working as a journalist with the magazine *Smash Hits*, caught the band's first ever live show, he was quick to condemn. "He said the worst thing about Culture Club is they use tapes," George recalled. "Then I went to see him about 10 years later, and I thought 'where's the band?'"

The group's first two singles, "White Boy" and "I'm Afraid of Me" echoed George's ambition. But, George continued, "somehow or other, Donald Fagen crept in, and things like that, Quincy Jones. Roy liked that stuff and it's good, but I don't know if it was really good for us."

The dub-lime skank of "Do You Really Want to Hurt Me" (#2 US, #1 UK), Culture Club's third single and first major hit, was the turning point, not only for the band's musical ambition, but also for George. Hitherto a subversive freak, the kind of creature people would back away from when they saw him on the street, George became the London media's house weirdo, always ready with a quick retort, and an opinion on absolutely everything.

Kissing to be Clever (#14 US, #5 UK), the group's debut album, and the single "Time (Clock of the Heart)" (#2 US,

#3 UK), were both swept along in the maelstrom; so was America, which regarded George as the safe face of counter-cultural excess. "Church of the Poisoned Mind" (#10 US, #2 UK) and "I'll Tumble 4 Ya" (#9 US) surrounded the band's second album, *Colour By Numbers* (US #2, UK #1).

Suddenly, what started as a twisted pop appraisal of the punk ethic which fired George's sense of outrage in the first place had become a part of society's furniture. The band ran away with Best New Act at the 1983 Grammys, George even raising a laugh when he thanked America for its taste and style, then added, "you know a good drag queen when you see one."

In later years, George admitted that Culture Club should have continued pushing the borders of acceptance. Instead, the Club bent to their audience's every whim — particularly after 1984's "Karma Chameleon" (#1 US, #1 UK) became the band's biggest hit yet. "When I wrote it I knew it was going to be huge," George admitted. "But I never understood its appeal."

"Miss Me Blind" (#5 US) and "It's a Miracle" (#13 US, #4 UK) followed "Karma Chameleon" into the charts, but then came "War Song" (#17 US, #2 UK), a heartfelt polemic which utterly misjudged the public's indulgence, and — despite charting high — would ensure the band never again received a fair hearing.

"We knew a lot of people thought we were a joke," George reflected later, "and in some ways we were. But what also happened was, we let the image get out of control. After *Colour By Numbers*, we just lost it. We lost our simplicity, everything became a bit too grand, too overproduced, we forgot about the songs." 1984's *Waking Up with the House on Fire* (#26 US, #2 UK) faltered despite the band's latest multi-million dollar tour extravaganza, and after watching both "The Medal Song" (#32 UK) and "Mistake #3" (#33 US) crash, the group announced they were taking a year off.

Then they came back in 1986 with *From Luxury to Heartache* (#32 US, #10 UK), and proved they hadn't learned a thing. Two singles "Move Away" (#12 US, #7 UK) and "God Thank You Woman" (#31 UK) utterly failed to recapture past glories, and George later admitted, "the last Culture Club album wasn't even us. Or rather, it was us, but it was us getting lost, doing all the stuff we thought we had to do to maintain the success we'd had, whereas if we'd just been honest with ourselves and said 'we hate this, let's do what we're good at....'"

By mid-1986, Culture Club was a dead issue, and though there was a disastrous attempt to reform in 1990, it would be 1997 before the four members were able to work with one another again.

Culture Club initially reformed for an episode of VH-1's *Storytellers*, released as a half-live, half-hits filled album

(#148 US), followed by a berth on the Big Rewind '80s revival tour, alongside Human League and Howard Jones (in the US; ABC in the UK). Performing both old and new material, the reunion was a huge success, paving the way for a return to the studio in 1998/99.

The 1998 single "I Just Wanna Be Loved" was followed in the new year by "Your Kisses Are Charity" and the album *Don't Mind If I Do*, while George proved he had lost none of his taste for controversy when he told *The Sun* newspaper that he was quitting music because of UK radio's lack of support for the band's latest single, "Cold Shoulder." Of course, he acknowledged later, he was lying. "Whenever I meet a *Sun* journalist, I always like to spin them a yarn." George hit the headlines again shortly before Christmas, when he narrowly escaped being hit on the head by a falling 62 lb. mirror ball, before Culture Club's show in Bournemouth, England.

Also see the entry for "BOY GEORGE" on page 218.

Culture Club LPs

7 Kissing to Be Clever (Virgin) 1982

6 Colour by Numbers (Virgin) 1983

5 Waking Up with the House on Fire (Virgin) 1984

3 From Luxury to Heartache (Virgin) 1986

8 VH-1 Storytellers/Greatest Moments (Virgin) 1998 Half live, half history, the best bet's to put the pair on random play and let fate play DJ...original hits from both Culture Club and a solo Boy George rotate with recent live versions of many of the same songs, while George's spoken word intros (storytellers, remember?) fire a fistful of memories themselves.

7 Don't Mind If I Do (Virgin) 1999 Astonishingly confident (not to mention competent) return, a dodgy remake of Bowie's "Starman" more than made up for by the miraculously slow burning "Strange Voodoo."

Selected Compilations and Archive Releases

7 12-Inch Remix Collection (Virgin) 1991 The Club never truly recovered from the brilliance of their first four singles, and the *Collection* damns them accordingly. "Poisoned Mind" and "Time" do escape the tyranny of hip memory and emerge as genuinely great, but it was daft extending "War Song" when the original was already overlong enough, and 12 inches of "Karma Chameleon" remain a classified secret weapon in the war against human intelligence.

8 At Best... The Worst (Virgin) 1993 Generally superior version of the hits disc appended to *Storytellers*.

Further Reading

Take It like a Man by Boy George and Spencer Bright (Harper Collins, 1995).

CURE

FORMED 1976 (Crawley, England)
ORIGINAL LINE UP Robert Smith (b. 4/21/59 — vocals, guitar); Lol Tolhurst (b. 2/3/59 — drums); Michael Dempsey (bass)

Robert Smith, Lol Tolhurst, and Michael Dempsey were 13 when they formed their first band, the Obelisks, which became Malice around 1975. They played their first live show at nearby Worth Abbey in December 1976, masquerading as a folk band in order to get the booking. They were so poorly received that within a month, the band had changed their name to Easy Cure (from one of the few original songs in their set, written by Tolhurst).

In April, fronted by the photogenic-sounding Peter O'Toole (no relation), Easy Cure answered an ad placed in the British music press by the German label, Ariola Hansa, calling for young, unsigned bands to enter a special talent contest; first prize — a record contract. Despite having taped their entry in Smith's front room, Easy Cure emerged first out of 1,400 entrants, and on May 18, they signed a £1,000 contract.

Throughout the fall of 1977, Easy Cure worked towards what they dreamed would be their first album. Overriding the departure of O'Toole by promoting guitarist Smith to lead vocals, the band recorded ten songs for the label's inspection. The label rejected them all, fuelling Smith's growing conviction that they had chosen the band on the strength of its photograph, and never once listened to their original tape.

It was the year of punk, and Easy Cure were very much a child of their times. Hansa, on the other hand, were old hands in the teenybop market. The relationship was doomed, and only got worse when Easy Cure announced their first single was going to be Smith's "Killing an Arab," based loosely on Albert Camus' novel, *The Stranger*.

Hansa were horrified, deadlock ensued; and a year after winning the talent contest, Easy Cure were dropped — and were almost immediately picked up by the newly-formed Fiction label. They celebrated by changing their name to the Cure. "Killing an Arab" remained their first choice for a single.

For reasons known only to themselves, the Cure intended releasing the single on December 22, only for Fiction's major label distributors, Polydor, to point out that it would be impossible to promote a record that close to Christmas. Instead, an alternative deal was worked out, whereby the tiny Small Wonder independent would issue the first 15,000 copies, after which the regular Fiction release would be unleashed. It finally appeared in February 1979.

The single was an immediate critical success; its makers, however, left many observers scratching their heads as they tried to pigeonhole this apparently image- and rootless band. When they failed, they coined the term "anti-image," and let that serve the same purpose. The Cure's debut album did not alleviate the confusion. Instead of a band photograph, *Three Imaginary Boys* (#44 UK) depicted three household appliances, a lamp stand, a vacuum cleaner, and a fridge. Musically, however, the record was peerless, short, tight, and at times verging on the same sense of minimalism as characterized early Talking Heads and Wire projects, and unleashed two powerpop classic singles, "Boys Don't Cry" and "Jumping Someone Else's Train," in the months before the band's first major UK tour, opening for Siouxsie and the Banshees. (The shock departure, four shows in, of the headliners' guitarist and drummer would see Smith also play with the Banshees throughout the remainder of the outing.)

Dempsey quit to join the Associates in November; he was replaced by bassist Simon Gallup (b. 6/1/60), and with keyboard player Matthieu Hartley following him in, the new-look Cure debuted at a Fiction label package designed to showcase all three of the label's principle signings — the Associates and the Passions opened the bill.

The Cure's second album, the monolithic *17 Seconds* (#20 UK), and single, "A Forest" (#31 UK), followed in 1980, a foreboding set which utterly eschewed the cute pop of its predecessor. The tour which followed, too, was characterized by its relentless doom, and when Hartley quit following the last show, his complaint was that the band's music was too dark — and getting even darker.

In fact, the Cure intended their third album to be a positive one. The death of Smith's grandmother, and news that Tolhurst's mother was terminally ill, however, altered the mood of the sessions entirely. Although the attendant single, "Primary" (#43) belied the mood, *Faith* (#14 UK) "became very morbid," Smith admitted, "and we then had to live with it for a year, in that we toured with it, and it was the one record we shouldn't have done that with, because for one year we lived with this doomy, semi-religious record. We sort of wore it everywhere we went, it was like sack cloth and ashes. It wasn't a very enjoyable year really."

It was, however, a magnificent record; its title track alone so potent that when the Cure finally dragged it out of mothballs in 1987, performing it live for the first time in five years, Smith found himself crying uncontrollably. Two years later, on the night the world learned of the Tiananmen Square massacre, in 1989, the Cure unleashed a 15-minute version of the song, dedicated to the dead.

A new single, "Charlotte Sometimes" (#44 UK) was followed by "Hanging Garden" (#34 UK), and *Pornography* (#8 UK), a harrowing album which Smith later acknowledged was born of fear. "I hate the idea that you'd die for your audience, [but] I was rapidly becoming enmeshed in that around the time of *Pornography*, the idea that Ian Curtis had gone first and I was soon to follow. I wasn't prepared for that to happen."

The tour which followed, however, was a nightmare. "We were cracking up, so all the people offstage began to fall

Robert Smith of the Cure   © Harold Sherrick/Chansley Entertainment

apart as well. Twenty-three people reverting to primitive is not a pretty sight." Gallup left the band following an onstage fight with Smith in Strasbourg, Germany (he would return to the Cure later in the band's career). He was replaced for the remainder of the tour by Steve Goulding, but by July 1982, the Cure were no more.

Smith rejoined the Banshees, and formed a side project with bassist Severin and vocalist Jeanette Landry, the Glove. Their album, *Blue Sunshine* (#35 UK) and single "Like an Animal" (#52 UK) were little more than an off-beat experiment in modern psychedelia, but they struck a resounding chord regardless, and within the year, Landray, too, had a full-time band, joining Lol Hammond in Kiss That.

In April 1983, Smith, Tolhurst, Andy Anderson (drums, ex-Brilliant), and Derek Thompson (bass, ex-SPK) appeared on television's *Oxford Road Show*; in May, with Phil Thornally replacing Thompson, they headlined the Elephant Fayre festival; and in October, Smith and Tolhurst were planning a full scale reunion, based around a trilogy of utterly un-Cure-like "fantasy" singles: "Let's Go to Bed" (#44 UK), "The Walk" (#12 UK) and "Love Cats" (#7 UK). All three were then compiled onto the EPs *The Walk* (#179 US) and *Japanese Whispers* (#181 US, #26 UK), and the Cure were back in business.

Still, it remained a very confused time for Smith. At the same time as preparing a new Cure album, he was also working on the Banshees' new album, *Hyaena*; and Tim Pope's "I Want to Be a Tree" solo single. One night in December 1983, he even appeared twice on the same episode of *Top of the Pops*, with the Banshees and then the Cure.

Preluded by the Cure's most bizarre single yet, the totally whacked out mock psychedelia of "The Caterpillar" (#14 UK), *The Top* (#180 US, #10 UK) was released in May 1984, on the eve of the band's biggest tour ever — captured on the *Concert* (#26 UK) live album. Anderson was sacked in October, on the eve of a US tour; he was replaced for the dates by Vince Ely (Psychedelic Furs), before former Thompson Twins drummer Boris Williams (b. 4/23/57, Versailles, France) was recruited. Finally, with the returning Gallup and Porl Thompson (b. 11/8/57, London) completing the line-up, work began on *The Head on the Door*.

Named for a nightmare which plagued Smith during his childhood, *The Head on the Door* (#59 US, #7 UK) was very much a return to past (pre-split) glories, at least in terms of musical intensity. The singles "In Between Days" (#99 US, #15 UK) and "Close to Me" (#24 UK) followed, themselves proving so successful on college radio that the group's US label, Elektra, immediately requested a greatest hits package — which Smith transformed into an unabridged recounting of all the band's singles to date, *Standing on the Beach* (#48 US, #4 UK). It became their biggest hit yet, even spawning a

hit of its own, when Smith rerecorded the vocals to 1979's "Boys Don't Cry" (#22 UK).

Again the band toured heavily, but not without some turmoil — in Los Angeles on July 27, 1986, a fan climbed onstage and stabbed himself repeatedly, after being jilted by his girlfriend. It was a sign of the band's "gothic" reputation that many of the 18,000 audience thought the bloodletting was a part of the show.

Kiss Me Kiss Me Kiss Me (#35 US, #6 UK), a double album set, was released in June, and finally broke the Cure in America. *Standing on the Beach* had breached the US Top 50, *Kiss Me* stormed the Top 40. MTV discovered the string of enchanting videos which paired the band with director Tim Pope; radio stumbled across the singles "Why Can't I Be You" (#54 US, #21 UK), "Just Like Heaven" (#40 US, #29 UK) and "Hot Hot Hot" (#65 US, #45 UK).

At a time when "alternative music" was still a media hype waiting to be created, and the mainstream muddied everything that crept close to success, the Cure was a self-sustaining anomaly — a band whose audience still regarded them as the world's best kept secret; whose detractors regarded every new hit a fluke; whose own record company essentially despaired of them. But when the Cure convened in mid-1988 to begin working on their next album, it was in the knowledge that the group's commercial standing was at an all time high.

Smith again intended an intense record, to mark his impending 30th birthday, describing his new songs as a thematic continuation of *17 Seconds* and *Pornography*, and adding to the tensions when he sacked Tolhurst, the only other constant member in the band's twelve year history. Tolhurst would go on to form his own band, Presence; he was replaced by Roger O'Donnell, and the new-look Cure emerged from isolation in April 1989, with the haunting "Lullaby" (#74 US, #5 UK).

The following month, as the Cure set out on the Prayer tour, *Disintegration* (#12 US, #3 UK) became their best-selling album yet, while the single "Love Song" (#2 US, #18 UK) astonished everyone with its performance. "Fascination Street" (#46 US) was featured in the hit movie *The Lost Angels*, "Pictures of You" (#71 US, #24 UK) kept the band on the chart a full year after the album was released — many of the US B-sides, incidentally, were culled from a Europe-only live album, *Entreat* (#10 UK), taken from the accompanying tour.

O'Donnell quit following the band's Glastonbury Festival show in June 1990; he was replaced by former roadie Perry Bamonte (b. 9/6/60, London) in time for an eastern European tour. The Cure then released their second hits album in November 1990; a series of contemporary remixes of past classics, suitably titled *Mixed Up* (#14 US, #8 UK), accompanied by two new singles, "Never Enough" (#72 US, #13 UK) and a remix of "Close to You" (#97 US), whose video carried on precisely where the earlier, 1986, video left off.

The band then retreated into silence for two more years. By the time of their March 1992 re-emergence, demand for new product was at fever pitch. A new single, "High" (#42 US, #8 UK), heralded the album *Wish* (#2 US, #1 UK); "Friday I'm in Love"(#18 US, #6 UK), and "A Letter to Elise" (#28 UK) followed, as the band launched a world tour which lasted so long that it spawned two new live albums, *Show* (#42 US, #29 UK), comprising a straightforward live "best of") and *Paris* (#118 US, #56 UK), a fans-only collection of older, more obscure songs.

Thompson quit the band following the tour, to work with Jimmy Page and Robert Plant (he took the Cure's "Lullaby" with him, adding it to the former Zeppelin men's live show). After two years of demoing without a drummer, the band finally enlisted Jason Cooper and resurfaced in January 1995, at the Hollywood Rock Festival in Brazil. Six months later, they headlined Glastonbury, and in May 1996, a new single, "13th" (#44 US, #15 UK), previewed the band's latest album.

Wild Mood Swings (#12 US, #9 UK) was released later that same month, again spawning a string of singles — "Mint Car" (#58 US, #31 UK) and "Gone" (#60 UK) followed "13th." But Smith admitted that the album's comparatively lowly chart placing "did prompt me to re-evaluate why I'm doing it, and the reasons why I started. And I decided I should just go back to pleasing myself."

Pausing to document the last ten years of the Cure with the *Galore* (#32 US, #37 UK) compilation, and a new single, "Wrong Number" (#62 UK), he then threw himself into *Blood Roses* (#16 US, #8 UK), an album which, as its February 2000 release date loomed, he swore would be the Cure's last album, before he launched an intentionally esoteric solo career.

"I hit 40 in 1999, and I've had this plan since I was in my early 30s, that if I was still going, still doing this, when I got to 40, that would be a perfect time to re-evaluate and re-think, and not quite too late to learn something new. I decided a long time ago that I'm not going to be sitting there at 47, strumming an acoustic guitar thinking about what the next single's going to be."

The Cure LPs

8 Three Imaginary Boys (Fiction — UK) 1979 The quintessential post-punk pop album, hinting ("Another Day," the title track) not only at the direction the band would take, but also at several they wouldn't ("So What," "Foxy Lady," "Boys Don't Cry").

9 Seventeen Seconds (Elektra) 1980 Smith's vision begins to implode — he still calls *17 Seconds* a 'catchy' album, but lyri-

cally, the rancor was starting to surface. Either that, or songs like "M," "The Final Sound," and "A Forest" really were his idea of a toe-tapping time.

10 Faith (Elektra) 1981 Of course, the ultimate cliché in the rock'n'wrist-slashing lexicon, the self-professedly Most Miserable Band in the World nailing their colors (black, usually) to the gallows and creating a record which sounds like it was recorded in a church.

In fact, *Faith* remains the perfect Cure album, a cathedral of dark sound which crystallized not only the band's internal despair (they were still selling no more than 50,000 albums worldwide), but also the post-punk scene's own gothic turn. Ian Curtis had just died and, Robert knew, the press wanted him to replace him. He just wasn't sure where — on stage or in the ground?

Everything about *Faith* seemed pre-ordained; seemed, also, to hinge around the spectral sleeve photograph of Bolton Abbey, near Shipworth in Yorkshire. Sliced into its composite parts, at least a couple of tracks ("Primary," "Doubt") are brighter and breezier than the album's reputation ever allows. But "Funeral Party" and "The Holy Hour" howl with inhuman hopelessness; the spectral, skeletal sound of the band echoes bleakly across just such a landscape, and the fading voice with which the record closes remains long after the disc has finished playing. There really is nothing left but faith, but what happens when you have none to begin with?

8 Carnage Visors (Fiction — UK) 1982 Drivingly hypnotic album-length instrumental movie soundtrack appended to cassette versions of *Faith*.

9 Pornography (Elektra) 1982 They reached the depths, then kept going. *Faith* was the perfect Cure album, *Pornography* was the ultimate, the sound of a band tearing itself to pieces and taking everybody with them. But "Siamese Twins" still emerged the wedding march of the early 1980s. "I chose an eternity of *this*."

7 The Top (Sire) 1984 Bouncing back from a string of hit singles, the Cure's first vaguely unsatisfying album as Robert's new-found persona of English eccentric with a bird's nest hair-do got the better of his lyrical abilities. "Bananafishbones" indeed.

6 Concert [LIVE] (Fiction — UK) 1984 The band's first live album, padded on cassette with the *Curiosity* collection of live and demo rarities.

8 Head on the Door (Elektra) 1985 Back on form, with "A Night Like This" quite unexpectedly establishing itself among Smith's greatest, gorgeously stupid compositions ever. "Close to Me," regarded without its over-played video, and the looming "The Blood" come close as well, and the novelty "Kyoto Song" long outlasts the joke.

6 Kiss Me Kiss Me Kiss Me (Elektra) 1987 No no no. Too long, too clichéd, two record set which caught Smith's hitherto concise vision spinning out at a dozen different directions at once, paving the way for the instability to come.

9 Disintegration (Elektra) 1989 "Love Song" and "Lullaby" were the ideal introductions into this dark, often symphonic, reminder of the Cure BLC (Before Love Cats); overall, the most Cure-like Cure album since *Pornography*, and their US breakthrough to boot.

8 Entreat [LIVE] (Fiction — UK) 1990 Essentially a live version of *Disintegration*, minus the biggest hits, but with plenty of room for "Homesick" and "Untitled" to spread out. The overall mood is similar to live tapes from the *Faith* era, marred only by an overly-joyous audience.

6 Mixed Up (Elektra) 1990 A largely redundant collection of largely redundant remixes which nevertheless sounded great on the dance floor. Pity no one lives in a disco, isn't it?

4 Wish (Elektra) 1992 "Friday I'm in Love," "Wendy Time," "Doing the Unstuck"... first impressions were of a Right Said Fred album mispressed to include one great Cure song ("From the Edge of the Deep Green Sea"). Second impressions recanted as they forgot "I'm Too Sexy." Fan club members were subsequently offered *Lost Wishes* (1994), comprising out-takes from this misbegotten pile. Lucky people.

5 Show [LIVE] (Elektra) 1993

6 Paris [LIVE] (Elektra) 1993 Live albums respectively recounting the poppy, and the miserable bits of the last tour.

5 Wild Mood Swings (Elektra) 1996 A year in the recording studio, Cure's most deliberately dishevelled album, packed with so many moments of wanton depravity that even Smith later regretted parts of it. The Latin lunacy of "13th," and the portentous "Jupiter Crash" offer opposing poles, but the pointlessly knockabout "Club America" strings the noose up between them.

9 Blood Roses (Elektra) 2000 Tracking back to *Pornography* and *Disintegration*, then feeding the despair through Smith's recent 40th birthday, the Cure's most intense offering in a decade — symphonic, sinister, and sensual.

Selected Compilations and Archive Releases

8 Boys Don't Cry (PVC) 1980 US compilation revising "Boys Don't Cry" to include non-LP singles.

9 Happy Ever After (A&M) 1981 US compilation drawing *17 Seconds* and *Faith* together as one unrelenting double album.

7 Japanese Whispers (Sire) 1984 Compilation pooling the "Let's Go to Bed," "The Walk," and "Love Cats" singles and B-sides.

9 Standing on the Beach (Elektra) 1987

7 Galore (Elektra) 1997 Taken together, an uncensored recounting of 20 years of Cure singles — wildly individualistic across the first album; increasingly bound to their conventional LP releases across *Galore*.

Presence LP

7 Inside (Island) 1992 There's no escaping the Cure comparisons, especially as Gary Biddles' intonations and Rob Stein's guitar are so Smith-like to start with, while Lol Tolhurst's very existence reminds us just how integral he was to the Cure's

sound. There's nods to a slew of post punk heroes, but Presence still sound most like the Cure with a not-so-brand new singer.

The Glove LP

8 Blue Sunshine (Polydor) 1984 The Cure without the pop hooks, the Banshees with less buzz and, on one track at least, New Order without the synths. Smith and Severin conjure up several atmospheric instrumentals, together with a clutch of dance-friendly(-ish) doompop songs, while future Kiss That vocalist Landry's strident etherealisms were to influence virtually every female singer in the late '80s goth pack.

Further Reading

The Cure: Faith by Dave Bowler/Bryan Dray (Pan, UK, 1995).

CURRENT 93

FORMED 1983 *(London, England)*
ORIGINAL LINE-UP *David Tibet (b. 3/5/60 — vocals, guitar, etc.)*

Formed by multi-instrumentalist David Tibet, a sonic potpourri into which he would cast esoteric ritual, personal mythology, and a menage of like-minded musicians, Current 93 debuted with *Lashtal*, a three-track EP featuring contributions from John Balance of Coil and 23 Skidoo's Fritz Haaman. Two years later, the *Nightmare Culture* LP turned over an entire album side to Coil, offering a sharp contrast to the eclectic chants and wails on Current 93's side.

As Dog's Blood Order, Current 93 made their live debut at the Equinox Event at the London Musician's Co-operative on June 21, 1983; accompanied by John Murphy, playing Tibetan thigh bone, it was at this show that Tibet met Nurse with Wound frontman Steven Stapleton, paving the way for a series of collaborations over the years. (The band's short performance later appeared on the EP *Current 93 Presents Dog Blood Order*). Four months later, within the less salubrious surroundings of London's Clarendon pub, the same pseudonym played its second show.

Launching a career sideline which would bedevil Current 93 collectors forever more, the band contributed to a string of compilations during this period; two full albums in 1984, *Nature Unveiled* and *Dog's Blood Rising*, however, indicated the true depth of Tibet's imagination. The backing tapes employed on these albums would then accompany Tibet, former Crass frontman Steve Ignorant, and John Balance on the road in December for a handful of European shows with Nurse With Wound. A sampling of the resultant soundscape appeared on 1986's *Live at Bar Maldoror* album — compensation, perhaps, for Tibet's decision not to play any shows whatsoever that year.

Released in time for Christmas 1986, the 12" single "Happy Birthday Pigface Christus" culminated a full year of entertainingly blasphemous contributions to sundry compilations ("Anti-Christ Anti Christian" and "Jesus Wants Me for a Moonbeam" among them). That year, however, also saw Tibet commence his slow shift into more pastoral sounds, with *In Menstrual Night* and *Imperium* (#22 UK indy) evincing an increased, if apocalyptic, awareness of the folk genre. Indeed, while *Dawn* and the "Crowleymass" 12" proved that Tibet could still be vicious when he wanted to, *Swastikas for Noddy* emerged in 1987 as the blueprint for his first masterpiece, a remixed and restructured version released the following year as *Crooked Crosses for the Nodding God.*

Noddy himself was a character created during the 1950s by English author Enid Blyton; Tibet's art-guerilla invocation of him as something other than a harmless wooden doll with a blue hat and a red car was an act of nostalgic sedition unparalleled in rock history. The addition of traditional folk songs and Vaudevillian jingles only heightened the sense of darkness which permeated this magnificent, and magnificently disturbing record.

Accompanied now by Boyd Rice collaborator Rose McDowall and Death in June's Douglas P (both guitar, vocals), Current 93 performed much of the *Noddy/Nodding God* material at the Indipenti Music Festival in San Giovanni Valdarno, Italy, on Halloween 1987; by 1989, this now-permanent trio had been joined by Boyd Rice (drums) and Tony Wakeford (bass), for a magnificent Japanese tour.

This outing, together with "The Red Face of God" 12", and the albums *Earth Covers Earth* and *As the World Disappears* marked the final progression of Tibet's folkie leanings, earning Tibet comparisons to '60s' esoterics the Incredible String Band — moods which he was still want to shatter through his still-prolific contributions to compilation albums, and such one-off singles as "Time Stands Still" (1988), "She is Dead and Fall Down" (1989), and "Broken Birds Fly" (1990).

A pair of patchy 1990 albums, *Horse* and *Looney Runes*, were contrarily followed by some of Tibet's best work yet, as he pieced together a new live band around Michael Cashmore (guitar), James Malindaine-Lafayette (harp), Joolie Wood (violin), and James Mannox (percussion), and played La Lune Des Pirates in Amiens, France, on December 15. The performance was recorded for *As the World Disappears*, the following year.

1991, the year which brought *Island*, a collaboration with Icelandic artist HOH, also saw the first ever Current 93 tours, through Germany and Austria in March, with Sol Invictus and Death in June. Lafayette had quit the band, to be replaced by Douglas P; by November, when Current 93 and

Death in June alone toured Italy and France, P was Tibet's sole on-stage collaborator. Plans to record a live album based around 1992's *Thunder Perfect Mind*, however, prompted the convening of the biggest Current 93 line-up yet, for shows in London and Paris during 1992–93 — P, McDowall, Wood, Cashmore, Stapleton, Mannox, John Balance, Karl Blake, and Bevis Frond's Nick Saloman (who lived just up the road from the first venue played, in Walthamstow, London).

Current 93 would not perform live again for three years, while Tibet pieced together his greatest work, *The Inmost Light*. Spread over three installments, the EP *Where the Long Shadows Fall*, the album *All the Pretty Little Horses* (highlighted by a terrifyingly sibilant rendition of the nursery rhyme of the same name) and a second EP, *The Starres Are Marching Sadly Home*, the full suite again drew upon all of Tibet's disparate cultural reference points to staggering effect. The album's penultimate track, a reprise of the title track, incidentally, represents one of Nick Cave's best ever vocal performances.

Accompanied by Cashmore, Blake, and Wood, Current 93 broke their live silence on June 2, 1996, at the Festival Musiques Ultimes II, in Nevers, France. October then brought Tibet, the band, and the returning McDowall to the US for the first time, for two shows at the Orensanz Foundation Synagogue in New York, on Halloween and All Saint's Day. Although the proceedings were tarnished when scheduled support act Tiny Tim suffered a heart attack shortly before the show (he died just weeks later), still the gigs were a triumph, eventually seeing release as *All Dolled Up Like Christ.*

The *Innermost Light* trilogy complete, 1997 brought the album *In a Foreign Town, In a Foreign Land*, a musical companion to the writings of Thomas Ligotti; the following years saw the *Gothic Love Song* EP, a self-titled collaboration with new bandmates Cashmore and Christopher Heeman, and the *Soft BlackStars* LP — three Current 93 shows in New York City were performed under that same name in March 1999. A new single, "Misery Farm," was produced for sale exclusively at those shows.

Current 93 LPs

6 Nature Unveiled (Laylah) 1984 Gregorian chants combine with Tibet's own interpretative meditations for a relaxing, if faintly disturbing, exercise in mantric madness.

7 Dog's Blood Rising (Laylah) 1984 Tibet's Eastern influences are allowed full reign, unimpeded by the use of non-original recordings. The album concludes with a Simon and Garfunkel medley, performed a cappella.

6 Nightmare Culture (With Coil) (Laylah) 1985 Hypnosis on Current 93's side, armageddon on Coil's.

5 Live at Bar Maldoror [LIVE] (Mi-Mort) 1985

6 In Menstrual Night (United Dairies) 1986

5 Dawn (Maldoror) 1987

6 Imperium (Madoror) 1987

7 Swastikas for Noddy (Laylah) 1987 A poor mix and a few weak songs cannot disguise the nightmarish power of Tibet's first full invocation of childhood's darkest corners. The forthcoming *Crooked Crosses* remix set is where the truth really lies, however.

5 Christ and the Pale Queens Mighty in Sorrow (Maldoror) 1988

6 Earth Covers Earth (United Dairies 1988) 1988

9 Crooked Crosses for the Nodding God (United Dairies) 1989 So much has changed, so much remains. You probably don't have to have grown up in the England of the '50s and '60s to understand all that's going on... but it surely helps. Sunday afternoons at grandma's by the radio, then down to the seaside for summer, *Two Way Family Favorites*, Punch and Judy, Enid Blyton, Noddy on his own in the woods with the golliwogs, whispered incantations from a mid-70s Steeleye Span album — an album of limited appeal, perhaps, but immense charm and unimaginable power; a talisman of terrors for an entire generation.

6 Horse (With Nurse With Wound, Sol Invictus) (Cerne) 1990

6 Looney Runes (Durtro) 1990

8 Island (With HOH) (Durtro) 1991

7 As the World Disappears [LIVE] (Durtro) 1991

9 Thunder Perfect Mind (Durtro) 1992 Increasingly portentous though Tibet was now becoming, still his subtle disturbances have the psyche on their side. A lot of mankind's greatest folk songs are about fairies — what are fairy folk songs about?

8 Hitler As Kalki [LIVE] (Durtro) 1993 Epic production from the *Thunder...* era.

7 Of Ruine or Some Blazing Starre 1994 (7)

10 All the Pretty Little Horses (Durtro) 1996 The centerpiece of Tibet's *The Inmost Light* trilogy (parts one and three exist on the EPs *Where the Long Shadows Fall* and *The Stars Are Marching Sadly Home*), Current 93's queer little world of traditional Englishness (so different to Blur's or even the Kinks'), omnipotent nodding boys, and the underlying wickedness of children never offered an easy entry for the uninitiated.

Taking its title track from a familiar lullaby, then rendering it faithfully via a guest-starring Nick Cave, Tibet created an almost pastoral scene over which his familiar whisper-whine then painted a litany of typical Tibetan themes. The deification of doomed artist Louis Wain's cats on the charming "Bloodbells Chime," ejaculating serpents, and the pain of Christ all played a part — if the genre hadn't been so successfully hijacked by other boys in black, Current 93 could well claim to be "gothic" in its truest, Shelley-esque, sense. Tibet might not have contracted consumption yet, but 200 years ago, at the height of that fever's fever, he'd have out-coughed Byron all the way to the bank.

A minimum of seismic experimentation ensures the attention remains unyieldingly on the songs, which themselves remain within the realms of musical convention. Some moments are genuinely beautiful, most are genuinely great. Either way, whatever you expect from Current 93, *All the Pretty Horses* will not disappoint.

7 Soft Black Stars (Durtro) 1998

7 Current 93/Michael Cashmore/Christoph Heeman (Durtro) 1999

8 All Dolled Up Like Christ (Durtro) 1999 Double live album, capturing the band's Halloween 1996 show in New York City.

Selected Compilations and Archive Releases

7 Emblems (Durtro) 1993

8 Calling for Vanished Faces (Durtro) 1999 Two double CDs rounding up lost singles, unreleased oddities, album-only gems, and the miraculously festive "Happy Birthday Pigface Christus" single.

D

DAFT PUNK

FORMED *[as Darling]* 1992 *(Paris, France)*
ORIGINAL LINE-UP *Thomas Bangalter (electronics); Guy-Manuel De Homem Christo (electronics)*

Thomas Bangalter and Guy-Manuel De Homem Christo began working and recording together in the early 1990s in a band they called Darlin', after the Beach Boys song. Bangalter recalled, "that was our first record as well, it was released as a split single with Stereolab, and an English reviewer said it was really horrible, just daft punk. And we liked that name better than ours."

Early Daft Punk releases entered Britain through the Glasgow underground label Soma, but while neither "New Wave," "Da Funk," nor "Indo Silver Club" received much attention, they did reach some influential ears. According to Bangalter, "the only people who heard them were the Chemical Brothers. They asked us to remix 'Life is Sweet' for them, and things started moving." By the time Daft Punk signed to Virgin and reissued the looping psychoses of "Da Funk," the original 12-inch had sold over 30,000. Sales for the two releases combined have since topped 100,000 in Britain alone.

For mainstream America, the introduction again came through "Da Funk," courtesy this time of late night MTV airings for Spike Jonze's brilliant video. "We were very excited to get him, it's the first music video he'd directed in over twelve months," Bangalter enthused, crediting Jonze with every last ounce of creativity in the video, "the whole thing was his idea, the dog headed man, the broken boom box, everything."

Three more Daft Punk singles, "Around the World," "Burnin'," and "Revolution 909" (taken from *Homework*), followed during 1997–98, but Bangalter and Christo would not be rushing to create a new Daft Punk release. For three years before "Da Funk," after all, the pair had been running their own network of French underground dance labels, and even as *Homework* took off, Bangalter was already preparing for a solo release on their own Roule label, the first of two volumes of "Trax on Da Rocks." He would also be recruited as producer by the Australian electro band Stardust, overseeing their acclaimed "Music Sounds Better with You" single.

De Homem Christo, too, would release a solo single, the festive "Santa Klaus."

Daft Punk LP
7 Homework (Virgin) 1979 Daft Punk's challenging assault on the European club scene was epitomized by "Da Funk" — grinding, contagious repetition looped around beats and diversions. The remainder of the album struggles to match the moment, but the scratchy "Around the World" comes close.

Thomas Bangalter LP
6 Trax on Da Rocks (Roule — France) 1996
6 Spinal Scratch (Roule) 1997

DAMNED

FORMED 1976 *(London, England)*
ORIGINAL LINE-UP *Dave Vanian (b. David Letts, 10/12/56, Hemel Hempstead, England — vocals); Brian James (b. Brian Robertson, 2/18/55 — guitar); Captain Sensible (b. Ray Burns 4/24/54, Balham, London — bass); Rat Scabies (b. Chris Miller 7/30/57, Kingston-upon-Thames, England — drums)*

The great survivors of punk, the Damned, formed in May 1976 when Brian James, after nearly a year spent rehearsing with basement proto-punk legends London SS, linked with Rat Scabies following an SS audition. Johnny Moped guitarist, Burns, followed and as a trio the band — dubbed the Subterraneans for the occasion — debuted in Cardiff, Wales backing journalist Nick Kent during one of his occasional forays into performance.

Returning to London, former gravedigger Dave Vanian was recruited as vocalist and the newly named Damned debuted at a gay club in Lissom Grove, West London. Of course, the impetus for the band was the Sex Pistols, although it was the impertinence of the band, rather than their iconoclasm, which appealed. Scabies later recalled, "they were the funniest group I'd ever seen. They were cartoon... you know what it was like the first time you saw the *Simpsons*, the first time you saw Bart, it was a bit like that; totally larger than life, animated, horrible little gits."

The Damned opened for the Sex Pistols at the 100 Club and in August 1976, featured at the first Mont de Marsen punk festival. Their appearance at the 100 Club punk festival in September brought tabloid notoriety after a girl lost an eye to a flying glass during their set, and while the band continued to balk at being termed "punk" (Scabies preferred "Dole Rock or Street Rock, cos that's where our roots are"), still they were a celebration of everything punk portended.

Following overtures from the indy label, Chiswick, the Damned signed to Stiff in September 1976 and in October, "New Rose" became the first "punk" single ever — a focal point for all the disparate streams filtering into the new music, and the absolute redefinition of all that rock'n'roll held dear.

The Damned toured constantly, but controversy was never far away. They walked out on the Flamin' Groovies' UK tour, complaining that the American cult heroes were simply hippies – thus condemning a hitherto respected R&B band (they were featured in the premier issue of the seminal *Sniffin' Glue* punkzine, after all) to Boring Old Fartdom, but were then themselves sacked from the Pistols' cancellation-wracked Anarchy tour after announcing — with little regard for punk solidarity — that they'd be happy to play even if the headliners were banned.

The Damned's second single, "Neat Neat Neat," arrived in February 1977, chalking up another first as the Damned became the first punk band to appear on Saturday morning pop TV's "Supersonic," while their debut album, *Damned Damned Damned* (#36 UK), of course, was the first ever punk LP.

The group visited the US for the first time in spring, playing CBGBs with the Dead Boys (17 years later, the Damned would be back at CBs, headlining one night of the venue's 20th anniversary festival). They then returned to London to celebrate their first anniversary with three sold-out nights at the London Marquee in July. Weeks later, the Damned augmented their line-up with a second guitarist, Robert "Lu" Edmunds — a sign of the band's accelerating ambition.

A month later, Scabies faked a suicide bid and quit the Damned in protest at the "hippy music" which he said they were now making (he subsequently formed Whitecats). *Music for Pleasure*, the Damned's sophomore album, bore him out. Produced by Pink Floyd's Nick Mason (after the band's initial demands for Syd Barrett were misheard), the set was written off by Scabies as an attempt to mimic the Rolling Stones' *Satanic Majesties* — a fair criticism as the album proceeded to alienate even the most faithful fan.

With former London (and future Culture Club) drummer Jon Moss replacing Scabies, and America's Dead Boys as the opening act, the Damned toured near-empty houses and in January, they were dropped by Stiff. A month later, the band broke up. James formed Tanz Der Youth and later the Lords of the New Church, Vanian joined the Doctors of Madness briefly, and Sensible joined the Softies. By year's end, however, Scabies, Sensible (now playing guitar), and Vanian were gigging again as the Doomed, and with bassist Algy Ward in tow, relaunched as the Damned soon after.

Signing to Chiswick, the group scored an immediate hit with "Love Song" (#20 UK) in April 1979, following it with

further excerpts from their *Machine Gun Etiquette* (#31 UK) comeback album: "Smash It Up" (#35 UK, since covered by the Offspring) and "I Just Can't Be Happy Today" (#46 UK). Ward quit following this to form Tank; his replacement, former Eddie and the Hot Rods bassist Paul Gray, would remain with the band for the next four years, during which *Untitled (Black Album)* (#29 UK) and the "History of the World Part One" (#51 UK) single would become the Damned's biggest sellers yet.

In June 1981, Scabies linked with James, Stiv Bators, and Dave Treganna, the gestating Lords of the New Church, for a one-off show as the Dead Damned Sham Band. The following month, James rejoined the Damned for a fifth anniversary show at the London Lyceum. It was purely a one-off, however. In November, with Gray back on board, the Damned released the *Friday the 13th* EP (#50 UK, #2 UK Indy), alongside the first in what would become a plague of compilations, *The Best of the Damned* (#43 UK, #3 UK Indy).

1982 opened with the launch of two extra-curricular projects as Scabies joined with former Rut Paul Fox as Rats and Foxes, and Sensible signed a solo deal with A&M. By mid-summer, Rats and Foxes had disbanded and Sensible was top of the UK charts with Rodgers and Hammerstein's "Happy Talk" (#1 UK), utterly dwarfing the Damned's own latest single, "Lovely Money" (#42 UK) He followed it with "Wot" (#26 UK) and a solo album, *Women and Captains First* (#64 UK), largely co-written with Robyn Hitchcock.

Ironically, on this occasion he was out-performed by a new Damned album, as the band signed to major label Bronze and unleashed *Strawberries* (#15 UK), but still Sensible would not remain with the Damned for much longer. He quit in 1984 (shortly after Gray departed) to continue a meandering and wholly idiosyncratic solo career, interspersed with periodic returns to the Damned.

Vanian and Scabies persevered, recruiting Roman Jugg (guitar, keyboards) and Bryn Gunn (bass), and launching the Damned in the faux-psychedelic direction hinted at over the course of *Strawberries* and the acclaimed garage rocker *Give Daddy the Knife*, (credited to Naz Nomad and the Nightmares). A new Damned album, 1985's *Phantasmagoria* (#11 UK), followed, accompanied by a string of hit singles — "Grimly Fiendish" (#21 UK), "The Shadow of Love" (#25 UK), and "Is It a Dream" (#34UK), with the band peaking with the early 1986 cover of Barry Ryan's majestic "Eloise" (#3 UK).

Unfortunately, monster success was followed by a rapid decline as the singles "Anything" (#32 UK), "Gigolo" (#29 UK), and "Alone Again Or" (#27 UK) and album, *Anything* (#40 UK), stumbled. One final 45, "In Dulce Decorum"

(#72 UK), followed before the band broke up in July 1989, with a farewell tour.

Of course the story did not end there. The Damned regrouped in 1991 to support the Ramones on a short UK tour, and again in 1992 for a pair of London shows. Another reunion in 1996 marked their 20th anniversary, while a succession of live and compilation albums ensured the band's name remained alive. Finally, a new Damned line-up formed around Vanian (hitherto working with his own band, the rockabilly Phantom Chords), Scabies, New Model Army guitarist Moose, Godfathers' bassist Chris Dolimore, and former Maniacs/Physicals guitarist Alan Lee Shaw, himself fresh from Brian James' latest band.

With Shaw and Scabies helping the songwriting, this line-up would record 1996's *Not of this Earth* — as worthy a Damned album as any. Business and personal wranglings would bury it, however, and the line-up shattered soon after. Shaw linked with fellow Damned escapee Paul Gray in a new band, Mischief, while Vanian and Scabies reunited with Sensible and relaunched the Damned onto the now-flourishing punk nostalgia circuit with a full US tour in early 1998, and a headline appearance at the fourth Holidays in the Sun festival. Drummer Spike Smith subsequently joined Morrissey's 1999 touring band.

Also see the entry for "LORDS OF THE NEW CHURCH" on page 466.

The Damned LPs

9 Damned Damned Damned (Stiff UK) 1977 Anarchy in action, the Damned reek of danger and destruction. Scabies' clattering, thrashing drums crash like a falling skyscraper, Sensible plays the bass like a jack hammer, and James's guitar scythes riffs through the turbulence. And above it all, Vanian sounds completely unperturbed. It's the frenetic pure punk of "New Rose" (oddly reminiscent of a lot of later Adam & the Ants) and "Neat Neat Neat" that engineered the Damned's pre-eminence; the bulk of the record is high energy pub rock mixed with a hefty dose of Stooges' threat — a glimmering of glam and the 99% proof Alice Cooper of "Feel the Pain." And then there's the dark oppression of "Fan Club" (gothic R&B) to add the finishing flourish to this album's explosive mix.

4 Music for Pleasure (Stiff UK) 1977 For once, received wisdom is right. Doomed prog-rock psychedelia and a near-total lack of worthwhile songs ("Problem Child" would disagree with that, though) was a bad move at the time and nothing has happened in the twenty years since to change that.

9 Machine Gun Etiquette (Chiswick UK) 1979 Deprived of their greatest songwriter, the Damned turn in some of their greatest songs: "Smash It Up," "I Just Can't Be Happy Today," "Love Song," and "Noise Noise Noise." The rest draws back from the brink a little, but still an astonishing comeback.

8 Black Album (Chiswick UK) 1980 Strung across four sides of vinyl, the ambitious first disc-and-a-half never bites off more than it can chew, even if a side-long Damned song ("Curtain Call") does sound odd on paper. The live fourth side is needless, but does remember past glories and would reappear as half of 1982's *Live at Shepperton.*

8 Strawberries (Bronze UK) 1982 Fashionably overlooked, any album which contains "Generals," "Don't Bother Me," and "Bad Time for Bonzo" can't be all bad.

5 Phantasmagoria (MCA) 1985 The vampire takes over. "Grimly Fiendish," "Is It a Dream," and "Sanctum Sanctorum" all feed into the band's now fully-realized gothic grandads reputation. It wasn't a bad album — just a very ordinary one.

6 Anything (MCA) 1986 The nastiness goes peace'n'love, as "Alone Again Or," "Psychomania," and the title track point a direction which really could have paid dividends.

7 Final Damnation [LIVE] (Restless) 1989 Abusing their past while reveling in their longevity, the Damned's 1988 reunion show offers up a 17-song summary of a career which went on forever.

9 Not of This Earth (Cleopatra) 1996 With Dolimore going out of his way to be the best Brian James shaped guitarist since James himself, with Scabies and Shaw pulling out the most convincing "true" Damned songs since the "Smash It Up" hey day, and Vanian singing better than the old ghoul's done in years, this seriously ranks alongside whatever your favorite Damned album might be.

Selected Compilations and Archive Releases

6 Damned But Not Forgotten (Castle UK) 1986 A gallant attempt to wring maximum mileage out of the band's then current revival; two "new" tracks mixed with Bronze-era singles, alternate takes, and the Captain's immortal "Nice Cup of Tea."

7 The Light at the End of the Tunnel (MCA) 1987 Career-spanning 27-song hits and rarities collection — slightly scarred by the lack of chronology.

8 Ballroom Blitz (Receiver UK) 1992 An upgrade of the earlier *Mindless Direction Less Energy* live set, with the full 15-song set and a sincere cover of the Ruts' "In a Rut" remembering Malcolm Owen died one year before.

6 Not the Captain's Birthday Party (Demon UK) 1992 Live in late 1977, with *Music for Pleasure* fresh on the racks, but a decent sound mix clearly beyond their requirements. A 23-minute muddy blurge which only occasionally resolves itself into a song, but does recapture some of the reasons why this band was so damned exciting.

7 Tales from The Damned (Cleopatra) 1993

7 Sessions of The Damned (Dutch East Ind) 1994

8 The Radio One Sessions (Night Tracks UK) 1996 Two discs worth of Peel and related BBC sessions, from the vibrant first (1976) to one of the last (1986) and rough enough that even the nadirs sound neat neat neat. "Nasty" is just that, "Fan Club" is fab, and "We Love You" is so good you want to return the compliment immediately.

8 Neat Neat Neat (Demon) 1996 Boxed set recreation of the Stiff Years, illogically using three discs where two would have comfortably fit. Nice booklet, though.

7 The Chaos Years (Cleopatra) 1997 Rarities and live cuts illustrate the band both rising towards its fiercest, snottiest peak (the Brian James era) and coming down again from its (first) commercial apex.

Dave Vanian and the Phantom Chords LP

7 Big Beat Presents (Big Beat UK) 1995 Surprisingly effective stab at an entire album's worth of the rock-psycho-punk-a-billy which the Damned occasionally yearned towards.

Naz Nomad and the Nightmares LP

7 Give Daddy the Knife (Big Beat) 1984

Captain Sensible LPs

5 Women and Captains First (A&M) 1982 "Happy Talk" and "Wot" were the hits; the remainder is a jockey cabaret distinguished by some suitably strange Robyn Hitchcock contributions.

5 Power of Love (A&M) 1983

8 Revolution Now (Deltic) 1989 Working now with ex-Cleaners from Venus vagabond Martin Newell, plus sundry former Damned mates, an intriguingly catchy commentary on the modern way of life. Buy this record.

7 Meathead (Humbug) 1995

6 Live at the Milky Way [LIVE] (Griffin) 1995

5 The Universe of Geoffrey Brown (Humbug) 1997 A sadly predictable set reprising themes and mannerisms already familiar from past albums, and trying just a little too hard to be the Captain.

Selected Compilations and Archive Releases

6 Day in the Life Of (A&M) 1984 Oddball compilation drawn from the first two albums.

8 The Best of: Sensible Lifestyles (Cleopatra) 1997 Despite substituting live recordings for the original hits, a suitably manic reminder of all that the Captain has achieved, from a sonic assault on the Damned's own "Smash It Up" through such unimpeachable gems of disaffected dementia as "Riot on Eastbourne Pier," "Revolution Now," and the immortally obscure "Jet Boy Jet Girl." Then there's "Smash It Up Part Four," which is Joe Meek goes Surf, and "Kamikaze Millionaire." The final track says "Glad It's All Over." Speak for yourself, Cap.

Further Reading

The Light at the End of the Tunnel by Carol Clerk (Omnibus, UK, 1987).

DANCE HALL CRASHERS

FORMED 1989 *(Berkeley, CA)*
ORIGINAL LINE-UP *Jason Hammon (guitar); Tim Armstrong (bass); Matt Freeman (drums)*

Unlike the bulk of bands queuing up to join the third wave of ska in the late 1980s, Dance Hall Crashers' premier debt was to the '60s American pop which formed the basis for their sound, as opposed to the Jamaican-style off-beat which underpinned their rhythms — a very unexpected change in direction for a group which began life as an Operation Ivy side project. (That said, their very name was taken from a vintage ska collection.)

Boasting a mid-tempo beat and strong, horn-drenched pop-rock melodies, DEC were formed by Ivy's Tim Armstrong and Matt Freeman in 1989. The group's line-up was never stable; indeed, Armstrong and Freeman themselves quit to form Rancid within months of the band launching. Hammon, however, opted to continue on, adding vocalist Elyse Rogers and a revolving door of drummers and bassists, and the band continued gigging around Berkeley where Rogers was studying political science.

Six months after Rogers joined, a second vocalist, Karina Denike, was added and with Alex Baker (bass) and Jason's brother, Gavin Hammon (drums), DHC recorded their debut album for proposed self-release. Instead they were picked up by Moon Records following a triumphant show opening for The Toasters, then broke up within days of the record's February 1991 issue.

It would be close to two years before DHC resurfaced, reuniting for a one-off show at the San Francisco club, Slim's, in 1992. After gigs with a succession of temporary musicians, the Hammons, Denike, and Rogers were joined by guitarist Scott Goodell and bassist Mikey Weiss, and the band agreed to reform permanently. To celebrate, Moon slipped one track onto the seminal *California Ska-quake* compilation, then re-released the group's debut discon CD with bonus tracks under the title *Dance Hall Crashers 1989–1992*.

Group and label parted company soon after and it would be two years more before Dance Hall Crashers reappeared on disc, the first act signed to MCA's new 510 subsidiary.

A single, "Enough," was followed by the band's debut album, 1995's *Lockjaw*, highlighting the group's new sound — punchier and moving in a more rock/punk direction (but still sporting those signature dual harmonies). Tim Armstrong contributed one song to the set.

DHC promptly toured with the Mighty Mighty Bosstones and a host of Epitaph punks, and being around that crowd certainly had a pronounced effect. Their third album, *Honey, I'm Homely!*, and the *Blue Plate Special* EP were both far more ska-driven than their predecessor, an attribute continued over 1999's *Purr*. Rogers agreed, "we've got upbeats and lots of ska influences. But if you ask the ska scene, the real traditionalists will say, 'nah, they're a fucking punk band.'"

Dance Hall Crashers LPs

7 Dance Hall Crashers (Moon) 1990 Driving ska-pop with just a touch of rock overtones. *DHC's* gleeful music is counterpointed by the angsty tongue-in-cheek lyrics which really add to the fun.

8 Lockjaw (510) 1995 Exuberantly poppy and eminently skankable, *Lockjaw* owes as much to the New Wave as to 2-Tone, but packing a punch which hindsight insists their debut lacked. Former member Tim Armstrong (Rancid) contributes one song.

7 Honey, I'm Homely (510) 1997 Further refining and polishing their sound and pushing the harmonies even further up front, the harmonies chime tart and tangy, and the band belt a heavily seasoned ska-heavy cacophony.

8 Purr (MCA) 1999 Consolidating the sound of *Honey* into a perfect blend of punk attitude powered by skanking rhythms, *Purr* delivers up a dozen fiery, melody-laden nuggets, with some of their best (and most serious) lyrics to date.

8 Live — Witless Banter and 25 Mildly Antagonistic Songs of Love (Pink & Black/Fat Wreck Chords) 2000

Selected Compilations and Archive Releases

7 1989–92 (Moon) 1992 The first album plus rarities.

DANDY WARHOLS

FORMED 1993 *(Portland, OR)*
ORIGINAL LINE-UP *Courtney Taylor (vocals, guitar); Zia McCabe (keyboards); Peter Holmstrom (guitar); Eric Hedford (drums)*

Formed by Courtney Taylor, former drummer with Oregon glam rockers Beauty Stab and an early incarnation of Nero's Rome, the Dandy Warhols were haunting the extremes of the Pacific Northwest grunge scene for some months before the local Tim/Kerr label noticed they were also a stupendous psychedelic band — a point hammered home by the group's self-released debut cassette, *The Instructions and Incidentals of Automotive Handling in Four*. The label dispatched the band to the studio in late 1994; they emerged first with a raw Christmas single, 1994's "Little Drummer Boy," swiftly following through with a new 45, re-recording the tape's "TV Theme" and their debut album, *Dandy's Rule OK!*

The set completely rewrote the group's reputation. "Imagine Jesus and Mary Chain if they'd been as good as people said they were," enthused *Alternative Press*. "Or Hawkwind, if they'd played low-fi Hammond organs." The

band embarked upon a similarly genre-crushing tour with Electrafixion, and with further singles "Ride" and "Nothing to Do" under their belt, the Dandys signed to Capitol in 1996.

Protracted sessions for their major label debut saw the band deliberately mythologizing themselves, dropping dark hints about all night studio drug parties and long days wasted getting stoned. Early sessions for the new album were scrapped at Capitol's insistence, but a tour with Love and Rockets that same year proved the band was fully functioning after all — a point overwhelmingly proven by 1997's *Come Down*.

Hedford quit to pursue a career as DJ Aquaman; he was replaced by Brent De Boer, and with the singles "Everyday Should Be a Holiday" (#29 UK), "Not If You Were the Last Junkie on Earth," and "Boys Better" breaching the UK chart during 1998, the Dandys toured Europe heavily before returning home to commence their third album. Featuring contributions from Brian Jonestown Massacre front man Anton Newcombe, the set was allegedly completed in February 1999. *13 Tales from Urban Bohemia* was released in summer 2000.

Dandy Warhols LPs

8 Dandy's Rule OK? (TK) 1995 Justine Frischmann had a baby and they called it Roger McGuinn. Then they force-fed it psychedelics, and the Dandys snailed the secret of full frontal sonic wallpaper before it had finished its first trip. Surf music for the end of the world; "Sister Ray" on a skateboard.

8 Come Down (Capitol) 1997 More of the same, only even more manic. A few of the titles reek of deliberate self-mythologizing, but the music more than compensates.

7 13 Tlaes from Urban Bohemia (Capitol) 2000

DB'S

FORMED 1978 *(Winston-Salem, NC)*
ORIGINAL LINE-UP *Chris Stamey (b. 12/6/54 — vocals, guitar, keyboards); Gene Holder (b. 7/10/54 — bass); Will Rugby (b. 3/17/56 — drums)*

All jangles and power-pop riffs, the dB's built a bridge across the crevice that separated crucial forbears Alex Chilton and Big Star from the likes of new boys on the block, REM. From 1975–1978, Stamey, Holder, and Rugby played the North Carolina club circuit as Sneakers, along with R. Keeley (ex-H-Bombs) and producer Mitch Easter. The band released two EPs, *Ruby* and *Red*, before disbanding after Easter's departure — undaunted, the trio regrouped and resurfaced as the dB's, joining forces with fellow ex-H-Bombs Peter Holsapple (b. 2/19/56 — guitar), with whom Stamey had worked in the early 1970s in another Easter-inspired band, Rittenhouse Square.

In late 1977, Stamey released a solo single, "Summer Fun," through New York's fabled Ork label; uprooting and relocating to that same city during 1978, the dB's released their first single "(I Thought) You Wanted to Know" on the indie Car label, but it was the UK which would first notice the band, as a second single on Shake, "Black and White," caught on and the dB's inked a two-record deal with the UK label Albion.

The dB's first full-length, *Stands for Decibels* (#16 UK Indy), was released in 1981. Produced in London by Scott Litt (later to produce REM and remix Nirvana), the uplifting and moody *Decibels* was followed one year later by *Repercussions* (#17 UK indy). Albion also released a handful of UK-only singles, "Amplifier," "Dynamite" (1980), "Big Brown Eyes," "Judy," "Living a Lie" (1981), and "Neverland" (1982), as well as teaming with Shake for a compilation album, *Shake to Date*, featuring early dB's and H-Bombs tracks.

Given a critical, if not financial, boost by the release of the two albums, the dB's signed Stateside to the Bearsville label in 1984 — just in time to see Stamey depart for a solo career which would include, among other things, a stint with the Golden Palominos.

Now a trio, Holsapple stepped up to the front. They recorded *Like This* (and single "Love Is for Lovers"), an album full of catchy hooks and countrified jangle-pop that poised them to step into the spotlight of commercial success. (The album also included the original version of "A Spy in the House of Love," a 1987 hit for Was Not Was.)

Recruiting bassist Rick Wagner for live work, the dB's' building momentum was, unfortunately, about to be crushed by the demise of Bearsville Records. This again left the band without a label and *Like This* passed quickly into remembrance, rather than placing them firmly in the commercial ranks they so deserved. The dB's wouldn't stay down for long, however. Replacing the soon-departing Wagner with Jeff Beninato, the band signed to IRS and released *The Sound of Music* (#171 US) in 1987. With a strong set, good promotion, and a well placed single, "I Lie," the album broke the Top 200, marking the dB's first ever chart appearance.

The band gained further visibility when they joined REM as opening band on their *Document* tour. But just when it seemed that everything was firmly cemented in place, Gene Holder left to join the Wygals. After touring, the dB's quietly disbanded in 1988.

The beginning of the 1990s saw the members of the dB's scattering. Holsapple guested with New Zealand's Chills before joining REM as a touring member and, along with his wife Susan Cowsill (of the Cowsills singing family), stepped into New Orleans-based Carlo Nuccio's band, the Continental Drifters, a roots-rock band formed with Mark Walton (ex-Dream Syndicate). Holsapple also reunited with Stamey in 1991, recording and releasing the acoustic-tinged *Mavericks*.

The dB's would have one last gasp. Holsapple, Rugby, and Beninato reunited in 1994, adding guitarist Eric Peterson (of Testament) and recording *Paris Avenue*. They then went their separate ways once more.

The dB's LPs

8 Stands for Decibels (Albion — UK) 1981 The dB's imbibe the sounds of their idols (Big Star to the Beatles) with an energy of their own, cutting through lyric, percussion, and arrangement to create a refreshingly unique sound.

7 Repercussions (Albion — UK) 1982 Still infused with the same energy, the band slicks up the sound somewhat, although the intensity wanes just a little.

8 Like This (Bearsville) 1984 Now a trio after Stamey's departure, the dB's revamp their sound, drop the odd angles to pursue purer pop, then shoot everything through with an essence of country sensibilities. The gems "Love Is for Lovers," "Lonely Is (As Lonely Does)," and "A Spy in the House of Love" emerge as powerful odes for a disgruntled generation.

6 The Sound of Music (IRS) 1987 Picking up precisely where *Like This* left off, even deeper country stylings are very well done, but lack the old-time swagger.

6 Paris Avenue (Monkey Hill) 1994

Selected Compilations and Archive Releases

7 The dB's Ride the Wild Tom Tom (Rhino) 1993 A delightful compilation of oddities, demos, and outtakes, plus singles for the completist.

Chris Stamey LPs

7 It's a Wonderful Life (dB) 1983 Like the dB's, but not really, as Stamey spins off in directions the band only hints at.

7 Christmas Time (Coyote) 1986 With extra tracks on the CD reissue; a wonderfully warm and humorous album. Extra festive!

5 It's Alright (A&M) 1987

8 Fireworks (Rhino) 1991 With two former dB's now in the band, a strong almost-rocker further dignified by the post-punk New York guitar strut of the title track, an inspired cover of William Bell's "You Don't Miss Your Water," and "On the Radio" which is as great as its subtitle ("For Ray Davies") demands it ought to be.

Chris Stamey and Peter Holsapple LP

7 Mavericks (Rhino) 1991

Chris Stamey and Kirk Ross LP

6 **Robust Beauty of Improper Models in Decision Making (East Side Digital) 1995**

Will Rugby LP

5 **Sidekick Phenomenon (Ego) 1985**

Peter Holsapple LP

6 **Out of My Way (Monkey Hill) 1997**

DEAD CAN DANCE

FORMED *1981 (London, England)*
ORIGINAL LINE-UP *Lisa Gerard (b. Australia — vocals, multi-instruments); Brendan Perry (b. Australia — vocals, multi-instruments)*

Lisa Gerrard and Brendan Perry began working together in the early 1980s, part of the remarkable clutch of groups which helped launch the infant 4AD label, and defined a sound quite unlike any other. Alongside the Cocteau Twins and the Wolfgang Press, Cindytalk, Colourbox, and X-mal Deutschland, Dead Can Dance were pioneers on the very fringe of the post-punk scene's mutation into darkness.

"We made medicine for ourselves and hopefully make medicine for other people, a way out, a way to the familiar," explained Gerrard, while Perry continued, "there's too much of an emphasis on [music] as an entertainment. It should be a necessary part of the culture. It should be part of communication, for education, therapy for meditation."

Signing to 4AD, 1984's *Dead Can Dance*, the duo's debut album, certainly lived up to such standards, a scintillating voyage of discovery — one which lies at the heart of so many subsequent journeys both by the duo and by those who admire them. They followed it with the *Garden of the Arcane Delights* EP (their only non-album release for almost a decade), crisper than the album, but no less dark and layered — a sound which would become a virtual trademark.

Spleen and Ideal, in 1985, was generally regarded as the album upon which Dead Can Dance came of age. Following on from the massive success of the collaborative This Mortal Coil, it paved the way for Dead Can Dance's subsequent explorations of medieval and classical themes, gothic in an historical/architectural sense, as opposed to the increasingly debased musical medium which the press still referred to. According to one critic, Dead Can Dance were already far more at home in cathedrals than clubs.

The group remained silent through 1986, although they would contribute an outtake from their gestating next album to 4AD's *Lonely Is an Eyesore* collection, before releasing *Within the Realm of a Dying Sun* in July 1987, the pair tak-ing one side of the album each, to explore personal ideals within the overall Dead Can Dance framework.

It was not necessarily a successful experiment, although the middle eastern cadences which permeated the record would follow through to 1988's *The Serpent's Egg* ("Severance," a track from this album, would be covered by former 4AD band mates Bauhaus during their 1998 reunion tour). Here, and across 1990's *Aion*, bagpipe vied with Gregorian chant, hurdy gurdy with Arabic cadence, to push the band to the very edge of unfathomable diversity. As the 1990s developed, the so-called new age movement would hijack many of these same ideals, but Dead Can Dance not only unearthed them first, they also utilized them to their greatest potential.

1991's *A Passage in Time* collection saw Dead Can Dance allow this new audience to play catch-up, rewarding them for the effort with two new songs, "Bird" and the intoxicating "Spirit," and it was a sign of just how successfully Dead Can Dance absorbed their new following that just three years later, the duo could repeat the retrospective exercise with a live album, *Toward the Within* (#131 US).

In between times, a new studio recording, 1993's *Into the Labyrinth* (#122 US, #47 UK), and their first ever single, "The Host of Seraphim," became Dead Can Dance's most successful releases yet — particularly in the United States, where the band's grasp on medieval music found an enormous audience of enraptured curiosity seekers. Mixing still more traditions into their brew, including Irish folk ballads and even a Bertolt Brecht cover, *Into the Labyrinth* peaked with Gerrard's mystifying "Yulunga (Spirit Dance)" and the contrarily off-set "The Carnival Is Over" — one of two tracks culled for US radio singles, alongside "The Ubiquitous Mr. Lovegrove."

Alongside the EP *Nierika* and single "The Snake and the Moon," the final Dead Can Dance album was *Spirit Chaser* (#75 US), released in 1996, at a time when both Gerrard and Perry seemed more intent on pursuing solo visions — Gerrard's *The Mirror Pool* appeared in 1995, while she would also collaborate with Soma Manstay Pieter Bourke on 1998's *Duality* and the 1999 soundtrack to Al Pacino's *The Insider*. Perry's *Eye of the Hunter* was released in 1999.

Dead Can Dance LPs

6 **Dead Can Dance (4AD) 1984** They slid so effortlessly into the esoteric bag that was the dawn of goth — an arcane Cocteau Twins for the cerebral crowd — that the true import of DCD was easily overlooked. Even so, the magical moods and movement of their first album only hinted at the brilliance to come.

7 **Spleen and Ideal (4AD) 1985** Shedding the anonymous band members in favor of musicians whose tastes were as esoteric as theirs' saw DCD begin to grasp the cross-cultural attitude

which would become their stock in trade. "Enigma of the Absolute," however, still sounds a lot like the Mission.

7 Within the Realm of a Dying Sun (4AD) 1987 Splitting the two members' vocals down either side of the album was a strangely divisive move. But still, outside of Current 93, no one was making music like this, so allow them their little quirks.

8 Serpent's Egg (4AD) 1988 Truly esoteric, with Gerrard's incredible vocals in particular tracing music back to some genuinely ancient sources, while the often portentous song titles disguise some genuinely lovely ("The Host of Seraphim") and powerful ("Ulysses") efforts.

7 Aion (4AD) 1990

8 Into the Labyrinth (4AD) 1993 Further absorbing middle-eastern exotica, clashed with tribal persistence; the best of *Labyrinth* beats like a heart — the rest is trance-like and tremulous.

7 Toward the Within [LIVE] (4AD) 1994

7 Spirit Chaser (4AD) 1996

Selected Compilations and Archive Releases

8 A Passage in Time (4AD) 1991 Smart compilation forgets the first album, but does add two new cuts, "Bird" and "Spirit."

Brendan Perry LP

9 Eye of the Hunter (4AD) 1999 A masterpiece, regaining the classic DCD's reliance upon moody textures and wide open imaginings. "Voyage of Bran," with its lonely wild calls and haunted birdsong; "Medusa," hot-wiring Leonard Cohen to a barren Celtic landscape; and the chilling "Archangel," lifting lyrics from old U2, are Perry at his best, while a supremely desolate reading of "I Must Have Been Blind," reiterates the infant 4AD community's fascination with composer Tim Buckley.

Lisa Gerrard LPs

7 The Mirror Pool (4AD) 1995

6 Duality (WB) 1997

6 The Insider (WB) 1998

DEAD KENNEDYS

FORMED 1978 *(San Francisco, CA)*

ORIGINAL LINE-UP *Jello Biafra (b. Eric Boucher, 6/17/58, Denver CO — vocals); East Bay Ray (b. Ray Pepperell — guitar); 6025 (guitar); Klaus Flouride (b. Geoffrey Lyall — bass); Ted (b. Bruce Slesinger — drums)*

America's finest, and favorite, punk band, the Dead Kennedys waged a near-decade long campaign of compulsive confrontation before messily imploding, never failing to push whichever buttons took their fancy and seldom delivering anything less than full frontal belligerence.

Even though their original modus operandi was pure Sex Pistols, a mood perfectly conjured by early singles "California Über Alles" (#4 UK indy), "Holiday in Cambodia" (#2 UK indy), and "Kill the Poor" (#1 UK indy); the group's musical brutality was always going to play second fiddle to their political acumen. That first 45, "California Über Alles," was a defiant attack on state governor Jerry Brown, and in 1979, Jello Biafra ran — not wholly facetiously — for mayor of San Francisco.

It took two years, and the departure of the mysterious 6025, for the group to release their debut album, 1980's *Fresh Fruit for Rotting Vegetables* (#33 UK, #2 UK indy), through IRS. The following year, they formed the Alternative Tentacles label and, with DH Peligro (born Darren Henley) replacing Ted (who formed the Wolverines), they released the eight track *In God We Trust* mini-album (#3 UK indy), dignifying their continued cult status when they scored UK Top 50 hits with "Kill the Poor" (#49 UK) and "Too Drunk to Fuck" (#36 UK, #1 UK indy).

Further singles, "Nazi Punks Fuck Off" (#11 UK indy) and "Bleed for Me" (#3 UK indy), maintained the band's profile through 1982 but *Plastic Surgery Disaster* (#2 UK indy), the band's second album, presaged a lengthy hiatus, during which all four band members pursued other projects.

East Bay Ray scored a cult hit with a solo single, "Trouble in Town" (#43 UK indy); while Biafra devoted himself to Alternative Tentacles, and during the three years before the Dead Kennedys reconvened, established it as one of the leading forces in the American underground. Hüsker Dü, DOA, TSOL, and No Means No would all have early releases on the label while it remains the vehicle for Biafra's continued solo career.

Frankenchrist (#1 UK indy), the Dead Kennedys' third album, was released in 1985, straight into a firestorm of opprobrium. The album included a free poster by Swiss artist HR Giger, *Penis Landscape #XX*, depicting ten sets of copulating genitalia, and following complaints from a woman whose 14-year-old daughter purchased the album for her 11-year-old brother, the Dead Kennedys were charged with "distributing harmful matter to minors."

The band would spend the next twelve months in and out of court, aware that the statute under which they were being charged — normally reserved for pornographers and drug dealers — carried a $2,000 fine and a one year jail sentence. Biafra fought back by arguing his First Amendment rights, adding that the album had been packaged with an advisory sticker, one of the first in fact to be employed following the success of the PMRC's campaign for music labeling.

The case ended in the summer of 1987 with a hung jury, but the strains of the past two years shattered the band. A new album, fittingly titled *Bedtime for Democracy* (#1 UK indy), had been released during 1986, but understandably suffered from under-promotion, particularly in the US. It was a sadly low key ending to such a high principled group.

While Alternative Tentacles bade the band farewell with the compilation *Give Me Convenience or Give Me Death* (#84 UK, #1 UK indy), Klaus Flouride resumed the solo career he launched with 1985's *Cha Cha* album; East Bay formed a new band, Scrapyard; Peligro joined the Red Hot Chili Peppers as they regrouped following the death of guitarist Hillel Slovak and the departure of drummer Jack Irons.

Biafra would retain the highest profile, however, issuing a string of often controversial solo albums, at the same time as maintaining his now-incontrovertible role as defender of the underground's freedom of speech.

Dead Kennedys LPs

9 Fresh Fruit for Rotting Vegetables (Alternative Tentacles) 1980 Dynamic debut dominated by the indy hits "Holidays in Cambodia," "Kill the Poor," and "California Über Alles."

6 In God We Trust, Inc. (Alternative Tentacles) 1981 Eight tracks, most of which clock in at well under two minutes of blistered hardcore — the 4.24 of "We've Got a Bigger Problem Now" sounds positively indulgent compared to the succinct thunder which preceded it.

7 Plastic Surgery Disasters (Alternative Tentacles) 1982 Expanding lyrical horizons, broadening musical vistas, but still the DKs we know and love — "Winnebago Warrior" will make you think twice about ever driving again.

7 Frankenchrist (Alternative Tentacles) 1985 The free poster got the most attention, but "MTV Get Off the Air" and "Stars and Stripes of Corruption" have been rated among the DKs' finest moments ever.

8 Bedtime for Democracy (Alternative Tentacles) 1986

Selected Compilations and Archive Releases

7 Give Me Convenience or Give Me Death (Alternative Tentacles) 1987 Rarities, live, and the best of — but 15 tracks only tell half the story.

Klaus Flouride LPs

7 Cha Cha Cha with Mr. Flouride (Alternative Tentacles) 1985 Down-home folkabilly with a grin the size of a dead prairie dog.

4 Because I Say So (Alternative Tentacles) 1988 Largely instrumental — almost ambient — but shot through with unexpected... noises.

6 Light Is Flickering (Virus) 1991

Jello Biafra LPs

7 No More Cocoons (Alternative Tentacles) 1987 Politically charged satire; Lenny Bruce's shoes indeed.

8 High Priest of Harmful Matter (Alternative Tentacles) 1989 The *Frankenchrist/Penis Landscapes* story.

8 Last Scream of the Missing Neighbors (Alternative Tentacles) 1990 High energy collaboration with DOA, but the DK sound is never far away.

6 I Blow Minds for a Living (Alternative Tentacles) 1991 Live rants flavored by the Gulf War.

6 The Sky Is Falling and I Want My Mommy (Alternative Tentacles) 1991 No Means No provide the musical mayhem.

6 Tumor Circus (Alternative Tentacles) 1991 Steel Pole Bath Tub and King Snake Roost's Charles Tolnay howl along with a fairly generic (but as usual, caustic) selection of Biafran rants.

8 Prairie Home Invasion (Alternative Tentacles) 1994 Oddly effective folk-blues union with Mojo Nixon. The excellent *Will the Fetus Be Aborted* EP pursues the same line of thought.

6 Beyond the Valley of the Gift Police (Alternative Tentacles) 1994 3 CDs of lectures reiterating Biafra's traditional bugbears — censorship and the problems of getting records into stores among them.

8 If Evolution Is Outlawed, Only Outlaws Will Evolve (Alternative Tentacles) 1998 Biafra berates the death penalty, censorship, and the space race.

Further Reading

The Unauthorized Version by Marian Kester (Last Gasp 1983).

DEAD OR ALIVE

FORMED 1981 *(Liverpool, England)*
ORIGINAL LINE-UP *Pete Burns (b. 8/5/59, Port Sunlight, Liverpool — vocals); Mitch (b. Mick Read — guitar); Marty Healey (keyboards); Sue James (bass); Joe Musker (drums)*

As a founding member of the Mystery Girls with Pete Wylie and Julian Cope, scouse androgyny Pete Burns was already a familiar figure on the Liverpool punk scene, long before he launched the proto-gothic disco band Nightmares in Wax. With the stated intention of becoming the worst group in history, Burns confessed, "we started because we had a stolen keyboard and thought we had to do something with it."

Nightmares in Wax issued one record, the *Birth of a Nation* EP, leading off with "Black Leather," a hectic blend of Iggy Pop's "Sister Midnight" and KC and the Sunshine Band's "That's the Way," revised as a sexually charged paean to greasy motorcycle riders. Considerably toned down, "Black Leather" would become the blueprint for much of what Burns would achieve over the next five years.

Retaining Marty Healey and Mitch from the ever changing line-up which characterized Nightmares, Burns formed Dead or Alive in April 1981, ten minutes before the band were due to appear on a radio program. Burns linked with the Inevitable label for the Ian Broudie produced "I'm Falling" (#22 UK indy) 45, then formed his own Black Eyes label for the swirling "Number 11" (#15 UK indy) and "The Stranger" (#7 UK indy) singles, and the EP *It's Been Hours Now* (#13 UK indy).

With guitarist Wayne Hussey (b. Jerry Lovelock, 5/26/58, Bristol) and bassist Mike Percy (b. 3/11/61) replacing Mitch and Sue James, such successes saw Dead or Alive begin attracting major label interest. The band headlined the Futurama festival in late 1982, then signed with Epic in December. With the band's sound gradually opening to embrace a dancier, club-friendly sound, playing down the original Doors-ish keyboards in favor of BPM percussion, the epic "Misty Circles" — quite feasibly Burns' greatest ever achievement — opened 1983 to enthusiastic reviews.

No matter that Burns had now been married (to Lynne) for three years, the media excitedly began linking his flamboyant image with the burgeoning gender-bender revolution forged by Boy George. Burns responded with devastating wit, establishing himself as one of the most quotable men of the era, and ensuring Dead or Alive would never be short of press.

Hits were harder to find, however. Over the next year, Dead or Alive released two further singles, "What I Want" and "I'd Do Anything," at the same time losing Hussey to the Sisters of Mercy in August 1983, and replacing Healey and Joe Musker with Tim Lever (b. 5/21/60) and Steve Coy (b. 3/15/62). And finally, their luck changed, as the band completed their debut album, *Sophisticated Boom Boom* (#29 UK), prefacing it with a full-fledged revival of "That's the Way (I Like It)" (#22 UK).

Linking with producers Stock, Aitken, and Waterman, Dead or Alive would lay silent through the remainder of 1984, but re-emerge shortly before Christmas with "You Spin Me Round (Like a Record)"(#11 US, #1 UK), a single championed furiously by *Melody Maker* for a full three months before it finally cracked the UK chart. Thereafter it was unstoppable, and with "Lover Come Back" (#75 US, #11 UK) following it into the Top 20, Dead or Alive unveiled *Youth Quake* (#31 US, #9 UK) — an album Burns mysteriously described as "our answer to the Stones' *Satanic Majesties.*"

Dead or Alive launched their first full UK and US tours that summer — Burns appearing with a live line-up of Lever, Percy, Coy, Russ Bell (guitar), and Chris Page (keyboards). Further singles from *Youth Quake* maintained the group's chart profile through 1985 — "In Too Deep" (#14 UK) and "My Heart Goes Bang" (#23 UK) — while they spent much of 1986 working on a new album, *Mad Bad and Dangerous to Know* (#52 US, #27 UK), again with Stock, Aitken, and Waterman. It would be released in February 1987 after two

new 45s, "Brand New Lover" (#15 US, #31 UK) and "Something in My House" (#85 US, #12 UK), heralded the group's re-emergence.

With Dead or Alive delving deeper into the Hi-NRG dance scene, British fans were fast losing interest in what had once been such an edgy, subversive club act, freeing the group to concentrate instead on the US and Japan. Two further singles, "Hooked on Love" (#69 UK) and "I'll Save You All My Kisses" (#78 UK), passed by all but unnoticed while the band embarked upon a summer tour of American stadia. But the *Rip It Up* remix collection (#195 US) failed and two years later, *Nude* (#106 US) effectively bombed everywhere bar the Far East, and following the singles "Turn Around and Count 2 Ten" (#70 UK) and "Come Home with Me Baby" (#69 US, #62 UK), Dead or Alive broke up in mid-1989.

Retaining Coy alone, Burns continued gigging through the early- and mid-1990s. He also embarked upon a very poorly planned America tour in fall 1992, performing to pre-recorded backing tapes with a cassette-only album, *Love Pete*, available only at the shows. It was a depressing exercise, and Burns would not resurface for another two years, when he teamed with Italian dance band Glam, for the "Sex Drive" single.

A sizeable club hit, as well as a return to the Dead or Alive sound of old, it prompted Burns and Coy to relaunch themselves in Europe as International Chrysis. This identity survived just one single — a cover of Bowie's "Rebel Rebel" — and the following year the pair returned as Dead or Alive, and released *Nukleopatra*.

A US tour in 1996 (a planned outing the previous year was cancelled) coincided with the Stateside release of *Nukleopatra*. Remixes of earlier material, including "Sex Drive" and "You Spin Me Round," have since maintained the band's presence in the clubs, while the band's contribution to the Madonna tribute, *Virgin Voices*, proved that the old Burns wit and wisdom is still alive and well.

Dead or Alive LPs

9 Sophisticated Boom Boom (Epic) 1984 DOA round up the last year or so of killer singles — "Misty Circles," "I'd Do Anything," and of course, "That's the Way") — which necessarily ensures it remains a creature of its time. A fevered mix of funk and synth-pop, then, insistent beats and catchy shout-along stompers, seductively coiled within Burns' tough soul tones — truly the best voice on the mid-'80s dance scene. Heavily indebted to funk and Motown, the band was equally in hock to early Spandau Ballet and Human League; about half of *Boom Boom*'s keyboard melodies were plundered from elsewhere... and the rest would provide fertile pickings for later groups.

6 Youth Quake (Epic) 1985 "You Spin Me Round" did more than make Burns a star, it unleashed dancing tendencies in the most left-footed wallflower. Add "Lover Come Back," "In Too

Deep," and "My Heart Goes Bang" to the brew and *Youth Quake*'s a virtual jukebox in itself — which makes it seem even stranger that the whole thing was so disappointing.

4 Mad Bad and Dangerous to Know (Epic) 1986 Only "Something in My House" touches the musical daring of classic DOA; only "Brand New Lover" had the subversive pop beat. The only way is down.

4 Nude (Epic) 1989

5 Fan the Flame (Epic — Japan) 1990

5 Love Pete (self-released) 1992

7 Nukleopatra (Cleopatra) 1995 Superficially, the DOA sound remains unchanged. But the post-techno apocalypse which swells around its best tracks proves that after a long, dodgy patch, Burns is back on track. So, still insisting he's a brand new species (early on in the opening title track), now he's messing with minds as well — modern remixes for "You Spin Me Round" and "Sex Drive" rewrite the rules around which both sounds revolved, while David Bowie's "Rebel Rebel" has not seemed this sordid since we thought Ziggy meant what he was singing.

Selected Compilations and Archive Releases

6 Rip It Up [REMIXES] (Epic) 1988

Further Reading

Dead or Alive by Jo-Ann Greene (Omnibus, UK, 1985).

DEATH IN VEGAS

FORMED *1995 (London, England)*
ORIGINAL LINE-UP *Richard Fearless (b. Richard Maguire, 1972, Zambia); Steve Hellier (b. 1966, South London)*

Job Club DJ and graphic artist, Richard Maguire became Richard Fearless while working alongside another DJ named Shameless in 1992. Building a reputation on the London club scene as one of the most enterprising DJs around and gleefully blending vintage Primal Scream with classic ska and reggae, he was also in demand as a remixer, executing radical reconstructions of St. Etienne's "People Get Real" and Ruby's "Paraffin."

In 1995, Fearless linked with BBC World Service engineer Steve Hellier to record the moody "Opium Shuffle," a ska-techno hybrid released through the Concrete label under the name Dead Elvis. They became Death in Vegas after learning of an Irish record label with prior claim on their original name.

Emboldened by the response to "Opium Shuffle," the pair issued their second single in January 1996, the rock-inflected "Dirt," following it up with "Rocco" in October and "Rekkit" in February 1997, just as Fearless and Monkey

Mafia's Jon Carter were recruited to take over the Chemical Brothers regular DJing slot at the Heavenly Social.

Dead Elvis, Death in Vegas' debut album, was recorded on a budget of $20,000 while Fearless was still attending college, working towards a degree in graphic art. Drawing upon his own musical background, growing up in Africa and the West Indies with a Blue Note jazz devotee for a father, *Dead Elvis* was a carnival ride through a slew of disparate musical influences (English Beat main man Rankin' Roger was notable among the contributors). It was not, he insisted, a techno album ("listen to our album and Daft Punk, and you'll hear quite a difference"), but still it would dominate dance floors across the UK and US, while "Dirt," its video directed by Andrea Giaconne, became a late-night MTV smash.

Impressions that Death in Vegas were just another couple of guys with computers and lots of flashing lights were further dispelled when the duo toured with the Chemical Brothers that summer; Rankin' Roger again appeared, together with live instrumentalists, and the minimum of pre-recorded trickery.

Fearless devoted the next two years to equipping his own studio, the Contino Rooms, before resuming Death in Vegas duties with new partner Tim Holmes (engineer on *Dead Elvis*). Acclaimed, in *Alternative Press*, among the year's most anticipated albums, *The Contino Sessions* (#19 UK) and accompanying "Aisha" single, was released in fall 1999, featuring guest appearances from Iggy Pop, Bobby Gillespie, Jim Reid, and Fearless' girlfriend Dot Allison.

The album also featured an audacious cover of the unreleased Rolling Stones' outtake "Aladdin's Story," discovered by Fearless on an old bootleg — unregistered as an official Jagger-Richard composition, the song was credited instead to "unknown," with two-thirds of the song's publishing royalties placed on account, ready for the day the authors came forward.

The accompanying world tour, meanwhile, included a handful of shows "supporting" Fearless' art work, alongside more conventional gigs, with a live line-up swollen by Matt Flint (bass), Ian Button, Danny Hammond (guitar), Shamus Beaghen (ex-Iggy Pop, keyboards), Jim Hunt, and Duncan Mackay (Primal Scream, horns).

Death in Vegas LPs

8 Dead Elvis (Concrete) 1997 Acid funk ("All That Glitters") and driving electro-dub stylings ("Opium Shuffle") dominate a genuinely apocalyptic march through the underbelly of modern junk culture.

8 The Contino Sessions (Time Bomb) 1999 Little here is as revolutionary as its predecessor's "Dirt," but the overall mood was even darker — "the influences on this album were the 13th Floor Elevators, Chocolate Watch Band, and on the other extreme a lot of Kraut Rock, Neu! Can, Harmonia," warned Holmes, and with guests ranging from Iggy Pop to Dot Allison (the terrifying "Dirge"), it was more open as well.

DEPECHE MODE

FORMED 1979 *(Basildon, England)*
ORIGINAL LINE-UP *Dave Gahan (b. 5/9/62, Basildon — vocals); Vince Clarke (b. 7/3/61, Basildon — keyboards); Martin Gore (b. 7/23/61, Basildon — keyboards); Andy Fletcher (b. 7/8/60, Nottingham — keyboards)*

School friends Vince Clarke and Andy Fletcher formed their first band, No Romance in China, in 1976; successive line-up changes followed. The band's initial ambition peaked with regular shows at a local youth club and it was there that they encountered Martin Gore, then guitarist with an acoustic duo, Norman and the Worms (Clarke also met Alison Moyet, his future partner in Yaz/Yazoo here).

By mid-1979, Clarke and Gore alone were rehearsing together as French Look, becoming Composition of Sound when Fletcher rejoined that summer. The group played three shows before Dave Gahan was recruited as vocalist, and with a unique line-up of three synthesizers and a singer, Depeche Mode (French for "fast fashion") debuted at their old high school before moving onto residencies at the Top Alex club in nearby South end, Crocs in Rayleigh, and the Bridgehouse in east London. A demo was sent to Rough Trade who passed it onto Mute head Daniel Miller.

He, too, rejected it (allegedly with a succinct "yeeeuch"), but the band did encounter Stevo, the London DJ then forming his own Some Bizzare label. One track from Depeche's demo, "Photographic," would appear on the label's debut *Some Bizzare Album*, alongside similar unknowns Soft Cell, The The, and Blancmange.

Miller rediscovered the band when they opened for Fad Gadget at the Bridgehouse in December 1981 and signed them to Mute soon after. Their debut single, Clarke's "Dreaming of Me" (#57 UK), was released in February 1982 — the first of four successive UK indy chart-toppers which the band would now enjoy.

With the band riding high on the new romantic boom now sweeping Britain, "New Life" (#11 UK) and the effervescent "Just Can't Get Enough" (#8 UK) previewed Depeche's first album, *Speak and Spell* (#192 US, #10 UK). Depeche toured the UK and were looking forward to a US visit (the album charted there purely on the strength of import sales) when Clarke — the band's only proven songwriter — quit. "We used to get letters from fans saying 'I like your records'," he mused. "A couple of hit singles later, we got letters saying 'I like your trousers.' Where do you go from there?" He linked with former Undertones vocalist Feargal Sharkey as

the Assemblage, before forming Yaz/Yazoo and later, Erasure.

Despite having never seriously considered such duties beforehand, Gore took over the songwriting and two new singles, "See You"(#6 UK) and "The Meaning of Love" (#12 UK), readily maintained the band's chart profile — although the latter became the first Depeche single ever to miss the top of the UK indy charts; it peaked at #2. "The Meaning of Love" (#12 UK) restored them to the top, however, while the trio hurriedly completed their second album, *A Broken Frame* (#177 US, #8 UK).

A new fourth member, ex-Hitmen/Daphne and the Tenderspots keyboard player Alan Wilder (b. 6/1/59, London), was initially recruited for TV and live work only. He was gradually eased into the studio setup, once the band proved it could continue without Clarke. His recorded debut would be 1983's "Get the Balance Right" (#13 UK). Two further singles that year, "Everything Counts" (#6 UK) and "Love, in Itself" (#21 UK), kept the band on the Top 20. Depeche also toured the US and the Far East before heading to Berlin to record their third album, the pivotal *Construction Time Again* (#6 UK).

Influenced both by the poverty they encountered while in Thailand and by the growing wave of "industrial" bands themselves moving out of Germany, the album's instrumentation was almost exclusively sample-driven, a dramatic move which pushed Depeche into the forefront of rock experimentalists, at the same time as retaining their pop flair — points proven by the similarly adventurous *Some Great Reward* (#51 US, #5 UK) and the singles "People Are People" (#13 US, #4 UK), "Master and Servant" (#87 US, #9 UK), and "Blasphemous Rumours" (#16 UK).

The band's live set, too, pushed frontiers even if Gore merely shrugged, "hitting bits of metal is very visual." Concerts sold out across Europe while the group's first US tour in two years, in March 1985, offered an even stronger gauge of their ascendancy — tickets for the 7,000 capacity Irvine Meadows show sold out within 30 minutes and they set a new 15 minute record at the L.A. Palladium. The release of a greatest hits collection, aptly titled *Catching Up with Depeche Mode* (#113 US), consolidated their position while the band worked on their next album. (A similar release, featuring all of the band's singles to date, was released in Britain as *Singles 81–85*, #6 UK.)

Reiterating the increasingly dark strains of the band's most recent singles, "Shake the Disease" (#18 UK) and "It's Called a Heart" (#18 UK), *Black Celebration* (#90 US, #4 UK) was again recorded in Berlin, echoing that city's division as the band attempted to balance their own progression with the marketplace's demands.

They failed. "Stripped" (#15 UK), "A Question of Lust" (#28 UK,#3 UK indy), and "A Question of Time" (#17 UK, #2 UK indy) all underperformed as singles, with the latter pair's failure to top the UK indy charts being the first such omissions in eight releases. But it was a glorious failure, as the album finally pushed Depeche Mode out of the teenybop cachet which had clung to them for so long and forced rock's cognoscenti to pay attention. The band later admitted that they had come close to scrapping *Black Celebration*, so concerned were they about its ultimate reception. They would not fall into that trap again.

1987's *Music for the Masses* (#35 US, #10 UK) would be the band's first without producer Daniel Miller, as he was replaced by David Bascombe (Peter Gabriel, Tears for Fears). Far more rock-inflected than ever before, *Music for the Masses* nevertheless pointed Depeche in yet another new direction, one well illustrated by the singles "Strangelove" (#76 US, #16 UK, #2 UK indy), "Never Let Me Down"(#63 US, #22 UK, #2 UK indy), and "Behind the Wheel" (#61 US, #21 UK, #1 UK indy — segued on the 12-inch mix with a dynamic version of "Route 66").

The devotion of the band's UK following, too, was proven by the domestic chart success of an imported European single, "Little 15" (#60 UK, #8 UK indy), while in the US, Depeche Mode's performance at the MTV Awards was so well received that a remix of "Strangelove" (#50 US) was promptly released to major radio success.

The most sensational development, however, was the band's 1988 US tour, climaxing at Pasadena's 70,000 capacity Rose Bowl, with a show filmed by DA Pennebaker for release the following year as *101* (#45 US, #5 UK, #2 UK indy). A single culled from the set, a live version of "Everything Counts" (#22 UK, #4 UK indy) was also a massive hit, but it was the movie which set the pace. In one weekend in August 1989, *101* was the tenth most profitable movie in America, out-performing *Ghostbusters II*, *Batman*, and *Turner and Hooch*.

While the movie and accompanying soundtrack album did the business in the stores, Gore and Wilder both recorded solo projects, Gore's *Counterfeit* (#156 US, #10 UK indy) covers EP and Wilder's *Hydrology* EP, released under the Recoil alias he debuted with a 1986 single.

Depeche, however, were soon stirring again. The launch of a new single, "Personal Jesus" (#28 US, #13 UK, #1 UK indy), in August 1989, was the cue for a near-riot when the band made an in-store appearance at Wherehouse in Hollywood, and while the single's progress was slow, by the new year "Personal Jesus" was on its way to giving the band their biggest American hit since "People Are People." Excerpted from the newly released *Violator* album (#7 US, #2 UK), "Enjoy the Silence" (#8 US, #6 UK) would do even better and over the next six months, two further singles would be culled from the new album, "Policy of Truth" (#15 US, #16 UK) and "World in My Eyes" (#52 US, #17 UK).

Violator itself would ship gold in April 1990, and of course their next (longest ever) tour was sold-out almost the moment it was announced. By the time it was over, however, the band's internal dynamics were so frayed that insiders doubted whether Depeche Mode would ever work together again. Gore was now married and a father and he talked of recording a solo album, but having a daughter "was just more enjoyable than going back into the studio." Fletcher, too, was married and planning to open a restaurant in St. John's Wood, London; Wilder was busying himself with another Recoil project.

That left Gahan, who was himself undergoing a total-transformation. Married (to the band's fan club secretary) since 1987 and already a father, in early 1992 he walked out on his family and relocated to Los Angeles with a new girl-friend, a beard, and a crop of tattoos. When Gore suggested that the quartet get back together to see what happened, Gahan later admitted he almost turned him down point-blank. Instead he decided to listen to the songs first — then turn him down.

Gore's new songs, however, matched Gahan's new-found mood perfectly — aggressive, riff-driven industrial rockers far removed from even Depeche Mode's mid-period neuroses. The studio set-up, too, was completely different, with live drums (Wilder) and guitars (Gore), and in February 1993 the first fruits of the reunion, a Brian Eno remix of "I Feel You" (#37 US, #8 UK), emerged with a grainy video introducing Gahan's new (albeit heavily Ministry-influenced) image. Again, it would be the first of four hits from the new album; "Walking in My Shoes"(#69 US, #14 UK), "Condemnation" (#9 UK), and "In Your Room" (#28 UK) all followed.

Songs of Faith and Devotion (#1 US, #1 UK) appeared in March 1993, while the monster tour which followed would spawn the band's second live album, a song-by-song recreation of the studio set, *Songs of Faith and Devotion — Live* (#193 US). Amusingly, German band Diesel Christ then paid tribute to Depeche Mode with their own version of that same album, performed in early 1980s synth-pop style.

Once again, however, the band came off the road in complete disarray. Fletcher retired from stage work in April 1994 to handle the band's business affairs; he was replaced for North and South American dates by Daryl Bamonte, brother of the Cure's Perry. The tour over, Wilder announced he was quitting the band in June 1995. Two months after that, Gahan was rushed to the hospital after attempting to slash his wrists. The following May, the singer was hospitalized again, following a massive drug overdose.

Pulling themselves back together via a series of sessions with Bomb the Bass mastermind Tim Simenon, Gore,

Gahan, and Fletcher reconvened for *Ultra* (#5 US, #1 UK) in April 1997, accompanying its release with two major hit singles, "Barrel of a Gun" (#47 US, #4 UK) and "It's No Good" (#38 US, #5 UK). "Useless" (#28 UK) and "Home" (#88 US) would follow but the band would not tour this latest album, preferring to wait until September 1998, which brought the release of their second singles collection, *86–98* (#38 US, #5 UK), a new 45, "Only When I Lose Myself" (#61 US, #17 UK), and finally, a US release for the earlier UK *81–85* collection (#114 US).

Performing only material from these latest collections, Gahan, Gore, and Fletcher were joined by Peter Gordeno (keyboards), Christian Eigner (drums), and backing vocalists Jordan Bailey and Janet Cooke, for a four-month outing widely predicted to be the band's farewell. Fittingly, then, May 1999 brought Gore an International Achievement Ivor Novello award from the British Academy of Composers and Songwriters.

Depeche Mode LPs

6 Speak and Spell (Sire) 1981 "Nigel wants to go and see Depeche Mode, because they play bland, unchallenging pop music, and Nigel likes bland, unchallenging pop music. That's why he likes Depeche Mode." — Attila the Stockbroker, 1981

7 A Broken Frame (Sire) 1982 With Clarke's departure, songwriting duties fall to Gore, who promptly responds with a myriad of classic tracks, gracing *Frame* with a depth of feeling utterly at odds with the one-dimensional debut. "See You" is truly majestic, but the future is best heard shimmering through the experimental blips and bleeps of "Monument," casting a haunting aura around "Leave in Silence" and even peeping through the synthi-ditty "Meaning of Love."

8 Construction Time Again (Sire) 1983 Depeche unveil a bigger, more layered sound, bolstered by the metal shop rhythms which pound across the grooves, from the construction site of "Pipeline" to the genuinely insidious pop which emanates from the corporate boardrooms of "Everything Counts." A rallying cry of revolution — from a totally unexpected quarter.

8 Some Great Reward (1984) 1984 Having explored global economics and politics, Depeche now turn to interpersonal relationships. Relentless, *Reward* drives from the poignant ballad "Somebody" to the industrial fantasy for fetishists of "Master and Servant," but it's the haunting "Blasphemous Rumours" which finally liberated Depeche from the constraints of teenybopperdom.

9 Black Celebration (Sire) 1986 There's little lyrical comfort from the emotional despair that spreads its tendrils throughout *Celebration*, although the music provides at least some tempered hope in the poignant, yearning ballads ("A Question of Lust" — maybe Gore's finest hour) and the driving force of "Here Is the House." The fear is palpable on "A Question of Time," though,

and much of the album is a gala of melancholy — a celebration of emotional misery and uncertainty.

9 Music for the Masses (Sire) 1987 Like a penitent seeking forgiveness, Depeche return with the more hopeful *Music* and the dream of salvation through love. A harbinger of things to come, there's an almost religious intensity to swathes of this album, from the choral harmonies which drench several tracks, to the unapologetic apocalypse of "Pimpf." That aura is heightened further by sundry classical piano passages, although it's not all sackcloth and ashes — the savage "Behind the Wheel" and the moody suckerpunch pop of "Strangelove" prove that.

7 101 [LIVE] (Sire) 1988

7 Violator (Sire) 1990 Producer Flood ensures an exquisite sounding album; awash in moods and atmospheres swinging from the gentle delicacy of "Waiting for the Night" to the tobacco spitting aggression of the industrial countrified "Personal Jesus," and reaching perfection on "Enjoy the Silence" — moody synths surrendering to the club rhythms.

7 Songs of Faith and Devotion (Sire) 1993
7 Songs of Faith and Devotion Live (Sire) 1993 Pulling away from the understated melancholy of its immediate predecessors and with Depeche no longer even pretending to drape their purgatory in pop's pretty clothing, this is not an album which sits lightly on the soul. So, live or in the studio, it's exactly what you'd expect — depressingly brilliant if you remain unconvinced, brilliantly depressing if you share their hurt.

7 Ultra (WB) 1997 Slimmed to a trio, but remaining on much the same course as before. Singles "Barrel of a Gun" and "Useless" are the first to resolve themselves beyond the general black moodiness.

Selected Compilations and Archive Releases

7 People Are People (Sire) 1984 Awkward US-make-weight set, designed to cash in on the title track hit by rounding up a few other recent singles.

7 Catching Up With (Sire) 1985
9 Singles 81–85 (Mute UK) 1985 Wrapping up the band's first five years, the UK collection reiterates all the singles so far; the US edition drops a few out of respect for *People Are People*. *81–85* would finally be released in America alongside *86–98*.

9 Singles Box (Sire) 1990 Actually three boxes, each stuffed with CD pressings of all the band's singles to date (almost — a few UK limited editions are absent).

9 Singles 86–98 (Sire) 1998 As a singles band through the 1980s, Depeche were practically peerless. The mood dissipates across the second half of *86–98*, though, as singles simply become recurrent trailers for whatever the latest album may be, but still the mood prevails — pop on the edge of paranoid pomp; adventurous despite both its own conditioning and that of the critics who once savaged them for kicks.

Vince Clarke/Yaz LPs

7 Upstairs at Eric's (Sire) 1982 Just three months after quitting Depeche Mode to escape pop fame and pursue a solo career, Clarke sailed even higher up the charts with Yaz (Yazoo in the UK), a voice and synth union with Alison Moyet — c'est la vie. Still working firmly within a pop framework, Clarke shifts direction slightly, maturing his melodies while retaining a keen eye for bubbles — dense, dark, and dancey, intensified by Moyet's stirring, deep vocals. Her songwriting contributions add gospel, disco, and soul to the brew while the driving, moodily militaristic "Goodbye Seventies" harshly reiterates the post-punk tendency suggested by the co-penned "Situation."

6 You and Me Both (Sire) 1983 Clarke and Moyet work hard to combine their diverse talents, as the former tries his hand at ballads and the latter has a go at pop (albeit within a funk and Motown context), and while these experiments are generally successful, the stretching takes it toll. Still a rewarding album, and a showcase for Moyet in particular, but Clarke's pop sensibilities are virtually lost.

Selected Compilations and Archive Releases

7 The Best Of (Reprise) 1999 From the first album, "Only You," "Don't Go," and the hideously intense "Winter Kills" are utterly peerless. Others, sadly, have been less fairly treated by the passing of time, and the 1999 remixes simply miss the point entirely.

Alan Wilder/Recoil LPs

6 Unsound Methods (Mute) 1997 An unsettled cover of Alex Harvey's "Faith Healer" launches Wilder into a series of psychotic sound scapes, all a million miles from the Mode he molded.

7 Liquid (Mute) 2000 Diamanda Galas, Rosa Torras, Nicole Blackman, and others guest on a second slab of driving electrofueled darkness.

Further Reading

Some Great Reward by Dave Thompson (St. Martin's Press, 1994).

DEUTSCHE-AMERIKANISCHE FREUNDSCHAFT

FORMED 1977 *(Dusseldorf, Germany)*
ORIGINAL LINE-UP *Robert Gorl (drums, keyboards); Gabi Delgado-Lopez (vocals); W Spelmans (guitar); Chrislo Haas (bass, keyboards)*

Although they broke up as early as 1982, Deutsche-Amerikanische Freundschaft joined Einsturzende Neubauten as prime movers on Britain's burgeoning industrial scene of the early- to mid-1980s. Formed at the height of the punk rush of 1977 and espousing similar DIY tendencies to the more conventional guitar-driven bands around them, DAF indeed began as just another gaggle of frenzied noise-merchants, shifting their focus towards calmer electronic dance music after hearing Donna Summer's "I Feel Love."

Their approach, however, was never conventional. First heard in the UK on the 1979 compilation *Earcom 3*, the band then released *Ein Produkt*, a riot of synth- and tape-powered heavy metal. To an electronic audience raised on Tangerine Dream and Kraftwerk, it represented armageddon.

Robert Gorl and Gabi Delgado alone moved to London in 1980 (Chrislo Haas later resurfaced in Crime and the City Solution), signing to Daniel Miller's Mute label and releasing the single, "Kebabtraume" (#15 UK indy). "Der Rauber Und Der Prinz" (#36 UK indy) followed.

Like the accompanying album *Die Kleinen Und Die Bosen* (#4 UK indy), it was a considerably more refined work than DAF's earlier material. Indeed, by the time of 1981's *Alles Ist Gut*, recorded with producer Connie Plank, the group was indeed moving in on Kraftwerk, albeit from a decidedly locker-room biology-influenced viewpoint.

A growing awareness of pure industrial music was demonstrated by the liberal use of found sounds (locomotives, etc.) although both *Gold Und Liebe* and *Fur Immer* in 1981 varied this approach considerably with the latter embracing a number of otherwise alien musical forms wholeheartedly: rock'n'roll, funk, and so on.

DAF were put on hold after that while both members attempted solo careers. Gorl's was the most eagerly awaited — shortly after arriving in London, he was invited to guest (as drummer) on the Eurythmics' *In the Garden* debut. With Annie Lennox now a media star, her appearance on Gorl's *Night Full of Tension* album was, however, generally disappointing. Delgado's *Mistress*, recorded with Can drummer Jaki Liebezeit and Connie Plank, was also poor and in 1985, the duo reunited. The project fizzled out before any recording could be accomplished and the pair returned to solo duties, Delgado fronting the evocatively named DAF Dos.

Deutsche-Amerikanische Freundschaft LPs

7 Ein Produkt Der Deutsche-Amerikanische Freundschaft (Warning — Germany) 1979 Heavy metal electro concerto clashing barely managed chaos with moments of viciously nihilistic overdub overkill. Utterly unlike anything else at the time, its impact remains brutal even now.

8 Die Kleinen Und Die Bosen (Mute) 1980 Still screaming, still grating, but allowing rhythm to march just below the surface in the spirit of a sometime Pere Ubu, or a more focussed Pop Group.

6 Alles Ist Gut (Virgin) 1981 With producer Conny Plank essentially erasing every last crust of abrasion — a definite improvement from a music standpoint — the use of found rhythms (passing trains, slamming doors) has a fascination of its own. The band's original vicious streak, however, will soon be sorely missed.

6 Gold Und Liebe (Virgin) 1981 A crushed Kraftwerk landscape of robot drums and bare bones instrumentation, while the vocals just hover over the glaciers. Delightfully spartan, but somewhat soul-less.

4 Fur Immer (Virgin) 1982 Either an experiment in sundry, different genres and styles, or the sound of a dying band having one last blowout. Patchy, ragged, and ultimately unfulfilling.

Selected Compilations and Archive Releases

6 Daf (Virgin) 1988 Reasonable stab at creating one cohesive album out of the band's final three.

Gabi Delgado LP

5 Mistress (Virgin) 1985 Sex-obsessed disco in a well-pressed cheap suit.

Robert Gorl LP

4 Night Full of Tension (Elektra) 1984
5 Psycho Therapie (Disko B) 1998
5 Watch the Great Copycat (Disko B) 1998

DEVO

FORMED *1972 (Akron, OH)*
ORIGINAL LINE-UP *Mark Mothersbaugh (keyboards); Bob Mothersbaugh (vocals, guitar); Bob Casale (guitar); Gerald Casale (bass); Jim Mothersbaugh (drums)*

Two sets of brothers formed what began as a deliberately anonymous quartet in 1972, chasing a vision of human de-evolution across acres of early cassette recordings, for little more than their own enjoyment.

The departure of drummer Jim Mothersbaugh in favor of Alan Myers was followed by Mark Mothersbaugh, too, quitting, to form Jackrabbit with local journalist/musician Chrissie Hynde. That outfit collapsed when Hynde relocated to the UK and Mark returned to brother Bob and the Casales, just as the group named itself the De-Evolution Band.

Clad in lab coats and patiently reducing their music into scientifically designed slabs of electronic sound, the De-Evolution Band's first public release was a 10-minute movie

short, *The Truth About De-Evolution*, an award winner at the 1976 Ann Arbor Film Festival. That same year, the band formed their own Booji Boy label and released the first in a trilogy of cult singles, "Jocko Homo"/"Mongoloid."

A radical rearrangement of the Rolling Stones' "Satisfaction" followed and in July 1977, the newly abbreviated Devo made their New York debut, introduced onstage by David Bowie. The band hit Britain the following spring, championed by indy label Stiff who promptly reissued both "Jocko Homo" (#51 UK) and "Satisfaction" (#41 UK), following through with "Be Stiff" (#71 UK), as Devo toured the country — a venture which peaked with June 1978's showing at the Knebworth festival.

A 1978 EP released through Elevator, *Mechanical Man*, increased interest in the band, and Devo signed to Warners in August (Virgin in the UK), scoring another British hit before year's end with "Come Back Jonee" (#60 UK; a US single, "Uncontrollable Urge," did little). Their Brian Eno produced debut album, *Q: Are We Not Men? A: We Are Devo!* (#78 US, #12 UK) scored on the back of another successful UK tour and was swiftly followed up with *Duty Now for the Future* (#73 US, #49 UK). The singles "The Day My

© Jim Steinfeldt/Chansley Entertainment Archives

Baby Gave Me a Big Surprise," "Secret Agent Man," and "Girl Want" followed to increasing applause.

Devo were already intriguing the US media and on October 14, 1978, they became the first homegrown "new wave" band ever to appear on *Saturday Night Live*. Their commercial breakthrough arrived in early 1980 with "Whip It" (#14 US, #51 UK), taken from their third album, *Freedom of Choice* (#22 US, #47 UK). Supported by a suitably wacky video — cartoon quirkiness had now replaced the original dark zaniness of their Booji Boy days — Devo suddenly found themselves lining up alongside the B-52's alone as the face of the American new wave. It was an honor they embraced wholeheartedly.

Collaborations with Neil Young in his *Rust Never Sleeps* and *Human Highway* movie projects readily established Devo as the Thinking Man's Favorite Weirdoes; Soundgarden's Kim Thayil would later describe Devo as the band kids got into if they were too smart for Kiss, and too hesitant for punk rock. But over the next five years, Devo would lock into an album-a-year routine utterly at odds with their original novelty and individuality, and one which certainly lost its appeal to the band members.

Although "Gates of Steel," "Beautiful World," and "Through Being Cool" all flopped, a version of "Working in a Coal Mine" (#43 US), cut for the National Lampoon movie *Heavy Metal*, became Devo's second US hit in late 1981, following up album successes *Devo Live* (#49 US) and *The New Traditionalists* (#23 US, #50 UK). "Jerkin' Back and Forth," "Peek a Boo," "That's Good," the album *Oh No! It's Devo* (#47 US) in 1982, and another soundtrack effort, "Doctor Detroit" (#59 US) succeeded it.

Warners dropped the band in 1985, following a surprising flop with the Devo-lved cover of Jimi Hendrix's "Are You Experienced" and the under-performance of their next album, *Shout* (#83 US); singles of the title track and "Here to Go" were equally unsuccessful. The group retaliated with the *E-Z Listening Disk*, a muzak revision of their greatest hits, released the same month as Mark Mothersbaugh staged an exhibition of postcards in L.A..

With new drummer David Kendrick on board, Devo signed to Enigma for the "Disco Dancer" and "Baby Doll" singles in 1988, followed by *Total Devo* (#189 US) and a live hits collection, the three-sided *Now It Can Be Told*. Another single, "Post Post-Modern Man" preceded the *Smooth Noodle Maps* album, but by the end of 1990, the party was over — Devo broke up, Mark Mothersbaugh later reflecting, "I don't like the lifestyle anymore."

Devo did not completely shatter. Bob Mothersbaugh, Bob Casale, and Kendrick would continue working together at Mark Mothersbaugh's Mutato Muzika composing corporation, creating TV themes and ad music, with Mark win-

ning an Emmy in 1992 for his theme for Disney's *Adventures in Wonderland*.

The team would also oversee the release of early archive material in the *Hardcore Devo* and *Mongoloid Years* series, while the band's memory would receive another fillip when Nirvana's version of the 1980 B-side, "Turnaround," was included on that band's *Incesticide* rarities collection. (Coincidentally, fellow Seattle-ites Soundgarden would record the other side of that same single, "Girl Want," for a 1995 B-side.)

Devo themselves would be revived for a contribution to the *Mighty Morphin Power Rangers* movie soundtrack and a CD-ROM game, *Devo Presents the Adventures of the Smart Patrol*. The group would also reunite for one show, in Clarkston, MI, during Lollapalooza '97.

Devo LPs

8 Q: Are We Not Men? A: We Are Devo (WB) 1978 It's hard to hear today just what was so shocking about Devo's debut, but in 1978, the Eno produced *Men* was the Battleship Potemkin of the punk revolution. A collision of rock riffs, pop melodies, synthi hooks, sci-fi feel, and jerking electronic rhythms made this album uniquely groundbreaking, as well as the impetus behind a plethora of "new wave" scenes across the US. Perhaps Americans really did need to devolve before punk could evolve here.

5 Duty Now for the Future (WB) 1979 As exposure increases, innovation subsides. Targets seem more obvious (Devo on sex... guess what?), the air of bemused observation is increasingly forced, the joke is almost over already.

7 Freedom of Choice (WB) 1980 "Girl Want," "Gates of Steel," and, of course, the super hit "Whip It" catch the spud boys as they realize their mistake. The hint of devolved über-menschen which remains in their imagery is now tempered by a growing awareness that perhaps we all aren't that different after all — so let's get down and have some fun!

6 Dev-O Live (WB) 1981

5 New Traditionalists 1981 (WB) But not too much fun. Embracing the reality of the electric revolution which their early recordings could simply imagine, Devo don't seem to have realized that sounds and effects which you really have to work to create, using whatever tools come to hand, are often a lot more productive than ones you get from pressing a button. There are a *lot* of pressed buttons here.

4 Oh No! It's Devo (WB) 1982 Oh no! is right.

4 Shout (WB) 1984

5 E-Z Listening Disc (Rykodisc) 1987 Awkwardly realized, but strangely successful, Devo reduce their greatest hits to near muzak standards — and not always in the song's best interests. Works better as a passing novelty than an album you may want to play more than twice (once for yourself, once for a friend), but the future was looking on regardless.

4 Total Devo (Enigma) 1988 Remembering the days when they were "weird" and "zany," Devo put the old hats back on and go hell for loony leather. But the sallow "Disco Dancer" and an obvious take on Presley's "Don't Be Cruel" are as good as it gets — they may sound forced but at least they're fleetingly funny.

4 Now It Can Be Told [LIVE] (Enigma) 1989

4 Smooth Noodle Maps (Enigma) 1990

Selected Compilations and Archive Releases

9 Be Stiff (Stiff UK) 1979 Six-track EP compiling all three original Booji Boy 45s.

6 Greatest Misses (WB) 1990

7 Greatest Hits (WB) Far-reaching collections documenting the WB/Virgin years.

6 Hardcore Devo I (Rykodisc) 1990

7 Hardcore Devo II (Rykodisc) 1991 Taken together, a 36-track collection of early 4-track recordings, including primitive takes on the three Booji Boy 45s, plus "Mechanical Man" and "Working in a Coal Mine." Enjoyable, but they'd have meant far more if they'd been released at the time.

8 Devo Live: The Mongoloid Years (Rykodisc) 1992 Highlighting shows in Cleveland 1975, Akron 1976, and New York (Max's) in May 1977, bootleggy sound cannot disguise the aura of mayhem which characterized the classic boojis.

DICKIES

FORMED 1977 (Los Angeles, CA)
ORIGINAL LINE-UP Leonard Phillips (vocals); Stan Lee (b. 9/24/56 — guitar); Chuck Wagon (b. Bob Davis — keyboards); Billy Club (bass); Karlos Kaballero (drums)

Absurdly costumed and given to supersonic covers of classic rock, the Dickies emerged from the wreckage of the punky Quick and blues-rocking Jerry's Kids in 1977. They were discovered by former Sparks manager John Hewlett at the end of his tenure with that band. Visiting L.A.'s Starwood Club with Mumps manager Joseph Fleury, Hewlett caught "the best band I've ever seen," completing only their second ever live show. Informing the somewhat shocked band members they were to music "what Spielberg and Lucas are to movies," Hewlett became the Dickies' manager and produced their first demo — breakneck renderings of Black Sabbath's "Paranoid" and two originals.

A deal with A&M followed and though the label clearly regarded the Dickies as little more than a novelty act — turning out mach ten renditions of further pop classics — still they were sent away to record their debut album, The Incredible Shrinking Dickies (#18 UK).

Following minor hits with "Paranoid" (#45 UK), "Eve of Destruction," "Give It Back," and "Silent Night" (#47 UK), the band scored their first major smash in April 1979. The Dickie-fied version of TV theme Banana Splits (#7 UK) was followed by a sold-out UK tour (their third in under a year) and a precipitous version of the Moody Blues' "Nights in White Satin"(#39 UK).

A sophomore album produced by prog rock veteran Robin Geoffrey Cable, Dawn of the Dickies (#60 UK), was disappointing, however, and while further singles, "Manny Moe and Jack," "Fan Mail" (#57 UK), and the theme from Gigantor (#72 UK) foundered, the band's support was further riven by the departure of multi-instrumentalist Chuck Wagon to pursue the solo career opened up by an earlier 45, "Rock and Roll Won't Go Away." The following week, Hewlett was fired as band manager and shortly after, A&M dropped the Dickies.

Hewlett and Wagon reunited in a new band (with Hewlett on vocals), the Four Squares, built around former Sparks members Adrian Fisher (guitar), Trevor White (bass) and Dinky Diamond (drums). An album was recorded, but scrapped following Wagon's suicide in June 1981.

The Dickies, however, regrouped around Phillips, Lee, Scott Sindon and Steve Hufsteter (guitar), Lorenzo Buhne (bass), and Jerome Angel (drums) and issued their third album, Stukas Over Disneyland in 1983, following a three-year delay. Thereafter, while the band would never officially disband, new releases became increasingly sporadic through the 1980s — the Killer Klowns from Outer Space EP and the live anthology We Aren't the World. However, a new line-up featuring Philips, Lee, Buhne, Enoch Hain (guitar), and ex-Red Hot Chili Peppers drummer Cliff Martinez formed in 1988 and the following year, brought Second Coming and a host of renewed live work. Live in London, in 1991, summed up this era of the band.

A constantly shifting line-up left Leonard Phillips and Stan Lee the only original members. Among the musicians passing through the band's ranks in the early 1990s, former Prince protege Jonathan Melvoin played keyboards for two years, his health-conscious lifestyle causing his bandmates to nickname him Mr. Perfect. Melvoin would later become touring pianist for the Smashing Pumpkins — ironically, he died from a heroin OD on July 11, 1996.

A third rebirth in 1995 brought the Idjit Savant album, well-received in the wake of punk's mainstream breakthrough via Green Day and the Offspring and in 1998, the band signed with Triple X for the Dogs from the Hair That Bit Us album; Fat Wreck Chords would release the single "My Pop the Cop" soon after.

Dickies LPs

9 The Incredible Shrinking Dickies (A&M) 1979 Incredible indeed. Speedball re-creations of rock's richest tapestries, interrupted by the band's own harebrained assaults on all the past held holy — a Roadrunner cartoon if the coyote won. Stunning.

6 Dawn of the Dickies (A&M) 1979 Prog producer Robin Geoffrey Cable tried, but somehow didn't realize that the Dickies' dream of sounding like Van Der Graaf Generator would only work if they had the songs to match. A garage punk prog masterpiece was not the end result. ("Gigantor" is great, though.)

8 Second Coming (Enigma) 1989 A song called "Goin' Homo" probably isn't the best way to reintroduce yourself to the PC-era, but the Dickies are such loveable scamps you can almost forgive them of anything. Especially when their comeback sees them sounding so bitingly, ferociously back to (near) best.

8 Live in London — Locked 'N' Loaded 1990 (Receiver UK) 1991

7 Idjit Savant (Relativity) 1995

7 Dogs from the Hair That Bit Us (Triple X) 1998 Another decade later, and they haven't changed a bit.

7 Still Live Even If You Don't Want It [LIVE] (Roir) 1999

Selected Compilations and Archive Releases

7 Stukas over Disneyland (Restless) 1983 Clashing demos for the band's unreleased third A&M album with more recent material; a return to first album form...too late. Led Zeppelin's "Communication Breakdown" gets a damned good kicking, though.

4 We Aren't the World (Roir) 1986 21-track live and demos cassette, with the best material dating back to 1978.

7 Great Dictations (A&M) 1989 The hits and misses, 1979 style.

DIE TOTEN HOSEN

FORMED *1983 (Dusseldorf, Germany)*

ORIGINAL LINE-UP *Campino (b. Andreas Frege, 6/22/62 — vocals); Breiti (b. Michael Breitkopf, 2/6/64 — guitar); Kuddel (b. Andreas Von Holst, 6/11/64 — guitar); Andi (b. Andreas Meurer, 7/24/62 — bass)*

Superstars in their native Germany; anti-establishment heroes elsewhere on the European mainland, Die Toten Hosen (literally the Dead Trousers, but in actuality a colloquialism for "all talk, no action") are almost single-handedly responsible for the continued life span enjoyed by such reformed first generation punks as The Buzzcocks, The Damned, and 999 on the continent.

Constantly paying tribute to the era which inspired their own career, Die Toten Hosen finally put their money where their mouths were on 1991's *Learning English: Lesson One*, a punk tribute which featured the band accompanying many of their own idols. TV Smith, Wreckless Eric, Sham 69's Jimmy Pursey, The Ramones' Joey Ramone, Johnny Thunders (at his last ever recording session), and many more re-created their own greatest hits, receiving what was, in many cases, their first ever silver disc award as a consequence. For a generation of Die Toten Hosen fans too young to have experienced these artists in their prime, *Learning English* was a history lesson as well.

Formed on Friday, February 13, 1983, when Kuddel delivered a pizza to Campino and Andi's shared apartment, Die Toten Hosen actually emerged from the wreckage of two earlier Dusseldorf bands, KFC and 2K. With three of the four founding members being named Andreas, they considered calling themselves the Andreas Band, opting out only when Breiti objected.

Die Toten Hosen signed with EMI Germany later that year and released their debut album, *Opel Gang*, soon after. Working with British engineer Jon Caffery, whose credentials included the Sex Pistols' "God Save the Queen," Die Toten Hosen followed up with *Unter Falscher Flagge*, and made their first appearances overseas, on British TV's *The Tube*, and radio's John Peel Show (the session subsequently reappeared on the *Liebesspieler* EP).

Constantly gigging, Die Toten Hosen signed to Virgin (Germany) in 1985, and issued the *Battle of the Bands* EP, a five-track collection featuring Hosen masquerading under such pseudonyms as Ricky Curl and the Standing Ovations, the Evel Kids and Little Pepito, and the Swinging Pesetas.

Joined by former Die Suurbiers drummer Wolli (b. Wolfgang Rhode, 1/9/63), Die Toten Hosen's third album, *Damenwahl* ("Ladies' Choice"), followed in 1986, bringing with it an excellent cover of The Vibrators' "Disco in Mosko." But it was an even more overt nod to British punk, 1987's *Never Mind the Hosen, Here's the Roten Rosen*, which broke the band in their homeland.

Packaged in a letter-perfect pastiche of the Sex Pistols' debut album, and opening with the semi-immortal "Itsy Bitsy Teenie Weenie Honolulu Strand Bikini," the album entered the German Top 20, with the band's popularity going into overdrive on the tour which followed. A live album, *Bis Zum Bitteren Ende* ("Until the Bitter End") was taped on this outing, capturing a rapid fire greatest hits set, interspersed with "Disco in Mosko" and another old-time favorite, The Clash's "Police on My Back." Gary Glitter's glam staple "Rock'n'Roll," too, got a workout, and the album eventually sold over 400,000 in Germany alone.

The newly composed soundtrack to a theatrical adaptation of *A Clockwork Orange, Ein Kleines Bischen Horrorschau* ("A Little Bit of Horror Show") the following year did even better, but it was with 1990's *Auf Dem Kreuzzug Ins Gluck* ("On a Crusade to Happiness") that Die Toten Hosen achieved what local radio programmers were still convinced was impossible — a #1 hit record.

Learning English followed, bringing Die Toten Hosen face to face with their own heroes — in most cases for the first time. "It was so important to meet [them]," Campino reflected later. "If I'm going to tell my grandchildren one day what I did with my life, this is the first album I would get out of the drawer to play." It would also be the first Die Toten Hosen album to be released in the lands of so much inspiration; *Learning English* appeared in the UK in late 1991 and the US early the following year. It saw little action, however — neither country was yet ready to reacquaint itself with punk and it would be another three years before Die Toten Hosen revisited either country.

1993 brought *Kauf MICH!* ("Buy ME!"), another massive hit (German sales topped 600,000), but the band's visibility no longer worked entirely in their favor. A far right-wing German politician convinced himself that the band's latest single, "Sascha, Ein Aufrechter Deutscher" ("Sascha, An Upstanding German"), incited physical action against his person — a complaint which, given the group's fervent anti-Nazi stance, might not have been too far from the truth. The matter went to court, where it was dismissed through lack of evidence; the band celebrated by pledging all proceeds from the single (some $330,000) to the Dusseldorf-based Appeal Against Action and Racial Prejudice.

"Sascha..." would reappear on the *Reich and Sexy* best of later in the year and with this set, too, selling over half a million copies, Die Toten Hosen received that year's Echo Award, presented annually to the most successful German band. A renewed attempt to broaden their appeal into English-speaking countries with the following year's *Love Peace and Money* (largely comprised of older material with new, English, lyrics), however, was again doomed to failure. Nevertheless, Die Toten Hosen toured both countries in support of the album's fall 1994 release, opening for Terror Vision in Britain, then — reversing a German bill from the previous April — Green Day in the US.

Touring to support their latest album, 1997's *Opium Fürs Volk* ("Opium for the People"), June 28, 1997, saw Die Toten Hosen play their 1,000th show at the Rheinstadion in Dusseldorf. They marked the achievement with their second live album, *Im Auftragdes Herrn* — covers this time included The Ramones' "Sheena Is a Punk Rocker," Iggy Pop's "The Passenger," and, oddly, Rodgers and Hammerstein's "You'll Never Walk Alone."

Even more bizarre, however, was the group's 1998 German Top 5 hit, *Wir Warten Auf's Christkind*, issued under the group's Die Roten Rosen (The Red Roses) identity, and devoted entirely to Christmas songs. Another album that same year paired Campino with former Boys members Casino Steel, John Plain, Matt Dangerfield, and Kid Reid for unplugged renditions of that band's greatest hits, aptly titled *Power Cut*.

1998 also saw Die Toten Hosen make a triumphant trip to Japan, Australia, and New Zealand aboard the first leg of the Vans Warped tour. In September, they would rejoin the

package for a string of European dates. The accompanying *Vans Warped Tour 98* compilation album included one cut, "Raise your Voice," pairing Campino with Bad Religion; Toten Hosen's own "No Escape" was also included.

In between times, the band commenced work on an ambitious new project, which itself grew out of *Learning English*. A songwriting collaboration with TV Smith saw a dozen tracks spread across 1998's *Soul Therapy* EP and the following year's *Crash Landing*, an English language "best of" intended for the band's growing Australian following. Smith also contributed one track, "Call of the Wild," to 1999's *Unsterblich* and the album entered the German chart at #1 immediately before Christmas, trailing the Top 10 hit "Schon Sein."

Die Toten Hosen LPs

7 Opel Gang (EMI — Germany) 1983 Raw power, savage energy, classic punk, if it hadn't detoured into hardcore. Die Toten Hosen's infant vision is part tribute, past ambition, and particularly strong on the faster numbers. And as there's plenty of them on board....

7 Unter Falscher Flagge (EMI — Germany) 1984

8 Damenwahl (Virgin — Germany) 1986

7 Ein Kleines Bisschen Horrorschau (Virgin — Germany) 1988

6 Bis Zum Bitteren Ende [LIVE] (Virgin — Germany) 1988

8 125 Jahre: Auf Dem Kreuzzug Ins Gluck (Virgin — Germany) 1990 Double-album showcasing Toten Hosen's extraordinary ability to reinvent the sounds of the past. From Sham to the Damned, the Boys to the Lurkers (both expertly covered within), hardcore to hip-hop, reggae to rock, Toten Hosen gives it all a new school twist; adding Bad Religion-ish harmonies to a hardcore song here, conjuring up a goth-esque atmosphere within a Social Distortion-like number there, anthemic and pop-punking elsewhere, to create one of the classic melodic punk records of all time.

9 Learning English: Lesson One (Charisma) 1991 Covering some of punk's greatest moments, and assisted by the 17 songs' original vocalists, we have the likes of Jimmy Pursey shouting along to "Kids Are United" and Joey Ramone bellowing "Blitzkrieg Bop," with the occasional original guitarist (including Johnny Thunders in his last recorded performance) joining in as well. As you'd expect, the renditions are pretty faithful to the originals, but not many bands get to record an album with so many of their heroes, and Toten Hosen make the most of it.

8 Kauf Mich! (Virgin — Germany) 1993 The notorious "Sascha" won the headlines, but the idiosyncratic "Hat-Clip-Video-Club" and "Katastrophenkommando" repay investigation with equal ferocity.

6 Love Peace and Money (Atlantic) 1994 Knowing their entire back catalog is a mystery to most English speakers, the bulk of the album was drawn from past Toten platters, then rendered into the new tongue. Unfortunately, it's not only language which is compromised — *Love Peace and Money* also sounds a little too much like Green Day for comfort.

8 Opium Fürs Volk (Virgin — Germany) 1996

7 Im Auftrag Des Herrn [LIVE] (Virgin — Germany) 1996

9 Crash Landing (Virgin — Australia) 1999 Another stab at reinventing Toten Hosen for an English-speaking audience, with new lyrics by TV Smith, but all the old power and individuality still intact. The thundering danceability of "Man," the viciously cynical "Hopeless Happy Song" (with an extended tribute to "Wild Thing" for an intro), and a rousing reworking of the classic "Bonnie and Clyde" rub shoulders with a positively blood-chilling "I Am the Walrus" (beat that, Oasis) and the more-Clash-than-Clash-like "I Fought the Law" on an album which generally stakes Toten Hosen's place alongside the best of the Anglo-American crew.

8 Unsterblich (Virgin — Germany) 1999 The hit "Schon Sein" and six near-symphonic minutes of "Helden und Deibe" power an anthem-packed epic. "Bayern," the band's ode to their most-hated German soccer team (and a hit single in spring 2000), offers listeners an even greater thrill.

Selected Compilations and Archive Releases

9 Reich and Sexy (Virgin — Germany) 1993 Excellent best of.

Die Roten Rosen LPs

7 Never Mind the Hosen, Here's Die Roten Rosen (Virgin — Germany) 1987 Christmas comes but once a year, so 24 tracks (two per month, all year round) about everything else the Hosen love. Including the bikini song.

8 Die Roten Rosen — Wir Warten Auf's Christkind (Virgin — Germany) 1998 From traditional jingles to Christian carols, and onto the new world of Xmas joy courtesy of Bing Crosby, Roy Wood, and Slade — the ultimate yuletide party experience.

Campino/The Boys LP

7 Power Cut (JPK — Germany) 1997 The Boys unplugged with Campino on hand to power through the classics.

DIED PRETTY

FORMED 1981 (Brisbane, Australia)
ORIGINAL LINE-UP Ron Peno (vocals); Brett Myers (guitar); Frank Brunetti (organ); Rob Younger (drums).

The 31st were a Brisbane garage band sundered in 1981 when bassist Tony Robertson quit to join the Hitmen, the lynchpin around which the Australian punk scene of the late 1970s revolved. His ex-bandmates, Ron Peno (vocals), Chris Welsh (drums), and Mike Medew (guitar) promptly regrouped, changing their name to Died Pretty — and then changing it again to the Screaming Tribesmen just months before Peno

quit to form his own new band, Final Solution, who in turn became the Died Pretty before the year was out.

A longtime proponent of Australian urban garage rock, Peno's first band, the Hellcats, were a Dolls/Stooges/Flamin' Groovies covers band especially beloved of Radio Birdman. That band's Rob Younger was a willing first recruit to Peno's next project, then, and with journalist Frank Brunetti and Brett Myers (ex-End) on board, Died Pretty began rehearsing and pursuing territory heavily influenced by New Yorkers Suicide.

Younger quit as drummer after two months, although he would remain on board as the band's producer. He was replaced by Colin Harwick (drums), around the same time as the band recruited Jonathan Lickliter (bass). Both had played with Myers in the End.

Having made their first live appearance in Brisbane in late 1983, following through with inroads into the Sydney scene through the patronage of the Celibate Rifles, Died Pretty signed to Citadel and debuted with the "Out of the Unknown" (#42 UK indy) debut 45 in early 1984, just weeks before Lickliter was replaced by former Dum Dum Boy Mark Lock (also ex-Swedish Rhythm Kings).

A successful Australian tour followed and in August 1984, the band recorded the 10-minute "Mirror Blues," to be split over both sides of their next single. It would be Harwick's final act with the band; he departed to live in India and a plethora of temporary drummers followed while the band tried to wrest Chris Welsh away from the Screaming Tribesmen. According to legend, the drummer did not actually have a kit of his own at that time, and played one financed by the Tribesmen. He could not quit, therefore, until the kit had been fully paid off!

With a settled line-up at last, the *Next to Nothing* EP and "Stone Age Cinderella" single confirmed Died Pretty's slow ascent and in the two years that they spent working towards their debut album, 1986's *Free Dirt*, the band was constantly on the road; still, well-received European and US releases for the album broadened their horizons considerably, and in 1987, the band made its first journey out of Australia.

It was a disaster. In London, Welsh broke two toes when a grocer's truck backed over his foot. In New Zealand, Brunetti broke his ankle. And Peno got mugged in New York. The band returned home to lick their wounds and supervise the release of the *Pre-Deity* compilation, before cutting 1988's "Winterland" single and *Lost* album, through Citadel's newly inaugurated Blue Mosque subsidiary.

Died Pretty returned to Europe the following spring, in the hope of landing a European release for *Lost*, remaining on the road there for close to four months while Australia was left with nothing more than the "Tower of Strength" and "Out of My Hands" singles and the promise of a six week tour in July. That fulfilled, it was back to Europe again for an outing marred by an appalling show at the Fulham Greyhound in London. Nervous at facing a solidly packed crowd, Peno got drunk and spent much of the set abusing an audience already hyped up by his "bastard son of Iggy Pop" reputation.

Despite his misgivings and the widespread opprobrium of the watching press, the gig convinced Beggars Banquet to pick the band up, and *Lost* was released in the US and UK in late 1989 (Died Pretty's sole Australian release that year was the "Everybody Moves" single). Further tours of both territories followed before Locke departed, to be replaced by Steve Clark (ex-the Glass). This line-up recorded one single, 1990's "Whitlam Square," before Brunetti, too, departed, unwilling to face any more touring. He was succeeded by John Hoey (ex-punk era heroes The Thought Criminals), before Died Pretty began work on their next album, *Every Brilliant Eye* and single, "True Fools Fall," in California.

Replacing producer Younger with Jeff Eyrich, the album found the band making a concerted stab for US approval, although not to the detriment of their sound and intensity — as they proved when they sanctioned an archival live EP, *Live Died*, for release alongside their own next single, an in-concert version of "Herr Godiva." Recorded during 1986, *Live Died* served up psychotic renderings of Lou Reed's "Wild Child" and Pere Ubu's "Final Solution." "Herr Godiva," meanwhile, hailed from a 1990 show in Odense, Denmark, and side by side they indicated just how consistent (and consistently brutal) Died Pretty had remained.

1991 opened with the *Stop Myself* EP and "DC Wonder" and "Sweetheart" singles, trailers for the *Doughboy Hollow* album; that was the band's last for Beggars Banquet, as they shifted to Columbia and unveiled new EPs, *Caressing Swine* and *Headaround*, alongside a new bassist, Robert Warren. *Harness Up* followed in mid-1993, with the *Trace* album hot on its heels, while the band also recorded a version of the Saints' "Eternally Yours" for the *Eternally Yours for Earth Music* benefit album, and reunited with producer Rob Younger for the *Good at Love* EP.

Chris Welsh left the band during 1994, just as Died Pretty departed Columbia for a return to Citadel — in his absence, the *Sold* album was recorded with two different drummers, Nick Kennedy and Shane Melder, before Simon Cox took over full time, for the *Deeper* EP in 1996. Since that time, Died Pretty have retained a constant line-up and a consistent policy of touring and recording, with the EPs and singles *Radio* (1997) and "Slide Song" (1998) preceding the acclaimed *Using My Gills as a Roadmap* album.

Died Pretty LPs

8 Free Dirt (Citadel — AUS) 1986 Considerably more introspective than the early singles suggested it might be, with the skewed country stylings (Triffid Graham Lee appears on one track, violin and mandolin on others) locking firmly into the lyrics' own sense of twisted romanticism.

7 Lost (Beggars Banquet) 1988 A delightfully misleading bright pop opening shatters into even darker vistas, punctuated by some genuinely slobbering mounds of blistered rock.

8 Every Brilliant Eye (Beggars Banquet) 1990 You can put the band into L.A., but you can never put L.A. into the band. "The Underbelly" churns with unbelievable passion — Died Pretty's finest since "Mirror Blues."

7 Doughboy Hollow (Beggars Banquet) 1991

7 Trace (Columbia — AUS) 1993 Very much the twin of its understated predecessor. Still *Trace* boasts "Caressing Swine," "Dreamaway," and the remarkable "A State of Graceful Mourning" — three more cuts for the Pretty hall of fame.

6 Sold (Columbia — AUS) 1995

7 Using My Gills As a Roadmap (Citadel — AUS) 1998 Keyboard-heavy set completely reinvents Died Pretty's trademark (guitar-led) sound, a sensation which takes a little getting used to, but bursts into life with "The Daddy Act" and "Paint It Black You Devils." A new direction or a fascinating diversion?

Selected Compilations and Archive Releases

9 Pre-Deity (Citadel) 1988 Essential collection wrapping up the *Next to Nothing* EP plus early singles.

8 Out of the Unknown (Citadel) 1999 Well-conceived 16-track collection, with limited bonus disc of unreleased and rare cuts.

DINOSAUR JR.

FORMED 1983 *(Amherst, MA)*

ORIGINAL LINE-UP *J Mascis (b. Donald Joseph Mascis, 12/10/65 — vocals, guitar); Lou Barlow (b. 7/17/66, Northampton, MA — bass); Patrick Murphy (b. Emmett Patrick Murphy, 12/21/64 — drums)*

The son of an Amherst dentist, J Mascis made his recorded debut at age 13, playing drums in the local youth orchestra on a live album available only to anybody involved in the show itself. Two years later, his drums had taken him to Deep Wound, a hardcore band also featuring Lou Barlow, vocalist Charlie Nakajima and bassist Scott Holland. The group recorded one EP, *I Saw It*, before Mascis tired of hardcore, and in 1984 he and Barlow formed first, Tunafist, then Mogo's Flute, with Patrick Murphy.

Signed to Homestead by Gerard Cosley, and changing their name to Dinosaur, the band debuted with an eponymous album in June 1985, following through with the single

"Repulsion" a year later. Mascis added "Jr." to the name after being contacted by a rival Dinosaur, featuring sundry former members of Country Joe's Fish and the Jefferson Airplane.

The new band name appeared first on a self-titled EP in March 1987, and with the band gigging around the east coast, loudly championed by Sonic Youth (whose Lee Ranaldo would guest with them in the studio), *You're Living All Over Me* in 1987 brought the band full underground attention. September 1988's "Freak Scene" (#7 UK indy) single became a college hit and an anthem of sorts for America's gradually coalescing rock underground, with the following month's *Bug* (#1 UK indy) readily consolidating this initial breakthrough. Constant friction between Mascis and Barlow, however, saw Dinosaur Jr. break up in early 1989 — only for Mascis to reform the band the following day without Barlow. The bassist subsequently formed Sebadoh and the Folk Implosion spin-off, also recording solo as Sentridoh.

With ex-Screaming Trees bassist Donna Biddell, Dinosaur Jr. returned to action in April 1989, with a new single covering the Cure's "Just like Heaven" (#2 UK indy); however, the group then vanished for over a year while Mascis produced fellow Amherst band Buffalo Tom, scored Allison Anders' movie *Gas, Food, Lodging* (Mascis would also have cameos in both this and a later Anders movie, *Grace of My Heart*), and collaborated with producer Don Fleming in the Velvet Monkeys. Fleming and Monkeys bassist Jay Spiegel would return the favor by guesting on a new Dinosaur Jr. single, June 1990's Sub Pop one-off, "The Wagon."

Dinosaur Jr. re-emerged again in the new year, sporting a major label deal (Sire's blanco y negro subsidiary), the album *Green Mind* (#168 US, #36 UK), and minor hits with a revival of "The Wagon" (#49 UK) and "Whatever's Cool with Me." With former Snake Pit bassist Mike Johnson joining Mascis and drummer Murphy, the band toured through the fall, supported by Nirvana, then awaiting the release of their *Nevermind* album. Later, in the wake of that band's breakthrough, many critics ranked Dinosaur Jr. the next underground band most likely to hit. Instead, there would be just one new single, "Get Me" (#44 UK), released during 1992 and it would be early 1993 before the album *Where You Been* (#50 US, #10 UK) arrived to capitalize on Mascis' burgeoning reputation.

While the singles, "Start Choppin'" (#20 UK) and "Out There" (#44 UK), climbed the college chart, Dinosaur Jr. toured as part of that year's Lollapalooza. The line-up remained in flux, however. Murphy was fired (he later joined the Lemonheads) following the tour; Mascis and Johnson alone would record the next album, *Without a Sound* (#44 US), released alongside the attendant college hits "Feel the Pain" (#25 UK) and "I Don't Think So" (#67 UK). The pair

then launched parallel solo careers — Johnson released his first effort, *Where Am I*, in 1994. Mascis' 1996 album, *Martin and Me*, was promoted with a solo acoustic tour. Mascis resumed Dinosaur duties in 1997, with the acclaimed *Hand It Over* and a single, "Take a Run at the Sun" (#53 UK), but announced the band's demise soon after. His second solo album, started in late 1999, featured contributions from My Bloody Valentine recluse Kevin Shields.

Dinosaur Jr. LPs

7 Dinosaur (Homestead) 1985 Dinosaur didn't have to choose between rock and punk, they just slaughtered them, then hung the bits from a raucous wall of noise.

8 You're Living All Over Me (SST) 1987 Loud, thrashed and smashed, *Living* took the noisy exuberance of the first album and added more distortion, more riffs, more guitar, and more guts, making punk and metal look like AOR. A CD-only cover of Peter Frampton's "Show Me the Way" seems almost sacrilegious.

7 Bug (SST) 1988 More of the same, although Mascis' melodic side bubbles under the roiling surface of the songs, most notably in the — dare we say — pop of "Freak Scene."

4 Green Mind (blanco y negro) 1991 Really doesn't have the same impact as earlier Dinosaur projects and, with Mascis' playing most of the instruments himself, this really should qualify as a solo record.

6 Where You Been? (blanco y negro) 1993 Although the band was ancestors of grunge, they now have to follow in its footsteps, and this well-crafted album is just that — too nice for its own good.

3 Without a Sound (blanco y negro) 1994 If a tree fell in the woods, and landed on a turntable playing this album, would anyone hear it, and would they care?

5 Hand It Over (blanco y negro) 1997

Selected Compilations and Archive Releases

7 Whatever's Cool with Me (Sire) 1991 Eight-track collection opening with the then-current single/title track, then plundering a host of Europe-only B-sides for the discerning US collector.

8 In Session (Fuel) 1999 Ten tracks from four BBC sessions, 1988–92, including a dynamic "Bulbs of Passion" and two acoustic performances from 1992.

J Mascis LP

6 Martin and Me (Reprise) 1996 Eeek! Acoustically inspired versions of old band songs plus odd covers. Kind of the Dinosaur lounge experience.

Mike Johnson LPs

8 Where Am I (Up) 1994
7 Year of Mondays (Atlantic) 1996

7 **I Feel Alright (Up) 1998** More like Nick Drake and Leonard Cohen on a bad day; Johnson shines across three delightfully gloomy solo albums of folky, bluesy songs.

Lou Barlow/Sebadoh LPs

5 **The Freed Man (Homestead) 1989**

7 **Weed Forestin' (Homestead) 1990** Redefining the concept of low-fi through the Dinosaur experience, generally brittle post-folk which actually improves with age — much of the superior *Weed Forestin'* was originally recorded three years before *The Freed Man.*

8 **III (Homestead) 1991** Sebadoh's earlier fascination with hiding their light beneath the bushel of zero production is pushed to one side by strong songs, clean sound, and astonishing diversity. The apparently anti-Mascis "Freed Pig" and Eric Gaffney's "Violet Execution" emerge as universal favorites.

7 **Bubble and Scrape (Sub Pop) 1993**

5 **In Tokyo [LIVE] (Bolide) 1994**

8 **Bakesale (Sub Pop) 1994** Another supremely delicate dose of melody, scratching (or bearing in mind the cover, maybe splashing) somewhere between Billy Childish blues and Billy Bragg folk.

7 **Harmacy (Sub Pop) 1996** Packing more in common with the Folk Implosion side project, itself raising the stakes high with the hit "Natural One," Sebadoh's most deliberately accessible release, and maybe a little on the disappointing side. The inconsistency, after all, was one of their brightest virtues.

7 **The Sebadoh (Sub Pop) 1999** Cohesion again, only this time it works, even when the songs (and there are several) seem less than fully realized. Jason Lowenstein's songs are generally the clearest, Barlow's unquestionably the weirdest.

Selected Compilations and Archive Releases

7 **Weed (Homestead) 1990** CD compilation of the first two albums.

6 **Smash Your Head on the Punk Rock (Sub Pop) 1992** Compilation pairing UK EPs *Rocking the Forest* and *Sebadoh vs Helmet.*

Folk Implosion LPs

7 **Dare to Be Surprised (Communion) 1997** Barlow and John Davis follow 1994's formative *Take a Look Inside* EP by omitting the "Natural One" hit single and concentrating on layering lots of guitars over some powerfully contagious hooks.

5 **One Part Lullaby (Interscope) 1999** Sounding more like a folky Beck than Barlow, a weaker set branded by the over-done reliance on cheapo guitars and synths. A handful of worthy songs try to ease it from the mire, but fail.

DISORDER

FORMED 1979 *(Bristol, England)*
ORIGINAL LINE-UP *Dean Curtis (vocals); Steve Allen (guitar); Mick (bass); Virus (drums)*

As punk swept the UK at the end of the 1970s, it hit the south-western city of Bristol hard. The first group to emerge was Vice Squad, swiftly followed by the Glaxo Babies and Essential Bop. Then came Chaos UK, one of the prime movers behind the then newly-emergent Oi! scene, and after them, Disorder.

Gigging furiously throughout 1980, Disorder released their first single, "Reality Crisis," via the tiny Durham Book Centre label towards the end of the year. By the time they approached Vice Squad's Riot City Records for a deal, Disorder was already the biggest band in Bristol, and Riot City the only label in town. The label turned the band down flat.

It wasn't hard to see why. Disorder represented a new breed of punk band, part of an up-and-coming generation which had sat back and watched while the last wave crashed fruitlessly, and which didn't intend letting that happen to them. Though less prone to mischief than Crass, the band with whom (primarily American) commentators have since seen fit to ally them, Disorder were not content simply to talk about anarchy, so much as put at least some of its principles into action. They responded to Riot City by forming their own Disorder label and by carrying on regardless.

A four-track EP, "Complete Disorder" (#29 UK indy), followed in May 1981; its arrival coincided with the first of the many line-up changes which would shake the group over the next five years, when bassist Mick quit, to be replaced by Steve Robinson — boyfriend of Vice Squad singer Beki Bondage. When he departed shortly after, Taff was drafted in from another local band, X-Certs.

Disorder followed up with "Distortion to Deafness" (#9 UK indy) in December, a second burst of violent call-to-arms which sent the group's reputation skyrocketing; while an appearance on the first "Punk and Disorderly" compilation early in the new year saw the band's fame spread to the US as well when Posh Boy picked it up in March 1982.

"Perdition" (#25 UK indy) debuted the band's latest vocalist, Boobs. Formerly the band's roadie, he stepped into the spotlight when Curtis quit during the summer of 1982, and Disorder roared on. Although Disorder had no problem selling out shows all around the UK, the band's greatest market was in Europe, where audiences were considerably less fashion conscious than their British counterparts. Not all the group's European excursions were happy, of course — original Disorder drummer, Virus, quit after what was said to be one "tragically comic European tour experience" too many. He was replaced by Glenn (ex-Dead Popstars).

The *Mental Disorder* EP (#16 UK indy) in March 1983 remains the high-water mark in Disorder's career. "Rampton," about one of Britain's top security prisons, and "Provoked War," lambasting Britain's recent conflict with Argentina over ownership of the Falkland Islands, both appeared on this milestone monster, establishing Disorder among the most literate and powerful of all punk's social commentators. Politics, of course, had always been a vital part of the Oi! experience, but Disorder boasted a verbal vehemence which left their compatriots reeling.

It is this vehemence, committed and fiery, which flavored the succession of studio albums which followed on either side of a short-lived break-up in 1989. The band unleashed four new albums: *Violent World, Sliced Punks on Meathooks*, the shared *One Day Son, All This Will Be Yours* (with Daska Process), and *Masters of the Glueniverse* (with Mushroom Attack). All resonated with the band's questioning and observations. Adopting targets far more varied than the standard punk whipping posts of general disaffection and dismay, Disorder attacked governmental repression at its most insidious.

"Driller Killer" took its title from the gory horror flick which Britain's censors had banned "just in case" it inspired copycat crimes; "Education" mourned the fact that it was becoming increasingly difficult to get one. Disorder's enemies lurked in the quieter corners of society...and didn't like it when they were dragged screaming into the sun. When the group finally called it a day, a lot of people slept a lot more peacefully at night.

Disorder LPs

🄶 **Under the Scalpel Blade (Disorder) 1984**

🄶 **Violent World (Disorder) 1985**

🄸 **Live in Oslo (Disorder) 1985**

🄶 **One Day Son, All This Will Be Yours (Aargh UK) 1986** Split LP with Kaska Process.

🄸 **Masters of the Glueniverse (Desperate Attempt — UK) 1994** Split LP with Mushroom Process.

🄶 **Sliced Punks On Meathooks (Anagram — UK) 1998**

Selected Compilations and Archive Releases

🄸 **Driller Killer (Cleopatra) 1996** Concentrating on the string of vital singles and EPs which preluded the band's first album, a demanding condemnation of punk mediocrity in all its guises.

DOCTORS OF MADNESS

FORMED 1975 (London, England)

ORIGINAL LINE-UP *Kid Strange (b. Richard Harding — vocals, guitar); Stoner (b. Colin Bentley — bass); Urban Blitz (b. Geoffrey Hickman – violin); Pete DiLemma (b. Peter Hewes — drums)*

The Doctors of Madness emerged in 1975 at a time when glam and its manifold roots were literally withering on the vine. More than a year had passed since the last significant new arrival on the scene, but Sparks and Cockney Rebel had already burned their best-made bridges, and now the rock intelligentsia was waiting...for the next E.L.P. album, for Genesis to announce Peter Gabriel's replacement, for Godot, for God knows what. What it wasn't waiting for was what it got — a band whom co-manager Justin DeVilleneuve was describing as "a reflection in the '70s of the decadence of Berlin in the '30s."

DeVilleneuve's partner in overseeing the Doctors' practice was former Pink Floyd/Tyrannosaurus Rex manager Bryan Morrison and his confidence knew no bounds either. "This band are going to be the biggest for ten years," he said, and the Doctors of Madness were not about to argue with him. "Kid" Richard Strange himself was curiously convincing when he explained that John Lennon and Bob Dylan alone were equal to him in the songwriting stakes, and even more so when he berated them both for deserting him. "They've really let me down," he complained. "And now I'm on my own. It's lonely at the top."

As Richard Harding, Strange first came to public attention as a member of the delightfully named Great White Idiot, a band whose solitary live show — at the 100 Club in London — coincided with what the audience thought was the venue's soul night. When it turned out to be anything but, the crowd rioted, the venue was stormed by the local police, and Great White Idiot shattered just as the record company bigwigs they'd invited along showed up at the door.

Not to be put off, Harding promptly threw himself into another band, comprising several former Idiots — Peter Hewes, Geoffrey Hickman, Martin (keyboards), Eddie Macaro (guitar), and a bassist who apparently believed he could write songs as well as the group's vocalist. Finally, the hapless imposter was sacked and Colin Bentley was recruited in his place. Then, with Martin and Macaro departing, the remaining quartet rented a rehearsal room at a nearby pub, the Cabbage Patch, and — in Bentley's words — "sat around plotting these absurd ideas, this really outrageous image that we wanted to create to match the type of songs Richard was writing."

"We are concerned with a kind of cinematographic style, where images come in and out," Harding confirmed, "not making much sense on a rational level, more on a sensory one. Our music, our show, has got this cold, sleazy feeling to it, of those old street corners. We are much more nasty than Alice Cooper, very sleazy, underground and outrageous."

A drunken, stoned evening ended with the rechristening of all four — Stoner (nothing more, nothing less), Kid Strange, Urban Blitz, and Pete DiLemma. Then, with the assistance of Mrs. Stoner, the grotesque make-up which was "to add something to our personalities" was created. "We are," Strange announced, "one of the few bands who get booed before we play a note. Not many others can get that reaction." And Stoner, resplendent in full zombied skeleton drag, told *NME*, "the make-up I wear puts the shits up people."

Weeks later, a talent scout for Bryan Morrison heard the band rehearsing while he was out walking his dog one evening. He alerted Morrison, Morrison brought in DeVilleneuve, and the Doctors were launched onto an unsuspecting nation in early 1976, as special guests on television's MOR *Twiggy Show*.

Rumors began flying immediately: record companies were allegedly offering up to £100,000 for the band's signature, NBC television were flying over from America to make a documentary on the band, the Doctors were going to steal the show at the Great British Music Festival. In truth, they signed to Polydor for considerably less money than that, the NBC documentary turned out to be a less than glowing chronicle on hype, and the festival gig ended when the band's PA broke down. But still there was a buzz about the Doctors, and one that was only going to get bigger.

A nationwide tour opening for Be Bop Deluxe earned the group a modicum of respect, if only for their dogged resistance to the total animosity of the dour headliners' audience. They were, indeed, getting booed before they played a single note and when Be Bop Deluxe were forced to reschedule one show for a few weeks later, the new support band reported back that they'd been met by the most hostile audience they'd ever faced in their lives —until they told the audience "it's okay, we're not the Doctors of Madness."

March 1976 saw the Doctors' first album, *Late Night Movies, All Night Brainstorms*, hit the stores. Bearing the legend "this record to be played with the gas full on," it fit neatly into the void existing between the original Velvet Underground and early Cockney Rebel, but few people looked beyond the band's make-up, and fewer still cared to actually play their record. People really did not like the Doctors of Madness.

The group marched on, gigging through the fall of 1976 with the End of the World tour, a wild extravaganza featuring exploding dummies and great swathes of the band's rush-released second album. *Figments of Emancipation* was issued in late November to catch the Christmas shopping rush — not even considering the possibility that the rush would immediately change direction the moment the album hit the stores. Winter 1976 was the season which ushered in the first bitter blasts of punk rock and if the Doctors had been ill-fitted to the last days of the Glam movement that they

were so obviously inspired by, they were totally out of step with punk — even though history can now look back and insist they helped predict the whole thing.

Having gigged through 1977, the Doctors released one further album, 1978's icily monochromatic *Sons of Survival* (and the "Bulletin" single), then replaced the outgoing Urban Blitz with Damned vocalist, Dave Vanian. Unfortunately, the Damned were no more in favor at this time than the Doctors, and though this line-up did record a projected single, a TV Smith song called "Don't Panic, England," even their record label rejected it. Soon after, the band announced they were breaking up, bowing out with one final show at the London Music Machine on October 26, 1978.

Strange and Stoner alone continued in music — the bassist with the Sadista Sisters, TV Smith's Explorers, and later, Daedalo; Strange as a solo performer.

Doctors of Madness LPs

10 Late Night Movies, All Night Brainstorms (Polydor — UK) 1976 Maggoty rancor at its pristine finest; suicidally doom-laden rock caught on the furthest edges of everywhere that Roxy Music, David Bowie, and the Velvet Underground ever threatened to go, but only if they could get a round trip ticket.

The Doctors didn't care for such niceties, welcoming first-time listeners with a side-long suite which relied upon brain-chilling violin and doomwatch bass to emphasize Strange's discomforted lyrics — "the nurse found a timebomb, it blew off her forearm" was one of his more overt observations and nastier stuff lay deeper within, usually within the sweetest sounding melodies. There again, a song called "The Noises of the Evening" is scarcely going to be about birdsong, is it?

Side two darkens perceptibly, despite kicking off with two relatively conventional numbers, "B-Movie Bedtime" and "Billy Watch Out," a mean streets epic which apparently begins with the plot already in full flow and ends before the action concludes — a mystery thriller with both the first and last pages torn out.

The centerpiece, however, is the concluding "Mainlines," 17 minutes which set the scene in the opening line — "this is the place where the rats come to die" — and goes steadily downhill from there. Again, the violin and bass duel at the forefront, and not for the first time on the album, one lengthy passage comes very close to rewriting every rules of rock instrumentation; so perfectly do the moods and momentum of the two dovetail together.

9 Figments of Emancipation (Polydor — UK) 1976 Two utterly spellbinding ballads, "Marie and Joe" and "Perfect Past," surface amid an electrifying recapitulation of *Brainstorms'* bitterest themes.

9 Sons of Survival (Polydor — UK) 1978 A frigid blast of proto-post-punk neurosis, Stoner's "No Limits" and the Strange/TV Smith composed "Back from the Dead" pinpointing a searchingly brittle new direction.

⑨ Doctors of Madness (UA) 1977 US double-album comprising the first two UK albums.

⑧ Revisionisms (Polydor — UK) 1980 Awkward collection designed to cash in on Richard Strange's solo revival, opening and closing with a bisected "Mainlines." Sacrilege!

Stoner/Daedalo LP

⑨ Walk Inside the Painting (Daedalo) 1995 With violin and bass (again) linking with a distinctly menacing vocal tone, a five-piece whose closest living relations are the Waterboys — if the Waterboys had a sinister side.

ANNA DOMINO

BORN *Anna Taylor (Tokyo, Japan)*

"When I was small, my family moved around a lot." With those words, Anna Domino explained a childhood which saw her art historian mother lead her family from Domino's birthplace, Tokyo, to Ann Arbor, MI, Florence (Italy), and Toronto, Canada, where Domino attended university. From there Domino alone moved to New York, where she briefly joined the band Polyrock; however, when she have first came to attention as a performer, it was in Belgium, after she signed with the Brussels-based Crepuscule in 1982.

Domino debuted with 1983's "Trust in Love" single. An EP, *East and West* followed in 1984, co-produced by Tuxedomoon's Blaine Reiniger — a dark, dreamy collection which received only glancing attention in the English-speaking world, but nevertheless anticipated the rise of fellow chanteuses Malka Spigel, Virna Lindt, Annie Lennox, and more. As *Smart* magazine put it, "the voice of the erotic, tense, despairing, Peggy Lee meets Nico, thinking woman — i.e. post-modern platinum."

A single "Zanna," recorded with Luc Van Acker (and taken from his second solo album, *The Ship*) was a major local hit that same year. Domino's own "Rhythm" and "Take That" singles were also successful, and 1986 brought Domino's self-titled debut album (co-produced by the Associates' Alan Rankine and Marc Moulin of Telex) highlighted by a dramatic reworking of "16 Tons." She also contributed vocals to The The's 1986 *Infected* album, while 1987 brought a union with producer Flood for the *This Time* album — Domino's first collaboration with future husband Michel Delory. Further singles "Lake" and "Tempting," and the EPs, *Colouring In the Edge of the Outline* and *L'Amour Fou*, appeared in 1988/89, but 1990's *Mysteries of America* was to prove Domino's final album for the Crepuscule label — and her last release for almost a decade.

Recorded in New York and Brussels, the downbeat set was produced by Delory, who also co-wrote all the album's originals with Domino (the exception was a Jesse Winchester cover). But the label's insistence that Domino involve herself more in the business side of her career instead prompted her to withdraw completely, and she and Delory returned to New York.

Domino finally resurfaced in 1996 with *Favorite Songs from the Twilight Years 1984–90*, a compilation drawing from her Crepuscule years and paving the way for her return to active recording. In 1997, Domino performed "Pome on Doctor Saxe" for the *Kerouac Kicks Joy Division* tribute album; she and Delory also began gigging around New York and looking for a deal for Domino's latest songs. None was forthcoming, so the pair turned their attention instead to a project which had been germinating for some time, another union with percussionist Hearne Gadbois and a dance-folk project called Snakefarm.

Previewed by a deeply atmospheric reworking of the old blues number "St. James' Infirmary," Snakefarm's *Songs From My Funeral* debut album mined a similar vein of inspiration to Nick Cave's recently released *Murder Ballads*, but with even darker intent and inspiration, drawing from the bottomless resource of American folk ballads for its content. In an interview with *Time Out* magazine, Domino herself described it as songs she'd grown up with, "the kind of Woody Guthrie, Leadbelly type stuff I'd heard even before I started taking guitar lessons in Ottawa." Through the years of moving around, "some of these songs were the only constants."

Anna Domino LPs

⑥ Anna Domino (Crepescule — Belg) 1986 A distinctly edgy, but sometimes overly polite set, Domino's chilled vocals setting up a vampiric boudoir mood which occasionally gets a little too self-conscious for its own good.

⑦ This Time (Mute) 1987 A vast improvement, although the semi-pop semi-melodies remain as intent on winning art rock plaudits as winning over the pop kids. Again, Domino's vocals sometimes seem to wonder what they're doing hanging round with songs (and arrangements) like these, but the overall effect is intriguing.

⑧ Mysteries of America (Crepescule — Belg) 1990 A deeply understated album, the first to place Domino in the best musical, as well as contextual light. Echoing some of Snakefarm's subsequent moodiness, with acoustic guitars and bongoes the most obtrusive backing, *Mysteries* is indeed mysterious — with the biggest question being, how did "Bonds of Love" (surely a hold-over from some mid-80s Frankensteinian synthipop experiment) get on it?

Selected Compilations and Archive Releases

⑧ Favorite Songs from the Twilight Years 1984–90 (Janken Pon/Cargo) 1996 A smattering of alternate takes and unreleased tracks further dignify a well-chosen trawl through the Crepuscule years.

Snakefarm LP

⑨ Songs From My Funeral (RCA) 1999 Domino genuinely sounds as disturbed as she should be, faced with having to sing such sadness. Against a somber semi-trip-hop backing, *Songs For My Funeral* rolls through ten melancholy slabs of broody American folk, most involving death, and a few about despair... betrayal... loss... all that good stuff. A purposefully edgy accompaniment removes any last remaining stigma from the songs' Peter, Paul, & Mary-shaped heritage, and the result is utterly irresistible.

DRAMARAMA

FORMED 1983 *(Wayne, NJ)*
ORIGINAL LINE-UP *John Easdale (vocals, guitar); Chris Carter (bass); Peter Wood (guitar); Mark Englert (guitar); Theothorous Athanasious Ellenis (keyboards); Jesse (drums)*

Criminally underrated throughout their nine-year career, Dramarama's attempt to meld classic British glam rock with current underground punk tendencies emerged from Wayne, NJ, after childhood friends John Easdale and Mark Englert recruited four friends, and began gigging locally.

Early recordings by the quartet would subsequently be released on the fan club CD *The Days of Wayne and Roses*; Dramarama's own first self-released EP, *You Drive Me*, appeared in 1983 on their own Questionmark label, to be followed by *Comedy* in 1984. (Questionmark released one other single, by In Colour, featuring future Easdale collaborator Nick Celeste.)

Cinema Verite, their band's first album, followed on Questionmark that same year; signing then to the French New Rose label, the single "It's Still Warm" followed. Dramarama's second album, *Box Office Bomb*, arrived in 1986 in Europe, but 1987 in the US — a situation rectified when Dramarama (with keyboard player Tommy T replacing Ellenis) signed with Chameleon in 1989.

With "Anything Anything," a cut from their debut album, featured in the latest *Nightmare on Elm Street* movie (#4), the *Stuck in Wonderamaland* album was followed by the singles, "Last Cigarette" and "Wonderamaland." CD reissues of the band's first two albums followed, while the in-concert *Live in Wonderamaland* set, originally produced for promotional purposes only, was then rushed out as the *Live at the China Club* EP to further applause.

In 1990, the group stepped out of their Dramarama roles, to release the *Looking Through...* label for New Rose, as the Bent Back Tulips. Comprising mainly *Stuck in Wonderland* outtakes, including a cover of Morrissey's "Last of the Famous International Playboys," and the single "Tie Me Down," the album would finally be released in the US in 1994, following Dramarama's demise.

1990 also saw drummer Jesse quit; he was replaced for the band's latest tour by Tim Edmondson and over subsequent releases, Wire Train's Brian McLeod, Rolling Stones sideman Jim Keltner and Blondie's Clem Burke would fill in.

"Anything Anything" had now resolved itself into something of an MTV staple, and with the band's line-up bolstered by former Tom Petty keyboard player Benmont Tench, Dramarama's next album, *Vinyl* (and the "Haven't Got a Clue" and "What Are We Gonna Do" singles) were hotly tipped for a breakthrough. They did not make it; another great 45, 1992's "I've Got Spies," was similarly overlooked and when 1993's *Hi Fi Sci Fi* also proved an honorable failure — despite some radio attention for both "Work for Food" and "Don't Feel Like Doing Drugs" — Dramarama broke up in 1994. Their final recordings were contributions to Bee Gees and T. Rex tribute albums.

Easdale moved into journalism and radio (he produced ex-Sex Pistol John Lydon's syndicated *Rotten Day* show) before re-emerging in 1999 with a new band, the Newcomes, and an album, *Bright Day*, featuring Englert and Clem Burke. Carter, too, moved into journalism and DJing, and played bass behind actor Mike Myers' Austin Powers alias at the 1999 MTV Video Awards.

Dramarama LPs

⑧ Cinema Verite (Questionmark) 1985 True to their name, Dramarama present human relationships at their most volatile, emotional dramas as vivid as the album's title; it's telling that *Cinema* contains both a Velvets and a Bowie cover. Their own songs are just as strong — an effervescent mix of frenetic poppy punk, flashy guitar leads, interstellar overdrive spacey-ness, and an all-conquering Byrdsy jangle.

⑧ Box Office Bomb (New Rose — France) 1986 Still determined to recast rock's rich past in their own mold — a darker concoction with nods to the Stones, the Stooges, Patti Smith (a pumping cover of "Pumpin'"), and even rockabilly. The increasingly personal lyrics no longer paint such vibrant dramas, but the music more than completes the picture — a sound whose influence will wash up as far afield as Jane's Addiction and Cracker.

⑥ Stuck in Wonderamaland (Chameleon) 1989 Contrary to what you'd expect, Wonderamaland is a pretty moody place where punks are apparently not welcome (although a few rockers do dot the neighborhood). The majority of the residents are midtempo tracks, some jangly pop, the rest just angsty indy and, while they do have some interesting tales to tell, few really grab your attention. Mellowamaland would be a more apt title.

8 Vinyl (Chameleon) 1991 Dramarama's cover of Mick Jagger's bluesy "Memo from Turner" tells you all you need to know about the group's current musical predilections, moving deep into Big Star country and steeped in the Southern rock tradition of R&B riffery, bluesy guitar leads, and a whiff of C&W.

7 Hi Fi Sci Fi (Chameleon) 1993

Selected Compilations and Archive Releases
8 The Best of — 18 Big Ones (Rhino) 1996

Bent Back Tulips LP
6 Looking Through... (Eggbert) 1979

DREAM SYNDICATE

FORMED 1981 (Los Angeles, CA)
ORIGINAL LINE-UP *Steve Wynn (b. 2/21/60 — vocals, guitar); Karl Precoda (b. 1961 — guitar); Kendra Smith (b. 3/14/60 — bass); Dennis Duck (b. 3/25/53 — drums)*

Steve Wynn and Kendra Smith were founding members of the Suspects (alongside True West's Russ Tolman and Gavin Blair), an L.A. punk band whose one single, 1979's "Talkin' Loud," belied a seriously ambitious band. Regularly gigging and recording, the band's 1979 demos included ferocious versions of the Rolling Stones' "19th Nervous Breakdown" and T. Rex's "Get It On (Bang a Gong)," and while the band broke up in 1980, their local fame was such that May 1981 brought a reunion at Orgis coffeehouse.

Wynn and Smith began scheming Dream Syndicate soon after and by the end of the year, the band was making their first local, live appearances. Epitomizing the Paisley Underground scene of early 1980s California, yet distancing themselves from it with their often obsessive sonic warscapes, Dream Syndicate debuted in early 1982 with a five-song EP released on Wynn's own Down There label. Aggressive garage pop, it was highlighted by "When You Smile," subsequently recorded by Concrete Blonde, and a version of Dylan's "Outlaw Blues" — itself soon to appear on the *Enigma* label sampler.

The band spent the next six months building their local live support with considerable success. *The Days Before Wine and Roses*, a posthumously released live album recorded in September 1982, found the band playing to a rabid audience and responding with similar zeal. Newly signed to Slash, they were already working on their debut album, the immortal *The Days of Wine and Roses* (#7 UK indy), and the energy was palpable.

A second EP (#11 UK indy), led off by title track "Tell Me When It's Over," but capturing three live cuts as well, followed, and toward the end of 1983, Dream Syndicate made the leap to a major label which their supporters had been demanding for so long.

Replacing Smith (who quit to form Opal with Rain Parade frontman David Roback) with former Droogs member Dave Provost and recruiting Blue Oyster Cult/Clash producer Sandy Pearlman to handle the sessions, Dream Syndicate cut *The Medicine Show* and were promptly nailed by their audience, who called the comparatively restrained record a sellout.

A single of the title track passed unnoticed; Provost quit to be replaced by Mark Walton, and with keyboard player Tommy Zvoncheckon board, the band hit the road in support of *Medicine Show*. Recorded at the Aragon ballroom in Chicago on July 7, 1984, the five-track EP, *This Is Not the New Dream Syndicate Album...Live*, was dominated by almost ten minutes of the album's "John Coltrane Stereo Blues," a driving masterpiece, but was also the band's swan song. Poor sales of their A&M releases saw the band dropped; Precoda quit and with Wynn, Duck, and Walton now joined by guitarist Paul B. Cutler (ex-45 Grave), producer of their debut EP, Dream Syndicate retired to reconsider their options.

The band was not idle during this apparent hiatus, recording much of the material which later surfaced on the *Lost Tapes 1985–88* compilation. Wynn and Duck also linked with Green on Red's Dan Stuart and Chris Cacavas, and Long Ryders' Sid Griffin and Tom Stevens, as Danny and Dusty, cutting the *Lost Weekend* album.

Dream Syndicate finally resurfaced in 1986 on Chrysalis with *Out of the Grey*. A considerably more aggressive, but simultaneously country-inflected outlook characterized the new line-up's approach, but *Out of the Grey* was well-received nevertheless and Dream Syndicate swiftly followed through with the *50 in a 25 Zone* EP of outtakes — Slim Harpo's "Shake Your Hips" included. There was also an attempt at introducing the band to the remix generation and the "50 in a 25 Zone Whodunnit Mix" 12-inch. It did little.

Extra tracks on the CD version of *Out of the Grey* pinpointed the band's continued outside obsessions — they joyously took on Alice Cooper's "Ballad of Dwight Frye," released as a single in mid-1986, and Eric Clapton's "Let It Rain" for a 45 the following year. But Neil Young remained their cover version of choice — a version of his "Cinnamon Girl" would be gifted to the British *Bucketful of Brains* fanzine in 1987 and in 1988, Young's own former producer, Elliot Mazer, was brought in to handle Dream Syndicate's Enigma label debut, *Ghost Stories*. The result was triumphant, with the old blues chest-beater "See That My Grave

Is Kept Clean" emerging the kind of performance Dream Syndicate had been hinting at since the beginning.

A single, "I Have Faith," appeared in Britain, but an American tour through late 1988/early 1989 was followed by the announcement that Dream Syndicate were no more. They bade farewell with *Live at Raji's*, taped in front of a delirious hometown audience in January 1989, and the *Weathered and Torn* tour documentary video.

Walton joined the Continental Drifters, with dB's frontman Peter Holsapple; Wynn launched a solo career, cutting the *Kerosene Man* EP and album in 1990 and maintaining a solid stream of releases in and around side projects with Gutterball, formed in 1993 alongside Long Ryders' Stephen McCarthy, Bob Rupe of the Silos, and House of Freaks' Johnny Hott and Bryan Harvey. He also hatched a revolutionary album-in-installments plan for 2000, releasing one new song a month via MP3 download.

Dream Syndicate LPs

8 The Days of Wine and Roses (Slash) 1982 Re-creating not so much the sound, but the atmosphere, of Haight-Ashbury and mixed with the rawness of a garage band, *Days* pulls together the threads of a myriad of '60s influences, twisting them into a skein of sounds that remains fresh, even amongst all the psychedelic flashbacks. There's the odd nod to the Velvets, but much of the album invokes *Berlin*-era Lou Reed. It's no wonder *Days* spearheaded the entire paisley underground.

9 Medicine Show (A&M) 1984 Subsequently reissued appended by the storming five-track *Live* EP; unquestionably the missing link in Neil Young's mid-'70s Crazy Horse catalog. Wynn later confessed this was his favorite Dream Syndicate album, and it's easy to agree.

9 Out of the Gray (Chrysalis) 1986 With the crazed guitars even further to the fore and the Crazy Horse running wilder than ever, another devastating glimpse into Wynn's crushed vision of lawless mid-western Americana.

8 Ghost Stories (Enigma) 1988 They got the sound down, now for the dynamics. Neil Young's own old producer, Elliot Mazer, moves into put the finishing touches to the vision — which means, of course, sounding less like the role model and more like themselves. So, no more extraneous attack, just solid playing, riffing, blasting, and a tension which is palpable.

7 Live at Raji's (Enigma) 1989

Selected Compilations and Archive Releases

8 It's Too Late to Stop Now (Normal) 1989 Out-takes and oddities from singles, flexidiscs, etc.

6 The Lost Tapes 1985-88 (Normal) 1993

7 The Days Before Wine and Roses [LIVE] (Normal) 1994

Kendra Smith LPs

7 The Guild of Temporal Adventures (Fiasco) 1992

7 Five Ways of Disappearing (4AD) 1995

Danny and Dusty LP

6 The Lost Weekend (A&M) 1985

Steve Wynn LPs

7 Kerosene Man (Rhino) 1990 Rootsy successor to the latter-day Dream Syndicate albums.

7 Dazzling Display (Rhino) 1992

8 Fluorescent (Mute) 1994 With Victoria Williams, John Wesley Harding, and Susan Cowsill among his conspirators — a darkly country-flavored set locked somewhere between early '70s Dylan and recent Neil Young.

7 Sweetness and Light (Zero Hour) 1997

8 My Midnight (Zero Hour) 1999

7 Live at the Ancienne Belgique (Zero Hour) 1999

Steve Wynn/Come LP

7 Melting in the Dark (Zero Hero) 1996 Back-handed remembrance of the early Dream Syndicate, with distortion and feedback (courtesy Come) to the fore.

Selected Compilations and Archive Releases

6 Take Your Flunky and Dangle (Return to Sender — Germany) 1994 Limited edition (2,000 copies) collection of unreleased demos recorded between 1986–92.

7 The Suitcase Sessions (Return to Sender — Germany) 1998 A selection of *Melting in the Dark* outtakes recorded with Eleventh Dreamday plus Wynn/Come's ferocious version of "John Coltrane Stereo Blues."

8 Advertisements for Myself (Fanclub Release) 1998 Limited edition 19-track career overview — highly recommended, even if there's only 1,000 of them out there.

6 Pick of the Litter (Glitterhouse) 1999 Drawing from the first aborted *My Midnight* sessions, a limited edition rarities collection issued to tie in with Wynn's 1999 tour of Germany.

Gutterball LPs

6 Gutterball (Brake Out — Germany) 1993

5 Weasel (Brake Out — Germany) 1995

Selected Compilations and Archive Releases

7 Turnyor Hedinkov (Normal) 1995 Demos and alternate versions of *Gutterball* material, plus some odd experimental efforts. Overall a loose, fun little effort.

DURAN DURAN

FORMED 1978 *(Birmingham, England)*
ORIGINAL LINE-UP *Stephen Duffy (vocals, guitar); Nick Rhodes (b. 6/8/62 Nick Bates — keyboards); John Taylor (b. 7/20/60 Nigel John Taylor, — bass); Simon Colly (clarinet)*

The early Duran Duran bore little resemblance to any subsequent model, physically, musically or in terms of future possibilities. A revolving door of musicians passed through before the arrival of Andy Taylor (b. 2/16/61, guitar) and Roger Taylor (b. 4/26/60), while a ceaseless string of would-be frontmen included at least one future star, Stephen "Tin Tin" Duffy. Music industry stalwart, Steve Gibbons Band drummer Bob Lamb, was intrigued enough to record a demo with the band, but still Duran Duran seemed doomed to forever stalk the halls of local cultdom, even after vocalist and would-be poet Simon Le Bon (b. 10/27/58) walked into their lives.

The first sign that their fate wasn't to be so straightforward came when John Taylor read an article in *Sounds* about an up-and-coming London band called Spandau Ballet, saw them tagged as "New Romantics," then rang up the paper in a fit of dudgeon to find out why Duran Duran weren't being given the same sort of coverage. After all, they were New Romantics too.

Of course they weren't, but having hastily dropped the phrase into one of their latest songs, "Planet Earth," they were ready for anything. Journalist Betty Page traveled to Birmingham to see the band, then published an article headlined, "we want to be the band to dance to when the bomb drops."

With a rhythm borrowed from Roxy Music and a riff which Billy Idol would later hijack for his own ends, the band's debut single, "Planet Earth," was originally intended for release on the band's own Tritec label. A tour opening for Hazel O'Connor, however, added fresh urgency to their strivings and in the fall of 1980, Duran Duran found themselves signing to EMI and preparing the most eagerly awaited debut single of the new decade so far.

Re-recording "Planet Earth" in a "proper" studio, and with EMI pulling out all the promotional stops for its March 1981 release, Duran Duran found themselves leaping from a back seat on the Spandau Ballet bandwagon to the driving seat of a movement of their own. "Planet Earth" (#12 UK) was followed into the chart by "Careless Memories" (#37 UK) and "Girls on Film" (#5 UK) and in June, Duran Duran's eponymous debut album (#3 UK) began a 118-week chart residency. The band had arrived, and in the process unleashed teen hysteria unseen in Britain since the heyday of the Bay City Rollers.

Europe and the Far East fell for Duran Duran across the course of the first album; America followed with the second, the epochal *Rio* (#6 US, #2 UK). Again, the album was backed by a string of majestic 45s: "My Own Way" (#14 UK), "Hungry like the Wolf" (#3 US, #5 UK), "Save a Prayer" (#16 US, #2 UK), and "Rio" (#14 US, #9 UK) itself. A collection of remixes, *Carnival* (#98 US), also did its bit to spread the word and in early 1983, the band's hitherto ignored debut album was reactivated (#10 US).

But the music wasn't working alone this time around. Video, via the newborn MTV, was also on their side. Suddenly, the short promo films which Duran Duran were shooting to save themselves from having to fly to Australia for occasional TV shows, were becoming an art form in their own right and the band responded with ever more extravagant big budget video epics, guaranteed to dominate MTV in its heyday.

"Is There Something I Should Know" (#4 US, #1 UK) gave Duran Duran their first British chart-topper in March 1983 while the band were in the US, performing on *Saturday Night Live*. In November 1983, the group began a lightning world tour taking in the UK, Japan, Australia, Canada, and finishing, in late December, at Madison Square Garden in New York City.

"Union of the Snake" (#3 US, #3 UK) previewed the group's third album, *Seven and the Ragged Tiger* (#8 US, #1 UK); "New Moon on Monday" (#10 US, #9 UK) and Nile Rodgers' hyper-quirk laden remix of "The Reflex" (#1 US, #1 UK) consolidated their success. Even the relatively patchy nature of the new album couldn't halt the juggernaut, while a pair of Grammys acknowledged Duran Duran's impact on the video world.

Duran Duran reached their peak as a pop phenomenon in 1984 with the *Arena* (#4 US, #6 UK) live album and accompanying movie charting the unparalleled hysteria with which the band was confronted every time they left the house. A new single, "Wild Boys" (#2 US, #2 UK), was extracted from the movie and it too documented Duran Duran's progress — a neo-industrial number which portrayed the band's own soaring ambitions as musicians first, showmen later. The accompanying video, depicting the band's battle with the "real" Duran Duran, actor Milo O'Shea reprising his role in the *Barbarella* movie, itself remains among the most impressive in Duran's entire canon.

Duran Duran followed up with the theme to the latest James Bond movie, 1985's "A View to a Kill" (#1 US, #2 UK) — and then the madness stopped. With the quintet desperate to regain their personal equilibrium, the band itself went on hiatus, allowing the members the chance to head off and try their hands at projects of their own, Andy and John Taylor as the Power Station, Le Bon, Rhodes, and Roger Taylor as Arcadia. By the time "the hulking, great beast that was Duran" as John Taylor put it, was ready to reconvene in 1986, the musical experiences of the previous year had given the group a whole new ethic.

Andy Taylor and Roger Taylor quit, reducing the band to a trio of Le Bon, Rhodes, and John Taylor. The errant pair was replaced with former Missing Persons guitarist Warren Cuccurullo and ex-Average White Band drummer Steve Ferrone before Duran Duran recorded their *Notorious* (#12 US, #16 UK) album with producer Nile Rodgers, beset on every side by predictions of their imminent demise. According to John Taylor, there could not have been any better incentive. "I thought, holy shit, we're fighting for our survival. We're fighting to keep Duran Duran in the hearts and minds of any audience. It seemed to me over the next five years, over the making of *Notorious*, *Big Thing* (#24 US, #15 UK), *Liberty* (#46 US, #8 UK), we were trying to keep an identity and keep an audience, just fighting to stay relevant."

That dilemma was apparent from their chart placings on both sides of the Atlantic. Following the comeback excitement of "Notorious" (#2 US, #7 UK) in 1986, over the next five years, Duran Duran scored just one more major hit single, "I Don't Want Your Love" (#4 US, #14 UK). Elsewhere, they scrapped with "Skin Trade" (#39 US, #22 UK), "Meet El Presidente" (#70 US, #24 UK), "All She Wants" (#22 US, #9 UK), and "Do You Believe in Shame"(#72 US, #30 UK). Even 1989's *Decade* (#67 US, #5 UK) greatest hits collection fared less well than anyone predicted.

Musically, however, Duran Duran were holding their own, a point proven when Capitol requested a remix of one of their old hits and Rhodes responded with "Burning the Ground" (#31 UK), a new song littered with reminders of Duran Duran's legacy, from the drum sounds from "The Wild Boys," through snippets of "Reflex" and backward lyrics from "Planet Earth." It would not be their biggest hit ever, but it embraced modern musical technology in away which few people expected to hear.

With new temporary drummer Sterling Campbell, 1990 saw Duran Duran release *Liberty* and the singles "Violence of Summer" (#64 US, #20 UK) and "Serious" (#48 UK) before embarking upon a three-year break which again saw the split rumors fly. Cuccurullo and the core trio regrouped, however, stronger than ever, and *Duran Duran — Wedding Album* (#7 US, #4 UK), in 1993, justified their confidence.

"Ordinary World" (#3 US, #6 UK) became Duran Duran's biggest US hit in five years. The album followed suit and when a second single, "Come Undone" (#7 US, #13 UK), kept the group in the Top 10, it was suddenly apparent that Duran Duran had done what no other band of their era — so irredeemably tarred with the "early '80s" brush as they all were — had managed to do. They had come back from the dead.

A third single from the album, "Too Much Information" (#45 US, #35 UK), appeared as the band launched their comeback tour — much of the outing would eventually be cancelled after Le Bon tore a vocal cord, but ticket sales had been healthy regardless. The revival even provoked a rush on past product. 1993 saw "Hungry like the Wolf," "Reflex," and "The Wild Boys" certified gold, to be joined almost immediately by both the new album and "Ordinary World" — itself set to be named Most Performed Work at the Ivor Novello Awards in London the following spring.

According to Rhodes, the inspiration behind the album was the departure of Campbell for Soul Asylum. "He got onto the cover of *Rolling Stone*. We couldn't, and we knew that however good the new album was, there was no way it was going to get heard, because radio was all hiphop or grunge. And we were neither of those, and didn't want to pretend to be either of them, even though there were elements of things we liked within them. We just knew there was no space for Duran Duran at the end of the '80s. Somebody wanted to shut us in and throw away the key. So we just got on with making the album."

The band relaunched their world tour in the new year, and once it was over, immediately began work on a new album — an all-covers collection dedicated to the bands they most admired. Lou Reed's "Perfect Day" (#28 UK), Grandmaster Flash's "White Lines" (#17 UK), and cuts by Sly Stone, Elvis Costello, Bob Dylan, Iggy Pop, and the Doors would feature on the aptly named *Thank You* (#19 US, #12 UK), as would Roger Taylor, returning after nearly a decade's absence to guest on three tracks. Yet even as the band's rise continued apace, discontent was setting in.

Having already partaken in an abortive Power Station reunion, and worked again outside the band in the part-time Neurotic Outsiders (with former Sex Pistol Steve Jones), John Taylor quit for a solo career just as the band were wrapping up the sessions for their next album. His bass parts were immediately replaced either by Cuccurullo or through programming and the album — dubbed by the errant Taylor as "trance punk" — emerged as one of the most entertaining, and certainly the most innovative in all of Duran Duran's long history.

"Out of My Mind" (#21 UK), from the soundtrack to *The Saint* movie, announced the band's comeback while the US release of *Medazzaland* (#58 US) was previewed with a genuine innovation as "Electric Barbarella" (#52 US) became the first 45 ever to be made available (for 99c) through the internet prior to hitting the stores.

However, the British release stalled when EMI, the band's label since the outset, first cancelled a domestic release of *Electric Barbarella*, then dropped Duran Duran altogether. It would be a full year before Britain finally received even a single of "Electric Barbarella" (#26 UK) after it was included on a new compilation, *Greatest* (#170 US, #15 UK). In the meantime, work on Duran Duran's own next scheduled album, *Pop Trash*, was completed in June 1999 for release the following summer.

Duran Duran LPs

9 Duran Duran (Capitol) 1981 In the five minutes before fame and five million screaming teenyboppers steamrollered the band and their reputation, it was possible to see Duran for what they were — an intelligent, innovative blend of all that made the late '70s pertinent. A hint of the early Damned ensured a shadowed, European twist which filled the album with almost gloomy atmospheres — indeed the entire second side wasn't far removed in mood from post-punk bands like The Cure, The Psychedelic Furs, and Echo and the Bunnymen. What spared Duran from living entombment were their dance-inducing rhythms and Nick Rhodes' often staggering electronics. What brought the screaming teens were those very same rhythms married to sublime dark pop melodies.

8 Rio (Capitol) 1982 Brasher than their debut and with a mostly brighter clutch of songs (although a few still carry an air of bittersweet melancholy), what makes *Rio* truly memorable is how easily and unaffectedly Duran showcase different aspects of their sound — slipping effortlessly across the pure pop of "Rio" to the dance-fired "Hold Back the Rain," from the funky "New Religion" to the very experimental "The Chauffeur."

7 Seven and the Ragged Tiger (Capitol) 1983 Branching into new musical territory, Duran strove to new heights, whilst at the same time pushing themselves creatively. From the funky rhythm wed to the latest electro-beats that was "The Reflex," through their excursions into glossy pop and their excavation of the '60s disinterred on an '80s dancefloor, *Tiger* polished each of the band's facets.

8 Arena [LIVE] (Capitol) 1984 Recorded live (bar the inclusion of the studio version of "Wild Boys") during their recent world tour, the band prove to the world what millions of fans already knew — that they were even more breathtaking onstage than on record.

6 Notorious (Capitol) 1986 The addition of horns couldn't cover the fact that Andy Taylor's departure had badly damaged the band. The ensuing departure into pure funk, then, was predictably far from successful.

7 Big Thing (Capitol) 1988 If John Taylor was the impetus behind the funk-riven *Notorious*, then *Big* was Rhodes' baby. Electro and jazzy piano heavy, Duran's sojourn into rave was lightyears ahead of its time, and suffered accordingly. There's echoes of their New Romantic past, while the hypnotic beat feeds through an acid house prism. Even at its most brooding ("...Shame"), the music is riotously infectious.

5 Liberty (Capitol) 1990 Duran seemed to lose not just the plot, but their confidence, and unsure what direction they want to take, *Liberty* emerges a muddle of pleasant funk, slick pop, and a stab at stadium rock that never quite coalesces. Stripping back the aural wallpaper that comprises most of this album comes the striking "My Antarctica," but there should be so much more.

8 Duran Duran — The Wedding Album (Capitol) 1993 A deliberately understated record, with the focus on melodies tailored towards Le Bon's strengths, rather than forcing him to stretch — a problem of late. With renewed confidence, Duran not only recreate that sublime group sound of the past, but now effortlessly tie together threads of other styles, without ever sounding forced. A welcome return to form.

6 Thank You (Parlophone UK) 1995 A mixed bag of covers which nicely sums up the varied influences on the band — Lou Reed, Sly and the Family Stone, The Temptations — the stylistic cornucopia which forged Duran's unique sound. "Perfect Day" was definitely the high point, but Le Bon comes a cropper on too many tracks, most seriously "Ball of Confusion" and "I Want to Take You Higher."

8 Medazzaland (Capitol) 1997 If *Rio* encapsulated the sound of the '80s, then *Medazzaland* does the same for the '90s, capturing the many threads of the decade's music, from electro-pop to industrial, all delivered in inimitable Duran pop-perfect style, and brimming with confidence. A truly of-its-time record, and all the more memorable for it.

7 Pop Trash (Hollywood) 2000

Selected Compilations and Archive Releases

8 Decade (Capitol) 1989

9 Night Versions (Capitol) 1998 Duran's singles, recounted on *Decade*, were great, but their 12-inch singles were better. *Night Versions'* grab-bag of extended remixes, from "Planet Earth" to "Wilder than Wild Boys," gives the most adoring palate a new lease on life.

9 Greatest Hits (EMI UK) 1999 Updating *Decade* with a bonus video disc for early bird purchasers.

Arcadia LP

8 So Red the Rose (Capitol) 1985 Exhilarating in its diversity and arty experimentation (from classical to the buzz and clatter of industrial), *Rose* embraces the quirky, yet insidiously catchy "Election Day," "Missing"'s exquisite dreamscapes, and "Rose Arcana"'s intriguing electro and rhythmic experiments... even Peruvian flutes. A captivating showcase for some genuinely mature musicianship and creativity.

Power Station LPs

7 The Power Station (Capitol) 1985 The two Taylors (John and Andy) meet up with Chic's Tony Thompson and Bernard Edwards and are joined by the debonair Robert Palmer. Then they let their funkified pop tendencies run riot.

6 Living in Fear (Chrysalis) 1996 Two years in the making, with John quitting and Bernie Edwards dying before they'd finished, *Fear* is a testament to the group's will and a fitting epitaph for Edwards' brilliant musicianship and production talents. Lacking the delirious pop sensibilities of a decade before, still *Fear* has its moments.

Andy Taylor LPs

4 Thunder (MCA) 1987 The guitarist hooks up with former Sex Pistol Steve Jones and elopes to Big Rock Land. Generic hard rock with a plastic L.A. flair; the playing's hot, but the songs are not. Taylor was never going to convince rockers that he was more than a pop star, and teenyboppers were never going to accept a pop-less record.

4 Dangerous (A&M) 1990

John Taylor LPs

5 Ambleside Days (Ah Um) 1992

6 Feelings Are Good and Other Lies (Demusik) 1997 The cutest one escapes the madding crowd for a quieter world of introspection. Amazingly, he's also joined by Steve Jones, who deserts his hard rock licks for *Feelings*' gentle ballads and soft rockers — all without a touch of pop or funk. The album is obviously John's way of not so much escaping his past, but of coming to terms with its emotional toll.

John Taylor/Neurotic Outsiders LPs

5 Neurotic Outsiders (Maverick) 1996 The Outsiders began life as a jokey onstage jam, but given a recording contract, it all gets a bit too serious. Everyone writes, everyone sings (regardless of ability), and the whole thing lost its sense of fun overnight. Charmless, finesse-less, maybe a live album would've been smarter.

DURUTTI COLUMN

FORMED *1978 (Manchester, England)*
ORIGINAL LINE-UP *Phil Rainford (vocals); Vini Reilly (b. 8/53 — guitar); Dave Rowbotham (guitar); Tony Bowers (bass); Chris Joyce (drums); Bruce Mitchell (percussion)*

Reilly was ex-Manchester punk pranksters Ed Banger and the Nosebleeds, the anarchic creators of the classic "Ain't Been No Music School" 45. The Nosebleeds also attracted the young Morrissey along to one of their auditions — he failed.

At the same time, Rowbotham, Joyce, and Mitchell were working together as Flashback (aka Fastbreeder), a somewhat directionless band managed by Granada TV presenter Tony Wilson. Aware that Reilly was keen to abandon the Nosebleeds' high octane punk stylings, Wilson contacted the guitarist and invited him to join Flashback. He accepted

in January 1978, just as Wilson rechristened the band Durutti Column — a name borrowed from a comic strip produced by 1960s German anarchist art movement Situationiste Internationale and a suitably portentous origin for what would become of the era's most challenging and obstinate acts.

Mitchell departed, but with vocalist Rainford and ex-Albertos Y Los Trios Paranoias bassist Bowers on board, Durutti Column were an immediate signing to Wilson's Factory label, alongside fellow Mancunians Joy Division and A Certain Ratio (the three bands frequently gigged together during 1978–79). Durutti Column made their live debut at Wilson's newly-opened Factory Club on May 19, 1978, but just weeks before the band was scheduled to begin recording, Rainford was sacked and Durutti Column entered the studio as a quartet, cutting two tracks ("No Communication" and "Thin Ice Detail") for the *Factory Sampler EP* collection.

The abridged line-up was no more stable than its predecessor; shortly after the session, Bowers, Joyce, and Rowbotham quit to form their own band, the Moth Men. Reilly opted not to replace them and instead linked with *Factory Sampler* producer Martin Hannett, to record Durutti Column's debut album, *The Return of the Durutti Column* (#7 UK indie).

It was an utterly uncompromising set, from its coarse sandpaper sleeve (another borrowing from Situationiste Internationale, who produced a book with similar packaging) to the nine slabs of echo-soaked guitar contained within. Still *The Return...* earned Reilly a string of delighted reviews in the music press and a host of complaints from record dealers and purchasers, as the sandpaper shredded every other record which came in contact with it. The sleeve was withdrawn, but the album went onto become one of the touchstones of what would, later in the decade, be termed ambient music.

Reilly explored this same arena with November 1980's "Lips That Would Kiss" 45, adding a simple drum machine to the guitar and echo, to create a soundscape which one critic described as "the sound of tears rolling off the record." However, an interlude which saw Reilly join future Mission frontman Wayne Hussey in the Invisible Girls, a session band formed by producer Hannett to back ex-Penetration vocalist Pauline Murray, apparently reawakened the guitarist's interest in volume. Three Durutti Column songs included on the *Factory Quartet* package at the end of the year featured a live drummer, Donald Johnson, and a guitar led savagery totally at odds with the tranquility of the earlier recordings.

Health problems did much to slow Durutti Column's progress during this period — Reilly was suffering from anorexia nervosa and was too ill to even consider a return to gigging. His relationship with Joy Division continued, however, when Reilly composed "Sleep Will Come" for their late vocalist, Ian Curtis; the track would appear on Factory Benelux's *From Brussels With Love* compilation cassette. Another European label, Sordide Sentimentale, also issued a new Durutti Column 45, the limited edition "Enigma." Compilations and one-offs notwithstanding, however, it would be Christmas 1981, before a second Durutti Column album emerged.

L.C. (#12 UK indie) was recorded in five hours on a four-track TEAC recorder Reilly had just purchased from Bill Nelson; indeed, much of the album was conceived as Reilly experimented with his new toy, feeding guitar and drum machine through his trusty echo unit. Accompanied by percussionist Bruce Mitchell, Reilly completed overdubbing and editing in a further two hours.

Its success made it imperative that Reilly finally returned to the road and, through early 1982, he and Mitchell gigged across North America, Spain, France, Italy, and Ireland. They also joined a European package tour featuring Tuxedomoon, former Skids vocalist Richard Jobson, the Names and the Rhythm of Life Organization (all captured on the 1982 live album *Some of the Interesting Things You See on a Long Distance Flight*) and, the following year, Durutti Column joined a similar outing pieced together by the Crepuscule label. Recordings, meanwhile, were limited to a single, "For Patti," and a trio of avant garde piano pieces released as the *Deux Trianges* EP.

By mid-1982, Reilly had expanded the band line-up to include A Certain Ratio's Simon Topping (trumpet), Maunagh Fleming (cor anglais), and vocalist Lindsay Wilson. This line-up would record the new year's "I Get Along Without You Very Well" single, with the third Durutti Column album, *Another Setting* (#4 UK indie), following in August. It was not, Reilly later admitted, the best realization of the material — the brass was at odds with much of Reilly's own works — but Durutti Column's live popularity remained unimpaired by the misadventure and, over the next six months, the band was on the road constantly. An official bootleg of a London show was released in June, while a trip to Portugal saw Reilly and his girlfriend record an entire album's worth of material for the local Fundacao Atlantica label.

Released only in Portugal, *Amigos En Portugal* (#11 UK indie) would become one of the year's top selling import albums. However, another album recorded that year, *Short Stories for Pauline*, would not appear for close to another decade — originally intended for release on Factory Benelux, the set remained archived until Les Disques Du Crepuscule compiled *Lips That Would Kiss*, otherwise a collection of assorted European-only singles and compilation tracks.

Away from the band, Reilly was heavily involved in two albums by singer Anne Clark, *Anne Clark* and *Changing Places*; his long time interest in a full-blown classical approach, meanwhile, was finally realized when Reilly, Mitchell, and Fleming set to work on 1984's *Without Mercy* (#8 UK indie), augmenting the core trio with saxophonist Mervyn Fletcher, Caroline Lavelle (cello), Richard Henry (trombone), and Tuxedomoon's Blaine Reininger. A companion six-track 12-inch single, "Say What You Mean, Mean What You Say" (#5 UK indie) followed, while further variations would be included on *Dome Arigato*, a live album recorded when Durutti Column toured Japan in April 1985.

With Reilly, Mitchell, and Fleming now joined by John Metcalfe (voila) and Tim Kellett (trumpet), 1986 brought a new single, "Tomorrow" (#15 UK indie), previewing the *Circuses and Bread* album (#11 UK indie). However, this latest line-up was swiftly sundered when Kellett quit to join fellow Durutti Column alumni Joyce and Bowers in Simply Red. Fleming, too, left, but Reilly, Mitchell, and Metcalfe persevered, releasing the *Greetings Three* EP in Italy in October 1986, while Factory compiled a box set of the band's finest moments to date, the *Valuable Passages* cassette package. (A second box, *The First Four Albums*, would arrive in March 1988.)

1987 saw Reilly and the returning Kellett travel to Los Angeles to cut the aptly titled *City of Our Lady of the Angels* EP (#46 UK indie) with vocalist Deb Diamond. Highlighted by a distinctly Durutti-ized version of Jefferson Airplane's "White Rabbit," the EP ushered in a new, up-beat era of Durutti Column, a mood which was only exaggerated by the album *The Guitar and Other Machines* (#13 UK indie). Recorded with producer Stephen Street, hitherto best known for his work with the Smiths and described as the world's first ever DAT rock album, *The Guitar* (and its accompanying single, "When the World") again veered towards a rock sound, a mood which Durutti Column retained first when they made their BBC session debut on the Andy Kershaw Show in January 1988, then when Reilly rejoined Street in the studio to work on former Smiths vocalist Morrissey's solo debut album.

With the singer himself still only tentatively exploring the horizons opened up by the demise of his band, Reilly's playing and arrangements were responsible for much of the ensuing album's musical success. Reilly's own attention, however, swiftly turned towards his latest play thing, the Akai sampler around which he planned building his own next album, 1989's *Vini Reilly* (#5 UK indie). (The ensuing silence was broken by the December 1988 release of a live

Durutti Column EP, *WOMAD Live*, recorded at the festival in 1987.)

It was a remarkable and remarkably audacious album — one track, "Otis," sampled soul giant Otis Redding's voice and later found fresh fame when it was employed for a northern California long distance telephone company's advertisements. Reuniting Reilly with Mitchell and Metcalfe, plus a host of guest and sampled vocalists, *Vini Reilly* would be further distinguished by the inclusion, as a limited edition bonus 3-inch single, of an out-take from the Morrissey sessions, the self-deprecating "I Know Very Well How I Got My Note Wrong," co-written by Morrissey and Reilly. Another nod towards Morrissey then surfaced the following year within the *Vini Reilly — The Sporadic Recordings* outtakes and demos collection, "For Stephen Patrick."

Durutti Column toured Britain during the summer of 1990, before Reilly formed a new partnership with Paul Miller for the next album, *Obey the Time*. Cut very much in the mold of the contemporary Madchester house scene, it was a very dance-oriented album and one which initially shocked the band's hardcore following. Neither was it a one-off deviation, as the "Contra Indications" single proved. Yet even as that hit the stores in February 1991, Reilly was moving again, recruiting a Chinese lute player alongside Mitchell and Miller, and performing a pair of heavily psychedelic shows in London and Paris.

These shows certainly informed the next Durutti Column album, 1991's Italy-only release, *Dry* — Reilly even included a rerecording of "The Beggar," from *Another Setting*, after noting how popular it was when he performed it as an encore. *Dry*, however, would be his last album for three years, prompting rumors that his continued health problems had finally prompted his retirement. The savage ax-murder of former guitarist Dave Rowbotham on November 8, 1991, had also disturbed his equilibrium, but finally 1994 saw Reilly resume action.

Tim Kellett, vocalist Ruth Ann Boyle, Martin Jackson, and New Order bassist Peter Hook joined Reilly for the *Sex and Death* album — released in a black sandpaper case and accompanied by a CD-ROM whose contents comprised, among other things, an overview of the various medications Reilly has been prescribed over the years, and included the revelation that Prozac rendered him suicidal. (Kellett and Boyle subsequently formed their own band, Olive, and scored a UK #1 with the haunting "You Are Not Alone.")

Two years more would elapse before the release of *Fidelity*, an album which Reilly himself considered little more than a demo, but which nevertheless featured some excellent sampling. Reilly's most recent album, *Time Was Gigantic... When We Were Kids*, appeared in 1997; since that time,

Reilly has been occupied with overseeing the remastering and reissue of the entire Durutti Column catalog.

Durutti Column LPs

8 The Return of the Durutti Column (Factory — UK) 1980 The archetypal DC album, as Hannett's characteristically spectral production feeds Reilly's guitar instrumentals into the echoplex and emerges the soundtrack to the best ghost story you've ever heard. *Return* was compared, at the time, to Mike Oldfield and Robert Fripp — a fair assessment, but a damaging one as well. Rather, Reilly was proving himself as individualistic as Oldfield and Fripp, which is another matter entirely.

6 L.C. (Factory — UK) 1981 Despite the not necessarily vital addition of drums and Reilly's vocals to the brew, *L.C.* emerged a classic of spontaneous improvisation — a return to the pastoral sounds of the first album, but even dreamier.

7 Another Setting (Factory — UK) 1983 More experimental variations, this time with a cor anglais taking center stage, adding an effective neo-classical edge to the proceedings. Again, a somewhat false step; imagine a sunny day in a peaceful park — suddenly dive-bombed by a flock of angry geese.

6 Live at the Venue, London (VU — UK) 1983

7 Amigos Em Portugal (Fundacao Atlantica — Port) 1983 A pointed and often whimsical set; hindsight insists it peaks with "Night Time Estoril" (see below); "Small Girl by a Pool" and "Favourite Descending Intervals" are also worthy of attention, however.

6 Without Mercy (Factory — UK) 1984 A seamless performance from themes originally (but so briefly) broached in one of the cuts from the Portuguese album, "Night Time Estoril."

9 Domo Arigato [LIVE] (Factory — UK) 1985 70-minute live album which not only captures the occasional majesty of a good DC show, it also preserves a career's worth of material in a form which doubles as the best compilation a band could ever ask for. A respectful audience adds to the magical ambience.

8 Circuses and Bread (Factory — UK) 1986 "Hilary" remains the most frightening sound ever found on a DC album, as Reilly's guitar cranks itself into a veritable frenzy. Elsewhere, varying degrees of mood and momentum seek out peaks which establish this as DC's most pioneering album since the debut and "Royal Infirmary" as their most atypical performance.

7 The Guitar and Other Machines (Factory — UK) 1987 Taking its impetus from material worked into the band's set during 1986, a dramatic shift which allows Reilly's co-workers almost as much space as he enjoys.

8 Vini Reilly (Factory — UK) 1988 When it appeared, *Vini Reilly* was an awkward sounding set, dividing its time between some genuinely fresh sounding dance-inflected pieces, and a few apparently meaningless doodles. Hindsight levels the aural playing field completely, and some altogether unexpected gems surface — "Opera I," "Love No More," and the funk frenzied "People's Pleasure Park."

7 Obey the Time (Factory — UK) 1990

7 Dry (Materiali Sonori — Italy) 1991

8 Sex and Death (London) 1994 A haunting and sometimes haunted set, sharpened by Peter Hook's trademark bass and Ruth-Ann Boyle's gorgeous vocals. "For Colette" and "My Irascible Friend" are especial highlights.

6 Fidelity (Les Disques Du Crepuscule — France) 1996

7 Time Was Gigantic... When We Were Kids (London) 1997

Selected Compilations and Archive Releases

8 Valuable Passages (Factory — UK) 1986 Much needed "best of," reprising some non-album material.

7 Live at the Bottom Line, New York (ROIR) 1987 Heralding elements of *Guitar...*, a 1986 live show featuring Metcalfe and Mitchell completing a surprisingly energetic trio.

7 The First Four Albums (Factory — UK) 1988

8 The Sporadic Recordings (Spore — UK) 1989 Wonderful glimpse behind the scenes of Reilly's restlessness, drawing on archive material dating back to the early days of DC.

7 Red Shoes (Materiali Sonori — Italy) 1992 Compilation of 1986–87 material.

8 Lips That Would Kiss (Crepescule — Belgium) 1994 Essential gathering of European rarities plus the bonus of an entire unreleased album.

IAN DURY

BORN 5/12/42 (Harrow, England)

Handicapped by a childhood attack of polio, Ian Dury was 28 and seemingly entrenched in a teaching career at Canterbury College when he formed Kilburn and the High Roads in 1970. Accompanied by saxophonist Davey Payne, future 999 guitarist Keith Lucas, bassist Charlie Hart, and drummer Louis Larose, and set to become a fixture on the British pub-rock circuit through the first half of the decade, the band's roughshod hybrid of vintage rock'n'roll and English vaudeville saw them swiftly elevated to critical favor, although record company interest rarely translated into anything tangible.

Early line-up changes saw artist Humphrey Ocean take over the bass slot for a time; he quit to return to his art (he would issue a solo single on Stiff, Dury's own "Whoops a Daisy," in 1978) and was replaced by Charlie Sinclair. Larose, too, departed, to be succeeded by George Butler and in this form Kilburn and the High Roads signed to Raft and cut a debut album, which was promptly shelved. (These tapes would subsequently appear as *Wotabunch*, following Dury's breakthrough in 1977–78.)

With new drummer David Rohoman and keyboard player Rod Melvin, Kilburn and the High Roads were then picked up by Dawn and released two cruelly under-promoted singles, "Rough Kids" and "Crippled with Nerves," before the June 1975, release of a similarly mistreated album, *Handsome*. The band broke up soon after and over the next year, Dury and a floating line-up continued gigging as the (abbreviated) Kilburns.

In mid-1976, Dury took the decision to go solo and signed with Stiff, releasing the now classic "Sex and Drugs and Rock and Roll" 45 the following summer. Recorded with Dury's new musical partner, former Byzantium keyboard player Chas Jankel, the single saw a new group coalesce around Dury: John Turnbull (guitar), Mickey Gallagher (keyboards), Norman Watt-Roy (bass), Charley Charles (drums) — all of whom had played together as Loving Awareness — and ex-Kilburn Payne.

An album was recorded, but scrapped, despite featuring most of what would become the *New Boots and Panties* album. This first effort was simply too slick, too clean, too funky for the punks of the age. Fresh sessions loosened everything up and *New Boots and Panties* (#168 US, #5 UK) emerged one of the crucial albums of the age.

Musically and visually, Dury and his newly named Blockheads were little more than a revised Kilburn and the High Roads, but still the act was swiftly embraced by the punk scene. Eccentric, scatological, and darkly humorous, the team was a runaway success on that fall's Live Stiffs tour, where they shared the billing with Nick Lowe, Elvis Costello, Larry Wallis, and Wreckless Eric (whose ultimately unreleased *Picadilly Menial* EP was produced by Dury). Both Eric and Costello, too, would include Kilburns material in their own repertoire, Eric recording "Rough Kids" for his debut album and Costello featuring "The Roadette Song" in his 1978 live show. British music hall veteran Max Wall also resurfaced with a Dury composition, "England's Glory."

"What a Waste" (#11 UK) in early 1978 formally introduced the Blockheads to the record-buying public, simultaneously launching Dury and the band into an era of almost unimagined success. In November, the deliciously punning "Hit Me with Your Rhythm Stick" (#1 UK) became the most unexpected monster smash of the year, *New Boots* was still selling strongly, and tours were colossal successes. Unfortunately, the Blockheads' hopes of moving away from what they saw as the formulaic mock Cockneyisms of *New Boots* were scuppered when the faux-funky *Do It Yourself* (#126 US, #2 UK) album proved a critical dud in spring 1979.

Since described as the first ever British rap record, "Reasons to Be Cheerful (Part 3)" (#3 UK) did much to alleviate the disappointment, but the band knew they'd let their fans down and it would be another year before a new Blockheads record appeared. "I Want to Be Straight" (#22 UK) faltered in

August 1980 and that same summer, Jankel quit for a solo career. He was replaced by former Dr. Feelgood guitarist Wilco Johnson and the Blockheads released their third album, *Laughter* (#159 US, #48 UK), together with a new single, "Sueperman's Big Sister" (#51 UK), backed by the symphonic and superlative "Fuckin' Ada." Again, however, the returns were dismal compared with what the band had once held in their hand. Finally, the band broke up, and Dury struck out alone.

A reunion with Jankel saw the *Lord Upminster* (#53 UK) album and a single originally written to protest the UN Year of the Disabled, "Spasticus Autisticus." The gesture was not appreciated; the single would be withdrawn within weeks. Cut in Jamaica with Sly and Robbie and keyboard player Tyrone Downie, the album, meanwhile, would be Dury's last for two years, before he resurfaced in 1983/84 with a new Jankel/Payne led outfit, the Music Students, and the album 4,000 *Weeks Holiday* (#54 UK).

Its failure, however, ensured that over the remainder of the decade, Dury concentrated on acting work, appearing in theater and television and also taking roles in Roman Polanski's *Pirates* and Peter Greenaway's *The Cook, the Thief, His Wife and Her Lover*. The success in early 1985 of a Paul Hardcastle remix of "Rhythm Stick" (#55 UK) did provoke some reaction, however, and Dury cut a new single, "Profoundly in Love with Pandora" (#45 UK), for the *Secret Diary of Adrian Mole* TV series and played a handful of shows with a reconstituted Blockheads. He also appeared in Bob Dylan's *Hearts of Fire* movie, scored the TV play "*Night Moves*, and in 1989 he delivered a new album, *Apples*, the soundtrack to a stage musical written with Blockhead Gallagher.

The death of Blockhead Charley Charles on September 5, 1990 from complications related to cancer prompted a full Blockheads reunion later that same month as a benefit for the drummer's family. A souvenir live album, *Warts 'n' Audience*, almost wholly comprised of vintage *New Boots*-era material, was released in April 1991, alongside another reissue of "Rhythm Stick" (#73 UK) and in November 1992, Dury released his first all-new "real" album in almost a decade, *The Bus Driver's Prayer and Other Stories*, and the band resumed more regular live work soon after.

In 1995, Dury was diagnosed with colon cancer and despite treatment, by May 1998, the disease had spread to his liver. Despite worsening health, however, he continued working both live and in the studio, with a new album, *Mr. Love Pants*, appearing later that same year. He also appeared in Clay Harper's *The Slippery Ballerina* project, alongside Wreckless Eric and former Velvet Underground drummer Maureen Tucker.

In 1999, Dury was honored for his achievements by the British Academy of Songwriters and Composers. He died

March 27, 2000 and was remembered with a gala tribute concert in London in June.

Ian Dury LPs

10 New Boots and Panties (Stiff) 1977 Despite adding nothing but a large, appreciative audience to Dury's talents; despite, too, omitting the already near-legendary joys of the "Sex and Drugs and Rock and Roll" comeback single, *New Boots* burst into punk with a swagger, a cackle, and such a boisterous sense of fun that even its caricatures soon came to life and there really were blockheads pissing in the swimming pool.

Dury's archetypes remained locked in the past, but they all seemed timeless anyway — the legend magic of "Sweet Gene Vincent" creating a new mythology around its own dreams, "Plaistow Patricia" with more rude words in its first nine syllables than the Sex Pistols squeezed into their entire career, "Clevor Trevor" and "Billericay Dickie" whose lives and times became legends overnight, and, of course, "Wake Up, Make Love to Me," the most libidinous song of its generation.

New Boots pandered, naturally, to the lowest common denominator — naturally, because the kind of people Dury sang about were the kind of people he was singing for, but also because in an industry which champions the working classes (ask John Lennon), Dury really did speak of what he knew: dads who worked on the local buses, scheming fathers and protective mothers, low-rent whores with distended orifices... and with an accent so broad you could set up a street market on it. And what would you sell when you'd done that? New boots and panties, of course.

7 Do It Yourself (Stiff) 1979 Deserting pub-rock, Dury and his Blockheads embark on a funk-fueled journey into further eccentricity — one which, ironically, closely echoed the scrapped first version of *New Boots and Panties*. Side one was the weird stuff — the jazzy piano and blaring horns moving far from the knees up Saturday night down the pub of yore — while the more traditional side two turned to the music hall for a trio of raucous yelling (shades of the Madness yet to come), before finishing off with a rocksteady lullaby. However, all the rude language and Cockney charm couldn't save this patchy album — an object lesson in why funk has no place on the Old Kent Road.

5 Laughter (Stiff) 1980 The majestic "Fuckin' Ada," "Hey Jude" meets a suicide note, rounded out *Laughter* with a pathos which would have distinguished even *New Boots*. Unfortunately, the rest of the album sagged horribly, Dury was clearly uncertain what he wanted to do, and with the band disintegrating so fast, there was no one around to tell him.

6 Lord Upminster (Polydor) 1981 Stopping the rot by at least reuniting with Jankel and poking a bit of personal fun with "Spasticus Autisticus," *Upminster* remained wrapped around the tears of a former clown.

5 4000 Weeks Holiday (Polydor) 1984

5 Apples (WEA) 1989

6 **Warts 'N' Audience [LIVE] (Demon) 1991** A night of passion with 2,000 strangers, reliving the old hits in buoyant style. Not the Blockheads of old, of course, but a reasonably close facsimile.

7 **Bus Driver's Prayer and Other Stories (Edsel) 1992** Reiterating one of the better tracks from *Apples* (the title cut), then building the rest of the album around its success, a return to the old-style narrative turns out not to be so old-style after all.

8 **Mr. Love Pants (Ronnie Harris Records) 1998** With Dury now under the shadow of inoperable cancer, *Mr. Love Pants* received more media attention than anything he'd done in 18 years. Thankfully, it deserved it — it was a triumph of warped logic, twisted humor, and a host of howling homespun epithets.

Selected Compilations and Archive Releases

7 **Jukebox Dury (Stiff) 1981**

9 **Sex'n'Drugs'n'Rock'n'Roll (Edsel) 1986** Reasonably similar trawls through the Stiff/Polydor catalogs, including non-album singles and rarities, with *Sex* triumphing largely through the inclusion of "Fuckin' Ada."

Kilburn and the High Roads LPs

9 **Handsome (Dawn) 1975** "Roadette Song," "Crippled with Nerves," "Rough Kids" — the Brit-pop prototype which nobody talked about; a vaudevillian twirling his figurative moustache and sniggering while the fire-eaters juggle and the fat lady sings; pure pantomime shot through with an honesty and simplicity which defies pop categorization.

Selected Compilations and Archive Releases

8 **Wotabunch (WEA) 1977** More magic, spread across an album's worth of cancelled magic.

E

ECHO AND THE BUNNYMEN

FORMED 1978 (Liverpool, England)
ORIGINAL LINE-UP Ian McCulloch (b. 5/5/59, Liverpool —
vocals); Will Sergeant (b. 4/12/58, Liverpool — guitar); Les Pattison (b. 4/18/58, Ormskirk, England — bass)

Contrary to popular rumor, the fourth founding member of the band, a drum machine, was *not* named Echo. "We just used to say that to shut people up," Sergeant later confessed. Emerging out of a chain reaction of low-key, low-action local bands, Echo and the Bunnymen formed around the nucleus of former Crucial Three/A Shallow Madness vocalist Ian McCulloch, Les Pattison — who had never played an instrument in his life prior to joining the group — and Will Sergeant, whose immediate past included an experimental noise band, Industrial Domestic, and a self-released cassette album, *Weird as Fish*.

The new group debuted at Eric's in Liverpool in November 1978, alongside Julian Cope's the Teardrop Explodes, themselves formed from the McCulloch-less remnants of A Shallow Madness. The Bunnymen had one song, a 20-minute piece called "Monkeys" and according to McCulloch, the moment they got offstage, the word began percolating around town about "this group that were weird, like nothing else. And obviously a great frontman who was making it up on the spot."

In March 1979, the Bunnymen were among a handful of Liverpool bands showcased in a *Sounds* feature on "The New Merseybeat," and on April 7, the Bunnymen signed to local indy label Zoo. The company had already signed Teardrop Explodes, and under Zoo's tutelage, the two bands would rapidly become figureheads of the entire city scene.

May 1979, brought the Bunnymen's first single, "Pictures on My Wall" (#24 UK indy) and an immediate barrage of applause. Single of the Week throughout the UK music press (the band hadn't even played eight gigs yet), the record alerted Sire Records to the Bunnymen's potential and in June, label head Seymour Stein came to London to check them out as they opened a Liverpool vs. Manchester Battle of the Bands at the London YMCA. Joy Division and A Certain Ratio were also on the bill.

Sire, however, had recently signed the Undertones, and could not actually afford to work another up and coming British band. Instead, the group was transferred to Warner

Brothers, who invented a new imprint for the group, Korova (named for the milk bar in *A Clockwork Orange*).

It was at Warners' insistence that the drum machine was replaced by a live drummer, Peter De Freitas (born 8/2/61, Port of Spain, Trinidad), a friend of Dave Balfe's brother. In this form, the group recorded their second single, "Rescue" (#62 UK), for an April 1980 release and in July, their debut album, *Crocodiles* (#17 UK), was released to immediate success.

"The Puppet," a non-album single, followed, and with tours of the UK that October and the US in March both selling out, the Bunnymen raced back to the studio to record *Heaven Up Here* (#184 US, #10 UK). It was released in June 1981, shortly after the semi-live *Shine So Hard* EP (#37 UK), the soundtrack to a short concert documentary of the same name. "The album was a consolidation," McCulloch reflected. "We kind of went off and proved we were going into uncharted territory, where no band of the time could even contemplate going." *NME* readers agreed, electing *Heaven Up Here* as the best album of the year.

"A Promise" (#49 UK) appeared in July 1981, and in September, the band played the Daze of Future Past festival in Leeds. Touring constantly both at home and abroad, the Bunnymen finally won their first UK Top 20 hit with May 1982's "The Back of Love"(#19 UK), the highlight, too, of an amazingly spirited showing at that summer's WOMAD Festival, backed by the African Drums of Burundi. A version of "Zimbo (All My Colours)," recorded at the show, would appear on the B-side of the band's next single, "The Cutter" (#8 UK).

McCulloch still believes "The Cutter" was "a big turning point. We just grew naturally as a band, we built up a following, it evolved and became a real group with real chemistry that knew no bounds. We were scared of doing uncool things and making crap music, which is fine, but we weren't scared of experimenting, possibly because musically, although individually we were all really good, we weren't that musical. We weren't accomplished musicians particularly, we worked within our own limitations, and we made them seem kind of limitless."

These attributes shone through the band's third album, *Porcupine* (#137 US, #2 UK), in the new year and the band's most extensive tour ever, from tiny village halls in the Scottish isles, to a stupendous climax at London's Royal Albert Hall on July 18, 1983 — a show recorded in part for the 1984 *Echo and the Bunnymen* EP (#188 US). If there were any doubts about the Bunnymen's rise to stardom, this put them to rest.

"Never Stop" (#15 UK) consolidated the group's achievements, as did a slew of indulgent reviews of Sergeant's *Themes for Grind* (#6 UK indy) solo album, the soundtrack to a movie which never quite got off the ground. But the greatest measure of the group's progress, they themselves knew, would be their fourth album, *Ocean Rain* (#87 US, #4 UK).

Recording in Paris, McCulloch explained "we knew from the start... it was going to be the most special thing we'd ever done up to that point. And I think that set us apart, because instead of going into the studio and trying to rewrite 'The Cutter' or whatever, we did 'The Killing Moon' (#9 UK) and the rest. I think a lot of people just went, 'What the hell is going on, this isn't the natural course.' And some people got it, and some people didn't; the ones that didn't were fools."

The band's most grandiose album was followed, naturally, by their most grandiose gesture — a day-long festival which took over the city of Liverpool for what the Bunnymen called A Crystal Day. The year then wrapped up with more touring, a new single ("Seven Seas," #16 UK), a video collection (*Pictures on the Wall*), and finally, a McCulloch solo single — a rendering of Kurt Weill's "September Song" (#51 UK). And while the Bunnymen initially planned taking the entire next year off to recover from such an exhausting period, by April they were back on the road, and in October 1985, a new single, "Bring on the Dancing Horses" (#21 UK), previewed the compilation *Songs to Learn and Sing* (#158 US, #6 UK).

"Dancing Horses" was also included in the hit movie soundtrack *Pretty in Pink*, but the band's upcoming US tour was thrown into total disarray when De Freitas suffered a nervous breakdown, which in turn gave rise to rumors that he'd quit the band. He even formed a new group, the Sex Gods, with Psychedelic Furs saxophonist Mars Williams and former Deaf School drummer Tim Wittaker.

In his absence, the Bunnymen recruited former Haircut 100/Aztec Camera drummer Blair Cunningham to cover their live schedule. Attempts to record a new album in this form, however, came to naught, and it would be September 1986, before De Freitas returned to the fold.

A new single, "The Game" (#28 UK), welcomed the band back to action, but the eponymous album (#51 US, #4 UK) that followed was a lifeless affair, even if did become their biggest hit yet. The near year of touring which succeeded it only exhausted the band further, and while two further singles, "Lips Like Sugar"(#36 UK) and a college hit cover of the Doors' "People Are Strange" (#29 UK), kept the pot boiling a little longer, the end of the band was clearly

imminent. Still, nobody could have predicted the sheer tragedy which would lead to their final demise.

In October 1987, the Bunnymen were forced to cancel their latest US tour after a fan threw McCulloch 12 feet into the orchestra pit in Santa Barbara; six months later, with McCulloch's father already dangerously ill, the band set out for a Japanese tour set to end in Osaka on April 26, 1988. The night of this final show, McCulloch Senior suffered another heart attack. The distraught singer got through the show, then sped to the airport to await the first flight out the following morning. He arrived in Liverpool just minutes after his father's death. He announced his decision to quit the band soon after.

McCulloch's solo debut, *Candleland* (#179 US, #18 UK), would appear the following summer; the remaining Bunnymen promptly began auditioning replacements, but fate was not finished with them yet. On June 14, 1989, De Freitas was killed when his motorcycle collided with a car in Rugley, Staffordshire, and another year would elapse before a new-look Bunnymen, featuring Sergeant and Pattison, former St. Vitus Dance vocalist Noel Burke, drummer Damon Reece, and keyboardist Jake Brockman, emerged with a single, "Enlighten Me." It failed to chart — a fate which was exacerbated by a March 1991, reissue of "People Are Strange"(#34 UK), drawn from the soundtrack to the movie *The Lost Boys*.

McCulloch's second album, *Mysterio* (#46 UK), and his erstwhile bandmates' first, *Reverberation*, sold poorly in early 1992 and with the Bunnymen splitting up shortly after, all three founding members were left to ponder the ironies of fate alone. Sergeant recovered first, returning to his old love of ambient sounds and releasing a trilogy of singles as Glide. McCulloch then announced a new band with former Smiths guitarist Johnny Marr which shattered when the pair fell out, and the master tape containing the three songs they had recorded ("Never Never Never," "Touchdown," and "Lowdown") mysteriously vanished.

McCulloch and Sergeant regrouped as Electrafixion in 1994. With bassist Leon De Silva and the returning Damon Reece, the band would cut one electrifying album before discovering midway through a 1996 US club tour that they'd been dropped by their label. Still keen to work together, McCulloch and Sergeant began discussing a Bunnymen reunion, and when Pattison (who had been working with ex-Specials Terry Hall) proved agreeable, the band signed to London in late 1996.

With new drummer Michael Lee (borrowed from Robert Plant and Jimmy Page's band) the Bunnymen made their live return in Liverpool on May 14, 1997. Three months later, their comeback album *Evergreen* (#8 UK) and single "Nothing Lasts Forever" (#8 UK) were stunning successes. The Bunnymen were back and though, by 1999, Pattison had quit, a virtual return to the Electrafixion format saw no decline in quality.

McCulloch co-wrote the official anthem of England's 1998 soccer World Cup campaign, "(How Does It Feel to Be) On Top of the World" (#9 UK), then regrouped with Sergeant alone to record 1999's single "Rust" and *What Are You Going to Do with Your Life?*, a profoundly mature, sober statement, but one which nevertheless retained the old Bunny magic. A US tour that fall did well, but modest sales sealed the band's fate. By the end of the year, the group's UK label, London, had dropped the Bunnymen from the roster.

Echo and the Bunnymen LPs

9 Crocodiles (Sire) 1980 One of the most dazzling debuts of the '80s, *Crocodiles* is powered by brooding insistence and an insatiable rhythm section, exquisitely moody melodies and McCulloch's almost childlike genius for saying precisely the right thing every time. Lush, atmospheric keyboards buffeted by the sheer weight of Sergeant's darting guitar are the backdrop to the dreams and fears, anger, and angst that fill the album, and though there is a fashionable sense of darkness pervading some of the textures, still McCulloch's ability to conjure up ghosts of rock's past — the Doors, Leonard Cohen, and the Beatles — makes a discomforting statement in itself.

7 Heaven Up Here (Sire) 1981 Less pop-driven than *Crocodiles*, the Bunnymen stray off the more traveled post-punk path into more experimental lands — the preserve of the Velvets and Siouxsie and the Banshees. *Heaven's* dense sound, underpinned by the fuzz guitar, was hypnotic, with only "A Promise" really linking the band to the accessible sounds of the past.

7 Porcupine (Sire) 1983 In a bold move, the Bunnymen pursue their musical explorations of styles and atmospheres in a more pop orientated format with much success, as *Porcupine* ignites darkness and light, psychedelia, and a personalized approximation of goth, subtly expanding into new styles on this ever intriguing album.

10 Ocean Rain (Sire) 1984 Few albums set out to become masterpieces and actually end up exceeding their brief. *Ocean Rain* managed it effortlessly. Beforehand, McCulloch couldn't stop talking about how brilliant this record would be — even he, however, could not have imagined just how inspired the ensuing mix of moody babble and exquisite melody would be.

Darkness ("The Killing Moon") and light ("Crystal Days") blend as effortlessly as the litany of styles at the Bunnymen's disposal. The thoughtful tribal beats, hints of Arabesque allure, and slivers of garage punk are gleefully combined and explored, while even some desperately portentous/silly lyrics ("c-c-c-cucumber") take on a life and meaning within the soundscapes. The album has the density of *Heaven Up Here*, the risk-taking of *Porcupine*, and the drive of *Crocodiles*. But it has so much more than that. Truly, a triumph.

7 Echo and the Bunnymen (Sire) 1987 Brighter and more upbeat than any of their previous albums, *Bunnymen* may not actually shine, but it is a solid set of strong driving tracks interspersed with infectious, glittering pop gems.

6 Reverberation (Sire) 1990 While not a bad record by any means, *Reverberation* is entirely inconsistent with past Bunnymen output. At best, the McCulloch-less band are simply treading water, and when they're not, they're merely resurrecting influences from Britain's rock past.

8 Evergreen (London) 1997 No classics, but no stinkers either; look elsewhere for "Bedbugs and Ballyhoo"; look elsewhere, too, for the stomach cramps of the band's final album. With songs with the strength of "I Want to Be There," "Altamont," and the yearning "Nothing Lasts Forever," *Evergreen* is at least as good as the bulk of the band's back pages. So it's not their best — but it is the Bunnymen.

7 What Are You Going to Do with Your Life (London) 1999 Melody and melancholy are the key words, with even the presence of the Fun Loving Criminals on a couple of cuts failing to imbibe the proceedings with more than a passing horniness. A distinctly post-modern MOR moods indelibly colors the album, offset by McCulloch's newly-found gruff'n'puff vocals and Sergeant's hypnotic guitars, but still encouraging the listener to go out and do something grown-up instead of listening to pop music. They apparently did.

Selected Compilations and Archive Releases

9 Songs to Learn and Sing (Sire) 1985 The best of the best, plus one new song (the surreal "Bring on the Dancing Horses").

6 BBC Radio 1 in Concert [LIVE] (Windsong) 1995 From 1987; sadly recorded some two or three years later than it ought to have been.

Ian McCulloch LPs

4 Candleland (Sire) 1989 Ian without the Bunnymen is like Hansel without Gretel — an easy target. But *Candleland* is genuinely light weight, foundering, and ultimately dull.

4 Mysterio (Sire) 1992 A few memorable moments ("Magical World," which sounds suspiciously like Teardrop Explodes) break through, but it's all so limp and lifeless again.

Will Sergeant LP

5 Themes for Grind (Happy Customer) 1982 Instrumental moodiness; themes for an imaginary Bunnymen rehearsal.

Electrafixion LP

8 Burned (WEA) 1995 Musically far removed from the Bunnymen's own unique sound, *Burned* has a startlingly symphonic quality, although what truly sets Electrafixion apart from the old job is Sergeant's raucous guitar, something never before heard in a Bunnymen context.

Further Reading

Never Stop by Tony Fletcher (Beekman 1990).

EINSTURZENDE NEUBAUTEN

FORMED 1980 *(Berlin, Germany)*
ORIGINAL LINE-UP *Blixa Bargeld (b. 1/12/59 — vocals, guitar); N.U. Unruh (b. Andrew Unruh, 6/9/57, New York, NY — percussion); Beate Bartel (percussion); Gudrun Gut (percussion); Alexander Van Borsig (engineer, percussion)*

If any band can be credited for welding together the entire would-be industrial scene of the early 1980s, it was Berlin conceptualists Einsturzende Neubauten (Collapsing New Buildings). Whilst not completely espousing conventional musical instrumentation, the group's calling card was a dense wall of pounding, screeching, and roaring, put together through the use of power tools, hammers, and sundry other gadgets. Concerts generally dissolved into enactments of blacksmith's forges or demolition squads, and while vinyl could scarcely capture the full howling power of Neubauten, their catalog shows a dexterity which is almost surprising in its complexity and diversity.

Although their first ever live show, in Berlin on April 1, 1980, was recorded and subsequently released as a cassette album, the group officially debuted with the "Fuer Den Untergang" single in 1980, together with tracks on a number of German compilations. Joined by F.M. Einheit (born Stuart Mufti, 12/18/58, Dortmund), following the departure of Bartel and Gut, Neubauten fell into the orbit of the Birthday Party, as they prepared to relocate in Berlin. The association carried over to Neubauten's next release, the *Schwarz* EP, itself showing Neubauten still to be coming to grips with their own unconventionality and offering up some genuinely strong melodies alongside the skull-crushing hammering. But vocalist Blixa Bargeld's collaboration with performance artist Suse, a 40-minute cassette called *Valium*, increased the band's own profile considerably and by the time the band's debut album, *Kollaps* (#21 UK indy), appeared in 1982, it was impossible to judge Neubauten on musical merits, a point which had much to do with their adoption by the UK press around 1983.

The arrival of bassist Marc Chung (born 6/3/57, Leeds, England) and electronics engineer Alexander Hacke (born 10/11/65) preceded Neubauten's UK debut as support on the latest Birthday Party tour. Critically acclaimed and signing to Some Bizzare, Neubauten became the band to watch throughout the country, yet only Depeche Mode truly latched on to their aural legacy, introducing to their arsenal many of the same sounds and devices as Neubauten was employing. Martin Gore began discussing the band at every opportunity, and when his band returned to the studio to record the epochal "People Are People," Neubauten's blueprint was all over the results.

Back in the collapsing new building, a brief union with Lydia Lunch and the Birthday Party's Rowland S Howard produced the magnificent *Thirsty Animal* EP. The following year, *Drawings of Patient OT*, the group's first UK album, was released, to be followed by the compilation *Strategies Against Architecture* (#3 UK indy). But fears that such exposure might be lessening Neubauten's attack were stilled by the inclusion on *Strategies* of three live cuts, violently highlighting the true nature of the Neubauten experience. The cassette-only *2x4* then brought an entire Neubauten concert into the living room.

With Bargeld now a full-time member of Nick Cave's Bad Seeds (both Van Borsig and Hacke would go on to Crime and the City Solution), Einsturzende Neubauten teetered on the brink of disintegration during 1984–85, and did in fact split following the release of their masterpiece, *Halber Mensch* (#2 UK indy), and the ultra-successful single, "Yu-Gung" (#5 UK indy), released with a stunning Adrian Sherwood remix.

Although the breach was mended the following year, another album *Fuenf Auf Der Nach Oben Offenen Richterskala* (#3 UK indy) emerged a considerable disappointment, having more in common with "I Want More"-era than anything in Neubauten's own repertoire. The final Neubauten album, in 1989, rectified the failings of *Fuenf* somewhat, but *Haus Der Luege* (#16 UK indy) was still a far cry from what Neubauten fans expected.

The group reformed in 1992, initially for live work, but sporadic new albums have followed, most notably *Ende Neu*, issued through Trent Reznor's Nothing label, and *Total Eclipse of the Sun*, an EP timed to coincide with the solar eclipse over Europe in August 1999 and introducing new collaborators Jochen Arbeit (guitar) and Rudolph Moser (drums) of Die Haut.

Einsturzende Neubauten LPs

2 **Liveaufnahme in Kunstkopfstereo [LIVE] (Eisengrau) 1980**
2 **Chaos, Sehnsucht/Energie [LIVE] (Eisengrau) 1980**
2 **Stahlmusik [LIVE] (Eisengrau) 1980** The all but unlistenable sound of unconstructed noise. Not yet writing "songs," not yet attempting even ghosts of melody, early Neubauten was a visual experience. Few people listened to the things they were breaking.

6 **Kollaps (Zick Zack) 1981** A lot of Neubauten's early work sounded like people just walking around dropping things. Which, presumably, is precisely what they were doing.

5 **Stahldubversions (Rip Off) 1982**

8 Durstiges Tier (Zick Zack) 1983

7 Portrait of Patient Ot (Some Bizzare) 1983 Less harrowing than its predecessors, a consequence perhaps of Neubauten trying to move away from the slavering dogs who now hung onto their every clatter as though it were a burning bush. Listened to almost 20 years later, it even seems melodic in places — that "Vanadium I-Ching"...what a toe-tapper.

5 2X4 (Roir) 1984 Brain-searingly mediocre quality live recording. They do remember their tunes, though.

8 Halber Mensch (Some Bizzare) 1985 Magnificently portentous, full-blooded battery, percussives as rhythms dictating the spectral melodies around which heavily harmonic vocals whisper and chant. Much of the sonic credit surely belongs to co-producer Gareth Jones, but still Neubauten display a grasp of gripping atmospherics which the past had barely hinted at.

8 Fuenf Auf Der Nach Oben Offenen Richterskala (Some Bizzare) 1987 Five on the Richter scale, a considerable downgrade on past Neubauten accomplishments, but as listenable as they get in a distinctly Nick Cave-y way. The opening "Zestoerte Zelle" is pure goth atmospherics and a rendering of Tim Rose's "Morning Dew" wouldn't have been out of place on Cave's *Kicking Against the Pricks*.

6 Haus Der Luege (Rough Trade) 1989 Close to a decade before, while the world played synth-pop, Neubauten hit anvils. Now, while the world embraces the industrial arena, Neubauten go all electro-burble, with only Bargeld's sinister Peter Lawrie vocals suggesting something else might be going on.

6 Der Hamlet Maschine (Rough Trade) 1991 Laibach and think of Shakespeare.

5 Tabula Rasa (Elektra) 1993

5 Ende Neu (Nothing) 1996 Locked firmly into the groove established by *Hans Der Luege* — nothing ventured, nothing gained.

6 Faustmusik (Mute — UK) 1996

8 Silence Is Sexy (Mute — UK) 2000 Understated and frequently underplayed, *Sexy* peaks with "Peli Kanol," 18 minutes of improvisation featuring jazz-tinged bass and a string section.

Selected Compilations and Archive Releases

8 Strategies Against Architecture I (Positive) 1984

7 Strategies Against Architecture II (Elektra) 1991 Volume one is the crucial introduction; volume two its lesser shadow. If there is no Neubauten in your life, these will fill the void.

6 Ende Neu Remixes (Mute) 1997 When Adrian Sherwood remixed "Yu-Gung," he unearthed the inherent pop ethic which was Neubauten's most discreet calling card. For further such excursions, come on in.

FM Einheit LPs

7 Stein (Our Choice) 1990

5 Steinzeit (Our Choice) 1992

7 Prometheus-Lear (Our Choice) 1993

FM Einheit/Andreas Ammer LPs

6 Radio Inferno (Our Choice) 1993

4 Apocalypse Live (Ego) 1995

FM Einheit/Casper Brotzmann LP

5 Merry Christmas (Our Choice) 1994

Blixa Bargeld LP

5 Commissioned Music (Ego) 1995

Further Reading

Headcleaner: Text for Collapsing New Buildings by Blixa Bargeld/Maria Zinfert (Die Gestalten Verlag, Germany, 1997).

ELASTICA

FORMED *[as Vaseline] 1992 (London, England)*
ORIGINAL LINE-UP *Justine Frischmann (b. 9/16/69, Twickenham, England — vocals, guitar); Donna Matthews (b. 12/2/71, Newport, Wales — guitar); Annie Holland (b. 8/26/65, Brighton, England — bass); Justin Welch (b. 12/4/72, Nuneaton, England — drums)*

Following a spell as second guitarist with London Suede, quitting shortly after the band recorded their "Be My God" debut single, Justine Frischmann linked with Justin Welch (who also played with Suede, guesting on the single) and Donna Matthews as Vaseline in 1992. Frischmann's then-boyfriend, Blur vocalist Damon Albarn, stood in on bass for a time; he was replaced by Annie Holland and late in the year Vaseline recorded a three-song demo for EMI Publishing.

The group's sound crystallized immediately — a harsh, minimalist jerk which owed much to Wire, but also possessed remarkable individuality. A second set of demos were recorded in March before the group changed their name to Onk and played their live debut in May 1993. They became Elastica immediately after, and by July, regular gigs had given them their first headline show at London's Powerhaus.

A John Peel session followed in August and three days later, Elastica signed to Deceptive Records. Elastica's debut single, "Stutter," arrived in the stores in November while the band toured the UK with Pulp. "Stutter" would also become Elastica's US debut, a limited edition released through Sub Pop's singles club and in early 1994, the band signed with Geffen for the US.

That year opened with a series of other achievements: Elastica's first television appearance, their first magazine cover (*Select*), victory as Best New Band in both *Melody*

Maker's readers' poll and at *NME*'s BRAT awards. "It was your typical British media avalanche," Frischmann modestly remarked, and it swept the group's second single, "Line Up" (#20 UK), along with it.

In March, Elastica embarked on their first headlining UK tour but the speed with which their career was moving was unbelievable — and disconcerting. "We were worried about it," Frischmann admitted, "so we decided we weren't gonna play the game and kinda went underground for the rest of 1994. People were just asking us about the hype, not the music, and it became a vicious circle."

It would be October 1994 before Elastica reappeared with their third single, "Connection" (#53 US, #17 UK). It would also prove to be their most controversial release yet, borrowing as it did the signature riff from Wire's "Three Girl Rumba." Wire's publishers swiftly moved in for a slice of the royalties. Nevertheless, the song would become Elastica's US breakthrough, its distinctive video dominating MTV through spring 1995.

Elastica's debut eponymous album (#66 US, #1 UK) hit the stores in March 1995, eclipsing Oasis' *Definitely Maybe* as the fastest-selling debut album in UK history. It was followed by "Waking Up" (#13 UK) and another legal headache, as the Stranglers' publishers spotted elements of "No More Heroes" in the song.

The group would spend the bulk of 1995 touring America in support of the album and the "Stutter" (#67 US) single, including a lengthy stint on Lollapalooza, where they replaced the pregnant Sinead O'Connor. They returned home to headline Glastonbury 95, a show which swiftly entered rock'n'roll legend for being disrupted midway through by a streaker — former Pulp keyboard player Anthony Genn, who would himself be joining Elastica early the following year.

However, the departure of Holland — citing exhaustion — seriously disturbed the group's equilibrium. She was replaced first by Abbey Travis (borrowed from Beck's band) and then Sheila Chipperfield, but with the band finally off the road, work on their proposed second album became secondary to holding the band together. Elastica played the V96 Festivals in August and then disappeared.

Over the next year, Frischmann would remain the most visible member of the band. She recorded a version of Frank and Nancy Sinatra's "Something Stupid" with Pavement's Steve Malkmus for the *Suburbia* movie soundtrack and in November, joined with Wire's Bruce Gilbert and Band of Susans' Susan Stenger for a one-off performance at the American Independents Festival in London, under the name the Brood.

Elastica, however, remained shrouded in disarray. Holland returned, but Matthews and Genn quit. Matthews later surfaced alongside Teenage Fanclub on the *Velvet Goldmine* movie soundtrack while Genn would produce Joe Strummer's *Rock Art and the X-Ray Style* album. The pair were replaced by Paul Jones (guitar) and two keyboard players, Dave Bush and Mew, and Elastica finally re-emerged in summer 1999 with a string of low-key/secret UK gigs leading up to their comeback at the Reading festival. The first of these shows, opening for the Fall, featured surprise covers of Trio's "Da Da Da" ("effectively reclaimed as the 'Louie Louie' of its day," insisted the *Manchester Guardian*) and Wire's "12XU."

With Frischmann now working with former Kingmaker frontman Loz Hardy, the sensibly titled *Six Track* EP followed in August 1999. Peculiarly, it was purposefully designed to be ineligible for the either the single or album charts (too many tracks for one, not long enough for the other). Work then resumed on the band's second album, Frischmann and producer Flood scrapping a set which had already been completed, and beginning again from scratch.

The band's departure from US label Geffen in late 1999 seemed to add further impetus to the band's strivings, while the album's commercial success was set by British radio's enthusiastic response to the two songs pre-released in the weeks ahead of the album's appearance — both "Mad Dog" and "Love Like Ours" became massive radio hits.

Elastica LPs

9 Elastica (Geffen) 1995 The Wire and Stranglers controversies devoured a lot of this album's initial magnificence, burying Elastica's light beneath the bushel of plagiarism. But dispassionately, what does it matter if this riff came from one place and that one from another — bands have been borrowing since time began, and they've been paying the consequences too. Regardless of who struck the first chord, *Elastica* is a triumph — staccato rock machine gun fired with relentless outrage, every song as short as it likes and even the classics, "Connection," of course, "Line Up," and "Stutter," are over before you even suspect their brilliance. And that, of course, was their brilliance. And then there's "2:1" which, if Elastica never recorded another note, would ensure they live forever.

8 The Menace (Deceptive — UK) 2000 Still cast firmly in the shadow of Wire, the Velvet Underground, and the Fall (whose "How I Wrote 'The Elastic Man'" was reprised from the EP), *The Menace* is also shot through the Frischmann's newly consummated love for early Eno. Much, of course, has changed in the five years since their debut, but Elastica at least proved — albeit belatedly — that they are not a one-trick pony.

EMF

FORMED 1989 (Cinderford, England)
ORIGINAL LINE-UP *James Atkin (b. 3/28/69, Cinderford — vocals); Ian Dench (b. 8/7/64, Cheltenham — guitar); Zak Foley (b. 12/9/70, Gloucester — bass); Derry Brownson (b. 11/10/70, Cheltenham — keyboards); Mark Decloedt (b. 6/26/69, Gloucester — drums)*

Ian Dench, whose band Apple Mosaic were signed to Virgin subsidiary MDM, met Derry Brownson when the latter auditioned for the band's vacant keyboard player slot. He failed the audition and promptly formed his own band, Light Aircraft Company. That outfit broke up in mid-1989 around the same time as Apple Mosaic — the cue for Dench and Brownson to pool their resources in a new band. Joined by Zak Foley, and plunging immediately into an exploration of the explosive rave scene, the new group — christened EMF, an acronym of Ecstacy Mother Fuckers — debuted at the Bilson pub in Cinderford on December 29, 1989.

With an ingeniously cute image of baseball caps and flappingly short trousers, a year of live work saw EMF establish a firm reputation within the psychedelic-tinged baggy circuit, through tours with Boo Yaa Tribe and Adamski. The band signed to EMI during the summer of 1990 and were launched via the televised *Smash Hits Party*, performing what would become their debut single, "Unbelievable" (#1 US, #3 UK).

Featuring a sample of US comedian Andrew Dice Clay, "Unbelievable" became an enviable, but pitfall-laced beginning for the band. While their own UK tour in the new year was a success, EMF were greeted with a hail of cans and insults when they guested with Carter the Unstoppable Sex Machine at a show in London in February, an early indication that their launch and subsequent success ("I Believe," #6 UK, followed "Unbelievable") left many onlookers convinced EMF were a callously manufactured cash-in band. This antagonism only rose after the band was voted best UK Newcomers at the DMC World DJ awards in April.

Heralded by a third successive Top 20 hit, "Children" (#19 UK), EMF's debut album, *Schubert Dip* (#12 US, #3 UK), arrived in May 1991 towards the end of another sold-out tour. It was a surefire hit, but was dogged by controversy as EMI was censured by the British government for failing to add Parental Advisory stickers to the album's artwork. A sample of John Lennon's murderer, Mark Chapman, would also cause problems and the band eventually recut the offending track, "Lies" (#18 US, #28 UK), after Lennon's widow, Yoko Ono, became indignantly involved in the fracas.

EMF made their North American debut in July 1991, performing at the New Music Seminar in New York, just as "Unbelievable" hit #1 in the US. *Schubert Dip* was certified platinum two months later, establishing EMF as the biggest British import since the heyday of Duran Duran — and setting a precedent which would mar Anglo-American musical relations for the next two years as a string of British bands (Jesus Jones, Ned's Atomic Dustbin, even Radiohead and Catherine Wheel) washed up on American shores with one signature hit, then promptly disappeared again. Radiohead, of course, soon recovered, but still their subsequent career would be informed by the days when they "did an EMF."

Work on EMF's next album, scheduled for fall 1992, was previewed in the spring with the *Unexplained* (#18 UK) EP, featuring an unexpected cover of the Stooges' "Search and Destroy." The *They're Here* (#29 UK) EP, in September, would similarly feature a revision of Traffic's "Low Spark of the High Heeled Boys," while Cream's "Strange Brew" was now a regular in the group's traditionally adventurous live set.

Such efforts did not dispel the suspicion with which EMF were still regarded, however; neither did *Stigma* (#19 UK) a second album patently colored by the band's attempts to retain their American success by tailoring the record towards that same audience. America, however, had already moved on, towards Nirvana and grunge, and *Stigma* was received coolly.

Remixes commissioned from Nirvana producer Butch Vig, Orbital, and Foetus did not salvage the band's reputation; "It's You That Bleeds Me Dry" (#23 UK) disappointed in late 1992 and following a short US tour in December, EMF faded from view.

The group relaunched in early 1995 with a new single, "Perfect Day" (#27 UK); remixers this time included Johnny Dollar and former Can mainman Holger Czukay. However, *Cha Cha Cha* (#30 UK) managed a mere week on the chart and while EMF would return to the top in July when they paired up with comedians Reeves and Mortimer for a cover of Neil Diamond's "I'm a Believer" (#3 UK), the group would release just one more single, "Afro King" (#51 UK), before fading again in late 1995.

EMF would resurface one last time to contribute a version of "We Are Glass" to the *Random* Gary Numan tribute album in 1997. By that time, however, all five members had new projects underway: Dench with Whistler, Foley with Carrie, and Brownson with LK (alongside brother Lee) and, following that band's early 1999 demise, Park. Atkins, meanwhile, became an occasional member of Bentley Rhythm Ace before forming his own Cooler dance project with Andrew Weatherall/Bocca Juniors vocalist Anna Haig. The duo's debut single, "Supersod," earned *NME*'s single of the week award in March 1999.

EMF LPs

⑧ Schubert Dip (EMI) 1991 The missing link between baggy/pop and house/rave, EMF's intriguing use of vocal samples and scratching, Joe Jackson-esque piano, and a decade's worth of influences were what grabbed the attention. The hip-hop and club beats did the rest. Oh, and "Unbelievable."

⑧ Stigma (EMI) 1992 EMF rave on, even as the guitars step into the spotlight and rock to the rafters. Their love affair with post-punk may be torrid, but still unsated, they embark on one night stands with glam, C&W, hard rock, and Eastern mystic melodies. Pulling pop's past into the present, decking it out in baggy beats, then pushing it center stage is EMF's goal, and they perform it flawlessly.

⑤ Cha Cha Cha (EMI) 1995

EUGENIUS

FORMED *1990 (Glasgow, Scotland)*
ORIGINAL LINE-UP *Eugene Kelly (vocals); Gordon Keen (guitar); James Sheenan (bass); Brendan O'Hare (drums)*

With co-vocalist Frances McKee, Kelly was leader of the Vaselines, a Bellshill-based band who released one album and a handful of singles for the local 53rd and 3rd label during 1986–87.

The band broke up in late 1987 and Kelly briefly joined go-getter garage pop band the Pastels, before forming Eugenius in 1990, just as the Vaselines' moribund star finally burst into view.

Though they never meant much during their own life-style, the Vaselines were undergoing a period of deification, thanks to the championing of Kurt Cobain. Nirvana recorded three Vaselines songs: "Son of a Gun" (originally a 1987 Vaselines single, #26 UK indy), "Molly's Lips" (later included on Nirvana's *Incesticide* rarities collection), and "Jesus Doesn't Want Me for a Sunbeam" (featured on the band's *MTV Unplugged* performance).

A compilation of the Vaseline's entire output would be released through Sub Pop in 1992. Included, of course, was the band's second hit, 1988's "Dying for It" (#11 UK indy); in the meantime, Kelly had formed the original ad hoc Eugenius line-up after he was invited to support the Lemonheads in Glasgow. Gordon Keen was a member of the BMX Bandits at the time, Brendan O'Hare played with Teenage Fanclub, and James Sheenan had recorded the "Molly's Lips" session with the Vaselines. A set was hastily written and rehearsed, and the band played the show as Captain America.

Word of at least a partial Vaselines reunion reached Cobain, and he invited Captain America to open for Nirvana during their 1991 European tour. With drummer Andy Bollen replacing O'Hare, two singles, "Wow" and "Flame On," preceded a deal with Creation before news of the band reached Marvel Comics, whose *Captain America* copyright was deemed threatened. They took legal action and Kelly renamed the group Eugenius.

With Roy Lawrence and Ray Boyle replacing Sheenan and Bollen, Eugenius cut their first album, *Oomalooma*, in three weeks. It was originally intended to be a mini-album but as more material presented itself, the band kept on recording. They toured the US in 1992 with audiences bolstered by the Cobain connection, then disappeared for a time to allow that particular hype to die down.

Eugenius returned with the singles "Caesar's Vein" (about the US tour) and "Easter Bunny" in 1993. However, the band's departure from Creation saw the album *Mary Queen of Scots* left to find its own cult niche and fail dismally. The band broke up soon after.

Kelly himself has laid very low since that time but did reappear in 1996 as keyboard player on Celtic traditionalists De Dannan's *Hibernian Rhapsody*. The following year, the Astro Chimp union with Teenage Fanclub's Raymond McGinley and Gerard Love spawned a single, "Draggin'."

Eugenius LPs

⑥ Oomalooma (Creation) 1992 Eleven tracks of solid easy-to-listen-to tunes. In a Teenage Fanclub mode, *Oomalooma* features a great, scratchy guitar sound, but lacks drive. With the exception of the title track, the songs are virtually indistinguishable, all blending and blurring into pleasant aural wallpaper. There are ones that jangle a bit, a few with a bit of heightened atmosphere, and several that are slightly rockier. So, a soft popster's dream, without a sharp edge or even a blunt one in sight.

⑧ Mary Queen of Scots (August) 1994 Stronger, more focussed, certainly brighter and cleaner – but delivered a year too late.

The Vaselines LP

⑧ Dum Dum (53rd & 3rd) 1987 Low-fi with a vengeance, but lovely harmonies and lilting melodies ensure a timelessness which rises above even the scrappiest sonic surroundings.

Selected Compilations and Archive Releases

⑧ All the Stuff and More (Sub Pop) 1992 Comprehensive rundown of the Vaselines' story, in all its scratchy glory.

F

FAITH NO MORE

FORMED 1980 (San Francisco, CA)
ORIGINAL LINE-UP *Jim Martin* (b. 7/21/61 — guitar); *Billy Gould* (b. 4/24/63, L.A. — bass); *Roddy Bottum* (b. 7/1/63, L.A. — keyboards); *Mike Bordin* (b. 11/27/62, San Francisco — drums)

L.A. punk graduates Gould and Bottum and Berkeley University student Bordin were already rehearsing together when Cliff Barton of Metallica recommended they audition Vicious Hatred guitarist Martin in 1980; the quartet would take their name from the winner of a greyhound race and over the next three years, a succession of vocalists would pass through their ranks (including the then-unknown Courtney Love), before Chuck Moseley emerged from the audience at one of the band's shows in mid-1983.

The group signed with local indy label, Mordam, and issued their eponymous debut album in 1985 — a unique, funk metal fusion which became a local radio hit and introduced the band to the Slash label. The following year, Faith No More's second album, *Introduce Yourself*, was released.

Constantly touring, often with the Red Hot Chili Peppers, Faith No More continued to build, scoring an MTV hit with the single "We Care a Lot," even as relations with Moseley declined. The singer was finally sacked following a European tour in spring 1988; Faith No More replacing him in November with Mr. Bungle vocalist Mike Patton (b. 1/27/68, Eureka). Patton would continue working with the masked and mysterious Mr. Bungle over the next decade, with the project ultimately outliving Faith No More.

A reactivated "We Care a Lot" (#53 UK) gave the band their UK chart debut that same month and Faith No More broke through in their homeland the following year with the release of their third album, *The Real Thing* (#11 US, #30 UK), although it would take close to a year to peak.

The singles "Epic" (#9 US, #25 UK) and "Falling to Pieces" (#92 US, #41 UK) were issued while the band toured the US with Metallica through late 1989 and Soundgarden the following year. They would subsequently be nominated for a Grammy in the Best Heavy Metal/Hard Rock category and through the summer of 1990, Faith No More were a featured attraction at the Reading festival in England and the Monsters of Rock show in Bologna, Italy. A 37-city tour with Billy Idol cemented their rise, and in January 1991, Faith No More played the massive Rock in Rio II festival in Brazil.

Work on the band's next album continued through 1991 and early 1992; *Angel Dust* (#10 US, #2 UK) was finally released in June 1992, while the band toured with Guns 'n' Roses and Metallica. Their European success, too, was now immense — 1991 saw them hit with a UK-only in-concert album, *Live at the Brixton Academy* (#20 UK) and Mr. Bungle's *Mr. Bungle* (#57 UK) debut while 1992 brought the successful singles "Midlife Crisis" (#10 UK), "A Small Victory" (#29 UK), and "Everything's Ruined" (#28 UK).

Touring continued to occupy the band through 1993. Patton also stopped off to drop some guest guitar and mandolin onto St. Etienne's *Tiger Bay* album. A cover of the Commodore's "Easy" (#58 US, #3 UK) kept the European pot boiling, even if its US performance was not so hot, while there was also a hit collaboration with Boo Yaa Tribe, "Another Body Murdered" (#26 UK). Yet another collaboration, with members of Tool and Rage Against the Machine, under the name of Shandi's Addiction, was included on the hit KISS tribute album *Kiss My Ass*.

However, sessions for Faith No More's next album were marred by the sacking of Martin and the temporary incapacitation of Gould, suffering from pneumonia. Trey Spruance of Mr. Bungle would replace Martin for *King for a Day, Fool for a Lifetime* (#31 US, #5 UK), and the hit singles "Digging the Grave" (#16 UK), "Ricochet" (#27 UK), and "Evidence" (#32 UK). On the road, Dean Mentia would take over, as Spruance returned to complete Bungle's gestating *Disco Volante* (#113 US).

Mentia in turn would be replaced by Jon Hudson for what became Faith No More's final album, *Album of the Year* (#41 US, #7 UK). Poorly received, the album nevertheless spawned two hit singles, "Ashes to Ashes" (#15 UK) and "Last Cup of Sorrow" (#51 UK), while an utterly unexpected union with Sparks saw Faith No More take part in a joyous remake of that band's 1974 hit "This Town Ain't Big Enough for Both of Us" (#40 UK), for inclusion on Sparks' *Plagiarism* album.

Faith No More toured the US and Europe through 1998, but even as a reissued "Ashes to Ashes" (#29 UK) took them back into the chart in the new year, the band split. Bottum, who formed his own side project, Imperial Teen, in 1996, would now work full time with that outfit; Patton formed Phantomas with the Melvins' Buzz Osborne, Slayer drummer Dave Lombardo, and Mr. Bungle bassist Trevor Dunn (Patton and Dunn would also convene a third Mr Bungle album in 1999). Faith No More, meanwhile, would be remembered with November 1998's *Who Cares a Lot?* (#37

UK) greatest hits package, and one final hit single, the excerpted Bee Gees cover, "I Started a Joke" (#49 UK).

Faith No More LPs

6 We Care a Lot (Mordam) 1985 Unfocused crashing throws hardcore, hip-hop, and sundry other devices into the air, without too much attention to where they land.

7 Introduce Yourself (Slash) 1987 Reprising the debut's title track (and getting it right this time), a distinctly hard-edged collection whose bludgeoning energies were more pleasing to metalheads than the rest of the band's apparent target audience.

8 The Real Thing (Slash) 1989 With Mike Patton now on board, the "real" Faith No More starts here — a joyously commercial realization of all that the first albums tried to accomplish, shot through with songs poised on the pop side of manic... "Epic" really was a classic.

6 Live at the Brixton Academy [LIVE] (Polygram) 1991

7 Angel Dust (Slash) 1992 Schizophrenic collection which tries to maintain the commercial momentum at the same time as pulling back from the breakthrough. "Midnight Cowboy" and "A Small Victory" are opposing poles around which the remainder hovers uncertainly.

8 King for a Day, Fool for a Lifetime (Slash) 1995 The stylistic abruptness of Patton and Spruance's Mr. Bungle alter-ego comes to the fore, but so does a warmer approach to songwriting, highlighted by the surprisingly mature "Evidence."

7 Album of the Year (WB) 1997

Selected Compilations and Archive Releases

6 Who Cares a Lot? (WB) 1998

Mike Patton/Mr. Bungle LPs

7 Mr. Bungle (WB) 1991 If the Residents were the Boredoms for a day...

6 Disco Volante (WB) 1995

7 California (WB) 1999 Breakneck lunacy lurches between Hawaiian breeze, Hollywood sleaze, and soulful yearning, all executed with an avant-garde cheerfulness lurking somewhere (sometimes) between Godley and Creme and a laidback Lawrence Welk. Supremely irritating and strangely grin-provoking in more or less equal doses.

Roddy Bottum/Imperial Teen LPs

7 Seasick (Slash) 1996 Glam-inflected grunge, shooting off at peculiar hookline tangents.

7 What is Not to Love 1998

Further Reading
The Real Story by Steffan Chirazi (Castle, UK, 1994).

FATBOY SLIM

BORN *Quentin Cook, aka Norman Cook , 7/31/63 (Brighton, England)*

Cook came to prominence as a bassist with Hull-based indy band the Housemartins, whose four-year career (1983–87) embraced one a cappella UK #1, "Caravan of Love," and two critically acclaimed hit albums before spawning three future worldwide chart-topping acts. The Beautiful South were formed by vocalist Paul Heaton and drummer Dave Hemmingway; Cook launched Beats International and Fatboy Slim.

With A Certain Ratio and Digital Underground already on his resume, Cook was already an in-demand remixer when, in 1989, he launched his solo career onto the dance floors. July's "Won't Talk About It" (#29 UK) featuring Billy Bragg, and October's "For Spacious Lies" (#48 UK), were both technically powerful, but typically lyrically facetious slices of danceable whimsy. "Freedom," Cook announced in the latter, "is just a song by Wham!"

In 1990, Cook surfaced with a new alias, Beats International, and a delicious dubbed-out remake of the SOS Band's "Just Be Good to Me," appropriately retitled "Dub Be Good to Me" (#76 US, #1 UK). Based around a bass line sampled from The Clash's "Guns of Brixton," the song was powered by Lindy Layton's seductive vocal line and what would become a Cook trademark — a mood-shattering mini-rap slogan hookline (from MC Wildski).

It powered to the top of the UK chart in February, setting up a pair of follow-ups — a reworked "Won't Talk About It" (#76 US, #9 UK) and the African percussive "Burundi Blues" (#51 UK) — and an album, *Let Them Eat Bingo* (#162 US, #17 UK).

The following year brought a second Beats International album, *Excursion on the Version*, and further hits "Echo Chamber" (#60 UK), "The Sun Doesn't Shine" (#66 UK), and "In the Ghetto" (#44 UK). None repeated the impact of "Dub," however, and Cook moved on to fresh territory.

With Cook disguising himself beneath an entire crop of new aliases, Pizzaman proved the most successful, especially after the Del Monte corporation picked up the single "Happiness" (#19 UK) to accompany a fruit juice commercial. A partnership with producers JC Reid and Tim Jefferey, Pizzaman continued their assault on the British chart with "Trippin' on Sunshine" (#18 UK), "Sex on the Streets" (#23 UK), and "Hello Honky Tonks" (#41 UK) during 1995/96.

Fried Funk Food, Cook's partnership with Ashley Slater, eschewed mainstream success for a monster club hit with "The Real Shit" and the *In Dub* EP. In late 1996, the Mighty Dub Katz hit with "Just Another Groove" (#43 UK), while Freakpower proved the most stalwart of them all when "Turn on Tune in Cop Out" made #29 in late 1993, then resurfaced 18 months later to breach the Top 3 ("Rush" and "New Direction," on either side of the smash, made #62 and #60 respectively).

Freakpower ended after their label, Island, dropped them. Encouraged by his friends, the Chemical Brothers, Cook returned to Brighton and set up his own Skint label with Damien Harris, debuting it with a new project, Fatboy Slim's "Santa Cruz" single.

"Going out of My Head," which threw the Who's "I Can't Explain" riff into the mix, was an even more powerful statement of intent; "Everybody Needs a 303" made the UK Top 10 and Fatboy Slim's debut album, *Better Living Through Chemistry* (titled from a 1950's American commercial, which suggested calming hyperactive children with valium) succeeded in creating a hybrid which even Prodigy had pulled short of, blending rock and rave into one seamless whole.

Fatboy's success, at first, seemed no greater than that attending any of Cook's other aliases. Indeed, a new Mighty Dub Katz single, the awesome "Magic Carpet Ride," was one of the club hits of 1997, while Cook's bi-weekly DJing exercises at Brighton's Big Beat Boutique Club would prove a testing ground for many of the techniques and remixes he intended unleashing on a wider public — the manic *On the Floor at the Boutique* mix album captures a typical set.

It was the Big Beat audience which first heard the mix he created (completely unofficially) for Cornershop's "Brimful of Asha" single, and whose response encouraged him to approach the band and its record company to ask if they wanted to release it. The result was an early 1998 UK chart topper, with a record which the band themselves had already given up on. Of the remixes which Cook would be offered in the wake of that one monster hit, he would accept the Beastie Boys' "Body Moving," but turned down chances to work with the Pet Shop Boys, U2, Madonna, and the Jungle Brothers.

1998 also brought a second Fatboy Slim album, *You've Come a Long Way* (#34 US, #1 UK), a set which included hits "Gangster Trippin'," the absurdly compulsive "Rockafeller Skank" (#78 US) and "Right Here Right Now" (#2 UK), and the magnificent "Praise You" (#36 US, #1 UK) — whose manic modern-dance troupe pastiche video would win three MTV awards the following fall (Breakthrough Video, Best Direction, and Best Choreography).

A summer 1999 US mini-tour included a performance at the Woodstock festival, while Cook's Brighton hometown would honor his achievements by giving him a star on the city's Walk of Fame, adjacent to Sir Winston Churchill's. Skint Records returned the favor by taking over the sponsorship of local soccer team Brighton and Hove Albion. Meanwhile, *You've Come a Long Way Baby* became the first mil-lion selling record in the US Astralwerks label's history, and was adjudged one of *Spin* magazine's Top 100 albums of the 1990s. Cook completed a memorable year with his marriage to Radio 1 DJ Zoe Ball.

Fatboy Slim LPs

🎵 Better Living Through Chemistry (Astralwerks) 1996 With its delirious mix of styles and flavors, Fatboy Slim's debut shook the club world — all the more so since Cook's forte had hitherto been killer singles wrapped in less-than-classic albums. Held together by some genuinely entertaining samples and ever-shifting beats, *Living* sucked in funk, soul, jazz, rock, and pop, put them through the blender, then poured out an exceptionally tasty electro-cocktail.

🎵 On the Floor at the Boutique (Skint) 1998 Breakneck mix tape collection.

🎵 You've Come a Long Way Baby (Astralwerks) 1998 The wry humor and ingenious perversion of innocent genres (check it out now — a funk/surf hit!) subverts everything you thought you knew about music as Cook flips traditional styles on their head, then cheekily snaps their garters. Rarely has electro-genius been so accessible and such outright fun.

Beats International LPs

🎵 Let Them Eat Bingo (Go! Discs) 1990 Where would we have been without "Dub Be Good to Me"? The rest of the album never catches up with the hit, but a few moments of Beats-inflected light-heartedness do try.

🎵 Excursion on the Version (Go! Discs) 1991

Freakpower LPs

🎵 Drive Through Booty (4th and Broadway) 1995

🎵 More of Everything for Everybody (4th and Broadway) 1996

🎵 Freak Power in Dub (4th and Broadway) 1997

Fried Funk Food LP

🎵 The Real Shit 1995

Pizzaman LP

🎵 Pizzamania (Cowboy Rodeo) 1995

Norman Cook All Stars LPs

🎵 All Star Breaks and Beats Volume One (Skint) 1996

🎵 Skip to My Loops (Skint) 1997

Norman Cook Selected Remixes
1988 VANESSA WILLIAMS — The Right Stuff (Wing)
1989 DIGITAL UNDERGROUND — Humpty Dance (Tommy Boy)
1989 FINE YOUNG CANNIBALS — Not the Man I Used to be (IRS)
1989 YOUNG MC — Bust a Move (Delicious Vinyl)

1990 KEITH SWEAT — Makes You Sweat (Elektra)

1990 LINDY LAYTON — Silly Games (Arista)

1990 A CERTAIN RATIO — Won't Stop Loving You (EMI)

1990 KINGS OF SWING — Nod Your Head to This (Atlantic)

1990 A TRIBE CALLED QUEST — I Left My Wallet in El Segundo (Jive)

1990 RUTHLESS RAP ASSASSINS — It Wasn't a Dream (Syncopate)

1990 AZTEC CAMERA — Good Morning Britain (Sire)

1990 KYM MAZELLE — Useless (Capitol)

1990 JUNGLE BROTHERS — Doing Our Own Dang (WB)

1990 A CERTAIN RATIO — Shack Up (EMI)

1990 STEREO MCS — I'm a Believer (4th and Broadway)

1990 DAVID GRANT — Life (4th and Broadway)

1990 RUTHLESS RAP ASSASSINS — Just Mellow (Syncopate)

1991 DEFINITION OF SOUND — Dream Girl (Cardiac)

1991 JEAN PAUL GAULTIER — How to Do Zat (Polydor)

1991 KID'N'PLAY — Do This My Way (Select)

1991 SCREAMING TARGET — Fallout (Island)

1991 NITRO DELUXE — This Brutal House (Cutting)

1991 LES NEGRESSES VERTES — Famile Heureuse (Virgin)

1991 PROFESSOR GRIFF — The Verdict (Effect)

1992 REAL ROXANNE — Roxanne's on a Roll (Contempo)

1992 JC LODGE — Pillow Talk (Tommy Boy)

1993 VANESSA PARADIS — Tandem (Polydor)

1993 BROTHERS LOVE DUBS — The Mighty Ming (Stress)

1993 ORIGINAL ROCKERS — What a Life (Rockers)

1994 JUDY CHEEKS — Reach (Positiva)

1995 YVONNE CHAKA CHAKA — Umqombothi (Polydor)

1995 WILDCHILD — Renegade Master (Hi Life)

1996 LATITUDE — Building a Bridge (Nude)

1996 CHRISSY WARD — Right and Exact (DDZ)

1996 URBAN COOKIE COLLECTIVE — Pressing on (Pulse 8)

1996 STRETCH N VERN — I'm Alive (ffrr)

1996 STRETCH N VERN — Get Up, Go Insane (ffrr)

1996 OSMONDS — One Bad Apple (Polygram)

1996 HEATWAVE — Ain't No Half Steppin' [NEW VERSION] (Legacy)

1996 MICROGROOVE — Walkin' (Alaska Deep)

1997 ERIC B AND RAKIM — I Know You Got Soul (4th and Broadway)

1997 JEAN JACQUES PERREY — E.V.A. (BGP)

1997 PEPLAB — Ride the Pony (Mr Cheng)

1997 MONDO GROSSO — Souffles H (King St)

1997 INXS — Elegantly Wasted (Polygram)

1997 MONDO GROSSO — Anger (King St)

1997 MIDFIELD GENERAL — Devil in Sports Casual (Skint)

1997 FLUKE — Absurd (Virgin)

1997 BASSBIN TWINS — Out of Hand (Southern Fried)

1998 DUKE — So in Love with You (Uptown)

1998 TRANQUILITY BASS — La La La (Astralwerks)

1998 JAMES BROWN — She's the One (Polygram)

1998 JAMES BROWN — The Payback Mix (Polygram)

1998 DARRYL PANDY — Love Can't Turn Around (Azuli)

1998 BEASTIE BOYS — Body Movin' (Grand Royale)

1998 CORNERSHOP — Brimful of Asha (Luaka Bop)

1998 LUNATIC CALM — Roll the Dice (City of Angels)

1998 CHRISTOPHER JUST — I'm a Disco Dancer (BMG)

1999 UNDERWORLD — King of Snake (V2)

9 Fatboy Slim's Greatest Remixes (BML) 2000 Remixes for Underworld, Wildchild, and Jean Jacques Perrey anthologized from rare UK singles.

Housemartins LPs

7 London 0 Hull 4 (Go! Discs) 1986 Revolutionary subversives extraordinaire, the Housemartins launch their plot to overthrow society from within, dispersing their radical message via wry, sing-along lyrics coated in radio friendly perfect pop that even your old Granny would adore, performed by a band brilliantly disguised as the nerds next door; resistance is fun, fun, fun.

7 The People Who Grinned Themselves to Death (Go! Discs) 1987

Selected Compilations and Archive Releases

8 Now That's What I Call Quite Good (Go! Discs) 1988

Beautiful South LPs

7 Welcome to the Beautiful South (Go! Discs) 1989

6 Choke (Go! Discs) 1990

7 0898 (Go! Discs) 1992

6 Miaow (Go! Discs) 1994

7 Blue is the Colour (Go! Discs) 1996

8 Quench (Polygram Int) 1998 No matter how much you want to hate the BS's squeaky clean, lushly produced, moistly melodic pap, there remains a nagging sense at the back of the mind that this is what true pop music sounds like — mature, reflective, orchestral, and utterly, unshakably sweet. With clever lyrics, of course. Hate... love... hate... love...

Selected Compilations and Archive Releases

8 Carry on Up the Charts (Go! Discs) 1994

FEELIES

FORMED 1977 *(Haledon, NJ)*
ORIGINAL LINE-UP *Glenn Mercer (vocals, guitar); Bill Million (vocals, guitar); John J (bass); Dave Weckerman (drums)*

Mercer, Million, and Weckerman were originally members of a high school punk band, the Outkids. They became the Feelies in 1977, but having debuted at Manchester High School in their NJ hometown, the original line-up played only a handful of shows before the rhythm section was replaced by bassist Keith Clayton and drummer Vincent

DeNunzio, and the band's sights raised toward nearby New York City.

Swiftly establishing themselves at such fashionable niteries as CBGBs and Max's Kansas City, the Feelies gigged through 1978 and 1979, overcoming the departure of DeNunzio with the recruitment of Anton Fier and (for live shows) original drummer Weckerman. By the end of 1979, the Feelies' odd policy of mainly playing shows on public holidays and dressing as high school nerds, saw them became one of those bands whom everyone seemed to have heard of, but few had ever heard — even after Rough Trade released a one-off single in 1979, the maddeningly Sparks-like "Fa Ce La."

Still, their recruitment to Stiff Records in early 1980 was feted by the label as a coup comparable to grabbing the unknown Ramones or Television — and Television were, in fact, one of the bands with whom the Feelies were most easily compared, assuming they'd first been indoctrinated by the Byrds. With hindsight, this combination conspired to ensure the band's debut album, *Crazy Rhythms* (and first single, a stylized cover of the Beatles' "Everybody's got Something to Hide Except for Me and My Monkey"), would age considerably better than many more fashionable bands of the era.

Nevertheless, Stiff — and the army of Stiff collectors who automatically pounced upon every record the label released — were disappointed with the album's reception and were even more horrified by the demos for the band's proposed second album. The band was dropped and by early 1981, the Feelies appeared to have sundered.

Back in NJ, Million and Mercer began working in film music, contributing soundtrack material to the Cannes Film festival hit, *Smithereens*, at the same time as recording with three new bands, the paisley-colored Trypes, the Eno-esque Yung Wu, and the instrumental Willies. The specter of the Feelies was never far away, however, and in 1983, the pair reunited with Weckerman to reform the band.

With Trypes alumni Stan Demeski (drums) and Brenda Sauter (bass), the Feelies embarked on their first ever tour of the US, before beginning work on their long-delayed second album, *The Good Earth*. Produced by Mercer, Million, and REM guitarist Peter Buck, both album and the EP *No-One Knows* re-established the Feelies as a potentially major player in the same post-Paisley pastures now being tilled by REM and a sensible Robyn Hitchcock.

Director Jonathan Demme was certainly impressed. He recruited the Feelies to play the high school reunion scene in his *Something Wild* movie; A&M, too, sensed the band's enormous potential and in 1988, the band cut the third Feelies album, *Only Life*, hot on the heels of the first Yung Wu set. A single, pairing "Away" with a delightful cover of

Patti Smith's "Dancing Barefoot," attracted some attention; so, later in the year, did "Higher Ground," with its live-at-the-L.A.-Roxy renditions of Jonathan Richman's "Egyptian Reggae" and a reprise of the Feelies' first Stiff single.

Only Life was followed by a major US tour with Lou Reed while the band returned to the studio in 1990 to record *Time for a Witness* and a string of devilish covers which A&M would squeeze out over the course of five promo singles in the next six months. The Rolling Stones' "Paint It Black," Neil Young's "Barstool Blues," Jonathan Richman's "Now I Wanna Sleep in Your Arms," Lou Reed's "White Light White Heat," and the Feelies' own "Sooner or Later" were all thrown at US radio, but to no avail.

The album, too, flopped and it was clear that the Feelies were fading. Finally, Million quit in mid-1991 once the latest tour was over; he subsequently left the music industry altogether. Demeski followed him out of the band, reappearing in the Galaxie 500 spin-off Luna, and the Feelies broke up. Sauter joined Speed the Plough (whose first two albums were produced by Million), and later, the Wild Carnation. Mercer and Weckerman formed the Wake Ooloo and when that band broke up, they gigged briefly as the True Wheel, then reunited with Demeski in Sunburst.

Feelies LPs

6 Crazy Rhythms (Stiff) 1980 Subtle and textured, the Feelies combined twangs of Television and the Velvets with burgeoning wave stirrings. The CD reissue includes a nifty cover of the Stones' "Paint It Black."

8 The Good Earth (Coyote) 1986 After making sure that everyone forgot them, the Feelies returned with the sleeper of the year — an album full of folk that only masked the underlying edge that still permeated their sound.

6 Only Life (A&M) 1988

7 Time for a Witness (A&M) 1991 The sound of the Feelies at their most relaxed.

Yung Wu LP

7 Shore Leave (Coyote) 1987 Vocalist Weckerman had already released the title track as a solo single in 1980; joined by the rest of the Feelies, plus Trypes keyboard player John Baumgartner, he continued in the same pleasantly acoustic vein across this entire album.

Wake Ooloo LPs

7 Hear No Evil (Pravda) 1994

6 What About It (Pravda) 1995

7 Stop the Ride (Pravda) 1996

Speed the Plough LPs

7 Speed the Plough (Coyote) 1989

8 Wonder Wheel (East Side Digital) 1991

7 Mason's Box (East Side Digital) 1993

6 Marina (East Side Digital) 1995

Wild Carnation LPs

6 Tricycle (Delmore) 1994

6 Live From Hamburg (Motorway — Japan) 1998

FELT

FORMED *1978 (Water Orton, England)*

ORIGINAL LINE-UP *Lawrence Hayward (vocals, guitar); Maurice Deebank (guitar); Nick Gilbert (bass)*

Hayward, Deebank, and Gilbert were schoolfriends in the village of Water Orton (near Birmingham, England) who formed their first loose band in 1978. Hayward and the classically trained Deebank then recorded some instrumentals together although, when Hayward conceived Felt, it was as a solo project. The first single released under that name, the spikey pop of September 1979's "Index," featured Hayward alone.

Self-released in a limited edition of 500, the single found its way to London after Hayward and Gilbert befriended Scritti Politti drummer Tom Morley. He encouraged Rough Trade's retail outlet to stock it and, with *Sounds* having already made "Index" their Single of the Week, the ensuing sales were sufficient to bring Felt to the attention of the Cherry Red label. Meanwhile, a second single on Hayward's Shanghai label, Gilbert's Versatile Newts' "Newtrition," brought the operation to the attention of the Fall's Mark E. Smith — he arranged for Felt to play their first ever live show opening for his band.

It would be mid-1981 before the next Felt release appeared through Cherry Red; "Something Sends Me to Sleep" was one of three songs recorded at the full band line-up's first ever demo session over a year before (one of the three, "Birdmen," was wiped immediately because the band hated it). The original demo was rejected by several labels before Cherry Red picked the band up; Felt were so confident with it, however, that both the demo version (featuring drummer Tony Race) and a rerecording (with new member Gary Ainge) were included on their Cherry Red debut, together with two versions of another song, "Red Indians."

The clash between Hayward's hybrid post-punk/proto-ambient writing and playing and Deeward's classical training was to flavor much of Felt's early work, with their next release, March 1982's six-song *Crumbling the Antiseptic Beauty* mini-album (#16 UK indie), especially benefitting from it. Even the partial loss of Hayward's vocals in the mix seemed both a deliberately atmospheric device (he has since admitted that given the chance, he would completely remix the record). However, the sessions were not easy — bassist Gilbert quit the band midway through the recording, while Deeward left soon after.

Hayward and new bassist Mick Lloyd alone recorded "Trails of Colour Dissolve" (#21 UK indie) the next Felt single; Deeward, however, returned for June 1983's "Penelope Tree" (#22 UK indie) and, in November, the reconstituted trio released *The Splendour of Fear* (#6 UK indie), another six-track collection of often atmospheric, and certainly surreal music which was distinctly at odds with the band's increasingly pop-inflected singles. Indeed, Hayward admitted that "when we started, one of our many plans was to release 30-minute reflective albums and then have pop 7-inchers at the same time, so there'd be two sides to the band." Such plans were scuppered, however, when Cherry Red decided to cull a single from the album, the twangy "Mexican Bandits" (#28 UK indie).

In its original form, "Sunlight Bathed Golden" (#6 UK indie), Felt's next single, was to feature strings arranged by Ivor Raymonde, the orchestral mastermind behind the Walker Brothers' greatest hits two decades previous. Cherry Red balked at his asking price, however and producer John Rivers took over, turning in a competent job, but by no means the majestic effort the band had dreamed of. (The arrangements' shortcomings were further illustrated on the B-side, a purely instrumental version of the song, retitled "Sunlight Strings".)

The experience certainly soured the band's ambitions; their next album, October 1984's *The Strange Idols Pattern and Other Short Stories* (#8 UK indie), dispensed with all the frills and a lot of Felt's past weirdness and concentrated on straightahead pop; Cherry Red, however, were unable to market it as anything more than another wacky Felt album and it was apparent that band and label were drifting apart.

For their next release, Felt — now featuring bassist Marco Thomas in place of Lloyd — recruited Cocteau Twins Robin Guthrie and Liz Fraser to help with their next single — the two bands toured together during 1984. Taking a lovely Deebank solo composition, "Primitive Painters" (#1 UK indie), Guthrie produced, Fraser added backing vocals, and Hayward was truly justified in telling the world, Felt had cut the perfect single — a record to play alongside his own ideals, the Wild Swans' "Revolutionary Spirit" and Joy Division's "Atmosphere." It became their first and only indie chart topper.

However, pride came before the fall. Despite retaining Guthrie as producer, *Ignite the Seven Cannons* (#4 UK indie), Felt's next album, was a vast disappointment with the long-threatened addition of a full-time organist, Martin Duffy, adding nothing more than an all-too-loud instrument to the previously well-balanced mix as he fought to fit into the line-up. (He would, of course, eventually succeed.)

Ignite the Seven Cannons was to end Felt's relationship with Cherry Red; it also marked Deebank's last recording with the band. He had recently moved to Barcelona, Spain, with his girlfriend and, though he talked of a solo career (in 1984, he released a low-key album in his own right, Inner Thought Zone), little more was heard of him. "Ballad of the Band" (#12 UK indie), Felt's next single, is widely rumored to be about the departing guitarist.

In Deeward's stead, Hayward, Thomas, Duffy, and Ainge recruited Tony Wille and Felt signed with Creation in 1985. The aforementioned "Ballad of the Band" followed in May 1986 while June brought Felt's latest album, the evocatively titled *Let the Snakes Crinkle Their Heads to Death* (#18 UK indie). All unsettlingly fragmentary instrumentals, it became their poorest selling yet. Just weeks later, however, a new, "conventional" Felt album was announced — *Forever Breathes the Lonely World* (#8 UK indie) was trailed by the "Rain Of Crystal Spires" (#11 UK indie) single and rewarded Creation for their patience with the album Felt had been threatening to make all along.

Yet Felt had still to peak. The arrival of a second guitarist, Neil Scott, in early 1987, encouraged the band to even greater heights with *Poem of the River* (#6 UK indie) in September 1987 — at the same time as returning to the original Felt format of six tracks in 30 minutes. An accompanying single, "The Final Resting of The Ark" (#10 UK indie), was recorded by Hayward and future Jesus and Mary Chain drummer Richard Thomas (on soprano sax) at Robin Guthrie's newly outfitted, but as yet untried, home studio.

While Cherry Red mourned the band's departure with the Hayward compiled *Goldmine Thrash* compilation (#11 UK indie), another Felt album followed in March 1988; *The Pictorial Jackson Review* (#9 UK indie) lifted its title from Jack Kerouac and featured eight short songs on one side, and one long Duffy instrumental on the other. Described by Hayward as two mini-albums in one, it was swiftly joined by a third, as Ainge and Duffy alone cut the instrumental *Train Above the City* (#9 UK indie). Hayward's contributions to what he subsequently described as his favorite Felt album were limited to the song titles — "Seahorses on Broadway," "On Weegee's Sidewalk," and "Press Softly on the Brakes, Holly" certainly reflect his own lyrical sensibilities.

Felt and Creation parted company following one further single, August 1988's "Space Blues" 45 (#9 UK indie), recorded by Hayward, Duffy and guest vocalist Rose McDowall (ex-Strawberry Switchblade). It was an amicable parting, brought on by the label's own scheduling problems — Hayward was adamant that what would become Felt's final album should appear in 1989, on the tenth anniversary

of "Index"; Creation, however, were unable to release it until early 1990. With guitarist John Mohan now on board, the band then turned near-full circle and linked with Cherry Red's el subsidiary for *Me and a Monkey on the Moon* (#18 UK indie), their tenth album in ten years. They split almost immediately after.

While Duffy moved on to Primal Scream, Hayward relocated to New York for a time, returning to Britain in 1992 to form a new band, Denim. Featuring bassist Siobhan and drummer Gerry Shepherd (ex-70s' glam superstars the Glitter Band), Denim's cunning re/deconstruction of the glam era would be spread across three albums, *Back In Denim*, *Denim On Ice*, and *Novelty Rock*, and a clutch of singles locked firmly into the '70s nostalgia market — 1993's "Middle of the Road" and 1996's "It Fell Off the Back of a Lorry." The following year, Denim signed with St. Etienne founders Bob Stanley and Pete Wiggs' shortlived Emi-Disc label, and cut the seasonally fashionable "Summer Smash" single. Denim folded in 1998, and Hayward next formed Go Kart Mozart. Their debut album, *Instant Wigwam and Igloo Mixture*, was a critical hit; the single "We're Selfish and Lazy and Greedy" and EP *Go Kart Mozart Tearing Up the Singles Chart* followed in 1999–2000.

Felt LPs

🎱 Crumbling the Antiseptic Beauty (Cherry Red — UK) 1982 An uneasily atmospheric blend of early Television with late Eno; once past the slipshod production, some moments of stunning inspiration leap out.

🎱 The Splendour of Fear (Cherry Red — UK) 1984 Mantric drones are the order of the day, although Felt do kick out the odd (very odd) memorable hookline, usually when you least expect it.

🎱 The Strange Idols Pattern and Other Short Stories (Cherry Red — UK) 1984 The band's most diverse album yet (flamenco guitar is an utterly unexpected bonus) is also their most guitar-driven, as the original Television comparisons come home to roost.

🎱 Ignite the Seven Cannons (Cherry Red — UK) 1985 Robin Guthrie's production understandably draws fresh nuances out of the band — most immediately, an oppressively obtrusive organ, but also some delicately lovely songs and melodies.

🎱 Let the Snakes Crinkle Their Heads to Death (Creation — UK) 1986 A set of ten instrumentals which range in length from 57 seconds to a little under three minutes, and never once settles down to a definable musical style.

🎱 Forever Breathes the Lonely Word (Creation — UK) 1986 A tight, well-produced and beautifully played set packed with some of the group's sharpest songs yet.

🎱 Poem of the River (Creation — UK) 1987 Brilliantly produced by Red Crayola's Mayo Thompson, a smooth but never featureless distillation of *Forever*'s beauty and *Snakes Crinkle*'s awkwardness.

4 The Pictorial Jackson Review (Creation) 1988 Half jazzy instrumentals, half neo-power-prog, and altogether half-baked.

5 Train Above the City (Creation — UK) 1988 In their rush to achieve Hayward's ten albums in ten years dictate, a sense of desperation seems to be creeping in, as another all-instrumental and all but Hayward-less set continues exploring Duffy's fascination with jazz stylings.

8 Me and a Monkey on the Moon (el — UK) 1989 Pure pop from start to finish, a harbinger of the Denim delight to come

Selected Compilations and Archive Releases

9 Goldmine Thrash (Cherry Red — UK) 1987

9 Bubblegum Perfume (Creation — UK) 1990 Demos, non-album cuts and the best of the rest make up two stunningly evenhanded overviews of Felt's finest.

9 Absolute Classic Masterpieces (Cherry Red — UK) 1992

9 Absolute Classic Masterpieces Vol 2 (Creation — UK) 1993 Overlook the duplication and ditto.

Denim LPs

8 Back In Denim (Boys Own — UK) 1992 "Fish and Chips," "Bubble Head," "Middle of the Road," "The Osmonds"... just four songs in and *Back In Denim* has already catapulted the listener so deep inside the Brit-glam 1970s that there will be no escape. The closing "I'm Against the Eighties" apparently disavows everything Felt ever stood for... and that was surely the point.

8 Denim On Ice (Echo — UK) 1996 Less precocious than its predecessor, but still a stunning exposition of all that is great, crass, and none-too-credible about '70s pop, progressing just enough to draw a bit of the Buzzcocks into the brew. "The Great Pub Rock Revival" would be infuriatingly rude if it wasn't so (sadly) true, and one can imagine the Auteurs spending some time with this album, as they prepared their own *Bootboys* masterpiece.

9 Novelty Rock (Emidisc — UK) 1998 Quite possibly the most deliberately and gloriously annoying record ever made; novelty rock by name and nature, an endless succession of grinning pap, with tongues so deep in cheeks that they look like extra arms.

Go Kart Mozart LP

7 Instant Wigwam and Igloo Mixture (Cherry Red — UK) 1999

Maurice Deebank LP

5 Inner Thought Zone (Cherry Red — UK) 1984

FIAT LUX

FORMED 1982 *(Wakefield, Yorkshire, England)*
ORIGINAL LINE-UP *Sebastian Barbaro [aka Steve Wright] (vocals); David Crickmore (keyboards, guitar, bass)*

Stepping out of the traditional synth-pop mode through their use of sometimes blurting saxophones, Fiat Lux was formed after drama student Wright joined the Yorkshire Actors group, a thespian body patronized by Be Bop Deluxe/Red Noise frontman Bill Nelson.

He occasionally supplied music to the Actors' productions and after hearing tapes Wright was recording with fellow drama student Crickmore, Nelson offered to release a single on his own Cocteau label (home, too, to the early A Flock of Seagulls).

As Fiat Lux (Latin for "let there be light"), the duo's "Feels Like Winter Again" (#10 UK indy) appeared in October 1982, and immediately earned *NME*'s Single of the Week award. With Nelson's brother Ian coming on board and Wright discarding his earlier alias of Sebastian Barbaro, Fiat Lux signed to Polydor that spring, and started work on their debut album.

Over the next year, too, the band toured with both Howard Jones and Blancmange and in January 1984, the single, "Secrets" (#65 UK), seemed to place the band on the edge of a step forward. Unfortunately, "Blue Emotion" (#59 UK), in May, failed to take advantage of the group's momentum and though a full album was recorded with producer Hugh Jones, it was never released. A European compilation, *Hired History*, was heavily imported into the UK and US in its stead, but when further singles achieved nothing, the band slowly dissolved.

Now a BBC librarian, Crickmore was rehearsing a new band in late 2000, hopefully a harbinger of a full return to action.

Selected Compilations and Archive Releases

8 Hired History (Polydor, UK) 1984 In lieu of a still archived album; "Secrets," "Blue Emotion," and more.

FISHBONE

FORMED 1979 *(San Fernando Valley, CA)*
ORIGINAL LINE-UP *Angelo Moore (b. 11/5/65 — vocals, sax); Norwood Fishbone (b. John Norwood Fisher, 12/9/65 — vocals, bass); Chris Dowd (b. 9/20/65 — trumpet); Kendall Jones (guitar); Walter Kibby II (trumpet); Phillip "Fish" Fisher (drums)*

The Fishbones were still in junior high when they began playing an explosive mix of music that crossed virtually every categorical barrier — ska and funk, rock and reggae, p-funk licks and teenage kicks. Gigging constantly around the L.A. club circuit, Fishbone wound up with a virtual residency at Madame Wong's and it was their frenetic live shows there that brought them to the attention of the major labels.

In 1985, the band inked a deal with Columbia and released their debut single, "Party at Ground Zero," instantly defining the band's hybrid sound. One side strolled from classical spoofs to 2-Tone with space rock overtones, interlaced with funk and gospel; the other ("Skanking to the Beat") was 2-Tone meets Devo, a blend which Fishbone would revisit on their second single, the oddly titled "Modern Industry (?)."

"Ugly" followed, completing a triptych so raucous, so breathtakingly creative, that Fishbone simply defied belief, swinging from silly to serious in the space of three minutes and crossing four musical genres en route.

After so much excitement, their 1986 debut album, *In Your Face* (and "When Problems Arise" single), was a slickly produced shock, and while 1987's *It's a Wonderful Life (Gonna Have a Good Time)* EP at least tried to return to basics, still it was live that Fishbone made the most sense.

Toasters' founder Bucket described them as "easily the best live ska band around at the time;" Mighty Mighty Bosstone Dickie Barrett confessed that "Fishbone almost made us say forget it. We heard the first Fishbone record, and we said, 'We're never gonna achieve this; these guys have got it all over us.'"

By the time of 1988's "Freddie's Dead," from the *Nightmare on Elm Street* sequel of the same name, and the *Truth and Soul* (#153 US) album, however, Fishbone were again eschewing the ska, in favor of the more commercial funk, soul, and clean production; while the two EPs which broke the three-year gap before the band's next album saw the band battling some serious creative confusion — *Ma and Pa* (1989) and *Set the Booty Upright Bonin' in the Boneyard* (1990).

Down quit, to be replaced by John Bigham shortly before work began on May 1991's belated third album, the double *The Reality of My Surroundings* (#49 US, #75 UK), the single "Everyday Sunshine," and two accompanying EPs *Sunless Sunday* and *Fight the Youth*. Jones, too, departed; Spacey T replaced him just as the band joined the 1993 Lollapalooza package, itself the prelude to the band's most eclectic album yet, *Give a Monkey a Brain and He'll Swear He's the Center of the Universe* (#99 US).

Presumably designed with the rock mainstream in mind, a string of accompanying singles hit radio — "Swim," "Black Flowers," "Servitude," and "Unyielding Conditioning" all missed the chart, however, just as the album itself missed the first stirrings of the ska third wave which Fishbone themselves had done so much to inspire.

Still, a measure of the affection with which Fishbone were regarded by their peers could be taken from the all-star turnout at a Norwood benefit at the Hollywood Palladium in

© Jim Steinfeldt/Chansley Entertainment Archives

January 1994. The singer had been charged with kidnapping after he attempted to abduct a friend who was reportedly suffering from mental problems and Porno for Pyros, Primus, Tool and, Alice in Chains all turned out to raise money for his defense. (The singer was eventually acquitted.)

Previewed by the single "Alcoholic," 1996's *Chim Chim's Bad Ass Revenge* (#158 US) landed some supportive reviews, but Fishbone's most essential release of the decade turned out to be their contribution to Island Records' 1998 *Ska Island* 40th anniversary compilation. Produced by Trojans' frontman Gaz Mayall, Fishbone's take on Bob Marley's "Crazy Bald Heads" was as revolutionary as anything the band produced during its heyday.

The decade-long retrospective *Fishbone 101: Nuttasaurusmeg Fossil Fuelin'* would be Fishbone's last for Sony; indeed, over the next five years, Fishbone themselves changed immensely. Though there was scarcely any let-up in the band's traditionally hectic live schedule, Fish departed and was replaced first by Cameron Clinton, then Deion; while former Untouchables keyboard player Anthony Brewster was on board briefly, before John McKnight was recruited.

Founding members Moore, Norwood, and Kibby, however, remained, and now signed with Hollywood, the band completed, *Fishbone and the Familyhood Nextperience Presents the Psychotic Friends Nuttwerx*, for March 2000 release. Band side projects Trulio Disgracios (which dated back to the late 1980s) and Dirty Walt and The Columbus Sanitations also had albums scheduled.

Fishbone LPs

4 **In Your Face (Columbia) 1986** Disappointment screams from every groove — a mellow moms'n'pops soul album with barely a hint of the early singles' madness.

8 **Truth and Soul (Columbia) 1988** A different band entirely! Screaming where the last disc whispered, blazing where it bumbled; hardcore, metal, and ska explode across a dam break of repressed energy and adrenaline.

8 **The Reality of My Surroundings (Columbia) 1991** "Everyday Sunshine" rewrites the book on subversive funk rock; "These Days Are Gone" blazes with psychedelic savagery.

6 **Give a Monkey a Brain (Columbia) 1993** Eclectic meltdown stylistically reminiscent of the MC5's attempt to blend hard-nosed political hard rock with free-form Sun Ra cacophony. And sometimes it almost works.

7 **Chim Chim's Bad Ass Revenge (Arista) 1996**

8 **Presents: The Psychotic Friends Nuttwerx (Hollywood) 2000** With guests from as far afield as No Doubt and the Peppers, George Clinton, and Donny Osmond (!), a dark, deep funk creation which defies both age and convention. Truly an unexpected triumph.

Selected Compilations and Archive Releases

8 **Fishbone 101: Nuttasaurusmeg Fossil Fuelin' (Sony) 1996** The whole story, rises and falls just like their career, but does round up the crucial earliest goodies.

FLAMING LIPS

FORMED 1983 *(Oklahoma City, OK)*
ORIGINAL LINE UP *Wayne Coyne (b. 3/17/65 — vocals, guitars); Mark Coyne (vocals); Michael Ivins (bass)*

According to legend, the Flaming Lips puckered up sometime in 1983 at a drunken house party given by Michael Ivins, whose parents were conveniently out of town for the weekend. Coyne gatecrashed, the two got talking and, when Coyne returned the following day with brother Wayne and an unnamed drummer in tow, the four jammed on the "Batman Theme."

This first drummer was duly succeeded by a steady stream of others, while the Coynes and Ivins continued jamming, occasionally stepping out of the rehearsal room for various gigs around town. Quickly realizing that the Lips were fast becoming a real band, the members cast their nets for a permanent drummer and reeled in Richard English in 1984, just in time for their first, self-financed, recording session.

The Flaming Lips — the band's self released debut EP, appeared late that same year, as the band continued gigging through 1985 and into 1986. Their semi-psychedelic classic rock initially incorporated a hefty punk-inflected nod in the direction of early idols Hüsker Dü, Black Flag, and Jesus and Mary Chain among others.

Mark Coyne quit in 1986 to get married; with Wayne taking over vocals, the three-piece Lips continued to tour and finally, on the west coast in late 1986 they came to the attention of Restless Records and were quickly signed.

The band recorded their debut album, *Hear It Is*, in a matter of days, a battery of blistering tracks which captured the maelstrom of punk which lurked even within the band's quieter moments. Teaming up with manager Michele Vlasimsky, the Lips showcased their unique sonics across the country, at times playing with the ubiquitous Butthole Surfers as they prepared for their sophomore set, the delightfully titled *Oh My Gawd!!! The Flaming Lips*. But the two weeks they spent recording it were devoted to shattering any preconceptions which others might have had of them, abandoning the earlier punk noise for an album of mind-blowingly odd pop.

Telepathic Surgery followed in 1988, but all was not well within the ranks. Frustrated with the tensions which had been bubbling within the band, English quit several dates into the Lips' latest US tour. Now a duo, Coyne and Ivins nevertheless refused to scuttle the outing and, instead, honored the rest of the dates using the adroit mixing technique of friend and soundman, Jonathan Donohue (himself a member of the nascent Mercury Rev). Donohue was finally drafted in as guitarist as the band crossed Canada.

The album spawned just one single, the band's first, "Drug Machine" in June 1989. The Lips also contributed a unique take on "After the Goldrush" to the Neil Young tribute album The Bridge, joining Sonic Youth, Nick Cave, Bongwater, and the Pixies to honor the man who would facilitate the rise of the next wave of alternative guitar bands just a few months later.

Joined now by new drummer Nathan Roberts, the Lips continued to tour Surgery through 1989. Returning home to Oklahoma, the quartet then began laying down what would eventually form their final record for Restless. 1991's In a Priest-Driven Ambulance was a mammoth effort which the band spent two months recording — setting, for themselves, a new record.

As their contract with Restless expired, the Lips found themselves at loose ends and, without label support, there would be no tour for Ambulance. Instead, the band contented themselves with gigging around Oklahoma and extending A&R invites to various record labels. Warner Brothers took the bait, and the band were duly signed and back in action.

Recorded in New York state and appearing in the stores in the summer of 1992, Hit to Death in the Future Head was as odd a masterpiece as its title promised. Musically diverse, strange, and filled with peculiar sonics, it was probably not quite what Warners had anticipated when they signed the Lips, but was fully in keeping with the band's credo of splitting sound, breaking barriers, and following whatever paths presented themselves.

Unfortunately, the past repeated hard as Donohue departed to focus on Mercury Rev and Nathan left amidst the now standard disputes over direction. Again, the Lips were reduced to a duo and again they had an album to promote. Ronald Jones (guitar) and Steven Drozo (drums) stepped in to fill the breach, remaining on board as the band quickly returned to the studio to cut 1993's Transmissions from the Satellite Heart, an album of dream-pop that garnered much critical acclaim.

Now, for the first time ever, the Lips were poised for some major success — albeit over a year after the album was released. With "She Don't Use Jelly" (#55 US) having already slipped into radio rotation, August 1994 saw the song hit the streets in single format and in November, it peaked just inside the Top 60. With this new-found visibility, the band made noteworthy appearances on both the David Letterman show and that venerable giant, Beverly Hills 90210;

they also toured with Seattle up-and-comers Candlebox and dropped in to MTV's Spring Break to soak up another shower of accolades.

Without any fresh material in the can, an eight-track odds and ends EP, Needles For Your Balloons, was swiftly compiled; a collection of demos, a cover of Suicide's "Ice Drummer," plus the stellar "Bad Days," which would appear not only on the Batman Forever soundtrack, but also on the Lips' own next album. The band also contributed "Turn It On" to the 1995 soundtrack Love & a .45.

But despite the rush of success, the Flaming Lips were tired, having been on the road almost longer than any of them could remember. They retreated to the shadows of the studio, this time in Chicago, to record Clouds Taste Metallic. Realizing that echoes of their sound had by now been fully co-opted by the post-grunge set, the Lips focused their attention on a classic rock sound — one which was fully realized when Metallic appeared in the fall of 1995. Three singles followed — "Bad Days" in December, "This Here Giraffe" in March 1996, and "Brainville" in August. But despite this smattering of releases, the band remained stubbornly out of sight — and seemed set to stay there.

In short succession, Jones quit to embark on some "spiritual" questing, while Drozd suffered a spider bite that almost took his hand. Coyne, meanwhile, utilized the down time to experiment with a pile of cars, prerecorded cassettes, and an empty lot in his "Parking Lot Experiment" — an excursion into the organic technology of sound which caused more than a few to wonder if he'd completely lost his mind.

He hadn't. Regrouping in 1997, the Lips cobbled an outstanding amalgamation of sound and song into Zaireeka — a wonderful effort which was, for the fans, a stellar success, if a somewhat costly one. According to Coyne's own specifications, the album was best heard if four separate copies were played — on four separate CD players — simultaneously. On the road, meanwhile, the principle was taken even further, rendering the latest Lips tour one of the grandest sonic experiments of the decade.

1998 heralded a juicy compilation of Restless years' material, A Collection of Songs Representing an Enthusiasm for Recording...By Amateurs as the band headed back into the studio to record 1999's The Soft Bulletin.

The Flaming Lips LPs

7 Here It Is (Pink Dust) 1986 The wacky cult starts here. Different ears hear different things, but basically, if you've ever wondered what might happen if Syd Barrett and Henry Rollins decided to form a guitar band, Flaming Lips could certainly sell you a car to get to their first gig. Make sure Mark Coyne's sole vocal spot, "My Own Planet," is playing on the 8-Track while you're driving, though.

7 Oh My Gawd!!!...The Flaming Lips (Restless) 1987 Settling down a little, in as much as such restless hyperactivity can ever be said to have done so, *Oh My Gawd!!!* finds the Lips concentrating as much on structure as dynamic, emerging with an album which wouldn't feel out of place at a Ween fan convention.

7 Telepathic Surgery (Restless) 1989 "Hell's Angel Cracker Factory," a bonus track on the CD release, is a 23-minute space jam which has nothing to do with the rest of the album but does, if played before the rest of the set, neatly pave the way for the shorter, sharper heart of the album.

9 In a Priest-Driven Ambulance (Restless) 1990 In the parallel universe which the Lips feel most at home in, "Unconsciously Screaming" could have slipped out behind "Cracker Factory" — shorter (a lot) but no less uncompromising, it lines up alongside the contrarily moody "Five Stop Mother Superior Rain" in positing the extremes which this band are capable of broaching.

6 Hit to Death in the Future Head (Warners) 1992 Another marathon bonus closes the album, although even *Metal Machine* afficianados would pull short of calling it music. Elsewhere, however, a strange form of restraint grips the Lips, as the most off-kilter moment emerges from the *Brazil* soundtrack.

8 Transmissions from the Satellite Heart (Warners) 1993 With "She Don't Use Jelly" buried beneath the knowing guffaws of the band's new-found jock audience, the subtler nuances of this essentially dream-soaked album are easily lost. So go out and find them.

6 Clouds Taste Metallic (Warners) 1995

7 Zaireeka (Warners) 1997 With nothing to match the last album's wonderful "Psychiatric Explorations of the Fetus with Needles," *Zaireeka* instead wanders into stereo-demonstration-record territory, with perhaps a little too much time spent on the sonics for the good of the songs. Perhaps.

7 The Soft Bulletin (Warners) 1999

FLESH FOR LULU

FORMED 1982 (London, England)
ORIGINAL LINE-UP *Nick "Nasty" Marsh (vocals, guitar); Rocco Barker (guitar); Glen Bishop (bass); James Mitchell (drums)*

"Rocco" Barker was fresh out of school in 1980 when he was invited to join Wasted Youth, a New York Dolls/Stooges-influenced band whose members emerged from punk hopefuls Cock Sparrer and the Tickets. Best associated with legendary east London pub club, the Bridgehouse, Wasted Youth would issue a handful of singles and one album, *Wild and Wandering* (#9 UK indy), during 1981/82, before breaking up following a tour with the Only Ones.

Immediately Barker linked with Nick Marsh, James Mitchell, and Glen Bishop to launch Flesh for Lulu, a horror movie name which slipped seamlessly into the gothic sensibilities of the day. Constant touring around the UK and Europe (they became particularly popular in Spain) led to a deal with Polydor and FFL's debut EP, *Roman Candle*, was released in late 1983.

Produced by Hein Hoven, the group's self-titled debut album and "Subterraneans" single appeared in 1984 to generally enthusiastic reviews. Their days "as a grim joke at the butt-end of goth are behind them," enthused *Melody Maker*, "in this mood, they could take on the world." The album did not take off, however, and following one final single for Polydor, the album's "Restless," Flesh for Lulu signed to Hybrid.

Bishop departed, to be replaced by ex-Specimen bassist Kevin Mills and keyboard player Derek Greening, and FFL released 1985's *Blue Sisters Swing* EP (#6 UK indy) and *Big Fun City* (#10 UK indy) album, recorded with New York punk veteran Craig Leon. The single "Baby Hurricane" (#8 UK indy), helped keep the band's domestic profile high, but an American tour that fall truly saw the group take off.

Now with Beggars Banquet, FFL's third album, *Long Live the New Flesh* (#89 US), and singles "Idol," "Postcards from Paradise," and "Siamese Twist" were recorded at Abbey Road studios with producer Mike Hedges. They bombed in Britain, but with the album emerging a major underground hit in the US, "as time went by," Barker recalled, "we just forgot about England. The English press just wouldn't give us a chance."

A tour with Gene Loves Jezebel in 1987 and the *Get Crazy* and *Flashback* movie soundtracks saw FFL verging on a major breakthrough. But the *Plastic Fantastic* album and singles "Decline and Fall" and "Time and Space," recorded at INXS' studio in Australia with producer Mark Opitz, were the sound, Barker mourned, of a group "putting our heads up our asses."

The album bombed, and the band effectively split up, reforming with a new rhythm section (bassist Mike Steed and drummer Hans Perrson) only for a tour with Public Image Ltd. during late 1989. Flesh for Lulu shattered again immediately after.

Barker and Marsh resurfaced in 1995 with a new band, Gigantic, featuring bassist Dave Blair and drummer Al Fletcher. Signing with Sony, an album, *Infidels/Disenchanted*, and accompanying single of Jacques Brel's "Seasons in the Sun," were completed and readied for release. Unfortunately, a dispute between band management and label saw the set scrapped just weeks before release, and Gigantic broke up.

Rumors of a Flesh for Lulu reunion before decade's end were eventually proven misguided; July 1999, however, saw Barker link with ragga toaster General Levy and programmer Dr. Cat as the Space Police, recording an album, *Money*

Maker, described by its makers as "electronic dancehall, a cross between the Prodigy and Yellowman."

Flesh for Lulu LPs

8 **Flesh for Lulu (Polydor) 1984** Ignore the cover which is hideous by any standards and make straight for the opening "Restless." A giant girly chorus wrapped around an impossible broad Psychedelic Furs meet Phil Spector wall of sound which doesn't let up, even when the band dip into the horror show hoe-down of the closing "Heavy Angel." There's nothing breathtakingly original about it, but "Subterraneans" set a standard which the rest of the pack still aspired to five years later, and Iggy-Lou Bowie had never sounded healthier.

8 **Big City Fun (Statik) 1985** A classic rock album in the tradition of mid-'60s Stones, the Lulus approaching near-perfection with a clutch of riffy R&B gems, as well as some blues, nods to Lou Reed, a hint of U2 and, in one of the several high points on the album, an exhilarating psychedelic Stones/Stooges/NY Dolls crossover that still defies belief.

8 **Long Live the New Flesh (Beggars Banquet/Capitol) 1987** The Lulus added synths — too late. Still they pull out all the stops and in a calculated attempt to lose the Stones comparisons, expanded their musical horizons. Soulful gospel, C&W twang, jangle guitars, screeching metal leads, Byrds-y pop, Gary Glitter stomp (rhythm section only), gothic atmospheres, you name it, the Lulus give it a go, with devastating results — "Postcards from Paradise," "Hammer of Love," "Siamese Twist"... an all-too easily overlooked gem.

7 **Plastic Fantastic (Beggars Banquet/RCA) 1989** Glitzy, slick, and pure plastic alt rock with dance beats, the band sidesteps into commercial big hair rock'n'roll. Which promptly sidesteps out of the way.

Wasted Youth LP

8 **Wild and Wandering (Bridge House, UK) 1981** Even the name conjured up images of spikey hair and sunken sharp cheekbones — a romanticized vision of what the Stones really meant, and a swaggering Stooges-on-dope riff mentality. Sloppy, debauched, and all slightly silly, but still high octane rock as the closet subversive's last resort.

Selected Compilations and Archive Releases

7 **From the Inner Depth (Bridge House, UK) 1984** Wild, wild youth, ragbag gathering of singles, out-takes, live cuts, and a pointlessly amusing collage of every mention of their name on BBC Radio 1.

FLIPPER

FORMED *1979 (San Francisco, CA)*
ORIGINAL LINE UP *Will Shatter (b. Russell Wilkinson, 1956 — bass, vocals); Ted Falconi (b. Laurence Falconi, 9/2/47 — guitar); Bruce Loose (b. Bruce Calderwood, 6/6/59 — bass, vocals); Steve DePace (b. 1/29/57 — drums)*

This Bay Area dirty punk band first surfaced in 1979 as Shatter and DePace regrouped following the demise of their last band, Negative Trend (their *We Don't Play, We Riot* EP appeared in 1978 on the Subterranean label). With former Rad Command drummer DePace also on board, the new group's name was one of two lasting contributions made by the duo's original choice for vocalist, Rickie Williams — the other was his recommendation of his replacement, Bruce Loose, like Shatter a bassist, and one whose addition would provide Flipper with a unique sub-level sound which defied belief, even when layered beneath the band's art-house hardcore appearance.

Having made violent appearances on the compilations *SF Underground* ("Earthworm") and *Live at Target*, Flipper then followed through with a single, "Love Canal," on the Thermidor label in 1980. Cuts on *Live at Kezar Pavilion* and Alternative Tentacles' *Let Them Eat Jellybeans* collections followed during 1981 and it wasn't until 1982 brought the "Sex Bomb" single that Flipper were fully thrust into the limelight.

The song was long — more than 3 regular punk numbers long — yet it embodied everything a great punk record stood for: blisteringly compelling, loud, and so relentless that critics across the US quickly took the band under their wing. Indeed, press adulation alone essentially created a Flipper fanclub which would propel the band for the remainder of their career. Flipper, however, never bowed to the accolades, not caring what anyone thought but simply playing music because it entertained them to do so.

Flipper's debut, *Album — Generic Flipper*, released in April 1982 was a sloppy and strangely positive masterpiece that would subsequently serve as a blueprint for any number of grunge proteges later that decade, including Seattle mainstays Nirvana and Tad.

The band followed up with *Blow'N Chunks*, a November 1983 cassette release of live material recorded in New York, and displaying the band at their intensive best, pulling material from their earlier songs as well as previewing those that would eventually appear on Flipper's second album.

Returning from tour, Flipper were soon back in the studio laying down tracks for 1984's *Gone Fishin'*. Without packing the same punch as *Album,* it was nevertheless a remarkable album, drawing in a host of contextually esoteric instruments (punks with clavinets). It was, however, very much a farewell disc. Although Flipper never did officially break up, gigs became increasingly sporadic, while new recordings were limited to a live retrospective, the thunderous *Public Flipper Ltd. (Live 1980–82)* — the title, of course, was a poke at PiL, who had (unfairly they thought) "borrowed" their own penchant for generics with their 1986 *Album*. At the same time, Shatter launched his own side project, Any Three Initials, cutting the oddball *Ruins of America* album.

This twilight era was finally closed when Shatter died from a heroin overdose in December 1987. His death split the band apart and they dissolved immediately, with just the posthumous *Sex Bomb Baby* compilation to mourn their departure.

The surviving members of Flipper remained out of sight until early 1991 when they reformed with John Dougherty (b. 4/20/61 — bass) taking Shatter's place. Signing to Rick Rubin's American label, the band's solitary comeback album, *American Grafishy* was released in June 1993.

Flipper LPs

9 Album — Generic Flipper (Subterranean) 1982 Heavyweight, hard-hitting artcore, an acquired taste for anybody not willing to be smacked around the head with something very loud and heavy, but it takes no more than a few listens to discern a lot more beneath the loudness than two bassists chasing one another into oblivion. With both Shatter and Loose taking vocals, there is a certain dislocation to the sound, but for once, the critics were correct. Flipper really were pursuing a new line of thought.

6 Blow'n Chunks [live] (ROIR) 1984 Thunderous lo-fi barrage, but no one can argue that it's at all unrepresentative.

6 Gone Fishin' (Subterranean) 1984 Distancing themselves from the visceral shock of old, cloaking their sound instead with ambitiously prog-inflected nuances, *Fishin'* emerges more shocking than earthshaking.

6 American Grafishy (American) 1993 Combining the promise of a comeback with the threat of continuation, but overlooking the decade that has elapsed in-between times, an unrecognizably competent Flipper add little to their legacy beyond a handful of okay songs and one definite classic, "Flipper Twist."

Selected Compilations and Archive Releases

7 Public Flipper Ltd. 1980–82 [LIVE] (Fundamental) 1986 A companion volume to *Chunks*, omitting any overlap and adding near-definitive renderings of "Sex Bomb" and "Brainwash."

9 Sex Bomb Baby (Subterranean) 1988 Crucial round-up of singles and compilation cuts, plus a limited edition Bruce Loose solo single.

7 Live at CBGBs 1983 (Overground — UK) 1997 Reissue of *Chunks*.

FOETUS

BORN *Jim Thirlwell, (Australia)*

Australia-born Jim Thirlwell arrived in England in 1978, falling from much the same boatload of Aussie punk invaders as the Birthday Party and The Saints. But he swiftly set himself apart from the rest of the scene, as his choice of aliases revealed: Foetus Under Glass, Foetus in Your Bed, Foetus Art Terrorism, Scraping Foetus off the Wheel, Foetus Over Frisco, Philip and His Foetus Vibrations, and — with the UK press wondering whether this was the most tasteless name in rock? — You've Got Foetus on Your Breath.

The names shocked, Thirlwell admitted. They turned people off before they'd even heard the music. But they were also the price of admission. If you could survive the name, you were ready for the music — a frenzied clash of performance art and practical dance music which was as compulsive as it was disturbing. Released as Foetus Under Glass, "OKFM," his first single in January 1981, was a cult hit in the UK, but the same year's "Wash It All Off," introducing the Breath alias to the public, remains Thirlwell's most startling statement of intent — pounding percussion, tortured rhythms, a snatch of *Mary Poppins*, and over it all Thirlwell snarled and yowled through the one musical soundtrack the '80s truly deserved.

In 1982, he linked with Soft Cell's Marc Almond for a one-off performance of Suicide's "Ghostrider" on British television's *The Tube*. It was a weird pairing, but it worked and before the year was out the pair had brought their act to America, linking with Birthday Party's Nick Cave and Lydia Lunch to perform as the Immaculate Consumptives.

Thirlwell and Almond would regroup for the "Slut" (#12 UK indy) single in 1988, this time in the guise of the Flesh Volcano. (Other Foetus collaborations include work with acts as disparate as Nurse with Wound and Brit rave-rockers EMF.)

Thirlwell, meanwhile, rolled on. Signing his own Self Immolation label to Some Bizzare, he flirted briefly with the UK pop mainstream — the Almond association had opened his name, if not his vision, to mass-consumption, even if 1983's *Hole* (#3 UK indy) and 1985's *Nail* (#1 UK indy) would prove nothing less than unpiloted juggernauts careening through residential streets. The kids couldn't dance to "The Theme From Pigdome Come" and they couldn't dance to "What is the Bane of Your Life?" either, but Phillip and his Foetus Vibrations still climbed to #30 on the UK indy charts in November 1984, one of four hit singles which Thirlwell would enjoy over the next year. Foetus Art Terrorism's "Calamity Crush" (#4 UK indy), Foetus over Frisco's "Finely Honed Machine" (#5 UK indy), and You've Got Foetus on

Your Breath's reactivated "Wash It All Off" (#5 UK indy) followed.

Thirlwell moved to New York City in 1984, linking with Roli Mossimann and Norm Westberg of the Swans for the Wiseblood project, while 1987 brought the somewhat chilling notion of the Foetus All Nude Review — an unfulfilled promise which nevertheless delivered a stunning mini-album, *Bedrock* (#2 UK indy). The following year, Foetus Interruptus released the shattering *Thaw* (#3 UK indy), a set so savage it could never be recaptured on stage, as Thirlwell acknowledged when he went out on tour. He was billed as Foetus Corruptus.

With Thirlwell backed by a band including Westberg and another former Swan, bassist Algis Kizys, Prong drummer Ted Parsons and Pig drummer Raymond Watts, the highlight of the show was a version of "Faith Healer," Alex Harvey's classic concert-opener (in common with fellow Australians Nick Cave, Chris Bailey, and The Church, Thirlwell cites Harvey as both an influence and an idol).

It was an inspired choice, for there were indeed precious few people around who could more easily fit into that role. Spray gunning his own personal philosophies, daubing them like graffiti then leaving them hanging unanswered in the air, Foetus is one of rock's last remaining visionaries, its last surviving exorcist. Like the song says, "Your spirit never has to grieve — all you have to do's believe." One show at CBGBs was recorded for the double live *Male*, credited to Foetus in Excelsis Corruptus Deluxe.

Thirlwell himself never took his role in rock too seriously. "I try to view my work as an entity unto itself, not that I am like one of many, or that I'm part of this big fucking dinosaural bureaucracy who are trying to sell jeans, or sell themselves or whatever. If I ever considered myself part of it I think I'd kill myself," he remarked in 1989, shortly before launching his next alias, the monolithic Foetus Inc.

Thirlwell opened the 1990s with some of his most readily accessible recordings yet, linking with Lydia Lunch for a stone age metal retread of Blue Oyster Cult's "Don't Fear the Reaper" and a grinding horror rerun of the Beatles' "Why Don't We Do It in the Road." As Steroid Maximus, that same year brought a collection of what he described as "ethnic music from a civilization yet to be invented," *Quilimbo*; while Wiseblood's *Pedal to the Metal* rounded off a remarkable year.

Thirlwell was constantly in demand as a remixer through the early 1990s, Foetus-izing artists ranging from Megadeth to the Red Hot Chili Peppers, The Cult to Nine Inch Nails, and seemingly edging ever closer to mainstream acceptance with each one. Finally, in 1995, he signed his first ever major deal, with Sony, delivering the album *Gash* and two EPs, *Null* and *Void*. It was a bizarre, and short-lived relationship,

and once it lapsed, he seemed most content reappraising his back catalog for reissue. 1997's Foetus Symphony Orchestra project marked a rare pre-millennial return to action.

Foetus LPs

You've Got Foetus on Your Breath

8 Deaf (Self Immolation) 1981 Murderously percussive, yelping, crashing, and defiantly brutal, *Deaf* describes itself as a series of "indiscretions before a microphone" and includes the lyrically powerful (if musically, all rather similar) "Why It Can't Happen to Me," "What Have you Been Doing," and "Thank Heaven for Push Button Phones." Quite.

8 Ache (Self Immolation) 1982 "Join the Church of the Immaculate Preconception," invites the opening "Dying with My Boots On" and the Foetus Experience just gets more intense, until "Instead...I Became Anenome" wraps up the madness...with more madness.

Foetus on the Beach LP

[UNRELEASED TRIPLE ALBUM] 1982 (Self Immolation)

Scraping Foetus off the Wheel LPs

7 Hole (PVC) 1984 Foetus' US debut. According to Marc Almond's autobiography, this was initially scheduled for release under the Breath alias until the label expressed concern about the name. "OK," replied Thirlwell, "I'll change it." That's about all that he changed, though.

9 Nail (Homestead) 1985 "Theme..." and "Overture from Pigdom Come" catch Foetus in almost Wagnerian mood, conjuring the sound, if not the stench, of burning cities from the cacophony — perhaps his most visual album, certainly his most disturbing.

The Foetus of Excellence LP

The Foetus of Excellence (Self Immolation) 1985 A boxed set... without the set, simply a box designed to hold all of the Foetus vinyl releases on Some Bizzare up to this point, as well as a t-shirt.

The Foetus All-Nude Revue LP

7 Bedrock (Self Immolation) 1987 "Bedrock Swing" is the shocker — Foetus Unplugged and growling like a grizzly bear. Elsewhere it's business as usual, although the vinyl is the essential purchase — side one plays at 45, side two plays at 33, and it's so easy to forget, and so hard to notice, that it's different. Four sides for the price of two.

Wiseblood LP

5 Dirtdish (Some Bizzare) 1987 Not the full frontal assault one would hope to find, as ex-Swan Roli Mosimann, Lou Reed sidekick Robert Quine, and others descend to dilute the damage before it gets out. Disappointing.

The Flesh Volcano LP

7 Slut (Some Bizzare) 1987 Purposefully unlistenable, the original 12-inch EP ran through three proto-industrial slabs of clamor and clatter, and essentially highlighted how self-indulgent Foetus and Marc Almond could be when they wanted. Upgraded with four other collaborations, however, it also proved how devastating the partnership had the potential to be.

Foetus Interruptus LP

7 Thaw (Self Immolation) 1988 Absurdly symphonic once you pass through the inevitable firestorm of percussion — which itself is nothing new for Foetus ("Pigdom Come" is still coming), with the slurred "English Faggot" almost literally pushing a deep-fried southern psychopath into your living room.

Foetus Corruptus LP

7 Rife [LIVE] (Invisible) 1988 Two discs of mania from the *Thaw* tour. Members of Pig, Prong, and the Swans keep the peace.

Steroid Maximus LPs

7 Quilombo (Big Cat) 1991
7 Gondwanaland (Big Cat) 1992

Foetus in Excelsis Corruptus Deluxe LP

8 Male [LIVE] (Big Cat) 1992

Foetus LPs

7 Gash (Sony) 1995
5 Boil [LIVE] (Cleopatra) 1996

Foetus Symphony Orchestra LP

**8 Featuring Lydia Lunch (aka First Exit to Brooklyn) [LIVE]
(Thirsty Ear) 1997**

Selected Compilations and Archive Releases

Foetus Inc. LPs

9 Sink (Wax Trax!) 1989 The ultimate experience, drawing album tracks and singles together across 20 slabs of whooping vandalism. Breath's immortal "Wash It All Off" (Mary Poppins as metal machine assassin), "Shut" (All Nude Revue), "Himmelfahrtstransport" (Foetus in Your Bed), and the well-titled "Anxiety Attack" (Scraping Foetus) serve up an indispensable primer. Foetus 101.

FOO FIGHTERS

FORMED 1995 (Seattle, Washington)
ORIGINAL LINE-UP *Dave Grohl (b. 1/14/69 — vocals, guitar); Pat Smear (guitar); William Goldsmith (drums); Nate Mendel (bass)*

Following the collapse of Nirvana in April 1994, drummer Dave Grohl toured with Tom Petty and the Heartbreakers and worked as part of the so-called Backbeat Band, providing the soundtrack for the movie *Backbeat*. Adamant throughout that he would not be remembered as simply a drummer for hire, however, he reunited with latter-day Nirvana (and ex-Germs) guitarist Pat Smear, and with the rhythm section from the newly disbanded Seattle outfit Green Apple Quickstep, debuted his new band, Foo Fighters, in Portland, OR in March 1995.

Grohl had already proven himself as a songwriter, with his pre-Nirvana band, Scream (whose final album, 1990's *Fumble*, featured several of his compositions). His "Marigold" was a highlight of Nirvana's *In Utero* sessions (it appeared as the B-side to "Heart Shaped Box"), while the independent Simple Machines label had already released an album-length cassette of his own songs, *Pocketwatch*.

The Foo Fighters' debut album, too, would showcase Grohl's abilities, not only as a writer but also as a musician. Released on the band's own Roswell label, *Foo Fighters* (#23 US) was originally recorded as a demo, produced by Barrett Jones and featuring Grohl playing virtually every instrument. The only other featured musician was Greg Dulli of the Afghan Whigs, but despite its humble origins, *Foo Fighters* proved one of the year's most enduring albums and one which proved so successful that Foo Fighters would spend much of the next year on the road.

In Europe, "This is a Call" (#5 UK) became a major hit, with "I'll Stick Around" (#18 UK), "For All the Cows" (#28 UK), and "Big Me" (#19 UK) following. The band would also confound *Billboard*'s chart compilers with the seven-track *Big Me* EP (#175 US) which, packing too many songs to be considered a single, was eventually listed on the albums chart.

Work began on the Foo Fighters' second album in mid-1996 with producer Gil Norton. Again, personal tragedy flavored the songs — Grohl's marriage to his former high school girlfriend had collapsed and he admitted that he had two choices when the sessions began. Either he could sing about the things that mattered most to him, like Kurt Cobain's death and his own divorce, "or I could do the same thing as the last record and deny everything all over again." He chose the first course and *The Color and the Shape* (#10 US) emerged a far louder, and sometimes more disturbing, effort than its predecessor.

Drummer William Goldsmith quit shortly before the album was completed, leaving Grohl to play many of the drum parts on the record before Taylor Hawkins was recruited from Alanis Morrissette's band. This line-up did some recording on the eve of their first tour together, banging out five songs in one day for what Grohl envisioned as an immediate follow-up album; in the event, the project would go on hold for the next two years, during which time Smear, too, quit the band.

Grohl alone contributed a moody soundtrack to Paul Schrader's *Touch* movie, before reassembling the Foo Fighters with Hawkins and guitarist Frank Stahl, to begin work on their third album. With the band having quit Capitol, the set was recorded independently with producer Adam Kaspar during spring 1999, then shopped around during the summer. The band — now a Grohl/Hawkins duo following Stahl's departure — eventually signed with BMG.

There's Nothing Left to Lose (#10 US, #10 UK) was released in fall 1999, accompanied by the "Learn to Fly" single (#20 US), itself notable for a B-side cover of Pink Floyd's "Have a Cigar" sung by drummer Hawkins. The accompany-

ing tour saw the line-up augmented with No Use for a Name guitarist Chris Shiflett.

Foo Fighters LPs

6 Foo Fighters (Roswell/Capitol) 1995 Pop tunes, straightforward delivery, and the near solo Grohl's oldtime punk ethics make for an interesting first set, quite removed from the N word's sound.

8 The Colour and the Shape (Capitol) 1997 Now with band, Grohl gets fast and furious — a brilliant album of alt/pop/indy/guitar (etc.) music that outshines almost all its ilk.

9 There's Nothing Left to Lose (Roswell/BMG) 1999 An abrasive opener, "Stacked Actors" gives way to a maturely magnificent collection, highlighted by the major hit "Learn to Fly" and the reflective "Ain't It the Life."

FRANKIE GOES TO HOLLYWOOD

FORMED 1980 *(Liverpool, England)*
ORIGINAL LINE-UP *Holly Johnson (b. William Johnson, 2/19/60, Khartoum, Sudan — vocals); Paul Rutherford (b. 12/8/59 — vocals); Brian Nash (b. 3/20/63 — guitar); Mark O'Toole (b. 1/6/64 — bass); Peter Gill (b. 3/8/64 — drums)*

Holly Johnson was the 17-year-old Judy Garland clone who played bass for Big in Japan, Bill Drummond's pre-KLF exercise in punk psychedelics. He quit that band in June 1978, announcing that, with a little help from Ian Broudie, BIJ's drummer (and the future founder of Lightning Seeds), he was going solo. Two singles, "Yankee Rose" (1979) and "Hobo Joe" (1980) did little, however, and by late 1980, he had a new band, Hollycaust, which became Frankie Goes to Hollywood after Johnson saw a magazine article of that title.

Early recruits to the line-up, Peter Gill and Brian Nash, were ex-Sons of Egypt (a band Johnson occasionally danced with); Mark O'Toole was the brother of the Sons' guitarist, Jed. With Lizard Woman on second vocals, this quartet worked up a repertoire which included "Relax," "Two Tribes," and "Love's Got a Gun" and played their first show opening for Hambi and the Dance.

Among that band's backing singers was Paul Rutherford, ex-Spitfire Boys, a band formed by drummer Budgie (later Siouxsie and the Banshees) in emulation of his recently signed flatmates, the Yachts. When they folded, he and Budgie linked with Broudie, alongside Pete Wylie, in the Opium Eaters. Wylie quit following a handful of rehearsals and Rutherford followed, eventually moving to California to stay with his elder sister. He returned and joined Hambi, moving onto Frankie immediately after that show.

Dave Grohl of Foo Fighters

© Jim Steinfeldt/Chansley Entertainment Archives

Rutherford's arrival was the cue for Frankie to delve deeper into onstage visuals. Two local sisters, the Leatherpets, were recruited to be tied to posts and writhe through the band's set; the band members themselves began wearing hardcore leather and studs and with word of their bizarre presentation spreading fast, they were offered demo time by a curious Arista label. A version of "Two Tribes" was recorded but the label's interest cooled after catching sight of the band's full stage performance. Shortly after, Phonogram, too, pulled out after financing a demo comprising "Get Out of My Way Arsehole (Junk Funk)" and "Love's Got a Gun."

DJ John Peel gave the band a session, however; fellow Radio 1 anchor Steve Blackwell aired the Arista demos; and in December 1982, Frankie were featured on television's *The Tube*, filmed in Liverpool performing an absolutely uninhibited rendition of "Relax." The response was immediate, but a London showcase at the Camden Palace was a disaster, and Frankie returned to Liverpool.

They did record a second Radio 1 session, however, and it was this which brought them to the attention of producer Trevor Horn and journalist Paul Morley, then establishing their ZTT label. Signing the group, the duo then put them on ice while they confirmed ZTT's viability with an Art of Noise single. It was a success, so Horn took Johnson and Rutherford into the studio to record "Relax" with sessionmen (drawn from Ian Dury's Blockheads). Horn had little faith in the remainder of the band's musical abilities.

A vast production job saw "Relax" consume some 70,000 pounds worth of studio time, and the single was launched over Halloween 1983. It crept up the charts over the next month, but it was a return engagement on *The Tube* which finally gave the record the push it needed. It promptly jumped to #35; the band appeared on *Top of the Pops* and by mid-January 1984, Frankie were #6. And then the record was banned, after BBC radio DJ Mike Read announced he took offense at the gratuitous use of the words "suck" and "come" in the lyric. The rest of the BBC fell in line behind him, and the ensuing publicity did the rest. "Relax" (#10 US, #1 UK) would top the UK listings for five weeks.

It was followed by "Two Tribes" (#43 US, #1 UK), a song written during the 1981 Falklands War, again backed by tremendous production and an eye-catching video. ZTT also released the first installment in one of the greatest marketing campaigns of the age, the "Frankie Say..." T-shirts, each bearing a different, generally incendiary, slogan.

Frankie were everywhere. In the record stores, fresh remixes of "Relax" were still appearing in prodigious quantities and formats, to be joined by a similar deluge of "Two Tribes" variations. On television, the band made their post-"Relax" live debut on *The Tube*'s midsummer night special,

and stole the show. Boy George wrote vituperative letters to *Record Mirror* condemning Frankie for "telling people that it's naughty to be gay," and while the Leatherpets — dropped from the line-up shortly before fame finally arrived — were venting their jilted spleen in one daily newspaper, Johnson's parents were standing up for their boy in another. "Two Tribes" entered the UK chart at #1 and stayed there for seven weeks; in its wake, "Relax" returned to #2.

On October 19, 1984, Frankie released their first album, the double *Welcome to the Pleasuredome* (#33 US, #1 UK), to advance sales of almost a million and a half. By the end of 1984, less than three months worth of sales had pushed *Welcome to the Pleasure Dome* into the Top Ten bestselling albums of the decade so far.

Frankie played their first live shows of the year in Canada in November, moving on to the US, where *Saturday Night Live* was awaiting them on November 14, 1984. They returned home for Christmas to unleash their next single, "Power of Love" (#1 UK), and to prepare for their first UK tour in March 1985 (Europe and Japan followed). That same month, the final single from the *Pleasure Dome* album would be a heavily edited version of the sidelong title track (#48 US, #2 UK).

Work on Frankie's second album began immediately after the tour — the three musicians in the group desperate to disprove the popular belief that they had played little part in creating their debut album, although Horn himself later acknowledged that Gill, Nash, and O'Toole themselves could be heard "live" on only a handful of tracks and that the remainder was accomplished with studio trickery.

This second album would redress the balance, but the sessions began disastrously in Ireland, shifted chaotically to Ibiza, and then returned bad-temperedly to Ireland. From there, a studio in Holland played host to the increasingly disgruntled group, after which it was off to the Channel island of Jersey and ultimately back to Holland where *Liverpool* (#88 US, #5 UK) was finally completed in mid 1986 — two years after *Pleasure Dome*.

Rumors of a major rift within the band accompanied its release and the album itself didn't seem to disagree. Three distinctly unimpressive singles, "Rage Hard" (#4 UK), "Warriors of the Wasteland" (#19 UK), and "Watching the Wildlife" (#28 UK) struggled to even begin to match their predecessors; *Liverpool* itself sold a mere fraction of *Pleasure Dome* and early in 1987, the curtain finally fell. "Frankie Goes to Hollywood have had enough of each other, at least for now," announced a ZTT press release. "They can't stand the sight of each other."

Plans to reconvene in 1988 to begin work on their third album, *Family Tension*, never materialized, although O'Toole, Nash, and Gill remained together as the Shuffle

Brothers, gigging with vocalist Dee Harris (ex-Fashion). Later, in 1992, Nash and Grant Boult released the "Tearing My Soul Apart" single and recorded an unreleased album, *Enter the Bigger Reality*. The pair then formed Dr. Jolly's Salvation Circus with Reg Ab Gwyneth (bass) and Paul Pridmore (drums); this band debuted with a self-released EP in 1995, following it with the album *Ripe* in 1999.

Gill moved into dance production, working with Eden, Slapback, and Love Station among others, while Johnson launched a solo career in 1989 and enjoyed a hit with "Love Train" (#65 US, #4 UK) and the album *Blast* (#1 UK). Further singles "Americanos" (#4 UK), "Atomic City" (#18 UK), and "Heaven's Here" (#62 UK) followed.

Rutherford also scored a minor hit in 1990 with "Oh World" (#61 UK); he then formed a new band, Pressure Zone, with Tommy Payne, Marco Perry, and Dave Clayton, but received little attention — a fate which also awaited Johnson's next album, *Dreams That Money Can't Buy* in 1992, and that despite a minor hit with the single "Where Has Love Gone' (#73 UK) in late 1991.

In 1993, the tenth anniversary of Frankie's emergence was celebrated with a string of reissued and remixed singles recreating the band's original glory — "Relax" (#5 UK), "Two Tribes" (#16 UK), "Power of Love" (#10 UK), and "Welcome to the Pleasuredome" (#18 UK) were joined by a greatest hits package, *Bang* (#4 UK), and a reactivated *Welcome to the Pleasuredome* (#24 UK; six years later, reissued once again, it climbed to #16 UK).

The year also saw Johnson announce that he had been diagnosed with AIDS, a discovery which prompted him to pen a hard-hitting and controversial autobiography. The singer later admitted he'd never have written it if he'd known he was going to live to see it published!

Frankie Goes to Hollywood LPs

8 Welcome to the Pleasuredome (ZTT) 1984 In the days when image was everything, Frankie briefly ruled the world... *not* via their image, but through their vision — which, of course, was the image. And though they required a lot of help bringing that vision to reality (not least of all from producer Trevor Horn), what a reality it became. Sexual fantasies (the title track, "Relax") came to life; war was reduced to surreal horror ("War," "Two Tribes"); love to religious intensity ("Power of Love"); and that was just the first four singles. But then came the rest of the double album and the momentum was quickly lost. A Springsteen cover, a C&W spacerocker, some funk, some soul...by the time they reached the ballads, Frankie seemed little more than a generic electro-pop group with better presentation than most. Which, of course, was what they were. For just a few magic moments, though, the world really was their oyster.

3 Liverpool (ZTT) 1986 Left to their own devices, divisive and destabilized, even the hits have been forgotten.

Selected Compilations and Archive Releases

8 Bang! The Greatest Hits (ZTT) 1994
8 Reload! Frankie the Whole 12 Inches (ZTT) 1995 All but interchangeable, although the 12-inchers are longer.

Holly Johnson LPs

7 Blast (UNI) 1989

4 Dreams That Money Can't Buy (MCA) 1991

5 Soulstream (Pleasuredome) 1999 Dance-heavy set featuring a powerful-but-needless remake of FGTH's "Power of Love."

Selected Compilations and Archive Releases

5 Hollelujah (MCA) 1990 *Blast*-heavy remix compilation.

Further Reading
A Bone in My Flute by Holly Johnson (Century Books, 1994)

FREESTYLERS

FORMED 1992 *(London, England)*
ORIGINAL LINE-UP *Aston Harvey (vocals, electronics); Matt Cantor (vocals, electronics)*

Aston Harvey and Matt Cantor first got together in 1992 with a series of studio experiments fusing electro, breakbeats, hip-hop, and Afrika Bambaataa, a blend which would emerge as the Freestylers' first single, "Drop the Boom." The band's name was a tribute to the first sample they ever used, Freestyle's "Don't Stop the Rock."

The duo's manifesto was to make "instant music" — as Aston complained, "too many dance artists are making jazz albums because they feel it's the mature thing to do." Taking their cue from the early Beastie Boys, Freestylers had no intention of seeming "mature," and their vision took off fast.

The *Uprock* EP, and the *FSUK2* remix compilation for the Ministry of Sound kept British dancefloors spinning, while "AK48," a retitled version of "Drop the Boom," was an American club hit.

It was the *Adventures in Freestyle* EP which broke the band in Britain. Grooverider, the Dub Pistols, and Robbie Hardkiss all turned in remixes for the club 12-inch of the self-defining "B Boy Stance," while the song was boosted further after the Freestylers were forced to re-record one lyric following complaints from Oasis' Noel Gallagher — the original lyric borrowed from his "Wonderwall."

Further singles "Ruffneck" and "Warning" followed "B Boy Stance" up the UK chart, while their US debut, "Here We Go," investigated the same Ultramagnetic MCs song Prodigy plundered for "Smack My Bitch Up" ("Give the Drummer Some"). The group's debut album rounded up all their 45s to date.

Freestylers LPs

8 We Rock Hard (Mammoth) 1999 True to their name, the Freestylers wheel freely through styles — hiphop, dancehall, rock, funk, and early electropop — cutting them up and mixing them down in a totally fresh way, then spinning them over old-school beats.

FRONT 242

FORMED 1980 *(Belgium)*
ORIGINAL LINE-UP *Jean-Luc de Meyer (vocals, drum machine); Patrick Codenys (keyboards); Daniel Bressanutti (keyboards)*

Originally formed as Prothese, Front 242 initially pursued a Euro-dance direction (the so-called New Beat sound), characterized by their "Principles" debut single, a club hit across Europe. Further singles "U Men," "Two in One" in 1982, and "Endless Riddance" in 1983, and the album *Geography* followed, but it was with the subsequent arrival of Richard 23 and the departure of Daniel Bressanutti that the band's sound begin to harden.

The restructured line-up debuted with the *No Comment* mini-album, while the club success of the singles "No Shuffle" and "Politics of Pressure" attracted the attention of Trevor Horn's ZTT label. Fearing that they would lose all independence if they accepted the offer, the band turned the label down and signed instead with Belgium's own Play It Again Sam, moving deeper into the still largely vacant industrial dance arena.

1987 saw the modern Front 242 finally emerge with *Official Version*, a record which the band claimed was the first to capture the true nature of their stage show. Signing to Wax Trax in the States, who promptly reissued the group's Belgian catalog, Front 242 immediately began picking up press in the US. A tour with Ministry (whose Revolting Cocks side project would also feature Jean-Luc De Meyer and 23) went down phenomenally well and in 1988, Front 242 scored a major club hit with "Headhunters (V1.0)" from their next album, *Front By Front*.

The band maintained the barrage onto *Tyranny for You* (#95 US, #49 UK), their first for Sony and their chart breakthrough in 1991. Two years later, Front 242 returned to the UK chart with the *Religion* EP (#46 UK), featuring three separate Prodigy remixes — including the premonitory "Bitch Slapper" mix.

The easily decoded 06.21.03.11. *Up Evil* (#166 US, #44 UK) and 05.22.09.12 *Off* (#46 UK) albums arrived in 1993 (a live album from the accompanying tour, *Live Code* would follow in 1994), but that same year saw the band members break apart temporarily, with De Meyer promptly forming two new projects.

Cobalt 60 linked him with Kriegsbereit mainstay Dominique Lallement and live guitarist Robert Wilcocks (ex-Sleeping Dogs Wake); the Cyber-Tech (C-Tec) project was a partnership with Jonathan Sharp (Bio-Tec) and Ged Denton (Crisis NTI). Sharp would be replaced by Cubanate's Marc Heal shortly before C-Tec's first album, *Darker*.

Front 242 reconvened in June 1997 for a European tour with Sabotage drummer Tim Kroker. The outing spread into the new year and a US tour with Project Pitchfork, documented on the *Re-Boot* live album (C-Tec would also tour America during the year). Front 242 would tour again in 1999 supporting the *Modem Angels* tribute album.

Front 242 LPs

9 Geography (New Dance — Belg) 1982 Drilling their own niche into the electronic scene, Front 242 place themselves on the extreme edge of accessibility, balancing precariously between experimentalism and pop. Incorporating the construction sounds of industrial, the keyboard wizardry of Krautrock, the dancefloor beats of the New Romantics, and the gloomy overtones of post-punk, Front 242 then finish the songs off with varying degrees of synthi-pop. *Geography* boasts three dancey gems still being sampled (or spun) today and a clutch of other crucial songs which would be equally influential outside the club scene.

7 No Comment (Another Side — Belg) 1984 Front 242 begin experimenting with a harder sound by toughening up the rhythms, giving much of this six track mini-LP a strident, almost militaristic quality. A few of the tracks still pull towards pop, but the rest are darker and much more aggressive.

7 Official Version (Wax Trax) 1987

8 Front by Front (Wax Trax) 1988 It was "Headhunter" that cemented Front 242's reputation at the head of the EBM pack, but most of this album is equally strong, splattering across the grooves like an anti-personal bomb. *Front* is inherently dance-friendly, but aggressive and threatening too, with lyrics attacking society's hypocrisy and power plays.

9 Tyranny (For You) (Epic) 1991 Duran Duran wanted to be the band you'd dance to when the bomb dropped, but it's Front 242 who captured the sound just seconds before the explosion. The single, "Tragedy for You," is a New Romantic club crowd preparing to go off to the killing fields while the rest of *Tyranny* reverberates with the sounds of the ensuing battle. Fired by the powerful rhythms — some dance floor orientated, others the drumbeats of war — all pound with the heart-clenching throb of a military tattoo. The songs themselves create vivid doomscapes where artillery and mortars seem to fall in the distance, and men march to death or glory as the sounds of a not-so-distant battle echoes in the dark. The album's release coincided with the Gulf War, to add ironic fuel to the already explosive ingredients.

7 06.21.03.11 Up Evil (Epic) 1993

8 05.22.09.12 Off (Epic) 1993 Two companion albums, *Off* includes the tracks considered too extreme for *Evil*, although the link between the two is made even clearer by some startling remixes of *Evil* tracks. Side by side, the two have an ebb and flow which is both consistent and disconcerting, as songs appear, disappear, then resurface in very different form. If *Evil* proved just how popular techno can sound, *Off* is the closing argument for Front 242's place on the cutting edge of industrio-techno.

8 Live Code (Play It Again Sam) 1995 Recorded live in Utrecht in October 1993, a tight set of classic songs old and new captures the intensity, energy and excitement of Front 242 onstage.

7 Re-Boot Live 98 (Metropolis) 1998 After five years of inactivity, Front 242 regrouped for a European tour during the winter of 1998, captured on *Re-Boot*, and proving that the band had lost none of its drive or power.

8 Headhunter 2000 (Metropolis) 1998

Selected Compilations and Archive Releases

8 Back Catalogue 1981–85 (Wax Trax!) 1987 Compiling material from the band's first years (1981–85) via tracks from their first four albums and EPs (the CD reissue adds two live tracks as well), *Catalogue* is best aimed at younger fans looking for an intro into the seminal early work.

6 Mut@ge Mix@ge (RRE) 1996

C-Tec LP

7 Cyber-Tech (Fifth Column) 1995 Front 242's Jean Luc DeMeyer gives voice to C-Tec, a project not entirely removed from his main gig. The insistent beats drive the record onto the dance floor, while the music cascades all around. Many of the (untitled) tracks are closer to songs than soundscapes, although there's plenty of those as well as the album sets off through a musical tour of electro moods and sub-genres from ambient to industrial.

FUGAZI

FORMED *1987 (Washington DC)*
ORIGINAL LINE-UP *Guy Picciato (b. 9/17/65, Washington DC — vocals); Ian MacKaye (4/16/62, Washington DC — guitar, vocals); Joe Lally (12/3/63, Rockville, MD — bass); Brendan Canty (3/9/66, Teaneck, NJ — drums)*

Former Minor Threat vocalist Ian MacKaye formed Fugazi following the break-up of his mid-1980s band Embrace, linking with Rites of Spring members Brendan Canty and Guy Picciato (MacKaye had produced that band for his Dischord label). The new group debuted in a church basement at the Wilson Center in Washington, DC on September 3, 1987; three weeks later, on September 26, they played a second ecclesiastical gig, at St. Stevens Church, and by the end of the year were regularly traveling around the north east for shows.

The band's name was taken from Mark Baker's Vietnamese war study *'Nam* — period slang for "a fucked up situa-tion" — a term which seemed increasingly appropriate as the band went on. Although Fugazi continued to espouse the cheap, all-ages admission policies which had characterized both Minor Threat and Rites of Spring, MacKaye was not afraid to condemn certain other of the rituals which accompanied so-called hardcore shows. He was a fierce opponent of slam dancing, not only for its brutality but also because, "if I was a teenager, I would not be doing a dance that's been going on for ten years." Youth, like music, he insisted, was about challenging the past — not falling meekly in line behind it. Fugazi's goal was to ensure that happened.

The band's first full US tour followed in April 1988 and Fugazi would end up spending close to a year on the road in the US and Europe before debuting a seven song EP, the Henry Rollins-produced *Fugazi* in fall 1988. *Margin Walker*, again overseen by Rollins, followed in the new year, reiterating its predecessor's insistence that Fugazi's first accomplishment had been to put the band members' individual pasts far behind them, musically and culturally.

MacKaye also launched a series of fascinating extra-curricular activities, linking with Ministry for the Pailhead project, producing Bikini Kill's eponymous EP, and collaborating with Sonic Youth. He was also heavily involved, of course, in the continued running and upkeep of Dischord. But still, like Minor Threat, Fugazi were devoted to live work, preferring to spend their time on the road around the world, rather than in the studio. Tours of America slipped into one another, European outings were exhaustive. Though another EP, *3 Songs*, did arrive in 1989, it would be early 1990 before the band released a full-length album of new material. And then it was back onto the road again.

With each new release selling in the region of 150,000 copies at a budget price little more than half the cost of a major label release, Fugazi — and Dischord — established themselves as a veritable anomaly, even within the world of alternative rock. The mainstream rock press was almost completely spurned; major label attempts to absorb Dischord were sent packing; the occasional claim that Fugazi were on the verge of "crossing over" would be met with undisguised disdain. It was a cliché to say that all Fugazi needed were "the kids," but it was true. The band were utterly self-sustaining, and owed absolutely nothing to the "conventional" music industry.

Over the next three years, *Repeater* would be followed by two further albums of blistered abrasion, *Steady Diet of Nothing* (#63 UK), which won them Best Album and Best Band WAMMIES from the Washington Area Music Association; and *In for the Kill Taker* (#153 US, #24 UK), in 1993, the year *Rolling Stone* readers voted them best Live Band.

Red Medicine (#126 US, #18 UK), in mid-1995, preceded the band's longest ever tour, a mammoth, two-year worldwide jaunt which wrapped up with the band's third, and longest, tour of Australia and New Zealand — 19 shows spread across four weeks. It was there that MacKaye caught pneumonia, and Fugazi were forced to cancel shows for the first time in their career.

It was becoming clear, however, that all four members had lives outside of the band — Canty and Joe Lally both married, with Canty becoming a father soon after. The band's lightest ever live schedule saw them play just a handful of US gigs during 1997, before rescheduling the lost Australian and New Zealand gigs in July, and making a short visit to South America. Then it was back to DC for an anniversary show in the church basement where they played their first ever live show, before lapsing into a very uncharacteristic silence.

It would be April 1998 before Fugazi re-emerged with a new album, *End Hits*, and US tours in May, July, and November; the band also announced the 1999 appearance of *Instrument*, a decade-spanning feature film (and accompanying soundtrack album) about the band directed by independent film maker Jem Cohen. Gigs arranged to follow the release, however, suffered a string of mid-December 1999 cancellations, brought on by a family medical emergency.

Also see the entry for "MINOR THREAT" on page 499.

Fugazi LPs

8 Repeater (Dischord) 1990 Ready...steady...flashpoint — this album takes off from track one and never slows down. The set is unrelenting in its immediacy and its post punky edge ensures that fast and furious is the way to go. More focused than the band's first two EPs, *Repeater* proves that the past can be pushed into the future and not become stillborn.

7 Steady Diet of Nothing (Dischord) 1991 Older but not softer, McKaye takes the band to new heights, razoring hardcore punk together with a rock diet and mashing it all up with his own manifestos, so deliberately placed to stick those who label him "preachy." From "Long Division" to "Exit Only" and "Latin Roots," Fugazi are doing fine.

7 In for the Kill Taker (Dischord) 1993 As raw as its predecessor was polished, *Kill Taker* is an intentionally slapdash affair, the DIY ethics not only a return to basics but also a refreshing blast in an overproduced world.

7 Red Medicine (Dischord) 1995 Possibly the oddest thing this band has done, as they pull in a myriad of sounds and styles from dub and middle east melody to jazz-tinged piano, and lighten their customary tendency to then ram the whole thing down your throat. Surprisingly accessible.

6 End Hits (Dischord) 1998 Intense, intense, and intense again, Fugazi go once more into the breach to bring that good old hardcore sound back to the masses.

Selected Compilations and Archive Releases

6 Combined (Dischord) 1989 A reissue of *Fugazi* and *Margin Walker*, the band's first two EPs.

6 Instrument Soundtrack (Dischord) 1999 The soundtrack to Jem Cohen's documentary, the album cobbles together old demos and practice tapes, all previously unreleased.

G

GADJITS

FORMED 1996 (Kansas City, MO)
ORIGINAL LINE-UP Brandon Phillips (vocals, guitar); Zachary Phillips (bass); Adam Phillips (drums)

Heralding the buoyant Kansas City ska scene of the early-mid 1990s, the Gadjits emerged in 1996 with the closing track on Jump Up's *Return of American Skathic* compilation (the fourth such volume). The children of a jazz teacher, the three brothers had an average age 15, and their solitary track, "Corpse I Fell in Love With," clashed lo-fi energy with rampant immature ambition.

Augmented by keyboard player Heidi Blobaum, the Gadgits followed through with their self-released debut album, *Da Gravy On Your Grits*, and with that under their belt, they were finally able to snag some gigs around their hometown, drawing large, increasingly vocal crowds as they opened for visiting heroes Let's Go Bowling, the Skatalites, and Rancid.

It was at the latter, where they threw a cover of Operation Ivy's "Unity" into their set, that they came to the attention of the headliners' Tim Armstrong, then in the process of establishing his Hellcat label. He signed the band, and the ensuing album, *At Ease* (recorded with Hillary Allen replacing the college-bound Blobaum), indicated how much the Gadgits had matured in a very short time — a process which was furthered by a powerful showing on the 1998 Warped tour, and 1999's *Wish We Never Met*.

The Gadjits LPs

8 Da Gravy On Yo Grits (Joco Ska) 1996 Playing to their strengths, The Gadjits' deceptively simple songs are fleshed out by tight musicianship and lyrics that go straight to the heart of teen life. Inevitably lo-fi and a bit immature, good time ska ingenuously spins rhythms through a lighthearted lyricism and irresistible get-up-and-skank joie de vivre. Half the songs start out like they want to be "Louie Louie" (or else "You're The One That I Want"), but they get distracted so quickly that you can't hold that against them.

8 At Ease (Hellcat) 1998 Lurching gracefully through the landscapes of lunacy, tackling "Mustang Sally" with joyous aplomb (and turning the otherwise harrowing "Beautiful Girl" into a gleeful bounce), the Gadjits are neither true to ska's first wave, nor traitors to its third. Rather, they are lovable lunks with an eye for manic melody, Aqua without the gimmicks, Hanson without the jockstraps, the Spice Girls without the chronological impairment. The sound of new America indeed.

7 Wish We Never Met (Hellcat) 1999

GALAXIE 500

FORMED 1987 (Boston, MA)
ORIGINAL LINE-UP Naomi Yang (b. 9/15/64 — bass); Damon Krukowski (b. 9/6/63 — drums); Dean Wareham (b. 8/1/63, New Zealand — guitar)

Having met at high school in New York in 1981, Dean Wareham, Damon Krukowski, and Naomi Yang first started playing together after all three relocated to Boston for college studies. Originally, Wareham and Krukowski gigged alone locally with a succession of punk-influenced student bands, before Wareham returned to New York. Yang took up bass following Wareham's return to form a new band with Krukowski in 1987.

Opting to remain a trio, the band named themselves after a mid-60s Ford, and played their first ever show at a party thrown to mark Wareham's permanent departure from Manhattan. On August 11, still in New York, the band cut their first demo tape, and on October 1, played their official first gig at Chet's Last Call in Boston.

The show was fairly disappointing — the Saturday night audience condemned the group as wimps, and treated them accordingly. However, with local radio picking up on their demo, Galaxie 500 linked with producer Kramer in February 1988, to record the single "Tugboat."

The reverb heavy sound would become a Galaxie 500 trademark, setting the stage for a debut album, *Today*, which Britain's *Melody Maker* hailed as "an astonishing debut by anyone's standards." The band toured the UK later that year, where local critics effortlessly included them in the so-called Boston sound characterized by the Pixies and Throwing Muses, irrespective of the band's inability to land a US record deal. The one label which did show an interest, Slash, pulled out when Galaxie 500 refused to augment their set with a light show.

In New York for the 1989 New Music Seminar, Galaxie 500 reunited with Kramer to record 1989's *Blue Thunder* EP and a new album, November's *On Fire* (#7 UK indy) — featuring an astonishing cover of Joy Division's "Ceremony." When the band appeared in Manchester during their next UK tour (opening for the Sundays), Peter Hook visited them backstage, and gave Yang a quick lesson in how to play the song correctly.

Over the next six months, the band toured Europe and Britain heavily, returning home only long enough to record their third album, *This is Our Music*. Then it was back to the

UK for a festival tour, followed by Galaxie 500's first ever American tour, opening for the Cocteau Twins in March 1991. Tours of Europe and Japan were next on the agenda, and thoughts were already turning towards a fourth album when Wareham — who had moved back to New York during the spring — announced he was quitting the band. Galaxie 500 played their final show at Bowdoin College, Maine.

Wareham would re-emerge alongside Chills bassist Justin Harwood and Feelies drummer Stan Demeski in Luna, while Yang and Krukowski continued on as Damon and Naomi. Galaxie 500, meanwhile, would be remembered through an all-encompassing 1996 box set — an indication of how thoroughly their sparse sound had influenced a new generation of low-fi performers. The wheel finally turned full circle in 1999, when the band that was named for a car suddenly found its music being used to sell cars — "Instrumental" (from *Today*) was picked up for use in an Acura commercial.

Galaxie 500 LPs

7 Today (Aurora) 1987 Re-introducing the art of dirgy guitar and honest emotion bungled by lo-fi production, to a generation spoon fed on slick packaging and the new wave's neon glitter. The cover of Jonathan Richman's "Don't Let Our Youth Go to Waste" really doesn't have much to worry about.

8 On Fire (Rough Trade) 1989 It's amazing just what ethereally-grounded magic can be conjured from plain ol' drums, guitar and bass, and a bucketful of reverb. Galaxie 500 settle into their sound, turning in a moody performance that still made toes tap.

7 This is Our Music (Rough Trade) 1990 A super confident 500 foundered just a little with a polished sound which — although good — does lack some of the verve of their earlier work. However, the dynamic percussion and dreamy melodic waves still ripple through layers of rich guitar — allowing the band to continue to soar where others lost their nerve.

Selected Compilations and Archive Releases

9 Galaxie 500 (Rykodisc) 1996 Rounding up the band's entire catalog, a voyage of rediscovery is flagged by some remarkable moments of wild premonition, and if the box serves any purpose whatsoever, it's a reminder that even in the '80s, failure was not necessarily a sign of failure.

7 Copenhagen [LIVE] (Rykodisc) 1997 Live set recorded in 1990 for Danish Public Radio is a mix of 500 classics plus covers of Yoko Ono's "Listen, The Snow is Falling", and the Velvet's "Here She Comes Now."

8 Portable Galaxie 500 (Rykodisc) 1998 On the heels of the box set comes, a well-designed best of highlighting a band who deserved much more. It's all here, from those honest vocal harmonies and that good indy guitar to the gorgeous sax on "Blue Thunder."

Luna LPs

6 Lunapark (Elektra) 1992
6 Bewitched (Elektra) 1994
5 Penthouse (Elektra) 1995
5 Pup Tent (Elektra) 1997
6 The Days of Our Nights (Jericho) 1999

Damon and Naomi LPs

7 More Sad Hits (Shimmy Disc) 1992
7 The Wondrous World of (Sub Pop) 1995
6 Playback Singers (Sub Pop) 1998

GANG OF FOUR

FORMED 1977 *(Leeds, England)*
ORIGINAL LINE-UP *Jon King (b. 6/8/55 — vocals); Andy Gill (b. 1/1/56 — guitar); Hugo Burnham (b. 3/25/56 — drums); Dave Allen (b. 12/23/55, Kendal, England — bass)*

Named, of course, for the leaders of China's cultural revolution, Gang of Four formed around fine art students Andy Gill, Hugo Burnham, and Jon King, plus Dave Allen, recruited through an ad calling for "a fast rivvum & blues bass player" for "a fast rivvum and blues band."

Debuting in the basement of Leeds Corn Exchange in May 1977, the group's first demos attracted Bob Last, head of the Edinburgh-based Fast label, home to another Leeds band, the Mekons. *Damaged Goods*, the band's 1978 debut EP, caused an immediate stir, a post-punk political manifesto which raised itself leagues above the now-traditional railing against unemployment and the government, set to a jerking, irregular funk soundtrack characterized by two, even three, voices working in strict counterpoint. It was a unique, and disconcerting approach, and within months, Gang of Four signed to EMI, and released the crucial "At Home He's a Tourist" (#58 UK).

With the single rising up the chart, the band were invited to perform on *Top of the Pops*, only to be informed at the last moment that they would have to change a lyric in the song, substituting "rubbish" for "rubbers (condoms)." The band refused; Dire Straits took their place (and scored their first hit as a consequence); and "Tourist" fell out of the chart.

Entertainment (#45 UK), the band's first album, followed, alongside their first American tour, opening for the Buzzcocks. History insists that Gang of Four never rose above cult status in the US, but the response to this first exposure to the band was so positive that, over the next two years, Gang of Four seemed constantly to be on the road in the US.

Their second album, 1981's *Solid Gold* (#190 US, #52 UK), too, had a definite Stateside sheen to it — recorded with American funk producer Jimmy Douglass, *Solid Gold* would spawn the club sensation "Paralyzed," and was swiftly followed by the *Another Day Another Dollar* mini-album (#195 US). However, the band's punishing live workload pushed Allen out in late 1981; he formed Shriekback, and was replaced first by ex-Talking Heads sideman Busta Jones, then by Sara Lee, from Robert Fripp's League of Gentlemen.

Early 1982 brought what threatened to be Gang of Four's most successful single yet, "I Love a Man in Uniform" (#65 UK). An instant club hit, it crossed effortlessly into both the gay and electro scenes, but earned the band another UK ban when the Falklands War rolled around, and the song's sentiments suddenly sounded sour against the required backdrop of patriotism.

The accompanying album, *Songs of the Free* (#175 US, #61 UK), too, collapsed early, and once again the bulk of the band's attention was directed towards the US. Gang of Four were one of the highlights of the 1982 US Festival and their tours were selling out larger venues every time. But a rift between Gill and King on the one hand, Burnham on the other, was growing — for 18 months, Burnham had been doubling as the band's manager, arousing conflicts which the group's principal writers no longer wished to contend with. The bassist quit, later resurfacing in Illustrated Man, with erstwhile Japan keyboard player Rob Dean, and Roger Mason of Tubeway Army. The band cut one self-titled EP for Capitol, in 1984, then disappeared.

Gang of Four continued on as a trio, recording the lush *Hard* (#168 US), highlighted by the inescapable "Woman Town," but the progressive dismantling of the band's original unity and ethic had gone too far. Gang of Four broke up in May 1983, following one last US tour — a live album, *At the Palace*, preserved their sadly ragged final show for posterity.

Gill moved immediately into production, overseeing the Red Hot Chili Peppers' debut album — and horrifying his clients when he dismissed their beloved *Entertainment* and *Solid Gold* by confessing that he didn't know what he was doing on either. In 1988, however, he and King reunited with a new Gang of Four record in mind, although it would be three years before the heavily programmed *Mall* appeared, with new bassist Gail Ann Dorsey replacing the B-52's-bound Lee. (Dorsey would subsequently join David Bowie's band).

A tour with Public Enemy and Sisters of Mercy followed through the summer of 1991, but poor ticket sales saw it curtailed early, and the King and Gill team returned to the studio to work on a movie soundtrack for director Peter Hall. This would eventually metamorphose into 1995's *Shrinkwrapped* album, Gang of Four's final statement.

King quit the music industry following *Shrinkwrapped*; Gill returned to production, handling Jesus Lizard's *Blue*; he would also co-write and co-produce INXS vocalist Michael

Hutchence's solo album, the post-humously (1999)-released eponymous set.

Original bassist Allen, meanwhile, relocated to Los Angeles, where he founded his own World Domination label, and led the bands Elastic Purejoy and Low Pop Suicide.

Gang of Four LPs

9 **Entertainment (WB) 1979** Savage convoluted rhythms dovetail with incendiary manifestos for the decade still to come — few proved workable, fewer still came true, but just for a moment ("Tourist," "Anthrax," "Damaged Goods"), Gang of Four were the future at hand.

8 **Solid Gold (WB) 1981** "Paralyzed" and "What We All Want" picked up where *Entertainment* stopped having fun, but the cracks in the make-up were already showing through.

7 **Songs of the Free (WB) 1982** The dance friendly "Man in Uniform" not withstanding, an oddly over-rated album — oddly, because less than half of it even sounded like the gang. Billy Idol fans, though, were happy.

4 **Hard (WB) 1983**

3 **At the Palace (Mercury) 1984** Recorded live on the last night of the band's final tour, the most quintessential dance band caught on a very bad night indeed. A hippo-like "Tourist" and a sonic boom "Poverty" are the twin peaks of the band's boredom, but "Damaged Goods" at least sounds sincere.

4 **Mall (Polydor) 1991** Occasionally workable reunion album, but Gill and King clearly yearn for something more than the anonymity of the music at hand.

3 **Shrinkwrapped (Castle — UK) 1995**

Selected Compilations and Archive Releases

8 **Peel Sessions (Dutch East Ind) 1990** Utterly uncompromising 11-track epic, undaunted by the passage of time.

6 **A Brief History of the 20th Century (WB) 1990** Reasonable smattering of the band's best, undermined by the inclusion of some of their worst.

9 **A Hundred Flowers Bloom (Rhino) 1998** A retrospective that never lets up. Previously unissued cuts from 1980/81 represent the Gang's musical peak, running older material through the wringer of discontent which would ultimately shatter the band; hits and bits from the remainder of the career pose a well-chosen study in priceless cynicism.

Dave Allen/Shriekback LPs

8 **Care (WB) 1983** Precisely the sum of its parts, XTC buzzing, Gang of Four crunching, drum machine precision, and an unforgettable post-punk fuzz frenzy.

6 **Jam Science (Arista — UK) 1984** A careless successor, forged in a deranged approximation of a Eurodisco factory — oddly reminiscent of Gang of Four's own latest convolutions, but not so tormented by slackness and polish.

6 **Oil and Gold (Island) 1985** The club hit "Nemesis," all big guitars and well-chosen title, bangs *Oil and Gold* into a league it might never otherwise have touched. Deceptive, then, but invigorating.

6 **Big Night Music (Island) 1986** Closer to an ambient jazz piano suite than the Shriekback of old, a weird but weirdly rewarding listen, with future Sky Cries Mary guitarist Mike Cozzi pulling some especially fascinating shadows into play.

7 **Go Bang (Island) 1988** Joined by Tackhead's Doug Wimbish, Andrews alone remains from the original guerilla pack, but somehow he scratches back the lost territory and turns in Shriekback's most consistently entertaining album since the beginning.

Selected Compilations and Archive Releases

7 **The Best Of (Kaz — UK) 1985**

6 **The Best of Vol. 2 (Kaz — UK) 1988**

7 **The Dancing Years (Island) 1990**

Dave Allen/King Swamp LPs

7 **King Swamp (Virgin) 1988**

6 **Wiseblood (Virgin) 1990**

Dave Allen/Low Pop Suicide LPs

7 **On the Cross of Commerce (World Domination) 1993**

7 **The Death of Excellence (World Domination) 1993**

Dave Allen/Elastic Purejoy LPs

7 **Elastic Purejoy (World Domination) 1994** Dave Allen and friends spin out an introspective album with an experimental edge, much influenced by the likes of Eno and *Low*-era Bowie — with a cover of the former's "Stiff" to drive home the point.

5 **Clutter of Pop (World Domination) 1996**

GARBAGE

FORMED *1994 (Madison, WI)*

ORIGINAL LINE-UP *Shirley Manson (b. Glasgow — vocals); Steve Marker (b. New York — guitar); Duke Erikson (b. Doug Erikson — bass, keyboards); Butch Vig (b. Brian Vig, Viroqua, WI — percussion)*

Butch Vig, Duke Erikson, and Steve Marker were already a highly respected production and remix team when they decided to form their own band in 1994. For the past two years, they had already been recording their own compositions, in the guise of remixes for other bands. From there, it was only a tiny step towards recording them for their own records. "It was really fun," Vig reflected, "and...that was the sensibility for us to start a band."

Vocalist Shirley Manson was recruited after the trio caught her band Angelfish's video, "Shock Me," on MTV —

previously, she sang back-up with '80s cult heroes Goodbye Mr. Mackenzie. Angelfish, in fact, was a MacKenzie spin-off, formed after the band was dropped by MCA in 1992.

Manson was originally flown over as just one of several different vocalists to contribute to the Smart Studios project — modestly named Garbage. She fit perfectly into the set-up, however, and the earlier plan was abandoned.

Intending never to work live, "because that would really free us up to record tons of... samples and loops and all sorts of strange, processed sound effects and weird guitar over dubs," as Vig put it, Garbage debuted with "Vow," included within Britain's *Volume* various artists series in March 1995. Once their first self-titled album was complete, however, the band realized the only way to promote it properly was to tour, and Garbage spent 14 months on the road, through 1995–96. Bassist Daniel Shulman joined the group for live work, which included appearances at the VH-1 Fashion Festival, the MTV Europe Music Awards, and a lengthy world tour with the Smashing Pumpkins.

Beginning in July 1996, four singles, "Vow" (#97 US), "Subhuman" (#50 UK), "Only Happy When It Rains" (#55 US, #29 UK), and "Queer" (#13 UK) proved hits through that first year of operations. *Garbage* (#20 US, #12 UK), backed

© Jim Steinfeldt/Chansley Entertainment Archives

up by slavering critical response, eventually went platinum, with "Stupid Girl" (#24 US, #4 UK) breaking the band into the singles chart in July 1996. Riding a sample of the Clash's "Train in Vain" with Manson ad-libbing lyrics (and originally recorded in Marker's basement), "Stupid Girl" would also top a number of critical year end best-of polls. (The band earned three 1997 Grammy nominations.)

"#1 Crush," contributed to the *Romeo and Juliet* soundtrack album, became a #1 Modern Rock hit in November 1996, while radical remixes from Tricky, Massive Attack, and Goldie saw "Milk" (#10 UK) give Garbage a second UK Top 10 hit that same month.

Garbage themselves would begin work on their second album during summer 1997 for a May 1998 release. "Push It" (#52 US, #9 UK) a single rooted around the refrain of the Beach Boys' "Don't Worry Baby," was an immediate hit. "I Think I'm Paranoid" (#9 UK) and "I'm Special" (#52 US, #15 UK) followed effortlessly, while the album itself, *Version 2.0* (#13 US, #1 UK), would go platinum in the UK that same summer (the US release received a similar award a year later).

On the road through 1998, Garbage continued touring the US and Europe — including first ever dates in Russia — into 1999. Two further singles, "When I Grow Up" (#12 UK) and "You Look So Fine" (#19 UK) were followed that winter by Garbage's specially commissioned theme to the latest James Bond movie, *The World is Not Enough* (#11 UK).

Garbage LPs

⑨ **Garbage (Almo Sounds) 1995** With "Stupid Girl" on everyone's best of list, *Garbage* was a shoo-in for 1995's Album of the Year awards... and rightfully so. Without a single look back at its composite parts, the band's electro-garage trash- rock-techno would be sensational even without Manson's Courtney Love out of Chrissie Hynde sensualities, while the sour "Vow" and shattered "Queer" punch fresh holes through the broadest expectations.

⑨ **Version 2.0 (Almo Sounds) 1998** "Special" really is, Manson teasing the Hynde traditions even further by throwing a slice of the Pretenders' "Talk of the Town" into the brew, while the band get back on the chain gang with a passion. Elsewhere, too, the band snap snatches of pop's pristine past ("Bend Me Shape Me" gets an airing in "I Think I'm Paranoid"), while the PJ Harvey meets Sonic Youth-like "Push It," and "Dumb" are equally powerful, supremely memorable.

Spooner LPs

⑥ **Every Corner Dance (Boat) 1982**
⑤ **Wildest Dreams (Boat) 1985**
⑤ **The Fugitive Dance (Dali) 1990**

Fire Town LPs

⑥ **In the Heart of the Heart Country (Boat/Atlantic) 1987**
⑥ **The Good Life (Boat) 1988**

Goodbye Mr Mackenzie LPs

⑦ **Good Deeds and Dirty Rags (Capitol) 1989**
⑥ **Now We Are Married (Radioactive) 1991**
⑥ **Live: On the Day of Storms (Blokskok — UK) 1993**

Selected Compilations and Archive Releases

⑦ **Fish Heads and Tails (Capitol) 1989** A collection of rare B-sides and live material .

⑥ **Hammer and Tongs (Radioactive) 1991** Unreleased 1989 album defies the major label's distaste.

Further Reading

A *Darker Religion* by Mark Freeth (Omnibus, UK, 1998).

GBH

FORMED 1980 (Birmingham, UK)
ORIGINAL LINE-UP Colin Abrahall (b. 12/5/61 — vocals); Colin "Jock" Blyth (b. 10/1/61 — guitar); Ross Lomas (b. 10/20/61 — bass); Wilf (b. Andrew Williams — drums)

Originally known as Charged GBH, to avoid confusion with a better established London metal band called GBH, the four midlands teens were unforgettable from the outset, an apocalypse of aggressive punk topped by vast fountains of violently colored hair, exploding in a razor straight mohawk down their scalps.

Readily championed by a street punk scene which had yet to start ossifying beneath the media banner of Oi!, GBH swiftly rose to the forefront of the movement — early gigs sharing a circuit with the Angelic Upstarts, Cockney Rejects, and the Exploited saw them develop a reputation far in excess of their experience, and by the time the band released their debut EP, *Leather, Bristles, Studs and Acne* (#8 UK indy), through Mike Stone's Clay label in 1981, even the band members were shocked by their success.

"It surprised me and all of us that we started to get coverage in mainstream music papers in the early '80s and our records got into the charts," Colin Blyth admitted years later. "It all came as a bit of shock when people had T-shirts with GBH all over them. We were quite happy playing in our local pub!"

There was to be no chance of that. In February 1982, GBH's first single, "No Survivors" (#63 UK, #4 UK indy) evidenced just how strong the band's grassroots support had grown. "Sick Boy" (#5 UK indy) and the quasi-bootleg *Live at the 100 Club* (#5 UK indy) were followed in August by the band's debut album, *City Baby Attacked By Rats* (#17 UK; #2 UK indy). In November, "Give Me Fire" (#69 UK, #2 UK indy) exploded onto the nation's television screens, via an incendiary performance on TV's *The Tube*.

"Catch 23," GBH's first — and only — single of 1983 sank without trace, even as a compilation of early singles, *Leather, Bristles, No Survivor and Sick Boy* (#5 UK indy) climbed the charts. The band's live schedule, meanwhile, barely let up (1989's *No Survivors* was recorded live around this time), and in December, their second album, *City Babies' Revenge* (#6 UK indy) also achieved stunning chart success.

The fiercely affirmative "Do What You Do" (#7 UK indy), however, would be their last hit for two years, as the band quit Clay; finally abbreviated their name (although nobody had ever used the full thing); then threw themselves into an onstage metamorphosis, from raucous Oi! to equally unrelenting speed metal.

By the time GBH resurfaced in August 1986, with *Midnight Madness and Beyond* (UK #12 indy) and the aptly titled *Oh No! It's GBH Again* EP (#29 UK indy), the transformation was complete.

Wilf left in late 1986, to be replaced by Kai Reder, and in July 1987, GBH released *No Need to Panic*. The *Wot a Bargain* EP followed, and over the next five years, the band would cut two more studio albums, before Reder was replaced by Joe Montero (aka Joseph Montanaro), for *Church of the Truly Warped*. A Japanese tour that same year would produce the career spanning *Live in Japan* set, but Montero left soon after, and GBH would record 1996's *Punk Junkies* with Scott Preece (ex-Bomb Disneyland).

Of course they continued touring (breaking to cut the festive "I'm Getting Pissed for Christmas" single with Peter and the Test Tube Babies), while 1998 and 1999 alike saw the band play throughout Eastern Europe and the US — home to some of their most devoted fans, as the rise of Rancid, the Offspring and co. made plain.

GBH LPs

7 Live at the 100 Club [CASSETTE] (Chaos) 1982 Archetypal GBH battering, although the sound quality doesn't need to be quite as punishing.

8 City Baby Attacked By Rats (Clay) 1982 The firestorm comes home, regardless of some occasionally brutish lyrical concerns.

8 City Babies Revenge (Clay) 1983 Other bands covering the Stooges' "I Feel Alright" usually live to regret it. GBH simply use it as an excuse to up their own potential somewhat, and the querulous "Diplomatic Immunity" sees them match the master blow for burning blow.

4 Midnight Madness and Beyond (Rough Justice) 1986 Oi! never sounded like a one-way street, but so many of its best bands just turned into rent a-speed-metal messes that maybe it was.

3 No Need to Panic (Rough Justice) 1987 No need to listen either.

4 A Fridge Too Far (Rough Justice) 1989

4 From Here to Reality (Restless) 1990

4 Church of the Truly Warped (Futurist) 1992

6 Live in Japan (Dojo) 1993 The revival starts here.

7 Punk Junkies (Triple X) 1996 Reclaiming their throne at the heart of Oi!, although time enough has passed to erase the divide with punk and hardcore...so, fast and loud and lively as ever. Welcome back.

Selected Compilations and Archive Releases

8 Leather, Bristles, No Survivors and Sick Boy (Clay) 1982 Essential collection housing the band's first EP and early singles.

8 The Clay Years 1981–84 (Clay) 1986

8 Punk Rock Hits (Cleopatra) 1999 Representative samplings of the pre-metal downfall days.

GENE

FORMED 1992 *(London, England)*

ORIGINAL LINE-UP *Martin Rossiter (b. 5/15/71, Cardiff, Wales — vocals); Steve Mason (b. 4/17/71, Pontypridd, Wales — guitar); Kevin Miles (b. 7/17/67, Sheffield, England — bass); Matt James (b. 10/29/66, High Wycombe, England — drums)*

Although their early press coverage obsessed upon the band's supposed similarity to The Smiths, over the course of just three albums, Gene would emerge as veritable giants on Britain's post-britpop scene. One of the first acts to prove that there was life after the initial blast of Britpop, Gene also rode the same wave of laconic literacy and musical adventure as catapulted Pulp to stardom around the same time. The difference was, Gene didn't spend a decade flapping around the indy scene beforehand.

In 1992, Steve Mason and Matt James were members of baggy hopefuls Spin, whose one album, *In Motion*, was still fresh on the racks when the band's van was involved in a serious collision with a truck. Although nobody was killed, the musicians' injuries essentially dashed the band's hopes of carrying on (bassist John Mason, Steve's brother, was in a coma for over a week). It would be some months before Mason and James were ready to resume, when they hooked up with Kevin Miles and longer still before they met with Martin Rossiter, one night at London's Underground club.

Rossiter's musical apprenticeship was divided between the teenage band Raintree County, alongside future Elevator guitarist James Elkington, and Drop, one of three bands of that name playing around Britain during the mid '80s ("ours was the one you wouldn't have heard of," Rossiter admitted). Since then, he had drifted in and out of various other groups, but almost immediately after joining what would become Gene, things began moving.

Discovered by journalists Roy Wilkinson and Keith Cameron, Gene signed to the duo's newly-formed Costermonger label in early 1993. It was third time's a charm for the pair — years earlier, they had attempted to sign the Pixies; more recently, they had gone after London Suede. In both instances, though, the objects of their desire had already been contracted.

Gene, however, would rapidly make up for the disappointments. The band's debut single, "For the Dead," was picked as *NME*'s Single of the Week, while the follow-up, "Be My Light, Be My Guide" (#54 UK) topped the indie chart. In its wake, Gene inked a worldwide deal with Polydor, and celebrated with "Sleep Well Tonight" (#36 UK, #1 UK indy).

"Haunted By You" (#32 UK) followed in February 1995, with Gene's debut album, *Olympian* (#8 UK) arriving the following month. A winsome disc whose most immediate attributes may have been somewhat disguised by Rossiter's pronounced vocal resemblance to Morrissey, *Olympian* nevertheless indicated that Gene's popularity far out-stripped the opinions of the critics. The singles "Olympian" (#18 UK), "For the Dead" (#14 UK), and "Fighting Fit" (#22 UK) pushed the band even higher, a streak of success which was only emphasized by the success of *To See the Lights* (#11 UK), a 1997 collection of B-sides and non-album material aimed specifically at the US market.

Drawn to the Deep End, the band's second full album, was the sound of Gene coming of age, a disc which matched the fire and commitment of the group's live sound to the studio. "I love *Olympian*, and it has charm, in the sense of naivety, that I think is quite appealing," Rossiter acknowledged. "But with this record, where a song was dark, now it's black, where it was gentle, it's now delicate."

At a time when the rate of attrition on mid-90s British bands was reaching Somme-like proportions, three Top 30 singles, "We Could be Kings," "Where Are They Now," and "Speak to Me Sometimes" proved that Rossiter's confidence in Gene was not misplaced.

Unreleased in the US, Gene's 1999 album *Revelations* (#25 UK) appeared in March, again attended by a bevy of hit singles, "As Good As It Gets" (#23 UK) on the eve of the LP release, "Fill Her Up" (#36 UK) shortly after. Touring and festivals occupied the group's summer, together with a contribution to the Jam tribute *Fire and Skill*, before the band quit Polydor in fall 1999. New material that debuted in concert through 1999, meanwhile, would flavor 2000's independently released live album, *Rising for Sunset* (#1 UK).

Gene LPs

🔟 **Olympian (A&M) 1995** A bit cynical, a tad broody, a touch cheeky, Gene's evocative angst is cocooned in some of the strongest melodies-in-a-melancholy-key ever written. Even the ballads are anthemic, while the rockabilly-tinged rockers are pure rabble rousers. Muted production does spoil the show a little, but still Gene's *Olympian* glory is there for all to hear.

🔟 **Drawn to the Deep End (A&M) 1997** ...then washed into a maelstrom of melodies, Gene don't disguise their lyrical trepidation as they enter the world of love and desire. But the guitars soar with delight, the rhythm section pulses expectantly, the organ sets the mood, and this time, the production does capture the sheer power of emotion.

🔟 **Revelations (Polydor — UK) 1999** Love battles politics, but the melodies conquer all as *Revelations* picks up where *End* left off, honing the band's fuller sound and style.

🔟 **Rising for Sunset [LIVE] (Contra — UK)** Peerless recounting of recent triumphs, early glories, and Rossiter's incandescent stage presence.

Selected Compilations and Archive Releases

🔟 **To See the Lights (A&M) 1996** Vivid, vital collection of non-album singles, radio sessions, and live performances, with a revealing barrage of Stones-inspired riffs proving that the most potent influences aren't necessarily the ones which everyone writes about.

GENE LOVES JEZEBEL

FORMED 1982 *(London, England)*
ORIGINAL LINE-UP *Michael Aston (b. 5/4/61 — vocals); Jay Aston (b. 5/4/61 — vocals); James Chater (drums); Steve Radwell (bass); Ian Hudson (guitar)*

From the moment they first appeared on a London stage, during the ICA Rock Week in 1982, Gene Loves Jezebel stood out like a sore thumb. There were, of course, two of them — Gene (Michael), who limped like rocker Gene Vincent, after breaking his leg playing football, and Jezebel, which is what a friend thought Jay's name was the first time they were introduced. And because they were twins and had always been close, Gene Loves Jezebel fell out of their mouths before they knew what they were saying, when they got that first gig and were stuck for a name.

The twins were captivating, prowling the stage, in lady's clothes and shocking bright hair, cackling, caterwauling, crazy as they could be, while behind them, James Chater,

Steve Radwell, and Ian Hudson laid down the ugliest barrage they could muster.

"Shaving My Neck," the band's first single, was originally intended as a demo; nevertheless, *Melody Maker* made it their single of the week, sensing then that even in an age of towering shadows (the era of Bauhaus and the Virgin Prunes, Southern Death Cult, and the Birthday Party), Gene Loves Jezebel were offering something unique — musically and visually.

A string of bass and drummer changes (among them All About Eve's Julianne Regan) did not dent the dementia, and the next two years saw the band unleash a string of classic proto-goth singles: "Screaming" (#18 UK indy), "Bruises" (#7 UK indy), "Influenza" (#11 UK indy), "Shame" (#14 UK indy), "Cow" (#9 UK indy), and an early version of what would become their signature hit, "Desire" (#4 UK indy).

This remarkable sequence was topped off by two classic albums, *Promise* (#8 UK indy) and *Immigrant*. In between times, the band worked with producers John Cale and Cockney Rebel's Steve Harley; and in 1986, Gene Loves Jezebel emerged with the sound which would reshape the decade.

With former Chelsea/Generation X guitarist James Stevenson filling the role which Ian Hudson vacated on the

© Jim Steinfeldt/Chansley Entertainment Archives

eve of a 60-date American tour, Peter Rizzo bringing some permanency to the bass position, and Chris Bell moving into the drum seat, Gene Loves Jezebel's third album, *Discover* (#155 US, #32 UK) was launched with a club-friendly, arena-shaking remake of "Desire."

Produced by Peter Walsh (the earlier version was recorded with Gary Lyons) and an instant American radio hit, "Desire"'s insistent yelping and compulsive riffing would provide the template for some of the broadest extremities of what would emerge from the late 1980s as Alternative Rock. From early Jane's Addiction (who opened several of the band's US dates, and were never afraid to wear their allegiance on their sleeve) to primal Guns n' Roses, from the bombast of the Cult to the bomb blast of Nirvana, "Desire" hangs over the age like a mortgage, a debt that will never be repaid. Simply, Gene Loves Jezebel reinvented excitement for the MTV generation, and the explosive "Heartache" (#71 UK) and the addictive "Sweetest Thing" (#75 UK) both proved that the initial breakthrough was no fluke.

Still the exposure came too quickly. Rushed back to the studio to record a follow-up album, Michael was miserable, Jay was jaundiced, and as what would eventually become *House of Dolls* (#108 US, #81 UK) took shape, Gene Loves Jezebel collapsed. Michael quit, and the remaining band now look back on the album as something which literally changed while they waited, from a dense, driven document of the life they wanted to lead, to a widescreen crash to follow up the smash.

"Motion of Love" (#87 US, #56 UK) started life sounding like Joy Division; it wound up something else entirely, and the album followed suit. With "Gorgeous" (#68 UK) proving an irresistible inducement both at home and abroad, *House of Dolls* became Gene Loves Jezebel's biggest seller, and was further from home than they'd ever wanted to go.

Although Michael Aston returned for the accompanying tour, the tensions which once fired the onstage act now fuelled the backstage battles as well. The shows over, Michael relocated to Los Angeles where he married and launched a solo career, while Jay returned to London, to join his bandmates in redesigning Gene Loves Jezebel.

1990's "Kiss of Life" (#123 US) was launched with "Jealous" (#68 US), a non-stop MTV favorite. But a projected American tour collapsed even as "Jealous" topped the US modern rock chart, and while Gene Loves Jezebel cooled their heels in Europe, America moved on to other fascinations. By the time the band were back in the States, in 1992, with the *Heavenly Bodies* album and new drummer, Robert Adam, the momentum had slipped away entirely. A single, "Josephina," was lost, and when the band's new US record company followed the album into the dumper, it was plain an era was approaching its end.

Jay followed Michael's lead into the land of solo recordings — his *Unpopular Songs* album was finally released four years after he started work on it. But a few archive releases kept Gene Loves Jezebel's name alive a little longer, and the twins' 15th anniversary reunion tour (featuring an all-new line-up, including Human Drama guitarist Michael Ciravolo) was an immense success.

Unfortunately, the tensions between the pair had not dissipated, and the moment the tour ended, the Astons separated again. Both set about forming their own very different versions of the band. The self-explanatorily named Michael Aston's Gene loves Jezebel joined with Triple X and released *Love Lies Bleeding*, forged in the clubs and bars of the west coast, and featuring the returning Ciravolo, Slobo Svrdlam (bass), and Michael Brahm (drums). Jay's unadorned Gene Loves Jezebel signed with the newly-founded Robison label, and cut their aptly-named seventh album, *VII*, with a line-up of Aston, Stevenson, Rizzo, and Bell. Joined by Jessica Blake (keyboards, guitar), this line-up also toured the US on the fall, 1999 Resurrection tour, with Alarm vocalist Mike Peters, and the revitalized Mission.

Gene Loves Jezebel LPs

7 Promise (Situation 2 — UK) 1983 Centered around nine minutes of "Screaming for Emmalene"/"Scheming," *Promise* veers from melody to experiment, ballad to brooding then closes with "Psychological Problems," a goth-rock kicker to disturb the most stubborn shroud.

8 Immigrant (Relativity) 1985 The band's third attempt at recording "Always a Flame" opens a shimmering, shuddering masterpiece, brought to fruition by producer John Leckie. The mysterious "Shame" and the thunderous "Stephen" maintain the momentum, before things peak with "Cow," all dark jangly guitars and a Celtic folk aura reminiscent of early U2, and "Worth Waiting For" — upbeat poprock bludgeoned by guitar.

9 Discover (Geffen) 1986 Dominated by "Desire," but by no means dwarfed by it, "Heartache," "Over the Rooftops," and "Kick" continue conjuring past dark auras. GLJ at their best, combining elements of the night, while allowing James Stevenson ample room for his searing stadium leads.

6 Glad to Be Alive [LIVE] (Beggars Banquet — UK) 1986 Eight tracks from a 1986 Nottingham show, a bonus disc with early copies of *Discover*. "It wasn't a bad show," Michael Aston recalled. "But it wasn't one of our best shows either. It wasn't mixed or anything, they just put out."

7 The House of Dolls (Geffen) 1987 The twins were separating, the producer was chafing, the band hated making it. But *Dolls* still includes "Motion of Love," and for that you can forgive it anything.

9 Kiss of Life (Geffen) 1990 From the powerful "Jealous" to the haunting title track ballad, a million moods and just as many mania. "Why Can't I?" is truly stygian, a classic beauty of love-

sex-death potency, and perhaps the archetypal post-Michael Jezzie gem.

8 Heavenly Bodies (Savage) 1993 Full frontal guitars and breathtaking poignancy, a poetic tour de force. From the ethereal "Josephina" to the joyous celebration of "Sweet Sweet Rain," *Heavenly* is an uncompromising vision of beauty, momentum, and melody.

8 VII (Robison) 1999 Opening with two tracks rerecorded from Jay's acoustic solo album, restructured around the Jezebel's own trademarks, a powerful offering serves tight, spiralling melodies, stomping pop ballads, and a reunion with *House of Dolls* producer Peter Walsh.

Selected Compilations and Archive Releases

6 From the Mouths of Babes (Avalanche) 1995 Two new songs don't heal the rift between the reunited brothers. Indeed, a painfully lopsided selection of older material make the greatest hits seem a personal battlefield.

8 In the Afterglow [LIVE] (Pink Gun) 1995 Disc one, Toronto 1988, catches the Aston roadshow wild in the disintegrating *House of Dolls*; disc two, Minneapolis 1993, is Jay versus James duelling through "Desire," and ad libbing an eternity.

9 Voodoo Dollies (Beggars Banquet) 1999 Dangerously powerful, carrer-spanning best of, barely missing an essential beat.

Michael Aston LPs

8 Edith Grove (Avalanche) 1993 A scorching tribute to T. Rex, "Cat Black," and the Mott the hoopling "Wheel" remark on Aston's influences; "Majik" nods to "Desire," but *Edith Grove's* roots are in the dulcimer driven "Venus in Rags," and the madrigal stomp of "Kings Horsemen." Seldom have mandolins been put to more raucous use.

8 Why Me Why This Why Now (Triple X) 1995 "Avalon SW10" opens the show with aching homesickness, name checking the same territory as brother Jay's "Jealous." But the lovers are memories now and, behind Aston's ineffably sad vocals, guitarist Mick Rossi raises ghosts of his own. It's a sparse album, acoustic in places, scratchy in others, but so intuitively dynamic that he could make you dance to your own funeral dirge.

Michael Aston's Gene Loves Jezebel LP

6 Love Lies Bleeding (Triple X) 1999

Jay Aston LPs

8 Unpopular Songs (Pink Gun) 1997 Remarkably powerful, even without the full weight of the band behind him; indeed, Aston's voice folds around the generally acoustic backing with distracting ease. Instantly recognizable, surprisingly, shockingly different.

7 Jezebel (Self-Released) 1999 Partially a demo-esque reworking of the Jezebels' *VII*, partly a glimpse into a possible future and, in the case of "White Car in Germany," an unexpected experimental journey unlike anything Aston's recorded since *Immigrant*.

GENERATION X

FORMED 1976 (London, England)
ORIGINAL LINE-UP *Billy Idol (b. William Broad, 11/30/55, Stanmore — vocals); Bob Andrews (guitar); Tony James (bass); John Towe (drums)*

Generation X emerged from the first line-up of Gene October's Chelsea, which splintered in late 1976. With Billy Idol switching from guitarist to frontman, the trio of Idol, Tony James, and John Towe, plus pub band guitarist Bob Andrews — took their new name from the cover of a swinging London paperback they found on Idol's mother's bookcase.

The band made their live debut on December 12, 1976 at London's Central College of Art & Design. Moving on to a near residency at the Roxy (which they opened, on January 15), by early 1977, Generation X were among the hottest unsigned bands around — a bootleg single of the band's first John Peel session was so popular that there were even rumors of an official release through the BBC's own label.

Towe departed for his own band, Rage, shortly before Generation X stepped in to replace the Clash supporting John Cale at the Roundhouse in April. He was replaced by Mark Laff (ex-Subway Sect) and in this form, the band signed to Chrysalis. Their first single, "Your Generation" (#36 UK) was released to much acclaim in September 1977, and while their next release, "Wild Youth," flopped dramatically, the band were swiftly back on track with first, "Ready Steady Go" (#47 UK), then with their self-named debut album (#29 UK).

It was a rushed recording — according to Idol, producer Martin Rushent was "trying to mix us, mix the Stranglers, run the United Artists A&R department, and do 999 all at the same time." But it was also a strong indication of the band's ideal, a collision between the power of punk, and the flash of glam rock.

It was that same ideal, of course, which prompted them to recruit former Mott the Hoople vocalist Ian Hunter to produce their sophomore album, 1979's *Valley of the Dolls* (#51 UK), a set which also spawned the band's biggest hit, Christmas 1978's "King Rocker" (#11 UK).

Again, Idol would attack the album — "It was," he said, "a disgusting display of a group who didn't understand why they were a group. Ian Hunter did his best... but he didn't know what the group was about." Two further singles, the title track (#23 UK) and "Friday's Angels" (#62 UK) failed to follow "King Rocker"'s success, while management problems added to the band's woes. Most damaging of all, however, was the conflict over the band's direction. Idol had formulated a whole new sound, but Andrews and Laff dismissed it out of hand. Finally, "I sat down and told them if they didn't do this 'Dancing With Myself'/'White Wedding' music, I was going to leave the group," Idol reflected.

In fact they quit, leaving Idol and James to piece together a new line-up around one-time Clash drummer Terry Chimes, and a steady stream of guest guitarists, all contributing to what was to become the third Generation X album: Steve New (Rich Kids), Danny Kustow (Tom Robinson Band), Steve Jones (Sex Pistols), and John McGeogh (Magazine) passed through, only for Chrysalis to announce they weren't even sure they wanted to release the album.

Kiss Me Deadly finally appeared in January 1981, as the band themselves fell apart, James Stevenson, recruited from Chelsea as a full-time member, joined for a British tour through December 1980, and there was a moment of hope with the release and subsequent reception of "Dancing With Myself" (#60 US, #62 UK) — remixed and reissued in the new year, the song became a firm club favorite in the US.

But *Kiss Me Deadly*, released under the abbreviated name Gen X, flopped, and any new lease on life which the single promised was ended that same month as Idol moved to New York to work with new manager Bill Aucoin and producer Keith Forsey in piecing together a band of his own. Together, they rerecorded "Dancing With Myself" as a solo single, and promptly introduced Idol to the audience which Gen X had just been flirting with. Months later, a cover of Tommy James' "Mony Mony" consolidated his standing as a superstar in waiting, and through the 1980s, Idol reigned supreme as one of Britain's most successful exports of the decade.

Over the next decade, James, too, remained in the spotlight, forming the outrageous Sigue Sigue Sputnik before joining the Sisters of Mercy in 1989. In fall 1993, however, he and Idol reunited with Laff and Andrews for a 7-song/30 minute encore following Idol's latest London show (promoting his *Cyberpunk* album) — the quartet refused, however, to consider expanding the event into a full-fledged revival.

Generation X LPs

🎵 **Generation X (Chrysalis) 1978** As exuberant as a pack of three years old on Christmas morning, if the Sex Pistols were the unacceptable face of punk destruction and anarchy, Gen X were their equally chaotic, but more cheerful counterpart. The Beatles compared to the wicked, hairy Stones... indeed, they cover a John Lennon song on US pressings of the original vinyl album, and continue enamored with Britain's pop past. From the tribute to '60s TV's *Ready Steady Go* to the glammy "Promises Promises," and onto the up-yours of "Your Generation," the group reel off a glorious celebration of rebellion past and present for youth (youth, youth).

5 Valley of the Dolls (Chrysalis) 1979 Years later, Billy Idol admitted that producer Ian Hunter didn't stand a chance — the band was crumbling, the songs were crummy and even the hit "King Rocker" wasn't that special really.

6 Kiss Me Deadly (Chrysalis) 1981 A distinct change of direction and wide hints of all the participants' future projects. "The Untouchables" and "Dancing With Myself" for Billy, the tranced riffs for guitarist McGeogh, the glam battery for James Stevenson... only Tony James didn't seem to be expecting his Sigue Sigue Sputnik future. But none of this had anything whatsoever to do with Gen X, so they did the smart thing and broke up within a week of release.

Selected Compilations and Archive Releases

5 Perfect Hits (Chrysalis) 1991 Two tracks from their pivotal debut Peel session and a third album outtake distinguish an otherwise mundane tramp through an unfulfilling sample of an unfulfilled band.

Billy Idol LPs

6 Billy Idol (Chrysalis) 1982
7 Rebel Yell (Chrysalis) 1984
7 Whiplash Smile (Chrysalis) 1986
6 Charmed Life (Chrysalis) 1990
7 Cyberpunk (Chrysalis) 1993

Selected Compilations and Archive Releases

8 Vital Idol (Chrysalis) 1985
7 Idol Songs (Chrysalis) 1988

Further Reading

Billy Idol by Jo-Ann Greene (Bobcat, UK, 1985).

LISA GERMANO

BORN *8/17/69 (Orange County, CA)*

Though her early ambition was to be a singer-songwriter, Germano played guitar in her first band, San Francisco-based Fisherman's Call — apparently she was fired after taking the microphone at a low-key local show, and singing one song herself.

She then came to notice as fiddle player with John Mellencamp's band, appearing on his *Big Daddy* and *Lonesome Jubilee* albums before Mellencamp persuaded her to use one of the breaks in their schedule to record her first demos.

Borrowing his drummer Kenny Aronoff, Germano recorded *On the Way Down from the Moon Palace* for release on her own Black Hole label in 1991. It was well-received, but attempts to land a full deal went nowhere, and in 1991, Germano returned to the road with Mellencamp.

Then, she recalled, "I wrote that stupid song about dresses..." — "The Dress Song" appeared on one of her demo tapes, and provoked a major label bidding war. She signed with Capitol in late 1991, and the following year released her first full album, *Happiness*.

"The Dress Song," of course, was selected as the first single, appearing in what she called "a horrible poppy version" before Germano persuaded the label to replace it with her original demo. Further conflicts over marketing followed, however, and in late 1993, Germano and Capitol parted company.

She moved immediately to 4AD, who'd been showing interest for some months, and a revised, resequenced, and slightly remixed version of *Happiness* was released to glowing praise, even as Germano began work on a new album, *Geek the Girl*.

Largely built around her original demos, *Geek the Girl* (and attendant the "Cry Wolf" single) was an intense confessional, numbering Germano's own experience of date rape and stalking among its subjects. She herself claimed "people who've never had a panic attack, never felt insecure, they're not gonna like my music," while her apparent role as spokesperson for the Neurotic Outsider even prompted one US magazine to invite her to a round table discussion on manic depression, following Kurt Cobain's suicide. She refused.

Trailed by the single "Small Heads," *Excepts from a Love Circus*, in 1996, saw Germano working for the first time with a full band, and also featured poetry read by her cats — albeit in very meow-y voices. It was followed by a union with Giant Sand mainstays Howie Gelb, Joey Burns, and John Convertino, under the OP8 alias.

Originally conceived as a one-off contribution towards a 4AD sampler, the project developed into a full album, *Slush* — which 4AD then passed on. Ultimately released by Thirsty Ear, it featured one song, "Tom, Dick, and Harry," which dated back to her Mellencamp days. Also, Germano's contributions to the album enabled her to stretch in directions her own albums had never permitted, a process which 1998's *Slide* certainly benefited from.

Lisa Germano LPs

7 On the Way Down from Moon Palace (Major Bill) 1991 8 Happiness (Capitol) 1993
10 Happiness (4AD) 1994 Two new tracks, two remixes, and one restructuring separate the pair, but the 4AD set's unquestionably superior, more in keeping with Germano's own vision and rid of the redundancies which caused her to quit Capitol in the first place.

A dark piece of work seeping gloomy introspection and lugubrious self-flagellation, even at its bounciest (as if a song called "Destroy the Flowers" could be termed bouncy), *Happiness* hangs on the edge of hope, and tears its nails as trust slips away.

Distractedly Lou Reed-like in its eye for dry detail ("you think you're pretty, but you're not, haha"), disturbingly bitter in its unrelenting fear of opening its heart to the possibility of hurt, *Happiness* defies traditional rock mopery by refusing to acknowledge that things could ever get better.

The Cure took off the sackcloth in the end, after all, and admitted they still had faith. Lou's *Berlin* ended with freedom and relief, even Nico cracked the occasional grin. *Happiness* sees no redemption, and even the token joke (the title, of course) isn't really funny. It is, however, horrifyingly honest.

8 Geek the Girl (4AD) 1994 Germano's most harrowingly real-life docudrama, *Geek* paints a sordid world of date rape lotharios and persistent real-life stalkers. Compiled from her original demos with little effort made to smooth the rough edges, *Geek* emerges music not as a purgative, but purgatory.

7 Excerpts from a Love Circus (4AD) 1996 With its full-band feel dominated by spectral violin (and her poetry-reciting cats), *Love Circus* retains Germano's homespun feel, but it's a lot less sparse and an awful lot less cranky than either of its predecessors. Boys are still beastly, of course, but Germano's gotten used to that. Now she's letting her hair down. A little.

7 Slide (4AD) 1998

OP8 LP

7 Slush (Thirsty Ear) 1997 Less a collaboration, more a series of maddening mood changes, with Giant Sand as cracked as ever and Germano simply being Germano. Her whispered take on Neil Young's "Round and Round" is terrifyingly tender; Lee Hazlewood's "Sand" is simply terrifying.

GERMS

FORMED *1977 (Los Angeles, CA)*
ORIGINAL LINE-UP *Darby Crash (b. Paul Beahm — vocals); Pat Smear (guitar); Lorna Doom (bass); Belinda Carlisle (drums)*

L.A.'s best known punk band grew out of an imaginary ensemble featuring University High student Darby Crash, Pat Smear, Lorna Doom, Belinda Carlisle, Michelle Baer, and Dinky — originally calling themselves Sophistif and the Revlon Spam Queens, they changed when they went to get T-shirts printed and discovered the printer charged by the letter. They became the Germs, Crash later said, because they made people sick.

Slowly taking things more seriously, and settling down briefly with a line-up of Crash, Smear, Doom, and Carlisle, the band was still untried — and largely unrehearsed — when Carlisle quit (she later joined the Go-Gos), to be replaced by a friend named Becky, aka Donna Rhia.

The Germs played their first show opening for the Weirdoes at the L.A. Orpheum, and caused an immediate sensation as Crash smeared his body in red liquorice, then melted under the lights. Behind him, his bandmates crashed through the only two songs they knew — the entire performance lasted five minutes. The Germs reappeared at the Roxy for another two song performance, during the filming of Cheech and Chong's *Up in Smoke* movie; they finally played a full show at the Whisky, a set recorded for posthumous release on the *Germicide* album.

The Germs were as apocalyptic as it was amateurish, and with an audience seemingly as bent on destruction as the band, a number of local venues were quick to ban them from performing. Still by July 1977, the Germs' debut single, "Forming," had been released on manager Chris Ashford's What? label. Recorded in Smear's garage, the song would emerge the first recorded manifestation of what would soon become the California hardcore sound.

Donna Rhia left to be replaced briefly by one Cliff Hanger; he rehearsed, but never gigged with the band, and when they did re-emerge onstage it was with ex-Eyes drummer Don "DJ" Bonebrake. Again, however, his time with the band was limited — he quit to join what became X, and was replaced by the Weirdos' Nicky Beat.

With rising producer Geza X behind them, the Germs signed to Slash and in May 1978, issued the "Lexicon Devil" 45; Beat departed to return to the Weirdos — his last act as a Germ was to teach ex-Exterminators drummer Don Bolles a Weirdos song, from which Bolles would extrapolate the Germs' repertoire. (Beat later re-emerged in the Cramps.)

Bolles arrived just in time to record the Germs' debut album, the Joan Jett produced *GI* — titled after the band decided to change their name to (GI) in an attempt to circumvent the various club bans they were subject to. The album was released in October 1979, and live work did increase even without the need for subterfuge; one show was filmed for inclusion in Penelope Spheeris' *Decline & Fall of Western Civilization* movie.

By summer 1980, however, things were on the edge of collapse. Doom quit, Bolles and manager Nicole Panter were sacked; and Crash headed over to London with the vague notion of forming a new band there. He returned home instead with a high mohawk haircut, and plans to form a new, eponymous band with Smear, bassist Bosco, and drummer Lucky Lehrer of the Circle Jerks.

The Darby Crash Band played a handful of poorly received live shows, before Crash and Smear reconvened Doom and new drummer Rob Henley for a reunion show on December 3, 1980, at the Starwood — one of the venues which had outlawed them in their prime, but had since relented. It was not a great show (excerpts would appear on the 1981 *What We Do is Secret* EP), and there were no tangible plans to repeat the exercise. Four days later, Crash died from a massive heroin overdose.

Smear would reappear 13 years later alongside that other doomed icon of American punk, Kurt Cobain, in Nirvana. The Germs, too, would become omnipresent, the subject of literally dozens of posthumous collections. A Germs tribute album featuring bands as far a field as NOFX, L7, Matthew Sweet, Meat Puppets, Free Kitten, the Melvins, Dinosaur Jr.'s J Mascis and Mike Watt, Red Hot Chili Pepper Flea, and D-Generation appeared in 1996.

The Germs LPs

7 (GI) (SLASH) 1979 The hardcore holocaust which is the Germs' reputation only partially hangs on their ability (or otherwise) to record; producer Joan Jett seems as uncertain as the band, and it's the nervous energy which carries *(GI)* — that, and Smear's seeming unwillingness to take his foot off the fuzz pedal. A ramblingly overlong live version of "Shut Down" spoils a lot of the album's impact, but that aside, it's as great as it should be... and probably about as good as it could have been.

Selected Compilations and Archive Releases

4 Germicide (Roir) 1982 Generally incomprehensible live recording from the Whiskey, the first in a long parade of sometimes legally dubious concert recordings.

5 Rock'n'Rule (XES) 1986

4 Media Blitz (Cleopatra) 1993 More in-concert tragedy.

8 M.I.A. (Slash) 1993 Wade through the myriad compilations, cash-ins and sub-bootleg live recordings out there, retire your *What We Do is Secret* mini-album anthology and this is all you really need, the story of the Germs in lovely, living mud.

GLAMPIRE

FORMED *1997 (New York, NY)*
ORIGINAL LINE-UP *David Michael Jahn (vocals, instruments)*

Glampire emerged from the New York nightclub Squeeze box, where Jahn spent two years as the increasingly theatrical house guitarist. A graduate of Robert Fripp's League of Crafty Guitarists, he linked with Psychotica frontman Patrick Briggs ("Breakable," from that band's *Espina* album, was a Glampire composition).

Signing with J-Bird soon after, Glampire then began work on his own first album, the self-played and co-produced 1998's *Beginning of Terror* album, a logical progression from the shock rock tactics of Marilyn Manson and Nine Inch Nails, fed through a hearty, guitar-driven appreciation for old glam (obviously) and futurist rock.

1998 brought *Pretty Scary*, a well-received sophomore set which saw one reviewer place Glampire alongside Prince and NIN's Trent Reznor in terms of artists blithely pursuing their own direction — the album was allegedly titled, inci-

dentally, because parts of it were pretty and parts of it were scary.

The EP *Glitta 99* followed, previewing two tracks from Glampire's third album, together with two past B-sides, and one cut a piece from the earlier albums. *The Heraldic Universe*, Glampire's self-proclaimed "Glambient" third album, emerged late in 1999. The first single, "My Own God," was released via the internet soon after.

Glampire LPs

7 Beginning of Terror (J-Bird) 1997 Even if the comparisons do ring true, still Glampire has a couple of tricks up his sleeve — he writes songs which aren't simply crashing manifestos, and he can play guitar like a devil. The single "Our Drugs" and the relentless "Bow Down" both stand high in the glam-industrial-metal lexicon, but elsewhere *Terror* throws such constraints away.

7 Pretty Scary (J-Bird) 1998 "Breakable" was already familiar from Psychotica's *Espina*, "Headspace" picked up from where *Terror* left off. But the push into deeper territory was on with a vengeance and even the self-mocking title has a truth of its own.

8 The Heraldic Universe (J-Bird) 1999 "My Own God," from the *Glitta* 99 EP, is the best indication of where Glampire now stands, some way past the Manson "Dope Show," in a scything psychotic circus of his own. ICP and Slipknot join the audience, but there's a seething viciousness here which really doesn't enjoy sharing.

7 The Soft White Ghetto (Muse Sick) 2000 Prince meets Depeche Mode in a jungle night club — it's time for a real celebrity death match!

GO-BETWEENS

FORMED *1978 (Brisbane, Australia)*
ORIGINAL LINE-UP *Grant McLennan (b. 2/12/58 — vocals, guitar, bass); Rob Forster (b. 6/29/57 — guitar); Dennis Cantwell (drums)*

It was in 1978 that Queensland University friends Grant McLennan and Rob Forster sowed the seeds for what would become one of the best loved Australian bands of the next decade. Co-opting the alternative sounds of America, the duo gave nods to contemporary idols Patti Smith and Television, as well as to the older brigade of Bob Dylan and the Velvet Underground — standard idols to be sure, but ones which would nevertheless conspire to give the Go-Betweens a unique slant.

Noodling turned into playing, songs were written and the pair, along with drummer Cantwell, cut their first single, "Lee Remick" for self-release that fall 1978. In the wave of enthusiasm which followed, the Go-Betweens came close to signing with US indie Beserkley, home to another band favorite, Jonathan Richman and the Modern Lovers. That deal fell through (a warning of things to come); instead, McLennan and Forster recruited a new drummer, Tim Mustafa, and organist Malcolm Kelly, and began writing the songs that would eventually appear on their debut album, 1982's *Send Me a Lullaby* (#28 UK indie).

Mustafa and Kelly, however, would stay only long enough to record one single, 1979's "People Say," before the band again rejuggled the players with drummer Lindy Morrison (b. 11/2/51) arriving and finalizing this incarnation as a trio.

Word of the Go-Betweens' magic continued to travel and, in summer 1980, Alan Horne, head of the Scottish indie label Postcard, invited the band to Britain. There they would record the singles "I Need Two Heads" and "Your Turn, My Turn," before the band returned to Australia and signed to Missing Link.

In June 1982, the Go-Betweens' debut album, *Send Me a Lullaby*, was released, swiftly followed by a non-album single, "Hammer the Hammer" and greeted with the news that another respected UK indie, Rough Trade, wanted to bring the band back to London. They swiftly accepted but it was not to be a happy move. Like so many other Australian bands of the period — most notably the Birthday Party (who they would accompany on an extensive tour of Australia), the Go-Betweens found themselves lauded by the local media, but greeted and treated as outsiders by the actual record-buying public. Even worse, however, was the knowledge that whereas the Birthday Party had made a positive musical virtue of their alien nature, the Go-Betweens' records really were tailor-made for the UK scene of the day.

Still the band persevered, adding bassist Richard Vickers (b. 11/25/59) and pushing forward despite the news that Rough Trade had also run into financial difficulties, a fact which made the recording and release of the Go-Betweens' second album, *Before Hollywood* (#2 UK indie) a somewhat tenuous affair.

Two singles, "Cattle and Cane" (#4 UK indie) in February 1983 and "Man O'Sand To Girl 'Sea" (#24 UK indie) in October, flanked the album's September release, closing the band's relationship with Rough Trade; in early 1984, the Go-Betweens signed with Sire, but this union, too, would be brief. The band released just one album, 1984's *Spring Hill Fair* and two accompanying singles, "Part Company" and "Bachelor Kisses," before this relationship, too, soured. Had Beggars Banquet not moved in almost immediately, with the offer of a new deal, the Go-Betweens would have returned to Australia on the spot.

Although the Go-Betweens had yet to break out into the mainstream, they remained critical darlings, and their decidedly post-punk ramblings were gathering speed not only in England, but in the college underground of the United States as well. There they would be scooped up and distributed by the indie Big Time.

Still gigging regularly, the Go-Betweens retained a recorded silence until February 1986, when Beggars released a taster, "Spring Rain," from March's *Liberty Belle and the Black Diamond Express* album, to be followed by "Head Full of Steam" (and, at year's end, a successful reissue of "Lee Remick" — #7 UK indie).

Joined now by Amanda Brown (b. 11/17/65) who added the additional lush elements of violin, oboe, and keyboards, the Go-Betweens re-emerged in early 1987 at the top of their game. February brought "Right Here," while May's "Cut It Out" was the perfect introduction to the band's most successful album to date, *Tallulah* (#91 UK). A further single, "Bye Bye Pride" was released in August, but it was also bye-bye Vickers — who quit to relocate to New York in 1987, shortly after completing work on *Tallulah*'s much anticipated follow up, *16 Lovers Lane* (#81 UK) and the attendant singles, "Streets of Your Town" and "Was There Anything I Could Do."

Vickers was replaced by fellow Australian John Willsteed (b. 2/13/57) and the band toured; however, *Lovers Lane* would be the last thing the band would record for over a decade. Despite a move to major label Capitol in the United States, despite all the media accolades which they continued to receive, and despite the cult status they attained around the world, mainstream fame remained damnably elusive. Although the band were pleased with what they'd achieved, so many years with so little recognition finally took their toll as the Go-Betweens caved in to the knowledge that they were still as far outside the mainstream music scene as they had been during their initial stint in London.

The band went their separate, solo, ways. Forster and McLennan both released a clutch of albums on Beggars; McLennan, along with the Church's Steve Kilbey, also formed the short lived Jack Frost. Morrison and Brown formed their own group, Cleopatra Wong and, while rumors of a Go-Betweens reunion were in constant circulation (most notably after McLennan and Forster reunited to support Lloyd Cole in Toronto in 1991), the band continued apart until 1997 when they reformed for a short series of live shows. 2000 finally confirmed the long-imminent reunion, with the release of the acclaimed *The Friends of Rachel Worth*.

The Go-Betweens LPs

🎵 **Send Me A Lullaby (Rough Trade) 1982** A rough album, poised teasingly on the edge of homespun and packing an effervescence which better production could never recreate — as the Go-Betweens themselves subsequently discovered.

9 Before Hollywood (Rough Trade) 1983 Belatedly, the band remember what they heard during their short stay at Postcard, turning in an album which could easily have been a reborn Josef K — and was surely a favorite of the early REM. "Cattle and Cane," the band's greatest UK hit, stands out loudest, but truly there is not a dull moment in sight.

7 Spring Hill Fair (Sire) 1984 Recorded in France and maybe, just a little too aware of the fact for its own good.... a little too thoughtful, a little too mannered, but hell, it's still a remarkable disc, chockful of intelligent pop and stretching out in whole new directions as strings, synth, and horns all pile in behind the melody.

8 Liberty Belle and the Black Diamond Express (Big Time) 1986 Backing down from *Spring Hill*'s occasional over-production, but no less ambitious (or precocious) because of that, *Liberty Belle* brings a wealth of fresh instrumentation to bear, but softens it with a gorgeous Tracey Thorn guest appearance.

7 Tallulah (Big Time) 1987 Perfecting the union of sound and musical vision, a grandiose effort — lush and loud at the same time and, while a couple of the songs do struggle to justify their appearance ("The House That Jack Kerouac Built"), the sheer dynamics of the album hold everything together.

8 16 Lovers Lane (Capitol) 1988 Ten crushingly heartbreaking/broken songs bring down the curtain as the band return towards the sparse production and sound of old — reinventing their own guitar magic as they do so.

9 The Friends of Rachel Worth (Jet Set) 2000 No great departure from anything the Go-Betweens have done in the past; ten lovely, largely introspective songs half-played, half-hinted, with sundry Sleater-Kinneys rattling around behind them. A stunning reminder, too, of just how much of their original sound currently haunts Arab Strap and Belle & Sebastian.

Selected Compilations and Archive Releases

8 Very Quick on the Eye — Brisbane 1981 (Man Made — Aus) 1982 Collection of outtakes and demos predating (but occasionally anticipating) *Lullaby*. The band's rawest ever release, later fans should approach with caution.

7 The Peel Sessions (Strange Fruit) 1989

8 The Go-Betweens 1979-1990 (Capitol) 1990 22-track compilation sprawling across singles, outtakes, radio and album cuts, most of which stands as a fine memorial.

Robert Forster Solo LPs

7 Danger in the Past (Beggars Banquet) 1990

6 Calling From a Country Phone (Beggars Banquet) 1993

7 I Had a New York Girlfriend (Atlantic) 1994

7 Warm Nights (Beggars Banquet) 1996

Grant McLennan Solo LPs

7 Watershed (Beggars Banquet) 1991

7 Fireboy (Atlantic) 1994

8 Horsebreaker Star (Beggars Banquet) 1994

6 In Your Bright Ray (Beggars Banquet) 1997

GOLDFINGER

FORMED 1994 (Los Angeles, CA)
ORIGINAL LINE-UP John Feldmann (vocals); Charlie Paulson (guitar); Simon Williams (bass); Darrin Pfeiffer (drums)

According to Simon Williams, Goldfinger began with the dream of becoming "a heavy [version of the] Police," an ambition which was skewered when a more meaningful ska-core hybrid popped into his head, one day at the shoe shop where Williams and Feldmann were then employed.

Having isolated their dream, Goldfinger began stockpiling the demos, from which their debut EP *Richter* would eventually be compiled. Recorded on a 12-track machine, just 2,000 copies were pressed up to be sold on the band's first west coast tour in 1995. A split single with Reel Big Fish followed, but then it was back to their day jobs, where one day — according to the legend — John Feldmann sold Mojo Records boss Jay Rifkin a pair of shoes. The label mogul reciprocated by giving Goldfinger a record deal.

Released in 1996, Goldfinger's self-titled album was an immediate hit, a self-confessed "pop-ska-core-skater" blend led by the MTV smash "Here in Your Bedroom" (and the immortally titled "Fuck You and Your Cat"), and supported by a truly tireless appetite for live work. Sometimes playing two shows a day, Goldfinger racked up 382 gigs in 1996 alone.

Hang Ups, an inevitably less successful, but nonetheless well-rounded follow-up album, arrived a year later, while 1999 brought the stupendous *Darrin's Coconut Ass*, an eight-track mini-album packed with covers. The Cure's "Just Like Heaven," Bad Company's "Feel Like Making Love," and the Buzzcocks' "You Say You Don't Love Me" ranked among the more audacious efforts. The band's fourth album, *Stomping Ground* brought a conventional follow-up in the new year.

Goldfinger LPs

6 Richter (Goldfinger) 1994 Semi-demo collection barely hints at what's to come, but a neat showcase for the band's potential for songwriting and innovative cross-over styles.

8 Goldfinger (Uptown) 1996 Chockablock with short, sharp songs dripping with melodies and hooks and spruced up with a grab bag of influences from the Sex Pistols to Green Day, Bad Religion to the Buzzcocks, Goldfinger's sound swings from hardcore to skacore with pop-rock seated firmly in the center of the dial. The quartet don't so much rip as drape their influences across their songs, a riff here, a harmony there, then a splash of jazz and some big hair for luck.

7 Hang Ups (Uptown) 1997 More cross-wired fun from the frolicsome foursome, Goldfinger drift further into the musical mainstream, but commercial accessibility (and acceptability) doesn't dampen their enthusiasm. *Hang-Ups'* part angsty/part self-deprecating lyrics tap every teen's secret dreams and fears, while the upbeat music pops, rocks, and skanks as vigorously as ever.

9 Stomping Ground (Mojo) 2000 Now firmly ensconced in the alternative mainstream, *Stomping's* magical mix of hardcore, hardrock, pop, hiphop and Third Wave ska/reggae has classic scrawled all over it. Fourteen tracks, half of which are obvious contenders for singles success, range from the anthemic "Counting the Days," the pounding pop waves of "San Simeon," and the NOFX-y "I'm Down." This is the perfect stomping ground for musical youth of all stylistic persuasions.

GOMEZ

FORMED *1996 (Sheffield, England)*
ORIGINAL LINE-UP *Tom Gray (vocals, guitar, keyboards); Ian Ball (vocals, guitar); Ben Ottewell (guitar, vocals); Paul Blackburn (bass); Olly Peacock (drums)*

Originally a quartet of school friends, joined by Ben Ottewell after they'd moved on to university in Sheffield, Gomez were content simply jamming in a basement and making tapes to pass around friends, when Ian Ball handed one to local record store owner Steve Fellows.

Completely unbeknownst to the band, Fellows was a former member of '80s cult heroes Comsat Angels, and still had contacts in the UK music industry. Within three weeks of receiving the tape, he was fielding offers from more than 30 UK labels, all of whom were invited to a special Gomez show in a Sheffield rehearsal studio, in October 1997.

Island and A&M were both especially keen, offering to fly the band to America to record and gig, but Gomez ultimately went with the smaller Hut label (distributed through Virgin), who offered total autonomy to continue doing what they'd always done — a condition which other suitors had been somewhat circumspect about. Lengthy blues-thrash-flavored space jazz, after all, has never been high on the majors' shopping lists, and Gomez themselves expected their bizarre concoctions to sell to no more than a handful of people.

Originally planned as an EP, the band's self-produced debut album, *Bring It On*, was released in April 1998; a low-key record which ended up winning three of the top music honors in Britain: the *Q* and *NME* Best New band awards and a Best Album at the Mercury Music Awards.

The band went on the road and stayed there. Festival dates through summer 1998, and a US tour before year's end won the band further converts, and in early 1999, the band retired to the house they'd rented on Ilkeley Moor, Yorkshire, to begin work on their sophomore effort. *Liquid Skin* (#2 UK) was confusingly previewed with a single titled "Bring It On," and became an immediate hit in September 1999, at the outset of the band's next US tour. A second single, "Rhythm and Blues Alibi" (#18 UK) wrapped up the year.

Gomez LPs

9 Bring It On (Virgin) 1998 An astonishing debut, all the more so because it emerged completely out of left field, from a happy land where maybe Ozric Tentacles and Phish are hard currency, but so are Beefheart, the Beatles, and the Beta Band. Something sent the critics into overdrive though — was it really just the mad simplicity of the music?

9 Liquid Skin (Virgin) 1999 Part psychedelic twangers, part space rock cowboys crossed with garage rockers, yet still refreshingly contemporary, Gomez have fattened their overall sound this time, experimenting with such controlled abandon that the outcome is glorious fun. "Hangover" is a mellow jam which sets the pace and "Bring It On" can only be described as grungefuzzy, while "Rhythm Blues and Alibi" is a modern anthem managing to blend acoustic guitar and folk-tinged lyrics with a drum machine.

ERIC GOULDEN

BORN *(Newhaven, England)*

Having previously played in the remarkably-named Addis and the Flip-Tops, lemonade factory quality control supervisor "Wreckless" Eric Goulden dropped a tape of his songs off at Stiff Records, quit his job — and then spent two days wondering what he was going to do next, before Stiff called and offered him a deal.

Produced by Nick Lowe, "Whole Wide World" was originally recorded for inclusion on the *Bunch of Stiffs* label sampler; response to the song was so powerful, however, that Stiff promptly had Goulden and Lowe record a B-side, the equally remarkable "Semaphore Signals," and released a single in August 1977.

Following up with a remarkable showing on the Live Stiffs tour in November, punctuating his short nightly set with a lewd helplessness so irresistible that he frequently threatened to upstage all three of the headlining acts (Lowe, Elvis Costello, and Ian Dury), Goulden came off the road to record an EP with Dury. The sessions ended with little more than a title ("Picadilly Menial"), while the chance for Goulden to work with Elton John apparently fell through when the pair were unable to agree on a suitable place to meet.

Elton wanted a swank London hotel, Goulden preferred his own "rotten little flat in some London back alley."

So it was Lowe again who handled both Goulden's second single, "Reconnez Cherie," and his debut album *Wreckless Eric* (#46 UK) — a set which revealed him to be one of the most observant songwriters around, capable of some crushingly accurate reports on the human condition ("Personal Hygiene"), and all a far cry from the image of dissolute drunkenness which Stiff's promotions department was hell bent on serving up to the public.

Following a backbreaking UK tour through the summer of 1978, Goulden and producer Pete Solley pieced together his second album, the modestly titled *Wonderful World of Wreckless Eric*. With the singer's fascination for '50s era atmospheres coming increasingly into play both musically (one critic called that world "a provincial English *American Graffiti*) and visually (the album's jacket aped a popular UK music TV show of the same era), *Wonderful World* was accompanied by two further singles, "Take the KASH," and a cover of Buddy Holly's "Crying, Waiting, Hoping."

Goulden headlined the second Stiff package tour that November, alongside Lene Lovich, country schoolgirl superstar Rachel Sweet, and pub veterans Mickey Jupp and Jona Lewie; it would be the following summer before Goulden resurfaced in record stores, with the raucous "Hit and Miss Judy," a trailer for the *Whole Wide World* compilation.

A stunning selection of remixes, oldies, and rarities, *Whole Wide World* was initially intended for release in America only, to follow a successful mini tour the previous December. So many copies were imported back to Britain, however, that Stiff — faced with the prospect of not actually releasing one of their best selling albums yet — promptly recast Goulden's own next album, *Big Smash* (#30 UK), as a double, with *Whole Wide World* making up sides two and four.

Though Goulden himself acknowledged it was not to be his best album, a fault which he himself has put down to a slowly worsening relationship with Stiff themselves, *Big Smash* nevertheless came closest to breaking his chart shutout, both in its own right and via the "A Pop Song" single. Another track, "Broken Doll," was covered by veteran Cliff Richard, but the glory came too late. In late 1980, Goulden quit Stiff for a job roadying for country star George Hamilton IV.

It would be another five years before he returned to his own music, signing to Go! Discs and forming the Captains of Industry with ex-Ian Dury and the Blockheads alumni Norman Watt-Roy and Mickey Gallagher. A *Roomful of Monkeys*, the band's May 1985, debut album and "Lifeline" single were released with Goulden having finally shrugged off the Wreckless identity. It was with the Captains, too, that he returned to the club scene, although neither of his bandmates were available, so he pieced together a new three-piece with former Billy Childish sidemen Russ Wilkins (bass) and Bruce Brand (drums), and debuted at London's Kennington Cricketers on August 11, 1985.

The defiantly low-fi *The Len Bright Combo Presents The Len Bright Combo, By the Len Bright Combo* was released

L to R: Eric Goulden, Russ Wilkins, Bruce Brand   Courtesy of Dave Thompson

on the band's own Empire label, in March 1986, together with a single, "Someone Must've Nailed Us Together," and with *Melody Maker* proclaiming it "the worst recorded record since the Velvets first turned everything up full blast and played till the recording heads broke," the Combo returned to the studio for October's sophomore *Combo Time*.

But disputes over the band's future direction — namely, whether the song was more important than the delivery (Goulden said yes, his bandmates disagreed) — were already puncturing the band's equilibrium. A projected EP, *Let's Make a Box*, was cancelled when Brand quit to get married shortly before Christmas 1986. He was replaced, fleetingly, by a roadie named Donald, but just weeks and a handful of contractual obligations later, the Combo split.

Goulden formed a new band, the Chicken Family, with ex-Men They Couldn't Hang bassist Shanne Bradley; however, he also suffered a nervous breakdown, and another two years passed before he resurfaced with a new album, *Le Beat Group Electrique*, and single "It's a Sick, Sick Sick World" — salvaged from the abortive Combo EP. Both were credited to Wreckless Eric.

Released only in France through New Rose, the records were barely promoted and scarcely sold, despite Goulden himself having relocated to that country. A second single, "Haunted House," passed unnoticed in May 1990, and finally tiring of the situation, Goulden taped an impromptu show at New Rose's storefront, and insisted the ensuing *At the Shop* become his next album. It did, and he left the label shortly after.

A self-released Christmas single, "Christmas," rounded out 1990, and it would be another three years before Goulden signed with SFTRI, with a new single eulogizing '60s producer "Joe Meek," and one final album as Wreckless Eric, *The Donovan of Trash*. He then formed the Hitsville House Band with Denis Baudrillart (b. Paris — drums — ex-Les Soucoupes Violents) and bassist Eduardo Leal de la Gala (b. Mexico), soon to be replaced by double bassist Farbice Lombardo, a member of Almost Presley.

Originally formed to accompany another British expatriate, Martin Stone, on a solo album which Goulden would be producing at his own Hitsville studio, the band slowly became Goulden's own, recording *12 o'Clock Stereo* during downtime in the sessions. The album would be released in the US in 1996 through Ottoman Empire frontman Clay Harper's Casino label, with a single, "The Girl With the Wandering Eye," becoming a radio hit in the UK that summer.

With Goulden having already returned to England to live, he immediately recorded a follow-up set, 1997's *Karaoke* mini-album, released as Eric Goulden ("The Artist Formerly

Known as Wreckless Eric"). A new band, the four piece Karaoke Car Crash was formed with Garry (guitar), Safi (bass), and Will (drums). However, the band played just two shows in May 1998 and by July, Will alone remained, to join Goulden, girlfriend Ina Weber, and bassist Andrew in a new band, Southern Domestic.

Their debut mini-album, *The Sound of Your Living Room (In a Dump Near Your Own Home)* was recorded in late 1999, following a string of gigs supporting the rejuvenated Ian Dury and the Blockheads. Goulden also recorded alongside Dury and former Velvet Underground drummer Mo Tucker, on *The Slippery Ballerina* childrens' story CD and appeard at the Dury tribute concert in London in June 2000.

Eric Goulden LPs

9 Wreckless Eric (Stiff) 1978 Joyously idiosyncratic, a rambling tour through a world of waxworks, Benny Hill, and personal hygiene (strong stomachs recommended) with an eye for detail which pre-Pulped Pulp. "Whole Wide World" and "Reconnez Cherie" are the best known points of entry; Ian Dury's "Rough Kids" and the monumental "Brain Thieves" among the most rewarding.

8 The Wonderful World of Wreckless Eric (Stiff) 1978 A more polished sound and delivery left *The Wonderful World* feeling less immediate than its predecessor, although the songs, if anything, are even stronger, and the mood less reliant on its roughshod charm.

7 Big Smash (Stiff) 1980 On paper and in isolation, another crop of classics — "Broken Doll," "Excuse Me," "A Pop Song." But the overall mood was just a little too despairing and any hopes of cohesion were hopelessly scattered by the insertion of a greatest hits collection.

8 Le Beat Group Electrique (New Rose) 1989 The deceptively buoyant "Tell Me I'm the Only One" and the merciless "Fuck By Fuck" characterize Goulden's most desolate album, produced with all the sonic warmth of toothache. The songwriter's vision remains undamaged, though, even when spitting "It's a Sick Sick World."

8 Donovan of Trash (Sftri) 1993 If you were to die within three seconds of this record beginning, the last sound you'd hear would be "plonk." Live on, and you might learn something. There's no crash for crunch's sake silliness, and while he might appear to be walking in Billy Childish's shoes, mood — even an exhilarating retro-'60s wall of noise mood — isn't everything. In hi-fi terms, this record is rubbish. But it's rubbish for people with brains, and the ability to think beyond the next knee-jerk spasm.

Captains of Industry LP

7 A Roomful of Monkeys (Go! Discs) 1986 For a man whose entire career had been spent dissecting the petty values of trash suburbia, it was bizarre that Eric should then up and move there.

But the Captains reflected what he found. "The check-out girls look just like pigs in our neck of the woods...."

Len Bright Combo LPs

10 **Len Bright Combo Presents the Len Bright Combo by the Len Bright Combo (Empire) 1987** Two intensive listens are required before the wall of noise even threatens to make sense, and when Goulden opens "Young, Upwardly Mobile and Stupid" a cappella, the moment when the band comes in sounds like an elevator full of fat people falling down a shaft.

In any other hands, the glorious "Someone Must Have Nailed Us Together" could win a Grammy. Here it sounds like it was recorded in a box. Even "Lureland," ostensibly a gentle song of childhood memories, is peopled by sinister old men in flapping raincoats and haunted by a tortured nostalgia which continuous oozing long into the night, to wash up in the stale family get-togethers at grandma's house reanimated by "The Golden Hour of Harry Secombe." And then there's "You're Gonna Screw My Head Off," which might be self-explanatory.

Not an album which sits easily on the turntable, then; even today, too many people will take it at face value and dismiss it as the lo-fi ramblings of a demented old rocker. But once you've unlocked the secrets of the sound, the Combo's psychotic beat-box stands revealed as an album of breathtaking purity. In 1986, there wasn't a soul on earth with the guts to release an album this grungey. By 1990, that's all people were doing. The modern world started here.

5 **Combo Time (Ambassador) 1987** Distinctly disappointing sophomore effort, apparently more intent on making the same noise as last time, but with some distinctly make weight songs.

Hitsville House Band LP

7 **12 o'clock Stereo (Casino) 1996** Simultaneously depressing, daunting, and utterly uplifting, from the opening "Killburn Lane" Goulden's cock-eyed squint on an anally-retentive world continues as funny (or rude and irreverent) as you want it to be. And if songs like "You Can't Be a Man (Without a Beer in Your Hand)" hint at a weariness with the common herd, what has Goulden's trademark always been if not a microscopic evaluation of the traumas of trendiness? It's not only the girl who's got a wandering eye.

GRANT LEE BUFFALO

FORMED 1989 (Los Angeles, CA)
ORIGINAL LINE-UP *Grant Lee Phillips (b. 9/1/63, Stockton CA — vocals, guitar); Paul Kimble (b. 9/24/60, Freeport, IL — bass); Joey Peters (b. 4/9/65, New York, NY— drums)*

Grant Lee Phillips emerged from King of the World, originally performing as Grant Lee Buffalo before full King sets, to run through his repertoire of country standards. The buf-

falo, he explained, represented all that had gone wrong with America.

When King of the World split, he linked with Paul Kimble and Joey Peters in Shiva Burlesque, a five-piece which was whittled down to three after the other members missed too many rehearsals. Reclaiming his earlier alias, Phillips set about creating a repertoire based upon pure Americana — "storytelling, and improvisation" — and in fall 1991, an eleven-track demo recorded at Kimble's home studio was passed onto Hüsker Dü's Bob Mould.

Mould released a single of "Fuzzy" on his Singles Only label; a month later, Grant Lee Buffalo signed to Slash and recorded their debut album, also titled *Fuzzy* (#74 UK) in two weeks. It was released in 1993, and was described by Michael Stipe as the year's "finest album, hands down."

A handful of EPs, led by the in-concert *Buffalondon* and *Blue Plate Special*, preluded the release of *Mighty Joe Moon* in 1994. Grant Lee Buffalo's sophomore album earned further accolades and thus emboldened, the band recruited violinist Bob Fergo, bass clarinetist Ralph Carney, and pedal steel guitarist Greg Leisz, and set to work on the heavily stylized *Copperopolis*, an ambitious (some said overly so) conclusion to what the members now considered a trilogy of folk/traditional excursions.

Stepping dramatically out of character, the group would next contribute a track to the *Velvet Goldmine* glam rock movie soundtrack; Kimble alone would be even more deeply involved, performing with the make-shift supergroup Venus in Furs, alongside Radiohead's Thom Yorke and Jonny Greenwood, ex-London Suede guitarist Bernard Butler, and original Roxy Music saxophonist Andy MacKay.

Citing musical differences, Kimble quit Grant Lee Buffalo later in 1997: Phillips and Peters alone would mastermind 1998's *Jubilee*, aided by Leisz, Dan Rothschild (ex-Tonic), Jon Brian (keyboards), and XTC/Sky Cries Mary producer Paul Fox. Other guests included Robyn Hitchcock playing harmonica, and Stipe. The band's next US tour, meanwhile, saw the core duo joined by the oddly pseudonymed Brian Bonk (bass) and Phil Parlapiano (keyboards).

The group announced its break up on June 9, 1999; Phillips pursuing a solo career, while Peters discussed a new band with Kimble. According to the official statement, "the possibility of a future Grant Lee Buffalo album exists."

Grant Lee Buffalo LPs

8 **Fuzzy (Slash) 1993** Loose and evocative Americana, the seemingly simple playing and production camouflaging dynamic strengths which trail from Neil Young to Jefferson Airplane, without ever once looking backwards.

8 Mighty Joe Moon (Slash) 1994 Wide screen variation on its predecessor, a sound as big as a Montana sky wrestling with Philips' grasp on both his lyrical and emotional abilities.

9 Copperopolis (Slash) 1996 Having seen *Joe Moon*'s virtues suddenly become current among a crop of other orchestral-rock bands, GLB scale back again, effortlessly placing themselves this time within a time-locked Sierra Nevada, chewing over past times and pains with a bunch of hoary old-timers. In lesser hands, a song like "Bethlehem Steel" would have wound up suffering from Springsteen-itus; here, it comes on like a lost Woody Guthrie.

7 Jubilee (Slash) 1998 Their most conventional album, returning to the symphonic production (Paul Fox) values of *Joe Moon*, but reining in some of their other, more laudable tricks. "Seconds" is sincere supersonic pop, though, and "Fine, How'd Ya Do" has a cracked Crackerish swagger to it.

GREEN DAY

FORMED 1989 *(Berkeley, CA)*
ORIGINAL LINE-UP *Billie Joe Armstrong (b. 2/17/72 — vocals, guitar); Mike Dirnt (b. Mike Pritchard, 5/4/72 — bass); John Kiffmeyer (drums)*

Bille Joe Armstrong and Mike Dirnt were friends hanging out within Berkeley's Gilman Street punk scene when they hooked up with John Kiffmeyer (ex-Isocracy) as Sweet Children in 1989. Quickly signing with the local Lookout label, after playing a show with labelhead Laryy Livermore's own band, the Lookouts, Sweet Children's *1000 Hours* EP, was just two weeks away from release when the band announced they were changing their name to Green Day, to avoid confusion with Slash/Warners act Sweet Baby (ex-Sweet Baby Jesus).

Despite Livermore's misgivings, the change was effected without any effect on the band's burgeoning live popularity and with the EP selling well, Green Day recorded their debut album, *39/Smooth*.

Green Day gigged regularly throughout the Bay Area; during a break in their own schedule, Dirnt and Armstrong also spent late summer 1989 touring as members, respectively, of Berkeley punk bands Crummy Musicians and Corrupted Morals. They returned in time for two new Green Day EPs, *Slappy* and *Sweet Children*, the latter including a frenzied cover of the Who's "My Generation."

While Green Day continued gigging over ever broader swathes of the US through the next few years, both Dirnt and Armstrong continued working outside the band format, Dirnt with Chicago punks Screeching Weasel, Armstrong on the final releases by The Lookouts and Gilman Street supergroup Pinhead Gunpowder. He also played some shows with Rancid, as they sought a second guitarist.

Green Day's first full national tour in 1991 was followed by Kiffmeyer's departure for college (he later resurfaced in the Ne'er Do Wells, for an EP on Lookout and a split album with Judy and the Loadies, *Gift of Knowledge*). Green Day promptly replaced him with Tre Cool (b. 12/9/72), out of work since the recent demise of the Lookouts, and recorded their second album, *Kerplunk!*.

Like its predecessor, *Kerplunk!* sold around 50,000 copies, sufficient to bring the first major label offers. The band opted for Reprise, then recruited that label's A&R man, Rob Cavallo, to produce their next album, 1993's *Dookie* (#2 US, #13 UK). Its success, opened up by the #1 Modern Rock hits and videos "Long View" (#30 UK), "Basketcase" (#7 UK), "When I Come Around" (#27 UK), and a re-recording of *Kerplunk!* stand-out "Welcome to Paradise" (#20 UK), was immediate. *Dookie* would sell over 8,000,000 copies in the US, earning the band a Grammy for Best Alternative Music Performance.

Touring kept Green Day on the road throughout 1993 and most of 1994. Crisscrossing the States as the album soared up the charts, the crowds grew and the band entered stadiumland. They toured Europe with Bad Religion, turned in a mud-spattered, show-stealing set at Woodstock '94 and,

Billie Joe Armstrong of Green Day

© Jim Steinfeldt/Chansley Entertainment Archives

in the new year, earned Best New Band, Best New Male Singer, Best Album, and Best Album Cover at the *Rolling Stone* Music Awards. In June — even as Green Day topped the modern rock chart with "J.A.R. (Jason Andrew Relva)," their contribution to the *Angus* movie soundtrack — the two Lookout albums were certified gold.

Perhaps inevitably, Green Day's fourth album, *Insomniac* (#2 US, #8 UK), sold no more than a quarter of its predecessor upon its release in October 1994 — although that would not stop it from spawning further radio monsters "Geek Stink Breath" (#16 UK), "Stuck With Me" (#24 UK), and "Brain Stew/Jaded" (#28 UK). Still, the record's comparative failure would cause the band to seriously reappraise their methods. A European tour in 1996 was cancelled, the band citing exhaustion, and in the year which followed, the band members opted to spend time instead with families the trio had barely seen in two years.

Green Day reconvened to record *Nimrod* (#10 US, #11 UK), an album which owed nothing to media or audience expectations and emerged so variety-packed that one cut, "Time of Your Life" (#11 UK), hit as a virtual Billie Joe solo project. The song also became a favorite of US TV producers, as background music for heart-wrenching scenes throughout the 1997–98 season.

Other singles from the album "Hitchin' a Ride" (#25 UK) and "Redundant" (#27 UK) were more in keeping with Green Day's reputation, of course; so were scenes on the band's next US tour, as media claims that their popularity had nose dived with their record sales were proven wrong on a nightly basis. Besides, the early 1999 news that *Dookie* had now sold over 10 million copies in the US proved they were doing something right — in an "alternative" rock market which had barely existed a decade before, Green Day were now the undisputed best selling band ever.

Green Day LPs

7 39/Smooth (Lookout) 1990 Crashing the Partridge Family into the Ramones, the band's concerns were mostly about girls and girl troubles — "At the Library," "Don't Leave Me," "Going to Pasalacqua," "Rest," and "The Judge's Daughter." But growing up and finding one's place in the world also gets a look-in, through "I Was There," "Disappearing Boy," and "Road to Acceptance." Finally there's "Green Day," ostensibly about what passes through one's mind after smoking good pot.

8 Kerplunk! (Lookout) 1992 Finding a happy medium between their punk/pop extremes (aside from Cool's sublimely silly hillbilly "Dominated Love Song"), *Kerplunk* has a sharper, punker sound than previous material. The strong melodies remain, but the guitar riffs have lost most of the '60s pop sound in favor of sharper riffery, and the energy level is much, much higher. There's also an edge to the songs that hadn't appeared before.

9 Dookie (Reprise) 1993 It sounds so familiar now, it's hard to remember that until Green Day made this record, no band sounded this dynamic and pure. Undiluted pop with an uninhibited punk edge, circus strongman melodies, harmonies and hooks, *Dookie* was a high gloss masterpiece. According to Armstrong, the songs "are about urban life and trying to find a solution to the whole thing within myself." And that perfectly sums it up.

8 Insomniac (Reprise) 1995 Mostly written late at night in Armstrong's basement, while he suffered the sleeplessness which accompanied the birth of his son, the been-there, heard-that mentality of the current youth market meant that this album's sales fell far below *Dookie's*, even though *Insomniac* was just as fast and furious. Lyrically, however, Billie Joe's angst reached K2 proportions, beating himself up in song after song — great fun for a handful of misunderstood and miserable kids, but a little exhausting for everyone else. Still, the music remains upbeat, catchy *In Excelsis*, and the band are tighter than ever.

8 Nimrod 1997 A purer '60s pop sound dominates, heavily influenced by the Byrds and the Beatles, but there's plenty of fire and fury left, and even some hardcore and old school punk. The band break new ground with the addition of strings, horns and harmonica, while lyrically Billie Joe also takes on some unexpected personas. Including, of course, the rapidly maturing songwriter responsible for the moody surf of "Last Ride In" and the melancholy string drenched "Good Riddance."

Selected Compilations and Archive Releases

8 1,039/Smoothed Out Slappy Hours (Lookout) 1991

The Ne'er Do Wells LP

6 Gift of Knowledge [SPLIT W/JUDY AND THE LOADERS] (Lookout) 1992

Pinhead Gunpowder LP

7 Jump Salty (Lookout) 1994

Screeching Weasel LPs

6 Screeching Weasel (Roadkill) 1987

6 Boogadaboogadaboogada! (Roadkill) 1988

7 My Brain Hurts (Lookout) 1991

7 Wiggle (Lookout) 1992 Across their first four albums, the prolific Weasels knockout a record shop's worth of fast and furious blasts of pop-punk. Faster than hardcore, more fervent than Fugazi, and even funnier than anyone you laugh at when they're not looking. Each new record somehow surpasses the last — the songs are just a bit sharper, the group (regardless of line-up shifts, revolving door bassists and regular band break-ups) a tad tighter, the lyrics even better, and the hooks more infectious.

8 Beat is On the Brat (Lookout) 1992 Breakneck recounting of the Ramones' first album — and if you thought that was fast....

7 Anthem for a New Tomorrow (Lookout) 1993

8 How to Make Enemies and Irritate People (Lookout) 1994
Weasel's track record continues unbroken. Not since the early
Buzzcocks has a band come up with so many ways to make you
smile, gaining new fans with each release. On *Enemies* they
reached even greater heights, helped by bassist Mike Dirnt, and
promptly broke up again.

8 Bark Like a Dog (Fat Wreck Chords) 1996 Reforming once
more, Weasel return with their poppiest album yet, melodies to
drool over accented by three-part harmonies and the best production the group's ever had.

7 Television City Dream (Fat Wreck Chords) 1998 All, apparently, has not been well in Weasel-land, and *Dream* is an outlet
for the ensuing tension. Bristling with anger and bitterness, a
much more aggressive approach than anything in the past,
although in typical Weasel fashion, the fury is still wrapped in
shiny melodies and harmonies.

8 EMO (Panic Button) 1990 Ben Weasel attempts to excise the
angst, anger, and confusion that's raged around the band for the
last few years. "I'm making my own rules. My own world," he
shouts in "The Scene," and that defiance reverberates across
EMO. Slammed down quickly, warts and all, Weasel's latest captures the fire and "fuck you" attitude that defined Old School
punk, the perfect answer to New School elitists and other detractors.

Further Reading
Green Day by Jon Ewing (MBS, 1995).

GREEN RIVER

FORMED 1984 *(Seattle, WA)*
ORIGINAL LINE-UP *Mark Arm (b. 2/21/62, CA — vocals); Steve
Turner (b. 3/28/65, Houston, TX — guitar); Jeff Ament (b.
3/10/63, Big Sandy, MT — bass); Alex Vincent (b. Alex Shum-
way — drums)*

Spiritual fathers of the entire Seattle explosion of the early
1990s, Green River combined the hardcore of visiting California bands like Flipper and Minor Threat with the classic
metal stylings which still dominated the PNW scene to devastating effect.

Growing out of an incestuous stream of local acts — Mr.
Epp and the Calculations, Limp Richard (Mark Arm and
Steve Turner), the Ducky Boys (Turner alone), Spluii Numa
(Alex Vincent), and Deranged Diction (Jeff Ament) —
Green River played their first show opening for PMA at a
party on Seattle's 12th Ave. in early 1984, with Arm on vocals
and guitar. Further gigs over the next six months, however,
convinced Arm that he wanted to concentrate on vocals
alone — he was replaced on guitar by Stone Gossard (b.
7/20/66, Seattle, WA — ex-Deranged Diction/March of
Crimes).

From the outset, Green River divided audiences neatly
down the center. When the quintet opened for the Dead
Kennedys at the local Moore Theatre, half the audience
pelted the band with popcorn, ice, and shoes. However,
Homestead A&R man Gerard Cosley was impressed and in
December 1984, Green River began work on the six-track
mini-album *Come On Down*. Completed in a matter of days,
it would not be released for close to a year, during which
time Green River continued playing around their hometown.

In January 1985, they opened for Sonic Youth and local
legends the U-Men at Gorilla Gardens; by summer, they
were gearing up for their first national tour, shedding Turner
in a dispute over musical direction shortly beforehand.
"Stoney and Jeff were like heavy metal kids. They were into
Motorhead and Stoney was really into Kiss," he explained
later, "I was into the California hardcore, but I also liked the
Clash, Devo, and 999."

Deranged Diction's Bruce Fairweather was quickly
drafted in to replace him, but the seven date tour proved
disastrous. Scheduling delays had pushed *Come On Down*
back yet again; the group toured without anybody knowing
who they were, with the final ignominy awaiting the band in
New York — where Green River headlined CBGBs to just
six people; four Japanese tourists and two people that worked
there. Gigs opening for Bad Brains were a bare improvement, while a Halloween show with Samhain in Detroit was
packed, but hostile.

Come On Down finally emerged before Christmas 1985
and in the new year, Green River returned to the road. A
meeting with Aerosmith's Joe Perry at a return date at
CBGBs provoked rumors that he would produce the group's
next record; in the event, the June 1986, *Dry as a Bone* EP
sessions were handled by local producer Jack Endino.

Again a year would elapse before the record saw release;
the band was now signed to the fledgling Sub Pop label and
needed to wait while the company geared itself up. They
killed time with November 1986's "Together We'll Never" 45
on their own ICP label (backed with a cover of the Dead
Boys' "Ain't Nothin' to Do") and also contributed to the now-
legendary *Deep Six* compilation (C/Z). *Dry As a Bone* finally
emerged a strong local seller and in August 1987, Green
River cut the *Rehab Doll* EP. However, their bad luck held
as once again the tape rotted in its case, while Sub Pop struggled with financing — and this time, the delay was too
much. By the time Sub Pop released the album, one year
and a desultory third tour later, later, Green River were history.

The split, again, was due to musical differences. Arm
complained, "they were trying to play Guns n' Roses and the
brand new Aerosmith. None of them had any interest in the

tape I wanted to play — rockabilly and Thee Milkshakes." Ament, Gossard, and Fair-weather were already jamming with Malfunkshun vocalist Andy Wood, planning what would become Mother Love Bone; Arm was soon reunited with Turner in Mudhoney.

Green River's own legacy, meanwhile, would carry on through the unearthing of previously unreleased material for such Seattle compilations as *Sub Pop 2000*, *Afternoon Delight* and, most apt of all, C/Z's *Another Pyrrhic Victory — The Only Compilation of Dead Seattle God Bands*.

Green River LP

🔲 **Come On Down (Homestead) 1985** Ambition flowers amid the road tapes, as one album slips effortlessly from "Swallow My Pride" to "Tunnel of Love," a multi-sectioned epic which borrowed more than its title from Dire Straits. Still a quivering slither of minimalist noise, but big rock ambitions were hoving into view, and Steve Turner could see them coming. So he quit.

Selected Compilations and Archive Releases

🔲 **Dry As a Bone/Rehab Doll (Sub Pop) 1988** 16-track collection combining both Sub Pop EPs, outtakes and alternate mixes.

GUN CLUB

FORMED 1980 *(Los Angeles, CA)*
ORIGINAL LINE-UP *Jeffrey Lee Pierce (b. 6/27/58, El Monte, CA — vocals, guitar); Kid Congo Powers (b. Brian Tristan — guitar); Brad Dunning (bass); Don Snowden (drums)*

Pierce was an occasional contributor to *Slash* magazine when he and guitarist Powers formed Creeping Ritual in 1980, partly inspired by a recent Damned concert and partly by a piece of advice a friend passed along when Pierce first started writing songs — "tell them what they don't want to hear."

As Pierce later noted in his autobiography, "as a rule, all of the [early] lyrics dealt with unpopular subjects, namely: Sex, Murder, Drugs, Insanity, Desperation, Loneliness, Suicide and just plain Bad Vibes. There is also a fair amount of Self-Destructive Serial Killer and Racist War Criminal mentality portrayed." It was around these admittedly promising roots that modern America's greatest urban blues band took shape — even as Pierce furiously shredded most people's concept of the blues.

Adding Dunning and Snowden, the band changed their name to Gun Club at the suggestion of Circle Jerks frontman Chris Morris and began gigging — their first ever show saw them opening for the Circle Jerks at a Chinese restaurant. However, by early summer, Dunning and Snowden had quit, to be replaced by Rob Ritter and Terry Graham, rhythm section with L.A. punk heroes The Bags — with

whom Gun Club's original line-up played their final show, at the Hong Kong Cafe.

The new members debuted at Madame Wong's in early summer; however, Gun Club's early momentum was to be seriously stifled by the gradual constriction of the L.A. club scene which was then in full swing. By the time Ritter quit in late 1980, complaining that the band was stagnating, they had not gigged in two months. Anna Statman replaced him for one show in Culver City — it was there, however, that Pierce learned Powers, too, was departing, to join the Cramps. By Christmas 1980, the Gun Club were no more.

Pierce, Ritter, and Graham reformed the band in the new year with guitarist Ward Dotson and began gigging regularly, often with the Cramps. They also linked with the Plugz' Fatima label, recording half a dozen songs before discovering the label didn't have the money to cut any more. Slash Records promptly stepped into the void and, with the Flesheaters' Chris Desjardins producing, Gun Club completed their debut album, *Fire of Love* (and the accompanying "Ghost on the Highway" single).

The album was an instant success, particularly outside of L.A.. Both New York and Boston became virtual second homes for Gun Club as they toured through 1982, while the UK Beggars Banquet label was sufficiently enthused to organize the album's UK release (#29 UK indie) — Britain, too, would remain loyal to Pierce over the next two decades.

Pierce's friendship with Blondie's Debbie Harry and Chris Stein doubtless influenced the band's next move, signing to Stein's own newly launched Animal label. Immediately, Stein returned Gun Club to the studio and, by August, a new single, "The Fire of Love," and album, *Miami*, were set for release.

Powers returned to the line-up in late 1982, around the same time as Ritter and Dotson departed. He left again after just a handful of gigs, however, but a new look Gun Club was already in place, as Pierce introduced Legal Weapon bassist Patricia Morrison to the brew — while admitting that Ritter taught her everything he knew before he left. Pierce took the opportunity now to completely revamp the line-up, recruiting drummer Dee Pop from the Bush Tetras and guitarist Jim Duckworth from Tav Falco's Panther Burns. (He also launched a side project, Tex and the Horseheads, with girlfriend Linda Jones. However, when the couple split up soon after, she took this new band with her.)

This line up debuted with the EP *Death Party* in April 1983; they also recorded a live album, *The Birth, The Death, and the Ghost* (#7 UK indie), for European release, but the band was again close to imploding. Duckworth quit at the start of an Australian tour — members of a local group, the Johnnys, augmented the disabled line-up for the remainder of the outing.

Back in L.A., Powers rejoined the band for their *Las Vegas Story* album, but the tensions and instability which had characterized the band's existence so far were not to be salved. Animal's parent label, Chrysalis, hated the new album and had already made it known that the release would be getting zero promotion. Gun Club's own latest tour was struggling, both musically and in terms of ticket sales — Pierce himself was more interested in an ad hoc free jazz trio he had formed with ex-Nerves frontman Peter Case and Masque club owner Brendan Mullen, the Astro Unicorn Jazz Ensemble.

In this state, Gun Club toured America and Europe for close to six months; with the 1981 live album *Sex Beat* (#6 UK indie) still on the shelves, their final show was at London's Dingwalls at Christmas 1984. Morrison promptly joined Powers' Fur Club before resurfacing first in the Sisters of Mercy and later, the Damned. Pierce, meanwhile, decamped to Egypt for a vacation, then returned to London where he signed a solo deal with Statik Records.

Vintage Gun Club material continued to appear — through 1985–86 the band enjoyed hits with *Two Sides of the Beast* collection (#16 UK indie), a reissue of *Fire of Love* (#19 UK indie), and a substandard live album, *Danse Kalinda* (#27 UK indie). Pierce himself formed a new band comprising Murray Mitchell (guitsr), John McKenzie (bass), and Andy Anderson (drums) and swiftly recorded his first solo album, *Wildweed*.

By summer, however, the singer was touring Europe and the US with a new line-up, featuring his Japanese guitarist girlfriend Romi Mori (ex-Red Zone, a Japanese Runaways tribute act) and the former Clock DVA rhythm section of Dean Dennis and Nick Sanderson. Two singles, "Love and Depression" and "Flamingo," followed, but by late 1985, Pierce's British visa had expired and he moved on to Tokyo, to live with Mori and her family. There he met future manager Haruko Minakami, the woman responsible for introducing her homeland to Nick Cave (the subject of Pierce's song "Bill Bailey"), Foetus, Lydia Lunch, and Einsturzende Neubauten.

Three months later, Pierce and Mori were back in Europe. In Amsterdam, Pierce took part in a series of readings given by Henry Rollins and William Burroughs (remarkably, punk poetess Joolz was the billed headliner). In London, he linked with long time admirer Robin Guthrie of the Cocteau Twins, who partially produced Pierce's next album and single, *Mother Juno* (#3 UK indie) and "Breaking Hands" (#18 UK indie). He continued touring, then returned to L.A. in 1988 — it was there that Pierce learned he was suffering from cirrhosis of the liver, malnutrition, and hypothrombosis, a surprising combination of ailments for a 29-year-old.

It was recommended that he give up music and file for a disability pension; instead he dried out and, reunited with Powers, launched another American tour, his first in almost four years. Gigs with Pussy Galore, Henry Rollins, and the Goo Goo Dolls among the most illustrious opening acts saw *Mother Juno* climb the CMJ chart — it eventually peaked at #1, while the band's next European tour saw them climbing the summer festival circuit.

However, European record label problems saw Gun Club weighed down by both legal and contractual difficulties — they signed a demo agreement with Island Records, then suffered an eight-month period during which they were prohibited from playing gigs in any major city, until they actually had new product to promote. Finally, Gun Club quit the label with nothing more than some demos and a few showcase gigs to show for their time.

With the band now signing to Fire, fall 1990 brought the album *Pastoral Hide and Seek* and single, "The Great Divide." The partial live album, *Divinity*, followed in 1991. Two years later, signed now to Triple X, the band released *Lucky Jim*. Pierce was again dividing his time between London, where he seemed to do his best work; L.A., where drink and, increasingly, drugs, devoured much of his time; and the far east, where an immune system long since shattered by hepatitis appeared to be a magnet for every nasty disease in creation.

The *In Exile* compilation (gathering up material from *Mother Juno* and *Pastoral Hide and Seek*) and a live set, *Ahmed's Wild Dream*, maintained the band's high profile; so did an American tour with Agent Orange. However, the appearance of stability was deceptive. Ever restless, Pierce was again contemplating a career away from Gun Club and, in early 1992, he formed a new band, Cypress Grove, to record the damaged swamp blues of *Ramblin' Jeffrey Lee With...* . He also turned his hand to writing, penning the semi-biographical *Go Tell the Mountain*. Indeed, the book occupied much of the last years of his life, in between occasional live shows and travelling in south-east Asia. He spent much of 1995 in Osaka, Japan, returning to L.A. in early 1996, aiming to complete the book before the publisher's deadline of April 1, 1996.

He never made it. On March 24, 1996 Pierce suffered a stroke; a week later, a blood clot reached his brain and killed him. Pieced together by Gun Club fan club president Gene Temesy, *Go Tell the Mountain* was finally published by Henry Rollins' 2.13.61 house in 1998.

Gun Club LPs

⑨ Fire of Love (Ruby) 1982 Unsettling, uncomfortable, and utterly anti-social, Gun Club burst out of L.A.'s already mutant underbelly with a cacophonous roar which made even the

Cramps (their closest living relatives) sound like a Rotary Club danceband. Violins and slide guitar echo where you least expect them and, though audiophiles run from the roughshod production, there is a majesty to the sound which neither years nor countless repeat plays can diminish. And if Robert Johnson has a record player, you know he'd agree.

8 Miami (Animal) 1982 Producer Stein cannot help but clean things up a little — he did the same to Iggy's *Zombie Birdhouse*. But Pierce is not to be denied, delving deeper into his knapsack of nasties in search of the ultimate twisted thrill. More vicarious than vicious in its overall delivery, *Miami* remains, nevertheless, a deeply twisted hitch-hike through the bowels of the American dream, and a journey which everyone should take.

9 The Birth, The Death, and the Ghost (ABC — UK) 1984 Gun Club on vinyl were powerful; Gun Club live were purging and, from the moment "Bo Diddley Is a Gunslinger" kicks in with all the menace which Bo is meant to encapsulate (but which his own records never, ever recreated — ain't that always the way?), Gun Club fill voids in your soul which you never even knew was there. Few live albums can be described as important; this one is actually essential.

8 The Las Vegas Story (Animal) 1984 Anyone who doubts Pierce wrote the Great American Novel need only dip into this, another psychotic journey around the country, and the fact that guitars replace the typewriter only adds emphasis to the cachet.

7 Mother Juno (Fundamental) 1987 With Robin Guthrie at the controls, but everybody drinking deep from the wellspring of hard rock inspiration, *Mother Juno* is initially confusing — where have all the blues songs gone? Then you realize they're still there, peeping out from behind the crunching chords and mutant solos, grinning like fiends and whispering... come on in. The water's lovely.

8 Pastoral Hide And Seek (Fire — UK) 1990 Of them all, this is the weirdest — a downbeat... yes indeed, pastoral collection, just the sort of thing to play when it's late at night and you want the kids to have really cool nightmares. If you've got kids. Otherwise, just scare yourself.

7 Divinity (Solid) 1991

7 Lucky Jim (Triple X) 1993 Superficially, here comes the new Gun Club, much the same as the old. But a basic reliance on

trusted truism quickly gives way to the need to discover what will happen if you push the barriers here, and punch them there, until the umpteenth variation on "Dust My Broom" (the closing "Anger Blues") collapses beneath its own redundancy and is reborn as something both stunning and, in ripping up the rule book, stentorian. In other words, imagine Bauhaus covering "Free Bird."

7 Live In Europe (aka Ahmed's Wild Dream) (Triple X) 1993

Selected Compilations and Archive Releases

8 Sex Beat — Live 1981 (Lolita — UK) 1984

5 Two Sides of the Beast (Castle — UK) 1985 Half live, half studio compilation, stunning in its diversity, but disappointingly redundant as well. If you really wanted to hear these songs, you'd already have the original albums.

7 Love Supreme (Offence — France) 1985 Live 1982; rotten sound but a great performance.

5 Dance Kalinda Boom (Roadrunner) 1985

7 In Exile (Triple X) 1992 Highlights from *Mother Juno* and *Pastoral Hide and Seek*, reprised for Americans who couldn't be bothered to buy the imports.

Jeffrey Lee Pierce LPs

7 Wildweed (Statik — UK) 1985 Precious, understated, dark, and delicious, Pierce strips away much of the surface electricity and emerges even more shocking than usual.

Ramblin' Jeffrey Lee & Cypress Grove with Willie Love LP

8 Ramblin' Jeffrey Lee & Cypress Grove with Willie Love (Triple X) 1992 Unwanted comparisons to Led Zeppelin notwithstanding, Pierce turns to a faithful recounting of the blues that matter most to him, stripping Chester Burnett's "Moanin' in the Moonlight" down to its composite nightmares while his own "Go Tell the Mountain" stands as possibly the greatest American blues song of the 30 years.

Further Reading

Go Tell The Mountain: The Stories and Lyrics of Jeffrey Lee Pierce by Jeffrey Lee Pierce (2.13.61, 1998).

H

LOL HAMMOND

BORN *(Stoke Newington, London)*

Hammond first came to attention as a guitarist with Kiss That, a London-based band featuring Karen Ware (percussion), Russell Crone (bass), David Long (drums), and Ginette (aka Jeanette) Landray, former vocalist with the Robert Smith/Steve Severin psychedelic project The Glove.

Formed in 1984, Kiss That played around London for close to a year before a chance encounter with former David Bowie guitarist Mick Ronson led to him producing their debut album, *Kiss and Tell*, in 1986. One of the year's most exciting proto-electro/rock albums, with the accompanying 12-inch single "March Out" already testifying to Hammond's vision as a remixer, *Kiss and Tell* was nevertheless completely overlooked and the band broke up in 1987.

Hammond re-emerged in 1991, linking with DJ Charlie Hall as the Drum Club, a production/remix act who toured with Orbital's 1993 MIDI Circus. The duo accomplished a number of spectacular remixes, including several for Lush (whose Emma Anderson would guest on Drum Club's own *Everything Is Now*) and in November 1993 Drum Club scored a memorable UK hit, "Sound System" (#62 UK). Unfortunately, their two studio albums never captured the excitement of the live show, a point exacerbated by their final offering, *Live in Iceland* and Drum Club broke up in 1995.

Hammond reinvented himself as Slab, releasing three solid singles on the Hydrogen Dukebox label, with remixes by Monkey Mafia, Andrew Weatherall, and others. Of these, "Rampant Prankster," Slab's second single, was a major club hit in 1996, while Hammond himself turned in remixes for Hardkiss, Psychick Warriors Ov Gaia, Alien Sex Fiend, and Steve Hillage and Miquette Giraudy's acclaimed System 7.

1998 brought a new Slab single, "Funked Up Kid," and album, *Ripsnorter*, even as Hammond — now DJ-ing at London's Funkt club — launched a fresh project, Girl Eats Boy, with Matt Rowlands and vocalist Mandy Wall. An album, *Thrilled by Velocity and Distortion*, was followed by the dance hits singles "Girl Eats Boy," "Napalm in Bohemia," "Cool Disco," and "Kamikaze."

An album, recorded with Brian Eno, *Beat Oblique*, has yet to appear; however, Hammond also recorded with Eno's brother, Roger, the results emerging as 1999's *Damage*.

Lol Hammond/Roger Eno LP

7 Damage (Thirsty Ear) 1999 Ravenous ambient album, melody lashed and quizzically organized — "Hip Hop Flipperty Flop" is actually a duet for piano and cicada, "Kinky Ink" a mesmerizing soundwash.

Kiss That LP

9 Kiss and Tell (Chrysalis) 1986 Pre-emptive strike on the fields of '90s electro-rock, majestically produced by Mick Ronson. Counterpoint vocals and scything dance guitars lead the way, while "I Can't Stand the Rain" is reinvented as torch for the blank generation.

Drum Club LP

8 Everything Is Now (Big Life) 1993
7 Drums Are Dangerous (Instinct) 1994
6 Live in Iceland (Instinct) 1995

Slab LP

6 Freeky Speed (Hydrogen Dukebox — UK) 1996
6 Ripsnorter (Hydrogen Dukebox — UK) 1998

Girl Eats Boy LP

8 Thrilled by Velocity and Distortion (Hydrogen Dukebox — UK) 1998

Selected Compilations and Archive Releases

8 Hydrogen Dukebox (Hypnotic) 1999 Ten-track collection of "Rare and Exclusive" remixes, featuring Girl Eats Boy, Drum Club, Slab, Dreamgrinder, and the Creatures.

HANOI ROCKS

FORMED 1980 *(Helsinki, Finland)*
ORIGINAL LINE-UP *Michael Monroe (b. Matti Fagerholm, 6/17/62 — vocals); Steffan Piesnack (guitar); Nasty Suicide (b. Jan Stenfors, 9/4/63 — guitar); Pasi Sti (bass); Peki Senola (drums)*

Michael Monroe was a saxophonist in Maukka Perujatka's band, whose sole recorded appearance was a lip-synced performance on YLE television. Linking with Nasty Suicide (ex-Briard), he formed Hanoi Rocks in blatant emulation of the New York Dolls, but with the added bite of recent punk, and the band debuted at Helsinki's Tavastia Club in summer 1980.

Regular gigs around Helsinki saw the band draw considerable attention to themselves — their already developed taste for make-up and leather was an open invitation to violence, all the more so since no Finnish band had ever paraded such an image before. Severely beaten on several occasions, Hanoi Rocks swaggered on and with such panache that both Sam Yaffa (b. Sami Takahaki, 8/4/63 — bass) and Andy McCoy (b. Antti Hulkko, 10/11/62 — guitar), were lured away from the chart-topping new wave act Pelle Miljoona Oy, to replace Steffan Piesnack and Pasi Sti. McCoy also played with Briard — Nasty, in fact, replaced him in the line-up.

Manager Seppo Vesterinen, too, was prompted to move away from the traditional rock bands he'd previously handled and take these vivacious upstarts under his wing. In late 1980, the band's first single, "I Want You," was released under the name of Hanoi Rocks with Andy McCoy — out of deference, of course, to McCoy's stint with PMO.

With half-Turkish drummer Gyp Casino replacing Sti, the band launched their first full Finnish tour on New Year's Eve 1980, eventually winding up in Sweden where they recorded their debut album. *Bangkok Shocks, Saigon Shakes, Hanoi Rocks* was released only in Finland and Sweden, but it was swiftly imported elsewhere as Hanoi Rocks themselves moved out of Scandinavia.

Three further singles through 1981, "Tragedy," "Desperadoes," and "Dead by Christmas," were imported into the UK and Japan in increasing numbers and by the end of the year, Hanoi Rocks were in London, recording their second album, *Oriental Beat*. Tours with Wishbone Ash and Twisted Sister followed, casting the band's glam punk savagery in a hair metal mold from which they would never truly escape.

Casino quit during the summer 1982; he was replaced by ex-Darkdrummer Razzle (b. Nicholas Dingley, Isle of Wight, UK) for the "Love Injection" 45 and by the end of the year, the band had landed a deal with Phonogram for Japan (following a wildly successful far Eastern tour) and Lick for the UK. Immediately, their new labels made plans to reissue the band's entire output to date, plus a compilation, *Self Destruction Blues*; in the meantime, Hanoi Rocks got to work on their first truly international release, the album *Back to Mystery City* (#87 UK) and singles, "Malibu Beach Nightmare" and "Until I Get You."

The British media never really took to Hanoi Rocks, but on the London club scene, they were ubiquitous. The Marquee Club became a home away from home, regardless of whether they were playing there — although when they did, they were a phenomenon. A live album and video recorded there in December 1983, *All Those Wasted Years*, would become one of Hanoi Rocks' most popular recordings, while Nasty, Yaffa, and Razzle were also gigging alongside Vibrators vocalist Knox Chandler as the Fallen Angels.

Hanoi Rocks signed with CBS in spring 1984 (just as Fallen Angels' eponymous debut album was released) and celebrated with the hit single the label had insisted they try for, a cover of Creedence Clearwater Revival's "Up Around the Bend" (#61 UK). It was followed by "Underwater World" and "Don't You Ever Leave Me," and in October 1984, the band's first hit album, the Bob Ezrin-produced *Two Steps from the Move* (#28 UK).

The following month, Hanoi Rocks set off for their first — and final — US tour. In Syracuse, New York, Monroe broke his ankle and with the band cancelling their next show in Athens, GA, they flew on to L.A., where Motley Crue's Vince Neil was preparing to throw a party in their honor.

On December 8, while taking Razzle for a spin in his sports car, Neil lost control and the vehicle spun into the oncoming traffic. It was hit twice by other cars and though Razzle was rushed to hospital, he never regained consciousness. He died at 7:12 that evening (Neil was charged with DWI and vehicular manslaughter; he was sentenced to 30 days imprisonment and fined $2.6 million.)

Immediately the remainder of Hanoi Rocks' tour was cancelled and the stunned band flew home to London. The only dates on their horizon were a pair of Helsinki gigs in January 1985 and after rehearsals with Motley Crue's Tommy Lee fell apart, the band picked up ex-Clash drummer Terry Chimes and played the shows. Yaffa quit immediately after.

He was replaced for a short Polish tour by Rene Berg (ex-Idle Flowers), before one of the band's road crew, Timo Kaltio, took over, but the heart had gone out of the band already. A live album, taken from the Polish tour, was scheduled, but by the time it was released, Monroe had already quit. The album appeared, appropriately, as *Rock and Roll Divorce*.

Monroe launched a solo career, sharing a London apartment with Lords of the New Church vocalist Stiv Bators and his wife, Stacey, and scheming a joint project which Bators would co-write and produce. In the event, his solo debut, 1988's *Nights Are So Long*, was produced by Craig Leon, but the Bators connection remained through the inclusion of two songs written by ex-Dead Boys guitarist Jimmy Zero — including one, "Nights Are So Long," which the reformed Dead Boys themselves would record the following year.

Mott the Hoople's Ian Hunter also guested on the album and a slew of good reviews saw Monroe sign to Polygram later in the year and release *Not Fakin' It*. Once again the reception was good, both critically and among Monroe's peers.

Aerosmith's Steve Tyler invited the singer to guest with his band at the New York Hard Rock Cafe, at a gig celebrating Les Paul's 75th birthday. Meanwhile, Guns n'Roses' Axl

Rose guested in the video for "Dead, Jail or Rock'n'Roll," and both he and Slash joined Monroe on stage at the Whisky A-Go-Go in L.A., at the conclusion of Monroe's first solo US tour. (Guns n'Roses would further acknowledge their debt to Hanoi Rocks by reissuing the band's entire back catalog on their own Uzi Suicide label, while Rose and Monroe duetted on a version of the Dead Boys' "Ain't It Fun," included on Guns n'Roses' *Spaghetti Incident* album.)

A second single from *Not Fakin' It*, "Man with No Eyes," followed its predecessor onto MTV, along with a paid commercial for the album, in which Monroe was described as "the brains behind Hanoi Rocks." The singer was touring Japan when the campaign was launched; immediately upon returning to the US, he tersely informed the label that Hanoi Rocks had no brains, which was the beauty behind the whole thing and demanded the ad be pulled. The label responded that if the one commercial went, all their other promotion would be pulled, but Monroe was adamant. He would not release another record for three years.

In the meantime, his bandmates, too, had led a checkered career. While Nasty and McCoy recorded a second Fallen Angels album with Knox, 1986's *In Loving Memory*, the pair also retained Kaltio and Chimes and linked with vocalist Anita Chellemah (ex-Toto Coelo), to relaunch as the Cherry Bombz. Immediately before commencing work on their debut single, Kaltio was replaced by ex-Lords of the New Church bassist Dave Treganna and "Hot Girls in Love" (#7 UK indy) appeared in February 1986. A second single, "House of Ecstasy" (#12 UK indy), followed and in March 1987, Cherry Bombz released a live debut album, *100 Degrees in the Shade*, before Chellemah was sacked.

McCoy and Nasty, meanwhile, were also operating a side project, the all-acoustic Suicide Twins, releasing one album in Finland, *Silver Missiles and Nightingales*. Like the Cherry Bombz' output, however, the album did little and in 1988, McCoy broke up both bands and returned to Finland.

His bandmates became the Wylde Things, with Nasty also recording a third Fallen Angels album, 1988's *Is That the Way Life's Supposed to Be?*. The new group never got off the ground though and in 1990, Nasty launched a new band, Cheap and Nasty. McCoy, meanwhile, recorded a solo album, 1988's *Too Much Ain't Anything*, before joining Iggy Pop's band.

Relocating to the US, McCoy and Treganna then formed a new band, Shooting Gallery, but after one album and a tour with KISS through 1992, McCoy split the group, went back to Finland and formed a new band, Live Ammo, with former Hanoi Rocks drummer Gyp Casino. He then reunited with Pete Malmi, his partner two decades before in Briard and recorded a new album under the old name.

Throughout this period, Hanoi Rocks reunions were never far from the individual members' activities. In 1988, Nasty and Monroe both appeared on Johnny Thunders' *Que Sera Sera* album, while Berg and Nasty formed their own band in the late 1980s, Gangbang (later, the Soho Vultures).

Nasty also guested on Monroe's 1989 *Not Fakin' It* album, while Yaffa was a member of Jerusalem Slim, the short-lived band Monroe and ex-Billy Idol guitarist Steve Stevens formed in 1993. When that project collapsed in acrimony, Monroe's own input into the record being utterly misrepresented by the bombastic metal production (three months of guitar overdubs, while Monroe pleaded for the project to be scrapped), the singer toured the US with Phil Grande (guitar), another Billy Idol sideman, Tommy Price (drums), and both Nasty and Yaffa.

In late 1993, Monroe and Yaffa formed a new band, Demolition 23, with Jimmy Clark (ex-Scandal, drums) and Jay Hening (ex-Star Star, guitar), recording an eponymous album with producer Little Steven for early 1994 release. When Hening was involved in an auto accident on the eve of the band's first tour, Nasty replaced him for tours of Finland and Japan. With a UK tour looming, however, Nasty quit and Monroe disbanded Demolition 23.

By 1997, the singer had returned to Finland to live, recording a new album, *Peace of Mind* and touring with a band comprising Olli Hilden (guitar) and ex-Demolition 23 member Clark. Live work, however, has been confined largely to Scandinavian shows. Nasty, too, was in Helsinki, recording under his given name; his solo debut, *Vinegar Blood*, was released in March 1996; Yaffa and wife Karmen Guy relocated to New York and formed Mad Juana.

Hanoi Rocks LPs

7 **Bangkok Shocks, Saigon Shakes, Hanoi Rocks (Johanna — Finland) 1981** Manic party time unleashed across the bones of old Rolling Stones, figurative New York Dolls, theoretical Mott the Hoople — if it rocked with attitude, Hanoi Rocks will do its makeup. Sleazy, slashing, squalid swagger, a few tracks echo the best of Briard (whose "I Really Hate You" single haunts this album like a watchful dead dowager), but Rocks' garage-choked grin had bigger fish to fry.

6 **Oriental Beat (Johanna — Finland) 1982** Perhaps allowing the sleaze and squalor to get the better of them, Rocks stall in mid-slash... although thankfully not until after they've finished "No Law or Order," the best reggae Clash song the Clash never dreamed of.

8 **Back to Mystery City (Lick — UK) 1983** And back to true heart basics, Stooges stoned immaculate — of course it's *nothing* like the real thing, but that wasn't the point. The greatest rock'n'roll legends develop an aura which the music can never get close to recapturing. But if you start out from where that aura begins...

6 All Those Wasted Years [LIVE] (Lick — UK) 1984 The only problem with wanting to be the new Dolls is you have to *really* want to be them. Which presumably means suffering some generally shoddy live albums.

7 Two Steps from the Move (CBS) 1984 Not quite the sell-out which the near hit "Up Around the Bend" suggested, but still the degeneracy starts to flag as the band get a whiff of the fortune to be made in America. Clean and sharper, a little better played, the least realized of Hanoi Rocks' albums is magically transformed into their best made.

6 Rock & Roll Divorce [LIVE] (Lick — UK) 1985

Selected Compilations and Archive Releases

7 Self Destruction Blues (Johanna — Finland) 1982 Though treated as a new album by US and UK fans, *SDB* actually originated as a Japanese stopgap, compiling out-takes and non-album singles. The classic "Kill City Kills" was the first ever B-side, "Dead by Christmas" a singularly unfestive Finnish Christmas single.

7 The Best Of (Lick — 1985) 1985

6 Tracks from a Broken Dream (Lick) 1990

6 True Live Rarities (Vodka — Finland) 1996

Michael Monroe LPs

6 Nights Are So Long (Yahoo — Finland) 1987

6 Not Fakin' It (Vertigo) 1989

5 Jerusalem Slim (Polygram — Japan) 1992

5 Demolition 23 (Music for Nations) 1994

7 Peace of Mind (Poko — Finland) 1996

Cherry Bombz LP

6 Coming Down Slow [LIVE] (High Dragon — UK) 1986

Suicide Twins LP

6 Silvermissiles and Nightingales (Lick — UK) 1986

Andy McCoy LPs

7 Too Much Ain't Enough (Amulet — Finland) 1988

7 Shooting Gallery (Polygram) 1992

6 Building on Tradition (AMT — Finland) 1995

6 Briard [WITH PETE MALMI] (BMG — Finland) 1996

Nasty Suicide LPs

6 Beautiful Disaster [AS CHEAP & NASTY] (China — UK) 1991

5 Vinegar Blood [AS JAN STENFORS] (Spinefarm — Finland) 1997

Sam Yaffa LPs

5 Skin of My Teeth [WITH MAD JUANA] (Spinefarm — Finland) 1997

Fallen Angels LPs

7 Fallen Angels (Quality) 1984 Vibrators frontman Knox and Rocks swagger through a high octane Aerosmith-cum-Stooges crasher.

6 In Loving Memory (Quality) 1986

4 Wheel of Fortune (Jungle) 1988 Knox and a new line-up essentially reinvent the Angels as a cracked bar band.

HAPPY MONDAYS

FORMED 1985 *(Manchester, England)*
ORIGINAL LINE-UP *Sean Ryder (b. 8/23/62 — vocals); Mark Day (b. 12/29/61 — guitar); Paul Ryder (b. 4/24/64 — bass); Paul Davis (b. 3/7/66 — keyboards); Bez (b. Mark Berry — percussion); Gary Whelan (b. 2/12/66 — drums)*

Born out of a combination of hometown Manchester's readily-linked football culture and club scene, Happy Mondays had already earned a reputation for drug-induced violence-stoked mania on and offstage when they were picked up by the Factory label in 1986 and given the chance to translate their live adrenaline onto vinyl. The group's first recordings, the "Delightful" and "Freaky Dancing" singles were produced, respectively, by Mike Pickering (of M People) and New Order's Bernard Sumner — neither, however, could harness the band's wildness, and Factory returned them to the studio with former Velvet Undergrounder John Cale.

A complete album was taped, then scrapped, Cale demanding that the band remake it in three days. The resultant *Squirrel and G-Man* (#4 UK indy) emerged one of the most overlooked, but subsequently crucial albums of the entire decade, one which would not only pinpoint the band's future direction, but also cast an inimitable shadow over the rest of the Manchester scene for a decade (or more) to come.

The singles "Tart Tart" (#13 UK indy) and "24 Hour Party People"(#10 UK indy) provided a soundtrack for countless warehouse parties, while live the Mondays were a revelation. With Sean Ryder's lascivious and perpetually seemingly-stoned persona hanging like a malignant ringmaster over the entire proceedings; Bez a demonic dancer guaranteed to turn the most up-tight gig into an all-night party; and the remainder of the band apparently lost in the cacophony of rhythm which was Happy Mondays' calling card, the group should have fallen to pieces every time they stepped on stage. Instead, their excesses (most publicly visible at Factory's Hacienda Club) simply made them stronger and by the time they recorded *Bummed* (#59 UK, #2 UK indy) with the legendary Martin Hannett, the group's fate was sealed.

"WFL" (#68 UK, #7 UK indy), from *Bummed*, in September 1989, "Lazyitus" (#6 UK indy) and the *Madchester Rave On* (#19 UK, #1 UK indy) EP in November were the band's first national chart entries — unrepentant dives into the heart of the country's rave culture which instantly titillated the national tabloids. Soon, Sean Ryder's alleged drug intake was as headline-worthy as the Mondays' music, and thus tarred, the group determined to blur the reality even further.

By early 1990, the pulsating "Step On" (#5 UK) a retitled cover of the 1971 John Kongos' hit "He's Gonna Step on You Again," had pushed the band to the very forefront of the Madchester scene (a second Kongos song, "Tokoloshe Man," would appear on the band's US label, Elektra's anniversary compilation, *Rubaiyat*). "Lazyitus" (#46 UK) was reissued; then, with Sean Ryder's slur seamlessly joined by backing vocalist Rowetta, "Kinky Afro," reappraised Labelle's "Lady Marmalade" (#5 UK) to devastating effect. In between times, the band's Hollywood-made third album, *Pills'n'Thrills' n' Bellyaches* (#89 US, #4 UK) took off trailing a host of cross-cultural psychedelic references — the inclusion of the lyrics to Donovan's "Sunshine Superman" in the song "Donovan" even led to the '60s singer-songwriter himself emerging from hibernation to side with the band.

Alongside Stone Roses — whose peace and love attitude was rapidly emerging as the absolute corollary of Happy Mondays' ethos — Sean Ryder and co. were arguably one of the biggest "young" bands in Britain as the new decade dawned. However, Sean Ryder's escalating drug use was now not only concerning the newspapers; it was impacting upon the band as well, coming to a head when the singer admitted a heroin addiction and entered detox.

Singles of "Loose Fit" (#17 UK), "Judge Fudge" (#24 UK) and a "91 Remix" of "Step in You" (#57 US), joined the stop-gap-but-stupendous *Live* (#21 UK) album in keeping the group's name on the chart. But attempts to record another studio album, in Barbados with Tom Tom Clubbers Tina Weymouth and Chris Frantz, were ill-tempered and scrappy.

Bez broke his arm in a car accident, which slowed things down further, while Sean Ryder at one point held the master tapes hostage, threatening to destroy them unless the record company wired him more money. "In the end," Frantz later mused, "we were lucky that nobody died." (Despite events in Barbados, Ryder would retain his producers' respect and was one of several guest vocalists on their 1996 *No Talking Just Head* album.)

Attended by the singles "Stinkin Thinkin" (#31 UK) and "Sunshine and Love" (#62 UK), the eventual *...Yes Please!* (#14 UK) was released in October 1992, just as the UK press began buzzing with rumors that the band was breaking up. In fact, the Happy Mondays' decline would be piecemeal through 1993, with the demise of the Factory label a key element in their eventual collapse. The end came when EMI offered the band a 2 million pound deal, only for Sean Ryder

to walk out of the contract-signing (before putting pen to paper) and never return.

Sean Ryder and Bez launched a new project, Black Grape, in 1995, signing to the Radioactive label. Featuring guitarist Paul Wagstaff (ex-Paris Angels); rappers Kermit (b. Paul Leveridge) and Ged Lynch from the Ruthless Rap Assassins; and producer/bassist Danny Saber, *It's Great When You're Straight... Yeah* (#1 UK) the new band's mockingly-titled debut, was very much the logical successor to the Mondays' sound and nature. Indeed, with an immediate hit single, "The Reverend Black Grape" (#9 UK) followed by further hits with "In the Name of the Father" (#8 UK) and "Kelly's Heroes" (#17 UK), it seemed Black Grape were destined to literally pick up where the Mondays left off.

However, luck was not to be on their side. Plans for a US tour in early 1996 were clouded when Kermit suffered a bout of septicemia, caused by bad water while vacationing in Mexico; he was still recovering when the band learned their visas had been denied due to prior drug convictions. Bez then quit the band following a financial dispute with Radioactive (he would return for Black Grape's Reading festival date) and all the while, Ryder recalled, "we went round Britain and Europe and Europe and Britain for 14 months, because they still wouldn't let us into the States."

With new member Psycho standing in for the still incapacitated Kermit, Black Grape released a new single, "Fat Neck" (#10 UK), featuring Smiths' Johnny Marr on guitar, in May 1996. The following month, they celebrated England's qualification for the European Championships soccer tournament with "England's Irie" (#6 UK), recorded with former Clash vocalist Joe Strummer. Black Grape then began work on their sophomore album at Peter Gabriel's Real World studios that fall.

The sessions were far looser than before: for *Straight*, Ryder revealed, the label kept a close eye on everything, in case he "decided to fuck off to India to build a house out of acid, to replace the one I built out of crack." This time around, the group followed its own instincts and emerged strongly, with 1997's *Stupid Stupid Stupid* (#11 UK) and the singles "Get Higher" (#24 UK) and "Marbles" (#46 UK).

Black Grape seemed to remain unstable, however; problems with management further disrupting their equilibrium — in December 1999, Ryder was ordered to pay managers Gloria and William Nicholl £160,000 in unpaid commissions after the Lord Justice Thorpe determined that Ryder was indeed in breach of contract. The "dyslexic drug abuser," as Thorpe described him, told the court "he was freaked out by paperwork and that it did his nut in."

By mid-1998, rumors of a Happy Mondays reunion were regularly surfacing, reaching fever pitch when the *Loads — Best Of* (#41 UK) album made its appearance towards the end of the year. The tales finally came to pass in January 1999, when the band re-emerged with a new single, an aptly-chosen cover of Thin Lizzy's "The Boys are Back in Town" (#35 UK) and a second *Greatest Hits* package (#11 UK).

Original members Sean Ryder, brother Paul, Gary Whelan, and Bez were joined by Rowetta, Wagstaffe, from Black Grape, Farm keyboard player Ben Leach and a friend of Ryder's named Nuts. Sean Ryder claimed he was only doing it for the money (he owed the taxman £400,000); Paul admitted "I'd have done it for ten bob. I had to see psychiatrists after the Mondays split up. They told me I should have had bereavement counseling. But now... it's like, mates again."

The band toured Britain through spring 1999, and joined the bill for August's Eclipse Festival; and in June, announced plans to release a new album, largely written by Nuts. Ryder, meanwhile, teamed up with Tricky to write further material for the album; however, the group's schedule was disrupted somewhat after Bez punctured a lung in a biking accident in November 1999.

Happy Mondays LPs

8 Happy Monday's Squirrel and G Man 24 Hour Party People Plastic Face Carnt Smile (White Out) 1987 (Factory) Party hard, heavy acid rock, pushed through the wringer of John Cale's manic production.

8 Bummed (Elektra) 1988 The missing link between post-punk and the burgeoning baggy scene, Sean Ryder does a fair impression of Mark E. Smith, percussionist and drummer Bez and Gary Wheelan respectively send their résumés to Adam Ant, guitarist Mark Day auditions for the Banshees, while Paul Davis' keyboards swirl ominously in the background... brilliant!

8 Pills'n'Thrills'n'Bellyaches (Elektra) 1990

9 Live (Elektra) 1991 This should be more a rave than a record, recorded in June, '91, at Elland Road (Leeds United's soccer stadium). Lining up with a grab-bag of hits and crowd pleasers old and new, all sound magnificent and must have driven the audience into a fever pitch. A few songs fall into an almost abrupt end, interrupting the flow and, at times, leaving the group foundering about a bit, but the dissolution was part of the charm as well. Treat this like a studio record, however, and it's brilliant.

7 Yes Please (Elektra) 1992 The soulful backing vocals steer the Mondays deeper into Funkytown, with the odd detour into the Wild West and rap, while still waving back at their own baggy past.

Selected Compilations and Archive Releases

8 Double Easy: The US Singles (Elektra) 1993 As the title states, a collection of US singles comprising all the A-sides and selected B-sides, including some culled from 12-inch white labels, promos, and the odd comp track.

9 Loads (And Loads More) (London) 1998

Black Grape LPs

8 It's Great When You're Straight — Yeah (Radioactive) 1995 It's great when you're straight, because then you can appreciate everything going on in Black Grape's eclectic debut, where toasters rap over sitars, guitars clash with horn sections and gospel goes clubbing. The influences are dizzying, the beats electrifying, and their sound defies description.

8 Stupid Stupid Stupid (Radioactive) 1997 More focused than last time, Black Grape distill their references and refine their sound down into a powerful funkadelic hybrid, powered by fat clubby beats.

PJ HARVEY

BORN *Polly Jean Harvey, 10/9/69 (Yeovil, England)*

Raised on a sheepfarm in the English west country whose regional burr still coats her accent, Harvey played in a succession of local bands before linking in 1988 with guitarist John Parish in Automatic Dlamini, a band who already had one album behind them (*The D Is for Drum*) and were now struggling to come up with a follow-up.

A single, "Water," was released in 1991, but a full album, taped in late 1989, *Here Catch Shouted His Father*, went unreleased — a compilation, *From a Diva to a Diver* would finally be released in 1992, following the band's demise and included a local radio session recorded during Harvey's tenure.

1991 also saw Harvey guest as backing vocalist with Bristol band The Family Cat on their "Colour Me Grey" single and one track from their *Furthest from the Sun* album; she would also sing the chorus of Grape's "Baby in a Plastic Bag" 45. Automatic Dlamini, however, split soon after this, when Parish quit to produce Wall of Voodoo. Harvey, bassist Ian Oliver, and an earlier Dlamini member, drummer Rob Ellis, then linked as PJ Harvey and played their live debut at a skittle alley in Charmouth.

Summer of 1991 also saw the group record their first demo, featuring "Dress" and "Sheela-Na-Gig" — a copy was sent to Too Pure label head Paul Cox, then booking shows at London's Moonlight Club, in the hope of getting a gig there. Cox offered both a gig and a deal and in October, the demo version of "Dress" became PJ Harvey's first single.

Oliver quit in November, to join a reformed Automatic Dlamini; he was replaced by fretless bassist Stephen Vaughan and the band continued gigging around London. Early in the new year, Island moved for the band, pledging to pick them up as soon as their two single/one album deal with Too Pure expired. "Sheela-Na-Gig" (#69 UK) and the *Dry* (#11 UK) album duly followed, together with a bonus album of demos, titled simply, *Demonstration*, and offered free with copies of *Dry*.

Overnight, PJ Harvey were being feted as superstars; more than that, Harvey herself was being regarded as a front-line warrior in the Women in Rock movement, a role she simultaneously rebelled from and, via her frequently charged lyrics, embraced. Certainly her writing for the group's second album would be flavored by this conflict and new songs were appearing in her live set a full nine months before the album's release.

Although they turned down an invitation to appear at Lollapalooza '92, tours through Britain and America took the band through the remainder of 1992; work on *Rid of Me* (#158 US, #3 UK) began in December, with producer Steve Albini. Two weeks later ,the record was completed; its May 1993 release was previewed by the uncompromising "50 Foot Queenie" (#27 UK) single (a second single, "Mansize" — #42 UK — followed). The album was a massive hit and again spawned a demos collection — issued separately this time, as *4 Track Demos* (#19 UK).

Again the group toured relentlessly, the outing climaxing at Wembley Stadium in London, opening for U2. Harvey, however, was tiring of the band format. The dates over, she dismissed first Ellis, then Vaughan and began planning a solo career — launched, after a fashion, at the 1994 BRITS awards, when she joined Björk for a ragged, wiry version of the Rolling Stones' "Satisfaction."

Harvey's third album, *To Bring You My Love* (#40 US, #12 UK), would be recorded with U2/Depeche Mode producer Flood — a violent, swamp-blues-inflected disc made possible, she insisted, by the freedom to write what she wanted, as opposed to what she thought her bandmates could play. Automatic Dlamini mainstay Parish and Bad Seed Mick Harvey were recruited to the sessions and over six weeks of recording (and four more mixing), Harvey would create her masterpiece, an album of unrelenting darkness and brittleness — a deserved bronze medallist, four years later, in *Spin* magazine's "album of the decade" poll (*Rid of Me* would make #37; "Sheela Na Gig" would be the #2 single.)

Again, successive singles — "Down by the Water" (#38 UK), "C'mon Billy" (#29 UK), and "Send His Love to Me" (#34 UK) — struggled to breach the UK top 30. But the album became Harvey's first sizeable US success and with a band comprising Parish, former Captain Beefheart/Frank Black collaborator Eric Drew Feldman (keyboards), Joe Gore (guitar), Fatima Mansions bassist Nick Bagnall, and drummer Jean Marc Butty, much of 1995 was spent on the road, in the US and Europe.

The following year, by contrast, was quiet — Harvey joined Parish (and drummer Ellis) on his *Dance Hall at Louse Point* (#178 US, #46 UK) album and played a handful of shows alongside Parish and the Mark Bruce Dance Company, in support of the record. (One single, "That Was My Veil" — #75 UK — accompanied the album.)

She also joined Nick Cave in the studio, to duet on "Henry Lee" (#36 UK) a track from his *Murder Ballads* album; while other performances over the next year or so included a version of Kurt Weill's "Ballad of the Soldier's Wife," for inclusion on the *September Songs* Weill tribute, and two songs to accompany her acting debut in the British TV movie *The Book of Life*.

1998 opened with Harvey and trip-hop maverick Tricky performing live on both British and US television (the pair had toured together in 1995), but hopes that the collaboration might lead to something more lasting were dashed when Harvey alone resurfaced in August, for her first full live shows in over three years. Accompanied by Feldman, Parish, Gore, Harvey and Ellis, Harvey then appeared at the V98 festival, previewing material destined for her fourth album.

Attended by the single "A Perfect Day Elise" (#25 UK), *Is This Desire?* (#54 US, #17 UK) followed in September 1998, another Flood production which early reports suggested would be heavily influenced by Garbage. Of course it wasn't and Harvey moved into the new century as stubbornly self-reliant as ever.

PJ Harvey LPs

8 Dry (Too Pure) 1992 A bleak rawness quite unlike anything else, bleeding on the edge of a nervous breakdown as Harvey rants and roils her way through powerful emotions, stronger and more real than any Riot Grrl manifesto. Shame she got so sick of the ferocious "Sheela-Na-Gig," though.

6 Rid of Me (Island) 1993 What should have been a superb follow-up fails. Rather than extending the images seen in *Dry*, Harvey trades in the beauty for utter grinding and vocal scaling that is grating rather than great. One can definitely feel producer Steve Albini's presence here.

10 To Bring You My Love (Island) 1995 The skeletal title track sets the scene, coiled rattlesnake drama in wind-whipped dry gulches — a litany of the tumbleweed terrors she encountered on her way. And it doesn't matter what she's brought you in the past, big-hipped seductress or sonic super-sexual, now she's crawling through the battle of the Somme, bruised and bleeding while the sky flashes purple and her words a death rattle... to bring you my love.

This is not a healthy album, these are not healthy songs, and the title track is only the curtain raising curse, Nick Cave's *Henry's Dream* in psilocybic overload. By the time you're at the halfway point, the haunted "Down by the Water" and the pounding "I Think I'm a Mother," Harvey is in it so deep that not even the acoustic spiral of "Send His Love to Me" can dispel the shifting shadow dance. Not when the whole thing shudders to a close with "The Dancer," but it's impossible to foxtrot for the bleached bones on the floor.

Flood's sparse production sets an effective counterpoint not only to the density of past Polly albums, but also to the richness of her lyrics. The result is primeval and ritualistic, dark red blues oozing black through the grooves, as *To Bring You My Love* steps out of that slice of deep south delta which white America has never truly comprehended, but which is writ large in the legends of rock regardless. Harvey just writes it in the mirror from *The Shining*.

9 Is This Desire? (Island) 1998 Building on the semi-experimental feel of *Love*, but substituting desolate clifftops for storm-blasted swamp, *Desire* is as concerned with musical dislocation as it is with songs. A few past Harvey trademarks eventually emerge from Flood's impenetrable mix (her continued obsession with water included), but for the most part *Desire* remains so mysterious it doesn't even answer its own title's question.

8 Stories from the City, Stories from the Sea (Island) 2000

PJ Harvey and John Parish LP

6 Dance Hall at Louse Point (Island) 1996 This is essentially a Parish solo album that Harvey walked her lyrics through. Should have been better.

Selected Compilations and Archive Releases

6 Demonstration (Too Pure) 1992

5 4 Track Demos (Island) 1993 The demos add little to the finished album beyond a certain ingenuous rawness, a little vocal clarity, and the unbidden image of Harvey in her portastudio screaming, "I'll rub it till it bleeds." Whatever must the neighbors have thought?

8 B-Sides (Island) 1995 Nine cuts, mostly *To Bring You My Love*-era B-sides (plus two *Rid of Me* era odds), and the best could have effortlessly fit on the parent album — that's the harmonium driven "Darling Be There," the lazy blues-fuzz "Goodnight," and the bellowing "Harder."

HELIUM

FORMED 1992 (Boston, MA)
ORIGINAL LINE-UP *Mary Timony (vocals, guitar); Brian Dunton (bass); Shane Devlin (drums)*

Washington, DC hardcore scenester Mary Timony was a founder member of proto Riot Grrl band Autoclave, alongside Christina Billotte (of Slant 6), Melissa Berkoff, and Nikki Chapman. The group released a single and an EP before Timony left DC for college in Boston; she continued writing with the band, before replacing Jason Hatfield (Julianna's brother) in Chupa, a band formed by Brian Dunton (ex-Dumptruck) and Shane Devlin.

Changing their name to Helium, the trio debuted with the "American Jean" single in 1992, signing with Pop Narcotic the following year for "Hole in the Ground" and a contribution to the *In a Little Box* label sampler. A flurry of press interest, beginning in the UK but rapidly returning across the Atlantic, greeted these early stirrings and following a triumphant (if poorly attended) showing at the 1993 New Music Seminar, Helium signed to Matador for the *Pirate Prude* mini-album.

The band launched a northeastern tour with Pavement and a brief (three show) visit to the UK before Dunton quit in a dispute over the band's future direction. As a duo, Timony and Devlin recorded a new single, "Pat's Trick," and album, *The Dirt of Luck*, but attempts to broaden the group's sound by replacing Dunton with Dambuilders violinist Joan Wasser collapsed after a few gigs. "Some woman named Lori," as Timony put it, came in for further live shows, before Polvo bassist Ash Bowie was debuted on the *Superball Plus* EP in 1995.

A handful of dates on the 1995 Lollapalooza prefaced a lengthy silence, although Helium continued to appear on compilations and soundtracks — "Magic Box" was included in *Half Cocked*, "Comet #9" featured in *Stealing Beauty*, Hole in the Ground in *All Over Me*. The band returned in 1997 with a new EP, *No Guitars* and album *Magic City*.

A European tour with Sleater Kinney preceded their own US headline outing; the following spring they toured the US again, opening for Sonic Youth. However, a two year silence was followed by news of a Timony solo album, apparently marking the demise of Helium.

Helium LPs

8 The Dirt of Luck (Matador) 1995 Zigzagged post-hardcore neuroses set to Mary Timony's sideways-shifting guitar, an expanded (welcome violin and keyboards) line-up and Timony's own savage lyricism. "Baby's Going Underground" and "Latin Song" are the skullbusters; "Pat's Trick," a stab at conventional (read Breeders-ish) pop. Everything else falls disconcertingly amidships, leaving Helium the kind of breath which won't just have you talking funny. You'll be thinking funny, too.

7 Magic City (Matador) 1997

Mary Timony LPs

8 Mountains (Matador) 2000

RICHARD HELL

BORN *Richard Meyers, 10/2/49 (Lexington, KY)*

Having seen his partnership with Tom Verlaine and the nascent Television established as one of the key influences on the nascent CBGBs scene during 1974, Richard Hell quit in a dispute over musical direction and linked with former New York Dolls guitarist Johnny Thunders in another new band, the Heartbreakers. This union, too, was short-lived, its demise hastened by Hell's "discovery" by former Dolls manager Malcolm McLaren.

Impressed both by the singer's attitude and wardrobe (the ripped T-shirts he habitually sported), McLaren invited Hell to return with him to London to form a new band with a group of young musicians he was involved with, either a pre-Rotten Sex Pistols or, according to Mick Jones, the pre-Joe Strummer Clash. Hell turned him down, then quit the Heartbreakers for a solo career.

Forming the Voidoids with guitarists Ivan Julian and Bob Quine and drummer Marc Bell, Hell then cut the *Blank Generation* EP for Terry Ork's Ork label, the song which kickstarted more dreams than all the anarchy in the world. Promptly reissued in the UK by Stiff Records, "Blank Generation" would then be swept up within the major label shopping spree which followed punk's emergence, as the Voidoids signed to Sire for an album titled after the hit.

Late in 1977, Hell finally made that long-delayed visit to the UK, to tour with the Clash. It was a violent and generally unproductive tour, as British audiences reacted poorly, and soon after returning to New York, the Voidoids began falling apart. They quit Sire, Bell joined the Ramones — he was replaced by Material drummer Fred Maher, and in early 1978, Hell signed with the UK label Radar and released a new single, the Nick Lowe-produced "Kid with the Replaceable Head."

It would be Hell's last recording for almost four years, although he continued gigging (the *R.I.P.* cassette compilation draws from several of these performances) and in 1982, he resurfaced with *Destiny Street*, a powerful collection which Hell promptly described as his farewell to the music industry.

He moved into writing and acting, starring in Susan Seidelman's *Smithereens* and also enjoying a cameo in Madonna's *Desperately Seeking Susan*. Occasional live gigs continued, however (again highlighted on a cassette-only album, *Funhunt*), and in 1991, he was lured out of the twilight as one quarter of Dim Stars — a band formed by Don Fleming and Steve Shelley and Thurston Moore of Sonic Youth.

Released through Moore's own Ecstatic Peace label, a triple single featured covers of Boston punks Unnatural Axe's "The Plug," Stickmen with Rayguns' "Christian Rat Attack," and Hell's own "You Gotta Lose." An album, *Dimstars*, followed two years later.

In its aftermath, Hell announced he was working on a new album of his own; since that time, however, his only reappearances were with the spoken word *Go Now* EP, a companion to the novel of the same name; and an appearance with the David Byrne-less Talking Heads, on 1996's *No Talking, Just Head* album.

Richard Hell LPs

9 Blank Generation (Sire) 1977 "Blank Generation" remains the ultimate anthem of disaffection with dignity; "Love Comes in Spurts" sex for an age where other things mattered. Occasionally arty (Hell writes lyrics like Burroughs' structured poetry), frequently abrasive (the band play like a chemical reaction), but never less than dynamic, Hell's masterpiece cannot be measured in songs, only in overall intent.

8 Destiny Street (Red Star) 1982 Rejoined by Voidoid Robert Quine, a less frantic album, but no less nasty — an inferior re-recording of the Nick Lowe produced "Kid with the Replaceable Head" single not withstanding, covers ranging from Kinks R&B to Dylan's most deliberate dirge ("Going Going Gone") reveal Hell has lost none of his cutting edge nihilism in the years since he last recorded.

6 Go Now (Tim/Kerr) 1995 With Quine now providing delightfully scratched background guitar, Hell reads the first two chapters of his debut novel, *Go Now*. One listen long, then start reading at chapter three.

Selected Compilations and Archive Releases

7 Rip (Roir) 1984 Sordid live diary trailing through nine years of favorites. The Stones' "Ventilator Blues" could have been written for him.

6 Funhunt 1990 (Roir) Three Stages of the Live Hell experience, typical bursts from 1978-79, and an oddly slick venture from 1985, promoting *R.I.P.* with Feelie Anton Fier and Jody Harris aboard.

Dim Stars LP

8 Dim Stars 1993 (Caroline) No great departure for any of the conspirators, although while Hell credited Sonic Youth with bringing more to rock than they've taken from it, still their antecedents were plainly visible, and the living hell of *Blank Generation* is high on their list of priorities. T. Rex's "Rip Off" is the only disaster; elsewhere, all concerned relive Hell's days in the Bowery with a sordid, churning passion.

HELMET

FORMED 1989 *(New York, NY)*
ORIGINAL LINE-UP *Page Hamilton (b. 5/18/60, Portland, OR — guitar); Henry Bogdan (b. 2/4/61, Riverside, CA — bass); Peter Mengede (b. Australia — guitar); John Stanier (b. 8/2/68, Baltimore, MD — drums)*

Jazz guitar student Page Hamilton moved to New York to pursue his studies, joining the Band of Susans in time to catch the latest wave of distortion-led guitar bands (Sonic Youth, Big Black) as they impacted the city's experimental scene. With Florida hardcore drummer John Stanier, he formed Helmet, intending a vicious contrast between the band's clean-cut, All-American appearance and the dense roar of their music, a dichotomy evidenced across the band's 1991 debut, *Strap It On* and the earlier singles "Born Annoying," "In the Meantime," and "Unsung."

Attracting both press and major label interest, Helmet gigged relentlessly and signed to Interscope for their sophomore set, *Meantime* (#68 US), the cue for another lengthy burst of gigging (including tours of Europe with Ministry and the US with Faith No More). Mengede quit to form Handsome during this period; he was replaced by Rob Echeverria (b. 12/15/67, New York, NY), who debuted on Helmet's contribution to the *Judgement Night* soundtrack (a collaboration with House of Pain): "Just Another Victim."

Betty (#45 US), launching the airplay hit "Wilma's Rainbow," and featuring a cover of Dizzy Gillespie's "Beautiful Love," saw the band's audience and appeal growing, a market increased by contributions to such soundtracks as *Jerky Boys*, *Feeling Minnesota*, and *Johnny Mnemonic*. But the departure of Echeverria (for Biohazard) saw the band fall into considerable disarray; a new album scheduled for fall 1996, was cancelled at the last minute (Hamilton recorded with Einsturzende Neubauten collaborator Caspar Brotzmann during the lay-off) and the remaining trio substantially reworked it before launching it in March as *Aftertaste*.

Chris Traynor (Orange 9mm) was recruited for live work and the band toured throughout the summer. The musicians themselves were becoming increasingly dissatisfied with Helmet's limitations. Finally the band split in September 1998, Hamilton explaining simply, "things weren't like they used to be," and the new year saw all four members embark on their own projects. Stanier teamed up with fellow Australians John and Kim Scott in Mark of Cain; Hamilton would guest on the latest Nine Inch Nails album, *The Fragile*, and also gigged and recorded with Ben Neil. Into 2000, Hamilton was working alongside David Bowie.

Helmet LPs

8 Strap It On (Amphetamine Reptile) 1991 To the uninitiated, a droning blast of minimalist fuzz, through which a National Guard instructor bellows odd commands and a guitar cuts loose for no reason at all. To initiates — much the same, and as good as it gets.

8 Meantime (Interscope) 1992 Stiffer production and better lyrics are the only real change, although "Unsung" packs a visceral bludgeon which its predecessor only alluded to.

6 Betty (Interscope) 1994 Edging into more experimental sonic pastures, but compensating with a wandering eye for conventional metal. It's not a happy mix — Coltrane jams with Corrosion of Coltrane — but "Milquetoast" burns with surprising ferocity.

7 Aftertaste (Interscope) 1997

Selected Compilations and Archive Releases

8 Born Annoying (Amphetamine Reptile) 1995 Band-approved collection of 1989-93 recordings.

Caspar Brotzmann and Page Hamilton LP

6 Zulutime (Blast First) 1996

ROBYN HITCHCOCK

BORN 3/3/53 (*East Grinstead, Sussex, England*)

The slow disintegration of the Soft Boys coincided naturally with the gradual creation of Hitchcock's solo debut, recorded with a floating line-up based around producer Pat Collier, Psychedelic Furs drummer Vince Ely, guitarist Knox (like Collier, ex-Vibrators), saxophonist and future Soft Cell collaborator Gary Barnacle, and a then-unknown Thomas Dolby.

Black Snake Diamond Role and the self-fulfilling "Man Who Invented Himself" single were released in May 1981, to a largely mystified audience and Hitchcock swiftly returned to the studio with producer Steve Hillage to begin work on his second solo album. Hillage's production of Simple Minds, on their epochal *Empire and Dance* album the previous year, had established the former Gong guitarist as a genuinely innovative studio maven, but what worked for the Scottish wunderkind was never going to be so successful for Hitchcock.

Recorded at the 24-track Ad Vision studio, with a £12,000 budget and a battery of session musicians (bassist Sara Lee would later join Gang of Four and the B-52's, saxophonist Anthony Thistlethwaite eventually became a Waterboy, drummer Rod Johnson would work with the Psychedelic Furs), *Groovy Decay* (#15 UK indy) revealed Hitchcock to be completely out of his depth. He subsequently released his original demos (recorded with Soft Boy Matthew Seligman) as the *Groovy Decoy* antidote.

Rejoined by Seligman and Andy Metcalfe, Hitchcock launched into another frenzied burst of recording, but remained disenchanted. Finally abandoning the sessions (they have since leaked out piecemeal over sundry compilations and reissues), he retired on the profits from his recent collaboration with Damned bassist Captain Sensible, the

Women and Captains First hit album, and dropped completely out of sight.

His silence was partially camouflaged by a string of singles — "It's a Mystic Trip," "America," and "Nightride to Trinidad" — and Hitchcock himself continued writing and recording. Finally, in May 1983, he resurfaced with James A. Smith and Simon Kunath and began demoing in earnest. The *I Often Dream of Trains* album took shape over the next year, while new sessions with Soft Boys Metcalfe and Morris Windsor — rechristened the Egyptians — saw another album, *Fegmania*, swiftly completed.

The new band (briefly augmented by saxophonist James Fletcher and keyboard player Roger Jackson) made its live debut at the London Hope & Anchor; further one-off gigs soon became a crowded diary and as the March 1985 release of his next album, *Fegmania*, approached, the band was seldom far from a stage. The *Gotta Let This Hen Out* (#6 UK indy) live album documented this period.

Following so hard on the heels of *Fegmania*, *Gotta Let This Hen Out* (and the accompanying *Exploding in Silence* mini-album) gave Hitchcock a visibility he had never previously imagined. He paid his first visits to the United States, gigged regularly to the kind of appreciation which the Soft Boys could only have dreamed about, and found people regularly queuing for his autograph.

Through 1985–86, four successive singles made the UK indy chart, "The Bells of Rhymney" (#39 UK indy),

"Heaven" (#21 UK indy), "Brenda's Iron Sledge" (#22 UK indy), and "If You Were a Priest" (#21 UK indy) — the first and only time Hitchcock scraped those listings. It was amidst this rarified atmosphere of imminent celebrity, then, that he and the Egyptians set to work on their next album, *Element of Light* (#11 UK indy), recording so much material that Hitchcock swiftly followed up with the out-takes and oddities collection, *Invisible Hitchcock*.

Although Hitchcock continued recording, usually with Chris Cox, the Egyptians themselves remained silent through 1987, finally resurfacing the following year to sign a major label deal with A&M. The group's popularity on the US college circuit had been growing for some time and for A&M, their recruitment finally signalled the label's acknowledgement of the fast-exploding grassroots alternative scene, as highlighted by the Smiths, REM, Billy Bragg, the Replacements and so on. "I think we were the last of the independent bands which were still independent," Hitchcock laughs. "So they had to sign us."

Two new albums, *Globe of Frogs* (#111 US) and *Queen Elvis* (#139 US), followed, accompanied by the singles "Balloon Man," "Globe of Frogs," and "Madonna of the Wasps." But though all certainly elevated Hitchcock's Stateside profile, the hardcore cognoscenti professed disappointment, their dourness shattered only when Hitchcock unleashed his first solo album, *Eye*, through the Minneapolis indy Twin/Tone.

Robyn Hitchcock with Peter Buck

© Jim Steinfeldt/Chansley Entertainment Archives

Then it was back to the Egyptians and A&M and a hefty dose of reality. The label insisted that the band's next album should be "properly produced" — which, Hitchcock pointed out, "was the complete opposite to what we'd been signed to do." In 1988, the Egyptians had been recruited for their ability not to sound like a mainstream act. By 1990, however, the mainstream was king once again and the Egyptians had to fall into line.

Recorded in L.A. with producer Paul Fox, *Perspex Island* was released in October 1991 and bolstered by the much-played "So You Think You're in Love," swiftly raced to the top of the American alternative charts. For a moment, it seemed as though A&M's insistence on a "proper" producer had not been so misguided after all.

But only for a moment. Barely had *Perspex Island* reached the top, when the entire music scene underwent one of its sudden, periodic shudders and the whole thing came tumbling down again. Hitchcock explained, "it's very significant that *Perspex Island* was knocked off the top of the alternative charts by Nirvana. I think other people who came through at the same time as us had all moved up a notch, to different planes — people like 10,000 Maniacs and REM and to a lesser extent the Replacements. But everyone else was just there to be scattered and that included us. We were still there as an alternative act, but it had altered, it all became 'rock' again, people were allowed to have long hair and punch the air again." The Egyptians' final A&M album, *Respect*, suffered accordingly, and so did the Egyptians. The group broke up shortly after the *Respect* tour finished.

Four years would elapse before Hitchcock returned to the fray, punctuating the silence with just one single, 1995's "Man with a Woman's Shadow," and the wholesale reissue of his entire (pre-A&M) catalog. 1996, however, brought two full new albums, a conventional set titled *Moss Elixir* and its spectral counterpart of demos and out-takes, *Mossy Liquor*. One, Hitchcock insisted, is "the one you put on your shelf as the new Robyn Hitchcock album. The other is the one you file away and never play again."

1996 also saw Hitchcock link with director Jonathan Demme, preparing to make an in-concert movie. Having established his reputation long before, as director of the Talking Heads' seminal *Stop Making Sense*, Demme had apparently been "monitoring" Hitchcock for some time and their eventual union was preserved both on celluloid and on disc — the soundtrack *Storefront Hitchcock* album was released in 1998 and rounded up both a handful of favorite old songs and acted as a taster for his next studio album, 1999's *Jewels for Sophia*. Moving quickly, Hitchcock then followed through with the *A Star for Bram* internet release.

Also see the entry for the "SOFT BOYS" on page 640.

Robyn Hitchcock LPs

7 Black Snake Diamond Role (Armageddon — UK) 1981
"The Man Who Invented Himself" still sounds an appropriate dawn for Hitchcock's solo career, for few people have so thoroughly created so pervasive a persona... a perceived lifestyle even... as Hitchcock began formulating around his debut album. Never as wacked-out funny as his reputation still insists, but "Brenda's Iron Sledge" and "Do Policemen Sing?" both come with high absurdity quotients.

6 Groovy Decay (Albion — UK) 1982 Nowhere near the disaster Hitchcock likes to claim, but the notion of combining the new king of English psychedelia with a man who once co-wrote songs about flying teapots was always a matter of chance. Steve Hillage's production is warm and rhythmic; Hitchcock on the other hand, was brittle as wit can be, and if the meeting did produce the miraculous "St. Petersburg," it also produced the desperate "Young People Scream."

8 I Often Dream of Trains (Midnight Music — UK) 1984
Returning from a little over a year out of circulation, the "classic years" start here — "It Sounds Great When You're Dead," the title track, and "Nocturne" all exhibit the first solid stirrings of the compulsive sharpness which remains Hitchcock's greatest ally... but his least reliable tool.

9 Fegmania (Slash) 1985 No need for comment, the songs speak for themselves. "Egyptian Cream," "The Man with the Lightbulb Head," "Insect Mother," "The Fly" and of course, "My Wife and My Dead Wife." And then there's "Heaven," a song so pure that *Melody Maker* was memorably moved to muse, Hitchcock had as much business writing it as George Michael would have penning "Layla."

9 Gotta Let This Hen Out [LIVE] (Relativity) 1985

9 Exploding in Silence [LIVE] (Relativity) Recorded live at the London Marquee in spring 1985, an effortless snapshot of Hitchcock howling his finest odds ever, rhyming "Norwich" with porridge, making coffee for his dead wife, and doing strange things in the shower while 500 rabid Egyptophiles howl their appreciation. One of the all-time classic live albums, with an offspring EP to finish the job.

8 Element of Light (Glass Fish — UK) 1986 Coming down gently from such a wild peak, the lustrous "Airscape" evinces the new maturity which made the album less of an instant howler; that and the unusually contemplative "Raymond Chandler Evening."

8 Globe of Frogs (A&M) 1988 Later all concerned pointed to the major label blues, but not so much that they scarred a fine album: the effervescing "Balloon Man," "Beatle Dennis," and "Trapped Flesh Mandela" had a unique charm, while "Flesh Number One" was once again, lovely.

7 Queen Elvis (A&M) 1989 The pickings get slimmer, but the great songs still keep coming — "Autumn Sea" and the roiling "Veins of the Queen," "Madonna of the Wasps"...

7 Eye (Twintone) 1990 A solo Hitchcock scratching at songs as opposed to performances, and contrarily emerging with a convincing performance, but not so much in the way of classic songs. Still, any album with "Glass Hotel" and "Queen Elvis" can't be all bad.

6 Perspex Island (A&M) 1991 And again... "Oceanside" is a symphonic masterpiece, "So You Think You're in Love" rivals "Heaven" in the magnificence stakes... the trouble is, you still have the rest of the album to get through, and it isn't half as pretty.

5 Respect (A&M) 1992 According to Hitchcock, he intended recording the album without overdubs, just a mike on the table and the band gathered round it. Unfortunately, they had a 24-track mobile studio parked outside, and things just vanished up their own rear ends....

8 Moss Elixir (WB) 1996 "It's not Julie Andrews running down the hillside saying 'sing, my little budgerigar, sing!' But it's got more life in it than anything I've done in a long time." — Robyn Hitchcock, 1996

7 Storefront Hitchcock [LIVE] (WB) 1998 The dead wife's absent from this movie soundtrack show, along with most of Hitchcock's other old hoaries. But the opening "1974," and the anti-autobiographical "No, I Don't Remember Guildford" take their places guilelessly, while a gorgeous rendition of Hendrix's "Wind Cries Mary" reminds us that Hitchcock isn't only one of the drollest men on earth, he is also one of the most gifted pop-stylists.

8 Jewels for Sophia (WB) 1999 Continuing many of the themes first addressed (or at least suggested) over the course of *Moss Elixir*, a string of informal sessions around the US and UK bring new diversity to the sound and songwriting.

8 A Star for Bram (Editions PAF) 2000

Selected Compilations and Archive Releases

7 Groovy Decoy (Glass Fish — UK) 1984 The demos for *Groovy Decay*, resurrected by Hitchcock to try and sponge away the memory of the Hillage sessions.

7 Invisible Hitchcock (Glass Fish — UK) 1986 Sprawling collection of unreleased material — some of it astonishingly good, some of it wishing it had stayed unreleased.

8 The Kershaw Sessions (Strange Roots — UK) 1994 Often wild BBC sessions, capturing some genuinely off-kilter moments and performances.

7 You and Oblivion (Rhino) 1995 Companion volume to *Invisible*, including tapes which even Hitchcock had forgotten he'd recorded. Further lost, forgotten, or just plain buried material would appear simultaneously as bonus tracks within a series of Hitchcock-approved reissues of his pre-A&M catalog.

7 Mossy Liquor (WB) 1996 *Moss Elixir*'s awkward twin, comprising demos, out-takes, and songs which simply never made it.

7 Live at the Cambridge Folk Festival (Fuel) 2000 Excellent Egyptians live set.

HOLE

FORMED 1989 (Los Angeles, CA)
ORIGINAL LINE-UP *Courtney Love (b. Love Michelle Harrison, 7/9/65 — vocals, guitar); Eric Erlandson (guitar); Jill Emery (bass); Caroline Rue (drums)*

The instant and largely unwanted celebrity which attended Courtney Love following her marriage to Kurt Cobain did much to obscure the fact that she had been performing around the US for close to a decade before that. An early member of Faith No More, she was then a member of Sugar Baby Doll with L7's Jennifer Finch and Kat Bjelland — when that band broke up, Love and Bjelland formed Babes in Toyland, before Love quit in 1989, to form Hole with Erlandson and former Super Heroines bassist Emery.

Formative singles "Retard Girl," "Dicknail," and "Teenage Whore" followed (the *First Session* EP, released in 1997, features early versions of the first named) and after a year of gigging, Hole signed with Caroline and recorded *Pretty on the Inside* (#59 UK), produced by Gumball's Don Fleming and Sonic Youth's Kim Gordon.

Swiftly pulled into the so-called Riot Grrl scene by virtue of Love's uncompromising lyrics and attitude, Hole ferociously — and successfully — resisted such pigeonholing, only for Love's relationship with Cobain to undo all their good work and paint the band instead as a mere plaything for a bored girlfriend. Blessed with a preternatural understanding of publicity and iconography, however, Love played along with much of the subsequent nonsense, painstakingly constructing a reputation as a manipulative super-bitch which may have been no more "real" than David Bowie's once-vaunted bisexuality, but was no less convincing because of it.

Unfortunately, Hole's own work would suffer accordingly. Despite the unimpeachable virtues of *Pretty on the Inside* (#59 UK) and the 1993 hit "Beautiful Son" (#54 UK), the rumor circulated that Cobain was, in fact, responsible for all of Hole's best songs, rumors which climaxed following the singer's death and the circulation of a home demo featuring him working with Love on several songs scheduled for Hole's sophomore album, *Live Through This* (#52 US). In fact, both "Violet" (#17 UK) and "Doll Parts" (#58 US, #16 UK) — two of the three hits culled from *Live Through This* — had been around long before Love met Cobain. They were originally recorded for a BBC John Peel session in November 1991 during Hole's first UK tour. (The third hit was "Miss World" — #64 UK.)

Recorded with a new rhythm section of Kristen Pfaff and Patty Schemel (b. 4/24/67), *Live Through This* (#55 US, #13 UK) was released just four days after the discovery of Cobain's body and an hitherto much anticipated album was largely obscured by the hail of recriminations and grief which followed. The overdose death of Pfaff two months later further derailed Hole, with rumor and coincidence — including Pfaff's imminent departure from the band — muddying the waters even more.

With Melissa Auf Der Maur (b. 3/17/72) replacing Pfaff, Hole toured constantly nevertheless, and finally saw *Live Through This* certified gold in summer 1995 — it would also top critics polls across the US, while a release for that 1991 BBC session, the *Ask for It* EP (#172 US), again reminded the Cobain conspiracists that Love had been writing great songs all along.

However, Love's capacity for outrage and controversy continued to trail the band through a flurry of increasingly hostile headlines. In January 1995, she was arrested for "offensive behavior" aboard a domestic Australian flight. In March, two teenaged concert goers accused her of punching them (the complaint was dismissed in court). In June, the media feasted on her accidental overdose of prescription medicine. In July, aboard Lollapalooza, she was charged with assault by Bikini Kill's Kathleen Hanna. In October, another fan claimed she kicked him in the groin after he leapt onstage during a concert and tried to dance with her.

Such lurid outrages, of course, were balanced by the quality of her work, musically (Hole's version of Stevie Nicks' "Gold Dust Woman" was a highpoint of the *Crow 2: City of Angels* soundtrack) and as an actress — she starred alongside Keanu Reeves in *Feelin' Minnesota*, then legitimized her ambitions with a triumphant starring role in the 1997 movie *The People vs. Larry Flint*.

With Smashing Pumpkins' Billy Corgan on board, Hole's long-awaited third album, *Celebrity Skin* (#9 US, #11 UK), arrived in September 1998, trailing new singles, "Celebrity Skin" (#85 US, #19 UK) and "Malibu" (#81 US). Of course, the attendant bout of rigorous touring was not to pass off without some controversy, most notably a string of fractious dates in early 1999 with Marilyn Manson, curtailed when Hole finally abandoned the tour early. On a happier note, the band would also appear at the Big Day Out festival in Australia (excerpts from the performance were included on the *Tour Edition* EP).

Auf Der Maur quit Hole for Smashing Pumpkins in October 1999, shortly after the band completed their contribution to the soundtrack of Oliver Stone's *Be a Man*.

Hole LPs

6 Pretty on the Inside (Caroline) 1991 Lots of screaming noise, sloppy punk ethics, and lyrics that could only have been written with "shock value" in mind — all honestly reflecting the band for the loud, scathing, embryonic misfits they apparently wanted to be.

9 Live Through This (Geffen) 1994 Toning down the out and out noise with melody and riffs, Hole found their form and the ensuing album was fabulous because of it. Still in your face, the songs now boast moments of almost graceful quiet, allowing the motion and emotions to build for that Courtney crescendo of rage and angst. "Doll Parts" and "Miss World" were masterly, but "Violet" took on even more vitality in the wake of recent events.

8 Celebrity Skin (Geffen) 1998 A much more mature album, the songs are bright, polished, and impeccably produced — so incredibly slick that Love comes dangerously close to emerging pop's diva rather than an idol for the discontent. Which may or may not be intention. Either way, it's an unsettling transition.

Selected Compilations and Archive Releases

7 My Body the Hand Grenade (City Slang) 1997 Collection of old and new material including the demo version of "Miss World," plus sundry live tracks.

Further Reading

Courtney Love: The Real Story by Poppy Z Brite (Touchstone, 1998).

HOVERCRAFT

FORMED 1993 *(Seattle, WA)*
ORIGINAL LINE-UP Campbell 2000 (b. Ryan — guitar); Karl 3-30 (b. Dave — drums); Sadie 7 (b. Beth Liebling — bass)

Built around lengthy soundscapes of rolling percussion and fragmented guitars and the sense that the musicians were making as much noise as they could, without quite descending into the tuneless clatter of improvisational hell, Hovercraft formed in 1994, wondering — as Campbell put it — "how people would react, if they'd have the patience to stand through 40 minutes of abstraction."

Early shows around Seattle, some featuring Sadie 7's husband Eddie Vedder as drummer, saw Hovercraft's original development tarred with the Pearl Jam spin-off brush; a tour opening for Mike Watt in 1995, continued the association. By 1996, however, Vedder had dropped out and with new drummer Karl onboard, the band's debut single, "Zero Zero Zero One" (on the Seattle label Repellant) proved Hovercraft's durability once and for all.

Habitually playing in darkness, illuminated only by slide shows and movie clips, Hovercraft continued playing, releasing a live 10" EP *Hovercraft* in fall 1996, and contributing a shock version of "Shutdown" to the *A Small Circle of Friends* Germs tribute album. The album *Akathisia* followed in 1997, with more of the same (only different) appearing on the attendant *Scanner Mixes* mini-album.

Hovercraft's second full album, March 1998's *Experiment Below*, was followed by touring and, through summer 1999, a collaboration with Stereolab's Mary Hanson.

Hovercraft LPs

8 Akathisia (Mute) 1997 Voiceless, wordless, and most of all screamless, Hovercraft make records for floating out to sea on, for drifting through the clouds to, and maybe, when the lights are out, and their astral pounding is all you can feel, sleepwalking into oblivion with. There isn't a tune in sight, but you'll never get it out of your head.

8 Experiment Below (Mute) 1998 Their second full-length album, but really just a continuation of their first, which itself took off from where Pink Floyd's *Saucerful of Secrets* left off. But if you've never heard Pink Floyd, picture this. Rhythms floating in a bottomless void; bass lines like ice flows leading nowhere in particular; fractured guitars like glasses in a bar fight; and over everything, the inescapable sense that someone is trying to tell you something, but they're doing it in morse code.

HUMAN DRAMA

FORMED *1985 (Los Angeles, CA)*

ORIGINAL LINE-UP *Salvador John Indovina Jr. (b. 8/5/57, New Orleans — vocals, guitar); Michael Ciravolo (guitar); CJ Eiriksson (drums)*

Alongside the late Rozz Williams, John Indovina's Human Drama project was the single most important act on the US gothic scene as it moved through the 1990s, and that despite Indovina himself (like Williams) purposefully distancing himself from his creation with a series of increasingly challenging new releases.

Human Drama began in New Orleans as the Models, self-releasing the singles "In the Red," "Child Star," and "Fool to Try," before Indovina alone relocated to L.A. in May 1985, changing the band's name after another Models, from Australia, landed a major label US deal. With Indovina joined by Michael Ciravolo (guitar) and drummer CJ Eiriksson, and emerging from the same L.A. scene that spawned Jane's Addiction and Guns 'n' Roses, Human Drama debuted on the 1987 *Scream* compilation with the self-defining "Wave of Darkness."

The following year, Human Drama's "Heaven on Earth" was included on The Album Network's *Unsigned Bands* sampler; a deal with RCA followed in November 1988 and Human Drama traveled to Wales to record the EP *Hopes, Prayers, Dreams, Heart, Soul, Mind, Love, Life, Death* for a May 1989 release. But the label buried their *Feel* debut in November and Indovina retired to reconsider his options.

It would be almost two years before Indovina and Eiriksson re-emerged with the single "This Tangled Web" on the indy Triple X (Jane's Addiction's original label), following up with "Fascination and Fear" and, in 1992, the album *The World Inside*.

Born out of an ad-hoc set performed at that album's launch party in 1993, *Pin Ups* was a cunning recreation of the David Bowie album of the same title, two decades previous, visually (the sleeve was a direct take-off) and aurally, as the set emerged packed with Indovina's interpretations of his own favorite influences — Joy Division, Lou Reed, John Lennon, Leonard Cohen and Bowie, of course, but also Pink Floyd, Peter Gabriel-era Genesis, Mink DeVille, and the Rolling Stones.

An out-take from these sessions, Nico's "60-40" (together with Greg Lake's "I Believe in Father Christmas," originally recorded for a 1990 festive sampler) would appear within 1995's *Songs of Betrayal/As Love Comes Tumbling* cycle, released following the *Human Drama* mini-album. A 23-song epic, *Songs* was nevertheless pruned for the occasion — it would be reissued in 1999 as two separate albums, with the missing tracks restored.

Now based in New York, Indovina spent much of the next year touring with a line-up comprising Ciravolo and Eiriksson, plus Mark Balderas (keyboards), Renelle LaPlanti (flute), Michael Mallory (bass), and Jamii Szmadzinski (violin). The itinerary included gigs in Germany and Mexico, before headlining L.A.'s Troubadour on December 21, 1996 for the show which would become the live *14,384 Days Later* album. Featuring material dating back to the *Scream* days ("Wave of Darkness," and "I Bleed for You," from the RCA EP), *14,384 Days Later* captured a virtual greatest hits set, Human Drama at their best.

Two years of apparent musical inactivity followed, during which Indovina published a collection of his lyrics, *My Bag of Secrets*, and began the upgrade of his back catalog. A new album, *Solemn Sun Setting*, appeared in 1999 featuring a dramatic remake of "The Great Pretender." (Ciravolo spent the hiatus touring and recording with Michael Aston's Gene Loves Jezebel.)

Human Drama LPs

7 Feel (RCA) 1989 Formative but vital collection capturing Indovina as he leaves the *Scream* scene behind, but has yet to be shunted into any other direction.

7 The World Inside (Triple X) 1992 Perfect for reminiscence and romance, *World* is soft music in a minor key, heavy with heartfelt emotion. The music and lyrics are all subtly nuanced, while the acoustic guitars, strings, and flute help to create that perfect aura of hopeful sorrow.

8 Pin Ups (Triple X) 1993 An astonishingly majestic album, revitalizing Bowie's original *Pin Ups* covers collection in sleeve art and contents alike. Reed, Gabriel, Nico, Pink Floyd, Leonard

Cohen and naturally, Bowie himself are under the microscope, but the peak is Joy Division's "Love Will Tear Us Apart," so desolate that even the original sounds jolly.

7 Songs of Betrayal (Projekt) 1997 Shorter songs make for a far greater impact, with instrumental interludes dividing the album into four sections, giving *Betrayal* the feel of an emotional feast. And that's precisely what the band had in mind, as Indovina dives deep into the human heart and psyche to reveal yet more very human dramas.

7 14,384 Days Later [LIVE] (Triple X) 1997

8 Solemn Sun Setting (Triple X) 1999 Johnny Indovina's tortured existence drags on, his umpteenth album of umpteen sorrowful songs, and if you want to be really cynical about it, you could say he's laughing all the way to the bank. Yet he's earned the right, not because anyone this lachrymose merits special treatment, but because he does it so stylishly that his beauty is wholly believable.

Selected Compilations and Archive Releases

8 Songs of Betrayal Vol 1 (Triple X) 1999

8 Songs of Betrayal Vol 2 (Triple X) Richly expanded version of the 1997 album.

9 ...In a Perfect World (Hollow Hills) 16-track "best of" doesn't put a foot wrong.

HUMAN LEAGUE

FORMED 1977 *(Sheffield, England)*
ORIGINAL LINE-UP *Martin Ware (b. 5/19/56, Sheffield — synth); Ian Craig Marsh (b. 11/11/56, Sheffield — synth); Adi Newton (synth)*

The Human League began life as Future, an exercise in electronics conceived by Martin Ware, Ian Craig Marsh, and Adi Newton. Though no music has ever been officially released (a projected archive EP in 1981 was blocked), the trio did a great deal of recording, including the tracks "Almost Medieval," "Blank Clocks," "Dancevision," "Future Religion," and "Looking for the Black Haired Girls." The trio also played a pair of now-legendary, but at the time, simply chaotic live shows — one as the Dead Daughters at a private party in June 1977; the other as the Studs, with a line-up completed by Glen Gregory (later to rejoin Ware and Marsh in Heaven 17), Haydn Boyes, and members of the similarly formative Cabaret Voltaire.

While Ware and Marsh were intent that Future's future rested solely in electronics, Newton was interested in incorporating other instruments and sounds; the conflict saw him quit to form Clock DVA in early 1978; he was replaced by vocalist Phil Oakey (b. 10/2/55, Sheffield), and with "director of visuals" Adrian Wright (b. Philip Wright, 6/30/56, Shef-

field) also on board, the newly-christened Human League became one of their hometown's closest watched bands.

Signing to Fast Product in early 1978, the League's debut single, "Being Boiled," would subsequently be regarded as one of the key building blocks in the development of electronic pop — even if Johnny Rotten did dismiss the band as "trendy hippies." In spring 1979, tours with Siouxsie and the Banshees and Iggy Pop confirmed the band's experimental credentials and following the ground-breaking *The Dignity of Labour Parts 1-4* EP, in 1979, the League were signed to Virgin Records.

"I Don't Depend on You," credited to The Men, debuted the band on their new label in July 1979; it was followed by the League's first album, *Reproduction*, itself highlighted by the "Empire State Human" single, which defied its parent's harsh angularism to establish the band firmly in the forefront of the burgeoning New Romantic movement, a trap which Ware and Marsh seemed to fear considerably more than Oakey.

A tour with the visiting Talking Heads ended when the headliners requested the League be removed; the group bounced back with the *Holiday 80* (#56 UK) EP and undertook their own UK tour in May, to coincide with the release of their second album, *Travelogue* (#16 UK) and reissues of both "Empire State Human" (#62 UK) and *Travelogue* (#49 UK).

The album caught the band in mid-split — Marsh and Ware now looking towards the direction they would take with their own British Electric Foundation/Heaven 17 project and doing their best to pull Oakey along with them. He wasn't listening, though and the resultant schizophrenia made for a considerably more uncomfortable album than anybody, the band and their record company included, expected. Marsh and Ware finally quit in October 1980, selling the rights to the Human League's name to Oakey in return for one percent of all future royalties.

With Wright learning synthesizer and Oakey pulling in bassist Ian Burden (b. 12/24/57, Sheffield) and joint vocalists Suzanne Sulley (b. 3/22/63, Sheffield), and Joanne Catherall (b. 9/18/62, Sheffield), the new look League debuted with "Boys and Girls" (#48 UK) in March 1981. It was followed by "Sound of the Crowd" (#12 UK), the first fruits of recent sessions with producer Martin Rushent (and the debut for second synth player, ex-Rezillos guitarist Jo Callis — b. 5/2/55, Glasgow).

"Love Action" (#3 UK) in August and "Open Your Heart" (#6 UK) in October led up to the band's next UK tour. Finally, with Oakey, Catherall, and Sulley now flirting with a seriously androgynous image, the League were ready to unveil *Dare* (#3 US, #1 UK), an album which would have irrevocably altered the prevailing musical mood even with-out the attendant "Don't You Want Me" (#1 US, #1 UK).

Single and album dominated the UK charts over Christmas 1981 pulling reissues of *Reproduction* (#34 UK), "Being Boiled" (#6 UK), and the *Holiday 80* (#46 UK) EP behind them. The *Love and Dancing* (#135 US, #3 UK) remix EP followed, but it would be close to a year before a genuine follow-up arrived, "Mirror Man" (#30 US, #2 UK), in November 1982. Another six months separated that hit from "(Keep Feeling) Fascination" (#8 US, #2 UK) — taken from the *Fascination* mini-album (#22 US) and while they, too, were a success, there was a distinct feeling abroad that the band had waited too long.

The departure of producer Rushent added to the sense of impending doom surrounding the band's next project; so did their refusal to tour again. "We thought we were so popular we didn't have to," Oakey later admitted. *Hysteria* (#62 US, #3 UK) in May 1984 unsurprisingly emerged a savage disappointment after the two-and-one-half years wait. The band's next single, the mildly political (and guitar led) "Lebanon" (#64 US, #11 UK) stumbled; "Life on Your Own" (#16 UK), and "Louise" (#13 UK) fared even worse and the group announced they were going on hiatus indefinitely.

Oakey recorded with German Motorik producer Giorgio Moroder, lending vocals to the title theme to the movie *Electric Dreams* (#3 UK) in late 1984; the pair would subsequently release a full album (#52 UK), even as attempts to record a new League album with producer Colin Thurston collapsed in disarray. Callis quit, to join former Undertone Feargal Sharkey's new band and early in 1986, the remainder of the League traveled to Minnesota for another attempt at an album.

Working with Jimmy Jam and Terry Lewis, masterminds behind Janet Jackson's *Control*, the band completed *Crash* (#24 US, #7 UK) before the sessions fell apart amidst fierce dispute over the amount of outside musical help brought into the sessions. However, "Human" (#1 US, #8 UK), the first single from the album, became a massive hit and while "I Need Your Loving" (#44 US, #72 UK) proved a weak follow-up, the band returned to the road for a lengthy tour, featuring Neil Sutton (keyboards) and Russell Dennett (guitar).

In 1988, a remix of "Love Is All That Matters" (#41 UK) from *Crash* preceded the compilation *Greatest Hits* (#3 UK). The League, however, again retreated from view, resurfacing briefly in 1990 with a low-key new album, *Romantic?* (#24 UK) and single "Heart like a Wheel" (#32 US, #29 UK), but again going underground — pursued, no doubt, by a savage reminder of their past glory, as the Farm's cover of "Don't You Want Me" (#18 UK) fearlessly outperformed their own new material.

Another hiatus, this time stretching to five years, was finally broken with the release of *Octopus* (#6 UK), a return to the old-style, synth-driven sound, updated through remix collaborations with Utah Saints, Red Jerry and the Development Corporation. However, while album and the "Tell Me When" (#31 US, #6 UK) single debuted high in the UK chart, both slipped quickly and *Octopus* was summed up by *Alternative Press'* caustic question, "what's that bumper sticker which [people] think will keep their children off drugs? *DARE* — the only decent Human League album ever."

Further singles "One Man in My Heart" (#13 UK), "Filling Up with Heaven" (#36 UK), and "Stay with Me Tonight" (#40 UK) were overshadowed by a remix of "Don't You Want Me" (#16 UK) in October 1995 and while the band toured briefly at the end of the year, it would be 1998 before the Human League finally came to terms with the reality of their predicament, when a new hits collection was released, to coincide with the band's appearance on the Big Rewind '80s revival tour, alongside Culture Club and Howard Jones (in the US; ABC in the UK).

Human League LPs

⑨ Reproduction (Virgin) 1979 So tight, so frigid, so utterly off the wall at the time, who would have believed that one day, everyone would be dancing to the same drum beat? Harshly proto-industrial, particularly across the premonitory "Empire State Human," but even without the benefit of hindsight, one of the finest electro albums ever made.

⑧ Travelogue (Virgin) 1980 The band tears in one direction, the singer in another, but the dynamic only adds an edge to the songs, pushing *Travelogue* into ever fresher territory.

⑨ Dare (A&M) 1981 Hands down *the* most influential electro-pop album to be released, today Human League's legacy has been overwhelmed by the strength of their singles (and "Don't You Want Me" in particular). *Dare's* status, however, is assured precisely because it wasn't a throwaway disc of singles, fleshed out by disposable fillers. Oakey's ability to create vivid vignettes with a minimum of words and then bring them to life almost defies belief, but the music was his match, a breathtaking blend of dance beats and pop melodies brought to maturity by the band's extraordinary talent for conjuring nuanced moods and atmospheres out of the cold hearts of synthesizers and keyboards.

⑤ Hysteria (Virgin) 1984 It wasn't as though they rushed it, but fame rushed them and nothing would ever be the same again. A smattering of unmemorable singles, a little bit of filler...

④ Crash (A&M) 1986 Massively successful reinvention, in commercial terms at least. But the Human League were never going to be the next Whitney Houston, and the bubble burst the moment they tried.

④ Romantic? (A&M) 1990

④ Octopus (East West) 1995

Selected Compilations and Archive Releases

8 **Greatest Hits (A&M) 1988**

8 **The Very Best Of (Ark 21) 1998** There's half a dozen League songs which nobody can live without — "Love Action," "Mirror Man," "Fascination"... but topping as many best-of lists today as it ever did back then, "Don't You Want Me," the touching tale of one man and his Machiavellian fantasy sums up New Romantic lives and loves better than any words ever could.

Phil Oakey and Giorgio Moroder LP

6 **Phil Oakey and Giorgio Moroder (A&M) 1985**

BEF LPs

7 **Music for Listening (Virgin) 1981** Combining tracks from the duo's first two EPs (*Music for Stowaways* and *Music for Listening*), Marsh and Ware pursue the electro experimentations they'd attempted with Human League, chasing their synthetic dreams through funky dance music, rich, ambient soundscapes and into bleak cyber-space, exploring rhythms, moods, and sounds along the way.

7 **Music of Quality and Distinction (Virgin) 1982** Classic set combining BEF's synthesized vision with a string of largely forgotten past icons — the album relaunched careers for Sandy Shaw and Tina Turner, among others.

5 **Music of Quality and Distinction Volume 2 (Arista) 1991** A less satisfying return to admittedly golden pastures, featuring Terence Trent D'Arby, Billy MacKenzie, and a second engagement with Tina Turner.

Heaven 17 LPs

7 **Penthouse and Pavement (Arista) 1981** Electro-funk pop monster distinguished by the crushing "Fascist Groove Thing" single. Recruiting vocalist Glenn Gregory, Heaven 17 is obviously BEF's more commercial alter-ego, and their debut album brilliantly blends a leftist political stance, provocative lyrics, funky rhythms, and strong pop melodies.

9 **The Luxury Gap (Arista) 1983** While *Penthouse* breached the heights of the UK album chart, single success eluded the band — a situation the trio were determined to remedy. *Luxury Gap* accordingly contained a trio of love lost and found songs, aimed directly at the British consumer. Their magnificent marketing scheme was so successful that in its wake, even the workers' rallying cry of "Crushed by the Wheels of Industry" would be dragged into the Top 20. From the joyous Motown soul of "Temptation" to the quiet desperation of "Let Me Go," *Luxury* smoothes down the more experimental edges found on *Penthouse*, while still agitating politically and pursuing musical adventure. Everything, however, was over shadowed by the masterful "Come Live with Me," the band's biggest hit yet (and their most mystifying video: did she jump? or did she just leave the old loser?).

7 **How Men Are (Arista) 1984**

6 **Pleasure One (Virgin) 1986**

5 **Teddy Bear, Duke and Psycho (Virgin) 1988**

7 **Bigger than America (Cleopatra) 1998** Pure pop, quirky rhythms with a hint of updated twist drive the album, beginning with the slightly sinister "Dive," then jumping straight to the upbeat tempos of "Designing Heaven" (reprised, on two bonus remixes, by Giorgio Moroder, and in German by "Gregorio." Elsewhere, the spacey trance of "Unreal Everything," the mellow "Maybe Forever," and the very aptly titled "Resurrection Man" prove the reunion might have unexpected legs.

Selected Compilations and Archive Releases

8 **Endless (Virgin) 1986** Essential collection of 12-inch remixes.

7 **Higher and Higher — The Best Of... (Virgin) 1993**

8 **The Remix Collection (Virgin — UK) 1995**

Further Reading

The Story of a Band Called... by Alaska Ross (Proteus, UK, 1982).

HUNDRED MILLION MARTIANS

FORMED 1991 *(Turku, Finland)*
ORIGINAL LINE-UP *Jyrki Makela (vocals); Seppo Lehdonkivi (guitar); Tuomas Peltarri (guitar); Pasi Hjerppe (bass); Jarkko Lehti (drums)*

One of the hardest hitting latter-day punk bands in Finland, characterized not only by their effortless encapsulation of all that keeps the genre alive in the 21st century, but also by their preference for English language lyrics, Hundred Million Martians spent close to three years in their rehearsal room before finally venturing out in public for the first time — by which time they had already written two albums' worth of material.

Early gigs around Turku saw them opening for the likes of 69 Eyes, Karkkiautomaatti, and Juliet Jones, and in 1996, the Martians made their recorded debut on the acclaimed *Return of the Babysitter* compilation. They contributed two tracks, "Something About You" and "Stupid Behaviour," and caused such a stir that by year's end, the Martians were regularly gigging elsewhere around the country.

That same year saw Hundred Million Martians take part in a talent contest organized by a local brewery, the Koff-Rock band competition — along with 600 other bands. They won, taking the first prize of studio time and 500 CD copies of the resultant music, and before Christmas, unleashed the four-track *Brighter Days* EP, a power-pop classic highlighted by "Damned," dedicated to the Martians' own favorite band.

Signing to the Tampere-based Hiljaiset Levyt label, the Martians linked with producer Jani Viitanen to rerecord "Brighter Days" (from the EP), together with a dozen other band originals. *Martian Arts* was released in 1997, and effortlessly established the Martians among the leading guitar-pop bands in Scandinavia. Surfing its success, the band spent much of the next year on the road.

The Martians' next release was, in their record company's own words, "an odd-ball" — a four-song EP, wherein every track shared the same title, "I Wanna Be Your Boyfriend." Three were covers, of the Ramones, the Pushtwangers, and the Rubinoos; the fourth was a band original, which would also appear on the Martians' long-awaited sophomore album, late 1999's *Mars Bars* .

Hundred Million Martians LPs

8 Martian Arts (Hiljaiset Levyt — Fin) 1997 The Martians land with a vengeance. In amidst the blistering power-punk pop and good time guitar-driven melodies, one track, "A Perfect Pop Song," absolutely lives up to its title.

9 Mars Bars (Hiljaiset Levyt — Fin) 1999 From the Buzzcocks to Cheap Trick, the Martians know their musical stablemates, but aren't afraid to tackle them on their own high ground. Contagiously fiery, blistered harmonies and singalong choruses result in such a great time that it's hard to believe that every song's an original. If the Martians came from Tampa rather than Turku, they'd already be enormous.

HÜSKER DÜ

FORMED *1978 (St. Paul, MN)*
ORIGINAL LINE-UP *Bob Mould (b. 10/12/60 — vocals, guitar, keyboard, percussion); Grant Hart (b. Grantzberg Vernon Hart, 3/18/61 — drums, keyboards, vocals); Greg Norton (b. 3/13/59 —bass)*

Hüsker Dü blasted out of the embryonic midwestern alternative scene and into the clubs fully formed, playing a perfect, pure punk and raging pop that would become standard for every band to follow in their wake.

With their name derived form a 1950s Norwegian game (translated, Do You Remember?), Hüsker Dü's genius evolved from the tight, complemented writing team of Bob Mould and Grant Hart, who circled each other then crashed together forming a perfect sonic mix, a wall of noise that reverberated across the city, daring anybody to forget the charisma that would shape the future of alternative rock.

As fast and furious as their songs were, so would Hüsker Dü's recording career become. Having had their initial demos turned down by Minneapolis' one significant independent label, Twin/Tone, the band released their first single, "Statues" in 1980 on their own Reflex label, following

through in 1982 with their live debut album, *Land Speed Record* — its 17 songs in 26 minutes certainly living up that title. Quickly following was the *In a Free Land* EP the same year.

Hüsker Dü stepped into the studio for the first time in summer 1983 to record July's *Everything Falls Apart*, before signing to Black Flag's SST label. The mini-album *Metal Circus* was released towards the end of the year.

Hüsker Dü set a precedent and a standard, creating a blueprint for the next generation. The band toured incessantly, hitting college after college in town after town, crisscrossing the US nonstop. They pushed to have their music played on college radio stations and continued to record apace, to ensure that no one would forget their crashing sounds. Of course no one could, and the band quickly became college favorites, rewarding the masses by releasing a version of the Byrds classic "Eight Miles High" (#22 UK indy) in April 1984.

In September the band once again sent the underground rumbling when they released the double album *Zen Arcade* (#11 UK indy), a deeply ambitious set which signaled a revolution in the Mould/Hart writing process — a loosely-veiled

© Jim Steinfeldt/Chansley Entertainment Archives

punk rock concept album, which added a little more pop to the punk.

But there were signs that all was not right. The grueling pace of the last five years was beginning to take its toll on the band. As fast as Hüsker Dü were rising to the top of the indie pile, Mould and Hart were succumbing to the ravages of drug and alcohol addiction. Seeding itself, too, was a vague tension between Mould and Hart, as the band's reputation spread and egos began to jostle.

Things would continue on as planned for a time. March 1985 brought *New Day Rising* (#10 UK indy), while a new single "Make No Sense at All" (#2 UK indy) hit the streets in August, in anticipation of October's *Flip Your Wig* (#1 UK indy). By the end of the year, Hüsker Dü were signing to major label Warner Brothers. *Candy Apple Grey* appeared in March 1986 and spawned two singles, "Don't Want to Know If You Are Lonely" in March and "Sorry Somehow" in September. The band then managed to do it all over again, releasing "Could You Be the One" and *Warehouse: Songs & Stories* (#72 UK) in January 1987. June's "Ice Cold Ice," however, would be the last new Hüsker Dü release ever.

By now, however, tensions between Mould and Hart had escalated to dangerous proportions, as addiction rubbed shoulders with recovery and ego, concocting a dangerous brew. And as if the band's own frictions weren't enough, tragedy would also drive Hüsker Dü closer to oblivion. On the eve of the band's spring 1987 album tour, longtime manager and friend David Savoy Jr. committed suicide. The tour went ahead, but it was apparent that the love affair had ended. Mould's new sobriety clashed with Hart's ever deepening dependency and finally, in early 1988, Hüsker Dü formally disbanded in shambles. Mould subsequently formed Sugar, Hart formed Nova Mob and, in 2000, was among the musicians featured on Patti Smith's *Gung Ho*.

Also see the entry for "BOB MOULD" on page 510.

Hüsker Dü LPs

4 Land Speed Record (New Alliance) 1982 Cheapo speedball live album, endearingly sloppy so long as you don't have to clean up afterwards.

6 Everything Falls Apart (Reflex) 1983 Donovan's "Sunshine Superman" stands out, not because it's necessarily the best song here, but it does have the best tune.

10 Zen Arcade (SST) 1984 Suddenly bursting with sonic ideas and conclusions, jamming them all into a double concept album probably wasn't the smartest move in the world. But it worked, both as a concept (which was rare enough) and also as a farewell to the one-dimensional reputation of old. Acoustic, psych, rock, pop — the moods shift by the moment and the rule book flew through the window.

Arguably, *Zen Arcade* could have been halved and still it would have made its point — but the fact that it wasn't is what made it important, not only in its own naïve right, but also as the benchmark which the rest of the '80s indy pack immediately sensed they, too, had to reach. Suddenly, anything went and everything goes, and if Hüsker Dü did themselves another disservice by banging the whole thing down so quickly (85 hours, including the mix), that too would power a lot of future dreaming.

"Turn on the News" and "Something I Learned Today" are the most potent rockers, "Never Talking to You Again" is the moment when sensitivity bites deep, even with a total length of barely one minute 40. But the heart of the album lies in the songs which are utterly unquantifiable, the almost-ethereal "Pink Turns to Blue" or "Hare Krsna"... or deeper still, across 1993's bizarro *The Twin Cities Replay Zen Arcade* tribute album, where the likes of Hammerhead and God's Favorite Band follow the paths which the original album mapped and find out precisely where they wound up. You'd be surprised at some of their findings.

9 New Day Rising (SST) 1985 A bit of a backward step, but only if you thought it'd be possible to take the last disc any further. Honing in on *Zen*'s tightest power pop punk, the hooks are spread thick and the melodies truly gell.

6 Flip Your Wig (SST) 1985 More of the same, but weaker, showcasing Mould's songwriting as opposed to the music.

8 Candy Apple Grey (WB) 1986 For their major label debut, the band polished their sound while retaining the hard thrash they were now famous for — and the result, oddly, was a success. Clean and — dare we say it — slick, Hüsker Dü crossed the gap from indy underground to radio friendly with ease, most notably on "Don't Want to Know (If You Are Lonely)", "Sorry Somehow," and "Too Far Down."

6 Warehouse: Songs and Stories (WB) 1987 Another double album with lots of guitars, occasionally bringing the harsher extremes of *Zen Arcade* to mind, but this time with a far friendlier edge.

Selected Compilations and Archive Releases

7 Everything Falls Apart and More (Rhino) 1993 Revisiting history for the masses, this album is a reissue of the 1982 album, plus a healthy handful of bonus tracks including early singles.

6 The Living End (WB) 1994 Live performance taken from the band's 1987 tour.

Grant Hart Solo LPs

6 All of My Senses (SST) 1987

7 Intolerance (SST) 1989

6 Ecce Homo (World Service) 1996

7 Good News for Modern Man (World Service) 1999

Nova Mob LPs

7 The Last Days of Pompeii (Rough Trade) 1991

7 Nova Mob (Restless) 1994

I

IMMACULATE CONSUMPTIVES

FORMED *1983 (New York, NY)*
ORIGINAL LINE-UP *Nick Cave (b. 9/22/57 — vocals, piano); Jim Thirlwell (vocals, drums); Lydia Lunch (b. 6/2/59 — vocals, guitar); Marc Almond (b. 7/5/59 — vocals)*

Emerging from the looming wreckage of two of the early 1980s' most innovative bands — Soft Cell and Birthday Party — Marc Almond and Nick Cave together with Foetus and Lydia Lunch, united for three shows in New York and Washington DC over Halloween 1983.

Cave recalled, "it was really Lydia's idea. She always had these grand ideas to do things, and she was always very much into roping other people in to do these things with her, and I think that was one of her better ideas." The quartet had already drifted in and out of one another's projects — Lunch and Cave had remained in touch since they met in New York on the Birthday Party's first American tour in 1981. Thirlwell and Cave had been friends since their days in Australia, and Almond and Thirlwell had been working together for a year or so on a project which would eventually blossom into the Flesh Volcanoes project.

The Immaculate Consumptive's set would be drawn from among all four musicians' latest compositions — with the collaborative "Body Unknown" closing the show, with Almond singing, Cave screaming, Thirlwell drumming and Lunch guitar picking. Around that centerpiece, the show divided into four inter-connected solo performances — all held together with backing tape recorded in one hectic week by Blixa Bargeld, Barry Adamson, Mick Harvey from the nascent Bad Seeds, and Annie Hogan from Marc and the Mambas.

It was a lot of work for not much return. Cave continued, "Lydia works in a kind of art-event area, and put a lot of effort into doing three shows that were never recorded, which is what this was about." Actually, it was recorded — Almond possessed a bootleg video of one show but never watched it, "because I've always liked the memory. If I watched it, I'd probably think 'oh God!'" And Cave agreed. "It was better to be left in that mythological state, without anyone actually hearing what it was like."

"Each of us did duets with each other," Almond remembered, "but Nick came on and stole the entire show..." Cave's set comprised of two songs: a cover of Elvis Presley's "In the Ghetto," and his own "A Box for Black Paul," a piano dirge for the morning after the Birthday Party. But "A Box for Black Paul" was doomed. The first night at New York's Danceteria, Thirlwell broke the piano. The second night Cave got bored, stopped singing and playing and told the audience instead, "then it goes on like that for another five minutes."

"I was really pissed off about it," Thirlwell complained later. "I thought it really broke the atmosphere." But he also admitted, "it was a lot of fun."

The Immaculate Consumptives never repeated the exercise. Cave later admitted, "it was Marc who intrigued me, who I was most interested in working with," but though he and Almond did discuss a Far Eastern tour together, playing only the sleaziest dives they could find, the project never went any further. And in the years since, the quartet's careers have only occasionally overlapped, usually around successive Foetus ventures.

Also see the entries for "MARC ALMOND" on page 153, "NICK CAVE" on page 245, "FOETUS" on page 371, and "LYDIA LUNCH" on page 476.

INSPIRAL CARPETS

FORMED *1983 (Oldham, England)*
ORIGINAL LINE-UP *Steve Holt (vocals); Graham Lambert (b. 7/10/64 — guitar); Craig Gill (b. 12/5/71 — drums)*

Originally formed as a garage punk band and named for a clothing store on the outskirts of nearby Manchester, Inspiral Carpets were a regular sight around that city through the 1980s, releasing two albums worth of demos for sale at shows — *Waiting for Ours* and *Songs of Shallow Intensity* — both including material which would later resurface in the band's repertoire.

Early line-ups were unstable, but by 1987, the band had settled down with the arrival of Clint Boon (keyboards) and Dave Swift (bass), and as the city club scene enlivened, so Inspiral Carpets moved with it, cranking up Boon's Farfisa organ and establishing their rave-friendly sound with the early 1987 "Garage Full of Flowers" flexidisc on the local Debris label.

The *Cow* cassette EP followed in May 1987, and by the new year, the band had signed with Playtime and in July 1988, released the *Planecrash* (#13 UK indy) EP, their first project to receive anything more than local attention. The following month, the band would make their first appearance on the John Peel Show.

The late 1988 collapse of Playtime's distributor, Red Rhino, prompted the band to form their own label, Cow, and in March 1989, the *Trainsurfing* (#5 UK indy) EP debuted the label as the band bade farewell to members Holt and Swift. They were replaced by Tom Hingley (ex-Too Much Texas) and Martyn "Bungle" Walsh (ex-Next Step), and with the Carpets now firmly locked into a swirling psychedelic groove, the group recorded "Joe" (#5 UK indy) for release in May 1989.

A second appearance on BBC John Peel's show in April 1989, spawned the band's next release, the sensibly titled *Peel Session* EP (#5 UK indy), and in September, "Find Out Why" (#1 UK indy — featuring a re-recording of "Planecrash") became the Carpets' biggest hit yet. Finally, after a year of gigging, the decade ended with "Move" (#49 UK, #1 UK indy), the band's first national hit, and their final independent release.

In early 1990, the Inspiral Carpets signed with Mute (although they would retain the Cow label identity), and in March, the anthemic "This Is How It Feels" (#14 UK) proved to be their breakthrough. The band's debut album, *Life* (#2 UK) followed, a hit which also included "She Comes in the Fall" (#27 UK), and the band's most dramatic moment yet, the mantric "Commercial Rain." The *Island Head* EP (#21 UK) in November kept the Inspiral Carpets in the Top 30, but the downbeat *Beast Inside* (#5 UK) album was a sour shock after the sparkling pop of its predecessor.

The singles "Caravan" (#30 UK) and "Please Be Cruel" (#50 UK) both performed comparatively poorly, while attempts to break the band in the US also fell short of expectations. *The Cool As* **** EP of early singles receiving far more attention for its title (taken from a popular band T-shirt, itself based on the Cow label's own motto) than its contents. Portugal, Germany and Argentina, contrarily, adored the band, and 1992's *Revenge of the Goldfish* (#17 UK) became the band's biggest hit yet in those territories.

Through 1992, Inspiral Carpets were seldom far from either the UK chart or MTV's 120 *Minutes*. Four singles that year — "Dragging Me Down" (#12 UK), "Two Worlds Collide" (#32 UK), "Generations" (#28 UK), and "Bitches Brew" (#36 UK) — maintained a seemingly constant presence while the band was on the road. A poor reception for summer 1993's "How It Should Be" (#49 UK), however, boded poorly for the band's next album, and so it turned out. The album *Devil Hopping* did not even chart in the UK.

Despite this, the Inspiral Carpets continued flirting with the Top 30 singles chart. "Saturn 5" (#20 UK) opened 1994 with some optimism, and March's "I Want You" (#18 UK)

achieved a milestone of sorts when it gave Fall vocalist Mark E. Smith his first ever appearance on *Top of the Pops*. Interestingly, Smith admitted that "when [Inspiral Carpets] first came along, I thought [they] were a right load of crap. But they called up and asked me to sing on a song with them, and it was good fun. They were great."

"I Want You" would be the Inspiral Carpets' last significant hit. "Uniform" (#51 UK) spent just one week on the chart, and in late 1995, following the release of the *Singles* collection, and a distinctly belated chart appearance for "Joe" (#37 UK), the group were dropped by Mute. They broke up soon after.

Hingley linked with Lotus Eaters mainstay Jerry Kelly in the Lovers, vowing never again to sign with a major label; the band's debut 45, "Work Rest and Play" was released on their own Poof Records. Boon formed the Clint Boon Experience and released a string of singles, also on his own label, Artful; Walsh moved into techno-dance production; and Gill formed a new band, Hustler.

The greatest post-Inspiral Carpets success, however, would fall to two of their roadies. Van driver Mark Collins had joined Charlatans UK in March 1991, and would soon be enjoying regular #1 albums. The other, Boon once shrugged, was "an arsehole who I love... but he's not to be trusted." His name was Noel Gallagher, and he quit the payroll to join his brother's band, Oasis.

Inspiral Carpets LPs

9 Life (Elektra) 1990 A glorious amalgamation of British Beat bands (think the Yardbirds) and the Teardrop Explodes, overlaid with Doors-esque keyboards. Rave central it is, then, as *Life* explodes with such jubilant glee, and is weighed down by so many hits-to-be, that even the loopy lyrics sound cool.

7 Beast Inside (Elektra) 1991 The Carpets reveal their (new) romantic side as keyboardist Clint Boon adds Ultravox to his repertoire, vocalist Tom Hingley has a go at becoming the new Tony Hadley, and the rest of the band embark on protracted jams notable not for their previous youthful exuberance, but their technical skills and sudden savoir faire flare.

6 Revenge of the Goldfish (Elektra) 1992 Having survived the angsty growing pains of *Beast*, the Carpets pull their influences together, refining and redefining their sound into a tightly hammered mold of rock, early new wave, and the faithful new romanticism, while placing the emphasis on more classic cross-generational pop songs.

5 Devil Hopping (Mute) 1994 The album's half over before the Carpets unearth any glimmers of *Life* or *Beast*, preferring to leap between late '60s classic Britrock and modern day adult-orientated pop. Such a decline was probably inevitable, but it's still all rather sad. They grow up so fast nowadays.

Selected Compilations and Archive Releases

8 **The Island Head EP (Mute — Island) 1990** 21-track compilation of early singles, B-sides, and rarities.

7 **Singles (Mute UK) 1995** Non-stop parade of the hits we hailed and the bits you missed.

7 **The Radio One Sessions 1999** 21-track anthology replacing the original John Peel Sessions EP on collectors' shelves.

J

JAM

FORMED 1974 (Woking, England)
ORIGINAL LINE-UP *Paul Weller (b. John Weller, 5/25/58 —
vocals, guitar); Bruce Foxton (b. 9/1/55 — bass); Rick Buckler
(b. 12/6/55 — drums)*

Although the band had been knocking around their native
suburbia for some four years, and making sporadic visits to
London for two, it took the emergence of the UK punk scene
to finally bring the Jam to attention, when the trio set up
their gear in Soho Market on October 16, 1976, and blasted
through a blistering set of proto-punk anthems and Mod
classic standards, before the astonished gaze of the afternoon
shoppers. Five days later, the band was asked to fill in as support on a Sex Pistols gig in Dunstable, and by the end of the
year, the Jam had a virtual residency at the Red Cow in
Hammersmith.

Weller formed what became the Jam while still at school
in 1972, playing his first gig at the school that November, a
six-song acoustic set with classmate Steve Brookes. Brookes
quit shortly after Foxton joined, with Buckler being recruited
during 1973, and over the next two years, the Jam played regularly around the Woking area, finally reaching London (or
at least, its outskirts), when they opened for Thin Lizzy at
Croydon Greyhound in November 1974.

By 1976, the band's grip on Weller's beloved
R&B/Motown Mod brew was water tight, with the associated
energy translating perfectly to the prevalent mood of early
punk. EMI turned them down, but Polydor — having been
jilted by both the Sex Pistols and the Clash — snapped the
band up in February 1977 and immediately sent them out on
the road with the Clash.

That venture ended in acrimony, a mood which would
repeat itself on several further occasions, as Weller struggled
to remove the band from beneath the shadow of punk, at the
same time as retaining sufficient credibility not to alienate
their fans. So, the Jam played the punk mecca Roxy Club,
but when *Sniffin' Glue* fanzine published a scathing review
of an earlier gig, Weller burned the offending issue onstage.
He spoke of doing things for the "kids" and the "street," but
when he was questioned about his personal politics, he
admitted he'd be voting Conservative at the next election.
And while the band's audience turned out in de rigueur
safety pins and bondage trousers, the band took the stage in
mohair suits and Beatleboots.

The Jam's first single, "In the City" (#40 UK) borrowed its
title and refrain from an old Who B-side; their debut album,
the high energy *In the City* (#20) followed in a similar vein.
But the band's first headlining UK tour was completely sold
out, a triumph soured only when, having completed 38 of
the scheduled 42 shows, the band withdrew, claiming
exhaustion.

But an American visit in November 1977 was less successful, and while the band's second single, "All Around the
World" (#13 UK) fared respectably, when "Modern World"
(#40 UK) faltered alongside the album *This Is the Modern
World* (#22 UK), it appeared as though the Jam's 15 minutes
were well and truly up.

Their next UK tour, in December, was highlighted by
Weller's arrest following a brawl with a bunch of rugby players at a Leeds hotel, while a return visit to the US in March
1978 saw the Jam billed alongside Blue Oyster Cult and dismissed accordingly. "News of the World" (#27 UK) barely
made the lower reaches of the Top 30, and work on the Jam's
third album was so ill-judged and disjointed that midway
through the sessions, Polydor insisted the band start again.

The Jam were at an all-time low. Weller was perfectly
aware that since the first flush of success and energy, the Jam
had been cruising; that their second album was distinctly
substandard; that subsequent singles did little more than go
through the motions. He also knew why — the compromise
between what he wanted to do, and what he thought his
audience wanted him to do, had sent the Jam careening up a
halfway course which satisfied nobody, least of all Polydor.
Which meant, if he was ever going to make the kind of music
he wanted to, he had to do it now. He might never get
another chance.

A cover of the Kinks' "David Watts" (#25 UK) served
notice of Weller's new intentions, the song's original '60s
Mod ethic fearlessly, and very poignantly, updated. The follow-up, "Down in the Tube Station at Midnight" (#15 UK),
was an original, but Weller's influences — Ray Davies, Pete
Townshend, John Lennon — peered out from the lyrics
regardless, mugging the last vestiges of Weller's punk pretensions as thoroughly as the song's protagonist is mugged on
the subway platform.

All Mod Cons (#6 UK) was released in November and
promptly acclaimed a masterpiece; overnight, the Jam were
transformed from punk flotsam into all-round winners in the
music papers' annual readers polls. Weller's now-legendary
cantankerousness was not to be stilled however, — a sparsely
attended show at Hamburg's Star Club ended with him

threatening to break up the group unless people started appreciating them. But his songwriting was now reaching new plateaus. "Strange Town" (#15 UK) and "When You're Young" (#17 UK) bracketed a sold-out UK tour through summer 1979, while the band's own standing was enhanced by what had suddenly, and swiftly, emerged as a full scale Mod revival.

The Chords, the Purple Hearts (both past Jam support acts), the Merton Parkas (featuring future Weller collaborator Mick Talbot), Secret Affair, and more exploded out of Weller's stylistic wardrobe, and though the Jam, again, tried hard to distance themselves from the phenomenon, there was as much pride as prejudice in their statements. A year earlier, after all, the Jam were still being accused of punk band wagon-jumping. Now they were leading a parade of their own.

The opening of the Who's *Quadrophenia* movie only added further emphasis to the Mod movement, and the Jam reflected their own role as Ace Faces of a generation with "Eton Rifles" (#3 UK), and "Going Underground," the first single to enter the UK chart at #1 since 1973. *Setting Sons* (#137 US, #4 UK), an album-length epic set in a post-imaginary war England, was hailed as Weller's second masterpiece, an even greater accomplishment given the cynicism which attended even the suggestion of "concept album" in post-punk Britain.

Reissues of the band's entire 45 catalog to date saw six of their earlier singles re-enter the chart during spring 1980 and while another US tour passed by unspectacularly, when the Beatles-esque "Start" (#1 UK) gave the band their second successive chart-topper in August, the Jam's triumph was complete.

Which was where the problems began. Now genuinely uninterested in conquering America, the only frontier left to a band who had subjugated Europe, Australia, and Japan (the Jam actually cut short their 1980 US tour, to fly home to appear on *Top of The Pops*) Weller had suddenly achieved everything he'd ever set out to do.

Another effortless smash, "A Town Called Malice" (#1 UK) saw the band assume a virtual residency in the UK Top 5 — "Funeral Pyre" (#4 UK), "Absolute Beginners" (#4 UK — titled for the Colin MacInnes' Mod novel of the same name), and "The Bitterest Pill" (#2 UK) all followed. Two further singles intended only for European release, "That's Entertainment" (#21 UK) and "Just Who Is the 5 o'Clock Hero" (#8 UK) charted on the strength of import sales alone.

Two more albums, *Sound Affects* (#72 US, #2 UK) and *The Gift* (#82 US, #1 UK) slid to the top as a matter of course. In October 1982 then, Weller announced that the Jam were going to do the only thing they hadn't yet done — and break up.

One final single, "Beat Surrender" (#1 UK); one last US EP, *Beat Surrender* (#171 US); one last album, the live *Dig the New Breed* (#131 US, #2 UK); one final tour, closing in Mod central Brighton on December 11, 1982; and that would be it. Weller formed Style Council; Foxton went solo briefly, then joined Stiff Little Fingers; Buckler formed Time UK.

A country mourned, and his bandmates weren't too happy either. But Weller was not only true to his word, he stuck to it as well. Even with a string of compilations and archive releases maintaining the band's name in the chart, beginning with 1983's *Snap* (#2 UK) and peaking with the 5-CD *Direction Reaction Creation* (#8 UK) box set, the Jam maintained their place among the ever declining number of punk bands who have steadfastly resisted the 1990s blandishments to regroup, reform, and rewrite their own epitaphs.

Also see the entry for "STYLE COUNCIL" on page 663.

The Jam LPs

7 In the City (Polydor) 1977 Proudly wearing their influences on their sleeves — the Beatles (whom they cover), the Small Faces, the Who, and old Motown — the Jam's strong lyrics and exhilarating delivery outweigh the many derivative moments here, while a few cuts offer proof of their budding songwriting talent. The title track, all crashing, thrashing power chords and '60s harmonies; and the mid-tempo "Bricks and Mortars" and "Away from the Numbers" underline the trio's potential for greatness.

7 This Is the Modern World (Polydor) 1977 From the explosive title track through the final dying chord, the Jam prove they're punks with a difference — and it's not just the Mod suits and skinny ties; nor the ability to recreate the '60s in their own image. In just a few verses, the songwriters Weller and Foxton create complete stories — perfect snapshots which bring the sights, sounds, and emotions to life.

9 All Mod Cons (Polydor) 1978 A masterpiece of time, place, mood, and music, *Cons* finds the Jam teetering on the edge of maturity. Still occasionally playing with punk's fast receding past ("Billy Hunt," "'A' Bomb," and the souped-up Kinks' cover "David Watts"), but simultaneously moving towards more complex and evocative numbers (the delicate "English Rose," the wistful "Fly," and "It's Too Bad") — then culminating in the epic "Down in a Tube Station at Midnight," an everyman classic of senseless violence.

8 Setting Sons (Polydor) 1979 Perhaps the most astonishing feature of Weller's talent is his seemingly effortless ability to create icons from ordinary events — "Eton Rifles'" rich kids versus poor punch-up transmutes into a manifest of class warfare; the drifting apart of young friends on "Thick as Thieves" transforms into the ultimate portrayal of childhood lost. With horns, strings, flute, and piano added to the brew, the Jam create a rich, mature pop-rock style rooted melodically in the '60s, but effortlessly forward-looking too.

7 Sound Affects (Polydor) 1980 An unexpected return to the derivative days of yore, climaxing with burglarizing the Beatles for "Start." At the time, Weller claimed he was trying to break the musical mode of *Sons*, and he succeeded. But *Sound* winds up their weakest album, as the lyrics deliberately avoid his strengths, and the music's little more than pastiche. However, there's still a host of evocative moods and songs, and "That's Entertainment" is worth waiting for.

9 The Gift (Polydor) 1982 The Jam's final studio album was a gift indeed of worthy and lasting proportions — a last look back at their past and present before embarking on their separate futures. Side one's a virtual travelogue of the trio's history, opening with the punky "Happy Together" then running through soul, funk (the rousing "Precious"), Kink-sy pop and, completing the tryptic, the pounding, driving ode to Motown, "Trans-Global Express." Side two reverts to the present, as the Jam haul their imagination around the American Southwest and the Caribbean, before returning home with the classic "A Town Called Malice" and title track's joyous initiation into an all night soul party. The perfect farewell.

7 Dig the New Breed [LIVE] (Polydor) 1982 "Best of" comp consisting of live performance from throughout the band's career.

Selected Compilations and Archive Releases

9 Snap! (Polydor) 1983 Weller-sanctioned hits and bits collection, packing in enough non-album B-sides and rarities to intrigue even casual observers.

8 Extras: A Collection of Rarities (Polydor) 1992 The creme-de-la-creme of unreleased Jam jams. A superb record that makes the perfect companion piece to *Snap*, *Extras* comprises a host of B-sides and rarities, fleshed out with unreleased gems and demos, including the long-fabled original version of "Solid Bond in Your Heart." Not so much extras as necessities.

7 Live Jam (Polydor) 1993 Live concert tracks taken from shows 1979–1982.

9 Direction Reaction Creation (Polydor) 1997 Boxed recounting of the band's entire output, plus a bonus disc appending *Extras*' generous helping of out-takes and oddities. Jewels range from their first Polydor demos, through a clutch of unheard alternates and undreamed of covers (the Beatles' "Rain," the Kinks' "Sunny Afternoon"), and a bunch which simply never made the grade. The addition of period singles to the regular albums, meantime, is long overdue.

Further Reading

Our Story by Bruce Foxton/Rick Buckler/Alex Ogg (Castle, UK, 1994).

JANE'S ADDICTION

FORMED 1986 (*Los Angeles, CA*)
ORIGINAL LINE-UP *Perry Farrell (b. Perry Bernstein, 3/29/59, New York, NY — vocals), Dave Navarro (b. 6/7/67, Santa Monica, CA — guitar), Eric Avery (b. 4/25/65, L.A., CA — bass), Stephen Perkins (b. 9/13/67, L.A., CA — drums)*

The son of a New York diamond merchant, raised in Florida, but relocating to Orange County, CA, in 1980, Farrell's first band, Psi Com, was formed a few months before his arrival by Vince Duran (guitar). The band were actually looking for a drummer when they encountered Farrell — he answered their ad, and without any prior musical experience whatsoever, announced he was a singer and songwriter. He was hired, and over the next two years, the band was recast to his own specifications, around Duran and Aaron Sherer (drums).

Drawing heavily from the UK goth scene, Psi Com's distinguishing features were Farrell's effects-laden vocal style, and, for close to a year (until the arrival of Kelly Wheeler), the absence of a bass player — hitherto considered a prerequisite in the gothic field. But that was enough to push them above the rank and file on the local scene. Gigs opening for the Cult (August 1984) and Kommunity FK raised their profile higher; Psi Com were also featured at the Gila Monster Jamboree in January 1985 when Sonic Youth made their west coast debut.

Psi Com self-released their debut, self-titled EP that summer; by early 1986, however, the band had drifted apart, and Farrell began jamming with Avery, a friend of the singer's flatmate, Jane — after whom, the pair named themselves. The pair made their live debut as a voice and bass duo in March 1986, opening for a Top 40 covers band at an Orange County bar. Weeks later, they recruited Perkins and Navarro, school friends of Avery, and the following month the newly reconstituted band opened for Gene Loves Jezebel at the Roxy.

Further high profile shows saw Jane's Addiction open for Peter Murphy, Nick Cave, and Dream Syndicate, with a set which already included the incendiary burst of covers and originals which would characterize the band's national emergence a year later — "Jane Says," "Ocean Size," "Whores," "Sympathy for the Devil." They became regulars at Scream alongside Human Drama, L.A. Guns, and Guns n'Roses, and contributed one track, "Pigs in Zen," to 1987's *Scream: The Compilation* compilation album. Suddenly, every label in L.A. wanted them, and while the band would sign to Warners as early as February 1987, still their first release, August's live *Jane's Addiction*, would be released through the band's management's own Triple X label.

With the local press now prostrate at Jane's altar, more prestigious shows followed, opening for X and the Psychedelic Furs in L.A., before the group were introduced to the rest of America on tour with Love and Rockets through December 1987. By the time the band's second album was ready for release, the whole country, it seemed, had opinions about Jane's Addiction.

They weren't all good. Farrell made no secret of his desire to employ shock and outrage as readily as music, and the cover of Jane's second album, *Nothing's Shocking* (#103 US) (a naked Siamese twin with her heads on fire) was designed to take that resolve to the limit. Seven major chain stores refused to stock the record before it was even released; others quickly followed, and before anybody had heard a note of the music, *Nothing's Shocking* was generating nationwide headlines.

In chart terms, however, the controversy did even less for the record's sales than the bans, and with the "Mountain Song" video banned by MTV due to Farrell and girlfriend Casey's on-screen nudity, all Jane's Addiction had to show for their efforts were headlines, and a long line of journalists murmuring "hype."

It was time to redress the balance. September saw Jane's Addiction tour the US opening for Iggy Pop — their first outing in a year. A couple of gigs with the Ramones, and three shows in the UK interrupted the schedule; they rejoined Iggy for the remainder of the month, and in the new year, joined

the headliner for an utterly unexpected honor, a nomination in the Grammy's newly-founded Heavy Metal category, alongside AC/DC, Metallica, and mystifyingly, Jethro Tull — the eventual victors.

Jane's Addiction remained on the road through 1989–90, touring now as headliners in their own right, while a second single, "Jane Says," made amends for past sins by finally giving radio and TV a Jane's Addiction track they could plunge into rotation. Farrell, meanwhile, began working on a full-length video (his second, following the previous year's *Soul Kiss*), *The Gift*, with the band's *Ritual De Lo Habitual* (#19 US, #37 UK) album finally arriving in September 1990.

Another sleeve controversy was this time dampened by Farrell's creation of an alternate version reprinting the First Amendment in lieu of the original's collage of drug paraphernalia and, glimpsed amidst the three bodies lying on a bed, Farrell's flaccid penis. This time, however, the fuss paid off. With the "banned" sleeve outselling its clean contemporary by five to one, *Ritual* at least breached the US Top 20, and made the Top 40 in Britain, where both "Been Caught Stealing" (#34 UK) and "Classic Girl" (#60 UK) garnered significant airplay. The following June, the album was certified gold in the US.

Again the band hit the road, through the US in late winter, Europe through the spring, and back to New York for a sold-out Madison Square Garden show in April. Then Farrell

© Jim Steinfeldt/Chansley Entertainment Archives

dropped his bombshell — the band's next tour would be their last. But it would also be their biggest.

Borrowing his concept in part from the Reading Festival, but more specifically from Cult frontman Ian Astbury's Gathering of the Tribes movable festival of the previous fall (which Jane's Addiction were initially scheduled to play), Lollapalooza was a massive package tour designed to showcase the best of contemporary 'alternative' talent. Its success, of course, would go on to dominate the American concert circuit for much of the next decade, and consume much of Farrell's time as well. Jane's themselves played their final live shows in Hawaii at the end of Lollapalooza, then shattered.

Navarro and Avery would reunite on Navarro's first solo album; the guitarist then formed Deconstruction with Michael Murphy, and filled in for Izzy Stradlin in Guns n'Roses, before joining the Red Hot Chili Peppers for the *One Hot Minute* album. Farrell and Perkins would resurface in late 1992, as Porno for Pyros, releasing two albums to mixed reception.

On January 20, 1997, Perkins and Red Hot Chili Peppers bassist Flea convened an ad hoc band (with Rage Against the Machine's Zack de la Rocha and Tom Morella) for the "Radio Free L.A." broadcast on January 20. Months later, Flea followed Navarro from the Peppers to replace the errant Avery in a Jane's Addiction reunion (or, in their parlance, relapse) for an appearance on MTV's *Live at the 10 Spot* in October.

The following month, the band launched the I-Itz M'My Party tour, supporting the *Kettle Whistle* (#21 US) collection of live, out-takes, and demo material, plus new tracks. Farrell then began working on material for his first solo album.

Jane's Addiction LPs

7 Jane's Addiction (Triple X) 1987 It's all about attitude and Janes' uncompromising stance was evident from day one, not only because they debuted with a live album (though that helped), but because they also served up a performance highlighting their deficiencies. While the slower acoustic numbers are gems in the rough, the rockers teeter precariously between mediocre punk and metal excess. Yet the group so obviously believe in their peculiar blend of hardcore, hardrock, and deathrock that the listener can't help but be convinced.

8 Nothing's Shocking (WB) 1988 Filing down the rough edges, Navarro's guitar screams and soars between evocative gloom and Led Zeppelin-ish screeches; the rhythm section preens with nonchalant elan, and Farrell is a demented warbling shaman. "Ocean Size" and "Mountain Song" invigorate, but the band's true strength lies in the acoustic guitars ("Jane Says"), where their talent finally gets a chance to shine through.

8 Ritual De Lo Habitual (WB) 1990 Rampant madness encompassing the band's constant questing, pursuing notions first hatched on *Shocking*, and embracing anything from funky

rhythms to Mediterranean melodies. "Been Caught Stealing," "Stop," "Classic Girl" — next time could have been the killer. But next time, of course, never happened.

Selected Compilations and Archive Releases

7 Live and Rare (WEA) 1991 Japanese collection of live cuts and demo versions.

8 Kettle Whistle (WB) 1997 Jam packed with band demos, previously unreleased live tracks and two new songs from Farrell and an ad hoc new generation Jane's.

Deconstruction LP

7 Deconstruction (WB) 1994

Further Reading

Saga of a Hypster by Dave Thompson (St Martin's Press, 1995).

JAPAN

FORMED 1977 *(London, England)*
ORIGINAL LINE-UP *David Sylvian (b. David Batt, 2/23/58, Lewisham — vocals); Rob Dean (guitar); Richard Barbieri (b. 11/30/57, London — keyboards); Mick Karn (b. Anthony Michaelides, 7/24/58, London — bass); Steve Jansen (b. Stephen Batt, 12/1/59, Lewisham — drums)*

Heavily influenced by the then-prevalent glam rock movement, brothers Jansen and Sylvian (named for a line in Bowie's "Drive in Saturday") formed the original four piece Japan while still at school, concentrating as much on breaking the establishment's gender-specific dress code, as on music. Not until the arrival of Dean, in early 1977, however, did the band members pay as much attention to their sound as their image and, by March, their camp stage show had already coaxed former Yardbirds manager Simon Napier Bell out of self-imposed retirement. The following month, Japan's studied glamor was sufficient for the band to be scooped up by the Ariola label, in a label-sponsored talent competition, first prize a record contract.

Out of 1,400 entrants and 60 finalists, Japan were one of just eight to make the final cut — an early incarnation of the Cure were numbered among the others. While that band left as quickly as they could, however, Japan hung around and in early 1978, the band cut their first single, "Don't Rain on My Parade."

It did nothing, a fate which also awaited "Be Unconventional" in August, and the band's debut album, *Adolescent Sex* — and that despite being described in *Sounds* as "by far the most interesting debut by a British band this year." The group's first nationwide tour, opening — absurdly — for the

Blue Oyster Cult, was similarly doomed, but a US release for the album brought some interest, while the Japanese market went mad for the band. *Obscure Alternatives*, the band's second album, went gold in Japan almost immediately upon its November 1978 release, and the group's first visit to the country saw them pack two nights at the Budokan — then return home to play a half-full London Rainbow.

Appearance aside, part of the reason for the band's warm reception in both the US and Japan was their disdain for the "punk" music which still held sway in their homeland, but had yet to make a major impression in those other markets. Rather, Japan pursued a dance- (if not disco-) oriented direction, one which would be effortlessly sharpened by a sojourn in Giorgio Moroder's Musicland Studios in Munich.

The ensuing "Life in Tokyo" single gave the group another Japanese hit, but American interest seemingly dipped so far that the band's US label would not even release Japan's next album, 1980's *Quiet Life* (#53 UK) — recorded back in England, with Napier Bell producing. Contrarily, this became the band's first UK hit, but the relationship with Ariola was now so poor that when Virgin Records showed signs of interest in the band, Japan not only quit Ariola, they also spent most of the Virgin advance buying their way out of their contract.

It was worth the expense. Japan's first single for Virgin, "Gentlemen Take Polaroids" (#60 UK) was followed by the album of the same name (#45 UK), and while Ariola immediately took advantage of their success by unleashing a string of singles from the band's earlier albums, three further hits with music previously deemed unsalable proved just how far Japan had come — the new album's "The Art of Parties" (#48 UK) would be followed by the reinvigorated "Quiet Life" (#19 UK), "European Son" (#31 UK), and "I Second That Emotion" (#9 UK). There was also success for the *Assemblage* (#26) compilation.

In October 1981, the band released "Visions of China" (#32 UK) as a taster for their new album, *Tin Drum* (#12 UK) — itself the first Japan album to utilize what critics called the band's penchant for Art School Orientalism, but which, with Karn's fretless bass sound to the fore, was to characterize and identify Japan for the remainder of their career. (It also indicated precisely how powerful an influence Eno had become; "Sky Saw," from his 1975 *Another Green World* album predicted much of what Japan would now be exploring.)

The loss of Dean (for Vivabeat, and later, Gary Numan's touring band) proved that the transformation was not altogether painless, but two further singles — "Cantonese Boy" (#24 UK) and the epic "Ghosts" (#5 UK) — thrust the band even further into the limelight. Yet once again, the album was not even released in the US. Instead, their next American

label, Epic, put together a compilation drawing from both Virgin albums.

In Japan, meanwhile, the band could do no wrong; their musical aspirations now taken so seriously that the band members' artwork, too, was accorded superstar status. An exhibition of Karn's sculptures opened in Tokyo, while Jansen negotiated a photography exhibition.

Such activity could not, of course, disguise the fact that musically, too, Japan were working apart from one another. Barbieri was actively seeking soundtrack work, while Karn collaborated with Gary Numan on a projected single which eventually evolved into the singer's *Dance* album; the bassist also cut a solo single, "Sensitive," in June 1982, a taster for the *Titles* (#74 UK) album later in the year. Barbieri and Jansen numbered among the guests on the album; Karn and Jansen would also record with Japanese vocalist Akiko Yana on her *Aiga Nakuchane* album, even as her husband, Ryuichi Sakamoto, recruited Sylvian to perform on his latest single, "Bamboo Houses" (#30 UK).

In the face of so much outside activity, split rumors were now swirling furiously around the band, but Japan reconvened for a fall 1982 UK tour (with Masami Tsuchiya, of Japanese band Ippu Do, replacing Dean), widely assumed to be the prelude to a new album. In fact, it really was the end — days after the final show, in London on November 22, Japan announced they had broken up. Their final release would be a recording from that final show, *Oil On Canvas* (#5 UK), accompanied by a live version of "Canton" (#42 UK).

Of the four surviving members of the original band, all launched careers as individualistic as their contributions to Japan. Commercial success, however, would prove elusive, with Karn's union with Peter Murphy, of the newly sundered Bauhaus, Dali's Car's *Waking Hour* (#84 UK), proving especially disappointing. He would score with another collaboration, joining Ultravox's Midge Ure for the single "After a Fashion" (#39 UK), but for the most part, Karn busied himself with a solo career, often working alongside Jansen and Barbieri — the Dolphin Brothers, as they now termed themselves; and occasionally, alongside Sylvian as well.

In fact, all four would pass through one another's orbit, the most crucial contact coming when the entire quartet reconvened to record two tracks for Karn's *Dreams of Reason Produce Monsters* album in 1987. One crept out as a single credited jointly to Karn and Sylvian, "Buoy" (#63 UK), and in 1989, 18 months of talk and speculation ended when the quartet entered the studio together to see, as Sylvian put it, "what happens."

It took two years, but the result was *Rain Tree Crow* (#24 UK), a Japan reunion in everything but name — the band, too, was dubbed Rain Tree Crow. Despite such anonymity, with a single, "Blackwater" (#62 UK) accompanying the album chartwards, a permanent regrouping seemed likely. Unfortunately, Karn reflected, "as we came to work together again, the gulf between David and the rest of us just widened." Since that time, only Jansen has worked again with Sylvian; the remainder of the band have continued on their own courses.

Japan LPs

8 **Adolescent Sex (Ariola) 1978** Predating the New Romantic movement by two years, Japan's debut is a groundbreaker, a fey fusion of funk-inspired rhythms, space-age synths, and guitars locked totally in a stygian glamrock madhouse. *Sex's* only concession to the contemporary post-punk powerhouse was its moody atmospheres.

7 **Obscure Alternatives (Ariola) 1978** With the electro-scene blossoming around them, Japan no longer sound quite so unique, and they couldn't be happier. *Obscure* replaces the funk with disjointed rhythms, brightens the guitars on some passages, then juxtaposes them with a Banshee-esque buzz.

7 **Quiet Life (Ariola) 1979** Half of *Life* is moody synthi-dance, predating the rise of Duran Duran and the rest of the dance floor electro acts; the remainder are lush and introspective keyboard heavy numbers,opening the door to the likes of the Midge Ure-led Ultravox.

5 **Live in Japan (Hansa) 1980** It's the album's rarity which makes this a must-have, not its contents. They were better in the studio.

8 **Gentlemen Take Polaroids (Virgin) 1980** The album that made Japan the heroes of the art crowd, the ultimate combination of rhythmic experiment and swooping keyboards stripping out virtually all past pop references. A little awkward and certainly pretentious, *Gentlemen* heralded Japan's arrival into adulthood.

9 **Tin Drum (Virgin) 1981** Journeying deep into the vagaries of musical structure, texture, and rhythm, weaving atmospheres as fine as gossamer, and dominated by the exotic Eastern themes. The chillingly evocative "Ghosts" may sound like a Roxy Music B-side, but "Canton," "Visions of China," and "The Art of Parties" are more than dilettante posturing.

6 **Oil On Canvas [LIVE] (Virgin) 1983** *"Plus ca change."* Three years on from the ropey *In Japan*, Japan stop trying to recreate their records, and concentrate instead on conjuring up their mystique. You can *hear* them standing around looking cool!

Selected Compilations and Archive Releases

8 **Assemblage (Hansa) 1981**

8 **Exorcising Ghosts (Virgin)** In the absence of an all-consuming box set, two discs sum up the (arguably) best of the band's development.

Mick Karn LPs

7 **Titles (Virgin) 1982**

7 **Dreams of Reason Produce Monsters (Virgin) 1987**

6 **Bestial Cluster (CMP) 1992**

4 **Tooth Mother (CMP) 1995** A studio counterpart to Karn's earlier US tour with Polytown, faintly King Crimson, fairly exotic, remarkable in its virtuosity but ultimately unmemorable.

5 **Liquid Glass (Resurgent) 1999**

Selected Compilations and Archive Releases

6 **The Collector's Edition (CMP) 1997**

Richard Barbieri LPs

6 **Flame (One Little Indian) 1994**

5 **Indigo Falls (Resurgent) 1998**

Steve Jansen LPs

5 **Other Worlds in a Small Room (Medium) 1996**

5 **Changing Hands (Resurgent) 1998**

6 **Pulse (Blueprint) 1999**

Dolphin Brothers LP

7 **Catch the Fall (Virgin) 1987**

Rain Tree Crow LP

7 **Rain Tree Crow (Virgin) 1990** Reunited and even more obscure than ever, little actually echoes anything one might have expected from such a regrouping, which was undoubtedly the reason they did it. A strong rebirth followed by a bitter sudden death.

Dali's Car LP

2 **Waking Hour (Beggars Banquet) 1984** How high hopes fly, and how quickly they are dashed. A trans-Japanese Bauhaus marriage made in heaven, but going straight to hell, a vaguely ambient groove, but two stars who were so busy making their individual presence felt that they forgot people might like to hear some songs as well.

PHILIP JEAYS

BORN *6/24/62 (Taunton, England)*

Singer-songwriter Jeays was living in France when he discovered Jacques Brel — just the latest in a long line of introspective troubadours to have fallen under the Belgian songwriter's spell in the years since Scott Walker snatched his muse back from the likes of Rod McKuen and reinvented Brel for the English-speaking doom-pop crowd. David Bowie, Alex Harvey, Marc Almond, and Momus have all acknowledged Brel's impact on their work, as both writer and performer. But only the pioneering Walker ever succeeded in truly translating homage into his own words, turning in a fourth album (1969's *Scott 4*) loaded with distinctly Brel-ian, but uniquely personal, self-compositions.

Jeays' debt to Brel, too, is heavy; like Walker, however, it would swiftly be amply repaid with a series of songs which, again, echoed but rarely aped the master's. After some years spent gigging around the southern English club circuit, Jeays' one man show erupted into mainstream consciousness in 1996, when he appeared at the Edinburgh Festival in Scotland. (He would make triumphant returns in 1998 and 1999.) There, the *Scotsman* newspaper raved, "Jeays has an avid, charismatic cabaret style all of his own, dipped in theatricality. Alternately casting himself as romantic fool, sneering devil, and irony-streaked sinner, Jeays produces a neat, hour-long set mixing wisdom and sarcasm, self-reflection and self-dramatization."

Other press was swift to follow. Comparisons with Bowie, Tom Waits, and even Stephen Sondheim, aside from the inevitable Brel and Walker, prompted *The Morning Star* to enthuse, "Jeays writes his own songs in a style quite unlike any other British songsmith I've heard. They are superbly crafted, written with poetic sensibility that is imbued with bitter irony and mordant wit. They can be funny and touching simultaneously and often carry in their subtext serious comment on human nature."

1997 saw Jeays make a similar impression at both the Salisbury Festival and the Canadian Vancouver Comedy Festival. Two years later, with a band comprising John Peacock (guitar), William George Q (bass), and Ditton Pye (drums), he released his now-much anticipated debut album, *October*, backing it up with a series of live shows climaxing at the Talk of London in early 2000. Summer then saw the release of Jeays' second album, *Cupid Is a Drunkard*, launched during the Edinburgh Festival in August.

Philip Jeays LPs

🔳 **October (DPR — UK) 1999** A staggering achievement, even once you know what's coming next. Ten songs range from the droll "Madame" to the shattered "Remember Me to the Roses," a rollercoaster of emotions which trips blithely from savage betrayal to unquestioning adoration, and still finds time to laugh at its own maudlinity.

🔳 **Cupid Is a Drunkard (DPR — UK) 2000** The title track is reprised from *October*; otherwise, more of the moody, maudlin, marvelous same.

JESUS AND MARY CHAIN

FORMED 1983 (*East Kilbride, Scotland*)
ORIGINAL LINE-UP *William Reid (b. 10/28/58, East Kilbride, Scotland — guitar, vocals); Jim Reid (b. 12/29/61, East Kilbride, Scotland — guitar, vocals); Douglas Hart (bass); Murray Dalglish (drums)*

After aborting their first musical venture, the Poppy Seeds duo — whose career comprised simply of recording demos and mailing them to London record labels — the Reid brothers recruited a rhythm section and set out on what amounted to a guerilla raid tour of East Kilbride, turning up at venues claiming to be the support band, and then unleashing an unrepentant wall of feedback until the plugs were pulled or the audience left.

Miraculously, their barrage earned a following, and by early 1984, the Jesus and Mary Chain (their name was allegedly taken from a line in a Bing Crosby movie) began playing their own shows, usually remaining on stage for no more than 20 minutes. They recorded another demo and mailed it to the then-tiny indy Creation records, in the hope of getting a gig at label head Alan McGee's Living Room club. He was impressed, not only booking the band, but also issuing their first single, "Upside Down" (#1 UK indy).

With the group's early impenetrable roar having now resolved itself into something at least approaching melody (particularly when they tackled such covers as the B-side, Syd Barrett's "Vegetable Man"), the single was picked up by DJ John Peel and, in November, the band visited London to perform at the 1984 ICA Rock Week. Dalglish had quit by now, to be replaced by Bobby Gillespie (b. 6/22/64, Scotland), and with the accolades of the well-received ICA showcase still ringing in their ears, the band spent the new year sifting through record company offers — most of which, oddly, contained a No Feedback clause.

Finally, they signed with the one label which did seem to want what they were already offering, and in February 1985, "Never Understand" (#47 UK) was released by blanco y negro.

With the press uncertain whether to describe them as the new Sex Pistols (for their apparent lack of conventional musical ability), or the new Velvet Underground (for their penchant for noise), the Jesus and Mary Chain attracted further controversy when a show at the north London Polytechnic ended in a riot, allegedly caused by "fans" furious at the brevity of the band's set. Press interviews saw the brothers court further outrage with a string of inflammatory remarks, while the group's third single, "You Trip Me Up" (#55 UK) was itself tripped up when no pressing plant would touch its intended B-side, "Jesus Suck." The offending song was replaced.

"Just Like Honey" (#45 UK) in October 1985 was followed in November by the band's debut album, *Psycho Candy* (#188 US, #3 1UK), which was promptly elected to *Sounds* magazine's Top 100 Albums of All Time.

The Jesus and Mary Chain's schedule through early 1986 was largely dependent on drummer Gillespie's availability — his own band, Primal Scream, was beginning to make some headway and, aside from some exploratory shows in the US, the Jesus and Mary Chain remained quiet until July brought "Some Candy Talking" (#13 UK) — its success surely aided by the popular suspicion that "candy" was an obscure drug reference. Finally replacing Gillespie with John Moore (b. 12/23/64) (who would later move to guitar, when James Pinko joined), the group followed up with what many observers noted — disappointedly — was the first "conventional" gig of their career, a 45-minute hit-heavy Hammersmith Palais show, opened by Sonic Youth and Pink Industry (Liverpudlian successors to Big in Japan).

"April Skies" (#8 UK), a song previewed at the Hammersmith show, became the Jesus and Mary Chain's next single in May 1987; "Happy When It Rains" (#25 UK) followed in August, on the eve of the band's second album, *Darklands* (#161 US, #5 UK). The ascent to mainstream approval appeared to have been completed — but of course it wasn't. Performing their next single, "Darklands" (#33 UK) itself, on TV's lip-synched *The Roxy*, the band found themselves banned from the show for not miming well enough, and embarrassing everyone who could.

There was also internal dissent over William Reid's reluctance to tour, particularly after a tempestuous US tour following the Stateside release of *Darklands*. Moore and Pink both quit to be replaced by Dave Evans and Richard Thomas; in the meantime, the band's time was spent compiling a collection of B-sides and rarities, *Barbed Wire Kisses* (#192 US, #9 UK), recording a new single, "Sidewalking" (#30 UK) and contemplating Jim's recent discovery of hip-hop. That never did manifest itself musically, although Hart — already a proven DJ — formed the Acid Angels house act and cut a single, "Speed Speed Ecstasy."

In August, the band resurfaced alongside the Sugarcubes on a reissue of the Icelandic band's "Birthday" single, the Jesus and Mary Chain's version, "Christmas," being accompanied by three further versions on the 12-inch pressing (#65 UK). Their own "Kill Surf City" single followed in November 1988, before Ben Lurie replaced Evans for 1989's "Blues From a Gun" (#32 UK) and the self-produced *Automatic* (#105 US, #11 UK) album, the group's most understated set yet.

"Head On" (#57 UK) followed, but the *Rollercoaster* EP (#46 UK), featuring a version of Leonard Cohen's "Tower of Song," saw the band back on form, as they proved when they toured through the fall of 1990 with My Bloody Valentine and the infant Blur. However, hopes for a stable line-up were punctured when Thomas quit for Renegade Soundwave, and Hart left to work in video.

Their replacements, ex-Starlings rhythm section Matthew Parkin and Barry Blacker, would see the Mary Chain return to the top with 1992's "Reverence" (#10 UK) and "Far

Out and Gone" (#23 UK), the first singles from *Honey's Dead* (#158 US, #14 UK) — itself the band's debut release for their new US label, American. And sure enough, the group's outlook would now become more "American," after years of merely deconstructing Americana. They appeared on Letterman, toured with Lollapalooza II, then launched immediately into their own headlining US tour, leaving the UK with nothing more than another single from the album, "Almost Gold" (#41 UK).

The loss of Parkin and Blacker did not slow the band — by December 1992, with the Reids accompanied now by Lurie and new drummer Steve Monti, the Mary Chain headlined London's Brixton Academy.

With 1993 marked only by the release of the *Sound of Speed* (#30 UK) EP and compilation album (#15 UK), the same team reconvened in 1994 to record *Stoned and Dethroned* (#98 US, #13 UK), a largely acoustic album featuring guest appearances from Pogue Shane MacGowan, and William Reid's girlfriend Hope Sandoval of Mazzy Star; their "Sometimes Always" (#96 US, #22 UK) would become the first single from the set, to be followed by "Come On" (#52 UK) and "I Hate Rock'n'Roll" (#61 UK).

Another two year hiatus followed, during which time the band — now featuring ex-Lush bassist Phil King — returned to the label where it all began, Creation (Sub Pop in the US), and in April 1998, released a new single, "Cracking Up" (#35 UK) on the eve of their first UK tour in three years. A new album, *Munki* (#47 UK) and a second single, "Iloverock-nroll" (#38 UK) followed, but a US tour in September 1998 fell apart after just three dates, when William Reid walked off stage at the L.A. House of Blues, and never returned.

The errant brother's first solo album was already recorded and awaiting release; the following week, Jim Reid announced that he, too, had a country-flavored solo project planned, with Lurie, and Spiritualized rhythm section Damon Reece and Sean Cook. He emphasized that the Mary Chain would continue, however, and in fact it would be close to a year before the band's final demise was announced.

In the meantime, William's solo album was held up indefinitely by the artist's insistence on a cover photograph depicting his erect penis, while Jim occupied himself guesting on Death in Vegas' *Contino Sessions* album.

Jesus and Mary Chain LPs

🎵 Psychocandy (blanco y negro) 1985 Their first and best, full of grinding melody and moping vocals. Perfect for the Reagan years, it gave the goths something to look forward to and even included a nifty ballad — "Just Like Honey."

🎵 Darklands (blanco y negro) 1987 The perfect postpunk album...seven years too late. Which doesn't make it a bad record, even if we've heard it all before, and we have — last time around, of course, but also through the Beach Boys, the Banshees, the Velvets et al. The Mary Chain are just shorter and noisier that's all.

6 Automatic (blanco y negro) 1989 Still full of fuzz and distorted guitar, *Automatic* is also backed by a (probably deliberately) annoying drum machine. However, the boys hit big with "Blues From a Gun".

7 Honey's Dead (blanco y negro) 1992 Holding tight to some newly- (too late) found baggy beats, the Reids link their chain to an ever widening array of influences and genres, the world's latest psychedelic-industrial-pop-punk-fuzz crossover. Still their continuing love affair with the Velvets guitar and New Order's melodies rein in the excesses and give the album coherency.

4 Stoned & Dethroned (American) 1994 Yes, they are. Jesus and Mary Chain go soft with upbeat toe-tappers and a silly lite delivery that washes out everything they were.

4 Hate Rock'n'roll (American) 1996 An ill-conceived attempt at a make-over, and although the Reids' don't entirely jettison their past, *Hate*'s stab at a more folky/indy style is truly hateful. Plus an up market production rips the heart out of any fuzzy/buzzy core sound they might have retained. You can stop any time.

4 Munki (Sub Pop) 1998

Selected Compilations and Archive Releases

9 Barbed Wire Kisses (blanco y negro) 1988 Non-album singles, B-sides, and bits, possibly the greatest imaginable introduction to the early wired world of the Mary Chain's dark psychoses, with the added bonus of "Sidewalkin'," their first genuinely great song (as opposed to fuzzy noise).

7 Sound of Speed (blanco y negro) 1993 More or less a companion to the above, although not half as visceral.

9 BBC Sessions (Strange Fruit) 2000 Unchained and churning, the early J&MC still sound like nothing on earth.

The Starlings LPs

7 Valid (Anxious) 1992

8 Too Many Dogs (Anxious) 1994 New Zealander Chris Sheehan's first album documented his withdrawal from heroin; his second, recorded after his rhythm section quit, chronicled his withdrawal from society in general. Vicious, dark, misanthropic gems which left him but one future option. He joined the Sisters of Mercy.

Further Reading

Jesus and Mary Chain by John Robertson (Beekman 1990).

JESUS LIZARD

FORMED *1987 (Chicago, IL)*
ORIGINAL LINE-UP *David Yow (vocals); Duane Denison (guitar); David Sims (bass)*

Sims and Yow were ex-Scratch Acid, an Austin hardcore band who broke up when Sims quit to join Steve Albini's Rapeman. While in Chicago, he reunited with Yow and having recruited Denison and a drum machine, launched Jesus Lizard with the Albini-produced *Pure* EP.

Fending off comparisons with Albini's own Big Black, Jesus Lizard added drummer Mac McNeilly shortly before starting work on their *Head* debut album — the single "Chrome," a medley of that band's "TV As Eyes" and "Abstract Nympho," debuted the full line-up, and revealed Jesus Lizard to be treading a fine conceptual line between the Butthole Surfers and the Birthday Party, a sensation which would be exacerbated over the course of both *Head*, and its follow-up, *Goat*.

The accompanying single, "Mouthbreaker," meanwhile, revealed a kitsch fascination for German pop band Trio — the B-side, "Sunday You Need Love," was a cover of one of their European hits, while another, "Anna," would be recorded with Big Black vocalist Santiago Durango.

With Jesus Lizard now accumulating a press following as rabid as their audience had become, Yow compounded his own uncompromising reputation by guesting on Pigface's *Gub* album in 1991 (Sims would appear on the same band's *Fook* the following year), then when Jesus Lizard themselves slammed out a cover of the Dicks' "Wheelchair Epidemic," a choice which hammered home the band's brutal, vulgar, and distinctly un-PC musical outlook.

A hit split single with Nirvana ("Puss," from the *Liar* album/ "Oh the Guilt" — #12 UK) in February 1993, preceded a three month US tour with Helmet and (on some dates) Therapy?; Jesus Lizard then opened for Nirvana in New York, during the 1993 New Music Seminar, following through with another new single, the triple 7-inch "Lash." A European tour immediately after included a showing at Britain's Reading Festival, the prelude to European and US tours which would take Jesus Lizard through until Christmas.

Still Denison found time to follow in Yow and Sims' footsteps by joining Pigface for the *Notes from Thee Underground* album. He would also guest with Ministry spin-off Revolting Cocks, on their *Linger Ficken' Good* album, before linking with former Laughing Hyenas/Mule drummer Jim Kimball in first, the Denison/Kimball Trio (actually a duo), then Firewater.

Jesus Lizard returned to the shelves in June 1994 with the *Show* live album. Recorded during CBGBs' 20th anniversary festival in December 1993 (where they were second billed to the Damned), *Show* was released through Capitol's Giant subsidiary, the first step towards the band re-emerging on the parent label later in 1995 — in turn, a cause for their break with lifelong producer Albini, a staunch supporter of indy bands.

Down (#64 UK), the band's final Touch and Go release, followed just six weeks later in August 1994 and still buoyed by the success of "Puss" a year earlier, Jesus Lizard found themselves with another UK hit.

With no new releases, Jesus Lizard were nevertheless one of the highlights of Lollapalooza '95; Yow alone also teamed with Helmet's Page Hamilton to contribute a raucous "Custard Pie" to the *Encomium* Led Zeppelin tribute. 1996's *Shot*, however, could not capitalize on either the publicity which Jesus Lizard's very name appeared to attract, or the band's ferocious live support — indeed, while three full US tours through 1997 were all sold out, 1998's *Jesus Lizard* EP (recorded with new drummer Kimball) and the *Blue* album both sank amid a sea of lukewarm reviews and poor sales.

Unperturbed, Jesus Lizard kept gigging. A US outing through January/February 1998 was followed by an Australian and New Zealand trip in April, before swinging back through Europe, the US, and Europe again, a solid ten months of roadwork. But in January 1999, Capitol dropped the band — who themselves played just one more major show, at the Umea Open festival in Sweden on March 26, then broke up on their tenth anniversary, 7/1/99. Their demise would be marked with a new year collection of rarities and live material.

Jesus Lizard LPs

8 Head (Touch & Go) 1990 Might as well start as you mean to go on, a bulbous barrage of noise, through which Yow vomits his near stream-of-consciousness babble of pop culture nightmares, neatly balanced between chaos and carnage. The CD appends the earlier *Pure* EP for even more of the miraculous same.

9 Goat (Touch & Go) 1991 Refining their vision at the same time as broadening their range, Jesus Lizard add increasingly poignant observation to their arsenal and edge perfection even closer.

8 Liar (Touch & Go) 1992 Basically *Goat* part two, with a little more yowling to prove Yow's been practicing.

5 Show (Giant) 1994 If you've never caught the Lizard live, this is not the same as being there; indeed, it's not even the same as thinking about being there. Disappointing.

6 Down (Touch & Go) 1994 Down by name and downcast by nature, the reflective side of the band is broken only by the scud-like "Mistletoe" — guitar-led garotting 101.

5 Shot (Capitol) 1996 "Skull of a German" plus way too many B-sides. If you know there's going to be a major label backlash, why bother trying to avoid it?

7 Blue (Capitol) 1998 Back to form, back to battle-readiness, ex-Gang of Four man Andy Gill inserts some dance sensibilities and "Post Coital Glow" is just as warm and fuzzy as its title.

Selected Compilations and Archive Releases

7 Bang! (Touch and Go) 2000 Long overdue collection of early singles.

Denison/Kimball Trio LPs

5 The Walls in the City (Skin Graft) 1994

6 Soul Machine (Skin Graft) 1995

5 Neutrons (Quarterstick) 1997

Firewater LPs

5 Get Off the Cross (We Need the Wood for Fire) (Jet Set) 1996

4 Ponzi Scheme (Universal) 1998

JOAN JETT

BORN 9/22/60 *(Philadelphia, PA)*

Following the break-up of the Runaways, and pausing only to produce the debut album by the Germs, Jett relocated to London, hooking up with ex-Sex Pistols Steve Jones and Paul Cook for the single "Right Now"/"Black Leather." She then linked with '60s bubblegum producers Kenny Laguna and Ritchie Cordell, and remaining in London, set about cementing a new power-punk sound with her solo debut album, *Joan Jett*.

Well-received in the UK, the album went unreleased in the US until 1981, when it was remixed and reissued as *Bad Reputation* (#51 US) — Jett, meanwhile, had convened a new band, the Blackhearts — Ricky Byrd (guitar), Gary Ryan (bass), and Lee Crystal (drums) — debuting them with a spirited performance on the *Urgh! A Music War* collection, then launching into a period of constant touring, eventually pushing *Bad Reputation* into the US chart.

Jett began work on *I Love Rock'n'Roll* (#2 US, #25 UK) in early 1982; excerpted as a single, (#1 US, #4 UK), the title cover of a mid-70s album track by British glam rock flotsam Arrows, singlehandedly thrust Jett into the forefront of '80s rock, and over the next year two further singles, Tommy James' "Crimson and Clover" (#7 US, #60 UK) and Gary Glitter's "Do You Wanna Touch Me" (#20 US) kept Jett at the top.

Jett's own label imprint, Blackheart, debuted with 1983's *Album* (#20 US), but the record struggled to make the Top 20, while two singles — "Fake Friends" (#35 US) and Sly Stone's "Everyday People" (#37 US) — were surprising under-achievers. 1984's *Glorious Results of a Misspent Youth*

(#67 US) fared even worse, and it would be two years before Jett resurfaced, with the album *Good News* (#105 US) and a Beach Boys-powered single (#83US) of the same name.

The following year, however, found Jett enjoying a reversal of sorts after her cover of Bruce Springsteen's "Light of Day" (#33US) became the theme to the Michael J. Fox movie of the same name. Still it came too late to prevent the dissolution of the Blackhearts; retaining only Bird, Jett formed a new band with Tommy Price (drums — ex-Billy Idol's band) and Casmin Sultan (bass — ex-Todd Rundgren's Utopia), and promptly scored a hit with 1988's "I Hate Myself for Loving You" (#8 US, #46 UK). "Little Liar" (#19 US) followed, with the *Up Your Alley* (#19 US) album giving Jett her first substantial hit in four years. But the audacious *Hit List* (#36 US) covers collection and an accompanying single of AC/DC's "Dirty Deeds" (#36 US, #69 UK) fared poorly, while *Notorious*, in 1992, missed the chart altogether — even as Jett herself was embraced as titular head of the burgeoning Riot Grrl movement.

She produced Olympia, WA-based Bikini Kill's "Rebel Girl" 45 (the band's Kathleen Hanna would co-write "Spinster" for Jett's own next album, *Pure and Simple*), and also fronted Seattle band the Gits, following the 1993 murder of vocalist, Mia Zapata. The live album *Evilstig* featured songs from both the Gits and Jett's career, including the self-defining "Activity GRRRL," co-written by Jett and Laguna, and "Last to Know," penned with the Gits themselves.

Jett and Tommy Price then formed a new generation of Blackhearts, and in 1999 released *Fetish*, a collection of new and old material.

Joan Jett LPs

7 Joan Jett (Ariola) 1980

8 Bad Reputation (Blackheart) Rampant joyous punk-glam party time, just a little too slickly produced for comfort.

9 I Love Rock & Roll (Blackheart) 1981 The title says it all!

7 Album (Blackheart) 1983

6 Glorious Results of a Misspent Youth (Blackheart) 1984 Reinventing the Runaways' "Cherry Bomb" was a good idea, the title was even better. But it's downhill from there.

6 Good Music (Epic) 1986

6 Up Your Alley (Epic) 1988

8 The Hit List (Epic) 1990 A traveling jukebox, Jett hammers through the real results of a misspent youth with dash, daring, and a dramatic "Roadrunner."

7 Notorious (Epic) 1991

5 Pure and Simple (WB) 1994

7 Fetish (Blackheart) 1999

Selected Compilations and Archive Releases

8 Flashback (Blackheart) 1994

8 Fit to Be Tied: Great Hits by Joan Jett (Blackheart) 1997

JOY DIVISION

FORMED 1977 *(Manchester, England)*
ORIGINAL LINE-UP *Ian Curtis (b. 7/15/56, Macclesfield — vocals); Bernard Dicken (b. 1/4/56, Salford — guitar); Peter Hook (b. 2/13/56, Manchester — bass); Steven Morris (b. 10/28/57, Macclesfield)*

"To a large extent," Genesis P-Orridge mused in 1982, "Joy Division evolved a unique sound of their own, a new sound amongst the sort-of progression of musical sound. They had their own, recognizable, individual style. And then suddenly there's 50 other groups who, because they like Joy Division, use the same style [but] can't have the content because they're not Ian Curtis."

Arguably, without Ian Curtis' tragic (but in terms of rock legend, romantic) suicide in May 1980, Joy Division would today be little more than a passing notation in history. Instead, they are widely regarded and regularly described, among the most influential bands of the age, founding fathers of the entire Positive Punk movement which swallowed the UK as the 1970s waited to die, and godfathers to a host of subsequent musical convolutions too.

Both the Cure and Bauhaus were put through the wringer of Joy Division copyists early on in their career, while the band's posthumous invulnerability can best be measured by the amount of substandard material released in their name in the two decades since the band's dissolution. Live recordings, out-takes, and studio oddities have seen Joy Division's catalog swell to encompass a four-CD boxed set, a double album, several bootlegs, and a 1999 live album whose own liner notes admitted that the gig itself was a shambles. Throughout their own lifetime, the band issued just two full albums.

Having been in the future-star-studded audience when the Sex Pistols played Manchester in 1976, and watched their own ambition unfold before their own eyes, Hook and Sumner pieced together their own band in early 1977. They were joined by Curtis and drummer John Tobac, the latter arriving just days before the Stiff Kittens (as Buzzcock Pete Shelley suggested they be called) became Warsaw, itself an event which occurred on the eve of the band's May 1977 live debut at the Electric Circus.

Warsaw owed little to the then-prevalent local scene, riding high as it was on the pure pop sensibilities of Slaughter and the Dogs and Buzzcocks, and the zanier, but still conventional Drones and Nosebleeds. Nevertheless, they persevered, replacing Tobac with first, Steve Brotherhood, and a month later, Steve Morris. (According to legend when Brotherhood quit to join Panik, he tried to take Curtis with him.)

Curtis' own interests and influences ran from Iggy Pop and the Velvet Underground, through to the harsher realities of Throbbing Gristle — he and P-Orridge became friends during 1977, after Curtis heard Gristle's *Second Annual Report* album. The following year, even as Joy Division honed their own studio sound, Curtis fell in love with "Weeping," from Gristle's *DOA* set — a suicide note, detailing betrayal and hopelessness.

The emergence of Howard Devoto's Magazine in January 1978 exerted further influence and, perhaps, pressure on a foursome whose only vinyl to date, the *Ideal for Living* EP, had shown them to be more in tune with mutant Bowie than the power of punk. Injecting into their sound the ragged despair which they later all but patented, Warsaw were close to signing to RCA when the local Factory label swooped.

Changing their name to Joy Division, the band initially made their mark on a string of compilations, the live *Short Circuit* 10-inch, capturing the last nights at Manchester's legendary Electric Circus club, the Factory *Sample* EP, and Fast Product's *Earcom 2*.

However, they also recorded their first album, *Unknown Pleasures* (#71 UK, #1 UK indy) in April 1979, releasing it into a hail of astonishment (but poor sales — it would be two years before it actually charted). *Sounds* described the album as the last record you'd play before committing suicide, and headlined its review "Death Disco" (Public Image Ltd would later turn that title into a hit single). *Melody Maker*, meanwhile, compared it to a tour of Manchester, "endless sodium lights and semis seen from a speeding car, vacant industrial sites... gaping like teeth from an orange bus."

Certainly their sudden elevation shocked the band, all the more so since they so disagreed with what was being said about them. "It was very unsettling," Hook reflected, "to go from being nothing, to being lauded as one of the darkest groups known to man, was a trifle confusing."

At P-Orridge's prompting, the band's next release was the Martin Hannett produced "Atmosphere," released as a limited edition through the Sordide Sentimental label; Joy Division also spent much of late 1979 touring, including a lengthy UK outing supporting the Buzzcocks. However, as their popularity increased, so did the awareness that the darkness of their music was not confined solely to their art.

Close to a year before, traveling home from Joy Division's first London show, Curtis was taken ill and subsequently diagnosed with epilepsy. Medication controlled his condition to a certain extent, but there was more going on in Curtis' mind than anybody realized, as Hook later pointed out.

"It wasn't as if it was just us four beer-swilling knobheads from Salford who couldn't see what was going on. There was a lot of professional people who didn't spot it either, and he was being treated by doctors and psychiatrists and they didn't seem to spot it either. And you can sit there now, and say 'fucking hell, how did you miss that, you dozy bastards?' But I think there's a lot more education these days, about depression and mental illness." At the time, Curtis' illness, and the side effects which were exacerbating it, passed by not without comment, but certainly withou effective treatment.

In January 1980 Joy Division's latest single, "Transmission" (#4 UK indy) came close to making the national chart, and through the spring of 1980, the band worked on their second album, *Closer*, and prepared for their American debut, scheduled for mid-May. Curtis was never enthusiastic about the prospects of visiting the US, but he went along with the plans regardless, concentrating his energies instead on the album, and a song which had already been selected for Joy Division's next single, the elegiac "Love Will Tear Us Apart" (#13 UK, #1 UK indy).

After the fact, the true meaning behind the song would be debated endlessly; Curtis' marriage to teen sweetheart Debbie was dangerously close to cracking, as his relationship with Annik Honore, who worked for Joy Division's Belgian record label, intensified. But there was also a chilling finality to the song — it was no coincidence whatsoever that the title would be engraved on Curtis' gravestone.

Curtis committed suicide on May 18, the evening before the band was due to leave for America. His body was found by his wife, hanged in the kitchen while Iggy Pop's *The Idiot* album still spun on the turntable. Tragically, Curtis had telephoned P-Orridge the previous evening, leaving his friend in doubt as to the state of Curtis' mind. "I phoned various people in Manchester and told them I really thought Ian was planning to kill himself," P-Orridge later said. "They basically ridiculed me and said 'Ian's always depressed and suicidal, that's how he is.' They persuaded me everything would be fine... that I was just panicking." (After a decade of silence on the subject, P-Orridge finally wrote Psychic TV's "I.C.Tears" about Curtis' death.)

After a suitable period of mourning, *Closer* (#6 UK, #1 UK indy) was finally released in August 1980, but the group itself broke up immediately, only regrouping as New Order some months later, and releasing their debut single, "Ceremony," almost precisely one year after Curtis' death. The song was one of two recorded at Joy Division's last ever session, two weeks before Curtis' death; the other, fittingly, was called "In a Lonely Place."

Over the next decade, two Joy Division compilations would appear, the rarities and live *Still* (#5 UK, #1 UK indy) and a straightforward best of, *Substance 1977-80* (#146 US, #7

UK, #1UK indy), along with 1988's reissued "Atmosphere" (#34 UK, #2 UK indy) single. All fed into a cult which had swollen to miraculous proportions — "Love Will Tear Us Apart" remained on the UK indy chart for 195 weeks following its June 28, 1980 entry, with ten of those at #1. "Transmission" stayed on the same listing for 77 weeks, a 1980 release of "Atmosphere" for 70, *Unknown Pleasures* for 136, *Closer* for 97. No other band in UK chart history has even come close to those tallies.

There would also be lengthy residencies for EPs of the band's two John Peel radio sessions (#4 UK indy, #3 UK indy), and a generally affable tribute album. There was even a remixed "Love Will Tear Us Apart" (#19 UK) to outrage purists, but delight an entire new generation in June 1995. A 1998 box set, *Heart and Soul* (#70 UK), however, firmly placed the group's legend in perspective, selling out its first pressing within weeks, and sending both the band's original albums back into the UK chart.

Joy Division LPs

10 Unknown Pleasures (Factory) 1979 In retrospect, this album is filled with portents of the onrushing tragedy; "Disorder" is a runaway train, while other songs are so distant and detached that one can't help but imagine the calm before the final storm. The lyrics, too, turned out to be highly prophetic, although like Nostradamus, hindsight and interpretation both play a major part in that.

Even before Curtis' suicide gave listeners new insight into *Pleasures*, however, it was still a discomforting album. The hollowness of the abyss echoes throughout, the vocals teetering in the empty space above — and that is not retrospect romanticizing. Peter Hook may later have balked at Joy Division's reputation as the most depressing band on the planet, but little about *Unknown Pleasures* (its ironic title notwithstanding) was lining up for a good time.

Admittedly still caught in the frantic guitars and drums of their Warsaw-era recordings, *Unknown Pleasures* is perhaps most indebted to Martin Hannett's production for the claustrophobia which is its most suffocating asset. But Joy Division nevertheless conjure an entire new mood from ingredients which Siouxsie and the Banshees had already toyed with and the Cure would bring to fruition (compare Joy Division's "Disorder" with *17 Seconds*' "A Forest"), one of tangibly bleak despair — salvation without redemption.

At the same time, "She's Lost Control" was a powerfully archetypal post-punk punch; "Insight" evinced an almost tongue-in-cheek playfulness; and "Shadowplay" brooded with such understated passion that it could have exploded into the daylight at a moment's notice. (Interestingly, the Eurythmics seemingly felt the same way — as "Sweet Dreams" unwittingly proves.) The end of the story, then, may not have been inevitable. But it may have been pre-ordained.

8 Closer (Factory) 1980 A denser, darker, but ultimately less-satisfying record than its predecessor; the demons which were gathering around Curtis were increasingly audible, but still unfocused — a sense of personal alienation which Joy Division were able to capture only in small bursts. "Isolation" is perhaps the ultimate Joy Division track, but others looked back to the debut for their impact.

Selected Compilations and Archive Releases

7 Still (Factory) 1981 Half live (horrible), half studio (patchy) collection rounding up everything which didn't make the albums. "Love Will Tear Us Apart," of course, is the icon, but "Dead Souls," "Something Must Break," and "The Kill" have their acolytes too.

8 Substance (Qwest) 1988 A well-designed "best of," concentrating on the most weighted material in the band's repertoire, but adding some rarities for the collectors' sake.

7 The Peel Sessions (Strange Fruit) 1990

9 Heart and Soul (London) 1998 No matter that they ultimately turned into New Order; nor that "Love Will Tear Us Apart" has since been subject to so many ernest dissertations that it has lost all its original meaning. Viewed with all the weight of hindsight behind us, Joy Division are revealed as: what Iggy should have done next, if he'd really meant "The Idiot," and what Bowie could have done, if he'd retired right after "'Heroes'." They're what the '80s wanted to be, and the '90s (Nine Inch Nails) tried so hard to be. And it's that which would have destroyed them, regardless of whether Curtis lived or not. No band can carry that much promise; no band should be expected to. "Heart and Soul" is more than a great boxed set; it's also a warning.

7 Live at Preston Warehouse (New Millennium) 1999 An even more chaotic show than they normally played, inadvertently captured on tape and released not for your listening pleasure, but to portray a moment in legend. It generally succeeds.

Further Reading

Touching from a Distance by Deborah Curtis (Faber & Faber 1995).

JUMP WITH JOEY

FORMED 1988 *(Los Angeles, CA)*
ORIGINAL LINE-UP *Joey Altruda (vocals, bass); Mike Boito (piano); Elliot Caine (trumpet); David Ralicke (trombone); Bill Ungerman (sax); Willie McNeil (drums)*

Following in Fishbone's footsteps, the majority of ska acts forming in the US throughout the 1980s entered the scene via 2-Tone. Altruda, however, arrived with a taste for jazz and jump blues, crossed with a healthy love of the recently reformed Skatalites — influences which were wholly to the fore when Jump with Joey formed in the late '80s, and landed a regular gig at Hollywood's now defunct King King club.

Things moved swiftly. Jason Mayall, brother of the Trojans' Gaz and an old friend of the band, introduced the boys to his boss, a Japanese promotor, who was in turn instrumental in their recruitment to the Japanese Quattro label. The Trojans themselves were huge in that country, and in 1989, the band released their debut long player, *Ska-Ba*, to a riotous reception.

Jump With Joey took their original vision even further on 1992's *Generations United*. The album featured guest appearances from across the historical divide: two original Skatalites, Roland Alphonso and Rico Rodriguez; the Trojans' Gaz Mayall; Johnnie T. of Bad Manners, and former Belle Star vocalist Jennie Mathias. Musically too, the record was true to its title, but better was still to come.

It was Roland Alphonso who introduced Jump with Joey to the legendary Sir Coxsone Dodd in 1993, igniting a collaboration which would result in one of the finest ska albums ever, *Strictly for You, Volume Two*. America began paying attention now. Although their full length albums remained Japanese imports alone, Jump with Joey had never been strangers to either the live circuit or the world of compilations, and finally, US labels began approaching them.

The group finally signed with Rykodisc, who reissued all three of their past records, although their own next new disc, the live *Swingin' Ska Goes South of the Border*, would not appear until 1999.

Jump with Joey LPs

7 **Ska-Ba (Quatro — Japan) 1989** Introducing the band's jumped up potpourri of ska, reggae, and jazz with a lounge lean... the title track was a cover of a Skatalites' oldie, but that's about the only non-original sound in sight.

7 **Generations Unlimited (Quatro — Japan) 1992** An exquisite blend of traditional ska, wrapped in a more modern jazzy swing sound, with a Latin beat for good measure.

8 **Strictly for You, Volume Two (Quatro — Japan) 1993** Crammed with superb covers, leaping from the Skatalites and sundry Studio One gems through Henry Mancini and even a James Bond theme. A magnificent blend of trad ska, jazz, and Latino further shot through with Roland Alphonso's sublime solos, while the very image of Dodd back at the controls remains a masterpiece.

7 **Swingin' Ska Goes South of the Border (Rykodisc) 1999**

K

KILLED BY DEATH
compilation

It was a simple concept, and it just got simpler. Around 1988, a Swedish record collector living in New York, the Mysterious Mr. Kugelburg (as he is remembered by the Frothy Snakes), gathered together 25 of his favorite punk-era obscurities, pressed up — estimates range between a few hundred and a couple of thousand — albums featuring all of them, then unleashed it onto a collecting scene which really didn't know what to do with it.

A few of the names were familiar — the Beastie Boys, from their hardcore *Pollywog Stew* days, the first Wipers B-side, the Slugs, featuring New York Doll Rick Rivits, California's Nuns, England's Users. But what even the "stars" of the showcase had in common was that these records were rare. More than rare, some were nigh on impossible to find, and slowly word began to circulate not only about the compilation, but also about the idea behind the compilation.

Killed by Death became a legend, the legend grew legs, and over the next two years or so, while one segment of the populace learned to love Obscure Punk as a collectible genre in its own rights, another got to work following up the original vision. While the long-anonymous founder of *Killed by Death* would pursue his vision across three more volumes, by the time of volumes five and six, the series was emanating out of Australia, while volume seven was compiled by somebody who happened to have most of the singles on the Australian's personal wants list!

Volumes 8.5 through 12 (and 19) concentrated exclusively upon American and a few Canadian bands, as the subtitle, "All American Punk, No Foreign Junk," made clear, although Volume 11 in fact served up just one band, Tennessee's mid-'90s outfit, Frothy Snakes. Few KBD fans were especially impressed.

Volumes 13 and 16 became even more specialized, seeking out Californian bands alone, preferably ones which had never actually released a record in their lives, and unearthing contributions from Rik Agnew (Adolescents) and Metal Mike (Angry Samoans) as well. And Volumes 17 and 18 did the series' own new collectors a favor by presenting virtual best-ofs of the volumes they'd missed. Later, Volume 200 concentrated on French punk bands and Volume 201 was exclusively Spanish, although the otherwise self-explanatory

British DIY Volume 1 did include one band from New Zealand. Maybe they emigrated.

By the end of the century, there were over 30 albums trading under the *Killed by Death* logo, a handful of which — the first few especially — rapidly became as hard to find as the oddities they were anthologizing.

Quality control was not always possible — or even desirable. Over the course of some 600 records, mostly mastered from vinyl, and some audibly demonstrating how much past owners loved them, a lot of rubbish made it into the series.

In terms of documenting punk rock as a worldwide phenomenon, however, *Killed by Death* has no peers, and probably never will. For the music did not flourish only in Britain, the US, and the handful of other lands where one successful export gave rise to strange whispers of an entire, flourishing scene. It really did get everywhere.

BIJOU — Ton No De Telephone (France, 1978) (V200)

BILLY KARLOFF BAND — Back Street Billy (UK, 1978) (V24)

BIRTHWARD 82 — The Greatest War/Idiots Power (Greece, 1983) (V40)

BLACK EASTER — What the Fuck (UK, 1982) (V5)

BLACKHOLES — Captain Payday (USA, 1979) (V999)

BLANK — [16 TRACKS, DEMOS/LIVE 1978] (V16)

BLANK STUDENTS — Underground Music (UK, 1979) (V20)

BLOWDRIERS — Berkeley Farms (USA C1979-80) (V13)

BRAIN POLICE — Kind of a Drag (USA, 1979) (V19)

BRAINIACS — Don't Tell Me Why (USA, 1979) (V15.5)

BREAKOUTS — In Vagueness Deal (USA, 1979) (V9)

BRIGADES — Riot & Dance (France, 1982) (V200)

BRONCS — Reason to Whine (USA, 1980) (V666)

BRULBAJZ — Eap (Sweden, 1980) (V4)

BUCKS — That Kind of Ohohoh (Switzerland, 1980) (V40)

BULLDOZER — J'suis Punk (France, 1978) (V200)

CADS — Do the Crabwalk (Canada, 1978) (V20)

CALCINATOR — Billard (France, 1980) (V200)

CARDBOARD BRAINS — Steppin' Stone (Canada, 1977) (V26)

CARDIAC KIDZ — Get Out (USA, 1979) (V12)

CARPETS — Kill Hirb Cane (USA, 1979) (V19)

CASTRATION SQUAD — The X Girlfriend (USA C1979-80) (V13)

CHAIN GANG — My Fly (USA, 1978) (V7)

CHAIN GANG — Son of Sam (USA, 1977) (V2)

CHAIN GANG — Cannibal Him (USA, 1978) (V17)

CHAIN GANG — Born in Brazil (USA, 1979) (V999)

CHAINSAW — [FOUR TRACKS] (Belgium, 1977) (V77)

CHEATERS — Ice Man (USA, 1980) (V12)

CHECKMATE — Weekend (France, 1979) (V200)

CHIEFS — Blues (USA, 1980) (V2)

CHILD MOLESTERS — (I'm The) Hillside Strangler (USA, 1978) (V1)

CHILD MOLESTERS — Don't Worry Kyoko (USA, 1978) (V2)

CHRONICS — Test Tube Baby (USA, 1978) (V999)

CIGARETTES — They're Back Again, Here They Come (UK, 1979) (V7)

CINECYDE — Underground (USA, 1978) (V24)

CITIZEN FEAR — We Need Another Vietnam (USA C1979-80) (V13)

CLAP — Killed by Kindness (USA, 1982) (V22)

CLOCKWORK CRIMINALS — No Future UK (UK, 1982) (V20)

COLD COCK — I Wanna Be Rich (USA, 1979) (V1)

COLORS — Growin' Up American (USA, 1980) (V20)

COMMERCIALS — Mein Kampf (Austria, 1981) (V22)

CONTROLLERS — (The Original) (V1) Neutron Bomb (USA, 1978) (V1)

CONTROLLERS — Do the Uganda (USA, 1979) (V15.5)

CORPSICLES — Big Doings (USA, 1982) (V9)

COSMETICS — Twinkie Madness (USA, 1980) (V8)

COUNT VERTIGO — X-Patriots (USA, 1979) (V10)

COUNT VERTIGO — I'm a Mutant (USA, 1979) (V17)

COWBOYS — Teenage Life (USA, 1980) (V5)

CRACKED ACTOR — Nazi School (USA, 1981) (V5)

CRAP DETECTORS — Intellectual Morons (USA, 1980) (V15.5)

CRAP DETECTORS — Police State (USA, 1979) (V9)

CRINGE — Spit on Your Grave (USA, 1981) (V10)

CRUCIFIED — Let the Kids Play (USA, 1977) (V8)

CULT HEROES — Amerikan Story (USA, 1981) (V12)

CURSE — Shoeshine Boy/Killer Bees (Canada, 1979) (V26)

DDT — I'm Walking Down the Psychopath (USA, 1983) (V7)

DEAF AIDS — Bored Christine (UK, 1980) (V20)

DECIBEL — Col Ditto (Italy, 1978) (V201)

DEFEX — Machine Gun Love (USA, 1979) (V18)

DEFNICS — 51 Percent (USA, 1981) (V3)

DEMENTS TRAGIQUES — 56e Etage (France, 1981) (V100)

DEMON PREACHER — Dead End Kidz (UK, 1978) (V666)

DENNIS MOST & THE INSTIGATORS — Excuse My Spunk (USA, 1979) (V18)

DEPRESSION — Moderne/Debout Papa (France, 1980) (V100)

DER STAB — Tracers/It's Gray (USA C1979-80) (V13)

DESCENDANTS — Unnational Anthem (USA, 1980) (V10)

DESTRY HAMPTON/WOLVES FROM HELL — Angel of Madness (USA, 1978) (V17)

DESTRY HAMPTON/WOLVES FROM HELL — Paradise (USA, 1978) (V18)

DETENTION — Dead Rock & Rollers (USA, 1983) (V2)

DIETER MEIER — Cry for Fame (Switzerland, 1978) (V5)

DIRT SHIT — Exit (Austria, 1979) (V6)

DISCO ZOMBIES — Drums over London (UK, 1979) (Vdiy 1)

DISCORDS — Dead Cubans (Canada, 1982) (V10)

DISHRAGS — Love Is Shit/Past Is Past (Canada, 1979) (V26)

DOA — Nazi Training Camp/Want Some Bondage (Canada, 1979) (V26)

DOGS — Slash Your Face (USA, 1978) (V1)

DOGS — Teen Slime (USA, 1977) (V18)

DOGS — Rot'n'roll (USA, 1977) (V999)

DOT VAETH GROUP — Armed Robbery (USA, 1978) (V7)

DOW JONES AND THE INDUSTRIALS — Ladies with Appliances (USA, 1981) (V15.5)

DOW JONES AND THE INDUSTRIALS — Can't Stand the Midwest (Us, 1980) (V8)

EAT — Doctor Tv/Kneecappin' (USA, 1980) (V3)

EAT — Jimmy B. Good (USA, 1980) (V18)

EAT — Communist Radio (USA, 1979) (V2)

EBENEZER & THE BLUDGEONS — Weekend Nazi (USA, 1978) (V12)

EBENEZER & THE BLUDGEONS — Oh I Love This Weather (USA, 1978) (V3)

EBENEZER & THE BLUDGEONS — Fake (USA, 1978) (V18)

ED NASTY & THE DOPEDS — I'm Gonna Be Everything (USA, 1978) (V7)

ED NASTY & THE DOPEDS — You Sucker (USA, 1978) (V6)

EDITH NYLON — Tank (France, 1979) (V200)

EDITH NYLON — Waldorf (France, 1979) (Vfu2)

EIGHTH ROUTE ARMY — Vice Presidente (USA, 1982) (V100)

ELECKTROSHOCK — Public Mores (Italy, 1977) (V201)

ELECTRIC DEADS — Mind Bomb/Screwball/Crossroad (Denmark, 1983) (V41)

ELECTRODES — Black Flag (France, 1983) (V200)

ELECTROFLEX — 8th Avenue (USA, 1979) (V19)

ELEKTROSHOCK — Fever of the Night (Italy, 1977) (V100)

END RESULT — Last Chance (UK, 1981) (V20)

ENDTABLES — Circumcision (USA, 1978) (V10)

EPICYCLE — Underground (USA, 1979) (V19)

EPICYCLE — You're Not Gonna Get It (USA, 1980) (V9)

ESPASMODICOS — [FIVE TRACKS] (Spain, 1983) (V202)

ESSENTIAL LOGIC — Aerosol Burns (UK, 1978) (V22)

EXECUTIVES — Jet Set (USA, 1980) (V10)

EXECUTIVES — Resistance (USA, 1980) (V19)

EXIT — Out in the Street (USA, 1979) (V19)

EXTRABALLE — Haute Tension (France, 1978) (V200)

FACTORY — Flesh (France, 1977) (V200)

FAST CARS — What Can I Do? (UK, 1979) (V20)

FEATURES — [THREE TRACKS] (New Zealand, 1980) (V69)

FEATURES — Drab City (UK, 1978) (V22)

FEEDERZ — Peter Gunn Theme (USA C1979-80) (V13)

FEEDERZ — Stop You're Killing Me (USA, 1981) (V14)

FENSICS — Full Time Job (USA, 1979) (V999)

FILTH — Don't Hide Your Hate (Holland, 1978) (V4)

FILTH — [THREE TRACKS] (Holland, 1978) (V77)

FIRE EXIT — Time Wall (UK, 1979) (V7)

FIRE EXIT — Time Wall (UK, 1979) (V6)

FLIRT — Don't Push Me/De-Generator (USA, 1978) (Vfu2)

FLYIN' SPIDERZ — S.O.S. (Holland, 1978) (Vfu2)

FORGOTTEN REBELS — Angry/National Unity (Canada, 1979) (V26)

FORT & GAELI — Nsb/Enveiskommunikasjon (Norway, 1981) (V40)

FRAEBBBLARNIR — No Friends/Critical Bullshit (Iceland, 1981) (V40)

FRANTIX — My Dad's a Fuckin' Alcoholic (USA, 1983) (V6)

FREESTONE — Bummer Bitch (USA, 1978) (V2)

FREEZE — I Hate Tourists (USA, 1980) (V2)

FRESH COLOR — The Source (Switzerland, 1978) (V7)

FRIED ABORTIONS — Joel Selvin (USA C1979-80) (V13)

FROTHY SHAKES — 13 Tracks (USA, 1996) (V11)

FU2 — Playin' My Guitar (UK, 1978) (Vfu2)

FUGITIVES — Mystery Girl (USA, 1980) (V22)

FUN 4 — Singing in the Shower (UK, 1979) (Vdiy 1)

FUNERAL DRESS — Army Life (Belgium, 1987) (V6)

FX — Slag (UK, 1979) (V100)

GANG GREEN/THE AMPUTATORS — I Hate You (USA, 1982) (V999)

GASOLINE — Killer Man (France, 1977) (V1)

GASOLINE — Radio Flic (France, 1977) (V200)

GENOCIDE — Renegade (UK, 1978) (V20)

GENRAL FOODZ — So Funny/Love Potion #9 (USA, 1980) (V69)

GENRAL FOODZ — So Funny (USA, 1980) (V12)

GENTLEMEN OF HORROR — God Knows You by Name (Canada, 1981) (V10)

GISM — Exclamations (Japan, 1983) (V6)

GIZMOS — Tie Me Up (USA, 1978) (V20)

GIZMOS — Amerika First (USA, 1978) (V9)

GIZMOS — Muff Divin' (USA, 1976) (V24)

GLI INCESTI — Sabato Midnight (Italy, 1978) (V201)

GLO — [SIX TRACKS] (Sweden, 1979) (V77)

GLOIRES LOCALES — Les Catalogues (France, 1980) (V200)

GLUEAMS — Mental (Switzerland, 1979) (V6)

GRIM KLONE BAND — Heat's Rising/Jehovah's Witness (USA, 1978) (V10)

GROUND ZERO — Nothing (USA, 1980) (V12)

GUILTY RAZORS — I Don't Wanna Be Rich (France, 1978) (V7)

GUILTY RAZORS — [THREE TRACKS] (France, 1978) (V77)

GYNACOLOGISTS — Sex Orgy with the Brady Bunch (USA, 1981) (V18)

HAMMER DAMAGE — Laugh (USA, 1978) (V9)

HASKELS — Taking the City by Storm (USA, 1980) (V8)

HATED — Seize the Middle East (USA, 1981) (V7)

HEART ATTACK — God Is Dead (USA, 1981) (V4)

HELEN KELLER — Surfin' with Steve & E.D. Amin (USA, 1978) (V999)

HITLER SS — Slave (Italy, 1979) (V6)

HITLER SS — No Solution (Italy, 1979) (V201)

HOLLYWOOD SQUARES — Hillside Strangler (USA, 1978) (V1)

HORNSEY AT WAR — Hornsey at War/U.C.2. Much 4 Me (UK, 1979) (Vdiy1)

HUBBLE BUBBLE — Look Around/Sweet Rot (Belgium, 1978) (V5)

HUNS — Glad He's Dead (USA, 1979) (V4)

ICE & THE ICED — [FOUR TRACKS] (Italy, 1981) (V77)

ICE 9 — Revolting Mess (USA, 1979) (V9)

INJECTIONS — Lies (USA, 1980) (V12)

INNOCENT VICARS — Antimatter/She's Here (UK, 1980) (V69)

INSULTS — Just a Doper (USA, 1979) (V6)

INSULTS — Zombie Lover (USA, 1979) (V19)

INSULTS — Population Zero (USA, 1979) (V8)

INVERTED TRIANGLE — White Night Riot (USA C1979-80) (V13)

ISM — I Think I Love You (USA, 1983) (V4)

IVAN/THE EXECUTIONERS — I Wanna Kill James Taylor (USA, 1979) (V999)

JACK RABBIT BAND — Revenge (Switzerland, 1979) (V41)

JACKIE SHARK/BEACH BUTCHERS — 2nd Generation Rising (USA, 1978) (V19)

JAYNE DOE — As the World Turns (USA, 1980) (V18)

JERKS — Get Your Woofing Dog off Me (UK, 1977) (V4)

JETSONS — Suicidal Tendencies (USA, 1981) (V9)

JIMI LALUMIA & THE PSYCHOTIC FROGS — Eleanor Rigby (USA, 1979) (V14)

JIMMY SMACK — The Scarlet Beast (USA C1979-80) (V14)

JOE SQUILLO ELETRIX — Skizzo, Skizzo (Italy, 1981) (V40)

JOHN BERENZY GROUP — Vice Verses (USA, 1978) (V3)

JOHN VOMIT & THE LEATHERSCABS — Punk Rock Star (USA, 1978) (V8)

JUDAS — Flashdown (Italy, 1978) (V201)

JUNIOR EXECUTIVES — Milo Buylow/Executive Washroom (USA, 1978) (V16)

JUST URBAIN — Everybody Loves (Australia, 1980) (V666)

K-TELS — Where Are You? (Canada, 1979) (V19)

KANDEGGINA GANG — Sono Cattiva (Italy, 1980) (V201)

KAOS ROCK — La Rapina (Italy, 1980) (V201)

KAOS — Alcoholiday (USA, 1980) (V4)

KEVIN SHORT & HIS PRIVATES — Punk Strut (UK, 1978) (V100)

KIDS — This Is Rock N Roll (Belgium, 1978) (V6)

KIDS — No Monarchy (Belgium, 1978) (V5)

KILLER BEES — TV Violence (USA, 1979) (V19)

KJOTT — Nei Nei Nei/Flue/Blalys/Ett Nytt Og Bedre Liv (Norway, 1979) (V77)

KOLLAA KESTAA — Kirjoituksia Kellarista (Finland, 1979) (V100)

KRAUT — Matinee (USA, 1981) (V1)

KRYPTON TUNES — Coming to See You (UK, 1978) (V24)

LA CAME AUX DAMELIAS — Le 5e Roue Du Systeme (France, 1978) (V200)

LA PESTE — Better Off Dead (USA, 1978) (V9)

LA BROMA DE SATAN — [SEVEN TRACKS] (Spain, 1982) (V202)

LARS LANG — Chartertont (Sweden, 1979) (V666)

LARSEN — Vomitas Sangre (Spain, 1983) (V22)

LARSEN — [FOUR TRACKS] (Spain, 1983) (V202)

LAST WORDS — Animal World (Australia, 1979) (V22)

LATIN DOGS — Killed in Jail (USA, 1983) (V8)

LEGIONAIRE'S DISEASE BAND — Downtown (USA, 1979) (V12)

LEPERS — Cops (USA, 1979) (V15.5)

LEPERS — Coitus Interruptus (USA, 1979) (V18)

LES FELES — Non Lycee (France, 1978) (V200)

LES ABLETTES — Spontaneite (France, 1982) (V200)

LEWD — Kill Yourself (USA, 1978) (V3)

LIKET LEVER — Hjartats Slag (Sweden, 1979) (V22)

LIXOMANIA — Fugitivo/Violencia & Sobrevivencia (Brazil, 1981) (V41)

LIZARDS — Is It Late? (USA, 1981) (V12)

LONDON PX — Orders (UK, 1981) (Vdiy 1)

LOS REACTORS — Laboratory Baby/Dead in the Suburbs (USA, 1980) (V100)

LOS NIKIS — Gamma Globulina/Amenaza Amarilla (Spain, 1982) (V41)

LOS VIOLADORES — Mirando La Guerra Por Tv/Represion (Argentina, 1983) (V40)

LOST KIDS — Cola Freaks (Denmark, 1979) (V7)

LOST GENERATION — Never Work (USA, 1982) (V14)

LUBRICANTS — Transformation Vacation (USA, 1980) (V18)

LUBRICANTS — Activated Energy (USA, 1980) (V12)

LUCY — Really Got Me Goin' (UK, 1977) (Vfu2)

LULLABIES — Junk/It Could Be You (Holland, 1980) (V41)

LULLABIES — Cops in the Street/Fashion Punx (Holland, 1980) (V41)

MACHINES — True Life (UK, 1978) (V2)

MACS — The Cowboy Song (USA, 1980) (V999)

MAD VIRGINS — Fuck & Suck (Belgium, 1978) (V4)

MAD — I Hate Music (USA, 1979) (V1)

MAD — Disgusting (USA, 1979) (V2)

MAD — Eye Ball (USA, 1979) (V17)

MAGGOTS — Tammy Wynette (USA, 1979) (V5)

MAGIC DE SPELL — Sweating All Over/Virgin Freedom (Greece, 1981) (V41)

MAIDS — Back to Bataan (USA, 1979) (V7)

MAIDS — I Do I Do (USA, 1979) (V17)

MARIE FRANCE — Dereglee (Belgium, 1977) (V41)

MARK TRUTH & LIARS — Prisoners of Time (USA, 1981) (V6)

MARY MONDAY — Pop Gun (USA, 1977) (V17)

MASS MEDIA — Das Jazz/Jag Vill Ingenting (Sweden, 1979) (V69)

MATCHHEADS — Pearl Harbor/Fat Bitch (USA, 1981) (V8)

MATT GIMMICK — Rag (USA, 1979) (V15.5)

MAX LOAD — X-Rod (USA, 1979) (V17)

MD — Manisch Depressiv (Switzerland, 1983) (V7)

MEATY BUYS — New Freedumb (USA, 1979) (V12)

MEATY BUYS — Criminal Mind (USA, 1979) (V18)

MECANO LTD — Face Cover Face (Holland, 1978) (V14)

MEN IN BLACK — Gypsy Lid (USA, 1979) (V999)

MENTALLY ILL — Gacy's Place (USA, 1979) (V2)

MENTALLY ILL — Padded Cell (USA, 1979) (V17)

MICHAEL LUCAS — Tearing Me Apart (USA, 1977) (V16)

MIRRORS — Mirrors (Japan, 1978) (V14)

MIZZ NOBODY — Smittad (Sweden, 1978) (V100)

MODS — Step Out Tonight (Canada, 1978) (V26)

MOLESTERS — Plastic/I Am (Holland, 1978) (V69)

MOLLS — White Stains (USA, 1979) (V5)

MOONDOGS — Make Her Love Me (N Ireland, 1981) (Vfu2)

MORDBUBEN AG — Bleib' Blod (Austria, 1980) (V22)

MUDHUTTERS — Water Torture (UK, 1979) (Vdiy 1)

MUTANTS — School Teacher (UK, 1978) (V24)

MX80 SOUND — Someday You'll Be the King (USA, 1980) (V20)

NAILS — Cops Are Punks (USA, 1977) (V20)

NAKED LADY WRESTLERS — William Tell Overture (USA C1979–80) (V13)

NCM — I Used to Know You (USA, 1981) (V24)

NEO PUNKZ — If I Watch TV (Holland, 1980) (V5)

NERVOUS EATERS — Just Head (USA, 1979) (V2)

NEXT — Monotony (USA, 1979) (V6)

NO FUN — Now I Ain't Got No Face (Canada, 1978) (V666)

NO SUBMISSION — The Degraded Men (Italy, 1981) (V201)

NOISE — Let's Have Some Fun Tonight (USA, 1979) (V19)

NORMALS — Almost Ready (USA, 1978) (V10)

NORMALS — Hardcore (USA, 1978) (V17)

NOTHING — Uniformz (USA, 1978) (V9)

NOW — I'm Eating off a Fashion Plate (USA, 1978) (V999)

NRG — Kulturel Forbaltnung (Denmark, 1983) (V22)

NUBS — I Don't Need You (USA, 1980) (V12)

NUBS — Little Billy's Burning (USA, 1980) (V18)

NUBS — Job (USA, 1980) (V5)

NUCLEAR CRAYONS — Outsider (USA, 1982) (V14)

NUCLEAR SOCKETTS — Pretenders Zeal (UK, 1980) (V24)

NUNS — Decadent Jew (USA, 1978) (V1)

NY NIGGERS — Headliner (USA, 1979) (V3)

NY NIGGERS — Just Like Dresden 45 (USA, 1979) (V19)

ONE GANG LOGIC — Who Killed Sex? (UK, 1980) (Vdiy 1)

OPUS — The Atrocity (USA, 1979) (V14)

OUTO ELAMA — Antero (Finland, 1980) (V666)

OX — Drugs (France, 1980) (V200)

PACK — Com' On/Nobody Can Tell Us (Germany, 1978) (V69)

PANICS — Drugs Are for Thugs (USA, 1981) (V15.5)

PANICS — Kill It (USA, 1979) (V19)

PANICS — I Wanna Kill My Mom (USA, 1980) (V9)

PANKRTI — Namesto Tebe (Yugoslavia, 1981) (V22)

PARAF — Rijeka/Moj Zivot Je Novi Val (Yugoslavia, 1979) (V69)

PATHETIX — Don't Touch My Machine (UK, 1978) (V100)

PATHETIX — Nil Carborundum (UK, 1979) (V666)

PEER PRESSURE — Sound of the 80s (USA, 1980) (V12)

PENETRATORS — Teenage Lifestyle (USA, 1979) (V19)

PETROLIO — Italia, Italia (Italy, 1983) (V201)

PETTICOATS — Normal (UK, 1980) (Vdiy 1)

PLASTIC IDOLS — Sophistication (USA, 1979) (V15.5)

PLASTIC IDOLS — Uncircumsised Twin (USA, 1980) (V14)

PLEEMOBIELZ — Troep/Dagenlang Balen (Holland, 1981) (V40)

PLUGZ — Let Go (USA, 1978) (V15.5)

PLUGZ — Mindless Contentment (USA, 1978) (V3)

POBEL — Es Lebe Hoch Die Perversion/Scheiss Auf's Bundesheer (Austria, 1981) (V40)

POINTED STICKS — What Do You Want Me to Do? (Canada, 1978) (V26)

PREFECTS — Things in General (UK, 1979) (V100)

PRIVATE DICKS — Green Is in the Red (UK, 1979) (V20)

PRLJAVO KAZALISTE — Moj Je Otac Bio U Ratu (Yugoslavia, 1979) (V40)

PROP SACK — Aujord'hui (France, 1982) (V22)

PSYCHO SURGEONS — Horizontal Action (Australia, 1978) (V2)

PSYCHOTIC PINEAPPLE — I Want Her So Bad (USA, 1978) (V15.5)

PSYKIK VOLTS — Totally Useless (UK, 1979) (V6)

PUBLIC DISTURBANCE — S&M (USA, 1983) (V8)

PUNCTURE — Mucky Pup (UK, 1977) (V14)

PURITAN GUITARS — 100 Pounds in 15 Minutes (UK, 1980) (Vdiy 1)

QUEERS — I Don't Wanna Work/I'm Useless/At the Mall (USA, 1984) (V3)

RAILBIRDS — Go to Hell (Holland, 1979) (V14)

RALPH & THE PONYTAILS — James Bond (UK, 1980) (Vfu2)

RANCID X — Get Someone to Love Me (Italy, 1978) (V201)

RATS — Come On Now (France, 1981) (V24)

RATTLERS — Meilla On Yhteinen Tuleveissus (Finland, 1980) (V41)

RAZORS — Subway (Germany, 1980) (Vfu2)

REACTORS — I Want Sex (USA, 1979) (V14)

REACTORS — I Want Sex/Seduction Center (USA, 1979) (V19)

REACTORS — I Am a Reactor (USA, 1979) (V17)

REACTORS — L.A. Sleaze (USA, 1979) (V8)

REALLY RED — Modern Needs (USA, 1980) (V4)

REALLY RED — Crowd Control (USA, 1979) (V2)

REALTORS — Guilt by Association (USA, 1979) (V999)

RED SQUARES — Time Change (USA, 1980) (V10)

RED SQUARES — Modern Roll (USA, 1980) (V666)

REJECTS — Eeg/Barbed Wire Baby (USA, 1980) (V12)

REMO VOOR — Toilet Love (Germany, 1979) (V40)

RENTALS — Gertrude Stein (USA, 1979) (V100)

RENTALS — Low Rent (USA, 1979) (V666)

REPULSIVE ALIEN — Say & Do (UK, 1980) (V22)

REVENGE 88 — Neon Lights (Belgium, 1981) (V6)

RIOT 303 — Drugs (Canada, 1982) (V5)

ROCK BOTTOM & THE SPYS — Rich Girl/No Good (USA, C1980) (V14)

ROTTERS — Sink the Whales (Buy Jap Goods)/Disco Queen (USA, 1979) (V4)

RPA — Shoot the Pope (USA, 1981) (V5)

RUDE NORTON — Tits on the Beach (Canada, 1980) (V7)

RUDE KIDS — Absolute Ruler (Sweden, 1979) (V2)

RUNE STRUTZ — A Knugen (Sweden, 1978) (V666)

S'NOTS — So Long to the Sixties (USA, 1977) (V2)

SADO-NATION — On Whom They Beat (USA, 1980) (V9)

SADONATION — Johnny Paranoid (USA, 1979) (V15.5)

SATAN 81 — Radioattivita (Italy, 1981) (V201)

SAUCERS — What We Do (USA, 1979) (V999)

SCABS — Amory Buildings (UK, 1979) (V22)

SCABS — Leave Me Alone (UK, 1979) (V666)

SCENE — High Numbers (UK, 1985) (Vfu2)

SCHEMATIX — Second Story (USA, 1980) (V999)

SCHUND — Schund (Austria, 1980) (V6)

SCREAMERS — If I Can't Have What I Want (USA C1979-80) (V13)

SCREAMING URGE — Homework (USA, 1980) (V6)

SCREAMING MEE MEES — Hot Sody (USA, 1977) (V3)

SE — Meilla Voisi Tunaau Olla Hauska (Finland, 1979) (V6)

SEIZURE — Frontline (USA, 1978) (V8)

SHELL SHOCK — Execution Time (USA, 1981) (V15.5)

SHELL SHOCK — My Way (USA, 1981) (V18)

SHIRKERS — Drunk & Disorderly (USA, 1978) (V9)

SHIRKERS — Suicide (USA, 1978) (V17)

SHITDOGS — Calling Dr. Modo (USA, 1981) (V15.5)

SHITDOGS — Reborn (USA, 1980) (V5)

SHITDOGS — World War Iii (USA, 1980) (V18)

SHITDOGS — Killer Cain (USA, 1981) (V8)

SHOCK — This Generation Is on Vacation (USA, 1978) (V3)

SHOCK — I Wanna Be Spoiled (USA, 1978) (V17)

SHOES THIS HIGH — The Nose One (New Zealand, C1980) (Vdiy 1)

SHRAPNEL — Way Out World (USA, 1981) (V24)

SIB — You/My Secret Life (Italy, 1981) (V201)

SICK & THE LAME — Ate Days a Week (USA, 1979) (V10)

SILLY KILLERS — Knife Manual (USA, 1982) (V12)

SINIESTRO TOTAL — Sexo Chungo (Spain, 1983) (V100)

SKABB — Tro Inte Dina Ogen (Sweden, 1978) (V666)

SKAMS — Konfirmationen/Sodertull (Sweden, 1979) (V40)

SKIANTOS — Io Sono Un Autonomo (Italy, 1978) (V41)

SKINNIES — Out of Order (USA, 1978) (V10)

SLEEPY SLEEPERS — Anarkiaa Karjalassa (Finland, 1977) (V40)

SLOBOBANS UNDERGANG — Maktgalen (Sweden, 1979) (V100)

SLUGS — Problem Child (USA, 1980) (V1)

SNOT PUPPIES — TV Tantrum/Towel Song (USA C1979-80) (V13)

SNUKY TATE — Can You Dance It (USA, 1979) (V18)

SNUKY TATE — Stage Speech (USA, 1979) (V8)

SNUKY TATE — High Hopes (USA, 1979) (V15.5)

SODS — Television Sect (Denmark, 1978) (V3)

SODS — No Pictures (UK, 1979) (Vdiy 1)

SODS — Mopey Grope (UK, 1979) (V666)

SOUND — Cold Beat (UK, 1979) (V24)

SOZZ — Law & Order (Switzerland, 1980) (V22)

SPELLING MISTEAKS — Pop Star (UK, 1979) (Vdiy 1)

SPERMA — Zuri Punx (Switzerland, 1979) (V7)

SPERMICIDE — Belgique (Belgium, 1979) (V100)

SPURTS — Je Suis Fier De Mon Grand Pere (France, C1978) (V200)

SQUAD — Flasher (UK, 1978) (V20)

STAINS — Feel Guilty (USA, 1980) (V12)

STAKANOV — Autonomie (France, 1981) (V100)

STALIN — [2 TRACKS] (Japan, 1981) (V41)

STALIN — [TITLE IN JAPANESE] (Japan, 1982) (V5)

STARSHOOTER — Quelle Crise Baby (France, 1978) (V14)

STARSHOOTER — Quelle Crise Baby (France, 1978) (Vfu2)

STERKE SVAKHETER — Trodde Vi Hadde Demokrati (Norway, 1982) (V41)

STIMULATORS — Run Run Run (USA, 1979) (V17)

STIPHNOYDS — Afraid of the Russians (USA, 1980) (V5)

STONED AKA ICE 9 — Nazi (USA, C1979-80) (V14)

STORMTROOPER — I'm a Mess (UK, 1975) (V100)

STRIKE UNDER — Context (USA, 1981) (V12)

STRIPES — Observer (Germany, 1980) (V22)

STRY OCH STRIPPARNA — Inte Intressant (Sweden, 1979) (V666)

STRYCHNINE — Ex-Bx (France, 1980) (V200)

STRYCHNINE — Pas Facile (France, 1980) (V40)

STRYCHNINE — C'est Pour Toi/Lache Moi (France, 1980) (Vfu2)

STUDS — Electric Chair (Holland, 1981) (V24)

STYPHNOIDS — Meat Is Rotten (USA, 1979) (V15.5)

STYPHNOIDS — Mom's a Fake (USA, 1980) (V8)

SUBHUMANS — No Productivity (Canada, 1980) (V4)

SUBVERTS — Can't Control Myself (USA, 1981) (V15.5)

SUBWAY — You Gotta Support (Holland, 1978) (V24)

SURPRISES — Flying Saucer Attack (UK, 1979) (V666)

SWINDLED — Who Wants Guns? (Canada, 1982) (V22)

SYPH — Industriemadchen (Germany, 1979) (V22)

SYSTEMI — Punk Nuorisoo (Finland, 1980) (V100)

TAMPAX — UFO Dictator (Italy, 1979) (V7)

TAMPAX — UFO Dictator (Italy, 1979) (V6)

TAMPAX — Tampax in the Cunt (Italy, 1979) (V201)

TANKS — Manifest Destiny (USA C1979-80) (V13)

TAPEWORM — Break My Face/Blues for an Insurance Salesman (USA, 1978) (V9)

TARTS — Terminal Romance/All the Girls.../Disposable Girl (USA C1979-80) (V13)

TEA SET — Sing Song (UK, 1978) (V666)

TEDDY & THE FRATGIRLS — Clubnite (USA, 1980) (V5)

TEENAGE PHDS — Punk Rock Is Dead (USA, 1982) (V12)

TEENAGE PHDS — Eat, Sleep & Fuck (USA, 1982) (V18)

TENANT — Manifestation of Your Sickness (USA, 1979) (V20)

TNT — Gilmore 77 (Spain, 1983) (V40)

TOLLWUT — Seuchen (Germany, 1981) (V40)

TOO MUCH — Photos, Photos (Belgium, 1978) (Vfu2)

TOREROS AFTER OLE — [FIVE TRACKS] (Spain, 1983) (V202)

TOXIN III — I Rock I Ran (USA, 1982) (V8)

TRACKS — Brakes on You (USA, 1977) (V666)

TRAGICS — Laughing Lover (USA, 1981) (V10)

TRASH — N-N-E-R-V-O-U-S (UK, 1978) (V24)

TRASH — Priorities (UK, 1977) (Vfu2)

TREND — Band Aid (USA, 1980) (V10)

TSUNEMATSU MASATOSHI — Do You Wanna Be My Dog? (Japan, 1978) (V22)

TUPPJUKK — Jag Vill Ma Bra (Sweden, 1980) (V666)

TURNBUCKLES — Super Destroyer Mark Ii (USA, 1981) (V8)

U-BOATS — Break Out Tonite (USA, 1982) (Vfu2)

UDS — Ma Che Belle Societa (Italy, 1983) (V201)

UGLY — To Have Some Fun (Canada, 1978) (V26)

UHF — Cacada (Portugal, 1979) (V40)

ULTIMO RESORTE — [FIVE TRACKS] (Spain, 1983) (V202)

UNCALLED 4 — Grind Her Up (USA, 1979) (V8)

UNIPLUX — Ux (Uniplux, 1982) (V201)

UNNATURAL AXE — The Creeper (USA, 1978) (V10)

USERS — Sick of You (UK, 1977) (V1)

V BABIES — Donna Blitzen (UK, 1980) (V20)

VAINS — The Fake (USA, 1980) (V15.5)

VAINS — The Loser (USA, 1980) (V2)

VAINS — School Jerks (USA, 1980) (V9)

VAST MAJORITY — I Wanna Be a Number (USA, 1980) (V8)

VECTORS — I Hate Myself (USA, 1979) (V999)

VERMINES — Rock in Belfond (France, 1982) (V200)

VERMINES — Another Place (France, 1982) (V100)

VICIOUS VISIONS — I Beat You (Sweden, 1982) (V1)

VICTIMS — TV Freak (Australia) (V4)

VICTIMS — Annette (USA, 1978) (V17)

VILETONES — Danger Boy/Backdoor to Hell (Canada, 1978) (V26)

VILLAGE PISTOLS — Big Money (USA, 1981) (V7)

VIOLATORS — NY Ripper (USA, 1980) (V3)

VIPERS — No Such Thing (Ireland, 1978) (V41)

VIVA! TEQUILA — Dime Que Me Quieres (Spain, 1980) (V20)

VOM — Punkmobile (USA, 1978) (V14)

VOMIT VISIONS — Punks Are the Old Farts of Today (Germany, 1979) (V14)

VOMIT VISIONS — Someone (Germany, 1981) (V14)
VOMIT PIGS — Useless Eater (USA, 1979) (V10)
VON GAM — Hasse Parasit/Mode (Sweden, 1980) (V41)
VONBRIDGI — Bornin Pin (Iceland, C1980) (V41)
VOODOO IDOLS — We Dig Nixon (USA, 1982) (V10)
VORES — Get Outta My Way (USA, 1978) (V17)
VORWARTS — Susie (Switzerland, 1983) (V22)
VOX POP — Cab Driver (USA, 1980) (V1)
WANNSKRAEK — Bla Heder (Norway, 1981) (V100)
WARM GUN — Broken Windows (France, 1977) (V200)
WARM GUN — Accident (France, 1977) (V24)
WASP WOMEN — Kill Me/I Don't Need Your Attitude (USA C1979-80)(V13)
WAYWARD YOUTH — Do You Wanna (USA, 1979) (V666)
WAYWARD YOUTH — Do You Wanna (USA, 1980) (V15.5)
WETNURSE — Bar Wars (USA, 1980) (V14)
WIDOWS — Overscrupulous (Finland, 1979) (V14)
WILD YOUTH — Wat 'Bout Me/Radio Youth (S. Africa, 1979) (V40)
WIPERS — [ONE TITLE] (USA, 1980) (V1)
X-X — You're Full of Shit (USA, 1979) (V9)
XTERMINATORS — Microwave Radiation (USA, 1980) (V5)
ZERO BOYS — [FOUR TRACKS] (USA, 1980) (V4)
ZERO ZERO — Chinese Boys (UK, 1979) (V24)
012 — Fish from Tahiti (UK, 1980) (Vdiy 1)
63 MONROE — Hijack Victim (Canada, 1980) (V10)
84 FLESH — D-Section (France, 1980) (V200)
84 FLESH — Salted City (France, 1980) (V3)

KILLING JOKE

FORMED 1979 (Notting Hill, London, England)

ORIGINAL LINE-UP Jaz Coleman (b. Jeremy Coleman, 2/26/60, Cheltenham — vocals); Geordie (b. Keith Walker, 2/18/58, Newcastle — guitar); Youth (b. Martin Glover, 12/27/60, Africa — bass); Paul Ferguson (b. 3/31/58, High Wycombe — drums)

Having met in a London unemployment office where both were queuing to register their claims, Jaz Coleman and Paul Ferguson formed Killing Joke after placing an ad in *Melody Maker*: "Want to be part of the Killing Joke? Total publicity, total anonymity, total exposure." What they actually wanted, Ferguson later admitted, was to find people interested in making music "which sounded like the earth vomiting." Geordie and Youth apparently fulfilled that desire.

Erupting out of London's post-punk apocalyptic scene, drawing in equal parts from the vivacious mind warp of the Birthday Party and the more ponderous savagery of the Pop Group, Killing Joke played a handful of shows purposely built to disorient — the Sex Pistols' brutal "Bodies" was a live favorite for some time, although only until the band had enough original material of similar jarring quality.

Killing Joke finally lurched into play with the self-financed *Almost Red*, a disquieting four-song EP in which music and melody were treated as two very separate notions, and scarcely allowed to touch.

An immediate underground success and highly praised by DJ John Peel, the group signed with Island for a reissue of their debut, but returned to their own Malicious Damage label for their third single, "Wardance" (#4 UK indy), in March 1980. Months later, the band signed with EG, home of Roxy Music and King Crimson (two more obvious, if barely recognizable, antecedents) and released *Killing Joke* (#39 UK).

With the band's live reputation as uncompromisingly bleak as their records, Killing Joke were soon being marked out among the UK media's most urgent tips for the new decade. Indeed, "Requiem" (#1 UK indy) and a reissue of "Wardance" (#18 UK indy) kept the band firmly on the chart while they set to work on their sophomore album, although neither could prepare the listener for what they would emerge with.

Noting the growing infusion of funk into the new wave's lexicon, *What's THIS For?* (#42 UK) was a considerably easier record than its predecessor, echoing in equal parts the seminal Gang of Four and, through the reggae-tinged ghosts which hung around the fringes, a controlled version of the Slits. But such reference points remained vague at best, despite the band landing an utterly unexpected US dance floor hit with the jerking "Follow the Leaders" (#55 UK).

Following a world tour, the band decamped for Germany. Produced by the now-fashionable Connie Plank, Killing Joke's third album, *Revelations* (#12 UK), marked both the high- and low-water mark in their career. Musically, it exceeded even the peaks to which Killing Joke customarily climbed; commercially, it was their best seller yet and spawned a pair of major hit singles, "Empire Song" (#43 UK) and "Birds of a Feather" (#64 UK).

However, it also precipitated a press backlash from which the band barely recovered — one of the sneering, seething, personal assaults at which the British media excel. Inflamed, and dreading another marathon world tour, Coleman and Geordie both quit the band following gigs in Iceland. They remained in that country, with the already occult-fixated Coleman apparently convinced of an impending worldwide apocalypse, which remote Iceland alone had a hope of evading.

Back home, Killing Joke's mysterious absence finally hit the headlines when Youth formed Brilliant with Paul Ferguson and Paul Raven (ex-Neon Hearts). It seemed the group had reached the end of the line.

Instead, it was Brilliant who split when Ferguson and Raven themselves decamped to Iceland, in search of Coleman and Geordie. Their quest was successful and in June 1983, Killing Joke re-emerged with Raven replacing Youth (who continued on with Brilliant). Tours of Europe and the US followed, with the *Ha!* live EP (#66 UK) proving a remarkable souvenir of the Toronto show.

The album, *Fire Dances* (#29 UK), followed and over the next year, the band would unveil four minor hit singles — "Let's All (Go to the Fire Dances)" (#51 UK), "Me or You?" (#57 UK), "A New Day" (#56 UK), and "Eighties" (#60 UK), with the latter subsequently attaining legendary status after Nirvana's "Come as You Are" was adjudged to have lifted its intro from the song.

Their most significant single release, however, was "Love Like Blood" (#16 UK) in January 1985 — like "Eighties," a trailer for the album *Night Time* (#11 UK) — and the band's biggest hit ever.

"Kings and Queens" (#58 UK) wrapped up this particular period of success, and for many onlookers, happily so. Much of the original line-up's menace and experimentalism had dissipated with the departure of Youth and as that acclaim faded, so Killing Joke themselves began to lose focus. 1986's *Brighter than a Thousand Suns* (#194 US, #54 UK) and the attendant "Adorations"(#42 UK) and "Sanity" (#70 UK) singles had little more than the band's name going for them; while matters reached a new nadir when Coleman announced he was taking time out to record a solo album, with Geordie alone.

Mid-session, Virgin (EG's parent label) announced they wanted another Killing Joke album instead and basically hijacked the tapes, giving Coleman two options. Either he could finish them up and let Virgin do what they wanted, or the label would release them as they were. Coleman acceded to their demands, but it was a futile effort all round. *Outside the Gate* (#92 UK) was almost completely overlooked and after a few gigs with ex-Smiths bassist Andy Rourke replacing Raven in 1988, Coleman and Geordie announced Killing Joke were going on hiatus. (Ferguson would eventually resurface with Warrior Soul.)

In late 1989, Coleman and Geordie re-emerged with a new Killing Joke line-up, featuring former PiL drummer Martin Atkins (b. Coventry, England, 8/3/59) and Taff (bass), and a handful of low-key US dates. A well-organized fan club was set up with a spoken word album, *The Courtauld Tapes*, offering purchasers a transcription of a post-split press conference.

Killing Joke finally signed with BMG in early 1990; the album *Extremities, Dirt and Various Repressed Emotions* followed, but while the group did play Finsbury Park, London, in June 1990, alongside New Model Army and the Mission, this latest union soon collapsed in vicious acrimony. Atkins, Geordie, and Raven formed a new band, Murder Inc.,

releasing a self-titled album on Atkins' own Chicago-based Invisible label (Raven later joined Prong); Coleman launched a solo career, recording an album, *Songs from the Victorious City*, with ex-Art of Noise pianist Anne Dudley. He also began work on a trilogy of EPs exploring his fascination with Arabic music (*Habebe, Minarets and Memories* and *Ziggarats of Cinnamon*).

The hiatus was short-lived. In 1992, Youth — now one of the UK's leading dance remixers — and Ferguson came together to oversee a Killing Joke compilation, *Laugh? I Nearly Bought One*. Coleman and Geordie followed, together with another Art of Noise alumni, Geoff Dugmore (drums) and in 1994, they released the *Pandemonium* album.

By now, Killing Joke's legend had been sealed — the Nirvana incident aside, bands as musically far afield as Soundgarden, Metallica, and Ministry were citing the group as an influence and the ensuing interest helped push *Pandemonium* into the UK Top 20, notch up US sales of 100,000+, and score British Top 40 singles with "Pandemonium" (#28 UK) and "Millennium" (#34 UK). Another track, "Exorcism, " was famously recorded in the King's Chamber of the Great Pyramid in Egypt.

Coleman was now spending much of his time in New Zealand where he was appointed Composer-in-Residence for the country's Symphony Orchestra. He and Youth were responsible for scoring vast orchestral renditions of hits by the Rolling Stones (Symphonic Music Of) and Pink Floyd (Us and Them) among others, released to considerable fanfare in the mid-1990s; Coleman alone would also compose two acclaimed symphonies, plus the equally well-received *Pacifica — Ambient Sketches*, performed by the New Zealand String Quartet. Thus, though Coleman would reconvene Youth and Geordie as Killing Joke for 1996's *Democracy* album (and attendant singles "Jana," #54 UK, and "Democracy," #39 UK), these other activities have conspired to keep the band silent since then.

Killing Joke LPs

8 Killing Joke (EG) 1980 KJ at their most primal; urgent rhythms and scathing chords collide in a statement of intent which basically left listeners with two choices. Either the world was ending — or they were.

7 What's This For? (EG) 1981 Like rabid wolves fighting over a bone, KJ wage internal war, Ferguson pounding a military tattoo, for Youth to echo then fracture; Geordie's guitar wails buzzing like a swarm of killer bees; Coleman's strident, snarling vocals, simultaneously aloof from and embedded in the battles raging around him.

7 Revelations (EG) 1982 The incoherency which would fracture the band sends *Revelations* skittering in a multitude of directions, only occasionally coming together through fragments of melodies, snatches of unity. Coleman's vocals echo the disconnection with even more clinical detachment than usual — this is the sound of world's end, when gravity is gone and everything spins uncontrollably into the sun.

7 Fire Dances (EG) 1983 The new-look KJ emerges little different from the old; the sound remains the same but the approach has dramatically changed. *Fire Dances* strives determinedly towards a more melodic style, hampered only by a lack of even halfway traditional songs. A lot of anthemic gloomrockers raise their heads, though.

8 Night Time (EG) 1985 The change is amazing, but other bands had already done the dirty work — breathlessly blending Siouxsie and the Banshees sepulchral leads, the Sisters of Mercy's big guitar sound and atmospheres, and The Cure's doom-pop, clashing them with a dance beat and emerging with *Night Time*. KJ brought little new to the Batcave festivities, but an anthemic and poppy sound was perfect for dancing the gloom away. And "Eighties" provided Nirvana with one of their most haunting melodies.

6 Brighter than a Thousand Suns (EG) 1986

7 Outside the Gate (EG) 1988

6 Extremities, Dirt and Various Repressed Emotions (Noise International) 1990 Minus precision drummer *extraordinaire* Ferguson, the new Joke builds around replacement Atkins' chaotic rage. *Extremities'* use of electronics, spoken passages, vocal samples, and aggressive guitar pulls the once gothy band wholly towards the still gelling paranoia of industrial angst — it isn't at all pretty, but is striking evidence of how closely the two genres are interwined on both an emotional and a musical level.

5 The Courtauld Tapes [SPOKEN WORD] (Invisible) 1990

8 Pandemonium (Zoo) 1994 Breathtaking in its vision and structure, *Pandemonium* completes the transformation which began with *Extremities*. Swirling and swooping, crashing and pounding, KJ weave a web of sound which stretches from industrial stompers to the darkly trance-whipped title track. Youth's production keeps the music under tight control, while enhancing the spellbound atmospheres — a genuine watershed.

6 Democracy (Zoo) 1996 And then the spell is broken. Swinging wildly between tired post-punk pop and reheated industrial aggro, *Democracy* is best compared to *17 Seconds*-era Cure crossed with Die Krupps, a genetically modified hybrid which takes on a monstrous quality. About half the songs work surprisingly well, but even Youth's production can't salvage the rest.

Selected Compilations and Archive Releases

8 An Incomplete Collection (EG) 1990 Boxed set rounding up the first five LPs on nifty colored vinyl.

7 Laugh? I Nearly Bought One! (Plan 9/Caroline) 1992 Band approved compilation, hits most of the high points.

7 Wilful Days (Caroline) 1995 Singles, B-sides, and remix collection

6 BBC Radio 1 Live in Concert (Windsong) 1996 Live from 1985/86 (Reading Festival).

6 Alchemy — The Remixes (Big Life) 1996 Collected remixes from the *Pandemonium/Democracy* period.

Youth/Brilliant LP

7 Kiss the Lips of Life (Atlantic) 1986

Jaz Coleman and Anne Dudley LP

6 Songs from the Victorious City (TVT) 1991

Jaz Coleman and the NZ String Quartet LP

8 Pacifica — The Ambient Sketches (Ode — NZ) 1996

Martin Atkins Etc/Murder Inc. LP

6 Murder Inc (Invisible) 1992

KLF

FORMED *1987 (Liverpool, England)*
ORIGINAL LINE-UP *Bill Drummond (b. William Butterworth, 4/29/53, South Africa); Jimmy Cauty (b. 1954)*

The hip-hop house acid-rave-thrash supergroup, KLF — also trading under the names Disco 2000, Space, The Orb, and the Justified Ancients of Mu Mu — was the brainchild of Zoo Records' boss and Liverpool scene-maker Bill Drummond (ex-Big in Japan), and former Brilliant guitarist Cauty. KLF stood for Kopyright Liberation Front and was originally designed to test Britain's rigorous copyright laws — could sampling, in more or less absurdly obvious chunks, hold up as art in a court of law?

A debut single titled after, and sampling, the Beatles' "All You Need is Love" (#3 UK indy) attacking the current climate of fear surrounding AIDS, passed by unscathed. But the Justified Ancients' 1987 (*What the Fuck's Going On*) (#5 UK indy) album, featuring a massive sample of Abba's "Dancing Queen" was utterly crushed by the Swedes in a settlement which saw the masters for the entire album surrendered to the BPI and Abba themselves.

The album was lost but the ensuing publicity enabled the duo to continue, reissuing 1987 as *The JAMS 45 Edits* EP (#35 UK indy), from which all unauthorized borrowings had been removed. The result was somewhat akin to a very funny joke being retold without its punchline and the following year the JAMS tried again, this time asking permission before creating their merry pop collage. "Whitney [Houston] Joins the JAMS" (#4 UK indy), "The Porpoise Song," in which disco queen Donna Summer was given the JAM treatment, and "Downtown" (#5 UK indy) duly followed during 1987.

February 1988's *Who Killed the JAMS?* (#3 UK indy) prefaced the release of the duo's greatest hit, a monstrous arrangement of Gary Glitter's "Rock'n'Roll," thematically reworked around the television program, Dr. Who. Released under the name of The Timelords, "Doctoring the Tardis" (#66 US, #1 UK) became a massive hit during the summer of 1988. The duo subsequently wrote a book, *The Manual*, offering would-be pop stars a step by step guide to having a #1 single, based on the experience.

With the duo having already inaugurated two new identities, the Timelords being joined by Disco 2000 (the "I Gotta CD" single, featuring Cauty's wife, Cressida), the JAMS passed away in March 1988, bowing out with the *Shag Times* (#5 UK indy) compilation and a collaboration with Wah's Pete Wylie, "It's Grim Up North."

Drummond and Cauty reassigned the KLF name to their own music and, retaining only the love of irreverent sampling which had made the JAMS so special, set off down a similar avenue. The single, "Burn the Beat" (#15 UK indy), debuted the project in April 1988.

While further Disco 2000 singles, "One Love Nation" and "Uptight," appeared, KLF was clearly to become the duo's principle outlet. Now firmly targeting Britain's dance scene, KLF's next project, in early 1990, was the "ultimate" ambient house album, *Chill Out*, featuring the sound of sheep bleating over a succession of rock samples.

Fresh pseudonyms emerged, including Space and The Orb, both uniting Cauty with Alex Paterson. KLF, meanwhile, unveiled a pastiche of Australian pop, "Kylie [Minogue] Said to Jason [Donovan]" (#6 UK indy), while multiple versions of "What Time Is Love" and "3 AM Eternal" appeared during late 1989/early 1990, each teasing dance floor collectors with another radically different mix. But despite the obvious parody which was KLF's chief objective, August 1990 brought the duo's next hit with the latest version of "What Time Is Love — Live at Trans-Central" (#5 UK).

They scored another major hit, "3AM Eternal — Live at SSL" (#5 US, #1 UK) in March 1991, and as the year wore on, KLF scored further massive UK hits, including "Last Train to Trans-Central" (#2 UK) and a revamped "It's Grim Up North" (#10 UK), this time minus the Wylie factor.

The *White Room* (#39 US, #3 UK) album, meanwhile remained on the British chart for 43 weeks and saw them follow up with the *Justified and Ancient* EP (#11 US, #2 UK), a set which brought country queen Tammy Wynette into the duo's lair for the classic "Stand by the Jams."

The EP also resulted in KLF receiving the Top British Group award at the 1992 BRIT awards — the cue for Cauty and Drummond's greatest publicity coup yet. First, they performed "3AM Eternal" as a thrash-metal outrage, accompanied by hardcore outfit Extreme Noise Terror, left the stage to the announcement "the KLF have now left the music business," and then deposited a freshly slaughtered sheep

outside the post-awards party with a note, "I died for you — Bon Appetit."

The band released one final musical question, "America: What Time Is Love?" (#57 US, #4 UK), then confirmed their resolution by deleting their entire back catalog and taking a full-page ad on the back page of the *New Musical Express*, explaining their decision.

They did continue recording — a version of "Que Sera Sera," featuring the Soviet Army Chorale, was taped in 1993, but would be released, they insisted, only when world peace was finally achieved; May 1996 brought "Ooh! Aah! Cantona" (#11 UK), a tribute to Manchester United soccer player Eric Cantona, as 1300 Drums Featuring the Unjustified Ancients of Mu.

The following year, KLF announced a one-off show in which "the next 480 days of our lives [leading up to the millennium] will be discussed." The gig, at London's Barbican Centre, was cancelled following the death of Diana, Princess of Wales, but still the duo prepared the world for the turn of the century with 2K's "Fuck the Millennium." (They also conducted a newspaper poll asking whether people agreed with them. The response was a massive 18,436 to 2,227 in favor.)

However, the duo achieved greater notoriety when they set up a challenge to the British art establishment's annual Turner Prize, awarded to the year's best original artwork — the K Foundation promised double the prize money (40,000 pounds) to the year's worst piece, published an identical shortlist to the Turner nominees, then gave the prize to the same winner, Rachel Whiteread.

KLF received even more attention after they nailed a million pounds cash to a board, paraded it in front of a specially convened London gathering of journalists and art world luminaries, then took it to a remote Scottish island and burned it. The destruction was video-recorded for future reference, and also spawned the 1997 book *K Foundation Burn a Million Quid*.

KLF currently function as K2 Plant Hire, a fictional company specializing in renting out heavy machinery (!). Their musical endeavors included contributing to a caustic Xmas single by comedian Fat Les.

KLF LPs

8 **What the Fuck Is Going On? (Jams) 1987** Legendary withdrawn juggernaut, slamming samples into sound shifts in search of absolute disorientation.

7 **Who Killed the Jams? (KLF Communications) 1988** Moving now closer to the wacked ambience which would make their fortune, but still slam-dunk with ear-twisting samples and effects.

10 **Chill Out (Wax Trax!) 1991** Their masterpiece; certainly one of the greatest ambient albums ever made, a smooth passage through the course of a day with oldies radio fading in and out of the ether, passing traffic passing sheep, and a succession of brilliantly obscure musical puns — Pink Floyd's "Echoes" cut off short of its opening lyric ("overhead the albatross..."), to drift into Fleetwood Mac's "Albatross" instead.

9 The White Room (Arista) 1991 Nine tracks spanning both the JAMS and KLF's past, *White Room* works both as an intro into the duo's electro-world or a revised and remixed greatest hits' package. Capturing the essence of KLF's creative oeuvre — their innovative cut and paste approach, brilliant breaks and deep beats, and constant recycling of key phrases and loops — *White Room* emerged a vivid pastiche of the very club sounds which pastiched the JAMS' own early enterprises.

Selected Compilations and Archive Releases

8 The History of the Jams A.K.A. The Timelords (TVT) 1988
8 Shag Times (KLF Communications — UK) 1989 Largely similar collections of singles and remixes to date.

8 The What Time Is Love Story (KLF Communications) 1989 Alex Paterson/Orb compiled collection of KLF related recordings.

7 MU (EMI — Japan) 1991 Remix compilation
8 This Is What the KLF Is About 1/2 (EMI — Japan) 1992 two 3CD singles box sets.

Bill Drummond LPs

6 The Man (Bar/None) 1986
5 Bill Drummond (Atlantic) 1987

Space LP

7 Space (KLF Communications — UK) 1990

KRAMER

BORN *Mark Stevan Kramer, 11/30/58 (New York, NY)*

A graduate of Ornette Coleman and Karl Berger's Creative Music Studio, where he encountered Eugene Chadbourne and former Fugs vocalist and author Ed Sanders, Kramer's first major musical work was the soundtrack to the latter's *Karen Silkwood Cantata*. In 1980, he became live sound engineer for the Waitresses, then joined Daevid Allen's floating New York Gong ensemble, alongside Fred Maher, Bill Laswell, and Michael Beinhorn. When that enterprise folded, in 1982, he was invited to join Chadbourne's eponymous country and western band, which in turn became Shockabilly.

It was while recording that band's *Dawn of Shockabilly* EP that Kramer first found himself producing. He would remain behind the desk for the band's debut album later that

same year, and its three successors, also working with Sanders again, when a reformed Fugs toured Europe in 1984. That project fizzled out after Sanders took to prefacing certain of the band's more inflammatory songs with onstage apologies, and Kramer quit in disgust. He left Shockabilly the following year to join the Butthole Surfers as resident producer.

He remained on board for two albums, but quit following a bout of serious food poisoning while touring the midwest, and returned to New York to establish his own Shimmy Disc label in 1987 as an outlet for his still-burgeoning appetite for production — one of his earliest "name" clients was former Velvet Underground drummer Maureen Tucker, whose *Life in Exile After Abdication* album proved one of the best Velvets-related solo albums of the entire decade.

1987 also saw Kramer launch another band of his own, Bongwater, with performance artist Ann Magnuson; he simultaneously commenced a string of collaborations with Penn and Teller's Penn Jillette (Captain Howdy), Mara Flynn (Milksop Holly), Jad Fair and John S. Hall (King Missile), Soft Machine alumnus Hugh Hopper, and a reunion with Daevid Allen. He also worked alongside auteur producer Don Fleming in BALL, recording a string of albums for Shimmy Disc between 1987 and 1991. *The Guilt Trip*, Kramer's first solo album, appeared in 1993 following Bongwater's acrimonious break-up.

Into this already savagely eclectic brew, Kramer continued to drop a string of outside productions, few of which (Urge Overkill notwithstanding) met with commercial success but generally received critical approval, while his nurturing of Galaxie 500 and Low indicated a depth of sonic grasp which the abrasion of his "typical" work rarely hinted at.

Also see the entry for "KRAMER PRODUCTIONS" on page 783 in "PRODUCERS & LABELS."

Kramer LPs

8 Guilt Trip (Shimmy Disc) 1992 Sprawling over six sides of vinyl, and maybe just a little over-long (???), dynamic guitar noise sonics cross most of Kramer's future paths, usually with a keen eye for wired psychedelic pop.

6 Secret of Comedy (Shimmy Disc) 1994
6 Let Me Explain Something to You About Art (Tzadik) 1998 Three lengthy tracks explain very little about art, but a lot about Kramer himself — wide ranging soundscapes shot through with noise, psychedelia and spooky violin.

7 Songs from the Pink Death (Knitting Factory) 1998 Half joking, half sensitive, Kramer's apparently most personal album could also be his most generally appealing.

Selected Compilations and Archive Releases

8 Music for Crying (Shimmy Disc) 1995 Sharp compilation of solo and collaborative work.

Shockabilly LPs

7 Earth vs Shockabilly (Rough Trade) 1983

7 Colosseum (Rough Trade) 1984

8 Vietnam (Fundamental) 1984

8 Heaven (Fundamental) 1985 The overall interchangeability of the Shockabilly catalog does not detract from the unearthly strength and adventure which characterized their assaults; a blend of ugly psych, spoken word horror, and vicious, driving jams.

Carny-Hild-Kramer LPs

8 Happiness Finally Came to Them (Shimmy Disc) 1987 Ralph Carny (sax), Daved Hild (drums), and Kramer make a lot of noise.

Jad Fair and Kramer LPs

6 Roll out the Barrel (Shimmy Disc) 1988 24-track collection of half-realized ideas and assaults on classic songbooks, each one short and sharp as you like.

John S. Hall and Kramer LPs

4 Real Men (Shimmy Disc) 1991 King Missile spin-off, apparently made because they could.

L

LA PESTE

FORMED 1977 *(Boston, MA)*
ORIGINAL LINE-UP *Peter Dayton (vocals, guitar); Mark Karl (bass); Roger Tripp (drums)*

Of all the bands operating out of Boston through the 1977–79 punk period, few emerged with the reputation, and legend of La Peste — a band whose vinyl legacy amounted to one and a half singles, a cut on a local compilation, and just enough demos and radio sessions to fill a CD — which finally emerged in 1996.

Their name, French for "the plague," forewarned of the sophistication and intensity which was this band's trademark, while the local *Subway News* claimed that "outside of Willie Alexander, they have the Boston underground's most distinctive and peculiar sound."

They were also among the city's most prolific — at one point, the band had a repertoire of 50 original songs, and in 1978, Backlash Records released two of them, "Better Off Dead" (subsequently included on Rhino's *Mass Ave* Boston punk compilation) and "Black Black" as the band's first single. Other tracks, "She's a Girl," "Rock Rots," and "Whites of Your Eyes," appeared on a local radio session late in 1978, and in February 1979, La Peste went into the studio with Ric Ocasek to record a three-track demo, "I Don't Know Right From Wrong," "Let Me Sleep," and "Don't Wanna Die in My Sleep."

A second single, 1979's "Computer Love," was split with the Neighborhoods and Lord Manuel, but the band's biggest moment would come in June 1979 when they entered the first Boston Rock'n'Roll Rumble. Fighting their way through a pool which included Unnatural Axe, the Lyres, Thrills, and the newly formed Mission of Burma, La Peste reached the finals, against the Neighborhoods. There their run finally ended, and just weeks later, Peter Dayton departed. "I read somewhere that the only escape from the plague is death or extreme purification," he mused. "So I quit the band and escaped to New York for two months."

He discussed a solo career, and moved into production, working with Boston all-girl group Bound and Gagged, and Mission of Burma; he also recorded with Negativland, appearing across their first three releases. Roger Tripp and Mark Karl tried to carry on without him, but eventually called a halt.

La Peste LP
8 Peste (Matador) 1996 21-track collection of demos and live material, edgy dance-inflected pop-punk infused with taut rhythms, angular guitars, and Dayton's quirky bark. If Brian Eno was a jittery rock three piece, *Tiger Mountain* might have sounded a lot like this.

LAIBACH

FORMED 1980 *(Trbovlje, Yugoslavia)*
ORIGINAL LINE-UP *Tomaz Hostnik (b. 1961 — vocals); Miran Hohar (guitar)*

Springing from the loins of Slovenian art collective NSK, Laibach was the musical expression of a seemingly Teutonic urge to establish the Slovenian capital of Ljubljana as the Athens of the modern age.

The band originally commenced operations around Yugoslavian army members Tomaz Hostnik and Miran Hohar. They played their first (banned) show at the Trbovlje Workers Center. Subsequent shows blended Laibach's music with other NSK exhibitions, but in July 1982, the band made its first tentative steps on its own, recording four songs "Death for Death," "State," "Triumph of Will," and "Jaruzelsky." The following year, they contributed to a cassette pairing them with The Last Few Days.

Having worked with a constantly fluctuating line-up, the group consolidated following Hostnik's 1982 suicide, around Ivan Novak, Milan Frez, Dejan Knez, and Ervin Markosek. Laibach then signed to RTV Ljubljana in May 1983 and recorded the unissued *The Sky Glows* album. Shortly after, they linked with the Belgian Laylah label for the *Boji* EP. From this same period, Laibach's characteristic version of the Yugoslavian national anthem appeared on an Italian compilation, *World National Anthems*, while the "Panorama" single was released in Britain. (Many of the band's earliest recordings, which fused jazz, rock, and disco into a strangely portentous whole, are collected together on the *Rekapitulation* double album.)

A European tour followed, from which the live albums *Through the Occupied Netherlands*, *Occupied Europe*, *Vstajenie v Berlinu*, *Life in Hell*, *Ein Schauspieler*, and *Neue Konservativ* emerged during 1984–1985. Another in concert recording, *Divergences/Divisions*, dated from a 1986 show in Bordeaux, France. The band's UK profile, meanwhile, was maintained by a flurry of 12" singles on Cherry Red ("Der Liebe Ist Die Grosse Kraft") and Mute ("Geburt Einer

Nation" — #8 UK indy, "Life is Life" — #5 UK indy), and two albums, *Nova Akropola* (#15 UK indy) and *Opus Dei* (#4 UK indy).

Of these, the former's use of Marshall Tito's speeches as lyrics for two of the songs prompted considerable controversy among critics unable to see past the band's iron cast grimaces — like Kraftwerk's experiments with robots, much of Laibach's work could be considered ironical, or at worst, allegorical, only to be hampered primarily by their audience's refusal to see more than was displayed.

While their UK albums tended to show the lighter side of Laibach's music, more atmospheric, and distinctly non-rock oriented efforts continued to appear on the continent — the German soundtrack *Baptism*, with its Wagnerian reworking of Queen's "One Vision" was another example of the band's playfulness.

Indeed, their occasional swipes at conventional rock soon came to epitomize the Laibach experience. 1988 caught the band tackling the Beatles' *Let It Be* album in its near-entirety (#3 UK indy), and releasing a single of "Across the Universe" (#12 UK indy). Later that same year, they delivered multiple mutilations of the Rolling Stones' "Sympathy for the Devil" (#5 UK indy). Both pinpointed the alien nature of western rock in eastern European culture, and were perhaps their most effective gestures yet. (1996's *Jesus Christ Superstar* would make a similar assault on the rock opera of the same name, together with metallic covers of Prince's "The Cross" and Reactor's "God Is God.")

These releases marked the conclusion, at least temporarily, of Laibach's most obvious pretensions towards rock music; their next album, in 1989, was the soundtrack to NSK's revolutionary production of Shakespeare's *MacBeth*, a set widely described as their best yet. 1992's *Kapital*, too, broke the mold, this time allying Laibach's traditional "sturm und drang" with the European dance club scene, at the same time as offering a violent (and with hindsight, deadly accurate) condemnation of post-Communist Eastern Europe's embracing of free market practices.

NATO, four years later, would follow a similar line of doomsday prophecy, itself born out by that organization's self-aggrandizing assault on the former Yugoslavia in early 1999. Included were covers of Europe's "Final Countdown," Zager & Evans' "In the Year 2525," and Edwin Starr's "War," all leading up towards the closing "Mars (On the River Drina)."

Laibach LPs

3 Through the Occupied Netherlands (Staal) 1984 The first of several dubious live albums dispensable even to fans of the studio material (much of which appears on *Laibach* and the *Rekapitulation* collection).

6 Vstajenje V Berlinu [LIVE] (Skuc) 1984

5 Laibach (Skuc) 1985 Generally formative set, offering hints of what was to come, pressed through a harsh, but already operatic industrial wringer. Recorded, as it was, as early as 1980, however, Laibach's efforts can at least claim to have made the whip for their own back.

5 Neue Konservativ [LIVE] (Cherry Red) 1985

8 Nova Akropola (Cherry Red) 1985 Laibach's terrifying symphony of the coming apocalypse, filled with images of battles fought long ago and vicious wars to come — with the use of sundry Tito speeches suggesting it'll be a state-sponsored bloodbath, so no surprises there. Chilling in the extreme, *Nova* acknowledges the nostalgia for a (usually mythical) golden age which lies at the core of every call-up, and the glory and grandeur which government wraps around warfare. Sadly, Laibach's concept was misinterpreted or lost as listeners were overwhelmed by the music and the group's iconography.

6 Occupied Europe Tour 1983-85 [LIVE] (Side Effects) 1986

7 Krst Pod Triglavom Baptism (Walter Ubricht — Germany) 1987 The avant-classically-informed soundtrack to an NSK theater production.

7 Slovenska Akropola [LIVE] (Skuc — Yugo) 1987 Interesting in concert set (probably their best) rearranges elements of both *Baptism* and *Nova Akropola*.

9 Opus Dei (Mute) 1987 Laibach's rendering of Queen's "One Vision" is almost a modern rock staple today; *Opus Dei*, however, offers plenty of similarly structured pieces, including an even more effective version of "Life Is Life," together with the frankly mystifying "How the West Was Won." Mystifying, that is, unless Laibach are freemasons.

8 Let It Be (Mute) 1988 Emerging more gimmicky than it was ever intended, the Beatles' final album re-enacted in its entirety, with a vicious, drunken approach which is probably truer to the original album than most fans would like to think.

8 Macbeth (Mute) 1989 A soundtrack to the NSK's radical new interpretation of the Shakespearean play, one of Laibach's most consistent, and consistently atmospheric, sets.

7 Sympathy for the Devil (Mute) 1990 Repeating the *Let It Be* experiment, only this time via half a dozen stylistic variations on the Rolling Stones' over-deified title track.

6 Kapital (Mute) 1992 Almost dance floor friendly, *Kapital* collides club beats into ominous soundscapes, Wagnerian operettas and hip-hop... for everything is interconnected in the New World Order's global economy. As conceptually obtuse as ever, but more musically accessible than usual, Laibach's mix of mutually exclusive club sounds, whilst not always successful, is certainly groundbreaking.

6 Ljubljana-Zagreb-Beograd [LIVE] (Grey Area) 1993

8 NATO (Mute) 1994 Laibach's finest yet assault on western musical values, an almost self-parodying array of covers include Edwin Starr's "War," Europe's "The Final Countdown," Status

Quo's "In the Army Now"... get the picture? Zager & Evans' "In the Year 2525" wraps things up, however, with imagery which even its concerned composers never dreamed of.

7 The Occupied Europe Nato Tour 1994-95 [LIVE] (Mute) 1996

8 Jesus Christ Superstar (Mute) 1996 With covers of the title track, Prince's "The Cross" and Juno Reactor's "God Is God" (reinvented as a Wagnerian recitation of Handel's "Messiah"), a fiendishly accessible set with the darker rock overtones which are truly one of Laibach's stronger points.

7 M.B. December 21, 1984 [LIVE] (Mute) 1997

Selected Compilations and Archive Releases

7 Rockapitulacija 1980-84 (Walter Ulbricht — Germany) 1985 Generally heavy duty compilation, ranging schizophrenically between basic noise and orchestrated slabs at sounding conventional.

Further Reading

Neue Slowenische Kunst (Amok Books, 1992).

THOMAS LEER

BORN *Thomas Wisharf, 1960 (Port Glasgow, Scotland)*

Utilizing his arsenal of primitive electronics in pure DIY fashion, Thomas Leer first emerged on the wide screen as one of several avant-gardists on Cherry Red's seminal *Business Unusual* compilation in January 1979, alongside Cabaret Voltaire, Robert Rental, and Throbbing Gristle. Leer's contribution was the insectoid "Private Plane," previously available (c/w "International") on a desperately obscure 1978 single.

The Bridge (#9 UK indy), Leer's groundbreaking collaboration with fellow electronics maven Rental, followed. Since cited as a major influence throughout the electronic underground, *The Bridge* was released on Throbbing Gristle's Industrial label in 1979.

Leer resurfaced on another pair of compilations, *Perspectivesand Distortions* and *Morocci Klung!*, before releasing the 4 *Movements* EP (#39 UK indy) in 1981. However, the double 12" single "Contradictions" completely shattered Leer's reputation as a minimalist and though the arrival of "All About You"/"Saving Grace" (#11 UK indy) in November 1981 rounded off Leer's most prolific year yet, it marked the storm before the quiet. In 1987, however, he resurfaced alongside Claudia Brucken of Propaganda as Act, purveyors of a sharp, frigid Eurodance opus for producer Trevor Horn's ZTT label. The duo's debut single, "Snobbery and Decay" (#60 UK) was moderately successful, but subsequent releases — "Absolutely Immune," " I Can't Escape From You," and

"Chance" — did little, and Act's debut album, *Laughter, Tears and Rage*, passed by unnoticed in July 1988. Brucken quit for a solo career and Leer returned to obscurity. It would be twelve years before he resurfaced with the internet-only *Future Historic* album.

Thomas Leer LPs

8 The Bridge (Industrial) 1979 An album of industrial ambience upon which furious guitar attack ("Monochrome Day") vied for superiority with the Cabaret Voltaire-esque pulsings of "Interferon." Neither won.

8 Future Historic (Parke) 1999 "Heroes and monsters. A sick thud then forever black." Leer's first assault in 12 years leaves an empty feeling as crushing as *The Bridge*, as brittle as Act, as remote as the future.

Act LP

7 Laughter Tears and Rage (ZTT) 1987 Linking with the incomparable Claudia Brucken, an awkward, icy creation, but one capable of moments of sublime beauty.

LEGENDARY PINK DOTS

FORMED 1981 *(East London, England)*
ORIGINAL LINE-UP *Edward Ka-Spel (vocals); Phillip Knight (keyboards)*

The Legendary Pink Dots were formed at the tail end of the punk era, during that difficult period when the goth and industrial scenes were still struggling to isolate themselves from the new wave's body politik, and the whimsical psychedelic revival which Tanz der Youth so boldly predicted in 1978 was finally taking hold. Isolating the mannerisms, if not the sheer musical genius, of the Barrett-era Pink Floyd, the Soft Boys' Robyn Hitchcock, Julian Cope, even XTC and the Cure's Robert Smith, the Legendary Pink Dots were sitting themselves comfortably cross-legged in the garden of English eccentricity.

The Pink Dots remained wholly out on a limb; they were strange, and they suffered for their strangeness. Following their debut at an east London folk club in October 1980, the group began releasing its music on home-made cassettes, sold at shows. Titles such as *Basilisk*, *Atomic Roses*, *Prayers for Arcadia*, *Apparition*, and the *Chemical Playschool* series would eventually see conventional release on CD in the 1990s; indeed, the band's first album, 1982's *Brighter Now*, too, was simply remixed from an earlier cassette.

Equally confusing was the band's permanently fluctuating line-up; only Edward Ka-Spel and Phillip Knight remained constant, with other musicians not only drifting in and out, but sharing pseudonyms as well. According to Ka-Spel, there was one month long period where he was actually fronting two different versions of the band simultaneously.

Largely overlooked at home, by the mid 1980s, the band had relocated to Amsterdam, Holland, the last surviving bastion of Europe's Stoned Immaculate, not returning their attention westwards until 1987's *Stone Circles* anthology, and the same year's *Tired Eyes* Tear Garden union between Ka-Spel and Canadian industrialists Skinny Puppy, won favorable receptions in both the UK and America.

The band took its first steps towards a settled line-up in 1988, following a wave of defections. Niels Van Hoornblower (horns) and guitarist Bob Pistoor joined shortly before the band's first US tour in 1988; but still the going was tough. Planning their second visit to America, the band believed they needed simply to apply for new work visas when it came time to tour again, following the release of 1990's *The Maria Dimension*.

It turned out that they also needed to have been making better records — the group's visa applications were rejected, Ka-Spel revealed, due to what officialdom deemed "a lack of artistic merit." The following year the band were approved, and Ka-Spel mused, "I can just see them all in the immigration department bopping away under their headphones, going 'ah, those Pink Dots, they've redeemed themselves!'"

Other tours have suffered for other reasons. According to Ka-Spel, he has learned of his own suicide on three separate occasions, including once from an Austrian promoter who refused to book the Pink Dots because he had it on very good authority that their singer was dead! And if it wasn't suicide, it was the persistent legends of his own acid-intake which continued to haunt him. "I don't know why people make up these stories about me!"

Since 1992, the Legendary Pink Dots line-up has remained constant, around Ka-Spel, Knight, and Van Hoornblower, guitarist Martyn de Kloor (enlisted following the death, from cancer, of Pistoor) and Canadian Ryan Moore — who was recruited in Vancouver, BC during the second US tour. This team has overseen a sequence of archive projects; they also headlined a massive (by Dots' standards) show in Mexico City in 1995 in front of 2,500 fans.

Legendary Pink Dots LPs

7 Brighter Now (Inphaze) 1982 Remixed from an earlier cassette release, the starting point in more than simple chronological/discographical terms; the dawn, too, of Ka-Spel's peculiar mythology of apocalypse, fed through an imagination straight out of Narnia.

6 Curse (Inphaze) 1983 "Stoned Obituary" would become a Dots classic, although the album itself is difficult.

6 Tower (Inphaze) 1984 The recurrent title track is the most lasting impression of a haunting, but somewhat downscaled set.

7 The Lovers (Ding Dong) 1985 Pursuing the tarot line, a more cluttered album highlighted by the astonishing "Geisha Mermaid."

6 Asylum (Play It Again Sam) 1985 Even by the Dots' standards, an ambitious set — although it probably didn't really need four sides of vinyl.

6 Island of Jewels (Play It Again Sam) 1986

6 Any Day Now (Play It Again Sam) 1988 Generally regarded as their first genuinely accessible album, with "Laguna Beach" and "The Peculiar Funfare" among several stand-out tracks. But still a morass of eclectic instrumentation and half-sung chants, poised on the most exciting edge of pretension.

7 The Golden Age (Play It Again Sam) 1989 Minimalist electronics accompany a creepy stalker drama.

6 Crushed Velvet Apocalypse (Play It Again Sam) 1990

7 The Maria Dimension (Play It Again Sam) 1991 While the Dots do enjoy disrupting otherwise lovely passages of music with dissonance and drastic sound effects, such devices can be effective, particularly throughout this, the band's most overtly commercial (if still distinctly Dotty) offering.

8 Shadow Weaver (Play It Again Sam) 1992 The opening "Zero Zero" suggests a brighter album than ultimately emerges — "Guilty Man," "Ghosts of Unborn Children," and "Twilight Hour" soon put you right on that score though.

7 Malachai (Shadow Weaver 2) (Play It Again Sam) 1993

8 9 Lives to Wonder (Play It Again Sam) 1994 Despite a guest appearance from Skinny Puppy's Cevin Key, the Dots continue pressing inwards, approaching an impenetrable darkness lightened only by the lunacy.

7 From Here You'll Watch the World Go By (Soleil Moon) 1995

7 It's Raining in Heaven (Soleil Moon) 1996

7 Hallway of the Gods (Soleil Moon) 1997 Impressive double album includes (on vinyl) an amazing live version of "9 Shades," one of the Dots' finest efforts.

8 Nemesis Online (Soleil Moon) 1998

8 Live at the Metro [LIVE] (SPV — Poland) 1999 From Chicago, 11/11/98, some dramatic improvisations and revisions include "Saucers Over Chicago" and "Fate's Faithful Punchline."

7 Farewell, Milky Way [LIVE] (Teka/World Serpent) 1999

Selected Compilations and Archive Releases

9 Stone Circles (Play It Again Sam) 1988 One unreleased track ("Gladiators Version Apocalypse") crowns a strong story-so-far set produced for the US market.

8 Legendary Pink Box (Play It Again Sam) 1991 Stunning three LP compilation, comprising one disc each of rerecordings, old cassette-only cuts, and new material.

6 Canta Mientras Pedas (Play It Again Sam) 1996 Anthology of 1990–95 material.

7 Lullabies for the New Dark Age (Soleilmoon) 1996 4-CD boxed set containing revised versions of earlier albums.

5 Under Triple Moons (Roir) 1997 One of several anthologies of cuts from early cassette releases.

7 Chemical Playschool 10 (Soleilmoon) 1997 Collection of new and unreleased material for sale on 1997 US tour.

Edward Ka-Spel LPs

6 Laugh China Doll (Inphaze) 1984

5 Eyes China Doll (Scarface) 1985

6 Chyekk China Doll (Torso) 1986

6 Aaazhyd China Doll (Torso) 1987

7 Apples (Big!) China Doll (Audiofile) 1987

6 Khataclimici China Doll (Dom) 1988

6 Tanith and the Lion Tree (Third Mind) 1991

5 The Scriptures of Illumina (Terminal Kaleidoscope) 1995

7 The Blue Room (Soleilmoon) 1998

Selected Compilations and Archive Releases

8 Perhaps We'll Only See a Thin Blue Line (Play It Again Sam) 1989 Collection of rarities from 12-inch singles, compilations etc.

7 Lyvv China Doll (Mirrordot) 1990 Live and studio rarities.

7 Down in the City of Heartbreak and Needles (Soleilmoon) 1995

Tear Garden LPs

6 Tired Eyes, Burning Slowly (Nettwerk) 1987 Moody electronics-heavy wash, not amazing but no disgrace either.

7 The Last Man to Fly (Nettwerk) 1992

6 Sheila Liked the Rodeo (Nettwerk) 1993

6 To Be an Angel Blind, the Cripple Soul Divide (Nettwerk) 1996

Selected Compilations and Archive Releases

8 Bouquet of Black Orchids 1993 Anthology of previously released material.

LESS THAN JAKE

FORMED *1992 (Gainesville, FL)*
ORIGINAL LINE-UP *Vinnie Balzano (drums); Chris Neil (guitar); Roger Sixx (bass)*

Founders Vince Balzano and Chris Neil played a handful of shows around their hometown Gainesville with a revolving door of part-timers, before finally recruiting Roger Sixx and a horn section in early 1993. Less Than Jake played what they consider their first show — or at least, their first gig with a sound of their own — in March 1993; according to Neil, "we

discovered a band called Snuff that rocked, which gave me a lot of inspiration, because our stuff without horns pretty much sounds like anybody else. The horns add that little bit to be distinct from everyone else."

Less Than Jake made their initial impact by guesting on as many compilations as they could — by 1998, their infectious punk-pop-ska hybrid had appeared on some 20 different collections, from Moon Ska's *Skarmaggeddon* and Stiff Dog's *Generic Skaca*, through to the *Misfits of Ska* and the *Scream 2* soundtrack, besides releasing a trio of 45s through the tiny Toy Box independent. In addition, the band also joined Asian Man label chief Mike Park in his kung-fu ska inspired B Lee band.

Less Than Jake debuted with the *Better Than Losers* tape, sold through various local record stores, then recorded a full album, *Pezcore*, for release that year through Dill. By the time of Less Than Jake's major label debut in spring 1998, *Pezcore* had sold close to 10,000 copies.

The group's switch to Capitol in 1997 initially provoked some underground hostility; Neil explained, "a lot of bands... say crap about us, call us sellouts... [but] they're sitting on their couch all day taking bong hits. They don't wake up in the morning and think about the band, they don't have the drive, they don't contact the people and try to work out what they have." A track on Less Than Jake's Capitol debut, *Losing Streak*, answered the nay-sayers — "Johnny Quest Thinks We're Sell Outs."

By that time, of course, the group had already proved that no amount of big league patronage could change their original attitude. A clause in their Capitol contract insisted that the A&R man who discovered them had to dress up as the Fonz when attending band functions.

Another guaranteed their freedom to continue gifting tracks to independent labels, even as they worked on their Capitol follow-up, 1998's *Hello Rockview* (#80 US). These included giving No Idea the single, "Rock-and-Roll Pizzeria," and the *Greased* mini-album (comprising eight covers from the famed movie soundtrack); and concocting the *Pesto* EP for Very Small. The band quit Capitol for a full-time return to indy-dom in 2000, signing with Fat Wreck Chords.

Less Than Jake LPs

6 Better Than Losers (No Idea) 1993

8 Pezcore (Dill) 1994 The first album suggested a live band who only recorded their songs to make sure they didn't forget them. The second album proves that a lot are already unforgettable.

8 Losing Streak (Capitol) 1996 Jake's move to a major label was met with trepidation by fans, a wariness which the band acknowledge on the self-mocking "Johnny Quest Thinks We're Sell Outs." But there was no need to worry, the group's loopy humor, party atmosphere, and poppy-punk-ska sound remains unaffected by the big time.

8 Hello Rockview (Capitol) 1998 Coming back better than ever, *Hello* is a shout-out to fans old and new, filled with fourteen new nuggets of high-energy fun time and even more absurd song titles (i.e. "Help Save the Youth of America From Exploding").

7 Live From Uranus [LIVE] (EMI) 1999

Selected Compilations and Archive Releases

8 Losers, Kings, and Things We Don't Understand (No Idea) 1995 Over the years, Jake have appeared on some twenty different compilations, as well as releasing a trio of 45s through the tiny ToyBox independent. Many of these tracks are bundled together here, a must for fan's collections.

JACKIE LEVEN

BORN *6/18/50 (Kirkcaldy, Scotland)*

Although he was a prolific composer and performer, Jackie Leven's earliest recordings would not see UK release until the mid-1990s — a BBC Newcastle radio session in 1969, with bassist Colin Sutter appeared in 1998 as the fan club only EP *St. Judas*; demos recorded during seven summers spent in the Greek islands appeared through the same outlet the following year as *Greek Notebook*.

In 1970, he recorded a full solo album at Mayfair Studios in London, under the name John St. Field — *Control* was released in Spain and Latin America only, and Leven relocated to Madrid that year. Never intending to make a career out of music, however, he was soon dividing his time between Berlin and Dorset, England, where he first linked with Joe Shaw (guitar) and Dave McIntosh (drums); with the addition of Robin Spreafico (bass), the trio moved to London in 1977 and began gigging as Doll by Doll.

With their menacing, angry post-rock sound, Doll by Doll slipped effortlessly into the burgeoning punk scene (whose simultaneous emergence took the band completely by surprise), although it would be two years before they signed a deal, with Warners' Automatic subsidiary. A single, "Palace of Love," was released simultaneously with the band's first album, *Remember*, and Doll by Doll launched their first national tour, supporting Devo. They survived two shows in Scotland, before being replaced by the Members — a group, Devo's management explained, who were far more in tune with Devo's idea of a "small, mindless punk combo."

A new single, "Teenage Lightning," preceded the release of the band's *Gypsy Blood* sophomore set (the title track would also become a 45) in February 1980. However, another major tour, supporting space rock mavens Hawkwind, through December 1979, also ended abruptly.

Buoyed by appearances at the Reading festival and Pink Pop in the Netherlands, Doll by Doll moved to the Magnet label later in the year, and in 1981, enjoyed their biggest success, when the single "Carita" received considerable airplay. However, when their eponymous third album, in May, and the "Main Traveled Roads" 45, failed to make the breakthrough the band were now expecting, Shaw, McIntosh and new bassist Tony Waite quit, leaving Leven to continue Doll by Doll alone. The band's fourth album, *Grand Passion*, was recorded with vocalist Helen Turner (later to collaborate with Paul Weller), and session musicians; a fifth set, *A Last Flick of the Golden Wrench*, went unreleased and Doll by Doll broke up soon after.

Leven moved to Charisma, and between 1982–83, recorded a pair of singles with producer Tom Newman, and a session team including former King Crimson saxophonist Mel Collins and drummer Graham Broad, "Love Is Shining Down on Me" and "Uptown," together with a further mini-album's worth of unreleased material. However, Leven was dropped when Charisma was purchased by Virgin, and further plans were put on hold after a brutal street attack left him with broken ribs and a severely damaged larynx. For a time, it seemed he would be unable to sing again, and a medical regimen which included anabolic steroids seemed only to worsen matters.

Leven turned to heroin for support, but also worked towards curing himself holistically, devising an approach (with his partner, Carol) which proved so successful that it became the basis of the CORE charity (Courage to stop, Order in life, Release from addiction, Entry into new life). This would develop into one of Britain's most successful and respected rehabilitation programs, even attracting the support, and heavy involvement, of Princess Diana.

In 1986, Leven returned to music with a new band, Concrete Bulletproof Invisible, built around former Doll by Doll members Shaw and McIntosh, and ex-Sex Pistols bassist Glen Matlock (who wanted to call the band Doll by Glen). Released through a Yorkshire indy, Radioactive, a single, "Big Tears," became *Melody Maker*'s Single of the Week, but CBI folded, and Leven began working instead with American poet Robert Bly in the so-called "Men's Movement," a calling which saw him become the movement's UK spokesman, and rack up a number of TV chat show appearances.

In 1993, a set of solo demos landed a deal with Cooking Vinyl, and the following year, the album *The Mystery of Love is Greater Than the Mystery of Death* (and single "I Say a Little Prayer") appeared, the first in a cycle of deeply atmospheric, darkly Celtic-tinged releases leading up to 2000's collaboration with David Thomas (Pere Ubu), *Defending Ancient Springs*, featuring a version of "You've Lost That

Loving Feeling." (Leven was previously involved in Thomas' acclaimed *Mirror Man* theatrical project.)

In between times, the EP *Songs From the Argyll Cycle* (1994) combined material from *Mystery* with Mike Scott's spoken word rendition of an Etheridge Knight poem; *The Right to Remain Silent* followed, and became a substantial German hit in 1995. Leven's own Haunted Valley label would also release three live "official bootlegs" during this period, to be sold through his fan club and on the road — in 1998, he played 185 shows; during 1999, he toured Britain three times, plus gigs across the Far East, Europe, and the Mountain Stage in California.

Jackie Leven LPs

⑧ **The Mystery of Love Is Greater Than the Mystery of Death (Cooking Vinyl — UK) 1994** Deservedly one of *Q* magazine's albums of the year, Leven's return found him tainted by his Celtic roots, darkly mysterious and deeply moving.

⑨ **The Forbidden Songs of the Dying West (Cooking Vinyl) 1995** No major stylistic changes, but guest appearances from Mike Scott, Richard Jobson, and Eddi Reader add to the windswept grandeur of the proceedings, while Leven's mountainous vocals soar high over moors even Clannad never imagined.

⑧ **Argyll Cycle (Cooking Vinyl — UK) 1996** No major departures, no major disappointments....

⑦ **For Peace Comes Dropping Slow [LIVE] (Haunted Valley — UK) 1996**

⑦ **Fairy Tales for Hard Men (Cooking Vinyl — UK) 1997** ⑥ **Man Bleeds in Glasgow [LIVE] (Haunted Valley — UK) 1997**

⑥ **Night Lilies (Thirsty Ear) 1999** Leven's weakest, verging at times on self-parody, but worth seeking out if only for the moving "Empty in Soho Square" and the amazing "Deep Choking Wooded Death Fix."

⑥ **The Wanderer (Haunted Valley — UK) 1999**

Jackie Leven/David Thomas LP

⑧ **Defending Ancient Springs (Cooking Vinyl — UK) 2000**

John St. Field LP

⑥ **Control (MCA — Spain) 1971**

Doll by Doll LPs

⑧ **Remember (Automatic) 1979** Although it sounds a lot tamer 20 years later, still Doll by Doll's softly spoken stalker rock has a bitter edge that even Joy Division would learn a little from.

⑦ **Gypsy Blood (Automatic) 1980** Still plowing the same murderous furrow, still rising above the rest of the pack through the strength of the songwriting.

⑥ **Doll by Doll (Magnet) 1981**

⑦ **Grand Passion (Magnet) 1982**

Selected Compilations and Archive Releases

⑧ **Greek Notebook (Haunted Valley — UK) 1999**

LONDON SS

FORMED 1975 *(London, England)*
ORIGINAL LINE-UP Brian James *(guitar)*; Mick Jones *(guitar)*; Tony James *(bass)*

Mick Jones and Tony James first came together in Kings Road haberdasher Malcolm McLaren's planned reformation of the Hollywood Brats — in their prime, the Norwegian answer to the New York Dolls, but doomed to even less commercial notice than their idols. McLaren himself had recently returned to London from the US, and a shortlived stint managing the Dolls themselves; there he encountered Richard Hell, and for a time considered recruiting him to front the new band. When Hell declined, McLaren left Jones and James to his assistant, Bernie Rhodes.

Abandoning the Brats concept, the duo renamed their band the London SS (a name first mooted for the Brats reunion), well aware that the suffix, with its Nazi-era connotations, was guaranteed to create a stir — despite it actually standing for Social Security — the English equivalent of Welfare. With Rhodes obtaining them a rehearsal space in the basement of a steak house in Praed Street, Paddington, the duo then began running weekly ads in *Melody Maker*; one of the earliest recruits was guitarist Brian James, himself fresh out of a Brighton-based dirty-ass rock'n'roll band called Bastard.

Through the glam rock era, Bastard had kept the faith in what Brian James insisted was the only exciting music around, the ghost of the MC5 and its reincarnation as the Pink Fairies. Short, hard, heavy, falling short of metal but certainly gutsier than anything which could even remotely have been called "commercial," Bastard apparently made it quite big in Belgium — which is where they finally broke up. James returned home to read the classifieds, co-guitarist Alistair Ward formed the Dirty Strangers, before rejoining James in a late incarnation of the Lords of the New Church.

In hindsight, the London SS represented what was surely the greatest lost opportunity in rock history. While Tony James exaggerated somewhat when he complained of the "thousands" of people claiming to have been fleeting members of the group, Brian James acknowledged that the queue outside the band's auditions did represent "a fairly good who's who" of British punk.

Chrissie Hynde of the Pretenders, future Clash members Terry "Tory Crimes" Chimes, Topper Headon and Paul Simenon, Chris "Rat Scabies" Miller, Matt Dangerfield and Casino Steel of the Boys (and themselves founder members of the original Hollywood Brats) all filed through, and with so much in-and-outing, it is ironic that the only person outside of the James-Jones-James gang to have had any longevity within the SS went on to do precisely nothing else of musical note, drummer Roland Hot. "He kept these at warm for three or four weeks," Brian James punned, adding that it was during Hot's tenure that the SS recorded their first, and only, demo, a couple of MC5 songs, and a Mick Jones number called "Protex Blue." (The song would subsequently reappear on the Clash's debut album; another SS standard, Brian James' "Fish," would be rerecorded for the first Damned LP.)

It was not the London SS's line-up which fascinated, however, so much as what its line-up represented. When Jones and Tony James first came together they were united primarily in their love for Mott the Hoople, the archetypal Nowhere Bar Band Made Astonishingly Good, and even when Brian James first met them, the pair still boasted long frizzy haircuts to match.

Moving ever closer into McLaren's orbit, however, and with Rhodes an ever-present task-master, the members' vision began to refine itself, and with that refining came the understanding that it was not music itself which was the issue, it was the attitude with which that music could be created. By mid-1976, Brian James was gigging with the Damned, Tony James was rehearsing with Chelsea, and Mick Jones was forming the Clash. They'd both got their hair cut as well.

Also see the entries for the "CLASH" on page 270, the "DAMNED" on page 311, and "GENERATION X" on page 389.

LONDON SUEDE

FORMED 1992 (London, England)
ORIGINAL LINE-UP Brett Anderson (vocals); Bernard Butler (guitar); Mat Osman (bass)

Suede grew out of a bedroom band called Geoff, formed by Brett Anderson, Mat Osman, vocalist Gareth Perry and drummer Danny Wilder in the late 1980s. Written off by Anderson as "sounding like nothing on earth... it probably sounded like Minipops, or something like that," Geoff recorded two demos then collapsed when Anderson and Osman moved to London in 1989.

Recruiting Bernard Butler from an NME ad calling for "a nonmuso guitarist," the pair formed a new band, Suave and Elegant, which became Suede around the same time they purchased a drum machine.

The group's first priority was to record an entire album's worth of demos, Specially Suede, and when the local GLR radio DJ Gary Crowley launched a talent contest for new bands, Suede entered one track from the set, "Wonderful Sometimes." In a competition judged by listeners' telephone votes, Suede won five weeks running, and in April 1990, the song was included on a cassette-only compilation of unsigned acts released by the Powerhaus club.

A second guitarist, Justine Frischmann, was introduced, but attempts to replace the drum machine were less successful, even after the band began negotiating with the newly-launched Brighton based RML label. That deal, too, was a non-starter from the beginning; RML were insisting Suede sign up for seven albums, Suede weren't even sure that they wanted to commit to a single. RML did provide sufficient studio time for the band to record two songs, "Be My God" (featuring drummer Justin Welch, who would later join Frischmann in Elastica) and "Art" (produced by and featuring former Smiths drummer Mike Joyce), but no more than a handful of white label 12" singles were ever produced.

Drummer Simon Gilbert was finally recruited through the band's manager in April 1991. Suede were his thirteenth band, and before the audition, Gilbert resolved, "this is the last band I'm ever going to play with. If I don't make it with this one, then I'm going to give up." Indeed, in a career which stretched back to his early teens, only once had Gilbert made it onto record, when his second group, Dead to the World, found their way onto the 1980 compilation *Bullshit Detector Volume One*.

Overcoming Frischmann's departure to form Elastica in October, Suede spent the next year rehearsing four or five hours every night, occasionally interrupting their schedule for what Gilbert called "crappy little gigs playing to one person. And it went on like that for a few months, and then all of a sudden our gigs were packed. I don't know what happened, but we suddenly became very hip."

Madness were early supporters; so was Morrissey, who later included the still unsigned Suede's "My Insatiable One" in his live set. By early 1992, Suede were recording demos for Island and East West, but when they finally signed a deal, it was with the independent Nude label. They celebrated by having their pictures taken for a *Melody Maker* story, and Gilbert remembered, "we expected to be on page 25 or something. So I went to the newsstand to get it in the morning, and there it was on the fucking front cover!"

Suede's first single, "The Drowners" (#49 UK) arrived a month later; it was followed in September by "Metal Mickey" (#17 UK), the cue for Britain to go Suede mad. By the end of the year, Suede had featured on 19 different magazine covers in the UK alone.

"I think for quite a while there, there hadn't been a decent British band, there really wasn't," Anderson mused. "The last decent band had been the Stone Roses, and then a whole bunch of people copied all the most obvious things about it and made crappy records." Now Suede came along with a brand new sound, a whole new look, and alongside the Auteurs, the blueprint, in fact, for what would soon be titled "Brit-pop" by a slavering media. How could they fail?

"Animal Nitrate" (#7) arrived in February 1993; two months later, Suede's eponymous debut album (#1 UK) became the fastest selling debut album in British chart history (an honor subsequently claimed first by Oasis, then Frischmann's Elastica).

"So Young" (#22 UK) and a sold-out UK tour were followed by barnstorming European and Japanese outings, leaving America alone immune to Suede's charms — as the band discovered when they visited that fall. Having headlined the Glastonbury Festival in England immediately before crossing the Atlantic, the band now found itself confronted with a date sheet full of half-full clubs, and a local media which was as suspicious of this latest Next Big Brit Thing as the UK media was welcoming. *Rolling Stone* summed up the general mood by electing Suede "hype of the year" in its year end polls.

Suede's frustrations were further exacerbated by an east coast performance artist who had already claimed the name "Suede" for herself, and was prepared to go to court to retain it. Suede — or London Suede, as they would henceforth be known in the US — would never again devote themselves to a full-length American tour.

With most of 1993 having been spent on the road, and any hopes of releasing a new album still months away, Suede opened 1994 with a new single, "Stay Together" (#3 UK) on Valentines' Day. But whereas Suede should have been celebrating, they were, in fact, falling apart.

The new album was being recorded on a knife's edge. Tensions within the band, notably between Anderson and Butler, were arising at every turn; both men saw themselves, in one way or another, as the band's heart — Anderson the widely-feted new rock god; Butler the unopposed heir to the guitar slinger's throne once occupied by the Smiths' Johnny Marr. Somehow the conflict was kept out of the media; somehow, too, Suede were able to maintain sufficient poise to release, and promote, a new single in September, the apocalyptic "We Are the Pigs" (#18 UK).

The following month, however, the entire situation exploded. Even as the alternately delicate and grandiose *dog man star* (#3 UK), Suede's second album, hit the streets, Butler hit the road.

His departure stunned the country, and Suede's immediate demise was not simply predicted, it was guaranteed. *dog man star*, an album which ordinarily would have confirmed Suede's ascendancy, was all but overlooked amidst the obitu-

aries, and Suede's own insistence that the band would continue were written off along with their masterpiece.

In fact, the band began auditioning for a new guitarist within days of Butler's departure, finally selecting 17-year-old Richard Oakes on the strength of a tape full of perfectly played Suede covers. Oakes made his live debut at a secret fanclub show in London on October 10, and three days later, he was playing to 4,000 people in Sweden, recording a radio concert. The band followed up with an eight date UK tour in November, in support of a new single, "The Wild Ones" (#18 UK); they would tour again in the spring, alongside the "New Generation" (#21 UK) single.

Despite playing well-received shows in the US, and a handful of UK festivals that summer, the band maintained a low profile throughout much of the rest of 1995, but Oakes' calm assurance when they did surface proved that they had not simply recovered from Butler's departure; they had been reinvigorated by it.

A guest appearance on the *Warchild* charity album, performing Elvis Costello's plaintive "Shipbuilding," broke Suede's silence, and in late 1995, the band — now swollen to a five piece by the recruitment of Gilbert's cousin, keyboardist Neil Codling — began work on their third album, *Coming Up* (#1 UK).

Although Suede premiered much of the new material at a fanclub show in January 1996, it would be July before the first single,"Trash" (#3 UK), was released, and a month more before *Coming Up* joined it. The band's most successful album yet, *Coming Up* sold over 1.4 million worldwide and spawned three further singles — "Beautiful Ones" (#8 UK), "Saturday Night" (#6 UK), and "Lazy" (#9 UK), all three trailing sufficient B-sides to create an entire new album, revealed in 1997 as one-half of the *Sci FiLullabies* (#9 UK) rarities collection.

Having recorded their three previous sets with former Psychedelic Furs keyboard player Ed Bueller, the recruitment of Perfecto mainman Steve Osborne to oversee their next album immediately dictated an abrupt change in style for the band, as Anderson cautioned towards the end of the sessions.

"It does sound pretty different. Steve's good with electronics and stuff, and we're using a lot more. I don't think the basics of it are different, it's still songs and dynamics, but the sound is different. A lot of the stuff is almost deliberately not what we normally do, it's quite cold, quite cool, not too passionate. We know how to do the big chorus, the sing-along end, we wanted to do something a bit cooler, a bit smaller scale."

Still, the first single, "Electricity" (#5 UK) remained indisputably Suede, while the *Head Music* album (#1 UK) proved that any other changes had not dented the group's popularity. Subsequent singles "She's in Fashion" (#13 UK), and "Everything Must Flow" all followed suit, with the latter making surprising inroads into the US dance chart.

Although the band would not visit the US, the accompanying world tour lasted into fall 1999, including a string of dates in Asia marred both by natural disasters and by Codling being diagnosed with exhaustion — he missed a handful of shows, while the UK music press mused the so-called "Curse of Suede"; he recovered to begin work on the band's fifth album in the new year, following the final *Head Music* show in Israel in late January.

London Suede LPs

9 Suede (Columbia) 1993 Ooh those vocals, wow that guitar, the androgynous cover, and oh, the songs... all sex and drugs and surreal imagery... meet Suede, who've just reinvented pop. Heralded with a string of cataclysmic singles — "So Young," "Animal Nitrate," "Metal Mickey," and "The Drowners" are all intact — then following through with further visions of darkness and disgrace Roxy Morrissey style, Suede didn't simply kickstart Britpop. They kicked British pop to its most invigorating high in years.

10 dog man star (Columbia) 1995 Portentous, pretentious, and a more than casual dry run for a future full of limp-wristed Britpop glamor pusses, Suede's sophomore album was Mission Impossible — how to follow-up a debut (*Suede*) which had already been acknowledged as the Second Coming?

Easy — crown it with the First Departure. Guitarist Bernard Butler quit within days of *dog man star*'s arrival, muttering darkly that his vision had been totalled. But it's hard to see what he means — through "We Are the Pigs," "This Hollywood Life," "Daddy's Speeding"... speeding indeed through the E-drenched detritus of a post-Bowie apocalypse, the darkest side of glam, and so edgy that it itched. It also made even more people wonder, how were they going to follow this one?

The stark *Coming Up* answered that question, as Brett Anderson pointed out. "After *dog man star*, everyone thought we were gonna do an operetta, or something like that. But you get things out of your system." Speak for yourself.

8 Coming Up (Columbia) 1997 Sans Butler, Suede resurface edgier than ever, their previous lush production hardened by Codling's sharp electronic fission, and dictated by the demands of "Trash," a boiling epitaph for doomed lovers everywhere. "Saturday Night" is so sexy it's surreal and though the rest of the set does falter in places, its high points more than compensate.

8 Head Music (Columbia) 1999 A new page? A new book. Departing regular producer Ed Buller for dance supremo Steve Osborne, Suede turn in an album high on electronics, but higher still on their musical freedom. Too much, sadly, falls by the wayside, unfulfilled even with regular listens, but again at its best, *Head Music* is savage, from the opening "Electricity," through the dreamy dance smash "Everything Will Flow" and onto the frankly surreal "Elephant Man."

Selected Compilations and Archive Releases

9 Sci Fi Lullabies (Columbia) 1998 Rampant B-sides collection which just happens to include two of Suede's best ever songs, "Killing of a Flash Boy" and "Europe Is Our Playground."

Bernard Butler LPs

7 The Sound of Mcalmont & Butler [WITH DAVID MCALMONT] (Gyroscope) 1995 Sweet '70s soul subverting everything the multi-instrumentalist Butler can throw at it, as McAlmont emotes to his heart's content. But Bernard is still glancing over his shoulder, desperate not to sound Suede-like for a second. The album works, but he could work harder.

8 People Move On (Columbia) 1998 We knew he could play guitar some; now he proves he can sing some as well. The opening "Woman I Know" borrows busloads of *Abbey Road*, but as the man who helped blueprint Britpop, if he can't bite the Beatles, who can? There are elements of Suede aboard, but there's just as much Neil Young and most of the songs fall midway. Plus "Autograph" is to pyrotechnic volume what Marilyn Manson is to the cosmetics industry.

6 Friends and Lovers (Columbia) 1999 Considerably more mature and, in parts, less satisfying set, recorded with a full band rather than the lonely tinkering of *People Move On*, and occasionally raising hell instead of heartbeats. More than competent, but less than expected.

Further Reading

The Illustrated Biography by York Membery (Omnibus, UK, 1996).

LONG BEACH DUB ALL-STARS

FORMED 1997 (*Los Angeles, CA*)
ORIGINAL LINE-UP *Opie Oritz (vocals); Jack Maness (keyboards); RAS-1 (guitar); Tim Wu (sax); Eric Wilson (bass); Bud Gaugh (drums); Marshall Goodman (percussion)*

Fast rising Los Angeles dub-punk trio Sublime had just completed their third and likely breakthrough album *Sublime*, when vocalist Brad Nowell died from a heroin overdose on May 25, 1996. Bandmates Eric Wilson and Bud Gaugh dissolved the group on the spot, resurfacing eight months later as the Long Beach Dub All-Stars, at the Enough Already benefit concert arranged (by themselves) as a benefit for the Musicians' Assistance Program and the Jacob James Nowell Scholarship fund, established for Nowell's young son.

The All-Stars were originally intended simply as a Sublime tribute band, playing a handful of shows for fans who missed the real thing. Several of the musicians had been involved with Sublime in the past — Jack Maness guested on their debut *40 oz to Freedom* album; Field Marshall Goodman was programmer and scratcher; Opie Oritz designed their album art, and the bandmembers' tattoos. When reaction to the shows convinced the septet to remain together, *Sublime* co-producer Miguel Happoldt, too, was recruited.

Recorded in early 1999, *Right Back* (#67 US) continued the earlier band's fascination with hip-hop, punk, and dub, and featured guest appearances from Tippa Irie, Barrington Levy, Bad Brains' vocalist HR and Pennywise guitarist Fletcher. Released as the band launched a major US tour, the "Trailer Ras" video gave a directorial debut to Bill Henderson.

Long Beach Dub All-Stars LPs

9 Right Back 1999 A continuation of the pair's fascination with musical crossovers. Few of the songs are proper dubs although reggae beats do power the album (bar the bit where the band breaks into hardcore), and considerably more laid back than Sublime ever were. But what is lost in punky dishevelment is more than repaid in atmosphere.

Sublime LPs

8 40oz to Freedom (Skunk) 1992 At heart, Sublime are a white reggae band, saddled with influences from rock and hip-hop to hardcore. The schizophrenia is initially revealed through covers as disparate as the Grateful Dead and Bad Religion, but the ensuing musical chaos is vibrant — a succession of classic songs surrounded by a myriad of musical touchstones.

7 Robbin' the Hood (MCA) 1994 This time around, dub predominates, the heavy, heavy beats the perfect backdrop for Sublime's electic tastes — and ever more bizarre rants and vocal samples. At times frustrating, at times just hilarious, *Hood* may try your patience (the rants are only funny once), but the negatives are overwhelmed by Sublime's frequent flashes of brilliance.

7 Sublime (MCA) 1996 Moving onto a major label forced the band to focus, and while long-time fans would inevitably miss the careening chaos of their indie releases, stripped of the more extraneous elements, Sublime not only emerge as a commercially viable band (who knew?), but a damned good one at that. Still an innovative hybrid, the songs are cleaner, clearer, and stronger and the only (minor) flaws are the melancholy tone of much of the album and the lyrical pessimism which permeates the songs. Still, few bands end on such a high note.

Selected Compilations and Archive Releases

6 Second Hand Smoke (MCA) 1997 Following the *What I Got* live and rarities EP, a full length collection of *Sublime* album out-takes, including Bob Marley's "Trenchtown Rock" and a remixed "Saw Red."

7 Stand by Your Van [LIVE] 1998 Mainly recorded in San Francisco in September, '94, *Live* goes a long way towards making sense of the trio's splatter approach to music, as the rhythm section valiantly provides a rhythmic framework for guitarist/singer Nowell to bounce off.

6 Greatest Hits (MCA) 1999 Ten-track sampler featuring "What I Got" and the Gwen Stefani duet "Saw Red" — that's the album title justified, now let's throw on a random selection of other cuts.

LOOKOUTS

FORMED 1985 (*Mendocino, CA*)
ORIGINAL LINE-UP *Larry Livermore (vocals, guitar); Kevin Kong (bass); Tre Cool (b. Frank Edwin Wright III — drums)*

Stalwarts of Berkeley's Gilman Street punk scene through the late 1980s, Larry Livermore's Lookouts were formed out of the 30-something guitarist's realization that if he didn't start the band he'd been dreaming of now, he never would. With a line-up completed by his then-girlfriend and a neighbor's junior high school kid, Kevin Kong, the band was further disadvantaged by location, in the Mendocino mountains, 45 dirt road minutes from the nearest town.

The girlfriend quit; she was replaced by another neighborhood kid, 12-year-old Tre Cool (a name dreamed up by Livermore), and the Lookouts debuted live in the summer of '85 at a campground on the side of the Highway 101. A tiny crowd gathered before an appalled onlooker unplugged the band.

At that point, Livermore was lead vocalist, but eventually all three members would share the mike. Other changes were equally dramatic, as Livermore surrendered his original domination of the songwriting, Kong and Cool updating Livermore's '60s aesthetic until the band's folk-punk approach earned its ultimate accolade — Dylan meets MDC.

Finally leaving the mountain, The Lookouts played their first Bay Area show in late 1985 and the following fall, they recorded their debut album, *One Planet, One People*. It was released, in the spring of 1987, on Livermore's own Lookout Records, a slowly gestating concern building around the simultaneously burgeoning Gilman Street scene. *Spy Rock Road*, the band's sophomore set, followed in 1989, by which time Lookout was firmly established as the area's leading punk outlet.

The *Mendocino Homeland* EP followed, but in the new year the band began to disintegrate. Kong was attending Humboldt State University in Arcata, California, Cool had passed his high school equivalency test and moved down to Berkeley where he was attending community college. But Livermore remained on the mountain. In different cities, the band members inevitably began drifting apart.

In June 1990, The Lookouts got together to record their farewell, the *IV* EP, and a clutch of songs gifted to sundry compilations. Three months later, Cool joined Green Day.

Also see the entry for "LOOKOUT RECORDS" on page 794 in "PRODUCERS & LABELS."

The Lookouts LPs

5 One Planet, One People (Lookout) 1987 "Not a very good record, some of the songs are pretty interesting, but we did a badly hashed version. We were trying too hard to be punk." — Larry Livermore

8 Spy Rock Road (Lookout) 1989 A long way from the formative first album, *Spy* boasts a diversity of style, from the slow stomper of "Red Sea" to the catchy "Living Behind Bars" with its strong melody and harmonic chorus. Tempo also varied dramatically from rapid-fire speed core to slower paced numbers like "Trees," while Livermore's guitar parts became equally adventurous.

LORDS OF THE NEW CHURCH

FORMED 1981 (London, England)
ORIGINAL LINE-UP *Stiv Bators (b. 1949, Youngstown, OH — vocals); Brian James (guitar); Dave Treganna (bass); Nicky Turner (drums)*

Stiv Bators and Brian James first met when the latter's Damned traveled to New York to make their debut at CBGBs in early 1977, and again when Bators' Dead Boys went to England to open for the Damned's *Music for Pleasure* tour later in the year.

Both bands broke up with the end of the decade. James launched into a series of solo projects, fronting such outfits as Tanz Der Youth, the Hellions, and Brian James' Brains; he also toured America with Iggy Pop. Bators, meanwhile, recorded a solo album, the pop classic *Disconnected*, before linking with the recently shattered remnants of Sham 69 in the Wanderers.

That band released one album, the darkly conspiratorial *Only Lovers Left Alive*, then broke up. Bators, now based in London, promptly linked with James and in early 1981, the pair began rehearsing with former Generation X bassist Tony James and ex-Clash drummer Terry Chimes, with Tony James leaving two great songs behind when he moved on a few weeks later, "Russian Roulette" and "Black Girl/White Girl."

Chimes, too, quit and by the summer of 1981, Wanderers bassist Dave Treganna and former Raincoats/Barracudas drummer Nicky Turner were in place. Just weeks before the quartet made their live debut, in Paris in late spring 1982, the band was named the Lords of the New Church — "it's a sort of swipe at Born Again Christians," Bators explained. "[Our manager] wanted to call us the Lords of Discipline; I liked the Lords bit, it put me in mind of a New York street gang. Then one day we were talking about religion, and how rock'n'roll has come to replace it in many ways, how it's like a New Church, and I just thought — the Lords of the New Church."

Two singles, "New Church" (#34 UK indy) and "Open Your Eyes" (#7 UK indy), previewed the band's eponymous debut album (#3 UK indy), a devastating statement which

Courtesy of Dave Thompson

attacked everything from organized religion in general, to Pope John Paul II's forthcoming world tour in particular. With Bators' imagination fuelled by a pre-internet network of conspiracy theorists, songs like "Apocalypso," "Open Your Eyes," "Living On Living," (about the faking of Jim Morrison's death) and the Coppola tribute "Russian Roulette" (#12 UK indy) found a ready audience among the disenfranchised post-punks of Margaret Thatcher's Britain.

The tribal identity which the Lords created around their name, their dress, and their lyrics, too, ensured that, for the first time since the Sex Pistols' original Bromley Contingent fanbase, a band had succeeded in grafting its own identity onto its audience without first paying obeisance to the gods of highstreet fashion.

Early in 1983, the Lords linked with producer Todd Rundgren to begin work on a new album. In fact, the union produced just one cut, a majestic cover of oldies radio favorite "Live for Today"; the Lords self-produced the remainder of *Is Nothing Sacred?* and came close to a hit with the infectious "Dance with Me" — until MTV pulled the Derek Jarman-directed video following accusations of child pornography.

The band responded by pinpointing one of America's own favorite sexual icons and lambasting her — Madonna, after all, never seemed to have her videos banned, not even when, as Bators once accused, "she does everything short of screwing the camera lens." Unfortunately, the Lords' version of "Like a Virgin" (#22 UK indy) was only ever released in Britain (over a year later, in early 1985), following the band's sadly rushed third album, *Method to Our Madness* (#158 US).

A new single, TV Smith's "The Lord's Prayer," was recorded with Miami Steve Van Zandt, but cancelled (the track eventually appeared on the *Killer Lords* compilation — #22 UK indy); by 1986, the Lords were surviving on live work alone.

In a bid to broaden the sound, James recruited second guitarist Alistair Ward, with whom he'd worked a decade previous in Bastard. However, the band was already in shreds. Treganna quit to join Cherry Bombz with Hanoi Rocks' Andy McCoy and Toto Coelo vocalist Anita Hahadervan. (A decade later, he resurfaced in Dog Kennel Hill, alongside Quireboys vocalist Guy Bailey.) He was replaced in the Lords by Grant Flemyng, Sham 69's old road manager, but no sooner was he settled in than Turner, too, departed to work with manager Miles Copeland's L.A.-based IRS label.

The Lords were dead, but they couldn't die. With drummer Danny, the band booked a European tour hoping to earn sufficient money to pay off a massive tax bill. They played ten shows in Spain before Bators quit.

Desperate to salvage the tour, the vacant position was offered to Jim Jones of Thee Hypnotics; he turned them down, and the band advertised for a new vocalist in *Melody Maker*. Nobody suitable came forward, however, and with the European dates finally abandoned, Bators agreed to return for one final show, in London in mid-1989. Then, resplendent in a home-made T-shirt emblazoned with the *Melody Maker* ad, he performed the last rites on the band, walking up to each member in turn, and telling them, "you're sacked." Then he walked offstage, never to return.

Bators moved to Paris, while planning a new band, the Whores of Babylon, with Dee Dee Ramone and former Dead Boy Cheetah Chrome; he died following a traffic accident, 6/4/90. James, too, relocated to France, reuniting with former Brian James Brains vocalist Alan Lee Shaw for the *Brian James* album; he subsequently formed a new band, Dripping Lips, before cutting his second solo album in L.A. in late 1999, with Blondie drummer Clem Burke, The Police's Stewart Copeland, and Duff McKagen of Guns n'Roses.

Lords of the New Church LPs

🎵 Lords of the New Church (IRS) 1982 If you have to stare the future in the face, "New Church" still stares right back at you. A defiant statement of conspiratorial intent, dire warnings heaped upon self-mythologizing madness, and a clarion call for the revolution which may still be just round the corner — "spanners in the works, go start your gang."

🎵 Is Nothing Sacred? (IRS) 1983 No one expected it, but with a second album as good as their first, the Lords suggested they were around for the long haul. True, "Tale of Two Cities" merely rewrote its predecessors' "Holy War," but the loping "Dance with Me" and soaring "Live for Today" bookended "World Without End," impassioned percussion and exhortation; "The Night Is Calling" — tenderness and virtue; and the nastier than nihilism of "Bad Timing." Solid and still super-smart.

🎵 Method to Our Madness (IRS) 1984 Too much, too soon. With no time on the road to write new songs, the Lords cruised through a no-surprises potpourri of darkness, disgrace, and civilization down the pan, spewed across titles like "Fresh Flesh," "Seducer," and the piano-sweet "When the Blood Runs Cold." Getting clichéd, then, but "Murder Style" flirts with post-modern funk, and l'il boys still play with Dolls.

🎵 Live at the Spit (Illegal) 1988 Dramatic in-concert set recorded in Boston and capturing most of the magic.

Selected Compilations and Archive Releases

🎵 Killer Lords (IRS) 1985 One for collectors who forgot to collect and, even when packed with B-sides and out-takes, the Lords burn with a passion which few other infant terribles could muster.

Stiv Bators/Dead Boys LPs

8 Young Loud and Snotty (Sire) 1977 The album which gave the world "Sonic Reducer." All attitude and aggression, the Dead Boys' scorching debut's blast of fiery punk was just as hot as that exploding on the other side of the Atlantic. What got lost in the ensuing debate over look, lyrics, and whether the mix was any good was the awesome scorching guitars, the haunting melodies, and pusillanimous pop mixed amidst the garage fury.

8 We Have Come for Your Children (Sire) 1978 More controlled and better sounding, *Children*'s production throws unexpected light on the band's dichotomous styles. The poppy numbers are even punchier, the harder-edged songs sizzle, and the darkly atmospheric ones (most notably "Son of Sam" and "Ain't It Fun") are mini-masterpieces of tension and ominous foreboding.

7 Night of the Living Dead Boys [LIVE] (Bomp) 1981 Documenting four March 1979 CBGBs shows (the 1990s reissue appends five tracks from their final "reunion" gig at the Ritz in April 1987). The sound's mediocre and three tracks are poor covers, but for all that, the record still does justice to the chaos, fun, and fury of the band's live performances. Plus, it's worth the pain for the searing "Sonic Reducer" and an all too poignant "Ain't It Fun."

Selected Compilations and Archive Releases

6 Younger Louder Snottier — The Rough Mixes (Necrophilia) 1989 Oft-reissued original mix of the band's debut album — more raw and closer to the band's live sound, but much too trebly.

2 Twistin' on the Devil's Fork [LIVE] (Bacchus) 1997 Absurdly poor quality live recording.

3 All This and More (Bomp) 1998 Chronologically confused album catches the Dead Boys in San Francisco in November, '77, and at three CBGB's gigs in April and August, '77 and March '78. The sound ranges from tinny-but-tolerable to utterly atrocious (the SF tracks are so muddy as to be worthless) and, even at its best, *All* is like hearing the band playing three floors down and four doors away.

Stiv Bators LP

9 Disconnected (Bomp) 1979 Dramatic, and utterly unexpected pop nugget offering from the former Dead Boys vocalist — how did he get from one to another? Equal parts '60s garage ("A Million Miles Away") and '70s suburbia ("I'm an Evil Boy"), Bators' passion for power pop at times outweighs even the best of the Boys' output.

Stiv Bators & Dave Treganna/Wanderers LP

7 Only Lovers Left Alive (Polydor) 1980 Neck deep in muddy waters, a semi-concept album built around the news bulletins of one Dr. Peter Beter, an American conspiracist whose regular cassette mailings were one of Bators' greatest joys. Much of the play-

ing has a distinctly post-punk tiredness to it, with the vocals alone geeing it along — Bators single-handedly carries the Dylan cover along, but a handful of tracks predict both the power and the diversity which the Lords would make their own.

Brian James LP

7 Brian James (New Rose) 1990 Reprising tracks dating back to his early '80s club days, then stretching forward to a future which Guns n'Roses only dreamed of subpoena-ing, this is the true sound of the rock'n'roll animal, playing guitar like a man on the run and only a few dodgy lyrics to spoil the show.

Dripping Lips LP

7 Ready to Crack (Bomp) 1997 Produced by former Stones overseer Jimmy Miller, and rooted in the same savage blues that were that band's coolest calling card, *Ready* makes no concessions to contemporary taste or decency. But anyone whose tastes stretch back to Gene Vincent, then on to the Stooges, will know precisely where the Lips are coming from.

Cherry Bombz LP

6 Coming Down Slow (High Dragon) 1987

Dog Kennel Hill LP

5 Sweethearts of the Rodeo (Whitelight) 1999

LOVE AND ROCKETS

FORMED 1984 *(London, England)*
ORIGINAL LINE-UP *Daniel Ash (b. 7/31/57, Northampton — vocals, guitar); David J (b. David Haskins, 4/24/57, Northampton — vocals, bass); Kevin Haskins (b. 7/19/56, Northampton — drums)*

Following the break-up of Bauhaus, all four members plunged immediately into new projects: vocalist Peter Murphy's shortlived Dali's Car, Ash and Haskins' Tones On Tail; J's collaborations with long time friend Jazz Butcher (aka Pat Fish). For the latter three, however, the separation was only temporary — they had already proven their own individual chemistry during the creation of the final Bauhaus album, *Burning From the Inside*, and by late 1984, the trio were rehearsing together, with a full band reunion in mind.

In the event, Murphy declined, but Ash, J and Haskins continued playing, catalyzing the following spring with a version of the Temptations' "Ball of Confusion" — one of J's all time favorite records. The band had already decided they wanted to relaunch themselves with a cover; with lyrics which were as pertinent to the mid-80s as they ever were to the '60s when it was originally written, "Ball of Confusion" fit the bill.

Weeks later, even as Love and Rockets — named for the Jaime and Gilbert Hernandez underground comic — were putting the finishing touches to their debut album, their debut single was tearing up every preconception a watching public might have had.

The mantric "If There's a Heaven Above" followed "Ball of Confusion" in September 1985 with *Seventh Dream of Teenage Heaven* arriving soon after. Eschewing the UK, Love and Rockets then made their live debut at Boston's Spit in September 1985 — they would, in fact, tour the US three times over the next year, while playing just two shows in the UK.

The strategy paid off however. Even without a domestic release for *Seventh Dream*, word spread fast, and by the time Love and Rockets' sophomore album, *Express* (#72 US), was ready for its September 1986, release, demand was at fever pitch. The album ultimately spent more than six months on the US chart, the singles "Kundalini Express" and "Yin and Yang" were college hits.

1988's *Earth-Sun-Moon* (#64 US), Love and Rockets' third album, typically presented listeners with a very different experience. Ash explained, "we did an electric album on *Express*. So then we said, 'let's do a strumming-guitars-in-the-country album!'" Still, the singles "Lazy," "No New Tale to Tell," and "Mirror People" streamed into college rotation, while the band also unleashed one of the most preposterous alter-egos in rock history, the bumble-bee bodied Bubblemen, whose cartoon visages were scribbled all over the liner notes for *Earth-Sun-Moon*, and who now unveiled their own single, "The Bubblemen Are Coming."

Love and Rockets themselves returned in January 1989 with the *Motorcycle* EP, cacophonous and electronic, guitar-driven and synth-laden, an intense combination of house meets the industrial nation cracked by Ash's scaling saxophone. It was followed that spring by "So Alive" (#3 US), a massive hit which inevitably hauled its parent album, *Love and Rockets* (#14 US), and the follow-up "No Big Deal" (#82 US) with it. Before Depeche Mode, before the Cure, before any of the acts who would soon be queueing to clog MTV's late night *120 Minutes* alternative video showcase, Love and Rockets took a mighty mouthful of mainstream America. And the taste almost killed them.

In the past, Love and Rockets had never undertaken anything longer than a two week tour. Now they had 45 theater shows mapped out for them between June and September, and climaxing with the chance to head out again in the fall, this time headlining stadiums. It was tempting, J reflected, "being offered huge amounts of money. But it just didn't feel right." Already the three band members could barely stand to be in the same room as one another. Another tour would

tear them apart completely. Instead, they announced they were taking a year off, to pursue other options.

In hindsight, Love and Rockets ended there and then. Of course, the band would regroup three years later, once Ash and J had both got their solo dreams out of their system, but from the outset, their reunion in 1992 was doomed. Subverting the sound of *Love and Rockets* in techno-trimmed electronics, keeping up the band's career long tradition of changing with every record without a single backward glance, the band completed some 70% of their projected new album, then played it to their US label, RCA. It was thrown back in their faces. "They couldn't see the single," J recalled, "they couldn't hear the guitars, they didn't know what we were doing. So they let us go."

Stunned, Love and Rockets came to a shuddering halt. J recorded a new solo album and toured with Jazz Butcher; Ash released his "traditional rock guitar" album *Foolish Thing Desire*. It would be eight months before the band were ready to reconvene, reworking the tapes into something at least approaching a compromise between the music they were making, and the music their audience expected; then, signing with Rick Rubin's American label, they delivered *Hot Trip to Heaven*.

While the *Body and Soul* EP foundered, *Hot Trip* sank like a stone, and for precisely the reasons RCA said it would. Love and Rockets' UK label, Beggars Banquet, didn't even bother releasing the album, so far removed from reality did it seem, and no matter that events elsewhere over the next three years would see the band's dream borne out in shattering commercial style, at the time, Ash mused, "we completely lost faith."

Love and Rockets' attempts to hit back quickly with a new, guitar-driven album were derailed when the house where they were recording was destroyed by fire. Instruments and tapes were lost, to be followed by their US label's patience. The band's recording budget was frozen, and while they finally completed the album in what Ash described as a friend's garage, *Sweet FA* (#172 US) emerged in 1996 as Love and Rockets' most fragmented, and unsatisfying album yet. An EP led off by the title track flopped in the UK, and the band's UK and US recording contracts followed it into the dumper soon after.

There would be one final Love and Rockets album. Signing to Red Ant, the group began working from some jam sequences which had emerged on stage during their last American tour, in the aftermath of *Sweet FA*.

Lift, a middle ground of sorts between its two predecessors, would appear in 1998, on the heels of that summer's Bauhaus reunion tour, and for a moment it looked as though the misfortunes of the five years had been put behind them. But "Resurrection Hex," the first single, never got beyond the cursory airplay stage, and in April 1999, at the conclusion of their latest tour, Love and Rockets broke up.

Love and Rockets LPs

10 Seventh Dream of Teenage Heaven (Beggars Banquet UK) 1985 Conceived at a time when the psychedelic dance craze of the late 1980s was still years away chronologically and light years away in terms of intent, *7th Dream* plopped into the decade like nothing else on earth.

Its components, '60s acid and '70s flash, were twisted, teased, and torn out of context; Bauhaus had hinted at similar plots, but they were only hints and besides, that band carried baggage which could never be unpacked. Love and Rockets represented a new start and not only for the musicians. Over the next five years, the stoned computers would go into overdrive, but nothing, not even the joyous Sigue Sigue Sputnik, could have breathed if *7th Dream* hadn't first filled the room with oxygen.

The club hit "Ball of Confusion" sets the scene, historically dated but ruthlessly updated, a pulsating mass which bleeds expectation through its solid funk trenches. Elsewhere, with its shifting vocal lines phasing through technology's Sunday-best hyperspace, *7th Dream* is mantric in some places, frantic in others, and almost childishly defiant ("The Game") in the rest. And today we can state that the trance stance started here. But so did a lot more besides.

9 Express (RCA) 1986 The driving "Kundalini Express" (the apparent role model for Jesus and Mary Chain's "Sidewalking") and the lasciviously laconic "Holiday on the Moon" highlight a tight, focused collection which isolates the band's penchant for filling dance floors with hazy acid, then compounds it with a funk heavy reprise of "Ball of Confusion."

8 Earth-Sun-Moon (RCA) 1987 Less cohesive than its predecessors, *Earth* delivers — albeit in a different direction. This strumming-guitars-in-the-country-album has a sun-drenched ebb and flow gathered best by "Lazy" and "Waiting for the Flood," but there's still the drastic punctuation of the all out ballbusting "No New Tale to Tell."

8 Love and Rockets (RCA) 1989 Carrying over the acid energy from the earlier *Motorcycle* EP, a brittle urban blues sound is crushed through the sound of industrial dance. The album is dominated by odd breaks and ricochets, its vision encapsulated by "So Alive" — the band's indelibly crafted tribute to Lou Reed's "Walk On the Wild Side."

9 Hot Trip to Heaven (American) 1994 "Body and Soul" starts slow, but at 14 minutes it can afford to, stretching like a giant awakening and then on with the boots and the soundscape is crushed. *Hot Trip* is Love and Rockets reclaiming their own, the looped psychedelia of *7th Dream* reassembled from the sidelines of all that followed, then recreating the modern electro-climate in its own deliciously looped image.

6 Sweet Fa (American) 1996 A tale of turgid woes surrounded this new disc's gestation and the wait made it weirder. Kicking off with vague acoustic whimsy, by the time we reach the end of the set, the signature triptych of "Clean," "Comedown," and "Spiked," L&R were suddenly the hardest, nastiest, loudest noise on earth, grinding out atmospherics, and not one riff in sight. Someone must have really pissed them off.

6 Lift (Red Ant) 1998 Sonically the son of both its predecessors, the tripped out techno of one, the grilled guitars of the other, but a strangely flaccid set nonetheless. "Deep Deep Down" floats on percussive waves of trance, "Resurrection Hex" has an edge of prodigious block rockers, and "Pink Flamingo" is bubbling dub. But so little else is going on that the band's break-up now seems inevitable.

Tones on Tail LPs

8 Pop (PVC) 1984 A very dry run for early Love and Rockets, in that the soundscapes drift from whispered to wired, and the dance instincts are at least primed to catch fire. More serviceable ideas than realized majesty, still an album which holds its place in time.

Selected Compilations and Archive Releases

8 Everything! (Beggars Banquet) 1998 Indeed it is — album, singles, B-sides, 12-inchers — amazing.

David J LPs

7 The Etiquette of Violence (Situation 2 — UK) 1983

7 Crocodile Tears and the Velvet Cosh (Glass) 1985

5 Songs from Another Season (RCA) 1990

4 Urban Urbane (MCA) 1992 The drummer plays with brushes, the bass is out smooching your mother, and J's vocals resonate like a naughty 1-900 line. 30-something melancholia, with a Pete Murphy cameo (on "Candy on the Cross") for the trivia freaks.

David J and Alan Moore LP

8 The Moon and Serpent Grand Egyptian Theatre of Marvels (Cleopatra) 1996 Astonishingly workable conceptual performance art beast, musically preposterous in all the right ways and swimming in death of goth atmospheres.

Selected Compilations and Archive Releases

7 On Glass: The Singles (Cleopatra) 1998 Rapid-fire succession of a sorely overlooked succession of great 45s.

Daniel Ash LPs

7 Coming Down (RCA) 1991

7 Foolish Thing Desire (Columbia) 1992 A lackluster opening salvo is forgotten the moment "Blue Bird" kicks in, like a crash on a fogbound highway, and *Foolish Thing* is transformed into an unremitting wall of feedback and fury, positively the nastiest record Ash has ever been involved in.

LOVE SPIT LOVE

FORMED 1992 *(New York, NY)*

ORIGINAL LINE-UP *Richard Butler (b. 6/5/56, Kingston Upon Thames, England — vocals); Richard Fortus (guitar); Tim Butler (b. 12/7/58, Kingston Upon Thames — bass); Frank Ferrer (drums)*

When the Psychedelic Furs went on hiatus following the completion of their *World Outside* tour in late 1991, Richard Butler originally planned a solo album, and began writing with former Furs stand-in guitarist, Knox Chandler (ex-Vibrators). "Then I thought, 'You know what Richard, this really isn't the way to go, you're going to end up with another Furs' album with the secondary members,' which is kind of ridiculous to do." He abandoned the project, and linked instead with Richard Fortus, guitarist with Pale Divine, support act on the final Furs tour.

Recruiting Butler's brother Tim as bassist and co-writer, and with the addition of Frank Ferrer, the quartet entered the studio with producer Dave Jerden, emerging with Love Spit Love's eponymous debut (#195 US), a record which both echoed the Butlers' past work, and distanced itself from anything which had gone before. "It's very difficult to pin exactly what's different," Richard Butler acknowledged, "because I was and still am the same person. I'm not going to go out and make a Spice Girls record."

Reluctant to commit to touring, Tim Butler quit (after several years' silence, he formed Feed with Don Yallech in 1997). He was replaced by Lonnie Hillyer and Love Spit Love launched their first headlining tour in the fall of 1994, followed by a spring outing opening for Live. "Am I Wrong" (#83 UK) hit in September 1994, but the collapse of the band's label, Imago, slowed momentum considerably.

Off the road, Love Spit Love continued working. Butler alone recorded "Shineaway" with dance band BT for inclusion in the *Jackyl* soundtrack; the full band (now with bassist Chris Wilson) then contributed a version of the Smiths' "How Soon Is Now" to the soundtrack, *The Craft*, and subsequently, TV's *Charmed*.

Trysome Eatone, Love Spit Love's second album, was released through Maverick in 1997 (1998 in the UK); it was followed by a triumphant club tour, which saw Butler performing both new and older, Furs-era material. But while the band did discuss releasing an internet-only acoustic album, there would be no rapid follow-up. Indeed, Fortus and Ferrer immediately launched into a new schedule with their side project, Honky Toast (with vocalist Eric J Toast and bassist E.Z. Bake), while Butler linked with keyboard player Jon Carin, to begin writing once again for a solo album.

Love Spit Love LPs

8 Love Spit Love (Imago) 1994 Mid-life apocalyptic grunge pop crisis a-go-go, poking the generation gap ("Seventeen"), anticipating uncertainty ("Am I Wrong"), then dancing with Christopher Isherwood through the leather-whipped carnival of the Brechtian "Jigsaw." An absolute rebirth, an enviable triumph.

9 Trysome Eatone (Maverick) 1997 Frantic and edgy, with percussion punching an unstated violence, Butler's first album to come to terms with his past is also his first to actually acknowledge he has one and, when "It Hurts When I Laugh" bites "Imitation of Christ," you can almost hear it giggle.

Selected Compilations and Archive Releases

8 Love Spit Love (New Millennium, UK) 1998 Double CD set repackaging first album with period B-sides and rarities, plus CD-Rom material.

Honky Toast LPs

6 Meet the Honky (Black Cat) 1997

5 Whatcha Gonna Do, Honky? (Sony) 1999

LENE LOVICH

BORN *Lili Marlene Premilovich, 3/30/50 (Detroit, MI)*

Although her shock vocal stylings and appearance would eventually relegate Lene Lovich to a mere novelty pop sideshow, her initial breakthrough in 1978 placed her firmly at the forefront of a new wave scene hitherto regarded as the sole preserve of Lydia Lunch, James Black, and sundry New York underground new wavers.

The daughter of a Yugoslavian father and English mother, Lovich arrived in Britain at 13, when her parents broke up. In 1968, she met future collaborator Les Chappell and the pair moved to London to attend art school. Over the next decade, both worked on the fringes of the rock mainstream — Lovich appeared as a dancer in one of Arthur Brown's stageshow extravaganzas, gigged with a succession of cabaret and bar bands, and was responsible for the English language lyrics to French disco star Cerrone's "Supernature" hit.

In 1975, Lovich and Chappell formed the Diversions, signing to Arthur Brown's Gull label and scoring an immediate hit with their cover of Carl Malcolm's "Fattie Bum Bum" (#34 UK). But two subsequent 45s, "But Is It Funky" and "Raincheck," failed and a name change, to the Commandos (for a cover of the Commodores' "The Bump") did nothing either. An unreleased album, *Soul Survivors*, and a version of "I Saw Mommy Kissing Santa Claus" (credited to Lovich alone) followed, and the Diversions broke up in mid-1977.

Lovich and Chappell resurfaced in the Carnival Orchestra dance band, before London DJ Charlie Gillett suggested they record a demo of the '60s bubblegum hit "I Think We're Alone Now"; he passed the results onto Stiff Records, who promptly commissioned a rerecording for release in June 1978.

Through fall 1978, Lovich was one of the attractions on the latest Stiff package tour, alongside Wreckless Eric, Rachel Sweet, Mickey Jupp, and Jona Lewie. Her debut album, *Stateless* (#137 US, #35 UK), was released simultaneously, packed with some of the most adventurous songwriting of the era (plus a seductive cover of Nick Lowe's "Tonight"), and backed by a publicity campaign which painted her background as mysteriously and undidentifiably eastern European.

By the new year, a new single, "Lucky Number" (#3 UK) was rerecorded from the "Alone Now" B-side to dramatic effect. "Say When" (#19 UK) followed it up the chart, but a third sure-fire hit, the non-album "Bird Song" (#39 UK) was abruptly drawn up short when Stiff switched pressing plants, early in production, leading to chronic delays in supplying the record to stores.

Such a "failure" was to have far-reaching consequences: UK radio at that time was very hit-driven, particularly where established artists were concerned. One flop, no matter what the reasons, would adversely effect the attention paid to their next 45; and so on. While the *Flex* album (#94 US, #19 UK) did well, "What Will I Do Without You" (#58 UK) peaked prematurely in March 1980; subsequent singles failed to chart altogether, and though the emergence of Hazel O'Connor proved that the UK public was still hungry for quirky sounding women with dynamic vocal ranges, Lovich and Chappell all but disappeared for the next year.

They re-emerged in 1981 with "New Toy" (#53 UK), and the following year with *No Man's Land* (#188 US) and the remarkable "It's You Only You" (#68 UK), but it would be five years before Lovich was again sighted, duetting with another sound-alike, German Nina Hagen, on a single benefitting the animal welfare organization, PETA, "Don't Kill the Animals." *March*, a full comeback album, was released to little response in 1990 and Lovich remained silent for much of the next decade. She finally resurfaced in 1999 as part of producer Mike Thorne's Thorn aggregation, alongside Chappell and co-vocalist Kit Hain.

Lene Lovich LPs

🮗 Stateless (Stiff) 1979 For a few years at the dawn of the '80s, Lovich's freaky whooping, wiry sexuality and utterly lustrous way with melodies was the sound of the future. "Lucky Number" and "Home" still have that quality; the bubblegum popster "I Think We're Alone Now," on the other hand, has transcended time and place, while her version of Nick Lowe's "Tonight" could well be the most seductive he's ever been.

🮗 Flex (Stiff) 1980 Falling back a little, too much of *Flex* recycled past innovations to the point where they verged on gimmickry — "MonkeyTalk," "Wonderful One," "You Can't Kill Me." At its best, however — the shrieking nervous "Bird Song" and a delicious cover of Frankie Valli's "The Night," the best of *Stateless* soon rushes back.

🮗 No Man's Land (Stiff) 1982 The minor hit "It's You (Only You)" pretended nothing had changed. And sadly, it was right, only this time there weren't even two great saving graces.

🮗 March (Pathfinder) 1990 Totally unexpected and utterly overlooked comeback, more competent than actually inspired, but enjoyable in a quirky way.

Lene Lovich/Kit Hain/Thorn LP

🮗 Thorn — Sprawl (Stereo Society) 1999 Near-eponymous producer Mike Thorne oversees the project, but leaves the musicianship to others, Lovich and early '80s "Coming Home" diva Kit Hain among them. Hain's techno take on the Sex Pistols' "Pretty Vacant" is truly radical, while Lovich's first new recordings in over a decade are a reminder of just how great a talent has been hibernating.

Selected Compilations and Archive Releases

🮗 The Stiff Years (Great Expectations — UK) 1990 Two discs rounding up all three albums, plus singles and oddities.

LOW

FORMED 1993 (*Duluth, MN*)
ORIGINAL LINE-UP Alan Sparhawk (guitar); John Nichols (bass); Mimi Parker (drums)

Formed by Alan Sparhawk and wife Mimi Parker, virtuoso of the one snare, one cymbal drum kit, in March 1993, Low cut their first demo within days of their first live show in May, and by August, they were signing a record deal and preparing to record their debut album with producer Kramer. He, in fact, was one of the recipients of Low's first demo, and *I Could Live in Hope* was originally scheduled for release on his Shimmy Disc label before Virgin subsidiary Vernon Yard made their own move for it.

Earning immediate comparisons to third album-era Velvet Underground and Joy Division, Low's bare bones approach came as a shock even in those days of low-fi extravagance, and their live show matched their minimalism. Regular gigging would eventually bolster their sound somewhat, as well as increasing their adventurousness, as evidenced by 1995's *Long Division* — the band's first with new bassist Zak Sally. (An out-take, "Tired," led off the band's 1994 *Low* EP, otherwise comprising cuts from the two albums.)

Pausing to cut the *Transmission* EP with producer Steve Albini (the title cut was a Joy Division cover, previously contributed to a tribute album), Low spent much of 1995–96 on the road, touring with Soul Coughing, Luna, Spectrum, and Pell Mell — it was through the latter that they met producer Steve Fisk, who handled the band's third album, *The Curtain Hits the Cask*, and the 1996 EPs *Finally* and *Over the Ocean*.

Following the collapse of Vernon Yard, Low resurfaced on Sub Pop for 1997's "Venus" single; Kranky then released the Albini produced *Songs for a Dead Pilot* EP. Further singles included the festive "If You Were Born Today (Song for Little Baby Jesus)" in December 1997, and a cover of the Beatles' "Long Long Long" the following year, before Low released the live *One More Reason To Forget* album, recorded in Louisville the previous November.

Spring 1999 finally brought the band's fourth album *Secret Name*; following European and US dates through early fall 1999, the band came off the road in October 1999, following the announcement of Parker's pregnancy. The eight-track *Christmas* EP was released at year's end.

Low LPs

9 I Could Live in Hope (Vernon Yard) 1994 If beautiful somnambulism could ever be described as exciting, Low's debut established the Minnesota three-piece as one of the most exhilarating groups around. Establishing their trademark sound of funereal drum, shapeshifting guitar, and ethereal harmonies, drifting dreamlike and uninterrupted through the disc, *I Could Live in Hope* also posed the question, where can they go from here?

6 Long Division (Vernon Yard) 1995 Twelve songs are recognizably Low, but unrecognizably fussier; guitarist Sparhawk admitted the group had tried some "different things" this time around; different as in waving goodbye to the sheer bleakness of *Hope*, for one, opening arms instead to a sense of wistful... dare we call it happiness? There is less reliance on counterpoint, more fiddling about during passages which *Hope* left echoingly silent, and a couple of songs — Mimi Parker's solo "Below and Above" especially — are genuinely substandard.

7 The Curtain Hits the Cast (Vernon Yard) 1996

8 Secret Name (Kranky) 1999 Despite past disappointments, the undisputed king (and queen) of sadcore return to near-basics to prove precisely how they earned that title. Even at its best, *Secret Name* remains a distillation of their debut, but the addition of orchestration lets the original sparseness breathe a little without once crowding out the crippling loneliness.

NICK LOWE

BORN 3/24/49 *(Woodbridge, Suffolk, England)*

In 1967, bassist Nick Lowe was a founder member of Kippington Lodge, a psychedelic pop band who evolved into pub rock champions Brinsley Schwarz (named for the band's guitarist), a testing ground for some of the most respected musicians of the late 1970s — Schwarz and Billy Rankin (drums) would later join Sean Tyla's Ducks Deluxe, before Schwarz joined Bob Andrews (keyboards) in Graham Parker's Rumour. Ian Gomm (vocals) would enjoy a short solo career; and Lowe would become one of Britain's most popular producers and best-loved songwriters.

Despite such a welter of talent, Brinsley Schwarz's six albums went nowhere and following the band's 1975 breakup, Lowe alone was retained by the band's UK label, UA — although nobody ever told him why. He finally broke away after delivering two utterly (and purposefully) wretched singles, a Bay City Rollers tribute, "Bay City Rollers We Love You," and a disco parody, "Let's Go to the Disco," recorded with Roogalator guitarist Danny Adler.

Linking next with pub rock entrepreneur Jake Riviera and producer Dave Robinson, Lowe helped form the Stiff label in spring 1976, and that summer the label debuted with Lowe's "So It Goes" 45. He would remain at the label for the next 18 months, releasing the *Bowi* EP (so-titled after David Bowie released the *Low* album), a second single, "Halfway to Paradise," and a clutch of tracks for Stiff compilations.

More importantly, however, he became the label's house producer, handling debuts by Elvis Costello, the Damned and Wreckless Eric, in addition to taking on a number of outside productions, for Graham Parker, Dr. Feelgood, the Pretenders, and Richard Hell. He also formed a partnership with Brinsley Schwarz's own ex-producer Dave Edmunds, the blistering Rockpile, and over the next five years, Rockpile acted as a live conduit for both Lowe and Edmunds' work — including Lowe's starring role in fall 1977's Live Stiffs package tour, alongside Costello, Ian Dury, Wreckless Eric, and Larry Wallis.

When the Stiff hierarchy broke apart in early 1978, Lowe followed Riviera to the newly formed Radar label, where he cut his first album, the effervescent *Jesus of Cool* (#127 US, #22 UK-retitled for the US, *Pure Pop for Now People*). His most successful British album, the set included the hit "I Love the Sound of Breaking Glass" (#7 UK), while Lowe would also score with "Crackin' Up" (#34 UK), and "Cruel to be Kind" (#12 US, #12 UK) — the latter charting in August 1979, the same month as Lowe married Carlene Carter. The accompanying video included scenes from the ceremony.

Labour for Lust (#31 US, #43 UK), Lowe's second solo album, was released that same year; almost three years (and a new label, FBeat) would separate it from its successor, *Nick the Knife* (#50 US, #99 UK), although Lowe was not idle in the meantime. The final Rockpile album, 1980's *Seconds of Pleasure*, was followed by one last, typically Rockpile-ian marathon US tour, and further production — two albums with Carter, two with Costello, and one apiece with the Feelgoods and John Hiatt.

He also landed a hit-by-proxy when Costello resurrected "What's So Funny 'Bout Peace, Love and Understanding" from Brinsley Schwarz's final album, *The New Favourites Of*; it would be another decade, however, before the song truly proved its worth, when Curtis Stigers covered it for inclusion on the best-selling soundtrack album of all time, *The Bodyguard*. In 1995, Lowe admitted that royalties from that single performance had made him a millionaire.

In 1981, Lowe formed a new band, the Chaps (later Noise to Go), around Martin Belmont (guitar — ex-Ducks Deluxe and the Rumour, and a former Brinsleys roadie), Paul Carrack (keyboards — ex-Ace) and Bobby Irwin (drums), but his solo career certainly suffered from the amount of extra-curricular work he was still taking on. Lowe later admitted that by the time of *Nick the Knife* and 1983's *The Abominable Showman* (#129 US), "I'd sort of lost the plot... I was burned out."

He continued producing, of course; through the first half of the 1980s, Lowe produced Carrack's eponymous debut album, plus sets by the Fabulous Thunderbirds, the Moonlighters, the Men They Couldn't Hang and Jimmy Cliff. He also cut two new solo sets, 1984's *Nick Lowe and His Cowboy Outfit* (#113 US) and 1985's *Rose of England* (#119 US), the latter the source of Lowe's first hit singles in five years, the UK success "Half a Boy Half a Man" (#53 UK), and a remake of Rockpile's "I Knew the Bride (When She Used to Rock'n'Roll)" (#77 US).

Pinker and Prouder Than Previous in 1987, continued what Lowe now regards as his rehabilitation (a process also enhanced by work on a second John Hiatt album, 1986's *Bring the Family*), and the following year he signed with Reprise for the Dave Edmunds produced *Party of One* (#182 US). Recorded with many of the musicians he encountered at the Hiatt sessions, including Ry Cooder and Jim Keltner, the album also spawned a new band, Little Village, featuring Hiatt and the *Bring the Family* session band.

Promising on paper, the collaboration was disastrous, with 1992's eponymous album (#66 US, #23 UK) an embarrassment which all concerned did their best to forget; Lowe for his part resolved to make his next album "as good as it possibly could be." Working now with Geraint Watkins (keyboards — ex-Dave Edmunds), Paul Riley (bass, ex-Roogalator) and Irwin, *The Impossible Band*, in November 1994

would be just that — *Q* magazine ad judged it one of the year's Top 10 releases.

Tours in support of this latest album spawned the *Live! on the Battlefield* EP, while further acclaim greeted *Dig My Mood*, in 1998, paving the way for the (solo) career-spanning *The Doings* boxed set in 1999.

Also see the entry for "NICK LOWE" on page 794 in "PRODUCERS & LABELS."

Nick Lowe LPs

9 Jesus of Cool (Radar UK) 1978 Unrelenting magpie pop, from the days when lawyers didn't care whether you wore your inspirations like a brightly colored shirt. "Nutted by Reality" clearly enjoyed some early Jackson 5, for example, but elsewhere, songs like "Tonight" (later covered by Lene Lovich), "Little Hitler" (a title borrowed from Elvis Costello — apparently without asking), and the amazing "Sound of the City" were classics all of his own making, while even the pun-packed comparative lightweights like "36 Inches High" seem imbibed with higher meaning.

8 Pure Pop for Now People (Columbia) 1978 Basically the same album, but with the Bay City irony of "Rollers Show" and a less gritty cut of "Shake and Pop," unceremoniously grafted into the running order. Still a magnificent record though.

8 Labour of Lust (Demon) 1979 Despite the hits (or near enough) "Cruel to Be Kind" and "American Squirm," a simultaneously darker ("Without Love," "You Make Me") and crasser ("Switchboard Susan") set. The period B-side "Basing Street," incidentally, could make an American (or anyone else) squirm.

7 Nick the Knife (Demon) 1982

5 The Abominable Showman (Demon) 1983 Not at all a classic Nick Lowe album, but a sign of the increasingly serious direction in which his pen is now moving.

8 Nick Lowe & His Cowboy Outfit (Demon) 1984 Cowboys, one presumes, as in the unlicensed handymen who make a mess of your double-glazing, as opposed to the midwest country rhinestone types who would probably take exception at even the vaguely Anglo Tex-Mexeries of "Half a Boy and Half a Man." A strong return to form.

8 The Rose of England (Demon) 1985 Rerecording Rockpile's "I Knew the Bride" was unnecessary, but Costello's "Indoor Fireworks" and his own "(Hope to God) I'm Right" are phenomenal, while the title track has a heartbeat all of its own.

6 Pinker and Prouder Than Previous (Demon) 1988 A roughshod smattering of sessions and gatherings, one of those albums which was probably more fun to make than it is to play consistently.

7 Party of One (Upstart) 1990

7 The Impossible Bird (Upstart) 1994 With Commander Cody mainstay Bill Kirchen leading the instrumental way, Lowe's most successful move yet towards sustaining a rock'n'country vibe.

"The Beast in Me," previously aired on Johnny Cash's Rick Rubin-produced comeback, joins a generous cover of Buck Owens' "True Love Travels On a Gravel Road" at the top of the pile.

7 Dig My Mood (Demon) 1998

Selected Compilations and Archive Releases

8 16 All Time Lowes (Demon — UK) 1984 Compilation drifting through the Stiff and Radar label years.

7 Nick's Knack (Demon — UK) 1986 Well-rounded follow-up which adds some rarities to the choice album cuts.

9 The Doings (Demon) 1999 Immaculate box set rounding up an unbeatable three disc summary of Lowe's entire solo career, plus a fourth of rarities, live and unreleased material.

Brinsley Schwarz LPs

5 Brinsley Schwarz (Capitol) 1970

6 Despite It All (Liberty — UK) 1971

6 Silver Pistol (UA) 1972

6 Nervous On the Road (UA) 1972

6 Please Don't Ever Change (UA — UK) 1973

7 New Favourites (UA — UK) 1974

Selected Compilations and Archive Releases

7 Surrender to the Rhythm (EMI) 1991

Dave Edmunds/Rockpile LPs

6 Subtle As a Flying Mallet (RCA) 1975

8 Get It (Swansong) 1977

7 Tracks On Wax (Swansong) 1978

6 Repeat When Necessary (Swansong) 1979

5 Seconds of Pleasure (Columbia) 1980

Selected Compilations and Archive Releases

7 The Best Of (Swansong) 1981

Little Village LP

4 Little Village (Reprise) 1992

L7

FORMED 1986 (Los Angeles, CA)

ORIGINAL LINE-UP Donita Sparks (b. 4/8/63, Chicago, IL — vocals, guitar); Suzi Gardner (b. 8/1/60 — guitar, vocals); Jennifer Finch (b. 8/5/66, Los Angeles, CA — bass, vocals); Roy Koutsky (drums)

Following a string of earlier bands, Gardner and Sparks met shortly after the latter relocated to Sacramento in 1985;

Finch joined the following year, having returned to L.A. from San Francisco, and with Roy Koutsky on drums the band began playing around the local club circuit.

Following a tour with Bad Religion, L7 became one of the first signings to that band's newly relaunched label Epitaph, releasing their eponymous debut in December 1988 before Koutsky left. A string of temporary drummers replaced him, before another Chicago native, Demetra Plaskas (b. 11/9/60), was recruited in 1989, and the band signed with Sub Pop. The group toured both the US and UK (supporting labelmates Nirvana), and in November 1989 released the *Smell the Magic* EP. "Shove" followed in January 1990.

The band signed with Slash in 1991, and in March 1992, "Pretend We're Dead" (#21 UK), gave L7 their first chart entry. Co-produced by Butch Vig, *Bricks Are Heavy* (#160 US, #24 UK) followed, together with further singles "Everglade" (#27 UK), "Monster" (#33 UK), and a reactivated "Pretend We're Dead" (#50 UK), coupled with a live version of "Fast 'N' Frightening". *Bricks Are Heavy* was later nominated among *Rolling Stone* magazine's essential albums of the 1990s.

By now, L7 were firmly entrenched as hard line Riot Grrls, coupling post-feminist manifestos with humorously vulgar stage antics that often created more buzz than their music. Not quick to let attention pass, L7 showed their serious side by forming the pro-abortion group Rock for Choice.

On the lighter side, the band briefly left the stage for the silver screen in 1994, stepping into the John Waters film *Serial Mom* under the auspices of their celluloid alter egos, Camel Lips. L7 would also appear in Krist Novoselic's indy film documentary *The Beauty Process*.

July 1994's *Hungry for Stink* (#117 US) was preceded by "Andres" (#34 UK). (Industro-techno gurus The Prodigy, would later reinvent the album's "Fuel My Fire" on their American breakthrough album, *Fat of the Land*.) Again the band toured heavily, but received a major blow when Finch departed in 1996. She was replaced by Greta Brinkman, and in this form, the band recorded 1997's *The Beauty Process: Triple Platinum* — Brinkman then quit; Gail Greenwood (ex-Belly) joined in time for the band's 1997 US tour with Marilyn Manson.

L7 Live: Omaha to Osaka followed in 1998, as the group linked with Bongload Records to form their own imprint, Wax Tadpole, named for a track on their first album, "Bite the Wax Tadpole." Overcoming Greenwood's departure, L7 recorded their label debut, *Slap Happy*, as a trio (with Sparks on bass); former StoneFox/Auntie Christ bassist Janis Tanaka would join the band as they set out on tour through summer/fall 1999.

L7 LPs

4 L7 (Epitaph) 1988 Short on melody and big on grunge — the stuff behind the fridge, not the genre — their debut is indeed fast and furious but lacks cohesion. "Bite the Wax Tadpole" would be recalled a decade later for their own record label, but "Metal Stampede" sums it all up best.

7 Smell the Magic (Sub Pop) 1990 Better and more coherent than its predecessor, with "Broomstick" and "Deathwish" offering glimpses of the future. *Magic* trades in some of the grinding guitar for melody and hooks, while still maintaining the rage against social mores and the conformity of the modern age.

9 Bricks Are Heavy (Slash) 1992 With all the charm of a High School Sex Change Prom Queen (at last, the Suzi Quatro revival!), there's a shadow of old-time Buzzcocks dancing around L7 — a comparison compounded by some cripplingly wry lyrics, but cemented by the band's effortless ability to locate the middle ground between Yoko Ono and Kylie Minogue. A selfless Butch Vig production, and possibly the most self-fulfilled collection of pop songs of the year.

6 Hungry for Stink (Slash) 1994

7 The Beauty Process: Triple Platinum (Slash) 1997 More of the same, lots of raunchy power punk blended with goodold hard rock riffs and a handful of genuine gems — "Non Existent Patricia" and the well-observed "Masses Are Asses."

6 Live: Omaha to Osaka (Slash) 1998

7 Slaphappy (Wax Tadpole Records) 1999 A solid set of crunchy guitar and heavy distorted rock — yet there is a strong sense of melody still buried under the surprisingly endearing mayhem — "Freezer Burn" seriously blisters.

LYDIA LUNCH

BORN *Lydia Koch, 6/2/59 (Rochester, NY)*

Lydia Lunch emerged in 1976 as the 16-year-old voice of Teenage Jesus and the Jerks, the key to what became the east coast no-wave scene of the late 1970s. Originally a collaboration between Lunch and saxophonist James Chance, the band was nevertheless confined, on vinyl, to a handful of releases — the single "Orphan," and the *Pre* EP before Chance quit to form the Contortions. (As Stella Rico, Lunch guested on their *Off White* album in 1978).

Teenage Jesus survived to cut a second EP, *Pink*, and deliver a starring four song role on the *No New York* compilation album (itself a statement of the city's post-punk intent). They brokeup in mid-1978, however, and Lunch resurfaced with Beirut Slump, cutting one single ("Try Me"), before issuing her solo debut, *Queen of Siam* — the first full-blooded examination of all that made her tick.

Released in 1980, *Queen of Siam* was well-received, even if the majority of reviews acknowledged their uncertainty of

Lunch's true musical mission; her later-stated belief that spoken word was the only true art shone through even the album's most musical moments.

Lunch maintained the dichotomy with her next project, 8 Eyed Spy. Reuniting with Teenage Jesus bassist Jim Sclavunos (on drums!), plus George Scott (ex-Contortions — bass), Michael Paumgardhen (guitar) and Pat Irwin (sax, guitar), 8 Eyed Spy would set a pattern which has since become Lunch's modus operandi — forming a band, disbanding it shortly after, and then releasing a record.

Premiered with a raw single covering Bo Diddley's "Diddy Wah Diddy," the blues-drenched *Live* and the half-live *8 EyedSpy* both hinted at the band's promise, but the death of Scott in 1980 saw the group dissolve, and Lunch linked next with the remnants of L.A. punk band, the Weirdos, to record a second solo album, 1982's *13: 13* (#19 UK indy). Announced as her vision of the new psychedelia, it was, in fact, closer to the thunder of *Metal Box*-era Public Image Ltd, an indication of both the musical and geographical directions in which Lunch's mood was shifting.

A collaborative book of poetry with Exene Cervenka (of X), *Adulterers Anonymous*, was followed by Lunch relocating to London, and becoming a regular sight at Birthday Party functions, and her next release, *The Agony Is the Ecstacy* was, in fact, split with that band. Lunch's side of the disc featured an impromptu London gig, pairing Lunch with Siouxsie and the Banshees bassist Steve Severin playing feedback guitar, while Lunch herself offered up one of her most extreme performances yet.

At the same time, she remained capable of some remarkably tender music, as when she paired with Birthday Party guitarist Rowland S. Howard for a single covering Lee Hazlewood's "Some Velvet Morning" (#26 UK indy). However, a full length collaboration with the Birthday Party (plus Thurston Moore of Sonic Youth, and Genevieve McGukin, later of Rowland Howard's These Immortal Souls), *Honeymoon in Red*, was cancelled when the band broke up.

Halloween 1983 saw Lunch compose her most audacious project yet, the Immaculate Consumptives partnership with Marc Almond, Nick Cave and Foetus; while she continued moving toward the now-burgeoning industrial movement via collaborations with Einsturzende Neubauten (the *Thirsty Animal* EP), Die Haut (the EP *Der Karibische Western*), and the Danish band Sol Sort (the 1983 album *Dagger and Guitar*).

Back in New York, Lunch's spoken word "Wet Me On a Dead Night" made up one side of the *Hard Rock* cassette (shared with Michael Gira of the Swans); she then signed with Cabaret Voltaire's Doublevision label for *In Limbo* (#19 UK indy), a six-track mini-album featuring Thurston Moore (Sonic Youth) and Pat Place (ex-Contortions, Bush Tetras), a grinding, guitar noise-heavy collection which wholly anticipated Sonic Youth's own later excursions — their own "Death Valley 69" (#32 UK indy) collaboration with Lunch, of course, included.

Her own Widowspeak label was reactivated (as Widowspeak Productions) for the first of Lunch's true spoken word releases, 1985's aptly-titled *Uncensored Lydia Lunch* cassette; the label would also release a brace of collaborations with No Trend, the album *A Dozen Dead Roses* and an EP, *Heart of Darkness*. Unwilling to follow any direction to its immediate conclusion, however, Lunch next linked again with Foetus to record the soundtrack to his first starring movie, Richard Kern's *The Right Side of My Brain*. Released on disc as *The Drowning of Lucy Hamilton*, the instrumental album featured actress Hamilton herself, on piano and bass clarinet.

Another spoken word effort, *The Intimate Diaries of the Sexually Insane* was followed, in 1986, by a momentary pause while Lunch considered precisely what she'd accomplished over the past decade — then served up the most representative moments on *Hysterie 1976–86* (#12 UK indy), a double album of rare and unreleased material dating back to Teenage Jesus. As an introduction to Lunch's work-to-date it was, in many ways, even more extreme than her regular albums, but it also inspired her next project, 1987's long-delayed release of *Honeymoon in Red*.

The album was remixed by Foetus and that same year he and Lunch paired up with twin percussionists Cliff Martinez (ex-Red Hot Chili Peppers) and D.J. Bonebrake (X), for 1989's *Stinkfist* EP (#18 UK indy) — one of the first Lunch collaborations, observers later remarked, which didn't see her overwhelm her partners. Much the same could be said for *Crumb* (#12 UK indy), an EP credited to Lunch, Moore, and the *Honeymoon in Red* Orchestra — which added Foetus and Howard to the brew.

Now maintaining a regular stream of spoken word appearances (1989's *Oral Fixation* featured a venomous solo performance recorded at the Detroit Institute of Art in January 1988; *Conspiracy of Women* saw Lunch launching a "13 step program" against men), Lunch next joined forces with Kim Gordon (Sonic Youth — bass), to form Harry Crews for a European tour through fall 1988 — source of the live album *Naked in Garden Hills*, recorded in London and Vienna.

Lunch spent part of 1990 shooting her starring role in Beth B's *Thanatopsis*, which premiered in 1991 at the Kitchen in New York — just as Lunch reunited with Rowland Howard and producer Foetus for a European tour and the album *Shotgun Wedding*, one of the crucial releases of the early 1990s — a full live recounting of the set featured on 1997's *Transmutations/Live in Siberia* retrospective.

She followed it with an audacious cover of Blue Oyster Cult's "Don't Fear the Reaper" cut with Foetus, then reunited briefly with Die Haut, to guest on their *Head On* album. 1992 also saw Lunch briefly relaunch her solo musical career with a pair of well-received singles, "Twisted" and "Unearthly Delights."

However, there would be only one more "new" release, 1996's "No Excuse" single; subsequent releases would see her concentrate on either collaborative work, including 1997's appearance alongside the Foetus Symphony Orchestra, on the *York (First Exit to Brooklyn)* album, or archive projects — Foetus' *Null and Void*, and her own *Widowspeak — The Original Soundtrack*. Summer 1993 brought the spoken word anthology *Crimes Against Nature*, while Widowspeak itself branched out to present solo recordings by poets Wanda Coleman, Exene Cervenka, and poet/playwright Emilio Cubeiro.

Her non-musical projects gathered pace amid this apparent inactivity. In 1992, Lunch recorded the spoken track and was featured in Sacred Cow Productions' *The Thunder*, which won a Louisiana Film Shorts Award; also that year, she published *Incriminating Evidence*, a collection of stories, rants, and scripts (Last Gasp); the same publisher also produced *AS-FIX-E-8*, a comic scripted by Lunch and illustrated by Mike Matthews; while Fantagraphics would be responsible for *Bloodsucker*, an adult comic collaboration with Bob Fingerman.

She appeared in eight of the films shown at the Whitney Museum of Art's Underground Film Festival (Oct. 96 to Jan. 97), including several shot with Richard Kern during the 1980s; October 1997 saw the publication of Lunch's harrowing novel *Paradoxia* (Creation Press, London), together with *Toxic Gumbo*, a prestige format graphic novel illustrated by Ted McKeever for DC Comics/Vertigo.

Lydia Lunch LPs

7 Queen of Siam (ZE) 1981 ⓪ Half Teenage Jesus-type dirges, half seductive big band extravaganzas (arranged by *Flintstones* composer Billy VerPlanck), the album Billie Holiday would have made if her modern reputation had translated into her own life.

6 13:13 (Line — Germany) 1982 Distinctly modern dance inflected, but otherwise a slightly punkier version of Teenage Jesus' more dissonant moments.

7 The Drowning of Lucy Hamilton (Widowspeak) 1985 Ghostly soundtrack, a duet for sparse clarinet, piano, and scratchy guitar.

10 Shotgun Wedding [w/Rowland Howard] (Triple X) 1991 The mid-1980s "Some Velvet Morning" single served notice that there was musical chemistry between Lunch and Howard which neither had enjoyed elsewhere; that it took close to six years more for them to bring it to fruition remains testament to their activities elsewhere.

Produced by Foetus with stunning understatement, *Shotgun Wedding* is first and foremost a strikingly musical album. No experimentation, no shrieking, not even too much damage, the duo let the songs speak through the textures as much as the lyrics, although there is no shortage of suitable subjects on board.

"In My Time of Dying" gets the definitive reading which neither Dylan nor Zeppelin were capable of delivering, Alice Cooper's "Black Ju Ju" restores the Dead Baby boy to his seething punk origins, and "Incubator" sounds almost Top 40. Elsewhere, the semi-rap "Pigeon Town" and the laconic "Cisco Sunset" prove the further versatility of the team's songwriting acumen, and though this is by far Lunch's most accessible album, if it wasn't by Lunch, that wouldn't seem surprising.

8 Eyed Spy LPs

6 8 Eyed Spy (Fetish) 1981

5 Live (Roir) 1981

Harry Crews LP

6 Harry Crews (Widowspeak) 1990 Hardnosed Sonic Youthisms upping the pressure to match Lunch's delivery.

Selected Compilations and Archive Releases

8 Hysterie 1976-86 (Widowspeak) 1987 Welcome career-so-far wrap up complete with rarities.

6 Honeymoon in Red (Widowspeak) 1987 Unreleased when first recorded, Lunch's collaboration with the Birthday Party doesn't quite match its made-in-hell potential.

7 Transmutations/Live in Siberia (Trident) 1995 Lunch and Howard take *Shotgun Wedding* on the road. Not quite as powerful as its studio counterpart, but the evolution is fascinating.

9 Widowspeak — The Original Soundtrack (NMC) 1998 Essential collection of Lunch collaborations and rarities, wrapping up a career's worth of non-CD singles and guest appearances.

Spoken Word Releases

5 The Uncensored Lydia Lunch (Widowspeak) 1985

5 Hard Rock (Ecstatic Peace) 1985

6 Oral Fixation (Widowspeak) 1988

5 Our Fathers Who Aren't in Heaven (Widowspeak) 1990 Double album shared with Henry Rollins, Hubert Selby Jr., Don Bajema

6 Conspiracy of Women (Widowspeak) 1990

6 South of Your Border (Widowspeak) 1991 From the play by Emilio Cubeiro.

6 Pow (Soyo) 1992

4 Rude Hieroglyphics [LIVE] (Rykodisc) 1995

4 Universal Infiltrators [LIVE] (Atavistic) 1996

6 Matrikamantra [LIVE] (Atavistic) 1997 Double CD recorded live in Prague and in the studio with Joseph Budenholzer.

Selected Compilations and Archive Releases

6 Crimes Against Nature (Triple X) 1994 3-CD box set including *Uncensored*, *Oral Fixation*, and *Conspiracy*, plus unreleased material.

LUSH

FORMED 1987 *(London, England)*
ORIGINAL LINE-UP *Meriel Barham (vocals); Miki Berenyi (b. 3/18/67, London — guitar); Emma Anderson (b. 6/10/64, London — guitar); Steve Rippon (bass); Chris Acland (b. 9/7/67, Lancaster — drums)*

College friends Emma Anderson and Miki Berenyi, daughter of a Hungarian father and Japanese mother, met in the early 1980s, publishing the *Alphabet Soup* fanzine together, before joining bands in 1986 — Anderson was bassist with the Rover Girls, Berenyi guitarist with the Bugs.

Neither group worked out, and by 1987, Berenyi, Anderson, Chris Acland, and vocalist Meriel Barham were rehearsing together as the Baby Machines. Steve Rippon followed, and the newly renamed Lush made their live debut at the Camden Falcon on March 6, 1988. Barham was sacked after her bandmates decided she wasn't committed enough (she later reappeared in Pale Saints), but still it took Lush more than a year to release their first record, the *Scar* EP (#3 UK indy) in October 1989 comprising six early band demos.

Following through with tours supporting Loop and the Darling Buds, Lush linked with producer Robin Guthrie (of 4AD labelmates the Cocteau Twins) for two further EPs in 1990 — *Mad Love* (#55 UK) in February, supported by a well received session for BBC radio's John Peel Show, and *Sweetness and Light* (#47 UK). The band also contributed a cover of Middle of the Road's "Chirpy Chirpy Cheep Cheep" to the *Alvin Lives in Leeds* anti-poll tax benefit album.

Constant touring, including an appearance at the Glastonbury Festival, and visits to Japan and the US (with Ride) ensured Lush's much anticipated debut album (released following yet another Top 50 EP, *Black Spring* — #43 UK) would become one of the new year's most analyzed releases — the general consensus was disappointed, largely due to Guthrie's production, but still *Spooky* (#7 UK) proved a monster.

Rippon quit during the final mixing of the album (he later wrote an unpublished novel about his time with the band, *Cold Turkey Sandwich*), and was replaced by ex-Biff Bang Pow bassist Phil King (b. 4/29/60, Chiswick). The *For Love* EP (#35 UK) broke Lush into the Top 40 for the first time in the new year, and their latest UK tour was their most successful yet. It was time to conquer the rest of the world.

For much of the next two years, Lush toured Europe, the Far East, and America. Having met Perry Farrell when Lush played a few gigs with Jane's Addiction in 1991, they were invited onto the 1992 Lollapalooza alongside Ministry, Soundgarden, and the Red Hot Chili Peppers. They also courted Bob Mould to produce their second album; he turned out to be too busy, and the band eventually went with Mike *Hedges* (Siouxsie and the Banshees, the Cure), and *Split* (#195 US) was released in June 1994, intriguingly promoted by two singles released on the same day: "Hypocrite" (#52 UK) and "Desire Lines" (#60 UK).

At their manager's prompting, the band all but ignored the UK in the aftermath of *Split*, again concentrating on the US. It was a decision they would swiftly regret; despite Lollapalooza, American interest was low, and when tours of both the UK and Japan were cancelled in the fall, Lush broke with their management, and began work immediately on a new album.

Lovelife (#189 US) would be a return to basics, and a return to home base, a very English sounding pop record, perfectly styled for the Britpop-crazed mid-90s, but utterly imbibed with Lush's own character too. Recorded in London, then mixed in Boston by Radiohead producers Paul Kolderie and Sean Slade, *Lovelife* featured a guest appearance from Pulp's Jarvis Cocker, "Ciao," and three successive singles which only narrowly missed the Top 20, "Single Girl" (#21 UK), "Ladykillers" (#22 UK), and "500" (#21 UK).

The band was riding these successes when Acland committed suicide in October. Rumors that the remaining band members were rehearsing with Stephen Albert (ex-Scarce) were put to rest before the end of the year and after a year's total silence, the band officially announced they were breaking up in March 1998. King moved onto the Jesus and Mary Chain; Anderson formed a new band, Sing Sing, with Joely Tonna and Lisa O'Neill, debuting at the University of London on July 29, 1998, and releasing their first album in late 1999 through Robin Guthrie's Bella Union label.

Lush LPs

8 Spooky (4AD/Reprise) 1992 Lush — mark one — with a definitive 4AD sound. All swirling guitars and ethereal melodies shot through with a suitably clear-murky production.

8 Split (4AD/Reprise) 1994 Still full of breathless guitar rushes, *Split* is generally a more rough-and-tumble experience, but packs an emotional punch lacking on their debut.

9 Lovelife (4AD/Reprise) 1996 Lush — mark two. Completely reinvented as Britpop darlings, Lush turn their attention to slickly polished songs, catchy hooks, and a snarling attitude best summed up on the acidly funny "Ladykillers" and "Single Girl." Elsewhere, Pulp's Jarvis Cocker turns in a great guest appearance on the scathingly lackadaisical "Ciao."

Selected Compilations and Archive Releases

7 Gala (4AD/Reprise) 1990 Collection comprising the band's first three Eps.

7 Topolino (4AD — Canada) 1998 B-sides and rarities collection.

M

KIRSTY MACCOLL

BORN 10/10/59 (England)

The daughter of folk singer Ewan MacColl made her recorded debut with the Drug Addix, a 1978 R&B band who adopted a punk image for their Chiswick Records EP *The Drug Addix Make a Record* in 1978. Leading off with the notorious "Gay Boys in Bondage," it featured MacColl under the name Mandy Doubt, the remainder of the group including such unlikely pseudonyms as Art Nouveau and Sterling Sterling.

Make a Record was only ever intended as a one-off. It garnered a fairly enthusiastic response, though, and towards the end of the year, Stiff Records made a tentative move for the Drug Addix, inviting them into the studio to record a demo. The results were less than satisfying, but MacColl herself attracted attention and when she was sacked from the Drug Addix, she was invited back to Stiff. She took with her the recently written "They Don't Know" and in June 1979, a new version, recorded with ex-Damned guitarist Lu Edmonds' band, the Edge, was released — on the eve of a distributors' strike which effectively killed the record.

A second single, "You Caught Me Out," was produced (its B-side, "Boys," paired MacColl with the Boomtown Rats), but MacColl and Stiff parted company shortly before its October 1979 release date and the record was shelved. She signed to Polydor the following year and in February 1981 released "Keep Your Hands off My Baby," followed by the hit "There's a Guy Works down the Chip Shop Swears He's Elvis" (#14 UK).

MacColl toured Ireland in the wake of "Chip Shop," but combining acute stage fright with near-total inexperience, she returned home vowing never to tour again, a resolution she kept until 1990. In the meantime, two further singles, "See That Girl" and a cover of the Beach Boys' "You Still Believe in Me," failed — a fate which also awaited her debut album, the Nick Lowe-produced *Desperate Character*.

Polydor promptly commissioned a second album, pairing MacColl with several different groups of musicians, including separate bands led by former Squeeze pianist Jools Holland and one-time Marmalade mainstay Junior Campbell. Edmonds returned to the fold as guitarist and occasional co-writer, together with bassist Pino Palladino (later to find fame in Paul Young's band), ex-Physical Alan Lee Shaw and ska legend, Rico. The album, tentatively titled *Real*, was completed and then Polydor dropped her.

Another year of comparative inactivity passed, during which MacColl resurfaced just once, in August 1983, with a re-recorded version of the abandoned *Real*'s "Berlin." Released by the tiny North of Watford independent, it did little sales-wise, but did remind Stiff Records that MacColl was still around, just as they were seeking material for comedienne Tracey Ullman's first album. A cover of "They Don't Know" hit #2 while MacColl also wrote (and co-produced) the album's title track, "You Broke My Heart in 17 Places" (#34 US). She then signed again with Stiff and released a new single, a cover of the '60s death song, "Terry."

Her follow-up, Billy Bragg's "New England" (#7 UK), appeared in summer 1984; MacColl was pregnant with her first child by husband Steve Lillywhite and was unable to promote the record heavily, but still it soared up the chart, peaking on the very day the couple's first son was born. Again, however, a follow-up proved elusive; "He's on the Beach" sank and so, the following year, did Stiff Records.

The company declared bankruptcy in early 1986 and MacColl was left unable to record until the receiver sold her contract. All she could do legally was session work and, between 1986 and 1989, she became one of the most in-demand session vocalists around, often (but not always) working in tandem with husband Lillywhite and recording with the Talking Heads, the Rolling Stones, The Smiths, Robert Plant, the Wonder Stuff, and Van Morrison.

She returned to the chart as special guest on Bragg's "Greetings to the New Brunette" (#58 UK); she also duetted with Shane MacGowan on The Pogues' "Fairytale of New York" (#2 UK) Christmas hit in 1987, touring Germany with the band in 1988, before returning home to demo new material with Lillywhite and Hitmen guitarist Pete Glenister.

The results were powerful enough for Virgin to promptly rescue her from the clutches of the receiver and in March 1989, "Free World" (#43 UK) became MacColl's first single in almost four years. A cover of the Kinks' "Days" (#12 UK) in June 1989 was followed by her much-delayed sophomore album, *Kite* (#34 UK), recorded with "Chipshop" co-writer Phil Rambow, Elvis Costello drummer Pete Thomas, Rumour guitarist Martin Belmont, plus Glenister, Bobby Valentino, Gavin Povey, and Paul Riley (ex-Roogalator).

Throughout 1990, MacColl gathered material for her next album, *Electric Landlady* (#17 UK). Contributors this time included ex-Smiths guitarist Johnny Marr, with whom she composed "Walking Down Madison" (#23 UK), her May 1991 US breakthrough. Two further singles, the Latin-esque "My Affair" (#56 UK) and "All I Ever Wanted," both flopped, however, and with *Electric Landlady's* sales failing to match those of *Kite*, MacColl was dropped towards the end of 1991.

Signing to IRS (ZTT in the UK), she pieced together a new band around Glenister and former Ruts rhythm section Dave Ruffy and Vince Seggs and continued working on the album she'd begun before Virgin let her go, *Titanic Days*. It finally appeared in fall 1993, her broadest and most developed album yet, but also her darkest — its creation coincided with the breakdown of her marriage.

Two singles from the album, "Can't Stop Killing You" (another MacColl/Marr composition) and "Angel," were followed by a collaboration with Morrissey mainstay Boz Boorer, "Perfect Day" (#75 UK), a duet with Lemonhead Evan Dando (Morrissey was originally intended to perform) and "Caroline" (#58 UK), recorded with producer Vic Van Vugt. Both were included on *Galore*, the first full MacColl retrospective (following several earlier, single-label collections) and her final album of the 1990s. MacColl finally broke a four-year silence in late 1999 with a new single, "Mambo De La Luna," a taster for the forthcoming *Tropical Brainstorm* — an exploration of her longstanding interest in Cuban music. A second single, "In These Shoes?" followed in the new year.

Kirsty MacColl LPs

7 Desperate Character (Polydor — UK) 1981 With MacColl already writing songs of incredible delicacy and excitement, the cow-punk drive of "Chip Shop" is not the best cut, but remains the best known.

8 Kite (Charisma) 1989 With Johnny Marr (Smiths) and Pete Glenister (Hitmen) on board, a powerful set highlighted by "Don't Come the Cowboy with Me, Sonny Jim," a lovely "Complainte Pour Ste Catherine," and the Smiths' "You Just Haven't Earned It Yet Baby."

7 Electric Landlady (Charisma) 1991 A not-too-successful amalgam of style and approach nevertheless scored with the hip-hop "Walking Down Madison" and the salsa "My Affair," but was best when it stuck to what it knew — the tremendous "All I Ever Wanted."

9 Titanic Days (IRS) 1993 MacColl's darkest revolves around the end of her marriage to producer Lillywhite; "Soho Square" is bag lady heartbreaking, while the colossal "Tomorrow Never Comes" conjures visions of a bitterly updated Shangri-Las. The semi-twee "Angel" lets the side down a little, but overall the entire thing is a triumph, with MacColl revealed among the UK's finest functioning songwriters.

9 Tropical Brainstorm (V2 — UK) 2000 The natural exuberance of MacColl's beloved Cuban musical styles forms a fascinating — and magnificent — partnership with her own lyrical sadness and cynicism. *Mojo* magazine called the album "grump a drole ole," and songs like "England 2 Colombia 0;" discussing a doomed one-night-stand and the painful "Wrong Again" live up

to that tag with bitter vengeance. Meanwhile, "Treachery," co-written with '60s hit-maker Graham Gouldman, is as good as its pedigree — the union of two of Britain's greatest ever songwriters — insists it should be.

Selected Compilations and Archive Releases

7 Kirsty MacColl (Polydor — UK) 1985 Rearranged version of *Desperate Character*, salvaging some of the cancelled second album.

8 Galore (IRS) 1995 A story-so-far compilation reaching back to her first UK hits ("Chip Shop," Billy Bragg's "New England," and MacColl's own original of Tracey Ullman's "They Don't Know"); embracing the Pogues-powered "Fairytale of New York"; then racing home with highlights from three last albums, and two last singles. A second version wrapping up further duets and sessions would be a rare treat indeed.

MADNESS

FORMED 1977 *(London, England)*
ORIGINAL LINE-UP *Suggs (b. Graham McPherson, 1/13/61, Hastings — vocals); Chas (b. Carl Smythe, 1/14/59 — guitar); Barso (b. Mike Barson, 5/21/58, London — keyboards); Billy Whizz (b. John Hasler — drums), Kix (b. Lee Thompson, 10/5/57, London — sax); Chrissy Boy (b. Chris Foreman, 8/8/58, London — guitar)*

Although they did not emerge on the national scene until 1979, following their absorption into the 2-Tone dynasty, Madness had been kicking around the north London circuit since June 1977 when a skinhead friend invited the North London Invaders to play a party at another friend's house. The quartet of Barso, Billy Whizz, Kix, and Chrissy Boy, plus vocalist Dikron, played rock'n'roll in the garden, the party went on indoors, and aside from the experience of actually playing live, the band also came away with two new members, Suggs and Chas.

According to legend, Suggs only knew the words to one song when he turned up at the next rehearsal, "See You Later Alligator." Such shortcomings initially didn't matter, as he was also more interested in going to soccer games than rehearsing. He was fired and the others continued to scour north London for further suitable nutty boys. So, it seems, did Suggs, but he never found any. He gave up the sport and returned to the Invaders.

Sporadic line-up changes continued to shape the band. Chas and Billy Whizz both departed; in their place came Mark "Bedders" Bedford (b. London, 8/24/61) and Daniel "Woody" Woodgate (b. London, 10/19/60), while horn player Chas Smash (b. Cathal Smyth, London, 1/14/59), too, contributed to the mutating brew.

The Invaders' ultimate shift from rock'n'roll to blue beat, however, was Barso's doing. His organ sound dominated the band, lending it a peculiarly carnival-like feel, which in turn slipped easily into a syncopated dance beat. Prince Buster songs began sliding into the set alongside their own early originals: "Madness," which they took for their new name and "One Step Beyond," which would become their second single. By the time the group ran into The Specials at a Rock Against Racism gig at the Hope and Anchor, Madness' direction was confirmed and the only surprise was, as Suggs later remarked, finding another band in Britain with the same tastes as their own.

Suggs and Jerry Dammers kept in touch and when The Specials next played the capital, a sold-out show at the Nashville on June 8, 1979, they asked the Londoners to be their support. Three weeks later, the same bill reconvened to serenade a sardine-solid crowd, while outside riot police and the ticketless hordes eyed one another distrustfully.

Madness joined the 2-Tone roster shortly after, offering up the fruits of a demo they'd recently recorded with producer Clive Langer — another tribute to Buster, "The Prince" (#16 UK). It was released at the end of July, just as "Gangsters" finally breached the British Top 30 and quickly followed The Specials into the chart.

Madness' deal with 2-Tone was for one single only; in October, they signed to Stiff Records, shortly before going out on the road again with The Specials, and scored instant Top 10 hits with "One Step Beyond (#7 UK) and "My Girl" (#3 UK). Their debut album, also titled One Step Beyond (#128 US, #2 UK), then soared two places higher in Britain than The Specials'.

Madness also got to America ahead of The Specials, in November 1979 and while it would be several years more before they translated live success into chart positions, still Madness' Python-esque Nutty Boy appeal was always closer to American hearts than The Specials' drier (if not deadpan) humor could ever hope to be. It was one thing, after all, for Terry Hall to announce a song as "the last dance before the Third World War," or to lead his fellows through a funereal dirge called "Enjoy Yourself," it was another for Madness to relive every great Buster Keaton film you've ever wanted to see, then round it out with the musical soundtrack to a hail of flying cream pies.

Touring the UK with The Specials, Madness encountered many of the same pressures that eventually spelled the end of the headlining group, most notably the violence of the "typical" 2-Tone audience. Where The Specials allowed the carnage to wear them down, however, Madness began to shift direction, retaining the nuttiness, but losing the ska. "Night Train to Cairo" (#6 UK) and "Baggy Trousers" (#3 UK), the latter heralding the band's second album, Abso-

lutely (#146 US, #2 UK), were Madness' vinyl farewell to the music; an appearance in the 2-Tone movie Dance Craze their visual departure.

Doubts that Madness' own creativity could sustain an abrupt lurch towards mainstream pop were dispelled by four successive Top 10 singles through 1981 — "Embarrassment" (#4 UK), the instrumental "Return of the Los Palmas Seven" (#7 UK), "Grey Day" (#4 UK), and "Shut Up" (#7 UK) — although an attempt to make celluloid stars of the boys through the Beatles-esque Take It Or leave It movie bombed.

A trip to Compass Point Studios in the Bahamas spawned Madness' next album, Seven (#5 UK), just in time for Christmas, while the new year brought with it a hit rendering of soul balladeer Labi Siffre's "It Must Be Love" (#4 UK), with Siffre himself conferring his approval by appearing in the attendant video. And while the follow-up, "Cardiac Arrest" (#14 UK) became the first Madness single since their debut not to make the Top 10, summer 1982 brought the band a remarkable triple crown as their new single, "House of Fun," the Complete Madness greatest hits album, and a video collection of the same name all topped their respective charts.

Two new songs, "Drivin' in My Car" (#4 UK) and "Our House" (#7US, #5 UK) pursuing the nutty sound into distinctly classic Kinks-ish territory, sandwiched the release of the Rise and Fall (#10 UK) album. "Our House" would also become the band's American breakthrough, two months after winning an Ivor Novello award for Best Pop Song of 1982.

"It Must Be Love" (#33 US) was hastily resurrected as a follow-up and the band toured to scenes reminiscent of their early days in the UK. Madness (#41 US), a compilation drawn in the main from Rise and Fall, plus attendant singles, coincided with the outing.

Madness powered upwards. Taken from 1984's Keep Moving album (#109 US, #6 UK), "Wings of a Dove" (#2 UK), "The Sun and the Rain" (#72 US, #5 UK), and the contrivedly Cockney "Michael Caine" (#11 UK) kept the band hot, while the news that Barso intended quitting for a new life in the Netherlands did not initially slow the momentum any. But "The Sun and the Rain" became the band's final American chart hit while "One Better Day" (#17 UK) in June, marked their final single for Stiff Records, before they located to their own Zarjazz label (the name was lifted from the 2000 AD comic). And it was tempting fate to title their next single "Yesterday's Men" (#18), because suddenly it seemed as though they were.

Although Zarjazz got off to a good start, with first signing (and former Undertones vocalist) Feargal Sharkey's rendition of Madness' own "Listen to Your Father" (#23 UK), Smash and Suggs' Fink Brothers' alias flopped with "Mutants in Mega City" (#50 UK) and a ska stars for Africa-type benefit single, "Starvation Tam Tam Pour L'Ethiope" (#33 UK), made a mockery of its makers' pedigree — UB40, General Public, and The Specials all joined Madness under the Starvation banner.

Madness' first self-released album, *Mad Not Mad* (#16 UK), was poorly received and though the band deliberately returned to the nutty sound of old for "Uncle Sam" (#21 UK), still the magic remained at arm's length. A cover of Scritti Politti's "Sweetest Girl' (#35 UK) fared even worse and the band began to prepare for the end. In July, Madness played their final show at the Docklands festival in Hartlepool and in September, the break-up was made public. Their final single, "Waiting for the Ghost Train" (#18 UK), was accompanied by a second hits collection, *Utter Madness* (#29 UK) in December 1986.

After 18 months of silence, Suggs, Chrissy Boy, Kix, and Smash reunited as The Madness, with Specials founder Jerry Dammers and former Elvis Costello/Attractions Steve Nieve, and Bruce Thomas. An eponymous album (#44 UK), however, was poorly received and though "I Pronounce You" (#44 UK) enjoyed a modicum of success, "What's That" became the band's first ever single not to make the Top 75. The group broke up again soon after.

Foreman and Thompson reconvened as the Nutty Boys and released the *Crunch* album in May 1990; Suggs resurfaced alongside Morrissey on one cut, "Piccadilly Palare," from the ex-Smith's *Bona Drag* compilation album, in 1990; Bedders played bass on the same singer's *Kill Uncle* album. The appearance of a third Madness compilation, *Divine Madness* (#1 UK) in early 1992, however, sparked a new flurry of interest in the band and with "It Must be Love" (#6 UK), "House of Fun" (#40 UK), and "My Girl"(#27 UK) all finding renewed life a decade on from their original release, the classic Madness line-up returned to headline their own Madstock Festival in London.

A live recording from that show, *Madstock* (#22 UK), appeared in November; a movie followed in the new year, while the reconstituted band's first studio recording in six years, a cover of Jimmy Cliff's "The Harder They Come" (#22 UK) was a surprise Christmas hit.

1993 saw Madness stage a string of sold-out Christmas concerts at Wembley Arena; 1994 brought a second Madstock festival and since that time, the band have remained a perennial live act — a second live album, *Universal Madness*, was recorded in Los Angeles in 1998. Meanwhile, Suggs also became the first ex-member to mount a convincing solo career when 1995 saw him launch a string of hits, beginning with a cover of the Beatles' "I'm Only Sleeping" (#7UK). Madness themselves finally returned to the studio in 1999 to cut their first all-new album in over a decade, *Wonderful* (#17 UK) and single "Lovestruck" (#10 UK). The

following June, Madness were among the highlights of the Ian Dury tribute concert in London.

Madness LPs

8 One Step Beyond (Sire) 1979 This is not your father's ska. Madness reinvent the popular island sound of the '60s, then carry on re-creating it in a madcap ride through musical mayhem, where rocksteady collides with ballerinas and boats on the Nile, pretty pop, and punk rock, pausing only to raise the Union Jack, salute Prince Buster, and grab some pints down the pub.

7 Absolutely (Sire) 1980 Slipping off the roller coaster, Madness' growing maturity means leaving wackiness behind and *Absolutely* leans towards more reflective numbers that trade exuberance for musical complexity. Among a heap of longer, more shaded, and serious tracks, only the rambunctious "Baggy Trousers" captures the infectious excitement of *Beyond*. No longer nutty boys, the band have transformed into introspective teens.

8 Seven (Stiff) 1981 Reflecting the more somber mood of the day, Madness expand their lyrical vision into socio-political concerns, making for a bleak album with only brief respites from adult issues. There's still some vaudevillian charm to be found — steel drums to lighten the mood and even a stab at reggae, but like The Specials' "Ghost Town," *Seven* is a sign of the times, magnificently catching the despair of the day on disc.

7 The Rise and Fall (Stiff) 1982 Madness' most personal album, *Rise* centers on the members' childhoods and is heavy with yearning and nostalgia. Expanding their sound in new directions, the album was compared at the time with *Sgt. Pepper*, but never reaches the surreal extremes of that record. Still, mature songwriting, elaborate instrumentation and a subtle blending of genres was equally astounding.

7 Keep Moving (Geffen) 1984 After the heights of *Rise*, *Moving* inevitably suffered disappointed fallout from the critics. But what it lacked in creative heights was offset by musical coherence. The album foreshadows the future eruption of Brit-pop — lush arrangements, the complexity of even the poppiest tracks, musical references to the past, melancholic tone, and, most tellingly, the lyrical suggestions that life really was once better then than now.

5 Mad Not Mad (Geffen) 1985 With melancholy fast turning to hopelessness and cynicism, lyrically much of *Mad* is depressing, an emotional sentiment which jars with the album's slick, glossy production and metronomic programmed drums. The new romantics would have given their wardrobes for this perfect funk-fired club sound, but it's sheer madness for a Madness album.

3 The Madness (Virgin, UK) 1988 Way past their sell-by date, an attempt to hang anything on the old brand name... with anything being the operative word.

7 Madstock! [LIVE] (Go! Discs,UK) 1992

7 Universal Madness [LIVE] (Golden Voice) 1999 Older, grayer, and far wrinklier than the perpetrators of all the memories served up here, Madness hone in on their Nutty Boy peak, and "Embarrassment" is the closest they get to past embarrassments. A cunningly clever return to glory.

8 Wonderful (Virgin) 1999 Powerful comeback acknowledges what was great about the old style Nuttiness, and what really should be left in the memory banks. A handful of genuinely great new songs rise above the odd bits of filler, and an inevitable comeback becomes an absolute delight.

Selected Compilations and Archive Releases

8 Complete Madness (Stiff) 1982 Non-stop hits collection... the first of many.

8 Madness (Geffen) 1983 US collection combines recent singles with the best of *Rise and Fall*.

8 Heavy Heavy Hits (EMI) 1999 Some half a dozen hits collections later, a solid — and solidly remastered — reflection on the band's biggest and best.

9 The Lot 1999 Box set of all six original albums, plus singles and 24 computer-powered videos.

Suggs LPs

7 The Lone Ranger (WEA) 1996
7 The Three Pyramids (WEA) 1998

MAGAZINE

FORMED *1977 (Manchester, England)*
ORIGINAL LINE-UP *Howard Devoto (vocals); John McGeogh (guitar); Barry Adamson (bass); Bob Dickinson (keyboards); Martin Jackson (drums)*

Though Howard Devoto's departure from The Buzzcocks paved the way for that band to unleash the most important sequence of singles in recent pop memory, his own vision — as exemplified by Magazine's debut single, "Shot by Both Sides" (#41 UK), was considerably darker. The song was originally written with Pete Shelley during their shared days as Buzzcocks, but while that band would record it as yet another shattered love song, "Promises," Magazine would turn it into a masterpiece of paranoid indecision.

"Shot by Both Sides" was released in January 1978, some four months after Magazine debuted at the last night of Manchester's legendary Electric Circus punk club. That night, as so many, the band's moody approach left much of the audience scratching their heads, but the single was a hit and in June, the band's debut album, *Real Life* (#29 UK), followed suit.

Line-up changes shook the band through 1978. Bob Dickinson quit shortly before the single was recorded; he was replaced for the album by Dave Formula, before Martin Jackson left after the band's first tour. Paul Spencer replaced

him through the summer, with John Doyle taking over in December. (Jackson later appeared in the Chameleons UK.)

Further singles "Touch and Go," and in the months leading up to Magazine's second album, "Give Me Everything" and "Rhythm of Cruelty," failed to chart, although *Secondhand Daylight* (#38UK), at least made the Top 40. Magazine gigged heavily, however, both at home and abroad, and while the failure of "Song from Under the Floorboards" and a cover of Sly Stone's "Thank You (Falettinme Be Mice Elf Again)" was mystifying, their third album, *The Correct Use of Soap* (#28 UK), returned the band to the chart with the "Sweetheart Contract" (#54 UK) single following soon after.

July 1980 saw John McGeogh quit to join Siouxsie and the Banshees as full time replacement for The Cure's Robert Smith; the guitarist also drew Barry Adamson and Formula into an *ad hoc* band formed by new romantic figureheads Steve Strange and Rusty Egan and Ultravox's Midge Ure and Billy Currie, and over the next three years, Visage would score half a dozen genre-defining hit singles, including the classic "Fade to Grey."

Magazine, meanwhile, continued on with former Ultravox guitarist Robin Smith and in November 1980 released *Play* (#69 UK), a live album recorded in Melbourne, Australia two months previous. It was to be Simon's sole release with the band; he quit in May 1981, and Magazine recorded their final album, *Magic, Murder and the Weather* (#39 UK) with Ben Mandelson (ex-Amazorblades).

The group split up shortly afterwards. Mandelson joined the Mekons, Doyle hooked up with the Armoury Show, Adamson joined Buzzcock Pete Shelley's solo band and later Nick Cave's Bad Seeds (he would also release a string of conceptual solo albums). Devoto launched a solo career with Formula and cut the well received *Jerky Versions of a Dream* with Neil Pyzer (keyboards) and Alan St Clair (guitar), both later of Spear of Destiny, Martin Heath (bass) and Pat Ahorn (drums).

When that project ended, the singer collaborated briefly with French electronic musician B. Szajner and appeared on 4AD collective This Mortal Coil's *It'll End in Tears*, before vanishing for close to four years. He resurfaced in January 1988 with Liverpudlian guitarist Noko, a new project, Luxuria, and the "Redneck" single. An album, *The Unanswerable Lust*, and a second single, "The Public Highway," followed in 1988; 1990 brought the album *Beast Box* and singles "The Beast Box Is Dreaming" and "Jezebel." Devoto would then effectively retire from the music industry; Noko subsequently formed Apollo 440.

Magazine LPs

8 Real Life (Virgin) 1978 Drenching its pop instincts in widescreen, sinister drama, so much of what would later lead the post-punk pre-goth pack emerged out of Magazine's early vision — primarily because most of the members were involved in those other bands somewhere down the line — supergroup super-embryo. It's Devoto's belligerent vocals which carry the show, though, with a re-recorded "Shot by Both Sides," the ugly glitter stomp of "The Light Pours out of Me" and the conspiratorial "Motorcade" leading the freak parade.

9 Secondhand Daylight (Virgin) 1979 Still heavy on keyboards and atmosphere, but with Devoto's naturally obtuse songwriting opening up to just a hint of daylight (secondhand or otherwise), "Feed the Enemy" and "Rhythm of Cruelty" open the album with devastating promise, while the brutal "Permafrost" closes it down with one of Magazine's finest moments.

8 The Correct Use of Soap (Virgin) 1980 "Song from Under the Floorboards" should have been a worldwide smash hit, a bub-bling almost-funk creation which fed directly into the album's other obsessions — Sly Stone's "Thank You," the playful "I Want to Burn Again," and the distinctly unreassuring "Because You're Frightened."

7 The Alternate Use of Soap (Virgin — UK) 1980 Utterly overlooked by the modern CD age, *Soap*'s limited edition dop-pelganger serves up highly serviceable demos and alternate takes, including a dramatic revision of the first album's "The Light Pours out of Me."

9 Play [LIVE] (IRS) 1980 The best live album of the entire UK new wave, running through a non-stop litany of Magazine's best. "The Light" and "Permafrost" effortlessly exceed their studio incarnations, "Give Me Everything" and "20 Years Ago" are revealed as unexpected classics and "Parade" is simply breathtaking.

7 Magic Murder & the Weather (IRS) 1981 Even before Devoto acknowledged the band's demise, *Murder* left no doubt that the chapter had ended. "Honeymoon Killers" isn't even the grimmest cut in sight and Devoto himself has never sounded so resigned.

Selected Compilations and Archive Releases

6 After the Fact (IRS US/Virgin UK) 1982 Two almost dissimi-lar collections with one title and just five tracks in common. The UK release is the most conventional, concentrating on albums and hits, the US hunts around for B-sides and odds. Neither, sadly, does the band much justice.

9 Rays & Hail (Virgin) 1987

9 Scree (Rarities 1978–81) (Virgin) 1991 Two sets wiping out the confusing patchiness of *After the Fact*, rounding up (almost) all you could need to know, including — for the first time — the single-only version of "Shot by Both Sides" (on *Rays*) and three more stunning live cuts (*Scree*).

8 BBC Radio 1 in Concert [LIVE] (Windsong) 1993

Howard Devoto LP

7 Jerky Versions of the Dream (Virgin) 1983 Working with a scratch semi-Magazine line-up, a deliberately cold and intellec-tual set which eschews the visceral thrill of Magazine for a more considered arty-awkwardness. Difficult.

Luxuria LPs

6 The Unanswerable Lust (Beggars Banquet) 1988

6 Beast Box (Beggars Banquet) 1990

Barry Adamson LPs

6 Moss Side Story (Mute) 1989 The explosive "Man with the Golden Arm" raises the curtain on what would become a fasci-nating (if occasionally overwrought) investigation of rock's most cinematic obsessions — one which has continued on over Adam-son's entire solo output.

5 Delusion — Original Motion Picture Soundtrack (Mute) 1991

6 Soul Murder (Mute) 1992 A B-movie who dunnit, sleuth Harry Pendulum as a flashy James Bond whose sense of self-gran-deur would be funny if the lynching near the end wasn't so hor-rifically lifelike. '60s TV cop show sound-a-likes muffle the conversations going on in the shadows, and the silhouettes dance against orchestral chintz.

4 The Negro Inside Me (Mute) 1993 Half film score, half dance record, a six-track, 31-minute mini-album highlighted by the least sexy version of "Je T'Aime" ever conceived.

6 A Prayer Mat of Flesh (Mute) 1995

6 Oedipus Schmoedipus (Mute) 1996 Nick Cave and Pulp's Jarvis Cocker guest, and sound as out of place as every other even marginally rock-related property on this supreme slab of distur-bance-with-a-(bit of a)-beat.

Selected Compilations and Archive Releases

8 The Murky World Of (Mute) 1999 Twelve-track collection cherry-picking an incontestable best of, including *Soul Murder*'s "007: A Fantasy James Bond Theme" and *Oedipus*'s carnivorous "Something Wicked This Way Comes."

MARILYN MANSON

FORMED 1989 *(Tampa Bay, FL)*

ORIGINAL LINE-UP *Marilyn Manson (b. Brian Warner, 1/5/69, Canton, OH — vocals, loops); Olivia Newton-Bundy (b. Brian Tutunick — bass); Daisy Berkowitz (b. Scott Putesky — gui-tar); Zsa Zsa Speck (b. Perry Pandrea — keyboards)*

Few people caught it, but Marilyn Manson — already an aspiring poet around Ft. Lauderdale — made his public debut with a bit part in *21 Jump Street* when he was 18. Then he started a band and nobody was able to miss anything he did again.

Formed by Manson and Daisy Berkowitz (a surname borrowed from another mass murderer, Son of Sam David) in Tampa Bay, FL, Marilyn Manson and The Spooky Kids made their live debut at Churchill's Hideaway in Miami in November 1989. From the start, the intention was to shock, the grotesquely androgynous Manson lashing together an act which drew as heavily from such adolescent preoccupations as Satanism and serial killers as it did from some remarkably well-ordered social commentary and a sense of shameless stagecraft.

Zsa Zsa Speck and Olivia Newton Bundy quit, to be replaced by Madonna Wayne Gacy (born Stephen Bier — keyboards) and Gidget Gein (born Brad Stewart — bass); by the time drummer Sara Lee Lucas (born Freddy Streithorst) joined in July 1990, the band's act had expanded to include a wealth of onstage props — chainsaws, fires, animals, cages, anything to provoke a reaction.

Certainly Trent Reznor was impressed when Marilyn Manson and the Spooky Kids opened a Nine Inch Nails show that summer and over the next year, the group continued to develop and refine their craft. A series of self-released

© Jim Steinfeldt/Chansley Entertainment Archives

cassettes was made available at shows, bearing such titles as *Meat Cleaver Beat*, *Grist-O-Line*, and *Snuffy's VCR* (all 1991), *After School Special*, *Lunchbox*, and *Family Jams* in early 1992.

That latter was the last to bear the Spooky Kids appellation; in August 1992, the group shortened its name to Marilyn Manson alone and the following January, released their final cassette album, *Refrigerator*. Four months later, the self-proclaimed Antichrist Superstars became the first band signed to Trent Reznor and manager John Malm's Nothing label.

Early recording sessions with former Swan Roli Mossiman were scrapped; Reznor himself would eventually take control, recording at Record Plant, before moving the mixing to his own studio in the same house on Cielo Drive, L.A., where actress Sharon Tate was murdered by the Charles Manson family in 1969. (Reznor's *Downward Spiral* album was also recorded there.) Then, pausing only to replace Gein with Twiggy Ramirez (born Jeordie White), Marilyn Manson prepared for their debut release with a handful of shows supporting NIN.

A single, "Get Your Gunn," was released in June 1994; the album, *Portrait of an American Family*, followed in July, but not before its original artwork — which included a nude photograph of the six-year-old Manson — was scrapped at the insistence of Nothing's parent label, Warner Brothers. The band returned to the road to promote the album, again opening for NIN, but were now flirting with notoriety on a major level.

In October, Anton LaVey ordained Manson a Reverend in the Church of Satan and during a performance in Salt Lake City that same month, Manson tore apart a copy of *The Book of Mormon*. Two months later, during the band's own American Family Tour, the singer was arrested in Jacksonville, FL and charged with violating the Adult Entertainment Code, after performing part of his set naked.

Still on the road in March, Manson set fire to Lucas' drum kit onstage; the drummer quit the band immediately the tour was over, to be replaced by Ginger Fish, just days before Marilyn Manson hit the road again, opening for Danzig (Korn were also on the bill). That tour ended in May and by September, the band were out again, for a five-month tour which ended with Berkowitz's departure in April. He was replaced by Zim Zum (ex-Life Sex and Death), shortly before the release of the EP *Smells Like Children* (#31 US) in June 1996.

With MTV hesitantly picking up on the band's latest video, a cover of the Eurythmics' "Sweet Dreams," Marilyn Manson was finally being catapulted into households which might never have gone near a NIN or Danzig concert. By the time the band returned to the road in September, however, a lot of people were heading for Manson gigs and not all of them were fans.

In much the same manner as Alice Cooper, Perry Farrell, and Courtney Love before him, Manson himself worked to create a public persona which was simultaneously utterly outrageous and, in the eyes of middle America, utterly believable, denying few rumors and starting many.

"I've at least brought a sense of humor to things," he reflected in late 1999. "I think people tend to be too serious when it comes to subjects of morality, subjects of human character, like violence and how man deals with those things. I try and point out the irony, point out things with sarcasm, so people don't get so caught up in it all. I think, like any good devil, it's about a sense of humor — not to say I don't take what I do seriously, but I think it's important to hold things up and laugh at them. Including yourself."

Not everybody saw the joke. The religious right, of course, loathed Manson with placard-waving passion; concerned parents joined them in their lobbying and soon Manson's lawyer Paul Cambrio would be almost as busy as the band, as he protected his clients' interests against a succession of suddenly outraged city elders, wanting to ban the band from their towns.

Into the midst of the gathering storm, *Antichrist Superstar* (#3 US, #73 UK) slammed onto the pre-Christmas 1996 buying market, bearing with it two new singles and videos, "Beautiful People" (#18 UK) and "Tourniquet" (#28 UK) and highlighted by "I Don't Like the Drugs (But the Drugs Like Me)," in concert the cue for a "give us a d..." cheer to rival anything Country Joe MacDonald did at Woodstock. (An album out-take, "Astonishing Panorama of the Endtimes," would become a hit in late 1999, after being included on the *Last Tour on Earth* live album.)

Headline, rumor, and debate followed the band everywhere, including the belief that Manson intended killing himself onstage in Asbury Park, NJ on Halloween 1996. Of course he didn't; rather, the band just kept on gigging, through Europe and the UK in November and December, back across the US in the new year, then onto the Pacific Rim in March.

The bans started in April 1997 when Columbia, SC legislators introduced a joint resolution to prohibit Marilyn Manson from performing on state property. Days later, lawyer Cambrio joined with the ACLU to contest Richmond, VA's decision to cancel the band's upcoming show; two weeks later, Marilyn Manson were taking on the New Jersey Sports and Exposition Authority, over their decision to cancel that summer's Ozzfest if Manson was on the bill.

Both Richmond and New Jersey were eventually forced to relent and following a short UK tour in May/June, the band joined Ozzy Osbourne and co. for a triumphant Giants Stadium performance. Then it was back to Europe for a string of further festivals.

Despite their successes, the band were not immune to misfortune and tragedy. On May 9, 1997, lighting technician Sean McGrann was killed after falling 90 feet to the ground while preparing the DC Armory venue for that evening's show, while both Gidget Gein and Daisy Berkowitz filed lawsuits against the band alleging breach of contract. And in November (just weeks after Manson bared his buttocks at the MTV Video Music Awards), a Senate committee investigating the effects of modern music on children heard testimony from a Burlington, ND father whose son, Richard, committed suicide after listening to *Antichrist Superstar*. Ironically, his appearance came just two weeks after Manson and Ramirez did their own bit for the children, by appearing at the Bridge School benefit to perform "Beautiful People" with Smashing Pumpkins.

Of course, the group continued working through the controversies which their very existence seemed to inspire, with Manson himself encouraging the outrage for all he was worth. His autobiography, *The Long Hard Road Out of Hell*, became a bestseller in early 1998, while some six months off the road had enabled the band to turn in its best album yet, September 1998's *Mechanical Animals* (#1 US, #8 UK).

Redesigning Manson as a glam rock monster, more than slightly reminiscent of '80s supergroup Sigue Sigue Sputnik — if they had mated with the cast of A *Clockwork Orange* — the album hosted the classic single, "The Dope Show" (#12 UK), a European hit even after the band's latest tour was cancelled when Fish was stricken with mononucleosis. It would be October before Marilyn Manson finally returned to the road for tours which carried them through to May 1999 and of course, controversy awaited them.

First came a highly publicized battle with *Spin* magazine editor Craig Marks, sparked after a run-in with Manson's security in New York in November. In January 1999, Manson himself walked off stage at the final night of the Australian Big Day Out traveling festival, after being pelted with missiles; another show, in Cedar Rapids, IA, in March, would be similarly curtailed after Manson spotted a smiley face stuck to one of his stage props; while a string of dates with Courtney Love and Hole was surely preordained to end with an ill-tempered severance.

But Manson's outspoken attack on corporate "sports metal" bands (naming, but not specifically targeting, Korn and Limp Bizkit) — "illiterate apes," as he described them — won him support from a number of hitherto unimpressed sources (although it was no coincidence that his latest UK single was "Rock Is Dead"). And further sympathy arose following the band's absurd implication-by-association in the April 1999 Columbine High School massacre.

Manson cancelled the last five dates of his US tour in the wake of the slaughter, "out of respect for those lost," as a cautious press release put it, and he remained sensitive in July when another American tragedy, the death of JFK Jr., prompted the withdrawal of Manson's next video, "Coma White."

The video, which featured Manson's girlfriend Rose MacGowan as Jackie Kennedy and dealt with President Kennedy's 1963 assassination, would eventually be premiered on the internet and led off the band's fall 1999 video collection *God Is in the TV*, itself heralding the band's first live album, *The Last Tour on Earth* (#82 US). It would be followed in 2000 by a new studio album, described by Manson himself as "the most dark and violent music we've ever done, probably because of the abuse in the media that I received last year. I thought if I was going to get blamed for something, I'd give them a real reason. This album will make them wish that I was never born."

Marilyn Manson LPs

6 Portrait of an American Family (Nothing/Interscope) 1994
America's master of schlock shock duly delivers, leaving American moms and dads wondering if they need to lock up their sons *and* daughters? They, of course, already know that there's little here that Nine Inch Nails haven't already foisted upon them, but the refreshed industrial attack and some deliciously nasty rumors go a long way.

8 Smells Like Children 1995 Dramatically overstated EP, ostensibly packing 15 tracks, but actually concentrating on sound-bites and collages designed to make middle America wet itself further. The Eurythmics' "SweetDreams," an appropriately over the top "I Put a Spell on You," and Patti Smith's always-controversial "Rock'n'Roll Nigger" join Manson's own "Diary of a Dope Fiend" in the parents-baiting stakes.

8 Antichrist Superstar (Nothing/Interscope) 1996

9 Mechanical Animals (Nothing/Interscope) 1998 The band's sound takes a dramatically different turn with the delicious "Dope Show," a frenetic nod to post-Sigue Sigue Sputnik techno-glam, lashed by Manson's effervescent persona. Full of tongue-in-cheeky-as-ever moments, and a lot funnier than a lot of people gave it credit for.

7 The Last Tour on Earth [LIVE] (Nothing/Interscope) 1999 Accompanied by a juicy video, this set of live performances is capable, but could have been better.

Further Reading
The Long Hard Road Out of Hell by Marilyn Manson/Neil Strauss (Harpercollins 1998).

MARINE GIRLS

FORMED 1980 (Hatfield, England)
ORIGINAL LINE-UP Tracey Thorn (b. 9/26/62 — vocals, guitar); Alice Fox (b. 1966 — vocals); Jane Fox (b. 1963 — bass)

Although Thorn would undoubtedly become better known as vocalist and one half of Everything But the Girl, whose near 20-year career has seen them drift through a variety of putatively alternative forms and guises, her own roots — and indeed, her reputation for both innovation and style — lay in the Marine Girls. The Marine Girls were a distinctly post-new wave trio whose own immediate antecedents lay in the punk aesthetics of the Slits and the Raincoats, but toned down to a level which often made '90s lo-fi sound technologically crass.

Comparable at the time to Young Marble Giants, but redolent, too, of the Velvet Underground's sleepier moments, Thorn and the Fox sisters debuted in 1980 with one cut, "A Day By the Sea," on a cassette-only compilation, *Shed Soundz Sampler*. The following year, having formed their own In-Phaze label, they released an entire album, *Beach Party — Catch the Cod*, a remarkable collection of self-composed songs which, with better production, could have given early Bananarama a run for their money.

Dan Treacy of the Television Personalities was especially impressed; he reissued the album on his own, better-distributed Whaam! label (#29 UK indie). In-Phaze then followed through with the Girls' first single, the sparse "On My Mind" in early 1982 and, in February, the band recorded a well-received session for the John Peel Show. By late spring, the trio had signed with Cherry Red.

The label clearly saw Thorn as the group's greatest asset; the deal provided both for a Marine Girls album and a Thorn solo set and August brought the singer's *A Distant Shore* (#2 UK indie). December 1982, saw a Thorn single, the album's "Plain Sailing" (#6 UK indie); the Marine Girls, meanwhile, returned to action in January 1983 with the release of "Don't Come Back" (#21 UK indie), a trailer for their sophomore album, *Lazy Ways* (#4 UK indie). With the line-up augmented by saxophonist Tim Hall, the Marine Girls toured briefly and, in April, returned to the BBC to record a second Peel session. It would be one of their final acts.

By now, Thorn was also working with fellow Cherry Red artist Ben Watt as Everything But The Girl — their debut, an adaptation of Cole Porter's "Night and Day" (#6 UK indie), would be released in August. Jane Fox, too, was planning an extra curricular career, linking with the singularly named Barton as Jane. In May 1983, the pair released the à cappella "It's a Fine Day" (#5 UK indie), a song which would, in the hands of Opus III, become a massive European hit in 1992. A second Jane single, "I Want To Be With You," and album, *Jane and Barton* followed, by which time the Marine Girls had officially disbanded.

With Jane returning to sister Alice, the pair launched a new band, Grab Grab The Haddock, in mid-1984. They cut just two singles, "I'm Used Now" and, aptly, "The Last Fond Farewell," before retiring from the music industry.

Thorn and Watt, meanwhile, were to go from strength to strength; their second single, "Each and Every One" (#28 UK) and first album, *Eden* (#14 UK), were hits, while a well-publicized union with ex-Jam frontman Paul Weller's newly launched Style Council saw Thorn contribute one of her finest ever vocals to the song "Paris Match."

The pair's subsequent musical meanderings, generally classy and seldom dull, have nevertheless taken them far from the naïve questing of their earlier work, ultimately placing Everything But The Girl (alongside the Pretenders, the Eurythmics, and Simple Minds, among others) in that awkward no-man's-land which firmly divides the alternative scene (and ethic) from its mainstream counterpart.

Marine Girls LPs

9 Beach Party — Catch the Cod (In Phase — UK) 1981
Naïve, innocent, raw, loose — the Marine Girls were all these things and more. But they were also bloody good fun, even when Thorn slipped into total heartbreak vocal mode and the only album's only real flaw was the omission of the delicious "On My Mind" single.

7 Lazy Ways (Cherry Red — UK) 1983 The title track is one of those period classics which the early '80s in general (and Cherry Red signings in particular) seemed to turn out with monotonous regularity. The remainder of the album doesn't quite live up to its allure (or its predecessor's promise), as Tracey and Jane both began eyeing other possibilities. But still *Lazy Ways* is worth owning, if only to hear all about "That Fink, Jazz-Me-Blues Boy."

Tracey Thorn LP

8 Distant Shore (Cherry Red — UK) 1982 Thorn's brief but beautiful debut album might be sonically sparse, but showcases that so-pure voice to quite devastating effect. Her reading of the Velvets' "Femme Fatale" in particular deserves attention.

Jane LP

8 Jane and Barton (Cherry Red — UK) 1983 The superb "It's a Fine Day" dominates the album — of course it does. There again, with just five other songs for company, including the two part "You Are Over There" and the caustic "Ha Bloody Ha," it didn't have to try too hard. A sadly overlooked classic.

MASSIVE ATTACK

FORMED 1988 *(Bristol, England)*
ORIGINAL LINE-UP *Robert "3D" del Naja (b. 1966 — vocals); Andrew "Mushroom" Vowles (b. 1968 — keyboards); Grant "Daddy G" Marshall (b. 1959 — keyboards)*

3D, Mushroom, Daddy G, and Nellee Hooper originally performed together as the Wild Bunch, an ad hoc hip-hop collective built around their DJ-ing skills. The Wild Bunch's first show was staged to welcome a friend home from prison, although by the mid-1980s, their reputation was such that local musicians actually — and loudly — accused Wild Bunch parties of destroying live music in the city.

By 1987, the Bunch had self-released their first club-only singles, "Tearing Down the House," "Fucking Me Up," and a totally tripped-out rap revision of Burt Bacharach's "The Look of Love." Diva Shara Nelson slipped in around the same time as Hooper slipped out to work with Soul II Soul and spread the Wild Bunch sound across the globe.

Hooper returned to Bristol to find the Bunch had metamorphosed into Massive Attack and promptly produced their first single, a cover of Chaka Khan's "Any Love," released in July 1988 via a one-off deal with Warner Brothers — the first UK hip-hop act to land a major label contract. Shortly after, a song 3D co-wrote with Neneh Cherry, "Manchild," was pulled from Cherry's *Raw Like Sushi* album and became a club hit on both sides of the Atlantic.

Massive Attack signed with Circa Records in 1990, completing their transition from sound system homeboys to a dynamic alt/dance group in November 1990 with the release of "Daydreaming." Months later, "Unfinished Sympathy" (#13 UK) gave them their first UK hit single under the abbreviated name of Massive — the Attack was dropped to avoid any untoward associations with the Gulf War then raging over Iraq.

The group's first album, *Blue Lines* (#13 UK), followed, a remarkable record whose freshness belied its makers' relative recording inexperience. It was, 3D explained, "extending other people's beats and putting vocals on top of that. Massive Attack was taking that idea into the studio and expanding it. Starting with a simple loop or bass line, or just a simple drum beat and then turning it into a whole landscape of ideas. Things we couldn't do live. We suddenly found we had all these ideas in the studio."

Friends dropped by the studio to further color the vision: Tricky Kid, who would re-emerge in 1995 as Tricky with his own smash, *Maxinquaye*; reggae legend Horace Andy; and Neneh Cherry's husband and producer Cameron McVey would also contribute to *BlueLines'* eclectic fusion of sound and style, while a list of inspirations published in the CD booklet only amplified Massive Attack's achievement: Wally

Badarou, Public Image Ltd, John Lennon, Herbie Hancock, and Joe Gibbs were all cited.

Blue Lines would be nominated for a prestigious Brit Award, while "Safe from Harm" (#25 UK) hit in June 1991. Tours of Britain and the US followed, the challenge of the latter amplified by the departure of Nelson and generally regarded as a disaster — in Minneapolis, the curtain was lowered upon the band, so disjointed was their performance.

In the studio, however, they could do no wrong. A Massive Attack remix of U2's "Mysterious Ways" (#9 US) in January 1992 brought their sound to a vast audience, just in time for the *Massive Attack* (#27 UK) EP, featuring material dating back to 1988's "Any Love," plus one new track; and thoughts were turning towards the group's next album.

Return appearances from Hooper, Andy, and Tricky (whose two songs on *Protection*, "Karmacoma" and "Eurochild," would resurface in different guises during *Maxinquaye*) were guaranteed, but replacing Nelson proved harder. The Cocteau Twins' Liz Fraser and Banshee Siouxsie Sioux both turned down invitations to guest with the band (Fraser would eventually appear on 1998's *Mezzanine*), but Everything but the Girl's Tracey Thorn was offered the lyrics to "Protection" (the new album's eventual title) and turned in a vocal performance which itself would completely reinvent her own band's direction.

Thorn was joined by the unknown Nigerian singer Nicolette, described by 3D as "Billie Holiday on acid" while another newcomer was Geoff Barrow, who in turn would quickly emerge with Portishead, his own take on the fledgling trip-hop wave.

Indeed, by the time *Protection* (#60 US, #4 UK) was released in October 1994, trip-hop (a term Massive Attack themselves despised) was already a mass marketable commodity. From Portishead and Morcheeba in the UK, to Japan where DJ Krush was ripping it up, syncopated hip-hop beats, loops, and samples abounded. Three singles from the album — Nicolette's showcase "Sly" (#24 UK), Thorn's "Protection" (#14 UK), and Tricky's "Karmacoma" (#28 UK) — ensured that Massive Attack remained at the forefront of the movement.

Further plaudits were garnered from 1995's *No Protection* (#10 UK), an audacious reassessment of the album by reggae maverick Mad Professor (born Neil Fraser), released the following year, while Madonna offered up her seal of approval when she collaborated with the band on a version of Marvin Gaye's "I Want You" for a forthcoming tribute album.

Yet amidst so much success, Massive Attack also knew that nothing short of a full scale reinvention of their music would suffice next time around — a process which commenced with the creation of their own genre-defying Melankolic label. Horace Andy, classical pianist Craig Arm-

strong, and the Bristol-based Alpha would all be recruited to the label and encouraged to produce anything which would shatter the parent band's stereotype — a pledge which Massive Attack, too, would make as they prepared their third album, 1998's *Mezzanine*.

A 1997 EP, *Risingson* (#11 UK), rushed out once it became apparent that the album itself would not meet its Christmas release deadline, paved the way; *Mezzanine* (#60 US, #1 UK) itself would emerge harder, heavier, and decidedly more sinister than anything Massive Attack had offered up before.

Post-punk guitars (and a Cure sample complimenting the Banshees and Velvet Underground lifts on *Risingson*) vied with the returning Horace Andy and a cover of the reggae standard "Man Next Door" owed as much to its 1980 reinvention by the Slits (and a 1993 version by On-U staple Bim Sherman), as it did to John Holt's original. Three singles — "Teardrop" (#10 UK), "Bring It On" (#52 UK), and "Angel" (#30 UK) — attended the album and would subsequently be compiled into a multi-disc box set of all the band's EPs and singles to date.

The accolades came flowing in — Album of the Year in *Q* magazine, Best International Group at the Dutch Edison Awards, Best Video (for "Teardrop") at the MTV Europe awards, and Godlike Genius Award for Unique Services to Music in the *NME* poll. Then, while (regularly denied) split rumors circled their heads, the band returned to the studio to begin work on their next album, jamming with members of Spiritualized's Lupine Howl side project. The band also joined with the Prodigy on that band's scheduled first single of 2000, "No Souvenirs," while another collaboration paired 3D with Blur's Damon Albarn on the movie soundtrack *Ordinary Decent Criminal*.

Massive Attack LPs

🎱 **Blue Lines (Virgin) 1991** More hip-hop than trip-hop, essentially a collaboration between Massive Attack, vocalist Shara Nelson, and reggae great Horace Andy. Completely defining what would happen to/become the Bristol sound, "Safe from Harm" and "Unfinished Sympathy" slid solid grooves and beats around a lustrous tripped up/stripped down sensuousness.

🎱 **Protection (Virgin) 1994** Trippier than its predecessor with additions from fellow Bristolian Tricky and Tracey Thorn's vocal jazz stylings, Attack create a dark psychedelic haze, all smoke and mirrors and an ambience of edgy rage bubbling just below an innocuous crust. A powerful album, it stands as one of the most wicked feel good sets of the decade.

🎱 **No Protection: Massive Attack vs. Mad Professor (Virgin) 1995** This is what happens when the Mad Professor gets his hands and equipment all over the master tapes. A tripped-out dub re-creation of *Protection* which takes on a whole new light and intent.

9 Mezzanine (Virgin) 1998 Edgier than its predecessor, and far more subtly ominous. From the opening "Angel" which sets the sinister tone, to the mesmeric "Rising Son" with its great beats and raw guitar, the album never falters. Cocteau Twin Liz Fraser is scattered throughout, a fitting guest patch in the Attack fabric. And for God's sake don't miss their cover of "Man Next Door."

Selected Compilations and Archive Releases

9 Singles 90/98 (Virgin) 1998 Groovy heat-sensitive packaging, stuffed with all the CD singles so far. Multiple remixes do not detract from the majesty.

MEAT BEAT MANIFESTO

FORMED *1988 (London, England)*
ORIGINAL LINE-UP *Jack Dangers (b. John Corrigan, 1965, Swindon, England — vocals, multi-instrumentalist); Jonny Stephens (programming)*

Growing out of an earlier Jack Dangers/Jonny Stephens project, Perennial Divide, who released an album and three singles between 1986 and 1987, Meat Beat Manifesto launched out of London's terminally turbulent acid rave scene in 1988 with a string of powerful dance singles, beginning with the acclaimed "I Got the Fear" and "Strap Down," each backed up with a similarly inventive series of live and video performances.

Originally the new group was a Perennial Divide side project, but the rapidity with which MBM made inroads soon saw the older band abandoned as MBM become a full time occupation. With non-musical members Marcus Adams and Craig Morrison emphasizing costume and choreography as an integral part of the band, and boasting a live show which involved up to 13 different musicians, dancers, and DJs, the band cut the *Suck Hard* EP and were about to release their debut album when the tapes were lost in a fire.

Instead, four past singles ("I Got the Fear" from *Suck Hard*, "Strap Down," "God OD," and "Reanimator") were substantially remixed to create 1989's double *Storm the Studio* album; further material surviving from various stages of the doomed first album was meanwhile cleaned up and released, with suitable warnings, as *Armed Audio Warfare*, an album whose unfinished nature in no way detracted from its power.

Signing to Wax Trax! and moving to the US, MBM joined a loose collective of industrial dance formed around Consolidated and the Disposable Heroes of Hip-Hoprisy, co-producing much of that band's early material. Through 1991 and 1992, MBM would also execute remixes for Coil, David Byrne, MC900 Ft. Jesus, Fatima Mansions, Orbital, and others. Their own releases included the *dog man star* EP and

the classic "Helter Skelter" and "Psyche Out" singles, trailing the US release of *Armed Audio Warfare*.

Concentrating as much on sampled and found sounds as they did on their own musical contributions, MBM fought hard to rise above accusations of simple plagiarism by the sheer inventiveness of their work. Like the Justified Ancients of Mu, Meat Beat Manifesto created dynamic sound sculptures, with 99%, the first MBM album to have been recorded and released according to plan (!) — a stark vindication of their chosen method of working.

Departing Wax Trax! for Mute shortly before 1992's *Satyricon* album, MBM toured the US with Orbital and Ultramarine and scored a minor UK hit with "Mindstream" (#55 UK); other singles from this period included September 1991's "I'm in Paradise Now," "Faster than the Speed of Love," "Edge of No Control," and into 1993, "Circles."

Following a lengthy world tour, MBM then withdrew from the fast-growing limelight, to concentrate on remixing for a variety of other artists, including David Bowie, Depeche Mode, Nine Inch Nails, Machines of Loving Grace, and State of Grace.

They returned in 1995 with the *Nuclear Bomb* EP; 1996 then saw MBM link with Trent Reznor's Nothing label, with the *Asbestos Lead Asbestos* EP and the *Subliminal Sandwich* 2-CD marathon; they also created an acclaimed jungle remix of Nine Inch Nails' "The Perfect Drug," a calling card for the duo's own current interests.

More remix work and the *Acid Again* and *Prime Audio Soup* EPs preceded *Actual Sounds and Voices*, in 1998, a well-received album which earned the band the Outstanding Electronic Album award at the California Music Awards and launched the band into a series of sporadic live shows in the US and Japan through 1999.

Meat Beat Manifesto LPs

8 99% (Wax Trax!) 1990 A bit more structured than the early singles would suggest, as the group moves towards more traditional song formats. The heavy, heavy beats still power the music, though, scattershot with innovative conversational snippets cleverly counterpointing Danger's own raps. Album highlight is definitely the massive club hit-to-be "Psyche-Out."

8 Satyricon (Mute) 1992

9 Subliminal Sandwich (Nothing) 1996 Another double-album, with disc one more groove orientated, all dancey hip-hop vying with light techno and dub; disc two is the more experimental side of the band, repetitive beats slowly hammering away while the electronics — beamed from another planet — melt your mind. Two hours and twenty minutes of electronic genius that leaves you wanting to play it over and over again.

8 Actual Sounds and Voices (Nothing) 1998 Drum and bass centric with ample doses of jungle, acid jazz, ambience, and even electro-pop and swing — a slathering of electro-weirdness and incongruous sampling which somehow slots together to create club music for the new millennia.

Selected Compilations and Archive Releases

8 Storm the Studio (Wax Trax!) 1989 A double-disc dose of high energy, hip-hop fueled and dub-heavy, sample-riven weirdness. Four early singles each remixed a minimum of three times, crafted for the dance floor, but filled with rampant angst and anger.

8 Armed Audio Warfare (Wax Trax!) 1990 Rarities, B-sides, and a host of unreleased tracks, together creating a facsimile of their lost debut album (which literally went up in flames) and launching two more club hits, "I Got the Fear" and "Mars Needs Women."

7 Peel Session (Strange Fruit UK) 1993 Recorded in December 1992, Meat Beat pull out the sample-heavy "Fire Number 9," the hypnotic "Soul Driver," the baggy pop-with-a-difference "Drop," and finish off with arguably the heaviest ever rendition of "Radio Babylon."

7 Original Fire (Nothing) 1997 Still haunted by the loss of their original *Warfare* album, Meat Beat revisit old favorites, reworking them in their current style with the classic "Radio Babylon," handed over to Luke Vibert and The Orb for remixes. The originals had a streetwise aggressive urban aura; the revitalized versions are more solid grooves, and far more accessible, but all remain fresh and edgy.

Perennial Divide LP

6 Purge (Sweatbox) 1986

Meat Beat Manifesto/Jack Dangers — Selected Remixes

1991 THE SHAMEN — Hyperreal [MULTIPLE] (One Little Indian)

1991 THE SHAMEN — En-tact [MULTIPLE MIXES] (One Little Indian)

1991 COIL — The Snow [MULTIPLE MIXES] (Wax Trax!)

1991 DAVID BYRNE — Ava (Luaka Bop)

1991 DAVID BYRNE — Ninevah (Luaka Bop)

1991 MC 900 FOOT JESUS — Killer Inside me [MULTIPLE MIXES] (IRS)

1992 CONSOLIDATED — Tool and Die [MULTIPLE MIXES] (IRS)

1992 FATIMA MANSIONS — Only Losers Take the Bus (Radioactive)

1992 ORBITAL — Oolaa (FFRR)

1992 THE SHAMEN — Ebenezer Good [MULTIPLE MIXES] (One Little Indian)

1992 CONSOLIDATED — You Suck [MULTIPLE MIXES] (Nettwerk)

1993 DHS — Bad Acid (Play It Again Sam)

1993 DAVID BOWIE — Pallas Athena (Savage)

1993 DAVID BOWIE — You've Been Around (Savage)

1993 DEPECHE MODE — Condemnation (Mute)

1994 NINE INCH NAILS — Closer (TVT)

1993 MACHINES OF LOVING GRACE — Butterfly Wings [MULTIPLE MIXES] (Mammoth)

1993 ETHYL MEATPLOW — Ripened Peach (Chameleon)

1994 CONSOLIDATED — Butyric Acid [MULTIPLE MIXES] (London)

1994 PAPA BRITTLE — Status Quo [MULTIPLE MIXES] (Nettwerk)

1994 BIGOD 20 — One [MULTIPLE MIXES] (Sire)

1994 SCORN — Silver Rain Fell (Earache)

1994 DAVID BYRNE — Back in the Box [MULTIPLE MIXES] (Luaka Bop)

1995 GROTUS — Ebola Reston (London)

1996 CONSOLIDATED — This Is Fascism (MC)

1996 YOUNG GODS — Kissing the Sun (Play It Again Sam)

1996 STATE OF GRACE — Hello [MULTIPLE MIXES] (3rd Stone)

1996 LAIKA — Looking for the Jackalope (TVT)

1996 GLOBO — Truly Independent (World Domination)

1996 EMPIRION — Narcotic Influence (XL)

1997 FUN LOVIN' CRIMINALS — King of NY [MULTIPLE MIXES] (Chrysalis)

1997 NINE INCH NAILS — Perfect Drug (1997)

1997 BUSH — Insect Kin (Trauma)

1997 PISTEL — 12 Skin Up (Baraka)

1998 AIR AND AUDIOACTIVE — Everything... (Polystar)

1998 BOOM BOOM SATELLITES — Moment of Silence (R&S)

1998 GOD LIVES UNDERWATER — Rearrange [MULTIPLE MIXES] (1500)

1998 MICKEY HART — Yabu [MULTIPLE MIXES] (Rykodisc)

1998 DHS — House of God (Space Children)

1998 CRASH WORSHIP — Pyru (Space Children)

MEAT PUPPETS

FORMED 1980 *(Phoenix, AZ)*

ORIGINAL LINE-UP *Curt Kirkwood (b. 1/10/59 — guitar); Chris Kirkwood (b. 10/22/60 — bass); Derrick Bostrom (6/23/60 — drums)*

Emerging out of Phoenix in 1980, the Meat Puppets prided themselves in looking like a conventional hardcore punk trio — an image which their debut EP, *In a Car*, and an eponymous album for SST were not about to shatter. The Puppets were feted as the new gods of the developing scene and dutifully worked that circuit for more than a year. But then, Curt Kirkwood recalled, "we discovered that most punks are just rednecks in disguise. By changing styles, we've successfully eliminated most of the idiots who might come to our shows."

"Changing styles" would subsequently become a way of life for the band. They opened a San Francisco show with the theme from *The King and I* and the entire audience bombarded them with beer cans. *Meat Puppets II* would not travel to the same extremes, but still its punk-folk hybrid stood at odds with the rest of the American underground and it would be close to a decade before the album was truly acknowledged for its undoubted influence, after the band members themselves joined Nirvana to perform three tracks during their *Unplugged* broadcast.

Constant live work saw the band break into the mainstream press consciousness with their third album, the semi-psychedelic *Up on the Sun* with the *Out My Way* (#15 UK indy) EP and albums *Mirage* (#14 UK indy) and the ZZ Top-inflected *Huevos*, in 1987, finding their way onto college radio, then still emerging as a genuine power in the land.

A live show from 1988, released a decade later as *Live in Montana*, captures the band at their absolute peak; by the time of 1989's hard rock *Monsters*, however, the Meat Puppets had apparently exhausted themselves and the band broke up shortly after its release.

They reformed in 1991 and signed to London; however, the comeback *Forbidden Places* and singles "Whirlpool" and "Sam" were widely regarded as a failure and the band retreated underground, surfacing only for occasional shows until 1993 saw them re-emerge as opening act on Nirvana's *In Utero* tour.

The next Meat Puppets album was timed for release just as Nirvana's much-anticipated *MTV Unplugged* performance was broadcast; a slow mover, *Too High to Die* (#62

US) was just finding its commercial feet when Cobain's suicide slammed all things Nirvana-related into the headlines.

MTV began airing *Unplugged* over and over and the Meat Puppets' sudden, if tragic, visibility saw their latest singles "We Don't Exist," "Tender Cuts," and "Backwater" (#47 US) pick up significant airplay, while *Too High to Die* eventually went gold. (The Nirvana-sponsored "Lake of Fire" was also reactivated as an EP in studio, live, and acoustic incarnations.)

The following year's *No Joke!* (#183 US) and *Taste of the Sun* EP did little to change their predecessor's format, an error of judgement which resulted in the band's worst received album yet. Again the band sank into seclusion, with reports of Cris Kirkwood's drug use insisting that they might never return. The overdose death of Cris' wife in 1998 consolidated his isolation.

However, Rykodisc's bonus stacked reissue of the first seven Meat Puppets albums (organized by Bostrom) won high praise and fall 1998 saw Curt Kirkwood alone relocate to Austin and return to gigging as the Royal Neanderthal Orchestra with ex-Pariahs Kyle Ellison (keyboards, guitar) and Shandon Sahm (son of Texan legend Doug, drums) and Andrew Duplantis (bass, ex-Bob Mould). The Orchestra reclaimed the Meat Puppets name in early 1999 and released an EP, *You Love Me*. That same year brought Bostrom's *Today's Sounds* covers EP, *Songs of Spiritual Uplift as Sung by Today's Sounds*. The Meat Puppets confirmed their return in summer 2000, signing with Hootie and the Blowfish's Breaking label and releasing the "I Quit" single ahead of their first new LP in five years.

Meat Puppets LPs

7 Meat Puppets (SST) 1982 Nobody had ever thought of blending hardcore with country before the Puppets came along, and no one needed to try afterwards. An album which is more audacious than enjoyable, but repeated plays do pull some marvels out of the blur.

9 Meat Puppets II (SST) 1983 Unquestionably the classic, thanks to the Nirvana connection, and ingenues won't find too much difference between the two bands' approaches. Strong songs and stark arrangements fit no stylistic bag, although the punk-Americana flavor remains strong.

8 Up on the Sun (SST) 1985

7 Mirage (SST) 1987

9 Huevos (SST) 1987 With its predecessors having pursued the Puppets into the musical equivalent of Joshua Tree national park, with all the (pre-U2) connotations that exudes, the *Huevos* sessions were nothing short of a solid 72-hour blast through rhythms as prickly as a cactus. The ensuing menage of ZZ Top rhythms and Gram Parsons attitudes taps *II* close for "best of" honors.

© Jim Steinfeldt/Chansley Entertainment Archives

6 Monsters (SST) 1989 Possibly *Huevos* took things as far as they could go; maybe the band just fancied a change. But *Monsters* was a letdown either way, more Bob Seger than Bob Willis, and recorded with a lot less panache than usual.

7 Forbidden Places (London) 1991

8 Too High to Die (London) 1994 *Forbidden Places* saw the Puppets nosedive into cliche; *Too High* pulls them out with a flourish, and into a new world where the Byrds fly overhead, flaming in their grooviness and, uplifted by such soaring harmonies, the guitars sparkle and jangle and occasionally twang (and the buffalos spring across the field). Nothing's ever so straightforward in Puppetland, though, so assaultive Who-esque power chords, wah-wah guitar, and a hefty dose of melancholy flit through as well.

6 No Joke! (London) 1995 The last album's "Severed Goddess Hand" perched the Puppets on the dangerous verge of REM tribute; *No Joke* just blunders straight in.

Selected Compilations and Archive Releases

8 No Strings Attached (SST) 1990 Solid retrospective ending with *Monsters*.

6 Live in Montana (RYKODISC) 1999 Entertaining late-1980s performance.

MEN THEY COULDN'T HANG

FORMED 1982 (London, England)
ORIGINAL LINE-UP *Cush* (vocals); *Shanne Bradley* (bass); *Paul Simmonds* (guitar); *Phil Odgers* (vocals, guitar); *John Odgers* (drums)

Spawned from the same mutant Gaelic punk bloodline as Shane McGowan's Pogues (Shanne Bradley was a former member of McGowan's Nipple Erectors, while Men They Couldn't Hang was a name McGowan had been considering for the Pogues), the Men formed after Cush met Bradley while busking in London's Shepherds Bush. Gathering together the remainder of the Men, the band debuted at the Alternative Country Music Festival in London over Easter 1984. There they were seen by Elvis Costello, who swiftly signed them to his new label, Imp, and issued their debut single, a cover of Eric Bogle's "The Green Fields of France" (#6 UK indy).

It remained on the UK indy chart for a full year, beginning November 1984, and was followed by the majestic "Iron Masters" (#1 UK indy) in June 1985. The group's debut album, *The Night of a Thousand Candles* (#91 UK, #1 UK indy), produced by Pogue Phil Chevron, was similarly successful the following month and the group's UK tour

through the fall climaxed with a solidly packed show at London's Electric Ballroom. Songs like "Wishing Well" and the unemployed drunkard's "Whiskey with My Giro" lament kept the band, as *Melody Maker* put it, "resolutely nailed down by the heartfelt sledgehammering of sub-political existentialism," an enviable role in the mid-1980s and one which the Nick Lowe-produced *Greenback Dollar* (#5 UK indy) EP only validated further. A June 1986 session for BBC radio's Janice Long soon established itself among that show's most popular broadcasts, and *How Green Is the Valley* (#68 UK) arrived in October.

Bradley left to form the Chicken Family with Eric Goulden; she was replaced by Ricky McGuire and the Men signed with Magnet in early 1987. They promptly scored a radio hit with "Island in the Rain," followed by their first national chart success, "Colours" (#61 UK). The *Waiting for Bonaparte* album (#41 UK) arrived in March 1988, but following the unsuccessful "The Crest" 45, the band switched to Silvertone (formed by ex-Radar/Demon/Imp A&R man Andrew Lauder) for 1989's Top 40 hit, *Silvertown* (#39 UK, #2 UK indy), and the "Rain, Steam and Speed" single.

Two further singles, "A Place in the Sun" and "A Map of Morocco," and a heavy metal/rap parody with poet Attila the Stockbroker, "The Iron Man of Rap," followed, before Nick Muir (keyboards) was recruited for the band's fifth album, *The Domino Club* (#53 UK), and their biggest gig yet, opening for David Bowie at the Milton Keynes Bowl that summer. However, the group announced its intention to split shortly after, launching a lengthy farewell tour and finally bowing out with the *Alive Alive O* live album.

The Men would reform in 1996 with drummer Kenny Harris (ex-Screaming Blue Messiahs), releasing a straightforward folk-rock album which was generally regarded as a competent — if not ambitious — comeback.

The Men They Couldn't Hang LPs

7 Night of 1000 Candles (Demon) 1985 They were never going to be more than a shadow cabinet Pogues — the Men's greatest virtue was that they didn't try to argue with that. Philip Chevron produced and "The Green Fields of France" was already a Pogues favorite. But the twinned vocals and powerful originals made *1000 Candles* less a substitute and more like a grand, rousing extension. The period B-side, "Donald, Where's Your Trousers?," really should have been included, though.

6 How Green Is the Valley (MCA) 1986

8 Waiting for Bonaparte (Magnet) 1988 No musical deviation, but "Dover Lights," "Life of a Small Fry," and "Smugglers" perfect the dramatic storytelling intimacy which *Valley*'s "Ghosts of Cable Street" only hinted at.

8 Silvertown (Silvertone) 1989 Biting, at times vicious, examination of the underdog experience, localized around London's homeless community and embellished with some genuinely moving music and vistas.

6 **Domino Club (Silvertone) 1990**

7 **Alive Alive O [LIVE] (Fun After All) 1991**

6 **Never Born to Follow (Demon) 1996** Relatively tame comeback; reminds one of the old band's passion, without really suggesting it'll be back any time soon.

Selected Compilations and Archive Releases

7 **Majestic Grill: The Best Of... (Demon) 1998** Welcome — if delayed — replacement for the withdrawn *Five Glorious Years* collection; hits most of the past highpoints plus a smattering of comeback cuts.

Paul Simmonds, Jon Odgers/Liberty Cage LP

8 **Sleep of the Just (Line — GERMANY) 1994** New name, new line-up, but same commitment and power — a worthy follow-up, in fact, to *Silvertown*.

MIGHTY MIGHTY BOSSTONES

FORMED 1985 *(Boston, MA)*

ORIGINAL LINE-UP *Dicky Barrett (vocals); Joe Gittleman (bass); Timothy Burton (saxophone); Nate Albert (guitar); Josh Dalsimer (drums); Dennis Brockenborough (trombone); Kevin Linear (saxophone); Ben Carr (Bosstone)*

The roots of what would become the Mighty Mighty Bosstones lay in the hardcore explosion of the early 1980s. Bassist Joe Gittleman played with Boston sensations Gang Green (he appears on at least two of their records, *Another Wasted Night* and *I81B4U*); Dickie Barrett played with Impact Unit, a low-fi, hardcore combo whose sole release during their lifetime was a single, "My Friend the Pit," on the German Critical Response label.

Then came the Cheap Skates, an ad hoc aggregation whose revolving door membership not only featured the occasional future Mighty Mighty Bosstone, but also hauled in guys from Gang Green and Stranglehold — just a bunch of kids from Boston High who were waiting to do something. Slowly, however, a line-up coalesced and it is indicative of the depth of friendship running through what became the Bosstones that since that time, there has been just one personnel change, when Joe Sirois replaced drummer Josh Dalsimer, shortly after the band's first album was recorded.

The music which the Cheap Skates and subsequently the Bosstones, played wasn't part of a revival. Ska lived on, in their hearts, in their minds, and on the radio. Madness were still releasing good records, the English Beat had yet to cover

Andy Williams, and Bad Manners were touring America with increasing vehemence. "We're talking a distance from the English 2-Tone movement of about four years, no more than that," Barrett reasoned. "So it was kind of: 'It's not over; keep it alive.' It wasn't a ska resurgence or anything; it was the tail end; guys hanging out, saying, 'The spirit is still alive.' When you have something you love so much, you want it to keep going."

The Bosstones made their recorded debut in 1986, when they were featured on the *Mash It Up* ska compilation. A remarkable document, *Mash It Up* also offered early vinyl appearances to the likes of Bim Skala Bim; the Bosstones' contribution was "The Cave" — a track which would later appear on their own *Devil's Night Out* album. Another early Bosstones recording, "Drums and Chickens," would appear on the *Mashin' Up the Nation* collection in 1989, again alongside some seminal talents — Bim again, Let's Go Bowling, the New York Citizens, and an early incarnation of The Toasters, Not Bob Marley.

The Bosstones had, in fact, broken up by the time *Mashin' Up the Nation* appeared, while Nate Albert and Gittleman finished high school. Immediately upon graduation, however, the group relaunched, adding Mighty Mighty to their name after learning about an earlier, '50s-era Boston band also called the Bosstones.

Slogging around New England's club circuit, entertaining audiences so small that occasionally there were more people onstage than off it, the Bosstones began dressing up in ever more bizarre costumes, simply to amuse themselves. At least one of these costumes, a plaid outfit which Barrett introduced one night, has since become a Bosstones' trademark — all the more so since the band was recruited to appear in a Converse sneaker commercial. It was only later, that the band realized why the Bosstones had such trouble persuading people to take them seriously. "Because we sold sneakers before we made an album!"

In fact, the band had already signed with the Taang! label, recording their debut album, *Devil's Night Out*, with producer Paul Kolderie. It was released to warm, but vague, applause, but at a time when ska itself was still struggling to move out of the American grassroots underground, little more. What complicated matters for the Bosstones was the fact that they weren't actually playing ska. Or rather, they were, but it had been through several kinds of mincer before it reached the outside world.

"It's ska music slammed together with hardcore music," Barrett once explained. "You know, everybody seems to need a label. The Mighty Mighty Bosstones didn't seem to be enough for people, they wanted to know exactly what kind of music it was. We certainly didn't know what we were doing, we were taking all the influences we had, all the things we loved and finally we gave them a label. I came up with the word ska-core and now there's actually other ska-core bands, which is pretty cool."

The problem in 1990–91, as Nate Alpert remembered, was that "the world really wasn't ready for ska-core. The ska kids hated us for years, because we weren't traditional. And then we got shit from punk rock people, because we were playing ska and metal (1991's *Where'd You Go* EP offered up covers of Aerosmith's "Sweet Emotion," Metallica's "Enter Sandman," and Van Halen's "Ain't Talkin' 'Bout Love"). We kind of got it from all angles."

Again produced by Paul Kolderie, the Bosstones' second album followed soon after. *More Noise and Other Disturbances* was, Gittleman still raves, "a great, great record" — marred, sadly, by a less than happy relationship with their record label. Quitting Taang!, the group signed to Mercury in 1992 and immediately set about proving who was boss, unleashing an EP's worth of hardcore covers — 1993's *Ska-core, the Devil and More*.

The band's next album, *Don't Know How to Party* (#187 US), followed shortly after, while their burgeoning public profile wasn't damaged by an appearance on 1993's *KISS My Ass* tribute to KISS, performing "Detroit Rock City." With the band touring constantly, too, it was suddenly of question not of if, but when, they were going to break through in a big way.

Question the Answers (#138 US), in the fall of 1994, was not the most obvious response to that question. Recorded over a three-month period, it featured the work of three different producers: the Philadelphia-based Butcher Brothers, whose credentials included Urge Overkill, Cypress Hill, and Aerosmith; Fort Apache mastermind Kolderie, whose time since he produced the first two Bosstones albums had been spent with Hole and Radiohead among others; and Ross Humphrey, the band's sound engineer (and supervisor of live broadcasts for Westwood One). Gittleman described the ensuing blend as an attempt to escape "the standard Mighty Mighty Bosstones formula," and its reception proved that the Bosstones' audience was as willing to move ahead as the band.

A string of singles spun into airplay and MTV — "Kinder Words," "Pictures to Prove It," and "Hell of a Hat"; a guest appearance in the summer hit movie *Clueless* and a slot on the 1995 Lollapalooza tour followed, together with a new EP, the *Here We Go Again* collection of what Barrett called "B-sides and shitty Mighty Mighty Bosstones experiments in the studio." The following year, the Bosstones scored another festival triumph, as they became one of the stars of Warped, setting the stage for their fifth album, 1997's *Let's Face It*, and UK chart breakthroughs with "The Impression I Get," "The Rascal King," and "Every Trick in the Book."

1998's *Live from the Middle East* (#144 US) set caught the band returning to one of the Boston area clubs which nurtured them, for a high energy live recording; an otherwise silent 1999 was broken by Barrett appearing as Bill Haley in the CBS mini-series *Shake, Rattle and Roll*. He also performed the title song. The Bosstones' eighth album, *Pay Attention*, followed in summer 2000.

Mighty Mighty Bosstones LPs

7 Devil's Nite Out (Taang!) 1990 The original ska-core holocaust, admittedly a lot more core than ska, but there's still a savagely enjoyable time to be had.

6 More Noise and Other Disturbances (Taang!) 1992

8 Skacore, the Devil and More (Mercury) 1993 An absolutely uncompromising collection of new songs and covers, with four of the seven tracks paying homage to the Bosstones' old heroes — the Angry Samoans, Minor Threat, SS Decontrol, and Bob Marley. Spectacular, self-defining, and defiantly uncommercial.

7 Don't Know How to Party (Mercury) 1993 Despite one of the most misleading titles ever, *Party*'s blistering blend of metal, old-school punk, and ska/rocksteady, brings to fruition the band's hybrid style, by always focusing on the songs' pop melody core.

8 Question the Answers (Mercury) 1994 The Bosstones go eclectic, delving into a melting pot of styles without ever leaving their roots behind. They may not have all the answers yet, but they certainly know how to mix it up.

9 Let's Face It (Mercury) 1997 *Face* sounds truly effortless, one great track after another slides by, as if this record just "magicked" itself together. The Bosstones sound utterly relaxed, yet in total control of the songs and the sound, while the songwriting is impeccable — all strong melodies, hooky choruses, and an exuberant mix of moods. The addition of dubby reggae to the sound is a welcome addition.

8 Live from the Middle East [LIVE] (Mercury) 1998 Recorded during their 1997 Hometown Throwdown, an annual five-day Bosstone event since '94, the tiny Middle East club provides an intimate setting for a 22-song set crammed with hits, crowd faves, and band picks.

7 Pay Attention (Island) 2000

MINISTRY

FORMED 1981 (*Chicago, IL*)

ORIGINAL LINE-UP *Al Jourgensen (b. 10/9/58, Cuba — guitar); Lamont Welton (bass); Preston (horns); Steve Brighton (backing vocals)*

Al Jourgensen was a year old when his family fled Cuba to escape the incoming Castro regime. His parents divorced soon after settling in Denver, Colorado, and following his mother's remarriage, the child took his stepfather's surname.

Moving to Chicago, Jourgensen joined his first band, Special Affect, in 1979, replacing guitarist Tom Hoffman. Also featuring Marty Sorensen (bass), Harry Rushakoff (drums), and Frank Nardiello (vocals), the band had already released an EP, *Mood Music*. With Jourgensen on board, they recorded one further single, 1980's "Empty Handed," before splitting in 1981. Nardiello subsequently resurfaced in My Life with the Thrill Kill Kult; Rushakoff was a member of the embryonic Concrete Blonde, Dream 6, and also played with Alice Cooper.

Jourgensen formed Ministry that same year, signing to Wax Trax! and cutting the "I'm Falling" single with drummer Stephen "Stevo" George. An immediate club hit, it led to Ministry signing to Arista in mid-1982.

Dovetailing perfectly with the incipient new romantic synth sound of the day, the group's major label premier, *With Sympathy* (#96 US), emerged a fascinating document, slickly co-produced by Psychedelic Furs' Vince Ely. (*With Sympathy* was released as *Work for Love* in the UK.) Ministry toured with some success, but chart success and heavy club play for the attendant singles "Revenge," "I Wanted to Tell Her," and "Work for Love," did not disguise Jourgensen's dislike for the project. "It's the same old story," he complained later. "They sign you because you're unique, then they try to make you sound like somebody else."

Jourgensen's relations with Arista finally soured when the label proposed a featherweight cover of Roxy Music's "Same Old Scene" for Ministry's next single; he balked, the label dropped him, and Ministry returned to Wax Trax!, relaunching with a reissue of "Cold life" (the B-side of "I'm Falling"). It was followed in 1984 by "Everyday is Halloween," later to be adopted as the anthem of America's disenfranchised gothic community and "Nature of Love."

Jourgensen spent the next year perfecting Ministry's sophomore album *Twitch* (#194 US) and organizing a new deal, with Sire. "All Day Remix," a 1984 single, bridged the gap, although the Adrian Sherwood-produced *Twitch* (and the accompanying "Over the Shoulder" single) would still baffle all expectations.

He hooked up with the Blackouts, a Seattle band based in Boston, whose "Lost Souls Club" single he produced in 1981. A short East Coast tour together in 1984 confirmed their chemistry and when that band broke up soon after, Jourgensen immediately recruited Paul Barker (b. Palo Alto, CA, 2/8/50 — bass), brother Roland (b. 6/30/57 — keyboards), and Bill Rieflin (b. Seattle, 9/30/60 — drums) to the new-look Ministry.

The band toured *Twitch* into 1986, again to widespread confusion, an emotion which was compounded when Jourgensen released what would become the first of many Ministry side projects, the Revolting Cocks' *Big Sexy Land* album

(and "No Devotion" single), recorded in London and Brussels the previous year, with Richard 23 and Luc Van Acker of Front 242.

A second Revco single followed — "You Often Forget" marked the debut of Rieflin and Paul Barker in this new band's ranks and like its predecessor, it presented a surprisingly lighthearted face to the increasingly belligerent Ministry. However, when Sire suggested that the follow-up to *Twitch* be similarly less abrasive, Jourgensen offered to break up the group instead. He'd already compromised once in his career — a point hammered home when the main band embarked on another two-year project, the *Land of Rape and Honey* (#164 US) album and two utterly un-single-like singles, "Stigmata" and "Burning Inside."

Lining up now as Jourgensen, Paul Barker, Rieflin (guitar, keyboards), and Jeff Ward (drums), Ministry toured extensively in the album's wake; in addition, Wax Trax! kept up a constant barrage of 12" singles by Ministry side projects, including 1000 Homo DJs (featuring Trent Reznor), Pailhead (with Fugazi's Ian MacKaye), Acid Horse (with Cabaret Voltaire), PTP (Chris Connolly), Lard (Dead Kennedy's Jello Biafra), and Barker's solo Lead into Gold. According to Rieflin, incidentally, "each name described a different musical category."

Ministry's own next album, 1989's *The Mind Is a Terrible Thing to Taste* (#163 US) was their breakthrough. A savage explosion of noise, battered into shape by some blistering guitar, it emerged an album of such relentless hatred and aggression that even the band's staunchest critics were shocked into silence.

The accompanying tour — with guitarist Mike Scaccia (b. Babylon, NY, 6/14/65) now on board — was similarly revolutionary. With the audience caged behind chain link fences, the band's pyro-technic live act was further enhanced by a string of guest appearances from the likes of David Yow (Jesus Lizard), Terry Roberts (Discharge), Martin Atkins (Public Image Ltd, Killing Joke), Ogre (Skinny Puppy), keyboard tech William Tucker (Scornflakes), and members of the support band, KMFDM. The brief hiatus between *The Mind* and the six-track *In Case You Didn't Feel Like Showing Up* live set only heightened awareness of the group's intent.

Musically, too, Jourgensen was being taken seriously. No longer in the shadow of Adrian Sherwood, whose electronics-whipped remix of "Over the Shoulder" was so highly acclaimed, Jourgensen himself was now being courted by remix-hungry pop kids; the Red Hot Chili Peppers would rank among his best-known clients.

Jourgensen's personal reputation, too, was by now as uncompromising as his music — a scenario which finally blew into epidemic proportions when Chicago poet Lorri Jackson ODed shortly after attending Jourgensen's birthday party. Rumors that Jourgensen was in some way responsible for her death made their way into print and even reached Jourgensen's daughter's private school. "They were going to kick her out," he later revealed, "just because of some unsubstantiated bullshit some guy wrote about me."

Jourgensen and wife Patti had to assure the school board "that we're not Satan and we don't have brain stew for dinner" before the school relented — at precisely the same time as he himself was convincing America's teens of something quite the contrary.

Ministry finally broke out of the cult circuit with the spring 1992 release of the tumultuous "Jesus Built My Hot Rod," featuring guest vocals by the Butthole Surfers' Gibby Haynes. The release swiftly became one of Warner Brothers' three bestselling CD singles of all time (behind Depeche Mode and Madonna) — an accolade which "floored" Jourgensen, even as it paved the way for both Ministry's appearance at that summer's Lollapalooza and their apocalyptic new album, *Psalm 69: The Way to Succeed and the Way to Suck Eggs* (#27 US, #33 UK).

Following the grinding "Just One Fix" single, "N.W.O." (#49 UK) (a ferocious attack on George Bush's "New World Order") was most people's introduction to Ministry's bestselling album, supported as it was by a Peter Christophersen/Coil video which mixed footage of the Los Angeles riots with a masturbating caricature of Bush himself. In its wake, Ministry found themselves touring to vast arenas, with Jourgensen himself feted, as *Rolling Stone* put it, as the "Phil Spector of industrial disco."

Having concluded a massively successful world tour, close to two years of comparative silence followed *Psalm 69*, a period which saw Jourgensen relocate to Austin, Texas and begin scheming a new image for himself in the heart of middle America. Rumors of a conversion to country music vied with escalating tales of personnel changes and personal problems.

Rieflin quit, allegedly after discovering the band intended recording Bob Dylan's "Lay Lady Lay." Turning his hand initially to sessions and production, he then re-emerged with 1999's critically acclaimed *Birth of a Giant* solo album.

Ministry themselves returned in January 1996 with *Filth Pig* (#19 US, #43 UK). Singles of "The Fall" (#53 UK) and the offending Dylan cover followed, but while the album enjoyed a reasonably high chart debut, it was very poorly received and swiftly dropped out of the chart.

Lining up now as Jourgensen, Paul Barker, Scaccia, Louis Svitek (ex-Mindfunk, guitar), Duane Buford (keyboards), and Ray Washam (ex-Scratch Acid, Rapeman; drums), Ministry toured during 1996, but swiftly went to ground again, Jourgensen recording a new Lard album, among other projects.

Again, four years would elapse before a new Ministry album emerged; previewed by the "Bad Blood" single, *Dark Side of the Spoon* (#92 US) was recorded during 1996 and 1997, then scrapped and almost completely reworked. Unfortunately, it would not reverse the band's apparently plunging fortunes.

Ministry LPs

8 With Sympathy (Arista) 1982 Across this fascinating attempt to blend New Romanticism electronics with shuddering dance floor beats, co-producer (Psychedelic Fur) Vince Ely brings an appropriately British doom-pop atmosphere, while holding tight to Jourgensen's triumphantly breezy electro hooks and melodies.

7 Twitch (Sire) 1984 Desperate to put as much distance between himself and his past, Jourgensen kicks out anything even vaguely resembling melody or music and exhales one of the most uncompromising albums of the early '80s. A new band and producer Adrian Sherwood add to the ferocity, ensuring Ministry's entrance to the construction site is utterly unpolluted by those toe-tapping tunes of old.

8 The Land of Rape and Honey (Sire) 1988 The modern Ministry's first "true" album is filled with anger, distortion, and a cacophonous wall of sound consisting of layer upon layer of electronics, and powered by Rieflin's metronomic pounding beats. The apocalypse caught on tape.

7 The Mind Is a Terrible Thing to Taste (Sire/WB) 1989

7 In Case You Didn't Feel Like Turning Up (Sire/WB) 1990 Six-track live album recorded during the band's North American tour showcases songs from both *Land* and its twisted sibling *Mind*.

8 Psalm 69: The Way to Succeed and the Way to Suck Eggs (WB) 1992 The soundtrack to armageddon, possibly the most cynical, nihilistic, and downright nasty album of the 1990s; a spite-drenched trawl through the most disgusting debris left behind by man's rise from the primordial soup of the late 1970s. Odd, then, that if you strip away the sound effects and scary voices, a lot of it is really rather pleasant.

3 Filth Pig (WB) 1995 Overlook the so-bad-it's-ghastly remake of Dylan's "Lay Lady Lay"; overlook, too, the fact that both Danzig and Sepultura had already made this kind of noise a million years before. *Filth Pig*, from its Reznor-baiting title on down, was less of an album and more of an attempt to do something really nasty — an unlistenable soup for sonic terrorists to play when they left the house unattended for a week. No jokes, no scary bits, no snatches of dislocated classical music jigging beneath the afterburn. Just an unrelenting blob of pain thresh-hold jelly, and a "fuck you" to Jesus and the hotrod he rode in on.

3 The Dark Side of the Spoon (WB) 1999 Presumably no-one got the joke last time out, so they tell it again with a little more regard for the attack which made Ministry seem important in the first place.

8 Twelve Inch Singles 1981–1984 (Wax Trax!) 1985 Compiling both original and remixed versions of "Cold Life," "All Day," "The Nature of Love," and the callous goth anthem of "Everyday is Halloween," this album sums up the transitional period between the sweetness of *No Sympathy* and the soul-sapping soup of *Twitch*.

Revolting Cocks LPs

6 Big Sexy Land (Wax Trax!) 1986 This offshoot brings together Al and Paul, occasional Ministry guest vocalist Chris Connelly, Lard guitarist Jeff Ward, Front 242's Richard 23, and producer Luc Van Acker. Their provocative debut album is the most industrial of all the Ministry spin-offs and the closest to that band's sound, minus the aggression, substituting a non-stop party atmosphere instead.

7 You Goddamned Son of a Bitch [LIVE] (Wax Trax!) 1988 Recorded live in September 1987, a raucous reprise for the best of *Big Sexyland*, with greater sonic appeal than the studio versions.

6 Beers Steers and Queers (Wax Trax!) 1990 A cock-eyed look at three of America's most powerful cultural icons maintains the sheer drive of *Bitch*, but falls down a little in its song selection.

6 Linger Ficken' Good… and Other Barnyard Oddities 1993 (Sire/Reprise) For Rev Co, the party never ends, it just gets more surreal. Be it Timothy Leary gently admonishing the crowd across the *Apocalypse Now*-flavored "Gila Copter," the PiL's in the house (that Jack built) of "Crackin' Up," or the slobbering cover of "Da Ya Think I'm Sexy?" that's truly threatening…until Chris Connelly dissolves into a giggle. The group may portray themselves as a limbo line with lampshade hats, but don't fall for that old party trick.

Lard LPs

7 The Last Temptation of Lard (Alternative Tentacles) 1990 Jourgensen, Barker, and Dead Kennedy Jello Biafra (plus drummer Jeff Ward) bring forth a ferociously pounding sound — Biafra's politically inflammable lyrics brilliantly combined with Ministry's customary nihilist clattering.

6 Pure Chewing Satisfaction (Alternative Tentacles) 1997

Paul Barker/Lead Into Gold LP

6 Age of Reason (Wax Trax!) 1990 Barker moves briefly into the spotlight with a fascinating solo album, distinguished more for its resemblance to Eno and Barker's pre-Ministry career (with Seattle art-experimentalists Young Scientists) than the Ministry mothership.

Bill Rieflin LP

9 Birth of a Giant (First World) 1999 Rieflin shakes off the shackles of his past with a mighty slab of post-modern prog-pop. Dramatic contributions from Robert Fripp and Trey Gunn are immediately identifiable, as Rieflin fashions a monstrous soundscape around an album which doesn't know whether it should dance or destroy. This is a cracking barrage and no mistake — Rieflin's vocals have a Hannibal Lecter calm (and Chris Connolly's harmonies add an eerie echo), while a host of fellow sinners contribute guitars which range from "shattered" to "duelling war" and onto "paranoid," "insect," and "supremes." And though it's hard to guess what any will sound like, once they start, you know.

MINOR THREAT

FORMED 1981 *(Washington DC)*
ORIGINAL LINE-UP *Ian MacKaye (b. 1963 — vocals); Lyle Preslar (guitar); Brian Baker (bass); Jeff Nelson (drums)*

Ted Nugent-loving teen skateboarder Ian MacKaye discovered punk rock in 1978 after going to a Cramps show with some likeminded friends. Exposure to the Sex Pistols, The Jam, and Generation X furthered his education and in 1979, as bassist, he formed his first band, the Slinkees.

That band immediately set out the confrontational attitude which would become an integral part of MacKaye's musical persona — their best known song was called "I Drink Milk"; another, "Deadhead," was about how boring pot smokers were. Add the ease with which nothing more threatening than a skinny tie and a pair of shades could send the adult world reeling in horror at the punk rock invasion and the future was at hand.

Recruiting new vocalist Nathan Strejcek, the Slinkees changed their name to the Teen Idles and began actively gigging, not only around DC, but as far afield as California. They played two shows, in L.A. and San Francisco, traveling aboard a Greyhound bus with roadie Henry Garfield, soon to return to the state as Henry Rollins.

In 1980, the Teen Idles cut their first EP, *Minor Disturbance*, for release on their own, newly formed Dischord label. The cover art, a pair of crossed hands with an X drawn on each, was intended as a tribute to the San Francisco club where underage audience members had their hands marked, to appease the local licensing laws. It was a system the Teen Idles had been trying to persuade DC bars to adopt; it would become the hallmark of the "straight edge" non-drinking (and later, non-smoking, non-meat-eating) scene which MacKaye himself never dreamed of when he wrote the song of the same name.

The Teen Idles broke up in November 1980 around the same time as MacKaye, the band's principal songwriter, decided he wanted to sing as well. With vocalist Strejcek now out of the way (he later joined Youth Brigade), MacKaye decided to make the move, forming a new band with Idles drummer, Jeff Nelson. Initial intentions of calling the band Straight were abandoned in favor of Minor Threat and with the Dischord label a ready outlet for their output, the band launched into an intense three years of gigging which saw them, knowingly, but nevertheless inadvertently, spreading the hardcore gospel far and wide.

The band's recorded legacy was small — just two EPs, *Filler* and *In My Eyes* (subsequently compiled on the *Minor Threat* album) and the *Out of Step* album, issued between 1981 and 1983. (The album included a cover of Wire's "12XU," disclosing just how great an influence that band's viscous minimalism had on the US hardcore scene.) But as with the case with the Sex Pistols, one of the few bands whose cultural significance parallelled Minor Threat's, the records were largely immaterial. It was the band's existence and the message which that existence represented, which mattered and few of the hardcore bands who would follow in their footsteps would ever be free of Minor Threat's influence.

That was the strain which ultimately shattered the band; as the straight-edge movement grew ever more intolerant, leaning evermore towards precisely the kind of cultural fascism which it was originally intended to oppose, MacKaye found himself losing patience with his mutant offspring. In 1983, he quit the band and, after laying low for two years, he linked with the recently sundered remains of brother Alex's band, Faith, as Embrace.

A deliberate reaction against the stringent rules of hardcore, Embrace debuted in August 1985 and played their final show in March 1986, a short existence during which they made a handful of recordings (posthumously released as *Embrace*) before breaking up for precisely the same reasons as Faith had broken up. The three musicians couldn't stand working with one another any longer. MacKaye reunited with Minor Threat drummer Nelson as Egg Hunt, cutting a solitary, eponymous, single, then formed Fugazi.

Also see the entry for "FUGAZI" on page 460.

Minor Threat LP

7 Out of Step (Dischord) 1983 The band lose the furious rush of the early EPs, but add things like hooks and punk stylings to their hardcore thrash. Still quick, but not dead.

Selected Compilations and Archive Releases

8 Minor Threat (Dischord) 1984 Welcome gathering of those first two EPs and crucial for "Minor Threat," "Filler," and "Straight Edge" — the song behind the movement.

8 Complete (Dischord) 1988 The perfect compilation collecting the band's whole canon in one handy package.

Embrace LP

6 Embrace (Dischord) 1987 A solid, intense, and unbridled slab of punk chronicling the beginning and end for this awkwardly hopeful aggregation.

MISFITS

FORMED 1977 (Lodi, NY)
ORIGINAL LINE-UP *Glenn Danzig (b. 6/23/55, Lodi, NY — vocals); Jerry Only (bass); Mannie (drums)*

Named for Marilyn Monroe's final movie, The Misfits were the B-Movie punk sensation which the New York underground had been waiting for; horror movie nuts whose idea of fun was to stage a horror movie for themselves. Originally a trio of Glenn Danzig, Jerry Only, and the short-lived Mannie, before recruiting Bobby Steele and Joey Image, The Misfits' early career would be dictated by their passion for B-movie-style artwork and the omnipresent Fiend skull logo which they applied to any surface it would stick to. More than any other band of their time and place, The Misfits understood the importance of image.

Forming their own Blank label, the band's debut single, "Cool Cough," was followed by the *Bullet* EP, before the band was offered free studio time, on the condition they changed the label's name — another Blank Records already existed. The Misfits agreed, renamed their label Plan 9 (for the classic movie *Plan 9 from Outer Space*) and recorded their first album, *Static Age*, in 1978, with a line-up now of Danzig, Only, Franche Come, and Mr. Jim.

The album would remain unreleased until 1997, as The Misfits lurched through a succession of line-up changes, releasing one further EP, *Night of the Living Dead*, before finally coalescing around Danzig, Only, Only's brother Doyle Von Frankenstein (guitar), and Eerie Von (b. Arthur Googy, Lodi, 8/25/64 — drums). This line-up would debut with the *Three Hits from Hell* in April 1981 and swiftly follow through with another EP, *Beware*, and the "Halloween" single.

Over the next two years, The Misfits would record two albums, *Walk Among Us* and *Earth AD/Wolf's Blood*, plus the in-concert set *Evil — Live*, but broke up following a Halloween 1983 show. Danzig immediately released a solo single, "Who Killed Marilyn," before reuniting with Eerie Von in Samhain, alongside Peter Marshall and Steve Zing. Samhain would pioneer America's black metal scene, transforming into Danzig in 1987 and slowly forcing their way into chart contention — 1994's *Danzig IV* album would breach the Top 30. The Only brothers regrouped as Kryst the Conquerer, with future Skid Row vocalist David Sabo, but broke up after just one EP.

The Misfits' legacy was made of stronger stuff. Two mid-'80s compilations, *Legacy of Brutality* and *Best of The Misfits* compiling some original releases which were already fetching large sums on the punk collectors circuit; in 1995, a full Misfits boxed set rounded up the band's entire output, including the unreleased *Static Age* album.

Meanwhile, a rising tide of late '80s bands gladly acknowledged their own personal debts to the band: Metallica covered "Last Caress," "Green Hell," and "Die, Die My Darling"; Guns n' Roses recorded "Attitude"; the Lemonheads covered "Skulls." Later, a 1997 tribute to the group would include contributions from Therapy?, Goldfinger, Pennywise, NOFX, Prong, and Sick of it All.

Throughout this period, the Only brothers pursued the right to reclaim The Misfits name from Danzig because, Jerry Only reflected, "I knew what we had was something special." The pair finally won through in January 1995 and began piecing together a new line-up. Michael Graves (vocals) was recruited some ten months and 200 auditions later, joining ex-Dan Kidney, Sacred Trash, and Sardonica drummer Dr. Chud.

The following year, The Misfits signed with Geffen and released the Daniel Rey produced *American Psycho* album, a full-blooded return to time-honored Misfits concerns: "Vampires, monsters, alien invasion, Frankenstein — we are The Misfits after all," warned Only.

The band broke with Geffen just months after the release of *American Psycho* and a tour with Megadeth; they eventually signed with Roadrunner in September 1998 and released *Famous Monsters* (#138 US) the following year, taking over Madison Square Garden for the early October release party. Other Misfits activities included the launch of band action figures and a link-up with the world of professional wrestling.

The Misfits LPs

9 Walk Among Us (Ruby) 1982 It took long enough, but The Misfits' debut emerges everything it should have been and more — a dense cinematic stew full of astro-zombies, skulls, and infant killers, but...maybe more surprisingly, given their low-rent punk reputation, some genuinely rocking songs and vocals that don't fall into the expected traps.

6 Earth A.D./Wolfsblood (Plan 9) 1983 Deviant dash into hardcore proves of use to no one, bar Metallica (they covered "Last Caress").

8 American Psycho (Geffen) 1997 Powerful comeback, concentrating wholly on the original band's greatest strengths — melody, songs, stuff like that — and on their reputation as the uncrowned kings of the cartoon horror monster show.

8 Famous Monsters (Roadrunner) 1999 Ripe as a bucketful of brains, the title comes from a '70s monster mag and "Fiend Club," "Living Hell," and "Scream" gnash their blood-soaked intent

before you've even cracked the shrink wrap. Tighter new punk disciplines wander into earshot occasionally, effortlessly absorbed into the trademark Misfits sound, and the comeback continues mighty.

Selected Compilations and Archive Releases

8 Legacy of Brutality (Caroline) 1986 Excellent outtakes collection dating back to late 1977's "She" — a time when the Misfits' sound was even more unique. The sound quality leaves something to be desired — a few studio cuts sound thuddingly live, but "American Nightmare" could have been the Stray Cats and "Who Killed Marilyn" would wind up in Danzig's repertoire.

7 Evil Live [LIVE] (Caroline) 1987 Henry Rollins is an unexpected guest star as The Misfits pound through *Walk Among Us*, live in New York, and San Francisco 1981.

7 Misfits (Caroline) 1988 20-track collection of alternate takes and remixes.

8 Coffin Box Set (Caroline) 1996 Magnificent rarities collection.

8 Evil Live II [LIVE] (Fiend Club) 1998 Amazing 19-track live set from 1997/98.

Glen Danzig and Eerie Von/Samhain LPs

7 Initium (Plan 9) 1984

6 November — Coming Fire (Plan 9) 1986

Selected Compilations and Archive Releases

7 Final Descent (Plan 9) 1990

Danzig LPs

5 Danzig (Def American) 1988

4 Danzig II: Lucifuge (Def American) 1990

5 Danzig III: How the Gods Kill (Def American) 1992

4 Thrall: Demonsweatlive [LIVE] (Def American) 1993

4 Danzig IV (American) 1994

6 Danzig V: Blackacidevil (Hollywood) 1996

5 Danzig 6: 66 Satan's Child (E-Magine) 1999

MISSION UK

FORMED 1985 *(London, England)*
ORIGINAL LINE-UP *Wayne Hussey (b. Jerry Lovelock, 5/26/58, Bristol, Avon — vocals, guitar); Simon Hinkler (guitar); Craig Adams (b. 4/4/62, Otley, Yorks — bass); Mick Brown (drums)*

Wayne Hussey and Craig Adams left the Sisters of Mercy in summer 1985 planning to form their own band. It was initially an amicable split, but much of the goodwill hinged upon an agreement that neither they nor surviving Sister Andrew Eldritch would invoke the old band's name in their future doings. When the pair announced that their new project was to be called the Sisterhood, in honor, insisted Hussey, of "a group of friends who followed us about," Eldritch immediately issued a terse press release and registered the Sisterhood name for himself.

Early in the new year, it must have appeared that Hussey and Adams had backed down. With Simon Hinkler (ex-Pulp, Artery) and Mick Brown (ex-Red Lorry Yellow Lorry) in tow, a Radio One session for Janice Long's show was taped under the name of the Wayne Hussey and Craig Adams Band. But shortly before its broadcast, on January 20, the band returned to the Sisterhood for their debut show at London's Alice in Wonderland, following up with a short European tour, opening for The Cult.

Again Eldritch blocked them, this time by releasing a single, itself credited to the Sisterhood. Hussey and co responded by announcing three UK shows, still under the Sisterhood name, but with a disclaimer noting this was not Eldritch's band. But Eldritch would not let the matter drop and on February 27, 1986, Hussey took the stage at London's Electric Ballroom and announced that, "thanks to Andrew Eldritch, we are no longer called the Sisterhood." The stage lights lit up a backdrop that proclaimed the band's new name — The Mission. Coincidentally, Eldritch's own next album currently had a working title of *Left on Mission and Revenge*.

In May, The Mission launched their first headlining UK tour, in support of their debut single, "Serpent's Kiss" (#70 UK, #2 UK indy). Released on the independent Chapter 22 label, both this and their follow-up, "Garden of Delight" (#50 UK, #1 UK indy), were only ever intended as shop windows for the band's wares — although this material would soon be gathered up as the *First Chapter* compilation (#35 UK).

By August, The Mission had signed with Mercury and following an appearance at the Reading festival, set to work on their debut album. Accompanied by the hits "Stay with Me" (#30 UK), the epic "Wasteland" (#11 UK), and "Severina" (#25 UK), *God's Own Medicine* (#108 US, #14 UK) saw The Mission take the Sisters' original goth image and imagery into entirely new territory, rooted in both pop and a new age sensibility which had never so successfully been woven into the music.

Tours of Europe and the UK through the first half of 1987 were spectacularly successful, while the band's US debut was marred first by the need to rename the band Mission UK, to avoid confusion with another band, then when Adams was diagnosed as suffering from physical and mental exhaustion and sent home early.

He recovered in time for a summer European tour, climaxed by another Reading appearance, before the band went into the studio with Led Zeppelin's John Paul Jones to record their sophomore album, *Children* (#126 US, #2 UK) — accompanied this time by the singles "Tower of Strength" (#12 UK), "Beyond the Pale" (#32 UK), and "Kingdom Come." A world tour kept the band on the road for much of 1988; 1989, on the other hand, would see them spend most of their time recording, emerging only to play Reading again and for a pair of benefit concerts, for victims of the Hillsborough soccer stadium disaster and the Lockerbie air crash.

They emerged from the studio in 1990 with two full albums, *Carved in Sand* (#101 US, #7 UK) and the out-takes collection *Grains of Sand* (#28 UK), and another run of classic singles, "Butterfly on a Wheel" (#12 UK), "Deliverance" (#27 UK), "Into the Blue" (#32 UK), and the Andy Partridge (XTC) produced "Hands Across the Ocean" (#28 UK).

Another US tour was stricken by illness, however, this time when Hinkler suffered rheumatic fever necessitating the cancellation of five opening shows. He returned, but in Canada in May, announced his departure. A stand-in, Red Lorry Yellow Lorry's Dave Wolfenden, was introduced, but Hussey was clearly shaken by events; in Toronto, he left the stage in tears after telling the audience the news.

Back in Europe, The Mission headlined Germany's Rocknight festival in August, moving on to full tours of Europe and the UK before wrapping up an eventful 12 months with a surprise mini-hit single, covering Slade's "Merry Christmas, Everybody" (#55 UK) as the Metal Gurus. (Slade's Noddy Holder and Jim Lea produced the record.)

With new guitarist Paul Etchells on board, The Mission's only live show in 1991 was alongside New Model Army and Killing Joke at London's Finsbury Park; they reappeared in May, with "Never Again" (#34 UK) and "Like a Child Again" (#30 UK), before the release of *Masque* (#23 UK), their most adventurous album yet, but also their most fraught. Much of the album was recorded in a home studio Hussey built in a barn, 50 miles from the nearest highway, at a time when he wanted to escape even from Adams and Brown. His new wife, Kelly, pulled him back on track, but *Masque* only papered over the cracks.

A final single, "Shades of Green" (#49 UK), preceded another lengthy hiatus, but when The Mission did reappear, Adams had departed for The Cult and Hussey and Brown were now accompanied by Mick Thwaite (ex-Spear of Destiny, guitar) and Andy Cousin (ex-All About Eve). The band debuted in August at an Off the Street homelessness benefit in London; Eldritch, too, was on the bill, performing with electronic band Utah Saints and the organizers hoped a reunion would happen. It didn't.

The Mission followed up with a 12-date UK tour in September 1993; Rik Carter (ex-Pendragon, keyboards) joined in the new year for a short tour promoting the forthcoming *Sum and Substance* (#49 UK) hits compilation and "Tower of Strength" remix (#33) and "Afterglow" (#53 UK) singles.

This line-up, too, soon collapsed; Mercury dropped the band and the next Mission album, *Neverland* (#58 UK), would be released by a duo of Hussey and Brown alone, through the indy Equator. The singles, "Rising Cain," "Swoon" (#75 UK), "Lose Myself in You," and the limited edition *Live* EP followed in mid-1995. Short UK and European tours followed and in summer 1996 came a new single, "Coming Home," and album, *Blue* (#73 UK). Neither was even noticed outside of The Mission's own fiercely dedicated following and after one final European tour and a single show in South Africa, the band broke up.

Two years passed before Hussey resurfaced at a Gary Numan show in L.A., then signed with Numan's US label, Cleopatra. At first he was content occupying himself as a remixer, gleefully stripping away all but the original vocals, then building entire new performances around the likes of Jay Aston (Gene Loves Jezebel), Rozz Williams (Christian Death), Bono (U2), and Brian Connolly (the Sweet). Soon, however, he was recording in his own right too. Recorded with Liar's Club drummer Dana, The Mission's version of the Stooges' "1969" appeared on *The Black Bible* Goth box set; a cover of Bowie's "After All" appeared on the *Goth Oddity* tribute album; and finally, an entire album of re-recorded Mission classics appeared in fall 1999, as Hussey reunited with Adams, Thwaite, and ex-Cult drummer Scott Garrett for the Resurrection tour of America (alongside Gene Loves Jezebel and Mike Peters).

The Mission UK LPs

8 God's Own Medicine (Mercury) 1986 From the opening chords of the glorious "Wasteland," through the anthemic "Severina" and onto "Island in a Stream," it's evident how The Mission differs from the Sisters they spun from — more optimistic, certainly less spartan, a celebration of the dawn after a long winter's night and no one's afraid to admit they like Led Zeppelin.

7 Children (Mercury) 1988 John Paul Jones produces, the band dip into the eclectic instrumentation bucket, and if parts of *Children* fall a bit flat, that's because other parts are so overpowering ("Tower of Strength," Aerosmith's "Dream On") that the rest just pale in comparison. It's a problem the band obviously recognized and the use of the briefer cuts as buffers did help. Besides, half a classic album is better than none.

7 Carved in Sand (Mercury) 1990 Learning from last time, Tim Palmer's production gives even the quietest numbers a big sound that's as effective on the rousing "Deliverance" as it is on the delicate "Butterfly...". *Sand*'s more coherent sound and the greater sonic qualities shine throughout the album, soaring and majestic.

7 Grains of Sand (Mercury) 1990 Mostly comprising songs recorded during the *Carved in Sand* sessions, including alternate versions of "Butterfly," "Kingdom Come," and "Tower of Strength" and two covers — a rollicking surreal Kinks' and a truly abysmal Beatles'. A powerful appendage.

6 Masque (Mercury) 1992 A *Joshua Tree* for the gloom set, *Masque* really does attain the same rabble-rousing height as U2 at their best, and with a similar reliance on glittering guitars and memorable melodies. Sadly, *Masque*'s attempt at diversifying The Mission's sound through eastern cadence, musical hall jaunt and lush ballad was just a fairy dance too far.

6 Neverland (Equator — UK) 1995 A dramatic departure from past albums — darker, moodier, and more introspective, it lacked either the sonic courage of *Sand* or the extremities of *Masque*, returning instead to Mission 101. None of the songs are The Mission at their best and, though the songwriting is actually more consistent than usual, there's a tiny hint of sameness.

6 Blue (Equator — UK) 1996

7 Resurrection (Cleopatra) 1999 Cheeky revision of the band's greatest hits, re-recorded and sometimes even reinvigorated. None will ever replace the originals in the true fan's heart, but one new track (the Stooges' "1969," reprised from Hussey's Sisters of Mercy days) and some dramatic new treatments at least keep things fresh.

Selected Compilations and Archive Releases

8 The First Chapter (Chapter 22) 1987 Essential early days wrap-up, featuring at least three of The Mission's finest ever performances, "Serpent's Kiss," "Garden of Delight," and the improbably magnificent "Wake (RSV)."

7 No Snow, No Show for the Eskimo [LIVE] (Windsong) 1993 Seven songs from 1988, four from 1990, originally recorded for the BBC.

9 Sum and Substance (Mercury) 1994 Broadside after broadside, bang-bang-bang, all the hits, a few 12-inch mixes — the ultimate primer of maximum goth.

7 Salad Daze (Night Tracks) 1994 Enjoyable BBC sessions collection, adding a sharp immediacy to otherwise familiar numbers.

Further Reading

Names Are for Tombstones, Baby by Martin Roach (IMP — UK).

MOBY

BORN *Richard Melville Hall, 9/11/65 (New York, NY)*

The great-great-grand nephew of *Moby Dick* author Herman Melville, Richard Hall was raised by his mother in Connecticut following the death of Hall Sr. in an auto accident when their child was two. In his teens and early 20s, Moby gravitated towards the east coast hardcore scene; his first band, the

Vatican Commandos, released a pair of EPs during 1983, while another early group, Peanuts, self-released an eponymous album's worth of untitled industrial noise shortly after. Fellow Peanut Paul Yates would continue collaborating with Moby through the Pork Guys punk sideline, well into the 1990s.

Moby would also spend some time with hardcore legends Flipper, but in 1989 he moved back to New York, intrigued by the incipient house boom. Quickly establishing himself as one of the city's top DJs, Moby released his first dance single, "Time's Up," under the name the Brotherhood, in September 1990.

He stepped out for the first time as Moby in November with "Mobility," following up with the first 12" by his Voodoo Child alias, "Voodoo Child" itself. It was with Moby's second single, however, that things took off — "Go" (#10 UK), built around a sample from the theme to TV's Twin Peaks, originally appeared on the B-side of "Mobility"; now it took on a life of its own, itself being sampled for a Toyota commercial.

Interspersing his own recordings with remix work for Depeche Mode, Erasure, Ajax, the B-52's, Brian Eno, Michael Jackson, Fierce Ruling Diva, Prodigy, the Pet Shop Boys, and Orbital, among others, Moby continued prolific through 1991. Brainstorm ("Rock the House," swiftly reissued as Mindstorm, after another dance act called Brainstorm made itself known), Barracuda ("Drug Fits the Face"), and UHF ("UHF3") would all release regularly, with the year wrapping up with an Instinct label sampler, Instinct Dance, compiled exclusively from Moby and his aliases.

Another compilation, Moby, would follow in June 1992, following the club success of "Drop the Beat," while a collaboration with David Sussman brought the Ecstasy anthem "Next Is the E" in October.

A second album titled Moby would be released in Europe in early 1993, again compiling single cuts, together with the American Early Underground and Ambient collections, before Moby returned to the UK chart in June with "I Feel It" (#38 UK) and another compilation, the helpfully titled The Story So Far. That summer, too, Moby played one of the best performances of the New Music Seminar in New York, marking his recent signing to Mute and in September, "Move (You Make Me Feel So Good)" (#21 UK) became his biggest British hit yet. Another honor came when the Guiness Book of Records featured Moby's "Thousands" as the fastest record ever made, one which reached an estimated 1060-1100 bpm, before it ended.

"Hymn" (#31 UK), "Feeling So Real" (#30 UK), and "Everytime You Touch Me" (#28 UK) followed, each one demonstrating another facet of Moby's songwriting abilities, at the same time as keeping him firmly in touch with the techno/acid scene. The album Everything Is Wrong, in March 1995, however, marked the apex of his techno ambitions.

Following the "Into the Blue" (#34 UK) single that summer, Moby joined the Lollapalooza tour with a solid return to his hardcore roots, followed through on 1996's "intentionally abrasive, misanthropic" Animal Rights (#38 UK). A statement of Moby's staunch veganism, it spawned one hit, "That's When I Reach for My Revolver" (#50 UK), but "Come on Baby" became his first ever British 45 not to chart and it was clear that Moby's own following had no time for this latest variation.

Proof that Moby was still interested in other musical forms, however, was gleaned from the ambient "Higher" single and orchestral The End of Everything, released as Voodoo Child in 1996, on Moby's own Trojan label.

Even more significant, however, was 1997's I Like to Score, a suggestively titled collection of movie themes which included, with exquisite timing, a version of the "James Bond Theme" just as a new Bond epic hit the theaters. While Sheryl Crow performed the "official" theme, "Tomorrow Never Dies," Moby's breathtaking rendition remains for many people a far stronger evocation of the movie.

Although he would remix Aerosmith, David Bowie, John Lydon, the Heads, Soundgarden, and Smashing Pumpkins during this period, over the next two years, Moby interested himself in researching historian Alan Lomax's field recordings of early blues, using them as a foundation first for the "Honey" single, in August 1998, and then the album Play (#66 US, #1 UK). A slow-burning set, the album took close to eight months to take off, finally peaking in spring 2000. The singles "Why Does My Heart Feel So Bad" (#16 UK) and "Natural Blues" (#11) also proved belated smashes.

Moby LPs

8 Everything Is Wrong (Elektra) 1995 Hero of the US club scene, Moby's greatest strength is his self-assurance across subgenres, as confident within ambient as house, as masterful at techno as electro-speed-punk, and equally dedicated and enthusiastic about each, making for a brilliant debut filled with crucial cuts.

5 Animal Rights (Elektra) 1996 Moby's interest in speed metal was evident from Everything, but no one expected an entire album of it, and not many people wanted it either.

7 I Like to Score (Elektra/Asylum) 1997 Impressive (if possibly jokey) assemblage of cinematic themes, fronted by the amazing hit James Bond reworking.

8 Play (V2) 1999 Making up for lost time, Play picks up where Everything Is Wrong left off, merging even more styles within the electro core, everything is, although only the authentically antiquated R&B cuts actually break new ground.

Selected Compilations and Archive Releases

6 Instinct Dance (Instinct) 1991 One man and his manifold dance floor aliases — essential compilation for the hotfooted collector.

7 Moby (Instinct) 1992
7 Moby (Instinct — Germany) 1993
6 Ambient (Instinct) 1993 Further compilations, drawing from singles, remixes and aliases. *Ambient*, of course, is true to its title.

8 The Story So Far (Instinct) 1993 15-track compilation comprises highlights of his '90-'91 EPs and 12-inch singles.

8 Rare: Collected B-Sides (Instinct) 1996 Frantic sibling to *Story So Far*, wrapping up with the indispensable "Thousands."

7 Everything Is Wrong: DJ Mix Album (Mute) 1996

Voodoo Child LPs

7 The End of Everything (Trojan) 1996

Moby — Selected Remixes
1991 LFO — Tan Ta Ra (Tommy Boy)
1991 ERASURE — Am I Right? (Mute)
1991 PET SHOP BOYS — Miserabalism [MULTIPLE MIXES] (Parlophone)
1991 ANDROMEDA — Gazza (Sonic)
1992 FIERCE RULING DIVA — You Gotta Believe [MULTIPLE MIXES] (React)
1992 RECOIL — Faith Healer (Mute)
1992 ORBITAL — Speed Freak (FFRR)
1992 ESKIMOS AND EGYPT — Fall from Grace [MULTIPLE MIXES] (One Little Indian)
1992 B-52's — Revolution Earth [MULTIPLE MIXES] (Reprise)
1992 B-52's — Good Stuff (Reprise)
1992 FORTRAN 5 — Heart on the Line [MULTIPLE MIXES] (Mute)
1992 MICHAEL JACKSON — Who Is It? [MULTIPLE MIXES] (Epic)
1992 SOHO — Ride [MULTIPLE MIXES] (Atco)
1992 JAM AND SPOON — Stella [MULTIPLE MIXES] (R&S)
1992 ENO — Fractal Dub [MULTIPLE MIXES] (Opal)
1992 SHAMEN — Make It Mine [MULTIPLE MIXES] (Sony)
1992 TEN CITY — Only Time Will Tell [MULTIPLE MIXES] (East West)
1992 B-52's — Is That You, Mo-Dean [MULTIPLE MIXES] (Reprise)
1992 PRODIGY — Everybody in the Place (Elektra)
1992 OPUS III — I Talk to the Wind [MULTIPLE MIXES] (Atlantic)
1993 MICHAEL JACKSON — Beat It (Epic)
1993 THE OTHER TWO — Moving On (Qwest)
1994 WESTBAM — Bam Bam Bam [MULTIPLE MIXES] (Low Spirit)
1994 DEPECHE MODE — Walking in My Shoes [MULTIPLE MIXES] (Sire)
1995 SMASHING PUMPKINS — 1979 (Virgin)
1995 YELLO — Lost Again (Motor Music)
1995 JON SPENCER BLUES EXPLOSION.. — Greyhound (Matador)
1996 SOUNDGARDEN — Dusty (A&M)
1996 HEADS — Damage I've Done [MULTIPLE MIXES] (Radioactive)
1996 METALLICA — Until It Sleeps (Vertigo)
1997 DAVID BOWIE — Dead Man Walking [MULTIPLE MIXES] (Virgin)
1997 BLUR — MOR [MULTIPLE MIXES] (Food)
1997 AEROSMITH — Falling in Love [MULTIPLE MIXES] (Columbia)
1997 JOHN LYDON — Grave Ride (Virgin)
1998 OMD — Souvenir [MULTIPLE MIXES] (Virgin)
1998 JON SPENCER — Wait a Minute (Au Go Go)

MONKEY MAFIA

BORN *Jon Carter, 1970 (Woodford, Essex, England)*

Jon Carter was studying philosophy at university in Southampton when he formed his first group, the Doors-and Hendrix-inflected jam band, Everything Burns. Regulars at early '90s free festivals and protest rallies, Everything Burns reached their peak during the 1991–92 campaign to prevent a motorway link carving through picturesque Twyford Down near Winchester. The night before the bulldozers finally moved in, after over a year of opposition, Everything Burns played a dynamic three-hour set.

The band's next regular gig was a residency at a local Irish pub, playing "funk stuff, Jah Wobble, and Beatles tunes to hardcore dockers." When the group broke up, Carter moved to London and took jobs with the dance labels Trouble on Vinyl and No U Turn, during the early days of drum'n'bass. Captivated by the possibilities, he made his own tape, "Dollar," released by Wall of Sound in 1994 under the name Artery. Label head Mark Jonesalso suggested Carter visit the newly opened Sunday Social, a dance club operating out of a London pub basement.

With the embryonic Chemical Brothers as house DJs, the Social styled itself as an anti-club club, eschewing dress, drug, and music codes, even as its reputation exploded. Carter became a regular DJ there, targeting his own recordings towards the kindred spirits who populated the Social. Released under his new Monkey Mafia alias, 1995's "Blow the Whole Joint Up," based around a loop from the Who's "Out in the Street," was an immediate hit and the following year brought Carter's *Live at the Social* mix album, featuring his own "Work Mi Body," the lead cut from the next Monkey Mafia EP and a showcase for scratcher Krash Slaughta.

Remix work for St. Etienne, the Prodigy, Kula Shaker, INXS, and more was followed by Carter (with Death in Vegas' Richard Fearless) being invited to take over the Chemical Brothers' regular slot at the Social. Monkey Mafia promptly went on hold and over the next year, just one further EP would emerge — 15 *Steps*.

Finally, 1998 brought the renegade ragga vision of *Shoot the Boss*, recorded with a rhythm section of Dan and Tom, keyboard players Lee Horsley and Lee Spencer, MCs Douge Reuben, Silva Bullet and Patra, and scratcher First Rate — released as a single, a cover of Creedence Clearwater Revival's "As Long as I Can See the Light" would become a dynamic highlight of the next few months.

Monkey Mafia LPs

🎵 **Live at the Heavenly Social (Deconstruction) 1996** One of the finest mix albums of the period, Carter's intuitive eye for dub potential ensuring the beats never let up.

🎵 **Shoot the Boss (Heavenly) 1998** Birthed in the dancehall, but raised on electro, Monkey Mafia's darkly dangerous sound is a sublime blend of toasting, tribal-industrio beats, scratching, and insidious, yet constantly surprising, electronics. The overall experience is more club-friendly than anything on On-U (with which the Mafia earned some comparisons), but it's just as groundbreaking.

MORRISSEY

BORN *Stephen Patrick Morrissey, 5/22/59 (Davyhulme, England)*

The final releases by The Smiths were still appearing when Morrissey launched his solo career in 1988, with a single, "Suedehead" (#5 UK), and an album, *Viva Hate* (aka *Education in Reverse*, for Australian release), working with producer Stephen Street, drummer Andrew Paresi, and former Durutti Column guitarist Vini Reilly.

Offering a continuation of, rather than a progression from, all he had accomplished with The Smiths, "Suedehead" took its title from a 1970s novel by author Richard Allen, one in a series of Youth Cult shockers, and quickly became Morrissey's biggest hit ever. *Viva Hate* (#48 US, #1 UK), too, was a major success, while the expected controversy arose with the song "Margaret on the Guillotine," an ode to British Prime Minister Thatcher, which essentially picked up where Morrissey had left off four years earlier when he publicly affirmed he wished she'd died in the IRA attack on the hotel where she was staying.

British MP Geoffrey Dickens promptly rushed to his leader's defense, contacting the police and charging Morrissey with "incitement to violence," an imprisonable offense. Nothing came of the ensuing investigation, although Morrissey subsequently wrote a song, "He Knows I'd Love to See Him," about his meetings with the police.

"Suedehead" was followed by another major hit, the evocative "Everyday Is Like Sunday" (#9 UK), and in December 1988, Morrissey played his first live show since the previous February, when he booked Wolverhampton

City Hall to film a video for "Last of the International Playboys" (#6 UK). Ex-Smiths Andy Rourke and Mike Joyce accompanied him on stage, as they would when he returned to the studio, to record the "Interesting Drug" (#9 UK) single which followed "Playboys" into the chart in April 1989.

A breach with producer Street after the producer filed an injunction against "Interesting Drug" in the hope of persuading Morrissey to "speed up the paperwork" saw Morrissey bring Clive Langer and Alan Winstanley (Madness, Elvis Costello) in for his next album. With a new band comprising Paresi, former Soft Boys bassist Matthew Seligman, Steve Hopkins (piano), and Kevin Armstrong (guitar, ex-Sandie Shaw, David Bowie), this line-up cut the "Ouija Board" single (#18 UK) but attempts to complete Morrissey's already overdue sophomore album were doomed to fail.

Instead, he released another new single, April 1990's unseasonal "November Spawned a Monster" (welcoming back Rourke and with spectral backing vocals from Mary Margaret O'Hara; #12 UK) and a compilation of singles, B-sides, and outtakes, *Bona Drag* (#59 US, #9 UK) in October. Four months later, the long-delayed, "real" second album, *Kill Uncle* (#52 US, #8 UK), emerged, introducing another Madness alumnus, Mark "Bedders" Bedford (bass) and Morrissey's latest songwriting partner, Mark Nevin (ex-Fairground Attraction, Kirsty MacColl).

It was not a successful partnership. While the album did well, its attendant singles, "Our Frank" (#26 UK) and "Sing Your Life" (#33 UK), foundered and Morrissey began the process of self-reinvention which would sustain him through the 1990s.

Key to this was the recruitment of guitarist Boz Boorer (ex-Polecats) and bassist Johnny Bridgewood, who joined Nevin and Paresi for the "Pregnant for the Last Time' single (#25 UK). Its recording coincided with the announcement that Morrissey was returning to live work in April 1991 with a new band built around Boorer — the Lads.

All three new musicians, Alain Whyte (guitar), Gary Day (bass), and Spencer Cobrin (drums), had previously played together in the rockabilly band, Bad Blood; prior to that, Whyte and Boorer had worked together as the Rugcutters, an ad hoc early-'80s outfit which featured Boorer's wife, Lynder, on stand-up bass (Boz and Lynder were also members of the Shillelagh Sisters, with future Bananarama vocalist Jacquie O'Sullivan).

The Lads made an immediate impression, touring the UK and Europe before making their first visit to the US that summer for a string of promotional shows. They returned in the fall for *Saturday Night Live* (11/14/92) and a tour marred by a near riot at the UCLA and the cancellation of 12 east coast dates after Morrissey was diagnosed with exhaustion. Then, with Whyte established as Morrissey's principal songwriting partner, they started work on Morrissey's next album, the Mick Ronson-produced *Your Arsenal* (#21 US, #4 UK).

Two singles, "We Hate It When Our Friends become Successful"(#17 UK) and "You're the One for Me, Fatty" (#19 UK), preceded the album, setting the scene for a rockabilly-tinged masterpiece. "Certain People I Know" (#35 UK) followed it in Britain, "Tomorrow" would top *Billboard's* Modern Rock chart, and David Bowie would cover "I Know It's Gonna Happen Someday" on his *Black Tie White Noise* album.

Tours of the UK and US exploded into scenes of mania, nowhere so much as in Seattle, where Whyte set fire to his guitar in tribute to local hero Jimi Hendrix, further choking a stage already awash with smoke bombs and feedback. It was a sensational act — a blend of rock and theater which knew few peers on the early 1990s scene, but certain elements would backfire. The inclusion on the album of the song "National Front Disco," seemingly a paean to the ultra-right wing political group and Morrissey's flag-draped appearance at Madness' Madstock festival the following summer both aroused accusations of racism — charges upon which Morrissey, uncharacteristically, remained silent.

A new album, the live *Beethoven Was Deaf* (#13 UK), was certainly caught up in the fallout, dropping out of the chart after just one week, and Morrissey maintained a low profile throughout 1993 before re-emerging in the new year with the defiantly titled modern rock chart-topper, "The More You Ignore Me, the Closer I Get" (#46 US, #8 UK).

Recorded with a new rhythm section — returning bassist Bridgewood and drummer Woodie Taylor — and produced by Steve Lillywhite, the album *Vauxhall and I* (#18 US, #1 UK) was similarly successful. A second single from the set, "Hold onto Your Friends" (#47 UK), performed less impressively, although any purchaser flipping the 12-inch would have been treated to the first indication of Morrissey's proposed next direction — a lengthy and extraordinarily emotional version of "Moon River." Coupled with his next release, a duet with Banshee Siouxsie on Timi Yuro's "Interlude" (#25 UK), Morrissey's embrace of music for the soul, as opposed to simply lyrics, was complete.

"Boxers" (#23, UK), reiterating his fascination for London "low-life" culture and backed by an assault on Natalie Merchant, one of several singers to have attempted covering "Everyday is Like Sunday" in recent years ("Have a Go Merchant"), prefaced a new compilation, the *World of Morrissey* (#134 US, #15 UK) round-up of recent singles and B-sides and in August 1995, with returning drummer Spencer James Cobrin on board, Morrissey's most audacious album yet, *Southpaw Grammar* (#64 US, #4 UK), was released to widespread confusion.

Opening and closing with the lengthiest tracks Morrissey had ever recorded, reveling in lengthy instrumental passages and with one cut beginning with a drum solo, the ensuing sonic stew was a shock to fans — but an even greater surprise to Morrissey's new label, RCA, who had signed him for one album only, but certainly foresaw a longer relationship than that unfolding. Instead, they received an album whose ultimate performance totally belied its maker's popularity and whose accompanying singles, "Dagenham Dave" (#26 UK) and "Boy Racer" (#36 UK), were scarcely noticed outside of the fan club. Equally damaging, a Morrissey-sanctioned single on his last label, "Sunny" (#42 UK) was released almost simultaneous to "Boy Racer."

Morrissey and RCA parted company and the singer moved to Island (Mercury in the US) in 1997. The "Alma Matters" (#16 UK) single in July marked a return of sorts to more familiar pastures; similarly, *Maladjusted* (#61 US, #8 UK) at least proved Morrissey's support had remained consistent. Two further singles followed — "Roy's Keen" (#42 UK), punning on the name of a popular Manchester United soccer player (Roy Keane) and "Satan Has Rejected My Soul" (#39 UK).

Tours of the UK and US were similarly successful, but once again, Morrissey seemed intent on spoiling his own chances, promptly following through with the British *Suedehead* (#26 UK) singles collection and the American *My Early Burglary Years* selection of B-sides and rarities.

Finally, Morrissey and Island parted company during 1998 and when he next resurfaced, for the Coachella Festival in California in October 1999, he remained without a label. However, a new rhythm section, comprising original bassist Day and ex-Damned drummer Spike Smith, new management (former Neil Young supremo Elliot Roberts) and a successful DVD collection of solo videos, *¡Oye Esteban!*, prompted understandable optimism.

Also see the entry for the "SMITHS" on page 637.

Morrissey LPs

🟤 **Viva Hate (Sire) 1988** Standing amid the ashes of pop music which he once claimed were "all around us," with a guilty smirk and a blowtorch in his pocket, Morrissey begins the reinvention with the sparkling "Suedehead," the sordid "Late Night, Maudlin Street," and the all but perfect "Everyday Is Like Sunday," a lament so lovely that ernest singer-songwriters have been queuing to dissect it ever since. When he first broke up The Smiths, few people understood why. Was this reason enough?

🟤 **Kill Uncle (Sire) 1991** A somewhat drier, more sober concoction than its predecessor, more concerned with mood than material, but still capable of breaking out with indelible magic ("The Harsh Truth of the Camera Eye" and "There's a Place in Hell for Me and My Friends") when it sees fit.

9 Your Arsenal (Sire) 1992 Orwellian in its vision, small-town English mundanities played out against a backdrop of relentless domestic violence, Morrissey responds with his first album ever to match his media rep — and the first to show what happens when you're abducted by rockabilly aliens.

7 Beethoven Was Deaf [LIVE] (EMI — UK) 1993 Recapturing most of *Arsenal*, plus selected B-sides, this live document of the 1992 tour invokes a new side of Morrissey — an abandoned wraith defying and decrying his "solitary" reputation.

10 Vauxhall & I (Sire) 1994 Returning to earth after the hyper-production of *Your Arsenal*, the boy with the tropical plant up his ass offers a markedly bitter recounting of a year's worth of media troubles and he doesn't forgive one of them. "I bear more grudges," he warns, "than lonely high court judges," but else-where, "hated for loving, I still don't belong" begs the question — loving what? Belonging to what?

The liberated consciousness of the early-mid '90s was never going to find a place for Morrissey, while the self-centered stormtroopers of intellectual Nazi-ism had an irony by-pass so long ago that even Morrissey's threat of retirement raised no more than an honorable shrug. So he delivered *Vauxhall* instead, flying through the face of reason like a body through a windshield, then going out with a bang — or at least, a chainsaw. The closing "Speedway" bellows betrayal, even as it slams the door shut on reconciliation.

At the end, though, what you get from *Vauxhall* is what you deserve and, when it ends, you have to choose your side. The "Lazy Sunbathers" have already selected theirs' and, though "a world war was announced days ago," they just carry on fid-dling...or maybe writing indignant letters about pop stars who dare to speak the unspeakable while the earth burns with genuine conflict. Morrissey spites their stupidity and he's suffered for his insights. *Vauxhall* ensures his pain is not for nothing.

8 Southpaw Grammar (Reprise) 1995 Several cuts shorter, but several minutes longer than Vauxhall, *Southpaw* kicks off with almost twelve heavily orchestrated minutes of foreboding and "The Teachers Are Afraid of the Pupils." Another track opens with a bona fide drum solo, while the whole thing closes with a 10-minute jam. The (absent) "Boxers" 45 set the conceptual stage for *Southpaw*, but even it offered no clues at all towards what emerged as Morrissey's most rebellious album yet.

8 Maladjusted (Polygram) 1997 Still the bard of questioning dementia, still touching with one line the kind of emotions which most people struggle to cram into a novel, then painting his band into the corners in between, Morrissey reclaims the crown of outsiders at the same time as refusing to wear it. Maybe bitter, sometimes savage, and endearingly confusing, living up to its title with a rude, rugged vengeance, *Maladjusted* is Morrissey crushing expectations by living far, far beyond them.

Selected Compilations and Archive Releases

9 Bona Drag (Sire) 1990 Frankly unbeatable collection of sin-gles, B-sides, odds and ends, and a post-Smiths greatest hits col-lection which cannot be faulted. "Ouija Board," "Interesting

Drug," and "November Spawned a Monster" were three of the most intelligent hits in recent history, while "Disappointed" is a moment of hope for everyone who wishes he'd just go away.

8 My Early Burglary Years (Reprise) 1998 Once more around the block for a batch of Morrissey B-sides and oddities which any self-respecting singles collector will already have two or three times already, a companion volume to *Bona Drag*, and the ghostly twin of both 1995's *The World of Morrissey* collection and the bonus track stacked reissued *Viva Hate*.

MOTHER LOVE BONE

FORMED 1988 *(Seattle, WA)*

ORIGINAL LINE-UP *Andrew Wood (b. 1966 — vocals); Stone Gos-sard (b. 7/20/66, Seattle, WA — guitar); Bruce Fairweather (guitar); Jeff Ament (b. 3/10/63, Big Sandy, MT — bass); Greg Gilmore (drums)*

Mother Love Bone formed from the wreckage of PNW glam metal mutants Malfunkshun, a Bremerton-based combo fronted by a vision named Andrew Wood — such a vision, in fact, that the first time the Melvins' Dale Crover saw them play, "there was this girl in a furry coat. She was walking up to the front of the stage, and people were trying to pick her up; I was looking at her, and she was pretty huge. Then she got on stage and started playing bass." "She" was Andrew Wood.

"We were the big flamboyant concert in a small club set-ting," drummer Regan Hagar recalled. "But we were really tongue-in-cheek; people found us amusing. I think people came to see Andy as much as to hear the music." Early in Malfunkshun's past (the band formed on Bainbridge Island in 1980, although it would take them five years to make an impact on the mainland), Wood had created "Landrew the Love Child," an onstage alter-ego who emerged, unan-nounced, swathed in a flowing cape, his face covered in white make-up — the living antithesis of all of rock's preoc-cupations with the Unholy.

"We were an anti-666 band," Landrew informed a puz-zled public in 1986, "because that's when the Satan thing was becoming really big. So we were a 333 band and did anti-devil songs. But it's called 'love rock' because we love to play it. I thought of what to call it today at work — we're a Deranged Gypsy Hard Rock band."

Play it they did, and they recorded prodigiously too, con-tributing to local label C/Z's crucial *Deep Six* compilation (alongside Green River, the Melvins, Soundgarden, the U-Men, and label founder Daniel House's Skin Yard), and lay-ing down the battery of demos which would emerge in 1995 as the intensely posthumous *Return to Olympus* album. But there, too, they demonstrated how Seattle maintained its individuality, the edge of darkness which established the most live-in-able city in the States, simultaneously, as the serial killer and suicide capital of America, was in its refusal to let ethics die with the ethos.

According to Soundgarden's Ben Sheppard, "most musicians in Seattle were Malfunkshun fans. Sometimes they were great, sometimes they weren't. They were cavemen on acid. Kevin (Wood's guitarist brother) used to solo the whole time, and Andy used to do his hair out, add glitter, and don a trenchcoat." It was only logical, then, that when Green River splintered, and Arm and Turner formed Mudhoney, that bandmates Ament and Gossard should make straight for Andrew Wood and drummer Hagar.

The hastily named Lords of Wasteland began gigging before the end of the year, in the basement of a local shoe store, Luna, with a set comprised exclusively of hard rock covers. Band chemistry, however, was strong and with the addition of another Green River alumni, Bruce Fairweather, and the arrival of Greg Gilmore in place of Hagar, the quintet became Mother Love Bone and in February 1988, they booked into Reciprocal Studios and recorded their first ten-song demo.

One tape landed them a manager, Kelly Curtis; a second reached one of Ament's friends, Geffen Records' Anna Statman. She convinced the label to finance another MLB demo, recorded in June. Geffen promptly offered the band a contract and the band returned to Seattle to await the paperwork.

It was a long wait. The contract never arrived, despite repeated assurances that it was on its way and as the summer drifted by, Mother Love Bone demos began making their way to other labels. According to Gilmore, "it took six months for a contract to arrive and when it did, it was from another label entirely." In December 1988, Mother Love Bone signed with Polydor.

Work began on their debut *Shine* EP in early 1989, for release (on their own Stardog imprint) in March, just as the band kicked off their first US tour, opening for Dogs D'Amour. Poor crowds marred the outing, but the band returned home to plan their debut album and cut a cover of Argent's 1972 hit, "Hold Your Head Up," for a forthcoming "tribute" to the 1970s. The tribute was never released and neither was funding for the band's album. Another summer of frustrating inactivity passed by, before September finally saw the sessions begin.

The album was completed by November 1989, but the waiting continued, as Polygram decided to hold *Apple* over for a spring release. A video for the first single, "Stardog Champion," was planned, while Wood's extravagant stage persona — a source of considerable discontent among the headliners crew on the Dogs D'Amour tour — so entranced

Polydor that talk was now turning towards allowing him to run a parallel solo career of songs recorded with his brother Kevin.

Wood, however, was fast losing touch with his career, as a longstanding drug habit grew deeper out of boredom and frustration at his continually stalled career, said friends. It was early March before the band began to stir again. A show at the Central Tavern in Seattle was scheduled to be their last before the album's release; a few days later, on March 15 1990, Wood gave what was intended to be the first of a battery of press interviews, with a local journalist. It would be his last — the following evening, his girlfriend returned home to find Wood had OD'd. Whisked to a hospital, he was placed on a life support machine, which two days later, his family had switched off.

A memorial service was held at the Paramount Theatre on March 24; *Apple* was delayed a few months more, but finally appeared in the early summer. It sank without trace, not re-emerging until October 1992 when interest in Ament and Stone's next project, Pearl Jam, saw the set retitled *Mother Love Bone* (#77US) and appended with bonus tracks drawn from the *Shine* EP. An archival video, *The Love Earth Affair*, would follow.

The greatest tribute to Wood, however, was Temple of the Dog, a collaboration between Ament and Gossard, Pearl Jam bandmates Eddie Vedder and Mike McCready, Chris Friel (drums; McCready's former bandmate in Shadow), and Soundgarden's Chris Cornell and Matt Cameron.

Taking its name from a lyric in MLB's "Man of Golden Words," Temple of the Dog was originally conceived by Cornell (Wood's former roommate) as a tribute single, coupling "Say Hello 2 Heaven" and "Reach Down." The sessions rapidly expanded, however, with material both dedicated to and inspired by Wood, recorded over a few weekends across November and December 1980. *Temple of the Dog* was released on Soundgarden's label, A&M, in April 1991 when the "band" played their only live show at the Off Ramp in Seattle; a full year on, again in the wake of Pearl Jam's breakthrough, the reactivated album climbed to #5 US.

Mother Love Bone LP

5 Apple (Stardog) 1990 An album rendered a bittersweet legend by its posthumous release, the music itself is a pushy morass of ragged, grungy rock in the style of the band's 1970 icons. Mother Love Bone themselves became a cornerstone in the annals of grunge. *Apple* was just the unfortunate side effect.

Selected Compilations and Archive Releases

7 Mother Love Bone (Polygram) 1992 Pulls together *Apple* plus the band's 1989 *Shine* EP.

BOB MOULD

BORN 10/16/60 (Malone, NY)

Following Hüsker Dü's 1987 demise, vocalist Mould spun around a full 360 degrees, retiring to Prince's Paisley Park studios to record his first solo album, while surrounding himself with a genre-shattering roster of musicians — Anton Fier (Pere Ubu, Golden Palominos; drums), Tony Maimone (Pere Ubu; bass), and cellist Jane Scarpantoni (Tiny Lights). The largely acoustic *Workbook* was released in July 1989, preceded in June by a single, "See a Little Light," both introducing a kinder, gentler, Mould to the world.

However, his next album, August 1990's *Black Sheets of Rain*, did welcome back the cacophony of powerhouse guitars that most people associated with Mould; a bracing collection which ran the gambit from bright pop to end of the world apocrypha and readily bridged the gap between Mould's solo canon and the more traditional sounds of his next project, Sugar.

Frustrated with major label politics, Mould split with Virgin in 1990 and hit the road, launching a quiet acoustic tour. He also formed his own imprint, SOL (Singles Only Label), which released material from up and comers as well as cult icons including William Burroughs. Emerging on the other side of this exorcism, Mould then linked with bassist Dave Barbe (ex-Mercyland) and drummer Malcolm Travis (ex-Zulus) as Sugar, a trio whose initial impetus seemed to build around much the same spark as Mould and Grant Hart had during the early days of Hüsker Dü.

Sugar's first release, a 12" EP, "Changes," was followed in September 1992 by their debut, *Copper Blue* (#10 UK). The album was well received both by critics and the listening public; indeed, thanks in part to the mainstream success of grunge, Mould was now considered all but godlike and though the expected comparisons to Hüsker Dü appeared, by this time it didn't matter at all. Mould was an untouchable, and *Copper Blue* readily jumped genres to become a mainstream hit as well. The album spawned two further singles, "A Good Idea" (#65 UK) in October and "If I Can't Change Your Mind" (#30 UK) in January 1993.

Mould continued to refuse to be defined, and stubbornly declined to become a pop guru as well. Sugar's next release, the mini-LP, *Beaster* (#130 US, #3 UK), was a dramatically noisy departure from the winsome sounds of *Copper Blue*. Still, two singles during 1993/94, "Tilted" (#48 UK) and "Your Favorite Thing" (#40 UK), proved that even reinvention could not dull Mould's edge, and the revelations continued across September 1994's *File Under Easy Listening* (#50 US, #7 UK).

Two further singles, "Believe What You're Saying" (#73 UK) and "Gee Angel," emerged, but with Mould sick of

touring and talking, the album was barely promoted and it became apparent that Sugar's ride was coming to an end. Mould, claiming that the band simply wasn't fun any more, split the trio in spring 1995.

But Mould wasn't through yet. While Sugar were remembered with the *Besides* (#122 US) live and rarities collection, Mould returned to action, recording what would eventually become 1996's *Bob Mould* (#52 UK) LP. Taking elements of Hüsker Dü, his previous solo inspirations, and Sugar, Mould emerged with a sound that was a smooth amalgam of everything he'd ever done. He would follow up in 1998 with the tight, listener-friendly *Dog & Pony Show* and the *Egoverride* EP, and gigged into summer 1999. He also became involved with wrestling's WCW, who hired him on board its booking committee as the organization's affiliation with rock music grew stronger. He quit in early 2000.

Also see the entry for "HÜSKER DÜ" on page 514.

Bob Mould LPs

7 Workbook (Virgin) 1989 Everything the music of Hüsker Dü was not — the perfect vehicle to showcase and shadow the melancholy air of Mould's songwriting, with only the closing "Whichever Way the Wind Blows" ringing with the blistered guitars of Mould's earlier sets.

6 Black Sheets of Rain (Virgin) 1990 Mould travels back from the acoustic land of nod, and back to the good old electric guitar — albeit in the guise of ambient fuzz. The songs follow suit, losing a lot of the intensity which once was his strongest point.

5 Bob Mould (Rykodisc) 1996 Competent alterna-rock from Mould in his first post Sugar effort. The sound is unmistakable, the style is just as expected. But the overall feel falls flat, and one wonders...is this album real? Or is it just a remembrance of past honesty?

7 The Last Dog & Pony Show (Rykodisc) 1998 More akin to earlier efforts, *Show* showcases a Mould who is polished, slick and sophisticated, while genuinely regaining the ragged glory of yesteryear.

Selected Compilations and Archive Releases

6 Poison Years (Virgin) 1994 Bits of the best of the first two albums.

Sugar LPs

7 Copper Blue (Rykodisc) 1992 A rip roaring rage of a good time. The sound is powerful yet melodic, the volume is almost over the top, and just when you think you've got a handle on it all, Sugar throw in the twangy "If I Can't Change Your Mind," just to shake things up.

7 File Under: Easy Listening (Rykodisc) 1994 Why yes — you almost could. Mellowed but still moving with distorted effect, Sugar do it one more (last) time.

7 Besides (Rykodisc) 1995 A collection of promos, B-sides, and live performances creating an alternative take on a "best of."

PETER MURPHY

BORN 7/11/57 (Northampton, England)

Peter Murphy's first step following the demise of Bauhaus was a dance routine with choreographer Annie Cox, performing to Bauhaus' "Hollow Hills" on British TV's *Riverside* on August 4 1983. He resurfaced again a year later, linking with former Japan bassist Mick Karn as Dali's Car; a single, "The Judgment Is in the Mirror" (#66 UK), and album, *The Waking Hour* (#84 UK), followed, but the duo made only one public appearance, on TV's *Old Grey Whistle Test* in November, before knocking the car on the head. Another twelve months then elapsed before Murphy launched his solo career in October 1985.

His first release was a cover of Magazine's "The Light Pours out of Me," included on the label sampler *One Pound Ninety Nine* and featuring former Magazine guitarist John McGeogh, Associates pianist L. Howard Hughes, and Bauhaus' sound engineer, Peter Edwards. Though the track was taken from Murphy's forthcoming *Should the World Fail to Fall Apart* (#82 UK) album, it would be July 1986 before the album materialized, by which time he had pieced together a new band around Hughes (guitar), Peter Bonas (guitar), Paul Statham (keyboards), Eddie Branch (bass), and Teri Bryant (drums). This line-up, soon to be dubbed the 100 Men, debuted with a short Italian tour in May; Murphy played his first solo UK shows in July.

Hughes quit the band following the band's Bela Lugosi Returns secret gig in London in November; he was not replaced in the line-up and in February 1987 Murphy played his first US tour. Yet another twelve-month break preceded his next single, February 1988's "All Night Long"; it was followed by the album *Love Hysteria* (#135 US) and in April, Murphy began another American tour, a week after erstwhile ex-Bauhaus bandmates Love and Rockets launched their latest outing. Shows in London, Europe, and Japan would follow, but by late summer, Murphy was back on the road in the US, establishing the fan base which would emerge in droves in 1990 with *Deep* (#44 US).

Supported again by two full US tours and with MTV rotating the "Cuts You Up" (#55 US) single, *Deep* poised Murphy on the brink of a breakthrough. He, however, withdrew once again. Now living in his wife's homeland, Turkey, reveling in his remove from the western music industry, it would be 1992 before *Holy Smoke* (#108 US) and the "You're So Close" single returned him to the stage. Murphy gigged through July, but following the final show in Seattle, he disbanded the 100 Men and returned to Turkey.

A reunion with Hughes saw Murphy and co-writer Statham piece together a new band in 1995, retaining Branch from the 100 Men, plus Ben Blakeman (guitar) and Mark Price (ex-All About Eve — drums). But neither the Pascal Gabriel-produced album *Cascade*, nor the accompanying tours recaptured the excitement of earlier outings, and the following summer Murphy parted company with Beggars Banquet, his label for the past 17 years.

Back in Turkey, Murphy worked with his wife, a modern dancer for whose productions he was an occasional co-writer; in spring 1998, however, he signed to Red Ant and returned to the studio with Tim Skold, Sasha (ex-KMFDM), and Bill Rieflin (ex-Ministry) for the *Recall* EP, a five-track set featuring an English language cover of Turkish supergroup MFO's "Buselik Makamina." Unfortunately, its fall 1998 release was somewhat overshadowed by the Bauhaus reunion tour which crossed the US and UK, and the ensuing *Gotham* live album, a set which also delayed release of Murphy's *Wild Birds* compilation. That finally arrived in early 2000, accompanied by Murphy's first solo US tour in five years.

Peter Murphy LPs

8 Should the World Fail to Fall Apart (Beggars Banquet) 1986 More accessible than Dali's Car, the former Bauhaus frontman's debut solo album still pushed hard at the edges of pop, whilst never quite stepping off the pavement. The staccato rhythms keep the record edgy throughout, while Murphy explores a plethora of musical themes — dancey pop, Middle Eastern melodies, majestic instrumental passages, and doompop (the 12-inch version of "Final Solution" was destined to become a Gothic classic). Fans expected nothing less, but this is still a remarkable achievement.

6 Love Hysteria (Beggars Banquet) 1988 Murphy shows off his gentler side, an overall mellowness which contrarily causes most of the record's sparks. Even an incendiary cover of Iggy Pop's ominous "Fun Time" comes off as simply an invitation to a carnival (the CD appends a wry cabaret mix) and only the rousing "Blind Sublime" and moody "All Night Long" truly break free.

7 Deep (Beggars Banquet) 1990 Now accompanied by the 100 Men (actually a quartet), Murphy moves closer towards the alternative mainstream with an even deeper warmth and lushness. The Middle East still softly calls, but the cry of the danceable, dark pop is louder, while an intriguing departure also sees him play with a funky rap track. The ever-shifting, musically adventurous "Roll Call" and the dramatic "Cuts You Up" round up the genuine developments.

7 Holy Smoke (Beggars Banquet) 1992 Two steps forward, one step back. Producer Mike Thorne brings a brighter and brasher sound, pulling Murphy further into commercialism, but adding some odd mid-'8os synthy stylings to conflict with the time warp wah-wah effects. Listen close, though, and hints of Bauhaus-ian experimentation ("Low Room") and a wicked twist of humor ("Hit Song") do surface.

G Cascade (Beggars Banquet) 1995

Selected Compilations and Archive Releases

S Wild Birds 2000 (Beggars Banquet) Titled from the best cut on the now forgotten *Cascade* transgression, a well-deserved career retrospective delivering (almost) exactly the tracks which one would hope to find.

MY BLOODY VALENTINE

FORMED 1984 (Berlin, Germany)
ORIGINAL LINE-UP *Kevin Shields (b. 5/21/63, Queens, NY — vocals, guitar); Dave Conway (vocals); Tina (keyboards); Colm O'Ciosoig (b. 10/31/64 — drums)*

Kevin Shields and Colm O'Ciosoig first united in Complex, gigging around Dublin, Ireland (where Shields' family moved when he was 6), through the early 1980s. In 1984, the pair recruited Dave Conway and briefly, a keyboardist named Tina, and relocated to Berlin, where My Bloody Valentine — the name borrowed from a horror movie — best echoed the Birthday Party, themselves residents in the city at that time. An EP, *This is Your Bloody Valentine*, released through the local Tycoon label, did little, however, and the band returned to the UK soon after.

Adding bassist Debbie Googe, the Valentines released a second EP, *Geek*, through Fever; then a third, *The New Record by My Bloody Valentine* (#22 UK indy) through Kaleidoscope Sound, refining their original cacophony into something which subsequent critics insisted resembled the early Jesus and Mary Chain.

Certainly the band was still seeking a sound of its own and the singles "Sunny Sundae Smile" (#6 UK indy) and "Strawberry Wine" (#13 UK indy) and the EP *Ecstasy* (#12 UK indy) all emphasized the struggle, as now the sound of the Primitives (whose Lazy label was the Valentines' latest home) was added to the brew. (A collection of this material, *Ecstasy and Strawberry Wine* (#2 UK indy), would be released following the band's 1989 breakthrough.)

Conway left the band in late 1987; he was replaced by Blinda Butcher and suddenly all the pieces fell into place. Signing to Creation, the Valentines' next two singles, "You Made Me Realise" (#5 UK indy) and "Feed Me with a Kiss" (#2 UK indy) both evinced a mantric collage of guitar-driven noise which, within a year, would hasten an entire new musi-

cal genre — the so-called Shoegazing movement, thus named for its creators' refusal to do anything on stage beyond gaze downwards.

Isn't Anything (#1 UK indy), the band's debut album, was released in November 1988 and over the next year, the Valentines remained locked in the studio, chasing Shields' vision of perfection through the *Glide* EP (the band's first UK chart entry, #41 in April), onto the following year's *Tremolo* (#29 UK) and finally, the group's second album, *Loveless* (#24 UK).

Two singles, "Soon" (#41 UK) and "To Here Knows When" (#29 UK), like the album, were moderate successes, but the total cost of the operation far outweighed its performance. Over half a million pounds was spent on the album — a figure which its ultimate chart placing and a modicum of US interest (the Valentines toured with Dinosaur Jr. during 1991) simply couldn't justify.

Creation dropped the band and though Island moved quickly to pick them up, two new albums recorded at Shields' newly built studios in Ireland were scrapped and the only fresh material to emerge was a cover of Wire's "Map Ref 41 Degrees North...," for the *Whore: Wire Tribute* album in 1996. That same year, Shields would contribute to Experimental Audio Research's *Beyond the Pale*; 1997 brought a Shields remix of Primal Scream's "If They Move, Kill 'Em," and in 1999 Shields reunited with Primal Scream to help with their sixth album. He also assisted with the latest solo album by Dinosaur Jr.'s J Mascis, at the same time scotching rumors that, having delivered 60 hours of guitar music to Island Records, he was now retiring from music to breed chinchillas.

O'Ciosoig and Googe quit the band and 1996 saw Googe resurface in Snowpony, an atmospheric electronics-driven band featuring Katharine Gifford (ex-Stereolab; vocals) and Max Corradi (ex-Rollerskate Skinny; drums). The singles "Evil Way Down" and "Chocolate in the Sun" followed, before 1998's *Slow Motion World of Snowpony* at least offered a hint of how the Valentines would have developed into the decade.

My Bloody Valentine LPs

B Isn't Anything (Creation) 1988 The Shoegazing movement starts here, dry ice-piercingly intense guitar drones and hefty nods to a miasmic hardcore soup, oozing a contrary trance-spun drone. Noise becomes beauty as feedback is layered over vocals over feedback ad infinitum, and nighttime takes on new meaning.

B Loveless (Sire) 1991 Worth the wait — after slogging through delays and roundabouts, evolution found the band more noisy, more beautiful, and more structured than ever.

N

NED'S ATOMIC DUSTBIN

FORMED 1988 (Stourbridge, England)
ORIGINAL LINE-UP John Penney (b. 9/17/68 — vocals); Rat
(b. Gareth Pring, 11/8/70, Sedgeley— guitar); Matt Cheslin
(b. Quarry Bank, 11/28/70 — bass); Alex Griffin (b. 8/29/71 —
bass); Dan Warton (b. 7/28/72, Sedgeley — drums)

With their two bassists, and absurdly eye-catching name
(borrowed from BBC radio's classic *The Goon Show*), Ned's
Atomic Dustbin first came to attention as local support for
fellow west midlanders the Wonder Stuff and Pop Will Eat
Itself.

Espousing a raucous variation on the punk-rave hybrid
which the UK press would label "grebo," the band's entire
approach seemed to be based around making their name
known. In their first three years together, Ned's themselves
produced a total of 86 different T-shirts, building a market in
consumer collectibles before they'd even released a record.
Their debut, the *Ingredients* EP, appeared in March 1990, on
the band's own Chapter 22 label; it was followed by "Kill
Your Television" (#53 UK), which promptly became one of
the new decade's most memorable catch phrases.

"Until You Find Out" (#51 UK) was followed by *Bite* (#72
UK), an imported European collection of this same mate-
rial, released shortly before the band signed to Columbia.
They immediately scored with "Happy" (#16 UK), released
on their own Furtive imprint. Their debut album, *God Fod-
der* (#91 US, #4 UK) was issued on the eve of a period of non-
stop gigging, highlighted by a triumphant showing at the
Reading Festival, and was punctuated by two further singles,
"Trust" (#21 UK) and the US radio smash "Grey Cell
Green." (The "Trust" video was voted #1 in the new year's
NME readers' poll; it was #2 in the rival *Melody Maker*.)

God Fodder managed US sales of 276,000, again on the
back of the band's tireless live work, touring with Jesus Jones.
On the last night of the band's next UK tour, however, John
Penney collapsed suffering from exhaustion, and the band
resolved never to tour so heavily again.

Returning to the studio to cut *Are You Normal* (#183 US,
#13 UK) in 1992, Ned's scored two further hits, "Not Sleeping
Around" (#19 UK) and "Intact" (#36 UK), then lapsed into a
three year hiatus, broken only by the "5.22" B-sides collection
in fall 1994. The band finally re-emerged with 1995's Tim
Palmer produced *Brainbloodvolume*, a powerful set which

was nevertheless utterly at odds with everything else happening on the UK scene.

Despite the promise of two singles, "All I Ask of Myself Is
that I Hold Together" (#33 UK) and "Stuck" (#64 UK), the
album failed to chart, largely as a consequence of it being
released several months earlier in the US (and consequently
selling heavily as an import). The band's American tour,
meanwhile, was thrown into momentary chaos when Rat
broke an arm snowboarding; he was replaced by Floyd Brennan and the tour went ahead. However, rumors that Rat had
quit the band were soon circulating (he was alleged to have
auditioned for the Wildhearts), adding to discord within the
group and just three months after the album's eventual UK
appearance, Ned's were dropped by Sony. The band broke
up soon after.

Dan Warton and Brennan subsequently formed a new
band, Floyd; Alex Griffin launched the techno project
Tickle, and signed to Gig Records. Penney and Rat would
resurface in 1997 with Groundswell UK, gigging around for a
year before Rat quit, on the eve of the band signing to the
Gig label. Their debut release, the *Corrode* EP two years
later, inspired a short fall 1999 American tour.

Ned's Atomic Dustbin LPs

⑨ God Fodder (Sony) 1991 The guitar, drummer, and bassist
thought they were a pop-punk band; the other bassist and the
singer thought the group were the kings of baggy and together,
Ned's achieved the impossible — a psychedelic punk sound with
nary a single reference to the '60s. Sheer brilliance indeed.

⑨ Are You Normal? (Sony) 1992 A bigger sound means more
space for Ned's roots to poke through, so this time the late '60s
space jams, the Beatles, the Who and even New Order poke their
heads above the surface. But they only make things more interesting, as Ned's follow through as strongly as they started.

⑦ Brainbloodvolume (Sony) 1995 Oops. Ned's desert punk for
a more mature rock style, and while they haven't completely severed their links with the past, the inclusion of achingly pretty ballads, bittersweet introspection, and rent-a-rally hard rockers is
definitely geared towards a whole new audience. Unfortunately,
they hadn't checked that to make sure that it actually existed.

Selected Compilations and Archive Releases

⑦ Bite (RTD) 1991 Round-up of the early frenetic singles.

⑥ 5.22 (Sony) 1994 A chunky collection of Ned's B-sides.

NERVOUS EATERS

FORMED 1974 (Boston, MA)
ORIGINAL LINE-UP Steve Cataldo (guitar, vocals); Scott Baerenwald (bass); Jeff Wikinson (drums)

Formed as the Psycho Punks, but changing their name at the suggestion of Jeff Wilkinson's mother, the Nervous Eaters owed much of their early energy to Boston legend Willie Alexander — "we saw [him] at Sandy's and we identified with him," Steve Cataldo recalled. "We asked him over to play with us in a cellar. He bought a lot of his songs down and we ran through them and put arrangements to them."

Alexander's scene-defining "Mass Ave" single was born out of a session at Moon Studios in Billerica, and the Nervous Eaters emerged alongside it, debuting at the Rat club later in 1976. A single on club owner Jim Harold's own Rat label, "Loretta," brought the band further local attention, and after a year of solid gigging, by 1978, the Nervous Eaters were one of the main attractions on the fiercely parochial Boston scene.

In common with so many other local bands, however, their undoubted promise was never captured on vinyl. A second single on Rat, the energetic new wave styles of "Just Head" was not released until 1979, while an ever-changing roster of sidemen passed through the band, including Matthew MacKenzie (of Ready Teddy), Andy and Jonathan Paley and guitarist Stanley Clarke.

They also shared manager Fred Lewis with fellow Bostonians the Cars, and in 1979, Ric Ocasek produced a ten-song demo with the band, telling *New York Rocker*, "we did a whole album's worth of stuff. It could be released as is. They're seeing if a label will get involved, which I think one will. They're getting some offers." Columbia were interested for a while, but the band eventually signed with Elektra.

There was also talk of a union with Lou Reed after Wilkinson handed him a tape of the band at one of Reed's Boston shows. According to Cataldo, "the next day Reed called him five times trying to find me. When he got hold of me we talked for a while... he told me he was looking for a guitar player and wanted me to come to New York. I wanted to get him to take [the rest of the band], it would have been good for him to jam with us three...." Nothing came of it, and Cataldo consoled himself by playing bass on the new Professor Anonymous album.

In 1980, Elektra finally released the Eaters' eponymous album, but it did little, and Cataldo disbanded the Eaters in 1981.

Nervous Eaters LPs

8 Nervous Eaters (Elektra) 1980 Sympathetically produced debut, Ocasek's ear for the group's quirky guitar-fired strengths

surpassing even the adventure implied by the band's early singles, demos, and live shows.

NEW ORDER

FORMED 1981 (Manchester, England)
ORIGINAL LINE-UP Bernard Sumner (b. Bernard Dicken, 1/4/56, Salford — guitar); Peter Hook (b. 2/13/56, Manchester — bass); Steven Morris (b. 10/28/57, Macclesfield)

Bernard Sumner, Peter Hook, and Steven Morris were three quarters of Joy Division, the blackest corner of their northern English hometown's late '70s' preoccupation with darkness, angst, and despair, and the most convincing as well. When vocalist Ian Curtis ended his own life in May 1980, he was not only killing himself, he was also killing the consumptive dreams of an entire generation of doomed romantics.

Nobody expected his bandmates to recover from the blow; however, with Sumner taking over on vocals, the trio rejected early names Khmer Rouge and the Witchdoctors of Zimbabwe, debuting as New Order on July 29, 1980, at the Beach Club, Manchester.

In September, the band fulfilled Joy Division's rescheduled US debut show, still working as a trio. In October, however, they recruited Gillian Gilbert (b. 1/27/61, Manchester), and in March 1981, New Order's first single, "Ceremony"/"In a Lonely Place" (#34 UK) resurrected the last ever songs Joy Division recorded.

New Order spent much of 1981 recording, interrupting the schedule for a short European tour in May, and a headline appearance at the Glastonbury festival. They also shot the *Celebration* TV documentary, while "Procession" (#38 UK) and the album *Movement* (#30 UK) painlessly established New Order's renewed viability, at the same time as indicating the direction in which Joy Division themselves might have gone, but for Curtis' death.

It was the March 1983 release of "Blue Monday" (#9 UK) which finally lifted the shroud of might-have-beens. The band had remained relatively quiet through 1982, releasing just one single ("Temptation" — #29 UK) and playing just a handful of live shows. Behind the scenes, however, New Order was plotting a musical revolution.

Musical perfection and dance floor success seldom walked hand in hand through the '80s. There were too many cooks serving too many broths, and the tyranny of the beats-per-minute ensured that even the best ideas would be syndrummed to death before they left the studio. Through the summer of 1983, however, "Blue Monday" not only made a mockery of received disco wisdom, it also hauled an entire musical genre out of the shadows of cult respectability, and into the Top 40 mainstream.

"Blue Monday" took everybody by surprise. It shocked the band's fans, who had long grown accustomed to blank looks and vague nods from anyone they mentioned them to. It shocked radio DJs, who simply couldn't perceive how a seven minute song slid so easily into three minute programming (the band refused to allow the song to be edited; refused, too, to release it on 7-inch vinyl. It existed exclusively as a 12-inch). And it shocked New Order themselves, as it catapulted four anonymous faces into the national headlines and ensured they would never return to normalcy again.

"Blue Monday" was recorded during the sessions for the band's second album, *Power, Corruption and Lies* (#4 UK), a dance heavy and synth-dominated set which proved, too, that the band's songwriting had suddenly emerged as an incontestable indication of their commercial intentions. New Order would become unstoppable.

Over the next two years, New Order would continue releasing perfectly conceived dance floor smashes. Linking with producer Arthur Baker in New York, they cut "Confusion" (#12 UK), following it with "Thieves Like Us" (#18 UK) and "The Perfect Kiss" (#46 UK), before February 1985 saw them sign to Quincy Jones' Qwest label in America, and unleash their first US hit, *Low Life* (#94 US, #7 UK).

The band's secret so far had been the ability to keep their singles and albums very separate — the inclusion of both "The Perfect Kiss" and "Sub-Culture" (#63 UK) on *Low Life* certainly contributed to the singles' poor chart showing. This pattern was repeated in 1986, when New Order scored Top 30 placings for "Shellshock" (#28 UK — taken from the soundtrack to *Pretty in Pink*) and "State of the Nation" (#30 UK — recorded during their Japanese tour in spring 1984), but barely scraped the chart with "Bizarre Love Triangle" (#56 UK), excerpted from the *Brotherhood* album (#117 US, #9 UK).

In July 1987, another non-album track, "True Faith" (#32 US, #4 UK) became the band's biggest ever hit. A singles-only retrospective, *Substance 1980–87* (#36 US, #3 UK) followed, debuting the new DAT audio tape format which the industry was then convinced was the medium of the future. Most of the album's 400,000 UK sales were traditional vinyl and the slowly emergent CD, however, and DAT returned to the recording studio where it belonged.

New Order wrapped up 1987 with a short European tour, and one more hit, "Touched by the Hand of God" (#20 UK); a handful of live appearances then previewed the early summer release of "Blue Monday 88" (#68 US, #3 UK), Quincy Jones' remix of the band's signature hit, but six more months would pass before New Order resurfaced, with "Fine Time" (#11 UK). A month later, *Technique* (#32 US, #1 UK) would become the band's first British chart-topper, as New Order

set out on the longest tour of their career. (Two further singles, "Round and Round" (#64 US, #21 UK) and "Run 2" (#49 UK), would hit while they were on the road.)

With New Order having closed the tour with a shaky headlining slot at the 1989 Reading Festival, the band scattered while Sumner unveiled his Electronic collaboration with Johnny Marr (ex-The Smiths) and Neil Tennant (Pet Shop Boys). News that New Order would be recording the official anthem for the England soccer team's assault on the 1990 World Cup was initially greeted with skepticism. The UK had a long history of soccer-related singles, few of which had much musical merit — which, Sumner later acknowledged, was why New Order agreed to do it in the first place, in the hope of bringing some respectability to an hitherto despised genre.

"World in Motion" (#1 UK), which featured guest appearances from several of the England players themselves, would top the UK chart for a month, and was indeed considered a rare oasis of quality in a sea of otherwise unrelenting vileness (six years later, Lightning Seeds would accomplish a similar feat with "Three Lions").

"World in Motion" would be New Order's last recording for close to three years; indeed, for a time, it seemed as though they might never reconvene. Sumner's Electronic had proven instantly successful, scoring a hit first time out with "Getting Away With It" (#12 UK), then following up through 1991–92 with a string of more singles, and an eponymous album (#109 US, #2 UK).

Morris and Gilbert's wryly named The Other Two, too, scored a minor hit with "Tasty Fish" (#41 UK); but Hook's Revenge was not so successful. Uniting him with vocalist Chris Hicks, Revenge released three singles and the album *One True Passion* (#190 US), before Hicks departed to be replaced by David Potts, engineer at Hook's studio. The pair completed the *Gun World Porn* EP in late 1991, but plans to continue the partnership were placed on hold when New Order began stirring again.

Much had changed since their last appearance; the demise of their career-long Factory label home, the elevation of Mad/Manchester as the music capital of the immediate universe — even before the emergence of Oasis, the spirit of the Happy Mondays and Stone Roses still roamed the streets. By their own confession, the group absorbed all this, then attempted to put their own spin on it, recruiting electro producer Stephen Hague, and settling down to make a record which would break radio wide open.

They succeeded — a single, the guitar-led "Regret" (#28 US, #4 UK) in April 1993 returned New Order to the forefront. "Ruined in a Day" (#22 UK), "World" (#92 US #13 UK), and "Spooky" (#22 UK), and the album *Republic* (#11 US, #1 UK) followed, all pushing the band into a whole new bracket of superstardom — yet immediately after the accompanying tour was over (including another Reading Festival finale), the band fell apart once again.

Sumner returned to Electronic; the Other Two released their debut album *The Other Two and You*; Hook reunited with Potts as Monaco, and this time, his success would become the benchmark for New Order's side projects. Both "What Do You Want From Me" (#11 UK) — a deliberately New Order-like single, and the album *Music for Pleasure* (#11 UK) were well-received hits; follow-up singles, "Sweet Lips" (#18 UK) and "Shine" (#55 UK), were similarly acclaimed.

Suddenly, New Order's continued existence — despite a new hits collection (#78 US) and a stream of remixed oldies — seemed faraway. A "second remix" of "Blue Monday" (#17 UK) in 1995 followed a restructured "True Faith" (#9 UK), while any hunger for "new" material was assuaged by "Nineteen 63" (#21 UK), a 20-minute, single track EP which essentially captured the band jamming a rhythm which might, one day, have resolved itself into "Blue Monday."

In January 1998, however, the four members met together to discuss a possible reunion, not only built around the band's own credibility, but also the recent release of the Joy Division boxed set *Heart and Soul*. The revitalized New Order was set to debut at the Phoenix Festival in July; when the event was cancelled due to low ticket sales, both New Order and co-headliners Prodigy, were promptly absorbed into the following month's Reading Festival.

Having recorded an all-oldies session for BBC DJ John Peel in December, New Order then played a second show in Manchester on New Year's Eve, reclaiming, as the *New Musical Express* put it, "their title as British rock's most erratic elder statesmen, speeding from banality to brilliance in the space of a heartbeat."

Plans to record a new album during the summer 1999, were disrupted by the unexpected death of the band's long-time manager Rob Gretton, from a heart attack in May. It would be October before the band completed any recording, a single track for the Leonardo DiCaprio vehicle *The Beach*.

New Order LPs

8 Movement (Factory) 1981 Focused on the rhythms, snaking and flowing like a fast moving current, building and ebbing like the tide, the album was true to its name, an odyssey of movement in its purest form, shifting across pulsing tribal beats, dance floor rhythms, and industrial clatter. Hook's bass pulses, intertwining and counterpointing Morris' drums; Sumner's guitar moves against the flow, all bright riffs and gloomy buzz, then shatters into shards of melody; and the keyboards conjure up the atmospheres. In under 40 minutes, New Order laid out their blueprint for the future, while still providing a link with their Joy Division past.

9 Power Corruption and Lies (Qwest) 1983 All the elements on *Movement* return, although *Power* is otherwise far removed, much more upbeat (at times almost jolly), the production concentrating on a fuller sound which encourages even the darkest corners to sparkle. Musical themes reappear throughout the record as melodies are revisited time and again, while the moods shift and the beats simmer underneath. From post-punk introspective gloom to glorious darkpop dance phenomenon in eight easy steps.

6 Low-Life (Qwest) 1985 Disappointing, with only the title track breaching the band's previous heights (and "Love Vigilantes" packing some truly excruciating lyrics). Cold production couples with excessive (post-"Blue Monday") commercial calculation for such over-stated delights as the disco dance of "Perfect Kiss," and the bloated "Sunrise" finds the guitar tripping over rock dinosaur powerchords, while ELP keyboards dance on the bones. However, even a bad New Order album sounds better than a lot of bands' best efforts, and the group still conjure up some intriguing moods amongst the dearth of memorable songs.

5 Brotherhood (Qwest) 1986 A fairly unmemorable collection of drab Euro-stylings, with the violent exception of the exquisite "Bizarre Love Triangle."

5 Technique (Qwest) 1989

6 Republic (Qwest) 1993 Embracing every rhythm pattern currently blaring out of club speakers (with jungle and drum & bass predominating), *Republic* is the ultimate disposable dance floor disc, so locked in time and place that in the fad-crazed early '90s scene, it already sounded dated the day of its release. New Order do explore some new territory (hip-hop, Arabesque melodies), but with these lands already well plundered by others before them, the album emerges as little more than a package tour, when it should have spent more time with "Regret."

Selected Compilations and Archive Releases

8 Substance (Qwest) 1987 A big fat compilation which has it all — album cuts, singles, and B-sides.

7 The Peel Sessions (Strange Fruit) 1990 Two previous EPs on one convenient disc, with the loose dub "Turn the Heater On" to ensure it's an essential purchase.

7 BBC Radio 1 Live (Windsong) 1992 Live set from 1987 includes a cover of "Sister Ray."

9 (The Best Of) (Qwest) 1995 Not until you hear the hits crashing one upon another does it become apparent just what a fine repertoire New Order developed. From the still-stunning "Age of Consent" through the corny (but okay, it's captivating) "Love Vigilantes," "True Faith," "World,"....Even 1988's misguided remix of the already perfect "Blue Monday" fits a pattern. A fresh take on "Let's Go," a 12-inch mix of "Bizarre Love Triangle" and "Touched by the Hand of God" lead the way, while a total disdain for chronology only adds to the album's constantly shifting moods.

Peter Hook/Revenge LPs

3 One True Passion (Capitol) 1990 Mindless self indulgent leather fantasies played out to less than stellar results.

4 Gun World Porn (Capitol) 1992

The Other Two LP

7 The Other Two and You (Qwest) 1993 These two are obviously the cheerful side of New Order, and left to their own devices, they conjure up a buoyant (if not exactly memorable) duet for ethereal vocals and cool driving club beats.

Monaco LP

9 Music for Pleasure (A&M) 1997 Monaco begins where Peter Hook's day job ended, but while some of the songs would slot nicely into New Order's lexicon, most are forays into unexpectedly new territory, all underpinned by some superbly melodic bass and the duo's unerring ear for hooks. The single "What Do You Want From Me" is up there with the best of New Order, and isn't alone. Exceptional.

Electronic LPs

7 Electronic (WB) 1991 Less a celebrity wedding than it is Smith Johnny Marr making a guest-shot with New Order, while Neil Tennant looks on and mutters. Moody synthpop at its belated best.

5 Raise the Pressure (WB) 1996

8 Twisted Tenderness (WB) 1999 It takes time, but an initially boring sounding eletroburble rewards perserverence with electricity and joy; play alongside contemporary efforts from Primal Scream and Ian Astbury and everything makes sense.

NINE INCH NAILS

FORMED 1988 *(Cleveland, OH)*
ORIGINAL LINE-UP *Trent Reznor (b. Michael Trent Reznor, 5/17/65, Mercer, OH)*

Having previously played in a string of local bands, such as Option 30, dating back to his school days, and on through Foreigner-sound-alikes the Innocent, a covers band called the Urge, and synthi-pop hopefuls Exotic Birds, Trent Reznor's first major public appearance came in the Michael J. Fox movie *Light of Day*, where he appeared (alongside fellow Exotic Birds Frank Vale and Mark Addison) in a band called The Problems, performing Buddy Holly's "True Love Ways."

A meeting with former Public Image Ltd drummer Martin Atkins, then touring with his band Brian Brain, saw Reznor join that band onstage as trumpeter (at school, he was a member of the marching band) whenever they played Cleveland; he was also gigging regularly with Slam Bam

Boo, described as Cleveland's answer to Duran Duran — he moved onto Lucky Pierre with Kevin McMahon and Tom Lash, a decade-old band which eventually metamorphosed into Prick. Reznor would produce their early demos and later helped with their debut album. (Lash's Hot Tin Roof would also receive Reznor's guidance.)

Reznor was now employed as an engineer at Right Track Studios in Cleveland, and during the summer of '88, he demoed three songs which friend and manager John Malm began shopping around for release as a 12-inch single. Ten small, mostly European, indie labels were approached, all ten offered contracts. Reznor immediately reconsidered his options, and began looking towards larger labels.

Nettwerk were interested, and offered Reznor the support slot on the forthcoming Skinny Puppy tour. Backed by a hastily compiled scratch band, Reznor's ill-rehearsed Nine Inch Nails lasted ten shows before they were asked to go home again. A TVT rep caught one of the shows, however, and was impressed enough to offer Reznor a deal. He took it.

A new batch of demos were sent out for remixes: NIN's first single, an Adrian Sherwood remix of "Down in It," would appear as the "Skin" 12-inch in 1989, to be followed by NIN's debut album *Pretty Hate Machine* (#75 US, #67 UK).

© Jim Steinfeldt/Chansley Entertainment Archives

Working with four different producers (including Sherwood, Flood, John Fryer, and Keith LeBlanc) and partner Chris Vrenna, Reznor completely restructured the recordings into what TVT head Steve Gottlieb called "an abortion — you'll be lucky if you sell 20,000 copies." And to begin with, he was right.

The album made no immediate mainstream impact, but the industrial community was intrigued. Further interest resulted from NIN's next live outings, opening first for Jesus and Mary Chain, then Peter Murphy, accompanied by Vrenna (drums), ex-Exotic Bird Richard Patrick (guitar), and David Hames (keyboards —replaced by Lee Mars later in the year). A new single, "Head Like a Hole" (#45 UK) was performing well, eventually topping *Rolling Stone*'s dance chart; while guest appearances on record and stage with Pigface, and Ministry's 1000 Homo DJs offshoot brought Reznor further exposure.

NIN's aptly-named Hate '90 North America tour kicked off in St.Louis on June 21, winding around the country to end on August 4 in Cleveland. Three days later, another Ministry side project, the Revolting Cocks, arrived in town and Reznor toured with them for a few weeks, before heading back out with NIN. By the end of the year, however, so much work paid off. Sales of *Pretty Hate Machine* were topping 150,000, and a new single, "Sin" (#35 UK), was doing well.

Summer 1991 brought a weary Lollapalooza, scarred both by a loss of power on the first night and the loss of Vrenna for several shows (he was replaced by Ministry associate Jeff Ward); NIN then headed to Europe for shows with Guns n'Roses in Germany, and the Wonder Stuff and Carter USM in Britain, mismatches which only heightened Reznor's determination.

A breakdown of relations with TVT, long fraught, saw Reznor sign instead with sister label Interscope, and launch his own Nothing label with manager Malm — home, immediately, to Prick, Pop Will Eat Itself, and the rising Marilyn Manson. NIN also returned to the studio for the 1992 EP *Broken* (#7 US, #18 UK). An instant hit — so unlike the painfully slow progress of *Pretty Hate Machine* — the EP also won a Grammy for Best Metal Performance With Vocal (a second EP, *Fixed*, would offer up remixes of much of *Broken*, by Coil and Foetus among others).

Work on NIN's second, full album began in New Orleans before shifting to L.A. and a dreamhouse which, apparently unbeknownst to Reznor, was the scene of the Sharon Tate murder in 1969. There he constructed the Pig studio (named for the blood scrawled word left on the wall by Mansonite Susan Atkins, and wrote and recorded 1994's *The Downward Spiral* (#2 US, #9 UK), a distinctly darker collection than its predecessor, but one which would assuredly launch NIN into the mainstream.

Previewing the album with the single "March of the Pigs" (#59 US, #45 UK), Reznor would also do remixes for a multitude of bands, including KMFDM, Megadeth, Machines of Loving Grace, the Wolfgang Press, and Queen, while he contributed backing vocals to a track on the latest Tori Amos album. Soundtrack work, too, would occupy him, as he recorded two new songs "Burn" (*Natural Born Killers* — a project he himself coordinated) and a cover of Joy Division's "Dead Souls" (*The Crow*), even as NIN traveled the US with their summer 1994 Self Destruct tour (and scored another hit single, "Closer" — #41 US, #25 UK).

Working now with a line-up comprising Robin Finck and Danny Lohner (guitars), James Wooley (keyboards) and Vrenna, NIN headlined Woodstock '94, then continued touring through the remainder of the year. The band made their Australian debut in May 1995, even as a new remix mini-album, *Further Down the Spiral* (#23 US) appeared in the US, before they moved into stadia via a scene stealing tour with David Bowie, through fall 1995.

Bowie's own career had been greatly reinvigorated by his recent 1: *Outside* album, itself reflecting the singer's own interest in Reznor's work, but in concert, he remained a shadow of his former self. NIN, with an audience salivating over their every move, effortlessly stole the show on a nightly basis. (There were no hard feelings — Reznor and Bowie would subsequently collaborate on Bowie's "I'm Afraid of Americans" single and video.)

Reznor remained relatively silent for much of the next four years. A single, "The Perfect Drug" (#46 US, #43 UK), was excerpted from the *Lost Highway* soundtrack in June 1997, but Reznor himself was occupied with the building a new studio in New Orleans, breaking with Vrenna, and working on his next album.

Contributors to the album would include former Ministry drummer Bill Rieflin, David Bowie pianist Mike Garson, and guitarist Adrian Belew, while Steve Albini, Alan Moulder, and Dave Ogilvie would all be involved in the recording. *The Fragile* (#1 US, #10 UK) was finally released in fall 1999 — a well received set which nevertheless established an unenviable record, when it became the fastest falling #1 album in *Billboard* chart history. Entering at #1, it then plunged to #16, topping a 25-year-old record set by the Beach Boys (#1–13). A single, "The Day the World Went Away" (#17 US), behaved equally precipitously.

Nine Inch Nails LPs

10 **Pretty Hate Machine (TVT) 1989** One of *the* defining moments in electro's history, *Machine* was the perfect collision of futurist synthi-melodies, the lyrical angst of '80s goth and slaverings of modern industrial — the clatter from its purist form, the layering of effects from the experimental edge, and the aggressive assaults that shaped the cold wave.

Stripped of the effects, the album would have been little more than a typical college radio-friendly release, more hooky than some if more self-immolating than most. But Trent's determination to recreate the swirl of noise he heard in his head surrounded the songs and translated the rage, a monster ultimately hacked out by a stellar cast of producers — Adrian Sherwood, Flood, John Fryer, and Keith LeBlanc.

In *Machine*'s wake, an entire generation who'd previously dismissed industrial as mere noise, blips, and bleeps, or just plain unlistenable, gradually found that the music was anything but. It would take some time, but as the hits started flying and word got around, the record would eventually change music as we know it.

8 The Downward Spiral (TVT) 1994 Deliberately less aggressive than last time, *Spiral* was simultaneously more commercially accessible, yet lyrically much bleaker. The dark moods are reminiscent of Bowie's *Low*, the album's most obvious influence, and the atmospheres are so dense and brooding as to make one pray for a cathartic release. But it never comes, and the tension is only heightened by Trent's lyrics, which move from the violently personal to a more objective reality. A bit like being in the eye of the hurricane, only the winds never return.

9 The Fragile (Nothing) 1999 When you hit the bottom of *The Downward Spiral*, then you fall into the abyss of *The Fragile* — a Dante's Inferno-esque pit of putrefaction, with only the promise of love as a means of escape. Musically more experimental than past releases, seamlessly blending in threads of other genres and refining snatches of NIN's own past, the first half of *Fragile* utilizes instrumentals as bridges between musical shifts; disc two is its apotheosis, deliberately disjointed, with a harsher sound stumbling into staccato beats and quirky rhythms. Certainly over-long, but cathartic in its corpulence.

The Innocent LP

5 Livin' in the Streets (Red Label) 1985 Wide-eyed electro, with Reznor little more than a witness to the witlessness.

Trent Reznor — Selected Remixes/Productions
1991 QUEEN — Stone Cold Crazy [REMIX] (Hollywood)
1992 MACHINES OF LOVING GRACE — Burn Like Brilliant Trash [REMIX] (Mammoth)
1992 MEGADETH — Symphony of Destruction [REMIX] (Capitol)
1992 CURVE — Missing Link [REMIX] (Charisma)
1993 BUTTHOLE SURFERS — Who Was in My Room? [REMIX] (Capitol)
1994 KMFDM — Light [REMIX] (Wax Trax!/TVT)
1994 MARILYN MANSON — Portrait of an American Family (Nothing) **6**
1995 PRICK — Prick [4 TRACKS] (Nothing/Interscope) **7**
1995 DAVID BOWIE — The Heart's Filthy Lesson [REMIX] (Virgin)
1995 MARILYN MANSON — Smells Like Children (Nothing) **8**
1996 MARILYN MANSON — Antichrist Superstar (Nothing) **8**

1997 DAVID BOWIE — I'm Afraid of Americans [REMIX] (Virgin)

Further Reading

Self Destruct by Martin Huxley (St. Martin's Press, 1997).

999

FORMED 1977 *(London, England)*
ORIGINAL LINE-UP *Nick Cash (b. 5/6/50 — vocals); Guy Days (guitar); Jon Watson (bass); Pablo Labritian (drums)*

Named for Britain's emergency telephone number, 999 formed from the partial wreckage of Ian Dury's Kilburn and the High Roads — under his given name of Keith Lucas, Cash was that band's guitarist, Days was a session guitarist who helped out on some of the band's demos. When the Kilburns disbanded, Cash and Days stayed together.

Auditions during late 1976 saw them turn away Chrissie Hynde, future Culture Club drummer Jon Moss, and Generation X's Tony James, before Watson and Pablo Labritian — an old schoolfriend of Joe Strummer's — were recruited. Sporadically known as 48 Hours, the Dials, and the Frantics, 999 became Monday night regulars at the legendary Hope and Anchor; opened for the Jam at the Red Cow in Hammersmith; and went on to star at most of London's prime punk niteries. They would eventually repay the Hope for its support by headlining the venerable old pub's Front Row festival the following spring.

999 signed to United Artists in the fall of 1977, around the same time as the Buzzcocks — and boasted a strong grip on the same vein in powerpop frenzy as them, an asset which they proved with their first single for the label, the speed-crazed "Nasty Nasty." Over the next twelve months, 999 then slammed through an unbroken string of garage classic anthems, each one bringing an ever more memorable chant: "Me and My Desire," "Emergency," and "Feeling Alright with the Crew."

The band's self-titled debut album (#53 UK) was launched with an extravagant punk rock art show in February 1978. Among the starring exhibits were one of Billy Idol's dirty T-shirts, Clash bassist Paul Simenon's still life of a junkyard, an abstract by ex-Sex Pistol Glen Matlock, and a Picasso print given the Damned treatment by Brian James; it was followed in October by 999's first hit, "Homicide" (#40 UK).

A second album, the Martin Rushent produced Separates, followed in September 1978, and in December, 999 unleashed their fifth monster single of the year, a rejuvenation of "I'm Alive." It would be their final UA release. Over the next couple of years, 999 would embark upon a nomadic existence which took them to three different labels: Radar, Polydor, and Albion.

They were, however, also establishing themselves as one of the leading bands on the live circuit, at home and in the United States. Indeed, since the band's first American tour, in 1978, 999's popularity had reached almost epidemic proportions. An album, *High Energy Plan*, was released in 1979, based around *Separates* and substituting various singles for album tracks, and while 999 would never score the hit which their live support insisted they deserved, still, the import racks bulged with their burgeoning catalog.

At a time when the "pure" punk of the Sex Pistols, Slits, and Siouxsie and the Banshees was considered too extreme for college radio tastes, 999's speed pop good humor stepped smartly into the breach: "Emergency" and "Homicide" remained firm favorites, to be joined by "Found Out Too Late" (#69 UK) in October 1979, "Trouble," and "Obsessed" (#71 UK, #4 UK indy) while fall 1980 saw Polydor release their second US album.

Recorded with Ed Case replacing Labritian, temporarily disabled by a car accident, *The Biggest Tour in Sport* was a live set, recorded during 999's recently completed two month American tour (the title punned on the band's last UK studio set, *The Biggest Prize in Sport* — #177 US). The whole thing lasted less than 20 minutes, but few better documents of 999's sheer sonic savagery exist.

1981–82 brought 999 a fresh string of British hits, including a pair of brilliant covers — Sam the Sham's "Lil Red Riding Hood" (#59 UK, #7 UK indy), and Paul Revere's "Indian Reservation" (#51 UK, #6 UK indy), and "Wild Sun" (#8 UK indy). With them came a fast broadening musical base: *Concrete* (#192 US, #4 UK indy), 999's fourth album, and *13th Floor Madness*, their fifth, both found the group's traditional punk sound mellowing. The British press (who never particularly liked the band anyway) actually hailed *Madness* as a stab at '80s disco, although all it really evinced was an attempt to keep up with the musical times, and a reasonably successful one at that.

Despite the band's obvious ambition, their label, Albion, seemed more interested in maintaining 999 as a nostalgia act than a going musical concern, and while they contended themselves with a 1984 greatest hits collection, 999 themselves revitalized their Labritian label, and ploughed on.

1985's *Face to Face* proved that the group was still a power in the land, while their latest British tour saw them headline the London Lyceum, on a bill which also featured the UK Subs and the Exploited. Two years later, following on from the band's first full-time personnel change (Danny Palmer replaced Watson), the live *Lust, Power and Money* only reaffirmed their continued prowess.

999 broke up shortly after, but the sundering was never likely to be permanent. In 1991, 999 were one of the classic punk acts invited to re-acquaint themselves with their legacy by guesting on Die Toten Hosen's *Learning English* punk tribute album. In 1993, they cut *You, Us, It*, and the following year, with the punk revival which that album presaged now burning up both the UK and US, 999 — featuring Cash, Labritian, Days and former Lurkers bassist Arturo Bassick — headlined the legendary Holidays in the Sun Punk festival in Blackpool, England.

999 were never the biggest punk band of their era, nor (in chart terms) the most successful. But they were one of the hardest working, and for many Americans, they were the first to actually bother with the backwoods, playing places which other Brit bands hadn't heard of, and returning to them again and again. And while no one knows how many American bands were first inspired to take up arms by 999, those that did still wear their loyalties loudly.

999 LPs

7 **999 (UA — UK) 1978**

7 **Separates (UA — UK) 1978**

6 **High Energy Plan (PVC/Radar) 1979** The punk do's and studded bracelets which the band habitually sported fooled few into believing that 999 were real punks. But two hit packed early albums and the surprisingly powerful *Plan* all proved that blinding conviction, tight songs, and a studiously raucous attitude can pay dividends — especially if you have more than a few good singles to your credit.

7 **The Biggest Prize in Sport (Polydor) 1980**

6 **The Biggest Tour in Sport [LIVE] (Polydor) 1980** Not quite getting the hang of what to do post-punk, 999 opt for aggressive pub rock crossed with pop (a la Eddie and the Hot Rods) and even some '60s garage, with the Buzzcocks an increasingly precarious touchstone.

5 **Concrete (Albion) 1981**

4 **13th Floor Madness (Albion) 1983**

6 **Face to Face (Labritian) 1985**

6 **Lust, Power & Money [LIVE] (ABC) 1987** Still high energy, still clinging rabidly to the creed...except no one remembered what the creed was anymore. 999's disillusion seems louder every time out.

4 **You Us It (Fan Club — France) 1993**

5 **Takeover (Takeover) 1998**

Selected Compilations and Archive Releases

9 **The 999 Singles Album (Liberty) 1980** Not until they're all laid out in front of one, does it become apparent just how many great 45s this band had!

5 **Live and Loud [LIVE] (Link) 1990**

7 **Cellblocks Tapes (Link) 1990** Early demos and live tracks.

8 The Albion Punk Singles Collection (Anagram) 1996 A companion volume to *Singles Album*, more hits and misses, but still a powerful saga.

6 Live at the Nashville 1979 (Anagram) 1997

8 Homicide: The Best of 999 (Cleopatra) 1997 20 three-minute anthems, chasing nearly two decades of 999 noises.

7 Slam (Overground) 1999 Unreleased 1982 album titled for the imported US hardcore dance craze — and scrapped when the English tabloids went into overdrive about the evils of punk. More or less worth waiting for.

NIPPLE ERECTORS

FORMED 1977 *(London, England)*
ORIGINAL LINE-UP *Shane O'Hooligan (b. Shane MacGowan, 12/25/57, Kent, England — vocals); Shanne Bradley (bass); Richard (guitar); Adrian Thrills (guitar); Arcane (drums)*

Born in England but raised in Tipperary, Ireland, Shane MacGowan was described as "the Face of '76" when his picture appeared on the front page of *Sounds*, a manically pogoing punk rocker representing the biggest kick in the ass British rock had received in a decade.

He was a legend in his own time. He might not have had his earlobe bitten off by Jane Modette when the Clash played the ICA; but it is true that he got so carried away by the Jam, that he smashed up their speakers at Ronnie Scott's; and he started a fanzine called *Bondage*, then cancelled it before he'd even finished photocopying the first issue. And he had a band he called the Nipple Erectors, whose other members were as motley an assortment as he could find — Shanne Bradley, who once had Captain Sensible as a bass tutor; a guitarist named Roger, who once played with the Tools; drummer Arcane who was replaced by someone named Gerry very early on, and guitarist Adrian Thrills, an *NME* journalist.

The band's first demo, "My Degeneration," was recorded in Bradley's bedroom, while their very name was a test of punk era morality, which backfired heavily on the band. Not only did the Nipple Erectors find it hard to get gigs, they also found it hard to get people to come to the gigs. Even at the height of 1977, their supporters could be counted on the fingers of one hand — *Sounds* writer Jane Suck was the loudest, the owners of the Rock On record store in Soho Market the most courageous.

In early 1978, with no other record company having shown even a token interest in the band, Rock On gave the Nipples a recording contract, kicking off the Soho label with "King of the Bop." It didn't sell, but undaunted the band tried again. Larry Hindricks (best known for his impromptu performance as Damned vocalist one night when Dave Vanian failed to turn up) replaced Roger on guitar; Gerry

had quit for an early incarnation of the Pretenders and was temporarily replaced by Phil Rowlands of Eater, and in this form, the Nipple Erectors recorded their second single, the R&B tinged "All the Time in the World."

By now the band was a surprisingly graceful musical powerhouse, but again their record didn't sell, so they tried a different tack — they shortened their name to the Nips. Then, having replaced Hindricks with Fritz, they set to work on their third single, "Gabrielle" (#30 UK indy). And it worked. Released in February 1980, amid a live schedule which included shows with the Jam, Dexy's Midnight Runners, the Purple Hearts, and the Dolly Mixtures, "Gabrielle" saw the band finally begin to attract attention.

Paul Weller talked of producing them, and their fourth single, "Only at the End of the Beginning," saw the band leaning towards a dramatic rockabilly style which would remain a London club fixture until well into the mid-1980s.

The Nips, however, would not be around to take advantage of it. By the time their final single, "Happy Song," appeared in late 1981, the Nips had already broken up, announcing their demise shortly before Bradley formed the Men They Couldn't Hang. MacGowan formed the Pogues. The group's entire catalog would subsequently form the basis of their one album.

Selected Compilations and Archive Releases

8 Bops, Babes, Booze & Bovver (Big Beat) 1990 The whole story, and what a wonder it was.

NIRVANA

FORMED 1987 *(Aberdeen, WA)*
ORIGINAL LINE-UP *Kurt Cobain (b. 2/20/67, Hoquiam, WA — vocals, guitar); Krist Novoselic (b. 5/16/65 — bass); Dale Crover (drums)*

Well-known local troublemaker Kurt Cobain and Croatian-American Krist Novoselic got together in 1987, after earlier bands — Fecal Matter and Brown Towel among them — fell apart. With a constantly revolving membership, their band's early shows in and around their logging hometown saw them appear under such names as Ted Ed Fred, Throat Oyster, Pen Cap Chew, and Windowframe, before they settled upon Nirvana.

Plowing a ragged furrow between punk and metal, the group recorded their first demo late in 1987, with drummer Dale Crover. Regular gigs throughout the Pacific Northwest brought them to the attention of Seattle's C/Z Records, who released one cut on the *Teriyaki Asthma* compilation; Sub Pop then asked the band for a single.

Crover quit in early 1988, going on to another Aberdeen band, the Melvins. He was replaced by Chad Channing (b.

1/31/67, Santa Rosa, CA), while a second guitarist, ex-Sound-garden Jason Everman, was also enlisted. In this form Nirvana recorded a cover of Dutchpop heroes Shocking Blue's "Love Buzz," and the following year Sub Pop released Nirvana's debut album, *Bleach* (#33 UK, #8 UK indy).

Barely noticed at home, *Bleach* and its attendant single, "Blew" (#15 UK indy), caused an instant sensation in the UK, where a handful of critics were already raving about the so-called Seattle scene: Mudhoney, Soundgarden, the Melvins, Green River, etc. Hijacking the term from an earlier musical movement, this new genre was termed grunge, and it stuck.

Nirvana toured constantly through 1990 and 1991, shedding Everman in the process. Channing, too, departed, to be replaced by Dan Peters (later of Mudhoney), who played on the band's next three singles, "Sliver," "Molly's Lips," and a cover of the Velvet Underground's "Here She Comes Now." When he left, the band recruited Dave Grohl (b. 1/14/69, Warren, OH), of Washington DC hardcore group Scream. Around the same time, the group left Sub Pop, and signed to Geffen.

Over-ruling Geffen's insistence that the band work with a bigger name producer, Nirvana retained faith in Butch Vig, with whom they'd already demoed much of the forthcoming

Kurt Cobain of Nirvana

© Jim Steinfeldt/Chansley Entertainment Archives

album. The result, *Nevermind* (#1 US, #7 UK) was released in fall 1991, with Geffen confidently expecting sales of around 250,000. But the first single, "Smells like Teen Spirit" (#6 US, #7 UK), took off immediately, slamming into rotation on MTV and alternative radio. By Christmas, *Nevermind* had displaced Michael Jackson at the top of the US chart.

Hurriedly revising a live schedule arranged months earlier — the band were opening for the Red Hot Chili Peppers when they learned they were #1 — Nirvana continued touring, while three more singles, "Come As You Are" (#32 US, #9 UK), "Lithium" (#64 US, #11 UK), and "In Bloom" (#28 UK), climbed charts around the world, and a reactivated *Bleach* (#89 US) marched toward its eventual platinum status.

They were invited onto *Saturday Night Live*'s January 11 show, and the ratings were the highest in months. The band's photographs adorned every magazine on the rack; when Cobain and Hole vocalist Courtney Love began dating, they instantly became America's most photographed couple. Rumors of drug and spousal abuse, however, were never far away, particularly after the birth of the couple's first child, Frances Bean — Cobain later equated the onset of fame to waking up to find local TV has named you as an escaped Nazi child killer, but the first you know of it is when the firebombs land on the bed. The relentless media spotlight which now followed Cobain would surely play a major part in his eventual death.

Nevermind was still high in the chart when Geffen — themselves as baffled by the phenomenon as anybody — released the *Incesticide* (#39 US, #14 UK) compilation of old singles and outtakes, a stop-gap Christmas best seller which gave Nirvana more time to work on their real next album. Nirvana also appeared on a split single with Jesus Lizard, "Oh the Guilt"(#12 UK), while Cobain alone would record a single with William Burroughs, for summer release, "The Priest, They Call Him By."

As the band geared up for the release of *In Utero* (#1 US, #1UK), they recruited second guitarist John Duncan from Goodbye Mr. Mackenzie — the same band that supplied former producer Vig's new project, Garbage, with vocalist Shirley Manson. In this form, Nirvana played that year's New Music Seminar, but a dynamic show did not still the doubters.

"Heart Shaped Box" (#5 UK), heralding the new album, was released as a single in Europe in August. It had been remixed by REM producer Scott Litt, fuelling media speculation that Nirvana's original choice of producer, Steve Albini, had conspired with them to make an album of such breath-taking ugliness it would completely destroy their fame. In fact, *In Utero* was the equal of its predecessor, and topped US and UK charts immediately upon its fall 1993 release.

The band followed the album release with, first, the season premiere of *Saturday Night Live*, then a majestic appearance on MTV's *Unplugged* — the logical conclusion to the short acoustic set Cobain had recently introduced to Nirvana's live show, and the opportunity for the band not only to show off their own songwriting skills, but to introduce the mainstream to some of their own favorites, the Meat Puppets, Leadbelly, and David Bowie among them. (Following the *Unplugged* performance's 1994 release, their version of Bowie's "The Man Who Sold the World" would top the Modern Rock charts, and when Bowie himself performed the song on his next tour that fall, more than one younger onlooker turned to a friend and said, "hey, he's doing a Nirvana cover.")

Through the fall of 1993, the Modern Rock chart topper "All Apologies" (#32 UK) held the European fort while Nirvana toured the US with Pat Smear (ex-Germs) now on second guitar. On January 8, 1994, the band played what would prove to be their last ever American show, at the Seattle Center Key Arena.

The band flew to Europe in February, opening their tour in Lisbon, Portugal. On March 1, they played their last ever show, in Munich, Germany. They traveled on to Rome, Italy, and it was there, on March 2, that Cobain suffered a coma-inducing overdose from prescription drugs and champagne.

He was discharged on March 8, and flew home, checking into the Exodus recovery center in Marina Del Rey, CA, on March 28. Ten days later, Cobain discharged himself and went missing for four days. The singer's body was discovered on the floor of a small apartment above the garage by an electrician working at the Cobains' Seattle home. The cause of death was a self-inflicted gunshot wound to the head.

Although increasingly wild speculation that the singer was murdered will never let Cobain himself rest, Nirvana ceased to exist immediately, with the surviving members both vowing not to use the band's own name and reputation to further their own career — vows they would adhere to.

Grohl and Smear reappeared the following year in the Foo Fighters; Novoselic moved into Seattle politics, before re-emerging with Sweet 75. Two subsequent Nirvana albums, the *Unplugged* (#1 US, #1 UK) performance and a live compilation, *From the Muddy Banks of the Wishkah* (#1 US, #4 UK), would maintain a respectful acknowledgement of Nirvana's continued importance; a career-spanning boxed set overseen by Novoselic would cement it.

Nirvana LPs

6 Bleach (Sub Pop) 1989 This aggressive assault of nascent grunge left nothing to the imagination. Now, of course, it's a venerable classic and history won't hear a word against it. But if one just came down from a few decades on Mars, 42 minutes of growly, low-fi probably wouldn't change your life too much.

10 Nevermind (DGC) 1991 Nirvana likened the two year lag between *Bleach* and *Nevermind* to looking for a job — "you get up at 2:30 and leave it till tomorrow." Constant touring consumed much of their time, but took some of the credit as well; refining the scraping of the sludge off *Bleach*, *Nevermind* was still readily identifiable Nirvana, but it was a sleeker, slicker-sounding model, hammered into shape by a hundred one night stands and bursting with head-haunting hooks. Even before it slammed into rotation, "Smells Like Teen Spirit" had radio-unfriendly-unit-shifter written all over it, while "Come As You Are" and "Lithium" even smiled while they smuggled the blueprint for the '90s into town.

It was, Cobain mused, the yawning gulf between "what people said was hip to listen to" and "the kind of stuff which we all really listened to," that *Nevermind* set out to bridge, so KISS were always a stronger influence than the Velvets and Cheap Trick were more fun than the beloved Sonic Youth. "We thought it would be funny to slip things in," Cobain explained, "to see if anyone noticed."

Killing Joke noticed, and won a settlement for the plundered riff of "Eighties" ("Come As You Are"); Boston didn't, but anyone who listened to "Teen Spirit" would have more than a feeling they'd heard it before. Such midwifery was barely relevant, however: of all the accolades cast at *Nevermind*, "original" was rarely top of the heap, as Cobain himself admitted. "Our songs have the standard pop format — verse, chorus, verse, chorus, verse, solo, bad solo. I think we sound like...." The Rollers being molested by Sabbath? "Or the Knack by Black Flag."

In fact, it sounded like all that put together, but finally, Cobain put it best of all. "We never set out to knock Michael Jackson off the top of the chart. We simply wanted something we could live with." Looks like they failed then.

8 In Utero (DGC) 1993 "Heart Shaped Box" may have smelled like teen spirit, but that's where the inevitable comparisons ended. What Nirvana needed was a well-rounded album, not a clutch of hit singles glued together with filler, and that's what they got — a surprisingly humorous and shockingly heartfelt collection boasting more variety than *Nevermind* and more archetypes than *Bleach*. And to think, when Steve Albini showed up at the sessions, the critics predicted commercial suicide.

Selected Compilations and Archive Releases

6 Incesticide (DGC) 1992 Six UK radio sessions are the nearest things come to vindicating some of the more outlandish claims made about the insurgent Nirvana. But highlights from past heydays (singles, comps, Chad Channing) took the edge off an increasingly surreal collectors' market and blazed with uncommon passion. Uncommon for out-takes and cast-offs, that is.

9 MTV Unplugged in New York [LIVE] (DGC) 1994 An unbelievable set stripping back the noise to reveal Cobain's vocal stylings in all their raw beauty. Emotive, emotional, and deceptively delicate, the band power through a set of hits — helped out by Pat Smear and most of the Meat Puppets. From "Come As You Are" and Bowie's "The Man Who Sold the World" to the wrenching "Where Did You Sleep Last Night," Nirvana are at their subtle best.

7 From the Muddy Banks of the Wishkah [LIVE] (Geffen) 1996 A posthumous collection of live material culled from shows between 1989 and 1994 and compiled by Novoselic and Grohl. All the expected cuts are here, from "Polly" to "Smells Like TeenSpirit" although "Spank Thru" is a pleasant surprise.

Further Reading

Come As You Are by Michael Azerrad (Doubleday, 1994).

NOFX

FORMED 1984 *(Berkeley, CA)*
ORIGINAL LINE-UP *Fat Mike (b. Mike Burkett — vocals, bass); Eric Melvin (guitar); Steve "Izzy" Kidwiler (guitar); Erik Ghint (drums)*

Four kids who initially set out to emulate R.K.L., then added Bad Religion to the recipe when they discovered they could sing harmonies, NOFX were heavily influenced by hardcore... with a twist — a sense of humor which was then virtually unheard of in the annals of American punk. Gigging constantly, they endured an unhappy spell on Mystic Records, through which they released several singles and their *Maximum Rock'n'Roll* debut album in 1986, before striking out alone, self-releasing *Liberal Animation*, and just plugging on as well as they could.

The 1987 EP *The PMRC Can Suck On This* bought the band a taste of notoriety, but despite touring constantly, NOFX's audiences remained small — five years into their career and they were still playing to a mere 40 or 50 people. But those low years helped NOFX hone their musical skills and learn the finer points of stage performance, an apprenticeship which helped turn them into one of the strongest live acts around.

It was that which first caught the attention of Brett Guerwitz in 1988, as he resurrected Bad Religion's Epitaph label. NOFX became the new company's first signing. Their first album for the label, *S&M Airlines*, arrived in 1989.

Both that record and its follow up, *Ribbed*, were firmly grounded in smash and grab hardcore. Across *White Trash, Two Heebs and a Bean*, however, NOFX expanded into a myriad of ever more varied sounds, culminating perhaps with the soul ballad "Straight Edge." By this time, 1992, Izzy had departed, to be replaced by the multi-instrumentalist El

Hefe (b. Aaron Abeyta), who took on backing vocals, guitar, and trumpet.

Fat Mike also founded his own Fat Wreck Chords label that year, initially releasing the NOFX singles "Liza and Louise" and "Don't Call Me White," and the *Longest Line* mini-album. But it was their 1994 Epitaph album, *Punk in Drublic*, which sent NOFX's comet streaking across the sky. Incessant touring definitely played a part in their growing success, but equally important was Guerwitz's decision to open Epitaph's catalog to the makers of sundry skate and snowboard videos; both NOFX and The Offspring would credit those videos in launching their rocket rides to fame.

Fame, however, was the last thing that NOFX wanted, and they grew increasingly nervous as the sales figures for *Drublic* rose. Stubbornly rejecting major label overtures, the band then began turning down any mass media approach — in the wake of both 1995's *I Hear They Suck Live* (#198 US), and 1996's *Heavy Petting Zoo* (#63 US), NOFX refused all further interviews with the national press, and even rejected MTV's request for a video.

To misquote one of NOFX's own lyrics, they weren't doing it for the fortune or the fame, they were doing it for the punk cause; and when supplicants demanded that the band think about "the kids" who were starving for information, their next Fat Wreck Chords single summed up that line of reasoning as well — "Fuck the Kids." It was the purity of that defiant ethos which kept NOFX on track.

1997's *So Long and Thanks for All the Shoes* album was followed by another string of singles, "Timmy the Turtle" and a reversal of their 1992 Fat debut, "Louise and Liza," leading up to 1999's *Decline EP* (#200 US) and the tempestuous new album *Pump Up the Valium*.

NOFX LPs

5 Maximum Rock'n'Roll (Mystic) 1986

6 Liberal Animation (Self-Released) 1987

6 S&M Airlines (Epitaph) 1989

8 Ribbed (Epitaph) 1991 After three albums of more-or-less unremarkable hardcore metal bellowing, *Ribbed* found NOFX putting the finishing touches to their sound — fiery leads played at hyperspeed, a banging beat, Bad Religion-ish harmonies, wave after wave of melodies and gleefully tossing a pie in the face of doo-wop, dinosaur rock, and pretty pop.

8 White Trash, Two Heebs and a Bean (Epitaph) 1992 With the arrival of axeman/trumpeter El Hefe, the quartet put a high gloss on their sound. Even more driving than *Ribbed*, *Trash* has the spit and polish of a band on a mission and the message is angstier and angrier. But as the album title makes clear, NOFX haven't lost their sense of humor, whether they're wheedling a sucker DJ into playing their song — only to fill it with banned words two thirds through; or puncturing the Minor Threat classic

"Straight Edge" by contorting it into a jazzy blues number. Nothing remains safe nor sacred in NOFX's hands, which is precisely their appeal.

9 Punk in Drublic (Epitaph) 1994 Who else but NOFX could write an ode to linoleum and produce a punk classic? Or a sarcastic gem to sheeplike behavior? Or the unforgettable and indignant demand, "don't call me white"? And so on across track after track of spot-on lyrical brilliance, peppered with harmonies, hooks, and humor, as the quartet defy gravity and take their music to an even higher pinnacle than *Trash*. Sex (of course), politics, economics, personal experiences, racism, and religion all come under NOFX's guns, now camouflaged under a battalion's worth of sing-a-long anthems that continue to remain live faves to this day.

8 I Heard They Suck Live [LIVE] (Far Wreck Chords) 1995 You heard wrong. Recorded over two nights in January, '95, NOFX slam through a seething set of hits and crowd pleasers, past and present. Some of the songs are just a tad ramshackle, but that doesn't lessen their power, while the comic chaos and self-deprecating insults between songs make this an experience not to be missed.

6 Heavy Petting Zoo (Epitaph) 1996 The success of *Drublic* brought NOFX increased fame and fortune, neither of which the band had actively sought or desired. The situation left a foul taste — *Zoo* was their way of exorcising it, an angry, pessimistic record without a joke song in sight.

7 So Long and Thanks for All the Shoes (Epitaph) 1997 Returning revitalized, and apparently "All Outta Angst," NOFX's short, sharp attacks on a diverse variety of societal and music industry ills are indeed less angsty, but they are angrier. The giddy goofs of yore may be gone for good, but *Shoes* radiates good humor even amid the world's ills, an optimistic take without rose-colored glasses.

8 Pump Up the Valium (Epitaph) 2000

Selected Compilations and Archive Releases
9 Ten Years of Fuckin' Up (Fat Wreck Chords) 1994

KLAUS NOMI

BORN *Klaus Sperber, 1945 (Bavaria, Germany)*

Of all the myriad artists to emerge from America's late 1970s new wave boom with the soubriquet "weird" firmly attached (and there were many, from the B-52's to Devo), few were weirder than Klaus Nomi, the sexually ambiguous New York via Berlin yodeler who burst into the mainstream consciousness when he and fellow artist Joey Arias accompanied David Bowie onstage at *Saturday Night Live* in November 1979.

Anticipating not only the bizarre antics and persona who would haunt Bowie's own "Ashes to Ashes" video the following year, but also an entire generation's worth of future new romantic freaks, Nomi was a former usher at the Deutsche Opera in Berlin, who arrived in New York in 1976, moving into the underground nightclub scene where his cabaret-inflected act caught Bowie's eye. (During the day, Nomi worked as a pastry chef, operating his own baking company.)

A 1979 show at Hurrah! in New York, released as a posthumous live album in 1986, highlighted Nomi's dexterity, including versions of Marlene Dietrich's "Falling in Love Again," Chubby Checker's "The Twist," and Donna Summer's "I Feel Love." Nomi remained beneath the major label radar, however, until the *SNL* performance.

A deal with Bowie's RCA label followed, together with a single, "You Don't Own Me" (backed by an audacious interpretation of Elvis Presley's "Can't Help Falling in Love"), while 1980 saw Nomi among the stars of the legendary *Urgh! A Music War* movie.

Nomi was self-consciously odd, but also possessed a miraculous voice — a counter tenor and baritone capable of swooping from opera to rock'n'roll without a second thought. This was brought fully to bear on his debut album, recorded live with Scott Woody (guitar), Jon Cobert (keyboards), Rick Pascual (bass), Julie Burgher (backing vocals), and Daniel Elfassy (drums); there, Nomi's inimitable style was brought to bear on everyone from Lou Christie ("Lightning Strikes") to Henry Purcell (a bass aria from the opera *King Arthur*). It was his second album, *Simple Man*, however, which included what had long been his live signature, a delirious rendition of "Ding Dong the Witch Is Dead," from *The Wizard of Oz*.

Unfortunately, illness kept Nomi out of the spotlight through late 1982 and early 1983 — ironically, his last single coupled the title track from *Simple Man* with another Purcell adaptation, "Death." He had contracted AIDS, and on August 6, he became one of the first public figures to succumb to the disease.

Klaus Nomi LPs

8 Klaus Nomi (RCA) 1981 Operatta superman, Nomi's distended takes on both pop and classical gems are shot through with his own, equally unique masterpieces.

9 Simple Man (RCA) 1982 "Ding Dong the Witch is Dead" was already a staple of his live performance. In the studio it became even more dramatic, but with the rest of the album screaming... whooping... yodelling just as loudly, even Dorothy wouldn't be able to play favorites.

Selected Compilations and Archive Releases

8 Encore — Nomi's Best (RCA) 1984 Short but stellar sampling.

8 In Concert (RCA) 1986 Had Nomi lived, this would still have been an inevitable release.

GARY NUMAN

BORN *Gary Webb, 3/8/58 (Hammersmith, England)*

A vision in black with a shock of blonde crop; cheekbones to die for and a pallor which already had, Gary Numan exploded onto the stage like a man from Mars — which is probably what he was. Glacial vocals over icicle synths, the last tango at the isolationist ball, Numan appeared from nowhere and invited everyone back there.

"I was just a guitarist that played keyboards," he explained. "I just turned punk songs into electronic songs." But no one else had ever done it like that, and few people would ever do it so well. Numan new man, of course new wave. By the spring of 1979, punk had long since run its course, and Numan knew, because he'd been running with it.

Having debuted with Mean Street, whose "Bunch of Stiffs" single preluded their appearance on the *Live at the Vortex* compilation, Numan then formed Tubeway Army with Paul Gardiner (bass) and Numan's uncle, Gerald Lidyard (drums). During 1978, the band released two singles, "That's Too Bad" and (with second guitarist Sean Burke and new drummer Barry Benn) "Bombers," together with an eponymous album. Numan, however, was already looking far beyond the band's buzzsaw punk for inspiration, and the following spring he suddenly found it, in the frozen warnings of electronics.

Gratefully, he still acknowledges the bands which made the movement possible, Ultravox, in their earliest, John Foxx-led incarnation and Rikki (Sylvain) and the Last Days of Earth — bands who saw the possibilities inherent in synthesizers, but allied them to those already rampant in guitars. All Numan did, he claimed, was take those possibilities to their furthest extent, and if he reinvented minimalism for the new decade, then that was simply a bonus.

With Lidyard returning to the band, three demos recorded in late 1978 introduced the synth to Tubeway Army's attack, and in March 1979, "Down in the Park" served warning of his intentions. Of course, his record label, Beggars Banquet, did their best to dissuade him from taking them any further, but Numan persevered, and "Are Friends Electric?" (#1 UK) proved he was right. A chart-topper across Europe, it was followed by an album which celebrated the outsider, and worshipped the machine — *Replicas* (#124 US, #1 UK) was part Kraftwerk, part David Bowie, but completely Gary Numan, and stated its intentions from the very first track: "Me," that disembodied voice announced, "me, I disconnect from you."

Abandoning the Tubeway Army alias, Numan's first solo album, *The Pleasure Principle* (#16 US, #1 UK), hauled Billy Currie out of the recently disbanded Ultravox, alongside Gardiner, Chris Payne (synth), and Cedric Sharpley (drums), in time for a Christmas release date. A world tour began, and as the 1970s finally lurched into history, Gary Numan was already poised on the edge of invincibility, the first superstar of a bright new decade.

There simply wasn't anyone like him, and though his detractors liked to paint a studious xerox of one of David Bowie's old images, Numan was always worth far more than that; so much more, in fact, that Bowie's own next album (and his best in three years, 1980's *Scary Monsters*) had far more in common with Numan's machinations than Numan ever had with him.

Elsewhere, too, the synthesized new romantic movement arose in his wake: Human League, OMD, Depeche Mode, Soft Cell — Numan's new men were suddenly everywhere, filing out of the minimoog store with their hearts and minds set on praying to the aliens. But no matter how far they went, Numan pressed his dream further. Onstage he drove an electric car; offstage, he passed his pilot's license, and took to the skies to survey his domain.

"Cars" (#9 US, #1 UK) gave him a second successive chart-topper in August 1979; "Complex" (#6 UK) followed in November. Currie quit the band to return to Ultravox; he was replaced by Dennis Haines, and with second guitar player Russell Bell on board, Numan's *Telekon* tour, built around his latest album (#64 US, #1UK), carried his cold dreams to their arctic limits; static movement, factory costumes, and the glaring white light of an industrial future.

It was akin to Metropolis — The Musical, and where could he go after that? Following a final blast of singles, "I Die You Die" (#6 UK) and "This Wreckage" (#20 UK), he slipped into studio seclusion, with one final extravagant concert in London, in April 1981. Gary Numan was 23 years old and he ruled the world.

Privately, he turned his attention to that other passion, flying, launching an ambitious attempt to fly round the world aboard his Cessna single engine plane. The trip ended with an unscheduled landing in India, where Numan and his co-pilot were arrested, finally returning home on December 24. (A second forced landing in January 1982, returning from Cannes, effectively ended Numan's aviation career.)

He continued to record. Two live albums, drawn from the 1979 and 1980 tours respectively, were his farewell to concert work — *Living Ornaments 1979–80* (#2 UK) was also available as two individual albums, *1979* (#47 UK) and *1980* (#39 UK). The band was dismissed to form their own concern, Dramatis (they would reunite with Numan for the joint credited "Love Needs No Disguise" (#33 UK) single in late 1981), and Numan called in Japan bassist Mick Karn, Queen drummer Roger Taylor, and mysterious Canadian violinist Nash the Slash for his next album, *Dance* (#167

US, #3 UK) and single, "She's Got Claws" (#6 UK). If there was any suggestion that the hysteria of the previous two years was beginning to die down, Numan's immediate chart placings did not show it.

However, there was a decline, and once it began, it proved very difficult to arrest the slide. A collaboration with Dollar vocalist Therese Bazar, "Music for Chameleons" (#19 UK) in March 1982 was followed by "We Take Mystery (To Bed)" (#9 UK) and "White Boys and Heroes" (#20 UK), while the album *I Assassin* (#8 UK) lasted just six weeks on the chart.

In April 1982, Numan announced he was leaving the UK to concentrate upon breaking the American market. In fact, the US was totally uninterested, and even as he packed his bags for his return to live work, an 18-date US tour, it transpired that the British were losing patience as well. The Bill Nelson-produced *Warriors* (#12 UK) was host to two distinctly weak singles, "Warriors" (#20 UK) and "Sister Surprise" (#32 UK), while *Berserker* (#45 UK) his first release on his own Numa label, bottomed out even faster than its attendant singles, "Berserker" (#32 UK) and the aptly titled "My Dying Machine" (#66 UK).

Numan tried to reinvent himself, collaborating with Shakatak dance maestro Bill Sharpe for spring 1985's "Change Your Mind" (#17 UK), while an attempt to reclaim former glories with the hit-heavy double live album *White Noise* (#29 UK) and the EP *Live* (#27 UK) appealed only to the resilient faithful. His next studio set, *The Fury* (#24) in September, was again accompanied by a string of poorly selling minor hit singles —"Your Fascination" (#46 UK), "Call Out the Dogs" (#49 UK), "The Miracle" (#49 UK), "This is Love" (#28 UK), and "I Can't Stop"(#27 UK).

A second union with Sharpe, "New Thing From London Town" (#52 UK) failed to rekindle the heights of its predecessor, and November, 1986's new album *Strange Charm* (#59 UK) and single "I Still Remember" (#74 UK) turned in Numan's worst chart performances to date. In February 1987, he closed the Numa label and began seeking a new deal.

Abandoning session musicians, Numan hooked up with the club band Radio Heart for the singles "Radio Heart" (#35 UK) and "London Times" (#48 UK). The project was not a success, however, a failing which was only exacerbated when former label Beggars Banquet unleashed a hit "E Reg Mix" remix of "Cars" (#16 UK). By fall, Numan was touring the UK in support of an entire album's worth of oldies, *Exhibition* (#43 UK).

Riding the surprising wave of support garnered from the tour, Numan and Sharpe scored another minor hit in early 1988 with "No More Lies" (#34 UK), and that summer, the singer signed with the Illegal label and released *Metal Rhythm* (#48 UK), home to two further singles, "New Anger"

(#46 UK) and "America" (#49 UK). The following year would repeat this pattern, as another collaboration with Sharpe, "I'm On Automatic" (#44 UK) was followed by a new album, *Automatic* (#59 UK), again featuring the Shakatak mainstay.

Preparing for the tenth anniversary of "Are Friends Electric," Numan reconvened many of the musicians who'd surrounded him during that first flush of success — Bell, Payne, and Sharpley (Gardiner died from a heroin overdose, 2/4/84) joined Numan's saxophonist brother John Webb (sax) for a string of late 1988 live shows preserved on the *Skin Mechanic* (#55 UK) album, and in March 1991, this line-up (plus former Kajagoogoo guitarist Nick Beggs) reconvened for the *Outland* (#39 UK) album.

Numan's best in some years, it was also his most successful since *The Fury*, spawning the minor hit "Heart" (#43 UK) on the back of well received UK and European tours. An audacious cover of Prince's "U Got the Look" accompanied a new single, "The Skin Game" (#68 UK); another Prince track, "1999," would appear on the *Machine + Soul* (#42 UK) album at the end of the year (the title track would also appear as a single — #72 UK).

1992 also brought the *Isolate* compilation of later material; it would be followed in late 1993 by a new collection of prime Numan, The Best Of 1979-83 (#70 UK) and a second reissue of "Cars" (#53 UK), and in December, Numan toured the UK with OMD — one of the few '80s synthesizer bands who couldn't be accused of borrowing all their best moves from him.

Despite so much activity, 1994's *Sacrifice* became Numan's first non-charting album since his debut; the *Dark Light* live album followed it. But aided by yet another appearance for "Cars," this time in a newly commissioned "Premier Mix" (#17 UK), the compilation *The Premier Hits* (#21 UK) suddenly saw Numan return to favor.

A slew of Numan covers — by Nancy Boy, Marilyn Manson, Information Society, Fear Factory, Foo Fighters, Smashing Pumpkins, and finally, a double CD's worth of top artists — saw him gradually gaining a new respect among the latest generation of music fans, and while 1996's *Techno Army* album did him few favors, a slew of reissues, remastering both his Beggars Banquet and Numa material, was followed by a very powerful new album. 1998's *Exile* brought him his best reviews in years, and further praise from unexpected quarters.

Both Afrika Bambaataa and Trent Reznor expressed interest in working with him, while Reznor and Manson joined Numan on stage in L.A., during the *Exile* tour. Numan accepted their accolades with convincing surprise. "For me to sit back and see that I had such an influence on such a cross section of bands is completely satisfying," he said, before adding, "but I still can't believe it."

Tubeway Army LPs

7 Tubeway Army (Beggars Banquet) 1978 If Ziggy hadn't played guitar, then he'd be Gary Numan. So went a popular joke at the time, although this early on, the electronics are sparse and the guitars buzz out like distress flares for wasps.

9 Replicas (Beggars Banquet) 1979 Far removed from *Tubeway Army*; far removed from Planet Earth, *Replicas* creates a chilling panorama of the future, a cyberworld of frosty sex and frigid violence, of people disconnected from each other and themselves. The synths bleep and blink then swell into black-heart symphonies, the metronome keeps merciless time and even the guitars are played by automatons. There is a tangible beauty to *Replicas*, but it's the beauty of a glacier from the bridge of the *Titanic*.

Selected Compilations and Archive Compilations

7 The Plan (Beggars Banquet) 1984 Demos cut in the full punk bloom of early 1978, bolstered with early singles for the CD reissue.

8 The Peel Session (Strange Fruit) 1989 First formative, then fully realized, 30 minutes of electro dreams take place before your ears.

Gary Numan LPs

8 The Pleasure Principle (Beggars Banquet) 1979 Richer and more textured than Numan's previous efforts, *The Pleasure Principle* has a greater depth of sound, even as the guitars are finally disposed of and the keyboards and synths take center stage.

7 Telekon (Beggars Banquet) 1980 Arguably Numan's most adventurous album, *Telekon* explores new electronic sounds, styles (from the jazzy "Panic in Detroit" piano to bass-driven melodies *a la* New Order), rhythms, and moods which swing dramatically from boisterously upbeat to opulent, soaring majesty.

8 Living Ornaments 1979 (Beggars Banquet) 1981
7 Living Ornaments 1980 (Beggars Banquet) 1981 Relatively calm live albums, simultaneously packaged together as a double and subsequently treated as CD bonus material.

7 Dance (Beggars Banquet) 1981

7 I Assassin (Beggars Banquet) 1981

6 Warriors (Beggars Banquet) 1982

7 Berserker (Numa) 1983 A brief recovery, if only with a title track which sounds like it means business, and the glowing "My Dying Machine."

8 White Noise — Live (Numa) 1984 Long regarded as one of the feathers in the electric friend's cap; a set which divorced him from the pure mechanoid-ics of the "Living Ornaments" live sets, at the same time as retaining the purity of thought and deed which made him matter in the first place. It was, of course, a sun-

set of sorts: nothing Numan did for the next dreadful decade ever caught up with this set for brilliance.

6 The Fury (Numa) 1985

6 Strange Charm (Numa) 1986

7 Ghost: Exhibition Tour 1987 (Numa) 1987 Fan club release recounting the fall 1987 tour supporting the *Exhibition* hits collection. The closing salvo — "Friends," "Down in the Park," "My Shadow in Vain," and "Berserker" is priceless. Subsequently given a full US release by Cleopatra.

5 Radio Heart (NBR) 1987 Stuttering collaboration with David and Hugh Nicholson, a little livelier than recent solo albums, but low on genuine interest.

4 Metal Rhythm (IRS UK) 1988 and **New Anger (IRS) 1989** Two tracks differentiate two versions of the same sad album.

6 The Skin Mechanic [LIVE] (IRS) 1989

4 Outland (IRS) 1991

4 Machine and Soul (Numa) 1992

4 Sacrifice (Numa) 1994

7 Live Dark Light [LIVE] (Numa) 1995 Generously packed concert set again breathes unexpected life into the mid-late '80s, but reserving its most powerful moments for the real oldies.

8 Exile (Cleopatra) 1998 In a decidedly unexpected move, Numan enters the darkside, emerging with the convincingly Gothesque *Exile*. It's filled with de rigeur religious imagery and iconographic lyrics, but the music is far from stereotypical, a blend of post punk, dark wave, and gothic influences. The tribal, clubby rhythms give an even more exciting sheen to the set.

Selected Compilations and Archive Releases

7 1978–1979, Vols. 1–3 (Beggars Banquet) 1985 Three mini-albums collecting *Plan*-era material.

8 Exhibition (Beggars Banquet) 1987 Far reaching hits and bits collection.

6 Isolate (Numa) 1992 Ten tracks offer highlights from the '80s.

3 Sacrifice [EXTENDED MIXES] (Numa) 1994

4 Archive (Rialto) 1996 Together with a second volume in 1998, deceptively packaged collection of live and latter-day versions of the hits.

7 Premier Hits (Beggars Banquet) 1997 Opens and closes with different style "Cars," but amidships, the transitional blast of "Bombers" bleeds chronologically into the desperate psychoses of "This Wreckage," and loses something in the process.

7 The Mix (Cleopatra) 1998 Old songs, new approaches, with contributions from Astralasia, Information Society, and Laeather Strip.

6 Remodulate: the Numa Chronicles (Cleopatra) 1998 Two-CD set sensibly documenting the Numa label material, including non-album mixes alongside a generally strong selection of LP material.

7 Exile Extended (Cleopatra) 1999 Seldom superior, but generally entertaining remixes from *Exile*.

6 New Dreams for Old: 1984–98 2000 A companion to *Remodulate*, concentrating exclusively on singles, B-sides, and a few 1998 reworkings.

Gary Numan and Bill Sharpe LP

6 Automatic (Polydor) 1989

SINEAD O'CONNOR

BORN *12/8/66 (Glenageary, Eire, Ireland)*

Raised in Dublin by an abusive mother following her parents' divorce when she was 8, Sinead O'Connor spent her early teens at a Dominican center for problem children. A natural singer, the 14-year-old O'Connor was asked to sing Barbra Streisand's "Evergreen" at a teacher's wedding, where she met the bride's brother, Paul Byrne, drummer with In Tua Nua. He encouraged the girl's musical interests — she co-wrote the band's "Take My Hand" single, and by 1985, after further academic mishaps, was attending Dublin's College of Music.

Originally gigging solo around Dublin, performing Bob Dylan covers, O'Connor joined her first band, Ton Ton Macoute, in 1985. There she met future manager Fachtna O'Ceallaigh, and in 1986, he arranged for O'Connor to appear on U2 guitarist The Edge's *Captive* solo soundtrack album (the first single, "Heroine," featured an O'Connor vocal), recorded at Dublin's Windmill Studio.

The following year, Ensign label executives Nigel Grainge and Chris Hill saw O'Connor performing with the band, and encouraged her to relocate to London. A number of friends, including U2 vocalist Bono, tried to discourage her, but she disregarded them and over the next year, she worked with producer Mick Glossop on her projected debut album, also guesting on World Party's *Private Revolution* album.

The album sessions were scrapped in April 1987, and O'Connor — now expecting her first child, Jake, by boyfriend and drummer John Reynolds — took over production herself, recruiting Enya, Ruts drummer Dave Ruffy, and former Adam and the Ants mainstay Marco Pirroni as guest musicians. Her first single, "Troy," appeared in October 1987 followed by the hit "Mandinka" (#17 UK) in the new year. With the media fascinated by this strident-voiced, shavenheaded, and vociferously opinionated figure, O'Connor's debut album *The Lion and the Cobra* (#36 US, #27 UK), its title a reference to Psalm 91, followed "Mandinka" into the chart.

O'Connor spent most of 1988 on the road in Britain, Europe, and the US, where *The Lion and the Cobra* became one of the year's most popular college radio hits. Two follow-up singles, "I Want Your Hands On Me" and "Jump in the River" (featuring rapper MC Lyte) failed to chart, but still

© Jim Steinfeldt/Chansley Entertainment Archives

O'Connor was nominated for a Best Female Singer at the Grammys, and in November 1989, the album would go gold in the US.

A home video release of O'Connor's London show the previous June, became a hit in April 1989 (the month after O'Connor and Reynolds married); she also guested on the new album by The The, *Mind Bomb*. Her own next release, however, was held back until the new year: "Nothing Compares 2 U" (#1 US, #1 UK) was a cover of a track from the 1985 Prince-produced Family album, rearranged by Jazzie B (Soul II Soul) and Massive Attack collaborator Nellee Hooper.

Over the next four months, it would top the chart in 18 different countries, including both the UK and US — where it was certified platinum even before it began its month long residency at the top. In addition, the John Murphy-directed video would become MTV's most requested of the year. The Modern Rock chart-topper "The Emperor's New Clothes" (#60 US, #31 UK) and "Three Babies" (#42 UK) followed, while O'Connor's sophomore album, *I Do Not Want What I Haven't Got* (#1 US, #1 UK), would top the US chart for six weeks, eventually going triple platinum.

In April 1990, O'Connor launched her *Year of the Horse* world tour — which, in turn, became her passport to tabloid infamy. Already notoriously outspoken on subjects ranging from politics and Irish nationalism, to religion and sex, O'Connor launched the first leg of her US tour in May by refusing to perform on *Saturday Night Live* due to the presence of host Andrew Dice Clay. She was replaced by Julee Cruise.

She returned to Europe to headline the Glastonbury Festival, and perform at Roger Waters' revival of Pink Floyd's *The Wall* in Berlin, then resumed her US tour with further headlines. Rumors that she had recently checked into a hospital for an abortion, and was leaving husband Reynolds for support act Black's vocalist Hugh Harris, were already setting tongues clucking when O'Connor refused to perform at the Garden State Arts Center in Holmdel, NJ, if the US national anthem was played before hand — a protest against both US jingoism and music censorship.

Reactionary radio stations immediately announced a ban on O'Connor's records, and a major protest was planned for O'Connor's show in Saratoga Springs, NY — one which she gleefully joined, in wig and make-up.

In September, O'Connor won three MTV video awards, and finally made it to *Saturday Night Live*, for the first show of the 1990–91 season. She also appeared alongside Sting and New Kids On the Block at the Amnesty International benefit for Chile...An Embrace of Hope; performed live at the launch of the AIDS benefit *Red Hot and Blue* album; and

during world AIDS Week in December, presented a series of televised *AIDS Update* infomercials.

However, she continued to court controversy, loudly opposing the Gulf War, and refusing to appear at either the BRITS or the Grammy ceremonies (where she received, respectively, Best International Artist and Best Alternative Music Performance awards). Further awards, including Blackwell's Worst Dressed Woman, the Hollywood Women's Press Club's Sour Apple and *Rolling Stone*'s Best *and* Worst Female Singer followed as the year wore on, and while two new singles, "My Special Child" (#42 UK) and "Silent Night" (#60 UK) fared poorly, still her next album, 1992's *Am I Not Your Girl* (#27 US, #6 UK), was widely regarded among the new year's most anticipated.

The single "Success has Made a Failure of Our Home" (#18 UK) arrived in September, and on October 3, O'Connor made her second appearance on *Saturday Night Live*, performing "Success" and an a cappella version of Bob Marley's "War" — climaxing in her tearing up a photograph of the Pope, and telling a stunned audience to "fight the real enemy."

The fall-out was immediate. *SNL* slapped a lifetime prohibition on her ever appearing on the program again, a fresh round of radio bans was followed by organized protests at which her records were smashed or burned, stores pulled her records off the shelves. The backlash reached its ironic peak, however, when O'Connor appeared at the Bob Dylan 30th Anniversary celebration concert at Madison Square Garden two weeks later, and was booed off stage by an audience gathered to honor one of rock's greatest advocates of free speech. O'Connor left the stage in tears, but remained unrepentant, attacking the Catholic Church afresh in a *Time* magazine interview in November.

A new single, a cover of "Don't Cry for Me, Argentina" (#53 UK) hit in the UK over Christmas, and was followed by her contribution to the soundtrack *In the Name of the Father*, "You Made Me the Thief of Your Heart" (#42 UK). O'Connor's silence through 1993, however, was compounded when she pulled out of both the massive Peace Together festival, and a role in the play Hamlet's Nightmare, claiming exhaustion.

In September, she was reported to have attempted suicide, and the following year, she entered a drug and alcohol rehab center in London. Public performances were restricted to a handful of TV dates, and an appearance at Roger Daltrey's 50th birthday gig at Carnegie Hall, and the release of her next album, *Universal Mother* (#36 US, #19 UK), in October 1994, was similarly low-key.

Singles "Thank You for Hearing Me" (#13 UK) and "Famine" (#51 UK), and a duet with ex-Pogues vocalist Shane MacGowan, "Haunted" (#30 UK), passed without fan fare, and through 1995, O'Connor concentrated only on high profile live shows, the London Irish Fleadh Festival, Glastonbury and, in July, Lollapalooza '95. She was, however, pregnant again, and after just eight dates, she pulled out of the tour and returned home, where her second child, daughter Roisin, was born in March 1996. In 1999, following a vituperative tabloid campaign against her, O'Connor handed custody of the child over to Dublin journalist father John Waters, from whom she separated just two months into her pregnancy.

Through the remainder of the 1990s, O'Connor's public appearances would be restricted largely to charity events and guest appearances; her recordings likewise. Only one EP of new material, 1997's *Gospel Oak* (#128 US, #28 UK), would appear, together with the single "This Is a Rebel Song" (#60 UK), although she would record with Pink Floyd's Rick Wright, Bono, Bomb the Bass, Sunhouse, Davy Spillane, Faithless, and the Chieftains. She also contributed new material to the Princess Diana memorial album, and the Omagh Benefit *Across the Bridge of Hope* — a spell binding version of Abba's "Chiquatita."

She also continued her sporadic acting career with a role in 1996's *The Butcher Boy*, but the most attention was paid to her ordainment by rebel Catholic Bishop Michael Cox, at the Latin Tridentine church at Lourdes — prompting O'Connor, in an interview soon after, to respond with the delightfully oxymoronic, "I can't answer that question, I'm a fucking priest." O'Connor returned to action in summer 2000 with *Faith and Courage*, drawn from sessions with Eno, Dave Stewart, Wyclef Jean, and Adrian Sherwood

Sinead O'Connor LPs

7 The Lion and the Cobra (Ensign) 1987 The rough presentation and less than stellar songs cannot hide a jewel of a voice, with the lengthy "Troy" and the single "Mandinka" spotlighting the first flash flood flourishes of the talent still to emerge.

9 I Do Not Want What I Haven't Got (Ensign) 1990 "Nothing Compares 2 U," of course, dominates, but little on this album cannot compete with it. The impossibly lovely "I Am Stretched on Your Grave" and the sharp "Emperor's New Clothes," come closest, but the whole album is a marvel.

9 Am I Not Your Girl? (Ensign) 1992 The critics swarmed all over it, but time has done the all-covers *Girl* many favors, including conferring modern standard status on "Don't Cry for Me, Argentina" and "Gloomy Sunday," while immortalizing the heartfelt "Success has Made a Failure of Our Home."

6 Universal Mother (Ensign) 1994 All original material pulls her back from the brink, but still relishing her reputation for "controversy" and "outspokenness," little about *Universal Mother* rests easy.

8 Faith and Courage (Atlantic) 2000

Selected Compilations and Archive Releases

9 So Far...The Best of Sinead O'Connor (Capitol) 1997 Away from the torn-up Pope pix, and the repressed Irish jingo-ism which were most outsiders' fondest memories, O'Connor was also responsible for the best Prince cover ever, the best debut single of the late 1980s, one of the hottest highlights on the best Bomb the Bass albums, and an eternally chilling rearrangement of the traditional "I Am Stretched on Your Grave." Oh, and she sings like an angel as well. What more could you want?

Further Reading

Her Life and Music by Jimmy Guterman (Warner Books, 1991).

OASIS

FORMED 1991 (Manchester, England)
ORIGINAL LINE-UP *Noel Gallagher (b. 5/29/67, Burnage — guitar); Liam Gallagher (b. 9/21/72, Burnage — vocals); Bonehead (b. Paul Arthurs, 6/23/65, Manchester — guitar); Paul McGuigan (b. 5/9/71, Manchester — bass); Tony McCarroll (drums)*

The Manchester band which would become the world-wide phenomenon began as Rain, a singer- and song-less trio formed by Paul Arthurs, Paul McGuigan, and Tony McCarroll. The first of their difficulties was solved when Liam Gallagher joined; the second when brother Noel, roadie for the Inspiral Carpets, returned from a European tour and caught the quartet (already renamed Oasis) opening for the Catchmen at Manchester's Boardwalk club on August 18, 1991. Noel joined the band on condition that he become principal song writer — in the absence of any competition whatsoever, the others agreed, and the quintet debuted, again at the Boardwalk, on October 19.

A year of gigging and demoing took the band nowhere; in May 1993, however, Oasis were invited to support 18 Wheeler at King Tut's Wah Wah Club in Glasgow, where they were seen by Creation Records chief Alan McGee. "He grabbed me by the collar as I came off stage," Noel reflected, "and asked if we had a record deal. It was dead simple, dead natural." They shook hands on the spot.

Oasis debuted in January 1994, with a 12-inch promo of their "Columbia" demo; four months later, their official first release, "Supersonic" (#31 UK) was Single of the Week in both *NME* and *Melody Maker*. Despite the group's obvious rawness and instability — the Gallagher brothers were regular sparring partners on and offstage — the UK media and public alike fell for Oasis in a big way.

Absurdly catchy songs seemed to ooze from every pore, while the Gallaghers' naive braggadocio remained charming, even when elements of those songs seemed somehow familiar — "Shakermaker" (#11 UK) had more than a touch of "I'd Like to Teach the World to Sing" about it; "Live Forever" (#10 UK), contrarily, sounded like two or three of Oasis' other songs. Noel, however, allowed such observations to pass by utterly unchallenged. "We're a rock band, a pop band, a punk band, but then we're something else altogether. If you go back through 30 years of music, we're the best bits, your favorite bits, all encompassed in one band. We're Oasis."

The August 1994 release of the *Definitely Maybe* (#58 US, #1 UK) album was the cue for all hell to break loose, at home of course, but also abroad. After a series of shows in Britain, Oasis headed for the US, where they played to sold-out crowds for five weeks. *Definitely Maybe* went gold shortly after (it hit double platinum in Britain), and even in the group's absence overseas, a new single, October 1994's "Cigarettes and Alcohol" (#7 UK) single (complete with the ghost of vintage T.Rex), was greeted with widespread glee. The band's final single of the year was "Whatever" (#3 UK), ensuring they were a shoo-in for the Best Newcomer award at the BRITS ceremony in the new year.

Oasis' second American tour opened in January 1995, running through to late March and characterized by increasingly over-subscribed venues. Trouble erupted occasionally, such as the Indianapolis show brought to a halt five songs in, after Liam was hit by a pair of glasses thrown from the audience; the band's own fraught make-up, however, exploded into the open in Paris the following month, when McCarroll was allegedly involved in a backstage fight with the brothers.

Although McCarroll has since denied that the brawl actually took place, and that other machinations were at work, he was sacked the following week, just as "Some Might Say" (#1 UK) became the group's first chart-topping single. (Five years later, on the morning of taking the matter before the high court, the drummer accepted an out of court settlement regarding his share of the band's fortune.)

McCarroll's replacement, Alan White, debuted at the Glastonbury Festival in May, the first in a string of summer festival dates, themselves coinciding with a massive media-fired feud with Blur, over who was the "biggest" band in Britain. Resolving to sort the matter out with their new singles, both groups scheduled new material — Oasis' "Roll with It" and Blur's "Country House" — for release on the same day, August 26.

Blur won, entering the chart at #1; "Roll with It" made #2. The two bands' new albums, on the other hand, would be staggered and *(What's the Story) Morning Glory* (#4 US, #1 UK) let nothing stand in its way. Oasis' UK tour that same month, however, was cancelled when McGuigan was diagnosed with exhaustion and he remained absent when the

band toured the US later in the year. Scott MacLeod of the Ya Yas deputized.

Effortlessly topping the Modern Rock chart, "Wonderwall" (#8 US, #2 UK) gave Oasis another smash in November, while the Gallaghers' now legendary antagonism came in for some unusual exposure that same month when a tape of a particularly vocal interview, "Wibling Rivalry" (#52 UK) was credited to O*sis and scored shortly before Christmas.

1996 began as 1995 ended, with another hit — "Don't Look Back in Anger" (#55 US, #1 UK) in February — and more controversy, when Noel turned down the Ivor Novello Award for songwriter of the year, after learning the honor was being shared with Blur. The band also caused a stir at the BRITS, when they accepted awards for Best Video, Best Group, and best Album, by describing their industry hosts as "corporate pigs."

Noel also stepped in to block a cover of "Wonder Wall" by the Smurfs, and forced the Freestylers to re-record their "B Boy Stance" after detecting a lyrical lift from "Wonderwall" (although he would endorse a lounge music rendition of the song by the Mike Flowers Pops).

August saw them headline their own two-day festival at Knebworth, setting a new UK attendance record, while September brought another hit for Noel alone, when he guested prominently on the Chemical Brothers' "Setting Sun" (#1 UK) single.

Nevertheless, "Oasis to Split" rumors flew wildly following events on the group's fall 1996 US tour — their eighth in two years. Liam had already missed the filming of Oasis' *MTV Unplugged* broadcast; three days later, he missed the plane to America, and the tour kicked off in Rosemont, IL, with Noel handling lead vocals. The errant brother rejoined the band two days later, but within a week, the tour itself was in shreds, apparently following an argument between the Gallaghers. The final five shows of the outing were cancelled, and when *NME* asked Noel if the shows would be rescheduled, the guitarist denied that Oasis would ever return to the US, with a terse "fuck 'em." In fact, they would be back the following June, opening for U2 in Oakland, California.

The bubble, however, was perilously close to bursting, creatively if not commercially. After the fact, even the Gallaghers acknowledged that the band's third album, August 1997's *Be Here Now* (#2 US, #1 UK) was rushed and underdone, that despite the simultaneous success of the attendant singles "D'You Know What I Mean" (#1 UK) and "All Around the World" (#1 UK). Although *Be Here Now* would become the fastest-ever selling album in UK chart history, shifting 750,000 units in three days, the speed with which both albums and singles dipped out of the charts was telling.

Pulling back from the massive exposure of the past five years was not easy — even when the Gallaghers were staying out of trouble, the vociferous UK tabloids found some to drop them in. Liam's marriage to actress Patsy Kensit was a particular source of media excitement (the couple's first child, Lennon, was born in September 1999), but when a bomb shell did finally explode out of the band's personal lives, in August 1999, few people truly saw it coming.

With the band and co-producer Mark Stent still some way from completing their fourth album, Oasis' only release in two years would be the *Masterplan* (#51 US, #2 UK) B-sides collection. In the midst of the sessions, however, Bonehead quit the band, saying he wanted to spend more time with his family. Two weeks later, McGuigan, too, quit, again citing personal reasons.

Split rumors were now circulating wildly, all the more so after the Gallaghers themselves recorded apart from one another, making individual contributions to the *Fire and Skill* Jam tribute album — highlighted by Noel's version of "Carnation" (#6 UK). The defiant brothers, however, insisted that Oasis would go on, and in late October announced replacements Andy Bell (ex-Ride, Gay Dad) and Gem (ex-Heavy Stereo), just weeks before launching their next American mini-tour. They began a full world mini-tour in support of *Standing on the Shoulder of Giants* in Japan in February, even as the single "Go Let It Out" (#24 US, #1 UK) proved that recent tribulation had in no way dented their flair for memorable pop.

Oasis LPs

⑨ **Definitely Maybe (Epic) 1994** One of the most accomplished debuts of the '90s, Oasis staked their claim to fame on a classic pop sound heavily influenced by British icons of the '60s and '70s, but fueled by strong melodies, baited with multitudes of hooks, and finished off with lyrics of universal appeal.

⑨ **(What's the Story) Morning Glory (Epic) 1995** The production brings out Oasis' heavier side, an apt alteration for teen screamers swiftly turned stadium idols. Increasingly lush arrangements, more anthemic choruses, big Stones-y rock riffs and omnipresent hooks (many lifted straight off *Maybe*) mean nothing's changed, it's just got bigger.

⑤ **Be Here Now (Epic) 1997** Maybe rushed, maybe simply rubbish, but the slick mega-production and clever arrangements can't hide the fact Oasis are still trotting out the same old hooks and even entire songs (with new lyrics) from their previous records — and on the occasions when they do break free, they're reduced to directionless rock riffing with not a melody to guide them.

⑦ **Standing On the Shoulders of Giants (Epic) 2000** The much-vaunted turnaround actually falls halfway, a few genuinely strong new songs, balanced by a few naggingly familiar hooks,

with a warm electro undercurrent driving even the lesser songs hard.

Selected Compilations and Archive Releases

⑨ **Definitely Maybe Singles Box Set (Creation) 1996**

⑨ **(What's the Story) Morning Glory? Singles... (Creation) 1996** Two multi-disc box sets rounding up all the band's singles (with B-sides) to date.

⑧ **The Masterplan (Sony) 1998** Surprisingly accomplished B-sides and rarities collection.

Further Reading

Brothers: From Childhood to Oasis by Paul Gallagher/Terry Christian (London Bridge, 1998).

OFFSPRING

FORMED 1985 *(Orange County, CA)*
ORIGINAL LINE-UP *Bryan "Dexter" Holland (b. 1966 — vocals); Greg Kriesel (b. 1/20/65 — bass); Noodles (b. Kevin Wasserman, 2/4/63 — guitar); James Lilja (drums)*

Bryan Holland and Noodles came together in 1983 as members of Garden Grove, Orange County punks the Clowns of Death (a name previously used for secret shows by Oingo Boingo); Holland and Greg Kriesel, meanwhile, played with Manic Subsidal, a similarly low-key punk band which was joined by Noodles following the Clowns' 1984 demise.

This line-up of Manic Subsidal debuted in March 1985 at Club Culture in Santa Cruz, opening for Scared Straight (now Ten Foot Pole) and White Flag; they became The Offspring that summer, after one too many club owners misnamed them on the billing, and by early 1987 the band were regulars at Berkeley's seminal Gilman Street, fitting in shows between their college studies.

That spring the band cut its debut single, "I'll be Waiting", self released on their own Black Label; James Lilja departed soon after, to be replaced by Ron Welty of FQX (Fuck Quality X-Rays), just as Offspring began taking their first serious steps out of California, playing as far a field as Salt Lake City, Las Vegas, Tuscon, and Phoenix.

In 1988, the band cut a five song demo (featuring a hardcore cover of the Sweet's "Ballroom Blitz"), intended for sale at shows. Attempts to interest independent punk labels like Alternative Tentacles and BYO failed, but the band did start receiving invitations to appear on compilations and by 1989, their fame had spread so far in these circles that they were ready to record an album of their own. Recorded with TSOL/Dead Kennedys' producer Thom Wilson, it was in the midst of the ten day sessions that The Offspring signed to Nemesis.

The Offspring's first full-length American tour followed, a four week outing crowned upon returning home by their biggest gig to date, opening for the TSOL reunion in Anaheim on December 29, 1989. A second tour in the summer, too, was successful, but money problems were souring the relationship with Nemesis and following one further EP, *Baghdad*, The Offspring broke away. They spent the next two years seeking a new label, finally linking with Epitaph after having already been turned away once before.

Ignition, the group's second album, appeared in late 1992, another high energy Wilson production which confirmed the band's support among the snowboard crowd. Several Offspring songs had already been used in snow boarding videos, and audiences were swift to respond to their apparent support for the sport, at home and abroad. A riotous five-week European tour, opening for label mates NOFX, was followed by a US outings with Lunachicks and Pennywise (with Rob Barton subbing for Noodles, who couldn't get the time off work!). *Smash* (#4 US), the band's third album, was released while The Offspring themselves were playing a snowboarding festival in Valdez, Alaska.

A new single, "Come Out and Play," was also attracting attention; it would soon be topping the Modern Rock chart, and by fall, with US tours alongside Guttermouth and Rancid under their belt, sales of *Smash* (#4 US, #21 UK) were still soaring towards their quadruple platinum peak. Further European tours, in summer 1994 and spring 1995, gave way to a summer of European festivals, and the band's first UK hits, "Self Esteem" (#37 UK) and "Gotta Get Away" (#43 UK).

Indeed, when the band was approached to contribute a new song to the *Batman Returns* sessions, they didn't even have time to write one. Instead, they covered the Damned's "Smash It Up" (#5 US), and created the first ever US radio hit for the first British punk band ever to play the US.

The Offspring's punk credentials would be sorely tested the following year, however, after the band succumbed to a prolonged bidding war, and signed with Sony. With the group heavily criticized throughout the punk community, Epitaph chief Brett Gurewitz joined the controversy when the label requested the L.A. Superior Court to hold the band's royalties in escrow while the terms of their existing contract were resolved — Epitaph had signed the band for three albums. It was finally agreed that Sony and Epitaph would jointly release the record, but still lower-than-expected sales for the Dave Jerden-produced *Ixnay On the Hombre* (#9 US, #17 UK) were blamed in part on their so-called defection.

Still, "All I Want" (#31 UK) and "Gone Away" (#42 UK) were hits, while a new year tour saw little reduction in the band's drawing power. Indeed, like Green Day before them,

the Offspring would not be ground down by the opposition, touring heavily in the wake of that album, then bouncing back even stronger in 1998–99.

An appearance in the movie *Idle Hands* was followed by the fall 1998, release of *Americana* (#2 US, #10 UK), the group's fifth album. Again produced by Jerden, the set included what turned out to be the Offspring's biggest hits since "Come Out and Play," the irresistible "Pretty Fly for a White Guy" (#53 US, #1 UK), "Why Don't You get a Job?" (#74 US, #2 UK), and "The Kids Aren't Alright" (#11 UK). 1999 would also see the band receive the on-line Artist Direct award for Top Alternative Artist.

The Offspring LPs

4 Offspring (Nemesis) 1989 The Offspring put the rawk in punk rock, but the best things about this album are the searing guitar leads... a bad sign for a punk band, and barely a hint of the melodic monsters to come.

7 Ignition (Epitaph) 1993 The Offspring learn quickly — they've tightened their songwriting light years beyond their debut, with strong melodies abounding and harmonies emerging. The raucous rock edge remains, but now neatly controlled within a pop-punk frame work.

9 Smash (Epitaph) 1994 If *Ignition* was the sketch, than *Smash* was the finished masterpiece, a ferocious mix of melodies, harmonies, and enough hooks to outfit an entire pirate ship. Best of all, though, are the lyrics — acerbic bites of real life drenched in sarcasm, but delivered positively po-faced.

7 Ixnay On the Hombre (Columbia) 1997 Moving to a major, The Offspring return to their rockier roots. *Ixnay* is almost *Ignition* part 2, although the lyrics now sound a little self-conscious — and worse, even preachy.

8 Americana (Columbia) 1998 After the brief identity crisis of *Ixnay*, the Offspring settle back down for a scorcher. The punk and rock are tightly intertwined, the excursions into other genres work a treat, and the lyrics return to their previous scathing and hilarious heights. "Don't blame me, I just work here," they announce, and though The Offspring lost a lot of indy-cred Brownie points when they wandered into major labeldom, fears that the Yankee dollar would distil their essential purity recede even further into the background.

ONLY ONES

FORMED 1976 *(London, England)*
ORIGINAL LINE-UP *Peter Perrett (b. 4/8/52, Camberwell, England — vocals, guitar); John Perry (guitar, keyboards); Alan Mair (bass); Mike Kellie (b. 3/24/47, Birmingham — drums)*

Like the Police, the Only Ones burst onto the punk scene in 1977 with a membership which blithely spanned the musical generations — drummer Kellie had a pedigree which stretched back to early '70s blues rockers Spooky Tooth; bassist Mair had played with '60s beat boom veterans the Beatstalkers — once unenviably tagged "The Scottish Beatles"! Even frontman Perrett could trace his professional career back to 1972, when he formed England's Glory with future wife Zena Kakoulli's brother Harry, drummer Jon Newey, and guitarist Dave Clarke — both past members of another '60s club band, They Bite.

Unlike the Police, however, the Only Ones' credentials were irrelevant in the face of their music. Undeniably influenced by Lou Reed's more decadent writing and David Bowie's less commercial recordings, the Only Ones played timeless, angular art rock, shot through with a healthy regard for the New York Dolls. Particularly in the years immediately following the first fiery blasts of punk, such a combination was irresistible.

England's Glory recorded an entire album, but split in 1974 when no record company interest was forthcoming (their album was finally released in 1987). Perrett lay low for a time, working with Zena as her career in S&M fashion design took off, but by mid-1975, he had rebounded sufficiently to book himself an appearance at the London Marquee — even though he didn't have a band to play with.

As the date approached, he found two options. The first, the Ratbites From Hell, were managed by one of Perrett's friends, but were essentially an acid-frenzied rock band best known for a myriad of festival shows and frequent gigs with Hawkwind; the second was a bunch of south London school-leavers named Squeeze, who Harry Kakoulli had recently hitched up with. Perrett finally opted for the latter and, on June 30, 1975, the hastily rehearsed group opened for Global Village Trucking Company.

The show was a surprising success — within days, entrepreneur Miles Copeland, who was in the audience that night, was offering the Perrett/Squeeze package a management deal. The band accepted, Perrett declined, but the union did persevere a little longer, with Squeeze joining Perrett in the studio during 1975 to cut some demos. Further recordings were made with guitarist Glenn Tilbrook alone.

However, Perrett was soon piecing together a new group with Ratbites From Hell guitarist John Perry. The pair recorded further demos together before Kellie and Mair were recruited and, by spring 1977, the regularly gigging Only Ones were recording their first single for self-release in June.

With the music press at least intrigued by Perrett's increasingly glam-androgynous image, "Lovers of Today" (backed by an old England's Glory number, "Peter and the Pets") appeared on Perrett and Zena's own Vengeance label in June, an immediate punk chart hit which naturally induced a storm of record company interest. In January 1978,

having already entertained offers from Sire, Anchor, and Island, the Only Ones signed with CBS.

A second single, the soon-to-be-classic "Another Girl, Another Planet," appeared in April, just ahead of the band's eponymous debut album (#56 UK). "Planet," in particular, established the Only Ones among the year's most promising bands — NME critic Nick Kent compared it to early Roxy Music, insisting its style was "so alien to the norm and yet so deadly effective that it knocked me back." Unwilling to accept that the single was not an instant chart hit, CBS would reissue it later in the year at a discounted price and with a new B-side. It flopped again.

Released in early 1979 while the Only Ones were playing their first US tour, a new single, "You've Got to Pay," heralded the band's second album, Even Serpents Shine (#42 UK) — an improvement in the band's chart fortunes, however, was not a sign that their profile was about to heighten. A UK tour through the spring was sparsely attended; another single, "Out There in the Night," bombed, together with the Special View compilation aimed at the US market (but released in the UK and Europe as well). Finally, CBS essentially slapped an injunction on the Only Ones ever returning to the studio again, unless they were accompanied by a name producer. After two attempts at self-production, the label had had enough of the amateur hour.

The group chose Colin Thurston and, in November 1979, released a new single, "Trouble in the World." It did nothing, but Thurston was retained for the album sessions and was rewarded when Baby's Got a Gun (#37 UK) saw the Only Ones finally breach the Top 40. However, the sessions were marred by in-fighting — Kellie all but quit after one fiery row and the other band members were constantly arguing. Yet another single, the album's "Fools," passed by unnoticed and it seemed likely that CBS would drop the group any day.

In fact, the label would hold onto them for another year, even advancing the band money for their fourth album, a collection of cover versions. Most of it was promptly plowed into paying off some of the band's outstanding debts elsewhere, but one track, the Small Faces' "What'cha Gonna Do About It," was recorded before the Only Ones set out on a summer 1980 American tour.

There they fell apart one more time. Perrett quit, a string of dates were cancelled, and all returned home. Reuniting to continue planning their next album, the band finally shattered in early 1981, when CBS suddenly dropped them. The Only Ones announced their immediate break-up, bowing out with a string of farewell shows in March. (The unused recording would eventually appear on the out-takes and demos collection Remains, together with older material dating back as far as Perrett's collaboration with Glenn Tilbrook.)

There would be little activity from the former band members. Perry formed a new band in May 1981 — Decline and Fall featured Douglas Bruce (ex-Snatch — bass) and Nick Howell (drums), but did little. Perrett, meanwhile, drifted through the 1980s, sometimes in the company of Douglas Bruce's former Snatch bandmate, Patti Paladin — the pair turned up at several Johnny Thunders shows during 1983, adding dischordant backing vocals to the ex-New York Doll's already dishevelled one man show. Attempted collaborations with ex-Rolling Stones guitarist Mick Taylor and producer Martin Hannett fell apart, but it would be 1988 before the long-circulating rumor that Perrett and wife Zena were heroin addicts was confirmed — when they announced that they'd cleaned up.

The first song Perrett wrote upon his recovery, "Baby Don't Talk," would become his comeback single in November 1994; it would be followed in April 1996, by an EP, *Woke Up Sticky* and, two months later, an album of the same title.

The Only Ones LPs

9 The Only Ones (CBS — UK) 1978 The best of the Only Ones' repertoire could have been made at any time in the past five years — or at any point in the next ten. That is how timeless this album emerged, from the insistent guitar-pop magnificence of "Another Girl" (blessed, incidentally, with one of the greatest opening lyrics ever written) through the partially self-fulfilling "Creature of Doom." Clearly in the thrall of Bowie, Reed, and such like, but effortlessly pre-empting the similar strivings of sundry later-70s art fops (Simple Minds fans start here), *The Only Ones* suffers only from the band's ambition — with a good, or even real, producer, it really could have been even better.

8 Even Serpents Shine (CBS — UK) 1979 Again self-produced, and lacking only the killer touch of the debut's most superlative moments, *Serpents* finds the band still working through a sizeable backlog of early songs. Lyrically, it can be a little silly at times, as the band's sense of mystic self-mythology moves to the fore — but there's nothing wrong with that.

7 Baby's Got a Gun (Epic) 1980 Nihilism merges with decadence to create an album whose rancorous shadow would enfold the band's reputation for the remainder of their career — "Why Don't You Kill Yourself," "Deadly Nightshade," and "Castle Built on Sand" are not, after all, the sound of a happy family.

Selected Compilations and Archive Releases

8 Special View (Epic) 1979 Concise "best of" the first 2 albums, featuring both sides of their debut single but not, oddly, the title track — also the B-side to the first "Another Girl" single.

8 Remains (Vengeance — UK) 1984 The unappetizing notion of wading through Perrett's back pages is salvaged considerably by the inclusion of "What'cha Gonna Do About It," realigned to a

doomed pop swagger, and the Tilbrook demos. Elsewhere, nods towards the Doctors of Madness and Peter Hammill indicate the other peaks Perrett was aiming for — and surprisingly, frequently attains.

7 Live (Mau Mau — UK) 1989

8 Double Peel Sessions (Strange Fruit — UK) 1989 John Perry once claimed that if anybody asks him what the Only Ones sounded like, he plays them the band's Peel sessions. The absence of a few of their stronger numbers notwithstanding, it's probably a smart decision.

9 The Immortal Story (CBS — UK) 1992 Marvelous retrospective which suffers from the absence of any unreleased gems, but does clean up the non-album B-sides.

6 In Concert (Windsong — UK) 1995 BBC broadcast capturing the band in indifferent form.

England's Glory

Selected Compilations and Archive Releases

6 The Legendary Lost Recordings (5 Hours Back — UK) 1987 Legendary... until you hear them. Part glam-soaked Bowie, part art-inflected Kursaal Fliers... hey, it's the Winkies revival!

Peter Perrett LP

7 Woke Up Sticky (Demon — UK) 1996

Further Reading

The One And Only: Peter Perrett — Homme Fatale by Nina Antonia (SAF, 1996).

OPERATION IVY

FORMED 1987 *(Berkeley, CA)*
ORIGINAL LINE-UP *Jesse Michaels (vocals); Tim Armstrong (guitar); Matt Freeman (bass); Dave Mello (drums)*

Childhood friends Tim Armstrong and Matt Freeman jammed their way through innumerable nameless bands before hooking up with drummer Dave Mello and singer Jesse Michaels as Operation Ivy, described by Freeman as a "punk-ska band" inspired by both the original 2-Tone bands and Berkeley's own infant ska scene. The band debuted live in April 1987, in Mello's garage, a dry run for the following day's official first show opening for MDC (Millions of Dead Cops) and Gang Green at Berkeley punk club Gilman Street. That opened the door for a truly hectic live schedule; over the next two years, Op Ivy would play 185 shows, or one every four days.

Two tracks on the *Maximum Rock'n'Roll* compilation EP *Turn It Around* gave the band their vinyl debut; soon after, they hooked up with local punk label Lookout Records, and in January 1988, released the *Hectic* EP, divided equally between hardcore and ska cuts — a blending, of course, which would one day be christened ska-core.

A six-week US tour followed in March; the band returned home to record their first album, *Energy*, for release in 1989. However, the band members themselves were becoming increasingly uncomfortable with their growing success. Freeman explained, "it just got too crazy. We started off as this little garage band, and then we got really popular, really quick. We had to start dealing with all sorts of crazy stuff. Before, if we showed up, it was, 'Great, here they are.' But later, if we didn't show up for some reason, it would be a tragedy."

On April 22, 1989, Op Ivy played Phoenix with The Offspring. Weeks later, the group broke up, following one final show at Gilman Street (supported by labelmates Green Day). Their reputation, however, never died. Lookout label head Larry Livermore reflected, "most people don't realize it, but Operation Ivy was our biggest band for years, Green Day existed in their shadow until *Dookie*. Operation Ivy is still selling more than ever, each year they sell twice as much as the year previous, and that's been going on since 1989." By 1998, sales of *Energy* topped 200,000.

Michaels went to Nicaragua and later became a Buddhist monk. Armstrong and later Freeman, threw themselves into the side band they'd created during the last days of Op Ivy, the Dance Hall Crashers, then reunited with Mello and his brother Pat (Op Ivy's roadie) as reggae-punks Downfall. Mello subsequently quit to join Schlong; Freeman resurfaced with MDC, appearing on their *Hey Cop If I Had a Face Like Yours* album, before quitting to form Rancid with Armstrong in late 1991.

Operation Ivy LPs

8 Energy (Lookout) 1989 A brilliant blend of hardcore and 2-Tone-flavored ska, by the time of their album debut Op Ivy were already maturing and diversifying their sound, replacing some of their original break-neck speed with tighter song writing, powerful guitar leads, and back-up vocals on even the most frenetic songs. Still ska-core at heart, Op Ivy were inventing a unique hybrid that will forever change the face of the American punk scene.

ORB

FORMED 1988 *(London, England)*
ORIGINAL LINE-UP *Alex Paterson (electronics); Jimmy Cauty (electronics)*

Former Killing Joke roadie Paterson was an A&R man at that band's EG label when he hooked up with KLF mainstay Jimmy Cauty to continue his home studio dabblings in ambient musical textures. The pair debuted as the Orb with a track, "Tripping On Sunshine," on the 1988 *Eternity*

Project One acid house compilation, and a single, "Let Jimi Take Over," released on a label Paterson and Killing Joke bassist Youth had established, WAU! Mr Modo.

It was followed in June 1989 by the EP *Kiss*, featuring station ID's from New York radio station KISS FM, and released under the name Rockman Rock and LX Dee. It became an instant hit in the chill-out rooms, with Paterson's own stint as chill DJ at Paul Oakenfeld's Land of Oz club helping it along. Another popular spin was former Gong guitarist Steve Hillage's *Rainbow Musick Dome*, and it was while sampling that during his DJ-ing set that Paterson met Hillage himself, and was invited to guest on Hillage and partner Miquette Giraudy's own new release, System 7 (aka 777)'s *Sunburst*.

The first Orb single, "A Huge Ever Growing Pulsating Brain That Rules from the Center of the Ultraworld," featuring lengthy samples from Minnie Ripperton's 1975 chart-topper "Loving You," appeared in October 1989, although it was a white label dance mix of "Brain" which set the pace for future Orb releases.

With the Ripperton sample excised, the track simply became one long slice of ambience, through which echoed and swirled every effect that could be wrung through the duo's own Trancentral studio (incredibly, "Brain" was created on an 8-track console, by an organ and a drum machine alone).

This release was eventually scrapped after recipients of the white label called up demanding to know "where's the sample?" But when the Orb's next single, "Little Fluffy Clouds," was hit by a writ from its sampled guest star, Rickie Lee Jones, the duo returned to the compositional purity of the remixed "Brain," leaving that other field open to the KLF (whose very name is an acronym — Kopyright Liberation Front).

The duo made their debut on the John Peel show on December 19, 1989, a compulsive performance made all the more attractive when a twenty minute version of "Brain" caught Paterson and Cauty reacting not only to their immediate surroundings (they redecorated the BBC studio as a living room), but also to a producer who clearly failed to understand the Orb. "I just started throwing all these samples at Jimmy," Paterson later explained, "waves, bird song, jets, old sci-fi experts, those 'aaahs' off Grace Jones' 'Slave to the Rhythm'... we were finding it so entertaining to defeat this producer bloke!"

In early 1990, the Orb scored their first hit when Paterson and Cauty remixed Dave Stewart's "Lilly Was Here," and made the Top 20. (Over the next two years, Paterson would perform remixes as far afield as Yello, Depeche Mode, and Primal Scream, before calling a halt in 1992, so he could concentrate again on the Orb.)

A Paterson/Cauty album was already under way when the pair split up in April 1990; minus Paterson's contributions, the projected set would become the rudiments of Cauty's Space album later in the year. Paterson, meantime, teamed with Kristian "Thrash" Weston (ex-Fortran 5) set to work on a new, sample-free, album.

The Orb originally intended their debut album, *Adventures Beyond the Ultraworld* (#29 UK), to be a triple. "But there was no way... anyone would release a triple album by an unknown artist," Paterson conceded. The Orb's new label, Big Life, conceded a mere double (plus a third, limited edition, disc of remixes), and the Orb scored another minor hit with "Perpetual Dawn (SolarYouth)" (#61 UK) in June 1991.

Following *The Aubrey Mixes* remix collection (#44 UK) in late 1991, the Orb released the single "Blue Room" (#8 UK). Co-written with Hillage, Giraudy, and ex-PiL bassist Jah Wobble, it clocked in at a marathon 39 minutes and 58 seconds, but still hit the UK charts in June 1992. It was followed by the chart-topping *UFOrb* (#1 UK), an album which maintained "Blue Room's" impact through a cycle of songs inspired by a small library of extra-terrestrial literature — Timothy Good's *Alien Liaisons* and *Above Top Secret*, Zecharia Witchin's *Genesis Revisited*, Bill Cooper's *Behold a Pale Face* and Frank Waters' *Book of the Hopi*.

Unlike conventional space rockers, however, whose invocation of their science fiction influences was expounded in lyrics and titles, the Orb's largely wordless explorations were relevant only in the eye of the beholder — "Close Encounters" and the title track alone made explicit reference to the UFO theme, while the Orb's most overt homage to the past, a cover of Hawkwind's "Silver Machine," not only remains unreleased, it was in any case counteracted by the brutal rendition of the Stooges' "No Fun," premiered on the band's third John Peel session in May 1992.

October 1992 brought a new single, "Assassin" (#12 UK), an instrumental version of a track originally intended to feature vocals from Primal Scream's Bobby Gillespie; its success prompted Big Life to reissue some of the Orb's earlier singles — at which point Paterson and Thrash announced they would release no fresh material until the label stopped. "Little Fluffy Clouds" (#10 UK) and a reactivated "Perpetual Dawn" (#18 UK) did make it out, but it was already too late. Summer 1994 saw the Orb sign to Island, and that fall they released *Live 93* (#23 UK), an in-concert stop gap which nevertheless included some of their most exciting performances yet. (A live EP, *absOrb*, also appeared, featuring versions of "Brain" and "Assassin.")

The EP *Pomme Fritz* (#6 UK) in early 1994, and the FFWD collaboration with Robert Fripp and Thomas Fehlmann that summer, marked the end of Paterson's work with

Thrash; marked, too, the end of his exploration of ambience. Thrash's final appearance with the Orb was on the rave bill at Woodstock 2, before Fehlmann and Andy Hughes moved in for the *Orbus Terrarum* album (#20 UK) and "Oxbow Lakes" single (#38 UK) in 1995.

Like *Pomme Fritz*, the record marked a strong progression away from traditional Orb territory, one which was exacerbated by the Orb's 1995 world tour. Fears that the Orb might turn into a straightforward techno act, however, were alleviated by the "Toxygene" (#4 UK) single, a homage to '70's ambient pioneer Jean Michel Jarre which became the Orb's biggest UK hit yet, and a new album, *Orblivion* (#19 UK).

The set seemed aptly named. Following one final single, "Asylum" (#20 UK), the Orb lapsed into a silence broken only by a bizarre collaboration with singer Robbie Williams for a tribute album version of the Bee Gees' "I Started a Joke," in 1998, and the *UF Off* compilation the following year — itself supported by an appearance at the Glastonbury Festival. By late 1999, however, Patterson had completed the Orb's next album, *Cydonia*, and also recorded a mix album, *Ambient Meditations 2* for the Return to the Source label.

The Orb LPs

9 The Orb's Adventures Beyond the Ultra World (Big Life) 1991 Steer past the dark side of the moon, turn right at Tiger Mountain, carry on for another 10,000 light years, pass the Ultraworld on your left, and it's there the Orb's adventures begin. This double album debut (aborted to a single disc in the US) is a journey into spacey, altered states with acid flash-back-like samples, warped by flickers of dub beats and hints of house, all spinning into soundscapes of magical proportions.

8 UFOrb (Big Life) 1992 The music starts and one is immediately teleported to a galaxy far, far away, an amorphous nebula where everyday objects and sounds suddenly transmute into very alien forms, and the familiar quickly becomes foreign. The songs spin out into infinity across the two discs... surrender yourself to the power of the Orb.

7 Live 93 (Island) 1993 Recorded during the band's European and Japanese tours, the double-disc *Live* includes greatest hits ("Blue Room," "Clouds," et al), tasters for *Orbvs Terrarvm* and more. On stage, the Orb transform their songs in weird and wonderful ways, some so transmuted as to be scarcely recognizable, rendering the record the ultimate remix trip.

6 Pomme Fritz (Island) 1995 Moving away from the evocative soundscapes of the past, the Orb journeys into much more experimental territory for this mini-album, leaving many outraged fans in its wake.

5 Orbvs Terrarvm (Island) 1995 Now straddling the line between the experimental sounds of *Fritz* and the more ambient stylings of the past, the Orb crashland their ship, pick their way through the wreckage and emerge on planet earth. Oops. More organic than their earlier records, but shot through with industrial clatter, *Terrarvm* is the sounds of the modern world, noisy one moment, calm the next — rivers bubble, machinery pounds, clouds drift by, and traffic roars. Neither ambient, nor industrial, the soundscapes reverberate with the buzz of life.

8 Orblivion (Island) 1997 Mostly true to its title, this Orb outing playfully skims across trance, all hypnotic rhythms and entrancing moods and melodies, before spinning into more aggressive numbers... winding back into poppy techno... and all the way back round again. Vocal passages spill out giving some clues to the album's obtuse themes, and *Orblivion* moves into a future that is already upon us.

Selected Compilations and Archive Releases

8 Peel Sessions (Strange Fruit — UK) 1991 Comprising two radio sessions recorded in 1989 and '90, *Peel* includes a phenomenal, possibly definitive rendering of "...Pulsating Brain..." ("Loving You") and masterful craftings of "Back Side of the Moon" and "Into the Fourth Dimension."

7 Aubrey Mixes: The Ultraworld Excursions (Caroline) 1992 Fulfilling Alex Patterson's dream of a triple album debut, *Aubrey* completes the *Ultraworld* set, and opened the door for thousands of cash-in copyists to now start compiling enough remixes for their own full length.

7 Auntie Aubrey's Excursions Beyond the Call of Duty 1996 (Deviant) Shape-shifting collection of Orb remixes for Bill Laswell's Material, Killing Joke, Primal Scream, Wir etc.

7 Peel Sessions 92-95 (Strange Fruit) 1996 Mini-album collection featuring two cuts from 1992 (including "No Fun"), two from 1995.

9 The UF OFF: The Best of Orb (Polygram) 1998 Two discs, one pursuing Patterson's decade long assault on the furthest limits of the three-minute pop single; the other, sundry remixes, rarities, and live cuts. The whole package totals nearly three hours. The Orb probably think it's an EP.

Orb/Alex Patterson — Selected Remixes

1989 KLF — 3am Eternal (KLF)

1989 DAVID STEWART — Lily Was Here [MULTIPLE MIXES] (Anxious)

1990 MARATHON — Love Park [MULTIPLE MIXES] (EG)

1990 SUN ELECTRIC — O'Locco [MULTIPLE MIXES] (Wau! Mr Modo)

1990 DEPECHE MODE — Happiest Girl (Reprise)

1990 MARATHON — Movin' [MULTIPLE MIXES] (EG)

1990 WEST INDIA CO — Oh Je Suis Seul (EG)

1990 SUN ELECTRIC — Red Summer (Wau! Mr Modo)

1990 JAM ON THE MUTHA — Hotel California [MULTIPLE MIXES] (M&G)

1990 PARADISE X — 2 Much (Wau! Mr Modo)

1990 READY MADE — Ambient State (Wau! Mr Modo)

1990 FISCHERMAN'S FRIEND — Money (EG)

1990 ERASURE — Ship of Fools (Mute)

1991 BIG AUDIO DYNAMITE — The Globe [MULTIPLE MIXES] (Columbia)

1991 LOVE KITTENS — What Goes On [MULTIPLE MIXES] (Sheer Joy)

1991 FORTRAN 5 — Groove (Mute)

1991 ZODIAC YOUTH — Fast Forward [MULTIPLE MIXES] (Eternal)

1991 TIME UNLIMITED — Men of Wadodem (ZTT)

1991 WENDY & LISA — Staring at the Sun (Virgin)

1991 FRONT 242 — Rhythm of Time [MULTIPLE MIXES] (Epic)

1991 U2 — Numb (Island)

1991 ZOE — Moonsister [MULTIPLE MIXES] (Polydor)

1991 WIR — So and Slow It Grows (Mute)

1991 PATO BANTON — Beams of Light [MULTIPLE MIXES] (IRS)

1991 PRIMAL SCREAM — Higher Than the Sun (Sire)

1992 DELKOM — Superjack (Wau! Mr Modo)

1992 YELLOW MAGIC ORCHESTRA — Tong Poo [MULTIPLE MIXES] (Internal)

1992 KEIICHI SUZUKI — Satellite Serenade [MULTIPLE MIXES] (Wau!)

1992 LISA STANSFIELD — Time to Make You Mine [MULTIPLE MIXES] (Arista)

1992 YOUNG GODS — Skinflowers (Play It Again Sam)

1992 MIKE OLDFIELD — Sentinel [MULTIPLE MIXES] (WEA)

1992 MAXIMUM BOB — Sucker [MULTIPLE MIXES] (Total)

1992 BLUE PEARL — Mother Dawn [MULTIPLE MIXES] (Big Life)

1992 MYSTIC KNIGHTS — Ragga-Nam-Poiser [MULTIPLE MIXES] (Wau! Mr Modo)

1992 MAURIZIO — Ploy (Wau! Mr Modo)

1993 YELLOW MAGIC ORCHESTRA — Hi Tech Hippies [MULTIPLE MIXES] (Toshiba)

1993 YELLOW MAGIC ORCHESTRA — Waterford [MULTIPLE MIXES] (Toshiba)

1993 FRONT 242 — Crapage [MULTIPLE MIXES] (RRE)

1993 MATERIAL — Mantra (Axiom)

1993 VOICES OF KWAHN — Third Whale Trip (Max Bilt)

1993 YELLOW MAGIC ORCHESTRA — Nanga Def [MULTIPLE MIXES] (Toshiba)

1993 ELECTROT'ETE — I Love You (Apollo)

1993 THE GRID — Crystal Clear [MULTIPLE MIXES] (Virgin)

1994 JUNO REACTOR — Luciana (Intermodo)

1994 SAXOPHONETTES — Secret Squirrel [MULTIPLE MIXES] (AO)

1994 HARUOMI HOSONO — Laughter Meditation [MULTIPLE MIXES] (Beachwood)

1994 GLOBAL COMMUNICATION — 7.39 (Dedicated)

1995 YELLO — Excess [MULTIPLE MIXES] (GE)

1995 LAIBACH — War (Mute)

1995 INNERSPHERE — Out of Body [MULTIPLE MIXES] (Sabrettes)

1995 POP WILL EAT ITSELF — Home (Infectious)

1996 KILLING JOKE — Democracy (Big Life)

1996 CRANBERRIES — Zombie (Island)

1996 PRONG — Rude Awakening [MULTIPLE MIXES] (Epic)

1996 GUT LANE — Firething [MULTIPLE MIXES] (Ocean Club)

1996 PENGUIN CAFE ORCHESTRA — Music for a Found Harmonium (Virgin)

1996 SPECTRE — Covert Dub (Nat Response)

ORBITAL

FORMED 1988 (Sevenoaks, England)

ORIGINAL LINE-UP *Phil Hartnoll* (b. 1/9/64 — keyboards); *Paul Hartnoll* (b. 5/19/68 — keyboards)

Confirmed rave-goers, the Hartnoll brothers united their fascination for electronics with the new musical scene in 1989, taking their name from the motorway ringroad which was the accepted route to the next party. Paul had previously played with a local band, Noddy and the Satellites — when they broke up, he and Phil began experimenting with a four-track recorder and a drum machine, and within months of forming, the first Orbital recording, "Chime" was receiving heavy air play on DJ Jazzy M's Jackin' Show house show.

A single appeared in January 1990 on Jazzy M's own Oh-Zine label, creating such a stir that by March 1990, the duo had been picked up by London records' ffrr subsidiary, for a reissue of "Chime" (#17 UK). One by-product of its success were the vast underground credos Orbital garnered after they appeared on *Top of the Pops* wearing T-shirts opposing the imminent Poll Tax.

"Omen" (#46 UK) followed in July 1990, and a year later "Satan" (#31 UK), featuring a dynamic Butthole Surfers sample, arrived on the eve of Orbital's untitled debut album (aka *Orbital I*) (#71 UK). A new single, "Midnight," missed the chart altogether, and the band hastily returned to the studio to organize the *Mutations* (#24 UK) remix EP, which featured remixes from Meat Beat Manifesto, Moby, and Joey Beltram.

A second EP, *Radiccio* (#37 UK), in September, and "Lush" (#43 UK) trailed a second untitled album (aka *Orbital II*) (#28 UK), as Orbital's live shows exploded out of the club and rave scene, to headline festivals and theaters. A US tour with Aphex Twin and Moby added to their reputation, Orbital standing almost alone on the dance circuit with their refusal to utilize DAT's, preferring to rely on sheer improvisation — a talent preserved on 1994's *John Peel Sessions* EP.

Summer 1994 saw Orbital emerge as one of the triumphs at both Woodstock 2 and Glastonbury, but it was with the bitter *Snivilization* (#4 UK) album that Orbital moved into the premier league, a biting combination of cutting dance and hard-edged politics, aimed at the British government's newly-formulated Criminal Justice Bill, legislation targeted firmly at the heart of the rave movement. The EP *Are We Here* (#33 UK) followed, effortlessly setting Orbital up for a second successive Glastonbury headline, the following summer.

Two low-key releases in 1995, an untitled EP featuring the club hit "Times Fly," and a split single with Therapy?, "Belfast"(#53 UK), interrupted an otherwise solid touring schedule. The following May, Orbital launched an ambitious tour of *seated* venues, including London's Royal Albert Hall, previewing their equally ambitious next single, the 28-minute "The Box" (#11 UK) and album, *Insides* (#5 UK).

A live EP, drawing from shows in Boston, MA and Chelmsford, England, followed in January 1997, uniquely charting on both Britain's singles and album listings (#3 and #48 respectively), due to its length; further live tracks would appear on the B-side of their soundtrack to the movie *The Saint* later in the year. (More soundtrack work would comprise the *Event Horizon* collaboration with Michael Kamen in August.)

Following on from the single March 1999 single "Style" (#13 UK), with its ear-catching Suzi Quatro and Dollar samples, the *Middle of Nowhere* album (#191 US, #4 UK), proved a worthy successor to the much-vaunted *Insides*, backed of course by a number of spectacular shows. Aside from the now-usual festival circuit, the duo played in the shadow of Edinburgh Castle in August, and also guested at the Edinburgh Festival that same month.

Orbital LPs

Orbital (ffrr) 1991 Balanced between ambience and all out rave, Orbital's "green" album weaves spell-binding beats across vivid and melody drenched soundscapes. From the rhythmic perfection of "The Moebius" to the epic "Desert Storm" with its strident, militaristic beats, and warscape electronics, Orbital conjure up a world all their own. Thinking man's dance music, *Orbital* is a brilliant debut.

Orbital II (ffrr) 1992 The "brown album" follows on from the *Halcyon* EP, adding ecology to their arsenal ("Impact — The Earth Is Burning"), but also taking time out simply to conjure effortless soundscapes —"Lush 3-1" and "Lush 3-2."

Snivilisation (ffrr) 1994 A snapshot of one particular moment in time and space, *Snivilisation* is a world of wonder and confusion, where questions are asked ("Are We Here?") and debated ("Philosophy by Numbers"), but ultimately remain unanswered and unresolved. Mostly it's an up beat excursion, but Orbital also journey to the dark side (the aggressive "Crash and

Carry" and speed-punk fire of "Quality Seconds"), as *Snivilisation* soars across moods and emotions, genres and styles.

9 **In Sides (ffrr/London) 1996** True to its title, *In Sides* is an album of many facets, containing six distinct soundscapes across eight tracks. The centerpiece is the marathon "The Box," Orbital's homage to '60s TV. Across the rest of the record, eclecticism reigns as Orbital shift from bright and breezy to dark and driving. A limited US edition includes a bonus disc comprising the European *Times Fly* EP and "The Box" single.

8 **Middle of Nowhere (Sire) 1999** A quasi-James Bond reminder of the Hartnolls' recent (successful) soundtrack work ("Way Out") and the dramatic techno of "I Don't Know You People" are the two extremes within which, presumably, nowhere is the middle.

Selected Compilations and Archive Releases
7 **Diversions/Peel Sessions (FFRR) 1998**

OZRIC TENTACLES

FORMED *1983 (Stonehenge, England)*
ORIGINAL LINE-UP *Ed Wynne (guitar); Joie Hinton (keyboards); Roly Wynne (bass); Gavin Griffiths (guitar); Nick Van Gelder(drums)*

Ozric Tentacles had been around for several years prior to their commercial acknowledgement; indeed, if their music can be compared to that of '70s space rock veterans Hawkwind, so their development, too, has much in common with that role model. The band formed at Stonehenge, during the 1983 free festival, and while their music promptly took a turn away from the hypnotic riffing of their best-known forebears, moving instead into more improvisational fields (which the media promptly dubbed "Space Jazz"), the similarities do not end there.

Like Hawkwind, the Ozrics managed to maintain a sense of humor lacking amongst many of their contemporaries. As *Vox* magazine explained, "while the Orb possess the pioneering spirit of...their idols, Soft Machine, Hawkwind, and Gong... the Ozrics play on their excesses." Soft Machine took their name from a William Burroughs book; Ed Wynne chose the Ozrics because he thought it sounded like a breakfast cereal — a decade later, reissuing their earliest cassette-only albums as a limited boxed set, the band did indeed design the package as though it were a new brand of corn flakes.

Having lost founding guitarist Gavin Griffiths, the Ozrics followed up a poor-sounding debut with the vastly improved *Tantric Obstacles*, and by the time of 1986's *Live Ethereal Cereal* (recorded, as it name suggests, in concert), the group's awareness of non-rock musical forms saw Arabia, the Far East, and even a hint of Kingston, Jamaica, creep into the sonic brew. For 1988's *Sliding Gliding Worlds*, *Record Collector* magazine was unable to distinguish where the Ozrics took most impetus from, outer Mongolia or outer space, and Joie Hinton admitted, "we find it amazing that we're getting away with it. It's a bit of a joke on the music industry, isn't it?"

From the beginning, the Ozrics were most at home amongst "their own people" — the New Age travelers and gypsy rave communities which littered the British landscape throughout the 1980's. The band themselves fed this imagery, and though the total opposite is now true, it is still widely believed, as Hinton explained, "that we all live together in a big house and take acid every day."

Even as they worked to maintain their caricature hippy image, however, the Ozrics' ambitions rocketed skywards. New members Merv Peopler (replacing Nick Van Gelder) and synth wizard Steve Everett broadened the sonics, while an ambitious slide and light show was pieced together from the proceeds from the sale of the band's jam tapes, and in 1991, the band formed their own label, Dovetail Records, and inked a US deal with IRS.

Strangeitude (#70 UK) was the first fruits of this new relationship, its success helping finance the opening of the band's own 24-track recording studio in a 16th century mill in rural Somerset. There they celebrated their absolute independence with the utterly unimagined success of 1993's *Jurassic Shift* (#11 UK).

The band's first US tour in 1994 was accompanied by a new album, *Arboresence*, but this period marked a commercial peak they couldn't consolidate, particularly after Hinton and Peopler departed to pursue their techno side project Eat Static. Still they continued to sell well, and following 1995's *Become the Other*, the Ozrics linked with Snapper for the *Curious Corn* album. 1999's *Waterfall Cities* continued in the traditional Ozrics vein, while a much-applauded internet broadcast produced 1997's ingeniously packaged *Spice Doubt*.

Ozric Tentacles LPs
5 **Erpsongs (Dovetail) 1984**

6 **Tantric Obstacles (Dovetail) 1985**

4 **Live Ethereal Cereal [LIVE] (Dovetail) 1986** The sound quality has always been the Ozrics' let down; even in the studio, they sound like they're jamming in a field beside a Walkman. *Ethereal Cereal*, contrarily, catches them when they're doing just that... and sounds even worse than usual.

6 **There Is Nothing (Dovetail) 1987**

7 **Sliding Gliding Worlds (Dovetail) 1988** The first of the Ozrics' truly listenable albums, although even they have acknowledged that this early on, much was interchangeable. The ideas are getting stronger, though, the jams becoming more focused...

7 Erpland (Dovetail) 1990

7 Pungent Effluent (Dovetail) 1990

8 Strangeitude (Dovetail) 1991 Take-off time. From here on in... they're still relatively interchangeable, but if you want textures and notions rather than tank tops and noodles, this is where it begins. The band's grasp of "world music" forms is peaking too, allowing for some increasingly audacious moves.

7 Afterswish (Dovetail) 199

6 Live Underslunky [LIVE] (Dovetail) 1992

8 Jurassic Shift (IRS) 1993 Epoch-sized leviathans of languid trancey jazz dance, littered with flutes and synths and samples, while insidious rhythms haunt the fringes of its consciousness. The songs are wordless, but the titles conjure images — "Stretchy," "Half Light in Thillai," "Pteranodon." Most of the time, they work as well.

7 Arboresence (IRS) 1994 "Yog-Bar-Og" is the centerpiece, almost 10 minutes of layered squeaking and squelching, building over an almost Kraftwerkian backing. Elsewhere, "Myriapod" is a solid dub freak out, and "Astro-Cortex" sends postcards to space rockers, from further out than they've ever strayed.

7 Become the Other (Dovetail) 1995

7 Curious Corn (Snapper) 1997

8 Spice Doubt [LIVE] (Streaming) 1998 Excellent live set taken from a pioneering internet broadcast, including the dynamite "Sploosh" and "Myriapod."

7 Waterfall Cities (Stretchy UK) 1999

8 Swirly Termination (Snapper) 2000

Selected Compilations and Archive Releases

6 Bits Between the Bits (Dovetail) 1989 Out-takes. Not that you'd notice.

7 Vitamin Enhanced (Dovetail) 1994 Boxed set featuring first six Ozrics albums on CD.

8 Floating Seeds — The Remix Album (Snapper UK) 1999 Propellerheads, Youth, System 7, and Space Raiders remake the Tentacles in an alternate image. Tripping ambience parexcellence.

Eat Static LPs

7 Implant (Planet Dog) 1994 A pair of former space rockers launch themselves into outer-space via cyberspace for this dance floor delight; Eat Static's mix of organic and electronic sounds married to hypnotic beats is totally entrancing, whilst avoiding the repetitive tedium of a lot of trance.

7 Epsylon (Planet Dog) 1995 Music to be played while dancing across the Milky Way, the seven-track (including two remixes of earlier songs) *Epsylon* rides insistent beats and cyber-space beeps.

8 Abduction (Mammoth) 1995

9 Science of the Gods [LIVE] Planet Dog 1997 In Eat Static's futuristic world, science and technology are one, practiced in a cyberlab workplace that's at times dark and ominous... but most days the machines pound away like warp engines as the scientists go about their ever more intricate musical experiments. The results are unexpected, as *Gods* harnesses the energy and aggression of industrial, mixes it with cybernetics, then carries some of the hybrids into outer space for further study.

8 B-World [LIVE] (Ultimate) 1998

P

PAVEMENT

FORMED 1989 (Stockton, CA)
ORIGINAL LINE-UP *Steve Malkmus (vocals, guitar); Scott Kannberg (guitar)*

The original two-piece Pavement reunited childhood friends, Steve Malkmus and Scott Kannberg, following Malkmus' history studies at the University of Virginia. They recorded their debut EP for $800 with Gary Young (b. 1954 — drums), owner of a local studio — released in 1989 as *Slay Tracks (1933–1969)*, its makers were credited as SM and Skystairs. Traveling the underground by word of mouth, it created a considerable stir by its very anonymity.

Opportunities to play live were passed by; instead Malkmus and Kannberg concentrated on recording a follow-up, joined again by Young. *Demolition Plot J-7* was released through Drag City in 1990, followed by the *Perfect Sound Forever* mini-album and the "Summer Babe" 45. That same year, Mark Ibold (bass) and second drummer Bob Nastanovich were added to the group as they began work on a full album. Pavement signed with Matador, and readied the heavily Fall-influenced *Slanted and Enchanted* (#72 UK) and "Trigger Cut" single for a spring 1992 release.

The band played their first gigs in the lead up to the album's release; a full national tour followed, and Pavement became critical darlings, all the more so since Young, in particular, behaved with such eccentric joie de vivre that he was frequently in danger of completely upstaging his companions. This, in fact, was why he was eventually eased out of the band, following the *Watery Domestic* EP (#58 UK) in late 1992; he was replaced by Steve West.

The compilation *Westing* (#30 UK) followed in early 1994, before Pavement released *Crooked Rain Crooked Rain* (#121 US, #15 UK). Critical magnaminity was joined by MTV support, and "Cut Your Hair" (#52 UK) climbed into the Modern Rock Top 10; subsequent singles, "Gold Soundz" and the anti-Smashing Pumpkin "Range Life," was similarly successful.

Following a brief hiatus, during which Malkmus and Nastanovich moonlighted on Silver Jews' *Starlight Walker* album, Pavement resurfaced in 1995 with *Wowee Zowee* (#117 US, #18 UK), and the singles "Rattled by the Rush" and "Father to a Sister of Thought." All alternately threatened to break the mainstream wide open, or alienate everybody who had ever supported the band in the past — certainly the critics loathed it, even criticizing Pavement's decision to perform on 1995's Lollapalooza, but other ears were paying attention.

Britpop heroes Blur encountered the band and borrowed much of their blueprint for 1997's change-of-direction *Blur* album ("at least it wasn't Hootie and the Blowfish," responded Nastanovich); Elastica's Justine Frischmann, Damon Albarn's then girlfriend, meanwhile, cut a version of Frank and Nancy Sinatra's "Something Stupid" with Malkmus for inclusion in the *Suburbia* movie soundtrack. With such strong British support, it was clear an entire new audience was now primed for Pavement.

Following the *Pacific Trim* EP, Pavement's new album, that same year's *Brighten the Corners* (#70 US, #27 UK) was accorded immense interest in the UK, while American audiences responded well, in dogged defiance of the critical backlash which was still underway. The singles "Stereo" (#48 UK) and "Shady Lane" (#40 UK) were also UK successes.

Another break in the band's schedule fermented rumors of a split, dispelled in summer 1999 by the release of Pavement's tenth anniversary album, *Terror Twilight* (#95 US, #19 UK), and the singles "Carrot Rope" and "Spit On a Stranger." Nodding back towards Blur's homeland, and recruiting former Radiohead producer Nigel Godrich, the album would become Pavement's most successful yet.

Pavement LPs

6 Slanted & Enchanted (Matador) 1992 With three tracks lifted bodily from old Fall records ("notebooks out, plagiarists," sniped that band's next album sleeve), a crunching low-fi monster, notable for its complete lack of bass — the instrument and the tone.

7 Crooked Rain, Crooked Rain (Matador) 1994 Too many Gram Parsons albums later, country rock shot through with signature guitar noise and some bad-tempered commentary on sundry other bands.

7 Wowee Zowee (Matador) 1995 Recorded in the belief that their audience comprised dope-hazed stoned philosophy students who enjoyed three or four disparate styles of music slamming into the same song.

8 Brighten the Corners (Capitol) 1997 A different band! Suddenly discovering lovely melodies and bright, happy lyrics, Pavement make a strong bid for the mantel of the new Mamas & Papas. Without the Mamas, of course.

8 Terror Twilight (Matador) 1999 Straight forward, uncomplicated, rocking...

Selected Compilations and Archive Releases

5 Westing (by Musket & Sextant) (Drag City) 1993 Collection of early EP tracks, primitive, brutal, and defiantly badly recorded. Although that was the point.

PERE UBU

FORMED 1975 *(Cleveland, OH)*
ORIGINAL LINE-UP *David Thomas (b. 6/14/53 — vocals); Peter Laughner (b. 1953 — guitar); Tom Herman (b. 4/19/49 — bass, organ); Tim Wright (guitar); Allen Ravenstine (b. 5/9/50 — keyboards); Scott Kraus (b. 11/19/50 — drums)*

Like the Dead Boys, the New York punk firestorm which unleashed two incendiary albums then swept vocalist Stiv Bators into the Lords of the New Church, Pere Ubu's roots lay in Rocket From the Tombs, the semi-legendary Cleveland, OH band formed by Peter Laughner (ex-Cinderella Backstreets) and David Thomas in 1973.

Future members of both bands would pass through Rocket's ranks, Cheetah Chrome (guitar) and Johnny Blitz (drums) would join Bators in first, Frankenstein, and then the Dead Boys — whose very name was adopted from an old Rocket number. Laughner promptly led the remainder of the group into Pere Ubu, sonic art terrorists whose own name was borrowed from a play by Frenchman Alfred Jarry, and whose initial statement of intent, "30 Seconds Over Tokyo," was regarded by the band members as the only record they would ever get the chance to make.

Released on the band's own Hearthan label in December 1975, the single percolated slowly through the underground in both the US and UK — itself becoming increasingly receptive to modern American music as the storm clouds of punk began to gather. In March 1976, Pere Ubu — now slimmed down to a quintet following Allen Ravenstine's New Year's Eve departure — released their follow-up, the now classic "Final Solution," and the following month Pere Ubu made their debut in New York, opening for Suicide at Max's Kansas City in New York City.

The appearance of "Final Solution" on the *Max's Kansas City* album in 1976 broadened the band's potential further; but rather than grabbing that straw, the band broke up in May 1976 — then reformed around Thomas, Tom Herman, Scott Kraus, the returning Ravenstine and new guitarist Alan Greenblatt. (Wright moved to New York, to join DNA; Laughner formed Friction, and later Peter and the Wolves, before years of drug and alcohol abuse hastened his death, on June 22, 1977, from acute pancreatitis.)

This line-up cut one track, "Untitled" (later retitled "The Modern Dance") before Greenblatt quit; he was replaced by Tony Maimone (bass) and in November, Pere Ubu released their third single, "Street Wave." It was followed by a rere-corded "The Modern Dance," and a well-received US tour through spring 1977, and in October, Pere Ubu signed to Mercury.

The Modern Dance, the band's first album, was released in early 1978, provoking what amounted to critical ecstasy — originally released on Mercury's specially formed Blank subsidiary, the response was so great that the album was switched to the parent label in April. A UK tour that same month saw Radar snatch up the rights to the early Hearthan singles, releasing the *Datapanik in the Year Zero* EP, and Pere Ubu returned home with the accolades of the British press, too, ringing in their ears. Mercury dropped them soon after.

They signed to Chrysalis, and over the next twelve months, released two albums, *Dub Housing* and *New Picnic Time* — critical favorites again, despite a pronounced lessening of the group's early punch. This softening was amplified further when Tom Herman quit following the band's fourth US tour in 1979, just as the band left Chrysalis; he was replaced by Rough Trade A&R man Mayo Thompson, the Red Crayola guitarist whom the band first met when Thomas guested on that band's own last album.

A far more "musical" musician than his predecessor, Thompson would lead Pere Ubu towards their most accomplished, yet simultaneously most obtuse album yet, 1980's *Art of Walking* (#3 UK indy) — a set which so polarized the band's own members that Krauss quit, to be replaced by the Feelies' Anton Fier, shortly before the group's appearance on the *Urgh! A Music War* feature.

Two years would elapse before the next Pere Ubu album, a period during which reissues of "Final Solution" (#12 UK indy) and *The Modern Dance* (#20 UK indy) would chart, alongside a live album, *390 Degrees of Simulated Stereo* (#6 UK indy). During this interim, Thomas recorded his first solo album, a reflection upon his recent religious conversion, *The Sound of the Sand and Other Sounds of the Pedestrians*. Pere Ubu then briefly reconvened in early 1982 for *Song of the Bailing Man*, but split before it was even released.

Krauss and Mamione formed their own band, Home and Garden; Thompson and Ravenstine reunited Red Crayola; Thomas continued solo, his backing band, the Pedestrians, drawn from a frequently intimidating meander through the backwaters of British experimentalism — contributors included former Henry Cow mavens Chris Cutler, John Greaves and Lindsay Cooper, Young Marble Giant Philip Moxham, guitarist Richard Thompson, and a revolving door of former Ubu members.

By 1985, both Maimone and Ravenstine were regular members of Thomas' live band, the Wooden Birds; when Krauss joined them on stage at a show in Cleveland the following year, the die was cast. With second drummer Cutler and local guitarist Jim Jones filling in the gaps, the reconstituted Pere Ubu launched a 14-city US tour in late 1987, followed by a UK visit in the newyear.

March 1988 brought the album *The Tenement Year*, and a near-breakthrough single, "We Have the Technology"; the following year, in the studio with Daniel Miller and Stephen Hague, Pere Ubu created *Cloudland*, a May 1989 release which came very close to charting.

The departure of Cutler and Ravenstine did not dampen the band's enthusiasm for their new life; *Worlds in Collision*, in 1991, and *The Story of My Life* two years later were both informed by the recruitment of former Captain Beefheart drummer Eric Drew Feldman to the brew. He subsequently departed to work with ex-Pixie Frank Black (the pair met when Pere Ubu toured with the Pixies in 1991), and in a surprising move, Pere Ubu replaced him with bassist and lute player Michele Temple, and Robert Wheeler, a theremin devotee. 1995's *Ray Gun Suitcase* (produced by Thomas) was a neo-concept album, built around the singer's visit to Memphis during the annual week of remembrance staged around the anniversary of Elvis Presley's death.

Again Pere Ubu would break up, with Thomas moving once more into solo work. His *Erewhon* set in 1996 was recorded with a new set of contributors, ex-Ubu member Jim Jones, bassist Paul Hamann, and trumpeter Andy Diagram, collectively the Two Pale Boys. Thomas then embarked upon an ambitious theatrical project, *Mirror Man*, staged in London and then released in 1999. Contributors included past collaborators Cutler and Diagram, plus Linda Thompson, Peter Hammill and Jackie Leven, with whom Thomas also recorded a full album for release the following year, *Defending Ancient Springs*.

A full-scale revitalization of Pere Ubu's back catalog, meanwhile, commenced with the acclaimed box set *Datapanik in the Year Zero*, the steady reissue of their individual albums, and a 1991 live album, *Apocalypse Now*.

Pere Ubu LPs

8 The Modern Dance (Blank) 1978 Post punk'n' Sex Pistols, Pere Ubu posture their way through true garage rock classic, incorporating punk, rock, and an essence of blues to their discordant didactic sound.

7 Dub Housing (Chrysalis) 1978 More polished than its predecessor, this album is a bitter foray into real life on the title track, "Caligari's Mirror" and the stunning "Codex" — a twisted little set.

6 New Picnic Time (Chrysalis) 1979 Pere Ubu ride the up swing into blues-ier territory with malevolent music for the everyman, the songs more often than not a vehicle for the band's views

and Thomas' strong religious bent — notably on "Goodbye" and "Kingdom Come."

6 The Art of Walking (Rough Trade — UK) 1980 Ubu branched out on *Walking*, beginning their experimentation with different musical sounds and style, adding a quiet ambience to the dissonance which hinted at a more pop-oriented sound — a transitional art rock album.

5 Song of the Bailing Man (Rough Trade — UK) 1982 Endless personnel changes cracked the tone of an album that otherwise continued on where *Walking* left off. Unfortunately, the band dropped their discordant riffing for a sound that was ultimately more art than rock.

4 The Tenement Year (Enigma) 1988 Returning to business after disbanding and hiatus, it's clear that the old spark is gone, replaced by self-indulgent noodling that barely contains the shell of what this band once were.

8 Cloudland (Mercury) 1989 It was clear something had to change — and what a change it was as Ubu returned to the spotlight with a brilliant interpretation of pop, helped in part by Pet Shop Boys producer Stephen Hague. Full of melodic hooks and catches and free of past baggage, the band turn in a stellar performance which masterfully incorporates the essence of what they used to be. Don't miss "Waiting for Mary," "Breath," and "Nevada." And if you think it's a sell-out — well, too bad for you.

7 Worlds in Collision (Mercury) 1991 More pop ethics, this time blended with old punk for a cocktail with some chunks.

7 The Story of My Life (Imago) 1993 Swinging in on an accordion, sliced through with sonic shards, and collapsing into the riffing "Coming Home," this is Pere Ubu returning to the bombast bomb blast which made them so vital in the first place, and permitted them to take all those fancy diversions of the past five years.

6 Ray Gun Circus (Cooking Vinyl — UK) 1995 More precise than they were at the beginning, Ubu again try their hand at the noise which set them apart from the pack at the end of the seventies. Raucous dissonance highlighted by the "30 Seconds Over Tokyo"-ish sound of "Vacuum in My Head," this album probably wasn't a hit with the new fans.

Selected Compilations and Archive Releases

7 Datapanik in the Year Zero (Rough Trade) 1978 Competent collection of early Hearthan sides including "30 Seconds Over Tokyo."

6 390 Degrees of Simulated Stereo [LIVE] (Rough Trade) 1981 Live performance from the US, UK, and Europe — 1976–79 era stuff.

6 Terminal Tower: An Archival Collection (Rough Trade) 1985 Archive collection with major liner notes.

6 One Man Drives While the Other Man Screams [LIVE] (Rough Trade) 1989 Live anthology.

8 Datapanik in the Year Zero (Cooking Vinyl) 1996 5-CD box set including rare pre-Ubu material, plus album selections.

7 **Apocalypse Now [LIVE] (Thirsty Ear) 1999** Chicago 1991 live recording, capturing the band with piano and acoustic guitars. "Non-Alignment Pact" unplugged!

David Thomas & The Pedestrians LPs

6 **The Sound of Sand and Other Songs of the Pedestrians (Roughtrade — UK) 1982** Definitely not Pere Ubu, Thomas' solo effort showcased an alternate plane, helped out by folkster Richard Thompson among others.

7 **Variations on a Theme (Rough Trade — UK) 1983** Another mix of a little bit of everything from jazz to crazy blues. Thomas has a few artistic screws loose and isn't scared to use them.

6 **More Places Forever (Rough Trade — UK) 1985**

David Thomas & His Legs LP

5 **Winter Comes Home [LIVE] (Rough Trade — UK) 1983**

David Thomas & The Wooden Birds LPs

7 **Monster Walks the Winter Lake (Rough Trade) 1986** Absolutely weird, yet stunning experiment with cello and accordion.

7 **Blame the Messenger (Rough Trade) 1987** Strong, a precursor to a reunited Pere Ubu.

David Thomas & Two Pale Men LP

6 **Erewhon (Cooking Vinyl) 1996**

David Thomas LP

7 **Mirror Man (Thirsty Ear) 1999** A wild journey, a twisted theatric combining ethereal antics, poetry, and a fine guest appearance from Linda Thompson.

David Thomas and Jackie Leven LP

8 **Defending Ancient Springs (Cooking Vinyl — UK) 2000** Supersonic sourpuss-ery; a beautiful, delicate set which tears reputations to shreds.

Peter Laughner LP

7 **Take the Guitar Player for a Ride (Tim/Kerr) 1994** Demos and oddities collection distinguished by early versions of "Ain't It Fun" and "Life Stinks," and a Robert Johnson cover recorded the night before Laughner's death.

PIXIES

FORMED *1986 (Boston, MA)*

ORIGINAL LINE-UP *Black Francis aka Frank Black (b. Charles Michael Kitridge Thompson IV, 1965 — vocals, guitar); Joey Santiago (b. 6/10/65 — guitar); Kim Deal (b. 6/10/61 — bass, vocals); Dave Lovering (b. 12/6/61 — drums)*

The Pixies broke onto the Boston scene snarling, screeching, and grinding their way to immediate cult status. Playing early shows with fellow Bostonians the Throwing Muses, the Pixies soon joined them as one of the elite few American bands on Britain's 4AD label. Their 1987 debut EP, *Come On Pilgrim* (#5 UK indy) was essentially a rough demo tape, but was powerful enough to unleash a immediate love affair that would change the face of alternative music.

Alternately explosively noisy and acoustically understated, schizophrenic and strikingly focused, the band quickly followed *Pilgrim* with the Steve Albini produced *Surfer Rosa* (#2 UK indy) — an album that remains, to this day, one of the most important and influential recordings of the age. Seemingly overnight, the Pixies had become a force to be reckoned with, drawing raves in the American college underground as well as pop adorations in Britain, and critical acclaim wherever their name hit paper. And while Francis was most often the focus, bassist Deal took the spotlight within the frame work of 1988's EP "Gigantic" (#4 UK indy), contributing heavily on all four tracks.

March 1989's "Monkey Gone to Heaven" (#60 UK, #1 UK indy) meanwhile, gave the Pixies their first chart position; it was followed by "Here Comes Your Man" (#54 UK, #1 UK indy). The wild rush continued when the band finally signed a US record deal with Elektra, and emerged with *Doolittle* (#98 US, #8 UK, #1 UK indy) in April 1989. And although the album was a relative commercial success, its tone chimed a warning bell for some. Slicker than its predecessors, *Doolittle* heavily reined in Black's psychosis, dimming the overall impact of the songs. The band, too, were reaching a crossroads. After grueling tours, they were ready for a break, and went on hiatus in the beginning of 1990.

Deal especially was aching for a change. With many songs written, but not appropriate for the Pixies' distinctive canon, she teamed up with Tanya Donelly (Throwing Muses) and Josephine Wiggs (Perfect Disaster) to form her own side project, The Breeders. Black, meanwhile, embarked on a solo tour before the Pixies reconvened in July, for the singles, "Velouria" (#28 UK) and "Dig for Fire' (#62 UK) and the album *Bossanova* (#70 US, #3 UK).

Reviews, however, were decidedly mixed, the album being heavily criticized as a vehicle for a solo Francis, rather than a Pixies effort. Indeed, Deal contributed very little to the album, and rumors of tension between Francis and Deal continued to grow, especially after the band's next American tour was canceled.

Despite the dirty linen, the band would pull together one more time for *Trompe Le Monde* (#92 US, #7 UK) in September 1991, a shallow effort masquerading as a pseudo-*Surfer Rosa*, and for the second time featuring very little material by Deal. (The album also spawned two singles, "Planet of Sound" (#62 UK), "Alec Eiffel.")

Despite the ever widening cracks within the band, the Pixies went out on the road with U2 on the opening leg of the Zoo TV tour; it would be the last time they would play together, as they again went on hiatus immediately after their stint in the Zoo was completed. Deal returned to the Breeders and began working on an album with them, while Francis embarked again on a solo career.

In late 1992, promoting his first solo album, Francis finally announced the Pixies' demise — albeit without having told his erstwhile bandmates the news. Shortly there after, Francis released a statement, rechristening himself as Frank Black, and effectively ensuring that the Pixies would remain as buried as his alter ego. The 1997 success of the compilations *Death to the Pixies* (#28 UK), *Death to the Pixies — Deluxe Edition* (#20 UK), and *At the BBC* (#45 UK), however, proved that the band would remain as highly regarded as ever.

Also see the entry for "FRANK BLACK" on page 202.

The Pixies LPs

10 Surfer Rosa (4AD) 1988 Eight little words — "You're so pretty when you're unfaithful to me" — spit out by Black Francis on this album's opening track let us know we were about to witness something unbelievable. 1988 was the year of the Pixies, and the consequences of their sound were to play a large part in changing the face of alternative music.

Infectiously heavy, with lots of fuzzy noise reigned in by snarling guitar (and a snarling lead singer), the Pixies didn't so much sing songs as expel them, each with a bite that simultaneously titillated and warned — even the apparent pop of "Gigantic" even has fangs.

From the opening "Bone Machine" to the closing "I'm Amazed," the Pixies brand of frantic, frenetic energy never lapsed. Joyously anti-social, *Rosa* waded into the maelstrom without excuse and emerged a blue print for the next generation of alt. rockers. The CD reissue also included the *Come On Pilgrim* EP.

9 Dolittle (Elektra) 1989 Without really changing their sound an iota, the Pixies unleash a little bit of everything — the undeniably pop of "Here Comes Your Man," the unease of "Monkey Gone to Heaven," and the utter nervous breakdown of "Debaser."

6 Bossanova (Elektra) 1990 Slump! Little new inspiration emerges beyond the essential "Velouria" and "Blown Away."

5 Trompe le Monde (Elektra) 1991 The ugly sounds of death throes.

Selected Compilations and Archive Releases

7 Death to the Pixies (Elektra) 1997 A double best of, two discs of everything Pixies, although without the addition of rarities and oddities.

8 At the BBC (Elektra) 1999 Career spanning sessions set.

PLACEBO

FORMED 1994 *(South London, England)*
ORIGINAL LINE-UP *Brian Molko (b. 1972 — vocals, guitar, bass); Stefan Olsdal (bass, keyboards); Robert Schultzberg (drums)*

Despite their UK origins, Placebo united one American and two Swedes, and a friendship forged at grade school (Brian Molko and Stefan Olsdal) in Luxembourg. Molko moved to London in his teens, Olsdal returned to Sweden, but they met again after Olsdal himself arrived in London, to study guitar at the Musicians' Institute.

Molko at the time was gigging with Breed drummer Steve Hewitt; joined by Olsdal, the trio promptly began work on Placebo's first demos. Hewitt's Breed commitments kept him too busy, however, and in late 1994, he was replaced by American Robert Schultzberg; in this form, Placebo debuted at London's Rock Garden in January 1995, and in November, released their first single "Bruise Pristine" (split with a track by Soup) on the Fierce Panda label. Months later, a second release on Deceptive, "Come Home," (#3 UK indy) reached well into the indy chart, and that spring, Placebo signed to Hut.

A single, "36 Degrees" (#80 UK), preceded the release of Placebo's self-titled debut album (#40 UK), with "Teenage Angst" (#30 UK) following in the fall. With Molko sporting an extraordinarily androgynous look (and possessing a voice to match), he was the source of much of Placebo's early recognition — all the more so after David Bowie, himself no stranger to blurring sexual boundaries, invited the band to join him for a handful of European dates.

Tours through the US (one with Weezer) and Britain, and a spell supporting U2's Pop Mart show in Europe, followed through 1996. When Hewitt returned to replace Schultzberg, it was with "Nancy Boy" (#4 UK — backed by a cover of the Smiths "Bigmouth Strikes Again") that Placebo's stock rocketed — the single peaked in Britain in January 1997, the same month as Placebo played Madison Square Garden on David Bowie's 50th birthday bash.

The following year, Placebo were invited to contribute to the *Velvet Goldmine* glam rock movie, turning in a version of T. Rex's "20th Century Boy," while scoring another UK hit single with the rerecorded "Bruise Pristine" (#14 UK).

Without You I'm Nothing, the band's second album, previewed by the "You Don't Care About Us" (#5 UK) and

"Pure Morning" (#4 UK) singles, was released in September 1998. The following year, the title track was released as a single with David Bowie guesting along side Molko. The band also scored with "Every You Every Me" (#11 UK).

Placebo LPs

◪ Placebo (Caroline) 1996 The most gloriously depressing pop since *Pornography*-era Cure, Brian Molko's adenoidal vocals quaver with intensity, the guitars quiver just this side of 4AD fuzz, and the melancholy melodies seep through the moody ballads and spit out of the angry, angst-filled rockers. "Nancy Boy" and "36 Degrees" stand out the furthest, but everything is ultimately rewarding.

◪ Without You I'm Nothing (Virgin) 1998 Retaining all the rough, androgynous values which made their debut so special, but upping the ante a little... again nothing leaps out with the same impact as "Nancy Boy," and singer Brian Molko still sings like a sheep. But a good grip of catchy guitar fuzz, and the conviction that Kula Shaker weren't the only sophomore outfit who could make stunning albums in 1998, ensured that "Without You" never let up, from the opening "Pure Morning," all drone and lackadaisical whine; through the lovably swirling title track; and on to the ripping trip-hop flavored "My Sweet Prince."

POGUES

FORMED 1983 (North London, England)
ORIGINAL LINE-UP Shane MacGowan (b. 12/25/57, Kent, England); Jem Finer (banjo); Caitlin O'Riordan (bass); Spider Stacey (tinwhistle); Andrew Ranken (drums); James Fearnley (accordion)

Following the 1981 break-up of the Nipple Erectors, and with his first choice of new band name, The Men They Couldn't Hang, having already been utilized for bassist Shanne Bradley's new band, Shane MacGowan's first stop was the Mill Wall Chainsaws, a band formed by friend Spider Stacy.

MacGowan and Stacy were also ring leaders of a group of London Irish musicians who played Richard Strange's Cabaret Futura in late 1983, performing a set of Irish rebel songs. The whole performance, MacGowan later revealed, was intended simply "to shock these ponces out of their smug synthesized heaven," but the presence in the audience of 20 British army soldiers turned the show into a riotous debacle, and the group decided to continue on, gigging around London's Irish pubs and busking outside tube stations.

At first the group had no name; they eventually settled upon Pogue Mo Chone (swiftly phoneticized to Mahone), Gaelic for "kiss my arse," and in May 1984, the band released their first single, "The Dark Streets of London" (#8 UK indy) on their own, eponymous record label. An immediate underground hit, the band were soon snapped up by Stiff, who promptly reissued the single. Airplay followed, and "Dark Streets of London" was already selling strongly when a BBC Scotland producer suddenly realized what the band's name meant.

He communicated his discovery to London, and "Dark Streets of London" was promptly banned from daytime airplay; Stiff then demanded the band shorten its name, and the Pogues debuted in October with a single, "Red Roses for Me," and the album of the same name (#89 UK). Tours with Elvis Costello and the Clash brought the band further recognition, with more following when Costello agreed to produce their next single, "A Pair of Brown Eyes" (#72 UK).

Costello would also perform with the band on occasion, prior to beginning work on the band's sophomore album; in the meantime, another single, "Sally MacLennane" (#51 UK) appeared in June 1985, with *Rum, Sodomy and the Lash* (#13 UK) (the title was Sir Winston Churchill's succinct summary of life in the navy) following in August. This proved the band's breakthrough, coming on the heels of a runaway success at the Cambridge Folk Festival. August, however, also saw the Pogues preside over a near riot at the Brixton Fridge, when they head lined a Nicaraguan benefit.

The Pogues were augmented on stage by several of the guest musicians involved in the album, including former Radiators From Space guitarist Phil Chevron. He would be recruited into the band as banjo player, and also produced their next single, a rendition of Ewan MacColl's "Dirty Old Town" (#62 UK).

With *Melody Maker* was already insisting that "if it hadn't been for Live Aid, then 1985 would surely have gone down as the year of the Pogues," the band ended 1985 with tours of Britain and Eire, and began 1986 in the US. There they were stunned by the exit of O'Riordan — she returned a few days later (roadie Darryl Hunt stood in for her), only for the band's next single, a cover of "Do You Believe in Magic," to be mysteriously withdrawn, in lieu of the *Poguetry in Motion* EP — their first Top 30 hit (#29 UK), but surely not as great a one as that fabled rendition of a much-loved oldie could have been.

"Haunted" (#42 UK), one of two songs contributed to the soundtrack of Alex Cox's *Sid and Nancy* followed — Cox directed the first ever Pogues video, and remained a staunch supporter; later in the year, the Pogues en masse would appear as the coffee-addicted McMahon family in Cox's *Straight to Hell* spaghetti western.

O'Riordan married Elvis Costello in May, the day before the Pogues played the unemployment benefit Self Aid in Dublin. A month later, they appeared at the Glastonbury CND rally and the YIVA benefit in Birmingham, O'Riordan's last major shows with the band. She quit in November, and Hunt again replaced her.

In March 1987, the new look Pogues appeared at the 25th anniversary of Irish TV's *Late Late Show*, alongside the Dubliners, U2, Christy Moore, and others. A version of "The Irish Rover" (#8 UK), recorded that night with the Dubliners, would become the band's first Top 10 hit later that month.

They followed it with "A Fairytale of New York" (#2 UK), a Christmas single cut with Kirsty MacColl — daughter of "Dirty Old Town" song writer Ewan, and herself a renowned singer-songwriter. Her duet with MacGowan on this tale of downtrodden street people remains one of the most unlikely festive hits ever — but is still regularly reissued and reprised on air.

In January 1988, the band's third album, the Steve Lillywhite-produced *If I Should Fall from Grace with God* (#88 US, #3 UK) entered the chart at its peak (Lillywhite, MacColl's husband, stepped in as producer after the band's first choice, David Byrne, dropped out).

On the heels of smashing success, the band embarked on their latest, and most successful US tour, a three-week outing which saw them introduce another new member to the line-up, former Clash vocalist Joe Strummer. He added two of his old band's songs to the repertoire, "I Fought the Law" and "London Calling," but his membership was not permanent, dropping out once the band returned to the UK, where the album's title track had just given them another hit (#58).

"Fiesta" (#24 UK) followed in July 1988, just as the band embarked upon their next US tour — without MacGowan. He collapsed at Heathrow Airport, and missed the first ten dates, including a San Francisco show opening for Bob Dylan. Rumors that his bandmates might be planning a coup against their hard-drinking frontman, however, were discounted, as two further singles, "Yeah Yeah Yeah" (#43 UK) and "Misty Morning Albert Bridge" (#41 UK) kept the band on the UK chart into 1989. Another successful US outing, the *Slaughtered Lambs of New Wave* tour, paired the Pogues with Violent Femmes.

Peace and Love (#118 US, #5 UK) was released in summer 1989; the following year, the Pogues made a raucous spectacle on *Saturday Night Live* (3/17/90), before returning home to record a single commemorating Ireland's qualification for the 1990 soccer World cup, "Jack's Heroes" (#63 UK). An Irish chart topper, it was followed by "Summer in Siam" (#64 UK) and in October 1990, the Strummer produced *Hell's Ditch* album (#187US, #12 UK).

Tours throughout the winter, and a string of shows through 1991 kept the band moving; "A Rainy Night in Soho" (#67 UK) in September, was desperately unlucky, as was a suitably damaged cover of the Rolling Stones' "Honky Tonk Women" (#56 UK), but a *Best of the Pogues* (#11 UK)

compilation made amends, and that same month, the Pogues returned to the US for some live shows with Joe Strummer. From there they traveled to Japan, and it was there that the ax fell on MacGowan. A sake drinking binge left him incapable of playing a show, and he was peremptorily sacked, to be replaced by Strummer — who committed to fulfilling the band's six month world tour at just three days notice.

The Pogues toured the UK through the winter, and in February 1992, Strummer was reported to be writing a new album with the band. The following month, however, he left the band, and Stacy took over as vocalist for 1993's *Waiting for Herb* album (#20UK) and the "Tuesday Morning" (#18 UK) and "Once Upon a Time"(#66 UK) singles. The resulting album, 1996's *Pogue Mahone* did little, and the band broke up following a performance at the Montreux Jazz festival in July 1996.

MacGowan, meanwhile, had launched a solo career, beginning with a duet with Nick Cave, covering Louis Armstrong's "What a Wonderful World" (#72 UK). (The pair later reconvened on Cave's acclaimed *Murder Ballads* album.) He also signed with ZTT, but rumors of a reconciliation with the Pogues were never far away, particularly after he joined them on stage at the Kentish Town Forum in December 1993.

By March, however, MacGowan was on the road in his own right, with a new band, the Popes, featuring Paul McGuinness (guitar), Bernie France (bass), Tom McManamon (banjo), and Danny Pope (drums), breaking the band in on the pub circuit, before unleashing their debut album, *The Snake*, in January 1995. Two years later, the almost exclusively Irish traditional *Crock of Gold* followed hit versions of "My Way" (#29 UK) and "Crock of Gold" (#59 UK) itself. In 1998, MacGowan was one of several family members to guest on sister Siobhan's solo debut, *Chariot*.

The Pogues LPs

7 Red Roses for Me (Enigma) 1984 Blurring the boundaries between traditional covers and original compositions, the Pogues' entire career was essentially based upon translating their phenomenal live presence onto vinyl... with varying success. "Dark Streets of London," "Greenland Whale Fisheries," and "Down in the Ground Where the Dead Men Go" are the stand-outs.

9 Rum Sodomy & The Lash (MCA) 1985 Their best album, the Elvis Costello production sensed intuitively how to present the band at its best, while a lachrymose selection of drunken drinking songs, dirges even when they rocked ("A Pair of Brown Eyes," "Wild Cats of Kilkenny," "Sally MacLennane," "Dirty Old Town") made the Pogues sound strongly original, even when they weren't. You'd have to go along way to hear "And the Band Played Waltzing Matilda" played like this.

8 If I Should Fall From Grace With God (Island) 1987
"Fairytale of New York," MacGowan's duet with Kirsty MacColl, might be the quint essential Pogues recording, but "Turkish Song of the Damned" and "The Broad Majestic Shannon" come close, while "Streets of Sorrow — Birmingham Six" leaps out to prove it's not only past injustices which make the Irish sing.

7 Peace and Love (Island) 1989 The first of the Pogues' formulaic albums, although a return engagement with MacColl, "Lorelei," is uncommonly lovely.

6 Hell's Ditch (Island) 1990 "The Sunny Side of the Street" opens in exactly the way you'd expect it to, and the rest of *Hell's Ditch* doesn't vary the approach.

5 Waiting for Herb (Chameleon) 1993

5 Pogue Mahone (WEA) 1996 MacGowan's departure deprived the Pogues of more than a vocalist; he also took the subversive streak with him, rendering the Pogues no better, no worse than any other Irish rock band on earth. Competent but lacking.

Selected Compilations and Archive Releases
9 The Best of the Pogues (WEA — UK)/Essential Pogues (Island) 1991
9 The Rest of the Best (WEA) 1994 Two discs round up virtually everything you could ever need...and then some.

The Popes LPs
7 The Snake (ZTT — UK) 1995 No real surprises, but more of the usual sozzled sardonicism, as "That Woman's Got Me Drinking" fills the ten bottles of beer with a smorgasbord of spirits and "The Song With No Name" doesn't really have a tune either. And when MacGowan steps away from the Gaelic gall bladdery, it's to prove that whatever else went wrong with the Pogues, it wasn't any dimming of his punk intuition.

6 Crock of Gold (ZTT) 1997

Further Reading
The Lost Decade by Ann Scanlon (Omnibus, UK, 1990).

POP GROUP

FORMED 1978 *(Bristol, England)*
ORIGINAL LINE-UP *Mark Stewart (vocals); Gareth Sager (guitar, keyboards, sax); John Waddington (guitar); Simon Underwood (bass); Bruce Smith (drums)*

Mark Stewart, Bruce Smith, and Gareth Sager formed The Pop Group in mid-1977, the name a pointedly ironic commentary on punk's already noticeable absorption into the mainstream — if that noise could "make it," what else could? "We couldn't play," Stewart admitted. "We were 16-year-old kids, friends from the youth club, mates from school, coming out of punk. We could only play three chords, and we were trying to play funk."

At their first ever rehearsal, the band jammed "My Generation" for three hours, but early shows proved just how far off base the band's visions were. When they opened for Otway-Barrett in London in early 1978, even the show's compere openly insulted them, while the uncomprehending audience simply threw things.

Stewart explained, "Punk became a new kind of orthodoxy and we wanted to experiment, and be as questioning with the music as we were with the lyrics and the ideas. The whole energy we got from punk was not just making a racket but being a little more imaginative. Editors from the *NME* and *Sounds* kept coming to the concerts and saying we were like Captain Beefheart, but we never heard of Captain Beefheart! The only reason why is we couldn't play, we were pushing the envelope of what we could do as far as possible."

A John Peel broadcast in August 1978 put the band on the air for the first time, while the Stranglers' Hugh Cornwell and former Velvet Underground-er John Cale both expressed an interest producing the group. Finally, the Pop Group linked with Dennis Bovell of UK dub reggae band Matumbi, and signed to Radar in late 1978.

A yowling single, "She Is Beyond Good and Evil," appeared in March 1979 followed by Y, in April. The Pop Group's first album was a collision of punk ethic and dub enterprise, a largely tuneless miasma which even shocked the band's supporters — who mis-guidedly imagined that once the band got into a studio with a producer, their onstage impressionism would be molded into something at least approaching a rough Joy Division.

Reviews were as uncertain and confused as the band was accused of being, but still the Pop Group toured vigorously (donating all their profits to Amnesty International) through the first half of 1979, before quitting Radar with a terse accusation, "they [Radar's Kinney Corporation parent company] are involved in things totally contrary to what we believe in."

Simon Underwood quit to be replaced by Dan Katsis and the band resurfaced on Rough Trade in October with the "We Are All Prostitutes" (#8 UK indy) single; they then set up their own Y label for their next album, *For How Much Longer Do We Tolerate Mass Murder?* (#1 UK indy), and a third single, "Where There's a Will, There's a Way" (#2 UK indy) — split between the Pop Group and the recently label-less Slits.

The records were as well-received as could be expected, but the group were not making money, a cause of increasing friction between the members. Smith was already moonlighting with the Slits, Sager was looking towards the urban funk of Rip Rig & Panic, Stewart was contemplating a solo career which would pursue the Pop Group's dub inclinations further. The Pop Group finally bowed out in December with the retrospective *We Are Time* (#4 UK indy).

Stewart was first to re-emerge with a new band, the Maffia, and a single reprising the hymn "Jerusalem," produced by Adrian Sherwood — Stewart and Sherwood would also work with Smith, his wife-to-be Neneh Cherry and Slits vocalist Ari Upp in the punk dub aggregation New Age Steppers. Smith, Sager, Cherry, Sean Oliver (bass), and Mark Springer (piano) then formed Rip Rig & Panic, a group which evolved into Float Up CP and God, Mother and Country, before Cherry launched out as a solo artist. Waddington formed Maximum Joy; while Underwood's Pigbag would score an utterly unexpected UK #3 with 1982's "Papa's Got a Brand New Pigbag."

The Pop Group LPs

8 Y (Radar) 1979 A gaggle of discomforting, discordant noise merchants churning the principle of skeletal dub through the bones of unsyncopated funk, the Pop Group's passion looms larger than their music, but there are moments when... there are moments when.

8 For How Much Longer Do We Tolerate Mass Murder? (Y) 1980 Louder, angrier, more inclined to polemic, but otherwise business as usual.

Selected Compilations and Archive Releases

7 We Are Time (Y) 1980 Wrapping up the non-album material alongside the "best" of the rest.

New Age Steppers LPs

9 New Age Steppers (On-U Sound — UK) 1980 The Steppers were an inspired cross of dub and experimental electronics, taken to the edge by the more extreme elements of punk — and "Fade Away" was even more inspired than that, drawing out Ari Up's finest vocals among everything else.

8 Action Battlefield (On-U Sound — UK) 1981

8 Foundation Steppers (On-U Sound — UK) 1983

7 Victory Horns (On-U Sound — UK) 1983

New Age Steppers/Creation LP

8 Threat to Creation (Cherry Red — UK) 1981 Dynamic collaboration owing everything... and nothing... to all that the two bands represented in the past.

Selected Compilations and Archive Releases

8 Massive Hits Volume 1 (On-U Sound — UK) 1994 Bundling up tracks from the group's albums, all of which featured the Slits' Ari Up and the Pop Group's Mark Stewart as primary vocalists, but included a host of guest stars; Neneh Cherry and reggae hero Bim Sherman among them.

Mark Stewart/The Maffia LPs

9 Learning to Cope with Cowardice (On-U Sound — UK) 1983

8 As the Veneer of Democracy Starts to Fade (Mute — UK) 1985

8 Mark Stewart (Mute — UK) 1987 Includes the exquisite "Stranger Than Love" — the trip-hop sound starts here.

7 Metatron (Mute — UK) 1990 Stewart moves into rock, and as the Maffia slash and burn their way across stadium riffs and big hair histrionics, the solid beats are sometimes the only thing holding the more extreme tracks together, while Stewart paints tense and threatening visions of potential disasters.

8 Control Data (Mute) 1996 A breathtaking album that incorporates techno's dance beats, dub's heavy rhythms, industrial's aggressive edge and mixes in large doses of electronic effects. Brooding, pulsing, angry, insightful... and even partly pop.

Pigbag LPs

6 Dr. Heckle and Mr. Jive (Y — UK) 1982

6 Lend an Ear (Y — UK) 1983

5 Live (Y — UK) 1983

Selected Compilations and Archive Releases

7 Favourite Things (Y — 1983) 1983

6 Discology (KAZ) 1987

7 BBC Sessions (Strange Fruit — UK) 1998

Rip Rig and Panic LPs

6 God (Virgin) 1981

6 I Am Cold (Virgin) 1982

5 Attitude (Virgin) 1983

Float Up CP

6 Kill Me in the Morning (Upside) 1985

PORNO FOR PYROS

FORMED 1992 *(Los Angeles, CA)*

ORIGINAL LINE-UP *Perry Farrell (b. Perry Bernstein, 3/29/59, Queens, NY — vocals); Peter Di Stefano (b. 7/10/65, L.A. — guitar); Martyn Le Noble (b. 4/14/69, Vlaardingen, Netherlands — bass); Stephen Perkins (b. 9/13/67, L.A. — drums)*

Following the demise of Jane's Addiction, Perry Farrell and girlfriend Kim Leung retired to Venice Beach, remaining out of sight through much of 1991 while the press ruminated on Farrell's supposedly ragged relations with the rest of the group. He nixed a proposed Jane's live album and kept counsel with a mere handful of musicians, Jane's drummer Stephen Perkins — now working with Mike Muir (Suicidal

Tendencies) in the Infectious Grooves and fresh off a tour with Ozzy Osbourne; and Peter DiStefano.

The three jammed together, and in early 1992, a friend of DiStefano's, Martyn Le Noble, was flown over from the Netherlands. DJ Skatemaster Tate completed the line-up (keyboard player Matt Hyde would later be added for live work), and Porno for Pyros debuted at a benefit for the Magic Johnson AIDS foundation on April 4. Speculation that the band might make it onto the bill for Lollapalooza '92 was denied, although they did play a few shows, including the opening day at Shoreline Amphitheater, CA on July 18.

Released in May 1993, Porno for Pyros' self-titled debut album (#3 US, #13 UK) had been recorded in three weeks the previous summer, and took no longer to go gold. "Pets" (#53 UK, #67 US), a Modern Rock chart topper, accompanied the album, but the full set was received poorly — *Alternative Press* counselled that without Farrell's celebrity status, it wouldn't even have been considered for review. The band's US tour that spring also attracted more than its share of negativity, as audiences struggled to adapt to Farrell's new art-for-art's-sake presentation and theatricality — clowns, dancers, fire-eaters, and a 6'2" hermaphrodite choked the stage, often to the detriment of the music.

Resurfacing only for the UK Reading festival, and the inevitable Lollapalooza rumors, Porno for Pyros remained silent through the remainder of 1993, but bounced back in January 1994, at a benefit for Fishbone's Norwood Fisher, recently charged with kidnapping after he attempted to abduct a former bandmate who was reportedly suffering from mental problems (the singer was eventually acquitted). The band would also play a stirring Woodstock '94 set, but it would be 1996 before Porno for Pyro's second album, *God's Good Urge* (#40 US, #20 UK), was released, by which time Le Noble had departed, to be replaced by Mike Watt (ex-Firehose, Minutemen).

The album fared poorly, its promotion further hampered when DiStefano was diagnosed with cancer in October. The band immediately cancelled all future engagements while he underwent chemotherapy, paving the way, the following year, for Farrell and Perkins to convene the Jane's Addiction "relapse" tour.

Despite Farrell's insistence that Porno for Pyros would continue, the appearance in 1999 of a career-spanning Farrell compilation, climaxing with two solo cuts (including Led Zeppelin's "Whole Lotta Love"), recorded with John Frusciante (Red Hot Chili Peppers) and Tom Morello (Rage Against the Machine), effectively closed the door on the prospect of a future revival. In November, Perkins joined Methods of Madness; LeNoble joined the reunited cult. Farrell's solo debut album followed in 2000.

Porno for Pyros LPs

7 Porno for Pyros (WB) 1993 Boomy atmospheric production and a guitarist with breathtaking technique provides Perry with a better palette to work from than Jane's Addiction ever were. Where Navarro screeched, DiStefano wah-wahs, but while Perkins continues to experiment with rhythm, and Farrell still flirts with styles, the anarchic two fingers in the air fun is gone. That and the climactic "Pets" probably account for this album's success.

5 God's Good Urge (WB) 1996 A softer, gentler Farrell plays up some pretty introspective melodies with lots of jangly acoustic guitars expanding the moodier passages, while even the rockers never reach their previous raucous heights.

Perry Farrell LP

7 Diamond Jubilee (Virgin) 2000

Selected Compilations and Archive Releases

7 Rev (WB) 1999 Jane's and Porno collection which includes hits, remixes, a few rarities, a cut off a soundtrack album, and two new songs, although disappointingly, one's a cover (Led Zep's "Whole Lott a Love," no less).

PORTISHEAD

FORMED 1992 *(Portishead, England)*
ORIGINAL LINE-UP *Beth Gibbons (b. 1/4/65, Devon, UK — vocals); Geoff Barrow (b. 12/9/71, Walton-in-Gordano, Avon, UK — keyboards); Adrian Utley (guitar); Dave McDonald (sound engineer)*

Geoff Barrow worked at Bristol's Coach House Studios as a tea boy and part-time tape operator, helping out on albums by Massive Attack (*Blue Lines*) and Neneh Cherry (*Homebrew*), and producing Tricky's contribution to the Bristol-based *Sickle Cell* album. He and pub band vocalist Beth Gibbons were already recording demos together, and through 1992, they worked alongside *Homebrew* producer Cameron McVey in his London studio, piecing together their ideas.

Nothing came of the sessions, and they returned to the Coach House, linking with Adrian Utley (ex-Jazz Messengers) for sessions which produced a demo of "Sour Times" (featuring samples from Lalo Schifrin's "More Mission Impossible"). Utley had been composing private film scores for several years, "and that," he recalled, "is what brought us together. Geoff came in from being a DJ, playing old soundtracks and sampling them, and I came in from always having an interest, and knowing how to write the music, and make the sounds."

A second demo featuring McDonald as the final integral member of Portishead secured the band a deal with Go!

Discs, and in May 1994, the mini-album *Numb* was released, followed by Portishead's dramatic soundtrack to Alexander Hemmings' short film, *To Kill a Dead Man*.

A second single, a re-recorded "Sour Times" (#57 UK), followed in August and gave Portishead their UK chart breakthrough. Her plaintive insistence that "nobody loves me" became one of the musical catchphrases of the early-mid 1990s, a gabba-gabba-hey for the confessional grunge generation. That same month, the band played their first live show, at London's Athletico Club. *Dummy* (#2 UK), their debut album, followed in September, pursuing the trip-hop style which Massive Attack had already hinted at, but which few other artists had ever taken so far. *Dummy* earned Album of the Year awards throughout the UK press, and scored both BRITS and (*NME* sponsored) BRATS honors.

"Glory Box" (#13 UK) became Portishead's biggest hit yet; while the band's first American tour quickly pushed both *Dummy* (#79 US) and a reissued "Sour Times" (#53 US, #13 UK) single into the chart during 1995.

Through 1996, Portishead worked at their sophomore set, emerging only to contribute one track, "Mourning Air," to the *War Child* charity album. *Portishead* (#21 US, #2 UK) was finally released in summer 1997, accompanied by the singles "All Mine" (#8 UK), "Over" (#25 UK), and "Only You" (#35 UK). While it was generally regarded as disappointing — an impression which the band themselves later acknowledged — the album was nevertheless the cue for an ambitious performance at New York's Roseland in July 1997, alongside a 30-piece orchestra. This performance would subsequently be released as the *PNYC* (#155 US, #40 UK) live album and video.

Silence again followed, although November 1999 saw Utley teamup with Lupine Howl (ex-Spiritualized) as the Creeping Meetball, at the Ochre Records festival in Gloucester, England.

Portishead LPs

🔟 Dummy (Polygram) 1994 Midnight on a mid-70's movie set, torch singers by torchlight and slow, panning break beats — Beth Gibbons and Geoff Barrow had been scheming what became *Dummy* for over a year. Adrian Utley had been composing private film scores for longer than that.

Barrow's love of hip-hop swept the soundscapes with a seductive pulse, shattered by Gibbons' haunted corncake husk — even without hearing the myriad remixes which spread "Sour Times" across the emotional spectrum.

Elsewhere, "Numb" and the closing "Glory Box" would assert themselves as the foundations upon which a new revolution was built. Subpoenaed by Tricky ("Hell Is Around the Corner"), and butchered by positively anyone else who could spell the words "trip-hop," "Box," in particular, remains the summation of all that Portishead promised and *Dummy* delivered in spades.

4 Portishead (London) 1997 The world kept turning, Portishead remained static — more than static, worse than static. "Cowboys," the opening cut, does not so much reaffirm *Dummy's* brilliance as repeat it. Ditto "All Mine," ditto "Undenied." Three tracks in and they've pulled out exactly the same stops as last time; the twisted spy themes, the scratchy record samples, the keening voice which kind of hurts. But unless modern dance music really does comprise a lot of funny sound effects with a bass line and vocals to separate songs, Portishead came up sorrowfully short.

7 PNYC [LIVE] (Polygram) 1998 Based around the band's July 1997 Roseland appearance, playing alongside a 30-piece orchestra — the video features 15 tracks, the album nine (plus two recorded "sans strings" elsewhere).

POSIES

FORMED 1987 *(Seattle, WA)*
ORIGINAL LINE-UP *Jonathan Auer (vocals, guitar); Ken Stringfellow (vocals, guitar)*

Ken Stringfellow and Jonathan Auer were high school friends whose earliest bands played in their parents' basements, recording on Auer's home studio set-up. Following college, the pair hooked up again in 1987, playing acoustic shows and recording what would become their debut album, *Failure*. Self-released on their own 23 label in March 1988, the cassette created a massive local stir, and was reissued by the PopLlama label in December.

The Posies played their first show at two weeks notice, joined by Rick Roberts (bass) and Mike Musburger (drums) — Stringfellow and Auer were also founder members of Roderick Wolmagott's Sky Cries Mary industrial project, appearing on the band's debut album *Until the Grinders Cease*, and one cut on the *Don't Eat the Dirt* EP, before quitting to concentrate on the Posies.

By mid-1989, the Posies were making regular trips to L.A., and late in the year, they signed with Geffen. Their sophomore album, *Dear 23*, and first single, "Golden Blunders" (later covered by Ringo Starr) appeared in late 1990, recorded with British producer John Leckie, himself fresh from the Stone Roses debut album. Gigs with Redd Kross and the Replacements, were followed by their first national headline tour. And after a second single, "Suddenly Mary," the band went to New York to begin work on their next album with Don Fleming.

Roberts quit early in the process; Auer, Stringfellow, and Musburger continued working as a trio, with Sky Cries Mary's Joe Howard (aka Joe Bass) guesting for live work, before Dave Fox was recruited. Recording and remixing through the remainder of the year, the Posies finally released *Frosting on the Beater* in early '93, and spent spring/summer on the road in the US; the fall in Europe. A single, "Dream All Day" became a major radio/MTV hit; it was followed by "Definite Door" (#67 UK).

Throughout this period, Auer and Stringfellow were also members of the reformed Big Star with Alex Chilton and Jody Stephens — their first gig together was staged the evening of the Posies' own album release party and was subsequently released as a live album. Only one other recording was made, however, a contribution to a Big Star tribute album, which was never released.

Both bands gigged through 1993, often on the same bill; Big Star headlined the Reading Festival, UK in 1993, with the Posies also high on the bill, while the Posies played their own US tour that fall, with Teenage Fanclub. Visits to Japan and Europe followed, before Fox quit. He was replaced by Mick Vee (Flop) for six shows, before Joe Bass returned — having already quit Sky Cries Mary, he had been playing with Pretty Mary Sunshine, whose producer, Keith Cleversley, would also come on board for the next Posies album.

Musburger quit shortly before work began on that set; he was replaced by Brian Young (drums), and *Amazing Disgrace* was released in early 1996, accompanied by the singles "Please Return It" and "Ontario"; European 45's included "Precious Moments" and "Everybody's a Fucking Liar" — a hit in Holland, Spain, and Scandinavia.

At the end of their 1996 tours, the Posies quit Geffen, taking the remainder of the year off to consider the band's future. They played a week of gigs through spring 1997; Stringfellow then cut a solo album, *This Sounds Like Goodbye* (Hidden Agenda) and played a handful of east coast dates with Juliana Hatfield before linking with Lagwagon to co-produce their *Double Plaid-inum* album and tour Europe. He and Young then joined with Bill Bartell (White Flag) and Alejandro Escovedo in Chariot, recording and mixing the *I Am Ben Hur* album in four days.

Work then began on the Posies' farewell album, *Success* (a corollary, of course, to their debut *Failure*), for release in February 1998 and the Posies played a handful of farewell shows around the Northwest, before Stringfellow and Young headed for Europe with Chariot. The Posies followed them, and the band played their final European date in Belgium in August 1998. Their last US dates included Seattle's Bumbershoot the next month. A live album from their final tour was released in Spain in late 1999, to be followed by a Geffen-era best of, and a boxed set of unreleased, live stuff, and rarities.

Howard went on to Sunny Day Real Estate; Stringfellow joined REM as auxiliary guitarist, and also formed his own band, Saltine, with Blake Wescott (guitar, keyboards), John Haslip (bass), and Paul Mumaw (drums). Their debut single, "Reveal Yourself," appeared in the UK and Spain in September 1999. The Posies themselves would return for occasional shows the following summer.

The Posies LPs

6 Failure (23/Popllama) 1988 Introduced an unsuspecting city to its power-pop gurus. Today Seattle, tomorrow — the world. Embryonic roughness wrapped up in pop goodness.

8 Dear 23 (Geffen) 1990 Auer and Stringfellow whip their sound into shape for their sophomore set, a gorgeous explosion packed with catchy harmonies and irresistible hooks while ghosts of the Move and Big Star percolate through the gems "My Big Mouth," "Suddenly Mary," and "Apology."

7 Frosting on the Beater (Geffen) 1993 The Posies flesh out their line-up and add some sonic aggression to their irrepressible pop overload, with big drums and bigger guitars to cut through their sweet exterior.

6 Amazing Disgrace (Geffen) 1996 More capable uplifting power pop, but one that retains the snarl.

7 Success (Popllama) 1998 An out-and-out return to the Posies sound, this album is crammed with all their best-loved attributes — the melody, hooks, and riffs. From "Somehow Everything" and "Fall Apart With Me" to "Fall Song," it's a cracker.

7 Alive Before the Iceberg [LIVE] (Houston Party — Spain) 1999

Selected Compilations and Archive Releases

6 Flavor of the Month (Geffen) 2000

7 At Least at Last (Not Lame) 2000

Ken Stringfellow LP

6 This Sounds Like Goodbye (Hidden Agenda) 1997

Chariot LP

6 I Am Ben Hur (Munster — Spain) 1998

Joe Bass/Skyward LP

7 Skyward (C/Z) 1998 An astonishing album ruled by unexpected instrumentation, slightly spacey production, and for much of the time, Brette Howard's liltingly appealing vocals. "If You Can" is the ghost of several Beatles songs, but hip-hop, funk, and Pink Floyd all get a look in, together with whatever ideas the guest list brought along... Bill Rieflin, sundry Sky Criers (past and present), Matt Chamberlain, Greg Gilmore, Jon Auer, and Amy Denio all take turns to play, and though there's a strong sense that half this album was intended for a different project entirely, the two parts are both complimentary and constant.

PRIMAL SCREAM

FORMED 1984 (Glasgow, Scotland)
ORIGINAL LINE-UP Bobby Gillespie (b. 6/22/64); Jim Beattie (guitar); Robert Young (bass); Martin St. John (tambourine); Tom McGurk (drums)

Ex-Wake vocalist Bobby Gillespie and Primal Scream were already gigging sporadically when he was recruited to play drums for the Jesus and Mary Chain in fall 1984. He quit the Mary Chain the following year, after their Creation label agreed to release Primal Scream's "All Fall Down" (#14 UK indy) single. Recruiting second guitarist Paul Harte, Primal Scream followed through with "Crystal Crescent" (#3 UK indy) in 1985.

By this time, Gillespie was a local figurehead of sorts, running Glasgow's popular Splash One Club, host to such local heroes as the BMX Bandits and the Pastels. Creation Records head (and band manager) Alan McGee moved Primal Scream to his Elevation label, now distributed by WB, and in June 1987, Gillespie unveiled a new line-up, featuring Stuart May (ex-Submarines — rhythm guitar), Andrew Innes (ex-Revolving Paint Dream — guitar) and Phil King (drums) for the "Gentle Tuesday" single. "Imperial" followed, and in October 1987, the band released their psychedelic debut album, *Sonic Flower Groove* (#62 UK). (Original guitarist Jim Beattie later formed Spirea X.)

Gigs (with Dave Morgan replacing King) followed, but by early 1989, further personnel shifts had reduced the band to a core trio of Gillespie, Innes, and Young, plus Jim Navajo (guitar), and Manchester rhythm section Henry Olsen and Philip Tomanov (ex-Nico's live band). The group were still struggling to find their musical feet though; now, Primal Scream's sound hardened around rock guitars and their second, eponymous, album (#1 UK indy) and single, "Ivy Ivy Ivy" (#3 UK indy) were released by Creation in September 1989.

It was the emergence of the British rave scene which finally pointed the band in the right direction, particularly after Gillespie, Young, and Innes met with dance producer Andrew Weatherall. The trio immersed themselves in the new culture and in March 1990, they unveiled an utterly hedonistic electro-rock anthem, "Loaded" (#16 UK); it was followed by the similarly intentioned "Come Together" (#26), both available in a string of often devastating remixes which provided the ultimate soundtrack to a winter of non-stop parties.

June 1991 brought an Orb remix of "Higher Than the Sun" (#40 UK), promoted by the band's first tour in 18 months with a line-up augmented with Denise Johnson (vocalist on much of the album), Hugo Nicolson (keyboards), Martin Duffy (keyboards — ex-Felt), and DJ's

Weatherall and Alex Paterson (the Orb). "Don't Fight It, Feel It" (#41) charted in August, and the following month the album Primal Scream had been threatening all year, *Screamadelica* (#8 UK) finally materialized. It would earn the band the inaugural Mercury Music Prize and while live appearances remained sporadic, a new EP, *Dixie Narco* (#11 UK), led off by the gospel-tinged "Movin' On Up," kept the band boiling.

Primal Scream spent much of the year in Nashville, TN, recording their next album — they returned home to headline a Miners Benefit show in Sheffield in November 1992, then headed back to the US, remaining out of sight throughout 1993 as they pieced together their next album from sessions with producers Jimmy Miller, Tom Dowd, and George Drakoulias. Finally March 1994 brought the George Clinton-led "Rocks" (#7 UK), and the latest Primal Scream line-up of Gillespie, Young, Innes, Duffy, and Johnson launched a 15-date UK tour in March, followed by a two month US tour opening for Depeche Mode.

Another dramatic reinvention of the band's sound and style, this time towards a bluesy (Stones-y) groove, *Give Out But Don't Give Up* (#2 UK) was followed by the singles, "Jailbird" (#29 UK) and "I'm Gonna Cry Myself Blind" (#49 UK), as Primal Scream continued gigging — by year's end, they would have played 100 shows, including the Reading and Strathclyde (Scotland) festivals, and a two night homecoming at Glasgow's Barrowlands.

1995 opened with an appearance at the Big Day Out festival in Melbourne, Australia; Primal Scream also contributed the title track to the *Trainspotting* movie soundtrack, then joined author Irvine Welsh and producer Adrian Sherwood on the expletive-packed "The Big Man and the Scream Team Meet the Barmy Army Uptown" (#17 UK) single. The group then returned to the studio.

With former Stone Roses bassist Gary "Mani" Mounfield now on board, Primal Scream's fifth album, *Vanishing Point* (#2 UK), was released in July 1997 surrounded by three hit singles, "Kowalski" (#8 UK), "Star" (#16 UK), and "Burning Wheel" (#17 UK). The *Echo Dek* remix EP (#43 UK) wrapped up another active year — and preluded another lengthy period of silence, while the group worked on their next album.

A short UK tour in February 1998 was followed in March by a benefit gig alongside Asian Dub Foundation. There would also be live appearances at the Creamfields and Glastonbury festivals, but the majority of the year was devoted to sessions with New Order's Bernard Sumner and My Bloody Valentine's Kevin Shields among others. Finally in October 1999, Creation's internet radio station aired a two song preview from the band's still-gestating sixth album. The single "Swastika Eyes," with production from the Chemical Brothers and a remix by Jagz Kooner (Sabres of Paradise) announced the band's rebirth in November; *XTRMNTR* (#3 UK) followed in February 2000.

Primal Scream LPs

6 Sonic Flower (Groove Elevation) 1987 Driving British beat-inflected takes on a merciless theme of sub-Stooges blues, immensely powerful, but wearing in large doses.

7 Primal Scream (Mercenary) 1989 "Gimme Gimme Teenage Head" pretty much encapsulates the pounding garage trash which are still the Scream's invigorating stock in trade.

9 Screamadelica (Sire) 1991 Suddenly sign posting the musical possibilities of the now-flourishing acid club scene, joyously careening across funk, house, R&B, gospel, and ambience, the experimental electro effects and Andy Weatherall's production makes each excursion sound more fabulous than the last.

7 Give Out But Don't Give Up (Sire) 1994 A more traditional Scream album — the adrenalin rock stomp of the early albums — heightened by an awareness of what made *Screamadelica* so great.

8 Vanishing Point (Reprise) 1997 The clubby beats and psychedelic guitar return, slamming into a distinctly dangerous liaison with a bunch of grooved-up Stones-y riffs and a defiant refusal to stick with any direction. Muddled, then, but the ever-changing, ever-intriguing electronics keep things astoundingly fresh.

9 XTRMNTR (Reprise) 2000 Dominated by the blistering "Swastika Eyes," *XTRMNTR* follows its predecessor into a ferocious rock/dance hybrid — on this evidence, Primal Scream might well be the most exciting British band of the century so far.

Further Reading

Primal Scream by Stuart Coles (Omnibus, UK, 1998).

PRODIGY

FORMED 1990 *(London, England)*
ORIGINAL LINE-UP *Liam Howlett (b. 8/21/71, Braintree, England — keyboards); Keith Flint (9/17/69, Braintree, England — vocals); Leeroy Thornhill (b. 10/8/68, Peterborough, England — dancer); MC Maxim (b. Keith Palmer, 3/21/67, Nottingham, England)*

Liam Howlett was 16 when he joined his first group, Cut to Kill, a local Essex hip-hop band, as their second DJ. He remained on board for two years, during which time he also studied graphic design, and built his reputation as a local club DJ. Eventually, Cut to Kill recorded a demo album and begun shopping it to labels, but Howlett quit when the band inked with Tam Tam Records on the strength of one of his songs, yet left him out of the deal. Around 1988, he walked out of the hip-hop scene and straight into rave.

Spending most of his time at the Barn, a favorite hangout of the then-chartbound Sunscreem, Howlett worked as a T-shirt designer in between DJ-ing gigs and, following victory in a Capital Radio mixing contest, recorded a ten-track demo and began shopping for a label. After a succession of rejections, XL finally took him on, and in November 1990, The Prodigy was signed.

Early in the new year Howlett met Keith Flint while DJ-ing at an after club party. Flint was another Barn regular and asked Howlett if he had a mix tape available — Howlett, who had never thought in those terms before, put together a cassette with his DJ set on one side and his own music on the other, and Flint returned several days later with a friend, Leeroy Thornhill, to ask Howlett if he was interested in playing live, and whether they could join him on stage as dancers.

The trio were joined by a third dancer, Sharky, and MC Maxim Reality (aka Keith Palmer), a 2-Tone/reggae buff who cut his rapping teeth with Sheik Yan Groove, and the Prodigy duly debuted with a 25-minute performance at the Labyrinth in Dalston, London, in February 1991. Four of the songs in the set had already been earmarked for their forthcoming debut EP, *What Evil Lurks*; the band would also release a single, "Android," to instant club success.

"Everybody in the Place" became another favorite, particularly after DJ Coldcut began working with it. According to Howlett, "for an hour during his set, he'd keep a copy of that record on one of [his three] decks the whole time. He'd mix off the other two turntables, and kept dropping it in over the top, because he liked it so much." The song would later be remixed and released as a single in its own right, selling over 7,000 copies on the underground dance scene.

The Prodigy stepped up their live work accordingly. Sharky quit, but Flint and Thornhill's performances remained breakneck extravaganzas, while Maxim began revising his original raps, simplifying his lyrics and letting them fall into the music's natural groove. Nevertheless, the Prodigy finally broke through in the most unexpected way, after Howlett sampled a popular public service TV commercial, "starring" a cat named Charly. Attached to the band's new single — aptly titled "Charly" (#3 UK).

The record topped the UK dance chart in August 1991, and inspired a major backlash throughout the rave community as a host of other electro-DJs began grafting their own favorite children's TV themes and slogans to their latest records. Suddenly the dance floors were swamped by "Charly" sound alikes, rave itself became synonymous with such monstrosities as "Sesame's Treat," and *Mixmag* spoke for many when it placed Howlett on its cover, holding a gun to his head over the caption "Did Charly Kill Rave?" The

Prodigy avenged themselves by burning a copy of the same issue in the video for their "Fire" single a year later.

The band continued gigging through the remainder of 1991, making their US debut at New York's Limelight, and taking advantage of the visit to film a video for the reissued "Everybody in the Place" (#2 UK). A return trip to America landed the group a deal with Elektra, while the summer was spent playing European festivals and recording their debut album, *Experience* (#12 UK). So long-awaited, the album would be released in October 1992, hot on the heels of "Fire" (#11); it went gold scant weeks later and, in commercial terms, did what no UK techno act had ever accomplished in the past — translating single hits into album successes.

For their next UK tour, The Prodigy introduced a live guitarist, Jim Davies, just as "Out of Space" (#5 UK) offered up another major hit. Successful tours of Australia in December, and the US in the new year, followed, but Howlett's personal musical tastes were beginning to change. Already disillusioned by the rave scene's sudden rush to emulate "Charly"; disgusted, too, with the way in which big business promoters had seized upon what had once been an essentially free, and certainly anarchic, movement, Howlett was leaving rave behind. The Prodigy, of course, had to follow.

"Wind It Up" (#11 UK), radically remixed from the album, was his first tentative step to the next level; but it was the release of two purposefully anonymous singles under the name Earthbound, which truly changed his perspective. Elitist club DJs who made a virtue of dismissing anything and everything by an "established" act went wild for Earthbound — only to choke on their enthusiasms when the new Prodigy single, "One Love" (#8 UK), emerged to inform them that Earthbound were Prodigy, and this was what they now sounded like.

Remixing songs for Jesus Jones and Front 242 added to Howlett's own musical palate, and introduced rockier elements to The Prodigy; a collaboration with Pop Will Eat Itself, "Their Law," and another new recording, "Rhythm of Life," expanded things further. By the time their second album, *Music for a Jilted Generation* (#198 US, #1 UK), was complete, the band were almost unrecognizable. Weeks later, Elektra dropped the band in America. (The album charted in the US following its reactivation by Madonna's Maverick label.)

Three singles, "No Good (Start the Dance)" (#4 UK), "Voodoo People" (#13 UK), and "Poison" (#15 UK), punctuated an intensive year of live work. The Prodigy performed live in some 25 different countries worldwide during 1994–95, a hectic schedule which precluded their return to the studio until early 1996 to work on a new single.

Howlett wrote "Firestarter" (#30 US, #1 UK) in two days; Flint slammed down his first ever vocal; and with its distinctive hook borrowed from The Art of Noise's "Close (To the Edit)" (prompting absurd rumors that the Prodigy were really a Trevor Horn invention), the band scored their biggest hit yet, a single which remained in the UK Top 75 for almost five months, topped the charts in seven other countries, and racked up worldwide sales of 750,000+. The song also became the first techno/electronica hit ever to make the US Top 30.

An incendiary video screened on *Top of the Pops* caused the BBC switchboards to light up in horror; one UK tabloid launched a campaign to "Ban This Sick Record" — which, of course, only increased the single's sales; and with the band (on the road all summer, with new guitarist Giz Butt on board) resisting a follow-up release until year's end, their back catalog went into overdrive. Eight earlier singles returned to the UK Top 75 during the summer; when "Breathe" (#1 UK) finally emerged in November 1996, it was the most predictable chart-topper of the year in nine different countries.

Maverick launched "Firestarter" in America in the new year, giving Howlett longer in which to complete the band's third album. The tactic paid off. Saturated by "Firestarter" and "Breathe," and tales of The Prodigy's manic hybrid of techno, punk, and armageddon, the US public and media alike were in a state of frenzy long before *The Fat of the Land* (#1 US, #1 UK) arrived in stores on June 30, 1997. Even before release it was a guaranteed hit in America and Britain alike; before release, too, the title of the album's first single, "Smack My Bitch Up" (#89 US, #8 UK), sampling the Ultramagnetics' "Give the Drummer Some," was guaranteed to raise temperatures even higher.

Of course, the song was not about wife-beating — it was, however, about getting a big reaction out of people with the minimum of effort. In the US, Wal-Mart and K-Mart both insisted on the title being amended, to "Smack My B**** Up" ("Funky Shit" was similarly altered). In the UK, MP Barry Gardiner fought to have the promotional poster campaign for the single withdrawn; and around the world, people looked askance at Jonas Akerlund's graphic accompanying video.

Even the band's contemporaries regarded the song with some distaste. When The Prodigy played the Reading Festival in August 1998, fellow headliners The Beastie Boys personally requested the band omit the song from their set, with Ad Rock insisting, "from where I'm from, it isn't cool." The Prodigy ignored them. "The track is probably the most pointless I've ever written," Howlett said. "It's almost too in your face to be offensive. But that's what's a shame about so many artists in our position, they become more boring the bigger they get. We want to keep it dangerous, because if it's not, it's not interesting anymore."

The Prodigy spent the summers of both 1997 and 1998 playing festivals; they also joined the Lollapalooza '97 caravan across the US. Fall, however, was devoted to lapping up the applause of the industry. In 1997 alone, "Breathe" won the Viewers Choice award at the MTV Video Awards in both the US and Europe; MTV Europe, in addition, crowned them Best Dance Act for the third time; *Q* magazine adjudged Prodigy the Best Live Act of the year; *Rolling Stone* readers voted them Best Electronic Act.

1999 brought a year of comparative silence; Howlett's *Dirt Chamber Sessions* (#136 US) remix album, and sessions with Massive Attack (for the spring 2000 single, "No Souvenir") were followed by both Maxim and Leeroy announcing solo albums.

The Prodigy LPs

8 Experience (Elektra) 1991 And what a prodigious experience it was, each song a masterpiece of samples and rhythms as the album shifts through a host of subgenres that include rave, house, drum & bass, and even proto-trip-hop, sublimely capturing on record the mood, feel, and pure exhilaration of the early UK club scene.

8 Music for the Jilted Generation (Elektra) 1994 The darker, angrier tone was a defiant dance-til-they-pull-the-plug roar, the songs first honed in front of live audiences — and sounding like it.

9 Fat of the Land (Maverick) 1997 Having gone as far as he could in one direction, programmer Howlett now doubles smartly back, returning to his own hip-hop and punk roots. The ensuing collision, characterized by "Firestarter" and the so-brutal-it's-brilliant "Smack My Bitch Up," is charring in its intensity.

Selected Compilations and Archive Releases

8 The Prodigy Presents the Dirt Chamber Sessions Vol 1 1999 (XL/Beggars Banquet) Bomb the Bass, Charlatans UK, Beastie Boys, Fatboy Slim, the Sex Pistols, Digital Underground, and the Jimmy Castor Bunch (yes, *that* Jimmy Castor Bunch) ride raucously through the mix, fading in and out of one another's best bits, and creating an ambience which is nothing short of riotous.

Giz Butt/Janus Stark LP

6 Great Adventure Cigar (Trauma) 1999 The title may come courtesy of the Wu-Tang Clan, but the Prodigy's live guitarist's own project is a bewildering mix of old school punk, new school melodies, and rock's greatest riffs and leads. There's lots of tasty tidbits, but squeezed together it's a rather unappetizing mishmash, even if the playing is at times breath-taking.

Further Reading

The Fat of the Land by Martin Roach (Omnibus, UK, 1997).

PSYCHEDELIC FURS

FORMED 1978 (London, England)
ORIGINAL LINE-UP Richard Butler (b. 6/5/56, Kingston Upon Thames, England — vocals); Tim Butler (b. 12/7/58, Kingston Upon Thames — bass); Simon Butler (guitar); Roger Morris (guitar); Duncan Kilburn (sax); Nick Sealy (drums)

Formed by the three Butler brothers, Richard, Tim, and Simon, the Psychedelic Furs suffered the first of a multitude of early line-up changes when Simon quit, fearing that with three siblings on board, the group would turn into the Bee Gees. A band whose first ever live show involved a ramshackle and apparently endless version of Jonathan Richman's "Roadrunner," however, was never going to attain those heights.

At the outset, the group's only real intention was to make as much noise as possible, in front of as many people as they could. To this end, they would tape songs off the radio, then send them to club owners in lieu of demos — hoping, of course, that the recipients didn't recognize the songs within. Few did, and so the band stumbled into life. One early gig was highlighted by the employment of an on-stage vacuum cleaner; others saw the group play just three songs for half an hour, because that's all they knew.

Not until the band was joined by former Unwanted drummer Paul Wilson and guitarist John Ashton (b. 11/30/57) in November 1978 did they take on a semblance of musical cohesion; with the addition of an increasingly ambitious light show giving credence to their name, by mid-1979 the Furs were one of the hottest attractions on the London pub circuit, feted by the press, watched by David Bowie (who would, 15 years later, record their "Pretty in Pink") and courted by every label in Britain.

Wilson quit; former Straight 8 drummer Rod Johnson stayed around long enough to play on the band's first John Peel session. Vince Ely (ex-Photons, and before that, a member of the short-lived Moors Murderers with Chrissie Hynde and Steve Strange) joined shortly before the band went into the studio to record their first single, "We Love You," for October 1979 release.

Originally signed to Epic, the band followed their A&R man Howard Thompson to CBS on the eve of the single's release — Thompson also produced "We Love You," but handed the reins to Steve Lillywhite before work began on the band's first album.

Designed to replicate their live show, *Psychedelic Furs* (#18 UK) was issued in March 1980, following a UK tour with Iggy Pop; with the album's success, the Furs then launched their first headline tour, before returning to the studio with Joy Division producer Martin Hannett, to record some extra songs for the American version of their debut album after US

CBS balked at the inclusion of the closing "Blacks" (#140 US).

The album's release preluded the band's first visit to the US in the summer; it was a success, and the band arranged a second visit that fall, first in their own right, then supporting Talking Heads.

So much live experience impacted heavily on the band's sound, trimming away their improvisational instincts and honing Richard Butler's songwriting. Two new singles in early 1981, "Mr. Jones" and "Dumb Waiters" (#59 UK), previewed a second Lillywhite-produced album, *Talk Talk Talk* (#89 US, #30 UK), while "Pretty in Pink" (#43 UK) would so impress actress Molly Ringwald that, in 1986, she had John Hughes write an entire movie around it — prompting the band to rerecord the track for the accompanying soundtrack album (#41 US, #18 UK).

Morris and Kilburn quit the band following a summer 1981 European tour; as a quartet of Ely, Ashton, and the Butlers, the Furs then traveled to Woodstock to record with producer Todd Rundgren (an earlier choice, David Bowie, was unavailable). He completely rejected the band's preferred method of working, jamming in the studio until something gelled, and instead forced them to go away until they had an album's worth of songs; the result was a lush, widescreen collection which augmented the band with cellist Ann Sheldon, and horn players Donn Adams, Mars Williamson, and Windo.

In July 1982, the first taster for the album, "Love My Way" (#44 US, #42 UK) was released as an instant hit single; the album, *Forever Now* (#61 US, #20 UK), followed in September, and with Ely replaced by former Birthday Party drummer Phil Calvert the band launched its first world tour in October. (From the album sessions, both Sheldon and Windo would join the group for the ensuing tour, together with future London Suede producer, pianist Ed Bueller.)

The Butlers moved to New York the following summer, while Ashton remained in the UK. Gestating songs would be sent back and forth by mail, and it would be close to a year before the band was ready to record again, with Billy Idol producer Keith Forsey. The group was now officially a trio — Calvert was sacked (on Forsey's recommendation), and replaced with session man Tommy Price; but still the resultant *Mirror Moves* (#43 US, #15 UK) would emerge the Furs' most clearly defined offering yet.

Hits "Heaven" (#29 UK) and "The Ghost in You" (#59 US, #68 UK) established the Furs as chart regulars through 1984; the accompanying tour, with guitarist Mike Mooney and drummer Paul Garristo, was similarly successful. In the US, the band had graduated to stadia, but the nine month outing left them exhausted. Their next album, the Chris Kimsey produced *Midnight to Midnight* (#29 US, #12 UK), wouldn't appear until 1987, by which time the Furs — by the members own admission — had lost all sense of themselves.

Having already broadsided the band's traditional audience with the punching "Heartbreak Beat" (#26 US), *Midnight to Midnight* was a bombastically produced set custom-built for the stadium show, with new second guitarist Marty Williamson and future Pink Floyd sideman Jon Carin (key-

© Jim Steinfeldt/Chansley Entertainment Archives

boards) contributing to the overwhelming wall of sound. Still the album entered the US Top 30, the only Furs' album to do so, and Richard Butler himself admitted, "it wasn't until six months later, on tour, I thought... 'Wow, I hate this'." Within weeks, he'd worried himself into such a state that his doctors initially thought he was having heart problems — not until the tour was over was his condition diagnosed as stress.

He was not alone in his distaste — the band almost broke up in the aftermath of *Midnight to Midnight*; instead, a scaled back line-up comprising the Butlers, Ashton, returning drummer Ely, and keyboardist Joe McGinty, returned to the studio to record a new single with Smiths' producer Stephen Street, the low-key "All That Money Wants" (#75 UK), for inclusion on the *All of This and Nothing* (#102 US, #64 UK) compilation.

A new album followed; *Book of Days* (#138 US, #74 UK), too, scaled the Furs back somewhat, reclaiming one of the band's earliest dreams of making an album without any (obvious) singles on it. It re-established, too, many of the precepts upon which the Furs were originally built; and looking back years later, all three core members acknowledged it should have been the band's final record — it would, indeed, have made a fine farewell.

Instead, coming off tour in 1990 (with drummer Don Yallech in for the non-touring Ely, and second guitarist, Knox Chandler), Ashton and McGinty joined the Butlers in New York, and work began on *World Outside* (#68 UK). Unfortunately, as Tim Butler reflected, "by then we'd lost grip of our audience, so when it came out and was lukewarmly received, even though it got great reviews, I think we saw it as a slap in the face, the audience saying we don't want you anymore." The Furs responded by breaking up.

The Butlers would remain together in an early incarnation of Love Spit Love (Tim Butler later withdrew); Ashton moved into sessions, working with Kristen Hall and Mercury Rev, among others. The Furs themselves would be remembered, appropriately, with the *Should God Forget* boxed set.

Also see the entry for "LOVE SPIT LOVE" on page 471.

Psychedelic Furs LPs

9 The Psychedelic Furs (CBS — UK) 1980
8 The Psychedelic Furs (Columbia) 1980 Brooding, hypnotic, yearning, bruised and bruising, the Furs' extraordinary debut showers down melancholy melodies which insidiously shift between the band members, before unleashing an avalanche of solos, riffs, and atmospheres. Producer Steve Lillywhite beautifully captures the band's own shimmering moods, from the trance-like "Sister Europe" to the anarchic medley of "Blacks" and "Radio," then completes the package with "Flowers," whose cacophonous conclusion is the closest the Furs ever come to rep-

licating their live sound on record. The US edition drops the medley, in favor of two distinctly lesser cuts recorded later with producer Martin Hannett.

8 Talk Talk Talk (Columbia) 1981 Kicking off with "Pretty in Pink," (*so* far removed from the later remake for the movie of the same name), Lillywhite graces the band with a sleeker, more sophisticated sound, while retaining their sonic density.

8 Forever Now (Columbia) 1982 Even tighter song structures, an even cleaner sound, filled with producer Todd Rundgren's keyboards and the slickly professional horn section. The title track and hit single "Love My Way" are the standouts, both totally accessible pop with just enough bittersweet edge to keep New Wavers happy, while "Danger," with its funk fired horns, clearly shows the band breaking with the past.

9 Mirror Moves (Columbia) 1984 Producer Keith Forsey encouraged the Furs to record *Mirror* with a drum machine, then created a glossy, slick sound to accompany it. There's still hints of the band's post-punk grandeur to be heard, most notably on "Highwire Days," but the silky "Heaven" and urban sax-drenched "Heartbeat" were more representative — the weird thing is, how magnificent it all ended up.

7 Midnight to Midnight (Columbia) 1987 Chris Kimsey's production is slick enough to slide down and clean enough to eat off, making *Midnight* the *Miami Vice* of albums — glossy, sleek, with expensive tastes and impeccable style. Huge drums, stadium guitars, and Pink Floyd's Jon Carin's keyboards fill gaps which are as effective blaring from disco or stadium speakers.

7 Book of Days (Columbia) 1989 After *Midnight's* excesses, *Book* was deliberately down played, a nearly lo-fi showcase for the Furs' return to their hypnotic, yearning sound of yore. The droney title track and the darkly driving "House" both recaptured the moods of 1979. Unfortunately, that was ten years ago.

7 World Outside (Columbia) 1991 *World* repeats the past by moving again in a much more pop direction. Incorporating hints of the orient (the multi-shaded "Valentine"), strong, haunting melodies, swirling atmosphere (all found on the bittersweet "Until She Comes," with its echoes of "Pretty in Pink") and even a nod to the driving rock of yesteryear ("In My Head"), the Furs recapture all their former glories — and a few of their mistakes.

Selected Compilations and Archive Releases

7 All of This and Nothing (Columbia) 1988 Random best of boasting two new songs, pre-empting the return to basics of *Book of Days*.

9 Radio One Sessions (Strange Fruit, UK) 1997 Manic, dense, psychedelic and furry, the early band occupied that peculiar void which the Velvets had exited and Bowie often dreamed of, but unless you caught them live at the time, you'd never know it from their records. Five Furs sessions, all but one dating from the band's first two years, help plug that gap in your learning, with the first actually predating their record deal. There, radical versions of "Imitation of Christ," "Fall," "Sister Europe," and "We

Love You" catch the band itself caught between the wanton expression of their fog and light-drenched stage set, and the sheer melodic majesty of their actual songs.

6 B-Sides and Lost Grooves (Columbia) 1994 Sweeping up the rarities, a jumble of radio edits and overlong 12-inchers does the band a fairly grim disservice. They were so much better than this.

9 Should God Forget: A Retrospective (Columbia) 1997 Double set offering up some great rarities, including — for the first time on CD — "Blacks"/"Radio," as well as two songs culled from Peel sessions ("Mack the Knife" and "Soap Commercial"), a previously unreleased alternate version of "Alice's House," and a keen selection of live tracks.

PSYCHIC TV

FORMED 1981 (London, England)
ORIGINAL LINE-UP Genesis P-Orridge (b. 1950, Manchester — vocals, instruments); Alex Fergusson (guitar); Peter Christopherson (tape, processors, trumpet); + others

Genesis P-Orridge and new wife Paula, having left Throbbing Gristle behind them, did not waste any time in continuing their musical career, immediately forming Psychic TV around what looked, on paper, to be a more musical collaboration — Alex Fergusson of Alternative TV joined TG's Peter Christopherson in the new group's ranks.

However, from the moment the group played its first live show in Manchester in November 1983, P-Orridge insisted that for all its apparent musicality, PTV was simply the musical wing of the quasi-religious Thee Temple of Psychic Youth, and would continue on from where Gristle left off — with an added pop super-consciousness.

Featuring contributions from wife Paula, Current 93's David Tibet and Marc Almond, PTV debuted with *Force the Hand of Chance* in 1982, quickly following through with *Dreams Less Sweet*, and the first of many PTV live albums, *NY Scum Haters*.

Christopherson quit in 1984 to devote himself to Coil; he was replaced by Fred Gianelli, who would also maintain a fairly high solo profile, debuting that same year with the Turning Shrines project (their self-titled album appeared on PTV's own Temple label). Such comings and goings did little to shake PTV's equilibrium, however — live shows tended to be fully improvised, albums only slightly less so.

At the same time, PTV were capable of creating some blistering pop music, and twice in 1984 the band found itself riding high on the chart, with "Roman P" (#13 UK indy) and the *Unclean* EP (#12 UK indy). In April 1986, they went even further with "Godstar" (#67 UK, #1 UK indy), dedicated to/written about the late Rolling Stone, Brian Jones, and a remarkably faithful cover of the Beach Boys' "Good Vibrations" (#65 UK).

Another bastion of establishment normalcy was breached when PTV bulldozed its way into the *Guinness Book of Records*, courtesy of a mind boggling collection of live albums, initially intended to be released on the 23rd of each month for 23 months. The series eventually petered out after 18 albums released between 1986–90, but 14 British albums in 18 months — including nine UK indy Top 30 hits — were enough for the record keepers.

Another successful PTV tactic was their infiltration of Britain's house and rave scene in 1988 — P-Orridge is generally credited with creating the term "acid house," after seeing "acid" alone on a Detroit record label. The PTV hit "Tune in (Turn On) to the Acid House" (#8 UK indy) announced his intentions in August 1988, and over the next three years, the band orchestrated a string of powerful techno/house compilation albums, purportedly featuring a plethora of unknown British and American artists, but actually all the work of P-Orridge and co. Such titles as *Jack the Tab, High Jack,* and *Tekno Acid Beat* saw PTV moving into areas where they might never have been welcomed under their own name.

PTV's adventures on the fringe of British society came to an end when one of P-Orridge's recently released performance art videos was excerpted, completely out of context, on a 1992 British TV program dealing with child abuse. The police raided his Brighton home, confiscating quantities of videos, books, and magazines whose content, of course, could be further used against P-Orridge and his chosen lifestyle, and later that year, he and Paula relocated to California. (The UK wing of PTV would release one album in his absence, 1993's *Peak Hour*.)

A collaboration with acid guru Timothy Leary followed, together with a brief liaison with Pigface. A new PTV album, however, would not emerge until 1996's *Trip Reset*, accompanied by a major US tour; other releases through the intervening years, tended to be either compilations or reissues. P-Orridge formally disbanded the group in 1997.

Psychic TV LPs

8 Force the Hand of Chance (Some Bizzare) 1982 The full Psychic TV experience previewed across one chaotic double album — lovely ballads, screaming noise, pristine pop, the lot.

7 Psychic TV Themes (Temple) 1982 Close in form to what Eno was doing, closer in intent to all Barry Adamson would go on to. Reissued in 1992 as *Cold Dark Matter* (Splinter Test)

9 Dreams Less Sweet (Some Bizzare) 1983 The moment "Hymn 23" and/or "White Nights" kicks in is the moment you lose all preconceptions about PTV. An avant-world music extravaganza, packed with moving soundscapes and dreamy savagery, musically it might be the most accomplished record P-Orridge ever made.

4 N.Y. Scum Haters [LIVE] (Temple) 1984

7 25 December 1984: A Pagan Day (Temple) 1984

7 Mouth Ov Thee Night (Temple) 1985

6 Those Who Do Not [LIVE] (Gramm — Iceland) 1985 An edited version of this set appeared in the Live 23 series.

6 Descending [LIVE] (Sordide Sentimental — France) 1985

5 Themes, Vol. 2 (Temple) 1985

6 Themes, Vol. 3 (Temple) 1987 Random soundtrack work, including a gallery exhibit of 20+ video monitors, all showing the people who were looking at them.

9 Allegory and Self (Temple) 1988 The staggering "Godstar" gets things underway, and things never let up from there. Pure modern psychedelic dance pop!

4 Kondole/Dead Cat (Temple) 1989 Deceptive timings see the promised 23 minutes of "Dead Cat" actually come in at less than ten, but it's so dull that it does seem that long.

8 Towards Thee Infinite Beat (Wax Trax!) 1990

6 Beyond Thee Infinite Beat [REMIXES] (Wax Trax!) 1990 With "Infinite Beat" and "Drone Zone" on board, another of PTV's wide-open dance monsters, powerful and even pretty in places. The remixes don't add too much, but are colorful.

5 Tarot Ov Abomination (Splinter Test) 1993 Meandering soundtrack to the movie *The Wanderer*.

7 A Hollow Cost (Invisible) 1994

8 Cathedral Engine (Dossier) 1998

4 Thee Fractured Garden (Invisible) 1995 Instrumental, ambient and spoken word versions of the same concept.

7 Breathe (Dossier) 1995 Live ambient music with tablas and spoken word improvisation by P-Orridge.

8 Trip Reset (Cleopatra) 1995 Rooted in a characteristically idiosyncratic middle ground between space rock and ambient, a delightfully dreamy journey which nods most publicly in the direction of early Pink Floyd (a cover of "Set the Controls," and a tribute to Syd Barrett).

7 Cold Blue Torch (Cleopatra) 1995

7 Brutal (Invisible) 1996 The "dark side" alternative to *Trip Reset*.

7 Beauty from Thee Beast (Visionary) 1996

6 Ov Power (Cold Spring) 1998

Live 23 Albums

#1: Live in Tokyo [1986] (Temple) 1986

#2: Live in Paris aka City Ov Paris [1986] (Temple) 1986

#3 Live in Heaven [London, 1986] (Temple) 1987

#4: Live in Glasgow [1986] (Temple) 1987

#5: Live in Reykjavik [1983] (Temple) 1987

#6: Live En Suisse [1986] (Temple) 1987

#7: Live in Gottingen [Germany, 1984] (Temple)1987

#8: Live in Toronto [1986] (Temple) 1987

#9: Temporary Temple [London, 1984] (Temple) 1987

#10: Thee Yellow Album/Psychedelic Violence (Temple) 1988

#11: Live at Mardi Gras [Nottingham, 1987] (Temple) 1988

#12: Live at Thee Circus [London, 1987–88] (Temple) 1988

#13: Live at Thee Ritz [Manchester, 1983] (Temple) 1989

#14: Live at Thee Pyramid [NYC, 1988] (Temple) 1989

#15: Live in Bregenz [Austria, 1985] (Temple) 1989

#16: A Real Swedish Live Show (Temple) 1989

#17: Live at Thee Berlin Wall Part 1 (Temple) 1990

#18: Live at Thee Berlin Wall Part 2 (Temple) (ave. 5) 1990

Selected Compilations and Archive Releases

4 City Ov London/City Ov Glasgow 1991 Reissue of *...Heaven/...Glasgow* volumes.

6 Stained by Dark Horses (Splinter Test) 1993 Anthology of PTV soundtracks to movies by Derek Jarman and P-Orridge.

5 Sugarmorphoses (Splinter Test) 1993 Soundtracks and tones dating back to 1965.

9 Hex Sex: The Singles, Pt. 1 (Cleopatra) 1994

8 Godstar: The Singles, Pt. 2 (Cleopatra) 1995 Stunning collections featuring the band's most accessible work.

4 Electric Newspaper, Issues 1–3 (Dossier — Germany) 1995 Collections of samples and loops from past PTV recordings.

8 The Best Of: Time's Up (Cleopatra) 1999 Collection drawing from similar sources to *Hex Sex/Godstar*.

Psychic TV/XKP LP

7 Al-Or-Al: Thee Transmutation of Mercury (Dossier) 1994 Steps 10–12 of an aural devotion to Alaura. The final step 13 appeared on the *From Here to Eternity* compilation (Silent).

Genesis P-Orridge & White Stains LP

6 At Stockholm (Psychick — Sweden) 1990

PTV3 LP

6 Directions Ov Travel (Topy) 1991 P-Orridge less UK wing of PTV.

Pseudo Compilations

8 Jack the Tab: Acid Tablets, Vol. 1 (Castalia) 1988 Excellent techno/acid album disguised as a compilation to hide the fact that it is all PTV/Genesis.

7 Tekno Acid Beat (Temple) 1988 Fred Gianelli's Sickmob and John Gosling's Sugardog line up alongside the rest of the japes.

8 High Jack: Politics of Ecstasy (Wax Trax) 1990 Remixes and samples of *Jack the Tab*.

8 Presents Ultrahouse: The La Connection (Wax Trax!) 1991

7 Ultradrug (Visionary) 1995 Remixes from the Ultrahouse album.

7 Sirens (Visionary — UK) 1995 The *Ultradrug* sequel, featuring tribal remixes by Andrew Weatherall.

8 The Origin of the Species (Invisible) 1998

8 Origin of the Species, Vol. 2 (Invisible) 1999 Double CD repackages of much of the above.

Fred Gianelli/Turning Shrines LPs

7 Turning Shrines (Temple) 1984

6 Fred (Wax Trax!) 1991

6 Painkiller (Telepathic) 1994

Peak Hour LP

7 Peak Hour (Temple) 1993

PUBLIC IMAGE LTD

FORMED 1978 *(London, England)*

ORIGINAL LINE-UP *John Lydon (b. 1/31/56, Finsbury Park, London — vocals); Keith Levene (guitar); Jah Wobble (b. John Wardle — bass); Jim Walker (drums)*

When John Lydon left the Sex Pistols following their American tour in January 1978, he had just three alternatives open to him.

The first, the easiest, was to sink into iconic oblivion, a specter to be invoked by future, awe-stricken critics, his untarnished punk purity an object lesson to everyone who tried carrying on past their sell-by date. The second, the saddest, was to form a new rock'n'roll band, and hope that public image and crowd credulity would be enough to sell a few more records. And the third was to stick with his public image alone, the antisocial outsider with chips on both shoulders, and deliver a gesture to match. Which, of course, is what he did.

Following a warm-up in Brussels, Belgium, on December 12, 1978, PiL debuted in London on Christmas Day, a deliberately spiteful gesture on a day when even public transport had the day off. 2,000 people poured out anyway to witness the Rotter's Return, and they poured away barely half an hour later, after a performance which made the Ramones look sluggish. PiL played for thirty minutes — time enough to air their debut single ("Public Image") twice, a few bass solos once, and a couple of songs from their forthcoming first album. And that was only the opening act in a career which would reduce most musicians' notions of rebellion to something akin to mild bellyache.

That first single came wrapped in a fake newspaper (#9 UK), but at least preluded an eponymous debut album (#22 UK) of more-or-less accessible post-punk dub funk. Lydon's love of Krautrock and reggae was no secret even at the height of the Pistols; by the time *Public Image* was released a year after Lydon quit the Pistols, the publicity machine had already stoked public anticipation to fever pitch.

Drummer Walker quit in January 1979; he was replaced first by Dave Crowe, then Richard Dudanski (ex-Raincoats) and PiL spent much of the year working on their sophomore album, a metal box containing three 12-inch singles — titled, of course, *Metal Box* (#18 UK. (The conventionally packed US edition was titled simply *Second Edition* — #171 US). Remixed from the album's "Swan Lake," PiL scored a second hit single with "Death Disco" (#20 UK), written for Lydon's mother while she was dying of cancer and documenting her suffering through his emotions. She apparently thought it was great. A second single, "Memories" (#60 UK) followed.

The addition of Jeanette Lee (keyboards) made little difference to the PiL attack — as proven by the *Paris Au Printemps* live album (#61 UK), recorded in France in spring 1980. Dudanski then quit, to be replaced by Martin Atkins (b. 8/3/59, Coventry), again without dire repercussions. The departure of Jah Wobble in July 1980, however, dealt a major body blow to the band's sound, and with a Far East tour looming, PiL relocated to Pasadena to audition for a replacement.

Of all the musicians who passed through the sessions, Atkins favored one Michael Balzary (aka Flea), then playing with L.A. punks Fear. He turned them down, while Atkins, too, was not long for the band. He was sacked midway through recording PiL's third album, and his drum parts replaced by Lydon and Levene for 1981's *Flowers of Romance* (#114 US, #11 UK), and the single of the same name (#24 UK).

Lydon relocated to New York in 1982, prompting at least partially justified rumors of a PiL split — Lee and Levene both quit, the latter midway through sessions for the band's next studio album, leaving Lydon and the returning Atkins to piece together a new line-up around Pete Jones (bass) and Ken Lockie (keyboards — ex-Cowboys International). This line-up would score PiL's biggest ever hit, the keening "This is Not a Love Song" (#5 UK), before Lydon and Atkins formed a live band from a pool of New Jersey sessionmen: Joseph Guida (guitar), Louie Bernardi (bass), and Tom Zvoncheck (keyboards).

This line-up would record the *Live in Tokyo* album (#28 UK) before being dismissed; Lydon and Atkins, meanwhile, completed the long-delayed *This Is What You Want* (#56 UK) album (and "Bad Life" single — #71 UK), for release in July 1984. Not surprisingly, it was a substantially different record to that which Keith Levene had worked on before his departure, a point he hammered home with the release of the markedly superior *The Commercial Zone*, a recreation of the album as he had left it.

It was apparent by now that PiL existed almost exclusively to annoy people who insisted on continuing to lionize Lydon for his Pistols past. A lounge version of "Anarchy in the UK" had already slipped into his live set (he also performed it on UK TV's *The Tube*), while his own interests were clearly moving in the direction of film (Lydon made his acting debut in 1983, alongside Harvey Keitel in *Cop Killer*) and hip-hop. In early 1985, a collaboration with Afrika Bambaataa, "World Destruction" (#44 UK) became his most convincing performance in years.

PiL, meanwhile, lumbered back into life for 1986's *Album* (#115 US, #14 UK), recorded with producer Bill Laswell, and an all-star session line-up, including Ryuichi Sakamoto (keyboards), Steve Vai (guitar — ex-Alcatrazz), Tony Williams (ex-Miles Davis — bass), Ravi Shankar (violin), and Ginger Baker (ex-Cream — drums). Miles Davis himself came into the studio during the sessions — Lydon recalled, "he said that I sang like he played the trumpet, which is still the best thing anyone's ever said to me."

The singles "Rise" (#11 UK) and "Home" (#73 UK) followed through 1986, successes which convinced Lydon to form a new band "to get away from the heady stuff." Reaching into punk's own past, he recruited Lu Edmonds (ex-Damned — guitar), John McGeogh (ex- Magazine, Siouxsie and the Banshees — guitar), Alain Dias (bass), and Bruce Smith (ex-Slits, Pop Group — drums). This line-up spent three months touring *Album*, opening for Big Country in Europe, and provoking a riot in Athens, where 500 fans — allegedly joined by shadowy Greek anarchists — caused over $1.5 million worth of damage to the venue and its surroundings.

Happy? (#169 US, #40 UK), and the singles "Seattle" (recorded in Seattle during a break in the band's latest US tour — #47 UK) and "The Body" (backed by a rerecording of the first album's "Religion" — #100 UK) followed before Edmonds quit. Lydon responded with a new single, "Disappointed" ("all about the... ways people let you down" — #38 UK), the first single from PiL's sensibly titled ninth album, 9 (#106 US, #36 UK).

A collaboration with remixer Dave Dotrrell (on the recommendation of Massive Attack/Soul II Soul producer Nellee Hooper) brought the acclaimed "Warrior" single. Ironically, this would become Lydon's first ever new single to miss the UK charts altogether, and while the defiant "Don't Ask Me" (#22 UK) would restore him to glory, Lydon's interest in PiL was at its nadir. Following tours with New Order and the Sugarcubes, and with the band's Virgin contract up for renewal, he pieced together 1990's *Greatest Hits... So Far* col-

lection (#20 UK), and spent the next year out of the public eye.

Lydon returned with a revised PiL line-up in early 1992, reuniting with Levene, plus Russell Webb (ex-Skids — bass), and Mike Joyce (b. 6/1/63, Manchester; ex-Smiths, Buzzcocks — drums). With producer Dave Jerden (who mischievously included a Sex Pistols sample into the final mix of "Acid Drops"), they recorded *That What Is Not* (#46 UK), the final PiL album. A well-received UK tour took the band to the Reading Festival, "Cruel" (#49 UK) restored them to the Top 50, and Lydon alone made a well-received appearance alongside Ian Dury at Madstock. But PiL folded following an ill-conceived appearance on MTV's *120 Minutes* US tour in September, Lydon still smarting from a German interviewer "who asked me why I was ripping off Nirvana. I politely told him that he was Very Mistaken Indeed."

Still, he was painfully aware that 15 years on from his initial breakthrough, time and temperament had indeed passed him by, and that when he performed now, the demand on his audience's lips was not "show us what you can do," but "let us show you what we've done since then." Nirvana were simply the latest manifestation of punk's ability to move on from *the* punks.

In 1993, Lydon collaborated with techno duo Leftfield on the astonishing "Open Up" (#13 UK); he also completed his autobiographical account of the Sex Pistols years, *No Irish, NoBlacks, No Dogs*, then reformed that band for the 1996 *Filthy Lucre* tour. But his solo debut, 1997's *Psycho's Path*, was a techno-tinged mess and Lydon settled into his fourth decade as a media celebrity, hosting his own syndicated radio show, and appearing as a plaintiff on *Judge Judy*.

The four-CD *Plastic Box* (as aptly named, of course, as the sophomore *Metal Box*) rounded up PIL's complete life and times, although Lydon's liner notes cautioned his audience not to think of it as the full stop at the end of the band's career. Rather, it was "just a comma, and there will be more in the future".

Public Image Ltd LPs

8 Public Image (Virgin) 1978 A dense, but utterly likeable collection which veered between the brilliantly fulfilled ("Public Image," "Annalisa") and the demoniacally self-indulgent ("Fodderstompf"), over which Lydon's patented yowling cut broad swathes through anything which stood in its way.

10 Metal Box (Virgin) 1979 Brilliant self invention cut through with stubbornly anti-commercial indulgence, but from start to finish an inescapable blast of chilled machinery, crying screeches, and dense metal dub loops.

Although sundry CD reissues are more convenient, the album was conceived as three 12-inch singles and does sound superior in that form, with Wobble's bass a subterranean rumble, Levene's guitar a bellowing hawk, and Lydon's scatman toasting ensuring that even when the band hits a groove, the listener never settles. Few actual songs emerge from the carnage — at his most melodic, Rotten chants and snarls while the band goes into paramilitary overdrive behind him.

"Swan Lake" — subsequently remixed for the grinding "Death Disco" — and "Poptones" are especially disorientating; one for the snatches of, indeed, "Swan Lake," which filter through the cacophony; the other, because it does come so close to resolving its internal strife. But the band's insistence on never surrendering their roost at the edge of the world wins through, there and elsewhere, leaving an album of relentless breathless sound which only proves how far Lydon had come in so short a time. *Bollocks* was only two years old — it might as well have been two lifetimes.

4 Paris Au Printemps [LIVE] (Virgin) 1980

7 The Flowers of Romance (WB) 1981 Wobble left and took the bass with him; PiL don't bother replacing it and the initial sense is of utter dislocation — the modern dance never sounded like this before.

3 Live in Tokyo (Virgin) 1983 With Lydon and Atkins joined by three anonymous minds from New Jersey and no more rehearsal time than they could squeeze into their carry-on, PiL were ill, greasily serenading their way through songs which once shook the earth, but now barely bothered the cocktail set. "Annalisa," performed with all the bloated fat which the subject matter denied herself; "Death Disco" reinvented with only the wettest elements of its Tchaikovsky genesis intact; and "This Is Not a Love Song" proving it wasn't a good song either.

5 This Is What You Want... This Is What You Get (Elektra) 1984 Colorless, humorless, faceless and Keith Levene's great guitar-less slab of bad-tempered yelling. Except that's not a good thing, this time.

6 Album/Cassette/Compact Disc (Elektra) 1986 Bill Laswell production which indulges Lydon's hip-hop world dub mess tendencies, but falls flat regardless.

5 Happy? (Virgin) 1987 The PiL punk supergroup, hamstrung by the increasingly formulaic songs and rock stylings which Lydon now believes passes for passable. "Hard Times" and "The Body" float above the mire, but it's lonely on the top.

6 9 (Virgin) 1989

7 That What Is Not (Virgin) 1992 "Acid Drops," with its stolen sample of "God Save the Queen," comes out hottest — initial impressions that the album marked a genuine return to form were sadly displaced by subsequent plays, although the end result is not as hollow as some of its sad predecessors.

Selected Compilations and Archive Releases

7 Greatest Hits, So Far (Virgin) 1990 Straight forward rampage through the singles.

9 Plastic Box (Virgin) 1999 Four CDs serving up the genuine best of PiL, plundering long legendary 12-inch mixes (the full-length "Death Disco" alone makes disc one essential), radio sessions and choice album tracks, rarities, and collaborations.

John Lydon LP

4 Psycho's Path (Virgin) 1991 What was once close to the edge is now on the green side of the landfill, so a loathsomely desperate game of keepsy-uppsy finds an erstwhile originator slumming with his post-graduate students (Moby, the Chemical Brothers, and Danny Saber all shake an ineffective stick in the remix room) and proving that not only does he have nothing to say, he doesn't even have an original way of saying it.

Keith Levene and PiL LP

6 Commercial Zone (XYZ) 1984 The original mix of the *This Is What You Want* sessions; different song titles but in terms of dynamic and electricity, genuinely preferable to the official album. Even "Love Song" sounds inspired.

Further Reading

Rise and Fall by Clinton Heylin (Omnibus, UK, 1991).

PULP

FORMED 1978 *(Sheffield, England)*
ORIGINAL LINE-UP *Jarvis Cocker (b. 9/62, Sheffield, England — vocals, guitar); Peter Dalton (keyboards); David Lockwood (bass); Mark Swift (drums)*

Taking their name from the commodities section of the *Financial Times*, Jarvis Cocker originally launched Arabiscus Pulp in 1978, recruiting David Lockwood, Mark Swift, and Peter Dalton to record the soundtrack to a movie shot by one of his school friends. Only slowly did the band become even a semi-permanent concern, while regular line-up changes ensured that the band's sound constantly evolved, even as Cocker's own vision sharpened.

Following their live debut at Rotherham Arts center in early 1980, the now-abbreviated Pulp played the Bouquet of Steel festival at Sheffield's Leadmill Club that August, but their first major break came after Cocker handed a demo to BBC DJ John Peel, while he was DJ-ing a road show gig in Sheffield in October 1981. Two weeks later, the band were in London recording a four-track session for Peel's radio show, with a line-up of Cocker, bassist Jamie Pinchbeck, and drummer Wayne Furniss.

In July 1982, the band broke up after Pinchbeck and Furniss left to attend university; Cocker resurfaced the following year with a new line-up comprising guitarist Simon Hinkler, his brother Dave on keyboards, bassist Peter Boam, drummer Gary Wilson, and Cocker's sister Saskia. In this form, Pulp signed to Fire, and recorded an album, *It*; a dark, neo-gothic collection which was to be this line-up's first and last hurrah.

Simon Hinkler quit for a career which would lead him to Artery and later, the Mission; the rest of the band followed him out, and by January 1984, Cocker was fronting an entirely new group: Russell Senior (guitar), Tim Allcard (keyboards), Peter Mansell (bass), and Magnus Doyle (drums). A handful of gigs later, Doyle's sister Candida moved in to replace Allcard; later, future Elastica keyboard player Anthony Genn would take over bass from Mansell.

In November 1985, Pulp released the *Little Girl and Other Pieces* EP, but further progress was halted when Cocker jumped out of a window to impress a girl, and sustained sufficient injuries to keep him confined to a wheelchair for the next twelve months. The group finally reappeared with the *Dogs Are Everywhere* EP, and over the next year, two minor classic singles, "They Suffocate at Night" and "Master of the Universe," paved the way for Pulp's second album, the moody *Freaks*, in May 1987.

Pulp took another vacation that fall when Cocker enrolled in St. Martin's Art College in London to study film. He returned to the band, and the loyal Senior and Candida Doyle, in 1989, and with a new rhythm section (bassist Steve Mackey, drummer Nick Banks), issued the single "My Legendary Girlfriend," and Pulp's best album yet, the introspective *Separations*.

Unfortunately, a falling out between Pulp and Fire Records kept the album on the shelf for close to two years — by which time the band were actively seeking a new deal. They signed with Gift in early 1992 and recorded three singles, "O.U. (Gone Gone)," "Babies," and "Razzamatazz"; months later, Island Records moved in for the group.

In November 1993, Pulp's debut single for the label, "Lipgloss" (#50 UK), saw them breach the UK chart for the first time. In April 1994, their follow-up, "Do You Remember the First Time?" (#33 UK) did even better. But still, nobody was prepared for the reception which awaited Pulp's fourth album, April 1994's *His'N'Hers* (#9 UK). Suddenly swept up by the Britpop movement and lauded in arenas which had hitherto pointedly ignored them, Pulp smashed into the Top Ten; the *Sisters* EP (#19 UK) hit the Top 20; and with the next six months devoted to often high profile live work, Pulp's next single, "Common People" (#2 UK) entered the chart at its peak position. (In October 1999, Cocker would nix a proposed cover of the song by children's television stars Teletubbies.)

Summer 1995 brought a second successive appearance at the Glastonbury festival, and amid a massively over-subscribed UK tour that fall, the double A-side "Misshapes" and the drug- and rave-flavored "Sorted for E's & Wizz" (#2 UK) was only held off the #1 slot by Simply Red's insidious "Fairground." The single's sleeve, incidentally, earned tabloid wrath after *The Sun* newspaper suggested that the Cocker-designed package offered purchasers a handy guide to hiding

their drugs (Es, of course, were Ecstasy; wizz was speed); the band, for their part, claimed total innocence.

In November 1995, Pulp's new album, *Different Class* (#1 UK) entered the UK chart at the top, selling 300,000+ within just two weeks. The following month, "Disco 2000" (#7 UK) offered Christmas record buyers an epic reflection on the deprecations of time. And 1996 commenced with further sensation when Cocker bared his buttocks on stage during Michael Jackson's BRITS Awards performance — a protest, he later explained, "at the way [Jackson] sees himself as some Christ-like figure with the power of healing."

Pulp toured the UK through the remainder of February before heading over to the US. American coverage of Cocker's BRITS behavior had been considerably less indulgent than the British press and despite an appearance on Letterman in early April, and a string of well-attended shows, attempts to introduce Pulp on a larger level constantly ran up against a wall of distaste. To add to the band's predicament, Cocker then succumbed to a tropical bug, and was forced to cancel part of the tour.

The band returned home for further festival shows during summer 1995 (Cocker alone would guest on albums by Barry Adamson and Lush); the following year, too, would see just one new single, "Something Changed" (#10 UK) in March, and another round of festivals. The remainder of their time was spent in the studio, working on their next album.

Senior quit to form his own band, Baby Birkin, in January 1997; Pulp continued out of sight until November 1997 brought the first fruits of their recent labors, the brutal "Help the Aged" (#8 UK) single. The following March, the band — augmented by Longpigs guitarist Richard Hawley — premiered six new songs before an invitation-only audience at the Park Lane Hilton in London, before the end of the month brought their new single, six intense minutes of "This Is Hardcore" (#12 UK).

An album of the same name (#114 US, #1 UK) followed in April 1998, and with the band launching out on tours of Europe, the UK, and Australia (plus a handful of select US dates), further singles "A Little Soul" (#22 UK) and "Party Hard" (#29 UK) appeared to belie the deliberate uncommerciality of the parent album. But *This Is Hardcore* would ultimately prove the band's least successful album since *Separations*, the musical embodiment of Cocker's own apparent determination to step back from his fame. Neither was there any haste to follow it up — a silent 1999 was punctuated by just two major appearances, presenting a stripped down set of almost exclusively new and decidedly experimental music as accompaniment for art installation shows in Venice, Italy, and Edinburgh, Scotland.

Pulp LPs

5 It (Fire, UK) 1983 Earnest indy singer-songwriter darkness, representative less of what Pulp would become than of a host of similarly cultish acts of the age.

8 Freaks (Fire, UK) 1987 Stronger and considerably more idio-syncratic, built around some affectedly atmospheric keyboard/bass tones and a well-crafted sense of menace ("Fairground," "Being Followed Home"). "Anorexic Beauty" has a strong touch of Robyn Hitchcock-esque macabre about it, while "They Suffocate by Night" could be a grim premonition of *This Is Hardcore*.

9 Separations (Fire, UK) 1991 While the group's pop twist remains to the fore, *Separations* is darker, deeper, and just a little camper than anything which had gone before; imagine Marc Almond's album of Jacques Brel covers without Almond. Or Brel. There's a hint of Leonard Cohen in there too, but the over-riding impression is straight out of Cocker's adolescent TV viewing, lugubrious mid-70's humorist Jack Thackeray's odd ball observations on death, doom, and dreadful people.

7 His'n'Hers (Island) 1994 More jaded than ever, Cocker's laconic delivery discovers a sardonic bent perfect for *His'n'Hers'* love- and lust-strewn world. Under-achieving, but terminally precocious, it was already clear that greater things are to come.

8 Different Class (Island) 1995 From the opening "Misshapes," through the vital "Common People," class tensions and pretensions provide Cocker with targets a plenty. Equal parts suave and savoir faire, wickedly observant and accurate ("Sorted for E's and Wizz" is spot on), but also capable of summoning genuine emotion out of the superficiality ("Disco 2000"). What's really different is the music, shifting from the background to center stage, dressed up in glittering hooks and sublimely catchy choruses.

10 This Is Hardcore (Island) 1998 "This is the sound of someone losing the plot," he sings on the opening "The Fear," and right away you know that Cocker did not react well to mega-fame. But who'd have expected him to shoot it in the foot? And with such unerring accuracy that not only would he conjure up an album which sold a mere fraction of its most recent predecessors, but also one whose total isolation (commercial, critical, and best of all, musical) lends it an almost super-heroic sense of futility.

Everything — from the dignity of age to the delights of sex — is reduced to the saddened, sleaze-ridden gutter of shame, and across the album's best tracks (the crippling "The Fear," the epic "This Is Hardcore"), optimism and hope creak like an over-worked gibbet. This isn't rock'n'roll, it's a collect call to the Samaritans.

Pulp should be an illness shared by a mere few, a guilty secret, a dirty desire, and there is something worrisomely wrong with a culture which would make a man like Cocker a superstar. In the real world, people are locked up for talking like he does. In Cocker's, they just go silently to pieces. This, as he points out, is the eye of the storm — "it's what men in stained raincoats pay for."

The slow burning "Help the Aged" sets the *Hardcore* scene, but barely hinted at the rancor in store. From the slimy spy theme of the title track to the on-the-ropes raggedness of "Sylvia"; from a super-Suede swagger which shatters all over, to the mock-Bowie petulance Cocker keeps for Sunday best... "Party Hard" stamps so doggedly around that you just *know* Cocker wanted to cover "Boys Keep Swinging," but didn't because that'd be too perfect for words.

And there's no room for perfection in the *Hardcore* world. If there was, he wouldn't be asking "how many of us have touched themselves?" Like Morrissey at his most uglily subversive, Cocker incites your confidence and you give it though you know it invites betrayal in return. Don't trust this man, don't love this man, but one listen to *Hardcore* and he'll have you regardless.

Jarvis Cocker isn't Jesus and admits it himself. But he has the same initials.

7 This Is Glastonbury [LIVE] (Island) 1998 *Hardcore* live. Twice as sick, half as slick, but some hits on the end to keep the pop fans happy.

Selected Compilations and Archive Releases

7 Intro — The Gift Recordings (Island) 1993 Wrap up of recent singles, the last gasp of the indy cred cult days.

7 Masters of the Universe (Fire) 1994 Sadly uneven round-up from the first three albums and attendant singles.

8 Countdown 1992–1983 (Nectar Masters) Doubtless intended for all the poor souls who want more Pulp, but are scared by the size of the catalog, *Countdown* reflects on the band's first decade and crams most of the best bits onto two discs. "My Lighthouse," "She's Dead," and "My Legendary Girlfriend" will need no introduction to anyone who's been paying attention — if the songs themselves are strange, the sentiments remain crucial to the core of the combo.

8 Second Class (Island) 1996 *Different Class*-era B-sides and oddities, highlighted by some genuinely crooked gems — "PTA," "Deep Fried in Kelvin," and "Your Sister's Clothes."

Further Reading

Pulp by Martin Aston (Plexus UK).

PUNK LUREX OK

FORMED 1993 *(Tampere, Finland)*
ORIGINAL LINE-UP *Ritta Suojanen (vocals, guitar); Jula Helminen (guitar); Tiina Wesslin (bass); Jyrki Siukonen (drums)*

Cut firmly in the mold of classic 1977-style punk, Punk Lurex OK were formed by Ritta Suojanen and Tiina Wesslin, devoted fans of their homeland's all-time greatest first wave band, Kollaa Kestaa. Between 1977–81, that band issued a string of singles, including a Finnish language version of the Adverts "One Chord Wonders," and "Kirjoituksia

Kellarista" — later to find fame in the US, following its inclusion on the *Killed by Death* volume 100 compilation.

Suojanen and Wesslin's first band, Porttikjelto, played almost exclusively Kollaa Kestaa material. It was only fitting, then, that the band should be discovered by KK's guitarist, Jula Helminen, who promptly joined — and brought KK drummer Jyrki Siukonen with him. In this form, Punk Lurex OK released their first single, "Paalimajassa," backed with a Finnish language version of another Adverts hit, "Gary Gilmore's Eyes" ("TappajanSilmat") in 1993.

By early 1994, the band's live schedule was accelerating fast. They played their first show outside of their native Tampere, in Helsinki, on February 19, with further gigs in Turku, Toijala, and Lahti following as the year continued. Indeed, the schedule grew so hectic that Siukonen, an established visual artist, was forced to quit for the sake of his "real" career; he was replaced by Sami Paivarinta.

With Suojanen and Wesslin now composing their own material, the band cut the eight-song mini-album *Veljet! Siskot!* ("Brothers! Sisters!"), for release in Finland in July 1995, and Germany two months later. However, Helminen also departed that fall, shortly before work was to begin on the band's first full-length album. A new guitarist, Kukka, was recruited from the local Tampere punk circuit, and the band continued gigging, even as they went into the studio with producer Jani Viitanen, to record *Hatut ja Myssyt* ("Hats and Caps"), a dynamic set which reprised their long-since out-of-print debut single, "Paalimajassa."

The album was released in Germany the following year, an other wise quiet time for the band — they played just four shows through 1997, and otherwise only two — in April — in 1998. A return to action in 1999, however, brought the acclaimed *Prolex* album, together with a short Finnish tour through April with TV Smith. The two also shared the bill at the Rovaniemi Festival in Lapland (the official home of Santa Claus, and the most northerly rock festival in the world) later in the year, before collaborating on an EP, comprising two new songs and the Adverts' classics, "One Chord Wonders" and a reprise of "Gary Gilmore's Eyes" for release in 2000.

Punk Lurex OK LPs

8 Hatut Ja Myssyt (Hiljaiset Levyt — Finland) 1996 Cut in classic Finnish punk mood (catch the *Bloodstains Over Finland* collection for a solid grounding in the old school best), a dashing throb through 14 succinct gems.

9 Prolex (Hiljaiset Levyt — Finland) 1999 Unafraid to wear their hearts very loudly on their sleeves, Punk Lurex resurrect the Buzzcocks "Ever Fallen in Love," then conjure up a dozen self-compositions to match it blow for blow. And yes, the clean-cut, folky-looking kids on the back cover did make this unrepentant noise.

PYLON

FORMED 1979 *(Athens, GA)*
LINE-UP *Vanessa Briscoe (vocals); Curtis Crowe (drums); Michael Lachowski (bass); Randy Bewley (guitar)*

Pylon remain one of the most underappreciated bands to come out of the early Athens scene; despite being hailed by both REM (who they pre-date) and the B-52's as veritable gurus, they remain largely unknown in the mainstream. Yet they completed that city's most venerable triumvirate, a staple within Athens and heroes in New York as well.

Formed by four University of Georgia (UGA) students, with a name lifted from a William Faulkner novel, Pylon started out playing parties and local clubs, before signing to the dB's DB label. Released in 1979, Pylon's debut single, "Cool," quickly became a club hit, topping *Rockpool's* dance chart and paving the way for their first LP, *Gyrate* (#26 UK indy).

Well received in Britain, the album was swiftly followed by two EP's, *Pylon* in fall 1980, and *10 Inch 45RPM* (#44 UK indy) in March 1981. Another single, "Crazy," followed — REM's Peter Buck later remarked, "I remember hearing ["Crazy"] on the radio the day that *Chronic Town* [REM's debut album] came out and being suddenly depressed by how much better it was than our record."

Though the band continued gigging regularly, Pylon's next release wouldn't appear until 1983 — *Chomp* (and the accompanying "Beep" single) was produced by dB's Chris Stamey and Gene Holder, and again proved to be an underground hit. Despite ever growing support for Pylon, they would disband following one final show at Athens' Mad Batter on December 3. Crowe and Bewley became cabinet makers, Lachowski went into bicycle repairs, Vanessa Hay (formerly Vanessa Briscoe) became a manager at Kinko's.

The spirit of Pylon, however, lived on. REM's version of Pylon's "Crazy" would be released in 1985, on the B-side of their "Driver 8" single, and would become a live staple through the band's next tour. Two years later, when *Rolling Stone* awarded REM the title of America's Best Rock'n'Roll Band, REM drummer Bill Berry promptly turned the honor over to Pylon, while "Stop It," from Pylon's first album, became a talking point of 1987's *Athens Inside-Out* documentary.

The following year Pylon reformed, rehearsing at REM's own practice space next door to the 40 Watt Club in Athens, and finally announcing their reunion by wandering unannounced into the club one night, and asking if they could play. Two weeks later they played a second, less-secret show, before moving on to a free gig at the university of Georgia.

DB promptly released a best of collection, *Hits*, while Pylon toured as the opening act on REM's *Green* tour. However, though a new album, *Chain*, would appear in 1990, the band broke up soon after.

Pylon LPs

8 Chomp (DB) 1983 Pylon's first album and swan song, *Chomp* was a quirky romp through the odd underbelly of this band's world and the resulting soundscape remains one of this country's best kept secrets. Gang of Four-esque guitars muscle in next to fat bass-lines and the whole thing is capped by Briscoe's delightfully eccentric vocals. Whether you think the album's tainted by psychedelics or psychosis, "Crazy," "Gyrate," and "Beep" are still masterpieces of the modern era.

7 Chain (Sky Records) 1990 Linking themselves firmly to the past while updating their sound with a new electronic sensibility, the band have a fun "comeback." The album is solid, especially on "Look Alive" and "Crunch" and although Pylon still impress, it's good to know that this album will remain a "one-off."

Selected Compilations and Archive Releases

8 Hits (DB) 1988 With only a handful of years comprising their career, *Hits* still manages to squeeze in twenty tracks, reaching back to the *Gyrate* EP, plus 1979's "Cool" and "Dub."

R

RADIO BIRDMAN

FORMED 1974 *(Sydney, Australia)*
ORIGINAL LINE-UP *Rob Younger (vocals); Deniz Tek (b. Ann Arbor, MI — guitar); Carl Rorke (bass); Pip Hoyle (keyboards); Ron Keeley (drums)*

Ann Arbor native Deniz Tek first visited Australia in 1967, moving there permanently in 1972 to study medicine. That same year he joined the Screaming White Hot Razor Blades, a band whose repertoire ranged from the Rolling Stones to the Bonzo Dog Doo Dah Band, and who would evolve over the next two years into the Cunning Stunts and, finally, TV Jones, where Tek was joined by Pip Hoyle, one of his fellow medical students.

Gigging around Sydney with their set slowly embracing The Stooges and MC5 material Tek had loved back in Michigan, TV Jones signed with the indy Earth label in 1974, and recorded a single. Unfortunately, the tape was erased and when the band couldn't afford to rerecord, they broke up.

Among the few local bands following a similar musical train as TV Jones were the Rats, an all-covers concern fronted by Rob Younger. They, too, broke up during 1974, with Younger, Tek, and Hoyle, immediately forming a new band together, Radio Birdman.

The original band line-up began splintering almost immediately, as Hoyle quit to pursue his studies; Rorke followed him in early 1975. The band was brought up to strength with the arrival of Chris Masuak (rhythm guitar), while Rats rhythm guitarist Warwick Gilbert was recruited as both bassist and resident graphic designer — he would become responsible for creating the visual image which sprung up around the band, nurtured by posters, buttons, and an almost militaristic love for uniforms and symbols.

By 1975, Radio Birdman's reputation — and audience — was sufficient to leave half of Sydney's club and bar owners dreading the very mention of their name. Some nights the band would have to pack their mike stands last in case they needed them to ward off hostile bouncers, but still, the local press found them impossible to ignore.

In December 1975, Radio Birdman won *RAM* magazine's presciently-titled RAM/Levis Punk Band Thriller and, in the new year, they found a regular venue, when they landed a residency at the Oxford Tavern in Darlinghurst — a veteran club with a rock'n'roll reputation as uncompromising as Radio Birdman's own. At the same time, Tek's medical studies were approaching their climax, severely restricting the amount of time he could spend playing music — a problem which Radio Birdman promptly turned to their advantage.

Sporadic gigs now became major events, with the highlights a pair of live broadcasts on 2JJ Radio in March and November 1976. Another now-legendary show found them playing the Lions Club in Armadale, to a hall full of pensioners who were as puzzled by the band as the band were by them. Radio Birdman played three songs before they were asked to stop, for fear of killing the feebler members of the audience.

Signing with the indy Trafalgar label, operating out of the studio of the same name, mid-1976 saw Radio Birdman — now celebrating Hoyle's return on keyboards — cut their debut EP, *Burn My Eye*, to be sold mail order through a solitary ad in *RAM*. The pressing sold out immediately and the band began planning their next release, the infectiously anthemic "New Race."

Joined now by backing singers Mark Sisto and Johnny Kannis, the band shot a promo film to accompany the song, an in-concert performance which rapidly developed into Nuremburg Rallies-esque fervor. Certainly that's what disapproving local critics said, anyway, with Radio Birdman's apparent alliance with fascist imagery only being exaggerated when they chose to title their late 1976 tour, "Blitzkreig."

The band took the first months of 1977 off, as Tek returned to the US to visit family. He returned in time for Radio Birdman to take over the running of the Oxford Tavern, renaming it the Oxford Funhouse, and filling it with any like-minded local bands they could find. The Hellcats, featuring Died Pretty's Ron Peno, the Mangrove Boogie Kings, and the Psycho Surgeons, became regulars at what one of the band's own ads described as "Sydney's only genuine rock'n'roll venue," home to Radio Birdman's definition of what a "good band" should be — "energetic, exciting, innovative (or unashamedly derivative) playing rock'n'roll with real manic fervor."

Tours of Victoria and New South Wales saw Radio Birdman pushing across the Australian continent in the run up to the release of *Radios Appear* — a title borrowed from Blue Oyster Cult's "Dominance and Submission." A new single, covering the Stooges' "TV Eye," followed.

Released again on Trafalgar, the original plan was to sell the album mail order with a handful of hipper record stores also supplied with copies. However, demand far outstripped the band's ability to package copies up for mailing and within a month of its release, WEA had offered to take up national distribution. Within weeks, *Radios Appear* was poised at #35 on the national chart — a feat made all the more amazing by the band's refusal to back the album up with any live work. They made just one appearance during that three month period, on the Australian Broadcasting Co's *Real Thing*, alongside the Saints.

In September, Radio Birdman launched the long-awaited *Aural Rape* tour, following through with more dates in November — compensation for the disappointment of Iggy Pop's first Australian tour being cancelled shortly after Radio Birdman were confirmed as support. Further proof of Radio Birdman's status was supplied when one of their Adelaide gigs was filmed by ABC's *Rockturnal* show, while the band also became the first Australian band ever to be subjected to a domestic bootleg album! *Eureka Birdman* was recorded in Victoria in late 1977; another show from this period would be excerpted on 1988's *More Fun* live EP.

In the midst of so much activity, the band signed with Sire. Of all the bands to emerge from the Australian punk scene, Radio Birdman's name and fame were now an international sensation, fitting labelmates indeed to the Ramones, Richard Hell, the Dead Boys, Talking Heads, the Rezillos, Plastic Bertrand, and the Undertones. *Radios Appear* would be released in the US and UK at the end of the year, appended with a few new songs, rerecordings and overdubs, and a new sleeve.

Released in Australia in the new year, it was the band's farewell to their homeland before they relocated to London in late February 1978, to launch their *Anglo Strike* tour. It was a disaster. Like the Saints before them, Radio Birdman discovered UK punk to be a completely different culture than that they had left behind — a fashion conscious sword fight in which even the length of a band's hair could count against them. And Birdman's hair was very long.

Departing London, the band retreated to Rockfield Studios to record their second album before launching a short European tour with the Flamin' Groovies — another band whose appearance had counted them out of the running in their spiritual homeland. Eighteen tracks were laid down, including reworkings of three of the songs from *Burn My Eye*, and the album was scheduled for release later in the year. However, relations in the band were souring. Local hostility and the need to begin working their way up a fresh ladder added to the band's discomfort, while the British leg of the Groovin' On the Road tour was poorly received and sparsely attended. On June 10, 1978, Radio Birdman played their last ever show, appropriately enough in their Sydney Funhouse's UK namesake city of Oxford.

The band returned to Australia piecemeal, turning their attention towards fulfilling the Funhouse's brief of nurturing new talent. In 1978, Tek produced Sydney rockers The Lip-

stick Killers, "Hindu Gods (Of Love)" debut 45, while Younger formed the Other Side — and so impressed Sydney native Mike Blood that he immediately went out and formed his own band, the Lime Spiders, subsisting on a diet of deranged '60s punk covers until it was time to record their own manic takes on the same sound. Younger — having since enjoyed a two month stint drumming with Died Pretty — produced their debut EP, 1983's *25th Hour*. Another fine tribute to Birdman's importance was delivered by Brisbane punks Just Urbain, whose laudatory "Everyone Loves" appeared in 1980. (It subsequently reappeared on *Killed By Death* vol. 666).

The aborted Rockfield album finally made it out in 1981, when 13 of the tracks appeared as the *Living Eyes* collection (one more appeared on a Tek solo B-side in 1982). But Radio Birdman themselves refused to take flight again, even after an Australian promoter even offered each member $3000 to reform and perform three gigs — one each in Sydney, Melbourne, and Adelaide in mid-1979. They turned him down.

Tek, Younger, and Gilbert would work together again, however, forming New Race with Ron Asheton (ex-Stooges) and Dennis Thompson (ex-MC5), and creating something of a stir in the early 1980s. Subsequently, Younger and Celibate Rifles guitarist Kent Steedman would reinforce those foundations with the New Christs, a supergroup of sorts formed in 1984 to keep the Hitmen busy after vocalist John Kannis suffered a near-fatal auto accident.

Mark Kingsmill, Birdman's own Masuak and the seemingly ubiquitous Tony Robertson all moonlighted from that band as the New Christs toured Australia with Iggy Pop, then (with Steedman replaced by Lime Spiders Richard Jakimayszyn) signed to Citadel to cut two crucial garage punk 45s, "Like a Curse" and "Born Out of Time." That line-up split in 1985; Younger, however, persevered and a decade (and innumerable line-up changes) later, the New Christs would still be on the front line of the Australian music scene — just as Radio Birdman reunited to tour Australia and cut the *Ritualism* album.

Radio Birdman LPs

8 Radios Appear (WEA — AUS) 1977

7 Radios Appear (Overseas Edition) (Sire) 1978 Powerful summary of the band's rise through the pariah ranks of the Australia pub scene, less purposefully misogynist than the Saints, but cut from a similar Stooges-blown cloth. The so-called overseas edition sheds some of the original madness in favor of a cleaner, (hopefully) more international barrage.

6 Ritualism 1996 Ten oldies and two new songs, recorded live in the studio.

Further Reading

Radio Birdman by Vivian Johnson (out of print).

RADIOHEAD

FORMED *[as On a Friday]* 1988 (Oxford, England)
ORIGINAL LINE-UP *Thom Yorke (vocals, guitar); Edward John O'Brien (b. 4/15/68 — guitar); Philip James Selway (b. 5/23/67 — drums); Jonathan Greenwood (b. 11/5/71); Colin Greenwood (b. 6/26/69)*

The members of Radiohead first started playing together at school when Thom Yorke left his first band, TNT, after accusing them of having no ambition. Initially he linked with Edward O'Brien "because he looked like Morrissey" and with Colin Greenwood because they always ended up at the same parties. They named the band On a Friday because that was the only day of the week when they could all get together to practice.

Although the band broke up in September 1989, when the members departed for various universities around the country, reunions took place during holidays, with a permanent reunion following in 1991. Yorke's work with the Exeter-based Headless Chickens, "I Don't Want To Go To Woodstock," is documented on *The Year Zero* punk compilation (Hometown Atrocities, 2000). The following year, a copy of On a Friday's demo was heard by Chris Hufford and Bryce Edge, owners of a recording studio and production company in nearby Sutton Courtenay, and with Hufford becoming the group's manager, they recorded *Manic Hedgehog*, a five-track demo sold through the local record store of the same name.

It was at another store, however, that the band came to the attention of the label which would eventually sign them, when a local sales rep dropped by to say goodbye, announcing he had just taken an A&R post at EMI's Parlophone subsidiary. As he was leaving, Greenwood handed him a tape and told him he should sign On a Friday. Weeks later, he did.

The group's first single, the *Drill* EP, was already scheduled for a May 1992 release when the band changed their name, at the suggestion of a review in *Melody Maker*. "Radio Head" came from a song on Talking Head's *True Stories* album.

Drill (#101 UK) was released as the band went into the studio with Fort Apache staffers Sean Slade and Paul Kolderie (then riding high on the success of Buffalo Tom's *Let Me*

© Henry Diltz/Chansley Entertainment Archives

Come Over album) to begin work on their *Pablo Honey* (#32 US, #25 UK) debut album. It was a confident set, but one track stood head and shoulders above the rest.

"Creep" (#34 US, #78 UK) would be released as a single in Britain in September 1992 and though it barely charted, it would appear in the *NME*'s end of year Best Singles poll and was also picking up airplay in the US, on San Francisco's LIVE 105. Radiohead themselves ended the year with a Christmas gig at the Jericho Tavern Oxford, where their set included covers of "Rhinestone Cowboy," the Motown classic "Money," and a disco-fied medley of classical tunes — a performance amusingly sampled seven years later by Oxford electro band SPU.N.K.L.E. All Stars, for their "Where Will You Be This Christmas" single.

Slowly, "Creep" began to move on America's west coast. By March 1993, while Radiohead's third single "Anyone Can Play Guitar" (#32) was staggering in Britain, "Creep" was breaking out all across the US. By May, when "Pop Is Dead" (#42 UK) returned Radiohead to the British Top 50, Beavis & Butthead conferred their mark of approval on "Creep," and MTV began paying attention. And by the time the band's American label, Capitol, realized what was going on, "Creep" was marching into the Top 40 and *Pablo Honey* (#32 US) was heading for gold.

The song struck a chord across society. Angst-ridden teens wrote the band fan letters; so, according to press reports, did convicted murderers. Still Radiohead didn't realize quite what they had wrought until, having made the decision to drop the song from their own live show, they played Las Vegas with Tears for Fears — and found it in *their* set instead!

Reissued and finally breaking in the UK, "Creep" (#7 UK) kept the band touring for close to 18 months; it would be April 1994 before Radiohead could finally get off the road and begin thinking about their next album and mid-summer before they had settled down enough to actually begin recording. But the sessions were disastrous. Everybody was looking for the next "Creep," from the band members to the label heads, and nothing would be good enough till they heard it.

Finally, after two months of total waste, producer John Leckie dismissed the entire band except Yorke from the sessions, and told the singer to just play him the new songs on an acoustic guitar. Next, he encouraged the whole group to devote their next major live show, the Glastonbury Festival, to their latest material.

Record company dreams of a new album for Christmas were shattered. Instead, Radiohead rescued a rough recording of "My Iron Lung" (#24 UK) from their recently released live video, Astoria 27.5.94 and, twelve months on from "Creep," finally released their follow-up single. Relieved, the band returned to the studio and this time, the album fell effortlessly into place.

February 1995 brought a new single, the remixed demo "High and Dry" (#78 US, #17 UK), with *The Bends* (#88 US, #6 UK) following in March. Neither did well to begin with, but when "Fake Plastic Trees" (#20 UK), the first video to be taken from the album, made a convincing dent in the MTV schedules, the tide turned completely. An American tour was a resounding success regardless of whether or not "Creep" appeared in the set, while a tour of Europe supporting REM prompted Michael Stipe to admit that his band came close to being blown off stage every night. Anything Radiohead had been in danger of losing as they made their initial dizzying ascent, was being restored by the bucket-load. They toured with Neil Young and Soul Asylum and all the while, *The Bends* continued leaking hit singles; "Just" (#19 UK) and "Street Spirit" (#5 UK), the album's moody and utterly uncharacteristic closing track, both scored. Another odd choice, "Lucky," led off the various artists charity disc *Help* EP (#51 UK), as Radiohead themselves returned to the studio to begin work on their third album.

OK Computer (#21 US, #1 UK) would emerge in 1997, one of the most eagerly awaited albums of the year and certainly the most appreciated. Topping most best-of-year polls, the album would also be dominating the best-of-decade lists three years later and again, the unlikeliest tracks were culled for hit single status "Paranoid Android" (#3 UK), "Karma Police" (#8 UK), "No Surprises" (#4 UK), and the *Airbag* EP (#56 US) while Radiohead themselves continued marching from strength to strength. In May 1997, the band debuted its new live set in Barcelona; in June, Radiohead were one of the star attractions at the Milarepa Tibetan Freedom concerts in New York, before setting off on their own latest American tour.

Extra curricular activities also loomed. In San Francisco, Yorke paired up with DJ Shadow, to record a track for the DJ's in-progress *UNKLE Psyence Fiction* album (#107 US); back home, he guested on the latest single by Drugstore, then joined Jonny Greenwood to record tracks for the acclaimed *Velvet Goldmine* movie soundtrack. Greenwood would also guest on Pavement's latest album, being recorded with *OK Computer* producer Nigel Godrich.

Live work dominated 1998, before Radiohead returned to the studio with Godrich in April 1999 to begin work on their next album. New material, meanwhile, would surface in September 1999, when the band contributed the instrumental soundtrack to the BBC TV drama *Eureka Street*. The band also debuted one new song, "Knives Out," during a three-and-one-half hour webcast through their official Web site in December 1999. *Kid A* finally arrived in fall 2000.

Radiohead LPs

7 Pablo Honey (Capitol) 1993 A confident, if hardly earth-shaking album, readily divided between the songs which would persevere within Radiohead's repertoire ("Stop Whispering," "You," "Blow Out"), those which were clearly land locked somewhere between youthful development and marginal filler, and one — "How Do You" — which was a dead ringer for a lost New York Dolls number. Within such surroundings, "Creep" stood out effortlessly.

8 The Bends (Capitol) 1995 The sheer enormity of what Radiohead had been faced with and the aplomb with which they pulled it off, both haunted Life After "Creep," the ghost of the hit hanging almost as heavy over the proceedings as a not-altogether healthy interest in Nirvana, as both "My Iron Lung" ("Heart-Shaped Box") and "Just" ("Smells Like Teen Spirit") readily testified. Other tracks, "High and Dry" and "Fake Plastic Trees" included, were allied with London Suede's recently released *dog man star* masterpiece, but if *The Bends* was, as many Stateside writers complained, the sound of the band treading water while it searched for the next masterpiece, at least they did go on to find one.

10 OK Computer (Capitol) 1997 Radiohead could not have spun further off the wall if they'd spent two years on the ceiling, and being given the room to maneuver in the studio removed any last barriers they may have run into.

Recording and touring in equal portions, breaking new songs on stage as they wrote them, then taping the carnage they could create from the pieces, Radiohead designed an album which not only belied their position as one of alternative radio's favorite picks, it questioned their membership in society too. Maggot-ridden, angst-driven, *OK Computer* was alternately powerful, profound, and powerfully, profoundly disturbing.

Extending themselves far from the norm (even *their* norm), even song structure was utterly redeveloped, a sequence of verse-, rhyme-, and chorus-less images with Yorke's pronunciation reducing even "Airbag's" portentous "I am back to save the universe" into one long word-less syllable. Other tracks touched on themes as disparate as Kurt Cobain ("No Surprises"), megalomania ("Paranoid Android"), and JG Ballard ("Let Down"). "Exit Music," meanwhile, subtitled itself "For a Film," which may be why something about the melody line suggested the closure of *Rosemary's Baby*.

Comparable in intent to some of Pink Floyd's later rage-driven albums, but in execution to... an execution, *OK Computer* could have been made by one of the album's own invented characters; someone who couldn't decide whether to top himself now, or take a few dozen passers-by out first. Making the record was his way of killing time while he made up his mind.

6 Kid A (Capitol) 2000 Low key escape from the grandiosity of its predecessor, songs interrupted by effects... even Pink Floyd were never this po-faced.

Selected Compilations and Archive Releases

My Iron Lung (Parlophone — Euro) 1994 Eight-track compilation comprising six *Bends*-era B-sides, plus the title track and an acoustic "Creep."

Further Reading

From a Great Height by Jonathan Hale (ECW 1999).

RAGE AGAINST THE MACHINE

FORMED 1991 *(Orange County, CA)*
ORIGINAL LINE-UP *Zack de la Rocha (b. 1971 — vocals); Tom Morello (b. 1965 — guitar); Tim Bob (bass); Brad Wilk (drums)*

Politically, Rage Against the Machine were hard hitters from the beginning — Tom Morello's uncle was former Kenyan president Jomo Kenyatta; Zack de la Rocha's father was Cuban political artist Beto. Musically, they were less impressive — Brad Wilk was a former bandmate of a pre-Pearl Jam Eddie Vedder; de la Rocha played with local concerns Farside and Inside Out.

Rage Against the Machine's first ever live show was in a friend's living room in 1991; a succession of less constrained performances followed, and in early 1992, the band self-released an eponymous cassette album featuring the visceral "Bullet in the Head." They followed up on July 13 by opening for Porno for Pyros official debut in L.A. and in September, the band joined the second stage at Lollapalooza '92.

High sales and stunned reviews brought Rage Against the Machine to Epic later in the year, prompting the band's by now notoriously radical political stance to be questioned by the more cynical observers. The group responded in November with their major label debut *Rage Against the Machine* (#45 US, #17 UK), a hard-hitting set which seemed to demand mainstream attention without offering any slackening of the band's attitude in return. Even the sleeve, a Vietnam War-era photograph of a self-immolating Buddhist monk, was guaranteed to outrage certain sensibilities — indeed, British band the Adverts had hoped to decorate their second album with that same picture back in 1979, only to be prevented by their horrified record label.

Rage Against the Machine played their first European dates in late 1992, opening for Suicidal Tendencies. They returned in May 1993, promptly scoring hits with the singles "Killing in the Name" (#25 UK) and "Bullet in the Head" (#16 UK). Indeed, Rage Against the Machine toured through much of 1993, continuing to ally their politics with the music — they headlined Rock for Choice benefits at the Hollywood Palladium in January and October, while their return to London in September included an Anti-Nazi benefit — and was greeted with another hit, "Bombtrack" (#37). The band also took a stand against censorship in Philadelphia during Lollapalooza '93, by standing naked and silent on stage for 15 minutes, gagged with duct-tape and with the initials "PMRC" spelled out across their chests.

A link with former Coil mainstay Peter Christopherson saw the band issue the long form *Freedom* video in December 1993, at the conclusion of their first headlining US tour. By the new year, it was the #1 video in America, although Rage Against the Machine themselves would remain silent through much of 1994, emerging only for a handful of festivals and benefit performances and to contribute a new song from their album-in-progress, "Year of the Boomerang," to the soundtrack of John Singleton's *Higher Learning*.

1995, too, was spent in the studio although Rage Against the Machine did appear at a Washington, DC benefit for the International Concerned Friends and Family of Mumia Abu-Jamal, the convicted cop killer whose proclaimed innocence was becoming an issue of national concern. During 1999, de la Rocha would address both the International Commission of Human Rights and a public rally for Abu-Jamal, and play a second benefit concert in East Rutherford, NJ.

The band's third album, *Evil Empire* (#1 US, #4 UK), was finally released in April 1996, an instant chart-topper which would eventually go double platinum and earn a Best Metal Performance Grammy for "Tire Me" (and Best Hard Rock nominations for "Bulls On Parade" and "People of the Sun"). Its release was accompanied by a free concert at the CSU Velodrome and a controversial appearance on *Saturday Night Live*, cut to just one song after the band tried to hang inverted American flags from their amplifiers.

A major European tour highlighted by both "Bulls in the Sun" (#8 UK) and "People of the Sun" (#26 UK) becoming international hits, was followed by an appearance at the Tibetan Freedom Concert, a full US tour, and a handful of guest appearances at Lollapalooza '96. The following April, the band undertook a full stadium tour, opening for U2. All Rage Against the Machine's profits from these dates would be donated to favored activist groups. (Morello and de la Rocha also appeared on the *Radio Free L.A.* broadcast, in a specially convened band featuring Red Hot Chili Peppers bassist Flea and Stephen Perkins of Porno for Pyros.)

In December 1997, Morello was arrested while taking part in a March of Conscience against sweatshop labor, prompting the infamous Rage Against Sweatshops advertising campaign, targeting Guess? Inc. Much of the next year, however, would be spent recording the band's next album, November 1999's *The Battle of Los Angeles* (#1 US) and single "Guerilla Radio" (#69 US). The set was preceded by

appearances at the Tibet Freedom Concert, Woodstock '99, and the Coachello Festival, plus shows in Mexico City, London, and Washington DC. The band also linked with Public Enemy to record a new version of the rap act's "It Takes a Nation of Millions to Hold Us Back."

Rage Against the Machine LPs

5 Rage Against the Machine (Self Release) 1991 Crossing metal, hard core, and rap, *Rage* debuted their crass, thrashed state of mind over twelve songs, some ("Darkness of Greed") great; others not quite up to speed.

8 Rage Against the Machine (Epic) 1992 Continuing their crusade against injustice, this sophomore set howled, fully formed, into the hearts of kids everywhere, causing their parents some discomfort. Apparently, children should be seen and not heard. And Rage were both, blistering through a powerful set made mightier by "Township Rebellion" and "Take the Power Back." Almost perfect, the band would benefit, however, from taking a stand against the clichés which pepper their songs. Sometimes the hit'em-with-a-brick approach isn't the most effective.

5 Evil Empire (Epic) 1996 More full-on assault, but a four year break didn't help their cohesion. Rather than take a raucous sonic step forward, Machine stayed still, gaining no new ground and losing much of the immediacy which invigorated their sound, which in turn, left the manifesto to founder.

7 The Battle of Los Angeles (Epic) 1999 Back in fine form — if only to stomp out sundry Limp Bizkit-shaped pretenders to their throne — Machine fused renewed energy to their sonic assault, staying focused and tight through a set which includes the gems, "Guerilla Radio," "Born of a Broken Man," and "Calm Like a Bomb."

Further Reading

Evil Empire by Rage Against the Machine (Hal Leonard 1997).

RAIN PARADE

FORMED 1982 *(Los Angeles, CA)*
ORIGINAL LINE-UP *David Roback (vocals, guitar); Matthew Piucci (guitar, sitar); Steve Roback (bass); Will Glenn (keyboards); Eddie Kalwa (drums)*

The inclusion of a sitar in Rain Parade's early arsenal immediately placed them into the burgeoning Paisley Underground neo-psychedelic scene, regardless of whether the band wanted to be there or not. As it turned out, of all the groups laboring beneath that epithet, Rain Parade were perhaps the most comfortable, genuinely drawing from a host of late '60s archetypes and influences to create a truly trippy miasma.

The band's own Llama label released Rain Parade's first single, "What She's Done to Your Mind," in mid-1982 — a local college hit — which brought the band to the attention of Enigma. Rain Parade then impacted with the album *Emergency Third Rail Power Trip*, a nine-track (10 in the UK) effort which featured Kendra Smith (ex-Dream Syndicate) as guest vocalist. Smith and Dream Syndicate's Dennis Duck would also appear on the Paisley supersession album, *Rainy Day*, organized by David and Steve Roback and featuring musicians across the underground scene — Matthew Piucci, Susanna Hoffs, and Michael Quercio were all involved in a loose aggregation that tackled a host of favorite (and self-defining) cover versions, from the Velvet Underground to the Beach Boys.

"You Are My Friend" gave Rain Parade another signature hit during summer 1983, but the *Explosions in the Glass Palace* EP marked the end of an era. David Roback and drummer Eddie Kalwa both departed; they were replaced by John Thoman and Mark Marcum and Rain Parade toured Japan, returning home with the live *Beyond the Sunset* collection, the debut for three of the new line-up's strongest tracks.

Certainly Island Records was impressed and Rain Parade cut their major label debut, the divisively minimalistic *Crashing Dream*. It would be their last gasp — the (poor) sales figures were barely even in before the band fell apart. Thoman and Steve Roback formed a new band, Viva Saturn; Piucci formed Gone Fishin' and also recorded with Neil Young's Crazy Horse.

David Roback, meanwhile, reunited with Kendra Smith as Clay Allison, cutting one single before changing their name to Opal. *Fell from the Sun*, an EP of Clay Allison material, appeared under this new name, followed by the *Northern Line* EP and in 1987, the *Happy Nightmare Baby* album. Kendra's departure during the tour that followed, however, ruptured the band and Roback linked with vocalist Hope Sandoval in Mazzy Star.

Rain Parade LPs

7 Emergency Third Rail Power Trip (Enigma) 1983 Trippy west coast psychedelia reigns here — a nice ambience, sweet pop, and Dream Syndicate's Kendra Smith guesting on "This Can't Be Today."

6 Beyond the Sunset [LIVE] (Restless) 1985 Strong set, well recorded in Japan with a new line-up and a clutch of cuts from *Emergency* and the *Explosions in the Glass Palace* EP, plus a nifty cover of Television's "Ain't That Nothin'."

4 Crashing Dream (Island) 1985 Overall a weak effort, scattered and false. *Crashing Dream* was a crashing bore, except for "Depending On You."

Rainy Day LP

8 Rainy Day (Enigma) 1984 David Roback-assembled supergroup-of-sorts, kicking back with an eclectic covers jam. Members of the Bangles, Dream Syndicate, Three O'Clock, and Rain Parade turn on to Dylan's "I'll Keep It With Mine," Alex Chilton's "Holocaust," the Who's "Soon Be Home," and, of course, Hendrix's "Rainy Day, Dream Away."

Steven Roback/Viva Saturn LPs

7 Soundmind (Heyday) 1992 Roback trades some hippy essence for pure power pop.

7 Brightside (Restless) 1995

Opal LP

5 Happy Nightmare Baby (SST) 1987 Nice and mellow, Velvet Underground lite.

Selected Compilations and Archive Releases

4 Early Recordings (Rough Trade) 1989 A best-of with outtakes, plus the Kendra Smith/David Roback/Keith Mitchell *Fell From the Sun* EP and more.

Mazzy Star LPs

7 She Hangs Brightly (Capitol) 1990 This is obviously where Roback had been leading. Mazzy Star is the culmination a decade of meandering. Singer Hope Sandoval replaces some of the Opal-esque psychedelics with utterly haunting delivery and helps create an ethereal soundscape.

6 So Tonight That I Might See (Capitol) 1993 More ragged than its predecessor, this set did reveal the diamond "Fade Into You."

5 Among My Swan (Capitol) 1996

RAINCOATS

FORMED 1977 *(London, England)*
ORIGINAL LINE-UP *Ana Da Silva (b. 1949, Madeira, Portugal); Gina Birch (b. 1956, Nottingham, England); Ross Crighton (guitar); Nick Turner (drums)*

The Raincoats played their first show in November 1977, opening for Doll by Doll at the Tabernacle, West London, a month after forming around a nucleus of Ana Da Silva and Gina Birch, plus Ross Crighton and future Barracudas/Lords of the New Church member Nick Turner. He remained on board for just a handful of shows; Kate Korus (ex-Slits, later of the Mo-Dettes) and Richard Dudanski (ex-101ers, later PiL) would also drum with the band through 1978 before another ex-Slit Palmolive joined in mid-1978. Ross Crighton also quit — he was replaced briefly by Jeremie Frank before, at Palmolive's suggestion, the band advertised for a woman musician and recruited the classically trained Vicky Aspinall (violin) in mid-1978.

Signing to Rough Trade, the band released their first single, "Fairytale in the Supermarket," in April 1979. Produced by Mayo Thompson (Red Crayola) and Rough Trade label head Geoff Travis, the single epitomized a band who one *NME* journalist later described as, "so bad… that every time a waiter drops a tray, we all get up and dance." At a time when punk was splintering into almost free-form territory, trivial rhythms were collapsing into the frail funk convolutions crowned by the Pop Group and the Slits, and the ethos of "play first, learn later," was still a healthy habit, the Raincoats evinced a shattering passion that eclipsed many of their better known contemporaries.

The Raincoats (#5 UK indy) arrived in January 1980. "We made our first album at precisely the right time," Gina Birch later reflected. "A couple of months on either side and it would have been totally different."

Palmolive quit in September following the band's latest tour — she subsequently left music, moving to Massachusetts with her family and embracing Christianity. She re-emerged in the mid-1990s with a new Christian Rock band, Hi Fi. The Raincoats, meanwhile, replaced her with Ingrid Weiss and continued gigging sporadically through 1980, touring with the Slits, among others, and performing at the Communist Party benefit at Alexander Palace in June alongside the Pop Group, the Slits, and John Cooper Clarke. In lieu of a new album, however, the band produced *The Raincoats Booklet*, a 32-page collection of photos, lyrics, and biography, which was distributed free and previewed several of the songs that would eventually appear on their second album, 1981's *Odyshape* (#5 UK indy), recorded with guests Robert Wyatt and Charles Hayward of This Heat.

Weiss quit shortly before the album's completion; Aspinall, too, seemed to be drifting away, appearing on the New Age Steppers debut album and Vivien Goldman's "Launderette" single. Meanwhile, Birch was now a de facto member of Red Crayola, alongside Thompson, Epic Soundtracks, and Laura Logic, contributing to 1979's "Microchips and Fish" and "Born in Flames" singles and 1981's *Kangaroo* LP. However, the Raincoats reconvened to tour through late 1981, and a new single appeared in July 1982 — the early live favorite "No-One's Little Girl," backed by a cover of Sly Stone's "Running Away" (#47 UK indy).

A live cassette, *The Kitchen Tapes*, followed in March 1983, a stop-gap while the Raincoats — with Dudanski back on drums, plus Paddy O'Connell (sax) and Derek Goddard (percussion) — worked on their third album. However, the group continued to splinter, a final 45, "Animal Rhapsody," in November 1983 prefacing the all but posthumous *The Moving* (#5 UK indy) in January 1984.

Birch formed a new band, Dorothy, with Aspinall but eventually moved into video production, working with the Pogues, New Order, and Daisy Chainsaw among others. Aspinall began working in dance music and Da Silva chose a career in an antiques store, which is where Nirvana's Kurt Cobain found her eight years later when he visited London. The Raincoat's first album had been one of his formative influences, as his liner notes to Nirvana's *Incesticide* compilation would make clear.

It was his interest that brought the band members back together — initially to supervise Geffen's planned reissues of their three albums, but also to consider a reunion. In 1993, da Silva and Birch reconvened the Raincoats with Anne Wood (violin) and Sonic Youth drummer Steve Shelley for shows in London and New York. The band recorded a John Peel session, later released as the *Extended Play* EP; this was followed by a new album, 1995's *Looking in the Shadows*, produced by Ed Buller (Psychedelic Furs, London Suede) and featuring Wood and Heather Dunn (drums).

Despite acknowledging an empathy with the Riot Grrrl movement with which the Raincoats were posthumously linked, however, Birch insisted that the band's aggression was targeted more at cerebral confrontation than sexual. "I never felt comfortable screaming 'fuck you' on stage. Although it was fun."

Raincoats LPs

🄋 The Raincoats (Rough Trade)1980 A purposefully awkward avant-shuffle, lurching between weighted philosophy and death dance rhythms, certainly cut in a less abrasive Pop Group mold, but blessed with an ecstatic harmonic tunefulness.

🄍 Odyshape (Rough Trade) 1981 Wider-ranging acoustics give the instruments and, more potently, the discordance more space to move in, with the violin in particular making its presence felt, both eerily and skull-splittingly.

🄋 Kitchen Tapes [LIVE] (Roir) 1983 Recorded in New York, December 1982, a rough snapshot of the band's true live intensity.

🄍 Moving (Rough Trade) 1984 A distant-sounding album, less a sign of the band's imminent split, however, than an indication of just how their early capacity for questioning had been crushed into rage and despair.

🄍 Looking in the Shadows (Geffen) 1996 A competent comeback, fully conscious of how and why they'd returned but bolstered by a burning desire not to simply relive old glories. The end result was more tuneful than anything they'd accomplished in the past, but maybe a little less exciting.

Selected Compilations and Archive Releases

🄍 Best Of (Tim/Kerr) 1995 Combining elements of all three Rough Trade albums.

RAMONES

FORMED *1974 (New York, NY)*

ORIGINAL LINE-UP *Joey Ramone (b. Jeff Hyman, 5/19/51, Forest Hills, NY — vocals); Johnny Ramone (b. John Cummings, 10/8/51, Long Island, NY — guitar); Dee Dee Ramone (b. Douglas Colvin, 9/18/52, Virginia — bass); Tommy Ramone (b. Thomas Erdelyi, 1/29/52, Budapest, Hungary — drums)*

The Ramones' first show was at a private party in Joey's native Forest Hills in early 1974; as a trio of Joey (drums), Johnny (guitar), and bassist Ritchie Ramone, they made their debut that spring, one "New Bands Night" at CBGBs in New York. Ritchie was replaced by Dee Dee soon after, with Tommy — already a successful recording engineer, with stints with Mountain, Herbie Hancock, and John McLaughlin to his credit — following, to allow Joey to take over on vocals. He and Johnny had previously played together in the Tangerine Puppets: Tommy on guitar, Johnny on bass.

In June 1975, the Ramones opened for Johnny Winter in Waterbury, CT, in hope of getting signed to the Blue Sky label. The company passed, but with former New York Dolls manager Marty Thau taking an interest in their development, the band recorded their first demos. Persistent calls to former Doors associate Danny Fields, too, paid off when he became their manager and landed a deal with Sire. The label originally wanted a single only; the Ramones turned them down, holding out for a full album. Finally Sire agreed

and, in May 1976, released *The Ramones* (#111 US), recorded for $6,400 in February 1976.

The Ramones' impact was immediate. Although they had steadfastly avoided inclusion on any of the New York compilations emerging at that time, word of their mach one bubblegum recreations had already leaked out — at least in the UK. A visit to London in July 1976 saw them regarded as arriving heroes, doing much to coalesce the already gathering forces of punk.

America, on the other hand, had very little time for the band. The Ramones spent a month in California in August, becoming the first studio guests on scene maker Rodney Bingenheimer's new *Rodney on the ROQ* show, but the city's old guard was distinctly unimpressed. Robert Hilburn, in the local *Times*, was one of the first to nail his colors to the flag post of Generation Gap infamy, complaining, "the songs are too short, the lyrics are dismal and the musicianship is rarely above that of the average garage band." What he didn't understand was that after the Ramones, there would no such thing as an average garage band anymore.

A single, "Blitzkrieg Bop," with its signature "hey ho let's go" rallying cry, accompanied the album; "I Wanna Be Your Boyfriend" followed, giving the Ramones a presence in the European marketplace that their homeland was still fiercely resisting. Even the band's withdrawal from the Sex Pistols "Anarchy" tour in November, an indication of the cultural void that — for all the superficial resemblances — existed

© Jim Steinfeldt/Chansley Entertainment Archives

between British and American punk ideals, could not dent their standing.

Accompanied by a new single, "I Remember You," *The Ramones Leave Home* (#148 US, #45 UK), the band's sophomore album, arrived in March 1977, running into immediate controversy in the US, where the Carbona company objected to the use of its trademarked name in "Carbona Not Glue," and in Britain, where the band's apparent obsession with sniffing anything whatsoever was attacked by political and moral guardians alike. But it was the May release of the epochal "Sheena Is a Punk Rocker" (#81 US, #22 UK) that catapulted the Ramones into the major leagues, a bona fide hit which established the band as superstars-in-waiting.

"Swallow My Pride" (#36 UK), "Rockaway Beach" (#66 US), and "Do You Wanna Dance" (#86 US) followed during late 1977/early 1978, with the band ending 1977 with a triumphant New Year's Eve show at the London Rainbow, recorded for the in-concert *It's Alive* (#27 UK) released 18 months later. In the meantime, the band's third album, the comparatively downbeat *Rocket to Russia* (#49 US, #60 UK) saw the band develop further from their original buzzsaw roar, at the same time retaining their breathless immediacy.

The Ramones' equanimity was shaken in May 1978, when Tommy "quit"; the errant brother would remain alongside the band in the studio, reverting to his given name, while his bandmates recruited Marky Ramone (b. Marc Bell, 7/15/56 — ex-Richard Hell).

That year's *Road to Ruin* (#103 US, #32 UK) represented a conscious attempt to break out of the two-minute buzzsaw anthem mold, a mood enhanced by the attendant single, "Don't Come Close" (#39 UK). However, the Ramones were back to their primal best for their movie debut, starring in Roger Corman's Rock'n'Roll High school. Then, with a Phil Spector remix of the title track maintaining their UK chart profile (#67 UK), the band and Spector got down to recording the Ramones' fifth album, January 1980's ambitious *End of the Century* (#44 US, #14 UK).

Despite the band's later reservations about the album as a whole and the very real strain between band and producer (Spector pulled a gun on Dee Dee and drove Johnny to briefly leave the band), "Baby I Love You" (#8 UK), Spector's reprise of the Ronettes' 1964 hit, became the band's biggest ever hit in February. "Do You Remember Rock'n'Roll Radio" (#54 UK) followed, and the Ramones were one of the hits of the 1980 Edinburgh Festival, as they toured the UK and Europe to rapturous acclaim. Plans to record their next album with the then–little known Steve Lillywhite were scotched by Sire, who instead teamed the band with '60s hitmaker/10cc mainstay Graham Gouldman. The resulting album, *Pleasant Dreams* (#58 US), again incurred the band's wrath, all the more so since it became their first album since

Ramones not to chart in the UK. Indeed, the band's UK fame would dip sharply over the next decade as the Ramones' music and attitude leaned further towards a domestic hard core sound.

In September 1981, the Ramones played the US Festival in San Bernadino, CA, their last significant outing for over a year — their silence through 1982 was broken only by Joey linking with Holly Beth Vincent of Holly & The Italians for a single of "I Got You, Babe." They re-emerged when May 1983 brought the *Subterranean Jungle* (#83 US) album, produced by '60s bubblegum maestro Ritchie Cordell and Glen Kolotkin. It was Marky Ramone's last record with the band. His departure was so sudden that a session man needed to be brought in to record the final track of the session. Marky was eventually replaced by Richie Ramone (b. Richard Beau — ex-Velveteens).

The Ramones themselves nearly came to an end in August after Joey was involved in a fight with Sub Zero Construction's Seth Micklaw; the singer was discovered unconscious on the street and rushed to hospital, where he underwent four hours of brain surgery to remove blood clots.

It would be over a year before the Ramones returned, in November 1984, with the aptly titled *Too Tough to Die* (#171 US, #63 UK), coproduced by Tommy ex-Ramone, and featuring guest appearances from Dave Stewart (Eurythmics), Benmont Tench (Tom Petty's Heartbreakers), and Jerry Harrison (Talking Heads). The album would not be released in the UK until the following January, after the band quit Sire and signed to Beggars Banquet (they remained with Sire in America); accompanied by the "Howling at the Moon" (#85 UK), it relaunched the band in Europe, with further attention garnered by their next single, "Bonzo Goes to Bitburg," condemning President Reagan's recent visit to Nazi war graves in Germany.

In June 1985, the band opened for U2 at Milton Keynes Bowl, while Joey alone scored a hit when he teamed with Little Steven's Artists United Against Apartheid for the self-explanatory "Ain't Gonna Play Sun City" (#38 US, #21 UK) in December. The next Ramones album, *Animal Boy* (#143 US, #38 UK), and single, "Somebody Put Something in My Drink" (#69 UK — based around a real-life incident suffered by Richie), saw the band's rejuvenation continue.

Richie quit in 1987 and was briefly replaced by Clem Burke (ex-Blondie), before Marky Ramone returned for *Halfway to Sanity* (#172 US, #78 UK); 1988, however, would bring only a Ramones greatest hits package, *Ramones Mania* (#168 US) and a joint single by Joey and Debbie Harry, "Go L'il Camaro Go." The band themselves returned in 1989 with *Brain Drain* (#122 US, #75 UK) and the title theme to the Stephen King movie *Pet Sematary*, but the biggest news of the year was the departure of Dee Dee for a new career in rap music. He became Dee Dee King (later reverting to his band name for further solo releases).

His replacement was a not-quite-former Marine, CJ Ramone (b. Christopher Ward, b. 10/8/65, Long Island); CJ was, in fact, AWOL when he auditioned for the band and was recaptured when he went home to visit his mother, whose illness had prompted him to desert in the first place. He spent three weeks in the brig before being discharged into the arms of the waiting Ramones.

Despite having to cancel a projected US tour in February, one of the highlights of the band's next album, *Mondo Bizarro*, was a cover of the Doors "Take It as It Comes"; an entire album of similarly themed covers appeared as *Acid Eaters* in early 1994 (#179 US), but the band's declining commercial standing — wholly overshadowed as they were by new punk talent like Green Day and Offspring — was taking its toll.

Early the following year, the band announced their intention to break up following one last album, 1995's *Adios Amigos* (#148 US), and what turned out to be a very lengthy farewell tour. Beginning in August 1995, it finally wrapped up in Seattle the following September, having taken the band around the world and across the US several times, including a headlining appearance on Lollapalooza '96. The Ramones finally bowed out with 1997's appropriately titled *We're Outta Here*. Joey was the first to resurface, as producer of Ronnie (ex-wife of producer Phil) Spector's 1998 comeback EP *She Talks to Rainbows*. The title track was a Ramones cover; another, "Bye Bye Baby," featured a duet with Joey. Joey would also appear live with Spector in New York and London.

The Ramones LPs

10 Ramones (Sire) 1976 Hey, ho! Let's go! And the Ramones do, blitzkrieging their way through a barrage of percussive assaults, blender guitars, and shotgun lyrics. With the hindsight induced by all that came after, *Ramones* no longer seems to be played at hyperspeed, and the songs aren't the least bit menacing. Times change, outrage shifts, and even "second verse, same as the first" sounds fairly standard these days. But in 1976, there was nothing like it on earth, and if Judy's no longer a punk… she was; the "Texas Chain Saw Massacre" was still a frightening concept and "Beat on the Brat" was an inducement to some quite savage amusement.

9 The Ramones Leave Home (Sire) 1977 Refining their sound, headbangers ("Glad to See You Go," the anthemic "Commando," et al.) vie with pop ("California Sun," "I Remember You," etc.) as *The Ramones Leave Home* but don't move far from their debut. But songs like the eventually withdrawn "Carbona Not Glue" and its replacement, "Babysitter," distill to further perfection their pop/punk mix.

8 Rocket to Russia (Sire) 1977 Completing the set (most of *Leave* and much of *Rocket* was written prior to the release of their debut album), the Ramones accept with open arms "Pinheads," "Cretins" (hopping or otherwise), "Teenage Lobotomies," and, of course, punk-rockers, all hitching a ride down to "Rockaway Beach" to catch the "Surfin' Bird" in action. But a growing maturity is peeking through, as the ballad "Here Today, Gone Tomorrow" proves.

8 Road to Ruin (Sire) 1978 Aggressive onstage, there was nothing remotely threatening (at least lyrically) on the band's first three albums. But with *Ruin* their anger and frustration leak through, vividly heard on… "Something to Do" and "Sedated." Still the exquisitely bittersweet "Don't Come Close" and the bright pop "She's the One" suggest the Ramones haven't reached the end of the road yet.

8 Rock 'N' Roll High School (Sire) 1979 Soundtrack to the movie of the same name, the Ramones contributed the anthemic title track and the ballad "I Want You Around," along with a duet with the Paley Brothers. A gathering of further fans faves — Devo, Eddie & The Hotrods, Nick Lowe, Alice Cooper, and others — add to the musical mayhem.

8 It's Alive [LIVE] (Sire) 1979 New Year's Eve in London. Where else could you be than at a Ramones gig?

8 End of the Century (Sire) 1980 Producer Phil Spector fulfills Joey's dream of finally achieving that '60s wall of sound, with the band even covering his old "Baby I Love You," before hitting new pop heights with "I Can't Make It on Time" and diving head first into the nostalgia of… "Rock'N'Roll Radio." Initially, many fans ran screaming from the band's perceived pop excesses, but eventually returned, muttering it was all Spector's fault.

6 Pleasant Dreams (Sire) 1981 Bringing in 10cc's Graham Gouldman to produce swung the pendulum too far in the other direction. While *Dreams* has some pleasant moments (notably, "She's a Sensation," whose '60s melody still melts through the hard rock, and the new schoolish "Not My Place"), only the angry "We Want the Airwaves" really works, with the rest just a bad rock dream.

6 Subterranean Jungle (Sire) 1983 Internal divisions saw Marky depart before the end of *Jungle*'s recording, as the Ramones return to both their punk roots (the searing "Psycho Therapy") and their pop past (the killer cover of "Time Has Come Today"). But it's evident that the group are struggling to overcome ever greater hurdles.

7 Too Tough to Die (Sire) 1984 And indeed they are, as the Ramones come back stronger than ever, with errant brother Tommy in the production seat. Much of *Tough* crackles with new found energy, from the sparkling pop of "Howling at the Moon" to the rockabilly snarl of "Mama's Boy," then takes their music into new depths with the moody "I'm Not Afraid of Life" and on to the speed core of "Endless Vacation…." … Speedcore?

5 Animal Boy (Sire) 1986 "Bonzo Goes to Bitburg" (retitled "My Brain…" on the album) is just one of the many stand-outs on an eclectic album that sees the Ramones reaching back to their pure punk past for "Eat That Rat," revisiting rock ("Somebody Put Something…"), before exploring Brit-pop ("Something to Believe In"), but the highlight, ironically, was saved for a B-side, the heartrending ode to Sid and Nancy, "I Don't Want to Live This Life."

4 Halfway to Sanity (Sire) 1987 The upbeat "I Wanna Live" nods to new romantic melodies, and *Sanity* plays with other '80s styles as well (including the Cult-ish gothesque "Garden of Serenity") before returning to format if not form, with a clutch of punk rockers and the bubbly pop of "Go Lil' Camaro Go."

2 Brain Drain (Sire) 1989 The album sounds unsure of itself, reflecting the internal divisions that resulted in Dee Dee's departure. The songs are there, including "Merry Christmas," "Pet Sematary," and the upbeat "I Believe in Miracles," but Bill Laswell's stultifying production scars an already mystifying union.

8 Loco Live [LIVE] (Sire) 1991 The fast fun and exhaustion; Coneheads with a gabba gabba banner and 15 years worth of mayhem to squeeze into a little over an hour. They'd better play really fast then.…

6 Mondo Bizarro (Radioactive) 1992 New bassist C.J. makes his recording debut and brings new life and blood to da bruddahs. More eclectic than most Ramones' albums, *Mondo* bounces from bright pop to hard rock, soars with the Byrds, slows down for the emotive "Poison Heart" (one of three songs written by the departed Dee Dee), pulls out the psychedelic keyboards for a Doors cover (courtesy of Psychedelic Fur Joe McGinty), then brings on Living Colour's Vernon Reid to knock out some searing big rock riffs. Best of all is the Beach Boysish "Touring," a joyous celebration of life on the road.

7 Acid Eaters (Radioactive) 1994 The Ramones versus a '60s jukebox and no points for guessing who wins. A dozen covers of pop, rock, surf, British invasion, and psychedelic classics, done in the expected inimitable style. Yet even a song as fragile as the Stones "Out of Time" sounds quite happy, and check out the special guest power chorder, Pete Townsend.

6 Adios Amigos (Radioactive) 1995 The Ramones return to their roots… in more ways than one, as Dee Dee comes home with six new songs (most cowritten with album producer Daniel Rey) for his former siblings. There's a real sense of homecoming weekend surrounding *Adios*, accentuated by the straight-ahead punk pound of the songs, the solid live-in-the-studio production, and even a nostalgic look back via a Johnny Thunders cover and the anthemic "Cretin Family."

7 Greatest Hits Live [LIVE] (MCA) 1996 Recorded at the Academy in front of a hometown crowd in February 1996, the Ramones run through the best bits of the past two decades, delivering up 16 songs in just over half an hour, then tossing on three bonus studio tracks for good measure.

6 We're Outta Here! [LIVE] (Radioactive) 1997 The farewell tour went on forever. Why shouldn't the live souvenirs?

Selected Compilations and Archive Releases

7 Ramones Mania (Sire) 1989 This 30-track compilation includes hits, crowd faves, and rarities (singles, a British B-side, and the odd previously unreleased track), but loses points for its bizarre refusal to sequence chronologically. Great liner notes, though.

9 All the Stuff & More, Vol. 1 (Sire) 1990 Bundles together the band's first two albums along with a B-side, two demos, and a pair of live cuts.

9 All the Stuff & More, Vol. 2 (Sire) 1990 The third and fourth albums compiled together, plus four bonus tracks.

8 Hey! Ho! Let's Go: The Anthology (Rhino) 1999 The Ramones box set was never going to be big enough to actually put in a box, but still, 58 tracks spread over two discs more than compensate for the lack of dead wood… which is what most boxed sets are all about. This one is just nonstop hey-ho-ing all the way, from the opening "Blitzkrieg Bop" and through those immaculate first four albums to the end of disc one; then on to the end, and the valedictory "R.A.M.O.N.E.S." — a Motorhead cover! There's not much room for rarities (although the once-banned "Carbona Not Glue" is reinstated from *Leave Home*); there's not really any need for them. After all, most Ramones songs sounded the same, which was the beauty of da bruddahs in the first place, and once you've beaten on one brat, you've beaten on them all.

Marky Ramone & The Intruders LP

7 Marky Ramone & The Intruders (Blackout) 1997 Once a Ramone, always a Ramone, even if he was a Voidoid first. From the cretin lyrics ("I lost my beer, I lost my beer") to the breakneck buzzsaw guitar and the drums that rise so high in the mix you spend half the first track answering the door, it's business as glorious usual.

Dee Dee Ramone LPs

4 Standing in the Spotlight (Sire) 1989 Dee Dee speaks: "after I left the Ramones, I went and got lots of Adidas gear and gold chains. I was just so happy. I thought that dance music was the only street thing happening." Dee Dee raps. Enough said.

6 I Hate Freaks Like You (World Domination) 1994

6 Ain't It Fun (Blackout) 1997

Further Reading

An American Band by Jim Bessman (St. Martin's Press, 1993).

RANCID

FORMED 1991 (Oakland, CA)
ORIGINAL LINE-UP Tim Armstrong (vocals, guitar); Matt Freeman (bass); Brett Reed (drums)

Following the break-up of Operation Ivy and short-lived stints with Dance Hall Crashers and Downfall, Tim Armstrong and Matt Freeman (also ex-MDC) recruited Gilman Street regular Brett Reed (ex-the even more short-lived Smog) and debuted as Rancid at a friend's house in Oakland in December 1991. They released the *I'm Not the Only One* EP the following year on Lookout Records — the five cuts indicating their intention to remain within the melodic punk/ska core frame that characterized the best of Op Ivy.

Having signed to Bad Religion's Epitaph label in late 1992 and looking to add a second guitarist before commencing work on their debut album, Rancid approached Green Day's Billie Joe Armstrong (no relation). He played one show with the band, but with Green Day also gathering speed, he turned down a full-time engagement. Work had already begun on the record when the UK Subs' Lars Fredericksen (whose last band, Slip, had opened one of Rancid's earliest shows) was recruited. Although he would not appear on the album, still he joined Rancid immediately.

Rancid's eponymous album arrived in April 1993, and in September, the band embarked on their first tours of the US (including gigs with Bad Religion and Green Day) and Europe, a seven week marathon which took them through Britain, Italy, Belgium, and Germany. A new EP, *Radio Radio Radio*, followed in early 1994, marking Fredericksen's debut on record; "Radio" itself was cowritten by Billie Joe Armstrong.

In February 1994, the band began recording *Let's Go* (#97 US), following through with close to six months of solid touring and festival dates, and the rewards began pouring in — a gold disc for *Let's Go*, an MTV hit with "Salvation," and a major label bidding war. Epic offered the band $1.5 million, while Madonna sent the band a pin-up, her way of inviting them to join her Maverick stable. Rancid, however, were happy where they were. "We made a band decision that we wanted to stay with Epitaph," said Freeman. "No matter what happened that's where we should be, just because all our friends were there."

A single, "Roots Radical," kept the pot boiling through early 1995; in March, Rancid began work on their next album, ...*And Out Come the Wolves* (#45 US), a wild ride through the underbelly of the mid-90s ska–punk explosion, complete with a look back at Operation Ivy, "Journey to the End of the East Bay."

With the singles "Ruby Soho" and "Time Bomb" (#56 UK) scoring across Europe, the ...*Wolves* tour finally ended with a berth on Lollapalooza '96, following which the band took a brief hiatus; Armstrong took the opportunity to launch his own Hellcat label through Epitaph, debuting it the following year with releases by the Gadjits, Hepcat, Dropkick Murphys, and more.

The band re-emerged briefly in 1997 for the Tibetan Freedom Concert in June; work on the next Rancid album, meanwhile, would be spread across studios in New York, New Orleans, Jamaica, San Francisco, and Armstrong's own Bloodclot Studios in L.A.; the finished product, 1998's *Life Won't Wait* (#35 US), would feature guest appearances from Marky Ramone (Ramones), Howie Pyro (D Generation), Buju Banton, Dickie Barrett (Mighty Mighty Bosstones), Dave Hillyard (Stubborn All Stars), Greg Lee (Hepcat), and the Specials' Neville Staples and Lynval Golding. Opening the year with the 1998 Vans Warped Tour, Rancid toured the US through November 1998, moving onto Australia and New Zealand before returning to the US for two December shows. The band then resurfaced in 1999 with a cover of Sham 69's "If the Kids Are United" on the Hellcat compilation *Give 'Em the Boot 2*. The group's fifth eponymous album followed during summer 2000.

Also see the entry for "OPERATION IVY" on page 537.

Rancid LPs

6 Rancid (Epitaph) 1993 People expected Operation Ivy — The Next Generation. Instead they were confronted with an anthemic, bass-driven, hard-core band whose brutally realistic snapshots of life in the gutter were tempered by the trio's love of melody.

8 Let's Go (Epitaph) 1994 With the enlistment of guitarist Fredricksen, Rancid crank up the melodies, slather on the harmonies, and spread the vocals around the band, spitting out 23 high-octane tracks with machine-gun precision and power.

9 ...And Out Come the Wolves (Epitaph) 1995 Rancid's self-assurance shines throughout *Wolves*. Armstrong's lyrics are much more upbeat and the mid-tempo numbers provide room for killer solos. Bright, brash, and heavily melodic, this remains one of the best sounding punk albums ever recorded.

9 Life Won't Wait (Epitaph) 1998 So Rancid get on with it in a glorious celebration of punk's present and precedents, a wild celebration of the *creme de la creme* of the ska, dance hall, and punk scenes, making for an exuberantly diverse album.

8 Rancid (Epitaph) 2000 Stipped-back return to formative hardcore/punk basics.

RAUNCHETTES

FORMED 1985 (Rochester, NY)
ORIGINAL LINE-UP Betsy Palmer (vocals, guitar); Janice Raunchette (guitar); Kiy Raunchette (bass); Joan Schopf (drums)

Formed in January 1985, the Raunchettes had been together just one month when they recorded their first demos, "Too Serious," and a version of the girl group classic "My Boyfriend's Back," before cutting their debut single, "Slaughter a Pig," for the local Jargon label. Following through with cuts on the compilations 9x9 and 8x4, the band's reputation for maniacal unconventionality seemed to grow with every show — at one, they staged a bake sale beside the stage, to raise money; at another, with all four band members suffering from flu, they played in their pajamas.

"Discovered" by Lords of the New Church vocalist Stiv Bators, Palmer, and Kiy Raunchette relocated to Hollywood the following year, completing the line-up with Gigi and Geolyn Raunchette. The Raunchettes signed to Bomp, and in 1987 released the Bators-produced self-titled debut EP.

Schopf rejoined the Raunchettes shortly after, and the band launched an east coast tour with the Lazy Cowgirls, as Jargon gathered together a clutch of demos and out-takes as the *Scrapbook* album. The Raunchettes return to Hollywood, however, saw a constantly fluctuating line-up finally shatter after Kiy quit. Schopf returned to the east coast and joined Lowell, MA-based Lawn Boy 2000; Palmer linked with Lazy Cowgirls Allen Clark and Keith Telligmann and Claw Hammer's Rob Walther and Chris Bagarozzi, as the psychedelia-fused Sacred Miracle Cave, in 1991. A handful of singles for SFTRI followed before the band, joined by Claw Hammer's John Wahl and Raunchette Schopf, went into the studio to cut their debut album.

Following early sessions with Rain Parade's Dave Roback, *Sacred Miracle Cave* was completed with Bad Religion's Brett Gurewitz and released by Bomp in 1991; however, the band themselves broke up soon after.

In 1995, Palmer and Schopf launched a new band, the Phenobarbidols, with Robin Clewell (bass) and Carmen Hillebrew (guitar). Hillebrew quit following the band's *Beyond the Valley of the Phenobarbidols* debut EP and a cut on SFTRI's *Happy Birthday Baby Jesus* Christmas album; enlisting Bibi McGill, the band recorded their first album, *Fish Lounge*, before McGill, too, quit, to be replaced by Pilar Stupa guitarist Delphine 13.

Anticipating the late 1999 revival of theremin (the world's first electronic musical instrument), the Phenobarbidols' next single, "Come Now," featured Spaceman 3's Sonic Boom playing that very instrument. However, the Phenobarbidols broke up before they could reap any relevant rewards,

Palmer moving on to work occasionally with L.A. band Satan's Cheerleaders.

Raunchettes LPs

Selected Compilations and Archive Releases
7 Scrapbook (Jargon) 1988 Sound quality varies, but there are few more invigorating rummages through the punk dustbin of demos, out-takes, and oddities than this.

Sacred Miracle Cave LP
8 Sacred Miracle Cave (Bomp) 1991 An extraordinary lyricist and so-seductive vocalist, Palmer leads the Cave through an album of tight, angular pysch awash in post-Americana emotion/art.

Phenobarbidols LP
8 Fish Lounge (SFTRI) 1995 Imagine your all-time favorite cross between psychedelia, pop, punk, acid rock, and prog, all wrapped up in a voice (Palmer again) to melt for… picture "Albert On His Bike" and Patti's "Rock'n'Roll Nigger," add on the fabulously scarce *Beyond the Valley of…* 10-inch EP, and if the mid-1990s had nothing else going for them, they still had the Phenobarbidols.

RED CRAYOLA

FORMED 1978 (New York, NY)
ORIGINAL LINE-UP 1966–69 [reunion] line-up: Mayo Thompson (guitar); Jesse Chamberlain (drums)

Although the original Red Crayola were a part of the Texas garage scene of the mid-1960s, creators of the immortal "Hurricane Fighter Plane" and a pair of snarling nuggets-stuffed fuzzy psych albums before the end of the decade, 10 years more would elapse before the band — long since splintered — emerged as anything more than a ghostly crackle on a string of garage archive collections.

In 1978, guitarist Mayo Thompson relocated to London as A&R man for the indy Rough Trade label; he produced a number of the company's early signings, including the Raincoats, Stiff Little Fingers, Scritti Politti, and the Fall, and also arranged for his old band's two albums to be reissued into a firestorm of critical approval. A single of "Hurricane Fighter Plane" (backed by the similarly vintage "Reverberation" by 13th Floor Elevators cut) appeared free with *Zig Zag* magazine, and with both original albums, *The Parable of Arable Land* and *God Bless the Red Krayola*, selling well, Thompson began contemplating a return to the stage.

Since Red Crayola's demise, his activities had been largely confined to recordings with the New York collective Art and Language (collected on the *Corrected Slogans* compilation)

and a much-overlooked solo album in 1970. Working now from a base loosely rendered from the platforms espoused by Pere Ubu in the US and Gang of 4 in the UK, Thompson and new partner Jesse Chamberlain signed with the Radar label.

By mid-1978, Red Crayola were gigging regularly, putting on a sensational show at the Hope & Anchor pub — later highlighted on the *Pink Stainless Hall* EP. They also cut the "Wives in Orbit" single, followed swiftly by *Soldier Talk*, an album that featured backing from Pere Ubu's David Thomas and X-RaySpex/Essential Logic saxophonist Laura Logic. (The album's title track would also appear on a single.)

In common with much of the music Thompson was pursuing outside of the band, it was a brutal, challenging work, delighting the critics but doing little else, and the 1979 single "Micro-Chips and Fish" marked the end of this incarnation of the band, as Thompson headed off to join Pere Ubu full time. Under his guidance, that band would emerge with their most accomplished, yet simultaneously most obtuse album yet, *Art of Walking* (#3 UK indy).

Pere Ubu went on hiatus soon after and in 1980, Thompson, Chamberlain, Pere Ubu keyboard player Allen Ravenstine, and the Raincoats' Gina Birch began working together under a reborn Red Crayola banner. A single, "Born in Flames" (#19 UK indy), appeared in October 1980, followed by "An Old Man's Dream" in July 1981. Renewing Thompson's acquaintance with Art and Language, this line-up would also cut two albums: May 1981's *Kangaroo?* (#22 UK indy) and *Black Snakes* — avant-garde theater soundtracks without the theater to explain what was happening. The single "Ratman the Rat Catcher" did not clarify matters.

The trio also toured, and in 1984, Red Crayola issued *Three Songs on a Trip to the United States*, an album-length EP that appended the title cuts with a hefty slice of live material recorded in Germany and featuring a truly manic version of "Wives in Orbit."

Red Crayola broke up again, freeing Thompson to oversee the reissue of his 1970 solo album, *Corky's Debt to His Father*. He continued in production, too, working with Primal Scream and the Chills among others, but in 1989, Red Crayola returned with *Malefactor; Ade*. The band would continue recording through the 1990s.

Red Crayola LPs

7 Soldier Talk (Radar — UK) 1979 A reconvened Red Crayola, aided by Pere Ubu, howling across a scorching garage rocker that was both retro and postmodern in scope.

6 Three Songs On a Trip to the United States (Recommended — UK) 1984 Essentially an EP, the set peaks across its second side and a hefty live slab of stripped-down psychedelics.

6 Malefactor; Ade (Glass — UK) 1989

6 The Red Crayola (Drag City) 1994 Rough reinvention of '90's style post-punk via Thompson's musical roots. Not bad on "Pride," although "Book of Kings" is silly.

2 Coconut Hotel (Drag City) 1995 Recorded in 1967 and turned down by Krayola's record label, this self-indulgent instrumental noodle finally sees the light of day. Not good enough then, it's not good enough now, and as far as the 36 "One Second Piece's" go — give us a break. There's not enough dope on earth to make this palatable.

5 Hazel (Drag City) 1996 A little Lou Reed, a little reggae, a little bit of this, a little bit of that… the mish mash is pleasant enough.

5 Fingerpainting (Drag City) 1999 Full of noise, from beginning to end, and as the point is to stretch sonic barriers, to experiment with sound, on that level, it's probably a success. Everyone else should skip straight to "Vile, Vile Grass."

Art & Language & The Red Crayola LPs

5 Kangaroo (Rough Trade) 1981

4 Black Snakes (Pure Freude — Germany) 1983

Selected Compilations and Archive Releases

6 The Parable of Arable Land [1967 REISSUE] (Radar — UK) 1978 Reissue of the band's first album. True psychedelics with an intelligent under tone.

6 God Bless the Red Krayola and All Who Sail With It [1968 REISSUE] (Radar — UK) 1979 The band's second album; more of the same.

5 Corrected Slogans [WITH ART & LANGUAGE] (Recommended — UK) 1982 Demos from 1976 studio session.

Mayo Thompson LP

5 Corky's Debt to His Father [1970 REISSUE] (Glass — UK) 1988 Easier on the stomach than a lot of Red Krayola's stuff, this will primarily appeal to die-hard fans and people who enjoy Skip Spence records. Charming in its own way.

RED HOT CHILI PEPPERS

FORMED 1983 *(Los Angeles, CA)*
ORIGINAL LINE-UP *Anthony Kiedis (b. 11/1/62, Grand Rapids, MI); Hillel Slovak (b. 4/13/62, Haifa, Israel — guitar); Flea (b. Michael Balzary, 10/16/62, Melbourne, Australia — bass); Jack Irons (b. 7/18/62, L.A., CA — guitar)*

Ex-Fear bassist Flea linked up with high school friends Anthony Kiedis and What is This? members Jack Irons and Hillel Slovak in April 1983 as Tony Flow and His Miraculous Majestic Masters of Mayhem. Their debut performance at L.A.'s Kit Kat Club was originally regarded as a one-off show, culminating with the band members appearing on stage naked, bar strategically placed socks. The show was such a success that the quartet continued on as the Red Hot Chili Peppers, landing a residency at the Cathay de Grand and swiftly becoming at least as big a local draw as What Is This?.

A deal with EMI America followed within six months of their debut show; What is This?, too, were offered a contract, and Slovak and Irons opted to remain with that band. In their stead, Kiedis and Flea recruited Jack Sherman (guitar) and Cliff Martinez (ex-Weirdos, drums), and in late 1983 recorded their hip-hop funk hybrid debut album with ex-Gang of 4 Andy Gill producing.

Slovak quit What Is This? following the release of *Red Hot Chili Peppers* in April 1984, replacing Sherman for the recording of *Freaky Styley* with producer and guru George Clinton. However, the band's early development was scarred by the escalating drug habits of Slovak and Kiedis, and the Peppers seemed forever doomed to remain a second division act. Nevertheless, Irons returned to replace Martinez in 1986, confirming the vitality of the original band line-up.

The Peppers' third album, *The Uplift Mofo Party* (#148 US), again stalled, despite the gratuitous publicity generated by the track "Party On Your Pussy." But the band's first full European tour — celebrated by the Beatle-esque sleeve to their *Abbey Road* EP — in early 1988 was a success and the band returned to L.A. prepared to begin work on their next album.

The death of Slovak from a heroin overdose on June 25, 1988, left the Peppers directionless for close to a year. Irons quit, winding up in hospital before being pulled back on the road by Joe Strummer and, later, former What Is This? front man Alan Johannes, with whom he formed Eleven (Irons joined Pearl Jam in 1994). Kiedis, too, went to ground, holing up on a beach in Mexico before returning to L.A. to reform the Peppers.

With Dead Kennedys drummer D.H. Peligro and P-Funk guitarist Duane McKnight on board, the band made a tentative return to live work; auditions then produced Chad Smith (b. 10/25/62, St. Paul, MN, ex-Toby Redd, drums) before Kiedis lured John Frusciante (b. 3/5/70, New York) from a Thelonious Monster audition. Reuniting with *Mofo* producer Michael Beinhorn, the reconstituted Peppers released *Mother's Milk* (#52 US) in September 1989, followed by the singles "Knock Me Down," which reached #6 on the US Modern Rock chart; "Higher Ground" (#55 UK); and "Taste the Pain" (#29 UK). By late March, *Mother's Milk* was gold in the US and early 1991 brought similar success for the *Psychedelic Sex Funk Live From Heaven* concert video.

The group signed to Warners that summer and recorded their new album, *Blood Sugar Sex Magic* (#3 US, #25 UK) with producer Rick Rubin — the perfect combination in every sense. A similar match was offered up by the Peppers' December tour, headlining over the fast-rising Nirvana and Pearl Jam. Both bands would leave the outing before it reached its end.

A string of consecutive hit singles followed — "Give It Away" (#73 US), the anti-drug ballad "Under the Bridge" (#2 US, #26 UK), and "Breaking the Girl" (#41 UK) all scored before *Blood Sugar* completed its rise up the US chart. The set eventually topped triple platinum, although the band's leap to superstardom was not without its casualties.

Frusciante quit the band midway through their Japanese tour; he was replaced by another Thelonious Monster graduate, Zander Schloss, who in turn gave way to Arik Marshall (b. 2/13/67 — ex-Marshall Law, and a session musician whose past credits included Tone Loc and Sting).

Amid this chaos, the Peppers headlined Lollapalooza '92 and won Best Art Direction, Breakthrough Video, and Viewers Choice categories at the MTV awards (for "Give It Away" and "Under The Bridge"); 1992 wrapped up with Top 30 placings for material the band once struggled to give away, as former label EMI released the career-spanning *What Hits?* (#22 US, #23 UK) compilation. A second compilation of B-sides and rarities, *Out in L.A.* (#82 US, #61 UK) would make further use of similar material.

Marshall quit in early 1993, having recorded the band's "Soul to Squeeze" single (#22 US) for the *Coneheads* soundtrack. He was replaced by Jesse Tobias (ex-Mother Tongue) for a handful of summer dates, including the Glastonbury Festival, but the new man lasted little more than a month before Dave Navarro (b. 6/7/67, Santa Monica — ex-Jane's Addiction) was drafted, as the Peppers launched into a period of comparative quiet — plugged with regular session work for Flea, a competent trumpeter as well as bassist, in particular.

A string of reissues — "Give It Away" (#9 UK) and "Under the Bridge" (#13 UK) — prefaced the band's return to action at Woodstock '94 and the Reading Festival that same year. The Peppers also opened two shows for the Rolling Stones in Pasadena in October before completing work on their long-anticipated next album, *One Hot Minute* (#4 US, #2UK).

"My Friends" (#29 UK) topped both the Modern Rock and Album Rock charts; "Warped" (#31 UK) and "Aeroplane" (#11 UK) were similar hits. The band's schedule was severely disrupted, however, when Smith broke his wrist playing baseball. Even as the airplay hit, "Love Rollercoaster" spun off the *Beavis and Butthead Do America* soundtrack, a full fall US tour was canceled, to be rescheduled for the new year, kicking off a well-received world tour.

Flea and Smith's Thermidor side project, formed with Robbie King and David Allen, released their *Monkey On Rico* album that same spring in 1996; the following year, Flea joined Navarro in the oft-rumored Jane's Addiction "relapse" reunion. (He and Jane's drummer Stephen Perkins had already convened an ad hoc band with Rage Against the Machine's Zack de la Rocha and Tom Morella for the "Radio Free L.A." broadcast on January 20.)

Jane's recorded four new songs for the *Kettle Whistle* compilation and toured extensively — an experience that left Navarro convinced that he no longer enjoyed life on the road. He quit the Peppers on April 3, 1998, although Spread, a side project he launched with Smith, would continue.

Navarro was replaced by the returning Frusciante, the new line-up making its comeback at the Tibetan Freedom Concert on June 13, 1998. Work then began on the new album, 1999's *Californication* (#3 US, #5 UK), followed by a prolonged bout of touring, which included Woodstock '99, the Reading Festival, and Baltimore's Festival. While they gigged, the single "Scar Tissue" (#9 US, #15 UK) established a new record stay at the top of Billboard's Modern Rock Tracks chart. The band was also nominated for three Grammy's and scored with further singles "Around the World" and "Otherside."

Red Hot Chili Peppers LPs

8 Red Hot Chili Peppers (EMI America) 1984 They just wanna rap, blitz, yell, and have fun. Nothing of consequence happens here, but it's raucous, loud, and completely uncontrollable. The funk-core revolution starts here.

8 Freaky Styley (EMI America) 1985 More of the same, only more controlled. Producer George Clinton doesn't let things get too chaotic, and the band respond by matching the music to their attitude. Juvenile smut still rocks their boat, but at least they can laugh while they're leering.

8 The Uplift Mofo Party Plan (EMI America) 1987 "Fight Like a Brave," "Party On Your Pussy," and then suddenly… a great song! Indeed, "Behind the Sun" so outclasses the rest of the album that the other songs probably beat it up later.

9 Mother's Milk (EMI America) 1989 "Higher Ground," "Taste the Pain," and the aptly named "Punk Rock Classic" fire the Peppers' most cohesive album yet… that's cohesive and genuinely listenable, by the way.

8 Blood Sugar Sex Magik (WB) 1991 Escape the interminable chain store rap of "Give It Away" and the bleeding heart emotions of "Under the Bridge" and the Peppers strike surprising gold again. Producer Rick Rubin reins in their last few stray weaknesses — it's PG party time from here on in.

7 One Hot Minute (WB) 1995 After the chaos of the last few years, "Aeroplane" at least flies off in a reasonably hopeful direction. Sadly, the rest of the album struggles to catch up.

6 Californication (WB) 1999 The Peppers continued slide into game show host sincerity is at least halted by the monster hit "Scar Tissue," though their peak days of danger seem a long way away now.

Selected Compilations and Archive Releases

7 What Hits!? (EMI America) 1992 Covering the band's pre–big time daze with all the expected chest-beaters, and little in the way of surprises. A helpful primer, but not much else.

8 Out in L.A. (EMI America) 1994 A random collection of 12-inch remixes, occasional B-sides, and the band's first-ever demo — kinda Clash meet Clinton, and his name isn't Bill. Flea and Kiedis' liner notes explain why.

7 Under the Covers: Essential (Capitol) 1998 Slick package wrapping up favorite covers — "Subterranean Homesick Blues," "Search and Destroy," "Fire" — caught live and otherwise. Two previously unreleased songs, "Dr Funkenstein" and "Tiny Dancer," add to the weirdness.

John Frusciante LPs

5 Niandra Ladies & Usually Just a T-Shirt (American) 1994

5 Smile From the Streets You Hold (Birdman) 1997

Thermidor LP

6 Monkey On Rico 1996

Toby Redd LP

5 Toby Redd (Epic) 1987

Further Reading

Red Hot Chili Peppers by Dave Thompson (St. Martin's Press, 1993).

REEL BIG FISH

FORMED 1990 *(Los Angeles, CA)*
ORIGINAL LINE-UP *Ben Guzman (vocals); Matt Wong (bass); Andrew Gonzales (drums) + others*

Reel Big Fish began life as a covers band dedicated to classic rock and glam metal hits, before ska fan Ben Guzman gradually weaned his bandmates onto the sound. He subsequently quit, bizarrely, for an REM-flavored confection, but the addition of singer/guitarist Aaron Barrett and an ever-shifting horn section more than fulfilled Guzman's original vision for the Fish's future.

Playing the club circuit around their native Orange County while an ever-changing horn section finally settled down to a stable quartet of Tavis Werts (trumpet), Scott Klopfenstein (trumpet), Grant Barry (trombone), and Dan Reagan (trombone), Reel Big Fish released two cassette-only releases before self-releasing the *Everything Sucks* album, a number one hit on Radio Free Hawaii.

Back on the mainland, Reel Big Fish opened a Skeletones show, where they met Goldfinger's John Feldmann; trumpeters Klopfenstein and Werts were promptly recruited to guest on Goldfinger's debut album, while Feldmann's enthusiasm for the rest of the band hooked Mojo chief Jay Rifkin as well. He signed Reel Big Fish, and following a national tour opening for Goldfinger (the two bands also shared a split single), *Turn the Radio Off* was released in summer 1996.

A monster hit video, "She Has a Girlfriend Now," followed on the eve of the band's first headlining tour, while spring 1997 brought a Modern Rock chart hit for "Sell Out" (from the *Keep Your Receipt* EP) and a Top 100 berth for the album. 1998's *Why Do They Rock So Hard* (#67 US) maintained the band's momentum. A reissue of *Everything Sucks* followed.

Reel Big Fish LPs

6 Everything Sucks (Self-Released) 1995

8 Turn the Radio Off (Uptown) 1996 This former covers band knows how to entertain and *Radio*'s all very pro and slick sounding. But the Fish are having such a grand time, the lyrics are so amusing (and never more so than when lampooning themselves), and the songs so damn infectious, that you can't help but join the party.

9 Why Do They Rock So Hard (Uptown) 1998 Good question, but the Fish decide not to answer. They do rock hard, and they skank harder too, although they don't *quite* match their previous pinnacle of delirious pop and so much more. *Why* is far more laid back than its predecessor, ofttimes utilizing an almost rock steady tempo and relying on the tart, biting lyrics to really turn up the heat.

REM

FORMED 1980 (Athens, GA)

ORIGINAL LINE-UP *Michael Stipe (b. 1/4/60 — vocals); Peter Buck (b. 12/6/56 — guitar); Mike Mills (b. 12/17/58 — bass, keyboards); Bill Berry (b. 7/31/58 — drums)*

Buck and Stipe originally met in 1978 at Wuxtry Records store in Athens. Buck worked behind the counter, picking out tunes on his guitar during the lulls; Stipe was a University of Georgia art student who spent hours in the store buying new singles.

Mills and Berry, meanwhile, had nurtured a mutual dislike through childhood, only connecting once they reached college and started to jam together. When Berry's girlfriend moved into the old church where Stipe and Buck were now sharing digs, it was only a matter of time before the quartet came together.

The fledgling REM made their live debut on April 5, 1980, at their friend Kathleen O'Brien's birthday party, playing as the Twisted Kites. Further gigs (with their new name) cemented the quartet's ambition and, as word of mouth drew increasing crowds to their shows, so things began to move. In

December 1980, REM opened for the Police in Athens, and the following year they entered the studio for the first time to capture their current live set on tape. Working first with Joe Perry and later with Mitch Easter, they emerged with a single, "Radio Free Europe," for release in July on the local Hib-Tone label.

The single only added to what was gearing up to become a monstrous cult following. "Radio Free Europe" was quickly adopted by college radio up and down the coast, while the band followed it in a battered van. They eventually rolled into New Orleans, where they played one of their worst sets ever — and one that would change their lives. Watching the band that night was Jay Boberg, then president of IRS Records. He liked what he saw and brought the band to the attention of label head Miles Copeland, who signed them immediately. Reuniting with Easter, the band recorded 1982's *Chronic Town* mini-album, following up in May 1983 with their debut album, *Murmur* (#36 US). Buoyed by their tireless live work, the album would spend thirty weeks on the US chart, a remarkable achievement for a band who were still virtually unknown outside the college underground.

Tours with the Police and the Cramps followed, sandwiching the release of a rerecorded "Radio Free Europe" (#78 US) and REM's television debut on *Late Night With David Letterman*. Their busy season ended in November 1983 with their live UK debut at London's Dingwalls, the dawn of a feverish love affair with the British music press.

REM began 1984 by taking the awards for Band of the Year, Best New Artist, and Album of the Year in the *Rolling Stone* poll. They also recorded with Warren Zevon, who had worked with the band in Athens and was now planning a comeback — the beginning of a long string of musical collaborations between the band and other musicians, a roll call that includes Robyn Hitchcock, Natalie Merchant (10,000 Maniacs), Neneh Cherry, Vic Chestnutt, Billy Bragg, The Troggs, Sweet 75, and Nikki Sudden (Swell Maps), among others.

The band's second album, *Reckoning* (#27 US, #91 UK) was released in April 1984, spawning two singles, "So. Central Rain (I'm Sorry)" (#85 US) and "Don't Go Back to (Rockville)"; touring in the album's aftermath spread into the new year before the band linked with legendary folk-rock producer Joe Boyd (Richard Thompson, Nick Drake) to record their next album.

Despite persistent rumors that Stipe was ill, both physically and emotionally, the sessions were completed and *Fables of the Reconstruction* (#28 US, #35 UK) was released in July 1985, trailing three singles, "Can't Get There From Here," "Driver 8," and "Wendell Gee." All three failed to chart, but REM maintained their now-predictable routine of touring and recording, returning to the studio in the new year to create *Life's Rich Pageant* (#21 US, #43 UK) with Don Gehman, (John Cougar, X) in Indiana, and interrupting the schedule only to allow Buck, Mills, and Berry to enjoy a little time away from the spotlight, gigging and recording as the Hindu Love Gods. Their most successful release yet, *Life's Rich Pageant* would be certified gold in January 1987, while the band's next tour would see them finally begin to break out of the mold by fashioning a set based on an old-time theatre, with images projected onto a screen behind the band. They were rewarded when "Fall On Me" (#94 US) became a minor hit (although "Superman" was a total bomb).

May 1987 brought *Dead Letter Office* (#52 US, #60 UK), a collector's paradise of old B-sides and non-album material, paving the way for the band's next new album, September's *Document* (#10 US, #28 UK), and the singles "The One I Love" (#9 US, #51 UK) and "Finest Worksong" (#50 UK).

Produced by Scott Litt, a long-time friend who would help craft the next generation sound of REM, *Document* would help the band sweep Rolling Stone's 1987 music awards, as they triumphed in six categories including "Best Band," "Artist of the Year," and "Best Video" for "The One I Love." *Document* went platinum in January 1988, while a celebratory single release, "It's the End of the World As We Know It (And I Feel Fine)" (#69 US), both rounded out the month and, aptly in view of its title, REM's relationship with the IRS. The band would join Warners that same year.

Through early 1988, the band members busied themselves with extracurricular activities — Buck teamed with Hüsker Dü founder Grant Hart to do some production work, Stipe recorded "Little April Showers" with Natalie Merchant for the Disney hits compilation *Stay Awake*. Then, with Litt again alongside, the band got on with their major label debut, *Green* (#12 US, #27 UK).

Released in November 1988, *Green* was the cue for REM's most ambitious outing yet: an arena tour which traveled the US and Europe while a chain of singles arrived at regular intervals — "Stand" (#6 US, #51 UK), "Orange Crush" (#28 UK), "Pop Song '89" (#86 US). However, when Berry collapsed on stage in Munich, Germany, in July, suffering from a bronchial infection, it was inevitable that the band would need to take a break from life on the road.

By August, REM had gone on hiatus, as band members scattered to work on their own projects. Mills did some soundtrack recording for friend Howard Libov, Buck recorded with Robyn Hitchcock, Stipe produced local band Chickasaw Mudpuppies; he also cofounded the company C-00 with film director Jim McKay. A nonprofit organization, C-00 provided a medium and platform for various Public Service Announcements, ranging from the homeless situation and the AIDS crisis, to race relations and political motivations in the United States.

C-00 also served another, more commercial purpose. Through the company, REM released a documentary of the *Green* tour, on- and offstage, released as *Tourfilm* within months of the final US dates. In August 1990, it was certified gold. 1990 also saw the resurrection of the Hindu Love Gods for the first time since 1985, and their "Narrator" single. They also teamed with Warren Zevon to record an album of blues covers — *Hindu Love Gods* was released in November along with a single, a cover of Prince's "Raspberry Beret."

REM reconvened in early 1991 with a string of low-key shows around the United States and England under another alias, Bingo Hand Job. They then returned to the studio to record what would become *Out of Time* (#1 US, #1 UK), the album that finally cemented the band as the first rock superstars of the 1990s. Single after single was peeled from the album: "Losing My Religion" (#4 US, #19 UK) would become the album's highlight, musically and visually — director Tarsem's video became one of the most talked-about efforts of the year, all the more so after its use of religious imagery prompted a ban in Ireland. "Shiny Happy People" (#10 US, #6 UK) followed, featuring B-52 Kate Pierson on vocals; "Near Wild Heaven" (#27 UK) and "Radio Song" (#28 UK), recorded with rapper KRS-1, wrapped up the hit factory in August and November 1991.

REM themselves boldly elected not to tour the album, preferring to stage a string of semi-secret shows around the country, with former dB Peter Holsapple, now ensconced as second guitarist. Higher profile performances came on *Saturday Night Live*, a much-lauded *MTV Unplugged* engagement, and Stipe and Mills' appearance at US president Clinton's inaugural ball, before the band returned to the studio for 1992's *Automatic for the People* (#2 US, #1 UK) in October. The album featured string arrangements from Led Zeppelin's John Paul Jones, and again unleashed a slew of accompanying singles — "Drive" (#28 US, #11 UK); a tribute to the late comedian Andy Kaufman, "Man On The Moon" (#30 US, #18 UK); "Nightswimming" (#27 UK); "Everybody Hurts" (#7 UK April, #29 US August); and finally, "Find the River"(#54 UK).

1994 began with Mills joining Sonic Youth's Thurston Moore, Dave Grohl (Nirvana, Foo Fighters), and Dave Pirner (Soul Asylum) on the score for the film *Backbeat* during the lull before REM's own next album appeared. Dedicated to the recently deceased River Phoenix, *Monster* (#1 US, #1 UK) reintroduced a harder sound thanks in part to input from Moore, a change laid bare across the now predictable plethora of singles — "What's the Frequency, Kenneth?" (#21 US, #9 UK), "Bang and Blame" (#19 US, #15 UK), "Crush With Eyeliner" (#23 UK), "Strange Currencies" (#47 US, #9 UK), and "Tongue" (#13 UK) — but most notable when the band kicked off their first major tour since *Green*, in January 1995.

The tour came to an abrupt halt in Lausanne, Switzerland, on March 1, when Berry suddenly left the stage, midway through the show, complaining of a migraine headache. Joey Peters of opening act Grant Lee Buffalo filled in for the remainder of the set, but two days later Berry was diagnosed with a brain aneurysm. The remainder of the tour was canceled, to resume in May, only for six more shows to be canceled in July, after Mills was stricken with an intestinal tumor.

The ill-starred tour resumed, but the band's fortunes did not improve. In Ireland, two fans drowned in the Boyne River during REM's performance at Slane Castle; in Czechoslovakia, Stipe discovered he was suffering from an inguinal hernia. The band finally wrapped up a nightmarish outing in November.

1996 began with a flurry of activity, as Stipe joined with writer William Burroughs for the X-Files inspired *Songs in the Key of X* album in March, while the full band contributed "Sponge" to the Vic Chestnutt tribute *Sweet Relief II: The Gravity of the Situation* in July. The band renewed their contract with Warner, shortly after breaking with long-time manager Jefferson Holt as the result of alleged sexual harassment charges. The fall then brought the band's latest album, *New Adventures in Hi Fi* (#2 US, #1 UK), featuring the recently revitalized Patti Smith as guest vocalist. The album's first single "E-Bow the Letter" (#49 US, #4 UK) debuted in August; two further singles, "Bittersweet Me" (#46 US, #19 UK) and "Electrolite" (#96 US, #29 UK), appeared later that year.

1997 saw the band again on hiatus, only regrouping in November to make the stunning announcement that Berry was leaving the band. Various musicians filled his shoes thereafter, including Barret Martin (Screaming Trees), while Scott McCaughey of Seattle's legendary Young Fresh Fellows was drafted in as second guitarist for a new burst of recording sessions soon after.

In this form, the band "came back" in 1998 with a new album, *UP* in November (#3 US, #2 UK). Three singles supported the album, "Daysleeper" (#57 US, #6 UK) and "Lotus" (#29 UK) in 1998 and "At My Most Beautiful" (#10 UK) and "Suspicion" in 1999; through the new year the band performed at events as disparate as the Tibetan Freedom Concert, *Sesame Street* (performing a revised "Shiny Happy People" — "Furry Happy Monsters"), Germany's Echo Awards ceremony and Fox TV's *Party of Five*.

With Ken Stringfellow (Posies) now a part of the band, REM also returned to touring that summer, fulfilling a year-old pledge to return to Europe with Teenage Fanclub — Catatonia and Wilco numbered among the support acts.

They then released *Man On the Moon* (#109 US), their soundtrack to Milos Foreman's biopic of Andy Kaufman, and the hit single "The Great Beyond" (#3 UK).

REM LPs

6 Murmur (IRS) 1983 After the embryonic *Chronic Town* EP, *Murmur* emerged competent and catchy and generally fine overall. The subsequent fame and applause of "Radio Free Europe" and "Talk About the Passion" flatters to deceive — even with two future monster hits on board, it's obvious that the band are still finding their songwriting feet.

10 Reckoning (IRS) 1984 This set explodes with an urgency and force that still manages to thrill — all the more so since it really wasn't expected. Although *Reckoning* was recorded in a very short time and is, essentially, a chronicle of the band live in the studio, it emerges cohesive, tight, and effervescent, with just enough edgy jangle to keep everyone on their toes.

Already the band are moving within the styles that would soon become "typical" REM. The driving insistence of "So. Central Rain" and "Pretty Persuasion" are tempered by the quiet introspection of "Camera," while the good ol' sing-along "(Don't Go Back to) Rockville" simultaneously celebrates everything that was good in '80s Americana, at the same time as imbibing it with their own unique sounds.

7 Fables of the Reconstruction (IRS) 1985 The album should have eclipsed its predecessor but instead slumped under everyone's expectations and sounded like a tired version of *Reckoning*. But still it gave us "Maps and Legends" and "Driver 8."

6 Lifes Rich Pageant (IRS) 1986 A reinvention of sorts for the band as their sound is refined and redirected, with pop stylings replacing edgy tension. The album also signaled the advent of what would become overt politicism in the band's songs, but for now, an innocuous effort.

7 Document (IRS) 1987 Scott Litt's eager production allowed the band to dabble more firmly in the mainstream with "The One I Love" and the ever-cheery "It's the End of the World As We Know It"; although it's stronger on its first side than the other, the second half does include a provocative cover of Wire's "Strange."

8 Green (WB) 1988 The sounds of REM firmly in the grips of mainstream success, but the band doesn't sell out. The songs on *Green* reflect a band comfortably maturing, full of understated political intent buffered by catchy hooks and sparkling pop.

7 Out of Time (WB) 1991 A rollicking good time full of bright songs, brighter production, and a sheen which even the moody "Losing My Religion" couldn't dampen. Unfortunately, it also involves guest vocalists KRS-1 on the overwrought "Radio Song" and B-52's Kate Pierson on the grotesque "Shiny Happy People."

8 Automatic for the People (WB) 1992 This set became the antithesis of *Out of Time*. Darker, deeper, and far more intense, the melancholy sweetness that permeates this album has a haunting ambience that drives the entire set — except for "Everybody Hurts," which whines way too much.

6 Monster (WB) 1994 From the opening redundancy of "What's the Frequency, Kenneth?," REM are what REM do. A total letdown in the wake of *Automatic*. Can anyone smell a pattern here?

8 New Adventures in Hi-Fi (WB) 1996 Extra chunky and massively textured, *Hi-Fi* is unlike anything the band have ever done before, as studio tracks mix with live performance, while Patti Smith guests on "E-Bow the Letter."

7 UP (WB) 1998 The first post-Bill Berry project finds them trying to redefine themselves as a band, and the overall sound suffers for it. Not a bad album though.

3 Man On the Moon 1999 Soundtrack by name, soundtrack by nature. Collaborations with Jim Carrey and great swathes of movie dialogue cannot disguise the fact that, an EP's worth of songs notwithstanding, anybody could have recorded these scrappy sketches, and with the album credited to REM and Friends, maybe anybody did.

Selected Compilations and Archive Releases

7 Dead Letter Office (IRS) 1987 A collection of B-sides, outtakes, and noodlings, plus the *Chronic Town* EP on the CD release.

7 Eponymous (IRS) 1988 Neat wrap up of the songs that would shape a generation.

8 In the Attic: Alternative Recordings... (Capitol) 1997 Surprisingly successful ragbag of alternative recordings of REM staples, 1985 to 1989; a mix of live tracks, B-sides, and studio noodling. "Gardening at Night" provides an alternative vocal take, while "Swan Swan H" marches in off the Athens, GA, *Inside Out* soundtrack. A cover of Aerosmith's hoary "Toys in the Attic," "Tired of Singing Trouble," and "Last Date" round out the B-sides. Scholars of the Georgia scene will also appreciate the cover of Pylon's "Crazy."

8 The Best of REM (EMI) 1998

Further Reading

From Chronic Town to Monster by Dave Bowler/Bryan Dray (Citadel 1995).

REPLACEMENTS

FORMED 1979 *(Minneapolis, MN)*
ORIGINAL LINE-UP *Paul Westerberg (b. 12/31/60 — vocals, guitar); Bob Stinson (b. 12/17/59 — guitar); Tommy Stinson (b. 10/6/66 — bass); Chris Mars (b. 4/26/61 — drums)*

Formed after songwriter Paul Westerberg linked with Mars and the Stinson brother's punk/hard rock combo Dogbreath — a band whose specialty was racing hard core versions of

old Yes and Ted Nugent numbers — the Replacements were gleefully bashing out drunken three-chord punk sets all over Minneapolis when they caught the attention of Peter Jesperson, head of the local Twin/Tone Records with a demo recorded in the Stinson family basement.

Taken immediately into Blackberry Way Studios, owned by Jesperson's Twin/Tone partner Paul Stark, the Replacements bashed out their debut album in as long as it took them to play the songs live. In early 1981, Twin/Tone released the hard-core holocaust *Sorry Ma, Forgot to Take Out the Trash* (and single, "I'm in Trouble") — its title, like its exuberance, reminding listeners that the band members' ages ranged from 21 (Bob Stinson) to just 14 (Tommy Stinson). Those ages, in turn, belied the band's already burgeoning notoriety for utter drunkenness.

Time and again shows would be disrupted, or even halted, as drunken members of the audience would find the band members even drunker than they were and just as ready for trouble; indeed, Bob Stinson's penchant for wearing women's clothing on stage was itself an open invitation for the average midwestern bar crowd to bombard the stage in beer and insults. Regardless of whether their music had any inherent worth, the Replacements attracted attention simply by existing.

Pushing on, the band quickly recorded and released an EP, 1982's *Stink*, in precisely the same vein as its predecessor. However, just when listeners thought they had the band pegged, the Replacements unleashed *Hootenanny* — still a barrage of noise, but one that suggested entirely new musical horizons lay at the band's fingertips: horizons that would be explored further on the early 1984 single "I Will Dare" and then explode into prominence on 1984's *Let It Be*. As Westerberg explained later, "we had a big dose of attitude in the early days. [But] on *Let It Be*... [we] let a little bit of music happen. And that was the right mixture."

Immediately, the Replacements found themselves the darlings of the underground; immediately, too, the major labels came to call. The band left Twin/Tone for Sire, and in November 1985, the Replacements released *Tim* (#183 US). Produced by ex-Ramone Tommy Erdelyi and featuring former Box Tops/Big Star icon Alex Chilton in a guest appearance on "Left of the Dial," *Tim* (and its attendant singles "Swingin' Party" and "Kiss Me On the Buss") made the transition from indy to major without compromising the band in any way. MTV even made a smash of the band's latest video, "Bastards of Young," despite the band themselves not even appearing in it — they were replaced by a phonograph speaker, in front of which a disembodied hand and foot occasionally strayed.

Behind the scenes, of course, little seemed to have changed. Rumor still insisted the band were out of control, that alcohol and drug use was rampant, that they weren't keeping it together. Indeed, the Replacements' live shows remained sloppy, chaotic affairs, often ending before they had really begun, and the band themselves seemed determined to perpetuate the legend when they appeared on *Saturday Night Live* on January 18, 1986, clearly out of control.

A European tour soon after brought matters to a head as Westerberg fired Bob Stinson, blaming the bassist's drug and alcohol abuse (Stinson would die on February 18, 1995, following an apparent drug overdose.)

Shaken but not beaten down, the band opted to remain a trio and retired to the studio to record April 1987's *Pleased to Meet Me* (#131 US). Far more commercial than its predecessor, the album was produced by Big Star producer Jim Dickinson and spawned two singles, the now classic "Alex Chilton" and "Can't Hardly Wait," which again featured Chilton on guitar.

Ready to tour, the Replacements replaced Stinson with guitarist Robert "Slim" Dunlap and hit the road. Touring gave way to recording as sessions for *Don't Tell a Soul* (#57 US) got underway. Coproduced this time by Matt Wallace, with Tom Waits as guest vocalist, the album showcased a softer side of the Replacements, one which ultimately added to the combustion of the band. Even more of a departure, it not only included the band's first-ever genuinely MTV-friendly songs but also became the band's first Top 100

album. April's "I'll Be You" (#51 US) followed, topping both the Modern Rock and Album Rock charts in the process.

Cleaned up and sober for the first time in their careers, Westerberg and the Replacements kicked off a US tour opening for Tom Petty in Florida on July 5, 1989. But the end of the band was looming; produced by Scott Litt, the Replacements swan song *All Shook Down* (#69 US), was released in September 1990, featuring guests ranging from John Cale to Terry Reid. But the album was derided by critics and fans alike, described more as a dry run for Westerberg's solo aspirations than a Replacements album.

By early 1991, Mars had left the group, apparently concerned over the control Westerberg had taken within the band. He would re-emerge as a solo artist, releasing four albums; he was replaced in the Replacements by Steve Foley as the band toured the album through the US and Europe, but it was a futile gesture. Returning home, disheartened by the relative failure of the tour, the Replacements disbanded in the fall of 1991.

Westerberg, Stinson, and Dunlap all went their own way; Dunlap recorded an LP for Twin/Tone; Stinson formed a new band, Bash and Pop; and Westerberg finally launched the solo career he'd apparently been longing for. The Replacements themselves were memorialized with 1997's hits- and rarities-packed collection *All for Nothing/Nothing for All* (#143 US).

Also see the entry for "PAUL WESTERBERG" on page 717.

© Jim Steinfeldt/Chansley Entertainment Archives

The Replacements LPs

③ Sorry Ma, Forgot to Take out the Trash (Twin/Tone) 1981

③ Hootenanny (Twin/Tone) 1983 Second-hand hard core scratching; an angry adolescent buzz over which Westerberg's snot-soaked gargle rings like a off-key car alarm. For insomniacs and completists only.

⑩ Let It Be (Twin/Tone) 1984 Waking up and discovering you're the brightest hope on the American gar[b]age scene of the mid-1980s, after three years and two albums of unrelenting noise-making, cannot be easy. But waking up to hear Springsteen-sing-Richman-sing-Boy George-sing-the-Stooges, while KISS' "Black Diamond" is steam rollered beneath a wall so blunt it makes the Sex Pistols sound like Fleetwood Mac… that must be even harder. So, put it all together and, congratulations, you've got the Replacements' third album, a record that was to American rock what Lee Harvey Oswald was to the White House.

"Tommy Has His Tonsils Out," "Gary's Got a Boner," and (again) "Black Diamond" prove that the band's infantile irrepressibility hasn't changed much since the early days. But Westerberg's handle on melody is peerless, and "(How Do You Say Goodnight to an) Answering Machine" is practically tender. Elsewhere, the barroom piano-led "Androgynous" swaggers with something more than the weight of a newly purchased dictionary, and "I Will Dare" isn't simply a pristine pop-funk romp, it also coaxes a killer klutz guitar solo out of guest Peter Buck (REM).

One assumes the band had been planning this album for years and just wanted to get the testosterone out first. But one hopes they just woke up and found it. Because then they'd have had the same thrill of discovery as everyone else did.

⑨ Tim (Sire) 1985 This album doesn't have half the balls of its predecessor but is still strong enough to kick any contenders firmly into the dirt and then laugh. Though the band have lost some of their urgency, the songs are still powerful, with a sharp quirk that sticks. "Left of the Dial," "Waitress in the Sky," and "A Little Mascara" all shine, while "Bastards of Young" could easily have been included on *Let It Be*. And, of course, there's the haunting "Here Comes a Regular," a poignant tearjerker guaranteed to bring a catch in even a cynic's throat.

⑤ Pleased to Meet Me (Sire) 1987 A major downturn for the band as this ragged, uneven set teeters precariously on the brink of ho-hum-dom. However, both "Alex Chilton" and "The Ledge" deserve accolades.

③ Don't Tell a Soul (Sire) 1989 An album that simply screams out to be lost in the left luggage box of life. What went wrong? Too much time spent dreaming of Alex Chilton for starters, and maybe too long spent reading their past press. But not only were the Replacements NOT, in any shape or form, the reincarnation of Chilton's Big Star, but Big Star weren't that good to begin with, which meant they were chasing a lost cause from the off. *Don't Tell a Soul* is simply the sound of them catching up with it… and wondering why they bothered.

④ All Shook Down (Sire) 1990 Essentially a Westerberg solo effort. There's no heart left in the Replacements' music, and the result is

the sorry sound of the Replacements simply going through the motions.

Selected Compilations and Archive Releases

⑨ All for Nothing/Nothing for All (Reprise) 1997 A must-have double CD with 16 remastered hits plus 17 previously unreleased tracks and multimedia with rare video footage.

Tommy Stinson/Bash and Pop LP

⑦ Friday Night Is Killing Me (Sire) 1993 Stinson dumps the bass, picks up the guitar, and records an admirable set in the vein of old Faces, with a little Westerberg thrown in for good measure.

Chris Mars Solo LPs

⑥ Horseshoes & Hand Grenades (Smash) 1992 Mars and bassist JD Foster turn in a deliciously bitter, biting tirade in "Popular Creeps" an anthemic cry against clique culture.

⑦ 75% Less Fat (Smash) 1993 More of the same, only a little more tightly focussed. It's obvious Mars still has stuff to get off his chest.

⑦ Tenterhooks (Bar/None) 1995 Mars replaces the angst with an odd amalgam of disco, jazz, strings, and more, all covered over with slabs of guitar.

⑦ Anonymous Batch (Bar/None) 1996

Slim Dunlap Solo LP

⑥ Times Like This (Restless) 1996 Good old rock and roll, something to drink beer to.

BOYD RICE

BORN *(San Francisco, CA)*

Having dropped out of school in tenth grade to avoid the daily beatings meted out by the local jocks, Rice grew up listening to pop and bubblegum music and contemplating the extraordinary hold on society that such supposedly lightweight music has; contemplating, too, how the removal, repetition, or manipulation of certain elements of those records could create a whole new meaning.

One of his earliest experiments involved sampling (long before samplers existed) every "cry" ever uttered by '60s sweetheart Lesley Gore, then stringing them together in one continuous collage; others would be gathered together on his first album, the limited edition (85 copies) *The Black Album*. It was, Rice believed, the ultimate easy listening record — one that "blanks out your brain, leaving a vacuum and allowing no new thoughts to form." In addition, the album was playable at any speed without any noticeable difference, "so you get four times as much for your [money]. " He found few people to agree with him. "People thought I was insane… this creative, talented guy who was just wasting my time pouring it into some kind of sociopathic attempt to inflict pain on people."

Among those who did understand were Throbbing Gristle. They brought Rice to London in 1978 after hearing him perform with avant-garde percussionist Z'ev at La Mamelles in San Francisco; he brought some unsold copies of *The Black Album* with him, and following his first-ever UK show at the London Film Makers Co-op, Rice dropped by the Rough Trade record store to try and interest them in the record. There he met Mute Records chief Daniel Miller; Rice signed with the label soon after and debuted with "Soundtracks 1–3," a split single with Smegma. He chose the name Non for the occasion.

Rice continued his experiments. His "Pagan Muzak" single that same year came with four holes drilled in the center for "multi-axial rotation"; "Rise" followed, while a reissue for *The Black Album* (as *Boyd Rice*) in 1981 became an integral building block in the noise experiments of later musicians.

Live, too, Rice developed an uncompromising reputation — "in New York," he revealed, "I was one of the first people in years to actually get cat calls. People were screaming 'I want my $7.50 back!' And in Den Haag, Holland, people were real angry. They really disliked me. I had these bright lights shining in their eyes so they could barely see me — they were trying to reach up and smash the lights, but the lights were just out of their reach." April 1982's *Physical Evidence* featured a number of concert recordings, although none featured audience reactions as radical as Rice had hitherto enjoyed.

Rice and Miller together recorded "Cleanliness and Order" for inclusion on the *Darker Scratcher* compilation; according to legend, another of the tracks, "Non Watusi," mysteriously changed sometime between the master tape leaving Rice's possession and the album being pressed. It became, Rice complained, a different song altogether.

With Mute as a regular outlet for his muse, Rice now had longer in which to concoct fresh unpleasantries. Many of these he then passed over to Frank Tovey (aka Fad Gadget), and the pair had a delightful time on the road in Europe during 1981/82 writing *Easy Listening for the Hard of Hearing*, a record that proudly boasted of using no musical instruments whatsoever. Instead, the duo retired to Blackwing Studios and "played" pipes, the furniture, the walls, and anything else that made a noise. The album would not be released until 1984, while Rice and Tovey tried to agree upon a suitable cover.

In the meantime, Rice wrote a pair of books for the San Francisco-based Re/Search company, *Pranks* and *Incredibly Strange Films*; he also collaborated with Current 93 and Coil as A Sickness of Snakes, while a rare European tour as Non

was documented on 1985's *Sick Tour*. He also began work on the next Non studio venture, 1987's *Blood and Flame* (#21 UK indy), an album that *NME*'s review admitted, "this… isn't intended to be sat down and listened to… more to be used and abused as the participants see fit."

Two years later, Rice released his second album under his own name, the delicate *Music Martinis and Misanthropy*. Recorded with Tony Wakeford of Sol Invictus, Rose McDowall of Strawberry Switchblade, and Doug Pierce of Death in June, the album shifted Rice some way closer toward "mainstream" tastes, although a subsequent appearance in an HBO special on Satanism and his well-publicized involvement with Anton La Vey's Church of Satan ensured he remained at arm's length from middle America and a favorite subject for evangelist Bob Larson.

1992's *In the Shadow of the Sword*, debating social Darwinism, evidenced Non *in extremis*; nevertheless, 1994 brought Rice's masterpiece, a collaboration with McDowell for a collection of '60s-era songs about death ("Terry," "Endless Sleep," "Stone Is Very Cold"), titled for Jacques Brel's *Seasons in the Sun*. Released under the name Spell, and accompanied by a single of Lee Hazlewood's "Big Red Balloon" (featuring a video directed by mondo trash master Ray Dennis Steckler), the album sadly disappeared after an Island Records act with the same name objected. A second Spell project was recorded in 1999, but remains unreleased.

Rice returned to both Non (the *Might* album) and his own self-named career, touring the US with Electric Hellfire Club in 1996, simultaneously juggling a welter of other projects, including the *Boyd Rice Presents* series of compilations and remix work. One audacious scheme, remixing the *A Clockwork Orange* soundtrack, was sadly buried, but other projects — including further links with Coil, Death in June, and Sol Invicta — continued. A new Non album, *Receive the Flame*, was released in December 1999 accompanied by a single, "Solitude," and a Non live show at the 1999 Stockholm Film Festival.

Boyd Rice LPs

🄶 **Boyd Rice (Mute) 1981** Noises, drones, hums, and buzzes, through which the ghosts of something you might vaguely recognize keep you from turning it off. The 45 RPM option is the best.

🄸 **Music Martini and Misanthropy (Bad) 1989** A lovely album; melody-drenched and delicately sung. The one Boyd album that you play when you don't want the party to end.

🄷 **Hatesville (World Serpent) 1996**

Non LPs

🄴 **Sick Tour [LIVE] (Staaltape) 1985**

🄶 **Blood & Flame (Mute) 1987**

7 In the Shadow of the Sword (Mute) 1992 Pulling back to the yowling mayhem of *Physical Evidence* and *Blood and Flame*, but heavy going for first-time listeners, regardless. Industrial-strength concepts and soundtracks; a case of preaching to the long-since converted.

7 Might (Mute) 1995 High conceptual, high experimental, the darkness on the edge of a very desperate town. Lyrics by 19th century philosopher Ragnar Redbeard; distortion by design.

7 God and Beast (Mute) 1997

8 Receive the Flame (Mute) 1999 Some records have great intros, rising blocks of sound that simply explode with the verse or the first slash of guitar. *Receive the Flame* is full of them… where it gets interesting is, that's all it is: eight killer intros, each one building up the tension and expectation — and then continuing on for three or four minutes. Masterful manipulation of one of modern rock's most trustworthy tricks.

Selected Compilations and Archive Releases

6 Physical Evidence (Mute) 1982 Collection of live and studio material trailing from the present backward.

7 Easy Listening for Iron Youth (Mute) 1991

Boyd Rice and Frank Tovey LP

7 Easy Listening for the Hard of Hearing (Mute) 1984 Banging and clattering on anything they can, neither an answer to Einsturzende Neubauten, nor an attempt to be one. Rather, a willfully eccentric exercise in making a noise and a tune at the same time.

Boyd Rice & Coil/Sickness of Snakes LP

6 Nightmare Culture (Laylah) 1985

Boyd Rice/Spell LP

9 Seasons in the Sun (Mute) 1994 A tribute to heartbreak and misery, '60s teen death style. "Johnny Remember Me," "Stone Is Very Cold," "This Little Bird," with MacDowell singing like a sultry angel and the arrangements effortlessly locked in time. They don't make them like that anymore, because if they did they'd be banned. Sick! Tasteless! Morbid! Naturally!

RIDE

FORMED 1988 (Banbury, England)
ORIGINAL LINE-UP *Mark Gardener (b. 12/6/69, Oxford — vocals, guitar); Andy Bell (b. 8/11/70, Oxford — guitar); Steve Queralt (b. 2/4/68, Oxford — bass); Laurence Colbert (b. 6/27/70, Oxford — drums)*

Andy Bell, Laurence Colbert, and Mark Gardener were attending Banbury Art College when they formed Ride with Steve Queralt (whose older brother was already a friend of the band's), initially jamming in Colbert's parents' garage.

Cultivating a dreamy, droning sound, highlighted by the show-stopping "Drive Blind," Ride began gigging around nearby Oxford, where promoter Dave Newton took them under his wing.

Over the next year, the band began making inroads to London venues, finally being picked up by Creation just as the My Bloody Valentine-led shoe gazing movement began to crest. Ride's incorporation into that scene, of course, was inevitable, but the band's first release, the *Ride* EP (#71 UK), was itself to become an archetype. Released in January 1990, the EP was followed by two further similar sets, *Play* (#32 UK) and *Fall* (#34), before Ride released their debut album, *Nowhere* (#11 UK).

Concentrating on the studio, the band rarely surfaced during 1991, although an appearance opening for the Pixies at the Crystal Palace Bowl was very well received, alongside the single "Today Forever" (#14 UK). The band's US profile also rose as "Taste," a track from the *Fall* EP, breached the US Modern Rock Tracks chart.

It was with the long-gestating *Going Blank Again* (#5 UK) album, prefaced by the eight-minute single "Leave Them All Behind" (#9 UK) that Ride fully established themselves, selling out tours in both the UK and US and scoring a further hit as "Twisterella" (#36 UK) climbed to 12 on the US Modern Rock chart.

However, live work and studio perfectionism were both taking their toll on the band, and following their Reading Festival date in August 1992, Ride announced a two-year sabbatical. They re-emerged in January 1994 with their first song ever to be credited to one member alone, Bell's "Birdman" (#38 UK). An even more disappointing performance by "How Does It Feel" (#58 UK), was, however, followed by a Top 5 entry for *Carnival of Light*, an album whose portentous air was compounded by the presence of Deep Purple organist Jon Lord.

A third single, "I Don't Know Where It Comes From" (#46 UK), featured Ride at the extremes of their influences — one B-side paired them with reformed '60s beat group The Creation (source, of course, for Alan McGee's label name); another featured a remix by Portishead, whose own trip-hop sound was widely regarded as a successor of sorts to the shoe gazing Ride had once espoused. But the band's future looked shaky, as Bell and Gardener continued to argue over lead vocal duties, and on August 4, 1995, Ride played what would become their last show, second-billed to the Charlatans at the Benicassim Festival in Spain. A live album, *Live Light*, would emerge from their last European tour, while the group returned to the studio to record what they already knew would be their final album.

Preceded by the "Black Night Crash" single (#67 UK), *Tarantula* peaked at #21 on the UK chart and was then deleted after just one week on sale. The band members promptly separated — Bell retained a solo deal with Creation before emerging in late 1997 with the highly rated Hurricane #1; he then joined Gay Dad in a blaze of publicity in October 1999, quitting just two weeks later to replace bassist Bonehead in Oasis.

Colbert joined a local Oxford band, Twist; Gardener formed Exile with George Vjestica (guitar), Gary Strange (bass), and Chris Kavanagh (ex-Big Audio Dynamite — drums), then reverted to his own name after discovering a US country band of the same title. A single, "Magdalen Sky," appeared in June 1997 before Gardener formed Animal House with Colbert, Super grass producer Sam Williams (vocals), Hari-T (keyboards), and Jason King (bass) in early 1998.

Ride LPs

7 Nowhere (Sire) 1990 Ride took the same musical mix of influences (Stones, Beatles, Byrds, Flaming Groovies) that the Stone Roses used to such devastating effect, added an equal proportion of fuzz guitars, and then evicted strong pop melodies in favor of atmosphere. The results were credible, if a little samey.

8 Going Blank Again (Sire) 1991 Jangly guitars and insistent bass lines now share equal billing with the My Bloody Valentine-esque guitars, as Ride themselves agree that atmosphere isn't everything and turn their hands to crafting songs drenched in melodies, harmonies, and hooks.

8 Carnival of Light (Sire) 1994 Ironic name for Ride's heaviest album, in which the quartet throw the spotlight on their previously dim rock roots, but lighten the mood with the inclusion of orchestral arrangements and a school choir. An unexpected mix of rock, Brit-pop, and their 4AD heritage make for another intriguing album.

7 Live Light (Elektra) 1995 Recording during the *Carnival of Light* tour and deliberately packaged to look like a bootleg but recorded with such perfectionist clarity it could have been made in the studio.

7 Tarantula (Sire) 1996 Hard, edgy rockers collide with acoustic ballads and jangly pop tracks, a diversity of styles and moods that remains unmistakably Ride, yet at the same time signifies major changes ahead.

Selected Compilations and Archive Releases

8 Smile (Sire) 1990 US-only compilation of first two UK EP's.

Hurricane #1 LPs

7 Hurricane #1 (Creation) 1997 With more clarity in the songwriting and less emphasis on the texture, a surprisingly crisp if Brit-poppy offering.

6 Only the Strongest Will Survive (Creation) 1999

TOM ROBINSON BAND

FORMED 1976 (London, England)
ORIGINAL LINE-UP *Tom Robinson (b. 6/1/50, Cambridge, England — vocals, guitar); Anton Mauve (b. Roy Butterfield — guitar); Bret Sinclair (guitar); Mark Griffiths (bass); Mick Trevisick (drums)*

Tom Robinson and Mick Trevisick were members of Cafe Society, a whimsical, folky band that had a brief flirtation with Ray Davies' Konk label. It was not a happy liaison — Robinson complained (loudly) that Davies never gave the band the chance to show what it could do. Davies replied that they weren't good enough to do anything. Only one Cafe Society album was ever released, allegedly to total sales of 600; in retaliation, the band took to performing Davies' own "Tired of Waiting for You" — dedicated to Davies — who responded with a new song, the scathing "Prince of the Punks," shortly after TRB scored their first successes on the club scene.

Robinson was already preparing for his next move during the last days of Cafe Society, penning future favorites "Martin," "Grey Cortina," "Glad to Be Gay," "Long Hot Summer," and most significantly, in commercial terms, "2-4-6-8 Motorway." When Café Society broke up in late 1976, Robinson and Trevisick immediately recruited Mauve, Sinclair, and Griffiths and debuted as the Tom Robinson Band (TRB) at the Hope & Anchor on November 28, 1976.

For their second gig, at the Fulham Golden Lion, Sinclair and Griffiths were absent, replaced by one of Robinson's boyhood friends, Danny Kustow; two months later, with Mark Ambler (keyboards) and Brian "Dolphin" Taylor (drums) replacing the remainder of the original group, the "classic" TRB debuted at the Sir George Robey in London's Finsbury Park.

A string of three- to four-week residences at any pub or club that would have them followed, but despite the strength of the band's show and the rabidity of their following, few labels wanted to know. Espousing a blatantly political stance, songs like "Glad to Be Gay," "I'm Alright Jack," and "Power in the Darkness" took murderously accurate swipes at the country's greatest evils, and in such a manner that even the crassest slogan was effective.

Virgin and Stiff turned them down, however, while the Jet label's interest was allegedly quashed by Robinson's ferocious gay stance. TRB finally signed with EMI in July 1977.

The distinctly apolitical "2-4-6-8 Motorway" (#5 UK) debuted the band in the public eye — a sound move that allowed Robinson and EMI to ease the band's true nature into the public eye via the media coverage that inevitably followed a hit single. The speed with which the message got through was evidenced when the *Rising Free* live EP (#18

UK) became TRB's second release and opened with "Glad to Be Gay" — already standing alongside "Anarchy in the UK" and "White Riot" among Britain's alternative national anthems. A nervous BBC opted for the safer "Don't Take No for an Answer" as the cut that would receive airplay, but their public spiritedness flung back in their faces as "Gay" became the hit, regardless, and sent TRB out headlining across the country.

"Up Against the Wall" (#33 UK) followed in May 1978 before the long-awaited and instantly successful arrival of TRB's debut album, *Power in the Darkness* (#144 US, #4 UK). Robinson traveled to the US, where the band had just been signed by Harvest, then returned for a summer schedule that saw TRB become regulars at Rock Against Racism shows across the country.

The band were on the brink of greatness, but suddenly, things started to sour. Ambler quit, to be replaced by ex-Roogalator pianist Nick Plytas in April 1978; now he, too, quit, and Ian Parker moved in. Dolphin then left in December 1978, to be replaced by former Brand X drummer Preston Heyman, while a month spent recording a second album at Rockfield Studios, again with Chris Thomas producing, came to naught. Over a year of constant touring had left no time whatsoever in which to work on new material.

Still EMI demanded a follow-up, and the band finally relocated to Woodstock, NY, to record with Todd Rundgren. There they created the critically slaughtered *TRB 2* (#163 US, #18 UK), a set that Robinson later acknowledged was primarily padding, with only three songs truly worthwhile — "Blue Murder," "Hold Out," and the single "Bully for You" (#68 UK) cowritten by Robinson and Peter Gabriel (with whom the band played a Christmas benefit gig).

Tours of Japan and Norway followed with the band lineup now in a seemingly permanent state of flux. Heyman left to join Kate Bush's band; Trevisick returned briefly before bowing out for Charlie Morgan. Kustow left in July to form the Spectres; Geoff Sharkey replaced him, but finally Robinson — who was "in no mood to carry on a Tom Robinson Band without any of the Tom Robinson Band in it" — called it a day.

A final TRB single was recorded with session men; "Never Gonna Fall in Love Again" was cowritten by Robinson and Elton John, and while it initially received a lot of airplay, Robinson still insists "it was dropped suddenly when somebody noticed the (distinctly gay) lyrics."

Robinson joined Sector 27, a trio comprising Steve Blanchard (guitar), Jo Birt (bass), and Derek Quinton (drums), whose career to date had amounted to one unreleased album for an EMI subsidiary Regal Zonophone. The band backed Robinson on the singles "Not Ready" (#4 UK indy) and "Invitation" before releasing an eponymous Steve Lilly-

white-produced debut album and two further singles, "Total Recall" and the purposefully post-TRB–flavored "Now Martin's Gone."

Sector 27 broke up in 1981 when their management company went bankrupt. Robinson, facing horrific debts, fled to Germany, moving first to Hamburg, then East Berlin, where he concocted Cabaret 79, a touring revue highlighted not only by a handful of TRB classics, but also the German-language "Tango Und Der Wand." A new solo album, *North by Northwest*, followed before Robinson returned to the UK to make what the media insisted was his comeback — a successful venture that saw him returning to the chart with the much-loved "War Baby" (#6 UK, #1 UK indy) in June 1983, "Listen to the Radio" (#39 UK, #4 UK indy), and a cover of Steely Dan's "Rikki Don't Lose That Number" (#58 UK).

The album *Hope and Glory* (#21 UK), featuring all three hits, arrived in September 1984, but Robinson lapsed back into comparative obscurity: the *Still Loving You* album scored in Italy alone, while a new cabaret revue, *A Private View*, played successfully at the 1986 Edinburgh Fringe Festival, then fell from view.

The most newsworthy event, then, came when the British tabloid *Sunday People* discovered that the man who performed "Glad to Be Gay" with such passion a decade previous had suddenly discovered bisexuality and married life. Headlines such as "Britain's #1 Gay in Love With Girl Biker" dominated the press for several weeks, although this time the exposure didn't translate into sales. A duet with Kiki Dee, "Feels So Good," in January 1987 went nowhere, while a collaboration with Level 42 guitarist Jakko Jaksysk spawned the well-received, but ultimately unsuccessful, *We Never Had It So Good*. (The pair also composed the theme to TV's *Hard Cases*).

An attempted TRB reunion in 1990 failed, Robinson reflected, "for exactly the same reasons we split up the first time." He and Kustow, he explained, first met in a home for problem children, "and it shows." Robinson returned to his solo career, and following the 1992 live album *Living in a Boom Time*, Robinson linked with fellow punk-era icon TV Smith for a series of tours that embraced both musicians' entire careers and two albums of new material: Smith's 1994 *The Immortal Rich* and Robinson's *Love Over Rage*, also featuring Sector 27 veteran Jo Birtand and TRB's Ambler. Smith and Robinson then teamed up for 1995's *Thin Green Line* EP, while Robinson's 1996 *Having It Both Ways* album also featured the singer.

Now a regular BBC radio presenter, 1997 saw Robinson form his own Castaway Northwest label with the intention of remastering and reissuing his back catalog, together with a series of archive collections, available only via Robinson's own fan club. He also received the Gay/Lesbian American

Music Awards Out Male Artist of the Year for the song "Blood Brothers," which also won Out Song of the Year and Out Recording of the Year.

A live album, *Holidays in the Sun*, was released in Japan in 1998; it would be released elsewhere in fall 1999 as one-half of the 2-CD set *Home From Home*. 2000 saw Robinson included among the highlights of the Ian Dury tribute concert. Fittingly, he performed Dury's "I Want To Be Straight."

Tom Robinson LPs

7 North by Northwest (IRS) 1982 "Now Martin's Gone" was Robinson's way of waving farewell to the TRB days, at the same time as keeping faith with one of that band's best-loved songs. The remainder of the album sees him delving into more mature territory ("Atmospherics," "Dungannon") but keeping his stylistic options open.

8 Cabaret '79 (Panic) 1982 Wicked live album, cabaret by name, but *Cabaret* in delivery, topped by the utterly wonderful "Tango Und Der Wand."

7 Hope and Glory (Castaway) 1984 Three hit singles peeled off one album, and though it was all getting very slick-sounding, it was hard not to be impressed. "War Baby" and the revisited "Atmospherics: Listen to the Radio" remain edgy soft rock classics.

4 Still Loving You (Castaway) 1986 Maybe allowing success to go to his head, certainly allowing the session men and '80s production to get inside his ears, a dispiritingly bland album.

9 Living in a Boom Time [LIVE] (Cooking Vinyl) 1992 A few singles and collaborations later, Robinson returns as a wandering minstrel, bitter again and sounding better for it. Revisiting many of the injustices unsolved by the first TRB album, especially those that have simply grown with their telling ("Yuppie Scum," the title track), Robinson dusts off just one key oldie, "War Baby" — but this time it sounds like he means it.

6 Love Over Rage (Scarface) 1994 Despite guests ranging from fellow troubadour TV Smith, Chris Rea, and old TRB-er Mark Ambler, another sadly inconsistent set.

5 Having It Both Ways (Cooking Vinyl) 1996

8 Home from Home [LIVE] (Oyster — Belgium) 1999 Even when the material lags, Robinson remains a captivating performer. Here, thankfully, the songs are as strong as he is.

Selected Compilations and Archive Releases

7 Castaway Club Volume 1 (Castaway Club) 1994 Features *Boomtime* out-takes, plus 1989/90 TRB reunion material.

6 Castaway Club Volume 2 (Castaway Club) 1995 *Love Over Rage* out-takes, plus material composed with Elton John in the late 1970s.

6 Castaway Club Volume 4 (Castaway Club) 1997 The earliest known version of "Motorway" joins post-TRB demos and out-takes.

Tom Robinson Band LPs

9 Power in the Darkness (Harvest) 1978 Much of the rhetoric sounds naive today, even if the problems remain unsolved. The punchy rock of "Up Against the Wall," "Long Hot Summer," and "Grey Cortina," of course, will never go out of date, while the just-this-side-of-dancey "Better Decide Which Side You're On" still sounds fresh. For first-time listeners, though, the title track remains the tour de force, its spoken word centerpiece proving that things really haven't changed in the intervening two decades. (The US vinyl includes a bonus 12-inch featuring "Motorway," "Glad to Be Gay," and others; CD reissues append the same tracks.)

3 TRB 2 (Harvest) 1979 *Power in the Darkness* worked because it acted first, thought about it later. *TRB 2* was created the other way around and is scarcely worth looking at. Only the truly majestic "Bully for You" stands out; indeed, it would have dignified its predecessor, too. The remainder clashes bland rock with crass catchphrases. A shame.

Selected Compilations and Archive Releases

7 The Collection 1977–1987 (EMI) 1987

6 The Gold Collection (EMI Gold) 1996

7 Rising Free: The Very Best Of (EMI) 1997 No TRB collection can exist without the hit singles or the bulk of *Power in the Darkness*. Where they go thereafter is immaterial, although the live "Waiting for the Man" is a nice touch.

Tom Robinson/Sector 27 LP

7 Sector 27 (Fontana) 1980 Recovering a little equilibrium, but still apparently uncertain, Robinson's rehab album actually emerges a lot stronger than anyone expected.

Selected Compilations and Archive Releases

6 Castaway Club Volume 3 (Castaway Club) 1996 Unreleased demos and out-takes from a once-proposed second S27 album.

Tom Robinson and Jakko M Jaksysk LP

6 We Never Had It So Good (Musidisc) 1990

HENRY ROLLINS

BORN *Henry Garfield, 2/13/61 (Washington DC)*

Although Henry Rollins had already indicated, through his career with Black Flag, that his talents were not confined wholly to hard core punk, still the variety of activities to consume him after he quit the band surprised many.

Fall 1983 saw him launch a parallel career as a spoken word performer; that same year, he launched his own publishing company, 2.13.61, and a self-described "low rent fanzine," 20.

The paperback *Two Thirteen Sixty One* followed. Since then, 2.13.61 has brought the writings of Nick Cave, the late Joe Cole and Jeffrey Lee Pierce, Roky Erickson, Iggy Pop, and Lydia Lunch to a wide American audience, together with regular volumes of Rollins' own, highly individual and frequently autobiographical work.

His 2.13.61 record label followed, featuring releases by TV Smith, Alan Vega, the Birthday Party, Gun Club, Hubert Selby Jr, Matthew Shipp, and, again, Rollins himself; he would also form the reissue/archive-intensive Infinite Zero with Rick Rubin, releasing classic recordings by Devo, the Monks, and Trouble Funk among others. In 1991, Rollins even launched an acting career with a role in Lydia Lunch's *Kiss Napoleon Goodbye* (1991), before entering more conventional pastures via *The Chase, Johnny Mnemonic*, and *Heat*. And of course, his Rollins Band established themselves as one of the hardest gigging groups on the circuit.

Formed around Chris Haskett (b. Leeds, England — guitar; ex-Surfin' Dave), Bernie Wandel (bass), and Mick Green (drums), the Rollins Band debuted in 1987 with a US club tour before flying to Holland to launch a 10-week European tour that summer. The band then traveled to Leeds, England, to record *Hot Animal Machine* with Fugazi front man Ian MacKaye producing.

Rollins had already recorded the *Big Ugly Mouth* spoken word live album during winter 1986 (he would do a similar tour of Europe that fall); a live musical album, split with Gore and featuring his regular band, appeared in Holland as *Live*. The EP *Drive by Shooting*, credited to Henrietta Collins and the Wifebeating Childhaters, also made it out in mid-1987.

A new Rollins Band line-up emerged during 1988, featuring Haskett, Andrew Weiss (bass), and Simeon Cain (drums), debuting with the Ian MacKaye-produced *Lifetime* album that fall. A second studio album, *Hard Volume*, would appear a year later, but the Rollins Band, like Rollins, were at their best in concert, touring tirelessly throughout this period and releasing just one further single, "I Know You" (Sub Pop). The band's live, in Vienna, *Turned On* collection, and Rollins spoken word *Readings; Switzerland* and *Live at McCabe's* set also emerged, plus an EP, *Fast Food for Thought*, credited to Wartime and featuring Rollins and Weiss.

The Rollins Band finally pushed into the public consciousness following a tour with Jane's Addiction, which led to them being invited onto Lollapalooza '91. Ironically, Roll-

ins' only recent release at that point was a collaboration with Australian punk legends, the Hard-Ons, *Let There Be Rock*.

Still a deal with Imago followed, and having scored an alternative radio hit with "Low Self Opinion," the Rollins Band released the aptly titled *End of Silence* (#160 US) in February 1992. A second single, "Tearing" (#54 UK), followed amid an 11-month world tour that took the Rollins Band to Japan for the first time. Rollins also compiled *The Boxed Life*, a collection of live spoken word performances.

Melvin Gibbs replaced Haskins during 1993; the Rollins Band would return to recording with April 1994's *Weight* (#33 US, #22 UK) and the single "Liar" (#27 UK). Another live album, *Electro Convulsive Therapy* was released in Japan as the band played Woodstock '94 and were nominated for a Grammy for Best Metal Band. But the collapse of the Imago label's distribution deal left the band's career in absolute limbo — the company claiming Rollins was still contracted to them, despite their total inability to release any records.

Rollins continued touring and performing; he would also win a Grammy for Best Audio Book with his Black Flag biography, *Get in the Van*. He produced Die Cheerleader's *Son of Filth* album, and in January 1996, he worked with the partially reformed Thin Lizzy at the *Vibe for Philo* gig, marking the 10th anniversary of vocalist Phil Lynott's death (Rollins also oversaw a new Lizzy compilation for US release).

Finally tiring of the group's inactivity, Rollins signed with Dreamworks in mid-1996, precipitating an ugly legal battle when the still-moribund Imago filed a $50 million breach of contract. Rollins responded with a counterclaim alleging fraud and deceit, undue influence, breach of fiduciary duty, and more.

The case was finally resolved the following year, and the first new Rollins Band album in three years, *Come in and Burn* (#89 US), appeared in April 1997, together with the single "The End of Something." Lower than expected sales and poorly attended shows, however, saw Rollins at least temporarily disband the group and concentrate further on his solo spoken word activities — the summer of 1998, he mourned, was the first since 1981 that he wasn't on the road with a band. "But I would as soon make music in a practice room in front of nobody, rather than risk another minute enduring someone else's apathy."

A new spoken word album, *Think Tank*, appeared in March 1998; Rollins would also tour heavily and undertake more film work before July 1999 brought the formation of a new Rollins Band, formed around the L.A. group Mother Superior. Their debut album, *Get Some Go Again*, was released in early 2000.

Also see the entry for "BLACK FLAG" on page 203.

Henry Rollins LPs

6 Hot Animal Machine (Texas Hotel) 1987 Rollins debut solo album is a beautifully raw, ragged affair, which includes Henrietta Collins and the Wifebeating Childhaters EP *Drive by Shooting*.

5 Live [SPLIT WITH GORE] (Eksakt — Holland) 1987

8 Life Time (Texas Hotel) 1998 Rollins and co. move away from his Black Flag parentage to the tight, exciting sounds of his own. The message here is alienation at full volume — "There's Nothing Like Finding Someone When You're Lonely to Make You Want to Be All Alone" really says it all.

7 Do It (Texas Hotel) 1989 Very cool collection. "Do It," "Move Right In," and "Next Time" are culled from sessions from the Rollins Band's 1988 *Life Time* sessions, plus live tracks from European performance.

7 Hard Volume (Texas Hotel) 1989 A funked up swagger that is moody and electrically eclectic. From "Hard" to "Down and Away" and "What Have I Got," Rollins is cranky and introspective while his band blissfully rocks on.

6 Turned On [LIVE] (Quarterstick) 1990 1989 concert in Vienna showcasing songs from 1987 onward.

8 The End of Silence (Imago) 1992 Incredibly intense, full of Rollins roiling, this album is a stellar, cohesive project that finds the band in fine fettle ready to kick you in the head — hard. Don't mess with Henry Rollins — he can, and will, bite, especially on "Low Self Opinion."

6 Electro Convulsive Therapy (Imago — Japan) 1994

8 Weight (Imago) 1994 Not quite as emotionally crippling as his past efforts, *Weight* reveals a remarkably chipper Rollins and a band that pulls out the stops to deliver some incredibly juicy sonics — the perfect balance between wit and wicked music.

6 Come in & Burn (Dreamworks) 1997 More of the same, but somehow disappointing this time, as it feels we've heard it all before on *Weight*.

7 Get Some Go Again (Dreamworks) 2000

Spoken Word LPs

8 Big Ugly Mouth (Texas Hotel) 1987

8 Sweat Box (Texas Hotel) 1988

7 Live at McCabe's (Texas Hotel) 1990

7 Human Butt (Quarterstick) 1990

8 The Boxed Life (Imago) 1993 A kinder, gentler, and much funnier Rollins than normally takes the stage, this double album recorded live at 10 spoken word shows reveals sheer comic genius. Even if his anecdotes are as everyman as most, Rollins' warped view will leave you gasping for breath; sex, hate, love, philosophy, bathos, and pathos are all grist for the mill, with many self-deprecating personal vignettes guaranteed to gain your sympathy and leave you guffawing.

8 Get in the Van [AUDIO BOOK] (Imago) 1994

7 Henry: Portrait of a Singer (Imago) 1994

6 Eye Scream [AUDIO BOOK] 1996

5 Everything (Thirsty Ear) 1996

5 Black Coffee Blues (Thirsty Ear) 1997

6 Think Tank (Dreamworks) 1998

6 Eric the Pilot (2.13.61) 1999

Selected Compilations and Archive Releases

7 Deep Throat (Quarterstick) 1992 Box set containing all four spoken word releases 1987–90.

ROOGALATOR

FORMED 1975 *(London, England)*
ORIGINAL LINE-UP *Danny Adler (b. Cincinnati, OH — vocals, guitar); Paul Riley (bass); Nick Plytas (keyboards); Dave Solomon (drums)*

A fixture on the Cincinnati club scene, guitarist Danny Adler cut his teeth working the same circuit as proto-funk heroes Dyke and the Blazers and Bootsy Collins' Pacesetters, frequently jamming with members of both bands. By 1971, however, he was based in the UK, a member of Smooth Loser, a group formed with fellow ex-pat Jeff Pasternak (bass) and Chris Gibbons (guitar). After their break up in 1972, Adler formed the first, very short-lived, incarnation of Roogalator.

Little came of it, and Adler moved into session work, highlighted by some monster jam sessions with drummer Ginger Baker's Nigerian group, Salt. He also spent time in Paris, studying jazz theory, then returned to London and suddenly, things started moving. Linking with drummer Bobby Irwin, pianist Steve Beresford, and keyboard player Nick Plytas, Adler recast Roogalator as an extraordinarily edgy funk-rock band, cut a demo, and immediately began to attract interest. Neither Beresford nor Irwin wanted to take things any further, however, and with their first live shows now coming up fast, Adler and Plytas rebuilt. Drummer Dave Solomon, a bandmate of both Plytas and Beresford in a Motown covers band, replaced Irwin; Irwin himself, introduced Paul Riley, a member of pub scene heroes Chilli Willi and the Red Hot Peppers. He joined shortly before Roogalator's September 1975 debut and, within weeks, the UK music press was feting the group as the next big thing — one paper even described them as "the future of rock'n'roll."

Neither was such applause simple hyperbole. At a time when British funk was still confined to the precise equations of Average White Band, Gonzalez *et al*, Roogalator played a jerky, minimalist stew which would, indeed, be absorbed by an entire future generation of local musicians. Like George Clinton five years before, and Prince five years hence, Roogalator isolated a funk which was utterly without precedent;

unlike Clinton and Prince, however, they would not be around to reap the rewards of their foresight.

Roogalator's precipitous ride ended as suddenly as it began, with a disastrous showcase gig in London in January, 1976, opening for R&B mavens Dr. Feelgood. Drummer Solomon quit, to be replaced with the session work, while his successor, Jeff Watts, lasted a matter of weeks. Irwin followed. Roogalator finally made their recorded debut in April with manager Robin Scott's brother Julian (bass) and Justin Hildreth (drums), cutting Adler's "Cincinnati Fatback" for the independent Stiff label.

A tumescent slab of triumphant, fractured funk, namechecking the sights and sounds Adler grew up with "on the banks of the O-Hi-O," sales of "Cincinnati Fatback" were sufficient to prompt interest from Virgin Records. Roogalator, however, balked at the label's demands that they sign a publishing contract as well as a record deal, and after just one 1977 single, Plytas' "Love and the Single Girl," the band backed away.

But time was passing them by. Britain was in the throes of the punk rock explosion now; it would be another two years before dexterous funk returned to even the grassroots club scene. By the time manager Scott launched his own Do It label, and Roogalator cut their debut album in mid-1977, Adler simply wanted to get the old songs down on tape before moving on to something else.

When Nick Plytas quit, an era had clearly ended. As a trio, Roogalator toured on through 1978, cutting one more single ("Zero Hero") and demoing a second album. But further line-up changes rocked the group and in July 1978, Roogalator came to the end of the line. Within twelve months, their praises were being played, if not overtly sung, by groups as far afield as Light of the World, the Gang of Four, and Spandau Ballet — spearheads of a Britfunk movement which Roogalator did not even know they were pioneering.

Striking out alone, Adler revived much of the projected second Roogalator album for his own solo debut, *The Danny Adler Story*. He subsequently worked with Rolling Stones drummer Charlie Watts' jazz band Rocket 88, reggae legend Niney the Observer, and James Brown drummer Tony Cook (1979's *Funky Afternoons* album), also recording a stream of extraordinarily eclectic albums over the past two decades.

Roogalator LP

6 Play It By Ear (Do It — UK) 1977 Road-weariness and too many line-up changes squeezed much of the soul out of Roogalator long before they cut their first album. More pop than stylish, a mere ghost of their early audacity flaps through.

Selected Compilations and Archive Releases

8 Cincinnati Fatback (Proper — UK) 1998 Think Chuck Berry's "Promised Land" tied to Hendrix's "Star Spangled Banner," or the Modern Lovers' "Roadrunner" if it raced down "Route 66." Think every thought you've ever dreamed when you're far away and homesick, then imagine what they'd sound like flooding out of a radio set halfway round the world. Congratulations: you've just heard "Cincinnati Fatback." A generous selection of the band's finest material, including demos and radio sessions.

Danny Adler LPs

8 The Danny Adler Story (Do It — UK) 1979

7 Gusha Gusha Music (Armageddon — UK) 1980

8 Live (Line — Germany) 1982 Excellent live in Switzerland recording.

8 Cincinatti's Finest (Flyright) 1988 Recorded under the alias Otis "Elevator" Gilmore, a fine, stomping blues monster masquerading as a long lost '50s-era master. A lot of people were fooled as well.

9 A 3-CD Trilogy (Line — Germany) 1989 Comprising three separately released discs, *Hometowns & High Iron, Hub Cap Heaven*, and *Night Shift*, a string of 1986–87 storytelling.

8 Mackinaw City (Line — Germany) 1989

8 Hometowns High Iron and Lakers (Roogalator) 1993 Cassette-only collection of traveling and railroad songs.

Selected Compilations and Archive Releases

8 Danny Adler Band (Line — Germany) 1988 Compilation of early '80s material.

7 Funky Afternoons (Line — Germany) 1990 Originally recorded in 1979, then updated in 1988.

9 Better Make a Move (Proper — UK) 1998 18-track collection drawing from Adler's entire post-Roogalator career — a stunning introduction to some very hard to find releases.

KEVIN ROWLAND

BORN 8/17/53 (*Wolverhampton, England*)

Kevin Rowland emerged as the front man of the Killjoys, a second-string punk act whose solitary single, "Johnny Won't Get to Heaven" created little interest upon release in late 1977, and the band — originally formed by Rowland and Heather Tonge (vocals), Gem (bass), Mark Phillips (guitar), and Joe 45 (drums) — broke up soon after.

Rowland and a latter day Killjoys member, Al Archer (guitar), formed a new band, Dexy's Midnight Runners, in July 1978, taking the group's name from the amphetamine Dexedrine. The original line-up of Rowland, Archer, Pete Saunders (keyboards), Pete Williams (bass), and Bobby Junior (drums), plus a brass section comprising Jimmy Patterson, JB Blyte, and Steve Spooner, gigged regularly around the English midlands and were soon swept up in the burgeoning mod revival.

A tentative link with the 2-Tone movement saw Dexy's included on a handful of ska concert bills; Rowland finally broke with the genre in mid-1979, when he withdrew Dexy's from an Electric Ballroom, London, gig with the Specials and Madness. The band signed with Parlophone and, with new drummer Andy Growcott in place, cut the "Dance Stance" single (#40 UK) in November.

Work then began on the band's first album, with former Merton Parka Mick Talbot replacing Saunders — the first single from the set, a tribute to '60s soul veteran Geno Washington, was an immediate smash — "Geno" (#1 UK) topped the UK chart in March 1980 and was swiftly followed by "There There My Dear" (#7 UK) and the album, *Searching for the Young Soul Rebels* (#6 UK) in July 1980.

The poor performance of two further singles, "Keep It Part Two" and "Plan B" (#58 UK), spelled the end of the band — citing Rowland's increasing autocracy, Archer, Growcott, and Talbot quit to form the Bureau (Talbot later surfaced in Paul Weller's Style Council), and Rowland and Patterson recruited a new band, comprising Billy Adams (guitar), Mickey Billingham (keyboards), Steve Wynne (bass), Seb Shelton (drums), and saxophonists Paul Speare and Brian Maurice.

Having signed now with Mercury, Dexy's June 1981 comeback began with the hit "Show Me" (#16 UK), but another flop, "Liars A to E," followed, and the group withdrew to reinvent itself. Out went the smart suits and mod sharpness; in came a rural gypsy look, exacerbated by the recruitment of violin trio Emerald Express — Helen O'Hara, Steve Brennan, and Roger MacDuff (Billingham quit at this time).

The new look band debuted with the self-affirming "Celtic Soul Brothers" (#45 UK), but again it was their sophomore single that was the charm — in June 1982, "Come on Eileen" (#1 US, #1 UK) topped charts around the world, and the following month, the album *Too Rye Aye* came close to repeating the feat (#14 US, #1 UK).

Again, however, dissension ripped the band. Patterson, Maurice, and Spear all quit within weeks of the hit, although the scaled-back Dexy's did not immediately notice. "Jackie Wilson Said" (#5 UK), "Let's Get This Straight from the Start" (#17 UK), and a reissue of "Celtic Soul Brothers" (#86 US, #20 UK) all ensured that Dexy's would remain chart contenders until mid-1983, but following a successful US tour highlighted by a May 14 *Saturday Night Live* appearance, Rowland again shattered the band.

More than two years would elapse before he re-emerged, with only O'Hara, Adams, and a returning Patterson comprising full-time Dexy's members. The remainder of the line-up was drawn from session men and while the *Don't Stand Me Down* (#22 UK) album — since acclaimed their best yet — would make a gallant appearance in the chart, a radically bisected version of the seven minute "This Is What She's Like" never stood a chance of returning the band to singles glory. "Because of You" (#13 UK) did hit, but it was too late. By October 1986, Dexy's had broken up yet again.

Rowland released a solo album in 1988, somewhat sadly credited to Kevin Rowland of Dexy's Midnight Runners, but neither *The Wanderer* nor its attendant singles, "Walk Away," "Tonight," and "Young Man," registered, and the singer faded away. He drifted into depression and drug dependency and in April 1991, declared bankruptcy with debts of over £100,000. Work was begun on a new album with Jimmy Patterson, and in March 1993, Rowland made his first TV appearance since 1985 on British television's *Saturday Zoo*. In 1994, however, Rowland entered rehab and it would be 1996 before he again began considering a comeback.

Upon hearing Rowland's latest demos, Creation label head Alan McGee offered him a deal — Rowland took it, then set about making an album quite unlike any he had discussed with his label, an all-covers set based around the songs that Rowland said had helped him through his recovery period. *My Beauty* was further distinguished by the 45-year-old Rowland's decision to make his public comeback in topless drag. "It's saying I have sexuality, I am a sexual being," he explained. "I am here and I can be sexy."

Unabashed by the barely concealed sniggering of the UK press, Rowland announced his live return on the largest stage he could find, at the Reading and Leeds festivals in August 1999, performing a three-song, 15-minute set, accompanied by a backing tape. His latest single, "Concrete and Clay," joined "The Greatest Love of All" and "You'll Never Walk Alone" in a purposefully confrontational performance, Rowland resplendent in a white mini-dress that afforded him several opportunities to flash his crotch at the audience. "It's borderline psychologically disturbed stuff," mused the *NME*. "Good or bad hardly seemed to matter."

Kevin Rowland LPs

❸ The Wanderer (Fontana) 1988 Distinctly underwhelming solo debut, devoid of even a hint of Dexy's pointed joy.

❽ My Beauty (Creation) 1999 From the crazed cover imagery through the histrionic recreations of a slew of classic oldies, a wildly unpredictable set that at least proves the voice and imagination are back.

Dexy's Midnight Runners LPs

7 Searching for the Young Soul Rebels (Parlophone) 1980
The soul-mod album, highlighted by the rambunctious "Geno" and some cogent lyrics elsewhere.

8 Too-Rye-Ay (Mercury) 1982 Excise "Come On Eileen" and the mood alters intensely; still folky-gypsy fiddle powered, but considerably darker and more serious.

6 Don't Stand Me Down (Mercury) 1985 Posthumous praise not withstanding, pristine production and portentous songs make for a distinctly soulless experience.

Selected Compilations and Archive Releases

7 The Very Best Of (Mercury) 1991
7 It Was Like This (Emi) 1996 Both stuffed with the hits and best bits.

RUNAWAYS

FORMED *1975 (Los Angeles, CA)*
ORIGINAL LINE-UP *Micki Steele (vocals, bass); Joan Jett (b. 9/22/60 — guitar); Sandy West (b. 1960 — drums)*

The Runaways were initially conceived as a teenaged female version of the Ramones. Joan Jett was the first musician to respond to manager Kim Fowley and songwriter Kari Krome's "musicians wanted" newspaper ad, followed by Sandy West and Micki Steele, and the Runaways played a handful of local shows as a trio in late 1975. Steele (who would later join the Bangles) quit to be replaced by Cherie Currie (b. 1960 — vocals) and Jackie Fox (bass); joined then by lead guitarist Lita Ford (b. 9/23/59), the band played a rooftop gig in L.A., landing a deal with Mercury soon after.

The group's debut album, *The Runaways* (#194 US), and the signature "Cherry Bomb" single were already in place when the band made its New York debut, supporting Television and the Talking Heads at CBGBs in summer 1976. They arrived at the club, stepped out of the car, and one of the area's notorious bums promptly threw up at Ford's feet.

The show was a success, but the band's potential was undermined by a marketing campaign that paid more attention to the musicians' ages (16, 17) than to their abilities. Still, the group's first UK visit in October was a success, the Runaways slipping readily into the burgeoning punk scene with the corseted Currie and leather-jacketed Jett — the visual and musical axis around which the band revolved — singled out for especial attention.

A second album, *Queens of Noise* (#172 US), undid much of the debut's goodwill, revealing the Runaways to be closer in spirit to heavy metal than punk, while the band's grueling live schedule was sufficient to push Fox out of the band, suf-

fering nervous exhaustion. She was replaced by Vicki Blue (ex-Venus and the Razorblades) before Currie, too, quit and Jett took over vocals. She led the band through their third album, *Waitin' for the Night*, by which time the Runaways were considered a joke everywhere but Japan, and when Ford quit following 1979's *And Now...* set, the group broke up.

Jett, Currie, and Ford would all go solo, targeting themselves toward distinctly polar audiences. Through the 1980s, Ford was the darling of the heavy metal set; Currie pursued a glammy singer-songwriter direction; Jett alone would remain pure to the ideals incited by the original line-up.

Also see the entry f or "JOAN JETT" on page 438.

The Runaways LPs

8 The Runaways (Mercury) 1976 The anthemic "Cherry Bomb" and the preposterous bad girls mini-opera "Dead End Justice" bookend an album, which really doesn't take itself too seriously but kicks out some convincing rockers regardless — "Blackmail," the super-coy "Secrets," and a remarkably convincing cover of the Velvets "Rock'n'Roll" included.

4 Queens of Noise (Mercury) 1977 There was "Queens of Noise" (to rhyme with "come and get it boys," or something equally erudite) and there was the rest. A great single....

4 Live in Japan (Mercury — UK) 1977 Recorded a year too late — first album Runaways put on one of the tightest shows around, even if the theatrics were a little naive. By 1977, however, Lita Ford already had her eyes on someone's metal guitar throne, and the second album proved that the songwriting had followed.

3 Waitin' for the Night (Mercury) 1977

5 And Now... The Runaways (Cherry Red — UK) 1978 A slew of covers and Jett's immortal "Black Leather" actually restore some dignity to the dying institution. Reissued as *Little Lost Girls*, which is quite an accurate summary as well.

2 Young and Fast (Allegiance) 1987 A disposable "reunion" album featuring no original members whatsoever, but masterminded again by Kim Fowley.

Selected Compilations and Archive Releases

4 Flaming Schoolgirls (Cherry Red — UK) 1980 Unreleased live and studio collection

7 The Best of the Runaways (Mercury) 1982

6 I Love Playing With Fire (Cherry Red — UK) 1982

6 Neon Angels (Mercury) 1992

Further Reading

Neon Angel: The Cherie Currie Story by Cherie Currie/Schusterman (Price Stern Sloan, 1989).

RUTS

FORMED *1978 (West London, England)*
ORIGINAL LINE-UP *Malcolm Owen (vocals); Paul Fox (guitar); John Jennings (bass); Dave Ruffy (drums)*

Formed by four west London school friends who were equally influenced by reggae as punk, the Ruts' first live show was supporting Wayne County's Electric Chairs at High Wycombe Town Hall in mid-1978. For much of the next year, they rarely played outside their local area, until a meeting with Southall-based reggae band Misty in Roots at a Rock Against Racism benefit gave them their first single, on Misty's own People Unite label. "In a Rut" appeared in late 1978, to be followed in January 1979 by the Ruts' first session for BBC radio's John Peel.

Virgin signed the band in spring, 1979 and promptly scored a hit when "Babylon's Burning" (#7 UK) rammed the Ruts into the UK Top 10. A tour with the Damned saw the follow-up, "Something That I Said" (#29), follow through in style, and in October, the Ruts released their debut album, *The Crack* (#16 UK), a rough set climaxed by its closing track — the culmination of the Ruts dubpunk hybrid, "Jah Wars" was written following the April 23, 1979, race riots, which shook the predominantly black Southall neighborhood.

Some 300 people were arrested that day, primarily members of the Anti Nazi League; there was also one death, a school teacher caught up in the police assault, and it was no coincidence at all that "Jah Wars," with its condemnation of both the police and the Fascists they had protected that day, should be released just as the first rioters went to trial. Unsurprisingly, the single was promptly slapped with an unspoken broadcast band.

The band's first headlining tour of Britain, the "Grin and Bear It" outing, followed, and a trip to France spawned a major television documentary on the band. In the spring of 1980, the Ruts were even recruited to back Jamaican legend Laurel Aitken on in what was confidently described as his "comeback" single, "Rudi Got Married," while the new year saw them restored to the UK Top 30 with the distinctly topical "Staring at the Rude Boys" (#22 UK).

Another British tour in early 1981 and a new single, "West One"(#43 UK), suggested that the Ruts were about to become the band of the new decade. Behind the scenes, however, all was not well. Malcolm Owen was a habitual heroin user, and in early 1981, with the singer now blowing off gigs because of his habit, his bandmates sacked him and went into the studio as a trio to begin work on a new album.

The shock treatment worked — Owen cleaned up, then went into rehab for a week. On July 11, 1981, he met with his estranged bandmates to discuss a reconciliation, won their approval, then went home and celebrated by getting high. His lifeless body was discovered in the bathtub the following morning.

The Ruts did carry on without him, regrouping as Ruts DC (Da Capo, or "new beginning"), while Virgin pieced together a posthumous second album of out-takes and non-album cuts, *Grin and Bear It* (#28 UK). When Ruts DC finally broke up, all three members would move into session work, with Dave Ruffy subsequently playing alongside Aztec Camera, Kirsty MacColl, and Joe Strummer, among many others.

Ruts LPs

8 The Crack (Virgin) 1979 Raised within equal reach of the punk and reggae communities, even the early Ruts' pounding hybrid was the equal of the Clash, both musically and spiritually. Owens' death renders discussion of their future academic, but across *The Crack* — and once past the handful of lesser ranters that did get on board — their brilliance is unquestionable.

Selected Compilations and Archive Releases

8 Grin and Bear It (Virgin) 1980 Respectful round-up of the non- and post-album singles.

6 The Ruts Live (Dojo) 1987

6 Live and Loud!! (Link) 1987 Thunderous concert recordings make up in energy what they lose in finesse but labor beneath such murky sound quality as to be practically worthless.

7 The Peel Sessions (Strange Fruit) 1990

9 Something That I Said (Caroline) 1995 The blueprint for everything the Clash had attempted to do and failed at very sadly, the Ruts are best remembered today for "Babylon's Burning," for "In a Rut," for the seven-minute dub epic "Jah Wars." Remember them for a lot more as well, though. Like the Tom Robinson Band just before them, the Ruts almost made a very big difference — to Punk, to the New Wave, to the rest of our lives.

Ruts DC LPs

6 Animal Now (Virgin) 1981 Sharp reinvention, retaining the reggae stylings but attempting something new with jazz-tinged funk — an admirable, if not always successful, attempt to move on.

7 Rhythm Collision (Bohemian) 1982 Playing to their true strengths again, with the Mad Professor at the controls.

S

SAINT ETIENNE

FORMED 1990 (London, England)
ORIGINAL LINE-UP Bob Stanley (b. 12/25/64, Peterborough, England — keyboards); Pete Wiggs (b. 5/15/66 — keyboards, synthesizers)

Bob Stanley and Pete Wiggs were childhood friends whose first collaboration was a fanzine, *Caff*, in 1986. Stanley also published *Pop Avalanche* with Andrew Midgley (aka Cola), and while at college in Peterborough in 1987, he began writing for the *New Musical Express*. He moved to *Melody Maker*, and in early 1989 he launched the Caff Corporation label, releasing 7" singles by bands he was interviewing.

By this time, he and Wiggs had already started recording as Next Projected Sound, working with Richard Norris (later of the Grid) on an aborted acid rave track, "Brutal Generation." The band lasted one recording session; in January 1990, the pair re-entered the studio to record what would become St. Etienne's first single, a cover of Neil Young's "Only Love Can Break Your Heart," with Faith over Reason vocalist Moira Lambert.

Signing with Heavenly Records (founder Jeff Barrett was a friend), the duo found themselves with a major club hit and began work on an album, intending to use a different vocalist on every track. September 1990's "Kiss and Make Up," their second single, featured Donna Savage of the New Zealand band Dead Famous People (their debut had recently been released through Billy Bragg's Utility label), and was released just as St. Etienne played their first live show at London's Heaven nightclub. They followed up with gigs at Subterrania with ex-Primal Scream guitarist Jim Beattie's new band, Spirea X, and Essex University with the Paris Angels, together with a lip-synced PA tour with model Stephanie Ansell fronting the group.

Next through the revolving door of vocalists was Sarah Cracknell, formerly a member of Prime Time and Lovecut DB (with whom she cut 1991's "Fingertips" single); Cracknell also self-released her own single on the 3 Bears label in 1987. She handled "Nothing can Stop Us" (#54 UK), St. Etienne's first UK hit in May 1991 and Wiggs and Stanley promptly halted their original plan, inviting Cracknell to join full-time. She accepted, and St. Etienne completed *Foxbase Alpha* (#34 UK) in time for a fall 1991 release.

A US deal with Warner Brothers saw a hit reissue for "Only Love Can Break Your Heart" (#97 US, #39 UK); it was followed by a single under the Cola Boy alias, "Seven Ways

of Love," which promptly emerged a major underground hit as a white label promo. The record was picked up for full release by Arista, with Wiggs and Stanley re-recording it with one of Cracknell's friends on vocals. It became their biggest hit yet (#8 UK), but a follow-up, "He Is Cola," flopped.

St. Etienne, in the meantime, scored further Top 40 entries in 1992 with a cover of Right Said Fred's "I'm Too Sexy" (#26 UK), recorded for the Terence Higgins AIDS trust, and two new songs, "Join Our Club" (#21 UK) and "Avenue" (#40 UK), previews for their in-progress sophomore set.

Loosely conceptual, March 1993's *So Tough* (#7 UK) was intended to illustrate a world tour beginning in London at "Mario's Cafe," each track linked either musically or with spoken samples in imitation of the band members beloved *Head* (the Monkees) and *Sell Out* (The Who) albums. It was an audacious effort, and wholly successful. The "You're in a Bad Way" (#12 UK) single accompanied the album and a collaboration with former Massive Attack vocalist Shara Nelson was followed by remixes for the Boo Radleys and Pizzicato Five and a session with Kylie Minogue, for her version of St. Etienne's own "Nothing Can Stop Me." They also recorded a new St. Etienne single with Charlatans vocalist Tim Burgess duetting with Cracknell on the "I Was Born on Christmas Day" (#37 UK) festive hit.

The band toured in the wake of *So Tough*, recruiting Heavenly label mates East Village and guitarist/engineer Ian Catt. (Supporting on this tour, incidentally, were Pulp). Another tour with DJ Kris Needs' Secret Knowledge project followed, before the band returned to the studio to record *Tiger Bay* (8# UK), an equally ambitious project revolving at least in part around short stories — two of these, "Pale Movie" (#28 UK) and "Like a Motorway" (#47 UK), would become hit singles, together with Cracknell's "Hug My Soul" (#32 UK).

The group parted with WB in the US after the label issued a mutilated version of *Tiger Bay* for bemused American consumption. When a fourth St. Etienne album, *Charlie Brown Music*, was conceived and just as quickly abandoned (elements subsequently appeared on the fan club only *I Love to Paint* album), rumors of a split began to circulate.

Over the next three years, the only new release would be an EP recorded with French singer Etienne Daho, logically titled *Saint Etienne Daho*. Released in mainland Europe only, it featured two re-recorded St. Etienne B-sides, a Daho oldie, and one new St. Etienne song, "Accident," which itself would reappear, in remixed form, as "He's on the Phone" (#11 UK) in October 1995.

The band's biggest UK hit was immediately followed by the singles collection *Too Young to Die* (#17 UK) and a year later, a companion collection of remixes, *Casino Classics* (#34), featuring contributions from Andrew Weatherall, Aphex Twin, Kris Needs, Autechre, David Holmes, Death in Vegas, Underworld, and more. Wiggs and Stanley, meanwhile, established their own Emidisc label — home to Denim and Kenickie, among others — and produced a comeback album by '60's veteran PJ Proby; Cracknell cut a solo album, *Lipslide*, and the single "Anymore" (#39 UK) during a short-lived alliance with the Gut label.

The trio reconvened in early 1998 at the Cardigans' studio in Malmo, Sweden, cutting the comeback "Sylvie" (#12 UK) and "Bad Photographer" singles, followed by *Good Humour* in September 1998. A new US deal with Sub Pop brought the band to American shores for two tours in 1998 and 1999, together with an EP, *Places to Visit*, and a rarities collection, *Fairfax High*. The band then decamped to Berlin to record *Sound of Water* with High Llamas frontman Sean O'Hagan among others.

St. Etienne LPs

7 Foxbase Alpha (WB) 1992 Classy dance floor '60's dream pop, distinctly formative compared to later efforts, but notable for the already classy sequence of singles and some surprising samples.

9 So Tough (WB) 1993 Equal parts Joe Meek, John Cale, and something sad by Kirsty MacColl, lush and hard and eminently fall-in-love able. "Mario's Cafe," "Join Our Club," and "Hobart Paving" top the pops, but nothing's less than sublime.

10 Tiger Bay (WB) 1994 St. Etienne's disco-llision of '50's romance, '60's pop, and '70's dance peaks with a piece of such consistent perfection that an uncaring label simply had to destroy it. US editions replaced subtlety with singles (two mixes each of "Hug My Soul" and "Motorway," and the utterly misplaced Christmas song), and should be treated with contempt; the never less-than-perfect original UK version wraps Cracknell around a chilling "Western Wind," feeds into the instrumental "Tanker-ville," and simply drifts on melancholia as far as the eye can see.

Everything St. Etienne promised is here. The mysteriously Kraftwerkian "Like a Motorway" bleeds onto the same tarmac as a string of '60's teen death songs — if the Leader of the Pack had a cell phone instead of a sad heart ("Look out! Look out!" "Shut up, I'm talking to my broker"); while four scene-setting instrumentals interlude the saddest seductions — "Motorway" is joined by Cracknell's Eurodisco "Hug My Soul" (and contrarily classical "Marble Lions") and the fetchingly yearning "Boy Scouts of America."

Odd lines leap out with precognitive clarity, so even when you're dancing, you're delving as well, into your heart, your soul, into all those secret corners where rock'n'roll rarely wanders.

Even in a nightclub, this is pure pop at its peak — the kind of sounds which two generations of Beatles wannabes have labored night and day to create, but which St. Etienne apparently knock off for fun. Captivating verses slide into divine imagery, and Cracknell's voice is the saddest, sexiest sound on earth.

8 Good Humour (Sub Pop), 1998 A gentler and initially more restrained effort than past albums, "Good Humour" grows slowly, but sticks. "Sylvie" and "Bad Photographer" both conjure heartbreaking melodies from Cracknell's voice, and while the remainder of the album is neither as hit-riddled or elusively pure as its predecessors, still it's as masterful as Etienne always should be — sugar which melts in your ears, not your deck.

8 Sound of Water (Sub Pop) 2000

Selected Compilations and Archive Releases

8 You Need a Mess of Help to Get By (Heavenly — UK) 1993 B-sides and rarities, with sufficient gems to make it irresistible.

9 Too Young to Die (Heavenly — UK) 1995 From "Only Love" to "He's on the Phone," the most perfect sequence of singles of the decade.

7 I Love to Paint (Fan Club — UK) 1995 Outtakes from the band's abandoned first attempt at a fourth album. Not all they could have been.

7 Casino Classics (Heavenly — UK) 1996 Two-CD remix collection, ranges between supreme (Underworld's "Cool Kids of Death") to the redundant, with a handful of new songs to set the pulse racing.

8 Continental (Heavenly — Japan) 1997

8 Fairfax High (Sub Pop) 1999 Two similar collections rounding up a host of non-album odds, but still omitting enough to keep the collectors hungry.

Sarah Cracknell LPs

7 Lipslide (Gut — UK) 1997

8 Lipslide (Instinct) 2000 Substituting four tracks and adding a video sees the (oddly belated) US edition squeeze ahead in the value stakes. Both versions, however, feature the crucial cuts, the lovely "Anymore" and "Coastal Town," as Cracknell moves away from Wiggs and Stanley, but keeps more than her fair share of the St. Etienne magic.

SCRITTI POLITTI

FORMED 1978 *(Leeds, England)*
ORIGINAL LINE-UP *Green (b. Green Strohmeyer-Gartside, 6/22/56, Cardiff — vocals); Tom Morley (linn drum); Nial Jinks (bass)*

Student and Young Communist Party member Green Gartside named his band from the writings of left-wing philosopher Gramsci, and initially intended his music to be an extension of his political beliefs. Self-releasing their debut single, "Skanc Blog Bologna," on the St. Pancras label, Scritti Politti became instant favorites with BBC DJ John Peel, who asked them to come into the studio to record a four-song session in December 1978. Scritti Politti, however, had only three songs, as they proved at their debut show at Acklam Hall in London, when they played all three twice. Rough Trade head Geoff Travis was impressed, however, and by the time Scritti Politti had learned a fourth song, they were already signed to his label. The 4 A-Sides EP (#11 UK indy) was released in September 1979; two months later, the band's second Peel session (from July 1979) was released as the Work in Progress EP (#13 UK indy).

Despite warm critical acclaim, Scritti Politti faded with the decade, and it would be some 18 months before the group resurfaced, with Mgotse (double bass) and Mike MacEvoy (synthesizers) widening the sound considerably. "The Sweetest Girl" (#64 UK, #3 UK indy) was a hit, but again Gartside retreated, to completely reinvent the band.

Out went Mgotse and founding member Jinks, replaced by Joe Cang (bass), Steve Sidwell (trumpet), and Jamie Talbot (sax) for the soulful "Faithless" (#56 UK, #2 UK indy). "Asylums in Jerusalem" (#43 UK, #2 UK indy) and the Songs to Remember album (#12 UK, #2 UK indy) followed, rounding up all three of the band's hits to date, but again Gartside restructured Scritti Politti, this time after a disastrous show in Brighton, while the band was touring with Gang of 4. He was hospitalized after suffering a panic attack and retired from live performance immediately.

The entire band was dismissed; henceforth, Scritti Politti would be Green and whoever else he felt like involving. Thus, a stellar line-up featuring the likes of Paul Jackson Jr. (guitar), Marcus Miller (ex-Miles Davis; bass), David Gamson (keyboards), Fred Maher (ex-New York Gong, Material; drums), Steve Ferrone (ex-Average White Band, Brian Auger; drums), and producer Arif Marden would convene for the March 1984 hit "Wood Beez (Pray like Aretha Franklin)" (#91 US, #10 UK), and a string of exquisitely crafted follow-ups. "Absolute" (#17 UK), "Hypnotise" (#69 UK), "The Word Girl" (#6 UK), and "The Perfect Way" (#11 US, #48 UK) were all taken from the band's second album, Cupid & Psyche 85 (#50 US, #5 UK).

The album sold over a million copies worldwide while Miles Davis covered "Perfect Way" on his Tutu album and offered his services for Green's next album. That was 1988's Provision (#113 US, #8 UK), produced by Green and Gamson and again featuring a line-up of sessionmen. The singles "Oh Patti" (#13 UK), "First Boy in Town" (#63 UK), and "Boom! There She Was" (#53 US, #55 UK) were hits, and Scritti Politti — Green, Gamson, and Maher — launched an arduous promotional tour (comprising radio and press interviews only) in support of the album.

Green returned to England to learn that his long-time manager Bob Last was retiring from the music industry, and decided to follow suit. He bought a cottage in the Usk Valley, close to his parents' home and by his own admission, "what was meant to be a couple of years chilling out in Wales turned into five or six...or was it six or seven?"

He did emerge briefly in 1991, linking with ragga star Shabba Ranks for a cover of the Beatles' "She's a Woman" (#20 UK), and a follow-up with Sweetie Irie, "Take Me in Your Arms and Love Me" (#47 UK). But it would be 1997 before Green contacted Gamson with a view to recording a new album. A band comprising Me'shell Ndegeocello (bass), Cato (guitar), and Abe Laboriel (drums) was swollen by Wendy Melvoin (of Wendy and Lisa), go-go drummer Juju House, and NYC reggae bassist Vere Isaacs, and hip-hop vocalists Mos' Def and Lee Majors. The resulting Anomie and Bonhomie (despair and delight) was released in early 2000.

Scritti Politti LPs

8 Songs to Remember (Rough Trade) 1982 After the often uncompromising offbeat of the early singles, songs like "Asylums in Jerusalem," "The Sweetest Girl," and the anthemic "Faithless" come as an utter — but utterly welcome — shock, marrying pop melody to passion while maintaining an almost homespun sound.

6 Cupid and Psyche (WB) 1985 Reinventing Scritti as a club concern, Cupid is precision crafted from dance beats, synth-sounds, and dazzling flashes of rock guitar...all of which are simply the backdrop for Green's unfathomably exquisite vocals. The presence of "Woodbeez" not withstanding, however, the song writing really isn't up to much.

6 Provision (WB) 1988 A stronger effort, but little more than a chance to tie up a few of Cupid's looser ends. "Boom! There She Was" is as good as it gets.

8 Anomie and Bonhomie (Virgin) 2000 After a decade away, reinvention was obvious. Delving into devilishly orchestrated hip-hop beats, while retaining the urban soul of old, Anomie emerges with unexpected power and persuasion, the epic "Brushed with Oil" and two sterling vocal offerings from Me'shell Ndegeocello.

SEX PISTOLS

FORMED 1975 (London, England)
ORIGINAL LINE-UP Johnny Rotten (b. John Lydon, 1/31/56, London — vocals); Steve Jones (b. 5/3/55, London — guitar); Glen Matlock (b. 8/27/56, London — bass); Paul Cook (b. 7/20/56, London — drums)

Steve Jones, Warwick "Wally" Nightingale (guitar), Jimmy Mackin (organ), and Stephen Hayes (bass) formed their first band, the Strand in 1974. Jones was the original drummer, but moved to vocals early on and Paul Cook replaced him. With equipment that Jones claimed was stolen from other bands backstage at various London venues, The Strand played a few rehearsals before Hayes and Mackin quit.

Glen Matlock, a part-time employee at the Chelsea boutique Sex, was recruited after the band met his employer, would-be rock entrepreneur, Malcolm McLaren. Rehearsing now at a disused BBC studio in Hammersmith, the band practiced for six months then sacked Nightingale. Jones would eventually take over guitar; in the interim, a number of musicians auditioned, including journalist Nick Kent.

The search for a vocalist to replace Jones was more problematic. Both Midge Ure (later of Ultravox) and Mike Spencer (Count Bishops) turned the band down. Finally, Jones and McLaren associate Bernie Rhodes approached an apparently hunchbacked, green-haired youth they had seen hanging around the store. In August 1975, John Lydon was invited to meet the band and McLaren at the nearby Roebuck Pub, then auditioned back at Sex, miming to Alice Cooper's "School's Out" on the jukebox.

Concerns about Jones' guitar playing also saw the band make attempts to recruit a new guitarist; a September 26 ad in Melody Maker called for a "whiz kid guitarist. Not older than 20, not worse looking than Johnny Thunders." Steve New (later of Glen Matlock's first post-Pistols band, the Rich Kids) turned up and rehearsed with the band for several weeks, but again nobody suitable came forward and the band remained a quartet.

Now renamed the Sex Pistols, the band's first show on November 6 1975 saw them opening for '50's revivalists Bazooka Joe (fronted by the future Adam Ant) at St. Martin's College of Art. The group played five songs before the plug was pulled on them. Other shows were more successful, despite the band's patent disregard for musicianship, and slowly an audience grew around what was clearly an irrepressible, if utterly unskilled, band.

The ringleaders were a cache of south Londoners, remembered today as the Bromley Contingent, and comprising such future heroes of the Punk movement as Steve Severin, Siouxsie Sioux, and Billy Idol. Utilizing Pistols shows as an excuse to dress themselves in increasingly bizarre costumes (purchased, or later borrowed from Sex), they created an image around the Pistols long before the band itself had begun to formulate a plan of its own.

Further gigs followed. The Pistols opened for Eddie and the Hot Rods at the Marquee in February and earned their first press mention. Ron Watts, promoter at the 100 Club in London, booked the band, insisting that whatever else was wrong with the Sex Pistols, "they did have a definite idea of presentation." Two kids in Manchester read about the group and promptly arranged for them to play that city; a month

later, the Pistols returned and found their erstwhile bookers had now formed a band themselves, the Buzzcocks.

The Pistols opened for pub rockers, the 101ers; vocalist Joe Mellor became Joe Strummer within days. They opened for metal band Budgie and a girl in the audience, Mari Elliott, went home and became Poly Styrene, vocalist with X-Ray Spex. Everywhere the Pistols played, they made converts; everywhere they played, too, there was controversy. A show at the Nashville in west London ended in fighting between band and audience. Venues banned the band without ever having heard them.

The band's first demos, in May 1976, were recorded with guitarist Chris Spedding at the helm; in July the band's own sound engineer, Dave Goodman, took a session. In September, the Pistols' made their television debut on future Factory Records boss Tony Wilson's So It Goes, and just days later, the Pistols headlined the first gathering of the putative tribes when the 100 Club gave itself over to a two-night Punk Festival. The following week, McLaren opened negotiations with EMI; the band signed the £40,000 deal on October 8 and immediately set about recording their debut single, "Anarchy in the UK" (#38 UK). EMI had specifically requested "Pretty Vacant."

Dave Goodman produced this session; six days later the band tried again with Mike Thorne; three days after that, they finally got it right with former Roxy Music producer Chris Thomas. "Anarchy in the UK" would be released on November 19; and on December 1, the band was invited to replace late withdrawals, Queen, on local London TV's nightly magazine show, Today, a live broadcast aired at 6 p.m. Three "fucks," two "shits," one "sod," and a "bastard" later, the Sex Pistols were public enemy #1 — and the greatest thing to hit rock'n'roll in five years.

The fallout was as dramatic as it was immediate. The following day's newspapers condemned the band with front page headlines. Dates on the band's Anarchy Tour were cancelled wholesale; "Anarchy in the UK" was banned from radio and television and EMI's own record packers refused to handle the single. But there would be anarchy in the UK regardless.

In January 1977, EMI finally bowed to public pressure and released the Pistols from their contract. The following month, just as Glen Matlock was replaced with one of Rotten's old friends, Sid Vicious (born John Beverley, London, 5/10/57), the group joined A&M, then were dropped within a week. In between times, the Pistols were implicated in a fracas which resulted in a friend of DJ Bob Harris being injured at a nightclub; London's Capital Radio threatened to boycott all A&M artists until the band was dropped and great swathes of A&M's own roster wrote letters of complaint to the UK office. The group were £75,000 richer, but homeless once again.

Vicious made his live debut with the Pistols on March 28, 1977 — it was, in fact, only the second live show he'd ever played, following a fumbling appearance as bassist for Siouxsie and the Banshees (making their own first ever appearance) at the 100 Club punk festival. He acquitted himself reasonably, but of course he was not recruited to the Pistols for his musical ability. He was recruited for an image which the band now needed to devote their career to upholding.

On May 12, 1977, the Pistols signed to Virgin; their long delayed new single, "God Save the Queen" (#2 UK), was released days later to coincide with HM Queen Elizabeth II's Silver Jubilee celebrations in June. Further uproar was inevitable. Selective misinterpretation of the song's lyrics made it apparent that the band was calling the Queen a moron, a scandal which the tabloids could not suppress, no matter (they said) how much they loathed giving publicity to these foul mouthed punk rockers. People heard what they wanted to hear, saw what they wanted to see, and reacted with violent predictability.

Radio and TV bans were immediate. Several chainstores announced they would not stock the record; some even deleted all reference to the single when they posted the weekly Top 30. Officially, "God Save the Queen" would peak at #2, behind Rod Stewart's "I Don't Want to Talk About It." In fact, the Pistols outsold every record in sight.

They were also marked men. Rotten, Cook, producer Chris Thomas, and designer Jamie Reid were attacked on the street by self-styled Royalist patriots, igniting a summer of attacks on punk fans and musicians. Later, when the band played its first gig in three months, on a boatcruise up the Thames on Jubilee night, the police were waiting at the dock when they disembarked. Eleven people were arrested, including McLaren.

Things settled down after that. On July 1, the Sex Pistols' third single, "Pretty Vacant" (#6 UK), moved into the market without a peep from the guardians of British morality — it was even featured on *Top of the Pops*, a show which had hitherto banned the band outright. Following the statements of civil disobedience which preceded it, however, even hardcore fans were disappointed.

Through August 1977, the Pistols played a handful of shows under a variety of aliases — the Spots (Sex Pistols on Tour), the Tax Exiles, the Special Guests, Acne Rabble, the Hamsters, even "a mystery band of international repute." Then it was back to the studio to complete their debut album, *Never Mind the Bollocks, Here's the Sex Pistols* (#106 US, #1 UK). Advance orders would top 125,000 before the record's October 24 release.

It could not go unremarked upon. Within four days of the album's release, Tory shadow Education Minister, Norman St. John Stevas announced, "[the] album has been produced deliberately to offend. It is the kind of music that is a symptom of the way society is declining. It could have a shocking effect on young people." The band's new single, "Holidays in the Sun" (#8 UK), was banned by Capitol Radio because it likened Belsen to a holiday camp; and the album's title, incorporating as it did a slang expression for testicles, was guaranteed to horrify societal mores — all the more so after an 88-year-old Indecent Advertising Act was invoked against a handful of stores which displayed posters for the record.

Unfortunately for the album's opponents, "bollocks" had a second meaning, originally applied to 19th century clergymen (of all people!) and their penchant for talking a lot of nonsense, or bollocks. With a battery of learned linguistic professors on their side, Virgin Records (standing firmly behind the persecuted store owners) were able to derail the prosecution by suggesting that in the context of the album title, "bollocks" did indeed mean nonsense — a lot of which had been hurled at the Pistols over the past twelve months. The court had no choice — "bollocks" was legitimized.

On December 5, the band departed Britain for a ten-day tour of Holland. A handful of UK dates followed, including a Christmas Day matinee for orphans in Huddersfield; and on December 29, they were to fly to New York to launch their first US tour with a stop in Pittsburgh and an appearance on *Saturday Night Live*. Delays in receiving their visas, however, necessitated cancelling these first shows (Elvis Costello replaced the group on *SNL*), and the tour eventually opened in Atlanta, GA, on January 5; swung through a succession of misbegotten southern state shows; then washed up in San Francisco on January 14. There, the Sex Pistols played their last ever show; the following day, Rotten flew home and announced he'd quit the band.

Jones, Cook, and Vicious remained behind, traveling to Rio De Janeiro to shoot scenes for McLaren's long dreamed of Sex Pistols movie (then titled *Who Killed Bambi?*), with escaped train robber Ronnie Biggs (he would sing lead on a new Sex Pistols single, "No-one Is Innocent (The Biggest Blow)," #7 UK).

It would be followed by Vicious' Eddie Cochran covers, "Something Else" (#3 UK) and "C'mon Everybody" (#3 UK), and Jones' "Silly Thing" (#6 UK); but by late 1978, with Rotten's Public Image Limited now up and running, Glen Matlock's Rich Kids touring their own first album, and Vicious in New York awaiting trial for the October 12, 1978 murder of girlfriend Nancy Spungeon, even the ghost of the Pistols was lain to rest. Vicious died from a heroin overdose on Feb 2, 1979, the month before the movie — now retitled *The Great Rock'n'Roll Swindle* — reached theaters.

Two further singles would be culled from the accompanying soundtrack album — the title track (#21 UK) and a Rotten-era outtake, "Stepping Stone" (#21 UK) — but the band was over. Cook and Jones would remain a double act through the early 1980s with their own band, the Professionals; subsequently, Jones launche d a solo career (as did Matlock, following the demise of the Rich Kids); Cook formed a new band, the Chiefs of Relief, and moved into production, handling early releases by Bananarama and future Damned guitarist Alan Shaw's Physicals.

Only Rotten/Lydon enjoyed any kind of commercial success, and in 1996, it was announced that the Sex Pistols were reforming for tours of America and the UK. The *Filthy Lucre* live album (and accompanying single, a live version of "Pretty Vacant," #18 UK) was an aptly named souvenir of the affair.

Also see the entry for "PUBLIC IMAGE LTD" on page 564.

Sex Pistols LPs

🔟 Never Mind the Bollocks Here's the Sex Pistols (WB) 1977 By the time the Sex Pistols finally got around to releasing their debut album, on October 28, 1977, much of its initial stated impact had long since been eroded. Four successive singles, three of them ("Anarchy in the UK," "God Save the Queen," and "Pretty Vacant") still rated amongst the most important noises ever consigned to vinyl, had already familiarized, even desensitized, the British public to the Pistols' sound; while the mainstream's absorption of punk music, personified by the now weekly appearance of one band or another on *Top of the Pops*, had removed the threat months before. Released a matter of weeks earlier, the legendary *Spunk* bootleg, too, had diluted the album's potential impact, serving up rougher and, perhaps, more vital early takes of many of the same songs, and reminding attentive listeners that there were, indeed, two Sex Pistols — the iconoclastic guerilla four-piece whose repertoire and reputation alike were forged in the undergrowth of word-of-mouth obscurity; and the fanciful media superstars who emerged foul-mouthed and attention-seeking in the aftermath of the *Today* interview. Neither was the distinction at all subjective. The Sex Pistols of 1976 would never have dreamed of recording the obscenity-laden anti-abortion rant "Bodies"; the Pistols of 1977 had no choice. *Spunk*, needless to say, was recorded by the first group, *Bollocks* by the second.

Still *Never Mind the Bollocks* impacted upon the British scene like no other album of the era, crashing into the national chart at #1; having its name dragged through the court system, as the greatest minds in the country debated the legal status of its title; and finally, confirming that after all the trials, traumas, and tribulations of the past ten months, the Sex Pistols really had been as great as everybody said they were — "had been," because all but two of the album's twelve tracks (the opening "Holidays in the Sun" and "Bodies") not only predated Glen Matlock's

replacement by Sid Vicious, but most of them were written before anybody outside of London even heard of the group.

The key to the record, of course, remained the unparalleled adrenalin rush of "Anarchy" — the 14-second intro which simultaneously defined and created this thing which the papers called Punk Rock; the sulphurous snarling of an opening verse which left listeners in no doubt which side of the incipient musical divide they stood on; the promise, through the chorus, of a holocaust to come.

Curiously scheduled almost midway through the original vinyl's second side, "Anarchy" lost none of its foreboding power in its new surroundings, and may indeed have gained some. Its fellow 45s not withstanding, afterall, the remainder of the album ranged from the petulant scorn of "New York" (a vitriolic riposte to manager McLaren's days with the Dolls) and "EMI" (a raspberry blown at the band's first label); through the nihilist nagging of "Problems," "No Feelings," and "17"; and on, again, to the sensationalist nadir of "Bodies."

Never Mind the Bollocks was a significant album, but it was its intent, not its contents, which made it so — the knowledge that with the Sex Pistols, rock'n'roll had not simply reached the end of a sentence. It had finally closed the book upon itself. And was it Lydon's luck or Johnny's judgement which demanded that the next volume should open where the last one left off?

Immediately following "Anarchy" in the running order, "Submission" was everything the rest of the album wasn't — a chilling mantra, an icy blast, a glimpse inside the parallel worlds of musical experiment which were already fermenting in Rotten's head. The rest of the band, he later claimed, hated the song, didn't understand it, or know what it portended. But the darkness which was already gathering over the fringes of the now year-old punk scene understood and would clasp "Submission" to its breast. And by the time Rotten re-emerged at the helm of Public Image Ltd., at the end of 1978, what had once appeared mere hubris had been recast as punk rock's destiny.

4️⃣ Filthy Lucre Live (Virgin) 1996 Money-spinning souvenir of the Sex Pistols' reunion tour.

Selected Compilations and Archive Releases

There are more Sex Pistols albums on the racks than the band itself had songs. The following notes key releases in the following categories:

> *(i)* Chris Spedding demos;
> *(ii)* Dave Goodman demos;
> *(iii)* live 1976;
> *(iv)* out-takes 1977;
> *(v)* live 1977–78;
> *(vi)* EMI/Virgin material compilations;
> *(vii)* miscellaneous.

All (bar section *vi*) should be approached with utmost caution; live recordings averaged **3**; studio averaged **5**.

(i) Chris Spedding Sessions
Pirates of Destiny (Skyclad — UK) 1988

(ii) Dave Goodman/Spunk Demos
The Mini Album (Chaos — UK) 1985

We Have Cum for Your Children... Wanted: (Skyclad — UK) 1988

The Swindle Continues (Restless) 1988

No Future UK? (Receiver — UK) 1989 Of varying completeness, the *Spunk* album and associated sessions.

(iii) 1976 Live
Original Sex Pistols Live (Castle — UK) 1985

The Original Pistols Live (Fame) 1986

Better Live than Dead (Restless) 1988

Early Daze — The Studio Collection (Streetlink — UK) 1992

Raw (Music Club) 1997 All live, Burton 9/76. Unanimously boasting scratchy sound, pissy vocals, and a mix mixed-up in a baboon's armpit, the majority of live Pistols shows are of purely academic interest. But the thrill of the moment is tangible.

After The Storm (Receiver — UK) 1985 Four tracks from Burton, others by New York Dolls.

Live Worldwide (Konnexion — UK) 1985

Tenth Anniversary Album (MBC — UK) 1986 Live Burton 9/76 + Goodman demos.

Live At Chelmsford Top Security Prison (Restless) 1988 Appalling sound quality.

(iv) 1977 Out-takes
Party Till You Puke (Discs Deluxe) 1991 Features cuts later issued as B-sides to the 1992 "Pretty Vacant" CD single (Virgin).

(v) 1977–78 Live
Never Trust a Hippy (Sex Pistols — UK) 1985 Lo-fi recordings from Sweden, Newport, and Atlanta.

Where Were You in 77? (77 — UK) 1985 Newport, Wales 12/23/77.

Anarchy in the UK (Sex Pistols — UK) 1985 Stockholm 1977 and San Francisco 1978.

The Best of the Sex Pistols Live (Bondage — UK) 1985 Side one — Burton 9/76; side two — San Francisco 1/78.

The Power of the Pistols (77 — UK) 1985 Side one — Halmsted 7/77; side two — Atlanta.

God Save the Sex Pistols (Konnexion — UK) 1985 Tracks from Halmstad, Uxbridge, Dallas, San Francisco, San Antonio, and Baton Rouge.

Cash from Chaos (SPCFC — UK) 1985 Side one — Goodman demos; side two — live Stockholm/San Francisco.

Anarchy Worldwide (Sex Pistols — UK) 1988 Side one — Goodman demos; side two — unspecified US live.

The Last Concert on Earth (Konnexion — UK) 1986

Live and Loud (Link — UK) 1989 San Francisco 1978.

(vi) Official (Virgin) Compilations
7 The Great Rock'n'Roll Swindle (Virgin) 1980 Original movie soundtrack including archive material from throughout the band's career, and released as both a double album recreating the full soundtrack, and a single disc concentrating only on the Pistols' own material.

8 Flogging a Dead Horse (Virgin) 1980 Indeed. The first Pistols compilation also stands as the only necessary one, a gathering of all the singles and attendant B-sides.

8 Kiss This (Virgin) 1992 The full Rotten repertoire, *Bollocks* plus B-sides and relevant *Swindle* material, plus a high quality live show from Trondheim 1977.

(vii) Miscellaneous
5 Some Product: Carri on Sex Pistols (Virgin) 1979 Radio interviews, TV and radio commercials, etc.

5 The Heyday (Factory — UK) 1980 Spoken word collection reprising TV and interview material.

Sid Vicious

Selected Compilations and Archive Releases
3 Sid Sings (Virgin) 1979

4 Drugs Kill (MBC — UK) 1986

3 Live at the Electric Ballroom (MBC — UK) 1986

2 The Real Sid And Nancy (MBC — UK) 1986

6 Sid Vicious vs Eddie Cochran (MBC — UK) 1986 Scrappy but indulgently entertaining selections of mainly live Vicious solo recordings. The Virgin album offers the best sound and range of material, with the *Swindle* cuts reprised alongside "I Wanna Be Your Dog," "Search and Destroy," and "Chinese Rocks." Can you spell self-mythology?

Glen Matlock LP
5 Who's He Think He Is When He's at Home? (Creation) 1996 Unfulfilling solo shot, although he can still write some memorable tunes.

Rich Kids LPs
7 Ghosts of Princes in Towers (EMI) 1978 Even Mick Ronson's eccentric production (which can be bettered by turning the treble way up) couldn't ruin this record, as Matlock draws a heavy veil across his Pistol past and delves into what the press would promptly christen power-pop. It wasn't, of course, but *Ghosts* nevertheless encompassed bright and chirpy hooks, the militaristically commercial "Marching Men," a clutch of punky pub

rockers, and even a glitter-filled rockabilly number. And the title track was a devastating statement of intent.

6 Burning Sounds (Revolver) 1999 Belated release for abortive second album demos and outtakes.

Steve Jones LPs
5 Mercy (Gold Mountain) 1987
5 Fire and Gasoline (Gold Mountain) 1989

Steve Jones & Paul Cook/The Professionals LPs
6 Professionals (Virgin) 1980 Surprisingly (?) competent and eminently likeable hard rock-inflected punk; no especially great songs, but no disgrace either.
6 I Didn't See It Coming (Virgin) 1981

Paul Cook/Chiefs of Relief LPs
7 Chiefs of Relief (Sire) 1988

Further Reading
No Irish, No Blacks, No Dogs by John Lydon/Keith Zimmerman/Kent Zimmerman (St. Martin's Press, 1994).

SHAM 69

FORMED *1976 (Hersham, England)*
ORIGINAL LINE-UP *Jimmy Pursey (vocals); Albie Slider (bass); Neil Harris (guitar); Johnny Good for nothing (guitar); Billy Bostik (drums)*

"Since I was a kid," Jimmy Pursey explained, "I used to go the discos regular. Then when I was about 14, I got really drunk and crawled up onstage and mimed to a couple of Stones songs. Well the geezer who ran the gaff really liked it, so...."

It became a regular gig and in late 1976, Pursey joined his first band, "local mates playing up a dead end. They were terrible before I joined. Hadn't a clue what was going on. We got our name when I was having a toilet at a football match, and there was this graffiti on the wall" — hometown Hersham's soccer team had a great year in 1969, but "Sham 69" was all that remained of a celebratory scrawl on the bathroom wall.

The original Sham line-up splintered in June 1977, after just a handful of shows had introduced them to the London punk scene; Albie Slider alone survived Pursey's night of the long knives. In came Dave Parsons — who quickly fell into the joint roles of guitarist and Pursey's songwriting partner — and drummer Mark Cain, and in this form, Sham and producer John Cale created the nihilistic snot classic "I Don't Wanna" for release on Miles Copeland's infant Step Forward label.

Slider quit the music business in October 1977; he was replaced by Dave Treganna and the new-look Sham debuted on a rooftop in central London — an alternative to the opening night of the Vortex Club. Of course the police intervened and when the band refused, in true Beatles fashion, to stop playing, Pursey was arrested. Rock's newest martyr got off with a £30 fine, but the exposure was priceless.

The Inner London Education Authority, planning a schools documentary on Punk, invited Sham to add two songs to *Confessions of a Music Lover*, and while the show never made it off the closed circuit educational broadcasting network, Polydor Records were sold. They signed the band in late 1977, and "Borstal Breakout," Sham's debut single, steamrollered into view in the new year.

Very early on, Sham's raucous chant- and stamp-along music brought them to the grateful attention of Britain's rising skinhead community. In their wake, the ultra right-wing National Front swiftly found in Sham the voice they had been looking for, regardless of Sham's own politics — Pursey himself was an extremely vocal supporter of Rock Against Racism.

Not that the ensuing controversy darkened Sham's commercial standing, as "Angels with Dirty Faces" (#19 UK) and the half-live *Tell Us the Truth* (#25 UK) continued the band's success, before the most eternal of itinerant soccer chants, "If the Kids Are United" (#9 UK), crystallized the band's yobbish charm in the mainstream during summer 1978.

A projected US tour was cancelled after the band failed to receive the requisite visas; Pursey's bitter "No Entry" documented the situation and appeared on the B-side of the band's next single, the oddly Ian Dury-esque "Hurry Up Harry" (#10 UK).

Sham's next move was equally bizarre — a concept album which Pursey insisted was "gonna be kinda like *Quadrophenia*, that album done by the Who. One song will be in a cafe with pinballs and so on, then a railway station, all sorts of places. It'll be like a concept, but it's things that mean something to people, about situations they can understand." Or, as *Spiral Scratch* magazine put it, *That's Life* (#27 UK) was the story of "a bloke who loses his job for bad time keeping, wins some money at the bookies, and spends it all on booze and birds."

Violence continued to haunt the band, with Pursey powerless to intercede as the bottles flew and seating was torn up. Matters reached a head at Middlesex Poly in January 1979; under the watchful eyes of a BBC camera crew, filming Sham for the arts show *Arena*, the gig was utterly trashed. A couple of nights later in Aylesbury, Pursey announced the band was retiring from live performance.

They continued recording. March 1979 brought "Questions and Answers" (#18 UK), but July's "Hersham Boys" (#6) was loudly trumpeted as the band's farewell. They split in June, then reformed a month later, to promote their next album, *The Adventures of the Hersham Boys* (#8 UK).

Tours of the UK and at last, the US, were set up. But although the album was a smash, appearances were deceptive and Sham remained at the end of their tether. An ill-conceived cover of The Yardbirds' "You're a Better Man than I" (#49 UK) indicated that the rot had set in commercially as well; "Tell the Children" (#45 UK), recorded with new drummer Mark Goldstein, sank similarly, and "Unite and Win" failed altogether. Pete Townshend rejected Sham for a role in the *Quadrophenia* movie "because the kids can't dance to them," and when *The Game*, Sham's fourth album, flopped, that really was the end.

Treganna, Parsons, and Goldstein joined Dead Boys vocalist Stiv Bators in the Wanderers; Pursey announced a solo career and produced early releases by the Cockney Rejects and Angelic Upstarts, two of the bands cut most accurately in Sham's own image. However, Polydor dropped him after the *Imagination Camouflage* album and "Lucky Man" single flopped, and a union with Epic was no happier, despite the presence of co-writer Peter Gabriel on the "Animals Have Fun" single in June 1981.

The *Alien Orphan* album in February 1982, ended Pursey's major label involvement, and over the next three years, he would drift between indy labels and a clutch of equally ill-starred singles, before reuniting with Parsons in early 1987 and relaunching Sham 69.

Working with full-time drummer Ian Whitewood and session musicians, the band debuted with the singles "Rip and Tear" and "Outside the Warehouse," before a new album, *Volunteer*, at least consolidated their revitalized live reputation. A trip to New York in 1988 reinforced this, and would be preserved in the *Live at CBGB's* set.

Another lengthy layoff followed, but reawakened by Pursey's starring role on Die Toten Hosen's *Learning English* punk tribute, Sham reconvened for 1992's *Information Libre*, a set which proved the group had lost none of its early abrasion.

Sham toured as far afield as Japan, then returned to the studio for *Kings and Queens*, mischievously recasting a clutch of the band's best known oldies with a raucous techno air. Scaling back the line-up from the often unwieldy mass of saxophones and keyboards which distinguished past efforts, Pursey, Whitewood, and Parsons, plus Matt Sargent (ex-Chelsea, bass) cut *Soapy Water and Marmalade*, and returned to the road in August 1995 (Pursey was also recruited as poster boy for The Gap). *The A Files*, in 1997, continued the band's growth.

Sham 69 LPs

8 Tell Us the Truth (Sire) 1978 Sham really weren't any better or worse than the scores of bands which formed in the Pistols' wake, but they had two qualities most of the others lacked — charisma, evident from the fervid response of fans on the live side of *Truth*, and anthemic songs, equally obvious across both sides of the record. There was indeed about to be a borstal breakout.

7 That's Life (Polydor — UK) 1978 A punk concept album is a novel idea to say the least, and Sham's day in the life of a typical working class kid certainly has a universal resonance. However, it was also utterly preposterous, a doomed attempt at bringing some meaning to the meaninglessness which induced punk in the first place. Nevertheless, Sham are unleashed across some of their mightiest songs... plus, "Hurry Up Harry" gave the Sham army a new refrain to roar — "we're going down the pub." As if they'd ever gone anywhere else.

7 The Adventures of the Hersham Boys (Polydor UK) 1979 A platform for Sham's now mature musicianship, the band returned to straightforward punk, albeit with the addition of some unusual elements — keyboards!

5 The Game (Polydor UK) 1980 Still defiant, but curiously unfocused, Jimmy and the boys seem to be losing touch with the very working class roots that had been their raison d'etre since day one. Musically they're evolving as well, away from the melodic anthems which once propelled so effortlessly and towards a hookless rock shout-along crossed with derivative Pistols riffing. Maybe we should all go down the pub.

3 Volunteer (Legacy UK) 1988 Scrappy comeback set picks up where *The Game* left off, with desperation now the loudest sound on show.

5 Live at CBGBS 1988 (Dojo UK) 1991

3 Information Libre (Rotate UK) 1992 The best cut is a cover of The Ramones' cover of the Doors' "Break on Through." Work that out, and you're welcome to the rest of it.

4 Live in Japan (Dojo UK) 1993

6 Kings and Queens (Creative Man) 1993 Entertaining attempt to revive old memories by re-recording old hits — their own ("Borstal Breakout," "Ulster Boy," "Hurry Up Harry," etc.) and others (ATV's "Action Time Vision"). Two new songs are alternately drab ("Bosnia"'s stab at social relevance) and entertaining ("Reggae Giro" could have been a dub outtake from *That's Life*).

5 Soapy Water and Mr. Marmalade (Plus Eye) 1995

5 The A Files (Cleopatra) 1997

4 Live in Italy 1997 (Essential — UK) 1999

Selected Compilations and Archive Releases

7 The First the Best and the Last (Polydor UK) 1980 Hits and live collection.

4 Live and Loud (Link UK) 1987

3 Live and Loud Vol 2 (Link UK) 1988

3 Sham's Last Stand (Link UK) 1989

3 Live at the Roxy 1977 (Receiver UK) 1990
7 BBC Radio 1 in Concert (Windsong UK) 1993 Largely inter-changeable live recordings from Sham's first reign, with the Roxy show oddly including keyboards — oddly, because they never used keyboards till long after the Roxy closed down.

8 The Punk Singles Collection (Cleopatra) 1997 Definitive collection of the band's A's and B's, from the essential "I Don't Wanna" through to the barely memorable "Unite and Win." The first half is as great as punk rock got.

SHONEN KNIFE

FORMED 1981 (Osaka, Japan)
ORIGINAL LINE-UP Naoko Yamano (b. 12/18/61, Osaka — vocals, guitar); Michie Nakatani (b. 10/8/61, Osaka — bass); Atsuko Yamano (b. 2/22/60, Osaka — drums)

Formed by the Yamano sisters, Naoko and Atsuko, who took their name from a popular pocket knife ("Shonen" translates as "boy"), Shonen Knife's distinctly Ramones-influenced take on power pop debuted live in their native Osaka in late 1981, and was followed by the *Minna Tanoshiku* ("everybody's happy") cassette album early the following year.

A late December 1982 show at Osaka's Studio One club was recorded for the band's next vinyl appearance, two tracks on the *Kotosho No Shimekukuriteki Festival* in early 1983, while an appearance on the *Aura Music* compilation celebrated their signing to the local Zero label, and the group's first full release, the *Burning Farm* album, was released in Japan in July 1983 (a mid-1990's Japanese reissue included a version of the Ramones' "I Wanna be Sedated" among its bonus tracks, the first in a long line of individual covers of the band's beloved western punk; the Rezillos "Flying Saucer Attack" was another early favorite).

Like its predecessor, sung almost entirely in Japanese (despite its western song titles), *Yama No Attchan* followed in 1984, and in 1986, *Pretty Little Baka Eyes*. Shonen Knife received their first notices in the US when Subversive released that same album later in the year. The fledgling Sub Pop, too, were paying attention, including a track from *Burning Farm*, "A Day at the Factory," on the seminal *Sub Pop 100* collection, and the following year, "Cycling Is Fun" from *Yama No Attchan*, was included on a *Flipside* compilation, *Vinyl Fanzine 3*.

The band's fame spread through the American underground at such a rate that 1989 saw the *Every Band Has a Shonen Knife Who Loves Them* tribute album. Featuring contributions from Death of Samantha, Babes in Toyland, Redd Kross (who also covered another Shonen Knife track on a contemporary B-side), Frightwig, Lunachicks, the Mr. T Experience, and more, the album's very existence took many people by surprise — its success even more so.

The US label Gasatanka promptly released the band's first two albums in a single collection, *Shonen Knife*, following up with *Pretty Little Baka Guy* appended by another album's worth of live material. The trio was also invited to contribute to Shimmy Disc's Rutles' tribute album, *Rutles Highway Revisited*, and with their 712 album imminent, Shonen Knife made their first visit to the US in 1990. A second Sub Pop appearance, for the "Neon Zebra" single, followed, while December 1991 also brought a Christmas 45 for the band's US and UK audience, "Space Christmas."

The single "Riding on the Rocket" would debut the band on the British label Creation early in 1992; that same year, a new album, *Let's Knife*, would be released in both Japanese and English language versions, as the band celebrated their new-found fame by signing with MCA Victor (Japan) and Virgin (US). Further European tours, meanwhile, were highlighted by an appearance on the BBC's John Peel show (one track from the session appeared on the UK *Get the Wow* EP in 1993), a UK-only live album, *We Are Very Happy You Came*, and a guest appearance on the latest single by the Sultans of Ping.

Meanwhile, the *Favorites* EP and *Rock Animals* album continued the band's homeland rise, particularly after the band was caught up in an admittedly overblown drugs controversy — the word "happa" (leaf) was cut from the song "Catnip Dream" because of its possible reference to marijuana — and seemingly overlooking its equal relevance to the song's actual title. Oddly, there were no such objections to the band's next release, "Brown Mushrooms" (released in the US on the *Brown Mushrooms and Other Delights* EP), with the zany vegetable theme continued on the *Tomato Head* EP in 1994. (A number of the band's English language versions and mixes would subsequently be gathered on the Japanese *Greatest History* collection.)

The band's appearance on the Carpenters' tribute album *If I Were a Carpenter*, would see them break into the US mainstream, as their distinctive version of "Top of the World" was selected to feature in a Microsoft Windows 95 TV commercial, and on the soundtracks to *The Last Supper* and *The Parent Trap*.

Shonen Knife's departure from Virgin was followed by the *The Birds and the B-Sides* collection of album tracks and rarities; the band themselves now signed to MCA Victor, launching with two new domestic singles, "Wonder Wine" and "ESP," previewing the *Brand New Knife* album in late 1996.

A second Shonen Knife tribute, the Japanese *Naritaina! Shonen Knife*, appeared alongside the remix retrospective *Super Mix*, a techno re-evaluation of the band's earlier recordings, through the eyes of Thurston Moore, Ryuichi Sakamoto, and others. *Brand New Knife*, meanwhile, finally reached the US early in 1997, and was followed by the *Explosion* EP. April also saw a new Japanese release, the *It's a New Find* mini-album, while later in the year MCA (now Universal) Victor released the *Ultramix* collection of *Brand New Knife*-era remixes, featuring contributions from Alex Empire, Stereolab, Bis, and Shonen Knife themselves.

1998's *Happy Hour!* brought a return to the "classic" Knife sound and was followed by an appearance at the Fuji Rock Festival in Tokyo; a version of April 1998's "Banana Chips" hit was included on the ensuing live souvenir album, alongside contributions from Prodigy, Nick Cave, Asian Dub Foundation, and Audio Active. Michie Nakatani quit the band in June 1999; the Yamanos, however, announced the band would continue with a new single, "Yamucha Rou De Umakarou" and in November, the launch of their own Burning Farm label with the *Wonder World Volume One* compilation of Japanese bands.

Shonen Knife LPs

5 Burning Farm (Zero — Japan) 1983 Cute punky-rock, as cuddly as it is razor sharp, the trio soothe raw sounds with lollipop reality.

4 Yama No Attchan (Zero — Japan) 1984 Like *Farm*, sung almost entirely in Japanese... so basically, more of the same.

6 Pretty Little Baka Guy (Subversive) 1986 More developed, but still retaining the whimsy of earlier efforts, the Knife turn in some not so shabby rock and roll sugared by their irresistible charm on "Public Bath" and "Ice Cream City."

4 712 (Gasatanka) 1991 Lennon's "The Luck of the Irish" kicked into the gutter then beaten to death with candy canes; the Beatles' "Rain" beneath Donald Duck umbrellas; Chip'n'Dale with a dentists' drill. A mystifying stab at demystifying the Knife.

7 Let's Knife [JAPANESE LANGUAGE] (MCA Victor — Japan) 1992
7 Let's Knife [ENGLISH LANGUAGE] (Virgin) 1992 Riding on the accolades of the Shonen Knife tribute *Every Band Has a Shonen Knife Who Loves Them*, the band return the kiss with an all English disc. Irresistible as an oddity, it was nevertheless a letdown for their true English speaking fans who loved them for what they were. Still, it's hard to grumble at "Twist Barbie" and "Flying Jelly Attack."

5 We Are Very Happy You Came [LIVE] (Creation — UK) 1993

3 Rock Animals [JAPANESE LANGUAGE] (MCA Victor — Japan) 1993
3 Rock Animals [ENGLISH LANGUAGE] (Virgin) 1993 Although this album boasts a guest appearance from Sonic Youth's Thurston Moore on "Butterfly" and they do branch out on "Music Square," Knife's bubblegum edge is beginning to get a little dull.

3 Brand New Knife [JAPANESE LANGUAGE] (MCA Victor — Japan) 1996
3 Brand New Knife [ENGLISH LANGUAGE] (Big Deal) 1997 Lots of filler punctuated by some gems, this new *Knife* retains some power-pop but really falls short of expectation. The US CD issue boasts seven bonus tracks in Japanese.

2 Happy Hour [JAPANESE LANGUAGE] (Universal Victor — Japan) 1998
2 Happy Hour [ENGLISH LANGUAGE] (Big Deal) 1998 It's run its course, enough is enough, and what once was catchy no longer appeals. Even their cover of the Monkees' "Daydream Believer" fails to invoke a tapping toe.

Selected Compilations and Archive Releases

6 Shonen Knife (Gasatanka) 1990 American repackaging of *Burning Farm* and *Yama No Attchan* with a booklet full of translated titles.

7 Pretty Little Baka Guy/Live in Japan (Gasatanka) 1990 *Baka* reissue with some track manipulation and 1990 concert track cobbled on.

7 Greatest History (MCA Victor — Japan) 1995

6 The Birds and the B-Sides (Virgin) 1996 Neat compilation with singles, B-sides, and live.

5 Super Mix (MCA Universal — Japan) 1997

SIGUE SIGUE SPUTNIK

FORMED 1981 *(London, England)*
ORIGINAL LINE-UP *Martin Degville (b. 1957 — vocals); Neal X (b. 1962 — guitar); Tony James (b. 1956 — bass); Yana (keyboards); Ray Mayhew (drums); Chris Kavanagh (b. 1964 — drums)*

Martin Degville was one of the post-punk drag queen shockers running on the same circuit as the then-unknown Boy George and Marilyn, when Tony James, fresh from the ruins of first wave punks Generation X, and a collaboration with the nascent Lords of the New Church, ran into him in 1982 working the YaYa clothes store in London's Kensington Market.

Having already linked with Neal X through a *Melody Maker* ad, James' first idea was to recruit Andrew Eldritch from the Sisters of Mercy; another scheme involved a pre-Eurythmics Annie Lennox. James, however, was immediately fascinated by the befeathered Degville dancing round the store to old Suicide records, and the search for a vocalist ended. YaYa became the new band's home base (and wardrobe supplier), and the band's early demos reflected their fascination with the more sordid aspects of the rock lifestyle — the Stones' "Memo from Turner," the New York Dolls' "Personality Crisis," and a self-composed song about penises, "Wang Wang Wang."

They developed an endless dub version of "Be Bop a Lula," watched a lot of John Waters movies, and toyed with names like Sperm Festival and Nazi Occult Bureau before playing their first gig, with no name at all, following a Johnny Thunders show in Paris. Former Generation X drummer Mark Laff (then part of Thunders' band) sat in for the three-song set.

Returning to London, the band recruited Ray Mayhew after he walked innocently into the store one day (he borrowed a drum kit from Topper Headon, ex-Clash; second drummer Chris Kavanagh got his from another Clash alumni, Terry Chimes, while the band's first sound engineer, Mick Jones, had just been sacked by the same band). Jones' first "appearance" with the band, manipulating their sound in the same way Brian Eno used to reshape Roxy Music's, was opening for New Model Army in Hastings.

Boomtown Rats manager Fatchner O'Kelly, who had already supplied much of the band's gear, finally named the group Sigue Sigue Sputnik from a Russian streetgang and with one of Degville's co-workers, Yana, brought in on keyboards, the band published their first T-shirts and began experimenting with what was, by now, a huge collection of synthesizers, tape machines, and electronics which none of them really knew how to operate.

According to James, the crucial moment came when he was bouncing bits of his favorite movies onto a homemade video compilation, over which he'd dubbed Sputnik's "Love Missile F1-11" demo. He hit the wrong button, and the movie's soundtracks — explosions, gunfire, and general destruction — was accidentally layered over the band's master tape. That tape was to shape the entire Sputnik sound. Before sampling had even got out of the laboratory, long before cut-ups of pre-existing speech and sound made it into mainstream rock'n'roll, Sputnik had a musical identity which would become unique.

An interview in the NME designed simply to catch Gen X fans up on James' latest doings precipitated a frenzy. Eleven record companies turned up to the band's next show at London's Electric Cinema, and the band were invited onto television's The Tube, a frenzied flurry of color, hair, and psychedelic Max Max imagery which blew that Friday evening into legend. Close to two years had elapsed since the band took its first steps — now it was to take a massive stride.

Linking with EMI for a reported four million pounds (in fact, the figure was vastly inflated, to match the hype already building around the group), Sputnik released their first single, the Giorgio Moroder-produced "Love Missile F1-11" (#3 UK) in February 1986. It was already selling 70,000 copies a day before anybody even thought about obtaining copyright clearance from the samples used in the record. (The UK single retains them, the US version replaced them with mimics.)

"21st Century Boy" (#20 UK), in June, was less successful, but the band's debut album, Flaunt It (#96 US, #10 UK), rode roughshod to glory over a crop of extraordinarily negative reviews. Amazingly, it even received flak for carrying out a lot of the things the members warned it would — the inclusion of advertising as an integral part of the album, for example, and the unrepentant plundering of movie and TV news for soundbytes. In fact, Sputnik's only significant error lay in allowing two years to elapse before following up this initial salvo, a period during which many of their original innovations had become so much a part of the musical furniture that even their image was no longer so futuristic.

"Success" (#31 UK), recorded with producer Pete Waterman, was released in November 1988 and limped out of the chart after just three weeks; "Dancerama" (#50 UK) in April 1989 and "Albinoni Vs. Space Wars" (#75 UK) in May fared even more poorly, and while the band's second album, Dress for Excess (#53 UK), sold very well in Brazil (prompting the "Rio Rocks" adaptation of "La Bamba" single), clearly Sputnik were crashing. The band broke up in July 1989 and by the end of the year James had joined the Sisters of Mercy — not quite what he'd had in mind when he first suggested to Eldritch they should play together.

1991 brought a release for the band's 1983 demos, the First Generation collection, but it would be 1995 before James and X reconvened, planning a new version of the band. Vocalist Christopher Novak was discovered via a video of a stillborn Prince project; John Green (keyboards) and former Gen X guitarist Derwood complete the line-up, and one of the band's earliest demos, "Cyberspace Party," went to #1 in Japan, after local star Hotei created a Japanese language re-recording.

With Marc Almond numbered among the guests (X was now a member of his Fantastic Star-era band), an album was recorded, Sputnik: The Next Generation. Unfortunately, band in-fighting, delays, and missed deadlines saw the project scrapped everywhere (bar Japan, where it sold 50,000 copies) and the group broke up. Another related project, Fin De Seicle, went unrecorded, but in June 1998, James, Degville, and X re-emerged as Sputnik 2.0, with Claudia Cujo (electronic drums), playing a London charity ball.

Versions of Madonna's "Ray of Light" and Prince's "I'll Never Take the Place of Your Man" followed for tribute albums, while James and X also remixed tracks by Faster Pussycat, Berlin, Warrant, and others.

Also see the entry for "GENERATION X" on page 389.

Sigue Sigue Sputnik LPs

10 Flaunt It (EMI America) 1986 A frantic and utterly unself-conscious melange of every triumphant glam guitar riff the band could remember, fed through the relentless motorik of Donna Summer and Suicide (*especially* Suicide), shatter-shocked with movie samples, blistered by sound effects and spoken word...if those were the only shells in Sputnik's sonic shotgun, still *Flaunt It* would have been a remarkable accomplishment.

But from the opening salvo of "Love Missile F1-11" and "Atari Baby," track followed track with savage elan, molten riffs running beneath the madness, Neal X staking his claim as THE rock guitarist of the post-rock age and — if Giorgio Moroder's production was thinner than it should have been — volume and bass boost compensate for that. By the time you hit the Wagner meets Vega "21st Century Boy," you're either sold for life — or running for it. Sigue Sigue Sputnik — "affordable fire power."

The electronics were a revelation. At a time when only Paul Hardcastle (of eternally annoying "19" fame) was truly confronting the mainstream with the technology, Sputnik recorded a solid album, then dubbed a veritable demonstration disc over it. The magic was in making it work; but the true splendor likes in the advisory notice plastered on the back cover. "Warning: Do Not Play If Accompanied by an Adult." Rock'n'roll returns to the kids — and joins in playing with their video games.

6 Dress for Excess (EMI America) 1988 More musical, less effects-driven, hollow flash, and yes, excess.

Selected Compilations and Archive Releases

7 First Generation (Cleopatra) 1991 The band's original demos add little more than a rough edge to the power of *Flaunt It*, although Bowie's "Rebel Rebel" sounds sexy in their grasp.

7 The Ultimate 12-Inch Collection (Sputnikworld — UK) 1998

6 F1rst Generation/2econd Edition (Cleopatra) 1999

Sputnik: The Next Generation LPs

4 Sputnik: The Next Generation (EMI — Japan) 1996

SIOUXSIE AND THE BANSHEES

FORMED 1976 (*London, England*)

ORIGINAL LINE-UP *Siouxsie Sioux (b. Susan Dallion, 5/27/57, London — vocals); Marco Pirroni (guitar); Two Tone Steve, aka Steve Severin (b. Steve Bailey, 9/25/55, London — bass); Sid Vicious (b. John Beverley, 5/10/57, London — drums)*

The Banshees formed in September 1976 as Siouxsie put it, "to fill in a gap at the 100 Club Punk Festival. We entered into the pure spirit of it, on the spur of the moment, forming a band to fill this slot then disbanding after it, one night only,

taking the Andy Warhol idea to its extreme, and also the idea that now's now, and it's important — no future, no past." The original line-up played just one piece, a storming, hypnotic medley of "Knocking on Heaven's Door," "Twist and Shout," and "The Lord's Prayer," improvised by musicians who'd never even appeared on stage before, let alone actually played together. Neither would they do so again — Vicious formed the Flowers of Romance, then joined the Sex Pistols and Pirroni went onto the Models and Adam and the Ants.

Sioux, Severin, and manager Nils Stevenson remained together, however, hoping to form a new line-up in time to join the Pistols' "Anarchy" tour in December. In the event, it would be July 1977 before a stable line-up emerged, around John McKay (guitar) and Kenny Morris (drums).

With this line-up, the Banshees became regulars at the Vortex club, and toured constantly, a string of revelatory shows which spotlighted Sioux, skinny, black, and bathed in make-up — the original Swastika girl barking songs like orders to the serried ranks of Punk. "Carcass," "Bad Shape," "Voices"...nightly the band's apocalyptic vision took shape — and not a record label in the land paid them any heed.

Even a graffiti campaign couldn't force the major labels' hands, despite the words SIGN THE BANSHEES NOW! being scrawled across their offices; at one point, DJ John Peel was even trying to persuade the BBC to place the band on its own label, hitherto the preserve of TV soundtrack music, simply to give them an outlet. Finally Polydor took the plunge, and were promptly rewarded when the band's first single, "Hong Kong Garden" (#7 UK), climbed the chart in August 1978.

The Scream (#12 UK) followed, and over the next year, two further Banshees singles would establish the band at the forefront of the dark, swirling, guitar-led sound which would subsequently influence an entire new generation: "The Staircase (Mystery)" (#24 UK) and "Playground Twist" (#28 UK) prefaced the band's second album, *Join Hands* (#13 UK), and in September 1979, the Banshees set out on their first headlining UK tour. Four nights later, they returned home after McKay and Morris walked out on the band. That evening's performance in Aberdeen was not cancelled — the opening Cure turned in a dramatically extended set before Sioux and Severin joined them for "The Lord's Prayer." Four subsequent shows were canned, however, while the duo tried to lure ex-Sex Pistols Steve Jones and Paul Cook into the breach, before the Banshees re-emerged with former Slits drummer, Budgie (b. Peter Clark, 8/21/57, St. Helens, England) and the Cure's Robert Smith; he would give way to Magazine's John McGeoch after the tour (then return to replace him in 1982).

"Happy House" (#17 UK) and "Christine" (#24 UK) from August 1980's *Kaleidoscope* (#5 UK) followed, opening doors into a brand new musical discipline even as they closed them on an older one. At a time when the media referred to them as Punks, the Banshees themselves moved towards the metal motorik of David Bowie's *Low* and Iggy Pop's *The Idiot*. They were present at the birth of goth, and were around for its immersion into industrial and ethereal. "We'd try to think up different labels for ourselves each month," recalled Severin. "Throughout our career, whenever anyone's tried to categorize us too much, we deliberately move away from it, twist people's preconceptions a bit."

"Israel" (#41 UK) followed in November 1980, its poor performance the responsibility of British radio programmers who remembered the band's former penchant for swastikas and assumed the song must be somehow anti-Semitic; in the new year, however, touring with rising Scots band Altered Images, the Banshees hit with "Spellbound" (#22 UK), "Arabian Nights" (#32 UK), and the *Juju* album (#7 UK), while the band undertook their longest UK tour yet — 30 shows which led directly into their first US visit in October. (Sioux and Budgie's Creatures side project was born during the *Juju* sessions).

December 1981 brought the Banshees' first compilation, the career-spanning *Once Upon a Time* (#21 UK) collection; it was swiftly followed by a new single, "Fireworks" (#22), before the band took a few months off to allow Sioux to recover from laryngitis. A proposed open-air show in London during the summer to follow festival appearances in Scandinavia, was cancelled by the local authorities; instead, the band's only UK appearance of note was the Elephant Fayre in Cornwall.

They bounced back in October 1982 with "Slowdive" (#41 UK) and the album *A Kiss in the Dreamhouse* (#11 UK), under-performers exacerbated by the near-total failure of "Melt" (#49 UK). A short British tour in December was then endangered when McGeoch was diagnosed with clinical depression; rather than cancel, the Banshees asked Robert Smith (from the newly moribund Cure) to return for the outing.

Aside from an Australian tour in March, 1983 was a quiet year for the band, although both the Creatures and Severin remained active. The Creatures' debut album, *Feast*, and accompanying single, "Miss the Girl," were the first releases on the Banshees' own newly formed Wonderland label; while Severin linked with Smith and singer Jeanette Landray in the psychedelically inspired Glove. (Severin also worked with Marc Almond's Marc and the Mambas project.)

The Banshees reconvened in September for a handful of shows in Europe and Israel, then returned to London for a Royal Albert Hall show almost seven years to the day since their 100 Club debut. A new single, a cover of the Beatles' "Dear Prudence" (#3 UK), welcomed them back, and in December 1983, a live album taken from the RAH show, *Nocturne* (#29 UK) was also a hot seller.

A new Banshees' album in January 1984, *Hyaena* (#157 US, #15 UK), was prefaced by two singles, the moody "Swimming Horses" (#28 UK) and "Dazzle" (#33). However, Smith's Cure were now swinging back into action as well, and the guitarist quit shortly before the Banshees' summer tour; he was replaced by John Carruthers (ex-Clock DVA), and in October a long-standing Banshees threat to re-record

© Jim Steinfeldt/Chansley Entertainment

some of their earlier B-sides was made good with the *Thorn* EP (#47 UK).

The band now entered a period of relative musical stability; their role as the (admittedly unwilling) godfathers of goth was assured and their commercial standing was strong enough to allow for a degree of relaxation. Spending 1985 in the studio, then, the band emerged that fall with "Cities in Dust" (#21 UK) and "Candyman" (#34 UK) — tasters for the band's first US hit, the esoteric *Tinderbox* (#88 US, #13 UK).

As far back as "Dear Prudence," the band had been discussing an EP of cover versions; their next project would take that notion to its logical extent — an entire album of covers, described by Severin as part homage, part sacrilege. Taking on Bob Dylan ("This Wheel's on Fire," #14 UK), Iggy Pop ("The Passenger," #41 UK), Kraftwerk, and John Cale among others, *Through the Looking Glass* (#188 US, #15 UK) arrived just as the band underwent its latest personnel change. Carruthers quit, to be replaced by Specimen's John Klein. Keyboard player Martin McCarrick was also drafted in — a former member of the Glove and Marc Almond's band, he had arranged strings on *Through the Looking Glass*.

This new line-up debuted in July 1987, with "Song from the Edge of the World" (#59 UK), premiered when the Banshees played the WOMAD Festival in 1986; the band would play the Finsbury Park super tent that same month, then returned to the studio to complete 1988's divisive *Peep Show* (#68 US, #20 UK) album, and the trans-Atlantic hit single "Peek a Boo" (#53 US, #16 UK). Further singles, "Killing Jar" (#41 UK) and "The Last Beat of My Heart" (#44 UK), followed, but following the inevitable world tour, the band drifted into silence, broken only by the 1989 revitalization of the Creatures.

June 1991 saw the Banshees return to action with the "Kiss Them for Me" single (#23 US, #32 UK), the first fruits of the band's studio liaison with Pet Shop Boys/New Order producer Stephen Hague. "Shadowland" (#57 UK) followed, and while the Banshees would subsequently disdain the cold, technological feel of *Superstition* (#65 US, #25 UK), unquestionably it launched them into their period of greatest trans-Atlantic success. The Banshees appeared on the inaugural Lollapalooza, then followed through with a sold-out tour in their own right in early 1992. They were invited to contribute a track, "Face to Face" (#21 UK), to the soundtrack of *Batman Returns* and in October, the *Twice Upon a Time* singles collection (#26 UK) was an alternative chart hit.

Again, however, the band backed away — a two-year silence broken only by Sioux's appearance on Morrissey's "Interlude" single (#25 UK) in August 1994. They re-emerged the following year with the *Rapture* album (#127 US, #33 UK), co-produced by John Cale, and featuring the hits "O Baby" (#34 UK) and "Stargazer" (#64) and lengthy tours of the UK and US.

However, despite good reviews, the Banshees had had enough. Although they actually broke up shortly after the tour was over, various legal matters ensured it would be another year before the split could be announced officially — just days after the Sex Pistols announced their reunion. The first reports of the Banshees' demise claimed that they were splitting up in protest.

Also see the entry for the "CREATURES" on page 297.

Siouxsie and the Banshees LPs

10 The Scream (Polydor — UK) 1978 It's the spaces in the songs which stun, the wide-open gaps which hang haunting between every note, it seems, awaiting the banshee wail of Siouxsie's first vocal ("Pure") or last cry; the depths of post-dirge density to which they drag the Beatles' "Helter Skelter."

A couple of reminders of their punk club rawness do surface — "Carcass" and "Nicotine Stain" — but with Steve Lillywhite's white light production isolating every nuance of sound, even they took on a new, eternally menacing aura. But the pounding "Metal Postcard," the desperate "Suburban Relapse" (the prototype for all that the Psychedelic Furs, first album went on to achieve), and the desolate "Switch" are more than a band's sonic reinvention. They are the moment when the phrase "post-punk" finally took on a true sound of its own.

7 Join Hands (Polydor — UK) 1979 Dense where *The Scream* was brittle, swampily blurred where it was abattoir sharp, *Join Hands* trademarked the swooping guitar roar which would live on in the goth world for the next 20 years, and its only mistake was adding the 14-minute "Lord's Prayer" to the brew. A live legend, its loose jam sensibilities were totally at odds with the focussed miasma of the rest of the set.

8 Kaleidoscope (Polydor — UK) 1980 Recent personnel problems disturbed the band's equilibrium some, but *Kaleidoscope* triumphed over instability regardless. The highlights, of course, were the doomily dancey "Happy House," the poppier "Christine," and the invocation of often ethereal acoustic guitars.

9 Juju (Polydor — UK) 1981 All shrouded atmospheres, melancholy melodies, and doomy, gloomy, spooky lyrics, *Juju* is the prototypical Goth record, which every band in the genre has since tried to equal. Few have. From the haunting opening "Spellbound" to the soaring, swirling *Scream*-esque "Halloween," *Juju* evokes the darkness in all its forms. Siouxsie's vocals are a wonder, the rhythms pulse and pound, the guitar shudders and shakes. And if you're looking for Christine, she's nowhere to be found.

6 Kiss in the Dream House (Polydor — UK) 1982 The heavenly "Slowdive" and the slow, creeping "Melt" distinguish an album which was strangely more style than substance.

7 Nocturne [LIVE] (Wonderland — UK) 1983

6 Hyaena (Geffen) 1984

5 Tinderbox (Geffen) 1986 The band which once danced at the end of the world now seems the band which jerks at the end of its tether, as the undisputed gems, "Cities in Dust" and "Lands End" are increasingly outweighed by the callous crowd pleasers, "Candyman," "The Sweetest Chill"....

8 Through the Looking Glass (Geffen) 1987 Drawing back from their looming self-destruction, time out with a boxful of covers and a chance to have some fun again. The audacious selection of "Trust in Me" (the snake's song from *The Jungle Book*), powered by entrancing harp and the juxtaposed culture shock of guitars on Kraftwerk's "Hall of Mirrors" prove the Banshees' can still surprise; while Dylan, the Doors, and Billy Holiday would turn up on few people's lists of likely Banshee covers.

7 Peep Show (Geffen) 1988 It was a great album until they added "Peek-A-Boo."

5 Superstition (Geffen) 1991 Generously, one could hope Stephen Hague's emotionless production was an attempt to update the lethal frigidity of *The Scream*. In fact, it simply strips the soul from Siouxsie's voice, the fun from the band's playing and the heart from their strongest crop of songs in a decade.

7 Rapture (Geffen) 1995 An unsettled — and just occasionally unsettling — swansong, the title track, and "Fall from Grace" both pushing the band towards fresh territory while partial producer John Cale certainly stretches even the familiar sounds.

Selected Compilations and Archive Releases

9 Once Upon a Time: The Singles (Geffen) 1981 With the addition of *The Scream*'s pristine "Mirage," the singles so far, and not a bum note in sight.

9 Peel Sessions (Dutch East Indies) 1991 Two timeless snatches of the Banshees at their 1977–78 most belligerent.

7 Twice Upon a Time: The Singles (Geffen) 1992 The singles brought up to date, and if you saw the disc in half ("Peek a Boo" is the cut-off point), we would all live happily ever after.

Steve Severin LP

8 Maldoror (RE) 1999 Art-gloom theatrical soundtrack with a dense beauty which — while it takes a while to sink in — reminds us where the Banshees' musical heart lay.

Further Reading

Entranced by Brian Johns (Omnibus, UK, 1990).

SISTERS OF MERCY

FORMED 1981 *(Leeds, England)*
ORIGINAL LINE-UP *Andrew Eldritch (b. Andrew Taylor, 5/15/59, Ely, England — vocals); Gary Marx (b. Mark Pearman — guitar); Doktor Avalanche (drum machine)*

The son of a Royal Air Force officer, Andrew Eldritch showed no interest in musicianship until a friend stored his drum kit in the basement of the family's Leeds home. Teaching himself to play (after a fashion), Eldritch graduated through a series of forgettable local bands before being asked to join a group which friend Gary Marx was putting together. Six months of rehearsal followed before the pair — already dubbed the Sisters of Mercy, in deference to a Leonard Cohen song — decided they needed a vocalist, and according to Eldritch, "purely by default, it turned out to be me. Because I can't drum and sing at the same time, we bought a machine [Doktor Avalanche]. Had we been able to buy a machine to do the singing, it might have turned out different."

In February 1981, the duo issued their debut single, "Damage Done," on their own Merciful Release label. It sank without trace, but the band returned to the studio to record the *Floorshow* EP, which was promptly scrapped when bassist Craig Adams (ex-Expelaires) joined the group and expanded their sound beyond all recognition.

The Sisters played their first gig on February 16, 1981, at the University of York's Alcuin College, opening for the Thompson Twins, with Mekons guitarist Jon Langford also on stage with them. It was his sole venture as a Sister; as a trio, the band continued playing sporadic shows to small but increasingly impressed crowds in Leeds. They appeared at the Futurama 3 Festival in September 1981 and made their London debut at the fashionable Embassy Club shortly after further swelling the sound with a second guitarist, Ben Gunn (born Ben Matthews).

Early 1982 finally delivered the Sisters second single, "Body Electric," released in April through Langford's CNT (Confederacio Nacional de Trabajo) label, and an instant *Melody Maker* Single of the Week. The band's continued inability to find many gigs to play was a curse, however, and when Adams quit to work as a photographer in the Canary Islands for a few months, he returned to find he'd only missed one show.

Eldritch, meanwhile, had recently signed his first band to Merciful Release, fellow Leedites the March Violets. The Violets' own career quickly took off and clashes between Eldritch and the Violets grew quickly into bitterness. The group released just one single on Merciful Release, and played a showcase gig alongside the Sisters at London's Clarendon in October, before Eldritch dropped them.

On June 7, 1982, the Sisters opened for former Velvet Underground chanteuse Nico at London's Venue — a prestigious billing which the band ensured would remain memorable by encoring with a blinding version of the Velvets' own "Sister Ray." The following month, they opened for the Birthday Party at the Zigzag Club, and in August, they recorded their first session for BBC radio's John Peel. Finally, people started taking notice, including Psychedelic

Furs guitarist John Ashton. He invited the Sisters to join the Furs' October 1982 UK tour (further dates with Nico also followed); he would also produce the band's next singles, "Alice" (#8 UK indy) and "Anaconda" (#3 UK indy). Ashton also financed the band's US debut, the 12" *Anaconda* EP on the Braineater label.

The Sisters reputation as new godheads of the British goth scene now confirmed, the band toured Britain through spring 1983. May brought the *The Reptile House* EP (#5 UK indy) while summer saw the band tour Europe, playing their first outdoor show at the Mallemont Festival in Brussels on August 5 before making their US debut with five East Coast shows.

They would return for two West Coast gigs in October, but the line-up was in shreds. Gunn quit, accusing the rest of the band of "taking things too seriously" and of "selling out" — an accusation aimed squarely at the new single, "Temple of Love" (#1 UK indy). He returned to school at Liverpool University and later started his own label, Flame on Records, and a band, Torch. "Temple of Love" spent one week atop the indy charts in October 1983 (it was displaced by The Smiths' "This Charming Man"); Gunn was replaced by ex-Dead or Alive guitarist Wayne Hussey, and the new line-up debuted on April 7, 1984, at the Tin Can Club in Birmingham with a set largely comprised of new material composed by Eldritch and Hussey.

The first release under a new distribution deal with the Warners group, the Sisters' next single, "Body and Soul" (#46 UK), made an immediate impact as the band toured the US, UK, and Europe before starting work on their debut album. More shows interrupted the recording before an exhausted Eldritch collapsed. Three weeks of hospital rest later, he was back inside the maelstrom; two German festivals in early September, the two-month Black October tour of Britain the following month, and two new singles, "Walk Away" (#45 UK) and "No Time to Cry" (#63 UK).

The *Tune in, Turn on, Burn Out* tour began in March, on the eve of the release of *First and Last and Always* (#14 UK), and again the band began to disintegrate. Marx quit immediately following the tour (he subsequently formed Ghost Dance with former Skeletal Family singer Anne-Marie); the remaining trio played a 25-date European tour, followed by another US outing, then returned home in June to find the media already composing the epitaphs.

The band played along with them, staging a one-off show at the Royal Albert Hall, "Altamont — A Festival of Remembrance," in June. Work then began on a second album, with the band intending to remain a trio. Constant fighting, however, proved too much for Adams; he quit during rehearsals, followed the next day by Hussey, with the pair announcing they were forming their own band, the Sisterhood. Eldritch

objected, pointing out that both parties had agreed not to invoke the Sisters of Mercy with their new projects; when Hussey persisted, Eldritch registered the Sisterhood name for himself.

Unabashed, Hussey and Adams played one show as the Sisterhood on January 20, 1986 — apparently unaware that Eldritch had chosen the same day to release his first single, under the same name, "Giving Ground (r.s.v.)" (#1 UK indy). Hussey and Adams became the Mission; Eldritch retained the Sisterhood. Recruiting Lucas Fox (ex-Motorhead, drums), James Ray (vocals), Patricia Morrison (ex-Gun Club, bass), and Alan Vega (ex-Suicide, vocals) he recorded July 1986's *The Gift* (#90 UK, #2 UK indy), but cancelled a scheduled second Sisterhood single, "This Corrosion," after relocating to Hamburg and reconsidering his position.

Retaining Morrison and Doktor Avalanche alone, Eldritch relaunched himself as the Sisters of Mercy in September 1987 with "This Corrosion" (#7 UK) — an epic production with Jim Steinman (of *Bat out of Hell* fame) at the controls. The album, *Floodland* (#101 US, #9 UK), followed, together with subsequent singles, "Dominion" (#13 UK) and "Lucretia, My Reflection" (#20 UK), in May 1988, but there would be no tour, and indeed no further action whatsoever for close to two years.

Then in February 1990, Eldritch announced the band was up to full strength with the addition of former Generation X/Sigue Sigue Sputnik bassist Tony James, Andreas Bruhn, and Tim Bricheno (ex-All About Eve, guitar). This new line-up debuted at the Loreley Festival in Germany that summer, releasing their first single, "More" (#14 UK), in October. The album *Vision Thing* (#136 US, #11 UK) followed, and another hit, "Dr. Jeep" (#37 UK), while the band — its line-up further swollen by the addition of Dan Donovan (ex-Big Audio Dynamite, keyboards) — spent the next twelve months touring the UK, Europe, and the US.

Tony James quit in late 1991; the rest of the band followed, and Eldritch alone supervised a new single, a remix of the album's "When You Don't See Me" (released in Germany alone). He then caught everybody off guard with a re-recording of "Temple of Love," featuring Yemenite vocal star Ofra Haza (#3 UK) in April 1992, a taster for the band's forthcoming *Some Girls Wander by Mistake* (#5 UK) collection of early singles and rarities. Gigs, however, were at a premium — just one in 1992 and one more in 1993, opening for Depeche Mode at London's Crystal Palace, the band lining up as Eldritch, Bruhn, Doktor Avalanche, and bassist Adam Pearson.

With Eldritch next teaming with former Berlin vocalist Teri Nunn, a new single, "Under the Gun" (#19 UK), and compilation, *A Slight Case of Overbombing* (#14 UK), followed that same fall, and rumor insisted Eldritch was preparing a new Sisters of Mercy album. Instead, he lapsed into a mammoth silence, as a dispute over future recordings with Warners saw Eldritch literally go on strike.

The Sisters would convene for occasional tours alone, Eldritch accompanied by a changing roster of musicians, opening with the *Roadkill* outing in 1996 and a short UK/European outing in summer 1997. Then, still stalemated with Warners, Eldritch finally recorded a new album in two days in mid-1997 with a group of unnamed friends.

Go Figure, however, was scarcely what Warners, or anybody else, was expecting, as Eldritch confirmed in a late 1997 press release. "Bearing no resemblance whatsoever to the Sisters of Mercy, this album will be released — if at all — under a completely different name, which is just as well... [because] the rather bad sub-techno music [within] was under-average and boring even before the drums were mysteriously removed." In fact, he intended the album to be released under the acronym SSV-NSMABAAOTW-MODAACOTIATW — "Screw Shareholder Value — Not So Much a Band as Another Opportunity to Waste Money on Drugs and Ammunition Courtesy of the Idiots at Time Warner."

With *Go Figure* still awaiting its fate, the Sisters toured Europe and briefly visited the US and Canada in January/February 1998, following through with a string of European festivals that summer. A second, lengthier US visit followed in in September/October 1999 with Pearson (guitar) and Mike Varjak (bass) joining Eldritch and Doktor Avalanche.

Also see the entry for "MISSION UK" on page 501.

Sisters of Mercy LPs

7 First and Last and Always (Elektra) 1985 A voice as deep as the grave, guitars howling and roaring at the night and a drum machine disguised as a drill instructor, the Sisters once staggering debut has been so mercilessly ravaged and plundered by the goths who followed that even the peerless beauties ("Marian" and "Some Kind of Stranger") now sound like warmed-over Rosetta Stone outtakes. Forget the indignities of the last 15 years, though, and it is breathtaking once again.

9 Floodland (Elektra) 1987 With Patricia Morrison and producer Jim Steinman to flesh out the sound, Eldritch heralds apocalypse with Wagnerian chorale, orchestrated bombast, and three truly epic masterpieces — "Dominion," "Mother Russia," and "This Corrosion." Elsewhere, emotional touchstones and whispers of love and life past simply dare the watchful hordes to try and duplicate this baby.

7 Vision Thing (Elektra) 1990 The Sisters put the rock back in goth, eschewing the epic operetta of *Floodland* ("More" not withstanding) in favor of crashing neo-industrial clatter, carnivore riffing, and sonic overkill. A few plays swiftly reveal "Dr Jeep," the title cut, and (again) "More" to be the songs with most substance, but the adrenaline doesn't stop pumping regardless.

Selected Compilations and Archive Releases

8 Some Girls Wander by Mistake (Elektra) 1992
7 A Slight Case of Overbombing: Greatest Hits,... (Elektra) 1993 The Sisters story at 45, suffering because their best moments were rarely selected as singles. And also because "Temple of Love" should never have been remade and "Under the Gun" should never have been issued.

Sisterhood LP

7 The Gift (Merciful Release) 1987 Closer to Suicide than the Sisters, an impression which Alan Vega's presence doesn't actually impact upon whatsoever. Very sparse, purposefully stark, less an album than a reminder that Eldritch still lives, there are no songs as such, just impressions, fragments and a few private jokes at the Mission's expense.

SKINNY PUPPY

FORMED 1983 *(Vancouver, Canada)*
ORIGINAL LINE-UP *Nivek Ogre (b. Kevin Ogilvie, 12/5/62 — vocals); ceVIN Key (b. Kevin Compton, 2/13/61 — keyboards)*

ceVIN Key was drummer with Canadian synth-pop band Images in Vogue when he moved beyond the constraints of the new wave to work on a solo project based around deeper, darker electronics. Taking the name Skinny Puppy, to suggest "life as seen through a dog's eyes," Key and Nivek Ogre came together at a party thrown by Images in Vogue member Gary Smith. Within days, Ogre had written the new band's first song, "Canine." A self-released cassette album, *Back and Forth*, quickly followed, initially in a limited edition of 35 copies. (It would be reissued in 1992). Signing with longtime friend Terry McBride's newly formed Nettwerk label and linking, too, with producer Dave "Rave" Ogilvie (no relation to Ogre), Puppy recorded the *Remission* EP. Their live debut followed after they broke into a Vancouver art gallery and at 3 am, played their first gig. Perhaps appropriately, goth faves Alien Sex Fiend were in the audience. (Another early performance saw Ogre and Key perform as Hell 'O' Death Day, opening for former Throbbing Gristle mainstays Chris and Cosey — it would be the first of many Puppy spin-offs over the next decade.)

With another keyboard player, Bill Leeb (born Wilhelm Schroeder), introduced for subsequent live work, Puppy's stageshow swiftly developed, with Ogre a consummate, if violent, frontman introducing a performance art aspect to the band which was quite unique, at least in North America. Indeed, at a time when true industrial music was still considered the preserve of unpronounceable German bands,

Puppy's assault was shattering, all the more so after it was captured on vinyl for their first full album, 1985's *Bites*.

The album's reception was sufficient to convince Key to quit Images in Vogue; he left following a Halloween 1985 show, the day of *Bites* release. Puppy went out on tour immediately after, then began work on their next album with Ogilvie and Adrian Sherwood. *Mind, the Perpetual Intercourse* would be followed by four months of solid gigging, the cue for Leeb to quit (he would subsequently form Frontline Assembly); he was replaced by Dwayne Goettel of Edmonton electronics duo Water.

1986 brought Key his first collaboration with Legendary Pink Dots frontman, Edward Ka-Spel; Tear Garden would emerge an oasis of relative calm amid the madness of Puppy's 72-date Ain't It Dead Yet tour, with two singles from *Mind*, "Dig It" and "Chainsaw," carving the band a new, and not wholly calculated niche in the dance world.

Cleanse, Fold, and Manipulate, in 1987, would be the group's first foray out of analogue and into the world of midi. This, too, would revolutionize their live show (Key was the first musician to tour Canada with an electronic drum kit, during the post-*Bites* outing), with Puppy peaking the following year with the stageshow which accompanied their next album, *VIVIsectVI*.

An overtly political attack on animal experimentation, Ogre explained the performance was intended "to personify an animal, and come from the point of view of a person experimenting on animals, who then slowly becomes the experiment." It was a realistic effort — in Cincinnati the band was actually arrested for animal abuse. When the authorities learned there were no live animals on the set, they changed the charges to disorderly conduct.

Elsewhere on the tour, a meeting with Al Jourgensen would draw Ogre into the Ministry camp, guesting with both that band and the Revolting Cocks spin-off. Despite such distractions, however, Puppy's own dynamic was becoming increasingly strained. While Key and Goettel remained close friends, Ogre — now nursing a growing drug problem — was constantly searching for new challenges, many of which brought him into conflict with his bandmates. Their next album, *Rabies*, in particular, was "a real dysfunctional record," reflected Ogre, "and I think that's how the group got to the point of absolute dysfunctional behavior."

The involvement of Jourgensen as guest and mixer added to the band tensions, particularly when — instead of touring with Puppy, as they had expected, he instead persuaded Ogre to tour with Ministry, leaving Key and Goettel to cool their heels with a succession of side projects — Cyberaktif (reuniting with Leeb), Doubting Thomas, Flu and Hilt, featuring Dave Ogilvie, Sons of Freedom member Don Harrison, and Al Nelson (with whom Key had recorded a one-off rap parody, "Yo Pusface," under the name Lee Chubby King, in 1987).

© Henry Diltz/Chansley Entertainment

A collection of Puppy's 12" singles, too, punctuated the band's silence, but finally the trio reunited to record *Too Dark Park*; the tour that followed was documented on the *Ain't It Dead Yet?* live album. From such a high, however, Skinny Puppy came down hard, as they struggled to record their next album, *Last Rights* (#193 US) — or Last Rites as Key preferred to call it.

Ogre was still using; he also refused to work in the studio if either of his bandmates were present. Yet the alienation fed the music; Key recalled, "I'd come in and hear [what he'd done] and I'd always be quite shocked or moved or disturbed by it. It wouldn't be hard for me to then take it to the next level. That's how we now worked." It took a total physical collapse, while vacationing in Sweden following the album's completion, to push Ogre into cleaning up; he emerged shortly before Puppy's next tour began, only for the European dates to be cancelled after he suffered a knee injury. Nobody knew it at the time, but Puppy had played their final concert.

The sessions for Skinny Puppy's final album — their first for new label American — were a disaster from the start. Completely misunderstanding the band dynamic, the label brought three separate producers in to the sessions, before finally acknowledging Puppy's own insistence that Ogilvie was the best man for the job. Relocating the group to L.A., too, was a mistake. The band essentially ceased to function mid-session — Ogre walked away; American froze the band's recording budget; finally Goettel and Key took the tapes home to Vancouver and tried finishing the album on their own, with Ogilvie. They were still putting the finishing touches to it when Goettel died of an overdose on August 23, 1995.

The Process (#102 US), the final Skinny Puppy album, was released in 1996, still incomplete but with nobody to mourn it. Key was working now with Download, a side project he and Goettel formed during the last months of Skinny Puppy; Ogre united with producer Mark Walk in WELT, a band name he'd been toying with since the early 1980's. Their eponymous debut album, set for release in 1997, would subsequently be canned by American.

Skinny Puppy LPs

6 Back and Forth (Self-Released) 1983 The very noisy sound of naive excitement, unbridled vision, and at least some of the ability to give it shape and substance.

7 Bites (Nettwerk) 1985 Although *Bites* does contain industrial elements, its focus was on atmospheres; dark and hovering, much of the album's influences can be traced either back to Britain's post-punk afterburn, or to Key's past in Images in Vogue. Only Ogre's gruff anti-melodic vocals seem determined to push Puppy into another dimension entirely.

8 Mind: The Perpetual Intercourse (Nettwerk) 1986 Taking the goth strand to its logical conclusion, *Mind* is a blissful union between Cabaret Voltaire and Einsturzende Neubauten, with a mind of its own throwing poisoned confetti. The effects are impressive, the atmospheres dense and provocative.

8 Cleanse, Fold, and Manipulate (Nettwerk) 1987 Moving the electronics into the forefront, Puppy desert their once accessible darkwave sensibilities behind, as Ogre launches lyrically from the personal to the public, addressing for the first time larger societal concerns. A pivotal album, both in the band's progress and on the industrial scene at large.

8 Vivisectvi (Nettwerk) 1988 Precision-crafted sterility dampens down Puppy's past power, but to devastating effect. Puppy's rage is growing too, barely remaining under control for this brilliantly furious stab at animal experiments, political conflicts, and government conspiracies. With hindsight, the lyrics are loaded with potent omens of the band's own future; at the time, the music was frightening enough.

6 Rabies (Nettwerk) 1989 For the first time, Puppy utilizes live guitar and guest vocals (Ministry's Al Jourgensen). Adored on the cold wave, but despised by electro-purists, *Rabies* remains a love or hate affair, even as it neatly weds two no longer disparate musical genres.

7 Too Dark Park (Nettwerk) 1990 A return to form of sorts, as Puppy turns full circle, from the chaotic sound collage of the opening "Convulsion," through their newfound love for more muted clatter, then back around to the atmospherics of the past. Ogre's increasingly literate lyrics are a searing indictment of planetary waste and pollution, and *Park* is a forceful new statement of intent.

5 Ain't It Dead Yet [LIVE] (Nettwerk) 1991

7 Last Rights (Nettwerk) 1992 The logical successor to *Park*, *Rights* features many of the heavy atmospheres and more melodic sounds of the past before unwinding it all into pure ambience. Of course Ogre's bitter lyrics stand in sharp contrast to the moody music.

8 The Process (American) 1996 A brilliant amalgamation of Puppy's hard hitting industrial edge, moody atmospherics, and even hints of pop, powered by concussive techno-esque beats and featuring a virtually unprocessed Ogre singing for the first time. The group's most accessible album (probably because the rest of the world has finally started catching up with them), *The Process* distills in 43 minutes everything Puppy was, and should have become.

Selected Compilations and Archive Releases

7 Twelve Inch Anthology (Nettwerk) 1990 Collecting four pre-1990 singles, *Anthology* illuminates the impact Puppy had on the industrial dance floors. Many of the A-sides are now club classics, so this album is not merely a collector's item, but a seminal greatest dance hits as well.

5 Back and Forth (Nettwerk) 1992 Coupling the group's debut album with live recordings and other very early material (circa 1981–1984). Chunks are virtually unlistenable, but still the band's schizophrenic sound (careening madly from danceable darkwave pop to very experimental electro) and power bleed forth.

8 Brap (Nettwerk) 1996 A double album of previously unreleased demos, outtakes, and live recordings from across the band's long history. Anything but a greatest hits collection, *Brap* is aimed at hardcore fans who can never get enough, and this won't disappoint.

5 Remix Dys Temper (Nettwerk) 1998 As if Puppy weren't disparate enough in their own right, a host of nearly name remixers descend to do their worst.

9 The Singles Collection (Nettwerk) 1999

8 The B-Sides Collection (Nettwerk) 1999

Download LPs

6 Furnace (Cleopatra) 1995 A love it or hate it affair, Download's debut sounded like a bunch of old tapes downloaded onto DAT, lacking an iota of focus, structure or sense, disconnected noises, rhythms, and soundscapes flitting through without rhyme or reason. Or maybe it was pure brilliance, deconstructing everything one ever knew about sound, form, and function. The dividing line seemed to fall between programmers (genius) and the general listening public (rip-off), but anything that evokes such extreme reactions obviously has something going for it.

7 The Eyes of Stanley Pain (Nettwerk) 1996 Still amorphous in form, *Eyes* is more focused by the simple addition of strong techno rhythms to Key's indescribable soundscapes, while Mark Spyvey hisses and threatens overhead. It's not quite noise, industrial, or techno, but a bizarre melding of all three; disturbing, glowering, driving, the sound of a danceclub down the road from hell.

Selected Compilations and Archive Releases

6 Microscopic (Cleopatra) 1996 Mini-album collecting *Furnace* remixes and reworkings, together with a handful of extreme new songs, recorded with Psychic TV's Genesis P-Orridge.

5 Charlie's Family (Metropolis) 1997 The 1995 soundtrack to the Jim VanBebber film, a disconcerting vista of vast soundscapes billowing like thunder clouds, only to be shredded by a cacophony of noise, effects, and vocal snippets. Rhythms appear, build, then vanish, and one feels there is a brilliant logic to it all, if only one could just work it out.

SKY CRIES MARY

FORMED 1988 (Seattle, Washington)

ORIGINAL LINE-UP *Roderick Wolgamott (b. 5/11/65, Seattle — vocals); Ken Stringfellow (guitar); Jon Auer (guitar)*

Sky Cries Mary began as a soundtrack vehicle for Roderick Wolgamott's theater work. Accompanied by Ken Stringfel-

low and Jon Auer, the first recordings were made on Wolgamott's 23rd birthday, shortly before he left Seattle to attend graduate school in Paris. There he landed a deal with the New Rose label and, upon his arrival back in Seattle in December, the band completed their first album in eight days. The harsh industrial soundscapes of *Until the Grinders Cease* appeared in Europe in 1989 (the album remained unreleased in the US for another decade).

SCM played three shows, including one opening for Pere Ubu, before Wolgamott returned to Paris to begin a follow-up EP, *Don't Eat the Dirt*, with a group of local musicians. One final cut was recorded in Seattle with Stringfellow and Auer, and again, the resultant clatter saw release in Europe only. Stringfellow and Auer bowed out of SCM soon after, to concentrate on their own band, the Posies, but the group's mood was shifting anyway. The emergence of a local rave scene connected Wolgamott with electronic whizz DJ Fallout (born Todd Robbins, aka TR), while the near-simultaneous arrival of the operatically-trained Anisa Romero (b. Olympia, WA, 5/14/68) both prompted, and coincided with, Wolgamott's own realization that he had more to say through his music than "a simple outpouring of 'this is shit, you are shit, I am shit....'"

Completing the line-up with bassist Joe Howard, drummer Ben Ireland, keyboard player Gordon Raphae,l and former Patti Smith Group guitarist Ivan Kral, the increasingly theatrical and ambitious band found a home at former Gang of Four bassist Dave Allen's World Domination label in 1991.

Sky Cries Mary debuted with the *Exit at the Axis* EP, recorded shortly before Kral quit for a solo career in late 1992. He was replaced by Marc Olsen of Sage and, with the EP picking up strong reviews, the band launched their first national tour, opening for Shriekback. The album *Return to the Inner Experience* followed in 1993, effortlessly aligning Sky Cries Mary with the resurgent space rock scene sweeping the American underground in the wake of Ozric Tentacles' recent breakthrough.

Howard quit shortly after *Inner Experience*, going on to Pretty Mary Sunshine, before joining fellow SCM alumni Auer and Stringfellow in the Posies (he also released his own *Skyward* album through Seattle's C/Z label). He was replaced by Juano (born John Davidson) and with Michael Cozzi (ex-Shriekback) in for Olsen, SCM recorded their masterpiece, *This Timeless Turning*. Appearances on network television's Conan O'Brien and John Stewart shows were followed by what history now remembers as the first ever rock concert to be broadcast over the internet — at a time when the internet itself was still little more than a playground for geeks and freaks. Finally, in 1996, SCM signed with Warners and began work on what should have been their breakthrough album, *Moonbathing on Sleeping Leaves*.

Instead, a complete breakdown of communication with every avenue within the record company left the band haplessly sitting on their hands. They appeared on the 1997 HORDE tour, but the album crashed unnoticed and Warners dropped the group soon after. For a time, SCM appeared to be on hold. Both Raphael and Cozzi quit the band altogether, while Wolgamott joined ex-Nirvana bassist Kris Novoselic and former Ministry drummer Bill Rieflin in a part-time project, Sunshine Cake, recording the soundtrack to the first of a projected trilogy of Novoselic's art movies.

Back briefly on World Domination, the group oversaw a well received compilation album, *Fresh Fruits for the Liberation — Ten Years of Musical Compost*, but despite regular local gigs (with William Bernhard replacing Cozzi), still the bulk of their attention appeared to be elsewhere. Wolgamott recorded a second Sunshine Cake soundtrack, with Ireland replacing Rieflin and Romero made an album with electronic composer Jeff Greinke (released on the First World label, co-founded by Greinke and Rieflin). SCM finally returned to full-time action in 1999. Demos recorded at Robbins' recently completed home studio, the Basement Audio Research Facility (BARF), bought the band to the attention of the Collective Fruit label, to be released as the *Seed* EP in September 1999. However, the band broke up four months later, their official statement simply paraphrasing Albert Camus, "it is just as important to know when to stop as to know when to begin."

Sky Cries Mary LPs

6 **Until the Grinders Cease (New Rose — France) 1989** An exotic amalgamation of samples, tribal drums, metallic clatter, and purposefully enigmatic lyrics, *Cease* centers around a haunting, tribal version of a song which would remain an SCM showstopper, "When the Fear Stops."

7 **Enter at the Axis EP 1992** An entirely new line-up saw the exit of SCM's early experimental sound and the entry of co-vocalist Romero's Eastern influences, alongside the band's own mix of swirling gothic drone, spacey prog-rock, and club sounds. A pivotal record, highlighted by the epic trance-story, "Elephant Song."

9 **Return to the Inner Experience (World Domination) 1993** Neo-space-rock at its best, with a modern, almost rave, twist. The vocals swoop and intertwine, the band ebb and flow and they meet near the center with heart-stopping power. From the delicate beauty of "Moving Like Water," the minimalistic sparseness of a revisited "When the Fear Stops," and on to the mystical trance of "Rain," *Return* reverberates with subtly shaped moods and shimmering atmospheres.

10 **This Timeless Turning (World Domination) 1994** Inextricably linked with the resurgent space rock of the early- to mid-

1990s, but unflinchingly eschewing all but the most superficial strands of the genre, SCM's trance-rave hybrid reaches a climax which even brought the major labels running. Twin vocals rise over hot electronic soup, space whisper bleeps in the dark behind the eyes, and a boiling, rolling soundtrack lends inexorable motion to the most stubbornly static of listeners.

Songs build from nothing, vague primitive chants which tap natural energies as yearning melodies ("These Old Bones") fade into fractured yowling ("Stretched"), and the band reach out for the spirit of pure improvisation ("4.00 AM"), which they hither to reserved for live performance. Indeed, there are moments not only of genre- but time-defying beauty — a communion of the ancient souls which dwell in Romero's unspeakably pure vocals, and the demons which live in TR's bank of electronic trickery. Space rock for the whole universe.

7 **Moonbathing on Sleeping Leaves (WB) 1997** Expanding their sound dramatically, SCM adds bright pop (the upbeat "Moonbathing") and surprisingly even hard rock (on the Black Sabbath-inspired "Breathe In") to their space/trance/prog rock core, to create a harder, more percussive-driven sound.

Selected Compilations and Archive Releases

7 **Fresh Fruits for the Liberation (World Domination) 1998** Coming full circle, *Fresh Fruits* pulls together songs spanning their entire career from their earliest industrial experimentations to their latest drum- and bass-heavy tracks. Sadly absent, a heavenly version of "California Dreaming," available through their website.

Anisa Romero and Jeff Greinke LP

6 **Hana (First World) 1999** Sadly unfocussed mix of Romero's spectral vocals and Greinke's ambient stylings.

SLEEPER

FORMED 1993 (London, England)

ORIGINAL LINE-UP *Louise Wener (b. 7/30/68, Gants Hill, London, England — vocals, guitar); Jon Stewart (b. 9/12/67, Sheffield, England — guitar); Diid Osman (4/10/68, Somalia); Andy McClure (b. 6/4/70, Manchester, England)*

Louise Wener met Jon Stewart at college in Manchester in 1992. They moved to London the following year, recruiting Diid Osman and Andy McClure (ex-The Crawl and the ten-piece ska orchestra The Mable String Quartet) and began gigging that summer as Surrender Dorothy. Signed to the Indolent label on the strength of one song, "Stay," the band became Sleeper after discovering, as Stewart said, "there are about a dozen Surrender Dorothys in America." Sleeper debuted late that year with a handful of gigs and the debut single, "Alice in Vain."

February 1994 bought the follow-up, "Swallow," while May delivered "Delicious" (#75 UK), the cue for Wener to unleash her own brand of sexual philosophy onto a nation lulled into soporific mateyness by the singing electricians of the Brit-pop rebirth. A tour with Blur confirmed Sleeper's ascendancy, for audiences gathered reverentially to hear about girls doing boys like they're girls. It was one thing for Damon Albarn to tell them to cut down on their pork life ("get a bit of exercise"); it was quite another for Wener to chastise them, "you're so dirty...make it dirtier." Sleeper need not have made another record; Wener was making headlines on her own.

Instead, the band hit out with "Inbetweener" (#16 UK), suburban angst in microcosmic detail; subsequently reborn for the *Get Real* movie soundtrack, "Inbetweener" smashed into the British Top 20 and Sleeper's *Smart* debut album (#5 UK) soared with it. The most eagerly awaited album of the year became the first to actually eclipse the hype, hope, and hubris which attended it — even if the tabloid press did spend most of its time searching for details of Wener's mid-album split with boyfriend Stewart.

Defying media predictions that Sleeper (like so many other emergent bands of the era) were unlikely ever to repeat the *Smart* experience, Wener lost no time debuting new material. Two more singles during 1995, "Vegas" (#33 UK) and "What Do I Do Now" (#14 UK), one of the most painfully perceptive mid-break-up narratives ever disguised as a pop song, kept the band in the UK Top 20, while their sophomore album, 1996's *The It Girl* (#5 UK), paired them with Smiths/Blur producer Stephen Street to devastating effect.

Marvelling in the mundanities of life, but without the exaggerated eccentricities of Blur and Pulp; with musical bases slipping from classic Blondie to mid-period Beatles, but avoiding the twin traps of affectation and retro posturing, *The It Girl* positioned Sleeper firmly on the brink of a major breakthrough. "Sale of the Century" (#10 UK), "Nice Guy Eddie" (#10 UK), and "Statuesque" (#17 UK) all charted, while an American tour with Elvis Costello in 1996 not only earned the group the maestro's applause, but also a B-side on his own latest single. Sleeper's cover of his "Other Side of the Telescope" backed the "Useless Beauty" 45, while a dramatic reworking of Blondie's "Atomic" was a key addition to the cult movie *Trainspotting* soundtrack.

It all came tumbling down with Sleeper's third album. While the UK media jokingly savaged Wener's newfound public preeminence, relegating the remainder of the band to the status of mere "Sleeper Blokes," the group fell apart during sessions for what Wener insisted was to be called *Cunt London*.

Bassist Diid was sacked in June 1997, to be replaced in the studio by Madder Rose bassist Chris Giammalvo, and with the album sessions dragging on, Sleeper cancelled a scheduled appearance at the Reading Festival. *Pleased to Meet You*

(#7 UK) finally emerged that fall, but sadly, few people returned the title's greeting. Wener's face alone appeared on the album cover, and despite entering the UK chart so high, it was swiftly apparent that sales of the record were never going approach the peaks of its predecessors.

With Dan Kauffman now on bass, Sleeper toured throughout the fall of 1997, while three successive singles, "She's a Good Girl" (#28 UK), "Romeo Me" (#39 UK), and "Motor Man" fared poorly. 1998 then opened with Wener angrily denying split rumors — only for Kauffman to quit in February. Giammalvo came back for a poorly attended second British tour, but news that their US label, Arista, had cancelled the Stateside release of *Pleased to Meet You* hit the band's future plans hard. So did the closure of Indolent in July, and five months later, on December 30, 1998, Wener announced Sleeper's demise. Stewart relocated to L.A. and joined a new band, UFO Bro; Wener and McClure announced plans to form a new band.

Sleeper LPs

7 Smart (Arista) 1995 Sleeper's quietly seething indy-pop nicely complements vocalist Louise Werner's tough vulnerability. Right now, the focus is squarely on the lyrics' vivid tales of sex, death, and the vanities and vagaries of modern life.

10 The It Girl (Arista) 1996 Moving self-assuredly forward, Sleeper keep their jagged lyrical edge, but the music slams up to join them. Too many promising mid-'90's Brit bands foundered after one album (remember Menswe@r?); the first signs that Sleeper weren't about to join them came with a late 1995 BBC session — four new songs, four new winners. "What Do I Do Now?," possibly the most perfect pop single of the post-*Parklife* '90s, followed; by the time Sleeper brought Stephen Street in to produce, they'd already proven their follow-up mettle. By that token, the unflinching triumph of *The It Girl* is simply a bonus.

First things first: just as she's turned down the occasional grungy grimaces which her guitar was once prone to produce, opting for a clearer, song-powered sound throughout, Wener also toned down her tongue, which meant that pound for pound, *The It Girl* offered considerably less headline-hogging sex than *Smart* — so if you got your kicks off "Delicious," savor them now. No longer bonking till they bleed, *The It Girl's* lovers are more content to repent their past and mourn their losses, and "What Do I Do Now" (again) offers a slant on break-ups which approaches pain threshold in its attention to detail.

That said, "Good Luck Mr. Gorsky" did take its title from the now-famous allusion to his neighbor getting a blow-job which Neil Armstrong allegedly uttered when he first walked on the moon, and "Dress like Your Mother" would have made a great intro tape for the Sex Pistols reunion. But at the end of the day, it's not what was said (or not) which really counted, it was the Brian Epstein quote which became Wener's guiding principle in the year following *Smart*. "The 'Next Big Thing'," the Beatles manager once said, "will be a great song." The It Girl was full of the things.

◐ Pleased to Meet You (Indolent UK) 1997 Still sharply pop bitter, brittle, and brutal in more or less equal mouthfuls, but the songs which sound like Sleeper are the ones that seem old-fashioned, out-numbered by an ambition which runs before it can wobble. "Rollercoaster" works, but someone's been listening to too much Costello. Stop it.

SLITS

FORMED 1977 (London, England)
ORIGINAL LINE-UP Ari Upp (b. Arianna Forster — vocals); Palmolive (b. Paloma Romero — drums); Kate Korus (rhythm guitar); Suzi Gutsy (bass)

Although word of an all-girl punk band called the Slits had already percolated into the punk underground, the band's original line-up had changed substantially by the time the group actually appeared in public. Ex-Castrator Suzi Gutsy had been replaced by bandmate Tessa Pollitt, and Kate Korus by Viv Albertine, ex-Flowers of Romance (where she'd played alongside Palmolive and Sid Vicious). This reformed line-up debuted opening for The Clash at the Harlesden Colosseum on March 11, 1977, following up as opening act on the same band's White Riot tour (alongside the Buzzcocks and Subway Sect).

Rolling Stone caught the Slits at the Vortex in August 1977 and described them as a band whose efforts "any current American audience would reward with a shower of bottles. The guitarist stops in the middle of the fourth song to announce, 'Fuckin' shit! Listen to this!' and plays an ungodly out-of-tune chord that no-one else had even noticed in the cacophony. The singer, apparently the only one with pitch, has to tune her guitar for her. 'Fuckin' shit!' explains the singer, plucking the strings. 'We never said we were musicians'."

Remaining musically unstable for much of the year — the *NME* called their earliest shows "shambolic and puerile with just a hint of something special [to] make these silly displays so frustrating" — the Slits first session for John Peel at the end of September suddenly saw them come of age. Primitive still, oft-times infuriating, the session was aired five times over the next three months, and closed '77 as perhaps the most popular of the year. When German vocalist Nina Hagen suggested the band lose Ari Upp and become her group instead, they swiftly turned her down.

The Slits repertoire — mostly original, but augmented by "I Heard It Through the Grapevine," "Louie Louie," and the Velvets Underground's "Femme Fatale" — was developing, too, and The Clash unhesitatingly invited the Slits back to open the Sort It Out tour in 1978. With Big in Japan drum-

mer Budgie replacing Palmolive (now with The Raincoats), the Slits also toured with the Buzzcocks, and came close to joining Malcolm McLaren's management roster.

The year's end *Zig Zag* readers poll placed the Slits firmly in the ascendant: #7 Best group, #1 Best Unsigned group, #1 Hot Tip For the Top, with Palmolive #10 Favorite Person. They signed with Island in early 1979, releasing the "Typical Girls" (#60 UK) single, followed quickly by an album, the Dennis Bovell-produced *Cut* (#30 UK). According to Budgie, "The [Slits] aspirations were so massive. When we went in to do 'Cut,' the brief to Dennis, if there was one, was a cross between *Saturday Night Fever* and *Spirits Having Flown*, the Bee Gees album. It's got to be dance, it's got to have reggae... this is a tall order, you know? But it was totally crazed, and it worked. The next thing I remember which caught me like that was the first PiL album, where you went 'whoops, what's this sound? What's all this about?'"

A tour followed with veteran trumpet player Don Cherry, an honorary Slit (his daughter, Neneh, also appeared as backing vocalist), but the band quit Island soon after, resurfacing in March 1980 with a new 45 on Rough Trade, the tribal "In the Beginning There Was Rhythm" (#2 UK indy), backed by a Pop Group track, "Where There's a Will, There's a Way." The Pop Group also lent their musical support to a second single, "Man Next Door" (#5 UK indy), which appeared later in the year on Y; that same label also released a ten-track Slits retrospective, combining early live and demo work (an epic "Sister Ray" included) with more recent material, under the title *The Bootleg Retrospective* (#1 UK indy). A brief stint with Human Records, for whom they cut the "Animal Space" (#10 UK indy) single, followed, but by mid-1981, the Slits were back on course. Budgie had quit by now, joining Siouxsie and the Banshees; he was replaced by the Pop Group's own Bruce Smith. Steve Beresford (keyboards) came in around the same time, fleshing out the Slits' sound further, and the band signed with CBS.

Sessions with Bovell, Pop Group manager Dick O'Dell, and engineer Nick Launay resulted in the Slits second "real" album, *Return of the Giant Slits*, previewed with a single of "Earth Beat." Again they toured, but the album was barely on the streets when the Slits split up. Upp and Smith joined producer Adrian Sherwood's New Age Steppers; Upp later relocated to Jamaica where her activities included fashion design; Pollitt and Albertine quit the music business.

Slits LPs

◐ Cut (Antilles) 1979 A reggae album by a punk band that can't play reggae or, conversely, a punk album by a reggae band which can't.... Utterly dislocating, frequently unfocussed, but walloping along on its own nerve and ambition, *Cut* defied both the band's limitations and the media's skepticism and emerged contagious, courageous, and — with the buoyant "Typical Girls" — commercial without a hint of compromise.

10 The Return of the Giant Slits (CBS — UK) 1981 The visceral dub of *Cut* was already three years old when the Slits convened for their major label debut — three years and a lifetime of activity on the furthest periphery of the white reggae punk experiment. The intervening years had muddied the waters, simultaneously portraying the band as rank musical auteurs whose only goal was to clatter and shriek a lot, and genuinely incisive pioneers, doggedly pursuing rhythms far beyond the established parameters of rock (or even reggae). The Slits were *not* great musicians. But their ideas could reach their dreams, and *Giant Slits* emerged the most obsessive major label release of the year.

The album's inspirations were all over the place. "Earthbeat," the haunting opener, was built upon similar foundations to the classical *Missa Luba* (famously the theme to Lindsay Anderson's movie epic of teen disaffection, *If*), insistent percussion and Ari's keening chant wrapped to a traumatic toast while the drums sought out a contradictory rhythm. It was savagely beautiful, the first putatively rock-related release to investigate such stylings at a time when "tribal" still meant labelmate Adam Ant, and "primitive" was a guitar tuning.

Preempting and predicting the violent shuddering of Kate Bush "Sat in Your lap" and "The Dreaming" (the most apparent of her several debts to the Slits); informing the ambitions of Peter Gabriel, whose WOMAD festival would be launched a year too late to benefit the Slits; *Giant Slits* was lauded for its bravery, applauded for its nerve, then lost beneath the apathy of a public whose taste for "World Music" needed to be coaxed into the light... not slammed naked onto the table.

Selected Compilations and Archive Compilations

2 Official Bootleg (Rough Trade) 1980 All but unlistenable sub-bootleg recordings through which an occasional hint of melody reminds you what they're meant to be playing.

8 The Peel Sessions (Dutch East Ind) 1989 The Slits in their native environment, messing around without a tune in the world. The original release features seven tracks, the reissue appends three from a magnificent 1981 session.

7 In the Beginning (A Live Anthology) (Cleopatra) 1997 An album wholly disoriented by the sonic shift from the punk buzz clatter of the early shows to the inspired blaze of the *Return*-era live shows. Both facets have their virtues, but unlike the similar blending on *The Peel Sessions*, their union is not a happy one.

SMASHING PUMPKINS

FORMED 1987 *(Chicago, IL)*

ORIGINAL LINE-UP *Billy Corgan (b. 3/17/67, Chicago, IL — vocals, guitar); James Iha (b. 3/6/68, Elk Grove, IL — guitar); D'arcy Wretzky (b. 5/1/68, South Haven, MI — bass, vocals); Jimmy Chamberlain (b. 6/10/64, Joliet, IL — drums)*

Smashing Pumpkins formed shortly after Billy Corgan returned to Chicago from Florida, where he played with goth band The Marked (named in honor of the distinctive birth marks that both Corgan and the drummer had); James Iha's previous band was the highly rated Snaketrain. Both, however, were consumed by a passionate desire which their last bands had been unable to fulfill — to try something different and blaze a new trail for themselves.

Unwilling to compromise their vision, the pair adamantly refused to bring anybody else into their dream group. Correspondingly, they made their live debut as a duo in a Chicago bar, meeting Wretzky that same evening. According to legend, she came over to fight Corgan over the merits of the evening's headline attraction, the Dan Reed Network. Corgan didn't like the way they bounced around on stage; Wretzky said that she enjoyed it, and mentioned she played bass as well. Corgan promptly handed her his phone number and asked if she'd like to try out for the Pumpkins. Anybody so forthright in their views would make an interesting addition to the line-up.

The three Pumpkins made their first appearance together in front of 50 people at the Avalon, a club in Chicago. It wasn't a great success but local promoter Joe Shanahan offered them another gig if they would replace the awful drum machine with a real musician. A friend promptly introduced the band to jazz drummer, Jimmy Chamberlain.

The Pumpkins rose quickly. Their fourth gig saw them open for Jane's Addiction, the first in what quickly became a succession of highly prestigious support slots for the nascent Pumpkins, a sequence which saw their reputation with audiences soar even as their popularity amongst other local bands plummeted. "We really rumpled the feathers of the local bands because we were getting the gigs that they wanted," Corgan admitted, and for years to come, hometown gigs remained fraught occasions as organized bands of hecklers congregated to accuse the Pumpkins of selling out.

By 1990, Smashing Pumpkins were ready to record — or at least, Corgan was. Echoing a plaintive complaint which would become a virtual war-cry as the band's success increased, he accused his bandmates of simply not being interested in embracing his ideas and refusing to motivate themselves to do the very best they could, whenever they could. Publicly, his bandmates dubbed him a total control freak; privately, all three threatened to quit the band unless Corgan cut them some slack. He responded by threatening to sack them. Something, however, kept them in place — a sense of destiny, Corgan once explained, and a belief that the Pumpkins were like a marriage; "we'll be together until death do us part."

"I Am One" (#73 UK) was the Pumpkins' first single, released in 1990 on Seattle's Sub Pop label. It, too, boasted its share of prescience — it was his work with the Pumpkins which introduced producer Butch Vig to the Seattle scene with which he would swiftly become inextricably entwined; the following year, the hitherto unknown Vig would produce Nirvana's mega-selling *Nevermind* album.

With the band moving from Sub Pop to the label's distributing company, Caroline, Smashing Pumpkins' debut album, *Gish* (#195 US), arrived in May 1991. The legacy of over a year spent touring solidly around the United States, *Gish* was an immediate hit, becoming the first independent album to top the *CMJ* album chart in over three years. Even more importantly, however, its dense, gritty sound ushered in a new era for the Pumpkins, and a new musical buzzword for the rest of the world.

Other bands, most of them hailing from Seattle of course, had been labelled grunge in the recent past. Smashing Pumpkins, however, were the first to illustrate what grunge was capable of becoming — a widescreen cacophony which owed as much to the classic rock sound of Corgan's 1970's childhood as it did the punk rock which fashionable journalists allied it to. *Gish* went on to sell over 700,000 copies. (The Pumpkin's "Drown" would subsequently be included in the *Singles* soundtrack, reinforcing the grunge linkage.)

Though the critical and public response to *Gish* made it seem that the band was on the fast track to success, the path would be uphill almost all the way. Smashing Pumpkins toured for a year and a half, lurching from crisis to crippling crisis. Iha and Wretzky, who were dating at the time, broke up while the band was still on the road. "All the normal stuff that would happen between a boyfriend and girlfriend who had broken up after a long time relationship was happening, " Iha reflected later, "only we were stuck together."

Chamberlain revealed his addiction to alcohol and drugs and announced that he wanted to quit the band to enter rehab. And with Corgan devoting all his spare emotional energy to holding his bandmates lives together, he completely neglected his own. After seven years together, Corgan and his girlfriend, Chris Fabian, split up. He later admitted he contemplated suicide. Instead, he started dating Courtney Love, remaining her companion until the night she met Kurt Cobain, in Chicago while visiting Corgan.

Despite the turmoil in their personal lives, on stage Smashing Pumpkins continued to amaze, and in spring 1992, the band signed to Virgin Records. Yet what should have been the happiest day of their lives instead plunged Corgan into a fresh trough of depression. "We barely had any songs written and the record company is saying you're going in the studio in two months. I was just standing there thinking, 'there's no way'."

Somehow, he pulled through.

With Vig again at the helm, Smashing Pumpkins returned to the studio to begin work on their major label debut, *Siamese Dream* (#10 US, #4 UK). Again, it was a depressing process, as Corgan grew accustomed to arriving at the studio to find his bandmates nowhere to be seen. Finally, he gave up, and began playing their parts himself.

Siamese Dream (#10 US) was finally released in July 1993; within less than a year, it had gone Double Platinum. In the UK, the singles "Cherub Rock" (#31 UK), "Today" (#44 UK), and "Diarm" (#11) accompanied the Pumpkins' ascent, and the band's breakthrough was confirmed the following summer, when they headlined Lollapalooza. They then returned to Chicago to write material for their next album.

It promised to be a lengthy process; so lengthy that Virgin, impatient for a Christmas bestseller, persuaded Corgan to sanction a stop gap compilation, the *Pisces Iscariot* (#4 US) collection of B-sides. The Pumpkins ended the year by running away with Spin magazine's Band of the Year award.

Meanwhile, the gestation of the band's next official album continued apace. Following the release of *Siamese Dream*, Corgan admitted that once he'd escaped his writer's block, he could not stop writing, and that the record could easily have been a double album. In 1993, Virgin had refused to even consider such a thing; by 1995, they had completely changed their minds.

A change of producer brought about its own changes. Under Butch Vig, Corgan's obsessions with such '70s heavyweights as the Electric Light Orchestra and Yes were given plenty of room to maneuver. For *Mellon Collie*, however, he opted to work with Alan Moulder and Flood, best known for their work with the cultish likes of Depeche Mode, Marc Almond, and Nick Cave. *Mellon Collie and the Infinite Sadness* (#1 US) was a better album for it. No longer feeling he had to cram every great idea into as short a time as possible, Corgan relaxed for the first time, and as he lightened up, so did his bandmates. Attitudes improved, relationships improved. For the first time, Smashing Pumpkins finally appeared to have triumphed over the collective and personal demons that had haunted them so vividly throughout the previous years.

The double CD was released in October 1995 and crashed into the charts at No. 1. A single, "Bullet with Butterfly Wings" (#20 UK), became a seemingly permanent fixture on MTV. American, British, European, and Far Eastern tours, scheduled to keep the band on the road for the next 18 months sold out in record time. "Tonight Tonight" (#7 UK) and "Thirty Three" (#21 UK) were hits; the mini-album, *Zero* (#46 US), was a hit. The Pumpkins were on top of the world, and then the crust crumbled beneath them.

The disasters began slowly. A video was shot for the band's next single, "1979" (#16 UK), only for a vital part of the footage to be lost when one of the production crew inadvertently drove off the set with the only copy of the shoot on the roof of his car. It was never recovered.

A week's worth of gigs were cancelled when Chamberlain's father died and the drummer flew home to be with his family; another gig in Dublin was scrapped after a fan was trampled in the mosh pit — Bernadette O'Brien died the following day from massive internal injuries. Twice, in Bangkok and Madrid, Chamberlain overdosed while hanging with the band's newly recruited fifth member, keyboardist Jonathan Melvoin, and while Melvoin was promptly sacked from the band, the need for a keyboard player could not be so easily solved.

He was reinstated for the American leg of the tour, through the summer of 1996, but the band's insistence that he clean up fell on deaf ears. On July 11, 24 hours before the first of three sold-out shows at Madison Square Garden, Melvoin died from a massive overdose in the hotel room he shared with Chamberlain. The shows were cancelled and the band returned to Chicago. Chamberlain was sacked from the band and when the tour resumed, drummer Matt Walker (of Filter) and Frogs keyboard player Dennis Flemion were on board.

Smashing Pumpkins remained relatively silent over the next two years, breaking cover only to contribute a couple of songs to the *Batman and Robin* soundtrack (Corgan alone featured on the *Ransom* soundtrack). Iha and Wretzky launched Scratchie Records, home to the renowned Chainsaw Kittens; Iha also cut a solo album, *Let It Come Down* (#171 US), released in February 1998, four months before the release of a new Smashing Pumpkins album, *Adore* (#2 US), and accompanying singles, "Ava Adore" (#42 US) and "Perfect" (#54 US).

With Kenny Aronoff now on drums, the band made it through their Adore tour unscathed, but thickening rumors regarding Wretzky's deteriorating relationship with Corgan were finally confirmed on September 10, 1999, when she quit the band.

Hole's Melissa Auf Der Mar was recruited in her stead; Jimmy Chamberlain, too, had returned to the band, and the band's fifth album, *Machina/The Machines of God*, was readied for February 2000 release. However, Wretzky was followed out by the band's manager, Sharon Osbourne, who had only joined the team a matter of months earlier. Osbourne's official statement claimed, "I must resign... due to medical reasons. Billy Corgan was making me sick." Shortly after, Corgan announced the end of the Smashing Pumpkins, bowing out with tours of Europe and the US.

Smashing Pumpkins LPs

7 Gish (Caroline) 1991 Smashing Pumpkins, mostly through Billy Corgan's odd vision, created an unusual hybrid of trippy psychedelics and goth. Immensely textured and layered, the songs draw you in, hold you tight, and let you experience the warm slipstream for yourself. Both "Siva" and "Tristess" gave the Pumpkins early cool status.

9 Siamese Dream (Virgin) 1993 Working with Butch Vig again, this time after grunge hit the windshield, the Pumpkins add an expected edge, but it can't totally suppress the quartet's 4AD-esque dream-pop atmospheres — and neither can they, although their fuzzy guitar roars as loud as the Jesus and Mary Chain. "Cherub Rock" opens the album — a scathing mockery of all indie rock — and that makes the album's commercial success even funnier.

8 Mellon Collie and the Infinite Sadness (Virgin) 1995 This double album is the ultimate journey through the psyche's dark underbelly, via all of its infinite undercurrents. From the melancholy title track and the dreamy "Tonight, Tonight" to the rage of "Jellybelly," although *Sadness* is depressing, obsessive, excessive, and emotionally exhausting, it's also a strangely entrancing excursion regardless. And maybe just a tad self-indulgent.

7 Adore (Virgin) 1998 After the emotional *Mellon Collie*, *Adore* seems positively upbeat — at least musically. The production and lush electronics free the sound from its former introspective claustrophobia, so morning dawns and the Pumpkins mood finally begins to lift and shift, highlighted on "Ava Adore" and "Tear."

8 Machina (Virgin) 2000 The Pumpkins' sharpest, most focused set since *Gish*, dominated by Corgon's waspish vocals and mud-soaked guitar buzz.

Selected Compilations and Archive Releases

7 Pisces Iscariot (Capitol) 1994 Big, fat odds and ends collection heavy on UK B-sides.

8 The Aeroplane Flies High (Virgin) 1996 Groovy box with singles, B-sides, and unreleased material.

James Iha LP

8 Let It Come Down (Virgin) 1998 Great songs, great style, verve and pluck, Iha's solo album is surely a response to Corgan intimation that his bandmate's musicianship was inferior. Who's laughing now?

Further Reading

Smashing Pumpkins by Jim Stapleton (MBS 1995).

PATTI SMITH

BORN *12/30/46 (Chicago, IL)*

Raised in New Jersey, Patti Smith arrived in New York at age 19, befriending art student Robert Mapplethorpe as they toiled at sundry, low-paying jobs together; and returned there after a three-month trip to Paris "in search of Rimbaud's ghost." She and Mapplethorpe shared a room at the Chelsea Hotel, and as his career in photography developed, she remained one of his favorite subjects.

In 1971, Smith began giving live poetry readings at the Mercer Arts Center and St. Mark's Church, occasionally backed by Lenny Kaye, a guitarist she met at the nearby Village Oldies record store. Pianist, Richard Sohl, followed, and over the next few years, Smith appeared on several Giorno Poetry Systems collections of modern poets. She also had a brief career as a nightclub chanteuse and a spell acting (she co-starred in several of Wayne County's off-off-Broadway productions during this period, and worked with the then-similarly obscure Sam Shepard).

Her writing, too, was appearing frequently, both in the mainstream music publications (*Creem, Crawdaddy, Rock Scene*) and in more specialist publications. She published a handful of poetry books — *Seventh Heaven, Kodak,* and *Witt*; while her now on-going relationship with Blue Oyster Cult's Allen Lanier saw her linked with that band as both a co-writer and a possible vocalist.

"Richard, Lenny and I were building what we were doing, which was essentially revolving around language," Smith explained later. "But we wanted to develop more

© Jim Steinfeldt/Chansley Entertainment

musically, and we decided to have another guitar player." She was already accruing considerable acclaim as a poet, but that wasn't what she wanted. "I'd rather be remembered as a great rock'n'roll star," she would tell journalists, and she meant it.

This early incarnation of what became the Patti Smith Group made their entrance into the CBGBs scene through Smith's friendship with fellow poet Richard Hell; he introduced her to Tom Verlaine, his bandmate in Television, and during early 1974, Smith opened several gigs for the better known band. Verlaine would also be on hand when the Group made their recorded debut, a single of "Piss Factory" and an idiosyncratic cover of "Hey Joe," self-released on the Mer label (financed by Mapplethorpe). It was the success of this venture which inspired Television manager Terry Ork to inaugurate his own Ork label with Television's "Little Johnny Jewel" 45.

The Patti Smith Group made their first trip to California in late 1974, headlining the Whisky a-Go-Go in L.A., then returning home convinced the band needed a second guitarist. Auditions revolved around a 40-minute version of Van Morrison's "Gloria," through which Smith would improvise a poem; they eventually settled on Ivan Kral (ex-Luger, Blondie — guitar) and in this form, the Group and Television took over CBGBs for a two month weekend residency through March/April 1975.

The arrival of Jay Dee Daugherty (ex-Mumps, drums) during that period completed the group, and in April, the Group signed with Arista. They chose John Cale to produce their first album and while Smith later played down his role in creating what became *Horses* (#47 US), at the time she acknowledged, "he helped just by being there." Packaged in one of Mapplethorpe's most striking images of Smith alone, the waif-like offspring of Keith Richard, Jim Morrison, and Bob Dylan, the album was released in November 1975 — the first fruit of the sea of creativity washing out of CBGB's.

The group's own commitments prevented Smith from accepting Bob Dylan's invitation to join his Rolling Thunder Tour, then itself just starting its gypsy trek across the US; instead, the Group launched a full national tour of their own, opening with three weekends at the Bottom Line in January 1976. Europe, primed by a single of "Gloria" (backed by an inflammatory live reading of "My Generation"), followed, Smith's appearance in London further polarizing a UK media already divided by the emergence of what would become punk rock. Smith's supporters — and detractors, for that matter — made no secret of which side of the divide she landed on. The new wave had its new Dylan.

On April 17, 1976, the Group became the first new wave act ever to appear on *Saturday Night Live* at a time when the very phrase "New Wave" was still waiting to be coined.

Weeks later, they linked with producer Jack Douglas to begin work on their second album. *Radio Ethiopia* (#122 US) was to prove as divisive as every other aspect of the band. It was released in October 1976 to generally unsympathetic press, with the British, in particular, coming down hard on it. The Sex Pistols and The Damned were both recording now and Smith's continued invocation of the idols of the past seemed strangely embarrassing, on vinyl and in concert.

In the event, the Group cut their European tour short because Andy Paley — deputizing for Sohl, himself suffering from exhaustion — had other commitments at home. He was replaced by Bruce Brody for a triumphant three-hour concert in Central Park and a week at the Bottom Line; Smith herself earned a ban from NY radio station WNEW for using the word "fuck" on air, but still the year wrapped up in triumph, with a Palladium show climaxed by Smith and Kral smashing their guitars up.

A new US tour commenced in late January 1977, opening in Florida. It was there, on the second night of the tour, that Smith fell off the stage during "Ain't It Strange," cracking two vertebrae in her neck, breaking some bones in her face, and splitting her head open. Later, she began suffering vision problems, but chose an intensive course of physical therapy over surgery, setting herself an Easter Sunday deadline for recovery. She made it as well, turning out in a neck brace for a special show at CBGB's, after the scheduled Dead Boys/Damned double-header. Further gigs at CBGB's in June, and the Elgin Theatre and the Village Gate in July, saw her regain strength and poise, and by fall, she was ready to begin work on the third Group album, with producer Jimmy Iovine.

The Group toured the US in January 1978 as they awaited the release both of *Easter* (#20 US, #16 UK), and a new single, pairing a Bruce Springsteen demo to Smith's lyric, "Because the Night" (#13 US, #5 UK). Both proved a crucial breakthrough in the US, pulling the Group out of the still misunderstood trough of punk and into a mainstream which happily welcomed the infusion of new talent emerging from the East Coast. The Talking Heads, Blondie, and Boston's Cars had all put their early allegiances behind them and were ready to embrace — or be embraced by — middle America. The Patti Smith Group, however, were not to prove quite so cuddly. Through August 1978, *Rolling Stone's* letters page overflowed with complaints about Smith's use and interpretation of language in the song "Rock'n'Roll Nigger." In Britain, her next single, a cover of Paul Jones' "Privilege (Set Me Free)" (#72 UK) was banned for its blasphemous employment of "goddamn." At the peak of her success, she continued to act like a cult.

Despite this, the Group's fourth album, *Wave* (#18 US, #41 UK), completed their transition from edgy punks to household names. Released in spring 1979, the songs on this Todd Rundgren production were dominated by Smith's love for future husband Fred Smith (ex-MC5) on the one hand and her growing disdain for stardom on the other. Three singles, "Frederick" (#90 US, #63 UK), "Dancing Barefoot," and "So You Want to Be a Rock'n'Roll Star" bombed, and while the Group remained a major live attraction, headlining massive arenas across Europe, it was obvious that Smith's heart was no longer on stage with her.

Finally, following an incendiary performance in Florence, in front of an all but rioting audience, and on a stage decked with American flags — strategically placed to further incense the crowd — she made her decision. Back at the hotel, she told the band she was quitting.

She remained true to her word for eight years. On March 11, 1980, Smith and Fred Smith married. The Patti Smith Group played one final show, an improvised jazz-influenced set at a benefit for the Detroit Symphony Orchestra in June 1980, but for the next six years, Patti Smith existed only in rumor. She and Smith did start work on a new album in 1980, tentatively titling it *Dream of Life*, but the project was abandoned. A son was born, Jackson, in 1982, and *Dream of Life* was briefly resuscitated. But they closed it down again and it would be 1986 before producer Iovine, and former Group mainstays Sohl and Daugherty were summoned to New York for a third attempt at recording an album.

The sessions were interrupted once again when Smith became pregnant with the couple's second child, Jesse; it would be spring 1988 before *Dream of Life* (#65 US, #70 UK) was finally released, but there would be no live performances and despite a flurry of interest, a new single, "People Have the Power," vanished and the album itself did poorly.

The Smiths returned to their seclusion, but it was to be a troubled period. Robert Mapplethorpe died from AIDS on March 9, 1989; Richard Sohl passed away from a cardiac seizure on June 3, 1990; Fred Smith's former MC5 bandmate Rob Tyner died of a heart attack on September 19, 1991. Fred appeared at an MC5 reunion benefit for Tyner's family in Detroit, he and Patti then played a pair of AIDS benefits, and in 1992, the pair contributed a song, "It Takes Time," to the soundtrack of Wim Wenders' *Until the End of the World*. Finally, the watching media convinced itself, the hermits were stirring.

Through 1993 and 1994, Patti Smith began writing and publishing again. She gave a poetry reading in Central Park on July 8, 1993, and arranged the publication of an anthology of her early writings. But on November 4, 1994 (Mapplethorpe's birthday), Fred Smith suffered a fatal heart failure. Six weeks later, Patti's brother Todd, too, was killed by a heart attack.

Alone, Smith made her first live appearance in 18 months with a poetry reading at St. Mark's Church on New Year's Day, 1995. The following month, she joined Allen Ginsberg at a Tibetan benefit in Ann Arbor and in April, she performed at a tribute to her late husband, again in Ann Arbor. She pieced together a new band around Carolyn Striho's Detroit Energy Asylum and on July 5, 1995, gave her first rock'n'roll performance since Florence at a small club in Toronto.

A reunion with Lenny Kaye followed at another Central Park reading on July 27 and, back in New York, she seemed reinvigorated. A second Central Park show was followed by a guest appearance at Lollapalooza 95, when the tour played Randall's Island, and with a new band built around Kaye, Daugherty, Oliver Ray (guitar), Tony Shanahan (bass), and Luis Resto (keyboards), work began on a new album. (Kral, the absent Group member, was now leading his own band, Native, and working largely in his native Czech Republic as a producer.) With Tom Verlaine added to the band, Smith toured first clubs, then, for eight dates through December, opening for Dylan around the East Coast. (This same bill would visit Australia in 1998.) *Gone Again* (#55 US, #44 UK) appeared in July, while the single, an old Fred Smith number called "Summer Cannibals," succeeded in seeming ubiquitous without actually making the chart. A second album, *Peace and Noise* (#152 US), followed in fall 1997 together with another burst of inspired gigging — she even returned to CBGB's, for four emotional nights in October 1997. Work then began on a new album, *Gung Ho*, for release in spring 2000; Smith saw in the new year with two shows at New York's Bowery ballroom, December 30–31, 1999, and a poetry reading at St. Mark's on January 1.

Patti Smith LPs

10 **Horses (Arista) 1975** She was a revelation. At a time when women in music were represented by the likes of rock chicks (Heart), biker babes (Suzi Quatro), and sex kittens (Linda Ronstadt), Patti Smith offered a real alternative. She was a true poet — angry, evocative, uplifting, depressing — not a whiny woman with an axe to grind.

What made *Horses* a classic wasn't only the emotional rawness and vividness of Patti's lyrics, however, but the music, soaring like Pegasus into a new world of edgy sound. From the melancholy spectral spaciness of "Birdland" to the triumph-of-love throb of "Free Money" and (especially) across the nine-minute masterpiece of "Land," the band created the perfect accompaniment to Patti's words. In a mere eight songs, *Horses* captured a myriad of moods and emotions, shifting effortlessly between musical styles and sounds.

Every nuance was open to interpretation. Was "Gloria" a lesbian revision of Van Morrison's original? Was Jimi Hendrix ("Elegy") a greater influence than Tom Verlaine (co-author of the peerless "Break It Up")? And who was the Johnny who the boy looked at? Patti never answered, but still *Horses* galloped across the spectrum, investigating raw reggae and dissolute funk, then reaching through time to snatch potent portents from rock'n'roll's past — "Gloria," of course, but also "Land of a Thousand Dances," Dylan's Mr. Jones and Brian Jones' fear of living, Charlie Parker and John Cale's cheekbones.

Less an album, more an experience; less eight songs, more the first eight commandments; '70's rock'n'roll as sonic salvation.

9 **Radio Ethiopia (Arista) 1976** A sidestep from the poetic dynamics of *Horses*, a denser album, deeper and darker — the viscous dub of "Ain't It Strange," the delicate beauty of "Pissing in the River," the sheer improv-inspiration of the title track, and while "Pumping" rocks, "Ask the Angels" is pop, a world of sinuous rhythms and smudged shadows which ensured Patti could never surprise us again.

7 **Easter (Arista) 1978** Unless, of course, she wrote a song with Bruce Springsteen and had a major hit all over the world. With her very delivery strangely lacking the old anger and passion, a reinvention of sound and dynamics which touched old heights only via the lethal live "Rock 'n' Roll Nigger." Elsewhere, the tender "Easter" and a gloriously blasphemous rendition of "Privilege" genuinely enthralled... but still it's sad to think that this is the album most people think of when the group's name is mentioned.

6 **Wave (Arista) 1979** This album should have been a stunner, but Smith rebounded a little too hard on the heels of her last three albums. That said, she still kicks on the unequaled "Dancing Barefoot" and "Frederick," but falls short with the Byrds cover, "So You Want to Be (A Rock and Roll Star)" and positively founders elsewhere.

5 **Dream of Life (Arista) 1988** A decade on, *Life* showcased a confident Smith, but while the album is competent and upbeat, it is also disappointing, toothlessly flailing in directions where she would once have bitten hard.

5 **Gone Again (Arista) 1996** More poetic than pop and a deeply somber affair — which adds a timbre to her work which had been lacking. From the title track to "Beneath the Southern Cross" and "Fireflies," Smith again is just giving from her gut, and it really doesn't matter what anyone thinks at all.

6 **Peace and Noise (Arista) 1997** "Death Singing," the one song Smith authored alone, is also the one song which harks back to past glories; elsewhere, conventional rock dirties the dirges, and even the ranting is kept to a minimum, saved to the end if she thinks we deserve it — thus a hint of "Howl," and thus ten minutes of the Cong-looked-at-Johnny "Memento Mori," with its discordant Stones riffing and reliable lyrical riffery, not quite parody but not the real thing either.

9 **Gung Ho (Arista) 2000** Without accomplishing anything of especial audacity, *Gung Ho* catches Smith in an odd state of transition — halfway between the half-decent highlights which gave *Gone Again* its peculiar charm, and the mantric calm which informed the best of *Easter* and *Wave*. "Lo and Beholden" and "New Party," in particular, are primal mystic body-checking

Smith, imbibing *Gung Ho* with the dynamism as youthful as Smith herself has ever been. And when it peaks, across the dark war-torn Namscape of the 11-minute title track, it's an achievement which she has not aspired to in years.

Selected Compilations and Archive Releases

8 Masters [BOX] (Arista) 1996 A magnificent opportunity crushed. All five of Smith's original albums with period B-sides appended as bonus tracks, plus a sixth...repeating the most radio friendly moments of the others. Pointless, bar the pristine remastering.

Ivan Kral/Eastern Bloc LP

7 Eastern Bloc (Paradox) 1987 Somewhat introspective melody-led rock, punctuated by a dreamy reprise of "Dancing Barefoot."

Ivan Kral/Native LPs

8 Native (Zensor — Germany) 1992 Low-key solo set, Kral is the sole musician on a distinctly European sounding album of moody rock cut in a very minor key.

7 Native (Indigo — Germany) 1993 With a band bringing the harder instincts back into focus, four of its predecessor's stand-out cuts are reprised, along with a driving version of the oldie "Slow Down" and a clutch of others which may, contrarily, have sounded better given the earlier approach.

Further Reading

Patti Smith by Victor Bockris/Roberta Bayley (Simon & Schuster 1999).

TV SMITH

BORN *Tim Smith, 4/5/56 (London, England)*

TV Smith was planning his next move even before he announced the end of the Adverts in November 1979. Retaining only Tim Cross (keyboards) from that band's final line-up and linking with Colin Stoner (born Colin Bentley, ex-Doctors of Madness; bass), another former Advert John Towe (ex-Chelsea, Generation X; drums) and Erik Russell (guitar) as TV Smith's Explorers. The group recorded their first demos in December 1979, just six weeks after the final Adverts show, and made their live debut at the London Marquee on March 13, 1980.

Cross left immediately after that show to rejoin Mike Oldfield's band (from whence he originally came); he was replaced by Mel Wesson, and the Explorers played three more shows through spring 1980 before Towe quit to join ex-Bay City Roller Ian Mitchell's new group, La Rox. Journalist David Sinclair (ex-London Zoo and, alongside Russell,

Blunder) replaced him and after a summer spent rehearsing, the Explorers re-emerged in October with a residency at the Fulham Greyhound.

Their first single, "Tomahawk Cruise" (#105 UK), was released in November through Chiswick's Big Beat subsidiary. An instant Single of the Week in *Sounds*, the record rose to its peak on the UK chart before it was transferred to the parent label and reissued; it did not chart any higher, but its success brought major label interest, and the Explorers signed with Epic's Kaleidoscope imprint.

A well-received single, "The Servant," appeared in April 1981 followed in June by the band's debut album, *Last Words of the Great Explorer*. However, two further singles, "Have Fun" and "The Perfect Life," sank, and a tour with the Undertones ended when the Explorers were asked to leave after just a handful of shows. One final major gig, supporting Iggy Pop in Manchester on July 4, brought a sympathetic review from *Record Mirror* correspondent Stephen Morrissey, before the Explorers broke up during an acrimonious German tour in October — just weeks after their album was given a belated US release.

Smith announced a solo career, and after several false starts, reunited with Cross and guitarist Tim Renwick (ex-David Bowie, Pink Floyd, Al Stewart) in 1983 to record *Channel Five*. Trailed by the "War Fever" single in June, the

Courtesy of Dave Thompson

album was withdrawn after just two months when the record company, Expulsion, folded. Under the name Party Line, Smith played a handful of London gigs through the remainder of the year, backed by Cross, Renwick, and Martin Noakes (keyboards) before adding future Fairground Attraction bassist Simon Edwards, Ginnie Clee (backing vocals), and Chris Wyles (drums) and forming a new band, 1984's short-lived TV Smith's High.

Over the next two years, Smith concentrated on writing, contributing the anthemic "The Lord's Prayer" to the Lords of the New Church (Smith and guitarist Brian James had discussed forming a band together in 1979), and self-releasing the "Coming Round" single, again recorded with Cross. In 1988, however, he formed a new band, Cheap, with Mik Heslin (guitar), Andy Bennie (ex-Last Touch, bass), and Simon Budd (drums), and began a relentless gigging schedule. Replacing Budd with Martin Deniz, Cheap recorded an epochal John Peel session in early 1988, before releasing a single, "Third Term," in April 1990. An album was recorded, but the band broke up before its release. It eventually appeared as *RIP! Everything Must Go* in 1991, by which time Smith had reinvented himself as a predominantly acoustic solo artist — a notion suggested to him by poet Attila the Stockbroker.

In 1991, Smith linked with German punks Die Toten Hosen to record a new version of The Adverts "Gary Gilmore's Eyes" for their *Learning English* album; the following year, his sophomore solo album, *March of the Giants* was released. Featuring Cross, Renwick, and Edwards, plus contributions from Clee and Deniz, the album was accompanied by the radio hit "Lion and the Lamb."

Smith hit the road with the similarly acoustic-based Tom Robinson, igniting a partnership which would prevail across both Smith's next album, 1995's *The Immortal Rich* (accompanied by the "We Want the Road" single), and Robinson's *Love over Rage*; the pair also began reaching into Smith's back catalog to reinvent old Adverts numbers acoustically — the first time Smith had touched those songs since 1979. 1995's *Thin Green Line* EP, credited jointly to Smith and Robinson, included a live version of "Gary Gilmore's Eyes," and the following year, Smith would perform the band's entire first album on acoustic guitar at the Holidays in the Sun punk festival in Blackpool. His refusal to take the easy option and simply put together a "punk" band for the occasion elevated him far above the other talent on display, and he emerged one of the very few heroes of a nostalgia-drenched weekend, and one of the few whose performance retained all the abrasive energy which characterized punk in the first place.

Now gigging regularly across Britain and Europe, as well as supervising the CD debut of much of his back catalog

through the Anagram, Essential, and Ozit labels, Smith linked again with Die Toten Hosen for a string of continental live shows and to co-write a dozen songs released across the German 1998 *Soul Therapy* EP, the following year's *Crash Landing* and 1999's chart-topping *Unsterblich*. Another collaboration would see him link with Finnish punk band Punk Lurex OK for an EP in 2000, combining two new songs with Adverts classics "One Chord Wonders" and "Gary Gilmore's Eyes."

Smith's own *Generation Y* album would be released through Die Toten Hosen's own JKP label in 1999, before he reconvened the *Channel 5* team to begin work on its successor. 2000 also saw Smith again extensively touring Europe and the UK; he also appeared at the Ian Dury tribute concert in June.

Also see the entry for "ADVERTS" on page 146.

TV Smith LPs

🮲 Channel Five (Expulsion) 1982 A tricky, twisted, nasty piece of work, embedded in ruthless percussion and tortured guitar sounds over which Smith unveiled his most apocalyptic lyrical visions yet — burning rain and beautiful bombs, necrophiliac lovers and disembodied stalkers, a man possessed by a suit of clothes and a more than credible stab at dub, delivered on a creaking door. Sparse instrumentation is remedied by a deep, dark production.

🮲 March of the Giants (Cooking Vinyl) 1991 Predominantly acoustic, but full-blooded regardless, *March* not only retains the raw shock of Smith's past, it enlarges and colors it. Sometimes (the title track, "Atlantic Tunnel" and "Free World") the effect is comforting, but still it skates by on such finely wrought blades that you're usually two songs further along before you suddenly do a double-take. What was that he just said? And more importantly, what did it mean?

🮲 Immortal Rich (2.13.61) 1995 Smith perfects the art of the acoustic vandal, although a wider taste in instrumentation broadens his broadsides considerably. Never preaching, avoiding polemic, his gleefully leprous lyrics lick the doorknobs in the corridors of power.

🮲 Generation Y (JKP — Germany) 1999 Smith usually sings for the underdog. Now he's singing for the dogs under them, and the view is his harshest yet. "Expensive Being Poor," "Momentous Changes," and "Happy Homeland" set the scene, although "I Know What You Want" is the key to the album, as he instructs himself to "stop depressing us and give us a specimen grin" and then rattles off his reasons to be cheerful. Hurrah, another multi-level parking garage.

TV Smith's Explorers LP

🮲 Last Words of the Great Explorer (Epic) 1981 A smorgasbord of solos, synths, and tempo changes, *Last Words* bristles with hooks, but it's a symphonic album as well, broad and sweeping in both vision and execution, and topped by some moments of devastating ambition. The title track, the bass-heavy "Unwelcome Guest" and the synth-led "Imagination" are the undisputed epics, but the shorter, sharp pop of "Have Fun," "Perfect Life," and "Servant" also remain both impressive and incredibly foresighted.

TV Smith's Cheap LP

🮸 **Rip: Everything Must Go (Humbug) 1991** Restoring the notion of melody to punk's frenzy-whipped rebirth, *RIP* is borne along by a thunderous rhythm section, while guitarist Heslin alternates between playing his brains out and kicking them around the floor. Smith then achieves the geometrically impossible and half sings, half spits, and half roars. Passion with a purpose.

SMITHS

FORMED *1982 (Manchester, England)*
ORIGINAL LINE-UP *Morrissey (b. Stephen Patrick Morrissey, 5/22/59, Davyhulme, Manchester — vocals); Johnny Marr (b. Johnny Maher, 10/31/63, Ardwick, Manchester — guitar); Andy Rourke (b. 1963, Manchester — bass); Mike Joyce (b. 6/1/63, Manchester — drums)*

Morrissey was already a cult author when the Smiths began, having published biographies of the New York Dolls and James Dean through the local Babylon Books imprint; he had also been contributing — to both the readers column and the reviews section — to various music magazines since 1977, when the *New Musical Express* published his defense of the Sex Pistols on the letters page.

Johnny Marr, through this same period, was a member of White Mice, a band which reached the finals of a talent contest run jointly by the *NME* and Elvis Costello's F-Beat label; when that band split, he formed Freaky Party with Andy Rourke before linking with Morrissey and first, Simon Wolstencroft (of the Fall, Colour Field, and the Patrol), then Joyce in The Smiths.

The band gigged around Manchester through the remainder of 1982, signing for a one-off single with Rough Trade following a show at the Manchester Hacienda in February 1983. That single, "Hand in Glove" (#3 UK indy), was released three months later as the band made their debut on the John Peel Show. It would remain on the indy chart for the next 59 weeks.

In July 1983, the Smiths signed a long-term deal with Rough Trade and in August received their first taste of tabloid publicity when they recorded "Reel Around the Fountain" for a session for BBC DJ David Jensen. According to *The Sun* newspaper, the song contained clear reference to paedophilia; it was immediately deleted from the session

broadcast (three other songs would be aired), while Rough Trade cancelled plans for the song to become The Smiths next single, replacing it with a new song, "This Charming Man" (#25 UK, #1 UK indy). Released in November 1983 and backed by a captivating string of flower-strewn TV appearances, the single would dominate the indy charts for the next 66 weeks, seven of them at the top.

The band's eponymous debut album (#150 US, #2 UK), featuring guest appearances from keyboard players Paul Carrack (ex-Ace, Nick Lowe) and Mick "Blue" Weaver (Lou Reed, Mott the Hoople) followed in February 1984. "What Difference Does It Make" (#12 UK) hit soon after, as The Smiths embarked upon their first UK tour.

Another taste of tabloid rage attended "Heaven Knows I'm Miserable Now" (#10 UK), The Smiths fourth single. The B-side, "Suffer Little Children," was inspired by the Moors Murderers case which horrified Britain in the early 1960's, and had been lurking on the fringe of shock-rock culture ever since. In 1978, Malcolm McLaren had placed Chrissie Hynde, Steve Strange, and future Psychedelic Furs drummer Vince Ely in a band called the Moors Murderers, only to drop it when the mother of one of the victims got wind of the scheme. Now a relative of another victim heard "Suffer Little Children," and within days the Smiths were at the center of a media storm unseen since the days of the Sex Pistols.

Two major high street retailers banned both the single and the album, and with the tabloid press in full cry, it took the intervention of Ann West — ironically, the woman who halted McLaren's earlier project — to salvage the situation, acknowledging that The Smiths intentions were to honor the dead, not glorify the killers, and persuading Morrissey and Marr, as co-writers, to donate a portion of their royalties to a children's charity.

Happier headlines arose from the band's next project, recording a single with '60s hit-maker, Sandy Shaw. In April 1984, her version of "Hand in Glove" (#27 UK) became Shaw's first hit since 1969, attended the following month by the Smiths' "William, It Was Really Nothing" (#17 UK).

Tours of Europe, Ireland, and the UK, and a show-stopping appearance at the 1984 CND festival led up to the Smiths' return to the studio. With their sophomore album not expected until mid-1985, Rough Trade rushed out a pre-Christmas collectors-only album comprising radio sessions and non-album singles and B-sides, *A Hatful of Hollow* (#7 UK). Predicting a marketing ploy which would benefit both Nirvana and Smashing Pumpkins a decade later, the album did relieve some of the pressure on the band, climbing the chart and spawning a single in the new year, an alternate take of "How Soon Is Now?" (#24 UK), originally the B-side to "William…" and already top of DJ John Peel's best of 1984 Festive 50 poll.

"Shakespeare's Sister" (#26 UK) prefaced February's *Meat Is Murder* (#110 US, #1 UK) album, proving that The Smiths were unquestionably the biggest "indy" band in the land. Beginning with "This Charming Man," they would score an unprecedented 14 successive No. 1s on the alternative chart — even as subsequent releases "That Joke Isn't Funny Anymore" (#49 UK), "The Boy with a Thorn in His Side" (#23 UK), and "Bigmouth Strikes Again" (#26 UK), struggled to make the national Top 30, a consequence, Morrissey insisted, of the BBC's refusal to play Smiths records ever since he criticized the annual BRITS awards.

However, the success of *The Queen Is Dead* (#70 US, #2 UK) in May 1986 and a new single, "Panic" (#11 UK), punctured all Morrissey's conspiracy theories — and that despite the latter's rousingly heartfelt chorus of "hang the DJ" scarcely being guaranteed to appeal to that particular breed. A British tour in spring 1986 was followed by the band's first full American outing, with Craig Gannon (ex-Terry Hall's Colour Field) on second guitar. He had originally been recruited to replace Rourke, however, the bassist was arrested for drug possession the following week and his bandmates reinstated him as a show of support. In the event, Gannon would remain with The Smiths for just eight months, and record one single ("Ask," #14 UK), before quitting, embarking instead on a five-year legal battle over disputed earnings.

1987 began with "Shoplifters of the World Unite" (#12 UK) and the band's second compilation, another round-up of non-album 45's, *The World Won't Listen* (#2 UK). Two months later, a superior US-only collection, *Louder than Bombs* (#62 US, #38 UK), gave the band their first American hit and sold in such quantities on import to the UK that it actually hit there as well.

In April 1987 Rough Trade released what would become the last single to be actively promoted by The Smiths, "Sheila, Take a Bow" (#10 UK). The band had, unbeknownst to anyone, already played their final show, at Italy's San Remo festival on February 7; on April 23, a performance on *Top of the Pops* would be their last TV appearance. Sessions for their new album were in absolute disarray; and when Morrissey called the band to the studio to record some possible B-sides, including a cover of Cilla Black's "Work Is a Four Letter word," Marr exploded. He didn't form a band, he announced, "just to play Cilla Black covers." The moment the sessions were complete, Marr boarded a plane for L.A. A single, "Girlfriend in a Coma," (#13 UK) followed in July; six weeks later, with *Strangeways, Here We Come* (#55 US, #2 UK) finally poised for release, it was announced that The Smiths had indeed broken up. Morrissey immediately launched a solo career, picking up the EMI contract which

The Smiths had signed shortly before their demise; the remainder of the band moved into session work, with Joyce and Rourke reuniting with Morrissey in late 1988 for the "Last of the International Playboys" and "Interesting Drug" singles — at the same time as two further singles, "I Started Something I Couldn't Finish" (#23 UK) and "Last Night I Dreamed That Somebody Loved Me" (#30 UK), and a live album, *Rank* (#77 US, #2 UK), kept the Smiths own name on the chart. The pair went on to work with Sinead O'Connor; Rourke subsequently recorded with The Pretenders; Joyce with The Buzzcocks, Public Image Limited, Julian Cope, and the nascent London Suede.

Marr, meanwhile, would work with Talking Heads, Kirsty MacColl, and The The, before convening the Manchester supergroup Electronic with Bernard Sumner (New Order) and Neil Tennant (Pet Shop Boys). He would also record with Bryan Ferry. The co-written title track to the resultant *The Right Stuff* album utilizes The Smiths instrumental "Money Changes Everything" (from *The World Won't Listen*) as its backing track.

Marr would also find himself involved again with Morrissey, when a protracted legal battle launched by Rourke and Joyce, again over past earnings, ended in defeat for the songwriters in 1996. According to a *New Musical Express* report, following Morrissey's final appeal in May 1999, the singer now faced "a pay out of millions to Joyce, Rourke having already settled for a one-off payment."

The band's story, meanwhile, would be told in Johnny Rogan's controversial *A Severed Alliance* biography, a distinctly weighted tome whose author, Morrissey hoped, would "end his days very soon in a [highway] pile-up."

Also see the entry for "MORRISSEY" on page 506.

The Smiths LPs

9 The Smiths (Sire) 1984 With Marr's guitar keeping things impossibly earthy, leaving Morrissey to spin off on deliciously anguished tangents, the combined styles defined a sound which would prevail through the rest of the decade. Here, Morrissey packs a ragged, devil-may-care delivery that renders each and every song utterly charming, from the sprightly "Hand in Glove" and the laconic "What Difference Does It Make" to "Still Ill" and, on the US issue, "This Charming Man." The Smiths would never sound so good again.

7 Meat Is Murder (Sire) 1985 This eagerly awaited follow-up lacked some of the exuberance of the first — and was almost certainly hurt by its proximity to *Hatful of Hollow*. But aside from the title track, with its overly self indulgent message (good only if you're 15 and take it literally), *Murder* does have high points in "Barbarism Begins at Home" and "That Joke Isn't Funny Anymore." Enhanced in the US by the addition of the cult/club favorite "How Soon Is Now?".

7 The Queen Is Dead (Sire) 1986 More knowing posturing by Morrissey over much of this record, as the band emerge as super tight, energetic, and fully fleshed out. "There Is a Light That Never Goes Out" is remarkable and although "Bigmouth Strikes Again" and "Some Girls Are Bigger than Others" are both throwaways, they remain amusingly true nonetheless.

5 Strangeways Here We Come (Sire) 1987 The album falters on all levels as the band itself was gasping their last breath — and the songs suffer for it. Morrissey is doing his own thing, seeming to leave the band somewhere else entirely. The melancholy has worn out it's welcome.

5 Rank [LIVE] (Sire) 1988 Could-have-been-better live show from 1986; heavy, obviously, on *Queen Is Dead*-era material.

Selected Compilations and Archive Releases

9 Hatful of Hollow (Sire) 1984 An amazing compilation, especially as it was only the band's second release. Full to brimful of the band's singles plus stellar BBC performances.

8 The World Won't Listen (Rough Trade) 1987 Compilation gathering singles, B-sides, and oddities plus the otherwise unreleased, "You Just Haven't Earned It Yet, Baby."

8 Louder than Bombs (Sire) 1987 The idiot's guide to The Smiths, following up the seminal *Hatful* with the remainder of the band's oft-aired, but never tiresome, BBC spots.

8 The Best, Vol. 1 (Sire) 1992

8 The Best, Vol. 2 (Sire) 1992

7 Singles (Reprise) 1995 18 tracks, all the singles in chronological UK order. The last one was called "There's a Light That Never Goes Out." It's the one in the vault where they keep The Smiths mastertapes.

Further Reading

Severed Alliance by Johnny Rogan (Omnibus, UK, 1992).

SOCIAL DISTORTION

FORMED 1978 *(Fullerton, CA)*
ORIGINAL LINE-UP *Mike Ness (vocals, guitar); Rikk Agnew (guitar); Frank Agnew (bass); Casey Royer (drums)*

Formed in the fiery first blast of L.A.'s punk scene of the late 1970s, Social Distortion nevertheless divorced themselves from the remainder of the pack very early on, by pursuing the distinctly individualistic style which, by 1981, already saw critics comparing them to an adrenalized Rolling Stones circa *Let It Bleed*.

By that time, the group had already changed beyond recognition — the first of a myriad of line-up changes occurring when all three of Mike Ness' co-founders quit to become the Adolescents in 1979. One of Ness' old schoolfriends, Dennis Danell (bass, later guitar), would be the longest serving

member during these earliest years, a period which also saw Social Distortion release the "Mainline" single on Posh Boy and contribute tracks to a variety of local compilations — *Rodney on the ROQ Vol. 2*, *The Future Looks Bright*, and the seminal *Hell Comes to Your House* collections in 1981 all featured Social Distortion tracks, many of which would be scooped up for the Posh Boy compilation, *Posh Boy EPs Volume One*, in 1981.

The following year, when the band was featured in the punk documentary *Another State of Mind*, the line-up had settled down to include a rhythm section of Brent Liles (bass) and Derek O'Brien (drums). Signing to 13th Floor, this team recorded Social Distortion's second album, 1983's *Mommy's Little Monster*, a set whose success was assured after the band shot an MTV-friendly video for the track "Another State of Mind."

Social Distortion found themselves something of a cause celebre through much of 1983 and 1984. Bad Religion, then taking their first steps out of the locale, would play a few gigs with them at this time, and believed that simply getting onto the bill was an accomplishment. Social Distortion's attempts to record a follow-up album, however, seemed doomed, thwarted by Ness' increasing drug dependency.

A new single, featuring remakes of the earlier cuts "1945" and "Playpen" and a raw version of the Stones' "Under My Thumb," appeared during 1985, but it would be 1988 before Ness recovered sufficiently to relaunch Social Distortion in earnest, recording the *Prison Bound* album with the ever-loyal Danell, John Maurer (bass), and Chris Reece (drums).

Two years later, with excitement again building around the band, the half million-selling *Social Distortion* (#128 US) saw the band shift to major label Epic and score college hits with a cover of Johnny Cash's "Ring of Fire" and their own "Ball and Chain." Other singles, "Let It Be Me" and the half-live *Story of My Life* EP, kept the band's profile high.

A tour with Neil Young brought the band massive exposure; 1992's *Somewhere Between Heaven and Hell* (#76 US) then followed through with the near-hit "Bad Luck," an MTV Buzz Bin favorite for 12 weeks. Follow-ups "Cold Feelings," "When She Begins," and "Born to Lose" were less successful, but still a well-received opening slot on the latest Ramones tour added to the urgency surrounding the band.

The departure of Reece did not shake the band's equilibrium; he was replaced by Chuck Biscuits, and 1996 saw the release of *White Light White Heat White Trash*, the band's most successful album yet, aided by the "I Was Wrong" and "When the Angels Sing" singles, and a 171-date world tour which played to 600,000 people in 13 countries.

They returned home, setting up three nights at the Roxy in April 1998 to be recorded for the band's first live album, *Live at the Roxy* (#121 US). The album took Social Distortion to their manager's own Time Bomb label; the same label would also release Ness' first solo album in 1999, a collection drawn largely from songs written around, but unsuitable for, Social Distortion.

The accompanying tour featured a backing band of Chris Lawrence (guitar, pedal steel), Sean Greaves (guitar), Brent Harding (bass), and Charlie Quintana (drums), a versatile unit which allowed the swift gestation of a second album, *Under the Influences* (#174 US), comprising many of the covers Ness slipped into his live set. "Before I ever heard the Sex Pistols, I was listening to Johnny Cash," Ness explained.

While he completed that, Maurer helped out with the Swingin' Utters' new album. Maurer also formed his own label, Slip, debuting it with psychobilly band, Hellbound Hayride's *Sinner*, and Huntington Beach's *Anyone*. Social Distortion's own immediate future was thrown into further doubt by the 2/29/00 death from a brain aneurysm of Danell.

Social Distortion LPs

8 **Mommy's Little Monster (13th Floor) 1983** Breaking the California hardcore mold somewhat, a strongly melodic blast equally informed by a rockabilly twang and a country Clash.

8 **Prison Bound (Sticky Fingers/Restless) 1988** The presence of the Rolling Stones' "Backstreet Girl" suggests something more than last time — excising a lot of the more fiery punk, *Prison Bound* hints at the darker country stylings which Uncle Tupelo would make their own.

8 **Social Distortion (Epic) 1990** Leaving the country behind again, Social D. trade their twang for riffs ripped by the roots of rock, a revival of the rockabilly flair powering through eleven high octane, anthemic tracks — which doesn't flinch even in the face of Johnny Cash's "Ring of Fire."

9 **Somewhere Between Heaven and Hell (Epic) 1991** With "Bad Luck" and "Cold Feelings" as dynamic foundations, a full-blooded return to the flair of *Mommy's Little Monster* — only this time they know what they're doing.

7 **White Light, White Heat, White Trash (550 Music/Epic) 1996**

8 **Live at the Roxy [LIVE] (Time Bomb) 1998**

Selected Compilations and Archive Releases

8 **Mainliner (Wreckage of the Past) (Time Bomb) 1995** Much needed round-up of early singles, compilation cuts, etc.

Mike Ness LPs

7 **Cheating at Solitaire (Time Bomb) 1999**

9 **Under the Influence (Time Bomb) 1999** Rockabilly swampa-punky, barrelling down the highway at 200 mph, the wind in your hair and the sun in your shades, relaxing through a bucketful of covers, there's not a wasted moment or a downbeat blip, just non-stop adrenalin until the laser falls off the edge of the disc, and you

have to play the whole thing again. Hank Williams, Bill Anderson, Marty Robbins, Carl Perkins, and Charlie McCoy rub shoulders with one mighty Mike original, and the whole thing sounds like the Pogues if they'd come out of Little Rock, rather than Limerick. If only all of America sounded like this.

SOFT BOYS

FORMED 1976 *(Cambridge, England)*
ORIGINAL LINE-UP *Robyn Hitchcock (b. 3/3/53, East Grinstead, Sussex — vocals, guitar); Alan Davis (guitar); Andy Metcalfe (bass); Morris Windsor (drums)*

Robyn Hitchcock was attending university in Cambridge in the early 1970's when he joined his first bands. None amounted to anything, although Hitchcock does remember making a few rough cassette recordings, "crossword clues set to music by Noel Coward. I don't think the songs were particularly good. They were fun at the time, but they're kind of hippy street theater folk club songs for the mid-1970s, and some of them are mine, some of them are joint compositions. I think the first listenable stuff I did was with the Soft Boys."

By the mid-1970's, Hitchcock was leading Dennis and the Experts, and with a permanent line-up coalescing around Alan Davis, Andy Metcalfe, and Morris Windsor, the band became the Soft Boys in 1976, punk's Year Zero.

Their musical hearts, however, were elsewhere, in the collections of Byrds, Beatles, and Syd Barrett records which all four had forgotten to throw away — a yearning which Raw Records discovered when they signed the band in early 1977. An EP released that spring, *Give It to the Soft Boys*, was an uncompromising and seemingly unrehearsed slab of exuberant thrashing, characterized not only by Hitchcock's already surreal lyricism (which was deliberate), but also by the band's equally unconventional accompaniment (which wasn't).

It would be another year before the Soft Boys — with Kimberley Rew having replaced Davis — again saw the inside of a recording studio, when they signed to the newly formed Radar label. Already an eclectic gathering of new talent and old, Radar seemed the perfect home for the band, particularly now that a year of almost solid gigging had ironed out most of their rougher musical edges. But the label's enthusiasm was grossly misplaced. According to Hitchcock, "Radar spent a lot of money and time trying to get us to sound right. We were very loud on stage, and it didn't really work in the studio [because] it was a very unstable outfit. I think we thrived off each others' bad vibes. We co-existed by trying to drown each other out."

Radar salvaged one single, "(I Want to Be An) Anglepoise Lamp," then dropped the group. They returned to the live circuit (1983's *Live at the Portland Arms* album dates from this period) and concentrated upon honing Hitchcock's increasingly idiosyncratic songs interspersed with a growing chain of gratuitously mutilated covers.

But they were also cultivating an audience, one which seemingly relied upon the Soft Boys for a slice of lyrical light relief at a time when elsewhere, the music scene was darkening daily. What better antidote to the mass catharsis of Joy Division than a grinning Hitchcock extolling the virtue of his favorite fruit — "I Like Bananas Because They Have No Bones."

Late 1979 saw the Soft Boys finally abandon their dream of being signed to somebody else's record label, and forming their own. 2 Crabs released the group's debut album, *A Can of Bees*, and with sales booming through mail order and gigs alone, early in the new year, it was reissued by the Aura label.

Metcalfe quit in 1980; he was replaced by former SW9 guitarist Matthew Seligman and the band released their definitive vision, the *Near the Soft Boys* EP (#23 UK indy). Comprising two Hitchcock originals, plus a version of Syd Barrett's "Vegetable Man," the EP was the cue for the trend-hungry UK music press to pinpoint what they hoped would become the Next Big Thing — a psychedelic revival.

Unfortunately, the press seemed to be the only people who did hope that. Released on latter-day Henry Rollins/Richard Butler manager Richard Bishop's Armageddon label, neither *Near the Soft Boys* nor the band's second album, *Underwater Moonlight* (#16 UK indy), took off. A new single, "I Want to Destroy You" (#39 UK indy) foundered, and over the next year, the Soft Boys essentially disintegrated — even if the musicians themselves did not exactly part company.

Hitchcock's first solo album would be co-produced by Matthew Seligman, and feature contributions from both Kimberley Rew and Morris Windsor; Rew would then join Katrina and the Waves, the band scoring a major hit with 1985's "Walking on Sunshine" and, 13 years later, winning the annual Eurovision Song Contest. Hitchcock and Rew reunited again later in the decade and, in late 2000, began rehearsing a full-blown Soft Boys reunion.

Also see the entry for "ROBYN HITCHCOCK" on page 414.

Soft Boys LPs

5 A Can of Bees (2 Crabs — UK) 1979 Passable power-pop dominates and it's clear that this band is still suffering birth pangs — the good songs are wonderful and the others...well, they're not quite as good. Hitchcock still hasn't gotten a handle on the Hitchcockiness that would render his songs super great or super grating.

6 A Can of Bees (Aura — UK) 1980 A reissue of the first album, but adding additional tracks including "Anglepoise Lamp."

8 Underwater Moonlight (Armageddon — UK) 1980 Draws all those embryonic urges together in a stellar set full of fat riffs and subtle quirk. Powered by the relentless "I Wanna Destroy You," *Moonlight*'s staccato drive is punctuated by "Insanely Jealous," the title track, and "Queen of Eyes."

Selected Compilations and Archive Releases

6 Only the Stones Remain (Armageddon) 1981 Mixed compilation of B-sides and oddities.

5 Two Halves for the Price of One (Armageddon — UK) 1982 A little live, a little studio — two very different sides.

6 Invisible Hits (Midnight Music — UK) 1983 A compilation of material recorded in 1978 and 1979.

6 Live at Portland Arms (Midnight Music — UK) 1983

6 Wading Through a Ventilator (Delaurean — UK) 1985

8 1976–81 (Rykodisc) 1993

SOFT CELL

FORMED 1980 (Leeds, England)
ORIGINAL LINE-UP Marc Almond (b. Peter Marc Almond, 7/9/59, Southport, England — vocals); Dave Ball (b. 5/3/59, Blackpool, England — keyboards)

The most innovative of all the so-called new romantic bands which erupted out of Britain during the early 1980's, Soft Cell represented the union of a self-confessed "horrible little boy with a lurid imagination" (Marc Almond) and the electronic maven (Dave Ball) who shared his unlikely dream of crossing Northern Soul with Can.

The duo's first performances were multimedia extravaganzas, staged to little more than local recognition during 1980. An appearance low on the bill at the Futurama festival in September drew a dismissive "an electronic band I think, although it might have been a loud buzz in the PA," from the *NME*, but while the best known song in Soft Cell's early set was Black Sabbath's "Paranoid," the group's own material was improving all the time. Towards the end of the year, Soft Cell recorded their first demos — a five-track session from which was culled the four-song *Mutant Moments* EP. The remaining cut, "Girl with the Patent Leather Face," was contributed to an electronic compilation being put together by the fledgling Some Bizzare label. Signing to that label in early 1981, Soft Cell then released the "Memorabilia" 12", a claustrophobic dance mutant whose theme, the joys of vacationing abroad, was utterly belied by the menacing instrumentation and Almond's pervertedly salacious vocals.

Described by journalist Chris Bohn as "Suicide made painless," Soft Cell continued eking out their dark vision with a medley of Ed Cobb's "Tainted Love" (#8 US, #1 UK) and the Supremes' "Where Did Our Love Go?" It was a brilliant record, but its progress was slow — for two months the single scratched at the UK chart before finally coming to rest at the top; in the US, it took four months to reach the Top 10.

Having arrived there, however, both it and Soft Cell seemed destined to stick around. "Bedsitter" (#4 UK) and "Say Hello Wave Goodbye" (#3 UK) ensured Soft Cell remained an odd, but inescapable, addition to the UK pop circus — just how odd was revealed by *Non Stop Erotic Cabaret* (#22 US, #5 UK), an anxiety-whipped adolescent's sleaze-ridden journey through the underbelly of London's red light district.

"Sex Dwarf," possibly the funniest comment on perversion ever committed to vinyl, was singled out for particular attention with the song's title drawn from a tabloid headline ("Sex dwarf leads 100 disco dollies to a life of vice"), it was accompanied by a video so explicit that it has still to be shown — if it even exists.

Introducing their New York drug dealer Cindy Ecstasy to the line-up, Soft Cell maintained their strangle hold on the Top 30 through singles "Torch" (#2 UK), "What?" (#3 UK), and "Where the Heart Is" (#21 UK) and the *Non Stop Ecstatic Dancing* remix EP (#57 US, #6 UK), at the same time as permitting their more adventurous notions to surface on B-sides and 12" mixes. The two sides collided, however, on the brooding hit "Numbers" (#25 UK), followed by Soft Cell's second album, *The Art of Falling Apart* (#84 US, #5 UK), an autobiographically titled set which simultaneously sent Almond alone spiralling away on his Marc and the Mambas sideline.

That band's two albums — the second subsequently described by Almond as "the sound of someone having a nervous breakdown on record" — highlighted his personal fascination with Jacques Brel, Peter Hammill, and flamenco music (among other things), linking him, too, with Siouxie and the Banshees Steve Severin and Foetus founder Jim Thirlwell. Almond further cemented his underground credentials through this period by guesting with Coil and Psychic TV and forming the Immaculate Consumptives Non Stop Revue with Nick Cave, Lydia Lunch, and Foetus.

The third Soft Cell album, *This Last Night in Sodom* (#12 UK), reflected these interests, albeit through the soft guaze of the band's (surprisingly) still intact reputation for pop music. Singles "Down in the Subway" (#24 UK) and "Soul Inside" (#16 UK) accompanied the album, but the band's demise was not far away. Soft Cell bowed out with two shows in London in January 1984.

Almond went solo; Ball's activities included work with Cabaret Voltaire and Stephen Mallinder's shortlived Love Street. He also cut a solo album, before pairing with Richard Norris as the techno duo, Grid. Ball and Almond, meanwhile, have reunited on a number of occasions since Soft Cell broke up, Ball co-writing and/or producing several of Almond's solo projects. The pair also wrote a full Soft Cell album in 1998, but scrapped it; according to Almond, "some of them we thought, these are great songs, and they were, but they'd have been really great in 1986, they would have been a great Soft Cell album in 1986, or... this is a great song, it sounds a little like 'Say Hello Wave Goodbye'...oooer."

Also see the entries for "MARC ALMOND" on page 153 and "IMMACULATE CONSUMPTIVES" on page 425.

Soft Cell LPs

⑧ Non-Stop Erotic Cabaret (Sire) 1981 The sordid sexual undertow and Almond's lascivious leering delivery knowingly subvert Soft Cell's position as squeaky pop hit-makers — and rightfully so. Indeed, alongside the sleazy "Seedy Films," the despairing "Youth," and of course, the mighty "Sex Dwarf," even "Tainted Love" sounds somehow...tainted.

⑦ Non-Stop Ecstatic Dancing (Sire) 1982 Club friendly reworkings of hits, B-sides, and "Sex Dwarf."

⑨ The Art of Falling Apart (Sire) 1983 Indeed. Half the album is divided equally between makeweight ditties ("Where the Heart Is," "Loving You Hating Me") and suburban secrets ("Forever the Same," "Kitchen Sink Drama"); the remainder is given over to a weighty examination not only of what fame portends, but also its consequences: the sexed-out jade of "Heat" and "Numbers," the ennui depravity of "Baby Doll," and finally, the title track, armageddon in a carry-on bag, an autobiographical catalog of chilling public disintegration — "my friends say I'm dying, but I do it so well." Originally appended as a bonus 12" single, a synthesized Hendrix medley proves that guitars aren't the only things that can riff in rock, while "Martin" is a preposterously overblown, but immensely entertaining, take on the horror film of the same name.

⑥ This Last Night in Sodom (Sire) 1984 Post-Marc's Mambas' excursions; a weak...exhausted...album barely bothers getting out of bed. But the epic, breathless "Soul Inside" and the labyrinthine squall of "L'Esqualita" are the equal of any past Soft Cell performance and "Where Was Your Heart" has a fierce undercurrent.

Selected Compilations and Archive Releases

⑦ The Singles 1981–1985 (Some Bizzare) 1986 Straightforward hits collection.

⑥ Memorabilia: Singles (Mercury) 1991 Latter-day remixes and Marc Almond solo pad out a reprise of *The Singles*.

⑨ Twelve Inch Singles Collection (Polygram) 1999 Excise the 1991 remixes and the true nature of Soft Cell's tainted love still leaves a salty taste in the mouth, and a faint feeling of dirtied disgust as well. The full-length "Numbers" had no business playing with the pop kids and the sublime "Say Hello" opens with a clarinet solo and has a very odd way of waving goodbye. Elsewhere, ten minutes of "Soul Inside" make prog-metal drum solos sound restrained, while a barrage of extended B-sides opens fresh doors into a very damaged notion of life, love, and loneliness.

Dave Ball LPs

❼ In Strict Tempo (Some Bizzare) 1983 Almond was the vocalist, Ball was the musician. Any questions?

SONIC YOUTH

FORMED *1981 (New York, NY)*

ORIGINAL LINE-UP *Thurston Moore (b. 7/25/58 — guitar, vocals); Kim Gordon (b. 4/23/53 — bass, vocals); Ann DeMarinis (keyboards); Richard Edson (drums); Lee Ranaldo (b. 2/3/56 — guitar, vocals)*

A battered combination of punk, hardcore, no wave, pure noise, and feedback, Sonic Youth built their career by pushing every musical boundary beyond its breaking point to a place where new sound erupted, widening the definition of what alternative sound could become.

One of the earliest and most influential progenitors of the hardcore/no wave scene, Sonic Youth's music created the blueprint for numerous bands to follow. The band, who took their name from two major musical hitters, MC5's Fred "Sonic" Smith and Reggae band Big Youth, consecrated their birth at the "Noise Festival," an avant garde music showcase co-founded by Kim Gordon to highlight bands from New York's East End scene.

Linking with avant garde composer and Neutral Records owner Glen Branca, the band patterned their now famous sound on his forays into feedback and discordant noise — Moore and Ranaldo had performed on Branca's *Symphony No. 3*. The band, meanwhile, would debut on Neutral in 1982, recording the live *Sonic Youth* at Radio City Music Hall in December 1981.

DeMarinis departed, leaving the remaining quartet to hone their sounds, formulate their style, and play gigs with a revolving door of drummers — Jon Sclavunos joined briefly, to be replaced by Bob Bert (ex-Lydia Lunch) in 1984.

1981–1984 were formative years for the band as they released two more albums, *Confusion Is Sex*, and the mini-LP *Kill Yr Idol*, before undertaking their first European tour in 1984. The American indie Ecstatic Peace! released a cassette-only album, *Sonic Death: Sonic Youth Live*, that year (reissued in the UK in 1988, it rose to #9 indy). Sonic Youth were also laying the groundwork for further releases, securing a deal with Blast First in the UK, where they quickly cultivated a very strong following (in common with several other East Coast bands of the era, Sonic Youth actually played Europe before they got to California — they made

© Jim Steinfeldt/Chansley Entertainment

their debut in that state in early 1985, at the Gila Music Festival).

In late 1984, the band teamed up with Lydia Lunch to record "Death Valley 69" (#4 UK indy); the track would also be included on March 1985's *Bad Moon Rising* (#14 UK indy), the band's first and only release for Homestead. It was that album which caught the attention of the indie press, spearheading a Sonic Youth revolution that would quickly break through the confines of the New York scene, as the band began to add elements of pure pop to the wall of grinding guitars that still dominated. Such interest quickly brought major labels sniffing around, although their advances were initially spurned by the band. After releasing two more singles for Homestead, "Halloween" (#4 UK indy) in January 1986 and "Halloween II" in March, Sonic Youth, joined now by drummer Steve Shelley, finally linked with SST, unleashing *Evol* (#2 UK indy) in May with "Star Power" (#4 UK indy) following in July.

Their next album, June 1987's *Sister* (#1 UK indy), would receive even more press and serious critical attention. The album's one single, "Master-Dik" (#3 UK indy), appeared in January 1988 and featured a B-side dedicated to one of the bands they had toured Britain with — "Under the influence of the Jesus and Mary Chain: Ticket to Ride." Sonic Youth were also busy collaborating with Mike Watt (Firehose), creating the Ciccone Youth alter-ego, whose twisted tribute to Madonna, "Into the Groovey," was released in November 1986. The song spread like wildfire, bringing swathes of new fans to the Sonic Youth camp. Nor would Ciccone Youth be forgotten, re-emerging in 1988 for the full-length *Whitey Album* (#63 UK), an experimental art/dance record that would put the band on Britain's national charts for the first time; a second Ciccone Youth single, "Stick Me Donna Magick Momma," followed.

By the October 1988 release of the double *Daydream Nation* (#99 UK, #1 UK indy), Sonic Youth had hit the big time. The album was a smash hit on the US college circuit and cuts were quickly becoming college radio standards. Unfortunately, the album suffered from poor distribution and often slipped in and out of stock at stores, much to the band's dismay.

Further signs that the band's attitude was changing came when a split single with Mudhoney (#2 UK indy) appeared in February 1989. The so-called "Seattle Sound" was already burgeoning across Europe, and Sonic Youth's acceptance as godfathers of the northwest's peculiarly earthy sound was already common knowledge; now, the band decided to turn their "fame" to their own advantage and accept the accolades they had previously ignored. They put together a deal with Geffen and in June 1990 released their major label debut, *Goo* (#96 US, #32 UK), with two singles following —

the MTV favorite "Kool Thing" in September and "Dirty Boots" (#69 UK) in April 1991.

1991 also saw the band join Neil Young's *Ragged Glory* tour — itself a direct repercussion of the grunge explosion. The tour, however, facilitated a crossover of unprecedented proportion, as Young introduced Sonic Youth to his fans with minor success, and Sonic Youth brought Young into the alternative camp. Young suddenly found himself the center of cool in a foreign world.

But all this mainstream action didn't mean that Sonic Youth weren't continuing to collaborate with the underground. In 1988, Gordon teamed up with Lydia Lunch and Sadie Mae for the one-off Harry Crews; three years later, Moore and Shelley joined Richard Hell and producer Don Fleming as the Dim Stars; indeed, 1991 continued at a furious pace, with tours that were punctuated by performances at the UK Reading Festival in August and a second union with Neil Young at the Bridge Tribute concert. The band also scored an unexpected hit with the EP *Dirty Boots* (#69 UK).

In 1992, Sonic Youth teamed with producer Butch Vig (Nirvana) to record *Dirty* (#83 US, #6 UK), released to rave reviews in July 1992 and trailing three singles, "100%" (#28 UK), "Youth Against Fascism" (#52 UK), and "Sugar Kane" (#26 UK). *Dirty* would eventually turn gold, marking a milestone for the band who brought underground music to the mainstream world.

Through 1993 and 1994 the band continued to tour and again teamed with Vig for a follow-up, *Experimental Jet Set, Trash and No Star* (#34 US, #10 UK), released in May 1994. The album's single, "Bull in the Heather" (#24 UK), again hit the charts in Britain; the band also co-ordinated and contributed a track, "Superstar" (#45 UK), to the Carpenters tribute album, *If I Were a Carpenter*.

1995, however, would make the last two years seem like vacation. Gordon formed a fresh side project, Free Kitten, while Moore released his first solo album, *Psychic Hearts*. He also began taking on outside remixes and over the next few years, he would work with artists as disparate as Blur, Yoko Ono, and Can. Sonic Youth themselves then accepted a headlining spot on Lollapalooza 95 and still found time to record and release October's *Washing Machine* (#58 US, #39 UK) and single, "Little Trouble Girl."

The following year would mark the first since 1993 that Sonic Youth didn't have a new album out; however, an appearance on TV's *The Simpsons* and a slot at the Beastie Boys Tibetan Freedom Concert in June were followed by a Reading festival date, and they contributed a whacked "Santa Don't Cop Out on Dope" for *Just Say Noel*, an album whose proceeds would benefit the Witness Program. January 1997 kicked off as the band joined veteran David

Bowie on stage to perform "The Voyeur of Utter Destruction (As Beauty)" and "I'm Afraid of Americans" at his 50th birthday concert at Madison Square Garden. They again participated in the Tibetan Freedom Concert in June, and later in the year Moore and Shelley joined the ad-hoc supergroup Wilde Rattz, to record soundtrack material for the forthcoming *Velvet Goldmine* movie (the Rattz also featured Mike Watt, ex-Stooges Ron Asheton, and Mudhoney's Mark Arm). Sonic Youth turned their attention behind the scenes as well, forming their own imprint SYR (Sonic Youth Records), primarily as a venue for their experimental releases which they didn't want to foist onto the mainstream market place.

The band were also busy preparing a new album, *A Thousand Leaves* (#85 US), released in 1998. The year's tour schedule again included Reading and the first day of the Tibetan Freedom Concert, where disaster awaited as lightning struck the venue, injuring eleven concert-goers. Saturday's performance was subsequently cancelled, although Sonic Youth did squeeze in on Sunday's bill.

June was capped with the band's first appearance at the Glastonbury Festival, to be followed in July by an appearance at John Peel's Meltdown '98 Festival. A single, "Sunday" (#72 UK), hit the charts, preluding another comparative silence, during which the band retired to their own Echo Canyon studio to record a new album for spring 2000 release. *NYC Ghosts and Flowers* was cited as the band's personal homage to their home town.

Sonic Youth LPs

4 Sonic Youth (Neutral) 1981 Embryonic noise, this one is best kept as memory, not reality.

5 Confusion Is Sex (Neutral) 1983 A small, dirty window to what Sonic Youth would become, this album is still headache-inducing and, for the most part, unlistenable. But "Making the Nature Scene" is fine and their cover of Iggy's "I Wanna Be Your Dog" is an enlightening, if not completely pleasurable, experience.

5 Bad Moon Rising (Homestead) 1985 Sonic Youth are gaining ground, clawing experience in and trading it for ragtag sonics — but they're still mighty loud. This album serves as an appetizer for what will come and includes the seminal Lydia Lunch collaboration, "Death Valley 69."

6 EVOL (SST) 1986 Adding Steve Shelly to the mix, *EVOL* is a blistering combination of avant art and heavy rock. The sonics are structured, but the overall effect is still brutal across "Secret Girls," "Expressway to Yr. Skull," and "Shadow of a Doubt." Do we smell just a whiff of mainstream crossover here?

8 Sister (SST) 1987 Better still, Sonic Youth evolve an entire era with this oft-times stunning collection of textured noise. What was once just noise, rumbling, screaming, dissonance, and distortion have become honest songs, complete with structure and

melodic twist. Although "Tuff Gnarl," "Hot Wire My Heart," and on the CD, "Master-Dik," are still difficult going, it's obvious that this band is easier to swallow.

10 Daydream Nation (Torso) 1988 "Teen Age Riot," "Silver Rocket," and "Eric's Trip" sit quivering on top of Sonic Youth's masterpiece. A sonic mountain of song — yes, that's song — which showcases the talents the band have finally brought to bear upon a complex wall of noise.

A masterful blend of art, rock, punk, and menace, *Nation* delivers on every level, from those who stuck with the band from early on to new fans titillated by the band's commercial crossover. Indeed, the closing "Trilogy: The Wonder/Hyperstation/Eliminator Jr," showcases even more than that. You can almost hear the majors come running forward as the final moments shudder to a close.

6 Goo (DGC) 1990 Takes an anti-mainstream music stance and puts it firmly into the commercial market via an album that is in the same vein as *Daydream Nation*. In comparison, however, the overall effect is relatively lackluster as it allows itself to become the very thing it attacks — mainstream. Public Enemy's Chuck D. guests on the MTV favorite "Kool Thing."

7 Dirty (DGC) 1992 Sonic Youth continue to hone their sound, shortening the jams, structuring the songs to punky perfection, stripping away the old — and if "100%" and "Youth Against Fascism" sound too commercial for you, well, Kim Gordon's "Swimsuit Issue" will put you in your place faster than you can say sellout.

5 Experimental Jet Set, Trash and No Star (DGC) 1994 The band seem to have forgotten that they were one with this lackluster set. The acoustic (!) "Winner's Blues" opens the album — and the door — for a foray into mellower music which still feels like it was telephoned in.

8 Washing Machine (DGC) 1995 Still experimenting, but returning to their '80's guitar ethics, an unexpected success. Not worrying about commercialism or the ragged wash of their early albums, Sonic Youth effortlessly blend everything they are into a solid set that is unpretentious, mellowed, and still full of ball-breaking sound.

4 Made in USA (Rhino) 1995 Sonic Youth shove themselves into the structured medium of film scoring.

6 A Thousand Leaves (DGC) 1998 Very mature and surprisingly warm, Sonic Youth retain their essence but add a subtlety that suits them.

7 NYC Ghosts and Flowers (DGC) 2000 New parents Moore and Gordon move to Massachusetts, then get all nostalgic for home.

Ciccone Youth LP

7 The Whitey Album (SST) 1988 A delightfully wicked side project with Mike Watt, reprising the stellar 1986 single "Into the Groovey" (a song that remains the brightest Madonna tribute ever) on an entire album of post modern experimentalism.

Further Reading

Confusion is Next by Alec Foege (St. Martin's Press, 1994).

SOUP DRAGONS

FORMED 1985 *(Bellshill, Lanarkshire)*
ORIGINAL LINE-UP *Sean Dickson (b. 3/21/67 — vocals, guitar);
Jim McCulloch (b. 5/19/66 — guitar); Sushill K Dade
(b. 7/15/66 — bass); Ross Sinclair (drums)*

Taking their name from a character on British children's TV show *The Clangers*, the Soup Dragons had just a few local gigs under their belt when they recorded their first demo album cassette, *You Have Some Too*, and a flexidisc single, "If You Were the Only Girl in the World."

Originally cut in a tight, Buzzcocks-esque punk mould, the group swiftly found favor with the *New Musical Express*, then engineering the so-called C-86 indy band explosion, and they signed to Subway in early 1986. The *Sun in the Sky* EP sold respectably, but it was "Whole Wide World" (#2 UK indy) which broke the band nationwide in June 1986, even as Sean Dickson and Jim McCulloch enjoyed similar success

as part-time members of Duglas Stewart's BMX Bandits (their "Sad" single climbed to #8 on the same chart in May).

Regular heroes at Bobby Gillespie's Splash One Club, the heart of the mid-'80's Glasgow scene, such activity did not go unnoticed in London and by September, the Soup Dragons had signed to Raw TV, the label operated by former Wham! co-manager Jaz Summers. Over the next two years, the band would place five singles in the indy Top 3: "Hang Ten!" (#2), "Head Gone Astray" (#3), "Can't Take No More" (#65 UK, #1 indy), "Soft as Your Face" (#66 UK, #2 indy), and "The Majestic Head?" (#4).

All five, too, traced the band's changing demeanor as they abandoned the breakneck punk of old, and embraced a mood more in common with the burgeoning Madchester sound — albeit one which was still developing in near isolation. In early 1988, the band signed with Sire, releasing their debut album, *This is Our Art* (#60 UK), in April. But a single, "Kingdom Chairs," flopped in 1988 and the band returned to Raw TV for "Backwards Dog" (#5 UK indy) and "Crotch Deep Trash" (#11 UK indy) in late 1989.

Ross Sinclair quit at the end of 1989; he was replaced by Paul Quinn and the band began work on their second album, *Lovegod* (#88 US, #7 UK), prefaced by yet another flop single, "Mother Universe." Constant gigging, however, and the now-endemic popularity of Madchester ensured that the Soup Dragons could not be ignored for long, the breakthrough finally coming when they linked with reggae star Junior Reid for a dynamic, tripped-out version of the Rolling Stones "I'm Free" (#79 US, #5 UK).

Despite widespread press comparisons with Primal Scream — fellow Scots, of course, and therefore an easy mark — American radio and MTV both seized upon both the single and the album. The group toured the US in response, but while a remix of "Mother Universe" (#26 UK) proved an adequate follow-up, there was no further US action, and the band returned to the studio.

In August 1991, a new single, "Electric Blues," flopped, but the following March brought the exquisite "Divine Thing" (#35 US, #53 UK). It proved a firm radio favorite, but the relative failure of the accompanying album, *Hotwired* (#97 US, #74 UK), dealt the band a fatal blow. After one further single, "Pleasure" (#69 US), Quinn quit to join Teenage Fanclub — he later released the superlative *Will I Ever Be Inside of You* album with his Independent Group. Dade followed, initially quitting the music industry, before returning with a new band, Future Pilot AKA; McCulloch and BMX Bandit Joe McAlinden formed Superstar.

Dickson alone continued the Soup Dragons name, recording the *Hydrophonic* album with Mickey Finn (drums, ex-T. Rex), Tina Weymouth (bass, Talking Heads), Bootsy Collins (rap) and Lynval Golding and Neville Staples (vocals, Specials). Released through the revitalized Raw TV label, the album spawned the singles "One Way Street" and "Mother Funker," but did nothing and the Soup Dragons faded away. Dickson resurfaced in 1999 with a new band, High Fidelity, releasing the acclaimed single "2 Up/2 Down."

Soup Dragons LPs

7 This Is Our Art (Sire) 1988

7 Lovegod (Big Life) 1990 Deserting their punky past for house's future, the Soup Dragons leap into the ecstasy-fueled world of dance, but even as the funky beats groove across the grooves, the group can't quite leave history behind...*Love God's* acid-drenched psychedelia swirls around the feet of *Sticky Fingers*-era Stones, whose blues-printed riffs and sinuous slide provide much of *Love God's* inspiration. Still, "Dream-E-Forever" emerges a twangy, gothy hybrid which suggests the Dragon's transformation is still far from complete.

9 Hotwired (Big Life) 1992 Suddenly the Dragons have it all — Stonesy rock riffs, honky tonk leads, samples and clubby beats, lush keyboards and wild harmonica, a hint of funk and a whiff of gospel, together they conjure a heart-stopping ride into the realm of the new psychedelia.

8 Hydrophonic (Phonogram) 1995 With the Dragons reduced to Sean Dickson alone, *Hydrophonic* becomes an excursion into altered realities — weird rap and weirder reggae, country, and even Brit-pop, although the core of the album is big, rootsy, rock riffs augmented by a gospel choir, an updated *Screamadelica*.

SPACE

FORMED *1992 (Liverpool, England)*
ORIGINAL LINE-UP *Tommy Scott (b. 2/18/67, Liverpool — vocals, bass); Jamie Murphy (guitar); Jamie Island (drums)*

Beginning in 1984, Tommy Scott ran through a string of local bands, including the Gary Numan-influenced Porcelain Touch and the largely acoustic Hello Sunset. The latter disbanded after being blown off stage by the rising La's, and Scott and bandmate Frannie Griffiths joined Adrian Crossan (bass, ex-Yeah Yeah Noh) and Jock Whelan (drums, ex-Pale Fountains) as the Australians in 1989.

The Australians made it onto a handful of compilations and recorded several demo tape cassettes for sale at gigs before Griffiths quit to live in Spain. Scott then joined the Substitutes, a Mod band led by Tim Smith (bass) and future Cast drummer Keith O'Neill; Smith quit after just two months in late 1992 and was replaced by Jamie Murphy (ex-Time). O'Neill was next to leave; he was replaced by Jamie Island and with Scott switching to bass to accommodate Murphy's abilities, the newly named Space began gigging around Liverpool.

Former Farm manager Mark Cowley took over the band's affairs in early 1993 and the band began preparing for their first single — by switching drummers. Andy Parle actually made his debut with the band playing on "If It's Real," self-released on the Hug label and clearly indebted to Scott's beloved '60's garage music. It was hearing a Cypress Hill album which turned Space's head musically; matching Hill's style of beats to Scott's already idiosyncratic songs and with Griffiths now back from Spain, and playing keyboards for the band, Space took six months off during 1994, to utterly rework their repertoire.

The band's first demo following their return, "Mr. Psycho," was rejected by record companies as "too weird"; in January 1995, however, Tug picked them up, signing Space to the Home imprint and releasing the "Home"/"Kill Me" single that fall. The band toured with Credit to the Nation and in spring 1996, their third single, "Neighbourhood" (#56 UK), was released on another Tug subsidiary, Gut.

For a moment, it looked as though Space were to have a hit; radio loved the single and sales were climbing. It had just entered the UK chart when the Dunblane school massacre occurred, and "Neighbourhood," with its single line about "Mr. Miller...the serial killer," was deemed too sensitive for a grieving nation. The record was quietly withdrawn and in June, Space released "Female of the Species" (#14 UK) in its stead. "Me and You Versus the World" (#9 UK) followed in August and as the band's debut album, *Spiders* (#5 UK), hit the streets in October, "Neighbourhood" (#11 UK) was reissued, to all the rewards it originally deserved.

January 1997 brought another hit, "Dark Clouds" (#15), but the tireless live work which had consumed the band for the best part of two years was finally taking its toll. A UK tour was cancelled, Parle quit, to be replaced by Leon McCaffrey, and slowly the band began recording again, adding bassist Dave Palmer to allow Scott to concentrate on vocals alone. Still the demand for new material was such that a remix/outtakes collection, *Invasion of the Spiders*, released in Japan earlier in the year and imported in increasing quantities ever since, was given a full UK release in November.

In the event, the next Space single was now just a month away — "Avenging Angels" (#6 UK) became the band's biggest hit yet, to be followed in the new year by "The Ballad of Tom Jones" (#4 UK), a duet between Scott and Cerys Matthews of Catatonia, themselves enjoying their first major hit, with "Mulder and Scully." (The record even appealed to Tom Jones himself. His 1999 *Reload* duets album would feature both Space and Matthews as singing partners.)

Two further space singles, "Begin Again" (#21 UK) and the *Bad Days* EP, featuring a cover of the Animal's "We Gotta Get Out of This Place" (#20), followed the March 1998 release of *Tin Planet*, Space's sophomore album, and the band embarked upon another major tour, including headlining V98 and a visit to China in summer 1999.

Space LPs

🟨 Spiders (Universal) 1996 Musically set in a spaceport lounge in a galaxy far, far away, Spider's sci-fi pop takes its cues from a dizzying array of sources — calypso, James Bond themes, and Burt Bacharach among them — which in turn revolve around an axis of dubby/clubby beats. Witty, sardonic lyrics conjure up twisted tales of unsavory characters — less imaginative critics compared them to the Kinks, but Graham Greene is closer to the mark.

🟨 Tin Planet (GUT — UK) 1998 "The Ballad of Tom Jones" pitched Space with Catatonia's Cerys Matthews, a highpoint which *Tin Planet* rarely recovered from. But "Avenging Angels" and "Begin Again" were close to equals and everything that *Spiders* brought into focus returns with charm and vigor.

Selected Compilations and Archive Releases

🟨 Invasion of the Spiders (Gut UK) 1997 Double CD compiling one disc's worth of remixes (also available in slightly different form as *The Web*); another of worthy B-sides.

SPAHN RANCH

FORMED 1992 *(Los Angeles, CA)*
ORIGINAL LINE-UP *Matt Green (keyboards); Rob Morton (keyboards)*

Matt Green and Rob Morton were based in New York when they first met Executive Slacks vocalist Athanasios Demetrios Maroulis in 1984 at the Danceteria in New York. It would be spring 1993, however, before the trio reunited in Los Angeles as Spahn Ranch, by which time Green and Morton had already released an eponymous EP under that name, with guest vocalist Scott Franklin of Murder in Exile. (Another cut, featuring Green and Morton alone, appeared on *The Whip* compilation in October.)

Maroulis, meanwhile, was working with Philadelphia based Tubalcain, alongside fellow Slacks John Young (keyboards) and Harry Lewis (drums), plus Rob Jordan (guitar) and Stephen Lentz (bass). An album, 25 *Assorted Needles*, was well received on the industrial scene, and when Maroulis himself relocated to L.A., he would retain interest in Tubalcain until that band's break-up in 1994.

Within three weeks of Maroulis' arrival in L.A. in April 1993, Spahn Ranch were recording their first album, 1993's *Collateral Damage*, released in October. The band made their live debut at the Hollywood Auditorium that same month and in November, launched a five-week US tour with STG and the Clay People. An appearance in the club scene in the movie *Separate Lives* coincided with the release of a second Spahn Ranch EP, *The Blackmail Starters Kit* remix collection in April 1994.

Again they toured heavily, before devoting six months to recording the decisive *The Coiled One*, Morton's final album with the band. He would be replaced for a handful of shows in Mexico City by former Christian Death drummer David Parkinson (aka David Glass), with Kent Bancroft (ex-Screams for Tina, guitar) and Maroulis Tubalcain/Executive Slacks bandmate Lewis (drums) following on the eve of the new album's September release.

This expanded line-up debuted at Sinamatic in L.A. and the CMJ conference in New York, before Parkinson pulled out due to prior commitments. As a quartet, the band embarked on a four-week US tour in November 1994, opening for the Electric Hellfire Club, but they parted with Bancroft soon after returning to L.A..

Parkinson returned, and with *The Coiled One* proving Spahn Ranch's most successful album yet, the group prepared the *In Parts Assembled Solely* remix collection, with contributions from Uberzone, Birmingham 6 and long-time band associate and engineer, Judson Leach. (Green also established himself as an in-demand remixer, working with Gene Loves Jezebel, Christian Death, Bow Wow Wow, Gary Numan, and Santana, among others.)

Gigs around L.A., including shows at the House of Blues and the Roxy's Electrofest, preceded the protracted recording of *Architecture*, the album which would see Spahn Ranch shed the last vestiges of their earlier industrial identity and embrace a new techno-powered sound. With contributions from guitarist Danny B. Harvey (guitar) and Paul Raven (ex-Killing Joke/Prong, bass), *Architecture* would be released in April 1997 on the eve of the band's longest ever tour, 45 dates in 50 days. Again Parkinson was unable to participate and the group decided to remain a trio.

Returning home from one tour, Spahn Ranch immediately launched another, visiting both coasts for shows with Electric Hellfire Club, Kervorkian Death Cycle, and the then-unsigned Rammstein. The schedule took them through the new year and in February 1998, the band began work on their fourth album, *Beat Noir* with assistance this time from 16 Volt frontman Eric Powell, and Love and Rockets/Bauhaus bassist David J.

Once again, they broke the silence with a remix EP, *Retrofit*, supporting its European release with their first ever visit to that continent, supporting Norwegian band Apoptygma Berzerk (who would then open for Spahn Ranch's winter 1998 US tour). Further US gigs opening for Frontline Assembly surrounded the release of *Beat Noir* (Mark Blasquez of Death Ride 69 deputized for Lewis on the second half of the tour). Spahn Ranch also returned to Europe for a two-week British tour in July/August 1999.

Spahn Ranch LPs

6 Collateral Damage (Cleopatra) 1993 Spahn Ranch create a hard-hitting and provocative indictment of life's injustices, filled with anger, angst, and bleakness. Far from pleasant it may be, but Ranch's industrial anguish and fury seethes with barely repressed emotion.

7 The Coiled One (Cleopatra) 1995 Tossing away much of their old sound (including the heavily processed vocals) for a sharp techno-industrial hybrid, the straight crossovers lack innovation. Move onto the goth-poppy "Locusts," the Laibachesque "Compression Test," the moody "Threnody," and the synthetic "Babel," however, and Spahn Ranch shine anew.

9 Architecture (Cleopatra) 1997 Imagine, perhaps, Psychic TV colliding with a dark night of Chic...Disco Noir, if you will, spread across a deliciously tight and seductive dance track. A cover of the Equals "Black Skinned Blue Eyed Boys" is positively ecstatic, pulsing sonics which throb with a literal passion. Several tracks (most notably "Futurist Limited") echo elements of Depeche Mode, *sans* that band's congealing precociousness, while "Incubate" takes Hammer's "Can't Touch This" motif into Kraftwerkian territory to stunning effect.

8 Beat Noir (Cleopatra) 1998 What started with *Architecture* continues on *Beat Noir*. From the infectious opening riff of "Fire Lives in the Hearts of All Men," to the near reverent melodies entwined within the synth structure of "Ride like Lightning Crash like Thunder," a tight, edgy, yet absolutely hummable album that is solid throughout. Love and Rockets bassist David J. leaves a fleeting and wonderfully indelible imprint on "Dubnosis" and "An Exit."

Selected Compilations and Archive Releases

8 Anthology (Cleopatra) 2000 Long over-due round-up of early EPs.

Athan Maroulis Solo LP

7 Blue Dahlia (Stardust) 2000

Matt Green — Selected Remixes
1992 ROBERT CALVERT — Freq LP (Cleopatra) **7**
1993 PENAL COLONY — Blue Nine (Cleopatra)
1995 PSYCHIC TV — I Believe What You Said (Cleopatra)
1995 CHRISTIAN DEATH — Death in Detroit (Cleopatra)
1995 CHRISTIAN DEATH — Cervix Couch (One by One) (Cleopatra)
1995 BIRMINGHAM 6 — Police State (Cleopatra)
1996 KRAFTWELT — Deranged (Cleopatra)
1996 THE DAMNED — No More Tears (Cleopatra)
1996 THE DAMNED — Shut It [W/PAUL RAVEN] (Cleopatra)
1996 SWITCHBLADE SYMPHONY — Sweet (Cleopatra)
1996 SWITCHBLADE SYMPHONY — Dollhouse [w/Rat Scabies] (Cleopatra)
1997 ELECTRIC HELLFIRE CLUB — ...Lightning Rod (Cleopatra)

1997 GARY NUMAN — Cars (Cleopatra)
1997 FLYS — Gods of Basketball [w/Paul Raven] (Cleopatra)
1997 PIGFACE — Burundi (Cleopatra)
1997 INFORMATION SOCIETY — Think (Cleopatra)
1998 GENE LOVES JEZEBEL — Motion of Love (Cleopatra)
1998 HEAVEN 17 — That's No Lie (Cleopatra)
1998 BOW WOW WOW — W.O.R.K. (Cleopatra)
1998 CINDERELLA — Gypsy Road (Cleopatra)
1999 A FLOCK OF SEAGULLS — Rainfall (Cleopatra)
1999 BOB MARLEY/WAILERS — Mr. Brown (Cleopatra)
1999 BERLIN — Dancing in Berlin (Cleopatra)
1999 BOB MARLEY/WAILERS — Mystic Mixes LP [NINE TRACKS] (Cleopatra)
1999 SANTANA — Jingo (Cleopatra)
1999 SANTANA — Neckbones (Cleopatra)
1999 MARILYN MONROE — Diamonds Are a Girl's Best Friend (Cleopatra)

SPEAR OF DESTINY

FORMED 1982 *(London, England)*
ORIGINAL LINE-UP *Kirk Brandon (b. 8/3/56 — vocals, guitar); Stan Stammers (bass); Lasette Ames (sax); Chris Bell (drums)*

Formed by Brandon and Stammers from the wreckage of Theatre of Hate and named, with characteristic grandeur, for the weapon with which the Roman centurion Longinus pierced the body of the crucified Christ, much of the group's debut album was already in place before Lasette Ames and Chris Bell joined. Released on the band's own Burning Rome label, through CBS, *The Grapes of Wrath* (#62 UK) and singles "Flying Scotsman" and "The Wheel" (#59 UK) echoed Theatre of Hate's final demos with astonishing precision.

This original quartet did not survive for long. Barely was the album on the streets when Ames and Bell quit, the latter citing both personal and religious reasons (he subsequently resurfaced in Gene Loves Jezebel). Theatre of Hate's Nigel Preston, fresh from a stint with Sex Gang Children, and Diodes saxophonist John Lennard were drafted in for live work, but by the time Spear began work on their second album, 1984's *One Eyed Jacks* (#22 UK), both had been replaced, by former Tom Robinson Band/Stiff Little Fingers drummer Dolphin Taylor, Case sax player Nick Donnelly, and Neil Pyzor and guitarist Alan St Clair, from Howard Devoto's first post-Magazine line-up.

This, the definitive Spear aggregation, toured constantly — three outings during 1984 saw them saturate the UK and incite *Melody Maker* to enthuse, "this time next year, [this band] should be huge...that they aren't already is down to nothing more than...criminal bad luck" — the bad luck which denied three successive 45's, "Rainmaker," "Prisoner of Love," (#59 UK) and "Liberator" (#67 UK), even a Top 50 berth.

The failure of *One Eyed Jacks* did much to knock Brandon back, a blow from which he would not recover even after 1985's *World Service* (#11 UK), a less cohesive, but occasionally superior, album just missed the Top ten. Two further indelible singles, "All My Love" (#61) and "Come Back" (#55 UK), were barely noticed and when attempts to record a new album on the Manor Mobile collapsed in bad-tempered disarray, Brandon sacked the entire group.

Spear of Destiny vanished for much of the next two years, and when the band did return, it was with a completely new line up of Brandon, bassist Chris Bostock, drummer Pete Barnacle, former Adam and the Ants guitarist Marco Pirroni, and keyboardist Volker Janssen. Ironically, it was now that Spear finally achieved the destiny which had evaded them for so long.

Released on Virgin's 10 subsidiary, *Outland* (#16 UK) spawned Spear of Destiny's biggest hits yet, "Stranger in Our Town" (#49 UK), "Never Take Me Alive" (#14 UK), "Was That You" (#55 UK), and "The Traveller" (#44 UK). The group also toured with U2, an outing which culminated at Wembley Stadium in June 1987, but before the group could capitalize on their sudden success, tragedy struck. Literally on the eve of an appearance at the Reading Festival, Brandon was diagnosed with Reiter's Syndrome and ordered to bed.

He spent a year flat on his back, barely able to move at a time when Spear of Destiny's commercial stock had never been higher — *Outland* was their biggest seller yet; their first tour of America was beckoning... and the brightest spot on Kirk's horizon was the possibility that he might be able to learn to walk again. He struggled back into action just in time to see Spear of Destiny fall apart; their 1988 album, *The Price You Pay* (#37 UK) and single, "So in Love With You" (#36 UK), foundered in the face of his inability to promote them, and while Brandon bravely tried to relaunch the group in 1990, reuniting with Stan Stammers, alongside drummer Bobby Rae Mayhem and guitarist Mark Thwaite, his future drifted even further out of reach when sundry legal problems meant he couldn't even continue using the band's name. Two largely unsatisfying albums document this era, the comeback *SOD's Law*, released in 1992, and *Live at the Lyceum* (1993).

Abandoning Britain, Brandon relocated to Philadelphia, where he hooked up with the two American musicians who would become the backbone of his future activities, guitarist John McNutt and drummer Art Smith. Demos recorded by this team, under the tentative name Elephant Daze, would subsequently be issued on the *Psalm One* archive collection;

they went unreleased at the time, however, and Brandon returned to Britain, bringing his new bandmates with him.

For a time, the team toured as Theatre of Hate; for a little longer, they worked under the unlikely name of 10:51, releasing the single "Children of the Damned" and album *Stone in the Rain*. Then Brandon took Spear back for himself, just in time to walk into another firestorm, an ultimately unsuccessful legal battle with Boy George, whose recently published autobiography alleged a homosexual relationship with Brandon.

But he also married and became a father, and in 1998, began work on a new album, "Religion" — "the first album I've done which says everything I want it to, all the way through. Even though there's stuff from the other Spear albums that I wouldn't want to forget about, and which still stands up, 'Religion' is the first one where I've actually been able to get on with what I wanted."

Spear of Destiny LPs

8 Grapes of Wrath (Burning Rome — UK) 1983 Roaring sax and Brandon's keening vocals collide with highway pile-up precision over songs written as anthems, performed as blessings. "Flying Scotsman" and the defining "The Wheel" have a commercial punch which defies the band's occasional moves towards more experimental passages and the album emerges a war whoop of ecstasy.

9 One Eyed Jacks (Burning Rome — UK) 1984 More of the same, only even more powerful. "Liberator" reiterated the band's strengths, "Prisoner of Love" and "Rainmaker" followed in its footsteps.

8 World Service (Epic — UK) 1985 Pausing for a moment at their peak, allowing a wider range of histrionics to filter into view — "Come Back" was another invigorating high.

7 Outlands (10:51) 1987 Calmer, more downbeat set, but conversely their most successful album. Little emerged truly stirring, but the highlights at least are memorable.

6 The Price You Pay (Virgin — UK) 1988

5 Sod's Law (Virgin — UK) 1992

6 Live at the Lyceum (10:51) 1993

7 Religion (Amsterdamned) 1999 A solid re-emergence, although mature reflection has replaced defiant whooping and the agitated edges have been smoothed out.

Selected Compilations and Archive Releases

8 The Epic Years (Epic — UK) 1987 Note perfect, but criminally short highlights collection.

7 BBC Radio One in Concert 1987 (Windsong — UK) 1994

7 Time of Our Lives (Virgin — UK) 1995

7 The Best of (Snapper — UK) 1998 Deceptive set, all-encompassing on first inspection, but weighted down with remakes, outtakes, and demos.

6 Psalm One (Amsterdamned) 1999 1990s demos and 1988 live material.

6 Psalm Two (Amsterdamned) 1999 *Outlands* demos and 1987 live.

7 Psalm Three (Amsterdamned) 1999 Powerful, but poorly recorded, 1985 live set and mid-1980's outtakes.

10:51 LP

6 Stone in the Rain (Anagram) 1995

SPECIALS

FORMED 1978 (Coventry, England)
ORIGINAL LINE-UP *Terry Hall (b. 3/19/59 — vocals); Neville Staples (vocals, percussion); Lynval Golding (b. 7/24/51 — vocals, percussion); Jerry Dammers (b. Gerald Dankin, 5/22/51 — guitar, vocals); Roddy Radiation (b. Byers — guitar); Sir Horace Gentleman (b. Horace Panter — bass), John Bradbury (drums)*

Formed as the Automatics in 1978, the band whose blending of ska and punk would completely rewrite Britain's musical mood at the end of the decade was the brainchild of clergyman's son Jerry Dammers, and friend, Neol Davies. Their first band, Night Train, was heavily soul-influenced but, inspired by the Clash's recent excursions into a punky reggae hybrid, the pair began recording their own experimental demos with Horace Panter, Golding, vocalist Tim Strickland and drummer Silverton Hutchinson. Davies dropped out

soon after, to concentrate on his own band, The Selecter, but the Automatics' line-up was crystallizing regardless. Terry Hall joined (replacing Strickland) after catching an early show and describing the band as a reggaefied Stranglers; Roddy Byers was recruited from a local punk band, Wild Boys.

Financed by the manager of Australian pub punks, The Saints, the Automatics recorded some demos and played a few shows as far south as London before a better established band of the same name forced them to find another name.

Dammers was still wrestling with that dilemma when he heard that Johnny Rotten had just walked out of the Sex Pistols. Immediately he decided to offer the singer a gig with the Automatics. Heading down to London, Dammers began infiltrating the ex-Pistols' circle, penetrating as far as Clash roadie Roadent before he realized that this was probably as good as it got. He left a tape of the band with Roadent, who passed it on to manager Bernie Rhodes, who in turn offered the band a couple of gigs supporting The Clash.

Originally billed as The Special AKA The Automatics, the band shortened their name to The Special AKA just four hours before the first gig, at Aylesbury Friars. That would then be shortened to The Specials, and while that first show was anything but special, Joe Strummer was sufficiently impressed to extend the group's contract to a full two-week tour (including a London date billed alongside visiting American minimalists Suicide). By the time the band returned to Coventry, confidence was high.

© Jim Steinfeldt/Chansley Entertainment

Still, it would take another couple more months, Silverton's replacement by John Bradbury, and the near collapse of the entire outfit, before The Specials finally found what they were looking for in Lynval Golding's collection of old blue beat singles. Other bands had already combined punk with reggae — but none had done it with ska.

Rhodes had long since vanished by now, walking away after his would-be proteges refused to sign a management contract with him. Dammers retaliated by writing a song about the band's experiences, "Gangsters," and in March 1979, that song became The Special's first single, on their own 2-Tone label. (The B-side, "The Selecter," debuted Neol Davies' own band.)

Opening with what would today be called a sample of the original "Al Capone" (although at the time, they simply dubbed it off a record), then tracing Prince Buster's own rhythm track through The Specials' own musical convolutions, "Gangsters" accomplished the impossible without even trying, fusing the energy of classic punk with the joy of early blue beat, then rising way above the sum of its parts. Certainly Rough Trade were impressed, ordering 5,000 copies on the spot. The first pressing was sold out within weeks, and when the band signed to Chrysalis in May, a reissue of "Gangsters" promptly soared to No. 6.

The Special's second single, a cover of Dandy Livingstone's "A Message to You Rudy" (#10 UK) consolidated the breakthrough; Dammer's own "Too Much Too Young" (#1 UK) confirmed it, and by the time the band's eponymous debut album (#84 US, #4 UK) was released, 2-Tone and ska ruled Britain. Yet when The Specials arrived in New York for their first US tour in January 1980, the first question they were asked was, "now you're in the States, are you going to continue playing Jamaican music?"

The six-week tour which followed did little to settle the band's rattled nerves, as they dutifully opened for the Police in the mid-west before returning to New York to play *Saturday Night Live* on April 19.

"Rat Race" (#5 UK), in May 1980, kept the band in the limelight, although events on their spring tour of Britain illustrated the darker side of The Specials' popularity. Violence seemed endemic, not only among the skinhead crowds attracted to the ska music which had, of course, provided the soundtrack to their movement's own genesis a decade before, but also among other factions — anyone, in fact, who wanted a good punch-up.

In July, the Greater London Council slapped an outright ban on a proposed 2-Tone festival, to be staged on Clapham Common to celebrate the label's first birthday, for fear of violence. When the Specials' fall tour, promoting the newly released sophomore album, *More Specials* (#98 US, #5 UK), and the "Stereotypes" (#6 UK) single, was marred by further outbreaks of trouble, the band announced they were going to take the next six months off to consider what they wanted to do next — and hope that tempers cooled in the meantime. Fittingly under the circumstances, plans for a "farewell — for now" showing at a C.N.D. rally in Trafalgar Square were cancelled when the local authorities refused permission.

While a cover of Bob Dylan's "Maggie's Farm" (#4 UK) soared up the chart, The Specials splintered. Staples established the Jah Baddis sound system and formed a label of his own, Shack Records. His first signing was a combo formed by two of The Special's roadies, 21 Guns. Bradbury also formed his own label, Race Records, and recruited Golding to produce a new aggregation called the People; the drummer would also join Sir Horace and Dammers in Rico's backing unit as the blue beat veteran toured around the UK and Europe.

The group would not completely disappear, however. Throughout the early part of 1981, The Specials reconvened for several low-key shows around England, usually allied to various political causes — sundry non-aligned anti-nuclear organizations, anti-racist and anti-Fascist benefits, and so forth. Fittingly, their first new single of the year, July's "Ghost Town" (#1 UK), topped the chart just as these latter concerns came to a head with a spate of rioting throughout England. The Specials broke up months after.

Dammers reverted to The Special AKA identity and over the next three years, maintained a constant presence, scoring hits with "The Boiler" (#35 UK, 1982), "Racist Friend" (#60 UK, 1983), "Free Nelson Mandela" (#9 UK, 1984), and "What I Like Most About You Is Your Girlfriend" (#51 UK, 1985), with the *In the Studio* album (#34 UK) following. He subsequently formed the crusading Artists Against Apartheid movement and remained instrumental in the international campaign to win Mandela's release from South African prison.

1982 also saw Hall, Golding, and Staples form the Fun Boy Three and enjoy a string of UK hits before Hall quit to form Colourfield in 1985 and subsequently go solo. In 1993, Hall joined Eurythmic Dave Stewart in Vegas, but returned to solo work soon after.

Byers formed a rockabilly band, Roddy Radiation and the Tearjerkers, while Sir Horace worked briefly with General Public before linking with Staples, Bradbury, and the Beat's Ranking Roger in Special Beat in 1989, a group whose very name summed up the ingredients and their promise — the recreation of two of the most compulsive catalogs in recent ska memory. All the hits, all the classics, and a firm grasp on the rudiments of everything that made ska so special in the first place.

With the line-up completed by former Fine Young Cannibals' trumpeter Graeme Hamilton, Bobby Bird, and two members of brave, but ultimately beleaguered, British hopefuls the Loafers, Sean Flowerdew, and Tony "Finny" Finn, the gathering never intended to be anything more than a touring party...with the emphasis on the word "party." In the studio, their triumph stretched little further than a remake of Prince Buster's "Time Is Longer than Rope," but across three continents Special Beat would remain the premier attraction on the live ska circuit until 1996, when — with the addition of Golding — the nucleus of the band reconvened as The Specials.

Buoyed by the "Hypocrite" (#66 UK) single, their first all new album in 15 years, *Today's Specials* was followed by a very successful US tour; indeed, when they played KROQ's Acoustic Christmas party at the end of 1997, the *L.A. Times* raved, "the Specials...show the depths possible in this genre"; when they played WBCN's Christmas Rave, the *Boston Globe* added, "the new material was consistent with their skanking gems from the late '70's." Audiences were equally appreciative when The Specials joined the 1998 Vans Warped tour and appeared at Reading in August, shortly before the release of their next album, *Guilty Til Proved Innocent*.

The Specials LPs

9 The Specials (2 Tone) 1979 Taking ska and rocksteady, setting them aflame with punk fury, and feeding the fire with insightful lyrics, The Special's wedding of the Caribbean's past and Britain's present did more than create a new musical style, it begot a revolution. On stage, the septet whipped crowds into a frenzy not felt since the early punk days and their eponymous album perfectly reproduced that exuberance. The revitalized covers of old Jamaican classics meld effortlessly into the band's own feverish compositions, while the slower, more thoughtful numbers (delivered in deadpan style by Terry Hall) were brilliant nuggets of teen angst and frustration.

7 More Specials (2 Tone) 1980 There are some lighthearted moments to be found here — the odd pop song, '60's rouser, East End vaudevillian night out, or holiday abroad — but the darker tracks are so ominous as to overwhelm the rest. From the opening warning of "Enjoy Yourself" onto the threatening "Man at C&A" and the despairing "Do Nothing," even the chirpiest songs here can't lift the mood. The mists of "Ghost Town" are already swirling at their feet.

3 Today's Specials (Virgin) 1996 With half the band missing, today's Specials are far removed from yesterday's 2-Tone heroes, and this MOR album of ska/reggae/punk/pop covers doesn't contain an iota of fire, energy, or anger. Meaning it's not very special at all.

5 Guilty 'Til Proved Innocent (MCA) 1998 With this album as Exhibit One, Judge Dread pronounced The Specials guilty, sentencing them to 500 years each. But when the blubbering rude boys appealed for mercy on the grounds that they'd shown some

rehabilitation since their last offence(ive) album, His Honor conceded that they had recovered a spark of old fire and even offered up some worthy tracks. But they were still guilty of writing too many lightweight songs, so sentence reduced to 450.

Special AKA LP

5 In the Studio (2 Tone) 1984 The Specials by any other name barely sound like The Specials at all. Instead *Studio* is Dammers' musical journey across a vast array of genres — funk, jazz, soul, reggae, and shreds of ska — oftentimes twinned with disconcerting rhythms and seemingly disembodied instrument parts, making for an intriguing, if jolting, sound. Lyrically, though, AKA have even more bite than their predecessor, taking uncompromising stances of a variety of socio-political issues.

The Specials with Desmond Dekker LP

4 King of Ska (Music Club) 1994 It should have been a marriage made in heaven, a joyous joining of the 2-Tone greats with ska's greatest legend. Instead, while Dekker does his best, The Specials disappoint, choosing not to revitalize the 11 classic numbers found here (as they'd always done in their heyday), but merely to recreate a "60's sound, and end up with this pleasant, but heavily MOR, record.

Selected Compilations and Archive Releases

8 The Singles Collection (2 Tone — UK) 1991

8 BBC Radio One Live (Split With Selecter) (Windsong — UK) 1992 Live in London, December 1979, raucous recountings of the kings (and Queen) of 2-Tone ska at their proto-nutty peak.

7 Live at the Moonlight Club (Chrysalis — UK) 1992 Recorded live in London in May 1979, *Moonlight* captures The Specials before they'd even released their first single, honing new material and searching for their true sound. Still loyal to their Blue Beat roots, the freneticism of their punk fired later gigs is yet to come, but their potential is more than evident.

5 Coventry Automatics AKA The Specials (Receiver) 1994 Early days, scampering across prototype versions of a few later classics, but for the most part trying harder to find out what they most want to do. One reaches the end just as mystified as they were.

8 BBC Sessions [LIVE] (EMI) 1998

4 1999 Ghost Town: Live at the Montreaux Jazz Festival, 1995 (Receiver UK)

Fun Boy Three LPs

9 Fun Boy Three (Chrysalis) 1983 One of the most interesting and adventurous albums of the '80's, the three former Specials explore musical styles from four continents in a totally unique, yet radio-friendly, fashion. The rhythms propel the songs, but the Fun Boys begin where Adam Ant ends, adding African tribal drumming and their old rocksteady beats. The music is equally diverse, encompassing ancient liturgical, rap, funk, reggae, gloomy post-punk pop, and a clutch which defy any attempt at categorization. The vocals are a further twist, and backed by Bananarama, they chant, rap, and sing in patterns as complex as the rhythms, alternately emphasizing and counterpointing the beats. Cleverly fleshed out by sparse instrumentation, *Fun Boy Three* delivers on its cover's promise to make you gasp, wonder, and thrill.

6 Waiting (Chrysalis) 1984 Last time around, it was "The Lunatics Have Taken over the Asylum" which stole the show, because no record on earth had ever sounded like that. This time, it was "Tunnel of Love" and "Our Lips Are Sealed" — both marvelous, both memorable, but even the Go-Go's weren't challenged by the latter.

English Beat LPs

7 I Just Can't Stop It (IRS) 1980 Dave Wakeling and Ranking Roger's sweet vocals immediately set the Beat apart from the rest of the 2-Tone set and, while their poppier hits defined their sound, *Stop* had an equal number of driving, punkier numbers, a clutch of great rocksteady covers and recreations and the powerful political plea of "Stand Down Margaret" to set against the lighter pop moments.

4 Wha'ppen? (IRS) 1981 It's hard to say precisely....the band makes all the right noises, Roger toasts away, Wakeling's dulcet tones provide perfect counterpoint — but the songs just aren't there, and *Wha'ppen* doesn't contain anything that remotely measures up to their earlier material. "Drowning" is the best of a mediocre bunch.

6 Special Beat Service (IRS) 1982 Having survived a bad case of sophomore slump, the Beat reinvent themselves as a pure party band. No punk or politics here, but a dozen glossy poppy songs (led off by "I Confess") guaranteed to keep everyone smiling and dancing.

Selected Compilations and Archive Releases

6 What Is Beat? (1983) (IRS) 1983

Further Reading

You're Wondering Now by Paul Williams (ST Publishing, UK, 1995).

STATE OF GRACE

FORMED 1979 (*Nottingham, England*)
ORIGINAL MEMBERS *Paul Arnall (guitar, keyboards); Sarah Simmonds (vocals)*

Paul Arnall was ex-The Secret, best remembered for touring with XTC (in the days when XTC still toured); he formed Fatal Charm in 1979 and released the "Paris" single before rebuilding the band around the newly recruited Simmonds. Signing to former Dozy, Beaky, Mick, and Tich mainman

Dave Dee's Double D label, Fatal Charm were promptly packaged as a proto-new romantic band and sent into the studio with producer Midge Ure (Visage, Ultravox). The sessions were aborted with just one track, "Christine," considered complete; it was released as a single in 1981, but failed, just as Double D folded.

Disbanding the group, Arnall and Simmonds returned to Nottingham to continue on as a duo and suddenly things began to pick up. In short succession, the reconstituted Fatal Charm — Arnall, Simmonds, a tape deck, and whoever they could draw in as drummer — opened local shows for Squeeze, Fad Gadget, and the then high-profile A Flock of Seagulls.

Their biggest break came when Echo and the Bunnymen's latest tour was rocked by the departure of the scheduled support band, Strawberry Switchblade, on the eve of their Nottingham show. Simmonds was working the bar at the club that night and was asked if Fatal Charm could step into the breach. They agreed, and were promptly offered the rest of the tour.

The band appeared on the first ever episode of British TV's *The Tube* and by mid-1984, with drummer Paul Richards brought on board full-time, Fatal Charm signed to the British wing of the European Carrere label. Their first single, "Summer Spies," was a radio hit, but did nothing chartwise, a fate suffered, too, by early 1985's "King of Comedy" — dedicated to the movie of the same name. Press and radio interest kept up, but the band's debut album, the ironically titled *Endangered Species I*, was delayed for six months; a new single, "You Know (You'll Never Believe)," went the same way as its predecessors and by mid 1986, the moment had passed. Following one final single on the Native indy, "Images of Fire" (#25 UK indy), Fatal Charm folded.

By the late 1980's, Arnall was immersing himself in club electronics and complaining, "there was nothing happening musically, and I knew that if I didn't like what anyone else was doing, I'd have to do it myself." In 1991, he and Arnall relaunched as State of Grace, a name Simmonds borrowed from Gabriel Garcia Marquez's *Love in the Time of Cholera*. The duo self-released their debut EP *Camden*, before signing to Third Stone and releasing two consecutive *Melody Maker* Single of the Weeks, the dreamy "Love, Pain and Passion," and the chunky guitar drone "Miss You." Irregular live shows followed and in 1994, State of Grace compiled together their singles to date for the album *Pacific Waves*, a well-received set which drew comparisons with One Dove and the Cocteau Twins.

Signing to RCA for the US and expanding the line-up to include Anthony Wheeldon (bass) and Tim Maddison (drums), State of Grace released a second EP, *Hello*, in 1995 with the acclaimed *Jamboreepop* album appearing in the UK that summer. It was released in the US in 1996 on the heels of the band's American breakthrough with a 12-minute version of "Hello," remixed by New York house producers Darrin Friedman and George Morel. That track spent four months on the *Billboard* club charts and reached No. 5 on CMJ's import chart, however, the group failed to follow through and have remained silent since.

State of Grace LPs

8 Jamboreepop (RCA) 1996 Drifting electro soundscapes, the occasionally abrasive textures constantly hauled back towards beauty by Simmond's haunting vocals and Arnell's inability to write a song without a killer hook.

Selected Compilations and Archive Releases

7 Pacific Waves (Third Stone — UK) 1994 UK singles and EPs round-up.

Fatal Charm LP

8 Endangered Species, I (Carrere — UK) 1986 Overflowing with nagging hooklines. At his most inspired, Arnell's songs unveil the melody first, then draw up the battle-lines with the lyrics, harsh radio benders whose impact is only accentuated by the lush symphonics. "Summer Spies" and "King of Comedy" should not be missed.

STIFF LITTLE FINGERS

FORMED 1977 *(Belfast, Ireland)*
ORIGINAL LINE-UP *Jake Burns (vocals, guitar); Henry Cluney (guitar, vocals); All McMordie (bass); Brian Faloon (drums)*

Jake Burns, Henry Cluney, and Brian Faloon had been playing together since they were 15, with Ali McMordie's arrival in the summer of 1977 completing the jigsaw. In November, a meeting with journalists Colin McClelland and Gordon Ogilvie gave Burns a fiery writing partner, Ogilvie, and the band a far-sighted management team which encouraged them to eschew the standard preoccupations of punk and concentrate on what they knew — life in occupied Belfast.

Within weeks, the first song under this new regime, "Suspect Device," was complete. Recorded at Downtown Radio's jingle studio, and manufactured at a Dublin studio, 350 copies of Stiff Little Finger's debut single were pressed for release in March 1978 on the band's own Rigid Digits label. The intention was to sell through mail order and gigs, but a copy sent to BBC DJ John Peel saw regular airings on the radio and by summer 1978, the single was long since sold-out.

By October, the band had already been contacted by Island Records, only for Rough Trade to step in offering financing and distribution for Rigid Digits. The band immediately accepted the proposal and that month "Alternative Ulster" — a song originally intended for a flexidisc to be given away with copies of the *Alternative Ulster* fanzine, a strong supporter of the group — was released on both Rigid Digits and Rough Trade.

Simultaneously, the band went out on a month-long tour with the Tom Robinson Band and commenced work on a debut album, *Inflammable Material* (#14 UK). "Suspect Device" was reissued by Rough Trade a full year after its original appearance, with the band swiftly following through with a new single, "Gotta Getaway," debuting new drummer Jim Reilly (previously a window cleaner in his hometown, Sheffield) — he replaced Faloon when the rest of the band decided to relocate to London from Belfast in May 1979.

With a hit album behind them, SLF were suddenly the darlings of the London scene. Burns appeared alongside Tom Robinson at a Rock Against Racism gig at Alexander Palace, in a band which also included Generation X's Tony James, and before the season had ended, the group was celebrating a new recording deal. After intense competition, Chrysalis won the band's hand and were immediately handed one of the hardest hitting singles of the year, the anti-mercenary "Straw Dogs" (#44 UK), the ideal introduction to the band's second album, *Nobody's Heroes* (#8 UK).

The Belfast angle to the band's material had long since dissipated; Burns and Ogilvie, the principal songwriters, now concentrated more on personal experience, a theme fully exploited by February 1980's "At the Edge" (#15 UK) — based, said Ogilvie, on "the kind of things [Jake's] parents used to say about him." With the band undertaking yet another sold-out UK tour, the double A-sided "Tin Soldiers"/"Nobody's Heroes" (#36 UK) followed and in August, "Back to Front" (#49 UK) aimed a very sharp barb in the direction of the skinhead revival which Britain was currently undergoing in the wake of the 2-Tone label's emergence.

Hanx (#9 UK), a dramatic live recording universally greeted as one of the year's more refreshing Christmas stocking fillers, peaked over Christmas 1980, despite having been conceived as a US-only release. Just four months later, *Go for It* (#14 UK), the band's fourth album, caught the band embracing at least a hint of the sparkling immediacy which characterized the best of the newfound '60s' soul revival — club favorites the Q-Tips were invited to appear on one track, "Silver Lining" (#68 UK) and "Just Fade Away" (#47 UK) became hits, while both the Wailing Souls' "Mr. Fire Coal-Man" and The Special's "Doesn't Make It Alright" became regulars in the band's live set.

But they could still punk out when they wanted to, all the more so after Reilly quit to form Red Rockers in September 1981, to be replaced by TRB's Dolphin Taylor. The *One Pound Ten or Less* EP (#33 UK), so named to protest the ever-increasing cost of a single, was dominated by the riotous "Listen" and the Clash-influenced "Two Guitars Clash," a sound gleefully reiterated for the band's next single, "Talkback," a trailer for their next album. Its failure to even breach the Top 75 would rank among 1982's greatest mysteries, particularly as the album itself, *Now Then*, was destined for No. 24.

The success and critical approval which greeted *Now Then*, however, was not enough to halt the fast-looming demise of the band. Burns was tiring of what he saw as the SLF formula and even as a new single, "Bits of Kids" (#73 UK), loomed, he and Dolphin were on their way out, forming a new band, Go West, with ex-Jam bassist Bruce Foxton.

The project fizzled out after just one three-song recording session, as Foxton decided he wanted to try a solo career (the Go West name, too, went elsewhere) and while Taylor joined Spear of Destiny, Burns formed a new band of his own, Big Wheel.

The rest of the band, too, found new occupations: McMordie formed the funk outfit Fiction Groove before joining Sinead O'Connor's band and Cluney was a founding member of Fairground Attraction. In November 1987, however, all three original members, plus Taylor, reformed for an excursion around the UK club scene, billed as the Final Reunion Tour, recorded for the following year's *Live and Loud* album.

Another outing, the Second Final Reunion Tour in the new year, was even more successful, slamming the band back into the same size venues they'd been playing before the split and spawning another live album, *See You Up There*, and the *Wild Rover* EP. By the time of the Third Final Reunion Tour, the band was selling out two nights at the 5,000 capacity Brixton Academy.

All four original SLF albums were reissued and the band's profile was soaring when Burns was offered a job as a producer at BBC Radio 1. He tried to juggle his new career with the band, but it didn't work — finally, he gave up the BBC job and SLF launched a European tour which consumed almost an entire year. It would be March 1991 before the band was back in Britain, and when McMordie quit to concentrate on the management company he'd recently established, the band barely paused as Bruce Foxton was drafted in to replace him.

Flags and Emblems, the new line-up's first studio album, was released in September 1991 and proved immediately that the band's eye for political statement remained unsubdued — the single "Beirut Moon," was banned for criticizing the British government's inactivity following the kidnapping of citizen John McCarthy.

Cluney's departure in early 1993 left SLF a trio for studio work with guitarists Ian McCallum and Dave Sharp coming in for live work. This line-up continued gigging and releasing live albums, but it would be January 1994 before any new studio material appeared — the single "Can't Believe in You," accompanied by unplugged versions of "Wasted Life," "Listen," and "Silver Lining" came close to giving the band a hit, while the *Get a Life* album (and a second single, "Harp"), were both well-received — again, SLF had proven that their rejuvenation was something far more meaningful than so many other of the reunions now gathering pace around them.

Taylor quit in 1996 to be replaced by Steve Grantley — ex-Burns' Big Wheel project — and the band returned to the studio to record 1997's *Tinderbox*, with guest appearances from the Kick Horns and Holly Roberts (keyboards), an unknown discovered playing in a pub by Burns and Foxton just three days before the sessions began. Two years later, *Hope Street* indicated how much farther the band's appeal had grown when it landed a US release — the first SLF album in 18 years to be issued there.

Stiff Little Fingers LPs

9 Inflammable Material (Rough Trade — UK) 1979 Raised amid the troubles of Northern Ireland, SLF seethe, spit, and snarl their way through a lethal cocktail of storming punk and roiling reggae, crowned by a barrage of in your face lyrics that mercilessly damn both sides of the conflict. The state of the union anthem "Alternative Ulster" is especially explosive.

8 Nobody's Heroes (Chrysalis) 1980 Fame's already taking its toll on SLF, as the title track's impassioned lyrics make clear. But "Wait and See," a nostalgic goodbye to departed drummer Falloon, documents the even higher personal cost, and although the energy level never flags, the introspection keeps up even across a Specials cover. Only "Fly the Flag" and "Tin Soldiers" look outwards, but the band remains impassioned and the music as powerful as ever.

7 Hanx [LIVE] (Chrysalis) 1980

7 Go for It (Chrysalis — UK) 1981 SLF do just that — their playing has come a long way from the early days and *Go for It* gives the members ample opportunities to show off their talent. The military precision of the title track and the flashy pop guitars on "Just Fade Away" are highlights; so, surprisingly, is a poppy C&W track, while reggae remains an understated forte as well.

6 Now Then (Chrysalis — UK) 1982 Great sounding set marred by a distinct lessening of focus and aggression. And songs.

6 Live and Loud/No Sleep Till Belfast [LIVE] (Link — UK) 1988

6 See You up There [LIVE] (Virgin — UK) 1989

6 Alternative Chartbusters [LIVE 1988] (Link — UK) 1991

5 Flags and Emblems (Essential — UK) 1991 From the opening Motorhead roar to the Irish drinking songs, through a homage to Gary Glitter, and onto a pair of '80's stadium rockers, *Flags* is far removed from expectations, with only two poppy-punky tracks waving a limp standard for the past. "It's all so different, I guess everything has to change," sings Burns, and judging by this, he's absolutely right.

4 Fly the Flags [LIVE 1991] (Dojo — UK) 1992

5 Get a Life (Essential — UK) 1994

5 Pure Fingers [LIVE 1993] (Dojo — UK) 1995

7 Tinderbox (EMI — UK) 1997 Grandmaster Flash's "The Message" is a shock highlight of a surprisingly fresh (and dramatically punk-punchy) album.

6 Hope Street (Oxygen) 1999

7 Hope Street Tour [LIVE 1998] (Oxygen) 1999

Selected Compilations and Archive Releases

9 All the Best (Chrysalis) 1983 Peerless two-disc collection of everything the original SLF should be remembered for.

9 The Peel Sessions (Strange Fruit) 1989 Far more than the endless stream of live albums, this is the sound of SLF in concert — without the concert setting to distract them. High energy, powerful punch, and a wrap-up of their very best.

6 BBC Radio 1 in Concert [LIVE 1981] (Windsong) 1992

6 BS, Live, Unplugged and Demos (Dojo) 1995

STONE ROSES

FORMED 1984 *(Manchester, England)*

ORIGINAL LINE-UP *Ian Brown (b. 2/20/63, Anacoats, Lancs — vocals); John Squire (b. 11/24/62, Broadheath, Lancs — guitar); Pete Garner (bass); Alan "Reni" Wren (b. 4/10/64, Manchester)*

Through the early 1980s, Ian Brown, then playing bass, led highly rated Manchester band, The Patrol, alongside Simon Wolstencroft (later original drummer for The Smiths) and Andy Couzens. The band played a handful of shows with punk band Corrosive Youth and recorded a handful of demos before breaking up. Childhood friends John Squire and Gary "Mani" Mounfield (b. 11/16/62, Crumpsall, Manchester), meanwhile, were members of Waterfront, with Chris Goodwin (bass) and Dave Cartey (vocals); Brown joined as joint vocalist in 1983, but by late 1984, he and Squire had broken away to form the Stone Roses.

With Alan Wren and Pete Garner, the Stone Roses' first show was an anti-heroin benefit staged by Pete Townshend at the Moonlight Club in West Hampstead, London, in December 1984. Mercenary Skank, High Noon, and Townshend himself also played. Other London shows followed, at the Embassy Club with ex-Sex Pistol Paul Cook's Chiefs of Relief and the Ad Lib, while the band also traveled south to Exeter for a university gig.

The following year, the band spent a month gigging in Sweden, returning to Manchester in time to sign to former Hacienda Club manager Howard Jones' Thin Line label. Cut with producer Martin Hannett, the band's first single, "So Young," would top Manchester's own local chart and Picadilly Radio DJ Tony the Greek began airing the band's demos. (A collection of this early material would be released in 1998 as *Garage Flower*, #58 UK,)

By 1986, Stone Roses were staging regular after hours shows beneath the railroad arches on Fairfield Street, Manchester. The Flower Shows became a regular part of the city's late nightlife, allowing the band to build both an audience and a repertoire. They broke with Thin Line and in 1987, manager Gareth Evans secured the band a new deal, with FM/Revolver; they quit the label after one single, "Sally Cinnamon" (#33 UK indy), in June 1987.

Garner quit to be replaced by Waterfront's Mani and Stone Roses spent another year gigging while seeking a new deal — they appeared with the La's at a one-day indie-fest at Sefton Park, Liverpool in June 1987 and highlighted an anti-(homosexuality legislation) Clause 28 benefit with James the following spring.

A proposed link with Rough Trade sent the band into the studio with New Order's Peter Hook to cut "Elephant Stone." Shortly before contracts were signed, however, Zomba/Silvertone stepped in with an eight-album contract (Rough Trade's was for one album only), purchased the "Elephant Stone" tape from Rough Trade, and sent the band into the studio in June 1988 to begin work on their debut with producer John Leckie.

"Elephant Stone" was released in October 1988 and with the album completed in January 1989, Stone Roses set out on their first full UK tour. "Made of Stone" (#4 UK indy), their next single, received thunderous media applause, while a show at the Middlesex Polytechnic, apparently attended by every journalist in the land, saw the band explode to press prominence.

The Stone Roses (#86 US, #19 UK) was released in May, an instant indy chart-topper, even if it did initially fail to breach the national Top 30, and after further UK dates, the band set out for their first European and Japanese shows. In their absence, "She Bangs the Drum" (#36 UK, #1 UK indy) scored, and on November 18, 1989, the band made further headlines when their performance on BBC TV's *The Late Show* ended after just 45 seconds, when their volume blew the studio fuses.

Two weeks later, the Stone Roses made their debut on *Top of the Pops*, performing "Fool's Gold" (#8 UK); coincidentally, Happy Mondays, too, were making their first appearance on the show, and for the first time, the music press insistence that Madchester was the Next Big Thing seemed justified. Both bands scored major hits and in the new year, *Stone Roses* re-entered the UK chart.

A reissued "Sally Cinnamon" (#46 UK) was followed by "Elephant Stone" (#8 UK), a saturating policy against which the Stone Roses themselves protested so bitterly that they led a paint attack on the FM label offices — and were fined £3,000 damages.

A new Stone Roses single, "One Love" (#4 UK), was scheduled for July release while the band staged a festival at Spike Island, Widnes, drawing a crowd of 30,000 plus. In the US, college radio play had pushed the album into the charts and the band's videos were becoming regular sights on MTV. Yet the bubble was perilously close to bursting. Again, against the band's own wishes, Silvertone continued repromoting past singles, "Made of Stone" (#20 UK) and "She Bangs the Drum" (#34 UK) in March and "Fools Gold" (#22 UK) in September.

By late fall the Stone Roses' wish to be freed from their contract was an open secret in the music industry. Silvertone hit back with an injunction on the band even entering a recording studio and while May 199, would see the High Court strike down the band's contract, citing it as an "unfair, unjustified and unjustifiable restraint of trade," still it would be close to another year before the band — having acrimoniously split with manager Evans as well — signed a new deal with Geffen. In the meantime, Silvertone scored further UK hits with "I Wanna be Adored" (#20 UK), "Waterfall" (#27 UK), and "I Am the Resurrection" (#33 UK), and a singles collection, Turn Into Stone (#32).

In March 1992, the Stone Roses and producer Leckie reunited to begin work on the band's eagerly awaited sophomore album, a period haunted by increasingly disquieting rumors — confirmed in February 1993, when a Geffen statement was released announcing "delays" in the recording. Leckie walked out of the sessions in July, to be replaced by Paul Schroeder and Simon Dawson; Schroeder, too, would leave the sessions before completion.

Second Coming (#47 US, #4 UK) was originally scheduled for release in March 1994; in fact, there would be no news from the studio until late fall, when the band announced a new single, "Love Spreads" (#2 UK). The album finally arrived in December, debuting at its peak before falling fast — after so much anticipation, Second Coming could not help but disappoint a media and audience long since primed to expect the new Stone Roses album to impact the scene as profoundly as their debut, five years before. And in March 1995, rumors of band disaffection were borne out by the departure of Wren.

He was replaced by Robbie Maddix and with a new single, "Ten Storey Love Song" (#11 UK), the band prepared to resume touring — even as Silvertone reactivated their earlier material once more. The remixed "Fool's Gold '95" single

(#25 UK) was followed by a compilation, The Complete Stone Roses (#4 UK).

The band made their US debut in late May, but played just eleven dates before Squire broke his collarbone while mountain biking near San Francisco. The rest of the tour was cancelled, together with a much-vaunted appearance at Glastonbury; it would be November 1995 before the band returned to the road, touring the UK for the first time in five years, behind a new single, "Begging You" (#15 UK).

Tickets for the 19 shows were sold out within 24 hours of going on sale, but the band was falling apart. Squire quit in spring 1996 and while Brown and Mounfield swiftly recruited a replacement, Aziz Ibrahim (ex-Simply Red), together with a keyboard player, Nigel Ippinson, an all-or-nothing performance at the Reading Festival ended in disaster. In October 1996, Mounfield quit to join Primal Scream and the Stone Roses were over.

Squire was first to re-emerge, with the Seahorses; their debut album, Do It Yourself (#2 UK), received a warm welcome in spring 1997, but the band broke up in February 1999, citing disputes over the direction their sophomore album should take. Vocalist Chris Helme would launch his own solo career the following month with a new band comprising fellow Seahorses Steve Fletcher (bass) and Dave Keegan (guitar). Drummer Mark Heaney, meanwhile, would remain with Squire, in an outfit formed with ex-Verve bassist Simon Jones, in October 1999.

Brown's first solo set, Unfinished Monkey Business (#4 UK), appeared in March 1998, a month after he hit the headlines following an airborne dispute with a flight stewardess and the plane's captain, while traveling from Paris to Manchester. The airline pressed charges and on October 23, Brown was sentenced to four months imprisonment. He was released on appeal after three days, but returned to jail on November 2 when the appeal failed. He would finally be released on December 24.

Brown's planned November 1998 UK tour was rescheduled for February 1999 — ironically coinciding with a hit remix of "Fool's Gold" (#25 UK), the first in a string of celebrations leading up to a tenth anniversary reissue of the Stone Roses' debut album. Brown also made a surprise appearance alongside UNKLE at London's Astoria (he guested on their "Be There" single), and contributed to Demons, the first solo album by Prodigy's Maxim, while preparing his own second album, Golden Greats (#14 UK), and "Love is Like a Fountain" single.

Outside attempts to reform the Roses, meanwhile, have consistently failed; according to Brown, they were offered £2 million to play the V99 Festival, "but wouldn't do it for ten. The Roses were 20th century."

Stone Roses LPs

9 Stone Roses (Silvertone) 1989 A magical mystery tour through Britain's pop past; the Stone Roses' psychedelic sound was surprisingly swirl-free, but heavily influenced by the Beatles, Byrds, Flaming Groovies, and the Stones — with just a soupçon of the Jesus and Mary Chain — making for a classic melody- and harmony-rich style that remains virtually timeless.

6 Second Coming (Geffen) 1994 Not as dreadful as history remembers, but a mere handful of fully realized cuts was several miles short of what the debut promised.

Selected Compilations and Archive Releases

7 Turn into Stone (Silverstone) 1992 Compilation comprising two non-album A-sides (both included as bonus tracks on later reissues of the eponymous album) and a round-up of B-sides.

8 Anniversary Edition (Silverstone — UK) 1999 Once more around an increasingly over-traveled block, the first album and attendant singles, plus enhanced disc featuring videos.

Seahorses LP

7 Do It Yourself (DGC) 1997 Oasis meet Matthew Sweet, a reflection on both ex-busker Helme's vocals and Squire's edgy guitar. A warm Tony Visconti production keeps things classic.

Ian Brown LPs

6 Unfinished Monkey Business (Polydor) 1998

8 Golden Greats (Polydor) 1999 After a less than convincing debut, Brown bounces back with genuine strength and emotion — the best post-Roses album yet.

Further Reading

Breaking into Heaven: The Rise and Fall by Mick Middles (Omnibus, UK, 1999).

RICHARD STRANGE

BORN *Richard Harding*

Strange began preparing for a solo career immediately following the break-up of the Doctors of Madness in October 1978, re-emerging on the London stage in late 1979, not as a performer, but a performance.

The Phenomenal Rise of Richard Strange was a revolving collection of songs which would, as Strange predicted at the time, ultimately evolve into one of the great (and less laudably, great lost) albums of the early 1980s, but which started life as a solo stageshow, Strange reclining in an armchair while a tape recorder stood in for a band, and movies and newsreels flickered around him.

A political satire in which the eponymous hero, a top performer, becomes titular head of a futuristic European federation, *The Phenomenal Rise* took the London club scene by storm. *Sounds* described it as "easily the most articulate and pertinent collection of songs ever attempted under the concept heading." And when Strange took the package to New York in the summer of 1980, the *Washington Spectator* went even further. "Pure vanguard stuff. Music about music that develops a critical consciousness in its audience."

A one-off single, "International Language," previewed the cycle, followed by a live album recorded at Hurrahs during his New York residency — *The Live Rise of Richard Strange* was released in fall 1980 and Strange continued honing the show in London, when he opened his own custom-designed nightclub, the Cabaret Futura. Although it was active just one night a week, it still played a dramatic role in the development of London's still embryonic Futurist scene. Eschewing conventional rock acts, Strange instead booked mixed-media mime acts, performance art poets, film shows, and plays, an esoteric bag which would be preserved on the acclaimed *Fools Rush In* collection.

A studio version of *The Phenomenal Rise of Richard Strange* was finally released in May 1981, featuring guest appearances from TV Smith (under the pseudonym Radio Jones), former Traffic percussionist Rebop Kwaku Ba, and early Supertramp saxophonist, Dave Winthrop. Repeating many of the live album's stand-out cuts, but equally notable for the strength of the songs which hadn't been a part of the New York stageshow, *The Phenomenal Rise* won sterling reviews in the British press and spawned a number of memorable performances at the Cabaret.

Courtesy of Dave Thompson

By early 1982, however, Strange had tired of both the show and his career as club owner; tired, too, of the progressive distillation of a musical mood which had promised so much, but had already been subverted into the new romantic flashflood which valued haircuts higher than hair shirts. The "Phenomenal Rise" ended there.

Strange continued to resurface on an unpredictable basis through the 1980's, most notably with Engine Room, while 1999 saw him re-record a handful of Doctors of Madness tracks as bonus material on a reissue of that band's debut album. For the most part, however, he has occupied himself elsewhere, adhering to a game plan which he first laid out at the end of the Doctors.

"Music is media, media is education. Bertolt Brecht once said if you've got a message, and I think I have, then it's got to be delivered in some way different from a political tract. It's got to be entertaining, otherwise you scare people off. They don't want to hear a political speech, or if they do, they'll go to [a political rally] or wherever. I don't just make records for the sake of it. I only want to do it when I have something to say."

Richard Strange LPs

7 The Live Rise of Richard Strange (PVC) 1980 A rough sketch of the main attraction — scratchy guitars and raw arrangements giving several songs a certain edge on the finished product.

9 The Phenomenal Rise of Richard Strange (Virgin) 1981 Possibly the best realized concept album ever made — a rich production which never gets in the way, a powerful narrative and some devastating songs. The opening title track and closing "I Won't Run Away" have a dramatic power which bookends the album to perfection, and while a couple of songs do seem to hang too heavily on the need for a plot, "Hearts and Minds," "International Language," and "Who Cries for Me" are Strange classics.

Engine Room LP

6 Going Gone (Side) 1987 1988

STRAY CATS

FORMED 1978 (Massapequah, NJ)

ORIGINAL LINE-UP Brian Setzer (b. 4/10/59, Massapequa, NJ — vocals, guitar); Lee Rocker (b. Leon Drucker, 1961, NY — string bass); Slim Jim Phantom (b. Jim McDonnell, 3/20/61, Brooklyn — drums)

Although he first came to prominence with New York new wavers, the Bloodless Pharoahs (stars of the unreleased Live at CBGB's Volume 2 album, recorded in 1979 and archived ever since), Brian Setzer's musical interests always reached back to an earlier age, to a time when rock'n'roll was still seriously young and deliciously rebellious; when Elvis really was

King; when the words "Be Bop a Lula" still meant something.

He had even gathered two likeminded rockabilly fans to his side, and as the Tom Cats, they'd been gigging sporadically around New York. But he was also convinced there was no real future in it, and remained convinced until a chance meeting with an ex-pat Briton named Tony Bidwell convinced Setzer to take the recently renamed Stray Cats to London, where they would find an audience, a country, an entire generation, for whom the sound of the Stray Cats was as fresh as tomorrow.

The band played their first major London show in September, opening for Elvis Costello. It was an incongruous pairing, but a deliriously triumphant one. Ever open to new music himself, Costello made no secret of his admiration for the Stray Cats, but what really set the pulse racing was the band's sheer strength of conviction.

No mucking around with scratchy old 45s rehearsed as close to the original as was humanly possible, the Stray Cats wrote their own material, then challenged the listener to spot the joins. Although they weren't averse to a handful of covers, and George Jones' "The Race Is On" (#34 UK) sounded superb in their clutches, in Setzer, the Stray Cats had one of the finest young songwriters around.

"Runaway Boys" (#9 UK), "Rock This Town" (#9 UK), "Stray Cat Strut" (#11 UK), "You Don't Believe me" (#57 UK) — the Stray Cats' music came straight from authentic rockabilly sources, but it was all theirs, and all current. "Storm the Embassy" was written about the SAS raid on the Iranian embassy in London; "Rumble in Brighton" picked up on the new tide of mods and rockers, battling it out on the southern English seafront.

A new single co-starring Dave Edmunds, "The Race Is On" (#34 UK), grew out of Edmunds' production of the Stray Cats' first two albums, Stray Cats (#6 UK) and Gonna Ball (#48 UK); both albums were already British hits when the band returned to their homeland, opening for the Rolling Stones in summer 1981, and angling to sweep up America as easily as they'd grabbed Britain and Europe.

They did it as well, and although it took a few months more, and another album, Rant'n'Rave (#14 US, #51 UK), by December 1982 — precisely two years on from hitting the UK chart — the band was enormous.

So were their ideas. Setzer recalled, "when [we] had 'Rock This Town' record, we almost got on the old Tonight show with Johnny Carson. And I thought, 'Wait a minute, let's get Doc Severinsen to have his big band, and 'Rock This Town' is a swing song, let's get him to play behind us. What a great idea.' All these bands go on there and Doc would take a powder. What a waste! So, that was our thing if we'd ever got on the Tonight show, we're going to use the big band. It never happened, [but] it was always in the back of my mind. What a great idea. It just took a while to put together."

A compilation drawn from the Stray Cats' two UK albums, *Built for Speed* (#2 US) stayed on the American chart for 74 weeks; "Rock This Town" (#9 US) was all over MTV. A few months later, in early 1983, it was the turn of "Stray Cat Strut" (#3 US), and by the end of the year, "Sexy and 17" (#5 US, #29 UK) had made it three Top 10 hits in a row, with two more singles, "I Won't Stand in Your Way" (#35 US) and "Look at That Cadillac" (#68 US), following during 1983.

The Stray Cats themselves, though, were getting restless. Just as rockabilly itself had grown and developed, peeled into other styles, turned around within and about itself, so the Stray Cats were looking to broaden their world. A little jazz, a little rock, a little swing — a lot of what Setzer would accomplish a decade or more on, with his Orchestra, was hinted at over the course of that second album, and the Stray Cats broke up in early 1984. "When I saw string basses and bowling shirts in the windows at Macy's, I thought well, it was nice while it lasted," Setzer explained.

Setzer went solo, and played his idol, Eddie Cochran, in the Ritchie Valens biopic *La Bamba*; he also cut two solo albums. Slim Jim (now, famously, husband of actress Britt Eckland) and Lee teamed with former David Bowie guitarist Earl Slick in a new band, Phantom Rocker and Slick, and like Setzer, enjoyed minor success. But it was always on the cards that the trio would get back together again, and in 1986, the reconvened Stray Cats released *Rock Therapy* (#122 US), mixed and recorded in a week. They reunited again in 1988 for *Blast Off* (#111 US, #58 UK) and scored a surprise hit with "Bring It Back Again" (#64 UK), then reformed one more time in 1992 for *Choo Choo Hot Fish*.

But time was moving on and so, again, were the members' own tastes and interests. By the mid-1990s, while Phantom and Lee remained together as the Stray Cats, Setzer finally realized the dream of his childhood by pushing an entire generation of Americans into something approaching a full fledged swing revival.

"When the Stray Cats were at their peak, there wasn't 5,000 rockabillies out there, but we were playing shows to thousands of people. It was always across the board, and it's like that with the big band. There's a bit of the rockabilly contingence, the hipster lounge scene, a bit of a swing scene, and the rest of it is just across the board people who just think it's great. I don't know what they look like, they're just people who don't belong to any particular group."

Stray Cats LPs

⑨ **Stray Cats (Arista — UK) 1981**
⑧ **Gonna Ball (Arista — UK) 1981**

⑧ **Rant'n'rave (EMI America) 1983** Three peas in a smartly bequiffed pod! The start of a new decade and time to turn to a musical past. But did rockabilly ever really sound like this? Perhaps, although the infusion of sound with punk's fire kept everything dynamically fresh. "Rock This Town," "Runaway Boys," "Sexy and 17,""Rumble on Brighton Beach" — barely a dull moment in sight.

⑥ **Rock Therapy (EMI America) 1986** Same sound, same intent, but sadly not the same quality.

⑥ **Blast Off (EMI America) 1989**

⑤ **Choo Choo Hot Fish (JRS) 1994**

Selected Compilations and Archive Releases

⑨ **Built for Speed (EMI America) 1982** Tight compilation from the first two (UK-only) albums, heavy on the hits.

⑧ **Runaway Boys — A Retrospective 1981–92 (Capitol) 1997**

⑥ **Live (Cleopatra) 1999**

Brian Setzer LPs

⑦ **The Knife Feels like Justice (EMI America) 1986**

⑦ **Live Nude Guitars (EMI America) 1988**

⑦ **The Brian Setzer Orchestra (Hollywood) 1994**

⑧ **Guitar Slinger (Interscope) 1995** Rockabilly meets swing is just-for-starters on this musical masterpiece. From jump to Latin, spy themes to soul, a Bobby Darin cover to a pair of Joe Strummer penned beauties, *Slinger* has it all, and is gunning for you.

⑦ **The Dirty Boogie (Interscope) 1998**

⑧ **Vavoom! (Interscope) 2000**

Phantom Rocker and Slick LPs

⑥ **Phantom Rocker and Slick (EMI) 1985**

⑥ **Cover Girl (EMI) 1986**

Swing Cats LP

⑥ **Swing Cats (Cleopatra) 1999**

JOE STRUMMER

BORN *John Graham Mellor, 8/21/52 (Ankara, Turkey)*

Departing the Clash in protest of the nature of their final album, 1985's *Cut the Crap* (#16 UK, #88 US), vocalist Joe Strummer was widely predicted to embark on a solo career at least as passionate and prolific as his years with the band. Instead, he reflected, "just hanging out's been my main achievement, gaining wisdom through patience."

Strummer's first port of call was the studio where ex-bandmate Mick Jones' Big Audio Dynamite were shooting the video for their "Medicine Show" single. He guested in the video; Jones reciprocated by playing guitar and producing

Strummer's debut solo single "Love Kills" (#69 UK) and by August, the pair were co-writing for the second B.A.D. album, *No. 10 Upping Street*. Strummer ultimately had a hand in five of the album's nine tracks, and shared the production credits as well, but hopes that the partnership might flourish further fell away as Strummer's interests turned more towards movies than music.

He appeared in (and scored) Alex Cox's spaghetti western *Straight to Hell*; he also composed the title theme for the same director's *Sid and Nancy* and scored *Walker* and Marisa Silver's *Permanent Record*, backed by a new band, Latino Rockabilly War. Reuniting Strummer with one of his *Straight to Hell* soundtrack collaborators, Zander Schloss (ex-Thelonious Monster, guitar), Jim Donica (bass), Tupelo Joe Altruda (guitar, keyboards), Willie McNeil (The Untouchables, drums), and percussionists Poncho Sanchez and Ramon Vanda, the outfit's efforts comprised one side of the soundtrack album and spawned a solitary single, "Trash City."

In early 1988, Strummer returned to the road as a member of The Pogues, remaining on board for a three-week US tour (during which two Clash numbers, "I Fought the Law" and "London Calling," were added to the repertoire) before dropping out when the band returned home, to launch his own *Rock Against the Rich* British tour.

Again convening Latin Rockabilly War, Strummer pieced together a set which traced his entire carerer from pub rockers the 101-ers, through The Clash and The Pogues, and onto the *Permanent Record* soundtrack. The moment he was off the road, however, he returned to the movie set, appearing as an Elvis impersonator in Jim Jarmusch's *Mystery Train*, remaining in L.A. piecing together a new band around Schloss and Lonnie Marshall (also ex-Thelonious Monster).

They recommended Jack Irons, the former Red Hot Chili Pepper whose shock at bandmate Hillel Slovak's recent death had landed him in a mental hospital — which is where Strummer called him, inviting him down to the studio to play. Hours later, the four were cutting tracks for Strummer's first solo album, *Earthquake Weather* (#58 UK); the finished album would also feature contributions from Latino Rockabilly drummer Willie McNeil, but still Irons would reflect, "I'll never forget what Joe did for me," reawakening his interest in music for the first time since Slovak's death.

Two singles from the album, "Gangsterville" and "Island Hopping," flopped and Strummer turned again to acting, despite swearing, after *Mystery Train*, that he was finished with the profession. Aki Kaurismaki's *I Hired a Contract Killer* was next, Strummer joining Nicky Tesco (ex-Members) as a pub entertainer and contributing two songs to the soundtrack, "Burning Lights" and "Afro-Cuban Be Bop."

Strummer would not reappear until September 1990 when he produced The Pogues' *Hell's Ditch*. The following year, he rejoined the band as vocalist at three days' notice, after Shane MacGowan was sacked during a Japanese tour. Strummer led the band through a January 1992 UK tour and by February, he was reported to be writing a new album with the band. He left the following month.

Although he spoke of recording a new solo album, it would be two more years before Strummer resurfaced, joining the Czech band Dirty Pictures at a Rock for Refugees benefit in Prague on April 16, 1994. A set full of Clash songs, however, gave no clue to his future direction and indeed, Strummer seemed content to appear directionless.

As pianist, he cut a single, "Just the One" (#12 UK), with the Levellers; and a second, "England's Irie" (#6 UK), with Black Grape. He began work on a new album, booking into Peter Gabriel's Real World with Richard Norris (of The Grid) and a new band called Strummerville. By the end of 1995, however, Strummer had returned to L.A. and the following year he linked with The Damned's Rat Scabies and the Ruts' Dave Ruffy in the Electric Dog House, to contribute the title track to the Amnesty benefit *Generations*.

He appeared on a tribute to Jack Kerouac and turned in a track for *South Park's Chef Aid* album; another movie project saw him score John Cusack's *Grosse Point Blank*, while he also contributed to Black Grape's *Stupid Stupid Stupid* sophomore set and co-wrote with ex-Stray Cat Brian Setzer. Other projects included recording with reggae star/Massive Attack collaborator Horace Andy, linking with DJ David Holmes, and hosting a BBC radio special, *London Calling*. He also scored a UK hit in 1998 as one of several superstars backing comedian Keith Allen's World Cup-themed Fat Les project; indeed, it was during those sessions that he linked with former Pulp/Elastica keyboard player Antony Genn and began work anew on his own second album.

Rock Art and the X-Ray Style finally appeared in October 1999. Recorded with Genn, Pablo Cooke (percussion), Black Grape sideman Martin Slattery (guitar), and Scott Shields (bass) — collectively, the Mescaleros — the album resurrected one song ("Yalla Yalla") from the aborted Real World sessions and another, "Forbidden City," which dated back to the period immediately following *Earthquake Weather*.

Although its release clashed with that of a new Clash archive release, the live *From Here to Eternity*, *Rock Art...* was well-received, and launched Strummer on his first full US tour in a decade, through November 1999.

Also see the entries for "BIG AUDIO DYNAMITE" on page 192 and "CLASH" on page 270.

Joe Strummer LPs

6 Walker [SOUNDTRACK] (Virgin) 1986

7 Earthquake Weather (Virgin) 1989 Oddly overlooked album sees Strummer merging his rock roots with a funky Latino mood, and songs at least the equal of middling Clash classics.

8 Rock Art and the X-Ray Scan (Epitaph) 1999 An eclectic offering of Latino, reggae, C&W, acoustic ballads, and rockers — no surprises there, then. Strummer's music has matured considerably since his days in The Clash, but he hasn't lost his punk edge; think a more focused, coherent *Sandanista*, or a marginally superior *Earthquake Weather*.

STYLE COUNCIL

FORMED 1983 *(London, England)*
ORIGINAL LINE-UP *Paul Weller (b. 5/25/58, Woking, England — vocals, guitar); Mick Talbot (b. 9/11/58, keyboards)*

As 1983 dawned, it appeared that the only person not mortally affected by the break-up of The Jam was the man who broke them up in the first place. Little more than three weeks after that band's final show, Paul Weller was onstage with Everything but the Girl at the ICA, duetting with vocalist Tracey Thorn on "The Girl from Ipanema" and Peggy Lee's "Fever," and adding guitar to Cole Porter's "Night and Day" and his own "English Rose." He had already expressed an interest in the jazzy pop sounds which the fledgling EBTG were thern exploring, and over the next two months, that interest was going to irredeemably flavor his own next project. (Thorn would appear as a guest vocalist on his next album.)

Linking with former Merton Parkas/Dexy's Midnight Runner Mick Talbot, Weller named his new band the Style Council and, from the outset, he appeared determined that they would live up to that title. The band's first photo shoot was a Euro-cafe flavored escapade in Boulogne, France, and in March 1983, "Speak like a Child" (#4 UK) became the band's first single.

A virtual duet between Weller and Tracie Young, the immensely talented 18-year-old vocalist currently languishing on Weller's ill-fated Respond label, "Speak like a Child" was not so far removed from latter-day Jam material. Its flip, "Party Chambers," however, sent the band spiralling off into new, swing-inflected territory and when Style Council made their live debut, at a CND May Day show in Liverpool, they debuted another new sound in the form of their next single, the driving funk rant "Money-Go-Round" (#11).

A second show at London's Brockwell Park gave Weller's old punk audience the opportunity to show him what they thought of his new direction — on a bill which also featured The Damned, Weller spent his set dodging handfuls of mud flying out of the crowd. But he remained undeterred.

In July, Style Council moved to Paris to record their next release, the *A Paris* EP (#3 UK), itself leading off with the mildly controversial video for the opening "Long Hot Summer." A scene featuring Weller and Talbot stroking one another's earlobes needed to be removed after Polydor (and the tabloids, of course) objected.

By now, the Style Council had broadened to include a new female vocalist, D.C. Lee, and drummer, Steve Wright. These "Honorary Councillors" were on board for the band's European tour that fall (accompanied by the *Introducing* mini album, #172 US, collecting all the band's singles to date) and of course, their fourth single, November 1983's "A Solid Bond in Your Heart" (#11 UK). A joyous precursor of the '60s mod soul recreations which Fine Young Cannibals would subsequently make their own, the track was, in fact, first recorded by The Jam as a possible final single, only to be discarded in favor of "Beat Surrender."

The Style Coucil returned to Britain to play the Big One charity concert in London; they were joined on stage by Elvis Costello to perform what would become the band's next single, "My Ever Changing Moods" (#56 US, #5 UK), itself a taster for their debut album, March 1984's *Cafe Bleu* (US title: *My Ever Changing Moods*) (#2 UK, #56 US). The band launched their first UK tour to coincide — an unusual presentation which saw them play one short set in between the support acts (the Questions and Billy Bragg), and then a full performance at the end.

Leading off the *Groovin'* EP in May, "You're the Best Thing" (#5 UK, #76 US) gave the band another signature hit, just as they departed for their first US and Far Eastern tours; "Shout to the Top" (#7 UK) and tours of Britain and Europe would follow, together with a pair of benefits for Britain's striking miners, a cause with which Weller was so concerned that in December, he convened the Council Collective, with Motown singer Jimmy Ruffin, funk hero Junior Giscombe, rapper Dizzy Hites, and DJ Vaughn Toulouse, to record "Soul Deep" (#24 UK), all proceeds going to the miner's fund.

Indeed, the Style Council were rapidly stepping into the political arena which Weller, with The Jam, had hitherto simply observed and occasionally spoken out about. They were regulars at CND benefits; while Weller attended a demonstration supporting the Youth Trade Union Rights Campaign, joining Billy Bragg in delivering a 50,000-signature petition to the Prime Minister's residence, before playing a free show across the river from the Houses of Parliament.

Later in the year, Weller would link again with Bragg to form Red Wedge, a coalition of left-wing musicians aiming to pave the way for a Socialist government to take power in Britain. With the Labour Party assisting with the financing and party leader, Neil Kinnock, pledging his personal support to a Red Wedge tour the following January, Weller's unflinching willingness to stand up for what he believed in would also see him elected joint President of the UN's International Year of Youth (alongside actress Julie Walters).

The band's music reflected these beliefs. "Walls Come Tumbling Down" (#6 UK) was a virtual call for revolution, a theme spread further across the band's second album, June 1985's *Our Favourite Shop*/US title *The Internationalists* (#123 US, #1 UK). There was also the sense, however, that Weller was occasionally over-reaching himself in his search for targets — "Welcome to Milton Keynes" (#23 UK), an assault upon one of Britain's "new town" conurbations, would become the first Style Council single not to hit the Top 20, although the band certainly redeemed themselves with a stunning performance at Live Aid, following a well-received UK tour in June. (Weller and Talbot both appeared on the earlier "Do They Know It's Christmas Time" Band Aid single).

A remix of "The Lodgers" (#13 UK) was released in September, alongside a solo single by vocalist Lee; "See the Day" (#3 UK), of course, featured her Council bandmates, and Weller would contribute an otherwise unheard song, "Just My Type," to Lee's 1986 solo album, *Shrine*. It came as no surprise when the pair announced soon after that they were intending to marry.

Red Wedge played their first short UK tour in January 1986, a bill split between Style Council, Bragg, and Jimmy Somerville's Communards, plus a host of special guests; the same team would headline a second tour in March. Style Council also played an Artists Against Apartheid festival in London in June, and amidst so much activity, there was little time for new recordings. In March, a single, "Have You Ever Had It Blue" (#14 UK), was culled from the soundtrack to *Absolute Beginners*, Julien Temple's wilful adaptation of Colin McInnes' mod classic novel of the same name; while May brought a live album, *Home and Abroad* (#8 UK), and a US-only single, a live version of "The Internationalists."

There was a new album in the pipeline, however, previewed in September on the *Rock Around the Dock* TV special and trailed by a new single, "It Didn't Matter" (#9 UK) in Januar, 1987. The album, *The Cost of Loving* (#122 US, #2 UK), followed, but a sense that the band's time was fast passing was inescapable — all the more so when, after all Red Wedge's efforts, the Labour Party was soundly routed by Thatcher's Conservatives at the General Election that same year.

A single, "Waiting" (#52), disappointed and when the band toured Britain in early 1987, energy and familiar faces

alike were absent — Steve White most notable among the latter. Nor was the future looking any better — two new singles, "Wanted" (#20 UK) in September and "Life at a Top People's Health Farm" (#28 UK), trailed the band's next album with surprisingly little elan and *Confessions of a Pop Group* (#174 US, #15 UK) emerged self-indulgent and generally disappointing.

The EP 1-2-3-4: *A Summer Quartet* (#41 UK) and single, "Promised Land" (#27), ensured Style Council remained chart contenders, but it was ironic that by the time Weller did find fresh inspiration, in the sounds of the acid house boom, even his record company had written him off.

In 1989, Polydor released *The Singular Adventures of the Style Council* (#3 UK) and a remix of "Long Hot Summer" (#48). But when Weller delivered a new Style Council album, the house-inflected *Modernism: A New Decade*, the label stripped two tracks for B-sides, then rejected the rest (the album would finally be released in 1998, within the Style Council box set). In March, 1990, Weller announced the Style Council had broken up, subsequently launching a solo career.

Also see the entry for the "JAM" on page 428.

Style Council LPs

8 **My Ever Changing Moods (Geffen) 1984**
8 **Cafe Bleu (Polydor — UK) 1984** An astonishing album and just for a moment, one could almost believe it was worthwhile breaking up The Jam. Although some of the Euro-jazz lite stylings can get tiresome, and the attempt at rap is risible, at its best *Moods* catches Weller in fine form, with Tracey Thorn's guest vocal on "Paris Match" a masterpiece. The re-recorded Jam outtake "A Solid Bond in Your Heart," the gentle US title track, and "You're the Best Thing" pack genuine class.

7 **Internationalists (Geffen) 1985**
7 **Our Favourite Shop (Polydor — UK) 1985** The US edition cuts the UK title track — it should have removed "All Gone Away," which sounds like a self-playing organ on autopilot, or "The Stand Up Comic's Instructions," which has no redeeming features whatsoever. At its best, however, as on "Walls Come Tumbling Down" and the CD bonus track "Shout to the Top" it's almost the equal of its predecessor.

6 **Home and Abroad [LIVE] (Geffen) 1986**
5 **Cost of Loving (Polydor) 1987** The whole point of the Style Council, as regular sleeve note readers will know, was to give voice to Weller's Capuccino Kid alter-ego. This, then, is it — a soundtrack for all the Parisian coffee bars he wishes he was hanging around.

4 **Confessions of a Pop Group (Polydor) 1988** "We confess we've lost it."

Selected Compilations and Archive Releases

7 The Singular Adventures of the Style Council (Polydor) 1989 But when they were good, they were astonishing. "Solid Bond," "Money-Go-Round," "Long Hot Summer," "My Ever Changing Moods," "Shout to the Top," and a load of later rubbish.

6 Here's Some That Got Away (Polydor) 1994 The Style Council outtakes collection.

7 The Complete Adventures of the Style Council (Polygram) 1998 Absurdly ambitious five-disc box repackaging every song they ever released, and an album's worth which wasn't — the group's final album wasn't as bad as Polydor seemed to think it was when they locked it in a box, but it doesn't add much to the Weller legend either.

Paul Weller LPs

7 Paul Weller (London) 1992 Tentative comeback finds Weller moving in a distinctly early-'70's "getting our heads together in the country, man" vibe; a generally pleasant set, although understated with a vengeance.

8 Wildwood (Polygram) 1993
8 Paul Weller Live Wood (Go! Discs — UK) 1994 Something is beginning to stir — maybe invigorated by the growing swell of support rising from the Brit-pop pack, or maybe just remembering what made him great in the first place, Weller turns in his best album in a decade, then reiterates it with a sternly determined live echo.

9 Stanley Road (London) 1995 From the opening "The Changingman," confidence and even a hint of old arrogance ooze from every moment. "You Do Something to Me" and the title track are genuinely impressive, but even more excitingly, Weller has found a sound which owes nothing to his past — but everything to what that past means.

8 Heavy Soul (Polygram) 1997 Consolidating *Stanley Road* — no great strides, but no disappointment either.

Selected Compilations and Archive Releases

8 Modern Classics: Greatest Hits (Polygram) 1998 Wrap-up of singles, most of which take on shades of greatness which will surprise even fans.

SUGARCUBES

FORMED 1986 *(Reykjavik, Iceland)*

ORIGINAL LINE-UP *Björk (b. Björk Godmundsdottir, 11/21/65, Reykjavik — vocals); Thor Eldon Jonsson (b. 6/2/62, Reykjavik — guitar); Einer Orn Benediktsson (b. 10/29/62, Copenhagen, Denmark — trumpet); Einar Mellax (keyboards); Bragi Olafsson (b. 8/11/62, Reykjavik — bass); Sigttryggur Baldursson (b. 10/2/62, Stavanger, Norway — drums)*

Child prodigy Björk Godmundsdottir was just eleven when she made her radio debut, a schoolteacher's cassette recording of her performing the 1976 Tina Charles' hit "I Love to Love" aired on Icelandic Radio 1 in 1977. The Falkkin label promptly signed her and released her all-covers debut album, *Björk*, in December 1977 — a family affair which included sleeve art by her mother, Hildur, and guitar from stepfather, Saevar Arnason. Other musicians on the album included two friends of her mother's and the disc's eventual producers, Palmi Gunnarsson (bass) and Sigurdur Karlsson (drums), who in turn recruited top Icelandic session guitarist, Bjorgvin Gislason.

Two years later, Björk formed Exodus, a punk-influenced band with Jakob Magnusson (bass), who managed a handful of appearances on Icelandic television; when that band broke up in early 1980, she joined Jam 80, before reuniting with Magnusson in Tappi Tikarrass. Signing to Spor, the band debuted with the EP *Bitid Fast I Vitid*, followed in 1983 by an album, *Miranda*.

Tappi Tikarras also appeared in the 1982 documentary *Rokk I Reykjavik*, a controversial effort which for the first time in Icelandic entertainment history, acknowledged that local youth might be prey to the same bad habits as music fans elsewhere in the west. All the participating bands performed live and a soundtrack album would be released later in the year.

1982 also saw Björk link with free-form jazz-rock outfit, Stifgrim, to take part in an Icelandic bid to get into the *Guinness Book of Records* — a source, apparently, of intense national frustration. Close to a hundred bands and performers took part in what was billed as the longest continuous live performance ever staged, a two-week event which saw many of the musicians playing for as much as 12 hours without a break.

Tappi Tikarrass broke up in late 1983, shortly after contributing two live tracks to the *Satt 3* compilation; Björk promptly formed a new group, Kukl, formed with the inflammatorily named God Krist (keyboards) and musicians from two of the other bands featured on *Rokk I Reykjavik*, Einer Orn Benediktsson (ex-Purrkurr Pillnikk) and Sigttryggur Baldursson (ex-Peyr).

Building on Peyr's already known profile in Britain, born of Killing Joke vocalist Jaz Coleman's recent patronage, Kukl landed European tours with Crass and Flux of Pink Indians, while maintaining a high and highly controversial reputation at home, courtesy of their outspoken political stance. The band's name translated as "sorcery," and much of their work discussed the pagan belief system which still dominated much of Iceland's culture.

The band's debut album, *The Eye*, would be released in Britain by the Crass' own label in 1984; two years later, *Holiday in Europe (Naughty Naught)* would join it and the band's stock increased even further when they toured the continent again with The Fall. However, the deadly seriousness of it all was fast wearing on the band members and in September 1986, shortly after Björk and Thor Eldon Jonsson married, Kukl announced a change in direction and a change in name.

Two years earlier, Björk had begun gigging, as drummer and backing vocalist, with Rokha Rokha Drum, a band led by Icelandic poet Johnny Triumph and featuring Jonsson and Einar Mellax. The band lasted around a year, mainly playing jazzy prog-rock around Reykjavik art galleries and coffee bars, before Björk and Jonsson, together with Kukl's Krist and Baldursson broke away as the Elgar Sisters in 1985.

The Sisters never gigged, but they wrote and recorded at least an album's worth of songs (unreleased at the time, three would subsequently surface as Björk solo B-sides). Krist pulled out of both the Sisters and Kukl; he would be replaced by Mellax, as the remaining members of the two bands recruited Bragi Olafsson and became Sykurmolarnir — in English, the Sugarcubes.

The band's attitude was the absolute reverse of Kukl's, mad fun and mischievousness, fronted by a squeaky, shrieking voice Björk had never previously unleashed. It was spattered all over their debut, the *Ein Mol a 'Mann* EP, released by Gramm that same month; the band's own increased dexterity was spotlighted with three instrumental contributions to the Icelandic movie soundtrack *Skytturnar*; and with the UK press following developments with interest, the band was signed to the UK label One Little Indian soon after.

A track from the EP, "Ammaeli" ("Birthday") (#65 UK, #2 UK indy), was selected for their first British single and the band recorded an English language version for the release; the accompanying video, however, remained in Icelandic, providing British TV watchers with an odd shock indeed. It was followed in February 1988 by "Cold Sweat" (#56 UK, #1 UK indy), performed only in English.

"Deus" (#51 UK, #2 UK indy) appeared in April 1988, backed by what had already become the group's best ever selling Icelandic single, "Luftgitar," recorded with former Rokha Rokha Drum vocalist, Triumph. Simultaneously, the Sugarcubes debut album, *Life's Too Good* (#54 US, #14 UK, #1 UK indy) was released; it would also make an impression in the US, where the band was signed with Elektra — the only major label move they made, despite spending most of 1987 listening to offers.

The group's decision to remain with One Little Indian, despite the blandishments of the majors, ensured their continued affair with the UK press; so did their next single, a reissue of "Birthday" paired with a version recorded by the Jesus and Mary Chain (#65 UK, #1 UK indy). But the band itself was experiencing problems. Mellax quit, to be replaced by Margret Ornolfsdottir (b. 11/21/67, Reykjavik), while Björk and Jonsson's marriage was beginning to crumble. The couple would divorce in 1988 and the following year, Jonsson and Ornolfsdottir would wed.

Two US singles, "Cold Sweat" and a live version of "Motorcrash," were unable to follow the album's performance, despite some support from radio and an October 15, 1988 appearance on *Saturday Night Live*. But "Regina" (#55 UK, #1 UK indy) proved a fine precursor to the band's second album, October 1989's *Here Today, Tomorrow, Next Week* (#70 US, #15 UK, #1 UK indy), proof that the group's wacky novelty had considerably more staying power than their detractors alleged.

Still, the failure of the "Planet" single in February 1990 justified complaints that the second Sugarcubes album was not up to the same standards as its predecessor and when work began on their third, the band itself knew that a lot was at stake. Much of their recent experimentalism was dropped, songs were tailored more towards a mainstream audience — there was even a song called "Hit," and few people were surprised, in February 1991, when that is what it became. The single rose to #17 UK, the band's biggest hit yet and while the follow-up, "Walkabout," again failed, *Stick Around for Joy* (#95 US, #16 UK) lived up to every expectation in February 1992.

Success, however, could not paper over the cracks now rending the band. Using the band's 1990 sabbatical to further her own ambitions, Björk had consummated a long-standing, if sporadic, relationship with the Icelandic bebop ensemble, Trio Gudmundar Ingolfssonar, by recording an entire album with them, a collection of jazz standards called *Gling Glo*.

She received further local plaudits when she guested on three successive albums by Megas, an artist whose epithets include such lofty titles as "The Icelandic Bob Dylan" and "The Grandfather of Icelandic Punk." His 1990 set, *Haettuleg Hljomsveit Og Glaepakendid Stella*, was a major hit, confirming Björk's status not only as a successful artist in her own right, but also one whom others took very seriously indeed.

Such success was one more spur to what appeared to be a veritable power struggle now unfolding between Björk and Benediktsson, whose penchant for onstage rapping and fooling around had already provoked a number of critics to suggest the band sack him.

While they considered this advice, the group concentrated on overseeing the remixing of great swathes of their back catalog, for two EPs, *Vitamin* and *Birthday* (#64 UK), and an album, *It's It* (#47 UK), released in the fall of 1992. Then, in September, Björk announced she was quitting for a solo career. The band disbanded on the spot.

Also see the entry for "BJÖRK" on page 244.

Sugarcubes LPs

8 Life's Too Good (Elektra) 1988 A little bit goth, a little bit wave, a healthy pinch of rock (but very little KUKL), are wrapped up and shoved alongside Björk's love-'em-or-get-used-to-them vocals, which themselves glimmer only when they're not revving up to a banshee roar. "Delicious Demon" and "Motorcrash" were only appetizers for the undeniably catchy "Birthday."

5 Here Today, Tomorrow, Next Week (Elektra) 1989 Lightning couldn't strike twice, and the Cubes' welcome shattered under the weight of this much anticipated, but ultimately disappointing, record. Despite the nuggets "Tidal Wave" and "Bee," the songs were unable to break new ground.

7 Stick Around for Joy (Elektra) 1992 Better than the last, even if the band couldn't pull in a winner like their first. Björk's vocals continue to soar, but so it seems do her solo ambitions.

Selected Compilations and Archive Releases

7 It's-It (Elektra) 1992 A remix album of songs from the band's three albums, that are considerably more miss than hit. An interesting, if dust-gathering, retrospective.

8 Great Crossover Potential (Elektra) 1998 Anything even remotely approaching a Best of the Sugarcubes had its work cut out to begin with, but somehow *Potential* pulls it off. Four tracks apiece from the band's three albums, and a couple of singles which never went any further. It's a remarkable record, and one which — like the Sugarcubes themselves — will divide or conquer all who come close. But yes, it is aptly titled. They did have great crossover potential...it just depends where you wanted them to cross over to.

SUICIDE

FORMED 1970 *(New York, NY)*
ORIGINAL LINE-UP *Alan Vega (b. 1948 — vocals); Martin Rev (keyboards)*

Visual artist Alan Vega met Martin Rev when the latter's band, the 15-piece jazz ensemble, Reverend B, performed at Vega's gallery space, the Project of Living Artists, in Manhattan.

Their vision of reintroducing pure minimalism to rock'n'roll was a radical one — long before New York City became a seething pre-punk cauldron, Suicide's first live show, in late 1970, was at an event presciently called Punk Best, staged in a loft on Broadway. According to Vega, how-

ever, they were so poorly received that it would be another year before they played another show.

The duo kept the audience waiting 45 minutes before taking the stage, setting the scene for a career in performance art torture. Vega, in his new guise of Alan Suicide, spent most of the band's set in the audience, doing his best to intimidate people — and usually succeeding. Daggers and bike chains were part of his stage wear and as early as 1972, Suicide were staging evenings of *Punk, Funk and Sewer Music* around Greenwich Village.

With the support of the New York Dolls, Suicide became semi-regulars at the Mercer Arts Center, behind the Broadway Central Hotel; other venues, however, were less impressed. It would be 1976 before Suicide played CBGBs, having played just one at owner Hilly Kristal's previous bar in late 1972; around the same time before they returned to Max's Kansas City, again after one early show let the management into the duo's dark secrets. (In fact, original Max's owner Mickey Ruskin never rebooked them. They had to wait until the place changed management.) By 1974, when they cut their first demos, Suicide were the synthesized equivalent of the similarly nascent Ramones — stark minimalism cut to its lowest possible pulse.

Introduced to the vinyl-buying public via a frantic "Rocket USA" on the 1976 *Max's Kansas City* album, Suicide signed with former New Yorks Dolls manager Marty Thau's Red Star in 1977, and an eponymous debut album in 1978 set the critical establishment raving, drawing comparisons with everything from an electro-Iggy and the Stooges, to an utterly misguided "American Kraftwerk."

American audiences, however, ignored the band, while British crowds loathed them — when Suicide toured Europe with The Clash and Elvis Costello, their very presence caused near-riots.

Shaken, but not perturbed, Suicide allowed one of their most-disturbed shows in Belgium to be released as *24 Minutes over Brussels*; a slightly later performance would be included on the *Half Live* cassette album, the other half comprising studio outtakes from 1974–75, a period when the duo really was at their peak.

In 1980, Rev and Vega released a second Suicide album, the misleadingly titled *Alan Vega and Martin Rev*. Produced by Cars mainstay Ric Ocasek, it owed little to Suicide's original power and vision and while it did spawn a near-hit single, "Dream Baby Dream" (belatedly following up the first album's "Cheree"), the band broke up shortly after its release.

Rev had already issued an eponymous solo EP by that time; Vega had his similarly self-titled debut solo album, quickly followed by a second set in a similar rockabilly inspired vein, *Collision Drive*, and while a 1981 reunion with

Rev for a tenth anniversary concert (later released as *Ghost Riders*) indicated that the duo's power to disturb was still intact, both men resisted the temptation to relaunch Suicide. Instead, Vega signed a major label deal with Elektra and with labelmate Ocasek again producing, recorded *Saturn Strip*.

The album sold poorly and Elektra's attempts to redirect Vega's interests and efforts led to an increasingly fraught relationship between artist and label. When 1985's *Just a Million Dreams* went the way of its predecessor, the two parted company and Vega linked again with Rev — who had finally issued a solo album, the Marty Thau-produced ambient set, *Clouds of Glory*, that same year — to reform Suicide.

Again, however, their own ambitions ran markedly contrary to anybody else's expectations and that despite signing to Wax Trax!, a label whose entire roster, it seemed, was by then in total awe of Suicide's original accomplishments. Their first single, "Rain of Ruin" (#13 UK indy), was never going to be a new "Cheree," and two late-1980s albums, *A Way of Life* (#11 UK indy) and *Why Be Blue*, could not help but disappoint.

Again the pair splintered temporarily, Vega reappearing briefly in Andrew Eldritch's Sisterhood project. Further solo albums were punctuated by Suicide's 20th anniversary reunion and the talking blues bubblegum album *YB Blue*. (A live album would follow.)

1996 brought a return from Rev, the *See Me Ridin'* album, while Vega was party to a fascinating, but ultimately disappointing, union with Alex Chilton 1997's *Cubist Blues*. The most significant development, then, would be Vega's re-emergence in 1999 with the Revolutionary Corps of Teenage Jesus, a collaboration with former Altered Images guitarist/Black Grape producer, Stephen Lironi. Having signed to Scotland's Creeping Bent label, three 12" singles garnered two Single of the Week awards from the *New Musical Express*, while the duo's debut album, *Righteous Lite*, returned Vega to pastures he truly had not visited since the halcyon days of Suicide.

Suicide LPs

8 **Suicide (Red Star) 1977** Stark, minimal, dark, economic. Few albums have been so lionized as Suicide's debut, but peculiarly, few turn out to be so disappointing. The immaculate "Cheree" notwithstanding, *Suicide* was important not for what it contained, but for what it ordained — tight, driving atmospheres, punks with synths, no sense of self-consciousness — a future began here.

6 **24 Minutes over Brussels (Bronze) (ZE) 1978** Typically chaotic live show, interesting more for the audience reaction than the band's performance, the show was curtailed by rioting Belgian Elvis Costello fans.

5 **Live (Franki) 1979**

6 **Alan Vega/Martin Rev (ZE) 1980** Ric Ocasek-produced slap at everyone expecting *Suicide II*. Far more musical, if equally understated, the album sounded a stark retreat from the freak-whisper weirdness of its predecessor, and ("Harlem" aside) served only to suggest a less than glowing future.

5 **Half Alive (Roir) 1981** Outtakes and live, of interest to completists only.

5 **Ghost Riders [LIVE] (Roir) 1986**

7 **A Way of Life (Wax Trax!) 1988**

6 **YB Blue (Brake Out) 1992** Walking a thin line between Vega's early talking blues rap and the intoxicating bubblegum of a butch Tom Tom Club, mindless pop perfection scarred only by the crass imbecility of "Flashy Love." The legend lurches towards the Top 40; the Top 40 goes on vacation.

6 **(Zero Hour) [LIVE] (Restless) 1997**

6 **Suicidal Days (Jamright) 1998** One more reunion, one more disappointment.

Selected Compilations and Archive Releases

8 **Suicide (Mute) 2000** The umpteenth repackaging of the band's debut, with a bonus live disc featuring a 1977 CBGBs show and the *24 Minutes* live album.

7 **The Second Album (Mute) 2000** Again, a straightforward reissue, appended with a bonus disc full of contemporary rehearsals.

Martin Rev LP

7 **Clouds of Glory (New Rose — France) 1985**

7 **See Me Ridin' (Roir) 1996**

Alan Vega LPs

5 **Alan Vega (ZE/PVC) 1980**

5 **Collision Drive (ZE/Celluloid) 1981**

6 **Saturn Drive (Elektra) 1983**

6 **Just a Million Dreams (Elektra) 1985**

6 **Vega (Celluloid — France) 1989**

4 **Deuce Avenue (Musidisc — France) 1990**

4 **New Raceion (WB) 1995**

5 **Dujang Prang (Thirsty Ear) 1996**

Alan Vega, Alex Chilton, Ben Vaughn LP

5 **Cubist Blues (Thirsty Ear) 1997**

Revolutionary Corps of the Teenage Jesus LPs

8 **Righteous Lite (Creepin' Bent — UK) 1999** Suicide never recaptured their debut power, but the Revolutionary Corps know exactly where it is — in the surreal subsonic landscapes, vocals cold as freezer burn, and dense, stygian passages of dance music at the wrong end of a cattle prod. Edgy, subversive, and blazing with scorn, this is the album which should have followed *Suicide*

— and twenty years later, it finally did. The difference is in the construction — RCTJ draw heavily from modern dance sensibilities, so while it is not easy listening by *any* standards whatsoever, it's also considerably less dislocated than *Suicide*, less intent on driving its audience out of the room, and a lot more disturbing because of it.

⑧ Daddy Died — A Brooklyn Nightmare (Creepin' Bent — UK) 1999 RCTJ's virtues become even more apparent across an eight-track collection of RCTJ remixes, including contributions by Mongoose, Future Pilot AKA, DJ Irn Clyde, and, in a neat reversal, an RCTJ assault on Suicide's own "Frankie Teardrop." If you thought the original was dramatic, you haven't heard anything yet.

SUNDAYS

FORMED 1988 (London, England)
ORIGINAL LINE-UP Harriet Wheeler (b. 6/26/63, Maidenhead, England — vocals); David Gavurin (b. 4/4/63, London — guitar); Paul Brindley (b. 11/6/63, Loughborough, England)

Wheeler was ex — the otherwise unremembered Jim Jiminee when she and future husband Gavurin left university in Bristol and moved to London with the express purpose of forming a band. Linking with Brindley and a drum machine as the Sundays, and offering up a distinctly Cocteau Twins/Smiths-flavored, guitar-drone-based sound, the trio debuted at the Camden Falcon pub's Vertigo Club in late 1988.

They ran immediately into a firestorm of media approbation. Other bands on the bill were completely overlooked and the following week, the Sundays found themselves proclaimed instant stars-in-waiting throughout the UK music press — within days, four record companies had offered the band a deal. What mystified the band, Wheeler later admitted, was "the gig was awful."

They eventually signed with Rough Trade and in February 1989, the Sundays — now joined by drummer Patrick Hannan (b. 3/4/66) — released their debut single, "Can't Be Sure" (#45 UK, #1 UK indie). It was an instant hit, but the perfectionist Sundays were not about to be rushed into a hasty follow-up. They toured Britain with the Throwing Muses and played a handful of provincial gigs in their own right, but it would be close to a year before the group returned, with their debut album, *Reading, Writing and Arithmetic* (#39 US, #4 UK) — and a *New Musical Express* cover story which proclaimed 1990 "The Year of The Sundays."

It would be, too. Newly signed to DGC in America, the album became a surprise Top 40 smash, largely on the strength of the utterly irresistible single (and similarly captivating video), "Here's Where the Story Ends."

The Sundays launched a major US tour in the album's wake, but the collapse of Rough Trade conspired again with their own relaxed attitude, and it would be over two years before the group resurfaced. "We weren't meant to be away that long," Wheeler explained, "but after Rough Trade folded, basically, we were trying to find a company that was as similar as possible to the company we hadn't wanted to leave." They ended up with EMI's Parlophone subsidiary in the UK, partly because "they'd let us do — or not do — whatever we wanted," but also — again according to Wheeler — because the art department was willing to resurrect Parlophone's old '60s logo for the band.

First undertaking a European tour, treating audiences to a lengthy preview of their then-unheard sophomore set; following through with the single "Goodbye" (#27 UK), the band arrived in the US on the eve of the release of *Blind* (#103 US, #15 UK).

The album offered little progression from its predecessor — deliberately, according to Gavurin, "because surely you only progress if you didn't do it properly last time." Still the album's American failure was a shock; although the band again toured heavily, promotion had been sorely misjudged and DGC's choice of single was especially disastrous. A version of the Rolling Stones' "Wild Horses," recorded for a throwaway UK B-side, was added to the album and accorded the full weight of the campaign, despite the band's own wishes.

Two American tours sandwiched another European outing, until the band had played over 100 shows in a year; they returned home in late summer 1993, and Gavurin reflected, "it was just an immediate sense of relief, going back to seeing our friends, sitting around the house, not having to think, breathe, and live music all the time." Just one new piece of music was recorded, an instrumental for television's Baddiel and Newman comedy team, then the Sundays lurched into hibernation. Wheeler and Gavurin had their first child, daughter Billie; they also began work building the home studio where the Sundays' third album would slowly gestate.

Static and Silence (#33 US, #10 UK) finally arrived in late 1997, trailing a new single, "Summertime" (#15 UK) whose success sincerely took the band by surprise — after so long away, "anything in the Top 30 would have been nice." (A second single from the album, "Cry" — #43 UK, was less successful.)

The Sundays LPs

⑨ Reading, Writing, and Arithmetic (Geffen) 1990 More than a decade on, it remains both a startling achievement and, more surprisingly, a still-breathtaking voyage, despite remaining locked into the Smiths/Cocteaus cocktail which was always the worst thing anyone could say about the band. A refreshing naivety still percolates through it, with "Can't Be Sure" and "I Kicked a Boy" rising even higher than the rest in assuring the Sundays' place among the decade's most mesmeric songwriters. But "Here's Where the Story Ends" remains the classic — a precious souvenir of an otherwise terrible year indeed.

8 Blind (Geffen) 1992 Responding to criticisms that *Blind* added little to the magic of its predecessor, Wheeler asked, "the last album had ten songs, the new one has twelve. How much more progress do you bastards want?" Subtract the faintly sickly "Wild Horses" from the equation and her meaning is only marginally jarred, but even perfection can be over-used. Still a lovely album, but if you've got the first, you've heard the second.

7 Static and Silence (Geffen) 1997 And if you have the first two, the third is fairly redundant. "Summertime" and "Monochrome" are the best cuts; otherwise, the recently converted are best pointed towards the accompanying "Cry" single, with two first album-era demos on the B-side.

SUPERGRASS

FORMED 1994 *(Oxford, England)*
ORIGINAL LINE-UP *Gaz Coombes (b. Gary Coombes, 1976 — guitar, vocals); Danny Goffey (b. 1975 — drums); Mickey Quinn (bass)*

Gaz Coombes was still at school when he and Danny Goffey began jamming together, in imitation of hometown heroes, Ride. Joined in early 1991 by bassist Andy Davie and Goffey's brother, Nick, on guitar, the pair formed the Jennifers, and with Ride's management behind them, landed a deal with Nude.

The Jennifers' debut single, "Just Got Back Today," sunk without trace in July 1992, and just as labelmates Suede shot through the roof, the shoe-gazing Jennifers disappeared through the floor. Eighteen months later, Coombes, Danny Goffey, and ex-5:30 frontman Tara Milton were regrouping (Nick Goffey remained on board as the band's video director, with partner Dominic Hawley); Milton then departed just as bassist Mickey Quinn joined and by early '94, the newly dubbed Theodore Supergrass were recording their first demos.

Sharing management with Radiohead, the group was signed to Parlophone just as they halved their name. In the meantime, local indie label Backbeat released the band's first single, a demo version of "Caught by the Fuzz," which garnered both *NME* and *Melody Maker* Single of the Week awards. Promptly Parlophone requested that the band re-record it and a new "Fuzz" (#43 UK) hit the shops in October, just as Backbeat released a second single, "Mansize Rooster," again taken from the demo. In response, Parlophone released a re-recorded version of "Rooster" (#20 UK), in April 1995, by Supergrass' third single, "Lenny" (#10 UK).

(In America, meanwhile, Sub Pop coupled an acoustic "Fuzz" with "Lose It.")

May 1995 saw the arrival of Supergrass' eagerly awaited debut album, *I Should Coco* (#3 UK), which smashed into the chart alongside a new single, "Alright" (#2 UK), and in June, Supergrass caused a stir when they arrived at the Glastonbury Festival aboard a helicopter, blasting Wagner's "Ride of the Valkyries" across the grounds as they landed.

Lauded both at home and abroad (*Coco* sold over a million worldwide; tours sold out across the US, Europe, and Far East), Supergrass nevertheless viewed their sophomore album as an opportunity to move away from the laddish pop of their debut; previewed by a rousing performance on BBC TV's *Later*, where they incorporated horns into the line-up, Supergrass re-emerged in April 1997 with another hit, "Richard III," (#2 UK) followed by the album, *In It for the Money*. Again the band committed close to two years to touring, breaking only to record their eponymous third album (#3 UK) previewed in May 1999 with the single, "Pumping (On Your Stereo)" (#11 UK), and a well-received appearance at the V99 festival. The band also headlined a webcast from the London Forum in mid-October as "Moving" (#9 UK) returned them to the Top 10.

Supergrass LPs

9 I Should Coco (Capitol) 1995 Supergrass' debut was a rabble-rousing masterpiece of pop-rock hammering, the aggression of punk, the melodic flair of glam, and the contagious hooks of a manic updated Monkees. Plus, "Caught by the Fuzz" laid the blueprint for every misbehaving teen song of the next five years (but Catch's "Bingo" is still great).

7 In It for the Money (Capitol) 1997 Sudden comedown? Or astonishing maturity? Wider instrumentation, songs which cook slowly instead of bursting into flames; horns, smart lyrics...nowhere near as madcap, but maybe more enduring.

8 Supergrass (Parlophone UK) 1999 Still pushing ahead, but a return to a little bit of old-style fun as well.

SWEET 75

FORMED 1994 *(Seattle, WA)*
ORIGINAL LINE-UP *Yva Las Vegas (b. Venezuela — vocals, bass) Kris Novoselic (b. 5/16/65 — guitar); Bobby Lurie (drums)*

The roots of Sweet 75 lay in a party staged by some of Novoselic's friends, in the aftermath of Kurt Cobain's death, in 1994. "[They] were trying to cheer me up," he reflected; instead, they set up the next stage of his career. Yva Las Vegas, a folk-inclined street performer who moved to the US at the age of 16, was hired as entertainment that night, and days later she joined Novoselic and fellow Nirvana survivor Dave Grohl at a rehearsal studio behind Seattle's Space

Needle. Within a week, she and Novoselic had written their first song together.

The original intention was for Novoselic to record a Las Vegas solo album, a plan abandoned following the recruitment of New York drummer, Bobby Lurie. Sweet 75 debuted at Seattle's RCKNDY on March 17, 1995, opening for Tad.

Following their festival debut at JAMPAC on July 22, 1995, Sweet 75 played a short California/southwestern tour through the fall, before Lurie quit to be replaced by former Ministry drummer Bill Rieflin, and the group recorded their first Novoselic/Las Vegas-composed demos in early 1996.

Hopes that the band might be launched immediately were postponed at the insistence of Geffen, still Novoselic's label, following the demise of Nirvana. "[They] were saying 'no, wait a while, let it develop.' But they were right. It would have been awful if we'd gone out then." Instead, the band would surface for a handful of shows, usually around Seattle, then head back into seclusion. Gigs with Sky Cries Mary and Hovercraft followed, but still things moved slowly. "We'd play, a few people would come to the show, we'd develop a core following and then we'd lose it again because we were away so long," Novoselic reflected. "But it was right. We could have gone out and created a buzz, been a local band again, but this way we were able to take our time and get everything right."

In fact, two years would elapse before Sweet 75 finally made their recorded debut, a self-titled set featuring guests Herb Alpert, REM's Peter Buck, and Sky Cries Mary vocalist Anisa Romero; with another twelve months elapsing before the album was actually released, by which time Rieflin had quit, in late 1996, to be replaced by Shudder to Think's Adam Wade (who would also play on one cut on the album). A summer 1997 tour with Dinosaur Jr. paved the way for the album's release and an Australia-only single of "Lay Me Down," but with the majority of reviews simply pointing out how little Sweet 75 resembled Nirvana (or even the Foo Fighters) and Geffen offering minimal support for the project, by late 1997, Sweet 75 were in tatters. Wade departed in October following a US tour with L7 and a handful of dates in Europe; by January 1998, Sweet 75 had disbanded.

Las Vegas and Novoselic reunited with Rieflin in May 1998 and further demos were recorded. By summer, however, Novoselic and Rieflin were more frequently working with Sunshine Cake, their side project with Sky Cries Mary's Roderick Romero and Jeff Grienke, and in mid-1999, Sweet 75 again collapsed.

Also see the entry for "NIRVANA" on page 521.

Sweet 75 LP

7 Sweet 75 (DGC) 1997 A smorgasbord of lighthearted edginess, mid-tempo rock splintering into as many genre-defying shards as it can. Most comfortable when Las Vegas unveils her Latin roots or Novoselic punches the hardcore button, still the relaxed ad-hoc atmosphere is contagiously delightful.

SWELL MAPS

FORMED 1972 *(Solihull, England)*
ORIGINAL LINE-UP *Nikki Sudden (b. Nicholas Godley, 7/18/56 — vocals, keyboards, guitar); Phone Sportsman (b. Dave Barrington — vocals); Epic Soundtracks (b. Paul Godley, 1960 — drums)*

If any band epitomized the DIY ethic and youthful exuberance of the early punk explosion, it was Swell Maps. Coupling that with an utter refusal to be bound by even the vaguest parameters of prevailing musical fashion, brothers Sudden and Soundtracks launched onto a short, but influential career at the furthest extremes of auteur experimentation. More than a decade later, Sonic Youth's Thurston Moore contributed liner notes to the band's *Collision Time Revisited* anthology, while both J. Mascis (Dinosaur Jr.) and Evan Dando (the Lemonheads) guested on Soundtracks' mid-1990s solo albums.

Devout Marc Bolan and T.Rex fans, the Godleys formed their first band in 1972 with Barrington; a year later, they were joined by bassist Jowe Head (b. Joe Hendon), while other members came and went with a frequency matched only by the band's name changes. Constantly recording tapes for their own amusement, the band's line-up and name finally stabilized around 1975; Sudden, Soundtracks, and Head were joined by vocalist/guitarist Richard Earl (another returning early member) and, on September 14, 1977, the quartet visited Cambridge's Spaceward Studios to cut their debut single, "Read About Seymour," for release on their own Rather label in the new year.

On December 26, the band made their live debut at Birmingham's Barbarellas club, playing a handful more shows before "Read About Seymour" was released. It caused an immediate stir — DJ John Peel played it regularly, while *Sounds* made it "Single of the Week," describing it as "more music to burn Yes albums to."

Swell Maps moved slowly. It would be October before they again made a national impact, when they recorded a stunning John Peel session — among the tracks previewed, "International Rescue" was scheduled for the band's next single, although by the time Swell Maps returned to the studio, in December, it had been replaced in the band's affections by "Dresden Style (City Boys)." Much of what would become Swell Maps' debut album was also recorded during that two day session.

Although several record labels had expressed an interest in the band, Swell Maps were in no hurry to sign — indeed, they had no intention of doing so, holding out instead for a leasing arrangement by which they would retain control of their master tapes, while the label simply handled manufacturing and distribution. In the new year, Swell Maps linked with Rough Trade and in February 1979, "Dresden Train" was released on the Rather/Rough Trade label.

Swell Maps' debut album was completed during a five day session in April; a new single, "Real Shocks," appeared in June; and in July, *A Trip To Marineville* (#10 UK indie) was released to a combination of wild praise and puzzled silence. Although both the band's singles had gleefully wandered around the stylistic spectrum, from tight pop to wild experimentation (usually in the space of one song), the album gave vent to a variety of influences and ideas, allowing the patient listener to discern everything from classic Kraut Rock to Bolan-flavored glam pop lurking within the grooves.

While the band members pumped out a steady string of extra-curricular releases — two EPs as the Cult Figures; a third, by the Phones Sportsman Band, with Barrington as the frontman — a second John Peel session in May saw the band joined by former X-Ray Spex saxophonist Laura Logic, together with backing vocalists Josi Munns and Andy Bean (later drummer with Sudden's French Revolution). Typically, neither of the new songs ("Armadillo" and "Bandits One Five") performed that day would make it onto vinyl during the band's lifetime; however, both became firm favorites as the band gigged through the summer of 1979, working up the material which would be featured on their second album.

Swell Maps entered 1980 with their finest single yet, the mighty "Let's Build a Car" (#6 UK indie); unfortunately, internal tensions were already gnawing at the band, finally coming to a head during a short Italian tour in March. Swell Maps effectively split immediately upon their return, reconvening only to oversee the mixing of their second album, *Jane From Occupied Europe* (#4 UK indie).

Both Sudden and Soundtracks now embarked upon their own wildly idiosyncratic careers, although they would frequently regroup. In 1984, following three solo albums recorded with a variety of collaborators (Hugo Burnham of Gang of Four, Swell Maps' Richard Earl, and Waterboys saxophonist Anthony Thistlethwaite among them), Sudden reunited with his brother to form the Jacobites with guitarist Dave Kusworth. Soundtracks, in the meantime, had released two singles, the *Popular Classical* EP and "Rain Rain Rain."

A sashaying glam rock'n'roll band, this original incarnation of the Jacobites peaked with the hit single "When the Rain Comes" (#43 UK indie) and album *Robespierre's Velvet Basement* (#8 UK indie), before Soundtracks joined ex-Birthday Party guitarist Rowland Howard's Crime and the City Solution.

He would nevertheless be on hand for the next Jacobites' album, 1986's *Texas*, with Howard also making a high-profile appearance, replacing the temporarily errant Kusworth. Indeed, 1987 saw Sudden and Howard officially team up for the "Wedding Hotel" single and *Kiss You Kidnapped Charabanc* album, before Sudden launched a new band, the French Revolution, for two albums during 1989–90. Another solo album, *The Jewel Thief*, found Sudden working with three-quarters of REM (vocalist Michael Stipe, of course, was not required); Sudden and Kusworth then reformed the Jacobites in 1994.

By that time, Soundtracks had relaunched his own solo career, releasing the voice and piano-led *Rise Above* shortly after his own latest band, another collaboration with Howard, These Immortal Souls, released their swansong *I'm Never Gonna Die Again*. Now a proven multi-instrumentalist, Soundtracks cut two further solo albums, *Sleeping Star* (1994) and *Change My Life* (1996), but the optimism which characterized his conversation when talking about his music disguised a dreadful battle with depression.

By mid-1997, Soundtracks was working on an album for the Chicago-based Idiot Savant label, but the last time Rough Trade chief Geoff Travis saw him, he was working in a record store in west London, simply to make ends meet. On November 22, 1997, Soundtracks' body was discovered lying in his apartment — the cause of death was a massive drug overdose. The surviving members of Swell Maps reunited to play a memorial concert; Sudden and Kusworth would also dedicate the Jacobites' next album, *God Save Us Poor Sinners*, to Soundtracks' memory.

Swell Maps LPs

🎱 **A Trip To Marineville (Rather/Rough Trade — UK) 1979** If punks played Kraut Rock, or psych bands went funk, Swell Maps might have been enormous. Instead, they dabbled their fingers into every conceivable style, then swirled their hands around very fast — somewhere in the ensuing vortex, a clutch of post-punk classics will be found.

🎱 **Jane From Occupied Europe (Rather/Rough Trade — UK) 1980** More of the same, only more so. Wildly extravagant, the sound of a band which knows it's over, so there's nothing to lose. (If only more would explore the same freedom.) Hard to take in in one sitting, *Jane* finally emerges a more thoughtful collection than its predecessor, but no less dramatic.

DAVID SYLVIAN

BORN *David Batt, 2/23/58 (Lewisham, England)*

Having already recorded the "Bamboo Houses" (#30 UK) single with former Yellow Magic Orchestra mainstay Ryuichi Sakamoto, it was no surprise when David Sylvian's first move following the demise of Japan was a second collaboration with the composer. Released in January 1983, "Forbidden Colours" (#16 UK) was the vocal theme to the movie *Merry Christmas Mr. Lawrence* and bolstered by its success, Sylvian and Sakamoto began work on the singer's own first solo album.

Recorded in Germany with fellow ex-Japan members, Steve Jansen (Sylvian's brother, drums) and Richard Barbieri (keyboards), plus Holger Czukay (Can), Danny Thompson (upright bass) and jazzmen Jon Hassell and Kenny Wheeler, *Brilliant Trees* (#4 UK) was released in June 1984, accompanied by the singles "Red Guitar" (#17 UK), "The Ink in the Well" (#36 UK), and "Pulling Punches" (#56 UK).

All confirmed the strength and the restless idiosyncrasy of Sylvian's abilities and, following a diversion into the visual arts with the *Perspectives* Polaroids book and accompanying photography exhibition in Tokyo, Sylvian linked with Robert Fripp, Wheeler, and Czukay to record "Steel Wheels." A reworking of the soundtrack (*Preparation for a Journey*) attached to a video of the Tokyo exhibition, the piece was released as part of a two-EP project, *Words with the Shamen* (#72 UK)/*Alchemy — An Index of Possibilities*.

Fripp and Wheeler would also be on board for Sylvian's next album, together with Be Bop Deluxe/Red Noise frontman Bill Nelson (guitar), Phil Palmer (guitar), and one of Fripp's old King Crimson allies, Mel Collins (sax). 1986's *Gone to Earth* (#24 UK) and the singles, "Taking the Veil" (#53 UK) and "Silver Moon," were all surprisingly well received — surprisingly, because Sylvian's reputation as a vocalist did not prevent the album from emerging predominantly instrumental.

Having guested on Virginia Astley's acclaimed "Some Small Hop," Sylvian immediately began work on his next album, with Sakamoto, Palmer, Jansen, and Thompson all returning from past projects, together with Mark Isham (trumpet), David Torn (guitar), and Anny Cummings (percussion). The ensuing *Secrets of the Beehive* (#37 UK) would be ranked Sylvian's masterpiece; the associated *In Praise of*

Shamans world tour, with Jansen, Barbieri, Torn, Isham, Robby Aledo (guitar), and Ian Maidman (percussion) among the most spectacular live outings of 1987.

Yet album and its two singles, "Let the Happiness In" (#66 UK) and "Orpheus," would be Sylvian's last solo projects for a decade, as he launched himself instead into a feverish rash of collaborations. "Music took a bit of a back seat in my life," he later reflected. "I was deeply troubled; there was a whole private search going on."

During 1988 and 1989, Sylvian linked with Czukay and his Can fellows Jaki Leibezeit and Michael Karoli, plus Markus Stockhausen (son of the legendary modern composer), to record two albums worth of largely improvised material, *Plight and Premonition* (#71 UK) and *Flux and Mutability*, and while some recent solo recordings would leak out across a new single, "Pop Song," Sylvian's only significant release at the end of the decade he had done so much to shape was a box set of his solo work to date, the five-disc *Weatherbox*.

In the meantime, he was concentrating on a Japan reunion, albeit one disguised beneath the pseudonym Rain Tree Crow. It was a difficult project, despite the presence of Bill Nelson in the studio and, by the time the album was actually released in April 1991, Sylvian had already moved on. In November, he released another one-off album, the soundtrack to a Russell Mills exhibition called *Ember Glance (The Permanence of Memory)* and by the new year, he was in New York, adapting a recent Sakamoto composition, "Tainai Kaiki," for a new Sylvian/Sakamoto single.

Recorded with Bill Frisell (guitar) and Sylvian's new wife Ingrid Chavez (vocals), "Heartbeat" (#58 UK) was released in June 1992; he and Chavez found new musical partners too, Fripp and latter-day King Crimsonite Trey Gunn (keyboards), and in spring 1993, the team toured Holland and Japan with David Bottrill (keyboards), Jerry Marotta (drums), and Marc Anderson (percussion), previewing music from their forthcoming album, *The First Day* (#21 UK), and single, "Jean the Birdman" (#68 UK).

A remarkable collaboration, *First Day* was followed by an EP of remixes, *Darshan*, in December 1993, and a second tour, documented on the *Damage* live album. Sylvian himself then defied the insecurities of over a decade and embarked on a solo acoustic tour, the first step towards a tentative comeback on the soundtrack to the movie *Marco Polo* in 1996, and his full scale emergence with *Dead Bees on a Cake*. Four years in the making and featuring returns for Jansen, Wheeler, and Frisell, plus Marc Ribot (guitar) and Talvin Singh (tabla), the self-produced set would finally be released in early 1999.

Also see the entry for "JAPAN" on page 432.

David Sylvian LPs

7 Brilliant Trees (Virgin) 1984 Working a ragtag assortment of renegades, Ryuichi Sakamoto and Holger Czukay included, Sylvian made his post-Japan visions reality, taking the first steps toward the organic jazz-inflected music that would define his sound.

7 Gone to Earth (Virgin) 1986 A sonic massage as Sylvian links with Robert Fripp, Bill Nelson, and Kenny Wheeler for four sides of often innovative exploration. "Taking the Veil" is wonderful and "Gone to Earth" and "Upon This Earth" are the sounds of a Fripp-ified Sylvian.

9 Secrets of the Beehive (Virgin) 1987 Working again with Sakamoto, a beautiful, delicate album takes some of the space out of Sylvian's rock and replaces it with a simpler acoustic vibe, highlighted by Sakamoto's string arrangements. "When Poets Dreamed of Angels," "Boy with the Gun," and "Orpheus" are particularly strong.

8 Dead Bees on a Cake (Virgin) 1999 Although the grim title suggests otherwise, this album is a deliciously palatable slab of what we've come to expect from Sylvian. Sakamoto adds his now customary bits, while Sylvian creates a dreamy tapestry punctuated by the edgy "God Man."

8 Approaching Silence (Shakki) 2000

Selected Compilations and Archive Releases

4 Alchemy — An Index of Possibilities (Virgin) 1985 Sylvian's ambience masquerades as movie soundtrack. Or maybe the other way around?

8 Weatherbox (5-CD) (Atlantic) 1989 The works...to date.

David Sylvian and Holger Czukay LPs

7 Plight and Premonition (Virgin) 1988

5 Flux and Mutability (Caroline) 1989

David Sylvian and Russell Mills LP

6 Ember Glance: The Permanence of Memory (Virgin) 1991 An interesting soundscape, but walking precariously close to the new age.

David Sylvian and Robert Fripp LPs

8 The First Day (Virgin) 1993 Funky, groovy album from two musicians who work well together. Fripp's guitar allows Sylvian to loosen up, while Sylvian's voice lets Fripp noodle in ways he often doesn't. Full of long, looming epics, this is a trip worth taking.

8 Damage [LIVE] (Virgin) 1994 Vastly entertaining exploration of the basic tenets of *First Day*, given renewed power by the live surroundings.

Further Reading

The Last Romantic by Martin Power (Omnibus, UK, 1999).

TALKING HEADS

FORMED 1974 *(New York, NY)*

ORIGINAL LINE-UP *David Byrne (b. 5/14/52, Dumbarton, Scotland — vocals, guitar); Martina Weymouth (b. 11/22/50, Coronado, CA — bass); Chris Frantz (b. Charlton Christopher Frantz, 5/8/51, Fort Campbell, KY — drums)*

Rhode Island School of Design students David Byrne (ex-Bizadi) and Chris Frantz (ex-Beans) were members of the Artistics/Autistics, a five-piece combo concentrating on '60s covers and the occasional original. When the band broke up upon graduation, Byrne, Frantz, and his girlfriend/cowriter Tina Weymouth moved to New York, sharing an apartment in the Lower East Side and planning a band together.

Early names like the Vague Dots and the Portable Crushers were finally discarded after the term "Talking Heads" was discovered in an issue of *TV Guide*, and in June 1975, the trio auditioned at CBGBs (the Shirts auditioned the same night) and were given a show opening for the Ramones, promptly ascending into local legend for possessing less equipment than any other band on the scene. They were also very fastidious, turning up for shows in neatly pressed clothes and cleaning off the usually filthy stage before playing.

In mid-July, the Heads played CBGBs three-week festival of unsigned talent alongside the Ramones, Johnny Thunders Heartbreakers, Television, Blondie, and the Tuff Darts and were promptly invited to reappear when the event was extended into August. They also made their television debut on the cable show *Rock From CBGBs*, but they rebuffed Sire Records when a deal was offered in October 1975, preferring to continue building an audience.

Gigs around the northeast saw the band joined by former Modern Lover Jerry Harrison (b. Jeremiah Harrison, 2/21/49, Milwaukee, WI — keyboards) after he caught them live in Boston in April 1976; he made his live debut with the Talking Heads in September, although he would not join full time until after completing an architecture course at Harvard the following spring. In the meantime, the band finally signed with Sire in November and released their debut single, "Love Goes to Building On Fire," in December.

The band toured the northeast again in support of the single, joined by Harrison in Boston and Providence; he then accompanied them into the studio to record their debut album, *Talking Heads 77* (#97 US, #60 UK) and on a European tour with the Ramones. The quartet returned to New York in mid-June, and on June 18, Weymouth and Frantz married. Five days later, the band opened for Bryan Ferry at the Bottom Line, then returned to the road in October to promote the album.

The band would remain on the road in the US and Europe until February, scoring a minor hit with "Psycho Killer" (#92 US) in March. The band were already recording their sophomore set by then, in the Bahamas with Brian Eno, emerging for more touring in the lead-up to the release of *More Songs About Buildings and Food* in July 1978 (#29 US, #21 UK). The album would be certified gold in the US in December 1983.

"Take Me to the River" (#26 US), an utterly characteristic cover of the Al Green oldie, followed through in early 1979, by which time the band's third album, *Fear of Music* (#21 US, #33 UK), and accompanying single "Life During Wartime" (#80 US) were already complete. They toured the Far East and Australia in June; a US tour included the Central Park Dr. Pepper festival in August; European shows were highlighted by an appearance at the Edinburgh Festival, alongside the Chieftains and Van Morrison; the nonstop touring would end in January, when the band announced a short sabbatical.

Byrne eventually plunged into a follow-up project with Eno, the *My Life in the Bush of Ghosts* (#44 US, #29 UK) album, before reconvening the Heads for the ambitious *Remain in Light* (#19 US, #21 UK). It would be another nine months before the album was released; in the meantime, the band previewed their new sound with an appearance at the Heatwave festival in Toronto, the debut of the new nine-piece line-up; Busta Jones (bass), Adrian Belew (guitar), Bernie Worrell (keyboards), Steven Scales (percussion), and Donette MacDonald joined the original quartet, and four days later, the same line-up appeared at Wollman Rink in Central Park.

These shows were intended to be the big band's only live appearances until the album's release, but an enthusiastic Sire immediately offered to underwrite a full European tour through the winter. The band complied (the support band in London was the then-unknown U2), and in March, "Once in a Lifetime" (#14 UK) previewed the new album with the first in what would prove a stream of increasingly innovative videos. In 1985, Byrne's pioneering input into the medium would see him join Godley and Creme and Russell Mulcahy to share the Video Vanguard Award at the second MTV Video Music Awards.

Remain in Light followed, together with the "Houses in Motion" single (#50 UK), but following another massive tour, the band announced another break to allow the members to pursue further solo projects.

Frantz and Weymouth's Tom Tom Club was the first off the mark, the pair teaming with Scales, Alex Weir (guitar), and Tyron Downie (keyboards) for the dance club smash "Wordy Rappinghood" (#7 UK). A smart follow-up, "Genius of Love" (#31 US, #65 UK) followed in October, together with the Club's million-selling eponymous debut album (#23 US, #78 UK); the following month, Harrison's *The Red and the Black* and Byrne's *The Catherine Wheel* (#104 US) would hit the streets, just as the Heads themselves reconvened for a show at the Pantages Theater in Hollywood, filmed by director Jonathan Demme for a projected concert movie. Creating one of the most potent images of the early 1980s, Byrne performed the show in an outsize suit.

The Name of This Band Is Talking Heads (#31 US, #22 UK), a compilation of live and unreleased material, was released in April 1982, not only sending the band back out on the road, but prompting Tom Tom Club to make their first live appearances as well — they opened for Talking Heads at Wembley Stadium, London, on July 13 and were rewarded with a new hit single, "Under the Boardwalk" (#22 UK).

Back home, the Talking Heads appeared at the US Festival in San Bernadino in September, before returning to Nassau to begin work on a new album — interrupted by the birth of Weymouth and Frantz's first child, Robert, on November 4, 1982. The set finally emerged in July 1983 as *Speaking in Tongues* (#15 US, #21 UK); a busy summer also saw the release of the Tom Tom Club's second album, *Close to the Bone* (#73 US) and the fruits of the Pantages Theater gig, the movie *Stop Making Sense*.

The band would also score two hit singles, "Burning Down the House" (#9 US) and "This Must be the Place" (#62 US, #51 UK) in early 1984, another year of comparative inactivity also being broken by the release of the *Stop Making Sense* soundtrack album (#41 US, #37 UK) and, in November, a new single covering the Staple Singers "Slippery People" (#68 US). The accompanying album, *Little Creatures* (#20 US, #10 UK) appeared in June, the sense that the Talking Heads were now little more than a commercial adjunct to Bryne's solo career in no sense assuaged by his near-100% writing credits.

That solo career was kept alive, too, by a show documenting a tour across the US, *The Tourist Way of Knowledge* at the New York Public Theater in January and a new album, *Music for the Knee Plays*, complimenting Robert Wilson's *The Civil Wars* opera — premiered in November 1986.

Singles from *Little Creatures* (#10 UK), meanwhile, turned up two of the band's biggest hits, "And She Was" (#54 US, #17 UK) and "Road to Nowhere" (#6 UK); there was also success for the live version of "Once in a Lifetime" (#91 US),

following its inclusion in the soundtrack to *Down and Out in Beverley Hills*, while "Wild Wild Life" (#25 US, #43 UK), excerpted from the band's most ambitious project yet, the *True Stories* cycle, won both Best Group Video and Best Video From a Film awards at the fourth MTV Video awards.

True Stories, a movie written by and starring Byrne, spawned two albums: the solo *Sounds From True Stories* and the band's *True Stories* (#17 US, #7 UK). Further singles, "Love for Sale" and "Radio Head" (#52 UK), would follow, while Byrne immediately began work on another movie project, collaborating with Cong Su and Ryuichi Sakamoto on the Oscar-winning soundtrack to *The Last Emperor*.

Talking Heads' final album, the Steve Lillywhite–produced *Naked* (#19 US, #3 UK) was released in March 1988; two singles, "Blind" (#59 UK) and "(Nothing But) Flowers," followed, but the band had already broken up — Byrne to continue pursuing his idiosyncratic solo career; Harrison to form a new band, the Casual Gods; and Weymouth and Frantz to devote themselves fully to the Tom Tom Club. Their third album, *Boom Boom Chi Boom Boom* (#114 US) was released in October 1988; the Casual Gods' *Walk On Water* (#188 US) in 1990. Byrne's Latin-influenced *Rei Mo Mo* (#71 US, #52 UK) appeared in-between times, christening the singer's own Luaka Bop label.

All three acts toured, but through early 1990, a Talking Heads reunion was on everybody's lips as the Ramones and Debbie Harry both pledged themselves to an upcoming CBGBs anniversary tour. In the event, Byrne refused to take part, but his bandmates joined the package, regardless; the following year, all four members convened in New York to compile a Talking Heads box set, the *Popular Favorites 1976–92* (#158 US, #7 UK) retrospective. Inevitably, they recorded some new material to round the set out, including the minor hit "Lifetime Piling Up" (#50 UK), but just weeks later, in December, Byrne announced the formal dissolution of the Talking Heads.

Again, solo activities would consume the members' time until 1996 saw Harrison, Weymouth, and Frantz unite again as the Heads. Despite objections from Byrne, who filed suit against the trio, claiming "wrong use in commerce of false designations of origin," the band's proposed album went ahead. They replaced Byrne with a succession of guest vocalists, including several with whom the trio had worked as producers over the past decade — Ed Kowalczyk from Live (Harrison) and Shaun Ryder from the Happy Mondays, whose swansong Weymouth and Frantz oversaw.

Debbie Harry and Richard Hell emerged from the days at CBGBs; Michael Hutchence, Andy Partridge, and Gavin Friday also appeared. Accompanied by the minor hit single, the Ryder-led "Don't Take My Kindness for Weakness" (#60 UK), *No Talking, Just Head* was released in October 1996.

Talking Heads LPs

8 Talking Heads '77 (Sire) 1977 Stellar debut from New York's premier art rockers includes the truly inspired "Psycho Killer" and "The Book I Read." Byrne's delivery seems perpetually uncertain, whether he's on the verge of a breakdown or has something so important to say that he can barely get the words out. Delightfully edgy!

8 More Songs About Buildings and Food (Sire) 1978 Less frantic delivery and more melody highlight the band, defining their sound. Al Green's "Take Me to the River" is particularly strong. Although without the intensity of the band's debut, one wonders if there should be warning bells sounding somewhere.

7 Fear of Music (Sire) 1979 Just two years after they toured with the Ramones and generally impressed the world with their post-Ubu dislocation, the Heads teamed up with Brian Eno, and you can hear them listening to what the critics say, getting cleverer by the chord sequence. In "Heaven" there resides quite a pretty little bleary ballad, but it's all getting dangerously samey.

7 Remain in Light (Sire) 1980 Belew, electro, and funk — oh my! Change is in the wind for the Talking Heads as they shift their sound quite dramatically, especially on "Once in a Lifetime," to the exuberant quirk that would come to dominate their music.

7 The Name of This Band Is Talking Heads [LIVE] (Sire) 1982 Talking Heads were always the odd boys (and girl) of the New York punk movement: the ones who carried a note to excuse them from sports and formed the band in chemistry class somewhere between splitting a frog and dissecting the atom. With a vastly expanded line-up, this set pull highlights from the canon so far.

6 Speaking in Tongues (Sire) 1983 With the first quirky head-kick of youthful zaniness out of their system, Talking Heads turn into the sort of preposterous art schoolers who never get laid because they seem so weird. So they just get weirder to compensate. But "Girlfriend Is Better" and "Burning Down the House" were still fresher than the sniveling droves of synthipop that saturated the airwaves.

6 Stop Making Sense [LIVE] (Sire) 1984 Concert soundtrack to accompany Jonathan Demme's sensational film of the band. It was the year of the Big Suit and a chunky reprisal of "Psycho Killer."

5 Little Creatures (Sire) 1985 Self-satisfying return to the "Talking Heads sound," but it isn't really. Far more mainstream than anything the band has done to date, it was a commercial success… and the token "hip" record for people who had no idea what made this band tick to begin with.

4 True Stories (Sire) 1986 Inspired, no doubt, by another night in the lab watching Byrne's test tubes swapping baseball cards, "Wild Wild Life" remains the catchy bit — the one that was hammered down everyone's throat, the one that sounded a bit like "Once in a Lifetime." You don't even need to remember it to recall just how jarringly annoying and preposterously overblown

the whole thing was, from the road trip video to the knowledge that swarming up behind the hit were another nine tracks that were just as irritating. Why can you never find a good psycho-killer when you need one?

5 Naked (Sire) 1988 Paris, Steve Lillywhite, the Smith's Johnny Marr… is it a bad dream, or is it *Naked* — a night spent looking at holiday snaps of the band's voyage from the swamps of excess they were mired in to the swamps of incidental music they landed in.

Selected Compilations and Archive Releases

7 Sand in the Vaseline: Popular Favorites 1976–92 (Sire) 1992 Big fat double career-spanning compilation, with a smattering of new songs to keep the comeback at bay.

Tom Tom Club LPs

6 Tom Tom Club (Sire) 1981 An outlet for Franz and Weymouth, the pure pleasure and sheer hell that was "Wordy Rappinghood" is followed by the tweaky dance beats that would characterize the band's further releases.

5 Close to the Bone (Sire) 1983

3 Boom Boom Chi Boom Boom (Red Eye) 1988

3 Dark Sneak Love Action (Sire) 1991

The Heads LP

2 No Talking Just Head (MCA) 1996 The Talking Heads without Byrne, the band teamed up with old New York peers Richard Hell and Debbie Harry, plus new friends Michael Hutchence, Gavin Friday, Happy Mondays' Sean Ryder, and Andy Partridge, among others. An odd album of collaborations. It probably wasn't a good idea.

David Byrne LPs

6 Songs From… The Catherine Wheel (Sire) 1982 Long before the Talking Heads imploded, Byrne was making dramatic forays into solo experimentalism. Gathering together Adrian Belew and Brian Eno, among others, Byrne scored a series of pieces to accompany dancer Twila Tharp for a Broadway Show. Surprisingly, it's not terribly different from Talking Heads output. The complete score was available on the *Catherine Wheel* cassette-only release.

5 Music for "The Knee Plays" (ECM) 1985 The sounds of David Byrne and horns.

4 Sounds From "True Stories" (Luaka Bop) 1986 Music to accompany the film.

6 Rei Momo (Luaka Bop) 1989 For his first actual "solo" effort, Byrne jumped head-on into Latin world beat music and added some of his own quirks to the beats. Some of his best solo work lies here, but for all the confidence one would assume he has, the songs sometimes seem a little uncertain.

2 The Forest (Luaka Bop) 1991 Eeek! An all instrumental set, and way too fussy to listen to for fun.

3 Uh-Oh (Luaka Bop) 1992

4 David Byrne (Luaka Bop) 1994

4 Feelings (WB) 1997 Having traveled the world over studying music and culture the last two decades, it all comes together on this album. Byrne looked at his handful of songs and demos and thought how much fun it would be to work with other musicians — Morcheeba, members of Devo, Seattle's Black Cat Orchestra, and DJ Hahn Rowe — and it may have been, but the album falls short.

6 Visible Mas (Luaka Bop) 1999 Box Set.

Jerry Harrison/Casual Gods LPs

4 The Red and the Black (Sire) 1981

6 Jerry Harrison/Casual Gods (Sire) 1988

5 Walk On Water (Sire) 1990

Further Reading

Talking Heads by Jerome Davis (Vintage, 1986).

TALL DWARFS

FORMED 1980 *(New Zealand)*
ORIGINAL LINE-UP *Chris Knox (b. 1952 — vocals, guitar, bass, keyboards); Alec Bathgate (b. 1956 — guitar, vocals)*

The Tall Dwarfs emerged from the musical hotbed of Dunedin, New Zealand. Previously, Knox and Bathgate had played alongside Mike Dawson and Mike Dooley in the Enemy, a late '70s band now widely credited as New Zealand's first punk outfit. Constant gigging earned them a fierce reputation, and they took that edge with them when they relocated to Auckland in 1978.

By the end of the year and early into 1979, however, the Enemy found themselves moving in another direction. They had (consciously or otherwise) anticipated the looming new wave explosion as they dropped the scathing punk snarl from their sound and picked up a punk-tinged pop ethic instead; the addition of new members Paul Kean (bass) and Jane Walker (keyboards) and a new name, Toy Love, only heightened the shift.

With a more commercially-viable sound and a strong fanbase carried over from Enemy, Toy Love were quickly snapped up by WEA New Zealand and, in July 1979, they released their first single, "Rebel" (#29 NZ). Gigging continued apace and, by the beginning of 1980, the kings (and queen) of New Zealand had relocated to Sydney, Australia, to conquer that country as well.

Their grueling tour schedule was punctuated the release of "Don't Ask Me" in January 1980 and their debut album, *Toy Love* (#4 NZ) in June. Aussie fame, however, proved elusive and the band returned to New Zealand to release one

final single, "Bride of Frankenstein" (#22 NZ) on the indie label Deluxe. Toy Love disbanded at the end of the year following a final, farewell gig in Auckland.

Knox and Bathgate alone remained together, continuing to work on new material, despite the fact that Knox was now living in Christchurch. Christening themselves the Tall Dwarfs, Knox experimented with sound and song on a battered 4-track, and quickly established the DIY formula that would become this new incarnation's trademark.

In 1981, Bathgate too moved to Christchurch, where Knox had assembled the rudiments of a repertoire on that tiny 4-track. With the (very) temporarily returning Dooley, the band recorded the 3 *Songs* EP, released in 1981 on the Furtive label. Henceforth, although the Dwarfs would be known as a duo, they would include a changing roster of musicians on their projects.

At the same time as the Tall Dwarfs were honing their blend of lo-fi, psych-tinged garage punk, spitefully avenging themselves on Toy Love's pop-soaked sheen, Roger Shepard was forming the Flying Nun label, solely to give alternative bands their own, good home. It was obvious that the Dwarfs were made for the label and vice versa, and the ensuing, enduring partnership between the two would not only popularize the Tall Dwarfs in Australia and England, but would help establish Flying Nun as a formidable label on both continents as well. (Knox would also become the label's house producer of sorts, working with the Chills, the Clean, the Verlaines, and sundry others. If there was a definable Flying Nun sound — and few would argue against it — Knox was probably responsible.)

By the end of 1981, the Tall Dwarfs had embarked on a four-year recording and gigging stint. They would record an EP, tour, break for a breather and then head back to the studio for another go round. *Louis Loves His Daily Dip* was released in 1982, the more experimental *Canned Music* in 1983, and finally *Slugbucket Hairybreath Monster* (featuring the legendary "The Brain That Wouldn't Die") in 1984, when the routine was broken by the appearance of a single as well, "Nothing's Going to Happen."

Knox also found time to work on his own projects, releasing the mini-LP *Songs For Cleaning Guppies* in 1983. (A solo cassette, *Monk III-AD 1987* followed in '87 and formally kicked off a solo career that only echoed the heavy release schedule of the Tall Dwarfs.) In 1985, though, it was uncertain what fate would befall the Tall Dwarfs. Bathgate was planning a move to London, which obviously would stymie the recording schedule. While they pondered the future, Knox and Bathgate convened to compile another EP's worth of outtakes, old Enemy-era songs, and live material which nicely showcased the addition of strings and wind instruments to their garage-y repertoire. *That's the Long and the Short of It*, an intended swansong, was released in 1985.

Bathgate, however, wasn't gone for as long as anticipated and, by 1986, he was back in New Zealand. The Tall Dwarfs were back in action. 1986 brought another EP, *Throw a Sickie*, recorded partially in the Auckland Play Centre while both band members were suffering from colds — hence the title. 1987 then saw the *Dogma* EP, widely publicized for the inclusion of "The Slide," a pro-euthanasia number which generated considerable controversy in New Zealand. The Dwarfs also finally agreed it was time for an album. *Hello Cruel World* duly appeared in December — a compilation of Tall Dwarfs material from 1981–1984 which, released in both the UK and the US, served as a global introduction to the band.

Through 1988 and 1989 the Tall Dwarfs were effectively on an extended hiatus. Knox resumed his solo career with *Seizure* (released 1989), but barely was that complete than the Tall Dwarfs were again in the studio, recording songs that would eventually become 1990's *Weeville*.

Released in New Zealand and in the US, *Weeville* was strong musically and was very well received, even if long-term fans did feel that time had finally taken its toll on Knox's biting lyrics. But no matter what grumbling reached their ears, the band bounded back in 1992 with another full length, *Forksongs* and embarked on a rigorous tour to support the album, complete with a Chris Knox solo support set.

The Tall Dwarfs, it seemed, were finally slowing down. 1993 was silent; 1994 brought the *3 E.P.s* album — a set cunningly divided into three sections and available either across three vinyl discs, or on CD with breaks in between movements. The band would then remain all but silent between 1994–1998 as Knox focused on his solo work — they could not, however, resist recording a version of "On and On and On" for Flying Nun's *Abbasalutely* Abba tribute album, while Bathgate took on art production for the project. (He also cut a solo album, *Gold Lame*.)

Adding Ivan Munjak to drums, the band returned in 1998 with a new album, *Stumpy: The Album*.

Tall Dwarfs LPs

7 Weeville (Homestead) 1990 It took a decade, but finally a full length — same as all the half lengths which preceded it. Standard Dwarfs psychedelia, best characterized by the fact that they did it better — and weirder — than almost anyone alive. The album as a whole does pale in comparison to earlier singles... one can't help wishing they'd thought of an LP back in 1984... but still, better late than never.

6 Forksongs (Flying Nun — NZ) 1992 "Boys" is the stand-out track, a seemingly deliberate attempt to drive everyone from the room, so they can get on with the quieter stuff unmolested. Subdued by the Dwarfs' best standards and, therefore, best experi-

enced bereft of all expectations, *Forksongs* is nevertheless a rewarding album. It's just not a rewarding Dwarfs album. Again.

7 3EPs (Flying Nun — NZ) 1994

8 Stumpy: The Album (Flying Nun — NZ) 1998 One hour, 22 songs, and enough nonsense to please even the most resigned Dwarfs fan. Most cuts weigh in at under two minutes, the second longest tops four... and then the whole things wraps up with 20 minutes of mayhem. In other words, this is what we wanted all along.

Selected Compilations and Archive Releases

9 Hello Cruel World (Homestead) 1987 All four EPs from 1981–84 lovingly repackaged for maximum madness.

Chris Knox Solo LPs

6 Seizure (Flying Nun — NZ) 1989

7 Song For 1990 + Other Songs (Flying Nun — NZ) 1990

5 Croaker (Flying Nun — NZ) 1991

5 Meat (Flying Nun — NZ) 1993

6 Songs of You & Me (Caroline) 1995

6 Yes!! (Flying Nun — NZ) 1997

7 Almost (Dark Beloved) 1999

8 Beat (Thirsty Ear) 2000

TEARDROP EXPLODES

FOUNDED *1978 (Liverpool, England)*
ORIGINAL LINE-UP *Julian Cope (b. 10/21/57, Tamworth, England — bass, vocals); Gary Dwyer (keyboards); Michael Finkler (guitar); Paul Simpson (organ)*

After more than a year spent working his way through the Liverpudlian punk underbelly in formative groups with fellow future heroes Ian McCulloch (Echo and the Bunnymen), Pete Wylie, Budgie (Siouxsie and the Banshees), and Pete Burns (Dead or Alive), Julian Cope linked with former Big in Japan roadie Gary Dwyer in fall 1978 as The Teardrop Explodes — a name lifted from a caption Cope found in a comic.

The group's original line-up would record the *Sleeping Gas* EP, released through the local Zoo label in February 1979. The first of many line-up changes then shook the group as Gerald Quinn replaced Paul Simpson shortly before the band recorded the instant classic "Bouncing Babies" (whose swift deletion was later immortalized by the Freshies' "I Can't Get 'Bouncing Babies' by The Teardrop Explodes" mini-hit). Quinn, in turn, was replaced by David Balfe (with Bill Drummond, one half of the partnership that owned the Zoo label), and in this form, The Teardrop Explodes recorded "Treason" (#3 UK indy).

In mid-1980, the band signed with Mercury and, maintaining the tradition of changing their line-up with every new single, replaced Martin Finkler with former Dalek I Love You guitarist Alan Gill. In the studio with producer Steve Hillage, the group recorded "When I Dream" (#47 UK) for release later in the year. Its B-side, "Kilimanjaro," would give its name to the group's debut album, released in October (#156 US, #24 UK), although the track itself would not be included.

With "Reward" (#6 UK) and "Treason" (#18 UK) finally giving the group Top 20 hits in early 1981, The Teardrop Explodes became one of the hottest commodities on the UK scene — even as Cope became one of its most discontented pop stars. Echoing his idol, '60s heartthrob Scott Walker, Cope reacted badly to the group's sudden elevation to near teenybopper status. He commissioned a complete repackaging and remixing of Kilimanjaro, then objected when a new single, "Ha Ha I'm Drowning," was pressed without his permission. The disc was promptly withdrawn, to be replaced with a new recording, "Passionate Friend" (#25 UK), featuring recently recruited guitarist Troy Tate.

Balfe was next to leave, to be replaced by Jeff Hammer, while bassist Alfie Agius was then enlisted, freeing Cope to concentrate on vocals alone. The singer's final change would be to the sound of the band itself, ditching the widescreen brass and hook-laden pop, which Balfe had made so integral, and replacing it with a dense, neo-psychedelic swirl wholly at odds with The Teardrop Explodes' reputation.

With subject matter ranging from the break-up of Cope's first marriage to his current confusion over his role in the music industry, Wilder (#176 US, #29 UK), the band's sophomore album, was released in November 1981 to generally baffled reviews — a fate that also attended the "Colours Fly Away" (#54 UK) single.

But Cope wasn't finished yet. The line-up lurched again, welcoming Balfe back into the fold and replacing Agius with Ron Francois (ex-Lene Lovich), but "Tiny Children" (#44 UK), the group's next single, was a purpose-built flop — a slow, organ-led number that defied easy listening.

Francois and Tate were dismissed, and the three-piece Teardrop Explodes began work on their third album, provisionally titled Everybody wants to Shag The Teardrop Explodes (a title originally intended for Kilimanjaro). Much to Cope's horror, Balfe was now writing the band's material, having dismissed Cope's efforts as suitable for a solo album alone — it was a sign of Cope's disillusion that he didn't object.

Mercury, however, did. The album was rejected and Teardrop Explodes finally broke up in October 1982, just months after playing the biggest gigs of their lives, opening for Queen at Leeds and Milton Keynes festival dates. One of Cope's final actions as a member of the band was to answer all his fan club mail: "Dear so-and-so. Julian is dead. He died yesterday. I'm sure he would have hated you anyway."

One track from the aborted third album sessions, "You Disappear From View" (#41 UK), would appear as a posthumous 45 in early 1983; the remainder of the set would finally be released in 1990, as the intended Everybody Wants to Shag The Teardrop Explodes (#72 UK).

Of the various band members, Cope would remain the best known, courtesy of a long and idiosyncratic solo career. Balfe would return to Zoo records, masterminding Cindy and the Saffrons' "Past Present and Future" (#56 UK), featuring future Art of Noise pianist Anne Dudley and model Joanne Whalley, before forming KLF with Drummond.

Also see the entries for "JULIAN COPE" on page 281 and "KLF" on page 451.

The Teardrop Explodes LPs

Kilimanjaro (Mercury UK) 1980

Kilimanjaro [REMIX] (Mercury UK) 1981

10 Kilimanjaro (US Version) (Mercury) 1981 The lyrics may occasionally err on the artsy side of surrealistic absurdity, but the music... oh the music! The pounding rhythm section sits defiantly on the fence between the dance floor and punk's roar; sizzling guitars slash through cocky rocky riffs, while keyboards bubbles with psychedelic effervescence.

Even in their original, brittle form, but all the more so across the two (noticeable) remixes, "Treason," "Reward," "Poppies in the Field," "Ha Ha I'm Drowning," and "Sleeping Gas" (musically, the bedrock upon which the entire Madchester sound would be grounded) — in other words, virtually all of side one — slam helter-skelter on top of one another, each bigger, brighter, punchier than the last. Listen on, and "Books" gives an indication of where the future might have played out, had Julian Cope and Ian McCulloch not found one band wasn't big enough for both of them.

Yet there can be no regrets or dreams of stolen promises, no matter what else befell Cope and Teardrop Explodes. So daybreak bright and brilliant, Kilimanjaro's antecedents may seem self-evident, but Teardrop Explodes crafts them into such a unique package that they make the past seem utterly irrelevant, simply by staying so firmly in the present. The perfect opening for a brand new decade.

8 Wilder (Mercury) 1981 The comedown hits hard, a darker, swirling, bad-tempered beast — not quite unable to exorcise the memory of the glory of the early hits, but doing its damnedest through keyboard jams and ugliness. But the song titles — "Like Leila Khaled Said," "Seven Views of Jerusalem," and "...and The Fighting Takes Over" — sound a lot more portentous than the music, while the Clive Langer production shimmers with life. Despite Cope's best wishes, a triumph.

7 **Everybody Wants to Shag The Teardrop Explodes (Mercury) 1990** Unreleased third album appears a decade late and proves that regardless of who did what on the songwriting front, Cope knew precisely what he was doing back then. "You Disappear From View" is magnificent — a forebear of several future solo creations, while "Count to Ten and Run From Cover" and "Terrorist" take no psychedelic prisoners.

Selected Compilations and Archive Releases
7 **Piano (Document) 1990**
9 **Floored Genius [INCLUDES COPE SOLO] (Island) 1992**

TEENAGE FANCLUB

FORMED *1989 (Glasgow, Scotland)*
ORIGINAL LINE-UP *Norman Blake (b. 10/20/65, Bellshill, Scotland — vocals, guitar); Raymond McGinley (b. 1/3/64, Glasgow — bass); Gerard Love (b. 8/31/67, Motherwell — bass); Francis MacDonald (b. 11/21/70, Bellshill, Scotland — drums)*

Teenage Fanclub formed around the ferment of musicians hanging out at Bobby Gillespie's Splash One Club in Glasgow in 1985–86 — a home away from home for the Pastels, the Soup Dragons, and the BMX Bandits, as well as Gillespie's own Primal Scream. Norman Blake, in fact, made his recording debut with the Bandits, a band formed by Duglas T. Stewart and Soup Dragons' Sean Dickson and Jim McCulloch.

Released on the Pastel's 53rd & 3rd label, the BMX Bandit's "Sad" (#8 UK indy) reached its peak on the chart in May 1986, and by the end of the year, Blake had teamed with fellow Splash One denizens Raymond McGinley, Francis MacDonald, Joe McAlinden (violin), and Jim Lambie (vibraphone) to form the Boy Hairdressers — named for an unpublished Joe Orton play.

The band gigged through 1987, including one show supporting Primal Scream and the visiting Dinosaur Jr. at the University of London; the latter would become a pronounced influence upon the Hairdressers, as at least partially evidenced by their debut single, the falsetto-led "Golden Showers," released through 53rd & 3rd in January 1988.

The single did nothing and the Boy Hairdressers broke up soon after. Blake joined the Pastels for a time but remained in contact with McGinley and MacDonald, and in 1989, the trio formed a new band, Teenage Fanclub. With the arrival of Gerard Love, Blake switched from bass to guitar and in July 1989, the band went into the studio for the six days of recording that would comprise the bulk of their debut album. It would be December before they could afford to return there; the band spent the interim gigging locally and breaking in new drummer Brendan O'Hare (b. 1/16/70, Bellshill) after MacDonald quit for the Pastels.

A rough tape of the album was sent to Fire Records' Dave Barker, then founding a new imprint, Paperhouse. He had already signed the Pastels (and Spaceman Three); immediately upon hearing Teenage Fanclub's tape, he added them to the roster, and in spring 1990, the band was dispatched to Abbey Road studios to complete their album. An American deal, too, was confirmed with Gerard Cosley's Matador label — he had signed Dinosaur Jr. back in 1985 and was now intent on capturing their Scottish counterparts.

A Catholic Education, the band's debut album, would appear simultaneously in the UK and US in July 1990 on the heels of the "Everything Flows" single in the UK and "Everybody's a Fool" in America. As heavily influenced by Alex Chilton's Big Star as by Dinosaur Jr, the album was well received but sold poorly — no more than 5,000 copies had been shifted before the band made their American debut at the New Music Seminar in New York. There they played two nights at CBGBs and spent a day in the studio with Don Fleming (whose Gumball were also signed with Paperhouse).

A version of the Beatles' "The Ballad of John and Yoko" was recorded and released as a limited edition single on the eve of the murdered Lennon's 50th birthday in October 1990 (the record was deleted after 24 hours); the next month, another Fleming production, "God Knows It's True," was released in the midst of Teenage Fanclub's latest UK tour, opening for Sonic Youth through late 1990, then headlining over Gumball in early 1991.

Teenage Fanclub quit Paperhouse and Matador in the new year, signing to Creation (UK) and Geffen (US), and in May, they spent four days recording their major label debut — an all-instrumental album, *The King* (#53 UK). Again cover heavy (Madonna's "Like a Virgin" and Pink Floyd's "Interstellar Overdrive" were among the tracks, while a band original, "Mudhoney," was a tribute to the Seattle band of the same name), this album, too, would be deleted quickly, but its chart breakthrough was the cue for the UK, at least, to go Fanclub crazy.

Singles "Star Sign" (#44 UK) and "The Concept" (#51 UK) were followed into the chart by their official new album, *Bandwagonesque* (#137 US, #22 UK). Again, the band's influences were to the fore, prompting US critics, too, to leap aboard, loudly touting Teenage Fanclub as the melodic face of the still-burgeoning grunge sound — a bizarre comparison, but one that did Teenage Fanclub little harm as they toured through 1991/92.

"What Do You Do to Me" (#31 UK), in January 1992, would be Teenage Fanclub's last release for a year; in the interim, the band gigged occasionally at home and abroad (they appeared on *Saturday Night Live* on February 15) but, most significantly, linked with Alex Chilton to record a session for Radio Scotland in July — Chilton had previously joined the band onstage in New Orleans after professing himself a fan of *Bandwagonesque.*

The band returned to action in July 1993, with the "Radio" (#31 UK) and "Norman 3" (#50 UK) singles, trailers for October's *Thirteen* album (#14 UK) — a tired set that the band would later acknowledge was overproduced and underplanned. Still, they worked hard in its wake, touring the US with the Posies and closing the year with a string of Christmas radio festivals in the company, among others, of Cracker, Catherine Wheel, and Lemonhead Evan Dando.

They would emerge one of the highlights of the Glastonbury festival, but once again, the band took a year out of the release schedules, breaking the embargo only to team up with De La Soul for the *Judgment Day* soundtrack. The ensuing "Fallin'" (#59 UK) hit as the band — now joined by former Soup Dragons drummer Paul Quinn, replacing O'Hare — began rehearsing for the next album.

Recording at the Manor Studio (the last band to do so before the studio was closed in late 1994), Teenage Fanclub again turned in a lustrous performance, a Top 10 album *Grand Prix* (#7 UK) spawning three hit singles, "Mellow Doubt" (#34 UK), "Sparky's Dream" (#40 UK), and "Neil Jung" (#62 UK). Critical disdain for the set, meanwhile, was met with the acoustic EP *Teenage Fanclub Have Lost It* (#53 UK) in December.

The band left Geffen and signed with Creation's US parent, Sony, before the release of *Songs From Northern Britain* (#3 UK) in July 1997. "Ain't That Enough," the album's first single, became their biggest hit yet (#17 UK); it was followed by "I Don't Want Control of You" (#43 UK) and "Start Again" (#54 UK), while the band's latest American tour saw them link up with the currently high-flying Radiohead for one of summer 1997's most eagerly anticipated outings.

The band's lengthiest sabbatical yet followed the six months of touring that accompanied the album. Teenage Fanclub released another limited edition single during summer 1998 — an unofficial theme to the soccer World Cup, "Longshot," and played a handful of European festival dates; 1999 brought an appearance at the Bowlie Weekender festival in April, with new keyboard player Finlay MacDonald making his live debut. Using the occasion to introduce some new material, it would be their only major gig of the year, although Blake would appear on Glasgow band High Fidelity's February 2000 single "Ithanku."

Teenage Fanclub LPs

8 A Catholic Education (Matador) 1990 Scottish version of indy power pop, Teenage Fanclub ditch the bagpipes for guitars; unfortunately, their debut took the idea of malformed, grunge-death nasties too seriously and merely hints at their successful rise.

8 Bandwagonesque (DGC) 1991 Lucky for the band (and, ultimately, for us), they slotted everything together in record time for their sophomore set. A true homage to '70's power pop, but one with a genuinely hooky, very '90's edge that both set the Fanclub apart from, and lumped them in with, the other leading contenders to the indy throne. Fun and funny with sharp barbs attached to the jokes ("The Concept"), this album is a triumph.

6 Thirteen (DGC) 1993 Excellent follow-though, totally in keeping with what one would expect. Still full of giggles and stabs, *Thirteen* pleases with "120 Minutes," "Radio," and "Cabbages."

7 Grand Prix (DGC) 1995 A lovely record, beautifully textured, gentle, warm, and sad in turns, scathingly humorous, engagingly derivative, and at its best ("I Gotta Know" and "Don't Look Back"), unlocking some positively labyrinthine harmonies.

8 Songs From Northern Britain (Sony) 1997 A hint of jangle and those ever-entangled choruses meander with mood-enhancing bombast through an album of almost impenetrably apocalyptic lushness.

Selected Compilations and Archive Releases

8 Peel Sessions (Strange Fruit) 1991

TELEVISION

FORMED 1974 *(New York, NY)*
ORIGINAL LINE-UP Tom Verlaine (b. Tom Miller, 12/13/49, Mt Morris, NJ — vocals, guitar); Richard Hell (b. Richard Myers, 10/2/49, Lexington, KY — vocals, bass); Richard Lloyd (guitar); Billy Ficca (drums)

Decade-old friends Tom Verlaine and Richard Hell formed Television from the wreckage of innumerable juvenile projects — Hell's poetry magazine *Genesis: Grasp*; a book of poetry called *Wanna Go Out?*; and the Neon Boys, a proto-prog rock band completed by one of Verlaine's schoolfriends, Ficca.

Attempts to add another guitar player repeatedly failed, despite the likes of Chris Stein and the future Dee Dee Ramone trying out. The Neon Boys folded with just a six-song demo to their name, regrouped briefly, and equally unsuccessfully, as Goo Goo, and another year would elapse before the trio reunited, under the aegis of New York entrepreneur Terry Ork.

He introduced the band to Richard Lloyd, a guitarist who perfectly fit Verlaine and Hell's specifications, and the newly named Television debuted at the Townhouse Theatre on March 2, 1974. It was Ork, too, who suggested the band take a leaf out of the early New York Dolls' book and find a small club to play on a regular basis. Verlaine promptly went out and discovered CBGBs OMFUG (Country, BlueGrass, and Blues and Other Music for Undernourished Gourmandizers); the band played there for the first time five days later.

By fall, Television were the uncrowned kings of the CBGBs scene, with Ork recruiting a string of upcoming bands to open for them — the Ramones, Blondie, Talking Heads, and Mink DeVille all served their apprenticeships supporting Television's Sunday night showcases. In addition, Verlaine would play guitar on the Patti Smith Group's first single, the self-released "Hey Joe."

In March 1975, with Brian Eno producing, the band cut demos for Island Records. "I didn't like what he did," Verlaine reflected, "which was basically set up a couple of mikes and record the band live. His heart was in the right place, but nobody in the band could stand listening to what he did with us. It just sounded like a piece of crap." Blue Oyster Cult frontman Allen Lanier, too, would work with the band, recording demos for Arista. Both labels rejected them and by the end of the month, Hell had quit to link with New York Doll Johnny Thunders in a new band, the Heartbreakers.

Fred Smith, from the fledgling Blondie, replaced Hell, and that fall Ork financed the release of Television's debut single, "Little Johnny Jewel" on his own Ork label. It would eventually sell 20,000 copies mail order, but its first consequence was to shatter the band, as Lloyd left in disgust at the choice of song. Verlaine rebilled the band's next scheduled show (at Mothers) as Tom Verlaine, then called Cleveland musician Peter Laughner to town to ask him to join the band.

Laughner's own band, Rocket From the Tombs, had just split; he accepted the invitation and was a member of Television for three days. Then Lloyd changed his mind; Verlaine welcomed him back and Laughner returned to Ohio to form Pere Ubu. Television resumed gigging, and with CBGBs' fame now spreading throughout the US music industry in the wake of Patti Smith and the Ramones' graduation to the major labels, Elektra moved for Television in mid-1976.

Television's debut album, *Marquee Moon* (#28 UK), was released in April 1977 to little attention in the US but immediate mass acceptance in Britain. A single of the epic title track made #30 UK, and the band's UK debut, supported by Blondie, at Hammersmith Odeon on May 28, 1977, was completely sold out. Seven further shows were similarly successful, as was "Prove It" (#25 UK), a second single from the album. The band returned to the US as conquering heroes, but played just three shows in their homeland between then and April 1978.

Television's second album, *Adventure* (#7 UK), was even more successful in the UK, despite less than laudatory reviews. Accompanied by the single, "Foxhole" (#36 UK), a second British mini-tour, seven shows in April 1978, followed

but shortly after returning to the US, Television announced their decision to split. The band bowed out following six shows at the Bottom Line in August 1978 — source of the posthumous *Blow Up* live album.

Verlaine and Lloyd immediately embarked upon critically acclaimed solo careers (Lloyd would go on to join Matthew Sweet's band in 1991), Ficca joined the Waitresses. In December 1990, however, the quartet reunited to discuss a reunion. Jamming proved successful, and in the new year, Television signed to Capitol, recording their comeback album even as Verlaine promoted his own new solo set, the all-instrumental *Warm and Cool* and underplayed the band project. "You'll hear it and you'll say 'oh God, not that old thing again.' It's two guitars, bass, and drums. Nothing's changed."

Debuting at Glastonbury in June 1992, Television toured the European festival circuit before moving on to Japan and the US through the remainder of the year. *Television*, the band's third album, was released in September alongside a single, "Call Mr. Lee." Despite critical rapture and receiving *Rolling Stone*'s Comeback of the Year award, however, both failed to chart, and the band were dropped by Capitol in early 1994. Television broke up again following spring shows in New York City.

Television LPs

10 Marquee Moon (Elektra) 1977 Unimaginative critics crowned them the Ice Kings of Rock; adrenalined punks called them the Dead of the New Wave. But Television were always a lot more than either, and *Marquee Moon* remains the only guitar solo wankfest of the Seventies that you don't need acid to appreciate.

A monolith guitar sculpture underpinned by a bass that assumed it was lead guitar, topped by a nasal whine that thought it could sing, Television emerged, of course, from CBGBs, but while everyone else got faster and louder, their best bits never exceeded their own funereal pace.

Entranced by songs as long as Broadway; enriched by rhythms as bleak as the Bowery; Television were mesmeric to watch, hypnotic to hear, and while they could rock out when they wanted, the short songs were never pressingly significant. "See No Evil," "Venus," and "Prove It," merely bookended the epics that were the essence of Television — the portentous "Torn Curtain," which closed on a guitar that sounded like a vacuum cleaner, and "Marquee Moon," ten minutes full of Cadillacs and graveyards and something very nasty going on, just around the corner. What's weird is, when you play it again, you know that it's still going on.

8 Adventure (Elektra) 1978 Defiant in the face of everything, a punk album without a single punk element. The band's virtuosity and intricate guitar leads call forth the most delicate of melody lines, flying in the face of the speed and aggression of the rest of the scene, while lyrically too, the band failed Punk 101 ("goodbye arms, so long head"). Still a fabulous album, though, built on relatively simple riffs and slightly quirky rhythms and gaining further points by eschewing any repetition of the debut's epics.

8 Television (Capitol) 1992 Lurching, searching, *Television* veers from the surreal to the simply unreasonable, screaming "no surrender" from the moment "1880 or So" kicks in. Shattered guitars tease the rhythm into following them; vocals lose the tune but pick up something even more worthwhile instead. "Shame She Wrote It" is the ghost of electricity that Dylan once captured; "Call Mr. Lee," "Rocket," and the molten "Careful" emerge fragments of songs nailed to fantastic ideas. *Television* completes Television's 15-year trilogy and emerges the antithesis of everything their reputation (but *only* their reputation) forged through the '90s.

Selected Compilations and Archive Releases

7 Blow Up [LIVE] (Roir) 1982 An epochal issue despite Verlaine's own dismissal of it. The better-than-bootleg rendering of a final Television live show captures a flawless "Marquee Moon" and "Little Johnny Jewel," plus unreleased epics "Satisfaction" and "Knocking On Heaven's Door."

Tom Verlaine LPs

8 Tom Verlaine (Elektra) 1979 A wonderful combination of Television-ish sensibility and Verlaine's own formidable solo chops, this debut has a desperate resonance accented on "Kingdom Come" (swiftly covered by David Bowie), and depending on who you talk to, the oddly zany "Yonki Time" is either the best or worst idea Verlaine ever had.

6 Always (WB) 1981

7 Dreamtime (WB) 1981

8 Words From the Front (WB) 1982 An album that's beautifully sparse yet pulls out the stops when it needs to. At times exuberant and melancholy, its finest moments ("Clear It Away") have the feel of a stand of barren trees in late winter twilight.

7 Cover (WB) 1984

6 Flash Light (IRS) 1987

6 The Wonder (Fontana) 1990

4 Warm and Cool (Rykodisc) 1992 Less assault than gratuitous battery, the man who reinvented the electric guitar as a lethal weapon, then kept on reinventing it for 15 years more, sits back to take stock on all he's accomplished. Recorded in two nights, largely live in the studio, an album of ugly instrumentals, unfortunately, was not the greatest resume he's written.

Selected Compilations and Archive Releases

8 The Miller's Tale: A Tom Verlaine Anthology (Virgin) 1996

Richard Lloyd LPs

6 Alchemy (Elektra) 1979

7 Field of Fire (Grand Slamm) 1985

6 Real Time [LIVE] (Grand Slamm) 1987

THEATRE OF HATE

FORMED 1980 (London, England)
ORIGINAL LINE-UP *Kirk Brandon (b. 8/3/56 — vocals, guitar); Stan Stammers (bass); Simon Werner (guitar); Jim Walker (drums)*

Theatre of Hate was the brainchild of vocalist/guitarist Kirk Brandon, a former art student who once attended the same classes as the Adverts bassist Gaye Advert. His last band, the Pack, had achieved a measure of recognition when it released a brace of well-received singles and an EP during 1979–80. Despite a measure of grassroots acclaim, though, the Pack went nowhere, and Brandon disbanded the group when he and manager Terry Razor met Straps' bassist Stan Stammers.

An early Theatre of Hate line-up featuring fellow Pack members Simon Werner (guitar) and future Public Image Limited drummer Jim Walker was dismissed, in favor of Nigel Preston (drums), Billy Duffy (guitar), and a classically trained saxophonist, Canadian squash champion John Lennard. In late 1980, Theatre of Hate took their first steps onto the London club circuit.

The noise the group made was swiftly matched by the noise made by its audience. Brandon was a born rabble-rouser, years before groups like U2 and the Alarm formulated the sound of marching men and battle cry guitars. Theatre of Hate's strident manifesto of human politics, coupled with a roar that was two parts dying punk, two parts embryonic goth and one part absolute chaos, was an instant magnet for madness.

Early shows, scarred by the total inability of passing journalists to understand what was happening, saw the group's audience swollen by what one might euphemistically describe as "troublemakers" — Rent-a-Fascist skinheads, Thugs 'R' Us bullies, and disenchanted soccer hooligans — an alarmingly combustible mixture that was the utter corollary to the band's own creed of tolerance.

The vaguely Communist overtones of the group's chosen logo and song titles such as "The Klan," "Judgement Hymn," "The Wake," and "Freaks" further singled Theatre of Hate out as a band who danced on the thin edge of the revolutionary blade. But the group was not initially concerned — it was not their music that needed to be toned down, it was their audience. But Theatre of Hate's dilemma was the same as that which eventually crippled Sham 69 — their fans' inability to distinguish militancy from moronity — and it would take a similar toll on the group.

In November 1980, Theatre of Hate released their first single, "Original Sin" (#5 UK indy), followed in the new year by the soul-shaking "Rebel Without a Brain" (#3 UK indy), debuting the band's own Burning Rome label. Their first album, *He Who Dares Wins — Live at the Warehouse* (#1 UK indy), followed — an odd, and poorly recorded choice of debut, but also a strong indication of the group's strengths. Bootleg tapes of Theatre of Hate shows were already widely circulated, and over the next year, several similar "official bootlegs" would be released to try and calm what remained a very active underground market. Demand for Theatre of Hate live recordings continued even after the group folded in late 1982.

The group's third single, "Nero" (#2 UK indy), was released in July 1981. Like its predecessors, it sold respectably, and as the band's live profile soared ever higher, Theatre of Hate attracted the attention of Clash guitarist Mick Jones. The Clash were on hiatus for much of 1981, leaving Jones plenty of time to join Theatre of Hate in the studio to record what would become one of the undisputable classic singles of 1981, the pulsating "Do You Believe in the Westworld?" (#40 UK, #1 UK indy).

A thunderous war cry, a patchwork of crashing percussion, tape effects, and backward masking, "Westworld" broke into the British Top 40, and suddenly Theatre of Hate was everywhere. The Clash connection remained strong as the two bands toured together; Jones stayed onboard to produce Theatre of Hate's *Westworld* (#17 UK) album; "Eastworld" (#3 UK indy) and "The Hop" (#70 UK) added to the band's attraction, and Theatre of Hate were thrust into a whole new dimension.

Their new-found chart success, however, never brought the band respite from the bully-boy reputation that continued to hover over their core audience; indeed, the bigger Theatre of Hate looked like becoming, the more menacing their audience appeared. Finally, despairingly, Theatre of Hate called it a day shortly before Christmas 1982. The band's projected second and third albums would subsequently be released within the three-volume/six-CD "Acts One–Three" collection.

While guitarist Duffy (and later, drummer Preston — already replaced in Theatre of Hate by Luke Rendle) would resurface in the Cult, Brandon and Stammers remained together as Spear of Destiny, a band that would eventually fulfill almost all the promise of Theatre of Hate.

Also see the entry for "SPEAR OF DESTINY" on page 649.

Theatre of Hate LPs
5 **He Who Dares Wins Live at the Warehouse (SS UK) 1981**
5 **Live at the Lyceum (Straight UK) 1982**

5 **He Who Dares Wins Live in Berlin (Straight UK) 1982** Three live albums account for ToH's massive concert popularity, but the proof of the band would be in the studio pudding. For vicarious thrill-seekers only.

8 **Westworld (Burning Rome UK) 1982** Pounding percussion, rebel yell saxes, and scything guitars undercut Brandon's triumphant war-whoop vocals in a literal dry run for the best of Big Audio Dynamite. Producer Mick Jones was obviously paying attention.

Selected Compilations and Archive Releases
6 **Revolution (Burning Rome) 1984** Poorly treated posthumous release for the band's second album — "Americanos" and "Eastworld," at least, deserved better.

7 **Act One (Amsterdamned) 1999** Remastered version of *Revolution* brings the brilliance belting out; twinned with a rough *Live in Sweden 81* recording.

8 **Act Two (Amsterdamned) 1999** Desk mixes for the band's abandoned third album, barely distinguishable from the finished mixes for Spear of Destiny's debut. An unretouched *He Who Dares Wins* rounds out the two-CD package.

6 **Act Three (Amsterdamned) 1999** *Live at Bingley Hall 82* captures the band as it makes the transition to Spear of Destiny, with several future songs already making their presence felt. The second disc, *Retribution*, immortalizes Brandon's brief 1996 return to the old brand name.

THROBBING GRISTLE

FORMED 1975 *(Hull, England)*
ORIGINAL LINE-UP *Genesis P-Orridge (b.2/22/50, Manchester — violin, vocals, bass); Cosey Fanni Tutti (guitar, cornet, effects); Peter Christopherson (tapes, trumpet); Chris Carter (synthesizer, rhythms)*

Six years after they met in the northern English city of Hull, performance artists Genesis P-Orridge and Cosey Fanni Tutti formed Throbbing Gristle, performing a musical hybrid that lay half in the still-embryonic punk rock camp and half in traditional performance art.

A minute and a half of the band's first live show was included on an Italian various artists' album, *Mission Is Terminated*, but it was to be a year before they first received any attention, when P-Orridge and Tutti (under the name Coum Transmissions) staged a retrospective exhibition, *Prostitute*, at London's ICA in October 1976 (support for the show was provided by the punk band Chelsea, making their first live performance). In the ensuing controversy, the couple's Art Council grant was terminated, and they were banned from exhibiting at any UK galleries.

The group's self-confessed interests included torture, cults, wars, venereology, concentration camp behavior,

Aleister Crowley, unusual murders, and unusual pornography; their work, of course, reflected most of these. Among their most noteworthy efforts, Chris Carter was "castrated" during *After Cease to Exist*, a 10-minute film for which Throbbing Gristle produced a 20-minute soundtrack, released over one side of their third album, February 1978's *2nd Annual Report*. (Its predecessors, *The Best of... Volumes One and Two* were limited editions of 12 and 30 cassettes, respectively, circulated among friends only.)

It was not necessarily sickness alone, however, that inspired the team. Rather, in latching onto some of society's greatest taboos, the group was arguably opening up areas in which understanding did not have to go hand in hand with outrage — or as P-Orridge once remarked, "we're just troublemakers really, cause otherwise the world's a very boring place to be."

Tutti made regular appearances in sundry men's magazines, while Coum's first US tour in November 1976 saw them link with Monte Cazazza for the inauguration of the Nazi Love and Gary Gilmore Society at Shattuck Studio in Berkeley.

Throughout the first year of the band's existence, almost every note they played at jams and rehearsals alike, seemed to have been recorded. *New TG Volumes One and Two*, *Nothing Short of a Total War*, *Time to Tell*, and *23 Drifts to Guestling*, all posthumous releases, document these formative months, although the latter also includes one track from P-Orridge's first recording, a 1969 album called *The Early Worm*. Just one copy of the record was pressed (it cost him eight pounds); a projected follow-up, *The Early Bird Catches*, was never completed.

Released through the band's Industrial label, *2nd Annual Report*, too, was a limited edition (785 copies, with a larger 2,000-strong reissue following on Fetish in December 1978); yet, Throbbing Gristle's grasp of both conventional music and marketing was indicated by "United" (#39 UK indy), a club hit single through spring 1978. The song also appeared, in remixed (or recalibrated — sped up until it lasted just 16 seconds) form on *DOA: The Third and Final Report*, the third Throbbing Gristle album.

This latest *Report* again combined live and studio work, although not without some surprises. One of the live tracks, "Wall of Sound," was pieced together from five separate performances, while four of the studio pieces were solo projects by the individual band members. Another cut, "Death Threats," was comprised of phone answering machine messages left by a writer for the UK magazine *Zig Zag* and Chris Carter's wife, Simone, who believed that Tutti (who had by now split up with P-Orridge) was leading her own husband astray. Her suspicions, incidentally, were later proven correct.

After three years spent as a potent, challenging, and often difficult underground force, 1979 saw Throbbing Gristle make what were apparently very genuine attempts to break out of the sick cult mode into which many people continued to cast them. *Twenty Jazz Funk Greats* (#6 UK indy) was accompanied by a series of gigs that saw the band trooping out in smiling white — a far cry from the scowling militaristic black of the past. Their reputation was seemingly assured when David Bowie announced on US radio that Throbbing Gristle was the most important thing then happening in the UK.

Throbbing Gristle were still aware of their heritage, however, as the release of the cassette-only *Pastimes/ Industrial Muzak* collection of unreleased material makes clear. (In 1982, future Psychic TV member Geoff Rushton released *Assume Power Focus*, which brought to light more unreleased studio material.) This particular aspect of the group's career was completed with the CD release of *TG CD!* in 1986, a collection of unreleased 1979 recordings.

Despite their growing reputation as a live act, Throbbing Gristle's first official live album, 1980's *Heathen Earth* (#10 UK indy), was recorded in the studio in front of a group of invited friends. The performance was also caught on video and released through Industrial. A second live album, *Psychic Rally in Heaven*, was recorded at the gay nightclub Heaven in January 1981. Later, following the band's breakup, this same period was documented by a slew of in-concert recordings.

The changing musical face of Throbbing Gristle was highlighted on the two double A-sided singles released simultaneously in September 1990. Techno-pop ("Adrenalin" — #26 UK indy), lilting synth music ("Distant Dreams"), reasonably straightforward rock ("Something Came Over Me" — #23 UK indy), and uncompromising industrial roar ("Subhuman") all raised their heads, with a third single, June 1981's live "Discipline" (#43 UK indy), blending all four styles into one lengthy, compulsive whole. (A studio version of this track, with vocals by Soft Cell's Marc Almond, was released by the *Flexipop* magazine.)

In May 1981, two months after P-Orridge married his latest girlfriend, Paula, Throbbing Gristle split up, bowing out with two shows in California. Carter and Cosey immediately formed their own band, the Creative Technology Institute; P-Orridge, Christopherson, and Paula remained together as Psychic TV, with P-Orridge reflecting, "assuming that Throbbing Gristle had no basic interest in making records, no basic interest in making music per se, it's pretty weird to think that we released something like 10 albums plus bootlegs; 40 cassettes... that have had an effect on the whole popular music scene, forever...."

Throbbing Gristle LPs

6 The Best of Volume One [CASSETTE] (Self-Released) 1975 A collection of jams, intended to be played very loudly "whilst driving through the ghettoes, factory areas, and malls of your town." It sounded like it as well.

6 The Best of... Volume Two [CASSETTE] (Self-Released) 1976

8 The Second Annual Report (Industrial Records) 1977 The crashing, droning soundtrack to *After Cease to Exist*, accompanied by four early live cuts and two studio takes. A new edition of this album was released following the band's demise, recut with the music playing backwards. A chamber music ensemble was also added to side two, creating a grotesque, but somehow very effective, collage of sound.

7 DOA: The Third and Final Report (Industrial Records) 1978

8 20 Jazz-Funk Greats (Industrial) 1979 Their most accessible album, although there were, in fact, only two songs that could even remotely be called jazz-funk, opening each side of the record.

7 Heathen Earth (Industrial Records) 1980

Selected Compilations and Archive Releases

1 – 6 24 Hours of TG (Industrial Records) 1979 A boxed set of unreleased recordings from 1976–79, presented as 24 60-minute cassettes.

7 Throbbing Gristle's Greatest Hits (Rough Trade) 1981 Compilation of the band's most listenable moments! Still difficult, but at least it tries....

5 Beyond Jazz Funk [LIVE] (Rough Trade) 1981

4 Fuhrer Der Menscheit [LIVE] (29861) 1981

8 Boxed Set (Fetish) 1982 Includes *2nd Annual Report/20 Jazz Greats/Heathen Earth* plus *Mission of Dead Souls* 12-inch single.

6 Journey Through a Body (Walter Ulbricht) 1982 The band's final studio recordings from March 1981, all instrumental and offering few clues as to the future.

6 Editions Frankfurt London [LIVE] (Phonograph — Sweden) 1983

7 Mission of Dead Souls [LIVE] (Mute) 1983 One of the better live albums, a vérité document of the band's last gig, in San Francisco.

6 In the Shadow of the Sun (Illuminated) 1984 Soundtrack to Derek Jarman movie.

6 Once Upon a Time [LIVE] (Casual Abandon) 1984

5 Nothing Short of a Total War (Cause for Concern) 1984 Unreleased recordings 1977–80.

5 Special Treatment [LIVE] (Decay) 1984

6 Throbbing Gristle CD1 (Mute) 1986 Unreleased recordings from 1979.

6 Live 1976–78 (Mute) 1993

6 Live 1977–78 (Mute) 1993

6 Live 1978–79 (Mute) 1993

7 Live 1979–80 (Mute) 1993

Further Reading

Wreckers of Civilization by Simon Ford (Black Dog, 1999).

JOHNNY THUNDERS

BORN *John Anthony Goenzale, 7/15/52 (New York, NY)*

As the stylish guitarist with the New York Dolls, Johnny Thunders was already a seminal figure when the first wave of punk broke over the US and, more particularly, the UK. His guitar sound dominated great swathes of the British movement, while his association with Sex Pistols manager Malcolm McLaren (who managed the Dolls briefly in 1975) also conferred punk credentials by association. When his post-Dolls band, the Heartbreakers, found it impossible to land a US record deal, manager Leee Black Childers promptly relocated the band to London.

The original Heartbreakers line-up featuring fellow Doll Jerry Nolan (b. 5/7/46 — drums) and Richard Hell (bass) formed in May 1975. Hell quit Television the same week as Thunders and Nolan left the Dolls, and the trio played one show in May before recruiting Walter Lure (b. 4/22/49 — guitar).

Described by future Stiff Records boss Jake Riviera as "the best rock'n'roll band I've ever seen" (Stiff would subsequently release Hell's first UK single, "Blank Generation"), the Heartbreakers' reputation as trouble makers and drug addicts nevertheless ensured that they were never going to get out of New York, and Hell left in July 1976 to form the Voidoids.

He was replaced by Billy Rath, and in November, the band flew to London to support the Sex Pistols' Anarchy tour. That outing fell apart in the wake of the Pistols' expletive-packed appearance on television's *Today* show, but the Heartbreakers remained in London, signing with Track Records and releasing the junkie anthem "Chinese Rocks" (cowritten by Thunders and Dee Dee Ramone) in May 1977.

The band's visas expired soon after, and they were forced to fly home, returning to the UK later that month for a tour. A second single, "One Track Mind," and their debut album, *L.A.M.F.*, were released in September — the latter a powerhouse set marred by such an atrocious mix that Nolan quit in protest. Sex Pistol Paul Cook replaced him for the opening night of the band's latest UK tour; former Clash drummer Terry Chimes also sat in before Nolan returned to complete the outing. (The band's own mix of the album would subsequently appear as *The Lost Mixes*).

The band quit Track and broke up soon after. Nolan formed the Idols with another ex-Doll, Arthur Kane; Rath and Lure, too, returned to New York, leaving Thunders in London, where he formed a floating pick-up band, the Living Dead, featuring Paul Gray (Eddie and the Hot Rods), Sid Vicious (Sex Pistols), Peter Perrett, Mike Kelly (Only Ones), and others. A few generally disheveled gigs later, he convened a Heartbreakers reunion, but it fell apart after just a handful of studio sessions, and in spring 1978, Thunders signed a solo deal with Real Records.

His first solo singles, "Dead Or Alive" and "You Can't Put your Arms Around a Memory," both came close to breaking into the UK chart, as did an album, *So Alone*, featuring several of the songs earmarked for the aborted Heartbreakers' sophomore set and recorded with many of the Living Dead sidemen, plus guests Chrissie Hynde, Patti Paladin, Phil Lynott, and Steve Marriott.

The album was a majestic accomplishment and a more coherent musician might have followed it up in triumph. Instead, Thunders modestly admitted he'd stolen the title for "Memory" from an episode of *The Honeymooners*, then returned to the US to reform the Heartbreakers one more time. With Lure, Rath, and drummer Styx on board, they played a handful of summer 1979 shows, including a Max's Kansas City gig recorded for the *Live At* album, then broke up once again, when Thunders joined Wayne Kramer's Gang War.

He re-emerged solo again in December 1982 with another clutch of great songs but little idea of how best to present them. The *In Cold Blood* album included Thunders' tribute to the late Sid Vicious, "Sad Vacation," together with classics "Diary of a Lover" and the title track but also featured a mess of sloppy live recordings (some with Lure).

Thunders gigged through 1983, often acoustically, with backing vocals from Peter Perrett and Patti Paladin. His time-keeping was appalling — one London show in December had him arrive at the venue two hours late, then play incoherently for another two; another Heartbreakers reunion in March 1984 saw all four original members reconvene for a handful of shows and a live album, *Live at the Lyceum* (#25 UK indy), all marred by Thunders wandering offstage for unspecified refreshment breaks.

A second album, *Hurt Me*, returned Thunders to solo pastures, before he launched a partnership with Patti Paladin, a debauched Sonny and Cher-type debacle fronted by a colossal new single in late 1985, "Crawfish" (#7 UK indy).

The solo *Que Sera Sera* (#6 UK indy) album and single followed 18 months apart, and an entire album with Paladin, *Yeah Yeah, I'm a Copy Cat*, appeared in mid-1988. However, Thunder's audience was unquestionably and irredeemably cult, seemingly more interested in the slew of often confusing compilations appearing in the guise of new product than in encouraging him to rise out of his self-imposed miasma,

and while Thunders was forever on the brink of forming a new band, January 1989's "Born to Cry" single (from *Copy Cat*) would be his final "new" release.

Thunders died from leukemia in New Orleans on April 23, 1991 — apparently he had been ill for some time, but the news never reached the general public.

Johnny Thunders LPs

🔟 So Alone (Real) 1978 In London with producer Steve Lillywhite and a roster of visiting/genuflecting musicians — Sex Pistols Cook and Jones, Thin Lizzy's Phil Lynott, Small Faces Steve Marriott, Patti Paladin and members of the Only Ones, and Eddie and the Hot Rods — Thunders had two choices: to make the album people expected, in which case, he could have just fallen over on the first day and let that be an end to it, or to make one which would force the world to pay attention. To the amazement of anybody who stumbles upon it after a lifetime listening to the Heartbreakers, he chose the latter course.

A tight warm-up slam through the surf gem "Pipeline" opens; from there on in, Thunders rides through an album that both refers back to his ancient history (the Dolls' unrecorded "Chatterbox" and "Subway Train") and present status (the Johnny Rotten riposte "London Boy"), but also opens up to a lot more besides — a delightfully hazy take on the Shangri-Las "Give Him a Great Big Kiss," a pub-inflected "Daddy Rolling Stone," and the big city soul of "(She's So) Untouchable."

The crowning achievement, however, was "You Can't Put Your Arms Around a Memory," a sentiment and a song that would pursue Thunders for the rest of his life and wrung a magnificent cover out of Ronnie Spector almost two decades later.

"One night Joey [Ramones] and I were sitting around talking about songs which might work for this record, and he played me 'You Can't Put Your Arms Around a Memory,' and I said 'that is so right, that is so me, I love this song.' At that time, my mother was in a nursing home, and I knew she didn't have much longer, so with that happening, 'You Can't Put Your Arms Around a Memory' was — boom, that's the song."

7️⃣ New Too Much Junkie Business (Roir) 1982 He was still writing great songs, it was just a matter of getting great recordings of them. Part studio demo, but mostly live, with later narration by Thunders, the Sid Vicious epitaph "Sad Vacation" joins reworkings of material dating back to the first Dolls album in a set whose patchiness is even more infuriating than its sound quality.

6️⃣ In Cold Blood (New Rose) 1983 Five new studio tracks cut with Heartbreaker Walter Lure, plus more live material.

7️⃣ Hurt Me (New Rose) 1984 More or less a full album, albeit one weighted down by covers and revivals — "Memory," "Ask Me No Questions" and "Sad Vacation" all resurface in fairly good shape, but so does a gruelling "Eve of Destruction."

8️⃣ Que Sera, Sera (Jungle) 1985 Thunders' best since *So Alone* — by a long chalk. Indeed, the presence of "Cool Operator," "MIA," "I Only Wrote This Song for You," plus the Thunders and David Johansen collaboration "Tie Me Up" suggest he may well have been saving songs for a moment like this.

7 Yeah Yeah I'm a Copycat (Restless) 1988 Riotous old-timey covers collection, with Patti Paladin a willing conspirator. Neither recorded too well nor performed too seriously, it winds up a lot more fun than it sounds.

Selected Compilations and Archive Releases

6 Diary of a Lover (PVC) 1983 Mini-album recycling the studio cuts from *In Cold Blood*.

5 Stations of the Cross [LIVE] (Combat) 1987 Amusing between-songs dialogue gives at least a little interest to an otherwise drab document of two 1982 New York shows.

6 Gang War [LIVE] (Zodiac-Demilo) 1990 In concert with Wayne Kramer.

4 Vive le Revolution (Skydog) 1995

5 Add Water & Stir Live Japan in 1991 (Castle) 1996

7 Have Faith [LIVE] Mutiny 1996 Recorded live in Tokyo in 1988, muddy sound and a mediocre recording cannot hide the fact that Thunders was on fire that night, running through a searing set of Dolls, Heartbreakers, and solo faves to the ecstasy of the audience.

5 Sad Vacation [LIVE] Imprint 1999

6 The Studio Bootlegs (Dojo) 1996

2 Saddest Vacation: Last Live Act, Vol. 1 Imprint 1998

2 Saddest Vacation: Last Live Act, Vol. 2 Imprint 1998

6 In the Flesh (Amsterdamned) 2000 Live in L.A., 1986.

7 Belfast (Amsterdamned) 2000

The Heartbreakers LPs

9 L.A.M.F. (Track) 1977 From the plaintive whine of "It's Not Enough" (teen angst to a tee) to the just (can't) say no of the ramshackle "Chinese Rocks," the Heartbreakers' total disregard for societal norms so perfectly encapsulated punk that they made the Pistols look like part-timers fresh off the production line. Whether they were thrashing out poppy punkers like "Get Off the Phone," adrenalized homages to fixing on "One Track Mind," or anthems like "Born Too Loose," nobody could equal *L.A.M.F.*'s raucous fire. People claim this record is badly produced and maybe it is, but it really couldn't have sounded any better.

7 Live at Max's Kansas City (Beggars Banquet) 1979 Sloppy, but endearingly raunchy, the Heartbreakers live were the greatest pub band in the world — assuming the pub sold smack instead of beer.

Selected Compilations and Archive Releases

6 D.T.K. [LIVE] At the Speakeasy (Jungle) 1982

7 L.A.M.F. Revisited (Jungle) 1984 Live and remixed versions of the band at its peak.

6 Live at the Lyceum (Receiver) 1984 The band's undeniably tight 1983 reunion, also available on video.

7 What Goes Around (Fan Club, France) 1991
7 Live at Mothers (Bomp) 1991 Amid the plethora of sordid 77-and-later live cuts, this pair of sub-bootleg sound sets recapture the original Hell-fired Heartbreakers, spread across 12 songs from three shows: CBGBs in July 1975 and Mothers in November 1975 and 1976. Scrappy, but vital documents of a dream that deserved better.

8 L.A.M.F.: The Lost '77 Mixes (Jungle) 1995 The band hated Speedy Keen's original production and spent their career insisting that there was a better version out there. It turned out that there wasn't, although this time you can hear the instruments a bit better.

6 Born Too Loose (Jungle) 1999 One disc of Thunders' "best," another of unreleased cuts and rarities, including a handful of band-fired previews for *So Alone*. Interesting, but hardly essential.

TINDERSTICKS

FORMED 1988 *(Nottingham, England)*
ORIGINAL LINE-UP *Stuart Staples (vocals); Dickon Hinchcliffe (violin); Dave Boulter (keyboards); Neil Frazer (guitar); Mark Colwill (bass); Al McCauley (drums)*

Following a musical train of thought suggested by Australian heroes the Triffids and the Go-Betweens, Stuart Staples, Dickon Hinchcliffe, and Dave Boulter originally played together as the Asphalt Ribbons, with musicians remembered only by their surnames, Fraser, Blackhouse, and Watt. Signed initially to the local Lily label, the Ribbons released the *Passion, Coolness, Indifference* EP in 1988, followed by two singles in 1989, *The Orchard* EP and "Good Love," and an album, the six-track *Old Horse*, in 1991.

By that time, however, Staples had already linked again with Neil Frazer, with whom he'd played in a short-lived (10 gigs) band called Desert Birds when they were 16; retaining Hinchcliffe and Boulter and adding the Colwill/McCauley rhythm section, Asphalt Ribbons drifted into Tindersticks during 1992, and in November, the band released "Patchwork," the first in a series of handmade limited edition singles.

"Marbles," "A Marriage Made in Heaven" (featuring Huggy Bear's Niki Sin), the *Unwired* EP, "City Sickness," and a cover of the James Bond theme, "All the Time in the World" (on the *Tindersticks Go to the Movies* EP, split with Gallon Drunk) were all released in limited editions of between 500 and 5,000 before the band released their debut album, *Tindersticks*, in 1993 on the heels of a European tour with Nick Cave. (Highlights of one show appeared on the mail-order *Live in Berlin* EP in November.)

Melody Maker's album of the year, *Tindersticks* (#56 UK) also earned the band a Top 3 place in *Rolling Stone's* Best New Band poll and set the stage for a new single, a cover of Townes van Zandt's "Kathleen" (#61 UK) in January 1994. That was the band's last release for a year, as they turned their attention first to touring (two European tours sold out) then to recording their second album in Cologne, again to be called *Tindersticks*. They highlighted the Roskilde Festival that summer, while another live recording from Amsterdam in February would appear as a limited edition release on the continent.

The band re-emerged in March 1995 with the album and two further hit singles, "No More Affairs" (#58 UK) and "Travelling Light" (#51 UK), featuring a duet with Walkabouts vocalist Carla Torgerson (Tindersticks reciprocated by contributing to Torgerson and bandmate Chris Eckman's *Chris & Carla* album), with the Pacific Northwest connection furthered by the release of Tindersticks' "Here" single by Sub Pop in June 1995.

A show at the Bloomsbury Theatre in London in March, accompanied by a 24-piece orchestra, prompted another live album, *The Bloomsbury Theatre* (#32 UK) in October 1995; another performance in Paris encouraged director Clair Denis to recruit the band to score her next movie, *Nenette Et Boni*. The soundtrack, which included two rearranged tracks from the second album, would appear in October 1996.

Following a summer of festival gigs, in November 1996, Tindersticks (with guests Belle and Sebastian) played a week-long season at the ICA in London, each show focusing on a different aspect of the band. One night was given over to older material, one to "talking songs," one evening was purely acoustic with St. Etienne's Bob Stanley as guest DJ, another featured keyboard music (DJ Andrew Weatherall), and one previewed music recorded in London, Berlin, and New York for Tindersticks' next album (DJ Jarvis Cocker — Pulp).

Curtains (#37 UK) would be accompanied by the "Bathtime" (#38 UK) and "Rented Rooms" (#56 UK) singles and was followed by a new version of "A Marriage Made in Heaven," recorded with Isabella Rosellini. (Another duet, with Bongwater's Ann Magnuson, featured on the album's "Buried Bones.")

1999's *Simple Pleasures* was previewed with the "Can We Start Again" single in July and appearances at the arts festivals staged by Nick Cave in Cork, Ireland, and London during the summer.

Tindersticks LPs

9 Tindersticks (Bar/None) 1993 This band doesn't so much write songs as create an aural backdrop for Stuart Staples' lyrics; it could be pretentious, but it isn't, as the listener is drawn ever deeper into Tindersticks' evocative world filled with melancholy late nights in smoky pubs whose faded denizens quietly impart their tales of woe, each polished by repeated retellings. A sly, moody and brooding masterpiece.

7 Amsterdam February 1994 (This Way Up — UK) 1994 So deep, so dark, so impossibly solitary, Tindersticks' live performance adds nothing more than a few extra bare bones to their normal unclothed skeleton.

7 Tindersticks [SECOND ALBUM] (Bar/None) 1995

8 The Bloomsbury Theatre, 12.3.95 [LIVE] (This Way Up — UK). 1995

8 Nenette Et Boni [OST] (Bar/None) 1996 Few British bands are so instinctively suited to continental soundtrack work as Tindersticks, primarily because it's what they were doing long before they got into movies. Primarily instrumental (seven recurrent themes precede the first vocal), the album's thunder-cloudy jazz feel never ages, an enthralling mental screenplay that really doesn't need the pictures.

8 Curtains (Polygram) 1997 A bit more accessible than their previous albums, if only for the increasing diversity of their music (hell, there's even a cacophonous fast track). But *Curtains'* intensity and densely textured arrangements evoke moods as spellbinding as ever, while Stuart's more confident vocals finally emerge from the dim, smoky recesses. Tindersticks remain defiantly in a world all their own, but at least they're letting folk look through the window now.

8 Simple Pleasure (Island — UK) 1999

Selected Compilations and Archive Releases

7 Donkeys 92–97 (Polygram) 1998 Rarities, singles, and B-sides compilation

TOASTERS

FORMED *1981 (New York, NY)*
ORIGINAL LINE-UP *Rob Hingley (vocals, guitar); Aid MacSpade (bass); Dan Johnson (drums) + others.*

British expatriate Rob "Bucket" Hingley was manager of the New York sci-fi comic shop Forbidden Planet and ringleader of a coterie of 2-Tone/ska devotees when he formed his first band, Not Bob Marley, in 1981. Featuring members of the Cooties, a troupe formed by friend Aid MacSpade, Not Bob Marley started life jamming at the 171A studio on the Lower East side, recording their first single, "The Beat," in 1983 for release on their own Ice Bear Records. (A third song from the same session, "No Respect," would appear a few years later on the first *Mashin' Up the Nation* compilation.)

The group became the Toasters in late 1983, and with the change in name, came a new sense of ambition. With no distribution and less money, the Toasters decided to try shopping for a label and returned to the studio with Bucket's old friend, new wave wonder Joe Jackson in tow. The union produced four songs, which were diligently played to every label in town… and rejected by every one of them. Finally, Bucket decided to scrounge up the money himself, and in 1985, the *Recriminations* EP appeared on the Toasters own, newly formed Moon label.

With *Recriminations* making a considerable splash locally, the Toasters grabbed a regular gig at CBGBs; they followed through with a new single, "Talk Is Cheap." Never stable, the Toasters' line-up now featured Bucket, drummer John McCain, Brian Emrich (bass), Steve Hex (keyboards), a horn section (John Dugan and Ann Hellandsjo), and the vocal duo Unity 2 (Sean Dinsmore and Lionel Bernard); in this form, the band returned to the studio with Jackson to begin work on their debut album.

Their debut album *Skaboom!* (released in the UK as *Pool Shark*) was the impetus for the Toasters' first national tour, an outing that was swiftly followed by a return engagement in the studio and their sophomore album, *Thrill Me Up* (and accompanying single, "Haitian Frustration").

Celluloid created the Skaloid imprint exclusively for the band, and with everything apparently falling into place, the Toasters embarked on another coast to coast tour, which is when the sky fell in. In swift succession, many of Moon's distributors went bankrupt, virtually wiping out both the label and the Toasters own finances. Celluloid followed and when both Unity 2 and Swedish trombonist Hellandsjo quit mid-tour, the Toasters abandoned the rest of the tour and retired home.

Vocalist Coolie Ranx and trombonist Vince Fossitt were recruited, and although the US shows remained lost, the Toasters headed off on a tour of Europe, signing to the German ska-centric Pork-Pie label. *Thrill Me Up* appeared in Germany soon after, while a reactivated Moon issued it on cassette in the US.

The following year, with a line-up now featuring Bucket, Hex, McCain, and Dugan, plus Matt Malles (bass), Cashew Myles, and Brandt Abner (keyboards), and a new horn section of Mike Christianson, Tim Champeau, and Erick Storckman, the Toasters' third album *This Gun for Hire*, won some of the best reviews of their career so far.

T-Time (1991) and *New York Fever* (1992) consolidated the Toasters' position, even as the third wave of ska began breaking around them; indeed Moon, its roster swollen primarily by bands Bucket himself discovered as the band toured, was instrumental in creating that wave in the first place. The traveling ska circus Skavoovie in late 1993, too, saw packed houses turn out to see the Toasters co-headline a bill, which included '60s heroes the Skatalites and 2-Tone staples Selecter and Special Beat. 1994's *Live in L.A.* EP captured one particularly rambunctious evening on the outing; the

same year's *Dub 56* album proved the thrill had not been forgotten.

As ska broadened, so did the Toasters' sound. 1996's *Hard Band for Dead* (a take-off on Prince Buster's "Hard Man Fe Dead") included a tribute to Chuck Berry (the band's latest single) and a couple of swing songs, alongside tracks inspired by the television classics "Get Smart" and "Secret Agent Man" (another track, "2-Tone Army," later metamorphosed into the theme song for the Nickelodeon show *Kablam!*).

This same eclecticism characterized *Don't Let the Bastards Grind You Down*, a one-stop amalgamation of all the band's musical experiments to date. With Coolie Ranx having been replaced by Jack Ruby Jr, son of the legendary Jamaican DJ, the album became their biggest hit yet and the source, too, of much of the following year's riotous *Live in London* album.

The Toasters LPs

7 Pool Shark (Unicorn) 1987

7 Skaboom (Celluloid) 1987 A truly innovative blend of 2-Tone, early new wave, and traditional Jamaican styles. The Toasters rekindle ska's flame, with nods to the Specials, the Skatalites, and, oddly, producer Joe Jackson in an upbeat album of pure fun. The UK edition contains four tracks absent from the original US, the CD consolidates them both.

8 Thrill Me Up (Moon) 1988 A fabulous blend of high energy beats and memorable melodies, with notable nods to Jamaica's musical past (from toasting to reggae). Producer Jackson coaxes the band to new heights, and some of these songs remain live favorites to this day.

7 Frankenska (Pork Pie) 1988 Recorded live during the band's 1988 European tour, *Frankenska* not only caught the band's frenetic live performances, but proved that even a major line-up change couldn't destroy their determination and drive.

7 This Gun for Hire (Moon) 1990 Despite continuing tribulations, the Toasters return stronger than ever, further diversifying their sound into Latin flavors and even electro-beats.

7 T-Time (Moon) 1991

8 New York Fever (Moon) 1992 Amid experiments with reggae and some light funk, *Fever* concentrates on exuberantly jumped up straightforward ska.

6 Skavoovie (Moon) 1994 Recorded live in L.A. during the first Skavoovie tour, this eight-track set bottles up all the excitement this tour entailed (among the Toasters and the audiences), shakes it up, and lets it explode.

8 Dub 56 (Moon) 1994 A rambunctious celebration of ska from the opening note to the closing refrain; 14 tracks draw the listener into an all-night party that just doesn't want to end.

7 Hard Band for Dead (Moon) 1996 A glorious tribute to the '60s, from Chuck Berry to hit TV shows, but the band still revel in 2-Tone, making this exhilarating album an eclectic one as well.

7 Don't Let the Bastards Grind You Down (Moon) 1997 Skillfully amalgamating sundry past musical excursions to create a surprisingly mature and adventurous sound.

7 Live in London (Moon) 1998

Selected Compilations and Archive Releases
9 History Book (Pork Pie — Germany) 1997

TOOL

FORMED *1991 (Hollywood, CA)*
ORIGINAL LINE-UP *Maynard James Keenan (b. 4/17/64, Ravenna, OH — vocals); Adam Jones (b. 1/15/65 — guitar); Paul D'Amour (b. 6/1/68, Spokane, WA — bass); Danny Carey (b. 5/10/61, Paola, KS — drums)*

A movie special effects designer whose work appeared in *Nightmare On Elm Street V*, *Ghostbusters 2*, and *Predator 2*, Adam Jones was ex-Electric Sheep, a high school band formed with Tom Morello of Rage Against the Machine. It was Morello who introduced him to ex-Green Jelly/Jello member Danny Carey, who was already jamming with former West Point student Maynard Keenan and former Kings of Oblivion/Replicants member Paul D'Amour. Jones' addition to the band was sufficient impetus for them to begin gigging around L.A. through 1991.

Attracting the attention of the local Zoo Records, the band produced a six-track mini-album comprising four-track demos in late 1991; it was their live reputation that sold them, however — an impact that can be gauged from the inclusion of the in-concert "Jerk Off" and "Cold and Ugly" on their debut EP, *Opiate*, in mid-1992. (Studio versions of both appeared on the demo album.)

Tours with Henry Rollins, Rage Against the Machine, and Helmet preceded 1993's *Undertow*, the band's first full album. Released on the eve of the band's breakthrough appearance on the third Lollapalooza (they moved from second stage to first as the tour progressed) and featuring a guest appearance from Rollins, *Undertow* (#50 US) went platinum, with two singles, "Prison Sex" and "Sober" keeping the band in the media spotlight while they continued to tour.

In September 1995, D'Amour quit over "creative differences"; he was replaced by Justin Chancellor (b. 11/19/71, New York), whose own last band, Peach, toured Europe with Tool in fall 1994. Work began on Tool's second album, *Aenima*, soon after; the set was finally released in October 1996.

A total of five singles would be released from the album: "Stinkfist," "H," the (purposefully misspelled) "Aenema" single, "46 and 2," and "Eulogy" appearing on either side of the band's return appearance at Lollapalooza in 1997. At one point, all, bar "Eulogy," were on the Active Rock Top 50, while 1998 dawned with the news that the "Aenema" single

and "Stinkfist" (directed by Jones and retitled "Track #1" by MTV) video had received Grammy nominations — the former won the Best Metal Performance category. The album itself was voted Best Sleeve in the *Rolling Stone* readers poll and registered double platinum in August 1999.

The band toured with Ozzfest through summer 1998, an outing swiftly followed by Jones and the Melvins, King Buzzo linking in a side project, Noiseland Arcade. Jones and Carey would also join the Melvins on the road at the conclusion of Tool's own headlining tour in September. Keenan's side project, Perfect Circle, was launched the following summer, shortly before Tool's re-emergence for the Coachella festival in October 1999.

Tool LPs

7 Undertow (ZOO) 1993 Grinding alterna-mosh metal that fleshes out the band's *Opiate* EP to mixed success — losing some immediacy, while gaining a lot of weight. Nevertheless, Tool blister through their set, a malevolent rush that is best appreciated on "Intolerance," "Prison Sex," and "Bottom" — a song cowritten and featuring Henry Rollins.

5 Aenima (Volcano) 1996 Experimental metal, thanks in part to production by Steve Botrill (King Crimson, Peter Gabriel), this long-anticipated sophomore album left fans either scratching their heads... or cheering this often monotonous, wrenching dive into very dark waters.

TRIFFIDS

FORMED *1981 (Perth, Australia)*
ORIGINAL LINE-UP *David McComb (b. 1962 — vocals, guitar); Byron Sinclair (guitar); Robert McComb (guitar); Richard Gunning (bass); Paul Kakulas (keyboards); Alsy MacDonald (drums)*

David McComb and Alsy MacDonald met at school in Perth, Australia, in 1978, where they pieced together an ambitious multimedia project called Daisy, whose remit included music, books, and photographs. Studying at Curtin University, the pair then formed Blok Music, followed by the first of several loose line-ups of Triffids (the name borrowed from author John Wyndham's *Day of the Triffids*) and debuting at Hernando's Hideaway, Perth, in April 1979.

In 1980, the Triffids released their debut single, "Stand Up," financed by victory in a local songwriting competition. The band also issued a series of half a dozen cassettes for sale at gigs. With regular performances at the Stoned Crow in North Freemantle and the Broadway Tavern in Nedlands, by summer 1981, the line-up had settled down around the McComb brothers, MacDonald, Byron Sinclair, Margaret Gillard (keyboards), and Will Akers (bass).

The *Reverie* EP followed in August, and after six more months playing around Perth, the band relocated to Melbourne in January 1982, where their biggest gig in six months was in front of 20 people. The group moved on to the Surrey Hills suburb of Sydney, 2,000 miles from home, and put together the "definitive" Triffids line-up, with Jill Birt replacing Gillard and Martyn Casey in for Akers.

The band was offered a deal with Mushroom's Hot subsidiary, on the strength of their proposed third single, "Spanish Blue"; the label, however, wanted it remixed, a demand the band would not accede to. Instead, they self-released it in April, and as sales began to mount, Hot returned, offering to simply reissue the single. This time their overtures were accepted, and the band returned to the studio to record the *Bad Timing* EP with producer Robert Ash.

The Triffids' debut album, *Treeless Plain* (#6 UK indy), was recorded in 12 midnight-to-dawn sessions during August/September 1983 and was released in Australia in December, by which time the band had already decided to follow upon wave of other Australian acts and move to the UK. They played their final hometown gig at the Red Parrot in Perth on August 24, 1984, and arrived in London the following month.

They left Australia with a seven-track mini-album, *Raining Pleasure* (#8 UK indy) and the "Beautiful Waste" 45 fresh in the stores; both of the group's albums would be released in the UK (through Rough Trade) over the next six months. Meanwhile, the band's first London shows, highlighting both albums, caused a riot of media interest. Gigs ranged from the sublime (opening for Echo and the Bunnymen) to the ridiculous (bottom of a bill topped by the Geisha Girls), but every one seemed to earn new friends.

A second EP, *Field of Glass* (#8 UK indy), was released in February 1985, while the band contributed one of their best-ever songs, "MGM," to the much-loved *Beyond the Southern Cross* compilation of Australian and New Zealand bands. They also recorded a wildly popular John Peel broadcast in May, after which the band recruited slide guitarist "Evil" Graham Lee in time for a triumphant Australian tour.

A new single, "You Don't Miss Your Water Till Your Well Runs Dry" (#3 UK indy) was released that summer, while the band themselves returned to London to cut their third album, the breakthrough *Born Sandy Devotional* (#2 UK indy). A lush, well-produced set highlighted by the single "Wide Open Road" (#19 UK indy), *Devotional* was rated Album of the Year in the Scandinavian rock press and ensured the Triffids' continental stock would soar.

The album was swiftly followed by *In the Pines* (#5 UK indy), subtitled "a woolshed recording" because it was actually recorded in one, during that most recent Australia tour. Rough and ragged, it answered complaints that the band had become too slick. The album also served to conclude the band's contract with Hot.

Adding guitarist Adam Peters, the Triffids signed to Island in late 1986, teaming with producer Gil Norton for *Calenture*, and the following year, the Triffids were one of the principal attractions at the 1987 Australia Made festival, co-headlining the Subiaco Oval with INXS, the Divinyls, and Mental As Anything. That year, too, saw the Triffids at last make a UK chart breakthrough with the Stephen Street–produced *The Black Swan* (#63 UK) and the singles "Bury Me Deep in Love" and "A Trick of the Light" (#73 UK).

However, the Triffids were in no position to take advantage of the breakthrough. Initially insisting they were simply taking three months off, the band played its final show at the Australian National University on August 14, 1989, MacDonald's 28th birthday. Their final release was the *Live in Stockholm* album.

The following year, the Western Australia Music Industry honored the Triffids for making the state's most outstanding contribution to the national and international music scene. Ironically, Birt was the only band member present at the event — she was now working at the Casino where the ceremony was held, on her way to qualifying as an architect.

Rob McComb, too, left the music industry, to become a teacher, while Dave McComb, MacDonald (now married to Birt), and original Triffid Paul Kakulas became founding members of the Black Eyed Susans, with Rob Snarski (ex-Chad's Tree — vocals, guitar) and Ross Bolleter (organ, accordion).

This line-up played just eight shows and cut the *Some Births Are Worse than Murders* EP, an Australian indy chart topper, before the band went on hiatus. MacDonald quit to become a lawyer with the Equal Opportunities Commission in Perth, and when the Susans reconvened, a floating line-up saw Snarski and McComb now joined by Casey and Adrian Wood (ex-the Fat — keyboards), another short-lived line-up fractured when Casey quit to join Nick Cave's Bad Seeds and McComb moved to London with his wife, Joanne.

Snarski joined him there, and with Kenny Davis Jr (ex-the Jackson Code — keyboards), the trio recorded the *Depends On What You Mean by Love* EP before Snarski and Davis returned to Australia and formed yet another line-up for the *Anchor Me* EP. Much of this material, together with further tracks from the London sessions, would comprise the Susans' debut album, *Welcome Stranger*, released in 1992.

McComb returned to Melbourne in 1993, straight into a new writing partnership with Snarski, composing eight of the songs that would feature on the Susans' next album, *All Souls Alive*, recorded with Dirty Three members Warren Ellis and Jim White (aka Venom P Stinger) and ex-Triffid Lee.

McComb's health, however, was failing — respiratory and circulatory problems that pointed toward a heart condition. Undeterred, he launched his long-planned solo career with 1994's *Love of the Will* album; he also formed a new backing band, the Red Ponies (named for an old Triffids favorite) and toured Europe before moving on to New York on a song writing expedition.

There he was taken ill and flown directly home, where he was admitted to a cardiac ward; the following year, 33 year old McComb underwent a heart transplant. The operation was a success, but McComb remained unwell. Putting on weight and forced to walk with sticks, he was constantly uncomfortable, but he continued working, as a guest film and TV critic on Radio National, and by 1997 he was working with a new band, Costar (named for one of his dogs) and gigging around Melbourne.

Hopes that he might reform the Triffids for the Mushroom label's 24th anniversary concert in 1998 went unfulfilled (instead, Chris Bailey and Paul Kelly performed "Wide Open Road" in their honor), but McComb was recording again and planning at least a new single when he was involved in a car accident on January 30, 1999. Although he was kept in hospital overnight, his injuries did not seem serious and he was released. He died two days later on February 2.

The Triffids LPs

9 Treeless Plain (Hot — Australia) 1983 Dark and disturbing, an album of promise. Startling and innovative, it is the sound of a band exploring their capabilities, toying with ideas, straining the limits — Dylan's "Lonesome Hobo" is mutilated in revenge for one critic calling the Triffids "folk rock"; elsewhere, a darkly disinherited second cousin of Tom Verlaine strolls through a doom-but-not-depression-laden landscape — a treeless plain indeed.

8 Raining Pleasure (Hot — Australia) 1984 "St James' Infirmary" is the old blues chestbeater, as melancholy as "Embedded" is sinister and "Property is Condemned" is maniacal. The title track, sung by Birt, naturally echoes Mo Tucker's Velvet vocals, and the Band Most Likely To for 1985 still sound that way today.

8 Born Sandy Devotional (Rough Trade) 1986 Without any definable change in focus, still the Triffids have moved on, away from the stark loneliness of the earlier releases and into a world of broad production and less excitable lyrics. The thoughtfulness doesn't hurt, but a little bit of roughness might not go astray.

8 In the Pines (Mushroom — Australia) 1986 Apparently feeling the same way, the Triffids decamp to a woolshed in the outback and bang out a virtual live album — no audience, but no distractions either, just a rudimentary recorder and a repertoire of classics. In years to come, this would be called unplugged. Right now, it's simply *au naturel.*

7 Calenture (Island) 1987

7 The Black Swan (Island) 1989 "Bury Me Deep in Love" and "Trick of the Light" finally gave the band the hits they deserved, but even a gorgeous Stephen Street production could not paper over the darkness, in either songs or performance. The end, and it knows it.

7 Stockholm [LIVE] (MNW) 1990

Selected Compilations and Archive Releases

9 Love in Bright Landscapes (Hot — Australia) 1986 Marvelous sampling of the band's first albums and rare singles, although the absence of "MGM" means it can never be perfect.

8 An Australian Melodrama (Mushroom — Australia) 1994

Black Eyed Susans LPs

8 All Souls Alive (Frontier) 1993 Dynamics and emotions come alive across a loose, but powerful, collection. Leonard Cohen has rarely sounded so despairing.

7 Mouth to Mouth (American) 1995

6 Spin the Bottle (American) 1997

Selected Compilations and Archive Releases

8 Welcome Stranger (Torn & Frayed) 1992 Collection combining the Susans' two essential EPs , plus further session material.

David McComb LP

7 Love of the Will (Mushroom — Australia) 1994 Understated solo album with some lovely melodies in the melancholy, but even its high notes miss the dramatic instrumental interplay that once so colored McComb's writing.

U

ULTRAVOX

FORMED 1976 (London, England)

ORIGINAL LINE-UP John Foxx (b. Dennis Leigh — vocals); Steven Shears (guitar); Chris St. John aka Chris Cross (b. Chris Allen, 7/14/52 — bass); Billy Currie (b. William Currie, 4/1/50, Huddersfield — keyboards); Warren Cann (b. 5/20/52, Victoria BC, Canada — drums)

The roots of Ultravox lay in John Foxx (ex-Wooly Fish) and Chris Cross (ex-Stoned Rose) discovering a shared preoccupation with Roxy Music. Having advertised in *Melody Maker* for fellow acolytes, Foxx recalled, "we must have auditioned every floater in London. People from Kilburn and the High Roads… The Motors…." Finally joined by Billy Curry, Warren Cann (ex-Thumper), and Steven Shears, Tiger Lily cut one single, a darkly camp version of Fats Waller's "Ain't Misbehavin'", released to mass apathy as the title song to a 1975 porn movie. (It was subsequently reissued in 1980 and reached #34 UK indy.)

The band followed through with a string of gigs, mainly at the King's Cross club The Dolls House, at the same time furiously writing the songs with which Ultravox! (the exclamation mark, "a silly ploy," according to Foxx, "to get us more publicity") were to erupt.

"The name was mine," Foxx said. "It means in Latin — 'ultra' means 'beyond all reasonable expectations' and 'vox' means voice, of course." He also admitted it was a name everybody hated, and that played a part as well. "Everyone disliked it, so we thought it must have some virtue. But we used to change the name every week…the Zips, the Innocents, London Soundtrack, Fire Of London…."

While most record companies, Foxx acknowledged, viewed the band as "NCV" (noncommercially viable), Island Records, still steering clear of punk but nevertheless intrigued by what was going on in the clubs, picked the band up toward the end of summer 1976 on the strength of a demo recorded with the then-unknown producer Steve Lillywhite.

It was a marriage made in heaven. Ultravox owed little more to the on-going live scene than a frenetic, electronic translation of punk's more refined elements. Island were still locked into their obsession with success Roxy Music/Sparks style — the self-same influences Ultravox were pinpointing in their interviews.

The choice of a "name" producer, too, reinforced the image. Although Lillywhite would remain on board, Brian Eno's reputation alone guaranteed Ultravox a more sympathetic hearing than might otherwise have been theirs', and reviews that greeted the band's January 1977 debut single, "Dangerous Rhythm," proved the decision-makers right.

The band's eponymous debut album followed, with a second single, the non-album "Young Savage," emerging in May 1977. Neither sold, however, and while the band were a highlight of the Reading Festival in August, even by the time of their second album in October, Ultravox were a considerably more sober — and sobering proposition — than they had appeared just nine months earlier.

The title was the most jocular thing about the Steve Lillywhite-produced *Ha Ha Ha*, and when "Rockwrock," the first single from the set, was released to little applause, Island all but let the album die in its tracks. *Retro*, a live EP released in January 1978, caught the band in savage form but failed likewise, and when — with ex-Neo guitarist Robin Simon now standing in for the errant Shears — Ultravox headed off to Germany to record with producer Connie Plank, it was very much make-or-break time.

Previewed by a second consecutive Reading Festival date and a five-night residency at the Marquee in London, *Systems of Romance* broke. Despite imbibing a heavy taste of Plank's better-known work with Kraftwerk, the album had little in common either with the Ultravox their fans remembered so fondly or the pre-Tubeway Army electro scene into which it wandered, and so it, too, perished, and the two singles it spawned, "Slow Motion" and "Quiet Men," could not dent the chart.

Island reacted in the only way they could think of — at the end of 1978, they washed their hands of the whole affair. So, it seemed, did Ultravox. Following two final Marquee shows over Christmas, Foxx was first to go, opting for a solo career which was to pay great, if brief, dividends in the wake of his "Underpass" debut. Cann joined Zaine Griff's band; Currie pledged his troth to Gary Numan, Simon joined Magazine, and Cross retired to his London home and a song-writing reunion with his brother Jeff Allen — himself an ex-pop star after a career with glam rockers Hello.

Behind the scenes, however, wheels were turning. Cann, Cross, and Currie remained intent on keeping the name of Ultravox alive, and in April 1979, they recruited Midge Ure (b. James Ure, 10/10/53, Glasgow) to replace the errant Foxx.

Ure was one of the great also-rans of '70s British rock. He first emerged as the vocalist with Slik (aka Salvation), a post-Bay City Rollers teenybopper act who scored one massive hit, "Forever and Ever," in early 1976, then crashed after a car accident incapacitated Ure. By the time the band was on their feet again, the fans had moved on, and the scene was shifting too. Slik regrouped as PVC2 and released one last punkish single, then split — three quarters of the band became the Zones; Ure joined ex-Sex Pistol Glen Matlock's Rich Kids. (Ure had, in fact, been offered a place in the Pistols before Johnny Rotten joined. He turned them down.)

The Rich Kids collapsed after one album, and for a time, Ure guested with Thin Lizzy (he would subsequently join Lizzy frontman Phil Lynott for the "Yellow Pearl" single), before trying his hand at production with State of Grace predecessors Fatal Charm. He was also a member of Visage, a synthi-pop combo being formed by club doorman Steve Strange, fellow Rich Kid Rusty Egan, three-quarters of Magazine, and Ultravox's Currie.

The new Ultravox debuted with four low-profile UK dates in November 1979 before heading to the US for a longer outing in December. A deal with Chrysalis followed, and in April 1980, the band released their latest single, "Sleepwalk" (#29 UK). Three months later, the *Vienna* (#164 US, #3 UK) album proved how suddenly the band had come to grips with the new synthi-pop scene by beginning a 72-week stay on the UK chart. "Passing Strangers" (#57 UK) followed and in January 1981, the atmospheric "Vienna" (#2 UK) was only held off the top by Joe Dolce's novelty song "Shaddap Your Face."

An EP of the band's Island material, *Slow Motion* (#33 UK), and Foxx's *Metamix* (#18 UK) and *The Garden* (#24 UK) proved that Ultravox's success was contagious. Visage were still going strong; Ultravox's own "All Stood Still" (#8 UK) and a return engagement with Connie Plank, "The Thin Wall" (#14 UK), proved that everything the band had done in the past was suddenly forgiven.

By 1981's end, Ultravox's own next album, *Rage in Eden* (#144US, #4 UK), and single, "The Voice" (#16 UK), had established them among the country's top acts, while Ure himself was planning his own solo breakout (following his departure from Visage) with a hit cover of the Walker Brothers "No Regrets" (#9 UK) in June 1982.

Ultravox traveled to Montserrat to record their next album, *Quartet* (#61 US, #6 UK), with Beatles producer George Martin. "Reap the Wild Wind" (#71 US, #12 UK) and "Visions in Blue" (#15 UK) were both hits; so was "Hymn" (#11 UK), a song that utilized the selfsame melody line as an earlier single by Ure's old friends in the Zones, "Mourning Star." Their version, however, had flopped completely.

Through 1983, "We Came to Dance" (#18 UK) and the live *Monument* (#9 UK) were joined on the UK chart by a second Ure solo effort, "After a Fashion," recorded with Japan's Mick Karn. The following year, the ambitious *Lament* (#115 US, #8 UK) album was responsible for three

more hits: "One Small Day" (#27 UK), "Dancing With Tears in My Eyes" (#3 UK), and "Lament' (#22 UK). Currie was involved in a third and final Visage album, and the year was about to wrap up with the much-anticipated *Collection* (#2 UK) hits compilation (and attendant single, "Love's Great Adventure" — #12 UK), when Boomtown Rats frontman Bob Geldof contacted Ure to co-write a song to raise funds for Ethiopian famine relief.

Band Aid's "Do They Know It's Christmas" (#1 UK) would become the biggest selling single in British history; it was followed by Live Aid, at which Ultravox turned in a triumphant set. In their moment of glory, however, the band were also nearing the end. Announcing an extended hiatus, Ultravox sundered, with Ure immediately launching his first solo album, *The Gift* (#2 UK), and his first chart-topper since the days of Slik, "If I Was" (#1 UK).

That latter band's drummer, Kenny Hyslop, would make a return on Ure's solo tour that winter, alongside former Sensational Alex Harvey Band guitarist Zal Cleminson, but by the New Year, the luster was beginning to fade. Two further Ure singles, "Wastelands" (#46) and "Call of the Wild" (#27 UK), performed poorly in early 1986, and Ultravox reunited that spring, with Mark Brzezicki (ex-Big Country) replacing Cann, now working alongside Kim Wilde.

U-Vox (#9 UK), the new line-up's debut, would also be Ultravox's last. After two final singles, "Same Old Story" (#31 UK) and "All Fall Down" (#30 UK), the band splintered — Currie launching a solo career; Ure continuing on with his.

In 1989, a new band — like the album, titled U-Vox — would form around Currie, pre-Ure guitarist Robin Simon, and Marcus O'Higgins (vocals), to tour an Ultravox-heavy show around the UK. It was an ill-starred venture — fan pressure allegedly persuaded Currie to rename the project Humania, before disbanding it. Three years later, however, he recruited Tony Fenelle (vocals, guitar) for a second revival, aiming this time to give the band their own identity.

Having debuted with an EP offering up a rerecording of "Vienna," the pair issued a second EP of new material, *I Am Alive*, in January 1993 before releasing an album, *Revelation*, hot on the heels of the compilation, *If I Was — The Very Best of Ultravox and Midge Ure* (#10 UK). A second album, 1995's *Ingenuity*, was recorded with new vocalist Sam Blue and guitarist Vinny Burns, although the lack of success — or even attention — meted out to the project left this new Ultravox with little option but to grind to a halt.

Ultravox LPs

🔟 **Ultravox! (Island — UK) 1977** "It's not like anything I've ever known before," John Foxx sings on "Dangerous Rhythms," and he's right...almost. Careful dissection reveals *Ultravox!* to be composed of equal parts Roxy Music's melodic genius (Brian

Eno produced) and Kraftwerkian electro-excellence, brought to life by punk's electric charge of aggression. The ensuing dichotomy is seen most vividly on the artsy "I Want to Be a Machine" — which perversely rides acoustic guitar and violin, but it's not all artsy experimentation either, as Ultravox! prove capable of flashes of assaultive fury as well, booming, crashing, thrashing drums propelling the beats, while sinuous bass add a palatable sensuality to the sound.

8 Ha Ha Ha (Island) 1977 Kicking off with the exuberant thrash of "Rockwrock," *Ha-Ha-Ha!* is a virtual homage to Roxy Music, without ever actually sounding remotely like them. The haunting perfection of "Hiroshima Mon Amour" and the barely contained chaos of "Fear in the Western World" dominate an eclectically varied set.

8 Systems of Romance (Antilles) 1978 — Filled with rich melodic wit and just a hint of gloomy melancholy, *Romance* furthers Ultravox's artier experimentation, albeit limiting their explorations to textures and rhythms in a highly accessible fashion.

8 Vienna (Chrysalis) 1980 Ure brings a more solid rock foundation, which nevertheless left room for gushing, lush keyboards raining atmospheres from above. A fistful of edgy rockers, glammy pop tracks, and the doomy, synthi-dance remain from earlier times, but there were new elements as well that melded in beautifully from the tinkling piano passages to Midge's more pop delivery. Then there's the epic title track itself, so far removed from anything previously attempted, yet the obvious culmination of so many of them.

8 Rage in Eden (Chrysalis) 1981 Divided between driving rockers wrapped in fleecy keyboard melodies and synth-heavy songs powered by the pulsing rhythms and fiery guitars, with the title track taking another tack entirely, all rat-a-tat-tat beats and Gregorian vocals. Together these highly divergent approaches combine seamlessly as Ultravox moves from strength to strength.

7 Quartet (Chrysalis) 1982 Rousing, stirring, soaring, reverential, *Quartet* incorporates ever more classical themes into their music (most noticeably on "Visions in Blue" and "Hymn"), pulling them dangerously close to the portentous pretensions of ELP et al. What saves the group is Currie's self-restraint and the band's ability to blend in modern elements — dance beats, palpitating bass, and the omnipresent guitar (which can be beautifully understated when necessary).

6 Monument [LIVE] (Chrysalis) 1983

6 Lament (Chrysalis) 1984 Pure dance floor beats emerge across "Dancing With Tears in My Eyes," "One Small Day," and "White China," but the brilliance of side one peters out quickly and, while the band keep making all the right noises, the music never quite gels. Some tracks are outright bland, with the only interesting touches deriving directly from Japan. Ominous to say the least.

5 U-Vox (Chrysalis) 1986

2 Revelation (Deutsche Schallplatten — Germany) 1993 The proto-industrial assault, the stadium rock riffs, the '80s noodle

leads, and a vocalist who apparently escaped from a mid-west stadium covers band audition...Currie destroys the band's legacy in one fell swoop.

1 Ingenuity (Resurgence) 1995 But wait, it gets worse! Dated house beats, archaic synthi-pop, Gary Glitter's cast-off drum beats.

Selected Compilations and Archive Releases

7 Three into One (Island) 1980 Highlights from the first three albums. In one, obviously.

8 The Collection (Chrysalis) 1984 The Midge years conveniently bundled up before further albums can start chipping away at the legend.

8 BBC Radio 1 in Concert [LIVE] (Windsong — UK) 1992 From 1981, a far tighter and considerably less po-faced concert broadcast than expected catches "Vienna" while it was still hot and fresh.

8 Ultravoxrare Vol. 1 (Chrysalis) 1993
7 Ultravoxrare Vol. 2 (Chrysalis) 1994 Rarities, 12-inch mixes, extended versions, two full discs of obscurities and vision.

8 Extended Ultravox (EMI) 1998 Hits heavy retrospective of some great 12-inch single mixes.

8 The Island Years (Island) 1999 Somewhat more generous reworking of *Three Into One*.

Midge Ure/Chris Cross LP

6 The Bloodied Sword [SOUNDTRACK] (Chrysalis) 1983 Pleasant mood music with little audible hints as to its makers.

Midge Ure LPs

3 The Gift (Chrysalis) 1985 Tiresomely bloated MOR, seemingly made up of the songs that were too soppy for the band. Jethro Tull's "Living in the Past" is utterly emasculated; Ure's own "If I Was" sounds like he has been as well.

3 Answers to Nothing (Chrysalis) 1988

3 Pure (Arista) 1991 The tunes are gone, along with the more innovative sounds that made his previous incarnation famous. Instead, one's left with an entire album of love songs, and gooey ones at that, and as for the synthesizers, they would probably sound great at strip mall cheese-tasting evenings.

2 Guns and Arrows (Arista) 1996

Billy Currie LPs

2 Transportation (Island) 1988
2 Stand Up and Walk (Hot Food Music) 1991

Visage LPs

8 Visage (Polydor) 1980 Superbly pretentious, magnificently ludicrous musical hybrids sprout across the album as the members jostle to get their own ideas/signature sounds in. A brave experiment and an arresting combination of styles and personalities still intrigues today, while "Fade to Grey" remains a timeless classic.

6 The Anvil (Polydor) 1982 More of the same, but the roots are showing.

3 Beat Boy (Polydor) 1984

Selected Compilations and Archive Releases
7 The Singles Collection (Polydor) 1983

UNCLE TUPELO

FORMED *1990 (Belleville, IL)*
ORIGINAL LINE-UP *Jay Farrar (b. 12/26/66 — guitar, vocals); Jeff Tweedy (b. 8/25/67 — bass, vocals); Mike Heidorn (drums)*

If any band can be said to have completely revolutionized American listening habits through the 1990s, it was Uncle Tupelo. Resurrecting country music for an audience too cool to listen to country; paving the way for full-scale revivals in the fortunes of Emmylou Harris, Johnny Cash, and the late Gram Parsons; even living to see the title of their debut album, *No Depression*, subpoenaed to describe an entire genre of what might other wise have been (and sometimes is) called alternative country, Uncle Tupelo take their place alongside Nirvana as the single most influential American act of the decade — and survived for about as long. Uncle Tupelo broke up within weeks of Kurt Cobain's suicide, a coincidence which will doubtless give 21st century rock historians plenty of pause for thought.

Tweedy, Farrar, and Heidorn first worked together as the Primitives, a punk band of such gritty purity that Tweedy wouldn't even talk to somebody unless they were fans of Black Flag. It was an uncompromising stance echoed in the band's music, but when fourth member Wade Tweedy (Jeff's brother) left to join the army, the remaining trio decided to reinvent themselves completely.

Toying with a country blues hybrid, the trio were certainly informed by their punk upbringing (one of their earliest songs was dedicated to the Minutemen's D. Boon), but they were open to darker, earlier, rural senses as well.

Armed with an arsenal of mandolins, fiddles, and old Carter Family records, Uncle Tupelo gigged sporadically but spent more time formulating their vision — it emerged, fully fledged, on 1990's *No Depression* (the title track was an AP Carter oldie), an album that began with raw guitars but swiftly developed into a naive, but credible, vision of the "good old days" of southern country singers, out on their porches, strumming their guitars.

The band's first single, "I Got Drunk" (backed by a rendering of the Gram Parsons' staple, "Sin City"), appeared in late 1990, recorded at Fort Apache in Boston with producer Sean Slade. The following year, Robyn Hitchcock's "I Wanna Destroy You" would visit the other extreme of the band's rural vision, on the flip of the "Gun" single.

1991's *Still Feel Gone* followed in a similar vein to its predecessor, although hindsight insists that the seeds of both Son Volt and Wilco, the two bands to emerge from the wreckage of Uncle Tupelo, can be detected as the album moves on.

Trailed by the "Sauget Wind" single, *March 16–20, 1992* would be the album with which Uncle Tupelo would make their greatest mark. It was indeed on March 20 that the band emerged from a four-day studio stint with REM's Peter Buck with an almost exclusively acoustic collection of traditional country and folk songs, squeezed through the disconcerting mangle of both the band's private vision and that intangible dream that Gram Parsons once called "Cosmic American music."

Heidorn quit to spend more time with his family; he was replaced by Ken Coomer (ex-Clockhammer), with the band's line-up expanding even further following the induction of John Sirratt (bass) and Max Johnston (multi-instrumentalist).

Building interest with live work, even as the albums were raised higher in the critical consciousness, Uncle Tupelo signed with Sire in late 1992 and, the following year, released *Anodyne* — the starting pistol for the entire alternative country scene to explode.

Suddenly, "Americana" was erupting everywhere, with Uncle Tupelo seemingly permanently at the center of the storm: their former guitar tech, Brian Henneman, formed the Bottle Rockets; Gary Louis, one of the guest musicians on *Still Feel Gone*, was leading the Jayhawks. Whiskey Town, the Old 97's, and the Blood Oranges emerged, and behind them, the flood gates were straining.

Despite such laudation, neither *Anodyne* nor the "Give Back the Key to My Heart" single sold well. A fall tour was sold out, though, and there was some talk of Uncle Tupelo's next album being live — the Vic Theater, Chicago, show on October 15 was recorded (five tracks appeared alongside *Anodyne* highlight "The Long Cut" on the EP *Long Cut and Five Live*). But it was not to be. For reasons neither Tweedy nor Farrar has ever felt the need to divulge, Uncle Tupelo broke up some time after the tour ended — they have never given a date, either, waiting until mid-1994 to even announce their dissolution.

Farrar reunited with Heidorn to form Son Volt; Tweedy and the remainder of Uncle Tupelo became Wilco.

Uncle Tupelo LPs

9 No Depression (Rockville) 1990 The band who took the country out of Nashville cracked it over the head with punk rush and suddenly made it cool to twang in the '90s. In fact, their debut is a glorious blur of thrash and threat: a dynamic blur that even the fiddles and banjos can't slow.

8 Still Feel Gone (Rockville) 1991 The band backslide a little on this one, splitting their cohesive sound as country and rock play king of the hill. "Gun" and "Punch Drunk" hint at good things to come, while "D. Boon" is a thrashing good tribute to the Minutemen's leader.

9 March 16–20 1992 (Rockville) 1992 REM's Peter Buck takes the band firmly in hand and wrenches out an absolutely stunning acoustic album, combining Tupelo's own songs with traditional cuts. A bitterly jagged, darkly melancholy examination of the hick's hick, those shadowy figures of American folk's past. "Wait Up" and "Grindstone" will define country's future.

8 Anodyne (Sire) 1993 Their most cohesive blend of rock and country — neither one nor the other, but a true hybridization best heard on "Give Back the Key to My Heart," "Acuff Rose," and "Steal My Heart." Too bad it was their last gasp.

Wilco LPs

5 Am (Sire) 1995 Jeff Tweedy drags dribs of Tupelo on in much the same vein, with solid countrified rock and roll.

7 Being There (Sire) 1996 Double set breaks down some rigid barriers for Tweedy, as he takes the opportunity to explore psychedelia, power pop, and R&B as he patches elements of all into the band's sound.

6 Summer Teeth (reprise) 1999

Wilco and Billy Bragg LP

9 Mermaid Avenue (Elektra) 1998

9 Mermaid Avenue Vol 2 (Elektra) 2000

Son Volt LPs

6 Trace (WB) 1995 Farrar's vision of life after Tupelo is a honky tonk version of American folk ethics, which largely continues on from where *Anodyne* left off.

7 Straightaways (WB) 1997

6 Wide Spring Tremolo (WB) 1998

UNDERTONES

FORMED 1975 *(Derry, North Ireland)*
ORIGINAL LINE-UP *Feargal Sharkey (b. 13/8/58, Londonderry — vocals); John O'Neill (b. 8/26/57, Londonderry — guitar); Damian O'Neill (b. 1/15/61, Belfast — guitar); Micky Bradley (b. 8/13/59 — bass); Billy Doherty (b. 7/10/58, Larne — drums)*

Although the O'Neill brothers formed the Undertones as early as fall 1975, it would be spring 1978 before the group made their presence felt outside of their Northern Ireland hometown, when they mailed a demo tape to Terri Hooley,

owner of the seminal Belfast record label Good Vibrations, and were offered a one-off single deal.

Despite their lack of past exposure, the group could already call on a great deal of experience; vocalist Sharkey was a veteran of countless childhood talent contests, while constant local live work had seen the 'tones, as they were affectionately known, build up both a stunning repertoire of pop covers and poppy originals, and an awful lot of self-belief.

For a while, they needed it. At least one wall in Derry was decorated with the spray-painted warning "The Undertones are shit," placed there by hands unknown, and across the Irish Sea in England, Stiff, Radar, and Chiswick had all rejected the band's early demos. Indeed, by early 1978, the band members had decided that if they didn't get a record out before the end of the year, they were going to call it quits. Good Vibrations finally came to the rescue and in June, the band booked £80 worth of studio time at Belfast's Wizard Studios and set to work on their debut, a four-track EP led off by the unspeakably effervescent "Teenage Kicks."

True Confessions, titled for the EP's second best track, was released in September, enclosed in a picture sleeve which saw the band posing against the "...are shit" graffiti. Events would prove, however, that they weren't. BBC DJ John Peel began playing the single regularly, singing the band's praises at every opportunity, and inviting them in to record their first Peel Session the following month. The band would ultimately make six appearances on the show, while Peel still ranks "Teenage Kicks" among his all-time favorite records.

At the same time, with the Good Vibrations single having easily sold out its original pressing of 7,000 copies, the band was snapped up by Sire and *True Confessions* was reissued — "Teenage Kicks" (#31 UK) became an immediate radio hit. A tour followed, opening for labelmates the Rezillos and, in January 1979, the 'tones' second single, "Get Over You" (#57 UK) at least consolidated their arrival. It would be with April's "Jimmy Jimmy" (#16 UK) however, that the band finally grasped the reputation which still enfolds them today, as one of Britain's premier singles bands. Indeed, of all their punk/post-punk era contemporaries, only the Buzzcocks can truly be rated alongside the 'tones in terms of sheer 45 rpm excellence and an unbroken sequence of hits which lasted almost until the band's demise.

The Undertones (#13 UK), the group's sensibly titled debut album, was released in the UK in May 1979 just ahead of the heatwave inducing "Here Comes Summer" single (#34 UK). The insistent "You've Got My Number" (#32) followed, but with the band's live schedule having precluded any more intensive recording, Sire prepared for the Christmas buying season by deleting the band's debut album, then reissuing it with a new cover and three extra tracks — thus bringing it in line with the forthcoming US release.

Feted as the (latest in a long line of) British Ramones, the Undertones spent much of early 1980 on the road in America, touring first with the Clash and later in their own right. They returned to the UK to watch their second album, *Hypnotised* (#6 UK) climb into the Top 10, while the superlative "My Perfect Cousin" (#9 UK) and "Wednesday Week" (#11 UK) singles both brought the band ever closer to British superstardom.

The US, however, proved utterly impervious to their charms — even Sharkey's habit of leaping into the audience to lead the applause for his band could not win the country over and, by summer, the Undertones' entire relationship with Sire was on the rocks. A five year deal negotiated by Sharkey himself was finally scrapped and, that fall, the Undertones formed their own label, Ardeck, and signed it to EMI. Subsequent recordings would not be given a US release until Rykodisc ambitiously reissued the band's entire catalog a decade later.

The band spent year's end in Holland, recording their third album, 1981's *Positive Touch* (#17 UK), and putting the finishing touches to their own drift away from the sharp pop of their earlier releases. Emboldened by the recent Mod revival, with its attendant soul and R&B overtones, the Undertones delved deep into influences which had barely been whispered in the past — the pounding horns of "It's Going to Happen" (#18 UK), the soft romance of "Julie Ocean" (#41 UK); audiences, however, were less impressed, and when tickets for the Undertones' spring 1981 UK tour went on sale, even middling-sized theaters were left half-empty.

Equally damaging, support act TV Smith's Explorers were getting as enthusiastic a response as the Undertones themselves — or at least, they did at the two shows they played before being dismissed from the outing. Matters did not improve, however, and the Undertones' misfortunes continued when their next single, the '60s psych-led "Beautiful Friend," became their first not to make the UK chart. Indeed, three further singles — "The Love Parade," "Got to Have You Back," and "Chain of Love" all followed it into oblivion, while the band's fourth album, the seemingly aptly named *The Sin of Pride* (#43 UK), was to be their last. Within weeks of the album's release, the band announced their decision to split — they broke up in July, following one final British tour.

The O'Neill brothers promptly formed a new band, That Petrol Emotion; Sharkey opted for a solo career, first uniting with ex- Depeche Mode songwriter Vince Clarke as the one-off Assembly and scoring with "Never Never" (#4 UK). A similarly shortlived alliance with Madness' Zarjazz label in

September 1984 saw Sharkey produce an excellent version of one of that band's better later songs, "Listen to Your Father" (#23 UK); and the following year, the singer signed with Virgin.

With Sharkey clearly aiming for a more mature audience than even the latter day Undertones had pursued, a reasonable first single, "Loving You" (#26 UK) was followed, in September, by an utterly unexpected smash, as Sharkey's cover of Maria McKee's "A Good Heart" (#1 UK) topped charts all over Europe. An eponymous album (#12 UK) recorded with Eurythmic Dave Stewart was next, while the deliciously spiteful "You Little Thief" (#5 UK) kept the ball rolling.

Yet as suddenly as Sharkey rocketed to the top, he plummeted back down again. In February 1986, his mother and sister were abducted by terrorists while spending time in Londonderry; they were swiftly released unharmed, but the shock certainly affected Sharkey's love of the limelight. April 1986's underperforming follow-up, "Someone to Somebody" (#64 UK), would be Sharkey's last hit for two years until "More Love" (#44 UK) in 1988. It would be three more years before "I've Got News for You" (#12 UK) and the *Songs from Mardi Gras* album (#27 UK) returned him to the public eye.

Soon after, Sharkey accepted an A&R position at Polydor records in London, turning down an offer to reform the Undertones because it would compromise his own position on the other side of the industry table. The reunion finally went ahead in July 1999, again without Sharkey — now working on the board of the UK Radio Authority. On July 17, the four remaining members played two songs at the end of a Saw Doctors show at the Galway Arts Festival in Ireland — the 16th anniversary of the original line-up's final show. Hours later, the band played a second show at a hotel in nearby Salthill, running through seven old favorites, then running through them again for an encore.

Vocalist, Paul McLoone, was recruited soon after and, in November 1999, the newly constituted Undertones debuted at the opening of a new multi-media arts center in Derry, the Nerve Center. Simultaneously, it was announced that all four original Undertones albums had been remastered for reissue in the new year.

The Undertones LPs

9 The Undertones (Sire) 1979 In under three minutes (and sometimes less than two), the Undertones perfectly encapsulate a mood, an emotion, or an entire teen-aged drama. Their biggest influence is obviously the Ramones, but the Derry boys used more chords and composed more complex songs than the Bruddahs, even if they are delivered just as fast and with equal punch. And like their idols, they're also indebted to '60s pop, but add Bolan, Bowie, and pub rock to their "I Wish I Could Be..." dreaming. But like all the best bands, the 'Tones are greater than the sum of their influences, with their debut rolling out sparkling pop rock gems, all catchy choruses and hooky melodies, one after another in perfect succession. True pop genius.

8 Hypnotised (Sire) 1980 A tad older and a lot wiser, the Undertones are growing up fast, as is evident from the opening track, "More Songs about Chocolate and Girls," a sardonic response to the press, wrapped round a Beach Boys meets Wire song. *Hypnotized* is filled with these weird, but wonderful crossovers, where early Kinks are stomped by Gary Glitter (Doherty's thumping drums often paid homage to the glam great, long before the 'tones included the Leader's "Rock'n'Roll" in a Peel session); The Animals go power pop; and post-punk collides with '60s garage... while still packing enough pure brilliance ("Wednesday Week," "My Perfect Cousin") to sate their less adventurous fans.

6 The Positive Touch (Ardeck — UK) 1981 Having set off down the path of musical experimentation, there's no turning back, and virtually every track on *Positive Touch* finds the Undertones exploring a fresh musical style. New homages to old heroes, new instruments (horns and piano), new genres (from ballads to swing), new extreme crossovers (the "Stranded in the Jungle" NY Dolls hook-up with the Ants and go glam of "Fascination")... and all adding up to a new problem. Rather than being impressed by the band's cleverness and breadth of musical range, fans and press alike were losing patience. But *Positive* isn't a total negative and, occasionally, the old magic came flooding back, just witness "It's Going to Happen." Sadly, these moments were few and far between.

8 The Sin Of Pride (Ardeck — UK) 1983 With an apt title and appropriately including covers of the Isley Brothers' "Got to Have You Back" and Dave Dee, Dozy, Beaky, Mick and Tick's "Save Me," the Undertones make amends for past mistakes. Squarely based on '60s pop, with other influences either kept to a minimum or expertly blended, *Sin* captures the group at their mature, melodic best. They still mixed it up a bit, but the gorgeous ballad "Love Before Romance," the funky Motown-esque "Conscious," and the psychedelic celebration of "The Love Parade" only liven up the proceedings even further, making this album the culmination of pop brilliance the 'tones had shown flashes of since their "Teenage Kicks" debut.

Selected Compilations and Archive Releases

8 All Wrapped Up (Ardeck — UK) 1983 All the singles, one after the other, bang-bang-bang. Early vinyl copies included all the B-sides as well, and a very odd sleeve of a lady draped in bacon.

7 Cher O'Bowlies — The Pick of the Undertones (Ardeck — UK) 1986

8 Double Peel Sessions (Strange Fruit — UK) 1989 Forget the singles, the 'tones were one of the most consistent Peel sessioneers as well, with their sterling take on "Rock'n'Roll" just one of the mighty treats within.

Feargal Sharkey LPs
4 Feargal Sharkey (A&M) 1985
4 Wish (Virgin) 1988
3 Songs From Mardi Gras (Virgin) 1991

That Petrol Emotion LPs
6 Manic Pop Thrill (Demon — UK) 1986
5 Babble (Polydor) 1987
6 End Of The Millennium Psychosis Blues (Virgin) 1988
6 Chemicrazy (Virgin) 1990

Selected Compilations and Archive Releases
7 Fireproof (Rykodisc) 1994

UNDERWORLD

FORMED 1987 (London, England)
ORIGINAL LINE-UP *Karl Hyde (vocals, guitar); Rick Smith (keyboards, vocals); Alfie Thomas (guitar); Baz Allen (bass); Bryn B. Burrows (drums)*

Rick Smith and Karl Hyde first worked together as Screen Gems, an early 1980s synth-pop band whose career never escaped their south Wales base. By 1983, the arrival of John Warwicker Le Breton (synth), together with Alfie Thomas and Bryn Burrows, saw the band — in a pre-Prince-ian flash of misguided inspiration — change their name to a simple symbol, which they insisted was pronounced Freur.

Signing to CBS in early 1983, the band's first single, "Doot Doot" (#59 UK), would be the peak of Freur's achievement. An eponymous album and the follow-up singles "Matter of the Heart," "Runaway," "Riders in the Night," and a repromoted "Doot Doot" all failed, and Freur moved into 1984 with their future looking increasingly bleak.

Rounding out the sound, Jake Bowie (bass) was added during the summer, debuting on the "Dark and Darkness" single. "Look in the Back for Answers" and the album *Get Us Out of Here* followed in February 1985, but Freur folded soon after.

Having relocated to the London suburb of Romford, Hyde and Smith were already establishing themselves as composers of TV breaks and commercial themes for MTV and others. In 1984, they scored the Clive Barker movie *Transmutations*, and when they reconvened Thomas and Burrows plus Baz Allen, they renamed themselves Underworld, from the movie's UK title.

With the band now concentrating on the UK dance club circuit, it would take close to three years before a new label deal arrived — Underworld signed with Sire in late 1987 and, in March 1988, released *Underneath the Radar* (#139 US). A US club tour pushed a single of the title track to #74

US in July, and the following month, "Show Some Emotion" made a similar splash on US dance floors.

Burrows departed to join World Electric and was replaced by Pascal Consou before Underworld scored a second US hit, "Stand Up" (#67 US) in August 1989. The album *Change the Weather* and title track single followed, but a tour with the disintegrating Eurythmics was to be Underworld's last stand. The band broke up in late 1989, and Smith and Hyde returned to TV work. Over the next few years, their Tomato company would become one of the UK's most successful composers of advertising music, scoring commercials for Nike, MTV, Levis, Tampax, and more.

In 1990, the pair recruited Darren Emerson (keyboards) and relaunched Underworld. An entire album was recorded, then scrapped, before they released a single, "Mother Earth," on their own Tomato label in 1992. Limited to just 5,000 copies, it coincided with their first live show, playing in the DJ booth at the Ministry of Sound club in London.

Masquerading under the name Lemon Interrupt, two singles, "Dirty" and "Bigmouth," emerged before "Mmm…Skyscraper I Love You" finally captured the sound Underworld were searching for. From the outset, the trio wanted to incorporate traditional rock instrumentation into dance. According to Hyde, "we threw away the first album trying to find the right spot [to place guitars and vocals]. I think 'Dark and Long' was the first one that we really clicked, that we felt we got something was going there; then 'Skyscraper,' and then a semiradical departure for 'Cowgirl.'

"We weren't treading on the groove, but at the same time we could still introduce these traditional elements that were fantastic, but still have to be approached in a different way." All three would be included on Underworld's next album in 1994; in the meantime, the absorption of Boys Own into parent label London saw Underworld follow label head Stephen Hall to Junior Boy's Own and release what swiftly became the club anthem of the year, "Rez," in September 1993.

Underworld resurfaced in December with "Spikee" (#63 UK), their first hit single, with *Dubnobasswithmyheadman* (#12 UK), the *Dark and Long* EP (#57 UK), and the US club smashes "Cowgirl" and "Dirty Guitar [Dirty Epic]" following. Underworld released the original mix of what would subsequently become their anthem, "Born Slippy" (#52 UK) in May 1995.

It would be another year before the band returned, by which time their reputation had truly exploded into the mainstream, thanks to the inclusion of "Born Slippy" in the *Trainspotting* soundtrack. A new album, *Second Toughest in the Infants* (#9 UK), and the singles "Pearl's Girl" (#24 UK) and "Juanita" were finally followed by a repromotion of "Born Slippy" (#2 UK) and a resurrected "Pearl's Girl" (#22 UK).

Underworld spent much of 1997 recording; they relaunched in summer 1998 with appearances at Glastonbury and V98, followed by European and US tours through the fall. (The band also opened for New Order in London on New Year's Eve.) Plans to release their third album at the same time, however, were placed on hold after Emerson premiered a new track, "King of Snake," at a DJ gig and immediately decided to remix the entire record. *Beaucoup Fish* (#93 US, #3 UK) finally appeared in March 1999, previewed by the "Push Upstairs" single (#12 UK).

UK, US, and European tours through spring 1999 were accompanied by the "Jumbo," "King of Snake" (#17 UK), and "Bruce Lee" singles, and in October, Underworld appeared at the Coachella Music Festival in California. They also prepared the *Everything, Everything* live album and DVD, drawn from these shows, for 2000 release.

Underworld LPs

6 Underneath the Radar (Sire) 1988 With Rupert Hine producing, a strong, but strangely muted pound through the halls of late '80s techno — if the Thompson Twins owned the house.

5 Change the Weather (Sire) 1989

9 Dubnobasswithmyheadman (Wax Trax!) 1993 It wasn't just Underworld's insistent, almost hypnotic, beats that set the club world on fire, nor the moody, textured atmospheres spun through with glorious melodies. It was the unique addition of guitar and vocals (the latter a series of mind-bending thought fragments), which were tightly interwoven into the songs. Amazing no one had thought of doing that properly before.

8 Second Toughest in the Infants (Wax Trax!) 1996 Pulsing rhythms, dark melodies, embedded guitars and Hyde's enigmatic vocals are the pillars upon which the trio's world rested, but this still left plenty of room for redecoration, as the group tweaked the beats; experimented with effects, instrumentation, and tempos; and broadened their horizons. Could "Pearl's Girl" have been any better?

8 Beaucoup Fish (V2) 1999 Perhaps the most surprising aspect of this album is the inclusion of guests contributing spoken word pieces on some tracks. But even this doesn't interrupt Underworld's core organic sound, as they amalgamate an array of electro-sub-genres into an exhilarating slamdance of styles, rhythms, and lyrics.

9 Everything, Everything (JBO) 2000

Freur LPs

3 Doot Doot (Epic) 1983 With "Doot Doot' itself saying more in four minutes than most new synthesizer mavens managed across entire albums, Freur were poised for a moment to redirect electronic music for the decade. But only for a moment, because the album had nothing even vaguely comparable.

Underworld — Selected Remixes

1992 SHAKESPEAR'S SISTER — Black Sky (London)

1992 108 GRAND — Te Queiro [MULTIPLE MIXES] (Brute)

1992 GAT DECOR — Passion (Effective)

1992 LEFTFIELD — Song of Life [MULTIPLE MIXES] (Hard Hands)

1992 ODD COUPLE — Swing in Trance [MULTIPLE MIXES] (Logic)

1992 EAGLE'S PREY — Tonto's Drum (Rumour)

1993 ORBITAL — Lush [MULTIPLE MIXES] (FFRR)

1993 DRUM CLUB — Sound System (Hypnotic)

1993 WILLIAM ORBIT — Water from a Vine Leaf [multiple mixes] (Virgin)

1993 BJÖRK — Human Behaviour [MULTIPLE MIXES] (Elektra)

1993 ONE DOVE — Why Don't You Take me? [MULTIPLE MIXES] (FFRR)

1993 SPOOKY — Schmoo [MULTIPLE MIXES] (Tribal)

1994 SVEN VATH — Beauty and the Beast [MULTIPLE MIXES] (Eye Q)

1994 ST ETIENNE — Urban Clearway (Heavenly)

1994 ST ETIENNE — Like a Motorway (Heavenly)

1994 ST ETIENNE — Pale Movie (Heavenly)

1995 MODEL 500 — The Flow (BE)

1995 DREADZONE — Zion Youth [MULTIPLE MIXES] (Virgin)

1995 ST ETIENNE — Cool Kids of Death (Heavenly)

1995 FRONT 242 — Happiness [MULTIPLE MIXES] (Red Rhino)

1995 CHEMICAL BROTHERS — Leave Home [MULTIPLE MIXES] (JBO)

1996 MENTAL GENERATION — Cafe del Mar [MULTIPLE MIXES] (JBO)

1997 MASSIVE ATTACK — Risingson (Virgin)

1997 BJÖRK — I Miss You (One Little Indian)

1997 ROB & GOLDIE — The Shadow [MULTIPLE MIXES] (Moving Shadow)

1997 DEPECHE MODE — Barrel of a Gun [MULTIPLE MIXES] (Mute)

1998 SIMPLY RED — Thrill Me [MULTIPLE MIXES] (JBO)

U2

FORMED 1978 (Dublin)

ORIGINAL LINE-UP Bono Vox (b. Paul Hewson, 5/10/60, Dublin — vocals); The Edge (b. David Evans, 8/8/61, Wales — guitar); Alan Clayton (b. 3/13/60, Chinnor, Oxfords, England — bass); Larry Mullen Jr. (b. 10/31/61, Dublin — drums)

Mount Temple High School student Larry Mullen brought the members of U2 together with a Musicians Wanted ad pinned to the school notice board. A five piece completed by The Edge's brother, Dick Evans (guitar), they took the name Feedback and concentrated on Beatles and Rolling Stones covers, rarely gigging outside of the school and party circuit, even after they changed their name, first to the Hype, then,

following Evans' departure in 1978 (he subsequently surfaced in the Virgin Prunes), to U2.

On March 18, 1978, U2 whizzed through to the finals of a talent contest sponsored by the *Evening Press* and Guinness, collecting 500 pounds prize money and an audition for CBS Ireland. They recorded two sets of demos, one with English journalist Chas de Whalley producing, and in September were signed to the label. A year later, the band members had left school and were concentrating exclusively upon building an audience. Their debut, the *U2: 3* EP, was released in fall 1979.

It swiftly topped the Irish chart, and in January 1980, U2 would sweep the annual *Hot Press* magazine readers' polls. Attempts to garner interest across the sea in Britain, however, seemed doomed to failure: CBS Ireland's UK wing had already passed on the band, and their first London shows in December attracted few customers — one gig, at the Hope & Anchor, saw the misbilled V2 play to just nine people.

In February, U2's second single, "Another Day," followed its predecessor to #1 in Ireland, and the band's latest Irish tour was completely sold out. The following month, Island Records picked the band up for the UK and US, but their debut British single, the Martin Hannett-produced "11 o'clock Tick Tock," failed to register, and the band's next British tour saw them still playing the pubs they'd visited last time.

Two further singles, "A Day Without Me" and "I Will Follow," sank, and in October, the band's biggest show yet, opening for glam rock survivors Slade at the London Lyceum, barely registered with the headliners' audience. By the time the band's debut album, the Steve Lillywhite-produced *Boy* (#63 US, #52 UK) was ready for release, the decision had already been taken to try and break the band in the US first and worry about Europe later.

The band paid their first visit to America in November, returning in February, following a British tour with Talking Heads. By March, *Boy* was climbing toward its eventual peak, but it would be mid-summer before U2 began making any impression in Britain, first when the single "Fire" (#35 UK) broke out, then when *Boy* finally scraped to its apex in August, just three months before the release of the band's next album.

Repeating the previous year's pattern, U2 toured the UK first, then headed to America, where *October* (#104 US, #11 UK), strangely, was not doing quite so well as expected. With two further hit singles, "Gloria" (#55 UK) and "A Celebration" (#47 UK), U2 would spend the next year consolidating their Irish and British support, with full tours of both countries, and recording their third album, *War* (#12 US, #1 UK).

U2's biggest hit yet, *War* quite unexpectedly burst into the UK chart at the top. A two-month tour of US arenas through the spring pushed "New Year's Day" (#53 US, #10 UK) into the chart. "Two Hearts Beat as One" (#18 UK) was remixed by Francis Kervorkian for a club smash, and at the end of May 1983, U2 were one of the headline attractions at the U.S. Festival in San Bernardino.

Even more essential to the U2 legend, however, was their performance at Red Rocks amphitheater in Colorado, filmed for a UK TV special and subsequently released as the *Under A Blood Red Sky* video and live album (#28 US, #2 UK) in November 1983. The movie excerpt, which accompanied the single "I Will Follow" (#81 US), would be elected to MTV's Top 100 Videos of All Time in 1999. The Red Rocks gig itself would rank 40th in *Entertainment Weekly*'s Great Moments in Rock survey that same year.

In December 1983, U2 toured Japan for the first time. They followed up with trips to Australia and New Zealand in August, but the majority of 1984 was spent ensconced within Slane Castle, Ireland, recording their fourth album with the most unexpected producer they could find, Brian Eno. Partnered by Daniel Lanois, Eno would utterly strip away every outward manifestation of U2's sound, rebuilding the band from the soul upward. It was, though history would swiftly absorb the shock, a stunningly courageous move, and if the album had bombed and the band broke up immediately, still *The Unforgettable Fire* (#12 US, #1 UK) was indeed unforgettable.

It was, however, an enormous hit, trailing the signature hits "Pride (In the Name of Love)" (#33 US, #3 UK) and the title track (#6 UK). A mini-album of album out-takes and live cuts, *Wide Awake in America* (#37 US, #11 UK) followed — a success despite being outlawed from the US listings for two years because it was considered too short to be an LP.

In the slipstream of *The Unforgettable Fire*, the band toured Britain in the winter, moving on to Europe and the US in early 1985, going back for festivals in England (Milton Keynes Bowl) and Ireland (Croke Park, Dublin), then returning to America to take part in Live Aid (Bono and Clayton both contributed to Band Aid's "Do They Know It's Christmas" single). Their set, one of the most dramatic of the day, would later be described as one of the most memorable as well.

The band spent much of 1986 working on private projects — The Edge recorded the soundtrack to the movie *The Captive*, with an unknown Sinead O'Connor among the guests; Bono appeared on Clannad's "Once in a Lifetime" (#20 UK) single; in May, however, the band convened to play the Self Aid unemployment rally in Dublin, and through June, they joined Lou Reed, Peter Gabriel, and Sting on Amnesty International's *A Conspiracy of Hope* US tour, before finally entering the studio, again with Eno and Lanois, to record their next album.

Released in March 1987, *The Joshua Tree* (#1 US, #1 UK) went platinum in 48 hours — the fastest-ever selling album in UK chart history. Around the world it spun off four hit singles, "With Or Without You" (#1 US, #4 UK), "I Still Haven't Found What I'm Looking For" (#1 US, #6 UK), "Where the Streets Have No Name" (#13 US, #4 UK), and "In God's Country" (#44 US, #48 UK), while the US leg of the band's 110-date world tour would see U2 swiftly follow through with the on-the-road *Rattle and Hum* documentary and accompanying soundtrack album (#1 US, #1 UK).

It, too, spawned a succession of hit singles — "Desire" (#3 US, #1 UK), "Angel of Harlem" (#14 US, #9 UK), "When Love Comes to Town" (#68 US, #6 UK), and "All I Want Is You" (#83 US, #4 UK), and again the band was able to relax through much of the next year, emerging only for benefits (Smile Jamaica in 1988, the Very Special Arts Festival benefit for handicapped artists in 1989) and one-off guest recordings, before launching an Australian tour in June 1989. (They would return to that country in November.)

1989 also saw both Bono and The Edge become fathers (The Edge for the third time, before his marriage to Aislinn broke down in 1990). But if two band members seemed to be settling down, a third was becoming increasingly wilder. In 1985, Adam Clayton was banned from driving for two years after pleading guilty to DWI; in August 1989, he was arrested for possession of marijuana, eventually having the conviction overturned when he agreed to pay $25,000 to the Dublin Women's Aid and Refuge Centre. Had he not had that option, the consequences for U2's continued ability to tour the world could have been disastrous.

1990 opened with the now almost-routine receipt of the Best International Group award at the BRIT awards — their third consecutive victory; their silence through the next 18 months, of course, would preclude a fourth such triumph, but in November 1991, a new single, the experimental "The Fly" (#61 US, #1 UK) announced a new album, and a new direction for the band. *Achtung Baby* (#1 US, #2 UK) would not be taken on the road for another four months, but further singles "Mysterious Ways" (#9 US, #13 UK) and "One" (#10 US, #7 UK) prepared the way for what would emerge as the band's most grandiose concept yet, Zoo TV.

A multimedia extravaganza, which included live telephone prank calls, a slew of special guests, and on one occasion, 10,000 pizzas to go, Zoo TV firmly divided the critics, but undoubtedly proved one of the live experiences of the age, all the more so at a time when other tours were being forced to cancel due to declining ticket sales. Equally remarkably, even as sales soared toward 7 million, *Achtung Baby* continued leaking singles — "Even Better Than the Real Thing" (#32 US, #12 UK) was followed by a remix of the same track (#8 UK) and "Who's Gonna Ride Your Wild Horses" (#35 US, #14 UK).

By the end of the year, Zoo TV grossed $67 million and produced a highly rated TV special, the Fox network's *U2 — Zoo TV* (directed by Kevin Godley). U2 had become the first rock band ever to play Yankee Stadium, and only the second ever musical performer (after Billy Joel). The "Even Better Than the Real Thing" video won the Best Group Video and best Special Effects categories at the MTV awards; the band picked up four trophies at the *Billboard* awards, Best Live Act at the BRITS, International Entertainer of The Year at Canada's Juno Awards, and Best Rock…Group at the Grammys, and Zoo TV had still to hit Europe.

Still evolving, the tour opened in Rotterdam in May, just as U2 released their next album, *Zooropa* (#1 US, #1 UK), recorded quickly during the hiatus between tours. Videos for "Lemon" and "Numb" became firm MTV favorites, and though the first retail single from the set, "Stay (Far Away So Close)" (#61 US, #4 UK) underperformed by the band's recent standards, still *Zooropa* would be registered double platinum in America some two months before the two-year tour finally ended in Japan. A video from the Sydney shows would go gold the following year and win the Best Music Video — Long Form category at the Grammys.

1994/95 were essentially given over to collecting awards, including a Special Award for International Achievements at the Ivor Novellos in London; in the meantime, the band's only recording would be one track for 1995's *Batman Forever* soundtrack, "Hold Me, Thrill Me, Kiss Me, Kill Me" (#16 US, #2 UK), and the latest in a long series of U2 benefit collaborations, dating back to Bono's involvement in the Artists Against Apartheid project in 1986. They joined Eno at the helm of the Passengers, a musical concept featuring guest appearances from Luciano Pavarotti, DJ Howie B., and Japanese singer Holi, to raise funds for the War Child charity.

An album, *Original Soundtracks 1* (#76 US, #12 UK) was followed by the "Miss Sarajevo" single (#6 UK) before U2 announced business as usual with a new album for 1997, the club-flavored *Pop*. Previewed by the pounding "Discotheque" (#10 US, #1 UK), the album was again a decisive moment in U2's development, but again their audience seemed willing to change with them.

The Popmart tour was as colossal an undertaking as its predecessor, the second highest grossing tour of the year, taking $79.9 million from 46 shows in 37 cities. "Staring at the Sun" (#26 US, #3 UK), "Last Night On Earth" (#57 US, #10 UK), "Please" (#7 UK), and "If God Will Send His Angels" (#12 UK), meanwhile, all spun off the album as hit singles, meaning U2 had now released almost as many singles from three albums in the 1990s as they had from seven in the 1980s — one reason, perhaps, that when 1999 brought U2's first greatest hits collection, it was restricted to their first decade's releases only.

Accompanied by a single, the 1987 B-side "Sweetest Thing" (#63 US, #3 UK), the two-CD collection *The Best of, 1980–90/The B-Sides* (#2 US, #1 UK) debuted at the top in 17 countries, selling over 237,000 copies in the US in its first week. This initial edition was deleted after just one week on sale, and the two discs were repackaged individually as *The Best Of, 1980–90* (#45 US, #4 UK) and *The B-Sides*.

The band's next all-new album, meanwhile, would be previewed in April 1999, with an appearance on BBC TV, performing "The Ground Beneath Her Feet." That same month, they contributed a cover of Johnny Cash's "Don't Take Your Guns to Town" to TNT's *All Star Tribute to Johnny Cash* television special. A new single, "Beautiful Day," preceded the October 2000 release of *All That You Can't Leave Behind*.

U2 LPs

9 Boy (Island) 1980 U2 exemplified the new wave of bands, coming of age at the dawn of the decade. The angst-soaked lyrics and Mullen's assaultive drumming kept punk's dying ember alight, and the moody instrumental passages echoed post-punk's gloom — not for nothing was their first UK recording session with Joy Division supremo Martin Hannett. But then the strong, shimmering melodies and The Edge's soaring, tingling guitar came to the fore, and though *Boy* still has echoes of that earlier flirtation, they would soon be gone forever.

7 October (Island) 1981 Opening with the deeply spiritual "Gloria," *October* further confounded critics who were already struggling to pigeonhole the band. Add a hint of Gaelic trad, some anthemic rabble rousers, a melancholy ballad, hauntingly beautiful instrumental passages, and a punk-fueled rhythm section battling The Edge's distinctive jangly guitar, and you can pity their plight.

9 War (Island) 1983 Mullen discovers the effectiveness of the military tattoo, adding further drama to U2's already rousing anthems, while "New Year's Day" and the dance-friendly "Two Hearts Beat As One" finally haul the group out into the open. And then there's "Sunday Bloody Sunday," assuredly not a rebel song, but powerful enough to rouse a few.

7 Under a Blood Red Sky [LIVE] (Island) 1983 Despite the all-pervading Red Rocks propaganda, only two of the eight tracks were taped in Colorado, and "Sunday Bloody Sunday" wasn't one of them. And it still wasn't a rebel song, so that's alright then.

9 The Unforgettable Fire (Island) 1984 After three LPs with producer Steve Lillywhite, U2 turned to Brian Eno and Daniel Lanois, who promptly graced the group with unimagined majesty, keyboards, and electronics, imbibing the proceedings with a deep, dense, more textured quality. With only "Pride" truly ringing the U2 bell of old and "Bad" pinpointing a move into almost ambient jam-type territory, it now seems such a logical step. At the time, though, it was a shocking and controversial move.

⏑⓪ The Joshua Tree (Island) 1987 After three years on the road and elsewhere, their latest lyrics reflected the kaleidoscope of loneliness, confusion, and fleeting exhilaration of such a life. The culmination of the band's early development encompassed *War*-like rousing rockers, *Fire*'s pervasive keyboards, and, though the familiarity of the hits defies such a thought, the addition of more introspective, almost experimental numbers.

The singles "With Or Without You," "Where the Streets Have No Name," and "I Still Haven't Found What I'm Looking For" were effortless classics, but the heart of *Joshua Tree* actually lay deeper, in the searing guitar of "Bullet the Blue Sky," the soaring lilt of "Red Hill Mining Town" and "In God's Country, "and the still jaunty weariness of "Trip Through Your Wires."

The album as a whole was a document of what the band themselves experienced as they traveled America, a theme they would return to when they filmed the accompanying tour. But the concerns (and indeed the themes) were universal, from the wide-ranging horrors of El Salvador ("Mothers of the Disappeared") to a personal tragedy in New Zealand — "One Tree Hill" remembered a band friend who died in a motorcycle smash.

On the down side, Bono's vocals had lost a lot of their early power, suddenly substituting heartfelt emotion for an almost automatic catch in the back of his throat, but though it was becoming very hip to feign fury at the way U2 had developed, after five albums in under seven years, they had yet to put a foot wrong — the most successful "new" band of the decade were also the most influential.

⑧ Rattle and Hum (Island) 1988 This 72-minute extravaganza includes live tracks recorded around the world, studio cuts, new songs, old faves, and covers in a celebration of passion and politics performed with the fervid urgency of a revivalist tent show. Occasionally Bono can get a little preachy, but *Rattle* is no less convincing for its excesses.

⑦ Achtung Baby (Island) 1991 If *Rattle* was U2's socio-political epic, then *Baby* is their opus to love lost and found, betrayed and abused; musically subtler than their previous releases, Lanois and Eno's production capturing the sultry sound of desire that bleeds through every track, Flood's mixes accentuate the pulsing rhythms and mood atmospheres, and Steve Lillywhite's pack an almost nostalgic punch.

⑦ Zooropa (Island) 1993 After the subtle nuances of *Baby*, *Zooropa* blows through like a fresh breeze. More diverse thematically and adventurous musically, the album journeys across moods and styles, with Clayton's prominent bass sinuously winding throughout. Still pushing forward, U2 redefine their sound and widen the boundaries of pop.

⑧ Pop (Island) 1997 From pounding techno to introspective ballads, U2 emerge in the most unexpected guise of all, fueled by dance floor beats that infuse all but the quietest numbers. Flood's production highlights the electronics, while Howie B's mix emphasizes the beats. There are some moments of self-consciousness, most notably in the "Discotheque" single, but the disc snaps and crackles regardless.

⑦ All That You Can't Leave Behind (Interscope) 2000

Selected Compilations and Archive Releases

⑨ Best of 1980–90 (Island) 1999 The first decade of hits, initially accompanied by a second album of B-sides (subsequently released separately).

U2/The Passengers LP
⑥ Original Soundtracks 1 (1995) 1995

The Edge LP
⑥ Captive (Virgin) 1986

Further Reading
Faraway So Close by BP Fallon (Little Brown & Co 1994).

V

VERVE

FORMED 1990 (Wigan, England)
ORIGINAL LINE-UP *Richard Ashcroft (b. 1971 — vocals, guitar); Nick McCabe (keyboards); Simon Jones (bass); Peter Salisbury (drums)*

Formed while all four members were still at school, Verve (the "The" was added later) made their live debut at a friend's birthday party at the local Honeysuckle pub, playing a set heavily influenced by the then-prevalent Madchester baggy scene, but characterized by Richard Ashcroft's wailing vocals over an effects-ridden sound track.

Immediately stepping onto the local live circuit, Verve were soon a regular attraction at the Boardwalk in Manchester and the Citadel in nearby St. Helens. The band's demo tapes were so well received that, within a year, Verve were widely regarded among the hottest unsigned bands in the UK.

They signed with Virgin's Hut subsidiary late in 1991, and in March 1992, with the British press hailing the band as the next London Suede, their debut single, "All in the Mind," was released to general confusion — after all the build up, the public was expecting a savage pop band. Instead, they got an atmosphere-laden funk cut, and when Verve followed through with the *Superstar* EP (#66 UK), even their staunchest fans whispered grimly of commercial suicide. Shoe-gazing was last year's thing.

Gravity Grave followed in October 1992, followed by a US-only compilation of the story-so-far, *The Verve EP*, which coincided with the band's first American tour and also debuted the band's name change, following complaints from the US jazz label of the same name.

In May 1993, the Verve finally released a record, "Blue" (#69 UK), which began to approach their much-vaunted potential. Their debut album, *A Storm in Heaven* (#27 UK) followed, with Ashcroft loudly proclaiming it to be a masterpiece. Unfortunately, few people agreed with him, and when the band's next single, the majestic "Slide Away," slid into oblivion, it was apparent that if the Verve were to survive, they needed to adapt quickly.

The band played Glastonbury before joining Lollapalooza 93 for a short run; in August, they played their first European tour, opening for the Smashing Pumpkins, before follow-up tours of America and the UK — supported on the latter by the infant Oasis. They continued gigging through 1994, returning to Lollapalooza through July and August. A handful of European dates was marred by an ugly incident in Sweden, where they joined forces with Oasis to wreck a hotel bar following their performance at the Hultsfred Festival.

Silent through the remainder of the year, the Verve reappeared in April 1995, when they opened for Oasis in Southend, England, and Paris, France. The intervening months had seen the band seriously rework their musical approach, creating a far harder, poppier sound, a move which paid immediate dividends when "This Is Music" made #35 in April. "On Your Own" (#24 UK) and "History" (#24 UK) followed, while the band's second album, *A Northern Soul* (#13 UK) and another Glastonbury appearance saw them finally reclaiming the "next big thing" tag they'd left behind in 1991.

A US tour, dubbed "Conquering America" by the band, took them through July, and on August 5, 1995, the band played Glasgow's T — In the Park Festival. Less than a month later, Ashcroft announced the band had broken up. "It no longer felt right."

In fact, Nick McCabe alone would be leaving; by the end of the year, the remainder of the band were working with new guitarist Simon Tong and considering relaunching under a new name. A handful of new songs was aired when Ashcroft played a solo acoustic show opening for Oasis in New York City in March 1996, and by the end of the year, it was clear that the band were recording again, with both Tong and the returning McCabe on board.

In June 1997, "Bitter Sweet Symphony" (#12 US, #2 UK), the first new Verve single in 18 months, soared on a wave of excitement and, perhaps, sympathy — the song was built around a sample from the Andrew Loog Oldham Orchestra's "The Last Time." When the band applied for clearance, the song's publisher, Allen Klein, wrested away all composer royalties, instead of the simple percentage normally applicable in such cases.

Further misfortune struck when Ashcroft contracted a viral infection, causing the postponement of the Verve's comeback tour until August. Better luck followed, however, climaxed by a triumphant Reading Festival showing, and in September, with their next single, "The Drugs Don't Work" (#1 UK) topping the UK chart, the band's third album, *Urban Hymns*, slammed straight in at #1.

The band opened for Oasis at Earl's Court and were generally described as stealing the show; a third single, "Lucky Man," was released amidst the band's latest, sold out, US tour through November 1997, with a UK outing in the new year including three massively oversubscribed dates at the

Brixton Academy and two more at the Manchester Apollo. (A fourth single from the album, "Sonnet," was released as a limited edition in March 1998 as part of a four 12-inch single boxed set, alongside its three predecessors.)

Despite a string of cancellations after Simon Jones fell ill, late spring 1998 still saw the Verve on the European festival circuit before they set out on another US tour — highlighted by news that *Urban Hymns* had been certified platinum. Just a month before the first show, however, McCabe quit the band (his first project was a remix for French band Mellow). Amid a swamp of rumors, he was replaced by veteran BJ Cole, and the tour went ahead as planned, wrapping up in Seattle, WA, on August 17.

The following weekend, the Verve headlined both days of Britain's V98 festival, ending their set with a spectacular 15-minute rendition of "Bitter Sweet Symphony." Those shows, in Chelmsford and Leeds, would be the last the Verve would play. Though it would take another eight months of speculation to bring the story out, in April, Ashcroft finally announced the end. Retaining Peter Salisbury alone, he began work on a solo album, and a single, "A Song for Lovers," for release in 2000.

The Verve LPs

7 A Storm in Heaven (Vernon Yard) 1993 Masters of mood and tension, Verve gust between fuzzy dream-pop ("The Sun, the Sea") and atmospheric roars ("See You in the Next One"), reaching a crescendo and then receding into quieter, pensive passages. A marvelously evocative album featuring the mini-hit "Blue."

8 A Northern Soul (Vernon Yard) 1995 Mixing the vocals up front subtly alters Verve's sound, while not compromising their flowing, dream-inducing style an iota. "Stormy Clouds" and "History" immediately benefit from the ensuing epic quality.

6 Urban Hymns (Virgin) 1997 With the increased use of orchestration and the soaring sample of "Bitter Sweet Symphony," the Verve aim for the heavens. A complete volte face stylistically, *Hymn's* dense textures are sprinkled with a dusting of pop but are still capable of conjuring that mood-altering feel.

Selected Compilations and Archive Releases

8 No Come Down (Vernon Yard) 1994 "Blue" resurfaces, this time in a "US mix," alongside EP cuts, an acoustic "Make It til Monday," and the live "Gravity Grave."

Richard Ashcroft LP

8 Alone with Everybody (Virgin) 2000

Further Reading

Crazed Highs & Horrible Lows by Martin Clarke (Plexus, UK, 1998).

VERVE PIPE

FORMED 1992 *(Grand Rapids, MI)*
ORIGINAL LINE-UP *Brian Vander Ark (vocals, guitar); Brad Vander Ark (bass); Donny Brown (drums)*

The Verve Pipe formed from the wreckage of two local bands, the Vander Ark brothers' Johnny With an Eye and Donny Brown's Water 4 the Pool. After considering such names as the Big Whoop and the Big To-Do, they opted for Verve Pipe one night at four in the morning and went into the studio almost immediately.

Within weeks of getting together, the band recorded a seven-track mini-album, *I've Suffered a Head Injury*. Their first live show, at the Hidden Shamrock, Chicago, on August 1, 1992 coincided with its release, and over the next six months the trio gigged locally, to mounting acclaim. Guitarist A.J. Dunning joined in April 1993, and with the band's own LMNO Pop! label up and running (the name was another discarded idea for the band's own), Verve Pipe's first full album, *Pop Smear*, was released in September.

Selling over 50,000 copies, *Pop Smear* couldn't help but bring the band to major label attention, and in February 1995, the band — now augmented by Doug Corella (keyboards) — signed with RCA. They would spend much of the next year recording (their sole release in 1995 was a version of XTC's "Wake Up," for the *Testimonial Dinner* tribute album). A return to the stage in January 1996 was followed by their debut single, "Photograph," which became February's #1 Most Added Single on Modern Rock radio — the track would spend more than two months on that chart in the lead-up to the release of *Villains* in March. (A second single, "Cup of Tea," followed in August.)

Over the next year, the Verve Pipe would play over 300 shows, beginning with two sold-out nights at the L.A. Troubadour in late April and including a three-month US and European stint tour with KISS beginning in September. They also co-headlined their own European dates with Imperial Drag, and in January 1997, their next single, "The Freshman," became the Verve Pipe's biggest yet, topping the Modern Rock chart for three weeks. It eventually went gold; *Villains* itself went platinum in July 1997.

The band continued touring the US through the summer; the outing finally ended with three sold-out shows in Kalamazoo, MI, in September, before the band moved on to their first Australian visit in October. Brian Vander Ark then went immediately to London to link with XTC main man Andy Partridge to write an album's worth of material. One track from this collaboration, "Blow You Away," would appear on the sound track to the *Avengers* movie. (Vander Ark also starred as a country singer in the movie *Road Kill*.)

With a clutch of other sound track appearances to their credit, the Verve Pipe began work on their third album in August 1998 with producer Michael Beinhorn; trailed by the "Hero" single in June 1999, *The Verve Pipe* (#158 US) was released in July, the cue for another protracted bout of touring.

Verve Pipe LPs

6 I've Suffered a Head Injury (LMNO Pop) 1992 The band's debut is full of nascent rumblings of pop riffing and rootsy indy guitar. Both "The Freshman" and "Brian's Song" impress.

7 Pop Smear (LMNO Pop) 1993 Slicker than *Injury*, Verve Pipe quickly got the hang of their sound and this package is full of meatier guitars. Add some Latin flair on "Honest" to round out the ballads and pop sonics that fill the rest of the album, and the result is a pleasant surprise.

8 Villains (RCA) 1996 Produced by Talking Heads Jerry Harrison, Verve Pipe really come into their own, emerging as a competent pop band whose songs are far deeper and more textured than they first appear. A re-recording of "The Freshman" turns what was a rough diamond into a sparkling hit single.

7 The Verve Pipe (RCA) 1999 Not a bad post-grunge grunge album, although the band are static, playing it safe and delivering a package that is so similar to their last album that first impressions are of a throwaway. The band do keep that from happening with an energetic second half, including the snappy "Kiss Me Idle," but one wonders why they saved their best for last.

VIBRATORS

FORMED 1976 (London, England)
ORIGINAL LINE-UP Ian "Knox" Carnochan (vocals); Pat Collier (bass); John Ellis (guitar); Eddie (drums)

Although the original Vibrators were closer to a pub rock R&B band than anything, early gigs opening for the likes of the Stranglers (at Hornsey College of Art in March 1976 — the Vibrators' debut) and the Sex Pistols saw them garner punk plaudits regardless, and in September, the quartet played the 100 Club Punk Festival, performing a covers-heavy set with veteran guitarist Chris Spedding (guitar).

It was he who brought the band to the attention of his record label, RAK, and in November, the Vibrators' debut single, "We Vibrate," was only narrowly beaten by the Damned's "New Rose" in the race to release the first-ever punk single. The Vibrators contented themselves with another accolade — the first punk band to release a second 45, when "Pogo Dancing," recorded with Spedding, hit the stores a mere two weeks later.

Neither hit, and plans for a third RAK single, "Bad Time"/"No Heart," were scrapped when the Vibrators signed to Epic in early 1977. There they unveiled what remains the all-time classic Vibrators single, the epic "Baby Baby," itself little more than a taster for what would become one of the benchmark punk albums, *Pure Mania* (#49 UK).

In March 1977, the Vibrators landed the coveted opening slot on Iggy Pop's comeback tour; they followed through with a longer outing, supporting Ian Hunter, while a new single, a live version of "London Girls," reinforced their credentials as tireless road warriors. Pat Collier's departure (to form the Boyfriends) was barely noticed; he was replaced by Gary Tibbs, and after a short sojourn in Berlin, the Vibrators returned home in time for their biggest hit yet — March 1978's "Automatic Lover" (#35 UK). The band's "Top of the Pops" TV debut followed, and the next month, the Vibrators proved that their recent success was not a fluke — their follow-up album, V2 (#33 UK) did even better.

Yet the Vibrators couldn't hold a line-up together. John Ellis was next to leave, heading off to join Peter Gabriel's band; he was replaced by Dave Birch and keyboard/saxophonist Don Snow. One single ("Judy Says" — #70 UK) later, Tibbs, Birch, and Snowall left — Tibbs joined Roxy Music and, later, Adam and the Ants. The band played a handful of shows with a new line-up, featuring Knox, Eddie, Greg Van Cook (from Wayne County's Electric Chairs — guitar) and Marianne Faithfull's husband Ben Brierley, before Knox quit toward the end of 1978.

Eddie and Van Cook tried to hold the band together, recruiting vocalist Kip and ex-Eater bassist Ian Woodcock, but by the time Epic dropped the band in mid-1979, the band themselves had all but broken up. Then, in early 1980, a new line-up built around Eddie, Woodcock, and Phil Ram and Adrian Wyatt (guitars), signed to Rat Race, released two singles, "Gimme Some Lovin'" (#5 UK indy) and the frankly amazing "Disco in Mosco" (#26 UK indy), and then split up...only for the original line-up to get back together again in mid-1982, sign to Anagram, and start their career all over again with a rerecording of "Baby Baby" (#10 UK indy).

Moving onto the UK punk circuit alongside fellow survivors Chelsea and the UK Subs, but coexisting, too, with the new Oi! community, the Vibrators' gradual ascent to Elder Statesmanhood was launched with a new single, the title track from the forthcoming *Guilty* album, before the band moved to Ram Records, releasing the singles "MX America" (#17 UK indy) and "Flying Home" and the album *Alaska 127* (#22 UK indy), named after Pat Collier's studio.

In mid-1985, the Vibrators signed to Carrere, but released just one single, "Baby Blue Eyes," before returning to Ram for the *Fifth Amendment* album and "Blown Away by Love" single.

Collier finally left to concentrate on his production career — he was replaced by Noel Thomson for the *Live* album, before Ellis, too, quit to join the Stranglers. Mickie

Owen replaced him; Mark Duncan succeeded the short-lived Thompson, and this new line-up promptly got to work on the aptly titled *Recharged* album and "String Him Along" single. Unfortunately, the next album, too, was aptly named — immediately following *Meltdown*, Owen quit. Nigel Bennett (ex-Members) was recruited for 1990's *Vicious Circle*.

Still touring regularly, the Vibrators were among the punk heroes sought out to accompany Die Toten Hosen on their 1991 *Learning English* punk tribute, while the band continued knocking out a steady stream of new albums — *Volume Ten* was followed by a collection of rerecorded older material, *The Power of Money* and *Hunting for You*, themselves interspersed by a number of archive releases on a variety of labels, few of which actually indicated whether or not they contained new material.

Finally tiring of this situation and anxious that fans should have some idea of what they were buying, the Vibrators launched their own, eponymous label in 1996 with *Unpunked*, an acoustic compilation.

1996, the band's 20th year, saw a new line-up briefly convene around Knox and Eddie, Darrell Bath (ex-UK Subs, Crybabies, Dogs D'Amour — guitar), and Nick Peckham (ex-Big Boy Tomato — bass); following Darrell's departure that May, the Vibrators opted to remain a trio and simply carried on touring. 1999 brought two visits to the US, alone: headlining their own outing in spring and then, through the summer, aboard the Social Chaos tour, with former UK Sub Gregor Kramer replacing the recently errant Peckham. A new bassist, Robbie, joined for the recording of *Buzzin'* later in the summer and a UK/European tour through the remainder of the year.

Vibrators LPs

8 Pure Mania (Epic) 1977 Reformed R&B band goes fashionably punky. The Vibrators' saving grace was to play as fast and furious as possible and not take things too seriously, which means *Pure Mania* was nothing if not unique, with flashes of sheer brilliance ("Whips & Furs"), weirdness (the many Ramones go down the pub songs), and endearing gaucheness (the perfect pop of "Baby Baby" pummeled by the Stones-whipped lead guitar).

8 V2 (Epic) 1978 The astonishing "Troops of Tomorrow" taps into the new wave's vague fascination with Teutonic regimentation, via drums and guitars; alongside the harder rocking "Nazi Baby" and "War Zone," the Vibrators hatch a powerful, but strongly melodic, album that should not be ignored.

7 Guilty (Anagram) 1982 Heavyweight punk, toying expertly with the fringes of oi!, but without ever losing their songwriting edge.

6 Alaska 127 (RAM) 1984

5 Fifth Amendment (RAM) 1985

6 Vibrators Live (Revolver) 1986 Never really accepted by the original punk crowd (too poppy, too riffy, too old, too clueless), the Vibrators were now poised in that awkward no-man's land of outlasting their cooler competition but outliving their usefulness. Still, the faithful remained, and the Vibrators can still play the old hits with panache.

6 Recharged (Revolver) 1988 A newly revised line-up produces the punchiest of the band's '80s albums.

5 Meltdown (Revolver) 1988

6 Vicious Circle (Revolver) 1989 Ex-Members guitarist Bennett brings a new dimension to the band's sound — more noticeable live than on record, unfortunately, but still there's a few new songs worth hanging on to.

5 Volume Ten (Revolver) 1990

6 Power of Money (Anagram) 1993 Competent reworkings of older material suffers by comparison with the out-of-print originals but did give a new audience the chance to catch up a little.

5 Hunting for You (Dojo) 1994

7 Unpunked (Vibrator) 1996

6 Rip Up the City [LIVE] (Receiver) 1999

5 Buzzin' (Raw Power) 1999

Selected Compilations and Archive Releases

8 Batteries Included (CBS) 1980 Singles and first two album cuts.

8 Live at the Marquee 1977 (Released Emotions) 1993 The best of all the Vibrators' live albums, even if the sound is a little ropey.

6 BBC Live in Concert [SPLIT WITH THE BOYS] (Windsong) 1993

6 Demos 1976/77 (Dojo) 1994

7 Independent Singles Collection (Anagram) 1996 Much-needed roundup of the band's post-Epic days.

7 We Vibrate: The Best Of (Cleopatra) 1997 Half 1990s rerecordings, half 1977 live and demo tracks — an adequate summation of the Vibrators' legacy, essential for its glimpse into moldy old punk rock archives, and entertaining because of the roots that now show. "Baby Baby" really was a great song, and now they're not afraid to play it properly (it is, of course, 1990s redux), they're not afraid who realizes that.

VIOLENT FEMMES

FORMED 1982 (Milwaukee, WI)
ORIGINAL LINE-UP *Gordon Gano (b. 6/7/63, New York, NY — vocals, guitar); Brian Ritchie (b. 11/21/60 — bass); Victor De Lorenzo (b. 10/25/54, Raccine, WI — drums)*

The Pretenders were making one of their regular sweeps through the US when guitarist James Honeyman-Scott discovered the Violent Femmes, sarcastic cow-punk rockers seemingly locked into the Wisconsin live circuit, but otherwise little further along than they had been a decade earlier, when Gano and ex-Plasticland bassist Ritchie first played together at high school.

Honeyman-Scott's enthusiasm for the band saw the London-based Rough Trade label pick them up (Slash quickly followed in the US) and, in September 1983, the Femmes' eponymous debut album arrived on a scene already bracing for what the media, at least, would soon be calling Indie Geek Rock — a not altogether disparaging term which swept up acts as far apart as the newly emergent Smiths and Australia's Go-Betweens.

Certainly the Femmes' grasp on sundry themes of adolescent angst would have an immediate impact; the non-album single "Ugly"/"Gimme the Car" was followed by "Gone Daddy Gone" into the realms of cult success, while *Violent Femmes*' opening track, "Blister in the Sun," was destined to become one of the most played and best loved songs of the era — an insistent, insidious, and delightfully ramshackle burst of kooky adrenalin which, in a nutshell, summed up the Femmes themselves. Indeed, almost two decades later, the band's apparent subsequent failure to improve upon the shocking frisson of their debut remains their greatest downfall.

Even without charting, *Violent Femmes* made an instant impression; within six months, with Slash (and, therefore, the Violent Femmes) now picked up by the London Records major, the band were working on their sophomore set, *Hallowed Ground* (and accompanying single, "It's Gonna Rain"). Predictably the subject of a major press backlash, the album was widely disregarded as little more than a pale imitation of its predecessor. In fact, it was its superior, but following the accompanying tour, the Femmes went to ground for close to a year.

Recording with the Talking Heads' Jerry Harrison producing, the Femmes re-emerged in early 1986 with a new single, covering T. Rex's "Children of the Revolution," a trailer for their forthcoming *The Blind Leading The Naked* album (#84 US, #81 UK).

Again the critics were unconvinced and, though the album was a hit, the Violent Femmes would not be following it up. By early 1988, the band had split; Ritchie for a sporadic solo career (his first album, *The Blend*, was released in 1987), Gano and De Lorenzo for a stint with former Shockabilly mainstay Eugene Chadbourne's new band. Gano also formed the shortlived gospel-based Mercy Seat for a single eponymous album in 1988.

Encouraged by college radio's continued support of "Blister in the Sun," the Femmes reformed in 1989 for *3* (#93 US), released all but simultaneously with Ritchie's own *Sonic Temple and the Court of Babylon*. The following year, the bassist's *I See a Noise* would keep the Femmes' name alive

while the band remained in the studio with producer Michael Beinhorn, completing their next album, *Why Do Birds Sing?* (#141 US). The "American Music" single did little, but September brought an audacious cover of Culture Club's "Do You Really Want To Hurt Me" and, suddenly, the band's fortunes began to reverse.

After eight years of steady sales, the Femmes' debut album finally nudged the US Top 200, coming to rest at #171 and, though the Femmes parted company with Slash/London in 1992, a compilation reprising almost every one of their best loved numbers, *Add It Up (1981–93)* (#146 US) raised their profile even higher. They signed to Elektra in 1993.

Having already released a solo album, *Peter Corey Sent Me* in 1991, De Lorenzo quit in 1993 to follow an acting career; he was replaced by ex-Bodeans drummer Guy Hoffman and the Femmes released the aptly titled *New Times* (#90 US) album, the "Machines" single and an intriguing cover of the Heartbreakers' smack anthem, "Chinese Rocks."

New Times would be the band's sole album for Elektra; when the group resurfaced the following year, it was with *Rock!!!*, an album intended for release in Australia only. (More so than any other, that country had long loved the Femmes, and had already been rewarded once, with an otherwise unavailable live album in 1992.)

A second live set, *Viva Wisconsin*, followed in the US in 1999 — recorded the previous fall in their home state, it featured the band performing all but unplugged and sounding surprisingly intimate because of it. The following year then brought the playful *Freak Magnet*, characterized by an excellent new single, "Sleepwalking," and a cover of jazzman Albert Ayler's "New Generation." The Femmes were joined by former Pink Floyd session saxophonist Dick Parry for tours of Europe, Australia, and North America through the late winter and spring 2000.

The Violent Femmes LPs

8 Violent Femmes (Slash) 1983 "Blister in the Sun" opens the album and ultimately devours it — although not before "Add It Up" and "Gone Daddy Gone" prove that whatever else the Femmes may be called, One Song Wonders is not part of it. One Album Wonders, on the other hand...?

9 Hallowed Ground (London) 1984 Again they open with the strongest number — indeed, "Country Death Song" might well be the band's best ever, just as *Hallowed Ground* digs deeper into the Femmes' gospel roots to create a denser, darker, and considerably less gimmick-laden set than its predecessor. The critics never understood, of course, but "Sweet Misery Blues," "Jesus Walking on the Water," and "I Know It's True" are all worth their weight in gold.

6 The Blind Leading the Blind (London) 1986 A cleaner production than either the Femmes' past or the "Children of The Revolution" taster ever let on, the album also suffers from a dearth of genuine feeling — "Old Mother Reagan" is amusing, of course, and "Candlelight Song" is as touching as the Femmes are ever likely to be in the future, but the album as a whole feels old and tired. Which may be why they stopped for a while.

7 3 (London) 1989 Back without too much fuss, or too many ideas — 3 treads water for much of its lifespan, although "Fat" and "See My Ships" have a certain cracked dignity.

8 Why Do Birds Sing (London) 1991 The opening "American Music" is big and bad, but the heart of this remarkable comeback lies in the Culture Club cover and the irresistible "Hey Nonny Nonny" — irresistible because, with a title like that, you know what it's going to sound like, right up until the first time you hear it.

7 Australian Tour (Mushroom — Aus) 1992 A riotous gathering, as triumphant as any hometown gig and packed to the gills with hits and humor. In terms of experiencing the Femmes in concert, this one beats *Viva Wisconsin* hands down.

6 New Times (Elektra) 1994

8 Rock!!! (Mushroom — Aus) 1995 Following an oddly disappointing major label interlude, another return to form. "Didgeri-blues" is a wonderful tribute to the album's intended audience, "Dahmer is Dead" an odd ode to one of their homeland's less appetizing citizens, and "Thanksgiving (No Way Out)" would make a great musical fridge magnet. Great sleeve, as well.

6 Viva Wisconsin (Beyond) 1999

7 Freak Magnet (Beyond) 2000

Selected Compilations and Archive Releases

6 Debacle — The First Decade (Liberation) 1990 Twelve-track compilation — worthy but worryingly brief.

8 Add It Up (1981–93) (London) 1993 Demos, live cuts, and non-album material bolster a genuinely powerful romp through the band's pack pages. "Do You Really Want To Hurt Me" is hurtfully absent, but its B-side, the immortal "Dance, Motherfucker, Dance," does make a welcome appearance.

Brian Ritchie LPs

6 The Blend (SST) 1987

8 Sonic Temple and the Court of Babylon (SST) 1989

6 I See a Noise (Dali) 1990

Victor De Lorenzo LP

6 Peter Corey Sent Me (Dali) 1991

VIRGIN PRUNES

FORMED *1977 (Dublin, Ireland)*
ORIGINAL LINE-UP *Gavin Friday (b. Fionan Hanvey — vocals); Dave-Id aka David Busaras Scott (b. David Watson — vocals); Guggi (b. Derek Rowan — vocals); Dik (b. Dick Evans — gui-tar); Strongman (b. Trevor Rowen — bass); Pod (b. Anthony Murphy — drums)*

Formed when Dick "Dik" Evans quit the nascent U2 in 1977, the Virgin Prunes began as a live fantasy, existing in a mythical place called Lypton Village, populated by Virgin Prunes — people, as Gavin Friday put it, "who are called ugly, but [with] a character that's strong." Although the village was also home to U2's Bono Vox and Dik's brother, The Edge, the Prunes fit far more appropriately in with the nature of its inhabitants, and following their debut at a private party in Glasneven, the Prunes concentrated on taking their ugliness out around Dublin.

Not surprisingly, gigs were hard to come by, with the experimental Project Arts Center proving the band's most reliable host. However, news of the band's activities had percolated across the Irish Sea, and in March 1980, the band played their first London show, opening for U2 and Berlin at Acklam Hall. (The U2 connection would deepen — Guggi's brother, Peter, would appear on the sleeve of U2's *Boy* and *War* albums, and Pod would occasionally roadie for U2.)

Joined now by Haa Lacka Bintii (keyboards) and Mary D'Nellon (guitar — moving to drums following Pod's departure), Virgin Prunes returned to London in February 1981 to back up their self-released debut EP *Twenty Tens* (#25 UK indy). An instant underground hit, *Twenty Tens* was picked up by Rough Trade in the UK, who also released the follow-up EPs *Moments and Mine* (#50 UK indy) and three volumes of *A New Form of Beauty* in 1981, the first two of which reached #44 and #47 UK indy, respectively. Two further parts of this cycle were a live performance at the Douglas Hyde gallery at Trinity College, Dublin, on November 8, 1981 (part 5), and a live cassette excerpting that performance (part 4); two projected concluding parts were never realized.

At this point, the Prunes were still regarded with some uncertainty by the UK media, a performance art freak show for whom the music was simply a sideline to the actual act. This perception changed in early 1982 following the release of "Pagan Lovesong" (#13 UK indy). The half studio/half live *Heresie* album followed, before November brought *If I Die I Die* (#8 UK indy), a remarkable album which also spawned the memorable "Baby Turns Blue" (#15 UK indy).

The band gigged steadily around the UK and Europe (they made their US debut at Danceteria, New York, in January 1983), but difficulty in completing their projected second album, *Sons Find Devils*, marked the end of the original band when Guggi and Dik quit in 1984. (An otherwise unconnected live video with the *Sons Find Devils* title made it out in 1985.)

With Pod returning to the line-up, O'Nellon turned back to guitar, but it would be July 1986 before the Prunes resurfaced with producer Dave Ball (ex-Soft Cell) and a considerably more musical attitude than onlookers might have expected. A new album, *The Moon Looked Down and Laughed* (#5 UK indy), and a single, "Love Lasts Forever" (#18 UK indy), followed, but by fall it was clear that the Prunes were on their last legs.

The group played their final live show at the Leopoldsville festival in Belgium on July 21, 1986, and though a live album, *The Hidden Lie*, was readied for 1987 release, when Friday quit for a solo career in November 1986, the band folded. Dik joined Debbie Skhow's Screech Owls for one single, "Desert"; Bintii formed Princess Tinymeat for a string of Rough Trade EP releases; Strongman and O'Nellon kept an abbreviated Prunes flag flying for three more years, but to little success.

Virgin Prunes LPs

6 New Forms of Beauty, Pt. 4 (Rough Trade) 1982 Rhythmic noise-scapes, a lot of screaming and a few snatches of melody floating through the agony.

6 Heresie (L'invitation) 1982 More of the same onstage and off.

9 If I Die I Die (Rough Trade) 1982 Eclectic Colin Newman production pushes the Prunes in directions that neither their live shows nor their media acolytes ever suggested they'd travel, into stirring almost-pop territory haunted by nagging chants and memorable rhythms. "Caucasian Walk," "Baby Turns Blue," and

"Baudachong" are unique (or at least, they were until a lot of later goth bands had the same ideas), but very catchy.

3 The Moon Looked Down & Laughed (Touch & Go) 1986 Ridiculous conceit, with producer Soft Cell's Dave Ball and a passing Foetus both powerless in the face of the remaining band members' Bowie-bound toothlessness. The album's release under the abbreviated Prunes band name suggests that even they were aware what an unworthy effort this was.

4 The Hidden Lie [LIVE] (Baby) 1986

Selected Compilations and Archive Releases

7 Over the Rainbow (Baby) 1985 Wonderful collection of rarities, singles, and out-takes includes the stirring "The Happy Dead" and "The King of Junk."

6 Sons Find Devils [LIVE] (Cleopatra) 1998

Gavin Friday LPs

8 Each Man Kills the Thing He Loves (Island) 1989 A demonic cabaret conceptual dip into the world of Piaf and Brel, so painfully executed that you feel dirtied even thinking about it.

4 Adam 'N' Eve (Island) 1992 Suddenly bright-eyed and bushy-tailed, unabashedly oozing "mature" MOR arrangements. By the time you hit "Melancholy Baby," the final shreds of sanity snap and you're lost in a world where virgins wear white, prunes are still grapes, and Friday falls just two days before Sunday.

5 Shag Tobacco (Island) 1996

4 The Boxer (MCA) 1998

WALL OF VOODOO

FORMED 1977 *(Los Angeles, CA)*
ORIGINAL LINE-UP *Stan Ridgway (b. 4/5/54 — vocals, harmonica, keyboards); Bill Noland (guitar); Charles T. Gray (bass, keyboards, synth); Joe Nanini (drums)*

Wall of Voodoo came directly from the steamy underbelly of the dying punk scene, dragging their own strange blend of beat noir around the L.A. underground for two years before being discovered by IRS founder Miles Copeland. He signed them in mid-1979, and Voodoo set about making their mark with a self-titled EP in September 1980.

A mini-hit with a cover of Johnny Cash's "Ring of Fire" ensured the band's local fame, and having adding Bruce Moreland (bass) and replaced Noland with Bruce's brother Marc (Noland resurfaced in Human Hands, with Dream Syndicate's Dennis Duck), Wall Of Voodoo were one of the high points at the US segment of Copeland's *Urgh! A Music War* event the following year.

The October 1981 release of *Dark Continent* (#177 US) was followed by Bruce Moreland's departure; without missing a beat, the band released their sophomore set, *Call of the West* (#45 US, #18 UK indy) in October 1982. The album spawned two singles: "On Interstate 15" in October and what became their signature recording, "Mexican Radio" (#58 US, #64 UK, #7 UK indy), the following January.

Wall of Voodoo capped this relative success with an appearance at the 1983 US Festival, but even with the band seemingly on the upswing, the revolving door once again began to spin as Ridgway left for a solo career and Ned Leukhardt replaced Nanini.

Voodoo persevered, recruiting Andy Prieboy to succeed Ridgway, but although the band had again effectively regrouped, they had indeed lost their momentum. With only a compilation, *Granma's House* to help break the silence between the beginning of January 1983 and March 1986, there would be just one release, 1984's overlooked "Big City" single.

Bruce Moreland returned to the fold for 1986's "Far Side of Crazy" single and *Seven Days in Sammystown* album; the following year brought a near-hit with an irreverent cover of the Beach Boys' "Do It Again" and the *Happy Planet* LP, but again Voodoo failed to recapture the magic of *Call of the West*, and the album sank into the gloom.

The last Wall of Voodoo recording would be released a year later, again without Bruce Moreland, the live *Ugly Americans in Australia and Bullshit City*.

Wall of Voodoo LPs

7 Dark Continent (IRS) 1981 Swinging to opposite ends of the musical spectrum from their L.A. contemporaries, Voodoo introduce their quirky hybridization of theatrical metallic wave and cowboy noir to a public who liked it…but weren't exactly sure what to do with it. The dichotomy of morose glee was puzzling.

8 Call of the West (IRS) 1982 The album that not only brought Voodoo a searing burst of fame with the catatonically jangly "Mexican Radio," but also confined them within their self-created genre. Stan Ridgway's vision was fully realized on *West* — a solid effort that is creepy as it is exuberant.

6 Seven Days in Sammystown (IRS) 1986 A dramatic disappointment on the heels of *West*, which is best only on its singles, "Far Side of Crazy" and "Big City." The first album post-Ridgway, the overall sound shifts dramatically and ultimately suffers without his deadpan twang.

4 Happy Planet (IRS) 1987 Another solidly proficient album, again without the spark that made the first two so snappy. The band still have an edge but can't push it far enough to make a difference, until even a cover of the Beach Boys' "Do It Again" founders.

7 The Ugly Americans in Australia and Bullshit City (IRS) 1988 A live album recorded in Melbourne and Arizona — hence the second half of the title — the band perk up a bit, bucking through hits and old standards including "Ring of Fire," from their 1980 eponymous debut EP.

Selected Compilations and Archive Releases

7 Granma's House (IRS) 1984 A best-of compilation.
6 Index Masters (RST) 1993

Stan Ridgway LPs

6 The Big Heat (IRS) 1986
7 Mosquitos (Geffen) 1989
7 Partyball (Geffen) 1991 Ridgway's solo career was defined by albums so incredibly textured, atmospheric, and packed with such strong musical and lyrical images, you could practically smell them. Specializing in vignettes rather than songs, Ridgway is the master of ceremonies, and one can't help but feel that Wall of Voodoo was his dress rehearsal.

7 Anatomy (New West) 2000

Andy Prieboy LPs

6 Upon My Wicked Dream (Doctor Dream) 1990

WATERBOYS

FORMED 1982 *(London, England)*
ORIGINAL LINE-UP *Mike Scott (b. Edinburgh, Scotland,
12/14/58 — vocals, guitars); Anthony Thistlethwaite (b. 8/8/55
— saxophone); Karl Wallinger (b. 10/19/57 — keyboards, bass)*

Following an aborted college career in the late 1970s, several fanzines, and non-starter musical projects, Scott formed Another Pretty Face in Edinburgh at the end of 1978, with old friend John Caldwell (guitar), Jim Geddes (bass), and Crigg (b. Ian Walter Greig — drums).

Paying homage to the great punk stars of the time, including Patti Smith and the Stooges, APF enjoyed a roller-coaster ride between 1978 and 1981, releasing several singles, including "All the Boys Love Carrie" and the cassette-only EP *I'm Sorry That I Beat You, I'm Sorry That I Screamed, For a Moment There I Really Lost Control*. However, having gone through several label and line-up changes and despite a successful tour with Stiff Little Fingers, Scott found himself becoming disillusioned with the business of rock and roll — a feeling that was only revoked after some sessions working with Nikki Sudden (Swell Maps) and a Scottish band, the One Takes.

With a new line-up of Scott, Alan Muir (bass), and Adrian Johnstone (drums), APF recorded their first John Peel session in June 1980, an experience that finally brought the band to the attention of the London-based music industry. It would take another year and further line-up convolutions, but by late 1981, Scott and the returning John Caldwell moved to London and signed with Ensign.

Changing their name to Funhouse to avoid conflict with an American Another Pretty Face, the duo released their debut single, "Out of Control," in February 1982. By the time Scott was ready to begin work on an album, however, he and Caldwell had drifted apart once again, and Scott launched a new project, the Red and the Black.

Teaming up with saxophonist Anthony Thistlewaite, who he met during the Sudden sessions, then recruiting Karl Wallinger through a musicians-wanted ad, Scott renamed the band the Waterboys from a lyric in Lou Reed's "The Kids." The band now began sessions for their debut LP. But while Ensign did shuttle the band to New York to work with Lenny Kaye (Patti Smith Group), the Waterboys' own vision of the album went no further than the rough demos they recorded in England.

The Waterboys' first single, "A Girl Called Johnny," appeared in March 1983 (the APF Peel session version of "Out of Control" appeared on the B-side). Four months later, *The Waterboys* was released, together with a second single, "December" — backed, already, by a taster from the band's second album. Immediately after *The Waterboys*

release, they returned to the studio, augmenting their sound with Kevin Wilkinson (drums), Roddy Lorimer (trumpet), and Tim Blanthorn (violin), as well as an assortment of backing vocalists.

A Pagan Place (#100 UK), released in May 1984, was both a widening exploration of Scott's newfound spirituality and an immediate critical hit. The Waterboys sound was growing, and the album's single "The Big Music" only reinforced the obvious. The Waterboys debuted live that spring, with a line-up boosted by Terry Mann (bass), In Tua Nua's Steve Wickham (violin), Charlie Whitten (drums), and Lorimer Delahaye (organ).

Solo European dates gave way to supporting spots with the Pretenders and U2; they then plunged back into the studio for September 1985's *This Is the Sea* (#37 UK) and the accompanying hit single, "The Whole of the Moon" (#26 UK).

But the immediate future of the band was about to take a shake. Egos were beginning to rub as Wallinger's compositions continued to be edged out in favor of Scott's ever-growing canon. Sessions for a live album were scrapped, and Wallinger left the band to form World Party.

Wickham, now a permanent member of the Waterboys (and former session player with Sinead O'Connor and U2) helped Scott forge a new direction for the band, as the sound took a dramatic turn toward traditional Irish music. Following a European tour with Simple Minds in early 1986, The Waterboys relocated to Ireland, regrouped, and began recording once again.

Anyone expecting a quick follow up to *This Is the Sea* would have a long wait, as sessions blended into sessions, and the Waterboys continued evolving over dozens of tracks. In 1987, however, Scott announced he was unhappy with the recordings to date and relocated the band from Dublin to Galway to record yet another slew of songs.

Fisherman's Blues (#76 US, #13 UK) was finally released in November 1988, this time spawning two hit singles, "Fisherman's Blues (#32 UK)" and "A Bang On the Ear" (#51 UK). Following a headline appearance at the Glastonbury Festival in June 1989, however, Scott again reshuffled the line-up and set out to record 1990's *Room to Roam* (#180 US, #5 UK).

Wickham quit during the short spell between the release of the album and the beginning of the band's next tour; Scott responded by trimming the band even further, acknowledging that much of the new material would be impossible to replicate on stage without such an integral member of the band. The Waterboys finally went out with a drastically pruned line-up built around Glastonbury Festival veterans Thistlewaite and Trevor Hutchinson (bass), and Ken Belvins (ex-John Hiatt Band — drums).

1991 brought the stop-gap *Best of the Waterboys* ('81–'90) (#2 UK) package, bearing with it reactivated singles of "Fisherman's Blues" (#75 UK) and "The Whole of the Moon" (#3 UK); the Waterboys' own era was over, however. The group disbanded shortly after the *Room to Roam* tour, as Thistlethwaite left and formed the Blue Stars. Scott took a break, then tried launching a new generation of Waterboys in 1991, with Chris Bruce (guitar), Scott Thunes (bass), American musician Jules Shear on backing vocals, and a quick guest appearance by comedian/sometime musician Billy Connolly.

The resulting album, 1993's *Dream Harder* (#171 US, #5 UK), and its two singles, "The Return of Pan" (#24 UK) and "Glastonbury Song" (#29), were successes, but when the sessions were over and Scott was unable to find a suitable line-up to continue with, he returned to Scotland to continue as a solo artist, releasing two acclaimed albums, 1995's *Bring 'Em All In* (#56 UK) and 1997's *Still Burning* (#34 UK). The Waterboys returned to action in late 2000, entering the studio to record their seventh album.

The Waterboys LPs

7 The Waterboys (Chrysalis) 1983 A musical outlet for Mike Scott's adoration of the whole New York wave scene, the tone is stripped, ballsy, and very much in keeping with the '70s ethics he espoused. The album's strongest track, "A Girl Called Johnny," was a very Patti Smith-y tribute to the goddess herself.

6 A Pagan Place (Chrysalis) 1984 With "Red Army Blues" a holdover from their debut, the Waterboy's second would become the bridge between the past and the future of the band's sound, as punky ethic was washed away and Scott's burgeoning exploration of folk spirituality began to bubble to the fore.

8 This Is the Sea (Chrysalis) 1985 A full-blooded assault of resonant dirge, sax, and Steve Wickham's violin, *This Is the Sea* swept the remnants of early Waterboys under the steps, cutting away some of the traditional rock and replacing it with eclectic Gaelic/Celtic folk. From "The Whole of the Moon," and "This Is the Sea" to "Be My Enemy," this album let Scott roil and spin to become new folk's organically spiritual dervish.

5 Fisherman's Blues (Chrysalis) 1988 What Scott began on *Sea* was fully realized here. In the wake of Karl Wallinger's departure for World Party, Scott shed the last remnants of the old for a complete neo-folk transformation. Unfortunately the sound suffered some and fans questioned Scott's sincerity and direction. However, there are good times to be had on "And A Bang On the Ear" and "When Will We Be Married?".

5 Room to Roam (Chrysalis) 1990 Fully entrenched in the grip of folk, Scott finally gets it out of his system with, among others, the ebullient "Raggle Taggle Gypsy."

6 Dream Harder (Geffen) 1993 Anyone expecting a continuation of *Roam* was sorely disappointed, as Scott traveled to his youthful mecca — New York — and returned to guitar-driven rock. Anyone hoping for a return to the band's early sounds

would be disappointed as well, as Scott's increasingly off-the-beaten-track fervor was still firmly rooted in-between riffs.

Selected Compilations and Archive Collections

7 The Best of The Waterboys (1981–1990) (Ensign) 1991

8 The Secret Life of The Waterboys 81–85 (Chrysalis) 1994 An important collection of alternative versions, demos, out-takes, and radio sessions.

7 Live Adventures of The Waterboys (Griffin) 1998

8 The Whole of the Moon: The Music of The... (Capitol) 1998 Chunky best-of compilation includes singles and B-sides, and because it is not in anything near to chronological order, the result is fresher than the average history.

Mike Scott Solo LPs

6 Bring 'Em All In (Chrysalis) 1995 A nice balance between acoustic folk and Scott's singer-songwriter instincts, best displayed on "She Is So Beautiful" and the title track.

7 Still Burning (Chrysalis) 1997

World Party LPs

8 Private Revolution (Chrysalis) 1986 Karl Wallinger made *Private Revolution* a public success, balancing what he contributed to the Waterboys with strong doses of Dylan-esque poetics, '60s British pop ethics, and a rollicking surf ethic. His effervescent pop came into its own on the standout "All Come True" and "Ship of Fools."

7 Goodbye Jumbo (Ensign) 1990 More good stuff, including the hooky "Put the Message in the Box."

7 Bang (Chrysalis) 1993

6 Egyptology (Chrysalis) 1997

WEEN

FORMED 1984 *(New Hope, PA)*
ORIGINAL LINE-UP *Mickey Melchiondo (vocals, guitar, etc.); Aaron Freeman (vocals, guitar, etc.)*

Just 14 years old when they first adopted the pseudonyms Dean (Melchiondo) and Gene Ween (Freeman), Mickey Melchiondo and Aaron Freeman's Ween started life as the archetypal bedroom project, recording ceaselessly, but seldom allowing outsiders to hear the fruit of their labor until 1987, when Freeman cut a solo cassette, *Synthetic Socks* (under the same name) on the Teenbeat label.

Emboldened, Ween formed their own Bird O'Pray label and swiftly followed through with the mini-album *The Crucial Squeegie Lip* that same year and two 1988 cassettes, *Axis Bold As Boognish* and their first full album, *Live Brain Wedgie*. A string of early singles furthered Ween's cult appeal: "Long Legged Sally Was a No-Necked Whore," "I'm

Fat," "Voodoo Lady," and "Sky Cruiser" linked the band with the labels C/Z, Vital, Flying Nun, and Sub Pop, respectively. 1989 then saw the duo sign with Twin/Tone and cut the 20-song double album, *God Ween Satan — The Oneness*.

With reviewers already tentatively comparing Ween's vision to the Residents or early Mothers of Invention and live performances fast outgrowing the simple drum machine that had backed them thus far, the band shifted to Kramer's Shimmy Disc label for 1991's *The Pod*, a set that saw the duo augmented for the first time by an outside musician, the mysterious — or maybe not so — Mean Ween (bass).

Further additions came when Ween went on the road that fall with Kramer on bass and Claude Coleman Jr. (drums). The band made their live debut at City Gardens, Trenton, NJ. Further shows around the metropolitan New York area were followed by a two-week UK tour in late 1991. With the album again winning a slew of good reviews, Ween signed to Elektra — a move that left industry observers shaking their heads in amazement and fans predicting the immediate downfall of Ween's surreal vision.

In fact, the move only encouraged Ween to greater excesses. Paying especially close attention to the most obvious outward manifestations of rap music, 1992's *Pure Guava* was purposefully insulting, ugly, and obscene, yet underpinned with such a sense of knowing nastiness that it was impossible to take the band's ramblings seriously. This, of course, was precisely what they expected, as they unveiled first *Chocolate and Cheese* and then the *Push th' Little Daisies* EP, further collections of genre-hopping music balanced neatly on the thin line between parody and purity — except in Europe, where a Ween tour was, according to Coleman, "irrefutably an absolute living nightmare."

In September 1995, Ween began work on what would become *The Mollusk*, a sprawling prog-rock epic recorded in the ocean-front town of Holgate, NJ, but interrupted first by the decision to visit Nashville to record another record entirely, then by a bitter northeastern winter.

A tour with the Foo Fighters in early 1996, followed by the release of the Nashville album *12 Golden Country Greats*, placed *Mollusk* on a back burner, and with good reason. *Country Greats* was a concept album recorded with a who's who of session giants who were apparently all in on the joke — the Jordanaires, Charlie McCoy, and Russ Hicks featured on the album, while country keyboard whiz Bobby Ogdin and the specially convened Shit Creek Boys would accompany Ween on tour that summer, a string of dates subsequently documented by several tracks on 1999's *Paintin' the Town Brown: Ween Live 1990–1998* retrospective.

Work on the *The Mollusk* resumed in late 1996, and Ween returned to action the following year, their latest guise furthered by a sleeve design by former Pink Floyd designer

Storm Thorgerson. American and European tours included festival dates as far afield as Budapest and Hamburg. The band then returned to New Jersey to jam the material intended for 2000's folk-pop opus *White Pepper*.

Ween LPs

6 Live Brain Wedgie (Bird o'Pray) 1988 Zappa-esque, in as much as it owes little to anything but laughs at a lot, Ween's actual mission remains unfocused (and noisy), but promising.

6 God Ween Satan: The Oneness (Twin/Tone) 1990 The drum machine gets tiresome, but with slow maturity comes a broadening humor.

7 The Pod (Shimmy Disc) 1991

7 Pure Guava (Elektra) 1992 Rap rhythms and purposefully foul lyrics crash across a gold mine of scatologia.

6 Chocolate & Cheese (Elektra) 1994

8 12 Golden Country Greats (Elektra) 1996 If it wasn't Ween, and therefore as sincere as a nightly news reader, this would not only live up to its title, it could even be the greatest greats. Nine out of ten rhinestone cowboys are already convinced.

8 The Mollusk (Elektra) 1997 Vast, sprawling, nightmarish, the prog-rock album to end them all; bloated and feeding on its own noodle-clever corpulence…there may be a concept; there has to be a mellotron. Perhaps it sounds like King Crimson. Ween's most twisted masterpiece yet.

7 White Pepper (Elektra) 2000 Bright, breezy, brash pop-folk weirdness…hey! It's the XTC revival!

Selected Compilations and Archive Releases

7 Paintin' the Town Brown: Ween Live 1990–1998 (Elektra) 1999 A handy introduction to the madness, following Ween's growth from a once-scratchy hall-emptier to a near orchestral monster.

PAUL WESTERBERG

BORN 12/31/59 *(Minneapolis, MN)*

Following the Replacements' disappointing final album in 1990, and even while the band were still grinding toward their ultimate demise, frontman Westerberg was busily creating his place in a post-Replacements world. In 1992 he contributed two songs, "Waiting for Somebody" and "Dyslexic Heart," to Cameron Crowe's grunge-ploitation film *Singles*. Both were very well received, and having primed an expectant audience, Westerberg returned to the studio to complete his first solo effort, *14 Songs* (#44 US).

Featuring contributions from Joan Jett, among others, and highlighted by the single "World Class Fad," *14 Songs* dispatched Westerberg onto a short solo tour through 1993.

However, it quickly became apparent that he didn't intend rushing back into the studio; by 1995, his only new release had been two songs contributed to the *Friends* TV sound track album, "Sunshine," and "Stain Yer Blood." Furthermore, attempts to begin a new album with Pearl Jam producer Brendan O'Brien foundered, and it would be April 1996 before Westerberg finally released the wryly titled *Eventually* (#50 US).

Westerberg toured in the album's aftermath, but it was a depressing experience as he realized "…that performing the same numbers for an audience night after night no longer made me happy. I always said I'd quit if it was no longer fun, and [touring] was no longer fun."

By 1997, Westerberg had broken his decade-long ties to Reprise Records, and under the auspices of long-time friend (14 *Songs*-era bassist) Darren Hill's indy Soundproof/Monolyth Records, he adopted the pseudonym Grandpaboy and released an EP, *Grandpaboy*, and the single "I Want My Money Back" that summer. By August however, Westerberg had inked a new deal with Capitol, and in early 1998, he re-entered the studio with producer Don Was and Benmont Tench of Tom Petty's Heartbreakers.

Describing his new work as "fucked-up folk music," Westerberg called *Suicaine Gratification* his darkest album ever, and as patently unsuitable for the live environment as its maker. Instead, Westerberg, Was, and filmmaker Ondi Timoner captured the evolution of the album on a 30-minute documentary — which promptly went unreleased. A single, "Whatever Makes You Happy," appeared in June 1999 to little attention.

Also see the entry for the "REPLACEMENTS," on page 591.

Paul Westerberg LPs

7 14 Songs (Sire) 1993 Despite the presence of a host of friends and guest stars, it's Westerberg's show through and through, showcasing his song-writing and guitar talents across a nice mix of moods and energies. Matters become especially stunning on "Even Here We Are" and "First Glimmer."

5 Eventually (Reprise) 1996 Now joined by Cracker's former rhythm section and reprising the last album's party's-worth of guests, Westerberg presents a set as diverse as its predecessor but exchanges the former's pop-rock heart for a healthy dose of Southern soul. There are a few great moments to be found, but the album lacks the spark of *14*.

4 *Suicaine Gratification* Capitol 1999 Westerberg's "comeback" is dark and broody, and although the sounds he captures with Don Was glimmer with promise (especially on "Whatever Makes You Happy"), it's hard not to feel let down.

WHAT IS THIS?

FORMED 1979 *(Los Angeles, CA)*
ORIGINAL LINE-UP *Alain Johannes (b. Chile, 1962 — vocals, guitar); Hillel Slovak (b. 4/13/62, Haifa, Israel — guitar); Michael Balzary (b. 10/16/62, Melbourne, Australia — bass); Jack Irons (b. 7/18/62, Los Angeles — drums); Anthony Kiedis (b. 11/1/62, Grand Rapids, MI — MC)*

Fairfax High School friends Alain Johannes, Hillel Slovak, and Jack Irons formed their first band, Chain Reaction, in late 1977, with classmate Tom Strasman (bass). With a prog-rock-heavy set highlighted by a cover of Queen's "Ogre Battle," the band played their first show in the school gymnasium shortly before Christmas 1977, then changed their name: first to Anthem then Anthym.

Two years of gigging around their and other schools ended when Strasman quit, to be replaced by Michael Balzary (aka Flea), three months before the band were due to compete in an inter-school Battle of the Bands. An accomplished trumpet player, the newcomer had never played bass before, but with a set now comprised largely of originals based around increasingly complicated time signatures, Anthym finished runners-up in the contest, and by early 1980, they were playing the Hollywood club scene, opening at the Troubadour and the Whiskey and headlining the Starwood's regular Young Nights.

Anthony Kiedis joined as MC shortly after graduation, by which time the band had outgrown their high school name — they became What Is This? after learning that was frequently the most commonly heard remark once they started playing. With Flea a committed punk fan and Kiedis introducing rap into their repertoire, What Is This? were developing a fusion all their own — one which received further plaudits when Flea and Slovak were invited to join a new band being formed by New York no wave superstar James White.

They turned him down, but Flea quit What is This? anyway, to join local punks Fear (he would also be invited to join Public Image Ltd); he was replaced by Hans Reunscheussel (b. Hamburg, Germany). Kiedis left around the same time, and What Is This? equilibrium would take another blow in spring 1983, when Slovak and Irons joined Kiedis and Flea in another project — Tony Flow and the Miraculously Majestic Masters of Mayhem, a guerilla-type joke band whose sporadic performances included campfire sing-alongs and frenzied raps and who encored naked, bar socks pulled over their genitalia. Changing their name to the Red Hot Chili Peppers, the act soon became a major draw, and as the summer passed, conflicts began arising.

Reunscheussel quit in protest at his bandmates' moonlighting; he was replaced by Chris Hutchinson, but matters nevertheless came to a head in November when the Peppers were offered a record deal by EMI America, just as MCA moved in for What Is This?. Forced to choose between the two, Slovak and Irons opted for the better established band (the Peppers would recruit Jack Sherman and Cliff Martinez in their stead), and in early 1984, What is This? cut their first EP, *Squeezed*.

A swift favorite on college radio, a Wayne Isham-directed video was shot for the lead track, "Mind My Have Still I," and the band returned to the studio with producer Todd Rundgren. It was an inspired but unhappy coupling, reaching its nadir when a team of MCA executives visited the studio to hear the band's progress and were played a tape of the band loosening up through a version of the Spinners' "I'll be Around." The label went wild for the song, ignored everything else they heard, and scheduled "I'll be Around" as the band's next single.

Slovak quit What Is This? in January 1985 to join the Peppers; the band opted to continue on as a trio, and with "I'll Be Around" (#62 US) giving them a summer hit, their self-titled debut album (#187 US) was released in August 1985. A US tour followed, with Johannes' girlfriend Natasha Schneider moving in on keyboards, but it was not a success. Too many nights the band found themselves facing audiences lured in by the hit and utterly unprepared for the funk-rap convolutions What is This? intended serving up elsewhere in the show.

Recorded during the tour, an EP, *Three Out of Five Live*, followed, and the band returned to L.A. in October to begin work on their next album; Irons completed his drum tracks then quit to join Slovak in the Peppers; Johannes and Schneider immediately convened a new outfit, Walk the Moon.

Working over the next two years and having salvaged what they could from the final What Is This? sessions, the pair traveled to England to complete their next album with producer David Lord; *Walk the Moon* passed by unnoticed in late 1988.

Irons, meanwhile, quit the Peppers following Slovak's death in June 1988, retiring from music for a year before being coaxed back into circulation by Clash vocalist Joe Strummer, who recruited him to play on 1989's *Earthquake Weather* solo album.

Reinvigorated, Irons rejoined Johannes and Schneider in a new band, Eleven, in 1990. Their 1992 debut album, *Awake in a Dream*, would be followed by two more powerful sets before Irons quit in 1994 to join Pearl Jam — who had, in fact, been trying to recruit him almost since the band formed. Johannes went on to play with Jason Falkner, and in 1998, he and Schneider linked with former Soundgarden vocalist Chris Cornell to record his solo debut, *Euphoria Morning* (#18 US).

What is This? LP

7 What Is This (MCA) 1985 Jerking, querulous, and seemingly purposefully obscure funk-rock crossover, lent even deeper obtuseness by the inclusion of the almost joyful "I'll be Around."

Walk the Moon LP

5 Walk the Moon (MCA) 1988 Heavily computerized textures clash with the natural soul of the original songs, an uneasy alliance that sees the band come off worse.

Eleven LPs

4 Awake in a Dream (Morgan Creek) 1992 Sadly murky metallic grunge, marred further when you remember its makers' pedigree.

5 Eleven (Hollywood) 1993

3 Thunk (Hollywood) 1995

WHITE TOWN

FORMED 1990 *(Derby, England)*
ORIGINAL LINE-UP Jyoti Mishra (b. 7/30/66, Rourkela, India — vocals, keyboards)

Mishra was a founding member of Daryl and the Chaperones, an early '80s keyboard-based band who became Whizz for Atoms around 1984, shortly before appearing on the UK children's TV show *Razzmatazz*. Mishra quit soon after, joining a handful of undistinguished pub bands before forming White Town in 1990 after seeing the Pixies — "I thought I could maybe go it alone; I'm a fat bastard, but when I saw Black Francis, I thought if a porker like him can get away with playing pop music, so can I. I still couldn't play the guitar, but I didn't let that stop me, so I booked a load of gigs before I'd roped in other band members on drums, guitar, and bass."

The first White Town gigs were around Derby; at their third, they opened for Primal Scream at the Dial, following up with slots supporting Cateran, the Family Cat, and the Sea Urchins. In 1990 too, White Town released their debut, an eponymous EP on Mishra's own Satya (Sanskrit for "truth") label. Later that year, a flexi, "Darby Abbey," appeared, and with White Town becoming popular on the UK fanzine scene, 1991 saw Mishra — now working alone, following the disintegration of the White Town band — contribute "We'll Always Have Paris" to the *Waah* compilations of local indy bands.

Shortly after, he signed with Illinois-based indy Parasol, debuting with "All She Said." Three EPs followed — *Alain Delon* in 1991, *Fairweather Friend* and *Bewitched* in 1992, and the beguilingly titled album, *Socialism, Sexism and Sexuality*, in 1994.

In 1996, White Town released the *Abort, Retry, Fail* EP, featuring the song "Your Woman," based around a sample of 1930's balladeer Al Bowlly's "My Woman." As usual, Parasol paid him with a box of ten copies of the finished record, but at his girlfriend's suggestion, Mishra sent one of the ten to BBC DJ Mark Radcliffe. Within days, "Your Woman" was airing on national radio.

Other DJs followed, and Mishra reflected, "the worst moment was when the BBC called back and said the record was getting an amazing response from listeners; they'd never had a reaction like this to a new release. I said 'well, what about Oasis?' and they said 'you don't understand, this is bigger than Oasis'."

A frantic call to Parasol elicited an offer to send over another 100 copies — Mishra responded, "I think we're going to need 100,000," at which point the label suggested he shop around for a major label deal. Copies were sent out to every major label — most passed on it, but finally, EMI stepped in, in January 1997, and by the end of the month, "Your Woman" was #1 in the UK. Amusingly, midway through the record's run at the top, Mishra received a letter from Island Records, informing him, "thank you for your submission; unfortunately, we do not think it fits into the current musical climate."

A follow-up single, "Undressed," and the album, *Women in Technology*, failed to repeat the success of "Your Woman"; indeed, Mishra had fiercely resisted even releasing a second single, already convinced that he was destined to be a one-hit wonder and not worrying about it, either. By 1999, he was back with Parasol, releasing the *Another Lover* EP that March and collaborating with David Devant and His Spirit Wife.

White Town LPs

7 Socialism, Sexism and Sexuality (Parasol) 1994 Low-rent sound, but sensational songs — even if there is nothing to touch "Your Woman."

8 Women in Technology (EMI) 1997 AOR dance pop with attitude, and while *Women* never really recovers from "Your Woman," the drifting gentility of "Undressed," "Thursday at the Blue Note," and "A Week Next June" paint a seriously grown-up canvas — Robert Miles with a rocking implant.

ROZZ WILLIAMS

BORN *Roger Painterz (Pomona, CA)*

Rozz Williams erupted out of the L.A. underground in the late 1970s, the transvestite 16-year-old figurehead of Christian Death. The original line-up of Williams, James, McGearthy (bass), and Jay (guitar) and George Belanger (drums) formed in Pomona as a relatively straightforward punk band, having relocated to L.A.; however, the band was swiftly absorbed into the local death/proto-goth rock scene alongside the likes of 45 Grave and the Super Heroines.

Replacing Jay with Rikk Agnew (ex-Adolescents/Social Distortion), Christian Death recorded their debut album, *Only Theatre of Pain*, with producer Thom Wilson in 1982; the *Deathwish* EP followed, based around tracks recorded for the seminal *Hell Comes to Your House* compilation, and over the next two years, constant live work perfected Christian Death's unique vision of B-movie snuff rock.

The line-up was rarely stable, however, and when Christian Death shattered on the eve of a major European tour, Williams was left with nothing more than the name, some songs, and an irate L.A.-based trio called Pompeii 99, who had been scheduled to support Death on the road. It was this band, with Williams (vocals), Gitane Demone (keyboards), and Valor Kand (guitar), that was to carry Christian Death into the second half of the decade.

A new album, *Catastrophe Ballet* was recorded at Rockfield Studios, Wales, in 1983, rerecording several tracks demoed by the "classic" line-up for their own projected sophomore album. The band toured throughout the UK and Europe, returning to L.A. in late 1984 and recording *Ashes*.

The band also designed an extravagant multimedia presentation for their next tour — in the event, it was performed just once, at the Roxy over Easter 1985, before a disillusioned Williams quit for Premature Ejaculation, an outfit he originally formed as a part-time project in 1981.

Purposefully over the top (one performance featured collaborator Chuck Collision eating and regurgitating a dead cat), the group was all but unbookable and concentrated instead on creating taped soundscapes. After several years spent out of sight, Williams resurfaced in 1989 at the helm of a temporary reunion of the Agnew/Belanger-era Christian Death, designed in part to quash escalating rumors of his own death — Kand and Demone had continued using the Christian Death name after Williams' departure and frequently explained the singer's absence away with such legends.

Recorded for the album *Sleepless Nights*, the tour prompted Williams and wife Eva O (ex-Super Heroines) to form a new band, Shadow Project, signing to Triple X and releasing their debut album, *Shadow Project*, the following year. Williams also found an outlet for further Christian Death material via the newly formed Cleopatra label, and by 1992, he had thoroughly reinvented that band's classic catalog, both on the road and via the *Iron Mask* collection of rerecorded material. Further Christian Death projects would include overseeing remixes and even recording new material.

Shadow Project, too, marched on, cutting the remarkable *Dreams for the Dying* in 1992 and also contributing an incredible revision of Alice Cooper's "Dead Babies"/"Killer" to an Alice tribute album.

Another Christian Death reunion in L.A. in 1993 saw Williams regroup with Belanger and Agnew, but an acrimonious end to the evening ensured the group would never work together again. When Shadow Project then broke up (along with his marriage), Williams began drifting. A succession of well-intentioned projects followed, including Heltir, Daucus Karota, a revived Premature Ejaculation (without the cat), a handful of spoken word recordings and so forth. But Williams was struggling with drugs, and many of the projects, he later admitted, were simply ways of making money to keep his habit happy. He was also ill — after years of hearing rumors insisting he had AIDS, Williams now believed he did, although he refused to visit a doctor to find out for sure.

Still, by 1997, he appeared to be back on course. He re-examined his early glam interests with an album cut with Gitane Demone, *Dream Home Heartache* (named for a Roxy Music track), while he and Eva O were discussing a planned Shadow Project reunion. Unfortunately, none of these plans would come to pass — on April 1, 1998, Williams' flatmate returned home to discover the singer had hanged himself.

Rozz Williams LPs

4 Every King a Bastard Son (Cleopatra) 1994 Spoken word set to a demolition derby; as interminable as it's intense.

3 The Whorse's Mouth (Cleopatra) 1995

Selected Compilations and Archive Releases

6 Live in Berlin (Triple X) 2000 1993 performance.

Rozz Williams/Christian Death LPs

8 Only Theatre of Pain (Frontier) 1982 Blasting L.A. death rock obsessing, of course, on religion and horror, but vastly influential on an entire nascent US goth scene.

7 Catastrophe Ballet (Nostradamus) 1983

5 Ashes (Nostradamus) 1984 More musical, if no less doomy collection, concentrating on medieval atmospheres but marred by a low vocal mix for Williams and a correspondingly high one for Demone.

7 Decomposition of Violets — Live in Hollywood (Roir) 1985 Cassette-only release highlighting "The Drowning," "Awake at the Wall," "The Blue Hour" and a ferocious "Cavity."

6 The Iron Mask (Cleopatra) 1992 Rerecording nine Death classics, an acknowledgement of the originals' shortcomings, and a neat reminder of where it all began.

6 The Rage of Angels (Cleopatra) 1993 A dramatic reworking of David Bowie's "Panic in Detroit," plus a welcome gathering of new material.

6 Iconologia: Dreams, Apparitions and Nightmares (Triple X) 1994 With guitarist Rikk Agnew disappearing offstage mid-set, then returning days later to dub his guitar lines, this document of the original line-up's 1993 reunion (with accompanying video) loses more from its survival than it gains from its memory. A virulent version of Lou Reed's "Kill Your Sons" is a remarkable highlight, though.

7 The Path of Sorrows (Cleopatra) 1995 A foreboding revision of the Velvet Underground's "Venus in Furs" winds up Williams' strongest Death album since *Ashes*.

Selected Compilations and Archive Releases

6 Invocations 1981–89 (Cleopatra) 1992

6 Tales of Innocence — A Continued Anthology [LIVE] (Cleopatra) 1993 Tight and well-recorded 1985 live set, heavy on the *Ashes* moods and momentum.

7 1994 Sleepless Nights [LIVE 1990] (Cleopatra) 1993

5 Death in Detroit (Cleopatra) 1995 Mini-album featuring three mixes of "Panic in Detroit" plus Death classics "Skeleton Kiss" and "Spiritual Cramp."

5 Death Mix (Cleopatra) 1996 Laibach, Matt Green, Frontline Assembly, and Die Krupps get to grips with the Death catalog.

8 The Best of (Cleopatra) 1999 Strong compilation drawn from both conventional and remixed sources; a beginners' guide to Christian Death.

Shadow Project LPs

7 Shadow Project (Triple X) 1991 Vastly more musical than Christian Death ever hoped to be, with the increasingly Bowie-esque Williams and wife O both taking song writing and vocal credits. Still distinctly goth-tinged, of course, but there are other musical powers in the mix.

8 Dreams for the Dying (Triple X) 1992 "Static Jesus" had Top 40 remix written all over it, while "Holding You Close" came as near to a love song as Shadow Project ever got — "I wish I was a coffin to hold you close." A deeper well than Williams' popular reputation allowed, *Dreams* closed with the passionate "The Circle and the Cross," an intense chest-beater unafraid to smirk behind its own hand.

6 In Tuned Out [LIVE] (Triple x) 1994 Posthumous live set touching most of the expected bases but losing a lot without the dry ice-fogged visuals.

Daucus Karota LP

7 Shrine (Triple X) 1994 Produced by Iggy sideman Hunt Sales and peaking with Pop's "Raw Power," a mini-album revealing

Williams' oft-confessed (but seldom-credited) love of the garage glam machine.

Rozz Williams/Gitane Demone LP
Dream Home Heartache (Triple X) 1997

Premature Ejaculation LP
8 Necessary Discomforts 1994 One of several dozen PE projects, many of which exist on limited edition cassette, only, but all of which follow the clattering, non-musical lead of this set.

WIRE

FORMED 1976 (London, England)
ORIGINAL LINE-UP *Colin Newman (b. 9/16/54 — guitar, vocal); George Gill (guitar); Bruce Gilbert (b. 5/18/46, Watford, England — guitar); Graham Lewis (b. 2/22/53 — bass, vocal); Robert Gotobed (b. Mark Field, 1951 — drums)*

From the outset, Wire made no secret of their fascination with the developing punk scene; nor were they shy of admitting that not one of them exactly knew his way around his chosen instrument. The experimentalism that naturally followed was a major part in both Wire's early sound and their early success. Having debuted in London on December 2, 1976, supporting the Derelicts, Wire moved on to the Roxy Club in the new year, shedding guitarist Gill in February. But by the time they were caught live at the Roxy, for the *Live at the Roxy, London WC2* compilation album in March 1977, the group had already developed the signal sound that would remain the band's trademark for the next three years.

Signing with Harvest Records — the only band on the Roxy compilation to remain with the label that released it — Wire immediately slammed out a single, the dissonant, but demandingly contagious, "Mannequin." *Pink Flag*, their debut album, followed, together with some shows opening for the visiting Tubes. And what a mismatch that was, with Fee Waybill and co. striking one final blow for the overblown glam that was America's late-in-the-day attempt to ride the last British rock wave, while Newman and his cohorts pointed the way to an inexorably more intense future. Even with a show that lasted barely as long as their album — 21 songs in less than 40 minutes — Wire blew the headliners off stage.

1978's *Chairs Missing* (#48 UK), produced by *Live at the Roxy* main man Mike Thorne, followed, introducing a more measured, if no less frenetic, assault. Songs were longer, more detailed, more challenging — three singles, "I Am the Fly," "Outdoor Miner" (#51 UK), and the non-album "Dot Dash," might not have flown by at the speed of light, but they still demanded total concentration from the listener and from the musicians. But after one further album, 154 (#39

UK) in September 1979, Wire were convinced that they had exhausted the pool of ideas that had sustained them.

The band returned to the studio following the album's release, debuting several new songs on tour and recording a number of others. However, the individual members were tiring of Wire's continued lack of commercial success; there was also, according to Bruce Gilbert, a need to "follow up the idea [on 154] in solo projects." In July 1980, following a show at London's Electric Ballroom, the band broke up.

The individual members went their separate ways, recording a string of releases that only occasionally followed the tracks laid down by Wire, with the most prolific being Gilbert and Graham Lewis' Dome partnership. Throughout the early 1980s, the pair maintained a prodigious output of work, generally characterized by its pioneering use of random electronics and white noise.

Newman, too, was active, producing the Virgin Prunes before October 1980's *A–Z* solo set offered freshly recorded versions of tracks originally intended for the fourth Wire album. The all-instrumental *Provisionally Entitled the Singing Fish* (#15 UK indy), *Not To* (#4 UK indy), and *Commercial Suicide* (#22 UK indy) would then appear within a year of one another.

Even in death, of course, Wire had not laid silent. Drawing further from the aborted fourth album sessions, a single

© Jim Steinfeldt/Chansley Entertainment Archives

of "Our Swimmer" (#13 UK indy) was released by Rough Trade in 1981; the same label's 1983 "Crazy About Love" (#28 UK indy) single was drawn from a BBC John Peel radio show in September 1979. Wire's last-ever live show, too, would be released on album, *Document and Eyewitness* (#3 UK indy).

Wire reunited in 1986, initially for the *Snakedrill* EP (#3 UK indy) alone. The set was so well received, that by early 1987 the band was recording their first new album in eight years, *The Ideal Copy* (#87 UK, #1 UK indy). An accompanying EP, *Ahead* (#2 UK indy), served up remixes of the title track, together with three tracks recorded live in Berlin, and joined the live-but-meddled-with *It's Beginning To and Back Again* (#135 US) in proving Wire had lost little of their early on-stage frenzy.

While *A Bell Is a Cup* (#2 UK indy), the out-takes EP *Kidney Bingos* (#8 UK indy), and the single "Silk Skin Paws" (#4 UK indy) maintained Wire's studio profile, it was "Eardrum Buzz" (#68 UK, #5 UK indy), excerpted from the live album, that finally returned the band to the national singles chart in April 1989. A new live album, *IBTABA* (*It's Beginning To and Back Again*) (#3 UK indy) also appeared that summer.

Follow-up singles "In Vivo" (#11 UK indy) and the studio "Life in the Manscape" were not so fortunate, however, and following 1990's Dave M. Allen-produced *Manscape*, drummer Richard Gotobed announced his departure. After contributing a remix of "Ambitious" to Stephen Petronio's *Middlesex Gorge* ballet at the London Queen Elizabeth Hall on October 12, the reborn Wire went out in much the same way as they came in, with *Drill*, a collection of out-takes from 1986's *Snakedrill*.

The survivors regrouped as Wir and recorded September's strangely dislocated *The First Letter* and "So and Slow It Goes" single, but by year's end, that project too had fizzled out — Wir's final act was to remix Erasure's 1995 single "Fingers and Thumbs" for release as an EP.

Again the members remained active, with Newman heading the revolutionary Swim electro-dance label with wife Malka Spigel and propagating ideals that remain as stand-alone in their own right as Wire ever were in their prime. "Where punk went wrong," he reflected, "was in thinking it could change music by playing the same guitars, bass, and drums like everybody else. When I understood that, I understood that the only way to go forward was to make music with machines."

Wire themselves regrouped for a US tour in spring 2000 to promote the wholesale reissue of their post-EMI catalog.

Wire LPs

9 Pink Flag (Harvest) 1977 A bit like sitting in the middle of No-Man's land during the battle of Verdun, *Pink's* 21 tracks rain down on the listener with the ferocity and chaos of an all-out

assault. Wire's splatter-spray attack is both their charm and their weakness, as the songs are so short, the band rarely follow them through to conclusion. Twisting pop like a pretzel and pushing punk inside out, then stapling the results together with lyrics that leap from sardonic to withering, peculiar to surreal, Wire rank among the most creative forces to hit disc since the Velvet Underground (their most obvious, yet subtly understated, influence). Other bands would be more overt in paying homage to Wire; Elastica being only the tip of the iceberg.

8 Chairs Missing (Harvest) 1978 Reinventing themselves as a purer pop-punk band (pop being a relative term, of course), the group concentrate on sharper, more coherent songs. Highlights include the maddeningly infectious "I Am the Fly," the moodily hypnotic "Heartbeat" (later rifled by U2), the pop-perfect "Outdoor Miner," and the edgily aggressive "Practice Makes Perfect."

7 154 (HARVEST) 1979 Packing even more variety, *154* divides its time between catchy pop, aggressive dark-dance, and sundry experiments with soundscapes.

9 The Ideal Copy (Enigma) 1987 The driving electro-dance-pop tracks are marvelous, grounded in the early '80s, but eschewing all the tell-tale markers of the era. Revisionist history at its best, Wire sweeps across the last decade of electro, deconstructs it to bits of bone, then rebuilds it to their own schematics.

8 A Bell Is a Cup Until It's Struck (Enigma) 1988 Slyly connects the dots between Bowie and the Batcave and mischievously links the mopey Morrissey to the earlier moody practitioners of gloom, but beyond that, the doomy atmospheres reek of decaying Banshees, Sisters, and Cure cast-offs; then they unveil the indy idiosyncrasies of "Kidney Bingos," with its delightfully ludicrous lyrics of totally disconnected words.

5 It's Beginning To and Back Again [LIVE] (Mute) 1989

7 Manscape (Mute) 1990

Selected Compilations and Archive Releases

5 Document and Eyewitness (Rough Trade) 1981 The original line-up's final gig, appended with a bonus EP featuring eight further live tracks, including one — from a gig in Montreux — upon which the loudest noise was what Newman called "the beautiful…sound of 8,000 Germans whistling and shouting 'Get off!'."

8 On Returning 1977–79 (Enigma) 1989 Compilation drawn from the first three albums, a dislocating journey from "12XU" on.

8 Double Peel Sessions (Strange Fruit) 1990 Bundling together three radio sessions recorded between January 1978 and September 1979, *Sessions* captures not only the true quirky creativity of Wire but also presents a time-lapse photo of how radically and quickly the band progressed and changed. From a truly peculiar version of "I Am the Fly" to radically revised "106 Beats," the band move toward more accessible pop melodies, at the same time zeroing in on a phenomenal 15-minute version of "Crazy About Love."

8 1985–90: The A List (Mute) 1993   Thirty-five friends and family members were asked to name their favorite Wire tracks, 1985–90. This album features the top 16.

7 Behind the Curtain (EMI) 1995   Harvest-era demos/live collection beginning with 1976 cover of "After Midnight."

7 Turns and Strokes (WMO) 1996   Compilation focusing on the period leading up to Wire's first demise (July 1979 through May 1980), featuring previously unavailable studio rarities and live material. Arranged chronologically and containing extremely informative liner notes, *Turns* captures a band in the process of disintegration, shattered by its own creativity and brilliance.

8 Coatings (WMO) 1997   Out-takes and archive material drawn from Wire's first three and last three albums, respectively.

Wir LPs

8 Wir   Edgy electronics and the percussive clatter of industrial join more traditional movements. Front 242 had traveled down a similar path years back, but Wir do it more adeptly, completing the circuit with skewered lyrics, repetitive phrases, and montages of banal cliches and overused expressions. What *Manscape* attempted, *Letter* pulls off.

Colin Newman LPs

8 A–Z (Beggars Banquet — UK) 1980   Comprising songs originally intended for the fourth (unrecorded) Wire album, strong keyboards and tightly abrasive lyrics crash into an album of almost unreasoning magnitude.

8 Provisionally Titled the Singing Fish (4AD — UK) 1981   Initially baffling, but ultimately magnificent instrumental set, largely retaining the melody he normally buries beneath the lyrics.

7 Not To (4AD) 1982

6 Commercial Suicide (Crammed — Belgium) 1986   Close enough to a collaboration with Sean Bonnar and Malka Spigel (the future Mrs. Newman) of Minimal Compact, a melancholy set overshadowed, seemingly, by a need to live up to its title.

7 It Seems (Crammed) 1988

9 Bastard (Swim — UK) 1997   A gorgeously varied, but utterly cohesive, collection of instrumental songs, moods, and textures, ranging in effect from the crunchy "May" (a postscript, perhaps, to Wir's mid-90s Erasure remix project) to the hypnotic "G-Deep" and onto "Spiked," which conjures up images of King Crimson without ever being so crass as to step on that band's toes. Raw guitars clashing with syncopated rhythms, riffs blending with repetition, "Bastard" is both bad-temperedly uncompromising and warm-heartedly inviting.

8 Vox Pop (Swim — UK) 1999

Colin Newman/Oracle LP

7 Tree (Swim — UK) 1993   Sweeping across electro barriers and juxtaposing genres with impunity, *Tree* has an exotic uniqueness rooted in the Arabesque but woven with diverse threads of intriguing contrasts and warped by unusual undercurrents from techno to industrial.

Colin Newman/Immersion LPs

7 Oscillating (Swim — UK) 1994

6 Low Impact (Swim — UK) 1999

Colin Newman/Malka Spiegel LPs

8 Rosha Ballata (Swim — UK) 1993   Twelve tracks are alternately moods and songs, calm and compulsion. Drifting dreams locked to the barest layers of percussion and keyboards are overlaid with haunting (Hebrew-language) vocals, then jarred by Newman's ever-edgy production.

8 My Pet Fish (Swim — UK) 1998

Bruce Gilbert LPs

5 To Speak (Uniton) 1983

7 This Way (Mute) 1984

6 Insiding (Mute) 1991

6 Music for Fruit (Mute) 1991

5 Ab ovo (Mute) 1996

Selected Compilations and Archive Releases

7 The Shivering Man (Mute) 1987   Collection of material from the first two solo albums.

6 The Haring (WMO) 1996   Anthology of unreleased material.

Gilbert & Lewis LPs

6 3R4 (4AD — UK) 1980

6 Dome 1 [AS DOME] (Dome — UK) 1980

5 Dome 2 [AS DOME] (Dome — UK) 1981

6 Dome 3 [AS DOME] (Dome — UK) 1981

6 MZUI (Waterloo Gallery) [WITH RUSSELL MILLS] (Cherry Red)   The most adventurous of Dome's output, being in part a recording of a London art gallery's patrons, taped through hidden mikes while viewing a Russell Mills exhibition. A second MZUI album, *MZUI Australia*, was recorded live via satellite from Sydney to London.

8 Or So It Seems [AS DUET EMMO] (Mute) 1983

6 Will You Speak This Word [AS DOME] (Dome — Norway) 1983

Selected Compilations and Archive Releases

6 Pacific/Specific [WITH RUSSELL MILLS] (WMO) 1995   Collection of radio sessions from 1980 and 1988.

5 P'O (WMO) 1996   Unreleased material from 1983 Gilbert/Lewis collaboration.

6 Y'clept [AS DOME] (WMO — UK) 1996   Unreleased studio/live from post-1985 unreleased Dome project.

Further Reading

Everybody Loves a History by Kevin S. Eden (SAF, UK, 1992).

WITCH HAZEL SOUND

FORMED *1992 (Kent, OH)*
ORIGINAL LINE-UP *Kevin Coral (b. 1/3/68 — guitar, keyboards, etc.); Mark F. (b. 4/12/71 — vocals); Mike Split (b. 8/26/71 — bass)*

Formed from the ashes of Second Skin, a gothic synth-drum machine band containing both Kevin Coral and Mike Split, the impossibly ambitious Witch Hazel Sound released their first single in fall 1993 on their own Bubblegum Smile label, following it in 1994 with a split single with San Francisco's Mommyheads, and in 1995, the *Beeswax* EP.

All three releases worked toward leader Coral's ideal of creating "classic" orchestral pop in the spirit of Brian Wilson and Phil Spector, reapplied to the auteur experimentalism of Joe Meek, a process that peaked with the release of the band's debut album, *Landlocked*. Packed with strings and brass and released at a time when the High Llamas, Eric Matthews, and Boo Radleys were all taking similar musical adventures into critical Top 10's, *Landlocked* earned unstinting praise from authorities as diverse as *Alternative Press*, *Mojo*, and Bevis Frond's *Ptolemaic Terrascope* (the UK trade paper *Music Week* even judged it their album of the week).

The group's momentum was slowed by mounting record company woes, however, and though Coral remained an active outside producer, based out of his own Waterloo Sound Recording studio, nothing more was heard from the band until mid-1998 unveiled their latest incarnation, the Witch Hazel Sound. Released by the resurrected Bubblegum Sound label, the *It's All True* mini-album picked up where its predecessor left off, and with such success that the UK monthly *Uncut* subsequently proclaimed Witch Hazel Sound one of the two best pop bands on the planet (the other was Canadians Sloan).

Witch Hazel Sound LPs

⑧ Landlocked (Flydaddy) 1995 A sound that harks directly back to the sound of classic, *Pet Sounds*-era Beach Boys, brought up to date with a healthy dose of Blur, Boo Radleys, and Brit-pop in general. Add a cornet which wandered in from a passing Caravan album, and you have an intriguingly eccentric, but eminently listenable, potpourri.

⑧ It's All True (Bubblegum Smile) 1998 Now seeking the missing link between a flugelhorn-laden Brit-pop prog band and some forgotten Morricone sound track, baroque ghosts stalk the sort of pastures Boo Radleys and High Llamas grazed on so stylishly, but

with an honesty (and lack of contrivance) that bigger names are rarely prone to.

PETE WYLIE

BORN *3/22/58 (Liverpool, England)*

After a musical apprenticeship that carried him through such seminal Liverpool acts as The Crucial Three (with Julian Cope and Echo and the Bunnymen vocalist Ian McCulloch) and the Mystery Girls (with Cope and Dead or Alive's Pete Burns), Wylie formed Wah! Heat in February 1979 with Rob Jones (drums) and Pete Younger (bass).

It would be ten months before the trio played its first show, at Liverpool's Everyman Theatre, in December; two shows opening for Pink Military in Manchester and Leeds then brought the band their first press attention, when *Sounds* announced the arrival of "three more Scouse rockers with infinite resourcefulness. They made a joyous New Wave sound pretty much along the lines of a happier, more effervescent Doll by Doll or Joy Division, and were best represented by 'Sleep,' a crisp 'Cold Turkey' and... 'Better Scream'."

"Better Scream" (#11 UK indy) would become Wah! Heat's first 45, an instant Single of the Week in *Sounds*, where it was described as "a lissom hybrid of 'Eve of Destruction' and 'Don't Fear the Reaper'." It was a smart comparison — Wylie actually wrote the song after reading a newspaper story about Howard Hughes' dream of deposing Fidel Castro. "The song's about how crazy people get over power; what lengths they'll go to."

The original Wah! Heat crumbled shortly before the single was released; by late February 1980, a new line-up — comprising Wylie, Jones, guitarist Colm Redmond, and bassist Oddball Washington — debuted at what would become the last show ever staged at the 'pool's most legendary nightclub, Eric's, opening for the Psychedelic Furs the night the local constabulary swooped to close the venue's doors forever.

Even as he worked to establish the band's name, Wylie was already plotting the nomenclatural convolutions of the future. Following "Seven Minutes to Midnight" (#3 UK indy) in November 1980, he recorded a new track for a forthcoming *New Musical Express* compilation, "The 7,000 Names of Wah!". Although the band's next single, "Forget the Down" (#7 UK indy), was credited to Wah! alone, the run-off groove carried such future possibilities as Wah! Scallies, and Athletico Wah! 82. In July, the band's debut album, *Nah-Poo: The Art of Bluff* (#33 UK), introduced Wah! Without End to the brew.

Described by *NME* as "one of the four or five best rock records of the year," *Nah-Poo* closed with the oddly prescient "The Death of Wah!" — three months after its release, Wylie, Washington, and a now regularly changing line-up had rechristened themselves the Mighty Wah!, and were back with a new single, rerecording the album's frantic "Somesay." By mid-1982, the band was Shambeko! Say Wah! and recorded a fantastic version of "You'll Never Walk Alone" for the John Peel show; in November, a return to the Mighty Wah! identity saw them score one of the most memorable hits of the era, the symphonic epic "Story of the Blues" (#3 UK).

It had been a year since the band's last new release, "but we needed to grow," said Wylie. "This record is a kind of link between the old and the new." But at over eight minutes in length, it was also a statement of bitter defiance, a slap back at the critics who had now started writing Wah! off because they had yet to scale the same heights as their fellow Liverpudlians. As if to prove his point, "Story of the Blues" rose higher than either the Bunnymen or Teardrop Explodes ever had.

With Britain's critics now rushing to reassess the group's achievements and potential, "Story of the Blues" established the Mighty Wah! as the band to watch in the new year. Wylie, however, had other plans, promptly deciding to take another year away from the studio while he sorted out Eternal's own future.

He eventually signed a distribution deal with WEA; in the meantime, just one new single, "Hope" (#37 UK), appeared during 1983, followed by the *Maverick Years Official Bootleg* (#2 UK indy), rounding up the band's earliest 45's and out-takes. But in July 1984, the Mighty Wah! was back and mightier than ever. "Come Back (The Story of the Reds)" (#20 UK) was everything one could want from a single. Another epic, another pop symphony, a glimpse into what might have happened if classic Phil Spector met a young Bruce Springsteen, "Come Back" melded every conceivable era of classic pop into one, and just for a few weeks, time stood still.

So, unfortunately, did sales — and was it twisted irony or bitter prescience? — but Wylie had already condemned the imbecility of the modern music consumer on the B-side of the 12-inch version, a gritty parody of "Come Back" called "From Disco Dickie to a Kid in Care." Presented as an entreaty from enthusiastic publicist to reluctant pop star, it hit out at everything from the children's TV puppet shows, which were an integral part of the promotional circuit ("come back — we'll get you on *The Sooty Show*"), to the kind of things one had to deal with once one got there. "Come back — Howard Jones is having hits."

Wah!'s second album, *A Word to the Wise Guy* (#28 UK) followed, blending "Come Back" and its follow-up, the masterful "Weekends," with a bizarre, attitude-laden, proto-rap landscape; and that winter, Wah! set out on a triumphantly sold-out British tour. Already, however, there were cracks appearing in the walls of Wah!. WEA were suddenly losing interest in the band; "Weekends" failed to follow up "Come Back," and *Melody Maker*'s review of the closing London show mourned, "Wah!'s undeniable talents are being absurdly squandered in the Sunday youth club surroundings of their present predicament." Weeks later, the Mighty Wah! broke up.

Wylie bounced back in 1986, heading the Oedipus Wrecks and sporting a solo album, *Sinful*. There was another pair of British hits as well, with the title track (#13 UK) and "Diamond Girl" (#57 UK). But the album itself did nothing, and Wylie remained out of sight until early 1989, when he resurfaced on the latest Justified Ancients of Mu/KLF single, "It's Grim Up North." The following year, he joined one of the latest wave of Liverpool bands, the Farm, on their hit "All Together Now," while 1991 saw the same partnership revive "Sinful" (#28 UK) for a surprise hit. Follow-ups "Don't Lose Your Dream" and "Long Tall Scally," however, failed, while a new Wylie album, *Infamy! Or I Didn't Get Where I Am Today* (credited this time to Wah! The Mongrel), also went nowhere. He played the Last Night of the Kop festival at Liverpool soccer stadium, immediately before the venue's historic terracing was torn down (Julian Cope and Ian McCulloch also appeared), but Wylie's bad luck continued when a 20-foot fall left him with a broken back and chestbone. His shattered sternum missed his heart by half a centimeter.

Early in 1998, it was reported that he was poised on the brink of a comeback, with a new deal with Sony and an album ready for release. Recorded with Mike Joyce (the Smiths), Mick Jones (the Clash), and a string of top producers, a new Mighty Wah! single, "Heart as Big As Liverpool," duly appeared in November before he was suddenly dropped by Columbia. Despite a crop of rave reviews for the now mothballed album, the only headlines Wylie earned were for an appearance at Liverpool Crown Court the following year, charged with making a string of threatening phone calls to a former girlfriend. He was sentenced to 150 hours of community service. The album, *Songs of Strength and Heartbreak*, was finally released in March 2000 through the Castle label.

Wah! LPs

🆖 (as Wah! Heat) Nah Poo! The Art of Bluff (Eternal) 1981
An uncommonly powerful album, stacked high with dark, but never gloomy, rockers and climaxing with the truly remarkable "Seven Minutes to Midnight."

8 (as Mighty Wah!) A Word to the Wise Guy (Beggars Banquet) 1984 The deceptively lovely "Come Back" camouflages an album of rap/hip-hop stylings, too early for the crossover and all the more dislocating because of it.

7 (as Wah! The Mongrel) Infamy — Or I Didn't Get Where I Am Today (Virgin) 1991

9 (as Mighty Wah!) Songs of Strength and Heartbreak (Castle) 2000 Wah! returns, as mighty as ever — if a shade more bitter(sweet). Still turning out classy class anthems and blessed with one of the most distinctive voices in modern British rock, Wylie's absorption of the past decade in pop combines with his own tight grasp on the classics to create a set ready to rival any past glories.

Pete Wylie LP

9 Sinful (Virgin) 1987 Genuinely sparkling rock'n'soul, the title track alone keeps things buoyant forever — which means the seven cuts that follow, the anthemic "Fourelevenfortyfour," and the triumphant "We Can Rule the World" are simply icing on the cake. A very 80's production (by Zeus B. Held) cannot smother the exuberance of the keyboards and harmony-heavy storm. Wylie's most defiantly upbeat album and one of the best British dance albums of the decade.

Selected Compilations and Archive Releases

8 The Maverick Years (Wonderful World) 1982 Round-up of the non-album singles that surfaced around *Nah Poo*.

9 The Way We Wah (WB) 1984 The epic "Story of the Blues" (part two is crucial to understanding Wylie) and Wah's recounting of Johnny Thunders "You Can't Put Your Arms Around a Memory" are just two of the classics gathered here.

X

X

FORMED *1977 (Los Angeles, CA)*
ORIGINAL LINE-UP *Exene Cervenka (b. Christine Cervenka, Chicago, 2/1/56 — vocals); John Doe (b. 2/25/53, Decatur, IL — bass, vocals); Billy Zoom (guitar); Mick Basher (drums)*

When John Doe and Exene Cervenka met at a Venice Beach writers workshop in early 1977, punk was still something L.A. could only dream about. Maybe, as Doe said later, there were other bands already playing around; maybe it was true that the Damned would be coming over from England sometime that spring. But there was little enough actually happening that two like-minded spirits instinctively acknowledged one another, particularly after Cervenka presented Doe with a poem she'd written, and he immediately recognized it as a song.

Exene Cervenka

© Jim Steinfeldt/Chansley Entertainment Archives

He was already rehearsing with rockabilly fan Billy Zoom and Mick Basher — who would be replaced by DJ Bonebrake long before the band left the rehearsal room — but when Doe offered to add the "song" to his band's repertoire, Cervenka refused, unless she could sing it herself. She had never been in a band before; "she got lucky," Doe later laughed. "Exene didn't have all the baggage of being in cover bands that [the rest of us] did. So we could recognize something as unique, because we'd done all the bullshit."

The moment X appeared in public, it was clear that they were special — a living clarification, as Doe put it later, that California really was "more than the Eagles and Linda Ronstadt and the excesses of the record industry." Twinning Doe and Cervenka's harmonies in what critics would describe as "Jefferson Airplane with a pogo beat," but which was otherworldly all the same, even after other bands began to rise around them, X remained far ahead of the pack.

X's first single, "Adult Books," was released through the local Slaughterhouse label in June 1978, and over the next two years, the band gigged relentlessly and recorded hopefully — a session at the Record Plant in 1979, subsequently released on the *Beyond and Back* anthology, showed that all the components of X's later sonic success were already in place, yet it would be early 1980 before they finally released another record, after they signed with Slash.

X's second single, "The World's a Mess," was released that June, alongside the band's debut album — titled for what would become their best-known number (but, surprisingly, never a single in either the US or UK), "Los Angeles" (#14 UK indy). Produced by former Doors keyboard player Ray Manzerek, the album defined X's development out of the narrow L.A. punk scene — and L.A.'s own development out of the cliches of the past.

Doe and Cervenka married, and howled on by their family/gang of fans, the Wolves, X became one of the smash hits of that summer's *Urgh; A Music War* movie festival. The group's personal empathy with their audience, however, was best confirmed by a show at the Whiskey in 1981.

Just minutes before the band commenced their second set, Cervenka learned that her sister Mirielle had been hit and killed by a drunk driver. Word of the tragedy spread through the crowd, and journalist Pleasant Gehman later described the scene as "one of the most painful moments I've witnessed ever, let alone in the realm of rock'n'roll."

X's bond with their audience spread into the critical establishment. 1981's *Wild Gift* (#165 US), accompanied by the singles "White Girl" and a remake of "We're Desperate," was Album of the Year in both the *L.A. Times* and *New York Times*; X's touring schedule had been increased with seemingly regular television appearances — *American Bandstand, Midnight Special*, even *Solid Gold* invited the band in, and by the end of the year, it was impossible for even the majors to ignore X any longer. They signed to Elektra, and with Manzerek still in tow, began work on their third album.

Previewed by the single "Blue Spark," *Under the Big Black Sun* (#76 US) in July 1982 gave X their first Top 100 chart hit; cut beneath the shadow of Doe and Cervenka's impending divorce, its follow-up, *More Fun in the New World* (#86 US), was widely regarded as a disappointment, and two successive underperforming singles, "Breathless" and "The New World," convinced everybody that X needed a breath of fresh air.

Separating from Manzerek, the band returned to the studio with Michael Wagener to cut "Wild Thing," a non-album single, for June 1984 release. Months later, following one final show at the Universal Amphitheater on November 1, X announced that they were taking a brief sabbatical while they considered their future.

Cervenka had already branched out into spoken word performances (*Twin Sisters*, recorded with Wanda Coleman, included excerpts from her X tour diaries), while continuing to write poetry – she now published *Adulterers Anonymous* with Lydia Lunch. Doe, too, had a heavy extracurricular work load, featuring in the movie *Great Balls of Fire*, among others.

Joined by Bonebrake, the pair had also been gigging as an acoustic country band, the Knitters (alongside Johnny Ray Bartel, Ethan James, and the Blasters' Dave Alvin) since the early 1980s; they took the opportunity now to record a full album, *Poor Little Critter On the Road* (an earlier Knitters track appeared on the *Radio Tokyo Tapes, Volume 3* compilation). When they finally returned to X in early 1985, Alvin was promptly drafted to replace the retiring Zoom.

X re-emerged in August 1985 with the "Burning House of Love" single and the album *Ain't Love Grand* (#89 US). The arrival in early 1986 of Lone Justice's Tony Gilkyson (guitar) saw the band briefly work as a quintet; the *See How We Are* album (#107 US) and "4th of July" single, however, failed to make an impression, and when Alvin quit soon after, the remaining members opted not to replace him. Instead, they cut a valedictory live album at their old hang-out, the Whiskey A-Go-Go (#175 US), then announced an indefinite break.

Over the next five years, both Doe and Cervenka would pursue solo careers — musical, spoken word, and, in Doe's case, thespian — with varying degrees of acceptance and success. In 1993, however, X reformed for *Hey Zeus*, and emboldened by its reception, followed through with 1995's

Unclogged live album, recorded the previous November at the Noe Valley Ministries Church in San Francisco.

It would be the final act, at least for the time being: "X is no more and not getting back together, and not on a hiatus, so we can do solo projects," Cervenka tersely announced, as if by so saying, she could rid herself and Doe of the reunion specter that had overhung their last attempts at working alone.

But it was not really the end. In December 1997, Doe, Cervenka, Bonebrake, and original guitarist Zoom reconvened at Tower Records' Hollywood branch for an in-store signing of the recently released *Beyond and Back* anthology; days later, the quartet announced a reunion mini-tour. "A bunch of people [700+] showed up at the Tower thing and it just started to seem like a good idea," Cervenka shrugged.

Returning to the club circuit that spawned them for a handful of warm-up shows, X followed up with performances on that summer's Guinness Fleadh festival tour, the Hootenanny Festival, before bowing out again with a stint opening for Pearl Jam in Las Vegas, L.A., and finally, Sacramento, on July 16, 1998.

Although they would subsequently regroup for one-off shows, the members then scattered again — Cervenka and Bonebrake to pursue their newly formed Auntie Christ project (with Rancid's Matt Freeman), Doe for his John Doe Thing (their 1998 EP *For the Best of Us* featured a collaboration with Foo Fighter Dave Grohl), and Zoom to complete the "Billy Zoom" Gretsch Silver Jet guitar he was commissioned to design. The Knitters, too, would continue to perform when the mood took them.

X LPs

10 Los Angeles (Slash) 1980 X were the West Coast punks' heaven on earth. Their hybridization of three-chord posturing and rockabilly sensibilities both rewrote punk's rule book and allowed the genre to diversify, all the while retaining the bite and spit necessary for street credibility.

Of course, it's true that the band's sound was vitally cohesive and that without Bonebrake and Zoom, X wouldn't have been nearly the band it was. What pushed them into mythic realms, however, was the duelling harmony of Doe and Cervenka — a discordant caterwauling that could be as abrasive as it was excruciatingly beautiful — and when the lyrics were shoved in front of the music, the sound was unlike anything else.

Los Angeles is the sort of album that comes along once in a lifetime. A furious rush of pure adrenaline that barely contains the urgency of the lyrics (yet allows the music and melody a tempered pace when necessary), it coalesced around the band's unique take on the Los Angeles scene, perfectly wrought on "Sex and Dying in High Society," "Los Angeles," and "Johnny Hit and Run Pauline." The American new wave crested here.

9 Wild Gift (Slash) 1981 X picked up straight where they left off, all grime coated with dirty glitter, but their sound has shifted slightly to something with more focus. The ragged tumble of their debut still punched through a fast-paced set however, which includes a rerecording of the excellent "We're Desperate" and "In That House That I Call Home."

8 Under the Big Black Sun (Elektra) 1982   X moved away from the urgency that dominated their first two, getting slicker as Doe and Cervenka continued to tinker. From "Motel Room in My Bed" and "The Have Nots" to the crushing "Dancing With Tears in My Eyes" and poignant — yes poignant — "Riding With Mary," X deliver.

5 More Fun in the New World (Elektra) 1983   Very similar in scope to its predecessor, one can't help but feel that by this time X have honed their sound to perfection, found a formula, and stuck to it. However, "I Must Not Think Bad Thoughts" is a standout, and a glorious romp is certainly to be had in "Breathless."

5 Ain't Love Grand (Elektra) 1985   An eclectic selection, highlighted by the Small Faces "All or Nothing," and "What's Wrong With Me," broken midway by John and Exene embarking into a B-52's type talkie, whose main purpose seems to be deciding whether that thing on Doe's shoulders is a head or a chip. There's also a track called "Love Shack," but (like the Ultravox premonition on *Big Black Sun*) four years early, that's probably just coincidence.

6 See How We Are (Elektra) 1987   Dave Alvin's "4th of July" is a stellar track on an album that is otherwise smarting without Zoom's guitar. It's still a good record but misses the mark.

8 Live at the Whiskey A Go Go A-Go-Go On the Fabulous Sunset Strip [LIVE] (Elektra) 1988

4 Hey Zeus (Phonogram) 1993   Doe and Cervenka prove that they've still got it, but the whole affair falls short.

3 Unclogged [LIVE] (Infidelity) 1995   X at their best were the best because they sounded so ragged and raucous. Here, they're Joni Baloney and Crosby-Stills-Slash, eleven old favorites (but no "Los Angeles" — some things are still sacred), and two new songs that are largely indistinguishable from the rest. Unclogged? Unfortunate.

Selected Compilations and Archive Releases

8 Beyond and Back (Elektra) 1997   A crucial double disc of album tracks, demos, rehearsal recordings, and live performance, this is an alternative take on the X-perience.

John Doe LPs

4 Meet John Doe (Geffen) 1990   John Doe as slick rocker — not bad but hard to swallow.

6 Kissingsohard (Rhino) 1995   Doe kick-starts his career with a much better sophomore set. Packed with energy, the album has a little bit of everything.

6 For the Rest of Us (Rhino) 1998

Exene Cervenka LPs

6 Old Wive's Tales (Rhino) 1989

6 Running Scared (Rhino) 1990   Cervenka proves herself to be quite a respectable solo artist, wrapping her trademarked voice around blues, country, and rock.

7 Surface to Air Serpents (2.13.61) 1996

Exene Cervenka/Wanda Coleman LP

6 Twin Sisters (Freeway) 1985

The Knitters LPs

5 Poor Little Critter On the Road (Slash) 1985   Essentially an X side-project but focusing on acoustic-driven, down-home, rootsy country.

Auntie Christ LPs

6 Auntie Christ (Lookout) 1998

X-RAY SPEX

FORMED   *1977 (London, England)*
ORIGINAL LINE-UP   *Poly Styrene (b. 1962, Marion Elliott — vocals); Jak "Airport" Stafford (guitar); Paul Dean (bass); Chris Chrysler (drums); Laura Logic (b. Susan Whitby — sax)*

X-Ray Spex were the brainchild of Marion Elliott, who cut one solo single as a schoolgirl in the mid-1970s but, by age 15, was selling sweets at Woolworths and planning to hitchhike around the UK. Then she discovered punk rock at a Sex Pistols gig in Hastings and decided to form a band instead.

Drawing the musicians from an early 1977 *Melody Maker* ad and changing her own name in accordance with current punk thinking, Styrene and X-Ray Spex became one of the most talked-about bands on the infant scene. The rendition of "Oh Bondage, Up Yours," which exploded midway through the *Live at the Roxy, WC1* album, was recorded at only the band's second-ever gig, but its aural impact alone was enough to win X-Ray Spex a residency at the Man in the Moon in Chelsea. That, in turn, led to both EMI and Virgin hotly pursuing the group (Virgin won), and in October 1977, the band released their debut single, a second epochal rendition of "Bondage."

Simultaneously, the rest of the band's repertoire hit the streets, courtesy of a nine-song bootleg of demos, while further accolades were drawn by a riotous performance of "Let's Submerge" on the *Front Row Festival* live compilation.

Virgin, however, remained strangely unimpressed, and by the end of the year, they had dropped the band. Now EMI could swoop, and X-Ray Spex — pausing only to sack Laura Logic and replace her with the equally characteristic, but noticeably less ebullient, Rudi Thompson — set about recording a new single.

Granted their own label identity, spun off from EMI International, X-Ray Spex released "The World Turned Day-Glo" (#23 UK) in March 1978 before making their first US visit with six nights at CBGB's in New York. The following month, X-Ray Spex previewed their next single "Identity" (#24 UK) and Styrene's newly shaven head at the Rock Against Racism gig at Victoria Park, Hackney.

It was becoming apparent, however, that all was not necessarily well in the X-Ray Spex camp; all the more so after Styrene's enthusiasm for a "natural" way of life, already marked by some increasingly eccentric remarks in the music press, hit the national tabloids. When she warned the *Daily Mirror* that she was under instructions from a pink flying saucer to tell her fans to "get rid of the synthetic life," the Loony Punk Chick headline writers really had something to get their teeth into.

For a while, Styrene all but disappeared from view, hiding out at manager Falcon Stuart's house and refusing to venture out the door. She finally re-emerged for the release of "Germ Free Adolescents" (#19 UK), a rallying call for personal hygiene freaks everywhere and the title track from the band's long-anticipated debut album, released in November 1978 (#30 UK).

The band undertook their first full UK tour that same month, closing with a sorely under-rehearsed show at the Hammersmith Odeon. It was plain already that they had run their course, a sad diagnosis hammered home by the relative underachievement of their final single, "Highly Inflammable" (#45 UK) in April 1979. It ground to a halt, and Spex broke up immediately.

Styrene immediately launched a sporadic solo career, built as much around her conversion to Hare Krishna as her music. The *Translucence* album in 1980 was followed by a six-year silence before the *Gods and Goddesses* EP. A decade further on, X-Ray Spex reformed around Styrene, Dean, and Logic, releasing an album, *Conscious Consumer*, but disappointing many when their projected comeback show at the Holidays in the Sun punk festival passed off without Styrene on board. Neither were the band to follow up *Conscious Consumer*, despite Styrene's insistence that it was the first of a projected trilogy.

X-Ray Spex LPs

5 Germ Free Adolescents (EMI International) 1978 Styrene's dentist drill shrill shriek was one of the most remarkable weapons in the early punk arsenal, and used sparingly — across a peerless run of singles through 1977–79 — it was devastating. Most of those tracks are repeated here, but the full feast gets wearing quickly, particularly as "Warrior in Woolworths" and "Plastic Bag" simply didn't have the class of the title track, "Identity," and "Oh Bondage! Up Yours."

4 Conscious Consumer (Receiver) 1995 Misjudged comeback sees Styrene's vocals remain an uncompromising bellow, but the band sound lifeless, and the songs really aren't very good.

Selected Compilations and Archive Releases

7 Live at the Roxy (Receiver) 1991 Low-fidelity but unmistakably high-energy performance; a duet between screeching cat and howling wolf.

Poly Styrene LP

4 Translucence 1980

XTC

FORMED 1976, (Swindon, England)
ORIGINAL LINE-UP *Steve Hutchins (vocals); Andy Partridge (b. 11/11/53, Malta — guitar); Colin Moulding (b. 8/17/55, Swindon — bass); Jon Perkins; Terry Chambers (b. 7/18/56, Swindon — drums)*

Andy Partridge, Colin Moulding, and Terry Chambers had a long history on Swindon's live circuit, individually and — as Star Park — collectively. When the first shock waves of glam hit the neighborhood in 1974, the trio immediately adapted, changing their name to the Helium Kidz and becoming XTC in mid-1975 (the name was lifted from a line in a Jimmy Durante movie, "dammit I'm in ecstasy.")

With Jon Perkins joining at the same time, the band was gigging regularly, and in early 1976, they cut a set of demos at a small studio in nearby Reading. The tape got them nowhere, but with the band's songwriting and sound fast evolving, they returned to the studio in August, without vocalist Hutchins. Instead, the more individualistic Partridge took over vocals, and toward the end of the year, the band was offered an audition by CBS.

Replacing Perkins with Barry Andrews (b. 9/12/56, West Norwood, London — keyboards) just days before the session, the band recorded three original compositions in January and were called back for a second audition in May. Club dates had tightened them even further, but the label wasn't impressed. In June, however, John Peel had the band in for a session, intrigued by a handbill he received in the mail that promised "Twilight! Insects! Iron! Lust! Rays!"

The following month, Virgin moved in and, in September, released XTC's debut, the *3D EP* — highlighted by "Science Friction," and offering up a blatant clue toward one of Partridge's own most significant influences, as "She's So Square" did its best to echo Be Bop Deluxe's "Maid in Heaven."

A single, "Statue of Liberty," followed in the new year, to be joined weeks later by the band's first album. Produced by John Leckie, *White Music* (#38 UK) was recorded in a week, and despite its superficial stylistic resemblance to the similarly quirk-laden Wire, it marked out the band in general, and songwriters Partridge and Moulding in particular, as a genuine cut above the New Wave rest. A second single, "This is Pop," consolidated the band's growing reputation, but it was with "Are You Receiving Me?" and the album *Go 2* (#21 UK) in fall 1978 that XTC truly came into their own.

Their initial hope was that Brian Eno would produce the album — he declined, telling them they should do it themselves. Uncertain, XTC instead returned to Leckie, turning in an album of monstrous ambition, then adding a disc of dub experiments to the main set and demonstrating an electronic imagination utterly at odds with their still punkish reputation.

The band's growth was precipitous; so were the problems associated with it. In January 1979, following a ten-date US tour, Andrews quit for Robert Fripp's League of Gentlemen (he later joined Shriekback). Auditions turned up one possible replacement in a young Thomas Dolby, but finally the band opted for familiarity and recruited a friend, Dave Gregory (ex-Ale House), from their days on the Swindon circuit.

Immediately, the band dynamic shifted, together with their sound. "Life Begins at the Hop" (#54 UK) in May 1979 moved firmly away from the darker elements associated with earlier releases, powering XTC toward the unique, and very English pop-rock format that would sustain them for the next two decades. The Steve Lillywhite-produced *Drums and Wires* (#176 US, #34 UK), released upon the band's return from a Far Eastern tour, spawned the band's biggest hit yet, Moulding's "Making Plans for Nigel" (#17 UK), and while successive US singles, "Nigel," "Ten Feet Tall," and "Love at First Sight," all bombed, still the band's Stateside fame was growing.

"Wait till Your Boat Goes Down," XTC's next UK single, failed as well, but an Andy Partridge solo album, credited to Mr. Partridge, *Take Away (The Lure of Salvage)* was warmly received, as was a solo single by Moulding and Chambers, "Too Many Cooks" (credited to The Colonel). The next few months, too, would see three new XTC singles make the chart — "Generals and Majors" (#32 UK), "Towers of London" (#31 UK), and "Sgt Rock" (#16 UK), alongside a second Lilywhite production, *Black Sea* (#41 US, #16 UK).

A BBC ban halted another hit, "Respectable Street" in March 1981 (the Corporation objected to the mention of Sony in the lyric), but still the band's biggest tour yet was also their most successful — their itinerary included visits to Venezuela, the US, the Middle East, Southeast Asia, and Australia through 1981 and Europe and the UK into 1982.

Another major hit with "Senses Working Overtime" (#10 UK) preceded the release of *English Settlement* (#48 US, #5 UK), and suddenly, XTC had risen to the very edge of UK superstardom. But twice during March and April, Partridge collapsed on stage – the first time from exhaustion, the second from a stomach ulcer. Friends counseled rest, but Partridge knew better. He hated touring, he was terrified of performing, and he had no intention of doing either, ever again.

In fact, he was persuaded to undertake one final US tour, but after one gig and a sound check, he knew he'd already made the right decision. The remainder of the tour was canceled, and XTC would never play another live show.

Coincidentally or otherwise, the band's next single, "Ball and Chain" (#58 UK) stalled, "No Thugs in Our House" bombed altogether, and even a compilation of the band's hits so far, *Waxworks* (#54 UK) (coupled with the *Beeswax* B-sides collection) showed poorly. By the end of the year, Chambers had quit, emigrating to Australia, and XTC were in ruins.

They recorded a new album with ex-Glitter Band drummer Pete Phipps — Virgin rejected it and suggested Partridge try writing more songs. They did accept a new single, but "Great Fire" flopped; so did "Wonderland" in July, and when a new XTC album did finally scrape out in August, neither band nor label seemed even half concerned with promoting it. *Mummer* (#145 US, #51 UK) and "Love On a Farm Boy's Wages" (#50 UK) crashed; so did a Christmas single, "Thanks for Christmas," released as the Three Wise Men.

XTC spent much of 1984 recording with producer David Lord, an electronics whiz currently fascinated by Linn drums. The result, *The Big Express* (#178 US, #38 UK), scarcely sold better than its predecessor, while an attempt to overcome XTC's refusal to tour with an expensive video failed alongside it — "All You Pretty Girls" (#55 UK) cost £33,000 and was scarcely seen by a soul.

Anxious to divert his attention away from XTC's sinking career, Partridge had recently been picking up production work with Thomas Dolby and Peter Blegvad, among others. He and Leckie were now scheduled to work with Mary Margaret O'Hara. When the project fizzled out (O'Hara claimed "the vibes weren't right"), the pair instead reconvened XTC and, having persuaded Virgin to give them £5,000 to cover recording costs, set about becoming the Dukes of Stratosphear, psychedelic revivalists to end all psychedelic revivals.

The resultant mini-album, *25 O'Clock*, and single, "The Mole From the Ministry," were issued on April Fool's Day 1985 and ended up outselling *The Big Express*, although they didn't chart at the time, and they couldn't help the band in their next battle — with the Inland Revenue. An unpaid tax bill forced the band into litigation with their manager; that, in turn, prompted Virgin to freeze all the band's income from royalties and publishing. The label then announced that its patience with the critically respected, but commercially suicidal, band was at an end. If XTC's next album didn't shift at least 70,000 units, they'd be dropped.

Acting on the suggestion of XTC's US label, Geffen, the band linked with Todd Rundgren for the series of increasingly uneasy and often explosive sessions, which resulted in *Skylarking* (#70 US, #90 UK). Singles from the set, "Grass" and "The Meeting Place" did nothing, but the album just kept on selling, even after concerned citizens began objecting to one of its finest tracks, the vaguely blasphemous "Dear God." The cut was eventually removed (to be replaced with "Mermaid Smiled"), and *Skylarking* went on to sell over 250,000 copies. The now legendary "Dear God" picked up further sales when it was released as a single; suddenly, and utterly despite themselves, XTC had discovered a whole new audience on American college campuses.

They responded first with a revival of the Dukes of Stratosphear album *Psonic Psunspot* and the single "You're a Good Man Albert Brown" then with a trip to L.A. to record 1989's *Oranges and Lemons* (#44 US, #28 UK) album. The single "The Mayor of Simpleton" (#72 US, #46 UK) gave them their first Top 100 Singles entry; other releases — "King for a Day" and "The Loving" — picked up US airplay, and XTC even managed a US tour of sorts, traveling around radio stations playing half-hour acoustic sets.

Work began on the next album immediately, but slowly. Virgin were pushing Partridge for more and better songs, and a stream of producers were either fired or rejected before getting into the studio; finally, Gus Dudgeon (Elton John, David Bowie) came on board, overseeing the production before being sacked early on in the mixing process. It would be three years before a single, "The Disappointed" (#33 UK) crept out, two months ahead of the album, *Nonsuch* (#97 US, #28 UK), while a second single, "The Ballad of Peter Pumpkinhead" (#71 US) actually topped the chart in Canada — albeit as a cover version by the Crash Test Dummies.

XTC's battles with Virgin, however, continued. A third single, "Wrapped in Grey," was released then withdrawn, and when Virgin rejected Partridge's next idea, an album of bubblegum pastiches, the band had had enough. Part of the legal settlement with their former manager — after five years of legal wrangling — had seen their already low royalty rate adjusted even lower. Aware that they might never clear their debt to Virgin, XTC took the only option they felt was open to them — they went on strike.

Moulding and Gregory both moved into session work, Partridge returned to production (including an ill-starred union with Blur) and a handful of collaborations. He recorded one album with Harold Budd, *Through the Hill*;

another with ex-Cleaners From Venus vocalist Martin Newell, *The Greatest Living Englishman*; and cowrote a track for the *Avengers* soundtrack with Verve Pipe vocalist Brian Vander Ark.

It would be four years before Virgin finally released the band from their contract, and with Partridge and Moulding alone reconvening, XTC signed with TVT in the US and Cooking Vinyl in the UK.

The deal was sealed with a box set of the band's BBC radio sessions (following on from the earlier *Drums'n' Wireless* set) while the band began recording. A double album's worth of songs had built up during their sabbatical, finally released as two volumes of *Apple Venus* in 1999 (#106 US, #42 UK) and 2000, plus a third disc of out-takes, *Homespun*. There would be no singles, no touring, no videos. But after a decade of near-total inactivity, that didn't seem to bother anybody.

XTC LPs

9 White Music (Geffen) 1978 Their own handbills put it best — "Twilight! Insects! Iron! Lust! Rays!" Plus, the unimaginable pop beauty of "This is Pop" and "Statue of Liberty," the crippling grinning death dance of "Neon Shuffle," and the most brutalized Bob Dylan cover of all time, "All Along the Watchtower," rearranged for a cat on a hot tin roof.

8 Go 2 (Geffen) 1978 Very much the son of *White Music*, but with less eye for quirky effect — a shift made all the more apparent by the inclusion of a bonus EP of sinister dub remixes.

8 Drums & Wires (Geffen) 1979 "Making Plans for Nigel" and "Life Begins at the Hop" proved there was indeed life after Barry Andrews — the same pop-inspired life that *White Music* had been too busy buzzing to snare.

7 Black Sea (Geffen) 1980 The self-consciousness that would scar the band's later albums begins to rise, as "Generals and Majors," "Tower of London," and "Respectable Street" begin tugging more on their odd delivery and unconventional structure than on the still-pristine tunes that are wrapped up in there somewhere.

6 English Settlement (Geffen) 1982 Double album once regarded as the summit of XTC's achievement, but subsequently revealed to be very much a child of its time; Partridge wasn't the only artist who suffered delusions of genius around this time.

6 Mummer (Geffen) 1983

7 The Big Express (Geffen) 1984

6 Skylarking (Geffen) 1986

7 Oranges & Lemons (Geffen) 1989

3 Nonsuch (Geffen) 1992 When in doubt, noodle! Most "clever" bands compound their art with humor. By 1992, XTC were compounding art with more art, as if obtuse eccentricity by itself is a viable alternative to making good records. It isn't, but so unrelenting is XTC's hatred of anything that contradicts that notion (good tunes, good lyrics, stuff like that) that not only have they painted themselves into a corner, they've painted themselves back to school. *Nonsuch* is the sound of the bad boys getting spanked.

8 Apple Venus Vol 1 (TVT) 1999

9 Wasp Star: Apple Venus Vol 2 (TVT) 2000 Remarkably lovely returns (to form), XTC strip away the convolutions and wackiness and prove that underneath the intellects working over-time, there really were some great songs scratching to be let out. Entertaining lyrics remain, of course, but there's a seductive calmness about it all, which makes this less a comeback and more a come-*on*.

Selected Compilations and Archive Releases

7 Beeswax: Some B-Sides 1977–1982 (Virgin) 1982

8 Waxworks: Some Singles 1977–1982 (Geffen) 1982

8 Explode Together (The Dub Experiments...) (Virgin) 1990 The *Go* bonus EP appended to Andy Partridge's solo *Take Away*

7 BBC Radio One in Concert (Windsong) 1992 A startling reminder of what was lost when Andy Partridge stopped gig-ging…startling, and even tear-inducing. Plus, the between-songs chatter is as good as some songs.

7 Drums and Wireless: BBC Live (Virgin) 1994 Equally enter-taining romp through the BBC vaults.

8 Fossil Fuel: The XTC Singles 1977–1992 (Virgin) 1996

7 Upsy Daisy Assortment (Selection of Sweetest...) (Geffen) 1997

9 Transistor Blast: Best of the BBC Sessions (TVT) 1998 XTC's late '70s BBC archives undergo a near-comprehensive overhaul for this four-CD package of both studio and live record-ings, tracking the band through the insane convolutions of their first three albums and reminding listeners that XTC were already weirdly wired long before they gained a reputation for wackiness. Near-definitive renderings of some excellent material.

7 Homespun (TVT) 1999 *Apple Venus* demos prove to be no less alluring (if a little less solid) than their album counterparts.

Dukes of Stratosphear LP

7 Psonic Psunspot (Geffen) 1987

Selected Compilations and Archive Releases

7 Chips From the Chocolate Fireball (Geffen) 1989

Andy Partridge/Mr. Partridge LP

8 Take Away (The Lure of Salvage) (Virgin) 1980 Incredible collection of *Drums and Wires* dub remixes.

Martin Newell Featuring the New, Improved Andy Partridge LP

8 1993 the Greatest Living Englishman (Pipeline) Actually, Partridge is fairly irrelevant to all this — the GLE of the title is Newell, former Cleaner From Venus and Brotherhood of Lizards boy, a Ray Davies/Roy Wood-shaped punk poet who is neither as punk or poetic as that suggests.

Further Reading

XTC: Chalkhills and Children — The Definitive Biography by Chris Twomey (Omnibus Press, 1992).

Y

YOUNG MARBLE GIANTS

FORMED 1978 (Cardiff, Wales)
ORIGINAL LINE-UP Alison Statton (b. 3/58 — vocals); Stuart
Moxham (guitar, organ, vocals); Philip Moxham (bass)

Although their legacy extended to no more than one album, two singles, an EP, and a solitary John Peel session, the Young Marble Giants remain one of the greatest bands spawned by Britain's post-punk ferment — a hauntingly skeletal sound which pre-empted much of what Galaxie 500 and Low would later accomplish, but stands so far from even those comparisons that it is not difficult to consider them truly unique.

Certainly there was nothing like them around in 1978–79, as the trio took their first steps out of their native Cardiff, a darkly minimalist concern which blended perfectly with the prevalent mood of the time. Echo and the Bunnymen, Joy Division, and Doll by Doll were all making their own presence felt at the same time, yet belonged to an entirely different musical discipline.

Young Marble Giants debuted with a cut on the Cardiff compilation Is the War Over? in 1979; perhaps unsurprisingly, the band signed with Rough Trade in late 1979, and debuted the following February with their first — and, as it transpired, only — album, Colossal Youth (#3 UK indie). Roundly adored by the UK music press, the album would remain on the independent chart for 57 weeks, while the band's apparently bottomless stockpile of songs swiftly prompted a follow-up single, the evocative "Radio Silents" (#6 UK indie).

The Peel session followed, a magnificent effort which left even the album in the shade; for all their recorded success (and despite their oft-remarked shyness), the Giants were at their best live, an environment which the BBC studios readily recaptured.

Yet Young Marble Giants were uncomfortable with their near-canonization and, in November, Stuart Moxham released a new single, "This is Love" (#42 UK indie) under the pseudonym, the Gist. Of course, the deception was swiftly unmasked and he returned to the Giants identity in time for a short visit to the US. There, however, the fairytale came off the rails. Returning to the UK, the band announced that they were splitting, even as Rough Trade readied their next release, the majestic Testcards EP (#10 UK indie).

Moxham continued working as the Gist; brother Philip would join him, at the same time working with Statton in her own new band, Weekend (Statton would also guest with Gist). Neither band lasted long — following the singles "Love at First Sight" (#14 UK indie) and "Fool for a Valentine" (#30 UK indie), the Gist broke up shortly after releasing a well-received album, Embrace the Herd (#10 UK indie) in March 1983. Stuart Moxham would, however, bequeath at least a little of his magic on the Marine Girls, producing their sophomore Lazy Ways.

The increasingly jazz-funk-tinged Weekend, meanwhile, debuted in May 1982, with "The View from Her Room" (#7 UK indie), following through with "Past Meets Present" (#6 UK indie) and "Drumbeat for Baby" (#8 UK indie), before they, too, broke up following the release of their album, November 1982's ambitious La Variete (#4 UK indie).

Statton and guitarist Simon Booth (b. 3/12/56) promptly convened a new Weekend vision, uniting with renowned jazz pianist Keith Tippett to record a live album, Live at Ronnie Scott's (#3 UK indie). Soon, however, Booth was forming a new band, Working Week, with fellow former Weekend-er Spike (viola, guitar), while Statton subsequently united with Ludus frontman Ian Devine for two albums, and Spike for one.

Young Marble Giants reformed in 1987 for a one-off single, "It Took You," for the Belgian Crepuscule label, but it made little impact and had even less to do with the intensity of their original incarnation. Since that time, Stuart Moxham (now a successful animator — he worked on Who Framed Roger Rabbit among others) has sporadically resurfaced, both with a new band, the Original Artists, and alongside Pacific Northwest low-fi mavens Beat Happening.

Young Marble Giants LP

🛢 **Colossal Youth (Rough Trade — UK) 1980** Colossal Youth slipped onto the nation's turntables like a corpse into a coffin. But it only lay there for a moment or two, and then it started kicking. The result was pandemonium. Brittle yet vivid, gentle yet brutal, Colossal Youth was quite unlike any other album of the age — any group of the age — and would remain so for at least the next four years, until Sad Lovers and Giants came to kick some similar ghosts around the mid-80s. Since that time, of course, half the world seems to have got stripped back and stark, but one cannot help but wonder, without Colossal Youth, would anyone ever have thought of it?

Stuart Moxham/The Gist LP
7 **Embrace the Herd (Rough Trade — UK) 1983**

Stuart Moxham and the Original Artists LPs
6 **Signal Path (Feels Good — UK) 1993**
6 **Cars In The Grass (Vinyl Japan) 1995**

Alison Statton/Weekend LPs
5 **La Variete (Rough Trade — UK) 1982**
7 **Live at Ronnie Scott's (Rough Trade — UK) 1983**

Alison Statton and Spike LP
6 **Tidal Blues (Vinyl Japan) 1994**

Z

ZODIAC MINDWARP AND THE LOVE REACTION

FORMED 1985 (Canada)

ORIGINAL LINE-UP *Zodiac Mindwarp (b. Mark Manning — vocals); Flash Evil Bastard (b. Jan Cyrka — guitar); Cobalt Stargazer (guitar); Haggis — aka Kid Chaos (bass); Boom Boom Kaboomski (drums)*

Though he argued convincingly to have descended to earth from another planet, Zodiac was actually former *Flexipop!* magazine art director Mark Manning, the man responsible for positioning each month's cover star's photograph so it would not be wholly obscured by the colored flexidisc given away free with every issue.

With a band built around a bunch of similarly fantastical alien pseudonyms (and equally down-to-earth professionals), Zodiac Mindwarp emerged in early 1985, relocating to the UK from their native Canada and swiftly earning a reputation for unrepentently loud and furious live shows. By spring, the band had signed to Food, the label started by former Teardrop Explodes' keyboard player Dave Balfe. In August, their first single, "Wild Child" (#9 UK indy) was released.

Produced by Balfe and partner Bill Drummond (later of KLF), "Wild Child" would be Kaboomski's sole-recorded appearance with the band; he quit to be replaced by Slam Thunderhide, shortly before the release of the band's mini-album, *High Priest of Love* (#1 UK indy). Haggis then quit to join The Cult; he was replaced by Paul Bailey just as the band signed to major label Mercury.

That fall, a UK tour opening for Alice Cooper was cancelled due to band illness (they were replaced on the bill by Alien Sex Fiend), but still Zodiac's momentum seemed unstoppable. The single "Prime Mover" (#19 UK) gave

Zodiac their UK chart breakthrough in April 1987, and was followed by hits "Backseat Education" (#49 UK) and "Planet Girl" (#63 UK). The band was one of the prime attractions at that year's Reading Festival, and their debut album, *Tattooed Beat Messiah* (#132 US, #20 UK), briefly established Zodiac at the pinnacle of Britain's deliberately-dumb metal explosion of the mid-1980's.

But the chronic, manic sloppiness which was so much a part of their stage act also informed the band's own internal dynamic. By the end of 1988, the group had crumbled.

In 1991, Mindwarp alone recorded a single with former Killing Joke/Brilliant bassist Youth, "Fast Forward — The Future" (released under the name Zodiac Youth), and the following year he reconvened the Love Reaction around Stargazer, Thunderhide and a new bassist, Suzy X (aka Richard). This line-up released the *Hoodlum Thunder* album, and the EPs *Elvis Died for You* and *My Life Story*, but interest was minimal. Following one final 45, 1994's "Too," the band folded.

Zodiac Mindwarp and the Love Reaction LPs

8 Tattooed Beat Messiah (Vertigo) 1988 Sheer, mindless nonsense, of course. A nigh-on, brain-dead cacophony which picked up where The Cult left off, then hammered even their lack of panache and subtlety into the ground with a sledge hammer. Which, of course, was what was so great about it — think the New York Dolls if they had liked Aerosmith instead of the Stones.

4 Hoodlum Thunder (Musidisc — UK) 1992

Selected Compilations and Archive Releases

7 The Friday Rock Show Live (Raw Fruit — UK) 1993 The Reading Festival at their peak, a field full of bikers who know every chord... paradise indeed.

PRODUCERS & LABELS

4AD

LABEL

4AD was formed by Ivo Watts-Russell in 1980, as an independently themed subsidiary to the burgeoning Beggars Banquet label. Early releases very much shadowed the parent label's own concerns, with Bauhaus actually transferring first to Situation 2 sister label, then Beggars itself. Birthday Party, too, would move to the larger concern.

It was the arrival in short succession of the Cocteau Twins, Dead Can Dance, X-Mal Deutschland, and Cindy Talk which saw a genuinely definable 4AD sound and ethos emerge, one which was crystallized by the first album by the This Mortal Coil collective — a frozen moment in time which even subsequent albums under the same name could not replicate. Building from the collision of minor chords, swirling guitars, and swooping vocals, TMC — and by association, 4AD itself — made musical miasma fashionable, all the more so since the ensuing blend was seldom less than spellbinding.

Unlike many labels of the era, 4AD would remain faithful to the majority of the bands who established its reputation — Dead Can Dance and Modern English would remain on board until their respective demises, and though the Cocteau Twins would depart in the early 1990s, still they left the label with a fine investment for the future, the Robin Guthrie produced Lush.

Also see the entry for "BEGGARS BANQUET" on page 743.

4AD Label Listing 1980–84

AXIS 1 THE FAST SET — Junction One 7-inch
AXIS 2 THE BEARZ — She's My Girl 7-inch
AXIS 3 BAUHAUS — Dark Entries 7-inch
AXIS 4 SHOX — No Turning Back 7-inch
BAD 5 REMA REMA — Wheels in the Roses 7-inch
AD 6 MODERN ENGLISH — Swans on Glass 7-inch
AD 7 BAUHAUS — Terror Couple Kills Colonel 7-inch
AD 8 IN CAMERA — Final Achievement 7-inch
BAD 9 CUPOL — Like This for Ages EP
AD 10 THE THE — Controversial Subject 7-inch
BAD 11 VARIOUS ARTISTS — Presages EP
AD 12 BIRTHDAY PARTY — The Friend Catcher 7-inch
CAD 13 BAUHAUS — In the Flat Field LP 🟪
AD 14 MASS — You and I 7-inch
AD 15 MODERN ENGLISH — Gathering Dust 7-inch

CAD 16 BC GILBERT/G LEWIS — 3R4 LP 🟦
AD 17 BAUHAUS — Telegram Sam 7-inch
AD 18 DANCE CHAPTER — Anonymity 7-inch
BAD 19 IN CAMERA — IV Songs EP
AD 101 SORT SOL — Marble Station 7-inch
AD 102 THE PAST SEVEN DAYS — Raindance 7-inch
AD 103 MY CAPTAINS — My Captains 7-inch
CAD 104 BIRTHDAY PARTY — Prayers on Fire LP 🟦
CAD 105 MODERN ENGLISH — Mesh and Lace LP 🟦
AD 106 BC GILBERT/G LEWIS — Ends with the Sea 7-inch
CAD 107 MASS — Labour of Love LP 🟦
CAD 108 COLIN NEWMAN — Provisionally Entitled the Singing Fish LP 🟦
BAD 109 DIF JUZ — Huremics EP
AD 110 MODERN ENGLISH — Smiles and Laughter 7-inch
AD 111 BIRTHDAY PARTY — Release the Bats 7-inch
AD 112 RENE HALKETT/DAVID J — Nothing 7-inch
CAD 113 MATT JOHNSON — Burning Blue Soul LP 🟦
AD 114 BIRTHDAY PARTY — Mr Clarinet 7-inch
BAD 115 DANCE CHAPTER — Chapter II EP
BAD 116 DIF JUZ — Vibrating Air EP
CAD 117 VARIOUS ARTISTS — Natures Mortes LP 🟦 12-track Japanese compilation, featuring the best of 4AD's output: Bauhaus, Birthday Party and In Camera, of course, but also future Eurythmic Rob Crash's Psychotic Tanks, with a magnificent quaaluded rendition of "Let's Have a Party" (from the BAD 11).
CAD 201 COLIN NEWMAN — Not To LP 🟦
JAD 202 BIRTHDAY PARTY — Drunk on the Pope's Blood EP
BAD 203 TONES ON TAIL — Tones on Tail EP
AD 204 THE HAPPY FAMILY — Puritans 7-inch
BAD 205 IN CAMERA — Fin EP
CAD 206 MODERN ENGLISH — After the Snow LP 🟦 The effervescent "I'll Melt with You" overshadows the remainder of the set, but still a clear pop collection with much to recommend it.
CAD 207 BIRTHDAY PARTY — Junkyard LP 🟩
BAD 208 MODERN ENGLISH — Life in the Gladhouse EP
AD 209 COLIN NEWMAN — We Means We Start 7-inch
BAD 210 ROWLAND HOWARD/LYDIA LUNCH — Some Velvet Morning EP
CAD 211 COCTEAU TWINS — Garlands LP 🟩
AD 212 MODERN ENGLISH — I Melt with You 7-inch
BAD 213 COCTEAU TWINS — Lullabies EP
CAD 214 HAPPY FAMILY — The Man on Your Street LP 🟦
BAD 215 COLOURBOX — Breakdown EP

BAD 301 BIRTHDAY PARTY — **Bad Seed EP**

CAD 302 X-MAL DEUTSCHLAND — **Fetisch LP 🎱** Despatching some of the harmonious drone which was their debut EP's calling card, still one of the quintessential building blocks around which the ethereal goth future would be coiled.

BAD 303 COCTEAU TWINS — **Peppermint Pig EP**

BAD 304 COLOURBOX — **Breakdown EP**

BAD 305 X-MAL DEUTSCHLAND — **Qual EP**

BAD 306 MODERN ENGLISH — **Gathering Dust EP**

BAD 307 BIRTHDAY PARTY — **Release the Bats EP**

CAD 308 WOLFGANG PRESS — **The Burden of Mules LP 7** Formative thrashing which hindsight insists was slowly moving in on X-Mal/Cocteau territory, although there's a sense of deliberate battery here which defies such logic.

BAD 309 MODERN ENGLISH — **Someone's Calling EP**

BAD 310 THIS MORTAL COIL — **16 Days/Gathering Dust EP**

BAD 311 X-MAL DEUTSCHLAND — **Incubus Succubus II EP**

BAD 312 BAUHAUS — **4AD EP**

CAD 313 COCTEAU TWINS — **Head Over Heels LP 7**

BAD 314 COCTEAU TWINS — **Sunburst and Snowblind EP**

MAD 315 COLOURBOX — **Colourbox LP 7**

BAD 401 MODERN ENGLISH — **Chapter 12 EP**

CAD 402 MODERN ENGLISH — **Ricochet Days LP 6**

BAD 403 COLOURBOX — **Say You EP**

CAD 404 DEAD CAN DANCE — **Dead Can Dance LP 8**

AD 405 COCTEAU TWINS — **Pearly Dew Drops Drop 7-inch**

BAD 405 COCTEAU TWINS — **Spanglemaker EP**

BAD 406 COLOURBOX — **Punch EP**

CAD 407 X-MAL DEUTSCHLAND — **Tocsin LP 7**

BAD 408 DEAD CAN DANCE — **Garden of the Arcane Delights EP**

BAD 409 WOLFGANG PRESS — **Scarecrow EP**

AD 410 THIS MORTAL COIL — **Kangaroo 7-inch**

CAD 411 THIS MORTAL COIL — **It'll End in Tears LP 🔟** Even if its long-term impact can now be narrowed down to a fairly small segment of the overall music scene, few albums released during the 1980s were so important, or so influential, as the first This Mortal Coil. Originally conceived by 4AD head Ivo Watts Russell as a collaborative showcase for the musicians signed to (or peripherally involved in/respected by) the label, TMC rapidly took on a life of its own, forging not only the future direction of 4AD itself, but also informing the reputation of its creators.

At the time, the Cocteau Twins and Modern English were the closest to even halfway household name status; of the others, Dead Can Dance, X-Mal Deutschland, Wolfgang Press, Colourbox, and Cindy Talk were still ingenue attractions working (or working towards) their debuts, while the only other contributors of note were ex-Magazine vocalist Howard Devoto, and Gini Ball and Martin McGarrick of Marc Almond's Mambas sideshow.

Nevertheless, the breadth and depth of *It'll End in Tears* was astonishing, even within the distinctly minor key parameters of the twelve songs and fragments. The late Tim Buckley's "Song to the Siren," by the Cocteaus' Fraser and Guthrie, and Devoto's "Holocaust" were immediately notable; Gordon Sharp (Cindy Talk)'s "Fond Affections" instantly heartbreaking. Elsewhere, the almost raucous "Not Me" (Guthrie and fellow Cocteau Simon Raymonde backing Modern English's Rob Grey) was built around a genuine abrasive guitar riff, to produce a hybrid of almost garage-goth proportions.

Much of the album's overall magic lay, of course, in John Fryer's production — a procedure in which he admitted recording the basic instruments "then fucking up the music." Across two subsequent TMC albums, the trick got very old very fast. But first time out, it was more than a breath of fresh air — it was positively reanimating.

CAD 412 Cocteau Twins — **Treasure LP 9**

STEVE ALBINI

PRODUCER
BORN *(Chicago, IL)*

Although Albini first came to attention as frontman with the purposefully abrasive Big Black, Rapeman, and late 1990s Shellac projects, it is as a producer that he has made the greatest impact. Fiercely independent, even when working with major label acts, his high principled attitude toward his work sees him eschewing even the conventional production credits normally accorded his profession — rather, he insists his clients simply state "recorded by...," believing that that is the extent of his contribution.

Readily acknowledging that it is the high profile commissions he takes on which finance his preferred independent activities, Albini has nevertheless had a hand in some of the most adventurous, and influential recordings of the late 1980s/early 1990s — the sonic sculptures of the Pixies' *Surfer Rosa* in 1987 arguably opened the door wide to a host of subsequent alternative rock bands, while Nirvana's decision to employ him to oversee their *In Utero* swansong gave rise to speculation that the group was deliberately pursuing an "unlistenable" follow-up to their *Nevermind* breakthrough. Record label Geffen's insistence on having REM producer Scott Litt remix the album's planned singles, "Heart Shaped Box" and "All Apologies," only added to the conspiracy theorists' glee.

Steve Albini — Selected Productions

6 URGE OVERKILL — Jesus Urge Superstar (Touch & Go) 1986 Gratuitous, distortion-torn hardcore battlefields highlighted not by the (after 18 tracks) predictable cover of "Wichita Linesman," but by the moral dilemma of "Very Sad Trousers."

5 SLINT — Tweez (Touch & Go) 1988 Sepulchral bass and toothache guitars clash in a soundscape — somewhere between a mud bath and the midwest.

6 TAD — Salt Lick (Sub Pop) 1988 Speed metal slowed to funereal proportions, you can turn it off but you still feel the vibrations. Bad-tempered braille for the hard of hearing.

10 PIXIES — Surfer Rosa (4AD) 1988

4 FLOUR — Luv 713 (Touch & Go) 1988 Industrial cowpunk a-go-go goes slow.

7 WEDDING PRESENT — Bizarro [FOUR TRACKS] (RCA) 1989 Shrugging off the Smiths comparisons which were the Wedding Present's finest calling card, an oddly belligerent blend of tender love and despairing dirges.

6 JESUS LIZARD — Head (Touch & Go) 1990

7 WRECK — Soul Train (Play It Again Sam) 1990 The modern dance on a red hot floor — jerking, awkward, but spitefully compelling.

4 BREEDERS — Pod (Elektra) 1990

6 PIGFACE — Gub (Invisible) 1990 Emerging from the loins of Ministry's 1990 tour, the ever-evolving entity that is Martin Atkins' Pigface initially featured a host of industrial greats brought together in one purposefully uncompromising, deliberately unlistenable, and always challenging creative spasm.

7 POSTER CHILDREN — Daisychain Reaction (Twin\Tone) 1990 Brittle, hard-nosed, space-inflected power pop, likeable despite its icy cold production, and splashed with wry humor — "If You See Kay" remains one of childhood's most pungent acronyms.

7 SILVERFISH — Fat Axl (Touch & Go) 1991 Lesley (Ruby) Rankine's caustic beauty overhangs the brutality of her bandmates, even while deconstructing Melle Mel's "White Lines" as a duet for ambulance and avalanche.

9 JESUS LIZARD — Goat (Touch & Go) 1991

5 POSTER CHILDREN — Flowerpower [FOUR TRACKS] (Frontier) 1991

5 JON SPENCER BLUES EXPLOSION — Jon Spencer... (Caroline) 1992 Low-fi urban blues shot through with the crassness of modern urbanity. Some records are purposefully unpleasant.

8 JESUS LIZARD — Liar (Touch & Go) 1992

5 WEDDING PRESENT — Sea Monsters (First Warning) 1992 More unwavering stubbornness, more classic pop buried in checkered shirt dissonance, and the epic "Octopussy" to prove that they really intend things to sound like this.

6 MURDER INC — Mania/Murder Inc (Invisible) 1992 Former Killing Jokers Martin Atkins, Raven, and Paul Ferguson, plus Revolting Cocks vocalist Chris Connolly serve a darkly threatening vision redolent, indeed, of early KJ, but much more driving and aggressive.

3 UNION CARBIDE PRODUCTIONS — Swing (Puppet — Sweden) 1992 Once hailed as the Swedish Stooges, and still blessed with the finesse of a viking at confessional. Lots of mindless rage and fury, then, but little in the way of tunes.

6 THINGS THAT FALL DOWN — Disbelief (Sonic Noise) 1992

3 BEWITCHED — Harshing My Mellow (Number 6) 1992 For those awkward days when Thurston Moore doesn't sound bored enough, early Sonic Youth drummer Bob Bert finds even drier pastures.

5 SCRAWL — Velvet Hammer (Simple Machines) 1993

6 PJ HARVEY — Rid of Me (Island) 1993

6 DQE — But Me, I Fell Down (Feel Good All Over) 1993

7 SHADOWY MEN ON A SHADOWY PLANET — Sport Fishin' (Jetpac) 1993 Twisted retro-modern guitar twangers, heavy on the reverb but twisted round some oddly dancey rhythms. "Spy School," incidentally, sums their name up completely.

8 NIRVANA — In Utero (DGC) 1993

7 USHERHOUSE — Molting (Cleopatra) 1993

4 DON CABALLERO — For Respect (Touch & Go) 1993

4 SPACE STREAKINGS — 7-Toku (Skin Graft) 1994

9 SILKWORM — Libertine (El Recordo) 1994 Cruelly underrated, with its makers poised for so long on the brink of something... anything... happening, Libertine lurches between the post-rock Television they wanted to be, and the more listener-friendly indy rock you could forgive them thinking they should turn to instead. "There is a Party in Warsaw" haunts like a murder; "Oh How We Laughed" could make you cry.

5 SHORTY — Fresh Breath (Skin Graft) 1994

2 JOHNBOY — Claim Dedications (Trance Syndicate) 1994 Mentor Butthole Surfers dynamics clash with left-over hardcore bellowing — aggression a-plenty, but a purpose? Never mind.

6 JESUS LIZARD — Down (Touch & Go) 1994

3 CRAW — Lost Nation Road (Choke) 1994 Down in the dirty grunge and grit.

4 DISTORTED PONY — Instant Winner (Trance Syndicate) 1994

6 RODAN — Rusty (Quarterstick) 1994

5 CRAIN — Heater (Restless) 1994

5 MOUNT SHASTA — Put the Creep On (Skin Graft) 1994 Slammed down live in under two hours, Creep eschews even unconventional notions of dissonance as it bids for a relentless vista of noise. It gets there, too.

6 BREADWINNER — Burner (Merge) 1994

7 GLAZED BABY — Squeeze the Tail (Allied) 1994

3 FLESHTONES — Laboratory of Sound (Ichiban) 1995 Two years divide this from the Peter Buck-produced marvel of Beautiful Light — two years during which the NY scene veterans apparently forgot every songwriting trick they ever knew. Albini tries hard to camouflage the void with a typically challenging sound, but even the hidden Hendrix massacre (track 69, "I Don't Live Today") falls flat.

5 ZENI GEVA — Freedombondage (Alternative Tentacles) 1995

8 MAN OR ASTROMAN — Experiment Zero (Touch & Go) 1996 Space rock from the edge of a deliciously deranged fantasy, most of which gets blamed on Coco the Electronic Monkey Wizard. All Astroman albums are more or less representative, but *Experiment Zero* suggests the mission is nearing its climax.

6 ROBBIE FULKS — Country Love Songs (Bloodshot) 1996 Sharp honky-tonking, nailed to a country cross which didn't take a wrong turn when the first folkies wound up in Nashville.

3 SMOG — Kicking Around (Drag City) 1996

4 LIZARD MUSIC — Fashionably Lame (World Domination) 1996

7 SILKWORM — Firewater (Matador) 1996 The first album recorded without founder Joel Phelps, and more melancholy than even he used to get. "Miracle Mile," Silkworm's vision of modern rock stardom, has a scent of sour grapes about it, while "Tarnished Angel" and "Drag the River" contemplate defeats of darker import.

7 LES THUGS — Strike (Sub Pop) 1996 As defiantly genre hopping as ever, this time around Les Thugs lean more towards the rock in punk rock, with a bit of pop and a dose of indy thrown in for good measure. Albini increases the roar, then roughens and muddies the edges in his usual manner.

5 BUSH — Razorblade Suitcase (Interscope) 1996

6 SCRAWL — Travel on Rider (Elektra) 1996

6 BIG'N — Discipline Through Sound (Gasoline Boost) 1996

3 FRED SCHNEIDER — Just Fred (Reprise) 1996

8 PALACE MUSIC — Arise Therefore (Drag City) 1996 Essentially a Will Oldham solo shot, low-key folk noir ghostliness haunted by saloon bar piano and western wind bass. Stark and lovely.

4 VERRUCA SALT — Blow It Out Your Ass (Geffen) 1996

3 MELT BANANA — Scratch Or Stitch (Skin Graft) 1996 Everything you have heard about Japanese noise rock is true. Albini just makes it even noisier.

6 THE AUTEURS — After Murder Park (Hut) 1996

2 CHEAP TRICK — Baby Talk (Sub Pop) 1997 It became dreadfully hip to like Cheap Trick in the late 1990s. But only if you liked them in the late 1970s.

6 SILKWORM — Developer (Matador) 1997

7 GREAT UNRAVELING — The Great Unraveling (Kill Rock Stars) 1997

4 STORM AND STRESS — Storm and Stress (Touch & Go) 1997

4 PW LONG — We Didn't See You on Sunday (Touch & Go) 1997

5 SPIDER VIRUS — Electric Erection (Volcano) 1997

4 PEG BOY — Cha Cha Da More (Quarterstick) 1997 Straight-ahead hardcore circa early SST. Is it time for the revival already?

5 CORDELIA'S DAD — Spine (Appleseed) 1998

7 ECLECTICS — Idle Worship (Jump Up) 1998 Skacore is too simple a label to hang on this Illinois apocalypse. Some of their songs do indeed blend ska and hardcore, but swing, heavy metal, pop-punk, and reggae also find their way into the melting pot.

7 PANSY DIVISION — More Lovin' from Our Oven (Lookout) 1998 Their reputation precedes them and their lyrics aren't too far behind, but still Pansy Division turn in some of the sharpest power punk pop joys around. Not their greatest album, but close.

4 SILVER APPLES — Beacon (Whirly Bird) 1998

7 PANSY DIVISION — Absurd Pop Romance (Lookout) 1998

7 PLUSH — More You Becomes You (Drag City) 1998 Less torch revival than revisionism, a stark stock of dark piano ballads.

6 EX — Starters Alternators (Touch & Go) 1998

5 JON SPENCER BLUES EXPLOSION — Acme (Matador) 1998

5 SILKWORM — Even a Blind Chicken Finds a Kernel (Matador) 1998

5 BEDHEAD — Transaction De Novo (Trance Syndicate) 1998

8 DIRTY THREE — Ocean Songs (Touch & Go) 1998 Full of sweeping melodies, dirgy, dirty guitars and heartbreaking violins, the Three have taken their vision to the seaside on this collection of sea shanty-inspired tunes that have just enough salt to be authentic, yet retain that otherworldly feel that this band captures so well.

8 LOW — Secret Name (Kranky) 1999

6 CHISEL DRILL HAMMER — Chisel Drill Hammer (Hefty) 1999

7 CHEVELLE — Point #1 (Squint) 1999 Deeply melodic post-Smashing Pumpkins Chicago indy rock. A beginning that deserves to go further.

5 PEZZ — Warmth & Sincerity (BYO) 1999

4 PHOENIX THUNDERSTORM — Phoenix Thunderstorm (Heyday) 1999

6 HOSEMOBILE — What Can and Can't Go On (Cuneiform) 1999 More or less instrumental post-rock à la John Mahonie and like-minded cohorts... think Gomez without the ambition.

9 NINE INCH NAILS — The Fragile (Interscope) 1999

ALTERNATIVE TENTACLES

LABEL

The Alternative Tentacles label was formed in June 1979 by Jello Biafra of the Dead Kennedys, initially as an outlet for that band's own debut single, "California Uber Alles." The success of that first single, however, soon saw the label expand its interests, whilst retaining an emphasis on the newly emergent hardcore scene.

The original plan was for a Europe-only label, the Dead Kennedys' profile across the Atlantic being infinitely higher than it ever seemed likely to become in the US. This prompted the compilation *Let Them Eat Jellybeans* — a collection of US hardcore bands who might otherwise never have seen a European release. The record also made inroads into the US market, however, and as the label picked up more bands, an American presence developed almost by default.

By 1981, Alternative Tentacles had grown into an astonishingly strong, and viable, alternative to the conventions of both major and other independent labels — its early emphasis on hardcore already expanding into more experimental underground areas. Alternative Tentacles would become the professed role model for a string of subsequent independents, Dischord and Epitaph among them. Prices were kept as low as possible, both domestically and abroad, while artists involved with the label were unilaterally guaranteed full control over their product.

Constantly positioned at the forefront of Biafra's own oft-times idealistic assaults upon the mores of modern America, Alternative Tentacles became the focus for free speech advocates in 1985, following the inclusion of a supposedly obscene poster in copies of the Kennedys' *Frankenchrist* album. The ensuing legal battle came close to taking the label down, before a mistrial was declared. Since that time, the label has maintained its position at the forefront of the US independent scene, and on the frontlines of American political expression.

Also see the essay "Art or Obscenity — Punk Rock Meets the PMRC" beginning on page 103 and the entry for the "DEAD KENNEDYS" on page 318.

Alternative Tentacles Label Listing 1979–87

1 DEAD KENNEDYS — Fresh Fruit for Rotting Vegetables LP 🔟

2 DEAD KENNEDYS — Too Drunk to Fuck 7-inch

3 WITCH TRIALS — Witch Trials EP

4 VARIOUS ARTISTS — Let Them Eat Jellybeans LP 🔟 Wide-ranging hardcore sampler featuring Flipper, DOA, Black Flag, Bad Brains, Circle Jerks, Really Red, The Feederz, the Subhumans, Germs producer Geza-X , B-People, the Wounds, the Offs, Anonymous, Half Japanese, Christian Lunch, Voice Farm, and the Dead Kennedys.

5 DEAD KENNEDYS — In God We Trust 🔟

6 DEAD KENNEDYS — Nazi Punks Fuck Off 7-inch

7 DOA — Positively DOA EP

8 FLIPPER — Ha Ha Ha 7-inch

9 BLACK FLAG — Six Pack EP (UK ONLY)

10 TSOL — Weathered Statues EP

11 CHRISTIAN LUNCH — Bites from Bait EP

12 KLAUS FLOURIDE — Shortnin' Bread 7-inch

13 BAD BRAINS — Bad Brains EP

14 VARIOUS ARTISTS — Not So Quiet on the Western Front LP 🔟 With a booklet provided by *Maximum Rock'n'Roll*, this remains the essential document of northern California- and Nevada-area hardcore bands — a total of 47 — including Flipper, the Dead Kennedys, 7 Seconds, MDC, MIA, and Demented Youth.

15 7 SECONDS — Skins, Brains and Guts EP

16 VOICE FARM — Double Garage 7-inch (UK ONLY)

17 THE FARTZ — World full of Hate EP

18 FLIPPER — Sex Bomb EP

19 TEDDY & THE FRAT GIRLS — I Wanna be a Man EP

20 GEZA-X — We Need More Power EP

21 THE FARTZ — Because This Fucking World Stinks EP

22 VARIOUS ARTISTS — Flex Your Head LP Licensed from the Dischord label, a 1982 survey of Washington DC hardcore — 11 bands including Minor Threat, the Teen Idles, SOA, Youth Brigade, and Government Issue.

23 DEAD KENNEDYS — Bleed for Me 7-inch

24 DOA — War on 45 EP

25 HÜSKER DÜ — Land Speed Record EP (UK only)

26 MDC — Millions of Dead Cops EP

27 DEAD KENNEDYS — Plastic Surgery Disasters LP 🔟

28 DEAD KENNEDYS — Halloween 7-inch

29 TSOL — Beneath the Shadows LP 🔟 Like Bad Religion's near-simultaneous *Into the Unknown*, the experimental face of hardcore, ambition lashed with pervasive organ, a firestorm for the futurists.

30 ERAZERHEAD — Original Soundtrack LP 🔟

31 DOA — Bloodied But Unbowed 1978-83 LP 🔟 Relentless collection of the Vancouver punks' early singles, B-sides, and adrenalin rushes.

32 BUTTHOLE SURFERS — A Brown Reason to Live EP 🔟

33 TRAGIC MULATTO — The Suspect 7-inch

34 EAST BAY RAY — Trouble in Town 7-inch

35 MIA — Murder in a Foreign Place EP

36 KLAUS FLOURIDE — Cha Cha Cha LP 🔟

37 TRAGIC MULATTO — Judo for the Blind EP

38 THE CRUCIFUCKS — Crucifucks LP 🔟

39 BUTTHOLE SURFERS — Live PCPP EP 🔟

40 PART TIME CHRISTIANS — Rock'n'Roll Is Disco EP

41 TOXIC REASONS — Kill by Remote Control LP 🔟

42 DOA — Don't Turn Your Back EP

43 THE DICKS — These People LP 🔟

44 DOA — Let's Wreck the Party LP 🔟 Aptly named partial change of direction as the traditional tirade of mach ten blisters is occasionally interrupted by.... well, not ballads, *per se*, but certainly slower mayhem.

45 DEAD KENNEDYS — Frankenchrist LP 🔟

46 AMEBIX — ARISE LP 🔟

47 EVAN JOHNS AND THE H-BOMBS — Rollin' Thru the Night LP 🔟 Awkwardly enjoyable Virginian roots rock, Woody Guthrie if he'd heard the Weirdos instead of the Wobblies.

48 FALSE PROPHETS — False Prophets LP **6**

49 GRONG GRONG — Grong Grong LP **3** Charles Tolnay (later King Snake Roost) diverts his psychotic bluesiness towards the urban squalling of a poorly rendered Birthday Party.

50 DEAD KENNEDYS — Bedtime for Democracy LP **3**

BEGGARS BANQUET

LABEL

The story of Beggars Banquet began in 1974, when London DJs Martin Mills and Nick Austin opened a record store in London's Earl's Court district. Dealing in both new and used vinyl, the store's immediate success saw the pair open further branches in Fulham and Ealing, and by 1976, the Beggars empire had expanded into tour promotion, handling the likes of the Crusaders, Lionel Ritchie's Commodores, and Southside Johnny — artists whose music reflected the stores' specialties.

The advent of punk changed all that. Sensing the way the wind was changing, the stores shifted their emphasis towards keeping up with the plethora of new 7-inch singles being released by major and indy labels at home and abroad; the promotions company followed suit, booking the Damned, the Stranglers, and Graham Parker. An empty room in the Fulham store's basement became one of the scene's most in-demand rehearsal spaces.

One of the bands using the area was the Lurkers, a local four piece whose obvious Ramones-ey pop influences were intriguingly clashed with a penchant for extraordinarily English humor and situations. Seeking management, they approached the Beggars team, who in turn went to work looking for a record label for the band. They never found one, so they started their own.

The Lurkers would be Beggars Banquet's premier release in 1978, followed by one-man-band Johnny G, and over the next year, the label developed a peerless reputation for left-of-center signings and, frequently, left-of-center hits. In September 1978 the supremely innuendo-laden "The Winker's Song (Misprint)" by Ivor Biggun, gave Beggars their first Top 30 hit, and while the label's finances were to wobble somewhat early in the new year, the emergence of the Doll, in January, and Gary Numan's Tubeway Army in April, brought security beyond the label's wildest dreams. Numan topped both the UK singles and album charts twice in less than a year, and with stability came expansion.

The 4AD label was launched in 1980, Situation 2 followed in 1983, both swiftly establishing their own identities away from the parent company, while Beggars' own signings continued successful. Bauhaus, the Associates, Icicle Works, and Pete Wylie's Wah! all scored hits during 1982–84; and in 1985, the Cult burst through with "She Sells Sanctuary," irre-

vocably establishing Beggars Banquet as an international independent label. Since that time, Love and Rockets, the Charlatans UK, Loop, Buffalo Tom, Mercury Rev, and Luna have all conspired to ensure they remain there.

Also see the entry for "4AD" on page 738.

Beggars Banquet Label Listing

1977–80 Singles

BEG 1 THE LURKERS — Shadow

BEG 2 THE LURKERS — Freak Show

BEG 3 JOHNNY G — Call Me Bwana

BEG 4 THE DOLL — Don't Tango on My Head

BEG 5 TUBEWAY ARMY — That's Too bad

BEG 6 THE LURKERS — Ain't Got a Clue

BEG 7 JOHNNY G — Hippy's Graveyard

BEG 8 TUBEWAY ARMY — Bombers

BEG 9 THE LURKERS — I Don't Need to Tell her

BEG 10 JOHN SPENCER — Natural Man

BEG 11 THE DOLL — Desire Me

BEG 12 JOHN SPENCER — Crazy for My Lady

BEG 13 JOHNNY G — Monophenia EP

BEG 14 THE LURKERS — Just 13

BEG 15 DUFFO — Give Me Back My Brain

BEG 16 JOHNNY G — The Golden Years

BEG 17 TUBEWAY ARMY — Down in the Park

BEG 18 TUBEWAY ARMY — Are "Friends" Electric?

BEG 19 THE LURKERS — Out in the Dark

BEG 20 DUFFO — Tower of Madness

BEG 21 JOHNNY THUNDERS & THE HEARTBREAKERS — Get off the Phone

EG 22 MERTON PARKAS — You Need Wheels

BEG 23 GARY NUMAN — Cars

BEG 24 RENTALS — I Got a Crush on You

BEG 25 MERTON PARKAS — Plastic Smile

BEG 26 THE DOLL — Cinderella with a Husky Voice

BEG 27 CARPETTES — I Don't Mean It

BEG 28 THE LURKERS — New Guitar in Town

BEG 29 GARY NUMAN — Complex

BEG 30 MERTON PARKAS — Give It to Me Now

BEG 31 THE DOLL — You Used to be My Hero

BEG 32 THE CARPETTES — Johnny Won't Hurt You

BEG 33 SHOX — No Turning Back

BEG 34 JOHN SPENCER — Natural Man

BEG 35 GARY NUMAN — We Are Glass

BEG 36 CHROME — New Age

BEG 37 BAUHAUS — Dark Entries

BEG 38 THE DOLL — Burning Up Like a Fire

BEG 39 COCKNEY & WESTERN — She's No Angel

BEG 40 JOHNNY G — Night After Night

BEG 41 PETE STRIDE & JOHN PLAIN — Laugh at Me

BEG 42 ANDDE LEEK — Move On

BEG 43 MERTON PARKAS — Put Me in the Picture

BEG 44 JOHNNY G — Blue Suede Shoes

BEG 45 SPIRIT — We've Got a Lot to Learn

BEG 46 GARY NUMAN — I Die You Die

BEG 47 THE CARPETTES — Nothing Ever Changes

BEG 48 COLIN NEWMAN — B

BEG 49 THE CARPETTES — The Last Lone Ranger

BEG 50 GARY NUMAN — This Wreckage

BOP 1 IVOR BIGGUN — The Winker's Song (Misprint)

BOP 2 IVOR BIGGUN — I've Parted (Misprint)

BOP 3 AKA — Space Age Lovers

BOP 4 REX BARKER & THE RICOCHETS — Jeremy is Innocent

BOP 5 IVOR BIGGUN — The W*nkers Rock'n'Roll

BOP 6 IVOR BIGGUN — Bras on 45

Beggars Banquet Albums

BEGA 1 VARIOUS ARTISTS — Streets 6   Primal punk comp led off by the Lurkers and Slaughter and the Dogs, but also offering space to the Drones, the Art Attacks, the Members, the Zeros, and poet John Cooper Clarke.

BEGA 2 THE LURKERS — Fulham Fallout 7   Tight Ramones-esque punk melodicism, shot through with a healthy love for pubs, guitars, and the Fulham Palace Road.

BEGA 3 JOHN SPENCER — John Spencer's Louts 5

BEGA 4 TUBEWAY ARMY — Tubeway Army 7

BEGA 5 DUFFO — Duffo 5   Best remembered for the near-hit "Give Me Back My Brain" and that, sadly, is exactly how it should be.

BEGA 6 JOHNNY G — G Sharp, G Natural 9   "Hippy's Grave-yard" remains one of the key commentaries on the wiles of the older generation, but just one of several acerbicfolk-fuzz gems at the great G's disposal. You really should own this record.

BEGA 7 TUBEWAY ARMY — Replicas 9

BEGA 8 THE LURKERS — God's Lonely Men 7

BEGA 9 JOHNNY THUNDERS & THE HEARTBREAKERS — Live at Max's Kansas City 7

BEGA 10 GARY NUMAN — The Pleasure Principle 8

BEGA 11 MERTON PARKAS — Face in the Crowd 7   With future Style Councillor Mick Talbot on board, a merry, Mod time is had by all.

BEGA 12 THE DOLL — Listen to the Silence 6 Another one-hit remembrance, although "Desire Me" was actually one of the band's lesser ideas. Once past the silly sultriness,they ran the Pretenders close for a moment.

BEGA 13 unissued

BEGA 14 THE CARPETTES — Frustration Paradise 6

BEGA 15 CHROME — Red Exposure 6

BEGA 16 JOHNNY G — G Beat

BEGA 17 PETE STRIDE & JOHN PLAIN — New Guitars in Town 6 Ex-Lurkers, ex-Boys... expect the expected.

BEGA 18 CHROME — Half Machine Lip Moves 7

BEGA 19 GARY NUMAN — Telekon 7

BEGA 20 COLIN NEWMAN — A–Z 8

BEGA 21 THE CARPETTES — Fight Amongst Yourselves 5

BOPA 1 IVOR BIGGUN — The Winker's Album (Misprint) 3
Comic Biggun — actually a well-loved UK TV satirist converting his lascivious smile into lavatory simile — had one good joke. The title of his first hit (and album).

BOPA 2 THE LURKERS — Last Will and Testament 8 The best of the brashest.

BOPA 3 IVOR BIGGUN — More Filth, Dirt Cheap 1

BOPA 4 CLAIRE HAMMILL — One House Left Standing 5

BOPA 5 CLAIRE HAMMILL — December 5

BELLA UNION

LABEL

Bella Union was formed by Robin Guthrie and Simon Raymonde in summer 1997 following the demise of the Cocteau Twins. Intended to give the duo (and their signings) a sense of personal musical control which their experiences with majors had long since disavowed them of, the label's initial signings echoed the Cocteaus' own esotericism — Australian instrumental moodists Dirty Three vied with French chanteuse Francoiz Breut; while the post-Lush outfit Sing Sing reunited Guthrie with Emma Anderson, whose very first recordings he produced.

Bella Union Label Listing 1997–2000

1 SIMON RAYMONDE — Blame Someone Else LP 7   Not too many surprises if you've followed Raymonde this far, a spooky middleground between ambience and miasma, and typically high on atmosphere.

2 SIMON RAYMONDE — It's a Family Thing 7-inch

3 DIRTY THREE — Ocean Songs LP 8

4 NANACO — Luminous Love in 23 LP 7

5 NANACO — Lick Your Footsteps to Clean My Room EP

6 DIRTY THREE — Ufkuko EP

7 FRANCOIZ BREUT — Ma Colere EP

8 SING SING — Feels Like Summer EP

9 FRANCOIZ BREUT — Francoiz Breut LP 7   Darkly textured Gallic pop for the post-Serge Gainsbourg generation.

10 SNEAKSTER — Pseudo Nouveau LP 🔳 See-feel electro king Mark Clifford and singer Sophie Hinkley link in trip-hop-inflected electronica cabaret.

11 SNEAKSTER — Splinters EP

12 SNEAKSTER & ROBIN GUTHRIE — 50:50 EP

13 RUSSELL MILLS — Pearl and Umbra LP 🔳 Though This Mortal Coil swiftly fell off the rails, Mills — with so many past collaborations already beneath his belt (most notably with David Sylvian) — effortlessly rekindles both the spirit and the mood of *It'll End in Tears*, drawing in Bill Laswell, Wire's Graham Lewis, Ian McCulloch, Thurston Moore, Hector Zazou, Harold Budd, Roger and Brian Eno, Peter Gabriel, and Sylvian himself for an eclectic passage of textures, moods, and torn emotions. Dazzling.

14 COCTEAU TWINS — BBC Sessions LP 🔳 After years of half-life on the underground circuit, the classic Cocteaus Peel sessions combine with a few latter-day shots for the one Twins album which never once goes off the rails. Plus, it's the closest we're likely to get to a live album.

16 DIRTY THREE — Whatever You Love, You Are LP 🔳 Definitely settling into a set groove, six instrumentals neither add nor subtract from any past (or, probably, future) Three album.

BOMP RECORDS

LABEL

A founding member of the now-legendary Underground Press Syndicate in late '60s San Francisco, Bomp Records founder Greg Shaw was already an established voice on the fanzine scene when he launched *Who Put the Bomp* in 1970 — indeed, an earlier Shawzine, *Mojo*, would subsequently lend its format to the early *Rolling Stone* (and its name to a more recent UK publication). It was an immediate hit — Charlie Gillett, doyen of British rock commentators, once described *WPTB* as the "only [rock fanzine] that can be unreservedly recommended to any music enthusiast regardless of his particular interest. It's edited... with energy, imagination, and a startling ambition to document even the most trivial details on virtually every record made since 1950."

Shaw was working as Assistant Head of Creative Services at United Artists in L.A. when he met the Flamin' Groovies, one of the hottest critical picks of the era, but utterly overlooked by the industry itself. He offered to release a Groovies' 45 through *WPTB*, knowing that the magazine's own subscriber base was at least sufficient for the enterprise to break even. But even he had no idea of just how successful it would prove. "You Tore Me Down," the first ever release on the Bomp label, became one of the radio hits of the year; the Groovies were promptly picked up by Sire; and Bomp Records was born.

Singles by the Wackers and New York beat-punk pioneers the Poppees had already confirmed the fledgling label's via-

bility, while a visit to Rockfield Studios in Monmouth (where Dave Edmunds was producing the Groovies' first Sire album) saw Shaw pick up another early Bomp release, the Rockfield Chorale's Christmas "Jingle Jangle." But Bomp's attentions were now fast focusing in on the punk and new wave spilling out across America. Singles by the Choir, journalist John Mendelssohn, Kim Fowley's Venus and the Razorblades and a second Poppees effort followed in quick succession, together with the debut release by Snatch, a duo formed by New Yorkers Patti Paladin and Judy Nylon — best known for later collaborations with Eno, John Cale, and Johnny Thunders.

Another city scene which fascinated Shaw was Boston, and 1977 saw Bomp release both Willie Alexander's genre-defining "Mass Ave" 45 and an EP by DMZ — shortly before drummer Dave Robinson left to join a new band, the Cars. L.A. punk and power pop moved heavily into focus too with the Zeros, the Weirdos, the Last, Australian ex-pats the Lipstick Killers, and 20/20. However, if any one release (or series of releases) truly moved Bomp into the international spotlight, it was Shaw's late 1977 acquisition of great swathes of the Stooges' unreleased catalog, the *Kill City* album, and later, the *Iguana Chronicles* live and out-takes collections.

Cut in a similar mold to Iggy and the Stooges were New York's Dead Boys, and 1979 saw Bomp strike up a relationship with vocalist Stiv Bators, on the run from that band's incendiary roar with the dream of becoming a pop singer. An album, *Disconnected* (and accompanying single, "The Last Year") launched a relationship which would subsequently see Bomp release the live *Night of the Living Dead Boys*; Bators would also introduce the label to the Raunchettes, an amazing all-girl group from Rochester, NY, whose self-titled 1987 EP he produced.

From 1978 on, Bomp maintained a frenetic release schedule, all the more so after mounting costs and business hassles persuaded Shaw to close *Who Put the Bomp* during 1979. Albums by Nikki and the Corvettes, the Sonics, the Nuns, and the Shoes all appeared, together with a string of compilations which remain the finest introductions available to all that was going on in the name of the American new wave underground as the 1970s wound down — *Vampires from Outer Space*, *No Disco*, *Experiments in Destiny*, *The Best of Bomp*, and two volumes of *Waves*.

Kim Fowley provided the label with their next archive classic, the long-forgotten tapes of his 1972–73 demo sessions with Jonathan Richman and the Modern Lovers — *The Original Modern Lovers* was originally released on Fowley's own Mohawk label, before being reissued (with some of Richman's own revisions) on Bomp in 1981. An even scarcer gem was supplied by L.A. scenemaker/KROQ DJ Rodney Bingenheimer, a version of "Little GTO" recorded with a helping hand (and voice) from Blondie. Debbie Harry lay down a guide vocal which Bingenheimer then sang over; unfortunately, Bomp's European licensees apparently got the wrong end of the stick entirely, and released the Harry version — complete with a tantalizing "featuring Madame X" credit. The record was withdrawn as soon as Blondie's lawyers got wind of it.

Another Bomp project which never got off the ground was a projected second volume of the legendary *Nuggets* collection, compiled by Lenny Kaye in the mid-1970s. Licensing problems saw the idea founder, but Shaw never let go of the dream and early in the 1980s, launched *Pebbles* — a multi (30+) volume series which restored some of the greatest, and most obscure garage records of all time to common currency. Further series *Highs in the Mid-Sixties* and the British psychedelia-themed *Electric Sugarcube Flashbacks* followed, while Shaw furthered his dreams of a full-scale garage revival by opening a venue off Hollywood Boulevard, suitably named the Cavern, devoted exclusively to the new generation of garage bands emerging through the mid-1980s.

The label lapsed into silence through the remainder of the decade, but re-emerged in the early 1990s, as Shaw set about reissuing the catalog on CD. Since that time, the careers and material which Shaw first began investigating during the late 1970s, from Iggy, Stiv Bators, and the MC5 to the Zeroes and the Pink Fairies have been chronicled with zealous efficiency, while a steady stream of new acts, led off by the immortally named Brian Jonestown Massacre, have ensured that the label's future remains as vibrant as its past.

Bomp Singles — 1974–80

101 FLAMIN GROOVIES — You Tore Me Down
102 WACKERS — Captain Nemo
103 POPPEES — If She Cries/ Love of the Loved
104 ROCKFIELD CHORALE — Jingle Jangle (unreleased)
104 CHOIR — I'd Rather You Leave EP
105 JOHN MENDELSSOHN'S THE PITS — Hollywood Can Be Cruel EP
106 POPPEES — Jealousy
107 VENUS & RAZORBLADES — Punk-O-Rama
108 SNATCH — IRT
109 WILLIE ALEXANDER — Kerouac/Mass Ave.
110 ZEROS — Don't Push Me Around
111 DMZ — EP
112 WEIRDOS — Destroy All Music
113 IGGY & THE STOOGES — Sick of You EP
114 IGGY POP/JAMES WILLIAMSON — Jesus Loves the Stooges EP
115 20/20 — Giving It All
116 SHOES — Okay

117 BOYFRIENDS — You're the One
118 ZEROS — Beat Your Heart Out
119 LAST — She Don't Know Why I'm Here
120 ROMANTICS — Tell It to Carrie
121 PERMANENT WAVE — Radar EP
123 B GIRLS — Fun at the Beach
124 STIV BATORS — It's Cold Outside
125 NIKKI & THE CORVETTES — Honey Bop
126 LAST — Every Summer Day
127 RODNEY BINGENHEIMER — Little GTO
128 STIV BATORS — Not That Way Anymore
129 REAL KIDS — She (unreleased)
129 STIV BATORS — I'll Be Alright (unreleased)
130 RANDY WINBURN — Sunshine USA

Bomp Albums

4001 IGGY POP/JAMES WILLIAMSON — Kill City **6**
4002 VARIOUS ARTISTS — The Best of Bomp **9** Crucial gathering of early singles — Willie Alexander, The Choir, DMZ, Flamin' Groovies, Rockfield Chorale, and more.
4003 SHOES — Black Vinyl (unreleased) **6** Power pop purity stumbles only in the absence of an album's worth of great tunes.
4003 VARIOUS ARTISTS — Waves, Vol. 1 **4** Subtitled "An Anthology of New Music," much is sadly somewhat old hat punk and power-pop — Blitzkrieg Bop, The Romantics, Tommy Rock, The Flashcubes....
4004 THE LAST — La Explosion **7**
4005 VARIOUS ARTISTS — Vampires from Outer Space **5**
4006 VARIOUS ARTISTS — No Disco! **6**
4007 The Weirdos — Who What Where When Why **8** Six-track sonic attack, pre-empting the punkabilly psycho-crash of the early 1980s with a truly deranged take on the classic "Jungle Rock."
4008 VARIOUS ARTISTS — Waves, Vol. 2 **6** More "new" music, this time from Pointed Sticks, The Toasters (no relation), The Dadistics, and Psychotic Pineapple. That's more like it.
4009 The Zantees — Out for Kicks **5**
4010 The Nuns — The Nuns **6** Punk always sounded different in San Francisco. Jennifer Miro's android delivery slashes through the band's paranoid thrash, rendering "Child Molester" and "Suicide Child" to icicle paeans of dispassionate observation.
4011 Sonics — Sinderella **5**
4012 Nikki and the Corvettes — Nikki and the Corvettes **4**
4013 unreleased
4014 Jimmy Lewis & Checkers — Yeah, Right **5**
4015 Stiv Bators — Disconnected **9**
4017 Dead Boys — Night of the Living Dead Boys **7**
4016/2 VARIOUS ARTISTS — Experiments in Destiny **8** A double-disc documenting the edgier pop/punk edge of the Bomp

roster. The Lipstick Killers, Rainbow Red Oxidizer, The Wombats, and the Jukebox Rebel Queens ensure the trash quotient never dips too low.

JOHN CALE

PRODUCER

Welsh-born Cale was a founder member of the Velvet Underground, departing in 1968 following the band's second album, *White Light White Heat*. Opting initially for a career in production, his first commissions were alongside fellow Velvets alumni Nico, and in 1969, the first Stooges album. He also cut a solo album, *Vintage Violence*, and collaborated with Terry Riley on *The Church of Anthrox* LP.

As a staff producer at Warners, where he replaced Van Dyke Parks in the role of what he later described as "house freak," Cale then recorded the Modern Lovers' label demos, before re-launching his own solo career with the *Paris 1919* album in 1972. In the UK through the early-mid '70s, his outside production took a backseat to his own career, and the albums *Fear*, *Slow Dazzler*, and *Helen of Troy*. In 1975, however, he was recruited to produce Patti Smith's debut album, and back in London, he became regular producer for Miles Copeland's IRS label group. His relationship with Squeeze, whose debut EP he produced, apparently soured after Cale insisted they title their first album *Gay Guys*.

Returning to New York, Cale established his own Spy label, planning to produce and record new talent — the venture fizzled out after just a handful of singles, including crucial releases by the Necessaries (featuring Red Crayola drummer Jesse Chamberlain, and British guitar hero Chris Spedding) and French hopes Marie et Les Garcons.

Cale spent much of the early 1980s again involved with his own recording career. However, sessions with Gene Loves Jezebel and the Happy Mondays have passed into legend — particularly after the Jezebel tracks disappeared. "It was a tragedy," Michael Aston mourned. "We tried to pick those tracks up for a comp, but I think Beggars had wiped all of them or lost them." Cale also produced what would become Nico's final album.

Maintaining this low-profile into the 1990s, he produced Siouxsie and the Banshees' swansong, and has remained in-demand, despite his apparent reluctance to take advantage of his reputation.

John Cale — Selected Productions

8 NICO — Marble Index (Elektra) 1969 Widely regarded among the most depressing albums ever made, but also one of the most discomfortingly beautiful.

9 THE STOOGES — The Stooges (Elektra) 1969 "No Fun," "I Wanna Be Your Dog," and "1969" ensure the album's immortal-ity; the ten minute "We Will Fall" prove its total disregard for compromise.

9 NICO — Desert Shore (Reprise) 1971 "Janitor of Lunacy" is so widely championed that it's almost a staple. But it's "Mutterlein" and "All That is My Own" which truly stake the album's claim to brilliance.

7 JENNIFER WARNES — Jennifer (Reprise) 1972

9 MODERN LOVERS — Demos 1972 Finally released in 1975 as the *Modern Lovers* album, Richman's juvenile genius crystallized in "Pablo Picasso," "She Cracked," and, of course, "Roadrunner."

6 NICO — The End (ISLAND) 1974 Simultaneously overlooked and over-rated — the production gives far too much room to co-conspirators Eno and Phil Manzanera, cluttering Nico's valkyrie delivery. "Das Lied DerDeutschland" notwithstanding, the version of The Doors' "The End" on the *June 1, 1974* live album demonstrates what this album should have sounded like.

10 PATTI SMITH GROUP — Horses (Arista) 1975

MENACE — Screwed Up EP (Illegal) 1977

SHAM 69 — Red London EP (Step Forward) 1977

SQUEEZE — A Packet of Three EP (Deptford Fun City) 1977

6 DAVE KUBINEC — Some Things Never Change (A&M) 1978

MARIE ET LES GARCONS — Attitudes 7-Inch (Spy) 1979

NECESSARIES — You Can Borrow My Car 7-Inch (Spy) 1979

GENE LOVES JEZEBEL — Demos [unreleased] 1984

6 NICO — Camera Obscura (Beggars Banquet) 1985 "My Funny Valentine" is beautiful, "... Einsamen Madchens" is heart-rending, but too much else is Nico-by-numbers, with a bland band barely adding anything by their presence.

8 HAPPY MONDAYS — Squirrel and G-man... (FACTORY) 1987

7 SIOUXSIE AND THE BANSHEES — Rapture [Five Tracks] (Geffen) 1995

7 MAIDS OF GRAVITY — The First Second (Vernon Yard) 1996

Further Reading

What's Welsh for Zen? by John Cale/Victor Bockris (Henry Holt, 1999).

IAN CAPLE

PRODUCER

As a teenaged engineer at EMI's west London studios, Caple cut his teeth with a string of visiting punk bands. He was part of the team which laid down the pounding percussives which took Adam and the Ants to stardom in 1979, while he would also engineer for Danse Society, Chameleons UK, the Mekons, and the 3 Mustaphas 3.

It was as engineer that Caple first stepped into the producer's seat, working with Shriekback in 1982. That experience marked the birth of a relationship which subsequently saw Caple return to work with band member Dave Allen's

World Domination label. There, he oversaw Sky Cries Mary's classic *This Timeless Turning* — one of the best sounding albums of the entire decade, while he would also engineer Tricky's acclaimed sophomore album. However, Caple's reputation was probably best confirmed by his sensitive treatment of Tindersticks' debut, and low-fi guru Baby Bird's major label debut.

Ian Caple — Selected Productions

SHRIEKBACK — Tench EP 1982

7 MEKONS — Fun 90 (Twin/Tone) 1990

9 TINDERSTICKS — Tindersticks (Bar None) 1993

10 SKY CRIES MARY — This Timeless Turning (World Domination) 1994

5 BABY BIRD — Ugly Beautiful (Echo) 1996 Steven Jones' first for a major label, reiterating a handful of past low-fi gems, but all clean and shiny now, and maybe more like Robyn Hitchcock than he ever set out to become.

7 MALACODA — Cascade (World Domination) 1997 Oddly overlooked Dave Allen effort, as slinkily graceful as ever.

6 VITRO — Distort (Sony) 1999 Competent industrial dance favoring electronics over aggression; a kinder, gentler Sister Machine Gun.

CHISWICK RECORDS

LABEL

Like so many other indy labels of the past 25 years, Chiswick Records was born out of a record store — or, in this case, a stall, set up in London's Soho Market in 1974 by owner Ted Carroll. Rock On specialized in '50s rarities, catering to much the same Teddy Boy contingent that was then frequenting Malcolm McLaren's Let It Rock clothes store across town in Chelsea. Little did those bequiffed and drain-piped retro casualties know, but within a year, their favorite tailor would be selling bondage gear to proto-punk rockers, and their favorite record shop would be issuing singles for the same crowd.

For both Carroll and his assistant, Roger Armstrong, the appeal of the rocking rarities they sold was not only rooted in the music. They were also fascinated by the very mechanics of the industry back then, the way independent entrepreneurs could simply find a band, find a studio, find a pressing plant, and within a matter of weeks, take delivery of a box of hot vinyl — the same hot vinyl which now paid Rock On's expenses. In spring 1975, they decided to see if it could still be done.

The first act "signed" to the new Chiswick label were the Hammersmith Gorillas, fronted by the monstrous sideburns of Jesse Hector, and already regarded as the wildest

rock'n'roll act in town — Hector was one of Rock On's most dedicated young customers, but away from his private record collection, he led his band through an ear-splitting set divided neatly between Gorilla originals, and ape shit classics. With Brinsley Schwarz manager Dave Robinson engineering the session, Carroll and Armstrong took the Gorillas into a tiny studio above the Hope & Anchor pub, and cut two songs — which promptly remained unreleased for another 25 years.

In fact, the first band to get a record out on Chiswick was the Count Bishops, fronted by a New Yorker named Mike Spenser — who himself would later ascend to punk immortality as one of the young vocalists who turned down the chance to sing lead with the Sex Pistols.

Chiswick launched with the Bishops' *Speedball* EP in November 1975, a full eight months before engineer Robinson got his Stiff Records off the ground, and though the record itself did little in commercial terms, culturally, its impact was immense. The first true "indy" label to get off the ground in Britain in almost a decade, Chiswick would suddenly find itself ideally placed to take advantage of an entire sub-genre of British rock, as the pub rock boom of the past few years girded itself to become the punk rock of the future.

The Bishops and the Gorillas were joined, in swift succession, by French rockers Little Bob Story — headline act at the first Mont De Marsen punk festival in France in August 1976; the 101ers — featuring a pre- Clash Joe Strummer and future Public Image Ltd drummer Richard Dudanski; Radio Stars, formed by ex-members of Sparks and John's Children; Greta Garbage and the Trash Cans, who changed their name to the Radiators from Space, Ireland's first ever punk band....

Stiff Records may, once it emerged, have been regarded as the more fashionable of the leading London indies; may, indeed, have had a more varied and commercially vital roster and certainly had a better eye for catchy slogans and publicity campaigns. But in terms of the two labels' actual output, there was little to choose between either of them.

Both labels, for instance, would sign Motorhead, before their speedfreak roar ossified into the metal madness of future renown; both would offer homes to the Damned, TV Smith, Kirsty MacColl, and Shane MacGowan; both would even pick up former members of '70s free festival favorites the Pink Fairies — Stiff got guitarist Larry Wallis, Chiswick got drummer Twink, who promptly linked with future Damned guitarist Alan Lee Shaw and Adverts drummer Rod Latter, in the first trans-generational supergroup, Rings. And both labels would discover that the major label distribution which came along once punk, and success, hit hard was a double-edged sword.

For Chiswick, the arrival of EMI in summer 1978 came just as the label's own fortunes were in something approaching free fall. Despite a handful of chart successes, most notably courtesy of Radio Stars, Chiswick's finances were weakening, resulting in a slew of cancelled results. EMI's offer might have cut the last links with the label's once stoutly defended indy roots (and forced a change in the label's cataloging system), but it brought Chiswick back to life, and with it, a new generation of potential hit-makers.

Chiswick finally folded in 1983, as Carroll and Armstrong made the decision to concentrate their attentions, and now encyclopediac experience, on the music which had got them into the record label business in the first place — a reissues-oriented label called Ace. It is still going strong today.

Chiswick Records Label Listing 1976–78

Singles/ EPs

SW1 COUNT BISHOPS — Route 66 EP
S2 VINCE TAYLOR — Brand New Cadillac
S3 101ERS — Keys to Your Heart
S4 GORILLAS — She's My Gal
S5 COUNT BISHOPS — Train Train
SW6 ROCKY SHARPE & THE RAZORS — Drip Drop EP
SW7 LITTLE BOB STORY — I'm Crying EP
S8 GORILLAS — Gorilla Got Me
S9 RADIO STARS — Dirty Pictures
S10 RADIATORS FROM SPACE — Television Screen
S11 SKREWDRIVER — You're So Dumb
S12 BISHOPS — Baby You're Wrong
S13 MOTORHEAD — Motorhead
S14 THE RINGS — I Wanna Be Free
S15 JOHNNY MOPED — No-One
NS16 JEFF HILL — I Want You to Dance with Me
SW17 RADIO STARS — No Russians in Russia EP
NS18 SKREWDRIVER — Anti-Social
NS19 THE RADIATORS — Enemies
NS20 AMAZORBLADES — Common Truth
NS21 THE STUKAS — Klean Livin' Kids
NS22 JOHNNY & THE SELF-ABUSERS — Saints and Sinners
NS23 RADIO STARS — Nervous Wreck
NS24 THE RADIATORS — Prison Bars (Unissued)
NS25 WHIRLWIND — Hang Loose
Ns26 TWINK — Do It 77
NS27 JOHNNY MOPED — Darling, Let's Have Another Baby
NS28 SKREWDRIVER — Streetfight
NS29 THE RADIATORS — Million Dollar Hero
NS30 THE JOOK — The Jook EP
NS31 THE TABLE — Sex Cells

NS32 LINK WRAY — Batman Theme (Unissued)
NS33 THE BISHOPS — I Take What I Want
SW34 RIFF RAFF — Cosmonaut EP
NS35 THE BISHOPS — Mr Jones (Unissued)
NS36 RADIO STARS — From a Rabbit
NS37 THE BISHOPS — I Want Candy
NS38 FRANKIE FORD — Sea Cruise
SW39 DRUG ADDIX — Gay Boys in Bondage EP
NS40 SNIFF'N'THE TEARS — Driver's Seat (Unissued)

Albums

CH1 VARIOUS ARTISTS — Hollywood Rock'n'Roll **7**
CH2 VARIOUS ARTISTS — Submarine Tracks and Fool's Gold **8** Count Bishops, Radio Stars, and Joe Strummer's 101ers head off a driving label rarities collection.
CH3 SKREWDRIVER — All Skrewed Up **5**
CH4 WHIRLWIND — 10" **7**
CH5 VARIOUS ARTISTS — Long Shots, Dead Certs & Odds On **8** Favorites subtitled "Chiswick Chart Busters Volume Two," more class singles from Johnny Moped, the Amazorblades, Motorhead, the Rings and more.
CH6 LINK WRAY — Link Wray **7**
CH7 COUNT BISHOPS — Live **8**
CH8 VARIOUS ARTISTS — Sound of Music (Unissued)
CH9 HUEY PIANO SMITH & THE CLOWNS — Huey Piano Smith & the Clowns **6**
CH10 unissued

WIK 1 COUNT BISHOPS — Count Bishops **9** Urban R&B with more energy than bands with twice their street cred.
WIK 2 MOTORHEAD — Motorhead **7** Not quite the guts'n'fire creation which was Motorhead's first stab at an album (*No Parole* would remain shelved till 1979), but an adequate recreation, launched with an admittedly definitive "Motorhead."
WIK 3 SKREWDRIVER — All Skrewed Up (Unissued)
WIK 4 RADIATORS FROM SPACE — TV Tube Heart **6**
WIK 5 RADIO STARS — Songs for Swinging Lovers **9**
Supreme power-pop punk with fiendishly witty lyrics, subject matter ranging from Greek restaurant menus ("Macaroni and Mice") to serial killers ("Beast of Barnsley"), and unrequited love ("Nervous Wreck"), nailed to some genuinely, memorably rocketing riffs.
WIK 6 LITTLE BOB STORY — Off the Rails **8** If the Count Bishops were French and had Eric Burdon on vocals..
WIK 7 WHIRLWIND — 12-Inch **7**
WIK 8 JOHNNY MOPED — Cycledelic **9** Absolute madness. The greatest songs, the sloppiest playing, a voice to make Billy Bragg feel grateful and the sheer immortality of the since-oft-covered "Darling, Let's Have Another Baby."
WIK 9 unissued
WIK 10 WHIRLWIND — Setting the Woods on Fire **7**

CITADEL RECORDS

LABEL

John Needham, guitarist with Australian post-punk legends Minuteman, launched Citadel in 1982, sweeping up the indisputable talents left behind (or ignored) by the better established Hot — and coming out on top more often than not. The label's first ten releases, by Minuteman, Screaming Tribesmen, Died Pretty, Lime Spiders, Angie Pepper and Radio Birdman offshoots New Race and Deniz Tek essentially spelled out the history of the Australian underground of the age, and also promised much for the future. In 1999, with Citadel still at the forefront of the national indy scene, the Divine Rites label released *Storming the Citadel*, a tribute album to the early days of the label.

Citadel Label Listing 1982–86

Singles

1 MINUTEMAN — Voodoo Slaves
2 NEW RACE — Crying Sun
3 DENIS TEK/RADIO BIRDMAN — 100 Fools
4 SCREAMING TRIBESMEN — Igloo
5 ANGIE PEPPER — Frozen World
6 NEW CHRISTS — Like a Curse
7 DIED PRETTY — Out of the Unknown
8 LIME SPIDERS — Slave Girl
9 SCREAMING TRIBESMEN — A Stand Alone
10 DIED PRETTY — Mirror Blues I
11 STEMS — Make You Mine
12 MOFFS — Another Day in the Sun
13 STEMS — Tears Me in Two
14 TRILOBITES — Venus in Leather
15 LIME SPIDERS — Out of Control
16 SUPER K — Recurring Nightmare
17 NEW CHRISTS — Born Out of Time
18 SOMELOVES — It's My Time
19 BAM BALAMS — Deliver My Love
20 DIED PRETTY — Stoneage Cinderella
21 PORCELAIN BUS — Indignation
22 INNER SLEEVES — End It All
23 TRILOBITES — American Tv
24 BAMBOOS — Snuff
25 BAM BALAMS — No-One Else

EPs

901 DIED PRETTY — Next to Nothing
902 SCREAMING TRIBESMEN — Date with a Vampire
903 STEMS — Love Will Grow

904 STONEFISH — From 2000 Fathoms

LPs

501 LIPSTICK KILLERS — Mesmerizer 5
502 VISITORS — Visitors 5
503 MOFFS — The Moffs 7
504 DIED PRETTY — Free Dirt 8

CLEOPATRA RECORDS

LABEL

Cleopatra was launched in 1992 by London-born, L.A. native Brian Perera, primarily as an outlet for two bands he was currently helping out: space rock figureheads Pressurehed, and industrial combo Spahn Ranch. Fully cogniscent, however, of the high attrition rate among even well-intentioned vanity labels, Perera opted to launch the label with a classic reissue, the first ever Motorhead album — oft-issued in the UK, but still awaiting a full US release.

A Pressurehed single, a cover of Hawkwind founder Robert Calvert's "The Right Stuff," duly followed, together with the band's debut album, *Infradrone*. But it was Cleopatra's next releases, compilations of rare Hawkwind and Kraftwerk material, and a set of new recordings by Christian Death founder Rozz Williams, which set the tone for Cleopatra's immediate future, establishing the label at the forefront of the then-burgeoning gothic and industrial booms.

In 1993, Perera and Cleopatra relaunched the career of former Hawkwind mainstay Nik Turner, uniting him with Pressurehed and Chrome guitarist Helios Creed, together with a number of fellow ex-Hawkwind members, for a handful of albums and two massively successful US tours, all recapturing the long-dormant spirit of Hawkwind at their very finest, and spear-heading a space rock revival which also brought success to non-Cleopatra acts Ozric Tentacles and Sky Cries Mary.

Despite now appearing the spearhead of three very successful genres, both via an eternally intelligent reissue program and some inspired new signings, Cleopatra continued to dodge pigeonholing, as a hectic monthly release schedule continued to expand.

Oi! acts Broken Bones, Discharge, and the Angelic Upstarts joined the catalog; former Velvet Underground chanteuse Nico, '80s techno-terrorists Sigue Sigue Sputnik, and glam-punk heroes the Adicts all numbered among the label's most inspired releases, while a link with legendary British entrepreneur Tony Secunda saw Cleopatra release "lost" albums by Motorhead and former T. Rex member Steve Peregrin Took, before Secunda's tragic death in 1995 severed the union.

In contrast, the majority of the label's "new" signings remained within Cleopatra's areas of greatest expertise — Usherhouse, Rosetta Stone, Digital Poodle, and Noisebox all made an impact in their chosen gothic/industrial genres, while the Electric Hellfire Club, formed by ex-Thrill Kill Kult legend Thomas "Buck Ryder" Thorn succeeded in crossing gothic sensibilities with hard-hitting industrial-electro sounds, to emerge one of the most fascinating bands of the 1990s. Licensing deals with European dance and electro labels, meanwhile, brought further talent to American ears, via the Hypnotic imprint (established 1994).

Irrevocably shaping the face of indy labeldom through the 1990s, simply by operating at a pace which few other companies could even dream of matching, Cleopatra celebrated its seventh birthday, in 1999, with a back catalog which now featured close to 1,200 releases (including new albums by Gary Numan, the Mission, Dead or Alive, and Yes), and two further imprints, the prog/classic rock specialist Purple Pyramid, and the glam metal-based Deadline.

Cleopatra Label Listing 1992–94

NOTE: Cleopatra's uniquely non-sequential numbering system cannot be relied upon for chronology.

0022 ANGELIC UPSTARTS — Kids on the Street [Compilation] 7 Excellent reminder of the UK Oi! pioneers, lacking only in one respect — the seminal "I'm an Upstart" is absent.

0023 TUBALCAIN — 25 Assorted Needles 7 Originally released 1992, industrial goth anticipating the later storm of loud guitars. Vocalist Maroulis later surfaced in Spahn Ranch.

0033 NOSFERATU — Legend [Reissued Cleo 1016] 6

0034 NICO — Chelsea Girl — Live [Reissued Cleo 6108] 7 The original goth, caught live and brutal in mid-80s England.

0036 KLUTE — Excepted [Reissued Cleo 9393] 7

0203 TUNNELMENTAL — The Demise Of 5

1017 PRESSUREHED — Sudden Vertigo 8

1019 VARIOUS ARTISTS — Gothic Rock 6

1022 CONTROLLED BLEEDING — Buried Blessings 5

1023 CONFLICT — Employing All Means Necessary [Compilation] 8 The best of the legendary UK anarcho-punks.

1029 THE DAMNED — Strawberries 8

1030 MARCH VIOLETS — The Botanic Verses 6 The first and last signing to the Sisters of Mercy's Merciful release label, walking very much in the shadow of their mentors.

1039 GITANE DEMONE — Facets in Blue 6

1079 NICO — Drama of Exile 9 From 1981, Nico's first true "rock" album, the blueprint for much of the next decade's darker dreamers.

1089 URBAN DOGS — Urban Dogs 3 Ill-conceived UK Subs spin-off.

1094 PENAL COLONY — Put Your Hands Down 5

1099 EVA O — Past Times 7

1182 TWO WITCHES — The Vampire Kiss 6

1257 CHRISTIAN DEATH — Invocations 7

1275 ROSETTA STONE — Adrenaline 9

1575 VARIOUS ARTISTS — The Whip 8 With Marc Almond and Andi Sex-Gang among the key inclusions, one of the leading goth compilations of the early 1980s, updated to include many of the '90s' leading underground lights.

1592 PROPHETESS — Prophetess 7

1593 PROPHETESS — Dichotomy 6

1844 VARIOUS ARTISTS — Space Daze 2000 8

2035 SIGUE SIGUE SPUTNIK — First Generation 7

2044 JOHNNY THUNDERS — LAMF: The Lost Mixes 8

2049 JOHNNY THUNDERS — Que Sera Sera 8

2129 BLITZ — The Killing Dream 5

2134 45 GRAVE — The Debasement Tapes 6

2135 NIK TURNER — Sphynx 7

2309 PSYCHOPOMPS — Pro-Death Ravers 6

2481 ADICTS — Songs of Praise 6

2756 KOMMUNITY FK — Enclose One Sad Eye 7

2833 KLUTE — Excluded 6

2899 X-MARKS THE PEDWALK — Human Desolation 5

3315 ADICTS — Sound of Music 6

3326 ADICTS — Smart Alex 6

3721 LEAETHER STRIP — Fit for Flogging 7

3731 THE GERMS — Media Blitz 4

3751 SUPER HEROINES — Love and Pain 7 Alongside 45 Grave and the original Christian Death, Eva O and future Hole bassist Jill Emery's Super Heroines epitomized the L.A. death rock scene of the early 1980s.

3993 CHRISTIAN DEATH — The Path of Sorrows 6

4139 SCREAMS FOR TINA — Screams for Tina 7

5000 THE EXPLOITED — Singles Collection [Compilation] 7

5100 VICE SQUAD — Live and Loud 8 With Beki Bondage among the most accomplished vocalists of the later UK punk scene, it was always frustrating that Vice Squad never rose to match her potential. This live disc, alongside a Peel Sessions collection in the late 1990s, represents the band at the peak of their achievement.

5185 NOSFERATU — Rise 7

5694 VARIOUS ARTISTS — The Industrial Revolution 7 Companion 2-CD set to the admittedly flawed encyclopedia of the same name, featuring cuts from Ministry, Einsturzende Neubauten, Throbbing Gristle, Laibach, Foetus, Brian Eno, Skinny Puppy, Spahn Ranch, and more.

5721 MOTORHEAD — On Parole 9 The first ever Cleopatra release, and a US debut for Motorhead's long-shelved first album.

5731 PRESSUREHED — Infradrone 8 In a quest to bring space-rock into the 21st century, Pressurehed's debut makes ample use of searing guitar solos, a throbbing bass, and genuinely clever samples, all coated with a searing industrial edge.

5741 HAWKWIND — Psychedelic Warlords 8

5751 CHRISTIAN DEATH — The Iron Mask 6

5761 KRAFTWERK — The Model EP

5771 SYD BARRETT — Octopus [Compilation] 8 Though his last album was released in 1970, former Pink Floyd founder Syd Barrett's music — and more importantly his legend — have drenched the modern era, attracting cover versions from as far a field as Jesus and Mary Chain, Love and Rockets, the Soft Boys, Camper Van Beethoven, and Electric Hellfire Club. *Octopus* draws from both Barrett's original solo sets, plus the *Opel* out-takes collection.

5773 HAWKWIND — Lord of Light (Compilation) 7

5811 VOICE OF DESTRUCTION — Steamroller Tactics 6

5841 CHRISTIAN DEATH — Skeleton Kiss 6

5853 ROZZ WILLIAMS — Every King a Bastard Son 5

5875 KRAFTWERK — Radio Activity 8

5876 KRAFTWERK — Trans-Europe Express 9

5877 KRAFTWERK — The Man Machine 9 The albums which sparked an electro-revolution, rerouting even the molten indiscipline of punk rock's electric guitars down a whole new track.

5901 USHERHOUSE — Molting 7 Surprisingly uncalculated latter-day goth, the rough edges obviously keeping the bats at bay.

5941 EXPLOITED — Don't Forget the Chaos 6

5951 ADICTS — 27 7 Classic English Oi!, the Exploited unrelenting in its commitment to "the cause"; the Adicts taking an artsier, *Clockwork Orange*-influenced approach.

6008 DIGITAL POODLE — Division 5

6115 OFRA HAZA — Yemenite Songs 5

6308 MEPHISTO WALTZ — The Eternal Deep 6

6408 BLITZ — Blitz Hits 7

6508 PSYCHIC TV — Hexsex — The Singles 1 9

6647 VARIOUS ARTISTS — First and Last and Forever 5

6675 BEAUTIFUL AUTHENTIC ZOO GODS — Birth 7

6808 VARIOUS ARTISTS — Mysterious Encounters 8 Genre-spanning collection, highlighting both older and forthcoming label releases, with essential contributions from Nik Turner, Aurora, Eva O, and more.

6843 KRAFTWERK — Showroom Dummies [Compilation] 8

6908 NIK TURNER — Prophets of Time 8

7036 BLOK 57 — Block 57 5

7109 SPAHN RANCH — Collateral Damage 6

7129 ADICTS — Live and Loud 5

7139 DAMNED — Tales from the Damned 7

7208 CHILDREN ON STUN — Tourniquets of Love's Desire 7 Featuring new material and reworkings of old, Children caught while turning from a sub-Sisters drone to a goth rock group with a uniquely diverse sound of their own.

7209 CHRISTIAN DEATH — Sleepless Nights — Live 1990 7

7269 ELECTRIC HELLFIRE CLUB — Burn Baby Burn 8

7279 ANTI-NOWHERE LEAGUE — Best Of 8 Crashing belligerence, righteous rage, and utter contempt for the "system," the League's bellicose rendering of "Streets of London" is worth the price of admission by itself.

7366 WRECKAGE — Crawling from the Wreckage 6

7519 PLAY DEAD — The First Flower 8

7593 PREMATURE EJACULATION — Necessary Discomforts 3

7693 LEAETHER STRIP — Solitary Confinement 8 A terrifying descent into homicidal madness, from the throbbing electronic to the hauntingly beautiful, each song draws you deeper into Strip's desolate vision.

7771 VARIOUS ARTISTS — Industrial Revolution (2nd ed.) 7 Revised reissue of earlier release.

7916 VARIOUS ARTISTS — Space Daze 8 Companion to the space rock history book of the same name.

8125 CHRISTIAN DEATH — Rage of Angels 7

9109 CHRISTIAN DEATH — Tales of Innocence 8

9119 ROSETTA STONE — Epitome EP

9187 THE WAKE — Masked 6

9243 VARIOUS ARTISTS — Trance Europe 6

9259 MEPHISTO WALTZ — Terra Regina 6

9309 BROKEN BONES — Death Is Imminent 7

9323 ROSETTA STONE — Foundation Stones 8

9400 VARIOUS ARTISTS — In Goth Daze 5

9402 VARIOUS ARTISTS — Trance-Europe 2.0 6

9404 RED LORRY YELLOW LORRY — Generation 7 Minor league pioneers of early '80s proto-goth, occasionally veering a little too close to Joy Division for comfort, but still purveying one true classic, "Hollow Eyes."

9405 BLITZ — Second Empire of Justice

9410 FRONTLINE ASSEMBLY — Total Terror I 8

9411 FRONTLINE ASSEMBLY — Total Terror II 7 Originally recorded back in '86/87, *I* is actually reminiscent of Bill Leeb's other project, Delirium; *II* is harder industrial dance, and together both are reminders of just where Frontline began and how far they've come.

9412 ALIEN SEX FIEND — Drive My Rocket 8

9413 MOTORHEAD — Iron Fist & the Hordes from Hell [Live] 7

9414 VARIOUS ARTISTS — Trance in Your Mind 6

9415 KOMMUNITY FK — The Vision and the Voice 7 Reissue of the band's 1983 debut, these early death rockers had an ear for gloom and a predilection for experimentation, amidst the more accessible poppy numbers.

9416 KRAFTWERK — The Capitol Years 9 Indispensable 3-CD box repackaging the three previous albums.

9417 AURORA — The Dimension Gate 7

9418 ELECTRIC HELLFIRE CLUB — Satan's Little Helpers 8

9419 X MARKS THE PEDWALK — Abattoir 6 Compiling 14 tracks from deleted vinyl and CD singles, Pedwalk's industrial dance is uncompromisingly electronic — no guitars, but some crossover pop melodies.

9460 THD — Mechanical Advantage 4

9461 USHERHOUSE — Flux 6

9463 EXECUTIVE SLACKS — Repressed 6

9465 HELIOS CREED — Busting Through the Van Allan Belt 8

9466 EVA O HALO EXPERIENCE — A Demon's Fall for an Angel's Kiss 8 Shadow Project co-founder O in reflective, if occasionally over-done goth overdrive.

9467 ROBERT CALVERT — Freq 7 1984 album from Hawkwind's on-board poet and vocalist, remixed by Spahn Ranch's Matt Green.

9469 PSYCHIC TV — A Pagan Day 7

9470 LEAETHER STRIP — Underneath the Laughter 7

9471 VARIOUS ARTISTS — Totentanz 7 Through the early-mid '90s, Germany's Zoth Ommog was one of the leading players on the European industrial scene. This "best of" the label's output shows how they did it.

9472 SPAHN RANCH — Blackmail Starters Kit EP

9473 X MARKS THE PEDWALK — The Killing Had Begun 6

9475 NOISE UNIT — Strategy of Violence 7 Bill Leeb and Rhys Fulber take time off from Frontline for this side project that sounds... Just like Frontline, perhaps a bit lighter, a wee more accessible, and a tad more trancey.

9476 VARIOUS ARTISTS — Influence 1.1 6

9479 PSYCHOPOMPS — Assassins DK United 7 Danish industrialists out to shock. Indeed, lyrically it's so over the top that it's obviously tongue in cheek — and eminently danceable.

9482 CLOCK DVA — Collective 88–93 7

9483 LAIBACH — Nova Akropola 8

9486 CONFLICT — Conclusion 6

9489 DIN — Decade of the Brain 6

9490 HELIOS CREED — X Rated Fairy Tales/Superior Catholic Finger 6 Back to back reissue for Creed's first two post Chrome albums.

9491 PSYCHIC TV — Allegory & Self-Thee Starlit Mire 6

9493 AURORA — Land of Harm and Apple Trees 5

9495 BIG ELECTRIC CAT — Dreams of a Mad King 8 This Aussie band's debut is the ultimate in goth pop, a drifting menage of melancholy melodies and surprisingly sparkling toe-tappers... with a light coating of funereal ash, of course.

9498 DIGITAL POODLE — Noisea 7 A rarities collection comprising remixes, a live cut, tracks from cassettes-only releases and two previously unreleased songs.

9501 VARIOUS ARTISTS — Trance Hardcore 5

9502 LEAETHER STRIP — Serenade for the Dead 8 A dramatic departure, *Serenade*'s melancholy mood transports the listener back to a distant age of tyrants slaughtering their way to the throne, while the boiling tides extinguish Atlantis' light. So, an aura of impending doom quickens and fades, filling the album with suppressed tensions and sound scapes of incredible power and depth.

9506 NIK TURNER — Space Ritual 1994 8

9507 NOSFERATU — Prophecy 7 A change in singers and a rejigging of style means that Nosferatu now sound more like the Mission than the Sisters, regardless, *Prophecy* is filled with darkly catchy songs, evocative lyrics, and a fog machine's worth of atmospheres.

9508 ALIEN SEX FIEND — I'm Her Frankenstein 7

9510 NOISE BOX — Monkey Ass 6

9511 MEPHISTO WALTZ — Thalia 7 Darker and more ominous than their previous albums, the airy lightness is now chased away by foreboding even on the featheriest of tracks, while a couple of songs cross over into unadulterated industrial territory, all harsh, metallic rhythms and ghostly effects.

9512 PENAL COLONY — 5 Man Job 6 A remix album of old and new, courtesy Bill Leeb, Genesis P-Orridge, Leaether Strip and more.

9518 PSYCHIC TV — Godstar — The Singles 2 8

9519 HELIOS CREED — Cosmic Assault 8

9520 VARIOUS ARTISTS — Enchantments 7

9523 LIGHTS OF EUPHORIA — Thought Machine 7 An intriguing blend of dark industrial dance tortured by techno-break beats, moving across gloomy, almost goth-esque dirges, then kicking in the rhythms — the dark corners in every discotheque.

9524 LEAETHER STRIP — Double Or Nothing 7 Disc one features four new songs combining the majestic soundscapes of *Serenade* with industrial dance; disc two wraps up some rare remixes and three live tracks.

9528 STEVE TOOK — Missing Link to Tyrannosaurus Rex 6

9529 ALIEN SEX FIEND — Inferno 6

PAT COLLIER

PRODUCER

BORN 1951 *(London, England)*

The original bassist with UK punk veterans the Vibrators, Collier quit the band to launch a power pop group, the Boyfriends, in early 1978. However, he also opened his own four track Alaska Studios beneath the railroad arches at south London's Waterloo Station, debuting as a producer in 1980, with Robyn Hitchcock's Soft Boys.

He rejoined the Vibrators in 1982, but departed within a couple of years, to concentrate on his newly opened 24 track

Greenhouse Studios, promptly enjoying commercial success when he produced ex-Soft Boy Kimberley Rew's new band, Katrina and the Waves' hit "Walking on Sunshine." Robyn Hitchcock meanwhile presented Collier with critical applause, while 1988 saw the produce combine both forms of success when he began working with the Wonder Stuff, formative masters of the UK baggy scene.

He also worked with Kingmaker, Adorable, and the Candyskins, the three finest representatives of that brittle pop scene which bridged the baggy and Britpop movements in the early 1990s, although the Hitchcock connection also remained strong, as Collier proved when he produced the singer's best album of the decade, 1999's *Jewels for Sophia*.

Pat Collier — Selected Productions

8 SOFT BOYS — **Underwater Moonlight (Armageddon) 1980**

7 ROBYN HITCHCOCK — **Black Snake Diamond Role (Armageddon) 1980**

7 VIBRATORS — **Guilty (Anagram) 1983**

5 THE SOUND — **Shock of Daylight (Statik) 1984**

6 KATRINA & THE WAVES — **Katrina & the Waves (Capitol) 1985** Ex-Soft Boy Kimberley Rew walking on sunshine at the head of an Anglo-American new wave-lite crusade. Nice.

8 ROBYN HITCHCOCK — **Fegmania (Slash) 1985**

5 KATRINA & THE WAVES — **Waves (Capitol) 1986**

7 SCREAMING BLUE MESSIAHS — **Gun Shy (Elektra) 1986**

7 ROBYN HITCHCOCK — **Element of Light (Glass) 1986**

SOUP DRAGONS — **Hang Ten [Three Tracks] (Sire) 1987**

8 JACK RUBIES — **See the Money in My Smile (TVT) 1988**

8 WONDER STUFF — **Eight Legged Groove Machine (Polydor) 1988** Best described as a punk Herman's Hermits, the Wonder Stuff are just as catchy, but exchange the kitschy tweeness for a demanding attitude and more assaulting sound. The melodies are a homage to the '60s, though, with nods to the New Wave and the obligatory wave to psychedelic excess — hence the title, presumably.

8 WONDER STUFF — **Hup (Polydor) 1989** An acid drenched journey into pop psychedelia, *Hup* divides its time between bubbling and swirling at hyper speed, and jangling along like an express train, while the addition of *Muswell Hillbilly*-ish banjo and fiddle makes a peculiar companion for the truly surreal lyrics.

6 DARLING BUDS — **Pop Said (Columbia) 1989**

7 NEW MODEL ARMY — **Impurity (EMI) 1990**

4 MODERN ENGLISH — **Life's Rich Tapestry (TVT) 1990**

6 MEN THEY COULDN'T HANG — **The Domino Club (Silvertone) 1990**

7 THE SEERS — **Psych Out (Relativity) 1990**

8 CANDYSKINS — **Space I'm In (DGC) 1991**

SCORPIO RISING — **Zodiac Killers EP (Sire) 1992**

5 FALLING JOYS — **Psychohum (IRS) 1992**

4 TWO LOST SONS — **Welcome to the World Of (Savage) 1992**

7 CANDYSKINS — **Fun? (DGC) 1993**

8 ADORABLE — **Against Perfection (SBK) 1993** An artful collision between early Psychedelic Furs and mid-period Cure, Adorable skip gaily between guitar drones and soaring dark-pop, moodily upbeat in a perfect post-punk pop way.

9 KINGMAKER — **Sleepwalking (Chrysalis) 1993** Taking the pop sensibilities which their unsung debut album hinted at, but adding a fresh sense of urgency and freneticism, *Sleepwalking* is a treasure chest of hooks, catchy tunes, raucous power chords, and an overwhelming joie de vivre guaranteed to make you smile. Best of the bunch — "Scrape the Sky," a ten star single in a five star world.

8 WONDER STUFF — **Construction for the Modern Idiot (Polydor) 1993** The official enlistment of Martin Bell during their last album, *Elvis*, aided the Wonder's bigger and more diverse sound, a strength even more evident on *Idiot*. Solidifying their changing style, adding harmonies, and flirtatiously playing the musical field, this year's Stuff moves effortlessly between exquisite ballads to adrenaline-drenched classic rockers.

6 ENGINE ALLEY — **Engine Alley (Mother) 1994**

6 OYSTER BAND — **Shouting End of Life (Cooking Vinyl) 1995** Without adding too much to a somewhat tired English folk rock genre, Oyster Band nevertheless captured some alternative ears through the mid-1990s. Collier's production certainly helped.

5 BANDIT QUEEN — **Hormone Hotel (Playtime) 1995**

4 MODERN ENGLISH — **Pillow Lips (Atlantic) 1996**

8 ROBYN HITCHCOCK — **Moss Elixir (WB) 1996**

6 MEN THEY COULDN'T HANG — **Never Born to Follow (Demon) 1996**

8 INMATES — **Silverio (Last Call) 1997** The phenomenal lungs of Bill Hurley head a pack of unrepentant blues men through tirelessly self-composed recreations of R&B's darkest, grungiest recesses.

8 ROBYN HITCHCOCK — **Jewels for Sophia (Reprise) 1999**

COP INTERNATIONAL

LABEL

America's premier dark wave/electro label of the late 1990s was launched in Frankfurt, Germany, in 1991 by Christian Koeppel — a US office was opened in Oakland, CA, soon after, and the label debuted with the *California Cyber-Crash* compilation of area industrial bands. Featuring contributions from the then red hot Consolidated, Switchblade Symphony, Xorcist, and Grotus, the set was followed by the first EP by Battery, themselves destined to score a major CMJ hit with the *Distance* album, and an on-board version of Coolio's "Gangsta's Paradise."

Deathline International, too, would score with a pair of audacious covers, of Soft Cell's "Tainted Love" and Duran Duran's "Wild Boys," stripping the latter back to its original mid-8os industrial archetype, then rebuilding from there. Originally formed as a COP label collective, featuring Consolidated's Mike Pistel, Don Gordon of Canadian extremists Numb, John Carson (Grotus) and Scott Holdergy (Mordred), Deathline eventually scaled back to Koeppel alone.

In addition to the COP label itself, the company was also responsible for bringing the European DDT label to America, as well as repackaging in-demand rarities from the Zoth Ommog and Flatline labels.

Cop International Label Listing 1991–99

001 VARIOUS ARTISTS — California Cyber Crash LP 7

002 BATTERY — Meat Market EP

003 DIATRIBE — Therapy EP

004 PAIN EMISSION — Fidget LP 6

005 BATTERY — Mutate LP 7

006 DEATHLINE INTERNATIONAL — Reality Check LP 8 Integrating diverse elements into a unique and unexpected whole, Deathline's synthi-techno-industrial-rock hybrid sound is surprisingly club-friendly, intriguing atmospheres, and totally unexpected genre blends.

007 PAIN EMISSION — Nudge EP

008 VARIOUS ARTISTS — Cyber Crash LP 6

009 BATTERY — Lilith 3.2 EP

010 DEATHLINE INTERNATIONAL — Venus Mind Trap EP

011 INDEX — Never This Infliction EP

012 PAIN EMISSION — The War Within LP 7 Leaving *Fidget*'s industrial dance behind, the group explore the darkness within the soul as the music winds through tribal rhythms, gothic gloom, spacey psychedelia, and thrash assault, all abetted by a multitude of effects and samples.

013 UNDER THE NOISE — Future Automatic EP

014 VARIOUS ARTISTS — Chaos LP 5

015 OF SKIN AND SALIVA — Sahul EP Looting far and wide for this cross-over masterpiece of jungle rhythms, hip-hop, and funk, layered with Arabesque melodies, goth atmospheres, and synthi-pop, rounded out by death metal vocals on two tracks accompanied by pure electro music — hybridization at its best.

016 BATTERY — NV LP 7 23 songs of anger, beauty, moody atmospheres, synthi-silliness, violent samples and much more, the tightly sequenced NV is a self-contained electro-encyclopedia, which miraculously holds together as a whole and never loses the band's own distinctive soul.

017 DEATHLINE INTERNATIONAL — Zarathoustra LP 8 Including new material, guest remixes of old and a searing cover of Soft Cell's "Tainted Love," Deathline continue down the road of electro-industrial mutant innovation.

018 INDEX — Sky Laced Silver LP 7 As cold as cyberspace, but burning with molten emotion, *Sky*'s melodies billow forth like gauze, softening the harsh edges of the mechanical beats and cyber blips, while dense atmospheres are conjured out of the cold heart of the electronics.

019 UNDER THE NOISE — Of Generation and Corruption LP 7 UTN's cross-genre juggling is a wonder to behold, guitars clash with jungle beats, cybersounds joust with ambient whooshes, cold wave confronts the Terminator.

020 VARIOUS ARTISTS — 13 Years of Electronic Lust LP 6

021 BATTERY — Distance LP 7 Melding together industrial, new wave, and electro-pop, *Distance* collides opposing moods, conjures up achingly poignant melodies and slides into cyber trance, while vocalist Maria Azevedo gives the album further emotive power.

022 SLAVE UNIT — Slave Unit LP 6

023 RAZOR SKYLINE — Journal of Trauma LP 8 Weaving together industrial, dark wave, gothic, and new wave, the core of TRS are the dark emotions that cast a shadowy spell across *Journal*, all wrapped in strong melodies and shrouded atmospheres, and driven by the powerful beats.

024 UNDER THE NOISE — Regeneration LP 6

025 INDEX — Black Light Twilight LP 6

026 VARIOUS ARTISTS — COP Compilation LP 7

027 VARIOUS ARTISTS — Diva X Machine Vol 1 LP 6 Intriguing collection of female-fronted goth-industrial-coldwave acts.

028 DEATHLINE INTERNATIONAL — Wild Boys EP

029 DEATHLINE INTERNATIONAL — Arashi Syndrome LP 8 Built around new wave synth melodies and atmospheres, but with edges sharp enough to shave with, *Arashi* features deft guitars, superb sampling, and a punk/industrial crunch of anger, plus the sublime cover of Duran Duran's "Wild Boys."

030 FISHTANK #9 — Itself LP 7

031 URANIA — Aquarious LP 5

032 VARIOUS ARTISTS — 14 Years of Electronic Challenge Vol 2 LP 6

033 SOIL & ECLIPSE — Necromancy LP 6

034 PULSE LEGION — Evolve LP 6

035 IVOUX — Frozen LP 5

036 INDEX — Faith in Motion LP 5

037 VARIOUS ARTISTS — Cop Vol 2 LP 7

038 IMBUE — Resurrected LP 7

039 VARIOUS ARTISTS — Diva X Machine Vol 2 LP 7

040 RINGTAILED SNORTER — Look Back in the Mirror LP 8

041 BATTERY — Momentum EP

042 VARIOUS ARTISTS — New Violent Breed LP 4

043 PAIN STATION — Disjointed LP 6

044 BATTERY — Aftermath LP 7

045 VARIOUS ARTISTS — 15 Years of Electronic Challenge Vol 3 LP 7

046 SOIL & ECLIPSE — Meridian LP [6]
047 SIGNAL 12 — Signal 12 LP [6]
048 RAZOR SKYLINE — Fade & Sustain LP [8]
049 unreleased
050 BIRMINGHAM 6 — Resurrection LP [8] Retrospective collection high-lighting rare and deleted material by Denmark's best loved electro warriors.

CRASS RECORDS

LABEL

No matter how uncompromising Crass might have seemed, their own label frequently went even further.

Also see the entry for "CRASS" on page 294.

Crass Records Label Listing 1977–84
1 CRASS — Reality Asylum 7-inch
621984 CRASS — The Feeding of the 5,000 LP [8]
521984/1 DONNA & THE KEBABS — You Can Be You 7-inch
521984 CRASS — Stations of the Crass LP [8]
421984/1 CRASS — Bloody Revolutions 7-inch
421984/2 POISON GIRLS — Chappaquidick Bridge 7-inch
421984/3 ZOUNDS — Can't Cheat Karma 7-inch
421984/4 VARIOUS ARTISTS — Bullshit Detector Volume I LP [8]
421984/5 CRASS — Nagasaki Nightmare 7-inch
421984/6 CRASS — Rival Tribal Rebel Revel 7-inch
421984/6f *TOXIC GRAFITY* FANZINE
421984/7 POISON GIRLS — Statement 7-inch
421984/8 POISON GIRLS — All Systems Go 7-inch
421984/9 POISON GIRLS — Hex LP [5]
321984/1f CRASS — Our Wedding (Flexi)
321984/1 CRASS — Penis Envy LP [9]
321984/2 FLUX OF PINK INDIANS — Neu Smell 7-inch
321984/3 ANNIE ANXIETY — Barbed Wire Halo 7-inch
321984/4 SNIPERS — Three Peace Suit 7-inch
321984/5 CAPTAIN SENSIBLE — This Is Your Captain Speaking 7-inch
321984/6 DIRT — Death Is Reality Today 7-inch
321984/7 MOB — No Doves Fly Here 7-inch
CTI 1 CRASS — Merry Crassmass 7-inch
221984/1 CONFLICT — The House That Man Built 7-inch
221984/2 RUDIMENTARY PENI — Farce 7-inch
Bollox2u2 CRASS — Christ: the Album LP [8]
221984/3 VARIOUS ARTISTS — Bullshit Detector Volume II LP [9]
221984/4 CRAVATS — Rub Me Out 7-inch
221984/5 AND Y — Weary of the Flesh LP [5]
221984/6 CRASS — How Does It Feel... 7-inch

221984/7 DIRT — Never Mind Dirt, Here's the Bollocks LP [7]
221984/8 ALTERNATIVE — In Nomine Patri 7-inch
221984/9 ANTHRAX — Capitalism Is Cannibalism 7-inch
221984/10 OMEGA TRIBE — Angry Songs 7-inch
221984/11 SLEEPING DOGS — Beware Sleeping Dogs 7-inch
221984/12 HIT PARADE — Bad News 7-inch
121984/1 D&V — The Nearest Door 7-inch
121984/2 CRASS — Yes Sir, I Will LP [8]
121984/3 CRASS — Sheep Farming in the Falklands 7-inch
121984/4 CRASS — Whodunnit? 7-inch
121984/5 MDC — Multi Death Corporation 7-inch
121984/6 LACK OF KNOWLEDGE — Grey 7-inch
1984 CRASS — You're Already Dead 7-inch
1984/1 KUKL — The Eye LP [6]
1984/207370 HIT PARADE — Plastic Culture 7-inch
1984/4 PENNY RIMBAUD — Acts of Love LP [8]
1 D&V — D&V LP [6]
2 JANE GREGORY — After a Dream LP [7]
3 VARIOUS ARTISTS — Bullshit Detector Volume III LP [8]
4 KUKL — Holidays in Europe LP [7]
5 CRASS — Best Before LP [9]
6 CRASS — Ten Notes on a Summer's Day EP
7 HIT PARADE — Nick Knack Paddy Whack LP [6]
8 VARIOUS ARTISTS — A-Sides 1979–82 LP [9]
9 VARIOUS ARTISTS — A-Sides 1982–84 LP [9] The Crass Label collection in all its shuddering glory!
10 PENNY RIMBAUD — Christ's Reality Asylum LP [5]
Spoken word.

C/Z RECORDS

LABEL

Alongside Sub Pop, Skin Yard bassist Daniel House's C/Z label was singlehandedly responsible for defining the sound and direction which the so-called grunge boom of the late 1980s would take.

Debuting with the retrospectively crucial *Deep Six* compilation, featuring early contributions from Soundgarden, Green River, Malfunkshun, the U-Men, and the Melvins, C/Z maintained a stream of genre-defining compilations through the late 1980s, most notably the *Teriyaki Asthma* collection of future Pacific Northwest heavyweights (see page 757), and *Another Pyrrhic Victory*, immortalizing some of the bands which didn't make it through. Other early recruits to the label included Hammerbox and Coffin Break, while producer Jack Endino, too, would become synonymous with C/Z.

By the early 1990s, C/Z was being distributed through A&M Records, raising the label's profile without necessarily providing any more muscle than word-of-mouth had already provided — tribute albums to KISS and the Buzzcocks, as usual featuring the crème de la local crème, both became regional smashes, while the classically trained Sara DeBell's much-applauded *GrungeLite* album paid tribute to another of the region's best-loved institutions, the Muzak corporation.

Several times in the mid-late 1990s, the label seemed to be stuttering, cutting back on releases, and foregoing new signings. New releases from Love Battery, Posies bassist Joe Howard, and a *Teriyaki Asthma* anthology, however, ensured C/Z's continued role in the development of local music.

C/Z Label Listing 1986–92

1 VARIOUS ARTISTS — Deep Six LP 7 Seminal premier compilation of Seattle rock circa 1986; Green River, the Melvins, Malfunkshun, Skinyard, and Soundgarden included.

2 MELVINS — 10 Songs [LIVE] EP

3 SKIN YARD — Skinyard LP 5

4 SKIN YARD — Gelatin Babies 7-inch

5 MY EYE — Empty Box 7-inch

6 VARIOUS ARTISTS — Secretions LP 6

7 COFFIN BREAK — Coffin Break EP

8 VEXED — Maybe 7-inch

9 VARIOUS ARTISTS — Teriyaki Asthma EP

10 COFFIN BREAK — Psychosis LP 5

11 SLACK — Deep Like Space LP 4

12 VARIOUS ARTISTS — Another Pyrrhic Victory LP 7 Or, Dead Seattle God Bands. A touching document, soon to become poignant.

13 VARIOUS ARTISTS — Teriyaki Asthma II EP

14 DADDY HATE BOX — Daddy Hate Box EP

15 YEAST — Crisco Wristwatch 7-inch

16 TONE DOGS — Ankety Low Day LP 5

17 VARIOUS ARTISTS — Teriyaki Asthma III EP

18 COFFIN BREAK — Pop Fanatic 7-inch

19 CRYPT KICKER FIVE — Crypt Kicker Five EP

20 COFFIN BREAK — Rupture LP 6

21 VEXED — The Good Fight LP 5

22 ICKY JOEY — Marron Marron 7-inch

23 VARIOUS ARTISTS — Teriyaki Asthma IV EP

24 VARIOUS ARTISTS — Hard to Believe: A Tribute to KISS LP 8 One of the first US tribute albums, and subsequently one of the most important — if only for the inclusion of the infant Nirvana. The other major selling point is, most of the bands here were KISS fans first.

25 VARIOUS ARTISTS — Teriyaki Asthma V EP

26 ICKY JOEY — Pooh 7-inch

27 THE HULLABALOO — Lubritorium LP 6

28 DOSE — Singleton

29 HAMMERBOX — Hammerbox LP 5

30 COFFIN BREAK — Kill the President 7-inch

31 JONESTOWN — Screw Crude 7-inch

32 DEADSPOT — Built in Pain LP 3

33 MY NAME — A Woman's Touch 7-inch

34 PAIN TEENS — Sacrificial Shack 7-inch

35 HENRY ROLLINS/HARD ONS — Let There Be Rock 7-inch

36 VARIOUS ARTISTS — Teriyaki Asthma VI EP

37 VARIOUS ARTISTS — Teriyaki Asthma I–V LP 8

38 COFFIN BREAK — No Sleep Till the Stardust Motel LP 7

39 PORN ORCHARD — Urges and Angers LP 7

40 TREEPEOPLE — Something Vicious for Tomorrow LP 8

41 VARIOUS ARTISTS — Teriyaki Asthma VII EP

42 VARIOUS ARTISTS — Something's Gone Wrong Again: A Tribute to the Buzzcocks LP 8 Again the fans turned up first, and though history doesn't resonate so powerfully, still the line-up (including the so aptly named Love Battery) impresses a sense of the city's true activities, even as "grunge" prepared to leak everywhere.

43 RHYTHM PIGS — Choke on This LP 6

44 GNOME — Six Hi Surprise Tower LP 6

45 7 YEAR BITCH — Loma 7-inch

46 MY NAME — Megacrush LP 4

47 MONKS OF DOOM — The Insect God EP

48 7 YEAR BITCH — Sick 'Em 7-inch

49 VARIOUS ARTISTS — Teriyaki Asthma VIII EP

50 TREEPEOPLE — Outside in LP 6

Teriyaki Asthma Anthology

A series of vinyl EPs, pressed in limited quantities ranging between 1,000 (volume I) and 2,500 (volumes VI through IX), giving early exposure to a host of then-unknown bands. Subsequently anthologized across two CDs in 1991 and 1999, the nine original releases were joined by a putative tenth, available only on the second CD.

ALICE DONUT — Mrs. Hayes

AMORPHOUS HEAD — Lonely Lonely

BABES IN TOYLAND — Fleshcrawl

COFFIN BREAK — Hole in the Ground

CRACKERBASH — Head Like a Weedeater

DADDY HATE BOX — Look Like Hell

DICKLESS — Sweet Teeth

DOSE — Eyesore

FRIGHTWIG — Highway to Hell

GAS HUFFER — Hijacked

GOD'S ACRE — Wood

HAMMERBOX — Promise to Never

HELIOS CREED — America Is in Good Hands
HULLABALOO — Kill Yr Parents
ICKY JOEY — Josephine
JONESTOWN — Fuck You High and Get You Up
LJ — Bloodstains
LOVE BATTERY — Commercial Suicide (Vol X)
MX 80 — Surfin' Pope
MY NAME — Hold On
NIRVANA — Mexican Seafood
OLIVE LAWN — You're a Dick and I'm Gonna Kill You
PAIN TEENS — Come Up and See Me Sometime
PITBULL BABYSITTER — Head Talks Cheese
PORN ORCHARD — What Kills
POSTER CHILDREN — It's True
SEMIBEINGS — Disco of Bums (Vol X)
SKYWARD — Masque Your Fear (Vol X)
STYMIE — One Proud Stout
SUPERCHUNK — Sister
SUPERCONDUCTOR — There She Goes
TFUL #282 — Wally & the Ghost (Vol X)
THROWN UPS — Walrus Head
TRASH CAN SCHOOL — Hobgoblins
TREEPEOPLE — Drawing Class
TSUNAMI — Punk Means Cuddle
UNREST — Caitlin Burns
VEXED — Gwym
WEEN — Long Legged Sally Was a No Necked Whore
YEAST — Solid Alligators

RHETT DAVIES

PRODUCER

Londoner Davies was engineer on Eno's crucial *Taking Tiger Mountain by Strategy* album in 1974, leading to a lengthy collaboration both with Eno, and with his former colleagues in Roxy Music.

An ambient pioneer through his work on Eno's seminal *Music for Films*, and engineer on Eno and David Byrne's tribal flavored *My Life in the Bush of Ghosts*, Davies could claim to be present at the birth of two of the most enduring musical forms of the 1990s.

However, Davies would be best associated over the next decade (he retired from music in 1990) with the increasingly sensuous layering of grooves and rhythms which characterized Roxy's later records, and despite such quirky (but effective) sidelines as the B-52's, Talk Talk, and Huang Chung, Davies' work through the 1980s would become synonymous with the big gloss sound of the decade, peaking with his 1986–88 union with 'Til Tuesday.

Rhett Davies — Selected Productions

6 BRIAN ENO — Another Green World (EG) 1975 "Somber Reptiles" adds to Eno's canon, "Skysaw" lent much to Japan's, but after the mania of his first two albums, *Another Green World* was a little grey pause.

9 ENO — Before and After Science (EG) 1977 Reacting to both the insurgence of punk and his recent experiences with David Bowie, Eno responds with what emerged as the center point around which much of 1977 (and beyond) would revolve — either rushing to, or emerging from the shattered fractures of Eno's (p)recognitions.

Kicking off with the white boy pop-funk of "No One Receiving" — soon to inspire the New Romantics, *Science* breezes into the art pop of "Kurt's Rejoinder," with the quirky rhythms which Wire will make their own; on into the soundscapes which are the starting point for the Orb and Aphex Twin, and "Here He Comes," the template for the '60s pop of Postcard; before the whole menage climaxes with the unexpected "King's Lead Hat," raucous aggression as a tribute to the Talking Heads (the title is anagram).

7 ENO — Music for Films (EG) 1978
6 AFTER THE FIRE — After the Fire (Epic) 1979
7 STARJETS — Starjets (Epic) 1979 Hopping happy power-pop with nothing to say, but a big grin while it does so.
7 B-52's — Wild Planet (WB) 1980
6 HITMEN — Torn Together (CBS) 1981
4 HUANG CHUNG — Torn Together (CBS) 1982
6 TALK TALK — The Party's Over (EMI America) 1982 Disappointing sophomore set from a band once poised to out-Duran Duran, and still awaiting the one great song ("It's My Life") which would prove they were actually capable of doing so.
5 OMD — Dazzle Ships (Virgin) 1983 "Genetic Engineering" was more than the best song, it was also the curse of an album which should have stayed in the studio's operating handbook. New technology is nice, but we don't need to hear people learning how it works.
6 ICEHOUSE — Measure for Measure (Chrysalis) 1986
4 'TIL TUESDAY — Welcome Home (Epic) 1986
4 'TIL TUESDAY — Everything's Different Now (Epic) 1988
3 THEN JERICHO — The Big Area (MCA)

DISCHORD

LABEL

Alongside Black Flag's SST and the Dead Kennedy's Alternative Tentacles, Dischord was the premier player on the early American hardcore scene. Launched by DC punk Ian MacKaye as a host for the first release by his own band, the

Teen Idles, Dischord followed through with the first release by Henry Rollins' SOA, before MacKaye's new band, Minor Threat, exploded into view with the *Filler* EP.

Dedicated exclusively to hardcore, Dischord's almost evangelical approach to the music saw the label encourage and develop scenes across the US, as well as spread the word about them once they had emerged — the *Flex Your Head* compilation issued jointly with Alternative Tentacles in 1982 did much to popularize Dischord's output on the west coast, long before the likes of SOA, Government Issue, and Iron Cross would be able to make it across country themselves.

Other key Dischord acts included Rites of Spring, whose members would eventually join MacKaye in Fugazi, Scream, from whence Dave Grohl (Nirvana/Foo Fighters) would emerge, and Boston straight-edge pioneers SS Decontrol.

Also see the entry for "FUGAZI" on page 378.

Dischord Label Listing 1980–85

1 TEEN IDLES — Minor Disturbance EP

2 SOA — No Policy EP

3 MINOR THREAT — Filler EP

4 GOVERNMENT ISSUE — Legless Bull EP

4 1/2 NECROS — Iq32 EP

5 MINOR THREAT — In My Eyes EP

6 YOUTH BRIGADE — Possible EP

7 VARIOUS ARTISTS — Flex Your Head LP 7 Album also released on Alternative Tentacles.

8 FAITH/VOID — Split LP 6

8 1/2 IRON CROSS — Skinhead Glory EP

9 SCREAM — Still Screaming LP 8 *Suburban Voice* magazine's Record of the Year, a violent but very thoughtful slab of aggression.

10 MINOR THREAT — Out of Step EP

10 1/2 DOUBLE O — You've Lost EP

10 3/4 GOVERNMENT ISSUE — Boycott Stabb EP

10 7/8 UNITED MUTATION — Fugitive Family EP

11 FAITH — Subject to Change EP

12 MINOR THREAT — 2 7-Inchers on a 12-Inch EP

13 MARGINAL MAN — Identity EP

14 VARIOUS ARTISTS — 4 Old 7-Inchers LP 8

15 MINOR THREAT — Salad Days EP

15 1/2 SCREAM — This Side Up LP 7

15 3/4 REPTILE HOUSE — I Stumble as the Crow Flies EP

16 RITES OF SPRING — Rites of Spring LP 7

17 BEEFEATER — Plays for Lovers LP 5

17 1/2 MISSION IMPOSSIBLE/LUNCHMEAT — Thanks EP

18 SNAKES — I Won't Love You Till You're More Like Me LP 6

19 DAG NASTY — Can I Say? LP 7 Ian MacKaye produced, Brian Baker led, DC hardcore at its mid-80s best.

20 EGG HUNT — Egg Hunt EP

21 GRAY MATTER — Take It Back EP

22 RITES OF SPRING — All Through a Life EP

22 1/2 SOUL SIDE — Less Deep Inside Keeps LP 6

23 BEEFEATER — House Burning Down LP 7

24 EMBRACE — Embrace LP 8

25 SCREAM — Banging the Drum LP 7

DUST BROTHERS

PRODUCERS

BORN *John King and Michael Simpson*

Having first met in 1983 at Pomona College, CA, the Dust Brothers came to note as producers of Delicious Vinyl label stars Tone Loc and Young MC in 1989, commissions which then saw them brought into the Beastie Boys' *Paul's Boutique* project.

Despite the album's landmark qualities, its success and influence did not immediately affect the Dust Brothers' work rate — most of their activities over the next five years centered around remix work, with their overseas fame resting on their request that another pair of Dust Brothers operating in the UK find themselves a new name.

In 1996, meanwhile, the Dust Brothers produced Beck's *O-de-lay*, after which their reputation soared, collectively and individually — as a staff producer at Dreamworks, Simpson alone would produce the Eels' acclaimed *Beautiful Freak*; King handled Porno for Pyros' contribution to TV host Howard Stern's *Private Parts* compilation. The Dust Brothers would also supervise the Rolling Stones' *Bridges to Babylon* set, and the debut album by Hanson.

They also launched their own recording career with the 1997 single, "Realize," appropriately released as a specially commissioned Chemical Brothers remix. The Dust Brothers for their part would remix the Chemicals' "Elektrobank." An album, the soundtrack to the Helena Bonham Carter vehicle *Fight Club*, followed in 1999.

Dust Brothers — Selected Productions

10 BEASTIE BOYS — Paul's Boutique (Capitol) 1989

7 TECHNOTRONIC — Trip on This (Capitol) 1990

3 WESLEY WILLIS — Feel the Power (American) 1996 A diagnosed schizophrenic, street performer Willis was thrust to mainstream attention with two near-simultaneous collections of raw, three-chord ranting, *Fabian Road Warrior* and *Feel the Power*. Production makes little difference to what are essentially 24 near identical songs about the people closest to him when they were recorded — label staff, other bands, the Dust Brothers themselves. Entertaining in short doses, but street performers are often performing on the street for a reason.

BECK — O-De-Lay (Geffen) 1996

7 BRIDGID BODEN — Oh, How I Cry (A&M) 1996

6 WHITE ZOMBIE — Supersexy Swingin' Sounds (DGC) 1996

6 SUGARTOOTH — The Sounds of Solid (Geffen) 1997

5 BECK — Midnight Vultures (DGC) 1999

MITCH EASTER

PRODUCER

BORN 11/15/54 (North Carolina)

Through the mid-late 1970s, Easter was a member of power-pop icons the Sneakers and Rittenhouse Square, bands formed with future dB's Chris Stamey and Peter Holsapple. Later, during a sojourn in New York, he would play with an early incarnation of future Twin/Tone signings, the Crackers.

Returning to N.C. in 1980, Easter established his own Drive-In Studio in his parents' garage in Winston-Salem, opening the doors to a string of local bands and friends. Early clients included the dB's, who used the Drive-In for mixing (Easter would later produce several albums for the band's own dB label). The Crackers did some recording there, while an unknown Athens band named REM would also avail themselves of Easter's expertise for their debut, "Radio Free Europe."

REM would become Easter's most regular clients through the early-mid-1980s; Game Theory through the remainder of the decade, confirming Easter's studios as ground zero for the jangle pop movement which swirled through the decade. Easter also launched his own new band, Let's Active, in 1986, but by 1988, he was concentrating exclusively on production, with a client base which subsequently included Pavement, Helium, Britain's momentarily hot Moose and Velvet Crush, who lured him back to performing following the completion of their *Teenage Symphonies* album.

Mitch Easter — Selected Productions

4 REM — Chronic Town (IRS) 1982

6 REM — Murmur (IRS) 1983

7 CHRIS STAMEY — It's a Wonderful Life (dB) 1983

6 RICHARD BARONE — Nuts and Bolts (Passport) 1983 Bongos frontman Barone and guitarist James Mastro recreating '60s American pop sounds in their own band's image.

10 REM — Reckoning (IRS) 1984

7 GAME THEORY — Real Nightmare (Enigma) 1984 Chronically Chilton-ian hangover from the paisley underground, digni-

fied by the stand-outs "Curse of the Frontierland" and near-hit "24."

7 GAME THEORY — Big Shot Chronicles (Enigma) 1985 Gritty sophomore set perched on the edge of a new breed of psychedelia (see "Crash Into June") which it never quite gets round to exploring. "I've Tried Subtlety," on the other hand, would have sounded great on English radio in 1972.

6 WINDBREAKERS — Run (dB) 1986

9 BOBBY SUTCLIFF — Only Ghosts Remain (Passport) 1987 With Richard Thompson's "Small Town Romance" joining the stunning *Another Jangly Mess* EP, even half of Sutcliff's first post-Windbreakers album would be a marvel. Add five more, and it's his most dramatic (lyrically and sonically) yet.

6 GAME THEORY — Lolita Nation (Enigma) 1987 Another shift in direction, caught maybe a little too early. A dramatically transitional double album, experimenting with both sound and spoken word, much of the record disconcerts in the same way as picking up cell phone transmissions on your stereo disconcerts. "We Love You Carol and Alice" is a marvel, however.

7 THE CONNELLS — Boylan Heights (TVT) 1987 Mature, graceful, cohesive and very, very college rock circa 1987. So it was just right.

7 WAXING POETIC — Hermitage (Emergo) 1987

6 GAME THEORY — Two Steps from the Middle Ages (Enigma) 1988

5 VELVET ELVIS — Velvet Elvis (Enigma) 1988

5 HUMMINGBIRDS — Love Buzz (Roo Art) 1989 Overly sweet and sickly Australian harmony band, making all the right sounds, hitting all the right notes, but at close to an hour... it's way too much.

5 LOVE TRACTOR — Themes from Venus (DB) 1989

5 WINDBREAKERS — At Home with Bobby & Tim (DB) 1990 Tim Lee and Bobby Sutcliff reunion under the old band name, but lacking a lot of their original fire. After Sutcliff's *Ghosts*, a real backward step.

5 JOHN AND MARY — Victory Gardens (Rykodisc) 1991

6 QUESTIONNAIRES — Anything Can Happen (EMI) 1991

4 LAVA LOVE — Aphrodisia (Sky) 1992

6 MOOSE — XYZ (Hut) 1992 Caught somewhere between the death of Britain's new wave of new wave fixation, and the birth of the somewhat more successful Brit-pop movement, an entertaining but ultimately unmemorable attempt to graft some of that there American-sounding magic onto a clutch of distinctly Anglo-themed songs.

5 LOUD FAMILY — Plants & Birds & Rocks & Things (Alias) 1993 Ex-Game Theory Scott pulls his title from America's "Horse with No Name" and his sound from *Lolita Nation*. So, a lot of unnecessary noodling goes on around the songs, but the writing is solid and the music is tight.

7 MOTOCASTER — Stay Loaded (Interscope) 1994

7 LOUD FAMILY — The Tape of Only Linda (Alias) 1994 This time named for a notorious Paul McCartney live bootleg, a sharper, and less gimmicky vision than last time out, but still wryly humorous.

6 VELVET CRUSH — Teenage Symphonies to God (550) 1994

5 GROVER — My Wild Life (Zero Hour) 1996

6 DRAG — Satellites Beaming Back at You (Island) 1996

7 HELIUM — The Magic City (Matador) 1997

8 PAVEMENT — Brighten the Corners (Matador) 1997

8 WASHINGTON SQUARES — From Greenwich Village (Razor & Tie) 1997

7 VELVET CRUSH — Heavy Changes (Action Musik) 1998

7 HANG UPS — Second Story (Restless) 1999

DAVE EDMUNDS

PRODUCER

BORN *4/15/44 (Cardiff, Wales)*

As guitarist with Welsh blues-psych rockers Love Sculpture, Edmunds first came to attention for "Sabre Dance," a break-neck guitar rendering of the classical staple, in 1968. He moved into production at the same time as launching a solo career, scoring immediate success in both capacities when his first single, "I Hear You Knocking," topped the UK chart in December 1970.

Obsessive beyond the point of perfection, Edmunds' production expertise would only occasionally be available for hire — working to standards which would make Phil Spector, Sam Phillips, and Joe Meek feel humble, Edmunds created a wall-of-sound technique that was utterly unique, vast swathes of orchestration swelling across spot-on pastiches of his beloved '50s rock. "Born to Be with You," a UK hit in 1973, might well be the best-sounding record ever made in Britain.

In 1974, Edmunds was employed to oversee the soundtrack to the rock movie *Stardust*, linking with singing actor David Essex and Nick Lowe's Brinsley Schwarz as the Stray Cats for an album's worth of painstakingly recreated Beat Boom-era material; six years later, an American band of the same name would come to Edmunds with a virtual carbon copy of the same material.

Edmunds' first outside production of note was the initial demos recorded by Motorhead, shelved by the band's label of the time and unreleased for another two decades. He followed up by reuniting with pub rockers Brinsley Schwarz, birthing a partnership with Lowe which would persist into the 1990s, then remained within that genre to produce Ducks Deluxe.

American retro-specialists Flamin' Groovies visited his Rockpile studios in 1976, and were gifted with their first album to actually match their ambitions and, while Edmunds' best-known work remained his own continuing career (both solo and alongside Lowe in Rockpile), he would also be instrumental in establishing the credentials of the Stiff label, following its inception in 1976. Released on the *Bunch of Stiffs* label sampler only, his production of Jill Read's "Maybe" so effortlessly updated the sound of the early '60s girl groups that the listener's first inclination was to check the record's copyright date.

Through the early 1980s, Edmunds worked successfully with the Stray Cats, Squeeze, and the Polecats, before 1984 brought what he considers his greatest accolade, producing the Everly Brothers' reunion album. Since that time, however, he has largely dropped out of sight, surfacing only occasionally (with kd lang, the Fabulous Thunderbirds and, of course, Nick Lowe), and releasing occasional new albums of his own.

Dave Edmunds — Selected Production

7 BRINSLEY SCHWARZ — New Favorites of (UA) 1974 "Peace, Love, and Understanding" now stands high above the rest of Nick Lowe's pre-solo output. At the time, however, it was just another song on an album riddled with similar class.

8 DUCKS DELUXE — Taxi to the Terminal Zone (RCA) 1975 Two years later, Ducks would have fit so effortlessly into the Lowe/Costello/Dury end of punk that their prescience still galls today. Driving R&B with a definitive snarl.

7 FLAMIN' GROOVIES — Shake Some Action (SIRE) 1976 The title track is a bona fide classic; elsewhere, the Groovies' approximation of the rock'n'roll high school at a Rolling Stones hop puts authenticity over excitement, and sometimes sounds just a little bit too perfect.

6 FLAMIN' GROOVIES — Now (Sire) 1978

8 POLECATS — Are Go (Mercury) 1981 Mercurial rockabilly revival act, whose take on Bowie's "John I'm Only Dancing" remains a genre-crushing classic. Four further tracks from these sessions appeared on the band's sophomore album, *Make a Circuit.*

8 STRAY CATS — Stray Cats (Arista) 1981

7 STRAY CATS — Gonna Ball (Arista) 1981

7 STRAY CATS — Rant 'n' rave (Emi America) 1983

7 KING KURT — Ooh Wallah Wallah (Stiff) 1983 Reformed madmen, hearty enough for the hottest hardcore party but stepping back, slowing down, and opting for undiluted lunacy instead. "Destination Zululand," an unforgettable UK hit single, torpedoes much of this album's attempts to impress, but still it's a riotous way of wasting half an hour.

6 FABULOUS THUNDERBIRDS — Tuff Enough (CBS) 1986

5 FABULOUS THUNDERBIRDS — Hot Number (Epic) 1987

6 KD LANG — Angel with a Lariat (Sire) 1987

6 STRAY CATS — Blast Off (EMI America) 1989

6 BREWERS DROOP — The Booze Brothers (Red Lightnin') 1989

7 NICK LOWE — Party of One (Reprise) 1990

JACK ENDINO

PRODUCER

If any one man can be said to have designed the Seattle sound of the late 1980s, it was Jack Endino. A fan and a musician, he originally fell into production through recording his own efforts on a primitive two tape deck set up, before graduating onto a four track machine and producing the seminal *Deep Six* compilation for the new-born *C/Z* label. Making a local household name from Endino's Reciprocal Studios, Green River, Soundgarden, the U-Men, the Melvins, and Malfunkshun all appeared on that album, and over the next two years, Endino produced Green River's *Dry as a Bone*, Mudhoney's *Superfuzz Bigmuff*, Soundgarden's *Screaming Life* EPs, and Nirvana's first demos.

He also cut two solo albums, *Angle of Attack* and *Jack Endino's Earthworm*, and formed Skin Yard with C/Z chief Daniel House. Their *Skin Yard* debut album was Endino's first experience of producing a full-length album.

With partner Chris Hensack, Endino upgraded to eight tracks in July 1986; by the time he came to produce Nirvana's *Bleach* debut album, the studio was ready to make the transition to 24 — still, the producer is adamant that the earlier set-up was all that the seminal late '80s C/Z and Sub Pop productions required. Nevertheless, the upgrade would not impair his ability to capture a band at their most primal, even away from the familiar surroundings of Reciprocal. As the Seattle scene exploded into major labeldom (an area Endino would for the most part keep away from), he found himself accepting invitations to travel as far afield as Australia and Argentina, to produce local bands.

Neither did the decline of the Seattle sound's popularity affect his work rate, although many of his best later productions maintained contacts he made back in the first flurry of grunge, producing latter-day albums by Mudhoney, Seaweed, Mark Lanegan and the Supersuckers.

Jack Endino — Selected Productions

5 SOUNDGARDEN — Screaming Life (Sub Pop) 1987

7 GREEN RIVER — Dry As a Bone (Sub Pop) 1987

5 SKIN YARD — Skin Yard (C/Z) 1987

6 SKIN YARD — Hallowed Ground (Toxic Shock) 1988

10 MUDHONEY — Superfuzz Bigmuff (Sub Pop) 1988 Like the "Touch Me, I'm Sick" single which preceded it, the six song *Superfuzz Bigmuff* stated in its very title all that listeners could

expect — assuming the very combination of Green River (Arm and Turner) and the Melvins (Lukin) did not cue them in first.

A colossal noise, slashing wah wah with feedback, Mudhoney drew their antecedents from garage rock's least frequented corners — they worshipped the Stooges, but were surely the only kids in class who thought "L.A. Jam" had a tune or a point; they were obsessed with old garage rock singles, but only the ones released on obscure backroom indies, and recorded for less than the cost of a pint.

And what the rest of the world called "grunge," and traced back through Aerosmith and Led Zeppelin, Mudhoney were still calling punk and blaming on Billy Childish. It was no coincidence whatsoever that at a time when most Brits didn't even know Childish had recorded 50 albums, there were people in Seattle who actually owned them — and based their entire vision upon his skewed perspective.

6 SWALLOW — Swallow (Tupelo) 1989

6 NIRVANA — Bleach (Sub Pop) 1989

8 MUDHONEY — Mudhoney (Sub Pop) 1989

5 HELIOS CREED — The Last Laugh (Amphetamine Reptile) 1989

4 TAD — God's Ball (Sub Pop) 1989

5 FLUID — Roadmouth (Sub Pop) 1989

7 SCREAMING TREES — Change Has Come EP (Sub Pop) 1989

6 SCREAMING TREES — Buzz Factory (SST) 1989

9 DWARVES — Blood, Guts & Pussy (Sub Pop) 1990 The Dwarves' rancid, nihilist, minimalist scampering was never going to impact on a larger scale, even before their label dropped them for pretending their singer was dead. But blasting through the ghosts of all that "big rock" held so holy, their sudden shock punk had an adrenaline pump mainlined to its heart. Exhausting to listen to, but impossible to resist.

6 LOVESLUG — Beef Jerky (Glitterhouse — Germany) 1990

8 MARK LANEGAN — The Winding Sheet (Sub Pop) 1990 Lanegan's cloaked, choked darkness owed much to Leonard Cohen, but even more to the crusted glamour of his assumed lifestyle. *The Winding Sheet* is sparse, gray, lonely. And very beautiful.

7 BABES IN TOYLAND — Spanking Machine (Twin/Tone) 1990 Psychopathic jack-hammering, screeching, yowling, motor-twin city madness.

5 ACCUSED — Grinning like an Undertaker (Nastymix) 1990

5 SOLOMON GRUNDY — Solomon Grundy (New Alliance) 1990

5 GRUNTRUCK — Inside Yours (Empty) 1990

6 OLIVELAWN — Sap (Cargo) 1990

6 SWALLOW — Sourpuss (Glitterhouse — Germany) 1990

6 DERELICTS — Love Machine (Penultimate) 1990

5 SKIN YARD — Fist Sized Chunks (Cruz) 1990

7 THROWN UPS — Thrown Ups (Glitterhouse — Germany) 1990 Pre-Green River/Mudhoney aggregation, reconvened to make a glorious noise.

6 COFFIN BREAK — Rupture (C/Z) 1990

8 AFGHAN WHIGS — Up in It (Sub Pop) 1990

6 GAS HUFFER — Janitors of Tomorrow (Empty) 1991

6 DON'T MEAN MAYBE — Real Good Life (Dr Dream) 1991

5 LOVE AND RESPECT — Love and Respect (Penultimate) 1991

7 COFFIN BREAK — Crawl (Epitaph) 1991

5 OLIVELAWN — Sophomore Jinx (Cargo) 1991

5 WEATHER THEATER — Dusk (Angry Fish) 1991

7 SKIN YARD — 1000 Smiling Knuckles (Cruz) 1991

6 COFFIN BREAK — No Sleep Till the Stardust Motel (C/Z) 1991

6 DERELICTS — Don't Wanna Live (Sub Pop) 1991

7 LOVE BATTERY — Between the Eyes (Sub Pop) 1992

4 WILLARD — Steel Mill (Roadrunner) 1992

3 BOGHANDLE — Step on It (Rock Owl — Denmark) 1992

6 HUNGRY CROCODILES — 100 Million Watts (Swamptown) 1992

6 SUPERSUCKERS — The Smoke of Hell (Sub Pop) 1992

5 VALENTINE SALOON — Super Duper (Pipeline) 1992

5 ZIP GUN — Eight Track Player (Empty) 1992

6 COFFIN BREAK — Thirteen (Epitaph) 1992

6 GAS HUFFER — Integrity Technology & Service (Empty) 1992

5 SEAWEED — Weak (Sub Pop) 1992

6 REIN SANCTION — Mariposa (Sub Pop) 1992

6 FALLOUTS — Here I Come and Other Hits (Sub Pop) 1993 Steve Turner side project, gratuitously loose and livid, but firmly locked back into those old Stooges albums again.

6 LOVESLUG — Circus of Values (Glitterhouse — Germany) 1993

7 DIRT FISHERMEN — Vena Cava (C/Z) 1993

6 VEXED — Cathexis (C/Z) 1993

6 BOGHANDLE — Worth Dying For (Sony — Denmark) 1993

5 UNEARTH — Everything Was Beautiful (New Rage) 1993

7 TITAS — Titanomaquia (Warner — Brazil) 1993

7 HAZEL — Toreador of Love (Sub Pop) 1993

4 GRUNTRUCK — Push (Roadrunner) 1993

4 SKIN YARD — Inside the Eye (Cruz) 1993

7 BABES IN TOYLAND — Painkiller (WB) 1993

7 POP SICKLE — Under the Influences (C/Z) 1993

6 BUCKET — Brother Fear (Bucket) 1994

4 KERBDOG — Kerbdog (Phonogram) 1994

5 MIKE JOHNSON — Where Am I? (Up) 1994

8 DANCING FRENCH LIBERALS OF '48 — Dancing French... (Broken) 1994 The Gits reconvene following the murder of vocalist Mia Zapata, redirecting their past punk energies towards more esoteric territory, but still dramatically engaging.

6 GUILLOTINA — Guillotina (WB — Mexico) 1994

7 SEVEN YEAR BITCH — Viva Zapata (C/Z) 1994 Mia Zapata's death haunts Bitch too, rousing the emotions, fears, and an anger which distinguished their finest album yet.

6 FITZ OF DEPRESSION — Let's Give It a Twist (K) 1994

8 MUDHONEY — My Brother the Cow (WB) 1995 That Mudhoney progressed (some said improved) to the point where, by the time of 1991's *Every Good Boy Deserves Fudge*, they seemed destined to follow Nirvana to nirvana, was beside the point. That they would eventually sign a major deal (in time for 1993's *Piece of Cake*) was an absolute irrelevance. What mattered was why "Cow" mattered. Because they still sounded like sludge on vacation, a glorious, retching racket; punk rock in excelsis.

5 TITAS — Domingo (Warner — Brazil) 1995

4 TAD — Infrared Riding Hood (Eastwest) 1995

4 SPIKE — Whelmed (Y) 1995

6 TEEN ANGELS — Daddy (Sub Pop) 1996

6 GUILLOTINA — Rock Mata Pop (WB — Mexico) 1996

5 BLUEBOTTLE KISS — Fear of Girls (Murmur — Australia) 1996

3 FITZ OF DEPRESSION — Swing (K) 1996

6 THROWN UPS — Seven Years Golden (Amp Reptile) 1997

5 AIN'T — If It's Illegal to Rock'n'roll (Gluttony) 1997

5 SHARK CHUM — Tres Homeboys (Rats Ass) 1997

4 MURDER CITY DEVILS — Empty Bottles, Broken Hearts (Sub Pop) 1998

4 DAY I FELL DOWN — Sweet to Be Strange (Gold Circus) 1998

6 SEAWEED — Actions and Indications (Merge) 1999

5 NEBULA — To the Center (Sub Pop) 1999

6 ZEN GUERILLA — Trace States in Tongues (Sub Pop) 1999

BRIAN ENO

PRODUCER

BORN 5/15/48 (*Woodbridge, England*)

Bryan Ferry's futuristic Edwardian glamor aside, Roxy Music's focal (and, in terms of gossip, vocal) point was synth player Brian Eno. How the rumors flew about him! He was heir to a vast pharmaceutical fortune — Eno's was a well-known indigestion remedy — he was gay, he was glam, he was (of course!) an alien, an emissary from God Himself... Eno is an anagram of One.

Actually, he was plain old Brian Peter George St. Baptiste de la Salle Eno, an East Anglian Catholic who never dreamed he was destined to bear the longest name in rock history. As a youth, he wanted to become a painter, but the art which he once slapped on canvas slowly gave way to the notions of sound as a painting in itself.

He studied electronics, and published a book, *Music for Non-Musicians*. He met saxophonist Andy MacKay in a tube station, and was enrolled into Roxy as their technical adviser. But he didn't do too much advising. While Roxy rehearsed, Eno would be behind the mixing desk, doing strange things to the sound from the back of the hall. His transition from soundboard to stage was as gradual as it was inevitable. His cold electronics projected the public face of Roxy Music, Ferry's fantasy of a world where all the men looked like Humphrey Bogart, and the women — all models, naturally — didn't have names, they had numbers. "The sweetest queen" Ferry had ever seen took her name from a 1962 British car number plate... CPL 593A.

Eno quit Roxy during the summer of 1973, but the fights with Ferry upon which the split was blamed were only part of the problem. Eno was growing bored with rock'n'roll in general, and though he immediately turned around and recorded two albums which still rank amongst the most important albums in the pre-punk almanac, *Here Come the Warm Jets* and *Taking Tiger Mountain by Strategy*, it was clear that his eyes were elsewhere.

But where? Successive Eno albums would prove as individual and, in their uniqueness, unphotographable as any other avant-gardist. It still seems improbable, if not impossible, that as early as 1972, he was recording what became the burps, bleeps, and blurts-laden *No Pussyfooting* with King Crimson's Robert Fripp. Impossible because when next the duo convened, in 1975, Evening Star was a positive step backwards. In 1978, the duo regrouped once more, following up Eno's reconstruction of David Bowie with a project called *Healthy Colours*.

Bare, bizarre, and repetitive, it would not be released until 1994 (when it appeared on the *Essential Fripp & Eno* compilation), where its resemblance to the later work of Japan, and Eno's own production of Talking Heads, was only its most remarkable achievement.

By then, of course, Eno's own solo work had moved further, much further, on from where he and Fripp left it. *Music for Airports*, *Music for Films*, *Possible Musics*, and a soundtrack for Al Reinert's movie of the American Apollo missions, *Atmospheres and Soundtracks*, not only defined, they *created* what would become Ambient Music. Indeed, Rob Brown, of '90s electronic band Autechre, later insisted, "there have only been five truly ambient records ever made — and two of them (*Airports* and *Atmospheres*) are by Eno."

Eno's first outside productions were for his own, short-lived Obscure label, followed by an abortive union with the hotly tipped New York guitar band, Television. There, and

on several occasions after, he proved that his much-vaunted dilettantism was not necessarily indicative of his working methods — Tom Verlaine was horrified to find that Eno simply wanted to hang some mikes over the rafters and record the band live!

Still, Eno remained many avant-garde rockers' first choice, and on the occasions he acceded to their entreaties, the results were seldom less captivating. Alongside Steve Lillywhite, he produced Ultravox's debut album in 1977; the following year, he opened what would prove a fruitful, long-term relationship with David Byrne and the Talking Heads. He also worked with Devo and the deliberately unmusical Portsmouth Sinfonia, and joined David Bowie in the studio for the three albums which, perhaps more than any, dictated the course of electronic rock over the next five years, *Low*, *"Heroes,"* and *Lodger*. Contrary to popular belief, however, he did not produce the albums, leaving that to long-time Bowie associate Tony Visconti.

Eno's most significant production, then, was the utter re-invention of U2 in 1984, across their *Unforgettable Fire* album — the source of another long-term partnership, and one whose impact (sonic and otherwise) has continued to inform both his and the band's subsequent work.

Although his continued involvement with U2 has tended to obscure much of Eno's other work since that time, he has remained an active and prolific figure, as a producer, a recording artist, and a label head. Three Eno-led labels have flourished over the years: Obscure, which brought the world the first recorded version of Gavin Bryars' seminal *Sinking of the Titanic*; Opal; and currently, All Saints.

Brian Eno — Selected Productions

7 ADAMS/BRYARS/HOBBS — Ensemble Pieces (Obscure) 1975

TELEVISION — Demos [unreleased] 1975

6 DAVID TOOP — New & Rediscovered... Adventures (Obscure) 1975

10 ULTRAVOX — Ultravox! (Antilles) 1977

8 TALKING HEADS — More Songs About Building & Food (Sire) 1978

7 TALKING HEADS — Fear of Music (Sire) 1979

7 PORTSMOUTH SINFONIA — Hallelujah (Transatlantic) 1979
The world's self-styled worst orchestra, butchering the classics in hilarious fashion.

6 LARAAJI — Days of Radiance (EG) 1980

7 TALKING HEADS — Remain in Light (Sire) 1980

8 DEVO — Are We Not Men (WB) 1980

7 HAROLD BUDD — Pavilion of Dreams (Obscure) 1980

5 PACE SETTERS — Edikanfo (EG) 1981

9 U2 — The Unforgettable Fire (Island) 1984

7 JOHN HASSELL — Power Spot (ECM) 1986

9 U2 — The Joshua Tree (Island) 1987

6 ZVUKI MU — Zvuki Mu (WB) 1989

5 JOHN CALE — Words for the Dying (WB) 1989 After half a decade of recorded silence, Cale made a portentously quasi-classical return built around the work of Poet Dylan Thomas. Valid in its own narrow world, but little further, it is very much an acquired taste. Alongside *Wrong Way Up*, a full-fledged collaboration with Eno, it paints its hero into a corner which not only has little to do with rock'n'roll (which was always one of Cale's ambitions), it has nothing to do with his reputation either.

7 U2 — Achtung Baby (Island) 1991

4 GEOFFREY ORYEMA — Exile (Real World) 1991

7 U2 — Zooropa (Island) 1993

6 JAMES — Laid (Fontana) 1993 Anxiously over-achieving pop, layered with more intelligent texture than the bulk of the songs deserve.

6 JANE SIBERRY — When I Was a Boy (Reprise) 1993

7 JOHN HASSELL — Flash of the Spirit (Intuition) 1993

6 NUSRAT FATEH ALI KHAN — The Last Prophet (Real World) 1994

8 JAMES — Wah Wah (Mercury) 1994

3 LAURIE ANDERSON — Strange Angels, Bright Red (WB) 1994

6 PASSENGERS — Passengers (Island) 1995

6 DAVID BOWIE — Outside (Virgin) 1995 Heavily indebted to Nine Inch Nails, a grating electronic soap opera, pitted by maybe half an album's worth of good songs. "Hello Spaceboy," later re-recorded with the Pet Shop Boys for a single, stands tallest even in edited company.

6 JAMES — Whiplash (Fontana) 1997

6 808 STATE — Lopez EP (ZTT) 1997

6 ROBERT WYATT — Shleep (Thirsty Ear) 1997

FACTORY RECORDS

LABEL

Chiswick and Stiff may have set the pace for British independent labels, but into the early 1980s, even they were no competition for Factory, the Manchester-based concern established by local scenemaker and TV host Tony Wilson (his *So It Goes* show in late 1976 gave broadcast debuts to the Sex Pistols, Wreckless Eric, Siouxsie and the Banshees and many more).

From the outset, the label's musical policy was beyond reproach — concentrating almost exclusively on Manchester and its environs, Factory's first signings represented a virtual who's who of local luminaries, including Joy Division, Cabaret Voltaire, John Dowie, and Durutti Column. Taking a leaf out of Stiff's book, Factory brought on board a house producer of soon-to-be-proven renown, Martin Hannett; taking another, Wilson also identified the collectors' need to be constantly challenged and entertained by a hobby.

Particularly through its first five years of activity, the Factory catalog would intersperse records with a plethora of other oddities, ranging from label stationery and posters, through to real estate. FAC 51 was the Hacienda nightclub, built and operated by Factory from May 1982, and soon to become the focal point for Manchester nightlife. FAC 98 was the hairdressing salon opened in the Hacienda's basement in October 1983. Even more bizarre was FAC 99, New Order manager Rob Gretton's dentistry bill, paid for by Factory after he was beaten up by associates of A Certain Ratio.

Few of these, of course, were obtainable by the average fan; through the label's 14-year history, however, until Steve Martland's *Wolfgang* (FAC 406) and the Happy Mondays' *...Yes Please!* (FAC 420) rang down the curtain on the company's output in 1992, the principles which guided the label's first releases were still firmly in place. The following discography tracks Factory through to 1984, when New Order's "Confusion" confirmed the stardom which the earlier "Blue Monday" had already suggested was imminent, launching Factory itself into a new era of prosperity. In addition, a full listing is provided for the short-lived Factory Benelux subsidiary, European home to a host of the label's most esoteric releases.

Factory Records Label Listing 1978–85

FAC 1 PETER SAVILLE — The Factory 5/78–6/78 May 78 (poster)

FAC 2 VARIOUS ARTISTS — A Factory Sampler EP Seminal compilation featuring Joy Division, Durutti Column, John Dowie and Cabaret Voltaire.

FAC 3 PETER SAVILLE — The Factory 20/10/78 (poster)

FAC 4 PETER SAVILLE — The Factory X-Mas 12/78 (poster)

FAC 5 A CERTAIN RATIO — All Night Party 7-inch

FAC 6 OMD — Electricity 7-inch

FAC 7 PETER SAVILLE — Factory Notepaper (stationery set)

FAC 8 LINDER — Factory Egg Timer (egg timer)

FAC 9 VARIOUS ARTISTS — The Factory Flick (8mm film)

FACT 10 JOY DIVISION — Unknown Pleasures LP **10**

FAC 11 X-O-DUS — English Black Boys 12-inch

FACT 12 DISTRACTIONS — Time Goes by So Slow 7-inch

FACT 13 JOY DIVISION — Transmission 7-inch

FACT 14 DURUTTI COLUMN — The Return of the... LP **8** Effective effects-heavy collection of (largely) guitar-based instrumentals, looking back towards early Mike Oldfield and forward to some of Eno's not-quite-ambient work.

FACT 14C MARTIN HANNETT — Testcard (flexi)

FAC 15 PETER SAVILLE — Zoo Meets Factory Halfway (poster)

FACT 16C A CERTAIN RATIO — The Graveyard and the Ballroom LP [7]

FAC 17 CRAWLING CHAOS — Sex Machine 7-inch

FAC 18 SECTION 25 — Girls Don't Count 7-inch

FAC 19 JOHN DOWIE — It's Hard to Be an Egg 7-inch

FAC 20 A CERTAIN RATIO — Too Young to Know, Too Wild to Care [UNMADE MOVIE]

FAC 21 PETER SAVILLE — Factory Badge (button)

FAC 22 A CERTAIN RATIO — Flight 12-inch

FAC 23 JOY DIVISION — Love Will Tear Us Apart 7-inch

FACT 24 VARIOUS ARTISTS — A Factory Quartet EP [5] Featuring Durutti Column, Kevin Hewick, Royal Family & the Poor, and the saxophone shrieking of Blurt, the most avant garde fun you can have with your ears turned off.

FACT 25 JOY DIVISION — Closer LP [8]

FAC 26 STEVE HORSFALL — Durutti in Paris (poster)

FAC 27 PETER SAVILLE — Sex Machine Alternative [unreleased picture sleeve for FAC 17]

FAC 28 JOY DIVISION — Komakino (flexi)

FAC 29 THE NAMES — Night Shift 7-inch

FACT 30 SEX PISTOLS — The Heyday [spoken word] LP [5]

FAC 31 MINNY POPS — Dolphin Spurt 7-inch

FAC 32 CRISPY AMBULANCE — Unsightly & Serene 7-inch

FAC 33 NEW ORDER — Ceremony 7-inch

FAC 34 ESG — You're No Good 7-inch

FACT 35 A CERTAIN RATIO — To Each... LP [5]

FAC 36 The US 'Closer' ad campaign

FACT 37 JOY DIVISION — Here are the Young Men VHS

FACT 38 A CERTAIN RATIO — Below the Canal [unreleased] VHS

FAC 39 TUNNELVISION — Watching the Hydroplanes 7-inch

FACT 40 JOY DIVISION — Still LP [7]

FAC 41 STOCKHOLM MONSTERS — Fairy Tales 7-inch

FACT 42 A CERTAIN RATIO — The Double 12-inch EP

FAC 43 ROYAL FAMILY & THE POOR — Art Dream Dominion 12-inch

FACT 44 DURUTTI COLUMN — LC LP [6]

FACT 45 SECTION 25 — Always Now LP [7]

FAC 46 VARIOUS ARTISTS — The Video Circus 81–84 (Collection of posters, advertisements, etc).

FAC 47 PETER SAVILLE — Factory Logo 1981 (new label logo)

FAC 48 KEVIN HEWICK — Ophelia's Drinking Song 7-inch

FAC 49 SWAMP CHILDREN — Little Voices 12-inch

FACT 50 NEW ORDER — Movement LP [8]

FAC 51 THE HACIENDA (Nightclub)

FAC 51b NEW ORDER — Merry Xmas from the Hacienda (flexi)

FAC 52 A CERTAIN RATIO — Waterline 12-inch

FAC 53 NEW ORDER — Procession 7-inch

FAC 54 Hacienda Construction Video (VHS)

FACT 55 A CERTAIN RATIO — Sextet LP [8]

FAC 56 VARIOUS ARTISTS — A Factory Video VHS

FAC 57 MINNY POPS — Secret Story 7-inch

FAC 58 STOCKHOLM MONSTERS — Happy Ever After 7-inch

FAC 59 52ND STREET — Look Into My Eyes 7-inch

FACT 60 THE WAKE — Harmony LP [6]

FAC 61 Hannett lawsuit (Stationery pertaining to a lawsuit concerning royalties).

FAC 62 A CERTAIN RATIO — Knife Slits Water 7-inch

FAC 63 NEW ORDER — Temptation 7-inch

FAC 64 DURUTTI COLUMN — I Get Along Without You Very Well 7-inch

FACT 65 A CERTAIN RATIO — I'd Like to See You Again LP [5]

FAC 66 SECTION 25 — The Beast 12-inch

FAC 67 QUANDO QUANGO — Go Exciting 12-inch

FAC 68 SECTION 25 — Back to Wonder 7-inch

FAC 69 unreleased

FACT 70 SWAMP CHILDREN — So Hot LP [6]

FACT 71 VARIOUS ARTISTS — A Factory Outing VHS

FAC 72 A CERTAIN RATIO — I Need Someone Tonight 7-inch

FAC 73 NEW ORDER — Blue Monday 12-inch

FACT 74 DURUTTI COLUMN — Another Setting LP [7]

FACT 75 NEW ORDER — Power, Corruption & Lies LP [9]

FACT 76 JAZZ DEFEKTORS — The Movie [unreleased movie]

FACT 77 NEW ORDER — Taras Shevchenko VHS

FAC 78 JAMES — Jimone 7-inch

FAC 79 QUANDO QUANGO — Love Tempo 12-inch

FACX 79 Feel Safe with Modern Music (earplugs)

FACT 80 STOCKHOLM MONSTERS — Alma Mater LP [7]

FAC 81 Factory 1st International Congress (notepaper)

FAC 82 CABARET VOLTAIRE — Yashar 12-inch

FAC 83 PETER SAVILLE Assoc — Hacienda 1 Year (poster card)

FACT 84 DURUTTI COLUMN — Without Mercy LP [6]

FACT 85 THICK PIGEON — Too Crazy Cowboys LP [5]

FAC 86 PETER SAVILLE Assoc. Christmas 1983 Hacienda (model)

FAC 87 KALIMA — The Smiling Hour 7-inch

FAC 88 THE WAKE — Talk About the Past 7-inch

FACT 89 JOHN DOWIE — Dowie VHS

FACT 90 SECTION 25 — From the Hip LP [6]

FAC 91 FACSOFT COMPUTER PROGRAMME [unreleased]

FAC 92 MARCEL KING — Reach for Love 7-inch

FAC 93 NEW ORDER — Confusion 7-inch

FAC 94 PETER SAVILLE Assoc — Factory Logo 1983 (logo)

FACT 95 ROYAL FAMILY & THE POOR — Temple of the 13th Tribe LP

FAC 96 AD INFINITUM — Telstar 7-inch

FAC 97 STREETLIFE — Act on Instinct 12-inch

FAC 98 Swing (hairdressing Salon in the Hacienda basement)

FAC 99 Rob Gretton's molar reconstruction (dentist bill)

FACT 100 NEW ORDER — Low Life LP **6**

Factory Benelux Complete Label Listing

FBN 1 A CERTAIN RATIO — Shack Up 7-inch

FBN 2 DURUTTI COLUMN — Lips That Would Kiss 7-inch

FBN 3 SECTION 25 — Charnel Ground 7-inch

FBN 4 CRISPY AMBULANCE — Live on a Hot August Night EP

FBN 5 SECTION 25 — Je Veux Ton Amour 7-inch

FBN 6 CRAWLING CHAOS — The Gas Chair LP **8**

FBN 7 VARIOUS ARTISTS — A Factory Complication VHS

FBN 8 NEW ORDER — Everything's Gone Green 12-inch

FBN 9 THE NAMES — Calcutta 7-inch

FBN 10 DURUTTI COLUMN — Deux Triangles 12-inch

FBN 11 MINNY POPS — Time 7-inch

FBN 12 CRISPY AMBULANCE — The Plateau Phase LP

FBN 13 VARIOUS ARTISTS — Vinyl Magazine Flexi

FBN 14 SECTION 25 — The Key of Dreams LP

FBN 15 MINNY POPS — Sparks in a Dark Room LP **6**

Dynamically noisy Dutch quartet, operating in similar (if less extreme) areas as Throbbing Gristle.

FBN 16 SWAMP CHILDREN — Taste What's Rhythm 12-inch

FBN 17 A CERTAIN RATIO — Guess Who 12-inch

FBN 18 CRISPY AMBULANCE — Sexus 12-inch

FBN 19 STOCKHOLM MONSTERS — Miss Moonlight 12-inch

FBN 20 52ND STREET — Cool as Ice 12-inch

FBN 21 SWAMP CHILDREN — So Hot LP

FBN 22 NEW ORDER — Murder 12-inch

FBN 23 QUANDO QUANGO — Love Tempo 7-inch

FBN 24 THE WAKE — Something Outside 12-inch

FBN 25 CABARET VOLTAIRE — Yashar 12-inch

FBN 26 SURPRIZE — In Movimento EP

FBN 27 VARIOUS ARTISTS — Factory Benelux Greatest Hits LP
7 Remixes of ACR, 52nd St, Quando Quango, Wake, Cabaret Voltaire, Stockholm Monsters.

FBN 28 NYAM NYAM — Fate/Hate 12-inch

FBN 29 (see FACT 60)

FBN 30 (see FACT 74)

FBN 31 (see FACT 80)

FBN 32 A CERTAIN RATIO — Brazilia 12-inch

FBN 33 SECTION 25 — From the Hip [unreleased] LP

FBN 34 LAVOLTA LAKOTA — Prayer 7-inch

FBN 35 THE WAKE — Talk About the Past [unreleased] 12-inch

FBN 36 DURUTTI COLUMN — Circuses and Bread LP

FBN 37 LIFE — Dites Moi 12-inch

FBN 38 LIFE — Dites Moi [unreleased]

FBN 39 LA COSA NOSTRA — Coming Closer 12-inch

FBN 40 LA COSA NOSTRA — Coming Closer 7-inch

FBN 41 SIMON TOPPING — Prospect Park 12-inch

FBN 42 LIFE — Better 12-inch

FBN 43 MARCEL KING — Reach for Love 12-inch

FBN 44 STANTON MIRANDA — Wheels Over Indian Trails 7-inch

FBN 45 SECTION 25 — Crazy Wisdom 12-inch

FBN 46 STOCKHOLM MONSTERS — How Corrupt is Rough Trade? 12-inch

FBN 47 THE EXECUTIONER — Executioner's Theme [unreleased]

FBN 48 THE EXECUTIONER — Executioner's Theme [unreleased] 12-inch

FBN 49 PLAYGROUP — Euphoria 12-inch

FBN 50 PLAYGROUP — Euphoria 7-inch

FBN 51 DURUTTI COLUMN — Tomorrow 7-inch

FBN 52 VARIOUS ARTISTS — Factory Complication 1 [unreleased LP]

FBN 53 unreleased

FBN 54 unreleased

FBN 55 VARIOUS ARTISTS — The Factory Complication 2 [unreleased LP]

FBN 100 DURUTTI COLUMN — For Patti 7-inch

FBN 100 NEW ORDER — Low Life LP **6**

FBN 123 NEW ORDER — Perfect Kiss 7-inch

FBN 150 NEW ORDER — Brotherhood LP **5**

FBN 153 NEW ORDER — State of the Nation 12-inch

FBN 839 NEW ORDER — Touched by the Hand of God 7-inch

DON FLEMING

PRODUCER

BORN *9/25/57 (Valdosta, GA)*

Fleming's first musical endeavors were as guitarist with the Valdosta, GA-based punk outfit the Stroke Band, who cut one single for the local Abacus label. From there, he moved to Washington DC and joined the Velvet Monkeys, producing their contributions to the *Connected* compilation album ("Drive In" and "Shadowbox") simply because the band couldn't afford to hire an outsider.

Finding he enjoyed the experience, Fleming began producing other local bands, before landing a job at a local studio, helping transfer ancient acetates to tape. He remained there through most of the 1980s, producing bands as a hobby, and working with the Velvet Monkeys until they broke up in 1986. The following year, he and drummer Jay Spiegel relocated to New York City, where they hooked up with fellow producer Kramer in the band BALL, recording four albums for Kramer's Shimmy Disc label.

In 1990, word of mouth introduced Fleming to the Scottish band Teenage Fanclub; he produced their *God Knows It's True* EP, and the following year handled their major label debut, *Bandwagonesque*. That album's success then introduced him to the Posies, the Seattle band who would frequently labor under the soubriquet of "America's Fannies." The PNW connection also saw Fleming work with Hole (co-producing with Sonic Youth's Kim Gordon) and the Screaming Trees.

Fleming and Spiegel reformed the Velvet Monkeys in 1990, with Dinosaur Jr.'s J. Mascis, Sonic Youth's Thurston Moore, and Pussy Galore's Julia Cafritz; they recorded one album, *Rake*, before Fleming launched a new band, Gumball, in 1991. Perhaps his greatest musical challenge arrived the following year, however, when he reunited with Moore and fellow Youth member Steve Shelley in Dim Stars, a band fronted by the long-retired Richard Hell. The quartet would release an EP and a full album, returning Hell to the public eye he had long since slipped out of.

1994 saw Fleming involved with two other sleeping legends: Alice Cooper, and the Beatles. Fleming joined Foo Fighter Dave Grohl, Thurston Moore, and Soul Asylum's Dave Pirner in the so-called Backbeat Band, handling the soundtrack to the movie retelling of the life and death of Stuart Sutcliffe. He would also launch a solo career following Gumball's demise that same year.

Don Fleming — Selected Productions

8 TEENAGE FANCLUB — Bandwagonesque (DGC) 1991
6 RUDOLPH GRAY — Mask of Light (New Alliance) 1991
6 HOLE — Pretty on the Inside (Caroline) 1991
7 SCREAMING TREES — Sweet Oblivion (Epic) 1992
8 POSIES — Frosting on the Beater (DGC) 1993
6 HOLLYFAITH — Purrrr (Epic) 1993
5 ALICE COOPER — The Last Temptation (Epic) 1994
7 ANN MAGNUSON — The Luv Show (Geffen) 1995
6 BRACKET — 4 Wheel Drive (Caroline) 1995
6 GRAVY — After That It's All Gravy (Fused Coil) 1996
5 HUNK — Hunk (Geffen) 1996
6 STEEL MINERS — All Hopped Up (Instant Mayhem) 1996
6 SLEEPINGTON — Sleepington (Instant Mayhem) 1996
5 GUV'NER — The Hunt (Merge) 1996
6 TRIPLEFASTACTION — Broadcaster (Capitol) 1996
6 JACK OFF JILL — Sexless Demons & Scars (Restless) 1997
7 DARK CARNIVAL — Last Great Ride (Sftri) 1997
6 CHOPPER ONE — Now Playing (Restless) 1997
7 SONIC YOUTH — A Thousand Leaves (Geffen) 1998
6 SMITHEREENS — God Save the Smithereens (Koch Int) 1999

FLOOD

PRODUCER
BORN *Mark Ellis (London, England)*

Bassist with Mod revival favorites, the Lambrettas, in 1979–80, Ellis was also working as a runner and teaboy at a London studio — where he earned his nickname, for constantly spilling the tea. Eventually rising to house engineer, he went freelance in 1981, and that same year he worked as assistant engineer on New Order's *Movement* debut album.

The following year, Flood was engineer on Ministry's epochal *With Sympathy* debut album, before he linked with Stevo's Some Bizzare label. He would work with most of that band's principal signings, most notably Marc Almond's Mambas sideline, and Cabaret Voltaire, before becoming producer of choice at Mute. There he would act as producer or engineer, with each of the label's major acts: Depeche Mode, Vince Clarke and Erasure, Nick Cave and Crime and the City Solution, contributing greatly to that so identifiable "sound" which permeated Mute's classic releases.

In 1987, Flood engineered U2's seminal *Joshua Tree* album; two years later, he would be one of several producers involved in creating Nine Inch Nails' *Pretty Hate Machine*. The partnership with Reznor would survive into the sessions for the *Broken*, although it was Flood's association with Cave which prompted perhaps his most powerful work, alongside PJ Harvey on *To Bring You My Love* — Harvey herself was a long time Cave fan.

Flood returned to performing in 1994, when he formed Node with London Suede producer Ed Bueller.

Flood — Selected Productions

10 MARC & THE MAMBAS — Torment & Torreros (Some Bizzare) 1982
6 CABARET VOLTAIRE — Micro-Phonies (Some Bizzare) 1984
8 MIGHTY WAH! — A Word to the Wise Guy (Beggars Banquet) 1984
9 NICK CAVE — The Firstborn is Dead (Mute) 1985
9 CRIME & THE CITY SOLUTION — Room of Lights (Mute) 1986
7 ERASURE — Wonderland (Sire) 1986 Yazoo with Moyet's bellowing soul replaced by Andy Bell's more calculated smoothness, and hits oozing from every orifice. This time it's "Heavenly Action" and "Oh L'Amour."
6 ERASURE — Circus (Sire) 1987
8 ERASURE — Two Ring Circus (Sire) 1987 "It Doesn't Have to Be" was a masterpiece; the remainder of *Circus* seemed gray and ill-considered — so they remixed and reissued it as a double 12-inch single, then threw on seven more new tracks when it was released on CD. That did the trick.
7 ANNA DOMINO — This Time (Mute) 1987
7 BOOK OF LOVE — Lullaby (WB) 1988

7 SILENCERS — **A Blues for Buddha (BMG) 1988**

6 WOLFGANG PRESS — **Bird Wood Cage (4AD) 1988** Deep and dark as ever, but deeply understated too, Wolfgang Press' interests expand to embrace a snatch of dub and even psychedelic guitars.

10 NINE INCH NAILS — **Pretty Hate Machine [Co-prod] (TVT) 1989**

8 POP WILL EAT ITSELF — **This is the Day... (RCA) 1989** And *This...* is PWEI evolving into a musical monster of magnificent proportions before our very ears — a seminal blend of every iota of indy-dom they can meld with hypnotic techno rhythms and hip-hop beats, pummelled by the hard-hitting rappy lyrics, then crushed under the cogs of the clattering and crashing industrial electronics.

6 RENEGADE SOUNDWAVE — **Soundclash (Elektra) 1989** Renegade's death-defying debut does precisely what it claims, clashing musical styles together then pounding them together with dubby, dance beats. Cat burglars prowl across "Probably a Robbery," all nocturnal guitar, stealthy keyboards, and irrepressible beats; hip-hop goes pop on "Biting My Nails"; and "Lucky Luke" pairs C&W with classical. A bold reinvention of the club scene.

7 WOLFGANG PRESS — **Kansas (4AD) 1989**

7 DEPECHE MODE — **Violator (Sire) 1990**

6 JAMES — **James (Fontana) 1990**

6 NITZER EBB — **Showtime (Sire) 1990** After three albums of harsh industrial anthems, a broader palette gives the Chelmsford, UK trio room to experiment with melody, format and even the blues.

7 POP WILL EAT ITSELF — **Cure for Sanity (RCA) 1990**

7 NITZER EBB — **Ebbhead (Sire) 1991**

7 CHARLATANS UK — **Between 10th and 11th (Beggars Banquet) 1992**

4 GAVIN FRIDAY — **Adam & Eve (Island) 1992**

6 CURVE — **Doppelganger (Anxious) 1992**

8 CURVE — **Cuckoo (Anxious) 1993** Warm intensity spilling out where once the band opted for cool, clinical distance; a swansong which also ranked as an utter reinvention.

7 DEPECHE MODE — **Songs of Faith & Devotion (Sire) 1993**

7 U2 — **Zooropa (Island) 1993**

8 NINE INCH NAILS — **Downward Spiral (Nothing) 1994**

10 PJ HARVEY — **To Bring You My Love (Island) 1995**

6 NITZER EBB — **Big Hit (Sire) 1995**

9 SMASHING PUMPKINS — **Mellon Collie and the Infinite Sadness (Virgin) 1995**

8 U2 — **Pop (Island) 1997**

4 NICK CAVE — **The Boatman's Call (Mute) 1997**

9 PJ HARVEY — **Is This Desire? (Island) 1998**

FLYING NUN

LABEL

New Zealand's Flying Nun can claim to be the southern hemisphere's most influential indy label, home to a low-fi psychedelic ethic which initially flavored a host of home-grown talent — the Clean, the Chills, the Tall Dwarfs, and the Verlaines — and then spread around the world.

Launched by Christchurch record store manager Roger Shepherd in 1981, Flying Nun's initial impetus was taken from the success of import releases on such UK indies as Factory and Beggars Banquet. Initially distributed through a loose network of friends and industry contacts, the first clutch of releases swiftly raised the label far above the auteur status Shepherd was expecting — a string of early singles proved major New Zealand hits, and though Shepherd himself would leave Flying Nun in 1997, still the company's original vision continues to inform its output.

Flying Nun Label Listing 1981–86

001 PIN GROUP — **Ambivalence 7-inch**
002 THE CLEAN — **Tally Ho! 7-inch**
003 THE CLEAN — **Boodle Boodle Boodle EP**
004 unreleased
005 unreleased
006 BUILDERS — **Schwimmin in der See 7-inch**
007 BALLON D'ESSAI — **Ballon D'essai EP**
008 RITCHIE VENUS — **Ritchie Venus EP**
009 25 CENTS — **The Witch 7-inch**
010 unreleased
011 THIS SPORTING LIFE — **Show Me to the Bellrope 7-inch**
012 unreleased
013 unreleased
014 VERLAINES — **Death and the Maiden 7-inch**
015 SNEAKY FEELINGS — **Be My Friend 7-inch**
016 unreleased
017 unreleased
018 unreleased
019 unreleased
020 BALLON D'ESSAI — **Grow Up EP**
021 unreleased
022 VERLAINES — **Ten O'clock EP**
023 THE RIP — **Timeless Piece EP**
024 BATS — **By Night EP**
025 EXPENDABLES — **The Flower 7-inch**
026 DOUBLEHAPPYS — **Double B-Side 7-inch**
027 PHANTOM FORTH — **Phantom Forth EP**
028 SCORCHED EARTH POLICY — **Scorched Earth Policy EP**

029 EXPENDABLES — Between Gears EP

030 CRYSTAL ZOOM — Uptown Sheep 7-inch

031 BATS — Music for the Fireside EP

032 unreleased

033 EXPLODING BUDGIES — Grotesque Singers EP

034 unreleased

035 THE FOLD — The Fold EP

036 NOT REALLY ANYTHING — Watched a World EP

037 unreleased

038 VIBRASLAPS — Vibraslaps EP

039 unreleased

040 VERLAINES — Hallelujah All the Way Home LP **7** Ragged and mournful with subject matter to match, the Verlaines' debut album is littered with strong melodies, mostly in search of a song to hang out with.

041 FROM SCRATCH — From Scratch LP **6**

042 SCORCHED EARTH POLICY — Going Through a Hole EP

043 ABLE TASMANS — Tired Sun 7-inch

044 BIRD NEST ROYS — Whack It All Down EP

045 VARIOUS ARTISTS — Tuatara LP **7**

046 GOBLIN MIX — Goblin Mix EP

047 ORANGE — Fruit Salad Lives EP

048 ERIC GLANDY MEMORIAL BAND — Eric Glandy Memorial Band EP

049 AXEMEN — Three Virgins LP **6**

050 ALPACA BROTHERS — Legless EP

Further Reading

Positively George St by Matthew Bannister (Reed Publishing — NZ).

PAUL FOX

PRODUCER
BORN 1954

After several years spent as a session keyboard player with the likes of the Pointer Sisters, Natalie Cole, Patti Labelle, and the Temptations, Fox made his production debut in 1987 with soul singer George McCrae, following that with Scarlet and Black's 1988 hit single "You Don't Know." He was, then, still comparatively unknown when Virgin Records recruited him first to work with Boy George, then going through a difficult musical rehabilitation following the demise of Culture Club; then with the equally difficult XTC as they strove to follow up the quarter-million selling *Skylarking*. *Oranges and Lemons* did not repeat the success of its predecessor, but Fox's involvement was above reproach and he found himself with an admirable reputation for being able to handle the "quirkier" kind of artist. Gene Loves Jezebel, Robyn Hitch-

cock, and the Sugarcubes would number among his clients through the next two years. Later, he would produce Sky Cries Mary, They Might Be Giants, and former Hawkwind mainstay Nik Turner during his early-mid 1990s renaissance.

Fox would also oversee former Nirvana bassist Krist Novoselic's sadly short-lived Sweet 75 project, although he did not shy away from more mainstream projects, as he proved with his handling of 10,000 Maniacs towards the end of Natalie Merchant's days with the group, Meredith Brooks, and the popular jam band Phish.

NOTE: Contrary to listings elsewhere, and despite sharing such an uncommon name, Paul Fox the US-born producer is in no way connected to Paul Fox, the UK-born former member of punk band the Ruts.

Paul Fox — Selected Productions

5 SCARLETT AND BLACK — Scarlett and Black (Virgin) 1987

7 XTC — Oranges and Lemons (Geffen) 1989

9 GENE LOVES JEZEBEL — Kiss of Life (Geffen) 1990

6 TOO MUCH JOY — Cereal Killers (Giant) 1991

6 ROBYN HITCHCOCK — Perspex Island (AandM) 1991

7 SUGARCUBES — Stick Around for Joy (Elektra) 1992

5 10,000 MANIACS — Our Time in Eden (Elektra) 1992

7 SUGARCUBES — It's It (Elektra) 1992

6 WALLFLOWERS — Wallflowers (Virgin) 1992

5 10,000 MANIACS — MTV Unplugged (Elektra) 1993

6 SUBJECT TO CHANGE — Womb Amnesia (Capitol) 1993

4 STRAITJACKET FITS — Blow (Arista) 1993 Disappointingly slick set from traditionally gritty New Zealand/Flying Nun outfit.

5 VICTORIA WILLIAMS — Loose (Mammoth) 1994

8 NIK TURNER — Prophets of Time (Cleopatra) 1994

4 THEY MIGHT BE GIANTS — John Henry (Elektra) 1994 The problem with everyone relying on you to be unselfconsciously wacky and weird is that sooner or later... Weak puns and flattened irony ricochet an album which seemed hell-bent on proving that humor doesn't always belong in music. Frank Zappa would be pleased.

5 TEXAS — Ricks Road (Mercury) 1994

3 PHISH — Hoist (Elektra) 1994

6 SARA HICKMAN — Necessary Angels (Discovery) 1994

6 ANUBIAN LIGHTS — Eternal Sky (Cleopatra) 1995 Heavily electronic set from many of the same musicians involved in Nik Turner's 1994 Hawkwind revival, pursuing a similar direction to his *Sphynx* album.

6 EDWIN MCCAIN — Honor Among Thieves (Lava) 1995

6 TINA AND THE B-SIDES — Salvation (Sire) 1996

6 REX DAISY — Guys and Dolls (Pravda) 1996

5 HOOKERS — Calico (MCA) 1996

7 SEMISONIC — Great Divide (MCA) **1996** Competent indy rock played with more feeling and energy than most bands of the genre, further enhanced by atmospheric moody melodies and catchy choruses.

7 SARA HICKMAN — Misfits (Shanachie) **1997**

6 NIELDS — Gotta Get Over Greta (Capitol) **1997**

8 SKY CRIES MARY — Moonbathing on Sleeping Leaves (World Domination) **1997**

8 GRANT LEE BUFFALO — Jubilee (WB) **1998**

7 MEREDITH BROOKS — Deconstruction (Capitol) **1999**

JOHN FRYER

PRODUCER

BORN *1958 (London, England)*

Giving up early dreams of becoming a successful rock musician in his late teens, Fryer moved into production after several years spent mixing live sound for a friend's band. In 1979, he began working as an assistant engineer at London's Blackwing Studios — it was there that he first met Mute label head Daniel Miller, and in 1981, he was recruited to produce Fad Gadget's *Incontinent* album, as well as engineer for Depeche Mode.

The 4AD label, too, used Blackwing on a regular basis, and in 1983, Fryer produced the Cocteau Twins' *Head Over Heels* and *Sunburst and Snowblind* EPs. More significantly, he would also helm the first 4AD collective This Mortal Coil album, 1984's *It'll End in Tears* (together with its less successful follow-ups), and through much of the decade, he vied with Flood as the architect of the soundtrack to an entire generation.

1989 saw Fryer oversee Love and Rockets' eponymous fourth album, source of the US hit "So Alive"; however, again like Flood, he was also to become involved in the sessions for Nine Inch Nails *Pretty Hate Machine* debut in 1989, and over the next decade, he continued to pursue the industrial option through later albums by Sister Machine Gun, Die Krupps, Course of Empire, Gravity Kills, and Stabbing Westward.

John Fryer — Selected Productions

8 FAD GADGET — Incontinent (Mute) **1981**

8 FAD GADGET — Under the Flag (Mute) **1982**

7 COCTEAU TWINS — Head Over Heels (4AD) **1983**

10 THIS MORTAL COIL — It'll End in Tears (4AD) **1984**

7 X-MAL DEUTSCHLAND — Tocsin (4AD) **1984**

7 HE SAID — Hail (Mute) **1985**

7 COLOURBOX — Colourbox (4AD) **1985**

6 THIS MORTAL COIL — Filigree & Shadow (4AD) **1986**

7 CLAN OF XYMOX — Medusa (4AD) **1986**

7 WOLFGANG PRESS — Standing Up Straight (4AD) **1986**

8 HE SAID — Take Care (Mute) **1988**

10 NINE INCH NAILS — Pretty Hate Machine (Tvt) **1989**

8 LUSH — Scar (4AD) **1989**

10 LOVE AND ROCKETS — Love and Rockets (RCA) **1989**

5 WIRE — It's Beginning to and Back Again (Restless) **1989**

7 DANIEL ASH — Coming Down (RCA) **1990**

8 PALE SAINTS — Comforts of Madness (4AD) **1990** Alongside fellow 4AD ingenues Lush, a rebirth for the original dream-laden 4AD sound at the same time as traditional sonic concerns are finally laid to rest in the face of the now-burgeoning shoe-gazing sound. A version of Opal's "Fell from the Sun" indicates another strong influence.

6 MOEV — Head Down (Nettwerk) **1990**

9 LUSH — Gala [SIX TRACKS] (4AD) **1990**

6 EASY — Magic Seed (Mute) **1991**

4 THIS MORTAL COIL — Blood (4AD) **1991**

6 HIS NAME IS ALIVE — Home is in Your Head (4AD) **1991** The 23 tracks are all too brief to settle — snapshots of leafy lanes, sunny days, grassy fields, and just enough menace in the guitar to suggest that something might happen soon. Unfortunately, it never does.

7 THE BEAUTIFUL — Storybook (Giant) **1992**

5 SWALLOW — Blow (4AD) **1992**

7 DIE KRUPPS — Die Krupps I (Rough Trade) **1992** Early German industrialists reform and evolve, leaving their original electro-purity behind to create industrio-rock instead. Insidious guitar draws further down the road to coldwave.

9 DIE KRUPPS — A Tribute to Metallica (Hollywood) **1992** A totally electronic tribute to vocalist Jurgen Engler's favorite band? Stranger things have happened, but not often, especially when it was meant for Metallica's ears alone, a gift from pupil to teacher. Metallica's label, though, felt otherwise and a whole generation of electro-geeks were suddenly introduced to the wonders of metal...without a guitar in sight!

8 STABBING WESTWARD — Ungod (Columbia) **1994** *Ungod's* theme of love lost and the resultant emotional turmoil of anguish, anger, and pain is given voice through the band's tribal tinged beats, swampy, dirty bass lines, and the swooping melodic guitars, then taken into the maelstrom by the cutting edge electronics.

8 SISTER MACHINE GUN — Burn (Wax Trax) **1995** Wrapped in a sinuous sensuality and driven by a funk feel, SMG soften their earlier harsh industrial inclinations, add a rock feel and a horn section — and presto! "Disease" pumps along, the guitars spike through like a fever, and though it's still palpably SMG, *Burn* melts into the soulful, moody, and magical melodies.

8 GRAVITY KILLS — Gravity Kills (TVT) **1996** Finely balanced between industrial and alternative rock, *Gravity's* starting point are strong pop-rock melodies *à la* the indy hit single "Guilty," over which is layered the subtle but powerful, skittering electro.

5 AC MARIAS — One of Our Girls (MUTE) **1996**

6 LOVE AND ROCKETS — Sweet FA [SEVEN TRACKS] (American) 1996

8 STABBING WESTWARD — Wither Blister Burn & Red (Columbia) 1996 While the pulsing "Shame" and the angst-laden "Why" remain tied to the band's past, *Wither...* reveals the group moving towards a much harder rock sound, with just enough dark electro-surged emotions to keep their own fans sweet. "What Do I Have to Do?" crosses moody melody with assaultive guitars and needles of electronic buzzing, while "Inside You" starts with pure electronics then bursts into hardrock. Where will it end?

7 RADIO IODINE — Tiny Warnings (Universal) 1997

9 SISTER MACHINE GUN — Metropolis (TVT) 1997 Initially conceived as a soundtrack to the silent movie of the same name, *Metropolis'* main theme takes the movie as a metaphor for the music industry, but twists off into further allegories from there. While keeping much of the soul-fired, swampy feel of *Burn*, most notably on "Temptation," the album is SMG's most diverse to date, with Bowie conspirator Reeve Gabrels supplying the fabulous guitar, and some amazing slide on "White Lightning."

7 COURSE OF EMPIRE — Telepathic Last Words (TVT) 1998 Cold wave based, but highly experimental, Empire's strongest suit is their penchant for occasional detours into Eastern modes — a blend of rhythms and moods which itself takes bewildering excursions into electronics.

5 LOVE IN REVERSE — Words Become Worms (WB) 1998

BRETT GUREWITZ

PRODUCER

Bad Religion frontman Gurewitz relaunched the band's Epitaph label in 1987 with the first album by L7 — the label had existed earlier in the decade as an outlet for Bad Religion alone; now it was to function on a far wider scale, concentrating upon local California punk and hardcore acts.

Having first worked in the studio with TSOL, 7 Seconds (mixing), and Chris Cacavas (engineer), Gurewitz would subsequently produce much of Epitaph's core output, including Bad Religion's own albums — he finally quit the band to concentrate fully on production and running the label.

Brett Gurewitz — Selected Productions (Non-Epitaph)

7 NO USE FOR A NAME — Incognito (New Red Archives) 1990

6 RUSS TOLMAN — Goodbye Joe (Skyclad) 1990

6 CLAWHAMMER — Ramwhale (Sftri) 1992

8 SACRED MIRACLE CAVE — Sacred Miracle Cave (Bomp) 1992

6 CHRIS CACAVAS & JUNKYARD LOVE — Good Times (Heyday) 1992

7 PONTIAC BROS — Doll Hut (Frontier) 1992

5 JUGHEAD'S REVENGE — It's Lonely at the Bottom (BYO) 1995

7 PIETASTERS — Willis (Hellcat) 1997 The Pietasters finally capture the power of their music on record (previous releases tended towards the lackluster), delving deep into R&B and soul with diversions into calypso and reggae, topped off by slatherings of the '60s, from the garage punk of "Crazy Monkey Woman" to their cover of "Time Won't Let Me."

8 PIETASTERS — Awesome Mix Tape Vol 6 (Hellcat) 1999 Even more diversified than last time out, *Awesome* is precisely that, a seething mix of dub, funk, and Latino-Western lunacy, with the rollicking "Somebody" — a stand-out in the new styles section. The instant classic "Take Some Time" and the soulful "Crying Over You" prove the Pietasters' heart still thumps achingly for the sounds of the '60s.

Brett Gurewitz/Epitaph Label Listing 1987–95

86401 L7 — L7 **4**

86402 VARIOUS ARTISTS — More Songs About Anger, Fear, Sex & Death **7**

86403 LITTLE KINGS — Head First **6**

86404 BAD RELIGION — Suffer **7**

86405 NOFX — S & M Airlines **7**

86406 BAD RELIGION — No Control **7**

86407 BAD RELIGION — 80–85 **6**

86408 INSTED — What We Believe **6**

86409 BAD RELIGION — Against the Grain **8**

86410 NOFX — Ribbed **8**

86411 DOWN BY LAW — Down by Law **6** Ex-DYS/Dag Nasty/All vocalist Dave Smalley returns with a new band and a refined variation on the punk rock theme, less metal than Nasty, more powerful than All, DBL is armageddon bashed by punchy pop.

86412 PENNYWISE — Pennywise **7** Crashing out of Southern California like a tidal wave, Pennywise wash over the punk scene soaking everything in their past. Across some of the best melodic hardcore ever made, the energy never flags.

86413 COFFIN BREAK — Crawl **7**

86414 BAD RELIGION — Along the Way (VHS)

86415 DAG NASTY — Four on the Floor **6**

86416 BAD RELIGION — Generator **8**

86417 NOFX — Liberal Animation **6**

86418 NOFX — White Trash, Two Heebs, & a Bean **8**

86419 DOWN BY LAW — Blue **7** Having established their sound, DBL now work on technique and *Blue* is a powerful blast, noticeably tighter and more cohesive than their debut.

86420 BAD RELIGION — Recipe for Hate **9**

86421 COFFIN BREAK — Thirteen **6**

86422 unreleased

86423 R.K.L. — Reactivate **5**

86424 THE OFFSPRING — Ignition **7**

86425 CLAW HAMMER — Pablum **5**

86426 R.K.L. — Rock & Roll Nightmare 6

86427 THELONIOUS MONSTER — Baby...You're Bummin' My Life Out in a Supreme Fashion 7

86428 RANCID — Rancid 6

86429 PENNYWISE — Unknown Road 8 The songs are sharper and the music varied, as Pennywise overcome hurdles both internal (the departure and return of vocalist Jim Lindberg) and external (mistaken for White Power supporters by passing media morons), resulting in a fervid album which proves the group are probably now unstoppable.

86430 SNFU — Something Green & Leafy This Way Comes 5 Canadian punk vets reform for a high energy, but slightly unfocused album.

86431 DOWN BY LAW — Punkrockacademyfightsong 8 Previously a cultish grassroots supergroup, Dave Smalley has finally decided to stop sharing members with other bands and keep them all to himself. So, an entirely new line-up and the change is obvious. Returning to old school roots, *Punk* is more melodic than previous releases, but equally raucous, a seething mix of early Jam and classic west coast hardcore, plus Smalley's own inimitable ear.

86432 THE OFFSPRING — Smash 9

86433 CLAW HAMMER — Thank the Holder-Uppers 7

86434 RANCID — Let's Go 8

86435 NOFX — Punk in Drublic 9

86436 TEN FOOT POLE — Rev 7 Changing their name (from Scared Straight), record label (previously with Mystic), and influences (they're now indebted to late '80s/early '90s Bad Religion), *Rev* is classic pop-punk — fast guitar assaults, revved up by the high energy rhythm section and lubricated with copious melodies and hooks.

86437 PENNYWISE — About Time 8 Moving from strength to strength, Pennywise's lyrics (arguably the band's forte) are even more scathing than usual, while remaining ultimately upbeat and uplifting. The addition of more harmonies makes *Time* virtually anthemic.

86438 TOTAL CHAOS — Pledge of Defiance 4 Agitpunk hardcore, with the group's radical message shouted over the roar of thrashing guitars (think Minor Threat taking a chainsaw to CRASS, with Henry Rollins trampling the severed limbs).

86439 GAS HUFFER — One Inch Masters 6 Not your typical Epitaph band, Gas Huffer hail from Seattle and, while *Masters* definitely fall into the punk category, there's more than a hint of grunge to be found in their sound. It's a unique one, however, living noisily in the cracks between pop-punk and hardcore.

86440 PENNYWISE — Home Movies (VHS)

86441 SNFU — The One Voted Most Likely to Succeed 6 Much sharper than *Green*, with shorter songs and more straightforward lyrics. It's even fairly cohesive.

86442 THE HUMPERS — Live Forever Or Die Trying 6

86443 BAD RELIGION — All Ages 7

86444 RANCID — ...And Out Come the Wolves 9

86445 R.K.L. — Riches to Rags 7 With the return of vocalist Jason Sears, RKL literally bristle with energy. The guitars are a roar of frenzied assault, the rhythm section slices and dices the beats, while Sears spits out "We're Back We're Pissed," an opener which aptly sums up the monster's intent.

86446 RED AUNTS — #1 Chicken 3 All girl group convinced that energy and anger can make up for a lack of musicianship. And maybe it can. But good ideas are definitely useful.

86447 WAYNE KRAMER — The Hard Stuff 6

86448 VARIOUS ARTISTS — Punk O Rama 7 The crucial first installment in a series of label samplers.

86449 THE CRAMPS — Flamejob 7

86450 TOTAL CHAOS — Patriotic Shock 6 Faster, angrier and heavier chords, the shout-along lyrics rise towards anthemhood... raw, violent mayhem for the next hardcore revival.

STEPHEN HAGUE

PRODUCER

BORN 1960 (*Portland, Maine*)

The 16-year-old Hague moved to Los Angeles in 1976 in search of a career in the music industry; he worked painting cars for a year, before being recruited to Walter Egan's band in time for the hit album *Not Shy* and single "Magnet and Steel," later forming Jules and the Polar Bears with songwriter Jules Shear. Hague would produce that band's first three albums, during 1978-80. Based now in Boston, Hague's first outside commission came after friend Peter Gabriel introduced him to the London-based Charisma label. They commissioned Hague to produce the Rock Steady Crew, and with a hit under his belt, paired him with former Sex Pistols manager Malcolm McLaren and the World Famous Supreme Team.

Having already handled OMD's *Crush* in 1985, Hague's major breakthrough, however, came when he linked with the Pet Shop Boys for their "West End Girls" debut; the union would remain solid for the next decade, establishing Hague as one of the leading exponents of "modern" production technology. Through the remainder of the decade, Hague's clinically precise methods would be brought to bear on artists as disparate as Marc Almond (the "A Lover Spurned" single), Siouxsie and the Banshees, New Order, and Sigue Sigue Sputnik.

His success and reputation were occasionally a double-edged sword. Utilizing up-to-date methods, after all, is only effective until even more up-to-date ones come along, and many of Hague's productions swiftly dated as technology moved on. The Banshees in particular noted that his aggressive programming on 1991's *Superstition* album did much to sour the album's memory for them, although other Hague productions from that era, the Pet Shop Boys, Public Image Ltd, and Flesh for Lulu among them, remain classics of their genre.

Into the 1990s, Hague's signature sound fell from fashion somewhat, as the earthier textures of grunge and punk moved back to center stage. He produced Blur's "To the End" single in 1994, however, further rehabilitating his methods via sterling work with the Manic Street Preachers, St. Etienne vocalist Sarah Cracknell, and post-Britpop icons Rialto.

Stephen Hague — Selected Productions

6 JULES & THE POLAR BEARS — Got No Breeding (Columbia) 1978

6 JULES & THE POLAR BEARS — Fenetics (Columbia) 1978

7 JULES & THE POLAR BEARS — Bad for Business (Columbia) 1980

6 SLOW CHILDREN — Slow Children (Ensign) 1981

3 OMD — Crush (Virgin) 1985 What was once edgy and subversive, iced electro-freakery on the brink of brilliance, topples over the edge into pretentious MOR artfulness, all studio perfection and not a drop of soul insight.

3 OMD — The Pacific Age (Virgin) 1986

8 PET SHOP BOYS — Please (EMI America) 1986 You've heard one, you've heard them all, but first time out, the Pet Shop's plaintive soulfulness clashed violently with the glacial electronics to poise enough pertinent questions to keep everything in the ascendant. Even in an idiot's hands, "West End Girls" would be a hard act to beat. For the Pet Shops, it was merely a difficult act to follow.

5 PETE SHELLEY — Heaven and the Sea (Mercury) 1986

4 MATTHEW SWEET — Inside (Columbia) 1986 Far from the heart-stopping indy guitar god of post-*Girlfriend* fame, Sweet's debut finds him little more than a fair singer-songwriter in desperate need of direction and drive.

4 HOLLYWOOD BEYOND — If (WB) 1987 Buoyed by the fabulous "What's the Color of Money," but sadly lacking much else of substance.

8 FLESH FOR LULU — Long Live the New Flesh (Beggars Banquet) 1987

6 COMMUNARDS — Red (London) 1987

6 HOUSE OF LOVE — House of Love (Creation) 1988

5 JANE WIEDLIN — Fur (EMI America) 1988

6 ERASURE — The Innocents (Sire) 1988

6 SIGUE SIGUE SPUTNIK — Dress for Excess (Atlantic) 1988

5 JIMMY SOMERVILLE — Read My Lips (London) 1990

5 SIOUXSIE AND THE BANSHEES — Superstition (Geffen) 1991

6 BANDERAS — Ripe (London) 1991

7 ONE DOVE — Morning Dove White (FFRR) 1993

5 NEW ORDER — Republic (Qwest) 1993

7 PET SHOP BOYS — Very (EMI) 1993 No reinvention, no change, no difference, but taking the Village People's "Go West" celebration of gay life by the bay and transforming it into a requiem for the victims of AIDS was an act of absolute genius.

7 THE OTHER TWO — And You (Qwest) 1994

6 PAPA WEMBA — Emotion (Real World) 1995

7 PET SHOP BOYS — Disco 2 (EMI) 1995

8 MANIC STREET PREACHERS — Everything Must Go (Epic) 1996 The assumption was that with vocalist Ritchey James having disappeared under still unsolved circumstances, Welsh megapunks the Manics were done for. Instead, they utterly reinvented themselves, a lot less abrasive, a lot more melodic, but still waving the same flag of sloganeering subversion.

6 JAMES — Whiplash (Fontana) 1997

7 DUBSTAR — Goodbye (Polydor) 1997

7 MANBREAK — Come and See (Almo) 1997

8 SPARKS — Plagiarism (Oglio) 1997

8 RIALTO — Rialto (Sire) 1998 First impressions are simply of a more precocious Pulp. But "Monday Morning 5.19" became one of the great love songs of the late 1990s, and Rialto weren't afraid to follow it either. The resultant album gets a little samey in places, but sufficient magic still shines through.

HANGMAN RECORDS

LABEL

Prolific label formed by the prodigious Billy Childish. Home to the Medway Beat and so much more.

Also see the entry for "BILLY CHILDISH" on page 256.

Hangman Records Label Listing

1 THEE MILKSHAKES — Milkshakes Revenge 7

2 BILLY CHILDISH — I've Got Everything Indeed 8

3 THEE MIGHTY CAESARS — Don't Give Any Dinner to Henry Chinaski 5

4 VARIOUS ARTISTS — Medway Powerhouse Vol 1 5

5 BILLY CHILDISH & Sexton Ming — Which Dead Donkey Daddy? 5

6 SEXTON MING — Old Horse of the Nation 6

7 THEE MIGHTY CAESARS — Punk Rock Showcase 7

8 VARIOUS ARTISTS — Medway Powerhouse Vol 2 5

9 BILLY CHILDISH — 1982 Cassettes 8

10 BILLY CHILDISH & Sexton Ming — Plump Prizes & Little Gems 6

11 THEE MILKSHAKES — Live in Chatham 7

12 BILLY CHILDISH & Sexton Ming — Ypres 1917 Overture 6

13 BILLY CHILDISH — I Remember 7

14 ROCKING RICHARD & WHISTLING VIC — Tea & Baccy 6

15 VARIOUS ARTISTS — The Medway Poets 8

MARTIN HANNETT

PRODUCER
BORN 1948 *(Wythenshaw, England)*

The architect of the Manchester/Factory Records sound of the late 1970s, Hannett was a local concert promotor whose first ever production, in 1976, was the debut album by the Belt and Braces Trucking Company, a band whose subsequent alliance with the Rock Against Racism organization would see them become one of Britain's hardest gigging bands. Their recording career, on the other hand, was extremely patchy (not to mention under-appreciated), but Hannett's deft handling of their agit-prop assault certainly deserved a fair hearing.

With that in mind, the producer landed an introduction to local scene-setter Tony Wilson, then hosting television's *So It Goes* new music showcase, in hopes of getting Belt and Braces a berth on the program. Wilson turned the band down, but intrigued by Hannett, agreed to attend an upcoming show by Slaughter and the Dogs, promoted by Hannett's Music Force company, and review it for one of the publications he was then writing for.

He didn't — and at the next Slaughter show, was forced to contend with Hannett's wrath. Days later, he was then confronted by another example of the man's talent, when a copy of the Buzzcocks' Hannett-produced *Spiral Scratch* EP landed on his desk, and over the next year, Wilson and Hannett continued orbiting one another; Wilson as he pieced together his Factory label, Hannett as he became the producer of choice for local bands.

Finally the two paired up, as Hannett was brought in to produce Factory's first release, a local compilation featuring Joy Division, Cabaret Voltaire, comedian John Dowie, and Durutti Column. In Joy Division's case, in particular, Hannett was to prove the catalyst in the band's own search for a sound, and during the four years which followed, he remained Factory's primary producer — reciprocating by seldom accepting commission from any other label, or even, any other city.

Those outsiders that he did work with, however, indicated the strength of his own eye for talent: U2's first British single, "11 O'Clock Tick Tock," was a Hannett production; while he came close to handling the Psychedelic Furs' second album, *Talk Talk Talk*, recording two tracks with them ("Soap Commercial" and "Susan Strange") which would then be grafted onto US editions of the band's first album. In both of these instances, incidentally, Hannett was succeeded by Steve Lillywhite.

An increasingly difficult private life, including serious dalliances with drink and drugs, saw Hannett move away from production in 1982 — over the next half-decade he would resurface just once, when he was persuaded to work with the then utterly unknown Stone Roses. Then he sank back into obscurity, before Factory recalled him to handle the Happy Mondays.

Seemingly reinvigorated by the experience, Hannett also worked with the Heart Throbs and the New Fast Automatic Daffodils. This new dawn, however, came too late — years of drug use had seriously weakened Hannett's system. He died of heart failure on 4/18/91.

Martin Hannett — Selected Productions

7 BELT AND BRACES TRUCKING CO — Belt and Braces (B&B) 1976

9 JOHN COOPER CLARKE — Disguise in Love (Epic) 1978
Genius colloquial punk poet, featuring the immortal "I Married a Monster from Outer Space," "Psycle Sluts," and "I Don't Want to Be Nice," with savage backing from the Invisible Girls.

10 JOY DIVISION — Unknown Pleasures (Factory) 1979

8 DURUTTI COLUMN — The Return Of (Factory) 1979

8 JOY DIVISION — Closer (Factory) 1980

8 MAGAZINE — Correct Use of Soap (Virgin) 1980

7 BASEMENT 5 — 1965-80 (Island) 1980

7 PAULINE MURRAY — ...& The Invisible Girls (RSO) 1980

9 JOHN COOPER CLARKE — Snap Crackle Bop (Epic) 1980
More of the same, only even more manic — "Beasley Street" is the nightmare mirror image of a 100 snapshots of suburban bliss from Blur, Madness, Space and co.; the classic "Twat," meanwhile, packs more smart ass, one-line insults into a song than you could wear out in a year.

5 A CERTAIN RATIO — To Each... (Factory) 1980

8 BASEMENT 5 — In Dub (Island) 1981 As much Hannett's baby as the band's (themselves members of Island Records' below-stairs art department!), and featuring future Big Audio Dynamite bassist Leo Williams, a collection of dub remixes/reinventions of Basement 5's debut.

8 ESG — ESG (99) 1981 Supremely edgy south Bronx quartet — the Raincoats with full no wave disdain — combining dub drum and bass with supremely lazy vocals, a half live/half studio six-track monster.

8 A CERTAIN RATIO — Sextet (Factory) 1981

7 SECTION 25 — Always Now (Factory) 1981

8 NEW ORDER — Movement (Factory) 1982

7 JOY DIVISION — Still (Factory) 1982

7 JOHN COOPER CLARKE — Zip Style Method (Epic) 1982

8 HAPPY MONDAYS — Bummed (Elektra) 1989

6 HEART THROBS — Cleopatra Grip (Elektra) 1990

JERRY HARRISON

PRODUCER
BORN 2/21/49 *(Milwaukee, MN)*

A member of Jonathan Richman's classic Modern Lovers, before joining Talking Heads in 1976, Harrison moved into production during one of the longer breaks in the Heads' schedule, handling recordings by Bonzo Goes to Washington and Elliott Murphy, then moving seriously into the arena with the Violent Femmes.

For much of the 1980s, he worked only sporadically; in 1991, however, Capitol Records contacted him regarding a young band they had recently signed, Live. Harrison became the band's first producer, and with that album's success, found his own phone ringing more and more. Poi Dog Pondering, Irish rockers Black 47, and Verve Pipe have since emerged among his more adventurous efforts; Crash Test Dummies, Noella Hutton, and return engagements with Live among his most successful — while he would also gallantly pull together the Duran Duran/Sex Pistols supergroup Neurotic Outsiders in 1996.

Also see the entry for the "TALKING HEADS" on page 675.

Jerry Harrison — Selected Productions

6 VIOLENT FEMMES — The Blind Leading the Naked (Slash) 1986

6 BO DEANS — Outside Looking In (Slash) 1987

4 LIVE — Mental Jewelry (Radioactive) 1991

5 PSYCHEFUNKAPUS — Skin (Atlantic) 1991

8 PURE — Purefunalia (Reprise) 1992 Hopping between Catherine Wheel, the Chameleons UK, and anything which else comes to mind, a rummage sale through the last 3 years of the UK Top 10.

6 POI DOG PONDERING — Volo Volo (Columbia) 1992

5 CRASH TEST DUMMIES — God Shuffled His Feet (Arista) 1993

4 LIVE — Throwing Copper (Radioactive) 1994 Sub-REM collegiate rockers discover a smidgen of originality amid the morass of old copies of *Monster*. Fans insist "Selling the Drama" was quite good.

8 BLACK 47 — Home of the Brave (SBK) 1994

5 FATIMA MANSIONS — Lost in the Former West (1995) 1995 It's a long way from minimalist terrors Microdisney, where vocalist Coughlan began his career... or is it?

5 BOGMEN — Life Begins at 40 Million (Arista) 1995

7 VERVE PIPE — Villains (RCA) 1996

6 RUSTED ROOT — Remember (Mercury) 1996

5 NEUROTIC OUTSIDERS — Neurotic Outsiders (Maverick) 1996

6 BIG HEAD TODD & THE MONSTERS — Beautiful World (Revolution) 1997

4 LIVE — Distance to Here (MCA) 1999

4 KENNY WAYNE SHEPHERD — Live On (WB) 1999

4 STROKE NINE — Nasty Little Thoughts (Uptown) 1999

MIKE HEDGES

PRODUCER

BORN 1953 (Nottingham, England)

Born in England but raised in Zambia, Africa, Hedges returned to the UK in 1969, playing in a succession of low-key bands before being offered a job as teaboy at London's Morgan Studios. Within three months he had risen to tape operator — his first credit came as assistant engineer on dance band Heatwave's *Central Heating* album in 1977; he also engineered Alex Harvey's swansong *The Mafia Stole My Guitar*, and the first singles by the Cure.

As producer, he worked alongside both the Cure and labelmates the Associates for three albums a piece, before going freelance in 1981, and opening his own Playground Studio. Among his earliest clients, Siouxsie and the Banshees, Southern Death Cult, and Pete Wylie set the stage for his best work: the succession of peerless Marc Almond albums released during 1984–87.

By 1992, Hedges was tiring of production and decided to retire to France. His resolution lasted less than a month — soon he was outfitting a new studio, Chateau Rouge Motte in Normandy, adding pro-tools to his arsenal. Crucial albums by Lush, the Manic Street Preachers, and Geneva followed, while 1995 also brought a reunion with Almond.

Mike Hedges — Selected Productions

8 THE CURE — Three Imaginary Boys (Fiction) 1979

8 ASSOCIATES — Affectionate Punch (Fiction) 1980 Broad, Bowie-esque strokes on the kind of canvas Eno's first two albums left littering the landscape; a joyously precocious romp.

9 THE CURE — 17 Seconds (Elektra) 1980

10 THE CURE — Faith (Elektra) 1981

7 ASSOCIATES — Fourth Drawer Down (Situation 2) 1981

7 ASSOCIATES — Sulk (Sire) 1982

7 SIOUXSIE AND THE BANSHEES — Kiss in the Dreamhouse (Geffen) 1982

7 SIOUXSIE AND THE BANSHEES — Nocturne (Geffen) 1983

7 CREATURES — Feast (Wonderland) 1983

9 UNDERTONES — Sin of Pride (Sire) 1983

6 MARC ALMOND — Vermin in Ermine (Some Bizzare) 1984

7 SIOUXSIE AND THE BANSHEES — Hyaena (Geffen) 1984

8 WAH! — A Word to the Wise Guy (Beggars Banquet) 1984

6 THREE O'CLOCK — Arrive Without Travelling (IRS) 1985

6 MARC ALMOND — Stories of Johnny (Some Bizzare) 1985

8 EVERYTHING BUT THE GIRL — Baby the Stars Shine (Sire) 1986 Tracey Thorn and Ben Watt come of age with a startlingly orchestral production, close to soul for the cocktail set.

8 SIOUXSIE AND THE BANSHEES- Through the Looking Glass (Geffen) 1987

7 SHAMEN — Drop (Communion) 1987

9 MARC ALMOND — Mother Fist... (Some Bizarre) 1987

7 SIOUXSIE AND THE BANSHEES — Peepshow (1988) 1988

7 CREATURES — Boomerang (Geffen) 1989

7 BEAUTIFUL SOUTH — Welcome To (Go! Discs) 1989

6 BEAUTIFUL SOUTH — Choke (Go! Discs) 1990

8 A HOUSE — I Want Too Much (Reprise) 1990 Slathering on the charm, *Want*'s ludicrously catchy, if somewhat ramshackle songs whine through the bare bones instrumentation, verging on lo-fi production. The stakes are raised considerably, though, by the band's Celtic lyrical wit and musical elan.

7 SENSATION — Burger Habit (550) 1994

8 LUSH — Split (4AD) 1994

7 THE CATCHERS — Mute (Discovery) 1995

8 MARC ALMOND — Fantastic Star (Some Bizzare) 1995

7 A HOUSE — No More Apologies (Setanta) 1996

6 TEXAS — White on Blonde (Mercury) 1997

7 GENEVA — Further (Work) 1997

STEVE HILLAGE

PRODUCER

BORN 8/2/51 (London, England)

Time and tradition play strange games on musical history, as one of the alternative era's most idiosyncratic producers/remixers (not to mention musicians) is revealed as one of the post-hippy underground's most dedicated. Hillage's first band of note, Uriel, flowered in London during 1967–68, recorded an eponymous album under the name Arzachel, then splintered when Hillage enrolled at the University of Kent.

His next band, Khan, locked into the prog rock boom to record the almost frighteningly po-faced *Space Shanties* (1972), before Hillage quit to join first, Kevin Ayers' Whole Wide World (also home to teen bassist Mike Oldfield at one point), then Gong, the space-age hippy commune best remembered for recording a trilogy of albums around the cosmic adventures of a flying teapot. (Fellow future producer Mike Howlett was also a memeber.)

Hillage quit Gong in 1976, shortly after founder Daevid Allen and both launched solo careers — Allen with a New York Gong whose floating membership at one point included producer Kramer; Hillage for a string of new age/ambient inflected albums with actress/partner Miquette

Giraudy. But he also worked briefly with Sham 69 (around the same time as he regaled a surprised *NME* journalist with a lengthy dissertation on the superior intelligence of cabbages), and after making his production debut on Nik Turner's *Sphinx Xitintoday*, he virtually abandoned his own recording career for life on the other side of the mixing desk.

A bizarrely successful production job on Simple Minds' *Sons and Fascination* album (during which Hillage reputedly kept a potted plant in the studio, to give him someone to talk to) and a less enjoyable union with Robyn Hitchcock followed, and through the remainder of the decade, his most notable work was with Cock Robin's European smash *Cock Robin*, and It Bites. A meeting with Orb frontman in 1989 then saw Hillage and Giraudy become ipso facto members of that group.

Hillage brought more than a weighty reputation to the Orb. He also introduced Paterson to the organic purity of Gong's original sonics, recreating in full the effects which Paterson, Thrash, and a growing coterie of attendant DJs had hitherto only been able to duplicate — glissando guitar and space whispers included. Past-time potheads who might never have looked at a 1990s copyright record flocked to the Orb's banner; the Orb responded by expanding their musical horizons via Hillage and Giraudy's own satellite project 777/System 7.

Steve Hillage — Selected Productions

⑧ **NIK TURNER — Sphynx (Charisma) 1978** The legendary original recording, superior to its 1990s Cleopatra remake only in that the concept was a lot fresher back then.

⑧ **SIMPLE MINDS — Sister Feelings Call (Virgin) 1981**

⑧ **SIMPLE MINDS — Sons & Fascination (Virgin) 1981** Two discs from the same session, Minds' slow shift towards brighter commercial pastures runs up against the mantric obstinacy of both Hillage's production and the band's own sense of rhythm. Few of the actual songs stand out, but the momentum of each is spellbinding.

⑥ **ROBYN HITCHCOCK — Groovy Decay (Albion) 1982**

⑤ **COCK ROBIN — Cock Robin (Columbia) 1985**

⑥ **IT BITES — Big Lad in the Windmill (Geffen) 1986**

⑥ **IT BITES — Once Around the World (Geffen) 1988**

⑥ **IT BITES — Eat Me in St Lous (Geffen) 1989**

⑨ **THE ORB — Adventures Beyond the Ultraworld (Big Live) 1991**

⑧ **THE ORB — Uforb (Big Life) 1992**

⑦ **CHARLATANS UK — Up to Our Hips (Beggars Banquet) 1994**

⑥ **BLINK — A Map of the Universe (Lime) 1995**

⑧ **RACHID TAHA — Ole Ole (Island) 1996**

⑦ **BLINK — Blink (Lime) 1998**

TREVOR HORN

PRODUCER
BORN *7/15/49 (Durham, England)*

An aspiring songwriter and studio musician through the 1970s, working with disco hitmaker Tina Charles among others, Trevor Horn first came to prominence in 1979 as a member of Bruce Wooley's highly-rated Camera Club (also featuring Thomas Dolby). By the end of the year, however, he and fellow Charles graduate Geoff Downes had broken away to form Buggles, the sci-fi duo whose "Video Killed the Radio Star" so presciently ushered in the age of MTV.

Revealed across the course of both single and the attendant *Age of Plastic* album as a producer and writer of astonishing vision and originality, Horn and Downes were invited first to produce, and then join '70s supergroup Yes, in time for their *90125*/"Owner of a Lonely Heart" renaissance. Horn alone would simultaneously become one of the UK's most in-demand producers.

Through 1982–83, hit singles with ABC ("Poison Arrow") and Dollar (the sumptuous "Give Me Back My Heart") persuaded Island Records to give Horn his own label. Teaming with journalist Paul Morley, Horn launched ZTT with Art of Noise, before dominating the UK chart as the sonic mastermind behind Frankie Goes to Hollywood. Other ZTT successes during 1984–85 included Propaganda and Grace Jones — later, the label would launch Seal, and relaunch both Kirsty MacColl and Pogues vocalist Shane MacGowan.

Still undertaking outside production, Horn linked with former 10cc mainstays and renowned video directors Godley and Creme for 1985's wildly ambitious *The History Mix*, an album which foreshadowed much of the following decade's sampling and programming technology. That duo's Lol Creme would later join Horn in British television's Glam Metal Detectives, and in 1998, the reborn Art of Noise. Simple Minds, Rod Stewart, Mike Oldfield, Paul McCartney, and Tina Turner have also numbered among Horn's most successful clients.

Also see the entry for "ZANG TUMB TUUM (ZTT)" on page 815.

Trevor Horn — Selected Productions (Non-ZTT)

⑥ **ABC — Lexicon of Love (Mercury) 1982** Their debut; we never would have made it though the year without "The Look of Love" and "Poison Arrow."

⑦ **MALCOLM MCLAREN — Duck Rock (Island) 1982** McLaren was the Sex Pistols' ex-manager, finally tiring of hiring musicians to conduct his odd little schemes. *Duck Rock* served up his take on hip-hop — oddly shot through with Appalachian cow-punk, and even more oddly spawning a massive hit single, "Buffalo Girls;" the world's first techno square dance.

7 **PHILIP JAPP** — **Philip Japp (A&M) 1983** One of those flighty new romantic types, making an album of ineffably camp synthi-Bowie rock, simply because all of his friends had. Did a good job of it, as well.

9 **GODLEY AND CREME** — **The History Mix (Polydor) 1985** Dynamic collage of the duo's past work (with Hotlegs, 10cc under their own name), merged into two long effects-heavy suites. Clumsy by modern technological standards, but remarkably strong regardless.

6 **ACT** — **Laughter Tears & Rage (AVI) 1987**

6 **PAUL MCCARTNEY** — **Flowers in the Dirt (Capitol) 1989**

5 **SIMPLE MINDS** — **Street Fighting Years (A&M) 1989**

8 **SEAL** — **Seal (Sire) 1991** Unpredictable post-Bryan Ferry type character, blessed however with a dynamic range, best witnessed across "Killer" (with Adamski) and "Crazy."

7 **SEAL** — **Seal (Second Album) (Sire) 1994**

8 **MARIE BRENNAN** — **Misty Eyed Adventures (Mesa) 1995**

7 **SHANE MACGOWAN** — **The Snake (ZTT) 1995**

6 **PATO BANTON** — **Stay Positive (Capitol) 1996**

7 **SEAL** — **Human Being (WB) 1998**

MIKE HOWLETT

PRODUCER

BORN *(Fiji Islands)*

The self-styled greatest Fijiian record producer of all time arrived in Britain in 1970, after his family moved to Australia and his first serious band, the Sydney based Affair, set out on tour. Remaining in London, Howlett was recruited to spac-erockers Gong, alongside Daevid Allen and Steve Hillage, staying on board throughout that group's period of greatest impact, then quitting in 1976.

With Gong's label Virgin encouraging Howlett to work in production and A&R, Howlett was instrumental in the birth of the Police — having "discovered" the future Sting playing with a jazz rock band called Last Exit. Howlett then paired him with veteran guitarist Andy Summers in Strontium 90, a band Howlett was piecing together with Nik Turner among others, to record on the political left of the rock protest circuit. With the line-up completed by drummer Stewart Copeland, and Howlett playing bass, Strontium 90 recorded a number of demos, including an early version of "Every Little Thing She Does Is Magic."

In 1977, Howlett produced Virgin's live sampler *Short Circuit at the Electric Factory*, a memorial to the influential Manchester punk club and featuring performances by the Buzzcocks, Joy Division, the Fall, and more. Thereafter, he would record vital albums by Penetration, the Comsat Angels, Fischer Z, and Punishment of Luxury, before scor-ing his first major hits with Martha and the Muffins' "Echo Beach" and OMD's "Enola Gay."

Howlett would then be recruited to mastermind A Flock of Seagulls' transition from dour electronic mavens to spar-kling pop superstars, but after five years spent on the cutting edge of new wave electronic, Howlett defected to hard rock production with generally unsatisfying consequences. Abandoning production, at least temporarily, he reunited with most of his old Gong bandmates (Hillage alone remained absent) in 1994, for one of the decade's most surprisingly enjoyable reinventions.

Mike Howlett — Selected Productions

8 **PENETRATION** — **Moving Targets (Virgin) 1978** Pauline Murray was blessed with one of the greatest voices in the entire first wave punk scene; her band with some of the sharpest songs. "Don't Dictate" remains their masterpiece, but they rarely put a foot wrong anywhere else.

8 **FISCHER Z** — **Word Salad (UA) 1979** Somewhat quirk-laden, but infinitely memorable stab at making the new wave sound even newer.

7 **COMSAT ANGELS** — **Land (Arista) 1979** Dramatically dark Sheffield-based band whose subsequent obscurity remains utterly baffling.

7 **PUNISHMENT OF LUXURY** — **Laughing Academy (UA) 1979**

7 **MARTHA AND THE MUFFINS** — **Metro Music (Virgin) 1979**

7 **HUNTERS & COLLECTORS** — **Hunters & Collectors (Virgin) 1980**

6 **STRAIGHT EIGHT** — **Shuffle &'Cut (Logo) 1980**

6 **REVILLOS** — **Rev Up (Dindisc) 1980** As the Rezillos, they were Scotland's punk trash finest; the B-52's with even more revved up zip. As the Revillos, the lunacy remained but the individuality sadly faded.

8 **FISCHER Z** — **Going Deaf for a Living (UA) 1980**

7 **MARTHA AND THE MUFFINS** — **Trance & Dance (Virgin) 1980**

8 **OMD** — **Organization (Virgin) 1980** Smart lyrics, sharp songs ("Enola Gay"), and genuinely innovative use of electronics bely the sad maudlinities which will scar the bulk of this band's career.

7 **SNIFF 'N' THE TEARS** — **Love Action (Chiswick) 1981**

6 **ANY TROUBLE** — **Wheels in Motion (Stiff) 1981**

8 **A FLOCK OF SEAGULLS** — **A Flock of Seagulls (Arista) 1981**

7 **ORIGINAL MIRRORS** — **Heart Twango (Phonogram) 1981**

8 **OMD** — **Architecture & Morality (Epic) 1981** Another winner, with "Joan of Arc" and "Souvenirs" both maintaining OMD's grasp on crystalline, evocative electro.

6 **BLANCMANGE** — **Happy Families (Island) 1982**

7 **GANG OF FOUR** — **Songs of the Free (WB) 1982**

7 **CHINA CRISIS** — **Working with Fire & Steel (Virgin) 1983**

6 A FLOCK OF SEAGULLS — Listen (Arista) 1983

4 BERLIN — Love Life (Geffen) 1984

7 THE ALARM — Strength (IRS) 1985

6 COMSAT ANGELS — 7 Day Weekend (Arista) 1985

6 SIREN — All Is Forgiven (Mercury) 1989

5 THE ALARM — Standards (IRS) 1990

INDUSTRIAL RECORDS

LABEL

Though it ultimately became much more than that, giving its very name to an entire (and not altogether related) musical genre, Industrial Records was formed in 1977, as part of Throbbing Gristle's investigation into the music industry — and also because a hoped-for deal with Virgin Records had eventually fallen apart.

"We wanted to... investigate music as a Business phenomenon, and propose models for entirely new and innovative modes of commercial operation," explained Genesis P-Orridge. Yet by 1981, when Industrial finally closed its doors, the label was one of the most successful operations of its kind in the country, and that despite a catalog almost utterly devoid of even vaguely popular music.

The first record released under Industrial's stylized logo — one of the main ovens at Auschwitz — was IR 002, in November 1977; over the next four years, the bulk of the label's output would be drawn from Throbbing Gristle's voluminous repertoire, although collaborator Monte Cazazza and the like-minded Cabaret Voltaire and Clock DVA would also see releases. TG-member Chris Carter, too, would release his first solo album through the label, prior to forming Chris and Cosey with bandmate Cosey Fanni Tutti.

Few of Industrial's releases were handled in a conventional manner. Cazazza's 1979 single "To Mom on Mother's Day," was recorded with the artist himself wearing earphones, in which a long electronic bleep ensured he could not hear his own vocals — the backing track was performed by Throbbing Gristle, to written instructions supplied by Cazazza one year later. Cazazza's contract with the label, incidentally, bound him to Industrial for life, and was signed in blood. It was, all agreed, the perfect parody of the modern, conventional record deal.

Also see the entry for "THROBBING GRISTLE" on page 685.

Industrial Records Label Listing 1976–81

001 unreleased

002 THROBBING GRISTLE — 2nd Annual Report 8

003 THROBBING GRISTLE — United 7-inch

004 THROBBING GRISTLE — DOA: The Third and Final Report 7

005 MONTE CAZAZZA — To Mom on Mother's Day 7-inch

006 LEATHER NUN — Slow Death EP

007 THOMAS LEER/ROBERT RENTAL — The Bridge 8

008 THROBBING GRISTLE — 20 Jazz Funk Greats 8

009 THROBBING GRISTLE — Hearthen Earth 7

010 MONTE CAZAZZA — Something for Nobody EP

011 SURGICAL PENIS KLINIK — Meat Processing Section 6

012 ELISABETH WELCH — Stormy Weather 7-inch

013 THROBBING GRISTLE — Subhuman 7-inch

014 DOROTHY — I Confess 7-inch

015 THROBBING GRISTLE — Adrenalin 7-inch

016 WILLIAM BURROUGHS — Nothing Here Now But the Recordings 6

Industrial Records Cassettes

1–26: THROBBING GRISTLE — Various Live/Outtake Collections 5   Above are all relatively poor quality live and out-take collections, released on cassette only during 1979–80, the so-called *Industrial Records Cassette Collection*.

27 LEATHER NUN — At Scala Cinema 6   Raw, in-concert recording, subsequently reissued by Wire Records. Guests include P-Orridge and Cazazza.

28 MONTE CAZAZZA — Live at Leeds Fan Club, Etc. 5   Good quality document of three UK shows during February/March 1980.

29 THROBBING GRISTLE — Live at Goldsmith's College 3

30 THROBBING GRISTLE — Live at Oundle Public School 3

31 CLOCK DVA — White Souls in Black Suits 6

32 CHRIS CARTER — The Space Between 5

33 THROBBING GRISTLE — Live at Sheffield University 3

34 RICHARD H KIRK — Disposable Half Truths 7

35 CABARET VOLTAIRE — 1974–76 6

DAVE JERDEN

PRODUCER

The son of a bass player, Jerden all but grew up in the studio environment, learning very early on to appreciate the man at the back with all the knobs and dials. Resolving to follow in such footsteps, Jerden made his engineering debut with Talking Heads' *Remain in Light* and Brian Eno and David Byrne's *My Life in the Bush of Ghosts* in 1980/81. That later year also saw him produce Jerry Harrison's 1981 debut album, while he continued engineering for such names as Herbie Hancock, Mick Jagger, and the Rolling Stones.

By the mid-1980s, Jerden's own interests had moved into the L.A. underground, producing What is This? and the Beat

Farmers, and engineering the Red Hot Chili Peppers. A familiar figure on the mid-80s Scream scene, Jerden would then oversee Jane's Addiction's major label debut, *Nothing's Shocking*, which in turn, led him as far a field as Alice in Chains, Social Distortion, Public Image Ltd, and the Offspring.

Dave Jerden — Selected Productions

6 **JERRY HARRISON** — The Red and the Black (Sire) 1981

7 **BEAT FARMERS** — Pursuit of Happiness (Curb) 1987

8 **JANE'S ADDICTION** — Nothing's Shocking (WB) 1988

8 **JANE'S ADDICTION** — Ritual De Lo Habitual (WB) 1990

8 **SOCIAL DISTORTION** — Social Distortion (Epic) 1990

3 **MARY'S DANISH** — Circa (Morgan Creek) 1991

4 **ALICE IN CHAINS** — Facelift (Columbia) 1991 Putting the lie to the "grunge is punk" debate, as Alice settles unapologetically in amid the big guitars and dumb defiance of Metal Any Era, swamped in fashionable distortion and mud.

4 **BULLET LAVOLTA** — Swandive (RCA) 1991

7 **PUBLIC IMAGE LTD** — That What Is Not (Virgin) 1992

9 **SOCIAL DISTORTION** — Between Heaven and Hell (Epic) 1992

6 **DIG** — Wasteland (Caroline) 1993

8 **LOVE SPIT LOVE** — Love Spit Love (Imago) 1994

4 **BIOHAZARD** — Mata Leao (WB) 1996

4 **EDNASWAP** — Wacko Magneto (Island) 1997

7 **OFFSPRING** — Ixnay on the Hombre (Columbia) 1997

7 **STABBING WESTWARD** — Darkest Days (Columbia) 1998

5 **ANGELIQUE** — Prsent (Red Ant) 1998

8 **OFFSPRING** — Americana (Columbia) 1998

5 **DISAPPOINTMENT INCORPORATED** — FO (Time Bomb) 1999

GARETH JONES

PRODUCER
BORN 1954 *(England)*

A former BBC technical operator and studio manager, Gareth Jones began working at London's Pathway Studios in 1980, engineering early recordings by Madness and ex-Ultravox vocalist John Foxx before joining the latter in a new studio venture, the Garden. Jones was employed as staff engineer, and it was there that he encountered Depeche Mode — a band he initially had no interest in working with. However, after the band's first choice of engineer didn't work out, Jones was brought in to handle the "Love in Itself" single, and by the end of the year, he was sufficiently involved to claim a co-production credit on their next album, *Construction Time Again*.

Working in Berlin with the band, Jones met his future wife Anete Humpe (of German new wave band Ideal); he relocated to the city, working at Hansa Studios and engineering and producing a string of native bands, including Ideal and Einsturzende Neubauten. His relationship with Depeche Mode flowered, while he would also work with fellow Mute label acts Nick Cave, Erasure, Inspiral Carpets, and Wire. Jones returned to the UK in 1992, maintaining his Mute links, and moving successfully into the techno field as producer of Sheep on Drugs.

Gareth Jones — Selected Productions

8 **DEPECHE MODE** — Some Great Reward (Mute) 1984

8 **EINSTURZENDE NEUBAUTEN** — Halber Mensch 1985

9 **DEPECHE MODE** — Black Celebration (Sire) 1986

9 **WIRE** — The Ideal Copy (Enigma) 1987

8 **TUXEDOMOON** — Suite En Sous Sol (Cram Boy) 1987

8 **WIRE** — A Bell Is a Cup (Enigma) 1988

7 **ERASURE** — Wild! (Sire) 1989 Or at least, as wild as Erasure ever get, with "Drama" and the supreme "You Surround Me" offering further invigorating slabs of the duo's electronic cabaret.

6 **HOUSE OF LOVE** — Spy in the House Of (Fontana) 1991

3 **SIMON BONNEY** — Forever (Mute) 1992

8 **SHEEP ON DRUGS** — Greatest Hits (Island) 1993 Manic acid rave techno excursions; a rapidfire beat and electronics blitzkrieg.

6 **PLAN B** — Cyber Chords & Sushi Stories (Imago) 1993

6 **DIAMANDA GALAS** — Masque of the Red Death (Mute) 1993

7 **SHEEP ON DRUGS** — From A to H (Smash) 1994

7 **ERASURE** — Erasure (Sire) 1995

7 **SIMON BONNEY** — Everyman (Mute) 1995

6 **IRWIN SCHMIDT** — Impossible Holidays (Fine Line) 1996

6 **ORIGINAL SOUNDTRACK** — To Have & to Hold (Mute) 1997
Nick Cave powered soundscapes, dignified by a rare appearance from Scott Walker.

7 **ERASURE** — Cowboy (Sire) 1997

HUGH JONES

PRODUCER
BORN *(London, England)*

As an apprentice engineer at London's IBC Studios in the early 1970s, Jones' first engineering commission was jazzman Chick Corea's *Light as a Feather* in 1972, although he was more likely to be found recording orchestral pop through the mid-1970s, before taking a year's sabbatical in 1977 while he contemplated his future plans.

In 1978, he moved across country to the rural Rockfield Studios in Monmouthshire, Wales, where he engineered early releases by Teardrop Explodes and Echo and the Bunnymen; he also produced ex-X-Ray Spex saxophonist Laura Logic, and in 1981 he handled the Bunnymen's *Heaven Up Here* album.

Bauhaus, the Damned, and the Undertones followed, before Jones joined with 4AD act Modern English for their *After the Snow* debut album, home to the international hit "I Melt with You." He followed through with another '80s anthem, Icicle Works' "Birds Fly (From a Whisper to a Scream)" before departing Rockfield in 1985 for Los Angeles. There he handled Wall of Voodoo frontman Stan Ridgway's *The Big Heat*, but he soon returned home, producing a string of classic, if under-appreciated albums by the Saints, James, Voice of the Beehive, and Kitchens of Distinction.

Still heavily involved with the 4AD/Beggars Banquet axis, Jones would also produce the Charlatans UK's *Between 10th and 11th* sophomore album, Died Pretty's *Doughboy Hollow*, and acclaimed sets by Heidi Berry, the Pale Saints, and the superlative Shack.

Hugh Jones — Selected Productions

6 ESSENTIAL LOGIC — Beat Rhythm News (Rough Trade) 1979

7 ECHO AND THE BUNNYMEN — Heaven Up Here (Sire) 1981

7 THE SOUND — From the Lion's Den (Korova) 1981

7 UNDERTONES — Positive Touch (Sire) 1981

6 MOTHMEN — One Black Dot (Do It) 1982

6 MODERN ENGLISH — After the Snow (Sire) 1983

7 MONSOON — Third Eye (MSC) 1983 Powerful sub-continental Indian-based pop, with vocalist Sheila Chandra a rising star.

8 CLOCK DVA — Advantage (Polydor) 1983

6 MODERN ENGLISH — Ricochet Days (Sire) 1984

7 ICICLE WORKS — Icicle Works (4AD) 1984

6 DEL AMITRI — Del Amitri (Chrysalis) 1985

6 COLOURFIELD — Virgins & Philistines (Chrysalis) 1985
After a promisingly sonic beginning, and the magnificent "Colourfield" debut single, disappointing first album from Terry Hall's first post-Fun Boy Three outfit.

6 STAN RIDGWAY — The Big Heat (IRS) 1986

5 THAT PETROL EMOTION — Manic Pop Thrill (Demon) 1986

5 DUMPTRUCK — For the Country (Big Time) 1987

8 THE SAINTS — All Fools Day (TVT) 1987

7 BALAAM & THE ANGEL — Greatest Story Ever Told (Virgin) 1987

7 JAMES — Strip-Mine (Sire) 1988 Second album from the original "new Smiths," with the title track suggesting they may shake the tag off. One day.

6 STUMP — Fierce Pancake (Chrysalis) 1988

6 DEL AMITRI — Waking Hours (A&M) 1990

5 KITCHENS OF DISTINCTION — Strange Free World (A&M) 1990

7 ULTRA VIVID SCENE — Joy 1967-90 (4AD) 1990

6 CONNELLS — One Simple Word (TVT) 1990

6 PARACHUTE MEN — Earth, Dogs & Eggshells (Fire) 1990

8 PALE SAINTS — In Ribbons (4AD) 1992

7 DIED PRETTY — Doughboy Hollow (Beggars Banquet) 1992

6 KITCHENS OF DISTINCTION — Death of Cool (A&M) 1992

7 DIED PRETTY — Trace (Columbia) 1993

6 HEIDI BERRY — Heidi Berry (4AD) 1993

6 GLEE CLUB — Mine (4AD) 1994

6 PALE SAINTS — Slow Buildings (4AD) 1994

7 BLUETONES — Expecting to Fly (A&M) 1996

6 HEIDI BERRY — Miracle (4AD) 1996

7 DODGY — Free Peace Sweet (Mercury) 1997

9 SHACK — HMS Fable (Sire) 1999 Former Pale Fountain Mike Head conjures emotive Brit post-pop masterpiece — varied moods, obtuse lyrics, powerful melodies, and superb sonics.

PAUL Q KOLDERIE & SEAN SLADE

PRODUCERS

BORN *(Minneapolis, MN and Rockland Co, NY, respectively)*

The masterminds behind Boston's famed Fort Apache studio set-up met at Yale in 1975, before relocating to Boston in the late 1970s, and establishing themselves as producers on the local punk scene.

By the end of the decade, having worked with the Lemonheads, the Mighty Mighty Bosstones, and Dinosaur Jr, the duo first came to international attention as producers of Radiohead's seminal *Pablo Honey* album and attendant "Creep" single — Radiohead, in turn, were alerted to the team by their work with Buffalo Tom.

Working first out of a converted laundry building in a run-down part of Roxbury, then from a new studio in Cambridge, the Fort Apache team landed a production deal with MCA in 1994, following hits with Hole, Juliana Hatfield, Echobelly, and more.

Showcasing both their own work and that of fellow Fort Apache producers Lou Giordano, Tim O'Heir, and Gary Smith, the duo released a powerful sampler, *This Is Fort Apache*, featuring many of the artists who worked at the studios — the Walkabouts, Billy Bragg, and Throwing Muses included. The Fort Apache label made a handful of signings, including Shatterproof, Cold Water Flat, and Speedball Baby, but there was little commercial success, and when the deal was dissolved, the duo returned to freelance status.

Paul Kolderie & Sean Slade — Selected Productions

7 DAS DAMEN — Mousetrap (Twin/Tone) 1989

5 LEMONHEADS — Lovey (Atlantic) 1990

7 MIGHTY MIGHTY BOSSTONES — Devil's Night Out (Taang!) 1990

9 UNCLE TUPELO — No Depression (Rockville) 1990

5 COCKHAMMER — Klinefelter (RCA) 1991

5 360S — Illuminated (Hollywood) 1991

8 UNCLE TUPELO — Still Feel Gone (Rockville) 1991

6 FIELD TRIP — Ripe (Slash) 1991

6 BUFFALO TOM — Let Me Come Over (Beggars Banquet) 1992

6 RADIOHEAD — Pablo Honey (Capitol) 1993

5 ORANGUTANG — The Rewards of Cruelty (Imago) 1993

6 BLACKFISH — Blackfish (Epic) 1993

6 TRIPMASTER MONKEY — Goodbye Race (Sire) 1994

5 ORANGUTANG — Dead Sailor Acid Blues (Imago) 1994

7 FAMILY CAT — Magic Happens (Arista) 1994 The Family Cat claw their way from the crunchy "Wonderful Excuse," to the stadium echoes of "Hamlet for Now," but the real standout is "Airplane Gardens" and all the corkscrew musical twists and swiftly banked rhythmic turns of a dogfight.

9 HOLE — Live Through This (Geffen) 1994

6 TACKLEBOX — Grand Hotel (Rockville) 1994

8 ECHOBELLY — On (550) 1995 Powerful, (vaguely) Sleeper-influenced Brit-grunge pop, initially highlighted by the titanic "Car Fiction," but there's a lot more to discover within.

7 WAX — 13 Unlucky Numbers (Interscope) 1995

6 UPPER CRUST — Let Them Eat Rock (Upstart) 1995

5 JULIANA HATFIELD — Only Everything (Mammoth) 1995

6 SPEEDBALL BABY — Fort Apache (1996) 1996

6 DINK — Blame It on Tito EP (Capitol) 1996

5 LIFTER — Melinda (Interscope) 1996

7 TRACY BONHAM — The Burdens of Being Upright (Island) 1996

7 BLAMELESS — The Sings Are All There (China) 1996

4 GOO GOO DOLLS — Lazy Eye (WB) 1997

6 RADISH — Restraining Bolt (Mercury) 1997

5 JAMIE BLAKE — Jamie Blake (A&M) 1997

9 MIGHTY MIGHTY BOSSTONES — Let's Face It (Mercury) 1997

8 LINOLEUM — Dissent (DGC) 1997 Fabulously dissonant Pavement-inflected sludge, building out of some decidedly unpromising beginnings into a charismatically uncompromising slab of unexpected melodicism.

7 STRETCH PRINCESS — Stretch Princess (Wind Up) 1998

8 GERALD COLLIER — Gerald Collier (WB) 1998 Former front man with the much-missed (but so daftly named) Best Kissers in the World, returning with a distinctly downbeat, vaguely Neil Young-ish sackful of sadness.

Paul Kolderie — Selected Productions

5 BULLET LAVOLTA — The Gift (Taang!) 1989

5 BLOOD ORANGES — Corn River (ESD) 1990

6 MIGHTY MIGHTY BOSSTONES — More Noise & Other... (Taang) 1991

4 FIREHOSE — Flyin' the Flannel (Columbia) 1991

6 THROWING MUSES — Red Heaven (Sire) 1992

7 MORPHINE — Good (Rykodisc) 1992 Two string bass and one dimensional vocals do not begin to describe the dense, low-key (low-fi) beauties which were Morphine's stock-in-trade.

6 VESTRYMEN — Ruby Ranch (Vertebrae) 1993

5 FIREHOSE — Big Bottom Pow Pow (Columbia) 1994

5 JALE — Promise (Sub Pop) 1994

5 GIGOLO AUNTS — Flippin' Out (RCA) 1994

6 MILES DETHMUFFEN — Clutter (Rainbow Quartz) 1994

8 MIGHTY MIGHTY BOSSTONES — Question the Answers (Mercury) 1994

6 SHATTERPROOF — Slip It Under the Door (Fort Apache) 1995

8 MORPHINE — Yes (Rykodisc) 1995

7 FUZZY — Electric Juices (Tag) 1996

7 MORPHINE — Like Swimming (Dreamworks) 1997

7 COME — Gently, Down the Stream (Matador) 1998

6 BIG DIPPER — Craps (Homestead) 1998

4 STRETCH PRINCESS — Stretch Princess (Wind Up) 1998

8 MIGHTY MIGHTY BOSSTONES — Live from the Middle East (Mercury) 1998

Sean Slade — Selected Productions

5 VOLCANO SUNS — Bumper Crops (Homestead) 1987

6 VOLCANO SUNS — Farced (SST) 1988

4 BUFFALO TOM — Buffalo Tom (Beggars Banquet) 1988

8 SEBADOH — III (Homestead) 1991

5 VANILLA TRAINWRECK — Sofa Livin' Dreamazine (Mammoth) 1991

5 360S — Supernatural (Hollywood) 1992

4 COLD WATER FLAT — Cold Water Flat (Fort Apache) 1995

KRAMER PRODUCTIONS

PRODUCER
BORN *Mark Stevan Kramer*

5 WHITE ZOMBIE — Psycho Head Blow Out (Caroline) 1986

6 HALF JAPANESE — Music to Strip By (50 Skidillion Watts) 1987

6 BALL — Period (Shimmy Disc) 1987

6 LARAAJI — Bring Forth (Shimmy Disc) 1987

5 KING MISSILE — Fluting on the Hump (Shimmy Disc) 1987

7 GALAXIE 500 — Today (Aurora) 1987

6 PUSSY GALORE — Right Now (Caroline) 1987

7 FRED FRITH — Technology of Tears (SST) 1988

6 DANIEL JOHNSTON — 1990 (Shimmy Disc) 1988

8 GWAR — Hell-O! (Shimmy Disc) 1988

6 UNREST — Malcolm X Park (Caroline) 1988

6 KING MISSILE — They (Shimmy Disc) 1988

5 HALF JAPANESE — The Band That Would Be King (50 Skidil-lion Watts) 1988

6 JAD FAIR — Roll out the Barrel (Shimmy Disc) 1988

6 BONGOS BASS & BOB — Never Mind the Sex Pistols (50 Skidillion Watts) 1988

5 BALL — Bird (Shimmy Disc) 1988

7 MAUREEN TUCKER — Life in Exile After Abdication (50 Skidillion Watts) 1989 Targeting an audience as opposed to any personal philosophies, an uncomplicatedly low-fi trawl through old legends, new acolytes, and common inspirations.

6 DOGBOWL — Tit (Shimmy Disc) 1989

7 LIDA HUSIK — Bozo (Shimmy Disc) 1989

6 BALL — Trouble Doll (Shimmy Disc) 1989

8 GALAXIE 500 — On Fire (Rough Trade) 1989

6 JELLYFISH KISS — Plank (Shimmy Disc) 1990

4 KING MISSILE — Mystical Shit (Shimmy Disc) 1990

5 DANIEL JOHNSTON — Artistic Vice (Shimmy Disc) 1990

5 BALL — Ball Four (Shimmy Disc) 1990

6 AC TEMPLE — Belinda Backwards (Blast First) 1990

5 JELLYFISH KISS — Stormy Weather (Shimmy Disc) 1991

5 DOGBOWL — Cyclops Nuclear Submarine (Shimmy Disc) 1991

6 REIN SANCTION — Broc's Cabin (Sub Pop) 1991

6 UNCLE WIGGLY — Across the Room... (Shimmy Disc) 1991

6 ALICE DONUT — Revenge Fantasies of the Impotent (Alternative Tentacles) 1991

5 PALEFACE — Paleface (Polydor) 1991

7 DAMON AND NAOMI — More Sad Hits (Shimmy Disc) 1992

6 KING MISSILE — Happy Hour (Atlantic) 1992

6 JON SPENCER BLUES EXPLOSION — A Reverse Willie Horton (PPC) 1992 Deliciously downplayed racket, purposefully recorded to sound like a pile of old blues records, rattling through the cheapest speakers in the world.

5 DOGBOWL — Flan (Shimmy Disc) 1992

5 DAEVID ALLEN — Who's Afraid? (Shimmy Disc) 1992

6 LIDA HUSIK — Your Bag (Shimmy Disc) 1992

5 JON SPENCER BLUES EXPLOSION — Jon Spencer Blues Explosion (Caroline) 1992

6 GRENADINE — Goya (Shimmy Disc) 1992

5 ALICE DONUT — Untidy Suicides... (Alternative Tentacles) 1992

4 EGOMANIACS — Egomaniacs (Shimmy Disc) 1993

5 DOGBOWL — Project Success (Shimmy Disc) 1993

7 DOGBOWL — Hot Day in Waco (Shimmy Disc) 1993

Kramer joins in for an unusually cohesive romp through Stephen Tunny's always appealingly twisted pop.

5 BARNYARD SLUT — Space Age Motel (Dutch East Indies) 1993

6 LIDA HUSIK — The Return of Red Emma (Shimmy Disc) 1993

3 DEEP JIMI AND THE ZEP CREAMS — Funky Dinosaur (East-west) 1993

5 ALICE DONUT — Medication (Alternative Tentacles) 1993

4 UNCLE WIGGLY — There Was an Elk (Shimmy Disc) 1993

4 SHERMAN — Transparent Extender (Shimmy Disc) 1993

6 RAYMOND LISTEN — Licorice Root Orchestra (Shimmy Disc) 1993

6 NOTHING PAINTED BLUES — Power Trips... (Kokopop) 1993

6 FALSE FRONT — Criminal Kind (Shimmy Disc) 1993

5 DOPES — Dawn of the Dopes (WDOP) 1994

6 JEHOVA'S WAITRESSES — Perfect Impossible (Shimmy Disc) 1994

5 VELVET CACTUS SOCIETY — Velvet Cactus Society (Shimmy Disc) 1994

4 ATS — Blood Drive (Shimmy Disc) 1994

7 OVARIAN TROLLEY — Crocodile Tears (Shimmy Disc) 1994

The erstwhile Glorious Clitoris clash the harmonic majesty of X with the downplayed drama which is always Kramer's strongest point.

5 FLY ASHTRAY — Tone Sensations of the Wonder Men (Shimmy Disc) 1994

9 LOW — I Could Live in Hope (Vernon Yard) 1994

7 DOGBOWL — Gunsmoke (Shimmy Disc) 1995

5 BLUEBERRY SPY — Sing (Shimmy Disc) 1995

7 DAMON AND NAOMI — The Wondrous World Of (Sub Pop) 1995

6 PALEFACE — Raw (Shimmy Disc) 1995

6 CAPTAIN HOWDY — Tattoo of Blood (Shimmy Disc) 1995

6 LOW — Long Division (Vernon Yard) 1995

7 CABLE — Whisper Firing Line (Mushroom — Australia) 1996

6 I SHARKO — I Sharko (Bomp) 1996

6 TADPOLES — Far Out (Bakery) 1996

6 SEMIBEINGS — Three Pawns Standing (C/Z) 1996

5 HONEYMOON KILLERS — Sing (Sftri) 1997

5 DANIELSON FAMILY — Tell Another Joke (Tooth & Nail) 1997

5 DANIELSON FAMILY — Tri-Danielson (Tooth & Nail) 1998

5 DRAZY HOOPS — Straight to Black (Shimmy Disc) 1998

7 GLEN OR GLENDA — Reasons in the Sun (Knitting Factory) 1998

6 CAPTAIN HOWDY — Money Feeds My Music Machine (Knitting Factory) 1998

8 BLUE WHALE — Congregation (Shimmy Disc) 1998 Slowly shifting psychedelic folk, haunted by ghosts which run from the Soft Machine to, of course, that entire vein of downbeat lysergia which Kramer mines so well.

7 HASIDIC NEW WAVE — Kabbalogy (Knitting Factory) 1999

CLIVE LANGER & ALAN WINSTANLEY

PRODUCERS

TW Studios engineer Winstanley and musician Langer met when the latter's band, Deaf School, visited the studio to record a set of demos in 1978. Winstanley had already earned a reputation for his willingness to work with passing punk and new wave bands — the Stranglers, Buzzcocks, and Generation X among them — and was dispatched to handle Deaf School as well. The pair remained in contact and, following the demise of both Deaf School and the subsequent Clive Langer & the Boxes, Langer made it known that he was interested in taking on production work.

His first clients were Madness, but aware that he was utterly unschooled in the business, he contacted Winstanley and suggested they pool resources. The duo would remain alongside the Nutty Boys throughout the remainder of the band's career. Teardrop Explodes and the recently rejuvenated Robert Wyatt also recorded with the pair (Winstanley alone co-produced Madness' Stiff Records labelmate Lene Lovich, among others; Langer alone would work with the Specials). 1982 saw them link with Kevin Rowland's Dexy's Midnight Runners as producers of the international smash "Come on Eileen."

Such an enormous success, coupled with the eternally buoyant Madness sound, marked the duo out as pop producers *par excellence*, and through the early-mid decade, they became adept at turning out hits for acts as far apart as Elvis Costello, Lloyd Cole, China Crisis, and Haysi Fantayzee — they also produced David Bowie and Mick Jagger's "Dancing in the Street" duet, released to raise funds for the Band Aid charity in 1985. The following year, they oversaw the *Absolute Beginners* movie soundtrack, again featuring Bowie.

As the decade progressed, the duo began to slow down their schedule; however, they were instrumental in the rise of Irish band Hothouse Flowers, and following Morrissey's departure from the Smiths, would be among the producers involved in his first album and early singles. Into the 1990s, their best known collaboration has been with Bush. The pair were also behind 1999's *Still Crazy* rock reunion movie.

Clive Langer & Alan Winstanley — Selected Productions

7 MADNESS — Absolutely (Sire) 1980

8 MADNESS — Seven (Stiff) 1981

6 BETTE BRIGHT/ILLUMINATIONS — Rhythm Breaks the Ice (Korova) 1981

6 THE NITECAPS — Go to the Line (Sire) 1982

8 DEXY'S MIDNIGHT RUNNERS — Too-Rye-Ay (Mercury) 1982

7 MADNESS — Rise and Fall (Stiff) 1982

7 ELVIS COSTELLO — Punch the Clock (Columbia) 1983

4 ELVIS COSTELLO — Goodbye Cruel World (Columbia) 1984

6 DEXY'S MIDNIGHT RUNNERS — Don't Stand Me Down (Mercury) 1985

5 MADNESS — Mad Not Mad (Geffen) 1985

6 LLOYD COLE — Easy Pieces (Geffen) 1985

4 CHINA CRISIS — What Price Paradise (A&M) 1986

5 NEVILLE BROTHERS — Uptown (EMI America) 1987

5 HOTHOUSE FLOWERS — People (London) 1988

6 THE ADVENTURES — Trading Secrets with the Moon (Elektra) 1989

6 SCHNELL FENSTER — The Sound of Trees (Atlantic) 1990

5 JEREMY DAYS — The Jeremy Days (Polydor) 1990

8 MORRISSEY — Kill Uncle (Sire/Reprise) 1991

7 TIM FINN — Before and After (Capitol) 1993

6 BUSH — Sixteen Stone (Elektra) 1994

7 AZTEC CAMERA — Frestonia (Reprise) 1995

6 DARLHOOD — Big Fine Thing (Reprise) 1996

6 HO HUM — Local (Universal) 1996

6 DRILL TEAM — Hope and Dream Explosion — (Reprise) 1997

5 SHIFT — Gen In (Columbia) 1997

4 SYMPOSIUM — Symposium (Red Ant) 1998

Clive Langer — Selected Productions

8 TEARDROP EXPLODES — Wilder (Mercury) 1981

7 AN EMOTIONAL FISH — Junk Puppets (Atlantic) 1993

Alan Winstanley — Selected Productions

4 J.J. BURNEL — Euroman Cometh (United Artists) 1979 Portentously over-reaching solo album from the Stranglers' bassist.

6 THE STRANGLERS — The Raven (United Artists) 1979 Massively ambitious, but only partially successful album capturing punk's favorite misogynist bully-boys as they began a surprise reinvention.

7 LENE LOVICH — Flex (Stiff) 1979

7 ORIGINAL MIRRORS — Original Mirrors (Mercury) 1980

4 FOUR OUT OF FIVE DOCTORS — 4 Out of 5 Doctors (Nemperor) 1980

3 THE RUMOUR — Purity of Essence (Stiff) 1980

5 FACE DANCE — About Face (Capitol) 1980

5 THE STRANGLERS — IV (United Artists) 1980

3 RACHEL SWEET — Protect the Innocent (Stiff) 1980 Following one of the most delightfully fresh country-pop albums of recent years (1978's *Fool Around*), schoolgirl Sweet aims for a raunchier adult sound and style. Big mistake.

5 CLIVE LANGER AND THE BOXES — Splash (F Beat) 1980

7 TV 21 — Thin Red Line (Deram) 1981 Dramatic Scot post-punk art rockers.

6 TENPOLE TUDOR — Let the Four Winds Blow (Stiff) 1981 Eddie Tudor starred in *Who Killed Bambi* and his title track made much of the soundtrack seem worthwhile. Unleashed across his own career, however, the buffoonery swiftly lost its allure.

6 TENPOLE TUDOR — Eddie, Old Bob, Dick and Gary (Stiff) 1981

DANIEL LANOIS

PRODUCER
BORN 9/19/51 (*Hull, Quebec, Canada*)

French-Canadian Lanois was just 15 when he opened his first studio, in the family basement in Hamilton, Ontario. The grandly named Mastersound recording played host to a steady stream of local bands, including several featuring the young Rick James. Lanois later estimated that he and brother Bob recorded "hundreds" of bands there, although their fame had apparently still to escape their immediate environs when Lanois was contacted by Brian Eno — to whom he had recently sent tapes of his own music.

The pair began collaborating on interpretations of some Harold Budd material, to be spread across Eno's albums *On Land*, *the Pearl*, *Plateau of Mirror*, and *Apollo*, and in 1981, Lanois was employed as engineer on Martha and the Muffins' *This Is the Ice Age* album. Two years later, when Eno was approached to produce U2's *Unforgettable Fire* album, he introduced Lanois to the set up, launching a relationship which has survived to this day.

In 1985, Lanois collaborated with Peter Gabriel on the *Birdy* soundtrack; the following year, he and Eno succeeded briefly in luring Scott Walker out of seclusion, for a set of recordings which would, however, then follow the singer back into obscurity.

Through the 1980s, Lanois worked primarily in tandem with Eno. Following the massive success of U2's *The Joshua Tree*, however, Lanois began stepping out alone, recording with Robbie Robertson, Bob Dylan, and the Neville Brothers. Since that time — both with and without Eno — Lanois has produced respected albums with Hothouse Flowers, Ron Sexsmith, Scott Weiland, Emmylou Harris, and Luscious Jackson. He launched his own parallel career in 1991, with a

contribution to Wim Wenders' *Until the End of the World* soundtrack.

Daniel Lanois — Selected Productions

5 PARACHUTE CLUB — The Parachute Club (Current) 1983

7 JON HASSELL — A.K.A. Darbari Java (EG) 1983

9 U2 — The Unforgettable Fire (Island) 1984

6 PETER GABRIEL — Music from the Film Birdy (Caroline) 1985

7 ROGER ENO — Voices (EG) 1985

6 JON HASSELL — Powerspot (ECM) 1986

3 PETER GABRIEL — So (Geffen) 1987 Vastly influential sound, but cripplingly MOR songs ensure that ultimately, the video for "Sledgehammer" is more memorable than the song. And as for that duet with Kate Bush...

10 U2 — The Joshua Tree (Island) 1987

6 NEVILLE BROTHERS — Yellow Moon (A&M) 1989

6 SYD STRAW — Surprise (Virgin) 1989

6 HOTHOUSE FLOWERS — Home (London) 1990

5 MICHAEL BROOK — Hybrid (Editions E.G.) 1990

7 U2 — Achtung Baby (Island) 1991

3 PETER GABRIEL — Us (Geffen) 1992

6 FARAFINA — Faso Denou (Realworld/Caroline) 1993

6 JON HASSELL — Flash of the Spirit (Intuition) 1993

6 PASSENGERS — Miss Sarajevo (Island) 1995

8 EMMYLOU HARRIS — Wrecking Ball (Elektra) 1995 Spellbinding reawakening. Much of Harris' career was spent carrying aloft the flame passed on by her mentor, Gram Parsons. Working alongside Lanois, she now lights an inspiring fire completely of her own.

7 COYOTE SHIVERS — Coyote Shivers (Mutiny) 1996

7 LUSCIOUS JACKSON — Fever in Fever Out (Grand Royal) 1996

6 GEOFFREY ORYEMA — Night to Night (Caroline) 1997

4 SCOTT WEILAND — 12 Bar Blues (Atlantic) 1998 Introspective solo meanderings from Stone Temple Pilot front man.

5 BRIAN BLADE — Brian Blade Fellowship (Blue Note) 1998

6 JIMMY CLIFF — Humanitarian (Universal) 1999

BILL LASWELL

PRODUCER

A funk session bassist through the 1970s, before forming his own studio supergroup Material in 1981 — originally as an offshoot of Daevid Allen's floating New York Gong set up. Forever exploring rhythms and textures today incorporated into "world music," Laswell's pioneering attitude towards dance music attracted a number of significant admirers — Mick Jagger, Herbie Hancock, and the Golden Palominos included.

It was his production of the John Lydon/Afrika Bambaataa Timezone collaboration, "World Destruction," which brought Laswell into collision with the "alternative" scene. He worked again with Lydon on Public Image Ltd's *Album* in 1986, while Iggy Pop, Motorhead, and the Ramones (somewhat surprisingly) sought him out before decade's end. He also produced albums for Yoko Ono, Ryuichi Sakamoto, and Jamaican rhythm masters Sly & Robbie, while his explorations of dub and rhythm unquestionably influenced another PiL alumni, Jah Wobble, as his career moved through the 1990s.

Laswell's Axiom label, an Island records subsidiary, devoured much of his attention through the early-mid 1990s, with his 1997 remix/reinvention of Bob Marley, *Dreams of Freedom: Ambient*, being described by many as the epitomization of Laswell's work elsewhere in that field. However, away from the apparently deeply meditative music which was his signature sound, Laswell was still capable of having fun, as he proved with the remarkable production of Mephiskapheles' *God Bless Satan* ska-metal masterpiece.

Bill Laswell — Selected Productions

6 GOLDEN PALOMINOS — The Golden Palominos (OAO/Celluloid) 1983 Heavily (obviously) influenced by Material, the revolving door supergroup piles Laswell, Anton Fier, Fred Frith, and John Zorninto — a heavily experimental hip-hop melange which is only occasionally successful.

6 GIL SCOTT-HERON — Re-Ron (Arista) 1984

6 THE LAST POETS — Oh My People (Celluloid) 1984

8 HERBIE HANCOCK — Sound System (Columbia) 1984

8 HERBIE HANCOCK & FODAY MUSO SUSO — Village Life (Columbia) 1985

3 MICK JAGGER — She's the Boss (Atlantic) 1985

7 MANU DIBANGO — Electric Africa (Celluloid) 1985

3 YOKO ONO — Starpeace (Polydor) 1985 Despite the presence of co-producer Laswell, the Sly & Robbie rhythm section and Anton Fier, a brew which could have ushered in untold magnificence, the queen of leftfield rock turns in a disc of unrelenting centralist mediocrity.

3 MOTORHEAD — Orgasmatron (GWR) 1986 Motorhead are Motorhead, Laswell is Laswell, and though both try hard to find some place to meet, they end up cancelling one another out. The first truly toothless Motorhead album was also their best sounding one. Hmmm.

6 PUBLIC IMAGE LTD — Album (Elektra) 1986

6 LAURIE ANDERSON — Home of the Brave (WB) 1986

8 RYUICHI SAKAMOTO — Neo Geo (Epic) 1987 With contributions from Iggy Pop and Sly Dunbar, Sakamoto's traditional eye for experimentation goes several steps further than usual, as Laswell drops some well-oiled funk into the normally delicate soundscapes.

8 SLY & ROBBIE — Rhythm Killers (Island) 1987

6 MANU DIBANGO — Afrijazzy (Urban) 1987

5 SONNY SHARROCK — Seize the Rainbow (Enemy) 1987

4 STEVIE SALAS — Colorcode (Island) 1988

7 SAMULNORI — Record of Changes (CMP) 1988

2 IGGY POP — Instinct (A&M) 1988 A pattern is beginning to emerge. Bill Laswell + Blistering Rock equals an Inexplicably Lifeless Plod.

6 LAST EXIT — Iron Path (Venture) 1988

8 BOOTSY COLLINS — What's Bootsy Doin'? (Columbia) 1988 Dynamic slab of true groove funk, Bootsy's most electrifying and eclectic in a decade.

6 HERBIE HANCOCK — Perfect Machine (Columbia) 1988

2 SWANS — The Burning World (Universal) 1989 A bizarre union foisted upon both parties by major label insistence. But even Michael Gira acknowledged that the union didn't work.

8 MATERIAL — Seven Souls (Virgin) 1989 Material's fourth album and the first with Laswell as essentially a solo operator, but much the same jazz-funk experimenting as before — with maybe a slightly clearer vision.

2 RAMONES — Brain Drain (Sire) 1989

6 JONAS HELLBORG — The Word (Mango) 1990

8 MATERIAL — The Third Power (Axiom) 1991

7 DEADLINE — Dissident (Day Eight) 1992

6 BLIND IDIOT GOD — Cyclotron (Avant) 1993

8 MEPHISKAPHELES — God Bless Satan (Pass the Virgin) 1994

7 JULIAN SCHNABEL — Every Silver Lining Has a Cloud (Island) 1995

9 AXIOM FUNK — Funkcronomicon (Axiom) 1995 Half Parliament/Funkadelic reunion, half tribute to the same, Laswell, Bootsy, George Clinton, Bernell Worrell, Sly Stone, and Sly & Robbie come together to see whether the mothership will still fire in the mid-1990s. It does... and it sounds even better than ever!

8 JAH WOBBLE — Heaven and Earth (Island) 1995

6 HENRY THREADGILL — Makin' a Move (Sony) 1995

7 BUCKETHEAD — Day of the World (Subharmonic) 1996

9 BOB MARLEY — Dreams of Freedom: Ambient Translations 1997 One of the most perfectly realized remix albums of an age when anything, it seems, is fair game for those tiresome studio-bound mouse potatoes with way too much computer-time on their hands. Never once departing from the subtlest intention of Marley's original recordings, Laswell lavishly draws them out of themselves, restructuring even the unlikeliest cuts ("Burnin' and Lootin'," "Heathen") into whole new experiences and rarely allowing them to get out of hand.

7 DEATH CUBE K — Disembodied (Ion) 1997

7 DUBADELIC — Bass Invaders (Wordsound) 1998

5 BUCKETHEAD — Colma (Cyber Octave) 1998

6 BUCKETHEAD — Monsters and Robots (EMI) 1999

NICK LAUNAY

PRODUCER

BORN 1960 *(London, England)*

Having spent much of his childhood in Spain, Launay returned to London in 1977, taking a job at Tape One studios, editing and mastering records to vinyl — it was there, during his spare time, that he hatched an extended remix of the recently delivered "Pop Musik" by M; playing the results back to M founder Robin Scott, he was gratified when Scott immediately suggested releasing the remix as a 12" single.

Launay moved to Virgin Records' Townhouse Studios later that same year as an engineer — in that capacity, he worked with the Jam, XTC, Simple Minds, and more, before John Lydon asked him to co-produce Public Image Ltd's third album, *Flowers of Romance*. Launay agreed, subsequently bringing a great deal of order to an otherwise dishevelled record, and earning himself engagements with a host of similarly edgy acts — Killing Joke, the Slits, Birthday Party, Spear of Destiny and the Gang of Four; amusingly, he was simultaneously working as Phil Collins' engineer of choice!

In 1983, Launay was recruited to produce Midnight Oil's *10, 9, 8, 7, 6...* album, their first to be recorded outside of Australia. A massive hit, it led to similar engagements with the Church and INXS, while Launay and Midnight Oil have since become virtually inseparable — Launay eventually settled in Australia himself.

He would resurface on the international scene in 1992, when he produced the three reunion tracks included in Talking Heads'*Sand in the Vaseline* collection, followed by band leader David Byrne's *Uh-Oh*; he also produced the Posies' *Amazing Disgrace* and Girls Against Boys' acclaimed *Freakonica*.

Nick Launay — Selected Productions

7 KILLING JOKE — What's This For? (EG) 1981

7 PUBLIC IMAGE LIMITED — The Flowers of Romance (WB) 1981

7 MIDNIGHT OIL — 10,9,8,7,6,5,4,3,2,1 (Columbia) 1983

8 SPEAR OF DESTINY — Grapes of Wrath (Burning Rome) 1983

7 THE CHURCH — Seance (Arista) 1983

6 INXS — The Swing (Atco) 1984

7 ARMOURY SHOW — Waiting for the Floods (EMI America) 1985 Trans-Magazine/Skids supergroup which really did sound like something halfway between the two of them.

6 MODELS — Out of Sight Out of Mind (Geffen) 1985

7 MIDNIGHT OIL — Red Sails in the Sunset (Columbia) 1985

7 BIG PIG — Bonk (A&M) 1988

6 TIM FINN — Big Canoe (Virgin) 1988

6 MARC ANTHONY THOMPSON — Watts and Paris (Reprise) 1989

4 STEPHEN BISHOP — Bowling in Paris (Atlantic) 1989

5 DAVID BYRNE — Uh-Oh (Luaka Bop/WB) 1992

7 MIDNIGHT OIL — Earth and Sun and Moon (Columbia) 1993

6 FOR SQUIRRELS — Example (550 Music) 1995

7 THE POSIES — Amazing Disgrace (DGC) 1996

6 SUBROSA — Never Bet the Devil Your Head (550 Music) 1997

5 SILVERCHAIR — Freak Show (Epic) 1997

6 AUTOMATIC — Transmitter (Sony) 1997

7 GIRLS AGAINST BOYS — FreaonOnIca (Geffen) 1998

7 SEMISONIC — Feeling Strangely Fine (MCA) 1998

5 SILVERCHAIR — Neon Ballroom (Epic) 1999

8 EARTH TO ANDY — Chronicle Kings (WB) 1999

PAUL LEARY

PRODUCER

A founding member of the Butthole Surfers, whose albums he co-produced, Leary's first outside productions were for Bad Livers and the Meat Puppets, helming their gold-selling *Too High to Die* in 1994 (and its 1996 successor *No Joke!*). He was also onboard for Sublime's 1996 breakthrough album.

Also see the entry for "BUTTHOLE SURFERS" on page 228.

Paul Leary — Selected Productions

5 BAD LIVERS — Delusions of Banjer (Quarterstick) 1992

7 MEAT PUPPETS — Too High to Die (London) 1994

4 DANIEL JOHNSTON — Fun (Atlantic) 1994

5 SUPERSUCKERS — Scrilicious Sounds (Sub Pop) 1995

6 MEAT PUPPETS — No Joke! (London) 1996

6 TOADIES — "Paper Dress" (Miramax/Hollywood) 1996

7 SUBLIME — Sublime (MCA) 1996

7 THE REFRESHMENTS — The Bottle and Fresh Horses (Mercury) 1997

JOHN LECKIE

PRODUCER

If any UK producer of the mid-1970s intuitively understood the direction in which the musical winds were blowing, it was John Leckie. A staff engineer at Abbey Road, where he worked with Beatles' Lennon, McCartney and Harrison, Pink Floyd and more, his first solo production job was with Be Bop Deluxe, one of the select handful of bands operating in the years before punk whose own direction and ambitions would be loudly echoed by events to come.

He followed this with the second album by the Doctors of Madness, 1976's *Figments of Emancipation*, a production which brought him to the attention of Adverts frontman TV Smith. Leckie would handle that band's *Crossing the Red Sea with the Adverts* album in late 1977, one of his last jobs at Abbey Road. In 1978, Leckie decided to go independent, promptly linking up with the infant XTC, Magazine, and Simple Minds, and leading all three through crucial debut albums, before nurturing XTC and Simple Minds on to the brink of stardom.

His workload slowed through the mid-late 1980s, but in 1989, Leckie produced the debut album by Stone Roses, and re-emerged as the producer of the moment. Radiohead, Ride, the Verve, and Curve would all approach him in that album's aftermath, while his talent for debuts was displayed again by recordings with Cast and Kula Shaker.

John Leckie — Selected Productions

6 BE BOP DELUXE — Modern Music (Harvest) 1976 Preposterous but oddly influential art-laden doom prog rockers emerged too late to impact on glam rock and too early to be taken to heart by the punks. *Modern Music* sounded strangely old-fashioned when compared to everything else that would soon be happening.

9 DOCTORS OF MADNESS — Figments of Emancipation (Polydor) 1976

7 ROY HARPER — One of These Days in England (Chrysalis) 1977

7 ROGER MCGOUGH — A Summer with Monika (Island) 1977

6 THE DOLL — Listen to the Silence (Beggars Banquet) 1977

7 BE-BOP DELUXE — Live in the Air Age (Harvest) 1977

10 THE ADVERTS — Crossing the Red Sea (Bright) 1978

7 BE-BOP DELUXE — Drastic Plastic (Harvest) 1978

6 ROY HARPER — Bullinamingvase (Harvest) 1978

9 XTC — White Music (Virgin) 1978

8 MAGAZINE — Real Life (Virgin) 1978

8 XTC — Go Too (Virgin) 1978

9 SIMPLE MINDS — Life in a Day (Zoom) 1979 Although their influences — Sparks, Velvets, Eno — are obvious, Simple Minds' debut is still startlingly original, perfectly poised between art rock extremism and sonic pop accessibility. It's a style which eminently suits them, swinging easily even from the derailed extremes of "Pleasantly Disturbed" to the jerky-quirk "Chelsea Girl" and even the mock Beatles epic title track.

7 SIMPLE MINDS — Real to Real Cacophony (Zoom) 1979

7 BILL NELSON — Sound on Sound (Harvest) 1979

6 AFTER THE FIRE — Laser Love (Epic) 1979

8 MR. PARTRIDGE — Take Away (Virgin) 1980

8 HUMAN LEAGUE — Travelogue (Virgin) 1980

6 PROOF — It's Safe (Nemperor) 1980

8 SIMPLE MINDS — Empires and Dance (Arista) 1980 The title perfectly sums up the album's lyrical themes (the disparate threads of European culture) and musical style; far more accessible than the preceding *Reel to Real*, *Empires* remains on the fringe of the club floor, caught in the eddies between the Scylla of proto-industrial dance and the Charybdis of the lush gloom of post-punk proto-Goth. Even there, Simple Minds' rudder remains their art rock sensibilities, now evolving in a Bauhausian-Wire direction.

7 CUBAN HEELS — Cuban Heels (Virgin) 1981

7 BILL NELSON — Quit Dreaming... (Enigma) 1981

6 BILL NELSON — The Love That Whirls (Enigma) 1982

8 THE FALL — Wonderful and Frightening World (PVC) 1984 Wildly prolific, execrably unstable, Fall albums fall distinctly into two camps — either they're good or they're not. With Mark E. Smith's wife Brix on board as co-writer and guitarist, this is one of the good ones.

8 THE FALL — This Nation's Saving Grace (PVC) 1985

8 GENE LOVES JEZEBEL — Immigrant (Beggars Banquet) 1985

7 LUCY SHOW — Mania (Big Time) 1986

6 BILL NELSON — Getting the Holy Ghost Across (Portrait) 1986

8 THE FALL — Bend Sinister (Beggars Banquet) 1986 Released (and slightly restructured) in the US as *Domesday Pay-Off* (although the UK title merely applies to a heraldic device), the Fall continue their most peerless sequence of albums.

7 DUKES OF THE STRATOSPHERE — Psonic Psunspot (Geffen) 1987

7 LET'S ACTIVE — Every Dog Has His Day (IRS) 1988 Kicking off with the bright and perky title track, slipping through stompers like "Ten Layers Down," gliding into the Beatlesque "Mr. Fool," brushing across C&W, then wagging everyone's tail with the instrumental "Orpheus in Hades Lounge," a non-ska ska song where 2-Tone keyboards are taken on a ride to hell.

9 STONE ROSES — The Stone Roses (Silvertone) 1989

7 HOUSE OF FREAKS — Tantilla (Rhino) 1989

8 LILAC TIME — And Love for All (Fontana) 1990

8 TRASH CAN SINATRAS — Cake (Go!) 1990

8 THE POSIES — Dear 23 (DGC) 1990

6 THEE HYPNOTICS — Soul, Glitter and Sin (Beggars Banquet) 1991

5 THE SILENCERS — Dance to the Holy Man (RCA) 1991

6 GRAPES OF WRATH — These Days (Capitol) 1991

5 FELT — Absolute Classic Masterpieces (Futurist) 1992

7 THE VERVE — A Storm in Heaven (Vernon Yard) 1993

7 ASHKHABAD — City of Love (Realworld/Caroline) 1993

5 ROBYN HITCHCOCK — Respect (A&M) 1993

8 RIDE — Carnival of Light (Reprise) 1994

8 RADIOHEAD — The Bends (Capitol) 1995

8 CAST — All Change (Polydor) 1996 Emerging out of the semi-legendary La's, Liverpool's Cast shift and blend styles at the drop of a hit, psychedelic guitars bleed into Merseyside pop, burbling riffs undercut glitter-strewn Monkees... from the glitterpop "Alright" on in, the emphasis of *Change* is on '60s-ish pop, but Cast wind and twine it into their own unique mold of chart busting songs.

7 KULA SHAKER — K (Columbia) 1996 Audaciously grabbing influences reaching back to '60s west coast psychedelia, Beatle George Harrison's Krishna kick (but forward through a touching affection for Britpop), Crispin (son of Hayley) Mills and co. debuted with an almost intentionally divisive album. Half built, indeed, around some seriously precocious raga-lite structures, but equally capable of degenerating into leaden Deadhead jam rock boogies, *K* could have been edited down into the best mini-album of the year.

5 MARK OWEN — Green Man (RCA) 1996

6 ANDY WHITE — Teenage (Cooking Vinyl) 1997

8 COWBOY JUNKIES — Mile from Our Home (Geffen) 1998

CRAIG LEON

PRODUCER
BORN *7/1/52 (Miami, FL)*

Leon moved into production in the early 1970s after tiring of playing in bands; aided by the legendary Alex Sadkin, he opened his first demo studio in 1972, meeting Sire Records' Richard Gottehrer when the latter brought the Climax Blues Band in for some preproduction work in 1974. Gottehrer persuaded Leon to relocate to New York and take an A&R post at Sire — he moved into production in 1975, after Gottehrer quit the label midway through producing a Chilliwack album.

It was as a Sire scout, of course, that Leon either discovered, or produced primal recordings by almost every key New York act of the new wave: Blondie, the Ramones, Richard Hell, Suicide, Mink DeVille, Tuff Darts, and the Shirts — indeed, the first time he saw the Ramones, on a CBGBs bill with Talking Heads, there were just four other people in the room. On a trip out of the city around the same time, he came across Willie Alexander; in L.A., he produced the Weirdos, 45 Grave, and the Bangles.

Small wonder that when Flesh for Lulu were seeking a producer who shared at least some of their formative influences, they picked Leon — he'd had a hand in creating almost all of them, but had now moved to London in search of the same indy scene excitement which New York and L.A. had patently stopped experiencing. It was there that Leon scored the biggest hit of his career so far, when he produced Doctor and the Medics' smash reworking of "Spirit in the Sky."

Through the 1990s, Leon worked regularly with the New FADS, the Fall, and Jesus Jones; he would also link with the Cowboy Junkies (string arrangements on the John Leckie-produced *Miles from Our Home*), the Chills, and Cobalt 60.

Craig Leon — Selected Productions

6 CHILLIWACK — Rockerbox (Sire) 1975

6 CITY LIGHTS — Silent Dancing (Sire) 1975

10 RAMONES — Ramones (Sire) 1976

7 MARTHA VELEZ — Escape from Babylon (Sire) 1976

8 SUICIDE — Suicide (Red Star) 1977

6 DEMONS — Demons (Mercury) 1977

8 WILLIE ALEXANDER — & The Boom Boom Band (MCA) 1978

6 WILLIE ALEXANDER — ...Back in the States (MCA) 1978

5 LISA BURNS — Lisa Burns (MCA) 1978

6 MOON MARTIN — Shots from a Cold Nightmare (Capitol) 1978 Reasonable singer-songwriter who emerged just in time to be saddled with an "American Elvis Costello"-type tag.

5 GARFEEL RUFF — Garfeel Ruff (Capitol) 1979

6 DWIGHT TWILLEY — Twilley (Arista) 1979 Highly-rated powerpop, but like so many of their contemporaries, better at *sounding* like they were creating joyful timeless classics than they were at actually delivering them.

6 MOON MARTIN — Escape from Demolition (Capitol) 1979

7 THE RECORDS — Crashes (Virgin) 1980 Sophomore set from sometimes supersonic Brit powerpoppers, comparable with Twilley except they had the great taste to cover the Searchers' "Hearts in Her Eyes."

6 SIR DOUGLAS QUINTET — Border Wave (Chrysalis) 1981

7 CRAIG LEON — Nommos (Takoma) 1982

6 THE KIND — Pain and Pleasure (Threesixty) 1983

4 45 GRAVE — Sleep in Safety (Enigma) 1983 Future Dream Syndicate guitarist Cutler fires L.A.'s leading death rockers through a shrill and generally discordant tribute to some of the world's worst Satanic metal bands. Whoever they may be.

7 THE POGUES — Red Roses for Me (Stiff) 1984

5 THE THOUGHT — The Thought (MCA) 1985

8 FLESH FOR LULU — Big City Fun (Statik/Caroline) 1985

8 JEFFREY LEE PIERCE — Wildweed (Statik) 1985

8 DOCTOR AND THE MEDICS — Laughing at the Pieces (IRS) 1986 Quite frankly, one of the greatest rock albums of the 1980s. No matter that the whole thing was sheer idiocy disguised in quasi-psychedelic clothing; nor that their hit version of "Spirit in the Sky" was simply a blurred carbon copy of the original... actually, that is precisely why this is so good. That and the fact that the accompanying Anadin Sisters made watching backing singers seem like fun again.

5 LAMARCA — Lamarca (Scotti Brothers) 1986

6 DOCTOR AND THE MEDICS — I Keep Thinking It's Thursday (IRS) 1987

7 THE GO-BETWEENS — Tallulah (Beggars Banquet) 1987

8 ADULT NET — Honey Tangle (Fontana) 1989 The recent Mrs. Mark E, Brix Smith links with ex-Blondie drummer Clem Burke and Smiths guitarist Craig Gannon for an album drawn equally from late '60s flower power, the early '80s paisley scene, and a dose of Brill Building Shangri-Las magic.

7 JESUS JONES — Liquidizer (Food/SBK) 1990 It all sounds fabulous; those burbling keyboards, that funky rhythm section, the guitar which soars into wild Hendrix wah-wahs, all delivered with unbridled enthusiasm. And it is...although, few of the melodies are particularly memorable. Is that a problem?

7 THE FALL — Extricate (Cog Sinister/Fontana) 1990

6 BEAT FARMERS — Van Go (Curb) 1991

7 THE FALL — Shift-Work (Cog Sinister/Fontana) 1991

8 THE FALL — Code: Selfish (Cog Sinister/Fontana) 1992

8 NEW FAST AUTOMATIC DAFFODILS — Body Exit Mind (Mute) 1993 Baggy based, but encompassing a wide range of other influences, the supple *Body* shifts through ambient soundscapes, dance floor trances, Velvet-y drones, and on into thundering hardrock. Your mind exits here.

6 THE KILLJOYS — Starry (Mushroom — Australia) 1994

8 EUGENIUS — Mary Queen of Scots (Atlantic) 1994

8 ANGEL CORPUS CHRISTI — White Courtesy Phone (Almo Sounds) 1995 Using an accordion as the perfect instrument of sedition, ACC's songs are twisted vignettes of real life, Lou Reed, but with a punk twist. Falling somewhere between the Velvets ("Big Black Cloud"), Suzanne Vega, and the early NY punk scene (there's even a touch of Suicide to "Candy"), *Phone* is like nothing you've ever heard or even imagined. It's ringing, pick it up.

6 COBALT 60 — Elemental (Edel America) 1996

5 MARTIN PHILLIPPS & THE CHILLS — Sunburnt (Flying Nun) 1996

6 MARK OWEN — Green Man (RCA) 1996

5 JUNIOR COTTENMOUTH — Bespoke (Atlantic) 1997

5 SIR DOUGLAS QUINTET — Live Texas Tornado (Takoma) 1998

STEVE LILLYWHITE

PRODUCER

BORN 1955 *(England)*

An engineer at the PolyGram studios in London (where he worked with Dutch rockers Golden Earring and the critically acclaimed Nucleus), Lillywhite made his production debut when Island Records picked up on the demos he had recorded with the then-unknown Ultravox — he wound up co-producing the band's eponymous debut album with Brian Eno, and was promptly offered a staff position at Island.

There, Lillywhite would handle pub-punks Eddie and the Hot Rods and critical favorite Snips, before being recruited to produce debuts by Siouxsie and the Banshees and (alongside John Leckie) XTC, the Members, the Leyton Buzzards, and the Psychedelic Furs, while his work with Johnny Thunders, the *So Alone* album, so impressed the Ramones that they requested him to work on their next album. According to Joey Ramone, "our label turned him down because they said he was an unknown" — and the next thing anybody knew, Lillywhite was top of the UK charts with Peter Gabriel, following that when he succeeded Martin Hannett with Irish up and comers U2.

Through the early 1980s, Lillywhite's now instantly identifiable sound aided Big Country, Simple Minds, and the Thompson Twins in their rise to the top, while he also produced the crucial debut singles by Chameleons UK, "In Shreds." Along the way, he met and married singer Kirsty MacColl, producing a string of her releases — she would also join him as a backing vocalist at a number of sessions, including that which produced the Pogues' immortal "Fairytale of New York."

The Rolling Stones employed Lillywhite (and MacColl) for their mid-1980s *Dirty Work* album; he would also oversee Talking Heads' final album, while the 1990s would pair him with Morrissey for three of the decade's most enigmatic albums.

Steve Lillywhite — Selected Productions

10 ULTRAVOX — Ultravox! (Island) 1977

7 EDDIE AND THE HOT RODS — Life on the Line (Island) 1977 Leapfrogging punk and diving straight into the pop end of the new wave, the Rods' biggest hit, "Do Anything You Wanna Do," dominates the shorter songs herein. The crucial moment, though, is the segued "We Sing... the Cross" instrumental and the epic "Beginning of the End" — lyrically fairly preposterous, but delivered with such power that it takes a while to twig that.

8 STEEL PULSE — Handsworth Revolution (Island) 1978 One of the crucial UK reggae albums of the era — burning frustration blending into almost accidental dub territory.

7 SNIPS — Video King (Jet) 1978

9 SIOUXSIE AND THE BANSHEES — The Scream (Polydor) 1978

10 JOHNNY THUNDERS — So Alone (Sire) 1978

9 XTC — White Music (Virgin) 1978

4 PENETRATION — Coming Up for Air (Virgin) 1979 Then going down for the last time. Penetration lose the plot even as producer Lillywhite tries to save the day with a spectacular wall-of-big-rock-noise. But the songs are beyond redemption — "Shout Above the Noise" and "Come Into the Open" deliver up some punch, but "Lifeline" is a throwaway, and the rest is spent flailing helplessly around in search of even half a hook.

8 XTC — Drums and Wires (Virgin) 1979

7 LEYTON BUZZARDS — Jellied Eels to Record Deals (Chrysalis) 1979 One of the bewildering platoon of vaguely interchangeable post-punk pop acts which emerged in the UK during 1978–79, usually with one signature smash hit single ("Saturday Night Beneath the Plastic Palm Trees" — a killer pre-sentiment of the 2-Tone boom to come), then vanished again.

8 MEMBERS — At the Chelsea Night Club (Virgin) 1979 The immediate power of "Sound of the Suburbs" made it look like the members were going to join the same club as the Buzzards (above); an unexpected ability to pen further such anthems saved them for a little while longer — and the sublime dub of "Offshore Banking Business" shows why.

7 SECTOR 27 — Sector 27 (Fontana/IRS) 1980

9 PSYCHEDELIC FURS — Psychedelic Furs (Columbia) 1980

8 PETER GABRIEL — Peter Gabriel (Mercury) 1980

7 XTC — Black Sea (Virgin) 1980

9 U2 — Boy (Island) 1980

6 BRAINS — Brains (Mercury) 1981

8 PSYCHEDELIC FURS — Talk Talk Talk (Columbia) 1981

7 URBAN VERBS — Early Damage (WB) 1981

7 U2 — October (Island) 1981

4 TOYAH — The Changeling (Safari) 1982

6 THOMPSON TWINS — In the Name of Love (Arista) 1982

7 BIG COUNTRY — The Crossing (Mercury/Sire) 1983 Adding a Celtic swirl to new wave, *The Crossing* is an inimitable collection of anthemic rabble rousers and yearning quieter numbers, all enhanced by the haunting sound of E-bows.

9 U2 — War (Island) 1983

7 SIMPLE MINDS — Sparkle in the Rain (Virgin/A&M) 1983 Having concluded their fascination with mesmeric rhythm with the breakthrough *New Gold Dream*, Simple Minds rebound to the broad, song-based pastures of their debut. The crystalline "Speed Your Love to Me" and "Up on the Catwalk" are livid snapshots of the band's destiny; while a limp take on Lou Reed's "Street Hassle" at least proves they still wear their hearts on their sleeve.

4 MARSHALL CRENSHAW — Field Day (WB) 1983

5 BIG COUNTRY — Steeltown (Mercury) 1984

4 FRIDA — Shine (Epic) 1984

8 BRUCE FOXTON — Touch Sensitive (Arista) 1984 The driving funk-based "Freak" proved that life didn't have to end with the Jam; indeed, over the course of this often enigmatic album, Foxton proves himself (at least temporarily) to be considerably closer to his natural abilities than his old bandmate Weller.

5 CROSSFIRE CHOIR — Crossfire Choir (Passport) 1986

6 THE PRETENDERS — Get Close (Real/Sire) 1986

9 U2 — The Joshua Tree (Island) 1987

5 TALKING HEADS — Naked (Sire) 1988

8 THE POGUES — If I Should Fall from Grace (Island) 1988

3 THOMPSON TWINS — Big Trash (Red Eye) 1989

7 THE POGUES — Peace and Love (Island) 1989

6 DAVID BYRNE — Rei Momo (Luaka Bob) 1989

7 KIRSTY MACCOLL— Kite (Charisma) 1990

9 THE LA'S — The La's (Go!) 1990 Devastating Liverpudlian acoustic pop quartet whose echoes of the Britpop past (or at least, what would eventually be termed such) ranged from Hollies harmony to Creation beat, but never sounded dated. With the band breaking up in 1991, guitarist John Powers subsequently formed the equally bright Cast.

7 KIRSTY MACCOLL — Electric Landlady (Charisma) 1991

7 U2 — Achtung Baby (Island) 1991

9 KIRSTY MACCOLL — Titanic Days (IRS) 1993

7 WORLD PARTY — Bang (Ensign) 1993

2 DAVE MATTHEWS BAND — Under the Table and Dreaming (RCA) 1994

6 ENGINE ALLEY — Engine Alley (Mother) 1994

10 MORRISSEY — Vauxhall and I (Sire/Reprise) 1994

8 MORRISSEY — Southpaw Grammar (Sire/Reprise) 1995

3 PHISH — Billy Breathes (Elektra) 1996

6 TRAVIS — Good Feeling (Independiente) 1997

8 MORRISSEY — Maladjusted (Mercury) 1997

3 DAVE MATTHEWS BAND — Before These Crowded Streets (RCA) 1998

SCOTT LITT

PRODUCER

BORN 1954 (New York , NY)

An engineer at New York's A-1 Sound and Power Station studios through the late 1970s/early 1980s, where he worked with Ian Hunter, Carly Simon, and more, Litt debuted as a producer on albums by former New York Doll Sylvain Sylvain and ex-Tuff Darts guitarist Robert Gordon, helming both with Lance Quinn. In 1980, he mixed the dB's *Stands for Decibels* debut, and the following year joined the band in London, as producer of their follow-up, *Repercussion*.

The relationship deepened as Litt was recruited to handle early recordings by Pylon and the newly solo Chris Stamey, and in 1987, dB's fans REM contacted Litt to produce their a cut intended for the *Made in Heaven* movie soundtrack, "Romance," launching a relationship which had remained intact ever since.

Litt was also involved (with co-producer Pat Collier) in Katrina and the Waves' rise to mid-80s fame, and Patti Smith's 1988 semi-comeback album, *Dream of Life*; while 1990 saw him launch a three-year partnership with Paul

Westerberg, when he produced the Replacements' *All Shook Down*.

Litt tasted a degree of controversy in 1993, after he was brought in to remix the projected singles from Nirvana's Steve Albini-produced *In Utero* album. According to that band's Krist Novoselic, "I'd been listening to [REM's] *Automatic for the People* and I really liked what Scott did with it. At the same time, there were a couple of things I didn't like on our album, so when we got the chance to take it back into the studio, I called Scott along." The following year, Litt would be re-engaged to handle Nirvana's MTV Unplugged album — 1998, meanwhile, would see him reunite with Chris Stamey for the Flat Duo Jets album.

Scott Litt — Selected Productions

7 **ROBERT GORDON — Are You Gonna Be the One? (RCA) 1981**

6 **ROBERT GORDON — Too Fast to Live, Too Young to Die (RCA) 1982**

7 **THE DB'S — Repercussion (Albion) 1982**

7 **CHRIS STAMEY — It's a Wonderful Life (dB) 1983**

6 **BEAT RODEO — Home in the Heart of the Beat (IRS) 1986**

4 **MATTHEW SWEET — Inside (Columbia) 1986**

7 **REM — Document (IRS) 1987**

6 **PAUL KELLY/MESSENGERS — Gossip (A&M) 1987**

5 **PATTI SMITH — Dream of Life (Arista) 1988**

6 **WOODENTOPS — Wooden Foot Cops on the Highway (Columbia) 1988**

8 **REM — Green (WB) 1988**

6 **RESTLESS SLEEPERS — Wake Up to the Big Boss Sounds (IRS) 1988**

5 **INDIGO GIRLS — Indigo Girls (Epic) 1989**

6 **PAUL KELLY/MESSENGERS — So Much Water So Close to Home (A&M) 1989**

8 **THAT PETROL EMOTION — Chemicrazy (Virgin) 1990** The departure of guitarist/songwriter Sean O'Neill forced a line-up reshuffle, but even so, Petrol manage to keep their old sound intact, with "Scumsurfin'" and "Blue to Black" capturing their rockier elements, "Another Day" showcasing their moodier side, and the sharply drawn "Hey Venus" and evocative "Compulsion" completing *Chemicrazy*'s package of Celto-alterno-pop rock.

5 **INDIGO GIRLS — Nomads Indians Saints (Epic) 1990**

6 **THE REPLACEMENTS — All Shook Down (Sire/Reprise) 1990**

7 **REM — Out of Time (WB) 1991**

4 **INDIGO GIRLS — Live: Back on the Bus Y'all (Epic) 1991**

8 **REM — Automatic for the People (WB) 1992**

6 **JULIANA HATFIELD 3 — Become What You Are (Mammoth) 1993**

6 **REM — Monster (WB) 1994**

9 **NIRVANA — MTV Unplugged in New York (DGC) 1994**

8 **REM — New Adventures in Hi-Fi (WB) 1996**

6 **DAYS OF THE NEW — Days of the New (Outpost) 1997**

6 **HAYDEN — The Closer I Get (Outpost) 1998**

4 **LIZ PHAIR — Whitechocolatespaceegg (Matador) 1998**

6 **FLAT DUO JETS — Lucky Eye (Outpost) 1998**

WARNE LIVESEY

PRODUCER
BORN *(London, England)*

An engineer at a succession of small London studios, undertaking what he later described as "very low level production work for very small labels" including the Higsons' 2-Tone label debut, Livesey's first major work was alongside Foetus on the genre-shattering *Hole* and *Nail* albums in 1984–85. Some Bizzare, Foetus' label at that time, promptly introduced him to The The's Matt Johnson for the classic *Infected*, while 1987 brought work with Midnight Oil and Julian Cope.

Into the early 1990s, Livesey seemed most active on the electro scene — he produced Jesus Jones' *Perverse*, and co-produced (with Trent Reznor) the debut album by Prick. However, he also handled House of Love's *Babe Rainbow* (co-writing two of the tracks with band leader Guy Chadwick), Whipping Boy's *Heartworm* masterpiece, and parts of the solo debut by St. Etienne vocalist Sarah Cracknell.

Warne Livesey — Selected Productions

7 **THE HIGSONS — Music to Watch Girls By (2-Tone) 1984**

7 **SCRAPING FOETUS OFF THE WHEEL — Hole (Some Bizzare) 1984**

9 **SCRAPING FOETUS OFF THE WHEEL — Nail (Some Bizzare) 1985**

7 **ICEHOUSE — Measure for Measure (Chrysalis) 1986**

7 **THE THE — Infected (Epic) 1986**

9 **JULIAN COPE — Saint Julian (Island) 1987**

7 **MIDNIGHT OIL — Diesel and Dust (Columbia) 1987**

6 **DEACON BLUE — When the World Knows Your Name (Columbia) 1989**

6 **MIDNIGHT OIL — Blue Sky Mining (Columbia) 1990**

5 **PAUL YOUNG — Other Voices (Columbia) 1990**

6 **ALL ABOUT EVE — Touched by Jesus (Vertigo) 1991**

6 **BIG DISH — Satellites (Eastwest) 1991**

8 **HOUSE OF LOVE — Babe Rainbow (Fontana) 1992** As eclectic as ever, *Rainbow*'s centerpiece is the psychedelic epic "Cruel," surrounded by the baggy hit "You Don't Understand," — melancholy ballads and moody pop, each a sublime experiment in sonics and style.

7 **JESUS JONES — Perverse (Food) 1993** The electronics may take center stage, but now they're an integral element of the songwriting process — which only partially explains why *Perverse* sounds so big. The guitars are huge, the drums boom... who says club pop can't translate from the dance floor to the stadium?

7 PRICK — **Prick [6 TRACKS] (Nothing/Interscope) 1995** This impressive debut features unusual song structures, strong melodies sprinkled with glam rock's glitter, and some of the most intriguingly witty word play around. Even the electronics of producers Livesey and Nine Inch Nails' Trent Reznor are unusually subtle and clever.

6 SUDDENLY TAMMY! — **We Get There When We Do (WB) 1995**

8 WHIPPING BOY — **Heartworm (Columbia) 1996** Melodic Irishmen whose view of the world is decidedly downbeat, half confessional, half secretive, but always nakedly brutal.

6 MATTHEW GOOD BAND — **Underdogs (Darktown) 1997**

6 MIDNIGHT OIL — **Redneck Wonderland (Columbia) 1998**

LOOKOUT RECORDS

LABEL

So-Cal punk specialist label founded by, and initially for, the band of the same name.

Also see the entry for the "LOOKOUTS" on page 465.

Lookout Label Listing 1987–94

1 LOOKOUTS — **One Planet One People LP** **5**

2 unreleased

3 OPERATION IVY — **Hectic EP**

4 CRIMPSHRINE — **Sleep? What's That? EP**

5 ISOCRACY — **Bedtime for Isocracy EP**

6 unreleased

7 PLAID RETNA — **Twelve Song Seven Inch EP**

8 SEWER TROUT — **Songs About Drinking EP**

9 YEASTIE GIRLZ — **Ovary Action EP**

10 OPERATION IVY — **Energy LP** **8**

11 VARIOUS ARTISTS — **The Thing That Ate Floyd LP** **8**

12 NEUROSIS — **Aberration EP**

13 SURROGATE BRAINS — **Surrogate Serenades EP**

14 EYEBALL — **Prosthetic Head EP**

15 CRIMPSHRINE — **Quit Talkin' Claude EP**

16 KAMALA & THE KARNIVORES — **Girlband EP**

17 GREEN DAY — **1000 Hours EP**

18 LOOKOUTS — **Spy Rock Road LP** **8**

19 CORRUPTIVE MORALS — **Cheese-It LP** **6**

20 unreleased

21 NEUROSIS — **Word As Law LP** **7**

22 GREEN DAY — **39/Smooth LP** **7**

23 unreleased

24 SAMIAM — **I Am EP**

25 CRINGER — **Karen EP**

26 FUEL — **Take Effect EP**

27 MONSULA — **Nickel EP**

28 LOOKOUTS — **Mendocino Homeland EP**

29 unreleased

30 FILTHY — **Live the Chaos EP**

31 THE BLATZ — **Cheaper Than Beer EP**

32 VAGRANTS — **Gone EP**

33 unreleased

34 FIFTEEN — **Fifteen EP**

35 GREEN DAY — **Slappy EP**

36 BRENT'S TV — **Lumberjack Days EP**

37 MR. T EXPERIENCE — **Making Things with Light LP** **8** If the Brady Bunch formed a punk band, and the Partridge Family wrote their songs, the Mr. T Experience would have a prime time TV series. This would be its soundtrack.

38 MONSULA — **Structure LP** **6** The bass guitar takes punk on a drive to the edge of world.

39 MR. T EXPERIENCE — **Everyone's Entitled to Their Own Opinion LP (1986) 7** The album which started the entire Bay Area explosion.

40 FIFTEEN — **Swain's First Bike Ride LP 7** *True Romance* magazine set to a real life rhythm.

41 SCHERZO — **Scherzo EP**

42 LOOKOUTS — **IV EP**

43 BLATZ/FILTH — **Shit Split EP**

44 VARIOUS ARTISTS — **Can of Pork LP**

45 unreleased

46 GREEN DAY — **Kerplunk LP** **8**

47 SCHERZO — **Suffering & Joy LP** **5**

48 NUISANCE — **Confusion Hill LP** **6**

49 MR. T EXPERIENCE — **Milk Milk Lemonade LP** **8**

50 SCREECHING WEASEL — **My Brain Hurts LP** **7**

NICK LOWE

PRODUCER

Nick Lowe — Selected Productions

8 GRAHAM PARKER/RUMOUR — **Howlin' Wind (Mercury) 1976** One of the albums around which punk would coalesce, "angry Motown" as its maker calls it, but scalding rock as well.

9 ELVIS COSTELLO — **My Aim Is True (Stiff) 1977**

9 THE DAMNED — **Damned Damned Damned (Stiff) 1977**

7 DR. FEELGOOD — **Be Seeing You (United Artists) 1977** The pub rock legends come to terms with punk by changing guitarists and turning up the snarl. Not their best.

8 GRAHAM PARKER/RUMOUR — **Stick to Me (Mercury) 1977**

7 CARLENE CARTER — Blue Nun (F-Bear/WB) 1977

10 ELVIS COSTELLO — This Year's Model (Columbia) 1978

9 WRECKLESS ERIC — Wreckless Eric (Stiff) 1978

8 ELVIS COSTELLO/ATTRACTIONS — Armed Forces (Columbia) 1979

6 DR. FEELGOOD — A Case of the Shakes (United Artists) 1980

7 ELVIS COSTELLO/ATTRACTIONS — Get Happy (Columbia) 1980

6 CARLENE CARTER — Musical Shapes (F-Beat) 1980

7 ELVIS COSTELLO — Trust (F-Beat/CBS) 1981

6 KIRSTY MACCOLL — Desperate Character (Polydor) 1981

6 DAVE EDMUNDS — Twangin' (Swan Song) 1981

5 PAUL CARRACK — Suburban Voodoo (Epic) 1982

5 FABULOUS THUNDERBIRDS — T-Bird Rhythm (Chrysalis) 1982

5 MOONLIGHTERS — Rush Hour (Demon) 1983

7 MEN THEY COULDN'T HANG — Night of 1,000 Candles (Demon) 1985

4 ELVIS COSTELLO/ATTRACTIONS — Blood and Chocolate (Columbia) 1986

5 KATYDIDS — Katydids (Reprise) 1990

5 RAIN — A Taste Of... (Columbia) 1992

6 JOHN HIATT — Living a Little, Laughing a Little (Raven) 1996

Also see the entry for "NICK LOWE" on page 473.

FRED MAHER

PRODUCER
BORN 12/3/62 (Manhattan, NY)

Just 16 years old, Maher was the child prodigy drummer in Daevid Allen's New York Gong, playing alongside Bill Laswell and Michael Beinhorn, graduating to Laswell's Material in 1979. He quit in 1981 attending architecture school at Cooper Union, until being introduced to Rough Trade signing David Gamson — that led to a union with Scritti Politti in 1985, by which time Maher had also been coaxed out of retirement to join Lou Reed's *Legendary Hearts* band. (He and Reed's guitarist, Robert Quine, also recorded an album together, 1984's *Basic*.)

Having co-produced much of Scritti Politti's *Cupid and Psyche* album, Maher then helmed Information Society's proto-techno debut album in 1988 and Matthew Sweet's *Earth*, before rejoining Reed for 1989's seminal *New York*. Alongside Quine, he would then link with Lloyd Cole and again, Matthew Sweet, for the latter's *Girlfriend*, followed by engagements with the Breeders, Ultra Vivid Scene, and 10,000 Maniacs.

Fred Maher — Selected Productions

7 ROBERT QUINE AND FRED MAHER — Basic (EG) 1984

6 INFORMATION SOCIETY — Information Society (Tommy Boy) 1988

9 LOU REED — New York (Sire) 1989

4 MATTHEW SWEET — Earth (A&M) 1989 A more mellow version of his Stephen Hague-produced debut, but still packing power pop guitar riffs plus a guest appearance from B-52's Kate Pierson.

6 KEVIN PAIGE — Kevin Paige (Chrysalis) 1989

8 LLOYD COLE — Lloyd Cole (Gold Rush) 1990

7 TRIP SHAKESPEARE — Across the Universe (A&M) 1990

9 LLOYD COLE — Don't Get Weird on Me Babe (Capitol) 1991

Love-lorn demons strewn over a post-coital languidity, with Cole raising himself just once, to unleash the devastating "She's a Girl and I'm a Man," then settling back for another cigarette because he knows that's all that's required. A work of utterly understated magnificence.

6 INFORMATION SOCIETY — Hack (Tommy Boy) 1991

10 MATTHEW SWEET — Girlfriend (Zoo) 1991 By far Sweet's greatest, and maybe Maher's too, combining the vicious kick first employed on Lou Reed's *New York*, adding Television's Richard Lloyd to the already murderous sonic soup, then kicking out some genuinely maladjusted arrangements and rhythms to ride roughshod over Sweet's traditional conventional delivery. Indeed, the ensuing crunch and jangle so mask the laid back, countrified air which permeate the songs that it's hard to imagine what the demos must have sounded like.

Honest and plaintive, but sometimes downright creepy, the opening "Divine Intervention" piledrives around the edgy, fractured guitars which would become a trademark of sorts, shot through with effects which raise the stakes even higher — snatched harmonies, muted solos, and somewhere in the distance, Lloyd's best interplay since *Marquee Moon*.

Elsewhere, "Girlfriend" and "Winona" and "Evangeline" unveil a maudlinity which would verge on despair if not for the disorientating up-tempo sound and while *Girlfriend* could be accused of going on just a little bit too long, one more track (the next album's "Someone to Pull the Trigger") would have raised it beyond even perfection.

6 ULTRA VIVID SCENE — Rev (Columbia) 1992

6 SUZANNE RHATIGAN — To Hell with Love (Imago) 1992

6 LUNA — Lunapark (Elektra) 1993

5 KATE CEBERANO — Globe (Elektra) 1994

5 KATELL KEINEG — O Seasons O Castles (Elektra) 1994

4 EVE'S PLUM — Cherry Alive (550 Music/Epic) 1995

5 GODS THUMB — Gods Thumb (Critique) 1996

4 10,000 MANIACS — Love Among the Ruins (Geffen) 1997

7 INFORMATION SOCIETY — Don't Be Afraid (Cleopatra) 1997

6 SEXPOD — Goddess Blues (Slab) 1997

6 DANIEL CARTIER — Avenue A (Rocket) 1997

5 VAST — Visual Audio Sensory Theater (Elektra) 1998

7 MARY LOU LORD — Got No Shadows (Work) 1998

6 DORO — Love Me in Black (Wea Germany) 1998

DANIEL MILLER

PRODUCER

It was the lowering price of synthesizers and their increased visibility in the rock scene, which first attracted Daniel Miller to the instrument. As guitarist in a school band, he had continually annoyed his fellow musicians with his insistence on trying to wring fresh sounds from his instrument, usually by hitting it with things. Later, as a DJ in Switzerland, he watched the burgeoning punk scene in England and prophesied that the synth would eventually replace the guitar as the ultimate punk instrument. Not only did you not have to be able to play an instrument, he argued, with a synth you didn't even need to know how to hold one.

He proved his point in 1978 when he recorded and self-released "TV OD," on his own Mute label (see following entry). Credited to The Normal, the single sold over 40,000 copies (and prompted Grace Jones to title her fourth album after its B-side, "Warm Leatherette"), persuading Miller that there was indeed a market for a label which released only experimental electronic sounds.

A new single, "First Frame," was abandoned; instead, the Normal followed up with the harsh *Live* EP (#14 UK indy), recorded at Rutland Pavilion in March 1979 with fellow electronics buff Robert Rental. Then, while Fad Gadget and Boyd Rice kept the early Mute catalog moving, Miller moved on to the Silicon Teens, a largely successful attempt to crush the essence of rock'n'roll into a tight electronic corner, via a succession of classic rock and pop covers reiterated through Miller's synthesizers.

Miller's discovery of the nascent Depeche Mode and their ensuing explosion into popularity (with Miller the band's producer until 1988) stripped much of the urgency from Miller's own work. While remaining a crucial producer through the remainder of the 1980s, he has not recorded in his own right since the Teens' album, although he has surfaced for occasional one off projects, including the "Or So It Seems" single and album recorded under the alias of Duet Emmo with Wire spin-off Dome.

Daniel Miller LPs

8 Music for Parties (As Silicon Teens) (Mute) 1980 As musical jokes go, this was a classic. Not only were the Silicons not Teens, they were actually non-existent, just a front for Miller to bubbly synthipopize 12 golden oldies and two originals songs.

8 Or So It Seems (As Duet Emmo) (Mute) 1983 Collaboration with Wire's Gilbert and Lewis.

Daniel Miller — Selected Productions

6 DEPECHE MODE — Speak and Spell (Sire) 1981

7 YAZOO — Upstairs at Eric's (Mute/Sire) 1982

7 DEPECHE MODE — A Broken Frame (Sire) 1982

8 DEPECHE MODE — Construction Time Again (Sire) 1983

8 DEPECHE MODE — Some Great Reward (Sire) 1984

9 DEPECHE MODE — Black Celebration (Sire) 1986

8 FRANK TOVEY — Snakes and Ladders (Sire) 1986

9 DEPECHE MODE — Music for the Masses (Sire) 1987

7 HOUSE OF LOVE — Spy in the House of Love (Fontana) 1991

MUTE RECORDS

LABEL

Would-be producer Daniel Miller (see previous entry) launched Mute records in mid-1978 with his own "TV OD" single, released under the name of The Normal — an unexpected hit on the experimental electronics circuit, it persuaded him that Mute should expand, and over the next few months the label was joined by San Francisco noise terrorist Boyd Rice, German electro-punks Deutsche Amerikanische Freundschaft, and Fad Gadget (aka Frank Tovey), the eccentric flatmate of *Sounds* cartoonist Edwin Pouncey. Together with Miller's own continued excursions as the Silicon Teens, this quartet would remain the heart of Mute Records until late 1980, when they were joined by Depeche Mode — discovered by Miller opening for Fad Gadget at the Bridgehouse pub in east London. He had already rejected the group once before, on encountering one of the early demos at the Rough Trade offices. This time, however, he was impressed and over a post-show drink, recruited the band to Mute.

"Daniel came along and said he could put out a record," Depeche Mode vocalist Dave Gahan recalled. "If after that we didn't want to stay, we didn't have to." Having already entertained offers from other interested record companies, "it was the most honest thing we had heard." Twenty years on, their relationship still based on a handshake, Depeche Mode (like Boyd Rice) remain part of the Mute set-up.

Depeche Mode's success was instantaneous; so, following Vince Clarke's departure after just three singles, were his subsequent enterprises — Yazoo, Assembly, and Erasure. However, they were not the only stars in the Mute firmament — the Birthday Party closed their recording career at the label, and vocalist Nick Cave continued his.

Former Pop Group vocalist Mark Stewart, Wire, and German pioneers Can all forged links with Miller and Mute, while label discoveries included He Said, Nitzer Ebb (proteges of Depeche Mode's Alan Wilder), and the highly rated mid-80s synth duo I Start Counting. Almost without exception, these acts, too, have retained relations with Mute, establishing the label among the most reliably self-contained record companies of the past 25 years.

Mute Records Label Listing 1981–89

Singles

1 DANIEL MILLER/THE NORMAL — TV OD
2 FAD GADGET — Back to Nature
3 SILICON TEENS — Memphis Tennessee
4 SILICON TEENS — Judy in Disguise
5 DAF — Kebabtraume
6 FAD GADGET — Ricky's Hand
7 NON — Sound Tracks 1-5
8 SILICON TEENS — Just Like Eddie
9 FAD GADGET — Fireside Favourite
10 ROBERT RENTAL — Double Heart
11 DAF — Der Rauber Und der Prinz
12 FAD GADGET — Make Room
13 DEPECHE MODE — Dreaming of Me
14 DEPECHE MODE — New life
15 NON — Rise, Out Out Out
16 DEPECHE MODE — Just Can't Get Enough
17 FAD GADGET — Saturday Night Special
18 DEPECHE MODE — See You
19 DIE DORAUS UND DIE MARINAS — Fred Vom Jupier
20 YAZOO — Only You
21 FAD GADGET — King of the Flies
22 DEPECHE MODE — Meaning of Love
23 LIAISONS DANGEREUSES — Los Ninos Del Parque
24 FAD GADGET — Life on the Line
25 DUET EMMO — Or So It Seems
26 FAD GADGET — For Whom the Bell Tolls
27 ROBERT GORL — Mit Dir
28 FAD GADGET — I Discover Love
29 BIRTHDAY PARTY — Mutiny EP
30 FAD GADGET — Collapsing New People
31 ROBERT GORL — Darling Don't Leave me
32 NICK CAVE — In the Ghetto
33 FAD GADGET — One man's Meat
34 I START COUNTING — Letters to a Friend
35 I START COUNTING — Still Smiling
36 CRIME AND THE CITY SOLUTION — The Dangling Man EP
37 MARK STEWART & THE MAFIA — Still Smiling
38 NICK CAVE — Tupelo
39 FRANK TOVEY — Luxury

40 ERASURE — Who Needs a Heart Like That
41 HE SAID — Only One I
42 ERASURE — Heavenly Action
43 HE SAID — Pump
44 FRANK TOVEY — Luddite Joe
45 ERASURE — Oh L'Amour
46 CRIME & THE CITY SOLUTION — Adventure
47 NICK CAVE — The Singer
48 HE SAID — Pulling 3 Gs
49 I START COUNTING — Catch That Look
50 AC MARIAS — Just Talk
51 ERASURE — Sometimes
52 NICK CAVE — The Mercy Seat
53 WIRE — Snakedrill EP
54 I START COUNTING — My Translucent Hands
55 HOLGER HILLER — Whippet
56 ERASURE — It Doesn't Have to Be
57 WIRE — Ahead
58 NITZER EBB — Let Your Body Learn
59 MARK STEWART — Stranger Than Love
60 LAIBACH — Geburt Einer nation
61 ERASURE — Victim of Love
62 LAIBACH — Life Is Life
63 THESE IMMORTAL SOULS — Marry Me
64 NITZER EBB — Join in the Chart
65 ANITA LANE — Dirty Sings
66 ERASURE — The Circus
67 WIRE — Kidney Bingoes
68 MKULTRA — Immobilise
69 I START COUNTING — Lose Him
70 AC MARIAS — Time Was
71 NITZER EBB — Control I'm Here
72 OHI HO BANG BANG — The Three
73 HE SAID — Could You
74 ERASURE — Ship of Fools
75 DIAMANDA GALAS — Double Barrel Prayer
76 CRIME & THE CITY SOLUTION — On Every Train
77 BARRY ADAMSON — Man with the Golden Arm
78 NITZER EBB — Hearts and Minds
79 FRANK TOVEY — Bridge Street Shuffle
80 LAIBACH — Sympathy for the Devil
81 I START COUNTING — Ra Ra Rawhide
82 RENEGADE SOUNDWAVE — Biting My Nails
83 ERASURE — Chains of Love
84 WIRE — Silk Skin Paws
85 ERASURE — A Little Respect
86 NICK CAVE — Deanna

87 WIRE — Eardrum Buzz

88 RENEGADE SOUNDWAVE — The Phantom, It's in There

89 ERASURE — Drama

90 THESE IMMORTAL SOULS — TVC

91 LAIBACH — Across the Universe

92 MARK STEWART — Hysteria

93 ERASURE — Crackers International

94 CRIME & THE CITY SOLUTION — The Shadow of No Man

95 I START COUNTING — Million Headed Monster

96 NITZER EBB — Shame

97 BARRY ADAMSON — Taming of the Shrewd

98 WIRE — In Vivo

99 unreleased

100 FRANK TOVEY — Sam Hall

NOTE: Follwing Mute 22 Depeche Mode singles were given BONG prefix numbers, beginning with: BONG 1 Leave in Silence

---

YAZ 001 YAZOO — Don't Go

YAZ 002 YAZOO — Other Side of Love

YAZ 003 YAZOO — Nobody's Diary

TINY 1 ASSEMBLY — Never Never

Albums

1 DAF — Die Kleinen Und Die Bosen **8**

2 SILICON TEENS — Music for Parties **8**

3 FAD GADGET — Fireside Favourites **8** Tearing a hole in synthi-pop and pouring in liters of undiluted industrial fluid, *Fireside* constructs a vividly grim surreal world, while reconstructing pop in Gadget's own skewered Punch-faced image.

4 BOYD RICE — Boyd Rice **6**

5 DEPECHE MODE — Speak and Spell **6**

6 FAD GADGET — Incontinent **7**

7 YAZOO — Upstairs at Eric's **7**

8 FAD GADGET — Under the Flag **8** *Flag*'s inspired musical lampoons of the dance floor vibe and style of New Romanticism are juxtaposed with a hurtfully accurate dissection of Thatcher's Britain.

9 DEPECHE MODE — A Broken Frame **7**

10 NON — Physical Evidence **7**

11 DUET EMMO — Or So It Seems **8**

12 YAZOO — You and Me Both **6**

13 DEPECHE MODE — Construction Time Again **8**

14 EINSTURZENDE NEUBAUTEN — Strategies Against Architecture **8**

15 FAD GADGET — Gag **8** Now expanded into a band, Gadget broadens the sound, laying the foundation for electro's future in the process and opening doors into guitar-led cold wave of future heroes Nine Inch Nails and Ministry.

16 ROBERT GORL — Night of Tension **4**

17 NICK CAVE — From Her to Eternity **8**

18 BRUCE GILBERT — This Way **7**

19 DEPECHE MODE — Some Great Reward **8**

20 BOYD RICE/FRANK TOVEY — Easy Listening for the Hard of Hearing

21 NICK CAVE — Firstborn Is Dead **9**

22 CRIME & THE CITY SOLUTION — Just South of Heaven EP

23 FRANK TOVEY — Snakes & Ladders **7**

24 MARK STEWART — As the Veneer of Democracy Starts to Fade **8**

25 ERASURE — Wonderland **7**

26 DEPECHE MODE — Black Celebration **9**

27 DIAMANDA GALAS — Divine Punishment **6**

28 NICK CAVE — Kicking Against the Pricks **8**

29 HE SAID — Hail **7**

30 I START COUNTING — My Translucent Hands **7**

31 RECOIL — 1&2 EP

32 NON — Blood & Flame **6**

33 DIAMANDA GALAS — Saint of the Pit **5**

34 NICK CAVE — Your Funeral My Trial **9**

35 ERASURE — The Circus **6**

36 CRIME & THE CITY SOLUTION — Room of Lights **9**

37 FRANK TOVEY — Fad Gadget Singles **8**

38 HOLGER HILLER — Oben Im Eck **6**

39 BRUCE GILBERT — The Shivering Man **7**

40 VARIOUS ARTISTS — International

41 VARIOUS ARTISTS — Nervous Systems

42 WIRE — The Ideal Copy **9**

43 MARK STEWART — Mark Stewart **8**

44 LAIBACH — Opus Dei **9**

45 NITZER EBB — That Total Age **7**

46 DIAMANDA GALAS — You Must Be Certain **5**

47 DEPECHE MODE — Music for the Masses **9**

48 THESE IMMORTAL SOULS — Get Lost **7**

49 unreleased

50 I START COUNTING — Fused **8**

GIL NORTON

PRODUCER

BORN *(Liverpool, England)*

Working from of a small Liverpool, England studio, and having engineered early releases by OMD, the March Violets, China Crisis, and Echo and the Bunnymen's landmark *Ocean Rain* album in 1984, Norton emerged out of obscurity when he produced Throwing Muses' eponymous debut album in 1986, following that with similarly impressive engagements with fellow 4AD Bostonians the Pixies and Australia's Triffids.

It was his work with the developing Catherine Wheel, however, which truly marked Norton out, as he enveloped the band in the dark, crunching guitar layers which would power "Black Metallic" to cult status — even as another Norton production, Belly's "Feed the Tree," soared into mainstream acceptance. He would then work with Counting Crows and Longpigs, before helming the second Foo Fighters album in 1997.

Gil Norton — Selected Productions

10 ECHO AND THE BUNNYMEN — Ocean Rain (Sire) 1984

8 AUTO DE FE — Tatitum (Spartan) 1985

7 THROWING MUSES — Throwing Muses (4AD) 1986

8 THE TRIFFIDS — Born Sandy Devotional (Hot) 1986

7 THE TRIFFIDS — Calenture (Island) 1987

5 HURRAH — Tell God I'm Here (Kitchenware) 1987

9 PIXIES — Dolittle (4AD/Elektra) 1989

6 PIXIES — Bossanova (4AD/Elektra) 1990

7 PALE SAINTS — The Comforts of Madness (4AD) 1990

5 BLUE AEROPLANES — Swagger (Ensign) 1990

7 DEL AMITRI — Waking Hours (A&M) 1990

6 BLUE AEROPLANES — World View Blue (Ensign) 1990

6 HEART THROBS — Cleopatra Grip (Elektra) 1990

5 PIXIES — Trompe Le Monde (4AD/Elektra) 1991

7 PERE UBU — Worlds in Collision (Fontana) 1991

6 TRIBE — Abort (Slash) 1991

7 DEL AMITRI — Change Everything (A&M) 1992

8 CATHERINE WHEEL — Chrome (Mercury) 1993

8 BLINK — A Map of the Universe (Lime) 1995 Not counting the band, 5 producers contributed to the making of *Map*, each obviously vying with the others to capture the group at their best. In Blink's universe ,everyone's a winner, as different facets of the group's pop-punk-rock-club-space sound are coaxed into the spotlight and encouraged to shine — a real aural treat.

7 CATHERINE WHEEL — Happy Days (Fontana) 1995

5 SEVEN DAY DIARY — Skin and Blister (WB) 1995

5 ROACHFORD — Permanent Shade of Blue (Epic) 1995

6 THE MEICES — Dirty Bird (London) 1996

6 COUNTING CROWS — Recovering the Satellites (Geffen) 1996

7 AGE OF ELECTRIC — Make a Pest a Pet (Universal) 1996

7 TERRORVISION — Regular Urban Survivors (EMI) 1996

8 FOO FIGHTERS — The Colour and the Shape (Roswell) 1997

RIC OCASEK

PRODUCER
BORN 3/23/49 (Baltimore, OH)

As a founding member of the Cars, the first new wave-era Boston band to break out of the city, Ocasek was swiftly established as a local guru of sorts, taking a number of aspiring bands under his wing as producer — Nervous Eaters and La Peste paramount among them. The Cars themselves had very quickly abandoned the stark, edgy style which characterized their earliest strivings — whether intentionally or otherwise, Ocasek's choice of production jobs ensured he retained some contact with his own roots.

Suicide's sophomore album debuted Ocasek in the public eye; he also recorded scene personality Bebe Buell, former La Peste vocalist Peter Dayton, and DC hardcore specialists Bad Brains (this team reunited in 1995), although his best known early work was with San Francisco's Romeo Void, whose signature "Never Say Never" was an early new wave classic. Two years later, he remixed tracks for Lloyd Cole's landmark *Rattle Snakes* album, before dropping out of sight for the remainder of the decade.

Ocasek re-emerged as producer with Suicide's late 1980's revival, before masterminding New York club heroes Black 47's earliest releases. His understanding of classic punk, meanwhile, was underlined by his mid-1990's handling of Bad Religion and D'Generation, although it was with Weezer that he scored his greatest success, producing their double platinum debut in 1994.

Ric Ocasek — Selected Productions

6 SUICIDE — Alan Vega and Martin Rev (ZE) 1980

8 NERVOUS EATERS — Nervous Eaters (Elektra) 1980

7 PETER DAYTON — Love at First Sight (Shoo Bop) 1981

6 ALAN VEGA — Saturn Drive (ZE) 1983

6 BAD BRAINS — Rock for Light (Abstract) 1983

7 SUICIDE — A Way of Life (Wax Trax!) 1989

8 BLACK 47 — Fire of Freedom (SBK) 1992

6 SUICIDE — Why Be Blue (Enemy) 1992

5 WEEZER — Weezer (DGC) 1994

4 BAD BRAINS — God of Love (Maverick) 1995

8 NADA SURF — High/Low (Elektra) 1996 "Popular" indeed was, a tongue-in-cheek lesson on achieving the teen-aged ideal status, wrapped around a melancholy riff which rips into sonic roars at the chorus — and shifting sonics is what Nada Surf are all about. Yearning, angsty melodies explode into resounding drone meltdowns, all cut through with punk fury, with Ocasek insuring things never melt into a wall of noise.

9 BAD RELIGION — The Gray Race (Atlantic) 1996

7 JOHNNY BRAVO — Then Again Maybe I Won't (Arista) 1996

7 D'GENERATION — No Lunch (Columbia) 1996 Featuring reworkings of four tracks from their aborted eponymous Chrysalis album, *No Lunch* is everything that record wasn't, as Ocasek puts the spotlight on D'Gen's innate power and aggression and the group run through a killer collection of punky pop rock, with the emphasis on speed, melody, and edge.

6 POSSUM DIXON — New Sheets (Interscope) 1998

6 JONATHAN RICHMAN — I'm So Confused (WB) 1998

7 GUIDED BY VOICES — Do the Collapse (TVT) 1999

DAVE OGILVIE

PRODUCER
BORN 1960 *(Montreal, Canada)*

As the *de facto* 4th member of Vancouver industrial icons Skinny Puppy, the bulk of Ogilvie's production career has been bound up in the music, and incidental soap operatics of that band's lengthy career. He linked with the band at the very dawn of their career, having previously engineered for producer Bruce Fairbairn, and produced the highly rated 54.40.

Puppy and sundry band spin-offs occupied Ogilvie through much of the '80s — he did maintain his relationship with 54.40, and engineered albums by Queensryche, Moev, Numb, Loverboy, and Ministry (*The Mind Is a Terrible Thing to Taste*). It would be the early 1990s, however, before Ogilvie truly branched out alone, producing and remixing Contagion, Die Krupps, Drown, Low Pop Suicide, and Epitaph punks SNFU among others, while also helming (along side Trent Reznor and Sean Beavan), Marilyn Manson's *Antichrist Superstar*.

Also see the entry for "SKINNY PUPPY" on page 622.

Dave Ogilvie — Selected Productions

6 54.40 — Set the Fire (Modamu) 1984

6 DEAD SURF KISS — Narcotic Nevada (Oceana) 1985

7 SKINNY PUPPY — Bites (Nettwerk) 1985

SKINNY PUPPY — Mind: The Perpetual Intercourse (Gold Rush) 1986

8 TEAR GARDEN — Tired Eyes (Nettwerk) **6** 1986

6 54.40 — 54.40 (Reprise) 1986

8 SKINNY PUPPY — Cleanse, Fold and Manipulate (Nettwerk) 1987

7 HILT — Orange Pony (Nettwerk) 1988

8 SKINNY PUPPY — Vivisect VI (Nettwerk) 1988

5 RIGOR MORTIS — Rigor Mortis (Capitol) 1989

5 54.40 — Fight for Love (Reprise) 1989

6 SKINNY PUPPY — Rabies (Nettwerk) 1989

5 HILT — Call the Ambulance Before I Hurt Myself (Nettwerk) 1990

4 CATERWAUL — Portent Hue (IRS) 1990

5 24 GONE — The Spin (Oceana) 1990

5 WATER WALK — Thingamajig (Nettwerk) 1990

7 SKINNY PUPPY — Too Dark Park (Nettwerk) 1990

5 SKINNY PUPPY — Ain't It Dead Yet? (Nettwerk) 1991

6 HILT — Journey to the Center of the Bowl (Nettwerk) 1991

3 THOUGHT INDUSTRY — Songs for Insects (Metal Blade) 1992

7 TEAR GARDEN — The Last Man to Fly (Nettwerk) 1992

7 SKINNY PUPPY — Last Rights (Nettwerk) 1992

6 PSYCLONE RANGERS — Feel Nice (World Domination) 1993

6 MYSTERY MACHINE — Glazed (Nettwerk) 1994

5 MALHAVOC — Get Down (Cargo) 1994

4 DROWN — Hold on to the Hollow (Elektra) 1994

5 HHEAD — Jerk (Capitol) 1995

6 SNFU — The One Voted Most Likely to Succeed (Epitaph) 1995

8 SKINNY PUPPY — The Process (American) 1996

ORK RECORDS

LABEL

As much as CBGBs, Ork Records would become a focal point for the burgeoning New York scene, and that despite releasing a mere handful of singles. Quality over quantity — four, at least, became undisputed classics. Television's "Little Johnny Jewel" would be followed by Richard Hell's "Blank Generation," the Marbles' "Red Light," and Mick Farren's frantic "Lost Johnny", recorded with future Voidoid/Ramone Marcy Bell and John Tiven, later of Jim Carroll's Band, and one of the great lost singles of the '70s.

"Terry (Ork) was an idealist, as true to the punk ethic as you could be," Farren enthused, "which means that when it all started getting slick, and the bands were getting deals, Terry got left behind." The label kept going through 1978, masterminding Alex Chilton's first come back, and also unleashing early stirrings by dB's frontman Chris Stamey, and the Feelies. But though Ork had the vision to succeed, he didn't have the venom, and though his deviant idealism nurtured the scene, the moment it could walk, he was off.

Ork Records Label Listing

1975 TELEVISION — Little Johnny Jewel

1976 RICHARD HELL — Another World EP

1978 ALEX CHILTON — Singer Not the Song EP

1979 MARBLES — Red Light

1980 MICK FARREN — Play with Fire

1981 LINK CORMWELL — Crazy Like a Fox

1982 CHRIS STAMEY — The Summer Sun

1983 ALEX CHILTON — EP

1984 FEELIES — Fa Ce La

1984 BLUE VEIN — Get off of My Cloud

MICK RONSON

PRODUCER
BORN *1946 (Hull, England)*

Though Ronson remains best remembered for the three years he spent as the mercurial guitarist alongside David Bowie's Ziggy Stardust persona, and for a patchy solo career thereafter, his career as a producer was responsible for some of the most individual sounding albums of the age. Alongside Bowie in 1972, he produced Mott the Hoople's *All the Young Dudes* and Lou Reed's *Transformer* albums, breakthrough sets which both, the artists concerned later acknowledged, owed far more to Ronson's influence than Bowie's.

After stints with Mott, Ian Hunter, and Bob Dylan, and two solo albums, Ronson returned to production in 1977, working with Manchester punk band Slaughter and the Dogs and Dead Fingers Talk, from his hometown Hull; he also produced ex-Sex Pistols Glen Matlock's Rich Kids before forming a new partnership with Ian Hunter, recording and gigging in their own right, and coproducing others — Ellen Foley, the Iron City Houserockers, and former New York Doll David Johansen included.

Solo again, Ronson worked alongside singer Sandy Dillon, and produced albums by Lol Hammond's Kiss That and the Sex Gang Children; he would also become very active on the Scandinavian rock scene through the late 1980's, before being diagnosed with liver cancer in 1991. His final production was Morrissey's *Your Arsenal*; Ronson died 4/29/93.

Mick Ronson — Selected Productions
(excluding David Bowie collaborations)

9 IAN HUNTER — Ian Hunter (CBS) 1975

7 ROGER MCGUINN — Cardiff Rose (Columbia) 1976

7 RICH KIDS — Ghost of Princes in Towers (Emi) 1978

6 DEAD FINGERS TALK — Storm the Reality Studios (Pye) 1978

5 DAVID JOHANSEN — In Style (Blue Sky) 1979 Swaggering, if heavily rock-oriented, sophomore set from the Doll who would be Buster Poindexter.

9 ELLEN FOLEY — Night Out (Epic) 1979 Foley's second solo set would be produced and largely written by boyfriend Mick Jones and the Clash. But it is her debut which remains her mas-

terpiece, as Ronson and Ian Hunter pair her with gems by one-time Max's Kansas City regular Phil Rambow, Graham Parker, and the Stones, for a driving new wave rock album.

7 IRON CITY HOUSEROCKERS — Have a Good Time (MCA) 1980

6 THE PAYOLAS — No Stranger to Danger (A&M) 1982 Middling Canadian new wave band, Ronson produced their demo and two albums.

6 THE PAYOLAS — Hammer on a Drum (A&M) 1983

5 LOS ILLEGALS — Internal Exile (A&M) 1983

6 IAN THOMAS — Riders on Dark Horses (Mercury) 1984

4 LISA DALBELLO — Who Man for Says (Capitol) 1984

SANDY DILLON — Sandy Dillon [unreleased] 1985

7 ONE THE JUGGLER — Some Strange Fashion (RCA) 1985 Post-"Come on Eileen" influenced cow-punks, mercifully blessed with a few convincing songs.

6 THE URGENT — Cast the First Stone (Manhattan) 1985

9 KISS THAT — Kiss and Tell (Chrysalis) 1986

6 DAVID LYNN JONES — Hard Times on Easy Street (Mercury) 1987

7 FATAL FLOWERS — Johnny B Is Back (Atlantic) 1988

4 ANDI SEXGANG — Arco Valley (Jungle) 1989 Former post-punk goth hero goes glam. At times ("Queen of Broken Dreams"), Sexgang suggests the sound of London Suede playing Bolan... no act of premonition, however, as Sexgang spends the entire album attempting to emulate either Bolan or Bowie, frequently both at once, but generally he just sounds Very Silly. One wonders what Ronson was thinking?

6 FATAL FLOWERS — Pleasure Ground (Atlantic) 1989

5 ROGER MCGUINN — Born to Rock and Roll (Columbia) 1991

9 MORRISSEY — Your Arsenal (Sire/Reprise) 1992

RICK RUBIN

PRODUCER
BORN *Frederick Jay Rubin, 1963 (Long Island, NY)*

As the mastermind behind the Def Jam label, co-founded with New York promotor Russell Simmons in 1984, Rubin had already cut his production teeth working with T La Rock and Jazzy Jay in a studio set up in his NYU dorm room. It was their "It's Yours" single which first introduced Rubin and Simmons; following the launch of Def Jam, Rubin continued utilizing his dorm room, this time as the label's head office and mail room.

Def Jam's first release, LL Cool J's "I Need a Beat" immediately established Def Jam on the infant US rap scene, but it was Rubin's production of the Beastie Boys *Licensed to Ill* which made household names of the operation in 1986. Work with Run DMC followed, together with the rap movie

Krush Groove, but Def Jam ran into problems after Rubin announced the next release would be by Slayer. Distributor Columbia refused to handle the record, and in the ensuing battle, Rubin and Simmons, too, split up.

Relocating to L.A., Rubin formed the Def American label (American only from 1991), an operation which would allow him to indulge all his private musical loves — over the next decade, the company's roster would include country star Johnny Cash, '60's singer/songwriter Donovan, Love and Rockets, Skinny Puppy, rapper Sir Mix-A-Lot, metal acts Danzig and Slayer, and comedian Andrew Dice Clay.

Rubin's production, too, would cross genres effortlessly — he oversaw the Cult's 1992 reinvention with the heavy electro beats of "The Witch," the Red Hot Chili Peppers monster hit *Blood Sugar Sex Magic*, and Joan Jett's "She's Lost You" comeback, while also working with older, established acts Aerosmith, Ozzy Osbourne, Mick Jagger, and Tom Petty.

American changed distributors from Warners to Sony in 1997; shortly after, the label ceased everyday operations. Rubin, however, remained an active producer, handling the Red Hot Chili Peppers' *Californication*, among others.

Rick Rubin — Selected Productions

9 THE BEASTIE BOYS — Licensed to Ill (Columbia) 1986
5 SLAYER — Reign in Blood (Def Jam) 1986
7 RUN D.M.C. — Raising Hell (Profile) 1986
8 THE CULT — Electric (Sire) 1987
4 MASTERS OF REALITY — Masters of Reality (Delicious Vinyl) 1988
5 DANZIG — Danzig (Def American) 1988
4 TROUBLE — Trouble (American) 1990
4 DANZIG II — Lucifuge (American) 1990
5 SLAYER — Live: Decade of Aggression (American) 1991
6 SIR MIX-A-LOT — Mack Daddy (Def American) 1991
8 RED HOT CHILI PEPPERS — Blood Sugar Sex Magik (WB) 1991
6 FOUR HORSEMEN — Nobody Said It Was Easy (American) 1991
5 RED DEVILS — King King (American) 1992
7 MICK JAGGER — Wandering Spirit (Atlantic) 1992
7 FLIPPER — American Grafishy (Def American) 1992
4 DANZIG — Thrall/Demonsweatlive (Def American) 1993
7 JOHNNY CASH — American Recordings (American) 1994
4 DANZIG — 4 (American) 1994
7 RED HOT CHILI PEPPERS — One Hot Minute (WB) 1995
7 DONOVAN — Sutras (American) 1996
6 SYSTEM OF A DOWN — System of a Down (Sony) 1998
6 RED HOT CHILI PEPPERS — Californication (WB) 1999
8 JOHNNY CASH — American Recordings III (Sony) 2000

ADRIAN SHERWOOD

PRODUCER
BORN *Adrian Maxwell, 1958 (London, England)*

Having already worked alongside UK DJ's Johnny Walker and Emperor Rosko at BBC roadshow performances and helped out at the UK reggae labels Pama and Vulcan, Adrian Sherwood was 17 when he co-founded Carib Gems in 1975, a London-based label which immediately came to prominence through early releases by Black Uhuru and Prince Far I. Three years later, Sherwood launched a new label, Hitrun, and produced Creation Rebel's *Dub from Creation* album; other releases included Far I's "Higher Field Marshall" 12-inch and *Crytuff Dub Encounter* album.

Sherwood and photographer Kishi Yamamoto launched ON-U Sounds in 1980 with Sherwood-produced releases by the New Age Steppers (featuring former members of the Pop Group and the Slits), London Underground, and Mark Stewart. Over the next three years, his revolutionary dub deconstructions graced a string of classic releases, attracting the likes of New York chanteuse Judy Nylon, the Fall, Little Annie, African Head Charge, and ex-Crass member Vivian Goldman to his table.

In 1984, Sherwood executed remixes of Depeche Mode's "People Are People" and "Master and Servant" singles, profoundly raising that band's underground credentials, at the same time as establishing his own name in a mainstream he had previously shunned. Subsequently, work with Einsturzende Neubauten, Ministry, KMFDM, and Nine Inch Nails saw him move into the proto-industrial arena, at the same time as maintaining a chart profile with Simply Red, EMF, and Living Colour remixes — few of which, of course, made any concessions whatsoever to their makers own commercial standing.

Adrian Sherwood — Selected Productions

7 ERIC CLARKE — Love That Grows and Grows (Hitrun) 1978
8 PRINCE FAR I — Message from the King (Virgin) 1978
7 SUNS OF ARQA — Revenge of the Mozabites (Rocksteady) 1980
8 LAST WORDS — Last Words (Armageddon) 1980
7 LONDON UNDERGROUND — Learn a Language (ON-U) 1980
7 AFRICAN HEAD CHARGE — My Life in a Hole in the Ground (ON-U) 1981
7 PRINCE FAR I — Cry Tuff Dub Encounter 3/4 (Trojan) 1981
6 PRINCE FAR I — Jamaican Heroes (Trojan) 1981
THE FALL — Slates Ep (Rough Trade) 1981
MEDIUM MEDIUM — Hungry, So Angry (Cherry Red) 1981

8 PRINCE FAR I & SINGERS & PLAYERS — Prince Far I &.. (Virgin) 1981

9 NEW AGE STEPPERS — New Age Steppers (ON-U) 1981

8 NEW AGE STEPPERS — Crucial 90 (Statik) 1981

8 NEW AGE STEPPERS — Action Battlefield (Statik) 1981

7 BIM SHERMAN — Across the Red Sea (ON-U) 1982

9 JUDY NYLON — Pal Judy (ON-U) 1982 New York chanteuse, ex-John Cale and Snatch, surfaces for a steaming, dub heavy album of sultry originals, plus a dispassionately sensual take on Presley's "Jailhouse Rock."

7 MAXIMUM JOY — Station M.X.J.Y (Y) 1982

7 NEW AGE STEPPERS — Victory horNs (ON-U) 1983

7 DUB SYNDICATE — One Way System (Roir) 1983

8 AFRICAN HEAD CHARGE — Drastic Season (EFA) 1983

6 NORTH OF THE RIVER THAMES (ON-U) 1984

7 DUB SYNDICATE — Pounding System 1984

6 CONGO ASHANTI ROY — Level Vibes (Sonic bOom) 1984

8 DUB SYNDICATE — Tunes from the Missing Channel (ON-U) 1985

7 NADJMA — Rapture in Baghdad (Crammed — Belgium) 1985

7 AFRICAN HEAD CHARGE — Off the Beaten Path (ON-U) 1986

7 MINISTRY — Twitch (Sire) 1986

7 CABARET VOLTAIRE — Code (Parlophone) 1987

6 FLUX — Uncarved Block (One Little Indian) 1987

8 DUB SYNDICATE — Pounding System (ON-U) 1988

5 KMFDM — Don't Blow Your Top (Skysaw) 1988

6 PANKOW — Freedom for the Slaves (Wax Trax!) 1988

10 NINE INCH NAILS — Pretty Hate Machine (TVT) 1989

7 KEITH LE BLANC — Stranger than Fiction (Nettwerk) 1989

8 COLDCUT — What's the Noise? (Ahead of Our Time) 1989

5 PANKOW — Gisela (Contempo) 1989

7 MARK STEWART — Metatron (Mute) 1990

7 AFRICAN HEAD CHARGE — Songs of Praise (1991) 1991

7 TWINKLE BROTHERS — Higher Heights (TwinkLe) 1992

6 SOFT BALLET — Alter Ego (Alpha) 1992

8 DUB SYNDICATE — Echomania (ON-U) 1993 A truly other worldly experience, the heavy dub rhythms pulse from the speakers, guest vocalists live and sampled rap and ramble, Akabu chime out the sweet choruses, as the guitar flits and soars riffs and roars, and surrounding it all are the futuristic electronics, strange samples, and burbling keyboards.

6 REVOLUTIONARY DUB WARRIORS — Reaction Dub Pt 1

6 DELIVERANCE (on-U) 1994 Fractured sounds of the Caribbean — roots, dub, reggae, steel drum calypso, rock, and trademark ON-U electronics.

8 BIM SHERMAN — Miracle (Talvin) 1994

6 LITTLE AXE — The Wolf That House Built (Wired) 1994

8 MARK STEWART — Control Data (Mute) 1995

7 LITTLE AXE — Slow Fuse (Wired) 1996

6 FIRE THIS TIME — Dancing on John Wayne's Head (Filter) 1998

4 BARMY ARMY — English Disease (EFA) 1998

6 AUDIO ACTIVE — Happy Happer (EFA) 1999

Adrian Sherwood — Selected Remixes

SHRIEKBACK — Hand on My Heart (Arista) 1984

DEPECHE MODE — People Are People (Mute) 1984

THE ENEMY WITHIN — Strike (Rough Trade) 1984

JAMES BLOOD ULMER — Eyelevel (Rough Trade) 1984

DEPECHE MODE — Master & Servant (Mute) 1984

UNKNOWN CASES — Masimbabele (Rough Trade) 1984

ATMOSFEAR — When Tonight Is Over (Elite) 1984

SIMPLY RED — Holding Back the Years (WEA) 1985

EINSTURZENDE NEUBAUTEN — Yu Gung (Some Bizzare) 1985

SUDDEN SWAY — Singsong (M-I-X-X-S-I-N-G) (Blanco) 1986

WOODENTOPS — Everyday Living (Rough Trade) 1986

CABARET VOLTAIRE — Here We Go (EMI) 1987

RINF — Bang Bang (Contempo) 1987

THE THREE JOHNS — Never and Always (Abstract) 1987

SIMPLY RED — Infidelity (WEA) 1987

SKINNY PUPPY — Addiction (Nettwerk) 1987

THE BEATINGS — Television (Alternative Tentacles) 1988

RINF — Rubber on Rider (Contempo) 1988

PULSE 8 — Radio Morocco (Mix Nation) 1989

THE FALL — Telephone Thing (Cog Sinister) 1990

DEPECHE MODE — Enjoy the Silence (Mute) 1990

STONE ROSES — Waterfall (Silvertone) 1991

POP WILL EAT ITSELF — Bulletproof (RCA) 1992

S.E.T. — Super Eccentric Theatre in the 90's (Alpha) 1992

DEEP JOY — Something Inside (Kinetix) 1992

JAH WOBBLE'S INVADERS... — Visions of You (Oval) 1992

BACK TO THE PLANET — Daydream (Parallel) 1993

TERMINAL POWER CO — Juggernaut (Beggars Banquet) 1993

BIG LIFE CASINO — My Ministry (Splash) 1993

LIVING COLOUR — Auslander (Epic) 1993

POP WILL EAT ITSELF — Get the Girl Kill the Baddies (RCA) 1993

WOLFGANG PRESS — Christianity (4AD) 1994

LIVING COLOUR — Sunshine of Your Love (Epic) 1994

SPEARHEAD — Hole in the Bucket (Capitol) 1995

DEEP FOREST — Bohemian Ballet (Epic) 1995

GARBAGE — Vow (Almo Sounds) 1995

NITZER EBB — Kick It (Mute) 1995

MAD CAPSULE MARKETS — Walk (YUI) 1996

SENSER — Charming Demons (Ultimate) 1996

THE CURE — Strange Attraction (Fiction) 1996

PRIMAL SCREAM — Scream Team and the Big Man (Creation) 1996

BIM SHERMAN — Simple Life (Mantra) 1996

CRAZY GODS OF ENDLESS NOISE — Trapped Water (Wired) 1996

PRIMAL SCREAM — Echo Dek (Creation) 1997

JEB LOY NICHOLLS — As the Rain (Capitol) 1997

THE CURE — Lime Green (Fiction) 1997

SLY & ROBBIE WITH SIMPLY RED — Night Nurse (East West) 1997

DEPECHE MODE — Useless (Mute) 1997

MANU DIBANGO — Popcorn (Mercury) 1997

SHANE MACGOWAN & THE POPES — Crock of Gold (ZTT)

LOOP LIZARD — Into the Sun (Double T) 1997

BLUR — Bustin' and Dronin' (Food) 1998

FRANTIC LANGUAGE — Move It (Arthrob) 1998

MONKEY MAFIA — Long as I Can See the Light (Heavenly) 1998

SST

LABEL

The pioneering hardcore label was launched in 1980 as an outlet for founder Greg Ginn's own band, Black Flag, with early releases alternating between new Black Flag product and releases by other local hardcore acts, the Minutemen, Saccharine Trust, and the Meat Puppets. The roster quickly grew, however, with the 1983 arrival of Minneapolis Hüsker Dü proving the national standing of both the label and the music it championed.

The break-up of Black Flag allowed Ginn to devote himself full-time to SST — Gone, Bad Brains, and the Leaving Trains all joined the label around this time, while later recruits included Pacific Northwest grunge pioneers Soundgarden and the Screaming Trees.

Also see the entry for "BLACK FLAG" on page 203.

SST Label Listing 1980–87

001 BLACK FLAG — Nervous Breakdown 7-inch

002 MINUTEMEN — Paranoid Time 7-inch

003 BLACK FLAG — Jealous Again EP

004 MINUTEMEN — The Punch Line EP

005 BLACK FLAG — Six Pack EP

006 SACCHARINE TRUST — Pagan Icons EP

007 BLACK FLAG — Damaged LP 9

008 OVERKILL — Hell's Getting Hotter

009 MEAT PUPPETS — Meat Puppets LP 7

010 STAINS — Stains 6 LP

011 WURM — I'm Dead 7-inch

012 BLACK FLAG — TV Party 7-inch

013 VARIOUS ARTISTS — The Blasting Concept LP 9 Excellent compilation drawn from the first 11 SST releases, including key singles by Wurm ("I'm Dead") and Saccharine Trust ("A Human Certainty"), plus Minutemen, Meat Puppets, Black Flag, Overkill, Stains, and an unreleased Hüsker Dü.

014 MINUTEMEN — What Makes a Man Start Fires? LP 7 18 songs, most of them more than a minute long — and as if that's not ambitious enough, blues and jazz stylings are creeping into the roar.

015 BLACK FLAG — Everything Went Black LP 6

016 MINUTEMEN — Buzz or Howl Under Influence of the Heat EP

017 DICKS — Kill from the Heart 7-inch

018 SUBHUMANS — No Wishes No Prayers 7-inch

019 MEAT PUPPETS — Meat Puppets II LP 9

020 HÜSKER DÜ — Metal Circus EP

021 BLACK FLAG — The First Four Years 7-inch

022 ST VITUS — St Vitus LP 6

023 BLACK FLAG — My War LP 3

024 SACCHARINE TRUST — Surviving You, Always LP 5

025 HÜSKER DÜ — Eight Miles High 7-inch

026 BLACK FLAG — Family Man LP 7

027 HÜSKER DÜ — Zen Arcade LP 8

028 MINUTEMEN — Double Nickels on the Dime LP [45 song double album]

029 BLACK FLAG — Slip It In LP 4

030 BLACK FLAG — Live 1984 LP 8

031 HÜSKER DÜ — New Day Rising LP 9

032 MINUTEMEN — My First Bells LP 7 Cassette-only release compiling 62 cuts from albums and EPs.

033 DC3 — This Is the Dream LP 7

034 MINUTEMEN — Project: Mersh EP

035 BLACK FLAG — Loose Nut LP 6

036 OCTOBER FACTION — October Faction EP

037 BLACK FLAG — The Process of Weeding Out EP

038 OVERKILL — Triumph of the Will LP 5

039 MEAT PUPPETS — Up on the Sun LP 8

040 DAS DAMEN — Das Damen EP

041 WURM — Feast LP 6

042 ST VITUS — The Walking Dead EP

043 VARIOUS ARTISTS — The Blasting Concept II LP 7

044 MEAT PUPPETS — In a Car 7-inch

045 BLACK FLAG — In My Head LP 5

046 SACCHARINE TRUST — World Broken LP 6

047 TOM TROCCOLI'S DOG — Tom Troccoli's Dog LP 6

048 SACCHARINE TRUST — We Became Snakes LP **5** Mike Watt (Minutemen)-produced set which touches on Stooges-esque jazz-jam intensity in places.

049 MEAT PUPPETS — Get Out of My Way LP **6**

050 MINUTEFLAG (Minute Men/Black Flag) — Minuteflag EP

051 HÜSKER DÜ — Makes No Sense at All 7-inch

052 SAINT VITUS — Hallow's Victim LP **7**

053 SWA — Your Future If You Have One LP **6**

054 ANGST — Lite Life LP **6**

055 HÜSKER DÜ — Flip Your Wig LP **6**

056 OCTOBER FACTION — Second Factionalization LP **6** Wildly divisive jamfest, two tracks merging into a hardcore guitar war of entertainingly epic (not to mention defiantly indulgent) proportions.

057 PAINTED WILLIE — Mind Blowing LP **6**

058 MINUTEMEN — 3 Way Tie LP **6**

059 unreleased

060 BLACK FLAG — Who's Got the 10 1/2 LP **4**

061 GONE — Let's Get Real Real Gone LP **7**

062 VARIOUS ARTISTS — Lovedolls Superstar Soundtrack LP **6**

063 DC3 — The Good Hex LP **6**

064 ANGST — Angst EP

065 BAD BRAINS — I Against I LP **9**

066 VARIOUS ARTISTS — Program; Annihilator LP **8**

067 SLOVENLY — Thinking of Empire LP **7**

068 MINUTEMEN — Ballot Result LP **7** Double album compiled from fans' write-in votes, rounding up radio and live recordings in varying states of sonic perfection.

069 VARIOUS ARTISTS — Chunks LP **6**

070 VARIOUS ARTISTS — The Wonders of the World LP **6**

071 LEAVING TRAINS — Kill Tunes LP **7**

072 VARIOUS ARTISTS — Desperate Teenage Lovedolls Soundtrack LP **6**

073 SWA — Sex Dr. LP **7**

074 ANGST — Mending Wall LP **5**

075 ALTER-NATIVES — Hold Your Tongue LP **6**

076 PAPER BAG — Ticket to Trauma LP **6**

077 ZOOGZ RIFT — Island of Living Puke LP **6**

078 ALWAYS AUGUST — Black Pyramid LP **5**

079 FIREHOSE — Ragin' Full On LP **8** The Minutemen reconvene following the death of D Boon, with vocalist Ed Crawford leading the band into a considerably calmer land where acoustic and atmospheric numbers peacefully co-exist with the expected blasts.

080 SONIC YOUTH — Starpower EP

081 BLACK FLAG — Annihilate This Week EP

082 ST VITUS — Born Too Late LP **7**

083 DC3 — You're Only as Blind as Your Mind Can Be LP **6**

084 SACCHARINE TRUST — The Sacramental Element LP **6**

085 PAINTED WILLIE — Live from Van Nuys LP **4**

086 GONE — Gone Ii: But Never Forgotten LP **5**

087 LAWNDALE — Beyond Barbeque LP **6**

088 ZOOGZ RIFT — Looser than Clams LP **5**

089 SLOVENLY — Riposte LP **6**

090 DIVINE HORSEMEN — Middle of the Night EP

091 DIVINE HORSEMEN — Devil's River LP **8**

092 VARIOUS ARTISTS — Cracks in the Sidewalk LP **7**

093 SWA — XCIII LP **6**

094 FLESH EATERS — Greatest Hits; Destroyed by Fire LP **7** Double album of album material and rarities.

095 DAS DAMEN — Jupiter Eye LP **6**

096 SONIC YOUTH — Confusion Is Sex LP **5**

097 SONIC YOUTH — Sonic Youth EP

098 PAINTED WILLIE — Upsidedowntown LP **6**

099 ZOOGZ RIFT — Water LP **6**

100 MEAT PUPPETS — Mirage LP **7**

STEPHEN STREET

PRODUCER

An assistant engineer and later novice producer at Island Record's Fallout Studios, Stephen Street's name first started getting noticed when he produced the Smith's "Girlfriend in a Coma" single (having earlier engineered *The Queen Is Dead*). Striking up a short, but fruitful relationship with the soon to be solo Morrissey, Street would both co-write and produce 1988's *Viva Hate* debut album. Though the partnership soured over money and paperwork, Street's work with Morrissey would remain a touchstone of sorts.

The young Blur, seeking a similarly decisive sound, recorded much of their *Leisure* album with Street, and would continue working with him for the next four albums; the Cranberries, too, would record their first two albums under Street's direction, while he was also behind Sleeper's best selling *The It Girl* album.

Stephen Street — Selected Productions

7 MIGHTY LEMON DROPS — Happy Head (Sire) 1986

5 THE SMITHS — Strangeways Here We Come (Sire) 1987

7 THE TRIFFIDS — The Black Swan (Island) 1988

9 MORRISSEY — Viva Hate (Sire) 1988

6 BRADFORD — Shouting Quietly (Sire) 1990

8 DANIELLE DAX — Blast the Human Flower (Sire) 1990

7 BLUR — Leisure [7 TRACKS] (SBK) 1991

7 PSYCHEDELIC FURS — World Outside (Columbia) 1991

7 THE DYLANS — The Dylans (Beggars Banquet) 1991 A dozen catchy songs immersed in waves of melodies, swirls of psychedelia and fetching harmonies, the Dylans recreate the sound of the '60's with a potent mix of swirling keyboards and powerful guitars.

6 **DARLING BUDS** — Erotica (Chaos) 1992

5 **THOUSAND YARD STARE** — Hands On (polydor) 1992

7 **FAT LADY SINGS** — The Fat Lady Sings (Atlantic) 1993

8 **CRANBERRIES** — Everybody Else Is Doing It (Island) 1993

8 **BLUR** — Modern Life Is Rubbish (SBK) 1993

6 **CRANBERRIES** — No Need to Argue (Island) 1994

10 **BLUR** — Parklife (SBK) 1994

5 **PRETENDERS** — Isle of View (WB) 1995

6 **KINGMAKER** — The Best Possible Taste (Chrysalis) 1995

6 **INTASTELLA** — What You Gonna Do (Planet 3) 1995

6 **LLOYD COLE** — Love Story (Rykodisc) 1995

7 **DURUTTI COLUMN** — Sex and Death (FFRR) 1995

8 **BLUR** — The Great Escape (Virgin) 1995

10 **SLEEPER** — The It Girl (Arista) 1996

8 **CATATONIA** — Way Beyond Blue (Blanco Y Negro) 1996

6 **BLUR** — Blur (Virgin) 1997

SUB POP

LABEL

Alongside the same city's C/Z label, Sub Pop was the driving force behind the PNW/Seattle Sound "grunge" movement of the late 1980s/early 1990s. Formed by Bruce Pavitt and Jonathan Poneman in the early 1980s, originally as a fanzine, Sub Pop dedicated itself to developing a label spirit which, in the alternative era, is analogous only with the early years of Stiff — acts seemed to be signed as much for what they could bring to Sub Pop, as for what Sub Pop could do for them.

During the five years of operation which preceded the explosion, almost every one of the acts who would eventually put Seattle on the musical map passed through Sub Pop — Green River, the first band to release a record on the label, were followed by Soundgarden, Mudhoney, Tad, the Walkabouts, and Nirvana. In addition, the label had strong ties with another underground concern, K Records in nearby Olympia (label head Calvin Johnson of Beat Happening was an early contributor to the Sub Pop fanzine).

The label did not, however, confine itself purely to local environs. Oklahoma City's Flaming Lips, Cincinnati's Afghan Whigs, San Francisco's Helios Creed, and Ann Arbor's Big Chief all released material through the label, while from even further afield, Les Thugs (France) and Billy Childish (UK) would be recruited.

Launched in November 1988, by the then unknown Nirvana, the much-collected Sub Pop Singles Club, too, brought fresh air to the US market, with limited edition 45's appearing every two months for the next five years — high-

lights included Smashing Pumpkins, Afghan Whigs, Rapeman, Elastica, Gene, and Rocket From the Crypt, before the series ended with Lou Barlow's "I Am Not Mocking You." (The Club was relaunched in April 1998, since when Luna, Jesus and Mary Chain, Dot Allison, and Imperial Teen have contributed.)

Amid such activities, Sub Pop first came to major attention in the UK, following well-received tours by Mudhoney, Soundgarden, and Nirvana (among others). Even before Geffen signed Nirvana in 1991, however, Sub Pop was already creeping into the American consciousness. Once *Nevermind* hit, however, it became ubiquitous, marketing its own name with merciless precision, particularly following the label's partial acquisition by Time Warner.

The decline of grunge's mainstream popularity naturally led to a downswing in the label's own visibility; however, intelligent signings continued to distinguish Sub Pop through the 1990's, with the 1998 capture of St. Etienne a particularly noteworthy accomplishment.

Sub Pop Label Listing 1979–92

1 **VARIOUS ARTISTS** — Subterranean Pop Fanzine

2 **VARIOUS ARTISTS** — Subterranean Pop Fanzine

3 **VARIOUS ARTISTS** — Sub Pop Fanzine

4 **VARIOUS ARTISTS** — Sub Pop Fanzine

5 **VARIOUS ARTISTS** — Sub Pop Cassette Fanzine

6 **VARIOUS ARTISTS** — Sub Pop Fanzine

7 **VARIOUS ARTISTS** — Sub Pop Cassette Fanzine

8 **VARIOUS ARTISTS** — Sub Pop Fanzine

9 **VARIOUS ARTISTS** — Sub Pop Cassette Fanzine

10 **VARIOUS ARTISTS** — SUB POP 100 LP 8

11 **GREEN RIVER** — Dry As a Bone EP

12 **SOUNDGARDEN** — Screaming Life EP

13 **BLOOD CIRCUS** — Two way Street 7-inch

14 **SWALLOW** — Guts 7-inch

15 **GREEN RIVER** — Rehab Doll EP

16 **FLUID** — Clear Black Paper LP 6

17 **SOUNDGARDEN** — Fopp EP

18 **MUDHONEY** — Touch Me I'm Sick 7-inch

19 **TAD** — Ritual device T 7-inch

20 **GIRL TROUBLE** — Hit It Or Quit EP

21 **MUDHONEY** — Superfuzz Bigmuff 7-inch

22 **BLOOD CIRCUS** — Primal Rock Therapy EP

23 **NIRVANA** — Love Buzz 7-inch

24 **SWALLOW** — Swallow 6

25 **VARIOUS ARTISTS** — SUB POP 200 LP 7

26 **MUDHONEY/SONIC YOUTH** — Halloween 7-inch

27 **TAD** — God's Balls LP 4 Tad's first album steamrolled a slack-jawed Seattle straight into the sidewalk, then pounded it

into submission with "Nipple Belt," "Behemoth," and "Satan's Chainsaw" — all heavy slabs of furious riffing.

28 FLAMING LIPS — Strychnine 7-inch

29 LES THUGS — Crime and Chess 7-inch

30 HELIOS CREED — Nothing Wrong 7-inch

31 WALKABOUTS — Cataract LP **7** Lots of texture and timbre drive this band's sound — a Pacific Northwest take on folk that is edgy and uniquely American, without being at all stereotypical. Chris Eckman and Carla Torgerson's vocals both play off and into each other — and that is what makes this band sound so good.

32 AFGHAN WHIGS — I Am the Sticks 7-inch

33 MUDHONEY — You Got It 7-inch

34 NIRVANA — Bleach LP **6**

35 MAD DADDIES — Alligator Wine 7-inch

36 FLUID — Road Mouth LP **5**

37 TAD/PUSSY GALORE — Damaged 7-inch

38 LES THUGS — Electric Troubles LP **7**

39 DAS DAMEN — Sad Mile 7-inch

40 RAPEMAN — Inki's Butt Crack 7-inch

41 CAT BUTT — Journey to the Center of Cat Butt EP

42 COSMIC PSYCHOS — Go the Hack LP **6**

43 LAZY COWGIRLS — Loretta 7-inch

44 MUDHONEY — Mudhoney LP **8**

45 LOVE BATTERY — Between the Eyes 7-inch

46 LONELY MOANS — Shoot the Cool 7-inch

47 SKIN YARD — Start at the Top 7-inch

48 SCREAMING TREES — Change Has Come 7-inch

49 TAD — Salt Lick EP

50 DWARVES — She's Head 7-inch

51 HONEYMOON KILLERS — Get It Hot 7-inch

52 FUGAZI — Joe 31 7-inch

53 BIG CHIEF — Blowout Kit 7-inch

54 THEE HYPNOTICS — Liv'r Than God LP **4** Their first US album, *Liv'r* cobbles together a UK EP plus a handful of studio cuts, wraps it up in a neat package — a perfect domestic introduction... except that the sound as transferred from vinyl to CD was pretty poor, and the overall result was like chewing tin foil.

55 TAD — Loser 7-inch

56 WALKABOUTS — Rag and Bone/Cataract EP

57 FLUID — Tin Top Toy 7-inch

58 L7 — Shove 7-inch

59 DICKLESS — I'm a Man 7-inch

60 AFGHAN WHIGS — Up in It LP **8**

61 MARK LANEGAN — The Winding Sheet LP **8**

62 MUDHONEY — Boiling Beef and Rotting Teeth EP

62A BEAT HAPPENING — Jamboree LP **8**

63 MUDHONEY — You're Gone 7-inch

64 FLUID — Glue LP

65 LUBRICATED GOAT — Meeting My Head 7-inch

66 BABES IN TOYLAND — House 7-inch

67 DWARVES — Blood, Guts & Pussy LP **8**

68 DINOSAUR JR — The Wagon 7-inch

69A LOVE BATTERY — Between the Eyes LP **7**

70 DERELICTS — Misery Maker 7-inch

71 THEE HEADCOATS — Time Will Tell

72 ROLLINS BAND — Earache My Eye 7-inch

73 NIRVANA — Sliver 7-inch

74 BEAT HAPPENING — Red Head Walking 7-inch

75 SISTER RAY — The King 7-inch

76 UNSANE — Vandal X 7-inch

77 SISTER DOUBLE HAPPINESS — Wheels a Spinnin' 7-inch

78A BEAT HAPPENING — Black Candy LP **4**

79 L7 — Smell the Magic EP

80 TAD — Jinx 7-inch

81 DWARVES — Drug Store 7-inch

82 THEE HEADCOATS — Heaven to Murgatroyd, Even! LP **7**

83 SOUNDGARDEN — Room a Thousand Years Wide 7-inch

84 AFGHAN WHIGS — Sister Brother 7-inch

85 COFFIN BREAK — Lies 7-inch

86 POISON IDEA — We Got the Beat 7-inch

87 THE FREEWHEELIN' MARK ARM — Masters of War 7-inch

88 POSTER CHILDREN — Thinner, Stronger 7-inch

89 TAD — 8 Way Santa LP **6**

90 SMASHING PUMPKINS — Tristessa 7-inch

91 REIN SANCTION — Creel 7-inch

92A REIN SANCTION — Broc's Cabin LP **6**

93 HOLE — Dicknail 7-inch

94 THIN WHITE ROPE — Ants Are Cavemen 7-inch

95 MUDHONEY — Let It Slide 7-inch

96 REV HORTON HEAT — Psychobilly Freakout 7-inch

97 FLUID/NIRVANA — Candy 7-inch

98A BEAT HAPPENING — Dreamy LP **8**

99B TAD — Jack Pepsi CD single

100 DICKLESS ALL STARS — Sex God Tad

MARTY THAU

PRODUCER

BORN *12/7/38 (Bronx, New York, NY)*

Like Craig Leon, Marty Thau is inextricably bound up in the story of the early-mid 1970s New York underground, not only as a producer, but also as one of the few industry insiders with the foresight to see what was going on, and the ability to help it. A veteran '60s era promo man, Thau was head of A&R at Paramount Records when he discovered the New York Dolls in 1972 — he promptly became their manager, producing their first demos (subsequently released as the *Lipstick Killers* album) and overseeing their career until early 1975.

He was replaced at the helm by future Sex Pistols manager Malcolm McLaren; Thau went to ground, only to be brought out again after Dolls drummer Walter Lure invited him down to CBGBs one evening. The Ramones asked him to manage them; Thau refused, but did produce their first demos, then hooked up with Richard Gottehrer in a production company, Instant Hits. Blondie, Robert Gordon, and Richard Hell numbered among their first clients, before Thau broke away to form his own Red Star label in late 1976. There he signed the Real Kids and Suicide, co-producing (with Leon) their debut album the following year.

Since that time, Thau has surfaced only infrequently, most notably working with the Fleshtones and producing Suicide's Martin Rev's *Clouds of Glory* solo album.

Marty Thau — Selected Productions

6 NEW YORK DOLLS — Demos [LP Lipstick Killers, 1981] 1972 Early recordings of the glam/punk heroes, known to fans as the Mercer St. sessions. As an archival item, it's of interest to the hardcore, but the low budget presentation and poor sound throw little light on the legends — except to suggest that offstage, at this point, they had little energy, flair, or charisma.

7 RAMONES — Demos [Released 1991] (TVT) 1975

8 REAL KIDS — The Real Kids (Red Star) 1977 Breezy pop buffeted by garage punk, producer Thau pulls the Kids' high energy delivery directly onto the record's grooves.

8 SUICIDE — Suicide (Red Star) 1977

7 FLESHTONES — Fleshtones (Red Star) 1982

7 MARTIN REV — Clouds of Glory (New Rose) 1985

MIKE THORNE

PRODUCER
BORN 1948 (*Sheffield, England*)

A classically trained musician and a physics BA, Thorne's studio career commenced in 1970 when he was hired as a tea boy at De Lane Lea Studios in London, rising to engineer and working with Deep Purple and Fleetwood Mac. By late 1971, however, he had turned to journalism, becoming editor of *Studio Sound* magazine before deciding to return to recording in 1976. He was hired as an A&R man at EMI, and was involved with both the Sex Pistols and Kate Bush, before early 1977 saw him commissioned to step into the lion's den of punk, to record a live album at the Roxy Club.

Live at the Roxy, London WC2 would become one of the seminal punk era recordings; a raw, harsh document of two weeks in the company of some of the movement's most savage auteurs. Of the bands on that album, however, almost all would land major label deals, with Wire going to EMI and working with Thorne again on their first three albums.

He would also be involved with ex-Sex Pistol Glen Matlock's Rich Kids, and in late 1977, Thorne quit EMI to go independent. Over the next three years, he would record with John Cale, Wire's Colin Newman, and American new wave-ers Human Sexual Response, but it was the northern English duo Soft Cell with whom he scored his biggest hit, producing the worldwide #1 "Tainted Love." As one of the few UK-based producers conversant with the recently developed Synclavier, he was the ideal producer for dance-oriented acts, and three years later, Thorne would helm another major dance hit, Bronski Beat's "Smalltown Boy." As with Soft Cell, he would continue working with the band into the future.

In 1986, Thorne opened his own studio, Stereo Society, one of the most advanced technological set-ups of its kind. Siouxsie and the Banshees, China Crisis, and Peter Murphy have all recorded there, together with Soft Cell's Marc Almond, with whom Thorne was reunited for 1995's *Fantastic Star* album. In addition, Thorne has also established his own Uptown Horns studio band, featuring vocalists Lene Lovich and Kit Hain, recording an ambitious solo album, *Sprawl*.

Mike Thorne — Selected Productions

9 VARIOUS ARTISTS — Live at the Roxy, London WC2 (Harvest) 1977 One of the most important (and poorest sounding) live albums ever made; a document of the Roxy Club from on- and off-stage (the mike in the bathrooms was a particularly nice touch). Despite being recorded at some of the first shows they ever played, the Buzzcocks, Wire, the Adverts, X-Ray Spex, and Slaughter and the Dogs would all live to tell the tale to major labels.

9 WIRE — Pink Flag (Harvest) 1977

7 TELEPHONE — Telephone (Marconi) 1977 French power-punkers get the garage sound down pat.

9 WIRE — Chairs Missing (Harvest) 1978

6 THE SHIRTS — The Shirts (Harvest) 1978

5 METRO — New Love (EMI) 1979

7 THE SHIRTS — Street Light Shine (Harvest) 1979

8 WIRE — 154 (Harvest) 1979

6 URBAN VERBS — The Urban Verbs (WB) 1980

6 BERLIN BLONDES — Berlin Blondes (EMI) 1980

8 COLIN NEWMAN — A–Z (Beggars Banquet) 1980

7 HUMAN SEXUAL RESPONSE — In a Roman Mood (Passport) 1981 Almost crushingly literate (but never crashingly boring), Boston's HSR were hung up on frantic rhythms, quirky dynamics, and jerky guitars. In other words, the musical equivalent of an ant farm having a panic attack.

7 JOHN CALE — Honi Soit (A&M) 1981

8 SOFT CELL — Non-Stop Erotic Cabaret (Some Bizarre) 1981

8 KIT HAIN — Spirits Walking Out (Mercury) 1981 Breaking up the "Dancing in the City" hitmaking duo of Marshall Hain, vocalist Kit trained the loveliest voice of the era on her own more balladic material. Never hitting the heights of the lustrous "Coming Home," she nevertheless cemented herself in place as a classic songwriter.

6 HOLLY AND THE ITALIANS — Holly and the Italians (Virgin) 1982

6 NINA HAGEN — Nunsex Monkrock (CBS) 1982 Quirky, stylized rock in a distinctly Lene Lovich-shaped vein.

7 KIT HAIN — Looking for You (Mercury) 1982 Another understated gem — the hit title track alone is worth its weight in vinyl.

7 SOFT CELL — Non-Stop Ecstatic Dancing EP (Some Bizzare) 1982

5 SHERRY KEAN — Mixed Emotions (Capitol) 1983

9 SOFT CELL — The Art of Falling Apart (Some Bizzare) 1983

7 KIT HAIN — School for Spies (Mercury) 1983

6 SHERRY KEAN — People Talk (Capitol) 1984

4 CARMEL — The Drum Is Everything (London) 1984

9 BRONSKI BEAT — The Age of Consent (London) 1984
Jimmy Somerville's emotion-packed falsetto defined the Bronski sound; his lyrical stance, their politics, and the music — running the gamut from Broadway to backroom — did the rest. The runaway "Smalltown Boy"'s poignancy captured people's heart, "Why?"'s defiance gave hope and the medley "I Feel Love"/"Johnny Remember Me" (featuring a delectably non-committal Marc Almond) was simply a joyous celebration.

7 THE REDS — Shake Appeal (Sire) 1984

5 'TIL TUESDAY — Voices Carry (Epic) 1985

8 BRONSKI BEAT — Hundreds and Thousands (London) 1985
Amazing remix collection, spreading six of the best of *Consent* cuts out to double the length.

7 COMMUNARDS — Communards (London) 1986

4 CARMEL — Everybody's Got a Little Soul (London) 1987

6 HOLLYWOOD BEYOND — If (WB) 1987

7 FURNITURE — Food, Sex, and Paranoia (Arista) 1989

7 CHINA CRISIS — Diary of a Hollow Horse (Virgin) 1989

6 BETTY — Hello Betty (Betty Rules) 1991

7 PETER MURPHY — Holy Smoke (RCA) 1992

6 INFORMATION SOCIETY — Peace and Love, Inc. (Tommy Boy) 1992

6 STRANGELOVE — Time for the Rest of Your Life (Food) 1994

7 HILLY KRISTAL — Mad Mordechai (Stereo Society) 1999
Unexpectedly entertaining debut album by the legendary CBGBs club owner — following on from a classic CBGBs Christmas single in the late 1970s.

6 JOHNNY REINHARD — Raven (Stereo Society) 1999

6 THE REDS — Cry Tomorrow (Stereo Society) 1999

9 LENE LOVICH/KIT HAIN/THORN — Sprawl (Stereo Society) 1999

TWIN/TONE RECORDS

LABEL

The Minneapolis/St. Paul based Twin/Tone was formed in January 1978, by engineer/producer Paul Stark, local sportswriter/music critic Charley Hallman, and Peter Jesperson, owner of the local record store Oar Folkjokeopus (Suicide Commandos frontman Chris Osgood was also an early participant) — the store itself was named for cult albums by Skip Spence and Roy Harper.

Early releases were strictly limited editions — 3,000 copies of the Suburbs' first in April 1978; 1,000 apiece of the next pair, and between 1,000 and 1,500 of the next four. In addition, the first three appeared on red vinyl, extra incentive to collectors.

Although most of the label's acts were the proverbial "big in Minneapolis," it would be 1981 before Twin/Tone signed the band whose name would subsequently become synonymous with the company, the Replacements. The Slickee Boys followed in 1983, Soul Asylum in 1984, and by 1985, the label put its original, all-local vision behind it with the recruitment of Pere Ubu frontman David Thomas, Jonathan Richman, Nikki Sudden, and Public Image Limited alumni Martin Atkins. Later, the Mekons, Babes in Toyland, Ween, and Robyn Hitchcock would also call Twin/Tone home.

Twin/Tone Label Listing 1978–84

7801 THE SUBURBS — The Suburbs EP

7802 CURTISS A — Spooks EP

7803 FINGERPRINTS — Fingerprints EP

7804 FINGERPRINTS — Christmas Down EP

7805 THE JETS — Paper Girl 7-inch

7906 THE SUICIDE COMMANDOS — Commit Suicide Dance Concert LP **8**

7907 VARIOUS ARTISTS — Big Hits of Mid-America Vol 3 LP **6**

7908 unreleased

7909 THE SUBURBS — World War III 7-inch

7910 ORCHID SPANGIAFORA — Flee Past Apes Alf LP **6**

7911 HYPSTYRZ — Hypstyrz LP **5**

7912 CURTISS A — I Don't Wanna Be President 7-inch

013 FINGERPRINTS — Smiles for Sale 7-inch

8014 THE SUBURBS — In Combo LP **6**

8015 CURTISS A — Courtesy LP **6**

8016 unreleased

8017 THE PISTONS — Investigations 7-inch

8018 THE OVERTONES — Red Checker Wagon 7-inch

8019 CURTISS A — Afraid 7-inch

8120 THE REPLACEMENTS — I'm in Trouble 7-inch

8121 THE PISTONS — Flight 581 LP **4**

8122 THE CRACKERS — Sir Crackers LP **5**

8123 THE REPLACEMENTS — Sorry Ma, Forgot to Take Out... LP **8**

8124 SAFETY LAST — Safety Last LP **5**

8125 THE SUBURBS — Credit in Heaven LP **5**

8126 unreleased

8127 THE SUBURBS — Music for Boys LP **6**

8128 THE REPLACEMENTS — Stink EP

8229 THE SUBURBS — Waiting EP

8230 THE SUBURBS — Dream Hog EP

8231 THE PHONES — Changing Minds LP **5**

8332 THE REPLACEMENTS — Hootenanny LP **8**

8333 JEFF WARYAN — Figures LP **4**

8334 SAFETY LAST — Struck by Love LP **5**

8335 CURTISS A — Damage Is Done LP **4**

8336 THE SLICKEE BOYS — When I Go to the Beach LP **6**

8337 THE SLICKEE BOYS — Cybernetic Dreams LP **6**

8438 THE PHONES — Blind Impulse LP **5**

8439 SOUL ASYLUM — Say What You Will LP **6** Spawned from the same formidable scene that gave us the Replacements and Hüsker Dü, this debut from the next generation of raw-cous showmen presented a lite version of that Minneapolis firestorm under the guise of new alterna-rock, as manipulated by hunky frontman Dave Pirner.

8440 THE REPLACEMENTS — I Will Dare 7-inch

8441 THE REPLACEMENTS — Let It Be LP **10**

8442 JESSE THE BODY — Picture Disc 7-inch

8443 THE REPLACEMENTS — The Shit Hits the Fans LP **6**

8544 THE SLICKEE BOYS — Uh Oh... No Breaks LP **7**

8545 unreleased

8546 FIGURES — In a Chalk Circle 7-inch

8547–50 unreleased

CONRAD UNO

PRODUCER

Seattle based Uno never thought of his home set-up of tape recorders as a studio, even after he began producing local bands — most notably the Young Fresh Fellows — in the early 1980s. Mudhoney's 1991 *Every Good Boy Deserves Fudge*, recorded by Uno on an eight track machine, brought him to national attention, however, as the Seattle grunge sound began to take off, and while he remained loyal to PNW bands, as their stock rose, so did his — he produced Mudhoney's major label debut *Piece of Cake* in 1992, together with a slew of Sub Pop classics by Love Battery,

Supersuckers, the Fastbacks, and the Mudhoney spin-off Monkeywrench.

Uno's greatest commercial success came in 1995, when he was brought in to helm the Presidents of the United States of America's eponymous multi-million seller; he would also produce their sophomore swansong.

Conrad Uno — Selected Productions

7 YOUNG FRESH FELLOWS — Fabulous Sounds of the Pnw (Popllama) 1984

8 YOUNG FRESH FELLOWS — Topsy Turvy (Popllama) 1985

8 YOUNG FRESH FELLOWS — The Men Who Loved Music (Frontier) 1987 This primarily wacky selection of songs may not rock out as much as other Fellow efforts, but remains an endearingly good time as the band chase genres with much success. From the frat rock of "I Got My Mojo Workin' (and I Thought You'd Like to Know)" to the ska-infused "TV Dream," the Fellows have come up with a winning combination. They found their mojo long before Mr. Powers and they wield it well.

8 YOUNG FRESH FELLOWS — Totally Lost (Frontier) 1988

7 YOUNG FRESH FELLOWS — This One's for the Ladies (Frontier) 1989

7 DHARMA BUMS — Haywire:Out Through the Indoor (Frontier) 1989

6 CAPPING DAY — Post No Bills (Popllama) 1990

8 THE SQUIRRELS — What Gives? (Popllama) 1990 Rob Morgan hi-jacks members of the Posies and the Young Fresh Fellows among others and makes them (willingly, of course!) do his bidding, resulting in a delightfully warped sophomore set, doing untold ridicule and damage to Gilbert O' Sullivan's "Get Down" and adding a little Alice Cooper to their take on Bill Withers' "Lean on Me."

8 MUDHONEY — Every Good Boy Deserves Fudge (Sub Pop) 1991

7 STUMPY JOE — One Way Rocket to Kicksville (Popllama) 1991

7 THE DERELICTS — Don't Wanna Live (Sub Pop) 1991

6 JIMMY SILVA AND THE GOATS — Heidi/Remnants of the Empty (Hollywood) 1991

7 LOVE BATTERY — Between the Eyes (Sub Pop) 1992

7 MUDHONEY — Piece of a Cake (Reprise) 1992

6 THE PICKETTS — Paper Doll (Popllama) 1992

7 YOUNG FRESH FELLOWS — It's Low Beat Time! (Frontier) 1992

8 THE MONKEYWRENCH — Clean As a Broke-Dick Dog (Sub Pop) 1992

6 THE SMUGGLERS — In the Hall of Fame (Popllama) 1993

5 BRATMOBILE — Pottymouth (Kill Rock Stars) 1993

5 SICKO — You Can Feel the Love in This Room (Empty) 1994

6 SUPERSUCKERS — La Mano Cornuda (Sub Pop) 1994

⑧ THE SQUIRRELS — Harsh Toke of Reality (Popllama) 1994

⑦ SHAME IDOLS — I Got Time (Frontier) 1995

⑦ THE PRESIDENTS OF THE U.S.A. — The Presidents of the U.S.A. (Columbia) 1995 Hooky and far more engaging than it has a right to be, the Presidents' debut shoved them into the spotlight of overnight success — something no one, including the band, expected. From "Kitty" to the Monkees' theme, this band (including Chris Bellew from Beck's breakthrough band) was flavor of the month for nigh on a year, and although they continued, they were smart enough to break up before the scoop fell out of the cone. Posterity alone will decide whether their 2000 reunion was as good an idea as their split.

⑦ THE FALL-OUTS — The Fall-Outs (Super Electro) 1995

⑥ THE PICKETTS — The Wicked Picketts (Rounder) 1995

⑦ SYMON-ASHER — Three Color Sun (Miramar) 1995

④ ZEKE — Flat Tracker (Scooch Pooch) 1996

⑤ LA DONNAS — Shady Lane (Scooch Pooch) 1996

⑤ GROOVY GHOULIES — World Contact Day (Lookout) 1996

⑥ GROOVY GHOULIES — Born in the Basement (Lookout) 1996

⑤ SHAME IDOLS — Rocket Cat (Frontier) 1997

⑦ MINUS 5 OF SCOTT MCCAUGHEY — My Chartreuse Opinion 1997

⑥ THE MAKERS — Hunger (Estrus) 1997

⑥ MUDDY FRANKENSTEIN — Dance with Evil (Rock Boss Intl) 1997

⑤ FLIPP — Flipp (Hollywood) 1997

④ THE PRESIDENTS OF THE U.S.A. — Pure Frosting (Columbia) 1998

⑦ THE POSIES — Success (Popllama) 1998

BUTCH VIG

PRODUCER
BORN *(Madison, WI)*

Wisconsin natives Butch Vig, Duke Erikson, Dave Benton, Jeff Walker, and Joel Tappero formed Spooner in 1978, a punk garage band whose eight-year career would never graduate from the Midwest club circuit. The band split in 1986, at which time Vig and Erikson linked with long-time friend Steve Marker to form Fire Town.

Working out of their own Madison, WI-based Smart Studios, this new act would echo Spooner in cutting two albums, one of which — *In the Heart of the Heart Country* — would see major label distribution through Atlantic. The group went nowhere, however, and following a 1989 Spooner reunion, Vig threw himself into full-time production work.

Killdozer, Sonic Youth, and Smashing Pumpkins all passed through Smart, along with Nirvana who recorded the demos for the pivotal *Nevermind* album there before moving

on to the LP itself. Of course, that album's success sent Vig's stock soaring, and over the next two years, he would produce L7, Sonic Youth, Don Fleming's Gumball, and Smashing Pumpkins' *Siamese Dream*.

By 1994, however, Vig was "kind of burned out on doing really long records." With Erikson and Marker, he began creating radical remixes for a number of bands (Depeche Mode, U2, and Nine Inch Nails among them), which usually involved erasing every last instrumental vestige of the original recording, then adding the trio's own music to the vocal track. From there, it was only a tiny step back into recording their own music for their own songs, and in 1994, they formed Garbage. His production schedule would decline accordingly.

Also see the entry for "GARBAGE" on page 383.

Butch Vig — Selected Productions

⑤ KILLDOZER — ...The Shoeshine Boys (Touch & Go) 1985

⑥ THE ROUSERS — In Without Knocking (Boat) 1986

⑥ FIRE TOWN — In the Heart of the Heart Country (Atlantic) 1987

⑤ SPOONER — Wildest Dreams (Boat) 1988

⑥ KILLDOZER — 12-Point Buck (Touch & Go) 1988

⑤ DIE KREUZEN — Century Days (Touch & Go) 1988

④ DIE KREUZEN — Gone Away (Touch & Go) 1989

⑤ LAUGHING HYENAS — Life of Crime (Touch & Go) 1990

⑤ THE FLUID — Glue (Sub Pop) 1990

⑤ SPOONER — The Fugitive Dance (Dali) 1990

④ URGE OVERKILL — Americruiser (Touch & Go) 1990

④ KILLDOZER — For Ladies Only (Touch & Go) 1990

⑦ SMASHING PUMPKINS — gish (Caroline) 1991

⑤ DIE KREUZEN — Cement (Touch & Go) 1991

⑥ COSMIC PSYCHOS — Blokes You Can Trust (Amphetamine Reptile) 1991

⑥ TAD — 8-Way Santa (Sub Pop) 1991

⑦ YOUNG FRESH FELLOWS — Electric Bird Digest (Frontier) 1991

⑩ NIRVANA — Nevermind (DGC) 1991

⑥ CHAINSAW KITTENS — Flipped Out in Singapore (Mammoth) 1992

⑦ OVERWHELMING COLORFAST — Overwhelming Colorfast 1992 (Relativity) Breezy pop-punk with hints of Bad Religion and a yen for melodies, Colorfast's forte is the brilliant guitar work which layers on the melodies; imagine chunky Flaming Groovies crossed with punk.

⑨ L7 — Bricks are Heavy (slash) 1992

⑦ SONIC YOUTH — Dirty (DGC) 1992

⑨ SMASHING PUMPKINS — Siamese Dream (Virgin) 1993

④ FREEDY JOHNSTON — Perfect World (Elektra) 1994

☐ KILLDOZER — Uncompromising War on Art... (Touch & Go) 1994

☐ UNREST — Fuck Pussy Galore and All Her Friends (Matador) 1994

☐ SONIC YOUTH — Experimental Jet Set and No Star (DGC) 1994

☐ SOUL ASYLUM — Let Your Dim Light Shine (Columbia) 1995

ANDREW WEATHERALL

PRODUCER
BORN *4/6/63 (Windsor, England)*

One of the best-known names on the UK electro dance scene, Weatherall first came to attention as an integral part of the fermenting Madchester scene. He worked on both Happy Mondays 1989 "Hallelujah" and New Order's "World in Motion" chart-topper, but it was his work with Primal Scream, producing and creating hit remixes from their *Screamadelica* album, that he truly made his name. He followed through with the debut album by Glasgow's One Dove featuring Dot Allison.

As part of the Boys Own label, Weatherall undertook a constant stream of releases through the first half of the 1990s — under his own name and in the guise of Sabres of Paradise (with Gary Burns and Jagz Kooner) and Two Lone Swordsmen (with Keith Tenniswood). He also found time to record a string of dance floor favorites of his own, under the names Bloodsugar, Bocca Juniors, the Lino Squares, the Lords of Afford, Meek, the Planet 4 Folk Quartet, and Rude Solo. In addition, Weatherall's Sabres of Paradise and Sabrettes labels have maintained a flow of crucial dance music through the decade.

Andrew Weatherall — Selected Remixes

NOTE: including Two Lone Swordsmen, Weatherall + Keith Tenniswood/Sabres of Paradise, Weatherall + Gary Burns, Jagz Kooner. Weatherall also records as above.

WORD OF MOUTH — What It Is (Urban) 1990

BIG HARD EXCELLENT FISH — Imperfect List (One Little Indian) 1990

THAT PETROL EMOTION — Abandon (Virgin) 1990

THERAPY? — Nowhere [MULTIPLE MIXES] (A&M) 1990

SLY & LOVECHILD — World According to (Heavenly) 1990

DEEP JOY — Fall [MULTIPLE MIXES] (Brainiak) 1990

GRID — Flotation [MULTIPLE MIXES] (East West) 1990

JAMES — Come Home [MULTIPLE MIXES] (Fontana) 1990

JAH WOBBLE — Bomba [MULTIPLE MIXES] (FFRR) 1990

MEAT BEAT MANIFESTO — Psyche Out [MULTIPLE MIXES] (Mute) 1990

WEST INDIAN CO — O Je Suis Suis [MULTIPLE MIXES] (EG) 1990

PRIMAL SCREAM — Come Together [MULTIPLE MIXES] (Creation) 1990

ST. ETIENNE — Only Love Can Break Your Heart [MULTIPLE MIXES] (Heavenly) 1990

HAPPY MONDAYS — Hallelujah (Factory) 1990

NEW ORDER — World in Motion [MULTIPLE MIXES] (Qwest) 1990

PRIMAL SCREAM — Loaded (Creation) 1990

MY BLOODY VALENTINE — Glider [MULTIPLE MIXES] (Creation) 1990

PRIMAL SCREAM — Higher Than the Sun (Creation) 1991

THE ORB — Perpetual Dawn [MULTIPLE MIXES] (Big Life) 1991

IMPOSSIBLES — The Drum (Fontana) 1991

JAH WOBBLE — Visions of You [MULTIPLE MIXES] (East West) 1991

A MAN CALLED ADAM — Chrono Psionic Interface (Big Life) 1991

FINITRIBE — 101 [MULTIPLE MIXES] (One Little Indian) 1991

S EXPRESS — Find 'Em Fool 'Em (Rhythm King) 1991

AIRSTREAM — Follow Through (One Little Indian) 1991

DUST [CHEMICAL] BROTHERS — Song to the Siren [MULTIPLE MIXES] (JBO) 1992

FLOWERED UP — Weekender [MULTIPLE MIXES] (Heavenly) 1992

ONE DOVE — Transient Truth [MULTIPLE MIXES] (London) 1992

BUMBLE — West in Motion [MULTIPLE MIXES] (Mother) 1992

GALLIANO — Skunk Funk [MULTIPLE MIXES] (Talkin' Loud) 1992

MOODY BOYS — Centre of the World (Polydor) 1992

YELLO — Jungle Bill [MULTIPLE MIXES] (Mercury) 1992

FSOL — Papua New Guinea (Jumpin' & Pumpin') 1992

UTAH SAINTS — I Want You [MULTIPLE MIXES] (FFRR) 1993

K KLASS — Let Me Show You (Deconstruction) 1993

ONE DOVE — Why Don't You Take Me (FFRR) 1993

STEREO MCS — Everything (4th & Broadway) 1993

HOLY GHOST — Mad Monks on Zinc (Holy Ghost) 1993

BROTHERS LOVE DUBS — The Mighty Ming (Stress) 1993

OHM — Tribal Tone [MULTIPLE MIXES] (Hubba Hubba) 1993

PEACE TOGETHER — Be Still (Island) 1993

NEW ORDER — Regret [MULTIPLE MIXES] (London) 1993

UZMA — Yab Yum (Nation) 1993

LEFTFIELD/JOHN LYDON — Open Up [MULTIPLE MIXES] (Hard Hands) 1993

JAMES — Jam J [MULTIPLE MIXES] (Fontana) 1994

INNERSPHERE — Necronomicon (Innersphere) 1994

PRIMAL SCREAM — Jailbird [MULTIPLE MIXES] (Creation) 1994

BJÖRK — Come to Me [MULTIPLE MIXES] (One Little Indian) 1994

ESPRITU — Conquistador [MULTIPLE MIXES] (Heavenly) 1994

ESPRITU — Bonita Manana (Heavenly) 1994

BOMB THE BASS — Dark Heart [MULTIPLE MIXES] (4th/Broadway) 1994

LMNO — Silcock Express (Vivatonal) 1994

BJÖRK — One Day [MULTIPLE MIXES] (One Little Indian) 1994

PSYCHIC TV — Reunited [MULTIPLE MIXES] (Visionary) 1995

TRANS-GLOBAL UNDERGROUND — International Times (Nation) 1995

CYMBOL — Crash (Deconstruction) 1995

SKYLAB — Indigo (L'attitude) 1995

RENEGADE SOUNDWAVE — Brixton (Mute)1995

INNERSPHERES — Out of Body (Sabrettes) 1995

FUNDAMENTAL — Mother India [MULTIPLE MIXES] (Mantra) 1995

DAVID HOLMES — Gone [MULTIPLE MIXES] (Go! Discs) 1995

RED SNAPPER — Hot Flush (Warp) 1995

ORB — Oxbow lakes (Island) 1995

CHEMICAL BROTHERS — Leave Home (JBO) 1995

WOLFGANG PRESS — 11 Years (4AD)1995

SLAB — Atomsmasher [MULTIPLE MIXES] (Hydrogen Dukebox) 1995

BLACK SHEEP — North South East West [MULTIPLE MIXES] (Heavenly) 1996

SLAB — Sonic Grudge [MULTIPLE MIXES] (Sabrettes) 1996

SNEAKER PIMPS — 6 Underground [MULTIPLE MIXES] (Clean Up) 1996

BETH ORTON — Touch Me with Your Love (Heavenly) 1996

BETH ORTON — It's This I Am I Find (Heavenly) 1996

BETH ORTON — Tangent (Heavenly) 1996

BETH ORTON — Galaxy of Emptiness (Heavenly) 1996

GALLIANO — Thunderhead (Mercury) 1996

DARK GLOBE — Take Me to the Sound (Hard Hands) 1996

ALTER EGO — Mescal [MULTIPLE MIXES] (Harthouse) 1996

AURAL EXPANSIONS — Freeform (Crammed) 1996

ATTICA BLUES — Blue print (Polygram) 1996

WAGON CHRIST — Floot (Rising High) 1996

JAZIAC SUNFLOWERS — Magic Flute (Black on Black) 1996

KROMOTONES — Forever (New Breed) 1996

SKYLAB — Indigo (Polygram) 1996

11.59 — Freemen (China) 1996

NANGPA — Ijakk (Malawi) 1996

IS — Lucy and the Mango Man (EAO) 1996

TEXAS — Put Your Arms Around Me [MULTIPLE MIXES] (Mercury) 1997

SCORN — Exodus [MULTIPLE MIXES] (Earache) 1997

RESTLESS SOUL — Psykodelik (Slip'n'slide) 1997

LOVE CORP — Give Me Some Love [MULTIPLE MIXES] (Creation) 1997

PRIMAL SCREAM — Stuka [MULTIPLE MIXES] (Creation) 1997

MUSIQUE TROPIQUE — 4am Kingston (GLASGOW U) 1997

MONEYPENNY PROJECT — Clarisse C [MULTIPLE MIXES] (Nuphonix) 1997

ALEX HANDLEY — Hypnotic Theory (EAO) 1997

GANGER — Trilogy (SOUL STATIC) 1997

ETIENNE DE CRECY — Le Patron... (Different) 1997

DEATH IN VEGAS — Rekkit [MULTIPLE MIXES] (Concrete) 1997

BALLISTIC BROS — Tuning Up [MULTIPLE MIXES] (Soundboy) 1997

HOWIE B — Angels Go Bald Too [MULTIPLE MIXES] (polydor) 1997

ALOOF — sinking (EAST west) 1997

TRANSIENT WAVES — Born with a Body (Fat Cat) 1998

SPIRITUALIZED — Come Together (Arista) 1998

RED SNAPPER — Bogeyman [MULTIPLE MIXES] (Warp) 1998

KLUTE — Silent Weapons (Cert 18) 1998

DAVID HOLMES — Rodney Yates (Go! Discs) 1998

16B — Falling (EYE Q) 1998

ELECTRONIC — Prodigal Son (EMI) 1999

CHIPET — Tik Tok (Phonograph) 1999

THOM WILSON

PRODUCER
BORN 11/16/51 (San Diego, CA)

In 1973, without any formal background in music, Wilson became a partner in the newly-built 24-track Davlen Studio in North Hollywood, working as an assistant engineer alongside such established names as Bill Schnee and Eric Prestridge. Having learned the basics, he moved first to Richard Perry's Studio 55, before joining producer Roy Halee at Dawnbreaker (owned by light rock duo Seals & Croft).

Debuting on an album by Chaka Khan's funk outfit Rufus, and sundry other radio staples of the day, Wilson was then asked to engineer the 1980 solo debut by former Dead Boys vocalist Stiv Bator, working so well alongside producer/Bomp Records supremo Greg Shaw that he was given a co-production credit. The following year, he followed Bomp's Lisa Fancher to the newly established Frontier label as house engineer, and again wound up as producer, this time with ex-Social Distortion guitarist Rikk Agnew's Adolescents.

Further hardcore productions for China White, TSOL, the Dead Kennedys, and the Vandals followed; Wilson was also in at the birth of American gothic rock when he helmed the debut album by Rozz Williams and Christian Death.

Through the mid-late 1980s, Wilson drifted away from the now moribund punk scene, working instead in movie soundtracks and television — he was Joan Rivers' music producer for a time, and sound engineer on shows ranging from *Roseanne* to the MTV Video Awards. In 1989, however, Offspring frontman Dexter Holland — a fan of so many of Wilson's "classic" productions — asked him to return to the battlefield to produce his band's debut album. Wilson would end up working alongside the band for the next six years, completely rediscovering his love of punk as he did so. Since that time, he has worked with Iggy Pop, Joykiller, the reformed Specials (mixing 1998's *Guilty 'Til Proved Innocent*) and Bouncing Souls.

Thom Wilson — Selected Productions

⑨ **STIV BATORS — Disconnected (Bomp) 1980**

⑥ **THE ADOLESCENTS — The Adolescents (Epitaph) 1981**

⑥ **JON AND THE NITERIDERS — Live at the Whiskey (Bomp) 1981**

⑦ **CHOIR INVISIBLE — Choir Invisible (Frontier) 1981**

⑥ **TSOL — Dance with Me (Frontier) 1981** Semi-fulfilling attempt to leap aboard the L.A. death rock band wagon, TSOL blend Misfits/Christian Death-themed horror lyrics with a solid hardcore roar.

⑥ **DEAD KENNEDYS — In God We Trust (Alternative Tentacles) 1981**

⑥ **RIKK AGNEW — All by Myself (Frontier) 1982**

⑦ **DEAD KENNEDYS — Plastic Surgery Disasters (Alternative Tentacles) 1982**

⑧ **CHRISTIAN DEATH — Only Theatre of Pain (Future) 1982**

⑤ **THE VANDALS — Peace Through Vandalism (Restless) 1982**

⑧ **TSOL — Beneath the Shadows (Alternative Tentacles) 1982**

⑥ **YOUTH BRIGADE — Sound and Fury (Byo) 1983**

⑦ **THE VANDALS — When in Rome Do As the Vandals (Nat Trust) 1984**

④ **THE OFFSPRING — The Offspring (Nemesis) 1989**

⑥ **D.I. — Ancient Artifacts (Triple X) 1989**

⑤ **THE VANDALS — Slippery When Ill (Restless) 1989**

⑥ **LEGAL WEAPON — Death of Innocence (Triple X) 1991**

⑦ **THE OFFSPRING — Ignition (Epitaph) 1992**

⑨ **THE OFFSPRING — Smash (Epitaph) 1994**

⑥ **FACE TO FACE — Big Choice (Victory) 1995**

⑧ **THE JOYKILLER — The Joykiller (Epitaph) 1995** The band's backgrounds (early TSOL, Gun Club, The Weirdos, and drummer's Chris Lagerborg's shopping list size resume) help explain their sound, a purist blend of punk roar and postpunk denseness, abetted by piano and keyboards that rip across the explosive guitar crush of "Unconscious" et al, before shredding the doom pop of one of the many standouts, "Seventeen."

⑤ **IGGY POP — Naughty Little Doggie (Virgin) 1996**

⑧ **BOUNCING SOULS — Maniacal Laughter (BYO) 1996** Kicking off with the fist in the air shout-along "Lamar Valley," the Bouncing Souls bash their way through a dozen high octane, old school inspired tracks — even their cover of Johnny Cash's "Born to Lose" is punk fuelled, with only the poignant surf instrumental "Moon Over Asbury" breaking pace. Tough, fast, and fun, the raw energy of early '80s hardcore resurrected with a passion.

⑤ **PHIL CODY — The Sons of Intemperance Offering (Interscope) 1996**

⑨ **THE JOYKILLER — Static (Epitaph) 1996** Adding a permanent second guitarist, as well as an octet of backing vocalists (including The Offspring's Dexter Holland), *Static* is a pop-punkers' dream come true, crackling with an energy that's as electrifying on the hardcore "Destroyer," as on more mid-tempo pop-punkers like "White Boy, White Girl." Drenched with harmonies and hooks, *Static* notches up more points with copious nods to pop/punk's past (from Black Flag to Bowie).

⑥ **SLUSH — North Hollywood (Discovery) 1997**

⑧ **THE JOYKILLER — Three (Epitaph) 1997** Unabashedly upbeat, *Three* offers up virtually every variation of pop-punk-rock one can imagine, as keyboard strings cross with C&W twang on "The Doorway" and Britpop emerges from "Your Girlfriend." But it's that classic old school melodic punk that Joykiller embrace the most, from the Clash-esque choruses of "Record Collection" and "Sex Attack" to the Buzzcocksish "Promises" — a celebration of melody and vivid lyrical vignettes, doused with adrenalin.

⑥ **STORM & HER DIRTY MOUTH — Storm & Her Dirty Mouth (Popmafia) 1998**

GEZA X

PRODUCER
BORN *Geza Gedeon (Los Angeles, CA)*

In 1976, Geza X was playing bass alongside Charlotte Caffey (later of the Go-Gos) and Joe Namini (later Wall of Voodoo) in Band X, an L.A. band who knew something was terribly wrong with the local music scene, but hadn't quite figured out what it might be. Not until the Ramones came to town in summer 1976, did the answer hit the trio — immediately following the Whiskey A-Go-Go show, the members of Band X began hurling themselves into the slowly igniting L.A. punk scene.

X himself enjoyed stints with the Bags and the Deadbeats, and took over as sound engineer at the Masque club. He was also working across the road at the Artists's Recording Studio, originally as a gopher, but with plenty of opportunity to learn his way around a control desk. By early 1978, with no major labels whatsoever showing any interest in the flood of punk talent exploding out of the city, X decided to set himself up as a producer to any band which asked him.

The Germs were his first client, coming off their "Foaming" debut to inaugurate the Slash label with "Lexicon

Devil." Singles for the Deadbeats, the Bags, and the Weirdos followed, and in 1980, he produced the Dead Kennedys' debut, "Holiday in Cambodia." Later, as the hardcore scene developed, he would work with Black Flag and Redd Kross, but by the mid-1980s, X had drifted out of production, to work as a music critic.

He returned to the desk in the late 1980s, after the rap scene piqued his attention, and in 1991, he opened the City Lab Sound Design studios and returned to action. His best-known work since then has been with Meredith Brooks, whose 1997 hit "Bitch" was a Geza X production.

Geza X — Selected Productions

7 REDD KROSS — Teen Babies from Monsanto (Gastanka) 1984

5 PAUL ROESSLER — Abominable (SST) 1988

6 CELEBRITY SKIN — Good Clean Fun (Triple X) 1991

5 BUTT TRUMPET — Primitive Enema (Chrysalis) 1994

5 OUTSIDEINSIDE — 6.6 (Hell Yeah) 1994

4 RIMITTI — Rimitti (Absolute) 1995

8 MICHAEL ASTON — Why Me Why This Why Now (Triple X) 1995

7 1000 MONA LISAS — New Disease (Rca) 1996

7 MAGNAPOP — Rubbing Doesn't Help (Play It Again Sam) 1996

ZANG TUMB TUUM (ZTT)

LABEL

Better known by the abbreviated ZTT, the label formed by producer Trevor Horn, wife Jill Sinclair, and journalist Paul Morley in 1983, emerged on the UK scene that August, with the first release by The Art of Noise, a team of studio/session musicians (joined by Horne and Morley).

It was, by subsequent ZTT standards, a very restrained release, appearing as a 12-inch single and cassette single only. Readily acknowledging the impact of record collectors on the marketplace, and with Marketing Executive Morley taking his lead from Italian futurist Russo's use of "zang tumb tuum" to describe the sound of rapid machine gun fire, ZTT would indeed spit out a stream of releases, remixing and reformatting individual singles to such an extent that even devoted ZTT collectors readily admit they still aren't sure whether every variant has been cataloged.

It was at times an unparalleled blitzkrieg, comparable only to Factory Records' penchant for slapping a catalog number on anything they could, from the label's Hacienda night club, to stationery, unreleased artwork, and advertising campaigns. ZTT did not go that far, but still they ventured to extremes.

Art of Noise's third single, "Close (to the Edit)" exists in seven separate versions; Frankie Goes to Hollywood's "Relax" debut in nine. (The following discography gives the primary number only. ZTT singles also bore irrelevant "Incidental Series" and "Action Series" numbers, a deliberate ploy to further intrigue collectors.)

The success of Frankie Goes to Hollywood, and the sheer weight of product released in that band's name, ensures that ZTT is primarily remembered for that one act alone. However, both Art of Noise and German electronic band Propaganda also enjoyed hit-making careers. Propaganda's Claudia Brucken would also cut several records for the label, under her own name and with her collaboration with Thomas Leer, Act. Other early signings, Andrew Poppy and Anne Pigalle, were less fortunate, however, their fates perhaps echoing the reasons behind Art of Noise's departure from the label —too much marketing, not enough promotion.

Originally distributed by Island Records, ZTT became a true independent until 1987, when the label severed its ties with the major. Subsequent releases would become considerably more modest.

Zang Tumb Tuum (ZTT) Label Listing 1984–87

Singles

ZTAS 1 FRANKIE GOES TO HOLLYWOOD — Relax

ZTAS 2 PROPAGANDA — Dr Mabuse

ZTAS 3 FRANKIE GOES TO HOLLYWOOD — Two Tribes

ZTAS 4 unreleased

ZTAS 5 FRANKIE GOES TO HOLLYWOOD — Power of Love

ZTAS 6 unreleased

ZTAS 7 FRANKIE GOES TO HOLLYWOOD — Welcome to the Pleasure Dome

ZTAS 8 PROPAGANDA — 13th Life of Dr Mabuse

ZTAS 9 CLAUDIA BRUCKEN — Wild Hearts

ZTAS 10–11 unreleased

ZTAS 12 PROPAGANDA — P Machinery

ZTAS 13–14 unreleased

ZTAS 15 CLAUDIA BRUCKEN/GLENN GREGORY — When Your Heart Runs Out

ZTAS 16–20 unreleased

ZTAS 21 PROPAGANDA — P Machinery

ZTAS 22 FRANKIE GOES TO HOLLYWOOD — Rage Hard

ZTAS 23 unreleased

ZTAS 24 DAS PSYCH-OH RANGERS — Essential Art of Communication

ZTAS 25 FRANKIE GOES TO HOLLYWOOD — Warriors of the Wasteland

ZTAS 26 FRANKIE GOES TO HOLLYWOOD — Watching the Wildlife

ZTAS 27 unreleased

ZTAS 28 ACT — Snobbery and Decay

ZTIS 100 THE ART OF NOISE — Into Battle EP

ZTIS 101–107 unreleased

ZTIS 108 THE ART OF NOISE — Beatbox

ZTIS 200 ANDREW POPPY — 32 Frames

ZTPS 01 THE ART OF NOISE — Close (To the Edit)

ZTPS 02 THE ART OF NOISE — Love Beat

CERT 1 ANNE PIGALLE — He Stranger

CERT 2 ANNE PIGALLE — Why Does It Have to be This Way?

DUEL 1 PROPAGANDA — Duel

WARTZ 3 FRANKIE GOES TO HOLLYWOOD — War

Albums

⑧ IQ 1 FRANKIE GOES TO HOLLYWOOD — Welcome to the Pleasuredome

⑦ IQ 2 THE ART OF NOISE — Who's Afraid of?

⑧ IQ 3 PROPAGANDA — A Secret Wish Propaganda explores electro-pop on their sophisticated and very European debut, traveling from the cut-and-paste sampling of "Jewel" to the dark lushness of the sinister "Dr. Mabuse."

⑥ IQ 4 INSIGNIFICANCE — The Shape of the Universe

⑤ IQ 5 ANDREW POPPY — The Beating of Wings

⑥ IQ 6 VARIOUS ARTISTS — Ztt Sampled

⑧ IQ 7 ANNE PIGALLE — Everything Could Be So Perfect

③ IQ 8 FRANKIE GOES TO HOLLYWOOD — Liverpool

⑤ IQ 9 ANDREW POPPY — Alphabed

⑦ AS 20 PROPAGANDA — Wishful Thinking

⑦ QLP 1 ACT — Laughter, Tears and Rage

ZOO RECORDS

LABEL

Shortlived but crucial Liverpool label formed in 1978 by Dave Balfe and Bill Drummond, initially to handle Drummond's own band, Big in Japan. As the pair moved towards management and production, other bands entered the picture, with two, Echo and the Bunnymen and Teardrop Explodes, going on to immediate international success, while Big in Japan would spawn Frankie Goes to Hollywood vocalist Holly Johnson and future Lightning Seeds frontman Ian Broudie.

With the success of the Bunnymen, Zoo was taken under the wing of their own Korova imprint at Sire, enjoying a minor hit in December 1979, with a reactivated version of Lori and the Chameleon's "Touch" (#70 UK). Drummond himself would re-emerge as one half of KLF; Balfe, after a spell as a member of Teardrop Explodes, subsequently formed the Food label, home of Blur and Zodiac Mindwarp.

Zoo Records Label Listing 1978–81

Singles

CAGE 001 BIG IN JAPAN — From Y to Z and Never Again EP

CAGE 002 THOSE NAUGHTY LUMPS — Iggy Pop's Jacket

CAGE 003 TEARDROP EXPLODES — Sleeping Gas

CAGE 004 ECHO AND THE BUNNYMEN — Pictures on My Wall

CAGE 005 TEARDROP EXPLODES — Bouncing Babies

CAGE 006 LORI & THE CHAMELEONS — Touch

CAGE 007 unreleased

CAGE 008 TEARDROP EXPLODES — Treason

Album

⑧ ZOO 4 VARIOUS ARTISTS — To the Shores of Lake Placid

Label rarities collection, offering a vivid snapshot of late '70s Liverpool. Unreleased cuts by Teardrop Explodes and the Bunnymen distinguish a lavishly packaged masterpiece.

10 Star Album List

(see individual entries for details/reviews)

THE ADVERTS   *Crossing the Sea with the Adverts*
CHRIS BAILEY   *Savage Entertainment*
BANANARAMA   *Deep Sea Skiving*
BAUHAUS   *The Sky's Gone Out*
BEASTIE BOYS   *Paul's Boutique*
BLUR   *Parklife*
KATE BUSH   *The Dreaming*
THE BUZZCOCKS   *A Different Music in Another Kitchen*
CARTER USM   *1992: The Love Album*
THE CLASH   *London Calling*
ELVIS COSTELLO   *This Year's Model*
WAYNE COUNTY & THE ELECTRIC CHAIRS   *Things Your Mother Never Told You*
THE CURE   *Faith*
CURRENT 93   *All the Pretty Little Horses*
DOCTORS OF MADNESS   *Late Night Movies, All Night Brainstorms*
IAN DURY   *New Boots and Panties*
ECHO AND THE BUNNYMEN   *Ocean Rain*
LISA GERMANO   *Happiness*
PJ HARVEY   *To Bring You My Love*
HÜSKER DÜ   *Zen Arcade*
JOY DIVISION   *Unknown Pleasures*
KLF   *Chill Out*
LEN BRIGHT COMBO   *Presents the Len Bright Combo by the Len Bright Combo*
LONDON SUEDE   *dog man star*
LOVE AND ROCKETS   *Seventh Dream of Teenage Heaven*
LYDIA LUNCH/ROWLAND HOWARD   *Shotgun Wedding*
MORRISSEY   *Vauxhall and I*

MARC AND THE MAMBAS   *Torment and Torreros*
MUDHONEY   *Superfuzz with Big Muff*
   (see entry under Jack Endino productions, page 762)
NINE INCH NAILS   *Pretty Hate Machine*
NIRVANA   *Nevermind*
THE PIXIES   *Surfer Rosa*
PORTISHEAD   *Dummy*
PUBLIC IMAGE LTD   *Metal Box*
PULP   *This is Hardcore*
RADIOHEAD   *Ok Computer*
THE RAMONES   *Ramones*
THE REPLACEMENTS   *Let it Be*
SAINT ETIENNE   *Tiger Bay*
THE SEX PISTOLS   *Never Mind the Bollocks, Here's the Sex Pistols*
SIGUE SIGUE SPUTNIK   *Flaunt It*
SIOUXSIE AND THE BANSHEES   *The Scream*
SKY CRIES MARY   *This Timeless Turning*
SLEEPER   *The It Girl*
SLITS   *Return of the Giant Slits*
PATTI SMITH GROUP   *Horses*
SONIC YOUTH   *Daydream Nation*
MATTHEW SWEET   *Girlfriend*
   (see entry under Fred Maher productions, page 795)
TEARDROP EXPLODES   *Kilimanjaro*
TELEVISION   *Marquee Moon*
THIS MORTAL COIL   *It'll End in Tears*
   (see entry under the 4AD label listing, page 739)
JOHNNY THUNDERS   *So Alone*
U2   *The Joshua Tree*
x   *Los Angeles*

The Top 40 Singles of the Alternative Era 1975–2000

B52'S "Rock Lobster" (Island)

BAUHAUS "Bela Lugosi's Dead" (Small Wonder)

BEASTIE BOYS "No Sleep Till Brooklyn" (Def Jam)

BLACK FLAG "TV Party" (SST)

BOOMTOWN RATS "Rat Trap" (Ensign)

CARTER USM "Only Living Boy in New Cross" (SBK)

CHAMELEONS "In Shreds" (Epic)

THE CLASH "White Man in Hammersmith Palais" (CBS)

CRANBERRIES "Zombie" (Island)

CULTURE CLUB "Do You Really Want to Hurt Me?" (Virgin)

DAMNED "New Rose" (Stiff)

DEAD KENNEDYS "California Uber Alles" (Alternative Tentacles)

DEVO "Jocko Homo" (Boojie Boy)

DOCTOR AND THE MEDICS "Spirit in the Sky" (IRS)

ELVIS COSTELLO "Watching the Detectives" (Stiff)

FRANKIE GOES TO HOLLYWOOD "Relax" (ZTT)

FUN BOY THREE "Tunnel of Love" (Chrysalis)

GARY NUMAN "Are 'Friends' Electric?" (Beggars Banquet)

GREEN DAY "Longview" (Reprise)

HOLE "Violet" (Geffen)

JOY DIVISION "Love Will Tear Us Apart" (Factory)

M "Pop Muzik" (Sire)

MIGHTY WAH "Come Back" (Beggars Banquet)

MINISTRY "NWO" (Sire)

NINE INCH NAILS "Closer" (Nothing)

NIRVANA "Smells Like Teen Spirit" (Geffen)

OFFSPRING "Come Out and Play" (Epitaph)

PATTI SMITH GROUP "Privilege" (Arista)

RADIOHEAD "Creep" (EMI)

REM "Radio Free Europe" (Hibtone)

RED HOT CHILI PEPPERS "Under the Bridge" (WB)

RICHARD HELL "Blank Generation" (Sire)

THE SEX PISTOLS "Anarchy in the UK" (EMI)

THE SMITHS "How Soon Is Now?" (Sire)

SONIC YOUTH AND LYDIA LUNCH "Death Valley 69" (Widowspeak)

THEATRE OF HATE "West World" (Burning Rome)

TIME ZONE "World Destruction" (Virgin)

TIMELORDS "Doctoring the Tardis" (TVT)

TV SMITH'S EXPLORERS "Tomahawk Cruise" (Chiswick)

WRECKLESS ERIC "Whole Wide World" (Stiff)

Index

Numerics

10,000 Maniacs 588, 770, 795
10.51 650–651
100 Club festival 128
1000 Homo DJs 497, 518
101ers 577
10cc 160, 778
120 Minutes 82, 469, 565
1984 224, 244
20/20 745
21 Guns 652
23 Skidoo 308
2-Tone 39, 43–45, 47, 110–113, 133, 135, 140, 366, 481–482, 537, 792
complete listing 48
31st 331
45 Grave 51, 720
4AD 277, 317, 390, 484, 547, 738, 743, 769, 771, 782, 799, 803
54.40 800
7 Seconds 51, 772
777 778
8 Eyed Spy 476, 478
808 State 200
999 125, 389, 519–521

A

A Certain Ratio 62, 140–141, 344–345, 350, 765, 776
A Flock of Seagulls 70, 79, 123, 142, 365, 654, 779
A Guy Called Gerald 235
A Wrinkle In Time 260
Abba 451, 532, 679
ABC 304, 778
Abdoujaparov 242
Acid Angels 436
Acid Horse 235, 497
acid house 562
Act 457
Adam and the Ants 29, 78, 142, 144–145, 176, 252, 530, 617, 650, 709, 747
Adamski 213, 356
Adamson, Barry 199, 247, 484, 562, 797
Adicts, The 750
Adler, Danny 600–601
Adolescents, The 639, 720
Adverts, The 13, 15, 24, 28, 40, 119, 132–133, 146–147, 162, 272, 568, 575, 635, 684, 748, 808
Afghan Whigs 147–148, 373, 763, 806–807

Afrika Bambaataa 376, 527, 565
Afrika Bambaataa Timezone 787
AFX 157–158
Agent Orange 403
"Agit-punk" 119
Aints, The 171–172
Air 149
Ajax 504
Alarm 119, 302, 388, 684
Albarn, Damon 209, 354, 490, 544
Albini, Steve 116, 162, 186, 194, 411, 437, 473, 518, 522–523, 547, 739, 741, 793
Ale House 732
Alexander, Willie 10, 13, 149–151, 455, 514, 745–746, 790
Alice in Chains 367, 781
Alien Sex Fiend 67, 82, 151–152, 177, 405, 622, 737, 752
All About Eve 387, 511
Allen, Daevid 777, 786, 795
Allen, Dave 747–748
Allison, Dot 125, 152–153, 321–322, 806
Almond, Marc 4, 153–157, 245, 279, 371–373, 425, 434, 476, 562, 616, 618, 630, 641–642, 686, 739, 751, 768, 773, 777, 808–809
Alphaphone label 237
Altered Images 152
Alternative Tentacles 49, 103–106, 167, 169, 228, 318–319, 370, 534, 741–742, 758–759
Alternative TV 562
Amazorblades 484
Amos, Matthew 83
Amos, Tori 227, 518
anarcho-pacifism 295
Andresen, Paul 83
Andrew Loog Oldham Orchestra 707
Andy, Horace 489
Angelfish 383
Angelic Upstarts 384, 613, 750
Another Pretty Face 715
Ant, Adam 100, 133, 151, 608, 653
Anthrax 224
Anti-Nowhere League, The 120, 253
Anxiety, Annie 279
Any Three Initials 371
Aphex Twin 125, 157–158, 162, 183, 541, 606
Apoptygma Berzerk 648
Aqua 159, 380
Arcadia 342–343

Armstrong, Tim 84
Arnell, Vaughn 84
Arnold, David 201
Art of Noise, The 80, 123, 160–161, 208, 236, 375, 450, 558, 680, 778, 815
Artery 502, 505, 566
Ash 125, 129, 161–162
Ash, Daniel 177, 470
Ashcroft, Richard 707–708
Asian Dub Foundation 556, 615
Asian Man label 115
Asphalt Ribbons 689
Ass Ponys 148
Assemblage 322
Assembly 700
Associates, The 184, 277, 305, 337, 743, 777
Astbury, Ian 124, 251, 300, 303, 432
Astley, Virginia 673
Aston, Jay 386
Aston, Michael 65, 386–387, 419
Atkins, Martin 84, 564
Attila the Stockbroker 119, 494
Attractions 284–285
ATV 22–23
Auntie Christ 475, 729–730
Autechre 157, 606
Auteurs, The 130, 162–163, 210, 365, 463, 741
Autoclave 412
Automatic Dlamini 410–411
Automatics 651
Avengers, The 163–164
Avis, Meiert 84
Ayers, Kevin 269
Aztec Camera 164–165, 193, 351, 361, 604, 785

B

B Lee band 459
B, Howie 201
B12 157
B-52's 130–131, 189–192, 214, 327, 382, 414, 504, 525, 569, 589, 758, 795
Baader Meinhof 162–163
Babes in Toyland 148, 417, 614
Baby Bird 748
Baby Birkin 567
Backstreet Boys 288
Bad Blood 506
Bad Brains 49–50, 111, 167–168, 401, 742, 799, 804

Daho, Etienne 605
Dalek I Love You 141, 680
Dali's Car 433–434, 468, 511
Daltrey, Roger 531
Dambuilders 412
Dammers, Jerry 483
Damned, The 13, 15, 18, 20, 24, 28, 44,
    49, 57, 63–64, 123, 128, 146, 167,
    204, 303, 311–313, 329, 336, 402–
    403, 414, 462, 466, 473, 480, 507,
    519, 521, 535, 565, 604, 610, 633,
    662–663, 709, 743, 748, 751, 782,
    794
Damon and Naomi 381, 784
Dance Hall Crashers 111, 126, 314–315,
    538, 583
Dando, Evan 481, 671
Dandy Warhols 130, 315
Danzig 71, 204, 486, 501, 802
Danzig, Glen 169, 500
Dark, Gregory 87
Darlin' 311
Darling Buds, The 478
Daucus Karota 721
Dave Vanian and the Phantom Chords 314
Davies, Ray 211, 428
Davies, Rhett 189, 758
Davis, Tamra 87
Days of the New 793
Dayton, Jonathan 87
dB's, The 260, 316, 340, 569, 589, 760,
    792–793, 800
De La Soul 193, 682
De Lorenzo, Victor 712
Dead Boys 312, 406, 466–468, 545, 572,
    613, 633, 745–746, 813
Dead Can Dance 67, 178, 317, 738
Dead Clergy 240
Dead Damned Sham Band 312
Dead Elvis 321
Dead Famous People 221
Dead Kennedys 103, 105, 108, 136, 167–
    169, 318–319, 401, 497, 534, 586,
    741, 758, 813, 815
Dead or Alive 123, 261, 319–320, 621,
    679, 725, 751
Dead Popstars 334
Dead to the World 224, 295, 462
Deadsy 277
Deaf School 785
Death Cult 300
Death in June 309, 594
Death in Vegas 125, 153, 321, 436, 505,
    606
Death Ride 69 648
Deathline International 755
Deconstruction 432
Deebank, Maurice 365

Deep Wound 332
Def Jam 801
Defects, The 253
Defenestration 248
Deftones, The 276
Del Amitri 239
Delany, Andy 85
Delgado, Gabi 326
Delory, Michel 337
Demme, Jonathan 87
Demon Preacher 151
Dempsey, Michael 304
Denim 364–365
Denison 437
Deniz Tek 750
Dennis and the Experts 640
Department S 175
Depeche Mode 29, 58–59, 69–70, 144,
    149, 197, 322–325, 353, 411, 469,
    491, 504, 526, 538, 556, 621, 630,
    700, 703, 768–769, 781, 796–798,
    802–803, 811
Depth Charge 213
Deranged Diction 401
Descendents, The 204
Desert Birds 689
Deutsche-Amerikanische Freundschaft
    325, 796
Deviants, The 7–8
DeVille, Mink 419, 683
Devlin, Barry 88
Devo 25, 111, 272, 326–328, 366, 525,
    581, 599, 678, 764
Devoto, Howard 230, 232, 440, 484
Dexy's Midnight Runners 47, 205, 521,
    601, 603, 663, 785
D-Generation 392
Dice Man 157
Dick, Nigel 88
Dickies, The 49, 328
Dickless 148
Dictators, The 12
Die Cheerleader 599
Die Haut 353
Die Roten Rosen 330–331
Die Toten Hosen 169, 220, 329–330,
    520, 613, 636, 710
Died Pretty 331–332, 571–572, 750
Diesel Christ 323
Diggle 231
Dill Records 111
Dim Stars 413, 768
Dinosaur Jr. 127, 138, 210, 223, 332–333,
    392, 512, 671, 681, 768, 782, 807
Dire Straits 165, 381
Dirty Pictures 662
Dirty Three 744
Dirty Walt 367

Discharge 49, 223, 497, 750
Dischord label 169, 742, 758–759
Disorder 334–335
Disposable Heroes of Hip-Hoprisy 491
Diversions, The 471
Divinyls, The 693
DJ Aquaman 315
DJ Coldcut began working with it. Accord-
    ing to Howlett, "for an 557
DJ Krush 490
DJ Shadow 574
DMZ 150, 745
DNA 545
DOA 318
Doane, Darren 88
Doctor and the Medics 790
Doctor Dre 179
Doctors of Madness 58, 312, 335–336,
    537, 635, 659, 789
Dodgy 239
Doe, John 730
Dog's Blood Order 308
Dogbreath 591
Dogs D'Amour 509, 710
Dolby, Thomas 732, 778
Dolezal, Rudi 88
Doll by Doll 123, 460–461, 577, 725,
    735
Dolly Mixtures, The 221, 521
Dolphin Brothers 433–434
Dom & Nic 88
Dome 722, 796
Domino, Anna 337
Donelly, Tanya 185–186, 245, 547
Donkey Show 197
Donovan 802
Doors, The 579, 581, 728
Doubting Thomas 623
Down By Law 773
Downfall 538, 583
Download 624–625
Dr. Feelgood 17, 348, 601
Dr. Jolly's Salvation Circus 376
Drain 230
Drake, Nick 588
Dramarama 338
Dramatis 526
Dreadzone 193–194, 703
Dream 6 497
Dream Syndicate 316, 339–340, 430,
    577, 714
Dripping Lips, The 467–468
Drones, The 234, 439
Dropkick Murphys 583
Drowning Craze 277
Drug Addix 480
Drugstore 574

Drum Club 405, 703
Drummond, Bill 282, 374
Dub Narcotic 182
Dub Pistols, The 376
Dubversive 218
Dudley, Anne 160
Duet Emmo 796–797
Duffy, Billy 300
Duffy, Stephen "Tin Tin" 341
Dukes of Stratosphear 732–734
Dumptruck 412
Duran Duran 57–59, 78–79, 81, 99,
    144, 208, 341–343, 356, 377, 434,
    517, 755, 776
Durutti Column 344–346, 506, 765,
    767, 775
Dury, Ian 24, 100, 125, 284, 347–349,
    375, 395–397, 473, 483, 519, 565,
    598, 612
Dust Brothers 117, 183–184, 254–255,
    759
Dylan, Bob 530–531, 550, 619, 632, 652,
    786, 801

E

Earwigs, The 151
Easdale, John 338
East Bay Ray 318
Easter, Mitch 315, 588, 760
Easy Cure 304
Eat Static 125, 542–543
Eater 521, 709
Echo and the Bunnymen 35, 62, 119, 123,
    125, 130, 136, 141, 177, 343, 350,
    352, 654, 679, 693, 725, 735, 782,
    799, 816
Ed Banger and the Nosebleeds 344
Eddie and the Hot Rods 312, 608, 688,
    791
Eddy, Clark 88
Eden 376
Edge, Damon 263–264
Edge, The 480, 704, 706
Edmunds, Dave 23–24, 473, 475, 660,
    745, 761
Edwards, Bernie 144, 208
Egan, Nick 89
Egg Hunt 500
Einsturzende Neubauten 69, 200, 298,
    325, 353–354, 403, 414, 476, 595,
    751, 781, 802–803
Elastic Purejoy 382
Elastica 125, 128–130, 161, 176, 211, 355,
    462, 544, 567, 662, 806
Eldritch, Andrew 501, 668
Electrafixion 315, 351–352
Electric Blood 274

Electric Chairs 38, 604
Electric Crayons 251
Electric Dog House 662
Electric Hellfire Club 71, 751
Electric Sheep 692
Electronic 141, 515, 517, 638
Electronic Eye 236
Elephant Daze 650
Elevator 197, 385
Eleven 719
Ellis, Mark
    See Flood
ELPH 280
E-Man 197
Embrace 500, 759
Emerald Express 602
EMF 7, 241, 356–357, 371, 802
End 331
Endino, Jack 401, 756, 762
Enemy, The 259, 678
Engine Room 660
England's Glory 536–537
English Beat 45, 495, 654
Eno, Brian 2, 55, 60, 134, 140, 157, 178,
    197, 213, 231, 236, 326–327, 405,
    433, 504, 562, 616, 677, 683, 695,
    697, 704–705, 732, 745, 747, 751,
    758, 763–764, 786
Epic Soundtracks 298–299, 578
Epitaph 168–169, 535, 742, 772, 800
Erasure 322, 504, 768, 781, 796
Erickson, Roky 282, 599
Escovedo, Alejandro 555
Essential Bop 334
Essential Logic 585
Eugenius 357
Eurythmics 175, 325, 486, 580, 615,
    652, 700
Everything Burns 505
Everything But the Girl 488, 490
Executive Slacks 648
Exodus 665
Exotic Birds 517
Experimental Audio Research 512
Exploited, The 204, 384, 520
Exterminators 391

F

Factory Records 140–141, 344, 408, 608,
    765, 775
    Benelux 140, 235, 765, 767
Fad Gadget 322, 594, 771, 796, 798
Fairground Attraction 506, 636, 656
Faith No More 129, 167, 358–359, 414,
    417
Faithfull, Marianne 709
Faithless 532

Fall, The 29, 119, 355, 426, 544, 584,
    637, 789
Fallen Angels 406–407
Family Cat, The 410, 719
Family Values tour 123
Faris, Valerie 87
Farm Aid 101
Farm, The 726
Farrell, Perry 123, 126, 128, 301, 430,
    479, 487, 552–553
Farren, Mick 7
Fashion 376
Fastbacks, The 182
Fatal Charm 654–655, 696
Fatboy Slim 125, 141, 221, 359–361, 559
Fatima Mansions 411, 491
Fear 564, 585, 718
Fearless, Richard 321
Feelies, The 361–362, 381, 545, 800
Felt 363–365, 556
Ferry, Bryan 675
festivals 123
Fiat Lux 365
Fibbers, Geraldine 183
Fiction Groove 656
Fier, Anton 362
Fierce Ruling Diva 504
Filter 299
Final Solution 331
Fine Young Cannibals 652, 663
Fink Brothers 482
Fire 811
Fire Town 811
Firehose 553
Firewater 437
Fishbone 108, 127, 365–367, 441, 553
Fisk, Steve 182, 473
Flag of Convenience 231
Flamin' Groovies 312, 331, 745, 761
Flaming Lips, The 248, 367–368, 806
Flansburgh, John 89
Flea 229, 392, 432, 564, 718
Fleming, Don 333, 413, 417, 453, 554,
    644, 681, 767–768, 811
Flesh for Lulu 65, 369–370, 673, 774,
    790
Flip City 284
Flipper 370–371, 401, 504
Float Up CP 552
Flood 324, 411, 518–519, 630, 706, 768,
    771
Flop 555
Flouride, Klaus 318–319
Flowers of Romance 617, 628
Floyd 513
Flu 623
Flying Lizards 288

Green, Matt
 remixes 649
Greenhaigh, Howard 90
Greinke, Jeff 626
Grid 605, 642
Grienke, Jeff 671
Griffin, Brian 91
Grohl, Dave 373–374, 522, 759
Grooverider 376
Groundswell UK 513
Gumball 214, 417, 681, 768
Gun Club 246, 292, 402–404, 599
Guns 'n' Roses 358
Gurewitz, Brett 584, 772
Guthrie, Robin 277, 744
Gutterball 340
Guttermouth 535

H

Hagen, Nina 472, 628
Haggerty, Mick 91
Hague, Stephen 210, 515, 546, 619–620,
 773–774
Hain, Kit 808
Haircut 100 164, 351
Hairdressers, The 681
Half Japanese 214
Hall, Kristen 561
Hall, Terry 351, 651
Halo Benders 182
Hambi and the Dance 374
Hamilton, Page 438
Hammer & Tongs 91
Hammerbox 756
Hammersmith Gorillas 748
Hammond, Lol 297, 306, 405, 801
Handsome 414
Hangman Records 256, 774
Hannett, Martin 140, 344, 408, 440, 537,
 559, 561, 657, 703, 705, 765, 775–
 776, 791
Hanoi Rocks 405–407, 467
Happy Mondays 35, 124, 152, 251, 408–
 410, 515, 657, 676–677, 747, 765,
 776, 812
Hardcastle, Paul 120
hardcore 49–54
 vs. Oi! 53
Harder, Philip 91
Hardkiss 405
Hardkiss, Robbie 376
Hard-Ons, The 599
Harper, Clay 348
Harper, Roy 809
Harris, Emmylou 786
Harrison, Jerry 678, 776, 780
Harry, Debbie 580, 676

See Blondie
Hart, Grant 423–424, 510, 589
Harvey, Alex 372, 434, 777
Harvey, Mick 299
Harvey, PJ 125, 247–248, 410–412, 740,
 768–769
Hatfield, Juliana 555, 782
Hawkwind 124, 151, 187, 263–264, 269,
 315, 536, 539, 542, 750, 770
Haynes, Gibby 228, 498
H-Bombs 315
Headcoat Sect 259
Headless Chickens 573
Heads, The 504, 676–677
Heartbreakers, The 123, 132, 413, 675,
 687, 689, 711
Heaton, Paul 359
Heaven 17 155, 234, 420, 422
Heavens to Betsy 196
Heavy Stereo 534
Hedges, Mike 153, 369, 479, 777
Helium 412, 760–761
Helium Kidz 731
Hell, Richard 25, 132, 207, 258, 412–413,
 461, 473, 572, 580, 632, 644, 676–
 677, 682, 687, 768, 790, 800, 808
Hellcats 331, 571
Hello 695
Helmet 414, 438, 692
Heltir 721
Henry Cow 214, 545
Hepcat 111, 583
Hersh, Kristin 185
Hi Fi 578
Hiatt, John 474
High Fidelity 682
High Llamas 725
Higher Intelligence Agency 198
Higsons 793
Hillage, Steve 251–252, 405, 414, 416,
 538, 680, 777–779
Hillcoat, John 91
Hillier, Dave 91
Hilt 623
Hilton, Simon 91
Hindu Love Gods 589
His Spirit Wife 720
Hitchcock, Robyn 27, 80, 312, 314, 362,
 398, 414–417, 457, 568, 588–589,
 640, 698, 748, 754, 770, 778
Hitmen 322, 331, 480, 572
Hitsville House Band 397
HOH 309
Hole 125, 128–129, 196, 417–418, 487,
 496, 522, 631, 751, 768, 782, 807
Holidays in the Sun festival 125
Holly & The Italians 580
Hollycaust 374

Hollywood Brats 219, 461
Holsapple, Peter 315–316
Holy Barbarians 302
Home and Garden 545
Honest 220
Honey Bane 204
Honky Toast 471
Hook, Peter 346, 380, 439, 514
Hooper, Nellee 201, 213
HORDE festival 125
Horn, Trevor 155, 160, 213, 375–377,
 457, 778, 815
Hothouse Flowers 785
House of Freaks 340
House of Love 239
Housemartins 359, 361
Houston, Penelope 163–164
Hovercraft 418–419, 671
Howl, Lupine 490
Howlett, Mike 262, 779
Howlin' Maggie 148
HR 167–168
Huggy Bear 196
Hugh Beaumont Experience 228
Human Drama 5, 388, 419, 430
Human League 59, 144, 234, 274, 304,
 320, 420–421, 526
Human Sexual Response 203
Human Waste 277
Humania 696
Hundred Million Martians 422–423
Hunter, Ian 220, 406, 792, 801
Hurricane #1 125, 596
Hüsker Dü 49, 244, 289, 318, 367, 398,
 423–424, 510, 589, 742, 804, 810
Hussey, Wayne 320, 501
Hutchence, Michael 217, 676
Hynde, Chrissie 193, 326, 461, 519, 559,
 688

I

I Start Counting 797
Ice Bear 114
Icicle Works 743, 782
Ideal 781
Idle Flowers 406
Idol, Billy 81, 133, 252–253, 341, 358,
 382, 389–390, 407, 439, 519, 560,
 608
Ignorant, Steve 295, 308
Iha, James 631
Illustrated Man 382
Images in Vogue 622
Immaculate Consumptives 245, 371, 425,
 476, 642
Impact Unit 495

MacInnes, Colin 429
MacKaye, Ian 50–53, 196, 203, 378, 497, 499, 599, 758
Mad Juana 407
Mad Professor 490
"Madchester" scene 251, 707
Madder Rose 627
Madness 25, 34, 44–45, 110, 136, 165, 210, 262, 348, 462, 481–484, 495, 506–507, 602, 700, 776, 781, 785
Madonna 360, 681
Magazine 57, 62, 136, 199, 231, 245, 250, 389, 484, 511, 565, 617, 649, 695–696, 739, 776, 789
Magick Heads 274
Magnuson, Ann 213
Maher, Fred 453, 607, 795
Mahurin, Matt 93
Major Thinkers 205
Makin' Time 251
Malfunkshun 402, 508, 756–757, 762
Mallet, David 93, 207
Mallinder, Kirk 234, 236
Mallinder, Stephen 234, 236
Maniacs 146
Manic Street Preachers 125, 243, 255
Manic Subsidal 534
Mansfield, Mike 93
Manson, Shirley 383, 522
Marc and the Mambas 5, 153, 156, 425, 618, 642, 768
March Violets 620, 798
Marching Girls 200
Marcy Playground 229
Marie et Les Garcons 747
Marilyn Manson 4, 72, 127, 130, 392, 418, 475, 485, 487–488, 518–519, 527, 800
Marine Girls 488–489, 735
Mark of Cain 414
Mark Stewart and the Mafia 797
Marley, Bob 40–42, 367, 531, 787
Marr, Johnny 463, 480, 515, 637
Marriott, Steve 688
Martha and the Muffins 786
Mascis, J 223, 333, 512
Massey, Graham 201
Massive Attack 116–118, 213, 219, 278, 384, 489–490, 531, 553–554, 559, 565, 662, 703
Massive Attack Sound System 125
Material 607, 787, 795
Matlock, Glen 460, 519, 607, 611
Matthews, Eric 725
Matumbi 551
Max's Kansas City 11, 13, 189, 545
Mazzy Star 255, 436, 577
MC5 571–572, 633, 643, 746

MC900 Ft. Jesus 491
McComb, David 692, 694
McCulloch, Ian 350, 352, 679–680, 745
McDowall, Rose 280, 309, 364, 594
McG 94
McGowan, Shane 494
McKee, Maria 700
McLaren, Malcolm 121, 135, 143, 303, 413, 461, 608, 687, 748, 773, 808
McLennan, Grant 394
MDC 537, 583
Meade, Tyson 248–249
Mean Street 526
Meat Beat Manifesto 128, 157, 159, 255, 491–492, 541
Meat Puppets 229, 392, 492–493, 523, 788, 804
Meek, Joe 725, 761
Megadeth 518
Mekons 381, 484
Mellow 708
Melvins, The 182, 358, 392, 508, 521–522, 692, 762
Members 662, 710
Men They Couldn't Hang, The 241, 397, 474, 494, 521, 549, 754
Men, The 420
Mental As Anything 693
Mephiskapheles 113, 787
Merchant, Natalie 221, 507
Mercury Rev 222, 255, 368, 561, 743
Mercy Seat 711
Mercyland 510
Merton Parkas, The 429
Metallica 358, 771
Methods of Madness 553
Mickey and the Milkshakes 256
Midnight Oil 788, 793
Mighty Dub Katz 359
Mighty Mighty Bosstones 80, 112, 125, 128, 314, 366, 495–496, 583, 782
Mighty Wah! 726, 768
Milkshakes, The 256
Mill Wall Chainsaws 549
Miller, Daniel 56, 60, 230, 235, 322, 325, 546, 594, 771, 796
Mills, Mike 94
Mills, Russell 674
Milne, Simon 94
Mindfunk 498
Mindstorm 504
Miner, Michael 94
Ming, Sexton 774
Ministry 59, 69–70, 116, 127, 223, 228, 235, 279, 323, 377–378, 414, 437, 450, 479, 497–498, 518, 623–624, 626, 671, 740, 751, 768, 798, 800, 802–803

Minogue, Kylie 247
Minor Threat 49–50, 169–170, 203, 378, 401, 500, 524, 742, 759
Minuteman 750
Minutemen 52, 553, 698, 804
Mischief 313
Misfits, The 7, 169, 500–501
Mishra, Jyoti 719
Missing Persons 342
Mission of Burma 150, 244, 455
Mission, The 7, 29, 44, 68, 129, 145, 302, 318, 344, 388, 450, 501–503, 566, 621–622, 751
Misty in Roots 604
Moby 123, 128, 158, 503–504, 541, 566 remixes 505
Mochnacz, Maria 94
Mod 47–48, 51, 136–137, 428–429 revival 47, 133, 429
Models 143, 199, 419
Modern English 277, 738, 782
Modern Lovers, The 9–10, 182, 675, 776
Mo-Dettes, The 577
Mojave Exodus 128
Momus 154, 434
Monaco 125, 516–517
Monkey Mafia 125, 405, 505–506, 804
Monks of Doom 238
Monochrome Set 143, 175
Monsterland 174
Mont de Marsen punk festival 128
Moon 110
Moon Ska 111–114
Moore, Thurston 413, 589, 643, 646, 745
Moors Murderers 559
Moped, Johnny 311
Morcheeba 490
Moroder, Giorgio 207, 433, 616
Morphine 783
Morris and the Minors 180
Morrison, Jim 632
Morrison, Sterling 3
Morrison, Van 480, 675
Morrissey 4, 123, 145, 243, 313, 338, 344–345, 386, 462, 481, 506–507, 573, 619, 635, 637, 785, 791, 801, 805
Morton, Rocky 94
Moth Men 344
Mother Love Bone 302, 402, 508–509
Mother Superior 599
Mothers of Invention 238, 717
Motorhead 23, 748–751, 761, 787
Motors, The 695
Mott the Hoople 269, 389, 406, 462, 637, 801
Mould, Bob 49, 398, 423, 479, 493, 510
Mould, David 94

Orchestral Manouvres in the Dark
    See OMD
Organic festival 128
Ork Records 316, 413, 632, 683, 800
Ork, Terry 682
Osborne, Joan 291
Other Side, The 572
Other Two, The 141, 515, 517
Ottoman Empire 397
Outkids, The 361
Outs, The 150
Outskirts of Infinity 187
Ozric Tentacles 125, 151, 283, 395, 542–543, 750

P

P 230
Pack, The 684
Pailhead 497
Paladin, Patti 537, 688, 745
Pale Divine 471
Pale Saints 478, 782
Panik 440
Pansy Division 182, 231, 741
Pariahs 493
Paris Angels 409
Parish, John 410
Parkas, Merton 663
Parker, Graham 18–19, 473, 743
Parsons, Gram 698
Partridge, Andy 676–677, 731, 734
Passengers, The 705–706
Passion Killers 266
Passions 305
Pastels, The 357, 556, 681
Patrol, The 657
Patterson, Alex 540
Patti Smith Group 129, 206, 269, 625,
    683, 715, 747
    See also Patti Smith
Patton, Mike 358
Paul K and the Weathermen 148
Pavement 123, 125, 128, 130, 212, 355,
    412, 544, 574, 760–761
Payne, Davey 347
Payolas, The 801
Peach 692
Peanuts 504
Pearl Harbor and the Explosions 263
Pearl Jam 169, 729
Peel, John 27–30, 35, 289, 699
    sessions index 30
Pell Mell 473
Pelle Miljoona Oy 406
Pellington, Mark 95
Pendragon 502

Penetration 344, 791
Pennywise 535, 772
Pepper, Angie 750
Pere Ubu 13, 60, 136, 202, 326, 332,
    460, 510, 545–546, 585, 625, 683,
    799, 809
Perennial Divide 491
Peretz, Jesse 95
Perfect Circle 692
Perfect Disaster 185, 547
Perrett, Peter 537
Perry, Brandon 318
Perry, Mark 22
Persistence of Memory Orchestra 150
Pet Shop Boys 141, 226, 266, 303, 360,
    504, 515, 619, 773
Peter Pan's Playground 240
Peters, Mike 388, 503
Petty, Tom 592, 718
Phantom Chord 313
Phantom Tollbooth 213
Phantomas 358
Phenobarbidols 584
Phillipps, Martin 261
Phones Sportsman Band 672
Photons 559
Physicals 480, 610
Pierce, Jeffrey Lee 402–404, 599
Pierson, Arthur 95
Pietasters 112, 772
Pig 372
Pigbag 552
Pigface 437, 518, 562, 740
PiL
    See Public Image Ltd
Pinhead Gunpowder 109, 399
Pink Fairies, The 461, 746
Pink Floyd 151, 238, 312, 335, 374, 419,
    450, 531–532, 560, 635, 681, 711,
    788
Pink Industry 436
Pirroni, Marco 143, 145, 176, 252, 530,
    617
Pixies, The 30, 129, 185, 202, 260, 290,
    368, 380, 386, 546–548, 595, 719,
    739–740, 799
Pizzaman 359
Placebo 4, 125, 548–549
Plank, Connie 325
Plant, Robert 480
Plasticland 711
Plastics, The 190
PMRC (Parental Music Resource Center)
    103–105, 576
Pogues, The 25, 129, 247, 285, 436, 480,
    494, 521, 531, 549–551, 578, 662,
    778, 791–792
Poi Dog Pondering 776

Poison Girls 295
Polecats, The 506
Police, The 253, 288, 394, 535, 588, 779
Polvo 412
Polygon Window 157–158
Pompeii 99 720
Pop Art Toasters 261
Pop Group 62, 116, 326, 449, 551–552,
    565, 578, 628, 796, 802
Pop Rivits 256–257, 775
Pop Will Eat Itself 241, 513, 518, 558
Pop, Iggy 3, 5–6, 15–16, 146, 177, 207–
    208, 218, 234, 269, 330, 342, 407,
    420, 431, 440, 559, 572, 599, 619,
    635, 709
Pope, Tim 95
Popes, The 550–551
Poppees, The 745
Poppy Seeds, The 435
Porcelain Touch 647
Pork Guys 504
"Porn Rock" 103–104
Porno for Pyros 127, 129, 131, 302, 367,
    432, 552–553, 575–576, 759
P-Orridge, Genesis 69–70, 263, 439,
    562–563, 685, 753, 780
Portishead 117–118, 125, 490, 553–554,
    595
Portsmouth Sinfonia 764
Posies, The 554–555, 590, 625, 682,
    757, 768, 810
Possession 279
"post-modern" viii
"post punk" viii
Postcard label 164
Power Station 342–343
Premature Ejaculation 69, 720–722, 752
Presence 306
Presidents of the United States of America
    183, 810–811
Pressure Zone 376
Pressurehed 263
Pretenders, The 193, 473, 521, 710
Pretty Mary Sunshine 555, 625
Prick 518
Primal Scream 125, 129, 141, 152, 252,
    254–255, 321, 364, 435, 512, 517,
    538–540, 556–557, 585, 646, 658,
    681, 719, 804, 812
Prime Movers 251
Prime Time 605
Primitives, The 512, 698
Primus 299, 367
Prince 527, 600, 616
Prince Buster 482, 691
Princess Tinymeat 713
Prisoners, The 256

Prodigy 125, 128–130, 160, 255, 299, 360, 370, 376–377, 475, 505, 516, 557–559, 615, 658
Professionals, The 174, 610, 612
Professor Anonymous album 514
Project Pitchfork 377
Prong 372, 450, 501
Propaganda 816
Prothese 377
Psi Com 430
Psychedelic Furs 123, 199, 224, 306, 343, 351, 370, 414, 431, 463, 471, 497, 559, 561, 578, 582, 619, 621, 637, 775, 791–792, 805
Psychic TV 70, 152, 279, 440, 562–563, 625, 642, 649, 686, 752
Psychick Warriors Ov Gaia 405
Psycho Punks, The 514
PTP 497
pub rock 17–19
Public Enemy 280, 382
Public Image Ltd 60, 193, 231, 275, 369, 371, 440, 450, 476, 490, 497, 517, 539, 564–566, 577, 609, 628, 638, 684, 718, 748, 774, 781, 788, 809
Pulp 125, 129, 354–355, 385, 397, 479, 485, 566–568, 627, 662, 690
Punk Lurex OK 568–569, 636
Purple Hearts, The 429, 521
Pursey, Jimmy 612
Pussy Galore 403
PVC2 696
Pylon 569–570, 591, 792

Q

Quango Quango 140
Quarks 168
Queen 518, 680, 718
Queen Elizabeth 288
Questions 663
Quick 328
Quine, Bob 413

R

R.K.L. 524
Rad Command 370
Radiators From Space 549
Radio Birdman 331, 571–573, 750
Radio Heart 527
Radio Hearts, The 150
Radio Stars 749
Radiohead 82, 125, 127, 129, 183, 239, 356, 398, 496, 544, 573–575, 670, 682, 782, 789
Rage Against the Machine 123, 125, 129, 131, 279, 358, 432, 553, 575–576, 587, 692

Rain 532
Rain Parade 339, 576–577, 584
Rain Tree Crow 433–434, 674
Raincoats, The 29, 466, 564, 577–578, 584–585, 628, 776
Raintree County 385
Rainy Day 577
Rambow, Phil 480
Ramone, Joey 791
Ramones, The 11, 13, 28, 49, 123, 127–128, 131–132, 134, 138, 143, 150, 167, 171–172, 203, 207, 219, 292, 313, 329, 362, 413, 423, 431, 564, 572, 579–583, 591, 603, 614, 639, 667, 675, 683, 688, 700, 790–791, 808, 814
Ranaldo, Lee 333, 646
Rancid 41, 107–108, 112, 128, 169, 314–315, 380, 385, 399, 535, 538, 583, 729, 773
Random, Eric 231, 234
Rankin' Roger 193, 321
Rankine, Alan 337
Raped, The 195
Rapeman 195, 437, 739, 806–807
Rats and Foxes 312
Raunchettes, The 584, 745
Raymonde, Simon 278, 744
Reading festival 128–129
Ready Teddy 149–150, 514
Real Kids, The 150
Recoil 325
Red and the Black 715
Red Crayola 151–152, 260, 364, 545, 578, 584–585, 747
Red Hot Chili Peppers 49, 101, 124, 126, 129–131, 134, 228–229, 319, 328, 358, 372, 382, 392, 432, 477, 479, 497, 522, 553, 576, 586–587, 662, 718, 781, 802
Red Lorry Yellow Lorry 502
Red Noise 365, 673
Red Ponies 694
Redd Kross 203, 554, 815
Redskins 220
Reed, Lou 3, 149, 234, 332, 342, 362, 372, 419, 514, 536, 637, 704, 715, 801
Reel Big Fish 394, 587–588
reggae 40–42
    and ska 44
    influence on punk 41
Reid, Jim 321
Reid, Terry 592
Reload 118, 158
REM 2, 83, 125, 169–170, 173, 221, 315, 362, 415, 522, 555, 569, 574, 587–590, 593, 671–672, 698–699, 760,

792–793
Renegade Soundwave 254, 436
Rental, Robert 780, 796
Replacements, The 289, 415, 554, 591, 593, 793, 809–810
    See also Paul Westerberg
Replicants, The 692
Resident Snakefinger 163
Residents, The 165, 263, 717
Rev, Martin 667–668, 808
Revenge 515
Revolting Cocks 377, 437, 497, 499, 518, 623, 740
Revolutionary Corps of the Teenage Jesus 668
Revolving Paint Dream 556
Rew, Kimberley 640
Rezillos, The 614, 699
Reznor, Trent 144, 279, 353, 486, 497, 517, 527, 793
    remixes and productions 519
Rhythm of Life Organization 345
Rialto 774
Rice, Boyd 69, 279–280, 309, 593–595, 796, 798
Rich Kids 389, 608, 611, 696, 801
Richardson, Garth 245
Richman, Jonathan 9, 149, 362, 559
Ricker D, Bob 96
Rico 652
Ride 214, 478, 534, 595–596, 670, 789
Ridgway, Stan 714, 782
Rieflin, Bill 235, 497, 518
Riff Raff 220
Right Said Fred 605
Riley, Paul 600
Rings 748
Riot Grrl scene 195–196, 412, 417, 439, 475
Rip Rig & Panic 551–552
Ritchie, Brian 712
Rites of Spring 378
Robinson, Dave 96
Robinson, Mark 96
Robinson, Tom 119, 122, 125, 597–598, 636, 655
    See also Tom Robinson Band
Rock Against Racism (RAR) 37–39, 42, 46
Rocket From the Crypt 806
Rocket From the Tombs 545, 683
Rockpile 473–475
Roddy Radiation and the Tearjerkers 652
Rodgers, Nile 208
Rollerskate Skinny 512
Rolling Stones 411, 419, 450, 562, 639, 660, 759, 780
Rollins Band 131, 204, 599, 807

Rollins, Henry 49–50, 120, 127, 203, 378, 403, 478, 499, 598, 600, 641, 692, 757, 759
Romanek, Mafk 96
Romeo Void 263
Romero, Anisa 626
Romhanyi, Pedro 96
Ronson, Mick 3, 193, 405, 507, 611, 801
Roogalator 18, 473–474, 480, 600–601
Rorschach, Poison Ivy 291
Rossacher, Hannes 88
Rotten, Johnny 1, 420, 607, 696
Rowland, Kevin 132, 205, 601–602
Roxy Music 144, 234, 398, 449, 497, 536, 616, 695, 709, 758, 763
Royal Neanderthal Orchestra, The 493
Rubin, Rick 302, 586–587, 801–802
Ruby 321
Ruffy, Dave 145, 164, 481, 530
Rugcutters, The 506
Rumour, The 19, 480
Run DMC 180
Runaways, The 5, 438, 603
Rundgren, Todd 439, 467, 560, 633, 733
Rushent, Martin 420, 519
Ruskin, Mickey 11
Ruthless Rap Assassins 409
Ruts DC 604
Ruts, The 30, 38, 41, 145, 164, 167, 312, 481, 530, 604, 662
Rybczynski, Zbigniew 96

S

Saber, Danny 409
Sabotage 377
Sabres of Paradise 254, 557
Saccharine Trust 804
Sacred Miracle Cave 584, 772
Sacred Trash 501
Sadista Sisters 336
Sadkin, Alex 790
Sage, Greg 182
Saints, The 28, 170, 172, 332, 371, 572, 651, 782
Sakamoto, Ryuichi 165, 433, 565, 673, 676
Saltine 555
Same, The 259
Samhain 169, 500
sampling 74–76
Sandoz 236
Santa 197
Sardonica 501
Sass and Susan 150
Sassi 236
Satan's Cheerleaders 292, 584

Saturday Night Live 78
Saw Doctors 700
Scab Aid 266
Scandal 407
Schenck, Rocky 97
Scornflakes 497
Scott, Jake 97
Scott, Mike 125, 716
Scrapyard 319
Scratch Acid 195, 437
Scream 373, 522
Screaming Blue Messiahs 494
Screaming Target 193, 361
Screaming Trees 148, 182, 333, 590, 768, 804
Screaming Tribesmen 331
Screaming White Hot Razor Blades 571
Screams for Tina 648
Screech Owls 713
Screeching Weasel 109, 399–400
Scritti Politti 363, 483, 584, 607, 795
Seahorses 658–659
Seal 213, 778–779
Seaweed 182
Sebadoh 130, 334
Secret Affair 429
Secret, The 654
Sector 27 597, 792
Sednaoui, Stephane 97
Seething Wells 119–120
Segel, Jonathan 238
Seggs, Vince 481
Selecter 691
Sensational Alex Harvey Band 154, 269, 696
Sentivan, Drew 97
Sergeant, Will 350, 352
Servants, The 162
Setzer, Brian 660–661
Sevendust 277
Severed Dwarves 146
Severin, Steve 297, 306, 405, 476, 608, 617
Sex Gang Children 65, 177, 649
Sex Gods 351
Sex Pistols viii, 13–14, 18–19, 40, 44, 55, 77, 121, 125, 128, 132, 135, 142, 147, 160, 163, 172, 174, 176–177, 203, 216, 230, 252, 254, 258, 270, 284, 288, 295, 303, 311, 318, 329, 338, 342, 344, 348, 389, 394, 413, 428, 435, 438–439, 449, 499, 519–520, 546, 559, 564, 579, 607–611, 617, 627, 633, 637, 640, 651, 657, 687–688, 696, 709, 748, 765, 776, 778, 801, 808
Seymour 209

Shack 782
Shadow 509
Shadow Project 720–721, 753
Shakatak 527
Shake Society 190
Shakespear's Sister 175–176
Shallow Madness, A 350
Sham 69 53, 125, 129, 133, 295, 329, 466, 583, 612–613, 684, 747, 778
Shampoo 176
Shandi's Addiction 358
Sharkey, Feargal 322, 482, 699–701
Shatterproof 782
Shaw, Alan Lee 146, 480
Shaw, Greg 745
She's In Pain 276
Sheep on Drugs 781
Shellac 195, 739
Shelley, Pete 230–231, 439, 484, 774
Shelley, Steve 413
Sherman, Bim 490
Sherwood, Adrian 41, 70, 116, 235, 353–354, 497, 517, 519, 552, 556, 623, 628, 802–803
Shields, Kevin 512, 556
Shillelagh Sisters 506
Shimmy Disc 213, 453, 614, 767
Shining Path 167
Shiva Burlesque 398
Shockabilly 213, 228, 238, 453–454, 711
Shoes 745
Shonen Knife 614–615
Shooting Gallery 407
Shriekback 260, 625, 747
Shudder to Think 671
Shuffle Brothers 375
Sick of it All 501
Sickness of Snakes 279
Sigismondi, Floria 97
Sigue Sigue Sputnik 57, 99, 120, 155, 192, 389, 470, 487, 615–617, 621, 750–751, 773–774
Silicon Teens 796–798
Silkworm 740
Silos 340
Silverhead 207
Simenon, Tim 212, 323
    productions 213
Simmons, Russell 801
Simple Minds 177, 261, 778, 789, 792
Simply Red 251, 345, 567, 658
Sing Sing 479, 744
singles
    top alternative 818
Sioux, Siouxsie 490, 507, 608, 617

Wanderers, The 466, 468, 613
Wareham, Dean 380
Warsaw 439
Was, Don 718
Wasted Youth 123, 168, 369
Waterboys 414, 672, 715–716
Watt, Ben 488
Watt, Matt 418
Watt, Mike 196, 553, 644
Watt-Roy, Norman 396
Weatherall, Andrew 152, 254, 356, 405, 556, 606, 690, 812–813
Wednesday, Jamie 240
Weekend 735–736
Ween 716–717, 758, 809
Weezer 799
Weill, Kurt 411
Weirdos 391
Weller, Paul 119, 125, 129, 175, 210, 224, 428, 460, 489, 521, 602, 663, 665
WELT 624
Wenders, Wim 98, 246, 285, 298
Wener, Louise 286, 626
Westerberg, Paul 591, 717–718, 793
Wham! 99, 144, 359
What is This? 585, 718–719, 780
Wheel, Catherine 799
Whipping Boy 793
White Flag 534, 555
White Town 719–720
White, Josh 98
Whitebloom, Monty 85
Who, The 47, 133, 505
Wilco 125, 221, 590, 698–699
Wild Bunch 489
Wild Carnation, The 362
Wilde, Kim 696
Wilder, Alan 325, 797
Wildhearts, The 513
Wildski, MC 359
Williams, Hype 98
Williams, Robbie 539
Williams, Rozz 66, 72, 419, 720–722, 750
Willing Sinners 153
Willson-Piper, Marty 270

Wilson, Brian 725
Wilson, Thom 534, 720, 813–814
Wilson, Tony 344, 775
Wind in the Willows 206
Winstanley, Alan 165, 262, 506, 785
Winter, Alex 98
Wipers, The 182, 443
Wir 540, 723–724
Wire 34, 197, 305, 354–355, 500, 512, 590, 722–724, 745, 771, 781, 796–797, 808
Wire Train 338
Wiseblood project 372
Witch Hazel Sound 725
Wiz 98
Wobble, Jah 125, 213, 787
Wolfgang Press, The 518
Wolverines 318
Wonder Stuff 480, 513, 518, 754
Wood, Andrew 508
Woodstock 131
Working Week 735
World Party 125, 530, 715–716
Worrell, Bernie 675
Wreckless Eric 18, 24, 253, 284, 329, 347–348, 395, 397, 472–473, 765, 775, 795
Wrestling Worms 237
Wu Tang Clan 201, 208
Wyatt, Robert 578
Wygals 316
Wylde Things 407
Wylie, Pete 30, 141, 261, 319, 374, 452, 679, 725–727, 743, 777
Wynn, Steve 340

X

X 134, 391, 431, 476–477, 589, 728–730, 784
X, Geza 391, 742, 814–815
X-Certs 334
X-Mal Deutschland 738
Xon 236
X-Ray Spex 132, 143, 220, 585, 608, 672, 730–731, 808

XTC 30, 136, 210, 261, 398, 457, 654, 708, 731–734, 770, 788–789, 791–792

Y

Y Criff 243
Ya Yas, The 533
Yachts, The 374
Yana, Akiko 433
Yang, Naomi 380
Yardbirds, The 613
Yaz 59, 322, 325
Yazoo 322, 796–798
Yeah Yeah Noh 647
Years, The 249
Yello 538
Yellow Magic Orchestra 673
Yellowman 370
Yes 751
Yobs, The 219
Young Aborigines 179
Young Fresh Fellows 590, 810
Young Marble Giants 275, 488, 545, 735
Young, Neil 1, 148, 327, 339, 362, 507, 574, 605, 639, 644
Young, Paul 480
Youth 151, 176, 449, 451, 538
Youth Brigade 499
Yow, David 437, 497
Yung Wu 362

Z

Zang Tumb Tuum
    See ZTT
Zapata, Mia 439
Zazou, Hector 198
Zeroes, The 746
Zodiac Mindwarp 301, 816
    and the Love Reaction 151, 737
Zombie, Rob 98
Zones, The 696
Zoo Records 350, 451, 679, 816
Zos Kia 279
ZTT 79, 160, 275, 375, 377, 481, 550, 778–779, 815–816
Zulus 510

 **Third Ear**

Fresh perspectives, new discoveries, great music.

Third Ear—The Essential Listening Companion is a new series of music guides exploring some of the most compelling genres in popular music. Each guide is written or edited by a leading authority in the field, who provides uncommon insight into the music. These books offer informed histories, anecdotal artist biographies, and incisive reviews and ratings of recordings. In-depth essays explore the roots and branches of the music. Easy to use and fun to browse, *Third Ear* guides are visually inviting as well, with evocative artist photos.

Swing
By Scott Yanow

Swing explores the musical phenomenon that has younger listeners up and dancing, and older ones fondly looking back. From the 1930s' classic sound of Duke Ellington through today's retro-swing movement with Big Bad Voodoo Daddy, this guide covers every era of swing. It profiles over 500 band leaders, players, vocalists, sidemen and composers, and the recordings that make (or don't make) the cut. Plus—it covers swing in the movies, books, hard-to-find recordings, and more.
Softcover, 514 pages, ISBN 0-87930-600-9, $22.95

Bebop
By Scott Yanow

On the heels of swing in 1945, bebop changed everything. This is the insightful guide to the innovators, tunes, and attitudes that evolved jazz from a dance music to an art form. *Bebop* portrays the lives and work of the daring musicians who became virtuosos in their own right: the bebop giants, like Charlie Parker and Dizzy Gillespie; the classic beboppers, like Sarah Vaughan and Dexter Gordon; and such later bebop figures as Oscar Peterson and Sonny Rollins.
Softcover, 391 pages, ISBN 0-87930-608-4, $19.95

Celtic Music
Edited by Kenny Mathieson

Today's Celtic music hails from its traditional homelands but also embraces new fusions from around the globe. Featuring 100 color photos, this guide captures the flavor of this widely enjoyed music in all its forms—traditional, new Celtic, and Celtic-influenced music. It describes known and lesser-known solo artists, groups, singers and players, ranging from Irish piper Johnny Doran to the Chieftains. Plus—essays explore Celtic's regional variations and unique instrumentation such as harp, pipe, fiddle, and squeezebox.
Softcover, 192 pages, ISBN 0-87930-623-8, January 2001, $19.95

Afro-Cuban Jazz
By Scott Yanow

This is the ultimate guide to the irresistible music that blends bebop with Cuban folk music and rhythms. Covering such early figures as Chano Pozo, Machito, Tito Puente, Cal Tjader and Willie Bobo, the book highlights today's leading artists—Poncho Sanchez, Chucho Valdes, Arturo Sandoval, Gato Barbieri, and many more. It also notes traditional jazz musicians who have frequently recorded Afro-Cuban jazz, and related strains of folk-influenced music by groups such as the Buena Vista Social Club.
Softcover, 240 pages, ISBN 0-87930-619-X, January 2001, $17.95

 **Miller Freeman Books**

AVAILABLE AT FINE BOOK AND MUSIC STORES EVERYWHERE. OR CONTACT:

Miller Freeman Books • 6600 Silacci Way • Gilroy, CA 95020 USA •
Phone: (800) 848-5594 • **Fax:** (408)848-5784 •
E-mail: mfi@rushorder.com • **Web:** www.books.mfi.com